A London
Bibliography of the
Social Sciences

BRITISH LIBRARY OF POLITICAL AND ECONOMIC SCIENCE

A London Bibliography of the Social Sciences

Thirteenth Supplement

1978

VOLUME XXXVI

MANSELL, LONDON, 1979

*This Bibliography has been computer typeset from
the machine-readable subject catalogue of the
British Library of Political and Economic Science by
Mansell Publishing, a part of Bemrose UK Limited,
3 Bloomsbury Place, London WC1A 2QA*

ISBN 0 7201 0929 9
ISSN 0076-051X
Library of Congress Card Number 31-9970

*Printed and bound in Great Britain by
The Scolar Press Ilkley West Yorkshire*

© *1979 The British Library of Political and Economic Science*

British Library Cataloguing in Publication Data

British Library of Political and Economic Science
    A London bibliography of the social sciences.
    Vol.36: 1978: 13th supplement.
    1. Social sciences - Bibliography
    I. Title
    016.3 Z7161 31-9970

ISSN 0076-051X

Preface

This annual supplement to *A London Bibliography of the Social Sciences* is the fifth to be produced by means of computer typesetting.

Readers are again referred to the 'List of subject headings used in the Bibliography arranged under topics' as an essential guide to related headings in their field. This is to be found at the end of the volume.

D. A. Clarke   *August* 1979

Contents

VOLUMES I-XXXVI

VOLUMES I–IV *Original Compilation*

Holdings up to 1929 of the
British Library of Political and Economic Science
Edward Fry Library of International Law
*Goldsmith's Library of Economic Literature,
    University of London*
National Institute of Industrial Psychology
Royal Anthropological Institute
Royal Institute of International Affairs
Royal Statistical Society

Special collections in the libraries of
The Reform Club (*political and historical pamphlets*)
University College, London (*the Hume, Ricardo and
    other economic and political collections*)
The University of London (*works on economics and
    related subjects*)

VOLUME V *First Supplement*

Additions from 1929 to 1931 to the collections
included in Volumes I–IV

VOLUME VI *Second Supplement*

Additions from 1931 to 1936 to the
British Library of Political and Economic Science
Edward Fry Library of International Law
Goldsmith's Library of Economic Literature

VOLUMES VII–IX *Third Supplement*

Additions from 1936 to 1950, other than works in
  the Russian language, to the
British Library of Political and Economic Science
Edward Fry Library of International Law

VOLUMES X–XI *Fourth Supplement*

Additions from 1950 to 1955 in all languages, and
  also from 1936 to 1950 in Russian, to the
British Library of Political and Economic Science
Edward Fry Library of International Law

VOLUMES XII–XIV *Fifth Supplement*

Additions from 1955 to 1962 to the
British Library of Political and Economic Science
Edward Fry Library of International Law

VOLUMES XV–XXI *Sixth Supplement*

Additions from 1962 to 1968 to the
British Library of Political and Economic Science
Edward Fry Library of International Law
Volume XXI contains indexes to Volumes XV–XXI

VOLUMES XXII–XXVIII *Seventh Supplement*

Additions from 1969 to 1972 to the
British Library of Political and Economic Science
Edward Fry Library of International Law
Volume XXVIII contains an index to
Volumes XXII–XXVIII

VOLUMES XXIX–XXXI *Eighth Supplement*

Additions from 1972 to 1973 to the
British Library of Political and Economic Science
Edward Fry Library of International Law
Volume XXXI contains an index to
Volumes XXIX–XXXI

VOLUME XXXII *Ninth Supplement*

Additions during 1974 to the
British Library of Political and Economic Science
Edward Fry Library of International Law
with index

VOLUME XXXIII *Tenth Supplement*

Additions during 1975 to the
British Library of Political and Economic Science
Edward Fry Library of International Law
with index

VOLUME XXXIV *Eleventh Supplement*
Additions during 1976 to the
British Library of Political and Economic Science
Edward Fry Library of International Law
with index

VOLUME XXXV *Twelfth Supplement*
Additions during 1977 to the
British Library of Political and Economic Science
Edward Fry Library of International Law
with index

VOLUME XXXVI *Thirteenth Supplement*
Additions during 1978 to the
British Library of Political and Economic Science
Edward Fry Library of International Law
with index

PERIODICALS LISTS

An alphabetical list of the periodicals in the British
Library of Political and Economic Science in 1929
is given in Volume IV; supplementary lists up to
1936 are given in Volumes V and VI, after which they
have been discontinued.

AUTHOR INDEX

Author indexes are given in Volumes IV (for Volumes
I–III), V, and VI, but not in later volumes.
Volumes I–XIV were published by the
British Library of Political and Economic Science,
Houghton Street, London WC2

A London
Bibliography of the
Social Sciences

ABBREVIATIONS.

FERLAND (LYSE) compiler. Sigles en usage au Québec. Québec, 1972. pp. 88. *bibliog. (Quebec (Province). Legislative Library. Bibliographie et Documentation. 2)*

DE SOLA (RALPH) Abbreviations dictionary. 5th ed. New York, [1978]. pp. 654.

ABELIAN GROUPS.

FUCHS (LÁSZLÓ) Infinite abelian groups. New York, 1970-73. 2 vols. *bibliogs.*

ABEOKUTA

— Population.

ADEPOJU (JOHN ADERANTI) Policy implications of migration into medium-sized towns: the case of Abeokuta, Nigeria. Ile-Ife, 1977. pp. 116. *bibliog.*

ABERHART (WILLIAM).

WILLIAM Aberhart and social credit in Alberta; edited by Lewis H. Thomas. Vancouver, [1977]. pp. 174. *bibliog.*

ABILITY GROUPING IN EDUCATION.

NEWBOLD (DAVID) Ability grouping: the Banbury enquiry. Windsor, 1977. pp. 125. *bibliog. Abbreviated version of the report of the Banbury Grouping Enquiry delivered to the Department of Education and Science.*

ABKHAZIA

— Politics and government.

ABKHAZIA. Verkhovnyi Sovet. Zasedaniia. Stenograficheskii otchet. sess., D 1974 (8th series, 8th session)- , with gaps. Sukhumi.

ABORTION

— Law and legislation — United States.

MOHR (JAMES C.) Abortion in America: the origins and evolution of national policy, 1800-1900. New York, 1978. pp. 331. *bibliog.*

— Germany.

GESELLSCHAFT ZUR UNTERSTÜTZUNG DER VOLKSKÄMPFE, HEIDELBERG. Weg mit dem [paragraph] 218e.: das Volk selber soll entscheiden. Plankstadt, 1975. pp. 54.

TALLEN (HERMANN) Die Auseinandersetzung über [Paragraph] 218 StGB: zu einem Konflikt zwischen der SPD und der Katholischen Kirche. München, 1977. pp. 376. *bibliog.*

— Hawaiian Islands.

STEINHOFF (PATRICIA G.) and DIAMOND (MILTON) Abortion politics: the Hawaii experience. Honolulu, [1977]. pp. 256.

— Italy.

LIBRO bianco sull'aborto: cronaca di un dramma della coscienza italiana; documenti dei dibattiti parlamentari nella VI e nella VII legislatura; a cura di Paolo Piccoli. Milano, 1977. pp. 384.

— New Zealand.

NEW ZEALAND. Royal Commission to Inquire into and Report upon Contraception, Sterilisation and Abortion, 1975. Contraception, sterilisation and abortion in New Zealand; report; [D.W. McMullin, chairman]. in NEW ZEALAND. General Assembly. House of Representatives. Journals...Appendix to journals, 1977, E.26.

— Rhodesia.

RHODESIA. Commission of Inquiry into Termination of Pregnancy. 1976. Report...; [William Adrian Pittman, chairman]. [Salisbury], 1976. pp. 39. *(Rhodesia. [Command Papers]. 1976. Cmd. R.R.2)*

— United Kingdom.

U.K. Office of Population Censuses and Surveys. Abortion statistics: legal abortions carried out under the 1967 Abortion Act in England and Wales. a., 1974(1st)- London. *Supersedes Supplement on abortion in Registrar General's statistical review of England and Wales.*

— United States.

RAMSEY (PAUL) Ethics at the edges of life: medical and legal intersections. New Haven, 1978. pp. 353. *(Columbia University. Bampton Lectures in America)*

ABSENTEEISM (LABOUR)

— New Zealand.

NEW ZEALAND. Department of Labour. Research and Planning Division. 1976. Absence from work in New Zealand. [Wellington], 1976. 1 vol.(various pagings). *bibliog.*

ACCADEMIA D'ITALIA.

FERRAROTTO (MARINELLA) L'Accademia d'Italia: intellettuali e potere durante il fascismo. Napoli, 1977. pp. 163.

ACCEPTANCE SAMPLING.

WETHERILL (GEORGE BARRIE) Sampling inspection and quality control. 2nd ed. London, [1977]. pp. 146. *bibliog.*

ACCOUNTANTS.

McKENNA (EUGENE F.) The management style of the chief accountant. Farnborough, Hants., [1978]. pp. 307. *bibliog.*

ACCOUNTING.

EDEY (HAROLD CECIL) Business budgets and accounts: an introduction to management accounting. 3rd ed. London, 1966 repr. 1972. pp. 176. *bibliog.*

VOPROSY sovershenstvovaniia khozraschetnykh otnoshenii v SSSR. Moskva, 1976. pp. 199. *(Akademiia Nauk SSSR. Problemy Sovetskoi Ekonomiki)*

BARTON (ALLAN DOUGLAS) The anatomy of accounting. 2nd ed. [St. Lucia, Queensland, 1977]. pp. 593.

STUDIES in accounting; edited by W.T. Baxter and Sidney Davidson. 3rd ed. London, 1977. pp. 426

STUDIES in the business economics; edited on behalf of [the] Institute of Industrial Research, Kwansei Gakuin University, by Osamu Kojima. Kyote, 1977. pp. 168.

EDEY (HAROLD CECIL) Introduction to accounting. 4th ed. London, 1978. pp. 192. *bibliog.*

— Law — Finland.

JÄGERHORN (REGINALD) Inflationen och vår nya bokföringslag. Helsingfors, 1974. fo. 76-85. *(Svenska Handelshögskolan. Företagsekonomiska Institutionen. Meddelanden. Nr. 9) (Särtryck ur Finlands Svenska Ekonomförbunds Kurskompendium kring den nya bokföringslagen 1973)*

— — United Kingdom.

CURRENT ACCOUNTING LAW AND PRACTICE. a., 1976- London.

— Social aspects.

LEVY (MORTON) Accounting goes public. [Philadelphia, 1977]. pp. 169.

— Study and teaching — United Kingdom — Mathematical models.

OSMAN (A.C.) A cybernetic paridigm for research and development in accountancy education and training. [London, 1972). pp. 24, fo. 6. *bibliog.*

ACCOUNTING AND PRICE FLUCTUATIONS.

GOLDSCHMIDT (YAAQOV) and ADMON (KURT) Profit measurement during inflation: accounting, economic and financial aspects. New York, [1977]. pp. 328. *bibliog.*

ACCREDITATION (EDUCATION).

See also the subdivision Accreditation under types of schools.

ACCULTURATION.

OLIVEIRA (ROBERTO CARDOSO DE) Do indio ao bugre: o processo de assimilação dos Terêna. Rio de Janeiro, 1976. pp. 149. *bibliog. Reprint of O processo de assimilação dos Terêna, published in 1960, with new preface.*

BERRY (JOHN WIDDUP) Human ecology and cognitive style: comparative studies in cultural and psychological adaptation. New York, [1976]. pp. 242. *bibliog.*

SCHADEN (EGON) ed. Leituras de etnologia brasileira. São Paulo, 1976. pp. 534.

ACHEAMPONG (IGNATIUS KUTU).

GHANA. Supreme Military Council. Office of the Press Secretary. 1976. Fourth year in office of Colonel Ignatius Kutu Acheampong, 13th January 1975 - 12th January 1976. [Accra, 1976]. pp. 306.

ACQUISITIONS (LIBRARIES).

HINDLE (ANTHONY) Developing an acquisitions system for a university library. London, 1977. pp. 45. *(British Library. Research and Development Department. Reports. 5351)*

ACQUITTALS

— United Kingdom.

McCABE (SARAH) and PURVES (ROBERT) By-passing the jury: a study of changes of plea and directed acquittals in higher courts. Oxford, [1972]. pp. 46. *(Oxford. University. Penal Research Unit. Occasional Papers. No. 3)*

ACRONYMS.

DE SOLA (RALPH) Abbreviations dictionary. 5th ed. New York, [1978]. pp. 654.

ACT (PHILOSOPHY).

PÖRN (INGMAR) Action theory and social science: some formal models. Dordrecht, [1977]. pp. 129. *bibliog.*

ACTON FAMILY.

GUNN (PETER) The Actons. London, 1978. pp. 212. *bibliog.*

ADAMS (HOWARD).

ADAMS (HOWARD) Prison of grass: Canada from the native point of view. Toronto, 1975. pp. 238. *bibliog.*

ADAMS (JOHN) President of the United States.

PETERSON (MERRILL DANIEL) Adams and Jefferson: a revolutionary dialogue. Oxford, 1978. pp. 146. *(Mercer University. Eugenia Dorothy Blount Lamar Memorial Lectures. No. 19)*

ADAPTABILITY (PSYCHOLOGY).

CORDIER (JEAN) Une anthropologie de l'inadaptation: la dynamique de l'exclusion sociale. Bruxelles, [1975]. pp. 240. *bibliog. (Brussels. Université Libre. Institut de Sociologie. Sciences Pédagogiques et Sociologie de l'Education)*

ADELAIDE

— Harbour.

SOUTH AUSTRALIA. 1952. Report on the slow turn round of ships at Port Adelaide, 1951. Adelaide, 1952. pp. 51.

ADENAUER (KONRAD).

KONRAD Adenauer und seine Zeit: Politik und Persönlichkeit des ersten Bundeskanzlers...; herausgegeben von Dieter Blumenwitz [and others]. Stuttgart, [1976]. 2 vols. *(Konrad-Adenauer-Stiftung für Politische Bildung und Studienförderung. Veröffentlichungen)*

STEHKAEMPER (HUGO) Konrad Adenauer als Katholikentagspräsident, 1922: Form und Grenze politischer Entscheidungsfreiheit im katholischen Raum: (Adenauer-Studien, IV; herausgegeben von Rudolf Morsey und Konrad Repgen). Mainz, [1977]. pp. 124. *bibliog. (Kommission für Zeitgeschichte. Veröffentlichungen. Reihe B: Forschungen. Band 21)*

ADJUSTMENT (PSYCHOLOGY).

CORDIER (JEAN) Une anthropologie de l'inadaptation: la dynamique de l'exclusion sociale. Bruxelles, [1975]. pp. 240. *bibliog. (Brussels. Université Libre. Institut de Sociologie. Sciences Pédagogiques et Sociologie de l'Education)*

LUNGHI (MARTIN EDWARD) Self identity, adaption to change and depression. 1977. fo. 257. *bibliog. Typescript. Ph.D. (London) thesis: unpublished. This thesis is the property of London University and may not be removed from the Library. Article in end pocket.*

EASTERBROOK (JAMES A.) and EASTERBROOK (PAMELA J.) The determinants of free will: a psychological analysis of responsible, adjustive behavior. New York, 1978. pp. 259. *bibliog.*

ADMINISTRATION.

GALY (PHILIPPE) Gérer l'État: corriger la déviation bureaucratique. [Paris, 1977]. pp. vii, 241. *bibliog.*

KAUFMAN (HERBERT) Red tape: its origins, uses, and abuses. Washington, D.C., [1977]. pp. 100.

CHEVALLIER (JACQUES) and LOSCHAK (DANIELE) Science administrative. Paris, 1978 in progress. *bibliogs.*

MIEWALD (ROBERT D.) Public administration: a critical perspective. New York, [1978]. pp. 272. *bibliogs.*

PETERS (B. GUY) The politics of bureaucracy: a comparative perspective. New York, [1978]. pp. 246.

— Bibliography.

SHELLEY (IVOR D.) British works on public administration since 1963. London, 1971. 2 pts. *(Extracted from British Book News, May and July, 1971)*

— Decision making.

GEARY (K.) Local authority resource allocation with multiple objectives: an education example. London, 1977. pp. 71. *bibliog. (Planning Research Applications Group. PRAG Technical Papers. TP 21)*

ONTARIO. Economic Council. 1977. The process of public decision-making. Toronto, 1977. pp. 68. *(Issues and Alternatives, 1977)*

POLICYMAKING in contemporary Japan; edited by T.J. Pempel. Ithaca, 1977. pp. 345. *bibliog. Based in part on papers presented at the 1974 annual convention of the Association for Asian Studies.*

BRUNEL UNIVERSITY. Department of Government. The working of the National Health Service. London, 1978. pp. 238. *bibliog. (U.K. Royal Commission on the National Health Service, 1976. Research Papers. No. 1)*

EDWARDS (GEORGE C.) and SHARKANSKY (IRA) The policy predicament: making and implementing public policy. San Francisco, [1978]. pp. 336.

— Study and teaching — United Kingdom.

THOMAS (ROSAMUND M.) The British philosophy of administration: a comparison of British and American ideas, 1900-1939. London, 1978. pp. 280. *bibliogs.*

— — United States.

THOMAS (ROSAMUND M.) The British philosophy of administration: a comparison of British and American ideas, 1900-1939. London, 1978. pp. 280. *bibliogs.*

ADMINISTRATIVE AGENCIES

— Australia.

NIEUWENHUYSEN (JOHN PETER) and DALY (ANNE ELIZABETH) The Australian Prices Justification Tribunal. [Carlton, Victoria, 1977]. pp. 234. *bibliog.*

— Barbados.

KHAN (JAMAL) Development administration: field research in Barbados. Bridgetown, Barbados, [1976]. pp. 203. *bibliogs.*

— United Kingdom — Scotland.

SCOTTISH DEVELOPMENT AGENCY. Report. a., 1975/76(1st)- Glasgow.

— — Wales.

WELSH DEVELOPMENT AGENCY. Report. a., Ja 1976/Mr 1977(1st)- Treforest.

— United States.

MARTIN (CURTIS H.) and LEONE (ROBERT ANTHONY) Local economic development: the federal connection. Lexington, Mass., [1972]. pp. 138.

STONE (ALAN) Economic regulation and the public interest: the Federal Trade Commission in theory and practice. Ithaca, [N.Y.], 1977. pp. 314. *bibliog.*

WEBER (ARNOLD R.) and MITCHELL (DANIEL J.B.) The Pay Board's progress: wage controls in Phase II. Washington, D.C., [1978]. pp. 454. *(Brookings Institution. Studies in Wage-Price Policy)*

ADMINISTRATIVE AND POLITICAL DIVISIONS

See also the subdivision Administrative and political divisions under names of countries, cities, etc.

ADMINISTRATIVE COURTS

— France.

PHYTILIS (JACQUES) Justice administrative et justice déléguée au XVIIIe siècle: l'exemple des commissions extraordinaires de jugement à la suite du conseil. Limoges, [1977]. pp. 250. *bibliog. (Limoges. Université. Faculté de Droit et des Sciences Economiques. Publications. 5)*

— United Kingdom.

FULBROOK (JULIAN) Administrative justice and the unemployed. London, 1978. pp. 338. *bibliog.*

ADMINISTRATIVE DISCRETION

— Denmark.

STORM (SUSANNE) A comparison between the administration of supplementary benefits in England and public assistance in Denmark with special reference to the exercise of discretion. 1977. fo. 313. *Typescript. Ph.D. (London) thesis: unpublished. This thesis is the property of London University and may not be removed from the Library.*

— United Kingdom.

STORM (SUSANNE) A comparison between the administration of supplementary benefits in England and public assistance in Denmark with special reference to the exercise of discretion. 1977. fo. 313. *Typescript. Ph.D. (London) thesis: unpublished. This thesis is the property of London University and may not be removed from the Library.*

ADMINISTRATIVE LAW

— France.

MELANGES offerts à Georges Burdeau: le pouvoir. Paris, 1977. pp. 1190.

— Germany.

LECHELER (HELMUT) Die Personalgewalt öffentlicher Dienstherren. Berlin, [1977]. pp. 280. *bibliog.*

— Poland.

GŁOWACKI (SŁAWOMIR) Terenowe organy a gospodarka narodowa: zagadnienia prawne organizacji i kierowania. Wrocław, 1977. pp. 260. *bibliog.*

— Russia.

IUSUPOV (VITALII ANDREEVICH) Pravo i sovetskoe gosudarstvennoe upravlenie: administrativno- pravovoi aspekt problemy. Kazan', 1976. pp. 263.

ALEKHIN (ALEKSEI PETROVICH) Predpriiatie v sisteme otraslevogo upravleniia: administrativno- pravovye voprosy. Moskva, 1977. pp. 191.

— — Tajikistan.

TAJIKISTAN. Statutes, etc. 1957-1975. Sobranie deistvuiushchego zakonodatel'stva Tadzhikskoi SSR. razdel 25(-27). Dushanbe, 1976. pp. 387.

— United Kingdom.

BAILEY (STEPHEN HENRY) and others. Cases and materials in administrative law. London, 1977. pp. 635.

WADE (HENRY WILLIAM RAWSON) Administrative law. 4th ed. Oxford, 1977. pp. 855.

ADMINISTRATIVE PROCEDURE

— Russia.

GALAGAN (IVAN ALEKSANDROVICH) Administrativnaia otvetstvennost' v SSSR: protsessual'noe regulirovanie. Voronezh, 1976. pp. 198.

ADMINISTRATIVE REMEDIES

— Canada.

CANADIAN LABOUR CONGRESS. Collective bargaining and the appeal procedures under the anti- inflation programme. [Ottawa], 1976. pp. 8,12.

— Hungary.

MARTONYI (JÁNOS) La protection du citoyen dans les procédures administratives à l'exclusion des recours juridictionnels: rapport national hongrois pour le sujet 3 du XIVe Congrès international des Sciences Administratives, Dublin, septembre 1968. Szeged, 1968. pp. 39. *(Szeged. Tudományegyetem. Acta Universitatis Szegediensis. Acta Juridica et Politica. tom. 15, fasc. 1)*

ADMINISTRATIVE RESPONSIBILITY

— Colombia.

ESGUERRA PORTOCARRERO (JUAN CARLOS) La responsabilidad del estado por falla del servicio publico. Bogota, 1972. pp. 239. *bibliog.*

— United Kingdom.

JONES (GEORGE WILLIAM) D.Phil.(Oxon.). Responsibility and government. London, [1977]. pp. 36. *An inaugural lecture delivered on 28 April 1977 at the London School of Economics.*

ADOLESCENCE.

LIPSITZ (JOAN) ed. Growing up forgotten: a review of research and programs concerning early adolescence. Lexington, Mass., [1977]. pp. 267. *bibliog. A report to the Ford Foundation.*

ADOLESCENT BOYS.

BELSON (WILLIAM A.) Television violence and the adolescent boy. Farnborough, Hants., [1978]. pp. 529.

ADOLESCENT PSYCHOLOGY.

LIPSITZ (JOAN) ed. Growing up forgotten: a review of research and programs concerning early adolescence. Lexington, Mass., [1977]. pp. 267. *bibliog. A report to the Ford Foundation.*

AGGRESSION and anti-social behaviour in childhood and adolescence; edited by L.A. Hersov and M. Berger. Oxford, 1978. pp. 171. *bibliogs.*

— United Kingdom.

IRWIN (EDNA M.) Growing pains: a study of teenage distress. Plymouth, 1977. pp. 310. *bibliogs.*

ADORNO (THEODOR WIESENGRUND).

BUCK-MORSS (SUSAN) The origin of negative dialectics: Theodor W. Adorno, Walter Benjamin, and the Frankfurt Institute. Hassocks, Sussex, [1977]. pp. 335. *bibliog.*

ADVERTISING.

McGRAW (JAMES HERBERT) Advertising and the maintenance of prosperity. New York, [1928?]. pp. 10.

HOOD (PETER) Ourselves and the press: a social study of news advertising and propaganda. London, [1939]. pp. 287.

SEDGWICK (ALASTAIR) Advertising and the competitive economy. [London, 1973]. pp. 10. *(Foundation for Business Responsibilities. Occasional Papers)*

ISSUES in advertising: the economics of persuasion; edited by David G. Tuerck. Washington, D.C., [1978]. pp. 284. *(American Enterprise Institute for Public Policy Research. AEI Symposia. 78D) Proceedings of a conference held by AEI.*

WORCESTER (DEAN A.) and NESSE (RONALD) Welfare gains from advertising: the problem of regulation. Washington, D.C., [1978]. pp. 134. *(American Enterprise Institute for Public Policy Research. AEI Studies. 188)*

ADVERTISING, CORRECTIVE.

The POLITICAL economy of advertising; edited by David G. Tuerck. Washington, D.C., [1978]. pp. 217. *(American Enterprise Institute for Public Policy Research. AEI Symposia. 78A). Papers presented at a conference held in Washington, D.C., in 1976.*

ADVERTISING, PUBLIC SERVICE.

The POLITICAL economy of advertising; edited by David G. Tuerck. Washington, D.C., [1978]. pp. 217. *(American Enterprise Institute for Public Policy Research. AEI Symposia. 78A). Papers presented at a conference held in Washington, D.C., in 1976.*

— United States.

PALETZ (DAVID L.) and others. Politics in public service advertising on television. New York, 1977. pp. 123.

ADVERTISING AGENCIES

— United Kingdom.

TREASURE (J.A.P.) The history of British advertising agencies, 1875-1939. Edinburgh, [1977]. pp. 20. *(Edinburgh. University. Commerce Graduates' Association. Jubilee Lectures. 1976)*

ADZHARIA

— Politics and government.

ADZHARIA. Verkhovnyi Sovet. Zasedaniia. Stenograficheskii otchet. sess., Je 1974 (series 8, session 7)- , with gaps. Batumi.

AERIAL PHOTOGRAPHY IN AGRICULTURE

— Brazil.

BRAZIL. Instituto Brasileiro do Cafe. Grupo Executivo de Racionalização da Cafeicultura. Serviço de Fotointerpretação. 1968. Inventario cafeeiro: pesquisa com fotografias aereas nas regiões cafeicultoras do estado de São Paulo, a este de 48 W. Rio de Janeiro, 1968. pp. 67. *bibliog. With summaries in English, French, Spanish and German.*

AERONAUTICS

— Accidents.

U.K. Civil Aviation Authority. Chief Scientist's Division. Directorate of Operational Research and Analysis. 1978. Fatal accident statistics for passenger air transport services, 1960-1976; compiled by S.J. Devon. London, 1978. pp. 5, (13). *(CAA Papers. 77027)*

— Russia.

SOVIET aviation and air power: a historical view; edited by Robin Higham and Jacob W. Kipp. London, 1978. pp. 328. *bibliogs.*

AERONAUTICS, COMMERCIAL.

INTERNATIONAL AIR TRANSPORT ASSOCIATION. Annual General Meeting. 1973. Auckland 73: the papers presented to a special session of the 29th Annual General Meeting, Auckland, November 1973. Montreal, [1973]. pp. 38.

SHAW (R.R.) The fuel situation: the airline viewpoint. [1974?]. pp. 7. *Typescript: unpublished.*

FOLLIOT (MICHEL G.) Le transport aérien international: évolution et perspectives. Paris, 1977. pp. 301.

— Statistics.

U.K. Civil Aviation Authority. CAA annual statistics. a., 1973- , with gap(1974, 1975) London.

— Canada — Statistics.

CANADA. Statistics Canada. Air carrier traffic at Canadian airports. a., 1976(1st)- Ottawa. *[in English and French] Supersedes in part CANADA. Statistics Canada. Airport activity statistics.*

— New Zealand.

NEW ZEALAND. Department of Civil Aviation. 1967. Introducing the Department of Civil Aviation. [Wellington, 1967]. pp. (10).

NEW ZEALAND. New Zealand National Airways Corporation. 1968. N[ational] A[irways] C[orporation]: twenty-one years. [Wellington, 1968]. pp. 15.

NEW ZEALAND. Tourist Facilities - Transport Working Party. Air Sub-Committee. 1968. Air transport development applicable to the non-resident tourist; report. [Wellington], 1968. fo. 14.

— United Kingdom.

EDWARDS (Sir RONALD STANLEY) The Edwards report in retrospect and prospect. [London], 1975. pp. 27. *Reprint from Aerospace, April 1975.*

TRAINING RESEARCH BULLETIN: [pd. by] Air Transport and Travel Industry Training Board. q. Staines. *Current issues only kept.*

— — Passenger traffic.

GREEN (J.H.T.) United Kingdom air traffic forecasting: research and revised forecasts. London, Department of Trade, 1978. pp. 24.

— — Statistics.

U.K. Civil Aviation Authority. CAA annual statistics. a., 1973- , with gap(1974, 1975) London.

— United States.

WYCKOFF (D. DARYL) and MAISTER (DAVID H.) The domestic airline industry. Lexington, Mass., [1977]. pp. 191.

— — Law and legislation.

AMERICAN ENTERPRISE INSTITUTE FOR PUBLIC POLICY RESEARCH. Legislative Analyses. 95th Congress. No. 25. Air transportation regulatory reform. Washington, D.C., 1978. pp. 26.

AERONAUTICS, MILITARY

— Russia.

BERMAN (ROBERT P.) Soviet air power in transition. Washington, D.C., [1978]. pp. 82. *(Brookings Institution. Studies in Defense Policy)*

SOVIET aviation and air power: a historical view; edited by Robin Higham and Jacob W. Kipp. London, 1978. pp. 328. *bibliogs.*

AEROPLANES

— Noise.

U.K. Department of Trade. 1976. Action against aircraft noise. [London, 1976]. pp. 25.

NOISE ADVISORY COUNCIL [U.K.]. Working Group on Noise from Air Traffic. Concorde noise levels: report; [G.M. Lilley, chairman]. London, H.M.S.O., 1977. pp. 9.

AEROSPACE INDUSTRIES

— United Kingdom.

ELLIOTT (DAVID) The Lucas Aerospace workers' campaign. London, 1977. pp. 20. *(Young Fabian Group. Young Fabian Pamphlets. 46)*

AESTHETICS.

VOLPE (GALVANO DELLA) Critique of taste; translated by Michael Caesar. London, 1978. pp. 272.

AFFIRMATIVE ACTION PROGRAMMES

— United States.

EQUALITY and preferential treatment: a Philosophy and Public Affairs reader; edited by Marshall Cohen [and others]; contributors Ronald Dworkin [and others]. Princeton, [1977]. pp. 209.

ROSENBLOOM (DAVID H.) Federal equal employment opportunity: politics and public personnel administration. New York, 1977. pp. 184. *bibliog.*

SOCIAL justice and preferential treatment: women and racial minorities in education and business; edited by William T. Blackstone and Robert D. Heslep. Athens, Ga., [1977]. pp. 216. *bibliog. Papers presented at a conference held at the University of Georgia, February 13-15, 1975, and sponsored by that university's Dept. of Philosophy and Religion and Dept. of History and Philosophy of Education, together with the Georgia State Committee for the Humanities.*

AFFORESTATION

— New Zealand.

NEW ZEALAND. Department of Lands and Survey. 1970. Maori land in a major development project. [Wellington], 1970. pp. (6).

AFGHANISTAN

AFGHANISTAN

— **Foreign relations.**

FOOT (ROSEMARY JUNE) New areas of tension and great power rivalry: central west Asia and Sino-Soviet relations, 1962-1974. 1976 [or rather 1977]. fo. 353. *bibliog.* Typescript. Ph.D. (London) thesis: unpublished. *This thesis is the property of London University and may not be removed from the Library.*

AFRICA

— **Bibliography.**

HELMREICH (WILLIAM B.) compiler. Afro-Americans and Africa: black nationalism at the crossroads. Westport, Conn., 1977. pp. 74. *(African Bibliographic Center. Special Bibliographic Series. New Series. No. 3)*

— **Colonization.**

GANN (LEWIS H.) and DUIGNAN (PETER) The rulers of German Africa, 1884-1914. Stanford, Calif., 1977. pp. 286.

— **Description and travel.**

GROVE (ALFRED THOMAS) Africa. 3rd ed. Oxford, 1978. pp. 337. *bibliog.*

— **Discovery and exploration.**

MURRAY-BROWN (JEREMY) Faith and the flag: the opening of Africa. London, 1977. pp. 238. *bibliog.*

— **Economic conditions.**

EUROPEAN COMMUNITIES. Directorate-General for Development and Cooperation. Les Conditions d'Installation d'Entreprises Industrielles dans les États Africains et Malgache Associés. 2nd ed. [Brussels], 1974.

GUTKIND (PETER C.W.) and WATERMAN (PETER) eds. African social studies: a radical reader. London, 1977. pp. 481. *bibliog.*

HARVEY (CHARLES) Macroeconomics for Africa: the elementary theory of the working of present-day African economics, illustrated by examples taken mainly from the economy of Zambia. London, 1977. pp. 240.

GROVE (ALFRED THOMAS) Africa. 3rd ed. Oxford, 1978. pp. 337. *bibliog.*

— **Economic history.**

The IMPERIAL impact: studies in the economic history of Africa and India; edited by Clive Dewey and A.G. Hopkins. London, 1978. pp. 409. *(London. University. Institute of Commonwealth Studies. Commonwealth Papers. 21)*

— **Economic integration.**

AKINTAN (S.A.) The law of international economic institutions in Africa. Leyden, 1977. pp. 222.

— **Economic policy.**

INTERREGIONAL SEMINAR ON DEVELOPMENT PLANNING, 4TH, ACCRA, 1968. Development prospects and planning for the coming decade, with special reference to Africa: report on the...Seminar...[held in] Accra, Ghana, 4 to 13 December 1968. (ST/TAO/SER.C/116) . New York, United Nations, 1970. pp. 38.

EUROPEAN COMMUNITIES. Directorate-General for Development and Cooperation. Les Conditions d'Installation d'Entreprises Industrielles dans les États Africains et Malgache Associés. 2nd ed. [Brussels], 1974.

MOBILIZATION of household savings: a tool for development; edited by Arnaldo Mauri. Milan, 1977. pp. 219. *(Cassa di Risparmio delle Provincie Lombarde. The Credit Markets of Africa. 14)*

— **Foreign economic relations.**

See also EUROPEAN ECONOMIC COMMUNITY — Africa.

— — **Arab countries.**

CHIBWE (EPHRAIM CHIPAMPE) Afro-Arab relations in the new world order. London, 1977. pp. 150.

— — **Communist countries.**

EKONOMICHESKIE otnosheniia sotsialisticheskikh gosudarstv so stranami Afriki. Moskva, 1973. pp. 235.

— **Foreign relations.**

MAZRUI (ALI AL'AMIN) Africa's international relations: the diplomacy of dependency and change. London, 1977. pp. 310.

See also EUROPEAN ECONOMIC COMMUNITY — Africa.

— — **Arab countries.**

CHIBWE (EPHRAIM CHIPAMPE) Afro-Arab relations in the new world order. London, 1977. pp. 150.

— — **China.**

ARMSTRONG (J.D.) Revolutionary diplomacy: Chinese foreign policy and the united front doctrine. Berkeley, [1977]. pp. 251.

— — **Communist countries.**

GREIG (IAN) The communist challenge to Africa: an analysis of contemporary Soviet, Chinese and Cuban policies. Richmond, Surrey, 1977. pp. 306. *bibliog.*

— **History.**

MURRAY-BROWN (JEREMY) Faith and the flag: the opening of Africa. London, 1977. pp. 238. *bibliog.*

DAVIDSON (BASIL) Africa in modern history: the search for a new society. London, 1978. pp. 431.

FAGE (JOHN DONNELLY) A history of Africa. London, 1978. pp. 534. *bibliog.*

— **Industries.**

EUROPEAN COMMUNITIES. Directorate-General for Development and Cooperation. Les Conditions d'Installation d'Entreprises Industrielles dans les États Africains et Malgache Associés. 2nd ed. [Brussels], 1974.

— **Kings and rulers.**

AFRICAN kingships in perspective: political change and modernization in monarchical settings; edited by René Lemarchand. London, 1977. pp. 325. *bibliog.*

— **Nationalism.**

SYLLA (LANCINE) Tribalisme et parti unique en Afrique noire: esquisse d'une théorie générale de l'intégration nationale. [Paris, 1977]. pp. 392.

— — **Bibliography.**

HELMREICH (WILLIAM B.) compiler. Afro-Americans and Africa: black nationalism at the crossroads. Westport, Conn., 1977. pp. 74. *(African Bibliographic Center. Special Bibliographic Series. New Series. No. 3)*

— **Politics and government.**

AFRO-ASIAN PEOPLES' SOLIDARITY ORGANIZATION. Presidium. Meeting, Aden, 1976. The third meeting of the A.A.P.S.O. presidium, etc. Cairo, 1976. pp. 33.

AFRICAN kingships in perspective: political change and modernization in monarchical settings; edited by René Lemarchand. London, 1977. pp. 325. *bibliog.*

CHIME (CHIMELU) Integration and politics among African states: limitations and horizons of mid-term theorizing. Uppsala, 1977. pp. 436.

GREIG (IAN) The communist challenge to Africa: an analysis of contemporary Soviet, Chinese and Cuban policies. Richmond, Surrey, 1977. pp. 306. *bibliog.*

GUTKIND (PETER C.W.) and WATERMAN (PETER) eds. African social studies: a radical reader. London, 1977. pp. 481. *bibliog.*

MAZRUI (ALI AL'AMIN) Africa's international relations: the diplomacy of dependency and change. London, 1977. pp. 310.

— **Relations (general) with Germany.**

GANN (LEWIS H.) and DUIGNAN (PETER) The rulers of German Africa, 1884-1914. Stanford, Calif., 1977. pp. 286.

— **Relations (general) with the United Kingdom.**

HETHERINGTON (PENELOPE) British paternalism and Africa, 1920-1940. London, 1978. pp. 196. *bibliog.*

— **Social conditions.**

GUTKIND (PETER C.W.) and WATERMAN (PETER) eds. African social studies: a radical reader. London, 1977. pp. 481. *bibliog.*

GROVE (ALFRED THOMAS) Africa. 3rd ed. Oxford, 1978. pp. 337. *bibliog.*

— **Social policy.**

INTERREGIONAL SEMINAR ON DEVELOPMENT PLANNING, 4TH, ACCRA, 1968. Development prospects and planning for the coming decade, with special reference to Africa: report on the...Seminar...[held in] Accra, Ghana, 4 to 13 December 1968. (ST/TAO/SER.C/116) . New York, United Nations, 1970. pp. 38.

— **Statistics.**

EUROPEAN COMMUNITIES. Statistical Office. ACP: statistical yearbook. a., 1970/76 (1st)- Luxembourg. *[in English and French]*

AFRICA, CENTRAL

— **Economic conditions.**

UNION GENERALE DES TRAVAILLEURS SENEGALAIS EN FRANCE. Qui est responsable du sous-développement? Paris, 1975. pp. 85.

AFRICA, EAST

— **Economic conditions.**

UNITED NATIONS. Eastern African Team. 1971. Co-operation for economic development of Eastern Africa. (ST/ECA/140). New York, 1971. 9 pts. (in 1 vol.)

KITCHING (GAVIN N.) Economic and social inequality in rural East Africa: the present as a clue to the past. [Swansea, 1977]. pp. 65. *(Wales. University. University College of Swansea. Centre for Development Studies. Monographs. No. 1)*

— **Economic integration.**

UNITED NATIONS. Eastern African Team. 1971. Co-operation for economic development of Eastern Africa. (ST/ECA/140). New York, 1971. 9 pts. (in 1 vol.)

— **Politics and government.**

LANGLANDS (B.W.) Nationalism, regionalism and federalism: the geographical basis to some conflicting political concepts in East Africa. 1964. pp. 55. *Typescript: unpublished. Paper presented to the Political Geography Seminar of the International Geographical Union at Sheffield in 1964.*

— **Rural conditions.**

KITCHING (GAVIN N.) Economic and social inequality in rural East Africa: the present as a clue to the past. [Swansea, 1977]. pp. 65. *(Wales. University. University College of Swansea. Centre for Development Studies. Monographs. No. 1)*

— Social conditions.

EAST African law and social change; edited by G.F.A. Sawyerr. [Nairobi, 1967]. pp. 307. *bibliogs.(East African Institute of Social and Cultural Affairs. Contemporary African Monograph Series. No.6) Proceedings of the Seminar on Law and Social Change in East Africa, held at University College Dar es Salaam, April 2nd to 5th, 1966.*

AFRICA, NORTH.

MAGHREB-MACHREK: monde arabe (formerly Maghréb: études et documents Algérie, Libye, Maroc, Tunisie); (bulletin rédigé par la Fondation Nationale des Sciences Politiques. ...et la Direction de la Documentation [France]). bi-m., Ja/F 1964 (no.1)- Paris. Index: 1973/1976 (nos. 55-74).

AFRICA, NORTHEAST

— History.

LEGUM (COLIN) and LEE (BILL) Conflict in the horn of Africa. London, 1977. pp. 95.

AFRICA, SUBSAHARAN

— Colonization.

DRANG nach Afrika: die koloniale Expansionspolitik und Herrschaft des deutschen Imperialismus...; herausgegeben von Helmuth Stoecker unter Mitwirkung von Jolanda Ballhaus [and others]. Berlin, 1977. pp. 375. *bibliogs.*

— Economic conditions.

O'CONNOR (ANTHONY MICHAEL) The geography of tropical African development: a study of spatial patterns of economic change since independence. 2nd ed. Oxford, 1978. pp. 229. *bibliogs.*

— Economic policy.

ROTHCHILD (DONALD SYLVESTER) and CURRY (ROBERT L.) Scarcity, choice, and public policy in middle Africa. Berkeley, [1978]. pp. 357.

— Foreign economic relations — Europe.

PROBLEMES de l'enseignement supérieur et de développement en Afrique centrale: recueil d'études en l'honneur de Guy Malengreau; [edited by Roman Iakemchuk]. [Paris, 1975]. pp. 227.

— Foreign relations.

LEGUM (COLIN) Southern Africa: the year of the whirlwind. New York, 1977. pp. 72.

— — United States.

COHEN (BARRY) The black and white minstrel show: Carter, Young and Africa. Nottingham, 1977. pp. 21. *(Spokesman, The. Pamphlets. No. 58)*

— Industries.

EDIAFRIC-SERVICE. Les projets industriels des pays d'Afrique noire. Paris, [1973]. pp. 252. *(Bulletin de l'Afrique Noire. Numéro Spécial)*

DIOP (CHEIKH ANTA) Les fondements économiques et culturels d'un état fédéral d'Afrique Noire. Paris, [1974]. pp. 126.

— Nationalism.

LEGUM (COLIN) Southern Africa: the year of the whirlwind. New York, 1977. pp. 72.

SYLLA (LANCINE) Tribalisme et parti unique en Afrique noire: esquisse d'une théorie générale de l'intégration nationale. [Paris, 1977]. pp. 392.

— Politics and government.

CALLINICOS (ALEX) and ROGERS (JOHN) Writer on Africa. Southern Africa after Soweto. London, 1977. pp. 229. *bibliog.*

LEGUM (COLIN) Southern Africa: the year of the whirlwind. New York, 1977. pp. 72.

MOORHOUSE (FRED) Politics, nonviolence and social justice: an African perspective. New Malden, [1977]. pp. 20. *(Fellowship of Reconciliation. Alex Wood Memorial Lectures. 1977)*

SOUTHERN AFRICA SOLIDARITY COMPAIGN. What's at stake?: Southern Africa. London, [1977?]. pp. 22.

SYLLA (LANCINE) Tribalisme et parti unique en Afrique noire: esquisse d'une théorie générale de l'intégration nationale. [Paris, 1977]. pp. 392.

VAN RENSBURG (ARRIE P.J.) The tangled web: leadership and change in Southern Africa. Cape Town, 1977. pp. 225. *bibliog.*

ROTHCHILD (DONALD SYLVESTER) and CURRY (ROBERT L.) Scarcity, choice, and public policy in middle Africa. Berkeley, [1978]. pp. 357.

— Race question.

CALLINICOS (ALEX) and ROGERS (JOHN) Writer on Africa. Southern Africa after Soweto. London, 1977. pp. 229. *bibliog.*

AFRICA, WEST

— Commerce — United Kingdom.

DAVIES (PETER N.) Sir Alfred Jones: shipping entrepreneur par excellence. London, [1978]. pp. 162. *bibliog.*

— Economic conditions.

AFANA (OSENDE) L'économie de l'Ouest africain: perspectives de développement. 2nd ed. Paris, 1977. pp. 209. *bibliog.*

— History.

ISICHEI (ELIZABETH ALLO) History of West Africa since 1800. London, 1977. pp. 380. *bibliog.*

— Politics and government.

WEST African states: failure and promise: a study in comparative politics; edited by John Dunn. Cambridge, 1978. pp. 259. *(Cambridge. University. African Studies Centre. African Studies Series. 23)*

— Social conditions.

AZARYA (VICTOR) Aristocrats facing change: the Fulbe in Guinea, Nigeria, and Cameroon. Chicago, [1978]. pp. 293. *bibliog.*

GUGLER (JOSEF) and FLANAGAN (WILLIAM G.) Urbanization and social change in West Africa. Cambridge, 1978. pp. 235. *bibliog.*

AFRICAN DEVELOPMENT BANK.

AMEGAVIE (YEWOU CHARLES) La Banque Africaine de Développement. Paris, [1977]. pp. 368. *bibliog.*

AFRICAN METHODIST EPISCOPAL CHURCH IN ZAMBIA.

JOHNSON (WALTON R.) Worship and freedom: a black American church in Zambia. London, [1977]. pp. 152. *bibliog.*

AFRICAN STUDIES.

GUTKIND (PETER C.W.) and WATERMAN (PETER) eds. African social studies: a radical reader. London, 1977. pp. 481. *bibliog.*

AFRICANS IN FRANCE.

N'DONGO (SALLY) "Coopération" et néo-colonialisme. Paris, 1976. pp. 199.

AFRICANS IN THE UNITED KINGDOM.

WEST African families in Britain: a meeting of two cultures; edited by June Ellis. London, [1978]. pp. 142. *bibliog.*

AFRO-AMERICANS.

AFRO-AMERICAN COLLEGE GRADUATES.

FREEMAN (RICHARD BARRY) Black elite: the new market for highly educated black Americans. New York, [1976]. pp. 246. *bibliog. A report prepared for the Carnegie Commission on Higher Education.*

AFRO-AMERICAN CRIMINALS.

BLACKS and criminal justice; edited by Charles E. Owens [and] Jimmy Bell. Lexington, Mass., [1977]. pp. 151. *bibliogs. Based on two conferences held in 1974 and 1975 by the University of Alabama, Department of Psychology, Center for Correctional Psychology.*

AFRO-AMERICAN FAMILIES.

GORDON (CHAD) Looking ahead: self-conceptions, race and family as determinants of adolescent orientation to achievement. Washington, D.C., [197-]. pp. 120. *bibliog. (American Sociological Association. Arnold and Caroline Rose Monograph Series in Sociology)*

GUTMAN (HERBERT GEORGE) The black family in slavery and freedom, 1750-1925. New York, [1976]. pp. 664.

SCANZONI (JOHN H.) The black family in modern society: patterns of stability and security. 2nd ed. Chicago, 1977. pp. 365.

MARTIN (ELMER P.) and MARTIN (JOANNE MITCHELL) The black extended family. Chicago, [1978]. pp. 129. *bibliog.*

AFRO-AMERICAN SOCIOLOGISTS.

— Bibliography.

CALIFORNIA UNIVERSITY. Center for Black Studies. (Bibliography of black sociologists; [compiled by] Gerald McWorter [and others]). Santa Barbara, [1977]. pp. 89.

AFRO-AMERICAN STUDIES.

MORRIS (SAM) The case and the course: a treatise on black studies. London, [1973]. pp. 37. *bibliog.*

AFRO-AMERICANS.

In previous volumes of the Bibliography similar material has been entered under NEGROES.

MYRDAL (GUNNAR) Race and class in a welfare state: introductory lecture to a symposium in a series entitled The national purpose reconsidered, 1776-1976 at Columbia University, October 28, 1976. 1976. pp. 57. *Unpublished: photocopy of typescript.*

GAITHER (GERALD H.) Blacks and the Populist revolt: ballots and bigotry in the "new south". University, Ala., [1977]. pp. 251. *bibliog.*

RABINOWITZ (HOWARD N.) Race relations in the urban south, 1865-1890. New York, 1978. pp. 441. *bibliog.*

— Bibliography.

CALIFORNIA UNIVERSITY. Center for Black Studies. (Bibliography of black sociologists; [compiled by] Gerald McWorter [and others]). Santa Barbara, [1977]. pp. 89.

HELMREICH (WILLIAM B.) compiler. Afro-Americans and Africa: black nationalism at the crossroads. Westport, Conn., 1977. pp. 74. *(African Bibliographic Center. Special Bibliographic Series. New Series. No. 3)*

— Civil rights.

WILLIAMS (ROBERT F.) Negroes with guns; edited by Marc Schleifer. Chicago, [1973]. pp. 128. *Originally published in 1962; reprinted 1973 with a new introduction.*

CAMEJO (PETER) Who killed Jim Crow?: the story of the civil rights movement and its lessons for today. New York, [1975]. pp. 29.

AFRO-AMERICANS. (Cont.)

SCOTT (JOSEPH WALTER) The black revolts: racial stratification in the U.S.A.: the politics of estate, caste, and class in the American society. Cambridge, Mass., [1976]. pp. 182. *bibliog.*

BLAIR (THOMAS LUCIEN VINCENT) Retreat to the ghetto: the end of a dream? New York, 1977. pp. 263. *bibliog.*

GAVINS (RAYMOND) The perils and prospects of southern black leadership: Gordon Blaine Hancock, 1884-1970. Durham, N.C., 1977. pp. 221. *bibliog.*

PIVEN (FRANCES FOX) and CLOWARD (RICHARD A.) Poor people's movements: why they succeed, how they fail. New York, [1977]. pp. 381. *bibliogs.*

— **Economic conditions.**

FREEMAN (RICHARD BARRY) Black elite: the new market for highly educated black Americans. New York, [1976]. pp. 246. *bibliog. A report prepared for the Carnegie Commission on Higher Education.*

COX (OLIVER CROMWELL) Race relations: elements and social dynamics. Detroit, 1976. pp. 337. *bibliog.*

RANSOM (ROGER L.) and SUTCH (RICHARD) One kind of freedom: the economic consequences of emancipation. Cambridge, 1977. pp. 409. *bibliog.*

WILSON (WILLIAM JULIUS) The declining significance of race: blacks and changing American institutions. Chicago, 1978. pp. 204. *bibliog.*

— **Education.**

SPIVEY (DONALD) Schooling for the new slavery: black industrial education, 1868- 1915. Westport, 1978. pp. 162. *bibliog.*

— **Employment.**

FREEMAN (RICHARD BARRY) Black elite: the new market for highly educated black Americans. New York, [1976]. pp. 246. *bibliog. A report prepared for the Carnegie Commission on Higher Education.*

— **History.**

GUTMAN (HERBERT GEORGE) The black family in slavery and freedom, 1750-1925. New York, [1976]. pp. 664.

PAINTER (NELL IRVIN) Exodusters: black migration to Kansas after Reconstruction. New York, [1976]. pp. 288. *bibliog.*

— **Housing.**

PHILPOTT (THOMAS LEE) The slum and the ghetto: neighborhood deterioration and middle- class reform, Chicago, 1880-1930. New York, 1978. pp. 428.

— **Politics and suffrage.**

SCOTT (JOSEPH WALTER) The black revolts: racial stratification in the U.S.A.: the politics of estate, caste, and class in the American society. Cambridge, Mass., [1976]. pp. 182. *bibliog.*

FONER (PHILIP SHELDON) American socialism and black Americans: from the age of Jackson to World War II. Westport, Conn., 1977. pp. 462. *bibliog.*

HOLT (THOMAS) Black over white: negro political leadership in South Carolina during reconstruction. Urbana, [1977]. pp. 269. *bibliog.*

NELSON (WILLIAM E.) of Ohio State University and MERANTO (PHILIP J.) Electing black mayors: political action in the black community. Columbus, Ohio, [1977]. pp. 403.

— **Social conditions.**

STAPLES (ROBERT) Introduction to black sociology. New York, [1976]. pp. 338. *bibliogs.*

CONNOLLY (HAROLD X.) A ghetto grows in Brooklyn. New York, 1977. pp. 248.

COX (OLIVER CROMWELL) Race relations: elements and social dynamics. Detroit, 1976. pp. 337. *bibliog.*

SCANZONI (JOHN H.) The black family in modern society: patterns of stability and security. 2nd ed. Chicago, 1977. pp. 365.

BUTTON (JAMES W.) Black violence: political impact of the 1960s riots. Princeton, [1978]. pp. 248. *bibliog.*

WILSON (WILLIAM JULIUS) The declining significance of race: blacks and changing American institutions. Chicago, 1978. pp. 204. *bibliog.*

— **Georgia.**

DITTMER (JOHN) Black Georgia in the progressive era, 1900-1920. Urbana, [1977]. pp. 239. *bibliog.*

— **Kansas — History.**

PAINTER (NELL IRVIN) Exodusters: black migration to Kansas after Reconstruction. New York, [1976]. pp. 288. *bibliog.*

AFRO-ASIAN-LATIN AMERICAN PEOPLES' SOLIDARITY CONFERENCE, HAVANA, 1966

AFRO-ASIAN-LATIN AMERICAN PEOPLES' SOLIDARITY CONFERENCE, HAVANA, 1966. Première Conférence de Solidarité des Peuples d'Afrique, d'Asie, d'Amérique Latine: documents. Paris, [1966?]. fo. 27.

AFRO-ASIAN PEOPLES' SOLIDARITY ORGANIZATION.

AFRO-ASIAN PEOPLES' SOLIDARITY ORGANIZATION. Presidium. Meeting, Aden, 1976. The third meeting of the A.A.P.S.O. presidium, etc. Cairo, 1976. pp. 33.

AGE (PSYCHOLOGY).

AGING into the 21st century: middle-ages today; edited by Lissy F. Jarvik; Helene Kratz, assistant editor. New York, [1978]. pp. 214. *bibliogs.*

RAYNER (ERIC) Human development: an introduction to the psychodynamics of growth, maturity and ageing. 2nd ed. London, 1978. pp. 208. *bibliogs.* (*National Institute for Social Work Training. National Institute for Social Work Training Series. No. 22*)

AGE AND EMPLOYMENT

— **Canada — Ontario.**

ONTARIO. Statutes, etc. 1966-68. The Age Discrimination Act, 1966...as amended by 1968, c.2: (office consolidation). Toronto, 1968. pp. (7).

— **Israel.**

HANDELMAN (DON) Work and play among the aged: interaction, replication and emergence in a Jerusalem setting. Amsterdam, 1977. pp. 193. *bibliog.*

— **New Zealand.**

NEW ZEALAND. Department of Labour. Research and Planning Division. 1977. The employment position of older workers in New Zealand. [Wellington], 1977. pp. 110. *bibliog.*

— **United States.**

SARASON (SEYMOUR BERNARD) Work, aging, and social change: professionals and the one life-one career imperative;...with a chapter, The Santa Fe experience; by David Krantz. New York, [1977]. pp. 298. *bibliog.*

SHEPPARD (HAROLD L.) and RIX (SARA E.) The graying of working America: the coming crisis in retirement- age policy. New York, [1977]. pp. 175.

AGE GROUPS.

STEWART (FRANK HENDERSON) Fundamentals of age-group systems. Oxford, [1977]. pp. 381. *bibliog.*

AGENCY (LAW)

— **Germany.**

STAUBACH (FRITZ) The German law of agency and distributorship agreements. London, 1977. pp. 267.

— **Italy.**

LA VILLA (G.) and CARTELLA (M.) The Italian law of agency and distributorship agreements. London, 1977. pp. 217.

AGGRESSION (INTERNATIONAL LAW).

STONE (JULIUS) Conflict through consensus: United Nations approaches to aggression. Baltimore, 1977. pp. 234.

AGGRESSIVENESS (PSYCHOLOGY).

LEARNING non-aggression: the experience of non-literate societies; edited by Ashley Montagu. New York, 1978. pp. 235. *bibliogs.*

MARSH (PETER) Aggro: the illusion of violence. London, 1978. pp. 165. *bibliog.*

AGING.

AGING into the 21st century: middle-ages today; edited by Lissy F. Jarvik; Helene Kratz, assistant editor. New York, [1978]. pp. 214. *bibliogs.*

BURNET (Sir MACFARLANE) Endurance of life: the implications of genetics for human life. Cambridge, 1978. pp. 230.

The SOCIAL challenge of ageing; edited by David Hobman. London, [1978]. pp. 286. *bibliogs.*

AGRICULTURAL ADMINISTRATION

— **Asia.**

GABLE (RICHARD W.) and SPRINGER (J. FRED) Administering agricultural development in Asia: a comparative analysis of four national programs. Boulder, Colo., 1976. pp. 398. *bibliog.*

AGRICULTURAL ASSISTANCE.

FAR NEWSBULLETIN: a m. review pd. by the Foreign Agricultural Relations Department, Ministry of Agriculture...Egypt. m., current issues only. Cairo.

AGRICULTURAL COLONIES

— **Paraguay.**

FOGEL (RAMON) Analisis de una pequeña comunidad rural: estudio de la Colonia Pirareta. Asunción, 1967. pp. 39.

— **Peru.**

JUELICH (VOLKER) Colonizacion como complemento de la reforma agraria en la selva peruana: el valle de Huallaga Central. Santiago de Chile, 1974. pp. 170. (*Instituto Latinoamericano de Investigaciones Sociales. Estudios y Documentos. 30*)

AGRICULTURAL CREDIT.

INTERNATIONAL BANK FOR RECONSTRUCTION AND DEVELOPMENT. Sector Policy Papers. Agricultural credit. [Washington], 1975. pp. 85.

— **Ethiopia.**

AGRICULTURAL AND INDUSTRIAL DEVELOPMENT BANK S.C. [ETHIOPIA]. Annual report. a., 1973/74(4th)- Addis Ababa. *[in English and Amharic]*

— **European Economic Community countries.**

SMITH (LOUIS P.F.) Comparison of certain finance costs in agriculture: Ireland and European Economic Community, 1961. Dublin, 1965. pp. 78.

— **India.**

GHOSH (BIDHU BHUSAN) Problems of agricultural credit in India. Calcutta, [1937]. pp. 139.

— **Ireland (Republic).**

SMITH (LOUIS P.F.) Comparison of certain finance costs in agriculture: Ireland and European Economic Community, 1961. Dublin, 1965. pp. 78.

— **Korea.**

KIM (IL-SUNG) On rural financial operations: (excerpts of the great leader comrade Kim Il Sung's teachings on rural financial operations). Pyongyang, 1977. pp. 38.

— **United Kingdom — Ireland, Northern.**

IRELAND, NORTHERN. Department of Agriculture. Accounts of the Agricultural Loans Fund. a., 1971/2- Belfast. *1945/6-1970/71 included in IRELAND, NORTHERN. Parliament. House of Commons. [Papers].*

AGRICULTURAL GEOGRAPHY.

MORGAN (WILLIAM BASIL) Agriculture in the Third World: a spatial analysis. Boulder, 1978. pp. 290. *bibliog.*

AGRICULTURAL INDUSTRIES

— **Russia.**

FESHCHENKO (PETRO STEPANOVYCH) Mizhvyrobnychi ekonomichni zv"iazky v sil's'komu hospodarstvi ta ïkh efektyvnist'. Kyïv, 1973. pp. 167.

PROKHORENKO (IVAN DENISOVICH) and VOLKOV (PETR DENISOVICH) Industrializatsiia sotsialisticheskogo sel'skogo khoziaistva na sovremennom etape. Minsk, 1974. pp. 175.

AGRICULTURAL INNOVATIONS.

RADICAL agriculture; edited by Richard Merrill. New York, 1976. pp. 459. *bibliogs.*

— **India — Bihar.**

The KOSI symposium: the rural problem in north-east Bihar: analysis, policy and planning in the Kosi area; by Stephen D. Biggs [and others]; edited by J.L. Joy and Elizabeth Everitt. [Brighton], 1976. pp. 277. *bibliog.*

— **Peru.**

COLLIN-DELAVAUD (CLAUDE) Consecuencias de la modernizacion de la agricultura en las haciendas de la costa norte del Peru. Lima, 1967. pp. 29. *(Instituto de Estudios Peruanos. Mesas Redondas y Conferencias. No. 10)*

AGRICULTURAL LABOURERS

— **America, Latin.**

LAND and labour in Latin America: essays on the development of agrarian capitalism in the nineteenth and twentieth centuries; edited by Kenneth Duncan and Ian Rutledge, with the collaboration of Colin Harding. Cambridge, 1977. pp. 535. *Based on papers of a symposium held in 1972 at Cambridge under the joint auspices of Cambridge University Centre of Latin American Studies and London University Institute of Latin American Studies.*

— **Canada.**

DAWSON (DONALD A.) and FRESHWATER (DAVID) Hired farm labour in Canada. [Ottawa, Food Prices Review Board, 1975]. pp. 30, 32. *bibliog. In English and French.*

— — **Bibliography.**

ARMSTRONG (DOUGLAS) and KRESTENSEN (KRISTEEN) compilers. Agricultural labour in Canada and the United States: a bibliography. [Toronto], Ontario Ministry of Labour Research Library, 1973. fo. 40.

— **Italy.**

MAGNO (MICHELE) La Capitanata dalla pastorizia al capitalismo agrario, 1400-1900. [Roma, 1975]. pp. 237. *bibliog.*

STEFANELLI (RENZO) Lotte agrarie e modello di sviluppo, 1947-1967. [Bari, 1975]. pp. 385.

FERRARESI (LUCIANO) and others. Riconversione professionale ed esodo programmato nel mondo agricolo. Milano, [1976]. pp. 181. *bibliog.*

TALAMO (MANLIO) and DE MARCO (CLARA) Lotte agrarie nel mezzogiorno, 1943-1944; prefazione di Enrico Pugliese. [Milano, 1976]. pp. 147.

— — **Calabria — History.**

ALCARO (MARIO) and PAPARAZZO (AMELIA) Lotte contadine in Calabria, 1943-1950. [Cosenza, 1976]. pp. 202.

— **Peru.**

COTLER (JULIO) and PORTOCARRERO (FELIPE) Organizaciones campesinas en el Peru. Lima, 1967. pp. 33. *(Instituto de Estudios Peruanos. Los Movimientos Campesinos en el Peru desde Fines del Siglo XVIII hasta nuestros Dias. No. 1)*

— **Poland.**

GRONIOWSKI (KRZYSZTOF) Robotnicy rolni w Królestwie Polskim, 1871-1914. Warszawa, 1977. pp. 275.

— **South Africa.**

FARM labour in South Africa; (edited by Francis Wilson [and others]). Cape Town, [1977]. pp. 226. *bibliog. Some of the papers presented at a conference convened by the Southern Africa Labour and Development Research Unit in 1976.*

— **United Kingdom.**

PLAN for the relief of the agricultural poor, with a view to diminish the poor-rates, and give permanent employment to the labourer, etc. Wycombe, printed by M.C. Morris, 1823. pp. 36.

BLACKER (WILLIAM) An essay on the best mode of improving the condition of the labouring classes of Ireland. London, R. Groombridge, 1846. pp. 56. *Revised version of an essay which won the Gold Medal of the Royal Agricultural Improvement Society of Ireland.*

LABOURING life on the Lincolnshire Wolds: a study of Binbrook in the mid-nineteenth century; edited by R. J. Olney. Sleaford, 1975. pp. 39. *bibliog. (Society for Lincolnshire History and Archaeology. Occasional Papers in Lincolnshire History and Archaeology. No. 2)*

TRINDER (CHRIS) and WINYARD (STEVE) A new deal for farmworkers: the case for an independent inquiry into the pay of farmworkers. London, 1975. fo. 7. *(Low Pay Unit. Low Pay Papers. No. 5)*

HUMPHRIES (BARBARA) The Tolpuddle martyrs: victims of the rich man's law. London, [1976]. pp. 8.

— **United States — Bibliography.**

ARMSTRONG (DOUGLAS) and KRESTENSEN (KRISTEEN) compilers. Agricultural labour in Canada and the United States: a bibliography. [Toronto], Ontario Ministry of Labour Research Library, 1973. fo. 40.

AGRICULTURAL LAWS AND LEGISLATION

— **America, Latin.**

MENDIETA Y NUÑEZ (LUCIO) Introduccion al estudio del derecho agrario. Mexico, 1975. pp. 251. *Reprint of second edition published in 1966.*

— **Italy.**

TAVOLA ROTONDA ITALO-SOVIETICA, 1A, FIRENZE, 1972. Esperienze e prospettive del diritto agrario in Italia e nell'U. R.S.S. Milano, 1975. pp. 193. *(Istituto di Diritto Agrario Internazionale e Comparato. Pubblicazioni. Nuova Serie. N.1)*

— **Russia.**

TAVOLA ROTONDA ITALO-SOVIETICA, 1A, FIRENZE, 1972. Esperienze e prospettive del diritto agrario in Italia e nell'U. R.S.S. Milano, 1975. pp. 193. *(Istituto di Diritto Agrario Internazionale e Comparato. Pubblicazioni. Nuova Serie. N.1)*

AGRICULTURAL MACHINERY

— **Sweden.**

ODENSTAD (GÖRAN) Jordbrukarnas utgifter för lejda maskinarbeten. Stockholm, 1976. pp. 41. *(Jordbrukets Utredningsinstitut. Meddelanden. 1976. Nr. 3) With English summary.*

HOLMSTRÖM (SVEN J.R.) Förskjutningen från manuellt arbete till maskinarbete i jordbruket. Stockholm, [1977]. pp. 73. *(Jordbrukets Utredningsinstitut. Meddelanden. 1976. Nr. 4) With English summary.*

AGRICULTURAL PRICE SUPPORTS

— **Canada — New Brunswick.**

SORFLATEN (ALLAN) Alternative approaches to New Brunswick farm price assurance and income stabilization: the second part of a two-part study; prepared for the New Brunswick Agricultural Resources Study. Bridgetown, N.S., 1976. fo. 107.

— **European Economic Community countries.**

COMMON prices and Europe's farm policy; by Theodor Heidhues [and others]. London, 1978. pp. 75. *bibliog. (Trade Policy Research Centre. Thames Essays. No. 14)*

AGRICULTURAL PRICES

— **European Economic Community countries.**

EUROPEAN COMMUNITIES. Statistical Office. EC-index of producer prices of agricultural products. a., 1968/75(1st)- Luxembourg. *[in Community languages] 1968/1975 figures included in Methodology of the EC-index of producer prices of agricultural products.*

U.K. Ministry of Agriculture, Fisheries and Food. Economics Division. EEC and common U.K. transition prices: agricultural commodities. a., 1968-69/1974-75- London.

EUROPEAN COMMUNITIES. Statistical Office. Agricultural prices: rapid information. irreg., current issues only. Luxembourg. *[in Community languages]*

— **Greece.**

GREECE. Ethnike Statistike Hyperesia. 1975. Agricultural price indices: 1966 [equals] 100. Athens, 1975. pp. 20. *([Publications]. O. Distribution and Prices. 1) In English and Greek.*

— **United Kingdom.**

U.K. Ministry of Agriculture, Fisheries and Food. Economics Division. EEC and common U.K. transition prices: agricultural commodities. a., 1968-69/1974-75- London.

AGRICULTURAL SOCIETIES

— **Austria.**

BRUCKMUELLER (ERNST) Landwirtschaftliche Organisationen und gesellschaftliche Modernisierung: Vereine, Genossenschaften und politischen Mobilisierung der Landwirtschaft Österreichs vom Vormärz bis 1914. Salzburg, [1977]. pp. 274. *(Arbeitsgemeinschaft für Historische Sozialkunde. Geschichte und Sozialkunde. Band I)*

— **Canada — New Brunswick.**

SORFLATEN (ALLAN) Farm organization policy study and recommended development plan; prepared for the New Brunswick Agricultural Resources Study. Bridgetown, N.S., 1977. fo. 122.

AGRICULTURAL WAGES

AGRICULTURAL WAGES

— Algeria.

BOURRINET (JACQUES) Salaires et revenus des travailleurs agricoles en Tunisie et en Algérie. Genève, Bureau International du Travail, 1975. pp. 144. *bibliog.*

— European Economic Community countries.

EUROPEAN COMMUNITIES. Statistical Office. Earnings in agriculture. a., 1975- Luxembourg. *[in Community languages].* 1974 figures included in EUROPEAN COMMUNITIES. Statistical Office. Social statistics, 1975, no. 5.

— Tunisia.

BOURRINET (JACQUES) Salaires et revenus des travailleurs agricoles en Tunisie et en Algérie. Genève, Bureau International du Travail, 1975. pp. 144. *bibliog.*

— United Kingdom.

U.K. Ministry of Agriculture, Fisheries and Food. Report on wages in agriculture. a., 1976- London. *Supersedes in part U.K. Ministry of Agriculture, Fisheries and Food. Report on safety, health, welfare and wages in agriculture.*

AGRICULTURE.

BOERMA (ADDEKE H.) Address to the eighteenth general conference of the International Federation of Agricultural Producers on the occasion of its twenty-fifth anniversary. Paris, 1971. pp. 22.

VRIES (EGBERT DE) and RICHTER-ALTSCHAFFER (J.H.) World food crisis and agricultural trade problems. Beverly Hills, [1974]. pp. 108. *bibliog. (Georgetown University. Center for Strategic and International Studies. Washington Papers. vol. 2/17)*

CONSERVATION and agriculture; edited by Joan Davidson and Richard Lloyd. Chichester, [1977]. pp. 252.

— Economic aspects.

ACCADEMIA NAZIONALE DEI LINCEI. Atti dei Convegni Lincei. 28. Convegno: agricoltura e industria e i loro rapporti nell'economia contemporanea. Roma, 12-13 aprile 1976. Roma, 1977. pp. 115.

GARREAU (GERARD) L'agrobusiness. [Paris, 1977]. 302.

NEW ZEALAND. Ministry of Agriculture and Fisheries. Economics Division. 1977. Cost-benefit procedures in New Zealand agriculture. [Wellington], 1977. pp. 111. *bibliogs.*

O'HAGAN (JAMES PATRICK) ed. Growth and adjustment in national agricultures: four case studies and an overview;...published by arrangement with the Food and Agriculture Organization of the United Nations. London, 1978. pp. 242.

— Energy consumption.

AGRICULTURE and energy; edited by William Lockeretz. New York, 1977. pp. 750. *bibliogs. Proceedings of a conference held at Washington University, St. Louis, Missouri, in 1976.*

— History.

HELLING (GERTRUD) Nahrungsmittel: Produktion und Weltaussenhandel seit Anfang des 19. Jahrhunderts. Berlin, 1977. pp. 383. *bibliog.*

NIALL (IAN) To speed the plough: mechanisation comes to the farm. London, 1977. pp. 231.

— Statistics.

PLANTATION CROPS: a review of production, trade, consumption and prices relating to coffee, cocoa, tea, sugar, spices, tobacco and rubber; compiled in the Commodities Division of the Commonwealth Secretariat. a., 1936- ; susp. pbln. 1939-1947. London.

SNEDECOR (GEORGE WADDEL) and COCHRAN (WILLIAM GEMMELL) Statistical methods. 6th ed. Ames, Iowa, 1967 reprinted 1976. pp. 593.

FAO MONTHLY BULLETIN OF STATISTICS; [pd. by] Food and Agriculture Organization. m., Ja 1978 (v. 1, no. 1)- Rome. *[in English, French and Spanish]*

— Africa, West.

FOOD crops of the lowland tropics; edited by C.L.A. Leakey and J.B. Wills. Oxford, 1977. pp. 345. *bibliogs. Based on a series of seminars held at the International Institute of Tropical Agriculture in Ibadan.*

— America, Latin.

FEDER (ERNEST) Dr., of the University of Nebraska, ed. La lucha de clases en el campo: analisis estructural de la economia agricola latinoamericana. Mexico, 1975. pp. 520. *bibliogs. (Fondo de Cultura Economica. Lecturas. 14)*

INTERNATIONAL CONGRESS OF AMERICANISTS. 42nd Congress. Actes du XLIIe Congrès International des Américanistes: Congrès du Centenaire, Paris, 2-9 septembre 1976. volume II. Paris, 1977. pp. 623. *bibliogs.*

— Australia.

AUSTRALIA. Bureau of Agricultural Economics. 1975. Rural industry in Australia. 2nd ed. Canberra, 1975. pp. 113. *bibliogs.*

AUSTRALIA. Bureau of Agricultural Economics. 1976. Rural income fluctuations: submission to the Industries Assistance Commission inquiry. Canberra, 1976. pp. 30. *(Occasional Papers. No. 39)*

— — Accounting.

AUSTRALIA. Commonwealth Bureau of Census and Statistics. Agricultural sector: financial statistics. a., 1974/75(1st)- Canberra.

— Belize.

AGRICULTURAL and economic studies in Belize; [by] J.R. Dunsmore [and others]. Tolworth, 1977. pp. 209. *bibliog. (U.K. Ministry of Overseas Development. Land Resources Division. Supplementary Reports. 16)*

— Brazil.

DE CASTRO ANDRADE (REGIS) On the relationship between the subsistence sector and the market economy in the Parnaiba Valley (Brazil). Glasgow, 1976. pp. 24. *(Glasgow. University. Institute of Latin American Studies. Occasional Papers. No.22)*

— — Economic aspects.

HALL (ANTHONY L.) Drought and irrigation in north-east Brazil. Cambridge, 1978. pp. 152. *bibliog.*

— Canada — Accounting.

CANADA. Statistics Canada. Farm cash receipts. a., 1976- Ottawa. *[in English and French]*

— — Alberta — Costs.

PORTER (K.D.) and McBAIN (B.J.) Final report: oil seeds and wheat, 1961-1963: a cost of production study on 104 farms: central Alberta, Peace River, southern Alberta. [Edmonton], Department of Agriculture, 1964. pp. 54,18.

— — Manitoba.

RYAN (JOHN) Professor of Geography, University of Winnipeg. The agricultural economy of Manitoba Hutterite colonies. Toronto, 1977. pp. 305. *bibliog. (Carleton University. Institute of Canadian Studies. Carleton Library. No. 101)*

— — Nova Scotia.

NOVA SCOTIA. Department of Agriculture and Marketing. Annual report. a., 1971/72- Halifax.

— — — Statistics.

NOVA SCOTIA. Department of Agriculture and Marketing. Agricultural statistics. a., 1972(v.8)- Halifax.

— — Quebec.

LESSARD (DIANE) L'agriculture et le capitalisme au Québec. [Montréal, 1976]. pp. 182. *bibliog.*

— — — History.

CHATILLON (COLETTE) L'histoire de l'agriculture au Québec. [Montréal, 1976]. pp. 127. *bibliog.*

— Communist countries.

SHMELEV (GELII IVANOVICH) and STARODUBROVSKAIA (VERA NIKOLAEVNA) Sotsial'no-ekonomicheskie problemy razvitiia sel'skogo khoziaistva evropeiskikh sotsialisticheskikh stran. Moskva, 1977. pp. 224.

— Europe — History.

KRIEDTE (PETER) and others. Industrialisierung vor der Industrialisierung: gewerbliche Warenproduktion auf dem Land in der Formationsperiode des Kapitalismus;...mit Beiträgen von Herbert Kisch und Franklin F. Mendels. Göttingen, 1977. pp. 393. *(Max-Planck-Institut für Geschichte. Veröffentlichungen. 53)*

— European Economic Community countries.

SPROTT (D.C.) and DICKIE (I.C.) The Common Agricultural Policy of the E.E.C. - a review of recent developments. Canberra, 1976. pp. 38. *(Australia. Bureau of Agricultural Economics. Occasional Papers. No. 41)*

— Finland — Accounting.

FINLAND. Tilastokeskus. Maatilatalous: maatilatalouden yritys- ja tulotilasto, etc. a., 1973(1st)- Helsinki. *[in Finnish and Swedish with summary and table heading in English]*

— — History.

ÅBO. Akademi. Acta Academiae Aboensis. Humaniora. 54. 4. Borgarna som lantbrukare i Finland under 1700-talet; av Oscar Nikula. Åbo, 1977. pp. 24. *bibliog.*

— France.

VIAU (PIERRE) L'essentiel sur l'agriculture française. Paris, [1978]. pp. 232. *bibliog.*

MEUVRET (JEAN) Le problème des subsistances à l'époque Louis XIV: la production des céréales dans la France du XVIIe et du XVIIIe siècle. Paris, [1977]. 2 vols. *(Paris. Ecole des Hautes Etudes en Sciences Sociales. Centre de Recherches Historiques. Civilizations et Sociétés. 50)*

— — Aquitaine — Accounting.

COMPTES AGRICOLES EN AQUITAINE, LES; [pd.by] Service Régional de Statistique Agricole Aquitaine, Ministère de l'Agriculture. a., 1970/74- Bordeaux.

— Germany — Statistics.

GERMANY (BUNDESREPUBLIK). Statistisches Bundesamt. 1972- . Landwirtschaftszählung 1971. Wiesbaden, 1972 in progress. *(Land- und Forstwirtschaft, Fischerei)*

GERMANY (BUNDESREPUBLIK). Statistisches Bundesamt. Pflanzliche Erzeugung. a., 1976- Wiesbaden. *(Land- und Forstwirtschaft, Fischerei. Reihe 3) Supersedes GERMANY (BUNDESREPUBLIK). Statistisches Bundesamt. Bodennutzung und Ernte and GERMANY (BUNDESREPUBLIK). Statistisches Bundesamt. Gartenbau und Weinbau.*

— Ghana — Bibliography.

VOLTA RIVER AUTHORITY. Library. Agricultural development on the Accra-Ho-Keta plains: [a bibliography]. Accra, 1972. pp. 12. *(Lists. No. 8)*

— Greece — History.

VERGOPOULOS (KOSTAS) Le capitalisme difforme et la nouvelle question agraire: l'exemple de la Grèce moderne. Paris, 1977. pp. 307. *bibliog.*

AGRICULTURE.

— India.

BURNS (WILLIAM) Technological possibilities of agricultural development in India: a note. Lahore, Superintendent of Government Printing, 1944. 1 vol. (various pagings).

INDIA. Ministry of Agriculture. Directorate of Economics and Statistics. 1971. Indian agricultural atlas. 3rd ed. [New Delhi, 1971]. pp. 76. *Index map in end pocket.*

BROEHL (WAYNE G.) The village entrepreneur: change agents in India's rural development. Cambridge, Mass., 1978. pp. 228.

— — Taxation.

KRISHNAN (S.N.) Agricultural taxation and states' resources. New Delhi, 1972. fo. 41. *(United States. Agency for International Development. USAID-New Delhi. Economic Affairs Division. Staff Papers)*

— — Assam.

GOSWAMI (PRABHAS CHANDRA) and BORA (C.K.) Studies in the economics of farm management in Nowgong district, Assam: combined report 1968-69 to 1970-71. [Delhi, Controller of Publications, 1977]. pp. 92.

GOSWAMI (PRABHAS CHANDRA) and BORA (C.K.) Studies in the economics of farm management in Nowgong district, Assam: report for the year 1970-71. [Delhi, Controller of Publications], 1977. pp. 283.

— — Bihar — History.

SCHWERIN (DETLEF) Graf. Von Armut zu Elend: Kolonialherrschaft und Agrarverfassung in Chota Nagpur, 1858-1908. Wiesbaden, 1977. pp. 551. *bibliog. (Heidelberg. Universität. Südasien-Institut. Beiträge zur Südasienforschung. Band 31) With English summary.*

— — Bombay.

DESAI (D.K.) Increasing income and production in Indian farming: possibilities with existing resource supplies on individual farms; application of linear programming technique. Bombay, 1963. pp. 200. *bibliog. Based on Ph.D. thesis, University of Illinois.*

— — Haryana — Accounting.

FARM ACCOUNTS IN HARYANA; [pd.by] Economic and Statistical Organisation, Haryana. a., 1965/66. Chandigarh.

— — Madras.

INDIA. Ministry of Agriculture and Irrigation. Directorate of Economics and Statistics. 1977. Studies in the economics of farm management in Coimbatore district, Tamil Nadu: report for the year 1971-72. [Delhi, Controller of Publications, 1977]. pp. 641.

RAJAGOPALAN (V.) and others. Studies in the economics of farm management in the Coimbatore district, Tamil Nadu: report for the year 1970-71. [Delhi, Controller of Publications, 1977]. pp. 422.

— — Maharashtra.

MAHARASHTRA ECONOMIC DEVELOPMENT COUNCIL. Agro-industries in Maharashtra: problems and prospects. Bombay, 1970. pp. 320.

DISKALKAR (P.D.) and PAWAR (JAGANNATHRAO R.) Studies in the economics of farm management in Ahmednagar district, Maharashtra State: combined report for the years 1969-70 to 1971-72. [Delhi, Controller of Publications, 1977]. pp. 256.

— Indonesia — Statistics.

CHANGING economy in Indonesia: a selection of statistical source material from the early 19th century up to 1940...; initiated by W.M.F. Mansvelt; re-edited and continued by P. Creutzberg. Amsterdam, 1975-77. 3 vols. (in 1). *bibliogs.*

INDONESIA. Biro Pusat Statistik. 1976. 1973 agricultural census:...number and area of crops by type of crops. Jakarta, 1976. 5 vols.(in 1). *In English and Indonesian.*

— — Sumatra — Statistics.

INDONESIA. Kantor Sensus dan Statistik Propinsi Sumatera Utara. 1974. Hasil sensus pertanian Sumatera Utara, Sept. 1973. [Medan, 1974?]. pp. 41.

— Iran.

GOLABIAN (HOSSEIN) An analysis of the underdeveloped rural and nomadic areas of Iran: a theoretical approach to the problems of social and economic development of rural and nomadic communities in Iran. Stockholm, 1977. pp. 279, 11. *(Stockholm. Tekniska Högskolan. School of Architecture. Department of Regional Planning. [Publications]. 1977. [No.] 4)*

— Iraq.

GABBAY (RONY E.) Communism and agrarian reform in Iraq. London, [1978]. pp. 240. *bibliog.*

— — Statistics.

IRAQ. Central Statistical Organization. 1973- . Results of 1971 census of agriculture. [Baghdad], 1973 in progress. *In English and Arabic.*

— Ireland (Republic).

NATIONAL ECONOMIC AND SOCIAL COUNCIL [EIRE]. Alternative growth rates in Irish agriculture; (by John A. Murphy [and others]). Dublin, Stationery Office, [1977]. pp. 182. *([Reports]. No. 34)*

— — Mathematical Models.

O'CONNOR (ROBERT) and others. A linear programming model for Irish agriculture. Dublin, 1977. pp. 156. *(Economic and Social Research Institute. Papers. No. 91)*

— Italy.

AVOLIO (GIUSEPPE) Agricoltura e sviluppo: la politica agraria del Partito Socialista dal 1973 al 1975. [Venezia, 1976]. pp. 364. *bibliog.*

BERTELÈ (UMBERTO) and BRIOSCHI (FRANCESCO) Il sistema agricolo-alimentare in Italia. Bologna, [1976]. pp. 204.

FORMICA (CARMELO) Lo spazio rurale nel Mezzogiorno: esodo, desertificazione e riorganizzazione. Napoli, [1976]. pp. 173.

ZAGARI (EUGENIO) Il problema agrario in trent'anni di meridionalismo. Napoli, [1976]. pp. 117.

— — History.

MAGNO (MICHELE) La Capitanata dalla pastorizia al capitalismo agrario, 1400-1900. [Roma, 1975]. pp. 237. *bibliog.*

STORIA dell'agricoltura italiana; [by Alvise Cornel and others]. Milano, [1976]. pp. 403. *bibliog.*

BERNARDI (ALBERTO DI) Questione agraria e protezionismo nella crisi economica di fine secolo. [Milano, 1977]. pp. 229. *bibliog.*

— — Piacenza (Province).

CONFERENZA ZONALE SULL'AGRICOLTURA DELLA VAL D'ARDA, 1972. Val d'Arda: conferenza zonale sull'agricoltura. Piacenza, 1974. pp. 88. *(Piacenza (Province). Ufficio Studi. Documenti e Notizie. 6)*

— Ivory Coast.

SAWADOGO (ABDOULAYE) L'agriculture en Côte d'Ivoire. [Paris, 1977]. pp. 367. *bibliog.*

— Malawi.

MALAWI. Lilongwe Land Development Programme. Evaluation Section. 1973. A socio-economic survey of agriculture in the Lilongwe Land Development Programme area 1971/1972. Lilongwe, 1973. 4 pts. (in 1 vol.) *(Reports. Nos. 10-13)*

MALAWI. Agro-Economic Survey. 1977. Agro-economic survey: report no. 21: Chisasa: a farm economic survey of oriental tobacco and food crop growers in the south-western part of Mzimba district, Malawi; prepared by G. Hendrix and J. Sterkenburg. Lilongwe, 1977. fo. 115.

MALAWI. Agro-Economic Survey. 1977. Agro-economic survey: report no. 23: Dowa West: a farm economic survey of dark fired tobacco growers and maize/groundnut growers in the western part of Dowa district, Malawi, prepared by I.M. Daniels. Lilongwe, 1977. fo. 63.

— Malaya.

LIM TECK GHEE Peasants and their agricultural economy in colonial Malaya, 1874- 1941. Kuala Lumpur, 1977. pp. 291. *bibliog.*

— Netherlands — History.

SLICHER VAN BATH (BERNARD HENDRIK) Mensch en land in de middeleeuwen: bijdrage tot een geschiedenis der nederzettingen in oostelijk Nederland. Arnhem, 1977. 2 vols. (in 1). *bibliog. Reprint of the first edition, Assen, 1944, with a new foreword by the author.*

— New Zealand.

NEW ZEALAND. Farm Advisory Division. 1970. Farming in Hawke's Bay; (with Statistical summary). [Hastings], 1970. 2 pts.

NEW ZEALAND. Ministry of Agriculture and Fisheries. Economics Division. 1977. Cost-benefit procedures in New Zealand agriculture. [Wellington], 1977. pp. 111. *bibliogs.*

— Pacific, The.

The SUBSISTENCE sector in the South Pacific; editor J.B. Hardaker. Armidale, 1975. pp. 210. *bibliogs. Selected papers presented at a seminar on the subsistence sector in the South Pacific, held at the University of the South Pacific, Suva, 12-23 August 1974.*

REGIONAL MEETING ON THE PRODUCTION OF ROOT CROPS, SUVA, 1975. Collected papers [of the Meeting], (24-29 October, 1975, Suva, Fiji). Noumea, South Pacific Commission, 1977. pp. 213. *(Technical Papers. No.174)*

— Paraguay.

ALVAREZ (LUIS ALBERTO) Prioridades nacionales en aspectos de produccion y productividad del sector agropecuario y forestal del Paraguay. Asuncion, 1976. fo. 142. *bibliog.*

— Poland.

KUBICA (JÓZEF) Rozmieszczenie i kierunki rozwoju produkcji rolniczej na terenie ziem górskich południowej Polski. Wrocław, 1962. pp. 80. *bibliog. (Polska Akademia Nauk. Oddział w Krakowie. Komisja Nauk Ekonomicznych. Prace. Nr. 5) With English summary.*

PRZEMIANY strukturalne w rolnictwie polskim; praca zbiorowa pod redakcją Zdzisława Grochowskiego. Warszawa, 1975. pp. 242.

JASSEM (GRA'ZYNA) Majątek smogulecki w latach 1918-1937; das Landgut Smogulec in den Jahren 1918-1937. Poznań, 1976. pp. 185. *bibliog. (Poznań. Poznańskie Towarzystwo Przyjaciół Nauk. Wydział Historii i Nauk Społecznych. Badania z Dziejów Społecznych i Gospodarczych. nr. 51) With German summary.*

POLSKA ZJEDNOCZONA PARTIA ROBOTNICZA. O dalszy rozwój rolnictwa: wybór materiałów i dokumentów, 1971-1976. Warszawa, 1976. pp. 197.

POLITYKA rolna PRL: wybrane problemy praca zbiorowa; pod redakcją Augustyna Wosia. 2nd ed. Warszawa, 1977. pp. 246. *bibliog.*

— Rhodesia.

SOUTHERN RHODESIA. Committee of Enquiry into the Economic Position of the Agricultural Industry. 1934. Report; [Max Danziger, chairman]. Salisbury, 1934. pp. 30. *(Legislative Assembly. [Sessional Papers]. 1934. C.S.R. 16)*

AGRICULTURE.(Cont.)

— Romania — History.

NEAMȚU (VASILE) La technique de la production céréalière en Valachie et en Moldavie jusqu'au XVIIIe siècle. București, 1975. pp. 270. *(Academia de Științe Sociale și Politice a Republicii Socialiste România. Bibliotheca Historica Romaniae. Studies. 52)*

CORFUS (ILIE) L'agriculture en Valachie depuis la révolution de 1848 jusqu'à la réforme de 1864. București, 1976. pp. 216. *(Academia de Științe Sociale și Politice a Republicii Socialiste România. Bibliotheca Historica Romaniae. Studies. 53)*

— Russia.

SEMIN (SERGEI IVANOVICH) and others. Razvitie sotsialisticheskikh proizvodstvennykh otnoshenii v sel'skom khoziastve. Moskva, 1977. pp. 277.

SOVIET agriculture: an assessment of its contributions to economic development; edited by Harry G. Shaffer. New York, 1977. pp. 166.

— — History.

SUSLOV (IURII PAVLOVICH) Leninskaia agrarnaia programma i bor'ba bol'shevikov Povolzh'ia za ee osushchestvlenie, mart 1917 - mart 1918 gg. Saratov, 1972. pp. 414.

HENNESSY (RICHARD) The agrarian question in Russia, 1905-1907: the inception of the Stolypin reform. Giessen, 1977. pp. 203. *bibliog. (Marburg. Universität. Arbeitsgemeinschaft für Osteuropaforschung. Marburger Abhandlungen zur Geschichte und Kultur Osteuropas. Band 16)*

— — Buryat Republic.

GALDANOV (TSYRETOR BIMBAEVICH) Ekonomicheskie problemy intensifikatsii sel'skogo khoziaistva Buriatskoi ASSR. Ulan-Ude, 1969. pp. 96.

— — Latvia — History.

KOZIN (MIKHAIL IVANOVICH) Latyshskaia derevnia v 50-70-e gody XIX veka. Riga, 1976. pp. 372.

— — Soviet North — Costs.

REZERVY sokrashcheniia zatrat v sel'skom khoziaistve Evropeiskogo Severa. Moskva, 1976. pp. 160. *(Akademiia Nauk SSSR. Problemy Sovetskoi Ekonomiki)*

— — Ural region — History.

VOPROSY agrarnoi istorii Urala. Sverdlovsk, 1975. pp. 142.

RUSAKOVA (LIDIIA MIKHAILOVNA) Sel'skoe khoziaistvo Srednego Zaural'ia na rubezhe XVIII- XIX vv.; otvetstvennyi redaktor…M.M. Gromyko. Novosibirsk, 1976. pp. 183.

— — White Russia — History.

LIPINSKII (LEONID PAVLOVICH) Stolypinskaia agrarnaia reforma v Belorussii. Minsk, 1978. pp. 223.

— Sahel.

BERG (ELLIOT J.) The economic impact of drought and inflation in the Sahel. Ann Arbor, 1976. fo. 35. *(Michigan University. Center for Research on Economic Development. Discussion Papers. No. 51)*

— Spain.

La CUESTION agraria en la España contemporanea; [by] Manuel Tuñon de Lara [and others]; (edicion a cargo de Jose Luis Garcia Delgado). Madrid, 1976. pp. 565. *Papers of the 6th Colloquium organized by the Centre de Recherches Hispaniques of the University of Pau.*

— — Accounting.

SPAIN. Ministerio de Agricultura. Secretaria General Tecnica. Las cuentas del sector agrario. irreg., 1975(no. 1)- Madrid.

— — Statistics.

SPAIN. Instituto Nacional de Estadistica. 1975. Censo agrario de España, 1972. Serie C. Resumenes nacionales. Madrid, 1975. pp. 64.

— Sudan.

SOCIETE D'ETUDES ET DE REALISATIONS ECONOMIQUES ET SOCIALES DANS L'AGRICULTURE. L'économie agricole soudanaise et ses conséquences: travaux préliminaires; tableaux de l'économie. [Paris?], 1959. fo. 202.

KISS (JUDIT) Will Sudan be an agricultural power? Budapest, 1977. pp. 50. *bibliog. (Magyar Tudományos Akadémia. Világgazdasági Kutató Intézet. Studies on Developing Countries. No. 94)*

— Sweden.

HOLMSTRÖM (SVEN J.R.) Jordbrukets möjligheter att anpassa sig till nya mönster för proteinförsörjningen. Stockholm, 1975. pp. 32. *(Jordbrukets Utredningsinstitut. Meddelanden. 1975. Nr. 4) With English summary.*

SAMBERGS (ÅKE) Producentpaneler i lantbruket: framtidsinriktade frågor till stående urval. Stockholm, 1975. pp. 59. *bibliog. (Jordbrukets Utredningsinstitut. Meddelanden. 1975. Nr. 3) With English summary.*

HOLMSTRÖM (SVEN J.R.) Förskjutningen från manuellt arbete till maskinarbete i jordbruket. Stockholm, [1977]. pp. 73. *(Jordbrukets Utredningsinstitut. Meddelanden. 1976. Nr. 4) With English summary.*

SWEDEN. Statistiska Centralbyrån, 1977. Lantbruksräkningen, 1976; Census of agriculture, 1976. Stockholm, 1977. 2 vols (in 1). *(Sveriges Officiella Statistik) In Swedish and English.*

— Switzerland — Statistics.

SWITZERLAND. Bureau Fédéral de Statistique. 1977- Eidgenössische Betriebszählung, 1975: Landwirtschaft. Bern, 1977 in progress. *(Statistiques de la Suisse. 580e fasc., etc.) In German and French.*

— Tanzania.

HALL (PETER KENNETH) African economic initiative and response in British Tanganyika. 1977 [or rather 1978]. fo.457. *bibliog.* Typescript. Ph.D. (London) thesis: unpublished. *This thesis is the property of London University and may not be removed from the Library.*

— Tunisia.

TUNIS. Ministère de l'Agriculture. 1957. Terre de Tunisie: problèmes de la mise en valeur. [Tunis, 1957?]. pp. 182. *(Bulletin du Ministère de l'Agriculture, juin 1957, no. 3)*

— Underdeveloped areas.

See UNDERDEVELOPED AREAS — Agriculture.

— United Kingdom.

ACLAND (Sir RICHARD THOMAS DYKE) and others. Common Wealth agricultural policy. London, C.W. Publishing, [1945?]. pp. 19. *(Common Wealth Popular Library. No.11)*

— — Accounting.

EXETER. University. Agricultural Economics Unit. Financial results of farming in the Exeter province, 1974/75 and 1975/76; based on an identical sample of 257 farms. Exeter, 1976. pp. 21.

MANCHESTER. University. Department of Agricultural Economics. Bulletins. No. 155. Farm management survey 1973-74 and 1974-75. Manchester, 1976. 1 pamphlet (various pagings).

— — History.

BOWEN (HARRIES COLLINS) Ancient fields: a tentative analysis of vanishing earthworks and landscapes. London, [1962?]. pp. 80. *bibliog.*

YELLING (J. A.) Common field and enclosure in England, 1450-1850. London, 1977. pp. 255. *bibliog.*

— — Ireland, Northern — Accounting.

FARM INCOMES AND INVESTMENT IN NORTHERN IRELAND (formerly NORTHERN IRELAND FARM MANAGEMENT SURVEY, THE); [pd. by] Economics and Statistics Division, Ministry of Agriculture, Northern Ireland. (Studies in Farm Economics). a., 1969/70- Belfast.

— — — Statistics.

STATISTICAL REVIEW OF NORTHERN IRELAND AGRICULTURE…with output forecasts (formerly Farming in Northern Ireland: statistical review); [pd. by] Economics and Statistics Division, Ministry of Agriculture [Northern Ireland]. a., 1969/70- Belfast.

— — Wales.

FROST (JOHN) of Newport. A second letter to Sir Charles Morgan of Tredegar, in the county of Monmouth, Baronet, M.P.;…also a letter to the farmers. Newport, the Author, 1822. pp. 39.

WELSH COUNCIL. Agriculture in the Welsh economy. [Cardiff], 1977. pp. 9.

— — — History.

HOWELL (DAVID W.) Land and people in nineteenth-century Wales. London, 1978. pp. 207. *bibliog.*

— United States.

O'ROURKE (ANDREW DESMOND) The changing dimension of U.S. agricultural policy. Englewood Cliffs, [1978]. pp. 241. *bibliog.*

— — Energy consumption.

AGRICULTURE and energy; edited by William Lockeretz. New York, 1977. pp. 750. *bibliogs. Proceedings of a conference held at Washington University, St. Louis, Missouri, in 1976.*

— — History.

DRACHE (HIRAM M.) Beyond the furrow: some keys to successful farming in the twentieth century. Danville, [1976]. pp. 551. *bibliog.*

— — New England — History.

RUSSELL (HOWARD S.) A long, deep furrow: three centuries of farming in New England. Hanover, N.H., 1976. pp. 672. *bibliog.*

— Upper Volta.

MÉTHODE de planification du développement rural: compte rendu du séminaire de Ouagadougou 2-5 mars 1976. Paris, 1977. pp. 100. *(France. Ministère de la Coopération. Méthodologie de la Planification. No. 11)*

— Yugoslavia — Bosnia — History.

POPOVIĆ (VASILJ) Agrarno pitanje u Bosni i turski neredi za vreme reformnog režima Abdul-Medžida, 1839-1861. Beograd, 1949. pp. 323. *(Srpska Akademija Nauka i Umetnosti. Posebna Izdanja. knj. 150 [being also] Odeljenje Društvenih Nauka. knj. 59) In Cyrillic.*

— Zambia.

RURAL DEVELOPMENT CORPORATION OF ZAMBIA LIMITED. Annual report and statement of accounts. a., 1974(6th)- Lusaka.

AGRICULTURE, COOPERATIVE.

RADICAL agriculture; edited by Richard Merrill. New York, 1976. pp. 459. *bibliogs.*

— Canada — New Brunswick.

LANTEIGNE (LEOPOLD) The agricultural co-operative in New Brunswick: report presented to the Agricultural Resources Study of New Brunswick. Nigadoo, 1976. fo. 100.

— **China.**

WALLACE (CHRISTOPHER ST. JOHN) Motivation and incentives in rural China. [n.p., 1977?]. fo.220. *bibliog.*

— **Germany, Eastern.**

KOOPERATION: Zeitschrift für die sozialistische Landwirtschaft und Nährungsgüterwirtschaft; (Herausgeber: Rat für landwirtschaftliche Produktion und Nährungsgüterwirtschaft der DDR). m., Ag 1967 (1)- Berlin. *Supersedes Deutsche Landwirtschaft (1947 - Je 1967, with gap)*

ZUR Agrar- und Bündnispolitik der SED bei der Gestaltung der entwickelten sozialistischen Gesellschaft; [by Dieter Sachse and others]. Berlin, 1977. pp. 255.

— **Iran.**

HANEL (ALFRED) and MUELLER (JULIUS OTTO) On the evaluation of rural cooperatives with reference to governmental development policies: case study Iran. Göttingen, 1976. pp. 298. *bibliog. (Marburg. Universität. Institut für Kooperation in Entwicklungsländern. Marburger Schriften zum Genossenschaftswesen. Reihe B. Band 15)*

— **New Zealand.**

STEPHENS (PATRICK RUSSELL) and CLARK (IAN NOEL) Co-operatives in New Zealand agriculture. [Wellington, Information Section, New Zealand Department of Agriculture, 1970]. pp. 44.

— **Peru.**

PADRON CASTILLO (MARIO) and PEASE GARCIA (HENRY) Planificacion rural, reforma agraria y organizacion campesina: programa de promocion campesina en el Valle del Santa 1971-1973. Lima, 1974. 2 vols. (in 1). *(Centro de Estudios y Promocion del Desarrollo. Cuadernos. 4)*

— **Poland.**

PRZEMIANY strukturalne w rolnictwie polskim; praca zbiorowa pod redakcją Zdzisława Grochowskiego. Warszawa, 1975. pp. 242.

GURNICZ (ANTONI) Franciszek Stefczyk: 'zycie, poglądy, działalność. Warszawa, 1976. pp. 204. *bibliog.*

— **Russia.**

FESHCHENKO (PETRO STEPANOVYCH) Mizhvyrobnychi ekonomichni zv"iazky v sil's'komu hospodarstvi ta ïkh efektyvnist'. Kyïv, 1973. pp. 167.

PROKHORENKO (IVAN DENISOVICH) and VOLKOV (PETR DENISOVICH) Industrializatsiia sotsialisticheskogo sel'skogo khoziaistva na sovremennom etape. Minsk, 1974. pp. 175.

— — **Russia (RSFSR).**

ANISKOV (VIKTOR TIKHONOVICH) S polei kolkhoznykh na polia srazhenii: partiino-organizatorskaia deiatel'nost' v iaroslavskoi i kostromskoi derevne v gody Velikoi Otechestvennoi voiny. Iaroslavl', 1975. pp. 208. *bibliog.*

— **Tanzania.**

CONNELL (JOHN) 1946- . The evolution of Tanzanian rural development. Brighton, [1973]. pp. 21. *bibliog. (Brighton. University of Sussex. Institute of Development Studies. Communications. 110)*

AGRICULTURE AND STATE

— **Asia.**

GABLE (RICHARD W.) and SPRINGER (J. FRED) Administering agricultural development in Asia: a comparative analysis of four national programs. Boulder, Colo., 1976. pp. 398. *bibliog.*

— **Bangladesh.**

KHATIB (A.L.) Two ears of rice. [Dacca], East Pakistan Agricultural Development Corporation, 1967. pp. 76.

— **Canada — New Brunswick.**

NEW BRUNSWICK. Department of Agriculture and Rural Development. Annual report. a., 1923- , with gaps. Fredericton. *[in English and French]*

— **China.**

STAVIS (BENEDICT) The politics of agricultural mechanization in China. Ithaca, [1978]. pp. 288. *bibliog.*

— **East (Near East).**

EXPERT GROUP MEETING ON PLANNING THE AGRICULTURAL SECTOR IN RELATION TO OVERALL PLANNING AND SECTORAL PROGRAMMING, BEIRUT, 1970. Report of the...Meeting...[held at] Beirut, Lebanon, 1-5 June 1970. (ST/TAO/SER.C/125). New York, United Nations, 1971. pp. 22.

— **Egypt.**

FAR NEWSBULLETIN: a m. review pd. by the Foreign Agricultural Relations Department, Ministry of Agriculture...Egypt. m., current issues only. Cairo.

— **European Economic Community countries.**

COMMON AGRICULTURAL POLICY, THE; [pd. by] Directorate General for Press and Information [European Communities]. irreg., 1972- Brussels.

MARSH (JOHN STANLEY) U.K. agricultural policy within the European Community. Reading, 1977. pp. 64. *bibliog. (Reading. University. Centre for Agricultural Strategy. CAS Papers. 1)*

COMMON prices and Europe's farm policy; by Theodor Heidhues [and others]. London, 1978. pp. 75. *bibliog. (Trade Policy Research Centre. Thames Essays. No. 14)*

CORRIE (JOHN ALEXANDER) and SCOTT-HOPKINS (JAMES SIDNEY RAWDON) Toward a community rural policy. London, [1978]. pp. 24. *bibliog.*

SCOTT-HOPKINS (JAMES SIDNEY AWDON) Food for thought: towards a better common agricultural policy. London, [1978]. pp. 51.

— **Pakistan.**

HAIDER (AGHA SAJJAD) and KHAN (DILAWAR ALI) Agricultural policy reconsidered. [Islamabad], United States Agency for International Development, Pakistan, 1976. pp. 28.

— **Russia.**

SOVIET agriculture: an assessment of its contributions to economic development; edited by Harry G. Shaffer. New York, 1977. pp. 166.

— **Seychelles.**

SEYCHELLES. 1972. A new deal for agriculture;...white paper, etc. [Mahé, 1972]. pp. 25.

— **Spain.**

BALDRICH CABALLE (JUAN) Programas agrarios de partidos politicos españoles: alternativa politico-economica para el sector agrario. Madrid, [1977]. pp. 235. *bibliog.*

— **United Kingdom.**

WILLIAMS (TOM) Baron Williams of Barnburgh. Labour shows the way. London, 1935. pp. 120.

GEORGE-BROWN (GEORGE ALFRED) Baron George-Brown. British farms: a new security. London, [1963]. pp. 4. *Reprint of a speech at Swaffham, Norfolk on 17 July 1963.*

MARSH (JOHN STANLEY) U.K. agricultural policy within the European Community. Reading, 1977. pp. 64. *bibliog. (Reading. University. Centre for Agricultural Strategy. CAS Papers. 1)*

WALKER (ADRIAN) One crust of bread: (new directions for food and agriculture policy in the UK in the context of world needs). London, [1977]. pp. 29. *bibliog. (Oxfam. Public Affairs Unit. Oxfam Public Affairs Reports. 4)*

— **United States.**

NATIONAL PLANNING ASSOCIATION. Reports. No. 145. A farm, food and land use policy for the future; by Harold F. Breimyer...with a statement by the NPA Agriculture Committee. Washington, 1976. pp. 24.

VALUES of growth. Lexington, Mass., [1976]. pp. 161. *(Commission on Critical Choices for Americans. Critical Choices for Americans. vol. 6)*

AMERICAN ENTERPRISE INSTITUTE FOR PUBLIC POLICY RESEARCH. Legislative Analyses. 95th Congress. No. 6. Farm policy proposals. Washington, 1977. pp. 49.

FOOD and agricultural policy; [papers of a conference held by the American Enterprise Institute for Public Policy Research in Washington, D.C., 1977]. Washington, D.C., [1977]. pp. 250. *(American Enterprise Institute for Public Policy Research. AEI Symposia. 77C)*

FOOD policy: the responsibility of the United States in the life and death choices; edited with an introduction by Peter G. Brown and Henry Shue. New York, [1977]. pp. 344. *bibliogs.*

U.S. farm policy: what direction?; (an [AEI] Round Table held on March 10, 1977...[in] Washington); John Charles Daly, moderator, etc. Washington, [1977]. pp. 40. *(American Enterprise Institute for Public Policy Research. Round Tables)*

O'ROURKE (ANDREW DESMOND) The changing dimension of U.S. agricultural policy. Englewood Cliffs, [1978]. pp. 241. *bibliog.*

AGRICULTURISTS

— **Russia.**

SAADANBEKOV (ZHUMAGUL) O sotsial'noi psikhologii sel'skoi intelligentsii. Frunze, 1975. pp. 88.

AIMS FOR FREEDOM AND ENTERPRISE.

AIMS FOR FREEDOM AND ENTERPRISE. The challenge and the change. London, [1975]. pp. 4.

AIR

— **Pollution.**

LAVE (LESTER BERNARD) and SESKIN (EUGENE P.) Air pollution and human health. Baltimore, [1977]. pp. 368. *bibliogs.*

— — **Economic aspects.**

PROBLEMES économiques de la pollution atmosphérique. Paris, 1975. pp. 127. *bibliogs. (Paris. Université de Paris I (Panthéon- Sorbonne). Centre de Recherche Environnement et Aménagement du Territoire. Série Environnement-Aménagement. 1)*

AIR LINES.

FOLLIOT (MICHEL G.) Le transport aérien international: évolution et perspectives. Paris, 1977. pp. 301.

— **United States.**

COMPETITION in the airlines: what is the public interest?; (an [AEI] Round Table held on July 12, 1977...[in] Washington); John Charles Daly, moderator, etc. Washington, [1977]. pp. 43. *(American Enterprise Institute for Public Policy Research. Round Tables)*

— — **Rates.**

JORDAN (WILLIAM A.) Ph.D. Some predatory practices under government regulation? Toronto, 1975. pp. 61. *(Toronto. University, and York University (Toronto). Joint Program in Transportation. Research Reports. No. 26) This is an amplified version of papers presented at the Seventh Annual Meeting of the Canadian Economics Association 1973, and at the 49th Annual Conference of the Western Economic Association, 1974.*

AIR POWER.

BERMAN (ROBERT P.) Soviet air power in transition. Washington, D.C., [1978]. pp. 82. *(Brookings Institution. Studies in Defense Policy)*

SOVIET aviation and air power: a historical view; edited by Robin Higham and Jacob W. Kipp. London, 1978. pp. 328. *bibliogs.*

AIR TRAFFIC CONTROL.

BRANCKER (JOHN W.S.) IATA and what it does. Leyden, 1977. pp. 257. *bibliog.*

AIRPORT NOISE

— New Zealand.

NEW ZEALAND. Valuation Department. Research Papers. 71-3. The effect of Boeing 737 jet noise on the value of houses near Wellington airport. Wellington, [1971]. fo. 37.

AIRPORTS

— Canada.

CANADA. Statistics Canada. Air carrier traffic at Canadian airports. a., 1976(1st)- Ottawa. *[in English and French] Supersedes in part CANADA. Statistics Canada. Airport activity statistics.*

— United Kingdom.

LEARMONTH (BOB) and NASH (JOANNA) The first Croydon airport 1915-1928; [edited by] Douglas Cluett. Sutton, 1977. pp. 87. *bibliog.*

AISHWARYA RAJYA LAXMI DEVI, Crown Princess of Nepal.

NEPAL. Department of Information. 1969. Short biographies of Their Royal Highnesses the Crown Prince and the Crown Princess. [Kathmandu, 1969?]. pp. 8, 3.

AKANS (AFRICAN PEOPLE).

PINE (FRANCES THERESA) Changes in the division of labour and sex roles among the Akan of Ghana. 1977. fo. 238. *bibliog. Typescript. Ph.D. (London) thesis: unpublished. This thesis is the property of London University and may not be removed from the Library.*

AKWE-SHAVANTE INDIANS.

GIACCARIA (BARTOLOMEU) and HEIDE (ADALBERTO) Xavante: reserva de brasilidade. São Paulo, 1975. pp. 8, 32 plates.

ALASKA

— Economic conditions.

KRESGE (DAVID T.) and others. Issues in Alaska development. Seattle, [1977]. pp. 223. *Based on studies carried out at the University of Alaska's Institute of Social and Economic Research.*

— Economic policy.

KRESGE (DAVID T.) and others. Issues in Alaska development. Seattle, [1977]. pp. 223. *Based on studies carried out at the University of Alaska's Institute of Social and Economic Research.*

ALATA (JEAN PAUL).

HAMON (HERVE) and ROTMAN (PATRICK) L'affaire Alata. Paris, [1977]. pp. 106.

ALBANY PRISON.

KING (ROY DAVID) and ELLIOTT (KENNETH W.) Albany: birth of a prison, end of an era. London, 1977 or rather 1978. pp. 378. *bibliog.*

ALBERTA

— Administrative agencies.

ALBERTA. Department of Advanced Education and Manpower. 1976. Alberta manpower committees: role and structure. [Edmonton], 1976. pp. 9.

— Economic conditions.

ALBERTA. Department of Business Development and Tourism. 1975. Industry and resources, 1975. [Edmonton], 1975. pp. 256.

— Executive departments.

ALBERTA. Department of Housing and Public Works. Annual report. a., 1975/76 [1st]- Edmonton.

ALBERTA. Department of Transportation. 1976. Re-organization study, November 1976. [Edmonton], 1976. 1 vol. (unpaged)

— Industries.

ALBERTA. Department of Business Development and Tourism. 1975. Industry and resources, 1975. [Edmonton], 1975. pp. 256.

— Legislative Assembly — Elections.

ALBERTA. 1975. Returns: Alberta provincial election held on March 26, 1975. [Edmonton], 1975. pp. 168.

— Population.

ALBERTA. Northern Development Group. 1974. Demographic trends and characteristics in census divisions 12-15, 1961-71. [Edmonton], 1974. fo. 86. *(Research Reports)*

— Population, Rural.

ALBERTA. Department of Municipal Affairs. Provincial Branch. Research Division. 1970. Population 3. Unincorporated communities. [Edmonton, 1970]. fo. 123.

— Public works.

ALBERTA. Department of Housing and Public Works. Annual report. a., 1975/76 [1st]- Edmonton.

ALBIGENSES.

SUMPTION (JONATHAN) The Albigensian Crusade. London, 1978. pp. 271. *bibliog.*

ALCOHOL AND YOUTH

— Ireland (Republic).

NATIONAL YOUTH COUNCIL OF IRELAND. Teenage Drinking Committee. Teenage drinking: a cause for concern. Dublin, [1976]. pp. 27. *bibliog.*

— United Kingdom.

O'CONNOR (JOYCE) The young drinkers: a cross-national study of social and cultural influences. London, 1978. pp. 312. *bibliog.*

ALCOHOLISM.

NELSON (JAMES) pseud. No more walls. London, 1978. pp. 92.

SWINSON (RICHARD P.) and EAVES (DEREK) Alcoholism and addiction. [Plymouth, 1978]. pp. 346. *bibliogs.*

— Treatment.

RESPONDING to drinking problems; [by] Stan Shaw [and others]. London, [1978]. pp. 269. *bibliog.*

— — United Kingdom.

ORFORD (JIM) and EDWARDS (GRIFFITH) Alcoholism: a comparison of treatment and advice, with a study of the influence of marriage. Oxford, 1977. pp. 175. *bibliog. (Bethlem Royal Hospital and Maudsley Hospital. Institute of Psychiatry. Maudsley Monographs. No. 26)*

OTTO (SHIRLEY) and ORFORD (JIM) Not quite like home: small hostels for alcoholics and others. Chichester, [1978]. pp. 218. *bibliog.*

U.K. Advisory Committee on Alcoholism. 1978. The pattern and range of services for problem drinkers; report; [W.I.N. Kessel, chairman]. [London, 1978]. pp. 52.

— United Kingdom.

CHRISTIAN ECONOMIC AND SOCIAL RESEARCH FOUNDATION. The differences between Scottish drunkenness and drunkenness in England and Wales. London, 1977. pp. 33.

ALCOHOLISM AND EMPLOYMENT.

ALCOHOLISM and its treatment in industry; Carl J. Schramm, editor. Baltimore, [1977]. pp. 191. *bibliogs.*

ALDRED (GUY ALFRED).

ALDRED (GUY ALFRED) Dogmas discarded;...rivised [sic], extended, and, in parts abridged from an autobiographical fragment published in 1908, author's trial for sedition affixed. London, 1913. pp. 31. *(Revolt Library. No. 6)*

ALEM (LEANDRO NICEFORO).

AVALLONE (CRISTOBAL) Leandro N. Alem: estudio critico historico. Buenos Aires, 1927. pp. 172.

ALEM: su vida, su obra, tragedia de su muerte, las doctrinas democraticas del fundador de la Union Civica Radical a traves de documentos, discursos y escritos. Buenos Aires, 1928. pp. 191.

FARIAS ALEM (ROBERTO) Alem y la democracia argentina. Buenos Aires, [1957]. pp. 201.

ALEMAN VALDES (MIGUEL).

ALEMAN VALDES (MIGUEL) Miguel Aleman contesta: ensayo. Austin, 1975. pp. 54. *(Texas University. Institute of Latin American Studies. Encuesta politica: Mexico. 4)*

ALGEBRA.

HERSTEIN (ISRAEL NATHAN) Topics in algebra. London, 1964 repr. 1976. pp. 342. *bibliogs.*

COHN (PAUL M.) Algebra. London, [1974 in progress].

JACOBSON (NATHAN) Basic algebra I. San Francisco, [1974]. pp. 472.

ALGEBRA, ABSTRACT.

McCOY (NEAL HENRY) and BERGER (THOMAS R.) Algebra: groups, rings, and other topics. Boston, Mass., [1977]. pp. 658. *bibliog.*

ALGEBRAS, LINEAR.

CURTIS (CHARLES WHITTLESEY) Linear algebra: an introductory approach. 3rd ed. Boston, [Mass.], 1974. pp. 337. *bibliog.*

HIRSCH (MORRIS W.) and SMALE (STEPHEN) Differential equations, dynamical systems, and linear algebra. New York, [1974]. pp. 358. *bibliog.*

NOBLE (BENJAMIN) and DANIEL (JAMES W.) Applied linear algebra. 2nd ed. Englewood Cliffs, [1977]. pp. 477.

ALGERIA

— Economic conditions.

LARABI (HACHEMI) Opinions sur l'économie algérienne, suivies de notes de voyages. Alger, 1973. pp. 269.

RAFFINOT (MARC) and JACQUEMOT (PIERRE) Le capitalisme d'état algérien. Paris, 1977. pp. 394. *bibliog.*

SCHLIEPHAKE (KONRAD) Oil and regional development: examples from Algeria and Tunisia; translated by Merrill D. Lyew. New York, 1977. pp. 203. *bibliog.*

— **Emigration and immigration.**

VILAR RAMIREZ (JUAN BAUTISTA) Emigracion española a Argelia, 1830-1900: colonizacion hispanica de la Argelia francesa. Madrid, 1975. pp. 537. *bibliog.*

— **Foreign relations — France.**

ADLER (STEPHEN) International migration and dependence. Farnborough, [1977]. pp. 235. *bibliog.*

— **Politics and government.**

LAZREG (MARNIA) The emergence of classes in Algeria: a study of colonialism and socio-political change. Boulder, Colo., 1976. pp. 252. *bibliog.*

ALGERIANS IN FRANCE.

Les DOSSIERS noirs du racisme dans le Midi de la France; ([by] François-Noël Bernardi [and others]). Paris, [1976]. pp. 203.

ADLER (STEPHEN) International migration and dependence. Farnborough, [1977]. pp. 235. *bibliog.*

ALGORITHMS.

MIYAKE (MARIO YOSHIKAZU) The quadratic assignment model applied to some facility location problems. 1977. fo. 190. *bibliog. Typescript. Ph.D. (London) thesis: unpublished. This thesis is the property of London University and may not be removed from the Library.*

ALIANZA POPULAR REVOLUCIONARIA AMERICANA.

HAYA DE LA TORRE (VICTOR RAUL) Carta a los jovenes de Indoamerica que me escriben: un documento trascendental. [Lima, 1968]. pp. 23.

ALICATA (MARIO).

ALICATA (MARIO) Lettere e taccuini di Regina Coeli. Torino, 1977. pp. 271.

ALIEN LABOUR.

PFLEGERL (SIEGFRIED) Gastarbeiter zwischen Integration und Abstossung. München, [1977]. pp. 223. *bibliogs.*

— **Austria.**

BEIRAT FÜR WIRTSCHAFTS- UND SOZIALFRAGEN. [Publikationen. 28]. Möglichkeiten und Grenzen des Einsatzes ausländischer Arbeitskräfte. Wien, 1976. pp. 95.

— **Germany.**

JEGODZINSKI (SYBILLE) Grundlagen und Konzepte einer strukturorientierten Ausländerpolitik: das Beispiel der Bundesrepublik Deutschland. Hamburg, [1977]. pp. 219. *bibliog.*

RIST (RAY C.) Guestworkers in Germany: the prospects for pluralism. New York, 1978. pp. 263. *bibliog.*

— **United Kingdom.**

SHAH (SAMIR) Immigrants and employment in the clothing industry: the rag trade in London's East End. London, 1975. fo.42

— **United States.**

BODNAR (JOHN E.) Immigration and industrialization: ethnicity in an American mill town, 1870-1940. Pittsburgh, [1977]. pp. 213. *bibliog.*

IMMIGRANTS in industrial America, 1850-1920; edited by Richard L. Ehrlich. Charlottesville, 1977. pp. 218. *Papers of a conference organised by the Eleutherian Mills- Hagley Foundation and the Balch Institute of Philadelphia and held in 1973.*

ALIEN LABOUR, AFRICAN

— **France.**

BAROU (JACQUES) Travailleurs africains en France: rôle des cultures d'origine. Grenoble, [1978]. pp. 162. *bibliog.*

ALIEN LABOUR, TURKISH

— **Germany.**

HOFFMEYER-ZLOTNIK (JUERGEN) Gastarbeiter im Sanierungsgebiet: das Beispiel Berlin- Kreuzberg. Hamburg, [1977]. pp. 191. *bibliog. (Hamburg. Hansische Universität. Seminar für Sozialwissenschaften. Beiträge zur Stadtforschung. Band 1)*

ALIENATION (SOCIAL PSYCHOLOGY).

HARTMAN (TOR) Uppsatser om alienation och kärlek: (three essays on alienation and love). Helsinki, 1977. pp. 62. *(Helsinki. Yliopisto. Research Group for Comparative Sociology. Research Reports. No.13) In Swedish, with English summaries.*

BRITTAN (ARTHUR) The privatised world. London, 1978. pp. 184. *bibliog.*

ALIENS.

GOODWIN-GILL (GUY S.) International law and the movement of persons between states. Oxford, 1978. pp. 324. *bibliog.*

— **Germany.**

LAMERS (KARL A.) Repräsentation und Integration der Ausländer in der Bundesrepublik Deutschland unter besonderer Berücksichtigung des Wahlrechts. Berlin, [1977]. pp. 164. *bibliog.*

ALIMONY.

GRAY (KEVIN JOHN) Reallocation of property on divorce. Abingdon, 1977. pp. 353.

ALLEGIANCE.

HART (VIVIEN) Distrust and democracy: political distrust in Britain and America. Cambridge, 1978. pp. 251. *bibliog.*

STEINBERG (JULIUS) 1940- . Locke, Rousseau, and the idea of consent; an inquiry into the liberal-democratic theory of political obligation. Westport, 1978. pp. 155. *bibliog.*

ALLENDE (SALVADOR).

GARCES (JOAN E.) Allende et l'expérience chilienne. [Paris, 1976]. pp. 286. *(Fondation Nationale des Sciences Politiques. Cahiers. 207)*

BOORSTEIN (EDWARD) Allende's Chile: an inside view. New York, 1977. pp. 277.

ALLOTMENTS

— **United Kingdom.**

NATIONAL LAND AND HOME LEAGUE. [Pamphlets]. No.2. Why you should join a land club. London, 1911. pp. 4.

ALMANACS, ENGLISH.

SOCIAL-DEMOCRATIC FEDERATION. Almanac for 1905. [London, 1905]. s.sh.

ALMANACS, IRISH.

ENGLISH REGISTRY, THE. a., 1816. Dublin. *Bound with the Gentleman's and Citizen's Almanack and Wilson's Dublin Directory for...1816. Title page has note "Fitted to be bound with Watson's Almanack, and making, with it, the present state of the United Kingdom.*

GENTLEMAN'S AND CITIZEN'S ALMANACK, THE. a., 1816. Dublin. *Bound with the English Registry for...1816 and Wilson's Dublin Directory for...1816 and engraved covering title page The Treble Almanack for the year 1816.*

ALPHAND (HERVE).

ALPHAND (HERVE) L'étonnement d'être: journal, 1939-1973. [Paris, 1977]. pp. 614.

ALTOPASCIO

— **Economic history.**

McARDLE (FRANK) Altopascio: a study in Tuscan rural society, 1587-1784. Cambridge, 1978. pp. 226. *bibliog.*

— **History.**

McARDLE (FRANK) Altopascio: a study in Tuscan rural society, 1587-1784. Cambridge, 1978. pp. 226. *bibliog.*

— **Social history.**

McARDLE (FRANK) Altopascio: a study in Tuscan rural society, 1587-1784. Cambridge, 1978. pp. 226. *bibliog.*

ALTRUISM.

HARDIN (GARRETT JAMES) The limits of altruism: an ecologist's view of survival. Bloomington, Ind., [1977]. pp. 154. *(Indiana University. Patten Foundation. Lectures. 1976)*

ALUMINIUM INDUSTRY AND TRADE

— **Australia.**

The CAPE York aluminium companies and the native peoples: Comalco, R.T.Z., Kaiser, C.R.A., Alcan, Billiton, Pechiney, Tipperary; [written by J. Roberts and D. McLean . Victoria, [1976]. pp. 104. *(International Development Action. Mapoon. Book 3)*

ALVEAR (MARCELO TORCUATO DE).

ARAMBURU (RICARDO H.) El Presidente Alvear. Paris, [1922?]. pp. 205.

BARROETAVEÑA (FRANCISCO ANTONIO) El gobierno del Dr. Alvear: post nubila Phoebus. Buenos Aires, 1923. pp. 147.

AMAZON VALLEY

— **Economic conditions.**

BATISTA (DJALMA DA CUNHA) O complexo da Amazônia: analise do processo de desenvolvimento. Rio de Janeiro, [1976]. pp. 292. *bibliogs.*

BOURNE (RICHARD) Assault on the Amazon. London, 1978. pp. 320. *bibliog.*

— **Economic history.**

BATISTA (DJALMA DA CUNHA) O complexo da Amazônia: analise do processo de desenvolvimento. Rio de Janeiro, [1976]. pp. 292. *bibliogs.*

— **Social conditions.**

BATISTA (DJALMA DA CUNHA) O complexo da Amazônia: analise do processo de desenvolvimento. Rio de Janeiro, [1976]. pp. 292. *bibliogs.*

AMBOINA

— **History.**

PENONTON (BUNG) De Zuidmolukse republiek: schets voor een beschrijving van de nieuwste geschiedenis van het Zuidmolukse volk. 4th ed. Amsterdam, 1977. pp. 299. *bibliog.*

— **Nationalism.**

PENONTON (BUNG) De Zuidmolukse republiek: schets voor een beschrijving van de nieuwste geschiedenis van het Zuidmolukse volk. 4th ed. Amsterdam, 1977. pp. 299. *bibliog.*

AMBULATORY MEDICAL CARE.

AMBULATORY care systems. Lexington, Mass., [1977 in progress].

AMERICA

AMERICA

— Antiquities — Bibliography.

COMAS CAMPS (JUAN) Cien años de Congresos Internacionales de Americanistas: ensayo historico-critico y bibliografico. Mexico, 1974. pp. 542. *bibliog.*

— Colonization.

POWELL (J.M.) Mirrors of the New World: images and image-makers in the settlement process. Folkestone, 1977. pp. 207. *bibliog.*

— Congresses.

COMAS CAMPS (JUAN) Cien años de Congresos Internacionales de Americanistas: ensayo historico-critico y bibliografico. Mexico, 1974. pp. 542. *bibliog.*

— Discovery and exploration — Norse.

JONES (GWYN) The Norse Atlantic saga, being the Norse voyages of discovery and settlement to Iceland, Greenland, America. London, 1964. pp. 246. *bibliog. Includes translations, by the author, of the more important early documents.*

— Historiography.

LOEWENBERG (BERT JAMES) American history in American thought: Christopher Columbus to Henry Adams. New York, 1973. pp. 731. *bibliog.*

— History.

POWELL (J.M.) Mirrors of the New World: images and image-makers in the settlement process. Folkestone, 1977. pp. 207. *bibliog.*

— Population.

The NATIVE population of the Americas in 1492; edited by William M. Denevan. [Madison, 1976]. pp. 353. *bibliog.*

AMERICA, LATIN.

PROBLEMES D'AMERIQUE LATINE; [pd. by] Direction de la Documentation [France]. 4 a yr., S 9 1966 (no.3)- Paris.

MARTÍ (JOSÉ) Our America: writings on Latin America and the struggle for Cuban independence; translated by Elinor Randall...; edited, with an introduction and notes, by Philip S. Foner. New York, [1977]. pp. 448.

— Armed forces — Political activity.

FUERZAS armadas, poder y cambio: ensayos; [edited by] Luis Mercier Vega. Caracas, [1971]. pp. 365. *bibliogs.*

LINDENBERG (KLAUS) La funcion politica de las fuerzas armadas en America Latina. Santiago de Chile, 1971. pp. 42. *(Instituto Latinoamericano de Investigaciones Sociales. Estudios y Documentos. 9)*

— Civilization.

ALEN LASCANO (LUIS C.) Hispanoamerica en el pensamiento de Yrigoyen. Buenos Aires, [1959]. pp. 88. *bibliog.*

FERREIRA (OLIVEIROS S.) Nossa America: Indoamerica; a ordem e a revolução no pensamento de Haya de la Torre. São Paulo, 1971. pp. 293.

ZEA (LEOPOLDO) Dependencia y liberacion en la cultura latinoamericana. Mexico, 1974. pp. 119.

RANGEL (CARLOS) Del buen salvaje al buen revolucionario: mitos y realidades de America Latina. Caracas, [1976]. pp. 261.

— Commerce.

LATIN America in the post-import-substitution era; edited by Werner Baer and Larry Samuelson. Oxford, 1977. pp. 168. *bibliogs. (World Development; incorporating New Commonwealth. vol. 5, nos. 1 and 2. Special Issue)*

— — United States.

STEWARD (DICK) Trade and hemisphere: the good neighbor policy and reciprocal trade. Columbia, Ma., 1975. pp. 307. *bibliog.*

— Discovery and exploration.

LIPSCHUTZ (ALEJANDRO) Marx y Lenin en la America Latina y los problemas indigenistas. La Habana, 1974. pp. 230.

— Economic conditions.

PINEDO (FEDERICO) La CEPAL y la realidad economica en America Latina. Buenos Aires, 1963. pp. 79.

NORTH AMERICAN CONGRESS ON LATIN AMERICA. Yanqui dollar: the contribution of U.S. private investment to underdevelopment in Latin America; contributors Susanne Bodenheimer [and others]. New York, [1971]. pp. 64.

MATOS MAR (JOSE) ed. La dominacion de America latina: [readings]. Buenos Aires, [1972]. pp. 181.

CARDOSO (FERNANDO HENRIQUE) Dependency revisited. Austin, 1973. pp. 35. *(Texas University. Institute of Latin American Studies. Charles W. Hackett Memorial Lectures. 1973)*

DAEMON (DALTON) Desenvolvimento das areas marginais latino-americanas. Petropolis, 1974. pp. 319. *bibliog.*

COLE (JOHN PETER) Latin America: an economic and social geography. 2nd ed. Totowa, N.J., 1975. pp. 470. *bibliogs.*

EN torno al capitalismo latinoamericano. Mexico, 1975. pp. 155. *(Mexico City. Universidad Nacional Autonoma de Mexico. Instituto de Investigaciones Economicas. Seminario de Teoria del Desarrollo. 1)*

FURTADO (CELSO) A economia latino-americana: formação historica e problemas contemporâneos. São Paulo, 1976. pp. 339.

POLITICA economica en centro y periferia: ensayos en homenaje a Felipe Pazos; seleccion de Carlos F. Diaz Alejandro [and others]. Mexico. 1976. pp. 751. *bibliogs. (Fondo de Cultura Economica. Lecturas. 16)*

LAGOS MATUS (GUSTAVO) and GODOY (HORACIO H.) Revolution of being: a Latin American view of the future. New York, [1977]. pp. 226.

LATIN America in the post-import-substitution era; edited by Werner Baer and Larry Samuelson. Oxford, 1977. pp. 168. *bibliogs. (World Development; incorporating New Commonwealth. vol. 5, nos. 1 and 2. Special Issue)*

— — Bibliography.

UNITED NATIONS. Economic Commission for Latin America. Library. 1973- . Bibliografia de la CEPAL, 1948-1972; ([with] Suplemento[s]). Santiago, 1973 in progress.

— Economic history.

VILLAMARIN (JUAN A.) and VILLAMARIN (JUDITH E.) Indian labor in mainland colonial Spanish America. Newark, Del., 1975. pp. 175. *bibliog.*

FURTADO (CELSO) A economia latino-americana: formação historica e problemas contemporâneos. São Paulo, 1976. pp. 339.

— — Bibliography.

LATIN America: a guide to economic history, 1830-1930; Roberto Cortés Conde [and others], editors;...sponsored by the Joint Committee on Latin American Studies of the American Council of Learned Societies and the Social Science Research Council and by the Consejo Latinoamericano de Ciencias Sociales. Berkeley, Calif., 1977. pp. 685.

— Economic integration.

INTERREGIONAL SEMINAR ON DEVELOPMENT PLANNING, 3RD, SANTIAGO, 1968. Policies of plan implementation, with special reference to Latin America; report on the...seminar...[held in] Santiago, Chile, 18-29 March 1968. (ST/TAO/SER.C/110). New York, United Nations, 1970. pp. 235.

NATHAN (ROBERT R.) ASSOCIATES. La integracion economica de Colombia y Venezuela...1967. Bogota, 1970. pp. 110.

KAPLAN (MARCOS) ed. Corporaciones publicas multinacionales para el desarrollo y la integracion de la America Latina. Mexico, 1972. pp. 369. *bibliog. Papers presented at the Seminario Regional de Derecho Internacional para la America Latina, Quito, 1969, organized by UNITAR.*

La INTEGRACION economica centroamericana; seleccion de Eduardo Lizano F. Mexico, 1975. 2 vols. (in 1). *(Fondo de Cultura Economica. Lecturas. 13)*

LATIN America and world economy: a changing international order; edited by Joseph Grunwald. Beverly Hills, [1978]. pp. 315. *bibliogs.*

— — Bibliography.

INSTITUTE FOR LATIN AMERICAN INTEGRATION. Documentation Service. Bibliographical Series. No. 1. Bilbiografia selectiva sobre integracion: Selective bibliography on integration. Buenos Aires, 1977. 1 vol.(various pagings). *bibliog.*

— Economic policy.

HALPERIN (MAURICE) Desarrollo economico y crisis en la America Latina. [Mexico?], 1961. pp. 47. *bibliog.*

INTERREGIONAL SEMINAR ON DEVELOPMENT PLANNING, 3RD, SANTIAGO, 1968. Policies of plan implementation, with special reference to Latin America; report on the...seminar...[held in] Santiago, Chile, 18-29 March 1968. (ST/TAO/SER.C/110). New York, United Nations, 1970. pp. 235.

CARDOSO (FERNANDO HENRIQUE) Dependency revisited. Austin, 1973. pp. 35. *(Texas University. Institute of Latin American Studies. Charles W. Hackett Memorial Lectures. 1973)*

CAMBRIDGE. University. Centre of Latin American Studies. Working Papers. No.18. The public sector in Latin America; by E.V.K. Fitzgerald. Cambridge, 1974. pp. 28. *bibliog.*

DAEMON (DALTON) Desenvolvimento das areas marginais latino-americanas. Petropolis, 1974. pp. 319. *bibliog.*

CARNEGIE-ROCHESTER CONFERENCE ON PUBLIC POLICY. 1976, April Conference. International organization, national policies and economic development; editors, Karl Brunner [and] Allan H. Meltzer. Amsterdam, 1977. pp. 240. *bibliogs. (Journal of Monetary Economics. Carnegie-Rochester Conference Series on Public Policy. vol. 6)*

— Emigration and immigration — Bibliography.

BAILEY (JOHN P.) Ph.D. and HEADLAM (F.) compilers. Immigration from overseas to Latin America;...a bibliography of works mainly in English. Bundoora, Vict., 1977. fo. 24. *(La Trobe University. Department of Sociology. Bibliographies in Social Research. No. 2)*

— Foreign economic relations.

MATOS MAR (JOSE) ed. La dominacion de America latina: [readings]. Buenos Aires, [1972]. pp. 181.

O'BRIEN (PHILIP J.) A critique of Latin American theories of dependency. Glasgow, [1974]. pp. 18. *(Glasgow. University. Institute of Latin American Studies. Occasional Papers. No.12)*

POLITICA economica en centro y periferia: ensayos en homenaje a Felipe Pazos; seleccion de Carlos F. Diaz Alejandro [and others]. Mexico. 1976. pp. 751. *bibliogs. (Fondo de Cultura Economica. Lecturas. 16)*

THEBERGE (JAMES DANIEL) and FONTAINE (ROGER W.) Latin America: struggle for progress. Lexington, Mass., [1977]. pp. 205. *(Commission on Critical Choices for Americans. Critical Choices for Americans. vol. 15)*

LATIN America and world economy: a changing international order; edited by Joseph Grunwald. Beverly Hills, [1978]. pp. 315. *bibliogs.*

— — **Communist countries.**

STRANY SEV i Latinskaia Amerika: problemy ekonomicheskogo sotrudnichestva. Moskva, 1976. pp. 335.

— — **United States.**

STEWARD (DICK) Trade and hemisphere: the good neighbor policy and reciprocal trade. Columbia, Ma., 1975. pp. 307. *bibliog.*

— **Foreign relations.**

DAVIS (HAROLD EUGENE) and others. Latin American diplomatic history: an introduction. Baton Rouge, [1977]. pp. 301. *bibliog.*

THEBERGE (JAMES DANIEL) and FONTAINE (ROGER W.) Latin America: struggle for progress. Lexington, Mass., [1977]. pp. 205. *(Commission on Critical Choices for Americans. Critical Choices for Americans. vol. 15)*

— — **United States.**

The AMERICAS in a changing world: a report of the Commission on United States-Latin American Relations...; selected papers by Kalman H. Silvert [and others]. New York, [1975]. pp. 248.

THEBERGE (JAMES DANIEL) and FONTAINE (ROGER W.) Latin America: struggle for progress. Lexington, Mass., [1977]. pp. 205. *(Commission on Critical Choices for Americans. Critical Choices for Americans. vol. 15)*

GASPAR (EDMUND) United States - Latin America: a special relationship? Washington, D.C., [1978]. pp. 90. *(American Institute for Public Policy Research and Stanford University. Hoover Institution on War, Revolution and Peace. AEI-Hoover Policy Studies. 26)*

— **History.**

FAGG (JOHN EDWIN) Latin America: a general history. 3rd ed. New York, [1977]. pp. 850. *bibliog.*

HENNESSY (ALISTAIR) The frontier in Latin American history. [London, 1978]. pp. 202. *bibliog.*

— **Industries.**

LATIN America in the post-import-substitution era; edited by Werner Baer and Larry Samuelson. Oxford, 1977. pp. 168. *bibliogs. (World Development; incorporating New Commonwealth. vol. 5, nos. 1 and 2. Special Issue)*

— **Intellectual life.**

MARINELLO VIDAURRETA (JUAN) Ocho notas sobre Anibal Ponce. La Habana, [1961]. pp. 45. *(Sobretiro de la revista "Islas", organo de la Universidad Central de las Villas)*

— **Native races.**

LIPSCHUTZ (ALEJANDRO) Marx y Lenin en la America Latina y los problemas indigenistas. La Habana, 1974. pp. 230.

— **Politics and government.**

ARISMENDI (RODNEY) America Latina: campo de lucha o base de agresion. [Montevideo, 1967]. 1 pamphlet (unpaged).

ARISMENDI (RODNEY) La izquierda uruguaya ante la hora de America latina. [Montevideo, 1967]. pp. 63.

COLLAZO (ARIEL B.) La OLAS: el camino revolucionario de los trabajadores. [Montevideo, 1968]. pp. 43.

FERREIRA (OLIVEIROS S.) Nossa America: Indoamerica; a ordem e a revolução no pensamento de Haya de la Torre. São Paulo, 1971. pp. 293.

RANGEL (CARLOS) Del buen salvaje al buen revolucionario: mitos y realidades de America Latina. Caracas, [1976]. pp. 261.

ALMEIDA (CANDIDO ANTONIO MENDES DE) Beyond populism;...translated by L. Gray Cowan. Albany, N.Y., 1977. pp. 112.

CLASES sociales y crisis politica en America Latina; seminario de Oaxaca;...coordinado por Raul Benitez Zenteno. Mexico, 1977. pp. 454.

FREI MONTALVA (EDUARDO) America Latina: opcion y esperanza. Barcelona, [1977]. pp. 299.

GERASSI (JOHN) Contemporary theories of revolution in Latin America with special reference to Venezuela, Colombia, Guatemala, Uruguay, Brazil and Chile. 1977. fo. 499. *bibliog.* Typescript. Ph.D. (London) thesis: unpublished. This thesis is the property of London University and may not be removed from the Library.

STATISTICAL ABSTRACT OF LATIN AMERICA. Supplement Series. 17. Money and politics in Latin America...; edited by James W. Wilkie. Los Angeles, 1977. pp. 92.

— **Population.**

POBLACION y desarrollo en America Latina; [papers prepared by the] Comision Economica para America Latina. Mexico, 1975. pp. 317. *Originally issued as a mimeographed document (E/CN.12/973) prepared by ECLA for members of the Reunion Preparatoria de la Conferencia Mundial de Poblacion, 15-19 April, 1974.*

MASS (BONNIE) Population target: the political economy of population control in Latin America. Toronto, [1976]. pp. 299.

— **Presidents.**

PRESIDENTIAL power in Latin American politics; edited by Thomas V. DiBacco. New York, 1977. pp. 122.

— **Public works — Finance.**

MACON (JORGE) and MERINO MAÑON (JOSE) Financing urban and rural development through betterment levies: the Latin American experience. New York, 1977. pp. 147. *bibliog.*

— **Rural conditions.**

FEDER (ERNEST) Dr., of the University of Nebraska, ed. La lucha de clases en el campo: analisis estructural de la economia agricola latinoamericana. Mexico, 1975. pp. 520. *bibliogs. (Fondo de Cultura Economica. Lecturas. 14)*

LAND and labour in Latin America: essays on the development of agrarian capitalism in the nineteenth and twentieth centuries; edited by Kenneth Duncan and Ian Rutledge, with the collaboration of Colin Harding. Cambridge, 1977. pp. 535. *Based on papers of a symposium held in 1972 at Cambridge under the joint auspices of Cambridge University Centre of Latin American Studies and London University Institute of Latin American Studies.*

— **Social conditions.**

COLE (JOHN PETER) Latin America: an economic and social geography. 2nd ed. Totowa, N.J., 1975. pp. 470. *bibliogs.*

SOLARI (ALDO E.) and others. Teoria, accion social y desarrollo en America Latina. Mexico, 1976. pp. 637.

IDEOLOGY and social change in Latin America; edited by June Nash [and others]. New York, [1977]. pp. 305. *bibliogs.*

LAGOS MATUS (GUSTAVO) and GODOY (HORACIO H.) Revolution of being: a Latin American view of the future. New York, [1977]. pp. 226.

AMERICAN FEDERATION OF LABOR AND CONGRESS OF INDUSTRIAL ORGANIZATIONS.

AMERICAN FEDERATION OF LABOR AND CONGRESS OF INDUSTRIAL ORGANIZATIONS. Executive Council. Statements and reports, 1956-1975; edited, with an introduction, by Gary M. Fink. Westport, Conn., 1977. 5 vols.

HOROWITZ (RUTH L.) Political ideologies of organized labor. New Brunswick, N.J., [1978]. pp. 260. *bibliog.*

AMERICAN FICTION

— **History and criticism.**

AUERBACH (NINA) Communities of women: an idea in fiction. Cambridge, Mass., 1978. pp. 222.

AMERICAN LITERATURE

— **History and criticism.**

CUNLIFFE (MARCUS) The literature of the United States. 3rd ed. Harmondsworth, 1967, repr. 1976. pp. 413. *bibliog.*

BARNETT (LOUISE K.) The ignoble savage: American literary racism, 1790-1890. Westport, Conn., 1975. pp. 220. *bibliog.*

PENKOWER (MONTY NOAM) The Federal Writers' Project: a study in government patronage of the arts. Urbana, Ill., [1977]. pp. 266. *bibliog.*

AMERICAN LOYALISTS.

COOKE (JACOB E.) Tench Coxe and the early Republic. Chapel Hill, [1978]. pp. 543. *bibliog.*

AMNESTY INTERNATIONAL

— **History.**

LARSEN (EGON) A flame in barbed wire: the story of Amnesty International. London, 1978. pp. 136.

AMSTERDAM

— **Population.**

AMSTERDAM. Bureau van Statistiek. Statistische Mededeelingen. No. 195. Migratie van beroepsbeoefenaren tussen Amsterdam en het omliggend gebied, 1961-1972. Amsterdam, 1973. pp. 51.

— **Prisons and reformatories.**

NEDERLANDS GENOOTSCHAP TOT RECLASSERING. Bijlmer Bajes: weg met de plannen. Amsterdam, [1974]. pp. 48.

ANALYSIS OF VARIANCE.

FISHER (LLOYD) and McDONALD (JOHN) Biostatistician. Fixed effects analysis of variance. New York, 1978. pp. 177.

ANARCHISM AND ANARCHISTS.

An ANARCHIST address to workingmen. [London, 188-?]. s.sh.

GALLEANI (LUIGI) Aneliti e singulti. Newark, N.J., [1935]. pp. 367. *Articles originally published between 1899 and 1920, mostly in Cronaca Sovversiva.*

ALDRED (GUY ALFRED) Dogmas discarded;...rivised [sic], extended, and, in parts abridged from an autobiographical fragment published in 1908, author's trial for sedition affixed. London, 1913. pp. 31. *(Revolt Library. No. 6)*

PUENTE (ISAAC) El comunismo libertario. Paris, 1969. pp. 32.

LEHNING (ARTHUR) Anarcho-syndikalisme: (tekst van een op November 1926 gehouden inleiding; [with] Anton Constandse, Syndikalisme en bedrijf, uit Grondslagen van het anarchisme...1938). Amsterdam, [197-]. pp. 31.

ANARCHISM AND ANARCHISTS. (Cont.)

ANARCHISMO '70: materiali per un dibattito; a cura de l'Antistato; con la partecipazione di Amedeo Bertolo [and others]. Cesena, 1970. pp. 71. *(Antistato. Quaderni. 1)*

CERRITO (GINO) Geografia dell'anarchismo: istantanee di mezzo secolo: (anarchismo '70: materiali per un dibattito). Pistoia, 1971. pp. 72. *(Antistato. Quaderni. 2)*

HOBSBAWM (ERIC JOHN ERNEST) Marxism and anarchism: are they compatible? London, [1972?]. pp. 6.

CIAURRO (GIAN FRANCO) ed. Anarchici e anarchia: antologia, etc. Roma, 1976. pp. 190. *bibliog.*

MALATESTA (ERRICO) and MERLINO (FRANCESCO SAVERIO) Gli anarchici e la questione elettorale: un dibatto. Roma, [1976]. pp. 144.

MELANGES d'histoire sociale offerts à Jean Maitron. Paris, [1976]. pp. 286. *bibliog.*

POLIANSKII (FEDOR IAKOVLEVICH) Kritika ekonomicheskikh teorii anarkhizma. Moskva, 1976. pp. 301.

CLARK (JOHN P.) The philosophical anarchism of William Godwin. Princeton, N.J., [1977]. pp. 343. *bibliog.*

LOESCHE (PETER) Anarchismus. Darmstadt, 1977. pp. 169.

ROCK (MARTIN) Anarchismus und Terror: Ursprünge und Strategien. Trier, 1977. pp. 105.

— **Germany.**

BECKER (JILLIAN) Hitler's children: the story of the Baader-Meinhof terrorist gang. Philadelphia, [1977]. pp. 322. *bibliog.*

— **Italy.**

STAJANO (CORRADO) Il sovversivo: vita e morte dell'anarchico Serantini. [Torino, 1975]. pp. 174.

— **Mexico.**

HART (JOHN MASON) Anarchism and the Mexican working class, 1860-1931. Austin, [1978]. pp. 249. *bibliog.*

— **Spain.**

HERNANDEZ (JESUS) Negro y rojo: los anarquistas en la revolucion española. Mexico, D.F., 1946. pp. 557.

CONFEDERACION REGIONAL DE ARAGON, RIOJA Y NAVARRA. Comarcal de Valderrobres, Teruel: sus luchas sociales y revolucionarias. [Royan, 1971?]. pp. 165.

ABAD DE SANTILLAN (DIEGO) El anarquismo y la revolucion en España: escritos 1930-38; seleccion y estudio preliminar de Antonio Elorza. Madrid, 1976. pp. 377.

BOOKCHIN (MURRAY) The Spanish anarchists: the heroic years 1868-1936. New York, [1977]. pp. 344. *bibliog.*

GOMEZ CASAS (JUAN) Historia de la FAI: aproximacion a la historia de la organizacion especifica del anarquismo y sus antecedentes de la Alianza de la Democracia Socialista. Madrid, 1977. pp. 304. *bibliog.*

— **United States.**

GOODMAN (PAUL) b. 1911. Drawing the line:...political essays...; edited by Taylor Stoehr. New York, 1977. pp. 272.

ANCESTOR WORSHIP

— **Taiwan.**

AHERN (EMILY M.) The cult of the dead in a Chinese village. Stanford, Calif., 1973. pp. 280. *bibliog.*

ANDALUSIA

— **Emigration and immigration.**

LARA SANCHEZ (FRANCISCO) La emigracion andaluza: analisis y testimonios. Madrid, [1977]. pp. 239. *bibliog.*

— **History.**

DOMINGUEZ ORTIZ (ANTONIO) Alteraciones andaluzas. Madrid, [1973]. pp. 237.

ANDEAN GROUP

— **Economic integration.**

ANDEAN GROUP; [pd. by] Junta, Acuerdo de Cartagena. m., Oc 1977 [no. 1]- Lima.

ANDERNACH

— **City planning.**

BUSE (MICHAEL) and others. Determinanten politischer Partizipation: Theorieansatz und empirische Überprüfung am Beispiel der Stadtsanierung Andernach. Meisenheim am Glan, 1978. pp. 410. *bibliog.*

ANDRYCHÓW

— **Economic history.**

KULCZYKOWSKI (MARIUSZ) Andrychowski ośrodek płócienniczy w XVIII i XIX wieku. Wrocław, 1972. pp. 238. *bibliog. (Polska Akademia Nauk. Oddział w Krakowie. Komisja Nauk Historycznych. Prace. nr.31) With French and Russian summaries.*

ANGOLA

— **Economic policy.**

EGERO (BERTIL) Mozambique and Angola: reconstruction in the social sciences. Uppsala, 1977. pp. 78. *(Nordiska Afrikainstitutet. Research Reports. No. 42)*

— **Nationalism.**

CENTRE D'ETUDES ANTI-IMPERIALISTES. Groupe Afrique Centrale. Angola: la lutte continue. Paris, 1977. pp. 221. *bibliog.*

— **Politics and government.**

PORTUGAL. Ministerio da Comunicação Social. 1975. Angola: the independence agreement. [Lisbon], 1975. pp. 31.

MOVIMENTO POPULAR DE LIBERTAÇÃO DE ANGOLA. Road to liberation: MPLA documents on the founding of the People's Republic of Angola. Richmond, B.C., [1976]. pp. 52.

CENTRE D'ETUDES ANTI-IMPERIALISTES. Groupe Afrique Centrale. Angola: la lutte continue. Paris, 1977. pp. 221. *bibliog.*

ANGUS.

SCOTTISH COUNCIL OF SOCIAL SERVICE. The Third Statistical Account of Scotland. The county of Angus; edited by William Allen Illsley. Arbroath, 1977. pp. 630. *bibliog.*

ANIMAL INDUSTRY.

SINGER (PETER) Animal liberation: towards an end to man's inhumanity to animals. London, 1977. pp. 285. *bibliog.*

— **European Economic Community countries.**

EUROPEAN COMMUNITIES. Statistical Office. Statistics of animal production. bien., 1965/75- Luxembourg. *[in Community languages]*

ANIMALS, TREATMENT OF.

SINGER (PETER) Animal liberation: towards an end to man's inhumanity to animals. London, 1977. pp. 285. *bibliog.*

ANSART (GUSTAVE).

ANSART (GUSTAVE) De l'usine à l'Assemblée nationale: entretien avec Jacques Estager. [Paris, 1977]. pp. 256.

ANSCHLUSS MOVEMENT, 1918-1938.

SCHAUSBERGER (NORBERT) Der Griff nach Österreich: der Anschluss. Wien, [1978]. pp. 666. *bibliog.*

ANTAISAKA.

EDHOLM (FELICITY ELIZABETH) Kinship and social change among the Antaisaka of coastal southeast Madagascar. [1976]. fo. 397. *bibliog. Typescript. Ph.D. (London) thesis: unpublished. This thesis is the property of London University and may not be removed from the Library.*

ANTHROPOGEOGRAPHY.

DIMENSIONS of human geography: essays on some familiar and neglected themes; Karl W. Butzer, editor. Chicago, 1978. pp. 190. *(Chicago. University. Department of Geography. Research Papers. No. 186) Based on a session held at the Salt Lake City meetings of the Association of American Geographers in 1977.*

GEOGRAPHY and the urban environment: progress in research and applications; edited by D.T. Herbert and R.J. Johnston. Chichester, [1978]. pp. 363. *bibliogs.*

GREGORY (DEREK) Ideology, science and human geography. London, [1978]. pp. 198. *bibliogs.*

SPENCER (JOSEPH EARLE) and THOMAS (WILLIAM L.) Introducing cultural geography. 2nd ed. New York, [1978]. pp. 428. *bibliog.*

— **Mathematical models.**

BRADFORD (MICHAEL G.) and KENT (WILLIAM ASHLEY) Human geography: theories and their applications. Oxford, 1977. pp. 180. *bibliogs.*

— **Africa.**

GROVE (ALFRED THOMAS) Africa. 3rd ed. Oxford, 1978. pp. 337. *bibliog.*

— **United Kingdom.**

COATES (BRYAN ELLIS) and RAWSTRON (ERIC MITCHELL) Regional variations in Britain: studies in economic and social geography. London, 1971 reprinted 1972. pp. 304. *Reprinted with minor revisions.*

— **United States.**

GERLACH (RUSSEL L.) Immigrants in the Ozarks: a study in ethnic geography. Columbia, [1976]. pp. 206. *bibliog. (Missouri University. Studies. vol. 64)*

HARRIES (KEITH D.) and BRUNN (STANLEY D.) The geography of laws and justice: spatial perspectives on the criminal justice system. New York, 1978. pp. 175. *bibliogs.*

ANTHROPOLOGICAL LINGUISTICS.

QUESTIONS and politeness: strategies in social interaction; edited by Esther N. Goody. Cambridge, 1978. pp. 324. *bibliog.*

ANTHROPOLOGY.

FOX (ROBIN) Encounter with anthropology. 2nd ed. New York, 1975. pp. 316. *bibliog. Reprint of the 1973 edition published New York, Harcourt Brace Jovanovich.*

COCHRANE (GLYNN) ed. What we can do for each other: an interdisciplinary approach to development anthropology. Amsterdam, 1976. pp. 85. *bibliogs.*

MEANING in anthropology; edited by Keith H. Basso and Henry A. Selby. Albuquerque, [1976]. pp. 255. *bibliog. (School of American Research. Advanced Seminar Series) Based on a conference held in 1974 in Santa Fe, New Mexico.*

GODELIER (MAURICE) Horizon, trajets marxistes en anthropologie. 2nd ed. Paris, 1977. 2 vols. (in 1). *bibliog.*

INTERNATIONAL CONGRESS OF ANTHROPOLOGICAL AND ETHNOLOGICAL SCIENCES. 9th Congress, 1973. The concept and dynamics of culture: [papers from the Congress]; editor Bernardo Bernardi. The Hague, [1977]. pp. 630. *bibliogs.*

HUMPHREYS (S.C.) Anthropology and the Greeks. London, 1978. pp. 357. *bibliog.*

NEEDHAM (RODNEY) Essential perplexities. Oxford, 1978. pp. 29. *An inaugural lecture delivered before the University of Oxford on 12 May 1977.*

The YEARBOOK of symbolic anthropology I; edited by Erik Schwimmer. London, 1978. pp. 230. *bibliogs.*

— Field work.

ENCOUNTER and experience: personal accounts of fieldwork; edited by André Béteille and T.N. Madan. Delhi, [1975]. pp. 225. *bibliogs.*

ANTHROPOMETRY
— Malawi.

NURSE (G.T.) Height and history in Malawi: an enquiry into the possible historical implications of contrasts in body-height among Malawians. Zomba, 1969. pp. 39. *(Malawi. Department of Antiquities. Publications. No. 5)*

ANTICLERICALISM
— France.

BERTOCCI (PHILIP A.) Jules Simon: republican anticlericalism and cultural politics in France, 1848-1886. Columbia, 1978. pp. 247. *bibliog.*

— Spain.

DIAZ MOZAZ (JOSE MARIA) Apuntes para una sociologia del anticlericalismo. [Madrid, 1976]. pp. 203.

ANTICOMMUNIST MOVEMENTS
— United States.

CAUTE (DAVID) The great fear: the anti-communist purge under Truman and Eisenhower. New York, [1978]. pp. 697. *bibliog.*

ANTINAZI MOVEMENT.

VERFOLGUNG und Widerstand unter dem Nationalsozialismus in Baden: die Lageberichte der Gestapo und des Generalstaatsanwalts Karlsruhe, 1933-1940; bearbeitet von Jörg Schadt. Stuttgart, [1976]. pp. 354. *bibliog. (Mannheim. Stadtarchiv. Veröffentlichungen. Band 3)*

Das "ANDERE Deutschland" im Zweiten Weltkrieg: Emigration und Widerstand in internationaler Perspektive: The "Other Germany" in the Second World War...; herausgegeben von Lothar Kettenacker. Stuttgart, 1977. pp. 258. *(Deutsches Historisches Institut in London. Veröffentlichungen. Band 2) In German or English, with summaries in the alternative language.*

BREITSCHEID (RUDOLF) Antifaschistische Beiträge, 1933-1939; ausgewählt und eingeleitet von Dieter Lange. Frankfurt am Main, 1977. pp. 136.

BOHN (WILLI) Stuttgart: geheim!: Widerstand und Verfolgung, 1933-1945. 3rd ed. Frankfurt am Main, [1978]. pp. 207. *bibliog.*

WIESNER (ERICH) Man nannte mich Ernst: Erlebnisse und Episoden aus der Geschichte der Arbeiterjugendbewegung. 4th ed. Berlin, 1978. pp. 316.

ANTIOQUIA
— Politics and government.

ABEL (CHRISTOPHER) Conservative politics in twentieth-century Antioquia, 1910-1953. Oxford, 1973. fo. 39. *(Oxford. University. St. Antony's College. Latin American Centre. Occasional Papers. 3)*

ANTISEMITISM.

SZEKELY (BELA) El antisemitismo: su historia, su sociologia, su psicologia; traduccion directa del hungaro por el doctor Olivier Brachfeld. Buenos Aires, [1940]. pp. 455. *bibliog.*

LOMBARDO TOLEDANO (VICENTE) Judios y mexicanos: razas inferiores? Montevideo, [1944]. pp. 44.

DRINAN (ROBERT F.) Honor the promise: America's commitment to Israel. Garden City, N.Y., 1977. pp. 250.

— Germany.

HAHN (FRED) Lieber Stürmer: Leserbriefe an das NS-Kampfblatt, 1924 bis 1945: eine Dokumentation aus dem Leo-Baeck-Institut, New York; Bearbeitung der deutschen Ausgabe von Günther Wagenlehner. Stuttgart, [1978]. pp. 263. *bibliog. (Studiengesellschaft für Zeitprobleme. Zeitpolitik. 19)*

— United Kingdom.

JEWRY UEBER ALLES; pd. by The Judaic Publishing Co., Ltd. a., Ap. 1920(vol. 1, no.3) London.

ANTITRUST LAW

MEESSEN (KARL MATTHIAS) Völkerrechtliche Grundsätze des internationalen Kartellrechts. Baden-Baden, [1975]. pp. 288.

— Canada.

GOFF (COLIN HARFORD) and REASONS (CHARLES E.) Corporate crime in Canada: a critical analysis of anti-combines legislation. Scarborough, Ont., [1978]. pp. 136.

— European Economic Community countries.

CONFEDERATION OF BRITISH INDUSTRY. Competition law in the European Community: a guide to investigation, procedure and enforcement. London, 1977. pp. 82. *bibliog.*

SEMAINE DE BRUGES, 1977. La réglementation du comportement des monopoles et entreprises dominantes en droit communautaire; [by] B. Baardman [and others]; edited by J.A. van Damme: Regulating the behaviour of monopolies and dominant undertakings in Community law. Bruges, 1977. pp. 578. *(College of Europe. Cahiers de Bruges. Nouvelle Série. 36) In English or French.*

BELLAMY (CHRISTOPHER WILLIAM) and CHILD (GRAHAM D.) Common Market law of competition. 2nd ed. London, 1978. pp. 492.

— United States.

WEAVER (SUZANNE) Decision to prosecute: organization and public policy in the Antitrust Division. Cambridge, Mass., [1977]. pp. 196. *(Massachusetts Institute of Technology. MIT Studies in American Politics and Public Policy. 2)*

AMERICAN ENTERPRISE INSTITUTE FOR PUBLIC POLICY RESEARCH. Legislative Analyses. 95th Congress. No. 22. Expanding the right to sue for antitrust violations: proposals to overrule the Illinois Brick decision. Washington, D.C., 1978. pp. 32.

ANTONICELLI (FRANCO).

ANTONICELLI (FRANCO) La pratica della libertà: documenti, discorsi, scritti politici, 1929-1974. Torino, 1976. pp. 257.

ANTWERP
— Commerce.

SOLY (HUGO) Urbanisme en kapitalisme te Antwerpen in de 16de eeuw: de stedebouwkundige en industriële ondernemingen van Gilbert van Schoonbeke. [Brussels], 1977. pp. 496. *bibliog. (Pro Civitate. Collection Histoire. Série in-8. No. 47) With summary in French.*

— Economic history.

BAETENS (ROLAND) De nazomer van Antwerpens welvaart: de diaspora en het handelshuis De Groote tijdens de eerste helft der 17de eeuw. [Brussels], 1976. 2 vols. *bibliog. (Pro Civitate. Collection Histoire. Série in-8. No. 45) Map in end pocket.*

SOLY (HUGO) Urbanisme en kapitalisme te Antwerpen in de 16de eeuw: de stedebouwkundige en industriële ondernemingen van Gilbert van Schoonbeke. [Brussels], 1977. pp. 496. *bibliog. (Pro Civitate. Collection Histoire. Série in-8. No. 47) With summary in French.*

— Growth.

SOLY (HUGO) Urbanisme en kapitalisme te Antwerpen in de 16de eeuw: de stedebouwkundige en industriële ondernemingen van Gilbert van Schoonbeke. [Brussels], 1977. pp. 496. *bibliog. (Pro Civitate. Collection Histoire. Série in-8. No. 47) With summary in French.*

— Poor.

ANTWERP. Commissie van Openbare Onderstand. Vijftig jaar Commissie van Openbare Onderstand Antwerpen 1915-1975. [Antwerp, 1975]. pp. 225.

— Social policy.

ANTWERP. Commissie van Openbare Onderstand. Vijftig jaar Commissie van Openbare Onderstand Antwerpen 1915-1975. [Antwerp, 1975]. pp. 225.

APARTMENT HOUSES
— United Kingdom — Manchester.

FLETT (HAZEL) and PEAFORD (MARGARET) The effect of slum clearance on multi-occupation. Bristol, Social Science Research Council Research Unit on Ethnic Relations, [1977]. pp. 53. *bibliog. (Working Papers on Ethnic Relations. No. 4)*

APHASIA.

LESSER (RUTH) Linguistic investigations of aphasia. London, 1978. pp. 222. *bibliog.*

APINAGE INDIANS.

MATTA (ROBERTO DA) Um mundo dividido: a estrutura social dos indios Apinaye. Petropolis, 1976. pp. 254. *bibliog.*

APOLOGETICS.

ROGERS (WALTER LACY) Evidences of Christianity: the Messianic prophecies. London, 1876. pp. 24.

APOSTASY.

CAPLOVITZ (DAVID) and SHERROW (FRED) The religious drop-outs: apostasy among college graduates. Beverly Hills, [1977]. pp. 199.

APPALACHIAN MOUNTAINS
— Economic conditions.

HAMMER, GREENE, SILER ASSOCIATES. Investment guidelines for the North Carolina Appalachian region; prepared for...North Carolina Department of Administration...[and] Appalachia Regional Commission. Washington, 1967. pp. 129.

— Economic policy.

PASCALE (RICHARD T.) and BARBOUR (GEORGE P.) Shared power: a study of four federal funding systems in Appalachia. Washington, [1977]. pp. 36. *(American Enterprise Institute for Public Policy Research. Special Analyses)*

APPELLATE PROCEDURE
— Egypt.

PALAGI (DARIO) L'appel et la requête civile dans la législation mixte: observations critiques et projet de modifications. Alexandrie, 1910. pp. 19.

APPENZELL-INNERRHODEN (CANTON).

TRIET (MAX) Der Sutterhandel in Appenzell Innerrhoden, 1760-1829: ein Beitrag zur Geschichte der politischen Unruhen in der Schweiz des Ancien Régime. Appenzell, 1977. pp. 279. *bibliog.*

APPLETON (NATHAN).

GREGORY (FRANCES W.) Nathan Appleton, merchant and entrepreneur, 1779-1861. Charlottesville, Va., 1975. pp. 358. *bibliog.*

APPRENTICES

APPRENTICES

— Canada — New Brunswick.

NEW BRUNSWICK. Department of Labour. 1970. Is apprenticeship seen as worthwhile?; (study designed and carried out by Ronald W. Johnson). [Fredericton, 1970]. pp. (26). *bibliog.*

— — Nova Scotia.

NOVA SCOTIA. Apprenticeship and Tradesmen's Qualifications Division. 1967. Apprenticeship training in Nova Scotia. [Halifax, 1967]. pp. 16.

— United Kingdom.

WHEATLEY (DAVID ERNEST) Apprenticeships in the United Kingdom. Brussels, 1976. pp. 199. *(European Economic Community. Studies. Social Policy Series. 30)*

AQUITAINE

— Economic conditions.

VUES SUR L'ECONOMIE D'AQUITAINE: revue bimestrielle; ([pd. by] Institut National de la Statistique et des Etudes Economiques,...Direction Régionale de Bordeaux [France]). bi-m., Ap 1973 (1973, no.2)- Bordeaux. *File includes L'année en Aquitaine, 1974- .*

ARAB COUNTRIES.

MAGHREB-MACHREK: monde arabe (formerly Maghréb: études et documents Algérie, Libye, Maroc, Tunisie); (bulletin rédigé par la Fondation Nationale des Sciences Politiques. ..et la Direction de la Documentation [France]). bi-m., Ja/F 1964 (no.1)- Paris. *Index: 1973/1976 (nos. 55-74).*

— Commercial policy.

NELSON (WALTER HENRY) and PRITTIE (TERENCE CORNELIUS FARMER) The economic war against the Jews. New York, [1977]. pp. 269.

— Economic conditions.

DIARUNA WAL-ALAM; pd. by Ministry of Finance and Petroleum, Qatar. m., Ag 1977(no. 20)- Doha.

EL MALLAKH (RAGAEI) and others. Capital investment in the Middle East: the use of surplus funds for regional development. New York, [1977]. pp. 194. *bibliog.*

SAYIGH (YUSIF ABDALLA) The determinants of Arab economic development. London, [1978]. pp. 181.

SAYIGH (YUSIF ABDALLA) The economics of the Arab world: development since 1945. London, [1978]. pp. 726.

— Economic integration.

EL MALLAKH (RAGAEI) and others. Capital investment in the Middle East: the use of surplus funds for regional development. New York, [1977]. pp. 194. *bibliog.*

— Foreign economic relations — Africa.

CHIBWE (EPHRAIM CHIPAMPE) Afro-Arab relations in the new world order. London, 1977. pp. 150.

— — Europe.

EURO-Arab cooperation; edited by Edmond Völker. Leyden, 1976. pp. 228. *Papers from a colloquium organized by the University of Amsterdam Europa Instituut in October 1975.*

— — Japan.

OPPORTUNITIES for cooperation between Japan and the Arab world: [proceedings of the OAPEC Tokyo seminar, November 11-12, 1976]. Kuwait, Organization of Arab Petroleum Exporting Countries, [1977]. pp. 250.

— Foreign relations — Africa.

CHIBWE (EPHRAIM CHIPAMPE) Afro-Arab relations in the new world order. London, 1977. pp. 150.

— History.

LAROUI (ABDALLAH) The crisis of the Arab intellectual: traditionalism or historicism?;...translated from the French by Diarmid Cammell. Berkeley, Calif., [1976]. pp. 180.

MANSFIELD (PETER) The Arabs. London, 1976 repr. 1977. pp. 572.

— Intellectual life.

LAROUI (ABDALLAH) The crisis of the Arab intellectual: traditionalism or historicism?;...translated from the French by Diarmid Cammell. Berkeley, Calif., [1976]. pp. 180.

— Nationalism.

ISMAEL (TAREQ Y.) The Arab left. Syracuse, N.Y., 1976. pp. 204. *bibliogs.*

— Politics and government.

ISMAEL (TAREQ Y.) The Arab left. Syracuse, N.Y., 1976. pp. 204. *bibliogs.*

HUDSON (MICHAEL CRAIG) Arab politics: the search for legitimacy. New Haven, 1977. pp. 434.

— Relations (general) with the United States.

CAN cultures communicate?; (an AEI Round Table held on September 23, 1976...); Edward Stewart, moderator, etc. Washington, 1976. pp. 33. *(American Enterprise Institute for Public Policy Research. Round Tables)*

ARABS.

MANSFIELD (PETER) The Arabs. London, 1976 repr. 1977. pp. 572.

ARAFAT (YASIR) pseud.

KIERNAN (THOMAS) Yasir Arafat: the man and the myth. London, 1976. pp. 223.

ARAUCANIAN INDIANS.

BERDICHEWSKY (BERNARDO) The Araucanian Indian in Chile. Copenhagen, 1975. pp. 38. *bibliog. (International Work Group for Indigenous Affairs. Documents. 20)*

ARBITRATION, INDUSTRIAL

— Australia.

AUSTRALIAN ARBITRATION INSPECTORATE. Annual report. a., 1972(1st)- Canberra. *Included in AUSTRALIA. Parliament. [Parliamentary papers].*

— Canada — Bibliography.

ARMSTRONG (DOUGLAS) and DWORACZEK (MARIAN) compilers. Industrial arbitration in Canada 1976-1974: a selective bibliography. [Toronto], Ontario Ministry of Labour Research Library, 1974. pp. 8.

— United Kingdom.

ADVISORY CONCILIATION AND ARBITRATION SERVICE [U.K.]. Press notices. irreg., current issues only. London.

DUFFRYN RHONDDA COLLIERY, CYMMER. Duffryn Rhondda Colliery, Cymmer: arbitration and award, May 1903: shorthand notes and transcript by D.M. Evans. Ystalyfera, 1903. fo.26.

GREAT EASTERN RAILWAY COMPANY. Wages and hours arbitration, 1909: award of...Lord Gorell of Brampton. [London, 1909]. pp. 25.

ADVISORY, CONCILIATION AND ARBITRATION SERVICE [U.K.]. Trade union recognition [under the] Employment Protection Act 1975, Section 12. Reports. irreg., [S 1976] (no.1)- [London].

ARBITRATION AND AWARD

— Germany.

HEIMANN (NORBERT) Die Schiedsgerichtsbarkeit der politischen Parteien in der Bundesrepublik Deutschland. Bonn, 1977. pp. 305. *bibliog. (Friedrich-Ebert-Stiftung. Forschungsinstitut. Schriftenreihe. Band 128)*

— Sweden.

STOCKHOLM. Handelskammare. Arbitration in Sweden. Stockholm, 1977. pp. 212. *bibliog.*

ARCHAEOLOGY, INDUSTRIAL

— United Kingdom — Scotland.

HUME (JOHN R.) The industrial archaeology of Scotland: 1: the Lowlands and Borders. London, 1976. pp. 279. *bibliog.*

DONNACHIE (IAN) and others. Scotland. Hartington, [1977]. pp. 112. *bibliog.*

ARCHITECTURE

— United Kingdom — Conservation and restoration.

WE WANT THE WEST PIER CAMPAIGN. The West Pier: a second report. Brighton, 1975. pp. 30. *bibliog.*

A REPORT on craft skills in the building industry; [by a working group, chairman Donald Ensom]. London, 1976. pp. 10.

— — — Finance.

THORNCROFT (M.E.T.) The economics of conservation. London, [1975]. pp. 12.

— United States.

HAYDEN (DOLORES) Seven American utopias: the architecture of communitarian socialism, 1790-1975. Cambridge, Mass., [1976]. pp. 401. *bibliog.*

ARCHITECTURE AND SOCIETY.

HAYDEN (DOLORES) Seven American utopias: the architecture of communitarian socialism, 1790-1975. Cambridge, Mass., [1976]. pp. 401. *bibliog.*

ARCHIVES

— Canada — Nova Scotia.

FERGUSSON (CHARLES BRUCE) The public archives of Nova Scotia. Halifax, N.S., 1963. fo. 27. *(Nova Scotia. Public Archives. Bulletins. No. 19).* Photocopy.

— Germany.

AUS der Arbeit des Bundesarchivs: Beiträge zum Archivwesen, zur Quellenkunde und Zeitgeschichte; herausgegeben von Heinz Boberach und Hans Booms. Boppard am Rhein, [1978]. pp. 568. *bibliog. (Germany (Bundesrepublik). Bundesarchiv. Schriften. 25)*

— United Kingdom.

LONDON. University. School of Oriental and African Studies. Library. Papers relating to the Chinese maritime customs, 1860-1943, in the library of the School of Oriental and African Studies. London, 1973. pp. 13.

LOCAL POPULATION STUDIES and CAMBRIDGE GROUP FOR THE HISTORY OF POPULATION AND SOCIAL STRUCTURE. The first supplement to Original parish registers in record offices and libraries. [Matlock], 1976. pp. 60.

LEEDS. University. Library. Handlists. 34. Political correspondence (1884-1897) of Louis Henry Hayter. [Leeds], 1977. pp. 16.

SWANN (BRENDA AUDREY SWANTON) and TURNBULL (MAUREEN) Records of interest to social scientists, 1919 to 1939: employment and unemployment. London, 1978. pp. 590. *(U.K. Public Record Office. Handbooks. No. 18)*

ARCTIC REGIONS.

CONFERENCE ON CANADA AND THE NORTHERN RIM, QUEEN'S UNIVERSITY, KINGSTON, ONTARIO, 1977. Report...; [edited by Nils Orvik]. Kingston, Ont., 1977. fo. 144. *(Kingston, Ontario. Queen's University. Centre for International Relations. National Security Series. No. 6)*

AREILZA (JOSE MARIA DE) Conde de Motrico.

AREILZA (JOSE MARIA DE) Conde de Motrico. Diario de un Ministro de la monarquia. Barcelona, 1977 repr. 1978. pp. 222.

ARGENTINE REPUBLIC

— Armed forces — Political activity.

ROUQUIE (ALAIN) Pouvoir militaire et société politique en République Argentine. [Paris, 1978]. pp. 772. *bibliog.*

— Boundaries — Chile.

MORZONE (LUIS ANTONIO) Cuestiones de limites con la Republica de Chile: el laudo arbitral en la region del Rio Encuentro. La Plata, 1967. pp. 31.

— Census.

GONZALEZ (JOAQUIN VICTOR) El censo nacional y la Constitucion. Buenos Aires, 1930. pp. 323.

— Civilization.

SOLHER (ANGEL RAUL) Biologia sociologica: evolucion de las fuerzas sociales argentinas. Buenos Aires, 1929. pp. 233.

— Constitutional law.

GONZALEZ (JOAQUIN VICTOR) El censo nacional y la Constitucion. Buenos Aires, 1930. pp. 323.

— Economic conditions.

TERRY (JOSE A.) La crisis, 1885-1892: sistema bancario. Buenos Aires, 1893. pp. 353.

SOARES (CARLOS F.) Economia y finanzas de la nacion argentina, [1903-1932, vols. 2 and 3]. Buenos Aires, [1922-32]. 2 vols.

ORTIZ PEREYRA (MANUEL) La tercera emancipacion: actualidad economica y social de la Republica Argentina. Buenos Aires, 1926. pp. 205.

SANGUINETTI (JULIO) Nuestro potencial economico industrial y la defensa nacional. Buenos Aires, 1946. pp. 323. *bibliog. (Circulo Militar. Biblioteca del Oficial. vol. 331)*

GRANCELLI CHA (NESTOR) De la crisis al desarrollo nacional; la UCRI y la realidad economica. [Buenos Aires, 1961]. pp. 134.

ECONOMIC INFORMATION ON ARGENTINA (formerly Economic information of Argentina); [pd. by] Secretaria de Programacion y Coordinacion Economica. m., Ag 1976(no. 63)- Buenos Aires.

— Economic history.

ARIAS (DAVID M.) Historia e influencia del papel moneda en el desenvolvimiento economico argentino. Buenos Aires, 1912. pp. 116.

FRIZZI DE LONGINI (HAYDEE E.) Rivadavia y la economia argentina. Buenos Aires, 1947. pp. 266. *bibliog.*

ALBARRACIN (JOSE MANUEL H.) Victorino de la Plaza y la crisis economica de 1875 a 1880. Buenos Aires, [1950]. pp. 155.

PANETTIERI (JOSE) La crisis ganadera: ideas en torno a un cambio en la estructura economica y social del pais, 1866-1871. La Plata, [1965]. pp. 123. *bibliog. (La Plata. Universidad Nacional. Facultad de Humanidades y Ciencias de la Educacion. Departamento de Historia. Monografias y Tesis. 6)*

RANDALL (LAURA REGINA ROSENBAUM) An economic history of Argentina in the twentieth century. New York, 1978. pp. 323. *bibliog.*

— Economic policy.

CATALANO (LUCIANO R.) Plan constructivo del radicalismo: el libro de las masas productoras. Buenos Aires, 1933. pp. 238. *bibliogs.*

BIDABEHERE (FERNANDO ARTURO) Accion de la economia dirigida en la Republica Argentina: control de cambios, juntas reguladoras. Buenos Aires, 1937. pp. 132. *bibliog.*

INSTITUTO ALEJANDRO E. BUNGE DE INVESTIGACIONES ECONOMICAS Y SOCIALES. Soluciones argentinas a los problemas economicos y sociales del presente. Buenos Aires, 1945. pp. 279.

GOMEZ MORALES (ALFREDO) Politica economica peronista. Buenos Aires, [1951]. pp. 230.

— Emigration and immigration.

ARGENTINE REPUBLIC. Oficina Sectorial de Desarrollo de Recursos Humanos. 1973. La inmigracion desde paises limitrofes hacia la Argentina: analisis estadistico. [Buenos Aires, 1973]. fo. 166.

— Foreign opinion, American.

CIRIA (ALBERTO) Estados Unidos nos mira. Buenos Aires, [1973]. pp. 258.

— Foreign relations.

DIAZ CISNEROS (CESAR) La Liga de las Naciones y la actitud argentina; con el texto del tratado. Buenos Aires, 1921. pp. 207.

MILENKY (EDWARD S.) Argentina's foreign policies. Boulder, Colo., 1978. pp. 345. *bibliog.*

— — United States.

CIRIA (ALBERTO) Estados Unidos nos mira. Buenos Aires, [1973]. pp. 258.

FRANCIS (MICHAEL J.) The limits of hegemony: United States relations with Argentina and Chile during World War II. Notre Dame, [1977]. pp. 292. *(Notre Dame. University. Committee on International Relations. International Studies)*

— History.

SOLHER (ANGEL RAUL) Biologia sociologica: evolucion de las fuerzas sociales argentinas. Buenos Aires, 1929. pp. 233.

SANTAYANA (MAURO) A tragedia argentina: poder e violência de Rosas ao Peronismo. Rio de Janeiro, 1976. pp. 202. *bibliog.*

— — 1817-1860.

ROSA (JOSE MARIA) Fraudes y adulteraciones documentales en "La caida de Rosas": respuesta a Jose Antonio Soares de Souza. [Buenos Aires, 1969]. pp. 37.

VARELA (FLORENCIO) Rosas y su gobierno: escritos politicos, economicos y literarios. Buenos Aires, 1975. pp. 211. *New edition of work published in 1927 which consisted of material first published in 1859.*

— — 1860-1910.

CARDENAS (EDUARDO J.) and PAYA (CARLOS M.) En camino a la democracia politica, 1904-1910. Buenos Aires, [1975]. pp. 417. *bibliog.*

— — 1890, Revolution.

MENDIA (JOSE M.) La revolucion del 90: la obra mas documentada, mas autentica y fidedigna para el conocimiento de la revolucion del 90. Buenos Aires, 1927. pp. 215. *At head of title: Jose M. Mendia - Luis O. Naon.*

VEDIA Y MITRE (MARIANO DE) La revolucion del 90: origen y fundacion de la Union Civica; causas, desarrollo y consecuencias de la revolucion de julio. Buenos Aires, 1929. pp. 271.

— — 1910-1943.

SOMMARIVA (J.O.) La republica federal, 1912-1936. [La Plata], 1955. pp. 327.

— Industries.

SANGUINETTI (JULIO) Nuestro potencial economico industrial y la defensa nacional. Buenos Aires, 1946. pp. 323. *bibliog. (Circulo Militar. Biblioteca del Oficial. vol. 331)*

— Politics and government.

FANELLI (VICENTE I.) Justificatio: la revolucion por la libertad es un derecho; causas y origen de los sucesos del 4 de febrero de 1905. Buenos Aires, 1905. pp. 144.

MORENO (RODOLFO) Enfermedades de la politica argentina. Buenos Aires, 1905. pp. 166.

CALLE (JORGE) Los iluminados: su encumbramiento y su fracaso en la politica argentina. Buenos Aires, 1922. pp. 339.

BARROETAVEÑA (FRANCISCO ANTONIO) El gobierno del Dr. Alvear: post nubila Phoebus. Buenos Aires, 1923. pp. 147.

PONSSA (JOSE M.) Principios y orientaciones del radicalismo. Cordoba, Argentine Republic, 1925. pp. 139.

BIANCO (JOSE) Don Bernardo de Irigoyen: estadista y pioneer, 1822-1906. Buenos Aires, 1927. pp. 333.

La OBRA de la Revolucion: [reseña sintetica de la labor desarrollada]. [Buenos Aires, 1931]. pp. 212.

OYHANARTE (RAUL F.) Radicalismo de siempre; exegesis doctrinaria por Adolfo Korn Villafañe. La Plata, 1932. pp. 108.

RODRIGUEZ YRIGOYEN (LUIS) Hipolito Yrigoyen, 1878-1933: documentacion historica de 55 años de actuacion por la democracia y las instituciones. Buenos Aires, 1934. pp. 543.

VILLAFAÑE (BENJAMIN) La ley suicida. Buenos Aires, 1936. pp. 157.

DAMONTE TABORDA (RAUL) Ayer fue San Peron: 12 años de humillacion argentina. [Buenos Aires], 1955. pp. 276.

REPETTO (NICOLAS) Mi paso por la politica: de Roca a Yrigoyen. Buenos Aires, [1956]. pp. 347.

FARIAS ALEM (ROBERTO) Alem y la democracia argentina. Buenos Aires, [1957]. pp. 201.

CODOVILLA (VICTORIO) Biografia politica de un revolucionario consecuente. Buenos Aires, 1964. pp. 16.

CODOVILLA (VICTORIO) Lo nuevo en la situacion nacional despues de las elecciones: informe presentado al pleno del Comite Central del Partido Comunista, realizado los dias 27 y 28 de marzo de 1965. Buenos Aires, 1965. pp. 39.

MALM GREEN (GUILLERMO) Revolucion nacional para la reconquista Argentina. [Buenos Aires?, 1968?]. pp. 12.

WORLD UNIVERSITY SERVICE. The present situation in Chile and Argentina. London, 1976. pp. 21. *bibliog.*

COMISION ARGENTINA POR LOS DERECHOS HUMANOS. Argentina: proceso al genocidio. Madrid, 1977. pp. 328.

ROUQUIE (ALAIN) Pouvoir militaire et société politique en République Argentine. [Paris, 1978]. pp. 772. *bibliog.*

— Population.

RECCHINI DE LATTES (ZULMA L.) and LATTES (ALFREDO E.) La poblacion de Argentina. [Buenos Aires, 1975]. pp. 212. *bibliog. (Committee for International Coordination of National Research in Demography. C.I.C.R.E.D. Series)*

ARGENTINE REPUBLIC (Cont.)

— Presidents — Election.

TORRE (LISANDRO DE LA) Las dos campañas presidenciales, 1916-1931. Buenos Aires, 1939. pp. 255. *(Escritos y Discursos. 1)*

— Relations (general) with the United States.

LIBRO azul y blanco de la prensa argentina; por cincuenta y tres periodistas argentinos. Buenos Aires, 1951. pp. 439.

— Rural conditions.

UNION CIVICA RADICAL. Comite Nacional. Congreso Agrario de la Union Civica Radical: "tierra y libertad". Buenos Aires, [1950]. pp. 126.

— Social life and customs.

BASUALDO (JOSE AGUSTIN DE) El gaucho argentino. Buenos Aires, [1942]. pp. 159.

— Social policy.

CATALANO (LUCIANO R.) Plan constructivo del radicalismo: el libro de las masas productoras. Buenos Aires, 1933. pp. 238. *bibliogs.*

INSTITUTO ALEJANDRO E. BUNGE DE INVESTIGACIONES ECONOMICAS Y SOCIALES. Soluciones argentinas a los problemas economicos y sociales del presente. Buenos Aires, 1945. pp. 279.

ARID REGIONS.

MAASS (ARTHUR AARON) and ANDERSON (RAYMOND LLOYD) ... And the desert shall rejoice: conflict, growth, and justice in arid environments. Cambridge, Mass., [1978]. pp. 447.

— United States.

URBAN planning for arid zones: American experiences and directions; Gideon Golany, editor. New York, [1978]. pp. 245.

ARISTOCRACY.

LUDOVICI (ANTHONY MARIO) A defence of aristocracy: a text book for Tories. London, 1915. pp. 459.

ARISTOTLE.

MULGAN (RICHARD G.) Aristotle's political theory: an introduction for students of political theory. Oxford, 1977. pp. 156. *bibliog.*

ARMAMENTS.

INTERNATIONAL INSTITUTE FOR STRATEGIC STUDIES. Adelphi Papers. No. 140. The future of land-based missile forces; by Colin S. Gray. London, 1977. pp. 36.

Les TRAFICS d'armes de la France: l'engrenage de la militarisation; étude réalisée par le Centre local d'information et de coordination pour l'action non violente. 2nd ed. Paris, 1977. pp. 335. *bibliog.*

INTERNATIONAL INSTITUTE FOR STRATEGIC STUDIES. Adelphi Papers. Nos. 144, 145. New conventional weapons and East-West security;...papers... given at the nineteenth annual conference of the IISS at Bruges, Belgium, in September 1977. London, 1978. 2 pamphlets.

ARMED FORCES.

FELD (MAURY D.) The structure of violence: armed forces as social systems. Beverly Hills, [1977]. pp. 203.

— Appropriations and expenditures.

BECKER (ABRAHAM S.) Military expenditure limitation for arms control: problems and prospects; with a documentary history of recent proposals. Cambridge, Mass., 1977. pp. 352. *bibliog.*

— Political activity.

MOVIMENTO GAETANO SALVEMINI. Forze armate e democrazia: [proceedings of two Round Tables held in Rome, 1971 and 1976]. [Roma, 1976?]. pp. 231. *(Movimento Gaetano Salvemini. Quaderni del Salvemini. 20/21)*

JANOWITZ (MORRIS) Military institutions and coercion in the developing nations. Chicago, 1977. pp. 211. *Expanded edition of The military in the political development of new nations.*

TRIMBERGER (ELLEN KAY) Revolution from above: military bureaucrats and development in Japan, Turkey, Egypt, and Peru. New Brunswick, [1978]. pp. 196. *bibliog.*

ARMENIA

— Industries.

ARMENIA. Tsentral'noe Statisticheskoe Upravlenie. 1973. Promyshlennost' Armianskoi SSR: statisticheskii sbornik. Erevan, 1973. pp. 235.

ARMENIAN QUESTION.

BRITISH ARMENIA COMMITTEE. Armenia and the Turkish settlement; memorandum submitted for the consideration of H.M. Government. London, 1920. pp. 8.

SONYEL (SALÂHI RAMSDAN) Greco-Armenian conspiracy against Turkey revived. London, 1975. pp. 28. *bibliog. (Cyprus Turkish Association. Publications. 1)*

ARMENIANS IN SYRIA.

KRIKORIAN (MESROB K.) Armenians in the service of the Ottoman Empire, 1860-1908. London, 1977. pp. 149. *bibliog.*

ARMENIANS IN TURKEY.

SHIRAGIAN (ARSHAVIR) The legacy: memoirs of an Armenian patriot; translated by Sonia Shiragian. Boston, Mass., 1976. pp. 217.

KRIKORIAN (MESROB K.) Armenians in the service of the Ottoman Empire, 1860-1908. London, 1977. pp. 149. *bibliog.*

ARMIES

— Staffs.

GENERAL staffs and diplomacy before the Second World War; edited by Adrian Preston. London, [1978]. pp. 138. *Essays originally read to the Fourth Annual Military History Symposium held at the Royal Military College of Canada in 1977.*

ARMS CONTROL

— Bibliography.

BURNS (RICHARD DEAN) compiler. Arms control and disarmament: a bibliography. Santa Barbara, [1977]. pp. 430. *(California University. Center for the Study of Armament and Disarmament. War/Peace Bibliography Series. 6)*

ARNO VALLEY

— Industries.

BUSINO (GIOVANNI) Vilfredo Pareto e l'industria del ferro nel Valdarno: contributo alla storia dell'impreditorialità italiana. Milano, 1977. pp. 922. *(Banco Commerciale Italiana. Studi e Ricerche di Storia Economica Italiana nell'Età del Risorgimento) A considerable appendix of Pareto's letters on the subject.*

ARNOLD (STANISLAW).

ZIEMIA i ludzie dawnej Polski: studia z geografii historycznej; redaktorzy Adam Galos i Julian Janczak. Wrocław, 1976. pp. 211. *(Wrocław. Wrocławskie Towarzystwo Naukowe. Prace. Seria A. Nr. 179) One article in Russian. With French summaries.*

ARREST

— United Kingdom.

U.K. Home Office. 1978. Evidence to the Royal Commission on Criminal Procedure: memorandum no. 3: the powers of the police to arrest or otherwise stop a person, to search him, to stop and search vehicles, and to enter and search premises. London, 1978. 1 vol. (various pagings).

ART

— History.

HADJINICOLAOU (NICOS) Art history and class struggle; translated from the French by Louise Asmal. London, [1978]. pp. 206.

— Canada — Galleries and museums.

CANADA. Statistics Canada. Culture statistics: museums, art galleries and related institutions. a., 1974(1st)- Ottawa. *[in English and French]*

— United Kingdom — Galleries and museums — Directories.

The LIBRARIES, museums and art galleries yearbook 1976; editors: Adrian Brink and Derry Watkins. Cambridge, 1976. pp. 254.

ART AND SOCIETY.

The ARTS and man: a world view of the role and functions of the arts in society. Paris, Unesco, 1969. pp. 175.

LE BRETON (ANDRE) Position politique du surréalisme. Paris, 1971. pp. 32. *(Bibliothèque Volante, La. No.2)*

HADJINICOLAOU (NICOS) Art history and class struggle; translated from the French by Louise Asmal. London, [1978]. pp. 206.

ART INDUSTRIES AND TRADE

— France.

FRANCE. Groupe sectoriel d'Analyse et de Prévision Arts- Création-Loisirs. 1976. Rapport...: préparation du 7e Plan. Paris, [1976]. pp. 95.

ART PATRONAGE.

ARTISTS NOW. Patronage of the creative artist. London, [1974]. pp.91,fo.(29).

ARTIFICIAL INTELLIGENCE.

THINKING: readings in cognitive science; edited by P.N. Johnson- Laird and P.C. Wason. Cambridge, [1977]. pp. 615. *bibliog.*

SLOMAN (AARON) The computer revolution in philosophy: philosophy, science and models of mind. Hassocks, 1978. pp. 304.

ARTIFICIAL SATELLITES.

REGIMES for the ocean, outer space, and weather; ([by] Seyom Brown [and others]). Washington, D.C., [1977]. pp. 257.

ARTIFICIAL SATELLITES IN TELECOMMUNICATION.

SMITH (DELBERT D.) Communication via satellite: a vision in retrospect. Leyden, 1976. pp. 335. *bibliog.*

ECONOMIC and policy problems in satellite communications; edited by Joseph N. Pelton [and] Marcellus S. Snow. New York, 1977. pp. 242.

MARTIN (JAMES THOMAS) Communications satellite systems. Englewood Cliffs, [1978]. pp. 398. *bibliogs.*

ARTISANS

— Kenya.

KING (KENNETH JAMES) The African artisan: education and the informal sector in Kenya. London, 1977. pp. 226. *bibliog.*

ASIA, SOUTHEAST

— Russia.

GRECHKINA (EL'ZA ROBERTOVNA) Srednie sloi na puti k sotsializmu. Tallin, 1976. pp. 187.

— United Kingdom.

A REPORT on craft skills in the building industry; [by a working group, chairman Donald Ensom]. London, 1976. pp. 10.

FEDERATION OF BRITISH CRAFT SOCIETIES. Income tax and the craftsman. London, 1977. pp. 14.

— United States — Political activity.

OLTON (CHARLES S.) Artisans for independence: Philadelphia mechanics and the American revolution. Syracuse, N.Y., 1975. pp. 172. *bibliog.*

ARTS

— Study and teaching — Canada.

CANADA. Statistics Canada. Culture statistics: the arts: education. a., 1974/75(1st)- Ottawa. *[in English and French]*

— United Kingdom.

WEINBERGER (BARBARA) Leisure and the arts in Birmingham: a pilot investigation. [Birmingham, 1974]. pp. 106. *(Birmingham. University. Centre for Urban and Regional Studies. Research Memoranda. No.47)*

LABOUR PARTY. The arts and the people: Labour's policy towards the arts. London, 1977. pp. 69.

— — Finance.

BROUGH (COLIN) As you like it: private support for the arts. London, [1977]. pp. 16. *bibliog.*

ARTS AND SOCIETY

— United Kingdom.

LLEWELYN-DAVIES WEEKS [AND PARTNERS]. Inner area study: Birmingham: you and me here we are: Artist Placement Group project. [London], Department of the Environment, [1977]. pp. 142.

ARUNACHAL PRADESH

— Population.

INDIA. Census, 1971. Series 24. Arunachal Pradesh: a portrait of population, [by] J. K. Barthakur. [Delhi, 1975]. pp. 128.

ASIA

— Economic conditions.

POVERTY and landlessness in rural Asia. Geneva, International Labour Office, 1977. pp. 288.

UPPAL (JOGINDAR S.) Economic development in south Asia. New York, [1977]. pp. 212. *bibliog.*

— Economic history.

UPPAL (JOGINDAR S.) Economic development in south Asia. New York, [1977]. pp. 212. *bibliog.*

— Economic policy.

UPPAL (JOGINDAR S.) Economic development in south Asia. New York, [1977]. pp. 212. *bibliog.*

— Foreign economic relations — United States.

SHAH (S.A.) ed. U.S. imperialism in modern Asia. Montreal, 1972. pp. 65. *bibliogs. (Afro-Asian-Latin American Peoples' Solidarity Committee. Pamphlet Series. No. 2)*

— Foreign relations.

ASIA AND THE WORLD FORUM. Sino-Korean forum on northeast Asia. Taipei, 1977. pp. 135. *(Asia and the World Forum. Asia and the World Monographs. 4)*

INTRA-Asian international relations; edited by George T. Yu. Boulder, Colo., 1977. pp. 172. *bibliog. Based on a panel organised for the 1976 annual conference of the Association for Asian Studies.*

— — Australia.

STARGARDT (A.W.) Australia's Asian policies: the history of a debate 1839-1972. Hamburg, [1977]. pp. 404.

— — China.

ARMSTRONG (J.D.) Revolutionary diplomacy: Chinese foreign policy and the united front doctrine. Berkeley, [1977]. pp. 251.

— — Russia.

SEN GUPTA (BHABANI) Soviet-Asian relations in the 1970s and beyond: an interperceptional study. New York, 1976. pp. 368.

TAN (SU-CHENG) The expansion of Soviet seapower and the security of Asia. Taipei, 1977. pp. 177. *bibliog. (Asia and the World Forum. Asia and the World Monographs. 3)*

— — United States.

SHAH (S.A.) ed. U.S. imperialism in modern Asia. Montreal, 1972. pp. 65. *bibliogs. (Afro-Asian-Latin American Peoples' Solidarity Committee. Pamphlet Series. No. 2)*

ASIA AND THE WORLD FORUM. Forum on the U.S. and east Asia [held in 1977: proceedings] . Taipei, 1977. pp. 157. *(Asia and the World Forum. Asia and the World Monographs. 7)*

HARRISON (SELIG S.) The widening gulf: Asian nationalism and American policy. New York, [1978]. pp. 468. *bibliog.*

— Historiography.

KRITIKA burzhuaznogo natsionalizma. Moskva, 1977. pp. 187. *bibliog. (Akademiia Nauk SSSR. Institut Vostokovedeniia. Sovremennaia Istoriografiia Stran Zarubezhnogo Vostoka. [vyp.6])*

— Nationalism.

KRITIKA burzhuaznogo natsionalizma. Moskva, 1977. pp. 187. *bibliog. (Akademiia Nauk SSSR. Institut Vostokovedeniia. Sovremennaia Istoriografiia Stran Zarubezhnogo Vostoka. [vyp.6])*

NATIONALISM and communism in Asia: the American response; edited and with an introduction by Norman A. Graebner. Lexington, Mass., [1977]. pp. 204. *bibliog.*

HARRISON (SELIG S.) The widening gulf: Asian nationalism and American policy. New York, [1978]. pp. 468. *bibliog.*

— Politics and government.

AFRO-ASIAN PEOPLES' SOLIDARITY ORGANIZATION. Presidium. Meeting, Aden, 1976. The third meeting of the A.A.P.S.O. presidium, etc. Cairo, 1976. pp. 33.

INTRA-Asian international relations; edited by George T. Yu. Boulder, Colo., 1977. pp. 172. *bibliog. Based on a panel organised for the 1976 annual conference of the Association for Asian Studies.*

ENDICOTT (JOHN E.) and HEATON (WILLIAM R.) The politics of east Asia: China, Japan, Korea. Boulder, Colo., 1978. pp. 323. *bibliog.*

RULE, protest, identity: aspects of modern south Asia; edited by Peter Robb and David Taylor. London, [1978]. pp. 234. *(London. University. School of Oriental and African Studies. Centre of South Asian Studies. Collected Papers on South Asia. 1)*

— Population.

POPULATION HEADLINERS; [pd. by] Division of Population and Social Affairs, Economic and Social Commission for Asia and the Pacific. irreg., current issues only. Bangkok.

— Religion.

EAST comes west: a background to some Asian faiths; [by] Peggy Holroyde [and others]. 2nd ed. London, Community Relations Commission, 1973. pp. 101. *bibliogs.*

— Rural conditions.

COMMUNICATION and rural change; edited by P.R.R. Sinha. Singapore, [1976]. pp. 230. *bibliog. Based on papers presented at a conference held by the Asian Mass Communication Research and Information Centre, in Bangalore, 1973.*

— Social conditions.

ASIAN values and modernization; [papers from a seminar]; edited by Seah Chee-Meow. Singapore, [1977]. pp. 100.

ASIA, SOUTHEAST

— Commerce — Canada.

HUGHES (WILLIAM) 1927- . Canada's exports to south-east Asia: a study of trade and transportation. Victoria, B.C., Bureau of Economics and Statistics, 1963. pp. 45.

— Defences.

INTERNATIONAL INSTITUTE FOR STRATEGIC STUDIES. Adelphi Papers. No. 142. The security of South-East Asia; by Bruce Grant. London, 1978. pp. 34.

— Economic conditions.

The ROLE of public enterprise in national development in southeast Asia: problems and prospects; edited by Nguyen Truong. Singapore, 1976. pp. 334. *bibliog.*

— Economic integration.

PAUKER (GUY JEAN) and others. Diversity and development in southeast Asia: the coming decade. New York, [1977]. pp. 190. *bibliog. (Council on Foreign Relations. 1980s Project Studies)*

— Economic policy.

PAUKER (GUY JEAN) and others. Diversity and development in southeast Asia: the coming decade. New York, [1977]. pp. 190. *bibliog. (Council on Foreign Relations. 1980s Project Studies)*

— Foreign economic relations.

FORUM on Australia, New Zealand and East Asia. [Taipei], 1977. pp. 109. *(Asia and the World Forum. Monograph Series. No. 5)*

— — Australia.

LOOKING north to south-east Asia: the view from Australia; edited by Edward P. Wolfers. Honolulu, [1976]. pp. 276. *Papers delivered to the 5th Annual Conference of the Australian Institute of International Affairs held in Melbourne in 1975.*

— Foreign relations.

COLBERT (EVELYN SPEYER) Southeast Asia in international politics, 1941-1956. Ithaca, 1977. pp. 372. *bibliog.*

AUSTRALIA. Prime Minister. 1974. Principal speeches made by the Prime Minister...during his visit to the countries of South East Asia, Malaysia, Thailand, Laos, Burma, Singapore, and the Philippines, from 28 January to 13 February 1974. Canberra, 1974. fo. 57.

— — United States.

FEDULOVA (NADEZHDA GEORGIEVNA) SSha: politika v Iugo-Vostochnoi Azii: sotsial'no- ekonomicheskie aspekty. Moskva, 1975. pp. 223.

BLAUFARB (DOUGLAS S.) The counterinsurgency era: US doctrine and performance, 1950 to the present. New York, [1977]. pp. 356. *bibliog.*

ASIA, SOUTHEAST (Cont.)

— Politics and government.

BLAUFARB (DOUGLAS S.) The counterinsurgency era: US doctrine and performance, 1950 to the present. New York, [1977]. pp. 356. bibliog.

ASIAN DOLLAR MARKET.

BHATTACHARYA (ANINDYA K.) The Asian dollar market: international offshore financing. New York, 1977. pp. 113. bibliog.

ASIATICS IN THE UNITED KINGDOM.

FENTON (MIKE) Asian households in owner-occupation: a study of the pattern, costs and experiences of households in Greater Manchester. Bristol, Social Science Research Council Research Unit on Ethnic Relations, [1977]. pp. 70. bibliog. (Working Papers on Ethnic Relations. No. 2)

ASQUITH (HERBERT HENRY) 1st Earl of Oxford and Asquith.

JENKINS (ROY HARRIS) Asquith. rev. ed. London, 1978. pp. 572.

ASSASSINATION

— Mexico.

FOURTH INTERNATIONAL. International Committee. How the GPU murdered Trotsky. London, [1976]. 1 pamphlet (unpaged).

FOURTH INTERNATIONAL. International Committee. Trotsky's assassin at large. London, [1977]. pp. 40.

— United States.

LANE (MARK) and GREGORY (DICK) Code name "Zorro": the murder of Martin Luther King, Jr. Englewood Cliffs, [1977]. pp. 314.

ASSESSMENT

— South Africa.

REINACH (S.C.) The effects of existing methods of property valuation and taxation on the ratepayer. Port Elizabeth, 1974. pp. 22. bibliog. (University of Port Elizabeth. Institute for Planning Research. Special Publications. No. 4)

— United Kingdom.

METCALF (B.W.) Valuation for rating, 1973. London, [1973]. pp. 30.

ASSIMILATION (SOCIOLOGY).

FEAGIN (JOE R.) Racial and ethnic relations. Englewood Cliffs, [1978]. pp. 392.

ASSISTANCE IN EMERGENCIES

— Australia.

GRIFFITHS (DAVID) Emergency relief: a report prepared for the Social Welfare Commission. [Canberra?], 1975. pp. 71. bibliog.

— United States — Mathematical models.

CARTER (GRACE M.) and others. Response areas for two emergency units. New York, 1971. pp. 47. bibliog. (Rand Corporation. [Rand Reports]. 532)

ASSOCIATED COUNTRY WOMEN OF THE WORLD.

SCARBOROUGH (NEVE) History of the Associated Country Women of the World...and of its member societies. London, 1953. pp. 403.

ASSOCIATIONS, INSTITUTIONS, ETC.

WEISBROD (BURTON ALLEN) The voluntary nonprofit sector: an economic analysis. Lexington, Mass., [1977]. pp. 179. bibliogs.

— Abbreviations.

BANCA COMMERCIALE ITALIANA. Il siglario mondiale de enti e imprese economiche. Milano, 1977. pp. 1253. bibliog.

— Denmark.

TEISEN (FLEMMING) Socialpolitiske aktiviteter gennem 75 år;... historien i korte uddrag og fire bilag. København, 1976. pp. 59. (Socialpolitisk Forening. Småskrifter. Nr.45)

— Finland.

PESTOFF (VICTOR ALEXIS) Voluntary associations and Nordic party systems: a study of overlapping membership and cross-pressures in Finland, Norway and Sweden. Stockholm, 1977. pp. 200. bibliog. (Stockholms Universitet. Statsvetenskapliga Institutionen. Stockholm Studies in Politics.10)

— Germany.

WEIDENFELLER (GERHARD) VDA, Verein für das Deutschtum im Ausland, Allgemeiner Deutscher Schulverein, 1881-1918: ein Beitrag zur Geschichte des deutschen Nationalismus und Imperialismus im Kaiserreich. Bern, 1976. pp. 507. bibliog.

— Norway.

PESTOFF (VICTOR ALEXIS) Voluntary associations and Nordic party systems: a study of overlapping membership and cross-pressures in Finland, Norway and Sweden. Stockholm, 1977. pp. 200. bibliog. (Stockholms Universitet. Statsvetenskapliga Institutionen. Stockholm Studies in Politics. 10)

— South Africa — Directories.

FELDBERG (LEON) compiler. South African Jewry: a survey of the Jewish community: its contribution to South Africa: directory of communal institutions: and a who's who of leading personalities. 3rd ed. Johannesburg, 1976-77. pp. 529.

— Sweden.

PESTOFF (VICTOR ALEXIS) Voluntary associations and Nordic party systems: a study of overlapping membership and cross-pressures in Finland, Norway and Sweden. Stockholm, 1977. pp. 200. bibliog. (Stockholms Universitet. Statsvetenskapliga Institutionen. Stockholm Studies in Politics.10)

— United Kingdom.

TEWSON (W.F.) The British Cotton Growing Association, incorporated by royal charter:...golden jubilee, [1904]-1954. [Manchester], [1954]. pp. 85, xiv.

SLADEN (EDWARD) Honorary officers and what they do. London, [1973]. pp. 15. bibliog.

JENKINS (ROY HARRIS) and others. The role of voluntary organisations in a recession; the address... to the 1975 annual meeting of the London Council of Social Service together with extracts from the address of...Lady Marre and from the vote of thanks by...Graham Lomas, etc. London, [1975]. pp. 4.

CIANO (J.L.D.) and PHILLIPS (R.F.R.) The Economics Association and the development of economics education. London, 1977. pp. 16.

— — Directories.

DIRECTORY of British associations and associations in Ireland... editors G.P. Henderson and S.P.A. Henderson. Edition 5, 1977-8. 5th ed. Beckenham, 1977. pp. 457.

— — Scotland.

ROWE (ANDREW J.B.) Co-operation among voluntary organisations in Scotland. [Edinburgh, 1975]. fo. 15.

— United States — New York (City).

KUO (CHIA-LING) Social and political change in New York's Chinatown: the role of voluntary associations. New York, 1977. pp. 160. bibliog.

ASSOCIAZIONE NAZIONALISTA ITALIANA.

DE GRAND (ALEXANDER J.) The Italian Nationalist Association and the rise of fascism in Italy. Lincoln, Neb., [1978]. pp. 238. bibliog.

ASTO INDIANS.

LAVALLEE (DANIELE) and JULIEN (MICHELE) Les établissements Asto à l'époque préhispanique. Lima, 1973. pp. 143. (Institut Français d'Etudes Andines. Travaux. 15) With Spanish and English summaries.

ASTRABAD

— History.

ABDULLAEV (IUSUF NEGMATOVICH) Astrabad i russko-iranskie otnosheniia, vtoraia polovina XIX - nachalo XX v. Tashkent, 1975. pp. 132. bibliog.

ASTURIAS

— History.

MIGUELEZ (FAUSTINO) La lucha de los mineros asturianos bajo el franquismo; prologo de Gerado Iglesias. Barcelona, 1977. pp. 309.

— Politics and government.

GONZALEZ MUÑIZ (MIGUEL ANGEL) Los asturianos y la politica: de las Cortes de Cadiz a nuestros dias. Salinas, Asturias, [1976]. pp. 231. bibliog.

ATHANASIAN CREED.

LAKE (JOHN W.) The Athanasian creed: a plea for its disuse in the public worship of the national church. London, 1875. pp. 26.

ATHEISM.

SAVEL'EV (SERGEI NIKOLAEVICH) Emel'ian Iaroslavskii - propagandist marksistskogo ateizma. Leningrad, 1976. pp. 104. bibliog.

ATLASES.

PHILIP (GEORGE) AND SON. The international atlas: Der internationale Atlas: El atlas internacional: L'atlas international. London, [1969]. 1 vol. (various pagings). In English, French, German and Spanish.

ATOMIC ENERGY.

INTERNATIONAL ATOMIC ENERGY AGENCY. General Conference. Resolutions and other decisions. a., 1961(5th)- [Vienna]. 1957-1960 (1st-4th) are bound with documents of the General Conference. Indexes: 1957/1971, 1972/1975, 1957/1976.

PATTERSON (WALTER C.) The fissile society. London, 1977. pp. 117. bibliog. Report prepared by the Energy Policy Unit of Earth Resources Research.

ATOMIC ENERGY INDUSTRIES

— Security measures.

INTERNATIONAL arrangements for nuclear fuel reprocessing; edited by Abram Chayes and W. Bennett Lewis. Cambridge, Mass., [1977]. pp. 251. Papers of a symposium held in Racine, Wisconsin, May 24-27, 1976, and sponsored by the Pugwash Conference on Science and World Affairs.

— Italy.

Lo SVILUPPO nucleare in Italia; di Gianni Cozzi [and others]. Milano, [1975]. pp. 253.

— United States.

COMMITTEE FOR ECONOMIC DEVELOPMENT. Research and Policy Committee. Nuclear energy and national security. New York, 1976. pp. 80.

MOORE (THOMAS GALE) Uranium enrichment and public policy. Washington, [1978]. pp. 64. *(American Enterprise Institute for Public Policy Research and Stanford University. Hoover Institution on War, Revolution and Peace. AEI-Hoover Policy Studies. 25)*

ATOMIC POWER.

SALAMON (BENJAMIN) Nuclear power plants and international politics. [1975]. fo.57. *Photocopy of typescript: unpublished.*

ROBERTS (ALAN) and MEDVEDEV (ZHORES ALEKSANDROVICH) Hazards of nuclear power. Nottingham, 1977. pp. 73.

— Economic aspects.

BURN (DUNCAN LYALL) Nuclear power and the energy crisis: politics and the atomic industry. London, 1978. pp. 348. *bibliog.*

— Security measures.

MYERS (DESAIX) The nuclear power debate: moral, economic, technical, and political issues. New York, 1977. pp. 153. *Based on a study undertaken by the Investor Responsibility Research Center.*

ATOMIC POWER INDUSTRY

— Costs.

MILLER (SAUNDERS) The economics of nuclear and coal power. New York, 1976. pp. 150. *bibliog.*

— France.

COLSON (JEAN PHILIPPE) Le nucléaire sans les Français: qui décide? qui profite? Paris, 1977. pp. 190. *bibliog.*

— United States.

GARVEY (GERALD) Nuclear power and social planning: the city of the second sun. Lexington, Mass., [1977]. pp. 159. *bibliog.*

MYERS (DESAIX) The nuclear power debate: moral, economic, technical, and political issues. New York, 1977. pp. 153. *Based on a study undertaken by the Investor Responsibility Research Center.*

ATOMIC POWER-PLANTS

— United States.

MOORE (THOMAS GALE) Uranium enrichment and public policy. Washington, [1978]. pp. 64. *(American Enterprise Institute for Public Policy Research and Stanford University. Hoover Institution on War, Revolution and Peace. AEI-Hoover Policy Studies. 25)*

ATOMIC WEAPONS.

ALBONETTI (ACHILLE) L'Italia e l'atomica: il governo, il parlamento, i partiti, i diplomatici, gli scienziati e la stampa. Faenza, [1976]. pp. 287.

BARNABY (CHARLES FRANK) Nuclear proliferation and the South African threat. Geneva, [1977]. pp. 22.

FRANK (LEWIS ALLEN) Soviet nuclear planning: a point of view on SALT. Washington, D.C., [1977]. pp. 63. *(American Enterprise Institute for Public Policy Research. AEI Studies. 140)*

— Environmental aspects.

WESTING (ARTHUR H.) Weapons of mass destruction and the environment. London, 1977. pp. 95. *bibliog.*

— International cooperation.

NUCLEAR weapons and world politics: alternatives for the future; [by] David C. Gompert [and others]. New York, [1977]. pp. 368. *(Council on Foreign Relations. 1980s Project Studies)*

ATOMIC WEAPONS AND DISARMAMENT.

JOHANSEN (ROBERT C.) The Vladivostok accord: a case study of the impact of U.S. foreign policy on the prospects for world order reform. Princeton, 1976. pp. 114. *(Princeton University. Center of International Studies. World Order Studies Program. Occasional Papers. No. 4)*

PFALTZGRAFF (ROBERT L.) and DAVIS (JACQUELYN K.) Salt II: promise or precipice? Coral Gables, Flor., [1976]. pp. 45. *(Miami (Florida). University. Center for Advanced International Studies. Monographs in International Affairs)*

FRANK (LEWIS ALLEN) Soviet nuclear planning: a point of view on SALT. Washington, D.C., [1977]. pp. 63. *(American Enterprise Institute for Public Policy Research. AEI Studies. 140)*

GREENWOOD (TED) and others. Nuclear proliferation: motivations, capabilities, and strategies for control. New York, [1977]. pp. 210. *bibliog. (Council on Foreign Relations. 1980s Project Studies)*

GRIFFITHS (DAVID) of the Campaign for Nuclear Disarmament. Labour and disarmament: a time for decision. London, 1977. pp. 22. *bibliog.*

GRIFFITHS (DAVID) of the Campaign for Nuclear Disarmament, and SMITH (DAN) of the Campaign for Nuclear Disarmament. How many more?: the spread of nuclear weapons. London, [1977]. pp. 30. *bibliog.*

INTERNATIONAL SCHOOL ON DISARMAMENT AND RESEARCH ON CONFLICTS, 6TH, NEMI, 1976. Arms control and technological innovation: [proceedings of the sixth course]; edited by David Carlton and Carlo Schaerf. London, [1977]. pp. 366.

NUCLEAR weapons and world politics: alternatives for the future; [by] David C. Gompert [and others]. New York, [1977]. pp. 368. *(Council on Foreign Relations. 1980s Project Studies)*

PUGWASH SYMPOSIUM, 25TH, KYOTO, 1975. A new design for nuclear disarmament: [proceedings of the Symposium held under the auspices of the Japanese Pugwash Group];...edited by William Epstein and Toshiyuki Toyoda. Nottingham, 1977. pp. 338.

WORLD disarmament kit...; (editor Robert Woito). Stockholm, [1977]. pp. 120. *bibliog. (World Without War Council. World Without War Publications)*

INTERNATIONAL INSTITUTE FOR STRATEGIC STUDIES. Adelphi Papers. No. 141. The future of arms control: part 1: beyond SALT II; (papers presented...at an International Arms Control Conference, Cumberland Lodge...1977); edited by Christoph Bertram. London, 1978. pp. 42.

— Bibliography.

BURNS (RICHARD DEAN) compiler. Arms control and disarmament: a bibliography. Santa Barbara, [1977]. pp. 430. *(California University. Center for the Study of Armament and Disarmament. War/Peace Bibliography Series. 6)*

ATROCITIES

— Rhodesia.

CATHOLIC COMMISSION FOR JUSTICE AND PEACE IN RHODESIA. Rhodesia: the propaganda war. Salisbury, 1977. 1 pamphlet (unpaged).

ATTITUDE (PSYCHOLOGY).

REICH (BEN) and ADCOCK (CHRISTINE) Values, attitudes and behaviour change. London, 1976. pp. 144. *bibliog.*

SOCIAL comparison processes: theoretical and empirical perspectives; edited by Jerry M. Suls [and] Richard L. Miller. Washington, D.C., [1977]. pp. 371. *bibliogs.*

AUCKLAND

— Social policy.

HAIGH (DAVID IAN) and GAVIN (DAVID CHARLES) Social planning for new communities in Auckland: a discussion document. [Auckland, Auckland Regional Authority], 1977. fo. 54. *bibliog.*

AUDITING.

UNITED NATIONS. Interregional Seminar on Government Auditing, Baden, 1971. Report of the...Seminar...[held in] Baden, Austria, 3 to 14 May, 1971. (ST/TAO/SER.C/136). New York, 1972. pp. 23. *bibliog.*

AUDITORY PERCEPTION.

MOORE (BRIAN CECIL JOSEPH) Introduction to the psychology of hearing. London, 1977. pp. 311. *bibliog.*

AUGSBURG

— History.

FISCHER (ILSE) Industrialisierung, sozialer Konflikt und politische Willensbildung in der Stadtgemeinde: ein Beitrag zur Sozialgeschichte Augsburgs, 1840-1914. Augsburg, [1977]. pp. 413. *bibliog. (Augsburg. Stadtarchiv. Abhandlungen zur Geschichte der Stadt Augsburg. Band 24)*

AUSTRALIA

— Administrative and political divisions.

AUSTRALIA. Department of Urban and Regional Development. 1975. Australian government regional boundaries. Canberra, 1975. pp. 27.

— Appropriations and expenditures.

AUSTRALIA. Department of Works. Civil works programme. a., 1963/64[1st]- Canberra. *[Included in AUSTRALIA. Parliament. [Parliamentary papers]*

— Armed forces.

The DEFENCE of Australia: fundamental new aspects: the proceedings of a conference organised by the Strategic and Defence Studies Centre, the Australian National University, October 1976; edited by Robert O'Neill. Canberra, 1977. pp. 143.

— Commerce.

AISLABIE (COLIN JAMES) and others. A statistical study of the comparative advantage of Australian industry: a report. Canberra, 1975. 1 vol. (various foliations) *(Australia. Department of Manufacturing Industry. Industry Research Series. 1975. No.1)*

— — Statistics.

AUSTRALIA. Commonwealth Bureau of Census and Statistics. Outward overseas cargo. a., 1974/75- Canberra.

— — New Zealand.

AUSTRALIA. Parliament. Senate. Standing Committee on Industry and Trade. 1972. Intirim report on Australia-New Zealand trade; [E.W. Prowse, chairman]. in AUSTRALIA. Parliament. Parliamentary papers, 1972, vol. 7.

— Commercial policy.

WISE (BERNHARD RINGROSE) Australia and preferential trade. Sydney, 1904. pp. 15.

— Constitution.

SAWER (GEOFFREY) The Australian constitution. Canberra, Australian Government Publishing Service, 1975. pp. 159.

GREENWOOD (GORDON) The future of Australian federalism: a commentary on the working of the constitution. 2nd ed. St. Lucia, Queensland, [1976]. pp. 361. *bibliog.*

CRISP (LESLIE FINLAY) Australian national government. 4th ed. Melbourne, 1978. pp. 523. *bibliog.*

AUSTRALIA (Cont.)

— Constitutional law.

GREENWOOD (GORDON) The future of Australian federalism: a commentary on the working of the constitution. 2nd ed. St. Lucia, Queensland, [1976]. pp. 361. *bibliog.*

— Economic history.

JACKSON (ROBERT VINCENT) Australian economic development in the nineteenth century. Canberra, 1977. pp. 175.

— Economic policy.

JOLLEY (AINSLEY) Macro-economic policy in Australia, 1972-1976. London, [1978]. pp. 261. *bibliog.*

— Emigration and immigration.

DIXON (R.) Secretary of the Australian Communist Party. Immigration and the "white Australia" policy. Sydney, [1945]. pp. 15.

CONFERENCE OF AUSTRALIAN AND STATE MINISTERS FOR IMMIGRATION, ADELAIDE, 1973. Report. Adelaide, 1973. fo. 26, 5.

CONFERENCE OF AUSTRALIAN AND STATE MINISTERS FOR IMMIGRATION, PERTH, 1975. Report. Perth, 1975. fo. 29.

WELFARE of migrants. Canberra, 1975. pp. 184. *bibliogs.* (Australia. Commission of Inquiry into Poverty. Research Reports)

AUSTRALIAN POPULATION AND IMMIGRATION COUNCIL. Immigration policies and Australia's population: a green paper. Canberra, Australian Government Publishing Service, 1977. pp. 101.

— Executive departments.

AUSTRALIA. Department of National Development. Report. a., 1970/71(1st)- Canberra. *Included in AUSTRALIA. Parliament. [Parliamentary papers].*

AUSTRALIA. Department of Science. Report. a., 1972/73 (1st)- Canberra. *Included in AUSTRALIA. Parliament. [Parliamentary papers].*

AUSTRALIA. Department of the Media. Report of activities. a., 1972/73(1st)- Canberra. *Included in AUSTRALIA. Parliament. [Parliamentary papers].*

AUSTRALIA. Department of Urban and Regional Development. Annual report. a., 1972/73(1st)- Canberra. *Included in AUSTRALIA. Parliament. [Parliamentary papers].*

— Foreign economic relations.

FORUM on Australia, New Zealand and East Asia. [Taipei], 1977. pp. 109. *(Asia and the World Forum. Monograph Series. No. 5)*

— — Asia, Southeast.

LOOKING north to south-east Asia: the view from Australia; edited by Edward P. Wolfers. Honolulu, [1976]. pp. 276. *Papers delivered to the 5th Annual Conference of the Australian Institute of International Affairs held in Melbourne in 1975.*

— — Japan.

CRAWFORD (Sir JOHN) and OKITA (SABURO) Australia, Japan and western Pacific economic relations: a report to the governments of Australia and Japan. Canberra, Australian Government Publishing Service, 1976. pp. 325.

— — Pacific, The.

CRAWFORD (Sir JOHN) and OKITA (SABURO) Australia, Japan and western Pacific economic relations: a report to the governments of Australia and Japan. Canberra, Australian Government Publishing Service, 1976. pp. 325.

— Foreign population.

JAKUBOWICZ (ANDREW) and BUCKLEY (BERENICE) Migrants and the legal system. Canberra, 1975. pp. 89. *bibliog.* (Australia. Commission of Inquiry into Poverty. Law and Poverty Series)

WELFARE of migrants. Canberra, 1975. pp. 184. *bibliogs.* (Australia. Commission of Inquiry into Poverty. Research Reports)

— Foreign relations.

ALBINSKI (HENRY STEPHEN) Australian external policy under Labor: content, process and the national debate. Vancouver, 1977. pp. 373. *bibliog.*

— — Asia.

STARGARDT (A.W.) Australia's Asian policies: the history of a debate 1839-1972. Hamburg, [1977]. pp. 404.

— — Asia, Southeast.

AUSTRALIA. Prime Minister. 1974. Principal speeches made by the Prime Minister...during his visit to the countries of South East Asia, Malaysia, Thailand, Laos, Burma, Singapore, and the Philippines, from 28 January to 13 February 1974. Canberra, 1974. fo. 57.

— — Europe.

AUSTRALIA. Prime Minister. 1975. Australia and Europe: principal speeches made during the visit to Europe by the Prime Minister...from 14 December 1974 to 21 January 1975. Canberra, 1975. pp. 78.

— Government publications.

AUSTRALIA. Parliament. Joint Committee on Publications. 1972. Report relating to departmental publishing activities; third special report; [G.D. Erwin, chairman]. in AUSTRALIA. Parliament. Parliamentary papers, 1972, vol.8.

— — Bibliography.

AUSTRALIA. Commonwealth Bureau of Census and Statistics. Catalogue of publications. a., current issue only. Canberra.

— History.

MANDLE (WILLIAM FREDERICK) Going it alone: Australia's national identity in the twentieth century. [London, 1978]. pp. 264. *bibliog.*

WARD (RUSSEL) The history of Australia: the twentieth century, 1901-1975. London, 1978. pp. 515. *bibliog.* Published in Australia as A nation for a continent: the history of Australia, 1901-1975.

— Industries.

AUSTRALIA. Commonwealth Bureau of Census and Statistics. Indexes of manufacturing production. a., 1968-69/1973-74(1st)- Canberra.

AUSTRALIA. Commonwealth Bureau of Census and Statistics. Manufacturing establishments: summary of operations by industry class. a., 1975/76- Canberra.

AISLABIE (COLIN JAMES) and others. A statistical study of the comparative advantage of Australian industry: a report. Canberra, 1975. 1 vol. (various foliations) *(Australia. Department of Manufacturing Industry. Industry Research Series. 1975. No.1)*

AUSTRALIA. Commonwealth Bureau of Census and Statistics. 1976. Australian national accounts: input-output tables, 1968-69. Canberra, [1976]. pp. 193.

— Military policy.

AUSTRALIA. 1975. Australian defence: major decisions since December 1972. Canberra, Australian Government Publishing Service, 1975. pp. 8.

The DEFENCE of Australia: fundamental new aspects: the proceedings of a conference organised by the Strategic and Defence Studies Centre, the Australian National University, October 1976; edited by Robert O'Neill. Canberra, 1977. pp. 143.

— Native races.

AUSTRALIA. Parliament. Senate. Standing Committee on Social Environment. 1972. Report on the environmental conditions of aborigines and Torres Strait Islanders and the preservation of their sacred sites; progress report; [C.L. Laucke, chairman]. in AUSTRALIA. Parliament. Parliamentary papers, 1972, vol. 8.

The SITUATION of aborigines on pastoral properties in the Northern Territory; report of the Committee of Review; [C. A.Gibb, chairman]. in AUSTRALIA. Parliament. Parliamentary papers, 1972, vol. 1.

— Navy — History.

AUSTRALIA. Department of Defence (Navy). 1976. An outline of Australian naval history. Canberra, 1976. pp. 90. *bibliog.*

— Parliament — Committees.

GREENWOOD (IVOR JOHN) and ELLICOTT (ROBERT JAMES) Parliamentary committees: powers over and protection afforded to witnesses. in AUSTRALIA. Parliament. Parliamentary papers, 1972, vol. 6.

— — Reporters and reporting.

BRIDGMAN (WILLIAM JOHN) Commonwealth Hansard: its establishment and development, 1901 to 1972; [a modernisation of J.S. Weatherston's work]. in AUSTRALIA. Parliament. Parliamentary papers, 1972, vol. 6.

— — Rules and practice.

ODGERS (JAMES ROWLAND) Australian Senate practice. 4th ed. in AUSTRALIA. Parliament. Parliamentary papers, 1972, vol. 6.

— Politics and government.

ALBINSKI (HENRY STEPHEN) Australian external policy under Labor: content, process and the national debate. Vancouver, 1977. pp. 373. *bibliog.*

HOLMES (MARJORIE JEAN) and SHARMAN (CAMPBELL) The Australian federal system. Sydney, [1977]. pp. 219. *bibliog.*

HUGHES (COLIN ANFIELD) A handbook of Australian government and politics, 1965-1974. Canberra, 1977. pp. 162.

CRISP (LESLIE FINLAY) Australian national government. 4th ed. Melbourne, 1978. pp. 523. *bibliog.*

— Prices Justification Tribunal.

NIEUWENHUYSEN (JOHN PETER) and DALY (ANNE ELIZABETH) The Australian Prices Justification Tribunal. [Carlton, Victoria, 1977]. pp. 234. *bibliog.*

— Public works.

AUSTRALIA. Department of Works. Civil works programme. a., 1963/64[1st]- Canberra. *[Included in AUSTRALIA. Parliament. [Parliamentary papers]*

— Rural conditions.

FINANCIAL aspects of rural poverty. Canberra, 1975. pp. 120. (Australia. Commission of Inquiry into Poverty. Research Reports)

— Social conditions.

AUSTRALIA. Cities Commission. 1975. Australians' use of time: a contribution of social planning to urban development and land use design. [Canberra], 1975. 1 vol. (unpaged). *Photocopy.*

— Statistics — Bibliography.

AUSTRALIA. Commonwealth Bureau of Census and Statistics. Catalogue of publications. a., current issue only. Canberra.

AUSTRALIAN ABORIGINES.

The SITUATION of aborigines on pastoral properties in the Northern Territory; report of the Committee of Review; [C. A.Gibb, chairman]. in AUSTRALIA. Parliament. Parliamentary papers, 1972, vol. 1.

AUSTRALIA. Aboriginal Land Rights Commission. Report. a., 1973(1st)- Canberra. *Included in AUSTRALIA. Parliament. [Parliamentary papers].*

AUSTRALIA. Department of Aboriginal Affairs. 1974. Selected policy statements on aboriginal affairs 1973-1974, [by] J.L. Cavanagh etc. Canberra, 1974. pp. 65.

BROWN (JILL W.) and others. Aboriginals and islanders in Brisbane: research report by Jill W. Brown, Roisin Hirschfeld and Diane Smith. Canberra, 1974. pp. 119. *(Australia. Commission of Inquiry into Poverty. Research Reports)*

HILL (KATHLEEN F.) A study of aboriginal poverty in two country towns. Canberra, 1975. pp. 89. *bibliog. (Australia. Commission of Inquiry into Poverty. Research Reports)*

The MAPOON story according to the invaders: church mission, Queensland government and mining company; [edited by J. Roberts and others]. Victoria, [1975]. pp. 112. *(International Development Action. Mapoon. Book 2)*

The MAPOON story by the Mapoon people; [edited by J.P. Roberts and others]. Victoria, [1975]. pp. 24. *(International Development Action. Mapoon. Book 1)*

The CAPE York aluminium companies and the native peoples: Comalco, R.T.Z., Kaiser, C.R.A., Alcan, Billiton, Pechiney, Tipperary; [written by J. Roberts and D. McLean . Victoria, [1976]. pp. 104. *(International Development Action. Mapoon. Book 3)*

GILBERT (KEVIN J.) Living black: blacks talk to Kevin Gilbert. London, 1977. pp. 305.

— **Antiquities — Conservation and restoration.**

AUSTRALIA. Parliament. Senate. Standing Committee on Social Environment. 1972. Report on the environmental conditions of aborigines and Torres Strait Islanders and the preservation of their sacred sites; progress report; [C.L. Laucke, chairman]. in AUSTRALIA. Parliament. Parliamentary papers, 1972, vol. 8.

AUSTRIA

— **Army — History.**

DUFFY (CHRISTOPHER) The army of Maria Theresa: the armed forces of imperial Austria, 1740-1780. Vancouver, [1977]. pp. 256. *bibliog.*

— **Biography.**

WHO'S who in Austria:...a biographical dictionary containing more than 4000 biographies of prominent personalities from and in Austria; edited by Otto J. Groeg. 9th ed. Munich, [1977]. pp. 600.

— **Constitutional history.**

STOURZH (GERALD) Kleine Geschichte des österreichischen Staatsvertrages; mit Dokumententeil. Graz, [1975]. pp. 255.

DOUIN (CLAUDE SOPHIE) Le fédéralisme autrichien. Paris, 1977. pp. 295. *bibliog.*

— **Constitutional law.**

ERMACORA (FELIX) Österreichischer Föderalismus: vom patrimonialen zum kooperativen Bundesstaat. Wien, [1976]. pp. 364. *bibliog. (Institut für Föderalismusforschung. Schriftenreihe. Band 3)*

— **Economic conditions.**

RENNER (KARL) Für Recht und Frieden: eine Auswahl der Reden des Bundespräsidenten. [Vienna], Verlag der Österreichischen Staatsdruckerei, [1951]. pp. 392.

— **Economic policy.**

OEHLINGER (THEO) and others. Institutionelle Aspekte der österreichischen Integrationspolitik. Wien, 1976. pp. 323. *bibliogs. (Österreichische Akademie der Wissenschaften. Philosophisch-Historische Klasse. Sitzungsberichte. 308. Band. 1. Abhandlung)*

— **Foreign relations.**

See also EUROPEAN COMMUNITIES — Austria.

— — **Treaties.**

STOURZH (GERALD) Kleine Geschichte des österreichischen Staatsvertrages; mit Dokumententeil. Graz, [1975]. pp. 255.

— — **United Kingdom.**

FEST (WILFRIED) Peace or partition: the Habsburg monarchy and British policy, 1914-1918. London, 1978. pp. 276. *bibliog.*

— **History.**

KREISSLER (FELIX) Histoire de l'Autriche. [Paris, 1977]. pp. 128. *bibliog.*

RAPE (LUDGER) Die österreichischen Heimwehren und die bayerische Rechte, 1920-1923. Wien, [1977]. pp. 457. *bibliog. (Ludwig Boltzmann Institut für Geschichte der Arbeiterbewegung. Veröffentlichungen)*

— — **1848-1867 — Sources.**

AUSTRIA. Ministerrat. 1852- . Das Ministerium Buol-Schauenstein...; bearbeitet von Waltraud Heindl, mit einer Einleitung von Friedrich Engel- Janosi. Wien, [1975 in progress]. *bibliog. (Die Protokolle des österreichischen Ministerrates, 1848-1867. Abteilung 3)*

AUSTRIA. Ministerrat. 1861- . Die Ministerien Erzherzog Rainer und Mensdorff...; bearbeitet von Horst Brettner-Messler, mit einer Einleitung von Friedrich Engel-Janosi. Wien, 1977 in progress. *(Die Protokolle des österreichischen Ministerrates, 1848- 1867. Abteilung 5)*

— — **1918-1938.**

GESCHICHTE der Republik Österreich; unter Mitwirkung von Walter Goldinger [and others]; herausgegeben von Heinrich Benedikt. Wien, 1954 repr. 1977. pp. 630. *bibliog.*

SCHAUSBERGER (NORBERT) Der Griff nach Österreich: der Anschluss. Wien, [1978]. pp. 666. *bibliog.*

— — **1938-1945.**

GESCHICHTE der Republik Österreich; unter Mitwirkung von Walter Goldinger [and others]; herausgegeben von Heinrich Benedikt. Wien, 1954 repr. 1977. pp. 630. *bibliog.*

— — **1945-1955, Allied occupation.**

STOURZH (GERALD) Kleine Geschichte des österreichischen Staatsvertrages; mit Dokumententeil. Graz, [1975]. pp. 255.

— **Militia.**

RAPE (LUDGER) Die österreichischen Heimwehren und die bayerische Rechte, 1920-1923. Wien, [1977]. pp. 457. *bibliog. (Ludwig Boltzmann Institut für Geschichte der Arbeiterbewegung. Veröffentlichungen)*

— **Politics and government.**

RENNER (KARL) Für Recht und Frieden: eine Auswahl der Reden des Bundespräsidenten. [Vienna], Verlag der Österreichischen Staatsdruckerei, [1951]. pp. 392.

VOM Justizpalast zum Heldenplatz: Studien und Dokumentationen, 1927 bis 1938: (Festgabe der Wissenschaftlichen Kommission des Theodor Körner-Stiftungsfonds und des Leopold Kunschak- Preises zur Erforschung der österreichischen Geschichte der Jahre 1927 bis 1938...; herausgegeben von Ludwig Jedlicka und Rudolf Neck). Wien, Verlag der Österreichischen Staatsdruckerei, 1975. pp. 588.

MOCK (ALOIS) Für eine menschenwürdige Gesellschaftsordnung: zur Neuauflage des "Wiener Programms" des OAAB. Wien, 1976. pp. 28. *(Österreichischer Arbeiter- und Angestelltenbund. Gesellschaftspolitische Informationen. 13)*

DOUIN (CLAUDE SOPHIE) Le fédéralisme autrichien. Paris, 1977. pp. 295. *bibliog.*

OBLER (JEFFREY) and others. Decision-making in smaller democracies: the consociational burden. Beverly Hills, [1977]. pp. 58. *bibliog.*

— **Social conditions.**

RENNER (KARL) Für Recht und Frieden: eine Auswahl der Reden des Bundespräsidenten. [Vienna], Verlag der Österreichischen Staatsdruckerei, [1951]. pp. 392.

— **Social life and customs.**

GRUENN (HELENE) Brauchtum der Fabriksarbeiter: Beobachtungen in der VOEST- Alpine AG. Wien, 1974. pp. 188-210. *(Österreichische Akademie der Wissenschaften. Institut für Gegenwartsvolkskunde. Mitteilungen. Nr. 2) (Sonderabdruck aus dem Anzeiger der phil.-hist. Klasse..., 111. Jahrgang 1974, So. 7)*

AUSTRIA-HUNGARY

— **Army.**

The HABSBURG empire in World War I: essays on the intellectual, military, political and economic aspects of the Habsburg war effort; edited by Robert A. Kann [and others] . New York, 1977. pp. 247. *(East European Quarterly. East European Monographs. 23) (City University of New York. Brooklyn College. Department of History. Studies on Society in Change. No. 2)*

— **Foreign relations.**

ERÉNYI (TIBOR) Die Sozialdemokratische Partei Ungarns und die Aussenpolitik der Österreichisch-Ungarischen Monarchie in den Jahren 1908- 1914. Budapest, 1970. pp. 397-426. *(Magyar Tudományos Akadémia. Studia Historica. 75)*

— **Intellectual life.**

The HABSBURG empire in World War I: essays on the intellectual, military, political and economic aspects of the Habsburg war effort; edited by Robert A. Kann [and others] . New York, 1977. pp. 247. *(East European Quarterly. East European Monographs. 23) (City University of New York. Brooklyn College. Department of History. Studies on Society in Change. No. 2)*

— **Politics and government.**

The HABSBURG empire in World War I: essays on the intellectual, military, political and economic aspects of the Habsburg war effort; edited by Robert A. Kann [and others] . New York, 1977. pp. 247. *(East European Quarterly. East European Monographs. 23) (City University of New York. Brooklyn College. Department of History. Studies on Society in Change. No. 2)*

AUSTRIAN SCHOOL OF ECONOMISTS.

LACHMANN (LUDWIG MORITZ) Capital, expectations, and the market process: essays on the theory of the market economy. Kansas City, [1977]. pp. 352. *bibliog.*

O'DRISCOLL (GERALD PATRICK) Economics as a coordination problem: the contributions of Friedrich A. Hayek. Kansas City, [1977]. pp. 172. *bibliog.*

AUTHORITARIANISM.

GERMANI (GINO) Autoritarismo, fascismo e classi sociali. Bologna, [1975]. pp. 306. *bibliog.*

SAHLIN (MICHAEL) Neo-authoritarianism and the problem of legitimacy: a general study and a Nigerian example. Stockholm, [1977]. pp. 240. *bibliog. (Uppsala. Statsvetenskapliga Föreningen. Skrifter. 77)*

AUTHORS, ENGLISH.

KNIGHTS (BEN) The idea of the clerisy in the nineteenth century. Cambridge, [1978]. pp. 274. *bibliog.*

AUTISM.

AUTISM.

NATIONAL SOCIETY FOR AUTISTIC CHILDREN. Nowhere to go: a report on the plight of autistic adolescents. London, 1973. pp. 10.

AUTOMATA.

LAING (RICHARD) and WRIGHT (JESSE B.) Commutative machines. Ann Arbor, 1962. pp. 46. *bibliog.* *(Michigan University. College of Literature, Science, and the Arts. Communication Sciences Program. Technical Notes)*

AUTOMATION

— **Social aspects.**

GALLIE (DUNCAN) In search of the new working class: automation and social integration within the capitalist enterprise. Cambridge, 1978. pp. 348. *bibliog.*

— **Sudan.**

EL MILIGI (IBRAHIM SAAD) National policies for computer applications in developing countries: a case study of the Sudan. 1977. fo. 317. *bibliog.* Typescript. Ph.D. (London) thesis: unpublished. This thesis is the property of London University and may not be removed from the Library.

AUTOMOBILE INDUSTRY AND TRADE.

JONES (D.T.) and PRAIS (SIGBERT JON) Plant-size and productivity in the motor industry: some international comparisons. London, 1977. pp. 26, 4. *(National Institute of Economic and Social Research. Discussion Papers. No. 8)*

COUNTER INFORMATION SERVICES. Anti-Reports. No. 20. The Ford Motor Company. Nottingham, [1978]. pp. 68.

— **Brazil.**

ALMEIDA (JOSE) A implantação da industria automobilistica no Brasil. Rio de Janeiro, 1972. pp. 90. *bibliog.*

— **France.**

ANGELI (CLAUDE) and BRIMO (NICOLAS) Une milice patronale: Peugeot;...avec la collaboration de Marc- Rémy Donnallin. Paris, 1975. pp. 105.

PAGANELLI (SERGE) and JACQUIN (MARTINE) Peugeot: la dynastie s'accroche. Paris, [1975]. pp. 156.

— **Germany.**

PORSCHE (FERDINAND ANTON ERNST) We at Porsche: the autobiography of Dr. Ing. h.c. Ferry Porsche; with John Bentley. Yeovil, [1976]. pp. 290.

DICKE (HUGO) Strukturwandel im westdeutschen Strassenfahrzeugbau. Tübingen, [1978]. pp. 171. *bibliog.* *(Kiel. Universität. Institut für Weltwirtschaft. Kieler Studien. 152)*

— **Italy.**

MILANACCIO (ALFREDO) and RICOLFI (LUCA) Lotte operaie e ambiente di lavoro: Mirafiori, 1968-1974. [Torino, 1976]. pp. 196.

GIOVANA (MARIO) Torino: la città e i "signori Fiat". Milano, [1977]. pp. 208.

— **Sweden.**

GYLLENHAMMAR (PEHR G.) People at work. Reading, Mass., 1977. pp. 164.

AUTOMOBILE INDUSTRY WORKERS

— **France.**

PAGANELLI (SERGE) and JACQUIN (MARTINE) Peugeot: la dynastie s'accroche. Paris, [1975]. pp. 156.

— **Italy.**

GAMBA (MARINO) Innocenti: imprenditore, fabbrica e classe operaia in cinquant'anni di vita italiana. [Milan, 1976]. pp. 207.

LA VALLE (DAVIDE) Le origini della classe operaia alla Fiat: salario e forza- lavoro dalla fondazione ai consigli di fabbrica. Roma, 1976. pp. 182.

— **Spain.**

SOLIDARITY (LONDON). Motor Bulletins. No. 5. Spain: struggle at SEAT Barcelona. London, 1976. pp. 12.

— **United Kingdom.**

JOHNS (STEPHEN) Victimization at Cowley. London, 1974. pp. 111. *(Workers' Revolutionary Party. Pocket Library. No. 11)*

AUTOMOBILE OWNERSHIP.

TANNER (JOHN CURNOW) Car ownership trends and forecasts. Crowthorne, 1977. pp. 117. *bibliog.* *(U.K. Transport and Road Research Laboratory. Reports. LR 799)*

AUTOMOBILE PARKING

— **United Kingdom — London.**

POWERS to control private non-residential parking; by a joint working party of the G[reater] L[ondon] C[ouncil] D[epartment] o[f the] E[nvironment]/L[ondon] B[oroughs] A[ssociation]. London, [1975]. pp. 12. *(London. Greater London Council. Research Memoranda. 483)*

AUTOMOBILES

— **Environmental aspects.**

EUROPEAN MOTOR VEHICLES SYMPOSIUM, BRUSSELS, 1975. Proceedings of the...Symposium and the Seminar on Accident Statistics. Brussels, European Communities, [1977]. 2 vols. (in 1). *bibliogs.*

— **Laws and regulations — Scandinavia.**

[SCANDINAVIA]. Nordiske Parlamentariske Komité for Friere Samfaerdsel. 1953. Betaenkning om lettelser i toldbehandlingen m.v. af motorkøretøjer i den internordiske trafik. Kóenhavn, 1953. pp. 40.

— **Safety measures.**

EUROPEAN MOTOR VEHICLES SYMPOSIUM, BRUSSELS, 1975. Proceedings of the...Symposium and the Seminar on Accident Statistics. Brussels, European Communities, [1977]. 2 vols. (in 1). *bibliogs.*

— **Social aspects — United Kingdom.**

BANISTER (DAVID) Car availability and usage: a modal split model based on these concepts. Reading, 1977. pp. 36. *bibliog.* *(Reading. University. Department of Geography. Reading Geographical Papers. No. 58)*

AUTONOMY.

ESCUDERO (MANU) and VILLANUEVA (JAVIER) La autonomia del Pais Vasco desde el pasado al futuro. San Sebastian, [1976]. pp. 259.

AUTONOMY (PSYCHOLOGY).

EASTERBROOK (JAMES A.) and EASTERBROOK (PAMELA J.) The determinants of free will: a psychological analysis of responsible, adjustive behavior. New York, 1978. pp. 259. *bibliog.*

AUVERGNE

— **Economic conditions.**

POINT ECONOMIQUE DE L'AUVERGNE, LE: revue mensuelle; ([pd. by] Institut National de la Statistique et des Etudes Economiques,...Direction Régionale de Clermont-Ferrand [France]). bi-m. (formerly m.), My 1971 (no.1)- Chamalières.

AVILA CAMACHO (MANUEL).

TARACENA (ALFONSO) La vida en Mexico bajo Avila Camacho. Mexico, 1976-77. 2 vols. (in 1).

AYMARA INDIANS

— **Religion and mythology.**

MONAST (JACQUES EMILE) On les croyait chrétiens: les Aymaras. Paris, 1969. pp. 493.

AZAD KASHMIR

— **Economic policy.**

PAKISTAN. Ministry of Information and Broadcasting. Directorate of Research, Reference and Publications. 1977. Achievements of the people's government, 1972-1976: Azad Kashmir. [Islamabad, 1977?]. pp. 6.

— **Politics and government.**

PAKISTAN. Ministry of Information and Broadcasting. Directorate of Research, Reference and Publications. 1977. Achievements of the people's government, 1972-1976: Azad Kashmir. [Islamabad, 1977?]. pp. 6.

— **Social policy.**

PAKISTAN. Ministry of Information and Broadcasting. Directorate of Research, Reference and Publications. 1977. Achievements of the people's government, 1972-1976: Azad Kashmir. [Islamabad, 1977?]. pp. 6.

AZERBAIJAN

— **Economic conditions.**

AKHUNDOV (VAID DZHUMSHUDOVICH) Sovershenstvovanie struktury obshchestvennogo vosproizvodstva: voprosy metodologii. Moskva, 1977. pp. 239.

AZIZ ISHAK (ABDUL).

AZIZ ISHAK (ABDUL) Special guest: the detention in Malaysia of an ex-cabinet minister. Singapore, 1977. pp. 210.

AZTECS.

CASTILLO FARRERAS (VICTOR M.) Estructura economica de la sociedad Mexica segun las fuentes documentales. Mexico, 1972. pp. 197. *bibliog.*

BAADER (ANDREAS).

BECKER (JILLIAN) Hitler's children: the story of the Baader-Meinhof terrorist gang. Philadelphia, [1977]. pp. 322. *bibliog.*

BACHELARD (GASTON).

LECOURT (DOMINIQUE) Marxism and epistemology: Bachelard, Canguilhem and Foucault; translated from the French by Ben Brewster. London, 1975. pp. 223. *bibliog.*

BACKHOUSE (Sir EDMUND TRELAWNY).

TREVOR-ROPER (HUGH REDWALD) Hermit of Peking: the hidden life of Sir Edmund Backhouse. [rev. ed.] Harmondsworth, 1978. pp. 391. *First published in 1976 under title A hidden life: the enigma of Sir Edmund Backhouse.*

BACON.

SPINK (REGINALD) DBC: the story of the Danish Bacon Company, 1902-1977. Welwyn Garden City, [1977]. pp. 96. *bibliog.*

BADEN

— **Economic history.**

STRAUB (ALFRED) Das badische Oberland im 18. Jahrhundert: die Transformation einer bäuerlichen Gesellschaft vor der Industrialisierung. Husum, [1977]. pp. 173. *bibliog.*

— **History.**

VERFOLGUNG und Widerstand unter dem Nationalsozialismus in Baden: die Lageberichte der Gestapo und des Generalstaatsanwalts Karlsruhe, 1933-1940; bearbeitet von Jörg Schadt. Stuttgart, [1976]. pp. 354. *bibliog.* (Mannheim. Stadtarchiv. Veröffentlichungen. Band 3)

Die SALPETERER...; herausgegeben von Thomas Lehner. Berlin, [1977]. pp. 125. *bibliog.*

BADEN-WUERTTEMBERG
— **Economic policy.**

BACKES (WIELAND) Planung und Raumentwicklung im mittleren Neckarraum: sozioökonomische Determinanten der Lebensbedingungen in einer verdichteten Region, dargestellt unter besonderer Berücksichtigung der Waiblinger Bucht. München, [1978]. pp. 426. *bibliog.*

BADER (ERNEST).

HOE (SUSANNA) The man who gave his company away: a biography of Ernest Bader, founder of the Scott Bader Commonwealth. London, 1978. pp. 242. *bibliog.*

BAGRAMIAN (IVAN KHRISTOFOROVICH).

BAGRAMIAN (IVAN KHRISTOFOROVICH) Tak nachinalas' voina. Kiev, 1975. pp. 510.

BAGRAMIAN (IVAN KHRISTOFOROVICH) Tak shli my k pobede. Moskva, 1977. pp. 608.

BAHAMAS
— **Appropriations and expenditures.**

BAHAMAS. Department of Statistics. 1976. Government revenue and expenditure, 1970-1973. Nassau, [1976]. fo. 18.

— **Population.**

BAHAMAS. Department of Statistics. 1976. Demographic aspects of the Bahamian population, 1901-1974. Nassau, [1976]. pp. 53. (Census Monographs. No. 2)

— **Statistics.**

BAHAMAS. Department of Statistics. Quarterly statistical summary. q., [Ap/Je] 1974- Nassau.

BAHRAIN
— **Economic conditions.**

RUMAIHI (M.G.) Bahrain: social and political change since the First World War. London, 1976. pp. 258. *bibliog.*

— **Politics and government.**

RUMAIHI (M.G.) Bahrain: social and political change since the First World War. London, 1976. pp. 258. *bibliog.*

— **Social conditions.**

RUMAIHI (M.G.) Bahrain: social and political change since the First World War. London, 1976. pp. 258. *bibliog.*

BAIKAL-AMUR RAILWAY.

PROBLEMY razvitiia raionov s ekstremal'nymi prirodnymi usloviiami; (Problems of developing districts with extremal natural conditions). Irkutsk, 1976. pp. 193. *bibliog. With English foreword, summaries and table of contents.*

BAIL
— **Australia.**

ESSAYS on law and poverty: bail and social security. Canberra, 1977. pp. 92. (Australia. Commission of Inquiry into Poverty. Law and Poverty Series)

BAIN (JOE STATEN).

ESSAYS on industrial organization in honor of Joe S. Bain; edited by Robert T. Masson and P. David Qualls. Cambridge, Mass., [1976]. pp. 277. *bibliog.*

BAKERS AND BAKERIES
— **United Kingdom.**

REEKIE (W. DUNCAN) Give us this day...; an economic critique of political intervention between men and women and their daily bread. London, 1978. pp. 78. *bibliog.* (Institute of Economic Affairs. Hobart Papers. 79)

BAKUNIN (MIKHAIL ALEKSANDROVICH).

HISTORIA i wolność: studia z dziejów ideologii XIX wieku, etc. Warszawa, 1961. pp. 299. (Polska Akademia Nauk. Instytut Filozofii i Socjologii. Archiwum Historii Filozofii i Myśli Społecznej. 7) *With Russian or German summaries.*

POLIANSKII (FEDOR IAKOVLEVICH) Kritika ekonomicheskikh teorii anarkhizma. Moskva, 1976. pp. 301.

BALANCE OF PAYMENTS.

JOHNSON (HARRY GORDON) Money, balance-of-payments theory, and the international monetary problem. Princeton, 1977. pp. 26. *bibliog.* (Princeton University. Department of Economics and Sociology. International Finance Section. Essays in International Finance. No. 124)

— **France — Mathematical models.**

SHEEN (JEFFREY RALPH) A study of monetary disequilibrium in open economies. 1977. fo. 330. *bibliog. Typescript. Ph.D. (London) thesis: unpublished. This thesis is the property of London University and may not be removed from the Library.*

— **Germany.**

EMMINGER (OTMAR) The D-mark in the conflict between internal and external equilibrium, 1948-75. Princeton, 1977. pp. 54. *bibliog.* (Princeton University. Department of Economics and Sociology. International Finance Section. Essays in International Finance. No. 122)

— **Mexico.**

VILLARREAL (RENE) El desequilibrio externo en la industrializacion de Mexico, 1929- 1975: un enfoque estructuralista. Mexico, 1976. pp. 281. *bibliog.*

WILFORD (D. SYKES) Monetary policy and the open economy: Mexico's experience. New York, 1977. pp. 152. *bibliog.*

— **Panama.**

PANAMA. Direccion de Estadistica y Censo. Estadistica panameña. Balanza de pagos. a., 1974/75- Panama.

— **United Kingdom.**

LECTURES on the U.K. balance of payments; [by] Ronald Shone [and others]; [presented at a conference held by the Scottish branch of the Economics Association and the Department of Economics of Stirling University at Stirling in 1977]; [edited by Peter Maunder]. [Stirling], 1977. pp. 40.

LOMAX (RACHEL) and MOWL (COLIN) Balance of payments flows and the monetary aggregates in the United Kingdom. London, Treasury, 1978. pp. 10,6. (Government Economic Service Working Papers. No.5)

— **United States.**

McALISTER (ANDREW MCDONALD) Overseas economic relations and foreign policy in the administration of President Kennedy, 1961-1963. [1977]. fo. 356. *bibliog. Typescript. Ph.D. (London) thesis: unpublished. This thesis is the property of London University and may not be removed from the Library.*

The PRESENTATION of the U.S. balance of payments: a symposium [by] Robert M. Stern [and others]. Princeton, 1977. pp. 64. (Princeton University. Department of Economics and Sociology. International Finance Section. Essays in International Finance. No. 123)

BALANCE OF POWER.

LISKA (GEORGE) Quest for equilibrium: America and the balance of power on land and sea. Baltimore, [1977]. pp. 254. (Johns Hopkins University. Washington Center of Foreign Policy Research. Studies in International Affairs)

BALFOUR (JABEZ SPENCER).

The STORY of the Liberator Crash with some account of the career and character of Jabez Spencer Balfour, with numerous illustrations. [London], 1893. pp. 44. (Westminster Gazette. Westminster Popular. No. 5)

BALI
— **Social life and customs.**

BOON (JAMES A.) The anthropological romance of Bali, 1597-1972: dynamic perspectives in marriage and caste, politics and religion. Cambridge, 1977. pp. 259. *bibliog.*

BALKAN STATES
— **History.**

ANALIS (DIMITRI T.) Les Balkans, 1945-1960: la prise du pouvoir. [Paris, 1978]. pp. 269. *bibliog.*

— — **1912-1913, War of — Atrocities.**

BALKAN ALLIES ATROCITIES PUBLICATION COMMITTEE. A Turkish appeal to the women and men of Great Britain. Constantinople, 1913. pp. (2).

— **Nationalism.**

JELAVICH (CHARLES) and JELAVICH (BARBARA) The establishment of the Balkan national states, 1804-1920. Seattle, [1977]. pp. 358. *bibliog.* (A History of East Central Europe. vol. 8)

— **Politics and government.**

JELAVICH (CHARLES) and JELAVICH (BARBARA) The establishment of the Balkan national states, 1804-1920. Seattle, [1977]. pp. 358. *bibliog.* (A History of East Central Europe. vol. 8)

BALTIC, THE.

GELBERG (LUDWIK) Problemy prawne współpracy państw bałtyckich. Wrocław, 1976. pp. 150. *With English table of contents.*

BALTIC STATES
— **History.**

VON den baltischen Provinzen zu den baltischen Staaten: Beiträge zur Entstehungsgeschichte der Republiken Estland und Lettland, 1918-1920; herausgeben im Auftrage der Baltischen Historischen Kommission von Jürgen von Hehn [and others]. Marburg/Lahn, 1977. pp. 447.

SOTSIALISTICHESKIE revoliutsii 1940 g. v Litve, Latvii i Estonii: vosstanovlenie Sovetskoi vlasti. Moskva, 1978. pp. 351.

— **Nationalism.**

NATIONALITY group survival in multi-ethnic states: shifting support patterns in the Soviet Baltic region; edited by Edward Allworth. New York, 1977. pp. 299. *bibliog.*

BALUCHISTAN
— **Appropriations and expenditures.**

ANNUAL BUDGET STATEMENT OF THE GOVERNMENT OF BALUCHISTAN; [pd. by] Finance Department. a., 1977/78- Quetta.

— **Economic policy.**

PAKISTAN. Ministry of Information and Broadcasting, Directorate of Research, Reference and Publications. 1977. Achievements of the people's government, 1972-1976: Baluchistan. [Islamabad, 1977?]. pp. 33.

BALUCHISTAN(Cont.)

— Politics and government.

PAKISTAN. Prime Minister. 1976. Speech in the parliament: situation in Baluchistan. [Islamabad, Directorate of Research, Reference and Publications, Ministry of Information and Broadcasting, 1976] . pp. 20.

PAKISTAN. Ministry of Information and Broadcasting, Directorate of Research, Reference and Publications. 1977. Achievements of the people's government, 1972-1976: Baluchistan. [Islamabad, 1977?]. pp. 33.

— Social policy.

PAKISTAN. Ministry of Information and Broadcasting, Directorate of Research, Reference and Publications. 1977. Achievements of the people's government, 1972-1976: Baluchistan. [Islamabad, 1977?]. pp. 33.

BALZAC (HONORÉ DE).

MEHLMAN (JEFFREY) Revolution and repetition: Marx, Hugo, Balzac. Berkeley, Calif., [1977]. pp. 132.

BANACH SPACES.

DIESTEL (JOSEPH) Geometry of Banach spaces: selected topics. Berlin, 1975. pp. 282. *bibliogs*.

LINDENSTRAUSS (JORAM) and TZAFRIRI (LIOR) Classical Banach spaces. Berlin, 1977 in progress. *bibliog*.

BANCO DE LA PROVINCIA DE BUENOS AIRES.

CUCCORESE (HORACIO JUAN) Historia del Banco de la Provincia de Buenos Aires. [Buenos Aires, 1972]. pp. 490. *bibliog*.

BANGLADESH

— Economic conditions — Statistics.

MONTHLY ECONOMIC SITUATION OF BANGLADESH; pd. by Bureau of Statistics. m., Jl 1977- Dacca.

— Economic policy.

NURUL ISLAM Development strategy of Bangladesh. Oxford, 1978. pp. 109.

— Foreign relations.

See also UNITED NATIONS — Bangladesh.

— History.

SALIK (SIDDIQ) Witness to surrender. Karachi, 1977. pp. 245.

RAHMAN (MATIUR) Bangladesh today: an indictment and a lament. London, [1978]. pp. 188. *bibliog*.

— — 1971, Revolution.

PAKISTAN. 1971. The present crisis in East Pakistan: a statement by an official spokesman of the government of Pakistan, May 5, 1971. [Karachi] 1971. pp. 8.

PAKISTAN. 1971. Summary of the White Paper on the crisis in East Pakistan. [Karachi], 1971. pp. 12.

PAKISTAN. Department of Films and Publications. 1971. East Pakistan crisis: answers to questions. [Karachi, 1971]. pp. 20.

PAKISTAN. Department of Films and Publications. 1971. Pakistan welcomes returning citizens. [Karachi, 1971]. pp. 14.

RADIO PAKISTAN. External Services. A tragedy in focus. [Karachi, 1971]. pp. 34.

A STATEMENT by East Pakistan scholars and artists. [Karachi, Department of Films and Publications, 1971]. pp. 8.

— Population policy.

BANGLADESH. Ministry of Information and Broadcasting. 1977. A comprehensive population communication strategy, Bangladesh: UNFPA/UNESCO project BGD/74/P12; testing, evaluation and development of a comprehensive population communication programme. [Dacca], 1977. 3 vols (in 1).

— Statistics.

MONTHLY STATISTICAL BULLETIN OF BANGLADESH; pd. by Bangladesh Bureau of Statistics. m., Mr 1972 (v.1, no.1)- Dacca. *Supersedes* BANGLADESH. Bureau of Statistics. Monthly bulletin of statistics (Oc 1950 - F 1969, with gaps)

STATISTICAL YEARBOOK OF BANGLADESH; [pd. by] Bureau of Statistics. a., 1975(1st)- Dacca. *Not pd.* *(1976). Supersedes* BANGLADESH. Bureau of Statistics. Statistical digest of Bangladesh.

STATISTICAL POCKET BOOK OF BANGLADESH; [pd. by] Bureau of Statistics. a., 1978- Dacca.

BANK DEPOSITS

— Netherlands — Mathematical models.

FASE (M.M.G.) Savings deposits, time deposits and interest rate differentials: an econometric analysis. Amsterdam, [1977]. pp. 15. *(Nederlandsche Bank. Reprints. No. 34) (Reprinted from Quarterly Statistics of the Nederlandsche Bank, 1977)*

— Turkey.

YASER (BETTY SLADE) Convertible foreign exchange deposit accounts and foreign private loans. Ankara, 1973. fo. 16. *(United States. Agency for International Development. USAID-Ankara. Economic Analysis Staff. Discussion Papers. No. 14)*

BANK EMPLOYEES

— United States.

SIMCICH (TINA L.) Women and minorities in banking: shortchanged/update. New York, 1977. pp. 173. *bibliog*. A survey of the Council on Economic Priorities.

BANK HOLDING COMPANIES

— United States.

BOCZAR (GREGORY E.) The growth of multibank holding companies: 1956-73. [Washington], 1976. pp. 27. *(United States. Board of Governors of the Federal Reserve System. Staff Economic Studies. No. 85)*

BANK INVESTMENTS.

ROUSSAKIS (EMMANUEL N.) Managing commercial bank funds. New York, 1977. pp. 180. *bibliog*.

BANK LOANS.

ROUSSAKIS (EMMANUEL N.) Managing commercial bank funds. New York, 1977. pp. 180. *bibliog*.

BANK-NOTES.

HANG SENG BANK. A guide to world banknotes regulations. Hong Kong, 1975. pp. 11.

FASE (M.M.G.) and NIEUWKERK (MARIUS VAN) The demand for bank notes in four countries: a statistical analysis for the Netherlands, the Federal Republic of Germany, Switzerland and the United States. Amsterdam, [1977]. pp. 22. *(Nederlandsche Bank. Reprints. No. 31) (Reprinted from Quarterly Statistics of the Nederlandsche Bank, June 1977)*

BANK VAN DE NEDERLANDSE ANTILLEN.

SOEST (JAAP VAN) Trustee of the Netherlands Antilles: a history of money, banking and the economy with special reference to the central Bank van de Nederlandse Antillen, 1828-6 February-1978. Zutphen, [1978]. pp. 422. *bibliog*.

BANK ZWIAZKU SPÓŁEK ZAROBKOWYCH.

SITAREK (HENRYK) Rola kredytu w rozwoju gospodarki Wielkopolski na przełomie XIX i XX wieku: Bank Związku Spółek Zarobkowych w Poznaniu, 1885-1918; Rolle des Kredits in der Entwicklung von Wielkopolska um die Wende des XIX. und XX. Jh. Warszawa, 1977. pp. 200. *bibliog.* (Poznań. Poznańskie Towarzystwo Przyjaciół Nauk. Wydział Historii i Nauk Społecznych. Badania z Dziejów Społecznych i Gospodarczych. nr.55) With German summary.

BANKING LAW

— Japan.

EXPORT-IMPORT BANK OF JAPAN. The Export-Import Bank of Japan law: [Law No. 268 of 1950, as amended]. [Tokyo], 1973. pp. 17.

— United Kingdom.

INSTITUTE OF BANKERS. Legal decisions affecting bankers, 1879-1966; edited and annotated by John R. Paget [and others]. London, 1900-1968. 8 vols.

CHORLEY (ROBERT SAMUEL THEODORE) 1st Baron Chorley, and SMART (PERCY EYNON) Leading cases in the law of banking. 4th ed. London, 1977. pp. 358.

BANKRUPTCY

— Canada.

CANADIAN LABOUR CONGRESS. Submission...to the Senate Committee on Banking, Trade and Commerce, respecting Bill C-60 (an act respecting bankruptcy and insolvency). Ottawa, 1975. fo. 4.

— United Kingdom.

FLETCHER (IAN F.) Law of bankruptcy. Plymouth, 1978. pp. 440.

BANKS AND BANKING.

BANCARI e banchieri: istituti finanziari e rapporti sociali di produzione; saggi a cura di Renzo Stefanelli. Bari, [1976]. pp. 223. *Essays by Renato Corsetti and others*.

— Bibliography.

ROCK (JAMES M.) compiler. Money, banking, and macroeconomics: a guide to information sources. Detroit, [1977]. pp. 281.

— Jews.

POLIAKOV (LEON) Jewish bankers and the Holy See from the thirteenth to the seventeenth century;...translated from the French by Miriam Kochan. London, 1977. pp. 275.

— Periodicals — Indexes.

CHESTERFIELD COLLEGES OF ART AND TECHNOLOGY. Library and Resources Centre. Bank reviews index; a subject index of articles from bank reviews published 1946-1975. Chesterfield, 1977. pp. 77.

— Africa, East.

ABDI (ALI ISSA) Commercial banks and economic development: the experience of eastern Africa. New York, 1977. pp. 148. *bibliog*.

— Argentine Republic.

TERRY (JOSE A.) La crisis, 1885-1892: sistema bancario. Buenos Aires, 1893. pp. 353.

BECU (CARLOS TEODORO) El control del dinero en la Argentina. Buenos Aires, [1953]. pp. 156. *bibliog*.

— Canada.

NAYLOR (R. TOM) The history of Canadian business, 1867-1914. Toronto, 1975. 2 vols.(in 1). *bibliog*.

— **Colombia — Statistics.**

COLOMBIA. Superintendencia Bancaria. Oficina Economica. Division Estudios Tecnicos. 1970. Estadisticas monetarias y financieras, 1963-1969; entidades: bancos, corporaciones financieras, compañias de seguros, sociedades administradoras, fondos de inversion y almacenes generales de deposito. [Bogota, 1970?]. pp. 100.

— **European Economic Community countries.**

EUROPEAN COMMUNITIES. Statistical Office. Labour costs in distributive trades, banking and insurance. trien., 1974(2nd)- Luxembourg. *[in Community languages] 1970(1st) included in EUROPEAN COMMUNITIES. Statistical Office. Social statistics, 1972(no. 4).*

EUROPEAN COMMUNITIES. Statistical Office. Special Series: Structure of Earnings in Wholesale and Retail Distribution, Banking and Insurance in 1974. Luxembourg, [1977] in progress.

— **Finland.**

OKSANEN (HEIKKI) Bank liquidity and lending in Finland, 1950-1973. Helsinki, 1977. pp. 138. *bibliog. (Societas Scientiarum Fennica. Commentationes Scientiarum Socialium. 8)*

— **Iran.**

ANAN'ICH (BORIS VASIL'EVICH) Rossiiskoe samoderzhavie i vyvoz kapitalov, 1895-1914 gg.: po materialam Uchetno-ssudnogo banka Persii. Leningrad, 1975. pp. 211.

— **Italy.**

BARCA (LUCIANO) and MANGHETTI (GIANNI) L'Italia delle banche. Roma, 1976. pp. 394.

— **Kenya.**

CENTRAL BANK OF KENYA. Money and banking in Kenya. [Nairobi, 1972?]. pp. 34.

— **Netherlands.**

LAAR (H.J.M. VAN DE) Opperbankier en wetenschapsman Willem Cornelis Mees, 1813-1884. 's Gravenhage, 1978. pp. 475. *bibliog.*

— **Netherlands Antilles.**

SOEST (JAAP VAN) Trustee of the Netherlands Antilles: a history of money, banking and the economy with special reference to the central Bank van de Nederlandse Antillen, 1828-6 February-1978. Zutphen, [1978]. pp. 422. *bibliog.*

— **Norway.**

NORWAY. Statistiske Centralbyrå. Kredittmarkedstatistikk: private og offentlige banker, etc. a., 1973/75(1st)- Oslo. *[in English and Norwegian] Supersedes in part NORWAY. Statistiske Centralbyrå. Kredittmarkedstatistikk.*

— **Russia.**

GARVY (GEORGE) Money, financial flows, and credit in the Soviet Union. Cambridge, Mass., 1977. pp. 223. *bibliog. (National Bureau of Economic Research. Studies in International Economic Relations. 7 [bis])*

KUSCHPÈTA (O.) The banking and credit system of the USSR. Leiden, 1978. pp. 284. *bibliog. (Tilburg. Katholieke Hogeschool. Tilburg Institute of Economics. Tilburg Studies on Economics. 18)*

— — **Kazakstan.**

FRIDMAN (TSEZAR' L'VOVICH) Banki i kredit v dorevoliutsionnom Kazakhstane, 1900-1914 gg. Alma-Ata, 1974. pp. 175.

— **South Africa.**

CLAIM against the imperial government in the matter of the specie commandeered by the government of the late South African Republic from British banks: further correspondence between the Colonial Office and the banks. [London?, 1904]. pp. 13.

— **Switzerland.**

BRODMANN (ROMAN) Der Un-Schweizer: was machen Eidgenossen mit einem Dissidenten?: vom "Fall Ziegler" zum Fall Schweiz. Darmstadt, [1977]. pp. 126.

— **Underdeveloped areas.**

See UNDERDEVELOPED AREAS — **Banks and banking.**

— **United Kingdom.**

DAVIS (STEVEN NORMAN) Banking in Boston. Boston, 1976. pp. 44. *(History of Boston Project. History of Boston Series. No.14)*

BANKS and the British exporter; based on the seminar held at... Cambridge, 11-16 September, 1977. London, 1977. pp. 86. *bibliog.*

MONTGOMERY (CHARLES JOHN) The clearing banks, 1952-77: an age of progress. London, 1977. pp. 16. *Presidential address to the Institute of Bankers, 18 May, 1977.*

The LONDON clearing banks: evidence by the Committee of London Clearing Bankers to the Committee to Review the Functioning of Financial Institutions. London, 1978. pp. 278.

— **United States.**

TALLEY (SAMUEL H.) Recent trends in local banking market structure. [Washington], 1977. pp. 28. *(United States. Board of Governors of the Federal Reserve System. Staff Economic Studies. No. 89)*

WEST (ROBERT CRAIG) Banking reform and the Federal Reserve 1863-1923. Ithaca, 1977. pp. 243. *bibliog.*

HENNING (CHARLES N.) and others. Financial markets and the economy. 2nd ed. Englewood Cliffs, [1978]. pp. 552. *bibliogs.*

BANKS AND BANKING, AMERICAN

— **United Kingdom.**

KELLY (JANET) Bankers and borders: the case of American banks in Britain. Cambridge, Mass., [1977]. pp. 226.

BANKS AND BANKING, CENTRAL

— **Colombia.**

IREGUI MEDINA (ENRIQUE) La Banca Central y sus controles. Bogota, 1972. pp. 102. *bibliog.*

BANKS AND BANKING, FOREIGN

— **South Africa.**

COUNTER INFORMATION SERVICES. Anti-Reports. Business as usual: international banking in South Africa. London, [1974?]. pp. 29. *bibliog.*

BANKS AND BANKING, INTERNATIONAL.

COUNTER INFORMATION SERVICES. Anti-Reports. Business as usual: international banking in South Africa. London, [1974?]. pp. 29. *bibliog.*

BANTU HOMELANDS, SOUTH AFRICA.

FAIR (T.J.D.) Some spatial aspects of black homeland development in South Africa. Johannesburg, 1975. pp. 22. *bibliog. (Johannesburg. University of the Witwatersrand. Urban and Regional Research Unit. Occasional Papers. No. 6)*

U.K. Foreign and Commonwealth Office. Research Department. 1978. The South African homelands. London, 1978. pp. 20, 1 map. *(Foreign Policy Documents. No. 1)*

BANTUS.

VAN DER MERWE (P.J.) Die Bantoe-mannekragpotensiaal van Suid-Afrika se Bantoevolke met verwysing na indiensnemingsmikpunte ten opsigte van elke volk. Pretoria, 1970. pp. 42. *(Africa Institute. Communications. No. 15)*

DAVIES (WILLIAM J.) A survey of consumer behaviour and shopping patterns amongst Bantu in Port Elizabeth. Port Elizabeth, 1972. fo. 31. *(University of Port Elizabeth. Institute for Planning Research. Information Bulletins. No. 5)*

ROGERS (BARBARA) Divide and rule: South Africa's Bantustans. London, 1976. pp. 86.

BARBADOS

— **Antiquities.**

HANDLER (JEROME S.) and others. Plantation slavery in Barbados: an archaeological and historical investigation. Cambridge, Mass., 1978. pp. 368. *bibliog.*

— **Economic policy.**

BARBADOS. 1969. Barbados development plan, 1969-72. [Bridgetown, 1969]. pp. 178.

BARBADOS. 1973. Development plan, 1973-77. [Bridgetown, 1973?]. 1 vol. (various pagings).

KHAN (JAMAL) Development administration: field research in Barbados. Bridgetown, Barbados, [1976]. pp. 203. *bibliogs.*

— **Emigration and immigration.**

BARBADOS. 195-. Information booklet for intending emigrants to Britain. [Bridgetown, 195-]. pp. 24.

— **House of Assembly — Elections.**

BARBADOS. Supervisor of Elections. 1976. Report...on the general election, 1976. [Bridgetown, 1976?]. 1 vol.(various foliations).

— **Parliament — Elections.**

BARBADOS. Supervisor of Elections. 1971. General election 1971 held 9th September, 1971: administrative report. [Bridgetown, 1971]. 1 pamphlet (various foliations).

— **Politics and government.**

KHAN (JAMAL) Development administration: field research in Barbados. Bridgetown, Barbados, [1976]. pp. 203. *bibliogs.*

— **Social policy.**

BARBADOS. 1969. Barbados development plan, 1969-72. [Bridgetown, 1969]. pp. 178.

BARBADOS. 1973. Development plan, 1973-77. [Bridgetown, 1973?]. 1 vol. (various pagings).

— **Statistics.**

BARBADOS. Statistical Service. Monthly digest of statistics. m., Ap 1974 (1st)- [Bridgetown]. *Supersedes its Quarterly digest of statistics (D 1956 - Je 1973)*

BARCELONA

— **Growth.**

FERRAS (ROBERT) Barcelone: croissance d'une métropole. Paris, 1977. pp. 616. *bibliog.*

BARCLAY (ALEXANDER).

HAMMOND (GEORGE PETER) The adventures of Alexander Barclay, mountain man...: a narrative of his career, 1810-1855, his memorandum diary, 1845 to 1850. Denver, Colo., 1976. pp. 246.

BARTELS (ADOLPHE).

BOLAND (ANDRE) Le procès de la révolution belge: Adolphe Bartels, 1802-1862. Namur, [1977]. pp. 316. *bibliog.* (Namur. Facultés Universitaires Notre-Dame de la Paix. Faculté de Philosophie et Lettres. Bibliothèque. fasc. 56)

BARTH (KARL).

GUNTON (COLIN E.) Becoming and being: the doctrine of God in Charles Hartshorne and Karl Barth. Oxford, 1978. pp. 236. *bibliog.*

BASILICATA

— **Economic conditions.**

CORTI (PAOLA) ed. Inchiesta Zanardelli sulla Basilicata. [Torino, 1976]. pp. 175. *bibliog.*

— **Economic policy.**

CAFIERO (SALVATORE) La pianificazione regionale in Basilicata: analisi di documenti e di proposte. [Milan], 1975. pp. 67. *(Associazione per lo Sviluppo dell'Industria nel Mezzogiorno. Centro per gli Studi sullo Sviluppo Economico. Collana Francesco Giordani)*

BASQUE PROVINCES

— **Nationalism.**

IBARRA ENZIONDO (LUIS DE) El nacionalismo vasco en la paz y en la guerra. n.p., [197-?]. pp. 285.

UGARANA LARRUN (ANDONI) La agonia del Franquismo: no hay mal que dure cien años. Saint Jean de Luz, 1975. pp. 208.

— **Politics and government.**

ESCUDERO (MANU) and VILLANUEVA (JAVIER) La autonomia del Pais Vasco desde el pasado al futuro. San Sebastian, [1976]. pp. 259.

PEREZ CALVO (ALBERTO) Los partidos politicos en el Pais Vasco: approximacion a su estudio. San Sebastian, 1977. pp. 119.

— **Social history.**

OLABARRI GORTAZAR (IGNACIO) Relaciones laborales en Vizcaya, 1890-1936. Durango, Spain, [1978]. pp. 532. *bibliog.*

BAUXITE

— **Guyana.**

GUYANA. Prime Minister. 1971. Control of our natural resources: address to the nation by the Hon. L.F.S. Burnham...on the occasion of Republic Day, February 23, 1971. [Georgetown, 1971]. pp. 12.

BAVARIA

— **History.**

BAYERN in der NS-Zeit: soziale Lage und politisches Verhalten der Bevölkerung im Spiegel vertraulicher Berichte; herausgegeben von Martin Broszat [and others]. München, 1977. pp. 712. *bibliog.*

RAPE (LUDGER) Die österreichischen Heimwehren und die bayerische Rechte, 1920-1923. Wien, [1977]. pp. 457. *bibliog. (Ludwig Boltzmann Institut für Geschichte der Arbeiterbewegung. Veröffentlichungen)*

— **Militia.**

RAPE (LUDGER) Die österreichischen Heimwehren und die bayerische Rechte, 1920-1923. Wien, [1977]. pp. 457. *bibliog. (Ludwig Boltzmann Institut für Geschichte der Arbeiterbewegung. Veröffentlichungen)*

BAYESIAN STATISTICAL DECISION THEORY.

MARITZ (J.S.) Empirical Bayes methods. London, 1970. pp. 159. *bibliog.*

ROSENKRANTZ (ROGER D.) Inference, method and decision: towards a Bayesian philosophy of science. Dordrecht,[1977]. pp. 262. *bibliogs.*

ROY (ANDREW DONALD) A Bayesian approach to the control of expenditure. [London], Department of Health and Social Security, 1978. pp. 13. *(Government Economic Service Working Papers. No. 9)*

BECHER (JOHANN JOACHIM).

VOLBERG (HEINRICH) Deutsche Kolonialbestrebungen in Südamerika nach dem Dreissigjährigen Kriege, insbesondere die Bemühungen von Johann Joachim Becher. Köln, 1977. pp. 223. *bibliog.*

BEDFORD PARK, LONDON

— **Social life and customs.**

BOLSTERLI (MARGARET JONES) The early community at Bedford Park: corporate happiness in the first garden suburb. London, 1977. pp. 136.

BEEF

— **Prices — Canada.**

CANADA. Food Prices Review Board. 1974. Beef pricing II. [Ottawa, 1974]. pp. 12, 13. *In English and French.*

CANADA. Food Prices Review Board. 1974. Retail beef prices and price spreads. [Ottawa, 1974]. pp. 41, 40. *In English and French.*

— **United States.**

AUSTRALIA. Bureau of Agricultural Economics. 1977. An econometric model of the United States beef market. Canberra, 1977. pp. 149. *bibliog. (Beef Research Reports. No. 20)*

BEEF CATTLE

— **Canada.**

CANADA. Food Prices Review Board. 1975. Market for heifer beef in Canada. [Ottawa, 1975]. pp. 28, 30. *In English and French.*

BEER.

U.K Food Standards Committee. 1977. Report on beer; [A.G. Ward, chairman]. London, 1977. pp. 59.

BEGGING

— **India — Uttar Pradesh.**

INDIA. Census, 1971. Series 21. The report on beggary in Uttar Pradesh. [Delhi, 1976]. pp. 49.

— **United Kingdom — Ireland.**

DUBLIN. Association for the Suppression of Mendicity in Dublin. Annual report. a., 1818-1819(1st-2nd). Dublin.

BEHAVIOUR THERAPY.

WACHTEL (PAUL L.) Psychoanalysis and behavior therapy: toward an integration. New York, [1977]. pp. 315. *bibliog.*

BELFAST

— **Social conditions.**

BURTON (FRANK PATRICK) The politics of legitimacy: struggles in a Belfast community. London, 1978. pp. 208. *bibliog.*

BELFAST UNIVERSITY.

DOWNING (JOHN DEREK HALL) Nothing to hide: the Boehringer case and academic freedom in Northern Ireland. London, [1975?]. pp. 19.

BELGIUM

— **History — 1830-1839, Revolution.**

BOLAND (ANDRE) Le procès de la révolution belge: Adolphe Bartels, 1802-1862. Namur, [1977]. pp. 316. *bibliog.* (Namur. Facultés Universitaires Notre-Dame de la Paix. Faculté de Philosophie et Lettres. Bibliothèque. fasc. 56)

— **Nationalism.**

FRANCIS (JEAN) Lettre ouverte à trois millions cent quatre-vingt mille cent dix- huit Wallons. [Bruxelles], 1974. pp. 71.

— **Politics and government.**

OBLER (JEFFREY) and others. Decision-making in smaller democracies: the consociational burden. Beverly Hills, [1977]. pp. 58. *bibliog.*

— **Population.**

POPULATION and family in the Low Countries, 1; edited by H.G. Moors [and others]. Leiden, 1976. pp. 179. *bibliogs. (Nederlands Interuniversitair Demografisch Instituut and Centre d'Etude de la Population et de la Famille [Belgium]. Publications. vol.1)*

— **Social history.**

NEUVILLE (JEAN) La condition ouvrière au XIXe siècle. Bruxelles, 1976-77. 2 vols.

— **Social policy.**

SENAEVE (PATRICK) De bestrijding van de armoede in België: analyse van het toekennen van een gewaarborgd inkomen en van de hervorming van de COO'S. Leuven, 1977. pp. 615. *(Katholieke Universiteit te Leuven. Instituut voor Sociale Zekerheidsrecht. [Publications]. Nr.27)*

BELIZE.

NEW BELIZE, THE; pd. m. by Government Information Service, Belize. m., Je 1974(v.4, no.2)- , with gaps. Belmopan.

BENES (EDVARD).

PRINZ (FRIEDRICH) Beneš, Jaksch und die Sudetendeutschen. Stuttgart, 1975. pp. 76.

BENGAL, WEST

— **Industries.**

KLASS (MORTON) From field to factory: community structure and industrialization in West Bengal. Philadelphia, [1978]. pp. 264. *bibliog.*

— **Rural conditions.**

KLASS (MORTON) From field to factory: community structure and industrialization in West Bengal. Philadelphia, [1978]. pp. 264. *bibliog.*

BENTHAM (JEREMY).

LONG (DOUGLAS G.) Bentham on liberty: Jeremy Bentham's idea of liberty in relation to his utilitarianism. Toronto, [1977]. pp. 294. *bibliog.*

ROSENBLUM (NANCY L.) Bentham's theory of the modern state. Cambridge, Mass., 1978. pp. 169.

BEREAVEMENT.

PINCUS (LILY) Death and the family: the importance of mourning. London, 1976. pp. 278.

BERIIA (LAVRENTII PAVLOVICH).

AVTORKHANOV (ABDURAKHMAN) Zagadka smerti Stalina: zagovor Beriia. [Frankfurt, 1976]. pp. 317.

BERLIN

— History — 1945- , Allied occupation.

BERLIN (WEST BERLIN). Senat. Schriftenreihe zur Berliner Zeitgeschichte. Band 9. Berlin: Chronik der Jahre 1959-1960;...bearbeitet durch Hans J. Reichhardt [and others]. Berlin, [1978]. pp. 949. *bibliog.*

— Social conditions.

HOFFMEYER-ZLOTNIK (JUERGEN) Gastarbeiter im Sanierungsgebiet: das Beispiel Berlin- Kreuzberg. Hamburg, [1977]. pp. 191. *bibliog. (Hamburg. Hansische Universität. Seminar für Sozialwissenschaften. Beiträge zur Stadtforschung. Band 1)*

BERLIN QUESTION (1945-).

GERLACH (HERIBERT) Die Berlinpolitik der Kennedy-Administration: eine Fallstudie zum aussenpolitischen Verhalten der Kennedy- Regierung in der Berlinkrise, 1961. Frankfurt/Main, [1977]. pp. 325. *bibliog.*

BERLINGUER (ENRICO).

GORRESIO (VITTORIO) Berlinguer. Milano, 1976. pp. 200. *bibliog.*

BERMUDA

— Statistics.

BERMUDA DIGEST OF STATISTICS: ([pd. by] Statistical Office, Finance Department [Bermuda]). a., Ap 1973 (no.1)- Hamilton, Bermuda.

BERN (CANTON)

— Appropriations and expenditures.

BERN (CANTON). Amt für Statistik. Die Ausgaben der bernischen Gemeinden. a., 1974- Bern.

BERNSTEIN (EDUARD).

MEYER (THOMAS) Writer on socialism. Bernsteins konstruktiver Sozialismus: Eduard Bernsteins Beitrag zur Theorie des Sozialismus. Berlin, [1977]. pp. 445. *bibliog.*

BESSARABIA

— History.

OKHOTNIKOV (J.) and BATCHINSKY (N.) La Bessarabie et la paix européenne. Paris, 1927. pp. 163. *Translated from the Russian.*

BEVERAGES.

ZAMBIA. Central Statistical Office. 1975. Food, beverages and tobacco industries. Lusaka, 1975. fo. 67. *bibliog. (Industry Monographs. No. 1)*

FOOD, DRINK AND TOBACCO INDUSTRY TRAINING BOARD [U.K.]. The Board's views on Training for vital skills. Gloucester, 1976. pp. 2. *(FDT News. Special Issues. November 1976)*

BHUTAN

— Constitution.

ROSE (LEO E.) The politics of Bhutan. Ithaca, 1977. pp. 237. *bibliog.*

— Politics and government.

ROSE (LEO E.) The politics of Bhutan. Ithaca, 1977. pp. 237. *bibliog.*

BHUTTO (ZULFIKAR ALI).

PAKISTAN INSTITUTE OF INTERNATIONAL AFFAIRS. Zulfikar Ali Bhutto and the third world's struggle for new economic order. Karachi, 1976. pp. 32.

PAKISTAN. National Committee. 1978. Bhutto: the truth about his rule and trial. Karachi, [1978]. pp. 59.

PUNJAB (PAKISTAN). High Court. 1978. Judgment in murder trial: state vs Zulfikar Ali Bhutto and others. [Lahore, 1978]. pp. 134.

QAYYUM (ABDUL) Bhutto and the demands of justice. [Islamabad, 1978]. pp. 15.

BIBLE

— Criticism, interpretation, etc.

PAINE (THOMAS) The age of reason;...with a biographical introduction by the Rt. Hon. J.M. Robertson. London, [193-?]. pp. 124. *The text is a reprint of Mrs. Bonner's edition (without the editor's notes), and is based directly upon that of Daniel Isaac Eaton's edition of 1795 (for the first part) and 1796 (for the second).*

— Evidences, authority, etc.

[SCOTT (THOMAS) of Mount Pleasant, Ramsgate] Thoughts on religion and the Bible; by a layman, an M.A. of Trin. Coll. Dub. 2nd ed. London, 1865. pp. 42.

BIBLIOGRAPHY

— Abbreviations.

ORNE (JERROLD) The language of the foreign book trade: abbreviations, terms, phrases. 3rd ed. Chicago, 1976. pp. 333.

— Bibliography — United States.

KANELY (EDNA A.) compiler. Cumulative subject guide to U.S. government bibliographies 1924- 1973; (with Superintendent of Documents classification number index to the...guide, etc.). Arlington, Va., [1976-77]. 7 vols.

— Dictionaries — Polyglot.

ORNE (JERROLD) The language of the foreign book trade: abbreviations, terms, phrases. 3rd ed. Chicago, 1976. pp. 333.

BIBLIOGRAPHY, NATIONAL

— Botswana.

NATIONAL BIBLIOGRAPHY OF BOTSWANA, THE; [pd. by] Botswana National Library Service. 3 a yr. (including annual cumulation), 1969 (v.1, no.2)- [Gaborone].

— Pakistan.

PAKISTAN NATIONAL BIBLIOGRAPHY, THE; [pd. by] Government of Pakistan Directorate of Archives and Libraries, National Bibliographical Unit. irreg., 1962 [1st issue]- Karachi.

— Russia.

LETOPIS' ZHURNAL'NYKH STATEI: organ gosudarstvennoi bibliografii SSSR; ([pd. by] Vsesoiuznaia Knizhnaia Palata [Russia]). w., 1957- , with gap (1975, no.26). Moskva.

— Singapore.

SINGAPORE NATIONAL BIBLIOGRAPHY; [pd. by] National Library, Singapore. trien. (formerly a.,) 1967 [1st issue]- Singapore.

— Taiwan.

CHINESE MATERIALS AND RESEARCH AIDS SERVICE CENTER. Western-language books from the Republic of China; [a] special list for the 28th International Congress of Orientalists, January 6-12 1971 at Australian National University, Canberra. Taiwan, [1971]. pp. 15.

— Tanzania.

PRINTED IN TANZANIA: a list of publications printed in mainland Tanzania and deposited with the Tanganyika Library Service and the Library of the University of Dar es Salaam...; printed...for the Tanganyika Library Services Board. a., 1969 [1st issue]-1970. Dar es Salaam.

— United Kingdom.

CHAPLIN (ARTHUR HUGH) New patterns of national published bibliographies. London, British Library, Bibliographic Services Division, 1976, pp. 10.

BIERMANN (WOLF).

EXIL: die Ausbürgerung Wolf Biermanns aus der DDR; eine Dokumentation, herausgegeben von Peter Roos. Köln, [1977]. pp. 319.

BIG BUSINESS

— United States.

THIMM (ALFRED L.) Business ideologies in the reform-progressive era, 1880-1914. University, Ala., [1976]. pp. 264. *bibliog.*

BIHAR

— Rural conditions.

The KOSI symposium: the rural problem in north-east Bihar: analysis, policy and planning in the Kosi area; by Stephen D. Biggs [and others]; edited by J.L. Joy and Elizabeth Everitt. [Brighton], 1976. pp. 277. *bibliog.*

BIKO (STEVEN).

NAPLEY (Sir DAVID) Steven Biko inquest. [1977]. fo. 26. *Unpublished: photocopy of typescript.*

BERNSTEIN (HILDA) No. 46 - Steve Biko. London, 1978. pp. 150.

WOODS (DONALD) Biko. New York, [1978]. pp. 288.

BILINGUALISM

— Mexico.

URIBE VILLEGAS (OSCAR) Un mapa del monolingüismo y el bilingüismo de los indigenas de Mexico en 1960. Mexico, 1970. pp. 33, with map.

— United Kingdom.

BILINGUALISM and British education: the dimensions of diversity; papers from a conference convened in January 1976. London, 1976. pp. 109. *bibliog. (Centre for Information on Language Teaching and Research. Reports and Papers. 14)*

KHAN (VERITY SAIFULLAH) Bilingualism and linguistic minorities in Britain: developments, perspectives. London, 1977. fo. 13. *(Runnymede Trust. Briefing Papers. 1977, No. 4)*

BILL DRAFTING.

DALE (Sir WILLIAM) Legislative drafting: a new approach; a comparative study of methods in France, Germany, Sweden and the United Kingdom. London, 1977. pp. 341.

BINBROOK

— Social history.

LABOURING life on the Lincolnshire Wolds: a study of Binbrook in the mid-nineteenth century; edited by R. J. Olney. Sleaford, 1975. pp. 39. *bibliog. (Society for Lincolnshire History and Archaeology. Occasional Papers in Lincolnshire History and Archaeology. No. 2)*

BIOGRAPHY.

GALLEANI (LUIGI) Figure e figuri. Newark, N.J., [1930]. pp. 235. *Articles reprinted from La questione sociale and Cronaca sovversiva for the years 1901 to 1920.*

TROTSKII (LEV DAVYDOVICH) Portraits: political and personal. New York, [1977]. pp. 237.

WHO's who in the socialist countries: a biographical encyclopedia of 10,000 leading personalities in 16 communist countries; edited by Borys Lewytzkyj and Juliusz Stroynowski. New York, [1978]. pp. 736.

BIOLOGICAL WARFARE.

WESTING (ARTHUR H.) Weapons of mass destruction and the environment. London, 1977. pp. 95. *bibliog.*

BIOLOGY

BIOLOGY

— Mathematical models.

THOM (RENÉ) Structural stability and morphogenesis: an outline of a general theory of models; translated...by D.H. Fowler. Reading, Mass., 1975. pp. 348.

— Statistics.

SNEDECOR (GEORGE WADDEL) and COCHRAN (WILLIAM GEMMELL) Statistical methods. 6th ed. Ames, Iowa, 1967 reprinted 1976. pp. 593.

BIOMETRY.

BAILEY (NORMAN THOMAS JOHN) The mathematical theory of infectious diseases and its applications. 2nd ed. London, 1975. pp. 413. *bibliog.*

BIRENDRA BIR BIKRAM SHAH DEVA, Crown Prince of Nepal.

NEPAL. Department of Information. 1969. Short biographies of Their Royal Highnesses the Crown Prince and the Crown Princess. [Kathmandu, 1969?]. pp. 8, 3.

BIRMINGHAM

— City planning.

LLEWELYN-DAVIES WEEKS (AND PARTNERS]. Inner area study: Birmingham: environmental action projects. [London], Department of the Environment, [1977-78]. 2 vols.

— Economic conditions.

BIRMINGHAM COMMUNITY DEVELOPMENT PROJECT. Youth on the dole; (by R. Dicker and A. Cochrane). [Oxford], 1977. pp. 24. *(Final Reports. No.4: Young Workers)*

— Economic policy.

SMITH (BARBARA M.D.) The inner city economic problem: a framework for analysis and local authority policy. Birmingham, 1977. pp. 104, xxii. *(Birmingham. University. Centre for Urban and Regional Studies. Research Memoranda. No. 56)*

— Industries.

BIRMINGHAM COMMUNITY DEVELOPMENT PROJECT. Driven on wheels. [Oxford], 1977. pp. 52. *(Final Reports. No. 1: the Transport Industry)*

BIRMINGHAM COMMUNITY DEVELOPMENT PROJECT. Workers on the scrapheap; (by A. Cochrane and R. Dicker). [Oxford], 1977. pp. 52. *(Final Reports. No. 2: Employment)*

— Playgrounds.

LLEWELYN-DAVIES WEEKS [AND PARTNERS]. Inner area study: Birmingham: Family Service Unit: 435 Neighbourhood Centre. [London], Department of the Environment, [1977]. pp. 63.

— Social conditions.

LLEWELYN-DAVIES WEEKS [AND PARTNERS]. Inner area study: Birmingham: circumstances of families. [London], Department of the Environment, [1977]. pp. 140.

BIRMINGHAM, ALABAMA

— Politics and government.

HARRIS (CARL VERNON) Political power in Birmingham, 1871-1921. Knoxville, Tenn., [1977]. pp. 318. *bibliog.*

BIRMINGHAM UNIVERSITY.

SMITH (BARBARA M.D.) Education for management: its conception and implementation in the Faculty of Commerce at Birmingham. Birmingham, 1974. pp. 55. *(Birmingham. University. Centre for Urban and Regional Studies. Research Memoranda. No. 37)*

BIRTH CONTROL.

[BRITISH birth control ephemera, 1870-1947: a collection by David Collis]. v.p., 1870-1947. 98 pamphlets (in 10 vols.). *(Collis Collections. 1) A catalogue compiled by Peter Fryer is kept with the collection.*

FRYER (PETER) compiler. British birth control ephemera, 1870-1947: a catalogue...; with an introduction by D.V. Glass. Leicester, 1969. pp. 42. *(Collis Collections. 1)*

HAIRE (NORMAN) The comparative value of current contraceptive methods. London, 1928. pp. 12. *(Reprinted from Proceedings of the First International Congress for Sexual Research, Berlin, October 10th-16th, 1926)*

SANGER (MARGARET) Woman of the future; including Margaret Sanger: crusader, by Mildred Adams. London, 1934. pp. 32.

DWYER (GEORGE PATRICK) Archbishop of Birmingham. Birth control. London, 1959. pp. 16.

UNITED NATIONS. Department of Economic and Social Affairs. Population Studies. No. 51. Measures, policies and programmes affecting fertility, with particular reference to national family planning programmes. (ST/SOA/SER.A/51). New York, 1972. pp. 162.

DEMERATH (NICHOLAS JAY) Birth control and foreign policy: the alternatives to family planning. New York, [1976]. pp. 228. *bibliog.*

KREAGER (PHILIP) Family planning drop-outs reconsidered: a critical review of research and research findings. London, 1977. pp. 162. *bibliog. (International Planned Parenthood Federation. Research for Action. No. 3)*

NEWLAND (KATHLEEN) Women and population growth: choice beyond childbearing. Washington, 1977. pp. 32. *(Worldwatch Institute. Worldwatch Papers. No. 16)*

— Bibliography.

INTERNATIONAL family planning programs, 1966-1975: a bibliography; edited by Katherine Ch'iu Lyle and Sheldon J. Segal. University, Ala., [1977]. pp. 207.

— Law and legislation — Europe, Eastern.

MAGGS (PETER B.) Law and population in Eastern Europe. 2nd ed. Medford, Mass., 1977. pp. 31. *(Tufts University. Fletcher School of Law and Diplomacy. Law and Population Monograph Series. No. 3)*

— — Malaysia.

IBRAHIM (AHMAD) Law and population in Malaysia. Medford, Mass., 1977. pp. 51. *(Tufts University. Fletcher School of Law and Diplomacy. Law and Population Monograph Series. No. 45)*

— America, Latin.

MASS (BONNIE) Population target: the political economy of population control in Latin America. Toronto, [1976]. pp. 299.

— Australia.

FAMILY planning and health care for infants and mothers. Canberra, 1977. pp. 88. *bibliog. (Australia. Commission of Inquiry into Poverty. Social/Medical Aspects of Poverty Series)*

— Bangladesh.

BANGLADESH. Ministry of Information and Broadcasting. 1977. A comprehensive population communication strategy, Bangladesh: UNFPA/UNESCO project BGD/74/P12; testing, evaluation and development of a comprehensive population communication programme. [Dacca], 1977. 3 vols (in 1).

— Belgium.

POPULATION and family in the Low Countries, 1; edited by H.G. Moors [and others]. Leiden, 1976. pp. 179. *bibliogs. (Nederlands Interuniversitair Demografisch Instituut and Centre d'Etude de la Population et de la Famille [Belgium]. Publications. vol. 1)*

— India.

INDIA. Office of the Registrar General. Vital Statistics Division. 1973. Survey on the extent of knowledge and practice of family planning methods in a sub-sample of units under sample registration system, 1971-72. New Delhi, 1973. pp. 81. *(S[ample] R[egistration] S[ystem] Analytical Series. No. 6)*

— — Kerala.

KURUP (R.S.) and others. Fact book on population and family planning. Trivandrum, Demographic Research Centre, 1974. pp. 77.

— Malaysia.

AZIZ (NOR LAILY) and others. The Malaysian national family planning programme: some facts and figures. [Kuala Lumpur], National Family Planning Board, Malaysia, 1977. pp. 53. *bibliog.*

— Netherlands.

POPULATION and family in the Low Countries, 1; edited by H.G. Moors [and others]. Leiden, 1976. pp. 179. *bibliogs. (Nederlands Interuniversitair Demografisch Instituut and Centre d'Etude de la Population et de la Famille [Belgium]. Publications. vol.1)*

— New Zealand.

NEW ZEALAND. Royal Commission to Inquire into and Report upon Contraception, Sterilisation and Abortion, 1975. Contraception, sterilisation and abortion in New Zealand; report; [D.W. McMullin, chairman]. in NEW ZEALAND. General Assembly. House of Representatives. Journals...Appendix to journals, 1977, E.26.

— Seychelles.

NATIONAL SYMPOSIUM ON LABOUR AND FAMILY WELFARE EDUCATION, VICTORIA, MAHE, 1975. National symposium on labour and family welfare education, Seychelles, August 26-30, 1975; organised by the Ministry of Labour and Social Security in collaboration with the International Labour Organisation, etc. Victoria, Mahé, [Government of Seychelles], 1975. pp. 74.

— Singapore.

SINGAPORE. Family Planning and Population Board. Annual report. a., 1972(7th)- Singapore.

— Underdeveloped areas.

See UNDERDEVELOPED AREAS — Birth control.

— United Kingdom.

CARTWRIGHT (ANN) Recent trends in family building and contraception. London, 1978. pp. 14. *bibliog. (U.K. Office of Population Censuses and Surveys. Studies on Medical and Population Subjects. No. 34)*

McLAREN (ANGUS) Birth control in nineteenth-century England. London, [1978]. pp. 263.

U.K. Social Survey. [Reports. New Series]. 1055. The family planning services: changes and effects; a survey carried out on behalf of the Department of Health and Social Security; [by] Margaret Bone. London, 1978. pp. 129.

— United States.

LITTLEWOOD (THOMAS B.) The politics of population control. Notre Dame, [1977]. pp. 232. *bibliog.*

REED (JAMES) From private vice to public virtue: the birth control movement and American society since 1830. New York, [1978]. pp. 456. *bibliog.*

— Uruguay.

ASOCIACION DE LOS ESTUDIANTES DE MEDICINA. Planificacion familiar y control de la natalidad como forma de la penetracion imperialista en el Uruguay: informe presentado en el Foro de la Facultad de Medicina en diciembre de 1969. [Montevideo?], 1970. pp. 16. *bibliog.*

BIRTH CONTROL CLINICS

— Australia.

FAMILY planning and health care for infants and mothers. Canberra, 1977. pp. 88. *bibliog. (Australia. Commission of Inquiry into Poverty. Social/Medical Aspects of Poverty Series)*

BISHOPS

— United Kingdom.

ROSENTHAL (JOEL THOMAS) The training of an elite group: English bishops in the fifteenth century. Philadelphia, 1970. pp. 54. *bibliog. (American Philosophical Society. Transactions. New Series. vol. 60, part 5)*

BISLEY, GLOUCESTERSHIRE

— History.

RUDD (MARY AMELIA) Historical records of Bisley with Lypiatt, Gloucestershire. Gloucester, [imprint, 1937?]. pp. 437. *Review by R.H. Tawney inserted at end.*

BISMARCK-SCHOENHAUSEN (OTTO EDUARD LEOPOLD VON) Prince.

STRIBRNY (WOLFGANG) Bismarck und die deutsche Politik nach seiner Entlassung, 1890- 1898. Paderborn, [1977]. pp. 359. *bibliog.*

BLACK NATIONALISM

— United States.

BLACK separatism and social reality: rhetoric and reason; editor Raymond L. Hall. New York, [1977]. pp. 280.

BLAIR (THOMAS LUCIEN VINCENT) Retreat to the ghetto: the end of a dream? New York, 1977. pp. 263. *bibliog.*

BLACK POWER.

MANN (ERIC) Comrade George: an investigation into the official story of his assassination: his work for the people and their response to his death. [Cambridge, Mass., 1972]. pp. 65.

JAMES (SELMA) and others. Sex, race and class;...with contributions from Barbara Beese, Mala Dhondy, Darcus Howe and correspondents to Race Today. Bristol, 1975. pp. 34.

— United States.

SMITH (BAXTER) Secret documents exposed: FBI plot against the black movement. New York, [1974]. pp. 23. *(Repr. from May 1974 issue of The Black Scholar)*

BLAIR (THOMAS LUCIEN VINCENT) Retreat to the ghetto: the end of a dream? New York, 1977. pp. 263. *bibliog.*

BLACKS

— Race identity.

BARKER (ANTHONY J.) The African link: British attitudes to the negro in the era of the Atlantic slave trade, 1550-1807. London, 1978. pp. 263. *bibliog.*

— Brazil, [Canada, South Africa, etc.].

In previous volumes of the Bibliography similar material has been entered under NEGROES IN BRAZIL, [CANADA, SOUTH AFRICA, etc.].

— Brazil.

NABUCO (JOAQUIM) Abolitionism: the Brazilian antislavery struggle;...translated and edited by Robert Conrad. Urbana, Ill., [1977]. pp. 186. *bibliog. Translation of O abolicionismo.*

— — Religion — Dictionaries.

CACCIATORE (OLGA GUDOLLE) Dicionario de cultos afro-brasileiros: com origem das palavras. Rio de Janeiro, 1977. pp. 279. *bibliog.*

— Canada.

HEAD (WILSON A.) The black presence in the Canadian mosaic: a study of perception and the practice of discrimination against blacks in metropolitan Toronto. [Toronto], Ontario Human Rights Commission, 1975. 1 vol. (various pagings). *bibliog.*

— Cuba — Religion.

CABRERA (LYDIA) El monte: Igbo-Finda, Ewe Orisha, Vititi Nfinda; notas sobre las religiones, la magia, las supersticiones y el folklore de los negros criollos y el pueblo de Cuba. Miami, 1975. pp. 564.

— Peru.

CUCHE (DENYS) Poder blanco y resistencia negra en el Peru: un estudio de la condicion social del negro en el Peru despues de la abolicion de la esclavitud. Lima, 1975. pp. 203. *bibliog.*

— Rhodesia.

GARGETT (ERIC) The administration of transition: African urban settlement in Rhodesia. Gwelo, 1977. pp. 104.

SITHOLE (NDABANINGI) Roots of a revolution: scenes from Zimbabwe's struggle. Oxford, 1977. pp. 142.

— South Africa.

HORWOOD (OWEN PIETER FAURE) The private budget of the urban natives. [Johannesburg, 1962]. pp. 138-145. *(Extracted from Optima, September, 1962).*

SOUTH AFRICA. Bureau of Statistics. Report on Bantu deaths in selected magisterial districts (formerly Bantu deaths in selected magisterial districts). a., 1968/71- Pretoria. *[in English and Afrikaans].*

BALDWIN (ALAN) The section ten people: a study of the urban Africans in South Africa. London, 1975. pp. 33. *(Africa Publications Trust. Studies in the Mass Removal of Population in South Africa. No. 4)*

MARKET RESEARCH AFRICA. Today's urban black household, fourth quarter 1975. Johannesburg, [1975]. 1 vol. (irregular paging). *Tables.*

SOUTH AFRICA. Census, 1970. Population census, 1970: [Bantu national units]. [Pretoria, 1976-77]. 12 pts. (in 2 vols.). *(Bureau of Statistics. Reports. Nos.02-02-03 to 02-02-14) In English and Afrikaans.*

BÖESEKEN (A.J.) Slaves and free blacks at the Cape, 1658-1700. Cape Town, 1977. pp. 208. *bibliog.*

GRANELLI (ROGER) Urban black housing: a review of existing conditions in the Cape peninsula with some guidelines for change. Cape Town, [1977]. pp. 79.

STARES (RODNEY) Black trade unions in South Africa: the responsibilities of British companies. London, 1977. pp. 82. *bibliog.*

VENTER (PAUL C.) Soweto: shadow city. Johannesburg, [1977]. pp. 193.

DAVIS (DAVID) Trade Unionist. African workers and apartheid. London, 1978. pp. 43. *(International Defence and Aid Fund. Fact Papers on Southern Africa. No. 5)*

LOMBARD (JOHANNES ANTHONIE) Freedom, welfare and order: thoughts on the principles of political co-operation in the economy of southern Africa. Pretoria, Bureau for Economic Research, Bantu Development, 1978. pp. 192. *bibliog.*

— United Kingdom.

UNDER heavy manners: report of the labour movement enquiry into police brutality and the position of black youth in Islington, held on Saturday July 23, 1977. London, 1977. pp. 23.

BARKER (ANTHONY J.) The African link: British attitudes to the negro in the era of the Atlantic slave trade, 1550-1807. London, 1978. pp. 263. *bibliog.*

LORIMER (DOUGLAS A.) Colour, class and the Victorians: English attitudes to the negro in the mid-nineteenth century. Leicester, 1978. pp. 300. *bibliog.*

BLACKSMITHS

— Italy.

TAVONI (MARIA GIOIA) Gli statuti della società dei Fabbri dal 1252 al 1579. Bologna, 1974. pp. 209. *(Deputazione di Storia Patria per le Province di Romagna. Documenti e Studi. vol.10)*

BLACKWELL (LESLIE).

BLACKWELL (LESLIE) Farewell to Parliament: more reminiscences of bench, bar, Parliament and travel. Pietermaritzburg, 1946. pp. 239.

BLANC (JEAN JOSEPH LOUIS).

MIRECOURT (EUGENE DE) pseud. [i.e. Charles Jean Baptiste JACQUOT] Louis Blanc. Paris, 1857. pp. 84. *(Les Contemporains) Bound with his Pierre Leroux, and other works.*

BLANCO (ANGEL SATURNINO).

HERRERA (MARIO A.) El Coronel Blanco: de la tradicion Radical, 1856-1919. Buenos Aires, 1930. pp. 422.

BLANQUI (LOUIS AUGUSTE).

MIRECOURT (EUGENE DE) pseud. [i.e. Charles Jean Baptiste JACQUOT] Blanqui. Paris, 1857. pp. 84. *(Les Contemporains) Bound with his Pierre Leroux, and other works.*

BLINDNESS

— Genetic aspects.

MORGAN (MICHAEL J.) Molyneux's question: vision, touch and the philosophy of perception. Cambridge, 1977. pp. 213.

BLOCH (JAN).

VAN DEN DUNGEN (PETER) compiler. A bibliography of the pacifist writings of Jean de Bloch. London, 1977. pp. 28.

BLOCH (JEAN DE).

See BLOCH (JAN).

BLOOD BANKS

— United States.

CONFERENCE ON BLOOD POLICY, WASHINGTON, D.C., 1976. Blood policy: issues and alternatives; edited by David B. Johnson. Washington, D.C., [1977]. pp. 212. *A conference sponsored by the American Enterprise Institute for Public Policy Research.*

BLUM (LEON).

LACOUTURE (JEAN) Léon Blum. Paris, [1977]. pp. 599.

BODY, HUMAN

— Social aspects.

POLHEMUS (TED) ed. Social aspects of the human body. Harmondsworth, 1978. pp. 336. *bibliog.*

BOEHRINGER (GILL HALE).

DOWNING (JOHN DEREK HALL) Nothing to hide: the Boehringer case and academic freedom in Northern Ireland. London, [1975?]. pp. 19.

BOFFI (LUIS LEOPOLDO).

BOFFI (LUIS LEOPOLDO) 1259 dias concejal de la ciudad de Buenos Aires: memorias de una epoca materialista. Buenos Aires, 1943. pp. 632.

BOHEMIANISM

BOHEMIANISM
— United States.

HUMPHREY (ROBERT E.) Children of fantasy: the first rebels of Greenwich Village. New York, [1978]. pp. 267. *bibliog.*

BOLIVAR (SIMON).

WORCESTER (DONALD EMMET) Bolivar. London, 1978. pp. 243. *bibliog.*

BOLIVIA
— Armed forces — Political activity.

MITCHELL (CHRISTOPHER) The legacy of populism in Bolivia: from the MNR to military rule. New York, 1977. pp. 167. *bibliog.*

— Economic conditions.

ECKSTEIN (SUSAN) The impact of revolution: a comparative analysis of Mexico and Bolivia. London, [1976]. pp. 53. *bibliog.*

— Economic policy.

BOLIVIA. Ministerio de Planeamiento y Coordinacion. 1976. Plan nacional de desarrollo economico y social, 1976-1980. La Paz, [1976]. 4 vols.

— Politics and government.

PARTIDO OBRERO REVOLUCIONARIO [BOLIVIA]. Congreso Nacional, 21, 1964. Abstencion electoral para desenmascarar las maniobras del oficialismo: hacia un frente revolucionario de izquierda: tesis politica. [La Paz?], 1964. pp. 34.

ANDRADE (VICTOR) Victor Andrade: su pensamiento politico pasado y presente. La Paz, 1966. pp. 21. *(Movimiento Nacionalista Revolucionario. [Publications]. No.1)*

OBLITAS FERNANDEZ (EDGAR) and BURGOA ALARCON (JORGE) Hacia una democracia cristiana boliviana: un analisis de una doctrina boliviana para uso de los bolivianos. La Paz, 1967. pp. 36. *bibliog.*

LORA (GUILLERMO) Bolivia y la revolucion permanente. [La Paz?], 1968. pp. 32.

ECKSTEIN (SUSAN) The impact of revolution: a comparative analysis of Mexico and Bolivia. London, [1976]. pp. 53. *bibliog.*

MITCHELL (CHRISTOPHER) The legacy of populism in Bolivia: from the MNR to military rule. New York, 1977. pp. 167. *bibliog.*

— Social policy.

BOLIVIA. Ministerio de Planeamiento y Coordinacion. 1976. Plan nacional de desarrollo economico y social, 1976-1980. La Paz, [1976]. 4 vols.

BOLOGNA
— Gilds.

TAVONI (MARIA GIOIA) Gli statuti della società dei Fabbri dal 1252 al 1579. Bologna, 1974. pp. 209. *(Deputazione di Storia Patria per le Province di Romagna. Documenti e Studi. vol.10)*

— Politics and government.

Il SINDACO di Bologna; Enzo Biagi intervista Renato Zangheri. Vaciglio, [1976]. pp. 190.

BOMBING, AERIAL.

POWERS (BARRY D.) Strategy without slide-rule: British air strategy, 1914-1939. London, [1976]. pp. 295. *bibliog.*

BONNOT DE MABLY (GABRIEL).

STIFFONI (GIOVANNI) Utopia e ragione in Gabriel Bonnot de Mably. Lecce, [1975]. pp. 391.

BOOK INDUSTRIES AND TRADE
— Dictionaries — Polyglot.

ORNE (JERROLD) The language of the foreign book trade: abbreviations, terms, phrases. 3rd ed. Chicago, 1976. pp. 333.

— Japan.

MAUGHAN (T.J.) An introduction to the market for British books and journals in Japan and South Korea, etc. Tokyo, 1976. pp. 255.

— Korea.

MAUGHAN (T.J.) An introduction to the market for British books and journals in Japan and South Korea, etc. Tokyo, 1976. pp. 255.

— Russia.

WALKER (GREGORY) Soviet book publishing policy. Cambridge, 1978. pp. 164. *bibliog. (National Association for Soviet and East European Studies. Soviet and East European Studies)*

— — Siberia.

POSADSKOV (ALEKSANDR LEONIDOVICH) Sibirskaia kniga i revoliutsiia, 1917-1918. Novosibirsk, 1977. pp. 285.

BOOKS
— Statistics.

WOOTTON (CHRISTOPHER B.) Trends in size, growth and cost of the literature since 1955. London, 1977. pp. 90. *(British Library. Research and Development Department. Reports. 5323)*

BOOKS AND READING.

NATIONAL BOOK LEAGUE. Conference, London, 1975. Books and undergraduates; proceedings...; edited by Peter H. Mann. London, 1976. pp. 132.

BOOTS AND SHOES
— Trade and manufacture — Turkey.

ÇAVUŞOĞLU (EMINE) The Turkish footwear industry. Istanbul, 1977. pp. 79. *(Türkiye Sinai Kalkinma Bankasi. Sector Research Publications. No. 12)*

BOPHUTHATSWANA
— Economic policy.

BUTLER (JEFFREY ERNEST) and others. The black homelands of South Africa: the political and economic development of Bophuthatswana and KwaZulu. Berkeley, Calif., [1977]. pp. 250. *bibliog.*

— Politics and government.

INTERNATIONAL DEFENCE AND AID FUND. Fact Papers on Southern Africa. No. 4. Bophuthatswana: South Africa's second independent Bantustan. London, [1977]. pp. 20.

BORDEN (Sir ROBERT LAIRD).

ENGLISH (JOHN) 1945- . Borden: his life and world. Toronto, [1977]. pp. 223. *bibliog.*

ENGLISH (JOHN) 1945- . The decline of politics: the Conservatives and the party system, 1901-20. Toronto, [1977]. pp. 237.

BORDER PATROLS
— Russia.

POGRANICHNYE voiska SSSR v Velikoi Otechestvennoi voine, 1942-1945: sbornik dokumentov i materialov. Moskva, 1976. pp. 975.

BORINAGE
— Politics and government.

MAHIEU-HOYOIS (FRANÇOISE) L'évolution du mouvement socialiste borain. Leuven, 1972. pp. xvi, 92. *bibliog. (Centre Interuniversitaire d'Histoire Contemporaine. Cahiers. 68)*

BORMANN (MARTIN).

LANG (JOCHEN VON) Der Sekretär: Martin Bormann: der Mann, der Hitler beherrschte. Stuttgart, [1977]. pp. 512. *bibliog.*

BORORO INDIANS.

VIERTLER (RENATE BRIGITTE) As aldeias Bororo: alguns aspectos de sua organização social. São Paulo, 1976. pp. 295. *bibliog. (Museu Paulista. Coleção Museu Paulista. Serie de Etnologia. 2)*

BOROUGH ROAD COLLEGE.

BARTLE (GEORGE FREDERICK) A history of Borough Road College. [London], 1976. pp. 114. *bibliog.*

BOSTON
— Economic history.

DAVIS (STEVEN NORMAN) Banking in Boston. Boston, 1976. pp. 44. *(History of Boston Project. History of Boston Series. No.14)*

BOSTON, MASSACHUSETTS
— Economic history.

TROUT (CHARLES H.) Boston: the great depression and the New Deal. New York, 1977. pp. 401. *bibliog.*

BOSTON UNIVERSITY.

BOSTON, MASSACHUSETTS. University. College of Business Administration. The story of C.B.A. Boston, 1927. pp. 16.

BOTANY
— Rhodesia.

TOMLINSON (R.W.) The Inyanga area: an essay in regional biogeography. Salisbury, 1973. pp. 67. *bibliog. (University of Rhodesia. Series in Science. Occasional Papers. No. 1)*

BOTEV (KHRISTO).

PETKO R. Slaveikov, Liuben Karavelov, Khristo Botev, Zakhari Stoianov v spomenite na suvremennitsite si. Sofiia, 1967. pp. 758.

BOTSWANA
— Commerce — Statistics.

BOTSWANA. Department of Customs and Excise. External trade statistics. a., 1976(2nd)- Gaborone.

— Economic policy.

BOTSWANA. Ministry of Finance and Development Planning. 1977. National development plan, 1976-81. Gaborone, 1977. pp. 401.

— Foreign relations.

CHIRENJE (J. MUTERO) Chief Kgama and his times, c. 1835-1923: the story of a Southern African ruler. London, 1978. pp. 140. *bibliog.*

— Politics and government.

CHIRENJE (J. MUTERO) Chief Kgama and his times, c. 1835-1923: the story of a Southern African ruler. London, 1978. pp. 140. *bibliog.*

— Rural conditions.

BOTSWANA. Central Statistics Office. 1976. The rural income distribution survey in Botswana, 1974/75. Gaborone, 1976. pp. 311. *bibliog.*

— **Social policy.**

BOTSWANA. Ministry of Finance and Development Planning. 1977. National development plan, 1976-81. Gaborone, 1977. pp. 401.

— **Statistics.**

BOTSWANA. Central Statistics Office. Statistical newsletter. irreg., Je 1973 (no.2)- Gaborone.

BOTTAI (GIUSEPPE).

GUERRI (GIORDANO BRUNO) Giuseppe Bottai, un fascista critico: ideologia e azione del gerarca che avrebbe voluto portare l'intelligenza nel fascismo e il fascismo alla liberalizzazione. Milano, 1976. pp. 277. *bibliog.*

BOUNDARIES.

TASMANIA. Law Reform Commission. 1976. Report on proof of boundaries. in TASMANIA. Parliament. Journals and Printed Papers. 1976, no.75.

PRESCOTT (JOHN ROBERT VICTOR) Boundaries and frontiers. London, [1978]. pp. 210. *bibliogs. Revised version of the author's The geography of frontiers and boundaries.*

BOUVERIE (WILLIAM PLEYDELL-) 3rd Earl of Radnor.

See PLEYDELL-BOUVERIE (WILLIAM) 3rd Earl of Radnor.

BOYCOTT

— **Arab countries.**

NELSON (WALTER HENRY) and PRITTIE (TERENCE CORNELIUS FARMER) The economic war against the Jews. New York, [1977]. pp. 269.

— **Netherlands.**

HASLEMERE DECLARATION GROUP and THIRD WORLD FIRST EDUCATIONAL TRUST. Coffee for Britain means blood for Angola. Birmingham, [1973?]. pp. 15.

— **United Kingdom.**

HASLEMERE DECLARATION GROUP and THIRD WORLD FIRST EDUCATIONAL TRUST. Coffee for Britain means blood for Angola. Birmingham, [1973?]. pp. 15.

BOYLE (JIMMY).

BOYLE (JIMMY) A sense of freedom. London, [1977]. pp. 264.

BOYS

— **Societies and clubs — United Kingdom.**

ENSOR (HOWARD) Paths to leadership. London, [1977]. pp. 11. *(National Association of Boys' Clubs. Basil Henriques Memorial Lectures. 1977)*

BRADFORD

— **Social conditions.**

ALLEN (SHEILA) and others. Work, race and immigration. [Bradford], 1977. pp. 415.

BRAIN DRAIN.

GLASER (WILLIAM A.) The brain drain: emigration and return; findings of a UNITAR multinational comparative survey of professional personnel of developing countries who study abroad;...with the assistance of G. Christopher Habers. Oxford, 1978. pp. 324. *bibliog. (United Nations Institute for Training and Research. Research Reports. No.22)*

— **Colombia.**

EUSSE HOYOS (GERARDO) The outflow of professional manpower from Colombia; [study... prepared at the request of the United Nations Institute for Training and Research]. Bogotá, 1969. fo. 91.

— **Israel.**

RITTERBAND (PAUL) Education, employment, and migration: Israel in comparative perspective. Cambridge, 1978. pp. 144. *(American Sociological Association. Arnold and Caroline Rose Monograph Series in Sociology)*

— **Sri Lanka.**

SRI LANKA. Cabinet Committee Inquiring into the Problem of Technologically, Professionally and Academically Qualified Personnel Leaving Sri Lanka. 1974. Report; [Maithripala Senanayeke, chairman]. Colombo, 1974. pp. 50. *(Sri Lanka. Parliament. Sessional Papers. 1974. No. 10)*

— **Underdeveloped areas.**

See UNDERDEVELOPED AREAS — Brain drain.

BRANCO (HUMBERTO DE ALENCAR CASTELLO).

See CASTELLO BRANCO (HUMBERTO DE ALENCAR).

BRAŞOV

— **Growth.**

PROCESUL de urbanizare în România: zona Braşov; coordonatori: Tiberiu Bogdan [and others]. Bucureşti, 1970. pp. 430. *With English summary.*

BRAZIL

— **Army — Military police.**

ANDRADE (PAULO RENE DE) Três revoluçoes: a atuação da Policia Militar de Minas Gerais, a antiga Força Publica, nos movimentos revolucionarios de 1924, 1930 e 1932; esboço historico. [Belo Horizonte, 1976]. pp. 538. *bibliog.*

— **Commerce.**

BRAZIL. Instituto Brasileiro do Cafe. Divisão de Mercados. 1968. Exportação brasileira de cafe, (periodo de 1900 a 1967). Rio de Janeiro, 1968. 1 pamphlet (unfoliated). *(Instituto Brasileiro do Cafe. Departamento Econômico. Boletins)*

BRAZIL. Instituto Brasileiro do Cafe. Divisão de Mercados. 1968. Importação de cafe nos principais mercados consumidores e participação do cafe brasileiro, (periodo 1955 a 1967). Rio de Janeiro, 1968. 1 pamphlet (unfoliated). *(Instituto Brasileiro do Cafe. Departamento Econômico. Boletins)*

— **Commercial policy.**

AMARAL (ADRIANO B. DO) Industrialisierung in Brasilien: zur Politik der Importsubstitution. Tübingen, [1977]. pp. 226. *bibliog. (Institut für Iberoamerika-Kunde. Schriftenreihe. Band 28)*

— **Discovery and exploration.**

HEMMING (JOHN) 1935- . Red gold: the conquest of the Brazilian Indians. Cambridge, Mass., 1978. pp. 677. *bibliog.*

— **Economic conditions.**

DALY (HERMAN E.) The population question in Northeast Brazil: its economic and ideological dimensions. Baton Rouge, 1969. pp. 47. *(Louisiana State University. Latin American Studies Institute. Working Papers. No. 1. Series 1)*

MAGALHÃES (JOÃO PAULO DE ALMEIDA) Modelo brasileiro de desenvolvimento: raizes do milagre e condições de sua continuidade. Rio de Janeiro, [1976]. pp. 219.

QUEM e quem na economia brasileira, 1976. São Paulo, 1976. pp. 818. *(Visão. vol. 49. no.5)*

BRESSER PEREIRA (LUIZ CARLOS) Estado e subdesenvolvimento industrializado: esboço de uma economia politica periferica. São Paulo, 1977. pp. 420. *bibliog.*

DAVIS (SHELTON H.) Victims of the miracle: development and the Indians of Brazil. Cambridge, 1977. pp. 205. *bibliog.*

INDICE O BANCO DE DADOS. Indice do Brasil: Brazilian index. [Rio de Janeiro, 1977]. pp. 322. *In Portuguese and English with summaries in various languages.*

— **Economic history.**

BUESCU (MIRCEA) Guerra e desenvolvimento: a economia brasileira durante a segunda guerra mundial. Rio de Janeiro, 1976. pp. 170. *bibliog.*

PRADO (CAIO) Historia econômica do Brasil. 3rd ed. São Paulo, 1977. pp. 364. *bibliog.*

— **Economic policy.**

BRAZIL. Superintendência do Desenvolvimento do Nordeste. 1964. Bases da politica de desenvolvimento do nordeste do Brasil e esquema do plano quinquenal da SUDENE. 2nd ed. [Recife], 1964. fo. 25.

MAGALHÃES (JOÃO PAULO DE ALMEIDA) Modelo brasileiro de desenvolvimento: raizes do milagre e condições de sua continuidade. Rio de Janeiro, [1976]. pp. 219.

BRESSER PEREIRA (LUIZ CARLOS) Estado e subdesenvolvimento industrializado: esboço de uma economia politica periferica. São Paulo, 1977. pp. 420. *bibliog.*

KATZMAN (MARTIN T.) Cities and frontiers in Brazil: regional dimensions of economic development. Cambridge, Mass., 1977. pp. 255.

BOURNE (RICHARD) Assault on the Amazon. London, 1978. pp. 320. *bibliog.*

— **Emigration and immigration.**

NOGUEIRA (ARLINDA ROCHA) A imigração japonesa para a lavoura cafeeira paulista, 1908-1922. São Paulo, 1973. pp. 255. *bibliog. (São Paulo. Universidade. Instituto de Estudos Brasileiros. Publicacões. 28)*

SALVADOR (JOSE GONÇALVES) Os cristãos-novos: povoamento e conquista do solo brasileiro, 1530-1680. São Paulo, 1976. pp. 406. *bibliog.*

— **Foreign economic relations — United States.**

COMMITTEE OF RETURNED VOLUNTEERS. Brazil: who pulls the strings?: or, Alliance for repression. Chicago, [1970?]. pp. 82.

— **Foreign relations.**

SCHNEIDER (RONALD M.) Brazil: foreign policy of a future world power. Boulder, Colo., 1976. pp. 236. *bibliog.*

— **Foreign relations administration.**

SCHNEIDER (RONALD M.) Brazil: foreign policy of a future world power. Boulder, Colo., 1976. pp. 236. *bibliog.*

— **History.**

FLYNN (PETER) Brazil: a political analysis. London, 1978. pp. 564. *bibliog.*

— — **To 1821.**

SALVADOR (JOSE GONÇALVES) Os cristãos-novos: povoamento e conquista do solo brasileiro, 1530-1680. São Paulo, 1976. pp. 406. *bibliog.*

— — **1763-1821.**

MOTA (CARLOS GUILHERME) Atitudes de inovação no Brasil, 1789-1801. Lisboa, [1977?.] pp. 133. *bibliog.*

BRAZIL (Cont.)

— — 1822-1889.

RODRIGUES (JOSE HONORIO) Independência: revolução e contra-revolução. Rio de Janeiro, [1975-76]. 5 vols.

— — 1889- .

DULLES (JOHN W.F.) Castello Branco: the making of a Brazilian president. College Station, Tex., [1978]. pp. 487. *bibliog.*

— — 1889-1930.

PINHEIRO (PAULO SERGIO DE M.S.) Politica e trabalho no Brasil dos anos vinte a 1930. Rio de Janeiro, 1977. pp. 191. *bibliog.*

— — 1924-1925, Revolution.

DANTAS (JOSE IBARÊ COSTA) O tenentismo em Sergipe: da revolta de 1924 a revolução de 1930. Petropolis, 1974. pp. 252. *bibliog.*

— — 1930, Revolution.

DANTAS (JOSE IBARÊ COSTA) O tenentismo em Sergipe: da revolta de 1924 a revolução de 1930. Petropolis, 1974. pp. 252. *bibliog.*

— — 1930-1954.

CARONE (EDGARD) compiler. A terceira republica, 1937-1945. São Paulo, 1976. pp. 585.

— — — Sources.

CARONE (EDGARD) compiler. A terceira republica, 1937-1945. São Paulo, 1976. pp. 585.

— — 1964, Revolution.

AGUIAR (HERNANI D') A Revolução por dentro. Rio de Janeiro, [1976]. pp. 342. *bibliog.*

— Industries.

BRAZIL. Instituto Brasileiro de Geografia e Estatistica. Pesquisa industrial: Brasil: dados gerais. a., 1972- Rio de Janeiro.

VON DOELLINGER (CARLOS) and CAVALCANTI (LEONARDO CASERTA) Empresas multinacionais na industria brasileira. Rio de Janeiro, 1975. pp. 158. *bibliog.* (*Brazil. Instituto de Planejamento Econômico e Social. Instituto de Pesquisas. Relatorios de Pesquisa. No. 29*)

— Politics and government.

WHAT is meant by Brazilian revolution?; [by] the team of observers of B.C. [Brazil Confidential]. [Rio de Janeiro], 1965. fo. 23.

PEREIRA PINTO (JUAN CARLOS) El Brasil en crisis. Buenos Aires, 1968. pp. 23.

COMMITTEE OF RETURNED VOLUNTEERS. Brazil: who pulls the strings?: or, Alliance for repression. Chicago, [1970?]. pp. 82.

RUSSELL TRIBUNAL II ON REPRESSION IN BRAZIL, CHILE AND LATIN AMERICA. The Bertrand Russell Tribunal on Brazil and Repression in Latin America; sponsored by the Bertrand Russell Peace Foundation. Nottingham, [1973]. pp. 43. *Reprint of first 3 issues of the Tribunal Bulletin.*

CRISPIM (JOSE MARIA) Sobre a estrategia global da revolução brasileira. Lisboa, 1975 in progress.

BARROS (ADIRSON DE) Março: Geisel e a Revolução brasileira. Rio de Janeiro, [1976]. pp. 283.

BENEVIDES (MARIA VICTORIA DE MESQUITA) O governo Kubitschek: desenvolvimento econômico e estabilidade politica, 1956-1961. Rio de Janeiro, 1976. pp. 302. *bibliog.*

ALMEIDA (CANDIDO ANTONIO MENDES DE) Beyond populism;...translated by L. Gray Cowan. Albany, N.Y., 1977. pp. 112.

ERICKSON (KENNETH PAUL) The Brazilian corporative state and working-class politics. Berkeley, Calif., [1977]. pp. 225. *bibliog.*

FLYNN (PETER) Brazil: a political analysis. London, 1978. pp. 564. *bibliog.*

— Population.

BRAZIL. Conselho Nacional de Estatistica. Laboratorio de Estatistica. 1958. A contribuição das diversas unidades da federação a regiões fisiograficas para a população do Distrito Federal; ...estudo redigido pelo Marcio R. Mota e Annibal R. Fontes. [Rio de Janeiro, 1958]. fo. 10. (*Estudos Demograficos. No. 247*)

BRAZIL. Conselho Nacional de Estatistica. Laboratorio de Estatistica. 1959. A contribuição das diversas unidades da federação e regiões fisiograficas para a população de São Paulo;... estudo redigido pelo Maria Cascaes Brasil. [Rio de Janeiro, 1959]. fo. 12. (*Estudos Demograficos. No. 246*)

DALY (HERMAN E.) The population question in Northeast Brazil: its economic and ideological dimensions. Baton Rouge, 1969. pp. 47. (*Louisiana State University. Latin American Studies Institute. Working Papers. No. 1. Series 1*)

— Presidents.

DULLES (JOHN W.F.) Castello Branco: the making of a Brazilian president. College Station, Tex., [1978]. pp. 487. *bibliog.*

— Rural conditions.

FREYRE (GILBERTO DE MELLO) A presença do açucar na formação brasileira. Rio de Janeiro, 1975. pp. 212.

— Social conditions.

SCHADEN (EGON) ed. Homem, cultura e sociedade no Brasil: seleções da Revista de Antropologia. Petropolis, 1972. pp. 450. *bibliogs.*

MACHADO (MARIA CHRISTINA RUSSI DA MATTA) Aspectos do fenômeno do cangaço no nordeste brasileiro. São Paulo, 1974. pp. 171.

OLIVEN (RUBEN GEORGE) Urbanization and social change in Brazil: a case study of Porto Alegre. 1977. fo. 424. *bibliog.* Typescript. Ph.D. (London) thesis: unpublished. This thesis is the property of London University and may not be removed from the Library.

— Social history.

FREYRE (GILBERTO DE MELLO) A presença do açucar na formação brasileira. Rio de Janeiro, 1975. pp. 212.

MOTA (CARLOS GUILHERME) Atitudes de inovação no Brasil, 1789-1801. Lisboa, [1977?.] pp. 133. *bibliog.*

BREAD

— Prices — Germany.

EBELING (DIETRICH) and IRSIGLER (FRANZ) Getreideumsatz, Getreide- und Brotpreise in Köln, 1368-1797. Köln, 1976-77. 2 vols. (*Cologne. Stadtarchiv. Mitteilungen. Hefte 65-66*) 9 graphs in end pocket of vol. 2.

BREAST FEEDING.

MULLER (MIKE) The baby killer: a War on Want investigation into the promotion and sale of powdered baby milks in the Third World. London, 1974. pp. 19.

BREEDER REACTORS.

ROBERTS (ALISON M.) The case against the fast breeder. [Milton Keynes, 1977]. pp. 75.

BREMEN

— History.

KAISEN (WILHELM) Zuversicht und Beständigkeit...: eine Dokumentation (herausgegeben und eingeleitet von Hans Koschnick). Bremen, [1977]. pp. 344.

ADAMIETZ (HORST) Freiheit und Bindung: Adolf Ehlers. Bremen, [1978]. pp. 208.

BRETT FAMILY.

BRETT (CHARLES EDWARD BAINBRIDGE) Long shadows cast before: nine lives in Ulster, 1625-1977. Edinburgh, 1978. pp. 162.

BREWING INDUSTRIES

— Law and legislation.

U.K Food Standards Committee. 1977. Report on beer; [A.G. Ward, chairman]. London, 1977. pp. 59.

BRIBERY.

JACOBY (NEIL HERMAN) and others. Bribery and extortion in world business: a study of corporate political payments abroad. New York, [1977]. pp. 294. (*Columbia University. Graduate School of Business. Studies of the Modern Corporation*)

— United States.

AMERICAN ENTERPRISE INSTITUTE FOR PUBLIC POLICY RESEARCH. Legislative Analyses. 95th Congress. No. 9. Criminalization of payments to influence foreign governments. Washington, 1977. pp. 34.

BRIGANDS AND ROBBERS

— Brazil.

MACHADO (MARIA CHRISTINA RUSSI DA MATTA) Aspectos do fenômeno do cangaço no nordeste brasileiro. São Paulo, 1974. pp. 171.

CARVALHO (RODRIQUES DE) Lampião e a sociologia do cangaço. Rio de Janeiro, [1976?]. pp. 385.

— Sardinia.

DESSY (UGO) Quali banditi?: controinchiesta sulla società sarda. Verona, [1977]. 2 vols.

BRIGHTON FREE SCHOOL.

BRIGHTON FREE SCHOOL. Brighton Free School. Brighton, [1973]. pp. 7.

BRISBANE

— Poor.

BROWN (JILL W.) and others. Aboriginals and islanders in Brisbane: research report by Jill W. Brown, Roisin Hirschfeld and Diane Smith. Canberra, 1974. pp. 119. (*Australia. Commission of Inquiry into Poverty. Research Reports*)

BRISTOL UNIVERSITY.

BRISTOL. University. University register III: (list of former and present officers, professors, honorary fellows and honorary graduates...with register of graduates...1909-1969). [Bristol, 1970?]. pp. 294.

BRITISH BROADCASTING CORPORATION.

MANSELL (GERARD) Broadcasting to the world: forty years of BBC external services. London, [1973]. pp. 8.

SCHLESINGER (PHILIP RONALD) Putting "reality" together: BBC news. London, 1978. pp. 303. *bibliog.*

BRITISH COLUMBIA

— Administrative and political divisions.

BRITISH COLUMBIA. Commission of Inquiry into Redefinition of Electoral Districts under the Public Inquiries Act, British Columbia. 1975. Report; [T.G. Norris, chairman]. [Vancouver], 1975. pp. 151. *bibliog.* 5 maps in end pocket.

— Commerce.

BRITISH COLUMBIA. Economics and Statistics Branch. 1971. Trade through British Columbia customs ports in the seventies. Victoria, [1971]. pp. 18.

BRITISH COLUMBIA. Department of Industrial Development, Trade and Commerce. 1972. The Pacific rim: an evaluation of British Columbia trade opportunities. Victoria, 1972. pp. 100.

— — European Economic Community countries.

BRITISH COLUMBIA. Economics and Statistics Branch. 1972. British Columbia's trade prospects with the New European Economic Community: a review of the principal factors involved in the entry of the United Kingdom into the E.E.C. Victoria, 1972. pp. 13.

— Economic conditions.

BRITISH COLUMBIA HYDRO AND POWER AUTHORITY. Industrial Development Department. The power of British Columbia. Vancouver, [1967]. pp. 27.

BRITISH COLUMBIA. Economics and Statistics Branch. 1971. British Columbia: manual of resources and development. Victoria, 1971. pp. 54.

BRITISH COLUMBIA. Department of Economic Development. 1975. British Columbia: manual of resources and development. [rev. ed.] Victoria, 1974 [or rather 1975]. pp. 55.

BRITISH COLUMBIA. Department of Economic Development. 1975. A summary report on development possibilities in the north east region of British Columbia, etc. [Victoria], 1975. pp. 125.

BRITISH COLUMBIA. Ministry of Economic Development. 1977. Manual of resources and development. Victoria, 1977. pp. 62.

BRITISH COLUMBIA. Ministry of Economic Development. 1977. The north west report '77: a summary report on development opportunities in the north west region of British Columbia. [Victoria], 1977. pp. 250.

— Economic policy.

BRITISH COLUMBIA. Department of Economic Development. 1975. A summary report on development possibilities in the north east region of British Columbia, etc. [Victoria], 1975. pp. 125.

— Emigration and immigration.

BRITISH COLUMBIA. Economics and Statistics Branch. 1971. Net migration to British Columbia, 1951-1970. Victoria, [1971]. pp. 26.

— Executive departments.

BRITISH COLUMBIA. Ministry of the Attorney-General. Annual report. a., 1976(3rd)- Vancouver.

— Government publications — Bibliography.

BRITISH COLUMBIA GOVERNMENT PUBLICATIONS: monthly checklist; [pd. by] Legislative Library. m., Ag 1977 (v.8, no. 8)- Victoria.

— Industries.

BRITISH COLUMBIA. Ministry of Economic Development. 1977. The north west report '77: a summary report on development opportunities in the north west region of British Columbia. [Victoria], 1977. pp. 250.

BRITISH COTTON GROWING ASSOCIATION.

TEWSON (W.F.) The British Cotton Growing Association, incorporated by royal charter:...golden jubilee, [1904]-1954. [Manchester], [1954]. pp. 85, xiv.

BRITISH EMPIRE EXHIBITION, 1924-1925.

CALDECOTT (Sir ANDREW) Report on the Malaya pavilion, British Empire Exhibition. Singapore, Government Printing Office, 1926. pp. 32.

BRITISH IN INDIA.

SPANGENBERG (BRADFORD) British bureaucracy in India: status, policy and the I.C.S., in the late 19th century. Columbia, Mo., 1976. pp. 380. *bibliog.*

BRITISH IN NEW ZEALAND.

NEW ZEALAND. Department of Social Welfare. 1972. Guide to the reciprocal agreement on social security between New Zealand and the United Kingdom. Wellington, [1972]. pp. 15.

BRITISH VIRGIN ISLANDS

— Commerce — Statistics.

TRADE REPORT FOR THE BRITISH VIRGIN ISLANDS; [pd. by Statistics Office]. a., 1971, 1974- Tortola.

BRITTANY

— Statistics.

OCTANT (formerly Sextant): cahiers statistiques de la Bretagne: revue trimestrielle; ([pd. by] Institut National de la Statistique et des Etudes Economiques, Direction Régionale de Rennes [France]). q., My 1971 (no.1)- Rennes.

BRNO

— Economic history.

FREUDENBERGER (HERMAN) of Tulane University. The industrialization of a central European city: Brno and the fine woollen industry in the 18th century. Edington, 1977. pp. 220. *bibliog.*

— Industries.

FREUDENBERGER (HERMAN) of Tulane University. The industrialization of a central European city: Brno and the fine woollen industry in the 18th century. Edington, 1977. pp. 220. *bibliog.*

BROADCASTING

— Guyana.

SANDERS (RON) Broadcasting in Guyana. London, 1978. pp. 77. *bibliog.* (*International Institute of Communications. Case Studies on Broadcasting Systems*)

— Ireland (Republic).

FISHER (DESMOND) Broadcasting in Ireland. London, 1978. pp. 120. *bibliog.* (*International Institute of Communications. Case Studies on Broadcasting Systems*)

— Japan.

ITO (MASAMI) Broadcasting in Japan. London, 1978. pp. 125. (*International Institute of Communications. Case Studies on Broadcasting Systems*)

— Netherlands.

HAAK (KEES VAN DER) and SPICER (JOANNA) Broadcasting in the Netherlands. London, 1977. pp. 93. *bibliog.* (*International Institute of Communications. Case Studies on Broadcasting Systems*)

— Underdeveloped areas.

See UNDERDEVELOPED AREAS — Broadcasting.

BROADCASTING POLICY

— United Kingdom.

INDEPENDENT BROADCASTING AUTHORITY. The Annual report: the Authority's comments. [London], 1977. pp. 42. *Special issue, No. 12, July 1977, of Independent Broadcasting.*

— United States.

GIBSON (GEORGE H.) 1932- . Public broadcasting: the role of the federal government, 1912-76. New York, [1977]. pp. 236.

BROCHER (VICTORINE).

[BROCHER (VICTORINE)] Souvenirs d'une morte vivante; [by] Victorine B...; préface de Lucien Descaves. Paris, 1976. pp. 246. *Reprint of 1909 Paris edition with a new introductory note.*

BROKERS

— Sri Lanka.

SRI LANKA. Commission of Inquiry on Agency Houses and Brokering Firms. 1974. Report; [B. Soysa, chairman]. Colombo, 1974. pp. 641. (*Sri Lanka. Parliament. Sessional Papers. 1974. No. 12*)

BRONCHITIS.

TOBACCO RESEARCH COUNCIL. Research Papers. 14. Part I. Report on a second retrospective mortality study in north-east England. Part I: Factors related to mortality from lung cancer, bronchitis, heart disease and stroke in Cleveland county, with particular emphasis on the relative risks associated with smoking filter and plain cigarettes. London, 1977. pp. 93. *bibliog. Report on the first study published as Research Paper. 8.*

BROOKES (EDGAR HARRY).

BROOKES (EDGAR HARRY) A South African pilgrimage. Johannesburg, 1977. pp. 158.

BROOKLYN

— History.

CONNOLLY (HAROLD X.) A ghetto grows in Brooklyn. New York, 1977. pp. 248.

BROTHERHOOD OF SLEEPING CAR PORTERS.

HARRIS (WILLIAM HAMILTON) Keeping the faith: A. Philip Randolph, Milton P. Webster and the Brotherhood of Sleeping Car Porters, 1925-1937. Urbana, Ill., [1977]. pp. 252. *bibliog.*

BROWN (MARY ANNE DAY).

ROSENBERG (DANIEL) Mary Brown: from Harpers Ferry to California. New York, [1975]. pp. 49. *bibliog.* (*American Institute for Marxist Studies. Occasional Papers. No. 17*)

BUBE (AFRICAN TRIBE).

CRESPO GIL-DELGADO (CARLOS) Conde de Castillo-Fiel. Notas para un estudio antropologico y etnologico del Bubi de Fernando Poo. Madrid, 1949. pp. 290. *bibliog.*

BUCHANS

— Economic conditions.

NEWFOUNDLAND. Buchans Task Force. 1976. Report; [Robert K. Langdon, chairman]. St. John's, 1976. pp. 249. *bibliog. 2 maps in end pocket.*

— Economic policy.

NEWFOUNDLAND. Buchans Task Force. 1976. Report; [Robert K. Langdon, chairman]. St. John's, 1976. pp. 249. *bibliog. 2 maps in end pocket.*

BUDDHA AND BUDDHISM

— Himalayas.

ORTNER (SHERRY B.) Sherpas through their rituals. Cambridge, 1978. pp. 195. *bibliog.*

BUDGET.

HARTLE (DOUGLAS G.) A theory of the expenditure budgetary process. Toronto, [1976]. pp. 98. *bibliog.* (*Ontario. Economic Council. Research Studies. 5*)

— Argentine Republic.

ZARACONDEGUI (CARLOS) Presupuestos nacionales, 1851-1853. Buenos Aires, 1933. pp. 267. *bibliog.*

BUDGET.(Cont.)

— Austria.

BEIRAT FÜR WIRTSCHAFTS- UND SOZIALFRAGEN. [Publikationen. 26]. Budgetvorschau, 1974-1978. Wien, 1974. pp. 62.

HENGSTSCHLAEGER (JOHANNES) Das Budgetrecht des Bundes: Gegenwartsprobleme und Entwicklungstendenzen. Berlin, [1977]. pp. 354. *bibliog.*

— Bangladesh.

BANGLADESH. Ministry of Finance. Annual budget: budget speech. a., 1976/77- Dacca. *Budget speech in 2 pts. File also includes Budget summary statements.*

— Belgium.

BELGIUM. Ministère des Affaires Economiques. Direction Générale des Etudes et de la Documentation. Essai de désagrégation sectorielle et régionale de quelques données du budget économique. a., 1975- Bruxelles. *1975 in 2 pts., Essai de désagrégation régionale du budget économique and Essai de désagrégation sectorielle du budget économique.*

— Canada.

CANADA. Department of Finance. Budget document: an elaboration by the Minister of Finance of the analysis and policies of the budget. a., 1977- Ottawa. *[in English and French] File includes Supplementary budget papers.*

HARTLE (DOUGLAS G.) The expenditure budget process in the government of Canada. [Toronto, 1978]. pp. 119. *(Canadian Tax Foundation. Canadian Tax Papers. No. 60)*

— — British Columbia.

BRITISH COLUMBIA. Department of Labour. 1969. The budget debate; an address by L.R. Peterson...third session of the 28th Legislative Assembly, 1969. Victoria, 1969. pp. 10.

— Denmark.

DENMARK. Finansministeriet. Finanslov. a., 1977/78- [København].

DENMARK. Budgetdepartementet. Oversigt over finanslovforslaget... og budgetoverslag. a., 1979- [København].

— European Economic Community countries.

SHAW (MICHAEL NORMAN) The European Parliament and the community budget. London, 1978. pp. 38.

— Gambia.

GAMBIA. Ministry of Finance, Trade and Development. 1969. Budget speech by S.M. Dibba, Minister of Finance, Trade and Development, 17th June, 1969, in the House of Representatives. Bathurst, 1969. pp. 14. *(Gambia. Sessional Papers. 1969. No. 3)*

— Germany.

WEILEPP (MANFRED) Der Full Employment Budget Surplus als Mass für die Wirkungen der Staatstätigkeit auf die volkswirtschaftliche Gesamtnachfrage: dargestellt am Beispiel der Bundesrepublik Deutschland. Hamburg, 1975. pp. 212. *bibliog. (Hamburg. Hamburgisches Welt-Wirtschafts-Archiv. Veröffentlichungen) Dissertation - Universität Hamburg.*

KONJUNKTURELLE Wirkungen öffentlicher Haushalte; ([by] Dieter Biehl [and others]). Tübingen, [1978]. pp. 257. *bibliog. (Kiel. Universität. Institut für Weltwirtschaft. Kieler Studien. 146)*

— Hong Kong.

HONG KONG. Budget: speech by the Financial Secretary, concluding the debate on the second reading of the Appropriation Bill. a., 1977/78- Hong Kong.

HONG KONG. Budget: speech by the Financial Secretary, moving the second reading of the Appropriation Bill. a., 1978/79- Hong Kong.

— India.

TARAPOREVALA (RUSSI JAL) The economic implications of the Union budget, 1976-77. Bombay, [1976]. pp. 31.

— Japan.

CAMPBELL (JOHN CREIGHTON) Contemporary Japanese budget politics. Berkeley, Calif., [1977]. pp. 308. *bibliog. (Columbia University. East Asian Institute. Studies)*

— Nigeria.

NIGERIA (KWARA STATE). Budget speech (formerly Budget broadcast). a., 1969/70[1st]- , with gaps (1974/75; 1976/77) Ilorin.

— Poland.

PIRO'ZYŃSKI (ZBIGNIEW) and WINTER (EMANUEL) Bud'zet państwowy Polski Ludowej. Warszawa, 1961. pp. 280. *bibliog.*

— Singapore.

SINGAPORE. Ministry of Finance. 1972. Economic pattern in the seventies: text of budget speech by Hon Sui Sen, Minister for Finance, March 7, 1972. [Singapore, 1972?]. pp. 58.

— Sri Lanka.

AMARASEKERA (ANIL) The crisis in Sri Lanka. [Colombo, 1975]. pp. 18.

— United Kingdom.

CONFEDERATION OF BRITISH INDUSTRY. The Budget 1974: representations to the Chancellor of the Exchequer. London, 1974. pp. 29.

CONFEDERATION OF BRITISH INDUSTRY. The Finance Act, 1976: an explanatory guide. London, 1976. pp. 34.

CONFEDERATION OF BRITISH INDUSTRY. The Budget 1977: CBI representations to the Chancellor of the Exchequer. London, 1977. pp. 36.

CONFEDERATION OF BRITISH INDUSTRY. The Finance Act, 1977: an explanatory guide. London, 1977. pp. 40.

HARTLEY (NICHOLAS) and BEAN (CHARLES) The standardised budget balance. London, Treasury, 1978. pp. 8. *(Government Economic Service Working Papers. No. 1)*

— — Guernsey.

GUERNSEY. States Office. Budget report. a., 1977- [St. Peter Port]. *Formerly included in GUERNSEY. Billet d'état, which see also.*

— United States.

PENNER (RUDOLPH GERHARD) and KORB (LAWRENCE J.) The 1978 budget in transition: from Ford to Carter to Congress. Washington, D.C., [1977]. pp. 144. *(American Enterprise Institute for Public Policy Research. AEI Studies. 177)*

The FEDERAL budget and social reconstruction: the people and the state; prepared for the Study Group on the Federal Budget, Institute for Policy Studies, Washington, D.C.; Marcus G. Raskin, editor in chief. New Brunswick, [1978]. pp. 470.

BUDGET IN BUSINESS.

EDEY (HAROLD CECIL) Business budgets and accounts: an introduction to management accounting. 3rd ed. London, 1966 repr. 1972. pp. 176. *bibliog.*

BRITISH INSTITUTE OF MANAGEMENT. Management Guides. No.4. Budgetary control for the smaller company. London, [1972]. pp. 31. *bibliog.*

BUENOS AIRES

— Foreign population.

NEWTON (RONALD C.) German Buenos Aires, 1900-1933: social change and cultural crisis. Austin, [1977]. pp. 225. *bibliog.*

— Growth.

JALIKIS (MARINO) Historia de los medios de transporte y de su influencia en el desarrollo urbano de la ciudad de Buenos Aires. Buenos Aires, 1925. pp. 65.

— History.

BESIO MORENO (NICOLAS) Buenos Aires: puerto del Rio de la Plata, capital de la Argentina; estudio critico de su poblacion, 1536-1936. Buenos Aires, 1939. pp. 500. *bibliog.*

— Hospitals.

BOFFI (LUIS LEOPOLDO) 1259 dias concejal de la ciudad de Buenos Aires: memorias de una epoca materialista. Buenos Aires, 1943. pp. 632.

— Politics and government.

BOFFI (LUIS LEOPOLDO) 1259 dias concejal de la ciudad de Buenos Aires: memorias de una epoca materialista. Buenos Aires, 1943. pp. 632.

— Population.

BESIO MORENO (NICOLAS) Buenos Aires: puerto del Rio de la Plata, capital de la Argentina; estudio critico de su poblacion, 1536-1936. Buenos Aires, 1939. pp. 500. *bibliog.*

— Social conditions.

NEWTON (RONALD C.) German Buenos Aires, 1900-1933: social change and cultural crisis. Austin, [1977]. pp. 225. *bibliog.*

— Transit systems.

COORDINACION o destruccion: el problema del transporte urbano de pasajeros en la ciudad de Buenos Aires. [Buenos Aires, 1936]. pp. 290.

BUFFALO

— Economic conditions.

YANS-McLAUGHLIN (VIRGINIA) Family and community: Italian immigrants in Buffalo, 1880-1930. Ithaca, N.Y., 1977. pp. 286. *bibliog.*

BUILDING

— Safety measures.

U.K. Health and Safety Executive. The construction industry: health and safety. a., 1976(1st)- London.

BUILDING AND LOAN ASSOCIATIONS

— United Kingdom.

The STORY of the Liberator Crash with some account of the career and character of Jabez Spencer Balfour, with numerous illustrations. [London], 1893. pp. 44. *(Westminster Gazette. Westminster Popular. No. 5)*

BUILDING FAILURES.

NIGERIA (WESTERN STATE). Commission of Inquiry into the Building Disaster at Oremeji, Ibadan. 1971. Report; [E.O. Fakayode, chairman]. [Ibadan, 1971?]. pp. 40.

BUILDING MATERIALS.

SEMINAR ON THE USE OF WOOD IN HOUSING, VANCOUVER, 1971. Report of the Seminar...with the emphasis on the needs of developing countries; organized jointly by the United Nations and the Government of Canada, [held in] Vancouver, Canada, 3-16 July 1971. (ST/TAO/SER.C/137). New York, United Nations, 1972. pp. 32. *bibliog.*

— Prices — Greece.

GREECE. Ethnike Statistike Hyperesia. 1976. Analysis of procedures of compiling construction price indices:... price index of the input of new dwelling buildings materials: 1971 [equals] 100. Athens, 1976. pp. 22. *([Publications] Z. Methodological Studies. 11) In English and Greek.*

BUILDING MATERIALS INDUSTRY.

WORKSHOP ON ORGANIZATIONAL AND TECHNICAL MEASURES FOR THE DEVELOPMENT OF BUILDING MATERIALS, MOSCOW, 1968. Report of the Workshop...organized jointly by the United Nations and the Government of the Union of Soviet Socialist Republics, Moscow, 25 September to 18 October, 1968. (ST/TAO/SER.C/123). New York, United Nations, 1970. pp. 130.

— Underdeveloped areas.

See UNDERDEVELOPED AREAS — Building materials industry.

BUILDING TRADES

— United Kingdom.

INSTITUTE OF BUILDING. Conference, 1972. Manpower crisis, 1973: [papers presented at the conference]. Ascot, Berks, [1973]. pp. 18.

HOPPÉ (MALCOLM) Is the party really over?: why rates rise in the North East. London, [1977]. pp. 11.

BUILDINGS, PREFABRICATED.

WORKSHOP ON ORGANIZATIONAL AND TECHNICAL MEASURES FOR THE DEVELOPMENT OF BUILDING MATERIALS, MOSCOW, 1968. Report of the Workshop...organized jointly by the United Nations and the Government of the Union of Soviet Socialist Republics, Moscow, 25 September to 18 October, 1968. (ST/TAO/SER.C/123). New York, United Nations, 1970. pp. 130.

— Norway.

MAGELI (JOHANNES) A/S Moelven Brug: karakteristika og synspunkter. Bergen, 1977. pp. 18. *(Norges Handelshøyskole. Kristofer Lehmkuhl Forelesninger. 1977)*

BUKHARA

— Economic history.

ISKANDAROV (BUKHODOR ISKANDAROVICH) Iz istorii proniknoveniia kapitalisticheskikh otnoshenii v ekonomiku dorevoliutsionnogo Tadzhikistana, vtoraia polovina XIX v.; otvet. redaktor Kh. Saidmuradov. Dushanbe, 1976. pp. 143.

— History.

ZIMANOV (SALYK ZIMANOVICH) Ot osvoboditel'nykh idei k sovetskoi gosudarstvennosti v Bukhare i Khive. Alma-Ata, 1976. pp. 220.

BULGARIA

— Commerce.

VUNSHNA TURGOVIIA: organ na Ministerstvoto na Vunshnata Turgoviia [Bulgaria]. m., 1965 (god.4)- Sofiia.

— Economic conditions.

PROBLEMI na ikonomicheskiia rastezh; Problems of economic growth. Sofiia, 1976. pp. 291. *With Russian and English summaries.*

— Foreign relations — Russia.

CHICHOVSKA (VESELA) Sobolevata aktsiia. Sofiia, 1972. pp. 109. *bibliog.*

DEVEDJIEV (HRISTO H.) Stalinization of the Bulgarian society, 1949-1953. Philadelphia, [1975]. pp. 216. *bibliog.*

— Historiography.

BULGARSKO ISTORICHESKO DRUZHESTVO. Nauchna Konferentsiia po Sluchai 70-godishninata ot Osnovavaneto, 1972. Problemi na bulgarskata istoriografiia sled Vtorata svetovna voina; materiali ot nauchnata konferentsiia, etc. Sofiia, 1973. pp. 701.

— History — Sources.

TODOROVA (TSVETANA) and STATELOVA (EL.) compilers. Dokumenti po obiaviavane na nezavisimostta na Bulgariia 1908 godina: iz tainiia kabinet na kniaz Ferdinand. Sofiia, 1968. pp. 238. *(Bulgarska Akademiia na Naukite. Institut za Istoriia. Dokumenti po Vunshnata Politika na Bulgariia) Some documents in the original French with Bulgarian translations. Appendix of facsimiles.*

— Occupations.

ATANASOV (ATANAS) and MASHIAKH (ARON) Promeni v sotsialnata prinadlezhnost na zaetite litsa v Bulgariia; Changements dans l'appartenance sociale des personnes occupées en Bulgarie. Sofiia, 1971. pp. 171. *bibliog. (Nauchnoizsledovatelski Institut po Statistika. Izdaniia. 3) With Russian and French summaries.*

— Politics and government.

IKONOMOV (TODOR) Memoari; (podbor i redaktsiia Toncho Zhechev). [Sofiia, 1973]. pp. 641.

DEVEDJIEV (HRISTO H.) Stalinization of the Bulgarian society, 1949-1953. Philadelphia, [1975]. pp. 216. *bibliog.*

BELL (JOHN D.) Peasants in power: Alexander Stamboliski and the Bulgarian Agrarian National Union, 1899-1923. Princeton, [1977]. pp. 271. *bibliog.*

— Relations (general) with Russia.

PAVLENKO (VIKTORIIA VIKTOROVNA) Solidarnost' trudiashchikhsia Ukrainskoi SSR s revoliutsionnoi bor'boi rabochikh i krest'ian Bolgarii, 1923-1934 gg. Kiev, 1977. pp. 140.

— Social conditions.

DEVEDJIEV (HRISTO H.) Stalinization of the Bulgarian society, 1949-1953. Philadelphia, [1975]. pp. 216. *bibliog.*

BULGARIAN LITERATURE

— History and criticism.

PETKO R. Slaveikov, Liuben Karavelov, Khristo Botev, Zakhari Stoianov v spomenite na suvremennitsite si. Sofiia, 1967. pp. 758.

BULGARIANS IN RUSSIA.

PAVLENKO (VIKTORIIA VIKTOROVNA) Solidarnost' trudiashchikhsia Ukrainskoi SSR s revoliutsionnoi bor'boi rabochikh i krest'ian Bolgarii, 1923-1934 gg. Kiev, 1977. pp. 140.

BULGARSKI ZEMEDELSKI NARODEN SUIUZ.

BELL (JOHN D.) Peasants in power: Alexander Stamboliski and the Bulgarian Agrarian National Union, 1899-1923. Princeton, [1977]. pp. 271. *bibliog.*

BUND.

LEVIN (NORA) Jewish socialist movements, 1871-1917: while Messiah tarried. London, 1978. pp. 554.

BUOL-SCHAUENSTEIN (CARL FERDINAND VON) Graf.

AUSTRIA. Ministerrat. 1852- . Das Ministerium Buol-Schauenstein...; bearbeitet von Waltraud Heindl, mit einer Einleitung von Friedrich Engel- Janosi. Wien, [1975 in progress]. *bibliog. (Die Protokolle des österreichischen Ministerrates, 1848-1867. Abteilung 3)*

BUREAUCRACY.

BALZANO (MICHAEL P.) Reorganizing the federal bureaucracy: the rhetoric and the reality. Washington, [1977]. pp. 43. *(American Enterprise Institute for Public Policy Research. AEI Studies. 165)*

FAMILY, bureaucracy and the elderly; edited by Ethel Shanas and Marvin B. Sussman. Durham, N.C., 1977. pp. 233. *bibliogs. Based on papers at a Conference on Older People, Family and Bureaucracy held at the Quail Roost Conference Center in Rougemont, N.C., in May 1973.*

GALY (PHILIPPE) Gérer l'État: corriger la déviation bureaucratique. [Paris, 1977]. pp. vii, 241. *bibliog.*

KAUFMAN (HERBERT) Red tape: its origins, uses, and abuses. Washington, D.C., [1977]. pp. 100.

FERNS (HENRY STANLEY) The disease of government. London, 1978. pp. 148. *bibliog.*

KAUFMAN (HERBERT) Fear of bureaucracy: a raging pandemic. Urbana, Ill., [1978]. pp. 30. *(Illinois University. Edmund J. James Lectures on Government. 1978)*

PETERS (B. GUY) The politics of bureaucracy: a comparative perspective. New York, [1978]. pp. 246.

BURMA

— Politics and government.

SILVERSTEIN (JOSEF) Burma: military rule and the politics of stagnation. Ithaca, N.Y., [1977]. pp. 224. *bibliog.*

BURROUGHS B1726 (COMPUTER).

ORGANICK (ELLIOTT I.) and HINDS (JAMES A.) Interpreting machines: architecture and programming B1700/B1800 series. New York, [1978]. pp. 315.

BURUNDI

— Statistics.

BURUNDI. Département des Statistiques. Bulletin (formerly Bulletin de statistique). q. (formerly bi-m.), N 1969 (no.22)- [Bujumbura]. *File includes Annuaire statistique 1972- .*

BUSINESS.

U.K. Central Statistical Office. 1971. Profit from facts. [London, 1971]. pp. 36.

STUDIES in the business economics; edited on behalf of [the] Institute of Industrial Research, Kwansei Gakuin University, by Osamu Kojima. Kyote, 1977. pp. 168.

— Data processing.

CLIFTON (HAROLD DENNIS) Business data systems: a practical guide to systems analysis and data processing. Englewood Cliffs, [1978]. pp. 336. *bibliogs.*

— Decision making.

LAPIN (LAWRENCE L.) Statistics for modern business decisions. 2nd ed. New York, [1978]. 1 vol. (various pagings).

— Dictionaries and encyclopedias.

AMMER (CHRISTINE) and AMMER (DEAN S.) Dictionary of business and economics. New York, [1977]. pp. 461. *bibliog.*

— History.

COCHRAN (THOMAS CHILDS) 200 years of American business. New York, [1977]. pp. 288. *bibliog.*

— Mathematical models.

KEMENY (JOHN G.) and others. Finite mathematics, with business applications. 2nd ed. Englewood Cliffs, 1962. pp. 529.

BUSINESS AND POLITICS

— Canada.

STANBURY (WILLIAM T.) Business interests and the reform of Canadian competition policy, 1971-1975. Toronto, [1977]. pp. 227.

BUSINESS AND POLITICS (Cont.)

— East (Near East).

HIRSCH (SEEV) Towards peace in the Middle East: how can business contribute? Tübingen, 1977. pp. 14. *(Kiel. Universität. Institut für Weltwirtschaft. Kieler Vorträge. Neue Folge. 83)*

BUSINESS CYCLES.

HENZEL (FRIEDRICH) Der Unternehmer in der Konjunktur: Richtlinien für die Praxis. Frankfurt am Main, 1959. pp. 79. *bibliog.*

KEINATH (KARL) Regionale Konjunkturschwankungen: eine empirische Analyse der Bundesrepublik Deutschland, 1950-1974. Tübingen, 1978. pp. 335. *bibliog.* *(Tübingen. Universität. Fachbereich Wirtschaftswissenschaft. Tübinger Wirtschaftswissenschaftliche Abhandlungen. Band 23)*

BUSINESS EDUCATION

— Rhodesia.

RHODESIA. Commission of Inquiry into Further Education in the Technical and Commercial Fields. 1974. Report...; [John Douglas Cameron, chairman]. [Salisbury], 1974. pp. 30.

— United Kingdom.

BUSINESS EDUCATION COUNCIL. Initial guidelines on the implementation of policy. London, 1977. pp. 39.

— United States.

BOSTON, MASSACHUSETTS. University. College of Business Administration. The story of C.B.A. Boston, 1927. pp. 16.

BUSINESS ETHICS.

ETHICAL perspectives on business and society; edited by Yerachmiel Kugel [and] Gladys W. Gruenberg. Lexington, Mass., [1977]. pp. 135.

BUSINESS RELOCATION

— Australia.

COMMITTEE OF COMMONWEALTH/STATE OFFICIALS ON DECENTRALISATION [AUSTRALIA]. Report. in AUSTRALIA. Parliament. Parliamentary papers, 1972, vol. 2.

— Rhodesia.

RHODESIA. 1974. Policy on decentralization. [Salisbury], 1974. pp. 10. *([Command Papers]. 1974. Cmd. R.R.31)*

— United Kingdom.

FIELD (A. MIRYAM) and CROFTS (C.) Some aspects of planned migration to new and expanding towns. London, [1977]. pp. 39. *bibliog.* *(London. Greater London Council. Research Memoranda. 527)*

HAYDEN (F.W.) Factors influencing the location of industry. London, [1978]. pp. 75. *(London. Greater London Council. Research Memoranda. 528)*

BUSINESS TAX

— Brazil.

SILVA (FERNANDO ANTONIO REZENDE DA) ed. O imposto sobre a renda das empresas. Rio de Janeiro, 1975. pp. 152. *bibliog.* *(Brazil. Instituto de Planejamento Econômico e Social. Instituto de Pesquisas. Monografias. No. 19)*

BUSINESS TRAVEL.

HENSHER (DAVID A.) Value of business travel time. Oxford, 1977. pp. 159. *bibliog.*

BUSINESSMEN

— Canada.

NEWMAN (PETER CHARLES) The Canadian establishment. Toronto, 1975 reprinted 1976, in progress.

— France.

HARRIS (ANDRE) and SEDOUY (ALAIN DE) Les patrons. Paris, [1977]. pp. 421.

— India.

BROEHL (WAYNE G.) The village entrepreneur: change agents in India's rural development. Cambridge, Mass., 1978. pp. 228.

— United States.

BROOKSTONE (JEFFREY M.) The multinational businessman and foreign policy: entrepreneurial politics in east-west trade and investment. New York, 1976. pp. 183. *bibliog.*

THIMM (ALFRED L.) Business ideologies in the reform-progressive era, 1880-1914. University, Ala., [1976]. pp. 264. *bibliog.*

PETERSON (RICHARD H.) The bonanza kings: the social origins and business behavior of western mining entrepreneurs, 1870-1900. Lincoln, Neb., [1977]. pp. 191. *bibliog.*

DAVIS (PATRICIA TALBOT) End of the line: Alexander J. Cassatt and the Pennsylvania Railroad. New York, [1978]. pp. 208. *bibliog.*

BUSONI (JAURÈS).

BUSONI (JAURÈS) Nel tempo del fascismo. Roma, 1975. pp. 241.

BUTLER (SAMUEL) Philosophical writer.

COLE (GEORGE DOUGLAS HOWARD) Samuel Butler. London, 1952. pp. 52. *bibliog.* *(British Book News. Bibliographical Series of Supplements: Writers and their Work. No. 30)*

BUYING.

CONSUMER and industrial buying behavior; edited by Arch G. Woodside [and others]. New York, [1977]. pp. 523. *bibliog.*

BYDGOSZCZ (PROVINCE)

— History.

GEY (THOMAS) Die preussische Verwaltung des Regierungsbezirks Bromberg, 1871-1920. Köln, [1976]. pp. 344. *bibliog.* Map in end pocket.

— Politics and government.

GEY (THOMAS) Die preussische Verwaltung des Regierungsbezirks Bromberg, 1871-1920. Köln, [1976]. pp. 344. *bibliog.* Map in end pocket.

BYZANTINE EMPIRE

— History.

INCONTRO DI STUDI BIZANTINI, 3, 1974. Calabria Bizantina: aspetti sociali ed economici; atti, etc. Reggio Calabria, 1978. pp. 119.

— Rural conditions.

LAIOU-THOMADAKIS (ANGELIKI E.) Peasant society in the late Byzantine Empire: a social and demographic study. Princeton, [1977]. pp. 332. *bibliog.*

— Social conditions.

PATLAGEAN (EVELYNE) Pauvreté économique et pauvreté sociale à Byzance 4e-7e siècles. Paris, [1977]. pp. 483. *bibliog.* *(Paris. Ecole des Hautes Etudes en Sciences Sociales. Centre de Recherches Historiques. Civilizations et Sociétés. 48)*

CABINET MINISTERS

— United States.

BIOGRAPHICAL directory of the United States executive branch, 1774-1977; Robert Sobel, editor in chief. Westport, 1977. pp. 503.

CABRERA (LUIS).

CABRERA (LUIS) Obras completas. vol. 4. Obra politica. Mexico, 1975. pp. 1074.

CADIZ

— History.

CONGRESO LUSO-ESPAÑOL PARA EL PROGRESO DE LAS CIENCIAS, 31ST, CADIZ. La burguesia mercantil gaditana, 1650-1868. Cadiz, 1976. pp. 322.

CAEN.

FRANCE. Direction de la Documentation. La Documentation Française. Notes et Etudes Documentaires. Nos. 4,401-4, 402-4,403. Les villes françaises: Caen et son agglomération; [by] Max André Brier [and others]. [Paris], 1977. pp. 97.

CAFFI (ANDREA).

BIANCO (GINO) Andrea Caffi: un socialista "irregolare"; intellettuale e politico d'avanguardia. Cosenza, [1977]. pp. 108.

CAIRO

— Social history.

STAFFA (SUSAN JANE) Conquest and fusion: the social evolution of Cairo, A.D. 642- 1850. Leiden, 1977. pp. 449. *bibliog.*

CALABRIA

— History.

ALCARO (MARIO) and PAPARAZZO (AMELIA) Lotte contadine in Calabria, 1943-1950. [Cosenza, 1976]. pp. 202.

INCONTRO DI STUDI BIZANTINI, 3, 1974. Calabria Bizantina: aspetti sociali ed economici; atti, etc. Reggio Calabria, 1978. pp. 119.

— Politics and government.

MULÉ (CESARE) Democrazia Cristiana in Calabria, 1943-1949: il movimento democratico-cristiano e le lotte contadine. Roma, [1975]. pp. 244. *bibliog.*

CORDOVA (FERDINANDO) Alle origini del PCI in Calabria, 1918-1926. [Roma, 1977]. pp. 174.

— Rural conditions.

SFRUTTAMENTO e subalternità nel mondo contadino meridionale; ([by] Pino De Angelis [and others]); con un intervento di Luigi M. Lombardi Satriani. Roma, 1975. 1 vol. (unpaged). *Photographs.*

CALCULUS.

AYRES (FRANK) Schaum's outline of theory and problems of differential and integral calculus. 2nd ed. New York, [1964]. pp. 345.

BOWMAN (FRANK) and GERARD (FITZGERALD ADOLPHUS) Higher calculus. Cambridge, 1967. pp. 416.

BAUMSLAG (GILBERT) and BAUMSLAG (BENJAMIN) Calculus. New York, [1976]. pp. 427.

BERS (LIPMAN) and KARAL (FRANK) Calculus. 2nd ed. New York, [1976]. pp. 783.

FREILICH (GERALD) and GREENLEAF (FREDERICK P.) Calculus: a short course with applications to business, economics, and the social sciences. San Francisco, [1976]. pp. 395.

MIZRAHI (ABE) and SULLIVAN (MICHAEL) Calculus with applications to business and life sciences. New York, [1976]. pp. 414.

CALCULUS, DIFFERENTIAL.

HILTON (PETER JOHN) Partial derivatives. London, 1960 repr. 1973. pp. 54.

FIELD (MICHAEL J.) Differential calculus and its applications. New York, [1976]. pp. 315. *bibliog.*

CALCULUS, INTEGRAL.

LEDERMANN (WALTER) Multiple integrals. London, 1966 repr. 1975. pp. 106.

CALI

— Economic conditions.

WALTON (JOHN) Elites and economic development: comparative studies on the political economy of Latin American cities. Austin, [1977]. pp. 257. *bibliog. (Texas University. Institute of Latin American Studies. Latin American Monographs. No. 41)*

CALIFORNIA

— Social history.

PETERSON (RICHARD H.) Manifest destiny in the mines: a cultural interpretation of anti-Mexican nativism in California, 1848-1853. San Francisco, 1975. pp. 126. *bibliog.*

— Social policy.

PASSELL (PETER) and ROSS (LEONARD) State policies and federal programs: priorities and constraints. New York, [1978]. pp. 168. *A Twentieth Century Fund Report.*

CAMBODIA

— Politics and government.

STEINBACH (JERÔME) and STEINBACH (JOCELYNE) Phnom Penh libérée. Paris, [1976]. pp. 165.

PONCHAUD (FRANÇOIS) Cambodia year zero; translated from the French by Nancy Amphoux. London, 1978. pp. 231.

CAMBRIDGE

— History.

MURPHY (MICHAEL JOSEPH) Cambridge newpapers and opinion, 1780-1850. Cambridge, [1977]. pp. 144. *bibliog.*

CAMDEN

— Politics and government.

BAKER (JOHN) of the Association for Neighbourhood Councils. The neighbourhood advice centre: a community project in Camden. London, 1978. pp. 310. *bibliog.*

CAMEROUN

— Constitution.

CAMEROUN. Constitution. 1961. Constitution de la République Fédérale du Cameroun: Constitution of the Federal Republic of Cameroon. [Yaoundé, 1961]. pp. 12. *In French and English.*

— Economic conditions.

CABOT (JEAN) Le bassin du moyen Logone. Paris, O.R.S.T.O.M., 1965. pp. 348. *Map in end pocket.*

FRANCE. Ministère de la Coopération. Service des Etudes Economiques et des Questions Internationales. 1976. Cameroun: données statistiques sur les activités économiques, culturelles et sociales. [Paris], 1976. pp. 205.

— Foreign relations — France.

BETI (MONGO) Main basse sur le Cameroun: autopsie d'une décolonisation. [2nd ed.] Paris, 1977. pp. 270.

— Politics and government.

FONLON (BERNARD) To every son of Nso. Yaoundé, 1965. fo. 41.

BETI (MONGO) Main basse sur le Cameroun: autopsie d'une décolonisation. [2nd ed.] Paris, 1977. pp. 270.

— Population.

CAMEROUN. Service de la Statistique Générale. 1962. Enquête démographique: Adamaoua, Sud Benoue: résultats principaux. [Paris], 1962. fo. 32.

— Social conditions.

FRANCE. Ministère de la Coopération. Service des Etudes Economiques et des Questions Internationales. 1976. Cameroun: données statistiques sur les activités économiques, culturelles et sociales. [Paris], 1976. pp. 205.

— Statistics.

CAMEROUN. Direction de la Statistique et de la Comptabilité Nationale. Note trimestrielle de statistique. q., 1968-1973; with gap (1970, no. 2, series A and B); ceased pbln. Yaoundé. *In 2 pts, series A and series B. Supersedes CAMEROUN. Service de la Statistique Générale. Note trimestrielle sur la situation économique. Superseded by CAMEROUN. Direction de la Statistique et de la Comptabilité Nationale. Bulletin mensuel de statistique.*

FRANCE. Ministère de la Coopération. Service des Etudes Economiques et des Questions Internationales. 1976. Cameroun: données statistiques sur les activités économiques, culturelles et sociales. [Paris], 1976. pp. 205.

CAMPAIGN FUNDS.

LABOUR RESEARCH DEPARTMENT. Political donations: an analysis of company donations made to the Conservative Party and allied organisations. London, [1973]. pp. 12.

MANITOBA. Law Reform Commission. 1977. Working paper on political financing and election expenses. Winnipeg, 1977. pp. 90. *bibliog.*

CANADA

— Administrative agencies.

GERIN-LAJOIE (PAUL) Developmental administration: C[anadian] I[nternational] D[evelopment] A[gency] in a changing government organization; paper delivered...to the Institute of Public Administration Conference in Regina, September 8, 1971. [Ottawa], 1971. pp. 15,16. *(Canadian International Development Agency. Thoughts on International Development. 4) In English and French.*

— Commerce.

HILL (O. MARY) Canada's salesman to the world: the Department of Trade and Commerce, 1892-1939. Montreal, 1977. pp. 631. *bibliog.*

— — Asia, Southeast.

HUGHES (WILLIAM) 1927- . Canada's exports to south-east Asia: a study of trade and transportation. Victoria, B.C., Bureau of Economics and Statistics, 1963. pp. 45.

— — Nigeria.

NIGERIA. Customs Department. 1920. Canada and Nigeria. Lagos, 1920. pp. 76, 1 map.

— Constitution.

MANS (ROWLAND) Canada's constitutional crisis: separatism and subversion. London, 1978. pp. 24. *(Institute for the Study of Conflict. Conflict Studies. No. 98)*

— Constitutional history.

FOX (PAUL WESLEY) Politics: Canada. 4th ed. Toronto, [1977]. pp. 653. *bibliogs.*

— Defences.

CONFERENCE ON CANADA AND THE NORTHERN RIM, QUEEN'S UNIVERSITY, KINGSTON, ONTARIO, 1977. Report...; [edited by Nils Orvik]. Kingston, Ont., 1977. fo. 144. *(Kingston, Ontario. Queen's University. Centre for International Relations. National Security Series. No. 6)*

— Description and travel.

FINCH (MARIANNE) An Englishwoman's experience in America. [London], 1853; New York, 1969. pp. 386. *Facsimile reprint.*

— Economic conditions.

MOORE (STEVE) and WELLS (DEBI) Imperialism and the national question in Canada. [Toronto, 1975]. *bibliog.*

ARMSTRONG (MURIEL) The Canadian economy and its problems. 2nd ed. Scarborough, Ont., [1977]. pp. 388.

CANADA and the burden of unity; edited by David Jay Bercuson. Toronto, [1977]. pp. 191.

IMPERIALISM, nationalism, and Canada: essays from the Marxist Institute of Toronto;...edited by Craig Heron. Toronto, [1977]. pp. 206.

McCREADY (GERALD B.) Profile Canada: social and economic projections. Georgetown, Ont., 1977. pp. 413. *bibliog.*

— — Mathematical models.

BOADWAY (ROBIN W.) and TREDDENICK (JOHN M.) The impact of the mining industries on the Canadian economy. Kingston, Ont., [1977]. pp. 115. *(Kingston, Ontario. Queen's University. Centre for Resource Studies. National Impact of Mining Series. 1)*

— Economic history.

NAYLOR (R. TOM) The history of Canadian business, 1867-1914. Toronto, 1975. 2 vols.(in 1). *bibliog.*

— Economic policy.

ARMSTRONG (MURIEL) The Canadian economy and its problems. 2nd ed. Scarborough, Ont., [1977]. pp. 388.

The CANADIAN state: political economy and political power; (edited by Leo Panitch). Toronto, [1977]. pp. 472.

GORDON (WALTER LOCKHART) A political memoir. Toronto, [1977]. pp. 395.

STONE (LEROY O.) and MARCEAU (CLAUDE) Canadian population trends and public policy through the 1980s. Montreal, 1977. pp. 109. *bibliog.*

WHICH way ahead?: Canada after wage and price control; contributors include Thomas Courchene [and others]; Michael Walker, editor. [Vancouver], 1977. pp. 291, 32.

GORDON (WALTER LOCKHART) What is happening to Canada. Toronto, [1978]. pp. 63.

REGIONAL economic policy: the Canadian experience; [edited by] N.H. Lithwick. Toronto, [1978]. pp. 368. *bibliog.*

— Emigration and immigration.

MANPOWER AND IMMIGRATION REVIEW: ATLANTIC REGION. (formerly Atlantic manpower review;) (pd. by the Manpower Information and Analysis Branch, Canada Department of Manpower and Immigration, Atlantic Region). q. (formerly bi-m.,) Jl/Ag 1969- Ja/Je 1976 (v.2, no.1- v.9, no.1) with gap Ja/Mr 1971 (v.4, no.1) ceased pbln. Halifax, N.S. *[in English and French] Jl-Oc 1969 in separate eds., English and French; N/D 1969 in English only; Ja/F 1970- in bilingual format.*

MANPOWER AND IMMIGRATION REVIEW: PRAIRIES AND NORTHWEST TERRITORIES (formerly Manpower review: Prairies and Northwest territories) ; ([pd. by] Manpower Information and Analysis Branch, Department of Manpower and Immigration [Prairies and Northwest Territories Regional Office, Canada]). q. (formerly bi-m.), Ja/F 1971 - Jl/S 1976 (v.4, no.1- v.9, no.3) ceased pbln. Winnipeg. *Not pd. N/D 1972 (v.5, no.6).*

— Executive departments.

HILL (O. MARY) Canada's salesman to the world: the Department of Trade and Commerce, 1892-1939. Montreal, 1977. pp. 631. *bibliog.*

CANADA (Cont.)

— Foreign economic relations.

MOORE (STEVE) and WELLS (DEBI) Imperialism and the national question in Canada. [Toronto, 1975]. *bibliog.*

PLUMPTRE (ARTHUR FITZGERALD WYNNE) Three decades of decision: Canada and the world monetary system, 1944-75. Toronto, [1977]. pp. 335. *bibliog.*

— Foreign population.

ONTARIO. Multicultural Development Branch. 1977. Papers on the Greek community. [Toronto, 1977]. pp. 26.

ONTARIO. Multicultural Development Branch. 1977. Papers on the Italian community. [Toronto, 1977]. pp. 7. *Consists solely of The quiet desperation of the immigrant, by Burt D'Antini.*

— Foreign relations.

CANADIAN foreign policy since 1945: middle power or satellite?; edited by J.L. Granatstein. 3rd ed. Toronto, 1973. pp. 246. *bibliog.*

STACEY (CHARLES PERRY) Canada and the age of conflict: a history of Canadian external policies. Toronto, [1977 in progress]. *bibliog.*

— — United States.

SWANSON (ROGER FRANK) Intergovernmental perspectives on the Canada-U.S. relationship. New York, 1978. pp. 278.

— Foreign relations administration.

SWANSON (ROGER FRANK) Intergovernmental perspectives on the Canada-U.S. relationship. New York, 1978. pp. 278.

— Full employment policies.

CANADA. Employment and Immigration Commission. Community employment strategy. a., 1976/77- Ottawa. *[in English and French]*

— History.

McNAUGHT (KENNETH) The Pelican history of Canada. rev. ed. London, 1978. pp. 350. *bibliog.*

— — 1837-1838, Rebellion.

PAPINEAU (LOUIS JOSEPH) Histoire de l'insurrection du Canada...en réfutation du rapport de Lord Durham; première partie. Burlington, Vt., 1839. pp. 38. *(Extraite de la Révue du Progrès, journal publié à Paris, 1839) Photographic reprint by Réédition Québec, 1968, from La Révue Canadienne, première livraison.*

— — 1914- .

CREIGHTON (DONALD GRANT) The forked road: Canada, 1939-1957. [Toronto, 1976]. pp. 319.

— — 1945- .

RESNICK (PHILIP) The land of Cain: class and nationalism in English Canada, 1945-1975. Vancouver, [1977]. pp. 297. *bibliog.*

— Industries.

CANADA. Statistics Canada. Industrial organization and concentration in the manufacturing, mining and logging industries. bien., 1972- Ottawa. *[in English and French].*

CANADA. Statistics Canada. Consumption of purchased fuel and electricity by the manufacturing, mining and electric power industries. a., 1975(1st)- Ottawa. *[in English and French]*

NAYLOR (R. TOM) The history of Canadian business, 1867-1914. Toronto, 1975. 2 vols.(in 1). *bibliog.*

ATLANTIC PROVINCES ECONOMIC COUNCIL. Background Papers. Industrial incentives programs in the Atlantic region: description, outlays and overview. Halifax, N.S., 1976. pp. 174.

WILLIAMS (JAMES RALLA) The Canadian-United States tariff and Canadian industry: a multisectoral analysis. Toronto, [1978]. pp. 174. *bibliog.*

— Nationalism.

MOORE (STEVE) and WELLS (DEBI) Imperialism and the national question in Canada. [Toronto, 1975]. *bibliog.*

ONTARIO. Legislative Assembly. Select Committee on Economic and Cultural Nationalism. 1975. Report...: final report on cultural nationalism; [Russell D. Rowe, chairman]. [Toronto], 1975. pp. 51.

DALY (D.J.) and GLOBERMAN (S.) Tariff and science policies: applications of a model of nationalism. Toronto, [1976]. pp. 125. *bibliog.* (Ontario. Economic Council. Research Studies. 4)

IMPERIALISM, nationalism, and Canada: essays from the Marxist Institute of Toronto;...edited by Craig Heron. Toronto, [1977]. pp. 206.

RESNICK (PHILIP) The land of Cain: class and nationalism in English Canada, 1945-1975. Vancouver, [1977]. pp. 297. *bibliog.*

— Politics and government.

MOORE (STEVE) and WELLS (DEBI) Imperialism and the national question in Canada. [Toronto, 1975]. *bibliog.*

APEX of power: the prime minister and political leadership in Canada;...Thomas A. Hockin, editor. 2nd ed. Scarborough, Ont., [1977]. pp. 359.

BOM (PHILIP C.) Trudeau's Canada: truth and consequences. St. Catharines, Ont., [1977]. pp. 173. *bibliog.*

The CANADIAN state: political economy and political power; (edited by Leo Panitch). Toronto, [1977]. pp. 472.

ENGLISH (JOHN) 1945- . Borden: his life and world. Toronto, [1977]. pp. 223. *bibliog.*

ENGLISH (JOHN) 1945- . The decline of politics: the Conservatives and the party system, 1901-20. Toronto, [1977]. pp. 237.

FOX (PAUL WESLEY) Politics: Canada. 4th ed. Toronto, [1977]. pp. 653. *bibliogs.*

GORDON (WALTER LOCKHART) A political memoir. Toronto, [1977]. pp. 395.

HARBRON (JOHN D.) Canada without Québec. Don Mills, Ont., [1977]. pp. 159. *bibliog.*

JENSON (JANE) and TOMLIN (BRIAN W.) Canadian politics: an introduction to systematic analysis. Toronto, [1977]. pp. 168.

LAXER (JAMES) and LAXER (ROBERT M.) The Liberal idea of Canada: Pierre Trudeau and the question of Canada's survival. Toronto, 1977. pp. 234.

MORRIS (RAYMOND N.) and LANPHIER (CHARLES MICHAEL) Three scales of inequality: perspectives on French-English relations. Don Mills, Ont., [1977]. pp. 303. *bibliog.*

MUST Canada fail?; edited by Richard Simeon. Montreal, [1977]. pp. 307.

PROSPECTS for a socialist Canada; edited by John Riddell and Art Young. Toronto, [1977]. pp. 127.

PUNNETT (ROBERT MALCOLM) The prime minister in Canadian government and politics. Toronto, [1977]. pp. 168.

WHITAKER (REGINALD) The government party: organizing and financing the Liberal Party of Canada, 1930-58. Toronto, [1977]. pp. 507.

ZINK (LUBOR J.) Viva Chairman Pierre. Toronto, 1977. pp. 150.

GORDON (WALTER LOCKHART) What is happening to Canada. Toronto, [1978]. pp. 63.

MANS (ROWLAND) Canada's constitutional crisis: separatism and subversion. London, 1978. pp. 24. *(Institute for the Study of Conflict. Conflict Studies. No. 98)*

— — Bibliography.

HEGGIE (GRACE F.) compiler. Canadian political parties, 1867-1968: a historical bibliography. Toronto, [1977]. pp. 603.

— Population.

STONE (LEROY O.) and MARCEAU (CLAUDE) Canadian population trends and public policy through the 1980s. Montreal, 1977. pp. 109. *bibliog.*

— Race question.

ADAMS (HOWARD) Prison of grass: Canada from the native point of view. Toronto, 1975. pp. 238. *bibliog.*

MORRIS (RAYMOND N.) and LANPHIER (CHARLES MICHAEL) Three scales of inequality: perspectives on French-English relations. Don Mills, Ont., [1977]. pp. 303. *bibliog.*

— Relations (general) with the United States.

RESNICK (PHILIP) The land of Cain: class and nationalism in English Canada, 1945-1975. Vancouver, [1977]. pp. 297. *bibliog.*

— Social conditions.

HILLER (HARRY H.) Canadian society: a sociological analysis. Scarborough, Ont., [1976]. pp. 200. *bibliog.*

McCREADY (GERALD B.) Profile Canada: social and economic projections. Georgetown, Ont., 1977. pp. 413. *bibliog.*

— Social history.

ESSAYS in Canadian working class history; editors: Gregory S. Kealey [and] Peter S. Warrian. Toronto, [1976]. pp. 231. *bibliog.*

SOCIETY and conquest: the debate on the bourgeoisie and social change in French Canada, 1700-1850; edited by Dale Miquelon. Vancouver, [1977]. pp. 219. *bibliog.*

— Social policy.

STONE (LEROY O.) and MARCEAU (CLAUDE) Canadian population trends and public policy through the 1980s. Montreal, 1977. pp. 109. *bibliog.*

CANBERRA

— Population.

AUSTRALIA. National Capital Development Commission. 1977. Canberra: demographic and social background. rev. ed. Canberra, 1977. pp. 38. *(Technical Papers. No. 7)*

— Social conditions.

AUSTRALIA. National Capital Development Commission. 1977. Canberra: demographic and social background. rev. ed. Canberra, 1977. pp. 38. *(Technical Papers. No. 7)*

CANCER

— Law and legislation — United States.

RETTIG (RICHARD A.) Cancer crusade: the story of the National Cancer Act of 1971. Princeton, N.J., [1977]. pp. 382.

CANGUILHEM (GEORGES).

LECOURT (DOMINIQUE) Marxism and epistemology: Bachelard, Canguilhem and Foucault; translated from the French by Ben Brewster. London, 1975. pp. 223. *bibliog.*

CANNING AND PRESERVING

— Industry and trade — Russia — Caucasus.

DANIIALOVA (NINA VASIL'EVNA) Ekonomicheskie problemy razmeshcheniia konservnoi promyshlennosti Severnogo Kavkaza. Moskva, 1976. pp. 198. *bibliog.*

CANNON (JAMES PATRICK).

CANNON (JAMES PATRICK) The struggle for socialism in the "American century": (writings and speeches, 1945-47). New York, [1977]. pp. 480.

CANTIMORI (DELIO).

CILIBERTO (MICHELE) Intellettuali e fascismo: saggio su Delio Cantimori. Bari, [1977]. pp. 264.

CAPE MACLEAR

— History.

COLE-KING (P.A.) Cape Maclear. Zomba, 1968. pp. 67. bibliog. (Malawi. Department of Antiquities. Publications. No. 4)

CAPE TOWN

— History.

BÖESEKEN (A.J.) Slaves and free blacks at the Cape, 1658-1700. Cape Town, 1977. pp. 208. bibliog.

CAPE VERDE ISLANDS

— Politics and government.

PORTUGAL. Statutes, etc. 1972. Estatuto politico-administrativo da provincia de Cabo Verde: decreto no. 541/72 de 22 de Dezembro. Lisboa, 1972. pp. 45.

CAPITAL.

BORELLI (GIANFRANCO) Teoria del valore e crisi sociale: sul concetto di capitale in generale. Napoli, [1975]. pp. 168.

CAPITAL market equilibrium and efficiency: implications for accounting, financial, and portfolio decision making; edited by James L. Bicksler. Lexington, Mass., [1977]. pp. 629. bibliogs.

LACHMANN (LUDWIG MORITZ) Capital, expectations, and the market process: essays on the theory of the market economy. Kansas City, [1977]. pp. 352. bibliog.

STATO e accumulazione del capitale; [by] Elmar Altvater [and others]; a cura di Alberto Martinelli. Milano, [1977]. pp. 287.

HARRIS (DONALD J.) Capital accumulation and income distribution. Stanford, 1978. pp. 313. bibliog.

MEACCI (FERDINANDO) La teoria del capitale e del progresso tecnico. Padova, 1978. pp. 379. (Padua. Università. Facoltà di Giurisprudenza. Pubblicazioni. 80)

STATE and capital: a Marxist debate; edited by John Holloway and Sol Picciotto. London, 1978. pp. 220. bibliog.

— America, Latin.

EN torno al capitalismo latinoamericano. Mexico, 1975. pp. 155. (Mexico City. Universidad Nacional Autonoma de Mexico. Instituto de Investigaciones Economicas. Seminario de Teoria del Desarrollo. 1)

— Argentine Republic.

SIMPOSIO de Buenos Aires, 1972; ([organized by the] Grupo Nacional Argentino [of the] Programa Latinoamericano para el Desarrollo de Mercados de Capital. [Buenos Aires, 1972]. pp. 37. (Programa Latinoamericano para el Desarrollo de Mercados de Capital. Grupo Nacional Argentino. [Publications]. 1)

El SISTEMA financiero argentino: documentos del Simposio de Buenos Aires, 1972 ([organized by the] Grupo Nacional Argentino [of the] Programa Latinoamericano para el Desarrollo de Mercados de Capital). Buenos Aires, 1973. 2 vols. (Programa Latinoamericano para el Desarrollo de Mercados de Capital. Grupo Nacional Argentino. [Publications]. 2)

— Brazil.

EVOLUCÃO do capitalismo no Brasil; ([by] Octavio Gouvêa de Bulhões [and others]). Rio de Janeiro, 1976. pp. 219.

— Italy.

FARINA (FRANCESCO) L'accumulazione in Italia, 1959-1972: un'interpretazione della crisi e della ristrutturazione capitalistica. [Bari, 1976]. pp. 188. bibliogs.

— Russia.

LARIONOV (IGOR' KONSTANTINOVICH) Stoimostnye rychagi v krugooborote fondov sotsialisticheskogo predpriiatiia. Moskva, 1976. pp. 151.

— South Africa.

NATTRASS (JILL) and BROWN (RICHARD P.C.) Capital intensity in South African manufacturing. Durban, 1977. pp. 44. (Natal University. Department of Economics. Black/White Income Gap Project. Interim Research Reports. No. 4)

— United States.

CAPITAL markets and water quality needs, 1975-1985...; [report of] a conference held...1975...New York City; (prepared for publication by Leonard Lund); a report from the Conference Board in cooperation with the National Commission on Water Quality. New York, [1975]. pp. 78. (National Industrial Conference Board. Conference Board Reports. No. 673)

CAPITAL ASSETS PRICING MODEL.

CAPITAL market equilibrium and efficiency: implications for accounting, financial, and portfolio decision making; edited by James L. Bicksler. Lexington, Mass., [1977]. pp. 629. bibliogs.

CAPITAL GAINS TAX.

AUSTRALIA. Commonwealth Treasury. 1974. Capital gains taxes. Canberra, 1974. pp. 35. (Treasury Taxation Papers. No. 10)

— United Kingdom.

U.K. Board of Inland Revenue. 1973. Capital gains tax. 2nd ed. [London], 1973. pp. 112.

CAPITAL INVESTMENTS.

BUSSEY (LYNN E.) The economic analysis of industrial projects. Englewood Cliffs, [1978]. pp. 491. bibliogs.

KOJIMA (KIYOSHI) Direct foreign investment: a Japanese model of multinational business operations. London, [1978]. pp. 246.

LEVY (HAIM) and SARNAT (MARSHALL) Capital investment and financial decisions. Englewood Cliffs, N.J., [1978]. pp. 354. bibliogs.

— Decision making.

BAKER (A.J.) Investment, valuation and the managerial theory of the firm. Farnborough, Hants., [1978]. pp. 321. bibliog.

— Mathematical models.

DORE (M.H.I.) Dynamic investment planning. London, [1977]. pp. 163. bibliog.

— Arab countries.

EL MALLAKH (RAGAEI) and others. Capital investment in the Middle East: the use of surplus funds for regional development. New York, [1977]. pp. 194. bibliog.

— Russia.

INVESTITSIONNYE problemy narodnokhoziaistvennykh kompleksov. Moskva, 1975. pp. 422. (Akademiia Nauk SSSR. Problemy Sovetskoi Ekonomiki)

STRUKTURA kapital'nykh vlozhenii v narodnoe khoziaistvo i puti ee sovershenstvovaniia. Kiev, 1977. pp. 226.

— Yugoslavia.

VOJNIĆ (DRAGOMIR) Investicije i društvena reprodukcija. Zagreb, 1977. pp. 219. bibliog.

CAPITAL LEVY.

ALLAIS (MAURICE) L'impôt sur le capital et la réforme monétaire. [Paris, 1977]. pp. 367.

CAPITAL PUNISHMENT

— Canada.

JAYEWARDENE (C.H.S.) The penalty of death: the Canadian experiment. Lexington, Mass., [1977]. pp. 125. bibliog.

— New Zealand.

ENGEL (PAULINE F.) The abolition of capital punishment in New Zealand, 1935-1961. [Wellington], Department of Justice, 1977. 1 vol. (various pagings). bibliog.

— United States.

BEDAU (HUGO ADAM) The courts, the constitution, and capital punishment. Lexington, Mass., [1977]. pp. 165.

CAPITALISM.

COMMUNIST PARTY OF GREAT BRITAIN. For a Marxist Leninist School. District School Material. Outlines. No.4. Period of temporary stabilization of capitalism, the second and third periods of post-war capitalism. [London, c. 1930]. pp. 16.

OELSSNER (FRED) Probleme der Krisenforschung. Berlin, 1959. pp. 20. (Deutsche Akademie der Wissenschaften zu Berlin. Sitzungsberichte. Klasse für Philosophie, Geschichte, Staats-, Rechts-, und Wirtschaftswissenschaften. 1959. Nr. 3)

BOYSON (RHODES) Youth and the image of free enterprise. London, [1973]. pp. 6. (Aims of Industry. The Future of Capitalism.)

ODEHNAL (EVA) The future of the businessman in a new Europe. [London, 1973]. pp. 13. (Aims of Industry. The Future of Capitalism)

AKADEMIIA NAUK SSSR. Institut Mirovoi Ekonomiki i Mezhdunarodnykh Otnoshenii. Materialy mezhdunarodnogo simpoziuma "Krizis i evoliutsiia mezhdunarodnoi valiutnoi sistemy kapitalizma", Leningrad, 1974. Moskva, 1975. 2 pts. (in 1).

L'ETAT contemporain et le marxisme; [by] J.-M. Vincent [and others]. Paris, 1975. pp. 235.

PERROTTA (COSIMO) La proletarizzazione contemporanea. Lecce, [1975]. 2 vols. (in 1).

[SANGUINETTI (GIANFRANCO)] Rapporto veridico sulle ultime opportunità di salvare il capitalismo in Italia: [by] Censor [pseud.]. [Milano, 1975]. pp. 143.

BOR'BA idei v sovremennom mire. Moskva, 1976 in progress.

L'AMBIVALENCE de la production: logiques communautaires et logique capitaliste. Paris, 1976. pp. 188. bibliog.

ANDREFF (WLADIMIR) Profits et structures du capitalisme mondial. [Paris, 1976]. pp. 285.

BRUNHOFF (SUZANNE DE) Etat et capital: recherches sur la politique économique. Grenoble, 1976. pp. 126.

CRISI della teoria economica e crisi del capitalismo; di Guido Carandini [and others]. Milano, [1976]. pp. 183. (Problemi del Socialismo. Quaderni. 1)

FANFANI (AMINTORE) Capitalismo, socialità, partecipazione. Milano, [1976]. pp. 225.

CAPITALISM.(Cont.)

INTERNATIONAL THEORETICAL CONFERENCE, 1976. Lenin's doctrine of imperialism and the contemporary stage of the general crisis of capitalism. Prague, 1976. pp. 109. *(Marxism-Leninism and Our Time)*

LESSARD (DIANE) L'agriculture et le capitalisme au Québec. [Montréal, 1976]. pp. 182. *bibliog.*

MIĘDZY feudalizmem a kapitalizmem: studia z dziejów gospodarczych i społecznych; prace ofiarowane Witoldowi Kuli. Wrocław, 1976. pp. 428. *Articles in French, English, German or Polish.*

SETTLE (TOM) In search of a third way: is a morally principled political economy possible? Toronto, [1976]. pp. 208. *bibliog.*

BEKHAR (NANSEN) Der Kapitalismus der Gegenwart: Faktoren und Widersprüche des Wirtschaftswachstums; aus dem Bulgarischen ([by] Burkhard Böttger). Berlin, 1977. pp. 165.

CARLI (GUIDO) Intervista sul capitalismo italiano; a cura di Eugenio Scalfari. Roma, 1977. pp. 131.

CAZZOLA (FRANCO) Lo sviluppo del capitalismo italiano, 1860-1914. Firenze, 1977. pp. 136. *bibliog.*

CORNWALL (JOHN) Modern capitalism: its growth and transformation. London, 1977. pp. 226.

CROMPTON (ROSEMARY) and GUBBAY (JON) Economy and class structure. London, 1977. pp. 248. *bibliog.*

DAVIS (WILLIAM) Editor of Punch. It's no sin to be rich: a defense of capitalism. Don Mills, [1977]. pp. 264.

HARRIS (STEPHEN E.) The death of capital. New York, [1977]. pp. 153.

LEMAITRE (JACQUES) Le chaos ou la troisième voie: ni capitalisme, ni socialisme étatiques, un système totalement différent: le libérisme. Paris, [1977]. pp. 324.

MANGENG (ELISABETH) Der Anachronismus in Theorie und Strategie der kommunistischen Partei: italienische Arbeiterwissenschaft gegen Theorie des Stamokap. Giessen, [1977]. pp. 285. *bibliog.*

MARKETS and morals; edited by Gerald Dworkin [and others]. Washington, [1977]. pp. 206. *bibliogs. Includes many of the papers presented at a three-day conference beginning May 9, 1974, at the Seattle Research Center of the Battelle Memorial Institute.*

NABUDERE (DAN) The political economy of imperialism: its theoretical and polemical treatment from mercantilist to multilateral imperialism. London, [1977]. pp. 293. *bibliogs.*

RAFFINOT (MARC) and JACQUEMOT (PIERRE) Le capitalisme d'état algérien. Paris, 1977. pp. 394. *bibliog.*

SPOHN (WILLFRIED) Weltmarktkonkurrenz und Industrialisierung Deutschlands, 1870-1914: eine Untersuchung zur...Geschichte der kapitalistischen Produktionsweise. Berlin, [1977]. pp. 452. *bibliog.*

GUINDEY (GUILLAUME) Vingt et une questions sur le capitalisme. [Paris, 1978]. pp. 94.

CAPITALISTS AND FINANCIERS

— France.

GRANOU (ANDRE) La bourgeoisie financière au pouvoir et les luttes de classes en France. Paris, 1977. pp. 306.

PLESHKOVA (SOF'IA LEONIDOVNA) K istorii kupecheskogo kapitala vo Frantsii v XV veke: Zhak Ker [i.e. Jacques Coeur] i ego deiatel'nost'. Moskva, 1977. pp. 181. *bibliog.*

— Spain.

TAMAMES GOMEZ (RAMON) La oligarquia financiera en España. Barcelona, 1977. pp. 262.

— United Kingdom.

CAMPLIN (JAMIE) The rise of the plutocrats: wealth and power in Edwardian England. London, 1978. pp. 340.

CAPITANATA

— History.

MAGNO (MICHELE) La Capitanata dalla astorizia al capitalismo agrario, 1400-1900. [Roma, 1975]. pp. 237. *bibliog.*

CAPODISTRIA (JOHN) Count.

CAPODISTRIA (JOHN) Count. John Capodistrias: some unpublished documents; [edited by] C.W. Crawley. Thessaloniki, 1970. pp. 109. *(Hidryma Meleton Chersonesou Tou Haimou. [Publications] . 114)*

CARACAS

— Economic conditions.

CARACAS. Oficina Municipal de Planeamiento Urbano. Estudio de base para la formulacion de una tesis sobre el area metropolitano de Caracas. [Caracas, 1966]. pp. 416. *bibliog.*

— Growth.

CARACAS. Oficina Municipal de Planeamiento Urbano. Estudio de base para la formulacion de una tesis sobre el area metropolitano de Caracas. [Caracas, 1966]. pp. 416. *bibliog.*

CARDENAS (LAZARO).

CARDENAS (LAZARO) Apuntes, 1913-1970. Mexico, 1972-74. 4 vols. (in 2).

PACHECO MENDEZ (GUADALUPE) and others. Cardenas y la izquierda mexicana: ensayo, testimonios, documentos. Mexico, [1976]. pp. 391. *bibliog.*

IANNI (OCTAVIO) El Estado capitalista en la epoca de Cardenas; [translated from the Portuguese by] Ana Maria Palos. Mexico, 1977. pp. 146.

CARIB INDIANS.

KLOOS (PETER) The Akuriyo of Surinam: a case of emergence from isolation. Copenhagen, 1977. pp. 31. *bibliog. (International Work Group for Indigenous Affairs. Documents. 27)*

CARIBBEAN AREA

— Commerce — History.

ANDREWS (KENNETH R.) The Spanish Caribbean: trade and plunder 1530-1630. New Haven, Conn., 1978. pp. 267.

— Economic conditions.

HAWKINS (IRENE) The changing face of the Caribbean. Barbados, 1976. pp. 271. *bibliog.*

KNIGHT (FRANKLIN W.) The Caribbean: the genesis of a fragmented nationalism. New York, 1978. pp. 251. *bibliog.*

— Economic integration.

CHARDON (CARLOS E.) Datos que sugieren la integracion economica de una parte de la region del Caribe: la Republica Dominicana y Puerto Rico: informe preliminar. San Juan, Banco Gubernamental de Fomento para Puerto Rico, 1962. fo. 105.

— Foreign economic relations.

HAWKINS (IRENE) The changing face of the Caribbean. Barbados, 1976. pp. 271. *bibliog.*

— Languages.

GOILO (ENRIQUE R.) Papiamentu textbook. Aruba, Netherlands Antilles, [1962]. pp. 150.

— Nationalism.

KNIGHT (FRANKLIN W.) The Caribbean: the genesis of a fragmented nationalism. New York, 1978. pp. 251. *bibliog.*

— Officials and employees.

PUBLIC SERVICES INTERNATIONAL. Regional Meeting for the Caribbean Area, Bridgetown, Barbados, 1966. Report of proceedings. London, [1966?]. pp. 74.

— Politics and government.

KNIGHT (FRANKLIN W.) The Caribbean: the genesis of a fragmented nationalism. New York, 1978. pp. 251. *bibliog.*

— Social conditions.

KNIGHT (FRANKLIN W.) The Caribbean: the genesis of a fragmented nationalism. New York, 1978. pp. 251. *bibliog.*

— Statistics.

EUROPEAN COMMUNITIES. Statistical Office. ACP: statistical yearbook. a., 1970/76 (1st)- Luxembourg. *[in English and French]*

CARICATURES AND CARTOONS

— United Kingdom.

WALKER (MARTIN) Daily sketches:...a cartoon history of twentieth century Britain. London, 1978. pp. 192. *bibliog.*

CARPENTER (EDWARD).

ROWBOTHAM (SHEILA) and WEEKS (JEFFREY) Socialism and the new life: the personal and sexual politics of Edward Carpenter and Havelock Ellis. London, 1977. pp. 198. *bibliog.*

CARPETS.

BARTLETT (JAMES NEVILLE) Carpeting the millions: the growth of Britain's carpet industry. Edinburgh, [1977]. pp. 296. *bibliog.*

CARTER (JAMES EARL) President of the United States.

SHOGAN (ROBERT) Promises to keep: Carter's first hundred days. New York, [1977]. pp. 300.

MELLOAN (GEORGE) and MELLOAN (JOAN) The Carter economy. New York, [1978]. pp. 312.

CASE GRAMMAR.

ANDERSON (JOHN M.) On case grammar: prolegomena to a theory of grammatical relations. London, [1977]. pp. 313. *bibliog.*

CASSATT (ALEXANDER JOHNSTON).

DAVIS (PATRICIA TALBOT) End of the line: Alexander J. Cassatt and the Pennsylvania Railroad. New York, [1978]. pp. 208. *bibliog.*

CASSIODORUS (MAGNUS AURELIUS).

SORACI (ROSARIO) Aspetti di storia economica italiana nell'età di Cassiodoro. Catania, [1974]. pp. 1 59. *bibliog.*

CASTE

— India.

CONLON (FRANK F.) A caste in a changing world: the Chitrapur Saraswat Brahmans, 1700-1935. Berkeley, Calif., [1977]. pp. 255. *bibliog.*

CASTELLO BRANCO (HUMBERTO DE ALENCAR).

DULLES (JOHN W.F.) Castello Branco: the making of a Brazilian president. College Station, Tex., [1978]. pp. 487.

CASTRO RUZ (FIDEL).

LLERENA (MARIO) The unsuspected revolution: the birth and rise of Castroism. Ithaca, 1978. pp. 324.

CATALAN NEWSPAPERS.

CULLA I CLARA (JOAN B.) El catalanisme d'esquerra: del Grup de "L'Opinio" al Partit Nacionalista Republica d'Esquerra, 1928-1936. Barcelona, 1977. pp. 428. *bibliog.*

CATALOGUES, BOOKSELLERS'.

GILHOFER UND RANSCHBURG. Catalogues. 74. Rare books:...manuscripts. Luzern, [1978?]. pp. 210.

CATALOGUES, LIBRARY.

FLORENCE. Biblioteca Nazionale Centrale. Pubblicazioni di società operaie italiane, 1881-1885: catalogo; a cura di Fabrizio Dolci. Firenze, [1973]. pp. 92.

CATALOGUING IN PUBLICATION.

SWINDLEY (L.R.) NATIS [National information systems]: cataloguing in publication: an international survey. (COM.75/WS/32). Paris, Unesco, 1975. 1 vol. (various pagings). *bibliog.*

CATALONIA

— Nationalism.

CRUELLS PIFARRE (MANUEL) El separatisme catala durant la guerra civil. Barcelona, 1975. pp. 248. *bibliog.*

CATASTROPHES (MATHEMATICS).

LU (YUNG-CHEN) Singularity theory and an introduction to catastrophe theory. New York, [1976]. pp. 199. *bibliog.*

ZEEMAN (E.C.) Catastrophe theory: selected papers, 1972-1977. Reading, Mass., 1977. pp. 674. *bibliog.*

CATERERS AND CATERING

— United Kingdom.

SERVICE: news-letter of the Hotel and Catering Industry Training Board [U.K.]. irreg. Wembley. *Current issues only kept.*

ERLAM (ANDREW) and BROWN (MARIE) Catering for homeless workers: a study of low pay and homelessness amongst casual catering workers [produced by the Low Pay Unit and the Campaign for the Homeless and Rootless]. [London, 1975]. fo. 13.

WINYARD (STEVE) Who will protect the low paid?; a submission to the Commission of Inquiry on the proposed abolition of the Industrial and Staff Canteen Undertakings Wages Council. London, 1975. fo. 8. (Low Pay Unit. Low Pay Papers. No. 7)

CATHOLIC CHURCH

— Historiography.

CHADWICK (WILLIAM OWEN) Catholicism and history: the opening of the Vatican archives. Cambridge, 1978. pp. 174. *bibliog.* (Oxford. University. Herbert Hensley Henson Lectures. 1976)

— Relations (diplomatic).

MASSARA (MASSIMO) La Chiesa cattolica nella seconda guerra mondiale, dallo scatenamento delle aggressioni hitleriane alla capitolazione della Francia, 1935-1940. Legnano, [1977]. pp. 377. *bibliog.*

CATHOLIC CHURCH AND CIVIL RIGHTS.

O'MAHONY (PATRICK J.) The fantasy of human rights. Great Wakering, Essex, 1978. pp. 192. *bibliog.*

CATHOLIC CHURCH IN CANADA.

DOUCET (PAUL) Quebec: secular and free. n.p., [c. 1970]. pp. 4.

CATHOLIC CHURCH IN FRANCE.

TACKETT (TIMOTHY) Priest and parish in eighteenth-century France: a social and political study of the curés in a diocese of Dauphiné, 1750- 1791. Princeton, N.J., [1977]. pp. 350. *bibliog.*

CATHOLIC CHURCH IN GERMANY.

MUCKERMANN (FRIEDRICH JOSEPH) Im Kampf zwischen zwei Epochen: Lebenserinnerungen; bearbeitet und eingeleitet von Nikolaus Junk. Mainz, [1973]. pp. 668. *(Kommission für Zeitgeschichte. Veröffentlichungen. Reihe A: Quellen. Band 15)*

STEHKAEMPER (HUGO) Konrad Adenauer als Katholikentagspräsident, 1922: Form und Grenze politischer Entscheidungsfreiheit im katholischen Raum: (Adenauer-Studien, IV; herausgegeben von Rudolf Morsey und Konrad Repgen). Mainz, [1977]. pp. 124. *bibliog. (Kommission für Zeitgeschichte. Veröffentlichungen. Reihe B: Forschungen. Band 21)*

TALLEN (HERMANN) Die Auseinandersetzung über [Paragraph] 218 StGB: zu einem Konflikt zwischen der SPD und der Katholischen Kirche. München, 1977. pp. 376. *bibliog.*

— Education.

KUEPPERS (HEINRICH) Der Katholische Lehrerverband in der Übergangszeit von der Weimarer Republik zur Hitler-Diktatur: zugleich ein Beitrag zur Geschichte des Volksschullehrerstandes. Mainz, [1975]. pp. 201. *bibliog. (Kommission für Zeitgeschichte. Veröffentlichungen. Reihe B: Forschungen. Band 18)*

CATHOLIC CHURCH IN ITALY.

ROSSI (MARIO VITTORIO) I giorni dell'onnipotenza: memoria di un'esperienza cattolica. Roma, 1975. pp. 204.

HAY (DENYS) The church in Italy in the fifteenth century. Cambridge, 1977. pp. 184. *bibliog.* (Cambridge. University. Trinity College. Birkbeck Lectures in Ecclesiastical History. 1971)

CATHOLIC CHURCH IN PERU.

KLAIBER (JEFFREY L.) Religion and revolution in Peru, 1824-1976. Notre Dame, Ind., [1977]. pp. 259. *bibliog.* (Notre Dame. University. Committee on International Relations. International Studies)

CATHOLIC CHURCH IN POLAND.

MAREK (RYSZARD) Kościół rzymskokatolicki wobec ziem zachodnich i północnych. Warszawa, 1976. pp. 358.

CATHOLIC CHURCH IN SPAIN.

PETSCHEN VERDAGUER (SANTIAGO) La iglesia en la España de Franco. Madrid, 1977. pp. 199.

CATHOLIC CHURCH IN THE UNITED STATES.

TOMASI (SILVANO M.) Piety and power: the role of the Italian parishes in the New York metropolitan area, 1880-1930. New York, 1975. pp. 201. *bibliog.*

CATHOLIC SCHOOLS

— United Kingdom.

HORNSBY-SMITH (MICHAEL P.) Catholic education: the unobtrusive partner: sociological studies of the Catholic school system in England and Wales. London, 1978. pp. 211. *bibliog.*

CATHOLICS IN FRANCE.

SUTTON (MICHAEL JOHN) Nationalism, positivism and Catholicism: a study of the controversy arising from the proposal of Charles Maurras for a political alliance between positivists and Catholics. [1978]. fo.431. *bibliog. Typescript. 2 pamphlets in end pocket. Ph.D. (London) thesis: unpublished. This thesis is the property of London University and may not be removed from the Library.*

CATHOLICS IN ITALY.

INTELLETTUALI cattolici tra riformismo e dissenso: polemiche sull'integrismo, obbedienza e fine dell'unità politica rifiuto dell'istituzione nelle reviste degli anni sessanta; a cura di Sergio Ristuccia. [Milano, 1975]. pp. 430. (Fondazione Adriano Olivetti. Programma di Ricerche di Cultura Politica. vol. 3)

ROSSI (MARIO VITTORIO) I giorni dell'onnipotenza: memoria di un'esperienza cattolica. Roma, 1975. pp. 204.

MURA (VIRGILIO) Cattolici e liberali nell'età giolittiana: il dibattito sulla toleranza. [Bari, 1976]. pp. 271.

PARTITO DI UNITÀ PROLETARIA PER IL COMUNISMO. Convegno, Roma, Dicembre 1975. I cattolici oltre la DC; atti del Convegno, etc. Roma, [1976]. pp. 247.

TASSANI (GIOVANNI) La cultura politica della destra cattolica. Roma, 1976. pp. 238.

I CATTOLICI dal fascismo alla resistenza; [by] Carlo F. Casula [and others]; a cura di Antonio Cucchiari. [Roma, 1977]. pp. 151. *bibliog.*

CUCCHIARI (ANTONIO) ed. Cattolici tra Togliatti e De Gasperi, 1937-45. Roma, [1977]. pp. 126.

CATHOLICS IN NORTHERN IRELAND.

BURTON (FRANK PATRICK) The politics of legitimacy: struggles in a Belfast community. London, 1978. pp. 208. *bibliog.*

CATHOLICS IN THE UNITED STATES.

SPALDING (JOHN LANCASTER) Bishop of Peoria. The religious mission of the Irish people and Catholic colonization. New York, 1880. pp. 339.

CROSBY (DONALD F.) God, church, and flag: Senator Joseph R. McCarthy and the Catholic church, 1950-1957. Chapel Hill, [1978]. pp. 307. *bibliog.*

CATIONS.

LONDON. University. London School of Economics and Political Science. Graduate School of Geography. Discussion Papers. No. 62. Water and cation movement in a tropical rainforest environment: I. Objectives, experimental design and preliminary results; [by] S. Nortcliff and J.B. Thornes. London, [1977]. pp. 30. *bibliog.*

CATTANEO (CARLO).

L'OPERA e l'eredità di Carlo Cattaneo: [proceedings of a Convegno held at Milan in 1974]; a cura di Carlo G. Lacaita. [Bologna, 1975 in progress].

DOTTI (UGO) I dissidenti del Risorgimento: Cattaneo, Ferrari, Pisacane. Roma, 1975. pp. 117. *bibliog.*

CATTLE TRADE

— Australia.

The SITUATION of aborigines on pastoral properties in the Northern Territory; report of the Committee of Review; [C. A.Gibb, chairman]. in AUSTRALIA. Parliament. Parliamentary papers, 1972, vol. 1.

— Rhodesia.

SOUTHERN RHODESIA. Commission of Enquiry into Certain Sales of Native Cattle in Areas occupied by Natives. 1939. Report; [Robert James Hudson, chairman]. [Salisbury], 1939. pp. 21. (Legislative Assembly. [Sessional Papers]. 1939. C.S.R. 24)

CAUCASUS

— Constitutional history.

SEMENTSOVA (VERA VLADIMIROVNA) and SUIAROVA (EVGENIIA VLADIMIROVNA) Partiinyi i gosudarstvennyi kontrol` na Severnom Kavkaze v 1923-1925 gg. Rostov-na-Donu, 1973. pp. 159.

— History — Sources.

DZIDZARIIA (GEORGII ALEKSEEVICH) F.F. Tornau i ego kavkazskie materialy. Moskva, 1976. pp. 130. *bibliog.*

CAYMAN ISLANDS.

CAYMAN ISLANDS. Report. a., 1974- [Grand Cayman]. *For 1918/19-1937, 1946-1973 see U.K. Foreign and Commonwealth Office. Cayman Islands: report.*

CEAUSESCU (NICOLAE).

CEAUSESCU (NICOLAE) Speeches and writings; selected and introduced by Stan Newens. 2nd ed. Nottingham, 1978. pp. 287.

CECIL (ROBERT ARTHUR TALBOT GASCOYNE) 3rd Marquess of Salisbury.

MARSH (PETER) of Syracuse University. The discipline of popular government: Lord Salisbury's domestic statecraft, 1881-1902. Hassocks, 1978. pp. 373. *bibliog.*

CECIL (WILLIAM) Baron Burghley.

HUME (MARTIN ANDREW SHARP) The great Lord Burghley (William Cecil): a study in Elizabethan statecraft. London, 1906. pp. 511.

CEMENT INDUSTRIES

— Russia — Mathematical models.

ROZANOV (GENNADII VLADIMIROVICH) Statisticheskoe modelirovanie razvitiia otrasli. Moskva, 1976. pp. 167. *bibliog.*

CENSORSHIP.

CENSORSHIP and obscenity; edited by Rajeev Dhavan and Christie Davies. London, 1978. pp. 187. *bibliogs.*

CENTRAL AFRICAN CUSTOMS AND ECONOMIC UNION.

See UNION DOUANIERE ET ECONOMIQUE DE L'AFRIQUE CENTRALE.

CENTRAL AMERICAN COMMON MARKET.

SALINAS ALVARADO (DOMINGO ALBERTO) El tratado general y la integracion economica de Centroamerica. Bogota, 1972. pp. 72. *bibliog.*

La INTEGRACION economica centroamericana; seleccion de Eduardo Lizano F. Mexico, 1975. 2 vols. (in 1). *(Fondo de Cultura Economica. Lecturas. 13)*

CENTRAL BUSINESS DISTRICTS

— Germany.

RHODE (BARBARA) Die Verdrängung der Wohnbevölkerung durch den tertiären Sektor: Strukturwandel in citynahen Stadtgebieten in Hamburg und Frankfurt/M., 1961-1970. Hamburg, [1977]. pp. 178. *bibliog. (Hamburg. Hansische Universität. Seminar für Sozialwissenschaften. Beiträge zur Stadtforschung. Band 2)*

— United States.

The FUTURE of urban centers: what are the policy options?; (a Round Table held on January 27, 1978...); John Charles Daly, moderator, etc. Washington, [1978]. pp. 38. *(American Enterprise Institute for Public Policy Research. Public Policy Forums. 15)*

CENTRAL PLACES.

CHRISTALLER central place structures: an introductory statement; [by] Nurudeen Alao [and others]. Evanston, 1977. pp. 311. *bibliog. (Northwestern University. Studies in Geography. No. 22)*

CENTRE PARTIES

— Colombia.

PARTIDO SOCIAL DEMOCRATA CRISTIANO [COLOMBIA]. Declaracion de principios; plataforma ideologica; programa de accion. Bogota, 1966. pp. 40.

— Germany.

SCHAUFF (JOHANNES) Das Wahlverhalten der deutschen Katholiken im Kaiserreich und in der Weimarer Republik: Untersuchungen aus dem Jahre 1928... ; herausgegeben und eingeleitet von Rudolf Morsey. Mainz, [1975]. pp. 214. *(Kommission für Zeitgeschichte. Veröffentlichungen. Reihe A: Quellen. Band 18)*

MITTMANN (URSULA) Fraktion und Partei: ein Vergleich von Zentrum und Sozialdemokratie im Kaiserreich. Düsseldorf, [1976]. pp. 455. *bibliog. (Germany (Bundesrepublik). Kommission für Geschichte des Parlamentarismus und der Politischen Parteien. Beiträge zur Geschichte des Parlamentarismus und der Politischen Parteien. Band 59)*

HOFMANN (JOSEF) Journalist in Republik, Diktatur und Besatzungszeit: Erinnerungen, 1916-1947; bearbeitet und eingeleitet von Rudolf Morsey. Mainz, [1977]. pp. 236. *(Kommission für Zeitgeschichte. Veröffentlichungen. Reihe A: Quellen. Band 23)*

MORSEY (RUDOLF) Der Untergang des politischen Katholizismus: die Zentrumspartei zwischen christlichem Selbstverständnis und "Nationaler Erhebung", 1932/33. Stuttgart, [1977]. pp. 279. *bibliog.*

PRIDHAM (GEOFFREY) Christian democracy in Western Germany: the CDU/CSU in government and opposition, 1945-1976. London, [1977]. pp. 371. *bibliog.*

— Italy.

ANDREOTTI (GIULIO) La Democrazia Cristiana, 1943-48. Roma, [1975]. pp. 70.

BASSO (LELIO) Fascismo e Democrazia Cristiana: due regimi del capitalismo italiano. Milano, [1975]. pp. 186. *bibliog.*

MULÉ (CESARE) Democrazia Cristiana in Calabria, 1943-1949: il movimento democratico-cristiano e le lotte contadine. Roma, [1975]. pp. 244. *bibliog.*

BASSETTI (PIERO) and others. DC: tra rifondazione e secondo partito. [Milano, 1976]. pp. 192.

DEMOCRAZIA CRISTIANA. Congresso Nazionale. 1954-1973, i Congressi della Democrazia Cristiana: (le relazioni dei Segretari politici). Roma, [1976]. pp. 615.

DEMOCRAZIA Cristiana, 1943-1976: una introduzione bibliografica; a cura dell'Istituto De Gasperi. Roma, [1976]. pp. 47.

MANTOVANI (GIOVANNI) Gli eredi di De Gasperi: iniziativa democratica e i "giovani" al potere. Firenze, [1976]. pp. 176.

MATTEUCCI (NICOLA) Dal populismo al compromesso storico. [Roma, 1976]. pp. 194.

ORFEI (RUGGERO) L'occupazione del potere: i democristiani '45-'75. Milano, [1976]. pp. 303.

PARTITO DI UNITÀ PROLETARIA PER IL COMUNISMO. Convegno, Roma, Dicembre 1975. I cattolici oltre la DC: atti del Convegno, etc. Roma, [1976]. pp. 247.

PROVASI (GIANCARLO) Borghesia industriale e Democrazia Cristiana: sviluppo economico e mediazione politica dalla Ricostruzione agli anni '70. Bari, [1976]. pp. 308. *bibliog.*

ZACCAGNINI (BENIGNO) Una proposta al paese. 2nd ed. [Firenze, 1976]. pp. 131.

BAGET-BOZZO (GIANNI) Il partito cristiano e l'apertura a sinistra: la Dc di Fanfani e di Moro 1954-1962. Firenze, [1977]. pp. 383.

Il COMPROMESSO storico; a cura di Luciano Gruppi. [Roma, 1977]. pp. 345.

MENIS (PIETRO) Dal Partito Popolare Italiano alla Democrazia Cristiana, 1918-1964: memorie di un politico di paese. [Udine, 1977]. pp. 95.

RODANO (FRANCO) Questione democristiana e compromesso storico. Roma, 1977. pp. 362.

— Venezuela.

PARTIDO SOCIALCRISTIANO "COPEI". Fracción Parlamentaria. Frente al acuerdo de Ginebra. Caracas, 1966. pp. 948-960. *(Publicaciones. No. 38)*

CEREAL PRODUCTS.

BRUSEKER (U.) Unilever, Meneba, Philips en de olieconcerns als inflatiemakers; een bestrijding van de looninflatie-theorie. [Amsterdam], 1974. pp. 133. *bibliog.*

CEREALS AS FOOD.

MYSORE. Directorate of Evaluation and Manpower. 1974. Report on a critical review of production and consumption of food grains in Mysore state, for the post-third five year plan period. Bangalore, [1974]. pp. 52.

CHAD

— Economic conditions.

CABOT (JEAN) Le bassin du moyen Logone. Paris, O.R.S.T.O.M., 1965. pp. 348. *Map in end pocket.*

CHAMBERLAIN (JOSEPH).

LIFE of Joseph Chamberlain; by Rt. Hon. Viscount Milner [and others]. [London, 1914?]. pp. 320.

POWELL (JOHN ENOCH) Joseph Chamberlain. London, [1977]. pp. 160.

CHAMBERS (WHITTAKER).

WEINSTEIN (ALLEN) Perjury: the Hiss-Chambers case. New York, 1978. pp. 674. *bibliog.*

CHAMBERS OF COMMERCE.

CHAMBER OF COMMERCE OF THE STATE OF NEW YORK. The chambers of commerce of the world, exclusive of the United States, etc. New York, 1923. pp. 43.

— Colombia.

MANTILLA SUAREZ (SERGIO) Las camaras de comercio en Colombia. Bogota, 1972. pp. 361. *bibliog.*

— United States.

HOWE (FREDERIC CLEMSON) Cleveland's education through its Chamber of Commerce. [New York], 1906. pp. 739-749. *(From the Outlook, July 28, 1906)*

CHAMPAGNE

— Economic history.

HAU (MICHEL) La croissance économique de la Champagne de 1810 à 1969. Paris, [1976]. pp. 179. *bibliog. Thèse de doctorat-Université de Strasbourg.*

CHAMPAGNE-ARDENNE

— Economic conditions — Statistics.

TABLEAUX DE L'ECONOMIE CHAMPENOISE; [pd. by] Direction Régionale de Reims, Institut National de la Statistique et des Etudes Economiques. a., 1978- Reims.

CHANCAY VALLEY

— Rural conditions.

MEJIA (JOSE MANUEL) and DIAZ SUAREZ (ROSA) Sindicalismo y reforma agraria en el valle de Chancay. Lima, 1975. pp. 151. *bibliog. (Instituto de Estudios Peruanos. Proyecto de Estudios Etnologicos del Valle de Chancay. Monografias. No. 5)*

CHANG (TSO-LIN).

McCORMACK (GAVAN) Chang Tso-lin in northeast China, 1911-1928: China, Japan, and the Manchurian idea. Stanford, 1977. pp. 334. *bibliog.*

CHANGKUFENG INCIDENT, 1938.

COOX (ALVIN D.) The anatomy of a small war: the Soviet-Japanese struggle for Changkufeng/Khasan, 1938. Westport, Conn., 1977. pp. 409. *bibliog.*

CHANNEL TUNNEL.

The CHANNEL Tunnel: England's chance to aid a great scheme. London, [1913]. pp. 17. *(Reprinted from the Daily Chronicle)*

FELL (Sir ARTHUR) The Channel Tunnel and food supplies in time of war. London, 1913. pp. 11.

TEMPEST (Sir PERCY CROSLAND) The Channel tunnel: memorandum...relating to the general aspects of the project of the Channel tunnel and its construction, as well as to the methods proposed for expediting the work and reducing its cost. 1923. pp. 3. *A paper of the House of Commons Channel Tunnel Committee.*

CHARENTES.

See also POITOU-CHARENTES (REGION).

CHARITABLE USES, TRUSTS AND FOUNDATIONS

— Italy.

FIORAVANTI (LUCIANO) La Fondazione Agnelli: cultura e potere nella strategia neo-capitalistica italiana. Rimini, 1976. pp. 162.

— United Kingdom.

PICARDA (HUBERT) The law and practice relating to charities. London, 1977. pp. 765.

— — Commonwealth.

COMMONWEALTH FOUNDATION. The first ten years, 1966-1976: a fifth report. [London, 1976]. pp. 97.

CHARITIES

— United Kingdom — Directories.

WELLS INTERNATIONAL DONORS ADVISORY SERVICES. Wells collection of U.K. charitable giving records. 2nd ed. London, 1973. pp. 33.

CHARITIES, MEDICAL

— United Kingdom.

TODD (ARMSTRONG) On the administration of medical charities, with suggestions for a more systematised plan of management: an extract from a paper read before...the Manchester Statistical Society...22nd of May, 1856. London, W. Davy, 1865. pp. 26.

CHARLEROI

— Economic history.

POTY (FRANCIS) Histoire de la démocratie et du mouvement ouvrier au Pays de Charleroi. Bruxelles, [1975 in progress]. *bibliog.*

CHARLES ROBERTS AND COMPANY.

CHARLES ROBERTS AND COMPANY. Charles Roberts and Company Limited, 1856-1956. [Wakefield, 1956]. pp. 52.

CHARTISM

— Bibliography.

HARRISON (JOHN FLETCHER CLEWS) and THOMPSON (DOROTHY K.G.) compilers. Bibliography of the Chartist movement, 1837-1976. Hassocks, Sussex, 1978. pp. 214.

CHASTENET DE GÉRY (J.)

CHASTENET DE GÉRY (J.) Les derniers jours de la Troisième République à Tahiti, 1938-1940: souvenirs d'un gouverneur. Paris, 1975. pp. 75. *(Reprinted from Bulletin de la Société des Etudes Océaniennes, Dec. 1974, no. 187-189)*

CHEGARAY (THOMAS and PIERRE ANTOINE).

CHARBONNEL (NICOLE) Commerce et course sous la Révolution et le Consulat à La Rochelle: autour de deux armateurs: les frères Thomas et Pierre-Antoine Chegaray. Paris, [1977]. pp. 103. *bibliog.* (Paris. Université de Paris II. Travaux et Recherches. Série Sciences Historiques. 12)

CHEMICAL INDUSTRIES.

UNITED NATIONS INDUSTRIAL DEVELOPMENT ORGANIZATION. Industrial Planning and Programming Series. No. 1. Techniques of sectoral economic planning: the chemical industries. (ST/CID/14) [(ID/SER.E/1)]. New York, United Nations, 1966. pp. 58. *bibliog.*

— France.

FRANCE. Groupe sectoriel d'Analyse et de Prévision Industries Chimiques. 1976. Rapport...: préparation du 7e Plan. Paris, [1976]. 2 vols. (in 1).

— United Kingdom.

GILL (COLIN) and others. Industrial relations in the chemical industry. Farnborough, Hants., [1978]. pp. 256.

— United States.

FORRESTAL (DAN J.) The story of Monsanto: faith, hope and $5,000: the trials and triumphs of the first 75 years. New York, [1977]. pp. 285.

CHEMICAL WARFARE.

WESTING (ARTHUR H.) Weapons of mass destruction and the environment. London, 1977. pp. 95. *bibliog.*

CHEROKEE INDIANS.

HALLIBURTON (R.) Red over black: black slavery among the Cherokee Indians. Westport, Conn., [1977]. pp. 218. *bibliog.*

CHESHIRE

— Economic conditions.

CHESHIRE. County Planning Department. County structure plan: report of survey. [Chester], 1977. 13 pts. (in 1 vol.).

— History.

MORRILL (JOHN STEPHEN) The Cheshire grand jury, 1625-1659: a social and administrative study. Leicester, 1976. pp. 60. (Leicester. University. Department of English Local History. Occasional Papers. 3rd Series. No. 1)

— Social conditions.

CHESHIRE. County Planning Department. County structure plan: report of survey. [Chester], 1977. 13 pts. (in 1 vol.).

CHESTERTON (GILBERT KEITH).

CANOVAN (MARGARET) G. K. Chesterton: radical populist. New York, [1977]. pp. 175. *bibliog.*

CHIANG MAI, THAILAND (PROVINCE)

— Social life and customs.

POTTER (JACK M.) Thai peasant social structure. Chicago, 1976. pp. 249. *bibliog.*

CHICAGO

— Race question.

SURGEON (GEORGE) and others. Race relations in Chicago: second survey: 1975. Chicago, [1976]. pp. 182. *bibliog.* (Chicago. University. Community and Family Study Center. Community and Family Monographs)

PHILPOTT (THOMAS LEE) The slum and the ghetto: neighborhood deterioration and middle-class reform, Chicago, 1880-1930. New York, 1978. pp. 428.

CHILD ABUSE

— United Kingdom.

KEMPE (RUTH S.) and KEMPE (C. HENRY) Child abuse. [London], 1978. pp. 157. *bibliog.*

CHILD DEVELOPMENT.

The ROLE of the father in child development; edited by Michael E. Lamb. New York, [1976]. pp. 407. *bibliogs.*

CULTURE and infancy: variations in the human experience; edited by P. Herbert Leiderman [and others]. New York, [1977]. pp. 615. *bibliogs.* Based on a conference held in 1973 by the Wenner-Gren Foundation for Anthropological Research.

DAMON (WILLIAM) The social world of the child. San Francisco, 1977. pp. 361. *bibliog.*

TUCKER (NICHOLAS) What is a child? [London], 1977. pp. 128. *bibliog.*

ENTWISLE (DORIS ROBERTS) and HAYDUK (LESLIE ALEC) Too great expectations: the academic outlook of young children. Baltimore, [1978]. pp. 193. *bibliog.*

HUMAN growth and development...; edited by Jerome S. Bruner and Alison Garton. Oxford, 1978. pp. 167. *bibliogs.* (Oxford. University. Wolfson College. Wolfson College Lectures. 1976)

MAIER (HENRY WILLIAM) Three theories of child development. 3rd ed. New York, [1978]. pp. 292. *bibliogs.*

CHILD PSYCHIATRY

— United Kingdom.

IRWIN (EDNA M.) Growing pains: a study of teenage distress. Plymouth, 1977. pp. 310. *bibliogs.*

CHILD PSYCHOLOGY.

PIAGET (JEAN) The essential Piaget; [selections from his works]; edited by Howard E. Gruber and J. Jacques Vonèche. London, 1977. pp. 881. *bibliog.*

TUCKER (NICHOLAS) What is a child? [London], 1977. pp. 128. *bibliog.*

AGGRESSION and anti-social behaviour in childhood and adolescence; edited by L.A. Hersov and M. Berger. Oxford, 1978. pp. 171. *bibliogs.*

MAIER (HENRY WILLIAM) Three theories of child development. 3rd ed. New York, [1978]. pp. 292. *bibliogs.*

NEWMAN (BARBARA M.) and NEWMAN (PHILIP R.) Infancy and childhood: development and its contents. New York, [1978]. pp. 619. *bibliog.*

CHILD WELFARE.

VIOLENCE and the family; edited by J.P. Martin. Chichester, [1978]. pp. 369. *bibliogs.*

— Canada — New Brunswick.

CANADIAN COUNCIL ON SOCIAL DEVELOPMENT. Child welfare services in New Brunswick; a report to the... Minister of Youth and Welfare, province of New Brunswick; by George Caldwell. Ottawa, 1965. fo. 28. *bibliog.* Photocopy.

— United Kingdom.

ABEL-SMITH (BRIAN) Child poverty; [address given to the annual general meeting of Family Service Units in 1971]. London, [1976]. pp. 22. *(Reprinted from Family Service Units Quarterly, No. 1)*

BRITISH ASSOCIATION OF SOCIAL WORKERS. Analysis of Children Bill. Birmingham, [1976]. pp. 39.

CHILD BENEFITS NOW CAMPAIGN. The great child benefit robbery. London, 1977. pp. 32.

DAVIES (HYWEL) Children in the care of the London boroughs, 1974 to 1976. London, 1977. pp. (118). (London. Greater London Council. Research Memoranda. 520)

CHILD WELFARE.(Cont.)

TRADES UNION CONGRESS. The under-fives; report of a TUC working party. London, [1977]. pp. 127.

FIELD (FRANK) 1942- . Children worse off under Labour?: an updating of the Secretary of State for Social Service's memorandum to the Cabinet. London, 1978. pp. 28. *(Child Poverty Action Group. Poverty Pamphlets. 32)*

HEYWOOD (JEAN SCHOFIELD) Children in care: the development of the service for the deprived child. 3rd ed. London, 1978. pp. 272. *bibliog.*

— — Ireland.

MONTEFIORE (DORA B.) Our fight to save the kiddies: smouldering fires of the Inquisition. London, [imprint, 1913]. pp. 16.

— United States.

GREENBLATT (BERNARD) Responsibility for child care: (the changing role of family and state in child development). San Francisco, [1977]. pp. 317. *bibliog.*

CHILDBIRTH.

MONNIER (ALAIN) La naissance d'un enfant: incidences sur les conditions de vie des familles; préface d'Alain Girard. [Paris], 1977. pp. 231. *(France. Institut National d'Etudes Démographiques. Travaux et Documents. Cahiers. No. 81)*

CHILDERS (ERSKINE).

BOYLE (ANDREW) The riddle of Erskine Childers. London, 1977. p. 351. *ibliog.*

CHILDREN

— Care and hygiene — Australia.

AUSTRALIA. Commonwealth Bureau of Census and Statistics. 1978. Child care, May 1977. Canberra, 1978. pp. 22.

— — United Kingdom.

FRANKLIN (ALFRED WHITE) Widening horizons of child health: a study of the medical health needs of children in England and Wales. Lancaster, [1976]. pp. 279. *bibliog. This study was originated in 1968 by a working party of the British Paediatric Association and the Royal College of General Practitioners.*

— Hospitals.

NATIONAL ASSOCIATION FOR THE WELFARE OF CHILDREN IN HOSPITAL. The fares enquiry; a NAWCH report prepared by Barbara Browse. London, 1972-73. pp. 25.

— Institutional care — Finland.

RAUHALA (URHO) Huostaanotto: Taking into custody. Helsinki, 1978. pp. 181. *bibliog. (Finland. Suomen Virallinen Tilasto. Finlands Officiella Statistik. 32. Sosiaalisia Erikoistutkimuksia. 54) With English summary.*

— Language.

CRYSTAL (DAVID) Child language, learning and linguistics: an overview for the teaching and therapeutic professions. London, 1976. pp. 106.

INGRAM (DAVID) Lecturer in linguistics. Phonological disability in children. London, 1976. pp. 167. *bibliog.*

UNDERSTANDING children talking; [by] Nancy Martin [and others]. Harmondsworth, 1976. pp. 208. *Derived from the 1971 conference of the National Association for the Teaching of English.*

BARON (NAOMI S.) Language acquisition and historical change. Amsterdam, 1977. pp. 320. *bibliog.*

CHILD discourse; edited by Susan Ervin-Tripp [and] Claudia Mitchell-Kernan. New York, 1977. pp. 266. *bibliog.*

CURTISS (SUSAN) Genie: a psycholinguistic study of a modern-day "wild child". New York, 1977. pp. 288. *bibliog.*

LINGUISTIC theory and psychological reality; edited by Morris Halle [and others]. Cambridge, Mass., [1978]. pp. 329. *bibliog. (Massachusetts Institute of Technology. M.I.T. Bicentennial Studies. 3)*

READINGS in language development; Lois Bloom, editor. New York, [1978]. pp. 506. *bibliogs.*

— Law — Canada — British Columbia.

BRITISH COLUMBIA. Royal Commission on Family and Children's Law, 1974-75. Reports 1-5, 7, 9-11, 13; [Thomas Rodney Berger, chairman]. Vancouver, 1974-75. 16 vols (in 5).

— — Russia.

SHEVCHENKO (IAROSLAVNA NIKOLAEVNA) Pravovoe regulirovanie otvetstvennosti nesovershennoletnikh. Kiev, 1976. pp. 189. *bibliog.*

— — United Kingdom.

BRITISH ASSOCIATION OF SOCIAL WORKERS. Analysis of Children Bill. Birmingham, [1976]. pp. 39.

HALL (Sir WILLIAM CLARKE) and MORRISON (ARTHUR CECIL LOCKWOOD) Law relating to children and young persons; ninth edition [by] Joseph Jackson [and others]. London, 1977. pp. 1295.

— Cyprus.

OMILOS PEDAGOGIKON EREVNON. The drama of Cyprus as it affects children and their education. Nicosia, 1974. pp. 7.

— Hungary.

HUNGARY. Központi Statisztikai Hivatal. Népességtudományi Kutató Intézet. Közlemények. 45. Az 1-60 hónapos Budapesti gyermekek testi fejlettsége, szociodemográfiai és morbiditási viszonyai: elozete jelentés. Budapest, 1977. pp. 237. *With separate English summary bound in.*

— United Kingdom.

WILSON (HARRIETT CHARLOTTE) and HERBERT (GEOFFREY WILLIAM) Parents and children in the inner city. London, 1978. pp. 248. *bibliog.*

CHILDREN, FIRST BORN.

NETHERLANDS. Centraal Bureau voor de Statistiek. 1974. De geboorte van het eerste kind, 1950-1972. 's-Gravenhage, 1974. pp. 20. *With English summary.*

CHILDREN OF ALIEN LABOURERS

— Education — Germany.

RIST (RAY C.) Guestworkers in Germany: the prospects for pluralism. New York, 1978. pp. 263. *bibliog.*

CHILDREN OF IMMIGRANTS

— Education — United Kingdom.

U.K. Department of Education and Science. 1971. Potential and progress in a second culture: a survey of the assessment of pupils from overseas. London, 1971. pp. 37. *(Education Surveys. 10)*

GILES (RAYMOND H.) The West Indian experience in British schools: multi-racial education and social disadvantage in London. London, [1977]. pp. 170.

— United Kingdom.

FISHER (THELMA) and FISHER (FRANK) Writer on social problems. All our children;...edited by Rachel Jenkins. London, [1976]. pp. 24. *bibliog.*

CHILDREN OF WORKING MOTHERS.

TRADES UNION CONGRESS. The under-fives; report of a TUC working party. London, [1977]. pp. 127.

CHILDS (MARQUIS WILLIAM).

CHILDS (MARQUIS WILLIAM) Witness to power. New York, [1975]. pp. 277.

CHILE

— Armed forces — Political activity.

REIMANN WEIGERT (ELISABETH) and RIVAS SANCHEZ (FERNANDO) Las fuerzas armadas de Chile: un caso de penetracion imperialista. La Habana, 1976. pp. 313. *bibliog.*

— Boundaries — Argentine Republic.

MORZONE (LUIS ANTONIO) Cuestiones de limites con la Republica de Chile: el laudo arbitral en la region del Rio Encuentro. La Plata, 1967. pp. 31.

— Commercial policy.

BEHRMAN (JERE R.) Foreign trade regimes and economic development: Chile. New York, 1976. pp. 408. *bibliog. (National Bureau of Economic Research. Special Conference Series on Foreign Trade Regimes and Economic Development. vol. 8)*

— Economic conditions.

KIRSCH (HENRY W.) Industrial development in a traditional society: the conflict of entrepreneurship and modernization in Chile. Gainesville, 1977. pp. 210. *bibliog. (Florida University. School of Inter-American Studies. Latin American Monographs. 2nd Series. 21)*

— Economic policy.

BEHRMAN (JERE R.) Foreign trade regimes and economic development: Chile. New York, 1976. pp. 408. *bibliog. (National Bureau of Economic Research. Special Conference Series on Foreign Trade Regimes and Economic Development. vol. 8)*

BOORSTEIN (EDWARD) Allende's Chile: an inside view. New York, 1977. pp. 277.

KOLM (SERGE CHRISTOPHE) La transition socialiste: la politique économique de gauche. Paris, 1977. pp. 212.

— Foreign relations.

TEORIA y praxis internacional del gobierno de Allende; [by] Leopoldo González Aguayo [and others]. Mexico, 1974. pp. 238. *bibliog. (Mexico City. Universidad Nacional Autonoma de Mexico. Centro de Relaciones Internacionales. Cuadernos. Nueva Epoca. 3)*

— — United States.

MARIN (GERMAN) Una historia fantastica y calculada: la CIA en el pais de los chilenos. Mexico, 1976. pp. 280.

FRANCIS (MICHAEL J.) The limits of hegemony: United States relations with Argentina and Chile during World War II. Notre Dame, [1977]. pp. 292. *(Notre Dame. University. Committee on International Relations. International Studies)*

— History — 1565-1810.

GONGORA (MARIO) Encomenderos y estancieros: estudios acerca de la Constitucion social aristocratica de Chile despues de la Conquista, 1580-1660. Santiago de Chile, 1970. pp. 244. *bibliog.*

— Industries.

KIRSCH (HENRY W.) Industrial development in a traditional society: the conflict of entrepreneurship and modernization in Chile. Gainesville, 1977. pp. 210. *bibliog. (Florida University. School of Inter-American Studies. Latin American Monographs. 2nd Series. 21)*

— Politics and government.

WORLD STUDENT CHRISTIAN FEDERATION. WSCF Dossiers. No.4. Chile. Geneva, 1974. 1 vol. (unpaged). *bibliog.*

GARCES (JOAN E.) Allende et l'expérience chilienne. [Paris, 1976]. pp. 286. *(Fondation Nationale des Sciences Politiques. Cahiers. 207)*

WORLD UNIVERSITY SERVICE. The present situation in Chile and Argentina. London, 1976. pp. 21. *bibliog.*

BOORSTEIN (EDWARD) Allende's Chile: an inside view. New York, 1977. pp. 277.

CASTEX (PATRICK) "Voie chilienne" au socialisme et luttes paysannes: approche théorique et pratique d'une transition capitaliste non révolutionnaire. Paris, 1977. pp. 296.

HIRSCH (FRED) and FLETCHER (RICHARD) The CIA and the labour movement. Nottingham, 1977. pp. 71.

DRAKE (PAUL W.) Socialism and populism in Chile, 1932-52. Urbana, [1978]. pp. 418. *bibliog.*

— Social conditions.

KIRSCH (HENRY W.) Industrial development in a traditional society: the conflict of entrepreneurship and modernization in Chile. Gainesville, 1977. pp. 210. *bibliog. (Florida University. School of Inter-American Studies. Latin American Monographs. 2nd Series. 21)*

— Statistics.

CHILE. Instituto Nacional de Estadisticas. Compendio estadistico. a., 1973- . *Not pd. 1975.*

CHINA.

KITAISKAIA Narodnaia Respublika: politicheskoe i ekonomicheskoe razvitie. a., 1973(1st)- Moskva.

— Armed forces — Political activity.

WOU (ODORIC YING-KWONG) Militarism in modern China: the career of Wu P'ei-Fu, 1916- 39. Folkestone, 1978. pp. 346. *bibliog. (Columbia University. East Asian Institute. Studies)*

— Army — History.

WOU (ODORIC YING-KWONG) Militarism in modern China: the career of Wu P'ei-Fu, 1916- 39. Folkestone, 1978. pp. 346. *bibliog. (Columbia University. East Asian Institute. Studies)*

— Boundaries — India.

EEKELEN (WILLEM FREDERIK VAN) Indian foreign policy and the border dispute with China. The Hague, 1964. pp. 220. *bibliog.*

— Commerce.

CHAN (WELLINGTON K.K.) Merchants, mandarins, and modern enterprise in late Ch'ing China. Cambridge, Mass., 1977. pp. 323. *bibliogs. (Harvard University. East Asian Research Center. Harvard East Asian Monographs. 79)*

HSIAO (GENE T.) The foreign trade of China: policy, law and practice. Berkeley, Calif., [1977]. pp. 291. *bibliog.*

SZUPROWICZ (BOHDAN O.) and SZUPROWICZ (MARIA R.) Doing business with the People's Republic of China: industries and markets. New York, [1978]. pp. 449.

— — Sweden.

LARSSON (JAN) Diplomati och industriellt genombrott: svenska exportsträvanden på Kina, 1906-1916. Uppsala, 1977. pp. 212. *bibliog. (Uppsala. Universitet. Historiska Institutionen. Studia Historica Upsaliensia. 94) With English summary.*

— — Thailand.

VIRAPHOL (SARASIN) Tribute and profit: Sino-Siamese trade, 1652-1853. Cambridge, Mass., 1977. pp. 419. *bibliog. (Harvard University. East Asian Research Center. Harvard East Asian Monographs. 76)*

— Constitution.

TAO-TAI (HSIA) and HAUN (KATHRYN A.) The 1975 revised constitution of the People's Republic of China. [Washington], Library of Congress, 1975. 1 vol. (various pagings).

— Economic conditions.

EKONOMIKA KNR: vozmozhnosti i real'nost'. Moskva, 1976. pp. 235.

WHITING (ALLEN SUESS) and DERNBERGER (ROBERT F.) China's future: foreign policy and economic development in the post-Mao era. New York, [1977]. pp. 202. *bibliog. (Council on Foreign Relations. 1980s Project Studies)*

HOWE (CHRISTOPHER) China's economy: a basic guide. London, 1978. pp. 248.

PRYBYLA (JAN S.) The Chinese economy: problems and policies. Columbia, S.C., 1978. pp. 258. *bibliogs.*

SZUPROWICZ (BOHDAN O.) and SZUPROWICZ (MARIA R.) Doing business with the People's Republic of China: industries and markets. New York, [1978]. pp. 449.

— Economic history.

SINGH (AJIT) Political economy of socialist development in China since 1949. Cambridge, 1974. 1 pamphlet (unpaged). *(Cambridge. University. Department of Applied Economics. Reprint Series. No. 395) Reprinted from Economic and Political Weekly, vol. 8. No. 47, November 24, 1973.*

MELIKSETOV (ARLEN VAAGOVICH) Sotsial'no-ekonomicheskaia politika gomin'dana v Kitae, 1927- 1949. Moskva, 1977. pp. 317. *bibliog.*

— Economic policy.

MAO (TSE-TUNG) A critique of Soviet economics;...translated by Moss Roberts, annotated by Richard Levy, with an introduction by James Peck. New York, [1977]. pp. 157.

HOWE (CHRISTOPHER) China's economy: a basic guide. London, 1978. pp. 248.

PRYBYLA (JAN S.) The Chinese economy: problems and policies. Columbia, S.C., 1978. pp. 258. *bibliogs.*

— — Bibliography.

BLAIR (PATRICIA WOHLGEMUTH) compiler. Development in the People's Republic of China; a selected bibliography...with an essay by A. Doak Barnett. Washington, [1976]. pp. 87. *(Overseas Development Council. Occasional Papers. No. 8)*

— — Mathematical models.

BERGMANN (THEODOR) The development models of India, the Soviet Union and China: a comparative analysis. Assen, 1977. pp. 255. *bibliog. (European Society for Rural Sociology. Publications. 1.)*

— Foreign economic relations.

HSIAO (GENE T.) The foreign trade of China: policy, law and practice. Berkeley, Calif., [1977]. pp. 291. *bibliog.*

— Foreign relations.

ARMSTRONG (J.D.) Revolutionary diplomacy: Chinese foreign policy and the united front doctrine. Berkeley, [1977]. pp. 251.

BARNETT (ARTHUR DOAK) China and the major powers in east Asia. Washington, D.C., [1977]. pp. 416.

DUNCANSON (DENNIS J.) The peacetime strategy of the Chinese People's Republic. London, [1977]. pp. 32. *bibliog. (Institute for the Study of Conflict. Special Reports)*

FITZGERALD (STEPHEN) China and the world. Canberra, 1977. pp. 126.

HARRISON (SELIG S.) China, oil, and Asia: conflict ahead? New York, 1977. pp. 317. *Based on a study for the International Fact-Finding Center of the Carnegie Endowment for International Peace.*

KOLOSKOV (BORIS TROFIMOVICH) Vneshniaia politika Kitaia, 1969-1976 gg.: osnovnye faktory i vedushchie tendentsii. Moskva, 1977. pp. 328.

WHITING (ALLEN SUESS) and DERNBERGER (ROBERT F.) China's future: foreign policy and economic development in the post-Mao era. New York, [1977]. pp. 202. *bibliog. (Council on Foreign Relations. 1980s Project Studies)*

SUTTER (ROBERT G.) Chinese foreign policy after the cultural revolution, 1966-1977. Boulder, Colo., 1978. pp. 176. *bibliog.*

WOU (ODORIC YING-KWONG) Militarism in modern China: the career of Wu P'ei-Fu, 1916- 39. Folkestone, 1978. pp. 346. *bibliog. (Columbia University. East Asian Institute. Studies)*

YAHUDA (MICHAEL B.) China's role in world affairs. London, [1978]. pp. 300. *bibliog.*

See also UNITED NATIONS — China.

— — Africa.

ARMSTRONG (J.D.) Revolutionary diplomacy: Chinese foreign policy and the united front doctrine. Berkeley, [1977]. pp. 251.

— — Asia.

ARMSTRONG (J.D.) Revolutionary diplomacy: Chinese foreign policy and the united front doctrine. Berkeley, [1977]. pp. 251.

— — India.

EEKELEN (WILLEM FREDERIK VAN) Indian foreign policy and the border dispute with China. The Hague, 1964. pp. 220. *bibliog.*

— — Japan.

JAIN (RAJENDRA KUMAR) China and Japan, 1949-1976. New Delhi, 1977. pp. 336. *bibliog.*

McCORMACK (GAVAN) Chang Tso-lin in northeast China, 1911-1928: China, Japan, and the Manchurian idea. Stanford, 1977. pp. 334. *bibliog.*

CHINA and Japan: search for balance since World War I; Alvin D. Coox and Hilary Conroy, editors. Santa Barbara, [1978]. pp. 468.

MENDL (WOLF) Issues in Japan's China policy. London, 1978. pp. 178. *bibliog.*

— — Korea.

CHUNG (CHIN O.) Pyongyang between Peking and Moscow: North Korea's involvement in the Sino-Soviet dispute, 1958-1975. University, Ala., [1978]. pp. 230. *bibliog.*

— — Russia.

[RUSSIA (U.S.S.R.). Soviet Embassy in London. Press Department]. Soviet Booklets. [2nd Series]. No. 120. On internationalism and nationalism; by L. Volodin. London, 1963. pp. 12.

FOOT (ROSEMARY JUNE) New areas of tension and great power rivalry: central west Asia and Sino-Soviet relations, 1962-1974. 1976 [or rather 1977]. fo. 353. *bibliog. Typescript. Ph.D. (London) thesis: unpublished. This thesis is the property of London University and may not be removed from the Library.*

HINTON (HAROLD CLENDENIN) The Sino-Soviet confrontation: implications for the future. New York, [1977]. pp. 71. *(National Strategy Information Center. Strategy Papers. No. 29)*

KERRY (TOM) The Mao myth and the legacy of Stalinism in China. New York, [1977]. pp. 190.

SUTTER (ROBERT G.) China-watch: toward Sino-American reconciliation. Baltimore, [1978]. pp. 155. *bibliog.*

— — United States.

WHITAKER (URBAN GEORGE) ed. The foundations of U.S. China policy; contributors, George E. Taylor [and others]. Berkeley, Calif., [1959]. pp. 136. *Transcript of a radio programme, 1959.*

VARG (PAUL A.) The closing of the door: Sino-American relations, 1936-1946. [East Lansing, Mich.], 1973. pp. 300.

CHINA.(Cont.)

THOMSON (JAMES C.) An anatomy of Chinese-American relations. Braamfontein, 1976. pp. 11. *(South African Institute of International Affairs. Occasional Papers)*

ASPECTS of Sino-American relations since 1784; edited by Thomas H. Etzold. New York, 1978. pp. 173. *bibliogs.*

COHEN (WARREN I.) The Chinese connection: Roger S. Greene, Thomas W. Lamont, George E. Sokolsky and American-East Asian relations. New York, 1978. pp. 322. *(Columbia University. East Asian Institute. Studies)*

SUTTER (ROBERT G.) China-watch: toward Sino-American reconciliation. Baltimore, [1978]. pp. 155. *bibliog.*

— History.

LATOURETTE (KENNETH SCOTT) A history of modern China. [Harmondsworth, 1954]. pp. 234.

The CAMBRIDGE history of China; (general editors Denis Twitchett and John K. Fairbank). Cambridge, 1978 in progress. *bibliogs.*

— — Sources.

MORRISON (GEORGE ERNEST) The correspondence of G.E. Morrison; edited by Lo Hui-Min. Cambridge, 1976-78. 2 vols.

— — 1900- .

HOWARD (ROGER) Mao Tse-tung and the Chinese people. London, [1977]. pp. 412. *bibliog.*

— — 1911-1912, Revolution.

YEN (CHING-HWANG) The overseas Chinese and the 1911 revolution. Kuala Lumpur, 1976. pp. 439. *bibliog.*

— — 1937-1945.

HISTORY of the Sino-Japanese War, 1937-1945; compiled [from the 100 volume History of the Sino-Japanese War, published by the Military History Bureau of the Ministry of National Defense, Republic of China] by Hsu Long-hsuen and Chang Ming-kai. 2nd ed. Taipei, 1972. pp. 642. *bibliog.*

— — 1945- .

MEISNER (MAURICE) Mao's China: a history of the People's Republic. New York, [1977]. pp. 416. *bibliog.*

CHINA: the impact of the cultural revolution; edited by Bill Brugger. London, [1978]. pp. 300. *bibliog.*

LEE (HONG YUNG) The politics of the Chinese cultural revolution: a case study. Berkeley, [1978]. pp. 369.

PEPPER (SUZANNE) Civil war in China: the political struggle, 1945-1949. Berkeley, [1978]. pp. 472. *bibliog.*

— — 1945- — Bibliography.

LUST (JOHN) and WOOD (FRANCES) B.A.(Cantab.) compilers. Catalogue of publications of translation and monitoring services and of periodicals dealing with the People's Republic of China in the library of the School of Oriental and African Studies. London, 1974. pp. 37.

— Industries.

AMERICAN RURAL SMALL-SCALE INDUSTRY DELEGATION. Rural small-scale industry in the People's Republic of China. Berkeley, Calif., [1977]. pp. 296.

CHAN (WELLINGTON K.K.) Merchants, mandarins, and modern enterprise in late Ch'ing China. Cambridge, Mass., 1977. pp. 323. *bibliogs. (Harvard University. East Asian Research Center. Harvard East Asian Monographs. 79)*

SZUPROWICZ (BOHDAN O.) and SZUPROWICZ (MARIA R.) Doing business with the People's Republic of China: industries and markets. New York, [1978]. pp. 449.

— Politics and government.

BRENDEL (CAJO) Theses on the Chinese revolution. 2nd ed. [London, 1974]. pp. 26. *(Solidarity: [for workers' power]. Pamphlets. [No.] 46)*

GYÖRGY (IMRE) Cherez prizmu Pekina; perevod s vengerskogo, etc. Moskva, 1975. pp. 284.

CHANG (YI-CHUN) Factional and coalition politics in China: the cultural revolution and its aftermath. New York, 1976. pp. 144.

HOFHEINZ (ROY) The broken wave: the Chinese Communist peasant movement, 1922- 1928. Cambridge, Mass., 1977. pp. 355. *bibliog. (Harvard University. East Asian Research Center. Harvard East Asian Series. 90)*

IDEINO-politicheskaia sushchnost' maoizma. Moskva, 1977. pp. 443. *bibliog.*

KERRY (TOM) The Mao myth and the legacy of Stalinism in China. New York, [1977]. pp. 190.

KHOR'KOV (VIKTOR IVANOVICH) Nankinskii gomin'dan i rabochii vopros, 1927-1932. Moskva, 1977. pp. 158. *bibliog.*

LAMPTON (DAVID M.) The politics of medicine in China: the policy process, 1949-1977. Boulder, Colo., 1977. pp. 301. *bibliog.*

LI (JUI) The early revolutionary activities of Comrade Mao Tse-tung; (translated by Anthony W. Sariti; edited by James C. Hsiung; introduction by Stuart R. Schram). White Plains, N.Y., [1977]. pp. 354.

MOODY (PETER R.) Opposition and dissent in contemporary China. Stanford, [1977]. pp. 342. *bibliog. (Stanford University. Hoover Institution on War, Revolution and Peace. Hoover Institution Publications. 177)*

RYCKMANS (PIERRE) The chairman's new clothes: ([by] Simon Leys [pseud.]) ; translated by Carol Appleyard and Patrick Goode. London, 1977. pp. 261.

WHITING (ALLEN SUESS) and DERNBERGER (ROBERT F.) China's future: foreign policy and economic development in the post-Mao era. New York, [1977]. pp. 202. *bibliog. (Council on Foreign Relations. 1980s Project Studies)*

BROYELLE (CLAUDIE) and BROYELLE (JACQUES) Le bonheur des pierres: carnets rétrospectifs. Paris, [1978]. pp. 197.

ENDICOTT (JOHN E.) and HEATON (WILLIAM R.) The politics of east Asia: China, Japan, Korea. Boulder, Colo., 1978. pp. 323. *bibliog.*

LEE (HONG YUNG) The politics of the Chinese cultural revolution: a case study. Berkeley, [1978]. pp. 369.

PEPPER (SUZANNE) Civil war in China: the political struggle, 1945-1949. Berkeley, [1978]. pp. 472. *bibliog.*

WOU (ODORIC YING-KWONG) Militarism in modern China: the career of Wu P'ei-Fu, 1916- 39. Folkestone, 1978. pp. 346. *bibliog. (Columbia University. East Asian Institute. Studies)*

YAHUDA (MICHAEL B.) China's role in world affairs. London, [1978]. pp. 300. *bibliog.*

— Relations (general) with Europe.

MURPHEY (RHOADS) The outsiders: the western experience in India and China. Ann Arbor, [1977]. pp. 299. *bibliog. (Michigan University. Center for Chinese Studies. Michigan Studies on China)*

— Relations (general) with New Zealand.

HOLYOAKE (Sir KEITH JACKA) New Zealand and China; an article by the Prime Minister. Wellington, Ministry of Foreign Affairs, 1971. pp. 13.

— Rural conditions.

DUMONT (RENE) Chine, la révolution culturale. Paris, [1976]. pp. 200. *bibliog.*

BERNSTEIN (THOMAS P.) Up to the mountains and down to the villages: the transfer of youth from urban to rural China. New Haven, 1977. pp. 371. *bibliog.*

AZIZ (SARTAJ) Rural development: learning from China. London, 1978. pp. 201. *bibliog.*

— Social conditions.

DEVIANCE and social control in Chinese society; edited by Amy Auerbacher Wilson [and others]. New York, [1977]. pp. 227. *Proceedings of a preliminary conference held at the International Center of Rutgers University in 1975.*

— Social policy.

AZIZ (SARTAJ) Rural development: learning from China. London, 1978. pp. 201. *bibliog.*

— — Bibliography.

BLAIR (PATRICIA WOHLGEMUTH) compiler. Development in the People's Republic of China; a selected bibliography...with an essay by A. Doak Barnett. Washington, [1976]. pp. 87. *(Overseas Development Council. Occasional Papers. No. 8)*

CHINANTEC INDIANS.

BARABAS (ALICIA) and BARTOLOME (MIGUEL) Hydraulic development and ethnocide: the Mazatec and Chinantec people of Oaxaca, Mexico. Copenhagen, 1973. pp. 20. *bibliog. (International Work Group for Indigenous Affairs. Documents. 15)*

CHINESE AMERICANS.

SUNG (BETTY LEE) A survey of Chinese-American manpower and employment. New York, 1976. pp. 247. *bibliog.*

KUO (CHIA-LING) Social and political change in New York's Chinatown: the role of voluntary associations. New York, 1977. pp. 160. *bibliog.*

ASPECTS of Sino-American relations since 1784; edited by Thomas H. Etzold. New York, 1978. pp. 173. *bibliogs.*

— Employment.

SUNG (BETTY LEE) A survey of Chinese-American manpower and employment. New York, 1976. pp. 247. *bibliog.*

CHINESE IN CUBA.

PÉREZ DE LA RIVA (JUAN) Demografia de los culies chinos en Cuba, 1853-74. [Havana], 1966. pp. 32. *(Separata de la Revista de la Biblioteca Nacional Jose Marti, año 57, No.4)*

CHINESE IN MALAYSIA.

YEN (CHING-HWANG) The overseas Chinese and the 1911 revolution. Kuala Lumpur, 1976. pp. 439. *bibliog.*

CHINESE IN SOUTHEAST ASIA.

WEE (MON-CHENG) The future of the Chinese in southeast Asia as viewed from the economic angle, and other articles on economic topics. Singapore, 1970 repr. 1972. pp. 116.

CHOCÓ, COLOMBIA

— Economic history.

SHARP (WILLIAM FREDERICK) Slavery on the Spanish frontier: the Colombian Chocó 1680- 1810. Norman, Okla., [1976]. pp. 253. *bibliog.*

— Social history.

SHARP (WILLIAM FREDERICK) Slavery on the Spanish frontier: the Colombian Chocó 1680- 1810. Norman, Okla., [1976]. pp. 253. *bibliog.*

CHOICE OF TRANSPORTATION

— Mathematical models.

BANISTER (DAVID) Car availability and usage: a modal split model based on these concepts. Reading, 1977. pp. 36. *bibliog. (Reading. University. Department of Geography. Reading Geographical Papers. No. 58)*

DETERMINANTS of travel choice; edited by David A. Hensher and Quasim Dalvi. Farnborough, Hants., [1978]. pp. 394. *bibliogs. A contribution to the US National Academy of Sciences Transportation Research Board Sub-Committee on the Value of Travel Time.*

CHOLERA, ASIATIC

— United Kingdom.

PELLING (MARGARET) Cholera, fever and English medicine, 1825-1865. Oxford, 1978. pp. 342. *bibliog.*

CHOTA NAGPUR

— Economic history.

SCHWERIN (DETLEF) Graf. Von Armut zu Elend: Kolonialherrschaft und Agrarverfassung in Chota Nagpur, 1858-1908. Wiesbaden, 1977. pp. 551. *bibliog.* (Heidelberg. Universität. Südasien-Institut. Beiträge zur Südasienforschung. Band 31) *With English summary.*

— Social history.

SCHWERIN (DETLEF) Graf. Von Armut zu Elend: Kolonialherrschaft und Agrarverfassung in Chota Nagpur, 1858-1908. Wiesbaden, 1977. pp. 551. *bibliog.* (Heidelberg. Universität. Südasien-Institut. Beiträge zur Südasienforschung. Band 31) *With English summary.*

CHOU (EN-LAI).

WE will always remember Premier Chou En-lai. Peking, 1977. pp. 196.

CHRISTIAN LIFE.

NANKIVELL (OWEN) All good gifts: a Christian view of the affluent society. London, [1978]. pp. 127.

CHRISTIAN PILGRIMS AND PILGRIMAGES.

TURNER (VICTOR WITTER) and TURNER (EDITH) Image and pilgrimage in Christian culture: anthropological perspectives. Oxford, 1978. pp. 281. *bibliog.*

CHRISTIANITY.

The NEW faith. London, 1876. pp. 11. *From 'The Index'. Signed J.L.S.*

— Controversial literature.

PAINE (THOMAS) The age of reason;...with a biographical introduction by the Rt. Hon. J.M. Robertson. London, [193-?]. pp. 124. *The text is a reprint of Mrs. Bonner's edition (without the editor's notes), and is based directly upon that of Daniel Isaac Eaton's edition of 1795 (for the first part) and 1796 (for the second).*

WHEELWRIGHT (G.) The "Edinburgh Review" and Dr. Strauss. London, 1873. pp. 14.

— Africa, Subsaharan.

CHRISTIANITY in independent Africa; [selected papers from a conference at Jos, Nigeria in 1975] edited by Edward Fasholé-Luke [and others]. London, 1978. pp. 630.

— France.

PHAYER (J. MICHAEL) Sexual liberation and religion in nineteenth century Europe. London, 1977. pp. 176. *bibliog.*

— Germany.

PHAYER (J. MICHAEL) Sexual liberation and religion in nineteenth century Europe. London, 1977. pp. 176. *bibliog.*

— Russia.

LANE (CHRISTEL OLGA) Christian religion in the Soviet Union: a sociological study. London, 1978. pp. 256. *bibliog.*

— Uganda.

PIROUET (M. LOUISE) Black evangelists: the spread of Christianity in Uganda, 1849- 1914. London, 1978. pp. 255. *bibliog.*

CHRISTIANITY AND ECONOMICS.

BEESON (TREVOR) Britain today and tomorrow. [London], 1978. pp. 284.

NANKIVELL (OWEN) All good gifts: a Christian view of the affluent society. London, [1978]. pp. 127.

CHRISTIANITY AND INTERNATIONAL AFFAIRS.

ECCLESTONE (GILES) and ELLIOTT (ERIC) The Irish problem and ourselves. London, [1977]. pp. 25. *bibliog. (Church of England. National Assembly. Board for Social Responsibility. Occasional Papers)*

SMITH (BERNARD) Monday Club member. The fraudulent gospel: politics and the World Council of Churches. Petersham, 1977. pp. 99.

CHRISTIANITY AND POLITICS.

SCIUBBA (ROBERTO) and PACE (ROSSANA SCIUBBA) Le communità di base in Italia. Volume primo: storia e cronaca. Roma, 1976. pp. 115.

HICK (JOHN) The new Nazism of the National Front and National Party: a warning to Christians. Birmingham, 1977. pp. 11.

JOHNSTON (W.B.) Church of Scotland minister, and others. Devolution and the British churches;...report to the spring 1977 assembly of the British Council of Churches. London, 1977. pp. 55.

SMITH (BERNARD) Monday Club member. The fraudulent gospel: politics and the World Council of Churches. Petersham, 1977. pp. 99.

STEHKAEMPER (HUGO) Konrad Adenauer als Katholikentagspräsident, 1922: Form und Grenze politischer Entscheidungsfreiheit im katholischen Raum: (Adenauer-Studien, IV; herausgegeben von Rudolf Morsey und Konrad Repgen). Mainz, [1977]. pp. 124. *bibliog. (Kommission für Zeitgeschichte. Veröffentlichungen. Reihe B: Forschungen. Band 21)*

BEESON (TREVOR) Britain today and tomorrow. [London], 1978. pp. 284.

KEE (ALISTAIR) ed. The scope of political theology. London, 1978. pp. 184. *bibliog.*

MARTIN (DAVID ALFRED) A general theory of secularization. Oxford, [1978]. pp. 353. *bibliog.*

CHRISTIANS IN CHINA.

CHRISTIANS in action: a record of work in war-time China; by seven missionaries. London, 1939. pp. 115. *Editor's preface signed: Ronald Rees.*

CHRONICALLY ILL

— United States — Socioeconomic status.

LUFT (HAROLD S.) Poverty and health: economic causes and consequences of health problems. Cambridge, Mass., [1978]. pp. 263. *bibliog.*

CHUBB AND SON'S LOCK AND SAFE COMPANY.

CHUBB AND SON'S LOCK AND SAFE COMPANY. Contemporary observations on security from the Chubb collectanea, 1818-1968; [edited by] Noel Currer-Briggs. London, [1970?]. 1 vol. (unpaged).

CHURCH AND LABOUR.

ANCEL (ALFRED) La mentalidad obrera. Bilbao, 1960. pp. 63.

ANCEL (ALFRED) El movimiento obrero. Bilbao, 1960. pp. 131.

— Germany.

BRACK (RUDOLF) Deutscher Episkopat und Gewerkschaftsstreit, 1900-1914. Köln, 1976. pp. 448. *bibliog.*

— Italy.

CULTURA cattolica e egemonia operaia; [by] G. Bianchi [and others]. Roma, 1976. pp. 191. *Proceedings of the conference of ACLI held at Bergamo, 1975.*

CHURCH AND RACE PROBLEMS.

RACISM in theology and theology against racism; report of a consultation organized by the Commission on Faith and Order and the Programme To Combat Racism. Geneva, 1975. pp. 21.

CHURCH AND SOCIAL PROBLEMS.

WORLD COUNCIL OF CHURCHES. Population policy, social justice and the quality of life: a report from the World Council of Churches. Geneva, 1973. pp. 12. *(Repr. from Study Encounter. vol. 9., no. 4, 1973)*

CLIFFORD (PAUL ROWNTREE) The death of the dinosaur: towards a co-operative society. London, 1977. pp. 143.

CULLINAN (THOMAS) O.S.B. The roots of social injustice. London, [1977]. pp. 19. *Address delivered at the Voluntary Housing Conference sponsored by the Catholic Housing Aid Society at Nottingham University in 1973.*

NANKIVELL (OWEN) All good gifts: a Christian view of the affluent society. London, [1978]. pp. 127.

— Catholic Church.

MARTI (CASIMIRO) Socializacion: que dice la Iglesia?. Barcelona, [1964]. pp. 51.

O'MAHONY (PATRICK J.) The fantasy of human rights. Great Wakering, Essex, 1978. pp. 192. *bibliog.*

— America, Latin.

CONSELHO EPISCOPAL LATINO-AMERICANO. Presença ativa da Igreja no desenvolvimento e na integração da America Latina: (conclusões da X assembleia extraordinaria do CELAM realizada em Mar del Plata (Argentina) de 11 a 16 de outubro de 1966). Petropolis, 1967. pp. 47. *(Conselho Episcopal Latino-americano. Departamento de Ação Social. Documentos Celam. No. 1)*

— Germany — Catholic Church.

BRAUNS (HEINRICH) Katholische Sozialpolitik im 20. Jahrhundert: ausgewählte Aufsätze und Reden...; bearbeitet von Hubert Mockenhaupt. Mainz, [1976]. pp. 209. *bibliog. (Kommission für Zeitgeschichte. Veröffentlichungen. Reihe A: Quellen. Band 19)*

— Peru — Catholic Church.

KLAIBER (JEFFREY L.) Religion and revolution in Peru, 1824-1976. Notre Dame, Ind., [1977]. pp. 259. *bibliog. (Notre Dame. University. Committee on International Relations. International Studies)*

— United Kingdom.

HOCKING (WILLIAM JOHN) Vicar of All Saints', Tufnell Park. The Church and sanitary progress: the annual sermon of the Church Sanitary Association, preached in All Saints Church, Tufnell Park, London, N., on Sunday morning, August 1, 1897. [London], 1897. pp. 15.

BEESON (TREVOR) Britain today and tomorrow. [London], 1978. pp. 284.

CHURCH AND STATE

— Catholic Church.

DUNN (DENNIS J.) The Catholic church and the Soviet government, 1939-1949. New York, 1977. pp. 267. *bibliog. (East European Quarterly. East European Monographs. 30)*

CHURCH AND STATE IN FRANCE.

SUTTON (MICHAEL JOHN) Nationalism, positivism and Catholicism: a study of the controversy arising from the proposal of Charles Maurras for a political alliance between positivists and Catholics. [1978]. fo.431. *bibliog.* Typescript. 2 pamphlets in end pocket. Ph.D. (London) thesis: unpublished. This thesis is the property of London University and may not be removed from the Library.

CHURCH AND STATE IN GERMANY.

BAUMGAERTNER (RAIMUND) Weltanschauungskampf im Dritten Reich: die Auseinandersetzung der Kirchen mit Alfred Rosenberg. Mainz, [1977]. pp. 272. *bibliog. (Kommission für Zeitgeschichte. Veröffentlichungen. Reihe B: Forschungen. Band 22)*

CHURCH AND STATE IN MALTA.

FENECH (DOMINIC) The making of Archbishop Gonzi. Valletta, 1976. pp. 50.

CHURCH AND STATE IN MEXICO.

OCAMPO (MELCHOR) Obras completas. Mexico, 1900-1901. 3 vols. *Tomo 1: Polemicas religiosas; Tomo 2: Escritos politicos; Tomo 3: Letras y ciencias.*

TORO (ALFONSO) La Iglesia y el Estado en Mexico: estudio sobre los conflictos entre el clero catolico y los gobiernos mexicanos desde la Independencia hasta nuestros dias. Mexico, 1927; 1975. pp. 502. *bibliog. Facsimile reprint.*

CHURCH AND STATE IN PERU.

KLAIBER (JEFFREY L.) Religion and revolution in Peru, 1824-1976. Notre Dame, Ind., [1977]. pp. 259. *bibliog. (Notre Dame. University. Committee on International Relations. International Studies)*

CHURCH AND STATE IN RUSSIA.

DUNN (DENNIS J.) The Catholic church and the Soviet government, 1939-1949. New York, 1977. pp. 267. *bibliog. (East European Quarterly. East European Monographs. 30)*

RÉVÉSZ (LÁSZLÓ) The Christian Peace Conference: human rights and religion in the USSR. London, [1978]. pp. 17. *(Institute for the Study of Conflict. Conflict Studies. No. 91)*

CHURCH AND STATE IN SPAIN.

COOPER (NORMAN B.) Catholicism and the Franco regime. Beverly Hills, [1975]. pp. 48. *bibliog.*

GOMEZ PEREZ (RAFAEL) Politica y religion en el regimen de Franco. Barcelona, 1976. pp. 380.

RUIZ RICO (JUAN JOSE) El papel politico de la Iglesia catolica en la España de Franco, 1936-1971. Madrid, [1977]. pp. 275.

CHURCH AND STATE IN THE UNITED KINGDOM.

UPTON (W. PRESCOTT) The King's Protestant declaration: why it must not be altered. London, 1910. pp. 16. *(Church Association. [Publications]. No. 404)*

MACHIN (GEORGE IAN THOM) Politics and the churches in Great Britain, 1832 to 1868. Oxford, 1977. pp. 438. *bibliog.*

CHURCH HISTORY.

JAY (ERIC G.) The church: its changing image through twenty centuries; volume two, 1700 to the present day. London, 1978. pp. 227. *bibliog.*

— Historiography.

CHADWICK (WILLIAM OWEN) Catholicism and history: the opening of the Vatican archives. Cambridge, 1978. pp. 174. *bibliog. (Oxford. University. Herbert Hensley Henson Lectures. 1976)*

— Primitive and early church.

MALHERBE (ABRAHAM J.) Social aspects of early Christianity. Baton Rouge, [1977]. pp. 98. *(Rice University. Rockwell Lectures on Religion. 1975)*

CHURCH OF ENGLAND

— History.

BENTLEY (JAMES) Ritualism and politics in Victorian Britain: the attempt to legislate for belief. Oxford, 1978. pp. 162. *bibliog.*

GREEN (I.M.) The re-establishment of the Church of England, 1660-1663. Oxford, 1978. pp. 263.

— Liturgy and ritual.

BENTLEY (JAMES) Ritualism and politics in Victorian Britain: the attempt to legislate for belief. Oxford, 1978 pp. 162. *bibliog.*

CHURCH RECORDS AND REGISTERS

— United Kingdom.

LOCAL POPULATION STUDIES and CAMBRIDGE GROUP FOR THE HISTORY OF POPULATION AND SOCIAL STRUCTURE. The first supplement to Original parish registers in record offices and libraries. [Matlock], 1976. pp. 60.

CHURCHILL (Sir WINSTON LEONARD SPENCER).

ROSKILL (STEPHEN WENTWORTH) Churchill and the admirals. London, 1977. pp. 351.

SMITH (ARTHUR LEE) 1927- . Churchill's German army: wartime strategy and cold war politics, 1943-1947. Beverly Hills, [1977]. pp. 158. *bibliog.*

TAYLOR (ALAN JOHN PERCIVALE) The war lords. London, 1977. pp. 189. *Transcripts of six lectures delivered on BBC Television in August 1976.*

CINCINNATI

— History.

CONDIT (CARL WILBUR) The railroad and the city: a technological and urbanistic history of Cincinnati. Columbus, Ohio, [1977]. pp. 335. *bibliog.*

CIPHERS.

LEWIN (RONALD) Ultra goes to war: the secret story. London, 1978. pp. 398. *bibliog.*

CITIES AND TOWNS.

DOXIADES (KONSTANTINOS A.) Ecology and ekistics. Boulder, [1977]. pp. 91.

FISHMAN (ROBERT) Urban utopias in the twentieth century: Ebenezer Howard, Frank Lloyd Wright and Le Corbusier. New York, [1977]. pp. 332. *bibliog.*

HALL (PETER GEOFFREY) The world cities. 2nd ed. London, 1977. pp. 271. *bibliog.*

MEDAM (ALAIN) Conscience de la ville. Paris, 1977. pp. 302.

PUBLIC economics and the quality of life; edited by Lowdon Wingo and Alan Evans. Baltimore, [1977]. pp. 327. *bibliogs. Mainly papers evolved from an International Research Conference on Public Policy and the Quality of Life in Cities, New Orleans, 1975, sponsored by Resources for the Future and the Centre for Environmental Studies.*

SMITH (PETER F.) The syntax of cities. London, 1977. pp. 271. *bibliog.*

CASTELLS (MANUEL) City, class and power; translation supervised by Elizabeth Lebas. London, 1978. pp. 198.

GEOGRAPHY and the urban environment: progress in research and applications; edited by D.T. Herbert and R.J. Johnston. Chichester, [1978]. pp. 363. *bibliogs.*

SYSTEMS of cities: readings on structure, growth, and policy; edited by L.S. Bourne and J.W. Simmons. New York, 1978. pp. 565. *bibliogs.*

TOWNS in societies: essays in economic history and historical sociology; edited by Philip Abrams [and] E.A. Wrigley. Cambridge, 1978. pp. 344. *bibliog. Papers of a Conference held in 1975 by the Past and Present Society, together with articles from Past and Present.*

— Growth.

DARIN-DRABKIN (HAIM) Land policy and urban growth. Oxford, 1977. pp. 442. *bibliog.*

SHAFER (THOMAS W.) Urban growth and economics. Reston, Va., [1977]. pp. 233. *bibliogs.*

— Planning.

See CITY PLANNING.

— America, Latin — Growth.

SINGER (PAUL ISRAEL) Economia politica de la urbanizacion; traduccion de Stella Mastrangelo. Mexico, 1975. pp. 178.

— Australia — Growth.

COMMITTEE OF COMMONWEALTH/STATE OFFICIALS ON DECENTRALISATION [AUSTRALIA]. Report. in AUSTRALIA. Parliament. Parliamentary papers, 1972, vol. 2.

— Brazil — Growth.

BERLINCK (MANOEL T.) Marginalidade social e relações de classes em São Paulo. Petropolis, 1975. pp. 152. *bibliogs.*

— Canada.

The CANADIAN city: essays in urban history; edited by Gilbert A. Stelter and Alan F.J. Artibise. Toronto, [1977]. pp. 452. *bibliog. (Carleton University. Institute of Canadian Studies. Carleton Library. No. 109)*

HIGGINS (DONALD J.H.) Urban Canada: its government and politics. Toronto, [1977]. pp. 322. *bibliog.*

— France — History.

PETIT-DUTAILLIS (CHARLES) The French communes in the middle ages;...translated by Joan Vickers. Amsterdam, 1978. pp. 165.

— India.

MITRA (ASOK) A functional classification of India's towns; [paper presented at the] (All India Seminar on Population, 12-14 March 1964). Delhi, [Controller of Publications, 1974]. pp. 76.

— Italy.

MERCANDINO (CESARE) and MERCANDINO (AUGUSTO) Storia del territorio e delle città d'Italia dal 1800 ai giorni nostri. Milano, [1976]. pp. 394. *bibliog.*

HEERS (JACQUES) Family clans in the middle ages: a study of political and social structures in urban areas. Amsterdam, 1977. pp. 266. *Translated by Barry Herbert.*

— Netherlands.

KNAAP (GIJSBERTUS ADRIANUS VAN DER) A spatial analysis of the evolution of an urban system: the case of the Netherlands. Utrecht, [1978]. pp. 242. *bibliog.*

— Poland.

JANICKA (KRYSTYNA) Ruchliwość międzypokoleniowa i jej korelaty: z badań nad ludnością miejską. Wrocław, 1976. pp. 233.

— — Growth.

SULIMSKI (JERZY) Kraków w procesie przemian: współczesne przeobra'zenia zbiorowości wielkomiejskiej. Kraków, [1976]. pp. 391. *bibliog. With English and Russian summaries.*

CITY PLANNING.

— — History.

CYNALEWSKA (URSZULA) Sytuacja społeczno-ekonomiczna miast wielkopolskich, 1918-1939. Warszawa, 1977. pp. 184. *bibliog. (Poznań (Province). Urząd Wojewódzki. Wydział Kultury i Sztuki. Biblioteka Kroniki Wielkopolski)*

— Romania — Growth.

PROCESUL de urbanizare în România: zona Brașov; coordonatori: Tiberiu Bogdan [and others]. București, 1970. pp. 430. *With English summary.*

— Russia — Buryat Republic.

BUIAEVA (NINA TSYRENBAZAROVNA) Ispol'zovanie trudovykh resursov malykh gorodov i rabochikh poselkov Buriatii. Ulan-Ude, 1969. pp. 44. *bibliog.*

— — Ukraine.

PITIURENKO (IUKHYM IVANOVYCH) Territorial'nye sistemy gorodskikh poselenii Ukrainskoi SSR: metodologiia i metodika issledovaniia, analiz sovremennogo sostoianiia, zakonomernosti i perspektivy razvitiia. Kiev, 1977. pp. 205.

— Senegal — Growth.

KEITA (ROKIATOU N'DIAYE) Kayes et le Haut Sénégal: les étapes de la croissance urbaine. T.1. [Bamako, 1972]. pp. 235.

— United Kingdom.

FIELD (A. MIRYAM) and CROFTS (C.) Some aspects of planned migration to new and expanding towns. London, [1977]. pp. 39. *bibliog. (London. Greater London Council. Research Memoranda. 527)*

ROSE (HILARY) Social welfare and the inner city. [Bradford, 1977?]. pp. 24. *An inaugural lecture delivered at the University of Bradford on 1st February 1977.*

SMITH (BARBARA M.D.) The inner city economic problem: a framework for analysis and local authority policy. Birmingham, 1977. pp. 104, xxii. *(Birmingham. University. Centre for Urban and Regional Studies. Research Memoranda. No. 56)*

— — History.

PATTEN (JOHN) English towns, 1500-1700. [Folkestone, 1978]. pp. 348.

— — Scotland.

ADAMS (IAN HUGH) The making of urban Scotland. Montreal, 1978. pp. 303.

— United States.

PADDOCK (JOHN) Pristine urbanism in Mesoamerica and the forgotten man. Mitla, Mexico, [1973]. pp. 27.

URBAN policymaking and metropolitan dynamics: a comparative geographical analysis; John S. Adams, editor. Cambridge, Mass., [1976]. pp. 576.

GOIST (PARK DIXON) From Main Street to State Street: town, city, and community in America. Port Washington, N.Y., 1977. pp. 180. *bibliog.*

SMALL cities in transition: the dynamics of growth and decline; edited by Herrington J. Bryce. Cambridge, Mass., [1977]. pp. 407. *Based on a forum held by the Joint Center for Political Studies, as part of its Public Policy Program.*

SWANSON (BERT E.) and SWANSON (EDITH) Discovering the community: comparative analysis of social, political, and economic change. New York, [1977]. pp. 391.

WHITE (MORTON GABRIEL) and WHITE (LUCIA) The intellectual versus the city: from Thomas Jefferson to Frank Lloyd Wright. Oxford, 1977. pp. 270.

MARXISM and the metropolis: new perspectives in urban political economy; edited by William K. Tabb and Larry Sawers. New York, 1978. pp. 376. *bibliogs. Based on a conference held in 1975 in New York City by the Union for Radical Political Economics.*

— — Growth — Management.

BURROWS (LAWRENCE B.) Growth management: issues, techniques and policy implications. New Brunswick, N.J., [1978]. pp. 141. *bibliog.*

CITIES AND TOWNS, ANCIENT.

THEMES de recherches sur les villes antiques d'occident; (actes du colloque international, Strasbourg, 1er-4 octobre, 1971). Paris, 1977. pp. 429. *(Centre National de la Recherche Scientifique. Colloques Internationaux. No. 542) In French, English, Italian or German.*

CITIES AND TOWNS, MEDIEVAL.

The MEDIEVAL city: ([essays] in honor of Robert S. Lopez) ; edited by Harry A. Miskimin [and others]. New Haven, 1977. pp. 345. *bibliog.*

CITIES AND TOWNS IN LITERATURE.

GOIST (PARK DIXON) From Main Street to State Street: town, city, and community in America. Port Washington, N.Y., 1977. pp. 180. *bibliog.*

CITIZENS' ASSOCIATIONS

— United States.

RODGERS (JOSEPH LEE) Citizen committees: a guide to their use in local government. Cambridge, Mass., [1977]. pp. 101. *bibliog.*

CITIZENSHIP

— United Kingdom.

DUMMETT (ANN) British nationality and the colonies. London, [1977]. fo. 10. *(Runnymede Trust. Briefing Papers. 1977, No. 7)*

— — Commonwealth.

DUMMETT (ANN) British nationality and the colonies. London, [1977]. fo. 10. *(Runnymede Trust. Briefing Papers. 1977, No. 7)*

CITIZENSHIP, LOSS OF

— Germany, Eastern.

EXIL: die Ausbürgerung Wolf Biermanns aus der DDR; eine Dokumentation, herausgegeben von Peter Roos. Köln, [1977]. pp. 319.

CITRUS FRUITS

— Australia.

AUSTRALIA. Bureau of Agricultural Economics. 1977. Australian citrus industry: B[ureau of] A[gricultural] E[conomics] submission to Industries Assistance Commission inquiry. Canberra, 1977. pp. 136. *(Industry Economics Monographs. No. 18)*

CITY CHILDREN.

GROWING up in cities: studies of the spatial environment of adolescence in Cracow, Melbourne, Mexico City, Salta, Toluca, and Warszawa; edited by Kevin Lynch from the reports of Tridib Banerjee [and others]. Paris, UNESCO, [1977]. pp. 177. *bibliog.*

WARD (COLIN) The child in the city. London, 1978. pp. 221. *bibliog.*

CITY PLANNING.

COBDEN-SANDERSON (THOMAS JAMES) The city planned. [London], 1911. pp. (3). *(Reprinted from the Westminster Gazette, 27 October 1910)*

BERRY (BRIAN JOE LOBLEY) Geography of market centers and retail distribution. Englewood Cliffs, [1967]. pp. 145.

UNITED NATIONS. Interregional Seminar on Development Policies and Planning in Relation to Urbanization, Pittsburgh, 1966. Report of the...seminar...Pittsburgh, Pennsylvania, 24 October to 4 November, 1966. (ST/TAO/SER.C/97). New York, 1967. pp. 74.

GANS (HERBERT J.) People and plans: essays on urban problems and solutions. New York, [1968]. pp. 395.

INTERREGIONAL SEMINAR ON THE FINANCING OF HOUSING AND URBAN DEVELOPMENT, COPENHAGEN, 1970. Report of the...Seminar...[held in] Copenhagen, 25 May to 10 June 1970. (ST/TAO/SER.C/134). New York, United Nations, 1972. pp. 94.

PERÉNYI (IMRE) Town centres: planning and renewal; (translated by K. Nagy). Budapest, 1973. pp. 199. *bibliog.*

DARIN-DRABKIN (HAIM) Land policy and urban growth. Oxford, 1977. pp. 442. *bibliog.*

FISHMAN (ROBERT) Urban utopias in the twentieth century: Ebenezer Howard, Frank Lloyd Wright and Le Corbusier. New York, [1977]. pp. 332. *bibliog.*

LOODMER (PATRICIA SIMONE) A geographical investigation of the social justice content of urban planning decisions, with special reference to the displacement of the population of St. Ebbe's Parish, Oxford, 1951-1961. [1977]. fo. 392. *Typescript. Ph. D. (London) thesis: unpublished. This thesis is the property of London University and may not be removed from the Library.*

MARKUSEN (JAMES R.) and SCHEFFMAN (DAVID T.) Speculation and monopoly in urban development: analytical foundations with evidence for Toronto. Toronto, [1977]. pp. 165. *bibliog. (Ontario. Economic Council. Research Studies. 10)*

PLANNING in turbulent environments; [edited by] John S. Western [and] Paul R. Wilson. St. Lucia, Queensland, 1977. pp. 206. *bibliogs.*

SMITH (PETER F.) The syntax of cities. London, 1977. pp. 271. *bibliog.*

UNITED NATIONS. Department of Economic and Social Affairs. 1977. Threshold analysis handbook. (ST/ESA/64). New York, 1977. pp. 167,48. *bibliog.*

GEOGRAPHY and the urban environment: progress in research and applications; edited by D.T. Herbert and R.J. Johnston. Chichester, [1978]. pp. 363. *bibliogs.*

ISSUES in urban society; edited by Ross Davies and Peter Hall. Harmondsworth, 1978. pp. 299. *bibliogs.*

POCOCK (DOUGLAS CHARLES DAVID) and HUDSON (RAY) Images of the urban environment. London, 1978. pp. 181. *bibliog.*

STRETTON (HUGH) Urban planning in rich and poor countries. Oxford, 1978. pp. 220. *bibliog.*

— Abstracts.

URBAN ABSTRACTS; (compiled in the Research Library of the Greater London Council). m., Ap 1974 (no.1)- London. *Supersedes Planning and transportation abstracts (Ag 1970 - F/Mr 1974, with gap)*

— Bibliography.

U.K. Department of the Environment. Library. 1976. New towns;...revised and index prepared by Pamela Johnstone. rev. ed. [London], 1976. pp. 406. *(Bibliographies. No. 65)*

SUTCLIFFE (ANTHONY) compiler. A history of modern town planning: a bibliographical guide. Birmingham, 1977. pp. 112. *(Birmingham. University. Centre for Urban and Regional Studies. Research Memoranda. No. 57)*

— Congresses.

INTERREGIONAL SEMINAR ON PHYSICAL PLANNING FOR URBAN, REGIONAL AND NATIONAL DEVELOPMENT, BUCHAREST, 1969. Report of the...Seminar...[held in] Bucharest, Romania 22 September to 7 October 1969. (ST/TAO/SER.C/132). New York, United Nations, 1971. pp. 43.

— Study and teaching.

FALUDI (ANDREAS K.F.) Essays on planning theory and education. Oxford, 1978. pp. 183. *bibliogs.*

CITY PLANNING.(Cont.)

— America, Latin.

ASENTAMIENTOS humanos, urbanismo y vivienda: cometido del poder publico en la segunda mitad del siglo XX; [by] Jesus Silva- Herzog Flores [and others]. Mexico, 1977. pp. 788.

— Australia.

AUSTRALIA. Department of Urban and Regional Development. Annual report. a., 1972/73(1st)- Canberra. *Included in* AUSTRALIA. Parliament. *[Parliamentary papers].*

MAUNSELL (G.) AND PARTNERS. New structures for Australian cities: main report. [Canberra], Cities Commission, 1975. pp. 205.

— Canada — British Columbia.

LOWER MAINLAND REGIONAL PLANNING BOARD OF BRITISH COLUMBIA. Land for living: the outlook for residential development in the lower mainland. New Westminster, 1963. pp. 32.

— — Ontario.

BOSSONS (JOHN) Reforming planning in Ontario: strengthening the municipal role. [Toronto, 1978]. pp. 231. *(Ontario. Economic Council. Discussion Paper Series)*

— — Quebec.

MARTIN (F.) La dynamique du développement urbain au Québec; [annexe du rapport sur l'urbanisation]. [Québec, Editeur officiel, 1976]. pp. 84. *bibliog.*

— France.

MAGNAN (RENE) and DRYJSKI (DOMINIQUE) Archipoles. [Paris, 1970]. pp. 93.

BUTLER (RÉMY) and NOISETTE (PATRICE) De la cité ouvrière au grand ensemble: la politique capitaliste du logement social, 1815-1975. Paris, 1977. pp. 193.

LOJKINE (JEAN) Le marxisme, l'état et la question urbaine. [Paris, 1977]. pp. 362.

BERTRAND (MICHEL JEAN) Pratique de la ville. Paris, 1978. pp. 212.

— Italy.

MARIANI (RICCARDO) Fascismo e "città nuove". Milano, 1976. pp. 340. *bibliog.*

— New Zealand.

HAIGH (DAVID IAN) and GAVIN (DAVID CHARLES) Social planning for new communities in Auckland: a discussion document. [Auckland, Auckland Regional Authority], 1977. fo. 54. *bibliog.*

— Russia.

LITOVKA (OLEG PETROVICH) Problemy prostranstvennogo razvitiia urbanizatsii. Leningrad, 1976. pp. 99.

— South Africa.

BROWETT (J.G.) Required and available data for town and regional planning in South Africa. Johannesburg, 1975. fo. 19. *bibliog. (Johannesburg. University of the Witwatersrand. Urban and Regional Research Unit. Occasional Papers. No. 8)*

— Underdeveloped areas.

See UNDERDEVELOPED AREAS — City planning.

— United Kingdom.

EDEN (GEORGE RODNEY) Bishop of Wakefield. Memorandum on the preparation of town planning schemes in anticipation of future developments. [London, 1917?]. pp. 3. *(National Housing and Town Planning Council. Reports and proceedings, 1916-1917)*

LABOUR PARTY. Advisory Committee on Local Government. Sub- Committee on Town Planning. Minutes, March 26th, 1920. [London, 1920]. 6 pts.

ENVIRONMENTAL BOARD [U.K.]. Sub Group on Older Areas. Interim report; [A.A. Wood, chairman]. [London, Department of the Environment], 1976. 1 vol. (unpaged).

FINLAYSON (JAMES) Urban devastation: the planning of incarceration. Oxford, [1976]. pp. 25. *(Solidarity (Oxford). Pamphlets. No. 2)*

PEOPLE and their settlements: aspects of housing, transport and strategic planning in the U.K.; papers for a conference held in London in January 1976, organised by the National Council of Social Service...as a contribution to the NGO Forum on Habitat, Vancouver, June 1976. London, [1976]. pp. 107.

U.K. Department of the Environment. 1976. Planning in the United Kingdom: national report (to Habitat: United Nations Conference on Human Settlements, Vancouver, 1976). London, [1976]. pp. 124. *bibliog.*

MANGAN (STEPHEN PAUL) Local housing and planning policies: a study of the south coast of England, 1961-1971. 1977. fo. 372. *bibliog.* Typescript. Ph. D. (London) thesis: unpublished. This thesis is the property of London University and may not be removed from the Library.

CHAPMAN (SYDNEY) Conservative. Town and countryside: future planning policies for Britain. London, 1978. pp. 37. *(Conservative Political Centre. [Publications]. No. 619)*

DOBBY (ALAN) Conservation and planning. London, 1978. pp. 173.

POUNTNEY (MELVILLE TREVOR) Planning and the concept of community: a brief assessment of the theory of community and the practice of community building in the setting of Washington New Town. Watford, [1978]. pp. 26. *(Building Research Establishment [U.K.]. Current Papers. 78/2).*

— — Bibliography.

U.K. Department of the Environment. Library. 1976. New towns;...revised and index prepared by Pamela Johnstone. rev. ed. [London], 1976. pp. 406. *(Bibliographies. No. 65)*

LAMBERT (CLAIRE M.) compiler. Structure and local plan documents. [2nd ed.]. [London, 1977]. pp. 107. *(U.K. Department of the Environment. Library. Bibliographies. No. 152A)*

U.K. Department of the Environment. 1978. Town and country planning: development plans, development control and associated matters, including community land scheme and land transactions: index to departmental circulars and other relevant publications as at 15 May 1978. London, 1978. 1 pamphlet (unpaged).

— — Citizen participation.

PLANNING EXCHANGE. Development control procedures and inquiries: a discussion paper. Glasgow, [1975]. pp. 27.

STRINGER (PETER) The press and publicity for public participation. [London], 1977. pp. 24. *(Linked Research Project into Public Participation in Structure Planning. Interim Research Papers. 12)*

— — Scotland.

SCOTLAND. Scottish Development Department. 1972. New Towns, Scotland, Act, 1968: draft new town, Stonehouse, designation order, 1972: memorandum by the Secretary of State for Scotland. Edinburgh, [1972]. pp. 15.

— — Wales.

DUMBLETON (BOB) The second blitz: the demolition and rebuilding of town centres in South Wales. Cardiff, [1977]. pp. 56.

— United States.

CITIZEN preferences and urban public policy: models, measures, uses; edited by Terry Nichols Clark. Beverly Hills, 1976. pp. 142. *Based on papers presented at a meeting of the Public Choice Society, Chicago, 1975, on Preference revelation for public goods.*

PLANNING the fourth migration: the neglected vision of the Regional Planning Association of America; edited by Carl Sussman. Cambridge, Mass., [1976]. pp. 277. *bibliogs.*

GILBERT (NEIL) and SPECHT (HARRY) Dynamics of community planning. Cambridge, Mass., [1977]. pp. 183.

BURROWS (LAWRENCE B.) Growth management: issues, techniques and policy implications. New Brunswick, N.J., [1978]. pp. 141. *bibliog.*

KAISER (HARVEY H.) The building of cities: development and conflict. Ithaca, [1978]. pp. 217.

PERSONALITY, politics, and planning: how city planners work; edited by Anthony James Catanese and W. Paul Farmer. Beverly Hills, [1978]. pp. 225.

URBAN planning for arid zones: American experiences and directions; Gideon Golany, editor. New York, [1978]. pp. 245.

— Venezuela.

APPLEYARD (DONALD) Planning a pluralist city: conflicting realities in Ciudad Guayana. Cambridge, Mass., [1975]. pp. 312. *bibliog. (Massachusetts Institute of Technology and Harvard University. Joint Center for Urban Studies. Publications)*

ROJAS (JOSE CUPERTINO) Litoral central: localizacion geografica de actividades urbanas. Caracas, 1976. pp. 309. *bibliog.*

CITY PLANNING AND REDEVELOPMENT LAW

— Russia.

EROFEEV (BORIS VLADIMIROVICH) Pravovoi rezhim zemel' gorodov. Moskva, 1976. pp. 200.

— United Kingdom.

HEAP (Sir DESMOND) An outline of planning law. 7th ed. London, 1978. pp. 344.

— United States.

AMERICAN BAR ASSOCIATION. Advisory Commission on Housing and Urban Growth. Housing for all under law: new directions in housing, land use and planning law...; edited by Richard P. Fishman. Cambridge, Mass., [1978]. pp. 635.

CITY PLANNING AND THE PRESS.

STRINGER (PETER) The press and publicity for public participation. [London], 1977. pp. 24. *(Linked Research Project into Public Participation in Structure Planning. Interim Research Papers. 12)*

CITY TRAFFIC.

MAGNAN (RENE) Equipements et déplacements urbains. [Paris, 1969]. pp. 65.

TAEBEL (DELBERT A.) and CORNEHLS (JAMES V.) The political economy of urban transportation. Port Washington, N.Y., 1977. pp. 218. *bibliog.*

CIUDAD GUAYANA

— City planning.

APPLEYARD (DONALD) Planning a pluralist city: conflicting realities in Ciudad Guayana. Cambridge, Mass., [1975]. pp. 312. *bibliog. (Massachusetts Institute of Technology and Harvard University. Joint Center for Urban Studies. Publications)*

CIVICS, AMERICAN.

DEMING (HORACE EDWARD) Public service by citizens in private station. 2nd ed. [Philadelphia], 1904. pp. 14. *(National Municipal League. Leaflets. No. 6)*

CIVICS, RUSSIAN.

BEZUGLOV (ANATOLII ALEKSEEVICH) Suverenitet sovetskogo naroda. Moskva, 1975. pp. 199.

KOREL'SKII (VIKTOR MIKHAILOVICH) Demokratiia i distsiplina v razvitom sotsialističeskom obshchestve. Moskva, 1977. pp. 136.

CIVIL ENGINEERING

— Canada.

CANADA. Statistics Canada. Heavy engineering contracting industry. a., 1975(1st)- Ottawa. *[in English and French]*

CIVIL LAW

— Luxembourg.

LUXEMBOURG. Statutes, etc. 1803-1975. Code civil en vigeur dans le Grand-Duché de Luxembourg annoté d'après la jurisprudence luxembourgeoise; mise à jour, législation jusqu'au 31 décembre 1975, etc. [Luxembourg, 1975]. 1 vol. (looseleaf).

— Poland.

POLAND. Statutes, etc. 1910. Grazhdanskie zakony Tsarstva Pol'skogo; s ob"iasneniiami po resheniiam Pravitel'stvuiushchego Senata so vsemi pozdneishimi izmeneniiami i dopolneniiami po 1910 g., sostavleno pod redaktsiei Nikolaia Sandlera. Varshava, [1910?]. pp. 592.

— Romania.

MIHUȚĂ (IOAN G.) Repertoriu de practică judiciară în materie civilă a Tribunalului Suprem și a altor instanțe judecătorești pe anii 1969-1975. București, 1976. pp. 430.

— Russia.

RUSSIA (RSFSR). Statutes, etc. 1927. Grazhdanskii kodeks Sovetskikh Respublik: tekst i prakticheskii kommentarii pod redaktsiei Al. Malitskogo. 3rd ed. [Khar'kov], 1927. pp. 774.

— — Ukraine.

RUSSIA (RSFSR). Statutes, etc. 1927. Grazhdanskii kodeks Sovetskikh Respublik: tekst i prakticheskii kommentarii pod redaktsiei Al. Malitskogo. 3rd ed. [Khar'kov], 1927. pp. 774.

CIVIL PROCEDURE

— Russia.

KOMMENTARII sudebnoi praktiki za 1974 god. Moskva, 1975. pp. 167. *Previous years have title Nauchnyi kommentarii sudebnoi praktiki, etc.*

— — Tajikistan.

TAJIKISTAN. Statutes, etc. 1959-1974. Sobranie deistvuiushchego zakonodatel'stva Tadzhikskoi SSR. razdel 28-29. Dushanbe, 1975. pp. 602.

TAJIKISTAN. Statutes, etc. 1975. Grazhdanskii protsessual'nyi kodeks Tadzhikskoi SSR: s izmeneniiami i dopolneniiami na 1 iiulia 1975 goda. Dushanbe, 1975. pp. 211.

— — White Russia.

TIKHINIA (VALERII GUR'EVICH) Primenenie kriminalisticheskoi taktiki v grazhdanskom protsesse: pri issledovanii veshchestvennykh dokazatel'stv. Minsk, 1976. pp. 159.

— United Kingdom.

BARNARD (DAVID NOWELL) The civil court in action. London, 1977. pp. 290.

CIVIL RIGHTS.

FERRARI (LEO C.) Human rights in a changing world; the problem of preserving human values in the upheavals caused by science and technology. Fredericton, New Brunswick Human Rights Commission, 1975. pp. 112.

LUCE (RICHARD) and RANELAGH (JOHN) Human rights and foreign policy. London, 1977. pp. 31. *(Conservative Political Centre. [Publications]. No. 614)*

SMALL comforts for hard times: humanists on public policy; Michael Mooney and Florian Stuber, editors. New York, 1977. pp. 402. *Papers from a conference series conducted under the auspices of Columbia's program of University Seminars.*

HUMAN rights; edited by Eugene Kamenka and Alice Erh-Soon Tay. [London, 1978]. pp. 148. *Based on a human rights symposium and a special working session on human rights held as part of the World Congress of the International Association for Philosophy of Law and Social Philosophy in Sydney and Canberra in 1977.*

OWEN (DAVID) Human rights. London, 1978. pp. 154.

— Bibliography.

DWORACZEK (MARIAN) compiler. Human rights: government documents held in the Research Library. 2nd ed. [Toronto], 1975. pp. 61. *(Ontario. Ministry of Labour. Research Library. Bibliography Series. No. 1)*

— Africa, East.

HUMAN rights in a one-party state: international seminar on human rights, their protection and the rule of law in a one-party state; convened by the International Commission of Jurists. London, 1978. pp. 133.

— Brazil.

RUSSELL TRIBUNAL II ON REPRESSION IN BRAZIL, CHILE AND LATIN AMERICA. The Bertrand Russell Tribunal on Brazil and Repression in Latin America; sponsored by the Bertrand Russell Peace Foundation. Nottingham, [1973]. pp. 43. *Reprint of first 3 issues of the Tribunal Bulletin.*

— Canada — Manitoba.

MANITOBA. Human Rights Commission. Annual report. a., 1974- Winnipeg.

MANITOBA. Law Reform Commission. 1976. Report on the case for a provincial bill of rights. [Winnipeg], 1976. pp. 66. *(Reports. 25)*

— — Nova Scotia.

NOVA SCOTIA. Statutes, etc. 1969. Nova Scotia Human Rights Act, 1969. Halifax, [1969?]. pp. 18.

NOVA SCOTIA. Human Rights Commission. Summary of activities. a., 1974- Halifax.

— — Ontario.

ONTARIO. Human Rights Commission. 1967. Human rights in Ontario. [Toronto, 1967]. pp. 16.

ONTARIO. Statutes, etc. 1961-67. The Ontario Human Rights Code, 1961-62...as amended by 1965, Chapter 85 and 1967, Chapter 66. Toronto, 1967. 1 pamphlet (unpaged).

— — Saskatchewan.

SASKATCHEWAN. Human Rights Commission. 1975. Report and summary of activities, November, 1972 to March 31, 1975. Regina, 1975. pp. 20.

— Communist countries.

EVERYDAY hazards under communist law. [London?], 1955. pp. 19.

— Czechoslovakia.

SLOVAK ACTION COMMITTEE. Demande addressée à l'Assemblée Générale des Nations Unies concernant la situation en Slovaquie et l'organisation d'un plébiscite dans ce pays. [New York, 1948?]. pp. (4).

— Europe.

EUROPEAN COMMISSION OF HUMAN RIGHTS. Decisions and reports. s-a., Jl 1975 (no.1)- Strasbourg. *[in English and French] Supersedes EUROPEAN COMMISSION OF HUMAN RIGHTS. Collection of decisions.*

EUROPEAN COMMISSION OF HUMAN RIGHTS. 1976. European Convention on Human Rights: collected texts. 11th ed. Strasbourg, Council of Europe, 1976. 1 vol. (various pagings). *In English and French.*

— France.

GUILBERT (FRANÇOISE) Liberté individuelle et hospitalisation de malades mentaux. Paris, 1974. pp. 381. *bibliog.*

— Italy.

ANTONICELLI (FRANCO) La pratica della libertà: documenti, discorsi, scritti politici, 1929-1974. Torino, 1976. pp. 257.

— Netherlands.

EUROPEAN COURT OF HUMAN RIGHTS. Publications. Series A: Judgments and Decisions. [A22]. ...Case of Engel and others. 1. Decision of 1 October 1975. 2. Judgment of 8 June 1976. 3. Judgment of 23 November 1976. Strasbourg, Council of Europe, 1977. pp. 71 [bis]. *In English and French.*

— Poland.

ASSOCIATION OF POLISH STUDENTS AND GRADUATES IN EXILE. Dissent in Poland: reports and documents in translation, December 1975-July 1977. London, [1977]. pp. 200.

RUCH oporu: Komitet Obrony Robotników; O powołanie komisji sejmowej; Za'zalenia i szykany; Kościół; Na Zachodzie; O naprawie Rzeczypospolitej; Sąsiedzi (Czechosłowacja); Ró'zne. Pary'z, 1977. pp. 285.

— Puerto Rico.

REVISTA DE DERECHOS HUMANOS: publicacion de la Comision de Derechos Civiles del Estado Libre Asociado de Puerto Rico. 3 a yr., Oc 1972- F/Je 1974 (v.3, no.1.-v.4, no. 2/3); ceased pbln. San Juan.

— Russia.

NATIONALISM and human rights: processes of modernization in the USSR; edited by Ihor Kamenetsky. Littleton, Colo., [1977]. pp. 243. *bibliog. (Association for the Study of the Nationalities (USSR and East Europe). Series in Issues Studies (USSR and East Europe). No. 1)*

RÉVÉSZ (LÁSZLÓ) Menschenrechte in der UdSSR. Bern, [1977]. pp. 320. *(Schweizerisches Ost-Institut. Tatsachen und Meinungen. TM 38)*

— — Estonia.

ESTONIAN INFORMATION CENTRE. Problems of the Baltic. 4. Documents from Estonia on the violation of human rights. Stockholm, 1977. pp. 72.

— — Lithuania.

LITHUANIAN CANADIAN COMMUNITY. The violations of human rights in Soviet occupied Lithuania: a report for 1974. [Toronto], 1975. pp. 112.

— Underdeveloped areas.

See UNDERDEVELOPED AREAS — Civil rights.

— United Kingdom.

LUCE (RICHARD) and RANELAGH (JOHN) Human rights and foreign policy. London, 1977. pp. 31. *(Conservative Political Centre. [Publications]. No. 614)*

STREET (HARRY) Freedom, the individual and the law. 4th ed. Harmondsworth, 1977. pp. 346.

CIVIL RIGHTS.(Cont.)

ANDERSON (Sir JAMES NORMAN DALRYMPLE) Liberty, law and justice. London, 1978. pp. 140. *(Hamlyn Lectures. 30th Series)*

NATIONAL COUNCIL FOR CIVIL LIBERTIES. Civil liberty: the NCCL guide to your rights; [edited by] Lawrence Grant [and others]. 3rd ed. Harmondsworth, 1978. pp. 618.

— United States.

NEWMAN (EDWIN STANLEY) ed. The freedom reader: a collection of materials on civil rights and civil liberties in America, etc. New York, 1955. pp. 256. *bibliog.*

CIVIL liberties and civil rights: edited...by Victor J. Stone. Urbana, [1977]. pp. 144. *bibliogs. (Illinois University. College of Law. David C. Baum Memorial Lectures on Civil Liberties and Civil Rights)*

LEBLANC (LAWRENCE J.) The OAS and the promotion and protection of human rights. The Hague, 1977. pp. 179.

SOCIAL justice and preferential treatment: women and racial minorities in education and business; edited by William T. Blackstone and Robert D. Heslep. Athens, Ga., [1977]. pp. 216. *bibliog. Papers presented at a conference held at the University of Georgia, February 13-15, 1975, and sponsored by that university's Dept. of Philosophy and Religion and Dept. of History and Philosophy of Education, together with the Georgia State Committee for the Humanities.*

McAULIFFE (MARY SPERLING) Crisis on the left: cold war politics and American liberals, 1947-1954. Amherst, 1978. pp. 204. *bibliog.*

CIVIL RIGHTS (INTERNATIONAL LAW).

SOHN (LOUIS BRUNO) and BUERGENTHAL (THOMAS) International protection of human rights. Indianapolis, [1973]. 2 vols. *With supplement: Basic documents, etc.*

CIVIL SERVICE

— Algeria.

REVIEW DE LA FONCTION PUBLIQUE, LA; ([pd. by] Direction de la Fonction Publique, Ministère de l'Intérieur, République Algérienne Démocratique et Populaire). q., 1966- Alger.

— France.

GALY (PHILIPPE) Gérer l'État: corriger la déviation bureaucratique. [Paris, 1977]. pp. vii, 241. *bibliog.*

PIQUEMAL (MARCEL) Les agents de l'Etat. [Paris, 1977]. pp. 128. *bibliog.*

— India.

INDIA. Administrative Reforms Wing. Report. a., 1973/74-1974/75. New Delhi. *From 1975/76 included in INDIA. Department of Personnel and Administrative Reforms. Report.*

INDIA. Department of Personnel and Administrative Reforms. Report. a., 1975/76- New Delhi. *File includes Supplement, 1976/77. From 1975/76 file includes report of Administrative Reforms Wing.*

SPANGENBERG (BRADFORD) British bureaucracy in India: status, policy and the I.C.S., in the late 19th century. Columbia, Mo., 1976. pp. 380. *bibliog.*

— Italy.

Il SERVIZIO civile in Italia: esperienze di alcuni collettivi di obiettori; a cura del Collettivo Obiettori in Servizio Civile a Vicenza. [Roma, 1976]. pp. 128. *bibliog.*

— Kenya.

JOURNAL OF THE KENYA INSTITUTE OF ADMINISTRATION, THE. irreg., D 1965 (no.1)- Lower Kabete. *no.1 entitled Administration in Kenya.*

— Nigeria.

ATTA (ABDUL AZIZI) The role of the civil service in the development process; a paper presented by Abdul Attah, Secretary to the Federal Military Government at the economic development plan seminar held in March, 1971 at the Nigerian Institute of International Affairs, Victoria Island, Lagos. [Lagos, 1971]. pp. 20.

— Rhodesia.

SOUTHERN RHODESIA. Commissioner appointed to Enquire into the Administrative System and Methods of the Government of Southern Rhodesia. 1936. Report; (by Alexander Glen). [Salisbury], 1936. pp. 17. *(Legislative Assembly. [Sessional Papers]. 1936. C.S.R. 1)*

— Sri Lanka.

WARNAPALA (W.A. WISWA) Civil service administration in Ceylon: a study in bureaucratic adaptation. [Colombo, Department of Cultural Affairs, 1974]. pp. 411. *bibliog.*

— Sudan.

AHMED (RAFIA HASSAN) Critical appraisal to the role of the Public Service Commission in the Sudan, 1954-1969. Khartoum, 1974. pp. 52. *bibliog.*

— United Kingdom.

CSD MANPOWER PLANNING NEWSLETTER; [pd. by Civil Service Department, U.K.]. s-a., Ja 1974 (no.1)- London.

LEE (JOHN MICHAEL) Reviewing the machinery of government 1942-1952: an essay on the Anderson Committee and its successors. n.p., 1977. pp. 176.

CHAPMAN (LESLIE) Your disobedient servant. London, 1978. pp. 206.

— — Study and teaching.

LINDLEY (P.D.) A short account of the administrative processes which led to the setting up of the Civil Service College. [rev. ed.] [London, Civil Service College, 1973]. pp. 30. *bibliog.*

U.K. Civil Service Department. Personnel Management (Training) Division. 1973. Review of civil service training: the history of civil service training; memorandum. [London], 1973. 1 pamphlet (various foliations).

U.K. National Council for the Administrative and Legal Departments of the Civil Service. Joint Committee on Training. Joint Review Sub-Committee. 1975. First report of the Joint Review Sub-Committee set up to consider the report on the review of civil service training by R.N. Heaton and Sir Leslie Williams. London, 1975. 1 pamphlet (unpaged).

U.K. National Council for the Administrative and Legal Departments of the Civil Service. Joint Committee on Training. Joint Review Sub-Committee. 1976. Final report of the Joint Review Sub-Committee set up to consider the report on the review of civil service training by R.N. Heaton and Sir Leslie Williams. London, 1976. pp. 6.

— United States.

BALZANO (MICHAEL P.) Reorganizing the federal bureaucracy: the rhetoric and the reality. Washington, [1977]. pp. 43. *(American Enterprise Institute for Public Policy Research. AEI Studies. 165)*

ROSENBLOOM (DAVID H.) Federal equal employment opportunity: politics and public personnel administration. New York, 1977. pp. 184. *bibliog.*

— Zaire.

MPINGA-KASENDA. L'administration publique du Zaïre: l'impact du milieu socio- politique sur sa structure et son fonctionnement. Paris, [1973]. pp. 316. *bibliog. (Bordeaux. Université. Centre d'Etude d'Afrique Noire. Bibliothèque. Série Afrique Noire. 3)*

CIVIL SERVICE PENSIONS

— Bangladesh.

BANGLADESH. Finance Department. Implementation Unit. 1966. Revision of pension rules and rates. Dacca, 1966. pp. 10.

— Colombia.

ESCALANTE MARTINEZ (FERNANDO) La pension de jubilacion de los empleados oficiales. Bogota, 1972. pp. 87. *bibliog.*

— New Zealand.

NEW ZEALAND. Government Superannuation Board. 1970. Government Superannuation Fund: actuarial examination as at 31 March 1964. Wellington, 1970. pp. 10.

— Rhodesia.

MACPHAIL AND FRASER, Consulting Actuaries. Report...on the valuation of the Southern Rhodesia Pension Fund as at 31st March, 1935. Salisbury, 1937. pp. 20. *(Southern Rhodesia. Legislative Assembly. [Sessional Papers]. 1937. C.S.R.1)*

— United Kingdom.

U.K. Civil Service Department. 1971. Allocation of pension: explanatory memorandum, rules, tables prepared by the Government Actuary: for female retiring officers. London, 1971. pp. 23. *(Booklets. A.P. (F))*

U.K. Civil Service Department. 1971. Allocation of pension: explanatory memorandum, rules, tables prepared by the Government Actuary: for male retiring officers. London, 1971. pp. 29. *(Booklets. A.P. (M))*

U.K. Civil Service Department. 1972. Allocation of pension: explanatory memorandum, rules, tables prepared by the Government Actuary: for pensioners. London, 1972. pp. 26. *(Booklets. A.P.(P))*

— — Scotland.

U.K. Government Actuary's Department. 1977. National Health Service, Scotland, Act, 1947: National Health Service Superannuation Scheme for Scotland, 1969- 1974; report by the Government Actuary. Edinburgh, 1977. pp. 24.

CIVIL SUPREMACY OVER THE MILITARY.

JANOWITZ (MORRIS) Military institutions and coercion in the developing nations. Chicago, 1977. pp. 211. *Expanded edition of The military in the political development of new nations.*

— Israel.

PERLMUTTER (AMOS) Politics and the military in Israel, 1967-1977. London, 1978. pp. 222.

— Russia.

DEANE (MICHAEL J.) Political control of the Soviet armed forces. London, [1977]. pp. 297.

CIVILIAN DEFENCE

— Europe.

INTERNATIONAL WORKING CONFERENCE ON VIOLENCE AND NON-VIOLENT ACTION IN INDUSTRIALIZED SOCIETIES, 2ND, BRUSSELS, 1976. Possibilities of civilian defence in western Europe; edited by Gustaaf Geeraerts. Amsterdam, 1977. pp. 172. *(Vrije Universiteit Brussel. Polemological Centre. Publications. vol. 6)*

CIVILIZATION.

WICKSTEED (PHILIP HENRY) [Review of Brooks Adams' Law of civilization and decay]. London, [1902]. pp. 29-33. *(From The Nationalist, No. 3)*

HUXLEY (ALDOUS LEONARD) The human situation: lectures at Santa Barbara, 1959; edited by Piero Ferrucci. London, [1977]. pp. 261.

— History.

HISTOIRE des idéologies; sous la direction de François Châtelet et Gérard Mairet. [Paris, 1978]. 3 vols. *bibliog.*

CIVILIZATION, ARAB.

LAROUI (ABDALLAH) The crisis of the Arab intellectual: traditionalism or historicism?;...translated from the French by Diarmid Cammell. Berkeley, Calif., [1976]. pp. 180.

CIVILIZATION, MODERN.

DUPUY (JEAN PIERRE) and ROBERT (JEAN) La trahison de l'opulence. [Paris, 1976]. pp. 256. *bibliog.*

BUCHANAN (GEORGE) Novelist. The politics of culture. London, 1977. pp. 54.

CLIFFORD (PAUL ROWNTREE) The death of the dinosaur: towards a co-operative society. London, 1977. pp. 143.

CULLINAN (THOMAS) O.S.B. The roots of social injustice. London, [1977]. pp. 19. *Address delivered at the Voluntary Housing Conference sponsored by the Catholic Housing Aid Society at Nottingham University in 1973.*

GOLDMAN (LUCIEN) Cultural creation in modern society; introduction by William Mayrl; translated by Bart Grahl, etc. Oxford, 1977. pp. 173. *bibliog.*

OGILVY (JAMES) Many dimensional man: decentralizing self, society and the sacred. New York, 1977. pp. 371.

BALLARD (EDWARD GOODWIN) Man and technology: toward the measurement of a culture. Pittsburgh, [1978]. pp. 251.

HAYEK (FRIEDRICH AUGUST) The three sources of human values. London, 1978. pp. 40. *(London. University. London School of Economics and Political Science. Hobhouse Memorial Trust Lectures. No. 44)*

HIGGINS (RONALD) The seventh enemy: the human factor in the global crisis. London, [1978]. pp. 303.

SIMON (ULRICH) Sitting in judgement, 1913-1963: an interpretation of history. London, 1978. pp. 166.

STASSINOPOULOS (ARIANNA) The other revolution. London, 1978. pp. 240.

CLANS AND CLAN SYSTEM.

HEERS (JACQUES) Family clans in the middle ages: a study of political and social structures in urban areas. Amsterdam, 1977. pp. 266. *Translated by Barry Herbert.*

CLARE

— History.

FITZPATRICK (DAVID) Politics and Irish life, 1913-1921: provincial experience of war and revolution. Dublin, 1977. pp. 394. *bibliog.*

CLARKE (JOHN SMITH).

CHALLINOR (RAYMOND) John S. Clarke: parliamentarian, poet and lion-tamer. London, 1977. pp. 85.

CLASS ACTIONS (CIVIL PROCEDURE)

— United States.

AMERICAN ENTERPRISE INSTITUTE FOR PUBLIC POLICY RESEARCH. Legislative Analyses. 95th Congress. No. 8. Consumer class actions. Washington, D.C., 1977. pp. 33.

CLASSIFICATION OF CRIMES.

SELLIN (JOHAN THORSTEN) and WOLFGANG (MARVIN EUGENE) The measurement of delinquency;...reprinted [from the 1964 edition] with a new introduction by Stanley Turner. Montclair, N.J., 1978. pp. 423.

CLAUSEWITZ (CARL VON).

KOERNER (THEODOR) Bundespräsident. Auf Vorposten: ausgewählte Schriften, 1928-1938; herausgegeben und kommentiert von Ilona Duczynska. Wien, [1977]. pp. 299.

CLAY

— Zambia.

LEGG (C.A.) and others. Brick clay in the Mansa area with special reference to the Loshi clay deposit. Lusaka, 1975. pp. 73. *(Zambia. Geological Survey Department. Economic Reports. No. 48)* 4 maps in end pocket.

CLAYBROOKE

— History.

PHYTHIAN-ADAMS (CHARLES) Continuity, fields and fission: the making of a Midland parish. Leicester, 1978. pp. 53. *(Leicester. University. Department of English Local History. Occasional Papers. 3rd Series. No. 4)*

CLEARING-HOUSE

— United Kingdom.

COMMITTEE OF LONDON CLEARING BANKERS. Preliminary submission to the Committee to Review the Functioning of Financial Institutions: channelling funds to industry and trade. London, 1977. fo. 59. *Bound with its Supplementary paper.*

COMMITTEE OF LONDON CLEARING BANKERS. Supplementary paper to the preliminary submission to the Committee to Review the Functioning of Financial Institutions: channelling funds to industry and trade. London, 1977. fo. 34. *Bound with its Preliminary submission.*

The LONDON clearing banks: evidence by the Committee of London Clearing Bankers to the Committee to Review the Functioning of Financial Institutions. London, 1978. pp. 278.

CLEATOR MOOR

— Economic history.

BARBER (ROSS) Iron ore and after: boom time, depression and survival in a West Cumbrian town, Cleator Moor, 1840-1960;...photographs prepared by Joseph Campbell, drawings by Joanna Pearce. [York, 1976]. pp. 71. *bibliog.*

CLEREL DE TOCQUEVILLE (CHARLES ALEXIS HENRI MAURICE) Comte.

LINARES (FILADELFO) Die Revolution bei Tocqueville und Marx. Percha am Starnberger See, [1977]. pp. 122.

CLERGY

— France.

TACKETT (TIMOTHY) Priest and parish in eighteenth-century France: a social and political study of the curés in a diocese of Dauphiné, 1750- 1791. Princeton, N.J., [1977]. pp. 350. *bibliog.*

— Russia.

FREEZE (GREGORY L.) The Russian Levites: parish clergy in the eighteenth century. Cambridge, Mass., 1977. pp. 325. *bibliog. (Harvard University. Russian Research Center. Studies. 78)*

— United States.

HATCH (NATHAN O.) The sacred cause of liberty: republican thought and the millennium in revolutionary New England. New Haven, 1977. pp. 197. *bibliog.*

CLEVELAND, UNITED KINGDOM

— Economic conditions.

CLEVELAND STRUCTURE PLANS: annual monitoring report; [pd. by] Cleveland County Planning Department. a., 1976- Middlesbrough.

— Social conditions.

CLEVELAND STRUCTURE PLANS: annual monitoring report; [pd. by] Cleveland County Planning Department. a., 1976- Middlesbrough.

CLIMATIC CHANGES.

BRYSON (REID A.) and MURRAY (THOMAS J.) Climates of hunger: mankind and the world's changing weather. Madison, 1977. pp. 171. *bibliog.*

GOUDIE (ANDREW S.) Environmental change. Oxford, 1977. pp. 243. *bibliogs.*

TICKELL (CRISPIN) Climatic change and world affairs. [Cambridge, Mass., 1977]. pp. 69. *bibliog. (Harvard University. Center for International Affairs. Harvard Studies in International Affairs. No. 37)*

CLIMATIC change and variability: a southern perspective; editors A.B. Pittock [and others] on behalf of the Australian Branch, Royal Meteorological Society. Cambridge, 1978. pp. 455. *bibliog.* Based on a conference at Monash University, Melbourne, Australia, 1975.

— Economic aspects — Europe.

POST (JOHN DEXTER) The last great subsistence crisis in the western world. Baltimore, [1977]. pp. 240. *bibliog.*

CLINICAL PSYCHOLOGY.

LADER (MALCOLM HAROLD) The psychophysiology of mental illness. London, 1975. pp. 270. *bibliog.*

CLOCK AND WATCH MAKING

— Switzerland.

BADER (URS G.) Die Exportförderungspolitik der schweizerischen Uhrenindustrie. Zürich, 1977. pp. 171. *bibliog.* Inaugural-Dissertation - Universität Bern.

CLOTHING TRADE

— Canada — Bibliography.

LYN (D.E.) and McDONALD (L.) compilers. A selective bibliography on the clothing and textile industry in Canada. [Toronto], Ontario Ministry of Labour Research Library, 1973. fo. 5.

— Germany.

FROEBEL (FOLKER) and others. Die neue internationale Arbeitsteilung: strukturelle Arbeitslosigkeit in den Industrieländern und die Industrialisierung der Entwicklungsländer. Reinbek bei Hamburg, 1977. pp. 654.

— United Kingdom.

HARTE (NEGLEY B.) A history of George Brettle and Co. Ltd., 1801-1964. [London, 1973]. fo. 165. *bibliog.*

SHAH (SAMIR) Immigrants and employment in the clothing industry: the rag trade in London's East End. London, 1975. fo.42

— Zambia.

ZAMBIA. Central Statistical Office. 1975. Textile, wearing apparel and leather industries. Lusaka, 1975. pp. 61. *bibliog. (Industry Monographs. No. 2)*

CLOTHING WORKERS

— India.

INDIA. Labour Bureau. 1971. Report on survey of labour conditions in clothing factories in India, 1965-66. [Delhi, 1971]. pp. 53.

— United Kingdom.

TRINDER (CHRIS) A stitch in time?: a proposal for the reform of the clothing wages councils. London, 1975. fo. 9. *(Low Pay Unit. Low Pay Papers. No. 4)*

WINYARD (STEVE) From rags to rags: low pay in the clothing industry. London, 1977. pp. 52. *(Low Pay Unit. Low Pay Pamphlets. No.7)*

CLOTHING WORKERS (Cont.)

— United States.

OUT of the sweatshop: the struggle for industrial democracy; edited by Leon Stein. New York, [1977]. pp. 367.

CLUTTERING (SPEECH PATHOLOGY).

DALTON (PEGGY) and HARDCASTLE (W.J.) Disorders of fluency and their effects on communication. London, 1977. pp. 161. *bibliog.*

COAL

— Costs.

MILLER (SAUNDERS) The economics of nuclear and coal power. New York, 1976. pp. 150. *bibliog.*

— Canada — Alberta.

ALBERTA. Department of Energy and Natural Resources. 1976. A coal development policy for Alberta. [Edmonton], 1976. 1 vol. (various pagings).

— China.

IKONNIKOV (ALEXANDER B.) The coal industry of China. Canberra, 1977. pp. 204. *bibliog.*

— European Economic Community countries.

COMITE D'ETUDE DES PRODUCTEURS DE CHARBON D'EUROPE OCCIDENTALE. Energy in western Europe: vital role of coal; a report... prepared in cooperation with the Association for Coal in Europe. [London, National Coal Board], 1977. pp. 42.

COAL MINERS

— Czechoslovakia — Czech Republic.

FRANĚK (OTAKAR) Oslavany obklíčují...: kronika prosincové generální stávky na Rosicku-Oslavansku. 2nd ed. Brno, 1976. pp. 143. *bibliog.*

— Germany.

HARTMANN (KNUT) Der Weg zur gewerkschaftlichen Organisation: Bergarbeiterbewegung und kapitalistischer Bergbau im Ruhrgebiet, 1851-1889. München, [1977]. pp. 415. *bibliog.*

— Spain.

MIGUELEZ (FAUSTINO) La lucha de los mineros asturianos bajo el franquismo; prologo de Gerado Iglesias. Barcelona, 1977. pp. 309.

— United Kingdom.

[LEWY (EMILE)] The Lewy scheme. [Durham, imprint, 1903]. s.sh.

NORTHUMBERLAND. Northumberland Miners' Mutual Confident Association. Rules [1911]. Newcastle-upon-Tyne, 1911. pp. 54.

DOUGLASS (DAVID) The miners of North Durham. [Doncaster, 1975]. pp. 38. *(Socialist Union (Internationalist). Pamphlets. No. 3)*

NEVILLE (ROBERT G.) The Yorkshire miners in camera. Nelson, Lancs., [1976]. 1 pamphlet (unpaged).

MINING and social change: Durham county in the twentieth century; edited by Martin Bulmer. London, [1978]. pp. 318.

— United States.

UNITED MINE WORKERS OF AMERICA. Coal miners and the economy. Washington, 1974. pp. 33.

COAL MINES AND MINING.

EZRA (Sir DEREK JOSEPH) Coal and energy: the need to exploit the world's most abundant fossil fuel. London, 1978. pp. 182.

— Environmental aspects — United States.

SCHLOTTMAN (ALAN M.) Environmental regulation and the allocation of coal: a regional analysis. New York, 1977. pp. 143. *bibliog.*

— Canada — British Columbia.

BRITISH COLUMBIA. Northeast Coal Study. Manpower Sub- committee on North East Coal Development. 1976. Report; [Ranjit Azad, chairman]. [Victoria], 1976. pp. 270.

— China.

IKONNIKOV (ALEXANDER B.) The coal industry of China. Canberra, 1977. pp. 204. *bibliog.*

KAILUAN WORKERS' WRITING GROUP. The Kailuan story: old mines into new. Peking, [1977]. pp. 74.

— Germany.

HARTMANN (KNUT) Der Weg zur gewerkschaftlichen Organisation: Bergarbeiterbewegung und kapitalistischer Bergbau im Ruhrgebiet, 1851-1889. München, [1977]. pp. 415. *bibliog.*

— United Kingdom.

DUFFRYN RHONDDA COLLIERY, CYMMER. Duffryn Rhondda Colliery, Cymmer: arbitration and award, May 1903: shorthand notes and transcript by D.M. Evans. Ystalyfera, 1903. fo.26.

[LEWY (EMILE)] The Lewy scheme. [Durham, imprint, 1903]. s.sh.

EZRA (Sir DEREK JOSEPH) More coal now to safeguard our future; address...to the annual conference of the National Union of Mineworkers at Tynemouth, July 5, 1977. London, [1977]. pp. 12.

KIRBY (M.W.) The British coalmining industry, 1870-1946: a political and economic history. London, 1977. pp. 278. *bibliog.*

— — Government ownership.

BERKOVITCH (ISRAEL) Coal on the switchback: the coal industry since nationalisation. London, 1977. pp. 237. *bibliogs.*

COAL TRADE

— India.

STATISTICS OF MINES IN INDIA: COAL; [pd. by] Directorate- General of Mines Safety. a., 1965- New Delhi. *Supersedes INDIAN COAL STATISTICS and includes data previously included in INDIA. Directorate General of Mines Safety. Annual report of the Director-General of Mines Safety.*

— United Kingdom.

ATCHESON (NATHANIEL) A letter addressed to Rowland Burdon, Esq., M.P., on the present state of the carrying part of the coal trade. London, printed by T. Davison, 1802. pp. 33, 2 fold. leaves.

COALITION (SOCIAL SCIENCES).

COALITIONS in British politics; edited by David Butler: essays by Robert Blake [and others]. London, 1978. pp. 128.

COALITION GOVERNMENTS

— United Kingdom.

COALITIONS in British politics; edited by David Butler: essays by Robert Blake [and others]. London, 1978. pp. 128.

COASTAL ZONE MANAGEMENT

— United Kingdom.

SHEAIL (JOHN) The impact of recreation on the coast: the Lindsey County Councils (Sandhills) Act, 1932. Amsterdam, 1977. pp. 19. *Reprinted from Landscape Planning, 4, 1977.*

COASTS

— Recreational use.

SHEAIL (JOHN) The impact of recreation on the coast: the Lindsey County Councils (Sandhills) Act, 1932. Amsterdam, 1977. pp. 19. *Reprinted from Landscape Planning, 4, 1977.*

COASTWISE SHIPPING.

UNITED NATIONS. Interregional Seminar on Coastal Shipping, Feeder and Ferry Services, Solstrand, 1969. Report of the...Seminar...[held at] Solstrand, OS per Bergen, Norway, 1-12 September 1969. (ST/TAO/SER.C/118). New York, 1970. pp. 35. *bibliog.*

COATICOOK VALLEY.

THORNES (JOHN B.) Some observations on the late-glacial stages in the Coaticook Valley, southern Quebec. Quebec, 1965. pp. 15. *(Reprinted from Cahiers de Géographie de Québec, no. 18, April-September, 1965)*

COBBETT (WILLIAM).

COBBETT (WILLIAM) M.P. Life and adventures of Peter Porcupine with other records of his early career in England and America; viz: Life and adventures, The scarecrow, etc. London, 1927. pp. 163. *Edited, with an introduction, by G.D.H. Cole.*

CLARKE (JOHN J.) The price of progress: Cobbett's England 1780-1835. London, 1977. pp. 200. *bibliog.*

COBOL (COMPUTER PROGRAM LANGUAGE).

YOURDON (EDWARD) and others. Learning to program in structured COBOL. New York, [1976]. pp. 250.

COCOA

— Congresses.

UNITED NATIONS. Cocoa Conference, Geneva, 1972. Summary of proceedings [of the conference held at Geneva, 6-28 March and 11-21 October, 1972]. (TD/COCOA. 3/9). New York, 1973. pp. 36.

— Africa, West.

AFANA (OSENDE) L'économie de l'Ouest africain: perspectives de développement. 2nd ed. Paris, 1977. pp. 209. *bibliog.*

COCOA TRADE.

SINGH (SHAMSHER) and others. Coffee, tea, and cocoa: market prospects and development lending. [Washington], International Bank for Reconstruction and Development, [1977]. pp. 129. *(World Bank Staff Occasional Papers. No. 22.)*

CODOVILLA (VICTORIO).

CODOVILLA (VICTORIO) Biografia politica de un revolucionario consecuente. Buenos Aires, 1964. pp. 16.

COEUR (JACQUES).

PLESHKOVA (SOF'IA LEONIDOVNA) K istorii kupecheskogo kapitala vo Frantsii v XV veke: Zhak Ker [i.e. Jacques Coeur] i ego deiatel'nost'. Moskva, 1977. pp. 181. *bibliog.*

COFFEE

— Prices.

CAMPAIGN CO-OP and WORLD DEVELOPMENT MOVEMENT. The world in your coffee cup: how the rich get richer and the poor get poorer on the coffee you drink. London, 1976. pp. 34. *bibliog.*

— Brazil.

STEIN (STANLEY J.) Vassouras: a Brazilian coffee county, 1850-1900. Cambridge, Mass., 1957. pp. 316. *bibliog.*

— — São Paulo.

BRAZIL. Instituto Brasileiro do Cafe. Grupo Executivo de Racionalização da Cafeicultura. Serviço de Fotointerpretação. 1968. Inventario cafeeiro: pesquisa com fotografias aereas nas regiões cafeicultoras do estado de São Paulo, a este de 48 W. Rio de Janeiro, 1968. pp. 67. *bibliog. With summaries in English, French, Spanish and German.*

— Ethiopia.

ETHIOPIA. Coffee and Tea Development and Marketing Authority. Planning and Programming Unit. Coffee statistics hand-book. irreg., 1961-62/1975-76- Addis Ababa.

— Malawi.

MALAWI. Agro-Economic Survey. 1976. Agro-economic survey: report no. 20: soil types and land suitability for coffee in the northern region of Malawi. Lilongwe, 1976. fo. 58. *bibliog.*

COFFEE TRADE.

BRAZIL. Instituto Brasileiro do Cafe. Divisão de Mercados. 1968. Importação de cafe nos principais mercados consumidores e participação do cafe brasileiro, (periodo 1955 a 1967). Rio de Janeiro, 1968. 1 pamphlet (unfoliated). *(Instituto Brasileiro do Cafe. Departamento Econômico. Boletins)*

CAMPAIGN CO-OP and WORLD DEVELOPMENT MOVEMENT. The world in your coffee cup: how the rich get richer and the poor get poorer on the coffee you drink. London, 1976. pp. 34. *bibliog.*

SINGH (SHAMSHER) and others. Coffee, tea, and cocoa: market prospects and development lending. [Washington], International Bank for Reconstruction and Development, [1977]. pp. 129. *(World Bank Staff Occasional Papers. No. 22.)*

— Angola.

HASLEMERE DECLARATION GROUP and THIRD WORLD FIRST EDUCATIONAL TRUST. Coffee for Britain means blood for Angola. Birmingham, [1973?]. pp. 15.

— Brazil.

STEIN (STANLEY J.) Vassouras: a Brazilian coffee county, 1850-1900. Cambridge, Mass., 1957. pp. 316. *bibliog.*

BRAZIL. Instituto Brasileiro do Cafe. Divisão de Mercados. 1968. Exportação brasileira de cafe, (periodo de 1900 a 1967). Rio de Janeiro, 1968. 1 pamphlet (unfoliated). *(Instituto Brasileiro do Cafe. Departamento Econômico. Boletins)*

BRAZIL. Instituto Brasileiro do Cafe. Divisão de Mercados. 1968. Importação de cafe nos principais mercados consumidores e participação do cafe brasileiro, (periodo 1955 a 1967). Rio de Janeiro, 1968. 1 pamphlet (unfoliated). *(Instituto Brasileiro do Cafe. Departamento Econômico. Boletins)*

BRAZIL. Instituto Brasileiro do Cafe. Divisão de Economia Rural. 1972. Boletim de informações econômicas, 1968/1971: objectivos e resultados. [Rio de Janeiro], 1972. fo. 44.

— Dominican Republic.

SHARPE (KENNETH EVAN) Peasant politics: struggle in a Dominican village. Baltimore, Md., [1977]. pp. 263. *bibliog.*

COGNITION.

BERRY (JOHN WIDDUP) Human ecology and cognitive style: comparative studies in cultural and psychological adaptation. New York, [1976]. pp. 242. *bibliog.*

SYMPOSIUM ON COGNITION, 11TH, CARNEGIE-MELLON UNIVERSITY, 1975. Cognition and social behavior; edited by John S. Carroll [and] John W. Payne. Hillsdale, N.J., 1976. pp. 290. *bibliog.*

COHEN (GILLIAN) The psychology of cognition. London, 1977. pp. 241. *bibliogs.*

COGNITION (CHILD PSYCHOLOGY).

TURNER (JOHANNA) Cognitive development. London, 1975. pp. 144. *bibliog.*

COGNITIVE learning in children: theories and strategies; edited by Joel R. Levin [and] Vernon L. Allen. New York, 1976. pp. 297. *bibliogs.*

The DEVELOPMENT of the cognitive processes; edited by Vernon Hamilton and Magdalen D. Vernon. London, 1976. pp. 772. *bibliogs.*

KOGAN (NATHAN) Cognitive styles in infancy and early childhood. Hillsdale, N.J., [1976]. pp. 146. *bibliog.*

PIAGET (JEAN) The grasp of consciousness: action and concept in the young child; ...translated by Susan Wedgwood. Cambridge, Mass., 1976. pp. 360.

AULT (RUTH L.) Children's cognitive development: Piaget's theory and the process approach. New York, 1977. pp. 193. *bibliog.*

FLAVELL (JOHN HURLEY) Cognitive development. Englewood Cliffs, [1977]. pp. 286. *bibliog.*

PIAGETIAN psychology: cross-cultural contributions; edited by Pierre R. Dasen. New York, [1977]. pp. 379. *bibliogs.*

ALTERNATIVES to Piaget: critical essays on the theory; edited by Linda S. Siegel [and] Charles J. Brainerd. New York, [1978]. pp. 262. *bibliogs.*

COGNITIVE STYLES.

KOGAN (NATHAN) Cognitive styles in infancy and early childhood. Hillsdale, N.J., [1976]. pp. 146. *bibliog.*

COINAGE

— New Zealand.

NEW ZEALAND. Post Office. 1966. Post Office training for decimal currency. [Wellington, 1966]. pp. 21.

COLBY (WILLIAM EGAN).

COLBY (WILLIAM EGAN) Honourable men: my life in the CIA. London, 1978. pp. 493.

COLD REGIONS.

PROBLEMY razvitiia raionov s ekstremal'nymi prirodnymi usloviiami; (Problems of developing districts with extremal natural conditions). Irkutsk, 1976. pp. 193. *bibliog. With English foreword, summaries and table of contents.*

COLLECTIVE BARGAINING.

La CONTRATTAZIONE collettiva: crisi e prospettive; ([by Luigi Mengoni [and others]). Milano, [1976]. pp. 304.

— Canada.

CANADIAN LABOUR CONGRESS. Collective bargaining and the appeal procedures under the anti- inflation programme. [Ottawa], 1976. pp. 8,12.

CANADA. Department of Labour. Labour data: wage developments resulting from major collective bargaining settlements. q., 1977 (no. 3)- Ottawa. *[in English and French]*

CANADA. Department of Labour. Wage developments...resulting from major collective bargaining settlements, construction industry excluded: (annual review). a., 1977 (incorporating 1976 revision)- Ottawa. *[in English and French]*

PHILLIPS (GERALD E.) The practice of labour relations and collective bargaining in Canada. Toronto, [1977]. pp. 266. *bibliogs.*

— — British Columbia.

BRITISH COLUMBIA. Department of Labour. 1968. Excerpts from remarks made by Leslie R. Peterson, Minister of Labour on second reading of Bill no. 33, an Act respecting Collective Bargaining and Mediation. [Victoria], 1968. pp. 20.

— — Ontario.

ONTARIO. Industrial Inquiry Commission into Bargaining Patterns in the Construction Industry. 1976. Report; [D.E. Franks, commissioner]. [Toronto], 1976. pp. 185.

— Europe.

ROJOT (JACQUES) International collective bargaining: an analysis and case study for Europe. Deventer, 1978. pp. 183. *bibliog.*

— Italy.

PIPAN (TATIANA) and SALERNI (DARIO) Il sindacato come soggetto di equilibrio: ricerca sulla politica contrattuale della FLM. Milano, [1975]. pp. 303.

— United Kingdom.

INDUSTRIAL studies, 2: the bargaining context; edited by Ed Coker and Geoffrey Stuttard. London, 1976. pp. 282. *bibliog.*

CONFEDERATION OF BRITISH INDUSTRY. The future of pay determination: a discussion document. London, 1977. pp. 56.

THOMSON (ANDREW W.J.) and BEAUMONT (P.B.) Public sector bargaining: a study of relative gain. Farnborough, Hants., [1978]. pp. 205.

— United States.

BROOKSHIRE (MICHAEL L.) and ROGERS (MICHAEL D.) Collective bargaining in public employment: the TVA experience. Lexington, Mass., [1977]. pp. 245.

GEORGE W. TAYLOR MEMORIAL CONFERENCE ON PUBLIC SECTOR LABOR RELATIONS, 1ST. Scope of public-sector bargaining: first George W. Taylor Memorial Conference on Public Sector Labor Relations; [edited by] Walter J. Gershenfeld [and others]. Lexington, Mass., [1977]. pp. 214. *Conference organised by Temple University Center for Labor and Human Resource Studies.*

HAGBURG (EUGENE C.) and LEVINE (MARVIN J.) Labor relations: an integrated perspective. St. Paul, [1978]. pp. 390. *bibliog.*

COLLECTIVE LABOUR AGREEMENTS

— Canada — New Brunswick.

NEW BRUNSWICK. Department of Labour. 1970. Collective agreement analysis. [Fredericton, 1970]. pp. 125.

COLLINS (JOHN) Canon.

See COLLINS (LEWIS JOHN).

COLLINS (LEWIS JOHN).

MAN of Christian Action: Canon John Collins: the man and his work; edited by Ian Henderson. Guildford, 1976. pp. 133.

COLOMBIA

— Appropriations and expenditures.

COLOMBIA. Contraloria General. Direccion de Analisis Financiero y Estadistica. Estadistica fiscal del estado. a., 1976- Bogota. *In 3 pts.*

— Census.

COLOMBIA. Census, 1973. XIV censo nacional de poblacion y III de vivienda: muestra de avance; poblacion. [Bogota], 1975. pp. 68. *Bound with Resultados provisionales.*

COLOMBIA. Census, 1973. XIV censo nacional de poblacion y III de vivienda: resultados provisionales. [Bogota, 1975]. pp. 40. *Bound with Muestra de avance: poblacion.*

— Commerce.

BETANCOURT L. (ENRIQUE) Algunos aspectos sobre las exportaciones agricolas colombianas. Bogota, [1972]. pp. 97. *bibliog.*

COLOMBIA (Cont.)

— Economic policy.

CUELLAR LOPEZ (LUIS) Comentarios al Articulo 32 de la Constitucion Nacional. Bogota, 1972. pp. 203. *bibliog.*

GOMEZ (MAURICIO) La planeacion: un derecho politico. Bogota, 1972. pp. 76. *bibliog.*

— Foreign economic relations — Venezuela.

NATHAN (ROBERT R.) ASSOCIATES. La integracion economica de Colombia y Venezuela...1967. Bogota, 1970. pp. 110.

— Foreign relations — United States.

RANDALL (STEPHEN J.) The diplomacy of modernization: Colombian-American relations, 1920-1940. Toronto, [1977]. pp. 239. *bibliog.*

— History.

ALFARO (RICARDO JOAQUIN) Vida del General Tomas Herrera;...prologo de Guillermo Andreve. Barcelona, 1909. pp. 351. *bibliog.*

— Industries.

COLOMBIA. Departamento Administrativo Nacional de Estadistica. Censo industrial, 1970. III censo industrial 1970. [Bogota, 1976]. pp. 111.

— Manufactures.

COLOMBIA. Departamento Administrativo Nacional de Estadistica. Censos economicos, 1970. Censos economicos 1970: comercio, industria, servicios; datos provisionales. Bogota, [1971?]. pp. 23.

— Politics and government.

OCAMPO (RODRIGO) Breves anotaciones historicas sobre el poder politico en Colombia. Bogota, 1972. pp. 71. *bibliog.*

ROBINSON (J.CORDELL) El movimiento gaitanista en Colombia, 1930-1948; traducido por Eddy Torres. Bogota, 1976. pp. 200. *bibliog.*

PEELER (JOHN A.) Urbanization and politics. Beverly Hills, [1977]. pp. 56. *bibliog.*

— Population.

ASOCIACION COLOMBIANA PARA EL ESTUDIO DE LA POBLACION. La poblacion de Colombia. [Bogota, 1975]. pp. 183. *(Committee for International Coordination of National Research in Demography. C.I.C.R.E.D. Series)*

— Social conditions.

LEYVA DURAN (ALVARO) Centros de integracion y de desarrollo de la comunidad. Bogota, 1972. pp. 139. *bibliog.*

— Social policy.

CUELLAR LOPEZ (LUIS) Comentarios al Articulo 32 de la Constitucion Nacional. Bogota, 1972. pp. 203. *bibliog.*

GOMEZ (MAURICIO) La planeacion: un derecho politico. Bogota, 1972. pp. 76. *bibliog.*

COLONIES.

MOVEMENT FOR COLONIAL FREEDOM. [Selected documents]. London, [1961-1965]. 16 parts (in 1 vol.). *Number of individual leaflets; includes proceedings of national conferences 1961-1965.*

COLONIES IN AFRICA.

N'DONGO (SALLY) "Coopération" et néo-colonialisme. Paris, 1976. pp. 199.

GRIMAL (HENRI) Decolonization: the British, French, Dutch and Belgian empires, 1919-1963;...translated by Stephan de Vos (from the third French edition). London, 1978. pp. 443. *bibliog.*

COLONIES IN ASIA.

GRIMAL (HENRI) Decolonization: the British, French, Dutch and Belgian empires, 1919-1963;...translated by Stephan de Vos (from the third French edition). London, 1978. pp. 443. *bibliog.*

COLONIZATION

— History.

PARRY (JOHN HORACE) The age of reconnaissance. 2nd ed. London, 1966 repr. 1973. pp. 366. *bibliog.*

SCHOTT (RUEDIGER) Consecuencias de la expansion europea para los pueblos del ultramar. [Mexico City], 1966. pp. 49. *(Mexico City. Colegio de Mexico. Centro de Estudios Sociales. Jornadas. 60)*

COLORADO

— History.

ATHEARN (ROBERT GREENLEAF) The Coloradans. Albuquerque, [1976]. pp. 430. *bibliog.*

COLOURED PEOPLE (SOUTH AFRICA).

SOUTH AFRICA. Administration of Coloured Affairs. Report. a., 1973/74- Pretoria. *1971/72-1972/73 included in SOUTH AFRICA. Parliament. House of Assembly. Votes and proceedings (with Printed annexures).*

COMBINATORIAL ANALYSIS.

KOLCHIN (VALENTIN FEDOROVICH) and others. Random allocations; translation editor A.V. Balakrishnan. Washington, D.C., 1978. pp. 262. *bibliog.*

COMMERCE.

POSTLETHWAYT (MALACHY) Selected works. Farnborough, [1968]. 2 vols. *Originally published between 1745 and 1759. Facsimile reprints.*

AMERICAN ECONOMIC ASSOCIATION. Readings in international economics, selected by a committee of the... Association; (selection committee for this volume, Richard E. Caves and Harry G. Johnson). London, 1968 repr. 1975. pp. 604. *bibliogs.*

GENERAL AGREEMENT ON TARIFFS AND TRADE. Studies in International Trade. Geneva, 1971 in progress.

JOHNSON (HARRY GORDON) Trade negotiations and the new international monetary system. Geneva, 1976. pp. 37. *(Geneva. Graduate Institute of International Studies, and Trade Policy Research Centre. Commercial Policy Issues. 1)*

DOBOZI (ISTVÁN) Forecasting structural changes in the international raw materials industries and markets. Budapest, 1977. pp. 85. *(Hungarian Scientific Council for World Economy. [Publications]. Trends in World Economy. No. 22)*

MACIEL (GEORGE ALVARES) The international framework for world trade: Brazilian proposals for GATT reform. London, [1977]. pp. 14. *(Trade Policy Research Centre. Lectures in Commercial Diplomacy. No. 3)*

NOBEL SYMPOSIUM, 35TH, STOCKHOLM, 1976. The international allocation of economic activity: proceedings of a Nobel Symposium held at Stockholm; edited by Bertil Ohlin [and others]. London, 1977. pp. 572.

ROBERTSON (DAVID) Economist. Fail safe systems for trade liberalisation. London, 1977. pp. 72. *(Trade Policy Research Centre. Thames Essays. No. 12)*

KINDLEBERGER (CHARLES POOR) and LINDERT (PETER H.) International economics. 6th ed. Homewood, Ill., 1978. pp. 562.

LONG (OLIVIER) International trade under threat: a constructive response. London, 1978. pp. 12. *(Trade Policy Research Centre. Lectures in Commercial Diplomacy. No. 4)*

COMMERCIAL AGENTS

— European Economic Community countries.

EUROPEAN COMMUNITIES. Commission. 1977. Equality of rights for commercial agents: proposal for a Council Directive to coordinate the laws of the member states relating to self-employed commercial agents; presented to the Council...on 17 December 1976. Luxembourg, 1977. pp. 26. *(Bulletin of the European Communities. Supplements. [1977/1]).*

— Germany.

GERMANY (BUNDESREPUBLIK). Statistisches Bundesamt. Kostenstruktur bei Handelsvertretern und Handelsmaklern (formerly Handelsvertreter und Handelsmakler). quadrennial. 1972- Wiesbaden. *(Unternehmen und Arbeitsstatten. Reihe 2.2)*

— Sri Lanka.

SRI LANKA. Commission of Inquiry on Agency Houses and Brokering Firms. 1974. Report; [B. Soysa, chairman]. Colombo, 1974. pp. 641. *(Sri Lanka. Parliament. Sessional Papers. 1974. No. 12)*

COMMERCIAL CRIMES

— Canada.

GOFF (COLIN HARFORD) and REASONS (CHARLES E.) Corporate crime in Canada: a critical analysis of anti-combines legislation. Scarborough, Ont., [1978]. pp. 136.

— United States.

CONKLIN (JOHN E.) Illegal but not criminal: business crime in America. Englewood Cliffs, [1977]. pp. 153.

COMMERCIAL LAW

— Argentine Republic.

ACEVEDO (CARLOS ALBERTO) Ensayo historico sobre la legislacion comercial argentina. Buenos Aires, 1914. pp. 172.

— Russia.

VORMS (AL'FONS ERNESTOVICH) and DANILOVA (ELIZAVETA NIKOLAEVNA) eds. Istochniki torgovogo prava za iskliucheniem morskogo prava: sbornik izvlechenii iz Svoda Zakonov po Prod. do 1917 g., postanovlenii Vrem. Prav.,...dekretov...Tsentr. Ispol. Komiteta...Soveta Nar. Khoz., mezhdunarodnykh konventsii, etc. 2nd ed. Moskva, 1918. pp. lxiv,592.

— United Kingdom.

SLATER (JOHN ARTHUR) Mercantile law; seventeenth edition [by] Lord Chorley and O.C. Giles. London, 1977. pp. 491.

SMITH (KENNETH) Barrister-at-Law, and KEENAN (DENIS J.) Mercantile law; fourth edition by D.J. Keenan. London, 1977. pp. 831.

STEVENS (THOMAS MOFFITT) and BORRIE (GORDON JOHNSON) Elements of mercantile law; seventeenth edition by J.K. Macleod and A.H. Hudson. London, 1978. pp. 788.

COMMERCIAL POLICY.

PŁOWIEC (URSZULA) Centralne sterowanie handlem zagranicznym. Warszawa, 1975. pp. 296. *bibliog.*

DIUMULEN (IPPOLIT IPPOLITOVICH) Bar'ery na torgovykh putiakh: imperialisticheskii protektsionizm v deistvii. Moskva, 1977. pp. 223.

COMMONWEALTH SECRETARIAT. Multilateral trade negotiations and relevant trends in international trade policy; paper. London, 1978. pp. 23.

MEYER (FREDERICK VICTOR) International trade policy. London, [1978]. pp. 234.

SCHIAVO-CAMPO (SALVATORE) International economics: an introduction to theory and policy. Cambridge, Mass., [1978]. pp. 398. *bibliog.*

COMMERCIAL PRODUCTS

— Classification.

PAKISTAN. Central Statistical Office. Economic Affairs Division. 1966. Pakistan standard trade classification, revised. [Karachi, 1966]. pp. 201.

CZECHOSLOVAKIA. Federální Statistický Úřad. 1976. Ekonomické klasifikace; [by] Jan Kazimour. Bratislava, 1976. pp. 186.

DMITRIEV (IL'IA DMITRIEVICH) Klassifikatsiia tovarov narodnogo potrebleniia. Moskva, 1976. pp. 176. *bibliog.*

— Canada.

CANADA. Statistics Canada. Products shipped by Canadian manufacturers. a., 1973- Ottawa. *[in English and French].*

— Japan.

MITUHASHI (SETUKO) Japanese commodity flows. Chicago, 1978. pp. 172. *bibliog. (Chicago. University. Department of Geography. Research Papers. No. 187)*

— Russia.

DZIUBYK (STEPAN DANYLOVYCH) Tovarnyi obih zasobiv vyrobnytstva v period pobudovy komunizmu. L'viv, 1971. pp. 202.

DMITRIEV (IL'IA DMITRIEVICH) Klassifikatsiia tovarov narodnogo potrebleniia. Moskva, 1976. pp. 176. *bibliog.*

COMMERCIAL TREATIES.

UNITED STATES. Treaties. 1827. Freundschafts-, Handels- und Schifffahrts-Vertrag zwischen den Senaten der freien und Hansestädte Lübeck, Bremen und Hamburg und den Vereinigten Staaten von Nord-Amerika unterzeichnet zu Washington am 20. December 1827. Hamburg, 1828. pp. 23. *In English, French and German. Facsimile reprint issued in 1976 by the Hamburg Chamber of Commerce.*

MACAVOY (PAUL WEBSTER) Economic perspective on the politics of international commodity agreements. Tucson, [1977]. pp. 36. *bibliog. (Arizona University. Gustavson Memorial Lectures. 1976)*

COMMODITY CONTROL.

MACAVOY (PAUL WEBSTER) Economic perspective on the politics of international commodity agreements. Tucson, [1977]. pp. 36. *bibliog. (Arizona University. Gustavson Memorial Lectures. 1976)*

COMMODITY EXCHANGES.

HART, BROWNE AND CURTIS. The commodity markets. London, [1974?]. fo. 8.

BEHRMAN (JERE R.) International commodity agreements: an evaluation of the UNCTAD integrated commodity programme. [Washington], 1977. pp. 93. *(Overseas Development Council. Monographs. No. 9)*

COMMON LAW.

HOLMES (OLIVER WENDELL) the Younger. The common law. Boston, Mass., 1948. pp. 422.

— United States.

BRIDWELL (RANDALL) and WHITTEN (RALPH U.) The constitution and the common law: the decline of the doctrines of separation of powers and federalism. Lexington, Mass., [1977]. pp. 206.

COMMONS.

KARL Marx über Formen vorkapitalistischer Produktion: vergleichende Studien zur Geschichte des Grundeigentums, 1879- 80; aus dem handschriftlichen Nachlass herausgegeben und eingeleitet von Hans-Peter Harstick. Frankfurt, [1977]. pp. 358. *bibliogs. (International Institute of Social History. Quellen und Studien zur Sozialgeschichte. Band 1) Includes extracts from M.M. Kovalevskii's Obshchinnoe zemlevladenie translated and annotated by Marx.*

COMMONWEALTH FUND FOR TECHNICAL CO-OPERATION.

COMMONWEALTH FUND FOR TECHNICAL CO-OPERATION. Commonwealth skills for Commonwealth needs. London, [1977]. pp. 24.

COMMUNES (CHINA).

DUMONT (RENE) Chine, la révolution culturale. Paris, [1976]. pp. 200. *bibliog.*

BERNSTEIN (THOMAS P.) Up to the mountains and down to the villages: the transfer of youth from urban to rural China. New Haven, 1977. pp. 371. *bibliog.*

COMMUNICABLE DISEASES.

BAILEY (NORMAN THOMAS JOHN) The mathematical theory of infectious diseases and its applications. 2nd ed. London, 1975. pp. 413. *bibliog.*

COMMUNICATION.

NEW models for communication research; Peter Clarke, editor. Beverly Hills, [1973]. pp. 307. *bibliogs.*

BRUDNYI (A.A.) ed. Filosofskie problemy psikhologii obshcheniia. Frunze, 1976. pp. 180.

EXPLORATIONS in interpersonnal communications; Gerald R. Miller, editor. Beverly Hills, [1976]. pp. 274. *bibliogs.*

CHERRY (EDWARD COLIN) On human communication: a review, a survey, and a criticism. 3rd ed. Cambridge, Mass., [1978]. pp. 374. *bibliog.*

— Social aspects.

CHERRY (EDWARD COLIN) World communication: threat or promise?: a socio-technical approach. rev. ed. Chichester, [1978]. pp. 229. *bibliog.*

— Asia.

COMMUNICATION and rural change; edited by P.R.R. Sinha. Singapore, [1976]. pp. 230. *bibliog. Based on papers presented at a conference held by the Asian Mass Communication Research and Information Centre, in Bangalore, 1973.*

COMMUNICATION AND TRAFFIC

— Australia.

AUSTRALIAN INFORMATION SERVICE. Transport and communications. [Canberra], 1974. pp. 27. *(Reference Papers)*

— Finland.

FINLAND. Tilastokeskus. Liikenteen yritystilasto. a., 1974- Helsinki.

— Russia.

POPKOVA (VALENTINA EVSTAF'EVNA) and others. Kreditovanie i raschety transporta i sviazi. Moskva, 1976. pp. 86.

— — Russia (RSFSR).

CHERVIAKOV (A.P.) Ekonomicheskie sviazi i razvitie zheleznykh dorog Urala. Moskva, 1976. pp. 87. *bibliog. (Akademiia Nauk SSSR. Problemy Sovetskoi Ekonomiki)*

COMMUNICATION IN MARRIAGE.

THOMAS (EDWIN JOHN) Marital communication and decision making: analysis, assessment and change. New York, [1977]. pp. 239. *bibliog.*

COMMUNICATION IN ORGANIZATIONS.

LAWLER (EDWARD E.) and RHODE (JOHN GRANT) Information and control in organizations. Pacific Palisades, [1976]. pp. 217. *bibliog.*

COMMUNICATION IN POLITICS.

LAUDON (KENNETH C.) Communications technology and democratic participation. New York, 1977. pp. 116.

HUDSON (KENNETH) The language of modern politics. London, 1978. pp. 167. *bibliog.*

— China.

HINIKER (PAUL J.) Revolutionary ideology and Chinese reality: dissonance under Mao. Beverly Hills, [1977]. pp. 320.

COMMUNICATION IN SCIENCE.

FRY (BERNARD MITCHELL) and WHITE (HERBERT S.) Publishers and libraries: a study of scholarly and research journals. Lexington, Mass., [1976]. pp. 166. *bibliog.*

COMMUNICATION IN THE SOCIAL SCIENCES.

GREIMAS (ALGIRDAS JULIEN) Sémiotique et sciences sociales. Paris, [1976]. pp. 219.

COMMUNICATIVE DISORDERS.

DALTON (PEGGY) and HARDCASTLE (W.J.) Disorders of fluency and their effects on communication. London, 1977. pp. 161. *bibliog.*

COMMUNISM.

COMMUNIST PARTY OF GREAT BRITAIN. For a Marxist Leninist School. District School Material. Outlines. No. 5. The transition period: an outline for students and party trainers. [London, 1932?]. pp. 16.

[RUSSIA (U.S.S.R.). Soviet Embassy in London. Press Department]. Soviet Booklets. [2nd Series]. No. 120. On internationalism and nationalism; by L. Volodin. London, 1963. pp. 12.

TROTSKII (LEV DAVYDOVICH) The basic writings of Trotsky; edited and introduced by Irving Howe. New York, 1976. pp. 427. *Reprint of the ed. published by Random House in 1963.*

BANDA (HASTINGS KAMUZU) What is communism?: speech...to Zomba Debating Society. [Blantyre, Ministry of Information], 1964. pp. 20.

NAUCHNYI KOMMUNIZM; ([pd. by] Ministerstvo Vysshego i Srednego Spetsial'nogo Obrazovaniia USSR). 6 a yr., 1974 [2nd yr.]- Moskva.

PROBLEMY istoricheskogo materializma...: nekotorye zakonomernosti razvitiia bazisa i nadstroiki etapa razvitogo sotsializma: tematicheskii sbornik. Dushanbe, 1975. pp. 179. *(Dushanbinskii Gosudarstvennyi Pedagogicheskii Institut. Uchenye Zapiski. t.96)*

THAELMANN (ERNST) Ausgewählte Reden und Schriften in zwei Bänden. Frankfurt am Main, 1976-77. 2 vols.

AKTIVNOST' lichnosti v sotsialisticheskom obshchestve. Moskva, 1976. pp. 278.

COLARIZI (SIMONA) Classe operaia e ceti medi. [Venezia, 1976]. pp. 172.

DIBATTITO sull'estremismo; [by] Herman Gorter [and others]; (introduzione di Silverio Corvisieri). Roma, 1976. pp. 219.

MELANGES d'histoire sociale offerts à Jean Maitron. Paris, [1976]. pp. 286. *bibliog.*

FABRE (JEAN) and others. Les communistes et l'état. Paris, [1977]. pp. 253. *bibliog.*

HEVESI (MARIA) Iz istorii kritiki filosofskikh dogm II Internatsionala. Moskva, 1977. pp. 207.

COMMUNISM.(Cont.)

KORSCH (KARL) Karl Korsch: revolutionary theory; edited by Douglas Kellner. Austin, Tex., [1977]. pp. 299.

KOSESKI (ADAM) Budowa rozwiniętego społeczeństwa socjalistycznego: zarys koncepcji politycznej. [Warszawa, 1977]. pp. 391. *bibliog.*

KRAUSE (GUENTER) Das Elend der "Linken": zur Kritik der politischen Ökonomie des Linksrevisionismus. Berlin, 1977. pp. 135. *bibliog.*

MANGENG (ELISABETH) Der Anachronismus in Theorie und Strategie der kommunistischen Partei: italienische Arbeiterwissenschaft gegen Theorie des Stamokap. Giessen, [1977]. pp. 285. *bibliog.*

POLITIKA KSČ: ciele a prostriedky. Bratislava, 1977. pp. 273. *(Komunistická Strana Slovenska. Ústredný Výbor. Ústav Marxizmu-Leninizmu. Zborník. roč.17, č.1)*

THAELMANN (ERNST) Über proletarischen Internationalismus: Reden und Artikel, [1925-1934]. Leipzig, 1977. pp. 250.

ZARODOV (KONSTANTIN IVANOVICH) Sotsializm, mir, revoliutsiia: nekotorye voprosy teorii i praktiki mezhdunarodnykh otnoshenii i klassovoi bor'by. Moskva, 1977. pp. 303.

ZARODOV (KONSTANTIN IVANOVICH) Tri revoliutsii v Rossii i nashe vremia. 2nd ed. Moskva, 1977. pp. 636.

KNEI-PAZ (BARUCH) The social and political thought of Leon Trotsky. Oxford, 1978. pp. 629. *bibliog.*

McMURTRY (JOHN MURRAY) The structure of Marx's world-view. Princeton, [1978]. pp. 269.

SOZIALISMUS in Theorie und Praxis: Festschrift für Richard Löwenthal zum 70. Geburtstag am 15. April 1978; herausgegeben von Hannelore Horn [and others]. Berlin, 1978. pp. 687. *bibliog. In various languages.*

WESSON (ROBERT GALE) Communism and communist systems. Englewood Cliffs, [1978]. pp. 227.

— History.

CORRIGAN (PHILIP R.D.) and others. Socialist construction and Marxist theory: Bolshevism and its critique. London, 1978. pp. 232. *bibliog.*

— Africa.

GREIG (IAN) The communist challenge to Africa: an analysis of contemporary Soviet, Chinese and Cuban policies. Richmond, Surrey, 1977. pp. 306. *bibliog.*

— America, Latin.

ARISMENDI (RODNEY) El pensamiento de Lenin y la revolucion latinoamericana. [Montevideo, Comision de Propaganda del Partido Comunista, 1968]. pp. 45.

— Argentine Republic.

ORTIZ (S.H.) El libro rojo de Rogelio Frigerio. Montevideo, 1962. pp. 125.

— Asia.

NATIONALISM and communism in Asia: the American response; edited and with an introduction by Norman A. Graebner. Lexington, Mass., [1977]. pp. 204. *bibliog.*

— Bulgaria.

PAVLENKO (VIKTORIIA VIKTOROVNA) Solidarnost' trudiashchikhsia Ukrainskoi SSR s revoliutsionnoi bor'boi rabochikh i krest'ian Bolgarii, 1923-1934 gg. Kiev, 1977. pp. 140.

— Cambodia.

STEINBACH (JERÔME) and STEINBACH (JOCELYNE) Phnom Penh libérée. Paris, [1976]. pp. 165.

— China.

GYÖRGY (IMRE) Cherez prizmu Pekina; perevod s vengerskogo, etc. Moskva, 1975. pp. 284.

CHANG (YI-CHUN) Factional and coalition politics in China: the cultural revolution and its aftermath. New York, 1976. pp. 144.

COMMUNIST LEAGUE. Ten years on: from revolution through counterrevolution to the consolidated rule of the national capitalist class in China. London, 1977. pp. 44.

DUNCANSON (DENNIS J.) The peacetime strategy of the Chinese People's Republic. London, [1977]. pp. 32. *bibliog. (Institute for the Study of Conflict. Special Reports)*

HINIKER (PAUL J.) Revolutionary ideology and Chinese reality: dissonance under Mao. Beverly Hills, [1977]. pp. 320.

HOFHEINZ (ROY) The broken wave: the Chinese Communist peasant movement, 1922- 1928. Cambridge, Mass., 1977. pp. 355. *bibliog. (Harvard University. East Asian Research Center. Harvard East Asian Series. 90)*

HOWARD (ROGER) Mao Tse-tung and the Chinese people. London, [1977]. pp. 412. *bibliog.*

IDEINO-politicheskaia sushchnost' maoizma. Moskva, 1977. pp. 443. *bibliog.*

MOODY (PETER R.) Opposition and dissent in contemporary China. Stanford, [1977]. pp. 342. *bibliog. (Stanford University. Hoover Institution on War, Revolution and Peace. Hoover Institution Publications. 177)*

— Cuba.

CRUZ COBOS (ARMANDO) Fidel Castro y su purga de Guignol: de Glassboro al "comunismo independiente" en Cuba. [Lima, 1968]. pp. 39.

— Czechoslovakia.

SLOVAK ACTION COMMITTEE. Demande addressée à l'Assemblée Générale des Nations Unies concernant la situation en Slovaquie et l'organisation d'un plébiscite dans ce pays. [New York, 1948?]. pp. (4).

MATĚJÍČEK (JAROSLAV) Politický systém socialismu a kritika pravicového revizionismu v ČSSR. Praha, 1976. pp. 251. *With Russian summary.*

ZÁBRAHOVÁ (LUDOSLAVA) Třídně sociální struktura ve výstavbě socialismu: východiska, kritéria a problémy ČSSR. Praha, 1976. pp. 153.

— East (Near East).

S"EZD NARODOV VOSTOKA. S"ezd 1-yi, Baku, 1920. Congress of the peoples of the East: Baku, September 1920; stenographic report translated and annotated by Brian Pearce. [London, 1977]. pp. 204.

— Europe.

CESARINI SFORZA (MARCO) and NASSI (ENRICO) L'eurocomunismo. Milano, 1977. pp. 192.

COMMUNIST power in Europe, 1944-1949; edited by Martin McCauley. London, 1977. pp. 242.

FONVIEILLE-ALQUIER (FRANÇOIS) L'Eurocommunisme: essai. [Paris, 1977]. pp. 288.

RIZZO (ALDO) La frontiera dell'eurocomunismo. Roma, 1977. pp. 240.

SEGRE (SERGIO) A chi fa paura l'eurocomunismo? [Rimini, 1977]. pp. 215.

CLAUDIN (FERNANDO) Eurocommunism and socialism; translated by John Wakeham. London, 1978. pp. 168.

EURO-Communism: its roots and future in Italy and elsewhere; edited by G.R. Urban. London, 1978. pp. 287. *Based on interviews broadcast in 1977 and 1978 by Radio Free Europe.*

The ITALIAN Communists speak for themselves; edited by Don Sassoon. Nottingham, 1978. pp. 195.

— Europe, Eastern.

Die WACHSENDE Rolle der Arbeiterklasse in den sozialistischen Ländern; ([by the] Parteihochschule beim ZK der KPdSU, Moskau [and others]). Berlin, 1974. pp. 359.

BAHRO (RUDOLF) Die Alternative: zur Kritik des real existierenden Sozialismus. Köln, 1977. pp. 543.

IZ istorii narodno-demokraticheskikh i sotsialisticheskikh revoliutsii v stranakh Tsentral'noi i Iugo-Vostochnoi Evropy. Moskva, 1977. pp. 391.

RAKOVSKI (MARC) Le marxisme face aux pays de l'Est. [Paris, 1977]. pp. 206.

SIKORA (FRANZ) Sozialistische Solidarität und nationale Interessen: Polen, Tschechoslowakei, DDR. Köln, [1977]. pp. 248. *(Bundesinstitut für Ostwissenschaftliche und Internationale Studien. Abhandlungen. Band 31)*

SOZIALISMUS in Theorie und Praxis: Festschrift für Richard Löwenthal zum 70. Geburtstag am 15. April 1978; herausgegeben von Hannelore Horn [and others]. Berlin, 1978. pp. 687. *bibliog. In various languages.*

— France.

ANSART (GUSTAVE) De l'usine à l'Assemblée nationale: entretien avec Jacques Estager. [Paris, 1977]. pp. 256.

LECOEUR (AUGUSTE) Le PCF : continuité dans le changement. Paris, [1977]. pp. 237.

ROBRIEUX (PHILIPPE) Notre génération communiste, 1953-1968: essai d'autobiographie politique. Paris, [1977]. pp. 351.

TROTSKII (LEV DAVYDOVICH) The crisis of the French section, 1935-36. New York, [1977]. pp. 286.

MONTALDO (JEAN) La France communiste. [Paris, 1978]. pp. 358.

— Germany.

FISCHER (RUTH) Stalin und der deutsche Kommunismus: der Übergang zur Konterrevolution; (translated from the English by H. Langerhans). Frankfurt am Main, [1950]. pp. 844.

THAELMANN (ERNST) Ausgewählte Reden und Schriften in zwei Bänden. Frankfurt am Main, 1976-77. 2 vols.

DOKUMENTE und Materialien zum gemeinsamen Kampf der revolutionären deutschen und polnischen Arbeiterbewegung, 1918- 1939; bearbeitet und eingeleitet von Franciszek Hawranek [and others]. Berlin, [1977]. pp. 335.

— Indonesia.

VAN DER KROEF (JUSTUS MARIA) The Indonesian Maoists: doctrines and perspectives. Baltimore, 1977. pp. 31. *(Maryland University. School of Law. Occasional Papers/Reprints Series in Contemporary Asian Studies. No. 3)*

— Israel.

GREILSAMMER (ALAIN) Les communistes israéliens. Paris, [1978]. pp. 415. *bibliog.*

— Italy.

PATITUCCI (RAFFAELE) No a Luigi Longo, no al comunismo: idee nuove, fatti nuovi, uomini nuovi. [Ferrara, 1958]. pp. 98.

PARTITO COMUNISTA ITALIANO. Comitato Centrale, [and] Commissione Centrale di Controllo. Sessione, 13-15 gennaio 1975. Battaglia delle idee e rinnovamento culturale: atti. [Roma, 1975]. pp. 308.

ALTERNATIVA ed elementi di socialismo nelle comunità locali; scritti di [Ernesto] Bettinelli [and others]: a cura di Ernesto Bettinelli ed Emilio Renzi. [Milano, 1976]. pp. 152. *Based on a conference organised by Azione e Ricerca per l'Alternativa, in Pavia, 1975.*

CAROLLO (VINCENZO) Borghesia rivoluzionaria per il comunismo. Milano, [1976]. pp. 211.

COLARIZI (SIMONA) Classe operaia e ceti medi. [Venezia, 1976]. pp. 172.

GIANNATTASIO (MARIO) Lettera a Saragat: l'incognita comunista e la dispersione socialista. [Napoli, 1976]. pp. 140. *bibliog.*

PARTITO DI UNITÀ PROLETARIA PER IL COMUNISMO. Federazione Milanese. Gruppo di Lavoro Teoria e Controinformazione. Convegno, Maggio 1975. Da Togliatti alla nuova sinistra: (atti). [Roma, 1976]. pp. 290.

ALICATA (MARIO) Lettere e taccuini di Regina Coeli. Torino, 1977. pp. 271.

PELLEGRINI (ROCCO) and PEPE (GUGLIELMO) Unire è difficile: breve storia del PdUP per il comunismo; (colloqui con V. Foa, etc.). Roma, [1977]. pp. 189.

SANTARELLI (ENZO) La revisione del marxismo in Italia: studi di critica storica. rev. ed. [Milano, 1977]. pp. 343.

The ITALIAN Communists speak for themselves; edited by Don Sassoon. Nottingham, 1978. pp. 195.

— Korea.

The FOUNDING of the anti-Japanese guerilla army, a historic event which brought about a great turn in the development of the Korean r[e]volution: [a commemoration of 40 years including extracts from speeches by Kim Il Sung]. [1972]. fo. 14. *Typescript.*

— Mexico.

CUADROS CALDAS (JULIO) El comunismo criollo. Puebla, 1930. pp. 265.

— Poland.

DOKUMENTE und Materialien zum gemeinsamen Kampf der revolutionären deutschen und polnischen Arbeiterbewegung, 1918- 1939; bearbeitet und eingeleitet von Franciszek Hawranek [and others]. Berlin, [1977]. pp. 335.

POLITYCZNA organizacja spøleczeństwa w Polsce w okresie budowy rozwiniętego społeczeństwa socjalistycznego; praca zbiorowa pod redakcją Mariana Szczepaniaka. Poznań, 1977. pp. 299.

STROITEL'STVO sotsializma v Pol'skoi Narodnoi Respublike: istoricheskie ocherki. Kiev, 1977. pp. 239.

— Romania.

CEAUSESCU (NICOLAE) Speeches and writings; selected and introduced by Stan Newens. 2nd ed. Nottingham, 1978. pp. 287.

— Russia.

KLIBANSKI (HERMANN O.) Der Kommunismus in Russland und die Diktatur des Proletariats: nach der Broschürenliteratur ihrer geistigen Urheber. Berlin, 1919. pp. 14. *(Generalsekretariat zum Studium und zur Bekämpfung des Bolschewismus. Revolutionäre Streitfragen. 7. Heft)*

BELOV (GENNADII ANATOL'EVICH) Politicheskie otnosheniia sotsialisticheskogo tipa: politicheskie otnosheniia v sisteme sotsialisticheskikh obshchestvennykh otnoshenii. Moskva, 1976. pp. 184.

KAISER (ROBERT G.) Russia: the people and the power. New York, 1976. pp. 499. *bibliog.*

ROGACHEV (SERGEI VLADIMIROVICH) and SHEKIR (N.S.) eds. Osobennosti deistviia ekonomicheskikh zakonov v usloviiakh razvitogo sotsializma. Moskva, 1976. pp. 180.

SOVETSKAIA demokratiia v period razvitogo sotsializma; otvetstvennyi redaktor D.A. Kerimov. Moskva, 1976. pp. 279.

AIMS FOR FREEDOM AND ENTERPRISE. 1917-1977: sixty years of communism: the age of the Gulag. London, [1977]. pp. 13.

BESANÇON (ALAIN) Les origines intellectuelles du léninisme. [Paris, 1977]. pp. 323. *bibliog.*

EKONOMICHESKIE problemy razvitogo sotsialisticheskogo obshchestva. Kiev, 1977. pp. 383.

GOSUDARSTVO, demokratiia i trudovoi kollektiv v razvitom sotsialisticheskom obshchestve. Moskva, 1977. pp. 200.

KOREL'SKII (VIKTOR MIKHAILOVICH) Demokratiia i distsiplina v razvitom sotsialisticheskom obshchestve. Moskva, 1977. pp. 136.

MATERIAL'NO-tekhnicheskaia baza kommunizma. Moskva, 1977. 2 vols. *bibliog.*

MEYER (GERD) Writer on Soviet affairs. Bürokratischer Sozialismus: eine Analyse des sowjetischen Herrschaftssystems. Stuttgart-Bad Cannstatt, 1977. pp. 331. *bibliog. With English summary.*

PARTIIA v period razvitogo sotsialisticheskogo obshchestva: materialy Vsesoiuznoi nauchno-teoreticheskoi konferentsii "XXV s"ezd KPSS i razvitie marksistsko-leninskoi teorii", Moskva, 4-6 oktiabria 1976 goda. Moskva, 1977. pp. 230.

PIECK (WILHELM) Wilhelm Pieck: ein unermüdlicher Streiter für die deutsch- sowjetische Freundschaft: ausgewählte Reden und Schriften... ; eingeleitet und zusammengestellt von Heinz Vosske. Berlin, 1977. pp. 159.

Die SOZIALISTISCHE Gesellschaft: Wesen, Entwicklung, Perspektiven; ([by] R. I. Kossolapow [and others]; Übersetzung [from the Russian]: Wolfgang Eckstein). Frankfurt am Main, 1977. pp. 327.

SZAMUELY (TIBOR) Socialism and liberty. London, [1977]. pp. 20. *Reprint with postscript of work first published in 1971.*

WODDIS (JACK) How October 1917 changed the world. London, [1977]. pp. 24. *(Communist Party of Great Britain. Communist Party Pamphlets)*

ZETKIN (CLARA) Für die Sowjetmacht: Artikel, Reden und Briefe, 1917-1933. Frankfurt am Main, 1977. pp. 485.

BESANÇON (ALAIN) The Soviet syndrome. New York, [1978]. pp. 103.

— — Baltic States.

SOTSIALISTICHESKIE revoliutsii 1940 g. v Litve, Latvii i Estonii: vosstanovlenie Sovetskoi vlasti. Moskva, 1978. pp. 351.

— Spain.

GRANDI (BLASCO) Togliatti y los suyos en España. Madrid, 1954. pp. 45.

INVESTIGACION Y DOCUMENTACION DE PROBLEMAS ACTUALES. Seccion de Temas Españoles. Planificacion comunista para España. Madrid, 1976. pp. 206.

BONAMUSA (FRANCESC) Andreu Nin y el movimiento comunista en España, 1930-1937. Barcelona, [1977]. pp. 521. *bibliog.*

— United Kingdom.

COMMUNIST WORKING MEN'S CLUB. Our May Day manifesto...1906. London, [1906?]. pp. 8.

STEWART-SMITH (DUDLEY GEOFFREY) Not to be trusted: left wing extremism in the Labour and Liberal Parties. Richmond, Surrey, 1974. pp. 24.

TRORY (ERNIE) Imperialist war: further recollections of a communist organiser. Brighton, 1977. pp. 242. *bibliog.*

WYATT (WOODROW LYLE) What's left of the Labour Party? London, 1977. pp. 183.

REBELS and their causes: essays in honour of A.L. Morton; edited by Maurice Cornforth. London, 1978. pp. 224.

— United States.

LARKIN (JAMES JOSEPH) The American trial of Big Jim Larkin, 1920. Belfast, 1976. pp. 106.

BELKNAP (MICHAL R.) Cold war political justice: the Smith Act, the Communist Party, and American civil liberties. Westport, Conn., 1977. pp. 322. *bibliog.*

DENNIS (PEGGY) The autobiography of an American communist: a personal view of a political life, 1925-1975. Westport, 1977. pp. 302.

FISH (HAMILTON) An American manifesto of freedom in answer to the manifesto on communism, 1848. New York, [1977]. pp. 209. *bibliog.*

— Yugoslavia.

DRASKOVICH (SLOBODAN M.) Tito, Moscow's Trojan horse. Chicago, 1957. pp. 357.

SAMOUPRAVLJANJE u Jugoslaviji, 1950-1976: dokumenti razvoja. Beograd, 1977. pp. 367.

SHER (GERSON S.) Praxis: Marxist criticism and dissent in socialist Yugoslavia. Bloomington, Ind., [1977]. pp. 360. *bibliog.*

COMMUNISM AND CHRISTIANITY.

BOURBECK (CHRISTINE) Kommunismus, Frage an die Christen: der angefochtene Mensch des technischen Zeitalters in Ost und West. Nürnberg, 1957. pp. 143.

RÉVÉSZ (LÁSZLÓ) The Christian Peace Conference: human rights and religion in the USSR. London, [1978]. pp. 17. *(Institute for the Study of Conflict. Conflict Studies. No. 91)*

— Catholic Church — Italy.

Il COMPROMESSO storico: contributi di Giorgio Amendola [and others]; a cura di Pietro Valenza. Roma, 1975. pp. 320.

ZUNINO (PIER GIORGIO) La questione cattolica nella sinistra italiana, 1919-1939. [Bologna, 1975]. pp. 503.

CASULA (CARLO FELICE) Cattolici-comunisti e sinistra cristiana (1938-1945). Bologna, [1976]. pp. 338. *bibliogs.*

— — Russia.

DUNN (DENNIS J.) The Catholic church and the Soviet government, 1939-1949. New York, 1977. pp. 267. *bibliog. (East European Quarterly. East European Monographs. 30)*

— France.

THOREZ (MAURICE) and others. Communistes et chrétiens. Paris, [1976]. pp. 135.

COMMUNISM AND CULTURE.

BUONFINO (GIANCARLO) La politica culturale operaia da Marx e Lassalle alla rivoluzione di novembre, 1859-1919. Milano, 1975. pp. 211.

COMMUNISM AND ECOLOGY.

MARX and Engels on ecology; edited and compiled by Howard L. Parsons. Westport, Conn., [1977]. pp. 262. *bibliog.*

COMMUNISM AND EDUCATION.

PRICE (RONALD FRANCIS) Marx and education in Russia and China. London, [1977]. pp. 376. *bibliog.*

COMMUNISM AND INTELLECTUALS.

BRYM (ROBERT J.) The Jewish intelligentsia and Russian Marxism: a sociological study of intellectual radicalism and ideological divergence. London, 1978. pp. 157. *bibliog.*

COMMUNISM AND LITERATURE.

RUEHLE (JUERGEN) Literature and revolution: a critical study of the writer and communism in the twentieth century. London, 1969. pp. 520. *bibliog. Translated and edited by Jean Steinberg.*

COMMUNISM AND LITERATURE.(Cont.)

MEHLMAN (JEFFREY) Revolution and repetition: Marx, Hugo, Balzac. Berkeley, Calif., [1977]. pp. 132.

SOTSIALISTICHESKII realizm segodnia: problemy i suzhdeniia. Moskva, 1977. pp. 396.

COMMUNISM AND MASS MEDIA.

HOGENKAMP (BERT) Worker's newsreels in the 1920's and 1930's. London, [1977?]. pp. 36. *(Communist Party of Great Britain. History Group. Our History. No. 68)*

COMMUNISM AND RELIGION.

BERAR (PETRU) Tineretul și religia. București, 1974. pp. 120.

NGUYEN NGOC VU. Idéologie et religion d'après Karl Marx et F. Engels. Paris, [1975]. pp. 219.

SAVEL'EV (SERGEI NIKOLAEVICH) Emel'ian Iaroslavskii - propagandist marksistskogo ateizma. Leningrad, 1976. pp. 104. *bibliog.*

COMMUNISM AND SOCIETY.

SOTSIOLOGIIA i sovremennost'. Moskva, 1977. 2 vols.

ROTHMAN (STANLEY) and BRESLAUER (GEORGE W.) Soviet politics and society. St. Paul, [1978]. pp. 341. *bibliog.*

COMMUNIST COUNTRIES

— Biography.

WHO's who in the socialist countries: a biographical encyclopedia of 10,000 leading personalities in 16 communist countries; edited by Borys Lewytzkyj and Juliusz Stroynowski. New York, [1978]. pp. 736.

— Economic conditions.

PUSENKOVA (IRINA VLADIMIROVNA) Neposredstvenno-obshchestvennyi trud i neobkhodimyi produkt pri sotsializme. Moskva, 1976. pp. 199.

— Economic integration.

DOLGIN (VENIAMIN GRIGOR'EVICH) V edinstve - sila sodruzhestva sotsialisticheskikh stran. Moskva, 1977. pp. 199.

EKONOMICHESKAIA integratsiia i material'no-tekhnicheskaia baza stran SEV; pod redaktsiei I.P. Oleinika i V.P. Sergeeva. Moskva, 1977. pp. 255.

EKONOMICHESKAIA integratsiia i material'no-tekhnicheskaia baza stran SEV; pod redaktsiei…I.P. Oleinika i V.P. Sergeeva. Moskva, 1977. pp. 255.

SEREGHYOVÁ (JANA) and others. Závazkové vztahy mezi hospodářskými organizacemi socialistických zemí. Praha, 1977. pp. 163.

— Economic policy.

EKONOMICHESKIE problemy nauchno-tekhnicheskoi revoliutsii pri sotsializme. Moskva, 1975. pp. 263.

ANCHISHKIN (ALEKSANDR IVANOVICH) The theory of growth of a socialist economy. Moscow, 1977. pp. 341.

— Foreign economic relations.

KRASNOV (IURII MATVEEVICH) Ot konfrontatsii k sotrudnichestvu: problemy ekonomicheskogo i nauchno-tekhnicheskogo sotrudnichestva kapitalisticheskikh i sotsialisticheskikh stran Evropy. Moskva, 1976. pp. 199.

ZUSAMMENARBEIT und Annäherung in der sozialistischen Gemeinschaft; (Autorenkollektiv unter Leitung von Joachim Krüger [and others]). Berlin, 1977. pp. 320.

— — Africa.

EKONOMICHESKIE otnosheniia sotsialisticheskikh gosudarstv so stranami Afriki. Moskva, 1973. pp. 235.

— — America, Latin.

STRANY SEV i Latinskaia Amerika: problemy ekonomicheskogo sotrudnichestva. Moskva, 1976. pp. 335.

— Foreign relations.

STOJIĆ-IMAMOVIĆ (EDITA) Stavovi socijalističkih zemalja istočne Evrope u medjunarodnim odnosima. Beograd, 1974. pp. 258. *bibliog.* With English and Russian summaries.

KUKUŁKA (JÓZEF) Współpraca polityczna państw wspólnoty socjalistycznej. Warszawa, 1976. pp. 259.

DOLGIN (VENIAMIN GRIGOR'EVICH) V edinstve - sila sodruzhestva sotsialisticheskikh stran. Moskva, 1977. pp. 199.

ZUSAMMENARBEIT und Annäherung in der sozialistischen Gemeinschaft; (Autorenkollektiv unter Leitung von Joachim Krüger [and others]). Berlin, 1977. pp. 320.

GARVEY (Sir TERENCE) Bones of contention: an enquiry into East-West relations. London, 1978. pp. 203. *bibliog.*

SOZIALISMUS in Theorie und Praxis: Festschrift für Richard Löwenthal zum 70. Geburtstag am 15. April 1978; herausgegeben von Hannelore Horn [and others]. Berlin, 1978. pp. 687. *bibliog.* In various languages.

— — Africa.

GREIG (IAN) The communist challenge to Africa: an analysis of contemporary Soviet, Chinese and Cuban policies. Richmond, Surrey, 1977. pp. 306. *bibliog.*

— — Yugoslavia.

SUKOB s Informbiroom; priredili Maroje Mihovilović, Mario Bošnjak, Sead Saračević. Zagreb, 1976. pp. 145.

— Politics and government.

AUTHORITARIAN politics in Communist Europe: uniformity and diversity in one-party states; Andrew C. Janos, editor. Berkeley, Calif., [1976]. pp. 196. *bibliogs.* *(California University. Institute of International Studies. Research Series. No. 28)* Essays from a colloquium held under the auspices of the Center for Slavic and East European Studies of the University of California, Berkeley in 1973.

IL'INSKII (IGOR' PAVLOVICH) Politicheskaia organizatsiia sotsialisticheskogo obshchestva. Moskva, 1976. pp. 255.

BERTSCH (GARY K.) Power and policy in communist systems. New York, [1978]. pp. 186. *bibliogs.*

— Presidents.

SZYMCZAK (TADEUSZ) Ewolucja instytucji prezydenta w socjalistycznym prawie państwowym. Łódź, 1976. pp. 180. *(Łódź. Łódzkie Towarzystwo Naukowe. Wydział 2 Nauk Historycznych i Społecznych. Prace. Nr.78)* With English summary.

— Relations (general) with Russia.

NA putiakh nerushimoi druzhby: materialy vsesoiuznoi nauchnoi konferentsii "Istoricheskoe znachenie ustanovleniia druzhby i sotrudnichestva mezhdu SSSR i sotsialisticheskimi stranami Evropy", g. Moskva, 24-25 fevralia 1975 g. Moskva, 1977. pp. 319.

COMMUNIST EDUCATION

— Germany.

GERHARD-SONNENBERG (GABRIELE) Marxistische Arbeiterbildung in der Weimarer Zeit: MASCH [Marxistische Arbeiterschule]. Köln, [1976]. pp. 206. *bibliog.*

— Russia.

AKADEMIIA OBSHCHESTVENNYKH NAUK. Kafedra Teorii i Metodov Ideologicheskoi Raboty. Voprosy Teorii i Metodov Ideologicheskoi Raboty. vyp. 7. Sotsial'no-psikhologicheskie aspekty ideologicheskoi deiatel'nosti. Moskva, 1977. pp. 279.

PAS'KO (NINA IVANOVNA) Sotsiologicheskie problemy kommunisticheskogo vospitaniia studencheskoi molodezhi. Kiev, 1977. pp. 191. *bibliog.*

SAFRAZ'IAN (NATALIIA LEONOVNA) Bor'ba KPSS za stroitel'stvo sovetskoi vysshei shkoly, 1921- 1927 gg. Moskva, 1977. pp. 159.

STRUKOV (EDUARD VLADIMIROVICH) Sotsialisticheskii obraz zhizni: teoreticheskie i ideino-vospitatel'nye problemy. Moskva, 1977. pp. 263. *bibliog.*

COMMUNIST PARTIES.

COMMUNISTS of the world about their parties. Prague, 1976. pp. 191. *(Marxism-Leninism and Our Time)*

MUCHAIDZE (GURAM O.) Formirovanie ucheniia marksizma o partii. Tbilisi, 1976. pp. 237.

COMMUNIST power in Europe, 1944-1949; edited by Martin McCauley. London, 1977. pp. 242.

— Congresses.

KONFERENZ der kommunistischen und Arbeiterparteien Europas, Berlin, 29. und 30. Juni 1976: Dokumente und Reden. Berlin, 1976. pp. 277.

— Europe, Eastern.

Die WACHSENDE Rolle der Arbeiterklasse in den sozialistischen Ländern; ([by the] Parteihochschule beim ZK der KPdSU, Moskau [and others]). Berlin, 1974. pp. 359.

COMMUNIST PARTY

— Argentine Republic.

CODOVILLA (VICTORIO) El movimiento sindical y la union nacional; tercera parte del informe rendido al Comite Central del Partido Comunista, el 12 de septiembre de 1942. Buenos Aires, 1942. pp. 38.

CODOVILLA (VICTORIO) Biografía politica de un revolucionario consecuente. Buenos Aires, 1964. pp. 16.

CODOVILLA (VICTORIO) Lo nuevo en la situacion nacional despues de las elecciones: informe presentado al pleno del Comite Central del Partido Comunista, realizado los dias 27 y 28 de marzo de 1965. Buenos Aires, 1965. pp. 39.

PARTIDO COMUNISTA DE LA ARGENTINA. Comité Central. Hacia el XIII congreso del Partido Comunista. Buenos Aires, 1968. pp. 61.

— Bulgaria.

CHICHOVSKA (VESELA) Sobolevata aktsiia. Sofiia, 1972. pp. 109. *bibliog.*

— Cambodia.

CARNEY (TIMOTHY MICHAEL) ed. Communist party power in Kampuchea (Cambodia): documents and discussion. Ithaca, 1977. pp. 76. *bibliog.* *(Cornell University. Department of Asian Studies. Southeast Asia Program. Data Papers. No. 106)*

— China.

BRITISH AND IRISH COMMUNIST ORGANISATION. Policy Statements. No. 3. The Communist Party of China and the 20th congress of the C. P.S.U. Belfast, 1970. pp. 20.

KERRY (TOM) The Mao myth and the legacy of Stalinism in China. New York, [1977]. pp. 190.

— — Congresses.

COMMUNIST PARTY OF CHINA. National Congress, 10th, 1973. [Proceedings]; press communique, report by comrade Chou En- lai, report on revision of party constitution by comrade Wang Hung-Wen, constitution of Communist Party of China. [Peking], 1973. pp. 20. *A supplement of New China News.*

COMMUNIST PARTY OF CHINA. National Congress, 11th, 1977. Documents. Peking, 1977. pp. 236.

— Czechoslovakia.

PŘEHLED dějin KSČ. Praha, 1976. pp. 375.

POLITIKA KSČ: ciele a prostriedky. Bratislava, 1977. pp. 273. *(Komunistická Strana Slovenska. Ústredný Výbor. Ústav Marxizmu-Leninizmu. Zborník. roč.17, č.1)*

— — Congresses.

AKTUÁLNE otázky ekonomického programu XV. zjazdu KSČ. Bratislava, 1977. pp. 252.

— Denmark.

KOMMUNISTISK FORBUND. Kritik af DKP. Aarhus, 1974 repr. 1976. pp. 195.

DANMARKS KOMMUNISTISKE PARTI. Programsamling: udtaleser, erklaeringer og programmer vedtaget på...kongresser, landskonferencer og landsmøder, 1952-1974. [Copenhagen], 1975. pp. 88.

MEIDELL (BJØRN) DKP og storstrejkerne i 1956. København, [1976]. pp. 106.

LUND (HENNING) Udviklingen i Danmarks Kommunistiske Parti, 1956-58: et studie i partisplittelse. Grenå, 1977. pp. 190. *bibliog.*

— France.

Les MILITANTS politiques dans trois partis français: Parti Communiste, Parti Socialiste, Union des Démocrates pour la République, [by] Jacques Lagroye [and others]. [Paris, 1976]. pp. 186. *bibliog. (Bordeaux. Université. Institut d'Etudes Politiques. Centre d'Etude et de Recherche sur la Vie Locale. Série Vie Locale. 5.)*

LECOEUR (AUGUSTE) Le PCF : continuité dans le changement. Paris, [1977]. pp. 237.

STIEFBOLD (ANNETTE EISENBERG) The French Communist Party in transition: PCF-CPSU relations and the challenge to Soviet authority. New York, [1977]. pp. 155.

TROTSKII (LEV DAVYDOVICH) The crisis of the French section, 1935-36. New York, [1977]. pp. 286.

— — History.

FAUVET (JACQUES) Histoire du Parti communiste français de 1920 à 1976;...en collaboration avec Alain Duhamel. 2nd ed. [Paris, 1977]. pp. 605. *bibliog.*

— Germany.

FISCHER (RUTH) Stalin und der deutsche Kommunismus: der Übergang zur Konterrevolution; (translated from the English by H. Langerhans). Frankfurt am Main, [1950]. pp. 844.

Die BOLSCHEWISIERUNG der KPD. 2nd ed. Berlin, 1970 repr. 1973-74. 2 vols. *Collection of documents most of which were originally published in 1925-26.*

KLINGEMANN (HANS DIETER) and PAPPI (FRANZ URBAN) Politischer Radikalismus:...dargestellt am Beispiel einer Studie anlässlich der Landtagswahl 1970 in Hessen. München, 1972. pp. 124. *bibliog.*

THAELMANN (ERNST) Ausgewählte Reden und Schriften in zwei Bänden. Frankfurt am Main, 1976-77. 2 vols.

DOKUMENTE und Materialien zum gemeinsamen Kampf der revolutionären deutschen und polnischen Arbeiterbewegung, 1918- 1939; bearbeitet und eingeleitet von Franciszek Hawranek [and others]. Berlin, [1977]. pp. 335.

EHRENBERG (ERNST N.) Die Bündnispolitik der Deutschen Kommunistischen Partei mit dem Deutschen Gewerkschaftsbund. Gerbrunn bei Würzburg, [1977]. pp. 306. *bibliog.*

EILDERMANN (WILHELM) Als Wanderredner der KPD unterwegs: Erinnerungen an die ersten Jahre der KPD, 1919-1920. Berlin, 1977. pp. 170.

EISNER (FREYA) Das Verhältnis der KPD zu den Gewerkschaften in der Weimarer Republik. Köln, [1977]. pp. 271. *bibliog. (Otto Brenner Stiftung. Schriftenreihe. 8)*

GERNS (WILLI) and STEIGERWALD (ROBERT REINHOLD) Für eine sozialistische Bundesrepublik: Fragen und Antworten zur Strategie und Taktik der DKP. 2nd ed. Frankfurt am Main, 1977. pp. 95.

HERLEMANN (BEATRIX) Kommunalpolitik der KPD im Ruhrgebiet, 1924-1933. Wuppertal, [1977]. pp. 339. *bibliog.*

SCHOECK (EVA CORNELIA) Arbeitslosigkeit und Rationalisierung: die Lage der Arbeiter und die kommunistische Gewerkschaftspolitik, 1920-28. Frankfurt, [1977]. pp. 280. *bibliog.*

THAELMANN (ERNST) Über proletarischen Internationalismus: Reden und Artikel, [1925-1934]. Leipzig, 1977. pp. 250.

— — History.

WIESNER (ERICH) Man nannte mich Ernst: Erlebnisse und Episoden aus der Geschichte der Arbeiterjugendbewegung. 4th ed. Berlin, 1978. pp. 316.

— Germany, Eastern.

OELSSNER (FRED) Die Sowjetunion, unser Vorbild und Freund: Festrede auf der Feier des Parteivorstandes der Sozialistischen Einheitspartei Deutschlands...am 6. November 1949...zu Berlin. Berlin, [1949]. pp. 41.

— — History.

GESCHICHTE der Sozialistischen Einheitspartei Deutschlands: Abriss; ([by] Ernst Diehl [and others]). Frankfurt am Main, 1978. pp. 677.

— India.

SAIYID (DUSHKA HYDER) The Comintern and the Communist Party of India, 1920-1929. 1977 [or rather 1978]. fo.203. *bibliog. Typescript. M.Phil. (London) thesis: unpublished. This thesis is the property of London University and may not be removed from the Library.*

— Iraq.

GABBAY (RONY E.) Communism and agrarian reform in Iraq. London, [1978]. pp. 240. *bibliog.*

— Israel.

GREILSAMMER (ALAIN) Les communistes israéliens. Paris, [1978]. pp. 415. *bibliog.*

— Italy.

CAMBONI (GIANFRANCO) and SAMSA (DANILO) PCI e movimento degli studenti, 1968-1973: ceti medi e strategi delle riforme. Bari, [1975]. pp. 208. *bibliog.*

MONTALDI (DANILO) Korsch e i comunisti italiani: contro un facile spirito di assimilazione. Roma, 1975. pp. 79.

PETTA (PAOLO) Ideologie costituzionali della sinistra italiana, 1892-1974. Roma, [1975]. pp. 239.

TOGLIATTI (PALMIRO) Togliatti e il centrosinistra: 1958-(1964). Firenze, [1975]. 2 vols.

BERLINGUER (ENRICO) La politica internazionale dei comunisti italiani, 1975-1976; a cura di Antonio Tatò. [Roma, 1976]. pp. 226.

BRANCOLI (RODOLFO) Gli USA e il PCI. Milano, 1976. pp. 197.

CRISI economica e stalinismo in occidente: l'opposizione comunista italiana alla "svolta" del '30; a cura di Ferdinando Ormea. Roma, 1976. pp. 230.

MATTEUCCI (NICOLA) Dal populismo al compromesso storico. [Roma, 1976]. pp. 194.

NAPOLITANO (GIORGIO) Intervista sul PCI; a cura di Eric J. Hobsbawm. Roma, 1976. pp. 132.

PARTITO DI UNITÀ PROLETARIA PER IL COMUNISMO. Federazione Milanese. Gruppo di Lavoro Teoria e Controinformazione. Convegno, Maggio 1975. Da Togliatti alla nuova sinistra: (atti). [Roma, 1976]. pp. 290.

La POLITICA militare dei comunisti: la difesa nazionale, l'ordinamento delle forze armate e i diritti democratici dei militari; [by Arrigo Boldrini and others]. [Roma, 1976]. pp. 233. *Papers presented at a conference held by the Centro di Studi e Iniziative per la Riforma dello Stato in 1974.*

TISO (AIDA) I comunisti e la questione femminile. Roma, 1976. pp. 151. *bibliog.*

VENÉ (GIAN FRANCO) La borghesia comunista. Milano, [1976]. pp. 199. *bibliogs.*

ZACCAGNINI (BENIGNO) Una proposta al paese. 2nd ed. [Firenze, 1976]. pp. 131.

ASOR ROSA (ALBERTO) and others. PCI, classe operaia e movimento studentesco; a cura di Gregorio Paolini e Walter Vitali. [Rimini, 1977]. pp. 250.

CHIAROMONTE (GERARDO) L'accordo programmatico e l'azione dei comunisti: (la relazione al Comitato centrale del PCI, 20 luglio 1977). Roma, [1977]. pp. 116.

EGEMONIA e democrazia: Gramsci e la questione comunista nel dibattito di Mondoperaio. Roma, 1977. pp. 249. *(Mondoperaio. Quaderni. Nuova Serie. 7)*

Il COMPROMESSO storico; a cura di Luciano Gruppi. [Roma, 1977]. pp. 345.

NAPOLITANO (GIORGIO) The Italian road to socialism: an interview by Eric Hobsbawm with Giorgio Napolitano of the Italian Communist Party. Westport, Conn., 1977. pp. 118.

OLTRE Gramsci? [Roma, 1977]. pp. 155. *Interviews on the subject, "Gramsci e il P.C.I. oggi", first published in Il Popolo, 1977.*

PONS (VITTORIO) The long-term strategy of Italy's communists. London, 1977. pp. 15. *(Institute for the Study of Conflict. Conflict Studies. No. 87)*

SECCHIA (PIETRO) Chi sono i comunisti: partito e masse nella vita nazionale, 1948- 1970; a cura e con prefazione di Ambrogio Donini. [Milano, 1977]. pp. 335.

— — History.

CORDOVA (FERDINANDO) Alle origini del PCI in Calabria, 1918-1926. [Roma, 1977]. pp. 174.

— — — Sources.

VIDOTTO (VITTORIO) compiler. Il Partito Comunista Italiano dalle origini al 1946: [a collection of documents]. [Bologna, 1975]. pp. 422. *bibliog.*

— Korea — History.

LEE (CHONG-SIK) The Korean Workers' Party: a short history. Stanford, [1978]. pp. 167. *bibliog. (Stanford University. Hoover Institution on War, Revolution and Peace. Hoover Institution Publications. 185)*

— Mexico.

PACHECO MENDEZ (GUADALUPE) and others. Cardenas y la izquierda mexicana: ensayo, testimonios, documentos. Mexico, [1976]. pp. 391. *bibliog.*

— Mongolia — Congresses.

MONGOL ARDYN KHUV'SGALT NAM. S″ezd, 17-yi, 1976. XVII s″ezd Mongol'skoi narodno-revoliutsionnoi partii, Ulan- Bator, 14-18 iiunia 1976 g.: osnovnye materialy i dokumenty. Moskva, 1977. pp. 175.

COMMUNIST PARTY (Cont.)

— Palestine.

BUDEIRI (MUSA KHALIL) The Palestine Communist Party: its Arabisation and the Arab Jewish conflict in Palestine, 1929-1948. 1977. fo. 321. *bibliog*. Typescript. *Ph.D. (London) thesis: unpublished. This thesis is the property of London University and may not be removed from the Library.*

— Poland.

KARTKI z dziejów KPP. Warszawa, 1958. pp. 499.

SYZDEK (BRONISŁAW) ed. Działalność PPR na ziemi Rzeszowskiej: szkice, opracowania, wspomnienia: zbiór. Warszawa, 1976. pp. 435.

DOKUMENTE und Materialien zum gemeinsamen Kampf der revolutionären deutschen und polnischen Arbeiterbewegung, 1918- 1939; bearbeitet und eingeleitet von Franciszek Hawranek [and others]. Berlin, [1977]. pp. 335.

— Portugal — Congresses.

PARTIDO COMUNISTA PORTUGUÊS. Congresso, 7 (Extraordinario), 1974. VII Congresso (Extraordinario), 20 de outubro de 1974: intervenções, saudações, documentos. [Lisboa], 1974. pp. 388.

PARTIDO COMUNISTA PORTUGUS Congresso, 8°, 1976. VIII congresso doPCP: 11 a 14 nov 1976. Lisboa. 1977. pp. 308.

— Romania.

PETRESCU (MIHAI M.) Partide, clase, naţiuni: originea şi rolul istoric al partidelor politice în perspectiva socialismului ştiinţific. Bucureşti, 1977. pp. 255.

— Russia.

OELSSNER (FRED) Die Sowjetunion, unser Vorbild und Freund: Festrede auf der Feier des Parteivorstandes der Sozialistischen Einheitspartei Deutschlands...am 6. November 1949...zu Berlin. Berlin, [1949]. pp. 41.

FISCHER (RUTH) Stalin und der deutsche Kommunismus: der Übergang zur Konterrevolution; (translated from the English by H. Langerhans). Frankfurt am Main, [1950]. pp. 844.

SEMENTSOVA (VERA VLADIMIROVNA) and SUIAROVA (EVGENIIA VLADIMIROVNA) Partiinyi i gosudarstvennyi kontrol' na Severnom Kavkaze v 1923-1925 gg. Rostov-na-Donu, 1973. pp. 159.

POTASHEV (FEDOR IVANOVICH) Reorganizatsiia Rabkrina i TsKK: tvorcheskoe razvitie i osushchestvlenie Kommunisticheskoi partiei leninskogo plana reorganizatsii Rabkrina. Rostov-na-Donu, 1974. pp. 216.

LEKTSII po istorii KPSS. vyp.3. 2nd ed. Moskva, 1975. pp. 552.

VO glave bor'by trudiashchikhsia za diktaturu proletariata i sotsialisticheskogo stroitel'stva: iz istorii partiinykh organizatsii Severo-Zapada RSFSR. Petrozavodsk, 1975. pp. 190.

NIKISHOV (PETR PETROVICH) Bor'ba bol'shevikov za uprochenie vlasti Sovetov v Kirgizii; pod redaktsiei V.V. Mirtova. Frunze, 1976. pp. 160. *(Kommunisticheskaia Partiia Kirgizii. Tsentral'nyi Komitet. Institut Istorii Partii. Bibliotechnaia Seriia)*

DVOINISHNIKOV (MIKHAIL ALEKSANDROVICH) Rukovodstvo KPSS vosstanovleniem i pazvitiem promyshlennosti v poslevoennyi period. Moskva, 1977. pp. 128.

PARTIIA v period razvitogo sotsialisticheskogo obshchestva: materialy Vsesoiuznoi nauchno-teoreticheskoi konferentsii "XXV s"ezd KPSS i razvitie marksistsko-leninskoi teorii", Moskva, 4-6 oktiabria 1976 goda. Moskva, 1977. pp. 230.

SAFRAZ'IAN (NATALIIA LEOŃOVNA) Bor'ba KPSS za stroitel'stvo sovetskoi vysshei shkoly, 1921- 1927 gg. Moskva, 1977. pp. 159.

STIEFBOLD (ANNETTE EISENBERG) The French Communist Party in transition: PCF-CPSU relations and the challenge to Soviet authority. New York, [1977]. pp. 155.

ZETKIN (CLARA) Für die Sowjetmacht: Artikel, Reden und Briefe, 1917-1933. Frankfurt am Main, 1977. pp. 485.

— — Congresses.

BRITISH AND IRISH COMMUNIST ORGANISATION. Policy Statements. No. 3. The Communist Party of China and the 20th congress of the C. P.S.U. Belfast, 1970. pp. 20.

NAUCHNO-ISSLEDOVATEL'SKII INSTITUT PLANIROVANIIA I NORMATIVOV. Nauchnye Trudy. Voprosy sovershenstvovaniia planirovaniia promyshlennosti v svete reshenii XXV s"ezda KPSS; pod redaktsiei N.M. Oznobina, A.I. Zalkinda. Moskva, 1976. pp. 182.

XXV s"ezd KPSS i razvitie marksistsko-leninskoi teorii: materialy Vsesoiuznoi nauchno-teoreticheskoi konferentsii, Moskva, 4-6 oktiabria 1976 goda: plenarnoe zasedanie; [doklady P.N. Fedoseeva, A.G. Egorova, N.N. Inozemtseva]. Moskva, 1977. pp. 110.

XXV s"ezd KPSS: osnovnye napravleniia ekonomicheskogo razvitiia. Kiev, 1977. pp. 208.

The TWENTY-fifth Congress of the CPSU: assessment and context; Alexander Dallin, editor. Stanford, Calif., 1977. pp. 127. *(Stanford University. Hoover Institution on War, Revolution and Peace. Hoover Institution Publications. 184) Papers presented at a conference held at Stanford University, April 2, 1976.*

— — History.

WESSON (ROBERT GALE) Lenin's legacy: the story of the CPSU. Stanford, [1978]. pp. 318. *bibliog.* (Stanford University. Hoover Institution on War, Revolution and Peace. Hoover Institution Publications. 192)

— — Party work.

AKADEMIIA OBSHCHESTVENNYKH NAUK. Kafedra Partiinogo Stroitel'stva. [Voprosy Teorii i Praktiki Partiinogo Stroitel'stva. vyp.2] Pervichnaia partiinaia organizatsiia - avangard trudovogo kollektiva Moskva, 1975. pp. 216.

ANISKOV (VIKTOR TIKHONOVICH) S polei kolkhoznykh na polia srazhenii: partiino-organizatorskaia deiatel'nost' v iaroslavskoi i kostromskoi derevne v gody Velikoi Otechestvennoi voiny. Iaroslavl', 1975. pp. 208. *bibliog.*

IDEOLOGICHESKAIA i organizatorskaia rabota KPSS v period stroitel'stva sotsializma i kommunizma. Leningrad, 1976. pp. 144.

PARTIIA vo glave narodnoi bor'by v tylu vraga, 1941-1944 gg. Moskva, 1976. pp. 325.

ANDRUKHOV (NIKOLAI ROMANOVICH) Partiinoe stroitel'stvo v period bor'by za pobedu sotsializma v SSSR, 1917-1937. Moskva, 1977. pp. 375.

BAIKOVA (VALENTINA GAVRILOVNA) Ideologicheskaia rabota KPSS v usloviiakh razvitogo sotsializma: nekotorye voprosy teoorii i praktiki. Moskva, 1977. pp. 214.

— — Azerbaijan — Party work.

NIKOLAEV (KONSTANTIN MIKHAILOVICH) Rost rabochego iadra Kompartii Azerbaidzhana, 1959-1970 gg. Baku, 1974. pp. 106.

— — Estonia — Congresses.

KOMMUNISTICHESKAIA PARTIIA ESTONII. S"ezd, 17-yi, 1976. XVII s"ezd Kommunisticheskoi partii Estonii, 28-30 ianvaria 1976 goda. Tallin, 1976. pp. 131.

— — Lithuania — Statistics.

KOMMUNISTICHESKAIA PARTIIA LITVY. Tsentral'nyi Komitet. Institut Istorii Partii. Lietuvos Komunistu partija skaičiais, 1918-1975: statistikos duomenu rinkinys; Kommunisticheskaia partiia Litvy v tsifrakh, 1918-1975: sbornik statisticheskikh dannykh. Vilnius, 1976. pp. 288. *With Russian table of contents.*

— — Tajikistan — History — Sources.

MATERIALY k istorii Kommunisticheskoi partii Tadzhikistana. vyp. 6. Dushanbe, 1975. pp. 391.

— — Ukraine — Congresses.

KOMMUNISTICHESKAIA PARTIIA UKRAINY. S"ezd, 25-yi, 1976. XXV s"ezd Kommunisticheskoi partii Ukrainy, 10-13 fevralia, 1976 goda: stenograficheskii otchet. Kiev, 1976. pp. 494.

— — — History.

NARYSY istoriï Mykolaïvs'koï oblasnoï partiinoï orhanizatsiï, 1897-1968 rr. Odesa, 1969. pp. 419.

OCHERKI istorii Kommunisticheskoi partii Ukrainy. 4th ed. Kiev, 1977. pp. 814.

— — White Russia — Party work.

VOPROSY istorii KPSS: nekotorye voprosy organizatorskoi i ideologicheskoi deiatel'nosti KPSS: mezhvedomstvennyi sbornik 8. Minsk, 1977. pp. 167.

— Sweden.

SVERIGES KOMMUNISTISKA PARTI. Kongress, 1876. Dokument från...andra kongress. Stockholm, [1976]. pp. 163.

— — History.

FRÅN SKP [Sveriges Kommunistiska Parti] till VPK [VÄnsterpartiet Kommunisterna]: en antologi redigerad av Sven E. Olsson. [Lund], 1976. pp. 276. *bibliog.*

— Switzerland.

LOERTSCHER (CLIVE) Le Parti communiste suisse et les syndicats, 1920-1921: stratégie de front unique en Suisse. Lausanne, 1977. pp. 219. *bibliog.*

HOFMAIER (KARL) Memoiren eines Schweizer Kommunisten, 1917-1947. Zürich, 1978. pp. 303.

— United Kingdom.

COMMUNIST PARTY OF GREAT BRITAIN. Central Committee. Copy of the application for affiliation made by the Communist Party to the Labour Party on November 25, 1935. London, 1935. s.sh. *Signed Harry Pollitt.*

COMMUNIST PARTY OF GREAT BRITAIN. London District Committee. Royal jubilee: 25 years of war and starvation. London, 1935. pp. 4.

SOCIALIST WORKER. Training Series. [No.] 3. The British Communist Party. London, [1976]. pp. 24.

JOURNES (CLAUDE) L'extrême gauche en Grande-Bretagne. Paris, 1977. pp. 229. *bibliog.*

MATTHEWS (BETTY) The revolutionary party. London, 1977. pp. 16.

COMMUNIST PARTY OF GREAT BRITAIN. The British road to socialism: programme of the Communist Party. 5th ed. London, 1978. pp. 61.

McSHANE (HARRY) and SMITH (JOAN) Harry McShane: no mean fighter. London, 1978. pp. 282.

— — Programme.

COMMUNIST PARTY OF GREAT BRITAIN. For Soviet Britain: the programme of the Communist Party adopted at the XIII Congress February 2nd, 1935; with a preface by R. Page Arnot. London, [1935?]. pp. 48.

— Uruguay.

ARISMENDI (RODNEY) La izquierda uruguaya ante la hora de America latina. [Montevideo, 1967]. pp. 63.

ARISMENDI (RODNEY) Conversando con los jovenes: algunos temas en debate acerca de nuestra revolucion. [Montevideo, 1968]. pp. (32).

[PARTIDO COMUNISTA DEL URUGUAY]. Congreso, 17, 1958. Declaracion programatica y plataforma politica inmediata del Partido Comunista; documento aprobado por XVII Congreso, 15-17 de Agosto de 1958. Montevideo, 1969. pp. 29.

— Venezuela.

CASTRO RUZ (FIDEL) Criticas a la direccion del Partido Comunista de Venezuela. Montevideo, Nativa Libros, 1967. pp. 39.

— Vietnam — History.

PIKE (DOUGLAS) History of Vietnamese communism, 1925-1976. Stanford, [1978]. pp. 181. bibliog. (Stanford University. Hoover Institution on War, Revolution and Peace. Hoover Institution Publications. 189)

— Yugoslavia.

KOMUNISTIČKA partija Jugoslavije u ratu i revoluciji: istina o navodno oslbodilačkoj [sic] borbi. [München], 1975. pp. 128.

COMMUNIST REVISIONISM.

BRITISH AND IRISH COMMUNIST ORGANISATION. Policy Statements. No. 3. The Communist Party of China and the 20th congress of the C. P.S.U. Belfast, 1970. pp. 20.

MATĚJÍČEK (JAROSLAV) Politický systém socialismu a kritika pravicového revizionismu v ČSSR. Praha, 1976. pp. 251. With Russian summary.

BEJDA (VASIL) Politika a ideológia: k vývoju v strane a spoločnosti v nedávnom období. Bratislava, 1977. pp. 235.

GREBING (HELGA) Der Revisionismus: von Bernstein bis zum "Prager Frühling". München, [1977]. pp. 281. bibliogs.

HEVESI (MARIA) Iz istorii kritiki filosofskikh dogm II Internatsionala. Moskva, 1977. pp. 207.

SANTARELLI (ENZO) La revisione del marxismo in Italia: studi di critica storica. rev. ed. [Milano, 1977]. pp. 343.

COMMUNIST STATE.

IL'INSKII (IGOR' PAVLOVICH) Politicheskaia organizatsiia sotsialisticheskogo obshchestva. Moskva, 1976. pp. 255.

GOSUDARSTVO, demokratiia i trudovoi kollektiv v razvitom sotsialisticheskom obshchestve. Moskva, 1977. pp. 200.

HOUGH (JERRY F.) The Soviet Union and social science theory. Cambridge, Mass., 1977. pp. 275. (Harvard University. Russian Research Center. Studies. 77)

KALENSKII (VALERII GEORGIEVICH) Gosudarstvo kak ob"ekt sotsiologicheskogo analiza: ocherki istorii i metodologii issledovaniia; otvetstvennyi redaktor V.E. Guliev. Moskva, 1977. pp. 182.

BERTSCH (GARY K.) Power and policy in communist systems. New York, [1978]. pp. 186. bibliogs.

COMMUNIST STRATEGY.

FREDERIK (HANS) Volksfront: der taktische Einsatz der Sowjetunion, um mit Hilfe der Einheitsfrontaktionen zwischen Sozialdemokraten und Kommunisten und der Bündnispolitik mit bürgerlichen Regierungen die materielle und politische Weltordnung des Westens abzulösen. Landshut, 1977. pp. 544.

GREIG (IAN) The communist challenge to Africa: an analysis of contemporary Soviet, Chinese and Cuban policies. Richmond, Surrey, 1977. pp. 306. bibliog.

CROZIER (BRIAN) Strategy of survival. London, 1978. pp. 224. bibliog.

CROZIER (BRIAN) The surrogate forces of the Soviet Union. London, 1978. pp. 20. (Institute for the Study of Conflict. Conflict Studies. No. 92)

COMMUNIST TEACHERS

— United Kingdom.

The ATTACK on higher education: where does it come from?; a reply to the Gould Report [by Anthony Arblaster and others]. [London, 1977]. pp. 24.

GOULD (JULIUS) The attack on higher education: Marxist and radical penetration; report of a study group of the Institute for the Study of Conflict. London, 1977. pp. 55. (Institute for the Study of Conflict. Special Reports)

COMMUNIST TRIALS

— United States.

BELKNAP (MICHAL R.) Cold war political justice: the Smith Act, the Communist Party, and American civil liberties. Westport, Conn., 1977. pp. 322. bibliog.

COMMUNISTIC SETTLEMENTS

— China.

WALLACE (CHRISTOPHER ST. JOHN) Motivation and incentives in rural China. [n.p., 1977?]. fo.220. bibliog.

— Israel.

ICHUD HABONIM. Kibbutz: a new society?: an anthology. Tel Aviv, [1971?]. pp. 222.

— Nigeria.

BARRETT (STANLEY R.) The rise and fall of an African utopia: a wealthy theocracy in comparative perspective. [Waterloo, Ont., 1977]. pp. 251. bibliog. (McGill University. Centre for Developing Area Studies. Development Perspectives. 1)

— United States.

HAYDEN (DOLORES) Seven American utopias: the architecture of communitarian socialism, 1790-1975. Cambridge, Mass., [1976]. pp. 401. bibliog.

HALL (JOHN R.) The ways out: utopian communal groups in an age of Babylon. London, 1978. pp. 269. bibliog.

COMMUNISTS

— Canada.

SMITH (ALBERT EDWARD) All my life: an autobiography. Toronto, 1949 repr. 1977. pp. 269.

— Italy.

GUARNIERI (SILVIO) L'intellettuale nel partito. [Venezia, 1976]. pp. 303.

FORNASIERO (FLAVIO) Cantavamo l'Internazionale. Milano, [1977]. pp. 159.

— Poland.

WYSZOMIRSKA-KUŹMIŃSKA (OTILDA) Aleksander Zawadzki. Warszawa, 1977. pp. 93.

— Russia — White Russia.

BERGMAN (ALEKSANDRA) Rzecz o Bronisławie Taraszkiewiczu. Warszawa, 1977. pp. 243.

— United States.

DENNIS (PEGGY) The autobiography of an American communist: a personal view of a political life, 1925-1975. Westport, 1977. pp. 302.

COMMUNITY.

FISCHER (CLAUDE S.) and others. Networks and places: social relations in the urban setting. New York, [1977]. pp. 229. bibliog.

GOIST (PARK DIXON) From Main Street to State Street: town, city, and community in America. Port Washington, N.Y., 1977. pp. 180. bibliog.

ROSS (JENNIE-KEITH) Old people, new lives: community creation in a retirement residence. Chicago, 1977. pp. 227. bibliog.

COMMUNITY AND SCHOOL.

FUENTES (LUIS) Puerto Rican, black and Chinese community control in New York city: the fight against racism in our schools. New York, [1973]. pp. 15.

— Bibliography.

RANDELL (SHIRLEY K.) and TURNBULL (JENNIFER M.) compilers. The school and the community: a bibliography. Canberra, Schools Commission, 1976. pp. 105.

COMMUNITY ANTENNA TELEVISION

— Social aspects — United States.

POWLEDGE (FRED) An A[merican] C[ivil] L[iberties] U[nion] guide to cable television. New York, [1972]. pp. 46. bibliog.

COMMUNITY-BASED CORRECTIONS

— United Kingdom.

HARDING (JOHN) Probation Officer, ed. Community service by offenders: the Nottinghamshire experiment. London, [1974]. pp. 63. bibliog. (National Association for the Care and Resettlement of Offenders. Papers and Reprints. No.9)

DURHAM (COUNTY). County Council. Community Service Committee. Annual report incorporating Progress report. a., 1976- Durham.

PEASE (KENNETH) and others. Community service assessed in 1976; a Home Office Research Unit report. London, 1977. pp. 26. bibliog. (U.K. Home Office. Home Office Research Studies. No.39)

SCULL (ANDREW T.) Decarceration: community treatment and the deviant: a radical view. Englewood Cliffs, [1977]. pp. 184. bibliog.

— United States.

SCULL (ANDREW T.) Decarceration: community treatment and the deviant: a radical view. Englewood Cliffs, [1977]. pp. 184. bibliog.

COMMUNITY CENTRES

— Australia — New South Wales.

HOROWITZ (LISA) A study of community aid centres in New South Wales. Canberra, 1975. pp. 50. (Australia. Commission of Inquiry into Poverty. Research Reports)

— United Kingdom.

SNAITH (JILL) An information service in a deprived housing estate. Glasgow, 1976. pp. 20. bibliog. (Glasgow. University. Department of Economic and Social Research. Discussion Papers in Social Research. No. 16)

LLEWELYN-DAVIES WEEKS [AND PARTNERS]. Inner area study: Birmingham: Family Service Unit: 435 Neighbourhood Centre. [London], Department of the Environment, [1977]. pp. 63.

OLDHAM COMMUNITY DEVELOPMENT PROJECT. Neighbourhood information and advice centres: Oldham C[ommunity] D[evelopment] P[roject]; edited by Neil Shenton and Pat Collis. [Oldham], 1977. pp. 83, xliv. bibliog.

COMMUNITY DEVELOPMENT.

COMMUNITY DEVELOPMENT.

ARMSTRONG (ROBERT) 1930- and others. Case studies in overseas community development; vol. 1. [Manchester, 1975]. pp. 122. *(Manchester. University. Department of Adult Education. Manchester Monographs)*

NORTON (MICHAEL) Community. London, 1977. pp. 250. *(The Directory of Social Change. vol.2)*

— Colombia.

LEYVA DURAN (ALVARO) Centros de integracion y de desarrollo de la comunidad. Bogota, 1972. pp. 139. *bibliog.*

— European Economic Community countries.

CORRIE (JOHN ALEXANDER) and SCOTT-HOPKINS (JAMES SIDNEY RAWDON) Toward a community rural policy. London, [1978]. pp. 24. *bibliog.*

— France.

AMENAGEMENT des zones rurales et de leur armature urbaine: rapport du groupe de travail de la Commission de l'Aménagement du Territoire et du Cadre de Vie; (préparation du 7e plan). Paris, [1976]. pp. 127. *Cover title reads Développement des zones rurales et de leur armature urbaine.*

— Rhodesia.

PROJECTS AND PEOPLE: community development and local government in Rhodesia; (pd. by the Branch of Community Development Training [Rhodesia]). 2 a yr., Ja 1971 (no.1)- Salisbury.

RHODESIAN COMMUNITY DEVELOPMENT REVIEW, THE; (pd. by the Branch of Community Development Training [Rhodesia]). a., Je 1971 - Je 1973 (v.3, nos.2-4); ceased pbln. [Salisbury].

— United Kingdom.

CRAWFORTH (JOHN) and others. Working in the community. Nottingham, [1975]. pp. 109. *bibliogs. (Nottingham. University. Department of Applied Social Science. Social Work Studies. No. 1)*

DAVIS (ALAN) and others. The management of deprivation: final report of Southwark Community Development Project. [London, 1977]. pp. 100.

— United States.

KAISER (HARVEY H.) The building of cities: development and conflict. Ithaca, [1978]. pp. 217.

COMMUNITY DEVELOPMENT CORPORATIONS

— United States.

BERNDT (HARRY EDWARD) New rulers in the ghetto: the community development corporation and urban poverty. Westport, Conn., 1977. pp. 161. *bibliog.*

KELLY (RITA MAE) Community control of economic development: the boards of directors of community development corporations. New York, [1977]. pp. 174.

COMMUNITY HEALTH SERVICES

— Asia.

COMMUNITY health in Asia: a report on two workshops; editor Susan B. Rifkin. Singapore, 1977. pp. 149. *bibliogs. (Christian Conference of Asia. Health Concerns)*

— Australia.

COMMUNITY health services. Canberra, 1977. pp. 130. *bibliog. (Australia. Commission of Inquiry into Poverty. Social/Medical Aspects of Poverty Series)*

— United States.

LOEWENTHAL (NORMAN H.) and BURBY (RAYMOND J.) Health care in new communities. Cambridge, Mass., [1976]. pp. 252. *bibliog. (North Carolina University. Center for Urban and Regional Studies. New Communities Research Series)*

— — Citizen participation.

PARKUM (VIRGINIA COHN) Efficacy and action: an extension of the efficacy concept in relation to selected aspects of citizen participation. Mannheim, 1976. pp. 198. *bibliog.*

COMMUNITY LEADERSHIP.

KELLY (RITA MAE) Community control of economic development: the boards of directors of community development corporations. New York, [1977]. pp. 174.

COMMUNITY LIFE.

GLASSER (RALPH) The net and the quest: patterns of community and how they can survive progress. London, 1977. pp. 263. *bibliog.*

COMMUNITY MENTAL HEALTH SERVICES.

SEGAL (STEVEN P.) and AVIRAM (URI) The mentally ill in community-based sheltered care: a study of community care and social integration. New York, [1978]. pp. 337. *bibliogs.*

— United Kingdom.

NATIONAL ASSOCIATION FOR MENTAL HEALTH. Mind Reports. 16. The next step: community care for former psychiatric patients in six towns. London, [1977?]. PP. 24.

— United States — California.

SEGAL (STEVEN P.) and AVIRAM (URI) The mentally ill in community-based sheltered care: a study of community care and social integration. New York, [1978]. pp. 337. *bibliogs.*

COMMUNITY NEWSPAPERS

— United Kingdom.

COMMUNITY work through a community newspaper; by YVFF workers in Stoke-on-Trent, John Armstrong, Peter Hudson, Michael Key and independent evaluators, John Whittaker and Marian Whittaker. London, [1976]. pp. 48. *(Young Volunteer Force Foundation. Community and Youth Work Papers)*

COMMUNITY ORGANIZATION.

BATLEY (RICHARD) and others. An evaluation of two neighbourhood schems in Liverpool and Teesside. Leeds, [1975?]. fo. 96. *(Centre for Environmental Studies. Working Papers)*

HOROWITZ (LISA) A study of community aid centres in New South Wales. Canberra, 1975. pp. 50. *(Australia. Commission of Inquiry into Poverty. Research Reports)*

GROSSER (CHARLES F.) New directions in community organization: from enabling to advocacy. [2nd ed.]. New York, 1976. pp. 286.

WOLF (STEPHANIE GRAUMAN) Urban village: population, community and family structure in Germantown, Pennsylvania 1683-1800. Princeton, N.J., [1976]. pp. 361. *bibliog.*

COCKBURN (CYNTHIA) The local state: management of cities and people. London, 1977, repr. 1978. pp. 207.

COMMUNITY or class struggle?; [by] John Cowley [and others]. London, 1977. pp. 246.

GILBERT (NEIL) and SPECHT (HARRY) Coordinating social services: an analysis of community, organizational, and staff characteristics. New York, 1977. pp. 84.

HUMAN services and resource networks; [by] Seymour B. Sarason [and others]. San Francisco, 1977. pp. 201. *bibliog.*

NORTON (MICHAEL) Community. London, 1977. pp. 250. *(The Directory of Social Change. vol.2)*

TOTTENHAM COMMUNITY PROJECT. A better place. London, 1977. pp. 77.

BAKER (JOHN) of the Association for Neighbourhood Councils. The neighbourhood advice centre: a community project in Camden. London, 1978. pp. 310. *bibliog.*

GRIMOND (JOSEPH) The common welfare. London, 1978. pp. 248.

POUNTNEY (MELVILLE TREVOR) Planning and the concept of community: a brief assessment of the theory of community and the practice of community building in the setting of Washington New Town. Watford, [1978]. pp. 26. *(Building Research Establishment [U.K.]. Current Papers. 78/2).*

COMMUNITY POWER.

BASSAND (MICHEL) and FRAGNIERE (JEAN PIERRE) Les ambiguités de la démocratie locale: la structure du pouvoir de deux villes jurassiennes. [n.p., 1976]. pp. 166. *bibliog.*

DOMHOFF (G. WILLIAM) Who really rules?: New Haven and community power reexamined. New Brunswick, N.J., [1978]. pp. 189.

COMMUNITY PSYCHOLOGY.

BENDER (M.P.) Community psychology. London, 1976. pp. 144. *bibliog.*

COMMUNITY SCHOOLS

— United States.

BOYD (JOHN) Community education and urban schools. London, 1977. pp. 82. *bibliog.*

COMMUTING

— Australia.

AUSTRALIA. Commonwealth Bureau of Census and Statistics. 1976. Journey to work and journey to school, August 1974. Canberra, 1976. pp. 28.

— United States.

KIRKWOOD (T.F.) Effects of a V/STOL commuter transportation system on road congestion in the San Francisco Bay area. Santa Monica, 1972. pp. 25. *bibliog. (Rand Corporation. [Rand Reports]. 1075)*

GILLARD (QUENTIN) Incomes and accessibility: metropolitan labor force participation, commuting and income differentials in the United States, 1960- 1970. Chicago, 1977. pp. 106. *bibliog. (Chicago. University. Department of Geography. Research Papers. No. 175)*

COMPAGNONNAGES.

PERDIGUIER (AGRICOL) Mémoires d'un compagnon. Paris, 1977. pp. 419. *bibliog. Reprint of 1854-55 Geneva edition with an introduction by Alain Faure.*

COMPENSATION (LAW)

— United Kingdom.

DAVIES (KEITH) Barrister-at-Law. Law of compulsory purchase and compensation. 3rd ed. London, 1978. pp. 398.

COMPETENCE AND PERFORMANCE (LINGUISTICS).

MUNBY (JOHN) Communicative syllabus design: a sociolinguistic model for defining the content of purpose-specific language programmes. Cambridge, 1978. pp. 232. *bibliog.*

COMPETITION.

DEREGULATING American industry: legal and economic problems; edited by Donald L. Martin [and] Warren F. Schwartz. Lexington, Mass., [1977]. pp. 120. *Papers of a conference sponsored by the Law and Economics Center, University of Miami School of Law, in May 1976.*

SCIBERRAS (EDMOND) Multinational electronics companies and national economic policies. Greenwich, Conn., [1977]. pp. 328. *bibliog.*

GREIPL (ERICH) Wettbewerbssituation und -entwicklung des Einzelhandels in der Bundesrepublik Deutschland. Berlin, [1978]. pp. 236. *bibliog. (Ifo-Institut für Wirtschaftsforschung. Schriftenreihe. Nr. 96)*

HAVEMAN (ROBERT H.) and KNOPF (KENYON A.) The market system: an introduction to microeconomics. 3rd ed. Santa Barbara, [1978]. pp. 272.

JORGE (ANTONIO) Competition, cooperation, efficiency, and social organization: introduction to a political economy. Rutherford, [1978]. pp. 89. *bibliog.*

VEREIN FÜR SOZIALPOLITIK. Schriften. Neue Folge. Band 93. Wettbewerbsprobleme der Versicherungswirtschaft; herausgegeben von Burkhardt Röper. Berlin, [1978]. pp. 168.

WORCESTER (DEAN A.) and NESSE (RONALD) Welfare gains from advertising: the problem of regulation. Washington, D.C., [1978]. pp. 134. *(American Enterprise Institute for Public Policy Research. AEI Studies. 188)*

COMPETITION, UNFAIR

— Canada.

STANBURY (WILLIAM T.) Business interests and the reform of Canadian competition policy, 1971-1975. Toronto, [1977]. pp. 227.

— European Economic Community countries.

BELLAMY (CHRISTOPHER WILLIAM) and CHILD (GRAHAM D.) Common Market law of competition. 2nd ed. London, 1978. pp. 492.

— United Kingdom.

HARVEY (BRIAN W.) The law of consumer protection and fair trading. London, 1978. pp. 327. *bibliog.*

COMPUTABLE FUNCTIONS.

INTERNATIONAL CONGRESS OF LOGIC, METHODOLOGY AND PHILOSOPHY OF SCIENCE, 5TH, LONDON, ONTARIO, 1975. Logic, foundations of mathematics, and computability theory: part one of the proceedings...; edited by Robert E. Butts and Jaakko Hintikka. Dordrecht, [1977]. pp. 406. *bibliogs. (Western Ontario. University. University of Western Ontario Series in Philosophy of Science. 9)*

COMPUTER ARCHITECTURE.

IFIP WORKING CONFERENCE ON MODELLING IN DATA BASE MANAGEMENT SYSTEMS, FREUDENSTADT, 1976. Modelling in data base management systems; proceedings of the... conference [organized by IFIP Technical Committee 2]...; edited by G.M. Nijssen. Amsterdam, 1976. pp. 418. *bibliogs.*

IFIP WORKING CONFERENCE ON MODELLING IN DATA BASE MANAGEMENT SYSTEMS, NICE, 1977. Architecture and models in data base management systems; proceedings of the...conference [organized by IFIP Technical Committee 2]...;edited by G.M. Nijssen. Amsterdam, 1977. pp. 326. *bibliogs.*

COMPUTER NETWORKS.

DATA COMMUNICATIONS SYMPOSIUM, 5TH, SNOWBIRD, UTAH, 1977. Fifth Data Communications Symposium...sponsored by the Association for Computing Machinery, Special Interest Group on Data Communications [and others: proceedings]. New York, [1977]. 1 vol. (various pagings). *bibliogs.*

DOLL (DIXON R.) Data communications: facilities, networks, and systems design. New York, [1978]. pp. 493. *bibliogs.*

COMPUTER PROGRAMS

— Evaluation.

CHARACTERISTICS of software quality; [by] Barry W. Boehm [and others]. Amsterdam, 1978. 1 vol. (various pagings) *bibliog.*

— Testing.

CURRENT trends in programming methodology. vol. 2. Program validation; Raymond T. Yeh, editor. Englewood Cliffs, [1977]. pp. 322. *bibliog.*

COMPUTER SIMULATION.

BECKER (H.A.) Simulatie en sociologie: rede uitgesproken bij het aanvaaden van het ambt van hoogleraar in de sociologie...aan de Rijksuniversiteit te Utrecht op 2 Juni 1969. 's-Gravenhage, 1969. pp. 23.

COATS (R.B.) and PARKIN (ANDREW) Computer models in the social sciences. London, 1977. pp. 184. *bibliogs.*

COMPUTER STORAGE DEVICES.

MATICK (RICHARD E.) Computer storage systems and technology. New York, [1977]. pp. 667. *bibliog.*

COMPUTERS.

BOEHM (B.W.) Computer systems analysis, methodology: studies in measuring, evaluating, and simulating computer systems. Santa Monica, 1970. pp. 42. *bibliog. (Rand Corporation. [Rand Reports]. 520)*

COMPUTING system design: proceedings of the joint IBM- University of Newcastle-upon-Tyne seminar held in the University Computing Laboratory, 7th-10th September 1976; edited by B. Shaw. Newcastle-upon-Tyne, 1977. pp. 260.

EL MILIGI (IBRAHIM SAAD) National policies for computer applications in developing countries: a case study of the Sudan. 1977. fo. 317. *bibliog.* Typescript. Ph.D. (London) thesis: unpublished. This thesis is the property of London University and may not be removed from the Library.

INTERNATIONAL COMPUTING SYMPOSIUM, 5TH, LIEGE, 1977. International computing symposium 1977; proceedings of the... symposium...organized by the European Chapters of the Association for Computing Machinery...; edited by E. Morlet and D. Ribbens. Amsterdam, 1977. pp. 613. *bibliogs.*

SOUTH EAST ASIA REGIONAL COMPUTER CONFERENCE, 1ST, SINGAPORE, 1976. Searcc 76; proceedings of the...conference...; edited by M. Joseph and F.C. Kohli. Amsterdam, 1977. pp. 781. *bibliogs.*

— Access control.

HOFFMAN (LANCE J.) Modern methods for computer security and privacy. Englewood Cliffs, [1977]. pp. 255. *bibliog.*

— Law and legislation — United Kingdom.

TAPPER (COLIN) Computer law. London, 1978. pp. 190. *bibliog.*

— Research.

ANDERSON (R.H.) Multi-access computing research at Rand. Santa Monica, 1971. pp. 16. *(Rand Corporation. [Papers]. 4738)*

— Social aspects.

GEORGE (FRANK HONYWILL) Machine takeover: the growing threat to human freedom in a computer-controlled society. Oxford, 1977. pp. 193. *bibliog.*

FABIAN SOCIETY. Fabian Tracts. [No.] 457. The computer and society; [by] Tom Crowe [and] John Hywel Jones. London, 1978. pp. 16.

— Study and teaching — Directories.

DIRECTORY of computer education and research, international edition. ..; edited by T.C. Hsiao. Washington, D.C., [1978]. 2 vols.

— Valuation.

WATSON (R.) Computer performance analysis: applications of accounting data. Santa Monica, 1971. pp. 61. *bibliog. (Rand Corporation. [Rand Reports]. 573)*

COMTE (ISIDORE AUGUSTE MARIE FRANÇOIS XAVIER).

INGRAM (JOHN KELLS) Human nature and morals according to Auguste Comte; with notes illustrative of the principles of positivism. London, 1901. pp. 115.

KENT (CHRISTOPHER) Brains and numbers: elitism, Comtism, and democracy in mid- Victorian England. Toronto, [1978]. pp. 212. *bibliog.*

CONCENTRATION CAMPS

— Germany.

KUEHNRICH (HEINZ) Der KZ-Staat: Rolle und Entwicklung der faschistischen Konzentrationslager, 1933 bis 1945. Berlin, 1960. pp. 144. *bibliog.*

CONCESSIONS

— Russia.

RUSSIA (RSFSR). Statutes, etc. 1920. O kontsessiiakh: dekret Soveta Narodnykh Komissarov ot 23 noiabria 1920 g.; tekst dekreta, ob"ekty kontsessii, karty. Peterburg, 1921. pp. 23.

CONCORDE (JET TRANSPORTS).

NOISE ADVISORY COUNCIL [U.K.]. Working Group on Noise from Air Traffic. Concorde noise levels: report; [G.M. Lilley, chairman]. London, H.M.S.O., 1977. pp. 9.

CONFÉDÉRATION DES SYNDICATS CHRÉTIENS DE BELGIQUE.

VERHOEVEN (JOSEPH) C.S.C., qui es-tu?: révolutionnaire dans l'évolution. Bruxelles, 1976. pp. 196.

CONFESSION

— Psychology.

ROGGE (OETJE JOHN) Why men confess. New York, 1975. pp. 298. *Reprint of the 1959 ed.*

CONFIDENTIAL COMMUNICATIONS

— United States.

SOCIAL research in conflict with law and ethics; Paul Nejelski, editor. Cambridge, Mass., [1976]. pp. 197. *Papers given at a conference held at the University of Bielefeld, 1974.*

CONFLICT OF LAW.

GRAVESON (RONALD HARRY) Comparative conflict of laws: selected essays, vol.1. Amsterdam, 1977. pp. 379. *(London. University. King's College. Centre of European Law. European Studies in Law. vol.1)*

— United States.

EHRENZWEIG (ALBERT ARMIN) and JAYME (ERIK) Private international law: a comparative treatise on American international conflicts law...vol.3. Special part: obligations (contracts, torts): an outline. Leyden, 1977. pp. 156. *bibliog.*

CONFORMITY.

PATTERSON (HORACE ORLANDO LLOYD) Ethnic chauvinism: the reactionary impulse. New York, 1977. pp. 346.

CONGRESS OF THE PEOPLES OF THE EAST, BAKU, 1920.

S"EZD NARODOV VOSTOKA. S"ezd 1-yi, Baku, 1920. Congress of the peoples of the East: Baku, September 1920; stenographic report translated and annotated by Brian Pearce. [London, 1977]. pp. 204.

CONJUGAL VIOLENCE.

VIOLENCE and the family; edited by J.P. Martin. Chichester, [1978]. pp. 369. *bibliogs.*

CONJUGAL VIOLENCE. (Cont.)

— United Kingdom.

COOTE (ANNA) and GILL (TESS) Battered women and the new law. London, 1977. pp. 32. *bibliog.*

RENVOIZE (JEAN) Web of violence: a study of family violence. London, [1978]. pp. 240. *bibliog.*

— — Ireland, Northern.

IRELAND, NORTHERN. Inter-departmental Committee on Family Problems. 1977- . Family problems: a guide to progress on the implementation in Northern Ireland of the recommendations of the Finer report on one parent families and of the report of the Select Committee on Violence in Marriage. [Belfast], 1977 in progress. 1 vol. (loose-leaf.)

CONNOLLY (JAMES).

BRITISH AND IRISH COMMUNIST ORGANISATION. Policy Statements. No. 1. Connolly and partition. Belfast, 1972. pp. 4.

CONSANGUINITY.

MITCHELL (Sir ARTHUR) Blood-relationship in marriage considered in its influence upon the offspring. Edinburgh, Oliver and Boyd, 1865. pp. 45. *(From the Edinburgh Medical Journal, March, April and June 1865)*

CONSCIENTIOUS OBJECTORS.

WAR RESISTERS' INTERNATIONAL. WRI statements: a selection of statements and resolutions from the WRI 1963-July 1972. London, [1972]. pp. 56.

CONSCIOUSNESS.

CONSCIOUSNESS and self-regulation: advances in research;... edited by Gary E. Schwartz and David Shapiro. London, 1976 in progress. *bibliogs.*

CONSENSUS (SOCIAL SCIENCES).

STEINBERG (JULIUS) 1940- . Locke, Rousseau, and the idea of consent; an inquiry into the liberal-democratic theory of political obligation. Westport, 1978. pp. 155. *bibliog.*

CONSERVATION OF NATURAL RESOURCES.

FANFANI (AMINTORE) Strategia della sopravvivenza: proposte degli anni 1970-1971. Roma, [1975]. pp. 53.

CONSERVATION and agriculture; edited by Joan Davidson and Richard Lloyd. Chichester, [1977]. pp. 252.

LEISS (WILLIAM) The limits to satisfaction: on needs and commodities. London, 1978. pp. 168.

— Rhodesia.

SOUTHERN RHODESIA. Commission to Enquire into the Preservation, etc. of the Natural Resources of the Colony. 1939. Report; [R. McIlwaine, chairman]. [Salisbury], 1939. pp. 76, 4 maps. *(Legislative Assembly. [Sessional Papers]. 1939. C.S.R. 40)*

— United Kingdom.

DOBBY (ALAN) Conservation and planning. London, 1978. pp. 173.

— United States.

HOUSE (PETER WILLIAM) and WILLIAMS (EDWARD R.) Planning and conservation: the emergence of the frugal society. New York, 1977. pp. 257. *bibliog.*

CONSERVATISM.

MIDDENDORP (C.P.) Progressiveness and conservatism: the fundamental dimensions of ideological controversy and their relationship to social class. The Hague, [1978]. pp. 457. *bibliog.*

— Colombia.

ABEL (CHRISTOPHER) Conservative politics in twentieth-century Antioquia, 1910-1953. Oxford, 1973. fo. 39. *(Oxford. University. St. Antony's College. Latin American Centre. Occasional Papers. 3)*

— Europe.

YOUNG (JOHN) Monday Club member. Europe: the unguarded legacy: a Conservative approach to European unity; (based on studies by members of the Monday Club's European Policy Group). London, [1977]. 1 pamphlet (unpaged).

— France.

RIOUX (JEAN PIERRE) Nationalisme et conservatisme: la Ligue de la Patrie Française, 1899-1904. Paris, [1977]. pp. 120.

— Germany.

PETZOLD (JOACHIM) Wegbereiter des deutschen Faschismus: die Jungkonservativen in der Weimarer Republik. Köln, 1978. pp. 410.

— Poland.

WŁADYKA (WIESŁAW) Działalność polityczna polskich stronnictw konserwatywnych w latach 1926-1935. Wrocław, 1977. pp. 253. *bibliog. With English summary.*

— United Kingdom.

THATCHER (MARGARET) Let our children grow tall; selected speeches, 1975-1977. London, 1977. pp. 114.

The RADICAL right and patriotic movements in Britain: [a collection of primary source material]. Hassocks. [1978 in progress]. *Microfiche. Microfiches 1a and 1b contain a bibliographical guide to 2-129.*

CONSERVATIVE essays; [by] Maurice Cowling [and others]; edited by Maurice Cowling. London, 1978. pp. 198.

QUINTON (ANTHONY MEREDITH) The politics of imperfection: the religious and secular traditions of conservative thought in England from Hooker to Oakeshott: the T.S. Eliot Lectures delivered at the University of Kent at Canterbury in October 1976. London, [1978]. pp. 105. *bibliog.*

WALDEGRAVE (WILLIAM) The binding of leviathan: conservatism and the future. London, 1978. pp. 162. *bibliog.*

— — Bibliography.

The RADICAL right and patriotic movements in Britain: [a collection of primary source material]; a bibliographical guide: an author, title and chronological index...; compiled by William Pidduck. Hassocks, 1978 in progress.

CONSERVATIVE PARTY (CANADA).

ENGLISH (JOHN) 1945- . The decline of politics: the Conservatives and the party system, 1901-20. Toronto, [1977]. pp. 237.

CONSERVATIVE PARTY (UNITED KINGDOM).

LABOUR RESEARCH DEPARTMENT. Political donations: an analysis of company donations made to the Conservative Party and allied organisations. London, [1973]. pp. 12.

LABOUR RESEARCH DEPARTMENT. Unfit to govern: the record of the Tory government. London, 1974. pp. 23.

BIFFEN (JOHN) Political office or political power?; six speeches on national and international affairs. London, 1977. pp. 46.

BOYSON (RHODES) Centre forward: a radical Conservative programme. London, 1978. pp. 192.

COSGRAVE (PATRICK) Margaret Thatcher: a Tory and her party. London, 1978. pp. 224.

FABIAN SOCIETY. Fabian Tracts. [No.] 459. Deserting the middle ground: Tory social policies. London, 1978. pp. 16.

LABOUR RESEARCH DEPARTMENT. Tories: new turn to the right. London, 1978. pp. 22.

NORTON (PHILIP) Conservative dissidents: dissent within the Parliamentary Conservative Party, 1970-74. London, 1978. pp. 331.

RUSSEL (TREVOR) The Tory party: its policies, divisions and future. Harmondsworth, 1978. pp. 176.

STEWART (ROBERT MACKENZIE) The foundation of the Conservative Party, 1830-1867. London, 1978. pp. 427. *bibliog.*

CONSOLIDATION AND MERGER OF CORPORATIONS

— Taxation — Netherlands.

FISCALE problemen rondom fusies 2: bespreking van het rapport van de Commissie voor de Bestudering van de Fiscale Problemen Rondom Fusies. Deventer, 1974. pp. 37. *(Vereniging voor Belastingwetenschap. Geschriften. No. 137)*

— Canada.

ANISMAN (PHILIP) Takeover bid legislation in Canada: a comparative analysis. Don Mills, Ont., [1974]. pp. 438.

— United Kingdom.

U.K. Office of Fair Trading. 1978. Mergers: a guide to the procedures under the Fair Trading Act 1973. London, 1978. pp. 45. *bibliog.*

CONSOLIDATION OF LAND HOLDINGS.

FOOD AND AGRICULTURE ORGANIZATION. Agriculture Division. Land and Water Use Branch. Working Party of specialists on the Consolidation of Fragmented Agricultural Holdings. 1954. Report of the Working Party...Rome...14-18 December, 1953 (FAO/54/6/3204). [Rome, 1954]. pp. 37.

FOOD AND AGRICULTURE ORGANIZATION. European Commission on Agriculture. Sub-Commission on Land and Water Use. Working Party on Consolidation of Holdings. 1956-61. Report[s], 1st (2nd, 3rd and 4th) session[s], 1956, (1957, 1959 and 1961). Rome, 1956-61. 4 pts.

CONSTITUTIONAL HISTORY.

POGGI (GIANFRANCO) The development of the modern state: a sociological introduction. Stanford, 1978. pp. 175.

CONSTITUTIONAL LAW.

MURPHY (WALTER F.) and TANENHAUS (JOSEPH) Comparative constitutional law: cases and commentaries. New York, 1977. pp. 754.

CONSTRUCTION EQUIPMENT

— Trade and manufacture — Norway.

MAGELI (JOHANNES) A/S Moelven Brug: karakteristika og synspunkter. Bergen, 1977. pp. 18. *(Norges Handelshøyskole. Kristofer Lehmkuhl Forelesninger. 1977)*

CONSTRUCTION INDUSTRY

— Canada — British Columbia.

BRITISH COLUMBIA. Special Commission of Inquiry into British Columbia Construction. 1975-76. First [and final] report[s]. [J. Kinnaird, commissioner] . [Victoria], 1975-76. 2 vols.

— — Ontario.

ONTARIO. Industrial Inquiry Commission into Bargaining Patterns in the Construction Industry. 1976. Report; [D.E. Franks, commissioner]. [Toronto], 1976. pp. 185.

— **Finland.**

HEIKKONEN (EERO) Talorakennusinvestoinnit ja talorakennuskanta Suomessa 1900-1970: (Building investment and building stock in Finland). Helsinki, 1977. pp. 43. *bibliog.* (*Suomen Pankki. Taloustieteellinen Tutkimuslaitos. Julkaisuja. Kasvututkimuksia. 9) With English summary.*

KOHI (PERTTI) Maa-ja vesirakennus-toiminta Suomessa 1900-1960: (Land and waterway construction in Finland). Helsinki, 1977. pp. 56. (*Suomen Pankki. Taloustieteellinen Tutkimuslaitos. Julkaisuja. Kasvututkimuksia. 8) With English summary.*

— — **Statistics.**

FINLAND. Tilastokeskus. Rakennustoiminnan yritystilasto. a., 1974- Helsinki. *[in Finnish and Swedish with English summary]*

— **Germany.**

GERMANY (BUNDESREPUBLIK). Statistisches Bundesamt. Bautätigkeit. a., 1956- Wiesbaden. (*Bautätigkeit und Wohnungen. Reihe 1*)

GERMANY (BUNDESREPUBLIK). Statistisches Bundesamt. Ausgewählte Zahlen für die Bauwirtschaft. m., Ja 1958(1st)- Wiesbaden.

GERMANY (BUNDESREPUBLIK). Statistisches Bundesamt. Kostenstruktur der Unternehmen im Baugewerbe (formerly Bauindustrie). a., 1974- Wiesbaden. (*Produzierendes Gewerbe. Reihe 5:3*)

— **New Zealand — Statistics.**

NEW ZEALAND. Department of Statistics. 1976. Census of building and construction, 1973-74. Wellington, 1976. pp. 38.

— **Nigeria.**

NIGERIA (WESTERN STATE). Commission of Inquiry into the Building Disaster at Oremeji, Ibadan. 1971. Report; [E.O. Fakayode, chairman]. [Ibadan, 1971?]. pp. 40.

— **United Kingdom.**

U.K. Construction Panel. 1974. Final report; [K.J. Johnson, chairman]. [London, 1974]. pp. 29.

ECONOMIC DEVELOPMENT COMMITTEE FOR BUILDING. Housing for all: a document for discussion. London, National Economic Development Office, 1977. pp. 50.

LABOUR PARTY. Building Britain's future: Labour's policy on construction. London, 1977. pp. 63.

BUILDING with direct labour: local authority building and the crisis in the construction industry; [written by the Direct Labour Collective]. London, 1978. pp. 115.

MORRIS (MICHAEL WOLFGANG LAURENCE) The disaster of direct labour: an examination of council building departments. London, 1978. pp. 43. (*Conservative Political Centre. [Publications]. No. 622*)

U.K. Department of the Environment. Housing and construction statistics. q., 1st quarter 1972 (1)- London. *Supersedes Housing statistics, Great Britain (Mr 1966 - F 1972) and Monthly bulletin of construction statistics (N 1942 - Je 1972).*

CONSTRUCTION WORKERS

— **United Kingdom.**

LATHAM (PETER) Labour historian. Rank and file movements in building 1910-1920. London, 1977. pp. 27. (*Communist Party of Great Britain. History Group. Our History. No. 69*)

CONSUMER CREDIT

— **United Kingdom.**

GUEST (ANTHONY GORDON) and LOMNICKA (EVA Z.) An introduction to the law of credit and security. London, 1978. pp. 382.

CONSUMER EDUCATION

— **European Economic Community countries.**

EUROPEAN COMMUNITIES. Commission. Consumer protection and information policy. irreg., 1977 (1st)- Brussels.

CONSUMER PROTECTION

— **Law and legislation — United Kingdom.**

CRANSTON (ROSS) Consumers and the law. London, [1978]. pp. 514.

HARVEY (BRIAN W.) The law of consumer protection and fair trading. London, 1978. pp. 327. *bibliog.*

PAINTER (A.A.) A guide to consumer protection law. Chichester, [1978]. pp. 173.

— — **United States.**

AMERICAN ENTERPRISE INSTITUTE FOR PUBLIC POLICY RESEARCH. Legislative Analyses. 95th Congress. No. 3. Consumer protection legislation. Washington, 1977. pp. 36.

— **European Economic Community countries.**

EUROPEAN COMMUNITIES. Commission. Consumer protection and information policy. irreg., 1977 (1st)- Brussels.

— **France.**

WIEVIORKA (MICHEL) L'état, le patronat et les consommateurs: étude des mouvements de consommateurs. [Paris, 1977]. pp. 271.

— **United Kingdom.**

NATIONAL GAS CONSUMERS' COUNCIL. Report. a., 1974/75 (2nd)- London.

NATIONAL CONSUMER COUNCIL. Annual report and accounts. a., 1975/76[1st]- London.

— **United States.**

CONSUMERISM: a new force in society; edited by Mary Gardiner Jones [and] David M. Gardner. Lexington, Mass., [1976]. pp. 179. *Proceedings of a symposium sponsored in 1974 by the University of Illinois and the James S. Kemper Foundation.*

AMERICAN ENTERPRISE INSTITUTE FOR PUBLIC POLICY RESEARCH. Legislative Analyses. 95th Congress. No. 8. Consumer class actions. Washington, D.C., 1977. pp. 33.

CONSUMERS.

CONSUMER and industrial buying behavior; edited by Arch G. Woodside [and others]. New York, [1977]. pp. 523. *bibliog.*

— **Mathematical models.**

RAY (RANJAN) Utility maximisation and consumer demand with an application to the United Kingdom, 1900-1970. 1977. fo. 174. *bibliog.* Typescript. Ph.D. (London) thesis: unpublished. *This thesis is the property of London University and may not be removed from the Library.*

— **America, Latin.**

MUSGROVE (PHILIP) Consumer behavior in Latin America: income and spending of families in ten Andean cities: an ECIEL study. Washington, D.C., [1978]. pp. 365.

— **France.**

WIEVIORKA (MICHEL) L'état, le patronat et les consommateurs: étude des mouvements de consommateurs. [Paris, 1977]. pp. 271.

— **South Africa.**

DAVIES (WILLIAM J.) A survey of consumer behaviour and shopping patterns amongst Bantu in Port Elizabeth. Port Elizabeth, 1972. fo. 31. (*University of Port Elizabeth. Institute for Planning Research. Information Bulletins. No. 5*)

MARKET RESEARCH AFRICA. Today's urban black household, fourth quarter 1975. Johannesburg, [1975]. 1 vol. (irregular paging). *Tables.*

— **United States.**

CONSUMERISM: a new force in society; edited by Mary Gardiner Jones [and] David M. Gardner. Lexington, Mass., [1976]. pp. 179. *Proceedings of a symposium sponsored in 1974 by the University of Illinois and the James S. Kemper Foundation.*

CONSUMERS' PREFERENCES.

TUCK (MARY) How do we choose?: a study in consumer behaviour. London, 1976. pp. 144. *bibliog.*

— **Netherlands — Mathematical models.**

MAKS (J.A.H.) Consistency and consumer behaviour in the Netherlands, 1921-1962. Groningen, 1977. pp. 23. *bibliog.* (*Groningen. Rijksuniversiteit. Economisch Instituut. Onderzoekmemoranda. No. 31*)

— **Rhodesia.**

SMOUT (M.A.H.) Commercial growth and consumer behaviour in suburban Salisbury, Rhodesia. Salisbury, 1974. pp. 69. (*University of Rhodesia. Series in Social Studies. Occasional Papers. No. 1*)

— **United Kingdom.**

BRITISH MARKET RESEARCH BUREAU. B[ritish] M[arket] R[esearch] B[ureau] housing consumer survey: a survey of attitudes towards current and alternative housing policies..., January 1976. London, National Economic Development Office, 1977. pp. 71.

CONSUMPTION (ECONOMICS).

PERROTTA (COSIMO) La proletarizzazione contemporanea. Lecce, [1975]. 2 vols. (in 1).

LLUCH (CONSTANTINO) and others. Patterns in household demand and saving; with contributions by Roger R. Betancourt [and others]; published for the World Bank. New York, [1977]. pp. 280. *bibliog.*

— **Mathematical models.**

THEIL (HENRI) Theory and measurement of consumer demand. Amsterdam, 1975-76. 2 vols. *bibliogs.*

MODIGLIANI (FRANCO) and TARANTELLI (EZIO) Mercato del lavoro, distribuzione del reddito e consumi privati. Bologna, [1975]. pp. 342.

— **America, Latin.**

MUSGROVE (PHILIP) Consumer behavior in Latin America: income and spending of families in ten Andean cities: an ECIEL study. Washington, D.C., [1978]. pp. 365.

— **Germany — Mathematical models.**

KRELLE (WILHELM) and PAULY (RALF) Konsum und Investitionen des Staates bis 1985. Göttingen, [1976]. pp. 181, A142. *bibliog.* (*Kommission für Wirtschaftlichen und Sozialen Wandel. Schriften. 130*)

— **Russia.**

DMITRIEV (IL'IA DMITRIEVICH) Klassifikatsiia tovarov narodnogo potrebleniia. Moskva, 1976. pp. 176. *bibliog.*

PROTSENKO (OLEG DMITRIEVICH) and SOLOVEICHIK (DAVID IZRAILEVICH) Planirovanie dolgovremennykh khoziaistvennykh sviazei. Moskva, 1976. pp. 143. *bibliog.*

SHIMANSKII (VSEVOLOD PAVLOVICH) and ORLOV (IAKOV L'VOVICH) Torgovlia i blago naroda. Moskva, 1977. pp. 272.

CONSUMPTION (ECONOMICS).(Cont.)

— — **Tajikistan.**

TOSHEV (O.) Material k lektsii: "Rost obshchestvennykh fondov potrebleniia i povyshenie urovnia zhizni trudiashchikhsia". Dushanbe, 1976. pp. 22.

— **United Kingdom — Mathematical models.**

BEAN (CHARLES) The determination of consumer's expenditure in the UK. London, Treasury, 1978. pp. 25. *bibliog. (Government Economic Service Working Papers. No. 4)*

CONTAINERS

— **Law and legislation — South Africa.**

SOUTH AFRICA. Parliament. House of Assembly. Select Committee on the Disposal of Containers Bill. 1977. Report...proceedings and evidence (S.C.14-1977). in SOUTH AFRICA. Parliament. House of Assembly. Select Committee reports.

CONTINENTAL SHELF.

FOOD AND AGRICULTURE ORGANIZATION. Legislative Series. No. 8. Limits and status of the territorial sea, exclusive fishing zones, fishery conservation zones and the continental shelf, with particular reference to fisheries. Rome, 1969. pp. 32.

CONTINGENCY TABLES.

EVERITT (B.S.) The analysis of contingency tables. London, 1977. pp. 128. *bibliog.*

FIENBERG (STEPHEN E.) The analysis of cross-classified categorical data. Cambridge, Mass., [1977]. pp. 151. *bibliog.*

CONTRACEPTIVES

— **Bibliography.**

INTERNATIONAL PLANNED PARENTHOOD FEDERATION. Bibliography Series. No. 3. Distribution of contraceptives. rev. ed. London, 1977. pp. 30.

CONTRACT SYSTEM (LABOUR)

— **United Kingdom.**

BRITISH STEEL SMELTERS, MILL, IRON, TINPLATE AND KINDRED TRADES ASSOCIATION. The truth about the dispute re contract system in the Staffordshire Mills at Hawarden Bridge Works. London, 1910. pp. 31.

CONTRACTS

— **Netherlands.**

PITLO (A.) and BOLWEG (M.F.H.J.) Het verbintenissenrecht naar het Nederlands Burgerlijk Wetboek: algemeen deel. 7th ed. Groningen, 1974. pp. 436.

— **New Zealand.**

NEW ZEALAND. Contracts and Commercial Law Reform Committee. 1976. Report on the effect of mistakes on contracts; [C.I. Patterson, chairman]. Wellington, 1976. pp. 24,6.

NEW ZEALAND. Contracts and Commercial Law Reform Committee. 1977. Credit contracts: report...presented to the Minister of Justice. Wellington, 1977. pp. 212. *bibliog.*

— **United Kingdom.**

YATES (DAVID) Exclusion clauses in contracts. London, 1978. pp. 197.

CONTROL THEORY.

FLEMING (WENDELL HELMS) and RISHEL (RAYMOND W.) Deterministic and stochastic optimal control. Berlin, 1975. pp. 222. *bibliog.*

APPLICATIONS of control theory to economic analysis; edited by John D. Pitchford and Stephen J. Turnovsky. Amsterdam, 1977. pp. 363. *bibliogs.*

CONVERTS, CATHOLIC.

The "CONFOUNDED" convert. London, 1876. pp. 40.

CONVEX FUNCTIONS.

CASTAING (CHARLES) and VALADIER (M.) Convex analysis and measurable multifunctions. Berlin, 1977. pp. 278. *bibliogs.*

CONVICT LABOUR

— **Russia.**

SUNDUROV (FEDOR ROMANOVICH) Sotsial'no-psikhologicheskie i pravovye aspekty ispravleniia i perevospitaniia pravonarushitelei. Kazan', 1976. pp. 144.

— — **Tajikistan.**

TAJIKISTAN. Statutes, etc. 1957-1975. Sobranie deistvuiushchego zakonodatel'stva Tadzhikskoi SSR. razdel 25(-27). Dushanbe, 1976. pp. 387.

COOPERATION.

ABRAHAMSEN (MARTIN ABRAHAM) Cooperative business enterprise. New York, [1976]. pp. 491. *bibliogs.*

L'AMBIVALENCE de la production: logiques communautaires et logique capitaliste. Paris, 1976. pp. 188. *bibliog.*

JORGE (ANTONIO) Competition, cooperation, efficiency, and social organization: introduction to a political economy. Rutherford, [1978]. pp. 89. *bibliog.*

— **Austria.**

KORP (ANDREAS) Der Konsumverein Teesdorf: ein Beitrag sur Frühgeschichte des österreichischen Genossenschaftswesens. Wien, [1977]. pp. 56. *bibliog.*

— **Bangladesh.**

BANGLADESH. Co-operative Directorate. 1967. Co-operative movement in East Pakistan. Dacca, 1967. pp. 53.

— **Brazil.**

BRAZIL. Superintendência do Desenvolvimento do Nordeste. Divisão de Organização Agraria. 1971. Avaliaçao preliminar do desenvolvimento do cooperativismo do nordeste, 1963-1968. Recife, 1971. fo. 66.

— **Colombia.**

CARDONA A. (ALDO A.) Formas de cooperacion en comunidades indigenas de Colombia. Bogota, 1974. pp. 139. *bibliog.*

— **Italy.**

GALETTI (VINCENZO) La cooperazione in Italia: novanta anni di storia. Roma, [1976]. pp. 101. *Collection of interviews.*

DEGL'INNOCENTI (MAURIZIO) Storia della cooperazione in Italia: la Lega nazionale delle cooperative, 1886-1925. Roma, 1977. pp. 461.

UNITI siamo tutto: il movimento cooperativo delle origini all'esperienza reggiana, 1815-1930; [an anthology]; a cura di Adolfo Zavaroni. Milano, [1977]. pp. 194.

— **Peru.**

GONZALES MAYORCA (GRIMALDO) Cooperativismo y revolucion. Lima, 1976. 2 vols.(in 1). *(Banco Nacional de las Cooperativas del Peru Ltdo. [Publicaciones]. No. 1)*

— **Russia.**

GRECHKINA (EL'ZA ROBERTOVNA) Srednie sloi na puti k sotsializmu. Tallin, 1976. pp. 187.

— **Tunisia.**

ALOUANE (YOUSSEF) Coopération et développement: l'expérience tunisienne à travers l'analyse des attitudes et comportements des cadres et des coopérateurs. Hannover, [1971]. pp. 159. *bibliog. (Friedrich-Ebert-Stiftung. Forschungsinstitut. Schriftenreihe. [Band 90])*

— **United Kingdom.**

GOYDER (GEORGE) The end of economic man. Wellingborough, [1977]. pp. 28. *(Scott Bader Commonwealth Centre. Ernest Bader Common Ownership Lectures. 1976)*

— **United States.**

ABRAHAMSEN (MARTIN ABRAHAM) Cooperative business enterprise. New York, [1976]. pp. 491. *bibliogs.*

COOPERATIVE COMMONWEALTH FEDERATION.

McHENRY (DEAN EUGENE) The third force in Canada: the Cooperative Commonwealth Federation, 1932-1948. Westport, Conn., 1976. pp. 351. *bibliog. Originally published by University of California Press in 1950.*

COOPERATIVE MARKETING OF FARM PRODUCE

— **Dominican Republic.**

SHARPE (KENNETH EVAN) Peasant politics: struggle in a Dominican village. Baltimore, Md., [1977]. pp. 263. *bibliog.*

COOPERATIVE SOCIETIES.

ABRAHAMSEN (MARTIN ABRAHAM) Cooperative business enterprise. New York, [1976]. pp. 491. *bibliogs.*

— **Law.**

HAZARD (JOHN NEWBOLD) Is private law becoming public?: the case of cooperatives. Athen, 1973. pp. 263-271. *(Offprint from Xenion: Festschrift für Pan.J. Zepos, II. Band)*

— **Canada — Ontario.**

O'MEARA (J.E.) Ontario's co-operatives, 1946-47: a survey of co-operative business organizations in the province of Ontario, 1946-47;... conducted jointly by Economics Division, Marketing Service, Dominion Department of Agriculture, and the Co-operation and Markets Branch, Ontario Department of Agriculture. [Toronto], Department of Agriculture, 1948. pp. 72.

— **Poland.**

ILO/UNDP REGIONAL SEMINAR ON THE ORGANISATION AND DEVELOPMENT OF DISABLED PERSONS' CO-OPERATIVES, WARSAW, 1974. ILO/UNDP Regional Seminar...16 September to 5 October 1974... regional Middle East; proceedings, conclusions and recommendations; report, etc. (REM/72/027). Geneva, International Labour Organisation, 1974. pp. 186.

ILO/UNDP REGIONAL SEMINAR ON THE ORGANISATION AND DEVELOPMENT OF COOPERATIVES FOR THE DISABLED, WARSAW, 1977. ILO/ UNDP Regional Seminar...Warsaw, Poland, 4 to 19 October, 1977...: regional Asia; proceedings, conclusions and recommendations, etc. (RAS/75/031). Geneva, International Labour Organisation, 1978. pp. 230.

— **Russia.**

[RUSSIA (U.S.S.R.). Soviet Embassy in London. Press Department]. Soviet Booklets. [2nd Series]. No.36. Co-operatives in the Soviet Union; by Israel E. Friedman. London, 1958. pp. 30.

— **United Kingdom.**

NEW CO-OPERATIVE QUARRIES (PIONEER SOCIETY). The New Co-operative Quarries (Pioneer Society), Limited: [prospectus]. [London, 1904?]. pp. (3).

PAISLEY COMMUNITY DEVELOPMENT PROJECT. Ferguslie community workshop: preparation and progress, September 1975-July 1976. [Paisley, 1976]. fo. 6.

COPARTNERSHIP.

EMPLOYEE partnership in Great Britain: £2,000,000 company - over 2000 partners. [Auckland?, 1929?]. pp. (3). *(Reprinted from the New Zealand National Review, August 15th, 1929)*

COPPER INDUSTRY AND TRADE.

BOWEN (ROBERT NAPIER CLIVE) and GUNATILAKA (ANANDA) Copper: its geology and economics. New York, [1977]. pp. 366. *bibliogs.*

— **Canada — British Columbia.**

BRITISH COLUMBIA. Copper Task Force. 1976. Report; [John E. McMynn, chairman]. [Victoria, 1976?]. fo. 83.

— **Europe.**

SCHWERPUNKTE der Kupferproduktion und des Kupferhandels in Europa, 1500-1650; herausgegeben von Hermann Kellenbenz. Köln, 1977. pp. 416. *(Cologne. Universität. Forschungsinstitut für Sozial- und Wirtschaftsgeschichte. Kölner Kolloquien zur Internationalen Sozial- und Wirtschaftsgeschichte. Band 3) In various languages.*

COPPER MINES AND MINING

— **Europe.**

SCHWERPUNKTE der Kupferproduktion und des Kupferhandels in Europa, 1500-1650; herausgegeben von Hermann Kellenbenz. Köln, 1977. pp. 416. *(Cologne. Universität. Forschungsinstitut für Sozial- und Wirtschaftsgeschichte. Kölner Kolloquien zur Internationalen Sozial- und Wirtschaftsgeschichte. Band 3) In various languages.*

COPPER ORES.

BOWEN (ROBERT NAPIER CLIVE) and GUNATILAKA (ANANDA) Copper: its geology and economics. New York, [1977]. pp. 366. *bibliogs.*

COPYRIGHT

— **Unauthorized reprints — United Kingdom.**

PHOTOCOPYING and the law: a guide for librarians and teachers and other suppliers and users of photocopies of copyright works. London, [1970]. pp. 16.

— **Russia.**

CHERTKOV (VLADIMIR LAZAREVICH) Avtorskoe pravo v periodicheskoi pechati. Moskva, 1977. pp. 103.

NEWCITY (MICHAEL A.) Copyright law in the Soviet Union. New York, [1978]. pp. 212. *bibliog.*

— **United Kingdom.**

CRABB (GEOFFREY) Copyright clearance: a practical guide. London, 1976. pp. 59. *(Council for Educational Technology for the United Kingdom. Guidelines. 2)*

WHITE (THOMAS ANTHONY BLANCO) and others. Patents, trade marks, copyright and industrial designs. 2nd ed. London, 1978. pp. 178.

CORAL INDUSTRY AND TRADE

— **United Kingdom.**

YOGEV (GEDALIA) Diamonds and coral: Anglo-Dutch Jews and eighteenth-century trade. Leicester, 1978. pp. 360. *bibliog.*

CORK (COUNTY)

— **History.**

BARRY (TOM) The reality of the Anglo-Irish war 1920-21 in West Cork: refutations, corrections and comments on Liam Deasy's Towards Ireland Free. Tralee, 1974. pp. 59.

CORN LAWS

— **United Kingdom.**

AUTHORITIES against the corn laws. Manchester, [imprint, 1842]. pp. 2.

CORNELL UNIVERSITY

— **Students.**

CONABLE (CHARLOTTE WILLIAMS) Women at Cornell: the myth of equal education. Ithaca, N.Y., 1977. pp. 211. *bibliog.*

CORNISHMEN IN MEXICO.

TODD (ARTHUR CECIL) The search for silver: Cornish miners in Mexico, 1824-1947. Padstow, [1977]. pp. 192. *bibliog.*

CORNWALL

— **Nationalism.**

TRURAN (LEN) For Cornwall: a future'. [Redruth, 1977]. pp. 20.

— **Politics and government.**

TRURAN (LEN) For Cornwall: a future'. [Redruth, 1977]. pp. 20.

CORONERS

— **South Africa.**

NAPLEY (Sir DAVID) Steven Biko inquest. [1977]. fo. 26. *Unpublished: photocopy of typescript.*

CORPORATE DIVESTITURE.

CONFERENCE ON HORIZONTAL DIVESTITURE IN THE OIL INDUSTRY, WASHINGTON, 1977. Horizontal divestiture; highlights of a conference on whether oil companies should be prohibited from owning nonpetroleum energy resources...; edited by W. S. Moore. Washington, [1977]. pp. 62.

— **United States.**

HOBBIE (BARBARA) Oil company divestiture and the press: economic vs. journalistic perceptions. New York, [1977]. pp. 167. *bibliog.*

CORPORATE PLANNING.

GLADWIN (THOMAS) Environment, planning and the multinational corporation. Greenwich, Conn., [1977]. pp. 295. *bibliog.*

STRATEGY plus structure equals performance: the strategic planning imperative; edited by Hans B. Thorelli. Bloomington, [1977]. pp. 310. *bibliog. Based on a conference held by the Graduate School of Business of Indiana University in 1975.*

BRIDGE (JOHN) M.A. and DODDS (JAMES COLIN) Planning and the growth of the firm. London, [1978]. pp. 211.

CORPORATE STATE.

PELLIZZI (CAMILLO) Una rivoluzione mancata. Milano, [1949]. pp. 279.

— **Denmark.**

LOGUE (JOHN) Trade unions in the corporate state: the effects of corporatism on party competition, contract referenda and internationalism in Danish trade unions. Gothenburg, 1976. pp. 65. *(Goteborgs Universitet. Historiska Institutionen. Research Section Post-War History. Publications. No. 5)*

CORPORATIONS.

CORPORATION LAW

— **Australia.**

STANDING COMMITTEE OF STATE AND COMMONWEALTH ATTORNEYS-GENERAL [AUSTRALIA]. Company Law Advisory Committee. Sixth interim report (and seventh interim report). in AUSTRALIA. Parliament. Parliamentary papers, 1972, vol. 2.

— **Canada — New Brunswick.**

NEW BRUNSWICK. Law Reform Division. Company Law Project. 1975. Report on company law; [Richard W. Bird, director]. [Fredericton], 1975. pp. 454.

— **Europe.**

KOLVENBACH (WALTER) Workers participation in Europe. Kluwer, 1977. pp. 79.

— **Italy.**

PROBLEMI giuridici dell'impresa: colloquio promosso dall'Accademia Nazionale dei Lincei in collaborazione con l'Università di Varsavia, Roma, 24-25 novembre 1975. Roma, 1976. pp. 159. *bibliogs. (Accademia Nazionale dei Lincei. Atti dei Convegni Lincei. 22)*

— **United Kingdom.**

FARRAR (HARRY) Company law;...eleventh edition by D.A. Thair. St. Albans, [1976]. pp. 324.

U.K. Department of Trade. 1977. Implementation of the second EEC directive on company law: an explanatory and consultative note. London, 1977. pp. (34).

MAGNUS (SAMUEL WOOLF) and ESTRIN (MAURICE) Companies: law and practice. 5th ed. London, 1978. pp. 1543.

SEALY (LEONARD SEDGWICK) Cases and materials in company law. 2nd ed. London, 1978. pp. 554.

TOPHAM (ALFRED FRANK) and IVAMY (EDWARD RICHARD HARDY) Company law; sixteenth edition by E.R. Hardy Ivamy. London, 1978. pp. 592.

CORPORATION REPORTS

— **United Kingdom.**

LEE (T.A.) and TWEEDIE (D.P.) The private shareholder and the corporate report: a report to the Research Committee of the Institute of Chartered Accountants in England and Wales. London, 1977. pp. 177. *bibliog.*

CORPORATIONS.

EILON (SAMUEL) On the corporate ethos. [London, 1973]. pp. 4. *(Foundation for Business Responsibilities. Discussion Papers)*

HARPER (JOHN DICKSON) A view of the corporate role in society. New York, [1977]. pp. 57. *(Carnegie-Mellon University. Benjamin F. Fairless Memorial Lectures. 1976)*

— **Corrupt practices.**

JACOBY (NEIL HERMAN) and others. Bribery and extortion in world business: a study of corporate political payments abroad. New York, [1977]. pp. 294. *(Columbia University. Graduate School of Business. Studies of the Modern Corporation)*

— **Finance.**

ALIBER (ROBERT ZELWIN) Exchange risk and corporate international finance. London, 1978. pp. 164.

BUSSEY (LYNN E.) The economic analysis of industrial projects. Englewood Cliffs, [1978]. pp. 491. *bibliogs.*

RICKS (DAVID A.) International dimensions of corporate finance. Englewood Cliffs, [1978]. pp. 143. *bibliog.*

— **Taxation.**

AUSTRALIA. Commonwealth Treasury. 1974. Company income tax systems. Canberra, 1974. pp. 44. *(Treasury Taxation Papers. No. 9)*

CORPORATIONS.(Cont.)

— **Valuation.**

FIRTH (MICHAEL A.) The valuation of shares and the efficient-markets theory. London, 1977. pp. 184.

— **Belgium.**

FEDERATION DES ENTREPRISES DE BELGIQUE. Belgian companies: their activities and professional organisation. Brussels, [1973]. pp. 57.

— **Brazil.**

QUEM e quem na economia brasileira, 1976. São Paulo, 1976. pp. 818. *(Visão. vol. 49. no.5)*

— — **Finance.**

EVOLUCÃO do capitalismo no Brasil; ([by] Octavio Gouvêa de Bulhões [and others]). Rio de Janeiro, 1976. pp. 219.

— **Canada — Taxation.**

CANADIAN TAX FOUNDATION. Corporate Management Tax Conference, 1976. Aspects of income tax compliance and administration: [papers of the conference; edited by Catherine Oswald]. Toronto, [1977]. pp. 139.

— **Japan.**

JOHNSON (CHALMERS) Japan's public policy companies. Washington, D.C., [1978]. pp. 173. *(American Enterprise Institute for Public Policy Research and Stanford University. Hoover Institution on War, Revolution and Peace. AEI-Hoover Policy Studies. 24)*

— — **Finance.**

INTERNATIONAL BUSINESS INFORMATION. Japanese corporate finance 1977-1980; report prepared by C. Tait Ratcliffe. Tokyo, [1977]. pp. 217.

— **Sweden — Finance.**

BERTMAR (LARS) and MOLIN (GÖRAN) Kapitaltillväxt, kapitalstruktur och räntabilitet: en analys av svenska industriföretag. Stockholm, 1977. pp. 645. *bibliog.*

— **United Kingdom.**

JORDAN DATAQUEST LTD. Britain's quoted industrial companies, 1976. [London, 1976]. pp. 122.

— — **Accounting.**

NATIONAL ECONOMIC DEVELOPMENT OFFICE. Financial statistics on manufacturing industry: suggestions for improvement; (Statistical Users Conference, 1977: financial statistics: [paper]). [London, 1977]. pp. 11.

— — **Finance.**

The STORY of the Liberator Crash with some account of the career and character of Jabez Spencer Balfour, with numerous illustrations. [London], 1893. pp. 44. *(Westminster Gazette. Westminster Popular. No. 5)*

CLARKSON (DEREK JOSHUA) and McKINLAY (KENNETH ALEXANDER) Edward Wood and Company Limited, Skibben Winton Construction Limited: investigations under section 165 of the Companies Act 1948. London, H.M.S.O., 1977. 1 vol. (various pagings).

KING (MERVYN A.) Public policy and the corporation. London, 1977. pp. 309. *bibliog. (Cambridge. University. Department of Applied Economics. Cambridge Studies in Applied Econometrics. 3)*

SHERRARD (MICHAEL) and DAVISON (IAN HAY) London Capital Group Limited, formerly British Bangladesh Trust Limited: investigation under section 165b of the Companies Act 1948; report. London, H.M.S.O., 1977. pp. 376.

COMYN (JAMES P.) and others. Court Line Limited: investigation under section 165b of the Companies Act 1948: final report. London, H.M.S.O., 1978. pp. 188, 167.

COOPERS AND LYBRAND ASSOCIATES LIMITED. Survey of investment attitudes and financing of medium-sized companies. London, 1978. pp. 46. *(U.K. Committee to Review the Functioning of Financial Institutions. Research Reports. No.1)*

— **United States.**

CONKLIN (JOHN E.) Illegal but not criminal: business crime in America. Englewood Cliffs, [1977]. pp. 153.

EWEN (LYNDA ANN) Corporate power and urban crisis in Detroit. Princeton, [1978]. pp. 312. *bibliog.*

— — **Corrupt practices.**

CORPORATE and governmental deviance: problems of organizational behavior in contemporary society; [edited by] M. David Ermann [and] Richard J. Lundman. New York, 1978. pp. 322.

— — **Statistics.**

CURHAN (JOAN P.) and others. Tracing the multinationals: a sourcebook on U.S.-based enterprises. Cambridge, Mass., [1977]. pp. 430.

— — **Taxation.**

NATIONAL MARINE ENGINEERS BENEFICIAL ASSOCIATION. The multi-billion dollar loopholes. New York, 1974. pp. 8.

CORPORATIONS, AMERICAN.

COMMITTEE OF RETURNED VOLUNTEERS. Gulf Oil Corporation: a study in exploitation. rev. ed. New York, 1971. pp. 48. *bibliog.*

WEISSKOPF (THOMAS E.) American economic interests in foreign countries: an empirical survey. Ann Arbor, 1974. pp. 56. *(Michigan University. Center for Research on Economic Development. Discussion Papers. No.35)*

BROOKSTONE (JEFFREY M.) The multinational businessman and foreign policy: entrepreneurial politics in east-west trade and investment. New York, 1976. pp. 183. *bibliog.*

AMERICAN ENTERPRISE INSTITUTE FOR PUBLIC POLICY RESEARCH. Legislative Analyses. 95th Congress. No. 9. Criminalization of payments to influence foreign governments. Washington, 1977. pp. 34.

RONSTADT (ROBERT) Research and development abroad by U.S. multinationals. New York, [1977]. pp. 127.

BERGSTEN (C. FRED) and others. American multinationals and American interests. Washington, D.C., [1978]. pp. 535.

— **Brazil.**

CONNOR (JOHN M.) The market power of multinationals: a quantitative analysis of U. S. corporations in Brazil and Mexico. New York, 1977. pp. 307. *bibliog.*

— **Mexico.**

CONNOR (JOHN M.) The market power of multinationals: a quantitative analysis of U. S. corporations in Brazil and Mexico. New York, 1977. pp. 307. *bibliog.*

CORPORATIONS, BRITISH

— **America, Latin.**

BUSINESS imperialism, 1840-1930: an inquiry based on British experience in Latin America; edited by D.C.M. Platt. Oxford, 1977. pp. 449.

— **Ghana.**

MILBURN (JOSEPHINE F.) British business and Ghanaian independence. London, [1977]. pp. 156.

— **South Africa.**

STARES (RODNEY) Poverty wages in South Africa: a review of the effectiveness of self-regulation and voluntary disclosure. London, [1976]. pp. 31, 16.

CORPORATIONS, CANADIAN

— **Brazil.**

PROJECT BRAZIL and LAST POST. The Brascan file: its friends in government: its record in Brazil. Toronto, [1973]. pp. 12. *(Reprinted from Last Post, vol. 3. no. 2., February 1973)*

CORPORATIONS, FOREIGN

— **Australia.**

AUSTRALIA. Commonwealth Bureau of Census and Statistics. Foreign ownership and control in manufacturing industry. a., 1972/73(1st)- Canberra.

SEMINAR ON THE FUTURE OF THE MULTINATIONAL CORPORATION, SYDNEY, 1976. Australia and the multinational; the proceedings of a seminar... edited by Michael T. Skully. Sydney, 1976. pp. 52.

— **Brazil.**

VON DOELLINGER (CARLOS) and CAVALCANTI (LEONARDO CASERTA) Empresas multinacionais na industria brasileira. Rio de Janeiro, 1975. pp. 158. *bibliog. (Brazil. Instituto de Planejamento Econômico e Social. Instituto de Pesquisas. Relatorios de Pesquisa. No. 29)*

VIEIRA (DORIVAL TEIXEIRA) and CAMARGO (LENITA CORRÊA) Multinacionais no Brasil: diagnostico e prognostico. São Paulo, 1976. pp. 389. *bibliog.*

— **Kenya.**

SWAINSON (NICOLA) Foreign corporations and economic growth in Kenya. 1977 [or rather 1978]. fo. 371. *bibliog. Typescript. Ph.D. (London) thesis: unpublished. This thesis is the property of London University and may not be removed from the Library.*

CORPORATIONS, NON-PROFIT.

WEISBROD (BURTON ALLEN) The voluntary nonprofit sector: an economic analysis. Lexington, Mass., [1977]. pp. 179. *bibliogs.*

CORPORATIONS, PUBLIC

— **America, Latin.**

KAPLAN (MARCOS) ed. Corporaciones publicas multinacionales para el desarrollo y la integracion de la America Latina. Mexico, 1972. pp. 369. *bibliog. Papers presented at the Seminario Regional de Derecho Internacional para la America Latina, Quito, 1969, organized by UNITAR.*

— **Asia.**

LAW and public enterprise in Asia. New York, [1976]. pp. 421. *Papers given at a colloquium held in Colombo, 1974, sponsored by the International Legal Center.*

— **Brazil.**

CARVALHO (GETULIO) Petrobras: do monopolis aos contratos de risco. Rio de Janeiro, 1976. pp. 250. *bibliog.*

— **Canada.**

PETRO-CANADA. Annual report. a., 1976(1st)- Ottawa. *[in English and French]*

— **New Zealand.**

NEW ZEALAND. New Zealand National Airways Corporation. 1968. N[ational] A[irways] C[orporation]: twenty-one years. [Wellington, 1968]. pp. 15.

— **Nigeria.**

NIGERIAN EXTERNAL TELECOMMUNICATIONS LIMITED. Annual report. a., 1963/64(1st)- , with gaps. Lagos.

NIGERIAN STEEL DEVELOPMENT AUTHORITY. Annual report and accounts. a., 1971/72(1st)- Lagos.

— Poland.

PROBLEMI giuridici dell'impresa: colloquio promosso dall'Accademia Nazionale dei Lincei in collaborazione con l'Università di Varsavia, Roma, 24-25 novembre 1975. Roma, 1976. pp. 159. *bibliogs. (Accademia Nazionale dei Lincei. Atti dei Convegni Lincei. 22)*

— United Kingdom.

NATIONAL ENTERPRISE BOARD [U.K.]. Annual report and accounts. a., 1976(1st)- London.

— United States.

WALSH (ANN MARIE HAUCK) The public's business: the politics and practices of government corporations. Cambridge, Mass., [1978]. pp. 436. *bibliog. A Twentieth Century Fund study.*

CORPORATIONS, SWISS

— Mexico.

IFFLAND (CHARLES) and GALLAND (ANTOINE) Les investissements industriels suisses au Mexique. Lausanne, 1978. pp. 155. *bibliog. (Lausanne. Université. Centre de Recherches Européennes. Publications. 4. L'Europe et les Pays Tiers)*

CORRECTIONS.

See PENOLOGY.

CORRÈZE

— Politics and government.

DENQUIN (JEAN MARIE) Le renversement de la majorité électorale dans le département de la Corrèze, 1958-1973. Paris, [1976]. pp. 90. *bibliog. (Paris. Université de Paris II. Travaux et Recherches. Série Science Politique. 6)*

CORRIENTES (PROVINCE)

— Politics and government.

HERRERA (MARIO A.) El Coronel Blanco: de la tradicion Radical, 1856-1919. Buenos Aires, 1930. pp. 422.

CORRUPTION (IN POLITICS)

— Canada — Nova Scotia.

NOVA SCOTIA. Royal Commission on the Sackville Land Assembly, 1968. Report; [William C. Dunlop, commissioner]. [Halifax, 1971]. pp. 70.

— Mexico.

La CORRUPCION; [by] Rosario Castellanos [and others]. 2nd ed. Mexico, 1970. pp. 162.

TARACENA (ALFONSO) La vida en Mexico bajo Avila Camacho. Mexico, 1976-77. 2 vols. (in 1).

— Pakistan.

PAKISTAN. 1978. White Paper on the conduct of general elections in March 1977 (with Summary). Rawalpindi, 1978. 2 vols.(in 1)

— Uganda.

UGANDA. Commission of Inquiry into the Kampala City Council. 1972. Part 1. Report; [P.A.P.J. Allen, chairman]. Part 2. Government decision on the Commission's recommendations. Entebbe, [1972]. pp. 126.

— United States.

AMICK (GEORGE) The American way of graft: a study of corruption in state and local government, how it happens, and what can be done about it. Princeton, [1976]. pp. 245.

CORSICA

— Economic conditions.

SUD: information économique Provence - Côte d'Azur - Corse: revue trimestrielle; ([pd. by] Institut National de la Statistique et des Etudes Economiques, Direction Régionale de man Marseille [France]). q., Jl 1971 (no.1)- Marseille. *Jl 1971 - F 1972 as Sud: information économique méditerranéenne; from Ap 1972 information on Languedoc-Roussillon pd. separately as Repères: économie du Languedoc-Roussillon.*

COSMOLOGY.

ZAHAVY (ZEV) Whence and wherefore: the cosmological destiny of man scientifically and philosophically considered. South Brunsick, [1978]. pp. 178. *"Comprising an analysis relating to the significant essay In the centre of immensities, by the distinguished Professor Sir Bernard Lovell, University of Manchester, England".*

COSSACKS.

LA CHESNAIS (PIERRE GEORGET) The defence of the Cossacks against Bolchevism. Paris, 1919. pp. 15.

COST ACCOUNTING.

HORNGREN (CHARLES T.) Introduction to management accounting. 4th ed. Englewood Cliffs, [1978]. pp. 714. *bibliogs.*

— Mathematical models.

CARSBERG (BRYAN VICTOR) An introduction to mathematical programming for accountants. London, 1969 repr. 1971. pp. 108.

COST AND STANDARD OF LIVING

— America, Latin.

MUSGROVE (PHILIP) Consumer behavior in Latin America: income and spending of families in ten Andean cities: an ECIEL study. Washington, D.C., [1978]. pp. 365.

— Bahamas.

BAHAMAS. Department of Statistics. 1972. Household budgetary survey report, 1970. Nassau, [1972]. 1 vol. (unpaged).

— Canada — Newfoundland.

NEWFOUNDLAND. Royal Commission on the Cost of Living in Newfoundland. 1950. Report; [F.S. Grisdale, chairman]. St. John's, 1950. fo. 111. *Photocopy.*

— Europe.

CONFEDERATION OF BRITISH INDUSTRY. West European living costs, 1977. London, 1977. pp. 31.

— Greece.

GREECE. Ethnike Statistike Hyperesia. 1977-78. Household expenditure survey, 1974. Athens, 1977-78. 2 pts. (in 1 vol.) ([Publications]. S. Levels of living, etc. 7-8) *In Greek with English introduction and translation of table headings.*

— Hong Kong.

HONG KONG. Census and Statistics Department. 1976. The household expenditure survey 1973/74 and the consumer price indexes. Hong Kong, [1976]. pp. 143.

— India — Maharashtra.

MAHARASHTRA ECONOMIC DEVELOPMENT COUNCIL. Evaluation of rural prosperity in Maharashtra: summary report. Bombay, 1973. pp. 73.

— Ireland (Republic).

EIRE. Central Statistics Office. Household budget survey: annual urban inquiry. a., 1974/75- Dublin.

— Japan.

WHITEPAPER ON NATIONAL LIFE; [pd. by] Economic Planning Agency, Japanese Government. a., 1973- Tokyo.

— Kenya.

KENYA. Central Bureau of Statistics. 1977. Consumer price indices, Nairobi. [Nairobi], 1977. 1 vol. (various pagings).

KENYA. Central Bureau of Statistics. 1977. Rural household survey, Nyanza province 1970/71. [Nairobi], 1977. 1 vol. (various pagings).

— Papua New Guinea.

PAPUA NEW GUINEA. Bureau of Statistics. 1976- . Household expenditure survey, 1975/76: bulletin[s]. Port Moresby, [1976 in progress].

— Russia — Tajikistan.

TOSHEV (O.) Material k lektsii: "Rost obshchestvennykh fondov potrebleniia i povyshenie urovnia zhizni trudiashchikhsia". Dushanbe, 1976. pp. 22.

— South Africa.

HORWOOD (OWEN PIETER FAURE) The private budget of the urban natives. [Johannesburg, 1962]. pp. 138-145. *(Extracted from Optima, September, 1962).*

POTGIETER (J.F.) The household subsistence level in the major urban centres of the Republic of South Africa, April, 1976. Port Elizabeth, 1976. pp. 56. *(University of Port Elizabeth. Institute for Planning Research. Fact Papers. No.16)*

POTGIETER (J.F.) The household subsistence level in the major urban centres of the Republic of South Africa, October 1977. Port Elizabeth, 1977. pp. 65. *(University of Port Elizabeth. Institute for Planning Research. Research Reports. No. 22.)*

— United Kingdom.

PRACTICAL estimates of household expenses, founded on economical principles, and adapted to families of every description, calculated according to income, etc. new ed. London, printed for Henry Colburn, 1824. pp. 77.

WILLSON (JOAN M.) Brent Cross shopping centre impact study: household income and expenditure in 1976. London, [1977]. pp. 7. *(London. Greater London Council. Research Memoranda. 526)*

WILSON (HARRIETT CHARLOTTE) and HERBERT (GEOFFREY WILLIAM) Parents and children in the inner city. London, 1978. pp. 248. *bibliog.*

— United States.

PERLMAN (ROBERT) and WARREN (ROLAND LESLIE) Families in the energy crisis: impacts and implications for theory and policy. Cambridge, Mass., [1977]. pp. 236.

COST EFFECTIVENESS.

ROBSON (PETER) Fiscal compensation and the distribution of benefits in economic groupings of developing countries. (TD/B/322/Rev.1). New York, United Nations, 1971. pp. 39.

JÖNSSON (BENGT) Cost-benefit analysis in public health and medical care. Lund, [1976]. pp. 141. *bibliog.*

MISHAN (EDWARD JOSHUA) Elements of cost-benefit analysis. 2nd ed. London, 1976. pp. 151. *bibliogs.*

MIKESELL (RAYMOND FRECH) The rate of discount for evaluating public projects. Washington, D.C., [1977]. pp. 64. *bibliog. (American Enterprise Institute for Public Policy Research. AEI Studies. 184)*

IRVIN (GEORGE) Modern cost-benefit methods: an introduction to financial, economic and social appraisal of development projects. London, 1978. pp. 257. *bibliog.*

SUGDEN (ROBERT) and WILLIAMS (ALAN) The principles of practical cost-benefit analysis. Oxford, 1978. pp. 275. *bibliog.*

COST EFFECTIVENESS.(Cont.)

YOSHIDA (TSUNEAKI) Applicability of project appraisal for developing countries with special reference to agricultural projects. 1977 [or rather 1978]. fo.115. Typescript. M.Phil. (London) thesis: unpublished. This thesis is the property of London University and may not be removed from the Library.

COSTA RICA

— Census.

COSTA RICA. Census, 1973. Vivienda, poblacion: ciudades capitales. San Jose, [1976?]. pp. 219. *(Costa Rica. Direccion General de Estadistica y Censos. Censos Nacionales de 1973. 11-12)*

COSTS, INDUSTRIAL

— Communist countries.

MATSKEVICHIUS (IONAS STANISLAVOVICH) Analiz kal'kulirovaniia sebestoimosti produktsii v stranakh SEV. Moskva, 1977. pp. 111.

COTTAGE INDUSTRIES

— India.

MEHTA (RATILAL) The story of Khadi. Bombay, Directorate of Publicity and People's Education, Khadi and Village Industries Commission, 1974. pp. 39.

INDIA. Khadi and Village Industries Commission. 1975. Patterns of assistance for Khadi and village industries. Bombay, [1975]. pp. 168.

— Indonesia.

INDONESIA. Biro Pusat Statistik. 1976-77. 1974/1975 industrial census;... household and cottage industries. Jakarta, 1976-77. 5 vols. (in 1). *In English and Indonesian.*

COTTON GROWING

— Argentine Republic.

CALVO (JORGE RAUL) El oro blanco en la Argentina: estudio economico-social del algodon. Buenos Aires, 1946. pp. 207.

— Tanzania.

SHAPIRO (KENNETH H.) Efficiency differentials in peasant agriculture and their implications for development policies. Ann Arbor, 1976. pp. 13. *bibliog. (Michigan University. Center for Research on Economic Development. Discussion Papers. No. 52)*

— United Kingdom.

TEWSON (W.F.) The British Cotton Growing Association, incorporated by royal charter:...golden jubilee, [1904]-1954. [Manchester], [1954]. pp. 85, xiv.

COTTON MANUFACTURE

— United Kingdom.

LONGMATE (NORMAN) The hungry mills: (the story of the Lancashire cotton famine, 1861-5). London, 1978. pp. 319. *bibliog.*

COTTON TRADE

— Argentine Republic.

CALVO (JORGE RAUL) El oro blanco en la Argentina: estudio economico-social del algodon. Buenos Aires, 1946. pp. 207.

— United States.

RICHARDS (FRANK A.) The marketing of cotton and the financing of cotton merchants. New York, 1949. pp. 50.

COUNCIL FOR MUTUAL ECONOMIC ASSISTANCE.

COUNCIL FOR MUTUAL ECONOMIC ASSISTANCE. Secretariat. Collected reports on various activities of bodies of the C.M.E.A. a., 1974- Moscow.

LASCELLES (DAVID) Comecon to 1980. London, [1976]. pp. 268.

PRAVOVYE voprosy deiatel'nosti SEV. Moskva, 1977. pp. 192.

COUNCIL OF EUROPE.

COUNCIL OF EUROPE. Directorate of Legal Affairs. Information bulletin on legal activities within the Council of Europe and in member states. 7 a yr., Je 1978(no. 1)- Strasbourg. *Supersedes COUNCIL OF EUROPE. Directorate of Legal Affairs. Bulletin on legislative activities.*

COUNCIL OF EUROPE FORUM; [pd.by] Council of Europe. q., 1978 (no.1/2)- Strasbourg. *Supersedes FORWARD IN EUROPE.*

COUNCILS AND SYNODS.

STAIR SOCIETY. [Publications]. 30. The records of the synod of Lothian and Tweeddale, 1589-1596, 1640-1649; edited with an introduction by James Kirk. Edinburgh, 1977. pp. 325.

COUNSELLING.

KENNEDY (EUGENE) On becoming a counsellor: a basic guide for non-professional counsellors. Dublin, 1977. pp. 337. *bibliogs.*

— United Kingdom.

TYLER (MARY) Writer on Counselling. Advisory and counselling services for young people. London, 1978. pp. 93. *bibliog. (U.K. Department of Health and Social Security. Research Reports. No. 1)*

COUNTERFEITS AND COUNTERFEITING

— Korea.

KOREA (REPUBLIC). 1964. Forgery and counterfeiting. Seoul, [1964]. pp. 24.

COUNTERINSURGENCY.

BLAUFARB (DOUGLAS S.) The counterinsurgency era: US doctrine and performance, 1950 to the present. New York, [1977]. pp. 356. *bibliog.*

COUPS D'ETAT.

FITCH (JOHN SAMUEL) The military coup d'état as a political process: Ecuador, 1948- 1966. Baltimore, Md., [1977]. pp. 243. *bibliog. (Johns Hopkins University. Studies in Historical and Political Science. Series 95. No. 1)*

COURT OF JUSTICE OF THE EUROPEAN COMMUNITIES.

EUROPEAN COMMUNITIES. Court of Justice. Formal hearings. a., 1974/75- Luxembourg.

BROWN (LIONEL NEVILLE) and JACOBS (FRANCIS GEOFFREY) The Court of Justice of the European Communities. London, 1977. pp. 254. *bibliog.*

VANDERSANDEN (G.) and BARAV (A.) Contentieux communautaire. Bruxelles, 1977. pp. 722. *bibliog.*

COURT RECORDS

— Poland.

KSIĘGA sądowa kresu klimkowskiego, 1600-1762; opracował i wydał Ludwik Łysiak. Wrocław, 1965. pp. 440. *(Polska Akademia Nauk. Instytut Historii. Starodawne Prawa Polskiego Pomniki. Seria 2. Pomniki Prawa Polskiego. dział 2: Prawo Wiejskie. t.4)*

— United Kingdom — Scotland.

STAIR SOCIETY. [Publications]. 30. The records of the synod of Lothian and Tweeddale, 1589-1596, 1640-1649; edited with an introduction by James Kirk. Edinburgh, 1977. pp. 325.

COURT RULES

— Nigeria.

NIGERIA (WESTERN STATE). 1971. Customary courts manual; incorporating customary courts law, customary courts rules and extracts from laws enforceable by customary courts;...issued for the guidance of customary courts. 2nd ed. [Ibadan, 1971]. pp. 170.

COURTS

— Canada — Ontario.

ONTARIO. Ministry of the Attorney General. 1976. White paper on courts administration. [Toronto], 1976. pp. 28.

— United Kingdom.

GILES (FRANCIS TRESEDER) The magistrates' courts: what they do, how they do it, and why. 2nd ed. Harmondsworth, [1951]. pp. 222.

GRIFFITH (JOHN ANEURIN GREY) The politics of the judiciary. Manchester, 1977. pp. 224.

— United States.

SUNDERLAND (LANE V.) Obscenity: the Court, the Congress and the President's Commission. Washington, 1975. pp. 127. *bibliog. (American Enterprise Institute for Public Policy Research. Domestic Affairs Studies. 27)*

JACOBSOHN (GARY J.) Pragmatism, statesmanship, and the Supreme Court. Ithaca, 1977. pp. 214. *bibliog.*

— — Bibliography.

NORRIS (LORETTA A.) and BOYER (LARRY M.) American colonial courts and lawyers: an annotated bibliography. [Washington], Library of Congress, 1976. pp. 24.

COVENTRY

— Economic history.

SEARBY (PETER) Coventry in crisis 1858-1863: ribbon factory, free trade and strike. Coventry, 1977. pp. 17. *bibliog. (Historical Association. Coventry Branch. Coventry and Warwickshire History Pamphlets. No. 10)*

COXE (TENCH).

COOKE (JACOB E.) Tench Coxe and the early Republic. Chapel Hill, [1978]. pp. 543. *bibliog.*

CRACOW (CITY)

— History.

CETERA (BRONISŁAW) Proletariacki nurt rewolucji krakowskiej 1848 roku. Kraków, [1977]. pp. 225. *bibliog.*

— Social conditions.

SULIMSKI (JERZY) Kraków w procesie przemian: współczesne przeobra'zenia zbiorowości wielkomiejskiej. Kraków, [1976]. pp. 391. *bibliog. With English and Russian summaries.*

CRACOW (PROVINCE)

— Appropriations and expenditures.

PAWLIK (JAN) Wydatki rad narodowych na usługi socjalno-bytowe na terenach o ró'znym charakterze gospodarczym i o ró'znym tempie rozwoju gospodarczego na przykładzie Województwa Krakowskiego. Kraków, 1964. pp. 199. *bibliog. (Zeszyty Naukowe Uniwersytetu Jagiellońskiego. Prace Prawnicze. zeszyt 16) With English and Russian summaries.*

CRAIOVA UNIVERSITY.

DINAMICA socială a învățămîntului i universitar: studiu pe modelul Universității din Craiova; coordonator... Aculin Cazacu. Craiova, 1973. pp. 278.

CREATIVE ABILITY.

ARIETI (SILVANO) The intrapsychic self: feeling and cognition in health and mental illness. New York, [1976]. pp. 350. *bibliog. Abridged version of the 1967 edition.*

CREDIT.

BEAUFORT WIJNHOLDS (J.A.H. DE) The need for international reserves and credit facilities. Leiden, 1977. pp. 251. *bibliog. (Nederlands Instituut voor het Bank- en Effectenbedrijf. Publikaties. No. 31)*

MATIUKHIN (GEORGII GAVRILOVICH) Problemy kreditnykh deneg pri kapitalizme. Moskva, 1977. pp. 224.

SHEFFER (CEES F.) The institutional organization of industrial investment credit throughout the world, with special reference to long-term credit banks. Leyden, 1977. pp. 490. *bibliogs.*

— Netherlands.

KORTEWEG (PIETER) and VAN LOO (PETER D.) The market for money and the market for credit: theory, evidence and implications for Dutch monetary policy. Leiden, 1977. pp. 105. *bibliog.*

— New Zealand.

NEW ZEALAND. Contracts and Commercial Law Reform Committee. 1977. Credit contracts: report...presented to the Minister of Justice. Wellington, 1977. pp. 212. *bibliog.*

— Poland.

SITAREK (HENRYK) Rola kredytu w rozwoju gospodarki Wielkopolski na przełomie XIX i XX wieku: Bank Związku Spółek Zarobkowych w Poznaniu, 1885-1918; Rolle des Kredits in der Entwicklung von Wielkopolska um die Wende des XIX. und XX. Jh. Warszawa, 1977. pp. 200. *bibliog. (Poznań. Poznańskie Towarzystwo Przyjaciół Nauk. Wydział Historii i Nauk Społecznych. Badania z Dziejów Społecznych i Gospodarczych. nr.55) With German summary.*

— Russia.

BARKOVSKII (NIKOLAI DMITRIEVICH) Problemy kredita i denezhnogo oborota v usloviiakh razvitogo sotsializma. Moskva, 1976. pp. 215.

KORNEICHEVA (TAT'IANA KONSTANTINOVNA) and NAZAROV (VALENTIN KONSTANTINOVICH) Kreditovanie legkoi promyshlennosti. Moskva, 1976. pp. 96.

POPKOVA (VALENTINA EVSTAF'EVNA) and others. Kreditovanie i raschety transporta i sviazi. Moskva, 1976. pp. 86.

DANILENKO (ANATOLII IVANOVICH) and others. Finansovo-kreditnye problemy sotsialisticheskoi promyshlennosti. Kiev, 1977. pp. 260. *bibliog.*

GARVY (GEORGE) Money, financial flows, and credit in the Soviet Union. Cambridge, Mass., 1977. pp. 2. *bibliog. (National Bureau of Economic Research. Studies in International Economic Relations. 7 [bis])*

PESSEL' (MARK ABRAMOVICH) Finansovo-kreditnyi mekhanizm intensifikatsii obshchestvennogo proizvodstva. Moskva, 1977. pp. 224.

KUSCHPÈTA (O.) The banking and credit system of the USSR. Leiden, 1978. pp. 284. *bibliog. (Tilburg. Katholieke Hogeschool. Tilburg Institute of Economics. Tilburg Studies on Economics. 18)*

— — Kazakstan.

FRIDMAN (TSEZAR' L'VOVICH) Banki i kredit v dorevoliutsionnom Kazakhstane, 1900-1914 gg. Alma-Ata, 1974. pp. 175.

— Turkey.

YASER (BETTY SLADE) Convertible foreign exchange deposit accounts and foreign private loans. Ankara, 1973. fo. 16. *(United States. Agency for International Development. USAID-Ankara. Economic Analysis Staff. Discussion Papers. No. 14)*

— United Kingdom.

COMMITTEE OF LONDON CLEARING BANKERS. Preliminary submission to the Committee to Review the Functioning of Financial Institutions: channelling funds to industry and trade. London, 1977. fo. 59. *Bound with its Supplementary paper.*

COMMITTEE OF LONDON CLEARING BANKERS. Supplementary paper to the preliminary submission to the Committee to Review the Functioning of Financial Institutions: channelling funds to industry and trade. London, 1977. fo. 34. *Bound with its Preliminary submission.*

— United States.

YEAGER (LELAND BENNETT) Proposals for government credit allocation. Washington, D.C., [1977]. pp. 75. *(American Enterprise Institute for Public Policy Research. AEI Studies. 181)*

CREOLE DIALECTS.

SOCIO-HISTORICAL factors in the formation of the Creoles; issue editor J.L. Dillard. The Hague, 1976. pp. 97. *bibliog. (International Journal of the Sociology of Language, no. 7)*

CRIME AND CRIMINALS.

MANNHEIM (HERMANN) ed. Pioneers in criminology. 2nd ed. Montclair, N.J., [1973]. pp. 505.

— Research — United Kingdom.

U.K. Home Office. Research Unit. Research bulletin. s-a., spring 1975 (no.1)- London.

— Puerto Rico.

TORO CALDER (JAIME) ed. Fundamentos para una sociologia penal en Puerto Rico. Rio Piedras, 1976. pp. 221.

— Russia.

TARARUKHIN (SVIATOSLAV ANDREEVICH) Ustanovlenie motiva i kvalifikatsiia prestupleniia. Kiev, 1977. pp. 151.

SOLOMON (PETER H.) Soviet criminologists and criminal policy: specialists in policy-making. London, 1978. pp. 253. *bibliog.*

— Switzerland.

CLINARD (MARSHALL BARRON) Cities with little crime: the case of Switzerland. Cambridge, 1978. pp. 208. *(American Sociological Association. Arnold and Caroline Rose Monograph Series in Sociology)*

— United Kingdom.

BRISTOW (EDWARD J.) Vice and vigilance: purity movements in Britain since 1700. Dublin, 1977. pp. 274. *bibliog.*

PHILIPS (DAVID) Crime and authority in Victorian England: the Black Country, 1835-1860. London, 1977. pp. 321. *bibliogs.*

SPARKS (RICHARD FRANKLIN) and others. Surveying victims: a study of the measurement of criminal victimization, perceptions of crime, and attitudes to criminal justice. Chichester, [1977]. pp. 276. *bibliog.*

— — Scotland.

BOYLE (JIMMY) A sense of freedom. London, [1977]. pp. 264.

— United States.

NELLI (HUMBERT STEVEN) The business of crime: Italians and syndicate crime in the United States. New York, 1976. pp. 314. *bibliog.*

IN fear of each other: studies of dangerousness in America; [edited by] John P. Conrad [and] Simon Dinitz. Lexington, Mass., [1977]. pp. 141.

SYKES (GRESHAM M'CREADY) Criminology. New York, [1978]. pp. 631. *bibliogs.*

— — Illinois.

BLOCK (RICHARD) Violent crime: environment, interaction, and death. Lexington, Mass., [1977]. pp. 121. *bibliog.*

CRIME AND THE PRESS.

LACOUMES (PIERRE) and MOREAU-CAPDEVIELLE (GHISLAINE) Image de la justice criminelle dans la société: rapport sur la phase qualitative de l'analyse de presse. Paris, S[ervice d']E[tudes] P[énales et] C[riminologiques], [1976]. 1 vol. (various pagings). *bibliog. (France. Service d'Etudes Pénales et Criminologiques. [Publications]. SEPC. 1976. 18) Front outer cover also has Déviance et contrôle social following the title and spells first author as LASCOUMES.*

CRIMEAN WAR, 1853-1856.

PROSECUTION of the war with Russia, and liberty of the press: a bill for the more effectual prosecution of the war...and for other purposes. [London], 1855. pp. 5.

BAYLEY (CHARLES CALVERT) Mercenaries for the Crimea: the German, Swiss, and Italian legions in British service, 1854-1856. Montreal, 1977. pp. 197. *bibliog.*

CRIMINAL COURTS

— United Kingdom.

ADVISORY COUNCIL ON THE PENAL SYSTEM. Powers of the courts dependent on imprisonment; report; [Baroness Serota, chairman]. London, H.M.S.O., 1977. pp. 19.

CRIMINAL INVESTIGATION.

GREENWOOD (PETER W.) and others. The criminal investigation process. Lexington, Mass., [1977]. pp. 326. *bibliog.*

POWIS (DAVID) The signs of crime: a field manual for police. London, [1977]. pp. 236. *bibliog.*

— Australia.

AUSTRALIA. Australian Law Reform Commission. 1975. Criminal investigation: an interim report. Canberra, 1975. pp. 224. *bibliog. (Reports. No. 2)*

— Colombia.

GARNICA QUINTERO (PABLO ENRIQUE) Investigacion criminal y policia judicial. Bogota, 1972. pp. 183. *bibliog.*

— Russia — White Russia.

TIKHINIA (VALERII GUR'EVICH) Primenenie kriminalisticheskoi taktiki v grazhdanskom protsesse: pri issledovanii veshchestvennykh dokazatel'stv. Minsk, 1976. pp. 159.

CRIMINAL JUSTICE, ADMINISTRATION OF.

ZIEGENHAGEN (EDUARD A.) Victims, crime, and social control. New York, 1977. pp. 156.

— France.

LACOUMES (PIERRE) and MOREAU-CAPDEVIELLE (GHISLAINE) Image de la justice criminelle dans la société: rapport sur la phase qualitative de l'analyse de presse. Paris, S[ervice d']E[tudes] P[énales et] C[riminologiques], [1976]. 1 vol. (various pagings). *bibliog. (France. Service d'Etudes Pénales et Criminologiques. [Publications]. SEPC. 1976. 18) Front outer cover also has Déviance et contrôle social following the title and spells first author as LASCOUMES.*

— Puerto Rico.

TORO CALDER (JAIME) ed. Fundamentos para una sociologia penal en Puerto Rico. Rio Piedras, 1976. pp. 221.

CRIMINAL JUSTICE, ADMINISTRATION OF. (Cont.)

— Switzerland.

CLINARD (MARSHALL BARRON) Cities with little crime: the case of Switzerland. Cambridge, 1978. pp. 208. *(American Sociological Association. Arnold and Caroline Rose Monograph Series in Sociology)*

— United Kingdom.

CONSPIRACY: notes; [by] Chris Bott [and others]. [London?, 1971?]. pp. 20.

U.K. Home Office. 1977. A review of criminal justice policy 1976. London, 1977. pp. 49. *(Working Papers)*

— — Research.

CROFT (IVOR JOHN) Research in criminal justice; a Home Office Research Unit report. London, 1978. pp. 11. *bibliog.(U.K. Home Office. Home Office Research Studies. No.44)*

— United States.

AMERICAN ASSEMBLY. 42nd Assembly, December 1972. Prisoners in America; [edited by Lloyd E. Ohlin]. Englewood Cliffs, N.J., [1973]. pp. 216. *bibliog.*

BLACKS and criminal justice; edited by Charles E. Owens [and] Jimmy Bell. Lexington, Mass., [1977]. pp. 151. *bibliogs. Based on two conferences held in 1974 and 1975 by the University of Alabama, Department of Psychology, Center for Correctional Psychology.*

SKOLER (DANIEL L.) Organizing the non-system: governmental structuring of criminal justice systems. Lexington, Mass., [1977]. pp. 309.

HARRIES (KEITH D.) and BRUNN (STANLEY D.) The geography of laws and justice: spatial perspectives on the criminal justice system. New York, 1978. pp. 175. *bibliogs.*

SYKES (GRESHAM M'CREADY) Criminology. New York, [1978]. pp. 631. *bibliogs.*

CRIMINAL LAW

— Communist countries.

EVERYDAY hazards under communist law. [London?], 1955. pp. 19.

— Italy.

VENDITTI (RODOLFO) Il diritto penale militare nel sistema penale italiano. 4th ed. Milano, 1978. pp. 456.

— Poland.

POLAND. Statutes, etc. 1969-1975. Kodeks karny, [1974]; Kodeks postępowania karnego, [1969]; Kodeks karny wykonawczy, [1975], oraz przepisy wprowadzające. 2nd ed. Warszawa, 1977. pp. 224.

— Romania.

ROMANIA. Statutes, etc. 1975-1976. Codul penal al Republicii Socialiste România, comentat şi adnotat: partea specială; [by] Teodor Vasiliu [and others]. Bucureşti, 1975-77. 2 vols.

— Russia — Tajikistan.

TAJIKISTAN. Statutes, etc. 1959-1974. Sobranie deistvuiushchego zakonodatel'stva Tadzhikskoi SSR. razdel 28-29. Dushanbe, 1975. pp. 602.

TAJIKISTAN. Statutes, etc. 1975. Ugolovnyi kodeks Tadzhikskoi SSR: s izmeneniiami i dopolneniiami na 1 iiunia 1975 goda. Dushanbe, 1975. pp. 172.

— United Kingdom.

GILES (FRANCIS TRESEDER) The criminal law: a short introduction. 3rd ed. [Harmondsworth, 1963]. pp. 300.

CROSS (Sir RUPERT) and JONES (PHILIP ASTERLEY) Cases and statutes on criminal law; [edited by] Richard Card. 6th ed. London, 1977. pp. 460.

RESHAPING the criminal law: essays in honour of Glanville Williams; edited by P.R. Glazebrook. London, 1978. pp. 492. *bibliog.*

SMITH (JOHN CYRIL) and HOGAN (BRIAN THOMAS) Criminal law. 4th ed. London, 1978. pp. 858.

— United States — California.

BERK (RICHARD A.) and others. A measure of justice: an empirical study of changes in the California panel code, 1955-1971. New York, 1977. pp. 312.

CRIMINAL PROCEDURE

— France.

FRANCE. Statutes, etc. 1957-58. Code de procédure pénale; première partie-législative; [and] ordonnance no. 58-1296 du 23 décembre 1958. Paris, 1959. pp. 204.

— Poland.

POLAND. Statutes, etc. 1962. Kodeks postępowania karnego: przepisy wprowadzające oraz wa'zniejsze przepisy szczególne, według stanu prawnego na dzień 30 czerwca 1962 r. Warszawa, 1962. pp. 343.

POLAND. Statutes, etc. 1969-1975. Kodeks karny, [1974]; Kodeks postępowania karnego, [1969]; Kodeks karny wykonawczy, [1975], oraz przepisy wprowadzające. 2nd ed. Warszawa, 1977. pp. 224.

— Russia.

KOMMENTARII sudebnoi praktiki za 1974 god. Moskva, 1975. pp. 167. *Previous years have title Nauchnyi kommentarii sudebnoi praktiki, etc.*

— — Tajikistan.

TAJIKISTAN. Statutes, etc. 1959-1974. Sobranie deistvuiushchego zakonodatel'stva Tadzhikskoi SSR. razdel 28-29. Dushanbe, 1975. pp. 602.

— United Kingdom.

THORNTON (PETER) Trial or error: a reply to the James Committee. London, [1976]. pp. 23. *(National Council for Civil Liberties. Reports. No. 16)*

U.K. Home Office. 1978. Evidence to the Royal Commission on Criminal Procedure: memorandum no.1: the background to the work of the Commission; memorandum no.2: the accountability of the police. London, 1978. pp. (72).

ZANDER (MICHAEL) Royal Commission on Criminal Procedure: (written) evidence of M. Zander. Part 1. London, 1978. pp. 167.

CRIMINAL PSYCHOLOGY.

SUNDUROV (FEDOR ROMANOVICH) Sotsial'no-psikhologicheskie i pravovye aspekty ispravleniia i perevospitaniia pravonarushitelei. Kazan', 1976. pp. 144.

CRIMINOLOGISTS

— Russia.

SOLOMON (PETER H.) Soviet criminologists and criminal policy: specialists in policy-making. London, 1978. pp. 253. *bibliog.*

CRISES.

OELSSNER (FRED) Probleme der Krisenforschung. Berlin, 1959. pp. 20. *(Deutsche Akademie der Wissenschaften zu Berlin. Sitzungsberichte. Klasse für Philosophie, Geschichte, Staats-, Rechts-, und Wirtschaftswissenschaften. 1959. Nr. 3)*

DELIBANES (DEMETRIOS) The repercussions of the international monetary crisis in the Balkans and a possible remedy. Thessalonika, 1972. pp. 10. *(Reprinted from Balkan Studies, vol. 13, No. 2, 1972)*

AKADEMIIA NAUK SSSR. Institut Mirovoi Ekonomiki i Mezhdunarodnykh Otnoshenii. Materialy mezhdunarodnogo simpoziuma "Krizis i evoliutsiia mezhdunarodnoi valiutnoi sistemy kapitalizma", Leningrad, 1974. Moskva, 1975. 2 pts. (in 1).

PARTITO DI UNITÀ PROLETARIA PER IL COMUNISMO. Convegno, Ariccia, Febbraio 1975. Uscire dalla crisi o dal capitalismo in crisi?: atti del Convegno, etc. [Roma, 1975]. pp. 238.

AGLIETTA (MICHEL) Régulation et crises du capitalisme: l'expérience des Etats-Unis. [Paris, 1976]. pp. 334.

ANGELOPOULOS (ANGELOS) Pour une nouvelle politique du développement international. Paris, [1976]. pp. 198.

AU-delà de la crise; ([by] Norman Birnbaum [and others]); présentation par Alain Touraine. Paris, [1976]. pp. 255.

BÀCULO (LILIANA) ed. La crisi degli anni '70 nel dibattito marxista: saggi di analisi e teoria economica. Bari, [1976]. pp. 298.

La CRISE de l'impérialisme et la troisième guerre mondiale; [by] Noam Chomsky [and others]. Paris, 1976. pp. 282.

L'EUROPE des crises; [by] Robert Triffin [and others]. Bruxelles, 1976. pp. 173. *(Fondation Paul-Henri Spaak. Bibliothèque) Mainly lectures given at the Institut des Etudes Européennes of the Université Libre of Brussels, in 1974 and 1975.*

VARGA (JENÖ) La crise économique, sociale, politique; introduction de Jean Charles et Serge Wolikow. Paris, [1976]. pp. 367. *Reprint of 1935 French edition with new introduction.*

BLAICH (FRITZ) Die Wirtschaftskrise 1925/26 und die Reichsregierung von der Erwerbslosenfürsorge zur Konjunkturpolitik. Kallmünz Opf., 1977. pp. 196. *bibliog.*

GESELLSCHAFT im Konkurs?: Handbuch zur Wirtschaftskrise 1973- 76 in der BRD; herausgegeben von Jörg Huffschmid und Herbert Schui. 2nd ed. Köln, 1977. pp. 538.

STEVENSON (JOHN) Historian, and COOK (CHRISTOPHER PIERS) The slump: society and politics during the depression. London, 1977. pp. 348. *bibliog.*

BOYER (ROBERT) and MISTRAL (JACQUES) Accumulation, inflation, crises. [Paris], 1978. pp. 260.

GOUX (CHRISTIAN) Sortir de la crise. [Paris, 1978]. pp. 163.

CRITICISM.

GONZALEZ (MICHAEL) Cambio de piel, or the myth of literature. Glasgow, [1974]. pp. 13. *(Glasgow. University. Institute of Latin American Studies. Occasional Papers. No. 10)*

GRAMSCI (ANTONIO) Letteratura e vita nazionale. Torino, 1972 repr. 1974. pp. 400. *bibliog. (Quaderni del Carcere. 5)*

CROATIA

— Economic conditions — Mathematical models.

STRUKTURNE karakteristike, dinamika rasta i akumulativnost privrede SR Hrvatske do 1985. godine: modelski pristup. Zagreb, 1977. pp. 266.

CROCE (BENEDETTO).

CARINI (CARLO) Benedetto Croce e il partito politico. Firenze, 1975. pp. 241. *(Pensiero Politico, Il. Biblioteca. 7)*

CROMWELL (OLIVER) Lord Protector.

SHERWOOD (ROY) The court of Oliver Cromwell. London, [1977]. pp. 194. *bibliog.*

CROMWELL (THOMAS) 1st Earl of Essex.

BECKINGSALE (BERNARD WINSLOW) Thomas Cromwell, Tudor minister. London, 1978. pp. 181. *bibliog.*

CROPS AND CLIMATE

— Europe.

POST (JOHN DEXTER) The last great subsistence crisis in the western world. Baltimore, [1977]. pp. 240. *bibliog.*

CROSS CULTURAL STUDIES.

WHYTE (MARTIN KING) The status of women in preindustrial societies. Princeton, 1978. pp. 222. *bibliog.*

CROWDS.

HAYTER (TONY) The army and the crowd in mid-Georgian England. London, 1978. pp. 239. *bibliog.*

CROWN LANDS

— New Zealand.

NEW ZEALAND. Committee of Investigation into Rentals and Freeholding of Crown Leases. 1968. Report...; chairman: W.R. Beattie. [Wellington], 1968. pp. 28.

CRUELTY TO CHILDREN.

INGLIS (RUTH) Sins of the fathers: a study of the physical and emotional abuse of children. London, 1978. pp. 220. *bibliog.*

— Canada — Nova Scotia.

NOVA SCOTIA. Family and Child Welfare Division. 1973. Child abuse in Nova Scotia: a research project about batteed and maternally deprived children. Halifax, 1973. pp. 295.

CRYONICS.

PEREZ GAVIRIA (JUAN DAVID) and GARCES HOLGUIN (JULIAN ALBERTO) La suspension artificial de la vida y el derecho. Bogota, 1972. pp. 115. *bibliog.*

CUBA.

CUBAN NEWS: information bulletin pd. by the Press and Information Department of the Cuban Embassy... London. bi-m., Mr/Ap 1974(v.1, no.1)- London.

— Census.

CUBA. Census, 1970. Censo de poblacion y viviendas, 1970. La Habana, 1975. pp. 1035.

— Economic conditions.

CASTRO RUZ (FIDEL) La experiencia cubana...; informe al Primer Congreso...del P. C.C. etc. Barcelona, 1976. pp. 317. *bibliog. Other documents included in appendices.*

BRUNNER (HEINRICH) 1945- . Cuban sugar policy from 1963 to 1970; translated by Marguerite Borchardt and H.F. Broch de Rothermann. Pittsburgh, [1977]. pp. 163. *bibliog.*

MESA LAGO (CARMELO) Cuba in the 1970s: pragmatism and institutionalization. rev. ed. Albuquerque, [1978]. pp. 187.

— Economic policy.

ROCA (SERGIO) Cuban economic policy and ideology: the ten million ton sugar harvest. Beverly Hills, [1976]. pp. 70. *bibliog.*

BRUNNER (HEINRICH) 1945- . Cuban sugar policy from 1963 to 1970; translated by Marguerite Borchardt and H.F. Broch de Rothermann. Pittsburgh, [1977]. pp. 163. *bibliog.*

— Foreign relations.

MESA LAGO (CARMELO) Cuba in the 1970s: pragmatism and institutionalization. rev. ed. Albuquerque, [1978]. pp. 187.

— — Venezuela.

CASTRO RUZ (FIDEL) Criticas a la direccion del Partido Comunista de Venezuela. Montevideo, Nativa Libros, 1967. pp. 39.

— History — 1810-1899.

FONER (PHILIP SHELDON) Antonio Maceo: the "Bronze Titan" of Cuba's struggle for independence. New York, [1977]. pp. 340. *bibliog.*

MARTÍ (JOSÉ) Our America: writings on Latin America and the struggle for Cuban independence; translated by Elinor Randall...; edited, with an introduction and notes, by Philip S. Foner. New York, [1977]. pp. 448.

— — 1933, Revolution.

DOLGOFF (SAM) The Cuban revolution: a critical perspective. Montréal, [1976]. pp. 200.

— — 1933-1959.

LLERENA (MARIO) The unsuspected revolution: the birth and rise of Castroism. Ithaca, 1978. pp. 324.

— — 1959- .

CASTRO'S Cuba in the 1970's; edited by Lester A. Sobel. New York, [1978]. pp. 244. *Based on records compiled by Facts on File.*

LLERENA (MARIO) The unsuspected revolution: the birth and rise of Castroism. Ithaca, 1978. pp. 324.

— Politics and government.

CUBA: revolution and counter-revolution; translated from Acción Libertaria, organ of the Argentine Libertarian Federation, etc. New York, [1961?]. s. sh.

POSADAS (J.) El asesinato de Guevara y el desarrollo de la revolucion politica en Cuba. Lima, [1967]. pp. xiv, 14.

CRUZ COBOS (ARMANDO) Fidel Castro y su purga de Guignol: de Glassboro al "comunismo independiente" en Cuba. [Lima, 1968]. pp. 39.

GOMEZ (JUAN GUALBERTO) Por Cuba libre; ... seleccion y prologo de Emilio Roig de Leuchsenring. La Habana, 1974. pp. 513.

CASTRO RUZ (FIDEL) La experiencia cubana...; informe al Primer Congreso...del P. C.C. etc. Barcelona, 1976. pp. 317. *bibliog. Other documents included in appendices.*

LEWIS (OSCAR) and others. Four men: living the revolution: an oral history of contemporary Cuba. Urbana, Ill., [1977]. pp. 538. *bibliog.*

LEWIS (OSCAR) and others. Neighbors: living the revolution: an oral history of contemporary Cuba. Urbana, [1978]. pp. 581. *bibliog.*

MESA LAGO (CARMELO) Cuba in the 1970s: pragmatism and institutionalization. rev. ed. Albuquerque, [1978]. pp. 187.

— Population.

HAVANA. Universidad. Centro de Estudios Demograficos. La poblacion de Cuba. La Habana, [1976]. pp. 236. *(Committee for International Coordination of National Research in Demography. C.I.C.R.E.D. Series)*

— Relations (general) with foreign countries.

CASTRO'S Cuba in the 1970's; edited by Lester A. Sobel. New York, [1978]. pp. 244. *Based on records compiled by Facts on File.*

— Social conditions.

CASTRO RUZ (FIDEL) La experiencia cubana...; informe al Primer Congreso...del P. C.C. etc. Barcelona, 1976. pp. 317. *bibliog. Other documents included in appendices.*

LEWIS (OSCAR) and others. Four men: living the revolution: an oral history of contemporary Cuba. Urbana, Ill., [1977]. pp. 538. *bibliog.*

LEWIS (OSCAR) and others. Four women: living the revolution: an oral history of contemporary Cuba. Urbana, [1977]. pp. 443. *bibliog.*

LEWIS (OSCAR) and others. Neighbors: living the revolution: an oral history of contemporary Cuba. Urbana, [1978]. pp. 581. *bibliog.*

MESA LAGO (CARMELO) Cuba in the 1970s: pragmatism and institutionalization. rev. ed. Albuquerque, [1978]. pp. 187.

CUIVA INDIANS.

ARCAND (BERNARD) The urgent situation of the Cuiva Indians of Colombia. Copenhagen, 1972. pp. 28. *bibliog. (International Work Group for Indigenous Affairs. Documents. 7)*

CULTURAL RELATIONS.

BUCHANAN (GEORGE) Novelist. The politics of culture. London, 1977. pp. 54.

CULTURE.

GRAMSCI (ANTONIO) Passato e presente. Torino, 1966 repr. 1974. pp. 273. *(Quaderni del Carcere. 6)*

ONTARIO. Legislative Assembly. Select Committee on Economic and Cultural Nationalism. 1975. Report...: final report on cultural nationalism; [Russell D. Rowe, chairman]. [Toronto], 1975. pp. 51.

GOLDMAN (LUCIEN) Cultural creation in modern society; introduction by William Mayrl; translated by Bart Grahl, etc. Oxford, 1977. pp. 173. *bibliog.*

INTERNATIONAL CONGRESS OF ANTHROPOLOGICAL AND ETHNOLOGICAL SCIENCES. 9th Congress, 1973. The concept and dynamics of culture: [papers from the Congress]; editor Bernardo Bernardi. The Hague, [1977]. pp. 630. *bibliogs.*

HARRIS (MARVIN) Cannibals and kings: the origins of cultures. London, 1978. pp. 239. *bibliog.*

CULTURE CONFLICT.

CULTURAL conflict and the Asian family; report of a conference organised by the National Association of Indian Youth [in Leicester in 1975]; edited by Pramila Parekh and Bhikhu Parekh. [London], 1976. pp. 13.

CUMBERLAND

— Industries.

LANCASTER (J.Y.) and WATTLEWORTH (D.R.) The iron and steel industry of West Cumberland: an historical survey. Workington, 1977. pp. 198. *bibliog.*

CUMBRIA

— Economic conditions.

CUMBRIA. Planning Department, and LAKE DISTRICT SPECIAL PLANNING BOARD. Choices for Cumbria: report of survey; technical analysis of the key issues for the structure plan and review of possible policies. [Kendal], 1976. pp. 244.

— Economic policy.

CUMBRIA. Planning Department, and LAKE DISTRICT SPECIAL PLANNING BOARD. Choices for Cumbria: report of survey; technical analysis of the key issues for the structure plan and review of possible policies. [Kendal], 1976. pp. 244.

— Social conditions.

CUMBRIA. Planning Department, and LAKE DISTRICT SPECIAL PLANNING BOARD. Choices for Cumbria: report of survey; technical analysis of the key issues for the structure plan and review of possible policies. [Kendal], 1976. pp. 244.

WEBBER (RICHARD J.) Cumbria social area analysis. London, 1977. pp. 40. *(Planning Research Applications Group. PRAG Technical Papers. TP 22)*

— Social policy.

CUMBRIA. Planning Department, and LAKE DISTRICT SPECIAL PLANNING BOARD. Choices for Cumbria: report of survey; technical analysis of the key issues for the structure plan and review of possible policies. [Kendal], 1976. pp. 244.

CUMMINGS (EDWARD ESTLIN).

FAIRLEY (IRENE R.) E.E. Cummings and ungrammar: a study of syntactic deviance in his poems. New York, 1975. pp. 191. *bibliog.*

CURAÇAOSCHE BANK.

See BANK VAN DE NEDERLANDSE ANTILLEN.

CURRICULUM PLANNING.

MUNBY (JOHN) Communicative syllabus design: a sociolinguistic model for defining the content of purpose-specific language programmes. Cambridge, 1978. pp. 232. *bibliog.*

CURVES, ALGEBRAIC.

FULTON (WILLIAM) Algebraic curves: an introduction to algebraic geometry. Reading, Mass., 1969 repr. 1978. pp. 226. *Notes written with the collaboration of Richard Weiss.*

CUSTODY OF CHILDREN

— United Kingdom.

CUSTODY after divorce: the disposition of custody in divorce cases in Great Britain; by John Eekelaar [and others]. Oxford, [1977]. pp. (92). *(U.K. Social Science Research Council. Centre for Socio- Legal Studies. Family Law Studies. No. 1)*

CUSTOMARY LAW.

LEACH (Sir EDMUND RONALD) Custom, law and terrorist violence. Edinburgh, 1977. pp. 37. *(Edinburgh. University. Munro Lectures on Anthropology and Prehistoric Archaeology. 1977)*

— Nigeria.

NIGERIA (WESTERN STATE). 1971. Customary courts manual; incorporating customary courts law, customary courts rules and extracts from laws enforceable by customary courts;...issued for the guidance of customary courts. 2nd ed. [Ibadan, 1971]. pp. 170.

CUSTOMS ADMINISTRATION

— China — History — Sources.

LONDON. University. School of Oriental and African Studies. Library. Papers relating to the Chinese maritime customs, 1860-1943, in the library of the School of Oriental and African Studies. London, 1973. pp. 13.

— New Zealand.

NEW ZEALAND. Customs Department. 1975. Customs administration in New Zealand. [Wellington, 1975]. pp. 28. *Photocopy.*

— Scandinavia.

[SCANDINAVIA]. Nordiske Parlamentariske Komité for Friere Samfaerdsel. 1952. Betaenkning om lettelser i toldbehandlingen af rejsende i den internordiske trafik: og Betaenkning om valutamaessige lettelser i rejsetrafikken mellem de nordiske lande. København, 1952. pp. 27,16.

[SCANDINAVIA]. Nordiske Parlamentariske Komité for Friere Samfaerdsel. 1953. Betaenkning om lettelser i toldbehandlingen m.v. af motorkøretøjer i den internordiske trafik. Kóenhavn, 1953. pp. 40.

CUSTOMS UNIONS.

LANGHAMMER (ROLF J.) Die Zentralafrikanische Zoll- und Wirtschaftsunion: Integrationswirkungen bei Ländern im Frühstadium der industriellen Entwicklung. Tübingen, [1978]. pp. 268. *bibliog. (Kiel. Universität. Institut für Weltwirtschaft. Kieler Studien. 151)*

CYBERNETICS.

GEORGE (FRANK HONYWILL) Machine takeover: the growing threat to human freedom in a computer-controlled society. Oxford, 1977. pp. 193. *bibliog.*

PÖRN (INGMAR) Action theory and social science: some formal models. Dordrecht, [1977]. pp. 129. *bibliog.*

CYPRUS

— Economic policy.

DELIBANES (DEMETRIOS) The prospects of the economic development of Cyprus on the basis of Greek experience. Leukosia, Cyprus, 1973. pp. 4.

— Foreign relations — Treaties.

PAPADOPOULOS (ANDRESTINOS N.) La pratique chypriote en matière de succession d'états aux traités. Nicosie, 1976. pp. 240. *bibliog. Thèse (docteur en droit) - Université de Genève.*

— — Greece.

MARKIDES (KYRIACOS C.) The rise and fall of the Cyprus Republic. New Haven, 1977. pp. 200.

— History.

CRAWSHAW (NANCY) The Cyprus revolt: an account of the struggle for union with Greece. London, 1978. pp. 447. *bibliog.*

— Industries.

CYPRUS. Statistics and Research Department. 1977- . Registration of establishments, 1976. [Nicosia], 1977 in progress.

— Nationalism.

CROSFIELD (Sir ARTHUR HENRY) An opportunity for the Peace League's leaders. [London, 1919?]. pp. 7. *(Reprinted from the Westminster Gazette, February 1919)*

— Politics and government.

NATIONAL DELEGATION OF CYPRUS. Memorandum; [to the Colonial Secretary, Arthur Creech Jones]. 1947. fo. 5.

CYPRUS. Public Information Office. 1969. The clearing up of certain misconceptions. Nicosia, 1969. pp. 11.

MARKIDES (KYRIACOS C.) The rise and fall of the Cyprus Republic. New Haven, 1977. pp. 200.

— Social conditions.

MARKIDES (KYRIACOS C.) The rise and fall of the Cyprus Republic. New Haven, 1977. pp. 200.

— Statistics.

CYPRUS. Statistics and Research Department. Quarterly statistical digest. q., Mr 1968 (no.1)- Nicosia.

CZECH LANGUAGE

— Dictionaries — Polyglot.

HEBÁK (PETR) and HUSTOPECKÝ (JIŘÍ) compilers. Šestijazyčný slovník termínů z regresní analýzy: [Czech, Russian, Polish, English, French, German]. Praha, 1978. pp. 211. *With preface and explanatory notes in each language.*

CZECHOSLOVAKIA

— Commerce.

ČESKOSLOVENSKÁ OBCHODNÍ KOMORA Facts on Czechoslovak foreign trade, [1977 ed.]. [Prague], 1977. pp. 225.

— Commercial policy.

HAMPL (JAROSLAV) and others. Zásady a zaměření zahraničně obchodní politiky ČSSR. Praha, 1976. pp. 123. *(Československá Obchodní Komora. Československé Hospodářství a Mezinárodní Obchod)*

— Constitutional history.

ROZVOJ socialistického štátu a práva v oslobodenom Československu: zborník referátov z vedeckej konferencie Ústavu štátu a práva SAV a Práavnickej fakulty Univerzity Komenského,...22.-24. apríla 1975 v Smoleniciach. [Bratislava], 1977. pp. 266.

— Defences.

VYSOCKY (MARTIN) Czechoslovakia and the Conference on Security and Cooperation in Europe. Bratislava, 1977. pp. 131.

— Economic conditions.

DEMOSTA: bulletin pro demografii a statistiku: bulletin for demography and statistics; [pd. by] Federální Statistický Úřad ČSSR, Institut Demografie. [in English, French, Russian and Spanish]. q., 1963 ([v.] 1)- Praha.

TEPLÝ (JAROSLAV) Economie nationale de la Tchécoslovaquie contemporaine. Paris, [1976]. pp. 219.

DAN'SHINA (VALENTINA NIKOLAEVNA) Ekonomicheskoe razvitie ChSSR. Moskva, 1977. pp. 223.

— Economic policy.

AKTUÁLNE otázky ekonomického programu XV. zjazdu KSČ. Bratislava, 1977. pp. 252.

— Foreign relations.

GLEICHGEWICHT, Revision, Restauration: die Aussenpolitik der Ersten Tschechoslowakischen Republik im Europasystem der Pariser Vorortevertträge; herausgegeben von Karl Bosl; Vorträge der Tagungen des Collegium Carolinum in Bad Wiessee...1976. München, 1976. pp. 424. *bibliog.*

SIKORA (FRANZ) Sozialistische Solidarität und nationale Interessen: Polen, Tschechoslowakei, DDR. Köln, [1977]. pp. 248. *(Bundesinstitut für Ostwissenschaftliche und Internationale Studien. Abhandlungen. Band 31)*

VYSOCKY (MARTIN) Czechoslovakia and the Conference on Security and Cooperation in Europe. Bratislava, 1977. pp. 131.

— — Germany.

JAWORSKI (RUDOLF) Vorposten oder Minderheit?: der sudetendeutsch Volkstumskampf in den Beziehungen zwischen der Weimarer Republik und der ČSR. Stuttgart, [1977]. pp. 240. *bibliog.*

— History — Chronology.

ČSSR 1974: kronika vnitropolitických událostí; zpracovalo vědeckoinformační středisko Ústavu marxismu- leninismu ÚV KSČ. Praha, 1975. pp. 181.

— — 1968- , Intervention.

MATĚJÍČEK (JAROSLAV) Politický systém socialismu a kritika pravicového revizionismu v ČSSR. Praha, 1976. pp. 251. *With Russian summary.*

PELIKÁN (JIŘÍ) Ein Frühling, der nie zu Ende geht: Erinnerungen eines Prager Kommunisten; (aus dem Französischen von Eva Moldenhauer). Frankfurt am Main, [1976]. pp. 332.

BEJDA (VASIL) Politika a ideológia: k vývoju v strane a spoločnosti v nedávnom období. Bratislava, 1977. pp. 235.

KUSIN (VLADIMIR V.) From Dubček to Charter 77: a study of 'normalisation' in Czechoslovakia, 1968-1978. Edinburgh, 1978. pp. 353. *bibliog.*

SKALA (JAN) Die ČSSR vom Prager Frühling zur Charta 77; mit einem dokumentarischen Anhang. Berlin, [1978]. pp. 197.

— Industries — Classification.

CZECHOSLOVAKIA. Federální Statistický Úřad. 1976. Ekonomické klasifikace; [by] Jan Kazimour. Bratislava, 1976. pp. 186.

— **Politics and government.**

GELLNER (ERNEST ANDRE) The pluralist anti-Levellers of Prague. n.p., [1970?]. fo. 20. *With ms. amendments.*

COMMITTEE TO DEFEND CZECHOSLOVAK SOCIALISTS. Pravda vitezi; truth will prevail. [London, 1973]. pp. 18. *No. 3 of the bulletin issued by the Committee.*

HUSÁK (GUSTÁV) Projevy a stati, únor 1972 - červen 1974. Praha, 1976. pp. 575.

MATĚJÍČEK (JAROSLAV) Politický systém socialismu a kritika pravicového revizionismu v ČSSR. Praha, 1976. pp. 251. *With Russian summary.*

PŘEHLED dějin KSČ. Praha, 1976. pp. 375.

BEJDA (VASIL) Politika a ideológia: k vývoju v strane a spoločnosti v nedávnom období. Bratislava, 1977. pp. 235.

POLITIKA KSČ: ciele a prostriedky. Bratislava, 1977. pp. 273. *(Komunistická Strana Slovenska. Ústredný Výbor. Ústav Marxizmu-Leninizmu. Zborník. roč.17, č.1)*

KUSIN (VLADIMIR V.) From Dubček to Charter 77: a study of 'normalisation' in Czechoslovakia, 1968-1978. Edinburgh, 1978. pp. 353. *bibliog.*

— **Population.**

DEMOSTA: bulletin pro demografii a statistiku: bulletin for demography and statistics; [pd. by] Federální Statistický Úřad ČSSR, Institut Demografie. [in English, French, Russian and Spanish]. q., 1963 ([v.] 1)- Praha.

— **Social conditions.**

ZÁBRAHOVÁ (LUDOSLAVA) Třídně sociální struktura ve výstavbě socialismu: východiska, kritéria a problémy ČSSR. Praha, 1976. pp. 153.

DAIRY LAWS

— **United States.**

FEDERAL milk marketing orders and price supports; edited by Paul W. MacAvoy. Washington, D.C., [1977]. pp. 166. *(American Enterprise Institute for Public Policy Research. AEI Studies. 176) A condensed and edited version of an earlier report by the U.S. Department of Justice.*

DAIRY PRODUCTS.

DAIRY PRODUCE: a review of production, trade, consumption...; pd. by the Commonwealth Secretariat. a., 1936- ; susp. pbln. 1939-1947-1954. London.

COMMONWEALTH SECRETARIAT. Meat and dairy products. s-a., N 1978(1st)- London.

— **European Economic Community countries.**

EUROPEAN COMMUNITIES. Statistical Office. Milk and milk products. a., 1977(1st)- Luxembourg. *[in Community languages]*

DAIRYING

— **Australia.**

AUSTRALIA. Bureau of Agricultural Economics. 1975. The Australian dairyfarming industry: report on an economic survey, 1971-72 to 1973-74. Canberra, 1975. pp. 116.

AUSTRALIA. Bureau of Agricultural Economics. 1975. Structural and farm adjustment in the Australian dairy industry. Canberra, 1975. pp. 68. *(Industry Economics Monographs. No. 10)*

AUSTRALIA. Bureau of Agricultural Economics. 1976. BAE submission to Industries Assistance Commission inquiry into the dairy industry: marketing arrangements. Canberra, 1976. pp. 62. *(Industry Economics Monographs. No. 12)*

— **Guyana.**

HUGGINS (H.D.) An economic survey of dairy-farming in east Demerara. [Georgetown], 1943 repr. 1944. pp. 40. *(Guyana. Department of Agriculture. Economic Intelligence Series)*

— **India.**

JONAS (PAUL) An analysis of bovine milk consumption in major Indian metropolitan areas. New Delhi, 1971. 1 vol. (various pagings). *bibliog. (United States. Agency for International Development. USAID-New Delhi. Economic Affairs Division. Staff Papers)*

— **New Zealand.**

NEW ZEALAND. Dairy Board. Investigation Section. 1971. The New Zealand dairy industry: a survey. Wellington, [1971]. fo. 28.

NEW ZEALAND. Dairy Board. Economics Section. 1977. The New Zealand dairy industry: a survey. 3rd ed. Wellington, 1977. fo. 50.

— **Rhodesia.**

SOUTHERN RHODESIA. Committee of Enquiry into Certain Aspects of the Dairy and Pig Industries. 1936. Report; [William Purdie Currie, chairman]. Salisbury, 1936. pp. 40. *(Legislative Assembly. [Sessional Papers]. 1936. C.S.R. 4)*

— **Tasmania.**

TASMANIA. Parliament. House of Assembly. Select Committee on the Dairy Industry. 1976. The dairy industry in Tasmania; report...with minutes of proceedings; [D.F. Clark, chairman]. in TASMANIA. Parliament. Journals and Printed Papers. 1976, no. 16.

— **United Kingdom — Costs.**

U.K. Milk Marketing Board and Ministry of Agriculture and Fisheries. 1951. National investigation into the economics of milk production: costs of milk production in England and Wales, October, 1949, to September, 1950. [London, 1951?]. pp. 44.

U.K. Milk Marketing Board and Ministry of Agriculture and Fisheries. 1952. National investigation into the economics of milk production: cost of milk production in England and Wales, October, 1950, to September, 1951. [London, 1952?]. pp. 39.

DALADIER (EDOUARD).

EDOUARD Daladier, Chef du Gouvernment, avril 1938 [to] septembre 1939; sous la direction de René Rémond et Janine Bourdin. [Paris, 1977]. pp. 320. *A colloque held at the Fondation Nationale des Sciences Politiques in December 1975.*

DANGEROUS GOODS

— **Transportation.**

INTER-GOVERNMENTAL MARITIME CONSULTATIVE ORGANIZATION. 1977- . International Maritime Dangerous Goods Code. London, 1977 in progress.

UNITED NATIONS. Committee of Experts on the Transport of Dangerous Goods. 1977. Transport of dangerous goods: recommendations, etc. (ST/SG/AC. 10/1/Rev.1). rev.ed. New York, 1977. pp. 377.

DANISH BACON COMPANY.

SPINK (REGINALD) DBC: the story of the Danish Bacon Company, 1902-1977. Welwyn Garden City, [1977]. pp. 96. *bibliog.*

DARDANELLES.

MORF (JUERG) Die Dardanellenfrage an der Konferenz von Montreux 1936. Bern, [1977]. pp. 243. *bibliog. (Zürich. Universität. Historisches Seminar. Geist und Werk der Zeiten. No.55)*

DASH (SAMUEL).

DASH (SAMUEL) Chief counsel: inside the Ervin committee: the untold story of Watergate. New York, [1976]. pp. 275.

DATA BASE MANAGEMENT.

TAYLOR (A.A.) and FOREMAN (E.K.) Integrated statistical data base systems. [Canberra, Australian Bureau of Statistics, 1975]. 1 vol. (unpaged).

IFIP WORKING CONFERENCE ON MODELLING IN DATA BASE MANAGEMENT SYSTEMS, FREUDENSTADT, 1976. Modelling in data base management systems; proceedings of the... conference [organized by IFIP Technical Committee 2]...; edited by G.M. Nijssen. Amsterdam, 1976. pp. 418. *bibliogs.*

IFIP WORKING CONFERENCE ON MODELLING IN DATA BASE MANAGEMENT SYSTEMS, NICE, 1977. Architecture and models in data base management systems; proceedings of the...conference [organized by IFIP Technical Committee 2]...;edited by G.M. Nijssen. Amsterdam, 1977. pp. 326. *bibliogs.*

INTERNATIONAL IFIP CONFERENCE ON VERY LARGE DATA BASES, 2ND, BRUSSELS, 1976. Systems for large data bases; proceedings of the...conference...; edited by P.C. Lockemann and E.J. Neuhold. Amsterdam, 1977. pp. 224. *bibliogs.*

WIEDERHOLD (GIO) Database design. New York, [1977]. pp. 658. *bibliog.*

CARDENAS (ALFONSO F.) Data base management systems. Boston, Mass., [1978]. pp. 519. *bibliogs.*

DATA STRUCTURES (COMPUTER SCIENCE).

MATICK (RICHARD E.) Computer storage systems and technology. New York, [1977]. pp. 667. *bibliog.*

WIEDERHOLD (GIO) Database design. New York, [1977]. pp. 658. *bibliog.*

DATA TRANSMISSION SYSTEMS.

BINGHAM (JOHN E.) and DAVIES (GARTH W.P.) Planning for data communications. London, 1977. pp. 218. *bibliog.*

CYPSER (R.J.) Communications architecture for distributed systems. Reading, Mass., [1978]. pp. 711.

DOLL (DIXON R.) Data communications: facilities, networks, and systems design. New York, [1978]. pp. 493. *bibliogs.*

DAY CARE AIDES

— **Canada — Manitoba.**

MANITOBA. Women's Bureau. Brandon Office. 1976. Employment in day care;...written by Joan Simpkins. Brandon, 1976. pp. 22.

DAY NURSERIES

— **Canada.**

CLIFFORD (HOWARD) Current trends and issues in day care in Canada; unpublished speech given at the 1973 Northwest Regional Conference of the Child Welfare League of America, June 10-13, 1973. Edmonton, 1973. fo. 32.

MANITOBA. Women's Bureau. 1974. Mothers in the labour force: their child care arrangements. Winnipeg, 1974. pp. (62). *bibliog.*

— **United Kingdom.**

ARMISTEAD (NIGEL) Data for 1975 on children's day care facilities in London. London, [1976]. pp. 26. *(London. Greater London Council. Research Memoranda. 493) Supplement to Research Memorandum 472.*

TRADES UNION CONGRESS. The under-fives; report of a TUC working party. London, [1977]. pp. 127.

DAY NURSERIES (Cont.)

— United States.

JOFFE (CAROLE E.) Friendly intruders: childcare professionals and family life. Berkeley, [1977]. pp. 172. *bibliog.*

DEAF

— Means of communication.

ON the other hand: new perspectives on American Sign Language; edited by Lynn A. Friedman. New York, 1977. pp. 245. *bibliog.* An outgrowth of a course on the structure of the American Sign Language (ASL) given at U.C. Berkeley in 1975.

DEATH.

RAMSEY (PAUL) Ethics at the edges of life: medical and legal intersections. New Haven, 1978. pp. 353. *(Columbia University. Bampton Lectures in America)*

— Causes.

JACOBS (G.D.) and BARDSLEY (MARGUERITE N.) Road accidents as a cause of death in developing countries. Crowthorne, 1977. pp. 18. *bibliog. (U.K. Transport and Road Research Laboratory. Supplementary Reports. 277)*

DEBRAY (REGIS).

DEBRAY (REGIS) Journal d'un petit bourgeois entre deux feux et quatre murs. Paris, 1976. pp. 170.

DEBTS, EXTERNAL

— Mexico.

GREEN (ROSARIO) El endeudamiento publico externo de Mexico, 1940-1973. Mexico, 1976. pp. 231. *(Mexico City. Colegio de Mexico. Centro de Estudios Internacionales. Coleccion. 15)*

— Underdeveloped areas.

See UNDERDEVELOPED AREAS — Debts, External.

DEBTS, PUBLIC.

CAVACO-SILVA (ANIBAL A.) Economic effects of public debt. London, 1977. pp. 147. *bibliog.*

DECEDENTS' ESTATES

— New Zealand.

NEW ZEALAND. Maori and Island Affairs Department. 1968. Estates and wills of Maoris. [Wellington, 1968]. pp. (6).

DECEMBRISTS.

LORER (NIKOLAI IVANOVICH) Zapiski dekabrista N.I. Lorera; pod redaktsiei M.N. Pokrovskogo; prigotovila k pechati i kommentirovala M.V. Nechkina. Moskva, 1931. pp. 448.

AGAPOVA (TAISIIA IVANOVNA) and SEROVA (MAIIA IGNAT'EVNA) Dekabristy na Kubani. Krasnodar, 1975. pp. 29.

DUM vysokoe stremlen'e. Irkutsk, 1975. pp. 335.

POSTNOV (IURII SERGEEVICH) Sibir' v poezii dekabristov. Novosibirsk, 1976. pp. 112. *(Akademiia Nauk SSSR. Sibirskoe Otdelenie. Institut Istorii, Filologii i Filosofii. Nauchno-Populiarnaia Seriia)*

DECENTRALIZATION IN GOVERNMENT

— France.

La DECENTRALISATION pour la rénovation de l'Etat: colloque sous la direction de Charles Debbasch,...organisé par la Faculté de Droit de l'Université d'Aix-Marseille d'Economie et des Sciences d'Aix-Marseille à Aix-en-Provence, les 23 et 24 mai 1975. [Paris], 1976. pp. 251.

GREMION (PIERRE) Le pouvoir périphérique: bureaucrates et notables dans le système politique français. Paris, [1976]. pp. 478. *bibliog.*

— Italy.

DELL'ACQUA (CESARE) Università, televisione e decentramento regionale: profili costituzionale e organizzativi. Napoli, 1974. pp. 157.

REGIONI e polizia locale. Milano, 1975. pp. 173. *(Istituto per la Scienza dell'Amministrazione Pubblica. Quaderni ISAP. 16)*

SVILUPPO delle autonomie e riforma dello Stato: relazioni presentate al seminario nazionale organizzato dalla Sezione centrale scuole di partito e dalla Sezione regioni e autonomie locali del Comitato centrale del PCI, etc. Roma, 1975. pp. 207. *bibliog.*

ROTELLI (ETTORE) L'alternativa delle autonomie: istituzioni locali e tendenze politiche dell'Italia moderna. Milano, 1978. pp. 340.

— Nigeria.

NIGERIA. Sessional Papers. 1948. No. 20. Statement of the policy proposed for the decentralization of the Nigeria Local Development Board. [Lagos], 1948. pp. 4.

— Sudan.

SALIH (GALOBAWI MOHAMMED) Patterns of decentralization in the republic of the Sudan: origins, characteristics and prospects. 2nd ed. [Khartoum, Institute of Public Administration, 1970]. pp. 93.

— United Kingdom.

DIVIDED loyalties: British regional assertion and European integration; edited by Martin Kolinsky, assisted by David Scott Bell. Manchester, 1978. pp. 216.

MERCER (JOHN) Scotland: the devolution of power. London, 1978. pp. 250. *bibliog.*

OSMOND (JOHN) Creative conflict: the politics of Welsh devolution. Llandysul, 1978. pp. 305.

— Zambia.

ZAMBIA. Division of Provincial Administration, National Guidance and Culture. Annual report. a., 1974- Lusaka.

DECIMAL SYSTEM.

NEW ZEALAND. Post Office. 1966. Post Office training for decimal currency. [Wellington, 1966]. pp. 21.

DECISION-MAKING.

DECISION making: an experimental approach to management education: (a report of a management education course run by B.I.M. (Luton Branch)...with the London School of Economics and Political Science); edited by Desmond Graves. Luton, 1969. fo. 62.

WAGNER (HARVEY M.) Principles of operations research, with applications to managerial decisions. 2nd ed. London, 1975. pp. 1039. *bibliog.*

BAILEY (FREDERICK GEORGE) Morality and expediency: the folklore of academic politics. Oxford, [1977]. pp. 230. *bibliog.*

FAIRWEATHER (GEORGE WILLIAM) and TORNATZKY (LOUIS G.) Experimental methods for social policy research. Oxford, 1977. pp. 420. *bibliog.*

JONES (HARRY) b. 1911 and TWISS (BRIAN CHARLES) Forecasting technology for planning decisions. [London, 1978]. pp. 263. *bibliogs.*

MANAGEMENT control and organizational democracy; editors Bert King [and others]. Washington, D.C., 1978. pp. 288. *bibliogs.* Papers presented at a conference held in Munich in 1976 by the Human Factors Division of the North Atlantic Treaty Organization.

— Mathematical models.

STEELE (JAMES D.) Markovian decision processes with limited state observability and unobservable costs. Santa Monica, 1972. pp. 13. *bibliog. (Rand Corporation. [Papers]. 4925)*

STEELE (JAMES D.) A model for the analysis of Markovian decision processes with unobservable states and unobservable costs. Santa Monica, 1972. pp. 8. *bibliog. (Rand Corporation. [Papers]. 4917)*

MULTIPLE criteria decision making, edited by James L. Cochrane and Milan Zeleny. Columbia, S.C., 1973. pp. 816. *bibliog.* Based on a seminar held at the University of South Carolina in 1972.

MENGES (GUENTER) Economic decision making: basic concepts and models. London, 1974. pp. 236. *bibliog.* English translation by G. Mschaty.

DELFT (AD VAN) and NIJKAMP (PETER) Multi-criteria analysis and regional decision-making. Leiden, 1977. pp. 135. *bibliog.*

SFEIR-YOUNIS (ALFREDO) and BROMLEY (DANIEL W.) Decision making in developing countries: multiobjective formulation and evaluation methods. New York, [1977]. pp. 200. *bibliog.*

— Methodology.

A DISCUSSION on the use of operational research and systems analysis in decision-making; [by] R.C. Tomlinson [and others]. London, 1977. pp. 193. *(London. Royal Society of London. Philosophical Transactions. Series A. vol. 287)*

DECISION-MAKING IN POLITICAL SCIENCE.

See POLITICAL SCIENCE — Decision making.

DECISION-MAKING IN PUBLIC ADMINISTRATION.

See ADMINISTRATION — Decision making.

DEFENCE (CRIMINAL PROCEDURE)

— United States.

HERMANN (ROBERT) and others. Counsel for the poor: criminal defense in urban America. Lexington, Mass., [1977]. pp. 243.

DEFICIT FINANCING

— Canada.

PATTISON (JOHN CHARLES) Government deficits and inflation reconsidered. [Toronto], Ontario Economic Council, 1976. fo. 7.

DEGRELLE (LEON).

DEGRELLE (LEON) Lettres à mon Cardinal. [Bruxelles, 1975]. pp. 341.

DE GROOTE (FIRM).

BAETENS (ROLAND) De nazomer van Antwerpens welvaart: de diaspora en het handelshuis De Groote tijdens de eerste helft der 17de eeuw. [Brussels], 1976. 2 vols. *bibliog. (Pro Civitate. Collection Histoire. Série in-8. No. 45)* Map in end pocket.

DELCEV (GOCE).

GOCE Delčev i makedonskoto nacionalno revolucionerno dviženje: materijali od Simpoziumot održan na 8, 9 i 10 noemvri 1972 godina vo Stip po povod 100-godišninata od ragjanjeto na Goce Delčev. Skopje, 1973. pp. 410.

DELEGATED LEGISLATION

— Italy.

CAZZOLA (FRANCO) and others. Il decreto legge fra governo e parlamento. Milano, 1975. pp. 339. *(Florence. Università degli Studi di Firenze. Istituto di Diritto Costituzionale Italiano e Comparato. Processo Legislativo nel Parlamento Italiano. 4)*

— United States.

GOVERNMENT regulation: where do we go from here?; (a Round Table held on December 19, 1977...); John Charles Daly, moderator, etc. Washington, [1977]. pp. 41. *(American Enterprise Institute for Public Policy Research. Public Policy Forums. 14)*

DELHI (UNION TERRITORY)

— Economic policy.

DELHI (UNION TERRITORY). Directorate of Public Relations. 1957. Second five year plan of Delhi Union Territory. Delhi, [1957]. pp. 321. *bibliog.*

— Social policy.

DELHI (UNION TERRITORY). Directorate of Public Relations. 1957. Second five year plan of Delhi Union Territory. Delhi, [1957]. pp. 321. *bibliog.*

DELIVERY OF GOODS (LAW)

— Russia.

EKONOMICHESKIE sanktsii i distsiplina postavok. Kiev, 1976. pp. 266.

DELORS (JACQUES).

BODMAN (ERIC DE) and RICHARD (BERTRAND) Changer les relations sociales: la politique de Jacques Delors. Paris, 1976. pp. 218. *bibliog.*

DEMOCRACY.

La DEMOCRAZIA nel sindacato; ([by] Guido Romagnoli [and others]). Milano, [1975]. pp. 133.

SOVETSKAIA demokratiia v period razvitogo sotsializma; otvetstvennyi redaktor D.A. Kerimov. Moskva, 1976. pp. 279.

CHISTIAKOV (OLEG IVANOVICH) Problemy demokratii i federalizma v pervoi Sovetskoi Konstitutsii. Moskva, 1977. pp. 125.

FISH (HAMILTON) An American manifesto of freedom in answer to the manifesto on communism, 1848. New York, [1977]. pp. 209. *bibliog.*

GOSUDARSTVO, demokratiia i trudovoi kollektiv v razvitom sotsialisticheskom obshchestve. Moskva, 1977. pp. 200.

GOVERNMENT secrecy in democracies; edited by Itzhak Galnoor. New York, 1977. pp. 313.

KAHN (JEAN FRANÇOIS) Complot contre la démocratie. [Paris, 1977]. pp. 235.

KOREL'SKII (VIKTOR MIKHAILOVICH) Demokratiia i distsiplina v razvitom sotsialisticheskom obshchestve. Moskva, 1977. pp. 136.

LAUDON (KENNETH C.) Communications technology and democratic participation. New York, 1977. pp. 116.

LIJPHART (AREND) Democracy in plural societies: a comparative exploration. New Haven, 1977. pp. 248.

MACPHERSON (CRAWFORD BROUGH) The life and times of liberal democracy. Oxford, 1977. pp. 120.

VACCA (GIUSEPPE) Quale democrazia: problemi della democrazia di transizione. Bari, [1977]. pp. 318.

WOLFE (ALAN) The limits of legitimacy: political contradictions of contemporary capitalism. New York, [1977]. pp. 432. *bibliog.*

BUULTJENS (RALPH) The decline of democracy: essays on an endangered political species. [Maryknoll, 1978]. pp. 150.

DEMOCRACY, consensus and social contract; editors Pierre Birnbaum [and others]. London, [1978]. pp. 357. *Based on the political theory workshops of the European Consortium for Political Research, held between 1975 and 1977.*

HART (VIVIEN) Distrust and democracy: political distrust in Britain and America. Cambridge, 1978. pp. 251. *bibliog.*

HOGG (QUINTIN McGAREL) Baron Hailsham. The dilemma of democracy: diagnosis and prescription. London, 1978. pp. 238.

IKE (NOBUTAKA) A theory of Japanese democracy. Boulder, 1978. pp. 178. *bibliog.*

KELSO (WILLIAM ALTON) American democratic theory: pluralism and its critics. Westport, Conn., 1978. pp. 288. *bibliog.*

RYN (CLAES G.) Democracy and the ethical life: a philosophy of politics and community. Baton Rouge, [1978]. pp. 208.

— Terminology.

STANKIEWICZ (WLADYSLAW JOZEF) A guide to democratic jargon. London, 1976. pp. 29.

DEMOCRATIC PARTY (UNITED STATES).

PARMET (HERBERT S.) The Democrats: the years after FDR. New York, 1977. pp. 371. *bibliog. First published in 1976.*

The LESSER evil?: the Left debates the Democratic Party and social change; [by] Michael Harrington, [and others]. New York, 1977. pp. 128.

FAIRLIE (HENRY) The parties: Republicans and Democrats in this century. New York, [1978]. pp. 236.

DEMOGRAPHY

— Mathematical models.

MODELIROVANIE sotsial'no-ekonomicheskikh protsessov: kachestvennye gipotezy i imitatsionnyi podkhod. Moskva, 1976. pp. 247. *bibliog.*

— Methodology.

COLLOQUE NATIONAL DE DEMOGRAPHIE, Vième, 1975. L'analyse démographique et ses applications; (actes du Colloque National...organisé...à Paris du 20 au 11 octobre, 1975); [edited by Paul Clerc]. Paris, 1977. pp. 548. *(Centre National de la Recherche Scientifique. Colloques Nationaux. No. 934)*

— Study and teaching.

INTERREGIONAL WORKSHOP ON PROGRAMMES OF TRAINING IN THE FIELD OF POPULATION, ELSINORE, 1967. Report of the...Workshop...[held at] Elsinore, Denmark, 19-30 June 1967. (ST/TAO/SER.C/98) (E/CN.9/207) (E/CN.9/CONF. 4/1). New York, United Nations, 1967. pp. 38. *bibliog.*

— — Netherlands.

PRAAG (PHILIP VAN) Het bevolkingsvraagstuk in Nederland: ontwikkeling van standpunten en opvattingen, 1918-1940. Deventer, [1976]. pp. 132. *bibliog. (Nederlands Interuniversitair Demografisch Instituut. NIDI-Publikaties. 1)*

DEMONSTRATIONS

— United Kingdom.

NATIONAL COUNCIL FOR CIVIL LIBERTIES. Reports. No. 11. Picketing and demonstrations...; briefing papers to the NCCL delegate conference on public order. London, 1975. 1 pamphlet (unpaged).

REPORT [of] independent trade union committee inquiry into events which occurred during the right-to-work march on Friday 19th March 1976; [chairman, Vincent Flynn]. London, 1976. pp. 7.

DEPRESSION, MENTAL.

MARSH (ALAN JOHN) Protest and political consciousness. Beverly Hills, [1977]. pp. 271. *bibliog.*

DENMARK

— Bibliography.

BRUUN (HENRY) and SIMON (GEORG) compilers. Dansk historisk bibliografi, 1913-1942; udgivet af Den danske historiske Forening. København, 1966-77. 6 vols. *vols. 1-4 were compiled by Henry Bruun only.*

— Defences.

LYKKEBO (LARS OLE) Det danske Socialdemokratis militaerpolitiske stilling, 1933-1937. Odense, 1976. pp. 117. *bibliog.*

— Economic history.

BOJE (PER) Det industrielle miljø, 1840-1940: kilder og litteratur. København, 1976. pp. 145. *(Københavns Universitet. Institut for Økonomisk Historie. Publikationer. Nr. 10)*

— Foreign relations — Poland.

CZAPLIŃSKI (WŁADYSŁAW) Polska a Dania XVI-XX w.: studia. Warszawa, 1976. pp. 356.

— History — Bibliography.

BRUUN (HENRY) and SIMON (GEORG) compilers. Dansk historisk bibliografi, 1913-1942; udgivet af Den danske historiske Forening. København, 1966-77. 6 vols. *vols. 1-4 were compiled by Henry Bruun only.*

— Politics and government.

LOGUE (JOHN) Trade unions in the corporate state: the effects of corporatism on party competition, contract referenda and internationalism in Danish trade unions. Gothenburg, 1976. pp. 65. *(Goteborgs Universitet. Historiska Institutionen. Research Section Post-War History. Publications. No. 5)*

— Social conditions.

FORDELINGEN af levekårene. København, 1978. 2 vols.(in 1). *(Socialforskningsinstituttet. Publikationer. 82)*

— Social history.

BOJE (PER) Det industrielle miljø, 1840-1940: kilder og litteratur. København, 1976. pp. 145. *(Københavns Universitet. Institut for Økonomisk Historie. Publikationer. Nr. 10)*

— Social policy.

TEISEN (FLEMMING) Socialpolitiske aktiviteter gennem 75 år;... historien i korte uddrag og fire bilag. København, 1976. pp. 59. *(Socialpolitisk Forening. Småskrifter. Nr.45)*

— Statistics, Vital.

DENMARK. Danmarks Statistik. 1973. Aegteskaber, fødte og døde, 1956-1969. København, 1973. pp. 107. *(Statistisk Tabelvaerk. 1973. 11)*

DENNIS (PEGGY).

DENNIS (PEGGY) The autobiography of an American communist: a personal view of a political life, 1925-1975. Westport, 1977. pp. 302.

DENTAL HYGIENISTS

— Canada.

CANADA. Statistics Canada. Health manpower: dental hygienists. a., 1976(1st)- Ottawa. *[in English and French]*

DEPRESSION, MENTAL.

LUNGHI (MARTIN EDWARD) Self identity, adaption to change and depression. 1977. fo. 257. *bibliog. Typescript. Ph.D. (London) thesis: unpublished. This thesis is the property of London University and may not be removed from the Library. Article in end pocket.*

DEPRESSION, MENTAL.(Cont.)

BROWN (GEORGE WILLIAM) Ph.D. and HARRIS (TIRRIL) Social origins of depression: a study of psychiatric disorder in women. London, 1978. pp. 399. *bibliog.*

DEPTH PERCEPTION.

BRAUNSTEIN (MYRON L.) Depth perception through motion. New York, [1976]. pp. 200. *bibliog.*

DERBY

— City planning.

DERBY AND DERBYSHIRE JUNIOR CHAMBER OF COMMERCE. Community Development Commission. Derby towards 2000: a project study report...1972-73. [Derby, 1973]. pp. 12.

DERBYSHIRE

— Economic conditions.

DERBYSHIRE. County Council. Derbyshire structure plan: report of survey. [Matlock], 1977. pp. 316.

— Economic policy.

DERBYSHIRE. County Council. Derbyshire structure plan: report of consultations. [Matlock], 1977. pp. 286.

DERBYSHIRE. County Council. Derbyshire structure plan: written statement. [Matlock], 1977. pp. 341. *2 maps in end pocket.*

— Social conditions.

DERBYSHIRE. County Council. Derbyshire structure plan: report of survey. [Matlock], 1977. pp. 316.

— Social policy.

DERBYSHIRE. County Council. Derbyshire structure plan: report of consultations. [Matlock], 1977. pp. 286.

DERBYSHIRE. County Council. Derbyshire structure plan: written statement. [Matlock], 1977. pp. 341. *2 maps in end pocket.*

DESCARTES (RENE).

WILLIAMS (BERNARD ARTHUR OWEN) Descartes: the project of pure enquiry. Harmondsworth, 1978. pp. 320. *bibliog.*

DESERTS.

COOKE (R.U.) An empty quarter. [London, 1977]. pp. 20. *bibliog. An inaugural lecture given at Bedford College, London University on 17 May 1976.*

ECKHOLM (ERIK P.) and BROWN (LESTER RUSSELL) Spreading deserts: the hand of man. Washington, 1977. pp. 40. *(Worldwatch Institute. Worldwatch Papers. No. 13)*

DETENTE.

DETENTE and peace in Europe; edited by Ruediger Juette. Frankfurt, [1977]. pp. 148. *bibliog.*

GATI (CHARLES) and GATI (TOBY TRISTER) The debate over detente. New York, 1977. pp. 63. *bibliog. (Foreign Policy Association. Headline Books. No. 234)*

WAJSMAN (PATRICK) L'illusion de la détente. [Paris, 1977]. pp. 288.

McWHINNEY (EDWARD) The international law of détente: arms control, European security, and East-West cooperation. Alphen aan den Rijn, 1978. pp. 259.

DETENTION OF PERSONS

— Netherlands.

EUROPEAN COURT OF HUMAN RIGHTS. Publications. Series B: Pleadings, Oral Arguments and Documents [B20]. Case of Engel and others. (1974-1976). Strasbourg, Council of Europe, 1977. pp. 306 [bis], 307-382.

DETROIT

— History.

DETROIT; edited by Melvin G. Holli. New York, 1976. pp. 291.

— Sources.

DETROIT; edited by Melvin G. Holli. New York, 1976. pp. 291.

— Social conditions.

EWEN (LYNDA ANN) Corporate power and urban crisis in Detroit. Princeton, [1978]. pp. 312. *bibliog.*

DEUTSCHE DEMOKRATISCHE PARTEI.

HESS (JUERGEN C.) "Das ganze Deutschland soll es sein": demokratischer Nationalismus in der Weimarer Republik am Beispiel der Deutschen Demokratischen Partei. Stuttgart, 1978. pp. 398. *bibliog.*

DEUTSCHE VOLKSPARTEI.

METHFESSEL (WERNER) Weg in den Abgrund: zur Geschichte der Deutschen Volkspartei, 1930-1933. [Berlin, 1978]. pp. 138. *(Liberal-Demokratische Partei Deutschlands. Schriften. Heft 18)*

DEUTSCHNATIONALE VOLKSPARTEI.

LEOPOLD (JOHN A.) Alfred Hugenberg: the radical nationalist campaign against the Weimar Republic. New Haven, 1977. pp. 298. *bibliog.*

DEVELOPMENT BANKS

— Africa.

AMEGAVIE (YEWOU CHARLES) La Banque Africaine de Développement. Paris, [1977]. pp. 368. *bibliog.*

— Arab countries.

BANQUE ARABE POUR LE DEVELOPPEMENT ECONOMIQUE EN AFRIQUE. Rapport annuel. a., 1975(1st)- Khartoum. *1975(1st) in English.*

— Ethiopia.

AGRICULTURAL AND INDUSTRIAL DEVELOPMENT BANK S.C. [ETHIOPIA]. Annual report. a., 1973/74(4th)- Addis Ababa. *[in English and Amharic]*

— Swaziland.

SWAZILAND DEVELOPMENT AND SAVINGS BANK. Annual report and financial statements (formerly Annual report and accounts). a., 1974(9th), 1976(11th)- Mbabane.

DEVELOPMENT CREDIT CORPORATIONS

— South Africa — Ciskei.

CISKEIAN NATIONAL DEVELOPMENT CORPORATION LTD. Annual report. a., 1976/77(1st)- King William's Town. *[in English, Afrikaans and Xhosa].*

DEVELOPMENTAL PSYCHOBIOLOGY.

MALNUTRITION, behavior, and social organization; edited by Lawrence S. Greene. New York, 1977. pp. 298. *bibliogs. Based on a symposium held at the Annual Meeting of the American Association for the Advancement of Science in 1976.*

DEVELOPMENTAL PSYCHOLOGY.

HAHNEMANN SYMPOSIUM, 35TH. Sex and the life cycle; edited by Wilbur W. Oaks [and others]. New York, [1976]. pp. 223.

RIEGEL (KLAUS F.) Psychology of development and history. New York, [1976]. pp. 263. *bibliog.*

DEVIANT BEHAVIOUR.

BLACK (DONALD J.) The behavior of law. New York, [1976]. pp. 175. *bibliog.*

DEVIANCE and social change; edited by Edward Sagarin. Beverly Hills, [1977]. pp. 317. *bibliogs.*

DEVIANCE and social control in Chinese society; edited by Amy Auerbacher Wilson [and others]. New York, [1977]. pp. 227. *Proceedings of a preliminary conference held at the International Center of Rutgers University in 1975.*

PATTERSON (HORACE ORLANDO LLOYD) Ethnic chauvinism: the reactionary impulse. New York, 1977. pp. 346.

MARSH (PETER) and others. The rules of disorder. London, 1978. pp. 140. *bibliog.*

DEVONSHIRE

— Economic conditions.

DEVONSHIRE. Planning Department. County structure plan: report of the survey. Exeter, 1977. pp. 184.

— Industries.

CHITTY (JEAN) Paper in Devon. Exeter, 1976. pp. 72. *bibliog.*

— Social conditions.

DEVONSHIRE. Planning Department. County structure plan: report of the survey. Exeter, 1977. pp. 184.

DIALECTIC.

GRASSI (ENRICO) L'"esposizione dialettica" nel Capitale di Marx; con introduzione di Luca Meldolesi. Roma, [1976]. pp. 102. *bibliogs.*

DIALECTICAL MATERIALISM.

See MARXISM.

DIAMOND INDUSTRY AND TRADE

— United Kingdom.

YOGEV (GEDALIA) Diamonds and coral: Anglo-Dutch Jews and eighteenth-century trade. Leicester, 1978. pp. 360. *bibliog.*

DIARIES

— Bibliography.

ZHITOMIRSKAIA (S.V.) ed. Vospominaniia i dnevniki XVIII-XX vv.: ukazatel' rukopisei, etc. Moskva, 1976. pp. 621.

DIAZ (PORFIRIO).

LOPEZ-PORTILLO Y ROJAS (JOSE) Elevacion y caida de Porfirio Diaz. Mexico, 1975. pp. 506. *Reprint of original published in 1921.*

DICTATORSHIP OF THE PROLETARIAT.

BALIBAR (ETIENNE) Sur la dictature du prolétariat. Paris, 1976. pp. 292.

BENOT (YVES) L'autre Italie, 1968-1976: problèmes de la dictature du prolétariat. Paris, 1977. pp. 319.

DIETZGEN (JOSEPH).

APEL (MAX) Einführung in die Gedankenwelt Josef Dietzgens: eine Kritik der materialistischen Weltanschauung. Berlin, 1931. pp. 79.

DIFFERENTIAL EQUATIONS.

ELSGOLTS (LEV ERNESTOVICH) Differential equations and the calculus of variations; translated from the Russian by George Yankovsky. Moscow, 1970 reprinted 1973. pp. 440.

WARGA (J.) Optimal control of differential and functional equations. New York, 1972. pp. 531. *bibliog.*

HIRSCH (MORRIS W.) and SMALE (STEPHEN) Differential equations, dynamical systems, and linear algebra. New York, [1974]. pp. 358. *bibliog.*

DRIVER (RODNEY DAVID) Ordinary and delay differential equations. New York, [1977]. pp. 501.

ROUCHE (NICOLAS) and others. Stability theory by Liapunov's direct method. New York, [1977]. pp. 396. *bibliog.*

— Delay equations.

DRIVER (RODNEY DAVID) Ordinary and delay differential equations. New York, [1977]. pp. 501.

DIFFERENTIAL EQUATIONS, LINEAR.

OPEN UNIVERSITY. Linear Mathematics Course Team. Unit 12: Linear functionals and duality: Unit 13: Systems of differential equations. Milton Keynes, 1972, repr. 1976. pp. 32. *(Open University. Mathematics: a second level course: linear mathematics. Units 12 and 13)*

DIFFERENTIAL MAPPINGS.

LU (YUNG-CHEN) Singularity theory and an introduction to catastrophe theory. New York, [1976]. pp. 199. *bibliog.*

DIFFERENTIAL TOPOLOGY.

HIRSCH (MORRIS W.) Differential topology. New York, 1976. pp. 221. *bibliog.*

DIFFUSION OF INNOVATIONS.

ZALTMAN (GERALD) and DUNCAN (ROBERT B.) Strategies for planned change. New York, [1977]. pp. 404. *bibliog.*

DIGITAL COMPUTER SIMULATION.

NAYLOR (THOMAS H.) and others. Computer simulation techniques. New York, [1968]. pp. 352. *bibliog.*

FISHMAN (GEORGE S.) Concepts and methods in discrete event digital simulation. New York, [1973]. pp. 385. *bibliog.*

DIMBAZA

— Social conditions.

BALDWIN (ALAN) and HALL (ANTHONY) A place called Dimbaza: a case study of a rural settlement township in South Africa. London, 1973. pp. 29. *(Africa Publications Trust. Studies in the Mass Removal of Population in South Africa. [No. 1])*

DINKAS.

DENG (FRANCIS MADING) Africans of two worlds: the Dinka in Afro-Arab Sudan. New Haven, 1978. pp. 244.

DIPLOMATS.

UNOFFICIAL diplomats; Maureen R. Berman and Joseph E. Johnson, editors. New York, 1977. pp. 268. *Based on a conference held at Bellagio, Italy, in 1973 by the Communications Institute.*

DIPLOMATS, FRENCH

— Correspondence, reminiscences, etc.

ALPHAND (HERVE) L'étonnement d'être: journal, 1939-1973. [Paris, 1977]. pp. 614.

DIRECT ACTION

— Italy.

TAKE over the city: community struggle in Italy. London, [1973]. pp. 36. *Based on articles in the newspaper of the revolutionary group Lotta Continua (Fight On).*

DIRECTORS OF CORPORATIONS

— United States.

KELLY (RITA MAE) Community control of economic development: the boards of directors of community development corporations. New York, [1977]. pp. 174.

DISARMAMENT.

UNITED NATIONS. Disarmament Affairs Division. 1970. The United Nations and disarmament, 1945-1970. New York, 1970. pp. 515.

UNITED NATIONS DISARMAMENT YEARBOOK, THE; [pd. by] United Nations Centre for Disarmament. a., 1976(1st)- New York.

BECKER (ABRAHAM S.) Military expenditure limitation for arms control: problems and prospects; with a documentary history of recent proposals. Cambridge, Mass., 1977. pp. 352. *bibliog.*

CONTROLLING future arms trade; [by] Anne Hessing Cahn [and others]. New York, [1977]. pp. 208. *bibliog. (Council on Foreign Relations. 1980s Project Studies)*

INTERNATIONAL INSTITUTE FOR STRATEGIC STUDIES. Adelphi Papers. No. 138. The role of arms control in the Middle East; by Yair Evron. London, 1977. pp. 43.

MACBRIDE (SEAN) Is nuclear survival possible? Bradford, [1977]. pp. 11. *An address delivered at the University of Bradford on 4 May 1977.*

WORLD disarmament kit...; (editor Robert Woito). Stockholm, [1977]. pp. 120. *bibliog. (World Without War Council. World Without War Publications)*

DISARMAMENT: a periodic review by the United Nations. 3 a yr., My 1978(v.1, no. 1)- New York.

DISARMAMENT and world development; edited by Richard Jolly. Oxford, [1978]. pp. 185. *bibliog. Based on a conference held by the UK Section of the United Nations Association and the Society for International Development.*

DOKUMENTE zur Abrüstung, 1917-1976; (bearbeitet und eingeleitet von Peter Klein). Berlin, 1978. pp. 475.

INTERNATIONAL INSTITUTE FOR STRATEGIC STUDIES. Adelphi Papers. No. 146. The future of arms control: part II: arms control and technological change: elements of a new approach; by Christoph Bertram. London, 1978. pp. 31.

— Bibliography.

BURNS (RICHARD DEAN) compiler. Arms control and disarmament: a bibliography. Santa Barbara, [1977]. pp. 430. *(California University. Center for the Study of Armament and Disarmament. War/Peace Bibliography Series. 6)*

— Economic aspects — Europe.

UDIS (BERNARD) From guns to butter: technology organizations and reduced military spending in western Europe. Cambridge, Mass., [1978]. pp. 368.

— — United Kingdom.

MILITARY spending and arms cuts: economic and industrial implications: alternative work for military industries;...[by] Dave Elliott [and others; edited by Dan Smith]. London, [1977]. pp. 68.

— — United States.

WAR, business, and American society: historical perspectives on the military-industrial complex; edited by Benjamin Franklin Cooling. Port Washington, 1977. pp. 203. *bibliogs.*

DISASTER RELIEF.

DAVIS (IAN THOMAS MAXWELL) Shelter after disaster. Oxford, 1978. pp. 127. *bibliog.*

DISASTERS: theory and research; edited by E.L. Quarantelli. Beverly Hills, [1978]. pp. 282. *Based on papers presented in 1974 at the Sociology of Disasters sessions of the Eighth World Congress of Sociology in Toronto.*

— France.

BROC (ANDRÉ PIERRE) La protection civile: la sécurité civile. [Paris, 1977]. pp. 128.

— New Zealand.

NEW ZEALAND. Ministry of Civil Defence. 1966. Civil defence: medical plan no. 1: natural disaster. [Wellington, 1966]. 1 pamphlet (various foliations). *bibliog.*

NEW ZEALAND. Ministry of Civil Defence. 1967. Civil defence: welfare plan. [Wellington, 1967]. 1 pamphlet (various foliations).

NEW ZEALAND. Ministry of Civil Defence. 1968. Civil defence handbook: welfare. Wellington, 1968. pp. 68.

DISASTERS.

DISASTERS: theory and research; edited by E.L. Quarantelli. Beverly Hills, [1978]. pp. 282. *Based on papers presented in 1974 at the Sociology of Disasters sessions of the Eighth World Congress of Sociology in Toronto.*

— Psychological aspects.

DISASTERS: theory and research; edited by E.L. Quarantelli. Beverly Hills, [1978]. pp. 282. *Based on papers presented in 1974 at the Sociology of Disasters sessions of the Eighth World Congress of Sociology in Toronto.*

DISCIPLINARY POWER

— Russia.

KOREL'SKII (VIKTOR MIKHAILOVICH) Demokratiia i distsiplina v razvitom sotsialisticheskom obshchestve. Moskva, 1977. pp. 136.

DISCONTENT.

ALLARDT (ERIK) On the relationship between objective and subjective predicaments. Helsinki, 1977. pp. 22. *bibliog. (Helsinki. Yliopisto. Research Group for Comparative Sociology. Research Reports. No. 16)*

DISCOVERIES (IN GEOGRAPHY).

PARRY (JOHN HORACE) The age of reconnaissance. 2nd ed. London, 1966 repr. 1973. pp. 366. *bibliog.*

DISCRIMINATION

— Canada — Ontario.

ONTARIO. Human Rights Commission. 1968. Case studies and community action programs under the Ontario Human Rights Code and the Age Discrimination Act. [Toronto, 1968]. pp. 27.

DISCRIMINATION IN EDUCATION

— United States.

FUENTES (LUIS) Puerto Rican, black and Chinese community control in New York city: the fight against racism in our schools. New York, [1973]. pp. 15.

DISCRIMINATION IN EMPLOYMENT.

INTERNATIONAL LABOUR OFFICE. 1975. Special national procedures concerning non-discrimination in employment, with particular reference to the private sector: a practical guide. Geneva, 1975. pp. 65.

— Law and legislation.

COMPARATIVE LABOUR LAW GROUP. Discrimination in employment: a study of six countries...; [by] Benjamin Aaron [and others]; [edited by] Folke Schmidt. Stockholm, [1978]. pp. 542.

— — Canada — Ontario.

ONTARIO. Statutes, etc. 1966-68. The Age Discrimination Act, 1966...as amended by 1968, c.2: (office consolidation). Toronto, 1968. pp. (7).

— — United Kingdom.

COMMISSION FOR RACIAL EQUALITY. A guide to the new Race Relations Act 1976: employment. [London, 1977]. pp. 8.

COMMISSION FOR RACIAL EQUALITY. Your rights to equal treatment under the new Race Relations Act 1976: employment. [London, 1977]. pp. 12.

DISCRIMINATION IN EMPLOYMENT.(Cont.)

— Canada.

NEW BRUNSWICK. Human Rights Commission. 1968. A study of the socially disadvantaged. Fredericton, [1968]. pp. 17.

— South Africa.

STARES (RODNEY) Black trade unions in South Africa: the responsibilities of British companies. London, 1977. pp. 82. *bibliog.*

— South West Africa.

RUBIN (NEVILLE) Labour and discrimination in Namibia. Geneva, International Labour Office, 1977. pp. 126.

— United Kingdom.

ALLEN (SHEILA) and others. Work, race and immigration. [Bradford], 1977. pp. 415.

— United States.

ALEXANDER (ARTHUR J.) Structure, income and race: a study in internal labour markets. Santa Monica, 1970. pp. 30. *(Rand Corporation. [Rand Reports]. 577)*

ROSENBLOOM (DAVID H.) Federal equal employment opportunity: politics and public personnel administration. New York, 1977. pp. 184. *bibliog.*

DISCRIMINATION IN HOUSING

— United Kingdom.

FENTON (MIKE) and COLLARD (DAVID) Do coloured tenants pay more?: some evidence. Bristol, Social Science Research Council Research Unit on Ethnic Relations, [1977]. pp. 9. *(Working Papers on Ethnic Relations. No. 1)*

— United States.

POLIKOFF (ALEXANDER) Housing the poor: the case for heroism. Cambridge, Mass., [1978]. pp. 216.

DISEASES

— Bibliography.

DONOVAN (J.W.) Bibliography of the epidemiology of New Zealand and its island territories; (a study in New Zealand mortality. 4). Wellington, 1969. pp. 94. *(New Zealand. Department of Health. Special Report Series. 33)*

DISRAELI (BENJAMIN) 1st Earl of Beaconsfield.

CLAYDEN (PETER WILLIAM) England under Lord Beaconsfield;...new introductory note by E. J. Feuchtwanger. Richmond, Surrey, 1971. pp. 542. *Reprint of original edition published in London in 1880 with subtitle: The political history of six years from the end of 1873 to the beginning of 1880.*

DISSENTERS

— Hungary.

HARASZTI (MIKLÓS) A worker in a worker's state: piece-rates in Hungary; translated by Michael Wright; with...a note about the author and a transcript of the author's trial. Harmondsworth, 1977. pp. 175.

— Poland.

ASSOCIATION OF POLISH STUDENTS AND GRADUATES IN EXILE. Dissent in Poland: reports and documents in translation, December 1975-July 1977. London, [1977]. pp. 200.

RUCH oporu: Komitet Obrony Robotników; O powołanie komisji sejmowej; Za'zalenia i szykany; Kościół; Na Zachodzie; O naprawie Rzeczypospolitej; Sąsiedzi (Czechosłowacja); Ró'zne. Pary'z, 1977. pp. 285.

— Russia.

CALDWELL (DAVID) Opposition, resistance, and political terror in the Soviet Union. [Coventry], 1976. pp. 19. *(University of Warwick. Department of Politics. Working Papers. No. 11)*

Une OPPOSITION socialiste en Union Soviétique aujourd'hui: (samizdat Vingtième siècle); introduction d'E. Bérard. Paris, 1976. pp. 205.

BLOCH (SIDNEY) and REDDAWAY (PETER B.) Russia's political hospitals: the abuse of psychiatry in the Soviet Union. London, 1977. pp. 510.

— Yugoslavia.

SHER (GERSON S.) Praxis: Marxist criticism and dissent in socialist Yugoslavia. Bloomington, Ind., [1977]. pp. 360. *bibliog.*

DISSENTERS, RELIGIOUS

— United Kingdom.

TOLMIE (MURRAY) The triumph of the saints: the separate churches of London, 1616- 1649. Cambridge, 1977. pp. 251. *bibliog.*

WATTS (MICHAEL R.) The dissenters. Oxford, 1978 in progress. *bibliog.*

LONDON. London Record Society. Publications. vol. 14. Committees for repeal of the Test and Corporation Acts: minutes 1786-90 and 1827-8; edited by Thomas W. Davis. London, 1978. pp. 126.

DISSERTATIONS, ACADEMIC

— United Kingdom — Bibliography.

GILBERT (VICTOR F.) and HOLMES (COLIN) compilers. Theses and dissertations in economic and social history in Yorkshire universities, 1920-74. 1975. pp. 154. *Typescript: unpublished.*

DISSONANCE (PSYCHOLOGY).

HINIKER (PAUL J.) Revolutionary ideology and Chinese reality: dissonance under Mao. Beverly Hills, [1977]. pp. 320.

DISTRIBUTION (ECONOMIC THEORY).

NEVIN (EDWARD THOMAS) The dilemma of distribution theory. London, [1977]. pp. 26.

DISTRIBUTION (PROBABILITY THEORY).

KALLENBERG (OLAV) Random measures. Berlin, 1976. pp. 104. *bibliog.*

MATHAI (A.M.) and PEDERZOLI (G.) Characterizations of the normal probability law. rev. ed. New Delhi, [1977]. pp. 149. *bibliog. Enlarged version of the authors' 1975 monograph.*

BARNDORFF-NIELSEN (OLE) Information and exponential families in statistical theory. Chichester, [1978]. pp. 238. *bibliog.*

KOLCHIN (VALENTIN FEDOROVICH) and others. Random allocations; translation editor A.V. Balakrishnan. Washington, D.C., 1978. pp. 262. *bibliog.*

DISTRITO FEDERAL, BRAZIL

— Census.

BRAZIL. Census, 1950. A composição da população do Distrito Federal segundo a idade e segundo a atividade, em 1.VII. 1950;...estudo redigido pelo Alceu Vicente de Carvalho. [Rio de Janeiro, 1959]. fo. 6. *(Estudos Demograficos. No. 250)*

— Population.

BRAZIL. Conselho Nacional de Estatistica. Laboratorio de Estatistica. 1958. A contribuição das diversas unidades da federação a regiões fisiograficas para a população do Distrito Federal; ...estudo redigido pelo Marcio R. Mota e Annibal R. Fontes. [Rio de Janeiro, 1958]. fo. 10. *(Estudos Demograficos. No. 247)*

— Statistics, Vital.

BRAZIL. Conselho Nacional de Estatistica. Laboratorio de Estatistica. 1951. A mortalidade infantil no Distrito Federal nos anos de 1939 a 1950;...estudo redigido por Giorgio Mortara. [Rio de Janeiro, 1951]. fo. 7. *(Estudos Demograficos. No. 8)*

BRAZIL. Conselho Nacional de Estatistica. Laboratorio de Estatistica. 1951. Tabua de sobrevivência para o Distrito Federal, conforme a mortalidade do ano de 1950;...planejada pelo Giorgio Mortara, calculada pelo Orêncio Longino de Arruda Gomes. [Rio de Janeiro, 1951]. fo. 10. *(Estudos Demograficos. No. 7)*

DIVIDENDS

— United Kingdom — Taxation.

ORHNIAL (ANTONY J.H.) and FOLDES (LUCIEN P.) Estimates of marginal tax rates for dividends and bond interest in the United Kingdom 1919-1970. London, 1976. pp. 33. *bibliog. (Papers on Capital and Risk. No. 4)*

DIVISION OF LABOUR.

PINE (FRANCES THERESA) Changes in the division of labour and sex roles among the Akan of Ghana. 1977. fo. 238. *bibliog. Typescript. Ph.D. (London) thesis: unpublished. This thesis is the property of London University and may not be removed from the Library.*

DIVORCE.

GRAY (KEVIN JOHN) Reallocation of property on divorce. Abingdon, 1977. pp. 353.

— Australia.

AUSTRALIA. Parliament. Senate. Standing Committee on Constitutional and Legal Affairs. 1972. Interim report on the law and administration of divorce and related matters; [P. D. Durack, chairman]. in AUSTRALIA. Parliament. Parliamentary papers, 1972, vol. 7.

— Europe.

DIVORCE in Europe; edited by Robert Chester, with the collaboration of Gerrit Kooy, on behalf of the Groupe International de Recherches sur le Divorce. Leiden, 1977. pp. 316. *(Nederlands Interuniversitair Demografisch Instituut and Centre d'Etude de la Population et de la Famille. [Belgium]. Publications. vol.3)*

— Italy.

RICHTER (GIOGIO STELLA) L'istituto del divorzio in Italia e l'esperienza giuridica dei principali ordinamenti europei. Milano, 1976. pp. 94.

— Netherlands.

NETHERLANDS. Centraal Bureau voor de Statistiek. 1976. Echtscheidingen in Nederland, 1900-1974. 's-Gravenhage, 1976. pp. 67. *With English summary.*

— Poland.

STOJANOWSKA (WANDA) Problematyka rozwodów w świetle badań. Warszawa, 1977. pp. 116. *(Instytut Badania Prawa Sądowego. Studia z Dziedziny Prawa Cywilnego)*

— Rhodesia.

RHODESIA. Commission of Inquiry into Divorce Laws. 1977. Report; [A.J.G. Lang, chairman]. [Salisbury], 1977. pp. 61. *(Rhodesia. [Command Papers]. 1977. Cmd. R.R. 16)*

— United Kingdom.

U.K. Office of Population Censuses and Surveys. Marriage and divorce statistics: review of the Registrar General on marriages and divorces in England and Wales. a., 1974(1st)- London. *Supersedes in part Registrar General's statistical review of England and Wales.*

CUSTODY after divorce: the disposition of custody in divorce cases in Great Britain; by John Eekelaar [and others]. Oxford, [1977]. pp. (92). *(U.K. Social Science Research Council. Centre for Socio- Legal Studies. Family Law Studies. No. 1)*

DJILAS (MILOVAN).

DJILAS (MILOVAN) Parts of a lifetime; edited by Michael and Deborah Milenkovitch. New York, [1975]. pp. 442.

DJUKAS.

GROOT (SILVIA W. DE) From isolation towards integration: the Surinam Maroons and their colonial rulers: official documents relating to the Djukas, 1845-1863. The Hague, 1977. pp. 113. bibliog. (Instituut voor Taal-, Land- en Volkenkunde. Verhandelingen. [Deel] 80)

DOCK WORKERS

— India.

INDIA. Tripartite Expert Committee for Calcutta Docks. 1970. Report; [N.N. Chatterjee, chairman]. [Delhi, 1970]. pp. 103.

— Singapore.

INTERNATIONAL LABOUR OFFICE. Development Programme: Technical Assistance Sector. [Singapore]. R.13. Report to the government of Singapore on training of port personnel. (ILO/TAP/Singapore/R.13). Geneva, 1973. pp. 119.

DOLLAR.

SCHMITT (BERNARD) L'or, le dollar et la monnaie supranationale. Paris, [1977]. pp. 227.

CHOLLET (ALEXANDRE) Faudra-t-il une supermonnaie pour stabiliser le dollar? Lausanne, 1978. pp. 44. (Lausanne. Université. Centre de Recherches Européennes. Publications. 6. Etudes Sectorielles)

DOMESTIC ECONOMY

POMPEI (GIULIANA) Wages for housework: with contributions from the feminist conference organised in Padova on the theme of wages for domestic work, in April 1972; translated by Joan Hall. Cambridge, [1972]. pp. 6.

— United Kingdom.

PRACTICAL estimates of household expenses, founded on economical principles, and adapted to families of every description, calculated according to income, etc. new ed. London, printed for Henry Colburn, 1824. pp. 77.

DOMESTIC RELATIONS

— Canada — British Columbia.

BRITISH COLUMBIA. Royal Commission on Family and Children's Law, 1974-75. Reports 1-5, 7, 9-11, 13; [Thomas Rodney Berger, chairman]. Vancouver, 1974-75. 16 vols (in 5).

— — Ontario.

ONTARIO. Ministry of the Attorney General. 1976. Family law reform. [Toronto, 1976]. pp. 70.

— Europe.

GLENDON (MARY ANN) State, law and family: family law in transition in the United States and Western Europe. Amsterdam, 1977. pp. 347.

— Italy.

BESSONE (MARIO) and ROPPO (ENZO) Il diritto di famiglia: evoluzione storica, principi costituzionali, lineamenti della riforma. Torino, [1977]. pp. 423.

— Malaysia.

IBRAHIM (AHMAD) Law and population in Malaysia. Medford, Mass., 1977. pp. 51. (Tufts University. Fletcher School of Law and Diplomacy. Law and Population Monograph Series. No. 45)

— Nigeria.

MULLER (JEAN CLAUDE) Chez les Rukuba: parenté et mariage (État Benue- Plateau, Nigeria). Paris, 1976. pp. 206. bibliog. (Paris. École Pratique des Hautes Études. Section des Sciences Economiques et Sociales. Cahiers de l'Homme. Nouvelle Série. 17) Cover bears title Parenté et mariage chez les Rukuba.

— Russia — White Russia.

WHITE RUSSIA. Statutes, etc. 1976. Kodeks o brake i sem'e Belorusskoi SSR: ofitsial'nyi tekst s izmeneniiami na 1 marta 1976 goda i s prilozheniem sistematizirovannogo materiala. Minsk, 1977. pp. 95.

— United Kingdom.

EEKELAAR (JOHN M.) Family law and social policy. London, [1978]. pp. 335. bibliog.

— United States.

GLENDON (MARY ANN) State, law and family: family law in transition in the United States and Western Europe. Amsterdam, 1977. pp. 347.

DOMESTIC RELATIONS COURTS

— Italy.

Un NUOVO giudice per la famiglia: atti del convegno nazionale di studi, Lucca, 24-25-26 Ottobre 1975. Lucca, 1977. pp. 254.

— United Kingdom.

SOCIETY OF CONSERVATIVE LAWYERS. The case for family courts: a report by a research sub-committee. London, 1978. pp. 47. bibliog. (Conservative Political Centre. [Publications] No. 631)

DOMINICAN REPUBLIC

— Economic conditions.

CHARDON (CARLOS E.) Datos que sugieren la integracion economica de una parte de la region del Caribe: la Republica Dominicana y Puerto Rico: informe preliminar. San Juan, Banco Gubernamental de Fomento para Puerto Rico, 1962. fo. 105.

— Emigration and immigration.

LLORENS (VICENTE) Memorias de una emigracion: Santo Domingo, 1939-1945. Barcelona, [1975]. pp. 214.

DORTMUND

— Social history.

KNIPPING (ULRICH) Die Geschichte der Juden in Dortmund während der Zeit des Dritten Reiches. Dortmund, 1977. pp. 255. bibliog. (Historischer Verein Dortmund. Monographien zur Geschichte Dortmunds und der Grafschaft Mark. Band 6)

DOUGLAS (WILLIAM ORVILLE).

WOLFMAN (BERNARD) and others. Dissent without opinion: the behavior of Justice William O. Douglas in Federal tax cases. Philadelphia, [1975]. pp. 204. bibliog.

DOWLAIS IRON COMPANY.

OWEN (JOHN A.) The history of the Dowlais iron works, 1759-1970. Risca, Mon., [1977]. pp. 161. bibliog.

DRAINAGE.

BLACKER (WILLIAM) An essay on the best mode of improving the condition of the labouring classes of Ireland. London, R. Groombridge, 1846. pp. 56. Revised version of an essay which won the Gold Medal of the Royal Agricultural Improvement Society of Ireland.

DROGHEDA (CHARLES GARRETT PONSONBY MOORE) 11th Earl of.

See MOORE (CHARLES GARRETT PONSONBY) 11th Earl of Drogheda.

DROPOUTS

— Canada — Manitoba.

SHARP (EMMIT F.) and KRISTJANSON (G. ALBERT) Manitoba high school students and drop-outs. [Winnipeg], Manitoba Department of Agriculture, [1967]. pp. 100. bibliog.

DROUGHTS.

BRYSON (REID A.) and MURRAY (THOMAS J.) Climates of hunger: mankind and the world's changing weather. Madison, 1977. pp. 171. bibliog.

— Brazil.

HALL (ANTHONY L.) Drought and irrigation in north-east Brazil. Cambridge, 1978. pp. 152. bibliog.

— Sahel.

BERG (ELLIOT J.) The economic impact of drought and inflation in the Sahel. Ann Arbor, 1976. fo. 35. (Michigan University. Center for Research on Economic Development. Discussion Papers. No. 51)

DRUG ABUSE.

SWINSON (RICHARD P.) and EAVES (DEREK) Alcoholism and addiction. [Plymouth, 1978]. pp. 346. bibliogs.

— Treatment — United States.

STUDIES of the effectiveness of treatments for drug abuse. vols. 1, 2, and 5. Cambridge, Mass., [1974-76]. 3 vols. Cover title: The effectiveness of drug abuse treatment.

SUGARMAN (BARRY) Daytop village: a therapeutic community. New York, [1974]. pp. 134. bibliog.

— United Kingdom — Scotland.

CONSULTATIVE COMMITTEE OF MEDICAL OFFICERS OF HEALTH [SCOTLAND]. Misuse of drugs in Scotland; the third report of a Sub- Committee; [J.A. Ward, chairman]. Edinburgh, H.M.S.O., 1975. pp. 12.

DRUG ABUSE AND EMPLOYMENT.

WARD (HUGH) Employment and addiction: overview of issues. Washington, 1973. pp. 52. (Drug Abuse Council. [Monographs]. 5)

DRUG TRADE.

HASLEMERE DECLARATION GROUP. Who needs the drug companies? London, [1975?]. pp. 44.

HELLER (TOM) Poor health, rich profits: multinational drug companies and the Third World. Nottingham, 1977. pp. 76.

LAZIO (JEAN PIERRE) La mafia du médicament. [Paris, 1977]. pp. 155.

— Australia.

SMITH (ROBERT GRENVILLE) and BARRIE (ALEXANDER) Aspro: how the family business grew up. Melbourne, 1976. pp. 182.

— Underdeveloped areas.

See UNDERDEVELOPED AREAS — Drug trade.

— United Kingdom.

SMITH (ROBERT GRENVILLE) and BARRIE (ALEXANDER) Aspro: how the family business grew up. Melbourne, 1976. pp. 182.

— United States.

The PHARMACEUTICAL industry: economics, performance and government regulation; [by] Erol Caglarcan [and others]; editor Cotton M. Lindsay. New York, [1978]. pp. 154.

DRUG UTILIZATION.

DRUG UTILIZATION.

CONTROLLING the use of therapeutic drugs: an international comparison; edited by William M. Wardell. Washington, D.C., [1978]. pp. 263. *(American Enterprise Institute for Public Policy Research. AEI Studies. 178)*

DRUGS.

CONTROL of medicines in hospital wards and departments; report of a joint group appointed by the Standing Pharmaceutical, Medical and Nursing and Midwifery Advisory Committees on control of medicines in hospital wards and departments; [A. Roxburgh, chairman]. Edinburgh, H.M.S.O., 1972. pp. 27.

LAZIO (JEAN PIERRE) La mafia du médicament. [Paris, 1977]. pp. 155.

LAURENCE (D.R.) and BLACK (J.W.) The medicine you take: benefits and risks of modern drugs. [London], 1978. pp. 190.

— **Laws and legislation.**

CONTROLLING the use of therapeutic drugs: an international comparison; edited by William M. Wardell. Washington, D.C., [1978]. pp. 263. *(American Enterprise Institute for Public Policy Research. AEI Studies. 178)*

— **Prices — United States.**

SCHWARTZMAN (DAVID) Innovation in the pharmaceutical industry. Baltimore, [1976]. pp. 399.

DUALITY THEORY (MATHEMATICS).

OPEN UNIVERSITY. Linear Mathematics Course Team. Unit 12: Linear functionals and duality: Unit 13: Systems of differential equations. Milton Keynes, 1972, repr. 1976. pp. 32. *(Open University. Mathematics: a second level course: linear mathematics. Units 12 and 13)*

DUBLIN

— **Benevolent and moral institutions and societies.**

DUBLIN. Association for the Suppression of Mendicity in Dublin. Annual report. a., 1818-1819(1st-2nd). Dublin.

— **Commerce.**

An ADDRESS to the committee of the Merchants Society. Dublin, 1761. pp. 16.

— **Directories.**

WILSON'S DUBLIN DIRECTORY. a., 1816. Dublin. *Bound with the Gentleman's and Citizen's Almanack and the English Registry for...1816.*

— **Social conditions.**

MONTEFIORE (DORA B.) Our fight to save the kiddies: smouldering fires of the Inquisition. London, [imprint, 1913]. pp. 16.

DU BOIS (WILLIAM EDWARD BURGHARDT).

RAMPERSAD (ARNOLD) The art and imagination of W.E.B. Du Bois. Cambridge, Mass., 1976. pp. 325.

DUISBURG

— **Economic history.**

BURKHARD (WOLFGANG) Abriss einer Wirtschaftsgeschichte des Niederrheins: strukturelle Wandlungen in Handel und Industrie in Duisburg und in den Kreisen Wesel und Kleve. Duisburg, 1977. pp. 173. *bibliog.*

DUKHOBORS.

CARSON (WILLIAM) Dear God! - how long - - -? n.p., [195-?]. s.sh. *Photocopy.*

UNION OF CHRISTIAN COMMUNITIES AND BROTHERHOOD OF REFORMED DOUKHOBORS. Petition to the government and the people of Canada from members of the...Community, etc. [Courtenay, B.C., imprint, 1954?]. pp. 54.

UNION OF CHRISTIAN COMMUNITIES AND BROTHERHOOD OF REFORMED DOUKHOBORS. A public indictment of J.J. Verigin, secretary of the Orthodox Doukhobors, for his deliberate distortion of the basic principles of the Doukhobor faith. [Krestova, 1954]. pp. 22.

FACTS about operation snatch: personal recordings of Doukhobour mothers whose children were taken away, and results of "successful" police raids in the Kootenays. n.p., [1955]. pp. 32.

[UNION OF CHRISTIAN COMMUNITIES AND BROTHERHOOD OF REFORMED DOUKHOBORS] Dogs used in apprehension of Doukhobor children. Trail, B.C., [imprint, 1955?]. pp. (4).

UNION OF CHRISTIAN COMMUNITIES AND BROTHERHOOD OF REFORMED DOUKHOBORS. Open letter to the Quakers. [Trail, B.C., imprint], 1955. pp. (8). *With leaflet attached on the use of police dogs to apprehend Doukhobor children.*

UNION OF CHRISTIAN COMMUNITIES AND BROTHERHOOD OF REFORMED DOUKHOBORS. Fraternal Council. Open letter to A.A. Gusskin, Sondalo, Italy, revised. [Crescent Valley, B.C., 1955?]. pp. 30.

SOROKIN (STEPHEN SAVELIEVICH) The epistle of S.S. Sorokin-Yastrebow to the Doukhobors; translated and released by the Fraternal Council, Christian Community and Brotherhood of Reformed Doukhobors. [Trail, B.C., imprint, 1956?]. pp. 19.

UNION OF CHRISTIAN COMMUNITIES AND BROTHERHOOD OF REFORMED DOUKHOBORS. Fraternal Council. Doukhobors reply to Rev. A. Dixon: an open letter. Trail, B.C., [imprint], 1956. pp. (3).

UNION OF CHRISTIAN COMMUNITIES AND BROTHERHOOD OF REFORMED DOUKHOBORS. Fraternal Council. The incident in the New Denver T.B. Sanatorium. [Trail, B.C. imprint, 1956?]. pp. (2).

SCHEIN (CHAIM) An open letter to B.C. Government: I accuse. Toronto, 1957. pp. 11.

SOROKIN (STEPHEN SAVELIEVICH) Further about Doukhobor affairs inside out;...translated and released by the Fraternal Council of Union of Christian Communities and Brotherhood of Reformed Doukhobors. Trail, B.C., [imprint, 1958?]. pp. 17.

SOROKIN (STEPHEN SAVELIEVICH) A letter to Bruce Larsen: more about Doukhobor affairs inside out; (translated from the original by J.E. Podovinikov). n.p., [1958]. pp. 8.

UNION OF CHRISTIAN COMMUNITIES AND BROTHERHOOD OF REFORMED DOUKHOBORS. Fraternal Council. The Messiah Day, November 27th. [Trail, B.C., imprint, 1958?]. pp. (5).

PEREPELKIN (JOHN J.) Doukhobor problem in Canada: a prototype copy of the Hebrew people in Egypt;...sequel to "Religious history of the Hebrews: prototype for the Doukhobors", part 1; by S.S. Sorokin, 26/3/53; translated and edited by J.E. Podovinikov. n.p., 1959. pp. 71. *Copy of open letter to Sir Thomas White from James Mavor attached.*

DULLES (JOHN FOSTER).

MOSLEY (LEONARD OSWALD) Dulles: a biography of Eleanor, Allen, and John Foster Dulles and their family network. London, 1978. pp. 530. *bibliog.*

DULLES FAMILY.

MOSLEY (LEONARD OSWALD) Dulles: a biography of Eleanor, Allen, and John Foster Dulles and their family network. London, 1978. pp. 530. *bibliog.*

DUMPING (COMMERCIAL POLICY).

LLOYD (PETER JOHN) Anti-dumping actions and the GATT system. London, 1977. pp. 54. *(Trade Policy Research Centre. Thames Essays. No. 9)*

WARES (WILLIAM A.) The theory of dumping and American commercial policy. Lexington, Mass., [1977]. pp. 130. *bibliog.*

ALLEN (GEORGE CYRIL) and OKANO (YUKIHIDE) How Japan competes: an assessment of international trading practices with special reference to dumping. London, 1978. pp. 74 *bibliog. (Institute of Economic Affairs. Hobart Papers. 81)*

DUNANT (JEAN HENRI).

HEUDTLASS (WILLY) J. Henry Dunant: Gründer des Roten Kreuzes, Urheber der Genfer Konvention: eine Biographie in Dokumenten und Bildern. 2nd ed. Stuttgart, 1977. pp. 225. *bibliog.*

DUPONT (PIERRE SAMUEL).

McLAIN (JAMES J.) The economic writings of Du Pont de Nemours. Newark, N.J., [1977]. pp. 244. *bibliog.*

DURHAM (COUNTY)

— **Economic conditions.**

DURHAM (COUNTY). County Council. County structure plan: report of survey 1976. [Durham], 1976. pp. 273,58.

— **Social conditions.**

DURHAM (COUNTY). County Council. County structure plan: report of survey 1976. [Durham], 1976. pp. 273,58.

— **Social life and customs.**

MINING and social change: Durham county in the twentieth century; edited by Martin Bulmer. London, [1978]. pp. 318.

DURKHEIM (EMILE).

FILLOUX (JEAN CLAUDE) Durkheim et le socialisme. Genève, 1977. pp. 388. *bibliog.*

GIDDENS (ANTHONY) Durkheim. [London], 1978. pp. 125. *bibliog.*

— **Bibliography.**

NANDAN (YASH) The Durkheimian school: a systematic and comprehensive bibliography. Westport, [1977]. pp. 458.

DURKHEIMIAN SCHOOL OF SOCIOLOGY

— **Bibliography.**

NANDAN (YASH) The Durkheimian school: a systematic and comprehensive bibliography. Westport, [1977]. pp. 458.

DUTCH GUIANA

— **Native races.**

GROOT (SILVIA W. DE) From isolation towards integration: the Surinam Maroons and their colonial rulers: official documents relating to the Djukas, 1845-1863. The Hague, 1977. pp. 113. *bibliog. (Instituut voor Taal-, Land- en Volkenkunde. Verhandelingen. [Deel] 80)*

DUTCH IN CANADA.

ISHWARAN (KARIGOUDAR) Family, kinship and community: a study of Dutch Canadians: a developmental approach. Toronto, [1977]. pp. 181. *bibliog.*

DWELLINGS

— **United Kingdom.**

WOODFORD (GEORGE P.) and others. The value of standards for the external residential environment. London, 1976. repr. 1977. pp. 108. *(U.K. Department of the Environment. Research Reports. 6)*

— — Maintenance and repair.

YEOMAN (ROD) Discount improvement?: a report on cost-saving approaches to housing improvement...for Oldham Community Development Project. [Oldham, Oldham Community Development Project, 1976]. pp. 51. *bibliog.*

— — Sscotland — Maintenance and repair — Bibliography.

PLANNING EXCHANGE. Housing improvement policies in Scotland: a guided bibliography of Scottish sources. Glasgow, 1976. fo. 27.

— Uruguay.

MONTEVIDEO. Universidad. Departamento de Extension Universitaria. Los rancherios y su gente: viviendas y familias. Montevideo, [1968]. pp. 115. *(Montevideo. Universidad. Departamento de Publicaciones. Coleccion Nuestra Realidad. 8)*

DYES AND DYEING.

GHIARA (CAROLA) L'arte tintoria a Genova dal 15 al 17 secolo: tecniche e organizzazione. [Bologna], 1976. pp. 96. *(Centro per la Storia della Tecnica in Italia. Pubblicazioni. Sezione 4. Vol. 8)*

DYNAMIC PROGRAMMING.

HASTINGS (NICHOLAS ANTHONY JOHN) Dynamic programming with management applications. London, 1973. pp. 173. *bibliog.*

NORMAN (JOHN M.) Elementary dynamic programming. London, 1975. pp. 92. *bibliog.*

BERTSEKAS (DIMITRI P.) Dynamic programming and stochastic control. New York, 1976. pp. 397. *bibliog.*

DORE (M.H.I.) Dynamic investment planning. London, [1977]. pp. 163. *bibliog.*

DZERZHINSKII (FELIKS EDMUNDOVICH).

DZERZHINSKII (FELIKS EDMUNDOVICH) Izbrannye proizvedeniia, (1897-1926). 3rd ed. Moskva, 1977. 2 vols.

EARTHQUAKES

— Italy.

FRIULI: immagini di una tragedia; a cura dei fotografi di Epoca, Sergio del Grande [and others]. Verona, 1976. pp. 212. *Collection of photographs originally published in the journal Epoca.*

EARTHWORKS

— United Kingdom.

BOWEN (HARRIES COLLINS) Ancient fields: a tentative analysis of vanishing earthworks and landscapes. London, [1962?]. pp. 80. *bibliog.*

EAST (FAR EAST)

— Foreign relations.

FORUM on northeast Asia; proceedings [of the forum held in 1976]. Taipei, 1977. pp. 62.

— — United Kingdom.

NYMAN (LARS-ERIK) Great Britain and Chinese, Russian and Japanese interests in Sinkiang, 1918-1934. [Lund], 1977. pp. 167. *bibliog. (Lund. Universitet. Historiska Institutionen. Lund Studies in International History. [No.] 8)*

— History — Sources.

MATTHEWS (NOEL) and WAINWRIGHT (MARY DOREEN) compilers. A guide to manuscripts and documents in the British Isles relating to the Far East; edited by J.D. Pearson. Oxford, 1977. pp. 182.

— Politics and government.

FORUM on northeast Asia; proceedings [of the forum held in 1976]. Taipei, 1977. pp. 62.

EAST (NEAR EAST)

— Commerce — Tasmania.

TASMANIA. Trade Mission of 1976 to Iran and the Arabian Peninsula. 1976. Report; [S.C.H. Frost, leader]. in TASMANIA. Parliament. Journals and Printed Papers. 1976, no. 51.

— Defences.

INTERNATIONAL INSTITUTE FOR STRATEGIC STUDIES. Adelphi Papers. No. 138. The role of arms control in the Middle East; by Yair Evron. London, 1977. pp. 43.

— Economic conditions.

OPEC and the Middle East: the impact of oil on societal development; edited by Russell A. Stone. New York, 1977. pp. 264.

VAN ARKADIE (BRIAN) Benefits and burdens: a report on the West Bank and Gaza Strip economies since 1967. New York, [1977]. pp. 164.

TUMA (ELIAS HANNA) and DARIN-DRABKIN (HAIM) The economic case for Palestine. London, [1978]. pp. 126. *bibliog.*

WATERBURY (JOHN) and EL MALLAKH (RAGAEI) The Middle East in the coming decade: from wellhead to well-being? New York, [1978]. pp. 217. *bibliog. (Council on Foreign Relations. 1980s Project Studies)*

— Economic integration.

EXPERT GROUP MEETING ON PLANNING THE AGRICULTURAL SECTOR IN RELATION TO OVERALL PLANNING AND SECTORAL PROGRAMMING, BEIRUT, 1970. Report of the...Meeting...[held at] Beirut, Lebanon, 1-5 June 1970. (ST/TAO/SER.C/125). New York, United Nations, 1971. pp. 22.

— Economic policy.

EXPERT GROUP MEETING ON PLANNING THE AGRICULTURAL SECTOR IN RELATION TO OVERALL PLANNING AND SECTORAL PROGRAMMING, BEIRUT, 1970. Report of the...Meeting...[held at] Beirut, Lebanon, 1-5 June 1970. (ST/TAO/SER.C/125). New York, United Nations, 1971. pp. 22.

HIRSCH (SEEV) Towards peace in the Middle East: how can business contribute? Tübingen, 1977. pp. 14. *(Kiel. Universität. Institut für Weltwirtschaft. Kieler Vorträge. Neue Folge. 83)*

— Foreign relations — Germany.

GERMANY and the Middle East, 1835-1939: international symposium, April 1975; Jehuda L. Wallach, editor. Tel-Aviv, [1975]. pp. 211. *(Tel-Aviv. University. Institute of German History. Jahrbuch des Instituts für Deutsche Geschichte. Beihefte. 1)*

FLEURY (ANTOINE) La pénétration allemande au Moyen-Orient, 1919-1939: le cas de la Turquie, de l'Iran et de l'Afghanistan. Genève, 1977. pp. 432. *bibliog. (Geneva. Graduate Institute of International Studies. Collection de Relations Internationales. 5)*

— — Pakistan.

PAKISTAN. President, 1958-1969 (Ayub Khan). 1967. Pakistan's support to the Arabs: speeches and statements by the President and the Foreign Minister of Pakistan, May- July 1967. [Karachi, 1967]. pp. 27.

— — Russia.

MANGOLD (PETER) Superpower intervention in the Middle East. London, [1978]. pp. 209. *bibliog.*

— — United States.

The MIDDLE East: critical choices for the United States; Eugene V. Rostow, editor. Boulder, Colo., 1976. pp. 211. *Papers of a symposium convened by the National Committee on American Foreign Policy, Inc.*

MANGOLD (PETER) Superpower intervention in the Middle East. London, [1978]. pp. 209. *bibliog.*

PRIMAKOV (EVGENII MAKSIMOVICH) Anatomiia blizhenevostochnogo konflikta. Moskva, 1978. pp. 374.

— History.

KIERNAN (THOMAS) Yasir Arafat: the man and the myth. London, 1976. pp. 223.

HIRST (DAVID) The gun and the olive branch: the roots of violence in the Middle East. London, 1977. pp. 367. *bibliogs.*

WAR or peace in the Middle East?; edited by Peggy Duff. London, 1978. pp. 199.

— Politics and government.

The MIDDLE East: critical choices for the United States; Eugene V. Rostow, editor. Boulder, Colo., 1976. pp. 211. *Papers of a symposium convened by the National Committee on American Foreign Policy, Inc.*

HIRSCH (SEEV) Towards peace in the Middle East: how can business contribute? Tübingen, 1977. pp. 14. *(Kiel. Universität. Institut für Weltwirtschaft. Kieler Vorträge. Neue Folge. 83)*

HIRST (DAVID) The gun and the olive branch: the roots of violence in the Middle East. London, 1977. pp. 367. *bibliogs.*

S"EZD NARODOV VOSTOKA. S"ezd 1-yi, Baku, 1920. Congress of the peoples of the East: Baku, September 1920; stenographic report translated and annotated by Brian Pearce. [London, 1977]. pp. 204.

FROM June to October: the Middle East between 1967 and 1973; edited by Itamar Rabinovich [and] Haim Shaked. New Brunswick, [1978]. pp. 412. *Based on the Shiloah Center (Tel-Aviv University) Annual Seminar for the academic year 1973/74.*

PRIMAKOV (EVGENII MAKSIMOVICH) Anatomiia blizhenevostochnogo konflikta. Moskva, 1978. pp. 374.

EAST AND WEST.

MURPHEY (RHOADS) The outsiders: the western experience in India and China. Ann Arbor, [1977]. pp. 299. *bibliog. (Michigan University. Center for Chinese Studies. Michigan Studies on China)*

EAST ANGLIA

— Commerce.

EAST ANGLIA ECONOMIC PLANNING COUNCIL. Seaports in East Anglia; a report. [London, 1977]. pp. 27.

— Industries.

SANT (MORGAN EUGENE CYRIL) and MOSELEY (MALCOLM J.) The industrial development of East Anglia. Norwich, [1977]. pp. 207. *bibliog.*

— Rural conditions.

PROPERTY, paternalism and power: class and control in rural England; [by] Howard Newby [and others]. London, 1978. pp. 432. *bibliog.*

EAST INDIANS IN EAST AFRICA.

TANDON (YASHPAL) Problems of a displaced minority: the new position of East Africa's Asians. [London, 1973]. pp. 31. *(Minority Rights Group. Reports. No. 16)*

EAST INDIANS IN FIJI.

GILLION (KENNETH LOWELL OLIVER) The Fiji Indians: challenge to European dominance, 1920-1946. Canberra, 1977. pp. 231. *bibliog.*

EAST INDIANS IN SOUTH AFRICA.

EAST INDIANS IN SOUTH AFRICA.

BÖESEKEN (A.J.) Slaves and free blacks at the Cape, 1658-1700. Cape Town, 1977. pp. 208. *bibliog.*

GINWALA (FRENE) Indian South Africans. London, 1977. pp. 20. *bibliog. (Minority Rights Group. Reports. No. 34)*

EAST INDIANS IN THE UNITED KINGDOM.

WANDSWORTH COUNCIL FOR COMMUNITY RELATIONS. Uganda Resettlement Unit. Uganda Asians in Wandsworth: a report produced...for Sir Charles Cunningham, chairman of the Uganda Resettlement Board. London, 1973. 1 vol.(unpaged).

CULTURAL conflict and the Asian family; report of a conference organised by the National Association of Indian Youth [in Leicester in 1975]; edited by Pramila Parekh and Bhikhu Parekh. [London], 1976. pp. 13.

ROMIJN (JAN) Tabu: Uganda Asians: the old, the weak, the vulnerable; a report on...work with the elderly and handicapped among the Uganda Asian evacuees in London...together with the LCSS's recommendations and suggestions for further action. London, 1976. pp. 41.

EAST INDIANS IN UGANDA.

WANDSWORTH COUNCIL FOR COMMUNITY RELATIONS. Uganda Resettlement Unit. Uganda Asians in Wandsworth: a report produced...for Sir Charles Cunningham, chairman of the Uganda Resettlement Board. London, 1973. 1 vol.(unpaged).

ROMIJN (JAN) Tabu: Uganda Asians: the old, the weak, the vulnerable; a report on...work with the elderly and handicapped among the Uganda Asian evacuees in London...together with the LCSS's recommendations and suggestions for further action. London, 1976. pp. 41.

EAST MIDLANDS STANDARD REGION (UNITED KINGDOM)

— **Economic conditions.**

EAST MIDLANDS ECONOMIC PLANNING COUNCIL. East midlands: a forward economic look. 2nd ed. [Nottingham], 1978. pp. 143.

EAST-WEST TRADE (1945-).

BROOKSTONE (JEFFREY M.) The multinational businessman and foreign policy: entrepreneurial politics in east-west trade and investment. New York, 1976. pp. 183. *bibliog.*

ENGLISH (FREDERICK C.) East-West trade: the French role. Loughborough, 1977. pp. 42. *bibliog.*

The INTERNATIONAL payments crisis and the development of East- West trade; translated from French. Brussels, 1977. pp. 150. *Proceedings of a colloquium held in 1975 under the auspices of the Centre for Research on International Institutions, Geneva.*

SEIDENFUS (HELLMUTH STEFAN) Ostverkehr: das Eindringen der östlichen Staatshandelsländer in die Verkehrswirtschaft der westlichen Welt. Berlin, [1977]. pp. 81. *(Adolf-Weber-Stiftung. Wirtschaftspolitische Kolloquien)*

EASTERN QUESTION (BALKAN).

TODOROVA (TSVETANA) and STATELOVA (EL.) compilers. Dokumenti po obiaviavane na nezavisimostta na Bulgariia 1908 godina: iz tainiia kabinet na kniaz Ferdinand. Sofiia, 1968. pp. 238. *(Bulgarska Akademiia na Naukite. Institut za Istoriia. Dokumenti po Vunshnata Politika na Bulgariia) Some documents in the original French with Bulgarian translations. Appendix of facsimiles.*

JELAVICH (CHARLES) and JELAVICH (BARBARA) The establishment of the Balkan national states, 1804-1920. Seattle, [1977]. pp. 358. *bibliog. (A History of East Central Europe. vol. 8)*

EBAN (ABBA SOLOMON).

EBAN (ABBA SOLOMON) An autobiography. London, 1978. pp. 628.

ECCLESIASTICAL COURTS

— **United Kingdom.**

SQUIBB (GEORGE DREWRY) Doctors' Commons: a history of the College of Advocates and Doctors of Law. Oxford, 1977. pp. 244. *bibliog.*

— — **Scotland.**

STAIR SOCIETY. [Publications]. 30. The records of the synod of Lothian and Tweeddale, 1589-1596, 1640-1649; edited with an introduction by James Kirk. Edinburgh, 1977. pp. 325.

ECOLOGY.

GORZ (ANDRE) Ecologie et politique. Paris, [1978]. pp. 249. *New edition of M. Bosquet's "Ecologie et politique", also containing A. Gorz's "Ecologie et liberté".*

ROBERTSON (JAMES HUGH) The sane alternative: signposts to a self-fulfilling future. London, 1978. pp. 151. *bibliog.*

— **Africa, North.**

MENSCHING (HORST) Mensch und Umwelt im Maghreb: L'homme et la biosphère au Maghreb. Hannover, 1972. pp. 23. *In German and French.*

— **Mediterranean.**

VADROT (CLAUDE MARIE) Mort de la Méditerranée. Paris, [1977]. pp. 253.

— **Peru.**

GADE (DANIEL W.) Plants, man and the land in the Vilcanota Valley of Peru. The Hague, 1975. pp. 240. *bibliog.*

ECONOMIC ASSISTANCE.

AID AND THE COMMONWEALTH: report by the Commonwealth Secretariat (formerly Flow of intra-commonwealth aid): report by the Commonwealth Secretary-General; pd. by the Commonwealth Secretariat. a., 1968 [3rd]- London. *Not pd. 1972.*

INTERREGIONAL SEMINAR ON DEVELOPMENT PLANNING, 2ND, AMSTERDAM, 1966. Planning domestic and external resources for investment; report of the...seminar...[held in] Amsterdam, Netherlands, 19-30 September, 1966. (ST/TAO/SER.C/109). New York, United Nations, 1969. pp. 198.

BHAGWATI (JAGDISH NATWARLAL) Amount and sharing of aid. Washington, D.C., [1970]. pp. 197. *(Overseas Development Council. Monographs. No. 2)*

INTERNATIONAL BANK FOR RECONSTRUCTION AND DEVELOPMENT. Sector Policy Papers. Rural development. [Washington], 1975. pp. 89.

OCHKOV (MIKHAIL SERGEEVICH) and others. "Filantropicheskie" fondy - vazhnoe ideologicheskoe oruzhie imperializma. Moskva, 1976. pp. 103. *(Akademiia Nauk SSSR. Institut Afriki. Nauchnyi Sovet po Problemam Zarubezhnykh Ideologicheskikh Techenii. Ideologicheskaia Bor'ba v Sovremennom Mire)*

SEWELL (JOHN WILLIAMSON) The United States and world development: agenda 1977. New York, 1977. pp. 245. *Written under the auspices of the Overseas Development Council.*

SINGH (SHAMSHER) and others. Coffee, tea, and cocoa: market prospects and development lending. [Washington], International Bank for Reconstruction and Development, [1977]. pp. 129. *(World Bank Staff Occasional Papers. No. 22.)*

Les SOCIALISTES et le Tiers Monde: éléments pour une politique socialiste de relations avec le Tiers Monde. [Paris, 1977]. pp. 251.

ECONOMIC ASSISTANCE, ARAB

— **Africa.**

BANQUE ARABE POUR LE DEVELOPPEMENT ECONOMIQUE EN AFRIQUE. Rapport annuel. a., 1975(1st)- Khartoum. *1975(1st) in English.*

ECONOMIC ASSISTANCE, AUSTRALIAN.

AUSTRALIA'S EXTERNAL AID; [pd. by Commonwealth Treasury]. a., 1973/74- Canberra. *Included in AUSTRALIA. Parliament. [Parliamentary papers].*

ECONOMIC ASSISTANCE, BRITISH

— **Asia.**

U.K. Central Office of Information. Reference Division. Reference Pamphlets. 147. Britain and the developing countries: Asia and the Pacific. London, 1977. pp. 52. *bibliog.*

— **Pacific, The.**

U.K. Central Office of Information. Reference Division. Reference Pamphlets. 147. Britain and the developing countries: Asia and the Pacific. London, 1977. pp. 52. *bibliog.*

ECONOMIC ASSISTANCE, CANADIAN.

DEVELOPMENT DIRECTIONS; [pd. by] Canadian International Development Agency. 9 a yr., Current issues only. Hull, Québec. *Supersedes COOPERATION CANADA.*

GERIN-LAJOIE (PAUL) Developmental administration: C[anadian] I[nternational] D[evelopment] A[gency] in a changing government organization; paper delivered...to the Institute of Public Administration Conference in Regina, September 8, 1971. [Ottawa], 1971. pp. 15,16. *(Canadian International Development Agency. Thoughts on International Development. 4) In English and French.*

GERIN-LAJOIE (PAUL) Journey to justice: reflections on a first year in office. [Ottawa], 1971. pp. 17,18. *(Canadian International Development Agency. Thoughts on International Development. 5) In English and French.*

ECONOMIC ASSISTANCE, DOMESTIC

— **United Kingdom.**

HIGGINS (JOAN) The poverty business: Britain and America. Oxford, [1978]. pp. 162. *bibliog.*

— **United States.**

A DECADE of federal antipoverty programs: achievements, failures and lessons; edited by Robert H. Haveman. New York, [1977]. pp. 381. *(Wisconsin University, Madison. Institute for Research on Poverty. Poverty Policy Analysis Series) Proceedings of a conference held in 1974.*

HALLMAN (HOWARD W.) Emergency employment: a study in federalism. University, Ala., [1977]. pp. 207.

MARTIN (CURTIS H.) and LEONE (ROBERT ANTHONY) Local economic development: the federal connection. Lexington, Mass., [1972]. pp. 138.

WAXMAN (CHAIM I.) The stigma of poverty: a critique of poverty theories and policies. New York, [1977]. pp. 148. *bibliog.*

AARON (HENRY J.) Politics and the professors: the Great Society in perspective. Washington, D.C., [1978]. pp. 185. *(Brookings Institution. Studies in Social Economics)*

BUTTON (JAMES W.) Black violence: political impact of the 1960s riots. Princeton, [1978]. pp. 248. *bibliog.*

HIGGINS (JOAN) The poverty business: Britain and America. Oxford, [1978]. pp. 162. *bibliog.*

ECONOMIC ASSISTANCE, EUROPEAN.

EUROPEAN MOVEMENT. Europe and you: the Common Market and the developing world. London, 1971. pp. 8.

WELLONS (P.A.) Borrowing by developing countries on the euro-currency market. Paris, Organisation for Economic Co-operation and Development, 1977. pp. 449. *(Development Centre. Studies)*

— **United Kingdom — Wales.**

WELSH COUNCIL. The operation of the European Regional Development Fund in Wales; report. [Cardiff], 1977. pp. (38).

ECONOMIC ASSISTANCE, NEW ZEALAND.

NEW ZEALAND. Department of External Affairs. 1966. New Zealand and the developing world: an outline of New Zealand aid abroad. [Wellington, 1966]. 1 pamphlet (unpaged).

ECONOMIC ASSISTANCE, NORWEGIAN.

STOKKE (OLAV) Norsk utviklingsbistand: målsettinger og retningslinjer for kanaliseringen; bistandsstrukturen. Uppsala, 1975. pp. 218. *bibliog. (Nordiska Afrikainstitutet. Biståndsstudier.1)*

ECONOMIC ASSISTANCE, RUSSIAN.

WOLYNSKI (ALEXANDER) Soviet aid to the third world: strategy before economics. London, 1977. pp. 13. *(Institute for the Study of Conflict. Conflict Studies. No. 90)*

ECONOMIC ASSISTANCE IN COSTA RICA.

DEWITT (R. PETER) The Inter-American Development Bank and political influence, with special reference to Costa Rica. New York, 1977. pp. 197. *bibliog.*

ECONOMIC ASSISTANCE IN GUATEMALA.

PLANT (ROGER) Guatemala: unnatural disaster. London, 1978. pp. 121.

ECONOMIC CONDITIONS.

ANGELOPOULOS (ANGELOS) Pour une nouvelle politique du développement international. Paris, [1976]. pp. 198.

CALDWELL (MALCOLM) The wealth of some nations. London, 1977. pp. 191. *bibliogs.*

— **Statistics.**

BIRLA INSTITUTE OF SCIENTIFIC RESEARCH. Economic Research Division. World economic profile: selected countries. Delhi, 1975. pp. 199.

ECONOMIC COUNCILS

— **Canada — Quebec.**

QUEBEC ECONOMIC ADVISORY COUNCIL. Status and work. [Montreal], 1966. 1 pamphlet (unpaged). *In English and French.*

— **Ireland (Republic).**

NATIONAL ECONOMIC AND SOCIAL COUNCIL [EIRE]. The work of the NESC: 1974-76. Dublin, Stationery Office, [1977]. pp. 171. *([Reports]. No. 32)*

NATIONAL ECONOMIC AND SOCIAL COUNCIL [EIRE]. The work of the NESC: 1977. Dublin, Stationery Office, [1978]. pp. 111. *([Reports]. No. 39)*

— **United States.**

NORTON (HUGH STANTON) The Employment Act and the Council of Economic Advisers, 1946-1976. Columbia, S.C., 1977. pp. 348. *bibliog.*

ECONOMIC DEVELOPMENT.

BONGOMA (JACQUES DANIEL) Indépendance économique et révolution. Kinshasa, [1969]. pp. 187. *bibliog.*

INTERREGIONAL SEMINAR ON DEVELOPMENT PLANNING, 2ND, AMSTERDAM, 1966. Planning domestic and external resources for investment; report of the...seminar...[held in] Amsterdam, Netherlands, 19-30 September, 1966. (ST/TAO/SER.C/109). New York, United Nations, 1969. pp. 198.

SECOMSKI (KAZIMIERZ) Factors of social development and economic growth. Warszawa, 1970. pp. 56. *(Instytut Gospodarki Krajów Rozwijających Się. Teaching Papers: Advanced Course in National Economic Planning. vol. 6)*

GERIN-LAJOIE (PAUL) The development officer: the role of human creativity and imagination in international development; text of a presentation... to...the Institute of International Cooperation of the University of Ottawa, etc. [Ottawa], 1971. pp. 10,10. *(Canadian International Development Agency. Thoughts on International Development. 2) In English and French.*

INTERREGIONAL SEMINAR ON PHYSICAL PLANNING FOR URBAN, REGIONAL AND NATIONAL DEVELOPMENT, BUCHAREST, 1969. Report of the...Seminar...[held in] Bucharest, Romania 22 September to 7 October 1969. (ST/TAO/SER.C/132). New York, United Nations, 1971. pp. 43.

SIMAI (MIHÁLY) Economic growth and the development level; translated by George Hajdu. Budapest, 1972. pp. 54. *(Hungarian Scientific Council for World Economy. [Publications]. Trends in World Economy. No. 7)*

TEMMAR (HAMID) Approche structurelle du phénomène du sous-développement: la structure de l'économie sous-développée. Alger, 1973. pp. 128. *bibliog.*

TAAKE (HANS-HELMUT) The implementation of development plans: organization and policies. Berlin, 1974. pp. 25.

UNITED NATIONS. Conference on Trade and Development. 1974. Problems of raw materials and development: report by the Secretary-General of UNCTAD prepared for the sixth special session of the General Assembly. (TD/B/488). New York, 1974. pp. 44.

La PLURALITE des mondes: théorie et pratiques du développement. [Genève, 1975]. pp. 139.

DIA (MAMADOU) Emancipation des économies captives. Paris, 1976 in progress.

The LIMITS to growth: a report for the Club of Rome's project on the predicament of mankind...; [by] Donella H. Meadows [and others]. 2nd ed. New York, 1976. pp. 205. *bibliog.*

PYATT (FRANK GRAHAM) and THORBECKE (ERIK) Planning techniques for a better future: a summary of a research project on planning for growth, redistribution and employment...; [with] foreword by Louis Emmerij, etc. Geneva, International Labour Office, 1976. pp. 91.

SCANTIMBURGO (JOÃO DE) Ilusões e desilusões do desenvolvimento. São Paulo, 1976. pp. 616.

SINGER (PAUL ISRAEL) Dinâmica populacional e desenvolvimento: o papel do crescimento populacional no desenvolvimento econômico. São Paulo, 1976. pp. 250. *bibliog.*

STRUKTURA materijalnih i novčanih tokova i njihov utjecaj na razvojnu politiku i opću privrednu ravnotežu. Zagreb, 1976. pp. 273. *bibliog.*

UNITED NATIONS EDUCATIONAL, SCIENTIFIC AND CULTURAL ORGANIZATION. Committee for the Furtherance of the Medium-Term Plan of Unesco. Bulletin. irreg., [1977, (no. 1)]- Paris.

AHARONI (YAIR) Markets, planning and development: the private and public sectors in economic development. Cambridge, Mass., [1977]. pp. 323.

ALTERNATIVES TO GROWTH CONFERENCE, 1ST, HOUSTON, TEXAS, 1975. Alternatives to growth-1: a search for sustainable futures; edited by Dennis L. Meadows. Cambridge, Mass., [1977]. pp. 405. *bibliog. Selection of papers presented at the conference including 4 prize-winning essays submitted to the Mitchell Prize competition.*

BEKHAR (NANSEN) Der Kapitalismus der Gegenwart: Faktoren und Widersprüche des Wirtschaftswachstums; aus dem Bulgarischen ([by] Burkhard Böttger). Berlin, 1977. pp. 165.

BLONDEL (DANIELE) and PARLY (JEANNE MARIE) L'inflation de croissance. [Paris, 1977]. pp. 295. *bibliog.*

CAIRE (GUY) Freedom of association and economic development. Geneva, International Labour Office, 1977. pp. 159. *bibliog.*

CARNEGIE-ROCHESTER CONFERENCE ON PUBLIC POLICY. 1976, April Conference. International organization, national policies and economic development; editors, Karl Brunner [and] Allan H. Meltzer. Amsterdam, 1977. pp. 240. *bibliogs. (Journal of Monetary Economics. Carnegie- Rochester Conference Series on Public Policy. vol. 6)*

DALY (HERMAN E.) Steady-state economics: the economics of biophysical equilibrium and moral growth. San Francisco, [1977]. pp. 185. *bibliogs.*

Der DIALOG Nord-Süd: Informationen zur Entwicklungspolitik;... ([edited by] Jan Tinbergen). Frankfurt am Main, [1977]. pp. 227.

DOBOZI (ISTVÁN) Forecasting structural changes in the international raw materials industries and markets. Budapest, 1977. pp. 85. *(Hungarian Scientific Council for World Economy. [Publications]. Trends in World Economy. No. 22)*

EQUALITY of opportunity within and among nations; edited by Khadya Haq. New York, [1977]. pp. 223. *Based on the fifteenth World Conference of the Society for International Development held in Amsterdam in 1976.*

KANGA (RUSTOM ADI) Economic evaluation of computer systems for developing countries. 1977. fo. 372,(73). *bibliog. Typescript. Ph.D. (London) thesis: unpublished. This thesis is the property of London University and may not be removed from the Library.*

KINDLEBERGER (CHARLES POOR) and HERRICK (BRUCE H.) Economic development. 3rd ed. New York, [1977]. pp. 397. *bibliogs.*

LLUCH (CONSTANTINO) and others. Patterns in household demand and saving; with contributions by Roger R. Betancourt [and others]; published for the World Bank. New York, [1977]. pp. 280. *bibliog.*

MEIER (GERALD MARVIN) Employment, trade, and development: a problem in international policy analysis. Leiden, 1977. pp. 80. *bibliog. (Geneva. Graduate Institute of International Studies. International Economics Series. 4)*

NEWLYN (WALTER TESSIER) The financing of economic development. Oxford, 1977. pp. 374. *bibliog.*

PERCEPTIONS of development; edited by Sandra Wallman. Cambridge, 1977. pp. 210. *bibliog. (McGill University. Centre for Developing- Area Studies. Perspectives on Development. 6)*

REDISTRIBUTION et croissance: politiques pour améliorer la répartition du revenu dans les pays en voie de développement dans le cadre de la croissance économique; étude faite par Hollis Chenery [and others]. [Paris, 1977]. pp. 408. *bibliog.*

REYNOLDS (LLOYD GEORGE) Image and reality in economic development. New Haven, [1977]. pp. 497. *bibliog.*

SALVATORE (DOMINICK) and DOWLING (EDWARD T.) Schaum's outline of theory and problems of development economics. New York, [1977]. pp. 229.

SCHWEFEL (DETLEF) Bedürfnisorientierte Planung und Evaluierung. Berlin, 1977. pp. 456. *bibliog. (Deutsches Institut für Entwicklungspolitik. Schriften. Band 50)*

The SUSTAINABLE society: implications for limited growth; edited by Dennis Clark Pirages. New York, 1977. pp. 338. *bibliogs.*

ECONOMIC DEVELOPMENT.(Cont.)

THEORY and practice of development in the third world; edited by Jozsef Nyilas. Leyden, 1977. pp. 298. *Part of a study undertaken by the Department of World Economy, Karl Marx University of Economics, Budapest, based on vol. 3 of Korunk Világgazdasága.*

UNITED NATIONS. Centre for Development Planning, Projections and Policies. 1977. Economic and social progress in the second development decade: assessment of progress made in the implementation of the international development strategy...; report of the Secretary-General. (E/5981/ST/ESA/68). New York, 1977. pp. 114.

INDUSTRY AND DEVELOPMENT; [pd. by] United Nations Industrial Development Organization. s-a., 1978(no.1)- New York.

WORLD DEVELOPMENT REPORT; [pd. by] International Bank for Reconstruction and Development. a., 1978 (1st)- Washington.

KEMP (TOM) Historical patterns of industrialization. London, 1978. pp. 183. *bibliog.*

O'HAGAN (JAMES PATRICK) ed. Growth and adjustment in national agricultures: four case studies and an overview;...published by arrangement with the Food and Agriculture Organization of the United Nations. London, 1978. pp. 242.

PEARSON (CHARLES S.) and PRYOR (ANTHONY) Environment: north and south: an economic interpretation. New York, [1978]. pp. 355. *bibliog.*

PRINGLE (LAURENCE P.) The economic growth debate: are there limits to growth? New York, 1978. pp. 86. *bibliog.*

SAYIGH (YUSIF ABDALLA) The determinants of Arab economic development. London, [1978]. pp. 181.

SAYIGH (YUSIF ABDALLA) The economics of the Arab world: development since 1945. London, [1978]. pp. 726.

THIRLWALL (ANTHONY PHILIP) Growth and development: with special reference to developing economies. 2nd ed. London, 1978. pp. 398. *bibliog.*

— Mathematical models.

BERGMANN (THEODOR) The development models of India, the Soviet Union and China: a comparative analysis. Assen, 1977. pp. 255. *bibliog. (European Society for Rural Sociology. Publications. 1.)*

LEVITSKII (EFIM MOISEEVICH) Adaptatsiia v modelirovanii ekonomicheskikh sistem; otvetstvennyi redaktor...B.B. Rozin. Novosibirsk, 1977. pp. 208.

— Research.

UNU NEWSLETTER; [pd. by] United Nations University. irreg., current issues only. Tokyo.

BATSCHA (ROBERT) The effectiveness of dissemination methods for social and economic development research. Paris, Organisation for Economic Co-operation and Development, 1976. pp. 201. *bibliog. (Development Centre. Technical Papers)*

— Social aspects.

PROSPECTS for growth: changing expectations for the future; edited by Kenneth D. Wilson. New York, 1977. pp. 343.

— Study and teaching.

GIFFEN (JANICE) and LOWRIE (MICK) Stuff the system. London, 1973. pp. 120. *bibliog.*

ECONOMIC FORECASTING.

KENDALL (Sir MAURICE GEORGE) Econometric forecasting from lagged relationships. Dublin, [1973]. pp. 15. *bibliog. (Economic and Social Research Institute. Geary Lectures. 1973)*

KAHN (HERMAN) and others. The next 200 years: a scenario for America and the world. New York, 1976. pp. 241. *bibliog.*

WORKSHOP ON ALTERNATIVE ENERGY STRATEGIES. Energy demand studies: major consuming countries: analyses of 1972 demand and projections of 1985 demand; first technical report of the Workshop...; Paul S. Basile, editor. Cambridge, Mass., [1976]. pp. 553.

DOBOZI (ISTVÁN) Forecasting structural changes in the international raw materials industries and markets. Budapest, 1977. pp. 85. *(Hungarian Scientific Council for World Economy. [Publications]. Trends in World Economy. No. 22)*

MEDIUM-term dynamic forecasting: proceedings of the 1975 London Conference; edited by W.F. Gossling, etc. London, 1977. pp. 292. *bibliogs. Sponsored by the Input-Output Research Association.*

The OPEC market to 1985; [by] Farid Abolfathi [and others]. Lexington, Mass., [1977]. pp. 406. *bibliog.*

ASCHER (WILLIAM) Forecasting: an appraisal for policy-makers and planners. Baltimore, [1978]. pp. 239.

FORECASTING and planning; edited by R. Fildes and D. Wood. Farnborough, Hants., [1978]. pp. 203.

MANAGEMENT for the future; edited by Lewis Benton. New York, [1978]. pp. 355.

ROSTOW (WALT WHITMAN) The world economy: history and prospect. Austin, [1978]. pp. 833. *bibliog.*

WORLD futures: the great debate; edited by Christopher Freeman and Marie Jahoda. London, 1978. pp. 416. *bibliog. Based on a programme of studies at the Science Policy Research Unit, University of Sussex.*

— Mathematical models.

LEDINGHAM (P.J.) Econometric model forecasts in New Zealand: a preliminary assessment. Wellington, 1976. pp. 24. *bibliog. (Reserve Bank of New Zealand. Research Papers. No. 20)*

CHETYRKIN (EVGENII MIKHAILOVICH) Statisticheskie metody prognozirovaniia. 2nd ed. Moskva, 1977. pp. 200. *bibliog.*

— Canada.

McCREADY (GERALD B.) Profile Canada: social and economic projections. Georgetown, Ont., 1977. pp. 413. *bibliog.*

— France.

FRANCE. Commissariat Général du Plan. 1976. Dossier quantitatif relatif aux perspectives de développement au cours du VIIe plan; (préparation du 7e plan). Paris, [1976]. pp. 138.

— Germany.

KRELLE (WILHELM) and PAULY (RALF) Konsum und Investitionen des Staates bis 1985. Göttingen, [1976]. pp. 181, A142. *bibliog. (Kommission für Wirtschaftlichen und Sozialen Wandel. Schriften. 130)*

— United Kingdom.

BROWN (C.J.F.) and SHERIFF (T.D.) Problems of medium term assessments: a postmortem on The British economy in 1975. London, 1977. pp. 89. *(National Institute of Economic and Social Research. Discussion Papers. No.11)*

OSBORN (DENISE RAE) National Institute gross output forecasts: a comparison with U. S. performance. London, 1977. pp. 24. *bibliog. (National Institute of Economic and Social Research. Discussion Papers. No. 1)*

OSBORN (DENISE RAE) and TEAL (FRANCIS) An analysis of NIESR forecasting error in 1975. London, [1977?]. pp. 46. *bibliog. (National Institute of Economic and Social Research. Discussion Papers. No. 2)*

OSBORN (DENISE RAE) and TEAL (FRANCIS) An analysis of N.I.E.S.R. forecasting error in 1976. London, 1977. fo. 25. *bibliog. (National Institute of Economic and Social Research. Discussion Papers. No. 6)*

— United States.

OSBORN (DENISE RAE) National Institute gross output forecasts: a comparison with U. S. performance. London, 1977. pp. 24. *bibliog. (National Institute of Economic and Social Research. Discussion Papers. No. 1)*

— — Mathematical models.

HOUSE (PETER WILLIAM) and WILLIAMS (EDWARD R.) The carrying capacity of a nation: growth and the quality of life. Lexington, Mass., [1976]. pp. 356. *bibliog.*

ECONOMIC HISTORY.

KAHN (HERMAN) and others. The next 200 years: a scenario for America and the world. New York, 1976. pp. 241. *bibliog.*

MIĘDZY feudalizmem a kapitalizmem: studia z dziejów gospodarczych i społecznych; prace ofiarowane Witoldowi Kuli. Wrocław, 1976. pp. 428. *Articles in French, English, German or Polish.*

CALDWELL (MALCOLM) The wealth of some nations. London, 1977. pp. 191. *bibliogs.*

GEURTS (P.A.M.) and MESSING (F.A.M.) compilers. Economische ontwikkeling en sociale emancipatie: 18 opstellen over economische en sociale geschiedenis, etc. Den Haag, 1977. 2 vols. (in 1). *bibliogs.*

HARRIS (STEPHEN E.) The death of capital. New York, [1977]. pp. 153.

MENON (BHASKAR P.) Global dialogue: the new international economic order. Oxford, 1977. pp. 110.

NABUDERE (DAN) The political economy of imperialism: its theoretical and polemical treatment from mercantilism to multilateral imperialism. London, [1977]. pp. 293. *bibliogs.*

POLANYI (KARL) The livelihood of man; edited [from unpublished manuscripts] by Harry W. Pearson. New York, 1977. pp. 280.

SINGH (JYOTI SHANKAR) A new international economic order: toward a fair redistribution of the world's resources. New York, 1977. pp. 135. *bibliog.*

ELSTER (JON) Logic and society: contradictions and possible worlds. Chichester, [1978]. pp. 235. *bibliog.*

GERSHUNY (JONATHAN I.) After industrial society?: the emerging self-service economy. London, 1978. pp. 181.

INDUSTRIELLE Gesellschaft und politisches System: Beiträge zur politischen Sozialgeschichte: Festschrift für Fritz Fischer zum siebzigsten Geburtstag; (Dirk Stegmann [and others], Hrsg.). Bonn, [1978]. pp. 464. *bibliog. (Friedrich-Ebert-Stiftung. Forschungsinstitut. Schriftenreihe. Band 137) In various languages.*

KEMP (TOM) Historical patterns of industrialization. London, 1978. pp. 183. *bibliog.*

LEAN (GEOFFREY) Rich world, poor world. London, 1978. pp. 352. *bibliog.*

LEWIS (Sir WILLIAM ARTHUR) Growth and fluctuations, 1870-1913. London, 1978. pp. 333.

MAGDOFF (HARRY) Imperialism: from the colonial age to the present: essays. New York, [1978]. pp. 279.

ROSTOW (WALT WHITMAN) Getting from here to there. New York, [1978]. pp. 271.

ROSTOW (WALT WHITMAN) The world economy: history and prospect. Austin, [1978]. pp. 833. *bibliog.*

TAWNEY (RICHARD HENRY) History and society: essays; edited and with an introduction by J.M. Winter. London, 1978. pp. 260.

— Bibliography.

GILBERT (VICTOR F.) and HOLMES (COLIN) compilers. Theses and dissertations in economic and social history in Yorkshire universities, 1920-74. 1975. pp. 154. *Typescript: unpublished.*

— **Methodology.**

O'BRIEN (PATRICK) The new economic history of the railways. London, [1977]. pp. 121. *bibliog.*

ECONOMIC INDICATORS

— **France.**

FRANCE. Groupe de Travail Indicateurs Sociaux et Economiques. 1976. Rapport; (préparation du 7e plan). Paris, [1976]. pp. 101.

— **Hong Kong.**

HONG KONG ECONOMIC TRENDS AND INDEXES (formerly Hong Kong economic indicators); [pd. by] Census and Statistics Department [Hong Kong]. m., Ja 1970- [Hong Kong].

— **India — Kerala.**

KERALA. Bureau of Economics and Statistics. 1977. Indicators of regional development: an appraisal. Trivandrum, 1977. pp. 103.

— **Korea.**

KOREA (REPUBLIC). Economic Planning Board. Major economic indicators. s-a., 1960/[Je]1971- Seoul. *[in Korean and English]*

— **Nigeria.**

NIGERIA. Federal Office of Statistics. Economic indicators. m., 1968 (v.4)- , with gaps. Lagos.

— **Pakistan.**

PAKISTAN'S KEY ECONOMIC INDICATORS; [pd. by] Statistical Division,...Government of Pakistan. m., 1970 (v.4)- Karachi.

— **Portugal.**

PORTUGAL. Instituto Nacional de Estatistica. Indicadores economico-sociais: Social-economic indicators. m., 1973 (ano 1)- Lisboa. *[in Portuguese and English] Supersedes its Indicadores estatisticos a curto prazo (1969-1972)*

— **Reunion.**

REUNION. [Secrétariat Général pour les Affaires Economiques. Documentation et Etudes]. Statistiques et indicateurs économiques. a., 1971 [1st issue]- [St. Denis].

— **South Africa.**

SOUTH AFRICA. Department of Statistics. Short-term economic indicators. m., Jl 1967 [1st issue]- Pretoria. *[in Afrikaans and English]*

— **Switzerland.**

BEGUELIN (JEAN PIERRE) Indicateurs statistiques de la conjoncture suisse: essai sur la signification conjoncturelle des statistiques économiques suisses. Berne, 1976. 1 vol. (various pagings). *bibliog. Thèse (docteur ès sciences économiques et sociales) - Université de Genève.*

— **Trinidad and Tobago.**

TRINIDAD AND TOBAGO. Central Statistical Office. Economic indicators. q., Ap/Je 1974 [1st issue]- Port of Spain.

— **United Kingdom.**

LONDON TRANSPORT EXECUTIVE. Planning Research Office. Economic Research. Economic indicators. (New series. No. 5). London, 1976. 1 pamphlet (unpaged).

— **Western Samoa.**

WESTERN SAMOA. Department of Economic Development. Economic indicators. a., 1977(2nd)- Apia.

ECONOMIC LEGISLATION

— **Belgium.**

ASPECTS juridiques de l'intervention des pouvoirs publics dans la vie économique: contributions belges à une enquête du Centre Français de Droit Comparé; par Jean-Michel Favresse [and others]. Bruxelles, 1976. pp. 355.

— **Italy.**

QUADRI (GIOVANNI) Diritto pubblico dell'economia. Napoli, 1977. pp. 378. *bibliog.*

— **Poland.**

GŁOWACKI (SŁAWOMIR) Terenowe organy a gospodarka narodowa: zagadnienia prawne organizacji i kierowania. Wrocław, 1977. pp. 260. *bibliog.*

— **Russia.**

ASKNAZII (SAMUIL ISAAKOVICH) Ocherki khoziaistvennogo prava SSSR. Leningrad, 1926. pp. 200.

— — **Tajikistan.**

TAJIKISTAN. Statutes, etc. 1932-1974. Sobranie deistvuiushchego zakonodatel'stva Tadzhikskoi SSR. razdel 2. Dushanbe, 1975. pp. 411.

TAJIKISTAN. Statutes, etc. 1957-1975. Sobranie deistvuiushchego zakonodatel'stva Tadzhikskoi SSR. razdel 25(-27). Dushanbe, 1976. pp..387.

— **United States.**

The INTERACTION of economics and the law: [lectures given at the University of San Diego School of Law]; edited by Bernard H. Siegan. Lexington, Mass., [1977]. pp. 175.

ECONOMIC POLICY.

UNITED NATIONS. Interregional Seminar on Development Policies and Planning in Relation to Urbanization, Pittsburgh, 1966. Report of the...seminar...Pittsburgh, Pennsylvania, 24 October to 4 November, 1966. (ST/TAO/SER.C/97). New York, 1967. pp. 74.

SYMPOSIUM ON SOCIAL POLICY AND PLANNING, COPENHAGEN, 1970. Report on the Symposium...[held at] Copenhagen, Denmark, 22 June to 2 July 1970. (ST/TAO/SER.C/128). New York, United Nations, 1971. pp. 26.

MYINT (MAUNG HLA) The economics of the developing countries. 4th ed. London, 1973 repr. 1977. pp. 160. *bibliog.*

JAŠIĆ (ZORAN) Nove tendencije u razvitku ekonomske politike u tržišnim privredama. Zagreb, 1975. pp. 30. *bibliog.*

SOCIETÀ ITALIANA DEGLI ECONOMISTI. Riunione Scientifica, 14a, Roma, 1973. Economia ed ecologia: [proceedings]. Milano, 1975. pp. 354.

AU-delà de la crise; ([by] Norman Birnbaum [and others]); présentation par Alain Touraine. Paris, [1976]. pp. 255.

PYATT (FRANK GRAHAM) and THORBECKE (ERIK) Planning techniques for a better future: a summary of a research project on planning for growth, redistribution and employment...; [with] foreword by Louis Emmerij, etc. Geneva, International Labour Office, 1976. pp. 91.

SETTLE (TOM) In search of a third way: is a morally principled political economy possible? Toronto, [1976]. pp. 208. *bibliog.*

STAPPO (ALESSANDRO FRANCHINI) Teoria del potere e politica economica: politica economica generalizzata. Padova, 1976. pp. 486.

RATHENAU (WALTHER) Walther Rathenau-Gesamtausgabe; herausgegeben von Hans Dieter Hellige und Ernst Schulin. München, 1977 in progress.

ALTERNATIVES TO GROWTH CONFERENCE, 1ST, HOUSTON, TEXAS, 1975. Alternatives to growth-1: a search for sustainable futures; edited by Dennis L. Meadows. Cambridge, Mass., [1977]. pp. 405. *bibliog. Selection of papers presented at the conference including 4 prize-winning essays submitted to the Mitchell Prize competition.*

AMERICAN ACADEMY OF POLITICAL AND SOCIAL SCIENCE. Annals. vol. 434. Social theory and public policy; special editor of this volume J. Rogers Hollingsworth. Philadelphia, [1977]. pp. 255.

BANKS (FERDINAND E.) Scarcity, energy, and economic progress. Lexington, Mass., [1977]. pp. 200. *bibliog.*

BLACK (STANLEY W.) Floating exchange rates and national economic policy. New Haven, 1977. pp. 204.

LEMAITRE (JACQUES) Le chaos ou la troisième voie: ni capitalisme, ni socialisme étatiques, un système totalement différent: le libérisme. Paris, [1977]. pp. 324.

SCHWEFEL (DETLEF) Bedürfnisorientierte Planung und Evaluierung. Berlin, 1977. pp. 456. *bibliog. (Deutsches Institut für Entwicklungspolitik. Schriften. Band 50)*

SHAW (GRAHAM KEITH) An introduction to the theory of macro-economic policy. 3rd ed. [London, 1977]. pp. 208. *bibliogs.*

BRETON (ALBERT) and SCOTT (ANTHONY) The economic constitution of federal states. Toronto, [1978]. pp. 166.

FORECASTING and planning; edited by R. Fildes and D. Wood. Farnborough, Hants., [1978]. pp. 203.

FREY (BRUNO S.) Modern political economy. Oxford, 1978. pp. 166. *bibliogs.*

GEORGE (KENNETH DESMOND) and SHOREY (JOHN CHARLES) The allocation of resources: theory and policy. London, 1978. pp. 275. *bibliogs.*

GRIMOND (JOSEPH) The common welfare. London, 1978. pp. 248.

KENESSEY (ZOLTÁN) The process of economic planning. New York, 1978. pp. 400. *bibliogs.*

ROLL (ERIC) Baron Roll. The uses and abuses of economics, and other essays. London, 1978. pp. 293.

ŠIK (OTA) Pour une troisième voie; traduit de l'allemand par Marcel Chabernaud. [Paris, 1978]. pp. 254.

TUFTE (EDWARD R.) Political control of the economy. Princeton, [1978]. pp. 168.

VEREIN FÜR SOZIALPOLITIK. Schriften. Neue Folge. Band 97. Ökonomische Verfügungsrechte und Allokationsmechanismen in Wirtschaftssystemen; von Rolf Eschenburg [and others]; herausgegeben von Karl-Ernst Schenk. Berlin, [1978]. pp. 205. *bibliogs.*

— **Mathematical models.**

MATEEV (EVGENI GEORGIEV) Automated system for national economic management: economic principles. Sofia, 1975. pp. 327.

CHESTNUT (HAROLD) Influence of technology on modern world evolution and use of dynamic models of macro-economic systems in development planning. Roma, 1976. pp. 61. *Paper read at a conference held by the Accademia Nazionale dei Lincei in Rome in 1972.*

MODELING for government and business: essays in honor of Prof. Dr. P.J. Verdoorn; edited by C.A. Van Bochove [and others]. Leiden, 1977. pp. 355. *bibliogs.*

ECONOMIC STABILIZATION

— **Mathematical models.**

STABILITY and inflation; edited by A.R. Bergstrom [and others]; ...a volume of essays to honour the memory of A.W.H. Phillips. Chichester, [1978]. pp. 323. *bibliogs.*

ECONOMIC ZONING

ECONOMIC ZONING
— Poland — Silesia.

BARTECZEK (ANDRZEJ) Integracyjna funkcja infrastruktury gospodarczej w świetle badań nad Górnośląskim Okręgiem Przemysłowym. Warszawa, 1977. pp. 138. *bibliog.* (Polska Akademia Nauk. Komitet Przestrzennego Zagospodarowahia Kraju. Studia. t.59) With Russian and English summaries.

— Russia.

AKHUNDOV (VAID DZHUMSHUDOVICH) Sovershenstvovanie struktury obshchestvennogo vosproizvodstva: voprosy metodologii. Moskva, 1977. pp. 239.

DOBRYNIN (ALEKSANDR IVANOVICH) Regional'nye proportsii vosproizvodstva. Leningrad, 1977. pp. 127.

— United States.

LAND use control: evaluating economic and political effects; [by] David E. Ervin [and others]. Cambridge, Mass., [1977]. pp. 182. *bibliog.*

ECONOMICS.

COLE (GEORGE DOUGLAS HOWARD) Some relations between political and economic theory. London, 1934. pp. 92. *Based on a course of lectures delivered in Oxford in 1933.*

BRUNHOFF (SUZANNE DE) Etat et capital: recherches sur la politique économique. Grenoble, 1976. pp. 126.

CHEVALIER (JEAN MARIE) L'économie industrielle en question. [Paris, 1977]. pp. 268. *bibliog.*

CIGNO (ALESSANDRO) The debate on natural resources and the fate of humanity; or, Do we need economists? Hull, 1977. pp. 24. *bibliog. An inaugural lecture delivered at the University of Hull on 4 May 1976.*

MARKETS and morals; edited by Gerald Dworkin [and others]. Washington, [1977]. pp. 206. *bibliogs. Includes many of the papers presented at a three-day conference beginning May 9, 1974, at the Seattle Research Center of the Battelle Memorial Institute.*

POLANYI (KARL) The livelihood of man; edited [from unpublished manuscripts] by Harry W. Pearson. New York, 1977. pp. 280.

WEBER (MAX) Critique of Stammler;...translated, with an introductory essay, by Guy Oakes. New York, [1977]. pp. 184.

FOURASTIE (JEAN) La réalité économique: vers la révision des idées dominantes en France. Paris, [1978]. pp. 364.

— Bibliography.

BELTON (E.J.) compiler. Bibliography of published writings to 1975 of Dr. Harry G. Johnson. [Ontario], 1976. pp. 60.

CENTRE FOR POLICY STUDIES. Bibliography of freedom. London, 1976. pp. 28.

— Dictionaries and encyclopedias.

MOSOLOVA (N.I.) compiler. Kratkii anglo-russkii slovar' ekonomicheskikh slov i vyrazhenii. Dushanbe, 1971. pp. 63.

AMMER (CHRISTINE) and AMMER (DEAN S.) Dictionary of business and economics. New York, [1977]. pp. 461. *bibliog.*

GILPIN (ALAN) Dictionary of economic terms. 4th ed. London, 1977. pp. 249. *bibliog.*

The PENGUIN dictionary of economics; by G. Bannock [and others]. 2nd ed. Harmondsworth, 1978. pp. 467.

— History.

FISTETTI (FRANCESCO) Critica dell'economia e critica della politica: Marx, Hegel e l'economia politica classica. Bari, [1976]. pp. 213. *bibliogs.*

DELFAUD (PIERRE) Keynes et le keynésianisme. [Paris, 1977]. pp. 128. *bibliog.*

HARRIS (STEPHEN E.) The death of capital. New York, [1977]. pp. 153.

KEYNES, Cambridge and The general theory: the process of criticism and discussion connected with the development of The general theory; proceedings of a conference held at the University of Western Ontario; ...edited by Don Patinkin and J. Clark Leith. London, 1977. pp. 182. *bibliog.*

MEEK (RONALD LINDLEY) Smith, Marx and after: ten essays in the development of economic thought. London, 1977. pp. 193.

MEHTA (GHANSHYAM) The structure of the Keynesian revolution. London, 1977. pp. 219. *bibliog.*

MODERN economic thought; edited by Sidney Weintraub. Oxford, 1977. pp. 584. *bibliogs.*

NENTJES (A.) Van Keynes tot Keynes: de ontwikkeling van het denken over geld en werkloosheid bij Keynes. Groningen, [1977]. pp. 357. *With summary in English.*

NEORICARDIANA: Sraffa e Graziadei; a cura di Roberto Finzi. Bologna, [1977]. pp. 258. *(Convegno Nazionale degli Storici del Pensiero Economico, 3 , 1974. Atti. vol. 2)*

O'DRISCOLL (GERALD PATRICK) Economics as a coordination problem: the contributions of Friedrich A. Hayek. Kansas City, [1977]. pp. 172. *bibliog.*

Il RUOLO dello Stato nel pensiero degli economisti; a cura di Roberto Finzi. Bologna, [1977]. pp. 249. *(Convegno Nazionale degli Storici del Pensiero Economico, 3 , 1974. Atti. vol.I)*

AMBIRAJAN (SRINIVASA) Classical political economy and British policy in India. Cambridge, 1978. pp. 301. *bibliog. (Cambridge. University. Centre of South Asian Studies. Cambridge South Asian Studies. 21)*

GERSHUNY (JONATHAN I.) After industrial society?: the emerging self-service economy. London, 1978. pp. 181.

PIĄTKOWSKI (WIESŁAW) J.C.L. Simonde de Sismondi : teoria ekonomiczna. Warszawa, 1978. pp. 320. *bibliog. With English and Russian summaries.*

WALTERS (ALAN A.) Economists and the British economy. London, 1978. pp. 31. *(Institute of Economic Affairs. Occasional Papers. 54)*

— — Austria.

MISES (LUDWIG VON) Erinnerungen...; mit einem Vorwort von Margit v. Mises und einer Einleitung von Friedrich August von Hayek. Stuttgart, 1978. pp. 112. *bibliog.*

— — France.

GUNASEKERA (MUAHANDORAMGE VICTOR AUGUSTUS) Some aspects of French classical economic thought. 1962. fo. 485. *bibliog. Typescript. Ph.D. (London) thesis: unpublished. This thesis is the property of London University and may not be removed from the Library.*

MAY (LOUIS PHILIPPE) Le Mercier de la Rivière, 1719-1801: aux origines de la science économique. Paris, [1975]. pp. 178. *bibliog.*

TURGOT (ANNE ROBERT JACQUES) Baron de l'Aulne. The economics of A.R.J. Turgot; edited and translated...by P.D. Groenewegen. The Hague, 1977. pp. 194.

— — Germany.

GRUNDLINIEN des ökonomischen Denkens in Deutschland: von den Anfängen bis zur Mitte des 19. Jahrhunderts; (Autorenkollektiv: Hermann Lehmann, Leitung und Gesamtbearbeitung). Berlin, [1977]. pp. 527. *bibliog. (Akademie der Wissenschaften der DDR. Zentralinstitut für Wirtschaftswissenschaften. Schriften. Nr.3)*

WAGNER (ADOLPH) Briefe, Dokumente, Augenzeugenberichte, 1851-1917; ausgewählt und herausgegeben von Heinrich Rubner. Berlin, [1978]. pp. 452. *With English summary.*

— — Italy.

CAFFÈ (FEDERICO) Frammenti per lo studio del pensiero economico italiano. [Roma, 1975]. pp. 130. *(Rome. Università. Istituto di Politica Economica e Finanziaria. Pubblicazioni. 18)*

— — Spain.

GRICE-HUTCHINSON (MARJORIE) Early economic thought in Spain, 1177-1740. London, 1978. pp. 189. *bibliog.*

— — United Kingdom.

APPLEBY (JOYCE OLDHAM) Economic thought and ideology in seventeenth-century England. Princeton, 1978. pp. 287.

ROBBINS (LIONEL CHARLES) Baron Robbins. The theory of economic policy in English classical political economy. 2nd ed. London, 1978. pp. 217.

— — United States.

WARD (DWAYNE) Toward a critical political economics: a critique of liberal and radical economic thought. Santa Monica, Calif., [1977]. pp. 334. *bibliog.*

DIGGINS (JOHN P.) The bard of savagery: Thorstein Veblen and modern social theory. New York, [1978]. pp. 257.

— Methodology.

MAYES (DAVID G.) Projects in economic and social statistics. Exeter, 1976. pp. 141.

SAWYER (JOHN A.) Stanley Jevons and the development of scientific method in economics. Toronto, 1976. pp. 39. *bibliog. (Toronto. University. Institute for the Quantitative Analysis of Social and Economic Policy. Working Paper Series. No. 7602)*

THOBEN (CHRISTA) Strukturdiagnose in der Marktwirtschaft. Berlin, [1977]. pp. 74. *bibliog. (Rheinisch-Westfälisches Institut für Wirtschaftsforschung, Essen. Schriftenreihe. Neue Folge. 40)*

— Miscellanea.

LEVI (GIUSEPPE) and WAGNEST (RODOLFO) eds. L'attività economica nei secoli: antologia del commercio e dell'industria. Torino, 1923. pp. 740.

— Periodicals — Indexes.

CONTENTS OF RECENT ECONOMICS JOURNALS; ([pd. by] Department of Industry, Library Services, Economics Division). w., Je 1 1973- London. *Not pd. Ap 12 1974. File includes Periodicals and their publishers, 1976-*

— Study and teaching — European Economic Community countries.

ASPECTS of upper secondary economics education in E.E.C. countries: containing selected papers presented at the First E. E. C. Working Conference on Economics Education, St. Ignatius University, Antwerp, September 1976; edited by Raymond Ryba and Brian Robinson. London, [1977]. pp. 178. *Published on behalf of the E.E.C. Working Committee on Economics Education in conjunction with the Economics Association.*

— — Italy.

Gli STUDI di economia in Italia; a cura di Augusto Graziani e Siro Lombardini. Milano, 1975. pp. 136. *bibliog.*

— — United Kingdom.

CIANO (J.L.D.) and PHILLIPS (R.F.R.) The Economics Association and the development of economics education. London, 1977. pp. 16.

— Terminology.

GILPIN (ALAN) Dictionary of economic terms. 4th ed. London, 1977. pp. 249. *bibliog.*

— 1776-1876.

LAFAURIE (ADOLF) Die materiellen Interessen: eine kritische Beleuchtung der politischen Oekonomie in ihrer gegenwärtigen Gestaltung als Wissenschaft. Kiel, Universitäts-Buchhandlung, 1841. pp. 32.

MARX (KARL) A contribution to the critique of political economy;...translated from the second German edition by N.I. Stone, with an appendix containing Marx's Introduction to the critique recently published among his posthumous papers. Chicago, [1904]. pp. 314.

BODEI (REMO) and others. Hegel e l'economia politica; a cura di Salvatore Veca. [Milano, 1975]. pp. 218.

BOSELLINI (CARLO) Opere complete; a cura di Miriam Rotondò Michelini. Torino, 1976. 2 vols. *(Fondazione Luigi Einaudi. Scrittori Italiani di Politica, Economia e Storia)*

FILANGIERI (GAETANO) Cavaliere. Scritti; a cura di Franco Venturi. [Torino, 1976]. pp. 139. *bibliog.*

— 1876-1976.

ROSCHER (WILHELM) System der Volkswirtschaft: ein Hand- und Lesebuch für Geschäftsmänner und Studierende. 1. Band. Grundlagen der Nationalökonomie;...ergänzt durch Robert Pöhlmann; fünfundzwanzigste Auflage mit Vorwort und Nachtrag von Adolf Weber. Stuttgart, 1918. pp. 942.

MISHAN (EDWARD JOSHUA) 21 popular economic fallacies. 2nd ed. New York, 1973 repr. 1974. pp. 235.

RICARDIENS, Keynésiens et Marxistes: essais en économie politique non-néoclassique: actes du colloque de Nice, septembre 1972; (édité par C. Berthomieu [and others]). [Grenoble, 1974]. pp. 405. *bibliogs.*

CAVALIERI (DUCCIO) Microeconomia politica. Milano, 1975. pp. 453. *bibliogs.*

25 years of economic theory: retrospect and prospect; edited by T.J. Kastelein [and others]. Leiden, 1976. pp. 143.

SHERMAN (HOWARD JAY) Stagflation: a radical theory of unemployment and inflation. New York, [1976]. pp. 252. *bibliogs.*

HUTCHISON (TERENCE WILMOT) Keynes versus the 'Keynesians'...?: an essay in the thinking of J.M. Keynes and the accuracy of its interpretation by his followers. London, 1977. pp. 83. *(Institute of Economic Affairs. Hobart Paperbacks. 11)*

LACHMANN (LUDWIG MORITZ) Capital, expectations, and the market process: essays on the theory of the market economy. Kansas City, [1977]. pp. 352. *bibliog.*

LEONTIEF (WASSILY W.) Essays in economics: theories, facts, and policies. vol. 2. Oxford, [1977]. pp. 161.

SOCIETE DU MONT-PELERIN. Congrès, 1976. Le libéralisme?: de Karl Marx à Milton Friedman; (edited by) Jacques Riboud. Paris, 1977. pp. 224. *In French or English.*

WEBER (ADOLF) Adolf Weber zum hundertsten Geburtstag: im Auftrage der Adolf-Weber-Stiftung herausgegeben von Otmar Issing. Berlin, [1977]. pp. 364. *bibliog. Selection of Weber's writings published between 1907 and 1963.*

SHAPIRO (EDWARD J.) Macroeconomic analysis. 4th ed. New York, [1978]. 1 vol. (various pagings).

— 1976- .

DRUMMOND (IAN MACDONALD) Economics: principles and policies in an open economy. Georgetown, Ont., 1976. pp. 612.

VITELLO (VINCENZO) Struttura e dinamica dell'economia: reddito nazionale, domanda effettiva e accumulazione. Roma, 1976. pp. 127.

BAUMOL (WILLIAM JACK) Economic theory and operations analysis. 4th ed. Englewood Cliffs, [1977]. pp. 695. *bibliogs.*

CHAÎNEAU (ANDRE) La mécanique du circuit économique. [Paris, 1977]. pp. 224.

FUNDAMENTALS of political economy; edited...by George C. Wang. [London, 1977]. pp. 505. *Translation from the Chinese.*

HARVEY (JACK) Modern economics: an introduction for business and professional students. 3rd ed. London, 1977. pp. 560.

HEERTJE (ARNOLD) Echte economie: misverstanden over en misstanden in de economie. Amsterdam, 1977. pp. 184.

HENSEL (K. PAUL) Systemvergleich als Aufgabe: Aufsätze und Vorträge;... herausgegeben von Hannelore Hamel. Stuttgart, 1977. pp. 254. *bibliog.*

HUTCHISON (TERENCE WILMOT) Keynes versus the 'Keynesians'...?: an essay in the thinking of J.M. Keynes and the accuracy of its interpretation by his followers. London, 1977. pp. 83. *(Institute of Economic Affairs. Hobart Paperbacks. 11)*

KLEIN (BURTON H.) Dynamic economics. Cambridge, Mass., 1977. pp. 289.

KORLIRAS (PANAYOTIS G.) The economics of disorder: a disequilibrium theoretical approach to the problems of inflation and unemployment. Athens, 1977. pp. 60. *bibliog. (Center of Planning and Economic Research [Athens]. Lecture Series. 29)*

KREHM (WILLIAM) Babel's tower: the dynamics of economic breakdown. Toronto, [1977]. pp. 131.

LINDAUER (JOHN) Economics: a modern view. Philadelphia, 1977. pp. 865.

LOWE (ADOLPH) On economic knowledge: toward a science of political economics. enlarged ed. White Plains, N.Y., [1977]. pp. 351.

LUNGHINI (GIORGIO) La crisi dell'economia politica e la teoria del valore. [Milano, 1977]. pp. 77. *bibliog. Text of the report to the sixteenth scientific meeting of the Società Italiana degli Economisti, 1975.*

MOTLEY (BRIAN) Money, income and wealth: the macroeconomics of a monetary economy. Lexington, Mass., [1977]. pp. 402. *bibliogs.*

NATURAL resources, uncertainty, and general equilibrium systems: essays in memory of Rafael Lusky; edited by Alan S. Blinder [and] Philip Friedman. New York, [1977]. pp. 255. *bibliogs.*

POSNER (RICHARD A.) Economic analysis of law. 2nd ed. Boston, Mass., [1977]. pp. 572.

BECK (ROGER) Microeconomic analysis of issues in business, government and society. New York, [1978]. pp. 274. *bibliog.*

BURSTEIN (MEYER LOUIS) New directions in economic policy. London, 1978. pp. 178. *bibliog.*

EQUILIBRIUM and disequilibrium in economic theory: proceedings of a conference organized by the Institute for Advanced Studies, Vienna, Austria, July 3-5, 1974; edited by Gerhard Schwödiauer. Dordrecht, [1978]. pp. 736. *bibliogs.*

FERGUSON (CHARLES E.) and MAURICE (S. CHARLES) Economic analysis: theory and application. 3rd ed. Homewood, Ill., 1978. pp. 520.

GEORGE (KENNETH DESMOND) and SHOREY (JOHN CHARLES) The allocation of resources: theory and policy. London, 1978. pp. 275. *bibliogs.*

HOWE (WILLIAM STEWART) Industrial economics: an applied approach. London, 1978. pp. 255.

KALDOR (NICHOLAS) Baron Kaldor. Further essays on applied economics. London, 1978. pp. 244.

KALDOR (NICHOLAS) Baron Kaldor. Further essays on economic theory. London, 1978. pp. 232.

LAYARD (PETER RICHARD GREVILLE) and WALTERS (ALAN A.) Microeconomic theory. New York, [1978]. pp. 498. *bibliog.*

MILLER (ROGER LEROY) Intermediate microeconomics: theory, issues and applications. [New York, 1978]. pp. 507.

PETERSON (WALLACE CARROLL) Income, employment, and economic growth. 4th ed. New York, [1978]. pp. 631.

PIONEERING economics: international essays in honour of Giovanni Demaria; edited by Tullio Bagiotti and Giampiero Franco. Padova, [1978]. pp. 1116. *bibliog. In English, French or Italian.*

ROBINSON (JOAN) Contributions to modern economics. Oxford, 1978. pp. 274. *bibliog.*

TUFTE (EDWARD R.) Political control of the economy. Princeton, [1978]. pp. 168.

VEREIN FÜR SOZIALPOLITIK. Schriften. Neue Folge. Band 97. Ökonomische Verfügungsrechte und Allokationsmechanismen in Wirtschaftssystemen; von Rolf Eschenburg [and others]; herausgegeben von Karl-Ernst Schenk. Berlin, [1978]. pp. 205. *bibliogs.*

ECONOMICS, COMPARATIVE.

BRD-DDR: die Wirtschaftssysteme: soziale Marktwirtschaft und sozialistische Planwirtschaft im Systemvergleich; mit Beiträgen von Hannelore Hamel [and others]; herausgegeben von Hannelore Hamel. München, [1977]. pp. 365.

HENSEL (K. PAUL) Systemvergleich als Aufgabe: Aufsätze und Vorträge;... herausgegeben von Hannelore Hamel. Stuttgart, 1977. pp. 254. *bibliog.*

LINDBLOM (CHARLES EDWARD) Politics and markets: the world's political-economic systems. New York, [1977]. pp. 403.

BERGSON (ABRAM) Productivity and the social system: the USSR and the West. Cambridge, Mass., 1978. pp. 256.

ECONOMICS, MATHEMATICAL.

KMENTA (JAN) Elements of econometrics. New York, [1971]. pp. 655. *bibliog.*

JOHNSTON (JOHN) Econometric methods. 2nd ed. New York, [1972]. pp. 437.

HILDENBRAND (WERNER) Core and equilibria of a large economy. Princeton, [1974]. pp. 251. *bibliog.*

MATHEMATICAL models in economics: editors, Jerzy Łoś and Maria W. Łoś; contributors, A. Anastasopoulos [and others]. Amsterdam, 1974. pp. 483. *bibliogs. Proceedings of the Symposium on Mathematical Methods of Economics, February-July 1972 and of the Conference on Von Neumann Models, 10-15 July 1972, organized by the Polish Academy of Sciences, Institute of Mathematics in Warszawa.*

BEILBY (M.H.) Economics and operational research. London, 1975. pp. 174. *bibliog.*

MELANGES offerts à Henri Guitton: le temps en économie, les mathématiques et l'économie, recherches pluridisciplinaires. [Paris, 1976]. pp. 503. *bibliog.*

MODELIROVANIE sotsial'no-ekonomicheskikh protsessov: kachestvennye gipotezy i imitatsionnyi podkhod. Moskva, 1976. pp. 247. *bibliog.*

STAPPO (ALESSANDRO FRANCHINI) Teoria del potere e politica economica: politica economica generalizzata. Padova, 1976. pp. 486.

AOKI (MASANAO) Optional control and system theory in dynamic economic analysis. New York, [1977]. pp. 400. *bibliog.*

APPLICATIONS of control theory to economic analysis; edited by John D. Pitchford and Stephen J. Turnovsky. Amsterdam, 1977. pp. 363. *bibliogs.*

ARROW (KENNETH JOSEPH) and others. Studies in resource allocation processes; edited by Kenneth J. Arrow and Leonid Hurwicz. Cambridge, 1977. pp. 482. *bibliogs.*

ECONOMICS, MATHEMATICAL. (Cont.)

BAUMOL (WILLIAM JACK) Economic theory and operations analysis. 4th ed. Englewood Cliffs, [1977]. pp. 695. *bibliogs.*

DUBOVSKII (SERGEI VASIL'EVICH) and others. Matematicheskie modeli ekonomicheskikh protsessov: obzor; pod nauchnoi redaktsiei D.M. Gvishiani i S.V. Emel'ianova. Moskva, 1977. pp. 61. *bibliog.*

ESPASA (ANTONI) The spectral maximum likelihood estimation of econometric models with stationary errors. Göttingen, [1977]. pp. 107. *bibliog.*

KOUTSOGIANNES (A.) Theory of econometrics: an introductory exposition of econometric methods. 2nd ed. London, 1977. pp. 681. *bibliog.*

LEVITSKII (EFIM MOISEEVICH) Adaptatsiia v modelirovanii ekonomicheskikh sistem; otvetstvennyi redaktor...B.B. Rozin. Novosibirsk, 1977. pp. 208.

MORALES (ROLANDO) Etude et analyse des modèles ARMA de Box-Jenkins en vue de leur utilisation en économétrie. Berne, [1977]. pp. 341. *bibliog. (Geneva. Université. Faculté des Sciences Economiques et Sociales. Collection des Thèses. No. 239)*

RAMB (BERND THOMAS) Zeitentwicklungsanalyse: eine ökonometrische Methode für die Untersuchung der zeitlichen Entwicklung makroökonomischer Zusammenhänge, etc. Berlin, [1977]. pp. 241. *bibliog.*

SOLARI (LUIGI) De l'économie qualitative à l'économie quantitative: pour une méthodologie de l'approche formalisée en science économique. Paris, 1977. pp. 313. *bibliogs.*

AYRES (ROBERT U.) Resources, environment, and economics: applications of the materials-energy balance principle. New York, [1978]. pp. 207.

DETERMINANTS of travel choice; edited by David A. Hensher and Quasim Dalvi. Farnborough, Hants., [1978]. pp. 394. *bibliogs. A contribution to the US National Academy of Sciences Transportation Research Board Sub-Committee on the Value of Travel Time.*

GLAISTER (STEPHEN) Mathematical methods for economists. 2nd ed. Oxford, [1978]. pp. 213.

GUJARATI (DAMODAR) Basic econometrics. New York, [1978]. pp. 462. *bibliog.*

HAINES (BRIAN) An introduction to quantitative economics. London, 1978. pp. 166. *bibliog.*

INTRILIGATOR (MICHAEL D.) Econometric models, techniques, and applications. Amsterdam, 1978. pp. 638. *bibliogs.*

SHAPIRO (EDWARD J.) Macroeconomic analysis. 4th ed. New York, [1978]. 1 vol. (various pagings).

SILBERBERG (EUGENE) The structure of economics: a mathematical analysis. New York, [1978]. pp. 543.

THEIL (HENRI) Introduction to econometrics. Englewood Cliffs, N.J., [1978]. pp. 447. *bibliog.*

ECONOMICS, PRIMITIVE.

GODELIER (MAURICE) Horizon, trajets marxistes en anthropologie. 2nd ed. Paris, 1977. 2 vols. (in 1). *bibliog.*

POLANYI (KARL) The livelihood of man; edited [from unpublished manuscripts] by Harry W. Pearson. New York, 1977. pp. 280.

PRYOR (FREDERIC L.) The origins of the economy: a comparative study of distribution in primitive and peasant economies. New York, [1977]. pp. 475. *bibliog.*

RELATIONS of production: Marxist approaches to economic anthropology; edited by David Seddon. London, 1978. pp. 414. *bibliog.*

ECONOMICS IN LITERATURE.

SHELL (MARC) The economy of literature. Baltimore, [1978]. pp. 176.

ECONOMISTS
— America, Latin.

O'BRIEN (PHILIP J.) A critique of Latin American theories of dependency. Glasgow, [1974]. pp. 18. *(Glasgow. University. Institute of Latin American Studies. Occasional Papers. No.12)*

— Italy.

CAFFÈ (FEDERICO) Frammenti per lo studio del pensiero economico italiano. [Roma, 1975]. pp. 130. *(Rome. Università. Istituto di Politica Economica e Finanziaria. Pubblicazioni. 18)*

— United Kingdom.

WALTERS (ALAN A.) Economists and the British economy. London, 1978. pp. 31. *(Institute of Economic Affairs. Occasional Papers. 54)*

ECUADOR
— Armed forces — Political activity.

FITCH (JOHN SAMUEL) The military coup d'état as a political process: Ecuador, 1948- 1966. Baltimore, Md., [1977]. pp. 243. *bibliog. (Johns Hopkins University. Studies in Historical and Political Science. Series 95. No. 1)*

— Census.

ECUADOR. Census, 1974. III censo de población 1974: resultados definitivos; resumen nacional. Quito, 1977. pp. 171.

— Commerce.

ECUADOR. Instituto Nacional de Estadistica. Encuesta anual de comercio interno. a., 1967- Quito.

— Executive departments.

ECUADOR. Junta Nacional de Planificacion y Coordinacion Economica. 1976. Guia institucional del sector publico. 2nd ed. Quito, 1976. pp. 553.

— Politics and government.

FITCH (JOHN SAMUEL) The military coup d'état as a political process: Ecuador, 1948- 1966. Baltimore, Md., [1977]. pp. 243. *bibliog. (Johns Hopkins University. Studies in Historical and Political Science. Series 95. No. 1)*

— Rural conditions.

REDCLIFT (MICHAEL R.) Agrarian reform and peasant organization on the Ecuadorian coast. London, 1978. pp. 186. *bibliog. (London. University. Institute of Latin American Studies. Monographs. 8)*

EDUCATION.

BESANT (ANNIE) Education for the new era; a lecture given at the Queen's Hall, London, on October 29th, 1919. London, Kelmscott Publishing Co., 1919. pp. 8. *(New Commonwealth. Supplements. No.11)*

CENTRO INTERCULTURAL DE DOCUMENTACION. Cidoc Documenta. Alternatives in education. July 1970-(June 1972). Cuernavaca, 1972. 4 vols. (in 1). *(Cidoc Cuadernos. Nos. 75-78)*

— Aims and objectives.

SPRING (JOEL) A primer of libertarian education. Montreal, [1975]. pp. 157. *bibliog.*

RAVEN (JOHN) Social psychologist. Education, values and society: the objectives of education and the nature and development of competence. London, 1977. pp. 351.

— Economic aspects.

ZYMELMAN (MANUEL) and others. The economic evaluation of vocational training programs. [Washington], International Bank for Reconstruction and Development, [1976]. pp. 122. *bibliog. (World Bank Staff Occasional Papers. No. 21)*

JASIĆ (ZORAN) Uvod u ekonomiku obrazovanja. Zagreb, 1978. pp. 311. *bibliog.*

— — United Kingdom.

ECONOMICS and education policy: a reader; edited by Carolyn Baxter [and others], at the Open University. London, 1977. pp. 378. *bibliogs.*

GEARY (K.) Local authority resource allocation with multiple objectives: an education example. London, 1977. pp. 71. *bibliog. (Planning Research Applications Group. PRAG Technical Papers. TP 21)*

— — United States.

ECONOMICS and education policy: a reader; edited by Carolyn Baxter [and others], at the Open University. London, 1977. pp. 378. *bibliogs.*

— — Yugoslavia.

JASIĆ (ZORAN) Uvod u ekonomiku obrazovanja. Zagreb, 1978. pp. 311. *bibliog.*

— History.

BARROW (ROBIN) Radical education: a critique of freeschooling and deschooling. London, 1978. pp. 207. *bibliog.*

— Philosophy.

DEVALDES (MANUEL) pseud. [i.e. Ernest LOHY]. L'éducation et la liberté. Bruxelles, 1958. pp. 21. *Last page signed and dated 1900.*

BARROW (ROBIN) Radical education: a critique of freeschooling and deschooling. London, 1978. pp. 207. *bibliog.*

ETHICS and educational policy; edited by Kenneth A. Strike and Kieran Egan. London, 1978. pp. 225. *bibliogs.*

— Australia.

CLAYDON (LESLIE FRANCIS) and others. Curriculum and culture: schooling in a pluralist society. Sydney, 1977. pp. 231.

— Bangladesh — Statistics.

PAKISTAN. Central Bureau of Education. 1967. Educational statistics for Pakistan, 1947-1957. [Karachi], 1967. pp. 29. *(Educational Statistics Bulletin Series. 1967/2)*

— Botswana.

BOTSWANA. National Commission on Education. 1977. Education for Kagisano: report...; [Torsten Husén, chairman]. Gaborone, 1977. 2 vols. *bibliog.*

— Canada — History.

PRENTICE (ALISON) The school promoters: education and social class in mid-nineteenth century Upper Canada. Toronto, [1977]. pp. 192.

— — Nova Scotia.

NOVA SCOTIA. Department of Education. Annual report. a., 1970/71- Halifax.

— — Ontario.

HALL (OSWALD) and CARLTON (RICHARD) Basic skills at school and work: the study of Albertown, an Ontario community. [Toronto, 1977]. pp. 326. *bibliog. (Ontario. Economic Council. Occasional Papers. 1)*

— Caribbean Area.

CARIBBEAN ECONOMIC DEVELOPMENT CORPORATION. Final report, C[aribbean] E[ducational] S[ervices] CO[ops] project. Hato Rey, 1968. 1 vol. (various pagings).

— China.

PRICE (RONALD FRANCIS) Marx and education in Russia and China. London, [1977]. pp. 376. *bibliog.*

— Cyprus.

OMILOS PEDAGOGIKON EREVNON. The drama of Cyprus as it affects children and their education. Nicosia, 1974. pp. 7.

— European Economic Community countries — Statistics.

EUROPEAN COMMUNITIES. Statistical Office. Education statistics. a., 1970/75(1st)- Luxembourg. *[in Community languages]*

— Finland — Statistics.

FINLAND. Tilastokeskus. Yleissivistävät oppilaitokset, etc. a., 1973/74- Helsinki. *[in Finnish and Swedish with summary in English]*

— France.

TANGUY (LUCIE) Le capital, les travailleurs et l'école: l'exemple de la Lorraine sidérurgique. Paris, 1976. pp. 226.

— Germany.

The BRITISH in Germany: educational reconstruction after 1945; edited by Arthur Hearnden. London, 1978. pp. 335. *Based on papers delivered at a conference held at St. Edmund Hall, Oxford in January 1975.*

— Gilbert Islands.

GILBERT ISLANDS. Ministry of Education, Training and Culture. 1975. Review of educational development. [Tarawa], 1975. pp. 32.

— Hong Kong.

HONG KONG. Education Department. Triennial survey. trien., 1955/58- Hong Kong.

— India.

HUSAIN BILGRAMI, Saiyid, 'Imad al-Mulk Bahadur. Presidential address...26th annual session of the All-India Muhammadan Educational Conference,...Lucknow, December, 1912. 2nd ed. Delhi, [imprint, 1913?]. pp. 44.

INDIA. Central Advisory Board of Education. 1944. Post-war educational development in India; report. 3rd ed. Delhi, 1944. pp. 93.

INDIA. National Council of Educational Research and Training. 1962. Review of education in India, 1947-1961. New Delhi, 1962. pp. 192. *(India. Ministry of Education. Publications. No. 588)*

— Italy.

PARTITO NAZIONALE FASCISTA. Manuale di educazione fascista; introduzione di Domenico De Masi; commento ai testi di Romolo Runcini. Roma, 1977. pp. 287. *Contains reprints of Il primo libro del fascista, and Il secondo libro del fascista.*

— Jamaica — Statistics.

JAMAICA. Ministry of Education. Education statistics: an annual review of the education sector. a., 1975/76(2nd)- Kingston.

— Kenya.

KING (KENNETH JAMES) The African artisan: education and the informal sector in Kenya. London, 1977. pp. 226. *bibliog.*

— Pakistan — Statistics.

PAKISTAN. Central Bureau of Education. 1967. Educational statistics for Pakistan, 1947-1957. [Karachi], 1967. pp. 29. *(Educational Statistics Bulletin Series. 1967/2)*

— Papua New Guinea.

AUSTRALIA. Advisory Committee on Education in Papua and New Guinea. 1969. Report; [W.J. Weedon, chairman]. Canberra, 1969. pp. 89.

PAPUA NEW GUINEA. Department of Education. 1973. Proposed five year plan. [Konedobu], 1973. fo. 109.

PAPUA NEW GUINEA. Five Year Education Plan Committee. 1974. Report; [A. Tololo, chairman]. [Konedobu], 1974. fo. 91.

— Poland.

OZGA (WŁADYSŁAW) Organizacja szkolnictwa w Polsce. Warszawa, 1960. pp. 424.

— Russia.

PRICE (RONALD FRANCIS) Marx and education in Russia and China. London, [1977]. pp. 376. *bibliog.*

— Scandinavia.

UUSITALO (HANNU) Education and welfare: some findings from the Scandinavian survey. Helsinki, 1977. pp. 28. *bibliog. (Helsinki. Yliopisto. Research Group for Comparative Sociology. Research Reports. No. 15) Paper prepared for the European Seminar on Measuring the Economic and Social Effects of Educational Inequalities held in Sigriswil in 1976.*

— Sierra Leone.

JOURNAL OF EDUCATION; [pd. by] Ministry of Education, Sierra Leone. s-a., Ap 1966 (v.1, no.1)- Freetown. *Not pd. Oc 1971 (v.6, no.2).*

— South Africa.

AUERBACH (F.E.) Education, 1961-1971: a balance sheet. Johannesburg, 1972. pp. 11. *(South African Institute of Race Relations. Topical Talks. 27)*

— Spain.

AVILA (JUSTO DE) Metodologia del nacional-sindicalismo. Valencia, 1942. pp. 48.

LERENA ALESON (CARLOS) Escuela, ideologia y clases sociales en España: critica de la sociologia empirista de la educacion. Barcelona, [1976]. pp. 465.

— Swaziland.

SWAZILAND TEACHERS' JOURNAL; (issued half-yearly by the Swaziland Ministry of Education). s-a., D 1971 (no.62)- Mbabane.

— Underdeveloped areas.

See UNDERDEVELOPED AREAS — Education.

— United Kingdom.

SECULAR EDUCATION LEAGUE. Tracts 4, 6, 7, 8, 10, 15, 16, 18, 21, 22. [London, 1905?-17]. 10 pts.

REPORTS ON EDUCATION: issued by the Department of Education and Science [U.K.]. m. (approx.) Ag 1963 (no.2: revised Ap 1966)- , with gaps (nos. 3,4,6-8, 11-13, 15, 17, 20, 24). *Certain issues are revised from time to time.*

BILINGUALISM and British education: the dimensions of diversity; papers from a conference convened in January 1976. London, 1976. pp. 109. *bibliog. (Centre for Information on Language Teaching and Research. Reports and Papers. 14)*

U.K. Commission for Racial Equality. Education journal. bi-m., Ap/My 1978 (v.1, no. 1)- London.

HOPKINS (ADAM) The school debate. Harmondsworth, 1978. pp. 233.

TAPPER (TED) and SALTER (BRIAN) Education and the political order: changing patterns of class control. London, 1978. pp. 250.

— — Finance.

TEACHERS' ACTION COLLECTIVE. Education cuts and teacher unemployment: a strategic analysis. London, [1976]. pp. 15.

— — History.

JONES (DONALD K.) The making of the education system, 1851-81. London, 1977. pp. 88. *bibliog.*

EDUCATION, HIGHER

SILVER (HAROLD) Nothing but the present, or nothing but the past? [London, 1977]. pp. 20. *Inaugural lecture at Chelsea College, University of London on 17 May 1977.*

— — Statistics.

U.K. Department of Education and Science. Statistical bulletin. m., current issues only. London.

— — Ireland — Statistics.

IRELAND. Census, 1851. The census of Ireland for the year 1851. Part 3. Report on the status of disease; (with Part 4: report on ages and education). Dublin, 1854-55. 2 pts. (in 1 vol.)

IRELAND. Census, 1861. The census of Ireland for the year 1861. Part 2. Report and tables on ages and education. Dublin, 1863. 2 vols.

— — Ireland, Northern — Statistics.

NORTHERN IRELAND EDUCATION STATISTICS; [pd. by] Ministry of Education, Northern Ireland. irreg., Oc 1965 (no.1)- , with gap (no.9, 1970). Belfast.

IRELAND, NORTHERN. Census, 1971. Census of population, 1971: education tables. Belfast, 1975. pp. 78.

— United States — Finance.

GARMS (WALTER I.) and others. School finance: the economics and politics of public education. Englewood Cliffs, [1978]. pp. 466.

RISING costs in education: the federal response?; (a Round Table held on March 20, 1978...); John Charles Daly, moderator, etc. Washington, [1978]. pp. 44. *(American Enterprise Institute for Public Policy Research. Public Policy Forums. 17)*

EDUCATION, COMPARATIVE.

COMPARATIVE perspectives on the academic profession; edited by Philip G. Altbach. New York, 1977. pp. 214. *bibliogs.*

EDUCATION, COOPERATIVE

— United Kingdom.

TRADES UNION CONGRESS. Paid release for union training. [London, 1978]. pp. 23.

EDUCATION, ELEMENTARY

— Cameroun.

CAMEROUN. Ministère de l'Education Nationale. 1977. Recommandations relatives à la réforme de l'enseignement primaire. [Yaoundé?, 1977?]. pp. 90.

— United States.

ENTWISLE (DORIS ROBERTS) and HAYDUK (LESLIE ALEC) Too great expectations: the academic outlook of young children. Baltimore, [1978]. pp. 193. *bibliog.*

EDUCATION, HIGHER

— Canada — Ontario.

BUTTRICK (JOHN A.) Who goes to university from Toronto. Toronto, 1977. pp. 188. *bibliog. (Ontario. Economic Council. Working Papers. 1977. No. 1)*

— Israel.

RITTERBAND (PAUL) Education, employment, and migration: Israel in comparative perspective. Cambridge, 1978. pp. 144. *(American Sociological Association. Arnold and Caroline Rose Monograph Series in Sociology)*

— Norway.

NORWAY. Statistiske Centralbyrå. 1978. Utdanningsstatistikk: utdanningen til personer 16 år og over, 1. oktober 1975, etc. Oslo, 1978. pp. 76. *(Norges Offisielle Statistikk. Rekke A.935) In Norwegian and English.*

EDUCATION, HIGHER (Cont.)

— Pakistan — Statistics.

STATISTICS ON HIGHER EDUCATION IN PAKISTAN; [pd. by] University Grants Commission [Pakistan]. a., 1973/74(1st)- Islamabad.

— Papua New Guinea.

PAPUA NEW GUINEA. Committee of Inquiry into Higher Education in Papua New Guinea. 1971. Report; [Sir Allen Brown, chairman]. Canberra, 1971. pp. 98.

— Russia — Economic aspects.

DAINOVSKII (ANATOLII BOLESLAVOVICH) Ekonomika vysshego obrazovaniia: planirovanie, kadry, effektivnost'. Moskva, 1976. pp. 156. *bibliog.*

— — History.

SAFRAZ'IAN (NATALIIA LEONOVNA) Bor'ba KPSS za stroitel'stvo sovetskoi vysshei shkoly, 1921- 1927 gg. Moskva, 1977. pp. 159.

— Underdeveloped areas.

See UNDERDEVELOPED AREAS — Education (Higher).

— United Kingdom.

PEDLEY (ROBIN) Towards the comprehensive university. London, 1977. pp. 111.

— — Curricula.

GIFFEN (JANICE) and LOWRIE (MICK) Stuff the system. London, 1973. pp. 120. *bibliog.*

— United States.

GRANT (GERALD) and RIESMAN (DAVID) The perpetual dream: reform and experiment in the American college. Chicago, 1978. pp. 474. *bibliog.*

PUSEY (NATHAN MARSH) American higher education, 1945-1970: a personal report. Cambridge, Mass., 1978. pp. 204.

EDUCATION, HUMANISTIC.

SMALL comforts for hard times: humanists on public policy; Michael Mooney and Florian Stuber, editors. New York, 1977. pp. 402. *Papers from a conference series conducted under the auspices of Columbia's program of University Seminars.*

— United Kingdom.

KNIGHTS (BEN) The idea of the clerisy in the nineteenth century. Cambridge, [1978]. pp. 274. *bibliog.*

EDUCATION, PRESCHOOL.

DEASEY (DENISON) Education under six. London, [1978]. pp. 130.

— New Zealand.

NEW ZEALAND. Committee of Inquiry into Pre-School Education. 1972. Report; [C.G.N. Hill, chairman]. Wellington, 1971 [or rather 1972]. pp. 141.

EDUCATION, SECONDARY

— France.

NORVEZ (ALAIN) Le corps enseignant et l'évolution démographique: effectifs des enseignants du second degré et besoins futurs; préface d'Alain Girard. [Paris], 1977. pp. 206. *bibliog.(France. Institut National d'Etudes Démographiques. Travaux et Documents. Cahiers. No. 82)*

— Italy.

La RIFORMA della scuola secondaria superiore e della formazione professionale: proposte e documenti, 1970-1976; a cura di Giorgio Franchi. [Milano, 1976]. pp. 273.

— United Kingdom.

WHITE (ROGER) and BROCKINGTON (DAVID) In and out of school: the ROSLA community education project. London, 1978. pp. 200.

— — Curricula.

HOLT (MAURICE) The common curriculum: its structure and style in the comprehensive school. London, 1978. pp. 198. *bibliog.*

— — Scotland.

MACKENZIE (R.F.) State school. Harmondsworth, 1970. pp. 140.

EDUCATION, URBAN

— United States.

BULLOUGH (WILLIAM S.) Cities and schools in the gilded age: the evolution of an urban institution. Port Washington, 1974. pp. 183.

BOYD (JOHN) Community education and urban schools. London, 1977. pp. 82. *bibliog.*

EDUCATION AND STATE

— Africa, Subsaharan.

NIGERIA. Sessional Papers. 1924. No.1. Educational policy in British dependencies in tropical Africa. [Lagos], 1924. pp. 5.

NIGERIA. Sessional Papers. 1926. No.42. Advisory Committee on Native Education in Tropical Africa. [Lagos], 1926. pp. 2.

— Botswana.

BOTSWANA. 1977. National policy on education. [Gaborone], 1977. pp. 18. *(Government Papers. 1977. No.1)*

— Canada.

PRENTICE (ALISON) The school promoters: education and social class in mid-nineteenth century Upper Canada. Toronto, [1977]. pp. 192.

— — Ontario.

CAMERON (DAVID M.) The northern dilemma: public policy and post-secondary education in northern Ontario. [Toronto, 1978]. pp. 198. *(Ontario. Economic Council. Discussion Paper Series)*

— Guyana.

GUYANA. Ministry of Education. 1968. First parliament of Guyana under the constitution of Guyana, second session 1967-1968: memorandum by the Minister of Education on education policy. [Georgetown], 1968. pp. 13. *(Parliament. Sessional Papers. 1968. No. 1)*

— Pakistan.

PAKISTAN. Ministry of Education. 1965. Achievement in education, 1958-1964. [Karachi, 1965?]. pp. 59.

— Seychelles.

SEYCHELLES. Ministry of Education and Social Development. 1975. Guidelines for a fourth development plan, 1975-85. [Victoria, Mahé], 1975. pp. 12.

— United Kingdom.

BOYLE (EDWARD CHARLES GURNEY) Baron Boyle. Parliament's views on responsibility for education policy since 1944. Birmingham, [1976]. pp. 20. *(Birmingham. University. Institute of Local Government Studies. Alfred G. Mays Memorial Lectures. No. 1)*

KOGAN (MAURICE) The politics of educational change. [London], 1978. pp. 172. *bibliog.*

— United States.

FINN (CHESTER E.) Education and the presidency. Lexington, Mass., [1977]. pp. 167.

FISHEL (ANDREW) and POTTKER (JANICE) National politics and sex discrimination in education. Lexington, Mass., [1977]. pp. 159.

AARON (HENRY J.) Politics and the professors: the Great Society in perspective. Washington, D.C., [1978]. pp. 185. *(Brookings Institution. Studies in Social Economics)*

GOVERNMENT regulation of higher education; edited by Walter C. Hobbs. Cambridge, Mass., [1978]. pp. 117. *Revised versions of papers presented to a conference held in 1977 by the Department of Higher Education at the State University of New York at Buffalo.*

PUBLIC policy and private higher education; edited by David W. Breneman [and others] and with contributions by Robert O. Berdahl [and others]. Washington, D.C., [1978]. pp. 468. *(Brookings Institution. Studies in Higher Education Policy. 1) Based on a Brookings conference held in 1976.*

EDUCATION OF ADULTS.

COLES (EDWIN KEITH TOWNSEND) Adult education in developing countries. 2nd ed. Oxford, 1977. pp. 199. *bibliog.*

— Africa, Central.

COLES (EDWIN KEITH TOWNSEND) Adult education in developing countries. 2nd ed. Oxford, 1977. pp. 199. *bibliog.*

— Canada — British Columbia.

BRITISH COLUMBIA. Committee on Continuing and Community Education. 1976. Report; [Ronald Faris, chairman]. [Victoria], 1976. pp. 82.

— Colombia.

COLOMBIA. Ministerio de Educacion Nacional. 1972. La educacion de adultos en Colombia, 1961-1971. Bogota, 1972. pp. 142.

— Germany.

BOMMERT (WILFRIED) Bestimmungsgründe der Weiterbildungsbereitschaft von Landfrauen: Befunde einer repräsentativen Befragung, etc. Bonn, 1977. pp. 185. *bibliog. (Forschungsgesellschaft für Agrarpolitik und Agrarsoziologie. [Publications]. 245)*

— Kenya.

KENYA JOURNAL OF ADULT EDUCATION: official jl. of the Board of Adult Education [Kenya]. 3 a yr., D 1971 (v.0); 1972 (v.1)- [Nairobi].

— Norway.

NORWAY. Statistiske Centralbyrå. Utdanningsstatistikk: vaksenopplaering, etc. a., 1975/76- Oslo. *[in English and Norwegian] Supersedes NORWAY. Statistiske Centralbyrå. Utdanningsstatistikk: vaksenopplaering og folkeopplysning.*

— United Kingdom.

ADULT LITERACY RESOURCE AGENCY. Management Committee. Adult literacy: developments: report to the Secretary of State for Education and Science...on the...year's operation. a., 1976/77(2nd)- London.

HUTCHINSON (ENID) and HUTCHINSON (EDWARD MOSS) Learning later: fresh horizons in English adult education. London, 1978. pp. 200.

SCHULLER (TOM) Education through life. London, 1978. pp. 28. *(Young Fabian Group. Young Fabian Pamphlets. 47)*

EDUCATION OF PRISONERS.

STRATTA (ERICA WENDY) The educational experience of boys admitted to borstal 1965-1966: a study of their background in relation to their prospects for education as part of borstal training. 1968. fo. 318. *bibliog. Typescript. Ph.D. (London) thesis: unpublished. This thesis is the property of London University and may not be removed from the Library.*

— United States.

BLACKS and criminal justice; edited by Charles E. Owens [and] Jimmy Bell. Lexington, Mass., [1977]. pp. 151. bibliogs. Based on two conferences held in 1974 and 1975 by the University of Alabama, Department of Psychology, Center for Correctional Psychology.

EDUCATION OF WOMEN

— Germany.

BOMMERT (WILFRIED) Bestimmungsgründe der Weiterbildungsbereitschaft von Landfrauen: Befunde einer repräsentativen Befragung, etc. Bonn, 1977. pp. 185. bibliog. (Forschungsgesellschaft für Agrarpolitik und Agrarsoziologie. [Publications]. 245)

— New Zealand.

ROMANOVSKY (P.C.) The education and employment of women graduates in New Zealand: the application of statistical and mechanical models to social structure studies. Wellington, 1975. pp. 36. (Victoria University of Wellington. Industrial Relations Centre. Industrial Relations Research Monographs. No. 2)

— Peru.

STEIN (WILLIAM W.) Modernization and inequality in Vicos, Peru: an examination of the "ignorance of women". Buffalo, 1975. fo. 56. (New York State University. Council on International Studies. Special Studies. No. 73)

— United States.

CONABLE (CHARLOTTE WILLIAMS) Women at Cornell: the myth of equal education. Ithaca, N.Y., 1977. pp. 211. bibliog.

EDUCATIONAL ACCOUNTABILITY

— United Kingdom.

BACON (WILLIAM) Public accountability and the schooling system: a sociology of school board democracy. London, [1978]. pp. 236. bibliog.

— United States.

FARQUHAR (JOHN A.) Accountability, program budgeting, and the California educational information system: a discussion and a proposal. Santa Monica, 1971. pp. 28. (Rand Corporation. [Rand Reports]. 637)

EDUCATIONAL ANTHROPOLOGY.

HOLBROOK (DAVID) Education, nihilism and survival. London, 1977. pp. 170. bibliog.

EDUCATIONAL ASSISTANCE, BRITISH

— Germany.

The BRITISH in Germany: educational reconstruction after 1945; edited by Arthur Hearnden. London, 1978. pp. 335. Based on papers delivered at a conference held at St. Edmund Hall, Oxford in January 1975.

EDUCATIONAL ASSISTANCE, CANADIAN.

GERIN-LAJOIE (PAUL) Educational innovation: new perspectives for Canada in international development; notes for a speech...prepared for the Canadian Council for Research in Education, etc. [Ottawa], 1971. pp. 11,13. (Canadian International Development Agency. Thoughts on International Development. 3) In English and French.

EDUCATIONAL ASSISTANCE, NEW ZEALAND.

NEW ZEALAND. External Aid Division. 1968. Handbook for students and trainees under New Zealand government aid programmes. [Wellington, 1968]. pp. 55.

NEW ZEALAND. External Aid Division. 1970. Handbook for students and trainees under New Zealand government aid programmes. [rev. ed.] [Wellington, 1970]. pp. 63.

EDUCATIONAL ASSOCIATIONS

— Germany.

KUEPPERS (HEINRICH) Der Katholische Lehrerverband in der Übergangszeit von der Weimarer Republik zur Hitler-Diktatur: zugleich ein Beitrag zur Geschichte des Volksschullehrerstandes. Mainz, [1975]. pp. 201. bibliog. (Kommission für Zeitgeschichte. Veröffentlichungen. Reihe B: Forschungen. Band 18)

EDUCATIONAL EQUALIZATION.

EQUALITY and social policy; (edited by Walter Feinberg). Urbana, [1978]. pp. 188. Papers from a conference held at the University of Illinois in 1976, sponsored by the National Institute of Education (Division of Equity).

— United Kingdom.

GILES (RAYMOND H.) The West Indian experience in British schools: multi-racial education and social disadvantage in London. London, [1977]. pp. 170.

— United States.

PERSELL (CAROLINE HODGES) Education and inequality: a theoretical and empirical synthesis. New York, [1977]. pp. 244. bibliog.

EDUCATIONAL INNOVATIONS.

DALIN (PER) Limits to educational change. London, 1978. pp. 112. Written under the auspices of the International Movement Towards Educational Change.

— United Kingdom.

KOGAN (MAURICE) The politics of educational change. [London], 1978. pp. 172. bibliog.

EDUCATIONAL LAW AND LEGISLATION

— United Kingdom.

NATIONAL UNION OF CONSERVATIVE AND UNIONIST ASSOCIATIONS. [Leaflets. 1909]. No.738. The Unionist position in educational politics. rev. ed. London, 1909. pp. 24.

EDUCATIONAL PLANNING.

ECONOMICS and education policy: a reader; edited by Carolyn Baxter [and others], at the Open University. London, 1977. pp. 378. bibliogs.

DAVID (MIRIAM E.) Reform, reaction and resources: the 3Rs of educational planning. [Windsor, 1977]. pp. 243. bibliog.

— United States.

FARQUHAR (JOHN A.) Accountability, program budgeting, and the California educational information system: a discussion and a proposal. Santa Monica, 1971. pp. 28. (Rand Corporation. [Rand Reports]. 637)

EDUCATIONAL PSYCHOLOGY.

FREEMAN (JOAN) In and out of school: an introduction to applied psychology in education. London, 1975. pp. 144. bibliog.

COGNITIVE learning in children: theories and strategies; edited by Joel R. Levin [and] Vernon L. Allen. New York, 1976. pp. 297. bibliogs.

EDUCATIONAL RESEARCH

— Europe.

EUDISED R AND D BULLETIN; [pd. by] Documentation Centre for Education in Europe, Council of Europe. q., current issues only. Strasbourg.

EDUCATIONAL SOCIOLOGY.

HARBISON (FREDERICK HARRIS) The connection between education and income distribution. [Princeton], 1974. pp. 36, 27. (Princeton University and Brookings Institution. Project on Income Distribution in Less Developed Countries)

SPRING (JOEL) A primer of libertarian education. Montreal, [1975]. pp. 157. bibliog.

POWER and ideology in education; edited and with an introduction by Jerome Karabel and A.H. Halsey. New York, 1977. pp. 670. bibliogs.

ENTWISTLE (HAROLD) Class, culture and education. London, 1978. pp. 214. bibliog.

PARELIUS (ANN PARKER) and PARELIUS (ROBERT J.) The sociology of education. Englewood Cliffs, [1978]. pp. 407.

REID (IVAN) Sociological perspectives on school and education. London, 1978. pp. 287. bibliog.

EDUCATORS

— Italy — Biography.

KRAMER (RITA) Maria Montessori. Oxford, 1978. pp. 410.

EDWARD WOOD AND COMPANY.

CLARKSON (DEREK JOSHUA) and McKINLAY (KENNETH ALEXANDER) Edward Wood and Company Limited, Skibben Winton Construction Limited: investigations under section 165 of the Companies Act 1948. London, H.M.S.O., 1977. 1 vol. (various pagings).

EENHEIDSVAKCENTRALE.

COOMANS (PAUL) and others. De Eenheidsvakcentrale (EVC), 1943-1948. Groningen, 1976. pp. 507. bibliog.(Rijksuniversiteit te Utrecht. Instituut voor Geschiedenis. Historische Studies. 30)

EFFICIENCY, INDUSTRIAL.

PROBLEMY effektivnosti i nauchno-tekhnicheskogo progressa: materialy rabochego soveshchaniia, Sofiia, 22-27 sentiabria 1975 g. Sofiia, 1976. pp. 131.

INDUSTRIAL efficiency and the role of government; edited by Colette Bowe. London, H.M.S.O., 1977. pp. 282.

EGGS

— Prices — Canada.

CANADA. Food Prices Review Board. 1974. Report on egg prices II. [Ottawa, 1974]. pp. 54, 58. In English and French.

EGO (PSYCHOLOGY).

HAAN (NORMA) Coping and defending: processes of self-environment organization. New York, 1977. pp. 346. bibliog.

EGYPT

— Foreign relations — Romania.

BOTORAN (CONSTANTIN) Relaţiile româno-egiptene în epoca modernă şi contemporană. Bucureşti, 1974. pp. 302. bibliog.

— — United Kingdom.

MELLINI (PETER) Sir Eldon Gorst: the overshadowed proconsul. Stanford, [1977]. pp. 315. bibliog. (Stanford University. Hoover Institution on War, Revolution and Peace. Hoover Colonial Studies)

— History — 1956, Intervention.

GEORGES-PICOT (JACQUES) The real Suez crisis: the end of a great nineteenth century work; translated from the French by W. G. Rogers. New York, [1978]. pp. 200.

LLOYD (SELWYN) Baron Selwyn-Lloyd. Suez, 1956: a personal account. London, 1978. pp. 282.

— Politics and government.

AL-SAYYID (AFAF LUTFI) Egypt's liberal experiment: 1922-1936. Berkeley, Calif., [1977]. pp. 276. bibliog.

EGYPT(Cont.)

— Social conditions.

BADAWI (W.A. ZAKI) The reformers of Egypt. London, [1978]. pp. 160.

— Statistics.

EGYPT. Central Agency for Public Mobilisation and Statistics. A.R.E. Statistical indicators. a., 1952/1972(11th)- Cairo.

EHLERS (ADOLF).

ADAMIETZ (HORST) Freiheit und Bindung: Adolf Ehlers. Bremen, [1978]. pp. 208.

EIGHTEENTH CENTURY.

Les PREOCCUPATIONS économiques et sociales des philosophes, littérateurs et artistes au XVIIIe siècle: colloque, Bruxelles, 26 et 27 mai 1975. Bruxelles, 1976. pp. 273. *(Brussels. Université Libre. Groupe d'Etude du XVIIIe Siècle. Etudes sur le XVIIIe Siècle. 3)*

EILDERMANN (WILHELM).

EILDERMANN (WILHELM) Als Wanderredner der KPD unterwegs: Erinnerungen an die ersten Jahre der KPD, 1919-1920. Berlin, 1977. pp. 170.

EINAUDI (LUIGI).

AROMA (ANTONIO D') Luigi Einaudi: memorie di famiglia e di lavoro. [Rome, 1975]. pp. 451. *(Ente per gli Studi Monetari, Bancari e Finanziari Luigi Einaudi. Quaderni di Ricerche. N.16)*

COMMEMORAZIONE di Luigi Einaudi nel centenario della nascita, 1874-1974. Torino, 1975. pp. 160. *(Fondazione Luigi Einaudi. Studi. 19) Held under the auspices of the Accademia delle Scienze di Torino and the Fondazione Luigi Einaudi.*

EISENHOWER (DWIGHT DAVID) President of the United States.

KILLIAN (JAMES RHYNE) Sputnik, scientists, and Eisenhower: a memoir of the first special assistant to the President for science and technology. Cambridge, [1977]. pp. 315. *bibliog.*

KINNARD (DOUGLAS) President Eisenhower and strategy management: a study in defense politics. Lexington, Ky., [1977]. pp. 169. *bibliog.*

CAUTE (DAVID) The great fear: the anti-communist purge under Truman and Eisenhower. New York, [1978]. pp. 697. *bibliog.*

EL SADAT (ANWAR).

EL SADAT (ANWAR) In search of identity. London, 1978. pp. 360.

ELDER (GLADYS).

ELDER (GLADYS) The alienated: growing old today. London, 1977. pp. 143.

ELECTION LAW

— Canada — Manitoba.

MANITOBA. Law Reform Commission. 1977. Working paper on controverted elections legislation. Winnipeg, 1977. pp. 32.

— — Ontario.

ONTARIO. Legislative Assembly. Select Committee on Election Laws. 1969-71. The first, second, third and fourth reports; [Edward Dunlop, chairman]. [Toronto], 1969-71. 4 pts.

ONTARIO. Municipal Elections Committee. 1970. [Report; F.A. Braybrook, chairman]. [Toronto], 1970. pp. 44.

— Colombia.

COLOMBIA. Statutes, etc. 1916-63. Codigo de elecciones: ley 85 de 1916, otras disposiciones concordantes; dirigido y elaborado por Alvaro Jaramillo Bohorquez. [Bogota, 1966]. pp. 169.

— Germany.

HIRSCH (PAUL) and LINDEMANN (HUGO) Das kommunale Wahlrecht. Berlin, 1911. pp. 51. *(Sozialdemokratische Gemeindepolitik. Heft 1)*

LAMERS (KARL A.) Repräsentation und Integration der Ausländer in der Bundesrepublik Deutschland unter besonderer Berücksichtigung des Wahlrechts. Berlin, [1977]. pp. 164. *bibliog.*

— India.

INDIA. Statutes, etc. 1860-1977. Manual of election law...; a compilation of the statutory provisions governing elections to parliament and the state legislatures. 8th ed. [Delhi, 1977]. pp. 365.

ELECTIONS.

MANITOBA. Law Reform Commission. 1976. Working paper on electoral systems. Winnipeg, 1976. pp. 92. *bibliog.*

ELECTIONS without choice; edited by Guy Hermet [and others]. London, 1978. pp. 250. *(International Political Science Association and International Sociological Association. Committee on Political Sociology. Publications. 15)*

— Argentine Republic.

CODOVILLA (VICTORIO) Lo nuevo en la situacion nacional despues de las elecciones: informe presentado al pleno del Comite Central del Pàrtido Comunista, realizado los dias 27 y 28 de marzo de 1965. Buenos Aires, 1965. pp. 39.

— Brazil.

LEAL (VICTOR NUNES) Coronelismo, enxada e voto: o municipio e o regime representativo no Brasil. São Paulo, 1975. pp. 270. *bibliog. Reprint, with new preface, of first edition published in 1949.*

— Canada — Quebec.

BERNARD (ANDRE) Québec: elections 1976. Montreal, [1976]. pp. 174. *bibliog.*

— France.

GAGNEUR (WLADIMIR) L'empire et la candidature officielle. Paris, 1875. pp. 36.

DENQUIN (JEAN MARIE) Le renversement de la majorité électorale dans le département de la Corrèze, 1958-1973. Paris, [1976]. pp. 90. *bibliog. (Paris. Université de Paris II. Travaux et Recherches. Série Science Politique. 6)*

— India.

INDIA. Election Commission. 1957. Results of bye-elections held between the 31st July, 1955 and the 31st October, 1956. Delhi, 1957. pp. 63.

INDIA. Election Commission. 1973. Report on the fifth general election to the House of the People in India, 1971. Vol 2. Statistical. [Delhi], 1973. pp. 598.

INDIA. Election Commission. 1976. Biennial elections brochure: an analysis: Council of States and Legislative Councils, 1966-1973. [Delhi, 1976]. pp. 381.

INDIA. Election Commission. 1976. Bye-elections brochure 1974: an analysis: House of the People and Legislative Assemblies, Council of States and Legislative Councils, 1-1-1974 to 31-12-1974. [Delhi, 1976]. pp. 140.

INDIA. Election Commission. 1976. Report on the general elections to the legislative assemblies in India, 1970-72. vol. 2, statistical...: statistical information relating to the general elections to the legislative assemblies of Kerala, 1970, Orissa, Tamil Nadu, West Bengal, 1971, and all states/union territories which went to poll in 1972 except Uttar Pradesh, Nagaland and Pondicherry. [Delhi], 1976. 5 pts. (in 4 vols).

INDIA. Election Commission. 1976. Report on the general elections to the legislative assemblies of Manipur, Nagaland, Orissa, Pondicherry and Uttar Pradesh in 1974, Gujarat in 1975 and the presidential and vice-presidential elections, 1974: narrative. [Delhi, 1976]. pp. 193.

INDIA. Election Commission. 1977. Bye-elections brochure 1975: an analysis: House of the People and Legislative Assemblies, Council of States and Legislative Councils, 1-1-1975 to 31-12-1975. [Delhi, 1977]. pp. 128. *In English and Hindi.*

— — Andhra Pradesh.

ANDHRA PRADESH. General Administration (Elections) Department. 1968. Report on the fourth general elections in Andhra Pradesh, 1967. [Hyderabad, 1968]. 2 vols.(in 1).

— Italy.

CANTALUPO (ROBERTO) Liberale a destra: a destra da liberale: lettera aperta. Roma, [1975]. pp. 215.

CATALANO (FRANCO) and BERNADINI (GIORGIO) L'Italia che cambia: voto e classi sociali. [Milano, 1975]. pp. 183.

— Korea.

KOREA (REPUBLIC). Ministry of Public Information. 1965. Question of Korean unification: why we insist on U.N.- supervised elections. [Seoul], 1965. pp. 7. *(Korean Information: Foreign Publicity Material Series. No. 5)*

— Malta.

MALTA. 1932. Il significato del trionfo nazionalista nelle ultime elezioni generali di Malta e Gozo, giugno 1932; presentato al Segretaria di Stato per le Colonie dalla delegazione Maltese recatasi a Londra nel luglio 1932, etc. [Valletta], 1932. pp. 95.

— Pakistan.

PAKISTAN. 1978. White Paper on the conduct of general elections in March 1977 (with Summary). Rawalpindi, 1978. 2 vols.(in 1)

— Trinidad and Tobago.

TRINIDAD AND TOBAGO. Elections Commission. 1972. Report on the local government elections, 1971. [Port of Spain], 1972. pp. 83.

TRINIDAD AND TOBAGO. Elections and Boundaries Commission. 1977. Report on the local government elections, 1977. [Port of Spain], 1977. pp. 174.

— United Kingdom.

ALDERMAN (GEOFFREY) British elections: myth and reality. London, [1978]. pp. 236. *bibliog.*

PUGH (MARTIN) Electoral reform in war and peace, 1906-18. London, 1978. pp. 228. *bibliog.*

— — Commonwealth — Bibliography.

BLOOMFIELD (VALERIE) compiler. Commonwealth elections, 1945-1970: a bibliography. London, 1976. pp. 306.

— United States.

DINKIN (ROBERT J.) Voting in provincial America: a study of elections in thirteen colonies, 1689-1776. Westport, Conn., 1977. pp. 284. *bibliog.*

The IMPACT of the electoral process; edited by Louis Maisel and Joseph Cooper. Beverly Hills, [1977]. pp. 302. *bibliogs.*

SEAGULL (LOUIS M.) Youth and change in American politics. New York, 1977. pp. 160. *bibliog.*

SMOLKA (RICHARD G.) Election day registration: the Minnesota and Wisconsin experience in 1976. Washington, D.C., [1977]. pp. 69. *(American Enterprise Institute for Public Policy Research. AEI Studies. 164)*

The HISTORY of American electoral behavior; edited by Joel H. Silbey [and others]. Princeton, [1978]. pp. 384. *(Mathematical Social Science Board. History Advisory Committee. Quantitative Studies in History). Based on a conference sponsored by the Committee at Cornell University in 1973.*

— — **Campaign funds.**

REGULATION of political campaigns: how successful; (a Round Table held on November 15, 1976 and sponsored by the Center for the Study of Government Regulation of the American Enterprise Institute for Public Policy Research [in] Washington); Lawrence Spivak, moderator, etc. Washington, [1977]. pp. 60. *(American Enterprise Institute for Public Policy Research. Round Tables)*

ELECTRIC INDUSTRIES.

BRUSEKER (U.) Unilever, Meneba, Philips en de olieconcerns als inflatiemakers; een bestrijding van de looninflatie-theorie. [Amsterdam], 1974. pp. 133. *bibliog.*

— **Netherlands.**

PHILIPS (FREDERIK) 45 years with Philips: an industrialist's life. Poole, 1978. pp. 280.

ELECTRIC MACHINERY INDUSTRY

— **France.**

FRANCE. Groupe sectoriel d'Analyse et de Prévision Biens d'Equipement Mécaniques et Electriques. 1976. Rapport...: préparation du 7e Plan. Paris, [1976]. pp. 72.

— **India.**

INDIA. Central Electricity Authority. 1968. Fifth annual electric power survey of India. Delhi, 1968. pp. 66.

ELECTRIC POWER-PLANTS

— **Costs.**

MILLER (SAUNDERS) The economics of nuclear and coal power. New York, 1976. pp. 150. *bibliog.*

— **Environmental aspects — United States.**

SCHLOTTMAN (ALAN M.) Environmental regulation and the allocation of coal: a regional analysis. New York, 1977. pp. 143. *bibliog.*

ELECTRIC POWER PRODUCTION.

ATOMIC ENERGY RESEARCH ESTABLISHMENT [U.K.]. Energy Technology Support Unit. The prospects for the generation of electricity from wind energy in the United Kingdom; a report prepared for the Department of Energy by J. Allen and R.A. Bird. London, 1977. pp. 67. *bibliog. (U.K. Department of Energy. Energy Papers. No. 21)*

ELECTRICITY SUPPLY.

PATTERSON (WALTER C.) The fissile society. London, 1977. pp. 117. *bibliog. Report prepared by the Energy Policy Unit of Earth Resources Research.*

— **Costs.**

UNITED NATIONS. Department of Economic and Social Affairs. Resources and Transport Division. 1972. Electricity costs and tariffs: a general study. (ST/ECA/156). New York, 1972. pp. 230.

— **Rates.**

UNITED NATIONS. Department of Economic and Social Affairs. Resources and Transport Division. 1972. Electricity costs and tariffs: a general study. (ST/ECA/156). New York, 1972. pp. 230.

— **Belgium.**

BELGIUM. Service Energie Electrique. Statistiques electricité: répertoire des centrales. a., 1957- Bruxelles.

— **Canada.**

CANADA. Statistics Canada. Consumption of purchased fuel and electricity by the manufacturing, mining and electric power industries. a., 1975(1st)- Ottawa. *[in English and French]*

— **European Economic Community countries.**

EUROPEAN COMMUNITIES. Statistical Office. Electrical energy: monthly bulletin. m., S 1977(no.9)- Luxembourg. *[in Community languages]. Supersedes in part EUROPEAN COMMUNITIES. Statistical Office. Quarterly bulletin of energy statistics.*

— **India.**

INDIA. Central Electricity Authority. 1968. Fifth annual electric power survey of India. Delhi, 1968. pp. 66.

— **Russia — Kazakhstan.**

ROMANOV (IURII IVANOVICH) Osushchestvlenie leninskikh idei elektrifikatsii v Kazakhstane. Alma-Ata, 1977. pp. 299.

— **United Kingdom — Mathematical models.**

RUFFELL (R.J.) An econometric analysis of the household demand for electricity in Great Britain. Edinburgh, 1977. pp. 157. *bibliog.*

ELECTRONIC APPARATUS AND APPLIANCES.

FRANCE. Groupe sectoriel d'Analyse et de Prévision Biens d'Equipement Electronique, Informatique et Télécommunications. 1976. Rapport...: préparation du 7e Plan. Paris, [1976]. pp. 62.

FRANCE. Groupe sectoriel d'Analyse et de Prévision sur les Composants Electroniques. 1976. Rapport...: préparation du 7e Plan. Paris, [1976]. pp. 53.

ELECTRONIC DATA PROCESSING.

INTERNATIONAL FEDERATION FOR INFORMATION PROCESSING. Congress, Stockholm, 1974. Information processing 74; proceedings of IFIP Congress 74...; editor, Jack L. Rosenfeld. Amsterdam, 1974. pp. 1107. *bibliogs.*

NAUR (PETER) Concise survey of computer methods. Lund, 1974. pp. 397. *bibliog.*

BOHL (MARILYN) Information processing. 2nd ed. Chicago, [1976]. pp. 438.

INTERNATIONAL COMPUTING SYMPOSIUM, 5TH, LIEGE, 1977. International computing symposium 1977; proceedings of the... symposium...organized by the European Chapters of the Association for Computing Machinery...; edited by E. Morlet and D. Ribbens. Amsterdam, 1977. pp. 613. *bibliogs.*

INTERNATIONAL FEDERATION FOR INFORMATION PROCESSING. Congress, Toronto, 1977. Information processing 77; proceedings of IFIP Congress 77...; edited by Bruce Gilchrist. Amsterdam, 1977. pp. 1004. *bibliogs.*

SOUTH EAST ASIA REGIONAL COMPUTER CONFERENCE, 1ST, SINGAPORE, 1976. Searcc 76; proceedings of the...conference...; edited by M. Joseph and F.C. Kohli. Amsterdam, 1977. pp. 781. *bibliogs.*

See also subdivision Data processing under subjects.

ELECTRONIC DATA PROCESSING PERSONNEL

— **United Kingdom.**

PACE (DAVID E.) and HUNTER (JOHN) of the Civil Service Job Satisfaction Team. Direct participation in action: the new bureaucracy. Farnborough, Hants., [1978]. pp. 119. *bibliogs.*

ELECTRONIC DIGITAL COMPUTERS.

INTERNATIONAL FEDERATION FOR INFORMATION PROCESSING. Congress, Stockholm, 1974. Information processing 74; proceedings of IFIP Congress 74...; editor, Jack L. Rosenfeld. Amsterdam, 1974. pp. 1107. *bibliogs.*

BOHL (MARILYN) Information processing. 2nd ed. Chicago, [1976]. pp. 438.

INTERNATIONAL FEDERATION FOR INFORMATION PROCESSING. Congress, Toronto, 1977. Information processing 77; proceedings of IFIP Congress 77...; edited by Bruce Gilchrist. Amsterdam, 1977. pp. 1004. *bibliogs.*

— **Evaluation.**

SVOBODOVA (LIBA) Computer performance measurement and evaluation methods: analysis and applications. New York, [1976]. pp. 146. *bibliogs.*

INTERNATIONAL WORKSHOP ON MODELLING AND PERFORMANCE EVALUATION OF COMPUTER SYSTEMS, 2ND, STRESA, 1976. Modelling and performance evaluation of computer systems; proceedings of the...workshop organized by the Commission of the European Communities Joint Research Centre...; edited by H. Beilner and E. Gelenbe. Amsterdam, 1977. pp. 515. *bibliogs.*

INTERNATIONAL WORKSHOP ON MODELLING AND PERFORMANCE EVALUATION OF COMPUTER SYSTEMS, 3RD, BONN-BAD GODESBERG, 1977. Measuring, modelling and evaluating computer systems; proceedings of the...symposium...organised by...Gesellschaft für Mathematik und Datenverarbeitung mbH...; edited by H. Beilner and E. Gelenbe. Amsterdam, 1977. pp. 470. *bibliogs.*

KANGA (RUSTOM ADI) Economic evaluation of computer systems for developing countries. 1977. fo. 372,(73). *bibliog. Typescript. Ph.D. (London) thesis: unpublished. This thesis is the property of London University and may not be removed from the Library.*

FERRARI (DOMENICO) Computer systems performance evaluation. Englewood Cliffs, [1978]. pp. 554. *bibliog.*

— **Mathematical models.**

INTERNATIONAL WORKSHOP ON MODELLING AND PERFORMANCE EVALUATION OF COMPUTER SYSTEMS, 2ND, STRESA, 1976. Modelling and performance evaluation of computer systems; proceedings of the...workshop organized by the Commission of the European Communities Joint Research Centre...; edited by H. Beilner and E. Gelenbe. Amsterdam, 1977. pp. 515. *bibliogs.*

INTERNATIONAL WORKSHOP ON MODELLING AND PERFORMANCE EVALUATION OF COMPUTER SYSTEMS, 3RD, BONN-BAD GODESBERG, 1977. Measuring, modelling and evaluating computer systems; proceedings of the...symposium...organised by...Gesellschaft für Mathematik und Datenverarbeitung mbH...; edited by H. Beilner and E. Gelenbe. Amsterdam, 1977. pp. 470. *bibliogs.*

ELECTRONIC INDUSTRIES.

BRAUN (ERNEST) and MACDONALD (STUART) Revolution in miniature: the history and impact of semi-conductor electronics. Cambridge, 1978. pp. 231.

— **France.**

FRANCE. Groupe sectoriel d'Analyse et de Prévision Biens d'Equipement Electronique, Informatique et Télécommunications. 1976. Rapport...: préparation du 7e Plan. Paris, [1976]. pp. 62.

FRANCE. Groupe sectoriel d'Analyse et de Prévision sur les Composants Electroniques. 1976. Rapport...: préparation du 7e Plan. Paris, [1976]. pp. 53.

— **United Kingdom.**

SCIBERRAS (EDMOND) Multinational electronics companies and national economic policies. Greenwich, Conn., [1977]. pp. 328. *bibliog.*

ELITE.

McCORD (WILLIAM MAXWELL) and McCORD (ARLINE F.) Power and equity: an introduction to social stratification. New York, 1977. pp. 316.

NAGLE (JOHN DAVID) System and succession: the social bases of political elite recruitment. Austin, [1977]. pp. 273. *bibliog.*

— America, Latin.

WALTON (JOHN) Elites and economic development: comparative studies on the political economy of Latin American cities. Austin, [1977]. pp. 257. *bibliog. (Texas University. Institute of Latin American Studies. Latin American Monographs. No. 41)*

— Europe.

EUROPEAN landed elites in the nineteenth century: [the James Schouler Lectures, 1974]; edited...by David Spring. Baltimore, [1977]. pp. 147. *bibliogs. (Johns Hopkins University. Department of History. Johns Hopkins Symposia in Comparative History)*

— France.

BIRNBAUM (PIERRE) Les sommets de l'État: essai sur l'élite du pouvoir en France. Paris, [1977]. pp. 188.

HUPPERT (GEORGE) Les bourgeois gentilshommes: an essay on the definition of elites in Renaissance France. Chicago, 1977. pp. 237.

— Germany.

BLEUEL (HANS PETER) Die Stützen der Gesellschaft: Unternehmer, Manager, Leitende, Akademiker: privilegiert durch Herkunft, Bildung und Einkommen? München, [1976]. pp. 200. *bibliog.*

HENKELS (WALTER) Neue Bonner Köpfe. 9th ed. Düsseldorf, 1978. pp. 368.

— India.

ROSENTHAL (DONALD B.) The expansive elite: district politics and state policy-making in India. Berkeley, Calif., [1977]. pp. 348.

— Peru.

BRAVO BRESANI (JORGE) Mito y realidad de la oligarquia peruana. Lima, 1966. pp. 51. *(Instituto de Estudios Peruanos. Mesas Redondas y Conferencias. No. 7)*

BONILLA MAYTA (HERACLIO) Guano y burguesia en el Peru. Lima, 1974. pp. 186. *bibliog. (Instituto de Estudios Peruanos. Peru Problema. 11)*

— United Kingdom.

ROSENTHAL (JOEL THOMAS) The training of an elite group: English bishops in the fifteenth century. Philadelphia, 1970. pp. 54. *bibliog. (American Philosophical Society. Transactions. New Series. vol. 60, part 5)*

ELIZABETH I, Queen of England.

JENKINS (ELIZABETH) Elizabeth the Great. London, 1958. pp. 336. *bibliog.*

ELLIS (HENRY HAVELOCK).

ROWBOTHAM (SHEILA) and WEEKS (JEFFREY) Socialism and the new life: the personal and sexual politics of Edward Carpenter and Havelock Ellis. London, 1977. pp. 198. *bibliog.*

EMBARGO.

The ARAB oil weapon; [compiled] by Jordan J. Paust [and] Albert P. Blaustein, with Adele Higgins. New York, 1977. pp. 370.

EMERGENCY COMMUNICATION SYSTEMS

— New Zealand.

NEW ZEALAND. Civil Defence Communications Planning Committee. 1966. Broad plan. [Wellington, 1966]. fo. 11. *(Communications Reports. No. 1)*

NEW ZEALAND. Civil Defence Communications Planning Committee. 1966. Communications for national and regional civil defence headquarters. [Wellington, 1966]. fo. 11. *(Communications Reports. No. 2)*

EMERGENCY MEDICAL SERVICES.

INTERNATIONAL CONFERENCE ON REMOTE EMERGENCY MEDICAL SERVICES, TEXAS TECH UNIVERSITY, 1975. Emergency medical care; edited by William M. Portnoy. Lexington, Mass., [1977]. pp. 193. *Proceedings of the conference organised by the Department of Electrical Engineering of Texas Tech University.*

— Planning — New Zealand.

NEW ZEALAND. Ministry of Civil Defence. 1966. Civil defence: medical plan no. 1: natural disaster. [Wellington, 1966]. 1 pamphlet (various foliations). *bibliog.*

NEW ZEALAND. Ministry of Civil Defence. 1971. Civil defence: medical plan no. 1: civil defence or national emergency. [rev. ed.]. [Wellington, 1971]. pp. 23.

— United States.

INTERNATIONAL CONFERENCE ON REMOTE EMERGENCY MEDICAL SERVICES, TEXAS TECH UNIVERSITY, 1975. Emergency medical care; edited by William M. Portnoy. Lexington, Mass., [1977]. pp. 193. *Proceedings of the conference organised by the Department of Electrical Engineering of Texas Tech University.*

EMERGENCY TRANSPORTATION.

NEW ZEALAND. Ministry of Civil Defence. 1966. Civil defence: transport plan no. 1: broad plan. [Wellington, 1966]. fo. 14.

EMIGRANT REMITTANCES

— Turkey.

YASER (BETTY SLADE) Some thoughts on the impact of remittances from Turkish workers abroad. Ankara, 1974. fo. 17. *(United States. Agency for International Development. USAID-Ankara. Economic Analysis Staff. Discussion Papers. No. 19)*

EMIGRATION AND IMMIGRATION.

HYMAN (GEOFFREY M.) and GLEAVE (D.) A reasonable theory of migration. London, 1976. pp. 41. *bibliog. (Centre for Environmental Studies. Research Papers. 22)*

ADLER (STEPHEN) International migration and dependence. Farnborough, [1977]. pp. 235. *bibliog.*

— Mathematical models.

CROSS (JOHN G.) A stochastic learning model of migration. Ann Arbor, 1977. pp. 17. *bibliog. (Michigan University. Center for Research on Economic Development. Discussion Papers. No.65)*

EMIGRATION AND IMMIGRATION LAW

— Canada.

CANADIAN LABOUR CONGRESS. Submission...to the House of Commons Standing Committee on Labour, Manpower and Immigration on Bill C-27, Employment and Immigration Reorganization Act. Ottawa, 1977. fo. 23.

— United Kingdom.

AGEE-HOSENBALL DEFENCE COMMITTEE. Scrap the act: empire and immigration: a historical background to the 1971 Immigration Act. London, [1976]. pp. 16.

U.K. Central Office of Information. Reference Division. 1977. Immigration into Britain. rev. ed. London, 1977. pp. 15. *bibliog.*

EMINENT DOMAIN

— Canada — Saskatchewan.

SASKATCHEWAN. Legislative Assembly. Special Committee on Expropriation. 1964. Report; [E.C. Whelan, chairman]. Regina, 1964. pp. 32.

— United Kingdom.

DAVIES (KEITH) Barrister-at-Law. Law of compulsory purchase and compensation. 3rd ed. London, 1978. pp. 398.

— United States.

ACKERMAN (BRUCE A.) Private property and the constitution. New Haven, 1977. pp. 303.

EMPLOYEE OWNERSHIP

— United Kingdom.

CONFEDERATION OF BRITISH INDUSTRY. Financial participation in companies: an introductory booklet. London, 1978. pp. 36.

FABIAN SOCIETY. Fabian Tracts. [No.] 455. Industrial common ownership; [by] David Watkins. London, 1978. pp. 24.

HOE (SUSANNA) The man who gave his company away: a biography of Ernest Bader, founder of the Scott Bader Commonwealth. London, 1978. pp. 242. *bibliog.*

EMPLOYEE RIGHTS

— United Kingdom.

HEWITT (PATRICIA) Your rights at work: a practical guide. London, [1978]. pp. 84. *(National Council for Civil Liberties. Know Your Rights Series. No. 2)*

EMPLOYEES, DISMISSAL OF

— United Kingdom.

ANDERMAN (STEVEN D.) The law of unfair dismissal; with appendices on procedure by John M. Angel. London, 1978. pp. 378.

EMPLOYEES, RATING OF.

MANSIONI e qualifiche dei lavoratori: evoluzione e crisi dei criteri tradizionali: atti delle Giornate di Studio di Pisa, 26-27 maggio 1973. Milano, 1975. pp. 230. *(Associazione Italiana di Diritto del Lavoro e della Sicurezza Sociale. Annuario di Diritto del Lavoro. N.7)*

EMPLOYEES, RELOCATION OF

— Russia.

ASTRAKHAN (EVGENII IVANOVICH) Perevod na druguiu rabotu. Moskva, 1977. pp. 63.

EMPLOYEES, TRAINING OF.

STAMMERS (ROBERT) and PATRICK (JOHN) The psychology of training. London, 1975. pp. 144. *bibliog.*

— Canada — Nova Scotia.

NOVA SCOTIA. Department of Labour. Economics and Research Division. 1967. Cosmos Imperial Mills: a case study in labour force recruitment and training. [Halifax, 1967]. pp. 12.

— Ethiopia.

TRAINING OF MANPOWER IN ETHIOPIA, THE; (pd. by) Employment and Manpower Division. a., 1974/75(7th)- Addis Ababa.

— Pakistan.

PAKISTAN. Basic Democracies Wing. Planning and Evaluation Unit. 1970. Training for local councils. [Karachi, 1970]. pp. 54.

— **United Kingdom.**

FOOD, DRINK AND TOBACCO INDUSTRY TRAINING BOARD [U.K.]. The Board's views on Training for vital skills. Gloucester, 1976. pp. 2. *(FDT News. Special Issues. November 1976)*

VITAL SKILLS TASK GROUP [U.K.]. Training for skills: a programme for action; [R. O'Brien, chairman]. [London, Manpower Services Commission, 1977]. pp. 51.

SERVICE: news-letter of the Hotel and Catering Industry Training Board [U.K.]. irreg. Wembley. *Current issues only kept.*

TRAINING RESEARCH BULLETIN: [pd. by] Air Transport and Travel Industry Training Board. q. Staines. *Current issues only kept.*

EMPLOYEES' REPRESENTATION IN MANAGEMENT.

TRUEB (A.) and BAUR (PETER) Dokumentation zur Mitbestimmung. Zürich, [1974]. pp. 50.

INTERNATIONAL CONFEDERATION OF FREE TRADE UNIONS. World Congress, 11th, Mexico City, 1975. Industrial democracy. Brussels, [1976]. pp. 43.

ABRAHAMSSON (BENGT) Bureaucracy or participation: the logic of organization. Beverly Hills, [1977]. pp. 240. *bibliog. Translation of his Organisationsteori.*

HEBDEN (JOHN E.) and SHAW (GRAHAM H.) Pathways to participation. London, [1977]. pp. 267. *bibliog.*

MANAGEMENT control and organizational democracy; editors Bert King [and others]. Washington, D.C., 1978. pp. 288. *bibliogs. Papers presented at a conference held in Munich in 1976 by the Human Factors Division of the North Atlantic Treaty Organization.*

POOLE (MICHAEL) Workers' participation in industry. rev. ed. London, 1978. pp. 198. *bibliog.*

— **Chile.**

ESPINOSA (JUAN G.) and ZIMBALIST (ANDREW S.) Economic democracy: workers' participation in Chilean industry. New York, [1978]. pp. 211. *bibliog.*

— **Europe.**

The ECONOMICS of co-determination; edited by David F. Heathfield. London, 1977. pp. 154. *bibliogs. Papers from the eighth annual joint seminar of the universities of Frankfurt and Southampton, in September 1975, sponsored by the Anglo-German Foundation for the Study of Industrial Society.*

KOLVENBACH (WALTER) Workers participation in Europe. Kluwer, 1977. pp. 79.

WORKER self-management in industry: the West European experience; edited by G. David Garson. New York, 1977. pp. 230.

CRISPO (JOHN H.G.) Industrial democracy in western Europe: a North American perspective. Toronto, [1978]. pp. 181. *bibliog.*

— **Germany.**

BADURA (PETER) and others. Mitbestimmungsgesetz 1976 und Grundgesetz: Gemeinschaftsgutachten. München, 1977. pp. 298.

ENGINEERING EMPLOYERS' FEDERATION. Co-determination in Germany; report on a visit by the... Federation. [London, 1977]. pp. 24.

— **Netherlands.**

WERKGROEP VOOR EEN MAATSCHAPPIJ KRITISCHE VAKBEWEGING. Naar werkelijke zeggenschap. Den Haag, [1972]. pp. 20.

— **New Zealand.**

NEW ZEALAND. Department of Labour. 1976. Worker participation: a New Zealand approach. Wellington, 1976. pp. 12.

NEW ZEALAND. Department of Labour. Research and Planning Division. 1976. Worker participation: (a study of worker participation in 65 manufacturing firms). [Wellington], 1976. pp. 47.

— **Sweden.**

LANDSORGANISATIONEN I SVERIGE. Företagsdemokratiska Råd. Solidariskt medbestämmande: rapport till LO-kongressen 1976. Stockholm, [1976]. pp. 121.

MEIDNER (RUDOLF) Employee investment funds: an approach to collective capital formation,...with the assistance of Anna Hedborg and Gunnar Fond. London, 1978. pp. 132. *Report of a study commissioned by the Swedish Confederation of Trade Unions (Landsorganisationen i Sverige).*

— **United Kingdom.**

BRITISH AND IRISH COMMUNIST ORGANISATION. Policy Statements. No. 6. Workers' control in Britain. Belfast, 1974. pp. 29.

AIMS FOR FREEDOM AND ENTERPRISE. Submission...to the committee of enquiry into employees' participation in major decisions affecting the future of their companies through representation at board level. London, 1976. fo. 4.

BRITISH AND IRISH COMMUNIST ORGANISATION. Workers' control now: evidence to the Committee of Inquiry on Industrial Democracy. London, [1976]. pp. 15.

CONFEDERATION OF BRITISH INDUSTRY. The full text of CBI's evidence to the Bullock Committee of Enquiry into Industrial Democracy, March 1976. London, 1976. pp. 28.

GENERAL AND MUNICIPAL WORKERS UNION. Industrial democracy;...[a] policy statement. [London], 1976. pp. 10.

The GREAT debate: report of the conference on industrial democracy held 18-19 May 1976; [edited by] Elizabeth B. Sharp. London, 1976. pp. 24.

INSTITUTE OF PERSONNEL MANAGEMENT. Industrial democracy: evidence from the Institute of Personnel Management to the Committee of Inquiry. London, 1976. pp. 63.

SCOTTISH COUNCIL (DEVELOPMENT AND INDUSTRY). Committee on Industrial and Social Conditions. Towards industrial democracy: [a] code of practice: some practical guidelines on employee participation. Edinburgh, [1976]. pp. 12.

ABEL (STEPHEN) Industrial democracy. London, [1977]. pp. 14. *(Liberal Party. Towards a New Political Agenda. No. 3)*

COATES (KEN) and TOPHAM (ANTHONY) The shop steward's guide to the Bullock Report. Nottingham, 1977. pp. 127.

CONFEDERATION OF BRITISH INDUSTRY. In place of Bullock. London, 1977. pp. 39.

ELLIOTT (DAVID) The Lucas Aerospace workers' campaign. London, 1977. pp. 20. *(Young Fabian Group. Young Fabian Pamphlets. 46)*

INCOMES DATA SERVICES LTD. IDS Handbook Series. No. 8. The machinery of industrial democracy. London, 1977. pp. 66.

ELLIOTT (JOHN) Journalist. Conflict or cooperation?: the growth of industrial democracy. London, [1978]. pp. 306. *bibliog.*

PACE (DAVID E.) and HUNTER (JOHN) of the Civil Service Job Satisfaction Team. Direct participation in action: the new bureaucracy. Farnborough, Hants., [1978]. pp. 119. *bibliogs.*

RADICE (GILES) The industrial democrats: trade unions in an uncertain world. London, 1978. pp. 241.

The RIGHT to useful work: planning by the people; edited by Ken Coates. Nottingham, 1978. pp. 287.

— **Yugoslavia.**

CHITTLE (CHARLES R.) Industrialization and manufactured export expansion in a worker- managed economy: the Yugoslav experience. Tübingen, [1977]. pp. 168. *bibliog.* (Kiel. Universität. Institut für Weltwirtschaft. Kieler Studien. 145)

ŠANE (DUŠAN PETROVIĆ) Self-management in Yugoslavia. London, [1977]. pp. 163.

EMPLOYERS' ASSOCIATIONS

— **Germany.**

GERHARDT (MICHAEL) Das Koalitionsgesetz: verfassungsrechtliche Überlegungen zur Neuregelung des Rechts der Gewerkschaften und der Arbeitgeberverbände. Berlin, [1977]. pp. 328. *bibliog.*

— **Italy.**

AMMASSARI (GLORIA PIRZIO) La politica della Confindustria: strategia economica e prassi contrattuale del padronato italiano. Napoli, 1976. pp. 354.

— **United Kingdom.**

U.K. Certification Office for Trade Unions and Employers' Associations. Annual report of the Certification Officer. a., 1976(1st)- London.

— — **Ireland, Northern — Directories.**

IRELAND, NORTHERN. Ministry of Health and Social Services. Industrial Relations Division. 1973. Directory of principal organisations of employers and workpeople in Northern Ireland. 17th ed. Belfast, 1973. pp. 39.

IRELAND, NORTHERN. Department of Manpower Services. Industrial Relations Division. 1975. Directory of principal organisations of employers and workpeople in Northern Ireland. 18th ed. Belfast, 1975. pp. 39.

EMPLOYMENT (ECONOMIC THEORY)

— **Mathematical models.**

HUTTON (JOHN P.) and others. Employment in manufacturing industry in a vintage capital model. London, Treasury, 1978. pp. 15,(2). *bibliog.* (Government Economic Service Working Papers. No. 10)

EMPLOYMENT FORECASTING

— **Ireland (Republic).**

NATIONAL ECONOMIC AND SOCIAL COUNCIL [EIRE]. Population and employment projections 1986: a reassessment. Dublin, Stationery Office, [1977]. pp. 87. *([Reports]. No. 35)*

— **New Zealand.**

NEW ZEALAND. Department of Labour. Research and Planning Division. 1977. Towards forecasting manpower requirements. Wellington, 1977. pp. 90.

— **United Kingdom.**

WEST MIDLANDS JOINT MONITORING STEERING GROUP. A developing strategy for the West Midlands: projection of labour supply and demand levels in the West Midlands at 1981. [Birmingham], 1976. pp. 8. *(Technical Reports)*

EMPLOYMENT MANAGEMENT.

See PERSONNEL MANAGEMENT.

ENCOMIENDAS (LATIN AMERICA).

GONGORA (MARIO) Encomenderos y estancieros: estudios acerca de la Constitucion social aristocratica de Chile despues de la Conquista, 1580-1660. Santiago de Chile, 1970. pp. 244. *bibliog.*

ENDOWMENTS.

ENDOWMENTS.

OCHKOV (MIKHAIL SERGEEVICH) and others. "Filantropicheskie" fondy - vazhnoe ideologicheskoe oruzhie imperializma. Moskva, 1976. pp. 103. *(Akademiia Nauk SSSR. Institut Afriki. Nauchnyi Sovet po Problemam Zarubezhnykh Ideologicheskikh Techenii. Ideologicheskaia Bor'ba v Sovremennom Mire)*

ENERGY

— United States.

CUNNINGHAM (WILLIAM HUGHES) and LOPREATO (SALLY COOK) Energy use and conservation incentives: a study of the Southwestern United States. New York, 1977. pp. 189. *bibliogs.*

ENERGY CONSERVATION.

LOVINS (AMORY BLOCH) Soft energy paths: towards a durable peace. Harmondsworth, 1977. pp. 231.

— Law and legislation — United States.

TETHER (IVAN J.) Government procurement and operations. Cambridge, Mass., [1977]. pp. 196. *A product of the Energy Conservation Project of the Environmental Law Institute.*

— Netherlands.

BEZ (KHAGESWAR) Demand for energy for transportation in the Netherlands. [Rotterdam, 1978]. pp. 93. *bibliog. Proefschrift (doctor) - Erasmus Universiteit Rotterdam. With summary in Dutch.*

— United Kingdom.

U.K. Department of Energy. Information Division. Energy management. m., current issues only. London.

ADVISORY COUNCIL ON ENERGY CONSERVATION [U.K.]. Freight transport: short and medium term considerations. London, H.M.S.O., 1977. pp. 22. *(Papers. 6)*

ENERGY CONSUMPTION.

WORKSHOP ON ALTERNATIVE ENERGY STRATEGIES. Energy demand studies: major consuming countries: analyses of 1972 demand and projections of 1985 demand; first technical report of the Workshop...; Paul S. Basile, editor. Cambridge, Mass., [1976]. pp. 553.

— United Kingdom.

U.K. Department of Energy. Economics and Statistics Division. 1977. Short term energy forecasts, 1977-8. [London, 1977]. pp. 3. *(Energy Commission [U.K.]. Papers. No. 3)*

— United States.

CUNNINGHAM (WILLIAM HUGHES) and LOPREATO (SALLY COOK) Energy use and conservation incentives: a study of the Southwestern United States. New York, 1977. pp. 189. *bibliogs.*

ENERGY POLICY.

CRISI dell'energia e crisi di miopia; a cura di Bruno de Finetti. [Milano, 1975]. pp. 254. *bibliogs. Convegno CIME di Economia Matematica, Urbino, 1974.*

DORAN (CHARLES F.) Myth, oil, and politics: introduction to the political economy of petroleum. New York, [1977]. pp. 226.

The ENERGY syndrome: comparing national responses to the energy crisis; edited by Leon N. Lindberg. Lexington, Mass., [1977]. pp. 383.

INTERNATIONAL studies of the demand for energy: selected papers presented at a conference in the International Institute for Applied Systems Analysis, 2361 Laxenburg, Austria. Amsterdam, 1977. pp. 340.

PATTERSON (WALTER C.) The fissile society. London, 1977. pp. 117. *bibliog. Report prepared by the Energy Policy Unit of Earth Resources Research.*

The SUSTAINABLE society: implications for limited growth; edited by Dennis Clark Pirages. New York, 1977. pp. 338. *bibliogs.*

ALTERNATIVES for growth: the engineering and economics of natural resources development: a conference of the National Bureau of Economic Research; edited by Harvey J. McMains and Lyle Wilcox. Cambridge, Mass., 1978. pp. 251. *Proceedings of the Charles Carter Newman Symposium on Natural Resources Engineering.*

CARR (DONALD EATON) Energy and the earth machine. London, 1978. pp. 430. *bibliog.*

— Bibliography.

BOLWIG (NIELS GEERT) and THOMSEN (ERIC STØTTRUP) compilers. The economics of raw materials, natural resources, energy, and related topics: a bibliography. Aarhus, [1977]. pp. 282. *(Aarhus. Universitet. Økonomiske Institut. Memos. 1977. 5)*

— Environmental aspects.

The ENERGY crisis and the environment: an international perspective; edited by Donald R. Kelley. New York, 1977. pp. 245.

— Social aspects — United States.

PROSPECTS for growth: changing expectations for the future; edited by Kenneth D. Wilson. New York, 1977. pp. 343.

ENERGY policy in the United States: social and behavioral dimensions; edited by Seymour Warkov. New York, 1978. pp. 235. *bibliogs. Based on a conference of the Energy Institute and the College of Social Sciences, University of Houston, held in 1977.*

— Canada — British Columbia.

BRITISH COLUMBIA. Energy Commission. 1976. British Columbia's energy outlook, 1976-1991. [Vancouver], 1976. 2 vols. (in 1).

— China.

SMIL (VACLAV) China's energy: achievements, problems, prospects. New York, 1976. pp. 246.

— Europe.

EURO-Arab cooperation; edited by Edmond Völker. Leyden, 1976. pp. 228. *Papers from a colloquium organized by the University of Amsterdam Europa Instituut in October 1975.*

ROBINSON (COLIN) and MORGAN (JON) North Sea oil in the future: economic analysis and government policy. London, 1978. pp. 216. *Written under the auspices of the Trade Policy Research Centre.*

— European Economic Community countries.

EUROPEAN COMMUNITIES. Commission. Periodical report on the Community action programme for the rational use of energy...and recommendations of the Council. irreg., 1975(1st)- Brussels.

U.K. Department of Energy. 1977. United Kingdom and Community energy policy: (a record of the UK presidency of the Energy Council, January-June 1977). [London, 1977]. pp. 31.

— France.

BOURGEOIS (BERNARD) Prix et coûts de l'énergie. Paris, 1976. pp. 184. *(Centre National de la Recherche Scientifique. Énergie et Société)*

— Germany.

MEYER-RENSCHHAUSEN (MARTIN) Energiepolitik in der BRD von 1950 bis heute: Analyse und Kritik. Köln, [1977]. pp. 165. *bibliog.*

— Ireland (Republic) — Mathematical models.

HENRY (EDMUND WILLIAM) and SCOTT (S.) A national model of fuel allocation: a prototype. Dublin, 1977. pp. 67. *bibliog. (Economic and Social Research Institute. Papers. No. 90)*

— Italy.

I PROBLEMI dell'energia in Italia; di Luciano Barca [and others]. [Milano, 1977]. pp. 311. *(Centro Studi di Politica Economica. Collana. Sezione 2: Industria Pubblica e Privata. 3) Proceedings of a seminar.*

— Underdeveloped areas.

See UNDERDEVELOPED AREAS — Energy policy.

— United Kingdom.

COOK (PAULINE LESLEY) and SURREY (A.J.) Energy policy: strategies for uncertainty. London, [1977]. pp. 240. *bibliog.*

ENERGY COMMISSION [U.K.]. Working document on energy policy for the Energy Commission. [London, 1977]. pp. 89. *(Papers. No. 1)*

FORMAN (NIGEL) Towards a more conservative energy policy. London, 1977. pp. 80. *bibliog. (Conservative Political Centre. [Publications]. No. 615)*

TRADES UNION CONGRESS. T.U.C. statements for the Energy Commission. [London, 1977]. pp. 5,(2). *(Energy Commission [U.K.]. Papers. No. 4)*

U.K. Department of Energy. 1977. United Kingdom and Community energy policy: (a record of the UK presidency of the Energy Council, January-June 1977). [London, 1977]. pp. 31.

U.K. Working Group on Energy Strategy. 1977. Report; [T.P. Jones, chairman]. [London], 1977. pp. 7, fo. 3. *(Energy Commission [U.K.]. Papers. No. 2)*

— United States.

HOLLOMON (JOHN HERBERT) and GRENON (MICHEL) Energy research and development. Cambridge, Mass., 1975. pp. 264. *bibliogs. A report to the Energy Policy Project of the Ford Foundation.*

COMMITTEE FOR ECONOMIC DEVELOPMENT. Research and Policy Committee. Nuclear energy and national security. New York, 1976. pp. 80.

LAIRD (MELVIN R.) Energy: a crisis in public policy. Washington, [1977]. pp. 21. *(American Enterprise Institute for Public Policy Research. AEI Studies. 157)*

PERLMAN (ROBERT) and WARREN (ROLAND LESLIE) Families in the energy crisis: impacts and implications for theory and policy. Cambridge, Mass., [1977]. pp. 236.

U.S. energy policy: which direction?; (an [AEI] Round Table held on June 27, 1977...[in] Washington); John Charles Daly, moderator, etc. Washington, [1977]. pp. 45. *(American Enterprise Institute for Public Policy Research. Round Tables)*

CONANT (MELVIN A.) and GOLD (FERN RACINE) The geopolitics of energy. Boulder, 1978. pp. 224.

MEADOR (ROY) Future energy alternatives: long-range energy prospects for America and the world. Ann Arbor, [1978]. pp. 197. *bibliogs.*

ENGEL (CORNELIS J.M.)

EUROPEAN COURT OF HUMAN RIGHTS. Publications. Series A: Judgments and Decisions. [A22]. ...Case of Engel and others. 1. Decision of 1 October 1975. 2. Judgment of 8 June 1976. 3. Judgment of 23 November 1976. Strasbourg, Council of Europe, 1977. pp. 71 [bis]. *In English and French.*

EUROPEAN COURT OF HUMAN RIGHTS. Publications. Series B: Pleadings, Oral Arguments and Documents [B20]. Case of Engel and others. (1974-1976). Strasbourg, Council of Europe, 1977. pp. 306 [bis], 307-382.

ENGELS (FRIEDRICH).

FRIEDRICH Engels: sein Leben und Wirken; (Autorenkollektiv: L.F. Iljitschow [and others; translated from the Russian by] N. Letnewa [and others]). Moskau, 1973 repr. 1975. pp. 624.

BERGER (MARTIN) 1942- . Engels, armies, and revolution: the revolutionary tactics of classical marxism. Hamden, Conn., 1977. pp. 239. *bibliog.*

McLELLAN (DAVID) of the University of Kent. Engels. Glasgow, 1977. pp. 79.

MARX and Engels on ecology; edited and compiled by Howard L. Parsons. Westport, Conn., [1977]. pp. 262. *bibliog.*

100 Jahre "Anti-Dühring": Marxismus, Weltanschauung, Wissenschaft; herausgegeben von R.Kirchhoff und T.I. Oiserman. Berlin, 1978. pp. 429. *(Akademie der Wissenschaften der DDR. Zentralinstitut für Philosophie. Schriften zur Philosophie und ihrer Geschichte. 17)*

— Bibliography.

PRIZHIZNENNYE izdaniia i publikatsii proizvedenii K. Marksa i F. Engel'sa: bibliograficheskii ukazatel'. Moskva, 1977. 2 vols.

ENGINEERING

— India.

THOMAS (PARAKUNNEL JOSEPH) Report on metallurgical and engineering industries, recent developments. Delhi, Department of Supply, [1944]. pp. 90.

— New Zealand.

NEW ZEALAND. Commission of Inquiry into the Heavy Engineering Industry. 1977. Report; [R.K. Davison, chairman]. [Wellington], 1977. pp. 170.

— United Kingdom.

EASTWOOD (GERRY) Skilled labour shortages in the United Kingdom with particular reference to the engineering industry. [Washington, D.C.], 1976. pp. 37. *(British-North American Committee. Publications. 18)*

ENGINEERS

— United Kingdom.

HOWIE (WILL) B.Sc., C. Eng., M.I.C.E. Trade unions and the professional engineer. London, 1977. pp. 76.

WABE (J. STUART) Manpower changes in the engineering industry. Watford, Engineering Industry Training Board, [1977]. pp. 141. *bibliog. (R[esearch] R[eports]. No. 5)*

ENGLAND IN LITERATURE.

COLMER (JOHN) Coleridge to Catch-22: images of society. [London, 1978]. pp. 240.

ENGLISH FICTION.

FERNANDO (LLOYD) "New women" in the late Victorian novel. University Park, Pa., [1977]. pp. 168.

COLMER (JOHN) Coleridge to Catch-22: images of society. [London, 1978]. pp. 240.

— History and criticism.

AUERBACH (NINA) Communities of women: an idea in fiction. Cambridge, Mass., 1978. pp. 222.

ENGLISH LANGUAGE

— Dictionaries — French.

COVENEY (JAMES) and MOORE (SHEILA J.) Glossary of French and English management terms: Lexique de termes anglais français de gestion. London, 1972. pp. 146.

— — Polyglot.

ORNE (JERROLD) The language of the foreign book trade: abbreviations, terms, phrases. 3rd ed. Chicago, 1976. pp. 333.

HEBÁK (PETR) and HUSTOPECKÝ (JIŘÍ) compilers. Šestijazyčný slovník termínů z regresní analýzy: [Czech, Russian, Polish, English, French, German]. Praha, 1978. pp. 211. *With preface and explanatory notes in each language.*

— — Russian.

MOSOLOVA (N.I.) compiler. Kratkii anglo-russkii slovar' ekonomicheskikh slov i vyrazhenii. Dushanbe, 1971. pp. 63.

— History.

SOCIOLINGUISTIC patterns in British English; edited by Peter Trudgill. London, 1978. pp. 186. *bibliog.*

— Jargon.

HUDSON (KENNETH) The jargon of the professions. London, 1978. pp. 146. *bibliog.*

— Phonology.

ANDERSON (JOHN M.) and JONES (CHARLES) Phonological structure and the history of English. Amsterdam, 1977. pp. 189. *bibliog.*

— Semantics.

READINGS in language development; Lois Bloom, editor. New York, [1978]. pp. 506. *bibliogs.*

ENGLISH LITERATURE

— History and criticism.

GROSSBRITANNIEN und Deutschland: europäische Aspekte der politisch-kulturellen Beziehungen beider Länder in Geschichte und Gegenwart: (Festschrift für John W.P. Bourke, München; herausgegeben von Ortwin Kuhn, Berlin). München, [1974]. pp. 691. *bibliogs. In German or English.*

KNIGHTS (BEN) The idea of the clerisy in the nineteenth century. Cambridge, [1978]. pp. 274. *bibliog.*

POCOCK (DOUGLAS CHARLES DAVID) The novelist and the north. Durham, 1978. pp. 41. *bibliog. (Durham. University. Department of Geography. Occasional Publications (New Series). No. 12)*

ENGLISH NEWSPAPERS.

HILL (DOUGLAS) ed. Tribune 40: the first forty years of a socialist newspaper. London, 1977. pp. 214.

MURPHY (MICHAEL JOSEPH) Cambridge newpapers and opinion, 1780-1850. Cambridge, [1977]. pp. 144. *bibliog.*

— History — Bibliography.

MADDEN (LIONEL) and DIXON (DIANA) compilers. The nineteenth-century periodical press in Britain: a bibliography of modern studies, 1901-1971. New York, 1976. pp. 280.

ENGLISH PERIODICALS

— History — Bibliography.

MADDEN (LIONEL) and DIXON (DIANA) compilers. The nineteenth-century periodical press in Britain: a bibliography of modern studies, 1901-1971. New York, 1976. pp. 280.

ENLIGHTENMENT.

VENTURI (FRANCO) Settecento riformatore. [Torino, 1969-76]. 2 vols.

DONAKOWSKI (CONRAD L.) A muse for the masses: ritual and music in an age of democratic revolution, 1770-1870. Chicago, 1977. pp. 435. *bibliog.*

ENTREPRENEUR.

ARE (GIUSEPPE) Industria e politica in Italia. Roma, 1975. pp. 211. *bibliog.*

PROVASI (GIANCARLO) Borghesia industriale e Democrazia Cristiana: sviluppo economico e mediazione politica dalla Ricostruzione agli anni '70. Bari, [1976]. pp. 308. *bibliog.*

ENVIRONMENTAL IMPACT ANALYSIS.

FRANKEL (MAURICE) The Social Audit pollution handbook: how to assess environmental and workplace pollution. London, 1978. pp. 210.

ENVIRONMENTAL LAW

— New Zealand.

NEW ZEALAND. Commission for the Environment. 1976. A guide to environmental law in New Zealand. Wellington, 1976. pp. 157.

ENVIRONMENTAL POLICY.

TECHNOLOGY AND THE ENVIRONMENT: reports from Scientific Counsellors; ([pd. by] Department of Industry) Overseas Technical Information Unit [U.K.]. q., N 1971 [1]- London.

ENVIRONMENTAL politics; edited by Stuart S. Nagel. New York, 1974. pp. 321.

FANFANI (AMINTORE) Strategia della sopravvivenza: proposte degli anni 1970-1971. Roma, [1975]. pp. 53.

SOCIETÀ ITALIANA DEGLI ECONOMISTI. Riunione Scientifica, 14a, Roma, 1973. Economia ed ecologia: [proceedings]. Milano, 1975. pp. 354.

[SELF-education packet; edited by Cally Abdulrazak and others. Cambridge, Mass., 1975?]. Looseleaf. *bibliog. A collection of articles from various sources on the subject of food supply and environmental policy.*

VALUES of growth. Lexington, Mass., [1976]. pp. 161. *(Commission on Critical Choices for Americans. Critical Choices for Americans. vol. 6)*

BARDE (JEAN PHILIPPE) and GERELLI (EMILIO) Economie et politique de l'environnement. [Paris, 1977]. pp. 210.

CIGNO (ALESSANDRO) The debate on natural resources and the fate of humanity; or, Do we need economists? Hull, 1977. pp. 24. *bibliog. An inaugural lecture delivered at the University of Hull on 4 May 1976.*

MANAGING the commons; edited by Garrett Hardin and John Baden. San Francisco, [1977]. pp. 294.

PLANNING in turbulent environments; [edited by] John S. Western [and] Paul R. Wilson. St. Lucia, Queensland, 1977. pp. 206. *bibliogs.*

PUBLIC economics and the quality of life; edited by Lowdon Wingo and Alan Evans. Baltimore, [1977]. pp. 327. *bibliogs. Mainly papers evolved from an International Research Conference on Public Policy and the Quality of Life in Cities, New Orleans, 1975, sponsored by Resources for the Future and the Centre for Environmental Studies.*

RESOURCE conservation: social and economic dimensions of recycling; edited by David W. Pearce and Ingo Walter. New York, 1977. pp. 383. *bibliogs. The outcome of an international symposium held at the Rockefeller Foundation's Study and Conference Center in Bellagio, Italy, in November 1976.*

The SUSTAINABLE society: implications for limited growth; edited by Dennis Clark Pirages. New York, 1977. pp. 338. *bibliogs.*

GORZ (ANDRE) Ecologie et politique. Paris, [1978]. pp. 249. *New edition of M. Bosquet's "Ecologie et politique", also containing A. Gorz's "Ecologie et liberté".*

PEARSON (CHARLES S.) and PRYOR (ANTHONY) Environment: north and south: an economic interpretation. New York, [1978]. pp. 355. *bibliog.*

ENVIRONMENTAL POLICY. (Cont.)

URBAN environmental indicators. Paris, Organisation for Economic Co-operation and Development, 1978. pp. 274.

— Africa, North.

MENSCHING (HORST) Mensch und Umwelt im Maghreb: L'homme et la biosphère au Maghreb. Hannover, 1972. pp. 23. *In German and French.*

— Austria.

BEIRAT FÜR WIRTSCHAFTS- UND SOZIALFRAGEN. [Publikationen. 27]. Probleme der Umweltpolitik in Österreich. Wien, 1976. pp. 54.

— Canada — North West Territories.

ALEXANDER (COLIN) Angry society...; new answers to a century of problems affecting all Canadians; a northern journalist tells the facts about Canada's northern colonies today. Saskatoon, [1976]. pp. 202.

— — Prince Edward Island.

PRINCE EDWARD ISLAND. Environmental Control Commission. Annual report. a., 1973/74 - 1974/75(3rd-4th). Charlottetown. *Superseded by PRINCE EDWARD ISLAND. Department of the Environment. Annual report.*

PRINCE EDWARD ISLAND. Department of the Environment. Annual report. a., 1975/76(2nd)- Charlottetown. *Supersedes PRINCE EDWARD ISLAND. Environmental Control Commission. Annual report.*

— New Zealand.

PHYSICAL ENVIRONMENT CONFERENCE, WELLINGTON, 1970. [Reports to the conference]. P.E.C. 1-5. [Wellington, Government Printer, 1970]. 5 pts.

— Philippine Islands.

MARLAY (ROSS) Pollution and politics in the Philippines. Athens, Ohio, 1977. pp. 121. *(Ohio University. Center for International Studies. Papers in International Studies. Southeast Asia Series. No. 43)*

— Underdeveloped areas.

See UNDERDEVELOPED AREAS — Environmental policy.

— United Kingdom.

ENVIRONMENTAL BOARD [U.K.]. Sub Group on New Development. Interim report; [Sir Hugh Wilson, chairman]. [London, Department of the Environment], 1976. pp. 15.

ENVIRONMENTAL BOARD [U.K.]. Sub Group on Older Areas. Interim report; [A.A. Wood, chairman]. [London, Department of the Environment], 1976. 1 vol. (unpaged).

PEOPLE and their settlements: aspects of housing, transport and strategic planning in the U.K.; papers for a conference held in London in January 1976, organised by the National Council of Social Service...as a contribution to the NGO Forum on Habitat, Vancouver, June 1976. London, [1976]. pp. 107.

WOODFORD (GEORGE P.) and others. The value of standards for the external residential environment. London, 1976. repr. 1977. pp. 108. *(U.K. Department of the Environment, Research Reports. 6)*

— United States.

HOUSE (PETER WILLIAM) Trading off environment, economics, and energy: EPA's strategic environmental assessment system. Lexington, Mass., [1977]. pp. 135.

HOUSE (PETER WILLIAM) and WILLIAMS (EDWARD R.) Planning and conservation: the emergence of the frugal society. New York, 1977. pp. 257. *bibliog.*

JOBS, money and pollution; edited by Lester A. Sobel. New York, [1977]. pp. 216. *Based on records compiled by Facts on File.*

MAGAZINE (ALAN H.) Environmental management in local government: a study of local response to federal mandate. New York, 1977. pp. 148. *bibliog.*

SCHLOTTMAN (ALAN M.) Environmental regulation and the allocation of coal: a regional analysis. New York, 1977. pp. 143. *bibliog.*

ENVIRONMENTAL POLICY RESEARCH

— United Kingdom.

NERC NEWS JOURNAL: the q. jl. of the Natural Environment Research Council [U.K.]). q. London. *Current issues only kept.*

ENVIRONMENTAL PROTECTION.

TECHNOLOGY AND THE ENVIRONMENT: reports from Scientific Counsellors; ([pd. by] Department of Industry) Overseas Technical Information Unit [U.K.]. q., N 1971 [1]- London.

ENVIRONMENTAL politics; edited by Stuart S. Nagel. New York, 1974. pp. 321.

NOBEL SYMPOSIUM, 29TH, STOCKHOLM, 1974. Man, environment, and resources: in the perspective of the past and the future; edited by Torgny Torgnysson Segerstedt and Sam Nilsson. [Stockholm, 1974]. pp. 111.

GLADWIN (THOMAS) Environment, planning and the multinational corporation. Greenwich, Conn., [1977]. pp. 295. *bibliog.*

— Australia.

AUSTRALIA. Department of the Environment, Aborigines and the Arts. 1972. Australian environment: commonwealth policy and achievements: ministerial statement, 24 May 1972. in AUSTRALIA. Parliament. Parliamentary papers, 1972, vol. 3.

TARRANT (VALERIE) and LYNE (ALEX) Conserving Australia. London, 1974. pp. 64. *bibliog.*

— Canada — Prince Edward Island.

PRINCE EDWARD ISLAND. Environmental Control Commission. Annual report. a., 1973/74 - 1974/75(3rd-4th). Charlottetown. *Superseded by PRINCE EDWARD ISLAND. Department of the Environment. Annual report.*

PRINCE EDWARD ISLAND. Department of the Environment. Annual report. a., 1975/76(2nd)- Charlottetown. *Supersedes PRINCE EDWARD ISLAND. Environmental Control Commission. Annual report.*

— Japan.

STRONG (KENNETH) Ox against the storm: a biography of Tanaka Shozo, Japan's conservationist pioneer. Tenterden, Kent, 1977. pp. 232. *bibliog.*

— United Kingdom — Scotland.

SCOTTISH DEVELOPMENT AGENCY. Report. a., 1975/76(1st)- Glasgow.

— — Wales.

WELSH DEVELOPMENT AGENCY. Report. a., Ja 1976/Mr 1977(1st)- Treforest.

ENVIRONMENTAL PSYCHOLOGY.

BERRY (JOHN WIDDUP) Human ecology and cognitive style: comparative studies in cultural and psychological adaptation. New York, [1976]. pp. 242. *bibliog.*

LEFF (HERBERT L.) Experience, environment, and human potentials. New York, 1978. pp. 523. *bibliog.*

NEWMAN (BARBARA M.) and NEWMAN (PHILIP R.) Infancy and childhood: development and its contents. New York, [1978]. pp. 619. *bibliog.*

EPIDEMICS

— Europe.

POST (JOHN DEXTER) The last great subsistence crisis in the western world. Baltimore, [1977]. pp. 240. *bibliog.*

EPIDEMIOLOGY.

PELLING (MARGARET) Cholera, fever and English medicine, 1825-1865. Oxford, 1978. pp. 342. *bibliog.*

EQUAL PAY FOR EQUAL WORK.

ONTARIO. Ministry of Labour. 1976. Equal pay for work of equal value: a discussion paper. [Toronto], 1976. pp. 106.

— Bibliography.

HAIST (DIANNE) compiler. Equal pay for work of equal value: a selected bibliography. [Toronto], 1976. pp. 15. *(Ontario. Ministry of Labour. Research Library. Bibliography Series. No. 3)*

— Law and legislation.

OSBORNE (RICHARD JOHN) Equal pay for equal work: a study of legislation in the United States, Canada, the United Kingdom, and New Zealand. Ann Arbor, 1977. fo. 479. *Thesis for the degree of Doctor of the Science of Law, Cornell University, presented 1976.*

— Canada.

MANITOBA. Women's Bureau. 1976. Working paper on equal pay for work of equal value. Winnipeg, 1976. fo. 18.

— United Kingdom.

MARSHALL (MARGARET) and ALDRED (CHRIS) The Equal Pay and Sex Discrimination Acts: report from Scotland. Aberdeen, [1977]. pp. 25.

— United States.

BLAU (FRANCINE D.) Equal pay in the office. Lexington, Mass., [1977]. pp. 158. *bibliog.*

SMITH (SHARON P.) Equal pay in the public sector: fact or fantasy. Princeton, N.J., 1977. pp. 177. *bibliog.* *(Princeton University. Department of Economics and Sociology. Industrial Relations Section. Research Report Series. No. 122)*

EQUALITY.

EVANS (STANLEY GEORGE) Equality. London, 1964. pp. 28. *(Christian Socialist Movement. Tawney Memorial Lectures. No. 1)*

BABEAU (ANDRE) and STRAUSS-KAHN (DOMINIQUE) La richesse des Français: épargne, plus-value, héritage: enquête sur la fortune des Français. [Paris, 1977]. pp. 287. *bibliog.*

COWELL (FRANK A.) Measuring inequality. Oxford, 1977. pp. 193. *bibliog.*

EQUALITY and preferential treatment: a Philosophy and Public Affairs reader; edited by Marshall Cohen [and others]; contributors Ronald Dworkin [and others]. Princeton, [1977]. pp. 209.

EQUITY, income, and policy: comparative studies in three worlds of development; edited by Irving Louis Horowitz. New York, 1977. pp. 293. *bibliogs. Based on a series of panels organised by the American Political Science Association in 1976.*

EUGENICS SOCIETY. Annual Symposium, 13th, 1976. Equalities and inequalities in family life: proceedings of the... symposium...; edited by Robert Chester [and] John Peel. London, 1977. pp. 200. *bibliogs.*

GIROD (ROGER) Inégalité-inégalités: analyse de la mobilité sociale;.. avec un groupe de recherche. Paris, 1977. pp. 183. *bibliog.*

McCORD (WILLIAM MAXWELL) and McCORD (ARLINE F.) Power and equity: an introduction to social stratification. New York, 1977. pp. 316.

SMALL comforts for hard times: humanists on public policy; Michael Mooney and Florian Stuber, editors. New York, 1977. pp. 402. *Papers from a conference series conducted under the auspices of Columbia's program of University Seminars.*

SOCIAL justice and preferential treatment: women and racial minorities in education and business; edited by William T. Blackstone and Robert D. Heslep. Athens, Ga., [1977]. pp. 216. *bibliog. Papers presented at a conference held at the University of Georgia, February 13-15, 1975, and sponsored by that university's Dept. of Philosophy and Religion and Dept. of History and Philosophy of Education, together with the Georgia State Committee for the Humanities.*

YANOWITCH (MURRAY) Social and economic inequality in the Soviet Union: six studies. London, 1977. pp. 196. *bibliog.*

BLUM (JOHN MORTON) The burden of American equality. Oxford, 1978. pp. 22. *An inaugural lecture delivered before the University of Oxford on 26 April 1977.*

EQUALITY and social policy; (edited by Walter Feinberg). Urbana, [1978]. pp. 188. *Papers from a conference held at the University of Illinois in 1976, sponsored by the National Institute of Education (Division of Equity).*

POLE (JACK RICHON) The pursuit of equality in American history. Berkeley, [1978]. pp. 380. *An expanded version of his Jefferson Memorial Lectures, 1971.*

ROTHMAN (ROBERT A.) Inequality and stratification in the United States. Englewood Cliffs, [1978]. pp. 243. *bibliogs.*

WEALE (ALBERT) Equality and social policy. London, 1978. pp. 149. *bibliog.*

EQUALITY BEFORE THE LAW.

ABU RANNAT (MOHAMMED AHMED) Study of equality in the administration of justice. (E/CN.4/Sub. 2/296/Rev.1). New York, United Nations, 1972. pp. 270.

EQUALITY OF STATES.

TUCKER (ROBERT W.) The inequality of nations. New York, [1977]. pp. 214.

EQUILIBRIUM (ECONOMICS).

HILDENBRAND (WERNER) Core and equilibria of a large economy. Princeton, [1974]. pp. 251. *bibliog.*

CHAÎNEAU (ANDRE) La mécanique de l'équilibre économique. [Paris, 1977]. pp. 137.

KLEIN (BURTON H.) Dynamic economics. Cambridge, Mass., 1977. pp. 289.

KORLIRAS (PANAYOTIS G.) The economics of disorder: a disequilibrium theoretical approach to the problems of inflation and unemployment. Athens, 1977. pp. 60. *bibliog. (Center of Planning and Economic Research [Athens]. Lecture Series. 29)*

NATURAL resources, uncertainty, and general equilibrium systems: essays in memory of Rafael Lusky; edited by Alan S. Blinder [and] Philip Friedman. New York, [1977]. pp. 255. *bibliogs.*

EQUILIBRIUM and disequilibrium in economic theory: proceedings of a conference organized by the Institute for Advanced Studies, Vienna, Austria, July 3-5, 1974; edited by Gerhard Schwödiauer. Dordrecht, [1978]. pp. 736. *bibliogs.*

— **Mathematical models.**

MARSCHAK (THOMAS) and SELTEN (REINHARD) General equilibrium with price-making firms. Berlin, 1974. pp. 246. *bibliog.*

SHEEN (JEFFREY RALPH) A study of monetary disequilibrium in open economies. 1977. fo. 330. *bibliog. Typescript. Ph.D. (London) thesis: unpublished. This thesis is the property of London University and may not be removed from the Library.*

EQUITY FUNDING CORPORATION OF AMERICA.

SEIDLER (LEE J.) and others. The Equity Funding papers: the anatomy of a fraud. Santa Barbara, [1977]. pp. 578.

ERHARD (LUDWIG).

LUDWIG Erhard: Erbe und Auftrag: Aussagen und Zeugnisse; (Karl Hohmann, Hrsg.). Düsseldorf, 1977. pp. 525. *(Ludwig-Erhard-Stiftung. Veröffentlichungen)*

ERIKSON (ERIK HOMBURGER).

MAIER (HENRY WILLIAM) Three theories of child development. 3rd ed. New York, [1978]. pp. 292. *bibliogs.*

ESCAPE (PSYCHOLOGY).

COHEN (STANLEY) and TAYLOR (LAURIE) Escape attempts: the theory and practice of resistance to everyday life. Harmondsworth, 1978. pp. 232.

ESKIMOS

— **Canada.**

SANDERS (DOUGLAS ESMOND) Native people in areas of internal national expansion: Indians and Inuit in Canada. Copenhagen, 1973. pp. 39. *(International Work Group for Indigenous Affairs. Documents. 14)*

ESPIONAGE, GERMAN

— **Brazil.**

HILTON (STANLEY E.) Suastica sobre o Brasil: a historia da espionagem alemã no Brasil, 1939-1944. Rio de Janeiro, 1977. pp. 357.

ESSEN

— **Politics and government.**

HORN (WOLFGANG) and KUEHR (HERBERT) Kandidaten im Wahlkampf: Kandidatenauslese, Wahlkampf und lokale Presse 1975 in Essen. Meisenheim am Glan, 1978. pp. 321. *bibliog.*

ESSLINGEN

— **Social history.**

SCHOMERUS (HEILWIG) Die Arbeiter der Maschinenfabrik Esslingen: Forschungen zur Lage der Arbeiterschaft im 19. Jahrhundert. Stuttgart, [1977]. pp. 353. *bibliog. (Arbeitskreis für Moderne Sozialgeschichte. Industrielle Welt. Band 24)*

ESTATE PLANNING

— **Australia.**

HARDINGHAM (IAN JAMES) and BAXT (ROBERT) Discretionary trusts. Sydney, 1975. pp. 235. *bibliog.*

ESTIMATION THEORY.

ROBUST estimates of location: survey and advances; [by] D.F. Andrews [and others]. Princeton, 1972. pp. 373. *bibliog.*

CASSEL (CLAES-MAGNUS) and others. Foundations of inference in survey sampling. New York, [1977]. pp. 192. *bibliog.*

MAASOUMI (ESFANDIAR) A study of improved methods of estimating reduced form coefficients based upon 3SLS estimators. 1977. fo. 244. *bibliog. Typescript. Ph.D. (London) thesis: unpublished. This thesis is the property of London University and may not be removed from the Library.*

SHENTON (L.R.) and BOWMAN (K.O.) Maximum likelihood estimation in small samples. London, 1977. pp. 186. *bibliogs.*

ESTONIA.

A CASE study of a Soviet republic: the Estonian SSR; edited by Tönu Parming and Elmar Järvesoo. Boulder, Colo., 1978. pp. 432. *bibliogs.*

— **Description and travel.**

ESTONIA: regional studies; (on the occasion of the 23rd International Geographical Congress). Tallinn, 1976. pp. 185, 16 plates. *bibliogs.*

— **Foreign population.**

RIKHTER (ELIZAVETA VLADIMIROVNA) Russkoe naselenie zapadnogo Prichud'ia: ocherki istorii, material'noi i dukhovnoi kul'tury. Tallin, 1976. pp. 292.

— **Nationalism.**

ESTONIAN INFORMATION CENTRE. Problems of the Baltic. 4. Documents from Estonia on the violation of human rights. Stockholm, 1977. pp. 72.

ESTONIANS IN RUSSIA.

MAAMIAGI (VIKTOR ANDREEVICH) Estonskie poselentsy v SSSR, 1917-1940 gg. Tallin, 1976. pp. 235.

ETHICS.

INGRAM (JOHN KELLS) Human nature and morals according to Auguste Comte; with notes illustrative of the principles of positivism. London, 1901. pp. 115.

MELDEN (ABRAHAM IRVING) Rights and persons. Oxford, [1977]. pp. 263.

FRIED (CHARLES) Right and wrong. Cambridge, Mass., 1978. pp. 226.

GEWIRTH (ALAN) Reason and morality. Chicago, 1978. pp. 393.

— **History — United Kingdom.**

SOFFER (REBA N.) Ethics and society in England: the revolution in the social sciences, 1870-1914. Berkeley, Calif., [1978]. pp. 325.

ETHICS, GREEK.

BRYSON, Neo-Pythagorean. Der Oikonomikoc des Neupythagoreers "Bryson" und sein Einfluss auf die islamische Wissenschaft; Edition und Übersetzung der erhaltenen Versionen...von Martin Plessner. Heidelberg, 1928. pp. 297. *Attributed also to Galen.*

ETHIOPIA

— **Economic policy.**

INTERNATIONAL LABOUR OFFICE. Exploratory Employment Policy Mission to Ethopia. 1974. Employment and unemployment in Ethiopia: report of the... Mission...financed by the United Nations Development Programme. Geneva, 1974. pp. 144. *bibliog.*

— **Full employment policies.**

INTERNATIONAL LABOUR OFFICE. Exploratory Employment Policy Mission to Ethopia. 1974. Employment and unemployment in Ethiopia: report of the... Mission...financed by the United Nations Development Programme. Geneva, 1974. pp. 144. *bibliog.*

— **History.**

MARKAKIS (JOHN) and AYELE (NEGA) Class and revolution in Ethiopia. Nottingham, 1978. pp. 191.

ETHNIC ATTITUDES.

COMMUNITY RELATIONS COMMISSION. Some of my best friends...: a report on race relations attitudes. London, [1976]. pp. 45.

URBAN ethnic conflict: a comparative perspective edited by Susan E. Clarke and Jeffrey L. Obler. Chapel Hill, 1976. pp. 257. *bibliogs. Proceedings of a conference held in Chapel Hill in 1975 by the University of North Carolina Institute for Research in Social Science.*

ETHNICITY.

CONFERENCE ON ETHNIC PLURALISM AND CONFLICT IN CONTEMPORARY WESTERN EUROPE AND CANADA, ITHACA, 1975. Ethnic conflict in the Western world: [papers presented at the Conference]; edited by Milton J. Esman. Ithaca, 1977. pp. 399. *bibliogs. Sponsored by the Western Societies Program of the Center for International Studies, Cornell University.*

ETHNICITY.(Cont.)

EXPERIMENTER effects and the ethnic cueing phenomenon; [by] A. Brah [and others]. Bristol, Social Science Research Council Research Unit on Ethnic Relations, [1977]. pp. 31. *bibliog. (Working Papers on Ethnic Relations. No. 3)*

HANSEN (HOLGER BERNT) Ethnicity and military rule in Uganda: a study of ethnicity as a political factor in Uganda, based on a discussion of political anthropology and the application of its results. Uppsala, 1977. pp. 144. *(Nordiska Afrikainstitutet. Research Reports. No. 43)*

IMMIGRANTS in industrial America, 1850-1920; edited by Richard L. Ehrlich. Charlottesville, 1977. pp. 218. *Papers of a conference organised by the Eleutherian Mills-Hagley Foundation and the Balch Institute of Philadelphia and held in 1973.*

PATTERSON (HORACE ORLANDO LLOYD) Ethnic chauvinism: the reactionary impulse. New York, 1977. pp. 346.

STEIN (HOWARD F.) and HILL (ROBERT F.) The ethnic imperative: examining the new white ethnic movement. University Park, Pa., [1977]. pp. 308.

EPSTEIN (ARNOLD LEONARD) Ethos and identity: three studies in ethnicity. London, 1978. pp. 181. *bibliog.*

— **Research — United Kingdom.**

A REPORT on the development of a standard research instrument for the study of identity structure; [by] R. Miles [and others]. [Bristol, Social Science Research Council Research Unit on Ethnic Relations], 1977. fo. 40. *(Research Notes)*

RESEARCH strategy in the identity structure research; [by] M. Fuller [and others]. [Bristol, Social Science Research Council Research Unit on Ethnic Relations], 1977. 1 vol. (various foliations). *(Research Notes)*

ETHNOCENTRISM.

SACHS (IGNACY) The discovery of the third world. [Cambridge, Mass., 1976]. pp. 287.

ETHNOLOGY.

HOEBEL (EDWARD ADAMSON) and FROST (EVERETT LLOYD) Cultural and social anthropology. New York, [1976]. pp. 442. *bibliogs. A revision of the cultural sections of E.A. Hoebel's Anthropology: the study of man, 4th ed.*

SAHLINS (MARSHALL DAVID) Culture and practical reason. Chicago, 1976. pp. 252. *bibliog.*

The ANTHROPOLOGY of power: ethnographic studies from Asia, Oceania, and the New World; edited by Raymond D. Fogelson [and] Richard N. Adams. New York, [1977]. pp. 429. *bibliogs. Based on a conference held under the auspices of the American Association for the Advancement of Science in San Francisco in 1974.*

HARRIS (MARVIN) Cannibals and kings: the origins of cultures. London, 1978. pp. 239. *bibliog.*

SPENCER (JOSEPH EARLE) and THOMAS (WILLIAM L.) Introducing cultural geography. 2nd ed. New York, [1978]. pp. 428. *bibliog.*

— **Methodology.**

MACFARLANE (ALAN DONALD JAMES) and others. Reconstructing historical communities;...in collaboration with Sarah Harrison and Charles Jardine. Cambridge, 1977. pp. 221. *bibliog.*

— **Africa.**

RELATIONS of production: Marxist approaches to economic anthropology; edited by David Seddon. London, 1978. pp. 414. *bibliog.*

— **Africa, Subsaharan.**

STEWART (FRANK HENDERSON) Fundamentals of age-group systems. Oxford, [1977]. pp. 381. *bibliog.*

— **America — Bibliography.**

COMAS CAMPS (JUAN) compiler. Bibliografia selectiva de las culturas indigenas de America. Mexico, Organization of American States, 1953. pp. 284, 4 fold. maps.

COMAS CAMPS (JUAN) Cien años de Congresos Internacionales de Americanistas: ensayo historico-critico y bibliografico. Mexico, 1974. pp. 542. *bibliog.*

— **Brazil.**

SCHADEN (EGON) ed. Homem, cultura e sociedade no Brasil: seleções da Revista de Antropologia. Petropolis, 1972. pp. 450. *bibliogs.*

— **Ghana.**

SCHILDKROUT (ENID) People of the zongo: the transformation of ethnic identities in Ghana. Cambridge, 1978. pp. 303. *bibliog.*

— **India.**

ENCOUNTER and experience: personal accounts of fieldwork; edited by André Béteille and T.N. Madan. Delhi, [1975]. pp. 225. *bibliogs.*

— **Indonesia — Bali.**

BOON (JAMES A.) The anthropological romance of Bali, 1597-1972: dynamic perspectives in marriage and caste, politics and religion. Cambridge, 1977. pp. 259. *bibliog.*

— **Norway.**

BRYN (HALFDAN) Der nordische Mensch: die Merkmale der nordischen Rasse mit besonderer Berücksichtigung der rassischen Verhältnisse Norwegens. München, 1929. pp. 166. *bibliog.*

— **Oceania.**

EXILES and migrants in Oceania; edited by Michael D. Lieber. Honolulu, [1977]. pp. 414. *bibliog. (Association for Social Anthropology in Oceania. ASAO Monographs. No.5) Based on a symposium held at the University of Washington in 1970.*

— **Sudan.**

AHMED (RAFIA HASSAN) Ethnic and socio-cultural pluralism in the Sudan: its manifestation and effects on national integration. Khartoum, [Institute of Public Administration], 1975. fo. 40. *(Occasional Papers)*

— **Thailand.**

POTTER (JACK M.) Thai peasant social structure. Chicago, 1976. pp. 249. *bibliog.*

— **United States.**

ETHNICITY and U.S. foreign policy; edited by Abdul Aziz Said. New York, 1977. pp. 180. *Based on a panel at the annual convention of the International Studies Association in Toronto, 1976.*

— **Zaire.**

DROOGMANS (HUBERT) Le Congo: quatre conférences publiques. Bruxelles, [1895]. pp. 122.

ETHNOPSYCHOLOGY.

STUDIES in cross-cultural psychology;... edited by Neil Warren. London, 1977 in progress. *bibliogs.*

GOODY (JOHN RANKINE) The domestication of the savage mind. Cambridge, 1977. pp. 179. *bibliog.*

LEARNING non-aggression: the experience of non-literate societies; edited by Ashley Montagu. New York, 1978. pp. 235. *bibliogs.*

EUGENE FRANCIS, Prince of Savoy.

McKAY (DEREK) Prince Eugene of Savoy. London, [1977]. pp. 288. *bibliog.*

EUGENICS.

KINOMETRICS: determinants of socioeconomic success within and between families; editor, Paul Taubman. Amsterdam, 1977. pp. 324. *bibliogs.*

EURODOLLAR MARKET.

BEKERMAN (GERARD) Les euro-dollars. [Paris, 1977]. pp. 128. *bibliog.*

EINZIG (PAUL) and QUINN (BRIAN SCOTT) The Euro-dollar system: practice and theory of international interest rates. 6th ed. London, 1977. pp. 124.

McKINNON (RONALD I.) The Eurocurrency market. Princeton, 1977. pp. 36. *bibliog. (Princeton University. Department of Economics and Sociology. International Finance Section. Essays in International Finance. No. 125)*

SCHMITT (BERNARD) La monnaie européenne. Paris, [1977]. pp. 229.

EUROPE.

SEVEN voices on Europe: symposium, Linköping University, Lund, 1972; edited by H. Peter Hallberg. [Lund, 1972]. pp. 106.

— **Civilization.**

RESZLER (ANDRE) L'intellectuel contre l'Europe. [Paris, 1976]. pp. 161. *bibliog.*

GERBOD (PAUL) L'Europe culturelle et religieuse de 1815 à nos jours. Paris, [1977]. pp. 384. *bibliog.*

— **Commerce.**

BAIROCH (PAUL) Commerce extérieur et développement économique de l'Europe au XIXe siècle. Paris, [1976]. pp. 355. *bibliog. (Paris. Ecole Pratique des Hautes Etudes en Sciences Sociales. Centre de Recherches Historiques. Civilisations et Sociétés. 53)*

KINDLEBERGER (CHARLES POOR) Economic response: comparative studies in trade, finance and growth. Cambridge, Mass., 1978. pp. 308. *bibliog.*

— — **Germany, Eastern.**

DEUTSCHES INSTITUT FÜR WIRTSCHAFTSFORSCHUNG. Sonderhefte. [Neue Folge]. 119. Der Handel der Deutschen Demokratischen Republik mit der Bundesrepublik Deutschland und den übrigen OECD-Ländern... ; ([by] Horst Lambrecht). Berlin, 1977. pp. 98.

— **Defences.**

PFALTZGRAFF (ROBERT L.) and DAVIS (JACQUELYN K.) The cruise missile: bargaining chip or defense bargain? Cambridge, Mass., 1977. pp. 53. *(Institute for Foreign Policy Analysis. Special Reports)*

VYSOCKY (MARTIN) Czechoslovakia and the Conference on Security and Cooperation in Europe. Bratislava, 1977. pp. 131.

GALLOIS (PIERRE MARIE) Soviet military doctrine and European defence: NATO's obsolete concepts. London, 1978. pp. 17. *(Institute for the Study of Conflict. Conflict Studies. No. 96)*

— **Economic conditions.**

KITZINGER (UWE WEBSTER) The new Europeans: a commentary on products and people, a marketing survey of the European Common Market and Britain, 1963. [London, 1963]. pp. 21.

L'EUROPE des crises; [by] Robert Triffin [and others]. Bruxelles, 1976. pp. 173. *(Fondation Paul-Henri Spaak. Bibliothèque) Mainly lectures given at the Institut des Etudes Européennes of the Université Libre de Brussels, in 1974 and 1975.*

EUROPEAN economic issues: agriculture, economic security, industrial democracy, the OECD. New York, 1977. pp. 263. *(Atlantic Institute. Atlantic Institute Studies. 3)*

EUROPE.

— — Sources.

CAMBRIDGE INFORMATION AND RESEARCH SERVICES LTD. Sources of European economic information. 2nd ed. Farnborough, Hants., [1977]. pp. 267.

— Economic history.

BAIROCH (PAUL) Commerce extérieur et développement économique de l'Europe au XIXe siècle. Paris, [1976]. pp. 355. bibliog. (Paris. Ecole Pratique des Hautes Etudes en Sciences Sociales. Centre de Recherches Historiques. Civilisations et Sociétés. 53)

FLAMANT (MAURICE) Histoire économique et sociale contemporaine. Paris, [1976]. pp. 647. bibliog.

HODGART (ALAN) The economics of European imperialism. [London, 1977]. pp. 88. bibliog.

KRIEDTE (PETER) and others. Industrialisierung vor der Industrialisierung: gewerbliche Warenproduktion auf dem Land in der Formationsperiode des Kapitalismus;...mit Beiträgen von Herbert Kisch und Franklin F. Mendels. Göttingen, 1977. pp. 393. (Max-Planck-Institut für Geschichte. Veröffentlichungen. 53)

MILWARD (ALAN S.) and SAUL (S.B.) The development of the economies of continental Europe, 1850-1914. London, 1977. pp. 555. bibliogs.

MISKIMIN (HARRY ALVIN) The economy of later renaissance Europe, 1460-1600. Cambridge, 1977. pp. 222. bibliog.

ALDCROFT (DEREK H.) The European economy, 1914-1970. London, [1978]. pp. 251. bibliog.

KINDLEBERGER (CHARLES POOR) Economic response: comparative studies in trade, finance and growth. Cambridge, Mass., 1978. pp. 308. bibliog.

— — Methodology.

An INTRODUCTION to the sources of European economic history, 1500-1800. volume 1. Western Europe; edited by Charles Wilson and Geoffrey Parker. London, [1977]. pp. 256.

— — Sources.

An INTRODUCTION to the sources of European economic history, 1500-1800. volume 1. Western Europe; edited by Charles Wilson and Geoffrey Parker. London, [1977]. pp. 256.

— Economic integration.

SHONFIELD (Sir ANDREW) European integration in the second phase: the scope and limitations of alliance politics. [Colchester], 1974. pp. 15. (University of Essex. Noel Buxton Lectures. 1974)

OEHLINGER (THEO) and others. Institutionelle Aspekte der österreichischen Integrationspolitik. Wien, 1976. pp. 323. bibliogs. (Österreichische Akademie der Wissenschaften. Philosophisch-Historische Klasse. Sitzungsberichte. 308. Band. 1. Abhandlung)

Die OSTBEZIEHUNGEN der Europäischen Gemeinschaft: von nationalstaatlicher Politik zu gemeinsamer Verantwortung; herausgegeben von Eberhard Schulz. München, 1977. pp. 272. (Deutsche Gesellschaft für Auswärtige Politik. Forschungsinstitut. Schriften. Band 40)

SZITA (JÁNOS) Perspectives for all-European economic co-operation. Leyden, 1977. pp. 371. bibliog.

— — Bibliography.

KUJATH (KARL) compiler. Bibliographie zur europäischen Integration, mit Anmerkungen: Bibliographie sur l'intégration européenne, annotée: Bibliography on European integration, with annotations. Bonn, [1977]. pp. 777.

— Economic policy.

SZITA (JÁNOS) Perspectives for all-European economic co-operation. Leyden, 1977. pp. 371. bibliog.

PLANNING in Europe; edited by Jack Hayward and Olga Narkiewicz. London, [1978]. pp. 199. bibliog.

— Emigration and immigration.

LUCAS (ULIANO) Emigranti in Europa. Torino, [1977]. pp. 127.

— Foreign economic relations — Africa, Subsaharan.

PROBLEMES de l'enseignement supérieur et de développement en Afrique centrale: recueil d'études en l'honneur de Guy Malengreau; [edited by Roman Iakemchuk]. [Paris, 1975]. pp. 227.

— — Arab countries.

EURO-Arab cooperation; edited by Edmond Völker. Leyden, 1976. pp. 228. Papers from a colloquium organized by the University of Amsterdam Europa Instituut in October 1975.

— — Japan.

JAPAN'S relations with Britain and Europe: the present and the future; [by] Roderick MacFarquhar [and others]. London, 1977. pp. 28. Six lectures given at the Japan Economic Journal symposium in 1977.

— Foreign population.

Les TRAVAILLEURS étrangers en Europe occidentale: actes du colloque organisé par la Commission Nationale pour les Etudes et les Recherches Interethniques, Paris-Sorbonne...1974; sous la direction de Philippe J. Bernard. Mouton, [1976]. pp. 416. (Nice. Université. Institut d'Etudes et de Recherches Interethniques et Interculturelles. Publications. 6) In English and French.

— Foreign relations.

The FOREIGN policies of West European socialist parties; edited by Werner J. Feld. New York, [1978]. pp. 149.

ZORGBIBE (CHARLES) La construction politique de l'Europe, 1946-1976. [Paris, 1978]. pp. 189. bibliog.

— — Australia.

AUSTRALIA. Prime Minister. 1975. Australia and Europe: principal speeches made during the visit to Europe by the Prime Minister...from 14 December 1974 to 21 January 1975. Canberra, 1975. pp. 78.

— — Japan.

JAPAN'S relations with Britain and Europe: the present and the future; [by] Roderick MacFarquhar [and others]. London, 1977. pp. 28. Six lectures given at the Japan Economic Journal symposium in 1977.

— — United States.

MENIL (LOIS PATTISON DE) Who speaks for Europe?: the vision of Charles de Gaulle. London, [1977]. pp. 232. bibliog.

WESTERN Europe: the trials of partnership; edited by David S. Landes. Lexington, Mass., [1977]. pp. 406. (Commission on Critical Choices for Americans. Critical Choices for Americans. vol. 8)

WILLIAMS (GEOFFREY LEE) The permanent alliance: the European-American partnership, 1945-1984. Leyden, 1977. pp. 407. bibliog.

— Historical geography — Maps.

HORRABIN (JAMES FRANCIS) An atlas of European history from the 2nd to the 20th century. London, 1935. pp. 159.

— History.

The GENERAL crisis of the seventeenth century; edited by Geoffrey Parker and Lesley M. Smith. London, 1978. pp. 283.

— — 476-1492.

ULLMANN (WALTER) Medieval foundations of renaissance humanism. London, 1977. pp. 212.

— — 1789-1900.

TAYLOR (ALAN JOHN PERCIVALE) Europe: grandeur and decline. Harmondsworth, 1967 repr. 1977. pp. 378. bibliog.

— — 1900- .

TAYLOR (ALAN JOHN PERCIVALE) Europe: grandeur and decline. Harmondsworth, 1967 repr. 1977. pp. 378. bibliog.

SPENDER (STEPHEN) The thirties and after: poetry, politics, people, 1933-75. Glasgow, 1978. pp. 286.

— — 1918-1945.

DOUGLAS (ROY) In the year of Munich. London, 1977. pp. 155. bibliog.

— — 1945- .

ZORGBIBE (CHARLES) La construction politique de l'Europe, 1946-1976. [Paris, 1978]. pp. 189. bibliog.

— Industries.

UNITED NATIONS. Conference of European Statisticians. Statistical Standards and Studies. No. 30. Standardized input-output tables of ECE countries for years around 1965. New York, 1977. 1 vol. (various pagings)

— Intellectual life.

BAUMER (FRANKLIN LE VAN) Modern European thought: continuity and change in ideas, 1600- 1950. New York, [1977]. pp. 541. bibliog.

BIDDISS (MICHAEL D.) The age of the masses: ideas and society in Europe since 1870. Harmondsworth, 1977. pp. 379. bibliog.

— Military policy.

GALLOIS (PIERRE MARIE) Soviet military doctrine and European defence: NATO's obsolete concepts. London, 1978. pp. 17. (Institute for the Study of Conflict. Conflict. Studies. No. 96)

— Nationalism.

CONFERENCE ON ETHNIC PLURALISM AND CONFLICT IN CONTEMPORARY WESTERN EUROPE AND CANADA, ITHACA, 1975. Ethnic conflict in the Western world: [papers presented at the Conference]; edited by Milton J. Esman. Ithaca, 1977. pp. 399. bibliogs. Sponsored by the Western Societies Program of the Center for International Studies, Cornell University.

— Nobility.

EUROPEAN landed elites in the nineteenth century: [the James Schouler Lectures, 1974]; edited...by David Spring. Baltimore, [1977]. pp. 147. bibliogs. (Johns Hopkins University. Department of History. Johns Hopkins Symposia in Comparative History)

— Politics and government.

CROZIER (MICHEL) The governability of West European societies. Colchester, [1977?]. pp. 15. (University of Essex. Noel Buxton Lectures. 1977)

DOUGLAS (ROY) In the year of Munich. London, 1977. pp. 155. bibliog.

JENKINS (PETER) Where Trotskyism got lost: the restoration of European democracy after the Second World War. Nottingham, [1977]. pp. 23. (Spokesman, The. Pamphlets. No. 59)

The OTHER Europe; edited by Gary L. Olson. Brunswick, Ohio, [1977]. pp. 339.

The GENERAL crisis of the seventeenth century; edited by Geoffrey Parker and Lesley M. Smith. London, 1978. pp. 283.

WOOD (DAVID MICHAEL) Power and policy in western European democracies. New York, [1978]. pp. 177. bibliogs.

EUROPE.(Cont.)

ZORGBIBE (CHARLES) La construction politique de l'Europe, 1946-1976. [Paris, 1978]. pp. 189. *bibliog.*

— Relations (general) with China.

MURPHEY (RHOADS) The outsiders: the western experience in India and China. Ann Arbor, [1977]. pp. 299. *bibliog. (Michigan University. Center for Chinese Studies. Michigan Studies on China)*

— Relations (general) with India.

MURPHEY (RHOADS) The outsiders: the western experience in India and China. Ann Arbor, [1977]. pp. 299. *bibliog. (Michigan University. Center for Chinese Studies. Michigan Studies on China)*

— Relations (general) with the United States.

ATLANTIS lost: U.S.-European relations after the Cold War; edited by James Chace and Earl C. Ravenal. New York, 1976. pp. 273.

— Religion.

GERBOD (PAUL) L'Europe culturelle et religieuse de 1815 à nos jours. Paris, [1977]. pp. 384. *bibliog.*

— Social conditions.

KITZINGER (UWE WEBSTER) The new Europeans: a commentary on products and people, a marketing survey of the European Common Market and Britain, 1963. [London, 1963]. pp. 21.

CONTEMPORARY Europe: social structures and cultural patterns; edited by Salvador Giner and Margaret Scotford Archer. London, [1978]. pp. viii, 323. *bibliog.*

— Social policy.

PLANNING in Europe; edited by Jack Hayward and Olga Narkiewicz. London, [1978]. pp. 199. *bibliog.*

EUROPE, EASTERN.

EUROPE DE L'EST, L'; [pd. by] Direction de la Documentation [France]. (La Documentation Française). a., 1970- Paris.

— Bibliography.

CENTRE FOR POLICY STUDIES. Bibliography of freedom. London, 1976. pp. 28.

INTERNATIONAL COMMITTEE FOR SOVIET AND EAST EUROPEAN STUDIES. European bibliography of Soviet, East European and Slavonic studies. vol.1. 1975; [editor Thomas Hnik]. Birmingham, 1977. pp. 437. *Compiled by joint Committee representing Birmingham University Library and Centre for Russian and East European Studies, and the Paris École des Hautes Études en Sciences Sociales, Centre d'Études sur l'URSS et l'Europe Orientale.*

— Civilization.

MIHAJLOV (MIHAJLO) Underground notes. London, 1977. pp. 204. *bibliog.*

— Commerce — France.

ENGLISH (FREDERICK C.) East-West trade: the French role. Loughborough, 1977. pp. 42. *bibliog.*

— — United States.

ATLANTIC COUNCIL OF THE UNITED STATES. Committee on East-West Trade. East-West trade: managing encounter and accommodation. Boulder, 1977. pp. 194.

— Constitutional history.

RENTSCH (NIKLAUS B.) Das System der Räte. Bern, [1976]. pp. 199.

— Economic integration.

BRABANT (JOZEF M.P. VAN) East European cooperation: the role of money and finance. New York, 1977. pp. 394. *bibliog.*

— Foreign economic relations.

HAYDEN (ERIC W.) Technology transfer to East Europe: U.S. corporate experience. New York, 1976. pp. 134. *bibliog.*

ECONOMIC relations between socialist countries and the third world; edited by Deepak Nayyar. London, 1977. pp. 265.

— Foreign relations.

STOJIĆ-IMAMOVIĆ (EDITA) Stavovi socijalističkih zemalja istočne Evrope u medjunarodnim odnosima. Beograd, 1974. pp. 258. *bibliog. With English and Russian summaries.*

The FOREIGN policies of Eastern Europe: domestic and international determinants; edited by James A. Kuhlman. Leyden, 1978. pp. 302. *(East-West Foundation. East-West Perspectives. 4) Includes papers presented at a Workshop Conference on the Comparative Study of Communist Foreign Policy held at the University of South Carolina in 1970.*

See also EUROPEAN ECONOMIC COMMUNITY — Europe, Eastern.

— — France.

KOMJATHY (ANTHONY TIHAMER) The crises of France's east central European diplomacy, 1933- 1938. New York, 1976. pp. 277. *bibliog. (East European Quarterly. East European Monographs. 21.)*

— History.

IZ istorii narodno-demokraticheskikh i sotsialisticheskikh revoliutsii v stranakh Tsentral'noi i Iugo-Vostochnoi Evropy. Moskva, 1977. pp. 391.

— Industries.

TURNOCK (DAVID) Eastern Europe. Boulder, Colo., 1978. pp. 273. *bibliog.*

— Nationalism.

SIKORA (FRANZ) Sozialistische Solidarität und nationale Interessen: Polen, Tschechoslowakei, DDR. Köln, [1977]. pp. 248. *(Bundesinstitut für Ostwissenschaftliche und Internationale Studien. Abhandlungen. Band 31)*

— Politics and government.

AUTHORITARIAN politics in Communist Europe: uniformity and diversity in one-party states; Andrew C. Janos, editor. Berkeley, Calif., [1976]. pp 196. *bibliogs. (California University. Institute of International Studies. Research Series. No. 28) Essays from a colloquium held under the auspices of the Center for Slavic and East European Studies of the University of California, Berkeley in 1973.*

COMMUNIST power in Europe, 1944-1949; edited by Martin McCauley. London, 1977. pp. 242.

POLITICAL development in Eastern Europe; edited by Jan F. Triska [and] Paul M. Cocks. New York, 1977. pp. 371.

RAKOVSKI (MARC) Towards an east European Marxism. London, 1978. pp. 140.

— Population.

MAGGS (PETER B.) Law and population in Eastern Europe. 2nd ed. Medford, Mass., 1977. pp. 31. *(Tufts University. Fletcher School of Law and Diplomacy. Law and Population Monograph Series. No. 3)*

POPULATION and migration trends in eastern Europe; edited by Huey Louis Kostanick. Boulder, Colo., 1977. pp. 247. *Proceedings of the Conference on Demography and Urbanization in Eastern Europe held in Los Angeles in 1976 and sponsored by the Center for Slavic and East European Studies of the University of California at Los Angeles.*

— Social policy.

SOCIAL scientists and policy making in the USSR; edited by Richard B. Remnek. New York, 1977. pp. 144.

EUROPEAN COAL AND STEEL COMMUNITY.

EUROPEAN COAL AND STEEL COMMUNITY. Consultative Committee. Handbook. a., current issue only. Luxembourg.

EUROPEAN COMMISSION OF HUMAN RIGHTS.

EUROPEAN COMMISSION OF HUMAN RIGHTS. Decisions and reports. s-a., Jl 1975 (no.1)- Strasbourg. *[in English and French] Supersedes EUROPEAN COMMISSION OF HUMAN RIGHTS. Collection of decisions.*

EUROPEAN COMMISSION OF HUMAN RIGHTS. 1976. European Convention on Human Rights: collected texts. 11th ed. Strasbourg, Council of Europe, 1976. 1 vol. (various pagings). *In English and French.*

EUROPEAN COMMUNITIES.

SWEET AND MAXWELL, LIMITED. European Community treaties, including the European Communities Act 1972...; advisory editor, K.R. Simmonds. 3rd ed. London, 1977. pp. 355.

— Bibliography.

JEFFRIES (JOHN) A guide to the official publications of the European Communities. London, 1978. pp. 178.

— Austria.

OEHLINGER (THEO) and others. Institutionelle Aspekte der österreichischen Integrationspolitik. Wien, 1976. pp. 323. *bibliogs. (Österreichische Akademie der Wissenschaften. Philosophisch-Historische Klasse. Sitzungsberichte. 308. Band. 1. Abhandlung)*

EUROPEAN CONVENTION ON HUMAN RIGHTS.

EUROPEAN COMMISSION OF HUMAN RIGHTS. 1976. European Convention on Human Rights: collected texts. 11th ed. Strasbourg, Council of Europe, 1976. 1 vol. (various pagings). *In English and French.*

EUROPEAN ECONOMIC COMMUNITY.

FEDERAL TRUST FOR EDUCATION AND RESEARCH. Research Committee. Britain in Europe: viewpoint for the labour movement. London, [1958]. pp. (11).

SEVEN voices on Europe: symposium, Linköping University, Lund, 1972; edited by H. Peter Hallberg. [Lund, 1972]. pp. 106.

SHONFIELD (Sir ANDREW) European integration in the second phase: the scope and limitations of alliance politics. [Colchester], 1974. pp. 15. *(University of Essex. Noel Buxton Lectures. 1974)*

MINNOCCI (GIACINTO) L'Europa che dobbiamo costruire: discorso pronunciato al Senato della Repubblica nella seduta del 6 maggio 1975. Roma, [1975]. pp. 23. politica regionale europea.

EDWARDS (GEOFFREY) and WALLACE (WILLIAM) Lecturer in government, University of Manchester. A wider European community?: issues and problems of further enlargement. London, [1976]. pp. 83.

Le REGIONI italiane e l'Europa: atti del convegno internazionale promosso e organizzato dalla Regione Piemonte, Torino, 22-24 Aprile, 1976. Milano, 1976. pp. 399.

EDWARDS (GEOFFREY) and WALLACE (HELEN) The Council of Ministers of the European Community and the President-in-Office. [London, 1977]. pp 113. *(Federal Trust for Education and Research. Federal Trust Papers)*

HEATH (EDWARD RICHARD GEORGE) Our community. London, 1977. pp. 23. *(Conservative Political Centre. [Publications]. No. 613)*

KERR (ANTHONY JOHN CRAWFORD) The Common Market and how it works. Oxford, 1977. pp. 210. *bibliog.*

Die SUED-Erweiterung der Europäischen Gemeinschaft: Wende oder Ende der Integration?; herausgegeben von Hajo Hasenpflug und Beate Kohler. Hamburg, 1977. pp. 319. *bibliog. (Hamburg. Hamburgisches Welt-Wirtschafts-Archiv. Veröffentlichungen)*

YOUNG (JOHN) Monday Club member. Europe: the unguarded legacy: a Conservative approach to European unity; (based on studies by members of the Monday Club's European Policy Group). London, [1977]. 1 pamphlet (unpaged).

MICHELMANN (HANS J.) Organisational effectiveness in a multi-national bureaucracy. Farnborough, Hants., [1978]. pp. 259. *bibliog.*

— **Foreign economic relations.**

EUROPEAN ECONOMIC COMMUNITY. Treaties. 1957-. Overseas countries and territories. French overseas departments; collected acts. [Brussels, 1977 in progress]. 2 vols. (loose-leaf).

TOVIAS (ALFRED) Tariff preferences in Mediterranean diplomacy. London, 1977. pp. 153. *bibliogs.*

— **Foreign relations.**

SJÖSTEDT (GUNNAR) The external role of the European Community. Farnborough, Hants, [1977]. pp. 273. *bibliog. (Utrikespolitiska Institutet. Swedish Studies in International Relations.7)*

— **Africa.**

MORINO (LINA) La Comunità Europea e l'Africa. [Bari, 1975]. pp. 367.

TWITCHETT (CAROL ANN COSGROVE) Europe and Africa: from association to partnership. Farnborough, [1978]. pp. 195. *bibliog.*

— **Europe, Eastern.**

Die OSTBEZIEHUNGEN der Europäischen Gemeinschaft: von nationalstaatlicher Politik zu gemeinsamer Verantwortung; herausgegeben von Eberhard Schulz. München, 1977. pp. 272. *(Deutsche Gesellschaft für Auswärtige Politik. Forschungsinstitut. Schriften. Band 40)*

— **Greece.**

HUMMEN (WILHELM) Greek industry in the European Community: prospects and problems. Berlin, 1977. pp. 88. *(Deutsches Institut für Entwicklungspolitik. (Occasional Papers. No. 45.)*

La GRÈCE et la Communauté: problèmes posés par l'adhésion; colloque organisé les 5 et 6 mai 1977 par l'Institut d'Etudes européennes. Bruxelles, 1978. pp. 344. *(Brussels. Université Libre. Institut d'Etudes Européennes. Colloques Européens) Articles in French or English.*

— **Israel.**

COHEN (YAACOV) Israel and the European Communities: political and economic implications of the free trade area agreement. n.p., [1977?]. pp. 52.

— **New Zealand.**

NEW ZEALAND. 1971. Britain, New Zealand and the EEC: a New Zealand government statement. [Wellington], 1971. pp. 12.

— **Norway.**

GLEDITSCH (NILS PETTER) and HELLEVIK (OTTAR) Kampen om EF. [Oslo, 1977]. pp. 339. *bibliog. (International Peace Research Institute. PRIO-Publikasjoner. 29-5)*

— **Portugal.**

RIBEIRO (SERGIO) O mercado comun: a integração e Portugal. 3rd ed. Lisboa, 1976. pp. 315.

— **United Kingdom.**

EGOSHIN (VALERII ALEKSANDROVICH) Rabochee dvizhenie Velikobritanii i zapadnoevropeiskaia integratsiia. Moskva, 1976. pp. 120.

EUROPEAN MOVEMENT. Britain in Europe since 1973: the benefits of membership. London, [1977]. pp. 53.

LABOUR PARTY. The EEC and Britain: a socialist perspective. London, 1977. pp. 75.

DIVIDED loyalties: British regional assertion and European integration; edited by Martin Kolinsky, assisted by David Scott Bell. Manchester, 1978. pp. 216.

RIPPON (AUBREY GEOFFREY FREDERICK) Our European future: speeches on Europe. London, [1978]. pp. 31.

EUROPEAN ECONOMIC COMMUNITY ASSOCIATED COUNTRIES.

EUROPEAN COMMUNITIES. Directorate-General for Development and Cooperation. Les Conditions d'Installation d'Entreprises Industrielles dans les États Africains et Malgache Associés. 2nd ed. [Brussels], 1974.

PROBLEMES de l'enseignement supérieur et de développement en Afrique centrale: recueil d'études en l'honneur de Guy Malengreau; [edited by Roman Iakemchuk]. [Paris, 1975]. pp. 227.

ACP-EEC COUNCIL OF MINISTERS. Annual report [and] Commission report...on the administration of financial and technical aid. a., 1976/77- Suva.

— **Economic policy.**

HENGSBACH (FRIEDHELM) Die Assoziierung afrikanischer Staaten an die Europäischen Gemeinschaften: eine Politik raumwirtschaftlicher Integration? Baden-Baden, [1977]. pp. 238. *bibliog. (List Gesellschaft. Monographien. Neue Folge. Band 1)*

EUROPEAN ECONOMIC COMMUNITY COUNTRIES

— **Commerce — Canada — British Columbia.**

BRITISH COLUMBIA. Economics and Statistics Branch. 1972. British Columbia's trade prospects with the New European Economic Community: a review of the principal factors involved in the entry of the United Kingdom into the E.E.C. Victoria, 1972. pp. 13.

— **Commercial policy.**

COMPETITION policy in the U.K. and EEC; edited by Kenneth D. George [and] Caroline Joll. Cambridge, 1975. pp. 220. *Papers presented at a Social Science Research Council conference held at Somerville College, Oxford in 1974.*

— **Economic conditions.**

ODEHNAL (EVA) The future of the businessman in a new Europe. [London, 1973]. pp. 13. *(Aims of Industry. The Future of Capitalism)*

MINSHULL (GORDON NEIL) The new Europe: an economic geography of the EEC. London, 1978. pp. 281. *bibliog.*

— **Economic policy.**

EUROPEAN COMMUNITIES. Commission. 1977. Guidelines for Community regional policy: communication and proposals submitted...to the Council on 3 June 1977. [Brussels], 1977. pp. 44. *(Bulletin of the European Communities. Supplements. [1977/2])*

SWIFT (MARK) A regional policy for Europe. London, 1978. pp. 23. *(Young Fabian Group. Young Fabian Pamphlets. 48)*

— **Foreign economic relations.**

ACP-EEC COUNCIL OF MINISTERS. Annual report [and] Commission report...on the administration of financial and technical aid. a., 1976/77- Suva.

SUTTON (MARY) The EEC and the developing world: a changing relationship. Dublin, 1976. pp. 59. *bibliog. (Trócaire and Irish Commission for Justice and Peace. Joint Development Education Programme)*

SHARP (ROBIN) and WHITTEMORE (CLAIRE) Europe and the world without: policies and programmes of the European Community and their impact on world poverty. London, [1977]. pp. 49. *bibliog. (Oxfam. Public Affairs Unit. Oxfam Public Affairs Reports. 3)*

— — **Germany, Eastern.**

JANSEN (BERNHARD) EWG und DDR nach Abschluss des Grundlagenvertrages. Baden-Baden, [1977]. pp. 133. *bibliog.*

— **Industries.**

CONFEDERATION OF BRITISH INDUSTRY. Europe Committee. Industrial policy in the European Community: reappraisal and priorities. London, 1976. pp. 33.

EUROPEAN COMMUNITIES. Statistical Office. Industrial short-term trends. m., 1978(no. 1)- Luxembourg. *[in Community languages]*

— **Population.**

EUROPEAN COMMUNITIES. Statistical Office. Population and employment. a., 1950/76(1st)- Luxembourg. *[in Community languages]*

EUROPEAN COMMUNITIES. Statistical Office. Demographic statistics. a., 1960/76- Luxembourg. *[in Community languages].*

— **Statistics, Vital.**

EUROPEAN COMMUNITIES. Statistical Office. Demographic statistics. a., 1960/76- Luxembourg. *[in Community languages].*

EUROPEAN FEDERATION.

HILBERT (LOTHAR W.) Droit écrit ou droit coutumier: problème de la construction institutionnelle de l'Europe. Luxembourg, 1962. fo. 21.

SHONFIELD (Sir ANDREW) European integration in the second phase: the scope and limitations of alliance politics. [Colchester], 1974. pp. 15. *(University of Essex. Noel Buxton Lectures. 1974)*

MINNOCCI (GIACINTO) L'Europa che dobbiamo costruire: discorso pronunciato al Senato della Repubblica nella seduta del 6 maggio 1975. Roma, [1975]. pp. 23. politica regionale europea.

MARC (ALEXANDRE) Révolution américaine - révolution européenne: message du fédéralisme. Lausanne, 1977. pp. 111. *(Lausanne. Université. Centre de Recherches Européennes. Publications. 2. Le Processus d'Union de l'Europe)*

YOUNG (JOHN) Monday Club member. Europe: the unguarded legacy: a Conservative approach to European unity; (based on studies by members of the Monday Club's European Policy Group). London, [1977]. 1 pamphlet (unpaged).

FEDERAL solutions to European issues; edited by Bernard Burrows [and others]. London, 1978. pp. 225.

ITALY. Senato. Segretariato Generale. Servizio Studi. 1978. L'unione politica europea: proposte, sviluppi istituzionali, elezioni dirette; a cura di Andrea Chiti-Batelli. [Roma], 1978. pp. 314. *bibliog. (Studi e documentazione)*

EUROPEAN PARLIAMENT.

FITZMAURICE (JOHN) The European parliament. Farnborough, Hants., [1978]. pp. 182.

HERMAN (VALENTINE) and LODGE (JULIET) The European Parliament and the European Community. [London, 1978]. pp. 199. *bibliog.*

SHAW (MICHAEL NORMAN) The European Parliament and the community budget. London, 1978. pp. 38.

EUROPEAN REGIONAL DEVELOPMENT FUND.

EUROPEAN REGIONAL DEVELOPMENT FUND.

WELSH COUNCIL. The operation of the European Regional Development Fund in Wales; report. [Cardiff], 1977. pp. (38).

EUROPEAN WAR, 1914-1918.

HERVE (GUSTAVE) La muraille: recueil in-extenso des articles publiés par Gustave Hervé dans la "Guerre Sociale" du 1er février 1915 au 1er mai 1915. Paris, [1916]. pp. 331.

MASARYK (THOMAS GARRIGUE) At the eleventh hour: a memorandum on the military situation. [London, 1916]. pp. 34.

— Aerial operations.

POWERS (BARRY D.) Strategy without slide-rule: British air strategy, 1914-1939. London, [1976]. pp. 295. *bibliog.*

— Causes.

SPITS (F.C.) Wilsvrijheid en onvermijdelijkheid: grensen van de mogelijkheid tot crisisbeheersing in Juli '14; rede uitgesproken bij de aanvaarding van het ambt van bijzonder hoogleraar aan de krijgsgeschiedenis aan de Rijksuniversiteit te Utrecht...1972. Assen, 1972. pp. 30.

STEINER (ZARA SHAKOW) Britain and the origins of the First World War. London, 1977. pp. 305. *bibliog.*

— Diplomatic history.

EMETS (VALENTIN ALEKSEEVICH) Ocherki vneshnei politiki Rossii v period pervoi mirovoi voiny: vzaimootnosheniia Rossii s soiuznikami po voprosam vedeniia voiny. Moskva, 1977. pp. 367.

GONDA (IMRE) Verfall der Kaiserreiche in Mitteleuropa: der Zweibund in den letzten Kriegsjahren, 1916-1918. Budapest, 1977. pp. 428.

LEMKE (HEINZ) Allianz und Rivalität: die Mittelmächte und Polen im ersten Weltkrieg, bis zur Februarrevolution. Wien, 1977. pp. 479. *bibliog. (Akademie der Wissenschaften der DDR. Zentralinstitut für Geschichte. Quellen und Studien zur Geschichte Osteuropas. Band 18)*

MUHR (JOSEF) Die deutsch-italienischen Beziehungen in der Ära des Ersten Weltkrieges, 1914-1922. Göttingen, [1977]. pp. 235. *bibliog.*

FEST (WILFRIED) Peace or partition: the Habsburg monarchy and British policy, 1914-1918. London, 1978. pp. 276. *bibliog.*

— Economic aspects.

LONDON. Chamber of Commerce and Industry. Special Circulars to Members. No. 7. The effect of the war upon business transactions. [London, 1914]. pp. 16.

SYDENHAM (A.) Capturing enemy's trade. [Birmingham?, 1916]. pp. 16.

— Food question — United Kingdom.

NEW STATESMAN. An alternative to food tickets. [London, 1917]. pp. 3.

— Influence and results.

LABOUR PARTY and TRADES UNION CONGRESS. Memorandum on war aims: to be presented to the Special Conference of the Labour Movement...December 28th, 1917. London, [1917?]. pp. 8.

COMMUNIST PARTY OF GREAT BRITAIN. For a Marxist Leninist School. District School Material. Outlines. No.4. Period of temporary stabilization of capitalism, the second and third periods of post-war capitalism. [London, c. 1930]. pp. 16.

— Peace.

INDEPENDENT LABOUR PARTY. Demand the terms of peace: manifesto. London, [191-]. s.sh.

The RESURRECTION of Poland. 2. For a lasting peace, etc. Paris, 1915. pp. 31.

LABOUR PARTY and TRADES UNION CONGRESS. Memorandum on war aims to be presented to the Special Conference of the Labour Movement...December 28th, 1917. London, [1917?]. pp. 8.

CHINA NATIONAL DEFENCE LEAGUE IN EUROPE, and others. Manifesto relating to Chinese aspirations at the final settlement of the war. [London?, 1918?]. s. sh.

NOEL-BUXTON (NOEL EDWARD) 1st Baron, and WEDGWOOD (JOSIAH CLEMENT) 1st Baron Wedgwood. A decisive settlement. [London, 1918?]. pp. 7.

JORDAN (W.M.) Great Britain, France, and the German problem, 1918-1939: a study of Anglo-French relations in the making and maintenance of the Versailles settlement. London, 1971. pp. 234. *Reprint of the 1943 edition, originally issued under the auspices of the Royal Institute of International Affairs.*

BARIETY (JACQUES) Les relations franco-allemandes après la première guerre mondiale, 10 novembre 1918 - 10 janvier 1925, de l'exécution à la négociation. Paris, 1977. pp. xix, 797. *(Paris. Université de Paris I (Panthéon-Sorbonne) and others. Publications de la Sorbonne. Série Internationale. 8)*

— Propaganda.

HASTE (CATE) Keep the home fires burning: propaganda in the First World War. London, 1977. pp. 230. *bibliog.*

— Reparations.

HOLZ (KURT A.) Die Diskussion um den Dawes- und Young-Plan in der deutschen Presse. Frankfurt/Main, [1977]. 2 vols. (in 1). *bibliog.*

— Sources.

MAYER (S.L.) and KOENIG (W.J.) The two world wars: a guide to manuscript collections in the United Kingdom. London, 1976. pp. 317.

— Supplies.

U.K. War Office. Contracts Department. 1916. Report on local purchases for the British expeditionary force in France; by E.M.H. Lloyd and G.U. Yule. [London, 1916]. pp. 44.

— Territorial questions — Bessarabia.

OKHOTNIKOV (J.) and BATCHINSKY (N.) La Bessarabie et la paix européenne. Paris, 1927. pp. 163. *Translated from the Russian.*

— — Romania.

[KRUPENSKII (ALEKSANDR NIKOLAEVICH) and SHMIDT (ALEKSANDR K.)] What is the "Bessarabian question"? Paris, [imprint, 1919?]. pp. 7.

— Women's work.

MARWICK (ARTHUR J.B.) Women at war, 1914-1918. London, 1977. pp. 176. *bibliog.*

— Austria.

GONDA (IMRE) Verfall der Kaiserreiche in Mitteleuropa: der Zweibund in den letzten Kriegsjahren, 1916-1918. Budapest, 1977. pp. 428.

— Austria-Hungary.

The HABSBURG empire in World War I: essays on the intellectual, military, political and economic aspects of the Habsburg war effort; edited by Robert A. Kann [and others]. New York, 1977. pp. 247. *(East European Quarterly. East European Monographs. 23) (City University of New York. Brooklyn College. Department of History. Studies on Society in Change. No. 2)*

— France.

BECKER (JEAN JACQUES) 1914: comment les Français sont entrés dans la guerre: contribution à l'étude de l'opinion publique printemps- été 1914. [Paris, 1977]. pp. 638. *bibliog.*

— Germany.

GONDA (IMRE) Verfall der Kaiserreiche in Mitteleuropa: der Zweibund in den letzten Kriegsjahren, 1916-1918. Budapest, 1977. pp. 428.

— India.

ROBERTS (CHARLES) M.P. The response of India;...being one of a series of lectures on the war organised by the University of Sheffield, 25th February, 1915. [Sheffield?, 1915?]. pp. 8.

— Poland.

LEMKE (HEINZ) Allianz und Rivalität: die Mittelmächte und Polen im ersten Weltkrieg, bis zur Februarrevolution. Wien, 1977. pp. 479. *bibliog. (Akademie der Wissenschaften der DDR. Zentralinstitut für Geschichte. Quellen und Studien zur Geschichte Osteuropas. Band 18)*

— Russia.

BRESHKO-BRESHKOVSKAIA (EKATERINA KONSTANTINOVNA) A message to the American people. New York City, 1919. pp. 20.

— United Kingdom.

LLOYD George and the war: a personal history of his part in Armageddon; by an independent Liberal. London, [1918?]. pp. 159.

STEINER (ZARA SHAKOW) Britain and the origins of the First World War. London, 1977. pp. 305. *bibliog.*

— United States.

GIFFIN (FREDERICK C.) Six who protested: radical opposition to the First World War. Port Washington, N.Y., 1977. pp. 158. *bibliog.*

EUTHANASIA.

EUTHANASIA. London, [1875?]. pp. 20.

EVACUATION OF CIVILIANS.

NEW ZEALAND. Ministry of Civil Defence. 1967. Civil defence: evacuation plan. [Wellington, 1967]. fo. 8.

EVALUATION RESEARCH (SOCIAL ACTION PROGRAMMES).

The EVALUATION of social programs; edited by Clark C. Abt. Beverly Hills, [1976]. pp. 503. *bibliog.*

The ETHICS of social intervention; edited by Gordon Bermant [and others]. Washington, [1978]. pp. 431. *bibliogs. Based on a conference held in 1973 at the Battelle Memorial Institute's Seattle Research Center.*

— United States.

MIKESELL (RAYMOND FRECH) The rate of discount for evaluating public projects. Washington, D.C., [1977]. pp. 64. *bibliog. (American Enterprise Institute for Public Policy Research. AEI Studies. 184)*

SCHULTZE (CHARLES L.) The public use of private interest. Washington, [1977]. pp. 93. *Revised and expanded version of the Godkin lectures delivered at the John F. Kennedy School of Government, Harvard University in Nov. and Dec. 1976.*

EVIDENCE (LAW).

COHEN (LAURENCE JONATHAN) The probable and the provable. Oxford, 1977. pp. 363.

— Canada — Ontario.

ONTARIO. Law Reform Commission. 1976. Report on the law of evidence. [Toronto], 1976. pp. 278.

— Europe.

LANGBEIN (JOHN H.) Torture and the law of proof: Europe and England in the ancien régime. Chicago, [1977]. pp. 229.

— **Netherlands.**

PITLO (A.) Bewijs en verjaring naar het Nederlands Burgerlijk Wetboek. 5th ed. Groningen, 1968. pp. 255.

— **New Zealand.**

NEW ZEALAND. Torts and General Law Reform Committee. 1977. Professional privilege in the law of evidence: report...presented to the Minister of Justice, March 1977; [I.L. McKay, chairman]. [Wellington], 1977. 1 vol. (various pagings)

— **Russia — White Russia.**

TIKHINIA (VALERII GUR'EVICH) Primenenie kriminalisticheskoi taktiki v grazhdanskom protsesse: pri issledovanii veshchestvennykh dokazatel'stv. Minsk, 1976. pp. 159.

— **Tasmania.**

TASMANIA. Law Reform Commission. 1976. Report on the taking of evidence on commission, together with a draft bill and notes thereon. in TASMANIA. Parliament. Journals and Printed Papers. 1976, no.4.

— **United Kingdom.**

PHIPSON (SIDNEY LOVELL) On evidence; twelfth edition by John Huxley Buzzard, [and others]. London, 1976. pp. 1014.

LANGBEIN (JOHN H.) Torture and the law of proof: Europe and England in the ancien régime. Chicago, [1977]. pp. 229.

EGGLESTON (Sir RICHARD MOULTON) Evidence, proof and probability. London, [1978]. pp. 226.

EVIDENCE, DOCUMENTARY

— **Tasmania.**

TASMANIA. Law Reform Commission. 1976. Report and recommendations on the Evidence Bill 1975, microfilm and other reproductions, together with draft bills and notes thereon. in TASMANIA. Parliament. Journals and Printed Papers. 1976, no.1.

EVOLUTION.

SOLOPOV (EVGENII FROLOVICH) Dvizhenie i razvitie. Leningrad, 1974. pp. 128.

SPENCER (JOSEPH EARLE) and THOMAS (WILLIAM L.) Introducing cultural geography. 2nd ed. New York, [1978]. pp. 428. *bibliog.*

EXAMINATIONS

— **United Kingdom.**

MONTGOMERY (ROBERT) A new examination of examinations. London, 1978. pp. 88. *bibliog.*

— — **Ireland, Northern.**

NORTHERN IRELAND SCHOOLS EXAMINATIONS COUNCIL. Report ([and] Accounts). a., 1970-71/1971-72(1st)- Belfast. *Accounts commence with year 1971/72.*

EXECUTIVE ABILITY.

BRECH (EDWARD FRANZ LEOPOLD) Restoring an ailing business: a review of improving management performance. London, [1970]. pp. 23. (*British Institute of Management. Occasional Papers. New Series. OPN.6*)

EXECUTIVE POWER

— **America, Latin.**

PRESIDENTIAL power in Latin American politics; edited by Thomas V. DiBacco. New York, 1977. pp. 122.

— **Australia.**

McNAIRN (COLIN H.H.) Governmental and intergovernmental immunity in Australia and Canada. Toronto, 1977 repr. 1978. pp. 205.

— **Canada.**

McNAIRN (COLIN H.H.) Governmental and intergovernmental immunity in Australia and Canada. Toronto, 1977 repr. 1978. pp. 205.

— **United States.**

KATZ (JAMES EVERETT) Presidential politics and science policy. New York, 1978. pp. 292. *bibliog.*

EXECUTIVE PRIVILEGE (GOVERNMENT INFORMATION).

GOVERNMENT secrecy in democracies; edited by Itzhak Galnoor. New York, 1977. pp. 313.

EXECUTIVES.

MACCOBY (MICHAEL) The gamesman: the new corporate leaders;...with a new preface for this [British] edition. London, 1977. pp. 285.

ORGANIZATIONAL careers: some new perspectives; edited by John Van Maanen. London, [1977]. pp. 199. *bibliog. Derives from an Industrial Liaison Program Symposium held at M.I.T. in 1974.*

PRIOR (PETER J.) Leadership is not a bowler hat. Newton Abbot, [1977]. pp. 64.

— **United Kingdom.**

MACKINTOSH (JOHN PITCAIRN) Britain's malaise: political or economic? Southampton, 1977. pp. 26. (*Southampton. University. Fawley Foundation. Lectures. 23*)

EXETER

— **Amusements.**

LEWES (FREDERICK MARTIN MEREDITH) and MENNELL (STEPHEN) Leisure, culture and local government: a study of policies and provision in Exeter. Exeter, [1976]. pp. 75.

EXMOOR NATIONAL PARK.

HERBERT (HENRY GEORGE REGINALD MOLYNEUX) Baron Porchester. A study of Exmoor; report...to the Secretary of State for the Environment and the Minister of Agriculture, Fisheries and Food. London, H.M.S.O., 1977. pp. 93. *bibliog. 4 maps in end pocket.*

EXPENDITURES, PUBLIC.

UNITED NATIONS. Interregional Seminar on Government Accounting and Financial Management, Beirut, 1969. Report of the...Seminar...[held at] Beirut, Lebanon, 8-19 December, 1969. (ST/TAO/SER.C/117). New York, 1970. pp. 31. *bibliog.*

HARTLE (DOUGLAS G.) A theory of the expenditure budgetary process. Toronto, [1976]. pp. 98. *bibliog.* (*Ontario. Economic Council. Research Studies. 5*)

U.K. Treasury. 1976. The presentation of public expenditure plans in selected countries; memorandum submitted...to the Expenditure Committee. [London], 1976. pp. 55.

MIKESELL (RAYMOND FRECH) The rate of discount for evaluating public projects. Washington, D.C., [1977]. pp. 64. *bibliog.* (*American Enterprise Institute for Public Policy Research. AEI Studies. 184*)

ORGANISATION FOR ECONOMIC CO-OPERATION AND DEVELOPMENT. Economic Policy Committee. Working Party No. 2. 1977. Public expenditure on health. [Paris], 1977. pp. 137. *bibliog.* (*Studies in Resource Allocation. No. 4*)

PUBLIC expenditure: allocation between competing ends; edited by Michael Posner. Cambridge, 1977. pp. 270. *bibliogs. This book arises from a Royal Economic Society Conference at Pembroke College.*

NUTTER (GILBERT WARREN) Growth of government in the West. Washington, D.C., [1978]. pp. 94. (*American Enterprise Institute for Public Policy Research. AEI Studies. 185*)

ORGANISATION FOR ECONOMIC CO-OPERATION AND DEVELOPMENT. Economic Policy Committee. Working Party No. 2. 1978. Public expenditure trends. [Paris], 1978. pp. 93. (*Studies in Resource Allocation. No. 5*)

— **Evaluation.**

WHOLEY (JOSEPH S.) Zero-base budgeting and program evaluation. Lexington, Mass., [1978]. pp. 157.

EXPERIENCE.

ADVANCES in experiential social processes; edited by Cary L. Cooper and Clayton P. Alderfer. Chichester, [1978 in progress]. *bibliogs.*

EXPERIMENTAL DESIGN.

BROWNLEE (KENNETH ALEXANDER) Statistical theory and methodology in science and engineering. 2nd ed. New York, [1965]. pp. 590. *bibliogs.*

EXPLOSIVES

— **Laws and legislation — Russia.**

TIKHII (VLADIMIR PAVLOVICH) Otvetstvennost' za khishchenie ognestrel'nogo oruzhiia, boevykh pripasov i vzryvchatykh veshchestv po sovetskomu ugolovnomu pravu. Khar'kov, 1976. pp. 128. *bibliog.*

EXPORT CREDIT.

INTERREGIONAL SEMINAR ON EXPORT CREDIT INSURANCE AND EXPORT CREDIT FINANCING, 1ST, BELGRADE, 1970. Report of the...Seminar...[held at] Belgrade, 28 September to 7 October 1970. (ST/TAO/SER.C/129). New York, United Nations, 1971. pp. 47.

EXPORT MARKETING.

EXPORT seminars, 1969: papers presented. [Wellington, New Zealand Department of Industries and Commerce, 1970]. 1 vol. (various pagings).

UNITED NATIONS. Conference on Trade and Development. 1970. Incentives for industrial exports: study, etc. (TD/B/C. 2/89/Rev.1). New York, 1970. pp. 64.

EXPORT PREMIUMS.

INTERNATIONAL trade and industrial policies: government intervention and an open world economy; edited by Steven J. Warnecke. [London, 1978]. pp. 245.

— **Underdeveloped areas.**

See UNDERDEVELOPED AREAS — Export premiums.

EXSERVICEMEN

— **Germany.**

DUNKER (ULRICH) Der Reichsbund jüdischer Frontsoldaten, 1919-1938: Geschichte eines jüdischen Abwehrvereins. Düsseldorf, [1977]. pp. 354. *bibliog.*

EXTERNALITIES (ECONOMICS).

MIKESELL (RAYMOND FRECH) The rate of discount for evaluating public projects. Washington, D.C., [1977]. pp. 64. *bibliog.* (*American Enterprise Institute for Public Policy Research. AEI Studies. 184*)

PUBLIC economics and the quality of life; edited by Lowdon Wingo and Alan Evans. Baltimore, [1977]. pp. 327. *bibliogs. Mainly papers evolved from an International Research Conference on Public Policy and the Quality of Life in Cities, New Orleans, 1975, sponsored by Resources for the Future and the Centre for Environmental Studies.*

CHEUNG (STEVEN N.S.) and others. The myth of social cost: a critique of welfare economics and the implications for public policy. London, 1978. pp. 93. *bibliog.* (*Institute of Economic Affairs. Hobart Papers. 82*)

FABIAN (WALTER).

ARBEITERBEWEGUNG, Erwachsenenbildung, Presse: Festschrift für Walter Fabian zum 75. Geburtstag;...herausgegeben von Anne-Marie Fabian. Köln, [1977]. pp. 240.

FABIAN SOCIETY.

YOUNG FABIAN GROUP. Constitution: [2 versions]. [London, 1960?]. 2 pts.

FACERIAS (JOSE LLUIS).

TELLEZ (ANTONIO) La guerrilla urbana. 1: Facerias. Paris, [1974]. pp. 350.

FACTORIES.

JONES (D.T.) and PRAIS (SIGBERT JON) Plant-size and productivity in the motor industry: some international comparisons. London, 1977. pp. 26, 4. *(National Institute of Economic and Social Research. Discussion Papers. No. 8)*

— Hong Kong.

SIT (VICTOR FUNG SHUEN) Factories in domestic premises: a case study of modern Hong Kong. 1977. fo. 356. *bibliog. Typescript. Ph.D. (London) thesis: unpublished. This thesis is the property of London University and may not be removed from the Library.*

— United Kingdom.

PRAIS (SIGBERT JON) The strike-proneness of large plants in Britain. London, 1977. pp. 28. *(National Institute of Economic and Social Research. Discussion Papers. No. 5)*

— — Location.

SMITH (BARBARA M.D.) Premises in manufacturing and related uses in the Small Heath planning district, Birmingham, 1958-75. Birmingham, 1977. pp. 187. *(Birmingham. University. Centre for Urban and Regional Studies. Research Memoranda. No. 59)*

FACTORY MANAGEMENT.

LOCKYER (KEITH GERALD) Factory and production management. 3rd ed. London, 1974 reprinted 1977. pp. 490. *Previous eds. entitled Factory management.*

FACTORY SYSTEM

— United States.

The FACTORY girls; edited by Philip S. Foner. Urbana, [1977]. pp. 360.

FAITH-CURE AND SPIRITUALISM.

HARWOOD (ALAN) Rx: spiritist as needed: a study of a Puerto Rican community mental health resource. New York, [1977]. pp. 251. *bibliog.*

FAMILY.

NEWSHOLME (HENRY PRATT) The population report and the survival of the Christian family. London, [1949]. pp. 15.

YOU as a product: an essay on the family as the key link between individual structure and socioeconomic reality and changes in family structure, cultural conditioning and sexual repression with economic changes in capitalism; [by members of Newcastle University Socialist Society]. [Newcastle, 1975?]. pp. 76.

EUGENICS SOCIETY. Annual Symposium, 13th, 1976. Equalities and inequalities in family life: proceedings of the... symposium...; edited by Robert Chester [and] John Peel. London, 1977. pp. 200. *bibliogs.*

FAMILY, bureaucracy and the elderly; edited by Ethel Shanas and Marvin B. Sussman. Durham, N.C., 1977. pp. 233. *bibliogs. Based on papers at a Conference on Older People, Family and Bureaucracy held at the Quail Roost Conference Center in Rougemont, N.C., in May 1973.*

ALDOUS (JOAN) Family careers: developmental change in families. New York, [1978]. pp. 358. *bibliogs.*

— Economic aspects.

KINOMETRICS: determinants of socioeconomic success within and between families; editor, Paul Taubman. Amsterdam, 1977. pp. 324. *bibliogs.*

— History.

LASCH (CHRISTOPHER) Haven in a heartless world: the family besieged. New York, [1977]. pp. 230.

— — Bibliography.

MILDEN (JAMES WALLACE) The family in past time: a guide to the literature. New York, 1977. pp. 200.

— Australia.

AUSTRALIAN COUNCIL OF SOCIAL SERVICE. Family welfare. Canberra, 1974. fo.48. *bibliog. (Australia. Social Welfare Commission. Occasional Papers) Photocopy.*

— Belgium.

POPULATION and family in the Low Countries, 1; edited by H.G. Moors [and others]. Leiden, 1976. pp. 179. *bibliogs. (Nederlands Interuniversitair Demografisch Instituut and Centre d'Etude de la Population et de la Famille [Belgium]. Publications. vol.1)*

— Cuba.

LEWIS (OSCAR) and others. Four men: living the revolution: an oral history of contemporary Cuba. Urbana, Ill., [1977]. pp. 538. *bibliog.*

LEWIS (OSCAR) and others. Four women: living the revolution: an oral history of contemporary Cuba. Urbana, [1977]. pp. 443. *bibliog.*

LEWIS (OSCAR) and others. Neighbors: living the revolution: an oral history of contemporary Cuba. Urbana, [1978]. pp. 581. *bibliog.*

— Europe.

INTERNATIONAL FAMILY RESEARCH SEMINAR, 13TH, PARIS, 1973. The family life cycle in European societies; Le cycle de la vie familiale dans les sociétés européennes; [papers presented at the seminar] edited by...Jean Cuisenier...[and] Martine Segalen. The Hague, [1977]. pp. 494. *bibliogs. In English and French.*

— France.

MONNIER (ALAIN) La naissance d'un enfant: incidences sur les conditions de vie des familles; préface d'Alain Girard. [Paris], 1977. pp. 231. *(France. Institut National d'Etudes Démographiques. Travaux et Documents. Cahiers. No. 81)*

— India.

BEBARTA (PRAFULLA C.) Family type and fertility in India. North Quincy, [1977]. pp. 147. *bibliog.*

— Ireland (Republic).

HANNAN (DAMIAN F.) and KATSIAOUNI (LOUISE A.) Traditional families?: from culturally prescribed to negotiated roles in farm families. Dublin, 1977. pp. 227. *bibliog. (Economic and Social Research Institute. Papers. No. 87)*

— Netherlands.

POPULATION and family in the Low Countries, 1; edited by H.G. Moors [and others]. Leiden, 1976. pp. 179. *bibliogs. (Nederlands Interuniversitair Demografisch Instituut and Centre d'Etude de la Population et de la Famille [Belgium]. Publications. vol.1)*

— Poland.

JANISZEWSKI (LUDWIK) Rodzina marynarzy i rybaków morskich: studium socjologiczne. Warszawa, 1976. pp. 363. *bibliog. (Wyższa Szkoła Pedagogiczna w Szczecinie. Rozprawy i Studia. t.7) With English summary.*

TYSZKA (ZBIGNIEW) Rodziny robotnicze w Polsce: różnice i podobieństwa. Warszawa, 1977. pp. 212. *bibliog.*

— Russia.

GERASIMOVA (IRINA ALEKSANDROVNA) Struktura sem'i. Moskva, 1976. pp. 168.

SKOL'KO detei budet v sovetskoi sem'e: rezul'taty obsledovaniia. Moskva, 1977. pp. 104.

— Thailand.

POTTER (SULAMITH HEINS) Family life in a northern Thai village: a study in the structural significance of women. Berkeley, [1977]. pp. 137. *bibliog.*

— United Kingdom.

BRITTON (EDWARD) The community of the vill: a study in the history of the family and village life in fourteenth-century England. Toronto, [1977]. pp. 291. *bibliog.*

LEVINE (DAVID) of the Ontario Institute for Studies in Education. Family formation in an age of nascent capitalism. New York, [1977]. pp. 194. *bibliog.*

MARPLAN LIMITED. The state of the family. [London, 1978?]. fo. 12.

RENVOIZE (JEAN) Web of violence: a study of family violence. London, [1978]. pp. 240. *bibliog.*

The VICTORIAN family: structure and stresses; edited by Anthony S. Wohl. London, [1978]. pp. 224.

— United States.

WOLF (STEPHANIE GRAUMAN) Urban village: population, community and family structure in Germantown, Pennsylvania 1683-1800. Princeton, N.J., [1976]. pp. 361. *bibliog.*

CLARK (JOHN G.) and others. Three generations in twentieth century America: family, community, and nation. Homewood, 1977. pp. 529. *bibliog.*

FAMILY and kin in urban communities, 1700-1930; edited with an introduction by Tamara K. Hareven. New York, 1977. pp. 214. *Based mainly on papers first presented at the National Conference on the Family, Social Change, and Social Structure, held at Clark University, 1972.*

PERLMAN (ROBERT) and WARREN (ROLAND LESLIE) Families in the energy crisis: impacts and implications for theory and policy. Cambridge, Mass., [1977]. pp. 236.

YANS-McLAUGHLIN (VIRGINIA) Family and community: Italian immigrants in Buffalo, 1880-1930. Ithaca, N.Y., 1977. pp. 286. *bibliog.*

— — Mathematical models.

DAVANZO (JULIE) A family choice model of U.S. interregional migration based on the human capital approach. Santa Monica, 1972. pp. 57. *bibliog. (Rand Corporation. [Papers]. 4815)*

FAMILY ALLOWANCES

— Belgium.

BOND VAN GROTE EN VAN JONGE GEZINNEN. Gemeentelijk gezinsbeleid: onderzoek naar de toelagenpolitiek van een aantal Limburgse gemeenten. Brussel, 1970. fo.52. *(Regionaal Gezinsbeleid. 2)*

FAMILY LIFE EDUCATION.

NATIONAL SYMPOSIUM ON LABOUR AND FAMILY WELFARE EDUCATION, VICTORIA, MAHE, 1975. National symposium on labour and family welfare education, Seychelles, August 26-30, 1975; organised by the Ministry of Labour and Social Security in collaboration with the International Labour Organisation, etc. Victoria, Mahé, [Government of Seychelles], 1975. pp. 74.

PAOLUCCI (BEATRICE) and others. Family decision making: an ecosystem approach. New York, [1977]. pp. 190. *bibliogs.*

FAMILY RESEARCH.

BEYOND the nuclear family model: cross cultural perspectives; edited by Luis Lenero-Otero. London, [1977]. pp. 226. *bibliogs. Selected papers presented in the working sessions of the Family Research Committee of the International Sociological Association in the 8th World Congress of Sociology, Toronto, August 1974.*

— **United States.**

HILL (REUBEN LORENZO) and others. Family development in three generations: a longitudinal study of changing family patterns of planning and achievement. Cambridge, Mass., [1970]. pp. 424. *bibliog.*

FAMILY SIZE.

SKOL'KO detei budet v sovetskoi sem'e: rezul'taty obsledovaniia. Moskva, 1977. pp. 104.

— **United Kingdom.**

CARTWRIGHT (ANN) Recent trends in family building and contraception. London, 1978. pp. 14. *bibliog. (U.K. Office of Population Censuses and Surveys. Studies on Medical and Population Subjects. No. 34)*

— **United States.**

LINDERT (PETER H.) Fertility and scarcity in America. Princeton, [1978]. pp. 395.

FAMILY SOCIAL WORK

— **Australia.**

AUSTRALIA. Family Services Committee. 1977. Families and social services in Australia: a report to the Minister for Social Security; [Marie Coleman, chairman]. Canberra, 1978. 2 vols.(in 1)

— **Belgium.**

BOND VAN GROTE EN VAN JONGE GEZINNEN. Gemeentelijk gezinsbeleid: onderzoek naar de toelagenpolitiek van een aantal Limburgse gemeenten. Brussel, 1970. fo.52. *(Regionaal Gezinsbeleid. 2)*

— **United Kingdom.**

The CYCLE of deprivation: papers presented to a national study conference, Manchester University, March 1974 [organized by the Child and Family Care Section of the British Association of Social Workers]. Birmingham, [1974?]. pp. 33.

SMITH (DONALD M.) Social worker, ed. Families and groups: a unit at work: a description and analysis of work with families, groups and the neighbourhood undertaken at the East London Family Service Unit. London, 1974. pp. 68. *(Family Service Units. Monographs. 2)*

MEANS (ROBIN) Social work and the 'undeserving' poor. Birmingham, 1977. pp. 125. *bibliog. (Birmingham. University. Centre for Urban and Regional Studies. Occasional Papers. No. 37)*

FAMINES.

FIGHT THE FAMINE AND EUROPEAN RECONSTRUCTION COUNCIL. Economic notes, nos. 3,5,6,7; [with two leaflets: Objects of the...Council, and Trade in Central Europe]. London, 1920. 6 pts.

FANTASY.

COHEN (STANLEY) and TAYLOR (LAURIE) Escape attempts: the theory and practice of resistance to everyday life. Harmondsworth, 1978. pp. 232.

FARM INCOME

— **Australia.**

AUSTRALIA. Bureau of Agricultural Economics. 1976. Rural income fluctuations: submission to the Industries Assistance Commission inquiry. Canberra, 1976. pp. 30. *(Occasional Papers. No. 39)*

— Canada — New Brunswick.

SORFLATEN (ALLAN) Alternative approaches to New Brunswick farm price assurance and income stabilization: the second part of a two-part study; prepared for the New Brunswick Agricultural Resources Study. Bridgetown, N.S., 1976. fo. 107.

— **India.**

DESAI (D.K.) Increasing income and production in Indian farming: possibilities with existing resource supplies on individual farms; application of linear programming technique. Bombay, 1963. pp. 200. *bibliog. Based on Ph.D. thesis, University of Illinois.*

— **New Zealand.**

NEW ZEALAND. Farm Incomes Advisory Committee. 1975. Report...to the Minister of Agriculture and Fisheries; [G.N. Zanetti, chairman]. Wellington, 1975. pp. 247.

FARM LIFE

— **Ireland (Republic).**

HANNAN (DAMIAN F.) and KATSIAOUNI (LOUISE A.) Traditional families?: from culturally prescribed to negotiated roles in farm families. Dublin, 1977. pp. 227. *bibliog. (Economic and Social Research Institute. Papers. No. 87)*

— **United Kingdom — Scotland.**

CAMERON (DAVID KERR) The ballad and the plough: a portrait of the life of the old Scottish farmtouns. London, 1978. pp. 253.

FARM MANAGEMENT.

DISKALKAR (P.D.) and PAWAR (JAGANNATHRAO R.) Studies in the economics of farm management in Ahmednagar district, Maharashtra State: combined report for the years 1969-70 to 1971-72. [Delhi, Controller of Publications, 1977]. pp. 256.

GOSWAMI (PRABHAS CHANDRA) and BORA (C.K.) Studies in the economics of farm management in Nowgong district, Assam: combined report 1968-69 to 1970-71. [Delhi, Controller of Publications, 1977]. pp. 92.

GOSWAMI (PRABHAS CHANDRA) and BORA (C.K.) Studies in the economics of farm management in Nowgong district, Assam: report for the year 1970-71. [Delhi, Controller of Publications], 1977. pp. 283.

INDIA. Ministry of Agriculture and Irrigation. Directorate of Economics and Statistics. 1977. Studies in the economics of farm management in Coimbatore district, Tamil Nadu: report for the year 1971-72. [Delhi, Controller of Publications, 1977]. pp. 641.

RAJAGOPALAN (V.) and others. Studies in the economics of farm management in the Coimbatore district, Tamil Nadu: report for the year 1970-71. [Delhi, Controller of Publications, 1977]. pp. 422.

FARM MECHANIZATION.

NIALL (IAN) To speed the plough: mechanisation comes to the farm. London, 1977. pp. 231.

— **China.**

STAVIS (BENEDICT) The politics of agricultural mechanization in China. Ithaca, [1978]. pp. 288. *bibliog.*

— **United States.**

DRACHE (HIRAM M.) Beyond the furrow: some keys to successful farming in the twentieth century. Danville, [1976]. pp. 551. *bibliog.*

FARM PRODUCE

— **Canada — Marketing.**

NATIONAL FARM PRODUCTS MARKETING COUNCIL [CANADA]. Annual report. a., 1976/77[5th]- Ottawa. *[in English and French].*

— — New Brunswick — Marketing.

RYLE (GERRY) The marketing of farm products in New Brunswick: an analysis of past trends, the present position and future options; prepared for Agricultural Resources Study. [Fredericton?], 1977. fo. 68.

— **European Economic Community countries — Marketing.**

ORGANIZZAZIONE del mercato agricolo nella Comunità economica europea: interventi di mercato e organismi di intervento; tavola rotonda, Firenze 28-30 gennaio 1976. Milano, 1977. pp. 365. *(Istituto di Diritto Agrario Internazionale e Comparato. Pubblicazioni. Nuova Serie. N.3) In various languages.*

— **Nigeria — Marketing.**

STATISTICAL INFORMATION ON WESTERN NIGERIA CONTROLLED PRODUCE; [pd. by] Statistics Division, Western Nigeria Marketing Board. s-a., Ag 1967 [no. 1], Oc 1968 (no. 3). [Ibadan].

— **United Kingdom.**

IMPORTS into the United Kingdom of food and animal feeding stuffs: annual average, 1934/38. [London, 1946]. pp. 171.

FARM TENANCY

— **United States — Maryland.**

STIVERSON (GREGORY A.) Poverty in a land of plenty: tenancy in eighteenth-century Maryland. Baltimore, [1977]. pp. 187. *bibliog. (Maryland Bicentennial Commission. Maryland Bicentennial Studies)*

FARMERS

— **Ireland (Republic).**

NATIONAL ECONOMIC AND SOCIAL COUNCIL [EIRE]. New farm operators, 1971 to 1975; (by Seamus J. Sheehy and Aidan Cotter). Dublin, Stationery Office, [1977]. pp. 86. *bibliog. ([Reports]. No. 27)*

FARMERS' WIVES

— **Poland.**

TRYFAN (BARBARA) Rola kobiety wiejskiej. Warszawa, 1976. pp. 166.

FARMS

— **Australia.**

AUSTRALIA. Commonwealth Bureau of Census and Statistics. Agricultural sector: structure of operating units. a., 1974/75(1st)- Canberra.

— — Western Australia.

AUSTRALIA. Bureau of Agricultural Economics. 1975. New land farms in Western Australia. Canberra, 1975. pp. 63. *(Wool Economic Research Reports. No. 26)*

— **Canada — Ontario.**

NOBLE (HENRY F.) Trends in farm abandonment. Toronto, Farm Economics and Statistics Branch, Ontario Department of Agriculture, [1962?]. pp. 69-77. *(Reprinted from Canadian Journal of Agricultural Economics, vol. 10, no. 1)*

— **Guyana.**

HUGGINS (H.D.) An economic survey of farming in east Demerara. [Georgetown], British Guiana Department of Agriculture, [1937?]. pp. 156. *(Reprinted from The Agricultural Journal of British Guiana, Vol. 8, No. 3, 1937)*

— **Malawi.**

MALAWI. Agro-Economic Survey. 1976. Agro-economic survey: report no. 18: Karonga North: a farm economic survey of agricultural households in the Karonga North Lakeshore Plain, Karonga district, Malawi; prepared by W. Chipeta and I.M. Daniels. Lilongwe, 1976. fo. 64.

FARMS(Cont.)

MALAWI. Agro-Economic Survey. 1976. Agro-economic survey: report no. 19: smallholder tea growers in Mulanje; a farm economic survey of smallholder tea growers in the southern part of Mulanje district, Malawi. Lilongwe, 1976. fo. 151.

MALAWI. Agro-Economic Survey. 1977. Agro-economic survey: report no. 21: Chisasa: a farm economic survey of oriental tobacco and food crop growers in the south-western part of Mzimba district, Malawi; prepared by G. Hendrix and J. Sterkenburg. Lilongwe, 1977. fo. 115.

MALAWI. Agro-Economic Survey. 1977. Agro-economic survey: report no. 23: Dowa West: a farm economic survey of dark fired tobacco growers and maize/groundnut growers in the western part of Dowa district, Malawi, prepared by I.M. Daniels. Lilongwe, 1977. fo. 63.

— New Zealand — Valuation.

NEW ZEALAND. Committee of Investigation into Rentals and Freeholding of Crown Leases. 1968. Report...; chairman: W.R. Beattie. [Wellington], 1968. pp. 28.

— United Kingdom.

SALES OF AGRICULTURAL LAND IN ENGLAND AND WALES: [pd. by] Ministry of Agriculture, Fisheries and Food, (Economic and Statistics Group and Agricultural Land Service) [U.K.]. s-a., Oc 1959/Ap 1969 [1st]- [London].

BOWEN (HARRIES COLLINS) Ancient fields: a tentative analysis of vanishing earthworks and landscapes. London, [1962?]. pp. 80. *bibliog.*

FARMS, SIZE OF

— Sweden.

ENEQUIST (GERD) Agricultural holdings in Sweden 1951-1966 and 1980. Helsinki, 1968. pp. 13. *bibliog. (Reprinted from Acta Geographica vol. 20)*

FASCISM.

FELICE (RENZO DE) ed. Il fascismo: le interpretazioni dei contemporanei e degli storici. Bari, 1970. pp. 702.

GERMANI (GINO) Autoritarismo, fascismo e classi sociali. Bologna, [1975]. pp. 306. *bibliog.*

DELARUE (JACQUES) Conquête du pouvoir et nazification de l'opinion publique. Bruxelles, 1976. pp. 77. *(Cercle d'Education Populaire. Cahiers. No. 60)*

MANTA (L.H. AFONSO) ed. A frente popular antifascista em Portugal: o primeiro esboço da unidade antifascista; documentos da historia do movimento operario portugês, 1935-1937. Lisboa, [1976]. pp. 206.

FELICE (RENZO DE) Interpretations of fascism. Cambridge, Mass., 1977. pp. 248. *bibliog.*

McKALE (DONALD M.) The swastika outside Germany. Kent, Ohio, [1977]. pp. 288. *bibliog.*

NOLTE (ERNST) Marxismus, Faschismus, Kalter Krieg: Vorträge und Aufsätze, 1964-1976. Stuttgart, [1977]. pp. 400. *bibliog.*

— Bibliography.

FASCISM: a reader's guide: analyses, interpretations, bibliography; edited by Walter Laqueur. London, 1976. pp. 478.

— Caricatures and cartoons.

C'ERA una volta il Duce: il regime in cartolina; a cura di Giuliano Vittori; saggio introduttivo di Carlo Arturo Quintavalle, nota di Luigi M. Lombardi Satriani. Roma, [1975]. 1 vol. (unpaged).

MICHELI (MARIO DE) Contro il fascismo: 50 anni di immagine satirico politica nel mondo. Milano, 1976. pp. 160. *bibliog.*

— Austria.

RAPE (LUDGER) Die österreichischen Heimwehren und die bayerische Rechte, 1920-1923. Wien, [1977]. pp. 457. *bibliog. (Ludwig Boltzmann Institut für Geschichte der Arbeiterbewegung. Veröffentlichungen)*

— France.

STERNHELL (ZEEV) La droite révolutionnaire, 1885-1914: les origines françaises du fascisme. Paris, [1978]. pp. 444. *bibliog.*

— Germany.

RAPE (LUDGER) Die österreichischen Heimwehren und die bayerische Rechte, 1920-1923. Wien, [1977]. pp. 457. *bibliog. (Ludwig Boltzmann Institut für Geschichte der Arbeiterbewegung. Veröffentlichungen)*

— Italy.

MATTEOTTI (GIACOMO) Reliquie. 2nd ed. Milano, 1946. pp. 247. *Most of the articles originally published in La Giustizia, 1922-24.*

PELLIZZI (CAMILLO) Una rivoluzione mancata. Milano, [1949]. pp. 279.

FELICE (RENZO DE) ed. Il fascismo: le interpretazioni dei contemporanei e degli storici. Bari, 1970. pp. 702.

AMENDOLA (GIORGIO) Fascismo e movimento operaio. Roma, 1975. pp. 258.

BUSONI (JAURÈS) Nel tempo del fascismo. Roma, 1975. pp. 241.

LALLA (MANLIO DI) Liberalismo e postfascismo. Roma, [1975]. pp. 291.

MICHELI (MARIO DE) La matrice ideologico-letteraria dell'eversione fascista. Milano, 1976. pp. 186. *bibliog. First published in 1975.*

AMENDOLA (GIORGIO) Intervista sull'antifascismo; a cura di Piero Melograni. Roma, 1976. pp. 221. *bibliog.*

ANTONICELLI (FRANCO) La pratica della libertà: documenti, discorsi, scritti politici, 1929-1974. Torino, 1976. pp. 257.

BERTOLDI (SILVIO) Salò: vita e morte della Repubblica Sociale Italiana. Milano, [1976]. pp. 432. *bibliog.*

CANTINI (CLAUDE) Le fascisme italien à Lausanne, 1920-1943. Lausanne, 1976. pp. 71.

CIANFLONE (GEPPINA) and SCAFOGLIO (DOMENICO) Fascismo sui muri: le scritti murali neofasciste di Napoli. Napoli, [1976]. pp. 119.

COLARIZI (SIMONA) ed. L'Italia antifascista dal 1922 al 1940: la lotta dei protagonisti. Roma, 1976. 2 vols. (in 1).

CRISI economica e stalinismo in occidente: l'opposizione comunista italiana alla "svolta" del '30; a cura di Ferdinando Ormea. Roma, 1976. pp. 230.

FASCISMO e antifascismo nell'Italia repubblicana; a cura di Guido Quazza. Torino, [1976]. pp. 189.

FASCISMO e capitalismo; [by] P. Alatri [and others]; a cura di Nicola Tranfaglia. Milano, 1976. pp. 225.

FEDELE (SANTI) Storia della concentrazione antifascista, 1927-1934. Milano, 1976. pp. 196.

FELICE (RENZO DE) ed. Antologia sul fascismo. Roma, 1976. 2 vols. (in 1).

GUALERNI (GUALBERTO) Industria e fascismo: per una interpretazione dello sviluppo economico italiano tra le due guerre. Milano, 1976. pp. 268.

GUERRI (GIORDANO BRUNO) Giuseppe Bottai, un fascista critico: ideologia e azione del gerarca che avrebbe voluto portare l'intelligenza nel fascismo e il fascismo alla liberalizzazione. Milano, 1976. pp. 277. *bibliog.*

LUSSO (EMILIO) Essere a sinistra: democrazia, autonomia e socialismo in cinquant'anni di lotte; a cura del Collettivo Emilio Lussu di Cagliari. Milano, [1976]. pp. 287.

MARIANI (RICCARDO) Fascismo e "città nuove". Milano, 1976. pp. 340. *bibliog.*

MURGIA (PIER GIUSEPPE) Ritorneremoe.: (storia e cronaca del fascismo dopo la Resistenza). Milano, [1976]. pp. 413.

NENNI (PIETRO) Storia di quattro anni, 1919-1922. 4th ed. Milano, [1976]. pp. 254. *bibliog.*

I CATTOLICI dal fascismo alla resistenza; [by] Carlo F. Casula [and others]; a cura di Antonio Cucchiari. [Roma, 1977]. pp. 151. *bibliog.*

CILIBERTO (MICHELE) Intellettuali e fascismo: saggio su Delio Cantimori. Bari, [1977]. pp. 264.

FELICE (RENZO DE) Interpretations of fascism. Cambridge, Mass., 1977. pp. 248. *bibliog.*

PARTITO NAZIONALE FASCISTA. Manuale di educazione fascista; introduzione di Domenico De Masi; commento ai testi di Romolo Runcini. Roma, 1977. pp. 287. *Contains reprints of Il primo libro del fascista, and Il secondo libro del fascista.*

POLCRI (ANDREA) Le cause della resistenza italiana. [Milano, 1977]. pp. 171. *bibliog.*

DE GRAND (ALEXANDER J.) The Italian Nationalist Association and the rise of fascism in Italy. Lincoln, Neb., [1978]. pp. 238. *bibliog.*

PALLA (MARCO) Firenze nel regime fascista, 1929-1934. Firenze, 1978. pp. 419. *(Unione Regionale delle Provincie Toscane. Biblioteca di Storia Toscana Moderna e Contemporanea. Studi e Documenti. 14)*

— Romania.

SIMA (HORIA) El hombre nuevo: elementos de doctrina legionaria. Muenchen, 1964. pp. 23.

— Russia.

STEPHAN (JOHN JASON) The Russian fascists: tragedy and farce in exile, 1925-1945. London, 1978. pp. 450. *bibliog.*

— Sicily.

MICCICHÈ (GIUSEPPE) Dopoguerra e fascismo in Sicilia, 1919-1927. Roma, 1976. pp. 232.

— Spain.

FUNDAMENTO de la Nueva España. [Bilbao, imprint, 194-?]. 1 pamphlet (unpaged).

AVILA (JUSTO DE) Metodologia del nacional-sindicalismo. Valencia, 1942. pp. 48.

— Switzerland.

CANTINI (CLAUDE) Le fascisme italien à Lausanne, 1920-1943. Lausanne, 1976. pp. 71.

FATHER AND CHILD.

The ROLE of the father in child development; edited by Michael E. Lamb. New York, [1976]. pp. 407. *bibliogs.*

FAULKNER (ARTHUR BRIAN DEANE) Baron Faulkner.

FAULKNER (ARTHUR BRIAN DEANE) Baron Faulkner. Memoirs of a statesman; edited by John Houston. London, 1978. pp. 306.

FAVOURED NATION CLAUSE.

UNITED NATIONS. Conference on Trade and Development. 1969. Rules of origin in the general scheme of preferences in favour of the developing countries: report by the secretariat of UNCTAD. (TD/B/AC.5/3/Rev.1). New York, 1969. pp. 22.

FEDERAL AID TO EDUCATION

— United States.

FINN (CHESTER E.) Education and the presidency. Lexington, Mass., [1977]. pp. 167.

GARMS (WALTER I.) and others. School finance: the economics and politics of public education. Englewood Cliffs, [1978]. pp. 466.

RISING costs in education: the federal response?; (a Round Table held on March 20, 1978...); John Charles Daly, moderator, etc. Washington, [1978]. pp. 44. *(American Enterprise Institute for Public Policy Research. Public Policy Forums. 17)*

FEDERAL GOVERNMENT.

MARC (ALEXANDRE) Révolution américaine - révolution européenne: message du fédéralisme. Lausanne, 1977. pp. 111. *(Lausanne. Université. Centre de Recherches Européennes. Publications. 2. Le Processus d'Union de l'Europe)*

BRETON (ALBERT) and SCOTT (ANTHONY) The economic constitution of federal states. Toronto, [1978]. pp. 166.

DAVIS (SOLOMON RUFUS) The federal principle: a journey through time in quest of a meaning. Berkeley, [1978]. pp. 237. *bibliog.*

VEREIN FÜR SOZIALPOLITIK. Schriften. Neue Folge. Band 96/I. Probleme des Finanzausgleichs I; von Dieter Bös [and others]; herausgegeben von Wilhelmine Dreissig. Berlin, [1978]. pp. 175. *In German, with summaries and table of contents in English.*

— Australia.

GREENWOOD (GORDON) The future of Australian federalism: a commentary on the working of the constitution. 2nd ed. St. Lucia, Queensland, [1976]. pp. 361. *bibliog.*

HOLMES (MARJORIE JEAN) and SHARMAN (CAMPBELL) The Australian federal system. Sydney, [1977]. pp. 219. *bibliog.*

— Austria.

ERMACORA (FELIX) Österreichischer Föderalismus: vom patrimonialen zum kooperativen Bundesstaat. Wien, [1976]. pp. 364. *bibliog. (Institut für Föderalismusforschung. Schriftenreihe. Band 3)*

DOUIN (CLAUDE SOPHIE) Le fédéralisme autrichien. Paris, 1977. pp. 295. *bibliog.*

— Canada.

LESAGE (JEAN) Un Québec fort dans une nouvelle confédération. Québec, [Office d'Information et de Publicité du Québec], 1965. pp. 51.

CANADA and the burden of unity; edited by David Jay Bercuson. Toronto, [1977]. pp. 191.

ONTARIO. Economic Council. 1977. Intergovernmental relations. Toronto, 1977. pp. 163. *bibliogs. (Issues and Alternatives, 1977)*

— Germany.

REICHOLD (HELMUT) Bismarcks Zaunkönige: Duodez im 20. Jahrhundert: eine Studie zum Föderalismus im Bismarckreich. Paderborn, [1977]. pp. 320. *bibliog.*

— Russia.

CHISTIAKOV (OLEG IVANOVICH) Problemy demokratii i federalizma v pervoi Sovetskoi Konstitutsii. Moskva, 1977. pp. 125.

— United States.

BRIDWELL (RANDALL) and WHITTEN (RALPH U.) The constitution and the common law: the decline of the doctrines of separation of powers and federalism. Lexington, Mass., [1977]. pp. 206.

HALLMAN (HOWARD W.) Emergency employment: a study in federalism. University, Ala., [1977]. pp. 207.

FEDERAL RESERVE BANKS.

WEST (ROBERT CRAIG) Banking reform and the Federal Reserve 1863-1923. Ithaca, 1977. pp. 243. *bibliog.*

FEDERAL reserve policies and public disclosure; edited by Richard D. Erb. Washington, D.C., [1978]. pp. 108. *(American Enterprise Institute for Public Policy Research. AEI Symposia. 78B) Papers from a conference held in 1977.*

FEDOSEEV (NIKOLAI EVGRAFOVICH).

NAFIGOV (RAFIK IZMAILOVICH) Revoliutsionnye sviazi kazanskogo podpol'ia 80-kh godov, kruzhkov N.E. Fedoseeva. [Kazan'], 1975. pp. 26.

FEEDS

— United Kingdom.

IMPORTS into the United Kingdom of food and animal feeding stuffs: annual average, 1934/38. [London, 1946]. pp. 171.

FEMINISM.

KOLLONTAI (ALEKSANDRA MIKHAILOVNA) International women's day; translated by Alix Holt [from a pamphlet written in 1920]. [London, 1972?]. pp. 6. *(North London Socialist Woman. Socialist Woman Specials)*

MOTHER was not a person; compiled by Margret Andersen. Montreal, [1972]. pp. 253. *bibliog. An anthology of writings by Montreal women as the result of a course on Women in Modern Society at Loyola of Montreal.*

UNION OF WOMEN FOR LIBERATION. Feminism and the women's liberation movement. [Hemel Hempstead, 1972?]. pp. 35.

FEMINISTS. Organizational principles and structure. New York, [1973?]. pp. 10.

ROBERTS (SABINA) Revolutionary dynamics of women's liberation. London, [1974?]. pp. 36.

JAMES (SELMA) and others. Sex, race and class;...with contributions from Barbara Beese, Mala Dhondy, Darcus Howe and correspondents to Race Today. Bristol, 1975. pp. 34.

ROWBOTHAM (SHEILA) and WEEKS (JEFFREY) Socialism and the new life: the personal and sexual politics of Edward Carpenter and Havelock Ellis. London, 1977. pp. 198. *bibliog.*

BIRMINGHAM. University. Centre for Contemporary Cultural Studies. Women's Studies Group. Women take issue: aspects of women's subordination. London, 1978. pp. 210. *bibliog.*

HAMILTON (ROBERTA) The liberation of women: a study of patriarchy and capitalism. London, 1978. pp. 117. *bibliog.*

— Canada.

ROBERTS (WAYNE) Honest womanhood: feminism, femininity and class consciousness among Toronto working women, 1893 to 1914. Toronto, [1976]. pp. 60.

— China.

CROLL (ELISABETH) Feminism and socialism in China. London, 1978. pp. 363.

— France.

TRISTAN (ANNE) and PISAN (ANNIE DE) Histoires du M[ouvement de] L[ibération des] F[emmes]. Paris, 1977. pp. 262.

— Italy.

TISO (AIDA) I comunisti e la questione femminile. Roma, 1976. pp. 151. *bibliog.*

— Russia.

KOLLONTAI (ALEKSANDRA MIKHAILOVNA) Selected writings...; translated with an introduction and commentaries by Alix Holt. London, [1977]. pp. 335. *bibliog.*

STITES (RICHARD) The women's liberation movement in Russia: feminism, nihilism and bolshevism, 1860-1930. Princeton, [1978]. pp. 464. *bibliog.*

— United Kingdom.

UNION OF WOMEN FOR LIBERATION. Lessons of Skegness; a brief account of the proceedings of the Women's National Co-ordinating Committee Conference at Skegness (October 15-17, 1971) and an exposure of the dirty role of the Trotskyites, revisionists and feminists. Hemel Hempstead, [1971]. pp. 60.

WOMEN'S RESEARCH AND RESOURCES CENTRE and others. Women's liberation: an introduction. [London], 1976. pp. 8.

A WIDENING sphere: changing roles of Victorian women; edited by Martha Vicinus. Bloomington, [1977]. pp. 326.

— United States.

VIDAL (MIRTA) and others. Chicanas speak out. New York, 1971. pp. 15.

BEAL (MARY F.) Safe house: a casebook study of revolutionary feminism in the 1970's. [Eugene, Or.], 1976. pp. 153. *bibliog.*

BERG (BARBARA J.) The remembered gate: origins of American feminism: the woman and the city, 1800-1860. New York, 1978. pp. 334. *bibliog.*

CAPITALIST patriarchy and the case for socialist feminism; edited by Zillah R. Eisenstein. New York, [1979 or rather 1978]. pp. 389.

DUBOIS (ELLEN CAROL) Feminism and suffrage: the emergence of an independent women's movement in America, 1848-1869. Ithaca, [1978]. pp. 220. *bibliog.*

— Vietnam.

BERGMAN (ARLENE EISEN) Women of Viet Nam. rev. ed. San Francisco, [1975]. pp. 255. *bibliog.*

FENCES

— Law — New Zealand.

NEW ZEALAND. Property Law and Equity Reform Committee. 1970. Fencing Act 1908: working paper [no. 1]. [Wellington, 1970?]. fo. 8, 13.

NEW ZEALAND. Property Law and Equity Reform Committee. 1971. Fencing Act 1908: working paper no. 2. [Wellington, 1971?]. pp. 5,12.

FERNANDO POO

— History.

UNZUETA Y YUSTE (ABELARDO DE) Geografia historica de la isla de Fernando Poo. Madrid, 1947. pp. 495.

FERRARI (GIUSEPPE).

DOTTI (UGO) I dissidenti del Risorgimento: Cattaneo, Ferrari, Pisacane. Roma, 1975. pp. 117. *bibliog.*

FERREIRA DA SILVA (VIRGOLINO) known as Lampião.

CARVALHO (RODRIQUES DE) Lampião e a sociologia do cangaço. Rio de Janeiro, [1976?]. pp. 385.

FERRIES.

UNITED NATIONS. Interregional Seminar on Coastal Shipping, Feeder and Ferry Services, Solstrand, 1969. Report of the...Seminar...[held at] Solstrand, OS per Bergen, Norway, 1-12 September 1969. (ST/TAO/SER.C/118). New York, 1970. pp. 35. *bibliog.*

FERRIES.(Cont.)

— United Kingdom — Scotland.

TRUSTEES OF THE FERRY BETWEEN LEITH AND PETTYCUR. Resolutions of a general meeting of the Trustees for carrying into execution the Act for improving the communication between the counties of Fife and Mid-Lothian, by the ferries of Kinghorn and Burntisland and Leith and Newhaven, etc. held at Cupar, on the 25th July, 1809. [Cupar?, 1809]. pp. 19. *Also contains the reports made by John Rennie, Civil Engineer. Without title-page. Caption title.*

FERTILITY, HUMAN.

UNITED NATIONS. Department of Economic and Social Affairs. Population Studies. No. 51. Measures, policies and programmes affecting fertility, with particular reference to national family planning programmes. (ST/SOA/SER.A/51). New York, 1972. pp. 162.

UNITED NATIONS. Department of Economic and Social Affairs. Population Studies. No. 52. Interim report on conditions and trends of fertility in the world, 1960-1965. (ST/SOA/SER.A/52). New York, 1972. pp. 89.

ZAMBIA. Central Statistical Office. 1975. Fertility data from census questions and from pregancy histories: a comparison. Lusaka, 1975. fo. 30. *bibliog. (Population Monographs. No. 1)*

ZAMBIA. Central Statistical Office. 1975. Inter-regional variations in fertility in Zambia. Lusaka, 1975. fo. 24. *bibliog. (Population Monographs. No. 2)*

DEMERATH (NICHOLAS JAY) Birth control and foreign policy: the alternatives to family planning. New York, [1976]. pp. 228. *bibliog.*

DUZA (M. BADRUD) and BALDWIN (C. STEPHEN) Nuptiality and population policy: an investigation in Tunisia, Sri Lanka, and Malaysia. New York, [1977]. pp. 83. *bibliog.*

The FERTILITY of working women: a synthesis of international research; edited by Stanley Kupinsky. New York, 1977. pp. 398. *bibliogs.*

ANDORKA (RUDOLF) Determinants of fertility in advanced societies. London, [1978]. pp. 431.

— Mathematical models.

SANTOW (GIGI) A simulation approach to the study of human fertility. Leiden, 1978. pp. 215. *bibliog. (Nederlands Interuniversitair Demografisch Instituut and Centre d'Etude de la Population et de la Famille [Belgium]. Publications. vol.5)*

— Research — Simulation methods.

SANTOW (GIGI) A simulation approach to the study of human fertility. Leiden, 1978. pp. 215. *bibliog. (Nederlands Interuniversitair Demografisch Instituut and Centre d'Etude de la Population et de la Famille [Belgium]. Publications. vol.5)*

— Finland.

FOUGSTEDT (GUNNAR) Trends and factors of fertility in Finland. Helsinki, 1977. pp. 138. *bibliog. (Societas Scientiarum Fennica. Commentationes Scientiarum Socialium. 7.)*

— France.

COLLOMB (PHILIPPE) and ZUCKER (ELISABETH) Aspects culturels et socio-psychologiques de la fécondité française: une enquête...1971. [Paris], 1977. pp. 322. *bibliog. (France. Institut National d'Etudes Démographiques. Travaux et Documents. Cahiers. No. 80)*

— India.

BEBARTA (PRAFULLA C.) Family type and fertility in India. North Quincy, [1977]. pp. 147. *bibliog.*

— Italy.

LIVI BACCI (MASSIMO) A history of Italian fertility during the last two centuries. Princeton, N.J., [1977]. pp. 311.

— Russia.

BONDARSKAIA (GALINA ALEKSEEVNA) Rozhdaemost' v SSSR: etnodemograficheskii aspekt. Moskva, 1977. pp. 127. *bibliog.*

— United States.

LINDERT (PETER H.) Fertility and scarcity in America. Princeton, [1978]. pp. 395.

FERTILIZER INDUSTRY.

INTERREGIONAL FERTILIZER SYMPOSIUM, 2ND, KIEV AND NEW DELHI, 1971. Recent developments in the fertilizer industry: report, etc. (ID/94) (ID/WG.99/113). New York, United Nations, 1972. pp. 118.

— Germany.

GERMANY (BUNDESREPUBLIK). Statistisches Bundesamt. Düngemittelversorgung. a., 1976/77- Wiesbaden. *(Produzierendes Gewerbe. Reihe 8.2) Earlier data pd. as Reihe 9.2 of GERMANY (BUNDESREPUBLIK). Statistisches Bundesamt. Industrie und Handwerk.*

FESTIVALS

— Peru.

SMITH (ROBERT J.) The art of the festival: as exemplified by the fiesta to the patroness of Otuzco: La Virgen de la Puerta. Lawrence, Kan., 1975. pp. 150. *bibliog. (Kansas University. Publications in Anthropology. 6)*

FEUDALISM.

MIĘDZY feudalizmem a kapitalizmem: studia z dziejów gospodarczych i społecznych; prace ofiarowane Witoldowi Kuli. Wrocław, 1976. pp. 428. *Articles in French, English, German or Polish.*

CRITCHLEY (JOHN S.) Feudalism. London, 1978. pp. 210. *bibliog.*

— Russia.

RAPOV (OLEG MIKHAILOVICH) Kniazheskie vladeniia na Rusi v X - pervoi polovine XIII v. Moskva, 1977. pp. 261.

FEUERBACH (LUDWIG ANDREAS).

WARTOFSKY (MARX W.) Feuerbach. Cambridge, 1977. pp. 460. *bibliog.*

FICTION

— History and criticism.

BERGER (MORROE) Real and imagined worlds: the novel and social science. Cambridge, Mass., 1977. pp. 303. *bibliog.*

ORR (JOHN M.) B.Sc. Ph.D. Tragic realism and modern society: studies in the sociology of the modern novel. London, 1977. pp. 202.

FIELD EXTENSIONS (MATHEMATICS).

NAGATA (MASAYOSHI) Field theory. New York, [1977]. pp. 268.

FIELD THEORY (SOCIAL PSYCHOLOGY).

RUMMEL (RUDOLPH JOSEPH) Field theory evolving. Beverly Hills, [1977]. pp. 531. *bibliog.*

FIELDS, ALGEBRAIC.

NAGATA (MASAYOSHI) Field theory. New York, [1977]. pp. 268.

FIJI.

FIJI. Report. a., 1972- Suva.

— Economic policy.

FIJI. Central Planning Office. 1975. Fiji's seventh development plan, 1976-1980. Suva, 1975. pp. 271.

— Government publications — Bibliography.

FIJI. Government publications. s-a., Ag 1977- Suva.

— Politics and government.

GILLION (KENNETH LOWELL OLIVER) The Fiji Indians: challenge to European dominance, 1920-1946. Canberra, 1977. pp. 231. *bibliog.*

— Social policy.

FIJI. Central Planning Office. 1975. Fiji's seventh development plan, 1976-1980. Suva, 1975. pp. 271.

FILE ORGANIZATION (COMPUTER SCIENCE).

MATICK (RICHARD E.) Computer storage systems and technology. New York, [1977]. pp. 667. *bibliog.*

WIEDERHOLD (GIO) Database design. New York, [1977]. pp. 658. *bibliog.*

FINANCE.

GENERAL AGREEMENT ON TARIFFS AND TRADE. Studies in International Trade. Geneva, 1971 in progress.

EUROPEAN FINANCE ASSOCIATION. Proceedings. a., 1974(1st)- Amsterdam.

FINANCIAL MARKET TRENDS; [pd. by] Organisation for Economic Co-operation and Development. 5 a yr., Je 1977 [preliminary issue]- Paris.

CAPITAL market equilibrium and efficiency: implications for accounting, financial, and portfolio decision making; edited by James L. Bicksler. Lexington, Mass., [1977]. pp. 629. *bibliogs.*

CAVACO-SILVA (ANIBAL A.) Economic effects of public debt. London, 1977. pp. 147. *bibliog.*

DAFFLON (BERNARD) Federal finance in theory and practice: with special reference to Switzerland. Berne, [1977]. pp. 229. *bibliog.*

FISCAL policy and labour supply. [London, 1977]. pp. 108. *(Institute for Fiscal Studies. Conference Series. No. 4) Papers presented at a conference organised jointly by The University of Stirling and the Institute and held at the University in 1976.*

The POLITICAL economy of fiscal federalism; edited by Wallace E. Oates. Lexington, Mass., [1977]. pp. 355. *bibliog. Papers presented at a conference sponsored by the International Seminar in Public Economics and the International Institute of Management, held in 1976 in Berlin.*

DORRANCE (GRAEME S.) National monetary and financial analysis. London, 1978. pp. 190.

POGUE (THOMAS F.) and SGONTZ (L.G.) Government and economic choice: an introduction to public finance. Boston, Mass., [1978]. pp. 514. *bibliogs.*

VAN HORNE (JAMES CARTER) Financial market rates and flows. Englewood Cliffs, [1978]. pp. 250. *bibliogs. Revised edition of his The function and analysis of capital market rates.*

— Accounting.

UNITED NATIONS. Department of Economic and Social Affairs. 1970. A manual for government accounting. (ST/ECA/130). New York, 1970. pp. 156.

— Mathematical models.

FINANCIAL decision making under uncertainty; edited by Haim Levy and Marshall Sarnat. New York, 1977. pp. 301. *bibliogs. Based on the 1975 Israel Scientific Research Conference held at Ein Bokek, Israel, by the National Council of Research and Development.*

FINANCE.

MOSSIN (JAN) The economic efficiency of financial markets. Lexington, Mass., [1977]. pp. 158. *bibliogs.*

BHASKAR (KRISH) Building financial models: a simulation approach. London, 1978. pp. 345. *bibliog.*

— Research — Simulation methods.

BHASKAR (KRISH) Building financial models: a simulation approach. London, 1978. pp. 345. *bibliog.*

— Statistics.

GOVERNMENT FINANCE STATISTICS YEARBOOK; [pd. by] International Monetary Fund. a., 1977 (v.1)- Washington.

— America, Latin.

STATISTICAL ABSTRACT OF LATIN AMERICA. Supplement Series. 17. Money and politics in Latin America...; edited by James W. Wilkie. Los Angeles, 1977. pp. 92.

— Argentine Republic.

SOARES (CARLOS F.) Economia y finanzas de la nacion argentina, [1903-1932, vols. 2 and 3]. Buenos Aires, [1922-32]. 2 vols.

SIMPOSIO de Buenos Aires, 1972; ([organized by the] Grupo Nacional Argentino [of the] Programa Latinoamericano para el Desarrollo de Mercados de Capital]. [Buenos Aires, 1972]. pp. 37. *(Programa Latinoamericano para el Desarrollo de Mercados de Capital. Grupo Nacional Argentino. [Publications]. 1)*

El SISTEMA financiero argentino: documentos del Simposio de Buenos Aires, 1972 ([organized by the] Grupo Nacional Argentino [of the] Programa Latinoamericano para el Desarrollo de Mercados de Capital). Buenos Aires, 1973. 2 vols. *(Programa Latinoamericano para el Desarrollo de Mercados de Capital. Grupo Nacional Argentino. [Publications]. 2)*

JORNADAS DE FINANZAS PUBLICAS, 9AS, CORDOBA. Trabajos de investigaciones presentados en las Novenas Jornadas de Finanzas Publicas; organizadas por la Facultad de Ciencias Economicas, Universidad Nacional de Cordoba. Cordoba, Argentine Republic, [1977]. 1 vol.(various pagings).

— — Bibliography.

SISTEMA financiero argentino: bibliografia. [Buenos Aires], 1975. pp. 56. *(Programa Latinoamericano para el Desarrollo de Mercados de Capital. Grupo Nacional Argentino. [Publications]. 6)*

— — Statistics.

IBARRA (FERNANDO A.) Estadisticas del sistema financiero argentino. [Buenos Aires], 1972. 1 vol. (unpaged) *(Programa Latinoamericano para el Desarrollo de Mercados de Capital. Grupo Nacional Argentino. [Publications]. 3)*

IBARRA (FERNANDO A.) and COLOMBO (CHRYSTIAN) Estadisticas del sistema financiero argentino. [Buenos Aires], 1975. 1 vol. (unpaged) *(Programa Latinoamericano para el Desarrollo de Mercados de Capital. Grupo Nacional Argentino. [Publications]. 5)*

— — Cordoba (Province).

ARNAUDO (ALDO ANTONIO) and others. El sector financiero en la provincia de Cordoba. [Buenos Aires?], 1975. pp. 19. *(Programa Latinoamericano para el Desarrollo de Mercados de Capital. Grupo Nacional Argentino. [Publications]. 4)*

— Austria.

DIWOK (FRITZ) and KOLLER (HILDEGARD) Reinhard Kamitz: Wegbereiter des Wohlstands. Wien, [1977]. pp. 192. *bibliog.*

— Bangladesh.

BANGLADESH. Ministry of Finance. Economic Adviser's Wing. Resume of the activities of the financial institutions of Bangladesh. a., 1971/73(1st)- Dacca.

— Canada.

POPKIN (JOHN W.) Developments affecting Canadian financial markets, 1975-1985. [Toronto], 1975. pp. 70.

— — Ontario.

BOADWAY (ROBIN W.) and others. Input-output analyses of fiscal policy in Ontario;...edited by John Bossons. [Toronto, 1978]. pp. 228. *bibliog. (Ontario. Economic Council. Occasional Papers. 3)*

— — Saskatchewan — Accounting.

SASKATCHEWAN. Legislative Assembly. Special Committee on Public Accounts Procedures. 1965. Report; [Eldon Johnson, chairman]. Regina, 1965. pp. 39.

— Europe.

KINDLEBERGER (CHARLES POOR) Economic response: comparative studies in trade, finance and growth. Cambridge, Mass., 1978. pp. 308. *bibliog.*

— Europe, Eastern.

BRABANT (JOZEF M.P. VAN) East European cooperation: the role of money and finance. New York, 1977. pp. 394. *bibliog.*

— Germany.

VEREIN FÜR SOZIALPOLITIK. Schriften. Neue Folge. Band 96/1. Probleme des Finanzausgleichs I; von Dieter Bös [and others]; herausgegeben von Wilhelmine Dreissig. Berlin, [1978]. pp. 175. *In German, with summaries and table of contents in English.*

— Hong Kong.

WU (CHING LUN) The public finances of Hong Kong in the post-war period. 1977. fo. 309. *bibliog. Typescript. M.Phil. (London) thesis: unpublished. This thesis is the property of London University and may not be removed from the Library.*

— India.

ALL INDIA CONGRESS COMMITTEE. Select Committee on the Financial Obligations between Great Britain and India. Report. vol.1. Bombay, [1931]. pp. 70,ix,ii.

GHOSH (O.K.) The Indian financial system. Allahabad, 1958. pp. 140, iv.

— Indonesia — Statistics.

CHANGING economy in Indonesia: a selection of statistical source material from the early 19th century up to 1940...; initiated by W.M.F. Mansvelt; re-edited and continued by P. Creutzberg. Amsterdam, 1975-77. 3 vols. (in 1). *bibliogs.*

— Italy.

MATTEOTTI (GIACOMO) Reliquiê. 2nd ed. Milano, 1946. pp. 247. *Most of the articles originally published in La Giustizia, 1922-24.*

FRASCANI (PAOLO) Politica economica e finanza pubblica in Italia nel primo dopoguerra, 1918-1922. Napoli, [1975]. pp. 378.

AMATO (GIULIANO) Economia, politica e istituzioni in Italia. [Bologna, 1976]. pp. 185.

ROSSIGNOLI (BRUNO) Il portafoglio di attività finanziarie delle famiglie italiane, 1964-1973: la domanda di impieghi liquidi e di titoli mobiliari. [Milano, 1976]. pp. 127. *bibliog.*

STRUTTURA finanziaria e politica economica in Italia; contributi di L.Izzo [and others]...; a cura di Franco Bernabè. [Milano, 1976]. pp. 179. *(Club Turati. Problemi della Società. 1)*

SVILUPPO economico e strutture finanziarie in Italia; a cura di Guido Carli. Bologna, [1977]. pp. 472.

— — Accounting.

SIESTO (VINCENZO) La contabilità nazionale. Bologna, [1977]. pp. 221. *bibliog.*

— Ivory Coast.

IVORY COAST. Ministère de l'Economie et des Finances. Bureau d'Etudes et de la Coordination. Etudes économiques et financières. q., D 1969 (no.2)- , with gap (Mr 1970). Abidjan.

— Mexico.

MEXICO. Direccion General de Estadistica. Censo de Servicios, 1971. VI censo de servicios, 1971; datos de 1970: instituciones de credito, organizaciones auxiliares e instituciones de seguros. Mexico, 1974. pp. 134.

WILFORD (D. SYKES) Monetary policy and the open economy: Mexico's experience. New York, 1977. pp. 152. *bibliog.*

— — Mexico (State).

FORUM HACENDARIO; [pd. by] Gobierno del Estado de Mexico, Direccion General de Hacienda. q., current issues only. [Toluca].

— Netherlands.

WYTZES (H.C.) Enkele beschouwingen inzake het groei-aandeel. 2nd ed. Haarlem, 1969. pp. 24.

— Nicaragua.

NICARAGUA. Ministerio de Hacienda y Credito Publico. Memoria. a., 1974- [Managua].

— Puerto Rico.

PUERTO RICO. Government Development Bank for Puerto Rico. 1962. A special report on the commonwealth of Puerto Rico. San Juan, 1962. pp. 24.

PUERTO RICO. Government Development Bank for Puerto Rico. 1969. A special report on the commonwealth of Puerto Rico. [rev.ed.]. San Juan, 1969. pp. 21.

— Russia.

VOLKOV (AL'FRED MIKHAILOVICH) Perspektivnoe planirovanie finansovykh resursov. Moskva, 1976. pp. 174.

DANILENKO (ANATOLII IVANOVICH) and others. Finansovo-kreditnye problemy sotsialisticheskoi promyshlennosti. Kiev, 1977. pp. 260. *bibliog.*

GARVY (GEORGE) Money, financial flows, and credit in the Soviet Union. Cambridge, Mass., 1977. pp. 223. *bibliog. (National Bureau of Economic Research. Studies in International Economic Relations. 7 [bis])*

PESSEL' (MARK ABRAMOVICH) Finansovo-kreditnyi mekhanizm intensifikatsii obshchestvennogo proizvodstva. Moskva, 1977. pp. 224.

— South Africa — Accounting.

SOUTH AFRICA. Department of the Auditor General. Report...on the accounts of the South-Western Cape Area Bantu Affairs Administration Board. a., 1973/75(1st)- Pretoria. *[in English and Afrikaans] Included in SOUTH AFRICA. Parliament. House of Assembly. Votes and proceedings (with Printed annexures).*

SOUTH AFRICA. Department of the Auditor General. Report...on the accounts of the Northern Cape Area Bantu Affairs Administration Board. a., 1975/76- Pretoria. *[in English and Afrikaans] Included in SOUTH AFRICA. Parliament. House of Assembly. Votes and proceedings [with Printed annexures].*

— Spain.

HACIENDA PUBLICA ESPAÑOLA (formerly Economia financiera española); [pd. by] Ministerio de Hacienda, Instituto de Estudios Fiscales [Spain]. bi-m., 1968-1969 (22-31/32); 1970 ([n.s.] no.1)- Madrid.

CRONICA TRIBUTARIA; [pd. by] Ministerio de Hacienda, Instituto Estudios Fiscales [Spain]. 3 a yr., 1972 (no.1)- , with gap (1974, no.8). Madrid.

FINANCE.(Cont.)

— Switzerland — Mathematical models.

DAFFLON (BERNARD) Federal finance in theory and practice: with special reference to Switzerland. Berne, [1977]. pp. 229. *bibliog.*

— Tanzania.

RASILIMALI: Tanzania investment outlook; [pd. by] Tanzania Investment Bank. 2 a yr., [1972 (no.1)]- Dar es Salaam.

— Trinidad and Tobago.

CENTRAL BANK OF TRINIDAD AND TOBAGO. Quarterly economic bulletin. q., S 1977(v. 2, no. 3)- Port of Spain.

— — Statistics.

CENTRAL BANK OF TRINIDAD AND TOBAGO. Statistical digest. m., F 1978(v. 11, no. 2)- Port of Spain.

— Turkey.

HEPLEVENT (NIMLA) and YASER (BETTY SLADE) Analysis of fiscal performance: Turkey. Ankara, 1973. fo. (27) *(United States. Agency for International Development. USAID-Ankara. Economic Analysis Staff. Discussion Papers. No. 13)*

— Underdeveloped areas.

See UNDERDEVELOPED AREAS — Finance.

— United Kingdom.

U.K. Committee to Review the Functioning of Financial Institutions. 1977. Progress report on the financing of industry and trade; (Sir Harold Wilson, chairman). London, [1977]. pp. 48.

HARTLEY (NICHOLAS) and BEAN (CHARLES) The standardised budget balance. London, Treasury, 1978. pp. 8. *(Government Economic Service Working Papers. No. 1)*

SANDFORD (CEDRIC T.) Economics of public finance: an economic analysis of government expenditure and revenue in the United Kingdom. 2nd ed. Oxford, 1978. pp. 301. *bibliog.*

U.K. Working Party on the Financing of North Sea Oil. 1978. The financing of North Sea oil; [A. D. Bain, chairman]. London, 1978. pp. 64. *(U.K. Committee to Review the Functioning of Financial Institutions. Research Reports. No. 2)*

— — Statistics.

U.K. Central Statistical Office. 1977. New contributions to economic statistics: eighth series. London, 1977. pp. 146. *(Studies in Official Statistics. No. 28) Reprinted from Economic Trends, January 1974-February 1975.*

U.K. Central Statistical Office. 1977. New contributions to economic statistics: ninth series. London, 1977. pp. 154. *(Studies in Official Statistics. No.33) Reprinted from Economic Trends, March 1975 - December 1976.*

— — London.

U.K. Department of the Environment. 1977. London Government Act 1963: the Greater London rate equalisation scheme, 1977. London, [1977]. pp. 2.

— United States.

HENNING (CHARLES N.) and others. Financial markets and the economy. 2nd ed. Englewood Cliffs, [1978]. pp. 552. *bibliogs.*

— — New York (City).

The FISCAL crisis of American cities: essays on the political economy of urban America with special reference to New York; edited by Roger E. Alcaly and David Mermelstein. New York, 1977. pp. 361.

FINANCE, PERSONAL.

ROSEFSKY (ROBERT S.) Personal finance and money management. New York, [1978]. pp. 613.

FINANCIAL INSTITUTIONS.

SMITH (PAUL F.) Money and financial intermediation: the theory and structure of financial systems. Englewood Cliffs, [1978]. pp. 370. *bibliogs.*

— Bangladesh.

BANGLADESH. Ministry of Finance. Economic Adviser's Wing. Resume of the activities of the financial institutions of Bangladesh. a., 1971/73(1st)- Dacca.

— Canada.

PESANDO (JAMES E.) The impact of inflation on financial markets in Canada. [Montreal, 1977]. pp. 80.

— Colombia — Statistics.

COLOMBIA. Superintendencia Bancaria. Oficina Economica. Division Estudios Tecnicos. 1970. Estadisticas monetarias y financieras, 1963-1969; entidades: bancos, corporaciones financieras, compañias de seguros, sociedades administradoras, fondos de inversion y almacenes generales de deposito. [Bogota, 1970?]. pp. 100.

— Europe.

The DEVELOPMENT of financial institutions in Europe, 1956-1976; edited by J.E. Wadsworth [and others]. Leyden, 1977. pp. 357. *Papers of a colloquium held by the Société Universitaire Européenne de Recherches Financières in Brussels in 1976. In English or French.*

— Underdeveloped areas.

See UNDERDEVELOPED AREAS — Financial institutions.

— United Kingdom.

CONFEDERATION OF BRITISH INDUSTRY. Industry and the city; the first-stage CBI evidence to the Committee to Review the Functioning of Financial Institutions (the Wilson Committee). London, 1977. pp. 40.

— United States.

HENNING (CHARLES N.) and others. Financial markets and the economy. 2nd ed. Englewood Cliffs, [1978]. pp. 552. *bibliogs.*

FINANCIAL STATEMENTS.

LEV (BARUCH) Financial statement analysis: a new approach. Englewood Cliffs, [1974]. pp. 262.

FINLAND

— Biography.

VEM är vem i Norden: biografisk handbok; huvudredaktör: Gunnar Sjöström. Stockholm, [1941]. pp. 1544.

— Census.

FINLAND. Census, 1975. Asunto- ja elinkeinotutkinus, 1975;...Population and housing census, 1975. Helsinki, 1978 in progress. *(Finland. Suomen Virallinen Tilasto. Finlands Officiella Statistik. 6.C. 105) In Finnish, Swedish and English.*

— Emigration and immigration.

WESTER (HOLGER) Innovationer i befolkningsrörligheten: en studie av spridningsförlopp i befolkningsrörligheten utgående från Petalax socken i Österbotten. Uppsala, 1977. pp. 218. *bibliog. (Uppsala. Universitet. Historiska Institutionen. Studia Historica Upsaliensia. 93) With English summary.*

— History.

FEDERLEY (BERNDT) Diktatur och lantdag: finländska opinioner, 1903-1905. Helsingfors, 1976. pp. 85. *(Societas Scientiarum Fennica. Bidrag till Kännedom av Finlands Natur och Folk. H. 118)*

— Statistics.

FINLAND. Tilastokeskus. 1977. Guide to Finnish statistics; [edited by Mauri Levomäki and Matti Kyrö]. Helsinki, 1977. pp. 51. *(Käsikirjoja. 8)*

FIREARMS

— Laws and legislation — Russia.

TIKHII (VLADIMIR PAVLOVICH) Otvetstvennost' za khishchenie ognestrel'nogo oruzhiia, boevykh pripasov i vzryvchatykh veshchestv po sovetskomu ugolovnomu pravu. Khar'kov, 1976. pp. 128. *bibliog.*

FIREARMS INDUSTRY AND TRADE

— Russia.

RABOCHIE oruzheinoi promyshlennosti v Rossii i russkie oruzheiniki v XIX - nachale XX v. Leningrad, 1976. pp. 144.

FIRMS.

TAVOLA rotonda sul tema: l'impresa alla luce dell'attuale giurisprudenza e dottrina del lavoro, Roma, 30-31 ottobre 1972. Roma, 1974. pp. 127. *(Accademia Nazionale dei Lincei. Problemi Attuali di Scienza e di Cultura. Quaderni. N. 196)*

WILLIAMS (PHILIP LAURENCE) The emergence of the theory of the firm: from Adam Smith to Alfred Marshall. 1977 [or rather 1978]. fo. 339. *bibliog. Typescript. Ph.D.(London) thesis: unpublished. This thesis is the property of London University and may not be removed from the Library.*

— History.

COUNTER INFORMATION SERVICES and TRANSNATIONAL INSTITUTE. Unilever's world. London, [1975?]. pp. 103. *bibliog. (Counter Information Services. Anti-Reports. No. 11)*

— — Australia.

SMITH (ROBERT GRENVILLE) and BARRIE (ALEXANDER) Aspro: how the family business grew up. Melbourne, 1976. pp. 182.

— — Belgium.

De GENTSE textielarbeiders in de 19e. en 20e. eeuw; [by] G. Avondts [and others]. Brussel, [1976]. 3 vols. (in 1). *bibliogs.*

— — China.

CHAN (WELLINGTON K.K.) Merchants, mandarins, and modern enterprise in late Ch'ing China. Cambridge, Mass., 1977. pp. 323. *bibliogs. (Harvard University. East Asian Research Center. Harvard East Asian Monographs. 79)*

— — Denmark.

SPINK (REGINALD) DBC: the story of the Danish Bacon Company, 1902-1977. Welwyn Garden City, [1977]. pp. 96. *bibliog.*

— — France.

PAGANELLI (SERGE) and JACQUIN (MARTINE) Peugeot: la dynastie s'accroche. Paris, [1975]. pp. 156.

— — Germany.

PORSCHE (FERDINAND ANTON ERNST) We at Porsche: the autobiography of Dr. Ing. h.c. Ferry Porsche; with John Bentley. Yeovil, [1976]. pp. 290.

FELLE (MANFRED) Schmidsfelden: eine Allgäuer Glashütte des 19. Jahrhunderts. München, [1977]. pp. 181. *bibliog.*

HANSSMANN (GEORG) Lud. Sartorius & Comp., 1777-1977: ein Oldenburger Handelshaus im Wandel der Zeiten. Oldenburg, [1977]. 1 vol. (various pagings).

HENTSCHEL (VOLKER) Wirtschaftsgeschichte der Maschinenfabrik Esslingen AG, 1846- 1918: eine historisch-betriebswirtschaftliche Analyse. Stuttgart, [1977]. pp. 170. *bibliog.* (*Arbeitskreis für Moderne Sozialgeschichte. Industrielle Welt. Band 22*)

HILLEGEIST (HANS HEINRICH) Die Geschichte der Lonauerhammerhütte bei Herzberg/Harz: ein Beitrag zur Wirtschaftsgeschichte der Eisenverhüttung und Eisenverarbeitung im Südharz. Göttingen, [1977]. pp. 193. *bibliog.*

— — Italy.

BONELLI (FRANCO) Lo sviluppo di una grande impresa in Italia: la Terni dal 1884 al 1962. [Torino, 1975]. pp. 360. *bibliog.*

— — Netherlands.

PHILIPS (FREDERIK) 45 years with Philips: an industrialist's life. Poole, 1978. pp. 280.

— — Norway.

MAGELI (JOHANNES) A/S Moelven Brug: karakteristika og synspunkter. Bergen, 1977. pp. 18. (*Norges Handelshøyskole. Kristofer Lehmkuhl Forelesninger. 1977*)

— — Poland — Silesia.

SZARANIEC (LECH) Załoga koncernu "Hohenlohe" i jej walka klasowa w latach 1905- 1939. Katowice, 1976. pp. 320. *bibliog.*

— — Switzerland.

HOTTINGER (MAX) 1879- . Geschichtliches aus der schweizerischen Metall- und Maschinenindustrie, etc. Frauenfeld, 1921. pp. 189.

[NESTLÉ]. A Swiss firm and its activities in developing countries: Nestlé's experience. [Lausanne, 1963]. 1 pamphlet (unpaged).

— — United Kingdom.

SIMPSON (STEPHEN) History of the firm of Stephen Simpson, 1829-1929. Preston, [1929]. pp. 74.

AND at Lloyd's: the story of Price, Forbes and Company Limited. London, [1955?]. pp. 71.

CHARLES ROBERTS AND COMPANY. Charles Roberts and Company Limited, 1856-1956. [Wakefield, 1956]. pp. 52.

CHUBB AND SON'S LOCK AND SAFE COMPANY. Contemporary observations on security from the Chubb collectanea, 1818-1968; [edited by] Noel Currer-Briggs. London, [1970?]. 1 vol. (unpaged).

HARTE (NEGLEY B.) A history of George Brettle and Co. Ltd., 1801-1964. [London, 1973]. fo. 165. *bibliog.*

MANAGEMENT strategy and business development: an historical and comparative study; edited by Leslie Hannah. [London, 1976]. pp. 267. *The present volume has its origins in a conference...held in London on 10 June 1975.*

SMITH (ROBERT GRENVILLE) and BARRIE (ALEXANDER) Aspro: how the family business grew up. Melbourne, 1976. pp. 182.

ESSAYS in British business history; edited for the Economic History Society by Barry Supple. Oxford, 1977. pp. 267.

GRIFFITHS (Sir PERCIVAL) A history of the Inchcape Group. London, 1977. pp. 211.

TREBILCOCK (CLIVE) The Vickers brothers: armaments and enterprise, 1854-1914. London, [1977]. pp. 181. *bibliog.*

HOE (SUSANNA) The man who gave his company away: a biography of Ernest Bader, founder of the Scott Bader Commonwealth. London, 1978. pp. 242. *bibliog.*

HUGILL (ANTONY) Sugar and all that: a history of Tate and Lyle. London, 1978. pp. 320. *bibliog.*

YOGEV (GEDALIA) Diamonds and coral: Anglo-Dutch Jews and eighteenth-century trade. Leicester, 1978. pp. 360. *bibliog.*

— — — Scotland.

ORBELL (JOHN) and others. From Cape to Cape: the history of Lyle Shipping Company. Edinburgh, 1978. pp. 239. *bibliog.*

— — — Wales.

OWEN (JOHN A.) The history of the Dowlais iron works, 1759-1970. Risca, Mon., [1977]. pp. 161. *bibliog.*

— — United States.

FORRESTAL (DAN J.) The story of Monsanto: faith, hope and $5,000: the trials and triumphs of the first 75 years. New York, [1977]. pp. 285.

SEIDLER (LEE J.) and others. The Equity Funding papers: the anatomy of a fraud. Santa Barbara, [1977]. pp. 578.

— Social aspects.

MEDAWAR (CHARLES) The Social Audit consumer handbook: a guide to the social responsibilities of business to the consumer. London, 1978. pp. 154.

— Germany.

LITTLE (ARTHUR D.) INCORPORATED. New technology-based firms in the United Kingdom and the Federal Republic of Germany: a report prepared for the Anglo-German Foundation for the Study of Industrial Society. [London], 1977. pp. 323.

— United Kingdom.

LITTLE (ARTHUR D.) INCORPORATED. New technology-based firms in the United Kingdom and the Federal Republic of Germany: a report prepared for the Anglo-German Foundation for the Study of Industrial Society. [London], 1977. pp. 323.

FISH-CULTURE.

BROWN (E. EVAN) World fish farming: cultivation and economics. Westport, Conn., [1977]. pp. 397.

FISHERIES

— Canada.

CANADA. Food Prices Review Board. 1975. Fish and fish products. [Ottawa, 1975]. pp. 43, 47. *In English and French.*

— — Newfoundland.

ALEXANDER (DAVID GEORGE) The decay of trade: an economic history of the Newfoundland saltfish trade, 1935-1965. Toronto, [1977]. pp. 173. (*St. John's. Memorial University of Newfoundland. Institute of Social and Economic Research. Newfoundland Social and Economic Studies. No. 19*)

— — Nova Scotia.

NOVA SCOTIA. Department of Fisheries. Annual report. a., 1964/65(1st)- , with gaps (1966/67, 3rd; 1970/71-1974/75, 7th-11th). Halifax.

— European Economic Community countries.

EUROPEAN COMMUNITIES. Statistical Office. Fishery: catches by fishing region. a., 1964/1976- Luxembourg. *[in Community languages]*

FISHERIES of the European Community. [Edinburgh, Fishery Economics Research Unit, White Fish Authority, 1977]. pp.16.

— India — Mysore.

PUTTASWAMAIAH (K.) An evaluation of fisheries development in Karnataka. Bangalore, 1976. pp. 52.

— New Zealand.

HAMPTON (WILLIAM F.) Observations on the N.Z. fishing industry; a report to the chairman, Commonwealth Scholarships and Fellowships Committee and to the chairman of the Fishing Industry Board. [Wellington, Fishing Industry Board, 1968]. pp. 27.

— Poland.

MACHALIŃSKI (ZBIGNIEW) Gospodarcza myśl morska II Rzeczypospolitej, 1919-1939. Wrocław, 1975. pp. 355. *bibliog. With English and Russian summaries.*

FISHERMEN

— Canada — Nova Scotia.

CAMERON (SILVER DONALD) The education of Everett Richardson: the Nova Scotia fishermen's strike, 1970-71. Toronto, [1977]. pp. 239.

— Poland.

JANISZEWSKI (LUDWIK) Rodzina marynarzy i rybaków morskich: studium socjologiczne. Warszawa, 1976. pp. 363. *bibliog.* (*Wy'zsza Szkøla Pedagogiczna w Szczecinie. Rozprawy i Studia. t.7*) *With English summary.*

FISHERY LAW AND LEGISLATION.

FOOD AND AGRICULTURE ORGANIZATION. Legislative Series. No. 8. Limits and status of the territorial sea, exclusive fishing zones, fishery conservation zones and the continental shelf, with particular reference to fisheries. Rome, 1969. pp. 32.

SCOVAZZI (TULLIO) Gli accordi bilaterali sulla pesca. Milano, 1977. pp. 118. *With English summary.*

— United States.

KNIGHT (HERBERT GARY) Managing the sea's living resources: legal and political aspects of high seas fisheries. Lexington, Mass., [1977]. pp. 140. *bibliog.*

FISHERY MANAGEMENT.

BELL (FREDERICK W.) Food from the sea: the economics and politics of ocean fisheries. Boulder, Colo., 1978. pp. 380. *bibliogs.*

FISHERY MANAGEMENT, INTERNATIONAL.

KNIGHT (HERBERT GARY) Managing the sea's living resources: legal and political aspects of high seas fisheries. Lexington, Mass., [1977]. pp. 140. *bibliog.*

FLATHER (HORACE).

FLATHER (HORACE) The way of an editor. Cape Town, 1977. pp. 209.

FLEMISH MOVEMENT.

De GROOTE Stooringe 1875: historische bijdrage tot de geschiedenis van de Vlaamse studenten-beweging; een realisatie van het Instituut Klein Seminarie te Roeselare. Gent, [1975?]. pp. 431.

FLOOD CONTROL.

PENNING-ROWSELL (EDMUND C.) and CHATTERTON (JOHN B.) The benefits of flood alleviation: a manual of assessment techniques;...with contributions from Stephen J. Farrell [and others]. Farnborough, Hants., [1977]. pp. 297. *bibliog.*

FLORENCE

— Economic history.

FIUMI (ENRICO) Fioritura e decadenza dell'economia fiorentina. Firenze, 1957 repr. 1977. pp. 216. *Reprinted from Archivio Storico Italiano, 1957.*

GOODMAN (JORDAN) The Florentine silk industry in the seventeenth century. [1977]. fo. 231. *bibliog. Typescript. Ph.D. (London) thesis: unpublished. This thesis is the property of London University and may not be removed from the Library.*

FLORENCE (Cont.)

— History.

RENOUARD (YVES) Histoire de Florence. Paris, 1964. pp. 127. *bibliog.*

MALANIMA (PAOLO) I Riccardi di Firenze: una famiglia e un patrimonio nella Toscana dei Medici. Firenze, 1977. pp. 271. *(Unione Regionale delle Provincie Toscane. Biblioteca de Storia Toscana Moderna e Contemporanea. Studi e Documenti. 15)*

KENT (DALE) The rise of the Medici: faction in Florence, 1426-1434. Oxford, 1978. pp. 389. *bibliog.*

PALLA (MARCO) Firenze nel regime fascista, 1929-1934. Firenze, 1978. pp. 419. *(Unione Regionale delle Provincie Toscane. Biblioteca di Storia Toscana Moderna e Contemporanea. Studi e Documenti. 14)*

FLOW OF FUNDS.

VAN HORNE (JAMES CARTER) Financial market rates and flows. Englewood Cliffs, [1978]. pp. 250. *bibliogs. Revised edition of his The function and analysis of capital market rates.*

— Trinidad and Tobago.

TRINIDAD AND TOBAGO. Central Statistical Office. 1977. Flow of funds for Trinidad and Tobago, 1966-1974. [Port of Spain, 1977]. pp. 176. *(Financial Statistics Reports. No. 2)*

FOLK LORE.

CULTURA popolare e marxismo; a cura di Raffaele Rauty. Roma, 1976. pp. 267. *bibliog.*

FOLK LORE, BLACK

— Cuba.

CABRERA (LYDIA) El monte: Igbo-Finda, Ewe Orisha, Vititi Nfinda; notas sobre las religiones, la magia, las supersticiones y el folklore de los negros criollos y el pueblo de Cuba. Miami, 1975. pp. 564.

FONDAZIONE GIOVANNI AGNELLI.

FIORAVANTI (LUCIANO) La Fondazione Agnelli: cultura e potere nella strategia neo- capitalistica italiana. Rimini, 1976. pp. 162.

FOOD (IN RELIGION, FOLK-LORE, ETC.).

ABDUL KARIM (WAZIR JAHAN BEGUM) The belief system of the Mak Betisek of Pulau Carey, Malaysia. 1977. fo. 430. *bibliog. Typescript. Ph.D. (London) thesis: unpublished. This thesis is the property of London University and may not be removed from the Library.*

FOOD ADDITIVES.

EUROPEAN COMMUNITIES. Scientific Committee for Food. Reports. irreg., 1975(1st)- Luxembourg.

— Law and legislation — United States.

The SACCHARIN ban: risks vs. benefits; (a Round Table held on April 21, 1977 and sponsored by the Center for Health Policy Research of the American Enterprise Institute for Public Policy Research [in] Washington); John Charles Daly, moderator, etc. Washington, [1977]. pp. 42. *(American Enterprise Institute for Public Policy Research. Round Tables)*

FOOD CONSUMPTION

— Australia.

FOOD consumption patterns. Canberra, 1975. pp. 51. *(Australia. Commission of Inquiry into Poverty. Research Reports)*

— Sweden.

HOLMSTRÖM (SVEN J.R.) and SJÖHOLM (BENGT) Livsmedlens andel i våra utgifter. 4th ed. Stockholm, 1976. pp. 67. *(Jordbrukets Utredningsinstitut. Meddelanden. 1976. Nr. 2) With English summary.*

FOOD HABITS

— United Kingdom.

WARDLE (CHRIS) Changing food habits in the U.K. London, 1977. pp. 98.

FOOD INDUSTRY AND TRADE.

GARREAU (GERARD) L'agrobusiness. [Paris, 1977]. pp. 302.

HEIDHUES (THEODOR) World food: interdependence of farm and trade policies. London, [1977]. pp. 48. *(Trade Policy Research Centre. International Issues. No. 3)*

HELLING (GERTRUD) Nahrungsmittel: Produktion und Weltaussenhandel seit Anfang des 19. Jahrhunderts. Berlin, 1977. pp. 383. *bibliog.*

— Canada.

CANADA. Food Prices Review Board. 1974. Food company profits and food prices. [Ottawa], 1974. pp. 33, 34. *In English and French.*

— — Newfoundland.

CANADA. Food Prices Review Board. 1974. Food prices in Newfoundland: comparison with mainland regions. [Ottawa, 1974]. pp. 52.

— Germany.

GERMANY (BUNDESREPUBLIK). Statistisches Bundesamt. Kostenstruktur der Unternehmen im Verbrauchsgüter produzierenden Gewerbe und im Nahrungs- und Genussmittelgewerbe (formerly Nahrungs- und Genussmittelindustrien). a. (formerly irreg.), 1970- Wiesbaden. *(Produzierendes Gewerbe. Reihe 4.3.3)*

— United Kingdom.

FOOD, DRINK AND TOBACCO INDUSTRY TRAINING BOARD [U.K.]. The Board's views on Training for vital skills. Gloucester, 1976. pp. 2. *(FDT News. Special Issues. November 1976)*

— Zambia.

ZAMBIA. Central Statistical Office. 1975. Food, beverages and tobacco industries. Lusaka, 1975. fo. 67. *bibliog. (Industry Monographs. No. 1)*

FOOD LAW AND LEGISLATION.

FOOD quality and safety: a century of progress: proceedings of the symposium celebrating the centenary of the Sale of Food and Drugs Act 1875, London, October 1975; chairman: Lord Zuckerman. London, H.M.S.O., 1976. pp. 243.

— United Kingdom.

U.K. Food Standards Committee. 1972. Report on the date marking of food; [A.G. Ward, chairman]. London, 1972. pp. 64.

FOOD quality and safety: a century of progress: proceedings of the symposium celebrating the centenary of the Sale of Food and Drugs Act 1875, London, October 1975; chairman: Lord Zuckerman. London, H.M.S.O., 1976. pp. 243.

FOOD PRICES

— Canada.

CANADA. Food Prices Review Board. 1974. Food company profits and food prices. [Ottawa], 1974. pp. 33, 34. *In English and French.*

CANADA. Food Prices Review Board. 1974. Food prices in Newfoundland: comparison with mainland regions. [Ottawa, 1974]. pp. 52.

CANADA. Food Prices Review Board. 1975. Food price comparisons: a report on an experiment in the publication of comparative food price information. [Ottawa, 1975]. pp. 61, 45. *In English and French.*

— — Newfoundland.

CANADA. Food Prices Review Board. 1974. Food prices in Newfoundland: comparison with mainland regions. [Ottawa, 1974]. pp. 52.

— France.

FRANCE. Centre d'Etude des Revenus et des Coûts. 1975. Les prix alimentaires en France, 1963-1975: vue d'ensemble sur la période et essai d'explication. Paris, 1975. pp. 58. *(Documents. No 28)*

FOOD RELIEF.

HUGUEL (CATHERINE) L'aide alimentaire: analyse comparative. Paris, [1977]. pp. 103. *bibliog. (Paris. Université de Paris II. Travaux et Recherches. Série Sciences Economiques. 3)*

— United States.

AMERICAN ENTERPRISE INSTITUTE FOR PUBLIC POLICY RESEARCH. Legislative Analyses. 95th Congress. No. 4. Food stamp reform. Washington, 1977. pp. 35.

OBERT (JESSIE CRAIG) Community nutrition. New York, [1978]. pp. 452. *bibliogs.*

FOOD RESEARCH.

EUROPEAN COMMUNITIES. Scientific Committee for Food. Reports. irreg., 1975(1st)- Luxembourg.

FOOD SUPPLY.

DRYSDALE (CHARLES VICKERY) Can everyone be fed?: a reply to Prince Kropotkin. London, 1913. pp. 14.

VRIES (EGBERT DE) and RICHTER-ALTSCHAFFER (J.H.) World food crisis and agricultural trade problems. Beverly Hills, [1974]. pp. 108. *bibliog. (Georgetown University. Center for Strategic and International Studies. Washington Papers. vol. 2/17)*

[SELF-education packet; edited by Cally Abdulrazak and others. Cambridge, Mass., 1975?]. Looseleaf. *bibliog. A collection of articles from various sources on the subject of food supply and environmental policy.*

CAMPBELL (KEITH O.) Constraints on future world food supply: real or imaginary? [Sydney], 1976. pp. 8. *(Sydney. University. Department of Agricultural Economics. Miscellaneous Papers. No. 71) (Reprinted from the Australian Quarterly, Sepstember 1976)*

VALUES of growth. Lexington, Mass., [1976]. pp. 161. *(Commission on Critical Choices for Americans. Critical Choices for Americans. vol. 6)*

CASTRO (JOSÚE DE) The geopolitics of hunger. rev. ed. New York, [1977]. pp. 524. *Published in 1952 under the title Geography of hunger.*

DIMENSIONS of world food problems; [edited by] E.R. Duncan. Ames, Iowa, 1977. pp. 309. *bibliogs.*

FOOD and agricultural policy; [papers of a conference held by the American Enterprise Institute for Public Policy Research in Washington, D.C., 1977]. Washington, D.C., [1977]. pp. 250. *(American Enterprise Institute for Public Policy Research. AEI Symposia. 77C)*

FOOD policy: the responsibility of the United States in the life and death choices; edited with an introduction by Peter G. Brown and Henry Shue. New York, [1977]. pp. 344. *bibliogs.*

HEIDHUES (THEODOR) World food: interdependence of farm and trade policies. London, [1977]. pp. 48. *(Trade Policy Research Centre. International Issues. No. 3)*

TALBOT (ROSS B.) ed. The world food problem and U.S. food politics and policies, 1972- 1976: a readings book. Ames, Iowa, 1977. pp. 381.

WALKER (ADRIAN) One crust of bread: (new directions for food and agriculture policy in the UK in the context of world needs). London, [1977]. pp. 29. *bibliog. (Oxfam. Public Affairs Unit. Oxfam Public Affairs Reports. 4)*

FOREST PRODUCTS

BELL (FREDERICK W.) Food from the sea: the economics and politics of ocean fisheries. Boulder, Colo., 1978. pp. 380. bibliogs.

MAREI (SAYED) The world food crisis. 2nd ed. London, 1978. pp. 134.

The POLITICAL economy of food; edited by Vilho Harle. Farnborough, Hants., [1978]. pp. 438. *A collection of papers presented to an international research seminar held in Tampere, Finland, in 1976 under the auspices of the Tampere Peace Research Institute and the Institute of Political Science, University of Tampere.*

— Arab countries.

MAREI (SAYED) The world food crisis. 2nd ed. London, 1978. pp. 134.

— Europe.

POST (JOHN DEXTER) The last great subsistence crisis in the western world. Baltimore, [1977]. pp. 240. bibliog.

— India.

BANSIL (PURAN CHAND) India's food resources and population: a historical and analytical study. Bombay, [1958]. pp. 252. bibliog.

— Italy.

BERTELÈ (UMBERTO) and BRIOSCHI (FRANCESCO) Il sistema agricolo-alimentare in Italia. Bologna, [1976]. pp. 204.

— Japan.

SANDERSON (FRED HUGO) Japan's food prospects and policies. Washington, D.C., [1978]. pp. 99. bibliog. *Published under the auspices of the Brookings Institution.*

— Netherlands.

Het VOEDEN van Nederland, nu en in de toekomst: (preadviezen voor het symposium, 14 oktober 1971); door M.J.L. Dols [and others]. 's-Gravenhage, 1971. pp. 70. *(Instituut van Ingenieurs. Stichting Toekomstbeeld der Techniek. Toekomstbeeld der Techniek. 9)*

— Solomon Islands.

SOLOMON ISLANDS. Committee on Food Supplies. 1974. Food and self-reliance: report; [S. Cheka, chairman]. Honiara, 1974. pp. 68. bibliog.

— United Kingdom.

LOSING ground: the first of three discussion papers on United Kingdom food prospects; [by] Michael Allaby [and others]. rev. ed. London, 1975. pp. 56.

WALKER (ADRIAN) One crust of bread: (new directions for food and agriculture policy in the UK in the context of world needs). London, [1977]. pp. 29. bibliog. *(Oxfam. Public Affairs Unit. Oxfam Public Affairs Reports. 4)*

WARDLE (CHRIS) Changing food habits in the U.K. London, 1977. pp. 98.

— United States.

TALBOT (ROSS B.) ed. The world food problem and U.S. food politics and policies, 1972-1976: a readings book. Ames, Iowa, 1977. pp. 381.

FORCED LABOUR

— Russia.

CONQUEST (ROBERT) Kolyma: the arctic death camps. London, 1978. pp. 256. bibliog.

FORD (GERALD RUDOLPH) President of the United States.

A DISCUSSION with Gerald R. Ford: the American Presidency. Washington, 1977. pp. 19. *(American Enterprise Institute for Public Policy Research. AEI Studies. 159)*

FORD MOTOR COMPANY.

COUNTER INFORMATION SERVICES. Anti-Reports. No. 20. The Ford Motor Company. Nottingham, [1978]. pp. 68.

FORECASTING.

KATERNEN 2000. Jaargang 1969, nummer 9/10. Balans der futurologie. Amersfoort, 1969. pp. 46.

DECOUFLE (ANDRE CLEMENT) Sociologie de la prévision: l'exemple de la prospective sociale en France. Paris, [1976]. pp. 144. bibliog.

EMERY (FREDERICK E.) Futures we are in. Leiden, 1977. pp. 230. bibliog.

POLITIKA KSČ: ciele a prostriedky. Bratislava, 1977. pp. 273. *(Komunistická Strana Slovenska. Ústredný Výbor. Ústav Marxizmu-Leninizmu. Zborník. roč.17, č.1)*

ASCHER (WILLIAM) Forecasting: an appraisal for policy-makers and planners. Baltimore, [1978]. pp. 239.

WORLD futures: the great debate; edited by Christopher Freeman and Marie Jahoda. London, 1978. pp. 416. bibliog. *Based on a programme of studies at the Science Policy Research Unit, University of Sussex.*

FOREIGN EXCHANGE.

DELIBANES (DEMETRIOS) Fluctuating exchange rates. Athen, 1972. pp. 15. *(Extract from Anamnestikos tomos Emmanouel Michelake)*

The EMERGING international monetary order and the banking system; editor, Yair Aharoni. Tel Aviv, [1976]. pp. 191. *Papers of a seminar held in Israel in 1975, sponsored by Tel Aviv University Top Executive Course.*

BLACK (STANLEY W.) Floating exchange rates and national economic policy. New Haven, 1977. pp. 204.

CLARKE (STEPHEN V.O.) Exchange-rate stabilization in the mid-1930s: negotiating the tripartite agreement. Princeton, 1977. pp. 59. bibliog. *(Princeton University. Department of Economics and Sociology. International Finance Section. Princeton Studies in International Finance. No. 41)*

The INTERNATIONAL payments crisis and the development of East-West trade; translated from French. Brussels, 1977. pp. 150. *Proceedings of a colloquium held in 1975 under the auspices of the Centre for Research on International Institutions, Geneva.*

PLUMPTRE (ARTHUR FITZGERALD WYNNE) Three decades of decision: Canada and the world monetary system, 1944-75. Toronto, [1977]. pp. 335. bibliog.

TOSINI (PAULA A.) Leaning against the wind: a standard for managed floating. Princeton, 1977. pp. 27. bibliog. *(Princeton University. Department of Economics and Sociology. International Finance Section. Essays in International Finance. No. 126)*

WILLETT (THOMAS D.) Floating exchange rates and international monetary reform. Washington, D.C., [1977]. pp. 146. *(American Enterprise Institute for Public Policy Research. AEI Studies. 172)*

ALIBER (ROBERT ZELWIN) Exchange risk and corporate international finance. London, 1978. pp. 164.

ARTUS (JACQUES B.) and CROCKETT (ANDREW) Floating exchange rates and the need for surveillance. Princeton, 1978. pp. 38. bibliog. *(Princeton University. Department of Economics and Sociology. International Finance Section. Essays in International Finance. No. 127)*

CONINX (RAYMOND G.F.) Foreign exchange today. Cambridge, 1978. pp. 167. bibliog.

HEYWOOD (JOHN) Foreign exchange and the corporate treasurer. London, 1978. pp. 160. bibliog.

ISARD (PETER) Exchange-rate determination: a survey of popular views and recent models. Princeton, 1978. pp. 52. bibliog. *(Princeton University. Department of Economics and Sociology. International Finance Section. Princeton Studies in International Finance. No. 42)*

McCUSKER (JOHN J.) Money and exchange in Europe and America, 1600-1775: a handbook. London, 1978. pp. 367. bibliog.

— Accounting.

HELLEMAN (JOHANNES VAN) Valutaproblemen bij bedrijfsbeleid en verslaggeving. [1977]. pp. 611. bibliog. *Proefschrift (doctor) - Erasmus Universiteit Rotterdam. With English summary.*

— Law — Chile.

BEHRMAN (JERE R.) Foreign trade regimes and economic development: Chile. New York, 1976. pp. 408. bibliog. *(National Bureau of Economic Research. Special Conference Series on Foreign Trade Regimes and Economic Development. vol. 8)*

— Europe, Eastern.

BRABANT (JOZEF M.P. VAN) East European cooperation: the role of money and finance. New York, 1977. pp. 394. bibliog.

— Turkey.

YASER (BETTY SLADE) Convertible foreign exchange deposit accounts and foreign private loans. Ankara, 1973. fo. 16. *(United States. Agency for International Development. USAID-Ankara. Economic Analysis Staff. Discussion Papers. No. 14)*

— United Kingdom.

ODLING-SMEE (JOHN) and HARTLEY (NICHOLAS) Some effects of exchange rate changes. 2nd ed. London, Treasury, 1978. pp. 12. *(Government Economic Service Working Papers. No. 2)*

FOREIGN TRADE PROMOTION.

UNITED NATIONS. Conference on Trade and Development. 1970. Incentives for industrial exports: study, etc. (TD/B/C. 2/89/Rev.1). New York, 1970. pp. 64.

— Switzerland.

BADER (URS G.) Die Exportförderungspolitik der schweizerischen Uhrenindustrie. Zürich, 1977. pp. 171. bibliog. *Inaugural-Dissertation - Universität Bern.*

FOREIGN TRADE REGULATION.

GENERAL AGREEMENT ON TARIFFS AND TRADE. Studies in International Trade. Geneva, 1971 in progress.

EXPERT GROUP MEETING ON PLANNING THE FOREIGN TRADE SECTOR IN RELATION TO OVER-ALL PLANNING, BEIRUT, 1971. Report of the Expert Group Meeting...[in] Beirut, Lebanon, 7 to 11 June, 1971. (ST/TAO/SER.C/135). New York, United Nations, 1971. pp. 16.

PŁOWIEC (URSZULA) Centralne sterowanie handlem zagranicznym. Warszawa, 1975. pp. 296. bibliog.

CARREAU (DOMINIQUE) and others. Droit international économique. Paris, 1978. pp. 513.

FOREST MANAGEMENT

— Nigeria.

NIGERIA. 1948. Forest administration plan, Nigeria, 1946-55, under a ten-year plan of development for Nigeria, 1946. Lagos, 1948. pp. 42. *(Sessional Papers. 1948. No. 13)*

FOREST PRODUCTS

— Canada — Nova Scotia.

NOVA SCOTIA. Department of Lands and Forests. 1968. Producers and production of forest products, 1967. [Halifax, 1968?]. fo. 29. *(Extension Notes. 50)*

— Europe.

TIMBER BULLETIN FOR EUROPE. Supplements; [pd. by] Economic Commission for Europe, United Nations. irreg., 1960/65- Geneva. *[in English with some issues in English, French and Russian].*

FOREST SURVEYS

— Canada — Nova Scotia.

NOVA SCOTIA. Department of Lands and Forests. 1958. The forest resources of Nova Scotia. [Halifax], 1958. pp. 171.

— Sudan.

FORESTRY development prospects in the Imatong central forest reserve, southern Sudan; by R.N. Jenkin [and others]. Tolworth, 1977. 2 vols (in 1). bibliog. (U.K. Ministry of Overseas Development. Land Resources Division. Land Resource Studies. 28) 7 maps in end pocket.

FORESTS AND FORESTRY

— Economic aspects — Canada — Ontario.

ONTARIO. Ministry of Natural Resources. Timber Sales Branch. 1977. The forest industry in the economy of Ontario. Toronto, 1977. fo. 63.

— — United States.

CLAWSON (MARION) The economics of national forest management. Washington, D.C., 1976. pp. 117. (Resources for the Future, Inc. Working Papers. EN-6)

— Australia — South Australia.

SOUTH AUSTRALIA. Woods and Forests Department. 1947. Empire forests and the war: statement prepared...for the fifth Empire Forestry Conference to be held in London, 1947. Adelaide, 1947. pp. 40.

— Canada — British Columbia.

BRITISH COLUMBIA. Task Force on Crown Timber Disposal. 1974. Forest tenures in British Columbia: policy background paper; [Peter H. Pearse, chairman]. Victoria, 1974 [repr. 1975]. pp. 131.

— — Newfoundland.

NEWFOUNDLAND. Forestry Division. 1947. Empire forests and the war: [statement prepared for the fifth Empire Forestry Conference, 1947]. [St. John's?, 1947?]. pp. (18).

— — Nova Scotia.

NOVA SCOTIA. Department of Lands and Forests. Annual report (formerly Report). a., 1957/58, 1962/63- , with gaps (1964/65, 1967/68-1971/72) Halifax. *File includes Interim report for 1966/67.*

— Europe.

TIMBER BULLETIN FOR EUROPE. Supplements; [pd. by] Economic Commission for Europe, United Nations. irreg., 1960/65- Geneva. [in English with some issues in English, French and Russian].

— Mauritius.

MAURITIUS. Forest Department. 1968. Progress report, 1961-65;... prepared for the Commonwealth Forestry Conference, 1968. Curepipe, 1968. pp. 18.

— New Zealand.

NEW ZEALAND. New Zealand Forest Service. 1968. Progress report, 1960-65;...prepared for the Commonwealth Forestry Conference, 1968. Wellington, 1968. pp. 30.

ALLSOP (FREDERICK) The first fifty years of New Zealand's forest service: a history from the time of its setting up in 1919 to the celebration of its fiftieth anniversary in 1969. Wellington, 1973. pp. 123. bibliog. (New Zealand. New Zealand Forest Service. Information Series. No. 59)

— Poland.

POLAND. Polish Information Center, New York. 1940. The German exploitation of Polish forests. New York, [1940?]. pp. 19. (Documents relating to the Administration of Occupied Countries in Eastern Europe. No.1)

— Russia — Mordvinian Republic.

TONKIKH (VLADISLAV SERGEEVICH) Lesa Mordovii: lesa Mordovskoi ASSR i perspektivy ikh uluchsheniia. Saransk, 1976. pp. 175.

— Sweden.

SWEDEN. Statistiska Centralbyrån. Arbetskraften i skogsbruket: definitiva uppgifter. a., 1972- Stockholm. [in Swedish with English summary and table heading]

FORGERY

— Korea.

KOREA (REPUBLIC). 1964. Forgery and counterfeiting. Seoul, [1964]. pp. 24.

FORMOSA

See TAIWAN.

FOS

— Economic conditions.

INDUSTRIE des fibres synthétiques: délocalisation en Méditerranée: conséquences pour Fos-Etang de Berre; [Yvon le Moal and others'. (Marseille', (Organisation d'Etudes d'A ménagement de l'Aire Metropolitaine Provence-Côte d'Azur), 1973. FO. 94. bibliog.

FOSTER (JOHN) 1740-1828.

MALCOMSON (A.P.W.) John Foster: the politics of the Anglo-Irish ascendancy. Oxford, 1978. pp. 504. bibliog.

FOSTER DAY CARE.

— United Kingdom.

SHANKLAND-COX PARTNERSHIP and INSTITUTE OF COMMUNITY STUDIES. Inner area study: Lambeth: the Groveway project: an experiment in salaried childminding. [London], Department of the Environment, [1977]. pp. 85.

— United States.

JOFFE (CAROLE E.) Friendly intruders: childcare professionals and family life. Berkeley, [1977]. pp. 172. bibliog.

FOSTER HOME CARE

— Sweden.

STYMNE (ANDERS) and SAMBERGS (ÅKE) Fosterbarn i lantbrukarfamiljer. Stockholm, [1977]. pp. 135. bibliog. (Jordbrukets Utredningsinstitut. Meddelanden. 1976. Nr. 5/6) With English summary.

— United States — New York (City).

YOUNG (DENNIS R.) and others. Foster care and nonprofit agencies. Lexington, Mass., [1977]. pp. 265.

FOUCAULT (MICHEL).

LECOURT (DOMINIQUE) Marxism and epistemology: Bachelard, Canguilhem and Foucault; translated from the French by Ben Brewster. London, 1975. pp. 223. bibliog.

FOUNDLINGS

— France.

APPLICATION du système de Mettray aux colonies agricoles d'orphelins et d'enfants trouvés. n.p. [185-?]. pp. 7.

FOUNDRIES

— Safety measures.

NATIONAL FOUNDERS' ASSOCIATION. N.F.A. safety code for foundries: prepared for the guidance of foundry managers, etc. Chicago, 1916. pp. 7.

FOUR-DAY WEEK

— United States.

MAKLAN (DAVID M.) The four-day workweek: blue collar adjustment to a nonconventional arrangement of work and leisure time. New York, 1977. pp. 204. bibliog.

FOURIER (FRANÇOIS CHARLES MARIE).

ACTUALITE de Fourier: colloque d'Arc-et-Senans sous la direction de Henri Lefebvre. Paris, [1975]. pp. 291.

FRANCE.

NEWS FROM FRANCE; [pd. by] French Embassy Press and Information Service...London. m. London. *Current issues only kept.*

— Armed forces — Political activity.

MALBOSC (FRANÇOIS) pseud. Civils, si vous saviez... Paris, 1977. pp. 178.

— Army — History.

SCOTT (SAMUEL F.) The response of the Royal Army to the French revolution: the role and development of the line army, 1787-93. Oxford, [1978]. pp. 243. bibliog.

— Biography.

FRITSCH (PIERRE) Les Wendel: rois de l'acier français. Paris, [1976]. pp. 280. bibliog.

MENDES-FRANCE (PIERRE) La vérité guidait leurs pas. [Paris, 1976]. pp. 261.

— Census.

FRANCE. Census, 1962. Recensement général de la population de 1962; résultats du dépouillement exhaustif: population, ménages, logements, immeubles; fascicules régionaux. Paris, 1967. 21 parts (in 2 vols.)

FRANCE. Census, 1975. Recensement général de la population en 1975: population de la France; départements, arrondissements, cantons, communes; ([with] Complément[s]). [Paris, 1976 in progress].

FRANCE. Census, 1975. Recensement général de la population de 1975: zones de peuplement industriel ou urbain: délimitation 1975: évolutions démographiques 1968-1975 et 1962-1968. [Paris], [1977]. pp. 947. *6 maps in end pocket.*

— Civilization.

ARDAGH (JOHN) The new France. 3rd ed. Harmondsworth, 1977. pp. 733. bibliog.

— Colonies.

SORUM (PAUL CLAY) Intellectuals and decolonization in France. Chapel Hill, N.C., [1977]. pp. 305. bibliog.

— — Administration.

DELAVIGNETTE (ROBERT) Robert Delavignette on the French Empire: selected writings; (edited by William B. Cohen, with the assistance of Adelle Rosenzweig); selections translated by Camille Garnier. Chicago, [1977]. pp. 148. bibliog.

— — History.

DELAVIGNETTE (ROBERT) Robert Delavignette on the French Empire: selected writings; (edited by William B. Cohen, with the assistance of Adelle Rosenzweig); selections translated by Camille Garnier. Chicago, [1977]. pp. 148. bibliog.

— Commerce.

PLESHKOVA (SOF'IA LEONIDOVNA) K istorii kupecheskogo kapitala vo Frantsii v XV veke: Zhak Ker [i.e. Jacques Coeur] i ego deiatel'nost'. Moskva, 1977. pp. 181. bibliog.

— — Europe, Eastern.

ENGLISH (FREDERICK C.) East-West trade: the French role. Loughborough, 1977. pp. 42. bibliog.

FRANCE.

— — Mediterranean.

DOSSIERS sur le commerce français en Méditerranée orientale au XVIIIe siècle; [by] Jean-Pierre Filippini [and others]. Paris, [1976]. pp. 251. *bibliog. (Paris. Université de Paris II. Travaux et Recherches. Série Sciences Historiques. 10)*

— Constitution.

BIRNBAUM (PIERRE) and others. Réinventer le Parlement. [Paris, 1977]. pp. 223.

— Constitutional history.

BURDEAU (GEORGES) Droit constitutionnel et institutions politiques. 18th ed. Paris, 1977. pp. 690.

— Constitutional law.

BURDEAU (GEORGES) Droit constitutionnel et institutions politiques. 18th ed. Paris, 1977. pp. 690.

MELANGES offerts à Georges Burdeau: le pouvoir. Paris, 1977. pp. 1190.

— Economic conditions.

FRANCE. Commissariat Général du Plan. 1976. Dossier quantitatif relatif aux perspectives de développement au cours du VIIe plan; (préparation du 7e plan). Paris, [1976]. pp. 138.

LAULAN (YVES) Physiologie de la France. Paris, [1976]. pp. 290.

ARDAGH (JOHN) The new France. 3rd ed. Harmondsworth, 1977. pp. 733. *bibliog.*

LE PORS (ANICET) ed. Immigration et développement économique et social; balance des paiements, bilan social, impacts sectoriels et macroéconomiques: rapport général. Paris, La Documentation Française, [1977]. pp. 364. *(Etudes Prioritaires Interministérielles)*

ALBERTINI (JEAN MARIE) L'economie française. Paris, [1978]. pp. 160.

GOUX (CHRISTIAN) Sortir de la crise. [Paris, 1978]. pp. 163.

— — Mathematical models.

BOYER (R.) and MISTRAL (J.) Inflation, investment and employment: a simple multisector model of the French economy with extension to some international comparisons. Paris, 1976. pp. 52. *(Centre d'Études Prospectives D'Économie Mathématique Appliquées à la Planification. [Publications]. No. 7608)*

— Economic history.

O'BRIEN (PATRICK) and KEYDER (CAGLAR) Economic growth in Britain and France, 1780-1914: two paths to the twentieth century. London, 1978. pp. 205.

— Economic policy.

FABRE-LUCE (ALFRED) Après la législature des dupes: le 22 avril. Paris, 1928. pp. 104.

FRANCE. Conseil Economique. 1949. Notes sur les travaux du Conseil Economique, 1947-1948-1949. Paris, 1949. pp. 150.

FRANCE. Commissariat Général du Plan de Modernisation et d'Equipement. 1953. Rapport sur la réalisation du plan de modernisation et d'équipement de l'Union française, année 1952. Paris, 1953. pp. 326.

FRANCE. Direction de la Documentation. La Documentation Française. Notes et Etudes Documentaires. Nos. 4,306-4, 307. Un essai de mesure anti-inflationniste: le prélèvement conjoncturel; par Jean-Paul Courthéoux. Paris, 1976. pp. 61. *bibliog.*

COHEN (STEPHEN S.) Modern capitalist planning: the French model. Berkeley, 1977. pp. 334. *bibliog. Reprint of the 1969 edition with additional preface and postscript.*

KOLM (SERGE CHRISTOPHE) La transition socialiste: la politique économique de gauche. Paris, 1977. pp. 212.

— Emigration and immigration.

N'DONGO (SALLY) "Coopération" et néo-colonialisme. Paris, 1976. pp. 199.

FRANCE. Secrétariat d'Etat aux Travailleurs Immigrés. 1977. La nouvelle politique de l'immigration. [Paris, 1977?]. pp. 165.

Les IMMIGRÉS du Maghreb: études sur l'adaptation en mili urbain; [by J.A. Carreno and others]. [Paris], 1977. pp. 411. *bibliog. (France. Institut National d'Etudes Démographiques. Travaux et Documents. Cahiers. No. 79)*

LE PORS (ANICET) ed. Immigration et développement économique et social; balance des paiements, bilan social, impacts sectoriels et macroéconomiques: rapport général. Paris, La Documentation Française, [1977]. pp. 364. *(Etudes Prioritaires Interministérielles)*

— Executive departments.

BIRNBAUM (PIERRE) Les sommets de l'État: essai sur l'élite du pouvoir en France. Paris, [1977]. pp. 188.

— Foreign economic relations.

LAULAN (YVES) Physiologie de la France. Paris, [1976]. pp. 290.

L'IMPERIALISME français aujourd'hui: journées d'étude de la Section de politique extérieure du Comité central du Parti communiste français, 22-23 mai 1976. [Paris, 1977]. pp. 190.

Les SOCIALISTES et le Tiers Monde: éléments pour une politique socialiste de relations avec le Tiers Monde. [Paris], 1977. pp. 251.

— — Vietnam.

FRONT SOLIDARITE INDOCHINE. Documents. No. 7. Le néo-colonialisme français: la France complice de Thieu. Paris, 1973. pp. 38. *bibliog.*

— Foreign relations.

ADAMTHWAITE (ANTHONY P.) France and the coming of the Second World War, 1936-1939. London, 1977. pp. 434. *bibliog.*

ALPHAND (HERVE) L'étonnement d'être: journal, 1939-1973. [Paris, 1977]. pp. 614.

L'IMPERIALISME français aujourd'hui: journées d'étude de la Section de politique extérieure du Comité central du Parti communiste français, 22-23 mai 1976. [Paris, 1977]. pp. 190.

MENIL (LOIS PATTISON DE) Who speaks for Europe?: the vision of Charles de Gaulle. London, [1977]. pp. 232. *bibliog.*

— — Algeria.

ADLER (STEPHEN) International migration and dependence. Farnborough, [1977]. pp. 235. *bibliog.*

— — Cameroun.

BETI (MONGO) Main basse sur le Cameroun: autopsie d'une décolonisation. [2nd ed.] Paris, 1977. pp. 270.

— — Europe, Eastern.

KOMJATHY (ANTHONY TIHAMER) The crises of France's east central European diplomacy, 1933-1938. New York, 1976. pp. 277. *bibliog. (East European Quarterly. East European Monographs. 21.)*

— — Germany.

L'HUILLIER (FERNAND) Dialogues Franco-Allemands, 1925-1933. Gap, 1971. pp. 175. *(Strasbourg. Université. Faculté des Lettres. Publications)*

Les RELATIONS franco-allemandes, 1933-1939; (actes du colloque international...organisé...à Strasbourg du 7 au 10 octobre, 1975). Paris, 1976. pp. 424. *(Centre National de la Recherche Scientifique. Colloques Internationaux. No. 563) Articles in French or German.*

BARIETY (JACQUES) Les relations franco-allemandes après la première guerre mondiale, 10 novembre 1918 - 10 janvier 1925, de l'exécution à la négociation. Paris, 1977. pp. xix, 797. *(Paris. Université de Paris 1 (Panthéon-Sorbonne) and others. Publications de la Sorbonne. Série Internationale. 8)*

BOISVERT (JEAN JACQUES) Les relations franco-allemandes en 1920. Montréal, 1977. pp. 283. *bibliog.*

POIDEVIN (RAYMOND) and BARIETY (JACQUES) Les relations franco-allemandes, 1815-1975. Paris, [1977]. pp. 373. *bibliogs.*

— — United Kingdom.

JORDAN (W.M.) Great Britain, France, and the German problem, 1918-1939: a study of Anglo-French relations in the making and maintenance of the Versailles settlement. London, 1971. pp. 234. *Reprint of the 1943 edition, originally issued under the auspices of the Royal Institute of International Affairs.*

SCHUMANN (MAURICE) Talleyrand, prophet of Entente Cordiale. Oxford, 1977. pp. 22. *(Oxford. University. Zaharoff Lectures. 1976-77)*

— — United States.

[TICKELL (RICHARD)] La cassette verte de Monsieur de Sartine, trouvée chez Mademoiselle du Thé. 6th ed. La Haye, chez la Veuve Whiskerfeld, 1779. pp. 76.

— History — 1500-1599.

MANDROU (ROBERT) Introduction to modern France, 1500-1640: an essay in historical psychology;...translated by R.E. Hallmark. London, 1975. pp. 285. *bibliog.*

HUPPERT (GEORGE) Les bourgeois gentilshommes: an essay on the definition of elites in Renaissance France. Chicago, 1977. pp. 237.

— — 1600-1699.

MANDROU (ROBERT) Introduction to modern France, 1500-1640: an essay in historical psychology;...translated by R.E. Hallmark. London, 1975. pp. 285. *bibliog.*

— — 1789-1799, Revolution.

GUIBERT (ELISABETH) Voies idéologiques de la Révolution française. Paris, [1976]. pp. 272. *bibliog.*

GAUTHIER (FLORENCE) La voie paysanne dans la Révolution française: l'exemple de la Picardie. Paris, 1977. pp. 241. *bibliog.*

GUERIN (DANIEL) Class struggle in the first French Republic: bourgeois and bras nus, 1793-1795; translated from the French by Ian Patterson. London, 1977. pp. 295.

PETERSON (MERRILL DANIEL) Adams and Jefferson: a revolutionary dialogue. Oxford, 1978. pp. 146. *(Mercer University. Eugenia Dorothy Blount Lamar Memorial Lectures. No. 19)*

ROBERTS (JOHN MORRIS) The French revolution. Oxford, [1978]. pp. 176. *bibliog.*

SCOTT (SAMUEL F.) The response of the Royal Army to the French revolution: the role and development of the line army, 1787-93. Oxford, [1978]. pp. 243. *bibliog.*

— — 1799-1815, Consulate and Empire.

MACAULAY (THOMAS BABINGTON) Baron Macaulay. Napoleon and the restoration of the Bourbons: the completed portion of Macaulay's projected History of France, from the restoration of the Bourbons to the accession of Louis Philippe; edited by Joseph Hamburger. New York, 1977. pp. 117.

— — 1814-1830, Restoration.

MACAULAY (THOMAS BABINGTON) Baron Macaulay. Napoleon and the restoration of the Bourbons: the completed portion of Macaulay's projected History of France, from the restoration of the Bourbons to the accession of Louis Philippe; edited by Joseph Hamburger. New York, 1977. pp. 117.

FRANCE.(Cont.)

— — 1848, February Revolution.

ZEVAES (ALEXANDRE) La chute de Louis-Philippe, 24 février 1848. [Paris, 1930]. pp. 128.

— — 1848-1870.

[BROCHER (VICTORINE)] Souvenirs d'une morte vivante; [by] Victorine B...; préface de Lucien Descaves. Paris, 1976. pp. 246. *Reprint of 1909 Paris edition with a new introductory note.*

— — 1851, Coup d'état.

SCHOELCHER (VICTOR) Dangers to England of the alliance with the men of the coup d'état; to which are added, the personal confessions of the December conspirators, and some biographical notices of the most notorious of them. London, 1854. pp. 194.

— — 1900- .

CONTEMPORARY France: illusion, conflict and regeneration; edited with an introduction by John C. Cairns. New York, 1978. pp. 270. *bibliog.*

— — 1914-1940.

BECKER (JEAN JACQUES) 1914: comment les Français sont entrés dans la guerre: contribution à l'étude de l'opinion publique printemps- été 1914. [Paris, 1977]. pp. 638. *bibliog.*

La FRANCE et les Français en 1938-1939; sous la direction de René Rémond et Janine Bourdin. [Paris, 1978]. pp. 365.

— — 1940-1945, German occupation.

ORY (PASCAL) Les collaborateurs, 1940-1945. Paris, [1976]. pp. 320. *bibliog.*

MENDÈS-FRANCE (PIERRE) Liberté, liberté chérie, 1940-42; suivi de Roissy-en- France: récit d'un vol du Groupe Lorraine, 3 octobre 1945. [Paris, 1977]. pp. 430.

DANK (MILTON) The French against the French: collaboration and resistance. London, 1978. pp. 365. *bibliog.*

— — 1945- .

LIMAGNE (PIERRE) L'éphémère IVe République. Paris, [1977]. pp. 406.

— Industries.

DUMARD (JEAN) and LETABLIER (MARIE THERESE) L'emploi industriel en France, fin 1968-fin 1971: modifications spatiales et structurelles. [Paris, 1976]. pp. 211. *(France. Centre d'Etudes de l'Emploi. Cahiers. 9) With English and German summaries.*

— — Bibliography.

ROSE (MICHAEL J.) compiler. French industrial studies: a bibliography and guide. Westmead, Hants., [1977]. pp. 142. *bibliog.*

— Intellectual life.

Les PREOCCUPATIONS économiques et sociales des philosophes, littérateurs et artistes au XVIIIe siècle: colloque, Bruxelles, 26 et 27 mai 1975. Bruxelles, 1976. pp. 273. *(Brussels. Université Libre. Groupe d'Etude du XVIIIe Siècle. Etudes sur le XVIIIe Siècle. 3)*

JULLIARD (JACQUES) Contre la politique professionnelle. Paris, [1977]. pp. 164.

Les DIEUX dans la cuisine: vingt ans de philosophie en France. [Paris, 1978]. pp. 251. *Based on articles published in Le Magazine Littéraire, septembre 1977, no. 127-128.*

— Nationalism.

ARNAUD (NICOLE) and DOFNY (JACQUES) Nationalism and the national question. Montreal, [1977]. pp. 134. *Translated by Penelope Williams.*

RIOUX (JEAN PIERRE) Nationalisme et conservatisme: la Ligue de la Patrie Française, 1899-1904. Paris, [1977]. pp. 120.

SUTTON (MICHAEL JOHN) Nationalism, positivism and Catholicism: a study of the controversy arising from the proposal of Charles Maurras for a political alliance between positivists and Catholics. [1978]. fo.431. *bibliog. Typescript. 2 pamphlets in end pocket. Ph.D. (London) thesis: unpublished. This thesis is the property of London University and may not be removed from the Library.*

— Navy.

FRANCE. Groupe sectoriel d'Analyse et de Prévision Construction Navale. 1976. Rapport...: préparation de 7e Plan. Paris, [1976]. pp. 138.

— Occupations.

FRANCE. Institut National de la Statistique et des Etudes Economiques, 1962. Nomenclature des métiers et des activités individuelles: index analytique; (code no. 2 du recensement de la population de 1962). 2nd ed. Paris, 1962. pp. 285.

— Officials and employees.

PIQUEMAL (MARCEL) Les agents de l'Etat. [Paris, 1977]. pp. 128. *bibliog.*

— Parliament — Assemblée Nationale — Rules and practice.

FRANCE. Assemblée Nationale, [1946- 1958]. 1947. Règlement...; constitution; lois organiques. Paris, 1947. pp. 327.

FRANCE. Assemblée Nationale, [1958-]. 1959. Règles provisoires de fonctionnement...; instruction générale du Bureau de l'Assemblée; assemblées européennes; constitution et textes intéressant l'Assemblée Nationale. [Paris, 1959]. pp. 341.

— Politics and government.

La DECENTRALISATION pour la rénovation de l'Etat: colloque sous la direction de Charles Debbasch,...organisé par la Faculté de Droit de l'Université de Droit, d'Economie et des Sciences d'Aix-Marseille à Aix-en-Provence, les 23 et 24 mai 1975. [Paris], 1976. pp. 251.

BIRNBAUM (PIERRE) Les sommets de l'État: essai sur l'élite du pouvoir en France. Paris, [1977]. pp. 188.

BIRNBAUM (PIERRE) and others. Réinventer le Parlement. [Paris, 1977]. pp. 223.

JULLIARD (JACQUES) Contre la politique professionnelle. Paris, [1977]. pp. 164.

KAHN (JEAN FRANÇOIS) Complot contre la démocratie. [Paris, 1977]. pp. 235.

ROSANVALLON (PIERRE) and VIVERET (PATRICK) Pour une nouvelle culture politique. Paris, [1977]. pp. 158.

FONTENEAU (JEAN) Les institutions politiques de la France. Paris, [1978]. pp. 110.

— — 1589-1789.

KLAITS (JOSEPH) Printed propaganda under Louis XIV: absolute monarchy and public opinion. Princeton, [1976]. pp. 341. *bibliog.*

BONNEY (RICHARD J.) Political change in France under Richelieu and Mazarin, 1624- 1661. Oxford, 1978. pp. 508. *bibliog.*

— — 1789-1900.

GAGNEUR (LOUISE MIGNEROT) Jean Caboche à ses amis les paysans: revu par M.-L. Gagneur. Paris, [imprint, 1871]. pp. 36.

GAGNEUR (LOUISE MIGNEROT) Mésaventure électorale de M. le baron Pirouëtt, député du centre droit. Paris, [1871]. pp. 32.

BERTOCCI (PHILIP A.) Jules Simon: republican anticlericalism and cultural politics in France, 1848-1886. Columbia, 1978. pp. 247. *bibliog.*

— — 1789-1799, Revolution.

GUERIN (DANIEL) Class struggle in the first French Republic: bourgeois and bras nus, 1793-1795; translated from the French by Ian Patterson. London, 1977. pp. 295.

— — 1848-1870.

MERRIMAN (JOHN M.) The agony of the Republic: the repression of the left in revolutionary France, 1848-1851. New Haven, 1978. pp. 298. *bibliog.*

— — 1870-1940.

LIGUE NATIONALE FRANÇAISE DE SAN FRANCISCO ET DU PACIFIQUE. Elections de 1876: les Français d'Amérique aux Français de France; avec une dédicace à MM. Thiers et Gambetta. Paris, 1876. pp. 36.

GAGNEUR (WLADIMIR) Le vrai péril social. Lons-le-Saunier, 1877. pp. 30.

BOURDE (GUY) La défaite du Front populaire. Paris, 1977. pp. 359. *bibliog.*

LACOUTURE (JEAN) Léon Blum. Paris, [1977]. pp. 599.

LEFRANC (GEORGES) Le mouvement socialiste sous la Troisième République. 2nd ed. Paris, [1977]. 2 vols. *bibliog.*

STERNHELL (ZEEV) La droite révolutionnaire, 1885-1914: les origines françaises du fascisme. Paris, [1978]. pp. 444. *bibliog.*

— — 1914-1940.

ADAMTHWAITE (ANTHONY P.) France and the coming of the Second World War, 1936-1939. London, 1977. pp. 434. *bibliog.*

EDOUARD Daladier, Chef du Gouvernment, avril 1938 [to] septembre 1939; sous la direction de René Rémond et Janine Bourdin. [Paris, 1977]. pp. 320. *A colloque held at the Fondation Nationale des Sciences Politiques in December 1975.*

La FRANCE et les Français en 1938-1939; sous la direction de René Rémond et Janine Bourdin. [Paris, 1978]. pp. 365.

— — 1945- .

DEJAY (EDOUARD) and others. Paris Mai/Juin 1968: 94 documents. [Paris, 1968?]. fos.(2), 45 plates. *Photographs.*

GISCARD d'Estaing, Mitterrand: 54,774 mots pour convaincre; by Jean-Marie Cotteret [and others]. Paris, [1976]. pp. 347. *bibliog.*

GREMION (PIERRE) Le pouvoir périphérique: bureaucrates et notables dans le système politique français. Paris, [1976]. pp. 478. *bibliog.*

SANGUINETTI (ALEXANDRE) Une nouvelle résistance. [Paris, 1976]. pp. 215.

BORNE (DOMINIQUE) Petits bourgeois en révolte?: le Mouvement Poujade. [Paris, 1977]. pp. 250. *bibliog.*

FREARS (JOHN RUSSELL) Political parties and elections in the French fifth republic. London, [1977]. pp. 292. *bibliogs.*

GRANOU (ANDRE) La bourgeoisie financière au pouvoir et les luttes de classes en France. Paris, 1977. pp. 306.

GRIMAUD (MAURICE) En mai, fais ce qu'il te plaît. [Paris, 1977]. pp. 345.

LIMAGNE (PIERRE) L'éphémère IVe République. Paris, [1977]. pp. 406.

MITTERRAND (FRANÇOIS) Politique. [Paris, 1977]. pp. 640. *bibliog.*

PETITFILS (JEAN CHRISTIAN) Le gaullisme. [Paris, 1977]. pp. 128. *bibliog.*

SAFRAN (WILLIAM) The French polity. New York, [1977]. pp. 332. *bibliog.*

TODD (OLIVIER) La marelle de Giscard, 1926-1974. Paris, [1977]. pp. 487. *bibliog.*

BAYNAC (JACQUES) Mai retrouvé: contribution à l'histoire du mouvement révolutionnaire du 3 mai au 16 juin 1968. Paris, [1978]. pp. 301.

COPIN (NOEL) La vie politique française: le Président, le gouvernement, le Parlement et les partis. Paris, [1978]. pp. 198.

DELALE (ALAIN) and RAGACHE (GILLES) La France de 68. [Paris, 1978]. pp. 238.

DESJARDINS (THIERRY) François Mitterrand: un socialiste gaullien. [Paris, 1978]. pp. 295. *bibliog.*

GUILLEBAUD (JEAN CLAUDE) Les années orphelines, 1968-1978. Paris, [1978]. pp. 109.

LIMAGNE (PIERRE) La Ve République de Charles de Gaulle et Georges Pompidou. Paris, [1978]. pp. 393.

PARTI REPUBLICAIN. Le Projet Républicain: programme du Parti Républicain. [Paris, 1978]. pp. 190.

TOUCHARD (JEAN) Le gaullisme, 1940-1969. Paris, [1978]. pp. 381. *bibliog.*

WINOCK (MICHEL) La République se meurt: chronique 1956-1958. Paris, [1978]. pp. 255.

WRIGHT (VINCENT) The government and politics of France. London, 1978. pp. 280. *bibliog.*

— Population.

FRANCE. Institut National de la Statistique et des Etudes Economiques. 1976- . Tableaux démographiques et sociaux: reliefs géographiques et historiques; [edited by] Marcel Croze. [Paris], 1976 in progress. *bibliogs.*

COLLOMB (PHILIPPE) and ZUCKER (ELISABETH) Aspects culturels et socio-psychologiques de la fécondité française: une enquête…1971. [Paris], 1977. pp. 322. *bibliog.* *(France. Institut National d'Etudes Démographiques. Travaux et Documents. Cahiers. No. 80)*

DYER (COLIN) Population and society in twentieth century France. London, 1978. pp. 247. *bibliog.*

— Presidents.

MASSOT (JEAN) La Présidence de la république en France. [Paris], La Documentation Française, [1977]. pp. 234. *bibliog.*

— Race question.

Les DOSSIERS noirs du racisme dans le Midi de la France; ([by] François-Noël Bernardi [and others]). Paris, [1976]. pp. 203.

— Relations (general) with Poland.

UNION DES FEDERALISTES POLONAIS. Manifestation franco-polonaise du centenaire de l'insurrection polonaise de 1863. [Paris], 1963. pp. 48.

— Social conditions.

ARDAGH (JOHN) The new France. 3rd ed. Harmondsworth, 1977. pp. 733. *bibliog.*

LE PORS (ANICET) ed. Immigration et développement économique et social; balance des paiements, bilan social, impacts sectoriels et macroéconomiques: rapport général. Paris, La Documentation Française, [1977]. pp. 364. *(Etudes Prioritaires Interministérielles)*

DYER (COLIN) Population and society in twentieth century France. London, 1978. pp. 247. *bibliog.*

GUILLEBAUD (JEAN CLAUDE) Les années orphelines, 1968-1978. Paris, [1978]. pp. 109.

— Social history.

ARC, L': revue trimestrielle. 65. Le Roy Ladurie. Aix-en-Provence, [1976]. pp. 85. *bibliog.*

— Social life and customs.

DUBY (GEORGES) Medieval marriage: two models from twelfth-century France; translated by Elborg Forster. Baltimore, [1978]. pp. 138. *(Johns Hopkins University. Department of History. Johns Hopkins Symposia in Comparative History)* Originally presented in French as lectures at Johns Hopkins University in 1977.

— Social policy.

FRANCE. Conseil Economique. 1949. Notes sur les travaux du Conseil Economique, 1947-1948-1949. Paris, 1949. pp. 150.

— Statistics, Vital.

FRANCE. Institut National de la Statistique et des Etudes Economiques. 1976- . Tableaux démographiques et sociaux: reliefs géographiques et historiques; [edited by] Marcel Croze. [Paris], 1976 in progress. *bibliogs.*

FRANCHE-COMTE
— Economic conditions.

REFLETS DE L'ECONOMIE FRANC-COMTOISE: revue mensuelle; ([pd. by] Institut National de la Statistique et des Etudes Economiques, Service Régional de Besançon [France]). m., Je 1971 (no.2)- Besançon.

FRANCHISES (RETAIL TRADE).

RAAD VOOR HET MIDDEN- EN KLEINBEDRIJF. Franchising II: modelcontract en arbitragereglement. 's-Gravenhage, 1975. pp. 41. *([Publikaties]. 1975, no. 3)*

FRANCISCANS IN BRAZIL.

WILLEKE (VENÂNCIO) Missões franciscanas no Brasil, 1500-1975. Petropolis, 1974. pp. 201. *bibliog.*

FRANKFURT AM MAIN
— Growth.

RHODE (BARBARA) Die Verdrängung der Wohnbevölkerung durch den tertiären Sektor: Strukturwandel in citynahen Stadtgebieten in Hamburg und Frankfurt/M., 1961-1970. Hamburg, [1977]. pp. 178. *bibliog.* *(Hamburg. Hansische Universität. Seminar für Sozialwissenschaften. Beiträge zur Stadtforschung. Band 2)*

FRANKLIN (BENJAMIN).

[TICKELL (RICHARD)] La cassette verte de Monsieur de Sartine, trouvée chez Mademoiselle du Thé. 6th ed. La Haye, chez la Veuve Whiskerfeld, 1779. pp. 76.

FREDERICK II, King of Prussia.

DUFFY (CHRISTOPHER) The army of Frederick the Great. Newton Abbot, [1974]. pp. 272. *bibliog.*

FREDERIK-HENDRIK ISLAND.

SERPENTI (L.M.) Cultivators in the swamps: social structure and horticulture in a New Guinea society (Frederik-Hendrik Island, West New Guinea). 2nd ed. Assen, 1977. pp. 308. *bibliog.*

FREE TRADE AND PROTECTION.

FIRTH (JOSEPH FIRTH BOTTOMLEY) Free trade: fair trade; depression of trade; speech… delivered at North Kensington on Saturday, October 17, 1885. [London], 1885. pp. 16. *(Reprinted from the West London Advertiser)*

HOWARD (JAMES) M.P. The science of trade: free trade, or fair trade?; an address at the Liberal Club, Luton…March 8th, 1887. Luton, 1887. pp. 20.

CHAMBERLAIN (JOSEPH) Fiscal policy: speech…Glasgow…October 6th, 1903. Birmingham, [1903]. pp. 30.

TARIFF REFORM LEAGUE. Fiscal facts, [No. 1]. London, [1903]. pp. 16.

[TARIFF REFORM LEAGUE]. Fiscal facts, No. 2. [London, 1903?]. pp. 16.

FREE TRADE UNION. Photographic reproductions of our brilliantly coloured picture and word posters. London, [1905]. pp. 16.

SMITH (FREDERICK EDWIN) 1st Earl of Birkenhead. Tariff reform:…speech delivered at…Hull, January 30th, 1914, etc. London, [1914]. pp. 14.

NATIONAL ASSOCIATION OF MERCHANTS AND MANUFACTURERS. National Association of Merchants and Manufacturers to Resist Interference with Trade. [London, 192-?]. pp. 4.

GENERAL AGREEMENT ON TARIFFS AND TRADE. Studies in International Trade. Geneva, 1971 in progress.

BERNARDI (ALBERTO DI) Questione agraria e protezionismo nella crisi economica di fine secolo. [Milano, 1977]. pp. 229. *bibliog.*

DIUMULEN (IPPOLIT IPPOLITOVICH) Bar'ery na torgovykh putiakh: imperialisticheskii protektsionizm v deistvii. Moskva, 1977. pp. 223.

CABLE (VINCENT) Developments in international trade policy and their implications for developing countries; paper. London, 1978. pp. 35.

FREE WILL AND DETERMINISM.

EASTERBROOK (JAMES A.) and EASTERBROOK (PAMELA J.) The determinants of free will: a psychological analysis of responsible, adjustive behavior. New York, 1978. pp. 259. *bibliog.*

FREEDMEN IN TEXAS.

WOOLFOLK (GEORGE RUBLE) The free negro in Texas, 1800-1860: a study in cultural compromise. Ann Arbor, 1976. pp. 240. *bibliog.*

FREEDOM OF ASSOCIATION.

CAIRE (GUY) Freedom of association and economic development. Geneva, International Labour Office, 1977. pp. 159. *bibliog.*

ERSTLING (JAY A.) The right to organise: a survey of laws and regulations relating to the right of workers to establish unions of their own choosing. Geneva, International Labour Office, 1977. pp. 82.

— Germany.

GERHARDT (MICHAEL) Das Koalitionsgesetz: verfassungsrechtliche Überlegungen zur Neuregelung des Rechts der Gewerkschaften und der Arbeitgeberverbände. Berlin, [1977]. pp. 328. *bibliog.*

— United Kingdom.

WORKERS' AND SOLDIERS' COUNCIL. Provisional Committee. Constitution of local councils. London, [192-?]. pp. (4).

FREEDOM OF INFORMATION
— United States.

FEDERAL reserve policies and public disclosure; edited by Richard D. Erb. Washington, D.C., [1978]. pp. 108. *(American Enterprise Institute for Public Policy Research. AEI Symposia. 78B)* Papers from a conference held in 1977.

FREEDOM OF THE SEAS.

DEUTSCHER VEREIN FÜR INTERNATIONALES SEERECHT. Schriften. Reihe A: Berichte und Vorträge. Heft 26. Schiffahrtsfreiheit und Gewerkschaften: Vortrag von Ingo von Münch gehalten am 29. Januar 1976. Hamburg, 1976. pp. 23, iii.

FREIBURG (CANTON)
— Politics and government.

VIAL (JEAN CLAUDE) Fribourg et la révision de la constitution fédérale de 1872. Fribourg, 1977. fo. 259. *bibliog.*

FREIE DEMOKRATISCHE PARTEI.

FREIE DEMOKRATISCHE PARTEI.

PROGRAMMATISCHE Entwicklung der FDP, 1946 bis 1969: Einführung und Dokumente; [edited by] Peter Juling. Meisenheim am Glan, 1977. pp. 209.

FREIGHT AND FREIGHTAGE.

UNITED NATIONS. Interregional Seminar on Containerization and other Unitized Methods for the Intermodal Movement of Freight, London, 1967. Report on the...seminar...[held in] London, England, 1-12 May 1967. (ST/TAO/SER.C/102). New York, 1968. pp. 61.

— Canada — Ontario.

BONSOR (N.C.) Transportation rates and economic development in northern Ontario. Toronto, [1977]. pp. 91. *bibliog. (Ontario. Economic Council. Research Studies. 7)*

— Japan.

MITUHASHI (SETUKO) Japanese commodity flows. Chicago, 1978. pp. 172. *bibliog. (Chicago. University. Department of Geography. Research Papers. No. 187)*

— United Kingdom.

ADVISORY COUNCIL ON ENERGY CONSERVATION [U.K.]. Freight transport: short and medium term considerations. London, H.M.S.O., 1977. pp. 22. *(Papers. 6)*

LONDON. Greater London Council. Freight policy for London. London, 1977. pp. 15.

FRENCH CANADIANS.

CONFERENCE ON ETHNIC PLURALISM AND CONFLICT IN CONTEMPORARY WESTERN EUROPE AND CANADA, ITHACA, 1975. Ethnic conflict in the Western world: [papers presented at the Conference]; edited by Milton J. Esman. Ithaca, 1977. pp. 399. *bibliogs. Sponsored by the Western Societies Program of the Center for International Studies, Cornell University.*

MAXWELL (THOMAS R.) The invisible French: the French in metropolitan Toronto. [Waterloo, Ont., 1977]. pp. 174. *bibliog.*

SOCIETY and conquest: the debate on the bourgeoisie and social change in French Canada, 1700-1850; edited by Dale Miquelon. Vancouver, [1977]. pp. 219. *bibliog.*

FRENCH IN RUSSIA.

PASCAL (PIERRE) En communisme: mon journal de Russie, 1918-1921. [Lausanne, 1977]. pp. 226.

FRENCH IN THE ARGENTINE REPUBLIC.

Les AVEYRONNAIS dans la Pampa: fondation, développement et vie de la colonie aveyronnaise de Pigüé-Argentine, 1884-1974; ([by] Jean Andreu [and others]). Toulouse, [1977]. pp. 325.

FRENCH LANGUAGE

— Dictionaries — English.

COVENEY (JAMES) and MOORE (SHEILA J.) Glossary of French and English management terms: Lexique de termes anglais français de gestion. London, 1972. pp. 146.

— — Polyglot.

HEBÁK (PETR) and HUSTOPECKÝ (JIŘÍ) compilers. Šestijazyčný slovník termínů z regresní analýzy: [Czech, Russian, Polish, English, French, German]. Praha, 1978. pp. 211. *With preface and explanatory notes in each language.*

FRENCH LANGUAGE IN CANADA.

LEBEL (CLEMENT) compiler. Documents de la Commission d'Enquête sur la Situation de la Langue Française et les Droits Linguistiques au Québec, Commission Gendron: bibliographie. Québec, 1974. pp. 206. *(Quebec (Province). Legislative Library. Bibliographie et Documentation. 3)*

RABOTIN (MAURICE) Le vocabulaire politique et socio-ethnique à Montréal de 1839 à 1842. Montréal, [1975]. pp. 123. *bibliog.*

FRENCH LITERATURE

— History and criticism.

LOUGH (JOHN) Writer and public in France: from the middle ages to the present day. Oxford, 1978. pp. 435. *bibliog.*

FRENCH WEST AFRICA.

POUQUET (JEAN) L'Afrique Occidentale française. Paris, 1954. pp. 128. *bibliog.*

FRIENDLY SOCIETIES

— Italy — Bibliography.

FLORENCE. Biblioteca Nazionale Centrale. Pubblicazioni di società operaie italiane, 1881-1885: catalogo; a cura di Fabrizio Dolci. Firenze, [1973]. pp. 92.

FRIENDS, SOCIETY OF.

SOCIETY OF FRIENDS. Friends Peace and International Relations Committee. Violence and oppression: a Quaker response. London, 1972. pp. 16.

FRIESLAND

— Social history.

FRIESWIJK (JOHAN) Socialisme in Friesland, 1880-1900. Amsterdam, 1977. pp. 270. *bibliog. (International Institute of Social History. De Nederlandse Arbeidersbeweging.2)*

FRIGERIO (ROGELIO).

ORTIZ (S.H.) El libro rojo de Rogelio Frigerio. Montevideo, 1962. pp. 125.

FRIULI

— Politics and government.

MENIS (PIETRO) Dal Partito Popolare Italiano alla Democrazia Cristiana, 1918-1964: memorie di un politico di paese. [Udine, 1977]. pp. 95.

FRIULI-VENEZIA GIULIA

— Economic conditions.

REGIONE FRIULI-VENEZIA GIULIA, LA: documentazione su fatti e problemi dell'economia italiana ed internazionale a cura della direzione regionale della programmazione studi e statistica [Friuli- Venezia Giulia]. bi-m. Trieste. *Current issues only kept.*

FRONDE.

KNECHT (ROBERT JEAN) The Fronde. London, 1975. pp. 30. *bibliog. (Historical Association. Appreciations in History. No. 5)*

FRONT DE LIBERATION QUEBECOIS.

FRONT DE LIBERATION QUEBECOIS. F.L.Q.: a translation. London, 1968. pp. 7.

FRONTIER AND PIONEER LIFE

— United States.

BARNETT (LOUISE K.) The ignoble savage: American literary racism, 1790-1890. Westport, Conn., 1975. pp. 220. *bibliog.*

HAMMOND (GEORGE PETER) The adventures of Alexander Barclay, mountain man...: a narrative of his career, 1810-1855, his memorandum diary, 1845 to 1850. Denver, Colo.; 1976. pp. 246.

LAMAR (HOWARD ROBERTS) The trader on the American frontier: myth's victim. College Station, Tex., [1977]. pp. 53.

FRONTIER THESIS.

NORDSTROM (CARL) Frontier elements in a Hudson river village. Port Washington, N.Y., 1973. pp. 199. *bibliog.*

FRUIT

— Marketing — Kenya.

WILSON (FRANK A.) Some economic aspects of the structure and organization of small scale marketing systems: a discussion of the research findings of a study into the marketing of fruit and vegetables in Kenya. 1973. fo. 21. *Unpublished: photocopy of typescript.*

— Canada.

CANADA. Department of Agriculture. Marketing Service. Annual unload report of fresh fruits and vegetables on 12 Canadian markets. a., 1977- Ottawa. *[in English and French]*

FRUIT CULTURE

— European Economic Community countries.

EUROPEAN COMMUNITIES. Statistical Office. Community survey of orchard fruit trees. a., 1976- Luxembourg. *[in Community languages].*

— Tasmania.

CUTHBERTSON (A.G.) and others. Income levels and adjustment patterns in a rural community: Huon valley, Tasmania. Canberra, 1974. pp. 134. *(Australia. Bureau of Agricultural Economics. Industry Economics Monographs. No. 2)*

FRUIT TRADE

— Colombia.

BETANCOURT L. (ENRIQUE) Algunos aspectos sobre las exportaciones agricolas colombianas. Bogota, [1972]. pp. 97. *bibliog.*

— Tasmania.

CUTHBERTSON (A.G.) and others. Income levels and adjustment patterns in a rural community: Huon valley, Tasmania. Canberra, 1974. pp. 134. *(Australia. Bureau of Agricultural Economics. Industry Economics Monographs. No. 2)*

FUEL.

SHAW (R.R.) The fuel situation: the airline viewpoint. [1974?]. pp. 7. *Typescript: unpublished.*

— Tables, calculations, etc.

U.K. Department of Energy. Economics and Statistics Division. 1977. Energy balances: some problems and recent developments; a paper prepared...by W.N.T. Roberts and W.A. Hawkins. London, 1977. pp. 37. *(Department of Energy. Energy Papers. No. 19)*

— Canada.

CANADA. Statistics Canada. Consumption of purchased fuel and electricity by the manufacturing, mining and electric power industries. a., 1975(1st)- Ottawa. *[in English and French]*

— Ireland (Republic).

HENRY (EDMUND WILLIAM) and SCOTT (S.) A national model of fuel allocation: a prototype. Dublin, 1977. pp. 67. *bibliog. (Economic and Social Research Institute. Papers. No. 90)*

— United Kingdom — Prices.

NATIONAL COUNCIL OF SOCIAL SERVICE. National Organisations Division. Fuel debts: an action guide. London, 1973. pp. 14.

FUENTES (CARLOS).

GONZALEZ (MICHAEL) Cambio de piel, or the myth of literature. Glasgow, [1974]. pp. 13. *(Glasgow. University. Institute of Latin American Studies. Occasional Papers. No. 10)*

FULAHS.

AZARYA (VICTOR) Aristocrats facing change: the Fulbe in Guinea, Nigeria, and Cameroon. Chicago, [1978]. pp. 293. *bibliog.*

FUNCTIONAL ANALYSIS.

OPEN UNIVERSITY. Linear Mathematics Course Team. Unit 12: Linear functionals and duality: Unit 13: Systems of differential equations. Milton Keynes, 1972, repr. 1976. pp. 32. *(Open University. Mathematics: a second level course: linear mathematics. Units 12 and 13)*

CASTAING (CHARLES) and VALADIER (M.) Convex analysis and measurable multifunctions. Berlin, 1977. pp. 278. *bibliogs.*

FUNCTIONAL ANALYSIS (SOCIAL SCIENCES).

ABRAHAMSON (MARK) Functionalism. Englewood Cliffs, [1978]. pp. 113.

FUNCTIONAL DIFFERENTIAL EQUATIONS.

HALE (JACK K.) Theory of functional differential equations. New York, [1977]. pp. 365. *bibliog.*

FUNCTIONAL EQUATIONS.

WARGA (J.) Optimal control of differential and functional equations. New York, 1972. pp. 531. *bibliog.*

FUNCTIONS.

HILTON (PETER JOHN) Partial derivatives. London, 1960 repr. 1973. pp. 54.

FUNCTIONS, EXPONENTIAL.

BARNDORFF-NIELSEN (OLE) Information and exponential families in statistical theory. Chichester, [1978]. pp. 238. *bibliog.*

FUNCTIONS OF COMPLEX VARIABLES.

FLEMING (WENDELL HELMS) Functions of several variables. 2nd ed. New York, [1977]. pp. 411.

FUND RAISING

— South Africa.

SOUTH AFRICA. Commission of Inquiry into the Collection of Voluntary Financial Contributions from the Public. 1977. Report (R.P.55/1977). in SOUTH AFRICA. Parliament. House of Assembly. Votes and proceedings; (with Printed annexures).

FUR TRADE.

PRENTICE (ARTHUR C.) A candid view of the fur industry. Bewdley, 1976. pp. 319. *bibliog.*

FURNITURE INDUSTRY AND TRADE

— Zambia.

ZAMBIA. Central Statistical Office. 1976. Wood, wood products and furniture industries. Lusaka, 1976. fo. 46. *bibliog. (Industry Monographs. No. 3)*

FUTURISM (ART).

L'AVANGUARDIA dopo la rivoluzione: le riviste degli anni Venti nell'URSS: "Il giornale dei futuristi", "L'arte della Comune", "Il Lef", "Il nuovo Lef"; introduzione e cura di Luigi Magarotto. Roma, 1976. pp. 304.

FUTURISM (LITERATURE).

L'AVANGUARDIA dopo la rivoluzione: le riviste degli anni Venti nell'URSS: "Il giornale dei futuristi", "L'arte della Comune", "Il Lef", "Il nuovo Lef"; introduzione e cura di Luigi Magarotto. Roma, 1976. pp. 304.

GABON

— Description and travel.

HOWE (RUSSELL WARREN) Theirs the darkness. London, 1956. pp. 190.

GAITAN (JORGE ELIECER).

ROBINSON (J.CORDELL) El movimiento gaitanista en Colombia, 1930-1948; traducido por Eddy Torres. Bogota, 1976. pp. 200. *bibliog.*

SHARPLESS (RICHARD E.) Gaitan of Colombia: a political biography. Pittsburgh, [1978]. pp. 229. *bibliog.*

GALICIA (EASTERN EUROPE)

— Economic history.

GURNICZ (ANTONI) Franciszek Stefczyk: 'zycie, poglądy, działalność. Warszawa, 1976. pp. 204. *bibliog.*

MENCEL (TADEUSZ) Galicja Zachodnia, 1795-1809: studium z dziejów ziem polskich zaboru austriackiego po III rozbiorze. Lublin, 1976. pp. 522. *bibliog. With Russian and German summaries.*

GALICIA (SPAIN)

— Rural conditions.

DURAN (JOSE A.) Historia de caciques, bandos e ideologias en la Galicia no urbana: Rianxo 1910-1914. Madrid, 1972. pp. 387.

— Social conditions.

LISON-TOLOSANA (CARMELO) Antropologia cultural de Galicia: moradas del vivir galaico. Madrid, 1971 repr. 1977. pp. 408.

GALLEANI (LUIGI).

FEDELI (UGO) Luigi Galleani: quarant'anni di lotte rivoluzionarie, 1891-1931. Forli, 1956. pp. 219. *bibliog.*

GALOIS THEORY.

STEWART (IAN) Galois theory. London, 1973 repr. 1976. pp. 226. *bibliog.*

GAMBIA

— Economic policy.

GAMBIA. 1971. Third development programme, 1971/72 to 1973/74. Bathurst, 1971. pp. 39. *(Sessional Papers. 1971. No. 2)*

— House of Representatives — Rules and practice.

GAMBIA. House of Representatives. 1965. The standing orders of the House of Representatives. Bathurst, [1965?]. pp. 29.

— Social policy.

GAMBIA. 1971. Third development programme, 1971/72 to 1973/74. Bathurst, 1971. pp. 39. *(Sessional Papers. 1971. No. 2)*

GAMBLING.

GAMBLING and society: interdisciplinary studies on the subject of gambling; edited by William R. Eadington. Springfield, Ill., [1976]. pp. 466.

— New Zealand.

NEW ZEALAND. Royal Commission on Gaming and Racing, 1946. Gaming and racing; report; [G.P. Finlay, chairman]. Wellington, 1948. pp. 150.

— United Kingdom.

CORNISH (D.B.) Gambling: a review of the literature and its implications for policy and research; a Home Office Research Unit report. London, 1978. pp. 281. *bibliog. (U.K. Home Office. Home Office Research Studies. 42)*

GAMES, THEORY OF.

AUBIN (JEAN PIERRE) Applied abstract analysis; translated by Carole Labrousse. New York, [1977]. pp. 263.

FRIEDMAN (JAMES W.) Oligopoly and the theory of games. Amsterdam, 1977. pp. 311. *bibliog.*

VOROB'EV (NIKOLAI NIKOLAEVICH) Game theory: lectures for economists and systems scientists; translated and supplemented by S. Kotz. New York, [1977]. pp. 178. *bibliog.*

FRYER (M.J.) An introduction to linear programming and matrix game theory. London, 1978. pp. 121.

GAMES OF CHANCE (MATHEMATICS).

EPSTEIN (RICHARD A.) The theory of gambling and statistical logic. rev.ed. New York, [1977]. pp. 450.

GANDHI (INDIRA).

HEREDIA (SUSANA) No kin to the Mahatma: a study of Indira Gandhi. New York, [1976]. pp. 127. *bibliog.*

KARLEKAR (HIRANMAY) Indira Gandhi: an interview. [New Delhi, 1976]. pp. 20. *(Repr. from the Hindustan Times of Feb. 8 1976)*

MURTHY (R.K.) The cult of the individual: a study of Indira Gandhi. New Delhi, 1977. pp. 152.

SELBOURNE (DAVID) An eye to India: the unmasking of a tyranny. Harmondsworth, 1977. pp. 561. *bibliog.*

SINHA (SACHCHIDANANDA) Emergency in perspective: reprieve and challenge. London, 1977. pp. 122.

DUBÉ (RANI) The evil within; edited by Timeri Murari. London, 1978. pp. 160.

GANDHI (MOHANDAS KARAMCHAND).

MEHTA (VED) Mahatma Gandhi and his apostles. Harmondsworth, 1977. pp. 260.

SHIMONI (GIDEON) Gandhi, satyagraha and the Jews: a formative factor in India's policy towards Israel. Jerusalem, 1977. pp. 60. *(Hebrew University. Leonard Davis Institute for International Relations. Jerusalem Papers on Peace Problems. 22)*

GARDEN CITIES

— United Kingdom.

SOCIETY FOR PROMOTING INDUSTRIAL VILLAGES. Address to the friends of social and industrial improvement. [London, c. 1885]. pp. 3. *Signed by Henry Solly and Thomas Fardon.*

WELWYN GARDEN CITY, LIMITED. Six and a half per cent debenture stock: prospectus. [Welwyn Garden City], 1927. pp. 3.

GARFIELD (JAMES ABRAM) President of the United States.

PESKIN (ALLAN) Garfield: a biography. [Kent, Ohio, 1978]. pp. 716. *bibliog.*

GARIBALDI (GIUSEPPE).

MIRECOURT (EUGENE DE) pseud. [i.e. Charles Jean Baptiste JACQUOT] Garibaldi. Paris, 1867. pp. 72. *(Histoire Contemporaine) Bound with his Pierre Leroux, and other works.*

GAS

— United Kingdom.

NATIONAL GAS CONSUMERS' COUNCIL. Report. a., 1974/75 (2nd)- London.

GAS, NATURAL

— Law and legislation — United States.

AMERICAN ENTERPRISE INSTITUTE FOR PUBLIC POLICY RESEARCH. Legislative Analyses. 93rd Congress. No. 13. Natural gas deregulation legislation. Washington, 1973. pp. 62.

— Transportation — United States.

MEAD (WALTER J.) and others. Transporting natural gas from the Arctic: the alternative systems. Washington, D.C., [1977]. pp. 111. *(American Enterprise Institute for Public Policy Research. AEI Studies. 171)*

— Canada.

LOUNSBURY (JOHN PATTON) The demand for Canadian crude and natural gas liquids, 1962-1967. [Toronto?, 1963]. pp. 5. *(Reprint from the Journal of Canadian Petroleum Technology, vol. 2, no. 1)*

PETRO-CANADA. Annual report. a., 1976(1st)- Ottawa. *[in English and French]*

— Europe, Eastern — Bibliography.

DARLINGTON (T.I.G.) and PARK (J.D.) compilers. Bibliographical guide to the political economy of oil and natural gas in the Soviet Union and Eastern Europe. Stone, Staffs., [1978?]. fo.67.

— Germany.

DEUTSCHES INSTITUT FÜR WIRTSCHAFTSFORSCHUNG. Sonderhefte. [Neue Folge]. 120. Untersuchung zu Fragen der Gaspreisbildung als Folge der Interdependenz zwischen dem internationalen Erdgasbeschaffungs- und Erdgasabsatzmarkt in der Bundesrepublik Deutschland; ([by] Urs Dolinski). Berlin, 1978. pp. 110.

— Russia — Bibliography.

DARLINGTON (T.I.G.) and PARK (J.D.) compilers. Bibliographical guide to the political economy of oil and natural gas in the Soviet Union and Eastern Europe. Stone, Staffs., [1978?]. fo.67.

— United States — Rates.

AMERICAN ENTERPRISE INSTITUTE FOR PUBLIC POLICY RESEARCH. Legislative Analyses. 93rd Congress. No. 13. Natural gas deregulation legislation. Washington, 1973. pp. 62.

GAS, NATURAL, IN SUBMERGED LANDS

— Law and legislation — Canada — Newfoundland.

NEWFOUNDLAND. Department of Mines and Energy. 1977. A white paper and draft regulations respecting the administration and disposition of petroleum belonging to Her Majesty in the right of the province of Newfoundland. [St. John's], 1977. 1 vol. (various foliations).

— Canada — Newfoundland.

NEWFOUNDLAND. Department of Mines and Energy. 1977. A white paper and draft regulations respecting the administration and disposition of petroleum belonging to Her Majesty in the right of the province of Newfoundland. [St. John's], 1977. 1 vol. (various foliations).

GAS INDUSTRY

— European Economic Community countries.

EUROPEAN COMMUNITIES. Statistical Office. Gas statistics. a., 1976- Luxembourg. *[in Community languages]*

— Russia.

OPTIMIZATSIIA razvitiia i razmeshcheniia neftegazovoi promyshlennosti; otvetstvennye redaktory Iu.I. Maksimov, Z.R. Tsimdina. Novosibirsk, 1977. pp. 181. *bibliog. (Akademiia Nauk SSSR. Sibirskoe Otdelenie. Institut Ekonomiki i Organizatsii Promyshlennogo Proizvodstva. Optimizatsiia Razvitiia i Razmeshcheniia Proizvodstva)*

GASP (COMPUTER PROGRAM LANGUAGE).

PRITSKER (A. ALAN B.) The GASP IV simulation language. New York, [1974]. pp. 451. *bibliog.*

GASPERI (ALCIDE DE).

PETRILLI (GIUSEPPE) La politica estera ed europea di De Gasperi. Roma, [1975]. pp. 90.

SPATARO (GIUSEPPE) De Gasperi e il Partito Popolare Italiano. Roma, [1975]. pp. 118.

GATESHEAD

— Social policy.

GATESHEAD COMPREHENSIVE COMMUNITY PROGRAMME. CCP: Comprehensive Community Programme: Gateshead project report. [Gateshead], 1977. pp. 14.

GAUCHOS.

BASUALDO (JOSE AGUSTIN DE) El gaucho argentino. Buenos Aires, [1942]. pp. 159.

GAULLE (CHARLES DE).

ARON (ROBERT) An explanation of De Gaulle;...translated from the French by Marianne Sinclair. New York, [1966]. pp. 210.

SANGUINETTI (ALEXANDRE) Une nouvelle résistance. [Paris, 1976]. pp. 215.

MENIL (LOIS PATTISON DE) Who speaks for Europe?: the vision of Charles de Gaulle. London, [1977]. pp. 232. *bibliog.*

PETITFILS (JEAN CHRISTIAN) Le gaullisme. [Paris, 1977]. pp. 128. *bibliog.*

LIMAGNE (PIERRE) La Ve République de Charles de Gaulle et Georges Pompidou. Paris, [1978]. pp. 393.

TOUCHARD (JEAN) Le gaullisme, 1940-1969. Paris, [1978]. pp. 381. *bibliog.*

GBARNGA

— Economic conditions.

HASSELMANN (KARL-HEINZ) Gbarnga (Liberia): an economic-geographic survey. Monrovia, 1975. fo. 45. *bibliog. (University of Liberia. Department of Geography. Occasional Research Papers. No. 8)*

GDANSK

— Economic conditions.

REPORT on visit to Germany, Polish Corridor and Danzig in September 1928; [by a delegation of Conservatives, led by Sir John Sandeman Allen]. 1928. fo. 6. *Typescript: unpublished.*

GDANSK (PROVINCE)

— Economic conditions.

PODOSKI (KAZIMIERZ) Czynnik ludzki w procesie zagospodarowania i przemian strukturalnych regionu gdańskiego. Gdańsk, 1976. pp. 270. *bibliog. (Gdańsk. Gdańskie Towarzystwo Naukowe. Wydział 1 Nauk Społecznych i Humanistycznych. Seria Monografii. Nr.56) With English and Russian summaries.*

— Population.

PODOSKI (KAZIMIERZ) Czynnik ludzki w procesie zagospodarowania i przemian strukturalnych regionu gdańskiego. Gdańsk, 1976. pp. 270. *bibliog. (Gdańsk. Gdańskie Towarzystwo Naukowe. Wydział 1 Nauk Społecznych i Humanistycznych. Seria Monografii. Nr.56) With English and Russian summaries.*

— Social history.

PRZEMIANY społeczne w regionie gdańskim w powojennym 30- leciu: referaty i materiały sesji naukowej; pod redakcją Kazimierza Podoskiego. Gdańsk, 1977. pp. 267.

GEDDES (Sir PATRICK).

BOARDMAN (PHILIP) The worlds of Patrick Geddes: biologist, town planner, re- educator, peace-warrior. London, 1978. pp. 528. *bibliog.*

GEISEL (ERNESTO).

BARROS (ADIRSON DE) Março: Geisel e a Revolução brasileira. Rio de Janeiro, [1976]. pp. 283.

GENERAL AGREEMENT ON TARIFFS AND TRADE.

LLOYD (PETER JOHN) Anti-dumping actions and the GATT system. London, 1977. pp. 54. *(Trade Policy Research Centre. Thames Essays. No. 9)*

MACIEL (GEORGE ALVARES) The international framework for world trade: Brazilian proposals for GATT reform. London, [1977]. pp. 14. *(Trade Policy Research Centre. Lectures in Commercial Diplomacy. No. 3)*

TOVIAS (ALFRED) Tariff preferences in Mediterranean diplomacy. London, 1977. pp. 153. *bibliogs.*

CLINE (WILLIAM R.) and others. Trade negotiations in the Tokyo Round: a quantitative assessment. Washington, D.C., [1978]. pp. 314.

GOLT (SIDNEY) Developing countries in the GATT system. London, 1978. pp. 36. *(Trade Policy Research Centre. Thames Essays. No. 13)*

GOLT (SIDNEY) The GATT negotiations 1973-79: the closing stage...; and, A policy statement by the British-North American Committee. [London], 1978. pp. 44. *(British-North American Committee. Publications. 22)*

GENERAL STRIKE, UNITED KINGDOM, 1926.

TROTSKII (LEV DAVYDOVICH) General strike 1926; [reprint of 3 articles first published in 1922 and 1926]. [Brighton], 1971. pp. 23.

UNION PLACE COMMUNITY RESOURCE CENTRE. Nine days 1926: the General Strike in Southwark. London, 1976. pp. 52. *bibliog.*

GENERAL STRIKE, UNITED STATES, 1877.

FONER (PHILIP SHELDON) The great labor uprising of 1877. New York, [1977]. pp. 288. *bibliog.*

GENERATIVE GRAMMAR.

HOOPER (JOAN B.) An introduction to natural generative phonology. New York, [1976]. pp. 254. *bibliog.*

SCHLESINGER (I.M.) Production and comprehension of utterances. Hillsdale, N.J., 1977. pp. 235. *bibliog.*

LINGUISTIC theory and psychological reality; edited by Morris Halle [and others]. Cambridge, Mass., [1978]. pp. 329. *bibliog. (Massachusetts Institute of Technology. M.I.T. Bicentennial Studies. 3)*

GENETIC PSYCHOLOGY.

McGURK (HARRY) Growing and changing: a primer of developmental psychology. London, 1975. pp. 142. *bibliog.*

GENETICS.

REILLY (PHILIP) Genetics, law and social policy. Cambridge, Mass., 1977. pp. 275.

GENOA

— Economic history.

GHIARA (CAROLA) L'arte tintoria a Genova dal 15 al 17 secolo: tecniche e organizzazione. [Bologna], 1976. pp. 96. *(Centro per la Storia della Tecnica in Italia. Pubblicazioni. Sezione 4. Vol. 8)*

GEOGRAPHICAL PERCEPTION.

GROWING up in cities: studies of the spatial environment of adolescence in Cracow, Melbourne, Mexico City, Salta, Toluca, and Warszawa; edited by Kevin Lynch from the reports of Tridib Banerjee [and others]. Paris, UNESCO, [1977]. pp. 177. *bibliog.*

DIMENSIONS of human geography: essays on some familiar and neglected themes; Karl W. Butzer, editor. Chicago, 1978. pp. 190. *(Chicago. University. Department of Geography. Research Papers. No. 186) Based on a session held at the Salt Lake City meetings of the Association of American Geographers in 1977.*

POCOCK (DOUGLAS CHARLES DAVID) The novelist and the north. Durham, 1978. pp. 41. *bibliog. (Durham. University. Department of Geography. Occasional Publications (New Series). No. 12)*

POCOCK (DOUGLAS CHARLES DAVID) and HUDSON (RAY) Images of the urban environment. London, 1978. pp. 181. *bibliog.*

GEOGRAPHY.

LACOSTE (YVES) La géographie, ça sert, d'abord, à faire la guerre. Paris, 1976. pp. 190.

— Data processing.

COX (NICHOLAS J.) and RHIND (DAVID W.) Geographical networks and automatic data processing. Durham, 1978. pp. 54. *bibliog. (Durham. University. Department of Geography. Occasional Publications (New Series). No. 11)*

— Methodology.

CHAPMAN (GRAHAM PETER) Human and environmental systems: a geographer's appraisal. London, 1977. pp. 421. *bibliog.*

— Network analysis.

COX (NICHOLAS J.) and RHIND (DAVID W.) Geographical networks and automatic data processing. Durham, 1978. pp. 54. *bibliog. (Durham. University. Department of Geography. Occasional Publications (New Series). No. 11)*

— Study and teaching.

FINK (L. DEE) Listening to the learner: an exploratory study of personal meaning in college geography courses. Chicago, 1977. pp. 186. *bibliog. (Chicago. University. Department of Geography. Research Papers. No. 184)*

GEOGRAPHY, ECONOMIC.

AKADEMIIA NAUK SSSR. Geograficheskoe Obshchestvo SSSR. S"ezd, 6- oi, 1975. Teoreticheskie aspekty ekonomicheskoi geografii: sbornik statei. Leningrad, 1975. pp. 151. *bibliog.*

PROBLEMY geografii naseleniia i ispol'zovaniia territorii; Problems of the geography of population and land utilization. Tbilisi, 1976. pp. 239. *bibliog. With English table of contents and brief summaries.*

LLOYD (PETER E.) and DICKEN (PETER) Location in space: a theoretical approach to economic geography. 2nd ed. New York, 1977. pp. 474. *bibliog.*

BOYCE (RONALD R.) The bases of economic geography. 2nd ed. New York, [1978]. pp. 433. *bibliogs.*

GEOGRAPHY, POLITICAL.

LANGLANDS (B.W.) Nationalism, regionalism and federalism: the geographical basis to some conflicting political concepts in East Africa. 1964. pp. 55. *Typescript: unpublished. Paper presented to the Political Geography Seminar of the International Geographical Union at Sheffield in 1964.*

GEOLOGY

— Brazil.

BRAZIL. Divisão de Fomento da Produção Mineral. 1970. Geologia econômica de parte da região do medio São Francisco, nordeste do Brasil. Rio de Janeiro, 1970. pp. 97. *bibliog. (Boletins. No. 140) 4 maps in end pocket.*

— — Bibliography.

IGLESIAS (DOLORES) and MENEGHEZZI (MARIA DE LOURDES) compilers. Bibliografia e indice da geologia do Brasil, 1951-1960. Rio de Janeiro, 1967. pp. 203. *(Brazil. Divisão de Geologia e Mineralogia. Boletins. No. 238)*

— — Goias (State).

MELLO (JOSE CARLOS RODRIGUES DE) and BERBERT (CARLOS OITI) Investigação geologico-econômica da area de Morro Feio- Hidrolândia, Goias. Rio de Janeiro, 1969. pp. 81, 4 maps. *bibliog. (Brazil. Divisão de Fomento da Produção Mineral. Boletins. No. 132)*

— Canada — Newfoundland and Labrador — Bibliography.

BAIRD (DAVID McCURDY) and others. Bibliography of the geology of Newfoundland, 1936-1954; [and] Bibliography of the geology of Labrador, 1814-1954. St. John's, 1954. pp. 47. *(Newfoundland. Department of Mines and Resources. Bulletins. No. 36)*

— — Ontario — Surveys.

THOMSON (JAMES E.) The Geological Branch: its history, services and operations. Toronto, 1970. pp. 31. *(Ontario. Department of Mines. Miscellaneous Papers. 40)*

— Sierra Leone.

ANDREWS-JONES (D.A.) Geology and mineral resources of the northern Kambui schist belt and adjacent granulites. Freetown, 1966. pp. 100. *bibliog. (Sierra Leone. Geological Survey. Bulletins. No. 6) 2 maps in end pocket.*

— Zambia.

VAVRDA (I.) The geology of the Chipata area: explanation of degree sheet 1332, SE quarter. Lusaka, 1974. pp. 22. *bibliog. (Zambia. Geological Survey Department. Reports. No. 41) 3 maps in end pocket.*

— — Bibliography.

ANNOTATED BIBLIOGRAPHY AND INDEX OF THE GEOLOGY OF ZAMBIA; [pd. by] Geological Survey Department. a., 1931/1959-1966/1967, 1972/1973- Lusaka. *The issue covering 1960/1961 forms part of Records of the Geological Survey, v. 9.*

GEOLOGY, STRATIGRAPHIC.

GOUDIE (ANDREW S.) Environmental change. Oxford, 1977. pp. 243. *bibliogs.*

GEOMORPHOLOGY.

ESTONIA: regional studies; (on the occasion of the 23rd International Geographical Congress). Tallinn, 1976. pp. 185, 16 plates. *bibliogs.*

GEORGE (DAVID LLOYD) 1st Earl Lloyd George.

LLOYD George and the war: a personal history of his part in Armageddon; by an independent Liberal. London, [1918?]. pp. 159.

FRY (MICHAEL GRAHAM) Lloyd George and foreign policy. Montreal, 1977 in progress.

ADAMS (R.J.Q.) Arms and the wizard: Lloyd George and the Ministry of Munitions, 1915-1916. London, [1978]. pp. 252.

GEORGE BRETTLE AND COMPANY.

HARTE (NEGLEY B.) A history of George Brettle and Co. Ltd., 1801-1964. [London, 1973]. fo. 165. *bibliog.*

GEORGIA

— Population.

PROBLEMY geografii naseleniia i ispol'zovaniia territorii; Problems of the geography of population and land utilization. Tbilisi, 1976. pp. 239. *bibliog. With English table of contents and brief summaries.*

GEORGIA (UNITED STATES)

— History.

SPALDING (PHINIZY) Oglethorpe in America. Chicago, [1977]. pp. 207.

— Race question.

DITTMER (JOHN) Black Georgia in the progressive era, 1900-1920. Urbana, [1977]. pp. 239. *bibliog.*

GEOTHERMAL RESOURCES.

UNITED NATIONS. Symposium on the Development and Utilization of Geothermal Resources, Pisa, 1970. United Nations Symposium...[held at] Pisa, Italy, 22 September to 1 October 1970. (ST/TAO/SER.C/126). New York, 1971. pp. 20.

GERMAN AMERICANS.

GERLACH (RUSSEL L.) Immigrants in the Ozarks: a study in ethnic geography. Columbia, [1976]. pp. 206. *bibliog. (Missouri University. Studies. vol. 64)*

BAYOR (RONALD H.) Neighbors in conflict: the Irish, Germans, Jews, and Italians of New York City, 1929-1941. Baltimore, [1978]. pp. 232. *bibliog. (Johns Hopkins University. Studies in Historical and Political Science. Series 96. No. 1)*

GERMAN LANGUAGE

— Dictionaries — Polyglot.

HEBÁK (PETR) and HUSTOPECKÝ (JIŘÍ) compilers. Šestijazyčný slovník termínů z regresní analýzy: [Czech, Russian, Polish, English, French, German]. Praha, 1978. pp. 211. *With preface and explanatory notes in each language.*

GERMAN LITERATURE

— History and criticism.

GROSSBRITANNIEN und Deutschland: europäische Aspekte der politisch-kulturellen Beziehungen beider Länder in Geschichte und Gegenwart: (Festschrift für John W.P. Bourke, München; herausgegeben von Ortwin Kuhn, Berlin). München, [1974]. pp. 691. *bibliogs. In German or English.*

GERMAN NEWSPAPERS.

VORWAERTS. Vorwärts, 1876-1976: ein Querschnitt in Faksimiles; herausgegeben von Günter Grunwald und Friedhelm Merz, etc. Berlin, [1976]. pp. 203.

TAUBERT (ROLF) Autonomie und Integration: das Arbeiter-Blatt Lennep: eine Fallstudie zur Theorie und Geschichte von Arbeiterpresse und Arbeiterbewegung, 1848-1850. München, 1977. pp. 215. *bibliog. (Institut für Zeitungsforschung derStadt Dortmund. Dortmunder Beiträge zur Zeitungsforschung. Band 24)*

GERMAN PERIODICALS.

HAHN (FRED) Lieber Stürmer: Leserbriefe an das NS-Kampfblatt, 1924 bis 1945: eine Dokumentation aus dem Leo-Baeck-Institut, New York; Bearbeitung der deutschen Ausgabe von Günther Wagenlehner. Stuttgart, [1978]. pp. 263. *bibliog. (Studiengesellschaft für Zeitprobleme. Zeitpolitik. 19)*

GERMAN REUNIFICATION QUESTION (1949-).

GERMAN REUNIFICATION QUESTION (1949-).

HESTERMANN (FERDINAND) Eine Rede, die nicht gehalten werden konnte. [Berlin, 1948]. pp. 16. *(Deutscher Volkskongress. Schriftenreihe für Einheit und Gerechten Frieden) Speech intended for the Volkskongress für Einheit und gerechten Frieden, Solingen, 1948, which was not allowed to take place.*

OELSSNER (FRED) Der Volkskammer-Appell und die Sozialistische Einheitspartei Deutschlands: Rede...auf der Tagung des Berliner Parteiaktivs am 28. Setember 1951. [Berlin, 1951]. pp. 47.

HERDE (GEORG) and WAGNER (ANKE) Revanchistische Politik: Einfluss, Kräfte, Gefahr. Frankfurt am Main, 1977. pp. 170.

WILKER (LOTHAR) Die Sicherheitspolitik der SPD, 1956-1966: zwischen Wiedervereinigungs- und Bündnisorientierung. Bonn-Bad Godesberg, [1977]. pp. 347. *bibliog. (Friedrich-Ebert-Stiftung. Forschungsinstitut. Schriftenreihe. Band 135)*

OVERESCH (MANFRED) Gesamtdeutsche Illusion und westdeutsche Realität: von den Vorbereitungen für einen deutschen Friedensvertrag zur Gründung des Auswärtigen Amts der Bundesrepublik Deutschland, 1946-1949/51. Düsseldorf, [1978]. pp. 204. *bibliog.*

GERMANS IN CZECHOSLOVAKIA.

PRINZ (FRIEDRICH) Beneš, Jaksch und die Sudetendeutschen. Stuttgart, 1975. pp. 76.

JAWORSKI (RUDOLF) Vorposten oder Minderheit?: der sudetendeutsch Volkstumskampf in den Beziehungen zwischen der Weimarer Republik und der ČSR. Stuttgart, [1977]. pp. 240. *bibliog.*

POZORNY (REINHARD) Wir suchten die Freiheit: Schicksalsweg der sudetendeutschen Volksgruppe. Vlotho/Weser, 1978. pp. 402. *bibliog.*

GERMANS IN ESTONIA.

GRUNDMANN (KARL HEINZ) Deutschtumspolitik zur Zeit der Weimarer Republik: eine Studie am Beispiel der deutsch-baltischen Minderheit in Estland und Lettland. Hannover-Döhren, 1977. pp. 741. *bibliog.*

GERMANS IN FOREIGN COUNTRIES.

WEIDENFELLER (GERHARD) VDA, Verein für das Deutschtum im Ausland, Allgemeiner Deutscher Schulverein, 1881-1918: ein Beitrag zur Geschichte des deutschen Nationalismus und Imperialismus im Kaiserreich. Bern, 1976. pp. 507. *bibliog.*

GERMANS IN HUNGARY.

SENZ (INGOMAR MANFRED) Die nationale Bewegung der ungarländischen Deutschen vor dem Ersten Weltkrieg: eine Entwicklung im Spannungsfeld zwischen Alldeutschtum und ungarischer Innenpolitik. München, 1977. pp. 306. *bibliog. (Südostdeutsche Historische Kommission. Buchreihe. Band 30)*

GERMANS IN LATVIA.

GRUNDMANN (KARL HEINZ) Deutschtumspolitik zur Zeit der Weimarer Republik: eine Studie am Beispiel der deutsch-baltischen Minderheit in Estland und Lettland. Hannover-Döhren, 1977. pp. 741. *bibliog.*

GERMANS IN POLAND.

GRZEŚ (BOLESŁAW) and others. Niemcy w Poznańskiem wobec polityki germanizacyjnej, 1815-1920; pod redakcją Lecha Trzeciakowskiego. Poznań, 1976. pp. 472. *bibliog. (Poznań. Instytut Zachodni. Studia Niemcoznawcze. Nr.29)*

JAKÓBCZYK (WITOLD) Pruska komisja osadnicza, 1886-1919. Poznań, 1976. pp. 200.

KOSIM (JAN) Okupacja pruska i konspiracje rewolucyjne w Warszawie, 1796-1806. Wrocław, 1976. pp. 272. *With French and German summaries.*

MENCEL (TADEUSZ) Galicja Zachodnia, 1795-1809: studium z dziejów ziem polskich zaboru austriackiego po III rozbiorze. Lublin, 1976. pp. 522. *bibliog. With Russian and German summaries.*

POŁOMSKI (FRANCISZEK) Aspekty rasowe w postępowaniu z robotnikami przymusowymi i jeńcami wojennymi III Rzeszy, 1939-1945. Wrocław, 1976. pp. 130. *bibliog. (Wrocław. Wrocławskie Towarzystwo Naukowe. Prace. Seria A. Nr. 185) With English summary.*

GERMANS IN ROMANIA.

BARCAN (MONICA) and MILLITZ (ADALBERT) Die deutsche Nationalität in Rumänien; (deutsche Fassung von Adalbert Millitz). Bukarest, 1977. pp. 150. *bibliog.*

GERMANS IN RUSSIA.

GRIDNEV (VIKTOR MIKHAILOVICH) Bor'ba krest'ianstva okkupirovannykh oblastei RSFSR protiv nemetsko-fashistskoi okkupatsionnoi politiki, 1941-1944. Moskva, 1976. pp. 231. *bibliog.*

GERMANS IN SILESIA.

MINCZAKIEWICZ (TADEUSZ) Stosunki społeczne na lasku Opolskim w latach 1922-1933. Wrocław, 1976. pp. 196. *bibliog. With Russian, German and English summaries.*

GERMANS IN THE ARGENTINE REPUBLIC.

NEWTON (RONALD C.) German Buenos Aires, 1900-1933: social change and cultural crisis. Austin, [1977]. pp. 225. *bibliog.*

GERMANTOWN, PENNSYLVANIA

— Social history.

WOLF (STEPHANIE GRAUMAN) Urban village: population, community and family structure in Germantown, Pennsylvania 1683-1800. Princeton, N.J., [1976]. pp. 361. *bibliog.*

GERMANY

— Appropriations and expenditures.

GERMANY (BUNDESREPUBLIK). Statistisches Bundesamt. Jahresabschlüsse: Öffentliche Finanzwirtschaft. a., 1959/62-1973. Wiesbaden. *(Finanzen und Steuern. Reihe 1.2) From 1965 file incorporates* GERMANY (BUNDESREPUBLIK). *Statistisches Bundesamt. Jahresabschlüsse: Staatsfinanzen.*

GERMANY (BUNDESREPUBLIK). Statistisches Bundesamt. Jahresabschlüsse: Staatsfinanzen. a., 1959-1964. Wiesbaden. *(Finanzen und Steuern. Reihe 1.2) From 1965 incorporated into* GERMANY (BUNDESREPUBLIK). *Statistisches Bundesamt. Jahresabschlüsse: Öffentliche Finanzwirtschaft.*

WEILEPP (MANFRED) Der Full Employment Budget Surplus als Mass für die Wirkungen der Staatstätigkeit auf die volkswirtschaftliche Gesamtnachfrage: dargestellt am Beispiel der Bundesrepublik Deutschland. Hamburg, 1975. pp. 212. *bibliog. (Hamburg. Hamburgisches Welt-Wirtschafts-Archiv. Veröffentlichungen) Dissertation - Universität Hamburg.*

— Armed forces.

WESTPHAL (SIEGFRIED) Der deutsche Generalstab auf der Anklagebank: Nürnberg, 1945- 1948; mit einer Denkschrift von Walther von Brauchitsch [and others]. Mainz, [1978]. pp. 152. *bibliog.*

— Army — History.

GRÜNBERG (KAROL) SS - czarna gwardia Hitlera. [Warszawa], 1975. pp. 558. *bibliog.*

— — — Sources.

ZWISCHEN Revolution und Kapp-Putsch: Militär und Innenpolitik, 1918-1920; bearbeitet von Heinz Hürten. Düsseldorf, [1977]. pp. 378. *bibliog. (Germany (Bundesrepublik). Quellen zur Geschichte des Parlamentarismus und der Politischen Parteien. 2. Reihe. Band 2)*

— — Officers.

WESTPHAL (SIEGFRIED) Der deutsche Generalstab auf der Anklagebank: Nürnberg, 1945- 1948; mit einer Denkschrift von Walther von Brauchitsch [and others]. Mainz, [1978]. pp. 152. *bibliog.*

— Bibliography.

EDGINGTON (PETER) The politics of the two Germanies...: a guide to sources and English-language materials. Ormskirk, 1977. pp. 80.

— Bundestag.

VITZTHUM (WOLFGANG) Graf. Parlament und Planung: zur verfassungsgerechten Zuordnung der Funktionen von Bundesregierung und Bundestag bei der politischen Planung. Baden-Baden, 1978. pp. 420. *bibliog.*

— — Elections.

INTER NATIONES E.V. Majorities, mandates, opinions: review of the election for the eighth German Bundestag on 3 October 1976. Bad Godesberg, 1976. pp. 23.

— Civilization.

GAY (PETER) Weimar culture: the outsider as insider. Harmondsworth, 1974. Originally published London, 1969. pp. 222. *bibliog.*

GROSSBRITANNIEN und Deutschland: europäische Aspekte der politisch-kulturellen Beziehungen beider Länder in Geschichte und Gegenwart: (Festschrift für John W.P. Bourke, München; herausgegeben von Ortwin Kuhn, Berlin). München, [1974]. pp. 691. *bibliogs. In German or English.*

— Colonies.

DRANG nach Afrika: die koloniale Expansionspolitik und Herrschaft des deutschen Imperialismus...; herausgegeben von Helmuth Stoecker unter Mitwirkung von Jolanda Ballhaus [and others]. Berlin, 1977. pp. 375. *bibliogs.*

GANN (LEWIS H.) and DUIGNAN (PETER) The rulers of German Africa, 1884-1914. Stanford, Calif., 1977. pp. 286.

VOLBERG (HEINRICH) Deutsche Kolonialbestrebungen in Südamerika nach dem Dreissigjährigen Kriege, insbesondere die Bemühungen von Johann Joachim Becher. Köln, 1977. pp. 223. *bibliog.*

— Commerce.

GERMANY (BUNDESREPUBLIK). Statistisches Bundesamt. Aussenhandel nach Ländern und Warengruppen: Spezialhandel, (formerly Spezialhandel nach Ländern und Warengruppen). q., 1976(1st)- Wiesbaden. *(Aussenhandel. Reihe 3)*

GERMANY (BUNDESREPUBLIK). Statistisches Bundesamt. Aussenhandel nach Waren und Ländern: Spezialhandel, (formerly Spezialhandel nach Waren und Ländern). m., Ja 1976- Wiesbaden. *(Aussenhandel. Reihe 2)*

GERMANY (BUNDESREPUBLIK). Statistisches Bundesamt. Durchfuhr in Seeverkehr und Seeumschlag. a., 1976- Wiesbaden. *(Aussenhandel. Reihe 6)*

GERMANY (BUNDESREPUBLIK). Statistisches Bundesamt. Foreign trade according to the Standard International Trade Classification (SITC)- special trade (formerly Special trade according to the Classification for Statistics and Tariffs (CST)). q., 1976(1st)- Wiesbaden. *(Aussenhandel. Reihe 5)*

GERMANY (BUNDESREPUBLIK). Statistisches Bundesamt. Zusammenfassende Übersichten für den Aussenhandel (formerly Zusammenfassende Übersichten). m., Ja 1976- Wiesbaden. *(Aussenhandel. Reihe 1)*

GERMANY

— — Statistics.

GERMANY (BUNDESREPUBLIK). Statistisches Bundesamt. Lagerverkehr, Übergang von Waren aus dem Veredelungsverkehr in den freien Verkehr, Zollerträge, Ausfuhr (Spezialhandel) von Waren ausländischen Ursprungs. a., 1976- Wiesbaden. (*Aussenhandel. Reihe 2.1*) *Supplementary volume to* GERMANY (BUNDESREPUBLIK). *Statistisches Bundesamt. Aussenhandel nach Waren und Ländern: Spezialhandel.*

— — Germany, Eastern.

DEUTSCHES INSTITUT FÜR WIRTSCHAFTSFORSCHUNG. Sonderhefte. [Neue Folge]. 119. Der Handel der Deutschen Demokratischen Republik mit der Bundesrepublik Deutschland und den übrigen OECD-Ländern... ; ([by] Horst Lambrecht). Berlin, 1977. pp. 98.

— — Japan.

MOERING (MARIA) Julius Simon: Jugend und Wanderjahre. [Hamburg, 1965?]. pp. 24.

— Constitution.

ELLWEIN (THOMAS) Das Regierungssystem der Bundesrepublik Deutschland. 4th ed. Opladen, [1977]. pp. 769. *bibliog.*

— Constitutional history.

REICHOLD (HELMUT) Bismarcks Zaunkönige: Duodez im 20. Jahrhundert: eine Studie zum Föderalismus im Bismarckreich. Paderborn, [1977]. pp. 320. *bibliog.*

— Constitutional law.

ANTIFASCHISTISCHE Politik heute: Verteidigung der demokratischen Grundrechte, Erfüllung antifaschistischer Verfassungsaufträge, etc.; ([by W.] Abendroth [and others]. Frankfurt/Main, [1975]. pp. 64. (*Vereinigung der Verfolgten des Naziregimes. Antifaschistische Arbeitshefte. 15*)

BADURA (PETER) and others. Mitbestimmungsgesetz 1976 und Grundgesetz: Gemeinschaftsgutachten. München, 1977. pp. 298.

BULL (HANS PETER) Die Staatsaufgaben nach dem Grundgesetz. 2nd ed. Kronberg, [1977]. pp. 468.

HEIMANN (NORBERT) Die Schiedsgerichtsbarkeit der politischen Parteien in der Bundesrepublik Deutschland. Bonn, 1977. pp. 305. *bibliog.* (*Friedrich-Ebert-Stiftung. Forschungsinstitut. Schriftenreihe. Band 128*)

VITZTHUM (WOLFGANG) Graf. Parlament und Planung: zur verfassungsgerechten Zuordnung von Bundesregierung und Bundestag bei der politischen Planung. Baden-Baden, 1978. pp. 420. *bibliog.*

— Defences.

BIELFELDT (CAROLA) Rüstungsausgaben und Staatsinterventionismus: das Beispiel der Bundesrepublik Deutschland, 1950-1971. Frankfurt/Main, [1977]. pp. 293. *bibliog.*

SMITH (ARTHUR LEE) 1927- . Churchill's German army: wartime strategy and cold war politics, 1943-1947. Beverly Hills, [1977]. pp. 158. *bibliog.*

WILKER (LOTHER) Die Sicherheitspolitik der SPD, 1956-1966: zwischen Wiedervereinigungs- und Bündnisorientierung. Bonn-Bad Godesberg, [1977]. pp. 347. *bibliog.* (*Friedrich-Ebert-Stiftung. Forschungsinstitut. Schriftenreihe. Band 135*)

— Economic conditions.

REPORT on visit to Germany, Polish Corridor and Danzig in September 1928; [by a delegation of Conservatives, led by Sir John Sandeman Allen]. 1928. fo. 6. *Typescript: unpublished.*

CLOZIER (RENE) L'économie de l'Allemagne de l'Ouest (R.F.A.). [Paris, 1977]. pp. 128.

A DISCUSSION with Herbert Giersch: current problems of the West German economy, 1976-1977. Washington, [1977]. pp. 30. (*American Enterprise Institute for Public Policy Research. AEI Studies. 147*)

— — Bibliography.

MERRITT (ANNA J.) and MERRITT (RICHARD LAWRENCE) compilers. Politics, economics and society in the two Germanies, 1945-75: a bibliography of English-language works. Urbana, [1978]. pp. 268.

— Economic history.

KELLENBENZ (HERMANN) Deutsche Wirtschaftsgeschichte. München, [1977 in progress]. *bibliog.*

GESELLSCHAFT im Konkurs?: Handbuch zur Wirtschaftskrise 1973- 76 in der BRD; herausgegeben von Jörg Huffschmid und Herbert Schui. 2nd ed. Köln, 1977. pp. 538.

SPOHN (WILLFRIED) Weltmarktkonkurrenz und Industrialisierung Deutschlands, 1870- 1914: eine Untersuchung zur...Geschichte der kapitalistischen Produktionsweise. Berlin, [1977]. pp. 452. *bibliog.*

INDUSTRIELLE Gesellschaft und politisches System: Beiträge zur politischen Sozialgeschichte: Festschrift für Fritz Fischer zum siebzigsten Geburtstag; (Dirk Stegmann [and others], Hrsg.). Bonn, [1978]. pp. 464. *bibliog.* (*Friedrich-Ebert-Stiftung. Forschungsinstitut. Schriftenreihe. Band 137*) *In various languages.*

KEINATH (KARL) Regionale Konjunkturschwankungen: eine empirische Analyse der Bundesrepublik Deutschland, 1950-1974. Tübingen, 1978. pp. 335. *bibliog.* (*Tübingen. Universität. Fachbereich Wirtschaftswissenschaft. Tübinger Wirtschaftswissenschaftliche Abhandlungen. Band 23*)

KITCHEN (MARTIN) The political economy of Germany, 1815-1914. London, 1978. pp. 304. *bibliog.*

— Economic policy.

RATHENAU (WALTHER) Walther Rathenau-Gesamtausgabe; herausgegeben von Hans Dieter Hellige und Ernst Schulin. München, 1977 in progress.

BLAICH (FRITZ) Die Wirtschaftskrise 1925/26 und die Reichsregierung von der Erwerbslosenfürsorge zur Konjunkturpolitik. Kallmünz Opf., 1977. pp. 196. *bibliog.*

BLUMENBERG (ROLF) Das System der Raumplanung in der Bundesrepublik Deutschland: eine Organisationsprüfung. Göttingen, 1977. pp. 447. *bibliog.* (*Münster in Westfalen. Westfälische Wilhelms- Universität. Institut für Verkehrswissenschaft. Beiträge. Heft 83*)

BRD-DDR: die Wirtschaftssysteme: soziale Marktwirtschaft und sozialistische Planwirtschaft im Systemvergleich; mit Beiträgen von Hannelore Hamel [and others]; herausgegeben von Hannelore Hamel. München, [1977]. pp. 365.

FROEBEL (FOLKER) and others. Die neue internationale Arbeitsteilung: strukturelle Arbeitslosigkeit in den Industrieländern und die Industrialisierung der Entwicklungsländer. Reinbek bei Hamburg, 1977. pp. 654.

KOMMISSION FÜR WIRTSCHAFTLICHEN UND SOZIALEN WANDEL. Wirtschaftlicher und sozialer Wandel in der Bundesrepublik Deutschland: Gutachten...; veröffentlicht durch die Bundesregierung; der Bundesminister für Arbeit und Sozialordnung. Göttingen, 1977. pp. 598.

KONJUNKTURPOLITIK: Zeitschrift für angewandte Konjunkturforschung. Beihefte. Heft 24. Die konjunkturpolitischen Lehren des letzten Jahrzehnts: Bericht über den wissenschaftlichen Teil der 40. Mitgliederversammlung der Arbeitsgemeinschaft deutscher wirtschaftswissenschaftlicher Forschungsinstitute...1977. Berlin, [1977]. pp. 173. *In German or English.*

MONETARY policy and economic activity in West Germany; compiled by S.F. Frowen [and others]. London, 1977. pp. 268. *bibliog.*

THOBEN (CHRISTA) Strukturdiagnose in der Marktwirtschaft. Berlin, [1977]. pp. 74. *bibliog.* (*Rheinisch-Westfälisches Institut für Wirtschaftsforschung, Essen. Schriftenreihe. Neue Folge. 40*)

Die ZERSTOERUNG der Weimarer Republik; [edited by] Reinhard Kühnl [and] Gerd Hardach]. Köln, [1977]. pp. 292.

LANGEN (WERNER) Unternehmensgrössenbezogene Wirtschaftspolitik in der Bundesrepublik Deutschland. Göttingen, 1978. pp. 605. *bibliog.* (*Institut für Mittelstandsforschung. Schriften zur Mittelstandsforschung. Nr. 74*)

— — Mathematical models.

KRELLE (WILHELM) and PAULY (RALF) Konsum und Investitionen des Staates bis 1985. Göttingen, [1976]. pp. 181, A142. *bibliog.* (*Kommission für Wirtschaftlichen und Sozialen Wandel. Schriften. 130*)

— Executive departments.

OVERESCH (MANFRED) Gesamtdeutsche Illusion und westdeutsche Realität: von den Vorbereitungen für einen deutschen Friedensvertrag zur Gründung des Auswärtigen Amts der Bundesrepublik Deutschland, 1946-1949/51. Düsseldorf, [1978]. pp. 204. *bibliog.*

— Foreign economic relations — Romania.

MARGUERAT (PHILIPPE) Le IIIe Reich et le pétrole roumain, 1938-1950: contribution à l'étude de la pénétration économique allemande dans les Balkans à la veille et au début de la Seconde Guerre mondiale. Leiden, 1977. pp. 231. *bibliog.* (*Geneva. Graduate Institute of International Studies. Collection de Relations Internationales. 6*)

— — United States.

LINK (WERNER) Deutsche und amerikanische Gewerkschaften und Geschäftsleute, 1945-1975: eine Studie über transnationale Beziehungen. Düsseldorf, [1978]. pp. 296. *bibliog.*

— Foreign population.

RIST (RAY C.) Guestworkers in Germany: the prospects for pluralism. New York, 1978. pp. 263. *bibliog.*

— Foreign relations.

TEXTE ZUR DEUTSCHLANDPOLITIK; hrsg. vom Bundesministerium für innerdeutsche Beziehungen [Germany]. irreg., D 13 1966/Oc 5 1967 (Bd.1)- [Bonn].

SCHENK (RAINER) Die Viermächteverantwortung für Deutschland als Ganzes, insbesondere deren Entwicklung seit 1969. Bern, 1976. pp. 199. *bibliog.*

RATHENAU (WALTHER) Walther Rathenau-Gesamtausgabe; herausgegeben von Hans Dieter Hellige und Ernst Schulin. München, 1977 in progress.

FRIEDMAN (ISAIAH) Germany, Turkey, and Zionism, 1897-1918. Oxford, 1977. pp. 461. *bibliog.*

GENSCHER (HANS DIETRICH) Deutsche Aussenpolitik. Bonn, [1977]. pp. 239. *Speeches, 1975-1977.*

HERDE (GEORG) and WAGNER (ANKE) Revanchistische Politik: Einfluss, Kräfte, Gefahr. Frankfurt am Main, 1977. pp. 170.

HERRSCHAFTSMETHODEN des deutschen Imperialismus, 1897/8 bis 1917: Dokumente zur innen- und aussenpolitischen Strategie und Taktik...; herausgegeben und eingeleitet von Willibald Gutsche. Berlin, 1977. pp. 295. (*Akademie der Wissenschaften der DDR. Zentralinstitut für Geschichte. Schriften. Band 53*)

HIDEN (JOHN) Germany and Europe, 1919-1939. London, 1977. pp. 205.

HILLGRUBER (ANDREAS) Deutsche Grossmacht- und Weltpolitik im 19. und 20. Jahrhundert. Düsseldorf, [1977]. pp. 389. *bibliog. Selected essays and articles originally published between 1964 and 1976.*

NOLTE (ERNST) Marxismus, Faschismus, Kalter Krieg: Vorträge und Aufsätze, 1964-1976. Stuttgart, [1977]. pp. 400. *bibliog.*

GERMANY (Cont.)

— — Czechoslovakia.

JAWORSKI (RUDOLF) Vorposten oder Minderheit?: der sudetendeutsch Volkstumskampf in den Beziehungen zwischen der Weimarer Republik und der ČSR. Stuttgart, [1977]. pp. 240. bibliog.

— — East (Near East).

GERMANY and the Middle East, 1835-1939: international symposium, April 1975; Jehuda L. Wallach, editor. Tel-Aviv, [1975]. pp. 211. *(Tel-Aviv. University. Institute of German History. Jahrbuch des Instituts für Deutsche Geschichte. Beihefte. 1)*

FLEURY (ANTOINE) La pénétration allemande au Moyen-Orient, 1919-1939: le cas de la Turquie, de l'Iran et de l'Afghanistan. Genève, 1977. pp. 432. bibliog. *(Geneva. Graduate Institute of International Studies. Collection de Relations Internationales. 5)*

— — France.

L'HUILLIER (FERNAND) Dialogues Franco-Allemands, 1925-1933. Gap, 1971. pp. 175. *(Strasbourg. Université. Faculté des Lettres. Publications)*

Les RELATIONS franco-allemandes, 1933-1939; (actes du colloque international...organisé...à Strasbourg du 7 au 10 octobre, 1975). Paris, 1976. pp. 424. *(Centre National de la Recherche Scientifique. Colloques Internationaux. No. 563)* Articles in French or German.

BARIETY (JACQUES) Les relations franco-allemandes après la première guerre mondiale, 10 novembre 1918 - 10 janvier 1925, de l'exécution à la négociation. Paris, 1977. pp. xix, 797. *(Paris. Université de Paris I (Panthéon-Sorbonne) and others. Publications de la Sorbonne. Série Internationale. 8)*

BOISVERT (JEAN JACQUES) Les relations franco-allemandes en 1920. Montréal, 1977. pp. 283. bibliog.

POIDEVIN (RAYMOND) and BARIETY (JACQUES) Les relations franco-allemandes, 1815-1975. Paris, [1977]. pp. 373. bibliogs.

— — Germany, Eastern.

RESS (GEORG) Die Rechtslage Deutschlands nach dem Grundlagenvertrag vom 21. Dezember 1972. Berlin, 1978. pp. 436. bibliog. *(Max-Planck-Institut für Ausländisches Öffentliches Recht und Völkerrecht, Heidelberg. Beiträge zum Ausländischen Öffentlichen Recht und Völkerrecht. 71)* With English summary.

— — Hungary.

SPIRA (THOMAS) German-Hungarian relations and the Swabian problem: from Károlyi to Gömbös, 1919-1936. New York, 1977. pp. 382. bibliog. *(East European Quarterly. East European Monographs. 25)*

— — Italy.

MUHR (JOSEF) Die deutsch-italienischen Beziehungen in der Ära des Ersten Weltkrieges, 1914-1922. Göttingen, [1977]. pp. 235. bibliog.

— — Japan.

DETERRENT diplomacy: Japan, Germany and the USSR 1935-1940: selected translations from Taiheiyo senso e no michi: kaisen gaiko shi; edited by James William Morley. New York, 1976. pp. 363. bibliog. *(Columbia University. East Asian Institute. Studies)*

— — Poland.

ARNDT (CLAUS) Die Verträge von Moskau und Warschau: politische, verfassungsrechtliche und völkerrechtliche Aspekte. Bonn, [1973]. pp. 216.

— — Russia.

ARNDT (CLAUS) Die Verträge von Moskau und Warschau: politische, verfassungsrechtliche und völkerrechtliche Aspekte. Bonn, [1973]. pp. 216.

BELETSKII (VIKTOR NIKOLAEVICH) Die Politik der Sowjetunion in den deutschen Angelegenheiten in der Nachkriegszeit, 1945-1976; übersetzt von Wolfgang Eckstein [and others]. Berlin, 1977. pp. 429.

SCHLESINGER (MORITZ) Erinnerungen eines Aussenseiters im diplomatischen Dienst; aus dem Nachlass herausgegeben und eingeleitet von Hubert Schneider. Köln, [1977]. pp. 315.

— — Sweden.

KARLSSON (RUNE) Så stoppades tysktågen: den tyska transiteringstrafiken i svensk politik, 1942-1943. Stockholm, 1974. pp. 363. bibliog. With English summary.

DRANGEL (LOUISE) Den kämpande demokratin: en studie i antinazistisk opinionsrörelse, 1935-1945. Stockholm, 1976. pp. 287. bibliog. With English summary.

— — United Kingdom.

ASPEKTE der deutsch-britischen Beziehungen im Laufe der Jahrhunderte: Ansprachen und Vorträge zur Eröffnung des Deutschen Historischen Instituts London: Aspects of Anglo-German relations through the centuries...; herausgegeben von Paul Kluke und Peter Alter. Stuttgart, 1978. pp. 83. *(Deutsches Historisches Institut. Veröffentlichungen. Band 4)* In German or English.

KRIEGER (WOLFGANG) Labour Party und Weimarer Republik: ein Beitrag zur Aussenpolitik der britischen Arbeiterbewegung zwischen Programmatik und Parteitaktik, 1918-1924. Bonn, [1978]. pp. 450. bibliog. *(Friedrich-Ebert-Stiftung. Forschungsinstitut. Schriftenreihe. Band 136)*

— — Uruguay.

MARQUEZ (JOAQUIN C.) Informe relativo a la reclamacion entablada ante el Gobierno de la Republica Oriental del Uruguay por las Compañias propietarias de los vapores alemanes requisados en 1917. Montevideo, 1922. pp. 36.

— Foreign relations administration.

OVERESCH (MANFRED) Gesamtdeutsche Illusion und westdeutsche Realität: von den Vorbereitungen für einen deutschen Friedensvertrag zur Gründung des Auswärtigen Amts der Bundesrepublik Deutschland, 1946-1949/51. Düsseldorf, [1978]. pp. 204. bibliog.

— Full employment policies.

WEILEPP (MANFRED) Der Full Employment Budget Surplus als Mass für die Wirkungen der Staatstätigkeit auf die volkswirtschaftliche Gesamtnachfrage: dargestellt am Beispiel der Bundesrepublik Deutschland. Hamburg, 1975. pp. 212. bibliog. *(Hamburg. Hamburgisches Welt-Wirtschafts-Archiv. Veröffentlichungen)* Dissertation - Universität Hamburg.

— History — Bibliography.

STACHURA (PETER D.) The Weimar era and Hitler, 1918-1933: a critical bibliography. Oxford, [1977]. pp. 276.

— — Chronology.

OSTERROTH (FRANZ) and SCHUSTER (DIETER) Chronik der deutschen Sozialdemokratie. 2nd ed. Berlin, 1975-78. 3 vols.

— — 1789-1900.

BOURGEOISIE und bürgerliche Umwälzung in Deutschland, 1789- 1871; herausgegeben von Helmut Bleiber. Berlin, 1977. pp. 525. bibliog. *(Akademie der Wissenschaften der DDR. Zentralinstitut für Geschichte. Schriften. Band 50)*

— — 1848-1870.

JACOBY (JOHANN) Briefwechsel, 1850-1877; herausgegeben und erläutert von Edmund Silberner. Bonn, [1978]. pp. 715. *(Institut für Sozialgeschichte Braunschweig. Veröffentlichungen)*

— — 1848-1849, Revolution.

AUFSTAND der Bürger: Revolution 1849 im westdeutschen Industriezentrum;...herausgegeben von Klaus Goebel und Manfred Wichelhaus. 3rd ed. Wuppertal, [1974]. pp. 317. bibliog.

JACOBY (JOHANN) Briefwechsel, 1816-1849; herausgegeben und erläutert von Edmund Silberner. Hannover, [1974]. pp. 669. bibliog. *(Institut für Sozialgeschichte Braunschweig. Veröffentlichungen)*

TAUBERT (ROLF) Autonomie und Integration: das Arbeiter-Blatt Lennep: eine Fallstudie zur Theorie und Geschichte von Arbeiterpresse und Arbeiterbewegung, 1848-1850. München, 1977. pp. 215. bibliog. *(Institut für Zeitungsforschung der Stadt Dortmund. Dortmunder Beiträge zur Zeitungsforschung. Band 24)*

— — — Sources.

VORMAERZ und Revolution, 1840-1849; herausgegeben von Hans Fenske. Darmstadt, 1976. pp. 449.

— — 1871- .

HILLGRUBER (ANDREAS) Deutsche Grossmacht- und Weltpolitik im 19. und 20. Jahrhundert. Düsseldorf, [1977]. pp. 389. bibliog. Selected essays and articles originally published between 1964 and 1976.

— — — Sources.

AUS der Arbeit des Bundesarchivs: Beiträge zum Archivwesen, zur Quellenkunde und Zeitgeschichte; herausgegeben von Heinz Boberach und Hans Booms. Boppard am Rhein, [1978]. pp. 568. bibliog. *(Germany (Bundesrepublik). Bundesarchiv. Schriften. 25)*

— — 1871-1918.

REICHOLD (HELMUT) Bismarcks Zaunkönige: Duodez im 20. Jahrhundert: eine Studie zum Föderalismus im Bismarckreich. Paderborn, [1977]. pp. 320. bibliog.

— — — Sources.

HERRSCHAFTSMETHODEN des deutschen Imperialismus, 1897/8 bis 1917: Dokumente zur innen- und aussenpolitischen Strategie und Taktik...; herausgegeben und eingeleitet von Willibald Gutsche. Berlin, 1977. pp. 295. *(Akademie der Wissenschaften der DDR. Zentralinstitut für Geschichte. Schriften. Band 53)*

— — 1918-1933.

GAY (PETER) Weimar culture: the outsider as insider. Harmondsworth, 1974. Originally published London, 1969. pp. 222. bibliog.

MUCKERMANN (FRIEDRICH JOSEPH) Im Kampf zwischen zwei Epochen: Lebenserinnerungen; bearbeitet und eingeleitet von Nikolaus Junk. Mainz, [1973]. pp. 668. *(Kommission für Zeitgeschichte. Veröffentlichungen. Reihe A: Quellen. Band 15)*

BIRD (KENNETH W.) Weimar, the German naval officer corps and the rise of national socialism. Amsterdam, 1977. pp. 313. bibliog.

Die ZERSTOERUNG der Weimarer Republik; ([edited by] Reinhard Kühnl [and] Gerd Hardach). Köln, [1977]. pp. 292.

— — — Sources.

LANE (BARBARA MILLER) and RUPP (LEILA J.) eds. Nazi ideology before 1933: a documentation. Manchester, [1978]. pp. 180. bibliog.

— — 1918-1919, Revolution.

Der JUELICHER Arbeiter- und Soldatenrat im November 1918: eine Dokumentation; ([edited by] Günter Bers). Jülich, 1974. pp. 31.

PIECK (WILHELM) Wilhelm Pieck: ein unermüdlicher Streiter für die deutsch- sowjetische Freundschaft: ausgewählte Reden und Schriften... ; eingeleitet und zusammengestellt von Heinz Vosske. Berlin, 1977. pp. 159.

GERMANY (Cont.)

— — Bibliography.

MEYER (GEORG P.) compiler. Bibliographie zur deutschen Revolution, 1918/19. Göttingen, 1977. pp. 188.

— — Sources.

ZWISCHEN Revolution und Kapp-Putsch: Militär und Innenpolitik, 1918-1920; bearbeitet von Heinz Hürten. Düsseldorf, [1977]. pp. 378. bibliog. *(Germany (Bundesrepublik). Quellen zur Geschichte des Parlamentarismus und der Politischen Parteien. 2. Reihe. Band 2)*

— — 1933-1945.

NAZISM and the Third Reich; edited with an introduction by Henry A. Turner. New York, 1972. pp. 262. bibliog.

MUCKERMANN (FRIEDRICH JOSEPH) Im Kampf zwischen zwei Epochen: Lebenserinnerungen; bearbeitet und eingeleitet von Nikolaus Junk. Mainz, [1973]. pp. 668. *(Kommission für Zeitgeschichte. Veröffentlichungen. Reihe A: Quellen. Band 15)*

DEUTSCHLAND im zweiten Weltkrieg; von einem Autorenkollektiv unter Leitung von Wolfgang Schumann [and others];... Herausgeberkollegium: Walter Bartel [and others]. Berlin, 1974 in progress.

Das "ANDERE Deutschland" im Zweiten Weltkrieg: Emigration und Widerstand in internationaler Perspektive: The "Other Germany" in the Second World War...; herausgegeben von Lothar Kettenacker. Stuttgart, 1977. pp. 258. *(Deutsches Historisches Institut in London. Veröffentlichungen. Band 2)* In German or English, with summaries in the alternative language.

HOEGNER (WILHELM) Flucht vor Hitler: Erinnerungen an die Kapitulation der ersten deutschen Republik, 1933. München, 1977 repr. 1978. pp. 296.

— — 1945-1955, Allied occupation.

SCHENK (RAINER) Die Viermächteverantwortung für Deutschland als Ganzes, insbesondere deren Entwicklung seit 1969. Bern, 1976. pp. 199. bibliog.

— Industries.

GERMANY (BUNDESREPUBLIK). Statistisches Bundesamt. Kostenstruktur der Unternehmen im Bergbau, Grundstoff- und Produktionsgütergewerbe (formerly Bergbau, Grundstoff- und Produktionsgüterindustrien). a. (formerly irreg.), 1970- Wiesbaden. *(Produzierendes Gewerbe. Reihe 4.3.1)*

GERMANY (BUNDESREPUBLIK). Statistisches Bundesamt. Kostenstruktur der Unternehmen im Investitionsgütergewerbe (formerly Investitionsgüterindustrien) . a.(formerly irreg), 1970- Wiesbaden. *(Produzierendes Gewerbe. Reihe 4.3.2)*

GERMANY (BUNDESREPUBLIK). Statistisches Bundesamt. Beschäftigung, Umsatz und Investitionen der Unternehmen in den Bergbau und im verarbeitenden Gewerbe (ohne Handwerk). a., 1975- Wiesbaden. *(Produzierendes Gewerbe. Reihe 4.2.1) File includes Vorbericht. Earlier data pd. as Reihe 1.2 of GERMANY (BUNDESREPUBLIK). Statistisches Bundesamt. Industrie und Handwerk.*

GERMANY (BUNDESREPUBLIK). Statistisches Bundesamt. Beschäftigung, Umsatz und Energieversorgung der Unternehmen und Betriebe im Bergbau und im verarbeitenden Gewerbe (ohne Handwerk). a. and m., 1976- Wiesbaden. *(Produzierendes Gewerbe. Reihe 4.1) File includes m. Vorbericht and annual in 2 pts., Teil 1, 1B-Systematik and Teil 2 SYPRO. Earlier data pd. as Reihe 1.1 of GERMANY (BUNDESREPUBLIK). Statistisches Bundesamt. Industrie und Handwerk.*

GERMANY (BUNDESREPUBLIK). Statistisches Bundesamt. Produktion im produzierenden Gewerbe. a., 1976- Wiesbaden. *(Produzierendes Gewerbe. Reihe 3) Supersedes GERMANY (BUNDESREPUBLIK). Statistisches Bundesamt. Industrielle Produktion.*

GERMANY (BUNDESREPUBLIK). Statistisches Bundesamt. Indizes der Produktion und der Arbeitsproduktivität, Produktion ausgewählter Erzeugnisse im Produzierenden Gewerbe. m., Ja 1977- Wiesbaden. *(Produzierendes Gewerbe. Reihe 2.1) File includes Eilbericht, Indizes der Produktion für das Produzierende Gewerbe. Earlier data pd. as Reihe 2 of GERMANY (BUNDESREPUBLIK). Statistisches Bundesamt. Industrie und Handwerk.*

GERMANY (BUNDESREPUBLIK). Statistisches Bundesamt. Indizes des Auftragseingangs, des Umsatzes und des Auftragsbestands für das verarbeitende Gewerbe und für das Bauhauptgewerbe. m., Ja 1977- Wiesbaden. *(Produzierendes Gewerbe. Reihe 2.2) Earlier data pd. as Reihe 6 of GERMANY (BUNDESREPUBLIK). Statistisches Bundesamt. Industrie und Handwerk.*

LANGEN (WERNER) Unternehmensgrössenbezogene Wirtschaftspolitik in der Bundesrepublik Deutschland. Göttingen, 1978. pp. 605. bibliog. *(Institut für Mittelstandsforschung. Schriften zur Mittelstandsforschung. Nr. 74)*

REFORM of statistics of production industries, etc; [by A. Sobotschinski and others]. Wiesbaden, 1978. pp. 38. *(Germany (Bundesrepublik). Statistisches Bundesamt. Studies on Statistics. No. 33) The original German articles were published in "Wirtschaft und Statistik", Vol. 7,8/1976 and Vol. 11/1977.*

— Intellectual life.

GAY (PETER) Weimar culture: the outsider as insider. Harmondsworth, 1974. Originally published London, 1969. pp. 222. bibliog.

— International status.

RESS (GEORG) Die Rechtslage Deutschlands nach dem Grundlagenvertrag vom 21. Dezember 1972. Berlin, 1978. pp. 436. bibliog. *(Max-Planck-Institut für Ausländisches Öffentliches Recht und Völkerrecht, Heidelberg. Beiträge zum Ausländischen Öffentlichen Recht und Völkerrecht. 71) With English summary.*

— Nationalism.

WEIDENFELLER (GERHARD) VDA, Verein für das Deutschtum im Ausland, Allgemeiner Deutscher Schulverein, 1881-1918: ein Beitrag zur Geschichte des deutschen Nationalismus und Imperialismus im Kaiserreich. Bern, 1976. pp. 507. bibliog.

HESS (JUERGEN C.) "Das ganze Deutschland soll es sein": demokratischer Nationalismus in der Weimarer Republik am Beispiel der Deutschen Demokratischen Partei. Stuttgart, 1978. pp. 398. bibliog.

SNYDER (LOUIS LEO) Roots of German nationalism. Bloomington, [1978]. pp. 309. bibliog.

— Navy — Officers.

BIRD (KENNETH W.) Weimar, the German naval officer corps and the rise of national socialism. Amsterdam, 1977. pp. 313. bibliog.

— Politics and government.

SNYDER (LOUIS LEO) Roots of German nationalism. Bloomington, [1978]. pp. 309. bibliog.

— — Bibliography.

EDGINGTON (PETER) The politics of the two Germanies...: a guide to sources and English-language materials. Ormskirk, 1977. pp. 80.

STACHURA (PETER D.) The Weimar era and Hitler, 1918-1933: a critical bibliography. Oxford, [1977]. pp. 276.

MERRITT (ANNA J.) and MERRITT (RICHARD LAWRENCE) compilers. Politics, economics and society in the two Germanies, 1945-75: a bibliography of English-language works. Urbana, [1978]. pp. 268.

— — 1789-1900.

JACOBY (JOHANN) Briefwechsel, 1816-1849; herausgegeben und erläutert von Edmund Silberner. Hannover, [1974]. pp. 669. bibliog. *(Institut für Sozialgeschichte Braunschweig. Veröffentlichungen)*

JACOBY (JOHANN) Briefwechsel, 1850-1877; herausgegeben und erläutert von Edmund Silberner. Bonn, [1978]. pp. 715. *(Institut für Sozialgeschichte Braunschweig. Veröffentlichungen)*

KITCHEN (MARTIN) The political economy of Germany, 1815-1914. London, 1978. pp. 304. bibliog.

— — 1871-1918.

WEIDENFELLER (GERHARD) VDA, Verein für das Deutschtum im Ausland, Allgemeiner Deutscher Schulverein, 1881-1918: ein Beitrag zur Geschichte des deutschen Nationalismus und Imperialismus im Kaiserreich. Bern, 1976. pp. 507. bibliog.

LAMBERTI (MARJORIE) Jewish activism in Imperial Germany: the struggle for civil equality. New Haven, 1978. pp. 235. bibliog.

SOCIETY and politics in Wilhelmine Germany; edited by Richard J. Evans. London, [1978]. pp. 305.

— — 1900- .

KITCHEN (MARTIN) The political economy of Germany, 1815-1914. London, 1978. pp. 304. bibliog.

— — 1918-1945.

NICHTS getan?: die Arbeit seit dem 9. November 1918. [Berlin, 1919]. pp. 32.

HITLER (ADOLF) The new Germany desires work and peace: speeches by Reich Chancellor Adolf Hitler, the leader of the new Germany. Berlin, [1933?]. pp. 66.

THAELMANN (ERNST) Ausgewählte Reden und Schriften in zwei Bänden. Frankfurt am Main, 1976-77. 2 vols.

STRESEMANN (GUSTAV) Schriften; mit einem Vorwort von Willy Brandt; herausgegeben von Arnold Harttung. Berlin, [1976]. pp. 438.

The SHAPING of the Nazi state; edited by Peter D. Stachura. London, [1978]. pp. 304.

— — 1918-1933.

DIEHL (JAMES M.) Paramilitary politics in Weimar Germany. Bloomington, Ind., [1977]. pp. 406. bibliog.

LEOPOLD (JOHN A.) Alfred Hugenberg: the radical nationalist campaign against the Weimar Republic. New Haven, 1977. pp. 298. bibliog.

— — 1945- .

DAHRENDORF (RALF) Die Regierbarkeit moderner Demokratien...; Vortrag...am 2. Dezember 1974 in München. Frankfurt (Main), [1974]. pp. 3-11. *(Extracted from Nr.13, Deutsche Bank, Beiträge zu Wirtschafts- und Währungsfragen und zur Bankgeschichte)*

ANTIFASCHISTISCHE Politik heute: Verteidigung der demokratischen Grundrechte, Erfüllung antifaschistischer Verfassungsaufträge, etc.; ([by W.] Abendroth [and others]). Frankfurt/Main, [1975]. pp. 64. *(Vereinigung der Verfolgten des Naziregimes. Antifaschistische Arbeitshefte. 15)*

REFORM in der Demokratie: theoretische Ansätze, konkrete Erfahrungen, politische Konsequenzen; (Wolfgang Schulenberg, Hrsg.). Hamburg, 1976. pp. 319. bibliogs.

ABENDROTH-Forum: Marburger Gespräche aus Anlass des 70. Geburtstags von Wolfgang Abendroth; herausgegeben von Frank Deppe [and others]. Marburg, [1977]. pp. 443. *(Studiengesellschaft für Sozialgeschichte und Arbeiterbewegung, Marburg. Schriftenreihe für Sozialgeschichte und Arbeiterbewegung. Band 6) Papers and discussion of four symposia held in May and June of 1976.*

ELLWEIN (THOMAS) Das Regierungssystem der Bundesrepublik Deutschland. 4th ed. Opladen, [1977]. pp. 769. bibliog.

HAEUSSERMANN (HARTMUT) Die Politik der Bürokratie: Einführung in die Soziologie der staatlichen Verwaltung. Frankfurt/Main, [1977]. pp. 146. bibliog.

GERMANY (Cont.)

HANDBUCH des politischen Systems der Bundesrepublik Deutschland; herausgegeben von Kurt Sontheimer und Hans H. Röhring. München, [1977]. pp. 761. *bibliogs.*

HERDE (GEORG) and WAGNER (ANKE) Revanchistische Politik: Einfluss, Kräfte, Gefahr. Frankfurt am Main, 1977. pp. 170.

NOLTE (ERNST) Marxismus, Faschismus, Kalter Krieg: Vorträge und Aufsätze, 1964-1976. Stuttgart, [1977]. pp. 400. *bibliog.*

PIRKER (THEO) Die verordnete Demokratie: Grundlagen und Erscheinungen der "Restauration". Berlin, [1977]. pp. 295.

Der SPD-Staat; herausgegeben von Frank Grube und Gerhard Richter. München, [1977]. pp. 351.

COBLER (SEBASTIAN) Law, order and politics in West Germany; translated [from the German] by Francis McDonagh. Harmondsworth, 1978. pp. 223.

VITZTHUM (WOLFGANG) Graf. Parlament und Planung: zur verfassungsgerechten Zuordnung der Funktionen von Bundesregierung und Bundestag bei der politischen Planung. Baden-Baden, 1978. pp. 420. *bibliog.*

— **Population.**

HISTORISCHE Demographie als Sozialgeschichte: Giessen und Umgebung vom 17. zum 19. Jahrhundert; (herausgegeben von Arthur E. Imhof). Darmstadt, 1975. 2 vols. *bibliog.* (*Hessische Historische Kommission, Darmstadt, and Historische Kommission für Hessen. Quellen und Forschungen zur Hessischen Geschichte. 31*)

BRUESE (RUDOLF) Mobilität der landwirtschaftlichen Bevölkerung: eine Analyse der Abwanderung und Statuszuweisung in der Bundesrepublik Deutschland. Bonn, 1977. pp. 416. *bibliog.* (*Forschungsgesellschaft für Agrarpolitik und Agrarsoziologie. [Publications]. 242*)

— **Reichstag — Elections.**

SCHAUFF (JOHANNES) Das Wahlverhalten der deutschen Katholiken im Kaiserreich und in der Weimarer Republik: Untersuchungen aus dem Jahre 1928... ; herausgegeben und eingeleitet von Rudolf Morsey. Mainz, [1975]. pp. 214. (*Kommission für Zeitgeschichte. Veröffentlichungen. Reihe A: Quellen. Band 18*)

WAEHLERBEWEGUNG in der deutschen Geschichte: Analysen und Berichte zu den Reichstagswahlen, 1871-1933; bearbeitet und herausgegeben von Otto Büsch [and others]. Berlin, [1978]. pp. 672. *bibliog.* (*Historische Kommission zu Berlin. Einzelveröffentlichungen. Band 20*)

— — **Rules and practice.**

MITTMANN (URSULA) Fraktion und Partei: ein Vergleich von Zentrum und Sozialdemokratie im Kaiserreich. Düsseldorf, [1976]. pp. 455. *bibliog.* (*Germany (Bundesrepublik). Kommission für Geschichte des Parlamentarismus und der Politischen Parteien. Beiträge zur Geschichte des Parlamentarismus und der Politischen Parteien. Band 59*)

— **Relations (general) with Africa.**

GANN (LEWIS H.) and DUIGNAN (PETER) The rulers of German Africa, 1884-1914. Stanford, Calif., 1977. pp. 286.

— **Relations (general) with foreign countries.**

DUEWELL (KURT) Deutschlands auswärtige Kulturpolitik, 1918-1932: Grundlinien und Dokumente. Wien, 1976. pp. 402. *bibliog.*

PEISERT (HANSGERT) Die auswärtige Kulturpolitik der Bundesrepublik Deutschland: sozialwissenschaftliche Analysen und Planungsmodelle; mit einem Vorwort von Ralf Dahrendorf. Stuttgart, [1978]. pp. 371.

— **Relations (general) with Russia.**

FRICKE (DIETER) and SHNEERSON (L.M.) eds. Iz istorii germanskogo rabochego dvizheniia i sovetsko-germanskogo internatsional'nogo sodruzhestva: sbornik statei. Minsk, 1975. pp. 208.

WEILL (CLAUDIE) Marxistes russes et social-démocratie allemande, 1898-1904. Paris, 1977. pp. 254. *bibliog.*

— **Relations (general) with the United Kingdom.**

GROSSBRITANNIEN und Deutschland: europäische Aspekte der politisch-kulturellen Beziehungen beider Länder in Geschichte und Gegenwart: (Festschrift für John W.P. Bourke, München; herausgegeben von Ortwin Kuhn, Berlin). München, [1974]. pp. 691. *bibliogs. In German or English.*

The BRITISH in Germany: educational reconstruction after 1945; edited by Arthur Hearnden. London, 1978. pp. 335. *Based on papers delivered at a conference held at St. Edmund Hall, Oxford in January 1975.*

PILLARS of partnership...; edited by Rolf Breitenstein. London, [1978]. pp. 103.

— **Social conditions.**

HANDL (JOHANN) and others. Klassenlagen und Sozialstruktur: empirische Untersuchungen für die Bundesrepublik Deutschland. Frankfurt/Main, [1977]. pp. 275. *bibliog.* (*Frankfurt am Main. Universität, and Mannheim. Universität. Sozialpolitische Forschergruppe. SPES- Projekt. Schriftenreihe. Band 9*)

LEBENSBEDINGUNGEN in der Bundesrepublik: sozialer Wandel und Wohlfahrtsentwicklung; (Wolfgang Zapf, Hg.). 2nd ed. Frankfurt/Main, 1978. pp. 947. *bibliog.* (*Frankfurt am Main. Universität, and Mannheim. Universität. Sozialpolitische Forschergruppe. SPES- Projekt. Schriftenreihe. Band 10*)

VEREIN FÜR SOZIALPOLITIK. Schriften. Neue Folge. Band 95. Zur Neuen Sozialen Frage; von Friedrich Buttler [and others]; herausgegeben von Hans Peter Widmaier. Berlin, [1978]. pp. 249.

— — **Bibliography.**

MERRITT (ANNA J.) and MERRITT (RICHARD LAWRENCE) compilers. Politics, economics and society in the two Germanies, 1945-75: a bibliography of English-language works. Urbana, [1978]. pp. 268.

— **Social history.**

GAY (PETER) Weimar culture: the outsider as insider. Harmondsworth, 1974. Originally published London, 1969. pp. 222. *bibliog.*

HISTORISCHE Demographie als Sozialgeschichte: Giessen und Umgebung vom 17. zum 19. Jahrhundert; (herausgegeben von Arthur E. Imhof). Darmstadt, 1975. 2 vols. *bibliog.* (*Hessische Historische Kommission, Darmstadt, and Historische Kommission für Hessen. Quellen und Forschungen zur Hessischen Geschichte. 31*)

SAGARRA (EDA) A social history of Germany, 1648-1914. London, 1977. pp. 473. *bibliog.*

INDUSTRIELLE Gesellschaft und politisches System: Beiträge zur politischen Sozialgeschichte: Festschrift für Fritz Fischer zum siebzigsten Geburtstag; (Dirk Stegmann [and others], Hrsg.). Bonn, [1978]. pp. 464. *bibliog.* (*Friedrich-Ebert-Stiftung. Forschungsinstitut. Schriftenreihe. Band 137*) *In various languages.*

SOCIETY and politics in Wilhelmine Germany; edited by Richard J. Evans. London, [1978]. pp. 305.

— **Social policy.**

BETHUSY-HUC (VIOLA VON) Gräfin. Das Sozialleistungssystem der Bundesrepublik Deutschland. 2nd ed. Tübingen, 1976. pp. 346. *bibliog.*

BRAUNS (HEINRICH) Katholische Sozialpolitik im 20. Jahrhundert: ausgewählte Aufsätze und Reden...; bearbeitet von Hubert Mockenhaupt. Mainz, [1976]. pp. 209. *bibliog.* (*Kommission für Zeitgeschichte. Veröffentlichungen. Reihe A: Quellen. Band 19*)

RATHENAU (WALTHER) Walther Rathenau-Gesamtausgabe; herausgegeben von Hans Dieter Hellige und Ernst Schulin. München, 1977 in progress.

KOMMISSION FÜR WIRTSCHAFTLICHEN UND SOZIALEN WANDEL. Wirtschaftlicher und sozialer Wandel in der Bundesrepublik Deutschland: Gutachten...; veröffentlicht durch die Bundesregierung; der Bundesminister für Arbeit und Sozialordnung. Göttingen, 1977. pp. 598.

GERMANY, EASTERN.

The GERMAN Democratic Republic: a developed socialist society; edited by Lyman H. Legters. Boulder, Colo., 1978. pp. 285. *bibliog.*

— **Appropriations and expenditures.**

GURTZ (JOHANNES) and KALTOFEN (GOTTHOLD) Der Staatshaushalt der DDR: Grundriss. Berlin, 1977. pp. 248. *bibliog.*

— **Bibliography.**

EDGINGTON (PETER) The politics of the two Germanies...: a guide to sources and English-language materials. Ormskirk, 1977. pp. 80.

— **Commerce — Europe.**

DEUTSCHES INSTITUT FÜR WIRTSCHAFTSFORSCHUNG. Sonderhefte. [Neue Folge]. 119. Der Handel der Deutschen Demokratischen Republik mit der Bundesrepublik Deutschland und den übrigen OECD-Ländern... ; ([by] Horst Lambrecht). Berlin, 1977. pp. 98.

— — **Germany.**

DEUTSCHES INSTITUT FÜR WIRTSCHAFTSFORSCHUNG. Sonderhefte. [Neue Folge]. 119. Der Handel der Deutschen Demokratischen Republik mit der Bundesrepublik Deutschland und den übrigen OECD-Ländern... ; ([by] Horst Lambrecht). Berlin, 1977. pp. 98.

— **Economic conditions.**

SCHNEIDER (EBERHARD) The G.D.R.: the history, politics, economy and society of East Germany;... translated by Hannes Adomeit and Roger Clarke. London, 1978. pp. 121. *bibliog.*

— — **Bibliography.**

MERRITT (ANNA J.) and MERRITT (RICHARD LAWRENCE) compilers. Politics, economics, and society in the two Germanies, 1945-75: a bibliography of English-language works. Urbana, [1978]. pp. 268.

— **Economic policy.**

BRD-DDR: die Wirtschaftssysteme: soziale Marktwirtschaft und sozialistische Planwirtschaft im Systemvergleich; mit Beiträgen von Hannelore Hamel [and others]; herausgegeben von Hannelore Hamel. München, [1977]. pp. 365.

PRODUKTIVITAET, Effektivität, Kontinuität; (Autorenkollektiv: Anneliese Braun [and others]). Berlin, 1977. pp. 261.

MATTERNE (KURT) and TANNHAEUSER (SIEGFRIED) Die Grundmittelwirtschaft in der sozialistischen Industrie der DDR. 2nd ed. Berlin, 1978. pp. 560. *bibliog.*

— **Foreign economic relations — European Economic Community countries.**

JANSEN (BERNHARD) EWG und DDR nach Abschluss des Grundlagenvertrages. Baden-Baden, [1977]. pp. 133. *bibliog.*

— **Foreign relations.**

SIKORA (FRANZ) Sozialistische Solidarität und nationale Interessen: Polen, Tschechoslowakei, DDR. Köln, [1977]. pp. 248. (*Bundesinstitut für Ostwissenschaftliche und Internationale Studien. Abhandlungen. Band 31*)

GEGEN den Rassismus, Apartheid und Kolonialismus: Dokumente der DDR, 1949-1977; (Dokumentenauswahl und Einführung: Alfred Babing). Berlin, 1978. pp. 703.

— — Germany.

RESS (GEORG) Die Rechtslage Deutschlands nach dem Grundlagenvertrag vom 21. Dezember 1972. Berlin, 1978. pp. 436. *bibliog.* (Max-Planck-Institut für Ausländisches Öffentliches Recht und Völkerrecht, Heidelberg. Beiträge zum Ausländischen Öffentlichen Recht und Völkerrecht. 71) With English summary.

— History.

REVOLUTIONAERER Prozess und Staatsentstehung. Berlin, 1976. pp. 184. *(Akademie der Wissenschaften der DDR. Institut für Theorie des Staates und des Rechts. Staats- und Rechtstheoretische Studien. 2)*

WEBER (HERMANN) Writer on Communism. DDR: Grundriss der Geschichte, 1945-1976. Hannover, [1976]. pp. 211. *bibliog.*

SCHNEIDER (EBERHARD) The G.D.R.: the history, politics, economy and society of East Germany;... translated by Hannes Adomeit and Roger Clarke. London, 1978. pp. 121. *bibliog.*

— Politics and government.

REVOLUTIONAERER Prozess und Staatsentstehung. Berlin, 1976. pp. 184. *(Akademie der Wissenschaften der DDR. Institut für Theorie des Staates und des Rechts. Staats- und Rechtstheoretische Studien. 2)*

EXIL: die Ausbürgerung Wolf Biermanns aus der DDR; eine Dokumentation, herausgegeben von Peter Roos. Köln, [1977]. pp. 319.

SCHNEIDER (EBERHARD) The G.D.R.: the history, politics, economy and society of East Germany;... translated by Hannes Adomeit and Roger Clarke. London, 1978. pp. 121. *bibliog.*

— — Bibliography.

EDGINGTON (PETER) The politics of the two Germanies...: a guide to sources and English-language materials. Ormskirk, 1977. pp. 80.

MERRITT (ANNA J.) and MERRITT (RICHARD LAWRENCE) compilers. Politics, economics and society in the two Germanies, 1945-75: a bibliography of English-language works. Urbana, [1978]. pp. 268.

— Social conditions.

POLICIES which put people first: life and social welfare in the G.D.R.; [written by Dr. Karl-Heinz Arnold]. Berlin, [1976]. pp. 96. *Based on policies outlined at the 9th Congress of the Socialist Unity Party of Germany, May 1976.*

SCHNEIDER (EBERHARD) The G.D.R.: the history, politics, economy and society of East Germany;... translated by Hannes Adomeit and Roger Clarke. London, 1978. pp. 121. *bibliog.*

— — Bibliography.

MERRITT (ANNA J.) and MERRITT (RICHARD LAWRENCE) compilers. Politics, economics and society in the two Germanies, 1945-75: a bibliography of English-language works. Urbana, [1978]. pp. 268.

— Social policy.

PRODUKTIVITAET, Effektivität, Kontinuität; (Autorenkollektiv: Anneliese Braun [and others]). Berlin, 1977. pp. 261.

GERTSEN (ALEKSANDR IVANOVICH).

PAVLOV (ALEKSEI TERENT'EVICH) Ot dvorianskoi revoliutsionnosti k revoliutsionnomu demokratizmu: ideinaia evoliutsiia A.I. Gertsena. Moskva, 1977. pp. 128. *bibliog.*

GHANA.

GHANA NEWS; (pd. by the Embassy of Ghana [United States]). bi-m. Washington. *Current yr.'s issues only kept.*

— Armed forces — Political activity.

OCRAN (A.K.) Politics of the sword: a personal memoir on military involvement in Ghana and of problems of military government. London, 1977. pp. 167.

— Constitution.

EPHSON (ISAAC S.) Reflections and refractions on the Ghana draft constitution. Part 1. Cape Coast, 1968. pp. 84.

— Economic conditions.

INVESTMENT JOURNAL; pd. by (Ghana Investment Centre,) the Capital Investments Board of Ghana. q., Oc/D 1970 (v.1, no.2), Ja/Mr 1971 (v.2, no.1)- , with gaps (Ja/Mr, Oc/D 1973: v.4, nos.1 and 4). Accra.

HOWARD (RHODA) Colonialism and underdevelopment in Ghana. London, [1978]. pp. 244. *bibliog.*

KILLICK (TONY) Development economics in action: a study of economic policies in Ghana. London, 1978. pp. 392. *bibliog.*

INVESTMENT TIT-BITS: opportunities and trends in Ghana; [pd. by] Capital Investments Board. bi-m., current issues only. Accra.

— Economic history.

MILBURN (JOSEPHINE F.) British business and Ghanaian independence. London, [1977]. pp. 156.

— Economic policy.

GHANA. Ministry of Economic Planning. 1977. Five-year development plan, 1975/76-1979/80. Accra, 1977. 3 pts.

STEEL (WILLIAM F.) Small-scale employment and production in developing countries: evidence from Ghana. New York, 1977. pp. 235. *bibliog.*

KILLICK (TONY) Development economics in action: a study of economic policies in Ghana. London, 1978. pp. 392. *bibliog.*

— Emigration and immigration.

SCHILDKROUT (ENID) People of the zongo: the transformation of ethnic identities in Ghana. Cambridge, 1978. pp. 303. *bibliog.*

— Foreign economic relations — United Kingdom.

MILBURN (JOSEPHINE F.) British business and Ghanaian independence. London, [1977]. pp. 156.

— Foreign relations.

GHANA. Supreme Military Council. Office of the Press Secretary. 1976. Fourth year in office of Colonel Ignatius Kutu Acheampong, 13th January 1975 - 12th January 1976. [Accra, 1976]. pp. 306.

— Politics and government.

NKRUMAH (KWAME) Voice from Conakry. London, 1967. pp. 73. *Broadcasts made to the people of Ghana in 1966 on Radio Guinea's 'Voice of the Revolution'.*

GHANA. Supreme Military Council. Office of the Press Secretary. 1976. Fourth year in office of Colonel Ignatius Kutu Acheampong, 13th January 1975 - 12th January 1976. [Accra, 1976]. pp. 306.

GHANA. Ad Hoc Committee on Union Government. 1977. Report; [G. Koranteng-Addow, chairman]. [Accra, 1977]. pp. 202.

OCRAN (A.K.) Politics of the sword: a personal memoir on military involvement in Ghana and of problems of military government. London, 1977. pp. 167.

RENNIE (RHODA ELIZABETH McKENZIE) Nkrumah, greatest of modern philosophers. New York, [1977]. pp. 125.

— Social policy.

GHANA. Ministry of Economic Planning. 1977. Five-year development plan, 1975/76-1979/80. Accra, 1977. 3 pts.

GIANNOTTI (DONATO).

GIANNOTTI (DONATO) Opere politiche ([and] Lettere italiane 1526-1571); a cura di Furio Diaz. Milano, [1974]. 2 vols. *bibliog.*

GIBBON (EDWARD).

EDWARD Gibbon and the Decline and fall of the Roman Empire; edited by G.W. Bowersock [and others]. Cambridge, Mass., 1977. pp. 257. *Proceedings of a conference held under the auspices of the American Academy of Arts and Sciences, Rome, 1976.*

GIESSEN

— Population.

HISTORISCHE Demographie als Sozialgeschichte: Giessen und Umgebung vom 17. zum 19. Jahrhundert; (herausgegeben von Arthur E. Imhof). Darmstadt, 1975. 2 vols. *bibliog. (Hessische Historische Kommission, Darmstadt, and Historische Kommission für Hessen. Quellen und Forschungen zur Hessischen Geschichte. 31)*

— Social history.

HISTORISCHE Demographie als Sozialgeschichte: Giessen und Umgebung vom 17. zum 19. Jahrhundert; (herausgegeben von Arthur E. Imhof). Darmstadt, 1975. 2 vols. *bibliog. (Hessische Historische Kommission, Darmstadt, and Historische Kommission für Hessen. Quellen und Forschungen zur Hessischen Geschichte. 31)*

GILBERT AND ELLICE ISLANDS COLONY

— Constitution.

GILBERT AND ELLICE ISLANDS COLONY. Legislative Council. Select Committee appointed...to review the Operation of the Constitution and to make Recommendations for Changes. 1973. Report; [R. Turpin, chairman]. Tarawa, 1973. 1 vol. (various pagings).

GILBERT ISLANDS.

GILBERT ISLANDS. Report. a., 1975- Tarawa.

GILDS

— Germany.

GOETTMANN (FRANK) Handwerk und Bündnispolitik: die Handwerkerbünde am Mittelrhein vom 14. bis zum 17. Jahrhundert. Wiesbaden, 1977. pp. 307. *bibliog.*

— Poland — Silesia.

TOMCZYK (DAMIAN) Pieczęcie górnośląskich cechów rzemieślniczych z XV- XVIII wieku i ich znaczenie historyczne. Opole, 1975. pp. 188. *bibliog. With English, German and Russian summaries.*

TOMCZYK (DAMIAN) Studia z dziejów rzemiosła Śląska Opolskiego przed epoką kapitalizmu. Opole, 1976. pp. 236.

GILL (ARTHUR ERIC ROWTON).

FAULKNER (PETER) William Morris and Eric Gill. [London], 1975. pp. 31.

GIPSIES

— Spain.

SANCHEZ (MARIA HELENA) Los gitanos españoles:[el periodo borbonico]. [Madrid, 1977]. pp. 554. *Map in end pocket.*

GISCARD D'ESTAING (VALERY).

GISCARD d'Estaing, Mitterrand: 54,774 mots pour convaincre; by Jean-Marie Cotteret [and others]. Paris, [1976]. pp. 347. *bibliog.*

TODD (OLIVIER) La marelle de Giscard, 1926-1974. Paris, [1977]. pp. 487. *bibliog.*

GLASGOW

GLASGOW

— Social conditions.

MACAULAY (RONALD K.S.) Language, social class, and education: a Glasgow study. Edinburgh, [1977]. pp. 179. *bibliog. Revised version of a report to the Social Science Research Council.*

— Transit systems.

A BETTER Glasgow: transport and environment; a statement issued jointly by Scottish Association for Public Transport [and others]. [Glasgow], 1974. fo.3.

GLASHUETTE SCHMIDSFELDEN.

FELLE (MANFRED) Schmidsfelden: eine Allgäuer Glashütte des 19. Jahrhunderts. München, [1977]. pp. 181. *bibliog.*

GLASS INDUSTRY AND TRADE

— Germany.

FELLE (MANFRED) Schmidsfelden: eine Allgäuer Glashütte des 19. Jahrhunderts. München, [1977]. pp. 181. *bibliog.*

GOA, DAMAN AND DIU

— Population.

INDIA. Census, 1971. Series 28. Goa, Daman and Diu: a portrait of population; [by] S.K. Gandhe. [Delhi, 1976]. pp. 186.

GOD.

MOST (JOHANN) La peste réligieuse; traduit de l'Allemand. Amiens, 1905. pp. 16.

GUNTON (COLIN E.) Becoming and being: the doctrine of God in Charles Hartshorne and Karl Barth. Oxford, 1978. pp. 236. *bibliog.*

— Attributes.

WHIPPLE (CHARLES KING) The good and evil in orthodoxy. London, 1876. pp. 16.

SWINBURNE (RICHARD) The coherence of theism. Oxford, 1977. pp. 302.

GODWIN (MARY).

DIURISI (MARIA) Mary Wollstonecraft e la rivendicazione dei diritti della donna. [Lecce], 1975. pp. 93. *bibliog.*

GODWIN (WILLIAM).

CLARK (JOHN P.) The philosophical anarchism of William Godwin. Princeton, N.J., [1977]. pp. 343. *bibliog.*

GOKHALE (GOPAL KRISHNA).

NANDA (B.R.) Gokhale: the Indian moderates and the British Raj. Delhi, 1977. pp. 520. *bibliog.*

GOLD.

SCHMITT (BERNARD) L'or, le dollar et la monnaie supranationale. Paris, [1977]. pp. 227.

GOLD MINERS

— South Africa.

LEGASSICK (MARTIN) The analysis of racism in South Africa: segregation, the state and the mining economy. [1976?]. 1 pamphlet (unpaged). *bibliog. Unpublished: photocopy of typescript. Paper presented at the Political Studies Association Conference, Nottingham, 1976.*

GOLD MINES AND MINING

— Colombia — Chocó.

SHARP (WILLIAM FREDERICK) Slavery on the Spanish frontier: the Colombian Chocó 1680-1810. Norman, Okla., [1976]. pp. 253. *bibliog.*

— United States — Colorado.

KING (JOSEPH E.) A mine to make a mine: financing the Colorado mining industry, 1859-1902. College Station, Tex., [1977]. pp. 209. *bibliog.*

GOLLANCZ (Sir VICTOR).

HODGES (SHEILA) Gollancz: the story of a publishing house, 1928-1978. London, 1978. pp. 256.

GOMEZ (JUAN GUALBERTO).

GOMEZ (JUAN GUALBERTO) Por Cuba libre; ... seleccion y prologo de Emilio Roig de Leuchsenring. La Habana, 1974. pp. 513.

GOMEZ (JUAN VICENTE).

RANGEL (DOMINGO ALBERTO) Gomez: el amo del poder. Valencia, Venezuela, 1975. pp. 411. *bibliog.*

GONZI (MICHAEL) Archbishop of Malta.

FENECH (DOMINIC) The making of Archbishop Gonzi. Valletta, 1976. pp. 50.

GOODMAN (PAUL).

GOODMAN (PAUL) b. 1911. Drawing the line:...political essays...; edited by Taylor Stoehr. New York, 1977. pp. 272.

GORDON (CHARLES GEORGE).

HAKE (ALFRED EGMONT) Events of the Taeping Rebellion, being reprints of Mss. copied by General Gordon, C.B. in his own handwriting. London, 1891. pp. 531. *Includes Reminiscences by one who served with Gordon in China [i.e. F.L. Story]*

GORDON (WALTER LOCKHART).

GORDON (WALTER LOCKHART) A political memoir. Toronto, [1977]. pp. 395.

GORE-BROWN (Sir STEWART).

ROTBERG (ROBERT IRWIN) Black heart: Gore-Brown and the politics of multiracial Zambia. Berkeley, [1977]. pp. 359. *bibliog.*

GORST (Sir ELDON).

MELLINI (PETER) Sir Eldon Gorst: the overshadowed proconsul. Stanford, [1977]. pp. 315. *bibliog. (Stanford University. Hoover Institution on War, Revolution and Peace. Hoover Colonial Studies)*

GORST (JOHN LOWNDES).

See GORST (Sir ELDON).

GOULD (JULIUS).

The ATTACK on higher education: where does it come from?; a reply to the Gould Report [by Anthony Arblaster and others]. [London, 1977]. pp. 24.

GOVERNMENT, COMPARATIVE.

LEGISLATURES in plural societies: the search for cohesion in national development; edited by Albert F. Eldridge. Durham, N.C., 1977. pp. 284. *bibliogs. (Consortium for Comparative Legislative Studies. Publications)*

LIJPHART (AREND) Democracy in plural societies: a comparative exploration. New Haven, 1977. pp. 248.

MAYER (LAWRENCE C.) Politics in industrial societies: a comparative perspective;... with John H. Burnett. New York, [1977]. pp. 388.

NAGLE (JOHN DAVID) System and succession: the social bases of political elite recruitment. Austin, [1977]. pp. 273. *bibliog.*

SIEGEL (RICHARD L.) and WEINBERG (LEONARD B.) Comparing public policies: United States, Soviet Union, and Europe. Homewood, Ill., 1977. pp. 430.

BERTSCH (GARY K.) and others. Comparing political systems: power and policy in three worlds. New York, [1978]. pp. 515. *bibliogs.*

CLARK (ROBERT P.) Power and policy in the Third World. New York, [1978]. pp. 159. *bibliogs.*

COLLIARD (JEAN CLAUDE) Les régimes parlementaires contemporains. [Paris, 1978]. pp. 369. *bibliog.*

PETERS (B. GUY) The politics of bureaucracy: a comparative perspective. New York, [1978]. pp. 246.

WEST African states: failure and promise: a study in comparative politics; edited by John Dunn. Cambridge, 1978. pp. 259. *(Cambridge. University. African Studies Centre. African Studies Series. 23)*

WOOD (DAVID MICHAEL) Power and policy in western European democracies. New York, [1978]. pp. 177. *bibliogs.*

GOVERNMENT, PRIMITIVE.

ORIGINS of the state: the anthropology of political evolution; edited by Ronald Cohen and Elman R. Service. Philadelphia, [1978]. pp. 233. *bibliogs.*

GOVERNMENT, RESISTANCE TO.

BAY (CHRISTIAN) and WALKER (CHARLES C.) Civil disobedience: theory and practice. Montreal, [1975]. pp. 50.

WEBER (DAVID R.) ed. Civil disobedience in America: a documentary history. Ithaca, 1978. pp. 318.

— Netherlands.

JOCHHEIM (GERNOT) Antimilitaristische Aktionstheorie, soziale Revolution und soziale Verteidigung: zur Entwicklung der Gewaltfreiheitstheorie...1890-1940, unter besonderer Berücksichtigung der Niederlande. Assen, [1977]. pp. 621. *bibliog.*

GOVERNMENT ADVERTISING.

The POLITICAL economy of advertising; edited by David G. Tuerck. Washington, D.C., [1978]. pp. 217. *(American Enterprise Institute for Public Policy Research. AEI Symposia. 78A). Papers presented at a conference held in Washington, D.C., in 1976.*

GOVERNMENT AND THE PRESS

— United States.

SMITH (CULVER HAYGOOD) The press, politics, and patronage: the American government's use of newspapers, 1789-1875. Athens, Ga., [1977]. pp. 351. *bibliog.*

GOVERNMENT ATTORNEYS

— New Zealand.

NEW ZEALAND. Crown Law Office. 1961. Crown law practice in New Zealand. Wellington, [1961]. pp. 46.

GOVERNMENT BUSINESS ENTERPRISES

— Law and legislation — Communist countries.

ČAPEK (KAREL) Jurist. Právní postavení socialistických podniků. Praha, 1976. pp. 478. *With Russian and German summaries.*

— Asia, Southeast.

The ROLE of public enterprise in national development in southeast Asia: problems and prospects; edited by Nguyen Truong. Singapore, 1976. pp. 334. *bibliog.*

— Austria.

RAMBOUSEK (HERBERT) Die "ÖMV Aktiengesellschaft": Entstehung und Entwicklung eines nationalen Unternehmens der Mineralölindustrie. Wien, 1977. pp. 225. *bibliog. (Wirtschaftsuniversität Wien. Dissertationen. 23) 2 maps in end pocket.*

— Europe.

RE (ALISA DEL) Il profitto differito: l'impresa di stato nello sviluppo e nella crisi in Italia e in Europa. [Venezia, 1974]. pp. 180. *bibliogs.*

— France.

SÈGRE (HENRI) ed. Les entreprises publiques en France: des entreprises comme les autres?, des entreprises pour quoi faire? Paris, [1975]. pp. 253. *bibliog.*

SAINT-JOURS (YVES) Les relations du travail dans le secteur public. Paris, 1976. pp. 450.

GALLAIS-HAMONNO (GEORGES) Les nationalisations: à quel prix? pour quoi faire?. [Paris, 1977]. pp. 238. *bibliog.*

— India.

INDIA. Ministry of Labour. Evaluation Wing. 1975. Labour in the public sector undertakings: basic information, 1974. [Delhi, 1975]. pp. 196.

— Italy.

RE (ALISA DEL) Il profitto differito: l'impresa di stato nello sviluppo e nella crisi in Italia e in Europa. [Venezia, 1974]. pp. 180. *bibliogs.*

SABATTINI (GIANFRANCO) and MORO (BENIAMINO) La crisi delle attività minerarie regionali ed il ruolo del settore pubblico. [Cagliari, 1975]. pp. 95. *bibliog.*

SARACENO (PASQUALE) Il sistema delle imprese a partecipazione statale nell'esperienza italiana. Milano, 1975. pp. 132. *(Associazione per lo Sviluppo dell'Industria nel Mezzogiorno. Centro per gli Studi sullo Sviluppo Economico. Collana Francesco Giordani)*

COLAJANNI (NAPOLEONE) Riconversione grande impresa partecipazioni statali. [Milano, 1976]. pp. 125.

CIANCI (ERNESTO) Nascita dello Stato imprenditore in Italia. Milano, [1977]. pp. 390. *bibliog.*

MERLONI (FRANCESCO) and URBANI (PAOLO) Il governo del territorio tra regioni e partecipazioni statali. Bari, 1977. pp. 222.

— Nigeria.

NEW NIGERIA DEVELOPMENT COMPANY. N.N.D.C.: New Nigeria Development Company Ltd.: a development agency owned by the governments of the northern states of Nigeria. Kaduna, 1971. pp. 15.

NEW NIGERIA DEVELOPMENT COMPANY. N.N.D.C. group. [Kaduna], 1971. pp. 52.

— United Kingdom — Wales.

U.K. Welsh Office. 1977. Guidelines for the industrial investment functions of the Welsh Development Agency. [Cardiff], 1977. pp. 8.

— Zambia.

RURAL DEVELOPMENT CORPORATION OF ZAMBIA LIMITED. Annual report and statement of accounts. a., 1974(6th)- Lusaka.

GOVERNMENT CONSULTANTS

— Russia.

SOLOMON (PETER H.) Soviet criminologists and criminal policy: specialists in policy- making. London, 1978. pp. 253. *bibliog.*

GOVERNMENT EXECUTIVES, TRAINING OF

— United Kingdom.

TRAINING in the civil service; [revised versions of papers presented at a conference held in 1977 in Birmingham, organized by the Public Administration Committee]; edited by R.A.W. Rhodes. London, 1977. pp. 85.

GOVERNMENT LAWYERS

— Italy.

L'AVVOCATURA dello Stato: studio storico-giuridico per le celebrazioni del centenario. Roma, Istituto Poligrafico dello Stato, 1976. pp. 615.

GOVERNMENT LIABILITY (INTERNATIONAL LAW).

DUDEK (WIESŁAW) Międzynarodowe aspekty nacjonalizacji w Polsce. Warszawa, 1976. pp. 310. *bibliog.* *With an appendix of treaties.*

GOVERNMENT LITIGATION

— New Zealand.

NEW ZEALAND. Crown Law Office. 1961. Crown law practice in New Zealand. Wellington, [1961]. pp. 46.

GOVERNMENT OWNERSHIP.

MURRAY (JOHN) M.P. for West Leeds. Nationalisation. London, [192-?]. pp. 7. *(League of Youth and Social Progress. [Pamphlets]. No. 5)*

NOVE (ALEXANDER) Efficiency criteria for nationalised industries. London, 1973. pp. 150.

— Austria.

OESTERREICHISCHER WIRTSCHAFTSBUND. Verstaatlichte wohin?: Struktur, Finanzierung, Konzentration. Wien, 1972. pp. 48. *(Informationen. IWB 8)*

— Guyana.

GUYANA. Prime Minister. 1971. Control of our natural resources: address to the nation by the Hon. L.F.S. Burnham...on the occasion of Republic Day, February 23, 1971. [Georgetown, 1971]. pp. 12.

— Poland.

DUDEK (WIESŁAW) Międzynarodowe aspekty nacjonalizacji w Polsce. Warszawa, 1976. pp. 310. *bibliog.* *With an appendix of treaties.*

— Underdeveloped areas.

See UNDERDEVELOPED AREAS — Government ownership.

— United Kingdom.

SLOMAN (MARTYN) Socialising public ownership. London, 1978. pp. 159. *bibliog.*

GOVERNMENT PUBLICITY

— Australia.

AUSTRALIA. Department of the Media. Report of activities. a., 1972/73(1st)- Canberra. *Included in AUSTRALIA. Parliament. [Parliamentary papers].*

— South Africa.

SOUTH AFRICA. Department of Information. Report. a., 1976. Pretoria. *These reports not for general distribution.*

GOVERNMENT PURCHASING OF REAL PROPERTY

— Canada — Nova Scotia.

NOVA SCOTIA. Royal Commission on the Sackville Land Assembly, 1968. Report; [William C. Dunlop, commissioner]. [Halifax, 1971]. pp. 70.

GOVERNMENT SPENDING POLICY.

NUTTER (GILBERT WARREN) Growth of government in the West. Washington, D.C., [1978]. pp. 94. *(American Enterprise Institute for Public Policy Research. AEI Studies. 185)*

— Tanzania.

CLARK (W. EDMUND) Socialist development and public investment in Tanzania, 1964-73. Toronto, [1978]. pp. 319. *bibliog.*

— United States.

SCHULTZE (CHARLES L.) The public use of private interest. Washington, [1977]. pp. 93. *Revised and expanded version of the Godkin lectures delivered at the John F. Kennedy School of Government, Harvard University in Nov. and Dec. 1976.*

The FEDERAL budget and social reconstruction: the people and the state; prepared for the Study Group on the Federal Budget, Institute for Policy Studies, Washington, D.C.; Marcus G. Raskin, editor in chief. New Brunswick, [1978]. pp. 470.

GOVERNMENTAL INVESTIGATIONS

— Canada — Nova Scotia.

NOVA SCOTIA. Legislative Library. 1973. Nova Scotia royal commissions and commissions of enquiry appointed by the province of Nova Scotia. Halifax, 1973. pp. 23.

— — Quebec.

QUEBEC (PROVINCE). Legislative Library. 1972. Commissions et comités d'enquêtes au Québec depuis 1867. Quebec, 1972. pp. 95. *bibliog. (Bibliographie et Documentation. 1)*

GRADING AND MARKING (STUDENTS).

U.K. Department of Education and Science. 1971. Potential and progress in a second culture: a survey of the assessment of pupils from overseas. London, 1971. pp. 37. *(Education Surveys. 10)*

GRADUATES

— Israel.

GLOBERSON (ARYÉ) Higher education and employment: a case study of Israel. Farnborough, Hants., [1978]. pp. 171. *bibliog.*

— Italy.

LAUREATI e disoccupati; a cura di R. Barbaresi [and others]. [Firenze, 1975]. pp. 249.

— United Kingdom.

BRIGHTON. University of Sussex. Appointments Advisory Service. The occupational choices of Sussex graduates. Brighton, 1972. pp. 20, 9.

CENTRAL SERVICES UNIT FOR CAREERS AND APPOINTMENTS SERVICES. First destination of university graduates. a., 1975/76- Manchester.

COMMITTEE OF VICE-CHANCELLORS AND PRINCIPALS OF THE UNIVERSITIES OF THE UNITED KINGDOM. Postgraduate education: report of a study group. [London], 1975. pp. 11.

— United States.

DAVIS (JAMES ALLAN) and others. Stipends and spouses: the finances of American arts and science graduate students. Chicago, 1962. pp. 294.

GRAFFITI

— Italy.

CIANFLONE (GEPPINA) and SCAFOGLIO (DOMENICO) Fascismo sui muri: le scritti murali neofasciste di Napoli. Napoli, [1976]. pp. 119.

GRAIN.

GRAIN CROPS: a review of production, trade, consumption and prices.. .; prepared in the Commonwealth Secretariat. a., 1936- ; susp. pbln. 1940-1949; 1950 contains figures for 1937- 1948; not pd. 1956. London.

GRAIN.(Cont.)

— China.

HOW China became self-sufficient in grain. Peking, [1977]. pp. 74.

— France.

MEUVRET (JEAN) Le problème des subsistances à l'époque Louis XIV: la production des céréales dans la France du XVIIe et du XVIIIe siècle. Paris, [1977]. 2 vols. *(Paris. Ecole des Hautes Etudes en Sciences Sociales. Centre de Recherches Historiques. Civilizations et Sociétés. 50)*

— India — Mysore.

MYSORE. Directorate of Evaluation and Manpower. 1974. Report on a critical review of production and consumption of food grains in Mysore state, for the post-third five year plan period. Bangalore, [1974]. pp. 52.

GRAIN TRADE.

JOHNSON (DAVID GALE) The Soviet impact on world grain trade. [London], 1977. pp. 55. *(British-North American Committee. Publications. 20)*

GRENNES (THOMAS) and others. The economics of world grain trade. New York, [1978]. pp. 129. *bibliogs.*

— Mathematical models.

GRENNES (THOMAS) and others. The economics of world grain trade. New York, [1978]. pp. 129. *bibliogs.*

— Canada.

CANADA. Statistics Canada. Grains and oilseeds review. m., My 1978 (no.1)- Ottawa. *[in English and French]. Supersedes CANADA. Statistics Canada. Coarse grains review, CANADA. Statistics Canada. Oilseeds review and CANADA. Statistics Canada. Wheat review.*

WILSON (CHARLES F.) A century of Canadian grain: government policy to 1951. Saskatoon, [1978]. pp. 1138. *bibliog.*

— Germany — Prices.

EBELING (DIETRICH) and IRSIGLER (FRANZ) Getreideumsatz, Getreide- und Brotpreise in Köln, 1368-1797. Köln, 1976-77. 2 vols. *(Cologne. Stadtarchiv. Mitteilungen. Hefte 65-66) 9 graphs in end pocket of vol. 2.*

— Russia.

JOHNSON (DAVID GALE) The Soviet impact on world grain trade. [London], 1977. pp. 55. *(British-North American Committee. Publications. 20)*

— Sweden.

SAMBERGS (ÅKE) Leveransförhållandena för spannmål i Sörmland, hösten 1974: resultat från en enkätundersökning. Stockholm, 1975. pp. 40. *(Jordbrukets Utredningsinstitut. Meddelanden. 1975. Nr. 5) With English summary.*

— United Kingdom.

MORRIS (EDWARD) M.P. A short enquiry into the nature of monopoly and forestalling; a third edition, with considerable additions. London, T. Adell and W. Davies, 1800. pp. 54.

GRAMMAR, CASE.

See CASE GRAMMAR.

GRAMMAR, COMPARATIVE AND GENERAL.

FORMAL syntax; edited by Peter W. Culicover [and others]. New York, 1977. pp. 500. *bibliog. Proceedings of a conference held by the Mathematics Social Science Board in Newport Beach, California, in 1976.*

— Honorific.

QUESTIONS and politeness: strategies in social interaction; edited by Esther N. Goody. Cambridge, 1978. pp. 324. *bibliog.*

— Interrogative.

QUESTIONS and politeness: strategies in social interaction; edited by Esther N. Goody. Cambridge, 1978. pp. 324. *bibliog.*

— Phonology.

HOOPER (JOAN B.) An introduction to natural generative phonology. New York, [1976]. pp. 254. *bibliog.*

SOMMERSTEIN (ALAN HERBERT) Modern phonology. London, 1977. pp. 282. *bibliog.*

SCHANE (SANFORD A.) and BENDIXEN (BIRGITTE) Workbook in generative phonology. Englewood Cliffs, [1978]. pp. 111.

— Sentences.

SENTENCE production: developments in research and theory; edited by Sheldon Rosenberg. Hillsdale, N.J., [1977]. pp. 323. *bibliogs.*

— Syntax.

FAIRLEY (IRENE R.) E.E. Cummings and ungrammar: a study of syntactic deviance in his poems. New York, 1975. pp. 191. *bibliog.*

MECHANISMS of syntactic change; edited by Charles N. Li. Austin, [1977]. pp. 620. *bibliogs. Papers presented at the Symposium on Mechanisms of Syntactic Change, Santa Barbara, 1976.*

SCHLESINGER (I.M.) Production and comprehension of utterances. Hillsdale, N.J., 1977. pp. 235. *bibliog.*

GRAMSCI (ANTONIO).

BADALONI (NICOLA) Il marxismo di Gramsci: dal mito alla ricomposizione politica. [Torino, 1975]. pp. 187.

BELLINGERI (EDO) Dall'intellettuale al politico: le "Cronache teatrali" di Gramsci. Bari, 1975. pp. 149.

GRAMSCI (ANTONIO) Scritti 1915-1921: (inediti dal Grido del Popolo e dall' Avanti...); a cura di Sergio Caprioglio. [Milano, 1976]. pp. 411.

TOSIN (BRUNO) Con Gramsci: ricordi di uno della "vecchia guarda". Roma, 1976. pp. 177.

EGEMONIA e democrazia: Gramsci e la questione comunista nel dibattito di Mondoperaio. Roma, 1977. pp. 249. *(Mondoperaio. Quaderni. Nuova Serie. 7)*

OLTRE Gramsci? [Roma, 1977]. pp. 155. *Interviews on the subject, "Gramsci e il P.C.I. oggi", first published in Il Popolo, 1977.*

PATERNOSTRO (ROCCO) Critica, Marxismo, storicismo dialettico: due note gramsciane. Roma, [1977]. pp. 147.

TAMBURRANO (GIUSEPPE) Antonio Gramsci. Milano, [1977]. pp. 337. *Reprint of the original ed. of 1963 with a new extensive preface.*

— Bibliography.

COZENS (PHIL) compiler. Twenty years of Antonio Gramsci; a bibliography of Gramsci and Gramsci studies published in English 1957-1977. London, 1977. pp. 12.

GRAND JURY

— United Kingdom.

LEACH-LEWIS (WILLIAM A.) The abolition of the grand jury in England. [Washington], Library of Congress, 1975. pp. 4. *bibliog.*

MORRILL (JOHN STEPHEN) The Cheshire grand jury, 1625-1659: a social and administrative study. Leicester, 1976. pp. 60. *(Leicester. University. Department of English Local History. Occasional Papers. 3rd Series. No. 1)*

GRANTS-IN-AID.

The POLITICAL economy of fiscal federalism; edited by Wallace E. Oates. Lexington, Mass., [1977]. pp. 355. *bibliog. Papers presented at a conference sponsored by the International Seminar in Public Economics and the International Institute of Management, held in 1976 in Berlin.*

— Canada — Nova Scotia.

NOVA SCOTIA. Department of Municipal Affairs. 1971. Financial assistance to municipalities of Nova Scotia from the federal and provincial governments. [4th ed.] [Halifax, 1971]. fo.26.

— United States.

PASCALE (RICHARD T.) and BARBOUR (GEORGE P.) Shared power: a study of four federal funding systems in Appalachia. Washington, [1977]. pp. 36. *(American Enterprise Institute for Public Policy Research. Special Analyses)*

GRAPH THEORY.

PRICE (W.L.) Graphs and networks: an introduction. London, 1971. pp. 108. *bibliogs.*

GRAZIADEI (ANTONIO).

NEORICARDIANA: Sraffa e Graziadei; a cura di Roberto Finzi. Bologna, [1977]. pp. 258. *(Convegno Nazionale degli Storici del Pensiero Economico, 3 , 1974. Atti. vol. 2)*

GRECO (JUAN).

GRECO (JUAN) Los sucesos de Alvear y la barbarie lencinista. Mendoza, Argentine Republic, 1929. pp. 188.

GREECE

— Armed forces — Political activity.

PAPACOSMA (S. VICTOR) The military in Greek politics: the 1909 coup d'état. Kent, Ohio, [1977]. pp. 254. *bibliog.*

— Economic conditions.

GREECE. Hypourgeion Syntonismou. 1969. Important speech by the Minister of Coordination, N. Makarezos, concerning the developments and prospects of the Greek economy; press conference of 4th October 1969. Athens, 1969. pp. 4. *(Greece: economic news. Special Issues)*

GREECE. Hypourgeion Syntonismou. 1971. The Minister of Coordination, N. Makarezos, talks on the progress of the Greek economy before representatives of the country's business world, on 18th January 1971. [Athens, 1971]. pp. 4.

VERGOPOULOS (KOSTAS) Le capitalisme difforme et la nouvelle question agraire: l'exemple de la Grèce moderne. Paris, 1977. pp. 307. *bibliog.*

MOUZELIS (NICOLAS PANAYIOTOU) Modern Greece: facets of underdevelopment. London, 1978. pp. 222.

— Economic policy.

DELIBANES (DEMETRIOS) The prospects of the economic development of Cyprus on the basis of Greek experience. Leukosia, Cyprus, 1973. pp. 4.

— Foreign economic relations.

For related material see EUROPEAN ECONOMIC COMMUNITY — Greece.

— Foreign relations — Cyprus.

MARKIDES (KYRIACOS C.) The rise and fall of the Cyprus Republic. New Haven, 1977. pp. 200.

— — United Kingdom.

KOLIOPOULOS (JOHN S.) Greece and the British connection, 1935-1941. Oxford, 1977. pp. 315. *bibliog.*

— History — Sources.

CAPODISTRIA (JOHN) Count. John Capodistrias: some unpublished documents; [edited by] C.W. Crawley. Thessaloniki, 1970. pp. 109. *(Hidryma Meleton Chersonesou Tou Haimou. [Publications] . 114)*

— — 1453-1821.

MANESES (ARISTOBOULOS I.) L'activité et les projets politiques d'un patriote grec dans les Balkans vers la fin du XVIIIe siècle. Thessalonique, 1962. pp. 75-118.

— — 1863-1913, George I.

PAPACOSMA (S. VICTOR) The military in Greek politics: the 1909 coup d'état. Kent, Ohio, [1977]. pp. 254. *bibliog.*

— Industries.

HUMMEN (WILHELM) Greek industry in the European Community: prospects and problems. Berlin, 1977. pp. 88. *(Deutsches Institut für Entwicklungspolitik. Occasional Papers. No. 45.)*

— Social conditions.

MOUZELIS (NICOLAS PANAYIOTOU) Modern Greece: facets of underdevelopment. London, 1978. pp. 222.

— Statistics.

GREECE. Ethnike Statistike Hyperesia. Meniaion statistikon deltion: Monthly statistical bulletin (formerly Bulletin mensuel de statistique). m., 1929 [t.1] - Mr 1940, with gaps (Ja 1930, Mr 1931); 1943/1944; 1956 ([n.s.] t.1)- Athenai.

GREECE, ANCIENT

— Economic history.

HUMPHREYS (S.C.) Anthropology and the Greeks. London, 1978. pp. 357. *bibliog.*

— History.

DAVIES (JOHN KENYON) Democracy and classical Greece. [London], 1978. pp. 284. *bibliog.*

— Social history.

HUMPHREYS (S.C.) Anthropology and the Greeks. London, 1978. pp. 357. *bibliog.*

GREEKS IN CANADA.

ONTARIO. Multicultural Development Branch. 1977. Papers on the Greek community. [Toronto, 1977]. pp. 26.

GREEKS IN THE NETHERLANDS.

GRIEKSE junta in Nederland: rapport n.a.v. de bezetting van de ruimte van de Griekse arbeidskommissie in Utrecht op 26-11-1973. Amsterdam, 1974. pp. 48.

GREEN (THOMAS HILL).

SMITH (CRAIG ALEXANDER) A critical study of T.H. Green's theory of political obligation. 1977. fo. 188. *bibliog.* Typescript. Ph.D.(London) thesis: unpublished. *This thesis is the property of London University and may not be removed from the Library.*

GREENE (ROGER SHERMAN).

COHEN (WARREN I.) The Chinese connection: Roger S Greene, Thomas W. Lamont, George E. Sokolsky and American-East Asian relations. New York, 1978. pp. 322. *(Columbia University. East Asian Institute. Studies)*

GREENLAND

— Discovery and exploration.

JONES (GWYN) The Norse Atlantic saga, being the Norse voyages of discovery and settlement to Iceland, Greenland, America. London, 1964. pp. 246. *bibliog. Includes translations, by the author, of the more important early documents.*

GREENWICH VILLAGE, NEW YORK CITY.

HUMPHREY (ROBERT E.) Children of fantasy: the first rebels of Greenwich Village. New York, [1978]. pp. 267. *bibliog.*

GREGORY I, Saint, surnamed the Great, Pope.

HOWORTH (Sir HENRY HOYLE) Saint Gregory the Great. London, 1912. pp. 340.

GRIBOEDOV (ALEKSANDR SERGEEVICH).

NECHKINA (MILITSA VASIL'EVNA) Griboedov i dekabristy. 3rd ed. Moskva, 1977. pp. 735.

GRIDS (CARTOGRAPHY)

— United Kingdom.

CRAIG (JOHN) Writer on population. Grid references of centres of population, Great Britain, 1971. [London?], 1977. pp. 39. *(U.K. Office of Population Censuses and Surveys. Occasional Papers. 1)*

GRIEF.

PINCUS (LILY) Death and the family: the importance of mourning. London, 1976. pp. 278.

GRISEBACH (EBERHARD).

RAUCHE (G.A.) The problem of truth and reality in Grisebach's thought. Pretoria, 1966. pp. 122. *bibliog. (South Africa. National Council for Social Research. Publication Series. No. 21)*

GROOTE (NICHOLAS DE).

BAETENS (ROLAND) De nazomer van Antwerpens welvaart: de diaspora en het handelshuis De Groote tijdens de eerste helft der 17de eeuw. [Brussels], 1976. 2 vols. *bibliog. (Pro Civitate. Collection Histoire. Série in-8 . No. 45) Map in end pocket.*

GROSS NATIONAL PRODUCT.

WORLD BANK ATLAS: population, per capita product and growth rates; pd. by International Bank for Reconstruction and Development. [sub-title varies]. a., [1966(1st)]- Washington.

HOLLARD (MICHEL) Les comptabilités sociales en temps de travail. Grenoble, [1976]. pp. 375. *bibliog. Thèse (Doctorat en Sciences Economiques)- Université de Paris I.*

— Australia.

AUSTRALIA. Department of Labor and Immigration. 1975. Labour's share of the national product: the post-war Australian experience: a discussion paper. Canberra, 1975. pp. 54. *bibliog.*

— Russia.

AKHUNDOV (VAID DZHUMSHUDOVICH) Sovershenstvovanie struktury obshchestvennogo vosproizvodstva: voprosy metodologii. Moskva, 1977. pp. 239.

— — Kirghizia.

SAIFULIN (RAVIL' ZINNATOVICH) Tempy, proportsii i effektivnost' obshchestvennogo proizvodstva v Kirgizskoi SSR. Frunze, 1976. pp. 159.

GROUP RELATIONS TRAINING.

ADVANCES in experiential social processes; edited by Cary L. Cooper and Clayton P. Alderfer. Chichester, [1978 in progress]. *bibliogs.*

GROWTH.

RAYNER (ERIC) Human development: an introduction to the psychodynamics of growth, maturity and ageing. 2nd ed. London, 1978. pp. 208. *bibliogs. (National Institute for Social Work Training. National Institute for Social Work Training Series. No. 22)*

GRUNWICK STRIKE, 1976.

ROGALY (JOE) Grunwick. Harmondsworth, 1977. pp. 199.

GUADALAJARA, MEXICO

— Economic conditions.

WALTON (JOHN) Elites and economic development: comparative studies on the political economy of Latin American cities. Austin, [1977]. pp. 257. *bibliog. (Texas University. Institute of Latin American Studies. Latin American Monographs. No. 41)*

GUANO.

BONILLA MAYTA (HERACLIO) Guano y burguesia en el Peru. Lima, 1974. pp. 186. *bibliog. (Instituto de Estudios Peruanos. Peru Problema. 11)*

GUARANTEED ANNUAL INCOME

— United States.

ANDERSON (MARTIN) Ph. D. Welfare: the political economy of welfare reform in the United States. Stanford, [1978]. pp. 251. *(Stanford University. Hoover Institution on War, Revolution and Peace. Hoover Institution Publications. 181)*

GUATEMALA

— Economic conditions.

PLANT (ROGER) Guatemala: unnatural disaster. London, 1978. pp. 121.

— Politics and government.

MOVIMIENTO REVOLUCIONARIO 13 DE NOVIEMBRE. Direccion. Primera declaracion de la Sierra de las Minas. Montevideo, 1965. pp. 47.

PLANT (ROGER) Guatemala: unnatural disaster. London, 1978. pp. 121.

— Population.

ARIAS (JORGE) La poblacion de Guatemala. [Guatemala, 1976]. pp. 154. *bibliog. (Committee for International Coordination of National Research in Demography. C.I.C.R.E.D. Series)*

GUERNSEY

— Census.

GUERNSEY. Census, 1976. Guernsey census, 1976. [St. Peter Port], 1976. pp. 58.

GUERRILLA WARFARE.

THAYER (CHARLES WHEELER) Guerrilla. New York, [1963]. pp. 195.

LORA (GUILLERMO) Revalorizacion del metodo de las guerrillas. [La Paz?, 1968?]. pp. 47.

— Bibliography.

SABLE (MARTIN HOWARD) compiler. The guerrilla movement in Latin America since 1950: a bibliography. Milwaukee, [1977]. pp. 57. *(Wisconsin University, Milwaukee. Center for Latin American Studies. Center Special Studies Series. No. 3)*

GUERRILLAS

— America, Latin — Bibliography.

SABLE (MARTIN HOWARD) compiler. The guerrilla movement in Latin America since 1950: a bibliography. Milwaukee, [1977]. pp. 57. *(Wisconsin University, Milwaukee. Center for Latin American Studies. Center Special Studies Series. No. 3)*

— Brazil.

CRISPIM (JOSE MARIA) Sobre a estrategia global da revolução brasileira. Lisboa, 1975 in progress.

GUERRILLAS(Cont.)

— Guatemala.

MOVIMIENTO REVOLUCIONARIO 13 DE NOVIEMBRE. Direccion. Primera declaracion de la Sierra de las Minas. Montevideo, 1965. pp. 47.

— Korea.

The FOUNDING of the anti-Japanese guerilla army, a historic event which brought about a great turn in the development of the Korean r[e]volution: [a commemoration of 40 years including extracts from speeches by Kim Il Sung]. [1972]. fo. 14. *Typescript.*

— Rhodesia.

NGOZI (Z.) and FANIKALO (V.) Zimbabwe: what is to be done now. n.p. [1972?]. pp. 14.

SITHOLE (NDABANINGI) In defence of a birthright. [Toronto], 1975. pp. 77.

RAEBURN (MICHAEL) Black fire!: accounts of the guerrilla war in Rhodesia; ... with an analysis by A.R. Wilkinson. London, 1978. pp. 243.

— Spain.

TELLEZ (ANTONIO) La guerrilla urbana. 1: Facerias. Paris, [1974]. pp. 350.

VIDAL SALES (JOSE ANTONIO) Despues del 39: la guerrilla antifranquista. Barcelona, 1976. pp. 241. *bibliog.*

PONS PRADES (EDUARDO) Guerrillas españolas, 1936-1960. Barcelona, 1977. pp. 460.

— Uruguay.

DIALOGUE before death: transcript from a tape recording of an English-language conversation between Dan Mitrione and an unidentified Uruguayan Tupamaro, August 1970. Washington, [1971]. pp. 19.

GUEVARA (ERNESTO).

POSADAS (J.) El asesinato de Guevara y el desarrollo de la revolucion politica en Cuba. Lima, [1967]. pp. xiv, 14.

GUIDED MISSILES.

INTERNATIONAL INSTITUTE FOR STRATEGIC STUDIES. Adelphi Papers. No. 140. The future of land-based missile forces; by Colin S. Gray. London, 1977. pp. 36.

PFALTZGRAFF (ROBERT L.) and DAVIS (JACQUELYN K.) The cruise missile: bargaining chip or defense bargain? Cambridge, Mass., 1977. pp. 53. *(Institute for Foreign Policy Analysis. Special Reports)*

GUINEA (REPUBLIC)

— Politics and government.

RIVIERE (CLAUDE) Sociologist. Guinea: the mobilization of a people; translated from the French by Virginia Thompson and Richard Adloff. Ithaca, 1977. pp. 262. *bibliog.*

GUJARAT

— Statistics, Vital.

INDIA. Office of the Registrar General. Vital Statistics Division. 1976. Report on sample registration system under Kaira project. [Delhi, 1976]. pp. 179. *bibliog.*

GULF OIL CORPORATION.

COMMITTEE OF RETURNED VOLUNTEERS. Gulf Oil Corporation: a study in exploitation. rev. ed. New York, 1971. pp. 48. *bibliog.*

GUROWSKI (ADAM).

STASIK (FLORIAN) Adam Gurowski, 1805-1866. Warszawa, 1977. pp. 420. *bibliog.*

GUYANA.

GUYANA. 1909. Handbook of British Guiana, 1909; comprising general and statistical information concerning the colony; edited and compiled by Geo. D. Bayley, etc. [Georgetown], 1909. pp. 606.

GUYANA. 1913. The British Guiana handbook, 1913; containing general and statistical information concerning the colony, its industries, manufactures and commerce; edited by Alleyne Leechman, etc. Georgetown, 1913. pp. 285. *bibliog.*

— Boundaries — Venezuela.

PARTIDO SOCIALCRISTIANO "COPEI". Fracción Parlamentaria. Frente al acuerdo de Ginebra. Caracas, 1966. pp. 948-960. *(Publicaciones. No. 38)*

— Constitution.

GUYANA. Constitution. 1966. The constitution of Guyana and related constitutional instruments. Georgetown, 1966. pp. 102.

GUYANA. Constitution. 1968-73. Laws of Guyana: constitution;...Act 16 of 1968 amended... [to] 1973. [Georgetown], 1973. pp. 119.

— Politics and government.

PEOPLE'S NATIONAL CONGRESS. [Pamphlets, including speeches by L.F.S. Burnham]. Georgetown, Guyana, 1961-62. 14 pts.

GUYANA LIBERATION FRONT. Manifesto and policy statement. 2nd ed. Georgetown, 1974. pp. 9.

HACIENDAS

— America, Latin.

HACIENDAS, latifundios y plantaciones en America Latina; coordinacion por Enrique Florescano. Mexico, 1975. pp. 667.

LAND and labour in Latin America: essays on the development of agrarian capitalism in the nineteenth and twentieth centuries; edited by Kenneth Duncan and Ian Rutledge, with the collaboration of Colin Harding. Cambridge, 1977. pp. 535. *Based on papers of a symposium held in 1972 at Cambridge under the joint auspices of Cambridge University Centre of Latin American Studies and London University Institute of Latin American Studies.*

HAITI

— Politics and government.

GARCIA ZAMOR (JEAN-CLAUDE) La administracion publica en Haiti. [Guatemala?, 1966]. pp. 186. *bibliog.*

HALFWAY HOUSES.

OTTO (SHIRLEY) and ORFORD (JIM) Not quite like home: small hostels for alcoholics and others. Chichester, [1978]. pp. 218. *bibliog.*

SEGAL (STEVEN P.) and AVIRAM (URI) The mentally ill in community-based sheltered care: a study of community care and social integration. New York, [1978]. pp. 337. *bibliogs.*

— United Kingdom — London.

OTTO (SHIRLEY) and ORFORD (JIM) Not quite like home: small hostels for alcoholics and others. Chichester, [1978]. pp. 218. *bibliog.*

HAMBURG

— Commerce.

MOERING (MARIA) Julius Simon: Jugend und Wanderjahre. [Hamburg, 1965?]. pp. 24.

— Growth.

RHODE (BARBARA) Die Verdrängung der Wohnbevölkerung durch den tertiären Sektor: Strukturwandel in citynahen Stadtgebieten in Hamburg und Frankfurt/M., 1961-1970. Hamburg, [1977]. pp. 178. *bibliog. (Hamburg. Hansische Universität. Seminar für Sozialwissenschaften. Beiträge zur Stadtforschung. Band 2)*

— History.

KROGMANN (CARL VINCENT) Es ging um Deutschlands Zukunft, 1932-1939: Erlebtes täglich diktiert von dem früheren Regierenden Bürgermeister von Hamburg. Leoni am Starnberger See, 1976 repr. 1977. pp. 372.

— Politics and government.

PUMM (GUENTER) Kandidatenauswahl und innerparteiliche Demokratie in der Hamburger SPD, etc. Frankfurt am Main, [1977]. pp. 501. *bibliog.*

HAMPSHIRE

— Economic policy.

HAMPSHIRE. County Council. South Hampshire structure plan for the south east part of the County of Hampshire, City of Portsmouth, City of Southampton; as approved by the Secretary of State for the Environment, March 1977. [Winchester, 1977]. 1 vol. (various pagings). *3 maps in end pocket.*

— Social policy.

HAMPSHIRE. County Council. South Hampshire structure plan for the south east part of the County of Hampshire, City of Portsmouth, City of Southampton; as approved by the Secretary of State for the Environment, March 1977. [Winchester, 1977]. 1 vol. (various pagings). *3 maps in end pocket.*

HANCOCK (GORDON BLAINE).

GAVINS (RAYMOND) The perils and prospects of southern black leadership: Gordon Blaine Hancock, 1884-1970. Durham, N.C., 1977. pp. 221. *bibliog.*

HANDICAPPED

— Employment — Poland.

ILO/UNDP REGIONAL SEMINAR ON THE ORGANISATION AND DEVELOPMENT OF DISABLED PERSONS' CO-OPERATIVES, WARSAW, 1974. ILO/UNDP Regional Seminar...16 September to 5 October 1974... regional Middle East; proceedings, conclusions and recommendations; report, etc. (REM/72/027). Geneva, International Labour Organisation, 1974. pp. 186.

ILO/UNDP REGIONAL SEMINAR ON THE ORGANISATION AND DEVELOPMENT OF COOPERATIVES FOR THE DISABLED, WARSAW, 1977. ILO/ UNDP Regional Seminar...Warsaw, Poland, 4 to 19 October, 1977...: regional Asia; proceedings, conclusions and recommendations, etc. (RAS/75/031). Geneva, International Labour Organisation, 1978. pp. 230.

— — United Kingdom.

BRIDGE (BRIAN) Employment service for the disadvantaged: a report to the Personal Social Services Council on current needs and provision including a study of supported employment. [London], Personal Social Services Council, 1977. pp. 43. *bibliog.*

— Psychology.

SHAKESPEARE (ROSEMARY) The psychology of handicap. London, 1975. pp. 143. *bibliog.*

— Australia.

TRELOAR (SUSAN) The relationship between poverty and disability in Australia. Canberra, 1977. pp. 72. *(Australia. Commission of Inquiry into Poverty. Social/Medical Aspects of Poverty Series)*

— Belgium.

BELGIUM. Fonds National de Reclassement Social des Handicapés. Rapport annuel. a., 1976- Bruxelles. *In 2 pts*

— United States — Socioeconomic status.

LUFT (HAROLD S.) Poverty and health: economic causes and consequences of health problems. Cambridge, Mass., [1978]. pp. 263. *bibliog.*

HANDICAPPED CHILDREN

— United Kingdom.

RUSSELL (PHILIPPA) The wheelchair child. London, 1978. pp. 388. *bibliog.*

HANDICRAFT

— Germany.

KUEFFNER (GERHARD) Das Gewerbezulassungsrecht der Handwerksordnung. Nürnberg, 1977. pp. 378. *bibliog.*

HANOVER

— Politics and government.

RABE (BERND) Der sozialdemokratische Charakter: drei Generationen aktiver Parteimitglieder in einem Arbeiterviertel. Frankfurt, [1978]. pp. 202. *bibliog.*

HARASZTI (MIKLÓS).

HARASZTI (MIKLÓS) A worker in a worker's state: piece-rates in Hungary; translated by Michael Wright; with...a note about the author and a transcript of the author's trial. Harmondsworth, 1977. pp. 175.

HARBORNE (WILLIAM).

SKILLITER (S.A.) William Harborne and the trade with Turkey, 1578-1582: a documentary study of the first Anglo-Ottoman relations. London, 1977. pp. 291. *bibliog.*

HARBOURS.

WANHILL (S.R.C.) The appraisal of port warehouse extensions. Bangor, [1973?]. fo. 7. *(Wales. University. University College of North Wales. Economic Research Papers. REG 7)*

— United Kingdom.

NATIONAL PORTS COUNCIL. Bulletin. irreg., spring 1972 (no.1)- London.

EAST ANGLIA ECONOMIC PLANNING COUNCIL. Seaports in East Anglia; a report. [London, 1977]. pp. 27.

— — Finance.

PORT FINANCIAL INFORMATION; [pd. by] Finance Division, National Ports Council. a., 1971 [1st issue]- London. *Previous information included in DIGEST OF PORT STATISTICS.*

— United States.

WINTERS (TOBEY L.) Deepwater ports in the United States: an economic and environmental impact study. New York, 1977. pp. 199. *bibliog.*

HARDIE (JAMES KEIR).

REID (FRED) Keir Hardie: the making of a socialist. London, [1978]. pp. 211. *bibliog.*

HARINGEY

— Social conditions.

WEBBER (RICHARD J.) The social structure of Haringey. London, 1977. pp. 59. *(Planning Research Applications Group. PRAG Technical Papers. TP 18)*

HARRISON (FREDERIC).

KENT (CHRISTOPHER) Brains and numbers: elitism, Comtism, and democracy in mid- Victorian England. Toronto, [1978]. pp. 212. *bibliog.*

HARTSHORNE (CHARLES).

GUNTON (COLIN E.) Becoming and being: the doctrine of God in Charles Hartshorne and Karl Barth. Oxford, 1978. pp. 236. *bibliog.*

HAUENSTEIN

— History.

Die SALPETERER...; herausgegeben von Thomas Lehner. Berlin, [1977]. pp. 125. *bibliog.*

HAWAIIAN ISLANDS

— Economic conditions.

TOURISM and regional growth: an empirical study of the alternative growth paths for Hawaii; edited by Moheb Ghali; contributors Robert Ebel [and others]. Leiden, 1977. pp. 121.

— Population.

NORDYKE (ELEANOR COLE) The peopling of Hawaii. Honolulu, [1977]. pp. 221. *bibliog.*

HAYA DE LA TORRE (VICTOR RAUL).

FERREIRA (OLIVEIROS S.) Nossa America: Indoamerica; a ordem e a revolução no pensamento de Haya de la Torre. São Paulo, 1971. pp. 293.

HAYEK (FRIEDRICH AUGUST).

MACHLUP (FRITZ) Würdigung der Werke von Friedrich A. von Hayek. Tübingen, 1977. pp. 75. *bibliog. (Walter Eucken Institut. Vorträge und Aufsätze. 62) The original English version was published in the Swedish Journal of Economics, vol. 76, December 1974, and reprinted in ESSAYS on Hayek.*

O'DRISCOLL (GERALD PATRICK) Economics as a coordination problem: the contributions of Friedrich A. Hayek. Kansas City, [1977]. pp. 172. *bibliog.*

HAYFIELD

— Economic history.

SMITH (JOHN H.) Local Historian, ed. Hayfield in 1851: a Derbyshire textile village as seen through the 1851 census. Manchester, 1972. pp. 24. *bibliog. Based on the work of a study group of the New Mills and Hayfield Branch of the Workers' Educational Association.*

— Social history.

SMITH (JOHN H.) Local Historian, ed. Hayfield in 1851: a Derbyshire textile village as seen through the 1851 census. Manchester, 1972. pp. 24. *bibliog. Based on the work of a study group of the New Mills and Hayfield Branch of the Workers' Educational Association.*

HAYTER (LOUIS HENRY).

LEEDS. University. Library. Handlists. 34. Political correspondence (1884-1897) of Louis Henry Hayter. [Leeds], 1977. pp. 16.

HEALTH ATTITUDES.

CONFERENCE ON THE REGIONAL HEALTH UNIVERSITY, PARIS, 1975. Health, higher education and the community: towards a regional health university; report of an international conference at OECD, Paris, 15th-18th December, 1975. Paris, Organisation for Economic Co-operation and Development, 1977. pp. 350.

HEALTH EDUCATION

— Nigeria.

BELLONCLE (GUY) and FOURNIER (GEORGES) Santé et développement en milieu rural africain: réflexions sur l'expérience nigérienne. Paris, [1975]. pp. 238. *bibliog.*

HEALTH MAINTENANCE ORGANIZATIONS.

AMBULATORY care systems. Lexington, Mass., [1977 in progress].

HEALTH PLANNING

— Underdeveloped areas.

See UNDERDEVELOPED AREAS — Health planning.

HEALTH SERVICES ADMINISTRATION

— Russia.

RYAN (MICHAEL) M.A., Ph.D. The organization of Soviet medical care. Oxford, 1978. pp. 168. *bibliog.*

— United Kingdom.

BROWN (RONALD GORDON SCLATER) The changing National Health Service. 2nd ed. London, 1978. pp. 109. *bibliogs.*

HELLER (TOM D.) Restructuring the health service. London, [1978]. pp. 114.

WATKIN (BRIAN) The National Health Service: the first phase: 1948-1974 and after. London, 1978. pp. 170. *bibliog.*

HEGEL (GEORG WILHELM FRIEDRICH).

BODEI (REMO) and others. Hegel e l'economia politica; a cura di Salvatore Veca. [Milano, 1975]. pp. 218.

FISTETTI (FRANCESCO) Critica dell'economia e critica della politica: Marx, Hegel e l'economia politica classica. Bari, [1976]. pp. 213. *bibliogs.*

KELLY (GEORGE ARMSTRONG) Hegel's retreat from Eleusis: studies in political thought. Princeton, [1978]. pp. 259.

MURE (GEOFFREY REGINALD GILCHRIST) Idealist epilogue. Oxford, 1978. pp. 180.

HEIDELBERG, VICTORIA

— Social conditions.

MORGAN (MARY) A study of the Heidelberg, Victoria, community. Canberra, 1976. pp. 85. *(Australia. Commission of Inquiry into Poverty. Research Reports)*

HEINEMANN (GUSTAV WALTER).

LINDEMANN (HELMUT) Gustav Heinemann: ein Leben für die Demokratie. München, [1978]. pp. 312. *bibliog.*

HEINITZ (FRIEDRICH ANTON VON) Freiherr.

WEBER (WOLFHARD) Innovationen im frühindustriellen deutschen Bergbau und Hüttenwesen: Friedrich Anton von Heynitz. Göttingen, 1976. pp. 309. *bibliog. (Fritz Thyssen Stiftung. Neunzehntes Jahrhundert. Studien zu Naturwissenschaft, Technik und Wirtschaft im Neunzehnten Jahrhundert. Band 6)*

HELMER (JEF).

WEG met het fascistiesje sjahregiem: (brochure...uitgegeven ter ondersteuning van de kampagne "Vrijspraak voor Jef Helmer"). Rotterdam, 1974. pp. 42.

HERBST (STANISLAW).

ZIEMIA i ludzie dawnej Polski: studia z geografii historycznej; redaktorzy Adam Galos i Julian Janczak. Wrocław, 1976. pp. 211. *(Wrocławskie Towarzystwo Naukowe. Prace. Seria A. Nr. 179) One article in Russian. With French summaries.*

HEREDITY.

LECOURT (DOMINIQUE) Lyssenko: histoire réelle d'une "science prolétarienne". Paris, 1976. pp. 257.

HEREFORDSHIRE

— Economic conditions.

HEREFORDSHIRE. County Planning Department. Herefordshire county structure plan: report of survey. [Hereford, 1973?]. pp. 82.

HEREFORDSHIRE(Cont.)

— Economic policy.

HEREFORDSHIRE. County Planning Department. Herefordshire county structure plan: report of survey. [Hereford, 1973?]. pp. 82.

HEREFORD AND WORCESTER [COUNTY]. Planning Department. Herefordshire structure plan: written statement. [Worcester, 1976]. pp. 67.

HEREFORD AND WORCESTER [COUNTY]. Planning Department. Herefordshire and Worcestershire structure plans: monitoring statement, July 1977. Worcester, 1977. pp. 119.

— Social conditions.

HEREFORDSHIRE. County Planning Department. Herefordshire county structure plan: report of survey. [Hereford, 1973?]. pp. 82.

— Social policy.

HEREFORDSHIRE. County Planning Department. Herefordshire county structure plan: report of survey. [Hereford, 1973?]. pp. 82.

HEREFORD AND WORCESTER [COUNTY]. Planning Department. Herefordshire structure plan: written statement. [Worcester, 1976]. pp. 67.

HEREFORD AND WORCESTER [COUNTY]. Planning Department. Herefordshire and Worcestershire structure plans: monitoring statement, July 1977. Worcester, 1977. pp. 119.

HEREN (LOUIS).

HEREN (LOUIS) Growing up on The Times. London, 1978. pp. 319.

HERESIES AND HERETICS

— Middle Ages, 600-1500.

MOORE (ROBERT IAN) The origins of European dissent. London, 1977. pp. 322.

HEROIN HABIT.

BULLINGTON (BRUCE) Heroin use in the barrio. Lexington, Mass., [1977]. pp. 179. *bibliog.*

HERON (HUGH).

The ARDBOE martyrs: John Pat Mullan: Hugh Heron. n.p., [1973?]. pp. 20.

HERR (LUCIEN).

LINDENBERG (DANIEL) and MEYER (PIERRE ANDRE) Lucien Herr: le socialisme et son destin. [Paris, 1977]. pp. 318.

HERREMA (TIEDE).

CONNOLLY (COLM) Herrema: siege at Monasterevin. Dublin, [1977]. pp. 116.

HERRERA (TOMAS).

ALFARO (RICARDO JOAQUIN) Vida del General Tomas Herrera;...prologo de Guillermo Andreve. Barcelona, 1909. pp. 351. *bibliog.*

HESS (MOSES).

FREI (BRUNO) pseud. [i.e. Benedikt FREISTADT] Im Schatten von Karl Marx: Moses Hess, hundert Jahre nach seinem Tod. Wien, 1977. pp. 189. *bibliog.*

LADEMACHER (HORST) Moses Hess in seiner Zeit. Bonn, 1977. pp. 194. *bibliog.* *(Bonn. Stadtarchiv. Veröffentlichungen. Band 17)*

HESSE

— Economic history.

MOEKER (ULRICH) Nordhessen im Zeitalter der industriellen Revolution. Köln, 1977. pp. 268. *bibliog.*

— Landtag — Elections.

KLINGEMANN (HANS DIETER) and PAPPI (FRANZ URBAN) Politischer Radikalismus:...dargestellt am Beispiel einer Studie anlässlich der Landtagswahl 1970 in Hessen. München, 1972. pp. 124. *bibliog.*

HEYDRICH (REINHARD).

DESCHNER (GUENTHER) Reinhard Heydrich, Statthalter der totalen Macht: Biographie. Esslingen am Neckar, [1977]. pp. 376. *bibliog.*

HEYNITZ (FRIEDRICH ANTON VON) Freiherr.

See HEINITZ (FRIEDRICH ANTON VON) Freiherr.

HIGH SCHOOL STUDENTS.

See SCHOOL CHILDREN.

HIGHWAY DEPARTMENTS

— United Kingdom — Isle of Man.

ISLE OF MAN. Local Government Districts (Administration) Commission. 1963. Interim report; [B.W. Macpherson, chairman]. [Douglas], 1963. pp. 30.

HIGHWAY LAW

— Australia.

BURKE (R.H.) History of Commonwealth government legislation relating to roads and road transport, 1900-1972. Canberra, 1977. pp. 25. *(Australia. Bureau of Transport Economics. Occasional Papers. No. 8)*

HINDI LANGUAGE

— Grammar.

McGREGOR (RONALD STUART) Outline of Hindi grammar, with exercises. 2nd ed. Delhi, 1977. pp. 261.

HINDMARSH

— Social conditions.

DUIGAN (M.G.) A study of the Hindmarsh, South Australia, community. Canberra, 1975. pp. 61. *(Australia. Commission of Inquiry into Poverty. Research Reports)*

HISS (ALGER).

WEINSTEIN (ALLEN) Perjury: the Hiss-Chambers case. New York, 1978. pp. 674. *bibliog.*

HISTORIANS

— Germany.

KRIEGER (LEONARD) Ranke: the meaning of history. Chicago, 1977. pp. 402. *bibliog.*

HISTORICAL GEOLOGY.

GOUDIE (ANDREW S.) Environmental change. Oxford, 1977. pp. 243. *bibliogs.*

HISTORICAL LIBRARIES

— Directories.

INTERNATIONAL ASSOCIATION OF LABOUR HISTORY INSTITUTIONS. Directory. [London?, 1977]. 1 pamphlet (unpaged).

HISTORICAL LINGUISTICS.

BYNON (THEODORA) Historical linguistics. Cambridge, 1977. pp. 301. *bibliog.*

HISTORICAL MATERIALISM.

MEHRING (FRANZ) On historical materialism. London, [1975]. pp. 63. *First published in German in 1893 as an appendix to Die Lessing-Legende.*

PROBLEMY istoricheskogo materializma...: nekotorye zakonomernosti razvitiia bazisa i nadstroiki etapa razvitogo sotsializma: tematicheskii sbornik. Dushanbe, 1975. pp. 179. *(Dushanbinskii Gosudarstvennyi Pedagogicheskii Institut. Uchenye Zapiski. t.96)*

WEBER (MAX) Critique of Stammler;...translated, with an introductory essay, by Guy Oakes. New York, [1977]. pp. 184.

HISTORICISM.

KRIEGER (LEONARD) Ranke: the meaning of history. Chicago, 1977. pp. 402. *bibliog.*

HISTORIOGRAPHY.

KRITIKA noveishei burzhuaznoi istoriografii: sbornik statei. Leningrad, 1976. pp. 267. *(Akademiia Nauk SSSR. Institut Istorii. Leningradskoe Otdelenie. Trudy. vyp.15)*

VOPROSY metodologii i istorii istoricheskoi nauki. Moskva, 1977. pp. 315.

HISTORY.

SILVER (HAROLD) Nothing but the present, or nothing but the past? [London, 1977]. pp. 20. *Inaugural lecture at Chelsea College, University of London on 17 May 1977.*

— Methodology.

HEXTER (JACK H.) The history primer. New York, [1971]. pp. 297.

ARC, L': revue trimestrielle. 65. Le Roy Ladurie. Aix-en-Provence, [1976]. pp. 85. *bibliog.*

VOPROSY metodologii i istorii istoricheskoi nauki. Moskva, 1977. pp. 315.

— Philosophy.

HISTORIA i wolność: studia z dziejów ideologii XIX wieku, etc. Warszawa, 1961. pp. 299. *(Polska Akademia Nauk. Instytut Filozofii i Socjologii. Archiwum Historii Filozofii i Myśli Społecznej. 7) With Russian or German summaries.*

HEXTER (JACK H.) The history primer. New York, [1971]. pp. 297.

HEGEL (GEORG WILHELM FRIEDRICH) Lectures on the philosophy of world history. Introduction: reason in history; translated from the German edition of Johannes Hoffmeister by H.B. Nisbet,...with an introduction by Duncan Forbes. Cambridge, 1975. pp. 252. *bibliog.*

MAFFESOLI (MICHEL) Logique de la domination. Paris, 1976. pp. 218. *bibliog.*

WODZYŃSKA (MARIA) Adam Mickiewicz i romantyczna filozofia historii w Collège de France. Warszawa, 1976. pp. 283. *With French summary.*

BULLOCK (ALAN LOUIS CHARLES) Baron Bullock. Is history becoming a social science?: the case of contemporary history. Cambridge, 1977. pp. 23. *(Cambridge. University. Sir Leslie Stephen Lectures. 1976)*

KRIEGER (LEONARD) Ranke: the meaning of history. Chicago, 1977. pp. 402. *bibliog.*

SAMARSKAIA (ELENA ALEKSANDROVNA) Poniatie praktiki u K. Marksa i sovremennye diskussii: o dialektike ob"ektivnogo i sub"ektivnogo v istoricheskom protsesse. Moskva, 1977. pp. 224.

CHESNEAUX (JEAN) Pasts and futures; or, What is history for? London, [1978]. pp. 150.

— — Bibliography.

CENTRE FOR POLICY STUDIES. Bibliography of freedom. London, 1976. pp. 28.

— Psychological aspects.

MANDROU (ROBERT) Introduction to modern France, 1500-1640: an essay in historical psychology;...translated by R.E. Hallmark. London, 1975. pp. 285. *bibliog.*

HISTORY, MODERN

— 20th century.

SIMON (ULRICH) Sitting in judgement, 1913-1963: an interpretation of history. London, 1978. pp. 166.

HITLER (ADOLF).

GRIMM (FRIEDRICH) Hitlers deutsche Sendung. Berlin, 1934. pp. 46.

HIDEN (JOHN) Germany and Europe, 1919-1939. London, 1977. pp. 183.

TAYLOR (ALAN JOHN PERCIVALE) The war lords. London, 1977. pp. 189. Transcripts of six lectures delivered on BBC Television in August 1976.

HAFFNER (SEBASTIAN) pseud. Anmerkungen zu Hitler. München, [1978]. pp. 204.

HÔ CHI MINH.

LACOUTURE (JEAN) Hô Chi Minh. Paris, [1977]. pp. 253. bibliog.

HODGSKIN (THOMAS).

OSIER (JEAN PIERRE) Thomas Hodgskin: une critique prolétarienne de l'économie politique. Paris, 1976. pp. 141.

HOEGNER (WILHELM).

HOEGNER (WILHELM) Flucht vor Hitler: Erinnerungen an die Kapitulation der ersten deutschen Republik, 1933. München, 1977 repr. 1978. pp. 296.

HOFMAIER (KARL).

HOFMAIER (KARL) Memoiren eines Schweizer Kommunisten, 1917-1947. Zürich, 1978. pp. 303.

HOFMANN (JOSEF).

HOFMANN (JOSEF) Journalist in Republik, Diktatur und Besatzungszeit: Erinnerungen, 1916-1947; bearbeitet und eingeleitet von Rudolf Morsey. Mainz, [1977]. pp. 236. (Kommission für Zeitgeschichte. Veröffentlichungen. Reihe A: Quellen. Band 23)

HOFMANNSTHAL (HUGO VON).

BURCKHARDT (CARL JACOB) Le souvenir de Hugo von Hofmannsthal. Lausanne, 1976. pp. 32. (Lausanne. Université. Centre de Recherches Européennes Publications. 1. Histoire, Précurseurs et Promoteurs de l'Union de l'Europe)

HOHENLOHE-WERKE, AKTIENGESELLSCHAFT.

SZARANIEC (LECH) Załoga koncernu "Hohenlohe" i jej walka klasowa w latach 1905- 1939. Katowice, 1976. pp. 320. bibliog.

HOLDING COMPANIES.

DAEMS (HERMAN) The holding company and corporate control. Leiden, 1978. pp. 145. bibliog.

— Belgium.

DAEMS (HERMAN) The holding company and corporate control. Leiden, 1978. pp. 145. bibliog.

HOLIDAYS.

INTERNATIONAL LABOUR CONFERENCE. 62nd Session. Reports. 2. Holidays with pay for seafarers: second item on the agenda; etc. Geneva, 1976. pp. 45.

HOLLAND MARSH

— Social conditions.

ISHWARAN (KARIGOUDAR) Family, kinship and community: a study of Dutch Canadians: a developmental approach. Toronto, [1977]. pp. 181. bibliog.

HOLMES (G.V.)

HOLMES (G.V.) The likes of us. London, [1948]. pp. 192.

HOLOCAUST, JEWISH (1939-1945).

DRUKS (HERBERT) The failure to rescue. New York, [1977]. pp. 108. bibliog.

GILBERT (MARTIN) The holocaust: a record of the destruction of Jewish life in Europe during the dark years of Nazi rule. London, [1978]. pp. 60.

HOME ACCIDENTS

— New Zealand.

FINDLAY (FREDERICK JOHN) Domestic accidents. Wellington, 1970. pp. 93. (New Zealand. Department of Health. Special Report Series. 35)

— United Kingdom.

ACCIDENTS in the home; edited by Sandra Burman and Hazel Genn; published for Centre for Socio-Legal Studies, a Research Unit of the Social Science Research Council. London, [1977]. pp. 140. bibliogs.

HOME AND SCHOOL.

IRELAND, NORTHERN. Working Party on Educational Welfare. 1976. Report: (home school links); [J. Ferguson, chairman]. Belfast, 1976. pp. 27. bibliog.

HOME LABOUR

— United Kingdom.

TRADES UNION CONGRESS. Homeworking: a TUC statement. London, [1978?]. pp. 38.

HOME OWNERSHIP.

OAKESHOTT (J.J.) A consideration of methods of extending owner occupation. London, [1976]. pp. 23. (London. Greater London Council. Research Memoranda. 495)

TUNNARD (JO) and WHATELY (CLARE) Rights guide for home owners. 2nd ed. London, 1977. pp. 80.

— United States.

PERIN (CONSTANCE) Everything in its place: social order and land use in America. Princeton, [1977]. pp. 291. bibliog.

HOME RULE

— Ireland.

PALL MALL GAZETTE. Extras. No. 25. Home rule for home reading: the best points of the best speeches. London, 1886. pp. 48.

PALL MALL GAZETTE. Extras. No. 28. For home rule and Gladstone̊': THE ELECTORS' CATECHISM. lONDON, 1886. PP. 16.

ANSON (Sir WILLIAM REYNELL) Objections of an Oxford Liberal to home rule. n.p., [1887?]. pp. 844-853.

REDMOND (JOHN EDWARD) Ulster and home rule: a speech...at Newcastle-on-Tyne, November 14th, 1913. [London, 1913?]. pp. 11. (Irish Press Agency. Leaflets. No. 53)

— Scotland.

U.K. Parliament. House of Commons. Library. Research Division. Background Papers. No. 63. The devolution debate: regional statistics, updated. [London, 1978]. pp. 17.

— Wales.

U.K. Parliament. House of Commons. Library. Research Division. Background Papers. No. 63. The devolution debate: regional statistics, updated. [London, 1978]. pp. 17.

HOMELESSNESS

— Australia.

SACKVILLE (RONALD) Homeless people and the law. Canberra, 1976. pp. 84. (Australia. Commission of Inquiry into Poverty. Law and Poverty Series)

— United Kingdom.

ERLAM (ANDREW) and BROWN (MARIE) Catering for homeless workers: a study of low pay and homelessness amongst casual catering workers [produced by the Low Pay Unit and the Campaign for the Homeless and Rootless]. [London, 1975]. fo. 13.

WAUGH (SARAH) Needs and provision for young single homeless people: a review of information and literature. London, 1976. pp. 56. bibliog.

DRAKE (MADELINE) and BIEBUYCH (TONY) Policy and provision for the single homeless: a position paper; a report to the Personal Social Services Council. [London], Personal Social Services Council, 1977. pp. 49. bibliog.

U.K. Department of the Environment. 1977. Housing, Homeless Persons, Act 1977: code of guidance, England and Wales. London, 1977. pp. 35.

WIDDOWSON (BOB) Hostel for a home. London, [1977]. pp. 21.

CARNWATH (ROBERT JOHN ANDERSON) A guide to the Housing, Homeless Persons, Act 1977. London, 1978. pp. 142.

PARTINGTON (MARTIN) The Housing (Homeless Persons) Act 1977 and the Code of Guidance. London, 1978. 1 pamphlet (unpaged).

— — Bibliography.

LONDON. Greater London Council. Research Library. Homelessness. London, 1972 repr. 1977. pp. 25. ([Research] Bibliographies. No. 34)

HOMICIDE

— New Zealand.

NEW ZEALAND. Criminal Law Reform Committee. 1976. Report on culpable homicide. [Wellington], 1976. 1 vol.(various pagings).

HOMOSEXUALITY

— United Kingdom.

WILDEBLOOD (PETER) Against the law. London, 1955. pp. 189.

HONDURAS

— Economic policy.

SANDOVAL C. (RIGOBERTO) Exposicion...ante el Comite Central del Partido Nacional de Honduras. Comayaguela, 1969. pp. 20. (Partido Nacional de Honduras. Comite Central. Publicaciones)

— Foreign economic relations — Salvador.

JIMENEZ (EDDY E.) La guerra no fue de futbol. La Habana, 1974. pp. 165.

HONG KONG

— Census.

HONG KONG. Census, 1976. Hong Kong by-census, 1976: a graphic guide. Hong Kong, [1977]. pp. 26. In English and Chinese.

HONG KONG. Census, 1976. Hong Kong by-census, 1976: basic tables. Hong Kong, [1977]. pp. 55.

— City planning.

LEEMING (FRANK) Street studies in Hong Kong: localities in a Chinese city. Hong Kong, 1977. pp. 182.

— Industries.

HONG KONG. Census and Statistics Department. 1976. 1973 census of industrial production. Hong Kong, [1976]. 2 vols.

HONG KONG (Cont.)

SIT (VICTOR FUNG SHUEN) Factories in domestic premises: a case study of modern Hong Kong. 1977. fo. 356. *bibliog. Typescript. Ph.D. (London) thesis: unpublished. This thesis is the property of London University and may not be removed from the Library.*

— Social conditions.

HAYES (JAMES) The Hong Kong region, 1850-1911; institutions and leadership in town and countryside. Hamden, Conn., 1977. pp. 289. *bibliog.*

— Social history.

HAYES (JAMES) The Hong Kong region, 1850-1911; institutions and leadership in town and countryside. Hamden, Conn., 1977. pp. 289. *bibliog.*

— Statistics.

HONG KONG MONTHLY DIGEST OF STATISTICS; [pd. by the Government Printing Department, Hong Kong]. m., Ja 1970- [Hong Kong]. *Supersedes Hong Kong government gazette: Suppl. no.4: Statistical tables (1951 - N 1969).*

— Statistics, Vital.

HONG KONG. Census and Statistics Department. 1975. Births, deaths and marriages, 1970-1973. Hong Kong, [1975]. pp. 110.

— Streets.

LEEMING (FRANK) Street studies in Hong Kong: localities in a Chinese city. Hong Kong, 1977. pp. 182.

HOOLIGANS

— United Kingdom.

INGHAM (ROGER) and others. "Football hooliganism": the wider context. London, 1978. pp. 151. *bibliog.*

HOOVER (HERBERT CLARK) President of the United States.

LERSKI (GEORGE JAN) ed. Herbert Hoover and Poland: a documentary history of a friendship. Stanford, 1977. pp. 128. *(Stanford University. Hoover Institution on War, Revolution and Peace. Hoover Institution Publications. 174)*

— Bibliography.

TRACEY (KATHLEEN) compiler. Herbert Hoover: a bibliography: his writings and addresses. Stanford, [1977]. pp. 202. *(Stanford University. Hoover Institution on War, Revolution and Peace. Bibliographical Series. 58)*

HORSE RACING

— New Zealand.

NEW ZEALAND. Royal Commission on Gaming and Racing, 1946. Gaming and racing; report; [G.P. Finlay, chairman]. Wellington, 1948. pp. 150.

HORSHAM

— Population.

CONSTABLE (DEREK) Household structure in three English market towns, 1851-1871. Reading, 1977. pp. 63. *(Reading. University. Department of Geography. Reading Geographical Papers. No. 55)*

— Social history.

CONSTABLE (DEREK) Household structure in three English market towns, 1851-1871. Reading, 1977. pp. 63. *(Reading. University. Department of Geography. Reading Geographical Papers. No. 55)*

HOSIERY INDUSTRY

— United Kingdom.

HARTE (NEGLEY B.) A history of George Brettle and Co. Ltd., 1801-1964. [London, 1973]. fo. 165. *bibliog.*

HOSIERY WORKERS

— United Kingdom.

The FRAMEWORK knitters and handloom weavers: their attempts to keep up wages; eight pamphlets, 1820-1845. New York, 1972. 1 vol.(various pagings). *Facsimile reprints.*

HOSPITAL CARE

— France — Costs.

DUMONT (JACQUES) and LATOUCHE (JEAN) L'hospitalisation malade du profit. [Paris, 1977]. pp. 222.

HOSPITAL PHARMACIES.

CONTROL of medicines in hospital wards and departments; report of a joint group appointed by the Standing Pharmaceutical, Medical and Nursing and Midwifery Advisory Committees on control of medicines in hospital wards and departments; [A. Roxburgh, chairman]. Edinburgh, H.M.S.O., 1972. pp. 27.

HOSPITALS

— France — Finance.

DUMONT (JACQUES) and LATOUCHE (JEAN) L'hospitalisation malade du profit. [Paris, 1977]. pp. 222.

— Nigeria — Finance.

NIGERIA (WESTERN STATE). Review Committee on Grants-in-Aid to Voluntary Agency Hospitals in Western Nigeria. 1969. Report; [T.O. Ogunlesi, chairman]. [Ibadan, 1969]. pp. 94.

— Spain.

SPAIN. Instituto Nacional de Estadistica. Estadistica de establecimientos sanitarios con regimen de internado. a., 1973(2nd)- Madrid.

— United Kingdom.

LABOUR PARTY. The hospital problem: the report of a special conference of labour, hospital, medical and kindred societies, held in Caxton Hall, Westminster, on April 28th and 29th, 1924. London, [1924?]. pp. 12. *(Reprinted...from supplement to the British Medical Journal, May 3rd, 1924)*

— — Administration.

SCHEME for the formation of a central hospital board for London, with a preliminary list of the general committee that have consented to promote such a scheme and the names of a large number of members of the staffs of hospitals, general practitioners, and others, who have expressed their approval of the movement. London, 1897. pp. 24.

U.K. Department of Health and Social Security. 1978. Future management of the London specialist postgraduate hospitals: a consultative document. [London], 1978. pp. 78.

— — Staff.

GORDON (HARVEY) and ILIFFE (STEVE) Pickets in white: the junior doctors dispute of 1975: a study of the medical profession in transition. London, [1977]. pp. 76.

— — Ireland, Northern.

IRELAND, NORTHERN. Department of Health and Social Services. Summary of accounts of endowments and gifts: Northern Ireland Hospitals Authority and Hospital Management Committees. a., 1970/71- Belfast. *1951/1956 [1st issue] - 1969/70 included in IRELAND, NORTHERN. Parliament. House of Commons. [Papers].*

— United States — Finance.

FEDER (JUDITH MORRIS) Medicare: the politics of federal hospital insurance. Lexington, Mass., [1977]. pp. 177. *bibliog.*

HOSPITALS, GYNAECOLOGIC AND OBSTETRIC.

RHODES (PHILIP) Doctor John Leake's hospital: a history of the General Lying-in Hospital, York Road, Lambeth, 1765-1971: the birth, life, and death of a maternity hospital. London, [1977]. pp. 400. *bibliog.*

HOTELS, TAVERNS, ETC.

— Barbados.

BARBADOS. Development Board. 1959. Barbados hotel development survey, 1958. [Bridgetown, 1959?]. pp. 11.

— Singapore.

SINGAPORE. Statistics Department. 1976. Report on the census of wholesale and retail trades, restaurants and hotels, 1973. Singapore, 1976. pp. 98.

SINGAPORE. Statistics Department. 1978. Report on the census of wholesale and retail trades, restaurants and hotels, 1975. Singapore, 1978. pp. 188.

— United Kingdom.

MARPLAN LIMITED. The British pub. [London, 1978?]. fo. 10.

MARPLAN LIMITED. Pub opening hours. [London, 1978?]. fo. 6.

SERVICE: news-letter of the Hotel and Catering Industry Training Board [U.K.]. irreg. Wembley. *Current issues only kept.*

— — Employees.

ECONOMIC DEVELOPMENT COMMITTEE FOR HOTELS AND CATERING. Employment policy and industrial relations in the hotels and catering industry. London, National Economic Development Office, 1977. pp. 64. *bibliog.*

HOURS OF LABOUR.

MARIC (D.) Adapting working hours to modern needs: the time factor in the new approach to working conditions. Geneva, International Labour Office, 1977. pp. 50. *bibliog.*

— Australia.

AUSTRALIA. Commonwealth Bureau of Census and Statistics. 1975. Earnings and hours of employees: distribution and composition, May 1975. Canberra, 1975. pp. 31.

— Canada.

CANADIAN LABOUR CONGRESS. Hours of work in the motor transport industry; submission...with respect to the inquiry pursuant to Part III of the Canada Labour Code. Ottawa, 1974. fo. 9.

— — British Columbia.

BRITISH COLUMBIA. Board of Industrial Relations. 1971. Summary of orders and regulations made pursuant to Male Minimum Wage Act, Female Minimum Wage Act, Annual and General Holidays Act, Hours of Work Act, Payment of Wages Act; compiled as at February 1, 1971. [Victoria], 1971. pp. 43.

— — Nova Scotia.

NOVA SCOTIA. Department of Labour. Economics and Research Division. 1969. Pilot survey: small firm wage rates, salaries and hours of labour, Nova Scotia, 1968: cleaners, laundries and pressers; fish products; general and variety stores; sawmills. Halifax, [1969]. pp. 34.

— European Economic Community countries.

EUROPEAN COMMUNITIES. Statistical Office. Hourly earnings: hours of work. s-a., 1975(no. 1)- Luxembourg. *[in Community languages]*

— Poland.

STRZEMIŃSKA (HELENA) Czas pracy i jego skracanie: etapy, metody, efekty. Warszawa, 1976. pp. 327. *bibliog. With Russian and English tables of contents.*

HOUSING.

— United States.

LEVITAN (SAR A.) and BELOUS (RICHARD S.) Shorter hours, shorter weeks: spreading the work to reduce unemployment. Baltimore, [1977]. pp. 94.

HOUSING.

INTERNATIONAL BANK FOR RECONSTRUCTION AND DEVELOPMENT. Sector Policy Papers. Housing. [Washington], 1975. pp. 74.

CHARLES (SUSAN) Housing economics. London, 1977. pp. 77. *bibliog.*

— Finance.

INTERREGIONAL SEMINAR ON THE FINANCING OF HOUSING AND URBAN DEVELOPMENT, COPENHAGEN, 1970. Report of the...Seminar...[held in] Copenhagen, 25 May to 10 June 1970. (ST/TAO/SER.C/134). New York, United Nations, 1972. pp. 94.

— Information services — United Kingdom.

HARLOE (MICHAEL) and others. Housing Advice Centres. London, 1976. pp. 28.

— America, Latin.

ASENTAMIENTOS humanos, urbanismo y vivienda: cometido del poder publico en la segunda mitad del siglo XX; [by] Jesus Silva-Herzog Flores [and others]. Mexico, 1977. pp. 788.

— Australia.

NATIONAL COUNCIL OF WOMEN OF AUSTRALIA. Flat survey report for the members of the National Council of Women. Canberra, 1959. fo. 5.

— — Finance.

AUSTRALIA. Department of Housing. States Grants (Dwellings for Aged Pensioners) Act 1969: annual statement. a., 1969/70(1st)- Canberra. *Included in AUSTRALIA. Parliament. [Parliamentary papers].*

— Austria — Statistics.

AUSTRIA. Statistisches Zentralamt. Wohnungsdaten. a., 1976/77- Wien. *Supersedes AUSTRIA. Statistisches Zentralamt. Wohnbautätigkeit and AUSTRIA. Statistisches Zentralamt. Wohnungen: Ergebnisse des Mikrozensus.*

— Barbados — Bridgetown.

BARBADOS. Committee appointed...to Advise on the Utilisation of the Pine Estate for Housing and Slum Clearance. 1947. Report; [L. De Syllas, chairman]. [Bridgetown, 1947]. pp. 11.

— Canada — Alberta.

ALBERTA. Department of Housing and Public Works. Annual report. a., 1975/76 [1st]- Edmonton.

ALBERTA. Department of Housing and Public Works. 1976. Housing for Albertans: a review of Alberta housing programs planned, administered and financed through Alberta government crown corporations. [Edmonton, 1976?]. pp. 21.

— — Nova Scotia.

NOVA SCOTIA. Housing Commission. 1974. Summary of building condition survey 1973. [Halifax, 1974?]. 1 vol. (various foliations)

— — Ontario.

MULLER (R.A.) The market for new housing in the metropolitan Toronto area. [Toronto, 1978]. pp. 220. *(Ontario. Economic Council. Occasional Papers. 5)*

— Colombia — Statistics.

COLOMBIA. Census, 1973. XIV censo nacional de poblacion y III de vivienda: resultados provisionales. [Bogota, 1975]. pp. 40. *Bound with Muestra de avance: poblacion.*

— Costa Rica — Statistics.

COSTA RICA. Census, 1973. Vivienda, poblacion: ciudades capitales. San Jose, [1976?]. pp. 219. *(Costa Rica. Direccion General de Estadistica y Censos. Censos Nacionales de 1973. 11-12)*

— Cuba — Statistics.

CUBA. Census, 1970. Censo de poblacion y viviendas, 1970. La Habana, 1975. pp. 1035.

— Ecuador — Statistics.

ECUADOR. Instituto Nacional de Estadistica y Censos. 1976. II censo de vivienda 1974: resultados definitivos; resumen nacional. Quito, 1976. pp. 77.

— Finland — Statistics.

FINLAND. Census, 1975. Asunto- ja elinkeinotutkinus, 1975;...Population and housing census, 1975. Helsinki, 1978 in progress. *(Finland. Suomen Virallinen Tilasto. Finlands Officiella Statistik. 6.C. 105) In Finnish, Swedish and English.*

— France.

BUTLER (RÉMY) and NOISETTE (PATRICE) De la cité ouvrière au grand ensemble: la politique capitaliste du logement social, 1815-1975. Paris, 1977. pp. 193.

— — Statistics.

FRANCE. Census, 1962. Recensement général de la population de 1962; résultats du dépouillement exhaustif: population, ménages, logements, immeubles; fascicules régionaux. Paris, 1967. 21 parts (in 2 vols.)

— Germany.

PELTZ-DRECKMANN (UTE) Nationalsozialistischer Siedlungsbau: Versuch einer Analyse der die Siedlungspolitik bestimmenden Faktoren am Beispiel des Nationalsozialismus. München, [1978]. pp. 547. *bibliog.*

— — Finance.

PALINKAS (PETER) Die Wohnungsbauinvestitionen in der BRD: eine theoretische und empirische Analyse. Hamburg, 1976. pp. 209. *bibliog. Dissertation - Universität Hamburg.*

— — Statistics.

GERMANY (BUNDESREPUBLIK). Statistisches Bundesamt. Bestand an Wohnungen: fortgeschriebene Ergebnisse. a., 1955/56- Wiesbaden. *(Bautätigkeit und Wohnungen. Reihe 3)*

— Israel — Statistics.

ISRAEL. Census, 1972. Census of population and housing, 1972: [publications]. Jerusalem, 1972 in progress. *In English and Hebrew.*

— Italy — Statistics.

DANDRI (GUIDO) Il deficit abitativo in Italia; saggio introduttivo di Roberto Mostacci. Milano, 1977. pp. irreg. *(Centro Ricerche Economiche, Sociologiche e di Mercato nell'Edilizia. Collana Cresme. 15)*

— — Bologna.

CESARI (CARLO) and GRESLERI (GIULIANO) Residenza operaia e città neo-conservatrice: Bologna caso esemplare. Roma, 1976. pp. 242. *bibliog.*

— — Lombardy.

MENEGHETTI (LODOVICO) Abitazioni in Lombardia: contraddizioni territoriali e sociali nell'interpretazione dei censimenti. Milano, 1976. pp. 144.

— Malaysia.

WEGELIN (EMIEL A.) Urban low-income housing and development: a case study in Peninsular Malaysia. Leiden, 1978. pp. 347. *bibliog.*

— — Statistics.

FEDERATION OF MALAYSIA. Census, 1970. 1970 population and housing census of Malaysia. Kuala Lumpur, 1971 in progress. *In English and Malay.*

FEDERATION OF MALAYSIA. Census, 1970. 1970 population and housing census of Malaysia: West Malaysia census of housing, 1970: final report. Kuala Lumpur, 1973. pp. 183. *In English and Malay.*

— Mexico.

ECKSTEIN (SUSAN) The poverty of revolution: the state and the urban poor in Mexico. Princeton, N.J., [1977]. pp. 300. *bibliog.*

— New Zealand — Finance.

NEW ZEALAND. Maori and Island Affairs Department. 1970. Housing for Maoris and Islanders: notes for social workers. [Wellington], 1970. fo. 7.

— Russia — Law.

SAWICKI (STANISLAW J.) Soviet land and housing law: a historical and comparative study. New York, 1977. pp. 199.

— South Africa.

DEWAR (DAVID) of Cape Town University, and UYTENBOGAARDT (ROELOF S.) Housing: a comparative evaluation of urbanism in Cape Town. Claremont, S.A., [1977]. pp. 207.

GRANELLI (ROGER) Urban black housing: a review of existing conditions in the Cape peninsula with some guidelines for change. Cape Town, [1977]. pp. 79.

HOUSING people: proceedings of the Housing 75 conference held in Johannesburg in October 1975, and arranged by the Institute of South African Architects; edited by Michael Lazenby. London, 1977. pp. 274. *bibliogs.*

— Underdeveloped areas.

See UNDERDEVELOPED AREAS — Housing.

— United Kingdom.

NATIONAL LABOUR HOUSING ASSOCIATION AND FEDERATION OF TENANTS' LEAGUES. Housing programme for town and district councils: to the workers of the United Kingdom of Great Britain and Ireland. [London, 189-?]. pp. 4.

GARDEN CITY TENANTS LIMITED. Rules. London, 1904. pp. 36.

RULES of the : [model for housing societies]. London, 1914. pp. 30.

NATIONAL HOUSING AND TOWN PLANNING COUNCIL. Housing and town planning after the war: memorandum, etc. London, 1917. pp. (3).

SHAWCROSS (HAROLD) Memorandum on housing and town planning after the war; prepared for the Conference of Workmen's Associations to be held at Manchester on March 31st 1917. n.p., [1917]. fo. 5.

LABOUR PARTY. Advisory Committee on Local Government. The position as to housing. [London, 1918?]. pp. 3.

WESTACOTT (A.G.) How to improve the government housing scheme: a really workable housing policy. n.p., 1919. pp. (3).

CONFERENCE OF SOCIALIST ECONOMISTS. Political Economy of Housing Workshop. Political economy and the housing question: papers presented at the...Workshop, etc. London, 1975. pp. 153.

CONFERENCE OF SOCIALIST ECONOMISTS. Political Economy of Housing Workshop. Housing and class in Britain: a second volume of papers presented at the...Workshop, etc. London, 1976. pp. 104.

HOUSING.(Cont.)

NATIONAL HOME IMPROVEMENT COUNCIL. Improvement of United Kingdom housing: a reappraisal: a discussion document, etc. London, 1976. 1 vol. (various pagings)

PEOPLE and their settlements: aspects of housing, transport and strategic planning in the U.K.; papers for a conference held in London in January 1976, organised by the National Council of Social Service...as a contribution to the NGO Forum on Habitat, Vancouver, June 1976. London, [1976]. pp. 107.

BAILEY (RON) The homeless and the empty houses. Harmondsworth, 1977. pp. 287.

BAYLY (RICHARD) and SWAIN (ANNE) Local authorities and building for sale: a handbook on local authority involvement in the provision of new housing for owner-occupiers. [London], Department of the Environment, 1977. pp. 42. *(HDD Occasional Papers. 77/1)*

ECONOMIC DEVELOPMENT COMMITTEE FOR BUILDING. Housing for all: a document for discussion. London, National Economic Development Office, 1977. pp. 50.

KELLY (FRANCES) and WINTOUR (JIM) The housing crisis nationwide. London, 1977. pp. 55.

BUILDING with direct labour: local authority building and the crisis in the construction industry; [written by the Direct Labour Collective]. London, 1978. pp. 115.

BURNETT (JOHN) Ph.D. A social history of housing, 1815-1970. Newton Abbot, [1978]. pp. 344.

U.K. Social Survey. [Reports. New Series]. 1091. Attitudes to letting in 1976; a survey of private landlords, private tenants and owner occupiers in areas of England and Wales which in 1971 were predominantly rented in the private sector; [by] Bobbie Paley. London, 1978. pp. 101.

—— Finance.

CLARK (STEVE) Who benefits?: a study of the distribution of public expenditure on housing; evidence to the House of Commons expenditure sub-committee submitted on behalf of Shelter...by the Housing Research Group. London, 1977. pp. 34. *bibliog.*

—— Law.

CARNWATH (ROBERT JOHN ANDERSON) A guide to the Housing, Homeless Persons, Act 1977. London, 1978. pp. 142.

HOATH (DAVID CHARLES) Council housing. London, 1978. pp. 169.

—— Statistics.

U.K. Department of the Environment. Housing and construction statistics. q., 1st quarter 1972 (1)- London. *Supersedes Housing statistics, Great Britain (Mr 1966 - F 1972) and Monthly bulletin of construction statistics (N 1942 - Je 1972).*

—— Ireland — Statistics.

IRELAND. Census, 1821. Abstract of the answers and returns made pursuant to an Act of the United Parliament, passed in the 55th year of the reign of His Late Majesty George the Third, intituled An Act to provide for taking an account of the population of Ireland, and for ascertaining the increase or diminution thereof: preliminary observations, enumeration abstract, appendix. (B.P.P. 1823, 577). [Dublin], 1823. pp. 393.

IRELAND. Census, 1831. Population, Ireland: abstract of answers and returns under the population acts...: enumeration 1831; (with Comparative abstract of the population in Ireland, as taken in 1821 and 1831, etc.) (B.P.P. 1833, 634 and 23). [Dublin], 1833. 2 pts.

IRELAND. Census, 1841. Report of the commissioners appointed to take the census of Ireland, for the year 1841. Dublin, 1843. 1 vol. (various pagings).

IRELAND. Census, 1851. The census of Ireland for the year 1851. Part 1, showing the area, population and number of houses, by townlands and electoral divisions. Vols 1-4: province [reports]. Dublin, 1852. 4 vols. (in 2).

IRELAND. Census, 1861. The census of Ireland for the year 1861. Part 1, showing the area, population and number of houses, by townlands and electoral divisions. Vols. 1-4: province [reports]. Dublin, 1863. 4 vols (in 2).

IRELAND. Census, 1871. Census of Ireland, 1871. Part 1. Area, houses and population: also the ages, civil condition, occupations, birthplaces, religion and education of the people. Vols 1-4: provinces of Leinster (C.662), Munster (C.873), Ulster (C.964), Connaught (C.1106). Dublin, 1873-75. 4 vols.

IRELAND. Census, 1891. Census of Ireland, 1891. Part 1. Area, houses and population: also the ages, civil or conjugal condition, occupations, birthplaces, religion and education of the people. Vols 1-2: provinces of Leinster (C.6515), Munster (C.6567). Dublin, 1891-92. 5 vols.

IRELAND. Census, 1901. Census of Ireland, 1901. Part 1. Area, houses and population: also the ages, civil or conjugal condition, occupations, birthplaces, religion and education of the people. Vols. 1-4: provinces of Leinster (C.847), Munster (Cd.1058), Ulster (Cd.1123), Connaught (Cd.1059). Dublin, 1902. 4 vols.

—— Ireland, Northern.

IRELAND, NORTHERN. Department of the Environment. 1976. The private rented sector in Northern Ireland: the government's proposals. [Belfast], 1976. pp. 22.

IRELAND, NORTHERN. Working Party on Tenant Participation and New Forms of Tenure. 1976. Report; [L.V.D. Calvert, chairman]. [Belfast], 1976. pp. 25.

—— Liverpool.

WILSON (HUGH) AND WOMERSLEY (LEWIS) Firm. Inner area study: Liverpool: social area analysis. [London], Department of the Environment, [1977]. pp. 71.

—— London.

ST. PANCRAS HOUSING ASSOCIATION IN CAMDEN. Servants of the manger. [London, c. 1925]. 1 pamphlet (unpaged).

BARCLAY (IRENE T.) The Chelsea housing problem: report for the Chelsea Housing Association. 2nd ed. London, 1926. pp. 12.

HOUSING FACTS AND FIGURES; (compiled by the Intelligence Unit of the Greater London Council). irreg., 1973 (no.1)- London.

SHELTER. Priorities for housing action; report 2, North Islington Housing Rights Project. London, [1973]. pp. 35.

WEBBER (RICHARD J.) The social structure of Haringey. London, 1977. pp. 59. *(Planning Research Applications Group. PRAG Technical Papers. TP 18)*

TROWBRIDGE (BARRY) Sample survey of borough housing waiting list applicants 1973-76. London, [1978]. 1 vol. (various pagings). *(London. Greater London Council. Research Memoranda. 533)*

—— Maidstone.

MAIDSTONE CITIZENS' UNION. The housing question in Maidstone: a statement and appeal submitted...to the Town Council, January, 1901. Maidstone, [imprint, 1901]. 1 pamphlet (unpaged).

—— Merseyside.

THOMPSON (ANDREW) The role of housing associations in major urban areas: a case study of Merseyside improved houses. Birmingham, 1977. pp. 113,26. *(Birmingham. University. Centre for Urban and Regional Studies. Research Memoranda. No. 60)*

—— Oldham.

GLODWICK ACTION GROUP. Evidence presented to the public inquiry on the Oldham - Waterloo Street compulsory purchase order, 1972. [Oldham, Oldham Community Development Project], 1973. 1 pamphlet (various foliations).

EAST GLODWICK GROUP. Do it our way: a report on the East Glodwick C[ompulsory] P[urchase] O[rder] prepared in conjunction with Oldham Community Development Project. [Oldham, Oldham Community Development Project, 1976]. 1 pamphlet (various pagings).

OLDHAM COMMUNITY DEVELOPMENT PROJECT. Fair rents and supplementary benefit rent allowances; or, How the Department of Health and Social Security supports slum landlords from public funds. Oldham, [1976]. 1 pamphlet (various pagings).

YEOMAN (ROD) Discount improvement?: a report on cost-saving approaches to housing improvement...for Oldham Community Development Project. [Oldham, Oldham Community Development Project, 1976]. pp. 51. *bibliog.*

BARR (ALAN) and URWIN (JAMES C.) Phased residential redevelopment: an account of a community based approach to redevelopment in Glodwick, Oldham. [Oldham], Oldham Community Development Project, [1977]. pp. 36.

EAST GLODWICK GROUP. How much longer?: a survey of conditions in the Bowden Street C[ompulsory] P[urchase] O[rder] area; prepared in conjunction with Oldham Community Development Project. [Oldham, Oldham Community Development Project, 1977]. 1 pamphlet (various pagings).

—— Scotland — Statistics.

HOUSING RETURN FOR SCOTLAND; ([pd. by] Scottish Development Department). q., D 1968- , with gap (D 1970). Edinburgh.

SCOTTISH HOUSING STATISTICS; [pd.by] Scottish Development Department. q., 1978(no.1)- Edinburgh. *Supersedes HOUSING RETURN FOR SCOTLAND.*

—— —— Glasgow.

WHEATLEY (JOHN) M.P. Eight-pound cottages for Glasgow citizens. Glasgow, [191-]. pp. 15.

—— West Midlands Standard Region.

WEST MIDLANDS JOINT MONITORING STEERING GROUP. A developing strategy for the West Midlands: general housing analysis, 1961-74. [Birmingham], 1976. pp. 113. *(Technical Reports)*

— United States.

NEIGHBORHOOD change: lessons in the dynamics of urban decay; [by] Charles L. Leven [and others]. New York, 1976. pp. 205.

The FORM of housing; edited by Sam Davis. New York, [1977]. pp. 282.

RESIDENTIAL location and urban housing markets; Gregory K. Ingram, editor. Cambridge, Mass., 1977. pp. 403. *bibliogs. (National Bureau of Economic Research. Conference on Research in Income and Wealth. Studies in Income and Wealth. vol. 43) Papers of a conference held in 1975.*

CONNECTICUT. Tri-State Regional Planning Commission. 1978. People, dwellings and neighbourhoods: the housing element of the regional comprehensive plan. New York, 1978. pp. 45.

MORRIS (EARL W.) and WINTER (MARY) Housing, family, and society. New York, [1978]. pp. 378. *bibliog.*

—— Finance.

CAPITAL markets and the housing sector: perspectives on financial reform; edited by Robert M. Buckley [and others]. Cambridge, Mass., [1977]. pp. 394. *bibliogs. Papers written for a study conducted by the Office of Economic Affairs of the U.S. Department of Housing and Urban Development.*

—— Law and legislation.

AMERICAN BAR ASSOCIATION. Advisory Commission on Housing and Urban Growth. Housing for all under law: new directions in housing, land use and planning law...; edited by Richard P. Fishman. Cambridge, Mass., [1978]. pp. 635.

— — Missouri.

NEIGHBORHOOD change: lessons in the dynamics of urban decay; [by] Charles L. Leven [and others]. New York, 1976. pp. 205.

— — New York (City).

TOLMAN (WILLIAM HOWE) Half a century of improved housing effort by the New York Association for Improving the Condition of the Poor: a paper. [New Haven, 1896]. pp. 287-402. *(From the Yale Review, November, 1896)*

— Western Samoa — Statistics.

WESTERN SAMOA. Census, 1971. Census of population and housing 1971. Apia, [1972?]. pp. 612.

HOUSING, COOPERATIVE

— Bibliography.

PUGH (HILARY A.) compiler. Housing co-operatives and co-ownership schemes. London, [1976]. pp. 11,5. *(U.K. Department of the Environment. Library. Bibliographies. No. 100)*

— Canada — Nova Scotia.

ROACH (WILLIAM M.) Co-operative housing in Nova Scotia, 1938-1973. [Halifax], Nova Scotia Housing Commission, [1974]. pp. 59.

— Russia.

GENDZEKHADZE (EKATERINA NIKOLAEVNA) Zhilishchno-stroitel'nye kooperativy v gorode i sele. Moskva, 1976. pp. 176.

— United Kingdom.

HOUSING CORPORATION. Housing policy: response by the Housing Corporation to the Secretary of State for the Environment on the government's consultative document. London, 1977. 1 pamphlet (unfoliated).

— — Scotland.

HOUSING CORPORATION. Housing policy: response by the Housing Corporation to the Secretary of State for Scotland on the government's consultative document. London, 1977. 1 pamphlet (unfoliated).

HOUSING, RURAL

— India.

INDIA. Study Group on Rural Housing. 1975. Report; [R. Gopalaswamy, chairman]. [Delhi], 1975. pp. 90.

— United Kingdom.

CONFERENCE ON THE HOUSING OF THE PEOPLE, 1891. Report of meeting; [and] paper on The home of the farm labourer; by E.O. Fordham. [London], 1891. pp. 19.

NATIONAL LAND AND HOME LEAGUE. [Pamphlets]. No. 5. Cottages for country people and how to get them. London, 1911. pp. (4).

RURAL housing: conference at Cambridge. [London, 1912]. pp. 6. *(Reprinted from Cambridgeshire Weekly News and Express, December 20th, 1912)*

HOUSING MANAGEMENT.

IRELAND, NORTHERN. Working Party on Tenant Participation and New Forms of Tenure. 1976. Report; [L.V.D. Calvert, chairman]. [Belfast], 1976. pp. 25.

LONDON. Greater London Council. Establishments Department. Behavioural Science Unit. The relationship between the GLC Housing Department, its tenants and the public; by the Behavioural Science Unit and an interdepartmental working party. London, [1977]. pp. 107. *(London. Greater London Council. Research Memoranda. 503)*

— Study and teaching — United Kingdom — Scotland.

SCOTLAND. Scottish Development Department. Scottish Housing Advisory Committee. 1977. Training for tomorrow: an action plan for Scottish housing; (report by a sub-committee); [W.A. Gordon Muir, chairman]. Edinburgh, 1977. pp. 64.

HOUSING POLICY

— France.

DUCLAUD-WILLIAMS (ROGER H.) The politics of housing in Britain and France. London, [1978]. pp. 280. *bibliog.*

— Italy.

ANGOTTI (THOMAS) Housing in Italy: urban development and political change. New York, 1977. pp. 106. *bibliogs.*

— United Kingdom.

KILLICK (ANGELA) Council house blues. London, [1976]. pp. 20.

BRITISH MARKET RESEARCH BUREAU. B[ritish] M[arket] R[esearch] B[ureau] housing consumer survey: a survey of attitudes towards current and alternative housing policies..., January 1976. London, National Economic Development Office, 1977. pp. 71.

ECONOMIC DEVELOPMENT COMMITTEE FOR BUILDING. Housing for all: a document for discussion. London, National Economic Development Office, 1977. pp. 50.

GILL (OWEN) Luke Street: housing policy, conflict and the creation of the delinquent area. London, 1977. pp. 207.

HOUSING CORPORATION. Housing policy: response by the Housing Corporation to the Secretary of State for the Environment on the government's consultative document. London, 1977. 1 pamphlet (unfoliated).

KIRBY (ANDREW) Housing action areas in Great Britain, 1975-77. Reading, 1977. pp. 31. *bibliog.* *(Reading. University. Department of Geography. Reading Geographical Papers. No.60)*

MANGAN (STEPHEN PAUL) Local housing and planning policies: a study of the south coast of England, 1961-1971. 1977. fo. 372. *bibliog.* Typescript. *Ph. D. (London) thesis: unpublished. This thesis is the property of London University and may not be removed from the Library.*

U.K. Housing Services Advisory Group. 1977. The assessment of housing requirements; [T.L. Jones, chairman] . [London, 1977]. pp. 67. *bibliogs.*

DUCLAUD-WILLIAMS (ROGER H.) The politics of housing in Britain and France. London, [1978]. pp. 280. *bibliog.*

LAMBERT (JOHN) Lecturer in Social Administration, and others. Housing policy and the state: allocation, access and control. London, 1978. pp. 178. *bibliog.*

NATIONAL UNION OF PUBLIC EMPLOYEES and SERVICES TO COMMUNITY ACTION AND TENANTS. Up against a brickwall: the dead-end in housing policy. London, 1978. pp. 60.

STAFFORD (D.C.) The economics of housing policy. London, [1978]. pp. 163. *bibliog.*

— — Birmingham.

LAMBERT (JOHN) Lecturer in Social Administration, and others. Housing policy and the state: allocation, access and control. London, 1978. pp. 178. *bibliog.*

— — London.

LONDON. Greater London Council. Inner London must live: a programme of action for housing and a better environment for the inner city. London, [1978]. pp. 11.

LONDON. Greater London Council. A new housing policy for London: inner London must live. [London, 1978]. pp. 35.

— — Scotland.

DUNCAN (T.L.C.) and COWAN (ROB H.) Housing action areas in Scotland. Glasgow, [1976]. pp. 39. *(Planning Exchange. Project: Housing Improvement Policies in Scotland. Research Papers. 3.)*

HOUSING CORPORATION. Housing policy: response by the Housing Corporation to the Secretary of State for Scotland on the government's consultative document. London, 1977. 1 pamphlet (unfoliated).

— United States.

A DECENT home and environment: housing urban America; edited by Donald Phares. Cambridge, Mass. [1977]. pp. 187. *bibliogs. Based on papers presented at a conference in Washington, D.C., in 1976, jointly sponsored by the American Real Estate and Urban Economics Association, and the Federal Home Loan Bank Board.*

The FORM of housing; edited by Sam Davis. New York, [1977]. pp. 282.

PHILPOTT (THOMAS LEE) The slum and the ghetto: neighborhood deterioration and middle- class reform, Chicago, 1880-1930. New York, 1978. pp. 428.

POLIKOFF (ALEXANDER) Housing the poor: the case for heroism. Cambridge, Mass., [1978]. pp. 216.

HOWARD (Sir EBENEZER).

FISHMAN (ROBERT) Urban utopias in the twentieth century: Ebenezer Howard, Frank Lloyd Wright and Le Corbusier. New York, [1977]. pp. 332. *bibliog.*

HOWARD LEAGUE FOR PENAL REFORM.

RYAN (MICK) The acceptable pressure group: inequality in the penal lobby: a case study of the Howard League and RAP. Farnborough, Hants., [1978]. pp. 165. *bibliog.*

HUALLAGA VALLEY

— Economic policy.

JUELICH (VOLKER) Colonizacion como complemento de la reforma agraria en la selva peruana: el valle de Huallaga Central. Santiago de Chile, 1974. pp. 170. *(Instituto Latinoamericano de Investigaciones Sociales. Estudios y Documentos. 30)*

HUASTEC INDIANS.

Los HUASTECAS en el desarrollo regional de Mexico; [by] Angel Bassols Batalla [and others]. Mexico, 1977. pp. 436. *bibliog.*

HUDDERSFIELD

— History.

STEPHENSON (CLIFFORD) The Ramsdens and their estate in Huddersfield: the town that bought itself. Almondbury, 1972. pp. 20.

HUGENBERG (ALFRED).

LEOPOLD (JOHN A.) Alfred Hugenberg: the radical nationalist campaign against the Weimar Republic. New Haven, 1977. pp. 298. *bibliog.*

HUGO (VICTOR MARIE) Vicomte.

MEHLMAN (JEFFREY) Revolution and repetition: Marx, Hugo, Balzac. Berkeley, Calif., [1977]. pp. 132.

HUMAN BEHAVIOUR.

HUMAN behavior and environment: advances in theory and research; edited by Irwin Altman and Joachim F. Wohlwill. New York, [1976] in progress. *bibliogs.*

COHEN (STANLEY) and TAYLOR (LAURIE) Escape attempts: the theory and practice of resistance to everyday life. Harmondsworth, 1978. pp. 232.

HUMAN CAPITAL.

HUMAN CAPITAL.

SHAEFFER (RUTH GILBERT) Monitoring the human resource system. New York, [1977]. pp. 41. *(National Industrial Conference Board. Conference Board Reports. No. 717)*

HUMAN ECOLOGY.

ACCADEMIA NAZIONALE DEI LINCEI. Atti dei Convegni Lincei. 16. Tavola rotonda: insediamenti territoriali e rapporti fra uomo e ambiente; criteri e metodologie. Roma, 9-10 dicembre 1974. Roma, 1976. pp. 218.

BOGUE (DONALD JOSEPH) and BOGUE (ELIZABETH J.) Essays in human ecology: 1. Chicago, [1976]. pp. 138. *bibliogs. (Chicago. University. Community and Family Study Center. Community and Family Monographs)*

DUPUY (JEAN PIERRE) and ROBERT (JEAN) La trahison de l'opulence. [Paris, 1976]. pp. 256. *bibliog.*

DOXIADES (KONSTANTINOS A.) Ecology and ekistics. Boulder, [1977]. pp. 91.

GUAY (LOUIS) The ecological differentiation of urban social space: Montreal, 1951-1971. 1976 [or rather 1977]. fo. 420. *bibliog.* Typescript. Ph.D. (London) thesis: unpublished. This thesis is the property of London University and may not be removed from the Library.

HARDIN (GARRETT JAMES) The limits of altruism: an ecologist's view of survival. Bloomington, Ind., [1977]. pp. 154. *(Indiana University. Patten Foundation. Lectures. 1976)*

SEMINAR ON SOCIAL WORK EDUCATION AND HUMAN SETTLEMENTS, VANCOUVER, 1976. People and places: social work education and human settlements. New York, [1977]. pp. 174. *Papers of a seminar sponsored by the International Association of Schools of Social Work.*

— Methodology.

CHAPMAN (GRAHAM PETER) Human and environmental systems: a geographer's appraisal. London, 1977. pp. 421. *bibliog.*

BENNETT (R.J.) and CHORLEY (RICHARD JOHN) Environmental systems: philosophy, analysis and control. London, [1978]. pp. 624. *bibliog.*

— Brazil.

DAVIS (SHELTON H.) Victims of the miracle: development and the Indians of Brazil. Cambridge, 1977. pp. 205. *bibliog.*

— Germany.

HOFFMEYER-ZLOTNIK (JUERGEN) Gastarbeiter im Sanierungsgebiet: das Beispiel Berlin- Kreuzberg. Hamburg, [1977]. pp. 191. *bibliog. (Hamburg. Hansische Universität. Seminar für Sozialwissenschaften. Beiträge zur Stadtforschung. Band 1)*

— Peru.

GADE (DANIEL W.) Plants, man and the land in the Vilcanota Valley of Peru. The Hague, 1975. pp. 240. *bibliog.*

HUMAN ENGINEERING.

McCORMICK (ERNEST JAMES) Human factors in engineering and design. 4th ed. New York, [1976]. pp. 491. *bibliogs.*

HUMAN GENETICS.

BURNET (Sir MACFARLANE) Endurance of life: the implications of genetics for human life. Cambridge, 1978. pp. 230.

HUMAN INFORMATION PROCESSING.

ANDERSON (JOHN ROBERT) Language, memory, and thought. New York, [1976]. pp. 546. *bibliogs.*

HUMANISM.

NAVASARDIAN (RAZMIK GAREGINOVICH) Formirovanie marksistskoi kontseptsii cheloveka: nachal'nyi period. Erevan, 1976. pp. 211. *bibliog.*

IDEI gumanizma v obshchestvenno-politicheskoi i filosofskoi mysli Belorussii: dooktiabr'skii period; redkollegiia K.P. Buslov [and others]. Minsk, 1977. pp. 279.

ULLMANN (WALTER) Medieval foundations of renaissance humanism. London, 1977. pp. 212.

HUMANITIES

— Study and teaching — Russia — Tajikistan.

RADZHABOV (ZARIF SHARIPOVICH) Ocherki istorii kul'turnogo stroitel'stva v Tadzhikistane; pod redaktsiei...G.A. Ashurova. Dushanbe, 1976. pp. 135.

HUME (DAVID).

BAGOLINI (LUIGI) David Hume e Adam Smith: elementi per una ricerca di filosofia giuridica e politica. Bologna, [1976]. pp. 106.

STROUD (BARRY) Hume. London, 1977. pp. 280. *bibliog.*

— Bibliography.

HALL (ROLAND) compiler. Fifty years of Hume scholarship: a bibliographical guide. Edinburgh, [1978]. pp. 150.

HUNGARIANS IN ROMANIA.

SCHÖPFLIN (GEORGE) The Hungarians of Rumania. London, 1978. pp. 20. *bibliog. (Minority Rights Group. Reports. No. 37)*

HUNGARY.

NEWS FROM HUNGARY; issued by Hungarian Embassy, London. bi-m. London. *Current issues only kept.*

— Census.

HUNGARY. Census, 1970. 1970 Hungarian census of population: information on the data collection and processing. Budapest, 1977. pp. 231. *Translation of vol. 31 of the 1970 census.*

— Constitutional history.

STROUP (EDSEL WALTER) Hungary in early 1848: the constitutional struggle against absolutism in contemporary eyes. Buffalo, N.Y., 1977. pp. 261. *bibliog. (New York State University. State University College, Buffalo. Program in East European and Slavic Studies. Publications. No.11)*

— Foreign relations — Germany.

SPIRA (THOMAS) German-Hungarian relations and the Swabian problem: from Károlyi to Gömbös, 1919-1936. New York, 1977. pp. 382. *bibliog. (East European Quarterly. East European Monographs. 25)*

— History — 1848-1849, Uprising of.

STROUP (EDSEL WALTER) Hungary in early 1848: the constitutional struggle against absolutism in contemporary eyes. Buffalo, N.Y., 1977. pp. 261. *bibliog. (New York State University. State University College, Buffalo. Program in East European and Slavic Studies. Publications. No.11)*

— — 1849-1867.

SZABAD (GYÖRGY) Hungarian political trends between the revolution and the compromise, 1849-1867. Budapest, 1977. pp. 184. *bibliog. (Magyar Tudományos Akadémia. Studia Historica. 128)*

— Politics and government.

SZABAD (GYÖRGY) Hungarian political trends between the revolution and the compromise, 1849-1867. Budapest, 1977. pp. 184. *bibliog. (Magyar Tudományos Akadémia. Studia Historica. 128)*

— Social conditions.

WORLD CONGRESS OF SOCIOLOGY, 8TH, 1974. Sociology in Hungary: recent issues and trends; ...Sociologie en Hongrie: sujets et tendances récents, etc. Budapest, 1974. pp. 176. *bibliog. (Magyar Tudományos Akadémia. Szociológia. 5. Supplement)*

WAYS of life: Hungarian sociological studies; edited by Miklós Szántó; (translated by Peter Szente). Budapest, [1977]. pp. 404. *bibliogs.*

HUNGER.

CASTRO (JOSÚE DE) The geopolitics of hunger. rev. ed. New York, [1977]. pp. 524. *Published in 1952 under the title Geography of hunger.*

HURRICANE PROTECTION

— Barbados.

BARBADOS. [Hurricane Relief Organisation]. 1947. Organisation of hurricane relief, 1947. [Bridgetown, 1947?]. pp. 13.

BARBADOS. [Hurricane Relief Organisation]. 1948. Handbook of the organisation of hurricane relief, 1948. [Bridgetown, 1948]. pp. 43.

BARBADOS. Hurricane Relief Organisation. 1949. The handbook of the...Organisation, 1949; (with Supplement: communications and legislation guide). Bridgetown, [1949]. 2 pts.

HUSÁK (GUSTÁV).

HUSÁK (GUSTÁV) Projevy a stati, únor 1972 - červen 1974. Praha, 1976. pp. 575.

HUTTERITES.

RYAN (JOHN) Professor of Geography, University of Winnipeg. The agricultural economy of Manitoba Hutterite colonies. Toronto, 1977. pp. 305. *bibliog. (Carleton University. Institute of Canadian Studies. Carleton Library. No. 101)*

HYDROCARBONS.

EUROPEAN COMMUNITIES. Statistical Office. Hydrocarbons: monthly bulletin. m., Ag 1977(no. 8)- Luxembourg. *Supersedes in part EUROPEAN COMMUNITIES. Statistical Office. Quarterly bulletin of energy statistics.*

HYDROGEN AS FUEL.

DICKSON (EDWARD M.) and others. The hydrogen energy economy: a realistic appraisal of prospects and impacts. New York, 1977. pp. 305.

HYGIENE, PUBLIC.

ORGANISATION FOR ECONOMIC CO-OPERATION AND DEVELOPMENT. Economic Policy Committee. Working Party No. 2. 1977. Public expenditure on health. [Paris], 1977. pp. 137. *bibliog. (Studies in Resource Allocation. No. 4)*

— Study and teaching.

CONFERENCE ON THE REGIONAL HEALTH UNIVERSITY, PARIS, 1975. Health, higher education and the community: towards a regional health university; report of an international conference at OECD, Paris, 15th-18th December, 1975. Paris, Organisation for Economic Co-operation and Development, 1977. pp. 350.

— Brazil.

BRAZIL. Superintendência do Desenvolvimento da Região Sul. Divisão de Saude. 1968. A saude no desenvolvimento da região sul; [by] Sergio Pacheco Ruschel [and] Natal Leonardelli. Pôrto Alegre, 1968. fo. 47. *bibliog.*

— Canada — Newfoundland.

NEWFOUNDLAND. Health Survey Committee. 1956. Newfoundland health survey report; [chairman, L.A. Miller]. [St. John's, 1956]. pp. 80. *bibliog.*

— — Saskatchewan.

SASKATCHEWAN. Department of Health. Annual report. a., 1976/77- Regina.

— France.

FRANCE. Ministère de la Santé Publique et de la Sécurité Sociale. Bulletin de statistiques de santé et de sécurité sociale. bi-m., Ja/F 1972 (no.1)- Paris.

— Germany.

GERMANY (BUNDESREPUBLIK). Statistisches Bundesamt. Ausgewählte Zahlen für das Gesundheitswesen. a., 1975- Wiesbaden. *(Gesundheitswesen. Reihe 1). Supersedes in part* GERMANY (BUNDESREPUBLIK). Statistisches Bundesamt. Gesundheitswesen.

— Italy.

TIMIO (MARIO) Classi sociali e malattie: per un nuovo rapporto medico-società. [Roma, 1976]. pp. 136.

— — Law and legislation.

CERBO (FERNANDO DI) La tutela della salute nell'ordinamento giuridico italiano. Roma, 1978. pp. 194.

— Japan.

JAPAN. Ministry of Health and Welfare. 1977. Guide to health and welfare services in Japan. Tokyo, 1977. pp. 59.

JAPAN. Ministry of Health and Welfare. 1977. Health and welfare services in Japan. Tokyo, 1977. pp. 170.

— New Zealand.

NEW ZEALAND. Department of Health. 1971. Chronological list of some noteworthy events in the history of New Zealand health services. [Wellington], 1971. pp. 26.

NEW ZEALAND. Department of Health. 1972. Department of Health: functions and responsibilities. [rev. ed.] Wellington, 1972. pp. 62.

— Nigeria.

BELLONCLE (GUY) and FOURNIER (GEORGES) Santé et développement en milieu rural africain: réflexions sur l'expérience nigérienne. Paris, [1975]. pp. 238. *bibliog.*

— Puerto Rico.

PUERTO RICO. Department of Health. 1971. Catalogo de programas y servicios. San Juan, [1971?]. pp. 69.

— Russia.

SOVETSKOE ZDRAVOOKHRANENIE; [pd. by] Ministerstvo Zdravookhraneniia [Russia]. m. (sometime bi-m.), 1943, nos. 1/2, 7/8-12; 1944, nos. 1/2-4/5, 7/8-12; 1945, 1950- with gap (My 1973). Moskva.

— — Uzbekistan.

KADYROV (ASADULLA ABDULLAEVICH) Stanovlenie i razvitie sovetskogo zdravookhraneniia v Uzbekistane; pod redaktsiei...B.D. Petrova. Tashkent, 1976. pp. 133. *bibliog.*

— Underdeveloped areas.

See UNDERDEVELOPED AREAS — Hygiene, Public.

— United Kingdom.

HOCKING (WILLIAM JOHN) Vicar of All Saints', Tufnell Park. The Church and sanitary progress: the annual sermon of the Church Sanitary Association, preached in All Saints Church, Tufnell Park, London, N., on Sunday morning, August 1, 1897. [London], 1897. pp. 15.

EUSTACE (G.W.) The effect of hygiene upon the wage-earning capacity of the people. London, 1910. pp. 385-395. *(Reprinted from vol. XXXI, No. 10 (1910) of the Journal of the Royal Sanitary Institute)*

HEALTH TRENDS: (a q. review for the medical profession issued by the Department of Health and Social Security and the Welsh Office [U.K.]). q., F 1971 (v.3, no.1)- London.

ROBINSON (DAVID) 1941- , and HENRY (STUART) Self-help and health: mutual aid for modern problems. London, 1977. pp. 164. *bibliog.*

PELLING (MARGARET) Cholera, fever and English medicine, 1825-1865. Oxford, 1978. pp. 342. *bibliog.*

— — Statistics.

HEALTH AND PERSONAL SOCIAL SERVICES STATISTICS FOR ENGLAND (formerly Digest of health statistics for England and Wales); ([pd. by] Department of Health and Social Security [U.K.]) . a., 1969 [1st]- London.

— — Wales — Statistics.

HEALTH AND PERSONAL SOCIAL SERVICES STATISTICS FOR WALES; ([pd. by] Welsh Office [U.K.]). a., 1974 (no.1)- London.

— United States — North Carolina.

NORTH CAROLINA. Office of Comprehensive Health Planning. 1969. Selected data for health planning in North Carolina; compiled by Alice M. Rupen. [Raleigh, 1969]. pp. 96.

HYPNOTISM.

FRANKEL (FRED H.) Hypnosis: trance as a coping mechanism. New York, [1976]. pp. 185. *bibliog.*

SHEEHAN (PETER W.) and PERRY (CAMPBELL W.) Methodologies of hypnosis: a critical appraisal of contemporary paradigms of hypnosis. Hillsdale, 1976. pp. 329. *bibliog.*

HYPOTHERMIA.

WICKS (MALCOLM) Old and cold: hypothermia and social policy. London, [1978]. pp. 208. *bibliog.*

IAGNOB RIVER.

See YAGNOB RIVER.

IAROSLAVSKII (EMEL'IAN MIKHAILOVICH).

SAVEL'EV (SERGEI NIKOLAEVICH) Emel'ian Iaroslavskii - propagandist marksistskogo ateizma. Leningrad, 1976. pp. 104. *bibliog.*

ICELAND

— Biography.

VEM är vem i Norden: biografisk handbok; huvudredaktör: Gunnar Sjöström. Stockholm, [1941]. pp. 1544.

— Discovery and exploration.

JONES (GWYN) The Norse Atlantic saga, being the Norse voyages of discovery and settlement to Iceland, Greenland, America. London, 1964. pp. 246. *bibliog. Includes translations, by the author, of the more important early documents.*

IDEALISM.

COUDENHOVE-KALERGI (RICHARD NICOLAUS) Count. Gebote des Lebens. Leipzig, [1931]. pp. 61. *Selected aphorisms.*

IDEALS (ALGEBRA).

GILMER (ROBERT) Multiplicative ideal theory. New York, 1972. pp. 609. *bibliog.*

IDENTITY.

The IDENTITIES of persons; edited by Amélie Oksenberg Rorty. Berkeley, Calif., 1976. pp. 333. *bibliog.*

CAUSEY (ROBERT L.) Unity of science. Dordrecht, [1977]. pp. 185. *bibliog.*

IDENTITY (PSYCHOLOGY).

LUNGHI (MARTIN EDWARD) Self identity, adaption to change and depression. 1977. fo. 257. *bibliog. Typescript. Ph.D. (London) thesis: unpublished. This thesis is the property of London University and may not be removed from the Library. Article in end pocket.*

— Research — United Kingdom.

A REPORT on the development of a standard research instrument for the study of identity structure; [by] R. Miles [and others]. [Bristol, Social Science Research Council Research Unit on Ethnic Relations], 1977. fo. 40. *(Research Notes)*

RESEARCH strategy in the identity structure research; [by] M. Fuller [and others]. [Bristol, Social Science Research Council Research Unit on Ethnic Relations], 1977. 1 vol. (various foliations). *(Research Notes)*

IDEOLOGY.

PLAMENATZ (JOHN PETROV) Ideology. London, 1971. pp. 148. *bibliog.*

BADIOU (ALAIN) and BALMES (FRANÇOIS) De l'idéologie. Paris, 1976. pp. 129.

POPOVICI (ELENA) Societate, ideologie, cunoaștere. București, 1976. pp. 248.

AKADEMIIA OBSHCHESTVENNYKH NAUK. Kafedra Teorii i Metodov Ideologicheskoi Raboty. Voprosy Teorii i Metodov Ideologicheskoi Raboty. vyp. 7. Sotsial'no-psikhologicheskie aspekty ideologicheskoi deiatel'nosti. Moskva, 1977. pp. 279.

BEJDA (VASIL) Politika a ideológia: k vývoju v strane a spoločnosti v nedávnom období. Bratislava, 1977. pp. 235.

IDEOLOGY and social change in Latin America; edited by June Nash [and others]. New York, [1977]. pp. 305. *bibliogs.*

SCHUBERT (GLENDON AUSTIN) Political attitudes and ideologies. Beverly Hills, [1977]. pp. 72. *bibliog.*

HISTOIRE des idéologies; sous la direction de François Châtelet et Gérard Mairet. [Paris, 1978]. 3 vols. *bibliog.*

MIDDENDORP (C.P.) Progressiveness and conservatism: the fundamental dimensions of ideological controversy and their relationship to social class. The Hague, [1978]. pp. 457. *bibliog.*

IGLESIAS POSSE (PABLO).

MARTINEZ DE SAS (MARIA TERESA) El socialismo y la España oficial: Pablo Iglesias, diputado a Cortes. Madrid, [1975]. pp. 358. *bibliog.*

IKONOMOV (TODOR).

IKONOMOV (TODOR) Memoari; (podbor i redaktsiia Toncho Zhechev). [Sofiia, 1973]. pp. 641.

ILE-DE-FRANCE

— Politics and government.

FRANC (MICHEL) and LECLERC (JEAN PIERRE) Les institutions de la région parisienne: du district à l'Ile-de-France. [n.p., 1977]. pp. 191. *bibliog.*

ILLEGITIMACY

— Canada — New Brunswick.

NEW BRUNSWICK. Law Reform Division. 1974. Status of children born outside marriage: their rights and obligations and the rights and obligations of their parents; a working report. [Fredericton], 1974. pp. 113.

ILLEGITIMACY(Cont.)

— New Zealand.

O'NEILL (DAVID P.) and others. Ex-nuptial children and their parents: a descriptive survey. Wellington, 1976. pp. 473. *(New Zealand. Department of Social Welfare. Research Section. Social Welfare Research Monographs. No. 2)*

— United Kingdom.

ONE-parent families; edited by Dulan Barber. [London, 1978]. pp. 179.

ILLICH (IVAN D.).

HORROBIN (DAVID FREDERICK) Medical hubris: a reply to Ivan Illich. Edinburgh, 1978. pp. 109.

ILLINOIS

— Politics and government.

WALLER (ROBERT A.) Rainey of Illinois: a political biography, 1903-34. Urbana, [1977]. pp. 260. *bibliog. (Illinois University. Illinois Studies in the Social Sciences. 60)*

ILLITERACY.

GOODY (JOHN RANKINE) The domestication of the savage mind. Cambridge, 1977. pp. 179. *bibliog.*

The POLITICS of literacy; edited by Martin Hoyles. London, 1977. pp. 211.

— Sudan.

SUDAN. National Council for Literacy and Adult Functional Education. 1974. National literacy programme, 1975-1979. [Khartoum, 1974?]. fo. 48.

— United Kingdom.

ADULT LITERACY RESOURCE AGENCY. Management Committee. Adult literacy: developments: report to the Secretary of State for Education and Science...on the...year's operation. a., 1976/7?(2nd)- London.

IMAGINARY WARS AND BATTLES.

HACKETT (Sir JOHN WINTHROP) and others. The Third World War: a future history. London, 1978. pp. 368.

IMAGINATION.

BRONOWSKI (JACOB) The origins of knowledge and imagination. New Haven, 1978. pp. 146. *(Yale University. Silliman Memorial Lectures. 1967)*

IMPEACHMENTS

— United States.

LABOVITZ (JOHN R.) Presidential impeachment. New Haven, 1978. pp. 268.

IMPERIAL PREFERENCE.

U.K. Customs and Excise Department. 1929. Imperial preference: history and results of existing preferences in the British tariff; note by the Board of Customs and Excise. [London], 1929. pp. 25.

IMPERIALISM.

COMMUNIST PARTY OF GREAT BRITAIN. For a Marxist Leninist School. District School Material. Outlines. No.2. Era of imperialism: the last phase of capitalism. [London, c. 1930]. pp. 24.

NCUBE (PATRICK D.) African socialism, imperialism, and a reconsidering of Trotsky's theory of the permanent revolution. Oslo, 1975. pp. 116, viii. *bibliog. (Oslo. Universitet. Instituttet for Sosiologi. Skriftserie. Nr. 29)*

La CRISE de l'impérialisme et la troisième guerre mondiale; [by] Noam Chomsky [and others]. Paris, 1976. pp. 282.

INTERNATIONAL THEORETICAL CONFERENCE, 1976. Lenin's doctrine of imperialism and the contemporary stage of the general crisis of capitalism. Prague, 1976. pp. 109. *(Marxism-Leninism and Our Time)*

OCHKOV (MIKHAIL SERGEEVICH) and others. "Filantropicheskie" fondy - vazhnoe ideologicheskoe oruzhie imperializma. Moskva, 1976. pp. 103. *(Akademiia Nauk SSSR. Institut Afriki. Nauchnyi Sovet po Problemam Zarubezhnykh Ideologicheskikh Techenii. Ideologicheskaia Bor'ba v Sovremennom Mire)*

AMIN (SAMIR) Imperialism and unequal development. Hassocks, [1977]. pp. 267. *Translation of his L'impérialisme et développement inégal.*

GEYER (DIETRICH) Der russische Imperialismus: Studien über den Zusammenhang von innerer und auswärtiger Politik, 1860-1914. Göttingen, 1977. pp. 344. *bibliog.*

HODGART (ALAN) The economics of European imperialism. [London, 1977]. pp. 88. *bibliog.*

LOUIS (WILLIAM ROGER) Imperialism at bay, 1941-1945: the United States and the decolonization of the British Empire. Oxford, 1977. pp. 595.

NABUDERE (DAN) The political economy of imperialism: its theoretical and polemical treatment from mercantilist to multilateral imperialism. London, [1977]. pp. 293. *bibliogs.*

WARREN (BILL) Imperialism and neo-colonialism. Belfast, 1977. pp. 32.

ARRIGHI (GIOVANNI) The geometry of imperialism: the limits of Hobson's paradigm; translated by Patrick Camiller. London, [1978]. pp. 160. *bibliog.*

ELDRIDGE (C.C.) Victorian imperialism. London, [1978]. pp. 248. *bibliogs.*

LEWIS (GORDON K.) Slavery, imperialism, and freedom: studies in English radical thought. New York, [1978]. pp. 346. *bibliog.*

MAGDOFF (HARRY) Imperialism: from the colonial age to the present: essays. New York, [1978]. pp. 279.

THORNTON (ARCHIBALD PATON) Imperialism in the twentieth century. London, 1978. pp. 363. *bibliog.*

— Congresses.

AFRO-ASIAN-LATIN AMERICAN PEOPLES' SOLIDARITY CONFERENCE, HAVANA, 1966. Première Conférence de Solidarité des Peuples d'Afrique, d'Asie, d'Amérique Latine: documents. Paris, [1966?]. fo. 27.

IMPORT SUBSTITUTION

— America, Latin.

LATIN America in the post-import-substitution era; edited by Werner Baer and Larry Samuelson. Oxford, 1977. pp. 168. *bibliogs. (World Development; incorporating New Commonwealth. vol. 5, nos. 1 and 2. Special Issue)*

INCENTIVES IN INDUSTRY

— Trinidad and Tobago.

ARMSTRONG (ERIC) Economist. An evaluation of incentive legislation in Trinidad and Tobago. [Mona], 1967. pp. 32. *(West Indies, University of the. Institute of Social and Economic Research. Studies in Regional Economic Integration. vol. 2, no. 5, part A)*

INCHCAPE GROUP.

GRIFFITHS (Sir PERCIVAL) A history of the Inchcape Group. London, 1977. pp. 211.

INCLOSURES.

YELLING (J. A.) Common field and enclosure in England, 1450-1850. London, 1977. pp. 255. *bibliog.*

INCOME

— Africa, East.

KITCHING (GAVIN N.) Economic and social inequality in rural East Africa: the present as a clue to the past. [Swansea, 1977]. pp. 65. *(Wales. University. University College of Swansea. Centre for Development Studies. Monographs. No. 1)*

— America, Latin.

MUSGROVE (PHILIP) Consumer behavior in Latin America: income and spending of families in ten Andean cities: an ECIEL study. Washington, D.C., [1978]. pp. 365.

— Australia — Tasmania.

CUTHBERTSON (A.G.) and others. Income levels and adjustment patterns in a rural community: Huon valley, Tasmania. Canberra, 1974. pp. 134. *(Australia. Bureau of Agricultural Economics. Industry Economics Monographs. No. 2)*

— Ireland (Republic).

NATIONAL ECONOMIC AND SOCIAL COUNCIL [EIRE]. Personal incomes by county in 1973; (by Miceal Ross and Roderick Jones, with the assistance of Eoin O'Malley). Dublin, Stationery Office, [1977]. pp. 93. *([Reports]. No. 30)*

— Israel.

HABIB (JACK) Poverty in Israel before and after receipt of public transfers. Jerusalem, 1974. pp. 129. *bibliog. (Israel. National Insurance Institute. Bureau of Research and Planning. Discussion Papers. 4)*

— Italy.

MODIGLIANI (FRANCO) and TARANTELLI (EZIO) Mercato del lavoro, distribuzione del reddito e consumi privati. Bologna, [1975]. pp. 342.

— New Zealand.

NEW ZEALAND. Department of Statistics. Statistics of incomes and income tax. a., 1971/72- Wellington. *Supersedes NEW ZEALAND. Department of Statistics. Incomes and income tax.*

NEW ZEALAND. Office of the Prime Minister. 1976. Incomes and prices. [Wellington], 1976. pp. 33.

— Poland.

KÜHNEMANN (ADOLF) Dynamika i struktura dochodów ludności województwa opolskiego w latach 1955-1972. Opole, 1976. pp. 187. *bibliog.*

— Russia.

MEHTA (VINOD K.) Soviet economic policy: income differentials in USSR. New Delhi, 1977. pp. 134. *bibliog.*

— Sweden.

GREVE (JOHN) Low incomes in Sweden;...background paper to Report No. 6: lower incomes. London, 1978. pp. 45. *(U.K. Royal Commission on the Distribution of Income and Wealth, 1974. Background Papers. No. 6) Report No. 6 published as British Parliamentary Paper Cmnd. 7175, Session 1977-78.*

— Trinidad and Tobago.

TRINIDAD AND TOBAGO. Central Statistical Office. 1973. Income; based on 1970 population census. [Port of Spain], 1973. pp. 88. *(Manpower Reports. vol. 1. no. 2)*

— United Kingdom.

SURVEY OF PERSONAL INCOMES, THE; ([pd. by] Board of Inland Revenue [U.K.]). a., 1969/70 [1st]- London.

U.K. Equal Opportunities Commission. 1977. Women and low incomes: a report based on evidence to the Royal Commission on Income Distribution and Wealth. [London], 1977. pp. 39.

INCOME TAX

U.K. Supplementary Benefits Commission. 1977. Low incomes: evidence to the Royal Commission on the Distribution of Income and Wealth. London, 1977. pp. 100. *(Supplementary Benefits Administration Papers. 6)*

U.K. Office of Population Censuses and Surveys. 1978. 1971 census: income follow-up survey. London, 1978. pp. 25. *(Studies on Medical and Population Subjects. No. 38)*

— **Yugoslavia.**

YUGOSLAVIA. Savezni Zavod za Statistiku. Studije, Analize i Prikazi. 83. Raspored opština u Jugoslaviji prema prosečnim neto ličnim primanjima po delatnostima januar-septembar 1973; Distribution of communes in Yugoslavia according to average net personal receipts by activities January-September 1973; [by] Božidar Stevanović. Beograd, 1976. pp. 79. *With English summary.*

YUGOSLAVIA. Savezni Zavod za Statistiku. Studije, Analize i Prikazi. 86. Prosečna neto lična primanja zaposlenih po opštinama u Jugoslaviji za period januar-septembar 1974. i njihov porast prema istom periodu 1973. godine; Average net personal receipts of the employed by communes in Yugoslavia for the period january-september [sic] 1974 and their increase compared with the same period 1973; [by] Božidar Stevanović. Beograd, 1977. pp. 72. *With English summary.*

INCOME DISTRIBUTION.

TINBERGEN (JAN) Income differences: recent research. Amsterdam, 1975. pp. 73. *bibliog. (Professor F. De Vries Foundation. Lectures)*

COWELL (FRANK A.) Measuring inequality. Oxford, 1977. pp. 193. *bibliog.*

EQUITY, income, and policy: comparative studies in three worlds of development; edited by Irving Louis Horowitz. New York, 1977. pp. 293. *bibliogs. Based on a series of panels organised by the American Political Science Association in 1976.*

STARK (THOMAS) The distribution of income in eight countries;...background paper to Report No. 5: third report on the standing reference. London, 1977. pp. 249. *(U.K. Royal Commission on the Distribution of Income and Wealth, 1974. Background Papers. No. 4) Report No. 5 published as British Parliamentary Paper Cmnd. 6999, Session 1977-78.*

UNITED NATIONS. Statistical Office. [Statistical Papers.] Series. M. No.61. Provisional guidelines on statistics of the distribution of income, consumption and accumuation of households. (ST/ESA/STAT/SER.M/61). New York, 1977. pp. 97.

HARRIS (DONALD J.) Capital accumulation and income distribution. Stanford, 1978. pp. 313. *bibliog.*

INCOME distribution and economic inequality; edited by Zvi Griliches [and others]. Frankfurt, 1978. pp. 335. *bibliogs. Papers of a symposium held in 1976 at Bad Homburg.*

— **Mathematical models.**

BARTELS (CORNELIS P.) Economic aspects of regional welfare: income distribution and unemployment. Leiden, 1977. pp. 261. *bibliog.*

HARTOG (JOOST) Personal income distribution: a multicapability theory with an application to tax incidence. 's-Gravenhage, 1978. pp. 296. *bibliog.*

— **Australia.**

AUSTRALIA. Commonwealth Bureau of Census and Statistics. 1975. Income distribution, 1968-69: consolidated and revised edition. Canberra, 1975. pp. 65.

— **Botswana.**

BOTSWANA. Central Statistics Office. 1976. The rural income distribution survey in Botswana, 1974/75. Gaborone, 1976. pp. 311. *bibliog.*

— **Brazil.**

BANCO DO NORDESTE DO BRASIL. Departamento de Estudos Econômicos do Nordeste. Distribuição e níveis da renda familiar no Nordeste urbano. [Fortaleza, 1969 or rather 1970]. pp. 45. *bibliog.*

CUPERTINO (FAUSTO) A concentração da renda no Brasil: o bolo esta mal dividido. Rio de Janeiro, 1976. pp. 123. *bibliog.*

— **Hong Kong.**

HSIA (RONALD) and CHAU (LAURENCE L.C.) Industrialisation, employment and income distribution: a case study of Hong Kong. London, [1978]. pp. 205. *bibliog. A study prepared for the International Labour Office within the framework of the Research Programme on Income Distribution and the World Employment Programme.*

— **Indonesia — Mathematical models.**

GUPTA (SYAMAPRASAD) and others. A model for income distribution, employment and growth: a case study of Indonesia. [Washington], International Bank for Reconstruction and Development, 1977. pp. 121. *bibliog. (World Bank Staff Occasional Papers. No. 24).*

— **Italy.**

SALARIO e crisi economica: dalla "ricetta Modigliani" al dopo- elezioni; interventi di [Nino] Andreatta [and others]; introduzione e cura di Ezio Tarantelli. Roma, [1976]. pp. 192.

— **Korea — Mathematical models.**

ADELMAN (IRMA) and ROBINSON (SHERMAN) Income distribution policy in developing countries: a case study of Korea. Stanford, 1978. pp. 346. *bibliog.*

— **Sahel.**

BERG (ELLIOT J.) The economic impact of drought and inflation in the Sahel. Ann Arbor, 1976. fo. 35. *(Michigan University. Center for Research on Economic Development. Discussion Papers. No. 51)*

— **South Africa.**

McGRATH (M.D.) Racial income distribution in South Africa. Durban, 1977. pp. 31. *(Natal University. Department of Economics. Black/White Income Gap Project. Interim Research Reports. No. 2)*

— **Sweden.**

SWEDEN. Statistiska Centralbyrån. Inkomstfördelningsundersökningen: [preliminary results]. a., 1974- Stockholm.

— **Underdeveloped areas.**

See UNDERDEVELOPED AREAS — Income distribution.

— **United Kingdom.**

DINWIDDY (ROBERT) and REED (DEREK) The effects of certain social and demographic changes on income distribution;...background paper to Report No. 5: third report on the standing reference. London, 1977. pp. 168. *bibliog. (U.K. Royal Commission on the Distribution of Income and Wealth, 1974. Background Papers. No. 3) Report No. 5 published as British Parliamentary Paper Cmnd. 6999, Session 1977-78.*

— — **Mathematical models.**

ARNOLD (BARRY C.) and LAGUNA (LEONOR) On generalized Pareto distributions with applications to income data. Ames, Iowa, 1977. pp. 48. *bibliog. (Iowa State University of Science and Technology. Department of Economics. International Studies in Economics. Monographs. No. 10)*

— **United States.**

ALEXANDER (ARTHUR J.) Structure, income and race: a study in internal labour markets. Santa Monica, 1970. pp. 30. *(Rand Corporation. [Rand Reports]. 577)*

CURTIN (RICHARD T.) Income equity among U.S. workers: the bases and consequences of deprivation. New York, [1977]. pp. 152. *bibliog.*

GARFINKEL (IRWIN) and HAVEMAN (ROBERT H.) Earnings capacity, poverty, and inequality. New York, [1977]. pp. 118. *bibliog. (Wisconsin University, Madison. Institute for Research on Poverty. Monograph Series)*

GILLARD (QUENTIN) Incomes and accessibility: metropolitan labor force participation, commuting and income differentials in the United States, 1960- 1970. Chicago, 1977. pp. 106. *bibliog. (Chicago. University. Department of Geography. Research Papers. No. 175)*

IMPROVING measures of economic well-being; edited by Marilyn Moon [and] Eugene Smolensky. New York, [1977]. pp. 239. *bibliogs. (Wisconsin University, Madison. Institute for Research on Poverty. Monograph Series)*

LINDERT (PETER H.) Fertility and scarcity in America. Princeton, [1978]. pp. 395.

— **Venezuela.**

URDANETA (LOURDES) Distribucion del ingreso: analisis del caso venezolano. [Caracas, 1977]. pp. 382. *bibliog. (Banco Central de Venezuela. Coleccion de Estudios Economicos. 5)*

INCOME MAINTENANCE PROGRAMMES

— **United States.**

The NEW Jersey income-maintenance experiment. New York, [1976-77]. 3 vols. *(Wisconsin University, Madison. Institute for Research on Poverty. Monograph Series)*

INCOME support policies for the aged; edited by G. S. Tolley [and] Richard V. Burkhauser. Cambridge, Mass., [1977]. pp. 194. *bibliogs. Papers presented at a conference held at the University of Chicago in 1976.*

WELFARE in rural areas: the North Carolina-Iowa Income Maintenance Experiment; editors John L. Palmer [and] Joseph A. Pechman. Washington, D.C., [1978]. pp. 273. *(Brookings Institution. Brookings Studies in Social Experimentation) Papers presented at a conference held in Washington, D.C., in 1977.*

INCOME TAX

— **Africa.**

SEMINAR ON ADMINISTRATION OF INCOME TAX IN AFRICAN COUNTRIES, DAKAR, 1968. Report of the Seminar...[held at] Dakar, Senegal, 25 March to 5 April 1968. (ST/TAO/SER.C/104). New York, United Nations, 1968. pp. 33. *bibliog.*

— **Australia.**

AUSTRALIA. Commonwealth Treasury. 1974. Personal income tax: personal allowances. Canberra, 1974. pp. 36. *(Treasury Taxation Papers. No. 7)*

AUSTRALIA. Commonwealth Treasury. 1974. Personal income tax: the income base. Canberra, 1974. pp. 56. *(Treasury Taxation Papers. No. 3)*

AUSTRALIA. Commonwealth Treasury. 1974. Personal income tax: the rate scale. Canberra, 1974. pp. 45. *(Treasury Taxation Papers. No. 4)*

AUSTRALIA. Commonwealth Treasury. 1974. Personal income tax: the tax unit. Canberra, 1974. pp. 20. *(Treasury Taxation Papers. No. 6)*

— **Austria.**

AUSTRIA. Statistisches Zentralamt. Lohnsteuerstatistik. a., 1973- Wien.

— **Ireland (Republic).**

DOWLING (BRENDAN R.) The income sensitivity of the personal income tax base in Ireland, 1947-1972. Dublin, 1977. pp. 82. *bibliog. (Economic and Social Research Institute. Papers. No. 86)*

INCOME TAX (Cont.)

NATIONAL ECONOMIC AND SOCIAL COUNCIL [EIRE]. Integrated approaches to personal income taxes and transfers; (by Brendan Dowling). Dublin, Stationery Office, [1977]. pp. 100. *bibliog.* ([Reports]. No. 37)

— Kenya.

KENYA. Central Bureau of Statistics. 1976. Income tax statistics report: year of income 1973. [Nairobi], 1976. 1 vol. (various pagings).

— New Zealand.

NEW ZEALAND. Department of Statistics. Statistics of incomes and income tax. a., 1971/72- Wellington. *Supersedes NEW ZEALAND. Department of Statistics. Incomes and income tax.*

— Poland.

GUTERMANN (CZESŁAW) Tabele podatków obrotowego i dochodowego dla rzemiosła i innej działalności zarobkowej według stanu prawnego na dzień 15 maja 1975 r. Warszawa, 1975. pp. 111.

— United Kingdom.

FEDERATION OF BRITISH CRAFT SOCIETIES. Income tax and the craftsman. London, 1977. pp. 14.

— — Isle of Man.

ISLE OF MAN. Income Tax Commission. 1957. Third interim report; [W.P. Cowley, chairman]. [Douglas, 1957]. pp. 7.

ISLE OF MAN. Income Tax Commission. 1964. Eighth interim report; [J.B. Bolton, chairman]. [Douglas, 1964]. pp. 8.

— United States.

COMPREHENSIVE income taxation; Joseph A. Pechman, editor: a report of a conference sponsored by the Fund for Public Policy Research and the Brookings Institution. Washington, D.C., [1977]. pp. 311. *bibliog.* (*Brookings Institution. Studies of Government Finance*)

— Yugoslavia.

YUGOSLAVIA. Savezni Zavod za Statistiku. Studije, Analize i Prikazi. 84. Obveznici poreza iz ukupnog prihoda građana u 1975. godini; Tax payers in 1975. Beograd, 1976. pp. 42. *With English summary.*

INCUNABULA

— Bibliography.

CATALOGUE of valuable printed books from the Broxbourne Library illustrating the spread of printing: (the first portion, Abbeville-Lyons); the property of John Ehrman. London, 1977. pp. 220.

INDEXATION (ECONOMICS).

JUD (G. DONALD) Inflation and the use of indexing in developing countries. New York, 1978. pp. 220. *bibliog.*

RAFFAY (HARALD VON) Erscheinungsformen und Auswirkungen von Indexkoppelungen. Berlin, [1978]. pp. 154. *bibliog.*

INDIA.

INDIA NEWS; [pd.by] Office of the High Commissioner for India. w., current issues only. London.

— Boundaries — China.

EEKELEN (WILLEM FREDERIK VAN) Indian foreign policy and the border dispute with China. The Hague, 1964. pp. 220. *bibliog.*

— Commerce.

INDIA. Office of the Economic Adviser. 1949. The review of the economic conditions of India with special reference to foreign trade in 1948-49. Delhi, [1949]. pp. 238.

VARSHNEY (ROSHAN LAL) A strategy for exports. Bombay, [1975]. pp. 16.

— — United Kingdom.

TOMLINSON (JAMES DAVID) Anglo-Indian economic relations, 1913 to 1928, with special reference to the cotton trade. [1977]. fo. 233. *bibliog.* Typescript: unpublished. Ph.D. (London) thesis. This thesis is the property of London University and may not be removed from the Library.

— Constitution.

INDIA. Constitution. 1975. The constitution of India, as modified up to the 1st August, 1975. [Delhi, 1975]. pp. 319.

KOGEKAR (S.V.) Revision of the constitution. Poona, [1976]. pp. 19. (*Gokhale Institute of Politics and Economics. R.R. Kale Memorial Lectures. 1976*)

INDIA. Constitution. 1977. The constitution of India, as modified up to the 1st June, 1977. [Delhi, 1977]. pp. 482.

TRIPATHI (P.K.) Amending the constitution. New Delhi, [1977]. pp. 19.

— Economic conditions.

INDIA. Office of the Economic Adviser. 1949. The review of the economic conditions of India with special reference to foreign trade in 1948-49. Delhi, [1949]. pp. 238.

SHARMA (SHYAM LAL) Some trends of capitalist concentration in India. Aligarh, [1955]. pp. 218,v. *bibliog.*

IENGAR (H.V.R.) Monetary policy and economic growth. Bombay, 1962. pp. 295. *bibliog. Speeches as Governor of the Reserve Bank of India, 1957-1962.*

GOPAL (LALLANJI) The economic life of northern India, c.A.D. 700-1200. Varanasi, [1965]. pp. 305. *bibliog.* Ph.D. thesis, University of London.

INDIAN INVESTMENT CENTRE. Restrictions on exports in foreign collaboration agreements in India. (TD/B/389). New York, United Nations, 1971. pp. 28.

LAMB (HELEN BOYDEN) Studies on India and Vietnam. New York, [1976]. pp. 267.

PACHAURI (RAJENDRA KUMAR) Energy and economic development in India. New York, 1977. pp. 185.

— — Statistics.

BIRLA INSTITUTE OF SCIENTIFIC RESEARCH. Economic Research Division. World economic profile: selected countries. Delhi, 1975. pp. 199.

— Economic history.

The IMPERIAL impact: studies in the economic history of Africa and India; edited by Clive Dewey and A.G. Hopkins. London, 1978. pp. 409. (*London. University. Institute of Commonwealth Studies. Commonwealth Papers. 21*)

— Economic policy.

INDIA. Planning Commission. 1953. The first five year plan, 1951-56: summary of recommendations. [Delhi, 1953]. pp. 130.

INDIA. Planning Commission. 1962. Second five year plan: progress report, 1959-60. Delhi, 1962. pp. 195.

GANDHI (INDIRA) Consolidating national gains: speeches. [Delhi, Directorate of Advertising and Visual Publicity, Ministry of Information and Broadcasting, 1976]. pp. 266.

INDIA. Planning Commission. 1976. Fifth five year plan, 1974-79. [Delhi, 1976]. pp. 162.

RAKSHIT (GANGADHAR) Poverty and planning in India. Calcutta, 1977. pp. 160. *bibliog.*

AMBIRAJAN (SRINIVASA) Classical political economy and British policy in India. Cambridge, 1978. pp. 301. *bibliog.* (*Cambridge. University. Centre of South Asian Studies. Cambridge South Asian Studies. 21*)

INDIA. Planning Commission. 1978. Draft five year plan, 1978-83. [New Delhi], 1978. pp. 276.

— — Mathematical models.

BERGMANN (THEODOR) The development models of India, the Soviet Union and China: a comparative analysis. Assen, 1977. pp. 255. *bibliog.* (*European Society for Rural Sociology. Publications. 1.*)

— Executive departments.

INDIA. Administrative Reforms Wing. Report. a., 1973/74-1974/75. New Delhi. *From 1975/76 included in INDIA. Department of Personnel and Administrative Reforms. Report.*

INDIA. Department of Personnel and Administrative Reforms. Report. a., 1975/76- New Delhi. *File includes Supplement, 1976/77. From 1975/76 file includes report of Administrative Reforms Wing.*

— Famines.

JAMES (S.H.) Letter to H.M. Secretary of State for India: subject: canals, irrigation, transport, etc., in connection with Indian famines. Uppingham, 1878. pp. 12.

WEDDERBURN (Sir WILLIAM) The skeleton at the "Jubilee" feast: being a series of suggestions towards the prevention of famine in India. London, 1897. pp. 20. (*Indian National Congress. British Committee. Congress Green Books. No. 1[a]*)

— Foreign economic relations — United Kingdom.

ALL INDIA CONGRESS COMMITTEE. Select Committee on the Financial Obligations between Great Britain and India. Report. vol.1. Bombay, [1931]. pp. 70,ix,ii.

— Foreign relations.

GANDHI (INDIRA) Consolidating national gains: speeches. [Delhi, Directorate of Advertising and Visual Publicity, Ministry of Information and Broadcasting, 1976]. pp. 266.

FOREIGN AFFAIRS RECORD; [pd. by] Ministry of External Affairs, External Publicity Division, India. m. n.p. *Current issues only kept.*

— — China.

EEKELEN (WILLEM FREDERIK VAN) Indian foreign policy and the border dispute with China. The Hague, 1964. pp. 220. *bibliog.*

— — Israel.

TAYAB (MOHAMMAD) Indo-Israel relations: a study of Indo-Israel collusion against the Arab world. Lahore, 1974. pp. 47.

— — Russia.

DRIEBERG (TREVOR) and others. Towards closer Indo-Soviet cooperation. Delhi, [1974]. pp. 182.

— Full employment policies.

INDIA. Committee on Unemployment. Working Group on Plan. 1974. Report...vol. 1; [Arjun Arora, chairman]. [Delhi, 1974]. pp. 425.

— History — To 1500.

GOPAL (LALLANJI) The economic life of northern India, c.A.D. 700-1200. Varanasi, [1965]. pp. 305. *bibliog.* Ph.D. thesis, University of London.

— — 1500-1765, European settlements.

MURPHEY (RHOADS) The outsiders: the western experience in India and China. Ann Arbor, [1977]. pp. 299. *bibliog.* (*Michigan University. Center for Chinese Studies. Michigan Studies on China*)

— — 1765-1947, British occupation.

SPANGENBERG (BRADFORD) British bureaucracy in India: status, policy and the I.C.S., in the late 19th century. Columbia, Mo., 1976. pp. 380. *bibliog.*

MURPHEY (RHOADS) The outsiders: the western experience in India and China. Ann Arbor, [1977]. pp. 299. *bibliog. (Michigan University. Center for Chinese Studies. Michigan Studies on China)*

—— 1857-1858, Sepoy Rebellion.

PEMBLE (JOHN) The Raj, the Indian Mutiny and the kingdom of Oudh, 1801- 1859. Rutherford, N.J., [1977]. pp. 303. *bibliog.*

HIBBERT (CHRISTOPHER) The Great Mutiny, India, 1857. London, 1978. pp. 472. *bibliog.*

— Industries.

SHARMA (SHYAM LAL) Some trends of capitalist concentration in India. Aligarh, [1955]. pp. 218,v. *bibliog.*

INDIA. Directorate of Exhibitions and Commercial Publicity. 1972. Profile of Indian industry. New Delhi, 1972. pp. 140. *Supplement to Economic and Commercial News.*

PENDSE (D.R.) Recession in Indian industry: causes, consequences and prospects. Bombay, 1975. pp. 12.

INDIA. Development Commissioner (Small Scale Industries). 1976- . All-India report on the census of small scale industries. [Delhi], 1976 in progress.

HAJRA (S.) and KUMAR (ASHOK) Production function in Indian industry. New Delhi, [1977]. pp. 321. *bibliog.*

— Nationalism.

BHUYAN (ARUN CHANDRA) The quit India movement: the Second World War and Indian nationalism. New Delhi, [1975]. pp. 262. *bibliog.*

KARUNAKARAN (KOTTA P.) Indian politics from Dadabhai Naoroji to Gandhi: a study of the political ideas of modern India. New Delhi, 1975. pp. 226. *bibliog.*

McLANE (JOHN R.) Indian nationalism and the early Congress. Princeton, [1977]. pp. 404. *bibliog.*

— Parliament.

INDIA. Ministry of Information and Broadcasting. Publications Division. 1977. The Indian parliament. 2nd rev. ed. [New Delhi, 1977]. pp. 52.

—— Rules and practice.

INDIA. Parliament. Lok Sabha. Secretariat. 1977. Directions by the Speaker under the rules of procedure and conduct of business in Lok Sabha. 3rd ed. New Delhi, 1977. pp. 125.

INDIA. Parliament. Lok Sabha. Secretariat. 1977. Rules of procedure and conduct of business in Lok Sabha. 6th ed. New Delhi, 1977. pp. 250.

—— Lok Sabha.

INDIA. Parliament. Lok Sabha. Secretariat. 1977. Directions by the Speaker under the rules of procedure and conduct of business in Lok Sabha. 3rd ed. New Delhi, 1977. pp. 125.

INDIA. Parliament. Lok Sabha. Secretariat. 1977. Rules of procedure and conduct of business in Lok Sabha. 6th ed. New Delhi, 1977. pp. 250.

— Politics and government.

GANDHI (INDIRA) Consolidating national gains: speeches. [Delhi, Directorate of Advertising and Visual Publicity, Ministry of Information and Broadcasting, 1976]. pp. 266.

ELDERSVELD (SAMUEL JAMES) and AHMED (BASHIRUDDIN) Citizens and politics: mass political behavior in India. Chicago, 1978. pp. 351.

—— 1765-1947.

KARUNAKARAN (KOTTA P.) Indian politics from Dadabhai Naoroji to Gandhi: a study of the political ideas of modern India. New Delhi, 1975. pp. 226. *bibliog.*

NANDA (B.R.) Gokhale: the Indian moderates and the British Raj. Delhi, 1977. pp. 520. *bibliog.*

—— 1800-1899.

McLANE (JOHN R.) Indian nationalism and the early Congress. Princeton, [1977]. pp. 404. *bibliog.*

—— 1919-1947.

BIJAY CHAND MAHTAB, Maharajadhiraja Bahadur of Burdwan. The Indian horizon. London, 1932. pp. 106.

BHUYAN (ARUN CHANDRA) The quit India movement: the Second World War and Indian nationalism. New Delhi, [1975]. pp. 262. *bibliog.*

—— 1947- .

HALAYYA (MUTHIA) Emergency: a war on corruption. New Delhi, 1975. pp. 164. *bibliog.*

KARLEKAR (HIRANMAY) Indira Gandhi: an interview. [New Delhi, 1976]. pp. 20. *(Repr. from the Hindustan Times of Feb. 8 1976)*

HENDERSON (MICHAEL DENNIS) Experiment with untruth: India under emergency. [Delhi, 1977]. pp. 250.

KAMAL (K.L.) and MEYER (RALPH C.) Democratic politics in India. New Delhi, [1977]. pp. 288.

MURTHY (R.K.) The cult of the individual: a study of Indira Gandhi. New Delhi, 1977. pp. 152.

SELBOURNE (DAVID) An eye to India: the unmasking of a tyranny. Harmondsworth, 1977. pp. 561. *bibliog.*

SINHA (SACHCHIDANANDA) Emergency in perspective: reprieve and challenge. London, 1977. pp. 122.

DUBÉ (RANI) The evil within; edited by Timeri Murari. London, 1978. pp. 160.

MEHTA (VED) The new India. Harmondsworth, 1978. pp. 174.

NARAYAN (JAYAPRAKASH) The essential JP: the philosophy and prison diary of Jayaprakash Narayan; edited by Satish Kumar. Dorchester, 1978. pp. 152.

— Population.

BANSIL (PURAN CHAND) India's food resources and population: a historical and analytical study. Bombay, [1958]. pp. 252. *bibliog.*

INDIA. Census. Papers. 1974. No.2. Census of India, 1971: series 1: India...: age and life tables; one per cent sample. [Delhi, 1974]. pp. 16. *(India. Census, 1971. Miscellaneous Studies)*

— Relations (general) with Europe.

MURPHEY (RHOADS) The outsiders: the western experience in India and China. Ann Arbor, [1977]. pp. 299. *bibliog. (Michigan University. Center for Chinese Studies. Michigan Studies on China)*

— Relations (general) with the United States.

KAMATH (MADHAV V.) The United States and India, 1776-1976. Washington, Embassy of India, [1976]. pp. 226. *bibliog.*

— Religion.

INDIA. Census. Papers. 1972. No. 2. Census of India, 1971: series 1: India...: religion. [Delhi, 1972]. pp. 110.

— Rural conditions.

ISHWARAN (KARIGOUDAR) A populistic community and modernization in India. Leiden, 1977. pp. 122.

SRINIVAS (MYSORE NARASIMHACHAR) Science, technology and rural development in India. [Poona], 1977. pp. 15. *(Gokhale Institute of Politics and Economics. R.R. Kale Memorial Lectures. 1977)*

INDIAN OCEAN REGION.

— Social conditions.

BIJAY CHAND MAHTAB, Maharajadhiraja Bahadur of Burdwan. The Indian horizon. London, 1932. pp. 106.

DIMENSIONS of social change in India; edited by M.N. Srinivas [and others]. Bombay, 1977. pp. 518. *bibliogs. Papers presented at a national seminar organized by the Institute for Social and Economic Change, 1972.*

— Social policy.

INDIA. Planning Commission. 1953. The first five year plan, 1951-56: summary of recommendations. [Delhi, 1953]. pp. 130.

INDIA. Planning Commission. 1962. Second five year plan: progress report, 1959-60. Delhi, 1962. pp. 195.

GANDHI (INDIRA) Consolidating national gains: speeches. [Delhi, Directorate of Advertising and Visual Publicity, Ministry of Information and Broadcasting, 1976]. pp. 266.

INDIA. Planning Commission. 1976. Fifth five year plan, 1974-79. [Delhi, 1976]. pp. 162.

INDIA. Planning Commission. 1978. Draft five year plan, 1978-83. [New Delhi], 1978. pp. 276.

INDIA-PAKISTAN CONFLICT, 1971.

FARUKI (KEMAL A.) India's role in East Pakistan crisis: an analysis of legal and political aspects; a talk delivered at the Pakistan Institute of International Affairs, Karachi, May 7, 1971. [Karachi, Department of Films and Publications, 1971]. pp. 14.

INDIA. Permanent Representative in the United Nations. 1971. U.N. Assembly session: statement of Shri Samar Sen... October 5, 1971. [New Delhi, 1971]. pp. 5.

HAENDEL (DAN) The process of priority formulation: U.S. foreign policy in the Indo-Pakistan war of 1971. Boulder, 1977. pp. 428. *bibliog.*

SALIK (SIDDIQ) Witness to surrender. Karachi, 1977. pp. 245.

INDIAN NATIONAL CONGRESS.

ARNOLD (DAVID) The Congress in Tamilnad: nationalist politics in south India, 1919-1937. London, 1977. pp. 252. *bibliogs. (Australian National University. Monographs on South Asia. No. 1)*

McLANE (JOHN R.) Indian nationalism and the early Congress. Princeton, [1977]. pp. 404. *bibliog.*

NANDA (B.R.) Gokhale: the Indian moderates and the British Raj. Delhi, 1977. pp. 520. *bibliog.*

INDIAN OCEAN REGION.

KUNERT (DIRK) Wars of national liberation, the super-powers and the Afro-Asian ocean region. Braamfontein, 1977. pp. 68. *(South African Institute of International Affairs. Special Studies)*

— Defences.

TAHTINEN (DALE R.) and LENCZOWSKI (JOHN) Arms in the Indian Ocean: interests and challenges. Washington, D.C., [1977]. pp. 84. *(American Enterprise Institute for Public Policy Research. AEI Studies. 145)*

— Foreign relations.

SHAW (K.E.) and THOMSON (GEORGE G.) The Straits of Malacca: in relation to the problems of the Indian and Pacific Oceans. Singapore, 1973. pp. 174.

—— United States.

BEZBORUAH (MONORANJAN) U.S. strategy in the Indian Ocean. New York, 1977. pp. 268. *bibliog.*

— Politics and government.

BEZBORUAH (MONORANJAN) U.S. strategy in the Indian Ocean. New York, 1977. pp. 268. *bibliog.*

INDIAN OCEAN REGION.(Cont.)

TAHTINEN (DALE R.) and LENCZOWSKI (JOHN) Arms in the Indian Ocean: interests and challenges. Washington, D.C., [1977]. pp. 84. *(American Enterprise Institute for Public Policy Research. AEI Studies. 145)*

INDIANS.

The NATIVE population of the Americas in 1492; edited by William M. Denevan. [Madison, 1976]. pp. 353. *bibliog.*

— Bibliography.

COMAS CAMPS (JUAN) compiler. Bibliografia selectiva de las culturas indigenas de America. Mexico, Organization of American States, 1953. pp. 284, 4 fold. maps.

— Religion and mythology.

LÉVI-STRAUSS (CLAUDE) The origin of table manners; introduction to a science of mythology, 3; translated from the French by John and Doreen Weightman. London, 1978. pp. 551. *bibliog.*

INDIANS, TREATMENT OF.

JORNADAS AMERICANISTAS DE LA UNIVERSIDAD DE VALLADOLID, 3AS, 1974. Estudios sobre politica indigenista española en America. Valladolid, 1975-77. 3 vols.

— America, Latin.

VILLAMARIN (JUAN A.) and VILLAMARIN (JUDITH E.) Indian labor in mainland colonial Spanish America. Newark, Del., 1975. pp. 175. *bibliog.*

— Ecuador.

BOSSANO (GUILLERMO) El Indio, problema olvidado. Quito, 1967. pp. 53.

INDIANS IN LITERATURE.

BARNETT (LOUISE K.) The ignoble savage: American literary racism, 1790-1890. Westport, Conn., 1975. pp. 220. *bibliog.*

INDIANS OF CENTRAL AMERICA

— Guatemala.

GUATEMALA INDIGENA: publicacion trimestral del Instituto Indigenista Nacional. irreg., Ag 1968 (2a epoca, v.4, no.1)- Guatemala. *Susp. pbln. Je 1963-Jl 1968.*

INDIANS OF MEXICO.

URIBE VILLEGAS (OSCAR) Un mapa del monolingüismo y el bilingüismo de los indigenas de Mexico en 1960. Mexico, 1970. pp. 33, with map.

— Dances.

BRICKER (VICTORIA REIFLER) Ritual humor in highland Chiapas. Austin, [1973]. pp. 257. *bibliog.*

— History.

CASTILLO FARRERAS (VICTOR M.) Estructura economica de la sociedad Mexica segun las fuentes documentales. Mexico, 1972. pp. 197. *bibliog.*

— Religion and mythology.

HUNT (EVA) The transformation of the hummingbird: cultural roots of a Zinacantecan mythical poem. Ithaca, 1977. pp. 312. *bibliog.*

— Rites and ceremonies.

VOGT (EVON ZARTMAN) Tortillas for the gods: a symbolic analysis of Zinacanteco rituals. Cambridge, Mass., [1976]. pp. 234. *bibliog.*

— Oaxaca.

BARABAS (ALICIA) and BARTOLOME (MIGUEL) Hydraulic development and ethnocide: the Mazatec and Chinantec people of Oaxaca, Mexico. Copenhagen, 1973. pp. 20. *bibliog. (International Work Group for Indigenous Affairs. Documents. 15)*

INDIANS OF NORTH AMERICA

— Languages.

STUDIES in American Indian languages; edited by Jesse Sawyer. Berkeley, [1971] repr. 1973. pp. 317. *(California University. Publications in Linguistics. 65)*

— Mixed bloods.

ADAMS (HOWARD) Prison of grass: Canada from the native point of view. Toronto, 1975. pp. 238. *bibliog.*

— Canada.

SANDERS (DOUGLAS ESMOND) Native people in areas of internal national expansion: Indians and Inuit in Canada. Copenhagen, 1973. pp. 39. *(International Work Group for Indigenous Affairs. Documents. 14)*

— — Law and legislation.

SANDERS (DOUGLAS ESMOND) Joint meeting on legal status of Indians in the Maritimes: address. Toronto, 1970. pp. 23.

— — British Columbia — Bibliography.

HOOVER (ALAN L.) and KEDDIE (GRANT R.) compilers. A selected list of publications on the Indians of British Columbia. Victoria, British Columbia Provincial Museum, 1976. pp. 30.

— — New Brunswick — Psychology.

NEW BRUNSWICK. Human Rights Commission. 1972. Some personality factors of matched groups of New Brunswick Indians and Whites. Frederiction, 1972. pp. 38. *bibliog.*

— Great Plains — Social life and customs.

STEWART (FRANK HENDERSON) Fundamentals of age-group systems. Oxford, [1977]. pp. 381. *bibliog.*

INDIANS OF SOUTH AMERICA.

INTERNATIONAL CONGRESS OF AMERICANISTS. 42nd Congress. Actes du XLIIe Congrès International des Américanistes: Congrès du Centenaire, Paris, 2-9 septembre 1976. volume II. Paris, 1977. pp. 623. *bibliogs.*

— Amazon Valley — Bibliography.

FUERST (RENÉ) compiler. Bibliography of the indigenous problem and policy of the Brazilian Amazon region, 1957-1972. Copenhagen, 1972. pp. 44. *(International Work Group for Indigenous Affairs. Documents. 6)*

— Brazil.

OLINTO (ANTONIO) Facts and ideas for a discussion on the problem of the Brazilian Indians at the present time. Oxford, 1972. pp. 16. *bibliog.*

SCHADEN (EGON) ed. Homem, cultura e sociedade no Brasil: seleções da Revista de Antropologia. Petropolis, 1972. pp. 450. *bibliogs.*

VILLAS BÔAS (ORLANDO) and VILLAS BÔAS (CLAUDIO) Indios do Xingu. São Paulo, [1975]. pp. 80. *Includes 35 pages of photographs. Text in Portuguese and English.*

MALHEIRO (PERDIGÃO) A escravidão no Brasil: ensaio historico, juridico, social. Petropolis, 1976. 2 vols. (in 1).

SCHADEN (EGON) ed. Leituras de etnologia brasileira. São Paulo, 1976. pp. 534.

COUDREAU (HENRI) Viagem ao Tapajos;...tradução Eugênio Amado. Belo Horizonte, 1977. pp. 162. *First published, in French, in Paris, 1897.*

COUDREAU (HENRI) Viagem ao Xingu;...tradução Eugênio Amado. Belo Horizonte, 1977. pp. 165. *First published, in French, in Paris, 1897.*

SILVA (ALCIONILIO BRÜZZI ALVES DA) A civilização indigena do Uaupes: observações antropologicas etnograficas e sociologicas. 2nd ed. Roma, [1977]. pp. 444. *bibliog. (Centro Studi di Storia delle Missioni Salesiane. Studi e Ricerche. 1)*

HEMMING (JOHN) 1935- . Red gold: the conquest of the Brazilian Indians. Cambridge, Mass., 1978. pp. 677. *bibliog.*

— — Bibliography.

FUERST (RENÉ) compiler. Bibliography of the indigenous problem and policy of the Brazilian Amazon region, 1957-1972. Copenhagen, 1972. pp. 44. *(International Work Group for Indigenous Affairs. Documents. 6)*

— — Government relations.

DAVIS (SHELTON H.) Victims of the miracle: development and the Indians of Brazil. Cambridge, 1977. pp. 205. *bibliog.*

HEMMING (JOHN) 1935- . Red gold: the conquest of the Brazilian Indians. Cambridge, Mass., 1978. pp. 677. *bibliog.*

— Colombia.

CARDONA A. (ALDO A.) Formas de cooperacion en comunidades indigenas de Colombia. Bogota, 1974. pp. 139. *bibliog.*

— Peru.

VARESE (STEFANO) The forest Indians in the present political situation of Peru. Copenhagen, 1972. pp. 28. *bibliog. (International Work Group for Indigenous Affairs. Documents. 8)*

SPALDING (KAREN) De indio a campesino: cambios en la estructura social del Peru colonial. Lima, 1974. pp. 258. *bibliog. (Instituto de Estudios Peruanos. Historia Andina. 2)*

BRUSH (STEPHEN B.) Mountain, field, and family: the economy and human ecology of an Andean valley. Philadelphia, Pa., 1977. pp. 199. *bibliog.*

— Venezuela.

JAHN (ALFREDO) Los aborigenes del occidente de Venezuela: su historia, etnografia y afinidades lingüisticas. Caracas, 1927 [repr. 1973]. 2 vols.(in 1). *bibliog. Facsimile reprint.*

INDIVIDUALISM.

FRIEDMAN (DAVID) The machinery of freedom: guide to a radical capitalism. New Rochelle, [1978]. pp. 240. *bibliog.*

INDIVIDUALITY.

KIRBY (RICHARD) and RADFORD (JOHN) Individual differences. London, 1976. pp. 144. *bibliog.*

INDOCHINA

— Foreign relations.

INDOCHINA: perspectives for reconciliation; edited...by Peter A. Poole. Athens, Ohio, 1975. pp. 84. *(Ohio University: Center for International Studies. Papers in International Studies. Southeast Asia Series. No.36).*

— — United States.

BRITISH CAMPAIGN FOR PEACE IN VIETNAM. Vietnam, Laos, Cambodia: Nixon get out!. Alkrington, Nr. Manchester, [1971?]. pp. (10).

— Politics and government.

INDOCHINA: perspectives for reconciliation; edited...by Peter A. Poole. Athens, Ohio, 1975. pp. 84. *(Ohio University: Center for International Studies. Papers in International Studies. Southeast Asia Series. No.36).*

INDONESIA

— Census.

INDONESIA. Census, 1971. A brief note on...1971 population census. Jakarta, 1976. pp. 14. *In English and Indonesian.*

INDUSTRIAL ORGANIZATION.

— Commerce — Japan.

PANGLAYKIM (JUSUF) Business relations between Indonesia and Japan: a view. Singapore, [1974]. pp. 43.

— Economic conditions.

PALMER (INGRID) The Indonesian economy since 1965: a case study of political economy. London, 1978. pp. 196. bibliog.

INDONESIA DEVELOPMENT NEWS; [pd. by] National Development Information Office. m. (formerly bi-m.) current issues only. London.

— — Statistics.

CHANGING economy in Indonesia: a selection of statistical source material from the early 19th century up to 1940...; initiated by W.M.F. Mansvelt; re-edited and continued by P. Creutzberg. Amsterdam, 1975-77. 3 vols. (in 1). bibliogs.

— Economic history — Sources.

CHANGING economy in Indonesia: a selection of statistical source material from the early 19th century up to 1940...; initiated by W.M.F. Mansvelt; re-edited and continued by P. Creutzberg. Amsterdam, 1975-77. 3 vols. (in 1). bibliogs.

— Economic policy.

CARLSON (SEVINC) Indonesia's oil. Boulder, Colo., 1977. pp. 257. bibliog. Prepared for the Center for Strategic and International Studies, Georgetown University.

GUPTA (SYAMAPRASAD) and others. A model for income distribution, employment and growth: a case study of Indonesia. [Washington], International Bank for Reconstruction and Development, 1977. pp. 121. bibliog. (World Bank Staff Occasional Papers. No. 24).

— Foreign relations — Netherlands.

SCHMUTZER (EDUARD J.M.) Dutch colonial policy and the search for identity in Indonesia, 1920-1931. Leiden, 1977. pp. 178. bibliog.

— History.

SCHMUTZER (EDUARD J.M.) Dutch colonial policy and the search for identity in Indonesia, 1920-1931. Leiden, 1977. pp. 178. bibliog.

MAY (BRIAN) The Indonesian tragedy. London, 1978. pp. 438.

— Industries.

INDONESIA. Biro Pusat Statistik. 1976-77. 1974/1975 industrial census:... household and cottage industries. Jakarta, 1976-77. 5 vols. (in 1). In English and Indonesian.

— Politics and government.

MAY (BRIAN) The Indonesian tragedy. London, 1978. pp. 438.

POLITICAL power and communications in Indonesia; edited by Karl D. Jackson and Lucian W. Pye. Berkeley, [1978]. pp. 424. bibliog.

INDUSTRIAL ACCIDENTS

— France.

HISTOIRE DES ACCIDENTS DU TRAVAIL; [published by] Centre de Recherches d'Histoire Economique et Sociale, Université de Nantes. Nantes, semi-annual, [1976]. (fasc.2).

— United Kingdom.

U.K. Health and Safety Executive. Health and safety statistics. a., 1975(1st)- London.

INDUSTRIAL CONCENTRATION.

CONNOR (JOHN M.) The market power of multinationals: a quantitative analysis of U. S. corporations in Brazil and Mexico. New York, 1977. pp. 307. bibliog.

— Canada.

CANADA. Statistics Canada. Industrial organization and concentration in the manufacturing, mining and logging industries. bien., 1972- Ottawa. [in English and French].

INDUSTRIAL EQUIPMENT

— United Kingdom — Scotland.

JOINT STANDING COMMITTEE OF THE SCOTTISH ECONOMIC COUNCIL AND THE OIL DEVELOPMENT COUNCIL FOR SCOTLAND. Scottish industry and offshore markets; (report by the Joint Standing Committee...: summary and government commentary). Edinburgh, H.M.S.O., 1977. pp. 18.

INDUSTRIAL HOUSING

— France.

MARION (E.) Institutions patronales créées par les grandes compagnies de chemins de fer en faveur de leur personnel. Paris, 1890. pp. 24. (Extrait du Soleil du Dimanche)

INDUSTRIAL HYGIENE

— Law and legislation.

INTERNATIONAL LABOUR CONFERENCE. 61st Session. Reports. 6. Working environment: sixth item on the agenda. Geneva, 1975-76. 2 pts.

— Denmark.

LANDSORGANISATIONEN I DANMARK. Fagbevaegelsen og arbejdsmiljøet: en redegørelse for LO's indsats for et bedre arbejdsmiljø i kongresperioden 1971-1975, etc. [Copenhagen, 1975]. pp. 56.

— Norway.

HANOA (ROLF) Fagbevegelsen og arbeidsmiljøet. [Oslo, 1974]. pp. 111.

— United States.

KOCHAN (THOMAS A.) and others. The effectiveness of union-management safety and health committees. Kalamazoo, 1977. pp. 127. bibliog.

INDUSTRIAL LAWS AND LEGISLATION.

INTERNATIONAL LABOUR CONFERENCE. 61st Session. Reports. 3. Third item on the agenda: information and reports on the application of conventions and recommendations. Geneva, 1976. 5 pts.

— Germany.

KUEFFNER (GERHARD) Das Gewerbezulassungsrecht der Handwerksordnung. Nürnberg, 1977. pp. 378. bibliog.

— Russia.

ALEKHIN (ALEKSEI PETROVICH) Predpriiatie v sisteme otraslevogo upravleniia: administrativno- pravovye voprosy. Moskva, 1977. pp. 191.

LAPTEV (VLADIMIR VIKTOROVICH) Pravovoe polozhenie promyshlennykh i proizvodstvennykh ob″edinenii. Moskva, 1978. pp. 247.

— United States.

DEREGULATING American industry: legal and economic problems; edited by Donald L. Martin [and] Warren F. Schwartz. Lexington, Mass., [1977]. pp. 120. Papers of a conference sponsored by the Law and Economics Center, University of Miami School of Law, in May 1976.

INDUSTRIAL MANAGEMENT.

LONDON. University. London School of Economics and Political Science. Seminar on Problems in Industrial Administration. Papers. Nos. 1-452. London, 1946-73. 19 vols. (including index vol.).

MACCOBY (MICHAEL) The gamesman: the new corporate leaders;...with a new preface for this [British] edition. London, 1977. pp. 285.

PRIOR (PETER J.) Leadership is not a bowler hat. Newton Abbot, [1977]. pp. 64.

STRATEGY plus structure equals performance: the strategic planning imperative; edited by Hans B. Thorelli. Bloomington, [1977]. pp. 310. bibliog. Based on a conference held by the Graduate School of Business of Indiana University in 1975.

MANAGEMENT control and organizational democracy; editors Bert King [and others]. Washington, D.C., 1978. pp. 288. bibliogs. Papers presented at a conference held in Munich in 1976 by the Human Factors Division of the North Atlantic Treaty Organization.

— Abstracts.

KEY TO TURKISH SCIENCE: industrial management (formerly: applied economics); (pd. by) Turkish Scientific and Technical Documentation Centre (Türdok). irreg., Ap 1969 (v.1, no.1)- Ankara.

— Bibliography.

ANDERER (JEANNE) compiler. Selected information sources on industrial administration. Farnborough, Hants., [1977]. pp. 148. Written under the auspices of the International Industrial Administration Centre, Vienna.

— Information services.

ANDERER (JEANNE) compiler. Selected information sources on industrial administration. Farnborough, Hants., [1977]. pp. 148. Written under the auspices of the International Industrial Administration Centre, Vienna.

— Russia.

OSTAPENKO (IVAN PROKOF'EVICH) Rabochii klass SSSR v upravlenii proizvodstvom, 1956-1970 gg. Moskva, 1976. pp. 483.

— Turkey — Abstracts.

KEY TO TURKISH SCIENCE: industrial management (formerly: applied economics); (pd. by) Turkish Scientific and Technical Documentation Centre (Türdok). irreg., Ap 1969 (v.1, no.1)- Ankara.

— United Kingdom.

The INDIVIDUAL, the enterprise and the state: a collection of ideas and insights from a series of seminars held at the Oxford Centre for Management Studies, England; edited by R. I. Tricker; with contributions from Lord Armstrong [and others]. London, 1977. pp. 170.

SYKES (ANDREW JAMES MACINTYRE) Industry: a career open to the talents. London, [1977]. pp. 10. bibliog.

— United States.

CHANDLER (ALFRED D.) The visible hand: the managerial revolution in American business. Cambridge, Mass., [1977] repr. 1978. pp. 608.

COCHRAN (THOMAS CHILDS) 200 years of American business. New York, [1977]. pp. 288. bibliog.

INDUSTRIAL NOISE

— United Kingdom.

INDUSTRIAL HEALTH ADVISORY COMMITTEE. Sub-Committee on Noise. Framing noise legislation; report; [Bryan Hugh Harvey, chairman]. London, H.M.S.O., [1976?]. pp. 8.

INDUSTRIAL ORGANIZATION.

LONDON. University. London School of Economics and Political Science. Seminar on Problems in Industrial Administration. Papers. Nos. 1-452. London, 1946-73. 19 vols. (including index vol.).

UNITED NATIONS INDUSTRIAL DEVELOPMENT ORGANIZATION. Industrial Planning and Programming Series. No. 1. Techniques of sectoral economic planning: the chemical industries. (ST/CID/14) [(ID/SER.E/1)]. New York, United Nations, 1966. pp. 58. bibliog.

INDUSTRIAL ORGANIZATION.(Cont.)

MILLER (ROGER EMILE) Entreprises et innovation: étude comparative de seize entreprises sidérurgiques européennes et américaines. Grenoble, 1975. pp. 124. *bibliog.*

CORIAT (BENJAMIN) Science, technique et capital. Paris, [1976]. pp. 250.

ESSAYS on industrial organization in honor of Joe S. Bain; edited by Robert T. Masson and P. David Qualls. Cambridge, Mass., [1976]. pp. 277. *bibliog.*

PREVOST (RENE) Les producteurs dans la civilisation industrielle. Lille, 1976. 1 vol. (various pagings). *bibliog.* Thèse - Université de Paris V.

CHEVALIER (JEAN MARIE) L'économie industrielle en question. [Paris, 1977]. pp. 268. *bibliog.*

GACHELIN (CHARLES) La localisation des industries. [Paris, 1977]. pp. 204.

GOODMAN (PAUL S.) and others. New perspectives on organizational effectiveness. San Francisco, 1977. pp. 275. *bibliog.*

WELFARE aspects of industrial markets; editors, A.P. Jacquemin and H.W. de Jong. Leiden, 1977. pp. 438. *bibliogs. (Instituut voor Bedrijfskunde. Nijenrode Studies in Economics. vol. 2) Essays based on conferences held at Nijenrode and Brussels in 1976.*

WORCESTER (DEAN A.) and NESSE (RONALD) Welfare gains from advertising: the problem of regulation. Washington, D.C., [1978]. pp. 134. *(American Enterprise Institute for Public Policy Research. AEI Studies. 188)*

— **European Economic Community countries.**

JACQUEMIN (ALEX P.) and JONG (HENDRIK WOUTER DE) European industrial organisation. London, 1977. pp. 269.

— **France.**

DUMARD (JEAN) and LETABLIER (MARIE THERESE) L'emploi industriel en France, fin 1968-fin 1971: modifications spatiales et structurelles. [Paris, 1976]. pp. 211. *(France. Centre d'Etudes de l'Emploi. Cahiers. 9) With English and German summaries.*

— **Germany, Eastern.**

MATTERNE (KURT) and TANNHAEUSER (SIEGFRIED) Die Grundmittelwirtschaft in der sozialistischen Industrie der DDR. 2nd ed. Berlin, 1978. pp. 560. *bibliog.*

— **Italy.**

LICHTNER (MAURIZIO) ed. L'organizzazione del lavoro in Italia. Roma, 1975. pp. 306. *bibliog.*

— **Russia.**

AKADEMIIA OBSHCHESTVENNYKH NAUK. Kafedra Partiinogo Stroitel'stva. [Voprosy Teorii i Praktiki Partiinogo Stroitel'stva. vyp.2] Pervichnaia partiinaia organizatsiia - avangard trudovogo kollektiva Moskva, 1975. pp. 216.

MAKAROV (STANISLAV PETROVICH) and SELEZNEV (ALEKSANDR ZAKHAROVICH) eds. Razvitie ob"edinenii v promyshlennosti. Moskva, 1976. pp. 215.

ALEKHIN (ALEKSEI PETROVICH) Predpriiatie v sisteme otraslevogo upravleniia: administrativno- pravovye voprosy. Moskva, 1977. pp. 191.

TAKSIR (KIM ISAEVICH) Nauchno-proizvodstvennye ob"edineniia. Moskva, 1977. pp. 160. *(Akademiia Nauk SSSR. Problemy Sovetskoi Ekonomiki)*

— **Sweden.**

GYLLENHAMMAR (PEHR G.) People at work. Reading, Mass., 1977. pp. 164.

WORK organization: Swedish experience and British context; papers and commentaries from a conference sponsored by the S[ocial] S[cience] R[esearch] C[ouncil] and held at the Imperial College of Science and Technology, London, March 1974, with a postscript on some subsequent changes to 1977; edited by Denis Gregory. London, Social Science Research Council, [1978]. pp. 267.

— **United Kingdom.**

The RIGHT to useful work: planning by the people; edited by Ken Coates. Nottingham, 1978. pp. 287.

— **United States.**

CHANDLER (ALFRED D.) The visible hand: the managerial revolution in American business. Cambridge, Mass., [1977] repr. 1978. pp. 608.

INDUSTRIAL PROJECT MANAGEMENT.

UNITED NATIONS INDUSTRIAL DEVELOPMENT ORGANIZATION. Industrial Planning and Programming Series. No. 1. Techniques of sectoral economic planning: the chemical industries. (ST/CID/14) [(ID/SER.E/1)]. New York, United Nations, 1966. pp. 58. *bibliog.*

INDUSTRIAL PROMOTION

— **Ethiopia.**

AGRICULTURAL AND INDUSTRIAL DEVELOPMENT BANK S.C. [ETHIOPIA]. Annual report. a., 1973/74(4th)- Addis Ababa. *[in English and Amharic]*

— **Nigeria.**

NEW NIGERIA DEVELOPMENT COMPANY. N.N.D.C.: New Nigeria Development Company Ltd.: a development agency owned by the governments of the northern states of Nigeria. Kaduna, 1971. pp. 15.

NEW NIGERIA DEVELOPMENT COMPANY. N.N.D.C. group. [Kaduna], 1971. pp. 52.

— **Philippine Islands.**

PHILIPPINE ISLANDS. Department of Industry. Report. a., 1976- Manila.

— **Underdeveloped areas.**

See UNDERDEVELOPED AREAS — Industrial promotion.

— **United Kingdom.**

NATIONAL ENTERPRISE BOARD [U.K.]. Investment potential in the north east and north west of England; report. [London, 1977]. fo. 17.

— — **Scotland.**

SCOTTISH DEVELOPMENT AGENCY. Report. a., 1975/76(1st)- Glasgow.

— — **Wales.**

WELSH DEVELOPMENT AGENCY. Report. a., Ja 1976/Mr 1977(1st)- Treforest.

U.K. Welsh Office. 1977. Guidelines for the industrial investment functions of the Welsh Development Agency. [Cardiff], 1977. pp. 8.

INDUSTRIAL PROPERTY

— **United Kingdom.**

WHITE (THOMAS ANTHONY BLANCO) and others. Patents, trade marks, copyright and industrial designs. 2nd ed. London, 1978. pp. 178.

INDUSTRIAL RELATIONS.

INTERNATIONAL LABOUR CONFERENCE. 61st Session. Reports. 5(1). Labour administration: role, functions and organisation; fifth item on the agenda. Geneva, 1975. pp. 170. *Report 5(2) was originally prepared for the 61st Session but held over for discussion at the 63rd Session (Report 5(2) of 63rd Session)*

ROSE (MICHAEL) Industrial behaviour: theoretical development since Taylor. Harmondsworth, 1978. pp. 304. *Reprint of the first edition published in London, 1975.*

BODMAN (ERIC DE) and RICHARD (BERTRAND) Changer les relations sociales: la politique de Jacques Delors. Paris, 1976. pp. 218. *bibliog.*

GRANT (JEANNE VALERIE) and SMITH (GEOFFREY JOHN) Personnel administration and industrial relations. 2nd ed. London, 1977. pp. 318. *bibliog.*

MORGAN (ALUN) and BLANPAIN (ROGER) The industrial relations and employment impacts of multinational enterprises: an inquiry into the issues. Paris, Organisation for Economic Co-operation and Development, 1977. pp. 42.

GALLIE (DUNCAN) In search of the new working class: automation and social integration within the capitalist enterprise. Cambridge, 1978. pp. 348. *bibliog.*

— **Australia.**

AUSTRALIA. Department of Employment and Industrial Relations. 1977. Australian industrial relations systems. Canberra, 1977. pp. 20.

— **Canada.**

PHILLIPS (GERALD E.) The practice of labour relations and collective bargaining in Canada. Toronto, [1977]. pp. 266. *bibliogs.*

CRISPO (JOHN H.G.) The Canadian industrial relations system. Toronto, [1978]. pp. 570.

— — **Newfoundland.**

NEWFOUNDLAND. Department of Manpower and Industrial Relations. Annual report. a., 1976- St. John's.

— **Europe.**

COMPARATIVE industrial relations in Europe; edited by Derek Torrington. London, 1978. pp. 270.

CRISPO (JOHN H.G.) Industrial democracy in western Europe: a North American perspective. Toronto, [1978]. pp. 181. *bibliog.*

— **France.**

ANGELI (CLAUDE) and BRIMO (NICOLAS) Une milice patronale: Peugeot;...avec la collaboration de Marc- Rémy Donnallin. Paris, 1975. pp. 105.

PAGANELLI (SERGE) and JACQUIN (MARTINE) Peugeot: la dynastie s'accroche. Paris, [1975]. pp. 156.

BODMAN (ERIC DE) and RICHARD (BERTRAND) Changer les relations sociales: la politique de Jacques Delors. Paris, 1976. pp. 218. *bibliog.*

CAILLE (MARCEL) Les truands du patronat. Paris, 1977. pp. 307. *bibliog.*

— **Germany.**

WALLRAFF (GUENTER) Neue Reportagen, Untersuchungen und Lehrbeispiele. Reinbek bei Hamburg, 1974 repr. 1978. pp. 144.

— **Italy.**

BONAZZI (GIUSEPPE) In una fabbrica di motori: organizzazione del lavoro, potere padronale e lotte operaie. Milano, 1975. pp. 273.

CORSO DI SPECIALIZZAZIONE PER DIRIGENTI AZIENDALI E CAPI DEL PERSONALE. N.3, [1974]. L'attività sindacale nei luoghi di lavoro; seminario di diritto sindacale con relazioni di G. Mazzoni [and others]. Milano, [1976]. pp. 246. *(Istituto di Studi Sindacali e del Lavoro. Collana. 3)*

GAMBA (MARINO) Innocenti: imprenditore, fabbrica e classe operaia in cinquant'anni di vita italiana. [Milan, 1976]. pp. 207.

GIUGNI (GINO) and others. Gli anni della conflittualità permanente: rapporto sulle relazioni industriali in Italia nel 1970-1971. [Milano, 1976]. pp. 209.

LA VALLE (DAVIDE) Le origini della classe operaia alla Fiat: salario e forza- lavoro dalla fondazione ai consigli di fabbrica. Roma, 1976. pp. 182.

— **Netherlands.**

BINNEVELD (JOHANNES MARTINUS WOUTER) De Rotterdamse metaalstaking van 1965. Amsterdam, 1977. pp. 175. *bibliog. Revised version of his De stakingen in de Rotterdamse metaalindustrie in 1965.*

— **Nigeria.**

ETUKUDO (AKANIMO J.) Waging industrial peace in Nigeria. Hicksville, [1977]. pp. 216. *bibliogs.*

— **Spain.**

OLABARRI GORTAZAR (IGNACIO) Relaciones laborales en Vizcaya, 1890-1936. Durango, Spain, [1978]. pp. 532. *bibliog.*

— **Sweden.**

LANDSORGANISATIONEN I SVERIGE. Företagsdemokratiska Råd. Solidariskt medbestämmande: rapport till LO-kongressen 1976. Stockholm, [1976]. pp. 121.

— **Switzerland.**

VETTERLI (RUDOLF) Industriearbeit, Arbeiterbewusstsein und gewerkschaftliche Organisation; dargestellt am Beispiel der Georg Fischer AG, 1890-1930. Göttingen, 1978. pp. 344. *bibliog.*

— **United Kingdom.**

ADVISORY, CONCILIATION AND ARBITRATION SERVICE [U.K.]. Reports. [London, 1975 in progress].

COATES (KEN) and TOPHAM (ANTHONY) The shop steward's guide to the Bullock Report. Nottingham, 1977. pp. 127.

DEMOCRACY at work: a book for active trade unionists. London, 1977. pp. 184. *Accompanies a series of ten Trade Union Studies programmes shown on BBC television.*

FRIEDMAN (ANDREW L.) Industry and labour: class struggle at work and monopoly capitalism. London, 1977. pp. 313. *bibliog.*

GLENDON (ALECK IAN) The participant observer and groups in conflict: a case study from industry. 1977. 2 vols. *bibliog. Typescript. Ph.D. (London) thesis: unpublished. This thesis is the property of London University and may not be removed from the Library.*

HUNT (DENNIS D.) Common sense industrial relations. Newton Abbot, [1977]. pp. 182. *bibliog.*

KEITHLEY (G.R.) and SAWBRIDGE (D.) The provision of industrial relations training for shop stewards. Durham, 1977. fo. 38. *(Durham. University. Business School. Working Papers. No. 2)*

ROGALY (JOE) Grunwick. Harmondsworth, 1977. pp. 199.

ELLIOTT (JOHN) Journalist. Conflict or cooperation?: the growth of industrial democracy. London, [1978]. pp. 306. *bibliog.*

GILL (COLIN) and others. Industrial relations in the chemical industry. Farnborough, Hants., [1978]. pp. 256.

HAWKINS (KEVIN H.) The management of industrial relations. [Harmondsworth, 1978]. pp. 265.

— — **Scotland.**

JOHNS (STEPHEN) Reformism on the Clyde: the story of UCS. London, [1973]. pp. 128. *(Workers' Revolutionary Party. Pocket Library. No. 7)*

— **United States.**

KOCHAN (THOMAS A.) and others. The effectiveness of union-management safety and health committees. Kalamazoo, 1977. pp. 127. *bibliog.*

BERG (IVAR E.) and others. Managers and work reform: a limited engagement. New York, [1978]. pp. 316.

HAGBURG (EUGENE C.) and LEVINE (MARVIN J.) Labor relations: an integrated perspective. St. Paul, [1978]. pp. 390. *bibliog.*

JENNINGS (KENNETH M.) and others. Labor relations in a public service industry: unions, management, and the public interest in mass transit. New York, 1978. pp. 323. *bibliog.*

RAMIREZ (BRUNO) When workers fight: the politics of industrial relations in the Progressive era, 1898-1916. Westport, [1978]. pp. 241. *bibliog.*

INDUSTRIAL SAFETY

— **Law and legislation.**

INTERNATIONAL LABOUR CONFERENCE. 61st Session. Reports. 6. Working environment: sixth item on the agenda. Geneva, 1975-76. 2 pts.

— **Russia — Law and legislation.**

BRAININ (MIKHAIL SEMENOVICH) and KVELIDZE (SERGEI ARKAD'EVICH) Ugolovno-pravovaia okhrana bezopasnosti truda v SSSR. Moskva, 1977. pp. 143.

— **United Kingdom.**

U.K. Health and Safety Commission. Report. a., 1974/76 (1st)- London.

LABOUR RESEARCH DEPARTMENT. LRD guide for safety representatives. London, 1978. pp. 43. *bibliog.*

— **United States.**

KOCHAN (THOMAS A.) and others. The effectiveness of union-management safety and health committees. Kalamazoo, 1977. pp. 127. *bibliog.*

INDUSTRIAL SOCIOLOGY.

BONZANINI (ANGELO) and SALERNO (FRANCO) Conflittualità e crisi nella società industriale. [Milano, 1976]. pp. 165.

GILBERT (JAMES BURKHART) Work without salvation: America's intellectuals and industrial alienation, 1880-1910. Baltimore, [1977]. pp. 240.

ORGANIZATIONAL careers: some new perspectives; edited by John Van Maanen. London, [1977]. pp. 199. *bibliog. Derives from an Industrial Liaison Program Symposium held at M.I.T. in 1974.*

SAINSAULIEU (RENAUD) L'identité au travail: les effets culturels de l'organisation. Paris, [1977]. pp. 487.

WATSON (TONY J.) The personnel managers: a study in the sociology of work and employment. London, 1977. pp. 246. *bibliog.*

WORK and technology; edited by Marie R. Haug and Jacques Dofny. London, [1977]. pp. 258. *bibliogs. Selected articles from papers presented at the sessions of the Research Committee on Work, of the Eighth World Congress of the International Sociological Association, held in Toronto, 1974.*

GALLIE (DUNCAN) In search of the new working class: automation and social integration within the capitalist enterprise. Cambridge, 1978. pp. 348. *bibliog.*

KUMAR (KRISHAN) Prophecy and progress: the sociology of industrial and post- industrial society. [London, 1978]. pp. 416. *bibliog.*

INDUSTRIAL STATISTICS.

UNITED NATIONS INDUSTRIAL DEVELOPMENT ORGANIZATION. First Ad Hoc Group of Experts on Industrial Programming Data. 1965. International comparisons of interindustry data: proceedings of the meeting of the...held in New York, November, 1965. New York, United Nations, 1969. pp. 270.

ROZANOV (GENNADII VLADIMIROVICH) Statisticheskoe modelirovanie razvitiia otrasli. Moskva, 1976. pp. 167. *bibliog.*

REFORM of statistics of production industries, etc; [by A. Sobotschinski and others]. Wiesbaden, 1978. pp. 38. *(Germany (Bundesrepublik). Statistisches Bundesamt. Studies on Statistics. No. 33) The original German articles were published in "Wirtschaft und Statistik", Vol. 7,8/1976 and Vol. 11/1977.*

INDUSTRIALIZATION.

EUROPEAN COMMUNITIES. Directorate-General for Development and Cooperation. Les Conditions d'Installation d'Entreprises Industrielles dans les États Africains et Malgache Associés. 2nd ed. [Brussels], 1974.

FRIEDMANN (JOHN REMBERT PETER) and WULFF (ROBERT) The urban transition: comparative studies of newly industrializing societies. London, 1976. pp. 96. *bibliog.*

KOBRIN (STEPHEN JAY) Foreign direct investment, industrialization and social change. Greenwich, Conn., [1977]. pp. 188. *bibliog.*

INDUSTRY AND DEVELOPMENT; [pd. by] United Nations Industrial Development Organization. s-a., 1978(no.1)- New York.

COMMONWEALTH TEAM OF INDUSTRIAL SPECIALISTS. Cooperation for accelerating industrialisation; final report; [L. K. Jha, chairman]. London, Commonwealth Secretariat, [1978]. pp. 54.

CONTEMPORARY industrialization: spatial analysis and regional development; edited by F.E. Ian Hamilton. London, 1978. pp. 203. *bibliogs. Based on the first conference of the International Geographical Union Working Group on Industrial Geography, held in London in 1974.*

INDUSTRIAL change: international experience and public policy; edited by F.E. Ian Hamilton. London, 1978. pp. 183. *bibliogs. Based on conferences of the International Geographical Union Working Group on Industrial Geography, held in London in 1974 and in Novosibirsk in 1976.*

— **History.**

KEMP (TOM) Historical patterns of industrialization. London, 1978. pp. 183. *bibliog.*

— **Mathematical models.**

HIRSCH (SEEV) Rich man's, poor man's and every man's goods: aspects of industrialization. Tübingen, 1977. pp. 150. *bibliog. (Kiel. Universität. Institut für Weltwirtschaft. Kieler Studien. 148)*

INDUSTRIEGEWERKSCHAFT DRUCK UND PAPIER.

BESTRAFTE Solidarität: Drucker und Journalisten im gewerkschaftlichen Kampf; ([by] Klaus Kräling [and others]). Berlin, [1973]. pp. 139.

INDUSTRIEGEWERKSCHAFT METALL FÜR DIE BUNDESREPUBLIK DEUTSCHLAND.

KRUSCHE (REINHARD) and PFEIFFER (DAGMAR) Betriebliche Gewerkschaftsorgane und Interessenvertretung: zur Betriebsräte- und Vertrauensleutepolitik der IG Metall. Berlin, [1975]. pp. 158. *bibliog.*

INDUSTRIES, LOCATION OF.

INDUSTRIES, LOCATION OF.

GACHELIN (CHARLES) La localisation des industries. [Paris, 1977]. pp. 204.

NOBEL SYMPOSIUM, 35TH, STOCKHOLM, 1976. The international allocation of economic activity: proceedings of a Nobel Symposium held at Stockholm; edited by Bertil Ohlin [and others]. London, 1977. pp. 572.

OPEN UNIVERSITY. Fundamentals of Human Geography [Course Team]. Values, relevance and policy: units 25-26, section III, D204. Milton Keynes, 1977. pp. 80. *bibliogs.*

BOYCE (RONALD R.) The bases of economic geography. 2nd ed. New York, [1978]. pp. 433. *bibliogs.*

CONTEMPORARY industrialization: spatial analysis and regional development; edited by F.E. Ian Hamilton. London, 1978. pp. 203. *bibliogs. Based on the first conference of the International Geographical Union Working Group on Industrial Geography, held in London in 1974.*

INDUSTRIAL change: international experience and public policy; edited by F.E. Ian Hamilton. London, 1978. pp. 183. *bibliogs. Based on conferences of the International Geographical Union Working Group on Industrial Geography, held in London in 1974 and in Novosibirsk in 1976.*

— Mathematical models.

MIYAKE (MARIO YOSHIKAZU) The quadratic assignment model applied to some facility location problems. 1977. fo. 190. *bibliog.* Typescript. *Ph.D. (London) thesis: unpublished. This thesis is the property of London University and may not be removed from the Library.*

— Brazil.

DICKENSON (JOHN P.) Brazil. Folkestone, 1978. pp. 246. *bibliog.*

— Europe, Eastern.

TURNOCK (DAVID) Eastern Europe. Boulder, Colo., 1978. pp. 273. *bibliog.*

— New Zealand.

THOMSON (JANET) Employment in the suburbs. [Wellington], Town and Country Planning Branch, Ministry of Works, 1969. pp. 8.

— United Kingdom.

SANT (MORGAN EUGENE CYRIL) and MOSELEY (MALCOLM J.) The industrial development of East Anglia. Norwich, [1977]. pp. 207. *bibliog.*

GUDGIN (GRAHAM) Industrial location processes and regional employment growth. Farnborough, Hants., [1978]. pp. 344. *bibliog.*

— United States.

LEONE (ROBERT ANTHONY) Location of manufacturing activity in the New York Metropolitan Area. 1971. fo. 194. *bibliog. Ph.D. (Yale) thesis: unpublished. Microfilm of typscript: 1 reel.*

— Zambia.

BHAGAVAN (M.R.) Zambia: impact of industrial strategy on regional imbalance and social inequality. Uppsala, 1978. pp. 76. *(Nordiska Afrikainstitutet. Research Reports. No. 44)*

INDUSTRIES, SIZE OF.

BRIDGE (JOHN) M.A. and DODDS (JAMES COLIN) Planning and the growth of the firm. London, [1978]. pp. 211.

LANGEN (WERNER) Unternehmensgrössenbezogene Wirtschaftspolitik in der Bundesrepublik Deutschland. Göttingen, 1978. pp. 605. *bibliog. (Institut für Mittelstandsforschung. Schriften zur Mittelstandsforschung. Nr. 74)*

INDUSTRY.

ACCADEMIA NAZIONALE DEI LINCEI. Atti dei Convegni Lincei. 28. Convegno: agricoltura e industria e i loro rapporti nell'economia contemporanea. Roma, 12-13 aprile 1976. Roma, 1977. pp. 115.

— Classification.

FRANCE. Institut National de la Statistique et des Etudes Economiques. 1974. Regroupements des nomenclatures d'activités et de produits 1973: niveaux 15 et 40. [Paris, 1974?]. pp. 45. *(Nomenclatures et Codes)*

FRANCE. Institut National de la Statistique et des Etudes Economiques. 1975. Table de correspondance n.a.e. (nomenclature des activités économiques 1959) - n.a.p. nomenclatures d'activités et de produits 1973. [Paris, 1975?]. pp. 161. *(Nomenclatures et Codes)*

— History.

ROMANO (RUGGIERO) Industria: storia e problemi. Torino, [1976]. pp. 78. *bibliog.*

— Social aspects.

PREVOST (RENE) Les producteurs dans la civilisation industrielle. Lille, 1976. 1 vol. (various pagings). *bibliog.* Thèse - Université de Paris V.

AHARONI (YAIR) and BADEN (CLIFFORD) Business in the international environment: a casebook. London, 1977. pp. 245.

WELFARE aspects of industrial markets; editors, A.P. Jacquemin and H.W. de Jong. Leiden, 1977. pp. 438. *bibliogs. (Instituut voor Bedrijfskunde. Nijenrode Studies in Economics. vol. 2) Essays based on conferences held at Nijenrode and Brussels in 1976.*

BEESLEY (MICHAEL R.) and EVANS (TOM) Corporate social responsibility: a reassessment. London, [1978]. pp. 211. *bibliog.*

KAPP (KARL WILHELM) The social costs of business enterprise. 3rd ed. [Nottingham, 1978]. pp. 348. *bibliog.*

— — Germany.

WALLRAFF (GUENTER) Industriereportagen: als Arbeiter in deutschen Grossbetrieben. Reinbek bei Hamburg, 1970 repr. 1978. pp. 118.

WALLRAFF (GUENTER) Neue Reportagen, Untersuchungen und Lehrbeispiele. Reinbek bei Hamburg, 1974 repr. 1978. pp. 144.

— — United Kingdom.

COMMUNITY DEVELOPMENT PROJECT. The costs of industrial change. London, 1977. pp. 96.

ELLIOTT (DAVID) The Lucas Aerospace workers' campaign. London, 1977. pp. 20. *(Young Fabian Group. Young Fabian Pamphlets. 46)*

The RIGHT to useful work: planning by the people; edited by Ken Coates. Nottingham, 1978. pp. 287.

— — United States.

BRUYN (SEVERYN TEN HAUT) The social economy: people transforming modern business. New York, [1977]. pp. 392.

INDUSTRY AND STATE.

FRANCE. Direction de la Documentation. La Documentation Française. Notes et Etudes Documentaires. Nos. 4,303-4, 304-4,305. Les transferts état-industrie en France et dans les pays occidentaux; par Anicet Le Pors. Paris, 1976. pp. 79.

AHARONI (YAIR) Markets, planning and development: the private and public sectors in economic development. Cambridge, Mass., [1977]. pp. 323.

INDUSTRIAL change: international experience and public policy; edited by F.E. Ian Hamilton. London, 1978. pp. 183. *bibliogs. Based on conferences of the International Geographical Union Working Group on Industrial Geography, held in London in 1974 and in Novosibirsk in 1976.*

— America, Latin.

CAMBRIDGE. University. Centre of Latin American Studies. Working Papers. No.18. The public sector in Latin America; by E.V.K. Fitzgerald. Cambridge, 1974. pp. 28. *bibliog.*

— Canada.

PROJECT BRAZIL and LAST POST. The Brascan file: its friends in government: its record in Brazil. Toronto, [1973]. pp. 12. *(Reprinted from Last Post, vol. 3. no. 2., February 1973)*

ATLANTIC PROVINCES ECONOMIC COUNCIL. Background Papers. Industrial incentives programs in the Atlantic region: description, outlays and overview. Halifax, N.S., 1976. pp. 174.

— Colombia.

CUELLAR LOPEZ (LUIS) Comentarios al Articulo 32 de la Constitucion Nacional. Bogota, 1972. pp. 203. *bibliog.*

— France.

FRANCE. Direction de la Documentation. La Documentation Française. Notes et Etudes Documentaires. Nos. 4,303-4, 304-4,305. Les transferts état-industrie en France et dans les pays occidentaux; par Anicet Le Pors. Paris, 1976. pp. 79.

— Germany.

BRANDT (MAXIMILIAN) and ECCIUS ( ) of Essen, defendants. Prozess Brandt und Genossen: der sogenannte Krupp- Prozess; Verhandlungsbericht, aus dem Reichstag, Zeitungsstimmen; mit einer Einführung herausgegeben von Ad. Zimmermann. Berlin, 1914. pp. 397.

— India.

INDIA. Khadi and Village Industries Commission. 1975. Patterns of assistance for Khadi and village industries. Bombay, [1975]. pp. 168.

MAHARASHTRA ECONOMIC DEVELOPMENT COUNCIL. The new industrial policy. Bombay, [1978?]. pp. 14.

— — Maharashtra.

MAHARASHTRA ECONOMIC DEVELOPMENT COUNCIL. Rehabilitation and expansion of industries in greater Bombay. Bombay, 1973. pp. 90.

MAHARASHTRA ECONOMIC DEVELOPMENT COUNCIL. State planning and industrial development in Maharashtra. [Bombay, 1974?]. pp. 222.

— Italy.

FABBRICA E STATO. No. 13/14. 1974/1975: crisi e lotte proletarie. Bari, 1975. pp. 270.

SARACENO (PASQUALE) Il sistema delle imprese a partecipazione statale nell'esperienza italiana. Milano, 1975. pp. 132. *(Associazione per lo Sviluppo dell'Industria nel Mezzogiorno. Centro per gli Studi sullo Sviluppo Economico. Collana Francesco Giordani)*

STATO e controllo dell'economia: democrazia politica e democrazia sociale. Bari, [1976]. pp. 193. *Proceedings of a conference held by the Istituto Gramsci in 1976.*

— Japan.

JOHNSON (CHALMERS) Japan's public policy companies. Washington, D.C., [1978]. pp. 173. *(American Enterprise Institute for Public Policy Research and Stanford University. Hoover Institution on War, Revolution and Peace. AEI-Hoover Policy Studies. 24)*

— Underdeveloped areas.

See UNDERDEVELOPED AREAS — Industry and state.

— United Kingdom.

NATIONAL ENTERPRISE BOARD [U.K.]. Annual report and accounts. a., 1976(1st)- London.

SELSDON GROUP. Briefs. No. 13. A smaller public sector: the priority for a free society. London, 1976. pp. 10.

The INDIVIDUAL, the enterprise and the state: a collection of ideas and insights from a series of seminars held at the Oxford Centre for Management Studies, England; edited by R. I. Tricker; with contributions from Lord Armstrong [and others] . London, 1977. pp. 170.

INDUSTRIAL efficiency and the role of government; edited by Colette Bowe. London, H.M.S.O., 1977. pp. 282.

KING (MERVYN A.) Public policy and the corporation. London, 1977. pp. 309. *bibliog. (Cambridge. University. Department of Applied Economics. Cambridge Studies in Applied Econometrics. 3)*

LABOUR PARTY. International big business: Labour's policy on the multinationals. London, 1977. pp. 135.

LIVINGSTONE (JAMES MACCARDLE) National government and the international enterprise. [Glasgow, 1977?]. pp. 70. *bibliog. (Glasgow. University of Strathclyde. Department of Marketing. Working Papers)*

SCIBERRAS (EDMOND) Multinational electronics companies and national economic policies. Greenwich, Conn., [1977]. pp. 328. *bibliog.*

FABIAN SOCIETY. Fabian Tracts. [No.] 453. Think small: enterprise and the economy; [by] Nicholas Falk. London, 1978. pp. 36.

REEKIE (W. DUNCAN) Give us this day...; an economic critique of political intervention between men and women and their daily bread. London, 1978. pp. 78. *bibliog. (Institute of Economic Affairs. Hobart Papers. 79)*

— United States.

GOVERNMENT regulation: what kind of reform?; (a round table held on 11 September 1975 and sponsored by the American Enterprise Institute for Public Policy Research and the Hoover Institution on War, Revolution and Peace); Eileen Shanahan, moderator, etc. Washington, [1976]. pp. 60. *(American Enterprise Institute for Public Policy Research. Round Tables)*

BRUYN (SEVERYN TEN HAUT) The social economy: people transforming modern business. New York, [1977]. pp. 392.

DEREGULATING American industry: legal and economic problems; edited by Donald L. Martin [and] Warren F. Schwartz. Lexington, Mass., [1977]. pp. 120. *Papers of a conference sponsored by the Law and Economics Center, University of Miami School of Law, in May 1976.*

WAR, business, and American society: historical perspectives on the military-industrial complex; edited by Benjamin Franklin Cooling. Port Washington, 1977. pp. 203. *bibliogs.*

INFANT PSYCHOLOGY.

KOGAN (NATHAN) Cognitive styles in infancy and early childhood. Hillsdale, N.J., [1976]. pp. 146. *bibliog.*

NEWMAN (BARBARA M.) and NEWMAN (PHILIP R.) Infancy and childhood: development and its contents. New York, [1978]. pp. 619. *bibliog.*

INFANTS

— Mortality.

ST. PANCRAS. [Public Health Department]. Progress in the prevention of infant mortality: (extract from the annual report of the Medical Officer of Health of the metropolitan borough of St. Pancras for the year 1906). [London, 1906]. pp. 14.

HAMPSTEAD. [Borough Council]. Infantile mortality. [London, 1908]. pp. 27-35. *Extract from report for 1908.*

BRAZIL. Conselho Nacional de Estatistica. Laboratorio de Estatistica. 1951. A mortalidade infantil no Distrito Federal nos anos de 1939 a 1950;...estudo redigido por Giorgio Mortara. [Rio de Janeiro, 1951]. fo. 7. *(Estudos Demograficos. No. 8)*

FOSTER (F. H.) Perinatal mortality in New Zealand, 1972-73. Wellington, 1977. pp. 99. *(New Zealand. Department of Health. Special Report Series. No. 50)*

— Nutrition.

MULLER (MIKE) The baby killer: a War on Want investigation into the promotion and sale of powdered baby milks in the Third World. London, 1974. pp. 19.

INFLATION (FINANCE).

BRUSEKER (U.) Unilever, Meneba, Philips en de olieconcerns als inflatiemakers; een bestrijding van de looninflatie-theorie. [Amsterdam], 1974. pp. 133. *bibliog.*

DEUTSCH (JOHN J.) The politics of inflation. Toronto, 1974. fo. 12. *(Ontario. Economic Council. Working Papers. 1974. No. 6)*

PATTISON (JOHN CHARLES) Adjustment to inflation. Toronto, 1974. fo. 25. *bibliog. (Ontario. Economic Council. Working Papers. 1974. No. 3)*

PATTISON (JOHN CHARLES) International inflationary linkages and the recent experience in individual countries. Toronto, 1974. fo. 35. *bibliog. (Ontario. Economic Council. Working Papers. 1974. No. 2)*

FARÈ (MAURIZIO) and others. Inflazione e mercato finanziario. Milano, 1975. pp. 188. *bibliogs.*

FRATIANNI (MICHELE) Inflazione, produzione e politica economica in Italia; (traduzione italiana di Franco Lucat). [Milano, 1975]. pp. 160. *(Centro Studi di Politica Economica. Collana. 2)*

HOTSON (JOHN H.) and others. Stagflation and the bastard Keynesians. Waterloo, Ont., [1976]. pp. 240.

BLONDEL (DANIELE) and PARLY (JEANNE MARIE) L'inflation de croissance. [Paris, 1977]. pp. 295. *bibliog.*

DENIZET (JEAN) La grande inflation: salaire, intérêt et change. [Paris, 1977]. pp. 159. *bibliog.*

GREENE (JAMES) International experiences in managing inflation. New York, [1977]. pp. 34. *(National Industrial Conference Board. Conference Board Reports. No. 729)*

NATIONAL BUREAU OF ECONOMIC RESEARCH. Conference on Research in Income and Wealth. Studies in Income and Wealth. vol. 42. Analysis of inflation, 1965-1974: [papers presented in 1974]; Joel Popkin, editor. Cambridge, Mass., 1977. pp. 487. *bibliogs. Proceedings of a Conference held in 1974 in Bethesda, Md. Tables on microfiche (1 card)*

PENSIONS and inflation: an international discussion [held at Geneva, May 1976]. Geneva, International Labour Office, 1977. pp. 136.

SOCIETE DU MONT-PELERIN. Congrès, 1976. Le libéralisme?: de Karl Marx à Milton Friedman; (edited by) Jacques Riboud. Paris, 1977. pp. 224. *In French or English.*

BOYER (ROBERT) and MISTRAL (JACQUES) Accumulation, inflation, crises. [Paris], 1978. pp. 260.

CARNEGIE-ROCHESTER CONFERENCE ON PUBLIC POLICY. 1977, April Conference. The problem of inflation; editors Karl Brunner [and] Allan H. Meltzer. Amsterdam, 1978. pp. 372. *bibliogs. (Journal of Monetary Economics. Carnegie- Rochester Conference Series on Public Policy. vol.8)*

The POLITICAL economy of inflation; edited by Fred Hirsch and John H. Goldthorpe. [London, 1978]. pp. 307. *bibliog.*

INFLATION (FINANCE).

— Mathematical models.

STABILITY and inflation; edited by A.R. Bergstrom [and others]; ...a volume of essays to honour the memory of A.W.H. Phillips. Chichester, [1978]. pp. 323. *bibliogs.*

— America, Latin.

WACHTER (SUSAN M.) Latin American inflation: the structuralist-monetarist debate. Lexington, Mass., [1976]. pp. 165. *bibliog.*

— Brazil.

CHACEL (JULIAN MAGALHÃES) and others. A correção monetaria. Rio de Janeiro, 1970. pp. 336. *(Columbia University. Inter-American Law Center. Estudos sôbre a propriedade privada nas Americas)*

— Canada.

PATTISON (JOHN CHARLES) Government deficits and inflation reconsidered. [Toronto], Ontario Economic Council, 1976. fo. 7.

PESANDO (JAMES E.) The impact of inflation on financial markets in Canada. [Montreal, 1977]. pp. 80.

— — Ontario.

ONTARIO. Ministry of Treasury, Economics and Intergovernmental Affairs. 1976. Anti-inflation program: the first six months. [Toronto], 1976. fo. 16.

ONTARIO. Ministry of Treasury, Economics and Intergovernmental Affairs. 1976. Anti-inflation program: the first year. [Toronto], 1976. fo. 16.

— France.

FABRE-LUCE (ALFRED) Après la législature des dupes: le 22 avril. Paris, 1928. pp. 104.

BOYER (R.) and MISTRAL (J.) Inflation, investment and employment: a simple multisector model of the French economy with extension to some international comparisons. Paris, 1976. pp. 52. *(Centre d'Etudes Prospectives d'Economie Mathematique Appliquées à la Planification. [Publications]. No. 7608)*

FRANCE. Direction de la Documentation. La Documentation Française. Notes et Etudes Documentaires. Nos. 4,306-4, 307. Un essai de mesure anti-inflationniste: le prélèvement conjoncturel; par Jean-Paul Courthéoux. Paris, 1976. pp. 61. *bibliog.*

BOYER (ROBERT) and MISTRAL (JACQUES) Accumulation, inflation, crises. [Paris], 1978. pp. 260.

— Germany.

HISTORISCHE Prozesse der deutschen Inflation, 1914 bis 1924: ein Tagungsbericht; bearbeitet und herausgegeben von Otto Büsch und Gerald D. Feldman...; mit Beiträgen von Werner Abelshauser [and others]. Berlin, 1978. pp. 466. *bibliogs. (Historische Kommission zu Berlin. Einzelveröffentlichungen. Band 21) Proceedings of a symposium held in Berlin in 1976; in German or English.*

— India.

WARREN (BILL) Inflation and wages in underdeveloped countries: India, Peru and Turkey, 1939-1960. London, 1977. pp. 285. *bibliog.*

— Italy.

ROTA (GIORGIO) L'inflazione in Italia, 1952-1974. Torino, 1975. pp. 146.

ROSSIGNOLI (BRUNO) Il portafoglio di attività finanziarie delle famiglie italiane, 1964-1973: la domanda di impieghi liquidi e di titoli mobiliari. [Milano, 1976]. pp. 127. *bibliog.*

TEORIA monetaria e struttura finanziaria in Italia; a cura di Gianluigi Mengarelli. Venezia, 1976. pp. 405.

La LOTTA all'inflazione. [Roma, 1977]. pp. 99. *Proceedings of the 1st meeting of the Comitato Direttivo, Centro Studi Politica Economica, Partito Comunista Italiano.*

INFLATION (FINANCE).(Cont.)

— Peru.

WARREN (BILL) Inflation and wages in underdeveloped countries: India, Peru and Turkey, 1939-1960. London, 1977. pp. 285. *bibliog.*

— Turkey.

WARREN (BILL) Inflation and wages in underdeveloped countries: India, Peru and Turkey, 1939-1960. London, 1977. pp. 285. *bibliog.*

— Underdeveloped areas.

See UNDERDEVELOPED AREAS — Inflation.

— United Kingdom.

INFLATION in the United Kingdom; edited by Michael Parkin and Michael T. Sumner. Manchester, 1978. pp. 181. *bibliog. (Manchester. University. Studies in Inflation) Derives from weekly meetings of the Manchester University-SSRC Inflation Workshop.*

— — Bibliography.

MACCAFFERTY (MAXINE) compiler. Inflation in the United Kingdom; [a bibliography]. London, [1977]. pp. 75. *(Association of Special Libraries and Information Bureaux. Aslib Bibliographies. 6)*

— United States.

COMMITTEE FOR ECONOMIC DEVELOPMENT. Research and Policy Committee. Fighting inflation and promoting growth. [New York], 1976. pp. 96.

SHERMAN (HOWARD JAY) Stagflation: a radical theory of unemployment and inflation. New York, [1976]. pp. 252. *bibliogs.*

DOES the government profit from inflation?; (an [AEI] Round Table held on May 25 1977...[in] Washington); John Charles Daly, moderator, etc. Washington, [1977]. pp. 42. *(American Enterprise Institute for Public Policy Research. Round Tables)*

NATIONAL BUREAU OF ECONOMIC RESEARCH. Conference on Research in Income and Wealth. Studies in Income and Wealth. vol. 42. Analysis of inflation, 1965-1974: [papers presented in 1974]; Joel Popkin, editor. Cambridge, Mass., 1977. pp. 487. *bibliogs. Proceedings of a Conference held in 1974 in Bethesda, Md. Tables on microfiche (1 card)*

CURING chronic inflation; Arthur M. Okun and George L. Perry, editors. Washington, D.C., [1978]. pp. 297. *Based on a special conference of the Brookings Panel on Economic Activity held in 1978.*

MILLER (ERVIN) Microeconomic effects of monetary policy: the fallout of severe monetary restraint. London, 1978. pp. 228.

INFLATION (FINANCE) AND ACCOUNTING.

JÄGERHORN (REGINALD) Inflationen och vår nya bokföringslag. Helsingfors, 1974. fo. 76-85. *(Svenska Handelshögskolan. Företagsekonomiska Institutionen. Meddelanden. Nr. 9) (Särtryck ur Finlands Svenska Ekonomförbunds Kurskompendium kring den nya bokföringslagen 1973)*

JÄGERHORN (REGINALD) Kan vi beakta inflationen i våra bokslut? Helsingfors, 1975. fo. 18. *(Svenska Handelshögskolan. Företagsekonomiska Institutionen. Meddelanden. Nr. 10)*

GOLDSCHMIDT (YAAQOV) and ADMON (KURT) Profit measurement during inflation: accounting, economic and financial aspects. New York, [1977]. pp. 328. *bibliog.*

INFLATION (FINANCE) AND UNEMPLOYMENT.

STAGFLATION: an international problem; edited by Randall Hinshaw. New York, [1977]. pp. 150. *Proceedings of the 5th Bologna-Claremont Conference on International Monetary Problems held at Claremont in 1975.*

— France.

MARCZEWSKI (JEAN) Inflation and unemployment in France. New York, 1978. pp. 200. *Translated by Marian Reeds.*

INFORMATION NETWORKS.

SAMUELSON (KJELL) and others. Information systems and networks: design and planning guidelines of informatics for managers, decision makers and systems analysts. Amsterdam, 1977. pp. 148. *bibliog.*

INFORMATION SCIENCE.

HICKEY (THOMAS J.) Introduction to metascience: an information science approach to methodology of scientific research. Oak Park, Ill., 1976. pp. 74.

INFORMATION SERVICES.

BATSCHA (ROBERT) The effectiveness of dissemination methods for social and economic development research. Paris, Organisation for Economic Co-operation and Development, 1976. pp. 201. *bibliog. (Development Centre. Technical Papers)*

— Directories.

INTER-ORGANIZATION BOARD FOR INFORMATION SYSTEMS. 1978. Directory of United Nations information systems and services. Geneva, 1978. pp. 267.

— France.

FRANCE. Groupe sectoriel d'Analyse et de Prévision Biens d'Equipement Electronique, Informatique et Télécommunications. 1976. Rapport...: préparation du 7e Plan. Paris, [1976]. pp. 62.

— Ireland (Republic).

ORGANISATION FOR ECONOMIC COOPERATION AND DEVELOPMENT. Information Policy Group. 1974. Ireland. Paris, 1974. pp. 82. *(Reviews of National Scientific and Technical Information Policy. [No. 2])*

— Spain.

ORGANISATION FOR ECONOMIC COOPERATION AND DEVELOPMENT. Information Policy Group. 1974. Spain. Paris, 1974. pp. 170. *bibliog. (Reviews of National Scientific and Technical Information Policy. [No.3])*

— Underdeveloped areas.

See UNDERDEVELOPED AREAS — Information services.

— United Kingdom.

SNAITH (JILL) An information service in a deprived housing estate. Glasgow, 1976. pp. 20. *bibliog. (Glasgow. University. Department of Economic and Social Research. Discussion Papers in Social Research. No. 16)*

LLEWELYN-DAVIES WEEKS [AND PARTNERS]. Inner area study: Birmingham: Family Service Unit: 435 Neighbourhood Centre. [London], Department of the Environment, [1977]. pp. 63.

OLDHAM COMMUNITY DEVELOPMENT PROJECT. Neighbourhood information and advice centres: Oldham C[ommunity] D[evelopment] P[roject]; edited by Neil Shenton and Pat Collis. [Oldham], 1977. pp. 83, xliv. *bibliog.*

— — Bibliography.

LUST (JOHN) and WOOD (FRANCES) B.A.(Cantab.) compilers. Catalogue of publications of translation and monitoring services and of periodicals dealing with the People's Republic of China in the library of the School of Oriental and African Studies. London, 1974. pp. 37.

INFORMATION STORAGE AND RETRIEVAL SYSTEMS.

LOCAL AUTHORITIES MANAGEMENT SERVICES AND COMPUTER COMMITTEE. Computer Panel. Census analysis. London, 1974. pp. 30.

STAMPER (RONALD) Informatics without computers? London, [1976]. pp. 14.

SAMUELSON (KJELL) and others. Information systems and networks: design and planning guidelines of informatics for managers, decision makers and systems analysts. Amsterdam, 1977. pp. 148. *bibliog.*

— Birth control clinics.

MOSSBERG (THOMAS) and others. ADDLIB: a packaged computer program for processing address and library information. Chicago, 1976. pp. 127. *(Chicago. University. Community and Family Study Center. R.F.F.P.I. Family Planning Evaluation Manuals. No. 9)*

— City planning.

SMEDLEY (B.S.) An Urban Management System and geographic data processing in urban planning. Peterlee, 1976. pp. 23. *bibliog. (IBM United Kingdom Limited. UK Scientific Centre. [Technical Reports]. 0079)*

— Education.

EUDISED R AND D BULLETIN; [pd. by] Documentation Centre for Education in Europe, Council of Europe. q., current issues only. Strasbourg.

— Evaluation.

UNIVERSITY OF BATH. Library. Design of Information Systems in the Social Sciences. Research Reports. Series A. No. 4. The evaluation of operational effectiveness and its use in the design of information systems. Bath, 1975. pp. 48. *bibliog.*

— Libraries.

MOSSBERG (THOMAS) and others. ADDLIB: a packaged computer program for processing address and library information. Chicago, 1976. pp. 127. *(Chicago. University. Community and Family Study Center. R.F.F.P.I. Family Planning Evaluation Manuals. No. 9)*

— Social sciences.

UNIVERSITY OF BATH. Library. Design of Information Systems in the Social Sciences. Research Reports. Series A. No. 4. The evaluation of operational effectiveness and its use in the design of information systems. Bath, 1975. pp. 48. *bibliog.*

SOCIAL SCIENCE RESEARCH COUNCIL SURVEY ARCHIVE. Catalogue; (with booklet, How to use the catalogue). 3 a yr. Colchester. *Current issue only kept, as each supersedes the previous one. File includes current issue of Inventory.*

— Study and teaching.

EDUCATION and large information systems: proceedings of the IFIP Working Conference organized by the Technical Committees for Education-TC3 and for Information Systems-TC8; edited by R.A. Buckingham. Amsterdam, 1977. pp. 197. *Conference held in The Hague, 1977 by the International Federation for Information Processing.*

INFORMATION THEORY IN SOCIOLOGY.

SHLIAPENTOKH (VLADIMIR EMMANUILOVICH) Problemy reprezentativnosti sotsiologicheskoi informatsii: sluchainaia i nesluchainaia vyborki v sotsiologii. Moskva, 1976. pp. 214. *bibliog.*

INHERITANCE AND SUCCESSION

— Russia — Soviet Central Asia.

KISLIAKOV (NIKOLAI ANDREEVICH) Nasledovanie i razdel imushchestva narodov Srednei Azii i Kazakhstana, XIX - nachalo XX v. Leningrad, 1977. pp. 131. *bibliog.*

— United Kingdom.

MELLOWS (ANTHONY ROGER) The law of succession. 3rd ed. London, 1977. pp. 843.

— **United States.**

BRITTAIN (JOHN A.) Inheritance and the inequality of material wealth. Washington, D.C., [1978]. pp. 102. *(Brookings Institution. Studies in Social Economics)*

INHERITANCE AND TRANSFER TAX

— **Australia.**

AUSTRALIA. Commonwealth Treasury. 1974. Estate duty and gift duty: purpose and rationale. Canberra, 1974. pp. 20. *(Treasury Taxation Papers. No. 11)*

— **Netherlands.**

VERENIGING VOOR BELASTINGWETENSCHAP. Commissie voor de Successie- en Registratiebelasting. Rapport inzake de Registratiewet 1917. Deventer, 1967. pp. 22. *(Vereniging voor Belastingwetenschap. Geschriften Nr. 117)*

— **United Kingdom.**

MORCOM (JOHN BRIAN) and PARRY (DAVID J.T.) Capital transfer tax. 2nd ed. Cambridge, 1978. pp. 496.

INLAND NAVIGATION

— **Laws and regulations.**

UNITED NATIONS. Interregional Symposium on Technico-Economic, Organizational and Administrative Aspects of Inland Waterborne Transport, Leningrad, 1968. Report of the...Symposium [held at] Leningrad, 9-29 September 1968. (ST/TAO/SER.C/114). New York, 1970. pp. 73.

INLAND WATER TRANSPORTATION.

UNITED NATIONS. Interregional Symposium on Technico-Economic, Organizational and Administrative Aspects of Inland Waterborne Transport, Leningrad, 1968. Report of the...Symposium [held at] Leningrad, 9-29 September 1968. (ST/TAO/SER.C/114). New York, 1970. pp. 73.

INSANE, CRIMINAL AND DANGEROUS.

SOCIETY FOR IMPROVING THE CONDITION OF THE INSANE. Rules and list of the present members of the Society;...and the prize essay entitled The progressive changes which have taken place since the time of Pinel in the moral management of the insane...; by Daniel H. Tuke; together with a short abstract or classification of cases contributed by Sir Alexander Morison. London, 1854. pp. 6, 122.

— **United Kingdom.**

HOWARD LEAGUE FOR PENAL REFORM. Procedure and resouces for mentally abnormal offenders. London, 1976. pp. 20.

— **United States.**

IN fear of each other: studies of dangerousness in America; [edited by] John P. Conrad [and] Simon Dinitz. Lexington, Mass., [1977]. pp. 141.

INSTITUT PROVINCIAL DES SCIENCES SOCIALES APPLIQUEES.

MAYENCE (SERGE) L'IPSSA à 25 ans: contribution à l'histoire de l'Institut et réflexions sur l'avenir des sciences sociales appliquées. [Marcinelle, 1970]. pp. 72. *biblog.*

INSTITUTIONAL CARE

— **Canada.**

CANADA. Statistics Canada. Special care facilities: residential facilities and services. a., 1974(1st)- Ottawa. *[in English and French]*

— — **Newfoundland.**

NEWFOUNDLAND. Commission of Enquiry into the Chafe's Nursing Home fire of December 26, 1976 and into the Safety Standards and Quality of Care in Homes for Special Care and Welfare Institutions in the Province of Newfoundland. Report...; J.R. Gushue, commissioner. [St. John's, 1977?]. pp. 252.

— **United Kingdom.**

LIVING and working in residential homes; interim report of a Working Group; [N.M.E. Eady, chairman]. [London], Personal Social Services Council, 1975. pp. 33.

RESIDENTIAL CARE WORKING GROUP [U.K.]. Residential care reviewed; the report of the...Working Group incorporating Daily living: questions for staff; [N.M.E. Eady, chairman]. [London], Personal Social Services Council, 1977. pp. 59.

INSURANCE.

BEARD (ROBERT ERIC) and others. Risk theory: the stochastic basis of insurance. 2nd ed. London, 1977. pp. 195. *biblog.*

NATURAL resources, uncertainty, and general equilibrium systems: essays in memory of Rafael Lusky; edited by Alan S. Blinder [and] Philip Friedman. New York, [1977]. pp. 255. *bibliogs.*

— **European Economic Community countries.**

EUROPEAN COMMUNITIES. Statistical Office. Labour costs in distributive trades, banking and insurance. trien., 1974(2nd)- Luxembourg. *[in Community languages] 1970(1st) included in EUROPEAN COMMUNITIES. Statistical Office. Social statistics, 1972(no. 4).*

EUROPEAN COMMUNITIES. Statistical Office. Special Series: Structure of Earnings in Wholesale and Retail Distribution, Banking and Insurance in 1974. Luxembourg, [1977] in progress.

— **France** — **Accounting.**

FRANCE. Direction des Assurances. Entreprises d'assurances et de capitalisation: principaux résultats comptables. a., 1975- Paris.

— **Germany.**

VEREIN FÜR SOZIALPOLITIK. Schriften. Neue Folge. Band 93. Wettbewerbsprobleme der Versicherungswirtschaft; herausgegeben von Burkhardt Röper. Berlin, [1978]. pp. 168.

— **Netherlands.**

BAKKER (VINCENT) Uw geld en uw leven: het verzekeringsbedrijf ontmaskerd. Bussum, 1978. pp. 272.

— **United States.**

POST (JAMES E.) Risk and response: management and social change in the American insurance industry. Lexington, Mass., [1976]. pp. 206. *biblog.*

— — **Social aspects.**

POST (JAMES E.) Risk and response: management and social change in the American insurance industry. Lexington, Mass., [1976]. pp. 206. *biblog.*

INSURANCE, AGRICULTURAL

— **European Economic Community countries.**

SMITH (LOUIS P.F.) Comparison of certain finance costs in agriculture: Ireland and European Economic Community, 1961. Dublin, 1965. pp. 78.

— **Ireland (Republic).**

SMITH (LOUIS P.F.) Comparison of certain finance costs in agriculture: Ireland and European Economic Community, 1961. Dublin, 1965. pp. 78.

INSURANCE, AUTOMOBILE

— **Tasmania.**

TASMANIA. Law Reform Commission. 1976. Report on motor vehicle insurance: right to sue insurance company direct. in TASMANIA. Parliament. Journals and Printed Papers. 1976, no. 12.

INSURANCE, LIFE

— **United Kingdom.**

IVAMY (EDWARD RICHARD HARDY) Fire and motor insurance. 3rd ed. London, 1978. pp. 498.

INSURANCE, EXPORT CREDIT

— **New Zealand.**

NEW ZEALAND. Export Guarantee Office. 1966. To assist you in the operation of your policy. [Wellington, 1966]. pp. 11.

NEW ZEALAND. Export Guarantee Office. 1967. Exporters' insurance. [Wellington, 1967]. pp. 12.

INSURANCE, FIRE

— **United Kingdom.**

IVAMY (EDWARD RICHARD HARDY) Fire and motor insurance. 3rd ed. London, 1978. pp. 498.

INSURANCE, HEALTH

— **Canada — British Columbia.**

BRITISH COLUMBIA. Provincial Secretary's Department. 1966. Twenty-second annual Western Conference of Pre-paid Medical Service Plans, November, 1966: who cares for people?. Panel: government and doctors: an effective co-operation. [Victoria, 1966]. fo. 16.

— — **Ontario.**

MANGA (P.) The income distribution effect of medical insurance in Ontario. [Toronto, 1978]. pp. 215. *biblog.* *(Ontario. Economic Council. Occasional Papers. 6)*

— **Germany.**

CARL-ZEISS STIFTUNG ZU JENA. Optische Werkstätte. Statut der Zuschusskrankenkasse der Optischen Werkstätte Carl Zeiss in Jena: eingeschriebene Hülfskasse. Jena, [imprint, 1902]. pp. 7.

— **Italy.**

CERBO (FERNANDO DI) La tutela della salute nell'ordinamento giuridico italiano. Roma, 1978. pp. 194.

— **Japan.**

NATIONAL FEDERATION OF HEALTH INSURANCE SOCIETIES (JAPAN). Health insurance and health insurance societies in Japan. Tokyo, 1976. pp. 26.

— **New Zealand.**

NEW ZEALAND. Department of Health. 1970. Health benefits in New Zealand. [Wellington], 1970. pp. 18.

— **United States.**

FEDER (JUDITH MORRIS) Medicare: the politics of federal hospital insurance. Lexington, Mass., [1977]. pp. 177. *biblog.*

FRECH (H.E.) and GINSBURG (PAUL B.) Public insurance in private medical markets; some problems of national health insurance. Washington, D.C., [1978]. pp. 93. *(American Enterprise Institute for Public Policy Research. AEI Studies. 201)*

INSURANCE, LIFE

— **Mathematics.**

NEILL (ALISTAIR) Life contingencies. London, 1977. pp. 452. *biblog.*

— **United Kingdom.**

HOUSEMAN (DAVID) Law of life assurance; ninth edition by B.P.A. Davies. London, 1978. pp. 428.

INSURANCE, MARINE

— New Zealand.

NEW ZEALAND. Contracts and Commercial Law Reform Committee. 1970. The Marine Insurance Act 1908: effect of Atkinson v. South British Insurance Co. Ltd.; report...presented to the Minister of Justice in November 1970; [M.F. Chilwell, chairman]. [Wellington], 1970. pp. 6.

INSURANCE, SOCIAL.

See SOCIAL SECURITY.

INSURANCE, UNEMPLOYMENT.

BLAUSTEIN (SAUL J.) and CRAIG (ISABEL) An international review of unemployment insurance schemes. Kalamazoo, Mich., 1977. pp. 267. *bibliog. (W. E. Upjohn Institute for Employment Research. Studies in Unemployment Insurance and Related Problems)*

— Canada.

CANADIAN LABOUR CONGRESS. Submission to the Parliamentary Committee on Labour, Manpower and Immigration on Bill C-69 (An Act to Amend the Unemployment Insurance Act, 1971). [Ottawa], 1975. fo. 10.

— United Kingdom.

BIRMINGHAM. Board of Guardians. Central Relief Committee. Report...16th November, 1927. [Birmingham, 1927]. fo.3.

FULBROOK (JULIAN) Administrative justice and the unemployed. London, 1978. pp. 338. *bibliog.*

INSURANCE COMPANIES

— Employees — Sweden.

STJERNBERG (TORBJÖRN) Organizational change and quality of life: individual and organizational perspectives on democratization of work in an insurance company. Stockholm, 1977. pp. 375. *bibliog. A research report of the Programme for Participation and Organization Development, Economic Research Institute, Stockholm School of Economics.*

— United Kingdom.

AND at Lloyd's: the story of Price, Forbes and Company Limited. London, [1955?]. pp. 71.

INSURANCE LAW

— United Kingdom.

IVAMY (EDWARD RICHARD HARDY) Fire and motor insurance. 3rd ed. London, 1978. pp. 498.

INSURGENCY

— Sri Lanka.

MILITANT: for labour and youth. Pamphlets. Which way forward for the workers and peasants of Ceylon?: a Marxist analysis of the insurrection. London, [1972?]. pp. 5.

INTEGRALS, GENERALIZED.

PFEFFER (WASHEK F.) Integrals and measures. New York, [1977]. pp. 259. *bibliog.*

INTELLECT.

The NATURE of intelligence; edited by Lauren B. Resnick. Hillsdale, N.J., 1976. pp. 364. *bibliogs. Papers presented at a conference held in 1974 at the Learning Research and Development Center, University of Pittsburgh.*

ZAHIRNIC (CONSTANTIN) Inteligența tehnică: studiu comparativ. București, 1976. pp. 179. *bibliog.*

INTELLECTUALS

— Europe.

RESZLER (ANDRE) L'intellectuel contre l'Europe. [Paris, 1976]. pp. 161. *bibliog.*

— France.

SORUM (PAUL CLAY) Intellectuals and decolonization in France. Chapel Hill, N.C., [1977]. pp. 305. *bibliog.*

— Italy.

INTELLETTUALI cattolici tra riformismo e dissenso: polemiche sull'integrismo, obbedienza e fine dell'unità politica rifiuto dell'istituzione nelle reviste degli anni sessanta; a cura di Sergio Ristuccia. [Milano, 1975]. pp. 430. *(Fondazione Adriano Olivetti. Programma di Ricerche di Cultura Politica. vol. 3)*

GUARNIERI (SILVIO) L'intellettuale nel partito. [Venezia, 1976]. pp. 303.

— Poland.

RAINA (PETER K.) Political opposition in Poland, 1954-1977. London, 1978. pp. 584. *bibliog.*

— Russia.

SAADANBEKOV (ZHUMAGUL) O sotsial'noi psikhologii sel'skoi intelligentsii. Frunze, 1975. pp. 88.

BESANÇON (ALAIN) Les origines intellectuelles du léninisme. [Paris, 1977]. pp. 323. *bibliog.*

PUZANEV (VLADIMIR SEMENOVICH) Sel'skii intelligent. Moskva, 1977. pp. 253.

— United States.

GILBERT (JAMES BURKHART) Work without salvation: America's intellectuals and industrial alienation, 1880-1910. Baltimore, [1977]. pp. 240.

HUMPHREY (ROBERT E.) Children of fantasy: the first rebels of Greenwich Village. New York, [1978]. pp. 267. *bibliog.*

INTELLIGENCE LEVELS.

PARTY FOR WORKERS POWER. Racism, intelligence and the working class. Boston, Mass., [1974?]. pp. 71.

— Afro-Americans.

PROGRESSIVE LABOR PARTY. Racism, IQ and the class society. London, [1974?]. pp. 75, xi.

INTELLIGENCE SERVICE

— Israel.

DEACON (RICHARD) The Israeli secret service. London, 1977. pp. 318. *bibliog.*

PEARSON (ANTHONY) Journalist. Conspiracy of silence. London, 1978. pp. 179.

— Italy.

PISANO (VITTORFRANCO S.) A study of the restructured Italian intelligence and security services. [Washington], Library of Congress, 1978. pp. 78.

— South Africa.

PENROSE (BARRIE) and COURTIOUR (ROGER) The Pencourt file. London, 1978. pp. 423.

— United Kingdom.

PENROSE (BARRIE) and COURTIOUR (ROGER) The Pencourt file. London, 1978. pp. 423.

— United States.

SMITH (BAXTER) Secret documents exposed: FBI plot against the black movement. New York, [1974]. pp. 23. *(Repr. from May 1974 issue of The Black Scholar)*

AGEE (PHILIP) Covert action: what next? London, [1976]. pp. 16. *(Agee-Hosenball Defence Committee. C.I.A. Briefings. No. 3)*

AGEE-HOSENBALL DEFENCE COMMITTEE. C.I.A. Briefings. No. 2. Jamaica destabilised: British Guiana repeated? London, [1976]. pp. 15.

MARIN (GERMAN) Una historia fantastica y calculada: la CIA en el pais de los chilenos. Mexico, 1976. pp. 280.

FREEDMAN (LAWRENCE DAVID) US intelligence and the Soviet strategic threat. London, 1977. pp. 235. *bibliog.*

HIRSCH (FRED) and FLETCHER (RICHARD) The CIA and the labour movement. Nottingham, 1977. pp. 71.

JEFFREYS-JONES (RHODRI) American espionage: from secret service to CIA. New York, [1977]. pp. 276. *bibliog.*

PAINE (LAURAN) The CIA at work. London, 1977. pp. 192. *bibliog.*

COLBY (WILLIAM EGAN) Honourable men: my life in the CIA. London, 1978. pp. 493.

PEARSON (ANTHONY) Journalist. Conspiracy of silence. London, 1978. pp. 179.

INTER-AMERICAN DEVELOPMENT BANK.

DEWITT (R. PETER) The Inter-American Development Bank and political influence, with special reference to Costa Rica. New York, 1977. pp. 197. *bibliog.*

INTERCULTURAL COMMUNICATION.

BUCHANAN (GEORGE) Novelist. The politics of culture. London, 1977. pp. 54.

MASS media policies in changing cultures; edited by George Gerbner. New York, [1977]. pp. 291. *bibliog.*

INTERCULTURAL EDUCATION

— United States.

OGBU (JOHN U.) Minority education and caste: the American system in cross-cultural perspective. New York, [1978]. pp. 410. *bibliog.*

INTEREST AND USURY.

VAN HORNE (JAMES CARTER) Financial market rates and flows. Englewood Cliffs, [1978]. pp. 250. *bibliogs. Revised edition of his The function and analysis of capital market rates.*

— France.

COTTA (ALAIN) Taux d'intérêt, plus-values et épargne en France et dans les nations occidentales. [Paris, 1976]. pp. 224.

— Italy.

POLIAKOV (LEON) Jewish bankers and the Holy See from the thirteenth to the seventeenth century;...translated from the French by Miriam Kochan. London, 1977. pp. 275.

— New Zealand.

DEANE (RODERICK S.) Interest rate policy: a New Zealand quandary. Wellington, 1975. pp. 36. *(Reserve Bank of New Zealand. Research Papers. No. 17)*

INTERGOVERNMENTAL FISCAL RELATIONS.

HUNTER (JAMES STUART HARDY) Federalism and fiscal balance: a comparative study. Canberra, 1977. pp. 271. *bibliog.*

The POLITICAL economy of fiscal federalism; edited by Wallace E. Oates. Lexington, Mass., [1977]. pp. 355. *bibliog. Papers presented at a conference sponsored by the International Seminar in Public Economics and the International Institute of Management, held in 1976 in Berlin.*

VEREIN FÜR SOZIALPOLITIK. Schriften. Neue Folge. Band 96/I. Probleme des Finanzausgleichs I; von Dieter Bös [and others]; herausgegeben von Wilhelmine Dreissig. Berlin, [1978]. pp. 175. *In German, with summaries and table of contents in English.*

— Brazil.

WIRTH (JOHN D.) Minas Gerais in the Brazilian Federation, 1889-1937. Stanford, 1977. pp. 322. *bibliog.*

— Canada.

BRITISH COLUMBIA. 1971. Opening statement of the province of British Columbia to the Constitutional Conference, Victoria, June 14 to 16, 1971. [Victoria, 1971]. fo. 7.

— Germany.

VEREIN FÜR SOZIALPOLITIK. Schriften. Neue Folge. Band 96/I. Probleme des Finanzausgleichs I; von Dieter Bös [and others]; herausgegeben von Wilhelmine Dreissig. Berlin, [1978]. pp. 175. *In German, with summaries and table of contents in English.*

— India.

KRISHNAN (S.N.) Agricultural taxation and states' resources. New Delhi, 1972. fo. 41. *(United States. Agency for International Development. USAID-New Delhi. Economic Affairs Division. Staff Papers)*

— United Kingdom — Isle of Man.

ISLE OF MAN. Commission on the Financial Relations between the Isle of Man Revenue and the Local Authorities and Public Services. 1931. Report; [R.D. Farrant, chairman]. [Douglas, 1931]. pp. 22.

— United States.

TAX FOUNDATION. Research Publications. New Series. No. 29. Federal grants: the need for reform. New York, [1973]. pp. 44.

PASCALE (RICHARD T.) and BARBOUR (GEORGE P.) Shared power: a study of four federal funding systems in Appalachia. Washington, [1977]. pp. 36. *(American Enterprise Institute for Public Policy Research. Special Analyses)*

PASSELL (PETER) and ROSS (LEONARD) State policies and federal programs: priorities and constraints. New York, [1978]. pp. 168. *A Twentieth Century Fund Report.*

INTERGOVERNMENTAL TAX RELATIONS

— Canada — Alberta.

ALBERTA. Provincial-Municipal Finance Council. 1976. A proposal for property tax growth-sharing. [Edmonton, 1976]. fo. 29. *bibliog.*

INTERINDUSTRY ECONOMICS.

UNITED NATIONS INDUSTRIAL DEVELOPMENT ORGANIZATION. First Ad Hoc Group of Experts on Industrial Programming Data. 1965. International comparisons of interindustry data: proceedings of the meeting of the...held in New York, November, 1965. New York, United Nations, 1969. pp. 270.

ZAJCHOWSKI (JÓZEF) The application of input-output analysis to planning. Warszawa, 1970. pp. 38. *bibliog. (Instytut Gospodarki Krajów Rozwijających Się. Teaching Papers: Advanced Course in National Economic Planning. vol.7)*

AUSTRALIA. Commonwealth Bureau of Census and Statistics. 1976. Australian national accounts: input-output tables, 1968-69. Canberra, [1976]. pp. 193.

MEDIUM-term dynamic forecasting: proceedings of the 1975 London Conference; edited by W.F. Gossling, etc. London, 1977. pp. 292. *bibliogs. Sponsored by the Input-Output Research Association.*

STUDIES in Soviet input-output analysis; edited by Vladimir G. Treml. New York, 1977. pp. 446. *bibliogs.*

UNITED NATIONS. Conference of European Statisticians. Statistical Standards and Studies. No. 30. Standardized input-output tables of ECE countries for years around 1965. New York, 1977. 1 vol. (various pagings)

BOADWAY (ROBIN W.) and others. Input-output analyses of fiscal policy in Ontario;...edited by John Bossons. [Toronto, 1978]. pp. 228. *bibliog. (Ontario. Economic Council. Occasional Papers. 3)*

INTERNAL SECURITY

— Germany.

COBLER (SEBASTIAN) Law, order and politics in West Germany; translated [from the German] by Francis McDonagh. Harmondsworth, 1978. pp. 223.

— Switzerland.

THUT (ROLF) and BISLIN (CLAUDIA) Aufrüstung gegen das Volk: (Staat und Staatsschutz in der Schweiz; zur Problematik der "inneren Sicherheit"). Zürich, [1977]. pp. 245. *bibliog.*

INTERNATIONAL, THE.

TRADES UNION CONGRESS and LABOUR PARTY. Joint International Department. International unity: the Berlin conference, 2nd-6th April, 1922; (and The Five Country International Conference,... Frankfurt, 25th, 26th and 27th February, 1922). [London, 1922]. 7 pts.

DONNEUR (ANDRE) Histoire de l'Union des partis socialistes pour l'action internationale, 1920-1923. [Geneva], 1967. pp. 434. *bibliog. Thèse (docteur ès sciences politiques)- Université de Genève.*

CONSTRUIRE le parti révolutionnaire: construire l'Internationale. Paris, 1969 in progress.

FOURTH INTERNATIONAL. International Committee. Accomplices of the GPU. London, [1976]. pp. 24.

FOURTH INTERNATIONAL. International Committee. How the GPU murdered Trotsky. London, [1976]. 1 pamphlet (unpaged).

HEVESI (MARIA) Iz istorii kritiki filosofskikh dogm II Internatsionala. Moskva, 1977. pp. 207.

HOFMAIER (KARL) Memoiren eines Schweizer Kommunisten, 1917-1947. Zürich, 1978. pp. 303.

SAIYID (DUSHKA HYDER) The Comintern and the Communist Party of India, 1920-1929. 1977 [or rather 1978]. fo.203. *bibliog.* Typescript. M.Phil. (London) thesis: unpublished. *This thesis is the property of London University and may not be removed from the Library.*

INTERNATIONAL AGENCIES.

UNITED NATIONS CONFERENCE ON THE REPRESENTATION OF STATES IN THEIR RELATIONS WITH INTERNATIONAL ORGANIZATIONS, VIENNA, 1975. Official Records. (A/CONF. 67/18). New York, 1976. 2 vols. (in 1)

AKINTAN (S.A.) The law of international economic institutions in Africa. Leyden, 1977. pp. 222.

BENNETT (ALVIN LEROY) International organizations: principles and issues. Englewood Cliffs, [1977]. pp. 440.

BISSELL (RICHARD E.) Apartheid and international organizations. Boulder, Colo., 1977. pp. 231. *bibliog.*

The FUTURE of international economic organizations; edited by Don Wallace [and] Helga Escobar. New York, 1977. pp. 184. *Papers of a colloquium held in Washington, 1975, and sponsored by the Institute for International and Foreign Trade Law and the Center for Strategic and International Studies of Georgetown University.*

WORK in intergovernmental organizations on transnational companies; proceedings of a seminar held in Jerusalem in 1976 during the 30th congress of the International Fiscal Association; edited by the International Fiscal Association. Deventer, [1977]. pp. 64.

INTERNATIONAL organisation: a conceptual approach; edited by Paul Taylor and A.J.R. Groom. London, 1978. pp. 464. *bibliogs.*

— Finance.

STEINBERG (ELEANOR B.) and YAGER (JOSEPH A.) New means of financing international needs; (with Gerard M. Brannon). Washington, D.C., [1978]. pp. 256.

INTERNATIONAL AND MUNICIPAL LAW

— Germany.

FONTES JURIS GENTIUM. Series A. Sectio 2. Tomus 5. Deutsche Rechtsprechung in völkerrechtlichen Fragen; Decisions of German courts relating to public international law... 1961-1965; bearbeitet im Max-Planck Institut für ausländisches öffentliches Recht und Völkerrecht von Albert Bleckmann [and others]. Berlin, 1978. pp. 1048.

INTERNATIONAL ATOMIC ENERGY AGENCY.

INTERNATIONAL ATOMIC ENERGY AGENCY. General Conference. Resolutions and other decisions. a., 1961(5th)- [Vienna]. *1957-1960 (1st-4th) are bound with documents of the General Conference. Indexes: 1957/1971, 1972/1975, 1957/1976.*

INTERNATIONAL BANK FOR RECONSTRUCTION AND DEVELOPMENT.

INTERNATIONAL BANK FOR RECONSTRUCTION AND DEVELOPMENT. Sector Policy Papers. Development finance companies. Washington, 1976. pp. 65.

INTERNATIONAL BROADCASTING.

MANSELL (GERARD) Broadcasting to the world: forty years of BBC external services. London, [1973]. pp. 8.

INTERNATIONAL BUSINESS ENTERPRISES.

COMMITTEE OF RETURNED VOLUNTEERS. Gulf Oil Corporation: a study in exploitation. rev. ed. New York, 1971. pp. 48. *bibliog.*

KAPLAN (MARCOS) ed. Corporaciones publicas multinacionales para el desarrollo y la integracion de la America Latina. Mexico, 1972. pp. 369. *bibliog. Papers presented at the Seminario Regional de Derecho Internacional para la America Latina, Quito, 1969, organized by UNITAR.*

BRUSEKER (U.) Unilever, Meneba, Philips en de olieconcerns als inflatiemakers; een bestrijding van de looninflatie-theorie. [Amsterdam], 1974. pp. 133. *bibliog.*

ACOCELLA (NICOLA) Imprese multinazionali e investimenti diretti: le cause dello sviluppo. Roma, 1975. pp. 262. *bibliog. (Rome. Università. Istituto di Politica Economica e Finanziaria. Pubblicazioni. 19)*

COUNTER INFORMATION SERVICES and TRANSNATIONAL INSTITUTE. Unilever's world. London, [1975?]. pp. 103. *bibliog. (Counter Information Services. Anti-Reports. No. 11)*

STREETEN (PAUL PATRICK) Policies towards multinationals. Oxford, 1975. pp. 6. *(Oxford. University. Institute of Commonwealth Studies. Reprint Series. No.77E) (Reprinted from World Development, vol.3, no.6, 1975)*

ANDREFF (WLADIMIR) Profits et structures du capitalisme mondial. [Paris, 1976]. pp. 285.

BROOKSTONE (JEFFREY M.) The multinational businessman and foreign policy: entrepreneurial politics in east-west trade and investment. New York, 1976. pp. 183. *bibliog.*

COLLOQUE DE LA FEDERATION DE PARIS DU PARTI SOCIALISTE, 1976. Socialisme et multinationales. Paris, [1976]. pp. 189. *bibliog.*

COMITO (VINCENZO) Multinazionali ed esportazione di capitale. Roma, 1976. pp. 385. *bibliogs.*

INTERNATIONAL BUSINESS ENTERPRISES. (Cont.)

GAMBA (MARINO) Innocenti: imprenditore, fabbrica e classe operaia in cinquant'anni di vita italiana. [Milan, 1976]. pp. 207.

HAYDEN (ERIC W.) Technology transfer to East Europe: U.S. corporate experience. New York, 1976. pp. 134. *bibliog.*

SEMINAR ON THE FUTURE OF THE MULTINATIONAL CORPORATION, SYDNEY, 1976. Australia and the multinational; the proceedings of a seminar... edited by Michael T. Skully. Sydney, 1976. pp. 52.

TEECE (DAVID J.) The multinational corporation and the resource cost of international technology transfer. Cambridge, Mass., [1976]. pp. 129. *bibliog.*

VIEIRA (DORIVAL TEIXEIRA) and CAMARGO (LENITA CORRÊA) Multinacionais no Brasil: diagnostico e prognostico. São Paulo, 1976. pp. 389. *bibliog.*

CONNOR (JOHN M.) The market power of multinationals: a quantitative analysis of U. S. corporations in Brazil and Mexico. New York, 1977. pp. 307. *bibliog.*

EDWARDS (ROBERT) Multinational companies and the trade unions. Nottingham, 1977. pp. 70.

GARREAU (GERARD) L'agrobusiness. [Paris, 1977]. pp. 302.

GLADWIN (THOMAS) Environment, planning and the multinational corporation. Greenwich, Conn., [1977]. pp. 295. *bibliog.*

HELLER (TOM) Poor health, rich profits: multinational drug companies and the Third World. Nottingham, 1977. pp. 76.

INTERNATIONAL resource flows; edited by Gerald Garvey and Lou Ann Garvey. Lexington, Mass., [1977]. pp. 178.

JACOBY (NEIL HERMAN) and others. Bribery and extortion in world business: a study of corporate political payments abroad. New York, [1977]. pp. 294. *(Columbia University. Graduate School of Business. Studies of the Modern Corporation)*

LABOUR PARTY. International big business: Labour's policy on the multinationals. London, 1977. pp. 135.

LEGAL problems of multinational corporations; edited by Kenneth R. Simmonds. London, 1977. pp. 233. *A selection from papers of an international conference held by the British Institute of International and Comparative Law in 1976.*

LIVINGSTONE (JAMES MACCARDLE) National government and the international enterprise. [Glasgow, 1977?]. pp. 70. *bibliog. (Glasgow. University of Strathclyde. Department of Marketing. Working Papers)*

MORGAN (ALUN) and BLANPAIN (ROGER) The industrial relations and employment impacts of multinational enterprises: an inquiry into the issues. Paris, Organisation for Economic Co-operation and Development, 1977. pp. 42.

SCIBERRAS (EDMOND) Multinational electronics companies and national economic policies. Greenwich, Conn., [1977]. pp. 328. *bibliog.*

THUNELL (L.H.) Political risks in international business: investment behavior of multinational corporations. New York, 1977. pp. 133. *bibliog.*

TSURUMI (YOSHIHIRO) Multinational management: business strategy and government policy. Cambridge, Mass., [1977]. pp. 604. *bibliog.*

WORK in intergovernmental organizations on transnational companies; proceedings of a seminar held in Jerusalem in 1976 during the 30th congress of the International Fiscal Association; edited by the International Fiscal Association. Deventer, [1977]. pp. 64.

BERGSTEN (C. FRED) and others. American multinationals and American interests. Washington, D.C., [1978]. pp. 535.

COUNTER INFORMATION SERVICES. Anti-Reports. No. 20. The Ford Motor Company. Nottingham, [1978]. pp. 68.

EUROPEAN research in international business; edited by Michel Ghertman and James Leontiades. Amsterdam, 1978. pp. 368. *bibliogs. Papers selected from four conferences held from 1973 to 1976 by the European Institute for Advanced Studies in Management, the Centre d'Enseignement Supérieur des Affaires, and the European International Business Association.*

KOJIMA (KIYOSHI) Direct foreign investment: a Japanese model of multinational business operations. London, [1978]. pp. 246.

TURNER (LOUIS) Oil companies in the international system. London, 1978. pp. 240. *bibliog.*

UNITED NATIONS. Centre on Transnational Corporations. 1978. National legislation and regulations relating to transnational corporations. (ST/CTC/6). New York, 1978. pp. 302. *bibliogs.*

— **Bibliography.**

HERNES (HELGA) compiler. The multinational corporation: a guide to information sources. Detroit, [1977]. pp. 197.

— **Finance.**

RICKS (DAVID A.) International dimensions of corporate finance. Englewood Cliffs, [1978]. pp. 143. *bibliog.*

— **Social aspects.**

BRUYN (SEVERYN TEN HAUT) The social economy: people transforming modern business. New York, [1977]. pp. 392.

— **Taxation — Communist countries.**

JONAS (PAUL) Taxation of multinationals in communist countries. New York, [1978]. pp. 88. *bibliog.*

— **Underdeveloped areas.**

See UNDERDEVELOPED AREAS — International business enterprises.

INTERNATIONAL COOPERATION.

BAILEY (ALICE ANNE) The coming world order. Bath, 1940. pp. 32.

KRASNOV (IURII MATVEEVICH) Ot konfrontatsii k sotrudnichestvu: problemy ekonomicheskogo i nauchno-tekhnicheskogo sotrudnichestva kapitalisticheskikh i sotsialisticheskikh stran Evropy. Moskva, 1976. pp. 199.

UNITED NATIONS CONFERENCE ON THE REPRESENTATION OF STATES IN THEIR RELATIONS WITH INTERNATIONAL ORGANIZATIONS, VIENNA, 1975. Official Records. (A/CONF. 67/18). New York, 1976. 2 vols. (in 1)

COMMONWEALTH TEAM OF INDUSTRIAL SPECIALISTS. Cooperation for accelerating industrialisation; final report; [L. K. Jha, chairman]. London, Commonwealth Secretariat, [1978]. pp. 54.

INTERNATIONAL ECONOMIC INTEGRATION.

FROEBEL (FOLKER) and others. Die neue internationale Arbeitsteilung: strukturelle Arbeitslosigkeit in den Industrieländern und die Industrialisierung der Entwicklungsländer. Reinbek bei Hamburg, 1977. pp. 654.

HENGSBACH (FRIEDHELM) Die Assoziierung afrikanischer Staaten an die Europäischen Gemeinschaften: eine Politik raumwirtschaftlicher Integration? Baden-Baden, [1977]. pp. 238. *bibliog. (List Gesellschaft. Monographien. Neue Folge. Band 1)*

— **Bibliography.**

INSTITUTE FOR LATIN AMERICAN INTEGRATION. Documentation Service. Bibliographical Series. No. 1. Bilbiografia selectiva sobre integracion: Selective bibliography on integration. Buenos Aires, 1977. 1 vol.(various pagings). *bibliog.*

INTERNATIONAL ECONOMIC RELATIONS.

AMERICAN ECONOMIC ASSOCIATION. Readings in international economics, selected by a committee of the.. .Association; (selection committee for this volume, Richard E. Caves and Harry G. Johnson). London, 1968 repr. 1975. pp. 604. *bibliogs.*

SÖDERSTEN (BO) International economics. London, 1971. pp. 554.

TEMMAR (HAMID) Approche structurelle du phénomène du sous-développement: la structure de l'économie sous-développée. Alger, 1973. pp. 128. *bibliog.*

ADLER-KARLSSON (GUNNAR) The political economy of East-West-South co-operation. Vienna, 1976. pp. 208. *(Wiener Institut für Internationale Wirtschaftsvergleiche. Studien über Wirtschafts-und Systemvergleiche. Band 7)*

ANGELOPOULOS (ANGELOS) Pour une nouvelle politique du développement international. Paris, [1976]. pp. 198.

CĂTRE o nouă ordine internaţională; coordonator Nicolae Ecobescu, cu un cuvînt înainte de Ştefan A. Andrei. Bucureşti, 1976. pp. 542. *With English, French, German and Russian tables of contents.*

FLAMANT (MAURICE) Histoire économique et sociale contemporaine. Paris, [1976]. pp. 647. *bibliog.*

HAQ (MAHBUB UL) The third world and the international economic order. Washington, 1976. pp. 56. *(Overseas Development Council. Development Papers. 22)*

KRASNOV (IURII MATVEEVICH) Ot konfrontatsii k sotrudnichestvu: problemy ekonomicheskogo i nauchno-tekhnicheskogo sotrudnichestva kapitalisticheskikh i sotsialisticheskikh stran Evropy. Moskva, 1976. pp. 199.

PAKISTAN INSTITUTE OF INTERNATIONAL AFFAIRS. Zulfikar Ali Bhutto and the third world's struggle for new economic order. Karachi, 1976. pp. 32.

SHONFIELD (Sir ANDREW) International economic relations: the Western system in the 1960s and 1970s. Beverly Hills, [1976]. pp. 88. *bibliog. (Georgetown University. Center for Strategic and International Studies. Washington Papers. vol. 4/42)*

BARON (STEFAN) and others. Internationale Rohstoffpolitik: Ziele, Mittel, Kosten. Tübingen, 1977. pp. 194. *bibliog. (Kiel. Universität. Institut für Weltwirtschaft. Kieler Studien. 150)*

BERGSTEN (C. FRED) Managing international economic interdependence: selected papers of C. Fred. Bergsten, 1975-1976. Lexington, Mass., [1977]. pp. 317.

BEYOND the crisis; edited by Norman Birnbaum; with essays by Hans Peter Dreitzel [and others]. London, 1977. pp. 232.

BOGNÁR (JÓZSEF) The fight for a new system of international relations. Budapest, 1977. pp. 28. *(Hungarian Scientific Council for World Economy. [Publications]. Trends in World Economy. No. 21)*

CALDWELL (MALCOLM) The wealth of some nations. London, 1977. pp. 191. *bibliogs.*

COPPOCK (JOSEPH DAVID) International trade instability. Farnborough, Hants., [1977]. pp. 218.

EGOM (PETER ALEX) Money in the theory of international economic activity: an inquiry into the nature and causes of the wealth and poverty of nations. Guderup, [1977]. pp. 155.

EQUALITY of opportunity within and among nations; edited by Khadya Haq. New York, [1977]. pp. 223. *Based on the fifteenth World Conference of the Society for International Development held in Amsterdam in 1976.*

The FUTURE of international economic organizations; edited by Don Wallace [and] Helga Escobar. New York, 1977. pp. 184. *Papers of a colloquium held in Washington, 1975, and sponsored by the Institute for International and Foreign Trade Law and the Center for Strategic and International Studies of Georgetown University.*

HEIN (JOHN) and MADRID (NORMAN R.) The changing world economy: problems of interdependence. New York, [1977]. pp. 51. *bibliogs. (National Industrial Conference Board. Conference Board Reports. No. 727)*

HUDSON (MICHAEL) Ph.D. Global fracture: the new international economic order. New York, [1977]. pp. 296.

INTERNATIONAL resource flows; edited by Gerald Garvey and Lou Ann Garvey. Lexington, Mass., [1977]. pp. 178.

ISSUES and prospects for the new international order; edited by William G. Tyler. Lexington, Mass., [1977]. pp. 195. *Derived from a conference organised by the International Studies Association/South held in Virginia in 1976.*

MALMGREN (HARALD B.) International order for public subsidies. London, 1977. pp. 74. *bibliog. (Trade Policy Research Centre. Thames Essays. No. 11)*

MEIER (GERALD MARVIN) Employment, trade, and development: a problem in international policy analysis. Leiden, 1977. pp. 80. *bibliog. (Geneva. Graduate Institute of International Studies. International Economics Series. 4)*

MENON (BHASKAR P.) Global dialogue: the new international economic order. Oxford, 1977. pp. 110.

The NEW international economic order: the North-South debate; Jagdish N. Bhagwati, editor. Cambridge, Mass., [1977]. pp. 390. *bibliogs. (Massachusetts Institute of Technology. M.I.T. Bicentennial Studies) Based largely on a workshop held at MIT in May 1976.*

The NEW international order: confrontation or cooperation between North and South?; edited by Karl P. Sauvant and Hajo Hasenpflug. Boulder, Colo., 1977. pp. 474.

The OPEC market to 1985; [by] Farid Abolfathi [and others]. Lexington, Mass., [1977]. pp. 406. *bibliog.*

Les RELATIONS internationales dans un monde en mutation. International relations in a changing world. Genève, 1977. pp. vi,434. *Articles in French or English.*

RESHAPING the world economic order: symposium 1976, ([held at] Institut für Weltwirtschaft an der Universität Kiel); edited by Herbert Giersch. Tübingen, [1977]. pp. 291.

ROTHSTEIN (ROBERT L.) The weak in the world of the strong: the developing countries in the international system. New York, 1977. pp. 384.

SINGH (JYOTI SHANKAR) A new international economic order: toward a fair redistribution of the world's resources. New York, 1977. pp. 135. *bibliog.*

SPERO (JOAN EDELMAN) The politics of international economic relations. London, 1977. pp. 326. *bibliog.*

THIRD world: change or chaos?; documents from the conference... called by Liberation and the World Development Movement... London...1976, and the speech of President Boumedienne...at the United Nations in April 1974; (edited by Stan Newens). Nottingham, 1977. pp. 96.

WHITMAN (MARINA VON NEUMANN) Sustaining the international economic system: issues for U.S. policy. Princeton, 1977. pp. 56. *bibliog. (Princeton University. Department of Economics and Sociology. International Finance Section. Essays in International Finance. No. 121)*

COMMONWEALTH SECRETARIAT. Review of progress in the implementation of recommendations of the report of the Commonwealth Experts' Group, Towards a new international economic order; paper. London, 1978. pp. 47.

FROM Marshall Plan to global interdependence: new challenges for the industrialized nations. Paris, Organisation for Economic Co-operation and Development, 1978. pp. 246.

GOMES (LEONARD) International economic problems. London, 1978. pp. 180.

INGRAM (JAMES CARLTON) International economic problems. 3rd ed. Santa Barbara, [1978]. pp. 174. *bibliogs.*

KALDOR (MARY) The disintegrating west. London, 1978. pp. 219.

LEAN (GEOFFREY) Rich world, poor world. London, 1978. pp. 352. *bibliog.*

LEWIS (Sir WILLIAM ARTHUR) The evolution of the international economic order. Princeton, [1978]. pp. 81. *(Princeton University. Woodrow Wilson School of Public and International Affairs. Eliot Janeway Lectures on Historical Economics. 1977)*

LEWIS (Sir WILLIAM ARTHUR) Growth and fluctuations, 1870-1913. London, 1978. pp. 333.

PEARSON (CHARLES S.) and PRYOR (ANTHONY) Environment: north and south: an economic interpretation. New York, [1978]. pp. 355. *bibliog.*

RICH and poor nations in the world economy; [by] Albert Fishlow [and others]. New York, [1978]. pp. 262. *bibliog. (Council on Foreign Relations. 1980's Project Studies)*

SCHIAVO-CAMPO (SALVATORE) International economics: an introduction to theory and policy. Cambridge, Mass., [1978]. pp. 398. *bibliog.*

— **Mathematical models.**

PROBLEMS of world modeling: political and social implications; edited by Karl W. Deutsch [and others]. Cambridge. Mass., [1977]. pp. 420. *bibliogs. Papers of a meeting of Research Committee 7 of the International Political Science Association.*

INTERNATIONAL FEDERATION OF COTTON AND ALLIED TEXTILE INDUSTRIES.

INTERNATIONAL FEDERATION OF COTTON AND ALLIED TEXTILE INDUSTRIES. Directory. 7th ed. Zürich, 1975. pp. 44.

INTERNATIONAL FEDERATION OF LIBRARY ASSOCIATIONS.

INTERNATIONAL FEDERATION OF LIBRARY ASSOCIATIONS. General Council Meeting, 41st., Oslo, 1975. Working documents for the...meeting, etc. The Hague, 1975. 1 pamphlet (various pagings).

INTERNATIONAL FEDERATION OF LIBRARY ASSOCIATIONS. Programme Development Group. Medium-term programme. The Hague, 1976. pp. 43.

INTERNATIONAL FINANCE.

BECSKY (GYÖRGY) The international monetary situation and the global economic strategy of the USA; translated by George Hajdu. Budapest, 1972. pp. 46. *(Hungarian Scientific Council for World Economy. [Publications]. Trends in World Economy. No. 8)*

AKADEMIIA NAUK SSSR. Institut Mirovoi Ekonomiki i Mezhdunarodnykh Otnoshenii. Materialy mezhdunarodnogo simpoziuma "Krizis i evoliutsiia mezhdunarodnoi valiutnoi sistemy kapitalizma", Leningrad, 1974. Moskva, 1975. 2 pts. (in 1).

AL-HAMAD (ABDLATIF Y.) Towards a reassessment of the recycling problem; (address to the Royal Institute of International Affairs, April 21, 1975). [Kuwait, Kuwait Fund for Arab Economic Development, 1975] . pp. 14.

ANDREFF (WLADIMIR) Profits et structures du capitalisme mondial. [Paris, 1976]. pp. 285.

DEANE (RODERICK S.) International monetary reform: content and perspective. Wellington, 1976. pp. 27. *bibliog. (Reserve Bank of New Zealand. Research Papers. No. 21)*

The EMERGING international monetary order and the banking system; editor, Yair Aharoni. Tel Aviv, [1976]. pp. 191. *Papers of a seminar held in Israel in 1975, sponsored by Tel Aviv University Top Executive Course.*

JOHNSON (HARRY GORDON) Trade negotiations and the new international monetary system. Geneva, 1976. pp. 37. *(Geneva. Graduate Institute of International Studies, and Trade Policy Research Centre. Commercial Policy Issues. 1)*

ZOLOTAS (XENOPHON) International monetary vacillations. Athens, 1976. pp. 48. *(Bank of Greece. Papers and Lectures. 35)*

BEAUFORT WIJNHOLDS (J.A.H.DE) The need for international reserves and credit facilities. Leiden, 1977. pp. 251. *bibliog. (Nederlands Instituut voor het Bank- en Effectenbedrijf. Publikaties. No. 31)*

BERGSTEN (C. FRED) Managing international economic interdependence: selected papers of C. Fred. Bergsten, 1975-1976. Lexington, Mass., [1977]. pp. 317.

CLARKE (STEPHEN V.O.) Exchange-rate stabilization in the mid-1930s: negotiating the tripartite agreement. Princeton, 1977. pp. 59. *bibliog. (Princeton University. Department of Economics and Sociology. International Finance Section. Princeton Studies in International Finance. No. 41)*

GUINDEY (GUILLAUME) The international monetary tangle: myths and realities;... translated by Michael L. Hoffman. Oxford, 1977. pp. 122.

INTERNATIONAL monetary relations after Jamaica; edited by Fabio Basagni. Paris, [1977]. pp. 82. *(Atlantic Institute. Atlantic Papers. 1976. 4)*

JOHNSON (HARRY GORDON) Money, balance-of-payments theory, and the international monetary problem. Princeton, 1977. pp. 26. *bibliog. (Princeton University. Department of Economics and Sociology. International Finance Section. Essays in International Finance. No. 124)*

SCHMITT (BERNARD) L'or, le dollar et la monnaie supranationale. Paris, [1977]. pp. 227.

SOLOMON (ROBERT) The international monetary system, 1945-1976: an insider's view. New York, [1977]. pp. 381.

WHITMAN (MARINA VON NEUMANN) Sustaining the international economic system: issues for U.S. policy. Princeton, 1977. pp. 56. *bibliog. (Princeton University. Department of Economics and Sociology. International Finance Section. Essays in International Finance. No. 121)*

WILLETT (THOMAS D.) Floating exchange rates and international monetary reform. Washington, D.C., [1977]. pp. 146. *(American Enterprise Institute for Public Policy Research. AEI Studies. 172)*

CHACHOLIADES (MILTIADES) International monetary theory and policy. New York, [1978]. pp. 516. *bibliogs.*

COHEN (BENJAMIN J.) Organising the world's money: the political economy of international monetary relations. [London, 1978]. pp. 310.

SCHIAVO-CAMPO (SALVATORE) International economics: an introduction to theory and policy. Cambridge, Mass., [1978]. pp. 398. *bibliog.*

STEINBERG (ELEANOR B.) and YAGER (JOSEPH A.) New means of financing international needs; (with Gerard M. Brannon). Washington, D.C., [1978]. pp. 256.

INTERNATIONAL LABOUR ACTIVITIES.

KERPER (MICHAEL) The international ideology of U.S. labor, 1941-1975. Gothenburg, 1976. pp. 42. *(Göteborgs Universitet. Historiska Institutionen. Research Section Post-War History. Publications. No. 6)*

INTERNATIONAL LABOUR CONFERENCE.

INTERNATIONAL LABOUR CONFERENCE. 5th Session. The fifth session of the International Labour Conference, October 1923. Geneva, 1923. pp. 24.

INTERNATIONAL LABOUR ORGANISATION.

INTERNATIONAL LABOUR ORGANISATION.

INTERNATIONAL LABOUR CONFERENCE. 61st Session. Reports. 8. Report of the working party on structure: eighth item on the agenda. Geneva, 1976. pp. 73.

— New Zealand.

NEW ZEALAND. [General Assembly]. House of Representatives. 1968. International Labour Organisation: report of the New Zealand government delegates on the fifty-second session of the International Labour Conference, Geneva, 5 June to 25 June 1968. Wellington, 1968. pp. 47.

INTERNATIONAL LAW.

PERETIATKOWICZ (ANTONI) Ogólne zasády prawa jako źródło prawa międzynarodowego a tendencje kosmopolityczne. Poznań, 1956. pp. 47. (*Poznań. Poznańskie Towarzystwo Przyjaciół Nauk. Wydział Historii i Nauk Społecznych. Komisja Nauk Społecznych. Prace. t.6, z.3*) With French and Russian summaries.

STONE (JULIUS) Of law and nations: between power politics and human hopes. Buffalo, 1974. pp. 484.

NGUYEN QUOC DINH. Droit international public; (with Supplement) by Patrick Daillier and Alain Pellet. Paris, 1975-77. 2 vols. *bibliog.*

MEESSEN (KARL MATTHIAS) Völkerrechtliche Grundsätze des internationalen Kartellrechts. Baden-Baden, [1975]. pp. 288.

MELANGES offerts à Georges Burdeau: le pouvoir. Paris, 1977. pp. 1190.

Les RELATIONS internationales dans un monde en mutation. International relations in a changing world. Genève, 1977. pp. vi,434. *Articles in French or English.*

McWHINNEY (EDWARD) The international law of détente: arms control, European security, and East-West cooperation. Alphen aan den Rijn, 1978. pp. 259.

— Cases.

FONTES JURIS GENTIUM. Series A. Sectio 2. Tomus 5. Deutsche Rechtsprechung in völkerrechtlichen Fragen; Decisions of German courts relating to public international law... 1961-1965; bearbeitet im Max-Planck Institut für ausländisches öffentliches Recht und Völkerrecht von Albert Bleckmann [and others]. Berlin, 1978. pp. 1048.

— History — China.

KAMINSKI (GERD) Die prinzipielle Haltung der VR China zu internationaler Ordnung und Völkerrecht. Wien, 1977. pp. 60. (*Oesterreichisches China Forschungsinstitut. Berichte. Nr. 9*)

— — Poland.

HUBERT (STANISŁAW) Poglądy na prawo narodów w Polsce czasów oświecenia. Wrocław, 1960. pp. 295. *bibliog.* (*Wrocław. Wrocławskie Towarzystwo Naukowe. Prace. Seria A. nr.66*) With French summary.

INTERNATIONAL LAW, PRIVATE

See CONFLICT OF LAW.

INTERNATIONAL MONETARY FUND.

INTERNATIONAL MONETARY FUND. 1976. Proposed second amendment to the articles of agreement of the International Monetary Fund: a report by the Executive Directors to the Board of Governors. Washington, 1976. pp. 371.

INTERNATIONAL OFFICIALS AND EMPLOYEES.

PLANTEY (ALAIN) Droit et pratique de la fonction publique internationale. Paris, 1977. pp. 499. *bibliog.*

INTERNATIONAL ORGANIZATION.

BENNETT (ALVIN LEROY) International organizations: principles and issues. Englewood Cliffs, [1977]. pp. 440.

CARNEGIE-ROCHESTER CONFERENCE ON PUBLIC POLICY. 1976, April Conference. International organization, national policies and economic development; editors, Karl Brunner [and] Allan H. Meltzer. Amsterdam, 1977. pp. 240. *bibliogs.* (*Journal of Monetary Economics. Carnegie-Rochester Conference Series on Public Policy. vol. 6*)

KEOHANE (ROBERT O.) and NYE (JOSEPH S.) Power and interdependence: world politics in transition. Boston, Mass., [1977]. pp. 268.

LAGOS MATUS (GUSTAVO) and GODOY (HORACIO H.) Revolution of being: a Latin American view of the future. New York, [1977]. pp. 226.

TUZMUKHAMEDOV (RAIS ABDULKHAKOVICH) Razvivaiushchiesia strany v mirovoi politike: mezhdunarodnye mezhpravitel'stvennye organizatsii razvivaiushchikhsia stran. Moskva, 1977. pp. 207.

INTERNATIONAL RELATIONS.

HANDBOOK of political science;...edited by Fred I. Greenstein [and] Nelson W. Polsby. Reading, Mass., [1975]. 9 vols. *bibliogs.*

BERLIA (GEORGES) Le maintien de la paix: doctrines et problèmes, 1919-1976. Paris, [1976]. pp. 341, vi.

CĂTRE o nouă ordine internațională; coordonator Nicolae Ecobescu, cu un cuvînt înainte de Ștefan A. Andrei. București, 1976. pp. 542. *With English, French, German and Russian tables of contents.*

HERZ (JOHN HERMANN) The nation-state and the crisis of world politics: essays on international politics in the twentieth century. New York, [1976]. pp. 307.

JOHANSEN (ROBERT C.) The Vladivostok accord: a case study of the impact of U.S. foreign policy on the prospects for world order reform. Princeton, 1976. pp. 114. (*Princeton University. Center of International Studies. World Order Studies Program. Occasional Papers. No. 4*)

LEBEDEV (NIKOLAI IVANOVICH) Novyi etap mezhdunarodnykh otnoshenii. Moskva, 1976. pp. 296.

MAYER (PIERRE) Le monde rompu. [Paris, 1976]. pp. 310.

WILLIAMS (P.M.) and SMITH (M.H.) The conduct of foreign policy in democratic and authoritarian states. [1976?]. 1 pamphlet (unpaged). *Unpublished: photocopy of typescript.*

BEYOND the crisis; edited by Norman Birnbaum; with essays by Hans Peter Dreitzel [and others]. London, 1977. pp. 232.

ERMOLENKO (DMITRII VLADIMIROVICH) Sotsiologiia i problemy mezhdunarodnykh otnoshenii: nekotorye aspekty i voprosy sotsiologicheskikh issledovanii mezhdunarodnykh otnoshenii. Moskva, 1977. pp. 232. *bibliog.*

ETHNIC conflict in international relations; edited by Astri Suhrke [and] Lela Garner Noble. New York, 1977. pp. 246.

KEOHANE (ROBERT O.) and NYE (JOSEPH S.) Power and interdependence: world politics in transition. Boston, Mass., [1977]. pp. 268.

KIM (SAMUEL S.) The Maoist image of world order. Princeton, 1977. pp. 51. (*Princeton University. Center of International Studies. World Order Studies Program. Occasional Papers. No. 5*)

PARKINSON (FRED) The philosophy of international relations. Beverly Hills, [1977]. pp. 243. *bibliog.*

PLISCHKE (ELMER) Microstates in world affairs: policy problems and options. Washington, D.C., [1977]. pp. 153. (*American Enterprise Institute for Public Policy Research. AEI Studies. 144*)

Les RELATIONS internationales dans un monde en mutation. International relations in a changing world. Genève, 1977. pp. vi,434. *Articles in French or English.*

STONE (JULIUS) Conflict through consensus: United Nations approaches to aggression. Baltimore, 1977. pp. 234.

UNOFFICIAL diplomats; Maureen R. Berman and Joseph E. Johnson, editors. New York, 1977. pp. 268. *Based on a conference held at Bellagio, Italy, in 1973 by the Communications Institute.*

ZIEGLER (DAVID W.) War, peace, and international politics. Boston, Mass., [1977]. pp. 444.

COULOUMBIS (THEODORE A.) and WOLFE (JAMES H.) Introduction to international relations: power and justice. Englewood Cliffs, [1978]. pp. 399. *bibliogs.*

INTERNATIONAL crises and crisis management: an East-West symposium; edited by Daniel Frei. Farnborough, Hants., [1978]. pp. 154. *bibliogs.*

KALDOR (MARY) The disintegrating west. London, 1978. pp. 219.

The REASON of states: a study in international political theory; edited by Michael Donelan. London, 1978. pp. 220.

ROGERS (CARL RANSOM) Carl Rogers on personal power. London, 1978. pp. 305. *bibliog.*

SPANIER (JOHN WINSTON) Games nations play: analyzing international politics. 3rd ed. New York, [1978]. pp. 628. *bibliog.*

WHY nations act: theoretical perspectives for comparative foreign policy studies; edited by Maurice A. East [and others]. Beverly Hills, [1978]. pp. 232. *bibliog.*

WIGHT (MARTIN) Power politics; edited by Hedley Bull and Carsten Holbraad. Leicester, 1978. pp. 317. *Revised and extended version of an essay published in 1946 by the Royal Institute of International Affairs.*

— Mathematical models.

MATHEMATICAL models in international relations; edited by Dina A. Zinnes [and] John V. Gillespie. New York, 1976. pp. 397.

MODELIROVANIE sotsial'no-ekonomicheskikh protsessov: kachestvennye gipotezy i imitatsionnyi podkhod. Moskva, 1976. pp. 247. *bibliog.*

PROBLEMS of world modeling: political and social implications; edited by Karl W. Deutsch [and others]. Cambridge, Mass., [1977]. pp. 420. *bibliogs. Papers of a meeting of Research Committee 7 of the International Political Science Association.*

— Psychological aspects.

RUMMEL (RUDOLPH JOSEPH) Field theory evolving. Beverly Hills, [1977]. pp. 531. *bibliog.*

— Research.

SNYDER (GLENN HERALD) and DIESING (PAUL) Conflict among nations: bargaining, decision making, and system structure in international crises. Princeton, N.J., [1977]. pp. 578. *bibliogs.*

APPROACHES and theory in international relations; edited by Trevor Taylor. London, [1978]. pp. 314. *bibliogs.*

DEUTSCH (KARL WOLFGANG) The analysis of international relations. 2nd ed. Englewood Cliffs, [1978]. pp. 312.

INTERNATIONAL RELIEF

— Bangladesh.

OLIVER (THOMAS W.) The United Nations in Bangladesh. Princeton, [1978]. pp. 231.

INTERNATIONAL WORKING UNION OF SOCIALIST PARTIES.

DONNEUR (ANDRE) Histoire de l'Union des partis socialistes pour l'action internationale, 1920-1923. [Geneva], 1967. pp. 434. *bibliog. Thèse (docteur ès sciences politiques)- Université de Genève.*

INTERNATIONALISM.

PERETIATKOWICZ (ANTONI) Ogólne zasády prawa jako źródło prawa międzynarodowego a tendencje kosmopolityczne. Poznań, 1956. pp. 47. *(Poznań. Poznańskie Towarzystwo Przyjaciół Nauk. Wydział Historii i Nauk Społecznych. Komisja Nauk Społecznych. Prace. t.6, z.3) With French and Russian summaries.*

INTEROCEANIC RAILWAY OF MEXICO.

FLEMING (ROBERT) Author of The Interoceanic Railway of Mexico, etc. The Interoceanic Railway of Mexico (Acapulco to Vera Cruz) Limited. London, 1892. pp. 12.

INTERPERSONAL ATTRACTION.

THEORY and practice in interpersonal attraction; edited by Steve Duck. London, 1977. pp. 438. *bibliog.*

INTERPERSONAL COMMUNICATION.

EADIE (WILLIAM F.) and KLINE (JOHN A.) Orientations to interpersonal communication. Chicago, [1976]. pp. 45. *bibliog.*

INTERPERSONAL RELATIONS.

EXPLORATIONS in interpersonal communications; Gerald R. Miller, editor. Beverly Hills, [1976]. pp. 274. *bibliogs.*

FISCHER (CLAUDE S.) and others. Networks and places: social relations in the urban setting. New York, [1977]. pp. 229. *bibliog.*

ADVANCES in experiential social processes; edited by Cary L. Cooper and Clayton P. Alderfer. Chichester, [1978 in progress]. *bibliogs.*

DOISE (WILLEM) Groups and individuals: explorations in social psychology. Cambridge, [1978]. pp. 226. *bibliog. Translated by Douglas Graham.*

INTERVENTION (INTERNATIONAL LAW).

The LIMITS of military intervention; edited by Ellen P. Stern. Beverly Hills, [1977]. pp. 399. *Based on papers presented at two conferences held in 1976.*

INTERVIEWING.

MATARAZZO (JOSEPH D.) and WIENS (ARTHUR N.) The interview: research on its anatomy and structure. Chicago, [1972]. pp. 183.

INVENTORY CONTROL.

HADLEY (GEORGE FRANCIS) and WHITIN (THOMSON M.) Analysis of inventory systems. Englewood Cliffs, 1963. pp. 452. *bibliogs.*

LEWIS (COLIN DAVID) Scientific inventory control. London, 1970. pp. 209.

— Mathematical models.

JOHNSON (LYNWOOD A.) and MONTGOMERY (DOUGLAS C.) Operations research in production planning, scheduling, and inventory control. New York, [1974]. pp. xiv,525.

INVESTMENT ANALYSIS.

SHARPE (WILLIAM F.) Investments. Englewood Cliffs, [1978]. pp. 617.

INVESTMENT OF PUBLIC FUNDS.

FRANCE. Direction de la Documentation. La Documentation Française. Notes et Etudes Documentaires. Nos. 4,303-4, 304-4,305. Les transferts état-industrie en France et dans les pays occidentaux; par Anicet Le Pors. Paris, 1976. pp. 79.

— France.

FRANCE. Direction de la Documentation. La Documentation Française. Notes et Etudes Documentaires. Nos. 4,303-4, 304-4,305. Les transferts état-industrie en France et dans les pays occidentaux; par Anicet Le Pors. Paris, 1976. pp. 79.

— Germany — Mathematical models.

KRELLE (WILHELM) and PAULY (RALF) Konsum und Investitionen des Staates bis 1985. Göttingen, [1976]. pp. 181, A142. *bibliog. (Kommission für Wirtschaftlichen und Sozialen Wandel. Schriften. 130)*

INVESTMENTS.

CAPITAL market equilibrium and efficiency: implications for accounting, financial, and portfolio decision making; edited by James L. Bicksler. Lexington, Mass., [1977]. pp. 629. *bibliogs.*

LORIE (JAMES HIRSCH) and BREALEY (RICHARD A.) Modern developments in investment management: a book of readings. 2nd ed. Hinsdale, [1978]. pp. 758.

SHARPE (WILLIAM F.) Investments. Englewood Cliffs, [1978]. pp. 617.

— Mathematical models.

FINANCIAL decision making under uncertainty; edited by Haim Levy and Marshall Sarnat. New York, 1977. pp. 301. *bibliogs. Based on the 1975 Israel Scientific Research Conference held at Ein Bokek, Israel, by the National Council of Research and Development.*

SAVAGE (DAVID) A comparison of accelerator models of manufacturing investment. London, 1977. fo. 10. *bibliog. (National Institute of Economic and Social Research. Discussion Papers. No. 9)*

— France.

BOYER (R.) and MISTRAL (J.) Inflation, investment and employment: a simple multisector model of the French economy with extension to some international comparisons. Paris, 1976. pp. 52. *(Centre d'Études Prospectives d'Économie Mathématique Appliquées à la Planification. [Publications]. No. 7608)*

MONNAIE, épargne, investissements. Paris, [1976]. pp. 204. *(Fondation Nationale des Sciences Politiques. Travaux et Recherches de Sciences Economiques. Série "Economie Française". 19)*

— Ghana.

INVESTMENT JOURNAL; pd. by (Ghana Investment Centre,) the Capital Investments Board of Ghana. q., Oc/D 1970 (v.1, no.2), Ja/Mr 1971 (v.2, no.1)- , with gaps (Ja/Mr, Oc/D 1973: v.4, nos.1 and 4). Accra.

INVESTMENT TIT-BITS: opportunities and trends in Ghana; [pd. by] Capital Investments Board. bi-m., current issues only. Accra.

— New Zealand.

NEW ZEALAND. Property Law and Equity Reform Committee. 1970. Trustees' statutory powers of investment; report; [C.P. Hutchinson, chairman]. [Wellington, 1970]. pp. 24.

NEW ZEALAND. Tourist and Publicity Department. 1971. Invest in the New Zealand tourist industry. Wellington, 1971. pp. 36.

— Nigeria.

NIGERIA (NORTH CENTRAL STATE). 1971. Industrial potentialities in the North Central State of Nigeria. [Kaduna, 1971]. pp. 57, 1 map.

— Underdeveloped areas.

See UNDERDEVELOPED AREAS — Investments.

— United Kingdom.

COOPERS AND LYBRAND ASSOCIATES LIMITED. Survey of investment attitudes and financing of medium-sized companies. London, 1978. pp. 46. *(U.K. Committee to Review the Functioning of Financial Institutions. Research Reports. No.1)*

U.K. Working Party on the Financing of North Sea Oil. 1978. The financing of North Sea oil; [A. D. Bain, chairman]. London, 1978. pp. 64. *(U.K. Committee to Review the Functioning of Financial Institutions. Research Reports. No. 2)*

INVESTMENTS, AMERICAN.

WEISSKOPF (THOMAS E.) American economic interests in foreign countries: an empirical survey. Ann Arbor, 1974. pp. 56. *(Michigan University. Center for Research on Economic Development. Discussion Papers. No.35)*

BRACEWELL-MILNES (JOHN BARRY) and HUISKAMP (JOHAN CHRISTIAAN LODEWIJK) Investment incentives: a comparative analysis of the systems of the EEC, the USA and Sweden. Deventer, 1977. pp. 143. *(Erasmus Universiteit Rotterdam. Fiscaal-Economische Instituut. International Series.3)*

ESSLEN (RAINER) The complete book of international investing: how to buy foreign securities and who's who on the international investment scene. New York, [1977]. pp. 368. *Updated and rewritten version of his How to buy foreign securities.*

— America, Latin.

NORTH AMERICAN CONGRESS ON LATIN AMERICA. Yanqui dollar: the contribution of U.S. private investment to underdevelopment in Latin America; contributors Susanne Bodenheimer [and others]. New York, [1971]. pp. 64.

INVESTMENTS, AUSTRALIAN

— Asia, Southeast.

LOOKING north to south-east Asia: the view from Australia; edited by Edward P. Wolfers. Honolulu, [1976]. pp. 276. *Papers delivered to the 5th Annual Conference of the Australian Institute of International Affairs held in Melbourne in 1975.*

INVESTMENTS, BRITISH

— Taxation.

UNITED NATIONS. Department of Economic and Social Affairs. 1972. Tax treatment of private investment in developing countries by the United Kingdom of Great Britain and Northern Ireland. (ST/ECA/163). New York, 1972. pp. 13.

— South Africa.

LEWIS-JONES (HELEN) South Africa: British involvement in apartheid. London, 1970. pp. 23. *bibliog.*

BAILEY (MARTIN DAWSON) Shell and BP in South Africa. London, 1977. pp. 44.

INVESTMENTS, EUROPEAN.

BRACEWELL-MILNES (JOHN BARRY) and HUISKAMP (JOHAN CHRISTIAAN LODEWIJK) Investment incentives: a comparative analysis of the systems of the EEC, the USA and Sweden. Deventer, 1977. pp. 143. *(Erasmus Universiteit Rotterdam. Fiscaal-Economische Instituut. International Series.3)*

INVESTMENTS, FOREIGN.

ACOCELLA (NICOLA) Imprese multinazionali e investimenti diretti: le cause dello sviluppo. Roma, 1975. pp. 262. *bibliog. (Rome. Università. Istituto di Politica Economica e Finanziaria. Pubblicazioni. 19)*

COMITO (VINCENZO) Multinazionali ed esportazione di capitale. Roma, 1976. pp. 385. *bibliogs.*

ESSLEN (RAINER) The complete book of international investing: how to buy foreign securities and who's who on the international investment scene. New York, [1977]. pp. 368. *Updated and rewritten version of his How to buy foreign securities.*

THUNELL (L.H.) Political risks in international business: investment behavior of multinational corporations. New York, 1977. pp. 133. *bibliog.*

INVESTMENTS, FOREIGN.(Cont.)

— **Law and legislation.**

CARREAU (DOMINIQUE) and others. Droit international économique. Paris, 1978. pp. 513.

— — **Korea.**

KOREA (REPUBLIC). Ministry of Finance. 1970. A guide for foreign investors. [Seoul, 1970]. pp. 54.

— — **Taiwan.**

CONFERENCE ON LEGAL ASPECTS OF UNITED STATES-REPUBLIC OF CHINA TRADE AND INVESTMENT, 1977. Proceedings...; editors: Hungdah Chiu and David Simon. Baltimore, 1977. pp. 217. *bibliog.* (*Maryland. University. School of Law. Occasional Papers/Reprints Series in Contemporary Asian Studies. No. 10*)

— **Social aspects.**

KOBRIN (STEPHEN JAY) Foreign direct investment, industrialization and social change. Greenwich, Conn., [1977]. pp. 188. *bibliog.*

— **Taxation.**

UNITED NATIONS. Department of Economic and Social Affairs. 1972. Tax treatment of private investment in developing countries by the United Kingdom of Great Britain and Northern Ireland. (ST/ECA/163). New York, 1972. pp. 13.

UNITED NATIONS. Department of Economic and Social Affairs. 1972. Taxation of private investments in developing countries by the Federal Republic of Germany. (ST/ECA/164). New York, 1972. pp. 45.

— **America, Latin.**

CAMBRIDGE. University. Centre of Latin American Studies. Working Papers. No. 23. Partners in dependency: the case of private foreign capital in the Andean group; by E. Floto. Cambridge, 1975. pp. 45. *bibliog.*

— **Asia.**

BANK OF JAPAN. Economic Research Department. Special Papers. No. 66. Trends in foreign investments in the Asian countries. Tokyo, 1976. pp. 13.

— **Australia.**

AUSTRALIA. Parliament. Senate. Select Committee on Foreign Ownership and Control of Australian Resources. 1972. Report No. 1; [R.G. Withers, chairman]. in AUSTRALIA. Parliament. Parliamentary papers, 1972, vol. 7.

FOREIGN INVESTMENT IN ENTERPRISES IN AUSTRALIA; (pd. by) Commonwealth Bureau of Census and Statistics. q., S 1976(1st)- Canberra.

— **Europe, Eastern.**

SPIGLER (IANCU) Direct western investment in East Europe. Oxford, 1975. pp. 346. *bibliog.* (*Oxford. University. St. Antony's College. Centre for Soviet and East European Studies. Papers in East European Economics. 48*)

— **France.**

EQUIPE DE RECHERCHES DE GEOGRAPHIE INDUSTRIELLE. Les investissements étrangers en France. Grenoble, 1975. pp. 217. *bibliog.*

— **Greece.**

GREECE. Hypourgeion Syntonismou. 1968. The protection of foreign investment in Greece. [Athens, 1968?]. pp. 4.

— **Italy.**

BENETTI (M.) and others. Il capitale straniero nel Mezzogiorno. [Roma, 1975]. pp. 127.

— **South Africa.**

COUNTER INFORMATION SERVICES. Anti-Reports. Business as usual: international banking in South Africa. London, [1974?]. pp. 29. *bibliog.*

LEGASSICK (MARTIN) and HEMSON (DAVID) Foreign investment and the reproduction of racial capitalism in South Africa. London, 1976. pp. 16. (*Anti-Apartheid Movement. Foreign Investment in South Africa. No. 2*)

— **Underdeveloped areas.**

See UNDERDEVELOPED AREAS — Investments, Foreign.

— **United Kingdom.**

LIVINGSTONE (JAMES MACCARDLE) National government and the international enterprise. [Glasgow, 1977?]. pp. 70. *bibliog.* (*Glasgow. University of Strathclyde. Department of Marketing. Working Papers*)

INVESTMENTS, GERMAN.

LAVES (WALTER HERMAN CARL) German governmental influence on foreign investments, 1871-1914. New York, 1977. pp. 235. *bibliog.* Ph.D. thesis - University of Chicago.

— **Taxation.**

UNITED NATIONS. Department of Economic and Social Affairs. 1972. Taxation of private investments in developing countries by the Federal Republic of Germany. (ST/ECA/164). New York, 1972. pp. 45.

INVESTMENTS, JAPANESE.

KOJIMA (KIYOSHI) Direct foreign investment: a Japanese model of multinational business operations. London, [1978]. pp. 246.

— **Indonesia.**

PANGLAYKIM (JUSUF) Business relations between Indonesia and Japan: a view. Singapore, [1974]. pp. 43.

INVESTMENTS, NORWEGIAN.

NORWAY. Statistiske Centralbyrå. Kredittmarkedstatistikk: fordringer og gjeld overfor utlandet, etc. a., 1973/75(1st)- Oslo. *[in English and Norwegian] Supersedes in part* NORWAY. Statistiske Centralbyrå. Kredittmarkedstatistikk.

INVESTMENTS, SWEDISH.

BRACEWELL-MILNES (JOHN BARRY) and HUISKAMP (JOHAN CHRISTIAAN LODEWIJK) Investment incentives: a comparative analysis of the systems of the EEC, the USA and Sweden. Deventer, 1977. pp. 143. (*Erasmus Universiteit Rotterdam. Fiscaal-Economische Instituut. International Series.3*)

MEYERSON (PER-MARTIN) Swedish companies' direct investment abroad: their motives and significance for employment. Stockholm, 1977. pp. 27. *bibliog.*

THUNELL (L.H.) Political risks in international business: investment behavior of multinational corporations. New York, 1977. pp. 133. *bibliog.*

INVESTMENTS, SWISS

— **Mexico.**

IFFLAND (CHARLES) and GALLAND (ANTOINE) Les investissements industriels suisses au Mexique. Lausanne, 1978. pp. 155. *bibliog.* (*Lausanne. Université. Centre de Recherches Européennes. Publications. 4. L'Europe et les Pays Tiers*)

IOWA

— **History.**

SCHWIEDER (ELMER) and SCHWIEDER (DOROTHY) A peculiar people: Iowa's Old Order Amish. Ames, Iowa, 1975 repr. 1977. pp. 188. *bibliog.*

IRAN

— **Constitutional history.**

HAIRI (ABDUL-HADE) Shi'ism and constitutionalism in Iran: a study of the role played by the Persian residents of Iraq in Iranian politics. Leiden, 1977. pp. 274. *bibliog.*

— **Economic conditions.**

IRAN ECONOMIC NEWS; (prepared by the Mission Economique de l'Iran [Belgium]). m., Ja 1975- Bruxelles.

IRAN: past, present and future: Aspen Institute/Persepolis symposium; edited by Jane W. Jacqz. New York, [1976]. pp. 481.

AMUZEGAR (JAHANGIR) Iran: an economic profile. Washington, D.C., 1977. pp. 280. *bibliog.*

LOONEY (ROBERT E.) A development strategy for Iran through the 1980s. New York, 1977. pp. 207. *bibliog.*

— — **Bibliography.**

U.K. Department of Trade. Statistics and Market Intelligence Library. 1977. Iran. London, 1977. pp. 14. (*Sources of Statistics and Market Information. 3*)

— **Economic policy.**

HANEL (ALFRED) and MUELLER (JULIUS OTTO) On the evaluation of rural cooperatives with reference to governmental development policies: case study Iran. Göttingen, 1976. pp. 298. *bibliog.* (*Marburg. Universität. Institut für Kooperation in Entwicklungsländern. Marburger Schriften zum Genossenschaftswesen. Reihe B. Band 15*)

IRAN: past, present and future: Aspen Institute/Persepolis symposium; edited by Jane W. Jacqz. New York, [1976]. pp. 481.

GOLABIAN (HOSSEIN) An analysis of the underdeveloped rural and nomadic areas of Iran: a theoretical approach to the problems of social and economic development of rural and nomadic communities in Iran. Stockholm, 1977. pp. 279, 11. (*Stockholm. Tekniska Högskolan. School of Architecture. Department of Regional Planning. [Publications]. 1977. [No.] 4*)

LOONEY (ROBERT E.) A development strategy for Iran through the 1980s. New York, 1977. pp. 207. *bibliog.*

— **Foreign relations.**

FOOT (ROSEMARY JUNE) New areas of tension and great power rivalry: central west Asia and Sino-Soviet relations, 1962-1974. 1976 [or rather 1977]. fo. 353. *bibliog.* Typescript. Ph.D. (London) thesis: unpublished. *This thesis is the property of London University and may not be removed from the Library.*

— — **Pakistan.**

PAKISTAN. Information and Broadcasting Division. Directorate of Research, Reference and Publications. 1975. Iran Pakistan friendship. [Islamabad, 1975?]. 1 vol. (unpaged).

— — **Russia.**

ABDULLAEV (IUSUF NEGMATOVICH) Astrabad i russko-iranskie otnosheniia, vtoraia polovina XIX - nachalo XX v. Tashkent, 1975. pp. 132. *bibliog.*

— **History.**

IRAN under the Pahlavis; George Lenczowski, editor. Stanford, [1978]. pp. 550. *bibliogs.* (*Stanford University. Hoover Institution on War, Revolution and Peace. Hoover Institution Publications. 164*)

— **Politics and government.**

WEG met het fascisties sjahregiem: (brochure...uitgegeven ter ondersteuning van de kampagne "Vryspraak voor Jef Helmer"). Rotterdam, 1974. pp. 42.

COMMITTEE AGAINST REPRESSION IN IRAN. Iran: the Shah's empire of repression. London, 1976. pp. 38. *bibliog.*

— **Rural conditions.**

GOLABIAN (HOSSEIN) An analysis of the underdeveloped rural and nomadic areas of Iran: a theoretical approach to the problems of social and economic development of rural and nomadic communities in Iran. Stockholm, 1977. pp. 279, 11. (*Stockholm. Tekniska Högskolan. School of Architecture. Department of Regional Planning. [Publications]. 1977. [No.] 4*)

IRAQ

— Economic conditions.

PENROSE (EDITH TILTON) and PENROSE (ERNEST FRANCIS) Iraq: international relations and national development. London, 1978. pp. 569. *bibliog.*

— History.

PENROSE (EDITH TILTON) and PENROSE (ERNEST FRANCIS) Iraq: international relations and national development. London, 1978. pp. 569. *bibliog.*

IRELAND

— Census.

IRELAND. Census, 1821. Abstract of the answers and returns made pursuant to an Act of the United Parliament, passed in the 55th year of the reign of His Late Majesty George the Third, intituled An Act to provide for taking an account of the population of Ireland, and for ascertaining the increase or diminution thereof: preliminary observations, enumeration abstract, appendix. (B.P.P. 1823, 577). [Dublin], 1823. pp. 393.

IRELAND. Census, 1831. Population, Ireland: abstract of answers and returns under the population acts...: enumeration 1831; (with Comparative abstract of the population in Ireland, as taken in 1821 and 1831, etc.) (B.P.P. 1833, 634 and 23). [Dublin], 1833. 2 pts.

IRELAND. Census, 1841. Report of the commissioners appointed to take the census of Ireland, for the year 1841. Dublin, 1843. 1 vol. (various pagings).

IRELAND. Census, 1851. The census of Ireland for the year 1851. Part 1, showing the area, population and number of houses, by townlands and electoral divisions. Vols 1-4: province [reports]. Dublin, 1852. 4 vols. (in 2).

IRELAND. Census, 1851. The census of Ireland for the year 1851. Part 3. Report on the status of disease; (with Part 4: report on ages and education). Dublin, 1854-55. 2 pts. (in 1 vol.)

IRELAND. Census, 1861. The census of Ireland for the year 1861. Part 1, showing the area, population and number of houses, by townlands and electoral divisions. Vols 1-4: province [reports]. Dublin, 1863. 4 vols (in 2).

IRELAND. Census, 1861. The census of Ireland for the year 1861. Part 2. Report and tables on ages and education. Dublin, 1863. 2 vols.

IRELAND. Census, 1861. The census of Ireland for the year 1861. Part 3. Vital statistics. Vol.1. Report and tables relating to the status of disease. Dublin, 1863. pp. 167.

IRELAND. Census, 1871. Census of Ireland, 1871. Part 1. Area, houses and population: also the ages, civil condition, occupations, birthplaces, religion and education of the people. Vols 1-4: provinces of Leinster (C.662), Munster (C.873), Ulster (C.964), Connaught (C.1106). Dublin, 1873-75. 4 vols.

IRELAND. Census, 1871. Census of Ireland, 1871. Part 2. Vital statistics. (C.876 and C.1000). Dublin, 1873-75. 2 vols.

IRELAND. Census, 1871. Census of Ireland, 1871. Part 3. General report, with illustrative maps and diagrams, summary tables and appendix. (C. 1177). Dublin, 1875. pp. 493.

IRELAND. Census, 1881. Census of Ireland for the year 1881: preliminary report with abstract of the enumerators' summaries. (C. 2931). Dublin, 1881. fo. 17. *Photocopy.*

IRELAND. Census, 1891. Census of Ireland, 1891. Part 1. Area, houses and population: also the ages, civil or conjugal condition, occupations, birthplaces, religion and education of the people. Vols 1-2: provinces of Leinster (C.6515), Munster (C.6567). Dublin, 1891-92. 5 vols.

IRELAND. Census, 1891. Census of Ireland, 1891: summary tables. Dublin, 1892. pp. 59.

IRELAND. Census, 1901. Census of Ireland, 1901. Part 1. Area, houses and population: also the ages, civil or conjugal condition, occupations, birthplaces, religion and education of the people. Vols. 1-4: provinces of Leinster (C.847), Munster (Cd.1058), Ulster (Cd.1123), Connaught (Cd.1059). Dublin, 1902. 4 vols.

IRELAND. Census, 1901. Census of Ireland, 1901. Part 2. General report, with illustrative maps and diagrams, tables, and appendix. (Cd. 1190). Dublin, 1902. pp. 641.

IRELAND. Census, 1911. Census of Ireland, 1911: general report, with tables and appendix. (Cd. 6663). London, 1913. pp. 605.

— Church history.

BOWEN (DESMOND) The Protestant crusade in Ireland, 1800-70: a study of Protestant-Catholic relations between the Act of Union and disestablishment. Dublin, 1978. pp. 412. *bibliog.*

— Economic history.

BURNS (ELINOR) British imperialism in Ireland. Dublin, 1931. pp. 66.

— Foreign relations.

KEATINGE (NEIL PATRICK) A place among the nations: issues of Irish foreign policy. Dublin, 1978. pp. 287. *bibliog.*

— Gazetteers.

NAMES of townlands and towns in Ireland, with the parliamentary county or borough in which situated. [Dublin, 1918]. pp. 215.

— History.

SPALDING (JOHN LANCASTER) Bishop of Peoria. The religious mission of the Irish people and Catholic colonization. New York, 1880. pp. 339.

BURNS (ELINOR) British imperialism in Ireland. Dublin, 1931. pp. 66.

BURNS (ELINOR) British imperialism in Ireland: a Marxist historical analysis. Cork, 1974. pp. 66. *(Cork Workers' Club. Historical Reprints. No. 2) Reprint of pamphlet first published in 1931.*

MAGNUSSON (MAGNUS) Landlord or tenant?: a view of Irish history. London, 1978. pp. 155. *bibliog. An expanded version of a series of programmes written for BBC Radio 4 and presented in 1977.*

— — Bibliography.

MORRALL (JOHN BRIMYARD) Kathleen ní Houlihan's new clothes: recent perspectives on Irish history. [Dublin], 1974. pp. 7. *bibliog. (Repr. from Studies, autumn 1974)*

— — Sources.

EMMET (THOMAS ADDIS) and others. The origin and progress of the Irish Union. Belfast, 1974. pp. 46. *(Reprint from Pieces of Irish History, edited by W.J. MacNeven, published in 1807)*

— — 1760-1820.

EMMET (THOMAS ADDIS) and others. The origin and progress of the Irish Union. Belfast, 1974. pp. 46. *(Reprint from Pieces of Irish History, edited by W.J. MacNeven, published in 1807)*

— — 1798, Rebellion of.

CORPORATION OF HOSIERS [DUBLIN]. Hosier's Hall. Dublin, 1798. pp. 15. *Signed Roger Gower, Clk. Gld.*

— — 1910-1921.

BOWDEN (TOM) The breakdown of public security: the case of Ireland, 1916-1921 and Palestine, 1936-1939. London, [1977]. pp. 342. *bibliog.*

FITZPATRICK (DAVID) Politics and Irish life, 1913-1921: provincial experience of war and revolution. Dublin, 1977. pp. 394. *bibliog.*

GAUGHAN (J. ANTHONY) Austin Stack: portrait of a separatist. Mount Merrion, Co. Dublin, [1977]. pp. 408. *bibliog.*

— Nationalism.

RONALD, pseud. Freedom's road for Irish workers. Cork, 1975. pp. 12. *(Cork Workers' Club. Historical Reprints. No. 14) Reprint of pamphlet first published in 1917.*

BRITISH AND IRISH COMMUNIST ORGANISATION. On the "historic Irish nation". Belfast, 1972. pp. 4.

BRITISH AND IRISH COMMUNIST ORGANISATION. The two Irish nations; an enlarged edition of the pamphlet first published in 1971 in answer to criticism of the two nations theory by the Peoples' Democracy. Belfast, 1975. pp. 72.

D'ANGELO (GIOVANNI) Italy and Ireland in the 19th centuries: contacts and misunderstandings between two national movements. Athlone, 1975. pp. 56.

COSTELLO (PETER) Author of In search of lake monsters. The heart grown brutal: the Irish revolution in literature, from Parnell to the death of Yeats, 1891-1939. Dublin, 1977. pp. 330. *bibliog.*

GAUGHAN (J. ANTHONY) Austin Stack: portrait of a separatist. Mount Merrion, Co. Dublin, [1977]. pp. 408. *bibliog.*

— Politics and government.

An ANTIDOTE to Dr. L.....s's address: addressed to the merchants of the City of Dublin. Dublin, 1766. pp. 14. *A reply to An address to the Lord Mayor and citizens of Dublin, by Charles Lucas, M.P.*

FITZPATRICK (DAVID) Politics and Irish life, 1913-1921: provincial experience of war and revolution. Dublin, 1977. pp. 394. *bibliog.*

— Relations (general) with Italy.

D'ANGELO (GIOVANNI) Italy and Ireland in the 19th centuries: contacts and misunderstandings between two national movements. Athlone, 1975. pp. 56.

— Statistics, Medical.

IRELAND. Census, 1851. The census of Ireland for the year 1851. Part 3. Report on the status of disease; (with Part 4: report on ages and education). Dublin, 1854-55. 2 pts. (in 1 vol.)

IRELAND. Census, 1861. The census of Ireland for the year 1861. Part 3. Vital statistics. Vol.1. Report and tables relating to the status of disease. Dublin, 1863. pp. 167.

IRELAND. Census, 1871. Census of Ireland, 1871. Part 2. Vital statistics. (C.876 and C.1000). Dublin, 1873-75. 2 vols.

— Statistics, Vital.

IRELAND. Census, 1871. Census of Ireland, 1871. Part 2. Vital statistics. (C.876 and C.1000). Dublin, 1873-75. 2 vols.

IRELAND (REPUBLIC)

— Constitution.

WORKERS' ASSOCIATION FOR THE DEMOCRATIC SETTLEMENT OF THE NATIONAL CONFLICT IN IRELAND. Why articles 2 and 3 must go. Dublin, [1974]. pp. 23.

— Description and travel.

O'BRIEN (EDNA) Mother Ireland;...with photographs by Fergus Bourke. Harmondsworth, 1978. pp. 89. *First published 1976.*

— Economic policy.

NATIONAL ECONOMIC AND SOCIAL COUNCIL [EIRE]. The work of the NESC: 1974-76. Dublin, Stationery Office, [1977]. pp. 171. *([Reports]. No. 32)*

IRELAND (REPUBLIC)(Cont.)

EIRE. 1978. National development 1977-1980. Dublin, [1978]. pp. 69.

NATIONAL ECONOMIC AND SOCIAL COUNCIL [EIRE]. The work of the NESC: 1977. Dublin, Stationery Office, [1978]. pp. 111. ([Reports]. No. 39)

— Foreign relations.

KEATINGE (NEIL PATRICK) A place among the nations: issues of Irish foreign policy. Dublin, 1978. pp. 287. bibliog.

— Full employment policies.

EIRE. 1978. Development for full employment; laid by the government before both Houses of the Oireachtas, June 1978. Dublin, [1978]. pp. 90.

— History — 1922-1923, Civil War — Sources.

O'MALLEY (ERNIE) The singing flame. Dublin, 1978. pp. 312.

— Languages.

BRITISH AND IRISH COMMUNIST ORGANISATION. Policy Statements. No. 5. The Irish language: revivalism and the Gaeltacht. rev. ed. Belfast, 1976. pp. 24.

— Nationalism.

BIRCH (ANTHONY HAROLD) Political integration and disintegration in the British Isles. London, 1977. pp. 183. bibliog.

— Rural conditions.

HANNAN (DAMIAN F.) and KATSIAOUNI (LOUISE A.) Traditional families?: from culturally prescribed to negotiated roles in farm families. Dublin, 1977. pp. 227. bibliog. (Economic and Social Research Institute. Papers. No. 87)

— Social policy.

NATIONAL ECONOMIC AND SOCIAL COUNCIL [EIRE]. The work of the NESC: 1974-76. Dublin, Stationery Office, [1977]. pp. 171. ([Reports]. No. 32)

EIRE. 1978. National development 1977-1980. Dublin, [1978]. pp. 69.

NATIONAL ECONOMIC AND SOCIAL COUNCIL [EIRE]. The work of the NESC: 1977. Dublin, Stationery Office, [1978]. pp. 111. ([Reports]. No. 39)

NATIONAL ECONOMIC AND SOCIAL COUNCIL [EIRE]. Universality and selectivity: social services in Ireland; (by Eithne Fitzgerald). Dublin, Stationery Office, [1978]. pp. 260. bibliog. ([Reports]. No. 38)

IRELAND, NORTHERN

— Census.

IRELAND, NORTHERN. Census, 1971. Census of population, 1971: education tables. Belfast, 1975. pp. 78.

— Economic conditions — Statistics.

SOCIAL AND ECONOMIC TRENDS IN NORTHERN IRELAND; ([pd. by] Department of Finance, Northern Ireland). a., 1975 (no.1)- Belfast.

— History.

CLARK (DENNIS J.) Irish blood: Northern Ireland and the American conscience. Port Washington, N.Y., 1977. pp. 97. bibliog.

BRETT (CHARLES EDWARD BAINBRIDGE) Long shadows cast before: nine lives in Ulster, 1625-1977. Edinburgh, 1978. pp. 162.

EVELEGH (ROBIN) Peace keeping in a democratic society: the lessons of Northern Ireland. London, [1978]. pp. 174.

— Parliament — Salaries, pensions, etc.

IRELAND, NORTHERN. Members' Contributory Pension (Northern Ireland) Fund accounts, together with the report of the Comptroller and Auditor-General thereon. a., 1971/72 [6th]- Belfast. *1966/67 1970/71 [1st-5th] included in IRELAND, NORTHERN. Parliament. House of Commons. [Papers].*

— Politics and government.

FIELDS (RONA M.) Society under siege: a psychology of Northern Ireland. Philadelphia, 1977. pp. 267.

GRAHAM (ALISTAIR) Northern Ireland: the unsolved problem; from civil rights to sectarianism. Leeds, [1977]. pp. 31.

— Social conditions — Statistics.

SOCIAL AND ECONOMIC TRENDS IN NORTHERN IRELAND; ([pd. by] Department of Finance, Northern Ireland). a., 1975 (no.1)- Belfast.

IRIGOYEN (BERNARDO DE).

BIANCO (JOSE) Don Bernardo de Irigoyen: estadista y pionero, 1822-1906. Buenos Aires, 1927. pp. 333.

IRIGOYEN (HIPOLITO).

GERCHUNOFF (ALBERTO) El nuevo regimen. Buenos Aires, 1918. pp. 199.

ATENEO RADICAL "BERNARDINO RIVADAVIA". El radicalismo americanista de Hipolito Yrigoyen. Buenos Aires, 1933. pp. 75.

RODRIGUEZ YRIGOYEN (LUIS) Hipolito Yrigoyen, 1878-1933: documentacion historica de 55 años de actuacion por la democracia y las instituciones. Buenos Aires, 1934. pp. 543.

RABUFFETTI (LUIS ERNESTO) El dogma radical. Buenos Aires, 1943. pp. 350.

CABALLERO (RICARDO) Yrigoyen: aspectos ignorados de una vida. [Rosario, Argentine Republic, 1957]. pp. 148.

IRISH AMERICANS.

SPALDING (JOHN LANCASTER) Bishop of Peoria. The religious mission of the Irish people and Catholic colonization. New York, 1880. pp. 339.

CLARK (DENNIS J.) Irish blood: Northern Ireland and the American conscience. Port Washington, N.Y., 1977. pp. 97. bibliog.

BAYOR (RONALD H.) Neighbors in conflict: the Irish, Germans, Jews, and Italians of New York City, 1929-1941. Baltimore, [1978]. pp. 232. bibliog. (Johns Hopkins University. Studies in Historical and Political Science. Series 96. No. 1)

IRISH LANGUAGE

— Revival.

BRITISH AND IRISH COMMUNIST ORGANISATION. Policy Statements. No. 5. The Irish language: revivalism and the Gaeltacht. rev. ed. Belfast, 1976. pp. 24.

IRISH LITERATURE.

COSTELLO (PETER) Author of In search of lake monsters. The heart grown brutal: the Irish revolution in literature, from Parnell to the death of Yeats, 1891-1939. Dublin, 1977. pp. 330. bibliog.

IRISH PRISONERS

— United Kingdom.

FEENEY (HUGH) In the care of Her Majesty's prisons: Irish P.O.W.s in England. Belfast, [1977]. pp. 16.

IRISH QUESTION.

ESCOPETTE, pseud. Dreyfusing a class. London, 1900. pp. 16.

BRITISH AND IRISH COMMUNIST ORGANISATION. On the "historic Irish nation". Belfast, 1972. pp. 4.

BRITISH AND IRISH COMMUNIST ORGANISATION. Policy Statements. No. 1. Connolly and partition. Belfast, 1972. pp. 4.

KAUTSKY (KARL) Ireland. Belfast, 1974. pp. 22.

WORKERS' ASSOCIATION FOR THE DEMOCRATIC SETTLEMENT OF THE NATIONAL CONFLICT IN IRELAND. Why articles 2 and 3 must go. Dublin, [1974]. pp. 23.

BRITISH AND IRISH COMMUNIST ORGANISATION. The two Irish nations; an enlarged edition of the pamphlet first published in 1971 in answer to criticism of the two nations theory by the Peoples' Democracy. Belfast, 1975. pp. 72.

The IRISH question: a socialist analysis; [edited by Adam Buick]. Brussels, [1976]. pp. 41.

CLARK (DENNIS J.) Irish blood: Northern Ireland and the American conscience. Port Washington, N.Y., 1977. pp. 97. bibliog.

COSTELLO (PETER) Author of In search of lake monsters. The heart grown brutal: the Irish revolution in literature, from Parnell to the death of Yeats, 1891-1939. Dublin, 1977. pp. 330. bibliog.

ECCLESTONE (GILES) and ELLIOTT (ERIC) The Irish problem and ourselves. London, [1977]. pp. 25. bibliog. (Church of England. National Assembly. Board for Social Responsibility. Occasional Papers)

LYONS (FRANCIS STEWART LELAND) Charles Stewart Parnell. London, 1977. pp. 704. bibliog.

TROOPS OUT MOVEMENT. Irish news-sheet: chronology Nov. '76-Jun. '77. London, [1977]. pp. 43.

IRON AND STEEL WORKERS

— Poland.

GAJEWSKI (ZDZISŁAW) Warszawscy hutnicy: narodziny i rozwój. Warszawa, 1977. pp. 144. bibliog.

— United Kingdom.

BRITISH STEEL SMELTERS, MILL, IRON, TINPLATE AND KINDRED TRADES ASSOCIATION. The truth about the dispute re contract system in the Staffordshire Mills at Hawarden Bridge Works. London, 1910. pp. 31.

— United States.

BODNAR (JOHN E.) Immigration and industrialization: ethnicity in an American mill town, 1870-1940. Pittsburgh, [1977]. pp. 213. bibliog.

IRON INDUSTRY AND TRADE.

ORGANISATION FOR ECONOMIC CO-OPERATION AND DEVELOPMENT. 1977. Emission control costs in the iron and steel industry. Paris, 1977. pp. 175.

— Europe.

MILLER (ROGER EMILE) Entreprises et innovation: étude comparative de seize entreprises sidérurgiques européennes et américaines. Grenoble, 1975. pp. 124. bibliog.

RIEBEN (HENRI) L'Europe sidérurgique au défi. Lausanne, 1977. pp. 83. (Lausanne. Université. Centre de Recherches Européennes. Publications. 5. L'Europe Face à la Concurrence Internationale)

— European Economic Community countries.

EUROPEAN COMMUNITIES. Statistical Office. Iron and steel: monthly bulletin (formerly Steel: monthly bulletin). m., S 1977 (no.9)- Luxembourg. [in Community languages]

— **Germany.**

HILLEGEIST (HANS HEINRICH) Die Geschichte der Lonauerhammerhütte bei Herzberg/Harz: ein Beitrag zur Wirtschaftsgeschichte der Eisenverhüttung und Eisenverarbeitung im Südharz. Göttingen, [1977]. pp. 193. *bibliog.*

— **Italy.**

BUSINO (GIOVANNI) Vilfredo Pareto e l'industria del ferro nel Valdarno: contributo alla storia dell'impreditorialità italiana. Milano, 1977. pp. 922. *(Banco Commerciale Italiana. Studi e Ricerche di Storia Economica Italiana nell'Età del Risorgimento) A considerable appendix of Pareto's letters on the subject.*

— **Nigeria.**

NIGERIAN STEEL DEVELOPMENT AUTHORITY. Annual report and accounts. a., 1971/72(1st)- Lagos.

— **Poland.**

ROLA (HENRYK) Przemysł hutniczy w Polsce Ludowej, 1944-1975. Katowice, 1977. pp. 400. *bibliog.*

— **Switzerland.**

HOTTINGER (MAX) 1879- . Geschichtliches aus der schweizerischen Metall- und Maschinenindustrie, etc. Frauenfeld, 1921. pp. 189.

— **United Kingdom.**

BARBER (ROSS) Iron ore and after: boom time, depression and survival in a West Cumbrian town, Cleator Moor, 1840-1960;...photographs prepared by Joseph Campbell, drawings by Joanna Pearce. [York, 1976]. pp. 71. *bibliog.*

AWTY (BRIAN GORDON) Force Forge in the seventeenth century. [Kendal], 1977. pp. 15. *(Reprinted from Transactions of the Cumberland and Westmorland Antiquarian and Archaeological Society, vol.77, 1977)*

LANCASTER (J.Y.) and WATTLEWORTH (D.R.) The iron and steel industry of West Cumberland: an historical survey. Workington, 1977. pp. 198. *bibliog.*

— — **Wales.**

OWEN (JOHN A.) The history of the Dowlais iron works, 1759-1970. Risca, Mon., [1977]. pp. 161. *bibliog.*

— — **United States.**

MILLER (ROGER EMILE) Entreprises et innovation: étude comparative de seize entreprises sidérurgiques européennes et américaines. Grenoble, 1975. pp. 124. *bibliog.*

INGHAM (JOHN N.) The iron barons: a social analysis of an American urban elite, 1874-1965. Westport, Conn., 1978. pp. 242. *bibliog.*

IRRIGATION.

MAASS (ARTHUR AARON) and ANDERSON (RAYMOND LLOYD) ... And the desert shall rejoice: conflict, growth, and justice in arid environments. Cambridge, Mass., [1978]. pp. 447.

— **Brazil.**

HALL (ANTHONY L.) Drought and irrigation in north-east Brazil. Cambridge, 1978. pp. 152. *bibliog.*

— **China.**

VERMEER (E.B.) Water conservancy and irrigation in China: social, economic and agrotechnical aspects. Leiden, 1977. pp. 350. *bibliog.*

— **Korea.**

UNION OF LAND IMPROVEMENT ASSOCIATIONS OF KOREA. U[nion of] L[and] I[mprovement] A[ssociations] and irrigation works in Korea. Seoul, 1969. pp. 38. *In English and Korean.*

— **Oman.**

WILKINSON (JOHN CRAVEN) Water and tribal settlement in South-east Arabia: a study of the Aflaj of Oman. Oxford, 1977. pp. 276. *bibliog.*

— **Russia.**

MAGAKIAN (GEORGII LUK'IANOVICH) Step' i voda: novoe v geografii irrigatsii v SSSR. Moskva, 1977. pp. 191.

— **Sudan.**

BARNETT (TONY) The Gezira scheme: an illusion of development. London, 1977. pp. 192. *bibliog.*

IRRIGATION CANALS AND FLUMES.

WILKINSON (JOHN CRAVEN) Water and tribal settlement in South-east Arabia: a study of the Aflaj of Oman. Oxford, 1977. pp. 276. *bibliog.*

ISLANDS.

GRØNNEBERG (ROY) Island governments: the experience of autonomous island groups in northern Europe in relation to Shetland's political future. Sandwick, Shetland, 1976. pp. 30. *bibliog.*

ISLE OF MAN

— **Statistics, Vital.**

ISLE OF MAN. General Registry. Chief Registrar's annual report and statistical review of births, marriages and deaths in the Isle of Man. a., 1975(99th)- Douglas.

ISLINGTON

— **Race question.**

UNDER heavy manners: report of the labour movement enquiry into police brutality and the position of black youth in Islington, held on Saturday July 23, 1977. London, 1977. pp. 23.

ISRAEL

— **Army.**

PERLMUTTER (AMOS) Politics and the military in Israel, 1967-1977. London, 1978. pp. 222.

— **Census.**

ISRAEL. Census, 1972. Census of population and housing, 1972: [publications]. Jerusalem, 1972 in progress. *In English and Hebrew.*

— **Commerce.**

ISRAEL. Central Bureau of Statistics. Foreign trade statistics quarterly. q. (in 2 pts.), Ja/Ap 1969 [v.1]- [Jerusalem]. *[in English and Hebrew]. 1969 (v.1) pd. as q. suppl. to its Monthly foreign trade statistics (1967-) but included in this file. Supersedes Israel's foreign trade (1951-1968, with gaps).*

— **Emigration and immigration.**

MOSSEK (MOSHE) Palestine immigration policy under Sir Herbert Samuel: British, Zionist and Arab attitudes. London, 1978. pp. 179. *bibliog.*

— **Foreign economic relations.**

For related material see EUROPEAN ECONOMIC COMMUNITY — Israel.

— **Foreign relations.**

PALESTINE: rule of the sword. n.p. [1973]. pp. 34.

See also EUROPEAN ECONOMIC COMMUNITY — Israel; UNITED NATIONS — Israel.

— — **India.**

TAYAB (MOHAMMAD) Indo-Israel relations: a study of Indo-Israel collusion against the Arab world. Lahore, 1974. pp. 47.

— — **United States.**

DRINAN (ROBERT F.) Honor the promise: America's commitment to Israel. Garden City, N.Y., 1977. pp. 250.

REICH (BERNARD) Quest for peace: United States-Israel relations and the Arab- Israeli conflict. New Brunswick, [1977]. pp. 495. *bibliog. (Tel-Aviv. University. Shiloah Center for Middle Eastern and African Studies. Monograph Series)*

SAFRAN (NADAV) Israel: the embattled ally. Cambridge, Mass., 1978. pp. 633. *bibliog.*

— **History.**

DAVIS (URIEL) Israel: Utopia Incorporated: a study of class, state, and corporate kin control. London, [1977]. pp. 182. *bibliog.*

SAFRAN (NADAV) Israel: the embattled ally. Cambridge, Mass., 1978. pp. 633. *bibliog.*

— **Politics and government.**

ISRAELI MIRROR: what Israelis are saying about themselves; pd. by Middle East International. f. 1973 (nos. 5, 9-16) London.

PALESTINE: rule of the sword. n.p. [1973]. pp. 34.

ETZIONI-HALEVY (EVA) and SHAPIRA (RINA) Political culture in Israel: cleavage and integration among Israeli Jews. New York, 1977. pp. 249. *bibliog.*

GREILSAMMER (ALAIN) Les communistes israéliens. Paris, [1978]. pp. 415. *bibliog.*

PERLMUTTER (AMOS) Politics and the military in Israel, 1967-1977. London, 1978. pp. 222.

— **Population.**

BENSIMON (DORIS) and ERRERA (EGLAL) Israel et ses populations. [Paris, 1977]. pp. 420. *bibliog.*

— **Social conditions.**

COHEN (CLAUDINE) Grandir au quartier kurde: rapports de générations et modèles culturels d'un groupe d'adolescents israéliens d'origine kurde. Paris, 1975. pp. 175. *bibliog. (Muséum National d'Histoire Naturelle. Institut d'Ethnologie. Mémoires. 12)*

ISRAEL-ARAB CONFLICT, 1948- .

WAR RESISTERS LEAGUE. Statement on the Middle East. New York, [1974]. pp. 9.

HIRST (DAVID) The gun and the olive branch: the roots of violence in the Middle East. London, 1977. pp. 367. *bibliogs.*

REICH (BERNARD) Quest for peace: United States-Israel relations and the Arab- Israeli conflict. New Brunswick, [1977]. pp. 495. *bibliog. (Tel-Aviv. University. Shiloah Center for Middle Eastern and African Studies. Monograph Series)*

ROSEN (STEVEN J.) Military geography and the military balance in the Arab-Israel conflict. Jerusalem, 1977. pp. 79. *(Hebrew University. Leonard Davis Institute for International Relations. Jerusalem Papers on Peace Problems. 21)*

PERLMUTTER (AMOS) Politics and the military in Israel, 1967-1977. London, 1978. pp. 222.

ISRAEL-ARAB WAR, 1967.

La CONFRONTATION Israélo-Arabe de juin 1967; traduit de l'anglais par Claude Triolet. Beyrouth, 1969. pp. 365. *(Palestine Research Centre. Palestine Monographs. 57) Reprinted from The Arab World, vol. 14, no. 10-11.*

ISRAEL-ARAB WAR, 1967.(Cont.)

— Naval operations.

PEARSON (ANTHONY) Journalist. Conspiracy of silence. London, 1978. pp. 179.

— Occupied territories.

GERSON (ALLAN) Israel, the West Bank and international law. London, [1978]. pp. 285.

ISRAEL-ARAB WAR, 1973.

VAN CREVELD (MARTIN L.) Military lessons of the Yom Kippur war: historical perspectives. Beverly Hills, [1975]. pp. 60. *bibliog.* (*Georgetown University. Center for Strategic and International Studies. Washington Papers. vol. 3/24*)

ISRAELI STUDENTS IN THE UNITED STATES.

RITTERBAND (PAUL) Education, employment, and migration: Israel in comparative perspective. Cambridge, 1978. pp. 144. (*American Sociological Association. Arnold and Caroline Rose Monograph Series in Sociology*)

ITALIAN AMERICANS.

AMFITHEATROF (ERIK) I figli di Colombo: storia degli Italiani d'America. Milano, 1975. pp. 331.

TOMASI (SILVANO M.) Piety and power: the role of the Italian parishes in the New York metropolitan area, 1880-1930. New York, 1975. pp. 201. *bibliog.*

NELLI (HUMBERT STEVEN) The business of crime: Italians and syndicate crime in the United States. New York, 1976. pp. 314. *bibliog.*

YANS-McLAUGHLIN (VIRGINIA) Family and community: Italian immigrants in Buffalo, 1880-1930. Ithaca, N.Y., 1977. pp. 286. *bibliog.*

BAYOR (RONALD H.) Neighbors in conflict: the Irish, Germans, Jews, and Italians of New York City, 1929-1941. Baltimore, [1978]. pp. 232. *bibliog.* (*Johns Hopkins University. Studies in Historical and Political Science. Series 96. No. 1*)

BRIGGS (JOHN WALKER) An Italian passage: immigrants to three American cities, 1890-1930. New Haven, 1978. pp. 348. *bibliog.*

ITALIAN LANGUAGE

— Grammar, Generative.

RADFORD (ANDREW) Italian syntax: transformational and relational grammar. Cambridge, 1977. pp. 271. *bibliog.*

— Syntax.

RADFORD (ANDREW) Italian syntax: transformational and relational grammar. Cambridge, 1977. pp. 271. *bibliog.*

ITALIAN LITERATURE

— History and criticism.

GRAMSCI (ANTONIO) Letteratura e vita nazionale. Torino, 1972 repr. 1974. pp. 400. *bibliog.* (*Quaderni del Carcere. 5*)

GATT-RUTTER (JOHN) Writers and politics in modern Italy. London, [1978]. pp. 66. *bibliog.*

ITALIAN NEWSPAPERS.

MARCO (MAURIZIO DE) Il Gazzettino: storia di un quotidiano. Venezia, 1976. pp. 223. *bibliog.*

VIOLI (PATRIZIA) I giornali dell'estrema sinistra: (i tranelli e le ambiguità della lingua e dell'ideologia). Milano, 1977. pp. 192.

ITALIANS IN CANADA.

ONTARIO. Multicultural Development Branch. 1977. Papers on the Italian community. [Toronto, 1977]. pp. 7. *Consists solely of The quiet desperation of the immigrant, by Burt D'Antini.*

ITALIANS IN THE UNITED STATES.

For related heading see ITALIAN AMERICANS.

ITALO-ETHIOPIAN WAR, 1935-1936.

ASANTE (SAMUEL KINGSLEY BOTWE) Pan-African protest: west Africa and the Italo-Ethiopian crisis, 1934-1941. London, 1977. pp. 243. *bibliog.*

ROBERTSON (ESMONDE MANNING) Mussolini as empire-builder: Europe and Africa, 1932-36. London, 1977. pp. 246. *bibliog.*

ITALY

— Appropriations and expenditures.

HOLMANS (STEPHANIE K.) The Italian public expenditure system. London, 1978. pp. 23. (*Government Economic Service Working Papers. No. 3*)

— Armed forces.

MOVIMENTO DEMOCRATICO DI SOLIDARIETÀ CON LE FORZE ARMATE. Dossier forze armate. Roma, [1975]. pp. 142.

CITTADINI in uniforme: il rinnovamento delle forze armate nel rinnovamento dello stato e del paese. [Cosenza, 1976]. pp. 311.

La POLITICA militare dei comunisti: la difesa nazionale, l'ordinamento delle forze armate e i diritti democratici dei militari; [by Arrigo Boldrini and others]. [Roma, 1976]. pp. 233. *Papers presented at a conference held by the Centro di Studi e Iniziative per la Riforma dello Stato in 1974.*

— Church history.

HAY (DENYS) The church in Italy in the fifteenth century. Cambridge, 1977. pp. 184. *bibliog.* (*Cambridge. University. Trinity College. Birkbeck Lectures in Ecclesiastical History. 1971*)

— Colonies — History.

DEGL'INNOCENTI (MAURIZIO) Il socialismo italiano e la guerra di Libia. [Roma, 1976]. pp. 341. *bibliogs.*

ROBERTSON (ESMONDE MANNING) Mussolini as empire-builder: Europe and Africa, 1932-36. London, 1977. pp. 246. *bibliog.*

— Commerce.

LEVI (GIUSEPPE) and WAGNEST (RODOLFO) eds. L'attività economica nei secoli: antologia del commercio e dell'industria. Torino, 1923. pp. 740.

— Constitution.

COMMENTARIO della costituzione; a cura di Giuseppe Branca. Bologna, 1975 in progress.

DELL'ACQUA (CESARE) Università, televisione e decentramento regionale: profili costituzionale e organizzativi. Napoli, 1974. pp. 157.

MANCINI (GIUSEPPE FEDERICO) Costituzione e movimento operaio. Bologna, [1976]. pp. 281.

La COSTITUZIONE italiana: i principi, la realtà; di Paolo Barile [and others]. Milano, [1977]. pp. 149.

LAVAGNA (CARLO) Costituzione e socialismo. Bologna, [1977]. pp. 100.

— Constitutional history.

PETTA (PAOLO) Ideologie costituzionali della sinistra italiana, 1892-1974. Roma, [1975]. pp. 239.

— Constitutional law.

SPAGNA MUSSO (ENRICO) Diritto costituzionale. Padova, 1976 in progress.

— Defences.

ALBONETTI (ACHILLE) L'Italia e l'atomica: il governo, il parlamento, i partiti, i diplomatici, gli scienziati e la stampa. Faenza, [1976]. pp. 287.

— Economic conditions.

LIBERTINI (LUCIO) and TRENTIN (BRUNO) L'industria italiana alla svolta: sindacato, partiti e grande capitale di fronte alla crisi. [Bari, 1975]. pp. 173. *Part of the proceedings of a conference "La struttura industriale del Piemonte e i problemi della sua trasformazione nella crisi dell'economia italiana" held in Turin by the Istituto Piemontese di Scienze Economiche e Sociali Antonio Gramsci in 1975.*

ALVARO (GIUSEPPE) La spirale del sottosviluppo: l'economia italiana al 1980. [Roma, 1976]. pp. 150.

COSTA (PAOLO) and others. Dalla crisi alla crisi: pianificazione sociale e nuovo modello di sviluppo; a cura di Giovanni Sarpellon. [Milano, 1976]. pp. 200. (*Padua. Università. Facoltà di Scienze Statistiche, Demografiche ed Attuariali. Contributi. Serie Pubblicazioni. N.4*)

CRISI economica e crisi politica: atti della tavola rotonda svoltasi a Roma il 17 marzo 1976. Roma, [1976]. pp. 59. (*Movimento Gaetano Salvemini. Quaderni del Salvemini. 22*)

CULTURA e democrazia: atti del Convegno "La cultura democratica di fronte alla crisi dello stato" Roma, 29-30 maggio 1975. [Roma, 1976]. pp. 405.

L'ECONOMIA italiana, 1975-1977;...secondo rapporto CEEP; [by] Pietro Armani [and others]. [Milano, 1976]. pp. 99. (*Centro Studi di Politica Economica. Collana. Sezione 1: Politica Economica. 7*)

FIACCAVENTO (CORRADO) Cronache di un capitalismo in declino. [Roma], 1976. pp. 346.

STRUTTURA finanziaria e politica economica in Italia; contributi di L.Izzo [and others]...; a cura di Franco Bernabè. [Milano, 1976]. pp. 179. (*Club Turati. Problemi della Società. 1*)

CARLI (GUIDO) Intervista sul capitalismo italiano; a cura di Eugenio Scalfari. Roma, 1977. pp. 131.

L'ECONOMIA italiana, 1976-1978: terzo rapporto CEEP; [by] Giorgio Basevi [and others]. [Milano, 1977]. pp. 100. (*Centro Studi di Politica Economica. Collana. Sezione 1: Politica Economica. 9*)

La LOTTA all'inflazione. [Roma, 1977]. pp. 99. *Proceedings of the 1st meeting of the Comitato Direttivo, Centro Studi Politica Economica, Partito Comunista Italiano.*

TRENTIN (BRUNO) Da sfruttati a produttori: lotte operaie e sviluppo capitalistico dal miracolo economico alla crisi. Bari, 1977. pp. 158, 356.

REGIONE FRIULI-VENEZIA GIULIA, LA: documentazione su fatti e problemi dell'economia italiana ed internazionale a cura della direzione regionale della programmazione studi e statistica [Friuli-Venezia Giulia]. bi-m. Trieste. *Current issues only kept.*

— — Mathematical models.

Il MODELLO econometrico dell'Università di Bologna: struttura e simulazioni; ([by] C. D'Adda [and others]). Bologna, [1976]. pp. 257. (*Bologna. Università. Istituto di Scienze Economiche. Gruppo di Lavoro del Modello Econometrico. Un Modello per l'Economia Italiano. 1*)

— Economic history.

SORACI (ROSARIO) Aspetti di storia economica italiana nell'età di Cassiodoro. Catania, [1974]. pp. 1 59. *bibliog.*

AMATO (GIULIANO) Economia, politica e istituzioni in Italia. [Bologna, 1976]. pp. 185.

FARINA (FRANCESCO) L'accumulazione in Italia, 1959-1972: un'interpretazione della crisi e della ristrutturazione capitalistica. [Bari, 1976]. pp. 188. *bibliogs.*

ITALY

GUALERNI (GUALBERTO) Industria e fascismo: per una interpretazione dello sviluppo economico italiano tra le due guerre. Milano, 1976. pp. 268.

MARUCCO (DORA) and TOS (ROSANNA) Capitalismo e lotte operaie in Italia, 1870-1970. Torino, [1976]. pp. 294. *Collection of documents.*

MERCANDINO (CESARE) and MERCANDINO (AUGUSTO) Storia del territorio e delle città d'Italia dal 1800 ai giorni nostri. Milano, [1976]. pp. 394. *bibliog.*

CAZZOLA (FRANCO) Lo sviluppo del capitalismo italiano, 1860-1914. Firenze, 1977. pp. 136. *bibliog.*

CIANCI (ERNESTO) Nascita dello Stato imprenditore in Italia. Milano, [1977]. pp. 390. *bibliog.*

MORI (GIORGIO) Il capitalismo industriale in Italia: processo d'industrializzazione e storia d'Italia. Roma, 1977. pp. 517.

— — Bibliography.

ANDREA (ANNA D') compiler. Il secondo dopoguerra in Italia, 1945-1960; proposte per una bibliografia ragionata. Cosenza, 1977. pp. 229.

— Economic policy.

SECCHI (BERNARDO) Squilibri regionali e sviluppo economico. [Padova, 1974]. pp. 300. *bibliogs.*

ABRAMI (ALBERTO) Comunità montane e sviluppo economico. [Milano], 1975. pp. 184. *(Associazione per lo Sviluppo dell'Industria nel Mezzogiorno. Centro per gli Studi sullo Sviluppo Economico. Collana Francesco Giordani)*

ARE (GIUSEPPE) Industria e politica in Italia. Roma, 1975. pp. 211. *bibliog.*

FERRARI AGGRADI (MARIO) La svolta economica della resistenza: primi atti della politica di programmazione. [Bologna, 1975]. pp. 202.

FRASCANI (PAOLO) Politica economica e finanza pubblica in Italia nel primo dopoguerra, 1918-1922. Napoli, [1975]. pp. 378.

FRATIANNI (MICHELE) Inflazione, produzione e politica economica in Italia; (traduzione italiana di Franco Lucat). [Milano, 1975]. pp. 160. *(Centro Studi di Politica Economica. Collana. 2)*

LEGA NAZIONALE DELLE COOPERATIVE E MUTUE. Consulta Economica. 2a Riunione, 1974. Il programma economico del governo; ([by] R. Antinolfi [and others]). Milano, 1975. pp. 78.

PARETO (VILFREDO) Lo sviluppo economico italiano [a collection of articles]; [with an introductory essay by] Lucio Avagliano. [Salerno, 1975]. pp. 219.

AMATO (GIULIANO) Economia, politica e istituzioni in Italia. [Bologna, 1976]. pp. 185.

CORTI (PAOLA) ed. Inchiesta Zanardelli sulla Basilicata. [Torino, 1976]. pp. 175. *bibliog.*

PETRICCIONE (SANDRO) Politica industriale e mezzogiorno. [Bari], 1976. pp. 161. *bibliogs.*

PROVASI (GIANCARLO) Borghesia industriale e Democrazia Cristiana: sviluppo economico e mediazione politica dalla Ricostruzione agli anni '70. Bari, [1976]. pp. 308. *bibliog.*

STATO e controllo dell'economia: democrazia politica e democrazia sociale. Bari, [1976]. pp. 193. *Proceedings of a conference held by the Istituto Gramsci in 1976.*

CINGARI (GAETANO) Nordisti, acciaio e mafia. Cosenza, [1977]. pp. 164.

MEZZOGIORNO e partiti politici; a cura di Domenico Novacco. [Milan, 1977]. pp. 498. *(Associazione per lo Sviluppo dell'Industria nel Mezzogiorno. Centro per gli Studi sullo Sviluppo Economico. Collana Rodolfo Morandi)*

MONTE (ALFREDO DEL) Politica regionale e sviluppo economico: un'analisi teorica ed econometrica degli effetti della politica degli incentivi nel Mezzogiorno, nell'Irlanda del Nord e in Scozia. Milano, [1977]. pp. 277. *(Naples. Università. Centro Studi di Economia Applicata all'Ingegneria. Studi Economici. 3)*

SVILUPPO economico e strutture finanziarie in Italia; a cura di Guido Carli. Bologna, [1977]. pp. 472.

— Emigration and immigration.

L'IMMIGRAZIONE in Svizzera: il lavoro straniero in Svizzera dalle origini ad oggi, con particolare riferimento all'immigrazione italiana; di S. Soldini [and others]. Milano, 1970 repr. 1975. pp. 202. *bibliog.*

L'EMIGRAZIONE italiana negli anni '70: antologia di studi sull'emigrazione; [by Claudio] Calvaruso [and others]. 2nd ed. Roma, 1975. pp. 270.

SAVONA (A. VIRGILIO) and STRANIERO (MICHELE L.) eds. Canti dell'emigrazione. Milano, [1976]. pp. 441.

SIGNORELLI (AMALIA) and others. Scelte senza potere: il ritorno degli emigranti nelle zone dell'esodo. Roma, 1977. pp. 328.

— Executive departments.

Le ISTITUZIONI in Italia: (otto conferenze curate dal Circolo Ottobre di Mantova); [by] Pio] Baldelli [and others]. Roma, [1976]. pp. 171. *bibliogs.*

— Foreign relations.

PETRILLI (GIUSEPPE) La politica estera ed europea di De Gasperi. Roma, [1975]. pp. 90.

GIORDANO (GIANCARLO) Il patto a quattro nella politica estera di Mussolini. [Bologna, 1976]. pp. 213. *bibliog.*

La POLITICA estera italiana: autonomia, interdipendenza, integrazione e sicurezza; a cura di Natalino Ronzitti. [Milano, 1977]. pp. 373. *Proceedings of an international convention held by the Istituto Affari Internazionali in 1976.*

ROBERTSON (ESMONDE MANNING) Mussolini as empire-builder: Europe and Africa, 1932-36. London, 1977. pp. 246. *bibliog.*

— — Germany.

MUHR (JOSEF) Die deutsch-italienischen Beziehungen in der Ära des Ersten Weltkrieges, 1914-1922. Göttingen, [1977]. pp. 235. *bibliog.*

— — United States.

BRANCOLI (RODOLFO) Gli USA e il PCI. Milano, 1976. pp. 197.

— History — 1400-1499.

PLUMB (JOHN HAROLD) and others. The Penguin book of the Renaissance; with essays by Garrett Mattingly [and others]. Harmondsworth, 1964 repr. 1978. pp. 333. *First published in Britain in 1961 under title The Horizon book of the Renaissance.*

— — 1500-1599.

PLUMB (JOHN HAROLD) and others. The Penguin book of the Renaissance; with essays by Garrett Mattingly [and others]. Harmondsworth, 1964 repr. 1978. pp. 333. *First published in Britain in 1961 under title The Horizon book of the Renaissance.*

— — 1700-1799.

VENTURI (FRANCO) Settecento riformatore. [Torino, 1969-76]. 2 vols.

— — 1815-1870.

GRAMSCI (ANTONIO) Il Risorgimento. Torino, 1972 repr. 1974. pp. 235. *bibliog. (Quaderni del Carcere. 3)*

LALLA (MANLIO DI) Storia del liberalismo italiano dal risorgimento al fascismo. Bologna, [1976]. pp. 341. *bibliogs. (Fondazione Luigi Einaudi. Il Liberalismo nel Mondo. 23)*

NEPPI MODONA (LEO) Correnti di libertà e di repressione tra Toscana e Piemonte dopo il 1831, con documenti su Tonduti, Manno, Giovannetti e Vieusseux. Milano, [1978]. pp. 63. *(Cagliari. Università. Facoltà di Scienze Politiche. Collectanea Caralitana. N.5)*

— — — Sources.

NEPPI MODONA (LEO) Correnti di libertà e di repressione tra Toscana e Piemonte dopo il 1831, con documenti su Tonduti, Manno, Giovannetti e Vieusseux. Milano, [1978]. pp. 63. *(Cagliari. Università. Facoltà di Scienze Politiche. Collectanea Caralitana. N.5)*

— — 1849-1870.

DOTTI (UGO) I dissidenti del Risorgimento: Cattaneo, Ferrari, Pisacane. Roma, 1975. pp. 117. *bibliog.*

— — 1870- .

LALLA (MANLIO DI) Storia del liberalismo italiano dal risorgimento al fascismo. Bologna, [1976]. pp. 341. *bibliogs. (Fondazione Luigi Einaudi. Il Liberalismo nel Mondo. 23)*

VALIANI (LEO) La lotta sociale e l'avvento della democrazia in Italia. Torino, [1976]. pp. 146. *bibliog.*

— — 1870-1915.

SAGRESTANI (MARCO) Italia di fine secolo: la lotta politico-parlamentare dal 1892 al 1900. [Bologna, 1976]. pp. 509.

— — 1914-1945.

DE BENEDETTI (AUGUSTO) La classe operaia a Napoli nel primo dopoguerra. Napoli, [1974]. pp. 197.

BERTOLDI (SILVIO) Salò: vita e morte della Repubblica Sociale Italiana. Milano, [1976]. pp. 432. *bibliog.*

FELICE (RENZO DE) ed. Antologia sul fascismo. Roma, 1976. 2 vols. (in 1).

I CATTOLICI dal fascismo alla resistenza; [by] Carlo F. Casula [and others]; a cura di Antonio Cucchiari. [Roma, 1977]. pp. 151. *bibliog.*

FERRAROTTO (MARINELLA) L'Accademia d'Italia: intellettuali e potere durante il fascismo. Napoli, 1977. pp. 163.

NORD e Sud nella crisi italiana, 1943-1945: atti della Tavola Rotonda, Catania 14-15 marzo 1975. Cosenza, 1977. pp. 285.

— — 1922-1945.

CUCCHIARI (ANTONIO) ed. Cattolici tra Togliatti e De Gasperi, 1937-45. Roma, [1977]. pp. 126.

— — 1945- .

PISCITELLI (ENZO) Da Parri a De Gasperi: storia del dopoguerra, 1945-1948. Milano, 1975. pp. 255.

L'ITALIA contemporanea, 1945-1975; a cura di Valerio Castronovo. Torino, [1976]. pp. 468. *bibliogs.*

SECCHIA (PIETRO) Chi sono i comunisti: partito e masse nella vita nazionale, 1948-1970; a cura e con prefazione di Ambrogio Donini. [Milano, 1977]. pp. 335.

— Industries.

LEVI (GIUSEPPE) and WAGNEST (RODOLFO) eds. L'attività economica nei secoli: antologia del commercio e dell'industria. Torino, 1923. pp. 740.

LIBERTINI (LUCIO) and TRENTIN (BRUNO) L'industria italiana alla svolta: sindacato, partiti e grande capitale di fronte alla crisi. [Bari, 1975]. pp. 173. *Part of the proceedings of a conference "La struttura industriale del Piemonte e i problemi della sua trasformazione nella crisi dell'economia italiana" held in Turin by the Istituto Piemontese di Scienze Economiche e Sociali Antonio Gramsci in 1975.*

COLAJANNI (NAPOLEONE) Riconversione grande impresa partecipazioni statali. [Milano, 1976]. pp. 125.

ITALY (Cont.)

PETRICCIONE (SANDRO) Politica industriale e mezzogiorno. [Bari], 1976. pp. 161. *bibliogs.*

MORI (GIORGIO) Il capitalismo industriale in Italia: processo d'industrializzazione e storia d'Italia. Roma, 1977. pp. 517.

— Intellectual life.

PARTITO COMUNISTA ITALIANO. Comitato Centrale, [and] Commissione Centrale di Controllo. Sessione, 13-15 gennaio 1975. Battaglia delle idee e rinnovamento culturale: atti. [Roma, 1975]. pp. 308.

CASSOLA (CARLO) Conversazione su una cultura compromessa: (militarismo e conformismo intellettuale a servizio del regime); a cura di Antonio Cardella. Palermo, [1977]. pp. 127.

CILIBERTO (MICHELE) Intellettuali e fascismo: saggio su Delio Cantimori. Bari, [1977]. pp. 264.

FERRAROTTO (MARINELLA) L'Accademia d'Italia: intellettuali e potere durante il fascismo. Napoli, 1977. pp. 163.

— Nationalism.

D'ANGELO (GIOVANNI) Italy and Ireland in the 19th centuries: contacts and misunderstandings between two national movements. Athlone, 1975. pp. 56.

— Nobility.

HEERS (JACQUES) Family clans in the middle ages: a study of political and social structures in urban areas. Amsterdam, 1977. pp. 266. *Translated by Barry Herbert.*

— Officials and employees.

POLI (ALBERTO) Pubblico impiego e classe operaia. Roma, 1977. pp. 159.

— Parliament.

Il PARLAMENTO nel sistema politico italiano; a cura di Alberto Predieri. Milano, [1975]. pp. 277. *bibliog. (Florence. Università degli Studi di Firenze. Facoltà di Scienze Politiche Cesare Alfieri. Studi Parlamentari. 1) Proceedings of a seminar held in 1975 and organized by the Istituto di Diritto Costituzionale Italiano e Comparato and the Fondazione Adriano Olivetti.*

AIMO (PIERO) Bicameralismo e regioni. Milano, 1977. pp. 216. *bibliog. (Fondazione Adriano Olivetti. Studi Parlamentari. 3)*

QUARANTA (GUIDO) Tutti gli uomini del Parlamento. Torino, [1977]. pp. 159.

— — Rules and practice.

CIOLO (VITTORIO DI) Le fonti del diritto parlamentare: appendice di aggiornamento al 30 aprile 1975. Milano, 1975. pp. 113. *bibliog.*

— Politics and government.

MATTEOTTI (GIACOMO) Reliquie. 2nd ed. Milano, 1946. pp. 247. *Most of the articles originally published in La Giustizia, 1922-24.*

L'ALTERNATIVA socialista: autogestione e riforme di struttura; [by] Claudio Signorile [and others], prefazione di Riccardo Lombardi. [Milano, 1976]. pp. 154.

CICCHITTO (FABRIZIO) La questione socialista: dall'autunno caldo all'alternativa. Venezia, [1976]. pp. 147.

ORDINE pubblico e sicurezza democratica: atti del convegno nazionale del PSI, Milano 7-9 marzo 1975. [Firenze, 1976]. pp. 414.

SCIUBBA (ROBERTO) and PACE (ROSSANA SCIUBBA) Le comunità di base in Italia. Volume primo. storia e cronaca. Roma, 1976. pp. 115.

— — Caricatures and cartoons.

CENTO anni di satira politica in Italia, 1876-1976; a cura di Enrico Gianeri e Andrea Rauch; interventi di Arduino Brizzi [and others]. Firenze, [1976]. pp.38,(111).

— — 1870-1915.

PARETO (VILFREDO) Lo sviluppo economico italiano [a collection of articles]; [with an introductory essay by] Lucio Avagliano. [Salerno, 1975]. pp. 219.

SAGRESTANI (MARCO) Italia di fine secolo: la lotta politico-parlamentare dal 1892 al 1900. [Bologna, 1976]. pp. 509.

— — 1900- .

BASSO (LELIO) Fascismo e Democrazia Cristiana: due regimi del capitalismo italiano. Milano, [1975]. pp. 186. *bibliog.*

COMPAGNA (FRANCESCO) Meridionalismo liberale. Milano, 1975. pp. 237.

CHIAROMONTE (NICOLA) Scritti politici e civili; a cura di Miriam Chiaromonte. Milano, [1976]. pp. 343.

LUSSO (EMILIO) Essere a sinistra: democrazia, autonomia e socialismo in cinquant'anni di lotte; a cura del Collettivo Emilio Lussu di Cagliari. Milano, [1976]. pp. 287.

— — 1914-1945.

GRAMSCI (ANTONIO) Passato e presente. Torino, 1966 repr. 1974. pp. 273. *(Quaderni del Carcere. 6)*

GRAMSCI (ANTONIO) Scritti giovanili, 1914-1918. Torino, 1972 repr. 1975. pp. 392. *(Opere. 8)*

PARETO (VILFREDO) Lo sviluppo economico italiano [a collection of articles]; [with an introductory essay by] Lucio Avagliano. [Salerno, 1975]. pp. 219.

GRAMSCI (ANTONIO) Scritti 1915-1921: (inediti dal Grido del Popolo e dall' Avanti...); a cura di Sergio Caprioglio. [Milano, 1976]. pp. 411.

NENNI (PIETRO) Storia di quattro anni, 1919-1922. 4th ed. Milano, [1976]. pp. 254. *bibliog.*

DE GRAND (ALEXANDER J.) The Italian Nationalist Association and the rise of fascism in Italy. Lincoln, Neb., [1978]. pp. 238. *bibliog.*

— — 1922-1945.

PELLIZZI (CAMILLO) Una rivoluzione mancata. Milano, [1949]. pp. 279.

— — 1945- .

CATALANO (FRANCO) and BERNADINI (GIORGIO) L'Italia che cambia: voto e classi sociali. [Milano, 1975]. pp. 183.

Il COMPROMESSO storico: contributi di Giorgio Amendola [and others]; a cura di Pietro Valenza. Roma, 1975. pp. 320.

CRISI politica: alternative di sinistra o involuzione autoritaria?: [proceedings of two Tavole Rotonde held in Rome, 1974]. [Rome, 1975]. pp. 99. *(Movimento Gaetano Salvemini. Quaderni del Salvemini. 16- 17)*

PANERAI (PAOLO) and DE LUCA (MAURIZIO) Il crack: Sindona, la DC, il Vaticano e gli altri amici. [Milan, 1975]. pp. 264.

PARTITO DI UNITÀ PROLETARIA PER IL COMUNISMO. Convegno, Ariccia, Febbraio 1975. Uscire dalla crisi o dal capitalismo in crisi?: atti del Convegno, etc. [Roma, 1975]. pp. 238.

PISCITELLI (ENZO) Da Parri a De Gasperi: storia del dopoguerra, 1945-1948. Milano, 1975. pp. 255.

[SANGUINETTI (GIANFRANCO)] Rapporto veridico sulle ultime opportunità di salvare il capitalismo in Italia: [by] Censor [pseud.]. [Milano, 1975]. pp. 143.

SINDACATO e sistema democratico; a cura del Centro Studi CISL. Bologna, [1975]. pp. 251. *Papers of a seminar organised by the Centro.*

TOGLIATTI (PALMIRO) Togliatti e il centrosinistra: 1958-(1964). Firenze, [1975]. 2 vols.

ALBONETTI (ACHILLE) L'Italia e l'atomica: il governo, il parlamento, i partiti, i diplomatici, gli scienziati e la stampa. Faenza, [1976]. pp. 287.

AMATO (GIULIANO) Economia, politica e istituzioni in Italia. [Bologna, 1976]. pp. 185.

AMENDOLA (GIORGIO) Gli anni della repubblica. Roma, 1976. pp. 356.

CULTURA e democrazia: atti del Convegno "La cultura democratica di fronte alla crisi dello stato" Roma, 29-30 maggio 1975. [Roma, 1976]. pp. 405.

FASCISMO e antifascismo nell'Italia repubblicana; a cura di Guido Quazza. Torino, [1976]. pp. 189.

GUIDUCCI (ROBERTO) La società dei socialisti. Milano, [1976]. pp. 206.

MANTOVANI (GIOVANNI) Gli eredi di De Gasperi: iniziativa democratica e i "giovani" al potere. Firenze, [1976]. pp. 176.

MURGIA (PIER GIUSEPPE) Ritorneremoë.: (storia e cronaca del fascismo dopo la Resistenza). Milano, [1976]. pp. 413.

STOLFI (EMANUELE) Da una parte sola: storia politica dello Statuto dei Lavoratori. Milano, [1976]. pp. 229.

BENOT (YVES) L'autre Italie, 1968-1976: problèmes de la dictature du prolétariat. Paris, 1977. pp. 319.

CASSOLA (CARLO) Conversazione su una cultura compromessa: (militarismo e conformismo intellettuale a servizio del regime); a cura di Antonio Cardella. Palermo, [1977]. pp. 127.

CHIAROMONTE (GERARDO) L'accordo programmatico e l'azione dei comunisti: (la relazione al Comitato centrale del PCI, 20 luglio 1977). Roma, [1977]. pp. 116.

MUZIO (PIER LUIGI) La crisi politica italiana: verso gli anni ottanta. Milano, [1977]. pp. 416.

NAPOLITANO (GIORGIO) The Italian road to socialism: an interview by Eric Hobsbawm with Giorgio Napolitano of the Italian Communist Party. Westport, Conn., 1977. pp. 118.

RADI (LUCIANO) Il voto dei giovani. Torino, [1977]. pp. 190.

VACCA (GIUSEPPE) Quale democrazia: problemi della democrazia di transizione. Bari, [1977]. pp. 318.

— Population.

La POPULATION de l'Italie. [Rome], 1974. pp. 188. *bibliog. (Committee for International Coordination of National Research in Demography. C.I.C.R.E.D. Series)*

LIVI BACCI (MASSIMO) A history of Italian fertility during the last two centuries. Princeton, N.J., [1977]. pp. 311.

— Relations (general) with Ireland.

D'ANGELO (GIOVANNI) Italy and Ireland in the 19th centuries: contacts and misunderstandings between two national movements. Athlone, 1975. pp. 56.

— Rural conditions.

FORMICA (CARMELO) Lo spazio rurale nel Mezzogiorno: esodo, desertificazione e riorganizzazione. Napoli, [1976]. pp. 173.

— Social conditions.

COSTA (PAOLO) and others. Dalla crisi alla crisi: pianificazione sociale e nuovo modello di sviluppo; a cura di Giovanni Sarpellon. [Milano, 1976]. pp. 200. *(Padua. Università. Facoltà di Scienze Statistiche, Demografiche ed Attuariali. Contributi. Serie Pubblicazioni. N.4)*

CULTURA e democrazia: atti del Convegno "La cultura democratica di fronte alla crisi dello stato" Roma, 29-30 maggio 1975. [Roma, 1976]. pp. 405.

ORDINE pubblico e sicurezza democratica: atti del convegno nazionale del PSI, Milano 7-9 marzo 1975. [Firenze, 1976]. pp. 414.

— Social history.

CERASE (FRANCESCO PAOLO) Sotto il dominio dei borghesi: sottosviluppo ed emigrazione nell'Italia meridionale, 1860-1910. Assisi, [1975]. pp. 164.

HEERS (JACQUES) Family clans in the middle ages: a study of political and social structures in urban areas. Amsterdam, 1977. pp. 266. *Translated by Barry Herbert.*

IVANOVO (OBLAST')

— Industries.

INDUSTRIAL'NOE razvitie Ivanovskoi oblasti, 1926-1941 gg.: sbornik dokumentov i materialov. Iaroslavl', 1976. pp. 215.

IVORY COAST

— Economic conditions.

IVORY COAST. Ministère de l'Economie et des Finances. Bureau d'Etudes et de la Coordination. Etudes économiques et financières. q., D 1969 (no.2)- , with gap (Mr 1970). Abidjan.

SAWADOGO (ABDOULAYE) L'agriculture en Côte d'Ivoire. [Paris, 1977]. pp. 367. *bibliog.*

JACKSON (ANDREW) President of the United States.

REMINI (ROBERT VINCENT) Andrew Jackson and the course of American empire, 1767-1821. New York, [1977]. pp. 502.

JACKSON (GEORGE LESTER).

MANN (ERIC) Comrade George: an investigation into the official story of his assassination: his work for the people and their response to his death. [Cambridge, Mass., 1972]. pp. 65.

JACOBS (ALETTA HENRIETTE).

JACOBS (ALETTA HENRIETTE) Herinneringen...; met een voorwoord van...J. Oppenheim. Amsterdam, 1924; Nijmegen, 1978. pp. 318.

JACOBY (JOHANN).

JACOBY (JOHANN) Briefwechsel, 1816-1849; herausgegeben und erläutert von Edmund Silberner. Hannover, [1974]. pp. 669. *bibliog. (Institut für Sozialgeschichte Braunschweig. Veröffentlichungen)*

JACOBY (JOHANN) Briefwechsel, 1850-1877; herausgegeben und erläutert von Edmund Silberner. Bonn, [1978]. pp. 715. *(Institut für Sozialgeschichte Braunschweig. Veröffentlichungen)*

JAKSCH (WENZEL).

PRINZ (FRIEDRICH) Beneš, Jaksch und die Sudetendeutschen. Stuttgart, 1975. pp. 76.

JAMAICA

— Politics and government.

STONE (CARL) Electoral behaviour and public opinion in Jamaica. [Kingston, Jamaica], 1974. pp. 107.

AGEE-HOSENBALL DEFENCE COMMITTEE. C.I.A. Briefings. No. 2. Jamaica destabilised: British Guiana repeated? London, [1976]. pp. 15.

— Social conditions.

BARRETT (LEONARD E.) The Rastafarians: the dreadlocks of Jamaica. Kingston, Jamaica, 1977. pp. 257. *bibliog.*

— Statistics.

STATISTICAL YEARBOOK OF JAMAICA; [pd. by] Department of Statistics. a., 1976(4th)- Kingston.

JAMMU AND KASHMIR

— Economic policy.

PAKISTAN. Ministry of Information and Broadcasting. Directorate of Research, Reference and Publications. 1976. Federal government's contribution to the progress of Azad Kashmir. [Islamabad, 1976?]. pp. 10.

— Politics and government.

BAZAZ (PREM NATH) The history of struggle for freedom in Kashmir; cultural and political from the earliest times to the present day. Islamabad, National Committee for Birth Centenary Celebrations of Quaid-i-Azam Mohammad Ali Jinnah, [1976]. pp. 744. *bibliog. Reprint of work first published commercially in 1954.*

— Social policy.

PAKISTAN. Ministry of Information and Broadcasting. Directorate of Research, Reference and Publications. 1976. Federal government's contribution to the progress of Azad Kashmir. [Islamabad, 1976?]. pp. 10.

JANSONISM.

ELMEN (PAUL) Wheat flour Messiah: Eric Jansson of Bishop Hill. Carbondale, Ill., [1976]. pp. 222. *bibliog.*

JANSSON (ERIK).

ELMEN (PAUL) Wheat flour Messiah: Eric Jansson of Bishop Hill. Carbondale, Ill., [1976]. pp. 222. *bibliog.*

JAPAN

— Civilization.

REED (JOHN PAUL) Kokutai: a study of certain sacred and secular aspects of Japanese nationalism. Chicago, 1940. pp. 274. *bibliog. Privately printed Ph.D. thesis, University of Chicago.*

MAINICHI NEWSPAPER PUBLISHING COMPANY, compilers. Japan and the Japanese. Tokyo, 1973. pp. 195. *Collection of essays submitted in a competition.*

FUKUTAKE (TADASHI) Japanese society today. Tokyo, [1974]. pp. 162.

POSTWAR trends in Japan: studies in commemoration of Rev. Aloysius Miller, S.J., edited by Shunichi Takayanagi and Kimitada Miwa. [Tokyo, 1975]. pp. 272. *bibliog.*

— Commerce.

MITUHASHI (SETUKO) Japanese commodity flows. Chicago, 1978. pp. 172. *bibliog. (Chicago. University. Department of Geography. Research Papers. No. 187)*

— — Germany.

MOERING (MARIA) Julius Simon: Jugend und Wanderjahre. [Hamburg, 1965?]. pp. 24.

— — Indonesia.

PANGLAYKIM (JUSUF) Business relations between Indonesia and Japan: a view. Singapore, [1974]. pp. 43.

— — New Zealand.

NEW ZEALAND ECONOMIC AND GOODWILL MISSION TO JAPAN AND TAIWAN. Report...October 1965. Wellington, Department of Industries and Commerce, [1966]. pp. 25.

— — United Kingdom.

JAPAN. Japanese Embassy, London. Information Centre. 1977. British trade with Japan. [London], 1977. pp. 33. *bibliog.*

— — United States.

SANDERSON (FRED HUGO) Japan's food prospects and policies. Washington, D.C., [1978]. pp. 99. *bibliog. Published under the auspices of the Brookings Institution.*

— Commercial policy.

ALLEN (GEORGE CYRIL) and OKANO (YUKIHIDE) How Japan competes: an assessment of international trading practices with special reference to dumping. London, 1978. pp. 74 *bibliog. (Institute of Economic Affairs. Hobart Papers. 81)*

— Constitutional law — Cases.

JAPAN. Supreme Court. 1978. The constitutional case law of Japan: selected Supreme Court decisions, 1961-70; [edited by] Hiroshi Itoh and Lawrence Ward Beer. Seattle, [1978]. pp. 283. *bibliog. (Washington University. School of Law. Asian Law Series. 6)*

— Economic conditions.

WHITEPAPER ON NATIONAL LIFE; [pd. by] Economic Planning Agency, Japanese Government. a., 1973- Tokyo.

ANGLO-JAPANESE ECONOMIC INSTITUTE. Japan: some of the problems of the seventies. London, [1973]. pp. 58.

MAINICHI NEWSPAPER PUBLISHING COMPANY, compilers. Japan and the Japanese. Tokyo, 1973. pp. 195. *Collection of essays submitted in a competition.*

MORINAGA (TEIICHIRO) Address...at the Thirtieth National Convention of Bankers, June 1, 1976. Tokyo, 1976. pp. 4. *(Bank of Japan. Economic Research Department. Special Papers. No. 63)*

FRANCE. Direction de la Documentation. La Documentation Française. Notes et Etudes Documentaires. Nos. 4,380-4, 381-4,382-4,383. Le Japon: maturité et vulnérabilité d'une expérience économique originale; par Edouard Maciejewski. [Paris], 1977. pp. 132. *bibliog.*

STUDIES in the business economics; edited on behalf of [the] Institute of Industrial Research, Kwansei Gakuin University, by Osamu Kojima. Kyote, 1977. pp. 168.

TSURU (SHIGETO) The mainsprings of Japanese growth: a turning point?; preface by Pierre Uri. Paris, [1977]. pp. 76. *(Atlantic Institute. Atlantic Papers. 1976. 3)*

— Economic history.

HANLEY (SUSAN B.) and YAMAMURA (KOZO) Economic and demographic change in preindustrial Japan, 1600-1868. Princeton, [1977]. pp. 409. *bibliog.*

— Economic policy.

JAPAN. Economic Planning Agency. 1975. Outlook and basic policy for the national economy, fiscal year 1975. [Tokyo], 1975. fo. 9.

CAMPBELL (JOHN CREIGHTON) Contemporary Japanese budget politics. Berkeley, Calif., [1977]. pp. 308. *bibliog. (Columbia University. East Asian Institute. Studies)*

WU (YUAN-LI) Japan's search for oil: a case study on economic nationalism and international security. Stanford, [1977]. pp. 116. *(Stanford University. Hoover Institution n War, Revolution and Peace. Hoover Institution Publications. 165)*

JOHNSON (CHALMERS) Japan's public policy companies. Washington, D.C., [1978]. pp. 173. *(American Enterprise Institute for Public Policy Research and Stanford University. Hoover Institution on War, Revolution and Peace. AEI-Hoover Policy Studies. 24)*

— Emigration and immigration.

NOGUEIRA (ARLINDA ROCHA) A imigração japonesa para a lavoura cafeeira paulista, 1908-1922. São Paulo, 1973. pp. 255. *bibliog. (São Paulo. Universidade. Instituto de Estudos Brasileiros. Publicacões. 28)*

— Foreign economic relations.

WU (YUAN-LI) Japan's search for oil: a case study on economic nationalism and international security. Stanford, [1977]. pp. 116. *(Stanford University. Hoover Institution n War, Revolution and Peace. Hoover Institution Publications. 165)*

JAPAN(Cont.)

— — Arab countries.

OPPORTUNITIES for cooperation between Japan and the Arab world: [proceedings of the OAPEC Tokyo seminar, November 11-12, 1976]. Kuwait, Organization of Arab Petroleum Exporting Countries, [1977]. pp. 250.

— — Australia.

CRAWFORD (Sir JOHN) and OKITA (SABURO) Australia, Japan and western Pacific economic relations: a report to the governments of Australia and Japan. Canberra, Australian Government Publishing Service, 1976. pp. 325.

— — Europe.

JAPAN'S relations with Britain and Europe: the present and the future; [by] Roderick MacFarquhar [and others]. London, 1977. pp. 28. *Six lectures given at the Japan Economic Journal symposium in 1977.*

— — Pacific, The.

CRAWFORD (Sir JOHN) and OKITA (SABURO) Australia, Japan and western Pacific economic relations: a report to the governments of Australia and Japan. Canberra, Australian Government Publishing Service, 1976. pp. 325.

— — United States.

JAPAN-U.S. ASSEMBLY, 1975. The Japan-U.S. Assembly. vol.2. Proceedings of a conference on the threat to the world economic order. Washington, D.C., [1976]. pp. 151. *Annual meeting of the Conference Board on U.S.-Japan Economic Policy in co-operation with the American Enterprise Institute for Public Policy Research.*

— Foreign relations.

POSTWAR trends in Japan: studies in commemoration of Rev. Aloysius Miller, S.J., edited by Shunichi Takayanagi and Kimitada Miwa. [Tokyo, 1975]. pp. 272. *bibliog.*

BLAKER (MICHAEL K.) Japanese international negotiating style. New York, 1977. pp. 253. *bibliog. (Columbia University. East Asian Institute. Studies)*

HORIUCHI (YOSHITAKA) Japan and mankind at the cross-roads. New York, [1977]. pp. 490.

— — China.

BARNETT (ARTHUR DOAK) China and the major powers in east Asia. Washington, D.C., [1977]. pp. 416.

JAIN (RAJENDRA KUMAR) China and Japan, 1949-1976. New Delhi, 1977. pp. 336. *bibliog.*

McCORMACK (GAVAN) Chang Tso-lin in northeast China, 1911-1928: China, Japan, and the Manchurian idea. Stanford, 1977. pp. 334. *bibliog.*

CHINA and Japan: search for balance since World War I; Alvin D. Coox and Hilary Conroy, editors. Santa Barbara, [1978]. pp. 468.

MENDL (WOLF) Issues in Japan's China policy. London, 1978. pp. 178. *bibliog.*

— — Europe.

JAPAN'S relations with Britain and Europe: the present and the future; [by] Roderick MacFarquhar [and others]. London, 1977. pp. 28. *Six lectures given at the Japan Economic Journal symposium in 1977.*

— — Germany.

DETERRENT diplomacy: Japan, Germany and the USSR 1935-1940: selected translations from Taiheiyo senso e no michi: kaisen gaiko shi; edited by James William Morley. New York, 1976. pp. 363. *bibliog. (Columbia University. East Asian Institute. Studies)*

— — Korea.

KOREA (REPUBLIC). Ministry of Public Information. 1965. End of long negotiation: signing of Korea-Japan talks. [Seoul], 1965. pp. 33. *(Korean Information: Foreign Publicity Material Series. No. 3)*

— — Russia.

DETERRENT diplomacy: Japan, Germany and the USSR 1935-1940: selected translations from Taiheiyo senso e no michi: kaisen gaiko shi; edited by James William Morley. New York, 1976. pp. 363. *bibliog. (Columbia University. East Asian Institute. Studies)*

— — United States.

COHEN (WARREN I.) The Chinese connection: Roger S. Greene, Thomas W. Lamont, George E. Sokolsky and American-East Asian relations. New York, 1978. pp. 322. *(Columbia University. East Asian Institute. Studies)*

— Nationalism.

REED (JOHN PAUL) Kokutai: a study of certain sacred and secular aspects of Japanese nationalism. Chicago, 1940. pp. 274. *bibliog. Privately printed Ph.D. thesis, University of Chicago.*

— Politics and government.

POLICYMAKING in contemporary Japan; edited by T.J. Pempel. Ithaca, 1977. pp. 345. *bibliog. Based in part on papers presented at the 1974 annual convention of the Association for Asian Studies.*

WATANUKI (JOJI) Politics in postwar Japanese society. Tokyo, [1977]. pp. 171. *bibliog.*

ENDICOTT (JOHN E.) and HEATON (WILLIAM R.) The politics of east Asia: China, Japan, Korea. Boulder, Colo., 1978. pp. 323. *bibliog.*

IKE (NOBUTAKA) A theory of Japanese democracy. Boulder, 1978. pp. 178. *bibliog.*

WARD (ROBERT EDWARD) Japan's political system. 2nd ed. Englewood Cliffs, [1978]. pp. 253. *bibliogs.*

— Population.

JAPAN. Bureau of Statistics. Population estimates. a., 1974(1st)- Tokyo. *[in English and Japanese] Not pd. in Census years. Supersedes JAPAN. Bureau of Statistics. Population estimates by age and sex and JAPAN. Bureau of Statistics. Population estimates by prefectures.*

HANLEY (SUSAN B.) and YAMAMURA (KOZO) Economic and demographic change in preindustrial Japan, 1600-1868. Princeton, [1977]. pp. 409. *bibliog.*

— Relations (general) with the United Kingdom.

MAUGHAN (T.J.) An introduction to the market for British books and journals in Japan and South Korea, etc. Tokyo, 1976. pp. 255.

— Rural conditions.

WASWO (ANN) Japanese landlords: the decline of a rural elite. Berkeley, Calif., [1977]. pp. 152. *bibliog.*

— Social conditions.

WHITEPAPER ON NATIONAL LIFE; [pd. by] Economic Planning Agency, Japanese Government. a., 1973- Tokyo.

ANGLO-JAPANESE ECONOMIC INSTITUTE. Japan: some of the problems of the seventies. London, [1973]. pp. 58.

MAINICHI NEWSPAPER PUBLISHING COMPANY, compilers. Japan and the Japanese. Tokyo, 1973. pp. 195. *Collection of essays submitted in a competition.*

FUKUTAKE (TADASHI) Japanese society today. Tokyo, [1974]. pp. 162.

— Social history.

STRONG (KENNETH) Ox against the storm: a biography of Tanaka Shozo, Japan's conservationist pioneer. Tenterden, Kent, 1977. pp. 232. *bibliog.*

— Social policy.

ORGANISATION FOR ECONOMIC CO-OPERATION AND DEVELOPMENT. 1977. Towards an integrated social policy in Japan. Paris, 1977. pp. 49.

— Statistics, Vital.

JAPAN. Bureau of Statistics. Population estimates. a., 1974(1st)- Tokyo. *[in English and Japanese] Not pd. in Census years. Supersedes JAPAN. Bureau of Statistics. Population estimates by age and sex and JAPAN. Bureau of Statistics. Population estimates by prefectures.*

JAPANESE AMERICANS.

MODELL (JOHN) The economics and politics of racial accommodation: the Japanese of Los Angeles, 1900-1942. Urbana, [Ill., 1977]. pp. 201.

— Evacuation and relocation, 1942-1945.

WEGLYN (MICHIKO NISHIURA) Years of infamy: the untold story of America's concentration camps. New York, 1976. pp. 351. *bibliog.*

JAPANESE IN BRAZIL.

NOGUEIRA (ARLINDA ROCHA) A imigração japonesa para a lavoura cafeeira paulista, 1908-1922. São Paulo, 1973. pp. 255. *bibliog. (São Paulo. Universidade. Instituto de Estudos Brasileiros. Publicacões. 28)*

JAPANESE IN CANADA.

BROADFOOT (BARRY) Years of sorrow, years of shame: the story of the Japanese Canadians in World War II. Toronto, 1977. pp. 370.

JAPANESE IN THE UNITED STATES.

For related heading see JAPANESE AMERICANS.

JEFFERSON (THOMAS) President of the United States.

McDONALD (FORREST) The presidency of Thomas Jefferson. Lawrence, Kan., [1976]. pp. 201. *bibliog.*

CUNNINGHAM (NOBLE E.) The process of government under Jefferson. Princeton, [1978]. pp. 357. *bibliog.*

PETERSON (MERRILL DANIEL) Adams and Jefferson: a revolutionary dialogue. Oxford, 1978. pp. 146. *(Mercer University. Eugenia Dorothy Blount Lamar Memorial Lectures. No. 19)*

JENSEN (ARTHUR R.)

PROGRESSIVE LABOR PARTY. Racism, IQ and the class society. London, [1974?]. pp. 75, xi.

JERN- OG METALINDUSTRIARBEJDSMAENDENES FAGFORENING.

JERN- OG METALINDUSTRIARBEJDSMAENDENES FAGFORENING. Århus Afdeling. Jern og metal igennem 75 år. [Århus, 1972]. pp. 44.

JERSEY

— Census.

JERSEY. Census, 1976. Report of the census for 1976. [St. Helier], 1977. pp. 62.

JERUSALEM

— History.

KOLLEK (TEDDY) and KOLLEK (AMOS) For Jerusalem: a life. London, [1978]. pp. 269.

JESUITS IN MEXICO.

PEREZ ALONSO (MANUEL IGNACIO) ed. La Compañía de Jesus en Mexico: cuatro siglos de labor cultural, 1572-1972. Mexico, 1975. pp. 645. *bibliogs.*

JET PLANES

— Noise.

NEW ZEALAND. Valuation Department. Research Papers. 71-3. The effect of Boeing 737 jet noise on the value of houses near Wellington airport. Wellington, [1971]. fo. 37.

JEVONS (WILLIAM STANLEY).

SAWYER (JOHN A.) Stanley Jevons and the development of scientific method in economics. Toronto, 1976. pp. 39. *bibliog. (Toronto. University. Institute for the Quantitative Analysis of Social and Economic Policy. Working Paper Series. No. 7602)*

JEWISH AMERICANS.

HIGHAM (JOHN) Send these to me: Jews and other immigrants in urban America. New York, 1975. pp. 259.

JICK (LEON A.) The Americanization of the synagogue, 1820-1870. Hanover, N.H., 1976. pp. 247. *bibliog.*

BAYOR (RONALD H.) Neighbors in conflict: the Irish, Germans, Jews, and Italians of New York City, 1929-1941. Baltimore, [1978]. pp. 232. *bibliog. (Johns Hopkins University. Studies in Historical and Political Science. Series 96. No. 1)*

LEVIN (NORA) Jewish socialist movements, 1871-1917; while Messiah tarried. London, 1978. pp. 554.

JEWISH CHRISTIANS.

SALVADOR (JOSE GONÇALVES) Os cristãos-novos: povoamento e conquista do solo brasileiro, 1530-1680. São Paulo, 1976. pp. 406. *bibliog.*

JEWISH-ARAB RELATIONS.

La CONFRONTATION Israélo-Arabe de juin 1967; traduit de l'anglais par Claude Triolet. Beyrouth, 1969. pp. 365. *(Palestine Research Centre. Palestine Monographs. 57) Reprinted from The Arab World, vol. 14, no. 10-11.*

COMMITTEES FOR SOLIDARITY WITH THE PALESTINIAN REVOLUTION. Palestinian revolution. Manchester, 1970. pp. 17.

PALESTINE: rule of the sword. n.p. [1973]. pp. 34.

JUREIDINI (PAUL A.) and HAZEN (WILLIAM EDWARD) The Palestinian movement in politics. Lexington, Mass., [1976]. pp. 139. *bibliog.*

The MIDDLE East: critical choices for the United States; Eugene V. Rostow, editor. Boulder, Colo., 1976. pp. 211. *Papers of a symposium convened by the National Committee on American Foreign Policy, Inc.*

The ARAB-Israeli conflict: readings and documents: abridged and revised version; edited by John Norton Moore. Princeton, N.J., 1977. pp. 1285. *bibliog.*

DRINAN (ROBERT F.) Honor the promise: America's commitment to Israel. Garden City, N.Y., 1977. pp. 250.

NELSON (WALTER HENRY) and PRITTIE (TERENCE CORNELIUS FARMER) The economic war against the Jews. New York, [1977]. pp. 269.

OUR roots are still alive: the story of the Palestinian people; written by the Palestine Book Project; Joy Bonds [and others]. San Francisco, 1977. pp. 189. *bibliog.*

PALESTINIAN impasse: Arab guerrillas and international terror; edited by Lester A. Sobel. New York, [1977]. pp. 282. *Based on records compiled by Facts on File.*

ASTOR (DAVID) and YORKE (VALERIE) Peace in the Middle East. London, 1978. pp. 174.

CAPLAN (NEIL) Palestine Jewry and the Arab question, 1917-1925. London, 1978. pp. 268. *bibliog.*

DOWNING (DAVID) and HERMAN (GARY) War without end, peace without hope. London, 1978. pp. 288. *bibliog.*

FROM June to October: the Middle East between 1967 and 1973; edited by Itamar Rabinovich [and] Haim Shaked. New Brunswick, [1978]. pp. 412. *Based on the Shiloah Center (Tel-Aviv University) Annual Seminar for the academic year 1973/74.*

KAYYALI (ABDUL-WAHHAB) Palestine: a modern history. London, [1978]. pp. 243. *bibliog.*

PRIMAKOV (EVGENII MAKSIMOVICH) Anatomiia blizhenevostochnogo konflikta. Moskva, 1978. pp. 374.

TUMA (ELIAS HANNA) and DARIN-DRABKIN (HAIM) The economic case for Palestine. London, [1978]. pp. 126. *bibliog.*

WAR or peace in the Middle East?; edited by Peggy Duff. London, 1978. pp. 199.

— Sources.

The ARAB-Israeli conflict: readings and documents: abridged and revised version; edited by John Norton Moore. Princeton, N.J., 1977. pp. 1285. *bibliog.*

JEWISH QUESTION.

JEWRY UEBER ALLES; pd. by The Judaic Publishing Co., Ltd. a., Ap. 1920(vol. 1, no.3) London.

SHIMONI (GIDEON) Gandhi, satyagraha and the Jews: a formative factor in India's policy towards Israel. Jerusalem, 1977. pp. 60. *(Hebrew University. Leonard Davis Institute for International Relations. Jerusalem Papers on Peace Problems. 22)*

— Bibliography.

SILBERNER (EDMUND) compiler. Western European socialism and the Jewish problem (1800-1918) : a selective bibliography. Jerusalem, 1955. pp. 61.

JEWS.

KRIEGEL (ANNIE) Les Juifs et le monde moderne: essai sur les logiques d'émancipation. Paris, [1977]. pp. 255.

— History.

COLLOQUE DES INTELLECTUELS JUIFS DE LANGUE FRANÇAISE. 16ième Colloque, 1975. La conscience juive face à la guerre: données et débats...; textes introduits, présentés et revus par Jean Halpérin et Georges Levitte. Paris, [1976]. pp. 163.

LEVIN (NORA) Jewish socialist movements, 1871-1917; while Messiah tarried. London, 1978. pp. 554.

— Identity.

HERMAN (SIMON N.) Jewish identity: a social psychological perspective. Beverly Hills, [1977]. pp. 262. *bibliog.*

— Persecution.

DRUKS (HERBERT) The failure to rescue. New York, [1977]. pp. 108. *bibliog.*

— Political and social conditions.

HERMAN (SIMON N.) Jewish identity: a social psychological perspective. Beverly Hills, [1977]. pp. 262. *bibliog.*

CARLEBACH (JULIUS) Karl Marx and the radical critique of Judaism. London, [1978]. pp. 466. *bibliog.*

LEVIN (NORA) Jewish socialist movements, 1871-1917; while Messiah tarried. London, 1978. pp. 554.

— Restoration.

DAVIS (URIEL) Israel: Utopia Incorporated: a study of class, state, and corporate kin control. London, [1977]. pp. 182. *bibliog.*

DRINAN (ROBERT F.) Honor the promise: America's commitment to Israel. Garden City, N.Y., 1977. pp. 250.

FRIEDMAN (ISAIAH) Germany, Turkey, and Zionism, 1897-1918. Oxford, 1977. pp. 461. *bibliog.*

FISCH (HAROLD) The Zionist revolution: a new perspective. London, [1978]. pp. 197.

GILBERT (MARTIN) Exile and return: the emergence of Jewish statehood. London, [1978]. pp. 364. *bibliog.*

KAYYALI (ABDUL-WAHHAB) Palestine: a modern history. London, [1978]. pp. 243. *bibliog.*

MOSSEK (MOSHE) Palestine immigration policy under Sir Herbert Samuel: British, Zionist and Arab attitudes. London, 1978. pp. 179. *bibliog.*

PRIMAKOV (EVGENII MAKSIMOVICH) Anatomiia blizhenevostochnogo konflikta. Moskva, 1978. pp. 374.

JEWS IN FRANCE.

ALAGNA (ANTONIO) Les Juifs dans la société française de la Révolution de 1789 à l'Affaire Dreyfus. [Naples, 1975]. pp. 133. *bibliog.*

ALBERT (PHYLLIS COHEN) The modernisation of French Jewry: consistory and community in the nineteenth century. Hanover, N.H., 1977. pp. 450. *bibliog.*

WEINBERG (DAVID H.) A community on trial: the Jews of Paris in the 1930s. Chicago, 1977. pp. 239. *bibliog.*

JEWS IN GERMANY.

FLIEDNER (HANS JOACHIM) Die Judenverfolgung in Mannheim, 1933-1945. Stuttgart, 1971. 2 vols. *bibliog. (Mannheim. Stadtarchiv. Veröffentlichungen. Bände 1-2)*

JUDEN im Wilhelminischen Deutschland, 1890-1914: ein Sammelband; herausgegeben von Werner E. Mosse, etc. Tübingen, 1976. pp. 786. *(Leo Baeck Institute. Schriftenreihe Wissenschaftlicher Abhandlungen. 33)*

DUNKER (ULRICH) Der Reichsbund jüdischer Frontsoldaten, 1919-1938: Geschichte eines jüdischen Abwehrvereins. Düsseldorf, [1977]. pp. 354. *bibliog.*

Das JUDENTUM in der deutschen Umwelt, 1800-1850: Studien zur Frühgeschichte der Emanzipation; herausgegeben von Hans Liebeschütz und Arnold Paucker. Tübingen, 1977. pp. 445. *bibliog. (Leo Baeck Institute. Schriftenreihe Wissenschaftlicher Abhandlungen. 35)*

KNIPPING (ULRICH) Die Geschichte der Juden in Dortmund während der Zeit des Dritten Reiches. Dortmund, 1977. pp. 255. *bibliog. (Historischer Verein Dortmund. Monographien zur Geschichte Dortmunds und der Grafschaft Mark. Band 6)*

LAMBERTI (MARJORIE) Jewish activism in Imperial Germany: the struggle for civil equality. New Haven, 1978. pp. 235. *bibliog.*

JEWS IN ITALY.

POLIAKOV (LEON) Jewish bankers and the Holy See from the thirteenth to the seventeenth century;...translated from the French by Miriam Kochan. London, 1977. pp. 275.

JEWS IN PALESTINE.

FRIEDMAN (ISAIAH) Germany, Turkey, and Zionism, 1897-1918. Oxford, 1977. pp. 461. *bibliog.*

JEWS IN POLAND.

BRONSZTEJN (SZYJA) Ludność 'zydowska w Polsce w okresie międzywojennym: studium statystyczne. Wrocław, 1963. pp. 295.

JEWS IN RUSSIA.

BRYM (ROBERT J.) The Jewish intelligentsia and Russian Marxism: a sociological study of intellectual radicalism and ideological divergence. London, 1978. pp. 157. *bibliog.*

KOCHAN (LIONEL EDMUND) ed. The Jews in Soviet Russia since 1917; edited by Lionel Kochan. Oxford, 1978. pp. 431.

LEVIN (NORA) Jewish socialist movements, 1871-1917; while Messiah tarried. London, 1978. pp. 554.

JEWS IN SOUTH AFRICA.

JEWS IN SOUTH AFRICA.

FELDBERG (LEON) compiler. South African Jewry: a survey of the Jewish community: its contribution to South Africa: directory of communal institutions: and a who's who of leading personalities. 3rd ed. Johannesburg, 1976-77. pp. 529.

DUBB (ALLIE A.) Jewish South Africans: a sociological view of the Johannesburg community. [Grahamstown, S.A., 1977]. pp. 190. *bibliog. (Rhodes University. Institute of Social and Economic Research. Occasional Papers. No. 21) A revised version of a doctoral thesis entitled A study of Jewish identification and commitment in Johannesburg, presented in the Department of Sociology at Rhodes University, 1973.*

JEWS IN THE UNITED KINGDOM.

FRAENKEL (JOSEF) The history of the British section of the World Jewish Congress. London, [1977?]. pp. 10.

YOGEV (GEDALIA) Diamonds and coral: Anglo-Dutch Jews and eighteenth-century trade. Leicester, 1978. pp. 360. *bibliog.*

JEWS IN THE UNITED STATES.

For related heading see JEWISH AMERICANS.

JINNAH (MOHAMED ALI).

ALI (MAHMUD) Quaid-i-Azam as a constitutionalist. Islamabad, National Committee for Birth Centenary Celebrations of Quaid-i-Azam Mohammad Ali Jinnah, 1976. pp. 88. *bibliog.*

WAHEED-UZ-ZAMAN. Quaid-i-Azam Mohammad Ali Jinnah: myth and reality. Islamabad, National Committee for Birth Centenary Celebrations of Quaid-i-Azam Mohammad Ali Jinnah, 1976. pp. 167. *bibliog.*

JIVARO INDIANS.

SALAZAR (ERNESTO) An Indian federation in lowland Ecuador. Copenhagen, 1977. pp. 68. *bibliog. (International Work Group for Indigenous Affairs. Documents. 28)*

JOB EVALUATION.

FRANKS (BERNARD) The measured day work and productivity deal swindle: how it works and how to fight it. London, 1970. pp. 157. *Articles originally published in the Workers Press, 1970.*

NIGERIA. Public Service Review Commission. 1974. Report on grading and pay, 1972-74. Lagos, 1974. 6 vols. (in 3).

JOB SATISFACTION

— **Bibliography.**

DWORACZEK (MARIAN) compiler. Job satisfaction: a selected bibliography. Toronto, Ontario Ministry of Labour Research Library, 1976. pp. 38.

— **Sweden.**

PALM (GÖRAN) The flight from work; translated by Patrick Smith. Cambridge, [1977]. pp. 204.

— **United States.**

SARASON (SEYMOUR BERNARD) Work, aging, and social change: professionals and the one life-one career imperative;...with a chapter, The Santa Fe experience; by David Krantz. New York, [1977]. pp. 298. *bibliog.*

BERG (IVAR E.) and others. Managers and work reform: a limited engagement. New York, [1978]. pp. 316.

JOB VACANCIES

— **United States.**

LECHT (LEONARD ABE) Occupational choice and training needs: prospects for the 1980's. New York, 1977. pp. 203.

JOHNSON (HARRY GORDON)

— **Bibliography.**

BELTON (E.J.) compiler. Bibliography of published writings to 1975 of Dr. Harry G. Johnson. [Ontario], 1976. pp. 60.

JONES (Sir ALFRED LEWIS).

DAVIES (PETER N.) Sir Alfred Jones: shipping entrepreneur par excellence. London, [1978]. pp. 162. *bibliog.*

JONES (REGINALD VICTOR).

JONES (REGINALD VICTOR) Most secret war. London, 1978. pp. 556.

JORDAN

— **Economic conditions.**

ASFOUR (BASSAM J.) The economic realities, Jordan, 1976-77. [Amman], 1977. fo. 20.

— **History — 1967- , Israeli occupation.**

GERSON (ALLAN) Israel, the West Bank and international law. London, [1978]. pp. 285.

— **Politics and government.**

MISHAL (SHAUL) West bank, east bank: the Palestinians in Jordan, 1949-1967. New Haven, 1978. pp. 129.

JOURNALISM

— **Canada.**

LAGRAVE (JEAN PAUL DE) Les journalistes-démocrates au Bas-Canada, 1791-1840. Montreal, [1975]. pp. 248.

— **United Kingdom — Social aspects.**

CRANFIELD (GEOFFREY ALAN) The press and society: from Caxton to Northcliffe. London, 1978. pp. 242. *bibliog.*

— **United States — Political aspects.**

SHAW (DONALD LEWIS) and McCOMBS (MAXWELL E.) The emergence of American political issues: the agenda-setting function of the press. St. Paul, [1977]. pp. 211. *bibliog.*

JOURNALISTS

— **Canada.**

LAGRAVE (JEAN PAUL DE) Les journalistes-démocrates au Bas-Canada, 1791-1840. Montreal, [1975]. pp. 248.

— **Germany.**

BESTRAFTE Solidarität: Drucker und Journalisten im gewerkschaftlichen Kampf; ([by] Klaus Kräling [and others]). Berlin, [1973]. pp. 139.

— **South Africa.**

WOODS (DONALD) Biko. New York, [1978]. pp. 288.

— **United Kingdom.**

HEREN (LOUIS) Growing up on The Times. London, 1978. pp. 319.

— **United States.**

CHILDS (MARQUIS WILLIAM) Witness to power. New York, [1975]. pp. 277.

JUDGES

— **United Kingdom.**

HEUSTON (ROBERT FRANCIS VERE) Judges and biographers: an inaugural lecture delivered at the University on 24th January, 1967. Southampton, 1967. pp. 27.

GRIFFITH (JOHN ANEURIN GREY) The pol judiciary. [London, 1977]. pp. 224.

— **United States.**

WOLFMAN (BERNARD) and others. Dissent v opinion: the behavior of Justice William O. Dou Federal tax cases. Philadelphia, [1975]. pp. 204.

WHITE (G. EDWARD) The American judicial t profiles of leading American judges. New York, reprinted 1978. pp. 441. *bibliog.*

JUDICIAL POWER

— **United Kingdom.**

GRIFFITH (JOHN ANEURIN GREY) The polit judiciary. Manchester, 1977. pp. 224.

— **United States.**

BERGER (RAOUL) Government by judiciary: th transformation of the Fourteenth Amendment. Ca Mass., 1977. pp. 483. *bibliog.*

JUDICIAL REVIEW

— **Russia.**

BROVIN (GEORGII IVANOVICH) and MIKHA (VLADIMIR TIMOFEEVICH) Prokurorskii nadz zakonnost'iu ispolneniia prigovorov. Moskva, 197 134.

— **United Kingdom.**

DENNING (ALFRED THOMPSON) Baron Denr Restraining the misuse of power. Birmingham, 19 14. *(Birmingham. University. Holdsworth Club. P. Addresses. 1978)*

JUDICIAL STATISTICS

— **Germany.**

GERMANY (BUNDESREPUBLIK). Statistische: Bundesamt. Ausgewählte Zahlen für die Rechtspfl 1975- Wiesbaden. *(Rechtspflege. Reihe 1) Supersed GERMANY (BUNDESREPUBLIK). Statistisches Bundesamt. Rechtspflege.*

— **Sweden.**

SWEDEN. Statistiska Centralbyrån. Rättsstatistisl etc. a., 1975(1st)- Stockholm. *[in English and Swec Supersedes SWEDEN. Statistiska Centralbyrån. Domstolarna and SWEDEN. Statistiska Centralby Kriminalstatistik.*

JUELICH

— **History.**

Der JUELICHER Arbeiter- und Soldatenrat im Nc 1918: eine Dokumentation; ([edited by] Günter Ber Jülich, 1974. pp. 31.

JÜLICH.

See JUELICH.

JURA

— **Nationalism.**

FLUECKIGER (FELIX) Jurassische Einheit: Volk und Staat im Jura: Vortrag, gehalten am 24. Februa anlässlich der Delegierten- Versammlung der Vereii der Freunde des Berner Jura in Bern. [Bern, 1977].

SCHWANDER (MARCEL) Jura: Konfliktstoff für Jahrzehnte. Zürich, [1977]. pp. 141.

JURISDICTION

— **European Economic Community cou**

HASFORD (HEINER) Die Jurisdiktion der Europä Gemeinschaften: zur extraterritorialen Wirkung des Gemeinschaftsrechts. Frankfurt am Main, [1977]. p *bibliog.*

JURISPRUDENCE.

CARDOZO (BENJAMIN NATHAN) Selected writings...; edited by Margaret E. Hall. New York, [1947]. pp. 456.

LEYTEN (J.C.M.) De rechter op de schopstoel: rede uitgesproken...aan de Katholieke Universiteit te Nijmegen...1970. Deventer, [1970]. pp. 35.

EHRENZWEIG (ALBERT ARMIN) Law: a personal view; edited by Max Knight. Leyden, 1977. pp. 163. *bibliog.*

KUBŮ (LUBOMÍR) Ryzí nauka právní v kontextu buržoazního právního myšlení. Brno, 1977. pp. 102. *bibliog.* With Russian summary.

PERSPECTIVES in jurisprudence: edited by Elspeth Attwooll. Glasgow, 1977. pp. 236.

SMITH (ADAM) LL.D., F.R.S. Lectures on jurisprudence; edited by R.L. Meek [and others]. Oxford, 1978. pp. 610. *bibliog.* (*Glasgow. University. Glasgow Edition of the Works and Correspondence of Adam Smith*)

JURY

— **United Kingdom.**

THORNTON (PETER) Trial or error: a reply to the James Committee. London, [1976]. pp. 23. (*National Council for Civil Liberties. Reports. No. 16*)

JUSTICE, ADMINISTRATION OF.

ABU RANNAT (MOHAMMED AHMED) Study of equality in the administration of justice. (E/CN.4/Sub. 2/296/Rev.1). New York, United Nations, 1972. pp. 270.

— **Canada — British Columbia.**

BRITISH COLUMBIA. Ministry of the Attorney-General. Annual report. a., 1976(3rd)- Vancouver.

DELISLE (A.O.) An organizational study of the Justice Councils Branch. Victoria, Department of the Attorney General, 1976. pp. 61. *bibliog.*

— — **Ontario.**

ONTARIO. Ministry of the Attorney General. 1976. White paper on courts administration. [Toronto], 1976. pp. 28.

— — **Prince Edward Island.**

MACKIMMIE (R. A.) Report made to Gordon L. Bennett, Minister of Justice and Attorney-General of the Province of Prince Edward Island on the constitution of the courts, judicial and quasi judicial institutions and certain other aspects of the administration of justice within the province. [Charlottetown, Department of Justice], 1973. fo.102. *Cover title begins: The McKimmie report.*

— **India — Gujarat.**

GUJARAT. Judicial Reforms Committee. 1976. Report of the...Committee appointed by the government of Gujarat; [P.N. Bhagwati, chairman]. [Gandhinagar], 1976. pp. 240.

— **Italy.**

Le ISTITUZIONI in Italia: (otto conferenze curate dal Circolo Ottobre di Mantova); [by Pio] Baldelli [and others]. Roma, [1976]. pp. 171. *bibliogs.*

RESTA (ELIGIO) Conflitti sociali e giustizia. Bari, [1977]. pp. 238.

SCHWARZENBERG (CLAUDIO) Diritto e giustizia nell'Italia fascista. Milano, [1977]. pp. 310.

— **Nigeria.**

ADEWOYE (OMONIYI) The judicial system in Southern Nigeria, 1854-1954: law and justice in a dependency. London, 1977. pp. 331. *bibliog.*

— **Russia.**

BUTLER (WILLIAM E.) ed. The Soviet legal system: selected contemporary legislation and documents. Dobbs Ferry, N.Y., 1978. pp. 733. (*Columbia University. Parker School of Foreign and Comparative Law. Studies in Foreign and Comparative Law*)

— **United Kingdom.**

JACKSON (RICHARD MEREDITH) The machinery of justice in England. 7th ed. Cambridge, 1977. pp. 627.

PHILLIPS (OWEN HOOD) A first book of English law; seventh edition by O. Hood Phillips and A.H. Hudson. London, 1977. pp. 389.

ZANDER (MICHAEL) Inequalities before the law. Milton Keynes, 1976. pp. 38. (*Open University. Social Science: a third level course: patterns of inequality. Unit 14*)

JUSTICES OF THE PEACE

— **United Kingdom.**

GILES (FRANCIS TRESEDER) The magistrates' courts: what they do, how they do it, and why. 2nd ed. Harmondsworth, [1951]. pp. 222.

JUTLAND

— **Economic history.**

SOCIAL forandring i Vestjylland: en samling originalartikler til belysning af nogle vigtige arbejdsmarkedsproblemer;...redigeret af Flemming Svejstrup. Esbjerg, 1976. 2 vols. (in 1). *Contributions by members of Projekt 1 at Sydjysk Universitetscenter.*

— **Social conditions.**

CHRISTENSEN (ERIK) Historian. Fagforeninger og lokalsamfund: en beskrivelse og analyse af 4 vestjyske fagforeninger. Esbjerg, 1977. pp. 384. *bibliog.*

— **Social history.**

SOCIAL forandring i Vestjylland: en samling originalartikler til belysning af nogle vigtige arbejdsmarkedsproblemer;...redigeret af Flemming Svejstrup. Esbjerg, 1976. 2 vols. (in 1). *Contributions by members of Projekt 1 at Sydjysk Universitetscenter.*

JUVENILE COURTS

— **United States.**

PURSUING justice for the child; edited by Margaret K. Rosenheim. Chicago, 1976. pp. 361. *bibliogs.*

JUVENILE DELINQUENCY.

MIDGLEY (JAMES) Children on trial: a study of juvenile justice. Cape Town, 1975. pp. 181. *bibliog.*

MARSH (PETER) and others. The rules of disorder. London, 1978. pp. 140. *bibliog.*

— **Canada — British Columbia.**

BRITISH COLUMBIA. Co-ordinator of Juvenile Delinquency Prevention Services. 1963. An interim report and recommendations on co-ordination of government and community resources in the treatment of juvenile delinquency for rural British Columbia; by C.W. Gorby. [Victoria], 1963. pp. 28.

BRITISH COLUMBIA. Co-ordinator of Juvenile Delinquency Prevention Services. 1965. A report and recommendations on co-ordination of youth services in Greater Vancouver and Greater Victoria; by C.W. Gorby. [Victoria], 1965. pp. 36. *bibliog.*

— **New Zealand.**

HAMPTON (ROSS E.) Sentencing in a children's court and labelling theory. [Wellington, 1976]. pp. 84. *bibliog.* (*New Zealand. Department of Justice. Research Section. Research Series. No. 5*)

— **South Africa.**

MIDGLEY (JAMES) Children on trial: a study of juvenile justice. Cape Town, 1975. pp. 181. *bibliog.*

— **Trinidad and Tobago.**

TRINIDAD AND TOBAGO. Central Statistical Office. 1975. Juvenile delinquency report, 1967-1972. Port of Spain, 1975. pp. 134.

— **United Kingdom.**

STRATTA (ERICA WENDY) The educational experience of boys admitted to borstal 1965-1966: a study of their background in relation to their prospects for education as part of borstal training. 1968. fo. 318. *bibliog.* Typescript. Ph.D. (London) thesis: unpublished. This thesis is the property of London University and may not be removed from the Library.

GILL (OWEN) Luke Street: housing policy, conflict and the creation of the delinquent area. London, 1977. pp. 207.

INTERMEDIATE treatment: 28 choices: a collection of papers on the projects described during the two seminars on intermediate treatment activities at Oxford and Clacton-on-Sea, November/December 1976. [London], Department of Health and Social Security, 1977. pp. 308.

CAWSON (PAT) Community homes: a study of residential staff. London, 1978. pp. 182. *bibliog.* (*U.K. Department of Health and Social Security. Research Reports. No. 2*)

— **United States.**

GIBBONS (DON C.) Delinquent behavior. Englewood Cliffs, [1970]. pp. 276.

JUVENILE JUSTICE, ADMINISTRATION OF

— **United Kingdom.**

PARSLOE (PHYLLIDA) Juvenile justice in Britain and the United States: the balance of needs and rights. London, [1978]. pp. 325. *bibliog.*

— — **Scotland.**

MORRIS (ALLISON) and McISAAC (MARY) Juvenile justice?: the practice of social welfare. London, 1978. pp. 186.

— **United States.**

PARSLOE (PHYLLIDA) Juvenile justice in Britain and the United States: the balance of needs and rights. London, [1978]. pp. 325. *bibliog.*

TWENTIETH CENTURY FUND. Task Force on Sentencing Policy Toward Young Offenders. Confronting youth crime: report;...background paper by Frankli E. Zimring. New York, [1978]. pp. 120.

KABRE (AFRICAN PEOPLE).

LUCIEN-BRUN (B.) La colonisation des terres neuves du Centre-Togo par les Kabrè et les Losso. [Bondy]. Office de la Recherche Scientifique et Technique Outre-Mer, [1974]. fo. 293. *bibliog.* Maps in end pocket.

KAISEN (WILHELM).

KAISEN (WILHELM) Zuversicht und Beständigkeit...: eine Dokumentation (herausgegeben und eingeleitet von Hans Koschnick). Bremen, [1977]. pp. 344.

KALISZ

— **Social history — Sources.**

BARANOWSKI (BOHDAN) Najdawniejsze procesy o czary w Kaliszu. Lublin, 1951. pp. 66. (*Polskie Towarzystwo Ludoznawcze. Archiwum Etnograficzne. nr.2*)

KAMAIURA INDIANS.

JUNQUEIRA (CARMEN) Os indios de Ipavu: um estudo sobre a vida do grupo Kamaiura. São Paulo, 1975. pp. 111. *bibliog.*

KAMCHATKA

KAMCHATKA
— Statistics.

KAMCHATKA. Statisticheskoe Upravlenie. Narodnoe khoziaistvo Kamchatskoi oblasti: statisticheskii sbornik. Petropavlovsk-Kamchatskii, 1971. pp. 203.

KAMITZ (REINHARD).

DIWOK (FRITZ) and KOLLER (HILDEGARD) Reinhard Kamitz: Wegbereiter des Wohlstands. Wien, [1977]. pp. 192. *bibliog.*

KAMPALA
— Officials and employees.

UGANDA. Commission of Inquiry into the Kampala City Council. 1972. Part 1. Report; [P.A.P.J. Allen, chairman]. Part 2. Government decision on the Commission's recommendations. Entebbe, [1972]. pp. 126.

KANO (STATE)
— Economic conditions.

HILL (POLLY) Population, prosperity and poverty: rural Kano, 1900 and 1970. Cambridge, 1977. pp. 240. *bibliog.*

— Population.

HILL (POLLY) Population, prosperity and poverty: rural Kano, 1900 and 1970. Cambridge, 1977. pp. 240. *bibliog.*

— Rural conditions.

HILL (POLLY) Population, prosperity and poverty: rural Kano, 1900 and 1970. Cambridge, 1977. pp. 240. *bibliog.*

KANSAS CITY, MISSOURI
— History.

BRIGGS (JOHN WALKER) An Italian passage: immigrants to three American cities, 1890- 1930. New Haven, 1978. pp. 348. *bibliog.*

KARAMZIN (NIKOLAI MIKHAILOVICH).

VOPROSY metodologii i istorii istoricheskoi nauki. Moskva, 1977. pp. 315.

KARAVELOV (LIUBEN).

PETKO R. Slaveikov, Liuben Karavelov, Khristo Botev, Zakhari Stoianov v spomenite na suvremennitsite si. Sofiia, 1967. pp. 758.

KASHMIR QUESTION.

DAULTANA (MIAN MUMTAZ MUHAMMAD KHAN) Kashmir dispute in present-day perspective; (text of the speech delivered...at a public meeting held under the auspices of the Punjab Literary League...November 2, 1965. Lahore, [1966]. pp. 18.

PAKISTAN. Department of Films and Publications. 1966. Kashmir in the Security Council: (a compilation of the texts of various resolutions tabled at the Security Council since 1948 until 5th November, 1965). [Karachi, 1966?]. pp. 49.

PAKISTAN. Department of Films and Publications. 1968. Story of Kashmir, (1947-68). rev. ed. [Karachi, 1968]. pp. 74.

PAKISTAN. Ministry of Foreign Affairs. 1977. White paper on the Jammu and Kashmir dispute. [Islamabad], 1977. pp. 137.

KATHOLISCHER LEHRERVERBAND DES DEUTSCHEN REICHES.

KUEPPERS (HEINRICH) Der Katholische Lehrerverband in der Übergangszeit von der Weimarer Republik zur Hitler-Diktatur: zugleich ein Beitrag zur Geschichte des Volksschullehrerstandes. Mainz, [1975]. pp. 201. *bibliog.* *(Kommission für Zeitgeschichte. Veröffentlichungen. Reihe B: Forschungen. Band 18)*

KATOWICE (PROVINCE)
— Industries.

SYREK (MIECZYSŁAW) Przemysł regionu katowickiego w latach 1945-1974. Katowice, 1976. pp. 240. *bibliog.*

KAYES.

KEITA (ROKIATOU N'DIAYE) Kayes et le Haut Sénégal: les étapes de la croissance urbaine. T.1. [Bamako, 1972]. pp. 235.

KAZAKSTAN
— Economic history.

PISHCHULINA (KLAVDIIA ANTONOVNA) Iugo-Vostochnyi Kazakhstan v seredine XIV - nachale XVI vekov: voprosy politicheskoi i sotsial'no-ekonomicheskoi istorii. Alma-Ata, 1977. pp. 288.

— History.

PISHCHULINA (KLAVDIIA ANTONOVNA) Iugo-Vostochnyi Kazakhstan v seredine XIV - nachale XVI vekov: voprosy politicheskoi i sotsial'no-ekonomicheskoi istorii. Alma-Ata, 1977. pp. 288.

— Statistics.

KAZAKSTAN. Tsentral'noe Statisticheskoe Upravlenie. 1975. Narodnoe khoziaistvo Kazakhstana v 1974 g.: statisticheskii sbornik. Alma-Ata, 1975. pp. 319.

KAZAN'
— Politics and government.

NAFIGOV (RAFIK IZMAILOVICH) Revoliutsionnye sviazi kazanskogo podpol'ia 80-kh godov, kruzhkov N.E. Fedoseeva. [Kazan'], 1975. pp. 26.

KELANTAN
— Politics and government.

KESSLER (CLIVE SAMUEL) Islam and politics in a Malay state: Kelantan, 1838-1969. Ithaca, [1978]. pp. 274. *bibliog.* Revised version of a doctoral thesis accepted by the University of London.

KELSEN (HANS).

RUSSO (FRANCO) Kelsen e il marxismo: democrazia politica e socialismo. [Firenze, 1976]. pp. 196.

KENNEDY (JOHN FITZGERALD) President of the United States
— Bibliography.

NEWCOMB (JOAN I.) compiler. John F. Kennedy: an annotated bibliography. Metuchen, N.J., 1977. pp. 143.

KENNEDY (ROBERT FRANCIS).

SCHLESINGER (ARTHUR MEIER) the Younger. Robert Kennedy and his times. London, 1978. pp. 1066.

KENT
— Economic conditions.

KENT. Planning Department. County structure plan: report of survey; ([with] Supplement). Maidstone, 1976-77. 2 vols. (in 1). *Cover title: Kent structure plan.*

— Economic policy.

KENT. Planning Department. County structure plan: report of survey; ([with] Supplement). Maidstone, 1976-77. 2 vols. (in 1). *Cover title: Kent structure plan.*

— History.

MOYLAN (PRUDENCE ANN) The form and reform of county government, Kent, 1889-1914. Leicester, 1978. pp. 96. *bibliog.* *(Leicester. University. Department of English Local History. Occasional Papers. 3rd Series. No. 3)*

— Politics and government.

MOYLAN (PRUDENCE ANN) The form and reform of county government, Kent, 1889-1914. Leicester, 1978. pp. 96. *bibliog.* *(Leicester. University. Department of English Local History. Occasional Papers. 3rd Series. No. 3)*

— Social conditions.

KENT. Planning Department. County structure plan: report of survey; ([with] Supplement). Maidstone, 1976-77. 2 vols. (in 1). *Cover title: Kent structure plan.*

— Social policy.

KENT. Planning Department. County structure plan: report of survey; ([with] Supplement). Maidstone, 1976-77. 2 vols. (in 1). *Cover title: Kent structure plan.*

KENYA
— Economic conditions.

SWAINSON (NICOLA) Foreign corporations and economic growth in Kenya. 1977 [or rather 1978]. fo. 371. *bibliog.* Typescript. Ph.D. (London) thesis: unpublished. This thesis is the property of London University and may not be removed from the Library.

— Economic policy.

SWAINSON (NICOLA) Foreign corporations and economic growth in Kenya. 1977 [or rather 1978]. fo. 371. *bibliog.* Typescript. Ph.D. (London) thesis: unpublished. This thesis is the property of London University and may not be removed from the Library.

— Politics and government.

MANS (ROWLAND) Kenyatta's middle road in a changing Africa: a model for the futuree? London, 1977. pp. 20. *(Institute for the Study of Conflict. Conflict Studies. No.85)*

— Population.

KENYA. Central Bureau of Statistics. 1975. Demographic baseline survey report, 1973. [Nairobi], 1975. pp. 70.

— Rural conditions.

KENYA. Central Bureau of Statistics. 1977. Rural household survey, Nyanza province 1970/71. [Nairobi], 1977. 1 vol. (various pagings).

— Social conditions.

SOCIAL PERSPECTIVES: technical bulletin; [pd. by] Central Bureau of Statistics. irreg., Jl 1977 (v. 1, no. 1)- Nairobi.

— Social policy.

SOCIAL PERSPECTIVES: technical bulletin; [pd. by] Central Bureau of Statistics. irreg., Jl 1977 (v. 1, no. 1)- Nairobi.

— Statistics, Vital.

KENYA. Central Bureau of Statistics. 1975. Demographic baseline survey report, 1973. [Nairobi], 1975. pp. 70.

KERALA
— Economic conditions.

KERALA. Bureau of Economics and Statistics. 1977. Indicators of regional development: an appraisal. Trivandrum, 1977. pp. 103.

— Officials and employees — Salaries, allowances etc.

KERALA. Commission of Enquiry into Scales of Pay and Related Matters. 1969. Report; [V.K. Velayudhan, chairman]. Trivandrum, 1969. pp. 443.

— Population.

KURUP (R.S.) and others. Fact book on population and family planning. Trivandrum, Demographic Research Centre, 1974. pp. 77.

KERALA. Bureau of Economics and Statistics. 1977. Indicators of regional development: an appraisal. Trivandrum, 1977. pp. 103.

— **Social conditions.**

KERALA. Bureau of Economics and Statistics. 1977. Indicators of regional development: an appraisal. Trivandrum, 1977. pp. 103.

KEYNES (JOHN MAYNARD) 1st Baron Keynes.

RICARDIENS, Keynésiens et Marxistes: essais en économie politique non-néoclassique: actes du colloque de Nice, septembre 1972; (édité par C. Berthomieu [and others]). [Grenoble, 1974]. pp. 405. bibliogs.

DELFAUD (PIERRE) Keynes et le keynésianisme. [Paris, 1977]. pp. 128. bibliog.

HUTCHISON (TERENCE WILMOT) Keynes versus the 'Keynesians'...?: an essay in the thinking of J.M. Keynes and the accuracy of its interpretation by his followers. London, 1977. pp. 83. (Institute of Economic Affairs. Hobart Paperbacks. 11)

JOHN Maynard Keynes nel pensiero e nella politica economica; a cura e con un'introduzione di Riccardo Faucci. [Milano, 1977]. pp. 242. bibliog.

KEYNES, Cambridge and The general theory: the process of criticism and discussion connected with the development of The general theory; proceedings of a conference held at the University of Western Ontario; ...edited by Don Patinkin and J. Clark Leith. London, 1977. pp. 182. bibliog.

MEHTA (GHANSHYAM) The structure of the Keynesian revolution. London, 1977. pp. 219. bibliog.

NENTJES (A.) Van Keynes tot Keynes: de ontwikkeling van het denken over geld en werkloosheid bij Keynes. Groningen, [1977]. pp. 357. With summary in English.

BUCHANAN (JAMES McGILL) and others. The consequences of Mr. Keynes: an analysis of the misuse of economic theory for political profiteering, with proposals for constitutional disciplines. London, 1978. pp. 88. bibliog. (Institute of Economic Affairs. Hobart Papers. 78)

KGAMA (BOIKANYO) Chief of the Ngwato.

See KHAMA (BOIKANYO) Chief of the Ngwato.

KHAMA (BOIKANYO) Chief of the Ngwato.

CHIRENJE (J. MUTERO) Chief Kgama and his times, c. 1835-1923: the story of a Southern African ruler. London, 1978. pp. 140. bibliog.

KHIVA KHANATE

— **History.**

ZIMANOV (SALYK ZIMANOVICH) Ot osvoboditel'nykh idei k sovetskoi gosudarstvennosti v Bukhare i Khive. Alma-Ata, 1976. pp. 220.

KIDNAPPING

— **Political aspects.**

CLUTTERBUCK (RICHARD LEWIS) Kidnap and ransom: the response. London, [1978]. pp. 192. bibliog.

KILLIAN (JAMES RHYNE).

KILLIAN (JAMES RHYNE) Sputnik, scientists, and Eisenhower: a memoir of the first special assistant to the President for science and technology. Cambridge, [1977]. pp. 315. bibliog.

KIM (IL-SUNG).

The FOUNDING of the anti-Japanese guerilla army, a historic event which brought about a great turn in the development of the Korean r[e]volution: [a commemoration of 40 years including extracts from speeches by Kim Il Sung]. [1972]. fo. 14. Typescript.

TAKAGI (TAKEO) Kim Il Sung: master of leadership. Pyongyang, 1976. pp. 241.

INTERNATIONAL SCIENTIFIC SEMINAR ON THE JUCHE IDEA, ANTANANARIVO, 1976. Juche: the banner of independence. Pyongyang, 1977. pp. 326.

JUCHE idea: the current thought of our present time. Pyongyang, 1977. pp. 265.

KING (MARTIN LUTHER).

LANE (MARK) and GREGORY (DICK) Code name "Zorro": the murder of Martin Luther King, Jr. Englewood Cliffs, [1977]. pp. 314.

— **Bibliography.**

FISHER (WILLIAM HARVEY) compiler. Free at last: a bibliography of Martin Luther King, Jr. Metuchen, 1977. pp. 169.

KINSHIP

— **Burma.**

SPIRO (MELFORD ELLIOT) Kinship and marriage in Burma: a cultural and psychodynamic analysis. Berkeley, Calif., [1977]. pp. 313. bibliog.

— **Israel.**

DAVIS (URIEL) Israel: Utopia Incorporated: a study of class, state, and corporate kin control. London, [1977]. pp. 182. bibliog.

— **Madagascar.**

EDHOLM (FELICITY ELIZABETH) Kinship and social change among the Antaisaka of coastal southeast Madagascar. [1976]. fo. 397. bibliog. Typescript. Ph.D. (London) thesis: unpublished. This thesis is the property of London University and may not be removed from the Library.

KIREEVSKII (IVAN VASIL'EVICH).

HISTORIA i wolność: studia z dziejów ideologii XIX wieku, etc. Warszawa, 1961. pp. 299. (Polska Akademia Nauk. Instytut Filozofii i Socjologii. Archiwum Historii Filozofii i Myśli Społecznej. 7) With Russian or German summaries.

KIRGHIZIA

— **Economic conditions.**

SAIFULIN (RAVIL' ZINNATOVICH) Tempy, proportsii i effektivnost' obshchestvennogo proizvodstva v Kirgizskoi SSR. Frunze, 1976. pp. 159.

— **History — 1917-1921, Revolution.**

NIKISHOV (PETR PETROVICH) Bor'ba bol'shevikov za uprochenie vlasti Sovetov v Kirgizii; pod redaktsiei V.V. Mirtova. Frunze, 1976. pp. 160. (Kommunisticheskaia Partiia Kirgizii. Tsentral'nyi Komitet. Institut Istorii Partii. Bibliotechnaia Seriia)

— **Industries.**

SELIKHOVA (OL'GA ROMANOVNA) Regional'nye osobennosti ekonomicheskogo razvitiia Kirgizii. Frunze, 1976. pp. 85.

KISSINGER (HENRY ALFRED).

SZULC (TAD) The illusion of peace: foreign policy in the Nixon years. New York, 1978. pp. 822.

KITCHENER

— **Economic history.**

INDUSTRIAL unionism in Kitchener, 1937-47; researched and written by students in the Department of History, Wilfrid Laurier University; edited by Terry Copp. Elora, Ont., [1976]. pp. 129.

KNOWLEDGE, SOCIOLOGY OF.

POPOVICI (ELENA) Societate, ideologie, cunoaștere. București, 1976. pp. 248.

BAUM (GREGORY) Truth beyond relativism: Karl Mannheim's sociology of knowledge. Milwaukee, Wis., 1977. pp. 83. (Marquette University. Theology Department. Pere Marquette Theology Lectures. 1977)

SIMONDS (A.P.) Karl Mannheim's sociology of knowledge. Oxford, 1978. pp. 205. bibliog.

KNOWLEDGE, THEORY OF.

LECOURT (DOMINIQUE) Marxism and epistemology: Bachelard, Canguilhem and Foucault; translated from the French by Ben Brewster. London, 1975. pp. 223. bibliog.

CAUSEY (ROBERT L.) Unity of science. Dordrecht, [1977]. pp. 185. bibliog.

PIAGET (JEAN) The essential Piaget; [selections from his works]; edited by Howard E. Gruber and J. Jacques Vonèche. London, 1977. pp. 881. bibliog.

RUBEN (DAVID HILLEL) Marxism and materialism: a study in marxist theory of knowledge. Hassocks, Sussex, 1977. pp. 199. bibliogs.

BRONOWSKI (JACOB) The origins of knowledge and imagination. New Haven, 1978. pp. 146. (Yale University. Silliman Memorial Lectures. 1967)

SOHN-RETHEL (ALFRED) Intellectual and manual labour: a critique of epistemology. London, 1978. pp. 216. bibliog.

SPENCE (LARRY D.) The politics of social knowledge. University Park, Penn., [1978]. pp. 374. bibliog.

KOLLEK (TEDDY).

KOLLEK (TEDDY) and KOLLEK (AMOS) For Jerusalem: a life. London, [1978]. pp. 269.

KOLLONTAI (ALEKSANDRA MIKHAILOVNA).

KOLLONTAI (ALEKSANDRA MIKHAILOVNA) Selected writings...; translated with an introduction and commentaries by Alix Holt. London, [1977]. pp. 335. bibliog.

KOMAROV (NIKOLAI PAVLOVICH) pseud.

KUTUZOV (VLADISLAV ALEKSANDROVICH) N.P. Komarov. Leningrad, 1976. pp. 208.

KONSUMVEREIN TEESDORF.

KORP (ANDREAS) Der Konsumverein Teesdorf: ein Beitrag sur Frühgeschichte des österreichischen Genossenschaftswesens. Wien, [1977]. pp. 56. bibliog.

KOOROKO (AFRICAN PEOPLE).

AMSELLE (JEAN LOUP) Les négociants de la Savane: histoire et organisation sociale des Kooroko (Mali). Paris, 1977. pp. 292.

KOREA

— **Economic conditions.**

BANK OF KOREA. The Korean economy: performance and prospect. [Seoul], 1976. pp. 52.

The FUTURE of the Korean peninsula; edited by Young C. Kim [and] Abraham M. Halpern. New York, 1977. pp. 193. Based on a conference held in 1975 at Arlington, Virginia, by the Institute for Sino-Soviet Studies of the George Washington University.

— — **Statistics.**

MAJOR STATISTICS OF KOREAN ECONOMY; [pd. by] Economic Planning Board. a., 1976- Seoul.

— **Economic history.**

SUH (SANG-CHUL) Growth and structural changes in the Korean economy, 1910-1940. Cambridge, Mass., 1978. pp. 227. bibliog. (Harvard University. East Asian Research Center. Harvard East Asian Monographs. 83)

KOREA(Cont.)

— Economic policy.

KOREA (REPUBLIC). Ministry of Public Information. 1966. Economic goals of the government in the year 1966. [Seoul], 1966. pp. 8. *(Korean Information: Foreign Publicity Material Series. No. 6)*

— Foreign relations.

The FUTURE of the Korean peninsula; edited by Young C. Kim [and] Abraham M. Halpern. New York, 1977. pp. 193. *Based on a conference held in 1975 at Arlington, Virginia, by the Institute for Sino-Soviet Studies of the George Washington University.*

See also UNITED NATIONS — Korea.

— — China.

CHUNG (CHIN O.) Pyongyang between Peking and Moscow: North Korea's involvement in the Sino-Soviet dispute, 1958-1975. University, Ala., [1978]. pp. 230. *bibliog.*

— — Japan.

KOREA (REPUBLIC). Ministry of Public Information. 1965. End of long negotiation: signing of Korea-Japan talks. [Seoul], 1965. pp. 33. *(Korean Information: Foreign Publicity Material Series. No. 3)*

— — Russia.

CHUNG (CHIN O.) Pyongyang between Peking and Moscow: North Korea's involvement in the Sino-Soviet dispute, 1958-1975. University, Ala., [1978]. pp. 230. *bibliog.*

— — United States.

DOCUMENTS on Korean-American relations, 1943-1976; editor Se-Jin Kim. Seoul, [1976]. pp. 558.

The US imperialists started the Korean war. Pyongyang, 1977. pp. 308.

— — Vietnam.

KOREA (REPUBLIC). Ministry of Public Information. 1965. Why do we send our troops to Vietnam? [Seoul], 1965. pp. 26. *(Korean Information: Foreign Publicity Material Series. No. 4)*

— History — Sources.

KOREAN unification: source materials with an introduction; editor Se-Jin Kim. Seoul, 1976. pp. 420.

— Industries.

KOREA DEVELOPMENT BANK. Industry in Korea, 1976. Seoul, [1976]. pp. 316.

— Politics and government.

KOREA (REPUBLIC). 1964. Forgery and counterfeiting. Seoul, [1964]. pp. 24.

KOREA (REPUBLIC). Ministry of Public Information. 1965. Question of Korean unification: why we insist on U.N.- supervised elections. [Seoul], 1965. pp. 7. *(Korean Information: Foreign Publicity Material Series. No. 5)*

KIM (SHIN-JO) An open letter to Kim Il-sung, together with the supplementary material concerning the raid on Seoul of January 21, 1968; a manifesto. [Seoul, Ministry of Public Information], 1968. pp. 31. *(Korea Information Series. 1968)*

KIM (SHIN-JO) Tool of tyranny: the story of a north Korean guerrilla terrorist. [Seoul, Ministry of Public Information, 1968]. pp. 38. *(Korea Information Series. 1968)*

KOREA (REPUBLIC). Ministry of Culture and Information. 1968. Plot set for renewed aggression: Red Korea girds for war: recent evidence shows plan for renewed attack. Seoul, 1968. pp. 29. *(Korea Information Series. 1968)*

KOREA (REPUBLIC). Ministry of Culture and Information. 1968. Red guerrilla threat in Korea blunted. Seoul, 1968. pp. 45. *(Korea Information Series. 1968)*

KOREA (REPUBLIC). Ministry of Public Information. 1968. Intensified aggression in Korea: a report on armed infiltrators sent by communists in the north. Seoul, 1968. pp. 46.

PARK (CHUNG-HEE) Let's "build while fighting": President Park meets with reporters on April 25, 1969. Seoul, Ministry of Culture and Information, 1969. pp. 16. *(Korea Information Series. 1969)*

KOREA (PEOPLE'S DEMOCRATIC REPUBLIC). Supreme People's Assembly. 1971. Appeal of the Supreme People's Assembly of the Democratic People's Republic of Korea to the South Korean fellow countrymen, brothers and sisters and the personages of political parties and public organisations. Pyongyang, [1971]. pp. 14.

KOREA (REPUBLIC). Ministry of Culture and Information. 1971. A break in the stalemate: Korea moves cautiously toward unity. Seoul, [1971]. pp. 40.

UNITED NATIONS. General Assembly. 1975. The question of Korea at the 30th session of the U.N. General Assembly: [collection of General Assembly documents]. Seoul, Republic of Korea Ministry of Foreign Affairs, 1975. 2 vols.(in 1).

TAKAGI (TAKEO) Kim Il Sung: master of leadership. Pyongyang, 1976. pp. 241.

The FUTURE of the Korean peninsula; edited by Young C. Kim [and] Abraham M. Halpern. New York, 1977. pp. 193. *Based on a conference held in 1975 at Arlington, Virginia, by the Institute for Sino-Soviet Studies of the George Washington University.*

JUCHE idea: the current thought of our present time. Pyongyang, 1977. pp. 265.

SIGNS of dictator's downfall: letters from South Korea; by T. K. Pyongyang, 1977. pp. 298.

ENDICOTT (JOHN E.) and HEATON (WILLIAM R.) The politics of east Asia: China, Japan, Korea. Boulder, Colo., 1978. pp. 323. *bibliog.*

— Relations (general) with the United Kingdom.

MAUGHAN (T.J.) An introduction to the market for British books and journals in Japan and South Korea, etc. Tokyo, 1976. pp. 255.

— Social conditions.

TAKAGI (TAKEO) Kim Il Sung: master of leadership. Pyongyang, 1976. pp. 241.

— Statistical services.

KOREA (REPUBLIC). Bureau of Statistics. 1967. Outline of statistical organization in Korea. [Seoul], 1967. pp. 35.

— Statistics.

GERMANY (BUNDESREPUBLIK). Statistisches Bundesamt. Länderkurzbericht: Republik Korea. a., 1978- Wiesbaden.

KOREAN RESISTANCE MOVEMENTS, 1905-1945.

The FOUNDING of the anti-Japanese guerilla army, a historic event which brought about a great turn in the development of the Korean r[e]volution: [a commemoration of 40 years including extracts from speeches by Kim Il Sung]. [1972]. fo. 14. *Typescript.*

KOREAN REUNIFICATION QUESTION (1945-).

KOREAN unification: source materials with an introduction; editor Se-Jin Kim. Seoul, 1976. pp. 420.

OPPRESSION and resistance movement in South Korea. Pyongyang, 1977. pp. 188. *Proceedings of the Emergency International Conference on Korea, Tokyo, 1976.*

KOREAN WAR, 1950-1953.

The US imperialists started the Korean war. Pyongyang, 1977. pp. 308.

KORSCH (KARL).

MONTALDI (DANILO) Korsch e i comunisti italiani: contro un facile spirito di assimilazione. Roma, 1975. pp. 79.

KORSCH: der Klassiker des Antirevisionismus ([by] Arbeitsgruppe Bewusstseinsformen;...Christoph Behrend [and others]). Westberlin, [1976]. pp. 165.

VACCA (GIUSEPPE) Criticità e trasformazione: Korsch teorico e politico, 1923-38. Bari, [1978]. pp. 123.

KOSI RIVER

— Regulation.

The KOSI symposium: the rural problem in north-east Bihar: analysis, policy and planning in the Kosi area; by Stephen D. Biggs [and others]; edited by J.L. Joy and Elizabeth Everitt. [Brighton], 1976. pp. 277. *bibliog.*

KOSSUTH (LAJOS).

SPENCER (DONALD S.) Louis Kossuth and Young America: a study of sectionalism and foreign policy, 1848-1852. Columbia, Miss., 1977. pp. 203. *bibliog.*

KOSTROMA (OBLAST')

— Economic history.

ANISKOV (VIKTOR TIKHONOVICH) S polei kolkhoznykh na polia srazhenii: partiino-organizatorskaia deiatel'nost' v iaroslavskoi i kostromskoi derevne v gody Velikoi Otechestvennoi voiny. Iaroslavl', 1975. pp. 208. *bibliog.*

KOT (STANISLAW).

PROFESOR Stanislaw Kot: 'zycie i dzieło [and other papers, by Franciszek Wilk and others]. London, 1976. pp. 53.

KRASNODAR (KRAI)

— Politics and government.

AGAPOVA (TAISIIA IVANOVNA) and SEROVA (MAIIA IGNAT'EVNA) Dekabristy na Kubani. Krasnodar, 1975. pp. 29.

KROGMANN (CARL VINCENT).

KROGMANN (CARL VINCENT) Es ging um Deutschlands Zukunft, 1932-1939: Erlebtes täglich diktiert von dem früheren Regierenden Bürgermeister von Hamburg. Leoni am Starnberger See, 1976 repr. 1977. pp. 372.

KROPOTKIN (PETR ALEKSEEVICH) Prince.

POLIANSKII (FEDOR IAKOVLEVICH) Kritika ekonomicheskikh teorii anarkhizma. Moskva, 1976. pp. 301.

KRUPP (FRIEDRICH) AKTIENGESELLSCHAFT.

BRANDT (MAXIMILIAN) and ECCIUS ( ) of Essen, defendants. Prozess Brandt und Genossen: der sogenannte Krupp- Prozess; Verhandlungsbericht, aus dem Reichstag, Zeitungsstimmen; mit einer Einführung herausgegeben von Ad. Zimmermann. Berlin, 1914. pp. 397.

KUBITSCHEK DE OLIVEIRA (JUSCELINO).

BENEVIDES (MARIA VICTORIA DE MESQUITA) O governo Kubitschek: desenvolvimento econômico e estabilidade política, 1956-1961. Rio de Janeiro, 1976. pp. 302. *bibliog.*

KULA (WITOLD)

— Bibliography.

MIĘDZY feudalizmem a kapitalizmem: studia z dziejów gospodarczych i społecznych; prace ofiarowane Witoldowi Kuli. Wrocław, 1976. pp. 428. *Articles in French, English, German or Polish.*

KULISHEVA (ANNA MIKHAILOVNA).

VALERI (NINO) Turati e la Kuliscioff. Firenze, 1974. pp. 214. *bibliog.*

KUMASI

— Foreign population.

SCHILDKROUT (ENID) People of the zongo: the transformation of ethnic identities in Ghana. Cambridge, 1978. pp. 303. *bibliog.*

KUOMINTANG.

KHOR'KOV (VIKTOR IVANOVICH) Nankinskii gomin'dan i rabochii vopros, 1927-1932. Moskva, 1977. pp. 158. *bibliog.*

MELIKSETOV (ARLEN VAAGOVICH) Sotsial'no-ekonomicheskaia politika gomin'dana v Kitae, 1927- 1949. Moskva, 1977. pp. 317. *bibliog.*

KURDS IN ISRAEL.

COHEN (CLAUDINE) Grandir au quartier kurde: rapports de générations et modèles culturels d'un groupe d'adolescents israéliens d'origine kurde. Paris, 1975. pp. 175. *bibliog. (Muséum National d'Histoire Naturelle. Institut d'Ethnologie. Mémoires. 12)*

KURUSU

— Social conditions.

SMITH (ROBERT JOHN) Kurusu: the price of progress in a Japanese village, 1951-1975. [Folkestone, 1978]. pp. 269. *bibliog.*

KUWAIT

— Constitution.

KUWAIT. Constitution. 1962. The constitution of the state of Kuwait. [Kuwait, 1962]. pp. 35, (79). *In English and Arabic.*

KWAZULU

— Economic conditions.

NATTRASS (JILL) Migrant labour and underdevelopment: the case of Kwazulu. Durban, 1977. pp. 29. *(Natal University. Department of Economics. Black/White Income Gap Project. Interim Research Reports. No. 3)*

— Economic policy.

BUTLER (JEFFREY ERNEST) and others. The black homelands of South Africa: the political and economic development of Bophuthatswana and KwaZulu. Berkeley, Calif., [1977]. pp. 250. *bibliog.*

LABOUR AND LABOURING CLASSES.

WELLWOOD (SAMUEL) A letter to Feargus O'Connor, Esq., against his plan of dividing the land, and in favour of the association of property, skill, and labour. London, [1842]. pp. 15.

LOUIS (PAUL) La puissance ouvrière. Paris, 1946. pp. 183.

VELASCO (GUSTAVO R.) Labor legislation from an economic point of view; edited...by B.A. Rogge. Indianapolis, [1973]. pp. 65. *bibliog.*

CASTORIADIS (CORNELIUS) L'expérience du mouvement ouvrier. [Paris, 1974]. 2 vols.

PERROTTA (COSIMO) La proletarizzazione contemporanea. Lecce, [1975]. 2 vols. (in 1).

MELANGES d'histoire sociale offerts à Jean Maitron. Paris, [1976]. pp. 286. *bibliog.*

PREVOST (RENE) Les producteurs dans la civilisation industrielle. Lille, 1976. 1 vol. (various pagings). *bibliog. Thèse - Université de Paris V.*

GALLIE (DUNCAN) In search of the new working class: automation and social integration within the capitalist enterprise. Cambridge, 1978. pp. 348. *bibliog.*

— Bibliography.

WOODBRIDGE (MARK E.) compiler. American Federation of Labor and Congress of Industrial Organizations pamphlets, 1889-1955: a bibliography and subject index to the pamphlets held in the AFL-CIO library. Westport, Conn., 1977. pp. 73.

INTERNATIONAL LABOUR OFFICE. Library. 1978. International labour documentation: cumulative edition, 1972-1976. Boston, Mass., 1978. 5 vols.

— Directories.

INTERNATIONAL ASSOCIATION OF LABOUR HISTORY INSTITUTIONS. Directory. [London?, 1977]. 1 pamphlet (unpaged).

— Education — France.

TANGUY (LUCIE) Le capital, les travailleurs et l'école: l'exemple de la Lorraine sidérurgique. Paris, 1976. pp. 226.

— — Germany.

GERHARD-SONNENBERG (GABRIELE) Marxistische Arbeiterbildung in der Weimarer Zeit: MASCH [Marxistische Arbeiterschule]. Köln, [1976]. pp. 206. *bibliog.*

ARBEITERBEWEGUNG, Erwachsenenbildung, Presse: Festschrift für Walter Fabian zum 75. Geburtstag;...herausgegeben von Anne-Marie Fabian. Köln, [1977]. pp. 240.

— — Ivory Coast.

MONSON (TERRY D.) and PURSELL (GARRY) An evaluation of expatriate labor replacement in the Ivory Coast. Ann Arbor, 1976. pp. 75. *bibliog. (Michigan University. Center for Research on Economic Development. Discussion Papers. No. 49)*

— — Russia — Siberia.

BUTORIN (VADIM PETROVICH) Prosveshchenie rabochikh Zapadnoi Sibiri, 1928-1933 gg. Novosibirsk, 1977. pp. 140.

— — United States — Bibliography.

DWYER (RICHARD E.) compiler. Labor education in the U.S.: an annotated bibliography. Metuchen, N.J., 1977. pp. 274.

— America, Latin.

VILLAMARIN (JUAN A.) and VILLAMARIN (JUDITH E.) Indian labor in mainland colonial Spanish America. Newark, Del., 1975. pp. 175. *bibliog.*

— Belgium.

POTY (FRANCIS) Histoire de la démocratie et du mouvement ouvrier au Pays de Charleroi. Bruxelles, [1975 in progress]. *bibliog.*

NEUVILLE (JEAN) La condition ouvrière au XIXe siècle. Bruxelles, 1976-77. 2 vols.

SEMAINE SOCIALE WALLONNE. 57me Semaine. Emploi et politique de développement en Wallonie, [by] A. Carton [and others]. Bruxelles, [1976]. pp. 135.

— Bolivia.

LORA (GUILLERMO) A history of the Bolivian labour movement, 1848-1971;...edited and abridged by Laurence Whitehead; translated by Christine Whitehead. Cambridge, 1977. pp. 408. *bibliog.*

— Brazil.

BRAZIL. Serviço Nacional de Aprendizagem Comercial. Divisão de Estudos e Pesquisas Sociais. 1963. Distribuição e composição ocupacional no comercio brasileiro. Rio de Janeiro, 1963. pp. (75). *(Estudos. No. 2)*

PINHEIRO (PAULO SERGIO DE M.S.) Politica e trabalho no Brasil dos anos vinte a 1930. Rio de Janeiro, 1977. pp. 191. *bibliog.*

— Bulgaria.

PAVLENKO (VIKTORIIA VIKTOROVNA) Solidarnost' trudiashchikhsia Ukrainskoi SSR s revoliutsionnoi bor'boi rabochikh i krest'ian Bolgarii, 1923-1934 gg. Kiev, 1977. pp. 140.

— Canada.

ESSAYS in Canadian working class history; editors: Gregory S. Kealey [and] Peter S. Warrian. Toronto, [1976]. pp. 231. *bibliog.*

INDUSTRIAL unionism in Kitchener, 1937-47; researched and written by students in the Department of History, Wilfrid Laurier University; edited by Terry Copp. Elora, Ont., [1976]. pp. 129.

— — British Columbia.

BRITISH COLUMBIA. Department of Labour. 1967. Excerpts from an address during debate on the speech from the throne; by L.R. Peterson...first session of the 28th Legislative Assembly, 1967. Victoria, 1967. pp. 14, 17.

BRITISH COLUMBIA. Department of Labour. 1968. Excerpts from an address during debate on the speech from the throne; by L.R. Peterson...second session of the 28th Legislative Assembly, 1968. Victoria, 1968. pp. 10.

BRITISH COLUMBIA. Department of Labour. 1969. Report on the Department of Labour; by L.R. Peterson;...third session of the 28th Legislative Assembly, 1969. Victoria, 1969. pp. 18.

LABOUR RESEARCH BULLETIN; produced by the Research Branch. British Columbia Department of Labour. m., 1973 (v.1)- Victoria, B.C.

— — Nova Scotia — Statistics.

SELECTED LABOUR STATISTICS FOR NOVA SCOTIA; [pd. by] Economics and Research Division, Nova Scotia Department of Labour. a. (formerly s-a.), Ap/S 1972 [1st issue]- Halifax, Nova Scotia.

— — Quebec (Province).

Les TRAVAILLEURS québécois, 1851-1896; par Noël Bélanger [and others]; sous la direction de Jean Hamelin. 2nd ed. Montréal, 1975. pp. 221. *bibliog. (Regroupement de Chercheurs en Histoire des Travailleurs Québécois. Collection Histoire des Travailleurs Québécois. 2)*

Les TRAVAILLEURS Québécois, 1941-1971: dossier; sous la direction de Jean Hamelin et Fernand Harvey. Québec, 1976. pp. xv, 547. *bibliog. (Québec. Université Laval. Institut Superieur des Sciences Humaines. Cahiers. 20)*

— China.

KHOR'KOV (VIKTOR IVANOVICH) Nankinskii gomin'dan i rabochii vopros, 1927-1932. Moskva, 1977. pp. 158. *bibliog.*

— Communist countries.

PUSENKOVA (IRINA VLADIMIROVNA) Neposredstvenno-obshchestvennyi trud i neobkhodimyi produkt pri sotsializme. Moskva, 1976. pp. 199.

— Europe, Eastern.

Die WACHSENDE Rolle der Arbeiterklasse in den sozialistischen Ländern; ([by the] Parteihochschule beim ZK der KPdSU, Moskau [and others]). Berlin, 1974. pp. 359.

LABOUR AND LABOURING CLASSES.(Cont.)

— France.

CONTRIBUTIONS à une prospective du travail; [report of a working group]. Paris, [1976]. pp. 267. *(France. Commissariat Général du Plan. Economie et Planification)*

ANSART (GUSTAVE) De l'usine à l'Assemblée nationale: entretien avec Jacques Estager. [Paris, 1977]. pp. 256.

CHOMBART DE LAUWE (PAUL HENRY) La vie quotidienne des familles ouvrières. 3rd ed. Paris, 1977. pp. 255.

LEQUIN (YVES) Les ouvriers de la région lyonnaise, 1848-1914. Lyon, [1977]. 2 vols. *bibliog.*

RUDE (FERNAND) C'est nous les canuts... Paris, 1977. pp. 263.

— — Dwellings.

BUTLER (RÉMY) and NOISETTE (PATRICE) De la cité ouvrière au grand ensemble: la politique capitaliste du logement social, 1815-1975. Paris, 1977. pp. 193.

— Germany.

WALLRAFF (GUENTER) Industriereportagen: als Arbeiter in deutschen Grossbetrieben. Reinbek bei Hamburg, 1970 repr. 1978. pp. 118.

GERMANY (BUNDESREPUBLIK). Bundesanstalt für Arbeit. Amtliche Nachrichten. m., 1973 (21.Jg.)- Nürnberg.

WALLRAFF (GUENTER) Neue Reportagen, Untersuchungen und Lehrbeispiele. Reinbek bei Hamburg, 1974 repr. 1978. pp. 144.

FRICKE (DIETER) and SHNEERSON (L.M.) eds. Iz istorii germanskogo rabochego dvizheniia i sovetsko-germanskogo internatsional'nogo sodruzhestva: sbornik statei. Minsk, 1975. pp. 208.

DOKUMENTE und Materialien zum gemeinsamen Kampf der revolutionären deutschen und polnischen Arbeiterbewegung, 1918- 1939; bearbeitet und eingeleitet von Franciszek Hawranek [and others]. Berlin, [1977]. pp. 335.

SCHOECK (EVA CORNELIA) Arbeitslosigkeit und Rationalisierung: die Lage der Arbeiter und die kommunistische Gewerkschaftspolitik, 1920-28. Frankfurt, [1977]. pp. 280. *bibliog.*

SCHOMERUS (HEILWIG) Die Arbeiter der Maschinenfabrik Esslingen: Forschungen zur Lage der Arbeiterschaft im 19. Jahrhundert. Stuttgart, [1977]. pp. 353. *bibliog. (Arbeitskreis für Moderne Sozialgeschichte. Industrielle Welt. Band 24)*

STILLER (KARL THEODOR) Gewerkschaftspolitik und Bewegungen in der Arbeiterschaft, 1914 bis 1920. Offenbach, 1977. pp. 111. *bibliog.*

TAUBERT (ROLF) Autonomie und Integration: das Arbeiter-Blatt Lennep: eine Fallstudie zur Theorie und Geschichte von Arbeiterpresse und Arbeiterbewegung, 1848-1850. München, 1977. pp. 215. *bibliog. (Institut für Zeitungsforschung derStadt Dortmund. Dortmunder Beiträge zur Zeitungsforschung. Band 24)*

RABE (BERND) Der sozialdemokratische Charakter: drei Generationen aktiver Parteimitglieder in einem Arbeiterviertel. Frankfurt, [1978]. pp. 202. *bibliog.*

— — Ruhr.

KLESSMANN (CHRISTOPH) and FRIEDEMANN (PETER) Streiks und Hungermärsche im Ruhrgebiet, 1946-1948. Frankfurt/Main, [1977]. pp. 163. *bibliog.*

— Hungary.

HARASZTI (MIKLÓS) Salaire aux pièces: ouvrier dans un pays de l'est; traduit du hongrois par Judit Svaradja et Joël Aizac. Paris, [1976]. pp. 188.

HARASZTI (MIKLÓS) A worker in a worker's state: piece-rates in Hungary; translated by Michael Wright; with...a note about the author and a transcript of the author's trial. Harmondsworth, 1977. pp. 175.

— India.

INDIA. Ministry of Labour. Evaluation Wing. 1975. Labour in the public sector undertakings: basic information, 1974. [Delhi, 1975]. pp. 196.

— Israel.

LABOR and society in Israel: a selection of studies; (editors Isaiah Avrech [and] Dan Giladi). Tel Aviv, 1973. pp. 258. *bibliog.*

— Italy.

AMENDOLA (GIORGIO) Fascismo e movimento operaio. Roma, 1975. pp. 258.

FABBRICA E STATO. No. 13/14. 1974/1975: crisi e lotte proletarie. Bari, 1975. pp. 270.

CULTURA cattolica e egemonia operaia; [by] G. Bianchi [and others]. Roma, 1976. pp. 191. *Proceedings of the conference of ACLI held at Bergamo, 1975.*

MANCINI (GIUSEPPE FEDERICO) Costituzione e movimento operaio. Bologna, [1976]. pp. 281.

MARUCCO (DORA) and TOS (ROSANNA) Capitalismo e lotte operaie in Italia, 1870-1970. Torino, [1976]. pp. 294. *Collection of documents.*

MORELLI (ALDO) and TOMASSINI (LUIGI) Socialismo e classe operaia a Pistoia durante la prima guerra mondiale. [Milano, 1976]. pp. 218.

MOVIMENTO operaio e organizzazione sindacale a Roma, 1860-1960; documenti per la storia della Camera di Lavoro; [by] F. Agostino [and others]. Roma, 1976. 2 vols.

STATO e controllo dell'economia: democrazia politica e democrazia sociale. Bari, [1976]. pp. 193. *Proceedings of a conference held by the Istituto Gramsci in 1976.*

ABRATE (MARIO) Lavoro e lavoratori nell'Italia contemporanea. Milano, [1977]. pp. 108.

ASOR ROSA (ALBERTO) and others. PCI, classe operaia e movimento studentesco; a cura di Gregorio Paolini e Walter Vitali. [Rimini, 1977]. pp. 250.

CAMMAROTA (ANTONELLA) Proletariato marginale e classe operaia: (un contributo al dibattito sulla cultura e l'unità di classe del proletariato). Roma, [1977]. pp. 156.

TRENTIN (BRUNO) Da sfruttati a produttori: lotte operaie e sviluppo capitalistico dal miracolo economico alla crisi. Bari, 1977. pp. 158, 356.

CIAULA (TOMMASO DI) Tuta blu: ire, ricordi e sogni di un operaio del Sud. Milano, 1978. pp. 174.

— — Statistics.

ITALY. Ministero del Lavoro e della Previdenza Sociale. Notiziario mensile "Statistiche del lavoro". m., Ja 1972 (anno 1, n.1)- Roma. *Supplements its Statistiche del lavoro.*

— — Calabria — History.

ALCARO (MARIO) and PAPARAZZO (AMELIA) Lotte contadine in Calabria, 1943-1950. [Cosenza, 1976]. pp. 202.

— — Naples.

DE BENEDETTI (AUGUSTO) La classe operaia a Napoli nel primo dopoguerra. Napoli, [1974]. pp. 197.

— Mexico.

SALAZAR (ROSENDO) Rosendo Salazar: [Las pugnas de la gleba; La Casa del Obrero Mundial; La C.T.M.]. Mexico, 1972. 2 vols.

HUITRON CHAVERO (JACINTO) Origenes e historia del movimiento obrero en Mexico. Mexico, 1974 repr. 1976. pp. 320.

BASURTO (JORGE) El proletariado industrial en Mexico, 1850-1930. Mexico, 1975. pp. 298.

PACHECO MENDEZ (GUADALUPE) and others. Cardenas y la izquierda mexicana: ensayo, testimonios, documentos. Mexico, [1976]. pp. 391. *bibliog.*

HART (JOHN MASON) Anarchism and the Mexican working class, 1860-1931. Austin, [1978]. pp. 249. *bibliog.*

— Netherlands.

JAARBOEK VOOR DE GESCHIEDENIS VAN SOCIALISME EN ARBEIDERSBEWEGING IN NEDERLAND. a., 1976- Nijmegen.

— Poland.

DOKUMENTE und Materialien zum gemeinsamen Kampf der revolutionären deutschen und polnischen Arbeiterbewegung, 1918- 1939; bearbeitet und eingeleitet von Franciszek Hawranek [and others]. Berlin, [1977]. pp. 335.

TYSZKA (ZBIGNIEW) Rodziny robotnicze w Polsce: róznice i podobieństwa. Warszawa, 1977. pp. 212. *bibliog.*

— — Silesia.

KLASA robotnicza na Śląsku. Opole, 1975 in progress. *bibliog. With German, Czech, Russian and English tables of contents.*

— Romania.

MOSHANU (ALEKSANDR KONSTANTINOVICH) Sotsialisticheskoe dvizhenie v Rumynii, seredina 70-kh - nachalo 90-kh gg. XIX v. Kishinev, 1977. pp. 272.

STOROZHUK (VLADIMIR PROKOF'EVICH) Rabochee dvizhenie v Rumynii i rumyno-russkie revoliutsionnye sviazi, 1893-1907. Kishinev, 1977. pp. 175. *bibliog.*

— — Transylvania.

CICALĂ (I.) Mişcarea muncitorească şi socialistă din Transilvania, 1901-1921. Bucureşti, 1976. pp. 289.

— Russia.

DEMESHINA (ELENA IVANOVNA) Rabochee dvizhenie na Donu v period imperializma, 1900-1914 gg. Rostov-na-Donu, 1973. pp. 201.

ZLOTNIKOV (RAFAIL ABRAMOVICH) Dukhovnye potrebnosti sovetskogo rabochego; pod red. N.A. Aitova. Saratov, 1975. pp. 236. *bibliog.*

IVANOVA (ROZA KONSTANTINOVNA) Nauchno-tekhnicheskaia revoliutsiia i razvitie obshchestvennogo truda v SSSR. Moskva, 1976. pp. 189. *(Akademiia Nauk SSSR. Problemy Sovetskoi Ekonomiki)*

OSTAPENKO (IVAN PROKOF'EVICH) Rabochii klass SSSR v upravlenii proizvodstvom, 1956-1970 gg. Moskva, 1976. pp. 483.

SUSLOV (VALENTIN IAKOVLEVICH) Trud v usloviiakh razvitogo sotsializma: sotsial'no-filosofskie voprosy. Leningrad, 1976. pp. 150.

GOSUDARSTVO, demokratiia i trudovoi kollektiv v razvitom sotsialisticheskom obshchestve. Moskva, 1977. pp. 200.

RAZZHIGAEV (ANATOLII FEDOROVICH) Ekonomicheskie problemy stanovleniia truda kak potrebnosti. Moskva, 1977. pp. 126.

SOBOLEV (PETR NIKIFOROVICH) Uprochenie soiuza rabochikh i krest'ian v pervyi god proletarskoi diktatury. Moskva, 1977. pp. 320.

SOTSIAL'NOE razvitie rabochego klassa SSSR: rost chislennosti, kvalifikatsii, blagosostoianiia rabochikh v razvitom sotsialisticheskom obshchestve: istoriko-sotsiologicheskie ocherki. Moskva, 1977. pp. 287.

SOTSIAL'NO-ekonomicheskie problemy truda: organizatsiia, planirovanie, upravlenie. Moskva, 1977. pp. 215.

TECKENBERG (WOLFGANG) Die soziale Struktur der sowjetischen Arbeiterklasse im internationalen Vergleich: auf dem Wege zur industrialisierten Ständegesellschaft?. München, 1977. pp. 228. *bibliog.*

— — **Siberia.**

CHISLENNOST' i sostav rabochikh Sibiri v usloviiakh razvitogo sotsializma, 1959-1975 gg.: materialy k "Istorii rabochego klassa Sibiri". Novosibirsk, 1977. pp. 191.

— — **Tajikistan.**

PROBLEMY istoricheskogo materializma...: nekotorye zakonomernosti razvitiia bazisa i nadstroiki etapa razvitogo sotsializma: tematicheskii sbornik. Dushanbe, 1975. pp. 179. *(Dushanbinskii Gosudarstvennyi Pedagogicheskii Institut. Uchenye Zapiski. t.96)*

— — **Ukraine.**

PROMYSHLENNOST' i rabochii klass Ukrainskoi SSR, 1933-1941: sbornik dokumentov i materialov v dvukh chastiakh. Kiev, 1977. 2 vols.

— — **White Russia.**

ABEZGAUZ (ZALMAN EVNOVICH) Rabochii klass Belorussii v nachale XX v., 1900-1913 gg. Minsk, 1977. pp. 168.

— **Senegal.**

UNION GENERALE DES TRAVAILLEURS SENEGALAIS EN FRANCE. Qui est responsable du sous-développement. Paris, 1975. pp. 85.

— **South Africa.**

DAVIS (DAVID) Trade Unionist. African workers and apartheid. London, 1978. pp. 43. *(International Defence and Aid Fund. Fact Papers on Southern Africa. No. 5)*

— **Spain.**

LUCHAS obreras en España. Lausanne, [1974]. pp. 177.

ZAGUIRRE (MANUEL) and HOZ (JOSE M. DE LA) eds. Presente y futuro del sindicalismo. Barcelona, 1976. pp. 217.

PICO LOPEZ (JOSEP) El moviment obrer al Pais Valencia sota el Franquisme. [Valencia, 1977]. pp. 222.

SONADELLAS (CONCEPCIO) Clase obrera y revolucion social en España, 1936-1939. Madrid, 1977. pp. 181. *bibliog.*

MARAVALL (JOSE ANTONIO) Dictatorship and political dissent: workers and students in Franco's Spain. London, 1978. pp. 199. *bibliog.*

— **Sweden.**

BÄCKSTRÖM (KNUT) Arbetarrörelsen i Sverige, etc. new ed. [Stockholm], 1977. 2 vols. (in 1). *bibliogs.*

KORPI (WALTER) The working class in welfare capitalism: work, unions and politics in Sweden. London, 1978. pp. 448. *bibliog.*

— **Switzerland.**

VETTERLI (RUDOLF) Industriearbeit, Arbeiterbewusstsein und gewerkschaftliche Organisation; dargestellt am Beispiel der Georg Fischer AG, 1890-1930. Göttingen, 1978. pp. 344. *bibliog.*

— **United Kingdom.**

EGOSHIN (VALERII ALEKSANDROVICH) Rabochee dvizhenie Velikobritanii i zapadnoevropeiskaia integratsiia. Moskva, 1976. pp. 120.

LAQUEUR (THOMAS WALTER) Religion and respectability: Sunday schools and working class culture, 1780-1850. New Haven, 1976. pp. 293. *bibliog.*

MEACHAM (STANDISH) A life apart: the English working class, 1890-1914. London, [1977]. pp. 272. *bibliog.*

SOCIAL control in nineteenth century Britain; edited by A.P. Donajgrodzki. London, 1977. pp. 258. *bibliog.*

WILLIAMS (GLANMOR) The general and common sort of people, 1540-1640. Exeter, 1977. pp. 32. *(Exeter. University. Harte Memorial Lectures in Local History. 1975)*

HEARN (FRANCIS) Domination, legitimation, and resistance: the incorporation of the nineteenth-century English working class. Westport, 1978. pp. 309. *bibliog.*

— — **Periodicals.**

WORKERS ILLUSTRATED NEWS. D. 13 1929 (vol. 1, no. 1) London.

— **United States.**

SCHLUETER (HERMANN) Lincoln, labor and slavery: a chapter from the social history of America. New York, 1913. pp. 237.

CURTIN (RICHARD T.) Income equity among U.S. workers: the bases and consequences of deprivation. New York, [1977]. pp. 152. *bibliog.*

GUÉRIN (DANIEL) Le mouvement ouvrier aux États-Unis 1866 à nos jours. 2nd. ed. Paris, 1977. pp. 218. *bibliog.*

BERG (IVAR E.) and others. Managers and work reform: a limited engagement. New York, [1978]. pp. 316.

GRIFFEN (CLYDE) and GRIFFEN (SALLY) Natives and newcomers: the ordering of opportunity in mid-nineteenth-century Poughkeepsie. Cambridge, Mass., 1978. pp. 291. *(Harvard University. Harvard Studies in Urban History)*

RODGERS (DANIEL T.) The work ethic in industrial America 1850-1920. Chicago, 1978. pp. 300.

SCHRANK (ROBERT) Ten thousand working days. Cambridge, Mass., [1978]. pp. 244. *bibliog.*

— — **Biography.**

WHO's who in labor. New York, 1976. pp. 807.

— — **Political activity.**

PIVEN (FRANCES FOX) and CLOWARD (RICHARD A.) Poor people's movements: why they succeed, how they fail. New York, [1977]. pp. 381. *bibliogs.*

— **Yugoslavia.**

BREKIĆ (JOVO) and JURINA (MILAN) Razvoj kadrova i organizacije kadrovske funkcije udruženog rada. Zagreb, 1977. pp. 115. *bibliog. (Zagreb. Ekonomski Institut. Centar za Kadrologiju i Poslovodne Kadrove. Kadrologijska Biblioteka. kolo 3)*

ŠANE (DUŠAN PETROVIĆ) Self-management in Yugoslavia. London, [1977]. pp. 163.

SISTEM kadrologije udruženoga rada; redaktor Jovo Brekić. Zagreb, 1977. pp. 132. *bibliog. (Zagreb. Ekonomski Institut. Centar za Kadrologiju i Poslovodne Kadrove. Kadrologijska Biblioteka. Kolo 5) With English table of contents and summary.*

SISTEM planiranja razvoja kadrova i obrazovanja samoupravno udruženog rada; redaktori Jovo Brekić i M. Jurina. Zagreb, 1977. pp. 305. *bibliog. (Zagreb. Ekonomski Institut. Centar za Kadrologiju i Poslovodne Kadrove. Kadrologijska Biblioteka. Kolo 4, svezak 1) With English table of contents and summary.*

LABOUR AND LABOURING CLASSES IN LITERATURE.

KJELLGREN (JOSEF) Jag är tusenden. [Stockholm, 1975]. pp. 88. *bibliog.*

LABOUR BUREAUS.

INTERNATIONAL LABOUR CONFERENCE. 61st Session. Reports. 5(1). Labour administration: role, functions and organisation; fifth item on the agenda. Geneva, 1975. pp. 170. *Report 5(2) was originally prepared for the 61st Session but held over for discussion at the 63rd Session (Report 5(2) of 63rd Session)*

LABOUR COSTS

— **Canada.**

CANADA. Statistics Canada. Labour costs in Canada: all industries. a., 1976(1st)- Ottawa. *[in English and French]*

LABOUR LAWS AND LEGISLATION.

— **European Economic Community countries.**

EUROPEAN COMMUNITIES. Statistical Office. Labour costs in distributive trades, banking and insurance. trien., 1974(2nd)- Luxembourg. *[in Community languages] 1970(1st) included in EUROPEAN COMMUNITIES. Statistical Office. Social statistics, 1972(no. 4).*

EUROPEAN COMMUNITIES. Statistical Office. Special Series: Structure of Earnings in Wholesale and Retail Distribution, Banking and Insurance in 1974. Luxembourg, [1977] in progress.

— **Germany — North Rhine-Westphalia.**

NORTH RHINE-WESTPHALIA. Landesamt für Datenverarbeitung und Statistik. Beiträge zur Statistik des Landes Nordrhein- Westfalen. Heft 387. Die Arbeitskosten im Produzierenden Gewerbe, 1975. Düsseldorf, 1978. pp. 327.

LABOUR DISPUTES

— **France.**

HELMICH (URSULA) Arbeitskämpfe in Frankreich: ein Beitrag zur Sozial- und Rechtsgeschichte, 1789-1939. Meisenheim am Glan, 1977. pp. 35 f. *bibliog.*

ADAM (GÉRARD) and REYNAUD (JEAN DANIEL) Conflits du travail et changement social. [Paris, 1978]. pp. 389.

— **United Kingdom.**

ADVISORY, CONCILIATION AND ARBITRATION SERVICE [U.K.]. Reports. [London, 1975 in progress].

LABOUR ECONOMICS.

KERR (CLARK) Labor markets and wage determination: the Balkanization of labor markets and other essays. Berkeley, Calif., [1977]. pp. 222.

— **Study and teaching — United States — Bibliography.**

DWYER (RICHARD E.) compiler. Labor education in the U.S.; an annotated bibliography. Metuchen, N.J., 1977. pp. 274.

LABOUR EXCHANGES

— **India — Mysore.**

PUTTASWAMAIAH (K.) Working of the employment exchanges in the state. Bangalore, Government Secretariat, 1976. pp. 39.

LABOUR LAWS AND LEGISLATION.

VELASCO (GUSTAVO R.) Labor legislation from an economic point of view; edited...by B.A. Rogge. Indianapolis, [1973]. pp. 65. *bibliog.*

— **Africa.**

EUROPEAN COMMUNITIES. Directorate-General for Development and Cooperation. Les Conditions d'Installation d'Entreprises Industrielles dans les États Africains et Malgache Associés. 2nd ed. [Brussels], 1974.

— **Brazil.**

VIANNA (LUIZ WERNECK) Liberalismo e sindicato no Brasil. Rio de Janeiro, 1976. pp. 288.

— **Canada.**

LEGISLATIVE REVIEW; [pd by] Canada Department of Labour, Legislative Research Branch. a., Je 30 1974 (no.3)- Ottawa.

CANADIAN LABOUR CONGRESS. Submission...to the House of Commons Standing Committee on Labour, Manpower and Immigration on Bill C-27, Employment and Immigration Reorganization Act. Ottawa, 1977. fo. 23.

— — **Nova Scotia.**

NOVA SCOTIA. General Assembly. House of Assembly. Select Committee on Labour Legislation. 1963. Report: [W.F. MacKinnon, chairman]. Halifax, 1963. fo. 27.

LABOUR LAWS AND LEGISLATION.(Cont.)

— France.

HELMICH (URSULA) Arbeitskämpfe in Frankreich: ein Beitrag zur Sozial- und Rechtsgeschichte, 1789-1939. Meisenheim am Glan, 1977. pp. 351. *bibliog.*

KAPP (BERNARD) and PETITGUYOT (BERNARD) Le bilan social, son application légale: loi du 12 juillet 1977; décret et arrêtés d'application du 8 décembre 1977. Paris, 1978. pp. 394.

— Germany.

BADURA (PETER) and others. Mitbestimmungsgesetz 1976 und Grundgesetz: Gemeinschaftsgutachten. München, 1977. pp. 298.

— India — Gujarat.

GUJARAT. Labour Laws Review Committee. 1974. Report; D.A. Desai, chairman. Gandhinagar, 1974. pp. 166.

— Iran.

JALIL (T.) Workers say no to the Shah: labour law and strikes in Iran. London, 1977. pp. 136.

— Italy.

TAVOLA rotonda sul tema: l'impresa alla luce dell'attuale giurisprudenza e dottrina del lavoro, Roma, 30-31 ottobre 1972. Roma, 1974. pp. 127. *(Accademia Nazionale dei Lincei. Problemi Attuali di Scienza e di Cultura. Quaderni. N. 196)*

Il NUOVO processo del lavoro; a cura del Anteo Genovese; (by V. Andrioli [and others]). Padova, 1975. pp. 199. *(Padua. Università. Facoltà di Giurisprudenza. Pubblicazioni. 75)*

PACIFICO (MARIO) and PACIFICO (ENRICO) Repertorio di giurisprudenza del lavoro, 1968-1975. Milano, 1976-77. 3 vols.

STOLFI (EMANUELE) Da una parte sola: storia politica dello Statuto dei Lavoratori. Milano, [1976]. pp. 229.

BRANCA (GIORGIO) Legislazione sociale: saggi. Padova, 1977. pp. 329.

LUCIFREDI (CLARA ENRICO) Evoluzione del potere direttivo nel rapporto di lavoro. Milano, 1977. pp. 138. *(Genoa. Università. Facoltà di Giurisprudenza. Annali. Collana. 42)*

PALMIERI (GERMANO) Lo statuto dei lavoratori commentato articolo per articolo. Firenze, 1977. pp. 246.

Lo STATUTO dei lavoratori: un bilancio politico; nuove prospettive del diritto del lavoro e democrazia industriale; scritti e interventi di Federico Mancini [and others]; a cura di Gianni Arrigo. Bari, [1977]. pp. 268.

— Mexico.

CUEVA (MARIO DE LA) El nuevo derecho mexicano del trabajo: historia, principios fundamentales, derecho individual y trabajos especiales. 4th ed. Mexico, 1977. pp. 639.

— New Zealand.

NEW ZEALAND. Department of Labour. 1968. Report on industrial relations legislation. Wellington, 1968. pp. 47.

— Nigeria.

DAVISON (R.B.) Industrial relations decrees in Nigeria: questions and answers to explain the law. Zaria, [1977]. pp. 83. *bibliog.*

— Russia.

CHALIDZE (VALERII N.) Lektsii o pravovom polozhenii rabochikh v SSSR. N'iu Iork, 1976. pp. 66.

SYMOROT (ZAKHAR KYRYLOVYCH) and MONASTYRS'KYI (IEVHEN OLEKSANDROVYCH) Problemy kodifikatsii zakonodatel'stva Soiuza SSR i soiuznykh respublik o trude. Kiev, 1977. pp. 300.

— Lithuania.

LITHUANIA. Statutes, etc. 1977. Kodeks zakonov o trude Litovskoi Sovetskoi Sotsialisticheskoi Respubliki: ofitsial'nyi tekst s izmeneniiami i dopolneniiami na 1 ianvaria 1977 g. Vil'nius, 1977. pp. 184.

— — Ukraine.

UKRAINE. Statutes, etc. 1973. Kodeks zakonov o trude Ukrainskoi SSR: ofitsial'nyi tekst s izmeneniiami i dopolneniiami na 1 noiabria 1975 goda. Kiev, 1976. pp. 126.

— Singapore.

JOSEY (ALEX) Industrial relations: labour laws in a developing Singapore. Singapore, 1976. pp. 305.

— South Africa.

DAVIS (DAVID) Trade Unionist. African workers and apartheid. London, 1978. pp. 43. *(International Defence and Aid Fund. Fact Papers on Southern Africa. No. 5)*

— Spain.

NORMAS y disposiciones sobre consejos de empresarios, consejos sindicales provinciales, congreso sindical. Madrid, 1965. pp. 32.

— United Kingdom.

WEDDERBURN (KENNETH WILLIAM) Baron Wedderburn. The worker and the law. 2nd ed. [Harmondsworth, 1971]. pp. 587. *bibliog.*

KAHN-FREUND (Sir OTTO) Labour and the law. London, 1972. pp. 270. *(Hamlyn Lectures. 24th Series)*

KAHN-FREUND (Sir OTTO) Labour and the law. 2nd ed. London, 1977. pp. 296. *(Hamlyn Lectures. 24th Series)*

HEWITT (PATRICIA) Your rights at work: a practical guide. London, [1978]. pp. 84. *(National Council for Civil Liberties. Know Your Rights Series. No. 2)*

SCHOFIELD (P.G.) and BURKE (C.) Cases and statutes on labour law. London, 1978. pp. 263.

— United States.

FRANK W. PIERCE MEMORIAL CONFERENCE, CORNELL UNIVERSITY, 1973. Union power and public policy; David B. Lipsky, editor. Ithaca, N.Y. 1975. pp. 131.

LABOUR law reform; (a Round Table held on March 21, 1978...); John Charles Daly, moderator, etc. Washington, [1978]. pp. 41. *(American Enterprise Institute for Public Policy Research. Public Policy Forums. 18)*

LABOUR LAWS AND LEGISLATION, INTERNATIONAL.

INTERNATIONAL LABOUR CONFERENCE. 61st Session. Reports. 4. Establishment of tripartite machinery to promote the implementation of international labour standards: fourth item on the agenda. Geneva, 1975-76. 2 pts.

INTERNATIONAL LABOUR CONFERENCE. 61st Session. Reports. 3. Third item on the agenda: information and reports on the application of conventions and recommendations. Geneva, 1976. 5 pts.

LABOUR MOBILITY.

SIMPSON (WAYNE DOUGLAS) Imperfect knowledge, urban structure and labour markets. [1978]. fo.289. *bibliog. Typescript. Ph.D. (London) thesis: unpublished. This thesis is the property of the Library and may not be removed from the Library.*

— Italy.

MORELLI (UGO) Classi e movimenti migratori. [Roma, 1976]. pp. 101. *bibliog.*

— Russia.

PAVLENKOV (VALERII ALEKSEEVICH) Dvizhenie rabochei sily v usloviiakh razvitogo sotsializma: voprosy teorii i metodologii. Moskva, 1976. pp. 222.

— United Kingdom.

EASTMAN (BYRON DELBERT) Voluntary labour mobility in manufacturing industries of Great Britain. 1976 [or rather 1977]. fo. 227. *bibliog. Typescript. Ph.D. (London) thesis: unpublished. This thesis is the property of London University and may not be removed from the Library.*

KENNETT (STEPHEN) Differential migration between British labour markets: some policy implications. [London], 1978. pp. 40.

LABOUR PARTY

— Australia.

MURPHY (DENIS J.) T.J. Ryan: a political biography. St. Lucia, Queensland, [1975]. pp. 596. *bibliog.*

ALBINSKI (HENRY STEPHEN) Australian external policy under Labor: content, process and the national debate. Vancouver, 1977. pp. 373. *bibliog.*

— New Zealand.

GOLDSTEIN (RAY) and ALLEY (ROD) eds. Labour in power: promise and performance: evaluations of the work of the New Zealand government from 1972 to 1975. [Wellington, N.Z., 1975]. pp. 200. *bibliogs.*

— United Kingdom.

LABOUR WHO'S WHO, THE: a biographical directory to the national and local leaders in the Labour and Co-operative movement. a., 1924(1st), 1927(2nd). London.

COMMUNIST PARTY OF GREAT BRITAIN. Central Committee. Copy of the application for affiliation made by the Communist Party to the Labour Party on November 25, 1935. London, 1935. s.sh. *Signed Harry Pollitt.*

LABOUR PARTY. What socialism will really mean to you. London, [1935]. pp. 16.

WILLIAMS (TOM) Baron Williams of Barnburgh. Labour shows the way. London, 1935. pp. 120.

LABOUR PARTY. Your Britain; nos. 2-4. London, [1938]. 3 pamphlets.

LABOUR PARTY. Go-ahead Britain. [London], 1965. pp. 16.

REVOLUTIONARY WORKERS PARTY (TROTSKYIST). The role of the Labour Party Young Socialists and the need to use the YS annual conference to prepare the LPYS to act as a revolutionary tendency in the Labour Party. London, 1974. pp. 11.

STEWART-SMITH (DUDLEY GEOFFREY) Not to be trusted: left wing extremism in the Labour and Liberal Parties. Richmond, Surrey, 1974. pp. 24.

AIMS FOR FREEDOM AND ENTERPRISE. A bombshell for the Labour Party; report on national opinion survey on trade unions and the Labour Party. London, [1977]. pp. 5.

COATES (KEN) Democracy in the Labour Party. [Nottingham, 1977]. pp. 116. *bibliog.*

COLE (HARRY B.) The British Labour Party: a functioning participatory democracy. Oxford, 1977. pp. 90. *bibliog.*

GRIFFITHS (DAVID) of the Campaign for Nuclear Disarmament. Labour and disarmament: a time for decision. London, 1977. pp. 22. *bibliog.*

JENKINS (PETER) The Labour Party and the politics of transition. Leeds, [1977]. pp. 24. *(Labour Party. Labour Party Discussion Series. No.1)*

JONES (BILL) The Russia complex: the British Labour Party and the Soviet Union. Manchester, [1977]. pp. 229. *bibliog.*

LABOUR PARTY. The arts and the people: Labour's policy towards the arts. London, 1977. pp. 69.

LABOUR PARTY. Building Britain's future: Labour's policy on construction. London, 1977. pp. 63.

LABOUR PARTY. The EEC and Britain: a socialist perspective. London, 1977. pp. 75.

LABOUR PARTY. International big business: Labour's policy on the multinationals. London, 1977. pp. 135.

MURGATROYD (STEPHEN J.) and others. Taking local decisions: the democratic reform of the Labour Party and local government. Leeds, [1977]. pp. 56. *bibliog.*

OSADCHAIA (ZHANNA FILIPPOVNA) Sovremennyi leiborizm: ideologiia i politika. Moskva, 1977. pp. 172.

WYATT (WOODROW LYLE) What's left of the Labour Party? London, 1977. pp. 183.

FABIAN SOCIETY. Fabian Tracts. [No.] 458. Labour and the social contract; [by] Robert Taylor. London, 1978. pp. 24.

KRIEGER (WOLFGANG) Labour Party und Weimarer Republik: ein Beitrag zur Aussenpolitik der britischen Arbeiterbewegung zwischen Programmatik und Parteitaktik, 1918-1924. Bonn, [1978]. pp. 450. *bibliog.* *(Friedrich-Ebert-Stiftung. Forschungsinstitut. Schriftenreihe. Band 136)*

RICHARDS (VERNON) The impossibilities of social democracy. London, 1978. pp. 142.

RIGHT turn: eight men who changed their minds; essays by Reg Prentice [and others]...; edited by Patrick Cormack. London, 1978. pp. 104.

TURNER (JOHN ELLIOT) Labour's doorstep politics in London. London, 1978. pp. 396. *bibliog.*

— — **History.**

MOORE (ROGER) The emergence of the Labour Party, 1880-1924. London, 1978. pp. 216. *bibliog.*

LABOUR POLICY

— **Asia.**

POVERTY and landlessness in rural Asia. Geneva, International Labour Office, 1977. pp. 288.

— **Ivory Coast.**

MONSON (TERRY D.) and PURSELL (GARRY) An evaluation of expatriate labor replacement in the Ivory Coast. Ann Arbor, 1976. pp. 75. *bibliog. (Michigan University. Center for Research on Economic Development. Discussion Papers. No. 49)*

— **United Kingdom.**

U.K. Central Office of Information. Reference Division. Reference Pamphlets. 152. Manpower and employment in Britain: the role of government. London, 1978. pp. 27. *bibliog.*

— **United States.**

HOROWITZ (RUTH L.) Political ideologies of organized labor. New Brunswick, N.J., [1978]. pp. 260. *bibliog.*

LABOUR SUPPLY.

ESSAYS in labor market analysis in memory of Yochanan Peter Comay; edited by Orley C. Ashenfelter and Wallace E. Oates. New York, [1977]. pp. 229. *bibliogs.*

FISCAL policy and labour supply. [London, 1977]. pp. 108. *(Institute for Fiscal Studies. Conference Series. No. 4) Papers presented at a conference organised jointly by The University of Stirling and the Institute and held at the University in 1976.*

— **Mathematical models.**

SIDDIQUI (FARID) Some concepts and methodologies in manpower forecasting. [Toronto], Ontario Ministry of Labour, Research Branch, 1974. pp. 47. *bibliog. ([Publications]. No. 9)*

MODIGLIANI (FRANCO) and TARANTELLI (EZIO) Mercato del lavoro, distribuzione del reddito e consumi privati. Bologna, [1975]. pp. 342.

TELLA (ALFRED) Cyclical behavior of bias-adjusted unemployment. Kalamazoo, Mich., 1976. pp. 23. *bibliog. (W.E. Upjohn Institute for Employment Research. Methods for Manpower Analysis. No. 11)*

SIMPSON (WAYNE DOUGLAS) Imperfect knowledge, urban structure and labour markets. [1978]. fo.289. *bibliog.* Typescript. Ph.D. (London) thesis: unpublished. *This thesis is the property of London University and may not be removed from the Library.*

— **Research** — **United Kingdom.**

COCKETT (IEN) compiler. Research projects on employment within the London boroughs, 1966- November 1976; compiled from the Register of Research in the London Boroughs. 2nd ed. London, 1976. pp. 13. *(London. Greater London Council. Research Library. Research Bibliographies. No. 76)*

— **America, Latin.**

SEMINARIO SOBRE PROBLEMAS DEL EMPLEO EN AMERICA LATINA, LA PLATA, 1975. El empleo en America Latina: problemas economicos, sociales y politicos; coordinacion por Victor E. Tokman y Paulo Renato Souza. Mexico, 1976. pp. 451. *bibliogs.*

— **Arab countries.**

CAIRO DEMOGRAPHIC CENTRE. Demographic aspects of manpower in Arab countries. Cairo, 1972. pp. 521. *bibliogs. (Research Monograph Series. No. 3)*

— **Australia.**

AUSTRALIA. Parliament. Joint Committee on the Australian Capital Territory. 1972. Report on employment opportunities in the Australian Capital Territory; [R.G. Withers, chairman]. in AUSTRALIA. Parliament. Parliamentary papers, 1972, vol. 7.

AUSTRALIA. Department of Labor and Immigration. 1975. Studies of displacement. Canberra, 1975. pp. 44. *(Employment and Technology. No. 16)*

AUSTRALIA. Commonwealth Bureau of Census and Statistics. 1976. Job tenure, August 1976. Canberra, 1976. pp. 11.

— **Brazil.**

BRAZIL. Serviço Nacional de Aprendizagem Comercial. Divisão de Estudos e Pesquisas Sociais. 1963. Distribuição e composição ocupacional no comercio brasileiro. Rio de Janeiro, 1963. pp. (75). *(Estudos. No. 2)*

BROEHL (ALLAN) Aspectos da fôrca de trabalho no Brasil: (analise dos resultados da pesquisa nacional por amostra de domicilios). Rio de Janeiro, Instituto de Planejamento Econômico e Social, Centro Nacional de Recursos Humanos, 1971. fo. 36.

FUNDAÇÃO GETULIO VARGAS. Centro de Estudos e Treinamento em Recursos Humanos. Força do trabalho do Brasil: resumo de dados censitarios; projeto realizado com os recursos assegurados pela Subsecretaria de Cooperação Economica e Tecnica Internacional, Secretaria de Planejament0. [Rio de Janeiro], 1974. fo. 91.

— **Canada.**

MANPOWER AND IMMIGRATION REVIEW: ATLANTIC REGION. (formerly Atlantic manpower review;) (pd. by the Manpower Information and Analysis Branch, Canada Department of Manpower and Immigration, Atlantic Region). q. (formerly bi-m.,) Jl/Ag 1969- Ja/Je 1976 (v.2, no.4 - v.9, no.1) with gap Ja/Mr 1971 (v.4, no.1) ceased pbln. Halifax, N.S. *[in English and French] Jl-Oc 1969 in separate eds., English and French; N/D 1969 in English only; Ja/F 1970- in bilingual format.*

MANPOWER AND IMMIGRATION REVIEW: PRAIRIES AND NORTHWEST TERRITORIES (formerly Manpower review: Prairies and Northwest territories) ; ([pd. by] Manpower Information and Analysis Branch, Department of Manpower and Immigration [Prairies and Northwest Territories Regional Office, Canada]). q. (formerly bi-m.), Ja/F 1971 - Jl/S 1976 (v.4, no.1- v.9, no.3) ceased pbln. Winnipeg. *Not pd. N/D 1972 (v.5, no.6).*

DODGE (WILLIAM) Skilled labour supply imbalances: the Canadian experience. [London], 1977. pp. 48.

LABOUR SUPPLY.

— — **British Columbia.**

BRITISH COLUMBIA. Northeast Coal Study. Manpower Sub- committee on North East Coal Development. 1976. Report; [Ranjit Azad, chairman]. [Victoria], 1976. pp. 270.

— — **Labrador.**

NEWFOUNDLAND. Industrial Commission of Inquiry into Employment Problems in the Labrador City-Wabush Area. 1977. Report. [St. John's, 1977]. fo. 69.

— — **Newfoundland.**

NEWFOUNDLAND. Department of Manpower and Industrial Relations. Annual report. a., 1976- St. John's.

— — **Ontario.**

EMPLOYMENT AND IMMIGRATION REVIEW: ONTARIO (formerly Manpower and immigration review: Ontario region (previously Manpower review: Ontario region [pd. by] Department of Manpower and Immigration, Manpower Information and Analysis Branch, Ontario Regional Office [Canada]. s-a. (formerly q.), (previously bi-m.), 1969 (v.2)- with gaps. Ottawa. *[in English and French] Ja/F 1969 - Jl/Ag 1970 in English only.*

MARR (WILLIAM L.) Labour market and other implications of immigration policy for Ontario. Toronto, 1976. pp. 1-98, 103-241. *bibliog. (Ontario. Economic Council. Working Papers. 1976. No. 1) Pages 99-102 were deleted for reasons of confidentiality.*

— — **Quebec (Province).**

MANPOWER AND IMMIGRATION REVIEW (formerly Manpower review: Quebec region (previously Québec manpower review); [pd. by] Department of Manpower and Immigration, Manpower Information and Analysis Branch, Québec Region [Canada] q. (formerly bi-m.), Ja/F 1969 (v.2, no.1)- , with gap (My/Je 1969: v.2, no.3). Montreal. *[in English and French] Ja/F 1969 in French only; Mr/Ap 1969 in English only.*

— **Denmark.**

SOCIAL forandring i Vestjylland: en samling originalartikler til belysning af nogle vigtige arbejdsmarkedsproblemer;...redigeret af Flemming Svejstrup. Esbjerg, 1976. 2 vols. (in 1). *Contributions by members of Projekt 1 at Sydjysk Universitetscenter.*

— **Ethiopia.**

ADDIS ABABA EMPLOYMENT SURVEY; [pd. by] Employment and Manpower Division. s-a., Mr/S 1974(8th)- Addis Ababa.

INTERNATIONAL LABOUR OFFICE. Exploratory Employment Policy Mission to Ethopia. 1974. Employment and unemployment in Ethiopia: report of the... Mission...financed by the United Nations Development Programme. Geneva, 1974. pp. 144. *bibliog.*

— **European Economic Community countries.**

EUROPEAN COMMUNITIES. Statistical Office. Population and employment. a., 1950/76(1st)- Luxembourg. *[in Community languages]*

EUROPEAN COMMUNITIES. Statistical Office. Labour force sample survey. a., 1975(7th)- Luxembourg. *[in Community languages] Earlier surveys included in the series EUROPEAN COMMUNITIES. Statistical Office. Social statistics.*

— **Fiji.**

EMPLOYMENT SURVEY, FIJI; [pd. by] Bureau of Statistics... Fiji. a., 1972[4th]- Suva.

— **France.**

BOYER (R.) and MISTRAL (J.) Inflation, investment and employment: a simple multisector model of the French economy with extension to some international comparisons. Paris, 1976. pp. 52. *(Centre d'Études Prospectives D'Économie Mathématique Appliquées à la Planification. [Publications]. No. 7608)*

LABOUR SUPPLY.(Cont.)

FRANCE. Direction Régionale du Travail et de la Main-d'Oeuvre de la Région Rhône-Alpes. 1977. Evolution des activités et des emplois dans l'agglomération lyonnaise, 1969-1974: analyse du développement d'une grande métropole régionale. [Lyons], 1977. pp. 127.

TRIVIDIC (J.Y.) Un marché local de l'emploi en période de crise: le cas de Fougères. [Rennes, Echelon Régional de l'Emploi, 1977]. fo. 36.

— — Statistics.

FRANCE. Ministère du Travail, de l'Emploi et de la Population. Bulletin mensuel des statistiques du travail. m., Ja 1972 [1st issue]- Paris. *Supersedes in part FRANCE. Ministère de la Santé Publique et de la Sécurité Sociale. Bulletin mensuel de statistiques sociales (1968-1971)*

— Gilbert and Ellice Islands Colony.

GILBERT AND ELLICE ISLANDS COLONY. Commissioner of Labour. 1970. Report on the manpower position in the Gilbert and Ellice Islands Colony. [Tarawa], 1970. 1 vol. (unpaged).

— India.

INDIA. Directorate of Employment, Training and Technical Education. 1964. Growth of employment in Delhi during the first three years of the third plan, 1961-64. New Delhi, 1964. pp. 58.

— — Maharashtra.

MAHARASHTRA ECONOMIC DEVELOPMENT COUNCIL. Study Group in Rural Employment in Maharashtra. Report; [S.K. Muranjan, chairman]. Bombay, 1966. pp. 37.

MAHARASHTRA ECONOMIC DEVELOPMENT COUNCIL. Manpower potential and business preferences in a rapidly developing economy: a case-study of Thana Taluka; summary report. Bombay, 1972. pp. 47.

— Indonesia.

INDONESIA. Biro Pusat Statistik. 1978. 1976 intercensal population survey:...Indonesian labour force. Jakarta, [1978]. pp. 174. *(1976 Intercensal Population Survey. Tabulation Series. No. 2) In English and Indonesian.*

— Ireland (Republic).

WHELAN (BRENDAN J.) and WALSH (BRENDAN M.) Redundancy and re-employment in Ireland. Dublin, 1977. pp. 119. *bibliog. (Economic and Social Research Institute. Papers. No. 89)*

— Italy.

MERCATO del lavoro, politiche sindacali, inflazione; a cura di Giancarlo Mazzocchi. Milano, 1975. pp. 252. *(Milan. Università Cattolica del Sacro Cuore. Pubblicazioni. Scienze Economiche. 2)*

MORELLI (UGO) Classi e movimenti migratori. [Roma, 1976]. pp. 101. *bibliog.*

OCCUPAZIONE e sottoccupazione femminile in Italia; ([by] Luigi Frey [and others]). Milano, [1976]. pp. 150.

— New Zealand.

THOMSON (JANET) Employment in the suburbs. [Wellington], Town and Country Planning Branch, Ministry of Works, 1969. pp. 8.

NEW ZEALAND. Department of Statistics. 1974. New Zealand labour force projections, 1971-2001. Wellington, 1974. pp. 44.

NEW ZEALAND. Department of Labour. Research and Planning Division. 1976. Employment distribution and potential in the King Country region. Wellington, 1976. pp. 16.

NEW ZEALAND. Department of Labour. Research and Planning Division. 1976. Employment distribution and potential in Southland. Wellington, 1976. pp. 31.

— Portugal.

FIALHO (JOSE ANTONIO SOUSA) Previsões regionais de emprego, continente. Lisboa, 1974. pp. 163. *(Portugal. Ministerio das Corporações e Previdência Social. Gabinete de Planeamento. Serie Estudos. 14) With abstracts in English, French and German.*

VIEGAS (VICTOR) Necessidades de mão-de-obra, 1967-1973. Lisboa, 1974. pp. 37. *(Portugal. Ministerio das Corporações e Previdência Social. Gabinete de Planeamento. Serie Estudos. 15) With abstracts in English, French and German.*

— Russia.

TRUDOVYE resursy : sotsial'no-ekonomicheskii analiz; pod red. V.G. Kostakova. Moskva, 1976. pp. 191.

— — Buryat Republic.

BUIAEVA (NINA TSYRENBAZAROVNA) Ispol'zovanie trudovykh resursov malykh gorodov i rabochikh poselkov Buriatii. Ulan-Ude, 1969. pp. 44. *bibliog.*

— South Africa.

SOUTH AFRICAN INSTITUTE OF RACE RELATIONS. Earnings and employment in various sectors of the economy, second quarter, 1976. Johannesburg, [1977]. pp. 8.

— Sweden.

SWEDEN. Statistiska Centralbyrån. Arbetskraftsundersökningarna. a., 1971- Stockholm. *[in Swedish with English summary]*

SWEDEN. Statistiska Centralbyrån. Förvärvsarbetande befolkning...enligt arbetskraftsundersökningarna: resultat anpassade till i folk- och bostadsräkningen...använda begrepp. a., 1971- Stockholm. *[in Swedish with English summary]*

SWEDEN. Statistiska Centralbyrån. Arbetskraften i skogsbruket: definitiva uppgifter. a., 1972- Stockholm. *[in Swedish with English summary and table heading]*

— Underdeveloped areas.

See UNDERDEVELOPED AREAS — Labour supply.

— United Kingdom.

INSTITUTE OF BUILDING. Conference, 1972. Manpower crisis, 1973: [papers presented at the conference]. Ascot, Berks, [1973]. pp. 18.

EASTWOOD (GERRY) Skilled labour shortages in the United Kingdom with particular reference to the engineering industry. [Washington, D.C.], 1976. pp. 37. *(British-North American Committee. Publications. 18)*

WEST MIDLANDS JOINT MONITORING STEERING GROUP. A developing strategy for the West Midlands: service industries in the West Midland Region. [Birmingham], 1976. pp. 15. *(Technical Reports)*

BIRMINGHAM COMMUNITY DEVELOPMENT PROJECT. Workers on the scrapheap; (by A. Cochrane and R. Dicker). [Oxford], 1977. pp. 52. *(Final Reports. No. 2: Employment)*

MANPOWER SERVICES COMMISSION [U.K.]. MSC review and plan, 1977. London, 1977. pp. 89.

U.K. Department of Employment. Unit for Manpower Studies. 1977. Employment in metropolitan areas; project report. London, [1977]. pp. 98. *bibliog.*

BUTLER (ROSEMARY) Employment of the highly qualified, 1971-1986; (Unit for Manpower Studies project report). [London], 1978. pp. 40. *(U.K. Department of Employment. Research Papers. No. 2)*

GUDGIN (GRAHAM) Industrial location processes and regional employment growth. Farnborough, Hants, [1978]. pp. 344. *bibliog.*

KENNETT (STEPHEN) Differential migration between British labour markets: some policy implications. [London], 1978. pp. 40.

— — Mathematical models.

JOSHI (HEATHER) Secondary workers in the cycle: married women and older workers in employment fluctuations, Great Britain 1961-74. London, Department of Health and Social Security, 1978. pp. 38. *bibliog. (Government Economic Service Working Papers. No. 8)*

— — Scotland.

HUNTER (LAURENCE C.) Labour shortages and manpower policy;...with P.B. Beaumont. London, H.M.S.O., 1978. pp. 107. *(Manpower Services Commission [U.K.]. Manpower Studies. No. 19782)*

SCOTLAND. Census, 1971. Census, 1971: Scotland: economic activity tables, 100 per cent. Edinburgh, 1978. pp. 126.

SCOTLAND. Census, 1971. Census, 1971: Scotland: qualified manpower tables, 100 per cent. Edinburgh, 1978. pp. 30.

— United States.

ALEXANDER (ARTHUR J.) Structure, income and race: a study in internal labour markets. Santa Monica, 1970. pp. 30. *(Rand Corporation. [Rand Reports]. 577)*

BLAU (FRANCINE D.) Equal pay in the office. Lexington, Mass., [1977]. pp. 158. *bibliog.*

LEVITAN (SAR A.) and BELOUS (RICHARD S.) Shorter hours, shorter weeks: spreading the work to reduce unemployment. Baltimore, [1977]. pp. 94.

— — South Carolina.

SOUTH CAROLINA. Employment Security Commission. Manpower Research and Analysis Section. 1976. Human resource requirements in South Carolina industry and occupation: 1975 with projection to 1979. Columbia, 1976. pp. 158.

SOUTH CAROLINA. Employment Security Commission. Manpower Research and Analysis Section. 1977. Employment projections for South Carolina's ten planning districts, 1974-1985, by occupation and industry. Columbia, 1977. pp. 175. *bibliog.*

SOUTH CAROLINA. Employment Security Commission. Manpower Research and Analysis Section. 1977. South Carolina employment projections 1974-1985: occupation and industry. Columbia, 1977. pp. 44.

— Yugoslavia.

PROJEKCIJA dugoročnog razvoja kadrova do 1985; redaktor Jovo Brekić. Zagreb, 1976. pp. 184. *bibliog. (Zagreb. Ekonomski Institut. Centar za Kadrologiju i Poslovodne Kadrove. Kadrologijska Biblioteka. Kolo 2)*

— Zambia.

ZAMBIA. Central Statistical Office. 1976. Projections of the labour force, 1969-84. Lusaka, 1976. fo. 26. *(Population Monographs. No. 3)*

LABOUR TURNOVER.

PRICE (JAMES L.) The study of turnover. Ames, Iowa, 1977. pp. 160. *bibliog.*

LA FOLLETTE (ROBERT MARION) the Younger.

MANEY (PATRICK J.) "Young Bob" La Follette: a biography of Robert M. La Follette, Jr., 1895-1953. Columbia, 1978. pp. 338. *bibliog.*

LAGOS

— Civilization.

ECHERUO (MICHAEL JOSEPH CHUKWUDALU) Victorian Lagos: aspects of nineteenth century Lagos life. London, 1977. pp. 124.

— **History.**

ECHERUO (MICHAEL JOSEPH CHUKWUDALU) Victorian Lagos: aspects of nineteenth century Lagos life. London, 1977. pp. 124.

— **Intellectual life.**

ECHERUO (MICHAEL JOSEPH CHUKWUDALU) Victorian Lagos: aspects of nineteenth century Lagos life. London, 1977. pp. 124.

— **Population.**

LAGOS. University. Human Resources Research Unit. Research Project No. 2. Population, employment and living conditions in Lagos. Research Bulletins. [No. 2]. Characteristics and changes of Lagos population. Lagos, 1972. fo. 7.

LAISSEZ-FAIRE.

BOYSON (RHODES) Youth and the image of free enterprise. London, [1973]. pp. 6. *(Aims of Industry. The Future of Capitalism.)*

IVENS (MICHAEL WILLIAM) and DUNSTAN (REGINALD ERNEST) eds. Freedom quotes. London, [1976]. pp. 45.

FRIEDMAN (DAVID) The machinery of freedom: guide to a radical capitalism. New Rochelle, [1978]. pp. 240. *bibliog.*

LITTLECHILD (STEPHEN CHARLES) The fallacy of the mixed economy: an Austrian critique of conventional mainstream economics and of British economic policy. London, 1978. pp. 83. *bibliog. (Institute of Economic Affairs. Hobart Papers. 80)*

LAITY

— **Church of England.**

CROSS (CLAIRE) Church and people, 1450-1660: the triumph of the laity in the English Church. Hassocks, 1976. pp. 272. *bibliog.*

LAMBETH

— **Civic improvement.**

SHANKLAND-COX PARTNERSHIP and INSTITUTE OF COMMUNITY STUDIES. Inner area study: Lambeth: multi-space project. [London], Department of the Environment, [1977]. pp. 14.

— **Politics and government.**

COCKBURN (CYNTHIA) The local state: management of cities and people. London, 1977, repr. 1978. pp. 207.

LAMBTON (JOHN GEORGE) 1st Earl of Durham.

PAPINEAU (LOUIS JOSEPH) Histoire de l'insurrection du Canada...en réfutation du rapport de Lord Durham; première partie. Burlington, Vt., 1839. pp. 38. *(Extraite de la Révue du Progrès, journal publié à Paris, 1839) Photographic reprint by Réédition Québec, 1968, from La Révue Canadienne, première livraison.*

LAMONT (DONAL) Bishop of Umtali.

LAMONT (DONAL) Bishop of Umtali. Speech from the dock. [Leigh-on-Sea, 1977]. pp. 143.

LAMONT (THOMAS WILLIAM).

COHEN (WARREN I.) The Chinese connection: Roger S. Greene, Thomas W. Lamont, George E. Sokolsky and American-East Asian relations. New York, 1978. pp. 322. *(Columbia University. East Asian Institute. Studies)*

LANCASHIRE

— **History.**

LONGMATE (NORMAN) The hungry mills: (the story of the Lancashire cotton famine, 1861-5). London, 1978. pp. 319. *bibliog.*

— **Politics and government.**

The HISTORY of Lancashire County Council, 1889 to 1974; edited by J.D. Marshall with the assistance of Marion E. McClintock. London, 1977. pp. 456. *bibliog.*

LAND

See LAND USE.

LAND, NATIONALIZATION OF

— **United Kingdom — Scotland.**

PLANNING EXCHANGE. Newsheets. 5. The community land scheme in Scotland. Glasgow, 1976. pp. 32.

SCOTLAND. Scottish Development Department. 1976. The community land scheme in Scotland: disposal notification areas. [Edinburgh, 1976]. pp. 9.

SCOTLAND. Scottish Development Department. 1976. The community land scheme in Scotland: planning applications and permissions for relevant development. [Edinburgh, 1976]. pp. 19.

LAND REFORM.

INTERNATIONAL BANK FOR RECONSTRUCTION AND DEVELOPMENT. Sector Policy Papers. Land reform. [Washington], 1975. pp. 73.

KING (RUSSELL) Land reform: a world survey. London, 1977. pp. 446.

— **America, Latin.**

MENDIETA Y NUÑEZ (LUCIO) Introduccion al estudio del derecho agrario. Mexico, 1975. pp. 251. *Reprint of second edition published in 1966.*

FEDER (ERNEST) Dr., of the University of Nebraska, ed. La lucha de clases en el campo: analisis estructural de la economia agricola latinoamericana. Mexico, 1975. pp. 520. *bibliogs. (Fondo de Cultura Economica. Lecturas. 14)*

— **Argentine Republic.**

UNION CIVICA RADICAL. Comite Nacional. Congreso Agrario de la Union Civica Radical: "tierra y libertad". Buenos Aires, [1950]. pp. 126.

— **Asia.**

LADEJINSKY (WOLF) Agrarian reform as unfinished business: (the selected papers of Wolf Ladejinsky); Louis J. Walinsky, editor; published for the World Bank. New York, [1977]. pp. 603. *bibliog.*

— **Chile.**

KAY (CRISTOBAL) Chile: an appraisal of Popular Unity's agrarian reform. [Glasgow, 1974]. pp. 21. *(Glasgow. University. Institute of Latin American Studies. Occasional Papers. No.13)*

STEENLAND (KYLE) Agrarian reform under Allende: peasant revolt in the south. Albuquerque, [1977]. pp. 241. *bibliog.*

— **China.**

WALLACE (CHRISTOPHER ST. JOHN) Motivation and incentives in rural China. [n.p., 1977?]. fo.220. *bibliog.*

— **Colombia.**

GONZALEZ MEJIA (LUIS VICENTE) Hacia un nuevo regimen agrario. Bogota, 1972. pp. 81. *bibliog.*

— **Ecuador.**

REDCLIFT (MICHAEL R.) Agrarian reform and peasant organization on the Ecuadorian coast. London, 1978. pp. 186. *bibliog. (London. University. Institute of Latin American Studies. Monographs. 8)*

— **Korea.**

KIM (IL-SUNG) On rural financial operations: (excerpts of the great leader comrade Kim Il Sung's teachings on rural financial operations). Pyongyang, 1977. pp. 38.

— **Mexico.**

MENDIETA Y NUÑEZ (LUCIO) El sistema agrario constitucional. 4th ed. Mexico, 1975. pp. 197.

— **Pakistan — Punjab.**

AHMAD (SAGHIR) Class and power in a Punjabi village. New York, [1977]. pp. 174. *bibliogs.*

— **Peru.**

JUELICH (VOLKER) Colonizacion como complemento de la reforma agraria en la selva peruana: el valle de Huallaga Central. Santiago de Chile, 1974. pp. 170. *(Instituto Latinoamericano de Investigaciones Sociales. Estudios y Documentos. 30)*

PADRON CASTILLO (MARIO) and PEASE GARCIA (HENRY) Planificacion rural, reforma agraria y organizacion campesina: programa de promocion campesina en el Valle del Santa 1971-1973. Lima, 1974. 2 vols. (in 1). *(Centro de Estudios y Promocion del Desarrollo. Cuadernos. 4)*

MEJIA (JOSE MANUEL) and DIAZ SUAREZ (ROSA) Sindicalismo y reforma agraria en el valle de Chancay. Lima, 1975. pp. 151. *bibliog. (Instituto de Estudios Peruanos. Proyecto de Estudios Etnologicos del Valle de Chancay. Monografias. No. 5)*

— **Portugal.**

CUNHAL (ALVARO) Contribuição para o estudo da questão agraria. Lisboa, 1976. 2 vols. (in 1).

LOPES CARDOSO (ANTONIO) Luta pela reforma agraria;...selecção e notas de J. Cândido de Azevedo. Lisboa, 1976 repr. 1977. pp. 246.

— **Uruguay.**

REFORMA agraria: falso planteo y falsa solucion para el Uruguay. Montevideo, 1967. pp. 39.

— **Venezuela.**

LOSADA ALDANA (RAMON) La tierra venezolana en la dialectica del subdesarrollo. Caracas, 1976. 2 vols. (in 1). *bibliog.*

LAND SETTLEMENT.

ACCADEMIA NAZIONALE DEI LINCEI. Atti dei Convegni Lincei. 16. Tavola rotonda: insediamenti territoriali e rapporti fra uomo e ambiente; criteri e metodologie. Roma, 9-10 dicembre 1974. Roma, 1976. pp. 218.

— **Brazil.**

KATZMAN (MARTIN T.) Cities and frontiers in Brazil: regional dimensions of economic development. Cambridge, Mass., 1977. pp. 255.

BOURNE (RICHARD) Assault on the Amazon. London, 1978. pp. 320. *bibliog.*

— **Italy.**

CECCHINI (DOMENICO) Trasporto stradale e struttura insediativa nel Mezzogiorno. [Milano, 1975]. pp. 191. *(Associazione per lo Sviluppo dell'Industria nel Mezzogiorno. Centro per gli Studi sullo Sviluppo Economico. Collana di Monografie)*

— **Netherlands.**

SLICHER VAN BATH (BERNARD HENDRIK) Mensch en land in de middeleeuwen: bijdrage tot een kennis der nederzettingen in oostelijk Nederland. Arnhem, 1977. 2 vols. (in 1). *bibliog. Reprint of the first edition, Assen, 1944, with a new foreword by the author.*

— **New Zealand.**

NEW ZEALAND. Department of Lands and Survey. 1968-70. Land development in the...land district[s]. [Wellington, 1968-70]. 11 pts.

LAND SUBDIVISION.

LAND SUBDIVISION.

MARKUSEN (JAMES R.) and SCHEFFMAN (DAVID T.) Speculation and monopoly in urban development: analytical foundations with evidence for Toronto. Toronto, [1977]. pp. 165. *bibliog.* (*Ontario. Economic Council. Research Studies. 10*)

— Canada — Ontario.

MARKUSEN (JAMES R.) and SCHEFFMAN (DAVID T.) Speculation and monopoly in urban development: analytical foundations with evidence for Toronto. Toronto, [1977]. pp. 165. *bibliog.* (*Ontario. Economic Council. Research Studies. 10*)

LAND TENURE.

KARL Marx über Formen vorkapitalistischer Produktion: vergleichende Studien zur Geschichte des Grundeigentums, 1879- 80; aus dem handschriftlichen Nachlass herausgegeben und eingeleitet von Hans-Peter Harstick. Frankfurt, [1977]. pp. 358. *bibliogs.* (*International Institute of Social History. Quellen und Studien zur Sozialgeschichte. Band 1*) *Includes extracts from M.M. Kovalevskii's Obshchinnoe zemlevladenie translated and annotated by Marx.*

— Australia.

AUSTRALIA. Aboriginal Land Rights Commission. Report. a., 1973(1st)- Canberra. *Included in AUSTRALIA. Parliament. [Parliamentary papers].*

ARCHER (R.W.) Leasehold and freehold urban land systems;...an amended version of the paper presented...to the Commission of Inquiry into Land Tenures. Canberra City, [1973]. fo. 13.

— — Queensland — Law.

QUEENSLAND. Department of Public Lands. 1960. Progressive land settlement and development in Queensland: a brief review of the more important provisions of recent land legislation...to give effect to the Government's land policy: the amending land acts of 1957, 1958 and 1959 reviewed...by A.G. Müller. Brisbane, [1960]. pp. 26.

— Chile.

KAY (CRISTOBAL) Chile: an appraisal of Popular Unity's agrarian reform. [Glasgow, 1974]. pp. 21. (*Glasgow. University. Institute of Latin American Studies. Occasional Papers. No.13*)

— China — Law.

CHINA. Statutes, etc. 1950. The land reform law of the People's Republic of China. 5th ed. Peking, 1976. pp. 52.

— Europe.

EUROPEAN landed elites in the nineteenth century: [the James Schouler Lectures, 1974]; edited...by David Spring. Baltimore, [1977]. pp. 147. *bibliogs.* (*Johns Hopkins University. Department of History. Johns Hopkins Symposia in Comparative History*)

— Finland.

ÅBO. Akademi. Acta Academiae Aboensis. Humaniora. 54. 4. Borgarna som lantbrukare i Finland under 1700-talet; av Oscar Nikula. Åbo, 1977. pp. 24. *bibliog.*

— India.

MONTAGU (EDWIN SAMUEL) India and the land: a paper read before the Liberal Colonial Club...19th February 1914. [London?, 1914?]. pp. 10.

STOKES (ERIC) The peasant and the Raj: studies in agrarian society and peasant rebellion in colonial India. Cambridge, 1978. pp. 308. (*Cambridge. University. Centre of South Asian Studies. Cambridge South Asian Studies. 23*)

— Italy.

TURRI (EUGENIO) Villa veneta. Verona, [1977]. pp. 209.

— Netherlands.

SLICHER VAN BATH (BERNARD HENDRIK) Mensch en land in de middeleeuwen: bijdrage tot een geschiedenis der nederzettingen in oostelijk Nederland. Arnhem, 1977. 2 vols. (in 1). *bibliog. Reprint of the first edition, Assen, 1944, with a new foreword by the author.*

— New Zealand — Law.

NEW ZEALAND. Department of Maori Affairs. 1967. Questions and answers on the Maori Affairs Amendment Bill, 1967, by the Minister of Maori Affairs. [Wellington, 1967?]. pp. 12.

— Poland — Silesia.

KAŃTOCH (F.) and others. Przemiany struktury agrarnej na Górnym Śląsku; Transitions in the agrarian structure in Upper Silesia. Katowice, 1962. pp. 88. *bibliog.* (*Śląski Instytut Naukowy w Katowicach. Biblioteczka Wiedzy o Śląsku. Seria Rolnicza. Nr.1*) *With English, French, German and Russian summaries.*

— Portugal.

MARTINS (JULIO SILVA) Estruturas agrarias em Portugal continental. Lisboa, [1973]-1975. 2 vols. *bibliog.*

— Russia.

RAPOV (OLEG MIKHAILOVICH) Kniazheskie vladeniia na Rusi v X - pervoi polovine XIII v. Moskva, 1977. pp. 261.

— — Law.

EROFEEV (BORIS VLADIMIROVICH) Pravovoi rezhim zemel' gorodov. Moskva, 1976. pp. 200.

SAWICKI (STANISLAW J.) Soviet land and housing law: a historical and comparative study. New York, 1977. pp. 199.

— United Kingdom.

YELLING (J. A.) Common field and enclosure in England, 1450-1850. London, 1977. pp. 255. *bibliog.*

MASSEY (DOREEN BARBARA) and CATALANO (ALEJANDRINA) Capital and land: landownership by capital in Great Britain. London, 1978. pp. 202. *bibliog.*

PROPERTY, paternalism and power: class and control in rural England; [by] Howard Newby [and others]. London, 1978. pp. 432. *bibliog.*

— — Law.

KOLBERT (COLIN FRANCIS) and MACKAY (NORMAN A.M.) History of Scots and English land law. Berkhamsted, [1977]. pp. 379. (*Cambridge. University. Department of Land Economy. Studies in Land Economy*) *Based on C.D'O. Farran, Principles of Scots and English land law.*

LAND TITLES

— Registration and transfer — Nigeria.

NIGERIA (WESTERN REGION). Committee appointed to consider the Registration of Title to Land in Western Nigeria. 1962. Report; [P.C. Lloyd, chairman]. [Ibadan], 1962. pp. 26. (*Nigeria (Western Region). Legislature. Sessional Papers. 1962. No. 2*)

— — United Kingdom.

ABRAHAM (ROBERT JOHN) A popular exploration of the system of land registration under Lord Westbury's Act; to which is added the report of the recent debate in the House of Lords, etc. London, Routledge, Warne, and Routledge, 1864. pp. 40.

LAND USE.

In earlier volumes of this Bibliography similar material is entered under LAND.

PROBLEMY geografii naseleniia i ispol'zovaniia territorii; Problems of the geography of population and land utilization. Tbilisi, 1976. pp. 239. *bibliog. With English table of contents and brief summaries.*

PUSHKAREV (BORIS SERGEEVICH) and ZUPAN (JEFFREY MICHAEL) Public transportation and land use policy. Bloomington, Ind., [1977]. pp. 242. *bibliog.*

DENMAN (DONALD ROBERT) The place of property: a new recognition of the function and form of property rights in land. Berkhamsted, [1978]. pp. 150. *bibliog.* (*Cambridge. University. Department of Land Economy. Studies in Land Economy*)

— Canada — Alberta.

ALBERTA. Land Use Forum. 1976. Report and recommendations; [V. A. Wood, chairman]. [Edmonton, 1976]. pp. 280.

— — British Columbia.

LOWER MAINLAND REGIONAL PLANNING BOARD OF BRITISH COLUMBIA. Land for living: the outlook for residential development in the lower mainland. New Westminster, 1963. pp. 32.

— India — Mysore.

MYSORE. Directorate of Evaluation and Manpower. Evaluation Unit. 1975. Report on land utilisation in Karnataka. Bangalore, 1975. pp. 163, 53.

— New Zealand.

NEW ZEALAND. Department of Lands and Survey. 1970. Maori land in a major development project. [Wellington], 1970. pp. (6).

NEW ZEALAND. Department of Lands and Survey. 1975. Activities of the Department of Lands and Survey. Wellington, 1975. pp. 21.

NEW ZEALAND. Department of Lands and Survey. 1976. The Department of Lands and Survey 1876-1976 centennial. Wellington, 1976. pp. 11.

— South Africa.

FAIR (T.J.D.) The Witwatersrand: its major socio-economic and land use trends, problems and prospects. Johannesburg, 1976. pp. 25. (*Johannesburg. University of the Witwatersrand. Urban and Regional Research Unit. Occasional Papers. No.12*)

— Tunisia.

TUNIS. Ministère de l'Agriculture. 1957. Terre de Tunisie: problèmes de la mise en valeur. [Tunis, 1957?]. pp. 182. (*Bulletin du Ministère de l'Agriculture, juin 1957, no. 3*)

— Underdeveloped areas.

See UNDERDEVELOPED AREAS — Land use.

— United Kingdom.

MASSEY (DOREEN BARBARA) and CATALANO (ALEJANDRINA) Capital and land: landownership by capital in Great Britain. London, 1978. pp. 202. *bibliog.*

— — Bibliography.

U.K. Department of the Environment. 1978. Town and country planning: development plans, development control and associated matters, including community land scheme and land transactions: index to departmental circulars and other relevant publications as at 15 May 1978. London, 1978. 1 pamphlet (unpaged).

— — Wales.

U.K. Land Authority for Wales. Land policy statement and rolling programme. a., 1977- [Cardiff].

— United States.

LAND use control: evaluating economic and political effects; [by] David E. Ervin [and others]. Cambridge, Mass., [1977]. pp. 182. *bibliog.*

LAND USE, RURAL

— Planning.

LASSEY (WILLIAM R.) Planning in rural environments. New York, [1977]. pp. 257. *bibliog.*

— Canada — Nova Scotia.

NOVA SCOTIA. Department of Lands and Forests. Annual report (formerly Report). a., 1957/58, 1962/63- , with gaps (1964/65, 1967/68-1971/72) Halifax. *File includes Interim report for 1966/67.*

— United Kingdom.

SALES OF AGRICULTURAL LAND IN ENGLAND AND WALES: [pd. by] Ministry of Agriculture, Fisheries and Food, (Economic and Statistics Group and Agricultural Land Service) [U.K.]. s-a., Oc 1959/Ap 1969 [1st]- [London].

LAND USE, URBAN.

DARIN-DRABKIN (HAIM) Land policy and urban growth. Oxford, 1977. pp. 442. *bibliog.*

OPEN UNIVERSITY. Fundamentals of Human Geography [Course Team]. Values, relevance and policy: units 25-26, section III, D204. Milton Keynes, 1977. pp. 80. *bibliogs.*

— United Kingdom.

KIRK (GWYNETH) Sociology of land use planning: Southwark's redevelopment plans. 1977 [or rather 1978]. pp. fo.537. *bibliog. Typescript. Ph.D. (London) thesis: unpublished. This thesis is the property of London University and may not be removed from the Library.*

— United States.

LEONE (ROBERT ANTHONY) Location of manufacturing activity in the New York Metropolitan Area. 1971. fo. 194. *bibliog. Ph.D. (Yale) thesis: unpublished. Microfilm of typscript: 1 reel.*

PERIN (CONSTANCE) Everything in its place: social order and land use in America. Princeton, [1977]. pp. 291. *bibliog.*

The SUBURBAN economic network: economic activity, resource use, and the great sprawl; edited by John E. Ullmann. New York, 1977. pp. 251.

AMERICAN BAR ASSOCIATION. Advisory Commission on Housing and Urban Growth. Housing for all under law: new directions in housing, land use and planning law...; edited by Richard P. Fishman. Cambridge, Mass., [1978]. pp. 635.

LANDLORD AND TENANT.

FLAT busted; [translated from a German pamphlet]. [London, c. 1973]. 1 vol. (unpaged)

— Australia.

BRADBROOK (ADRIAN J.) Poverty and the residential landlord-tenant relationship. Canberra, 1975. pp. 157. *(Australia. Commission of Inquiry into Poverty. Law and Poverty Series)*

CONSUMER groups and their views on welfare services and rented housing. Canberra, 1975. pp. 111. *(Australia. Commission of Inquiry into Poverty. Research Reports)*

— Japan.

WASWO (ANN) Japanese landlords: the decline of a rural elite. Berkeley, Calif., [1977]. pp. 152. *bibliog.*

— Netherlands.

PROFESSOR MR. B.M. TELDERSSTICHTING. Geschriften. 19. Modernisering van de pachtwetgeving. 's-Gravenhage, 1970. pp. 36.

— United Kingdom.

HARPER (MICHAEL) Landlord v. tenant. London, 1977. pp. 149.

LABOUR PARTY. Home, secure home: a charter for private tenants. London, [1977]. pp. (8).

LONDON. Greater London Council. Establishments Department. Behavioural Science Unit. The relationship between the GLC Housing Department, its tenants and the public; by the Behavioural Science Unit and an interdepartmental working party. London, [1977]. pp. 107. *(London. Greater London Council. Research Memoranda. 503)*

PETTIT (PHILIP HENRY) Landlord and tenant under the Rent Act 1977. London, 1978. pp. 317.

U.K. Social Survey. [Reports. New Series]. 1091. Attitudes to letting in 1976; a survey of private landlords, private tenants and owner occupiers in areas of England and Wales which in 1971 were predominantly rented in the private sector; [by] Bobbie Paley. London, 1978. pp. 101.

LANGUAGE AND LANGUAGES.

SAMPSON (GEOFFREY) Natural language and the paradox of the liar. The Hague, [1972]. pp. 18. *(Reprinted from Semiotica vol. 5. No. 4, 1972)*

LANGUAGE and speech; edited by Edward C. Carterette and Morton P. Friedman. London, 1976. pp. 501. *bibliogs.*

CHERRY (EDWARD COLIN) On human communication: a review, a survey, and a criticism. 3rd ed. Cambridge, Mass., [1978]. pp. 374. *bibliog.*

— Origin.

STAM (JAMES H.) Inquiries into the origin of language: the fate of a question. New York, [1976]. pp. 307.

— Variation.

LINGUISTIC variation: models and methods; edited by David Sankoff. New York, [1978]. pp. 296.

LANGUAGES

— Philosophy.

KEMPSON (RUTH M.) Semantic theory. Cambridge, 1977. pp. 216. *bibliog.*

BRONOWSKI (JACOB) The origins of knowledge and imagination. New Haven, 1978. pp. 146. *(Yale University. Silliman Memorial Lectures. 1967)*

— Physiological aspects.

SENTENCE production: developments in research and theory; edited by Sheldon Rosenberg. Hillsdale, N.J., [1977]. pp. 323. *bibliogs.*

— Political aspects.

RABOTIN (MAURICE) Le vocabulaire politique et socio-ethnique à Montréal de 1839 à 1842. Montréal, [1975]. pp. 123. *bibliog.*

LAITIN (DAVID D.) Politics, language, and thought: the Somali experience. Chicago, [1977]. pp. 268. *bibliog.*

LANGUAGES, MODERN

— Study and teaching.

MUNBY (JOHN) Communicative syllabus design: a sociolinguistic model for defining the content of purpose-specific language programmes. Cambridge, 1978. pp. 232. *bibliog.*

LANGUEDOC-ROUSSILLON (REGION)

— Economic conditions.

REPERES: économie du Languedoc-Roussillon: revue bimestrielle; ([pd. by] Institut National de la Statistique et des Etudes Economiques, Direction Régionale de Montpellier [France]. q. (formerly bi-m.), Ap 1972 (no.1)- Montpellier. *Formerly included in Sud: information économique méditerranéenne, afterwards Sud: information économique Provence - Côte d'Azur - Corse.*

LARKIN (JAMES JOSEPH).

LARKIN (JAMES JOSEPH) The American trial of Big Jim Larkin, 1920. Belfast, 1976. pp. 106.

LA ROCHELLE.

FRANCE. Direction de la Documentation. La Documentation Française. Notes et Etudes Documentaires. Nos. 4,394-4, 395. Les villes françaises: La Rochelle; par Jacques Pinard. [Paris], 1977. pp. 66. *bibliog.*

— Commerce.

CHARBONNEL (NICOLE) Commerce et course sous la Révolution et le Consulat à La Rochelle: autour de deux armateurs: les frères Thomas et Pierre-Antoine Chegaray. Paris, [1977]. pp. 103. *bibliog. (Paris. Université de Paris II. Travaux et Recherches. Série Sciences Historiques. 12)*

LASKI (HAROLD JOSEPH).

EASTWOOD (GRANVILLE G.) Harold Laski. London, [1977]. pp. 173.

LASSALLE (FERDINAND JOHANN GOTTLIEB).

BUONFINO (GIANCARLO) La politica culturale operaia da Marx e Lassalle alla rivoluzione di novembre, 1859-1919. Milano, 1975. pp. 211.

LATIFUNDIO

— America, Latin.

HACIENDAS, latifundios y plantaciones en America Latina; coordinacion por Enrique Florescano. Mexico, 1975. pp. 667.

LATIN AMERICAN FREE TRADE ASSOCIATION.

CARDENAS (GONZALO HORACIO) Origenes, evolucion y futuro de la A.L.A.L.C. (Asociacion Latinoamericana de Libre Comercio). Buenos Aires, 1968. pp. 32.

LATVIA

— Economic conditions — Mathematical models.

ADIRIM (ITSKHOK GIRSHEVICH) Prognozno-planovye modeli ekonomiki respubliki. Riga, 1977. pp. 255. *bibliog. With English table of contents.*

— Rural conditions.

KOZIN (MIKHAIL IVANOVICH) Latyshskaia derevnia v 50-70-e gody XIX veka. Riga, 1976. pp. 372.

— Statistics.

NARODNOE KHOZIAISTVO LATVIISKOI SSR: statisticheskii ezhegodnik; [pd. by] Tsentral'noe Statisticheskoe Upravlenie [Latvia]. a., 1970- Riga.

LAW.

PERETIATKOWICZ (ANTONI) Ogólne zasády prawa jako źródło prawa międzynarodowego a tendencje kosmopolityczne. Poznań, 1956. pp. 47. *(Poznań. Poznańskie Towarzystwo Przyjaciół Nauk. Wydział Historii i Nauk Społecznych. Komisja Nauk Społecznych. Prace. t.6, z.3) With French and Russian summaries.*

KAHN-FREUND (Sir OTTO) Selected writings: published under the auspices of the Modern Law Review. London, 1978. pp. 381. *bibliog.*

LAW. (Cont.)

LAW in social context: Liber Amicorum honouring Professor Lon L. Fuller; edited by Thomas W. Bechtler. Deventer, 1978. pp. 227. *bibliog.*

— **International unification.**

GRAVESON (RONALD HARRY) One law: on jurisprudence and the unification of law; selected essays, vol.2. Amsterdam, 1977. pp. 287. *(London. University. King's College. Centre of European Law. European Studies in Law. vol.2)*

— **Periodicals — Bibliography.**

LONDON. University. Institute of Advanced Legal Studies. Union catalogues. No.1. Union list of legal periodicals : a location guide to holdings of legal periodicals in libraries in the United Kingdom. 4th ed. London, 1978. pp. 316.

— **Philosophy.**

COHEN (LAURENCE JONATHAN) The probable and the provable. Oxford, 1977. pp. 363.

LONG (DOUGLAS G.) Bentham on liberty: Jeremy Bentham's idea of liberty in relation to his utilitarianism. Toronto, [1977]. pp. 294. *bibliog.*

WEBER (MAX) Critique of Stammler;...translated, with an introductory essay, by Guy Oakes. New York, [1977]. pp. 184.

ROSENBLUM (NANCY L.) Bentham's theory of the modern state. Cambridge, Mass., 1978. pp. 169.

— **Study and teaching — South Africa.**

LABUSCHAGNE (J.M.T.) Bantoereg: 'n vakwetenskaplike terreinverkenning;...rede uitgespreek by die aanvaarding van die professoraat in die Departement Bantoereg...1973. Pretoria, 1973. pp. 10. *(Pretoria. University of Pretoria. Publications. New Series. No. 79) With English summary.*

— **Africa — Codification.**

VARGA (CSABA) Modernization of law and its codificational trends in the Afro- Asiatic legal development. Budapest, 1976. pp. 45. *(Magyar Tudományos Akadémia. Világgazdasági Kutató Intezet. Studies on Developing Countries. No. 88)*

— **Africa, East.**

EAST African law and social change; edited by G.F.A. Sawyerr. [Nairobi, 1967]. pp. 307. *bibliogs.(East African Institute of Social and Cultural Affairs. Contemporary African Monograph Series. No.6) Proceedings of the Seminar on Law and Social Change in East Africa, held at University College Dar es Salaam, April 2nd to 5th, 1966.*

— **Asia — Codification.**

VARGA (CSABA) Modernization of law and its codificational trends in the Afro- Asiatic legal development. Budapest, 1976. pp. 45. *(Magyar Tudományos Akadémia. Világgazdasági Kutató Intezet. Studies on Developing Countries. No. 88)*

— **Asia, Southeast — History and criticism.**

HOOKER (MICHAEL BARRY) A concise legal history of South-East Asia. Oxford, 1978. pp. 289. *bibliog.*

— **Austria.**

OESTERREICHISCHER GEMEINDEBUND. Prise de position de l'Association des pouvoirs locaux autrichiens en face du questionnaire sur les réformes de la collectivité territoriale et sur la planification dans les différents pays d'Europe. Wien, [196-?]. fo.16.

— **Czechoslovakia.**

ROZVOJ socialistického štátu a práva v oslobodenom Československu: zborník referátov z vedeckej konferencie Ústavu štátu a práva SAV a Práavnickej fakulty Univerzity Komenského,...22.-24. apríla 1975 v Smoleniciach. [Bratislava], 1977. pp. 266.

— **Europe.**

HILBERT (LOTHAR W.) Droit écrit ou droit coutumier: problème de la construction institutionnelle de l'Europe. Luxembourg, 1962. fo. 21.

— — **History and criticism.**

TIGAR (MICHAEL E.) and LEVY (MADELEINE R.) Law and the rise of capitalism. New York, [1977]. pp. 346. *bibliog.*

— **European Economic Community countries.**

SCHMIDT (REIMER) Zu den rechtlichen Grundfragen des Gemeinsamen Marktes, unter besonderer Berücksichtigung der Kredit- und Versicherungswirtschaft. Karlsruhe, 1962. pp. 67. *(Karlsruhe. Juristische Studiengesellschaft Karlsruhe. Schriftenreihe. Heft 52/53)*

PROBLEME des europäischen Gemeinschaftsrechts; herausgegeben von Fritz Schwind. Wien, 1976. pp. 411. *(Österreichische Akademie der Wissenschaften. Philosophisch-Historische Klasse. Sitzungsberichte. 302. Band)*

HASFORD (HEINER) Die Jurisdiktion der Europäischen Gemeinschaften: zur extraterritorialen Wirkung des Gemeinschaftsrechts. Frankfurt am Main, [1977]. pp. 253. *bibliog.*

— — **Interpretation and construction.**

BREDIMAS (ANNA) Methods of interpretation and Community law. Amsterdam, 1978. pp. 219. *bibliog. (London. University. King's College. Centre of European Law. European Studies in Law. 6)*

— **France — History and criticism.**

PHYTILIS (JACQUES) Justice administrative et justice déléguée au XVIIIe siècle: l'exemple des commissions extraordinaires de jugement à la suite du conseil. Limoges, [1977]. pp. 250. *bibliog. (Limoges. Université. Faculté de Droit et des Sciences Economiques. Publications. 5)*

— **Italy.**

BOSELLINI (CARLO) Opere complete; a cura di Miriam Rotondò Michelini. Torino, 1976. 2 vols. *(Fondazione Luigi Einaudi. Scrittori Italiani di Politica, Economia e Storia)*

CANOSA (ROMANO) Diritto e rivoluzione. Milano, [1977]. pp. 168.

— — **History and criticism.**

SCHWARZENBERG (CLAUDIO) Diritto e giustizia nell'Italia fascista. Milano, [1977]. pp. 310.

— **Netherlands.**

LEYTEN (J.C.M.) De rechter op de schopstoel: rede uitgesproken...aan de Katholieke Universiteit te Nijmegen...1970. Deventer, [1970]. pp. 35.

— **Russia.**

LEIDEN. Rijks Universiteit. Documentation Office for East European Law. Law in Eastern Europe. No. 20/1. Soviet law after Stalin. Part 1. The citizen and the state in contemporary Soviet law; edited by Donald D. Barry [and others]. Leyden, 1977, pp. 303.

BUTLER (WILLIAM E.) ed. The Soviet legal system: selected contemporary legislation and documents. Dobbs Ferry, N.Y., 1978. pp. 733. *(Columbia University. Parker School of Foreign and Comparative Law. Studies in Foreign and Comparative Law)*

— — **Codification.**

SYMOROT (ZAKHAR KYRYLOVYCH) and MONASTYRS'KYI (IEVHEN OLEKSANDROVYCH) Problemy kodifikatsii zakonodatel'stva Soiuza SSR i soiuznykh respublik o trude. Kiev, 1977. pp. 300.

— — **Interpretation and construction.**

KOMMENTARII sudebnoi praktiki za 1974 god. Moskva, 1975. pp. 167. *Previous years have title Nauchnyi kommentarii sudebnoi praktiki, etc.*

— **United Kingdom.**

GRAVESON (RONALD HARRY) One law: on jurisprudence and the unification of law; selected essays, vol.2. Amsterdam, 1977. pp. 287. *(London. University. King's College. Centre of European Law. European Studies in Law. vol.2)*

PHILLIPS (OWEN HOOD) A first book of English law; seventh edition by O. Hood Phillips and A.H. Hudson. London, 1977. pp. 389.

CARD (RICHARD) and JAMES (JENNIFER) Law for accountancy students. London, 1978. pp. 660.

KAHN-FREUND (Sir OTTO) Selected writings: published under the auspices of the Modern Law Review. London, 1978. pp. 381. *bibliog.*

— — **Bibliography.**

RAISTRICK (DONALD) and REES (JOHN) Lawyers' law books: a practical index to legal literature. Abingdon, 1977. pp. 576.

— — **Dictionaries and encyclopedias.**

JOWITT (WILLIAM ALLEN) 1st Earl Jowitt, and WALSH (CLIFFORD) Dictionary of English law;...second edition by John Burke. London, 1977. 2 vols. *bibliog.*

— — **History and criticism.**

BABINGTON (ANTHONY) The rule of law in Britain from the Roman occupation to the present day. Chichester, 1978. pp. 313.

— — **Study and teaching.**

SOCIETY OF PUBLIC TEACHERS OF LAW. Working Party on Law Publishing. Final report on law publishing and legal scholarship. n.p., 1977. pp. 45.

— **United States.**

CARDOZO (BENJAMIN NATHAN) Selected writings...; edited by Margaret E. Hall. New York, [1947]. pp. 456.

IAKOVLEV (ALEKSANDR MAKSIMOVICH) Pravo i sotsiologiia: krizis zakonnosti v SShA. Moskva, 1975. pp. 112.

POSNER (RICHARD A.) Economic analysis of law. 2nd ed. Boston, Mass., [1977]. pp. 572.

ROSTOW (EUGENE VICTOR) The ideal in law. Chicago, [1978]. pp. 305.

— — **History and criticism.**

HORWITZ (MORTON J.) The transformation of American law, 1780-1860. Cambridge, Mass., 1977. pp. 356.

LAW, BANTU.

LABUSCHAGNE (J.M.T.) Bantoereg: 'n vakwetenskaplike terreinverkenning;...rede uitgespreek by die aanvaarding van die professoraat in die Departement Bantoereg...1973. Pretoria, 1973. pp. 10. *(Pretoria. University of Pretoria. Publications. New Series. No. 79) With English summary.*

LAW, COMPARATIVE.

EHRMANN (HENRY WALTER) Comparative legal cultures. Englewood Cliffs, N.J., [1976]. pp. 172. *bibliog.*

GRAVESON (RONALD HARRY) One law: on jurisprudence and the unification of law; selected essays, vol.2. Amsterdam, 1977. pp. 287. *(London. University. King's College. Centre of European Law. European Studies in Law. vol.2)*

DAVID (RENÉ) and BRIERLEY (JOHN E.C.) Major legal systems in the world today: an introduction to the comparative study of law. 2nd ed. London, 1978. pp. 584. *bibliog.*

— **Study and teaching.**

HAZARD (JOHN NEWBOLD) Comparison in preparation for statesmanship. Padova, 1973. pp. 359-367.

LAW, PRIMITIVE.

MOORE (SALLY FALK) Law as process: an anthropological approach. London, 1978. pp. 270. *bibliog.*

LAW AND ETHICS.

ROSTOW (EUGENE VICTOR) The ideal in law. Chicago, [1978]. pp. 305.

LAW AND SOCIALISM.

KUBŮ (LUBOMÍR) Ryzí nauka právní v kontextu buržoazního právního myšlení. Brno, 1977. pp. 102. *bibliog.* With Russian summary.

LAW REFORM

— Canada — Manitoba.

MANITOBA. Law Reform Commission. 1971. Reports and recommendations; [Francis C. Muldoon, chairman]. [Winnipeg], 1971. pp. 37. *(Reports. 1-6)*

— — Nova Scotia.

NOVA SCOTIA. Law Reform Advisory Commission. Annual report. a., 1972(1st)- Halifax.

— Tasmania.

TASMANIA. Law Reform Commission. Report. a., 1975 (1st)- Hobart. *Included in TASMANIA. Parliament. Journals and printed papers.*

— United Kingdom.

EDMUND-DAVIES (HERBERT EDMUND) Baron Edmund-Davies. Ferment in the law. Birmingham, 1977. pp. 19. *(Birmingham. University. Holdsworth Club. Presidential Addresses. 1977)*

LAW REPORTS, DIGESTS, ETC.

— Czechoslovakia.

SBÍRKA SOUDNÍCH ROZHODNUTÍ A STANOVISEK; vydává Nejvyšší soud ČSSR. [title varies slightly]. 10 a yr., 1969 (roč. 21)- Praha.

— Germany.

FONTES JURIS GENTIUM. Series A. Sectio 2. Tomus 5. Deutsche Rechtsprechung in völkerrechtlichen Fragen; Decisions of German courts relating to public international law... 1961-1965; bearbeitet im Max-Planck Institut für ausländisches öffentliches Recht und Völkerrecht von Albert Bleckmann [and others]. Berlin, 1978. pp. 1048.

— Romania.

MIHUȚĂ (IOAN G.) Repertoriu de practică judiciară în materie civilă a Tribunalului Suprem și a altor instanțe judecătorești pe anii 1969-1975. București, 1976. pp. 430.

— United Kingdom.

SELDEN SOCIETY. Publications. vol. 93. The reports of Sir John Spelman. vol. 1; edited...by J.H. Baker. London, 1977. pp. 238.

LAW SCHOOLS

— Russia.

OCHERKI po istorii iuridicheskikh nauchnykh uchrezhdenii v SSSR. Moskva, 1976. pp. 238.

LAWYERS

— Russia.

COLLIGNON (JEAN GUY) Les juristes en Union Soviétique. Paris, 1977. pp. 555. *bibliog.* (*Centre National de la Recherche Scientifique. Service de Recherches Juridiques Comparatives. Travaux*)

— United Kingdom.

BAR ASSOCIATION FOR COMMERCE, FINANCE AND INDUSTRY. Barristers in business. 2nd ed. London, 1973. pp. 16.

ZANDER (MICHAEL) Lawyers and the public interest...; notes to bring the book up to date. 1976. fo. 91.

ASSOCIATION OF LIBERAL LAWYERS. Reform of legal services: (the evidence of the Association...to the Royal Commission on Legal Services). London, 1977. pp. 12. *(Liberal Publication Department. Study Papers. No. 8)*

LABOUR PARTY. The citizen and the law;...evidence to the Royal Commission on Legal Services. London, 1977. pp. 47.

FABIAN SOCIETY. Fabian Tracts. [No.] 454. Legal services for all; [by a sub-committee of the] Society of Labour Lawyers [under the chairmanship of Ben Hooberman]. London, 1978. pp. 28.

ZANDER (MICHAEL) Legal services for the community. London, 1978. pp. 416.

SOLICITORS' DIARY, THE: almanac and legal directory incorporating the Law Society lists of practising solicitors. a., current issue only. London.

— United States.

BRUGGER (ROBERT J.) Beverley Tucker: heart over head in the old south. Baltimore, [1978]. pp. 294. *bibliogs.* (*Johns Hopkins University. Studies in Historical and Political Science. Series 96. No.2*)

— — Bibliography.

NORRIS (LORETTA A.) and BOYER (LARRY M.) compliers. American colonial courts and lawyers; an annotated bibliography. (Washington), Library of Congress, 1976. pp. 24.

LAYAWAY PLAN

— New Zealand.

NEW ZEALAND. Contracts and Commercial Law Reform Committee. 1969. Layby sales; report...presented to the Minister of Justice in August 1969; [M.F. Chilwell, chairman]. [Wellington], 1969. pp. 19.

LEADERSHIP.

ENSOR (HOWARD) Paths to leadership. London, [1977]. pp. 11. *(National Association of Boys' Clubs. Basil Henriques Memorial Lectures. 1977)*

MACCOBY (MICHAEL) The gamesman: the new corporate leaders;...with a new preface for this [British] edition. London, 1977. pp. 285.

PAIGE (GLENN D.) The scientific study of political leadership. New York, [1977]. pp. 416. *bibliog.*

PRIOR (PETER J.) Leadership is not a bowler hat. Newton Abbot, [1977]. pp. 64.

CARTWRIGHT (JOHN R.) Political leadership in Sierra Leone. London, [1978]. pp. 308.

McKENNA (EUGENE F.) The management style of the chief accountant. Farnborough, Hants., [1978]. pp. 307. *bibliog.*

MANAGEMENT control and organizational democracy; editors Bert King [and others]. Washington, D.C., 1978. pp. 288. *bibliogs. Papers presented at a conference held in Munich in 1976 by the Human Factors Division of the North Atlantic Treaty Organization.*

LEAGUE OF ARAB STATES.

GOMAA (AHMED MAHMOUD H.) The foundation of the League of Arab States: wartime diplomacy and inter-Arab politics, 1941 to 1945. London, 1977. pp. 323. *bibliog.*

TUZMUKHAMEDOV (RAIS ABDULKHAKOVICH) Razvivaiushchiesia strany v mirovoi politike: mezhdunarodnye mezhpravitel'stvennye organizatsii razvivaiushchikhsia stran. Moskva, 1977. pp. 207.

LEAGUE OF NATIONS.

DIAZ CISNEROS (CESAR) La Liga de las Naciones y la actitud argentina; con el texto del tratado. Buenos Aires, 1921. pp. 207.

LEARNING, PSYCHOLOGY OF.

SEGERSTEDT (TORGNY TORGNYSSON) Symbolmiljö, mening och attityd: ett forskningsprojekt. Uppsala, 1956. pp. 55. *(Uppsala. Universitet. Årsskrifter. 1956:4)*

BANDURA (ALBERT) Social learning theory. Englewood Cliffs, [1977]. pp. 247. *bibliog.*

LEARNING ABILITY.

CARRIER (JAMES GOLDEN) Social influence on the development of scientific knowledge: the case of learning disabilities. 1977. fo. 361. *bibliog. Typescript. Ph.D. (London) thesis: unpublished. This thesis is the property of London University and may not be removed from the Library.*

LEARNING AND SCHOLARSHIP

— Poland.

DZIESIEC lat rozwoju nauki w Polsce Ludowej. [Warszawa], 1956. pp. 725.

— United Kingdom.

KNIGHTS (BEN) The idea of the clerisy in the nineteenth century. Cambridge, [1978]. pp. 274. *bibliog.*

LEASES

— Netherlands.

PITLO (A.) and KASDORP (J.E.) Het erfrecht naar het Nederlands Burgerlijk Wetboek. 4th ed. Haarlem, 1971. pp. 388.

— New Zealand.

NEW ZEALAND. Committee of Investigation into Rentals and Freeholding of Crown Leases. 1968. Report...; chairman: W.R. Beattie. [Wellington], 1968. pp. 28.

LEATHER INDUSTRY AND TRADE.

UNITED NATIONS. Conference on Trade and Development. 1971. Leather and leather products: report, etc. (TD/B/387). New York, 1971. pp. 90.

— Zambia.

ZAMBIA. Central Statistical Office. 1975. Textile, wearing apparel and leather industries. Lusaka, 1975. pp. 61. *bibliog. (Industry Monographs. No. 2)*

LEBANON

— Economic conditions.

OWEN (EDWARD ROGER JOHN) ed. Essays on the crisis in Lebanon. London, [1976]. pp. 91. *bibliogs. Papers originally presented to a seminar at the Middle East Centre, St. Antony's College.*

— History.

OWEN (EDWARD ROGER JOHN) ed. Essays on the crisis in Lebanon. London, [1976]. pp. 91. *bibliogs. Papers originally presented to a seminar at the Middle East Centre, St. Antony's College.*

VOCKE (HARALD) The Lebanese war: its origins and political dimensions; (translated from the German by A.K.H. Weinrich and Ilse Fisher). London, 1978. pp. 81. *bibliog.*

— Politics and government.

OWEN (EDWARD ROGER JOHN) ed. Essays on the crisis in Lebanon. London, [1976]. pp. 91. *bibliogs. Papers originally presented to a seminar at the Middle East Centre, St. Antony's College.*

LEBER (JULIUS).

LEBER (JULIUS).

LEBER (JULIUS) Schriften, Reden, Briefe; herausgegeben von Dorothea Beck und Wilfried F. Schoeller; mit einem Vorwort von Willy Brandt und einer Gedenkrede von Golo Mann. München, [1976]. pp. 327.

LE BRUN (JOYCE).

HERTSLET (MARY) From pain to purpose: the story of Joyce Le Brun as told to Mary Hertslet. Plumstead, South Africa, [1975]. pp. 61.

LE CORBUSIER ( ) pseud. [i.e. Charles Edouard JEANNERET].

FISHMAN (ROBERT) Urban utopias in the twentieth century: Ebenezer Howard, Frank Lloyd Wright and Le Corbusier. New York, [1977]. pp. 332. *bibliog.*

LEGA NAZIONALE DELLE COOPERATIVE E MUTUE.

DEGL'INNOCENTI (MAURIZIO) Storia della cooperazione in Italia: la Lega nazionale delle cooperative, 1886-1925. Roma, 1977. pp. 461.

LEGACIES

— New Zealand.

NEW ZEALAND. Contracts and Commercial Law Reform Committee. 1971. Nominations in respect of savings bank accounts; report... presented to the Minister of Justice in July 1971; [M.F. Chilwell, chairman]. [Wellington], 1971. pp. 10.

LEGAL AID

— Canada.

NATIONAL CONFERENCE ON LAW AND POVERTY, OTTAWA, 1971. The law and the poor in Canada; edited by Irwin Cotler and Herbert Marx. Montréal, [1977]. pp. 143.

— — Ontario.

ONTARIO. Task Force on Legal Aid. 1974- . Report; [John H. Osler, chairman]. [Toronto], 1974 in progress.

— India.

INDIA. Expert Committee on Legal Aid. 1974. Processual justice to the people: report; [V.R. Krishna Iyer, chairman]. [Delhi, 1974]. pp. 275.

— Ireland (Republic).

EIRE. Committee on Civil Legal Aid and Advice. 1978. Report. Dublin, [1978]. pp. 289.

— South Africa.

ELLUM (PATRICK) Legal aid developments in South Africa, July 1973-June 1975. Durban, 1975. pp. 75.

— United Kingdom.

ASSOCIATION OF LIBERAL LAWYERS. Reform of legal services: (the evidence of the Association...to the Royal Commission on Legal Services). London, 1977. pp. 12. *(Liberal Publication Department. Study Papers. No. 8)*

BYLES (ANTHEA) and MORRIS (PAULINE J.) Unmet need: the case of the neighbourhood law centre. London, [1977]. pp. 95. *bibliog. A study by the Legal Advice Research Unit.*

LABOUR PARTY. The citizen and the law;...evidence to the Royal Commission on Legal Services. London, 1977. pp. 47.

FABIAN SOCIETY. Fabian Tracts. [No.] 454. Legal services for all; [by a sub-committee of the] Society of Labour Lawyers [under the chairmanship of Ben Hooberman]. London, 1978. pp. 28.

ZANDER (MICHAEL) Legal services for the community. London, 1978. pp. 416.

LEGAL ETHICS

— United States.

HAZARD (GEOFFREY C.) Ethics in the practice of law: (report of a symposium held in 1976 at Seven Springs Center). New Haven, 1978. pp. 159.

LEGISLATION.

FILANGIERI (GAETANO) Cavaliere. Scritti; a cura di Franco Venturi. [Torino, 1976]. pp. 139. *bibliog.*

— Europe.

COUNCIL OF EUROPE. Directorate of Legal Affairs. Information bulletin on legal activities within the Council of Europe and in member states. 7 a yr., Je 1978(no. 1)- Strasbourg. *Supersedes* COUNCIL OF EUROPE. *Directorate of Legal Affairs. Bulletin on legislative activities.*

— Russia.

DREISHEV (BORIS VLADIMIROVICH) Pravotvorchestvo v sovetskom gosudarstvennom upravlenii. Moskva, 1977. pp. 159.

— Scandinavia.

TÖTTERMAN (RICHARD) Lawmaking and Nordic co-operation. London, 1976. pp. 14. *(London. University. University College. Lectures in Nordic History. 1976)*

— United Kingdom.

U.K. Statutes, etc. The local and personal acts: tables and index (formerly Supplementary index to the local and personal acts, previously Index to local and personal acts consisting of classified lists of the local and personal and private acts and special orders and special procedure orders). a., (formerly irreg.), 1801/1947, 1948/1966, 1967- London.

— United States.

MILLER (JAMES CLIFFORD) Regulatory reform: some problems and approaches. Washington, 1977. pp. 11. *(American Enterprise Institute for Public Policy Research. Reprints. No. 72)*

RALPH NADER CONGRESS PROJECT. Ruling Congress: how the House and Senate rules govern the legislative process; [edited by] Ted Siff and Alan Weil, directors. Harmondsworth, 1977]. pp. 299.

LEGISLATIVE BODIES.

ALBUM François Dumont. Bruxelles, 1977. pp. 317. *(International Commission for the History of Representative and Parliamentary Institutions. Studies. 60) In French, English and German.*

The HISTORY of parliamentary behavior; edited by William O. Aydelotte. Princeton, [1977]. pp. 321. *(Mathematical Social Science Board. History Advisory Committee. Quantitative Studies in History) Papers presented at a conference held at the University of Iowa, 1972, by the Committee.*

LEGISLATURES in plural societies: the search for cohesion in national development; edited by Albert F. Eldridge. Durham, N.C., 1977. pp. 284. *bibliogs. (Consortium for Comparative Legislative Studies. Publications)*

COLLIARD (JEAN CLAUDE) Les régimes parlementaires contemporains. [Paris, 1978]. pp. 369. *bibliog.*

ELECTIONS without choice; edited by Guy Hermet [and others] . London, 1978. pp. 250. *(International Political Science Association and International Sociological Association. Committee on Political Sociology. Publications. 15)*

— Congresses.

AUSTRALIAN PARLIAMENTARY SEMINAR, 1ST, CANBERRA, 1972. Summary report of proceedings. in AUSTRALIA. Parliament. Parliamentary papers, 1972, vol. 8.

— Australia — Congresses.

AUSTRALIAN PARLIAMENTARY SEMINAR, 1ST, CANBERRA, 1972. Summary report of proceedings. in AUSTRALIA. Parliament. Parliamentary papers, 1972, vol. 8.

— France.

BIRNBAUM (PIERRE) and others. Réinventer le Parlement. [Paris, 1977]. pp. 223.

— Poland.

KRAJOWA Rada Narodowa; pod redakcją Andrzeja Burdy. Wrocław, 1976. pp. 250.

— Russia.

IROSHNIKOV (MIKHAIL PAVLOVICH) Vo glave Sovnarkoma: gosudarstvennaia deiatel'nost' V.I. Lenina v 1917-1922 gg. Leningrad, 1976. pp. 216. *(Akademiia Nauk SSSR. Seriia "Istoriia Nashei Rodiny")*

SOVERSHENSTVOVANIE raboty Sovetov v sovremennykh usloviiakh. Moskva, 1976. pp. 116.

ZNAMENSKII (OLEG NIKOLAEVICH) Vserossiiskoe Uchreditel'noe sobranie: istoriia sozyva i politicheskogo krusheniia. Leningrad, 1976. pp. 364.

RAZGON (ANATOLII IZRAILEVICH) VTsIK Sovetov v pervye mesiatsy diktatury proletariata. Moskva, 1977. pp. 335.

— — Moldavian Republic.

ORGANY gosudarstvennoi vlasti i upravleniia Moldavskoi SSR. Kishinev, 1976. pp. 206.

— — White Russia.

SLOBODCHIKOV (NIKOLAI AFANAS'EVICH) Sovet Narodnykh Komissarov BSSR v 1920-1936 gg.: pravovye voprosy organizatsii i deiatel'nosti. Minsk, 1977. pp. 166. *bibliog.*

LEGISLATORS.

The HISTORY of parliamentary behavior; edited by William O. Aydelotte. Princeton, [1977]. pp. 321. *(Mathematical Social Science Board. History Advisory Committee. Quantitative Studies in History) Papers presented at a conference held at the University of Iowa, 1972, by the Committee.*

— Canada — Saskatchewan.

SASKATCHEWAN. Committee on the Role and Remuneration of Members of the Legislative Assembly of Saskatchewan. 1976. Interim report; [Edward N. Hughes, chairman]. [Regina], 1976. fo. 48.

SASKATCHEWAN. Committee on the Role and Remuneration of Members of the Legislative Assebmbly of Saskatchewan. 1976. Second interim report; [Edward N. Hughes, chairman]. [Regina], 1976. fo. 6.

— United Kingdom.

MELLORS (COLIN) The British MP: a socio-economic study of the House of Commons. [Farnborough, Hants., 1978]. pp. 146.

— — Correspondence, reminiscences, etc.

MORRELL (FRANCES) From the electors of Bristol: the record of a year's correspondence between constituents and their member of parliament. Nottingham, [1977]. pp. 36. *(Spokesman, The. Pamphlets. No. 57)*

LEGITIMACY OF GOVERNMENTS.

STEINBERG (JULIUS) 1940- . Locke, Rousseau, and the idea of consent; an inquiry into the liberal-democratic theory of political obligation. Westport, 1978. pp. 155. *bibliog.*

LEICESTER

— City planning.

LEICESTER. City Council, and LEICESTERSHIRE. County Council. Leicester and Leicestershire structure plan: written statement. Leicester, 1974. pp. 109. *Two maps in end pocket.*

LEICESTERSHIRE

— Economic policy.

LEICESTER. City Council, and LEICESTERSHIRE. County Council. Leicester and Leicestershire structure plan: written statement. Leicester, 1974. pp. 109. *Two maps in end pocket.*

— Social policy.

LEICESTER. City Council, and LEICESTERSHIRE. County Council. Leicester and Leicestershire structure plan: written statement. Leicester, 1974. pp. 109. *Two maps in end pocket.*

LEIDEN UNIVERSITY

— Libraries.

QUAESTIONES Leidenses: twelve studies on Leiden University Library and its holdings published on the occasion of the quater-centenary of the University; by Quaerendo. Leiden, 1975. pp. 227. *Published in English with contributions in French, accompanied by English summaries.*

LEISURE

— Belgium.

DU LAING (M.) and MARIVOET (M.) Situationele benadering van de werkende jongeren in Vlaanderen. Leuven, 1976. 2 vols. (in 1). *bibliog.*

— United Kingdom.

WEINBERGER (BARBARA) Leisure and the arts in Birmingham: a pilot investigation. [Birmingham, 1974]. pp. 106. *(Birmingham. University. Centre for Urban and Regional Studies. Research Memoranda. No.47)*

LEWES (FREDERICK MARTIN MEREDITH) and MENNELL (STEPHEN) Leisure, culture and local government: a study of policies and provision in Exeter. Exeter, [1976]. pp. 75.

LEISURE and the quality of life: the report of a central steering group of officials on four local experiments; [W.M. Fox, chairman] . London, H.M.S.O., 1977. 2 vols.(in 1).

LE MERCIER DE LA RIVIERE (PIERRE FRANÇOIS JOACHIM HENRI).

MAY (LOUIS PHILIPPE) Le Mercier de la Rivière, 1719-1801: aux origines de la science économique. Paris, [1975]. pp. 178. *bibliog.*

LENCINAS (JOSE NESTOR).

OLGUIN (DARDO) Lencinas, el caudillo radical: historia y mito. Mendoza, Argentine Republic, 1961. pp. 566.

LENIN (VLADIMIR IL'ICH).

ARISMENDI (RODNEY) El pensamiento de Lenin y la revolucion latinoamericana. [Montevideo, Comision de Propaganda del Partido Comunista, 1968]. pp. 45.

LIPSCHUTZ (ALEJANDRO) Marx y Lenin en la America Latina y los problemas indigenistas. La Habana, 1974. pp. 230.

STASOVA (ELENA DMITRIEVNA) Uchitel' i drug. Moskva, 1975. pp. 32.

INTERNATIONAL THEORETICAL CONFERENCE, 1976. Lenin's doctrine of imperialism and the contemporary stage of the general crisis of capitalism. Prague, 1976. pp. 109. *(Marxism-Leninism and Our Time)*

IROSHNIKOV (MIKHAIL PAVLOVICH) Vo glave Sovnarkoma: gosudarstvennaia deiatel'nost' V.I. Lenina v 1917-1922 gg. Leningrad, 1976. pp. 216. *(Akademiia Nauk SSSR. Seriia "Istoriia Nashei Rodiny")*

KOVALENKO (DMITRII ALEKSANDROVICH) Lenin i sotsialisticheskie preobrazovaniia v promyshlennosti Sovetskoi Rossii, 1917-1920 gg. Moskva, 1976. pp. 368. *bibliog.*

MOSKOVSKII GOSUDARSTVENNYI ISTORIKO-ARKHIVNYI INSTITUT. Trudy. t. 32. Tri sostavnye chasti marksizma v knige V.I. Lenina "Chto takoe "druz'ia naroda" i kak oni voiuiut protiv sotsial-demokratov?": istochniki, istoriografiia. Moskva, 1976. pp. 205.

HARDING (NEIL) Lenin's political thought. London, 1977 in progress. *bibliog.*

APPIGNANESI (RICHARD) and ZARATE (OSCAR) Lenin for beginners. [London, 1977]. pp. 176. *bibliog.*

BESANÇON (ALAIN) Les origines intellectuelles du léninisme. [Paris, 1977]. pp. 323. *bibliog.*

HEVESI (MARIA) Iz istorii kritiki filosofskikh dogm II Internatsionala. Moskva, 1977. pp. 207.

LENIN (VLADIMIR IL'ICH) Wladimir Iljitsch Lenin: Dokumente seines Lebens, 1870-1924.. .; ausgewählt und erläutert von Arnold Reisberg. Leipzig, 1977. 2 vols.

LENIN: dedicated Marxist or revolutionary pragmatist; edited with an introduction by Stanley W. Page. 2nd ed. St. Louis, Mo., [1977]. pp. 114. *bibliog.*

S Leninym vmeste: vospominaniia, dokumenty. 3rd ed. Petrozavodsk, 1977. pp. 430.

SHISHKIN (VALERII ALEKSANDROVICH) V.I. Lenin i vneshneekonomicheskaia politika Sovetskogo gosudarstva, 1917-1923 gg. Moskva, 1977. pp. 371.

CRISENOY (CHANTAL DE) Lénine face aux moujiks. Paris, [1978]. pp. 379. *bibliog.*

V.I. Lenin i "Soiuzy bor'by". Moskva, 1978. pp. 303. *bibliog.*

WESSON (ROBERT GALE) Lenin's legacy: the story of the CPSU. Stanford, [1978]. pp. 318. *bibliog. (Stanford University. Hoover Institution on War, Revolution and Peace. Hoover Institution Publications. 192)*

LENNEP.

See REMSCHEID.

LEOPOLD I, Emperor of Germany.

SPIELMAN (JOHN P.) Leopold I of Austria. London, [1977]. pp. 240. *bibliog.*

LEROUX (PIERRE) Socialist.

MIRECOURT (EUGENE DE) pseud. [i.e. Charles Jean Baptiste JACQUOT] Pierre Leroux. Paris, 1856. pp. 96. *(Les Contemporains) Bound with his Garibaldi, and other works.*

LE ROY LADURIE (EMMANUEL).

ARC, L': revue trimestrielle. 65. Le Roy Ladurie. Aix-en-Provence, [1976]. pp. 85. *bibliog.*

LESOTHO

— Politics and government.

BURMAN (SANDRA B.) The justice of the Queen's government: the Cape's administration of Basutoland, 1871-1884. Leiden, 1976. pp. 131. *bibliog.*

LEVITTOWN, PENNSYLVANIA

— Social conditions.

POPENOE (DAVID) The suburban environment: Sweden and the United States. Chicago, [1977]. pp. 275.

LEWIS (JOHN LLEWELLYN).

LEWIS (JOHN LLEWELLYN) Papers, 1879-1969. Madison, Wis., 1970. Microfilm: 4 reels. With printed guide to the microfilm edition.

LEWIS (JOHN LLEWELLYN) Papers of John L. Lewis: guide to a microfilm edition; edited by Eleanor Niermann. Madison, Wis., 1970. pp. 12. *bibliog. (State Historical Society of Wisconsin. Guides to Historical Resources)*

LIABILITY FOR ANIMALS

— New Zealand.

NEW ZEALAND. Torts and General Law Reform Committee. 1975. The law relating to liability for animals: report...presented to the Minister of Justice in September 1975; [I.L. McKay, chairman]. [Wellington], 1975. pp. 52.

LIAPUNOV FUNCTIONS.

ROUCHE (NICOLAS) and others. Stability theory by Liapunov's direct method. New York, [1977]. pp. 396. *bibliog.*

LIBEL AND SLANDER

— United Kingdom.

DUNCAN (COLIN) and NEILL (BRIAN) Defamation. London, 1978. pp. 219.

LIBELT (KAROL).

HISTORIA i wolność: studia z dziejów ideologii XIX wieku, etc. Warszawa, 1961. pp. 299. *(Polska Akademia Nauk. Instytut Filozofii i Socjologii. Archiwum Historii Filozofii i Myśli Społecznej. 7) With Russian or German summaries.*

LIBERAL PARTY

— Canada.

LAXER (JAMES) and LAXER (ROBERT M.) The Liberal idea of Canada: Pierre Trudeau and the question of Canada's survival. Toronto, 1977. pp. 234.

WHITAKER (REGINALD) The government party: organizing and financing the Liberal Party of Canada, 1930-58. Toronto, [1977]. pp. 507.

— Colombia.

ROBINSON (J.CORDELL) El movimiento gaitanista en Colombia, 1930-1948; traducido por Eddy Torres. Bogota, 1976. pp. 200. *bibliog.*

— Italy.

CORTESE (GUIDO) Concretezza liberale per il mezzogiorno. Firenze, 1975. pp. 228.

— Spain.

PARTIDO Liberal; [by] Enrique Larroque [and others]. Bilbao, 1977. pp. 143.

— United Kingdom.

[RICH (Sir HENRY)] Yes or no? London, J. Ridgway, 1852. pp. 13.

STEWART-SMITH (DUDLEY GEOFFREY) Not to be trusted: left wing extremism in the Labour and Liberal Parties. Richmond, Surrey, 1974. pp. 24.

CAVENDISH (RUPERT) Differences and similarities between radical liberalism and Plaid Cymru. Manchester, [1977]. pp. 15.

STEEL (DAVID) 1938- . Militant for the reasonable man; addresses...at the Brighton assembly, 1977. London, [1977]. pp. 23.

BANKS (DESMOND) Baron Banks. Your future with the Liberals: a summary of Liberal policies. London, [1978]. pp. 32.

PENROSE (BARRIE) and COURTIOUR (ROGER) The Pencourt file. London, 1978. pp. 423.

LIBERALISM.

LIBERALISM.

KAHN (JEAN FRANÇOIS) Complot contre la démocratie. [Paris, 1977]. pp. 235.

SALVADORI (MASSIMO L.) The liberal heresy: origins and historical development. London, 1977. pp. 248. *bibliog.*

SOCIETE DU MONT-PELERIN. Congrès, 1976. Le libéralisme?: de Karl Marx à Milton Friedman; (edited by) Jacques Riboud. Paris, 1977. pp. 224. *In French or English.*

WOLFE (ALAN) The limits of legitimacy: political contradictions of contemporary capitalism. New York, [1977]. pp. 432. *bibliog.*

HOWARD (MICHAEL ELIOT) War and the liberal. conscience. London, 1978. pp. 143. *(Cambridge. University. Trevelyan Lectures. 1977)*

MIDDENDORP (C.P.) Progressiveness and conservatism: the fundamental dimensions of ideological controversy and their relationship to social class. The Hague, [1978]. pp. 457. *bibliog.*

MOREAU (PIERRE FRANÇOIS) Les racines du libéralisme: une anthologie. Paris, [1978]. pp. 186. *bibliog.*

— Brazil.

VIANNA (LUIZ WERNECK) Liberalismo e sindicato no Brasil. Rio de Janeiro, 1976. pp. 288.

— Europe.

STEED (MICHAEL) Who's a liberal in Europe?. Manchester, [1975?]. pp. 25.

— Italy.

CANTALUPO (ROBERTO) Liberale a destra: a destra da liberale: lettera aperta. Roma, [1975]. pp. 215.

FRANCHINI (RAFFAELLO) Il dissenso liberale: politica e cultura. Firenze, [1975]. pp. 241.

LALLA (MANLIO DI) Liberalismo e postfascismo. Roma, [1975]. pp. 291.

LALLA (MANLIO DI) Storia del liberalismo italiano dal risorgimento al fascismo. Bologna, [1976]. pp. 341. *bibliogs. (Fondazione Luigi Einaudi. Il Liberalismo nel Mondo. 23)*

MURA (VIRGILIO) Cattolici e liberali nell'età giolittiana: il dibattito sulla toleranza. [Bari, 1976]. pp. 271.

— United Kingdom.

FREEDEN (MICHAEL) The new liberalism: an ideology of social reform. Oxford, 1978. pp. 291. *bibliog.*

— United States.

PINE (R. DEAN) Beginning the third century: the liberal-led march to communism. New York, [1977]. pp. 68.

McAULIFFE (MARY SPERLING) Crisis on the left: cold war politics and American liberals, 1947-1954. Amherst, 1978. pp. 204. *bibliog.*

LIBERALISM (RELIGION)

— Protestant churches.

LIBERAL Protestantism: what is it?; by J.W. London, 1876. pp. 15.

LIBERIA

— Statistics.

QUARTERLY STATISTICAL BULLETIN OF LIBERIA; ([pd. by] Republic of Liberia Ministry of Planning and Economic Affairs). q., D 1970 (no.3, covering 1st and 2nd quarters 1970)- Monrovia. *Each issue contains statistics for earlier years.*

LIBERTY.

DEVALDES (MANUEL) pseud. [i.e. Ernest LOHY]. L'éducation et la liberté. Bruxelles, 1958. pp. 21. *Last page signed and dated 1900.*

LIBERAL LIBERTY LEAGUE. Declaration of principle. London, [1944?]. pp. (4).

IVENS (MICHAEL WILLIAM) and DUNSTAN (REGINALD ERNEST) eds. Freedom quotes. London, [1976]. pp. 45.

DICKINSON (H.T.) Liberty and property: political ideology in eighteenth-century Britain. London, [1977]. pp. 369.

KAHN (JEAN FRANÇOIS) Complot contre la démocratie. [Paris, 1977]. pp. 235.

LONG (DOUGLAS G.) Bentham on liberty: Jeremy Bentham's idea of liberty in relation to his utilitarianism. Toronto, [1977]. pp. 294. *bibliog.*

FRIEDMAN (DAVID) The machinery of freedom: guide to a radical capitalism. New Rochelle, [1978]. pp. 240. *bibliog.*

IN defence of freedom; edited by Dr. K.W. Watkins; essays by Winston S. Churchill, M.P. [and others]. London, 1978. pp. 180.

LIBERTY OF CONSCIENCE.

MELVILLE (DAVID) The conscience clause: its meaning, its authority, its use. London, Rivingtons, 1865. pp. 30.

LIBERTY OF SPEECH.

TUSSMAN (JOSEPH) Government and the mind. New York, 1977. pp. 175.

— United Kingdom.

FREEDOM of speech in tertiary education;...background papers [for] a conference...held in...London...[in] 1974. 1974. pp. 58. *Unpublished: typescript.*

LIBERTY OF THE PRESS.

LAMBRICHS (NATHALIE) La liberté de la presse en l'an IV: les journaux républicains. Paris, [1976]. pp. 112. *bibliog. (Paris. Université de Paris II. Travaux et Recherches. Série Sciences Historiques. 11)*

— Argentine Republic.

LIBRO azul y blanco de la prensa argentina; por cincuenta y tres periodistas argentinos. Buenos Aires, 1951. pp. 439.

MIRI (HECTOR F.) Yrigoyen, Peron, Frondizi y el cuarto poder. Buenos Aires, 1959. pp. 111.

— Canada — Quebec.

QUEBEC (PROVINCE). Assemblée Nationale. Commission Parlementaire Spéciale sur les Problèmes de la Liberté de Presse. 1973-75. La liberté de presse au Québec; [François Cloutier, président]. [Québec, 1973-75]. 5 vols. (in 2).

— France.

BESSON (ALAIN) La presse locale en liberté surveillée: diagnostic et propositions pour les journaux de province. Paris, [1977]. pp. 256.

HAMON (HERVE) and ROTMAN (PATRICK) L'affaire Alata. Paris, [1977]. pp. 106.

DAVILLE (DENIS PERIER) La liberté de la presse n'est pas à vendre. Paris, [1978]. pp. 254.

— United Kingdom.

PROSECUTION of the war with Russia, and liberty of the press: a bill for the more effectual prosecution of the war...and for other purposes. [London], 1855. pp. 5.

WHITEHORN (KATHARINE) Whose news? London, [1978]. pp. 16. *(Unservile State Group. Unservile State Papers. No. 23)*

LIBRARIES

— Canada — British Columbia.

BRITISH COLUMBIA. Committee on Library Development. 1971. A proposal for province-wide organization of library services in British Columbia; [Daphne Parr, chairman]. Victoria, 1971. pp. 50.

— New Zealand.

NEW ZEALAND. Department of Statistics. 1976. Census of libraries, 1974. Wellington, 1976. pp. 67.

— Sabah.

SABAH STATE LIBRARY. Annual report. a., Current issue only. Kota Kinabalu. *[in English and Malay].*

— United Kingdom.

O'KELLY (JOSS) The political role of public libraries. Brighton, 1977. pp. 15.

— — Directories.

KNOCK (ANN) compiler. Library resources in psychology: a directory of libraries in the Greater London area with a specialist interest in psychology, etc. London, 1974. pp. 16. *(London. University. Birkbeck College. Library. Publications. No. 47)*

The LIBRARIES, museums and art galleries yearbook 1976; editors: Adrian Brink and Derry Watkins. Cambridge, 1976. pp. 254.

— — Special collections.

LONDON. University. School of Oriental and African Studies. Library. Papers relating to the Chinese maritime customs, 1860-1943, in the library of the School of Oriental and African Studies. London, 1973. pp. 13.

KNOCK (ANN) compiler. Library resources in psychology: a directory of libraries in the Greater London area with a specialist interest in psychology, etc. London, 1974. pp. 16. *(London. University. Birkbeck College. Library. Publications. No. 47)*

LIBRARIES, PRIVATE

— United States.

WRIGHT (LOUIS BOOKER) Of books and men. Columbia, S.C., [1976]. pp. 179.

LIBRARIES, UNIVERSITY AND COLLEGE

— United Kingdom.

LONDON. University. London School of Economics and Political Science. British Library of Political and Economic Science. Outline of the resources of the library. 3rd ed. London, 1976. pp. 43.

NATIONAL BOOK LEAGUE. Conference, London, 1975. Books and undergraduates; proceedings...; edited by Peter H. Mann. London, 1976. pp. 132.

COPING with cuts: proceedings of a conference (to examine the problems facing academic libraries in the late 1970's) held at Holborn Library 13 July 1977. [London, 1977]. pp. 98.

HINDLE (ANTHONY) Developing an acquisitions system for a university library. London, 1977. pp. 45. *(British Library. Research and Development Department. Reports. 5351)*

NATIONAL BOOK LEAGUE. University library expenditure 1969-1975: results of a six-year survey. [London], 1977. pp. 20.

LIBRARIES AND PUBLISHING.

FRY (BERNARD MITCHELL) and WHITE (HERBERT S.) Publishers and libraries: a study of scholarly and research journals. Lexington, Mass., [1976]. pp. 166. *bibliog.*

LIBRARIES AND STUDENTS.

NATIONAL BOOK LEAGUE. Conference, London, 1975. Books and undergraduates; proceedings...; edited by Peter H. Mann. London, 1976. pp. 132.

LIBRARY FINANCE

— United Kingdom.

NATIONAL BOOK LEAGUE. University library expenditure 1969-1975: results of a six-year survey. [London], 1977. pp. 20.

LIBYA

— Politics and government.

EL FATHALY (OMAR I.) and others. Political development and bureaucracy in Libya. Lexington, Mass., [1977]. pp. 122.

— Statistics.

LIBYA. Census and Statistical Department. Quarterly bulletin of statistics. q., Ja/Mr 1970 [no.1?]- [Tripoli]. *[in English and Arabic].*

LICENCES

— India.

SATYANARAYANA (Y.) Impact of G[overnment] o[f] I[ndia]'s liberalised licencing policy on industrial output. New Delhi, 1972. pp. 97. *(United States. Agency for International Development. USAID-New Delhi. Economic Affairs Division. Staff Papers)*

LIEBKNECHT (WILHELM PHILIPP MARTIN CHRISTIAN LUDWIG).

150 Jahre Wilhelm Liebknecht, 29. März 1826, Giessen; herausgegeben von der Wilhelm-Liebknecht-Gesellschaft, Giessen. Frankfurt am Main, 1976. pp. 59.

LIFE IMPRISONMENT

— Germany.

ALBRECHT (PETER ALEXIS) Zur sozialen Situation entlassener "Lebenslänglicher". Göttingen, [1977]. pp. 449. *bibliog.*

LIFE SPAN, PRODUCTIVE.

NEW ZEALAND. Department of Statistics. 1970. New Zealand tables of male working life, 1966. Wellington, [1970?]. pp. 8. *(Monthly abstract of statistics. Special supplement, [ ])*

LIGUE DE LA PATRIE FRANÇAISE.

RIOUX (JEAN PIERRE) Nationalisme et conservatisme: la Ligue de la Patrie Française, 1899-1904. Paris, [1977]. pp. 120.

LIMOUSIN

— Economic conditions.

LIMOUSIN. Préfecture. 1976. Le Limousin et ses institutions régionales. Limoges, 1976. pp. 67.

— Executive departments.

LIMOUSIN. Préfecture. 1976. Le Limousin et ses institutions régionales. Limoges, 1976. pp. 67.

— Social conditions.

LIMOUSIN. Préfecture. 1976. Le Limousin et ses institutions régionales. Limoges, 1976. pp. 67.

LINCOLN (ABRAHAM) President of the United States.

SCHLUETER (HERMANN) Lincoln, labor and slavery: a chapter from the social history of America. New York, 1913. pp. 237.

OATES (STEPHEN B.) With malice toward none: the life of Abraham Lincoln. London, 1978. pp. 492.

LINCOLNSHIRE

— Religion.

OBELKEVICH (JAMES) Religion and rural society: South Lindsey 1825-1875. Oxford, 1976. pp. 353. *bibliog.*

LINEAR PROGRAMMING.

FRYER (M.J.) An introduction to linear programming and matrix game theory. London, 1978. pp. 121.

LINEN

— Poland.

KULCZYKOWSKI (MARIUSZ) Andrychowski ośrodek płócienniczy w XVIII i XIX wieku. Wrocław, 1972. pp. 238. *bibliog. (Polska Akademia Nauk. Oddział w Krakowie. Komisja Nauk Historycznych. Prace. nr.31) With French and Russian summaries.*

LINGUISTIC ANALYSIS (LINGUISTICS).

TESTING linguistic hypotheses; edited by David Cohen and Jessica R. Wirth. Washington D.C., [1975]. pp. 228. *Papers from a symposium held at the University of Wisconsin-Milwaukee, May 10-11, 1974.*

LINGUISTIC CHANGE.

BARON (NAOMI S.) Language acquisition and historical change. Amsterdam, 1977. pp. 320. *bibliog.*

LINGUISTIC GEOGRAPHY.

BRETON (ROLAND J.L.) Géographie des langues. [Paris, 1976]. pp. 128. *bibliog.*

LINGUISTICS.

ASSESSING linguistic arguments; edited by Jessica R. Wirth. Washington D.C., [1976]. pp. 280. *Papers from a symposium held at the University of Wisconsin-Milwaukee, May 9-10, 1975.*

CURRENT themes in linguistics: bilingualism, experimental linguistics, and language typologies; edited by Fred R. Eckman. Washington, D.C., [1977]. pp. 277. *Papers from a symposium held at the University of Wisconsin-Milwaukee, March 26-28, 1976.*

FORMAL syntax; edited by Peter W. Culicover [and others]. New York, 1977. pp. 500. *bibliog. Proceedings of a conference held by the Mathematics Social Science Board in Newport Beach, California, in 1976.*

INTERNATIONAL CONGRESS OF LOGIC, METHODOLOGY AND PHILOSOPHY OF SCIENCE, 5TH, LONDON, ONTARIO, 1975. Basic problems in methodology and linguistics: part three of the proceedings...; edited by Robert E. Butts and Jaakko Hintikka. Dordrecht, [1977]. pp. 321. *bibliogs. (Western Ontario. University. University of Western Ontario Series in Philosophy of Science. 11)*

LINGUISTIC INSTITUTE, UNIVERSITY OF SOUTH FLORIDA, 1975. Current issues in linguistic theory; edited by Roger W. Cole. Bloomington, Ind., [1977]. pp. 303. *bibliogs.*

— Bibliography.

GAZDAR (GERALD) and others, compilers. A bibliography of contemporary linguistic research. New York, 1978. pp. 425.

LIQUOR PROBLEM

— Canada — Saskatchewan.

DEWAR (ROBERT) M.A., Psychologist, and SOMMER (ROBERT) The consumption of alcohol in a Saskatchewan community before and after the opening of a new liquor outlet. Regina, Bureau on Alcoholism, Department of Social Welfare and Rehabilitation, 1962. pp. 59. *bibliog.*

LITERARY FORGERIES.

TREVOR-ROPER (HUGH REDWALD) Hermit of Peking: the hidden life of Sir Edmund Backhouse. [rev. ed.] Harmondsworth, 1978. pp. 391. *First published in 1976 under title A hidden life: the enigma of Sir Edmund Backhouse.*

LITERATURE.

GONZALEZ (MICHAEL) Cambio de piel, or the myth of literature. Glasgow, [1974]. pp. 13. *(Glasgow. University. Institute of Latin American Studies. Occasional Papers. No. 10)*

— History and criticism.

GRAMSCI (ANTONIO) Letteratura e vita nazionale. Torino, 1972 repr. 1974. pp. 400. *bibliog. (Quaderni del Carcere. 5)*

SOCIOLOGICAL REVIEW, THE; [published by] University of Keele. Monographs. [No.] 26. The sociology of literature: applied studies; issue editor, Diana Laurenson. Keele, 1978. pp. 283.

LITERATURE AND POLITICS.

SPENDER (STEPHEN) The thirties and after: poetry, politics, people, 1933-75. Glasgow, 1978. pp. 286.

LITERATURE AND REVOLUTIONS.

MEHLMAN (JEFFREY) Revolution and repetition: Marx, Hugo, Balzac. Berkeley, Calif., [1977]. pp. 132.

LITERATURE AND SOCIETY.

ZERAFFA (MICHEL) Fictions: the novel and social reality; translated by Catherine Burns and Tom Burns. [Harmondsworth, 1976]. pp. 153.

BERGER (MORROE) Real and imagined worlds: the novel and social science. Cambridge, Mass., 1977. pp. 303. *bibliog.*

ORR (JOHN M.) B.Sc. Ph.D. Tragic realism and modern society: studies in the sociology of the modern novel. London, 1977. pp. 202.

SOCIOLOGICAL REVIEW, THE; [published by] University of Keele. Monographs. [No.] 25. The sociology of literature: theoretical approaches; issue editors, Jane Routh and Janet Wolff. Keele, 1977. pp. 180. *bibliogs.*

LOUGH (JOHN) Writer and public in France: from the middle ages to the present day. Oxford, 1978. pp. 435. *bibliog.*

SOCIOLOGICAL REVIEW, THE; [published by] University of Keele. Monographs. [No.] 26. The sociology of literature: applied studies; issue editor, Diana Laurenson. Keele, 1978. pp. 283.

LITHUANIA

— Nationalism.

LITHUANIAN CANADIAN COMMUNITY. The violations of human rights in Soviet occupied Lithuania: a report for 1974. [Toronto], 1975. pp. 112.

LITHUANIAN AMERICANS.

GREENE (VICTOR R.) For God and country: the rise of Polish and Lithuanian ethnic consciousness in America, 1860-1910. Madison, Wis., 1975. pp. 202. *bibliog.*

LITTER (TRASH)

— South Africa.

SOUTH AFRICA. Parliament. House of Assembly. Select Committee on the Disposal of Containers Bill. 1977. Report...proceedings and evidence (S.C.14-1977). in SOUTH AFRICA. Parliament. House of Assembly. Select Committee reports.

LITTLE ENTENTE, 1920-1939.

IORDACHE (NICOLAE) La Petite Entente et l'Europe. Genève, 1977. pp. 397. *bibliog. (Geneva. Graduate Institute of International Studies. Publications. No. 52)*

LIVERPOOL

LIVERPOOL
— Social conditions.
WILSON (HUGH) AND WOMERSLEY (LEWIS) Firm. Inner area study: Liverpool: social area analysis. [London], Department of the Environment, [1977]. pp. 71.

— Social policy.
BATLEY (RICHARD) and others. An evaluation of two neighbourhood schems in Liverpool and Teesside. Leeds, [1975?]. fo. 96. (Centre for Environmental Studies. Working Papers)

LIVERPOOL UNIVERSITY.
SAVILLE (JOHN) The Wakstein case at the University of Liverpool. London, [1973]. pp. 12.

LIVINGSTONE (DAVID).
COLE-KING (P.A.) The Livingstone search expedition, 1867. Zomba, 1968. pp. 12. bibliog. (Malawi. Department of Antiquities. Publications. No. 2)

LOANS, FOREIGN.
INTERNATIONAL BANK FOR RECONSTRUCTION AND DEVELOPMENT. Sector Policy Papers. Urban transport. [Washington], 1975. pp. 103.

— America, Latin.
DEWITT (R. PETER) The Inter-American Development Bank and political influence, with special reference to Costa Rica. New York, 1977. pp. 197. bibliog.

LOBBYING
— Law and legislation — United States.
EASTMAN (HOPE) Lobbying: a constitutionally protected right. Washington, D.C., [1977]. pp. 35. (American Enterprise Institute for Public Policy Research. Studies in Legal Policy)

— United States.
BERRY (JEFFREY M.) Lobbying for the people: the political behavior of public interest groups. Princeton, [1977]. pp. 311. bibliog.

GREENWALD (CAROL SCHIRO) Group power: lobbying and public policy. New York, 1977. pp. 372. bibliog.

LOCAL ELECTIONS
— Germany.
DOLIVE (LINDA L.) Electoral politics at the local level in the German Federal Republic. Gainesville, 1976. pp. 110. bibliog. (Florida University. Monographs. Social Sciences. No. 56)

HORN (WOLFGANG) and KUEHR (HERBERT) Kandidaten im Wahlkampf: Kandidatenauslese, Wahlkampf und lokale Presse 1975 in Essen. Meisenheim am Glan, 1978. pp. 321. bibliog.

— United Kingdom.
CLARK (DAVID M.) Battle for the counties: guide to the county council elections May 1977. Newcastle, 1977. pp. 100. bibliog.

— — Ireland, Northern.
ELLIOTT (S.) and SMITH (F.J.) The Northern Ireland local government elections of 1977: results and transfer analysis. Belfast, 1977. pp. 182.

— — Scotland.
BOCHEL (J.M.) and DENVER (D.T.) The Scottish district elections 1977: results and statistics. Dundee, 1977. pp. 96.

LOCAL FINANCE
— Austria.
OESTERREICHISCHER WIRTSCHAFTSBUND. Kommunale Finanzpolitik: Finanzplanung, Verschuldung, Kontrolle. Wien, 1973. pp. 52. (Informationen. IWB 9)

— Canada — Ontario.
AULD (D.A.L.) Fiscal knowledge and preferences in Ontario. Toronto, 1977. 1 vol. (various pagings). (Ontario. Economic Council. Working Papers. 1977. No. 2)

KITCHEN (HARRY M.) Public finance in metropolitan Toronto: a study for the Royal Commission on Metropolitan Toronto. [Toronto], 1977. pp. 247. bibliog.

— Colombia.
COLOMBIA. Contraloria General. Direccion de Analisis Financiero y Estadistica. Estadistica fiscal del estado. a., 1976- Bogota. In 3 pts.

— Finland.
FINLAND. Tilastokeskus. Kuntien talous. a., 1973- Helsinki. [in Finnish and Swedish with English summary and table headings].

— Germany.
GERMANY (BUNDESREPUBLIK). Statistisches Bundesamt. Jahresabschlüsse: Kommunalfinanzen. a., 1959-1973, with gap (1962). Wiesbaden. (Finanzen und Steuern. Reihe 1.2) Superseded by GERMANY (BUNDESREPUBLIK). Statistisches Bundesamt. Rechnungsergebnisse der kommunalen Haushalte.

GERMANY (BUNDESREPUBLIK). Statistisches Bundesamt. Rechnungsergebnisse der kommunalen Haushalte. a., 1974- Wiesbaden. (Finanzen und Steuern. Reihe 3.3) Supersedes GERMANY (BUNDESREPUBLIK). Statistisches Bundesamt. Jahresabschlüsse: Kommunalfinanzen.

— Ireland (Republic).
EIRE. Department of Local Government. Local authority estimates...with provisional outturn figures. a., 1977- Dublin.

— Netherlands.
NETHERLANDS. Werkgroep Middellange Termijnplanning Provincies [en] Gemeenten. 1976. Rapport; [J. Mulder, voorzitter]. 's-Gravenhage, 1976. pp. 67. bibliog.

— New Zealand.
NEW ZEALAND. Local Authority Finance Committee. 1977. Local authority finance in New Zealand: report; [Sir Patrick O'Dea, chairman]. [Wellington], 1977. pp. 60.

— Poland.
PAWLIK (JAN) Wydatki rad narodowych na usługi socjalno-bytowe na terenach o różnym charakterze gospodarczym i o różnym tempie rozwoju gospodarczego na przykładzie Województwa Krakowskiego. Kraków, 1964. pp. 199. bibliog. (Zeszyty Naukowe Uniwersytetu Jagiellońskiego. Prace Prąwnicze. zeszyt 16) With English and Russian summaries.

— South Africa.
REINACH (S.C.) The effects of existing methods of property valuation and taxation on the ratepayer. Port Elizabeth, 1974. pp. 22. bibliog. (University of Port Elizabeth. Institute for Planning Research. Special Publications. No. 4)

— United Kingdom.
COSTELLO (BRIAN) Local rates: a viable alternative. London, [1977]. pp. 4.

HOPPÉ (MALCOLM) Is the party really over?: why rates rise in the North East. London, [1977]. pp. 11.

O'CLEIREACAIN (CAROL CHAPMAN) The determinants of local government expenditure in English and Welsh county boroughs, 1971. 1977. fo. 288. bibliog. Typescript. Ph.D. (London) thesis: unpublished. This thesis is the property of London University and may not be removed from the Library.

FREEMAN (ROLAND) The rates riddle. London, [1978]. pp. 20.

HEPWORTH (NOEL PEERS) The finance of local government. 4th ed. London, 1978. pp. 320. bibliog.

MINNS (RICHARD) and THORNLEY (JENNIFER) State shareholding: the role of local and regional authorities. London, 1978. pp. 159.

— — Isle of Man.
ISLE OF MAN. Commission on the Financial Relations between the Isle of Man Revenue and the Local Authorities and Public Services. 1931. Report; [R.D. Farrant, chairman]. [Douglas, 1931]. pp. 22.

— — Scotland — Accounting.
SCOTLAND. Accounts Commission. 1976. First report of the Commission for Local Authority Accounts in Scotland. Edinburgh, 1976. pp. 21.

— — Wales.
WELSH LOCAL GOVERNMENT FINANCIAL STATISTICS; [pd. by] Welsh Office. a., 1977(no. 1)- Cardiff. Data on Welsh local government financial statistics also available in LOCAL GOVERNMENT FINANCIAL STATISTICS, ENGLAND AND WALES.

LOCAL GOVERNMENT
— Economic aspects — United Kingdom.
GEARY (K.) Local authority resource allocation with multiple objectives: an education example. London, 1977. pp. 71. bibliog. (Planning Research Applications Group. PRAG Technical Papers. TP 21)

— Africa, West.
CAMERON (IAN DONALD) and COOPER (BASIL KEITH) The west African councillor. 2nd ed. London, 1961. pp. 224.

— Australia.
BOWMAN (MARGARET) Local government in the Australian states. Canberra, 1976. pp. 106. (Australia. Department of Environment, Housing and Community Development. Urban Papers)

— — New South Wales.
LARCOMBE (FREDERICK ARTHUR) The stabilization of local government in New South Wales, 1858- 1906. Sydney, 1976. pp. 339. bibliog. (A history of local government in New South Wales. vol.2)

— Austria.
OESTERREICHISCHER GEMEINDEBUND. Prise de position de l'Association des pouvoirs locaux autrichiens en face du questionnaire sur les réformes de la collectivité territoriale et sur la planification dans les différents pays d'Europe. Wien, [196-?]. fo.16.

— Canada — Alberta.
ALBERTA. Department of Business Development and Tourism. Northern Development Branch. 1977. Local government structure and organization in northern Alberta. [Edmonton], 1977. fo. 69.

— — British Columbia.
BRITISH COLUMBIA. Department of Municipal Affairs. 1973. Statistics relating to regional and municipal governments in British Columbia. [Victoria], 1973. pp. 67.

— — Nova Scotia.
NOVA SCOTIA. Department of Municipal Affairs. Annual report. a., 1973/74(1st)- Halifax.

— **European Economic Community countries.**

HULL (CHRIS) and RHODES (R.A.W.) Inter-governmental relations in the European Community. Westmead, Hants., [1977]. pp. 87. *bibliog.*

— **France.**

COUNCIL OF EUROPEAN MUNICIPALITIES. French Section. La réforme communale en France. [Paris?], 1968. pp. 16.

GREMION (PIERRE) Le pouvoir périphérique: bureaucrates et notables dans le système politique français. Paris, [1976]. pp. 478. *bibliog.*

CITOYEN dans sa commune: propositions municipales socialistes. Paris, [1977]. pp. 159.

FRANC (MICHEL) and LECLERC (JEAN PIERRE) Les institutions de la région parisienne: du district à l'Ile-de-France. [n.p., 1977]. pp. 191. *bibliog.*

— **Germany.**

KOMMUNALPOLITIK und Sozialdemokratie: der Beitrag des demokratischen Sozialismus zur kommunalen Selbstverwaltung; ([edited by] Karl-Heinz Nassmacher). Bonn-Bad Godesberg, [1977]. pp. 256.

— — **Ruhr.**

HERLEMANN (BEATRIX) Kommunalpolitik der KPD im Ruhrgebiet, 1924-1933. Wuppertal, [1977]. pp. 339. *bibliog.*

— **Ghana.**

NTI (JAMES) Local administration in Ghana: an analytical survey of administrative reform reports made in Ghana from 1950-1971. 1976 [or rather 1977]. fo. 271. *bibliog. Typescript. Ph.D. (London) thesis: unpublished. This thesis is the property of London University and may not be removed from the Library.*

— **Italy.**

COUNCIL OF EUROPEAN MUNICIPALITIES. Italian Section. Conseil de l'Europe...: Conférence européenne des pouvoirs locaux...: note redigée par la section italienne...en réponse au questionnaire concernant l'adaptation des structures locales à l'unification européenne. Roma, [1969?]. pp. 9.

ALTERNATIVA ed elementi di socialismo nelle comunità locali; scritti di [Ernesto] Bettinelli [and others]: a cura di Ernesto Bettinelli ed Emilio Renzi. [Milano, 1976]. pp. 152. *Based on a conference organised by Azione e Ricerca per l'Alternativa, in Pavia, 1975.*

ROTELLI (ETTORE) L'alternativa delle autonomie: istituzioni locali e tendenze politiche dell'Italia moderna. Milano, 1978. pp. 340.

— **Kenya.**

JOURNAL OF THE KENYA INSTITUTE OF ADMINISTRATION, THE. irreg., D 1965 (no.1)- Lower Kabete. *no.1 entitled Administration in Kenya.*

— **Netherlands.**

ANTI-REVOLUTIONAIRE PARTIJ. College van Advies, and VERBAND VAN VERENIGINGEN VAN ANTIREVOLUTIONAIRE GEMEENTE- EN PROVINCIEBESTUURDERS. Bestuurlijke vormgeving: preadvies van een werkgroep...voor de openbare partijconferentie op 13 oktober 1969. 's-Gravenhage, [1969]. pp. 36.

— **New Zealand.**

NEW ZEALAND. Local Government Commission. 1977- . [Establishment of regional government]: provisional scheme[s] and explanatory statement[s]. [Wellington, 1977 in progress].

NEW ZEALAND. Local Government Commission. 1978. Nelson region: decision on objections to provisional regional scheme. [Wellington], 1978. fo. 27.

— **Nigeria.**

NIGERIA (WESTERN STATE). 1971. Proposals for the reorganisation of local government councils in the Western State of Nigeria. [Ibadan], 1971. pp. 26. *(Official Documents. 1971. No. 4)*

— **Poland.**

GEBERT (STANISŁAW) and HATTOWSKI (TADEUSZ) Komisje rad narodowych podstawy prawne i zadania. Warszawa, 1957. pp. 140.

RADY narodowe i terenowe organy administracji po reformach; praca zbiorowa pod redakcją Zbigniewa Leońskiego. Warszawa, 1976. pp. 169.

GŁOWACKI (SŁAWOMIR) Terenowe organy a gospodarka narodowa: zagadnienia prawne organizacji i kierowania. Wrocław, 1977. pp. 260. *bibliog.*

TERENOWE organy administracji i rady narodowe po reformie; redaktor naukowy Jerzy Słu'zewski. Warszawa, 1977. pp. 432.

— **Rhodesia.**

PROJECTS AND PEOPLE: community development and local government in Rhodesia; (pd. by the Branch of Community Development Training [Rhodesia]. 2 a yr., Ja 1971 (no.1)- Salisbury.

— **Russia.**

SOVERSHENSTVOVANIE raboty Sovetov v sovremennykh usloviiakh. Moskva, 1976. pp. 116.

KORENEVSKAIA (ELENA IGNAT'EVNA) Mestnye Sovety i sotsial'noe planirovanie. Moskva, 1977. pp. 104.

— **Spain.**

DURAN (JOSE A.) Historia de caciques, bandos e ideologias en la Galicia no urbana: Rianxo 1910-1914. Madrid, 1972. pp. 387.

— **Switzerland.**

BASSAND (MICHEL) and FRAGNIERE (JEAN PIERRE) Les ambiguités de la démocratie locale: la structure du pouvoir de deux villes jurassiennes. [n.p.], 1976]. pp. 166. *bibliog.*

— **Thailand.**

BUNNAG (TEJ) The provincial administration of Siam, 1892-1915: the Ministry of the Interior under Prince Damrong Rajanubhab. Kuala Lumpur, 1977. pp. 322. *bibliog.*

— **United Kingdom.**

LOCAL AUTHORITIES MANAGEMENT SERVICES AND COMPUTER COMMITTEE. Computer Panel. Census analysis. London, 1974. pp. 30.

BAYLY (RICHARD) and SWAIN (ANNE) Local authorities and building for sale: a handbook on local authority involvement in the provision of new housing for owner- occupiers. [London], Department of the Environment, 1977. pp. 42. *(HDD Occasional Papers. 77/1)*

COCKBURN (CYNTHIA) The local state: management of cities and people. London, 1977, repr. 1978. pp. 207.

GRANT (WYN P.) Independent local politics in England and Wales. Farnborough, Hants., [1977]. pp. 112.

GRANT (WYN P.) The role perceptions of rural councillors: a study of two non- metropolitan districts. [Coventry], 1977. pp. 24. *(University of Warwick. Department of Politics. Working Papers. No. 12)*

MURGATROYD (STEPHEN J.) and others. Taking local decisions: the democratic reform of the Labour Party and local government. Leeds, [1977]. pp. 56. *bibliog.*

BAKER (JOHN) of the Association for Neighbourhood Councils. The neighbourhood advice centre: a community project in Camden. London, 1978. pp. 310. *bibliog.*

CROSS (MARTIN) and MALLEN (DAVID) Local government and politics. [London, 1978]. pp. 144. *bibliog. (Politics Association. Political Realities)*

HAMBLETON (ROBIN) Policy planning and local government. London, 1978. pp. 268.

KEITH-LUCAS (BRYAN) and RICHARDS (PETER GODFREY) A history of local government in the twentieth century. London, 1978. pp. 266. *bibliog.*

RICHARDS (PETER GODFREY) The reformed local government system. 3rd. rev. ed. London, 1978. pp. 192. *bibliog.*

— — **Bibliography.**

SHELLEY (IVOR D.) British works on public administration since 1963. London, 1971. 2 pts. *(Extracted from British Book News, May and July, 1971)*

— — **Information services — Bibliography.**

SCOTT (GAY) compiler. Information for members. 2nd ed. London, 1976. pp. 9. *(London. Greater London Council. Research Library. Research Bibliographies. No. 64)*

— — **Isle of Man.**

ISLE OF MAN. Local Government Districts (Administration) Commission. 1963. Final report; [B.W. Macpherson, chairman]. [Douglas], 1963. pp. 25, 2 maps.

ISLE OF MAN. Local Government Districts (Administration) Commission. 1963. Interim report; [B.W. Macpherson, chairman]. [Douglas], 1963. pp. 30.

— — **Scotland.**

PLANNING EXCHANGE. Newsheets. 1. The new structure of local government in Scotland. [Glasgow, 1975]. pp. 32.

YOUNG (RONALD GEORGE) The search for democracy: a guide to and polemic about Scottish local government. [Milngavie, 1977]. pp. 135. *bibliog.*

— **United States.**

AMICK (GEORGE) The American way of graft: a study of corruption in state and local government, how it happens, and what can be done about it. Princeton, [1976]. pp. 245.

KAPLAN (SAMUEL) The dream deferred: people, politics and planning in suburbia. New York, 1977. pp. 242. *bibliog.*

MAGAZINE (ALAN H.) Environmental management in local government: a study of local response to federal mandate. New York, 1977. pp. 148. *bibliog.*

RODGERS (JOSEPH LEE) Citizen committees: a guide to their use in local government. Cambridge, Mass., [1977]. pp. 101. *bibliog.*

HAMBLETON (ROBIN) Policy planning and local government. London, 1978. pp. 268.

— **Yugoslavia.**

RADUSINOVIĆ (MILENKO) The commune in the Yugoslav socio-economic system. Beograd, 1965. pp. 37.

LOCAL GOVERNMENT OFFICIALS AND EMPLOYEES

— **Caribbean Area.**

PUBLIC SERVICES INTERNATIONAL. Regional Meeting for the Caribbean Area, Bridgetown, Barbados, 1966. Report of proceedings. London, [1966?]. pp. 74.

— **Pakistan.**

PAKISTAN. Basic Democracies Wing. Planning and Evaluation Unit. 1970. Training for local councils. [Karachi, 1970]. pp. 54.

LOCAL GOVERNMENT OFFICIALS AND EMPLOYEES(Cont.)

— United Kingdom.

U.K. Committee of Inquiry into the System of Remuneration of Members of Local Authorities. 1977. Remuneration of councillors. Vol. 2. The surveys of councillors and local authorities. London, 1977. pp. 65. *Vol. 1 published as British Parliamentary Paper Cmnd. 7010, 1977.*

POOLE (K.P.) The local government service in England and Wales. London, [1978]. pp. 245. *bibliog.*

— United States.

CHUTE (CHARLTON F.) Modern ideas for administrative assistants to the Mayor in large American cities. Detroit, 1971. pp. 63. *(Citizens' Research Council of Michigan. Memoranda. No. 220)*

LOCAL TAXATION

— United States.

MACMANUS (SUSAN A.) Revenue patterns in U.S. cities and suburbs: a comparative analysis. New York, 1978. pp. 265. *bibliog.*

METROPOLITAN financing and growth management policies: principles and practice; edited by George F. Break. Madison, 1978. pp. 329. *bibliogs. (Committee on Taxation. Resources and Economic Development. Publications. 9) Proceedings of a symposium sponsored by the Committee at the University of Wisconsin, Madison, 1974, part of the Thirteenth Annual Conference of the Committee.*

LOCAL TRANSIT.

COORDINACION o destruccion: el problema del transporte urbano de pasajeros en la ciudad de Buenos Aires. [Buenos Aires, 1936]. pp. 290.

— Australia.

AUSTRALIA. Commonwealth Bureau of Census and Statistics. 1976. Journey to work and journey to school, August 1974. Canberra, 1976. pp. 28.

— Hong Kong.

HONG KONG. Transport Department. Research and Development Section. 1976. Public transport in the New Territories: Part 2. Development of Kowloon-Canton railway, British section. [Hong Kong], 1974 repr. 1976. pp. 25. *(Studies Reports. No. 74/2) Reprint updates to 1976.*

HONG KONG. Transport Department. Research and Development Section. 1976. Public transport in Oi Man and Ho Man Tin estates. [Hong Kong], 1976. pp. 34. *(Studies Reports. No. 76/5)*

HONG KONG. Transport Department. Research and Development Section. 1976. Public transport in Sha Tin. [Hong Kong], 1976. pp. 11. *bibliog. (Studies Reports. No. 76/7)*

HONG KONG. Transport Department. Research and Development Section. 1976. Public transport in Wong Chuk Hang estate. [Hong Kong], 1976. pp. 23. *(Studies Reports. No. 76/6)*

HONG KONG. Transport Department. Research and Development Section. 1977. Public transport in Wang Tau Hom and Lok Fu. [Hong Kong], 1977. 1 vol. (various pagings). *(Studies Reports. No. 77/1)*

— Underdeveloped areas.

See UNDERDEVELOPED AREAS — Local transit.

— United Kingdom.

WEBSTER (F.V.) Urban passenger transport: some trends and prospects. Crowthorne, 1977. pp. 49. *bibliog. (U.K. Transport and Road Research Laboratory. Reports. LR 771)*

LOCKE (JOHN).

FRANKLIN (JULIAN HAROLD) John Locke and the theory of sovereignty: mixed monarchy and the right of resistance in the political thought of the English revolution. Cambridge, 1978. pp. 146. *bibliog.*

STEINBERG (JULIUS) 1940- . Locke, Rousseau, and the idea of consent; an inquiry into the liberal-democratic theory of political obligation. Westport, 1978. pp. 155. *bibliog.*

LOCKS AND KEYS

— United Kingdom.

CHUBB AND SON'S LOCK AND SAFE COMPANY. Contemporary observations on security from the Chubb collectanea, 1818-1968; [edited by] Noel Currer-Briggs. London, [1970?]. 1 vol. (unpaged).

ŁÓDŹ

— Economic conditions.

ŁÓDŹ. Rada Naukowa. Przegląd ekonomiczno-społeczny miasta Łodzi. [nr.3]. Łódź, 1976. pp. 208. *bibliog.*

ŁÓDŹ (PROVINCE)

— History.

REWOLUCJA 1905-1907 w Lodzi i okręgu: studia i materiały; pod red. Barbary Wachowskiej. Łódź, [1975]. pp. 302.

LOGIC.

ELSTER (JON) Logic and society: contradictions and possible worlds. Chichester, [1978]. pp. 235. *bibliog.*

LOGIC, SYMBOLIC AND MATHEMATICAL.

BELL (JOHN LANE) and MACHOVER (MOSHE) A course in mathematical logic. Amsterdam, 1977. pp. 599. *bibliog.*

INTERNATIONAL CONGRESS OF LOGIC, METHODOLOGY AND PHILOSOPHY OF SCIENCE, 5TH, LONDON, ONTARIO, 1975. Historical and philosophical dimensions of logic, methodology and philosophy of science: part four of the proceedings...; edited by Robert E. Butts and Jaakko Hintikka. Dordrecht, [1977]. pp. 336. *bibliogs. (Western Ontario. University. University of Western Ontario Series in Philosophy of Science. 12)*

INTERNATIONAL CONGRESS OF LOGIC, METHODOLOGY AND PHILOSOPHY OF SCIENCE, 5TH, LONDON, ONTARIO, 1975. Logic, foundations of mathematics, and computability theory: part one of the proceedings...; edited by Robert E. Butts and Jaakko Hintikka. Dordrecht, [1977]. pp. 406. *bibliogs. (Western Ontario. University. University of Western Ontario Series in Philosophy of Science. 9)*

RAMSEY (FRANK PLUMPTON) Foundations: essays in philosophy, logic, mathematics and economics...; edited by D.H. Mellor. rev.ed. London, 1978. pp. 287. *bibliogs. A revision of The foundations of mathematics and other logical essays. Includes new material.*

LOGISTICS.

ROSTKER (BERNARD) Logistics: its planning, programming and budgeting in the Office of the Secretary of Defense, 1968-1970. [Santa Monica], 1972. pp. 15. *(Rand Corporation. [Papers]. 4881)*

— Mathematical models.

FOX (B.L.) and ROLPH (JOHN) Adaptive policies for Markov renewal programs. Santa Monica, 1971. pp. 17. *bibliog. (Rand Corporation. [Rand Reports]. 838)*

LOGONE BASIN.

CABOT (JEAN) Le bassin du moyen Logone. Paris, O.R.S.T.O.M., 1965. pp. 348. *Map in end pocket.*

LOLLARDS.

CAMDEN SOCIETY. [Publications]. 4th Series. vol. 20. Heresy trials in the diocese of Norwich 1428-31; edited for the Royal Historical Society from Westminster Diocesan Archives MS.B.2 by Norman P. Tanner. London, 1977. pp. 233.

LOMBARDY

— Economic history.

KLANG (DANIEL M.) Tax reform in eighteenth century Lombardy. Boulder, Colo., 1977. pp. 110. *bibliog. (East European Quarterly. East European Monographs. 27)*

— Social conditions.

MENEGHETTI (LODOVICO) Abitazioni in Lombardia: contraddizioni territoriali e sociali nell'interpretazione dei censimenti. Milano, 1976. pp. 144.

LOMÉ, CONVENTION OF.

ACP-EEC COUNCIL OF MINISTERS. Annual report [and] Commission report...on the administration of financial and technical aid. a., 1976/77- Suva.

LONAUERHAMMERHUETTE.

HILLEGEIST (HANS HEINRICH) Die Geschichte der Lonauerhammerhütte bei Herzberg/Harz: ein Beitrag zur Wirtschaftsgeschichte der Eisenverhüttung und Eisenverarbeitung im Südharz. Göttingen, [1977]. pp. 193. *bibliog.*

LONDON.

LONDON FACTS AND FIGURES; (compiled by the Intelligence Unit of the Greater London Council). irreg. London. *Current issues only kept.*

— Canals.

LONDON CANALS CONSULTATIVE COMMITTEE. London's canal. [London], Greater London Council, [1976]. pp. 21. *bibliog.*

— Church history.

TOLMIE (MURRAY) The triumph of the saints: the separate churches of London, 1616- 1649. Cambridge, 1977. pp. 251. *bibliog.*

— City planning.

HOLDEN (CHARLES HENRY) and HOLFORD (WILLIAM GRAHAM) Baron Holford. Reconstruction in the City of London: final report to the Improvements and Town Planning Committee by the Joint Consultants. [London], 1947. pp. 64.

LONDON. Corporation. Improvements and Town Planning Committee. Report [of the]...Committee to be presented, 14th July 1947, to the Right Honourable the Lord Mayor, Aldermen and Commons of the City of London in Common Council assembled. [London], 1947. pp. 24.

HALL (JOHN M.) London: metropolis and region. Oxford, 1976. pp. 48. *bibliog.*

LONDON. Greater London Council. The Greater London Council, Covent Garden, GLC action area plan: written statement, incorporating the proposals map. [London, 1976]. pp. 153.

LONDON. Greater London Council. King's Cross/St. Pancras action area; report of survey. [London], 1977. pp. 78.

— Description.

LONDON. Greater London Council. Survey of London. vol. 39. The Grosvenor estate in Mayfair. Part I. General history. London, 1977. pp. 236, 56. *2 maps in end pocket.*

— Economic policy.

HALL (JOHN M.) London: metropolis and region. Oxford, 1976. pp. 48. *bibliog.*

— Gilds — Vintners' Company.

CRAWFORD (ANNE) A history of the Vintners' Company. London, 1977. pp. 319. *bibliog.*

— History.

LONDON. Greater London Council. Survey of London. vol. 39. The Grosvenor estate in Mayfair. Part I. General history. London, 1977. pp. 236, 56. *2 maps in end pocket.*

— — Sources.

LONDON. London Record Society. Publications. vol. 14. Committees for repeal of the Test and Corporation Acts: minutes 1786-90 and 1827-8; edited by Thomas W. Davis. London, 1978. pp. 126.

— Hospitals.

LONDON HOSPITAL. Rules and orders of the London Infirmary. London, printed by H. Woodfall, 1745. pp. 23.

SCHEME for the formation of a central hospital board for London, with a preliminary list of the general committee that have consented to promote such a scheme and the names of a large number of members of the staffs of hospitals, general practitioners, and others, who have expressed their approval of the movement. London, 1897. pp. 24.

RHODES (PHILIP) Doctor John Leake's hospital: a history of the General Lying-in Hospital, York Road, Lambeth, 1765-1971: the birth, life, and death of a maternity hospital. London, [1977]. pp. 400. *bibliog.*

U.K. Department of Health and Social Security. 1978. Future management of the London specialist postgraduate hospitals: a consultative document. [London], 1978. pp. 78.

— Industries.

WEATHERITT (L.) and LOVETT (A.F.) Manufacturing industry in Greater London. London, [1975]. pp. 26. *(London. Greater London Council. Research Memoranda. 498)*

FIELD (A. MIRYAM) and CROFTS (C.) Some aspects of planned migration to new and expanding towns. London, [1977]. pp. 39. *bibliog. (London. Greater London Council. Research Memoranda. 527)*

HAYDEN (F.W.) Factors influencing the location of industry. London, [1978]. pp. 75. *(London. Greater London Council. Research Memoranda. 528)*

— Libraries.

KNOCK (ANN) compiler. Library resources in psychology: a directory of libraries in the Greater London area with a specialist interest in psychology, etc. London, 1974. pp. 16. *(London. University. Birkbeck College. Library. Publications. No. 47)*

— Maps.

AGAS (RALPH) Plan of London, circa 1560-1570. London, 1905. 8 sheets. *(London. London Topographical Society. [Publications. No. 17])*

— Moral conditions.

SPARKS (RICHARD FRANKLIN) and others. Surveying victims: a study of the measurement of criminal victimization, perceptions of crime, and attitudes to criminal justice. Chichester, [1977]. pp. 276. *bibliog.*

— Office buildings.

KERR (DEREK) An assessment of development potential in London's commercial property sector. London, [1977]. pp. 44. *(London. Greater London Council. Research Memoranda. 505)*

— Officials and employees.

THOMPSON (RICHARD) of the Greater London Council. Staff of local authority residential and day care establishments for the mentally disordered in the London boroughs, 1966-1973. London, [1975]. pp. (80). *(London. Greater London Council. Research Memoranda. 492)*

— Politics and government.

COMMUNIST PARTY OF GREAT BRITAIN. London District Committee. A Labour L.C.C.: what now?; a call to action. London, [1934?]. s.sh.

— — Bibliography.

WRIGHT (N.H.) compiler. Publicly available Research Memoranda Nos. 31 to 530: a contextual index of titles and authors. London, 1978. pp. 32. *(London. Greater London Council. Research Memoranda. 530)*

— Population.

HOLLIS (JOHN) Writer on Population, and FIELD (A. MIRYAM) Mid-year population estimates: a commentary. London, [1976]. pp. 18. *bibliog. (London. Greater London Council. Research Memoranda. 494)*

DEAKIN (NICHOLAS) and UNGERSON (CLARE) Leaving London: planned mobility and the inner city. London, 1977. pp. 194.

FIELD (A. MIRYAM) and CROFTS (C.) Some aspects of planned migration to new and expanding towns. London, [1977]. pp. 39. *bibliog. (London. Greater London Council. Research Memoranda. 527)*

HOLLIS (JOHN) Writer on Population, and others. Population and household projections for London: 1976. London, [1977]. 3 pts. *bibliog. (London. Greater London Council. Research Memoranda. 506-508)*

PERMANAND (R.) London's institutional population: a look at the future. London, [1977]. pp. 47. *bibliog. (London. Greater London Council. Research Memoranda. 521)*

FIELD (A. MIRYAM) compiler. Index to published and unpublished work of the Population Studies Section;...revised by Sandra Strachan. 3rd ed. London, 1977. 1 pamphlet (unpaged). *(London. Greater London Council. Research Library. Research Bibliographies. No. 53)*

— Recreational activities.

CHARLTON (JOHN) and CAMPBELL (LORNA) Preparation and contents of basic data from G[reater] L[ondon] R[ecreation] S[tudy] and S[urvey of] I[nformal] R[ecreation in] S[outh] E[ast] E[ngland]. London, [1977]. pp. 62. *bibliog. (London. Greater London Council. Research Memoranda. 523)*

— Statistics, Vital.

PRICE (RICHARD) D.D. Observations on the expectations of lives, the increase of mankind, the influence of great towns on population and particularly the state of London with respect to healthfulness and number of inhabitants; in a letter...to Benjamin Franklin, etc. [London, W. Bowyer and J. Nichols, 1769]. pp. 89-126. *(From the Philosophical Transactions of the Royal Society, vol. 59)*

HAMPSTEAD. [Borough Council]. Infantile mortality. [London, 1908]. pp. 27-35. *Extract from report for 1908.*

— Stores, shopping centres, etc.

BRUCE (A.J.) and MANN (H.R.) The Brent Cross shopping centre impact study: results of the first diary study of household shopping trips. London, [1977]. pp. 59, 1 map. *(London. Greater London Council. Research Memoranda. 522)*

DOWNEY (P.) Brent Cross shopping centre impact study: preliminary analysis of shop vacancies and changes in NW London, 1971-76. London, [1977]. pp. 13. *(London. Greater London Council. Research Memoranda. 525)*

WILLSON (JOAN M.) Brent Cross shopping centre impact study: household income and expenditure in 1976. London, [1977]. pp. 7. *(London. Greater London Council. Research Memoranda. 526)*

— Suburbs and environs.

BOLSTERLI (MARGARET JONES) The early community at Bedford Park: corporate happiness in the first garden suburb. London, 1977. pp. 136.

— Transit systems.

DAOR (E.) and GOODWIN (P.B.) Variations in the importance of walking as a mode of transport. London, [1976]. pp. 16. *(London. Greater London Council. Research Memoranda. 487)*

LONDON TRANSPORT EXECUTIVE. Planning Research Office. Economic Research. Economic indicators. (New series. No. 5). London, 1976. 1 pamphlet (unpaged).

ROSE (J.S.) A study of violence on London Transport. [London], Greater London Council Establishments Department, Behavioural Science Unit, 1976. 1 vol.(various pagings). *bibliog.*

LONDON. Greater London Council. Department of Planning and Transportation: departmental performance review of transportation work. London, 1977. pp. 10.

LONDON UNIVERSITY

— School of Oriental and African Studies.

RUSSELL (RALPH) Oriental despotism: a report on the School of Oriental and African Studies, University of London. London, [1973]. pp. 10.

LONDONDERRY

— Bridges.

LONDONDERRY BRIDGE TRUST. Report of the trustees of the Londonderry Bridge. Londonderry, 1852. pp. 13.

LONG MARCH, 1934-1935.

WILSON (RICHARD GARRATT) The Long March, 1935: the epic of Chinese communism's survival. rev. ed. Harmondsworth, 1977. pp. 380. *bibliog.*

LORER (NIKOLAI IVANOVICH).

LORER (NIKOLAI IVANOVICH) Zapiski dekabrista N.I. Lorera; pod redaktsiei M.N. Pokrovskogo; prigotovila k pechati i kommentirovala M.V. Nechkina. Moskva, 1931. pp. 448.

LOS ANGELES

— History.

LOS Angeles: biography of a city; [edited by] John and Laree Caughey. Berkeley, 1977. pp. 509. *bibliog.*

— Race question.

MODELL (JOHN) The economics and politics of racial accommodation: the Japanese of Los Angeles, 1900-1942. Urbana, [Ill., 1977]. pp. 201.

LOUGHLIN (ANNE).

NATIONAL UNION OF TAILORS AND GARMENT WORKERS. An International Women's Year tribute to an outstanding pioneer woman member and leader on the occasion of the naming ceremony of Anne Loughlin Room at Union Headquarters, 21st March 1975. Milton Keynes, [1975]. pp. 4.

LOVE.

HARTMAN (TOR) Uppsatser om alienation och kärlek: (three essays on alienation and love). Helsinki, 1977. pp. 62. *(Helsinki. Yliopisto. Research Group for Comparative Sociology. Research Reports. No.13) In Swedish, with English summaries.*

LOWTHER (Sir CHRISTOPHER).

SURTEES SOCIETY. Publications. vol. 189. Commercial papers of Sir Christopher Lowther, 1611-1644; edited by D.R. Hainsworth. Gateshead, 1977. pp. 250.

LUCCA

— History.

MEEK (CHRISTINE) Lucca, 1369-1400: politics and society in an early Renaissance city-state. Oxford, 1978. pp. 427. *bibliog.*

LUCCA(Cont.)

— Politics and government.

MEEK (CHRISTINE) Lucca, 1369-1400: politics and society in an early Renaissance city-state. Oxford, 1978. pp. 427. *bibliog.*

LUD. SARTORIUS & COMP.

See SARTORIUS (LUD.) & COMP.

LUNGS

— Cancer.

TOBACCO RESEARCH COUNCIL. Research Papers. 14. Part I. Report on a second retrospective mortality study in north-east England. Part 1: Factors related to mortality from lung cancer, bronchitis, heart disease and stroke in Cleveland county, with particular emphasis on the relative risks associated with smoking filter and plain cigarettes. London, 1977. pp. 93. *bibliog. Report on the first study published as Research Paper. 8.*

LUSSO (EMILIO).

LUSSO (EMILIO) Essere a sinistra: democrazia, autonomia e socialismo in cinquant'anni di lotte; a cura del Collettivo Emilio Lussu di Cagliari. Milano, [1976]. pp. 287.

LUXEMBOURG

— Economic conditions.

POOS (JACQUES FRANÇOIS) Crise économique et petites nations: le modèle luxembourgeois. Lausanne, 1977. pp. 75. *(Lausanne. Université. Centre de Recherches Européennes. Publications. 3. Les Politiques Nationales Face au Processus d'Intégration)*

LUXURY.

SEKORA (JOHN) Luxury: the concept in Western thought, Eden to Smollett. Baltimore, [1977]. pp. 340.

LYLE SHIPPING COMPANY.

ORBELL (JOHN) and others. From Cape to Cape: the history of Lyle Shipping Company. Edinburgh, 1978. pp. 239. *bibliog.*

LYNCHING

— United States.

GRANT (DONALD L.) The anti-lynching movement, 1883-1932. San Francisco, 1975. pp. 205. *bibliog.*

LYONS

— Economic conditions.

FRANCE. Direction Régionale du Travail et de la Main-d'Oeuvre de la Région Rhône-Alpes. 1977. Evolution des activités et des emplois dans l'agglomération lyonnaise, 1969-1974: analyse du développement d'une grande métropole régionale. [Lyons], 1977. pp. 127.

— Economic history.

LEQUIN (YVES) Les ouvriers de la région lyonnaise, 1848-1914. Lyon, [1977]. 2 vols. *bibliog.*

— Politics and government.

PICKVANCE (CHRISTOPHER GEOFFREY) Marxist approaches to the study of urban politics: divergences among some recent French studies. Canterbury, 1976. fo. 52. *Paper for the Political Studies Association Conference, Nottingham, 1976.*

— Riots, 1831.

RUDE (FERNAND) C'est nous les canuts... Paris, 1977. pp. 263.

— Social history.

GARDEN (MAURICE) Lyon et les Lyonnais au XVIIIe siècle. [Paris, 1975]. pp. 374.

LYSENKO (TROFIM DENISOVICH).

LECOURT (DOMINIQUE) Lyssenko: histoire réelle d'une "science prolétarienne". Paris, 1976. pp. 257.

McCARTHY (JOSEPH RAYMOND).

CROSBY (DONALD F.) God, church, and flag: Senator Joseph R. McCarthy and the Catholic church, 1950-1957. Chapel Hill, [1978]. pp. 307. *bibliog.*

MACCHIAVELLI (NICCOLÒ).

GUILLEMAIN (BERNARD) Machiavel: l'anthropologie politique. Genève, 1977. pp. 403. *bibliog.*

MACEDONIA

— History.

STOJANOVSKI (ALEKSANDAR) Dervendžistvoto vo Makedonija. Skopje, 1974. pp. 362. *bibliog. With Russian and French summaries.*

— Nationalism.

KATARDŽIEV (IVAN) Serskiot okrug od Kresnenskoto vostanie do Mladoturskata revolucija: nacionalno-politički borbi. Skopje, 1968. pp. 469. *bibliog.*

MACEDONIAN QUESTION.

GOCE Delčev i makedonskoto nacionalno revolucionerno dviženje: materijali od Simpoziumot održan na 8, 9 i 10 noemvri 1972 godina vo Stip po povod 100-godišninata od raganjeto na Goce Delčev. Skopje, 1973. pp. 410.

MACEO (ANTONIO).

FONER (PHILIP SHELDON) Antonio Maceo: the "Bronze Titan" of Cuba's struggle for independence. New York, [1977]. pp. 340. *bibliog.*

McGOVERN (GEORGE STANLEY).

McGOVERN (GEORGE STANLEY) Grassroots: (the autobiography of George McGovern). New York, [1977]. pp. 307.

MACHINE TRACTOR STATIONS

— Russia.

VINOGRADOV (IVAN IVANOVICH) Politotdely MTS i sovkhozov v gody Velikoi Otechestvennoi voiny, 1941-1943 gg. Leningrad, 1976. pp. 128.

MACHINERY

— Trade and manufacture — France.

FRANCE. Groupe sectoriel d'Analyse et de Prévision Biens d'Equipement Mécaniques et Electriques. 1976. Rapport...: préparation du 7e Plan. Paris, [1976]. pp. 72.

— — Germany.

HENTSCHEL (VOLKER) Wirtschaftsgeschichte der Maschinenfabrik Esslingen AG, 1846- 1918: eine historisch-betriebswirtschaftliche Analyse. Stuttgart, [1977]. pp. 170. *bibliog. (Arbeitskreis für Moderne Sozialgeschichte. Industrielle Welt. Band 22)*

— — Russia — Ukraine.

BEM (IHOR SERHIIOVYCH) and DEMIDION (VOLODYMYR OLEKSANDROVYCH) Problemy rozvytku i rozmishchennia mashynobuduvannia ta metaloobrobki v Ukraïns'kii RSR. Kyïv, 1977. pp. 311. *bibliog.*

— — Switzerland.

HOTTINGER (MAX) 1879- . Geschichtliches aus der schweizerischen Metall- und Maschinenindustrie, etc. Frauenfeld, 1921. pp. 189.

MACHINERY IN INDUSTRY.

GYLLENHAMMAR (PEHR G.) People at work. Reading, Mass., 1977. pp. 164.

MACKIEWICZ (STANISLAW).

JARUZELSKI (JERZY) Mackiewicz i konserwatyści: szkice do biografi. Warszawa, 1976. pp. 231.

McSHANE (HARRY).

McSHANE (HARRY) and SMITH (JOAN) Harry McShane: no mean fighter. London, 1978. pp. 282.

MADAGASCAR

— History.

HATZFELD (OLIVIER) Madagascar. Paris, 1952. pp. 127. *bibliog.*

— Industries.

MADAGASCAR. Institut National de la Statistique et de la Recherche Economique. 1975. Recensement industriel. (Tome 2). 1973-1974. [Antananarivo?, 1975?]. pp. 473.

— Social conditions.

EDHOLM (FELICITY ELIZABETH) Kinship and social change among the Antaisaka of coastal southeast Madagascar. [1976]. fo. 397. *bibliog. Typescript. Ph.D. (London) thesis: unpublished. This thesis is the property of London University and may not be removed from the Library.*

MADRAS

— City planning.

MADRAS. Rural Development and Local Administration Department. 1971. Madras metropolitan plan, 1971-1991. [Madras], 1971. pp. 132.

— Nationalism.

ARNOLD (DAVID) The Congress in Tamilnad: nationalist politics in south India, 1919-1937. London, 1977. pp. 252. *bibliogs. (Australian National University. Monographs on South Asia. No. 1)*

— Politics and government.

ARNOLD (DAVID) The Congress in Tamilnad: nationalist politics in south India, 1919-1937. London, 1977. pp. 252. *bibliogs. (Australian National University. Monographs on South Asia. No. 1)*

MAHARASHTRA

— Economic policy.

MAHARASHTRA ECONOMIC DEVELOPMENT COUNCIL. State planning and industrial development in Maharashtra. [Bombay, 1974?]. pp. 222.

— Industries.

MAHARASHTRA ECONOMIC DEVELOPMENT COUNCIL. Rehabilitation and expansion of industries in greater Bombay. Bombay, 1973. pp. 90.

— Politics and government.

ROSENTHAL (DONALD B.) The expansive elite: district politics and state policy-making in India. Berkeley, Calif., [1977]. pp. 348.

— Population.

MAHARASHTRA ECONOMIC DEVELOPMENT COUNCIL. Manpower potential and business preferences in a rapidly developing economy: a case-study of Thana Taluka; summary report. Bombay, 1972. pp. 47.

— Rural conditions.

MAHARASHTRA ECONOMIC DEVELOPMENT COUNCIL. Study Group in Rural Employment in Maharashtra. Report; [S.K. Muranjan, chairman]. Bombay, 1966. pp. 37.

MAHARASHTRA ECONOMIC DEVELOPMENT COUNCIL. Evaluation of rural prosperity in Maharashtra: summary report. Bombay, 1973. pp. 73.

MALAYSIA

PUNEKAR (S.D.) and GOLWALKAR (ALKA R.) Rural change in Maharashtra: an analytical study of change in six villages in Konkan. Bombay, 1973. pp. 138.

MAISEL (KARL).

MAGAZINER (ALFRED) Ein Sohn des Volkes: Karl Maisel erzählt sein Leben. Wien, [1977]. pp. 123.

MAIZE.

The DEVELOPMENT and production of soy-ogi, a corn based complete protein food; [by] I.A. Akinrele [and others]. Lagos, Federal Ministry of Industries, 1970. pp. 63. *bibliog.* *(Federal Institute of Industrial Research [Nigeria]. Research Reports. No.42)*

— Rhodesia and Nyasland, Federation of.

FEDERATION OF RHODESIA AND NYASALAND. Federal Ministry of Agriculture. Economics and Markets Branch. 1957. Maize production costs on some European farms in Northern and Southern Rhodesia for the 1955-56 and 1956-57 crops: interim report on the results for 1955-56. [Salisbury, 1957]. pp. 9. *([Sessional Papers]. 75)*

MAKHNO (NESTOR).

PALIJ (MICHAEL) The anarchism of Nestor Makhno, 1918-1921: an aspect of the Ukrainian revolution. Seattle, [1976]. pp. 428. *bibliog.* *(Washington State University. Institute for Comparative and Foreign Area Studies. Publications on Russia and Eastern Europe. No. 7)*

MALACCA, STRAIT OF.

SHAW (K.E.) and THOMSON (GEORGE G.) The Straits of Malacca: in relation to the problems of the Indian and Pacific Oceans. Singapore, 1973. pp. 174.

MALAWI

— Administrative and political divisions.

MALAWI. Electoral Commission on Delimitation of Constituencies. 1976. The third report...; [A.L. Mwenifumbo, chairman]. Zomba, 1976. 1 vol. (various foliations)

— Economic conditions.

MALAWI. National Statistical Office. 1966. Budget 1966: background information. Zomba, [1966]. pp. 89. *(Malawi. Treasury. Documents. No. 5)*

— Foreign relations.

MALAWI. Prime Minister. 1964. Malawi admitted to United Nations: address to the General Assembly by the Prime Minister, Ngwazi Dr. Kamuzu Banda, December 2nd 1964. [Blantyre, 1964]. pp. 12.

MALAWI. Prime Minister. 1965. Speech of the Prime Minister of Malawi, Ngwazi Dr. Kamuzu Banda, to the General Assembly of the United Nations, delivered by Hon. A.M. Nyasulu, M.P., on September 27, 1965. [Blantyre, 1965]. pp. 10.

MALAWI. Delegation to the 23rd Session of the General Assembly of the United Nations. 1968. An address to the 23rd session of the General Assembly, 1968: Malawi and the United Nations; (delivered by the Hon. Alec Nyasulu on the behalf of the President of Malawi). [Blantyre, 1968]. pp. (5).

See also UNITED NATIONS — Malawi.

— — South Africa.

MALAWI. Department of Information. 1970. Pioneers in inter-African relations: (speeches by the President of Malawi and the Prime Minister of South Africa at State House, Zomba, 20 May 1970). [Blantyre, 1970]. pp. 18.

— — Taiwan.

FORMOSA. Ministry of Foreign Affairs. 1968. Press conferences made by the Chinese Vice-Minister for Foreign Affairs, H.K. Yang, on his arrival and before his departure, at Chileka airport on August 25-27, 1968. Blantyre, Malawi Department of Information, [1968]. pp. 4, 2.

— History.

FEDERATION OF RHODESIA AND NYASALAND. Central African Archives. 1951. The story of Nyasaland told in a series of historical pictures to commemorate the Diamond Jubilee of Nyasaland, 1891-1951: descriptive souvenir and catalogue. [Salisbury, 1951]. pp. 95.

— Parliament — Elections.

MALAWI. Department of Information. 1971. The general elections, 1971: guide for the selection of candidates. Blantyre, [1971]. 1 pamphlet (unpaged). *In English and Chichewa.*

MALAWI. Department of Information. 1971. The general elections, 1971: historical background. Blantyre, [1971]. 1 pamphlet (unpaged).

— Relations (general) with South Africa.

MALAWI. Department of Information. 1968. Speeches by G.W. Kumtumanji, Minister of Local Government, Health and Education, and H. Muller, the South Africa's Foreign Minister, made at Ryall's Hotel, Blantyre, during his visit to the Republic of Malawi, August 27, 1968. Blantyre, [1968]. pp. 7,8.

— Statistics.

MALAWI. National Statistical Office. Monthly statistical bulletin. m., Ja 1971- Zomba.

MALAY RACE.

ABDUL KARIM (WAZIR JAHAN BEGUM) The belief system of the Mak Betisek of Pulau Carey, Malaysia. 1977. fo. 430. *bibliog. Typescript. Ph.D. (London) thesis: unpublished. This thesis is the property of London University and may not be removed from the Library.*

THAM SEONG CHEE. Malays and modernization: a sociological interpretation. Singapore, [1977]. pp. 319. *bibliog.*

MALAYA.

CALDECOTT (Sir ANDREW) Report on the Malaya pavilion, British Empire Exhibition. Singapore, Government Printing Office, 1926. pp. 32.

— Commerce.

MALAYA: the making of a neo-colony; edited by Mohamed Amin and Malcolm Caldwell. Nottingham, 1977. pp. 265.

— History.

MALAYA: the making of a neo-colony; edited by Mohamed Amin and Malcolm Caldwell. Nottingham, 1977. pp. 265.

— Officials and employees — Salaries, allowances, etc.

REPORT of the Commission appointed by His Excellency the Governor of the Straits Settlements and High Commissioner for the Malay States to inquire into...the temporary allowances paid to officers and retired officers of the public service of the Straits Settlements and Federated Malay States, etc.; [W.C. Huggard, chairman]. [Kuala Lumpur], 1931. pp. 27. *(Federated Malay States. Federal Council. Papers to be laid before the...Council, etc. 1931. No. 22)*

FEDERATION OF MALAYA. Legislative Council. Special Committee on Salaries in the Federation of Malaya. 1950. Report; [F.C. Benham, chairman]. Kuala Lumpur, 1950. pp. 114. *(Legislative Council. Papers to be laid before the...Council, etc. 1950. No.54)*

MALAYSIA

— Census.

FEDERATION OF MALAYSIA. Census, 1970. 1970 population and housing census of Malaysia. Kuala Lumpur, 1971 in progress. *In English and Malay.*

— Constitution.

SUFFIAN (MOHAMED) An introduction to the constitution of Malaysia. 2nd ed. Kuala Lumpur, Government Printer, 1976. pp. 407.

— Economic conditions.

FEDERATION OF MALAYSIA. Ministry of Finance. Economic report. a., 1975/76(4th)- Kuala Lumpur.

THAM SEONG CHEE. Malays and modernization: a sociological interpretation. Singapore, [1977]. pp. 319. *bibliog.*

— Economic policy.

RUDNER (MARTIN) Nationalism, planning, and economic modernization in Malaysia: the politics of beginning development. Beverly Hills, [1975]. pp. 85. *bibliog.*

WEGELIN (EMIEL A.) Urban low-income housing and development: a case study in Peninsular Malaysia. Leiden, 1978. pp. 347. *bibliog.*

— Historical geography.

HILL (R.D.) Rice in Malaya: a study in historical geography. Kuala Lumpur, 1977. pp. 234. *bibliog.*

— History.

BARR (PAT) Taming the jungle: the men who made British Malaya. London, 1977. pp. 172. *bibliog.*

— Nationalism.

RUDNER (MARTIN) Nationalism, planning, and economic modernization in Malaysia: the politics of beginning development. Beverly Hills, [1975]. pp. 85. *bibliog.*

— Politics and government.

FEDERATION OF MALAYSIA. Department of Information. 1967. The challenging decade: a review of Malaysia's ten years of independence based on a Radio Malaysia broadcast highlighting the major political and constitutional developments from 1957 to 1967. [Kuala Lumpur, 1967]. pp. 24.

RUDNER (MARTIN) Nationalism, planning, and economic modernization in Malaysia: the politics of beginning development. Beverly Hills, [1975]. pp. 85. *bibliog.*

MILNE (ROBERT STEPHEN) and MAUZY (DIANE K.) Politics and government in Malaysia. Singapore, 1978. pp. 406. *bibliog.*

— Population.

FEDERATION OF MALAYSIA. Census, 1970. 1970 population and housing census of Malaysia: age distributions. Kuala Lumpur, 1973. pp. 198. *In English and Malay.*

FEDERATION OF MALAYSIA. Department of Statistics. 1973. An interim report on the post enumeration survey. Kuala Lumpur, [1973]. pp. 8. *In English and Malay.*

IBRAHIM (AHMAD) Law and population in Malaysia. Medford, Mass., 1977. pp. 51. *(Tufts University. Fletcher School of Law and Diplomacy. Law and Population Monograph Series. No. 45)*

— Population, Rural.

MALAYSIAN CENTRE FOR DEVELOPMENT STUDIES. A study of the value orientation of the rural population towards change in peninsular Malaysia: report of phase 1 of the study; published...in cooperation with Friedrich-Naumann-Stiftung. Kuala Lumpur, [1975]. pp. 88. *bibliog.*

— Rural conditions.

MALAYSIAN CENTRE FOR DEVELOPMENT STUDIES. A study of the value orientation of the rural population towards change in peninsular Malaysia: report of phase 1 of the study; published...in cooperation with Friedrich-Naumann-Stiftung. Kuala Lumpur, [1975]. pp. 88. *bibliog.*

MALAYSIA (Cont.)

GRIJPSTRA (B.G.) Common efforts in the development of rural Sarawak, Malaysia. Assen, 1976. pp. 231. *bibliog.* (Studies of Developing Countries. 20)

— **Social conditions.**

THAM SEONG CHEE. Malays and modernization: a sociological interpretation. Singapore, [1977]. pp. 319. *bibliog.*

— **Social policy.**

WEGELIN (EMIEL A.) Urban low-income housing and development: a case study in Peninsular Malaysia. Leiden, 1978. pp. 347. *bibliog.*

— **Statistics.**

STATISTICAL HANDBOOK OF PENINSULAR MALAYSIA; [pd. by] Department of Statistics. a., 1974(8th)- Kuala Lumpur. *[in English and Malay].*

MALI (REPUBLIC)

— **Commerce.**

AMSELLE (JEAN LOUP) Les négociants de la Savane: histoire et organisation sociale des Kooroko (Mali). Paris, 1977. pp. 292.

— **Economic conditions.**

FRANCE. Ministère de la Coopération. Service des Etudes Economiques et des Questions Internationales. 1977. Mali: données statistiques sur les activités économiques culturelles et sociales. Paris, 1977. pp. 165.

— **Social conditions.**

FRANCE. Ministère de la Coopération. Service des Etudes Economiques et des Questions Internationales. 1977. Mali: données statistiques sur les activités économiques culturelles et sociales. Paris, 1977. pp. 165.

— **Statistics.**

FRANCE. Ministère de la Coopération. Service des Etudes Economiques et des Questions Internationales. 1977. Mali: données statistiques sur les activités économiques culturelles et sociales. Paris, 1977. pp. 165.

MALNUTRITION.

MALNUTRITION, behavior, and social organization; edited by Lawrence S. Greene. New York, 1977. pp. 298. *bibliogs. Based on a symposium held at the Annual Meeting of the American Association for the Advancement of Science in 1976.*

MALNUTRITION IN CHILDREN.

MALNUTRITION, behavior, and social organization; edited by Lawrence S. Greene. New York, 1977. pp. 298. *bibliogs. Based on a symposium held at the Annual Meeting of the American Association for the Advancement of Science in 1976.*

MALRAUX (ANDRE).

MALRAUX (ANDRÉ) Le miroir des limbes: hôtes de passage. [Paris, 1975]. pp. 238.

MALTA

— **Constitutional history.**

CREMONA (JOHN J.) From the declaration of rights to independence: an English translation of the public address delivered in the Palace Square, Valletta, on the 17th September, 1964, on the occasion of the official celebrations of Malta's independence. [Valletta], Department of Information, 1965. pp. 11.

— **Economic policy.**

JOINT MISSION FOR MALTA. Report, 18th July 1967; [Robens of Woldingham, chairman]. [Valletta], Department of Information, [1967]. pp. 70.

— **Industries.**

JOINT MISSION FOR MALTA. Report, 18th July 1967; [Robens of Woldingham, chairman]. [Valletta], Department of Information, [1967]. pp. 70.

— **Politics and government.**

MALTA. 1932. Il significato del trionfo nazionalista nelle ultime elezioni generali di Malta e Gozo, giugno 1932; presentato al Segretaria di Stato per le Colonie dalla delegazione Maltese recatasi a Londra nel luglio 1932, etc. [Valletta], 1932. pp. 95.

MALTHUSIANISM.

LEDBETTER (ROSANNA) A history of the Malthusian League, 1877-1927. Columbus, Ohio, [1976]. pp. 261. *bibliog.*

MAN.

SHOTTER (JOHN) Images of man in psychological research. London, 1975. pp. 144. *bibliog.*

CHELOVEK kak ob"ekt sotsiologicheskogo issledovaniia; pod redaktsiei L.I. Spiridonova i Ia.I. Gilinskogo. Leningrad, 1977. pp. 197.

OGILVY (JAMES) Many dimensional man: decentralizing self, society and the sacred. New York, 1977. pp. 371.

GORDON (MILTON MYRON) Human nature, class and ethnicity. New York, 1978. pp. 302.

KOESTLER (ARTHUR) Janus: a summing up. London, 1978. pp. 354. *bibliog.*

ZAHAVY (ZEV) Whence and wherefore: the cosmological destiny of man scientifically and philosophically considered. South Brunsick, [1978]. pp. 178. *"Comprising an analysis relating to the significant essay In the centre of immensities, by the distinguished Professor Sir Bernard Lovell, University of Manchester, England".*

— **Influence of climate.**

TICKELL (CRISPIN) Climatic change and world affairs [Cambridge, Mass., 1977]. pp. 69. *bibliog. (Harvard University. Center for International Affairs. Harvard Studies in International Affairs. No. 37)*

MAN-MACHINE SYSTEMS.

MURRELL (KENNETH FRANK HYWEL) Men and machines. London, 1976. pp. 144. *bibliog.*

MANAGEMENT.

OPTIMUM: a forum for management; [pd. by] Bureau of Management Consulting, Department of Supply and Services (Canada). q., 1970 (v.1, no.2)- Ottawa. *[articles in English or French with a summary in the alternative language]*

GUPTA (SHIV KUMAR) and COZZOLINO (JOHN M.) Fundamentals of operations research for management: an introduction to qualitative methods. San Francisco, [1975]. 2 vols. *The second volume consists of Solutions manual with supplementary problems for Fundamentals, etc.*

ROSE (MICHAEL) Industrial behaviour: theoretical development since Taylor. Harmondsworth, 1978. pp. 304. *Reprint of the first edition published in London, 1975.*

TABATONI (PIERRE) and JARNIOU (PIERRE) Les systèmes de gestion: politiques et structures. Paris, [1975]. pp. 233.

HERBERT (THEODORE T.) Dimensions of organizational behavior. New York, [1976]. pp. 530.

MANAGEMENT strategy and business development: an historical and comparative study; edited by Leslie Hannah. [London, 1976]. pp. 267. *The present volume has its origins in a conference...held in London on 10 June 1975.*

ABRAHAMSSON (BENGT) Bureaucracy or participation: the logic of organization. Beverly Hills, [1977]. pp. 240. *bibliog. Translation of his Organisationsteori.*

BEDRIFTSØKONOMI i teori og praksis: artikler skrevet av Johan Arndt [and others]. Bergen, 1977. pp. 275. *bibliogs. Essays offered to Olav Harald Jensen on his 60th birthday.*

BRUNEL UNIVERSITY. Department of Government. The working of the National Health Service. London, 1978. pp. 238. *bibliog. (U.K. Royal Commission on the National Health Service, 1976. Research Papers. No. 1)*

DAMACHI (UKANDI GODWIN) Theories of management and the executive in the developing world. London, 1978. pp. 163. *bibliog.*

MANAGEMENT for the future; edited by Lewis Benton. New York, [1978]. pp. 355.

— **Bibliography.**

HAIST (DIANNE) compiler. Women in management: a selected bibliography, 1970-1975. [Toronto], 1976. pp. 18. *(Ontario. Ministry of Labour. Research Library. Bibliography Series. No. 4)*

— **Dictionaries and encyclopedias.**

COVENEY (JAMES) and MOORE (SHEILA J.) Glossary of French and English management terms: Lexique de termes anglais français de gestion. London, 1972. pp. 146.

— **Mathematical models.**

HASTINGS (NICHOLAS ANTHONY JOHN) Dynamic programming with management applications. London, 1973. pp. 173. *bibliog.*

— **Study and teaching.**

DECISION making: an experimental approach to management education: (a report of a management education course run by B.I.M. (Luton Branch)...with the London School of Economics and Political Science); edited by Desmond Graves. Luton, 1969. fo. 62.

— — **United Kingdom.**

SMITH (BARBARA M.D.) Education for management: its conception and implementation in the Faculty of Commerce at Birmingham. Birmingham, 1974. pp. 55. *(Birmingham. University. Centre for Urban and Regional Studies. Research Memoranda. No. 37)*

MANAGEMENT INFORMATION SYSTEMS.

BURCH (JOHN G.) and STRATER (FELIX R.) Information systems: theory and practice. Santa Barbara, [1974]. pp. 494.

MANAGEMENT RIGHTS.

LUCIFREDI (CLARA ENRICO) Evoluzione del potere direttivo nel rapporto di lavoro. Milano, 1977. pp. 138. *(Genoa. Università. Facoltà di Giurisprudenza. Annali. Collana. 42)*

MANAGERIAL ACCOUNTING.

HORNGREN (CHARLES T.) Introduction to management accounting. 4th ed. Englewood Cliffs, [1978]. pp. 714. *bibliogs.*

INFORMATION analysis in management accounting; [edited by] Donald L. Anderson and Donald L. Raun. Santa Barbara, [1978]. pp. 706.

MANCHESTER

— **Industries.**

ABELL (APUL HENRY) Transport and industry in Greater Manchester. Barnsley, 1978. pp. 84. *bibliog.*

— **Population — Maps.**

WILLIAMS (GWYN) 1946- . Metropolitan Manchester: a social atlas. Manchester, [1975]. fo. 41.

— Race question.

FLETT (HAZEL) Council housing and the location of ethnic minorities. Bristol, Social Science Research Council Research Unit on Ethnic Relations, [1977]. pp. 52. *(Working Papers on Ethnic Relations. No. 5)*

— Social conditions — Maps.

WILLIAMS (GWYN) 1946- . Metropolitan Manchester: a social atlas. Manchester, [1975]. fo. 41.

MANCHURIA

— History.

McCORMACK (GAVAN) Chang Tso-lin in northeast China, 1911-1928: China, Japan, and the Manchurian idea. Stanford, 1977. pp. 334. *bibliog.*

MANDEVILLE (BERNARD DE).

HORNE (THOMAS A.) The social thought of Bernard Mandeville: virtue and commerce in early eighteenth-century England. London, 1978. pp. 123. *bibliog.*

MANITOBA

— Economic policy.

INCENTIVES, location and regional development: proceedings of a conference sponsored by the Manitoba Economic Development Advisory Board and the Department of Industry and Commerce, Winnipeg, January 28-29, 1975; edited by Paul Phillips. [Winnipeg, 1975]. pp. 220.

— Industries.

ECONOMIC DEVELOPMENT ADVISORY BOARD OF MANITOBA. Manufacturing nationalization trends in Manitoba. Winnipeg, 1976. pp. 280. *bibliog.*

— Officials and employees.

MANITOBA. Planning and Priorities Committee. Women in the Manitoba civil service. [Winnipeg], 1973. pp. 124.

MANNHEIM (KARL).

BAUM (GREGORY) Truth beyond relativism: Karl Mannheim's sociology of knowledge. Milwaukee, Wis., 1977. pp. 83. *(Marquette University. Theology Department. Pere Marquette Theology Lectures. 1977)*

SIMONDS (A.P.) Karl Mannheim's sociology of knowledge. Oxford, 1978. pp. 205. *bibliog.*

MANNHEIM

— Social history.

FLIEDNER (HANS JOACHIM) Die Judenverfolgung in Mannheim, 1933-1945. Stuttgart, 1971. 2 vols. *bibliog. (Mannheim. Stadtarchiv. Veröffentlichungen. Bände 1-2)*

MANORS

— Poland.

JASSEM (GRA'ZYNA) Majątek smogulecki w latach 1918-1937; das Landgut Smogulec in den Jahren 1918-1937. Poznań, 1976. pp. 185. *bibliog. (Poznań. Poznańskie Towarzystwo Przyjaciół Nauk. Wydział Historii i Nauk Społecznych. Badania z Dziejów Społecznych i Gospodarczych. nr. 51) With German summary.*

MANPOWER

— South Africa.

VAN DER MERWE (P.J.) Die Bantoe-mannekragpotensiaal van Suid-Afrika se Bantoevolke met verwysing na indiensnemingsmikpunte ten opsigte van elke volk. Pretoria, 1970. pp. 42. *(Africa Institute. Communications. No. 15)*

MANPOWER POLICY.

AD HOC MEETING OF EXPERTS ON THE ROLE OF ADVANCED SKILLS AND TECHNOLOGIES IN INDUSTRIAL DEVELOPMENT. NEW YORK, 1967. Planning for advanced skills and technologies: studies presented at the Ad Hoc Meeting...New York, 22-29 May 1967. (ID/SER.E/3). New York, United Nations, 1969. pp. 225. *(United Nations Industrial Development Organization. Industrial Planning and Programming Series. No.3)*

— Australia.

AUSTRALIA. Parliament. Joint Committee on the Australian Capital Territory. 1972. Report on employment opportunities in the Australian Capital Territory; [R.G. Withers, chairman]. in AUSTRALIA. Parliament. Parliamentary papers, 1972, vol. 7.

AUSTRALIA. Department of Labour and Immigration. 1975. Manpower policy in Australia: a report to the Organisation for Economic Co-operation and Development. Canberra, 1975. pp. 114.

— Canada.

BAETZ (REUBEN C.) and COLLINS (KEVIN) Manpower programs: equity and integration;...submission to the Standing Senate Committee on National Finance (Manpower Programs) [on behalf of] the Canadian Council on Social Development. Ottawa, [1975]. pp. 72.

— — Alberta.

ALBERTA. Department of Advanced Education and Manpower. 1976. Alberta manpower committees: role and structure. [Edmonton], 1976. pp. 9.

— — British Columbia.

BRITISH COLUMBIA. Northeast Coal Study. Manpower Sub- committee on North East Coal Development. 1976. Report; [Ranjit Azad, chairman]. [Victoria], 1976. pp. 270.

— France.

FRANCE. Groupe Technique de Prévision Emploi-Formation. 1976. Rapport; (Préparation du 7e plan). Paris, [1976]. pp. 395. *bibliogs.*

— New Zealand.

NEW ZEALAND. Department of Labour. Research and Planning Division. 1972. Manpower planning: a discussion of aspects of manpower forecasting and manpower planning, and a description of the work of the Manpower Planning Unit. Wellington, 1972. pp. 22.

— United Kingdom.

MANPOWER SERVICES COMMISSION [U.K.]. MSC review and plan, 1977. London, 1977. pp. 89.

O'BRIEN (RICHARD) 1920- . Education, industry and people. [Birmingham, 1978]. pp. 16. *(Birmingham. University. Sir Josiah Mason Centenary Memorial Lectures. 1977)*

SWANN (BRENDA AUDREY SWANTON) and TURNBULL (MAUREEN) Records of interest to social scientists, 1919 to 1939: employment and unemployment. London, 1978. pp. 590. *(U.K. Public Record Office. Handbooks. No. 18)*

U.K. Central Office of Information. Reference Division. Reference Pamphlets. 152. Manpower and employment in Britain: the role of government. London, 1978. pp. 27. *bibliog.*

— — Scotland.

HUNTER (LAURENCE C.) Labour shortages and manpower policy;...with P.B. Beaumont. London, H.M.S.O., 1978. pp. 107. *(Manpower Services Commission [U.K.]. Manpower Studies. No. 19782)*

— United States.

LECHT (LEONARD ABE) Occupational choice and training needs: prospects for the 1980's. New York, 1977. pp. 203.

MANUAL TRAINING

— United States.

SPIVEY (DONALD) Schooling for the new slavery: black industrial education, 1868- 1915. Westport, 1978. pp. 162. *bibliog.*

MANUFACTURES.

AQUINO (ANTONIO) Technical progress and international specialization in manufactures, 1951-1974. 1977. fo. 373. *bibliog. With two previously published articles by the author. Typescript. Ph.D. (London) thesis: unpublished. This thesis is the property of London University and may not be removed from the Library.*

MANUSCRIPTS

— United Kingdom — Catalogues.

BRITISH MUSEUM. Department of Manuscripts. 'Rough register' of acquisitions of the Department of Manuscripts, British Library, 1961-1965. London, 1974. pp. 172. *(List and Index Society. Special Series. vol. 7)*

MANUSCRIPTS, AZTEC.

CASTILLO FARRERAS (VICTOR M.) Estructura economica de la sociedad Mexica segun las fuentes documentales. Mexico, 1972. pp. 197. *bibliog.*

MAO (TSE-TUNG).

HOWARD (ROGER) Mao Tse-tung and the Chinese people. London, [1977]. pp. 412. *bibliog.*

IDEINO-politicheskaia sushchnost' maoizma. Moskva, 1977. pp. 443. *bibliog.*

KERRY (TOM) The Mao myth and the legacy of Stalinism in China. New York, [1977]. pp. 190.

KIM (SAMUEL S.) The Maoist image of world order. Princeton, 1977. pp. 51. *(Princeton University. Center of International Studies. World Order Studies Program. Occasional Papers. No. 5)*

LI (JUI) The early revolutionary activities of Comrade Mao Tse-tung; (translated by Anthony W. Sariti; edited by James C. Hsiung; introduction by Stuart R. Schram). White Plains, N.Y., [1977]. pp. 354.

RYCKMANS (PIERRE) The chairman's new clothes: ([by] Simon Leys [pseud.]) ; translated by Carol Appleyard and Patrick Goode. London, 1977. pp. 261.

MAORIS.

NEW ZEALAND. Department of Maori Affairs. 1962. Integration of Maori and pakeha. Wellington, 1962. 1 pamphlet (unpaged). *(Series of Special Studies. No. 1)*

NEW ZEALAND. Department of Maori Affairs. 1964. The Maori today. 3rd ed. [Wellington, 1964]. 1 vol. (unpaged).

NEW ZEALAND. Maori and Island Affairs Department. 1968. Estates and wills of Maoris. [Wellington, 1968]. pp. (6).

ROSE (RICHARD JOHN) Maori-European comparisons in mortality. Wellington, 1972. pp. 188. *(New Zealand. Department of Health. Special Report Series. No. 37)*

POOL (D. IAN) The Maori population of New Zealand, 1769-1971. Auckland, 1977. pp. 266. *bibliog.*

— Education.

The EDUCATION of non-European children: proceedings of a national in-service course for secondary teachers, held at Lopdell House, 12-16 May, 1969. [Wellington, Department of Education, 1969]. pp. 63.

— — Bibliography.

McKENZIE (MARY BEEBAN) compiler. Maori education 1960-1969: a bibliography. Wellington, New Zealand Council for Educational Research, 1970. fo. 53.

MAORIS.(Cont.)

— Government relations.

NEW ZEALAND. Department of Maori Affairs. 1967. Questions and answers on the Maori Affairs Amendment Bill, 1967, by the Minister of Maori Affairs. [Wellington, 1967?]. pp. 12.

NEW ZEALAND. Department of Lands and Survey. 1970. Maori land in a major development project. [Wellington], 1970. pp. (6).

NEW ZEALAND. Maori and Island Affairs Department. 1970. Housing for Maoris and Islanders: notes for social workers. [Wellington], 1970. fo. 7.

NEW ZEALAND. Maori and Island Affairs Department. 1970. The work of the Maori and Island Affairs Department. Wellington, 1970. pp. 24. *bibliog*.

MAPOON

— Industries.

The CAPE York aluminium companies and the native peoples: Comalco, R.T.Z., Kaiser, C.R.A., Alcan, Billiton, Pechiney, Tipperary; [written by J. Roberts and D. McLean . Victoria, [1976]. pp. 104. *(International Development Action. Mapoon. Book 3)*

— Social conditions.

The MAPOON story according to the invaders: church mission, Queensland government and mining company; [edited by J. Roberts and others]. Victoria, [1975]. pp. 112. *(International Development Action. Mapoon. Book 2)*

The MAPOON story by the Mapoon people; [edited by J.P. Roberts and others]. Victoria, [1975]. pp. 24. *(International Development Action. Mapoon. Book 1)*

MARGINAL UTILITY.

SOCIETÀ ITALIANA DEGLI ECONOMISTI. Riunione Scientifica, 10a, Roma, 1969. Essenza e limiti del marginalismo nelle teorie economiche. Milano, 1974. pp. 279.

SCHICCHI (SIMONE) Il Marxismo e la reazione dell'utilità marginale. Catania, 1977. pp. 191. *bibliog*.

MARIHUANA.

GRAHAM (J.D.P.) Cannabis now. [Aylesbury, 1977]. pp. 122. *bibliog*.

MARINE POLLUTION

— Mediterranean.

VADROT (CLAUDE MARIE) Mort de la Méditerranée. Paris, [1977]. pp. 253.

MARINE RESOURCES.

REGIMES for the ocean, outer space, and weather; ([by] Seyom Brown [and others]). Washington, D.C., [1977]. pp. 257.

— Law and legislation.

The LAW of the sea: issues in ocean resource management; edited by Don Walsh. New York, [1977]. pp. 268.

— Poland.

MACHALIŃSKI (ZBIGNIEW) Gospodarcza myśl morska II Rzeczypospolitej, 1919-1939. Wrocław, 1975. pp. 355. *bibliog*. *With English and Russian summaries*.

MARITIME LAW.

BURKE (WILLIAM THOMAS) A report on international legal problems of scientific research in the oceans; prepared for the National Council on Marine Resources and Engineering Development. [Washington], 1967. pp. 143.

HENKIN (LOUIS) Law for the sea's mineral resources; ...prepared for the National Council on Marine Resources and Engineering Development. [Washington, 1968]. pp. 108,83.

DROIT de la mer; [by] Guy de Lacharrière [and others]. Paris, [1977]. pp. 256. *(Paris. Université. Institut des Hautes Etudes Internationales. Cours et Travaux)*

The LAW of the sea: issues in ocean resource management; edited by Don Walsh. New York, [1977]. pp. 268.

INTERNATIONAL INSTITUTE FOR STRATEGIC STUDIES. Adelphi Papers. No.143. A sea of troubles?: sources of dispute in the new ocean regime; by Barry Buzan. London, 1978. pp. 50.

— Baltic States.

GELBERG (LUDWIK) Problemy prawne współpracy państw bałtyckich. Wrocław, 1976. pp. 150. *With English table of contents*.

MARKET SURVEYS

— United Kingdom.

ASSOCIATED TELEVISION. Media and Marketing Surveys. 4. Media and marketing survey of the London T.V. area. London, [1960]. pp. 158.

ASSOCIATED TELEVISION. Media and Marketing Surveys. 5. Media and marketing survey of the Midlands T.V. area; prepared for Associated Television Limited. London, [1960]. pp. 192.

MARKETING.

WILSON (FRANK A.) Some economic aspects of the structure and organization of small scale marketing systems: a discussion of the research findings of a study into the marketing of fruit and vegetables in Kenya. 1973. fo. 21. *Unpublished: photocopy of typescript*.

— Mathematical models.

MODELING for government and business: essays in honor of Prof. Dr. P.J. Verdoorn; edited by C.A. Van Bochove [and others]. Leiden, 1977. pp. 355. *bibliogs*.

— Japan.

DENTSU INCORPORATED. Marketing Division. Marketing opportunities in Japan. London, [1978]. pp. 194.

MARKETING BOARDS.

IZRAELI (DOV) and ZIF (JAY JEHIEL) Societal marketing boards. New York, [1977]. pp. 265. *bibliogs*.

— Israel.

IZRAELI (DOV) and ZIF (JAY JEHIEL) Societal marketing boards. New York, [1977]. pp. 265. *bibliogs*.

MARKETING MANAGEMENT.

EILON (SAMUEL) and others. Distribution management: mathematical modelling and practical analysis. London, 1971. pp. 240.

— Mathematical models.

EILON (SAMUEL) and others. Distribution management: mathematical modelling and practical analysis. London, 1971. pp. 240.

MARKETING RESEARCH

— Netherlands.

MARKET research in the Netherlands; special issue [of] (Marktonderzoek kwartaalschrift). Rotterdam, 1969. pp. 48. *bibliogs*. *Published on the occasion of the 22nd congress of European Society for Opinion Surveys and Marketing Research, Rotterdam, 1969*.

MARKOV PROCESSES.

FOX (B.L.) and ROLPH (JOHN) Adaptive policies for Markov renewal programs. Santa Monica, 1971. pp. 17. *bibliog*. *(Rand Corporation. [Rand Reports]. 838)*

STEELE (JAMES D.) Markovian decision processes with limited state observability and unobservable costs. Santa Monica, 1972. pp. 13. *bibliog*. *(Rand Corporation. [Papers]. 4925)*

STEELE (JAMES D.) A model for the analysis of Markovian decision processes with unobservable states and unobservable costs. Santa Monica, 1972. pp. 8. *bibliog*. *(Rand Corporation. [Papers]. 4917)*

FLEMING (WENDELL HELMS) and RISHEL (RAYMOND W.) Deterministic and stochastic optimal control. Berlin, 1975. pp. 222. *bibliog*.

ISAACSON (DEAN L.) and MADSEN (RICHARD W.) Markov chains: theory and applications. New York, [1976]. pp. 256. *bibliog*.

MARKS OF ORIGIN.

UNITED NATIONS. Conference on Trade and Development. 1969. Rules of origin in the general scheme of preferences in favour of the developing countries: report by the secretariat of UNCTAD. (TD/B/AC.5/3/Rev.1). New York, 1969. pp. 22.

MAROONS.

GROOT (SILVIA W. DE) From isolation towards integration: the Surinam Maroons and their colonial rulers: official documents relating to the Djukas, 1845-1863. The Hague, 1977. pp. 113. *bibliog*. *(Instituut voor Taal-, Land- en Volkenkunde. Verhandelingen. [Deel] 80)*

MARRIAGE.

LASCH (CHRISTOPHER) Haven in a heartless world: the family besieged. New York, [1977]. pp. 230.

WORKING couples; edited by Rhona Rapoport and Robert N. Rapoport with Janice M. Bumstead. London, 1978. pp. 191. *bibliogs*.

— Burma.

SPIRO (MELFORD ELLIOT) Kinship and marriage in Burma: a cultural and psychodynamic analysis. Berkeley, Calif., [1977]. pp. 313. *bibliog*.

— France.

DUBY (GEORGES) Medieval marriage: two models from twelfth-century France; translated by Elborg Forster. Baltimore, [1978]. pp. 138. *(Johns Hopkins University. Department of History. Johns Hopkins Symposia in Comparative History) Originally presented in French as lectures at Johns Hopkins University in 1977*.

— Malaysia.

DUZA (M. BADRUD) and BALDWIN (C. STEPHEN) Nuptiality and population policy: an investigation in Tunisia, Sri Lanka, and Malaysia. New York, [1977]. pp. 83. *bibliog*.

— Nigeria.

MULLER (JEAN CLAUDE) Chez les Rukuba: parenté et mariage (État Benue- Plateau, Nigeria). Paris, 1976. pp. 206. *bibliog*. *(Paris. École Pratique des Hautes Études. Section des Sciences Économiques et Sociales. Cahiers de l'Homme. Nouvelle Série. 17) Cover bears title Parenté et mariage chez les Rukuba*.

— Sri Lanka.

DUZA (M. BADRUD) and BALDWIN (C. STEPHEN) Nuptiality and population policy: an investigation in Tunisia, Sri Lanka, and Malaysia. New York, [1977]. pp. 83. *bibliog*.

— Tunisia.

DUZA (M. BADRUD) and BALDWIN (C. STEPHEN) Nuptiality and population policy: an investigation in Tunisia, Sri Lanka, and Malaysia. New York, [1977]. pp. 83. *bibliog*.

— United Kingdom.

U.K. Office of Population Censuses and Surveys. Marriage and divorce statistics: review of the Registrar General on marriages and divorces in England and Wales. a., 1974(1st)- London. *Supersedes in part Registrar General's statistical review of England and Wales*.

LEVINE (DAVID) of the Ontario Institute for Studies in Education. Family formation in an age of nascent capitalism. New York, [1977]. pp. 194. *bibliog.*

ORFORD (JIM) and EDWARDS (GRIFFITH) Alcoholism: a comparison of treatment and advice, with a study of the influence of marriage. Oxford, 1977. pp. 175. *bibliog. (Bethlem Royal Hospital and Maudsley Hospital. Institute of Psychiatry. Maudsley Monographs. No. 26)*

MARRIAGE LAW
— Colombia.

JARAMILLO SALAZAR (PABLO) Epitome de la Ley Concha: la ley 54 de 1924 ante la constitucion; solucion juridica al problema. Bogota, 1972. pp. 168. *bibliog.*

MARRIED PEOPLE.

The COUPLE; edited by Marie Corbin. Harmondsworth, 1978. pp. 248.

— Employment.

WORKING couples; edited by Rhona Rapoport and Robert N. Rapoport with Janice M. Bumstead. London, 1978. pp. 191. *bibliogs.*

MARRIED WOMEN
— United States.

WOMEN into wives: the legal and economic impact of marriage; edited by Jane Roberts Chapman and Margaret Gates. Beverly Hills, [1977]. pp. 320. *bibliogs.*

MARSH (Sir RICHARD WILLIAM).

MARSH (Sir RICHARD WILLIAM) Off the rails: an autobiography. London, 1978. pp. 214.

MARTIAL LAW
— Pakistan.

PAKISTAN. Statutes, etc. 1977-1978. Martial law regulations. [Islamabad], 1978. pp. 67.

MARX (KARL).

MARX (KARL) A contribution to the critique of political economy;...translated from the second German edition by N.I. Stone, with an appendix containing Marx's Introduction to the critique recently published among his posthumous papers. Chicago, [1904]. pp. 314.

MARX (KARL) Karl Marx on value:...comments on Adolph Wagner's "Lehrbuch der politischen Ökonomie"...; translated by Angela Clifford. Belfast, 1971. pp. 37.

LIPSCHUTZ (ALEJANDRO) Marx y Lenin en la America Latina y los problemas indigenistas. La Habana, 1974. pp. 230.

BUONFINO (GIANCARLO) La politica culturale operaia da Marx e Lassalle alla rivoluzione di novembre, 1859-1919. Milano, 1975. pp. 211.

CENCINI (ALVARO) and SCHMITT (BERNARD) La pensée de Karl Marx: critique et synthèse. Albeuve, [1976 in progress].

BAGATURIIA (GEORGII ALEKSANDROVICH) and VYGODSKII (VITALII SOLOMONOVICH) Ekonomicheskoe nasledie Karla Marksa: istoriia, soderzhanie, metodologiia. Moskva, 1976. pp. 325.

FISTETTI (FRANCESCO) Critica dell'economia e critica della politica: Marx, Hegel e l'economia politica classica. Bari, [1976]. pp. 213. *bibliogs.*

GRASSI (ENRICO) L'"esposizione dialettica" nel Capitale di Marx; con introduzione di Luca Meldolesi. Roma, [1976]. pp. 102. *bibliogs.*

Il MARXISMO e lo stato: il dibattito aperto nella sinistra italiana sulle tesi di Norberto Bobbio. [Roma], 1976. pp. 215. *(Mondoperaio. Quaderni. Nuova Serie. 4)*

ORFEI (RUGGERO) Marx: il regno della libertà. Roma, 1976. pp. 255. *bibliogs.*

RIO (EDUARDO DEL) Marx for beginners; (English translation by Richard Appignanesi). London, [1976]. pp. 155.

KARL Marx: Biographie; (Autorenkollektiv: P.N. Fedossejew [and others]...; aus dem Russischen übersetzt von Hans Zikmund). 3rd ed. Berlin, 1977. pp. 896.

KARL Marx über Formen vorkapitalistischer Produktion: vergleichende Studien zur Geschichte des Grundeigentums, 1879-80; aus dem handschriftlichen Nachlass herausgegeben und eingeleitet von Hans-Peter Harstick. Frankfurt, [1977]. pp. 358. *bibliogs. (International Institute of Social History. Quellen und Studien zur Sozialgeschichte. Band 1)* Includes extracts from M.M. Kovalevskii's *Obshchinnoe zemlevladenie* translated and annotated by Marx.

LINARES (FILADELFO) Die Revolution bei Tocqueville und Marx. Percha am Starnberger See, [1977]. pp. 122.

MARX and Engels on ecology; edited and compiled by Howard L. Parsons. Westport, Conn., [1977]. pp. 262. *bibliog.*

MEHLMAN (JEFFREY) Revolution and repetition: Marx, Hugo, Balzac. Berkeley, Calif., [1977]. pp. 132.

PREYER (GERHARD) Untersuchung zu Voraussetzungen und zur Systematik der "Kritik der politischen Ökonomie" von Karl Marx. Frankfurt am Main, [1977]. pp. 228. *bibliog.*

ROSDOLSKY (ROMAN) The making of Marx's 'Capital'; translated by Pete Burgess. London, 1977. pp. 581. *bibliog.*

SAMARSKAIA (ELENA ALEKSANDROVNA) Poniatie praktiki u K. Marksa i sovremennye diskussii: o dialektike ob"ektivnogo i sub"ektivnogo v istoricheskom protsesse. Moskva, 1977. pp. 224.

ASSOUN (PAUL LAURENT) and RAULET (GERARD) Marxisme et théorie critique. Paris, [1978]. pp. 248.

BERLIN (Sir ISAIAH) Karl Marx: his life and environment. 4th ed. Oxford, 1978. pp. 228. *bibliog.*

CARLEBACH (JULIUS) Karl Marx and the radical critique of Judaism. London, [1978]. pp. 466. *bibliog.*

McMURTRY (JOHN MURRAY) The structure of Marx's world-view. Princeton, [1978]. pp. 269.

PADOVER (SAUL KUSSIEL) Karl Marx: an intimate biography. New York, [1978]. pp. 667. *bibliog.*

PEREZ-DIAZ (VICTOR) State, bureaucracy and civil society: a critical discussion of the political theory of Karl Marx. London, 1978. pp. 117.

— Bibliography.

PRIZHIZNENNYE izdaniia i publikatsii proizvedenii K. Marksa i F. Engel'sa: bibliograficheskii ukazatel'. Moskva, 1977. 2 vols.

MARXIAN ECONOMICS.

BORCHARDT (JULIAN) Die volkswirtschaftlichen Grundbegriffe nach der Lehre von Karl Marx. 2nd ed. Berlin, 1923. pp. 138.

POLITISCHE Ökonomie: (Lehrbuchwerk...unter der Gesamtredaktion...[of] G.A. Kozlov; [revised translation from the Russian]. Berlin, 1974-77. 4 vols.

RICARDIENS, Keynésiens et Marxistes: essais en économie politique non-néoclassique: actes du colloque de Nice, septembre 1972; (édité par C. Berthomieu [and others]). [Grenoble, 1974]. pp. 405. *bibliogs.*

CENCINI (ALVARO) and SCHMITT (BERNARD) La pensée de Karl Marx: critique et synthèse. Albeuve, [1976 in progress].

BAGATURIIA (GEORGII ALEKSANDROVICH) and VYGODSKII (VITALII SOLOMONOVICH) Ekonomicheskoe nasledie Karla Marksa: istoriia, soderzhanie, metodologiia. Moskva, 1976. pp. 325.

BRUNHOFF (SUZANNE DE) Marx on money; translated by Maurice J. Goldbloom. New York, [1976]. pp. 139.

Il COMUNISMO difficile: i comunisti dei consigli e la teoria marxiana dell'accumulazione e delle crisi; ([by Mario] Cogoy [and others]); a cura di Claudio Pozzoli. Bari, 1976. pp. 239. *bibliog.*

CRISI della teoria economica e crisi del capitalismo; di Guido Carandini [and others]. Milano, [1976]. pp. 183. *(Problemi del Socialismo. Quaderni. 1)*

GRASSI (ENRICO) L'"esposizione dialettica" nel Capitale di Marx; con introduzione di Luca Meldolesi. Roma, [1976]. pp. 102. *bibliogs.*

PUSENKOVA (IRINA VLADIMIROVNA) Neposredstvenno-obshchestvennyi trud i neobkhodimyi produkt pri sotsializme. Moskva, 1976. pp. 199.

ROGACHEV (SERGEI VLADIMIROVICH) and SHEKIR (N.S.) eds. Osobennosti deistviia ekonomicheskikh zakonov v usloviiakh razvitogo sotsializma. Moskva, 1976. pp. 180.

STRUKTURA materijalnih i novčanih tokova i njihov utjecaj na razvojnu politiku i opću privrednu ravnotežu. Zagreb, 1976. pp. 273. *bibliog.*

CUTLER (ANTONY J.) and others. Marx's 'Capital' and capitalism today. London, 1977-78. 2 vols. *bibliog.*

AMIN (SAMIR) Imperialism and unequal development. Hassocks, [1977]. pp. 267. *Translation of his L'impérialisme et développement inégal.*

ANCHISHKIN (ALEKSANDR IVANOVICH) The theory of growth of a socialist economy. Moscow, 1977. pp. 341.

BECKER (JAMES F.) Marxian political economy: an outline. Cambridge, 1977. pp. 326.

COMMUNITY or class struggle?; [by] John Cowley [and others]. London, 1977. pp. 246.

EKONOMICHESKIE zakony sotsializma i ikh ispol'zovanie v praktike kommunisticheskogo stroitel'stva. Minsk, 1977. pp. 271. *bibliog.*

FUNDAMENTALS of political economy; edited...by George C. Wang. [London, 1977]. pp. 505. *Translation from the Chinese.*

KOLM (SERGE CHRISTOPHE) La transition socialiste: la politique économique de gauche. Paris, 1977. pp. 212.

MEEK (RONALD LINDLEY) Smith, Marx and after: ten essays in the development of economic thought. London, 1977. pp. 193.

NABUDERE (DAN) The political economy of imperialism: its theoretical and polemical treatment from mercantilist to multilateral imperialism. London, [1977]. pp. 293. *bibliogs.*

PREYER (GERHARD) Untersuchung zu Voraussetzungen und zur Systematik der "Kritik der politischen Ökonomie" von Karl Marx. Frankfurt am Main, [1977]. pp. 228. *bibliog.*

RAZZHIGAEV (ANATOLII FEDOROVICH) Ekonomicheskie problemy stanovleniia truda kak potrebnosti. Moskva, 1977. pp. 126.

STEEDMAN (IAN) Marx after Sraffa. London, [1977]. pp. 218.

WARD (DWAYNE) Toward a critical political economics: a critique of liberal and radical economic thought. Santa Monica, Calif., [1977]. pp. 334. *bibliog.*

HARRISON (JOHN) Economist. Marxist economics for socialists: a critique of reformism. [London, 1978]. pp. 169. *bibliogs.*

MARXISM and the metropolis: new perspectives in urban political economy; edited by William K. Tabb and Larry Sawers. New York, 1978. pp. 376. *bibliogs. Based on a conference held in 1975 in New York City by the Union for Radical Political Economics.*

ŠIK (OTA) Pour une troisième voie; traduit de l'allemand par Marcel Chabernaud. [Paris, 1978]. pp. 254.

SOHN-RETHEL (ALFRED) Intellectual and manual labour: a critique of epistemology. London, 1978. pp. 216. *bibliog.*

MARXIAN ECONOMICS.(Cont.)

STATE and capital: a Marxist debate; edited by John Holloway and Sol Picciotto. London, 1978. pp. 220. *bibliog.*

WALKER (ANGUS) Marx: his theory and context: politics as economics: an introductory and critical essay on the political economy of Karl Marx. London, 1978. pp. 241. *bibliog.*

MARXISM.

NIEDER mit dem Marxismus. [Bern?, 1933?]. pp. 48. *(Separatdruck aus der Schweiz. Metallarbeiter-Zeitung)*

LORA (GUILLERMO) Bolivia y la revolucion permanente. [La Paz?], 1968. pp. 32.

PLAMENATZ (JOHN PETROV) Ideology. London, 1971. pp. 148. *bibliog.*

GRAMSCI (ANTONIO) Scritti giovanili, 1914-1918. Torino, 1972 repr. 1975. pp. 392. *(Opere. 8)*

HOBSBAWM (ERIC JOHN ERNEST) Marxism and anarchism: are they compatible? London, [1972?]. pp. 6.

BADALONI (NICOLA) Il marxismo di Gramsci: dal mito alla ricomposizione politica. [Torino, 1975]. pp. 187.

DUMENIL (GERARD) La position de classe des cadres et employés: la fonction capitaliste parcellaire. Grenoble, 1975. pp. 120.

L'ETAT contemporain et le marxisme; [by] J.-M. Vincent [and others]. Paris, 1975. pp. 235.

BÀCULO (LILIANA) ed. La crisi degli anni '70 nel dibattito marxista: saggi di analisi e teoria economica. Bari, [1976]. pp. 298.

BADALONI (NICOLA) and others. Problemi teorici del marxismo. Roma, 1976. pp. 248. *bibliogs.*

BADIOU (ALAIN) and BALMES (FRANÇOIS) De l'idéologie. Paris, 1976. pp. 129.

BATALOV (EDUARD IAKOVLEVICH) Philosophie de la révolte: critique de l'idéologie du gauchisme; (traduit du russe). Moscou, [1976]. pp. 332.

CULTURA popolare e marxismo; a cura di Raffaele Rauty. Roma, 1976. pp. 267. *bibliog.*

INTERNATIONAL THEORETICAL CONFERENCE, 1976. Lenin's doctrine of imperialism and the contemporary stage of the general crisis of capitalism. Prague, 1976. pp. 109. *(Marxism-Leninism and Our Time)*

KORSCH: der Klassiker des Antirevisionismus ([by] Arbeitsgruppe Bewusstseinsformen;...Christoph Behrend [and others]). Westberlin, [1976]. pp. 165.

MAFFESOLI (MICHEL) Logique de la domination. Paris, 1976. pp. 218. *bibliog.*

MUCHAIDZE (GURAM O.) Formirovanie ucheniia marksizma o partii. Tbilisi, 1976. pp. 237.

NAVASARDIAN (RAZMIK GAREGINOVICH) Formirovanie marksistskoi kontseptsii cheloveka: nachal'nyi period. Erevan, 1976. pp. 211. *bibliog.*

PICKVANCE (CHRISTOPHER GEOFFREY) Marxist approaches to the study of urban politics: divergences among some recent French studies. Canterbury, 1976. fo. 52. *Paper for the Political Studies Association Conference, Nottingham, 1976.*

ROVATTI (PIER ALDO) and others. Bisogni e teoria marxista. Milano, [1976]. pp. 246.

SAHLINS (MARSHALL DAVID) Culture and practical reason. Chicago, 1976. pp. 252. *bibliog.*

ZOLO (DANILO) Stato socialista e libertà borghesi: una discussione sui fondamenti della teoria politica marxista. Roma, 1976. pp. 189.

XXV s"ezd KPSS i razvitie marksistsko-leninskoi teorii: materialy Vsesoiuznoi nauchno-teoreticheskoi konferentsii, Moskva, 4-6 oktiabria 1976 goda: plenarnoe zasedanie; [doklady P.N. Fedoseeva, A.G. Egorova, N.N. Inozemtseva]. Moskva, 1977. pp. 110.

BALL (TERENCE) ed. Political theory and praxis: new perspectives. Minneapolis, Minn., [1977]. pp. 281. *Essays dedicated to the memory of Hannah Arendt.*

BLACKBURN (ROBIN) ed. Revolution and class struggle: a reader in Marxist politics. [London], 1977. pp. 444. *bibliog.*

The CANADIAN state: political economy and political power; (edited by Leo Panitch). Toronto, [1977]. pp. 472.

CHELOVEK kak ob"ekt sotsiologicheskogo issledovaniia; pod redaktsiei L.I. Spiridonova i Ia.I. Gilinskogo. Leningrad, 1977. pp. 197.

FISH (HAMILTON) An American manifesto of freedom in answer to the manifesto on communism, 1848. New York, [1977]. pp. 209. *bibliog.*

GODELIER (MAURICE) Horizon, trajets marxistes en anthropologie. 2nd ed. Paris, 1977. 2 vols. (in 1). *bibliog.*

HEVESI (MARIA) Iz istorii kritiki filosofskikh dogm II Internatsionala. Moskva, 1977. pp. 207.

JOURNES (CLAUDE) L'extrême gauche en Grande-Bretagne. Paris, 1977. pp. 229. *bibliog.*

KRAUSE (GUENTER) Das Elend der "Linken": zur Kritik der politischen Ökonomie des Linksrevisionismus. Berlin, 1977. pp. 135. *bibliog.*

LENIN: dedicated Marxist or revolutionary pragmatist; edited with an introduction by Stanley W. Page. 2nd ed. St. Louis, Mo., [1977]. pp. 114. *bibliog.*

MAKAROV (MIKHAIL GEORGIEVICH) Kategoriia "tsel'" v marksistskoi filosofii i kritika teleologii. Leningrad, 1977. pp. 188.

MANGENG (ELISABETH) Der Anachronismus in Theorie und Strategie der kommunistischen Partei: italienische Arbeiterwissenschaft gegen Theorie des Stamokap. Giessen, [1977]. pp. 285. *bibliog.*

NOLTE (ERNST) Marxismus, Faschismus, Kalter Krieg: Vorträge und Aufsätze, 1964-1976. Stuttgart, [1977]. pp. 400. *bibliog.*

PAPERS on class, hegemony and party; edited by Jon Bloomfield. London, 1977. pp. 125. *Papers originally delivered at the Communist University, held in London in 1976.*

PRICE (RONALD FRANCIS) Marx and education in Russia and China. London, [1977]. pp. 376. *bibliog.*

RAKOVSKI (MARC) Le marxisme face aux pays de l'Est. [Paris, 1977]. pp. 206.

RUBEN (DAVID HILLEL) Marxism and materialism: a study in marxist theory of knowledge. Hassocks, Sussex, 1977. pp. 199. *bibliogs.*

SAMARSKAIA (ELENA ALEKSANDROVNA) Poniatie praktiki u K. Marksa i sovremennye diskussii: o dialektike ob"ektivnogo i sub"ektivnogo v istoricheskom protsesse. Moskva, 1977. pp. 224.

SANTARELLI (ENZO) La revisione del marxismo in Italia: studi di critica storica. rev. ed. [Milano, 1977]. pp. 343.

SCHICCHI (SIMONE) Il Marxismo e la reazione dell'utilità marginale. Catania, 1977. pp. 191. *bibliog.*

SHER (GERSON S.) Praxis: Marxist criticism and dissent in socialist Yugoslavia. Bloomington, Ind., [1977]. pp. 360. *bibliog.*

VARIETIES of Marxism; edited by Shlomo Avineri. The Hague, 1977. pp. 404. *Based on papers delivered at an international symposium dedicated to the memory of George Lichtheim and held at the Van Leer Jerusalem Foundation, 1974.*

VECA (SALVATORE) Saggio sul programma scientifico di Marx. Milano, 1977. pp. 184. *bibliog.*

100 Jahre "Anti-Dühring": Marxismus, Weltanschauung, Wissenschaft; herausgegeben von R.Kirchhoff und T.I. Oiserman. Berlin, 1978. pp. 429. *(Akademie der Wissenschaften der DDR. Zentralinstitut für Philosophie. Schriften zur Philosophie und ihrer Geschichte. 17)*

ASSOUN (PAUL LAURENT) and RAULET (GERARD) Marxisme et théorie critique. Paris, [1978]. pp. 248.

AUSTRO-Marxism; texts translated and edited by Tom Bottomore and Patrick Goode. Oxford, 1978. pp. 308. *bibliog.*

CORRIGAN (PAUL) and LEONARD (PETER TERRANCE) Social work practice under capitalism: a marxist approach. London, 1978. pp. 161.

GRUNDBEGRIFFE der marxistischen Theorie: Handbuch zur Theorie der bürgerlichen Gesellschaft; (Joachim Bischoff, Hrsg.). Hamburg, [1978]. pp. 264.

KISSIN (S.F.) Farewell to revolution: Marxist philosophy and the modern world. London, [1978]. pp. 256.

McMURTRY (JOHN MURRAY) The structure of Marx's world-view. Princeton, [1978]. pp. 269.

RAKOVSKI (MARC) Towards an east European Marxism. London, 1978. pp. 140.

RELATIONS of production: Marxist approaches to economic anthropology; edited by David Seddon. London, 1978. pp. 414. *bibliog.*

SEVE (LUCIEN) Man in marxist theory and the psychology of personality;... translated from the French by John McGreal. Hassocks, Sussex, 1978. pp. 508.

THERBORN (GÖRAN) What does the ruling class do when it rules?: state apparatuses and state power under feudalism, capitalism and socialism. London, [1978]. pp. 290.

— **Dictionaries and encyclopedias.**

DIZIONARIO dei termini marxisti; [by] Paolo Biazzi [and others]; a cura di Ernesto Mascitelli. Milano, [1977]. pp. 437. *bibliog.*

MASCHINENFABRIK ESSLINGEN AG.

HENTSCHEL (VOLKER) Wirtschaftsgeschichte der Maschinenfabrik Esslingen AG, 1846- 1918: eine historisch-betriebswirtschaftliche Analyse. Stuttgart, [1977]. pp. 170. *bibliog. (Arbeitskreis für Moderne Sozialgeschichte. Industrielle Welt. Band 22)*

MASOWE APOSTLES.

DILLON-MALONE (CLIVE MARY) The Korsten basketmakers: a study of the Masowe Apostles, an indigenous African religious movement. Manchester, [1978]. pp. 169. *bibliog.*

MASS MEDIA.

MASS media policies in changing cultures; edited by George Gerbner. New York, [1977]. pp. 291. *bibliog.*

SMITH (ANTHONY) 1938- . The politics of information: problems of policy in modern media. London, 1978. pp. 252.

— **Political aspects — India.**

INDIA. 1977. White Paper on misuse of mass media during the internal emergency. [Delhi], 1977. pp. 87.

— — **Pakistan.**

PAKISTAN. 1978. White Paper on misuse of media, December 20, 1971-July 4, 1977 (with Summary). [Islamabad], 1978. 2 vols. (in 1).

— — **United Kingdom.**

WHALE (JOHN) The politics of the media. Glasgow, 1977. pp. 176. *bibliog.*

— **Social aspects.**

MASS communication and society; edited by James Curran [and others]. London, [1977]. pp. 479. *bibliogs.*

— Australia.

AUSTRALIA. Department of the Media. Report of activities. a., 1972/73(1st)- Canberra. *Included in AUSTRALIA. Parliament. [Parliamentary papers].*

— United Kingdom.

PIEPE (ANTHONY) and others. Mass media and cultural relationships. Farnborough, Hants., [1978]. pp. 168.

MASS SOCIETY.

BIDDISS (MICHAEL D.) The age of the masses: ideas and society in Europe since 1870. Harmondsworth, 1977. pp. 379. *bibliog.*

MASSACHUSETTS

— Politics and government.

SOCIETY, freedom, and conscience: the American revolution in Virginia, Massachusetts, and New York; [by] Jack P. Greene [and others]; edited by Richard M. Jellison. New York, [1976]. pp. 233. *(Miami University (Ohio). McClellan Lectures. 1973, 1974, 1975)*

MASTER AND SERVANT

— Germany.

LECHELER (HELMUT) Die Personalgewalt öffentlicher Dienstherren. Berlin, [1977]. pp. 280. *bibliog.*

MATACO INDIANS.

RODRIGUEZ (NEMESIO J.) Oppression in Argentina: the Mataco case. Copenhagen, 1975. pp. 39. *(International Work Group for Indigenous Affairs. Documents. 21)*

MATERIALISM.

GREGORY (FREDERICK) Scientific materialism in nineteenth century Germany. Dordrecht, [1977]. pp. 279. *bibliog.*

MATERNAL AND INFANT WELFARE

— Australia.

FAMILY planning and health care for infants and mothers. Canberra, 1977. pp. 88. *bibliog. (Australia. Commission of Inquiry into Poverty. Social/Medical Aspects of Poverty Series)*

— France.

MONNIER (ALAIN) La naissance d'un enfant: incidences sur les conditions de vie des familles; préface d'Alain Girard. [Paris], 1977. pp. 231. *(France. Institut National d'Etudes Démographiques. Travaux et Documents. Cahiers. No. 81)*

— United Kingdom.

MILSOM (PENNY) Unsupported mothers on social security. London, [1972]. pp. 9. *(Mothers in Action. Study Pamphlets. No.2)*

CO-OPERATIVE WOMEN'S GUILD. Maternity: letters from working-women; collected by the Women's Co-operative Guild; edited and introduced by Margaret Llewelyn Davies; new introduction by Gloden Dallas. London, 1978. pp. 212. *Reprint of the book first published in 1915, with a new introduction.*

MATHEMATICAL ANALYSIS.

An INTRODUCTION to linear analysis; [by] Donald L. Kreider [and others]. Reading, Mass., [1966]. pp. 773. *bibliog.*

BURKILL (JOHN CHARLES) and BURKILL (HARRY) A second course in mathematical analysis. Cambridge, 1970. pp. 526. *bibliog.*

BAUMOL (WILLIAM JACK) Economic theory and operations analysis. 4th ed. Englewood Cliffs, [1977]. pp. 695. *bibliogs.*

BINMORE (KENNETH GEORGE) Mathematical analysis: a straightforward approach. Cambridge, 1977. pp. 257. *bibliog.*

MATHEMATICAL MODELS.

MODELING for government and business: essays in honor of Prof. Dr. P.J. Verdoorn; edited by C.A. Van Bochove [and others]. Leiden, 1977. pp. 355. *bibliogs.*

MORALES (ROLANDO) Etude et analyse des modèles ARMA de Box-Jenkins en vue de leur utilisation en économétrie. Berne, [1977]. pp. 341. *bibliog. (Geneva. Université. Faculté des Sciences Economiques et Sociales. Collection des Thèses. No. 239)*

WILLIAMS (H.P.) Model building in mathematical programming. Chichester, [1978]. pp. 330. *bibliog.*

MATHEMATICAL OPTIMIZATION.

ROSS (SHELDON M.) Applied probability models with optimization applications. San Francisco, [1970]. pp. 198.

FLEMING (WENDELL HELMS) and RISHEL (RAYMOND W.) Deterministic and stochastic optimal control. Berlin, 1975. pp. 222. *bibliog.*

ARROW (KENNETH JOSEPH) and others. Studies in resource allocation processes; edited by Kenneth J. Arrow and Leonid Hurwicz. Cambridge, 1977. pp. 482. *bibliogs.*

AUBIN (JEAN PIERRE) Applied abstract analysis; translated by Carole Labrousse. New York, [1977]. pp. 263.

MATHEMATICAL STATISTICS.

RAO (CALYAMPUDI RADHAKRISHNA) Linear statistical inference and it applications. 2nd ed. New York, [1973]. pp. 625. *bibliogs.*

ROHATGI (VIJAY K.) An introduction to probability theory and mathematical statistics. New York, [1976]. pp. 684. *bibliog.*

LEAMER (EDWARD E.) Specification searches: ad hoc inference with nonexperimental data. New York, [1978]. pp. 370. *bibliog.*

MATHEMATICS.

KEMENY (JOHN G.) and others. Finite mathematics, with business applications. 2nd ed. Englewood Cliffs, 1962. pp. 529.

— Dictionaries — Polyglot.

HEBÁK (PETR) and HUSTOPECKÝ (JIŘÍ) compilers. Šestijazyčný slovník termínů z regresní analýzy: [Czech, Russian, Polish, English, French, German]. Praha, 1978. pp. 211. *With preface and explanatory notes in each language.*

— Philosophy.

INTERNATIONAL CONGRESS OF LOGIC, METHODOLOGY AND PHILOSOPHY OF SCIENCE, 5TH, LONDON, ONTARIO, 1975. Logic, foundations of mathematics, and computability theory: part one of the proceedings...; edited by Robert E. Butts and Jaakko Hintikka. Dordrecht, [1977]. pp. 406. *bibliogs. (Western Ontario. University. University of Western Ontario Series in Philosophy of Science. 9)*

LAKATOS (IMRE) Mathematics, science and epistemology: philosophical papers, vol. 2; edited by John Worrall and Gregory Currie. Cambridge, [1978]. pp. 285. *bibliogs.*

MATHER (COTTON).

MIDDLEKAUFF (ROBERT) The Mathers: three generations of Puritan intellectuals, 1596- 1728. New York, 1971. pp. 440.

MATHER (INCREASE).

MIDDLEKAUFF (ROBERT) The Mathers: three generations of Puritan intellectuals, 1596- 1728. New York, 1971. pp. 440.

MATHER (RICHARD).

MIDDLEKAUFF (ROBERT) The Mathers: three generations of Puritan intellectuals, 1596- 1728. New York, 1971. pp. 440.

MATRICES.

FRYER (M.J.) An introduction to linear programming and matrix game theory. London, 1978. pp. 121.

MATTEI (ENRICO).

GALLI (GIORGIO) La sfida perduta: biografia politica di Enrico Mattei. Milano, [1976]. pp. 261.

MAURITANIA.

TOUPET (CHARLES) and PITTE (JEAN ROBERT) La Mauritanie. [Paris, 1977]. pp. 128. *bibliog.*

— Census.

MAURITANIA. Census. 1976. Seconds résultats provisoires du recensement général de la population: population au 1 er janvier, 1977. Nouakchott, [1977?]. fo. 54.

— Statistics.

MAURITANIA. Direction de la Statistique et des Etudes Economiques. Bulletin mensuel statistique. m., 1968 [no.1]-, with gap (Ja 1970). Nouakchott. *Supersedes MAURITANIA. Service de la Statistique. Bulletin statistique (Mr 1970 - Mr 1962, with gaps).*

MAURITIUS

— Constitutional history.

NAPAL (D.) ed. Les constitutions de l'île Maurice: documents (1723- 1961). Port Louis, 1962. pp. 151. *(Mauritius. Mauritius Archives. Publications. No. 6)*

— Economic policy.

MAURITIUS. Ministry of Information and Broadcasting. 1973. Le développement: engagement et participation. Port Louis, 1973. pp. 44.

MAURITIUS. 1976. 1975-1980 5-year plan for social and economic development. [Port Louis, 1976]. pp. 203.

— Social policy.

MAURITIUS. Ministry of Information and Broadcasting. 1973. Le développement: engagement et participation. Port Louis, 1973. pp. 44.

MAURITIUS. 1976. 1975-1980 5-year plan for social and economic development. [Port Louis, 1976]. pp. 203.

MAURRAS (CHARLES MARIE PHOTIUS).

SUTTON (MICHAEL JOHN) Nationalism, positivism and Catholicism: a study of the controversy arising from the proposal of Charles Maurras for a political alliance between positivists and Catholics. [1978]. fo.431. *bibliog. Typescript. 2 pamphlets in end pocket. Ph.D. (London) thesis: unpublished. This thesis is the property of London University and may not be removed from the Library.*

MAYAS.

ANTHROPOLOGY and history in Yucatán; edited by Grant D. Jones. Austin, Tex., [1977]. pp. 344. *bibliog.*

— Housing.

CAMBRIDGE. University. Centre of Latin American Studies. Working Papers. No.19. Ethnographic notes on the Maya of Belize, Central America; [by] J.C.H. King. Cambridge, [1974]. pp. 43. *bibliog.*

MAYORS

— United States.

ALLSWANG (JOHN M.) Bosses, machines, and urban voters: an American symbiosis. Port Washington, 1977. pp. 157. *bibliog.*

NELSON (WILLIAM E.) of Ohio State University and MERANTO (PHILIP J.) Electing black mayors: political action in the black community. Columbus, Ohio, [1977]. pp. 403.

MAZATEC INDIANS.

BARABAS (ALICIA) and BARTOLOME (MIGUEL) Hydraulic development and ethnocide: the Mazatec and Chinantec people of Oaxaca, Mexico. Copenhagen, 1973. pp. 20. *bibliog. (International Work Group for Indigenous Affairs. Documents. 15)*

MEANING.

SEGERSTEDT (TORGNY TORGNYSSON) Symbolmiljö, mening och attityd: ett forskningsprojekt. Uppsala, 1956. pp. 55. *(Uppsala. Universitet. Årsskrifter. 1956:4)*

SAMPSON (GEOFFREY) Natural language and the paradox of the liar. The Hague, [1972]. pp. 18. *(Reprinted from Semiotica vol. 5. No. 4, 1972)*

MEANING in anthropology; edited by Keith H. Basso and Henry A. Selby. Albuquerque, [1976]. pp. 255. *bibliog. (School of American Research. Advanced Seminar Series) Based on a conference held in 1974 in Santa Fe, New Mexico.*

MEANING (PHILOSOPHY).

PUTNAM (HILARY) Meaning and the moral sciences. London, 1978. pp. 145.

WEINSTEIN (MICHAEL A.) Meaning and appreciation: time and modern political life. West Lafayette, Ind., 1978. pp. 155.

MEASURE THEORY.

FADEN (ARNOLD M.) Economics of space and time: the measure-theoretic foundations of social science. Ames, 1977. pp. 703.

PFEFFER (WASHEK F.) Integrals and measures. New York, [1977]. pp. 259. *bibliog.*

MEAT.

COMMONWEALTH SECRETARIAT. Meat and dairy products. s-a., N 1978(1st)- London.

— Prices — Australia.

AUSTRALIA. Bureau of Agricultural Economics. 1973. A consideration of movements in meat prices: a paper submitted to the Joint Parliamentary Committee on Prices. Canberra, 1973 repr. 1975. pp. 48. *bibliog. (Occasional Papers. No. 16)*

MEAT INDUSTRY AND TRADE

— Denmark.

SPINK (REGINALD) DBC: the story of the Danish Bacon Company, 1902-1977. Welwyn Garden City, [1977]. pp. 96. *bibliog.*

MECHANICAL ENGINEERING

— Italy.

FEDERMECCANICA. Dalla conflittualità al consenso: opinioni e proposte degli imprenditori sulla crisi attuale. Milano, [1976]. pp. 129. *Proceedings of a conference held at Rome, 8 March 1976.*

MEDELLIN, COLOMBIA

— Economic conditions.

WALTON (JOHN) Elites and economic development: comparative studies on the political economy of Latin American cities. Austin, [1977]. pp. 257. *bibliog. (Texas University. Institute of Latin American Studies. Latin American Monographs. No. 41)*

MEDIATION AND CONCILIATION, INDUSTRIAL

— Canada — British Columbia.

BRITISH COLUMBIA. Department of Labour. 1968. Excerpts from remarks made by Leslie R. Peterson, Minister of Labour on second reading of Bill no. 33, an Act respecting Collective Bargaining and Mediation. [Victoria], 1968. pp. 20.

— United Kingdom.

ADVISORY, CONCILIATION AND ARBITRATION SERVICE [U.K.]. Reports. [London, 1975 in progress].

MEDICAL APPOINTMENTS AND SCHEDULES.

AMBULATORY care systems. Lexington, Mass., [1977 in progress].

MEDICAL CARE.

MEDICAL encounters: the experience of illness and treatment; edited by Alan Davis and Gordon Horobin. London, [1977]. pp. 223. *bibliogs.*

BASCH (PAUL F.) International health. New York, 1978. pp. 380. *bibliogs.*

— Canada.

SODERSTROM (LEE) The Canadian health system. London, [1978]. pp. 271. *bibliog.*

— Russia — Uzbekistan.

KADYROV (ASADULLA ABDULLAEVICH) Stanovlenie i razvitie sovetskogo zdravookhraneniia v Uzbekistane; pod redaktsiei...B.D. Petrova. Tashkent, 1976. pp. 133. *bibliog.*

— Underdeveloped areas.

See UNDERDEVELOPED AREAS — Medical care.

— United Kingdom.

GAMMON (MAX) Public and private provision for medical care in Great Britain. London, 1976. pp. 10.

— United States.

FORD (AMASA B.) Urban health in America. New York, 1976. pp. 294. *bibliog.*

KLAW (SPENCER) The great American medicine show: the unhealthy state of U.S. medical care, and what can be done about it. [Harmondsworth, 1976]. pp. 316.

ENOS (DARRYL D.) and SULTAN (PAUL) The sociology of health care: social, economic, and political perspectives. New York, 1977. pp. 420. *bibliogs.*

HEALTH services: the local perspective; edited by Arthur Levin. New York, 1977. pp. 262. *bibliog. Based on a conference held by the Academy of Political Science, New York City.*

TOWARD a national health policy: public policy and the control of health-care costs; edited by Kenneth M. Friedman [and] Stuart H. Rakoff. Lexington, Mass., [1977]. pp. 257. *Papers delivered at two meetings sponsored by the Committee on Health Politics at the 1975 Annual Meeting of the American Political Science Association in San Francisco.*

MEDICAL CARE, COST OF

— Canada — Ontario.

MANGA (P.) The income distribution effect of medical insurance in Ontario. [Toronto, 1978]. pp. 215. *bibliog. (Ontario. Economic Council. Occasional Papers. 6)*

— France.

DUMONT (JACQUES) and LATOUCHE (JEAN) L'hospitalisation malade du profit. [Paris, 1977]. pp. 222.

— United States.

HAVIGHURST (CLARK C.) Controlling health care costs: strengthening the private sector's hand. Washington, 1977. pp. 27. *(American Enterprise Institute for Public Policy Research. Reprints. No.68)*

TOWARD a national health policy: public policy and the control of health-care costs; edited by Kenneth M. Friedman [and] Stuart H. Rakoff. Lexington, Mass., [1977]. pp. 257. *Papers delivered at two meetings sponsored by the Committee on Health Politics at the 1975 Annual Meeting of the American Political Science Association in San Francisco.*

MEDICAL CENTRES

— United Kingdom.

SCOTTISH HOSPITAL CENTRE. Centrepiece Series. Health centres: design-in-use study. Edinburgh, 1974. pp. 72. *bibliog.*

MEDICAL ECONOMICS.

JÖNSSON (BENGT) Cost-benefit analysis in public health and medical care. Lund, [1976]. pp. 141. *bibliog.*

— France.

DUMONT (JACQUES) and LATOUCHE (JEAN) L'hospitalisation malade du profit. [Paris, 1977]. pp. 222.

— Sweden.

JÖNSSON (BENGT) Cost-benefit analysis in public health and medical care. Lund, [1976]. pp. 141. *bibliog.*

— United Kingdom.

CLINICAL practice and economics; edited by C.I. Phillips and J. N. Wolfe. Tunbridge Wells, 1977. pp. 216. *bibliogs.*

ECONOMIC aspects of health services; edited by A.J. Culyer and K.G. Wright. London, 1978. pp. 190. *bibliogs.*

— United States.

KLAW (SPENCER) The great American medicine show: the unhealthy state of U.S. medical care, and what can be done about it. [Harmondsworth, 1976]. pp. 316.

BURROW (JAMES GORDON) Organized medicine in the progressive era: the move toward monopoly. Baltimore, [1977]. pp. 218.

ENOS (DARRYL D.) and SULTAN (PAUL) The sociology of health care: social, economic, and political perspectives. New York, 1977. pp. 420. *bibliogs.*

MEDICAL ETHICS.

RAMSEY (PAUL) Ethics at the edges of life: medical and legal intersections. New Haven, 1978. pp. 353. *(Columbia University. Bampton Lectures in America)*

MEDICAL FEES

— Australia — New South Wales.

MASON (Sir ANTHONY FRANK) General practitioner fees in New South Wales: inquiry into the fees to be adopted for general practitioner medical services in New South Wales, items 1 and 4, for the purpose of the National Health Act. in Australia. Parliament. Parliamentary papers, 1972, vol. 5.

MEDICAL GEOGRAPHY.

LEARMONTH (ANDREW T.A.) Patterns of disease and hunger. Newton Abbot, [1978]. pp. 256. *bibliog.*

MEDICAL LAWS AND LEGISLATION

— United States.

REILLY (PHILIP) Genetics, law and social policy. Cambridge, Mass., 1977. pp. 275.

RAMSEY (PAUL) Ethics at the edges of life: medical and legal intersections. New Haven, 1978. pp. 353. *(Columbia University. Bampton Lectures in America)*

MEDICAL PERSONNEL

— New Zealand.

NEW ZEALAND. Department of Health. Management Services and Research Unit. Health manpower resources. irreg., 1978- Wellington.

— Underdeveloped areas.

See UNDERDEVELOPED AREAS — Medical personnel.

— United Kingdom.

CUMING (MAURICE WILLIAM) Personnel management in the National Health Service. London, [1978]. pp. 270.

— — Scotland — Salaries, pensions, etc.

U.K. Government Actuary's Department. 1977. National Health Service, Scotland, Act, 1947: National Health Service Superannuation Scheme for Scotland, 1969- 1974; report by the Government Actuary. Edinburgh, 1977. pp. 24.

— United States.

GOLDSTEIN (HAROLD M.) and HOROWITZ (MORRIS AARON) Entry-level health occupations: development and future. Baltimore, [1977]. pp. 100. *bibliog.*

SORKIN (ALAN L.) Health manpower: an economic perspective. Lexington, Mass., [1977]. pp. 175.

MEDICAL PERSONNEL AND PATIENT

— United Kingdom.

PATIENTS ASSOCIATION. Can I insist? London, [1974]. pp. 13.

MEDICAL POLICY.

ROEMER (MILTON IRWIN) Comparative national policies on health care. New York, [1977]. pp. 252. *bibliogs.*

— China.

LAMPTON (DAVID M.) The politics of medicine in China: the policy process, 1949-1977. Boulder, Colo., 1977. pp. 301. *bibliog.*

— United Kingdom.

WATKIN (BRIAN) The National Health Service: the first phase: 1948-1974 and after. London, 1978. pp. 170. *bibliog.*

— United States.

HEALTH services: the local perspective; edited by Arthur Levin. New York, 1977. pp. 262. *bibliog.* Based on a conference held by the Academy of Political Science, New York City.

KRAUSE (ELLIOTT A.) Power and illness : the political sociology of health and medical care. New York, [1977]. pp. 383.

TOWARD a national health policy: public policy and the control of health-care costs; edited by Kenneth M. Friedman [and] Stuart H. Rakoff. Lexington, Mass., [1977]. pp. 257. *Papers delivered at two meetings sponsored by the Committee on Health Politics at the 1975 Annual Meeting of the American Political Science Association in San Francisco.*

DAVIS (KAREN) and SCHOEN (CATHY) Health and the war on poverty: a ten-year appraisal. Washington, D.C., [1978]. pp. 230. *(Brookings Institution. Studies in Social Economics)*

MEDICAL RESEARCH

— Pacific, The.

HODGE (JAMES VINCENT) Reports to the South Pacific Medical Research Committee, Medical Research Council of New Zealand, on visits to 1. The Cook Islands. 2. Fiji and Western Samoa. [Wellington?], 1970. fo. 10, 16.

— United Kingdom.

U.K. Advisory Panel on Health and Health Policy. 1977. Health and health policy: priorities for research;...report... to the Research Initiatives Board; [M. Kogan, chairman]. [London, 1977]. 1 vol. (various pagings). *bibliog.*

MEDICAL SOCIETIES

— United States.

BURROW (JAMES GORDON) Organized medicine in the progressive era: the move toward monopoly. Baltimore, [1977]. pp. 218.

MEDICAL STATISTICS.

BAILEY (NORMAN THOMAS JOHN) Mathematics, statistics, and systems for health. Chichester, [1977]. pp. 222. *bibliog. Based on his The mathematical approach to biology and medicine, published in 1967.*

MEDICI FAMILY.

KENT (DALE) The rise of the Medici: faction in Florence, 1426-1434. Oxford, 1978. pp. 389. *bibliog.*

MEDICINE

— Mathematics.

BAILEY (NORMAN THOMAS JOHN) Mathematics, statistics, and systems for health. Chichester, [1977]. pp. 222. *bibliog. Based on his The mathematical approach to biology and medicine, published in 1967.*

— Political aspects.

The CULTURAL crisis of modern medicine; edited by John Ehrenreich. New York, [1978]. pp. 300.

— Practice.

BOTHA (HOWARD P.) Die magisterstudie in geneeskundige praktyk (M. Prax. Med.) van die Universiteit van Pretoria. Pretoria, 1971. pp. 60. *bibliog. (Pretoria. University of Pretoria. Publications. New Series. No. 64) With English summary.*

— Study and teaching — South Africa.

BOTHA (HOWARD P.) Die magisterstudie in geneeskundige praktyk (M. Prax. Med.) van die Universiteit van Pretoria. Pretoria, 1971. pp. 60. *bibliog. (Pretoria. University of Pretoria. Publications. New Series. No. 64) With English summary.*

— — United States.

KAUFMAN (MARTIN) American medical education: the formative years, 1765-1910. Westport, Conn., 1976. pp. 208. *bibliog.*

— United States — History.

BURROW (JAMES GORDON) Organized medicine in the progressive era: the move toward monopoly. Baltimore, [1977]. pp. 218.

MEDICINE, CLINICAL

— Decision making.

SHAPIRA (EDGAR) Systems analysis of clinical decision-making: a suggested approach. 1977. fo. 155. *bibliog. Typescript. Ph.D. (London) thesis: unpublished. This thesis is the property of London University and may not be removed from the Library.*

MEDICINE, PRIMITIVE

— South Africa.

NGUBANE (HARRIET) Body and mind in Zulu medicine: an ethnography of health and disease in Nyuswa-Zulu thought and practice. London, 1977. pp. 184. *bibliog.*

MEDICINE, STATE

— Canada.

SODERSTROM (LEE) The Canadian health system. London, [1978]. pp. 271. *bibliog.*

— — Saskatchewan.

SASKATCHEWAN. Department of Health. Annual report. a., 1976/77- Regina.

— New Zealand.

NEW ZEALAND. Department of Health. 1976. Functions and responsibilities. Wellington, 1976. pp. 73. *bibliog.*

— Russia.

SOVETSKOE ZDRAVOOKHRANENIE; [pd. by] Ministerstvo Zdravookhraneniia [Russia]. m. (sometime bi-m.), 1943, nos. 1/2, 7/8-12; 1944, nos. 1/2-4/5, 7/8-12; 1945, 1950- with gap (My 1973). Moskva.

— United Kingdom.

NORTHERN REGIONAL HEALTH AUTHORITY. Regional strategic plan, 1977-1986. [Newcastle upon Tyne], 1977. pp. 185.

RADICAL STATISTICS HEALTH GROUP. In defence of the NHS. London, 1977. pp. 41.

ABEL-SMITH (BRIAN) National Health Service: the first thirty years. London, H.M.S.O., 1978. pp. 66. *bibliog.*

BROWN (RONALD GORDON SCLATER) The changing National Health Service. 2nd ed. London, 1978. pp. 109. *bibliogs.*

BRUNEL UNIVERSITY. Department of Government. The working of the National Health Service. London, 1978. pp. 238. *bibliog. (U.K. Royal Commission on the National Health Service, 1976. Research Papers. No. 1)*

HELLER (TOM D.) Restructuring the health service. London, [1978]. pp. 114.

U.K. Department of Health and Social Security. 1978. Health and personal social services in England: DHSS planning guidelines for 1978/79. [London, 1978]. pp. 26.

WATKIN (BRIAN) The National Health Service: the first phase: 1948-1974 and after. London, 1978. pp. 170. *bibliog.*

— — Ireland, Northern.

IRELAND, NORTHERN. Department of Health and Social Services. Summary of health and personal social services accounts...together with the reports of the Comptroller and Auditor-General; (formerly Summary of health services accounts). a., 1971/72- Belfast. *Mr 24 1948/Mr 31 1949 [1st issue]- 1970/71 included in IRELAND, NORTHERN. Parliament. House of Commons. [Papers].*

— — Scotland.

PLANNING EXCHANGE. Newsheets. 3. Reorganization of the National Health Service in Scotland. Glasgow, [1975]. pp. 33. *bibliog.*

MEDICINES, PATENT, PROPRIETARY, ETC.

I PREZZI d'imperio delle specialità medicinali: atti del Convegno di Pavia del 23 gennaio 1976 ordinati e presentati dai professori A. Grisoli e G. Manera. Padova, 1976. pp. 245. *bibliog. (Pavia. Università. Centro Studi sulle Comunità Europee. Pubblicazioni. 4)*

MEDITERRANEAN.

VADROT (CLAUDE MARIE) Mort de la Méditerranée. Paris, [1977]. pp. 253.

— Commerce — France.

DOSSIERS sur le commerce français en Méditerranée orientale au XVIIIe siècle; [by] Jean-Pierre Filippini [and others]. Paris, [1976]. pp. 251. *bibliog. (Paris. Université de Paris II. Travaux et Recherches. Série Sciences Historiques. 10)*

— Economic conditions.

L'INDUSTRIALIZZAZIONE del Mediterraneo: movimenti di manodopera e capitali; a cura di Roberto Aliboni. Roma, [1977]. pp. 193. *bibliog. (Istituto Affari Internazionali. Collana "Lo Spettatore Internazionale".42)*

MEDITERRANEAN.(Cont.)

— Foreign relations.

COOPERAZIONE e sicurezza nel Mediterraneo. [Roma, 1976]. pp. 173. *(Istituto per le Relazioni tra l'Italia e i Paesi dell'Africa, America Latina e Medio Oriente. Collana Atti e Documenti. 8) Papers in Italian and French with English summaries.*

— Industries.

DEMAILLY (SERGE) and LE MOAL (YVON) Avenir industriel du Bassin Méditerranéen: bilan d'une recherche exploratoire: portée et sens des actions des firmes. Marseille, [Organisation d'Etudes d'Aménagement de l'Aire Metropolitaine Provence-Côte d'Azur], 1973. 1 vol. (various pagings).

MEDVEDEV (ROI ALEKSANDROVICH).

Une OPPOSITION socialiste en Union Soviétique aujourd'hui: (samizdat Vingtième siècle); introduction d'E. Bérard. Paris, 1976. pp. 205.

MEDWAY VALLEY

— Industries.

PRESTON (J.M.) Industrial Medway: an historical survey;... the industrial development of the Lower Medway Valley with special reference to the nineteenth and early twentieth centuries. Rochester, [1977]. pp. 218. *bibliog.*

MEES (WILLEM CORNELIS).

LAAR (H.J.M. VAN DE) Opperbankier en wetenschapsman Willem Cornelis Mees, 1813-1884. 's Gravenhage, 1978. pp. 475. *bibliog.*

MEGHALAYA

— Economic policy.

MEGHALAYA. Planning Department. 1976. Mid-term review of fifth five year plan: revised outlays and targets. [Shillong, 1976]. pp. 230.

— Social policy.

MEGHALAYA. Planning Department. 1976. Mid-term review of fifth five year plan: revised outlays and targets. [Shillong, 1976]. pp. 230.

MEHINACU INDIANS

— Social life and customs.

GREGOR (THOMAS) Mehinaku: the drama of daily life in a Brazilian Indian village. Chicago, [1977]. pp. 382. *bibliog.*

MEINHOF (ULRIKE MARIE).

BECKER (JILLIAN) Hitler's children: the story of the Baader-Meinhof terrorist gang. Philadelphia, [1977]. pp. 322. *bibliog.*

MEMORY.

PIAGET (JEAN) and INHELDER (BÄRBEL) Memory and intelligence;...in collaboration with Hermine Sinclair-de Zwart; translated from the French by Arnold J. Pomerans. London, [1973] repr. 1978. pp. 414.

SHORT-term memory; edited by Diana Deutsch [and] J. Anthony Deutsch. New York, 1975. pp. 411. *bibliogs.*

ANDERSON (JOHN ROBERT) Language, memory, and thought. New York, [1976]. pp. 546. *bibliogs.*

MENDÈS-FRANCE (PIERRE).

MENDÈS-FRANCE (PIERRE) Liberté, liberté chérie, 1940-42; suivi de Roissy-en- France: récit d'un vol du Groupe Lorraine, 3 octobre 1945. [Paris, 1977]. pp. 430.

MENDOZA (PROVINCE)

— Politics and government.

GRECO (JUAN) Los sucesos de Alvear y la barbarie lencinista. Mendoza, Argentine Republic, 1929. pp. 188.

OLGUIN (DARDO) Lencinas, el caudillo radical: historia y mito. Mendoza, Argentine Republic, 1961. pp. 566.

MENGER (ANTON).

HOERNER (HANS) Anton Menger: Recht und Sozialismus. Frankfurt am Main, [1977]. pp. 217.

MENNONITES IN IOWA.

SCHWIEDER (ELMER) and SCHWIEDER (DOROTHY) A peculiar people: Iowa's Old Order Amish. Ames, Iowa, 1975 repr. 1977. pp. 188. *bibliog.*

MENSDORFF (ALEXANDER) Graf.

See MENSDORFF-POUILLY (ALEXANDER) Graf.

MENSDORFF-POUILLY (ALEXANDER) Graf.

AUSTRIA. Ministerrat. 1861- . Die Ministerien Erzherzog Rainer und Mensdorff...; bearbeitet von Horst Brettner-Messler, mit einer Einleitung von Friedrich Engel-Janosi. Wien, 1977 in progress. *(Die Protokolle des österreichischen Ministerrates, 1848- 1867. Abteilung 5)*

MENTAL HEALTH LAWS

— France.

GUILBERT (FRANÇOISE) Liberté individuelle et hospitalisation de malades mentaux. Paris, 1974. pp. 381. *bibliog.*

MENTAL HEALTH SERVICES.

MAGARO (PETER A.) and others. The mental health industry: a cultural phenomenon: alternate solutions generated from an empirical evaluation of the cultural determinants, vested interests, and treatment effectiveness of the current mental health establishment. New York, [1978]. pp. 272. *bibliog.*

— United Kingdom.

THOMPSON (RICHARD) of the Greater London Council. Residential and day care services for the mentally handicapped and mentally ill in the London boroughs, 1966-1974. London, [1976]. 1 vol. (various pagings). *(London. Greater London Council. Research Memoranda. 489)*

MENTAL ILLNESS.

COOPER (DAVID GRAHAM) The language of madness. London, 1978. pp. 182.

McCULLOCH (JAMES WALLACE) and PRINS (HERSCHEL A.) Signs of stress: the social problems of psychiatric illness. London, 1978. pp. 207. *bibliogs.*

WING (JOHN KENNETH) Reasoning about madness. Oxford, 1978. pp. 265. *bibliog.*

— United Kingdom.

IRWIN (EDNA M.) Growing pains: a study of teenage distress. Plymouth, 1977. pp. 310. *bibliogs.*

MENTAL TESTS.

ZAHIRNIC (CONSTANTIN) Inteligenţa tehnică: studiu comparativ. Bucureşti, 1976. pp. 179. *bibliog.*

MENTALLY HANDICAPPED

— Care and treatment — United Kingdom.

OFFICE OF HEALTH ECONOMICS. [Studies in Current Health Problems]. No. 61. Mental handicap: ways forward. London, [1978]. pp. 49. *bibliog.*

— Employment — United States.

MENTAL retardation: social and educational perspectives; [edited by] Clifford J. Drew [and others]. Saint Louis, 1977. pp. 248. *bibliogs.*

— Rehabilitation — United States.

MILIEU rehabilitation for physical and mental handicaps: [by] Robert W. Hyde [and others]. Providence, 1962. pp. 106. *bibliog.*

MENTALLY HANDICAPPED CHILDREN

— Education — United States.

MENTAL retardation: social and educational perspectives; [edited by] Clifford J. Drew [and others]. Saint Louis, 1977. pp. 248. *bibliogs.*

MENTALLY ILL

— Care and treatment.

SOCIETY FOR IMPROVING THE CONDITION OF THE INSANE. Rules and list of the present members of the Society;...and the prize essay entitled The progressive changes which have taken place since the time of Pinel in the moral management of the insane...; by Daniel H. Tuke; together with a short abstract or classification of cases contributed by Sir Alexander Morison. London, 1854. pp. 6, 122.

— — United Kingdom.

BRITISH ASSOCIATION OF SOCIAL WORKERS. Aspects of the social care of the mentally ill; a discussion paper. [London, 1976]. pp. 20. *bibliogs.*

— Rehabilitation.

SEGAL (STEVEN P.) and AVIRAM (URI) The mentally ill in community-based sheltered care: a study of community care and social integration. New York, [1978]. pp. 337. *bibliogs.*

— — United Kingdom.

McCOWEN (PETER) and WILDER (JOHN) Lifestyle of 100 psychiatric patients: some cost and policy implications for rehabilitation. London, 1975. pp. 62. *bibliog.*

NATIONAL ASSOCIATION FOR MENTAL HEALTH. Mind Reports. 15. Room to let: a report on nine social service lodgings schemes. London, [1976]. pp. 14.

— Australia.

POVERTY and mental illness. Canberra, 1977. pp. 78. *(Australia. Commission of Inquiry into Poverty. Social/Medical Aspects of Poverty Series)*

MERCANTILE SYSTEM.

JENETZKY (JOHANNES) System und Entwicklung des materiellen Steuerrechts in der wissenschaftlichen Literatur des Kameralismus von 1680-1840, etc. Berlin, 1978. pp. 298. *bibliog.*

MERCATOR (GERARDUS).

OSLEY (ARTHUR SIDNEY) Mercator: a monograph on the lettering of maps, etc. in the 16th century Netherlands, with a facsmile and translation of his treatise on the italic hand and a translation of Ghim's Vita Mercatoris. London, 1969. pp. 209. *bibliog.*

MERCENARY TROOPS.

BAYLEY (CHARLES CALVERT) Mercenaries for the Crimea: the German, Swiss, and Italian legions in British service, 1854-1856. Montreal, 1977. pp. 197. *bibliog.*

BURCHETT (WILFRED G.) and ROEBUCK (DEREK) The whores of war: mercenaries today. Harmondsworth, 1977. pp. 240. *Written under the auspices of the International Commission of Inquiry on Mercenaries.*

HALLIDAY (FRED) Mercenaries "counter-insurgency" in the Gulf. Nottingham, 1977. pp. 80.

MERCHANT MARINE

— Finland.

BJÖRKQVIST (HEIMER) Handelsflottan och dess betydelse för sysselsättningen i de svensk-österbottniska städerna åren 1815-1858. Åbo, 1970. pp. 195-240. *(Åbo. Akademi. Handelshögskolan. Nationalekonomiska Institutionen. Meddelanden. Nr. 17) (Särtryck ur Österbotten 1970)*

— Poland.

MACHALIŃSKI (ZBIGNIEW) Gospodarcza myśl morska II Rzeczypospolitej, 1919-1939. Wrocław, 1975. pp. 355. *bibliog. With English and Russian summaries.*

— United Kingdom.

GRIFFITHS (Sir PERCIVAL) A history of the Inchcape Group. London, 1977. pp. 211.

— United States.

SAFFORD (JEFFREY J.) Wilsonian maritime diplomacy, 1913-1921. New Brunswick, [1978]. pp. 282. *bibliog.*

MERCHANTS

— China.

CHAN (WELLINGTON K.K.) Merchants, mandarins, and modern enterprise in late Ch'ing China. Cambridge, Mass., 1977. pp. 323. *bibliogs. (Harvard University. East Asian Research Center. Harvard East Asian Monographs. 79)*

— France.

PLESHKOVA (SOF'IA LEONIDOVNA) K istorii kupecheskogo kapitala vo Frantsii v XV veke: Zhak Ker [i.e. Jacques Coeur] i ego deiatel'nost'. Moskva, 1977. pp. 181. *bibliog.*

— Netherlands.

MULLER (HENDRIK) Muller: een Rotterdams zeehandelaar Hendrik Muller Szn, 1819-1898. Schiedam, 1977. pp. 467. *(Rotterdam. Historisch Genootschap Roterodamum. [Publications]. 18)*

— Switzerland.

MONDADA (GIUSEPPE) Commerci e commercianti di Campo Valmaggia nel Settecento, dalle lettere dei Pedrazzini e di altri conterranei attivi in Germania e in Italia. Lugano, 1977. pp. 247.

— United Kingdom.

EMMISON (FREDERICK GEORGE) Elizabethan life: wills of Essex gentry and merchants proved in the Prerogative Court of Canterbury. Chelmsford, 1978. pp. 361. *(Essex. Records Committee. Essex Record Office Publications. No. 71)*

— — Ireland.

An ADDRESS to the committee of the Merchants Society. Dublin, 1761. pp. 16.

— United States.

GREGORY (FRANCES W.) Nathan Appleton, merchant and entrepreneur, 1779-1861. Charlottesville, Va., 1975. pp. 358. *bibliog.*

COOKE (JACOB E.) Tench Coxe and the early Republic. Chapel Hill, [1978]. pp. 543. *bibliog.*

DECKER (PETER R.) Fortunes and failures: white-collar mobility in nineteenth-century San Francisco. Cambridge, Mass., 1978. pp. 336.

MERCIER (HONORE).

RUMILLY (ROBERT) Honoré Mercier et son temps (1840-1894). Montréal, [1975]. 2 vols.

MERTHYR TYDFIL

— Riot, 1831.

WILLIAMS (GWYN ALFRED) The Merthyr rising. London, [1978]. pp. 237.

MESSIAH

— Prophecies.

ROGERS (WALTER LACY) Evidences of Christianity: the Messianic prophecies. London, 1876. pp. 24.

MESSIANISM.

QUEIROZ (MARIA ISAURA PEREIRA DE) O messianismo no Brasil e no mundo. 2nd ed. São Paulo, 1977. pp. 441. *bibliog.*

MESSIANISM, AMERICAN.

MOORHEAD (JAMES H.) American apocalypse: Yankee Protestants and the Civil War, 1860-1869. New Haven, 1978. pp. 278. *bibliog.*

MESSIANISM, BRAZILIAN.

QUEIROZ (MARIA ISAURA PEREIRA DE) O messianismo no Brasil e no mundo. 2nd ed. São Paulo, 1977. pp. 441. *bibliog.*

METAL TRADE.

The PRICING and marketing of metals; proceedings of a meeting held in London in November 1971, organized by the Institution of Mining and Metallurgy. London, [1972]. pp. 46. *(Reprinted from Transactions of the Institution of Mining and Metallurgy-Section A: Mining Industry, vols. 80 and 81, 1971- 1972)*

— Italy.

FEDERMECCANICA. Dalla conflittualità al consenso: opinioni e proposte degli imprenditori sulla crisi attuale. Milano, [1976]. pp. 129. *Proceedings of a conference held at Rome, 8 March 1976.*

METAL WORKERS

— Denmark.

JERN- OG METALINDUSTRIARBEJDSMAENDENES FAGFORENING. Århus Afdeling. Jern og metal igennem 75 år. [Århus, 1972]. pp. 44.

— Italy.

PIPAN (TATIANA) and SALERNI (DARIO) Il sindacato come soggetto di equilibrio: ricerca sulla politica contrattuale della FLM. Milano, [1975]. pp. 303.

— Netherlands.

BINNEVELD (JOHANNES MARTINUS WOUTER) De Rotterdamse metaalstaking van 1965. Amsterdam, 1977. pp. 175. *bibliog. Revised version of his De stakingen in de Rotterdamse metaalindustrie in 1965.*

— Poland — Silesia.

SZARANIEC (LECH) Załoga koncernu "Hohenlohe" i jej walka klasowa w latach 1905- 1939. Katowice, 1976. pp. 320. *bibliog.*

— Switzerland.

VETTERLI (RUDOLF) Industriearbeit, Arbeiterbewusstsein und gewerkschaftliche Organisation; dargestellt am Beispiel der Georg Fischer AG, 1890-1930. Göttingen, 1978. pp. 344. *bibliog.*

METALLURGY.

THOMAS (PARAKUNNEL JOSEPH) Report on metallurgical and engineering industries, recent developments. Delhi, Department of Supply, [1944]. pp. 90.

— Russia — Ukraine.

BEM (IHOR SERHIIOVYCH) and DEMIDION (VOLODYMYR OLEKSANDROVYCH) Problemy rozvytku i rozmishchennia mashynobuduvannia ta metaloobrobki v Ukraïns'kii RSR. Kyïv, 1977. pp. 311. *bibliog.*

METALS

— Prices.

The PRICING and marketing of metals; proceedings of a meeting held in London in November 1971, organized by the Institution of Mining and Metallurgy. London, [1972]. pp. 46. *(Reprinted from Transactions of the Institution of Mining and Metallurgy-Section A: Mining Industry, vols. 80 and 81, 1971- 1972)*

METAPHOR.

The SOCIAL use of metaphor: essays on the anthropology of rhetoric; edited by J. David Sapir and J. Christopher Crocker. Philadelphia, [1977]. pp. 249. *bibliog. Based on papers presented at a symposium held at the 1970 annual meetings of the American Anthropological Association.*

METAYER SYSTEM

— Peru.

MUÑOZ (ERASMO) Erasmo Muñoz, yanacon del valle de Chancay: biografia organizada por Jose Matos Mar [and] Jorge A. Carbajal H. Lima, 1974. pp. 168. *(Instituto de Estudios Peruanos. Proyecto de Estudios Etnologicos del Valle de Chancay. Monografias. No. 4)*

METHODOLOGY.

CLARK (PETER JAMES) Thermodynamics and the kinetic theory in the late nineteenth century: a case study in the methodology of scientific research programmes. [1977]. fo. 393. *bibliog. Typescript. Ph.D.(London) thesis: unpublished. This thesis is the property of London University and may not be removed from the Library.*

METHODS ENGINEERING.

HAWKINS (PETER JAMES LETHAM) Role conflict and the work study engineer: a study of role consensus in industry. [1977]. fo. 322. *bibliog. Typescript. Ph.D. (London) thesis: unpublished. This thesis is the property of London University and may not be removed from the Library.*

METRIC SPACES.

AUBIN (JEAN PIERRE) Applied abstract analysis; translated by Carole Labrousse. New York, [1977]. pp. 263.

METRIC SYSTEM.

— Canada.

CANADIAN LABOUR CONGRESS. Submission...to the Standing Committee on Finance, Trade and Economic Affairs. [Ottawa], 1975. fo. 5,4,3.

— United Kingdom.

GOING METRIC; [pd. by] Metrication Board [U.K.]. q., Jl 1971 (no.1)- London.

U.K. Department of Prices and Consumer Protection. Metrication: report to Parliament. a., [1976](1st)- London.

METRIC MEMO; ([pd. by] Metrication Board [U.K.]). irreg. London. *Current issues only kept.*

METRICATION BOARD [U.K.] News release. irreg. London. *Current issues only kept.*

— United States.

THOMSON (WILLIAM) Baron Kelvin. Extracts from the evidence...before the Committee on coinage, weights and measures...House of Representatives...United States...April 24, 1902. [Washington?, 1902?]. pp. 8.

METRIC SYSTEM.(Cont.)

HOLT (SUSAN FRAKER) The United States and the metric system; revised by Gretchen Borges. rev. ed. Minneapolis, 1976. pp. 40. *bibliog.* (*Federal Reserve Bank of Minneapolis. Ninth District Exponent. No. 10*)

— Zambia.

PROGRESS TOWARDS METRICATION: (news letter issued by the Metrication Board [Zambia]). irreg., My 5 1970 (no.1)- Lusaka.

METROPOLITAN AREAS.

HALL (PETER GEOFFREY) The world cities. 2nd ed. London, 1977. pp. 271. *bibliog.*

— South Africa.

HART (T.) and LOURENS (I.K.) The demographic structure of black and white populations in the Witwatersrand metropolitan region, 1970. Johannesburg, 1977. pp. 30. *bibliog.* (*Johannesburg. University of the Witwatersrand. Urban and Regional Research Unit. Occasional Papers. No. 18*)

— United Kingdom.

U.K. Department of Employment. Unit for Manpower Studies. 1977. Employment in metropolitan areas; project report. London, [1977]. pp. 98. *bibliog.*

— United States.

URBAN policymaking and metropolitan dynamics: a comparative geographical analysis; John S. Adams, editor. Cambridge, Mass., [1976]. pp. 576.

The SOCIAL burdens of environmental pollution: a comparative metropolitan data source; Brian J.L. Berry, ed.; contributing authors Susan Caris [and others]. Cambridge, Mass., [1977]. pp. 613. *bibliog.*

METROPOLITAN FINANCE

— United States.

METROPOLITAN financing and growth management policies: principles and practice; edited by George F. Break. Madison, 1978. pp. 329. *bibliogs.* (*Committee on Taxation, Resources and Economic Development. Publications. 9*) Proceedings of a symposium sponsored by the Committee at the University of Wisconsin, Madison, 1974, part of the Thirteenth Annual Conference of the Committee.

METROPOLITAN GOVERNMENT

— United States.

HALLMAN (HOWARD W.) Small and large together: governing the metropolis. Beverly Hills, [1977]. pp. 308. *bibliog.*

PALLEY (MARIAN LIEF) and PALLEY (HOWARD A.) Urban America and public policies. Lexington, Mass., [1977]. pp. 277. *bibliogs.*

MEXICAN AMERICANS.

VIDAL (MIRTA) and others. Chicanas speak out. New York, 1971. pp. 15.

PETERSON (RICHARD H.) Manifest destiny in the mines: a cultural interpretation of anti- Mexican nativism in California, 1848-1853. San Francisco, 1975. pp. 126. *bibliog.*

BULLINGTON (BRUCE) Heroin use in the barrio. Lexington, Mass., [1977]. pp. 179. *bibliog.*

MEXICAN FICTION

— History and criticism.

GONZALEZ (MICHAEL) Cambio de piel, or the myth of literature. Glasgow, [1974]. pp. 13. (*Glasgow. University. Institute of Latin American Studies. Occasional Papers. No. 10*)

MEXICANS IN THE UNITED STATES.

COALSON (GEORGE O.) The development of the migratory farm labor system in Texas, 1900- 1954. San Francisco, 1977. pp. 132. *bibliog.*

The POLITICS of Chicano liberation; Olga Rodríguez, editor. New York, [1977]. pp. 159. *The Socialist Workers Party (United States) program for Chicano liberation. Contains documents accepted at national conventions in 1971 and 1976.*

See also MEXICAN AMERICANS.

MEXICO.

MEXICAN NEWSLETTER; [pd. by] Office of the President [Mexico]. m. (approx.) Mr 31 1971 (no.1)- Mexico.

— Armed forces — Political activity.

PANI (ALBERTO J.) El cambio de regimenes en Mexico y las asonadas militares: sintesis historica. Paris, 1930. pp. 20.

— Commercial policy.

VILLARREAL (RENE) El desequilibrio externo en la industrializacion de Mexico, 1929- 1975: un enfoque estructuralista. Mexico, 1976. pp. 281. *bibliog.*

— Constitution.

MENDIETA Y NUÑEZ (LUCIO) El sistema agrario constitucional. 4th ed. Mexico, 1975. pp. 197.

— Description and travel.

OCAMPO (MELCHOR) Obras completas. Mexico, 1900-1901. 3 vols. *Tomo 1: Polemicas religiosas; Tomo 2: Escritos politicos; Tomo 3: Letras y ciencias.*

— Economic conditions.

ECKSTEIN (SUSAN) The impact of revolution: a comparative analysis of Mexico and Bolivia. London, [1976]. pp. 53. *bibliog.*

IFFLAND (CHARLES) and GALLAND (ANTOINE) Les investissements industriels suisses au Mexique. Lausanne, 1978. pp. 155. *bibliog.* (*Lausanne. Université. Centre de Recherches Européennes. Publications. 4. L'Europe et les Pays Tiers*)

— — Statistics.

MEXICO. Secretaria de Programacion y Presupuesto. Boletin mensual de informacion economica. m., Jl 1977(v.1, no. 2)- Mexico.

— Economic history.

VILLARREAL (RENE) El desequilibrio externo en la industrializacion de Mexico, 1929- 1975: un enfoque estructuralista. Mexico, 1976. pp. 281. *bibliog.*

— Economic policy.

HELLMAN (JUDITH ADLER) Patterns of power and manipulation in the Mexican political system. 1976. fo. 316. *bibliog.* Typescript. Ph.D. (London) thesis: unpublished. *This thesis is the property of London University and may not be removed from the Library.*

— Foreign relations — Treaties.

ENRIQUEZ COYRO (ERNESTO) El tratado entre Mexico y los Estados Unidos de America sobre rios internacionales: una lucha nacional de noventa años. Mexico, [1976]. 2 vols. (in 1). (*Mexico City. Universidad Nacional Autonoma de Mexico. Facultad de Ciencias Politicas y Sociales. Serie Estudios. 47-48*)

— — United States.

SCHOONOVER (THOMAS DAVID) Dollars over dominion: the triumph of liberalism in Mexican- United States relations, 1861-1867. Baton Rouge, [1978]. pp. 316. *bibliog.*

— Government publications — Bibliography.

FERNANDEZ DE ZAMORA (ROSA MARIA) compiler. Las publicaciones oficiales de Mexico: guia de publicaciones periodicas y seriadas, 1937-1970. Mexico, 1977. pp. 239. (*Mexico City. Universidad Nacional Autonoma de Mexico. Instituto de Investigaciones. Bibliograficas. Serie: Guias. 5*)

— History.

MAYO (SAMUEL H.) A history of Mexico from pre-Columbia to the present. Englewood Cliffs, [1978]. pp. 454. *bibliog.*

— — 1540-1810, Spanish colony.

BEYOND the codices: the Nahua view of colonial Mexico; translated and edited by Arthur J.O. Anderson [and others]. Berkeley, [1976]. pp. 235. *bibliog.* (*California University. Latin American Center. Latin American Studies. vol. 27*)

— — 1910-1946.

AGUILAR CAMIN (HECTOR) La frontera nomada: Sonora y la Revolucion mexicana. Mexico, 1977. pp. 450. *bibliog.*

— Industries.

VILLARREAL (RENE) El desequilibrio externo en la industrializacion de Mexico, 1929- 1975: un enfoque estructuralista. Mexico, 1976. pp. 281. *bibliog.*

NACIONAL FINANCIERA. Mexico: una estrategia para desarrollar la industria de bienes de capital; proyecto conjunto de bienes de capital NAFINSA-ONUDI. Mexico, 1977. pp. 490.

— Languages — Maps.

URIBE VILLEGAS (OSCAR) Un mapa del monolingüismo y el bilingüismo de los indigenas de Mexico en 1960. Mexico, 1970. pp. 33, with map.

— Politics and government.

OCAMPO (MELCHOR) Obras completas. Mexico, 1900-1901. 3 vols. *Tomo 1: Polemicas religiosas; Tomo 2: Escritos politicos; Tomo 3: Letras y ciencias.*

PANI (ALBERTO J.) El cambio de regimenes en Mexico y las asonadas militares: sintesis historica. Paris, 1930. pp. 20.

GOBIERNO MEXICANO, EL; ([pd. by] Presidencia de la Republica, Estados Unidos Mexicanos). m., Ja 1971 (2nd s., [no.] 2)- Mexico.

CARDENAS (LAZARO) Apuntes, 1913-1970. Mexico, 1972-74. 4 vols. (in 2).

ALEMAN VALDES (MIGUEL) Miguel Aleman contesta: ensayo. Austin, 1975. pp. 54. (*Texas University. Institute of Latin American Studies. Encuesta politica: Mexico. 4*)

CABRERA (LUIS) Obras completas. vol. 4. Obra politica. Mexico, 1975. pp. 1074.

ECKSTEIN (SUSAN) The impact of revolution: a comparative analysis of Mexico and Bolivia. London, [1976]. pp. 53. *bibliog.*

HELLMAN (JUDITH ADLER) Patterns of power and manipulation in the Mexican political system. 1976. fo. 316. *bibliog.* Typescript. Ph.D. (London) thesis: unpublished. *This thesis is the property of London University and may not be removed from the Library.*

TARACENA (ALFONSO) La vida en Mexico bajo Avila Camacho. Mexico, 1976-77. 2 vols. (in 1).

HELLMAN (JUDITH ADLER) Mexico in crisis. New York, 1978. pp. 229. *bibliog.*

— Population.

ALBA-HERNANDEZ (FRANCISCO) La poblacion de Mexico. [Mexico, 1976]. pp. 122. *bibliog.* (*Committee for International Coordination of National Research in Demography. C.I.C.R.E.D. Series*)

— Race question.

LOMBARDO TOLEDANO (VICENTE) Judios y mexicanos: razas inferiores? Montevideo, [1944]. pp. 44.

— Social conditions.

La CORRUPCION; [by] Rosario Castellanos [and others]. 2nd ed. Mexico, 1970. pp. 162.

— Social history.

BEYOND the codices: the Nahua view of colonial Mexico; translated and edited by Arthur J.O. Anderson [and others]. Berkeley, [1976]. pp. 235. *bibliog. (California University. Latin American Center. Latin American Studies. vol. 27)*

— Social policy.

ECKSTEIN (SUSAN) The poverty of revolution: the state and the urban poor in Mexico. Princeton, N.J., [1977]. pp. 300. *bibliog.*

— Statistics.

MEXICO. Direccion General de Estadistica. Revista de estadistica. m., Mr 1938 (v.1, no.1)- , with gaps (Ja-Ag 1946; 1947; Je 1962); susp. pbn. Ja-Mr 1941. Mexico.

MEXICO UNIVERSITY.

RAMIREZ GOMEZ (RAMON) and CHAPOY BONIFAZ (ALMA) Estructura de la Universidad Nacional Autonoma de Mexico: ensayo socio-economico. Mexico, 1970. pp. 105.

MIAO PEOPLE.

KEEN (FRANCIS GRAHAME BELLINGHAM) The Meo of northwest Thailand. [Wellington, Government Printer, 1966]. pp. 48. *Prepared and originally published as a Post-Primary School Bulletin by the Department of Education.*

MICHELET (JULES).

WODZYŃSKA (MARIA) Adam Mickiewicz i romantyczna filozofia historii w Collège de France. Warszawa, 1976. pp. 283. *With French summary.*

MICKIEWICZ (ADAM).

WODZYŃSKA (MARIA) Adam Mickiewicz i romantyczna filozofia historii w Collège de France. Warszawa, 1976. pp. 283. *With French summary.*

MIDDLE AGES

— Social conditions.

MOLLAT (MICHEL) Les pauvres au Moyen Age: étude sociale. [Paris, 1978]. pp. 395. *bibliog.*

MIDDLE CLASSES.

ELGOZY (GEORGES) Le bourgeois socialiste; ou, Pour un post-libéralisme. [Paris, 1977]. pp. 310.

— Finland.

ÅBO. Akademi. Acta Academiae Aboensis. Humaniora. 54. 4. Borgarna som lantbrukare i Finland under 1700-talet; av Oscar Nikula. Åbo, 1977. pp. 24. *bibliog.*

— Germany.

BOURGEOISIE und bürgerliche Umwälzung in Deutschland, 1789- 1871; herausgegeben von Helmut Bleiber. Berlin, 1977. pp. 525. *bibliog. (Akademie der Wissenschaften der DDR. Zentralinstitut für Geschichte. Schriften. Band 50)*

HENNIG (EIKE) Bürgerliche Gesellschaft und Faschismus in Deutschland: ein Forschungsbericht. Frankfurt am Main, 1977. pp. 424. *bibliog.*

— Italy.

CERASE (FRANCESCO PAOLO) Sotto il dominio dei borghesi: sottosviluppo ed emigrazione nell'Italia meridionale, 1860-1910. Assisi, [1975]. pp. 164.

MANACORDA (GASTONE) Rivoluzione borghese e socialismo: studi e saggi. Roma, 1975. pp. 403.

CAROLLO (VINCENZO) Borghesia rivoluzionaria per il comunismo. Milano, [1976]. pp. 211.

PROVASI (GIANCARLO) Borghesia industriale e Democrazia Cristiana: sviluppo economico e mediazione politica dalla Ricostruzione agli anni '70. Bari, [1976]. pp. 308. *bibliog.*

VENÉ (GIAN FRANCO) La borghesia comunista. Milano, [1976]. pp. 199. *bibliogs.*

— Poland.

ZIENKOWSKA (KRYSTYNA) Sławetni i urodzeni: ruch polityczny mieszczaństwa w dobie Sejmu Czteroletniego. Warszawa, 1976. pp. 357.

— Russia.

GRECHKINA (EL'ZA ROBERTOVNA) Srednie sloi na puti k sotsializmu. Tallin, 1976. pp. 187.

— United States.

RODGERS (DANIEL T.) The work ethic in industrial America 1850-1920. Chicago, 1978. pp. 300.

MIDI-PYRENEES

— Economic conditions.

BONNAUD (JACQUES) Panorama et structures économiques de la région Midi- Pyrénées. Toulouse, Echelon Régional de l'Emploi, 1976. pp. 128.

— — Statistics.

STATISTIQUES ET ETUDES MIDI-PYRENEES: revue trimestrielle; [pd. by] Institut National de la Statistique et des Etudes Economiques,...Direction Régionale de Toulouse [France]. q., Mr 1972 (no.1)- Toulouse.

MIDWIVES

— Nigeria.

MIDWIVES SEMINAR, ENUGU, 1965. Official report, etc. [Lagos, Federal Ministry of Information, 1966]. pp. 83.

— United Kingdom — Ireland, Northern.

NORTHERN IRELAND COUNCIL FOR NURSES AND MIDWIVES. Statement of accounts...together with the report of the Comptroller and Auditor-General. a., 1971/72 [2nd]- Belfast. *1971 [1st] included in IRELAND, NORTHERN. Parliament. House of Commons. [Papers].*

MIGRANT AGRICULTURAL LABOURERS

— United States.

COALSON (GEORGE O.) The development of the migratory farm labor system in Texas, 1900- 1954. San Francisco, 1977. pp. 132. *bibliog.*

MIGRANT LABOUR.

ADLER (STEPHEN) International migration and dependence. Farnborough, [1977]. pp. 235. *bibliog.*

INTERNATIONAL LABOUR OFFICE. 1977. Social security for migrant workers. Geneva, 1977. pp. 154. *bibliog.*

— Europe.

Les TRAVAILLEURS étrangers en Europe occidentale: actes du colloque organisé par la Commission Nationale pour les Etudes et les Recherches Interethniques, Paris-Sorbonne...1974; sous la direction de Philippe J. Bernard. Mouton, [1976]. pp. 416. *(Nice. Université. Institut d'Etudes et de Recherches Interethniques et Interculturelles. Publications. 6) In English and French.*

— European Economic Community countries.

INTERNATIONAL CATHOLIC MIGRATION COMMISSION. Migration: Informative Series. No. 11. Migration in the Europe of nine. Geneva, [1973]. pp. 64.

EUROPEAN COMMUNITIES. Social Security for Migrant Workers. Guides. No. 1. Guide...concerning the rights and obligations with regard to social security of employed persons going to work in...[European Economic Community countries]. Brussels, 1975. 9 parts (in 1 vol.)

— France.

UNION GENERALE DES TRAVAILLEURS SENEGALAIS EN FRANCE. Qui est responsable du sous-développement. Paris, 1975. pp. 85.

N'DONGO (SALLY) "Coopération" et néo-colonialisme. Paris, 1976. pp. 199.

— South Africa.

NATTRASS (JILL) Migrant labour and underdevelopment: the case of Kwazulu. Durban, 1977. pp. 29. *(Natal University. Department of Economics. Black/White Income Gap Project. Interim Research Reports. No. 3)*

— South West Africa.

GORDON (ROBERT J.) Ph.D. Mines, masters and migrants: life in a Namibian mine compound. Johannesburg, [1977]. pp. 276. *bibliog. Based on a dissertation submitted at the University of Illinois.*

MIGRATION, INTERNAL.

INTERNAL migration: a comparative perspective; edited by Alan A. Brown [and] Egon Neuberger. New York, [1977]. pp. 508. *bibliogs.*

— Africa.

CAIRO DEMOGRAPHIC CENTRE. Urbanization and migration in some Arab and African countries. Cairo, 1973. pp. 528. *bibliogs. (Research Monograph Series. No. 4)*

— Arab countries.

CAIRO DEMOGRAPHIC CENTRE. Urbanization and migration in some Arab and African countries. Cairo, 1973. pp. 528. *bibliogs. (Research Monograph Series. No. 4)*

— Europe, Eastern.

POPULATION and migration trends in eastern Europe; edited by Huey Louis Kostanick. Boulder, Colo., 1977. pp. 247. *Proceedings of the Conference on Demography and Urbanization in Eastern Europe held in Los Angeles in 1976 and sponsored by the Center for Slavic and East European Studies of the University of California at Los Angeles.*

— Italy.

TREVES (ANNA) Le migrazioni interne nell'Italia fascista: politica e realtà demografica. Torino, [1976]. pp. 201. *bibliogs.*

— Kenya.

KENYA. Central Bureau of Statistics. 1975. Internal migration patterns in a selected area in Kenya. [Nairobi], 1975. pp. 13. *(Demographic Working Papers. No. 1)*

— Oceania.

EXILES and migrants in Oceania; edited by Michael D. Lieber. Honolulu, [1977]. pp. 414. *bibliog. (Association for Social Anthropology in Oceania. ASAO Monographs. No.5) Based on a symposium held at the University of Washington in 1970.*

— Peru.

MARTINEX (HECTOR) Las migraciones internas en el Peru. [Lima, 1968]. pp. 15. *bibliog. (Centro de Estudios de Poblacion y Desarrollo. Estudios de Poblacion y Desarrollo. vol. 2, no. 1)*

— Philippine Islands.

PERNIA (ERNESTO DEL MAR) Urbanization, population growth, and economic development in the Philippines. Westport, Conn., 1977. pp. 213. *bibliog.*

MIGRATION, INTERNAL.(Cont.)

— Spain.

SPAIN. Instituto Nacional de Estadistica. 1974. Las migraciones interiores en España, decenio 1961-1970. [Madrid, 1974]. pp. 141.

— United Kingdom.

FIELD (A. MIRYAM) and CROFTS (C.) Some aspects of planned migration to new and expanding towns. London, [1977]. pp. 39. *bibliog. (London. Greater London Council. Research Memoranda. 527)*

U.K. Census, 1971. Census, 1971: England and Wales: migration regional report[s], 10 per cent sample..., as constituted on 1st April 1974. London, 1978 in progress.

— United States.

CONNECTICUT. Tri-State Regional Planning Commission. 1975. Regional migration, 1970. [New York], 1975. 1 pamphlet (unpaged) *(Regional Profiles. Vol. 2. No. 7)*

MORGAN (DAVID J.) Patterns of population distribution: a residential preference model and its dynamic. Chicago, 1978. pp. 200. *bibliog. (Chicago. University. Department of Geography. Research Papers. No. 176)*

WEINSTEIN (BERNARD L.) and FIRESTINE (ROBERT E.) Regional growth and decline in the United States: the rise of the sunbelt and the decline of the northeast. New York, 1978. pp. 151.

MILITARISM

— Netherlands.

JOCHHEIM (GERNOT) Antimilitaristische Aktionstheorie, soziale Revolution und soziale Verteidigung: zur Entwicklung der Gewaltfreiheitstheorie...1890-1940, unter besonderer Berücksichtigung der Niederlande. Assen, [1977]. pp. 621. *bibliog.*

MILITARY ART AND SCIENCE.

The LIMITS of military intervention; edited by Ellen P. Stern. Beverly Hills, [1977]. pp. 399. *Based on papers presented at two conferences held in 1976.*

MILITARY ASSISTANCE, AMERICAN.

FARLEY (PHILIP J.) and others. Arms across the sea. Washington, D.C., [1978]. pp. 134.

— Chile.

REIMANN WEIGERT (ELISABETH) and RIVAS SANCHEZ (FERNANDO) Las fuerzas armadas de Chile: un caso de penetracion imperialista. La Habana, 1976. pp. 313. *bibliog.*

— Korea.

McGOVERN (GEORGE STANLEY) and STILWELL (RICHARD GILES) Withdrawal of U.S. troops from Korea? Washington, [1977]. pp. 28. *(American Enterprise Institute for Public Policy Research. AEI Defense Reviews. No. 2)*

MILITARY ASSISTANCE, NEW ZEALAND

— Malaysia.

NEW ZEALAND. Ministry of Foreign Affairs. 1971. Five power defence arrangements. Wellington, [1971]. pp. 42. *(Publications. No. 410)*

— Singapore.

NEW ZEALAND. Ministry of Foreign Affairs. 1971. Five power defence arrangements. Wellington, [1971]. pp. 42. *(Publications. No. 410)*

MILITARY DISCIPLINE

— Netherlands.

EUROPEAN COURT OF HUMAN RIGHTS. Publications. Series A: Judgments and Decisions. [A22]. ...Case of Engel and others. 1. Decision of 1 October 1975. 2. Judgment of 8 June 1976. 3. Judgment of 23 November 1976. Strasbourg, Council of Europe, 1977. pp. 71 [bis]. *In English and French.*

EUROPEAN COURT OF HUMAN RIGHTS. Publications. Series B: Pleadings, Oral Arguments and Documents [B20]. Case of Engel and others. (1974-1976). Strasbourg, Council of Europe, 1977. pp. 306 [bis], 307-382.

MILITARY GEOGRAPHY

— East (Near East).

ROSEN (STEVEN J.) Military geography and the military balance in the Arab-Israel conflict. Jerusalem, 1977. pp. 79. *(Hebrew University. Leonard Davis Institute for International Relations. Jerusalem Papers on Peace Problems. 21)*

MILITARY GOVERNMENT.

PHILIP (GEORGE D.E.) The rise and fall of the Peruvian military radicals, 1968-1976. London, 1978. pp. 178. *bibliog. (London. University. Institute of Latin American Studies. Monographs. 9)*

MILITARY HISTORY, MODERN.

SMOKE (RICHARD) War: controlling escalation. Cambridge, Mass., 1977. pp. 419. *bibliogs.*

MILITARY INTELLIGENCE.

LEE (WILLIAM THOMAS) The estimation of Soviet defense expenditures, 1955-75: an unconventional approach. New York, 1977. pp. 358. *bibliog.*

LEWIN (RONALD) Ultra goes to war: the secret story. London, 1978. pp. 398. *bibliog.*

MILITARY LAW

— Germany.

SCHWELING (OTTO PETER) Die deutsche Militärjustiz in der Zeit des Nationalsozialismus;...bearbeitet, eingeleitet und herausgegeben von Erich Schwinge. Marburg, 1978. pp. 407.

— Italy.

La RIFORMA della giustizia militare: prospettive e orientamenti per la riforma democratica delle forze armate e della giustizia militare; il nuovo regolamento di disciplina militare; atti del seminario organizzato dal Centro studi e iniziative per la riforma dello Stato, Roma...1975. Roma, 1976. pp. 178. *Contributions by Arrigo Boldrini and others.*

VENDITTI (RODOLFO) Il diritto penale militare nel sistema penale italiano. 4th ed. Milano, 1978. pp. 456.

MILITARY SERVICE, COMPULSORY

— Canada.

GRANATSTEIN (JACK LAWRENCE) and HITSMAN (J. MACKAY) Broken promises: a history of conscription in Canada. Toronto, 1977. pp. 281. *bibliog.*

MILITARY SERVICE, VOLUNTARY

— United States.

BACHMAN (JERALD G.) and others. The all-volunteer force: a study of ideology in the military. Ann Arbor, [1977]. pp. 210. *bibliog.*

LEVITAN (SAR A.) and ALDERMAN (KAREN CLEARY) Warriors at work: the volunteer armed force. Beverly Hills, [1977]. pp. 215.

MILITARY UNIONS

— France.

MALBOSC (FRANÇOIS) pseud. Civils, si vous saviez... Paris, 1977. pp. 178.

— United States.

UNIONIZING the armed forces; edited by Ezra S. Krendel and Bernard Samoff. [Philadelphia], 1977. pp. 198.

MILK

— European Economic Community countries.

EUROPEAN COMMUNITIES. Statistical Office. Milk and milk products. a., 1977(1st)- Luxembourg. *[in Community languages]*

MILK, DRIED.

MULLER (MIKE) The baby killer: a War on Want investigation into the promotion and sale of powdered baby milks in the Third World. London, 1974. pp. 19.

MILK CONSUMPTION

— India.

JONAS (PAUL) An analysis of bovine milk consumption in major Indian metropolitan areas. New Delhi, 1971. 1 vol. (various pagings). *bibliog. (United States. Agency for International Development. USAID-New Delhi. Economic Affairs Division. Staff Papers)*

MILK SUPPLY

— Sweden.

SAMBERGS (ÅKE) Mjölkproducenternas avsikter, 1971-74 och 1974-77: resultat från två planeringsenkäter. Stockholm, [1976]. pp. 66. *(Jordbrukets Utredningsinstitut. Meddelanden. 1975. Nr.6) With English summary.*

MILK TRADE

— New Zealand.

NEW ZEALAND MILK BOARD. Organisation and administration of the town milk industry in New Zealand; (with Supplement: The town milk industry in New Zealand: statistical information to 31st August, 1968). Wellington, [1969]. 2 pts.

— Underdeveloped areas.

See UNDERDEVELOPED AREAS — Milk trade.

MILLEDGEVILLE

— History.

BONNER (JAMES CALVIN) Milledgeville: Georgia's antebellum capital. Athens, Ga., [1978]. pp. 307. *bibliog.*

MILLENNIUM

— History of doctrines.

HATCH (NATHAN O.) The sacred cause of liberty: republican thought and the millennium in revolutionary New England. New Haven, 1977. pp. 197. *bibliog.*

MOORHEAD (JAMES H.) American apocalypse: Yankee Protestants and the Civil War, 1860-1869. New Haven, 1978. pp. 278. *bibliog.*

MILTON KEYNES

— City planning.

MILTON KEYNES DEVELOPMENT CORPORATION. The plan for Milton Keynes; main consultants, Llewelyn-Davies Weeks Forestier-Walker and Bor; technical supplements, nos. 2-7,9. Wavendon, Bucks., 1970. 8 vols. (in 1).

MINAS GERAIS

— History.

ANDRADE (PAULO RENE DE) Três revoluçoes: a atuação da Policia Militar de Minas Gerais, a antiga Força Publica, nos movimentos revolucionarios de 1924, 1930 e 1932; esboço historico. [Belo Horizonte, 1976]. pp. 538. *bibliog.*

WIRTH (JOHN D.) Minas Gerais in the Brazilian Federation, 1889-1937. Stanford, 1977. pp. 322. *bibliog.*

— Politics and government.

WIRTH (JOHN D.) Minas Gerais in the Brazilian Federation, 1889-1937. Stanford, 1977. pp. 322. *bibliog.*

MIND AND BODY.

SLOMAN (AARON) The computer revolution in philosophy: philosophy, science and models of mind. Hassocks, 1978. pp. 304.

MINERAL INDUSTRIES.

BOSSON (REX) and VARON (BENSION) The mining industry and the developing countries. Washington, International Bank for Reconstruction and Development, 1977. pp. 292. *bibliog.*

TILTON (JOHN E.) The future of nonfuel minerals. Washington, D.C., [1977]. pp. 113.

— Statistics.

WORLD MINERAL STATISTICS: production: exports: imports; [pd. by] Mineral Statistics and Economics Unit, Institute of Geological Sciences. irreg., 1970/74(1st)- London. *Supersedes U.K. Institute of Geological Sciences. Statistical summary of the mineral industry: world production, exports and imports.*

— Taxation — Bolivia.

GILLIS (MALCOLM) and others. Taxation and mining: nonfuel minerals in Bolivia and other countries. Cambridge, Mass., [1978]. pp. 358.

— Asia.

WANG (KUNG-PING) and CHIN (EDMOND) Mineral economics and basic industries in Asia. Boulder, 1978. pp. 358. *bibliog.*

— Canada — Mathematical models.

BOADWAY (ROBIN W.) and TREDDENICK (JOHN M.) The impact of the mining industries on the Canadian economy. Kingston, Ont., [1977]. pp. 115. *(Kingston, Ontario. Queen's University. Centre for Resource Studies. National Impact of Mining Series. 1)*

— France.

FRANCE. Groupe sectoriel d'Analyse et de Prévision Minerais, Métaux et demi-Produits non-Ferreux. 1976. Rapport...: préparation du 7e Plan. Paris, [1976]. pp. 234.

— India.

STATISTICS OF MINES IN INDIA: NON COAL; [pd. by] Directorate- General of Mines Safety. a., 1974- New Delhi. *Data previously included in INDIA. Directorate-General of Mines Safety. Annual report of the Director-General of Mines Safety.*

— Malaysia.

BULLETIN OF STATISTICS RELATING TO THE MINING INDUSTRY, MALAYSIA (formerly Bulletin of statistics relating to the mining industry of Malaya); [pd. by] Department of Mines, West Malaysia. a., 1949, 1956/60- Kuala Lumpur.

FEDERATION OF MALAYA. Department of Mines. Quinquennial report. quinquennial. 1955 [covering 1950/1955]. Kuala Lumpur.

— Peru.

ANUARIO DE LA MINERIA DEL PERU; [pd. by] Unidad de Estadistica, Direccion General de Mineria. a., 1973- [Lima].

— Underdeveloped areas.

See UNDERDEVELOPED AREAS — Mineral industries.

— United States.

PETERSON (RICHARD H.) The bonanza kings: the social origins and business behavior of western mining entrepreneurs, 1870-1900. Lincoln, Neb., [1977]. pp. 191. *bibliog.*

MINERAL WATERS

— Law and legislation — Brazil.

BRAZIL. Statutes, etc. 1940-45. Codigo de minas...29.1.1940; codigo de aguas minerais...8.8.1945; como requerer pesquisa de jazida mineral. 3rd ed. Rio de Janeiro, 1966. pp. 116. *(Brazil. Divisão de Fomento da Produção Mineral. Avulsos. 91)*

LABORATORIO DA PRODUÇÃO MINERAL [BRAZIL]. Como obter autorização para exploração de fontes hidrominerais: dados informativos. rev.ed. Rio de Janeiro, 1967. pp. 23. *(Avulsos. 14)*

MINERS

— Mexico.

TODD (ARTHUR CECIL) The search for silver: Cornish miners in Mexico, 1824-1947. Padstow, [1977]. pp. 192. *bibliog.*

— Rhodesia — Diseases and hygiene.

SOUTHERN RHODESIA. Commission appointed to Enquire into the Possible Prevalence and Origin of Cases of Silicosis and other Industrial Pneumonoconioses in the Industries of the Colony of Southern Rhodesia, and of Pulmonary Tuberculosis in such industries. 1938. Report; [Louis Godfrey Irvine, chairman]. Salisbury, 1938. pp. 96. *(Legislative Assembly. [Sessional Papers]. 1938. C.S.R. 28)*

— South West Africa.

GORDON (ROBERT J.) Ph.D. Mines, masters and migrants: life in a Namibian mine compound. Johannesburg, [1977]. pp. 276. *bibliog. Based on a dissertation submitted at the University of Illinois.*

— United States.

LEWIS (JOHN LLEWELLYN) Papers, 1879-1969. Madison, Wis., 1970. Microfilm: 4 reels. With printed guide to the microfilm edition.

LEWIS (JOHN LLEWELLYN) Papers of John L. Lewis: guide to a microfilm edition; edited by Eleanor Niermann. Madison, Wis., 1970. pp. 12. *bibliog. (State Historical Society of Wisconsin. Guides to Historical Resources)*

MINES, SUBMARINE.

HENKIN (LOUIS) Law for the sea's mineral resources; ...prepared for the National Council on Marine Resources and Engineering Development. [Washington, 1968]. pp. 108,83.

MINES AND MINERAL RESOURCES.

HENKIN (LOUIS) Law for the sea's mineral resources; ...prepared for the National Council on Marine Resources and Engineering Development. [Washington, 1968]. pp. 108,83.

TILTON (JOHN E.) The future of nonfuel minerals. Washington, D.C., [1977]. pp. 113.

— Asia.

WANG (KUNG-PING) and CHIN (EDMOND) Mineral economics and basic industries in Asia. Boulder, 1978. pp. 358. *bibliog.*

— Bolivia — Government ownership.

AGUILAR PEÑARRIETA (ANIBAL) Revolucion y derecho de huelga: debe irse a la huelga en las minas nacionalizadas? La Paz, [1960?]. pp. 23.

— Brazil.

BRAZIL. Departamento Nacional da Produção Mineral. 1969. Contribuição do Departamento Nacional da Produção Mineral no desenvolvimento geo-econômico da região norte: documento basico. Rio de Janeiro, 1969. pp. 105. *bibliog. (Publicações Especiais. No. 7)*

BRAZIL. Departamento Nacional da Produção Mineral. 1969. Contribuição do Departamento Nacional da Produção Mineral no desenvolvimento geo-econômico do Rio Grande do Sul e Santa Catarina: documento basico. Rio de Janeiro, 1969. pp. 123, 1 map. *bibliog. (Publicações Especiais. No. 8)*

BRAZIL. Departamento Nacional da Produção Mineral. 1970. Contribuição ao desenvolvimento geo-econômico de São Paulo e Parana: documento basico. Rio de Janeiro, 1970. pp. 111. *bibliog. (Publicações Especiais. No. 10)*

BRAZIL. Divisão de Fomento da Produção Mineral. 1970. Geologia econômica de parte da região do medio São Francisco, nordeste do Brasil. Rio de Janeiro, 1970. pp. 97. *bibliog. (Boletins. No. 140) 4 maps in end pocket.*

— — Goias (State).

MELLO (JOSE CARLOS RODRIGUES DE) and BERBERT (CARLOS OITI) Investigação geologico-econômica da area de Morro Feio- Hidrolândia, Goias. Rio de Janeiro, 1969. pp. 81, 4 maps. *bibliog. (Brazil. Divisão de Fomento da Produção Mineral. Boletins. No. 132)*

— Canada — British Columbia.

BRITISH COLUMBIA HYDRO AND POWER AUTHORITY. Industrial Development Department. The mining industry of British Columbia and the Yukon. 3rd ed. [Vancouver], 1968. pp. 53.

— — Ontario.

LEITH (J. CLARK) Exploitation of Ontario mineral resources: an economic policy analysis. Toronto, 1976. pp. 93. *bibliog. (Ontario. Economic Council. Working Papers. 1976. No. 2)*

— — Yukon.

BRITISH COLUMBIA HYDRO AND POWER AUTHORITY. Industrial Development Department. The mining industry of British Columbia and the Yukon. 3rd ed. [Vancouver], 1968. pp. 53.

— Iran.

MINING STATISTICS OF IRAN; ([pd. by] Bureau of Statistics [Iran]). a., 1968 [1st issue]- Tehran. *Supersedes Iran. Ministry of Industry and Mines. Industry and mines statistical yearbook (1958/9, 1960/61, 1962/3)*.

— Italy.

SABATTINI (GIANFRANCO) and MORO (BENIAMINO) La crisi delle attività minerarie regionali ed il ruolo del settore pubblico. [Cagliari, 1975]. pp. 95. *bibliog.*

— Rhodesia.

SOUTHERN RHODESIA. 1933. Copy of correspondence, opinions by counsel, documents and returns relating to the question of the ownership of the mineral rights in Southern Rhodesia. Salisbury, 1933. pp. 34, 5. *(Legislative Assembly. [Sessional Papers]. 1933. C.S.R. 18)*

— Russia — Tajikistan.

MADALIEV (NARIMON) Nedra Iagnoba - na sluzhbu narody. Dushanbe, 1976. pp. 130.

— Sierra Leone.

ANDREWS-JONES (D.A.) Geology and mineral resources of the northern Kambui schist belt and adjacent granulites. Freetown, 1966. pp. 100. *bibliog. (Sierra Leone. Geological Survey. Bulletins. No. 6) 2 maps in end pocket.*

MINES AND MINERAL RESOURCES.(Cont.)

— South Africa.

VAN RENSBURG (W.C.J.) and PRETORIUS (DESMOND A.) South Africa's strategic minerals: pieces on a continental chess board. Johannesburg, 1977. pp. 156. *bibliogs.*

MINING CORPORATIONS

— Australia.

The MAPOON story according to the invaders: church mission, Queensland government and mining company; [edited by J. Roberts and others]. Victoria, [1975]. pp. 112. *(International Development Action. Mapoon. Book 2)*

MINING INDUSTRY AND FINANCE

— United States — Colorado.

KING (JOSEPH E.) A mine to make a mine: financing the Colorado mining industry, 1859-1902. College Station, Tex., [1977]. pp. 209. *bibliog.*

MINING LAW.

HENKIN (LOUIS) Law for the sea's mineral resources; ...prepared for the National Council on Marine Resources and Engineering Development. [Washington, 1968]. pp. 108,83.

— Brazil.

BRAZIL. Statutes, etc. 1940-45. Codigo de minas...29.1.1940; codigo de aguas minerais...8.8.1945; como requerer pesquisa de jazida mineral. 3rd ed. Rio de Janeiro, 1966. pp. 116. *(Brazil. Divisão de Fomento da Produção Mineral. Avulsos. 91)*

BRAZIL. Statutes, etc. 1967-68. Codigo de mineração e legislação correlativa. [rev.ed.]. Rio de Janeiro, 1970. pp. 122. *(Brazil. Departamento Nacional da Produção Mineral. Publicações Especiais. No. 11)*

MINORITIES.

BERTELSEN (JUDY S.) The Palestinian Arabs: a non-state nation systems analysis. Beverly Hills, [1976]. pp. 81. *bibliog.*

— Education — United States.

PERSELL (CAROLINE HODGES) Education and inequality: a theoretical and empirical synthesis. New York, [1977]. pp. 244. *bibliog.*

OGBU (JOHN U.) Minority education and caste: the American system in cross-cultural perspective. New York, [1978]. pp. 410. *bibliog.*

— Employment — United Kingdom.

MONCK (ELIZABETH M.) and LOMAS (GLENYS BARBARA GILLIAN) The employment and socio-economic conditions of the coloured population. London, 1975. pp. 33. *(Centre for Environmental Studies. Research Papers. 21)*

— — United States.

KAPLAN (H. ROY) ed. American minorities and economic opportunity. Itasca, Ill., [1977]. pp. 387. *bibliogs.*

LECHT (LEONARD ABE) Occupational choice and training needs: prospects for the 1980's. New York, 1977. pp. 203.

SIMCICH (TINA L.) Women and minorities in banking: shortchanged/update. New York, 1977. pp. 173. *bibliog. A survey of the Council on Economic Priorities.*

WILLIAMS (WALTER E.) Youth and minority employment. Stanford, [1977]. pp. 44. *(Stanford University. Hoover Institution on War, Revolution and Peace. Hoover Institution Studies. 61)*

— Housing — United Kingdom.

FENTON (MIKE) Asian households in owner-occupation: a study of the pattern, costs and experiences of households in Greater Manchester. Bristol, Social Science Research Council Research Unit on Ethnic Relations, [1977]. pp. 70. *bibliog. (Working Papers on Ethnic Relations. No. 2)*

FLETT (HAZEL) Council housing and the location of ethnic minorities. Bristol, Social Science Research Council Research Unit on Ethnic Relations, [1977]. pp. 52. *(Working Papers on Ethnic Relations. No. 5)*

— — — Bibliography.

BUSH (MARTHA) compiler. Immigrant housing. London, 1976. pp. 15. *(London. Greater London Council. Research Library. [Research] Bibliographies. No. 74)*

— — United States.

PHILPOTT (THOMAS LEE) The slum and the ghetto: neighborhood deterioration and middle-class reform, Chicago, 1880-1930. New York, 1978. pp. 428.

— — — Bibliography.

BUSH (MARTHA) compiler. Immigrant housing. London, 1976. pp. 15. *(London. Greater London Council. Research Library. [Research] Bibliographies. No. 74)*

— Canada.

MAXWELL (THOMAS R.) The invisible French: the French in metropolitan Toronto. [Waterloo, Ont., 1977]. pp. 174. *bibliog.*

— Europe.

CHITI-BATELLI (ANDREA) Terze variazioni in tema di politica regionale europea: nazioni proibite e lingue tagliate; note presentate al convegno dell'Associazione internazionale per la difesa delle lingue e culture minacciate, 1975. Roma, 1975. fo. 14.

CONFERENCE ON ETHNIC PLURALISM AND CONFLICT IN CONTEMPORARY WESTERN EUROPE AND CANADA, ITHACA, 1975. Ethnic conflict in the Western world: [papers presented at the Conference]; edited by Milton J. Esman. Ithaca, 1977. pp. 399. *bibliogs. Sponsored by the Western Societies Program of the Center for International Studies, Cornell University.*

— France.

Les DOSSIERS noirs du racisme dans le Midi de la France; ([by] François-Noël Bernardi [and others]). Paris, [1976]. pp. 203.

— Russia.

LENINSKAIA natsional'naia politika i bor'ba protiv ee fal'sifikatorov; redaktsionnaia kollegiia M.B. Mitin [and others]. Ashkhabad, 1975. pp. 423.

NATIONALISM and human rights: processes of modernization in the USSR; edited by Ihor Kamenetsky. Littleton, Colo., [1977]. pp. 243. *bibliog. (Association for the Study of the Nationalities (USSR and East Europe). Series in Issues Studies (USSR and East Europe). No. 1)*

NATIONALITY group survival in multi-ethnic states: shifting support patterns in the Soviet Baltic region; edited by Edward Allworth. New York, 1977. pp. 299. *bibliog.*

NEKRICH (ALEKSANDR MOISEEVICH) The punished peoples: the deportation and fate of Soviet minorities at the end of the Second World War; translated from the Russian by George Saunders. New York, [1978]. pp. 238.

— United Kingdom.

MONCK (ELIZABETH M.) and LOMAS (GLENYS BARBARA GILLIAN) The employment and socio-economic conditions of the coloured population. London, 1975. pp. 33. *(Centre for Environmental Studies. Research Papers. 21)*

BETWEEN two cultures: migrants and minorities in Britain; edited by James L. Watson. Oxford, [1977]. pp. 338. *bibliogs.*

RUNNYMEDE TRUST. Briefing Papers. 1977, No. 6. Ethnic minorities in Britain: a select bibliography. London, 1977. fo. 43.

IMMIGRANTS and minorities in British society; edited by Colin Holmes. London, 1978. pp. 208. *bibliog.*

— United States.

GERLACH (RUSSEL L.) Immigrants in the Ozarks: a study in ethnic geography. Columbia, [1976]. pp. 206. *bibliog. (Missouri University. Studies. vol. 64)*

WOOLFOLK (GEORGE RUBLE) The free negro in Texas, 1800-1860: a study in cultural compromise. Ann Arbor, 1976. pp. 240. *bibliog.*

KAPLAN (H. ROY) ed. American minorities and economic opportunity. Itasca, Ill., [1977]. pp. 387. *bibliogs.*

STEIN (HOWARD F.) and HILL (ROBERT F.) The ethnic imperative: examining the new white ethnic movement. University Park, Pa., [1977]. pp. 308.

FEAGIN (JOE R.) Racial and ethnic relations. Englewood Cliffs, [1978]. pp. 392.

MISES (LUDWIG VON).

MISES (LUDWIG VON) Erinnerungen...; mit einem Vorwort von Margit v. Mises und einer Einleitung von Friedrich August von Hayek. Stuttgart, 1978. pp. 112. *bibliog.*

MISSIONS

— Africa.

MURRAY-BROWN (JEREMY) Faith and the flag: the opening of Africa. London, 1977. pp. 238. *bibliog.*

— Australia.

The MAPOON story according to the invaders: church mission, Queensland government and mining company; [edited by J. Roberts and others]. Victoria, [1975]. pp. 112. *(International Development Action. Mapoon. Book 2)*

— China.

CHRISTIANS in action: a record of work in war-time China; by seven missionaries. London, 1939. pp. 115. *Editor's preface signed: Ronald Rees.*

MISSOURI

— Social life and customs.

GERLACH (RUSSEL L.) Immigrants in the Ozarks: a study in ethnic geography. Columbia, [1976]. pp. 206. *bibliog. (Missouri University. Studies. vol. 64)*

MITRIONE (DAN).

DIALOGUE before death: transcript from a tape recording of an English-language conversation between Dan Mitrione and an unidentified Uruguayan Tupamaro, August 1970. Washington, [1971]. pp. 19.

MITTERRAND (FRANÇOIS).

GISCARD d'Estaing, Mitterrand: 54,774 mots pour convaincre; by Jean-Marie Cotteret [and others]. Paris, [1976]. pp. 347. *bibliog.*

MITTERRAND (FRANÇOIS) Politique. [Paris, 1977]. pp. 640. *bibliog.*

TAÏX (GABRIEL) Monsieur Mitterrand vous n'êtes pas socialiste. Paris, 1977. pp. 179.

DESJARDINS (THIERRY) François Mitterrand: un socialiste gaullien. [Paris, 1978]. pp. 295. *bibliog.*

MOATS.

MEDIEVAL moated sites; edited by F.A. Aberg. London, 1978. pp. 93. *bibliog. (Council for British Archaeology. Research Reports. No. 17)*

MOBILE HOMES

— United Kingdom.

BIRD (BARBARA) and O'DELL (ALAN) Mobile homes in England and Wales, 1975: report of surveys. [Watford], Building Research Establishment, [1977]. pp. 144.

PICK (JOYCE) No caravan: no home. London, 1977. pp. 63.

MODULES (ALGEBRA).

BLYTH (T.S.) Module theory: an approach to linear algebra. Oxford, 1977. pp. 400.

MOELVEN BRUG, AKSJESELSKAPET.

MAGELI (JOHANNES) A/S Moelven Brug: karakteristika og synspunkter. Bergen, 1977. pp. 18. (Norges Handelshøyskole. Kristofer Lehmkuhl Forelesninger. 1977)

MOHAMMEDAN COUNTRIES

— Foreign relations — Pakistan.

PAKISTAN. Ministry of Foreign Affairs. 1977. Pakistan's relations with the Islamic states: a review. [Islamabad], 1977. pp. 34.

MOHAMMEDANS AND SOCIAL PROBLEMS

— Egypt.

BADAWI (W.A. ZAKI) The reformers of Egypt. London, [1978]. pp. 160.

MOHAMMEDANS IN MALAYSIA.

KESSLER (CLIVE SAMUEL) Islam and politics in a Malay state: Kelantan, 1838-1969. Ithaca, [1978]. pp. 274. *bibliog. Revised version of a doctoral thesis accepted by the University of London.*

MOLDAVIAN REPUBLIC

— Executive departments.

ORGANY gosudarstvennoi vlasti i upravleniia Moldavskoi SSR. Kishinev, 1976. pp. 206.

MOLUCCANS IN THE NETHERLANDS.

PENONTON (BUNG) De Zuidmolukse republiek: schets voor een beschrijving van de nieuwste geschiedenis van het Zuidmolukse volk. 4th ed. Amsterdam, 1977. pp. 299. *bibliog.*

SMEETS (HENK) Lunetten, kroniek van een failliet beleid: het overheidsbeleid ten aanzien van de Molukse gemeenschap in Vught. Vught, 1977. pp. 207.

MOLYNEUX (WILLIAM).

MORGAN (MICHAEL J.) Molyneux's question: vision, touch and the philosophy of perception. Cambridge, 1977. pp. 213.

MONARCHY.

ECCLESHALL (ROBERT) Order and reason in politics: theories of absolute and limited monarchy in early modern England. Oxford, 1978. pp. 197. *bibliog.*

FRANKLIN (JULIAN HAROLD) John Locke and the theory of sovereignty: mixed monarchy and the right of resistance in the political thought of the English revolution. Cambridge, 1978. pp. 146. *bibliog.*

MONARCHY, SPANISH.

TARRAGO (JAIME) La monarquia que quiso Franco. Madrid, 1976. pp. 159.

MONASTERIES

— United Kingdom.

MORIMOTO (NAOMI) The sheep farming of Norwich Cathedral Priory in the 13th and 14th centuries. Aichi, [1977]. pp. 37. (Nagoya Gakuin University. Institute of Industrial Sciences. Discussion Papers. No. 2)

MONASTIC LIBRARIES

— Russia.

KUKUSHKINA (MARGARITA VLADIMIROVNA) Monastyrskie biblioteki Russkogo Severa: ocherki po istorii knizhnoi kul'tury XVI-XVII vekov. Leningrad, 1977. pp. 223.

MONASTICISM AND RELIGIOUS ORDERS

— Canada — Quebec.

DENAULT (BERNARD) and LEVESQUE (BENÔIT) Eléments pour une sociologie des communautés religieuses au Québec. Sherbrooke, 1975. pp. 220. *bibliog.*

MONETARY POLICY.

SLOVIN (MYRON B.) and SUSHKA (MARIE ELIZABETH) Money and economic activity: an analytical approach. Lexington, Mass., [1977]. pp. 220. *bibliog.*

— Bibliography.

ROCK (JAMES M.) compiler. Money, banking, and macroeconomics: a guide to information sources. Detroit, [1977]. pp. 281.

— Germany.

EMMINGER (OTMAR) The D-mark in the conflict between internal and external equilibrium, 1948-75. Princeton, 1977. pp. 54. *bibliog.* (Princeton University. Department of Economics and Sociology. International Finance Section. Essays in International Finance. No. 122)

— India.

SIDDIQI (A.A.) Indian currency policy, 1872-1914. Aligarh, 1973. pp. 39.

— Mexico.

WILFORD (D. SYKES) Monetary policy and the open economy: Mexico's experience. New York, 1977. pp. 152. *bibliog.*

— United Kingdom.

LYFORD (KENNETH) Monetary policy in Britain since 1951. [1976]. fo. 127. *bibliog. Typescript. M.Sc. (London) thesis: unpublished. This thesis is the property of London University and may not be removed from the Library.*

— United States.

BECSKY (GYÖRGY) The international monetary situation and the global economic strategy of the USA; translated by George Hajdu. Budapest, 1972. pp. 46. (Hungarian Scientific Council for World Economy. [Publications]. Trends in World Economy. No. 8)

BROCK (LESLIE V.) The currency of the American colonies, 1700-1764: a study in colonial finance and imperial relations. New York, 1975. pp. 602. *bibliog. Originally presented as a thesis, University of Michigan, 1941.*

FEDERAL reserve policies and public disclosure; edited by Richard D. Erb. Washington, D.C., [1978]. pp. 108. (American Enterprise Institute for Public Policy Research. AEI Symposia. 78B) *Papers from a conference held in 1977.*

MILLER (ERVIN) Microeconomic effects of monetary policy: the fallout of severe monetary restraint. London, 1978. pp. 228.

MONETARY UNIONS.

ONE money for Europe; edited by Michele Fratianni and Theo Peeters. London, 1978. pp. 224. *bibliogs.*

MONEY.

McGREGOR (L.) and WALTERS (ALAN A.) Real balances and output: a productivity model of a monetary economy. [Amsterdam, 1973]. pp. 26. *bibliog. Photocopy from Econometric studies of macro and monetary relations: papers presented at the Second Australasian Conference of Econometricians, 1971.*

AKADEMIIA NAUK SSSR. Institut Mirovoi Ekonomiki i Mezhdunarodnykh Otnoshenii. Materialy mezhdunarodnogo simpoziuma "Krizis i evoliutsiia mezhdunarodnoi valiutnoi sistemy kapitalizma", Leningrad, 1974. Moskva, 1975. 2 pts. (in 1).

ACCADEMIA NAZIONALE DEI LINCEI. Atti dei Convegni Lincei. 12. Il problema della moneta oggi: (convegno internazionale) indetto nel centenario della nascita di Luigi Einaudi, Roma, 6-8 febbraio 1975. Rome, 1976. pp. 211.

BRUNHOFF (SUZANNE DE) Marx on money; translated by Maurice J. Goldbloom. New York, [1976]. pp. 139.

DEANE (RODERICK S.) International monetary reform: content and perspective. Wellington, 1976. pp. 27. *bibliog.* (Reserve Bank of New Zealand. Research Papers. No. 21)

The EMERGING international monetary order and the banking system; editor, Yair Aharoni. Tel Aviv, [1976]. pp. 191. *Papers of a seminar held in Israel in 1975, sponsored by Tel Aviv University Top Executive Course.*

TEORIA monetaria e struttura finanziaria in Italia; a cura di Gianluigi Mengarelli. Venezia, 1976. pp. 405.

ALLAIS (MAURICE) L'impôt sur le capital et la réforme monétaire. [Paris, 1977]. pp. 367.

BINN (FELIX G.) Konjunkturpolitik am Scheideweg: Fiskalismus oder Monetarismus?. Zürich, [1977]. pp. 19. *Revised version of address given at the Parteitag of the Liberalsozialistische Partei der Schweiz, Bern, 16th April, 1977.*

CHICK (VICTORIA) The theory of monetary policy. rev. ed. Oxford, 1977. pp. 163. *bibliog.*

EGOM (PETER ALEX) Money in the theory of international economic activity: an inquiry into the nature and causes of the wealth and poverty of nations. Guderup, [1977]. pp. 155.

FRANKEL (SALLY HERBERT) Money: two philosophies: the conflict of trust and authority. Oxford, [1977]. pp. 163. *bibliog. Published in the United States as Two philosophies of money.*

MAKINEN (GAIL E.) Money, the price level, and interest rates: an introduction to monetary theory. Englewood Cliffs, [1977]. pp. 446. *bibliogs.*

MATIUKHIN (GEORGII GAVRILOVICH) Problemy kreditnykh deneg pri kapitalizme. Moskva, 1977. pp. 224.

MOTLEY (BRIAN) Money, income and wealth: the macroeconomics of a monetary economy. Lexington, Mass., [1977]. pp. 402. *bibliogs.*

NENTJES (A.) Van Keynes tot Keynes: de ontwikkeling van het denken over geld en werkloosheid bij Keynes. Groningen, [1977]. pp. 357. *With summary in English.*

PLUMPTRE (ARTHUR FITZGERALD WYNNE) Three decades of decision: Canada and the world monetary system, 1944-75. Toronto, [1977]. pp. 335. *bibliog.*

SCHMITT (BERNARD) L'or, le dollar et la monnaie supranationale. Paris, [1977]. pp. 227.

SLOVIN (MYRON B.) and SUSHKA (MARIE ELIZABETH) Money and economic activity: an analytical approach. Lexington, Mass., [1977]. pp. 220. *bibliog.*

CONGDON (TIM) Monetarism: an essay in definition. London, 1978. pp. 88.

DAVIDSON (PAUL) Money and the real world. 2nd ed. London, 1978. pp. 428.

JOHNSON (HARRY GORDON) Selected essays in monetary economics. London, [1978]. pp. 275. *bibliogs.*

KLEIN (JOHN JACOB) Money and the economy. 4th ed. New York, [1978]. pp. 598. *bibliogs.*

MORGAN (BRIAN) Monetarists and Keynesians: their contribution to monetary theory. London, 1978. pp. 183. *bibliog.*

NEWLYN (WALTER TESSIER) Theory of money. 3rd ed. Oxford, 1978. pp. 204.

MONEY.(Cont.)

NIEHANS (JUERG) The theory of money. Baltimore, [1978]. pp. 312. *bibliog.*

SIMMEL (GEORG) The philosophy of money; translated by Tom Bottomore and David Frisby. London, 1978. pp. 512.

SMITH (PAUL F.) Money and financial intermediation: the theory and structure of financial systems. Englewood Cliffs, [1978]. pp. 370. *bibliogs.*

WILCZYNSKI (JOZEF) Comparative monetary economics: capitalist and socialist monetary systems and their interrelations in the changing international scene. London, 1978. pp. 270. *bibliogs.*

— Bibliography.

ROCK (JAMES M.) compiler. Money, banking, and macroeconomics: a guide to information sources. Detroit, [1977]. pp. 281.

— History.

McCUSKER (JOHN J.) Money and exchange in Europe and America, 1600-1775: a handbook. London, 1978. pp. 367. *bibliog.*

— Mathematical models.

SHEEN (JEFFREY RALPH) A study of monetary disequilibrium in open economies. 1977. fo. 330. *bibliog. Typescript. Ph.D. (London) thesis: unpublished. This thesis is the property of London University and may not be removed from the Library.*

FISHER (DOUGLAS) Monetary theory and the demand for money;...mathematical appendices by Jeffrey I. Bernstein. London, 1978. pp. 278. *bibliog.*

— Argentine Republic.

LAMAS (DOMINGO) Reforma monetaria; investigacion de la Honorable Camara de Diputados de la Nacion. Buenos Aires, 1913. pp. 166.

CARRANZA PEREZ (RICARDO) El sistema monetario argentino. Buenos Aires, 1943. pp. 195.

BECU (CARLOS TEODORO) El control del dinero en la Argentina. Buenos Aires, [1953]. pp. 156. *bibliog.*

— Balkan States.

DELIBANES (DEMETRIOS) The repercussions of the international monetary crisis in the Balkans and a possible remedy. Thessalonika, 1972. pp. 10. *(Reprinted from Balkan Studies, vol. 13, No. 2, 1972)*

— Brazil.

CHACEL (JULIAN MAGALHÃES) and others. A correção monetaria. Rio de Janeiro, 1970. pp. 336. *(Columbia University. Inter-American Law Center. Estudos sôbre a propriedade privada nas Americas)*

— Europe.

L'EUROPE des crises; [by] Robert Triffin [and others]. Bruxelles, 1976. pp. 173. *(Fondation Paul-Henri Spaak. Bibliothèque) Mainly lectures given at the Institut des Etudes Européennes of the Université Libre of Brussels, in 1974 and 1975.*

EINZIG (PAUL) and QUINN (BRIAN SCOTT) The Euro-dollar system: practice and theory of international interest rates. 6th ed. London, 1977. pp. 124.

— Europe, Eastern.

BRABANT (JOZEF M.P. VAN) East European cooperation: the role of money and finance. New York, 1977. pp. 394. *bibliog.*

— European Economic Community countries.

SCHMITT (BERNARD) La monnaie européenne. Paris, [1977]. pp. 229.

ONE money for Europe; edited by Michele Fratianni and Theo Peeters. London, 1978. pp. 224. *bibliogs.*

— France.

SADRIN (JEAN) Monnaie et politique monétaire. Paris, [1974]. pp. 150.

— — Mathematical models.

MODELES monétaires de l'économie française; [by] V. Lévy-Garboua [and others]. Paris, [1976]. pp. 356. *bibliogs. (France. Commissariat Général du Plan. Economie et Planification) Summaries in English, French and German.*

SHEEN (JEFFREY RALPH) A study of monetary disequilibrium in open economies. 1977. fo. 330. *bibliog. Typescript. Ph.D. (London) thesis: unpublished. This thesis is the property of London University and may not be removed from the Library.*

— Germany.

MONETARY policy and economic activity in West Germany; compiled by S.F. Frowen [and others]. London, 1977. pp. 268. *bibliog.*

— India.

IENGAR (H.V.R.) Monetary policy and economic growth. Bombay, 1962. pp. 295. *bibliog. Speeches as Governor of the Reserve Bank of India, 1957-1962.*

— Italy — Mathematical models.

TEORIA monetaria e struttura finanziaria in Italia; a cura di Gianluigi Mengarelli. Venezia, 1976. pp. 405.

— Netherlands.

KORTEWEG (PIETER) and VAN LOO (PETER D.) The market for money and the market for credit: theory, evidence and implications for Dutch monetary policy. Leiden, 1977. pp. 105. *bibliog.*

TIMMERMAN (P.C.) The intervention policy of the Netherlands bank in the money market. Amsterdam, [1977]. pp. 26. *(Nederlandsche Bank. Reprints. No. 33)*

— Netherlands Antilles.

SOEST (JAAP VAN) Trustee of the Netherlands Antilles: a history of money, banking and the economy with special reference to the central Bank van de Nederlandse Antillen, 1828-6 February-1978. Zutphen, [1978]. pp. 422. *bibliog.*

— Russia.

BARKOVSKII (NIKOLAI DMITRIEVICH) Problemy kredita i denezhnogo oborota v usloviiakh razvitogo sotsializma. Moskva, 1976. pp. 215.

GARVY (GEORGE) Money, financial flows, and credit in the Soviet Union. Cambridge, Mass., 1977. pp. 223. *bibliog. (National Bureau of Economic Research. Studies in International Economic Relations. 7 [bis])*

— Spain.

BARTHE Y BARTHE (ANDRES) Cuales son los medios que podrian ponerse en practica para mejorar nuestra circulacion monetaria: memoria premiada en el certamen celebrado por la Asociacion de Profesores Mercantiles de Madrid en 1892. Madrid, 1893. pp. 15.

BARTHE Y BARTHE (ANDRES) Estudio critico de la crisis monetaria: memoria presentada...al quinto concurso extraordinario abierto por la Real Academia de Ciencias Morales y Politicas, etc. Madrid, 1905. pp. 107.

— Switzerland.

LIBERALSOZIALISTISCHE PARTEI DER SCHWEIZ. 25 Jahre später: zur Abstimmung über die Kaufkraft-Initiative vom 15. April 1951. Zürich, 1976. pp. 28.

SIEBER (HANS) Der flottierende Schweizerfranken: ein Befund. Zürich, 1978. pp. 360. *bibliog. (Hochschule St. Gallen. Schweizerisches Institut für Aussenwirtschafts-, Struktur- und Marktforschung. Veröffentlichungen. Band 30)*

— United Kingdom.

JACOB (CLAUD P.G.) Economic salvation: a treatise on unemployment, taxation, debt: the cause and a remedy. London, 1933. pp. 142. *With a typescript letter in end pocket, from the author to the Review Editor of the Economist, replying to criticism.*

BRITAIN's money puzzle: are we on target for economic stability?; [by] Brian Scott Quinn [and others]. London, [1977]. pp. 20.

NEWLYN (WALTER TESSIER) Theory of money. 3rd ed. Oxford, 1978. pp. 204.

— United States.

KEMMERER (EDWIN WALTER) High prices and deflation. Princeton, 1920 repr. 1921. pp. 86. *A revision and enlargement of three articles published 1919-1920 by the Bankers' Statistics Corporation of New York City.*

CHOLLET (ALEXANDRE) Faudra-t-il une supermonnaie pour stabiliser le dollar? Lausanne, 1978. pp. 44. *(Lausanne. Université. Centre de Recherches Européennes. Publications. 6. Etudes Sectorielles)*

HENNING (CHARLES N.) and others. Financial markets and the economy. 2nd ed. Englewood Cliffs, [1978]. pp. 552. *bibliogs.*

MONEY SUPPLY.

SLOVIN (MYRON B.) and SUSHKA (MARIE ELIZABETH) Money and economic activity: an analytical approach. Lexington, Mass., [1977]. pp. 220. *bibliog.*

— America, Latin.

WACHTER (SUSAN M.) Latin American inflation: the structuralist-monetarist debate. Lexington, Mass., [1976]. pp. 165. *bibliog.*

— Mexico.

WILFORD (D. SYKES) Monetary policy and the open economy: Mexico's experience. New York, 1977. pp. 152. *bibliog.*

— United Kingdom.

LOMAX (RACHEL) and MOWL (COLIN) Balance of payments flows and the monetary aggregates in the United Kingdom. London, Treasury, 1978. pp. 10,6. *(Government Economic Service Working Papers. No.5)*

MONGOLIA

— Economic conditions.

ZAGASBALDAN (D.) Razvitie proizvoditel'nykh sil v MNR: opyt ekonomiko- statisticheskogo analiza; perevod s mongol'skogo avtora; nauchnyi redaktor...V.E. Adamov. Moskva, 1977. pp. 147.

— Foreign relations — Russia.

MATERIALY po istorii russko-mongol'skikh otnoshenii. Moskva, 1974 in progress.

MONOPOLIES.

MORRIS (EDWARD) M.P. A short enquiry into the nature of monopoly and forestalling; a third edition, with considerable additions. London, T. Adell and W. Davies, 1800. pp. 54.

CLARKE (ROGER) Ph.D. Four classical views of monopoly: Ricardo, McCulloch, Bailey and Senior. Sheffield, [1977]. pp. 23. *bibliog.*

— United States.

SHERMAN (HOWARD JAY) Stagflation: a radical theory of unemployment and inflation. New York, [1976]. pp. 252. *bibliogs.*

MONSANTO COMPANY.

FORRESTAL (DAN J.) The story of Monsanto: faith, hope and $5,000: the trials and triumphs of the first 75 years. New York, [1977]. pp. 285.

MONTERREY, MEXICO

— Economic conditions.

WALTON (JOHN) Elites and economic development: comparative studies on the political economy of Latin American cities. Austin, [1977]. pp. 257. *bibliog.* (*Texas University. Institute of Latin American Studies. Latin American Monographs. No. 41*)

MONTESSORI (MARIA).

KRAMER (RITA) Maria Montessori. Oxford, 1978. pp. 410.

MONTREAL

— Languages.

RABOTIN (MAURICE) Le vocabulaire politique et socio-ethnique à Montréal de 1839 à 1842. Montréal, [1975]. pp. 123. *bibliog.*

— Social conditions.

GUAY (LOUIS) The ecological differentiation of urban social space: Montreal, 1951-1971. 1976 [or rather 1977]. fo. 420. *bibliog.* Typescript. Ph.D. (London) thesis: unpublished. This thesis is the property of London University and may not be removed from the Library.

MONTREUX, SWITZERLAND, TREATY OF, 1936.

MORF (JUERG) Die Dardanellenfrage an der Konferenz von Montreux 1936. Bern, [1977]. pp. 243. *bibliog.* (*Zürich. Universität. Historisches Seminar. Geist und Werk der Zeiten. No.55*)

MOORE (CHARLES GARRETT PONSONBY) 11th Earl of Drogheda.

MOORE (CHARLES GARRETT PONSONBY) 11th Earl of Drogheda. Double harness: memoirs. London, [1978]. pp. 387.

MORGAN (Sir CHARLES).

FROST (JOHN) of Newport. A second letter to Sir Charles Morgan of Tredegar, in the county of Monmouth, Baronet, M.P.;...also a letter to the farmers. Newport, the Author, 1822. pp. 39.

MORLEY (JOHN) Viscount Morley of Blackburn.

KENT (CHRISTOPHER) Brains and numbers: elitism, Comtism, and democracy in mid- Victorian England. Toronto, [1978]. pp. 212. *bibliog.*

MORO (ALDO).

PALLOTTA (GINO) Moro: ritratto di un leader. [Isola del Liri, 1975]. pp. 182.

MOROCCO

— Constitution.

MOROCCO. Constitution. 1970. Texte intégral de la nouvelle constitution marocaine. Bruxelles, Ambassade du Royaume du Maroc, [1970]. fo. 17.

MOROCCO. Constitution. 1972. La constitution marocaine. Bruxelles, Ambassade du Royaume du Maroc, 1972. fo. 25.

— Economic policy.

MOROCCO. Division du Plan et des Statistiques. 1965. Projections de population: répercussions sur certains aspects de l'économie du pays et solutions proposées. [Rabat], 1965. pp. 25.

— Foreign relations.

PRICE (D.L.) Morocco and the Sahara: conflict and development. London, 1977. pp. 16. *bibliog.* (*Institute for the Study of Conflict. Conflict Studies. No. 88*)

MORPHOGENESIS

— Mathematical models.

THOM (RENÉ) Structural stability and morphogenesis: an outline of a general theory of models; translated...by D.H. Fowler. Reading, Mass., 1975. pp. 348.

MORRIS (WILLIAM).

LEATHAM (JAMES) William Morris, master of many crafts: a study. 2nd ed. Peterhead, 1903. pp. 129.

FAULKNER (PETER) William Morris and Eric Gill. [London], 1975. pp. 31.

MORRISON (GEORGE ERNEST).

MORRISON (GEORGE ERNEST) The correspondence of G.E. Morrison; edited by Lo Hui-Min. Cambridge, 1976-78. 2 vols.

MORTALITY

— Tables.

PRICE (RICHARD) D.D. Observations on the expectations of lives, the increase of mankind, the influence of great towns on population and particularly the state of London with respect to healthfulness and number of inhabitants; in a letter...to Benjamin Franklin, etc. [London, W. Bowyer and J. Nichols, 1769]. pp. 89-126. (*From the Philosophical Transactions of the Royal Society, vol. 59*)

IRELAND. Census, 1871. Census of Ireland, 1871. Part 2. Vital statistics. (C.876 and C.1000). Dublin, 1873-75. 2 vols.

BRAZIL. Conselho Nacional de Estatistica. Laboratorio de Estatistica. 1951. Tabua de sobrevivência para o Distrito Federal, conforme a mortalidade do ano de 1950;...planejada pelo Giorgio Mortara, calculada pelo Orêncio Longino de Arruda Gomes. [Rio de Janeiro, 1951]. fo. 10. (*Estudos Demograficos. No. 7*)

WATANABE (SADAMU) Old people in transitional Japan with activities of gerontology of Japan and mortality trends in selected countries. [Tokyo], 1960. pp. 78. *bibliog.*

SOUTH AFRICA. Bureau of Statistics. Report on Bantu deaths in selected magisterial districts (formerly Bantu deaths in selected magisterial districts). a., 1968/71- Pretoria. [in English and Afrikaans].

ROSE (RICHARD JOHN) Maori-European comparisons in mortality. Wellington, 1972. pp. 188. (*New Zealand. Department of Health. Special Report Series. No. 37*)

NETHERLANDS. Centraal Bureau voor de Statistiek. 1976. Onderzoek naar de sterfte onder overlevenden uit concentratiekampen, 1945-1968. 's-Gravenhage, 1976. pp. 63. *With English summary.*

U.K. Office of Population Censuses and Surveys. 1978. Trends in mortality, 1951-1975. London, 1978. pp. 44. *bibliog.* ([*Publications*]. *Series DH1. No.3*)

MORTGAGE LOANS

— United States.

CAPITAL markets and the housing sector: perspectives on financial reform; edited by Robert M. Buckley [and others]. Cambridge, Mass., [1977]. pp. 394. *bibliogs.* Papers written for a study conducted by the Office of Economic Affairs of the U.S. Department of Housing and Urban Development.

MORTGAGES

— United Kingdom.

FISHER (WILLIAM RICHARD) and LIGHTWOOD (JOHN MASON) Law of mortgage; ninth edition by E.L.G. Tyler. London, 1977. pp. 771.

TUNNARD (JO) and WHATELY (CLARE) Rights guide for home owners. 2nd ed. London, 1977. pp. 80.

MOSCA (GAETANO).

LOMBARDO (ANTONIO) Teorie del potere politico: Mosca e Pareto. Bologna, [1976]. pp. 146.

MOSCOW

— History.

MOSKOVSKIE bol'sheviki v ogne revoliutsionnykh boev: vospominaniia. Moskva, 1976. pp. 415.

— Statistics.

MOSCOW. Statisticheskoe Upravlenie. Moskva v tsifrakh, 1917-1977 gg.: statisticheskii sbornik. Moskva, 1977. pp. 192.

MOSSI (AFRICAN PEOPLE).

SCHILDKROUT (ENID) People of the zongo: the transformation of ethnic identities in Ghana. Cambridge, 1978. pp. 303. *bibliog.*

MOTHER AND CHILD.

CULTURE and infancy: variations in the human experience; edited by P. Herbert Leiderman [and others]. New York, [1977]. pp. 615. *bibliogs.* Based on a conference held in 1973 by the Wenner- Gren Foundation for Anthropological Research.

MOTHERS

— Employment — Canada — Manitoba.

MANITOBA. Women's Bureau. 1974. Mothers in the labour force: their child care arrangements. Winnipeg, 1974. pp. (62). *bibliog.*

MOTIVATION (PSYCHOLOGY).

EVANS (PHIL) Motivation. London, 1975. pp. 143. *bibliog.*

MURRELL (KENNETH FRANK HYWEL) Motivation at work. London, 1976. pp. 144. *bibliog.*

WALLACE (CHRISTOPHER ST. JOHN) Motivation and incentives in rural China. [n.p., 1977?]. fo.220. *bibliog.*

MOTIVATION RESEARCH (MARKETING).

CONSUMER and industrial buying behavior; edited by Arch G. Woodside [and others]. New York, [1977]. pp. 523. *bibliog.*

MOTIVE (LAW)

— Russia.

TARARUKHIN (SVIATOSLAV ANDREEVICH) Ustanovlenie motiva i kvalifikatsiia prestupleniia. Kiev, 1977. pp. 151.

MOTOR BUS LINES

— Hong Kong.

HONG KONG. Transport Department. Research and Development Section. 1976. Lantao Island bus service. [Hong Kong], 1976. pp. (51). (*Studies Reports. No. 76/1*)

HONG KONG. Transport Department. Research and Development Section. 1976. Public transport in Wong Chuk Hang estate. [Hong Kong], 1976. pp. 23. (*Studies Reports. No. 76/6*)

— United Kingdom.

PEAT, MARWICK, MITCHELL AND COMPANY. An initial report on minimum levels of service for rural public transport; prepared for the National Bus Company. [London], 1977. fo. 124,(5). *bibliog.*

— — Employees.

TRANSPORT AND GENERAL WORKERS' UNION. To the members of the London Bus Section, Central Area. London, 1937. pp. 6.

MOTOR BUSES

— Bibliography.

COLLINS (JUDITH) compiler. Buses in urban areas, 1970-1976;...edited by Claire M. Lambert. [London], 1976. pp. 60. (*U.K. Department of the Environment. Library. Bibliographies. No. 17C*)

MOTOR VEHICLES

— United Kingdom — Fuel.

ADVISORY COUNCIL ON ENERGY CONSERVATION [U.K.]. Energy for transport: long-term possibilities. London, H.M.S.O., 1978. pp. 20. *bibliog*. (*Papers. 8*)

MOUNTAIN ECOLOGY

— Peru.

BRUSH (STEPHEN B.) Mountain, field, and family: the economy and human ecology of an Andean valley. Philadelphia, Pa., 1977. pp. 199. *bibliog*.

MOVEMENT (PHILOSOPHY).

SOLOPOV (EVGENII FROLOVICH) Dvizhenie i razvitie. Leningrad, 1974. pp. 128.

MOVEMENT, PSYCHOLOGY OF.

BRAUNSTEIN (MYRON L.) Depth perception through motion. New York, [1976]. pp. 200. *bibliog*.

MOVIMIENTO DE LA IZQUIERDA REVOLUCIONARIA.

MOVIMIENTO DE LA IZQUIERDA REVOLUCIONARIA. MIR: Movimiento de Izquierda Revolucionaria Chileno. Bilbao, 1976. pp. 458. *Cover subtitle: seleccion de documentos, declaraciones publicas y discursos, emitidos durante los dos años posteriores al golpe militar.*

MOVIMIENTO NACIONALISTA REVOLUCIONARIO.

ANDRADE (VICTOR) Victor Andrade: su pensamiento politico pasado y presente. La Paz, 1966. pp. 21. (*Movimiento Nacionalista Revolucionario. [Publications]. No.1*)

MITCHELL (CHRISTOPHER) The legacy of populism in Bolivia: from the MNR to military rule. New York, 1977. pp. 167. *bibliog*.

MOVING PICTURE JOURNALISM

— United States.

FIELDING (RAYMOND) The March of Time, 1935-1951. New York, 1978. pp. 359. *bibliog*.

MOVING PICTURES

— Censorship.

BRODY (STEPHEN) Screen violence and film censorship: a review of research; a Home Office Research Unit report. London, 1977. pp. 176. *bibliog*. (*U.K. Home Office. Home Office Research Studies. No. 40*)

— Psychological aspects.

JARVIE (IAN CHARLES) Movies as social criticism: aspects of their social psychology. Metuchen, N.J., 1978. pp. 207. *bibliog*.

— Social aspects.

SORLIN (PIERRE) Sociologie du cinéma: ouverture pour l'histoire de demain. Paris, 1977. pp. 315. *bibliog*.

JARVIE (IAN CHARLES) Movies as social criticism: aspects of their social psychology. Metuchen, N.J., 1978. pp. 207. *bibliog*.

— Italy.

SORLIN (PIERRE) Sociologie du cinéma: ouverture pour l'histoire de demain. Paris, 1977. pp. 315. *bibliog*.

MOZAMBIQUE

— Economic conditions.

COSTA RODRIGUES (RUI) As assimetrias espaciais do desenvolvimento socio-economico em Moçambique. Lourenço Marques, [1966?]. pp. 26.

— Economic policy.

EGERO (BERTIL) Mozambique and Angola: reconstruction in the social sciences. Uppsala, 1977. pp. 78. (*Nordiska Afrikainstitutet. Research Reports. No. 42*)

— History.

HENRIKSEN (THOMAS H.) Mozambique: a history. London, [1978]. pp. 276.

— Nationalism.

INTERNATIONAL CONFERENCE IN SOLIDARITY WITH MOZAMBIQUE, ANGOLA, GUINEA BISSAU, CAPE VERDE, SÃO TOME AND PRINCIPE, LOURENÇO MARQUES, 1975. Solidarity with Mozambique. Cairo, [1975]. pp. 230. (*Afro-Asian People's Solidarity Organization. Afro-Asian Publications. 72*)

— Social conditions.

COSTA RODRIGUES (RUI) As assimetrias espaciais do desenvolvimento socio-economico em Moçambique. Lourenço Marques, [1966?]. pp. 26.

MUCKERMANN (FRIEDRICH JOSEPH).

MUCKERMANN (FRIEDRICH JOSEPH) Im Kampf zwischen zwei Epochen: Lebenserinnerungen; bearbeitet und eingeleitet von Nikolaus Junk. Mainz, [1973]. pp. 668. (*Kommission für Zeitgeschichte. Veröffentlichungen. Reihe A: Quellen. Band 15*)

MUELLER VON NITERSDORF (ADAM HEINRICH).

HISTORIA i wolność: studia z dziejów ideologii XIX wieku, etc. Warszawa, 1961. pp. 299. (*Polska Akademia Nauk. Instytut Filozofii i Socjologii. Archiwum Historii Filozofii i Myśli Społecznej. 7*) *With Russian or German summaries.*

MUGGING

— United Kingdom.

POLICING the crisis: mugging, the state, and law and order; [by] Stuart Hall [and others]. London, 1978. pp. 425.

MULDOON (ROBERT DAVID).

MULDOON (ROBERT DAVID) Muldoon. London, 1978. pp. 224.

MULLAN (JOHN PAT).

The ARDBOE martyrs: John Pat Mullan: Hugh Heron. n.p., [1973?]. pp. 20.

MULLER SZN. (HENDRIK).

MULLER (HENDRIK) Muller: een Rotterdams zeehandelaar Hendrik Muller Szn, 1819-1898. Schiedam, 1977. pp. 467. (*Rotterdam. Historisch Genootschap Roterodamum. [Publications]. 18*)

MULTIVARIATE ANALYSIS.

FIENBERG (STEPHEN E.) The analysis of cross-classified categorical data. Cambridge, Mass., [1977]. pp. 151. *bibliog*.

WEBBER (RICHARD J.) and CRAIG (JOHN) Writer on population. Socio-economic classification of local authority areas. London, 1978. pp. 117. (*U.K. Office of Population Censuses and Surveys. Studies on Medical and Population Subjects. No.35*)

MUNICH FOUR POWER AGREEMENT, 1938.

DOUGLAS (ROY) In the year of Munich. London, 1977. pp. 155. *bibliog*.

MUNICIPAL BONDS

— United States.

WALSH (ANN MARIE HAUCK) The public's business: the politics and practices of government corporations. Cambridge, Mass., [1978]. pp. 436. *bibliog*. *A Twentieth Century Fund study*.

MUNICIPAL FINANCE

— Canada — Quebec.

BELANGER (GERARD) Le financement municipal au Québec; [annexe du rapport sur l'urbanisation]. [Québec, Editeur officiel, 1976]. pp. 73.

— Finland.

FINLAND. Tilastokeskus. Kuntien tabus...kunnittaiset tiedot, etc. a., 1973- Helsinki. *[in Finnish and Swedish]*

— Norway.

NORWAY. Statistiske Centralbyrå. Strukturtall for kommunenes økonomi, etc. a., 1974- Oslo.

— United States.

The FISCAL crisis of American cities: essays on the political economy of urban America with special reference to New York; edited by Roger E. Alcaly and David Mermelstein. New York, 1977. pp. 361.

MACMANUS (SUSAN A.) Revenue patterns in U.S. cities and suburbs: a comparative analysis. New York, 1978. pp. 265. *bibliog*.

MUNICIPAL GOVERNMENT.

MADDICK (HENRY) Problems facing local government in metropolitan areas: a one-day seminar organized by the Auckland City Council, held at the Logan Park Motor Hotel, Auckland, Monday 29th October, 1973; speaker Professor Henry Maddick. Auckland, 1973. 1 vol. (various pagings).

PICKVANCE (CHRISTOPHER GEOFFREY) Marxist approaches to the study of urban politics: divergences among some recent French studies. Canterbury, 1976. fo. 52. *Paper for the Political Studies Association Conference, Nottingham, 1976*.

— Brazil.

LEAL (VICTOR NUNES) Coronelismo, enxada e voto: o municipio e o regime representativo no Brasil. São Paulo, 1975. pp. 270. *bibliog*. *Reprint, with new preface, of first edition published in 1949*.

— Canada.

HIGGINS (DONALD J.H.) Urban Canada: its government and politics. Toronto, [1977]. pp. 322. *bibliog*.

— — Quebec.

LORD (GUY) and CHENARD (DANIEL) Les structures politiques et administratives des municipalités urbaines du Québec; [annexe du rapport sur l'urbanisation]. [Québec, Editeur officiel, 1976]. pp. 156. *bibliog*.

— France.

PETIT-DUTAILLIS (CHARLES) The French communes in the middle ages;...translated by Joan Vickers. Amsterdam, 1978. pp. 165.

— Italy.

FERRARESI (FRANCO) and KEMENY (PIETRO) Classi sociali e politica urbana: destra e sinistra nelle amministrazioni locali. Roma, 1977. pp. 160.

— Netherlands.

VERENIGING VAN NEDERLANDSE GEMEENTEN. Extract from the constitution of the Kingdom of the Netherlands, 1956: provisions relating to municipalities and municipal government. [The Hague?], 1963. pp. 3.

— **United Kingdom.**

ROEBUCK (JOHN ARTHUR) A letter to the electors of Bath, on the Municipal Corporation Reform Bill; with a postscript on the conduct of Sir Robert Peel and others, on the discussion of the question. London, J. Longley, [1835]. pp. 16.

— **United States.**

URBAN administration: management, politics, and change; edited by Alan Edward Bent and Ralph A. Rossum. Port Washington, N.Y., 1976. pp. 385.

ALLSWANG (JOHN M.) Bosses, machines, and urban voters: an American symbiosis. Port Washington, 1977. pp. 157. *bibliog.*

DORSETT (LYLE W.) Franklin D. Roosevelt and the city bosses. Port Washington, N.Y., 1977. pp. 134. *bibliog.*

SWANSON (BERT E.) and SWANSON (EDITH) Discovering the community: comparative analysis of social, political, and economic change. New York, [1977]. pp. 391.

YATES (DOUGLAS) The ungovernable city: the politics of urban problems and policy making. Cambridge, Mass., [1977]. pp. 219. *(Massachusetts Institute of Technology. MIT Studies in American Politics and Public Policy. 3)*

MUNICIPAL OFFICIALS AND EMPLOYEES

— **Switzerland.**

TRABER (ALFRED) Geschichte des V[erbandes des] P[ersonals] O[effentlicher] D[ienste], Sektion Zürich, städtische Arbeiter und Angestellte, 1893-1953. [Zürich, 1953]. pp. 229.

MUNICIPAL OWNERSHIP

— **United Kingdom.**

HOPPÉ (MALCOLM) Is the party really over?: why rates rise in the North East. London, [1977]. pp. 11.

BUILDING with direct labour: local authority building and the crisis in the construction industry; [written by the Direct Labour Collective]. London, 1978. pp. 115.

MORRIS (MICHAEL WOLFGANG LAURENCE) The disaster of direct labour: an examination of council building departments. London, 1978. pp. 43. *(Conservative Political Centre. [Publications]. No. 622)*

MUNICIPAL SERVICES

— **Mathematical models.**

BELTRAMI (EDWARD J.) Models for public systems analysis. New York, 1977. pp. 218.

— **Canada — Quebec.**

DIVAY (GERARD) Les niveaux de services municipaux au Québec; [annexe du rapport sur l'urbanisation]. [Québec, Editeur officiel, 1976]. pp. 79.

— **United States.**

INNOVATION and implementation in public organizations; edited by Richard R. Nelson [and] Douglas Yates. Lexington, Mass., [1978]. pp. 186.

— — **Mathematical models.**

CARTER (GRACE M.) and others. Response areas for two emergency units. New York, 1971. pp. 47. *bibliog. (Rand Corporation. [Rand Reports]. 532)*

LARSON (RICHARD C.) and STEVENSON (KEITH A.) On insensitivities in urban redistricting and facility location. New York, 1971. pp. 24. *(Rand Corporation. [Rand Reports]. 533)*

— — **Maryland — Baltimore.**

ANDERSON (ALAN D.) The origin and resolution of an urban crisis: Baltimore, 1890-1930. Baltimore, [1977]. pp. 143. *bibliog.*

MUNITIONS.

CONTROLLING future arms trade; [by] Anne Hessing Cahn [and others]. New York, [1977]. pp. 208. *bibliog. (Council on Foreign Relations. 1980s Project Studies)*

COUNCIL ON CHRISTIAN APPROACHES TO DEFENCE AND DISARMAMENT. The sale and transfer of conventional arms, arms systems and related technology; a report of a working party...[convenor, Barrie Paskins]. London, 1977. pp. 19.

— **Laws and legislation — Russia.**

TIKHII (VLADIMIR PAVLOVICH) Otvetstvennost' za khishchenie ognestrel'nogo oruzhiia, boevykh pripasov i vzryvchatykh veshchestv po sovetskomu ugolovnomu pravu. Khar'kov, 1976. pp. 128. *bibliog.*

— **East (Near East).**

SNIDER (LEWIS W.) Arabesque: untangling the patterns of supply of conventional arms to Israel and the Arab states and the implications for United States policy on supply of "lethal" weapons to Egypt. [Denver, Colo., 1977]. pp. 151. *(Denver. University. Social Science Foundation and Graduate School of International Studies. Monograph Series in World Affairs. vol. 15, no. 1)*

— **Europe.**

UDIS (BERNARD) From guns to butter: technology organizations and reduced military spending in western Europe. Cambridge, Mass., [1978]. pp. 368.

— **France.**

CHARBONNEL (NICOLE) Commerce et course sous la Révolution et le Consulat à La Rochelle: autour de deux amateurs: les frères Thomas et Pierre-Antoine Chegaray. Paris, [1977]. pp. 103. *bibliog. (Paris. Université de Paris II. Travaux et Recherches. Série Sciences Historiques. 12)*

Les TRAFICS d'armes de la France: l'engrenage de la militarisation; étude réalisée par le Centre local d'information et de coordination pour l'action non violente. 2nd ed. Paris, 1977. pp. 335. *bibliog.*

— **Germany.**

BRANDT (MAXIMILIAN) and ECCIUS ( ) of Essen, defendants. Prozess Brandt und Genossen: der sogenannte Krupp- Prozess; Verhandlungsbericht, aus dem Reichstag, Zeitungsstimmen; mit einer Einführung herausgegeben von Ad. Zimmermann. Berlin, 1914. pp. 397.

— **Russia.**

RABOCHIE oruzheinoi promyshlennosti v Rossii i russkie oruzheiniki v XIX - nachale XX v. Leningrad, 1976. pp. 144.

— **Sweden.**

OLSSON (ULF) The creation of a modern arms industry, Sweden, 1939-1974. Göteborg, 1977. pp. 207. *bibliog. (Göteborgs Universitet. Ekonomisk-Historiska Institutionen. Meddelanden. 37)*

— **United Kingdom.**

TREBILCOCK (CLIVE) The Vickers brothers: armaments and enterprise, 1854-1914. London, [1977]. pp. 181. *bibliog.*

ADAMS (R.J.Q.) Arms and the wizard: Lloyd George and the Ministry of Munitions, 1915-1916. London, [1978]. pp. 252.

— **United States.**

SNIDER (LEWIS W.) Arabesque: untangling the patterns of supply of conventional arms to Israel and the Arab states and the implications for United States policy on supply of "lethal" weapons to Egypt. [Denver, Colo., 1977]. pp. 151. *(Denver. University. Social Science Foundation and Graduate School of International Studies. Monograph Series in World Affairs. vol. 15, no. 1)*

FARLEY (PHILIP J.) and others. Arms across the sea. Washington, D.C., [1978]. pp. 134.

MUÑOZ (ERASMO).

MUÑOZ (ERASMO) Erasmo Muñoz, yanacon del valle de Chancay: biografia organizada por Jose Matos Mar [and] Jorge A. Carbajal H. Lima, 1974. pp. 168. *(Instituto de Estudios Peruanos. Proyecto de Estudios Etnologicos del Valle de Chancay. Monografias. No. 4)*

MURCIA

— **Gilds.**

GARCIA ABELLAN (JUAN) Organizacion de los gremios en la Murcia del siglo XVIII y recopilacion de ordenanzas. Murcia, 1976. pp. 323.

MURDER

— **Canada.**

JAYEWARDENE (C.H.S.) The penalty of death: the Canadian experiment. Lexington, Mass., [1977]. pp. 125. *bibliog.*

MURMANSK (OBLAST')

— **Economic policy.**

EKONOMICHESKIE problemy razvitiia Murmanskoi oblasti. Apatity, 1976. pp. 117. *bibliog.*

MUSEUMS

— **Canada.**

CANADA. Statistics Canada. Culture statistics: museums, art galleries and related institutions. a., 1974(1st)- Ottawa. *[in English and French]*

— **United Kingdom — Directories.**

The LIBRARIES, museums and art galleries yearbook 1976; editors: Adrian Brink and Derry Watkins. Cambridge, 1976. pp. 254.

MUSEUMS IN EDUCATION.

U.K. Department of Education and Science. 1971. Museums in education. London, 1971. pp. 55. *(Education Surveys. 12)*

MUSIC

— **Economic aspects.**

ATTALI (JACQUES) Bruits: essai sur l'économie politique de la musique. [Paris], 1977. pp. 303. *bibliog.*

— **History and criticism.**

DONAKOWSKI (CONRAD L.) A muse for the masses: ritual and music in an age of democratic revolution, 1770-1870. Chicago, 1977. pp. 435. *bibliog.*

MUSIC, POPULAR (SONGS, ETC.)

— **Italy.**

SAVONA (A. VIRGILIO) and STRANIERO (MICHELE L.) eds. Canti dell'emigrazione. Milano, [1976]. pp. 441.

MUSIC AND SOCIETY.

GAGNEUR (WLADIMIR) Toast composé pour la solennité musicale de Poligny 20 août 1848. Arbois, Javel, 1848. pp. 18.

MUSIC FESTIVALS.

LONDON. Greater London Council. Code of practice for pop concerts: a guide to safety, health and welfare at one day events. [London, 1976]. 1 pamphlet (unpaged).

— **United Kingdom.**

U.K. Working Group on Pop Festivals. 1978. Pop festivals and their problems; second report of the Working Group; [Baroness Stedman, chairman]. London, 1978. pp. 38.

MUSSOLINI (BENITO).

GIORDANO (GIANCARLO) Il patto a quatro nella politica estera di Mussolini. [Bologna, 1976]. pp. 213. *bibliog.*

MUSSOLINI (BENITO) Mussolini e "La Voce"; a cura di Emilio Gentile. Firenze, [1976]. pp. 239. *Consists of letters to Giuseppe Prezzolini and of articles by Mussolini and by Prezzolini.*

ROBERTSON (ESMONDE MANNING) Mussolini as empire-builder: Europe and Africa, 1932-36. London, 1977. pp. 246. *bibliog.*

TAYLOR (ALAN JOHN PERCIVALE) The war lords. London, 1977. pp. 189. *Transcripts of six lectures delivered on BBC Television in August 1976.*

MUTINY

— United Kingdom.

LAMB (DAVE) Mutinies, 1917-1920. Oxford, [1977]. pp. 32.

MUTTON

— Marketing.

NEW ZEALAND MEAT PRODUCERS' BOARD. A common sense approach to the EEC sheepmeat market. London, 1978. pp. 17.

MYSORE

— Economic conditions.

MYSORE. 1970. A brief report on the economy of Mysore State, 1969-70. Bangalore, 1970. pp. 34.

PUTTASWAMAIAH (K.) Indicators of development, with reference to Mysore's economy, India. Bangalore, Directorate of Evaluation and Manpower, 1972. pp. 86.

— Economic policy.

PUTTASWAMAIAH (K.) Evaluation of plan programmes in Karnataka. Bangalore, Government Secretariat, 1976. pp. 14.

— Social policy.

PUTTASWAMAIAH (K.) Evaluation of plan programmes in Karnataka. Bangalore, Government Secretariat, 1976. pp. 14.

MYSORE (CITY)

— Social conditions.

VENKATARAYAPPA (K.N.) Slums: a study in urban problem. New Delhi, 1972. pp. 105.

MYTHOLOGY.

LÉVI-STRAUSS (CLAUDE) The origin of table manners; introduction to a science of mythology, 3; translated from the French by John and Doreen Weightman. London, 1978. pp. 551. *bibliog.*

NAHUAS.

BEYOND the codices: the Nahua view of colonial Mexico; translated and edited by Arthur J.O. Anderson [and others]. Berkeley, [1976]. pp. 235. *bibliog. (California University. Latin American Center. Latin American Studies. vol. 27)*

— Religion and mythology.

LEON-PORTILLA (MIGUEL) Religion de los Nicaraos: analisis y comparacion de tradiciones culturales nahuas. Mexico, 1972. pp. 117. *bibliog. (Mexico City. Universidad Nacional Autonoma de Mexico. Instituto de Investigaciones Historicas. Serie de Cultura Nahuatl. Monografias. 12)*

NA'INI (MIRZA MUHAMMAD HUSAYN).

HAIRI (ABDUL-HADE) Shi'ism and constitutionalism in Iran: a study of the role played by the Persian residents of Iraq in Iranian politics. Leiden, 1977. pp. 274. *bibliog.*

NAMIBIA.

See SOUTH WEST AFRICA.

NAPLES

— Economic history.

ROMANO (RUGGIERO) Napoli: dal viceregno al regno: storia economica. Torino, [1976]. pp. 370.

— History.

GHIRELLI (ANTONIO) Napoli italiana: la storia della città dopo il 1860. Torino, [1977]. pp. 314.

— Social history.

DE BENEDETTI (AUGUSTO) La classe operaia a Napoli nel primo dopoguerra. Napoli, [1974]. pp. 197.

NAPOLEON I, Emperor of the French.

MACAULAY (THOMAS BABINGTON) Baron Macaulay. Napoleon and the restoration of the Bourbons: the completed portion of Macaulay's projected History of France, from the restoration of the Bourbons to the accession of Louis Philippe; edited by Joseph Hamburger. New York, 1977. pp. 117.

NARAYAN (JAYAPRAKASH).

NARAYAN (JAYAPRAKASH) The essential JP: the philosophy and prison diary of Jayaprakash Narayan; edited by Satish Kumar. Dorchester, 1978. pp. 152.

NARCOTIC ADDICTS

— Rehabilitation — United States.

WARD (HUGH) Employment and addiction: overview of issues. Washington, 1973. pp. 52. *(Drug Abuse Council. [Monographs]. 5)*

NARCOTIC HABIT

— Treatment — United States.

SUGARMAN (BARRY) Daytop village: a therapeutic community. New York, [1974]. pp. 134. *bibliog.*

— — — California.

BULLINGTON (BRUCE) Heroin use in the barrio. Lexington, Mass., [1977]. pp. 179. *bibliog.*

NARCOTIC LAWS

— Ireland (Republic).

EIRE. Dail Eireann. Special Committee on the Misuse of Drugs Bill, 1973. 1975-76. Parliamentary debates. Dublin, 1975-76. 11 pts. (in 1 vol.) *(Dail Eireann. Parliamentary Debates: Official Report. 1975-76. D 19. Nos. 1-11)*

NASSER (GAMAL ABDEL).

VATIKIOTIS (PANAYIOTIS J.) Nasser and his generation. London, [1978]. pp. 375.

NATAL, BRAZIL

— Commerce.

BANCO DO NORDESTE DO BRASIL. Departamento de Estudos Econômicos do Nordeste. Mercado consumidor de aves e ovos em Natal. Fortaleza, 1969. pp. 47.

NATIONAL FRONT.

SOCIALIST WORKER. Pamphlets. Organise against the National Front: the new Nazis. [London, 1975?]. pp. 13.

COOK (DAVE) A knife at the throat of us all: racism and the National Front. London, [1977]. pp. 31. *(Communist Party of Great Britain. Communist Party Pamphlets)*

EYRES (STEPHEN) The National Front is a socialist front. London, [1977]. pp. 17. *(Aims for Freedom and Enterprise. Studies of the Left. No. 1)*

FIELDING (NIGEL GOODWIN) The National Front: a sociological study of political organization and ideology. 1977. fo. 523. *bibliog.* Typescript. Ph. D. *(London) thesis: unpublished. This thesis is the property of London University and may not be removed from the Library.*

HICK (JOHN) The new Nazism of the National Front and National Party: a warning to Christians. Birmingham, 1977. pp. 11.

LABOUR RESEARCH DEPARTMENT. The National Front investigated. London, 1978. pp. 28.

SHIPLEY (PETER) The National Front: racialism and neo-fascism in Britain. London, [1978]. pp. 16. *(Institute for the Study of Conflict. Conflict Studies. No. 97)*

TAYLOR (STAN) Writer on politics. The National Front: a contemporary evaluation. [Coventry], 1978. pp. 38. *(University of Warwick. Department of Politics. Working Papers. No. 16)*

NATIONAL INCOME.

BECKERMAN (WILFRED) An introduction to national income analysis. 2nd ed. London, 1976. pp. 308.

NUTTER (GILBERT WARREN) Growth of government in the West. Washington, D.C., [1978]. pp. 94. *(American Enterprise Institute for Public Policy Research. AEI Studies. 185)*

— Accounting.

ORGANISATION FOR ECONOMIC CO-OPERATION AND DEVELOPMENT. Quarterly national accounts bulletin. q., 1976(no.3)- [Paris]. *[in English and French] File includes supplement, Historical statistics, 1960-1971.*

KURABAYASHI (YOSHIMASA) Collection of national accounts studies. Tokyo, 1977 in progress. *bibliogs. (Tokyo. Hitotsubashi University. Institute of Economic Research. Economic Research Series. No. 16 etc.)*

UNITED NATIONS. Statistical Office. Statistical Papers. Series M. No.60. Provisional international guidelines on the national and sectoral balance-sheet and reconciliation accounts of the system of national accounts. (ST/ESA/STAT/SER.M/60). New York, 1977. pp. 117.

— Canada — Nova Scotia — Accounting.

CZAMANSKI (STANISLAW) Structure of the Nova Scotia economy: analysis of income and product accounts; commissioned by Nova Scotia Department of Trade and Industry. Halifax, 1970. pp. 129. *bibliog. (Dalhousie University. Institute of Public Affairs. [Current Publications]. No.82)*

— Finland — Accounting.

FINLAND. Tilastokeskus. Aluetilinpito: tuotanto, työllisyys ja kiinteän pääoman bruttomuodostus lääneittäin, etc. a., 1973- Helsinki. *[in Finnish and Swedish with summary in English].*

— Mauritania — Accounting.

BARROT (ANDRE) Les comptes spéciaux du Trésor en Mauritanie. Nouakchott, Ecole Nationale d'Administration, 1976. fo. 39.

— Norway — Accounting.

NORWAY. Statistiske Centralbyrå. Fylkesfordelt nasjonalregnskap. a., 1973- Oslo. *[in Norwegian with English summary]*

— Portugal — Accounting.

PILAR (JULIETA) A distribuição funcional dos rendimentos. [Lisbon, 1972]. pp. 36. *(Portugal. Instituto Nacional de Estatística. Estudos. 44) With summaries in English and French.*

— Spain.

BARTHE Y BARTHE (ANDRES) El aumento de la riqueza en España desde 1795. Madrid, 1907. pp. 47.

— Sri Lanka — Accounting.

PYATT (FRANK GRAHAM) and ROE (ALAN R.) Social accounting for development planning with special reference to Sri Lanka. Cambridge, [1977]. pp. 190. *bibliog. Based on an International Labour Office World Employment Programme Research Branch mission to Sri Lanka in 1973.*

— Underdeveloped areas.

See UNDERDEVELOPED AREAS — National income.

— United Kingdom.

UNITED KINGDOM. Board of Inland Revenue. 1929. Inland revenue report on national income, 1929. Cambridge, 1977. pp. 17. *bibliog. Reprint of unpublished report of 1929.*

— — Accounting.

U.K. Central Statistical Office. 1978. Regional accounts. London, 1978. pp. 52. *(Studies in Official Statistics. No. 31)*

— Yugoslavia — Accounting.

YUGOSLAVIA. Savezni Zavod za Statistiku. Studije, Analize i Prikazi. 85. Privredni bilansi Jugoslavije, 1975; Economic balances of Yugoslavia, 1975. Beograd, 1976. pp. 202. *With English and Russian summaries.*

NATIONAL MARITIME MUSEUM.

GUIDE to the manuscripts in the National Maritime Museum; edited by R.J.B. Knight. London, 1977 in progress.

NATIONAL PARKS AND RESERVES

— United Kingdom.

FABIAN SOCIETY. Fabian Tracts. [No] 456. National parks; [by] Chris Smith. London, 1978. pp. 24.

NATIONAL SOCIALISM.

HITLER (ADOLF) The new Germany desires work and peace: speeches by Reich Chancellor Adolf Hitler, the leader of the new Germany. Berlin, [1933?]. pp. 66.

GRIMM (FRIEDRICH) Hitlers deutsche Sendung. Berlin, 1934. pp. 46.

KUEHNRICH (HEINZ) Der KZ-Staat: Rolle und Entwicklung der faschistischen Konzentrationslager, 1933 bis 1945. Berlin, 1960. pp. 144. *bibliog.*

FLIEDNER (HANS JOACHIM) Die Judenverfolgung in Mannheim, 1933-1945. Stuttgart, 1971. 2 vols. *bibliog. (Mannheim. Stadtarchiv. Veröffentlichungen. Bände 1-2)*

NAZISM and the Third Reich; edited with an introduction by Henry A. Turner. New York, 1972. pp. 262. *bibliog.*

Der AUFSTIEG der NSDAP in Augenzeugenberichten; herausgegeben und eingeleitet von Ernst Deuerlein. München, 1974 repr. 1976. pp. 459. *bibliog.*

GRÜNBERG (KAROL) SS - czarna gwardia Hitlera. [Warszawa], 1975. pp. 558. *bibliog.*

DELARUE (JACQUES) Conquête du pouvoir et nazification de l'opinion publique. Bruxelles, 1976. pp. 77. *(Cercle d'Education Populaire. Cahiers. No. 60)*

KROGMANN (CARL VINCENT) Es ging um Deutschlands Zukunft, 1932-1939: Erlebtes täglich diktiert von dem früheren Regierenden Bürgermeister von Hamburg. Leoni am Starnberger See, 1976 repr. 1977. pp. 372.

POŁOMSKI (FRANCISZEK) Aspekty rasowe w postępowaniu z robotnikami przymusowymi i jeńcami wojennymi III Rzeszy, 1939-1945. Wrocław, 1976. pp. 130. *bibliog. (Wrocław. Wrocławskie Towarzystwo Naukowe. Prace. Seria A. Nr. 185) With English summary.*

ABENDROTH-Forum: Marburger Gespräche aus Anlass des 70. Geburtstags von Wolfgang Abendroth; herausgegeben von Frank Deppe [and others]. Marburg, [1977]. pp. 443. *(Studiengesellschaft für Sozialgeschichte und Arbeiterbewegung, Marburg. Schriftenreihe für Sozialgeschichte und Arbeiterbewegung. Band 6) Papers and discussion of four symposia held in May and June of 1976.*

ADAM (UWE DIETRICH) Hochschule und Nationalsozialismus: die Universität Tübingen im Dritten Reich. Tübingen, 1977. pp. 240. *bibliog. (Tübingen. Universität. Contubernium. 23)*

BAUMGAERTNER (RAIMUND) Weltanschauungskampf im Dritten Reich: die Auseinandersetzung der Kirchen mit Alfred Rosenberg. Mainz, [1977]. pp. 272. *bibliog. (Kommission für Zeitgeschichte. Veröffentlichungen. Reihe B: Forschungen. Band 22)*

BAYERN in der NS-Zeit: soziale Lage und politisches Verhalten der Bevölkerung im Spiegel vertraulicher Berichte; herausgegeben von Martin Broszat [and others]. München, 1977. pp. 712. *bibliog.*

BEYERCHEN (ALAN D.) Scientists under Hitler: politics and the physics community in the Third Reich. New Haven, 1977. pp. 287. *bibliog.*

BIRD (KENNETH W.) Weimar, the German naval officer corps and the rise of national socialism. Amsterdam, 1977. pp. 313. *bibliog.*

BREITSCHEID (RUDOLF) Antifaschistische Beiträge, 1933-1939; ausgewählt und eingeleitet von Dieter Lange. Frankfurt am Main, 1977. pp. 136.

HENNIG (EIKE) Bürgerliche Gesellschaft und Faschismus in Deutschland: ein Forschungsbericht. Frankfurt am Main, 1977. pp. 424. *bibliog.*

HOEGNER (WILHELM) Flucht vor Hitler: Erinnerungen an die Kapitulation der ersten deutschen Republik, 1933. München, 1977 repr. 1978. pp. 296.

McKALE (DONALD M.) The swastika outside Germany. Kent, Ohio, [1977]. pp. 288. *bibliog.*

SAAGE (RICHARD) Faschismustheorien: eine Einführung. 2nd ed. München, 1977. pp. 184. *bibliog.*

Die ZERSTOERUNG der Weimarer Republik; ([edited by] Reinhard Kühnl [and] Gerd Hardach). Köln, [1977]. pp. 292.

HAHN (FRED) Lieber Stürmer: Leserbriefe an das NS-Kampfblatt, 1924 bis 1945: eine Dokumentation aus dem Leo-Baeck-Institut, New York; Bearbeitung der deutschen Ausgabe von Günther Wagenlehner. Stuttgart, [1978]. pp. 263. *bibliog. (Studiengesellschaft für Zeitprobleme. Zeitpolitik. 19)*

LANE (BARBARA MILLER) and RUPP (LEILA J.) eds. Nazi ideology before 1933: a documentation. Manchester, [1978]. pp. 180. *bibliog.*

PELTZ-DRECKMANN (UTE) Nationalsozialistischer Siedlungsbau: Versuch einer Analyse der die Siedlungspolitik bestimmenden Faktoren am Beispiel des Nationalsozialismus. München, [1978]. pp. 547. *bibliog.*

The SHAPING of the Nazi state; edited by Peter D. Stachura. London, [1978]. pp. 304.

— Caricatures and cartoons.

HEARTFIELD (JOHN) Photomontages of the Nazi period. London, 1977. pp. 143. *bibliog.*

NATIONAL UNION OF DISTRIBUTIVE AND ALLIED WORKERS.

NATIONAL UNION OF DISTRIBUTIVE AND ALLIED WORKERS. Circulars 1925-(1946). Manchester, 1925-46. 2 loose-leaf binders.

PETCH (ARTHUR W.) A manual of branch administration; prepared and issued by authority of the Executive Council for the guidance of N.U.D.A.W. branch officials ([with] Supplement). Manchester, 1925. pp. 117.

NATIONALDEMOKRATISCHE PARTEI DEUTSCHLANDS [BUNDESREPUBLIK].

KLINGEMANN (HANS DIETER) and PAPPI (FRANZ URBAN) Politischer Radikalismus:...dargestellt am Beispiel einer Studie anlässlich der Landtagswahl 1970 in Hessen. München, 1972. pp. 124. *bibliog.*

NATIONALISM.

LENINSKAIA natsional'naia politika i bor'ba protiv ee fal'sifikatorov; redaktsionnaia kollegiia M.B. Mitin [and others]. Ashkhabad, 1975. pp. 423.

KRITIKA burzhuaznogo natsionalizma. Moskva, 1977. pp. 187. *bibliog. (Akademiia Nauk SSSR. Institut Vostokovedeniia. Sovremennaia Istoriografiia Stran Zarubezhnogo Vostoka. [vyp.6])*

SETON-WATSON (GEORGE HUGH NICHOLAS) Nations and states: an enquiry into the origins of nations and the politics of nationalism. London, 1977. pp. 563. *bibliog.*

NATIONALISM AND SOCIALISM.

NATIONALISM and communism in Asia: the American response; edited and with an introduction by Norman A. Graebner. Lexington, Mass., [1977]. pp. 204. *bibliog.*

NATIONALISM and human rights: processes of modernization in the USSR; edited by Ihor Kamenetsky. Littleton, Colo., [1977]. pp. 243. *bibliog. (Association for the Study of the Nationalities (USSR and East Europe). Series in Issues Studies (USSR and East Europe). No. 1)*

NATIONALITIES, PRINCIPLE OF.

BERTELSEN (JUDY S.) The Palestinian Arabs: a non-state nation systems analysis. Beverly Hills, [1976]. pp. 81. *bibliog.*

NATIVE RACES.

SANDERS (DOUGLAS ESMOND) The formation of the World Council of Indigenous Peoples. Copenhagen, 1977. pp. 27. *(International Work Group for Indigenous Affairs. Documents. 29)*

NATIVISM.

PETERSON (RICHARD H.) Manifest destiny in the mines: a cultural interpretation of anti- Mexican nativism in California, 1848-1853. San Francisco, 1975. pp. 126. *bibliog.*

NATURAL LAW.

MELDEN (ABRAHAM IRVING) Rights and persons. Oxford, [1977]. pp. 263.

NATURAL RESOURCES.

NOBEL SYMPOSIUM, 29TH, STOCKHOLM, 1974. Man, environment, and resources: in the perspective of the past and the future; edited by Torgny Torgnysson Segerstedt and Sam Nilsson. [Stockholm, 1974]. pp. 111.

ACCADEMIA NAZIONALE DEI LINCEI. Atti dei Convegni Lincei. 7. Convegno internazionale: utilizzazione ottimale ed economia delle risorse naturali; Roma, 3-4 maggio 1974. Roma, 1975. pp. 221.

SOCIETÀ ITALIANA DEGLI ECONOMISTI. Riunione Scientifica, 14a, Roma, 1973. Economia ed ecologia: [proceedings]. Milano, 1975. pp. 354.

BANKS (FERDINAND E.) Scarcity, energy, and economic progress. Lexington, Mass., [1977]. pp. 200. *bibliog.*

CIGNO (ALESSANDRO) The debate on natural resources and the fate of humanity; or, Do we need economists? Hull, 1977. pp. 24. *bibliog. An inaugural lecture delivered at the University of Hull on 4 May 1976.*

INTERNATIONAL resource flows; edited by Gerald Garvey and Lou Ann Garvey. Lexington, Mass., [1977]. pp. 178.

PROSPECTS for growth: changing expectations for the future; edited by Kenneth D. Wilson. New York, 1977. pp. 343.

NATURAL RESOURCES.(Cont.)

ALTERNATIVES for growth: the engineering and economics of natural resources development: a conference of the National Bureau of Economic Research; edited by Harvey J. McMains and Lyle Wilcox. Cambridge, Mass., 1978. pp. 251. *Proceedings of the Charles Carter Newman Symposium on Natural Resources Engineering.*

PRINGLE (LAURENCE P.) The economic growth debate: are there limits to growth? New York, 1978. pp. 86. *bibliog.*

— **Bibliography.**

BOLWIG (NIELS GEERT) and THOMSEN (ERIC STØTTRUP) compilers. The economics of raw materials, natural resources, energy, and related topics: a bibliography. Aarhus, [1977]. pp. 282. *(Aarhus. Universitet. Økonomiske Institut. Memos. 1977. 5)*

— **Australia.**

AUSTRALIA. Department of National Development. Report. a., 1970/71(1st)- Canberra. *Included in AUSTRALIA. Parliament. [Parliamentary papers].*

— **Canada — Alberta.**

ALBERTA. Department of Business Development and Tourism. 1975. Industry and resources, 1975. [Edmonton], 1975. pp. 256.

— — **British Columbia.**

BRITISH COLUMBIA. Economics and Statistics Branch. 1971. British Columbia: manual of resources and development. Victoria, 1971. pp. 54.

BRITISH COLUMBIA. Department of Economic Development. 1975. British Columbia: manual of resources and development. [rev. ed.] Victoria, 1974 [or rather 1975]. pp. 55.

BRITISH COLUMBIA. Ministry of Economic Development. 1977. Manual of resources and development. Victoria, 1977. pp. 62.

BRITISH COLUMBIA. Ministry of Economic Development. 1977. The north west report '77: a summary report on development opportunities in the north west region of British Columbia. [Victoria], 1977. pp. 250.

— **Rhodesia.**

OTTAWA conference: report of the Committee appointed to investigate and report to the government on certain matters relating to the natural resources and industries of Southern Rhodesia, their present position and future prospects, and their relation to empire and world trade; [H. Bertin, chairman]. Salisbury, 1933. pp. 65. *(Southern Rhodesia. Legislative Assembly. [Sessional Papers]. 1933. C.S.R.1)*

— **Underdeveloped areas.**

See UNDERDEVELOPED AREAS — Natural resources.

NATURAL THEOLOGY.

JAKI (STANLEY L.) The road of science and the ways to God. Edinburgh, 1978. pp. 478. *(Gifford Lectures. 1974-76)*

NATURALIZATION

— **Switzerland — Basel-Stadt (Canton).**

PFISTER (WILLY) Die Einbürgerung der Ausländer in der Stadt Basel im 19. Jahrhundert: Basler Bürgerbuch III. Basel, 1976. pp. 487. *bibliog. (Basel-Stadt (Canton). Staatsarchiv. Quellen und Forschungen zur Basler Geschichte. 8)*

NAUDEBA (AFRICAN PEOPLE).

LUCIEN-BRUN (B.) La colonisation des terres neuves du Centre-Togo par les Kabrè et les Losso. [Bondy], Office de la Recherche Scientifique et Technique Outre-Mer, [1974]. fo. 293. *bibliog. Maps in end pocket.*

NAVAL STRATEGY.

LEUTZE (JAMES R.) Bargaining for supremacy: Anglo-American naval collaboration, 1937-1941. Chapel Hill, [1977]. pp. 328. *bibliog.*

NEDERLANDS VERBOND VAN VAKVERENIGINGEN.

De BEHEERSTE vakbeweging: het NVV tussen loonpolitiek en loonstrijd, 1959-1973; ([by] Kees van Doorn [and others]). Amsterdam, 1976. pp. 568.

NEDERLANDSCHE BANK.

TIMMERMAN (P.C.) The intervention policy of the Netherlands bank in the money market. Amsterdam, [1977]. pp. 26. *(Nederlandsche Bank. Reprints. No. 33)*

NEGATIVE INCOME TAX

— **United States.**

The NEW Jersey income-maintenance experiment. New York, [1976-77]. 3 vols. *(Wisconsin University, Madison. Institute for Research on Poverty. Monograph Series)*

NEGLIGENCE

— **Russia.**

DAGEL' (PLEKHAN SERGEEVICH) Neostorozhnost': ugolovno-pravovye i kriminologicheskie problemy. Moskva, 1977. pp. 143.

— **United Kingdom.**

CHARLESWORTH (JOHN) LL.D. On negligence; sixth edition by R. A. Percy. London, 1977. pp. 955.

NEGOTIABLE INSTRUMENTS

— **New Zealand.**

NEW ZEALAND. Working Party on Negotiable Instruments. 1977. Report; [C.I. Patterson, chairman]. [Wellington, 1977]. 1 vol. (various pagings).

NEGOTIATION.

FOX (ARNOLD JEFFREY) Role-reversal: an aid to resolving conflict. [1978]. fo.102. *bibliog. Typescript. M.Phil. (London) thesis: unpublished. This thesis is the property of London University and may not be removed from the Library.*

NEGROES.

See AFRO-AMERICANS.

NEGROES IN BRAZIL, [CANADA, SOUTH AFRICA, ETC.]

See BLACKS — Brazil, [Canada, South Africa, etc.]

NEIGHBOURHOOD.

NEIGHBORHOOD change: lessons in the dynamics of urban decay; [by] Charles L. Leven [and others]. New York, 1976. pp. 205.

NATIONAL CONFERENCE ON NEIGHBORHOOD COMMERCIAL REVITALIZATION, 2ND, 1976. Neighborhoods in the urban economy: the dynamics of decline and revitalization; edited by Benjamin Goldstein [and] Ross Davis. Lexington, Mass., [1977]. pp. 160.

NENNI (PIETRO).

TAMBURRANO (GIUSEPPE) ed. Pietro Nenni: intervista sul socialismo italiano. Roma, 1977. pp. 170.

NEPAL.

NEPAL. Department of Information. 1970. Facts about Nepal. [Kathmandu], 1970. pp. 53.

— **Census.**

NEPAL. Census, 1971 Population census, 1971. Kathmandu, 1975. 7 pts. (in 5 vols.)

— **Foreign relations.**

NEPAL. King, 1955-72 (Mahendra). Address by His Majesty King Mahendra to the third non- aligned summit conference, (Lusaka, 1970). [Kathmandu, 1970]. pp. 14.

BIRENDRA BIR BIKRAM SHAH DEVA, Crown Prince of Nepal. His Royal Highness the Crown Prince has said-. 2nd ed. Kathmandu, Department of Information, 1971. pp. 30.

— **Politics and government.**

KHATRI (PADMA BAHADUR) Nepal: towards prosperity. Kathmandu, Department of Information, 1969. pp. 9.

NEPAL. King, 1955-72 (Mahendra). Royal address at the constitution day function organised to celebrate the tenth anniversary of the partyless democratic panchayat system. [Kathmandu, 1970?]. pp. 18.

BIRENDRA BIR BIKRAM SHAH DEVA, Crown Prince of Nepal. His Royal Highness the Crown Prince has said-. 2nd ed. Kathmandu, Department of Information, 1971. pp. 30.

NEPAL. Department of Information. 1971. The panchayat democracy. [Kathmandu], 1971. pp. 40.

SHAHA (RISHIKESH) Nepali politics: retrospect and prospect. 2nd ed. Delhi, 1978. pp. 291. *bibliog.*

— **Statistics.**

NEPAL INDUSTRIAL DEVELOPMENT CORPORATION. Statistical abstract. s-a., Jl/D 1970 ([n.s.] no.1)- Kathmandu.

NESTLÉ.

[NESTLÉ]. A Swiss firm and its activities in developing countries: Nestlé's experience. [Lausanne, 1963]. 1 pamphlet (unpaged).

NETHERLANDS

— **Appropriations and expenditures.**

PRIORITEITEN in de besteding van het nationaal inkomen; (met bijdragen van G.M.V. van Aardenne [and others]). Baarn, [1978]. pp. 105.

— **Civilization.**

NEWTON (GERALD) The Netherlands: an historical and cultural survey, 1795-1977. London, 1978. pp. 300. *bibliogs.*

— **Colonies.**

SCHMUTZER (EDUARD J.M.) Dutch colonial policy and the search for identity in Indonesia, 1920-1931. Leiden, 1977. pp. 178. *bibliog.*

— **Constitution.**

VERENIGING VAN NEDERLANDSE GEMEENTEN. Extract from the constitution of the Kingdom of the Netherlands, 1956: provisions relating to municipalities and municipal government. [The Hague?], 1963. pp. 3.

NETHERLANDS. Ministerie van Binnenlandse Zaken. 1974. Nota inzake het grondwetsherzieningsbeleid. 's-Gravenhage, 1974. 1 vol. (various pagings).

— **Economic history.**

GEURTS (P.A.M.) and MESSING (F.A.M.) compilers. Economische ontwikkeling en sociale emancipatie: 18 opstellen over economische en sociale geschiedenis, etc. Den Haag, 1977. 2 vols. (in 1). *bibliogs.*

— **Economic policy.**

WYTZES (H.C.) Enkele beschouwingen inzake het groei-aandeel. 2nd ed. Haarlem, 1969. pp. 24.

NETHERLANDS. Ministerie van Economische Zaken. 1977. Nota regionaal sociaal-economisch beleid 1977 t/m 1980. ['s-Gravenhage, 1977]. pp. 127.

— **Foreign relations.**

KERSTEN (A.E.) and MANNING (A.F.) eds. Documenten betreffende de bujtenlandse politiek van Nederland, 1919-1945; periode C 1940-1945. 's-Gravenhage, 1976 in progress. *bibliogs. (Nederland. Commissie voor's Rijks Geschiedkundige Publicatiën. Rijks Geschiedkundige Publicatiën. 157 [etc.])*

WOLTRING (J.) ed. Documenten betreffende de buitenlandse politiek van Nederland, 1919-1945; periode A 1919-1930. 's-Gravenhage, 1976 in progress. *(Netherlands. Commissie voor's Rijks Geschiedkundige Publicatiën. Rijks Geschiedkundige Publicatiën. 156 [etc.]*

— — **Indonesia.**

SCHMUTZER (EDUARD J.M.) Dutch colonial policy and the search for identity in Indonesia, 1920-1931. Leiden, 1977. pp. 178. *bibliog.*

— **History.**

NEWTON (GERALD) The Netherlands: an historical and cultural survey, 1795-1977. London, 1978. pp. 300. *bibliogs.*

— — **1556-1648, Wars of Independence.**

SWART (KOENRAAD WOLTER) William the Silent and the revolt of the Netherlands. London, [1978]. pp. 40. *bibliog. (Historical Association. General Series. G. 94)*

— **Parliament.**

VONDELING (ANNE) Tweede Kamer: lam of leeuw? Amsterdam, [1976]. pp. 276. *bibliog.*

RAALTE (ERNST VAN) Het Nederlandse Parlement. 6th ed. 's-Gravenhage, Staatsuitgeverij, 1977. pp. 350. *bibliog. (Parlementaria. 3)*

— **Politics and government.**

OBLER (JEFFREY) and others. Decision-making in smaller democracies: the consociational burden. Beverly Hills, [1977]. pp. 58. *bibliog.*

— **Population.**

NETHERLANDS. Centraal Bureau voor de Statistiek. 1976. De toekomstige demografische ontwikkeling in Nederland na 1975; aansluitend op De toekomstige nederlandse bevolkingsontwikkeling na 1972. 's-Gravenhage, 1976. pp. 127. *With English summary.*

POPULATION and family in the Low Countries, I; edited by H.G. Moors [and others]. Leiden, 1976. pp. 179. *bibliogs. (Nederlands Interuniversitair Demografisch Instituut and Centre d'Etude de la Population et de la Famille [Belgium]. Publications. vol.1)*

PRAAG (PHILIP VAN) Het bevolkingsvraagstuk in Nederland: ontwikkeling van standpunten en opvattingen, 1918-1940. Deventer, [1976]. pp. 132. *bibliog. (Nederlands Interuniversitair Demografisch Instituut. NIDI-Publikaties. 1)*

— **Social history.**

ANGLO-DUTCH HISTORICAL CONFERENCE, 6TH, 1976. Britain and the Netherlands:...war and society: papers delivered to the...Conference; edited by A.C. Duke and C.A. Tamse. The Hague, 1977. pp. 256.

GEURTS (P.A.M.) and MESSING (F.A.M.) compilers. Economische ontwikkeling en sociale emancipatie: 18 opstellen over economische en sociale geschiedenis, etc. Den Haag, 1977. 2 vols. (in 1). *bibliogs.*

— **Social policy.**

NETHERLANDS. Ministerie van Economische Zaken. 1977. Nota regionaal sociaal-economisch beleid 1977 t/m 1980. ['s-Gravenhage, 1977]. pp. 127.

— **Statistics.**

STATISTICAL STUDIES; ([pd. by] Centraal Bureau voor de statistiek, Netherlands). irreg., Ag 1953 (no.1)- Utrecht.

— **Statistics, Vital.**

NETHERLANDS. Centraal Bureau voor de Statistiek. 1974. De geboorte van het eerste kind, 1950-1972. 's-Gravenhage, 1974. pp. 20. *With English summary.*

NETHERLANDS. Centraal Bureau voor de Statistiek. 1976. Onderzoek naar de sterfte onder overlevenden uit concentratiekampen, 1945-1968. 's-Gravenhage, 1976. pp. 63. *With English summary.*

NETHERLANDS ANTILLES

— **Economic history.**

SOEST (JAAP VAN) Trustee of the Netherlands Antilles: a history of money, banking and the economy with special reference to the central Bank van de Nederlandse Antillen, 1828-6 February-1978. Zutphen, [1978]. pp. 422. *bibliog.*

NETWORK ANALYSIS (PLANNING).

PRICE (W.L.) Graphs and networks: an introduction. London, 1971. pp. 108. *bibliogs.*

SYMPOSIUM ON MODELING AND ANALYSIS OF DATA NETWORKS, WASHINGTON, D.C., 1976. Symposium on Modeling and Analysis of Data Networks: [report and proceedings]; principal organizers: R.L. Pickholtz [and] M. Schwartz. Washington, D. C., [1976]. pp. 95. *Symposium sponsored jointly by George Washington University and Columbia University.*

NEW BRUNSWICK

— **Administrative and political divisions.**

NEW BRUNSWICK. Representation and Electoral Districts Boundaries Commission. 1975. Further considerations and recommendations...; [G.E. Graham, chairman]. [Fredericton], 1975. fo. 57,66. *In English and French.*

— **Economic conditions — Statistics.**

NEW BRUNSWICK ECONOMIC STATISTICS; [pd. by] Office of the Economic Advisor. 3 a yr. (formerly q.), Je 1970- [Fredericton]. *Not pd. Ja 1974.*

— **Executive departments.**

NEW BRUNSWICK. Department of Agriculture and Rural Development. Annual report. a., 1923- , with gaps. Fredericton. *[in English and French]*

NEW COMMUNIST PARTY OF BRITAIN.

NEW COMMUNIST PARTY OF BRITAIN. The case for the New Communist Party. London, [1977]. pp. 14.

NEW CO-OPERATIVE QUARRIES (PIONEER SOCIETY).

NEW CO-OPERATIVE QUARRIES (PIONEER SOCIETY). The New Co-operative Quarries (Pioneer Society), Limited: [prospectus]. [London, 1904?]. pp. (3).

NEW GRANADA (VICEROYALTY)

— **Commerce.**

McFARLANE (ANTHONY) Economic and political change in the Viceroyalty of New Granada, with special reference to overseas trade, 1739-1810. 1977. fo. 413. *bibliog. Typescript. Ph.D. (London) thesis: unpublished. This thesis is the property of London University and may not be removed from the Library.*

— **Economic history.**

McFARLANE (ANTHONY) Economic and political change in the Viceroyalty of New Granada, with special reference to overseas trade, 1739-1810. 1977. fo. 413. *bibliog. Typescript. Ph.D. (London) thesis: unpublished. This thesis is the property of London University and may not be removed from the Library.*

— **Politics and government.**

McFARLANE (ANTHONY) Economic and political change in the Viceroyalty of New Granada, with special reference to overseas trade, 1739-1810. 1977. fo. 413. *bibliog. Typescript. Ph.D. (London) thesis: unpublished. This thesis is the property of London University and may not be removed from the Library.*

NEW GUARD.

AMOS (KEITH WILLIAM) The New Guard movement, 1931-1935. Carlton, Victoria, 1976. pp. 142. *bibliog.*

NEW GUINEA

— **Social conditions.**

SERPENTI (L.M.) Cultivators in the swamps: social structure and horticulture in a New Guinea society (Frederik-Hendrik Island, West New Guinea). 2nd ed. Assen, 1977. pp. 308. *bibliog.*

NEW HARMONY

— **History.**

BROWN (PAUL) Twelve months in New-Harmony: presenting a faithful account of the principal occurrences which have taken place there within that period; interspersed with remarks. Philadelphia, 1972. pp. 128. *Reprint of the 1827 ed.*

[PEARS (THOMAS) and PEARS (SARAH PALMER)] New Harmony: an adventure in happiness: papers of Thomas and Sarah Pears; edited by Thomas Clinton Pears, Jr. Clifton, N.J.,1933, repr. 1973. pp. 101. *(Indiana Historical Society. Publications. vol.11. no.1)*

NEW HAVEN

— **Politics and government.**

DOMHOFF (G. WILLIAM) Who really rules?: New Haven and community power reexamined. New Brunswick, N.J., [1978]. pp. 189.

NEW SPAIN (VICEROYALTY)

— **Economic history.**

SEMO (ENRIQUE) Historia del capitalismo en Mexico: los origenes, 1521-1763. Mexico, 1973. pp. 281.

NEW TOWNS

— **United Kingdom.**

CORDEN (CAROL) Planned cities: new towns in Britain and America. Beverly Hills, [1977]. pp. 220. *bibliog.*

DEAKIN (NICHOLAS) and UNGERSON (CLARE) Leaving London: planned mobility and the inner city. London, 1977. pp. 194.

— **United States.**

LOEWENTHAL (NORMAN H.) and BURBY (RAYMOND J.) Health care in new communities. Cambridge, Mass., [1976]. pp. 252. *bibliog. (North Carolina University. Center for Urban and Regional Studies. New Communities Research Series)*

CORDEN (CAROL) Planned cities: new towns in Britain and America. Beverly Hills, [1977]. pp. 220. *bibliog.*

ZEHNER (ROBERT B.) Access, travel, and transportation in new communities. Cambridge, Mass., [1977]. pp. 217. *bibliog. (North Carolina University. Center for Urban and Regional Studies. New Communities Research Series)*

KAISER (HARVEY H.) The building of cities: development and conflict. Ithaca, [1978]. pp. 217.

NEW YORK (CITY)

— **Fires and fire prevention — Mathematical models.**

CARTER (GRACE M.) and others. Response areas for two emergency units. New York, 1971. pp. 47. *bibliog. (Rand Corporation. [Rand Reports]. 532)*

NEW YORK (CITY)(Cont.)

— Foreign population.

BAYOR (RONALD H.) Neighbors in conflict: the Irish, Germans, Jews, and Italians of New York City, 1929-1941. Baltimore, [1978]. pp. 232. *bibliog. (Johns Hopkins University. Studies in Historical and Political Science. Series 96. No. 1)*

— Industries.

LEONE (ROBERT ANTHONY) Location of manufacturing activity in the New York Metropolitan Area. 1971. fo. 194. *bibliog.* Ph.D. (Yale) thesis: unpublished. Microfilm of typescript: 1 reel.

— Politics and government.

KUO (CHIA-LING) Social and political change in New York's Chinatown: the role of voluntary associations. New York, 1977. pp. 160. *bibliog.*

BAYOR (RONALD H.) Neighbors in conflict: the Irish, Germans, Jews, and Italians of New York City, 1929-1941. Baltimore, [1978]. pp. 232. *bibliog. (Johns Hopkins University. Studies in Historical and Political Science. Series 96. No. 1)*

— Population.

BURSTEIN (ABRAHAM C.) Residential mobility in New York City, 1965-1970: movement of population within and into New York City during the period 1965-1970. New York, 1975. 4 vols. (in 3).

— Schools.

FUENTES (LUIS) Puerto Rican, black and Chinese community control in New York city: the fight against racism in our schools. New York, [1973]. pp. 15.

NEW YORK (STATE)

— Economic history.

RITCHIE (ROBERT C.) The Duke's province: a study of New York politics and society, 1664-1691. Chapel Hill, [1977]. pp. 306. *bibliog.*

— Politics and government.

NEW YORK (STATE). Governor, 1973- .(Wilson). Public papers of Malcolm Wilson, fiftieth Governor of the State of New York. 1973- . [Albany, 1975 in progress].

SOCIETY, freedom, and conscience: the American revolution in Virginia, Massachusetts, and New York; [by] Jack P. Greene [and others]; edited by Richard M. Jellison. New York, [1976]. pp. 233. *(Miami University (Ohio). McClellan Lectures. 1973, 1974, 1975)*

RITCHIE (ROBERT C.) The Duke's province: a study of New York politics and society, 1664-1691. Chapel Hill, [1977]. pp. 306. *bibliog.*

— Social history.

RITCHIE (ROBERT C.) The Duke's province: a study of New York politics and society, 1664-1691. Chapel Hill, [1977]. pp. 306. *bibliog.*

NEW ZEALAND.

THIRTEEN facets: essays to celebrate the Silver Jubilee of Queen Elizabeth the Second, 1952-1977; edited by Ian Wards. Wellington, Government Printer, 1978. pp. 388. *bibliogs.*

— Administrative and political divisions.

NEW ZEALAND. Local Government Commission. 1976. Regions of New Zealand: preliminary appraisal. [Wellington], 1976. pp. 6. *2 maps in end pocket.*

— Census.

NEW ZEALAND. Department of Statistics. Census, 1976. Census of population and dwellings 1976: provisional population and dwellings statistics. [Wellington, 1976]. pp. 52.

NEW ZEALAND. Department of Statistics. Census, 1976. 1976 census of population and dwellings: [volume series]. [Wellington, 1977 in progress].

— Civil defence.

NEW ZEALAND. Civil Defence Communications Planning Committee. 1966. Broad plan. [Wellington, 1966]. fo. 11. *(Communications Reports. No. 1)*

NEW ZEALAND. Civil Defence Communications Planning Committee. 1966. Communications for national and regional civil defence headquarters. [Wellington, 1966]. fo. 11. *(Communications Reports. No. 2)*

NEW ZEALAND. Ministry of Civil Defence. 1966. Civil defence: government action in major disaster. [Wellington, 1966]. 1 pamphlet (various foliations).

NEW ZEALAND. Ministry of Civil Defence. 1966. Civil defence: medical plan no. 1: natural disaster. [Wellington, 1966]. 1 pamphlet (various foliations). *bibliog.*

NEW ZEALAND. Ministry of Civil Defence. 1966. Civil defence: supply plan. [Wellington, 1966]. 1 pamphlet (various foliations).

NEW ZEALAND. Ministry of Civil Defence. 1966. Civil defence: transport plan no. 1: broad plan. [Wellington, 1966]. fo. 14.

NEW ZEALAND. Ministry of Civil Defence. 1967. Civil defence: evacuation plan. [Wellington, 1967]. fo. 8.

NEW ZEALAND. Ministry of Civil Defence. 1967. Civil defence: welfare plan. [Wellington, 1967]. 1 pamphlet (various foliations).

NEW ZEALAND. Ministry of Civil Defence. 1968. Civil defence: traffic control plan. [rev. ed.] Wellington, 1968]. fo.(18).

NEW ZEALAND. Ministry of Civil Defence. 1968. Civil defence handbook: general information. Wellington, 1968. pp. 86.

NEW ZEALAND. Ministry of Civil Defence. 1968. Civil defence handbook: welfare. Wellington, 1968. pp. 68.

NEW ZEALAND. Ministry of Civil Defence. 1971. Civil defence: medical plan no. 1: civil defence or national emergency. [rev. ed.]. [Wellington, 1971]. pp. 23.

NEW ZEALAND. Ministry of Civil Defence. 1971. Civil defence handbook: functions and organisation of a local civil defence headquarters. Wellington, 1971. pp. 27.

— Commerce.

EXPORT seminars, 1969: papers presented. [Wellington, New Zealand Department of Industries and Commerce, 1970]. 1 vol. (various pagings).

— — Australia.

AUSTRALIA. Parliament. Senate. Standing Committee on Industry and Trade. 1972. Interim report on Australia-New Zealand trade; [E.W. Prose, chairman]. in AUSTRALIA. Parliament. Parliamentary papers, 1972, vol. 7.

— — Japan.

NEW ZEALAND ECONOMIC AND GOODWILL MISSION TO JAPAN AND TAIWAN. Report...October 1965. Wellington, Department of Industries and Commerce, [1966]. pp. 25.

— — Taiwan.

NEW ZEALAND ECONOMIC AND GOODWILL MISSION TO JAPAN AND TAIWAN. Report...October 1965. Wellington, Department of Industries and Commerce, [1966]. pp. 25.

— Economic conditions.

NEW ZEALAND. Ministry of Transport. Economics Division. 1974. The effects of regional development on transport. Wellington, 1974. fo. 32.

— — Mathematical models.

LEDINGHAM (P.J.) Econometric model forecasts in New Zealand: a preliminary assessment. Wellington, 1976. pp. 24. *bibliog. (Reserve Bank of New Zealand. Research Papers. No. 20)*

The RESERVE Bank's model of the New Zealand economy; [by] J. Gallacher [and others]. Wellington, 1977. pp. 44. *(Reserve Bank of New Zealand. Research Papers. No. 22)*

— Economic policy.

NATIONAL DEVELOPMENT CONFERENCE, WELLINGTON. 1971. Recommendations: action taken as at 25 November 1970. [Wellington, Government Printer, 1971]. pp. 50. *([Reports]. N.D.C. 23 Add. 2)*

NEW ZEALAND. Task Force on Economic and Social Planning. 1976. New Zealand at the turning point: report...; [Frank Holmes, chairman]. [Wellington], 1976. pp. 414.

— Executive departments.

NEW ZEALAND. Department of Civil Aviation. 1967. Introducing the Department of Civil Aviation. [Wellington, 1967]. pp. (10).

NEW ZEALAND. Ministry of Transport. 1968. Why a Ministry of Transport. Wellington, [1968?]. pp. 6. *(News Backgrounders)*

NEW ZEALAND. Maori and Island Affairs Department. 1970. The work of the Maori and Island Affairs Department. Wellington, 1970. pp. 24. *bibliog.*

NEW ZEALAND. Department of Health. 1972. Department of Health: functions and responsibilities. [rev. ed.] Wellington, 1972. pp. 62.

NEW ZEALAND. Department of Labour. Research and Planning Division. 1972. Manpower planning: a discussion of aspects of manpower forecasting and manpower planning, and a description of the work of the Manpower Planning Unit. Wellington, 1972. pp. 22.

ALLSOP (FREDERICK) The first fifty years of New Zealand's forest service: a history from the time of its setting up in 1919 to the celebration of its fiftieth anniversary in 1969. Wellington, 1973. pp. 123. *bibliog. (New Zealand. New Zealand Forest Service. Information Series. No. 59)*

NEW ZEALAND. Department of Lands and Survey. 1975. Activities of the Department of Lands and Survey. Wellington, 1975. pp. 21.

NEW ZEALAND. Department of Health. 1976. Functions and responsibilities. Wellington, 1976. pp. 73. *bibliog.*

NEW ZEALAND. Department of Lands and Survey. 1976. The Department of Lands and Survey 1876-1976 centennial. Wellington, 1976. pp. 11.

— Foreign economic relations.

FORUM on Australia, New Zealand and East Asia. [Taipei], 1977. pp. 109. *(Asia and the World Forum. Monograph Series. No. 5)*

— Foreign relations.

See also EUROPEAN ECONOMIC COMMUNITY — New Zealand.

— — United Kingdom.

ADAMS (PETER) Fatal necessity: British intervention in New Zealand, 1830- 1847. Auckland, 1977. pp. 308. *bibliog.*

— — Vietnam.

NEW ZEALAND. 1966. Vietnam: questions and answers. [Wellington], 1966. pp. 40.

— History.

ADAMS (PETER) Fatal necessity: British intervention in New Zealand, 1830- 1847. Auckland, 1977. pp. 308. *bibliog.*

— Native races.

NEW ZEALAND. Department of Maori Affairs. 1964. The Maori today. 3rd ed. [Wellington, 1964]. 1 vol. (unpaged).

NEW ZEALAND. Maori and Island Affairs Department. 1970. Housing for Maoris and Islanders: notes for social workers. [Wellington], 1970. fo. 7.

— Parliament — Rules and practice.

NEW ZEALAND. [General Assembly]. House of Representatives. 1969. Standing orders of the House of Representatives relating to public business; brought into force 28 June 1951; reprinted and renumbered April 1969 incorporating amendments made since 28 June 1951. Wellington, 1969. pp. 147.

— Politics and government.

MULDOON (ROBERT DAVID) Muldoon. London, 1978. pp. 224.

— Population.

POOL (D. IAN) The Maori population of New Zealand, 1769-1971. Auckland, 1977. pp. 266. *bibliog.*

— Population policy.

ENVIRONMENTAL COUNCIL [NEW ZEALAND]. Report of the Environmental Council and the Social Development Council on public submissions on population matters. [Wellington], 1975. pp. 36. *(Occasional Papers. No. 1)*

ENVIRONMENTAL COUNCIL [NEW ZEALAND]. Sub-Committee on Population. Crisis or choice?: questions on a population policy for New Zealand. Wellington, 1975. 1 pamphlet (unpaged)

NEW ZEALAND. Interdepartmental Committee on Population Questions. 1975. New Zealand population policy guidelines: to assist in the formation of a population policy for New Zealand; report etc. Wellington, 1975. pp. 95.

— Public buildings.

NEW ZEALAND. Ministry of Works. 1970. A brief history of public buildings in New Zealand. [Wellington, 1970]. 1 pamphlet (unpaged).

— Race question.

NEW ZEALAND. Department of Maori Affairs. 1962. Integration of Maori and pakeha. Wellington, 1962. 1 pamphlet (unpaged). *(Series of Special Studies. No. 1)*

— Relations (general) with China.

HOLYOAKE (Sir KEITH JACKA) New Zealand and China; an article by the Prime Minister. Wellington, Ministry of Foreign Affairs, 1971. pp. 13.

— Relations (general) with the United States.

HARLAND (W. BRYCE) New Zealand's relations with the United States of America: text of an address...at the fifth Foreign Policy School, University of Otago, Department of University Extension, Dunedin, 15-19 May 1970. [Wellington, Ministry of Foreign Affairs, 1970]. pp. 16. *(Reprinted from Foreign Affairs Review, May 1970)*

— Social policy.

NATIONAL DEVELOPMENT CONFERENCE, WELLINGTON. 1971. Recommendations: action taken as at 25 November 1970. [Wellington, Government Printer, 1971]. pp. 50. *([Reports]. N.D.C. 23 Add. 2)*

NEW ZEALAND. Task Force on Economic and Social Planning. 1976. New Zealand at the turning point: report...; [Frank Holmes, chairman]. [Wellington], 1976. pp. 414.

— Statistics, Vital.

NEW ZEALAND. Department of Statistics. 1970. New Zealand tables of male working life, 1966. Wellington, [1970?]. pp. 8. *(Monthly abstract of statistics. Special supplement, [ ])*

ROSE (RICHARD JOHN) Maori-European comparisons in mortality. Wellington, 1972. pp. 188. *(New Zealand. Department of Health. Special Report Series. No. 37)*

FOSTER (F. H.) Perinatal mortality in New Zealand, 1972-73. Wellington, 1977. pp. 99. *(New Zealand. Department of Health. Special Report Series. No. 50)*

NEW ZEALANDERS IN THE UNITED KINGDOM.

NEW ZEALAND. Department of Social Welfare. 1972. Guide to the reciprocal agreement on social security between New Zealand and the United Kingdom. Wellington, [1972]. pp. 15.

NEWFOUNDLAND

— Economic conditions.

NEWFOUNDLAND. Royal Commission on the Economic State and Prospects of Newfoundland and Labrador. 1967. Report; [Gordon F. Pushie, chairman]. St. John's, 1967. fo. 494. *Photocopy.*

— Economic history.

ALEXANDER (DAVID GEORGE) The decay of trade: an economic history of the Newfoundland saltfish trade, 1935-1965. Toronto, [1977]. pp. 173. *(St. John's. Memorial University of Newfoundland. Institute of Social and Economic Research. Newfoundland Social and Economic Studies. No. 19)*

— Economic policy.

NEWFOUNDLAND. Royal Commission on the Economic State and Prospects of Newfoundland and Labrador. 1967. Report; [Gordon F. Pushie, chairman]. St. John's, 1967. fo. 494. *Photocopy.*

— Executive departments.

NEWFOUNDLAND. Department of Manpower and Industrial Relations. Annual report. a., 1976- St. John's.

NEWSPAPER PUBLISHING

— Italy.

La STAMPA quotidiana tra crisi e riforma: problemi giuridici e organizzativi; a cura di Enzo Cheli e Paolo Barile. Bologna, [1976]. pp. 635. *Based on papers presented at a conference held in Florence in 1975.*

— South Africa.

FLATHER (HORACE) The way of an editor. Cape Town, 1977. pp. 209.

— United Kingdom.

THOMSON ORGANISATION. The Thomson Organisation in Great Britain; [including a statement of Roy Thomson circulated with the report and accounts for the year ended 31 December, 1959]. [London, 1960]. pp. 32.

CLEVERLEY (GRAHAM) The Fleet Street disaster: British national newspapers as a case study in mismanagement; with a preface by Rex Winsbury. London, [1976]. pp. 175. *bibliog.*

NEWSPAPER READING.

NEWSPAPER SOCIETY. Regional Readership Surveys among Housewives. No. 4. Southern region. London, 1958. pp. 131-172.

NEWSPAPER SOCIETY. Regional Readership Surveys among Housewives. No. 7. South western region. London, 1959. pp. 257-298.

NEWSPAPER SOCIETY. Regional Readership Surveys among Housewives. No. 9. Eastern region. London, 1959. pp. 341-382.

NEWSPAPER SOCIETY. Regional Readership Surveys among Housewives. No. 10. North Midland region. London, 1959. pp. 383-424.

READERSHIP survey of Wales; commissioned by the Thomson Organisation Limited and conducted by Marplan Limited. London, 1961. 1 vol (various pagings)

NEWSPAPERS

— History.

DESMOND (ROBERT WILLIAM) The information process: world news reporting to the twentieth century. Iowa City, 1978. pp. 495. *bibliog.*

— — United Kingdom.

NEWSPAPER history from the seventeenth century to the present day; edited by George Boyce [and others]. London, 1978. pp. 423. *bibliog. Published on behalf of the Acton Society Trust's Press Group.*

NEWSREEL

— History.

HOGENKAMP (BERT) Worker's newsreels in the 1920's and 1930's. London, [1977?]. pp. 36. *(Communist Party of Great Britain. History Group. Our History. No. 68)*

NGUYEN THI DINH.

NGUYEN THI DINH. No other road to take; memoir...translated by Mai Elliott. Ithaca, N.Y., 1976. pp. 77. *(Cornell University. Department of Asian Studies. Southeast Asia Program. Data Papers. No. 102)*

NICARAGUA

— Appropriations and expenditures.

NICARAGUA. Ministerio de Hacienda y Credito Publico. Memoria. a., 1974- [Managua].

— Executive departments.

NICARAGUA. Ministerio de Hacienda y Credito Publico. Memoria. a., 1974- [Managua].

— Guardia Nacional.

MILLETT (RICHARD) Guardians of the dynasty. Maryknoll, [1977]. pp. 284. *bibliog.*

— Politics and government.

MILLETT (RICHARD) Guardians of the dynasty. Maryknoll, [1977]. pp. 284. *bibliog.*

— Relations (general) with the United States.

MILLETT (RICHARD) Guardians of the dynasty. Maryknoll, [1977]. pp. 284. *bibliog.*

NICARAO INDIANS

— Religion and mythology.

LEON-PORTILLA (MIGUEL) Religion de los Nicaraos: analisis y comparacion de tradiciones culturales nahuas. Mexico, 1972. pp. 117. *bibliog. (Mexico City. Universidad Nacional Autonoma de Mexico. Instituto de Investigaciones Historicas. Serie de Cultura Nahuatl. Monografias. 12)*

NICHOLAS INTERNATIONAL LIMITED.

SMITH (ROBERT GRENVILLE) and BARRIE (ALEXANDER) Aspro: how the family business grew up. Melbourne, 1976. pp. 182.

NIELSEN (FRITZ WALTER).

NIELSEN (FRITZ WALTER) Emigrant für Deutschland, in der Tschechoslowakei, in England und in Kanada: Tagebuchaufzeichnungen, Aufrufe und Berichte aus den Jahren 1933-1943; mit einem Sonderband, Zitate und Kommentare. Darmstadt, [1977]. 2 vols. *bibliog.*

NIETZSCHE (FRIEDRICH WILHELM).

STERN (JOSEPH PETER) Nietzsche. [London], 1978. pp. 159. *bibliog.*

NIEVRE.

FRANCE. Direction de la Documentation. La Documentation Française. Notes et Etudes Documentaires. Nos. 4,283-4, 284-4,285. Les départements français. 58. Nièvre, Bourgogne; (document...réalisé...par Philippe Sanmarco et Philippe Parini). Paris, 1976. pp. 100. *bibliog.*

NIGER

NIGER
— Economic policy.

FUNEL (JEAN MARIE) Le développement régional et sa problématique étudiés à travers l'expérience de Tahoua, Niger. Paris, 1976. pp. 336. *bibliog.* (France. Ministère de la Coopération. Méthodologie de la Planification. No. 9)

NIGER COMPANY.

GOLDIE (Sir GEORGE DASHWOOD TAUBMAN) The false allegations against the Niger Company. n.p., 1892. pp. 4.

NIGERIA.

NIGERIA TODAY; (pd. by the Nigeria High Commission, London) . m., Ag 1970 (no.1)- , with gaps (Jl 1975, no.58, F 1977, no.76). London.

— Armed forces — Political activity.

SOLDIERS and oil: the political transformation of Nigeria; edited by Keith Panter-Brick. London, 1978. pp. 375.

— Census.

NIGERIA. National Census Board. 1973. Your guide to the census: Federal Republic of Nigeria 1973 population census. Lagos, [1973?]. pp. 7.

— Commerce.

BRITISH EMPIRE EXHIBITION, 1924. Nigeria: its history and products. [London, 1925?]. pp. 106.

— — Canada.

NIGERIA. Customs Department. 1920. Canada and Nigeria. Lagos, 1920. pp. 76, 1 map.

— Economic conditions.

NIGERIA (NORTH-WESTERN STATE). Department of Information. 1968. Introducing the North Western State of Nigeria. [Sokoto, 1968]. pp. 34, 2 maps.

NIGERIA (KWARA STATE). Budget speech (formerly Budget broadcast). a., 1969/70[1st]- , with gaps (1974/75; 1976/77) Ilorin.

NIGERIA: economy and society; edited by Gavin Williams. London, 1976. pp. 226.

BARRETT (STANLEY R.) The rise and fall of an African utopia: a wealthy theocracy in comparative perspective. [Waterloo, Ont., 1977]. pp. 251. *bibliog.* (McGill University. Centre for Developing Area Studies. Development Perspectives. 1)

SOLDIERS and oil: the political transformation of Nigeria; edited by Keith Panter-Brick. London, 1978. pp. 375.

— Economic policy.

NIGERIA. Sessional Papers. 1948. No. 20. Statement of the policy proposed for the decentralization of the Nigeria Local Development Board. [Lagos], 1948. pp. 4.

NIGERIA (NORTHERN REGION). Public Works Department. 1952. Report on the work under the development plan carried out by the Public Works Department in the northern provinces, 1946-51. Kaduna, 1952. pp. 11.

MIDWEST ADVISORY COUNCIL [NIGERIA (WESTERN REGION)]. Report on the activities of the...Council together with statements of government action in the midwest. [Ibadan, 1960]. pp. 57. *(Nigeria (Western Region). Legislature. Sessional Papers. 1960. No. 3)*

MIDWEST ADVISORY COUNCIL [NIGERIA (WESTERN REGION)]. Second memorandum by the Council on its activities, [with report of government action, etc.]. [Ibadan, 1961]. pp. 76. *(Nigeria (Western Region). Legislature. Sessional Papers. 1961. No. 11)*

ATTA (ABDUL AZIZI) Philosophy of development; an address by A.A. Atta, Secretary to the Federal Military Government at the Federal Palace Hotel, Lagos. [Lagos, 1971?] pp. 18.

ATTA (ABDUL AZIZI) The role of the civil service in the development process; a paper presented by Abdul Attah, Secretary to the Federal Military Government at the economic development plan seminar held in March, 1971 at the Nigerian Institute of International Affairs, Victoria Island, Lagos. [Lagos, 1971]. pp. 20.

NEW NIGERIA DEVELOPMENT COMPANY. N.N.D.C.: New Nigeria Development Company Ltd.: a development agency owned by the governments of the northern states of Nigeria. Kaduna, 1971. pp. 15.

NEW NIGERIA DEVELOPMENT COMPANY. N.N.D.C. group. [Kaduna], 1971. pp. 52.

NIGERIA. National Youth Service Corps. 1973. Lectures for the orientation course. [Lagos, 1973]. pp. 227.

NIGERIA. Central Planning Office. 1976. First progress report on third national development plan, 1975-80. Lagos, [1976?]. pp. 508.

— Foreign relations.

ASOBIE (HUMPHREY ASSISI) Domestic political structure and foreign policy: the Nigerian experience, 1960-1974. 1977. fo. 489. *bibliog. Typescript. Ph.D. (London) thesis: unpublished. This thesis is the property of London University and may not be removed from the Library.*

STREMLAU (JOHN J.) The international politics of the Nigerian Civil War, 1967- 1970. Princeton, [1977]. pp. 425. *bibliog.*

— History.

BRITISH EMPIRE EXHIBITION, 1924. Nigeria: its history and products. [London, 1925?]. pp. 106.

NIGERIA. National Youth Service Corps. 1973. Lectures for the orientation course. [Lagos, 1973]. pp. 227.

IKIME (OBARO) The fall of Nigeria: the British conquest. London, 1977. pp. 232. *bibliog.*

— — 1967-1970, Civil War.

STREMLAU (JOHN J.) The international politics of the Nigerian Civil War, 1967- 1970. Princeton, [1977]. pp. 425. *bibliog.*

— Industries.

NIGERIA (NORTH CENTRAL STATE). 1971. Industrial potentialities in the North Central State of Nigeria. [Kaduna, 1971]. pp. 57, 1 map.

— — Directories.

NIGERIA. Federal Ministry of Labour. 1967. Directory of business establishments in Nigeria. Lagos, 1967. pp. 128.

NIGERIA. Federal Ministry of Industries. 1971. 1971 industrial directory. 6th ed. Lagos, 1971. pp. 93.

— Officials and employees.

NIGERIA. Public Service Review Commission. 1974. Report on grading and pay, 1972-74. Lagos, 1974. 6 vols. (in 3).

— — Salaries, allowances, etc.

NIGERIA. Federal Ministry of Pensions. Federal Establishment Office. 1960. 1960 revision of salaries and wage rates in the federal public service; (with Review of salaries and wage rates in the federal public service, 1959: distribution and amendment). [Lagos], 1960. 1 vol. (various foliations). *(Circulars. No. 1960/20-21)*

NIGERIA. Federal Ministry of Information. 1971. Better conditions for you: twenty questions and answers on Adebo report and government decisions. [Lagos, 1971]. pp. 12.

— Politics and government.

NIGERIA (KANO STATE). Military Governor, 1967- (Bako). Policy statement broadcast...1st April, 1968. [Kano, 1968]. pp. 12. *In English and Hausa.*

NIGERIA (NORTH-WESTERN STATE). Department of Information. 1968. Introducing the North Western State of Nigeria. [Sokoto, 1968]. pp. 34, 2 maps.

NIGERIA (KWARA STATE). Budget speech (formerly Budget broadcast). a., 1969/70[1st]- , with gaps (1974/75; 1976/77) Ilorin.

NIGERIA (KANO STATE). Military Governor, 1967- (Bako). Policy statement broadcast...April 1969. [Kano, 1969]. pp. 26. *In English and Hausa.*

STOKKE (OLAV) Integration and disintegration: the case of the Nigerian Federation up to June 1967. Uppsala, 1970. fo.32.

GOWON (YAKUBU) New year of great hopes: New Year message to the nation...on January 1, 1973. [Lagos, Federal Ministry of Information, 1973]. pp. 8.

GOWON (YAKUBU) Nigeria on the threshold of socio-economic revolution; [message to the nation on the occasion of the 13th independence day anniversary celebration on the 1st of October, 1973]. [Lagos, Government Printer, 1973]. pp. 12.

NIGERIA. National Youth Service Corps. 1973. Lectures for the orientation course. [Lagos, 1973]. pp. 227.

MUHAMMED (MURTALA) Drift and chaos arrested; [text of first broadcast to the nation... July 30, 1975]. [Lagos, Federal Ministry of Information, 1975]. pp. 12.

NIGERIA: economy and society; edited by Gavin Williams. London, 1976. pp. 226.

ASOBIE (HUMPHREY ASSISI) Domestic political structure and foreign policy: the Nigerian experience, 1960-1974. 1977. fo. 489. *bibliog. Typescript. Ph.D. (London) thesis: unpublished. This thesis is the property of London University and may not be removed from the Library.*

SAHLIN (MICHAEL) Neo-authoritarianism and the problem of legitimacy: a general study and a Nigerian example. Stockholm, [1977]. pp. 240. *bibliog.* (Uppsala. Statsvetenskapliga Föreningen. Skrifter. 77)

SOLDIERS and oil: the political transformation of Nigeria; edited by Keith Panter-Brick. London, 1978. pp. 375.

— Public works.

NIGERIA (NORTHERN REGION). Public Works Department. 1952. Report on the work under the development plan carried out by the Public Works Department in the northern provinces, 1946-51. Kaduna, 1952. pp. 11.

— Social conditions.

REHFISCH (FARNHAM) The social structure of a Mambila village. Zaria, 1972. pp. 197. *bibliog.* (Ahmadu Bello University. Sociology Department. Occasional Papers. No. 2)

NIGERIA: economy and society; edited by Gavin Williams. London, 1976. pp. 226.

— Social life and customs.

REHFISCH (FARNHAM) The social structure of a Mambila village. Zaria, 1972. pp. 197. *bibliog.* (Ahmadu Bello University. Sociology Department. Occasional Papers. No. 2)

— Social policy.

MIDWEST ADVISORY COUNCIL [NIGERIA (WESTERN REGION)]. Report on the activities of the...Council together with statements of government action in the midwest. [Ibadan, 1960]. pp. 57. *(Nigeria (Western Region). Legislature. Sessional Papers. 1960. No. 3)*

MIDWEST ADVISORY COUNCIL [NIGERIA (WESTERN REGION)]. Second memorandum by the Council on its activities, [with report of government action, etc.]. [Ibadan, 1961]. pp. 76. *(Nigeria (Western Region). Legislature. Sessional Papers. 1961. No. 11)*

NIGERIA. National Youth Service Corps. 1973. Lectures for the orientation course. [Lagos, 1973]. pp. 227.

NIGERIA. Central Planning Office. 1976. First progress report on third national development plan, 1975-80. Lagos, [1976?]. pp. 508.

NIGERIAN EXTERNAL TELECOMMUNICATIONS LIMITED.

NIGERIAN EXTERNAL TELECOMMUNICATIONS LIMITED. Annual report. a., 1963/64(1st)- , with gaps. Lagos.

NIGERIAN STEEL DEVELOPMENT AUTHORITY.

NIGERIAN STEEL DEVELOPMENT AUTHORITY. Annual report and accounts. a., 1971/72(1st)- Lagos.

NIGHT LABOUR.

CARPENTIER (JAMES) and CAZAMIAN (PIERRE) Night work: its effects on the health and welfare of the worker. Geneva, International Labour Office, 1977. pp. 82. *bibliog.*

NIHILISM.

HOLBROOK (DAVID) Education, nihilism and survival. London, 1977. pp. 170. *bibliog.*

STITES (RICHARD) The women's liberation movement in Russia: feminism, nihilism and bolshevism, 1860-1930. Princeton, [1978]. pp. 464. *bibliog.*

NIKOLAEV (OBLAST')

— Politics and government.

NARYSY istoriï Mykolaïvs'koï oblasnoï partiinoï orhanizatsiï, 1897-1968 rr. Odesa, 1969. pp. 419.

NIN (ANDREU).

BONAMUSA (FRANCESC) Andreu Nin y el movimiento comunista en España, 1930-1937. Barcelona, [1977]. pp. 521. *bibliog.*

NIUE

— Constitution.

QUENTIN-BAXTER (ROBERT QUENTIN) Report to the Niue Island Assembly on the constitutional development of Niue. Wellington, Government Printer, 1971. pp. 20.

NIXON (RICHARD MILHOUS) President of the United States.

HALDEMAN (HARRY R.) and DIMONA (JOSEPH) The ends of power. London, 1978. pp. 326.

LABOVITZ (JOHN R.) Presidential impeachment. New Haven, 1978. pp. 268.

SZULC (TAD) The illusion of peace: foreign policy in the Nixon years. New York, 1978. pp. 822.

NKRUMAH (KWAME).

RENNIE (RHODA ELIZABETH McKENZIE) Nkrumah, greatest of modern philosophers. New York, [1977]. pp. 125.

NOISE CONTROL

— Economic aspects.

NELSON (JON P.) Economic analysis of transportation noise abatement. Cambridge, Mass., [1978]. pp. 264. *bibliog.*

— United States.

SELECTED papers from the Washington hearings on noise abatement and control, November 9-12, 1971, U.S. Environmental Protection Agency. n.p. 1971. 15 parts (in 1 vol.)

NOMADS

— Iran.

GOLABIAN (HOSSEIN) An analysis of the underdeveloped rural and nomadic areas of Iran: a theoretical approach to the problems of social and economic development of rural and nomadic communities in Iran. Stockholm, 1977. pp. 279, 11. *(Stockholm. Tekniska Högskolan. School of Architecture. Department of Regional Planning. [Publications]. 1977. [No.] 4)*

— Sahel.

MARNHAM (PATRICK) Nomads of the Sahel. London, 1977. pp. 19. *bibliog. (Minority Rights Group. Reports. No. 33)*

NOMINATIONS FOR OFFICE

— Germany.

HORN (WOLFGANG) and KUEHR (HERBERT) Kandidaten im Wahlkampf: Kandidatenauslese, Wahlkampf und lokale Presse 1975 in Essen. Meisenheim am Glan, 1978. pp. 321. *bibliog.*

NONFERROUS METALS

— France.

FRANCE. Groupe sectoriel d'Analyse et de Prévision Minerais, Métaux et demi-Produits non-Ferreux. 1976. Rapport...: préparation du 7e Plan. Paris, [1976]. pp. 234.

NONMETALLIC MINERALS

— France.

FRANCE. Groupe sectoriel d'Analyse et de Prévision Minerais, Métaux et demi-Produits non-Ferreux. 1976. Rapport...: préparation du 7e Plan. Paris, [1976]. pp. 234.

NONPARAMETRIC STATISTICS.

HÁJEK (JAROSLAV) A course in nonparametric statistics. San Francisco, [1969]. pp. 184. *bibliog.*

LEHMANN (ERICH LEO) Nonparametrics: statistical methods based on ranks. San Francisco, [1975]. pp. 457.

RUNYON (RICHARD PORTER) Nonparametric statistics: a contemporary approach. Reading, Mass., [1977]. pp. 218.

NONTARIFF TRADE BARRIERS.

CLINE (WILLIAM R.) and others. Trade negotiations in the Tokyo Round: a quantitative assessment. Washington, D.C., [1978]. pp. 314.

NONVIOLENCE.

MOORHOUSE (FRED) Politics, nonviolence and social justice: an African perspective. New Malden, [1977]. pp. 20. *(Fellowship of Reconciliation. Alex Wood Memorial Lectures. 1977)*

NORFOLK

— Economic policy.

NORFOLK. County Council. Norfolk structure plan: statement on public participation and consultation. [Norwich], 1977. pp. 259.

NORFOLK. County Council. Norfolk structure plan: written statement. [Norwich], 1977. pp. 170.

— Social conditions.

SOCIAL issues in rural Norfolk; edited by Malcolm J. Moseley. Norwich, 1978. pp. 192. *bibliog.*

— Social policy.

NORFOLK. County Council. Norfolk structure plan: statement on public participation and consultation. [Norwich], 1977. pp. 259.

NORFOLK. County Council. Norfolk structure plan: written statement. [Norwich], 1977. pp. 170.

NORMANDY

— Economic conditions — Statistics.

STATISTIQUES POUR L'ECONOMIE NORMANDE: revue trimestrielle; ([pd. by] Institut National de la Statistique et des Etudes Economiques,... Direction Régionale de Rouen [France]). bi-m. (formerly q.), Je 1971 (no.1)- Rouen.

NORRIS (GEORGE WILLIAM).

LOWITT (RICHARD) George W. Norris: the triumph of a progressive, 1933-1944. Urbana, [1978]. pp. 493. *bibliog.*

NORSK POLITIFORBUND.

RASMUSSEN (SIGURD) Norsk Politiforbund gjennom 50 år, 1905-1955. Oslo, 1955. pp. 258.

NORSK TREINDUSTRIARBEIDERFORBUND.

OUSLAND (GUNNAR) Norsk Treindustriarbeiderforbund 50 år. [Oslo, 1954]. pp. 438.

NORSKE VIDENSKAPS-AKADEMI I OSLO.

AMUNDSEN (LEIV) Det Norske Videnskaps-Akademi i Oslo, 1857-1957. Oslo, 1957-60. 2 vols. *bibliog.*

NORTH AFRICANS IN FRANCE.

Les IMMIGRÉS du Maghreb: études sur l'adaptation en mili urbain; [by J.A. Carreno and others]. [Paris], 1977. pp. 411. *bibliog. (France. Institut National d'Etudes Démographiques. Travaux et Documents. Cahiers. No. 79)*

NORTH ATLANTIC TREATY, 1949.

REID (ESCOTT) Time of fear and hope: the making of the North Atlantic Treaty, 1947-1949. Toronto, [1977]. pp. 315.

NORTH ATLANTIC TREATY ORGANIZATION.

REID (ESCOTT) Time of fear and hope: the making of the North Atlantic Treaty, 1947-1949. Toronto, [1977]. pp. 315.

WILLIAMS (GEOFFREY LEE) The permanent alliance: the European-American partnership, 1945-1984. Leyden, 1977. pp. 407. *bibliog.*

COOK (ROBERT FINLAYSON) and SMITH (DAN) of the Campaign for Nuclear Disarmament. What future in NATO? London, 1978. pp. 27. *(Fabian Society. Research Series. [No.] 337)*

GALLOIS (PIERRE MARIE) Soviet military doctrine and European defence: NATO's obsolete concepts. London, 1978. pp. 17. *(Institute for the Study of Conflict. Conflict. Studies. No. 96)*

HILL (ROGER) Political consultation in NATO. Toronto, 1978. pp. 143. *bibliog. (Canadian Institute of International Affairs. Wellesley Papers, 6)*

HILL-NORTON (Sir PETER J.) No soft options: the politico-military realities of NATO. London, [1978]. pp. 172.

— Turkey.

EREN (NURI) Turkey, NATO and Europe: a deteriorating relationship? Paris, [1977]. pp. 54. *(Atlantic Institute. Atlantic Papers. No. 34)*

NORTH CAROLINA

— Economic conditions.

HAMMER, GREENE, SILER ASSOCIATES. Investment guidelines for the North Carolina Appalachian region; prepared for...North Carolina Department of Administration...[and] Appalachia Regional Commission. Washington, 1967. pp. 129.

NORTH CAROLINA. Governor's Council for Economic Development. 1968. The economic performance of North Carolina; a report; (with Summary). Raleigh, 1968. 2 pts.

NORTH CAROLINA(Cont.)

— Social conditions.

NORTH CAROLINA. Office of Comprehensive Health Planning. 1969. Selected data for health planning in North Carolina; compiled by Alice M. Rupen. [Raleigh, 1969]. pp. 96.

NORTH RHINE-WESTPHALIA

— Industries.

NORTH RHINE-WESTPHALIA. Landesamt für Datenverarbeitung und Statistik. Beiträge zur Statistik des Landes Nordrhein- Westfalen. Heft 386. Die Einheitswerte der gewerblichen Betriebe und der Mineralgewinnungsrechte, 1972. Düsseldorf, 1978. pp. 199.

NORTH WEST TERRITORIES

— Economic policy.

ALEXANDER (COLIN) Angry society...; new answers to a century of problems affecting all Canadians; a northern journalist tells the facts about Canada's northern colonies today. Saskatoon, [1976]. pp. 202.

— Native races.

ALEXANDER (COLIN) Angry society...; new answers to a century of problems affecting all Canadians; a northern journalist tells the facts about Canada's northern colonies today. Saskatoon, [1976]. pp. 202.

— Politics and government.

ALEXANDER (COLIN) Angry society...; new answers to a century of problems affecting all Canadians; a northern journalist tells the facts about Canada's northern colonies today. Saskatoon, [1976]. pp. 202.

— Social policy.

ALEXANDER (COLIN) Angry society...; new answers to a century of problems affecting all Canadians; a northern journalist tells the facts about Canada's northern colonies today. Saskatoon, [1976]. pp. 202.

NORTHUMBERLAND

— Economic conditions.

NORTHUMBERLAND. County Planning Department. Northumberland county structure plan: report of survey for consultation. Newcastle upon Tyne, 1976. pp. 264.

— Social conditions.

NORTHUMBERLAND. County Planning Department. Northumberland county structure plan: report of survey for consultation. Newcastle upon Tyne, 1976. pp. 264.

NORTHUMBERLAND MINERS' MUTUAL CONFIDENT ASSOCIATION.

NORTHUMBERLAND. Northumberland Miners' Mutual Confident Association. Rules...[1911]. Newcastle-upon-Tyne, 1911. pp. 54.

NORWAY

— Commerce.

NORWAY. Departementet for det Indre. Statistiske tabeller for Kongeriget Norge: tabeller vedkommende Norges handel og skibsfart. a., 1851, 1853, 1855-1858. Christiania.

— Economic policy.

HANISCH (TED) Hele folket i arbeid: et essay om sysselsettingspolitikken i Norge. Oslo, 1977. pp. 108. *bibliog.*

— Foreign relations.

For related heading see EUROPEAN ECONOMIC COMMUNITY — Norway.

— Full employment policies.

HANISCH (TED) Hele folket i arbeid: et essay om sysselsettingspolitikken i Norge. Oslo, 1977. pp. 108. *bibliog.*

— Learned institutions and societies.

AMUNDSEN (LEIV) Det Norske Videnskaps-Akademi i Oslo, 1857-1957. Oslo, 1957-60. 2 vols. *bibliog.*

— Population.

NORWAY. Statistiske Centralbyrå. 1977. Flyttemotivundersøkelsen, 1972: Survey of migration motives, 1972. Oslo, 1977. pp. 321. *bibliog. (Samfunnsøkonomiske Studier. 35) With English summary and table headings.*

DYRVIK (STÅLE) Utviklingstendensar i 1976 i Norges befolking. Oslo, 1978. pp. 36. *(Norway. Statistiske Centralbyrå. Artikler. 106) With English headings.*

— Social policy.

CHRISTIANSEN (VIDAR) and JANSEN (EILEV S.) Implicit social preferences in the Norwegian system of indirect taxation. Oslo, 1977. pp. 88. *bibliog. (Oslo. Universitet. Socialøkonomiske Institutt. Memoranda)*

NORWEGIAN SEA REGION.

SJAASTAD (ANDERS C.) and SKOGAN (JOHN KRISTEN) Politikk og sikkerhet i Norskehavsområdet: om de enkelte land og våre felles problemer. Oslo, 1975. pp. 301. *(Norsk Utenrikspolitisk Institutt. Utenrikspolitiske Studier. Nr.18)*

NORWICH (DIOCESE)

— History.

CAMDEN SOCIETY. [Publications]. 4th Series. vol. 20. Heresy trials in the diocese of Norwich 1428-31; edited for the Royal Historical Society from Westminster Diocesan Archives MS.B.2 by Norman P. Tanner. London, 1977. pp. 233.

NOVA SCOTIA

— Bibliography.

VAISON (ROBERT) compiler. Nova Scotia past and present: a bibliography and guide. Halifax, Department of Education, 1976. pp. 164.

— Executive departments.

NOVA SCOTIA. Department of Lands and Forests. Annual report (formerly Report). a., 1957/58, 1962/63- , with gaps (1964/65, 1967/68-1971/72) Halifax. *File includes Interim report for 1966/67.*

NOVA SCOTIA. Department of Fisheries. Annual report. a., 1964/65(1st)- , with gaps (1966/67, 3rd; 1970/71-1974/75, 7th-11th). Halifax.

NOVA SCOTIA. Department of Education. Annual report. a., 1970/71- Halifax.

NOVA SCOTIA. Department of Agriculture and Marketing. Annual report. a., 1971/72- Halifax.

NOVA SCOTIA. Department of Municipal Affairs. Annual report. a., 1973/74(1st)- Halifax.

— Fishermen's Strike, 1970-1971.

CAMERON (SILVER DONALD) The education of Everett Richardson: the Nova Scotia fishermen's strike, 1970-71. Toronto, [1977]. pp. 239.

— Government publications — Bibliography.

PUBLICATIONS OF THE PROVINCE OF NOVA SCOTIA: a check list compiled in the Legislative Library of documents received. a., 1968(2nd)- , with gaps (1969(3rd); 1971(5th); 1973(7th)). Halifax.

NOVA SCOTIA. Legislative Library. 1973. Nova Scotia royal commissions and commissions of enquiry appointed by the province of Nova Scotia. Halifax, 1973. pp. 23.

— Population.

SELIG (BRIAN M.) and HARVEY (ANDREW S.) Nova Scotia population projections 1972-81 (by age and sex for province, counties and Halifax metro)...; prepared for Economics and Statistics Division, Department of Development. [Halifax], 1975. fo.39. *bibliog.*

— Social conditions — Statistics.

NOVA SCOTIA. Department of Development. Economics and Statistics Division. 1976. Perspective Nova Scotia: a compendium of social statistics. [Halifax, 1976?]. pp. 185.

NOYES (JOHN HUMPHREY).

THOMAS (ROBERT DAVID) The man who would be perfect: John Humphrey Noyes and the utopian impulse. [Philadelphia], 1977. pp. 199. *bibliog.*

NSO (AFRICAN PEOPLE).

FONLON (BERNARD) To every son of Nso. Yaoundé, 1965. fo. 41.

NUBIA

— Antiquities.

ADAMS (WILLIAM Y.) Nubia: corridor to Africa. London, 1977. pp. 797.

— History.

ADAMS (WILLIAM Y.) Nubia: corridor to Africa. London, 1977. pp. 797.

NURSERY SCHOOLS.

JOFFE (CAROLE E.) Friendly intruders: childcare professionals and family life. Berkeley, [1977]. pp. 172. *bibliog.*

NURSES AND NURSING.

INTERNATIONAL LABOUR CONFERENCE. 61st Session. Reports. 7. Employment and conditions of work and life of nursing personnel: seventh item on the agenda. Geneva, 1975-76. 2 pts.

— United Kingdom — Ireland, Northern.

NORTHERN IRELAND COUNCIL FOR NURSES AND MIDWIVES. Statement of accounts...together with the report of the Comptroller and Auditor-General. a., 1971/72 [2nd]- Belfast. *1971 [1st] included in IRELAND, NORTHERN. Parliament. House of Commons. [Papers].*

NURSING HOME ACCIDENTS

— Canada — Newfoundland.

NEWFOUNDLAND. Commission of Enquiry into the Chafe's Nursing Home fire of December 26, 1976 and into the Safety Standards and Quality of Care in Homes for Special Care and Welfare Institutions in the Province of Newfoundland. Report...; J.R. Gushue, commissioner, [St. John's, 1977?]. pp. 252.

NURSING HOMES

— Canada — Newfoundland.

NEWFOUNDLAND. Commission of Enquiry into the Chafe's Nursing Home fire of December 26, 1976 and into the Safety Standards and Quality of Care in Homes for Special Care and Welfare Institutions in the Province of Newfoundland. Report...; J.R. Gushue, commissioner, [St. John's, 1977?]. pp. 252.

— United States.

MANARD (BARBARA BOLLING) and others. Better homes for the old. Lexington, Mass., [1977]. pp. 152.

NUTRITION.

THOMPSON (BENJAMIN) Count Rumford. Essay on food, and particularly on feeding the poor; published in the year 1795, and now reprinted for the Friends of the Poor. Youghal, printed by J.W. Lindsay, 1847. pp. 51.

AKOI (STEPHEN) and HASSELMANN (KARL-HEINZ) Youth and environment: a Liberian case study on food and nutrition in Buzzi-quarter, Monrovia. [Monrovia], 1975. fo. 32. *bibliog.* (*University of Liberia. Department of Geography. Occasional Research Papers. No. 9*)

CASTRO (JOSÚE DE) The geopolitics of hunger. rev. ed. New York, [1977]. pp. 524. *Published in 1952 under the title Geography of hunger.*

— Underdeveloped areas.

See UNDERDEVELOPED AREAS — Nutrition.

NUTRITION POLICY.

REUTLINGER (SHLOMO) and SELOWSKY (MARCELO) Malnutrition and poverty: magnitude and policy options. [Washington], International Bank for Reconstruction and Development, [1976]. pp. 82. (*World Bank Staff Occasional Papers. No. 23*)

— United States.

NATIONAL PLANNING ASSOCIATION. Reports. No. 145. A farm, food and land use policy for the future; by Harold F. Breimyer...with a statement by the NPA Agriculture Committee. Washington, 1976. pp. 24.

OBERT (JESSIE CRAIG) Community nutrition. New York, [1978]. pp. 452. *bibliogs.*

NYACK, NEW YORK

— Economic history.

NORDSTROM (CARL) Frontier elements in a Hudson river village. Port Washington, N.Y., 1973. pp. 199. *bibliog.*

— History.

NORDSTROM (CARL) Frontier elements in a Hudson river village. Port Washington, N.Y., 1973. pp. 199. *bibliog.*

— Social history.

NORDSTROM (CARL) Frontier elements in a Hudson river village. Port Washington, N.Y., 1973. pp. 199. *bibliog.*

OAXACA

— Social history.

CHANCE (JOHN K.) Race and class in colonial Oaxaca. Stanford, 1978. pp. 250. *bibliog.*

O'BRIEN (CONOR CRUISE).

LYSAGHT (D.R.O'CONNOR) End of a liberal: the literary politics of Conor Cruise O'Brien. Dublin, [1977]. pp. 56.

O'BRIEN (EDNA).

O'BRIEN (EDNA) Mother Ireland;...with photographs by Fergus Bourke. Harmondsworth, 1978. pp. 89. *First published 1976.*

OBSCENITY (LAW).

CENSORSHIP and obscenity; edited by Rajeev Dhavan and Christie Davies. London, 1978. pp. 187. *bibliogs.*

— United States.

SUNDERLAND (LANE V.) Obscenity: the Court, the Congress and the President's Commission. Washington, 1975. pp. 127. *bibliog.* (*American Enterprise Institute for Public Policy Research. Domestic Affairs Studies. 27*)

OCAMPO (MELCHOR).

OCAMPO (MELCHOR) Obras completas. Mexico, 1900-1901. 3 vols. *Tomo 1: Polemicas religiosas; Tomo 2: Escritos politicos; Tomo 3: Letras y ciencias.*

OCCITANE MOVEMENT.

ARNAUD (NICOLE) and DOFNY (JACQUES) Nationalism and the national question. Montreal, [1977]. pp. 134. *Translated by Penelope Williams.*

OCCUPATIONAL DISEASES.

U.K. Health and Safety Executive. Health and safety statistics. a., 1975(1st)- London.

OCCUPATIONAL MOBILITY

— United States.

HAUSER (ROBERT MASON) and FEATHERMAN (DAVID L.) The process of stratification: trends and analyses. New York, [1977]. pp. 372. *bibliog.*

DECKER (PETER R.) Fortunes and failures: white-collar mobility in nineteenth-century San Francisco. Cambridge, Mass., 1978. pp. 336.

GRIFFEN (CLYDE) and GRIFFEN (SALLY) Natives and newcomers: the ordering of opportunity in mid-nineteenth-century Poughkeepsie. Cambridge, Mass., 1978. pp. 291. (*Harvard University. Harvard Studies in Urban History*)

OCCUPATIONAL PRESTIGE.

COXON (ANTHONY PETER MACMILLAN) and JONES (CHARLES L.) The images of occupational prestige. London, 1978. pp. 226. *bibliog.*

OCCUPATIONAL THERAPY.

WANSBROUGH (NANCY) Contract and pay questions in industrial therapy units: report of an investigation into some technical aspects of the operation of industrial units. London, 1971. fo.50.

OCCUPATIONAL TRAINING

— Ghana.

BOAKYE (KWESI J.A.) Occupational activities of rural youth and their attitudes towards craft training: an exploratory study. Cape Coast, 1973. pp. 64, vii. (*University of Cape Coast. Centre for Development Studies. Research Report Series. Papers. No. 16*)

OCCUPATIONS

— Classification.

FRANCE. Institut National de la Statistique et des Etudes Economiques, 1962. Nomenclature des métiers et des activités individuelles: index analytique; (code no. 2 du recensement de la population de 1962). 2nd ed. Paris, 1962. pp. 285.

PAKISTAN. Central Statistical Office. Economic Affairs Division. 1965- . Pakistan standard classification of occupations: PSCO. [Karachi, 1965 in progress].

OCEAN BOTTOM (MARITIME LAW).

LUARD (DAVID EVAN TRANT) The control of the sea-bed: who owns the resources of the oceans? rev. ed.. London, 1977. pp. 315.

INTERNATIONAL OCEAN SYMPOSIUM, 2ND, TOKYO, 1977. (Proceedings): marine technology and law; development of hydrocarbon resources and offshore structures. Kasumigaseki, 1978. pp. 191. *With 11 maps and diagrams in end-pocket.*

OCEANIA

— Social conditions.

EXILES and migrants in Oceania; edited by Michael D. Lieber. Honolulu, [1977]. pp. 414. *bibliog.* (*Association for Social Anthropology in Oceania. ASAO Monographs. No.5) Based on a symposium held at the University of Washington in 1970.*

OCEANOGRAPHIC RESEARCH.

BURKE (WILLIAM THOMAS) A report on international legal problems of scientific research in the oceans; prepared for the National Council on Marine Resources and Engineering Development. [Washington], 1967. pp. 143.

ODESSA

— History — Chronology.

KHRONIKA revoliutsionnykh sobytii na Odesshchine v gody pervoi russkoi revoliutsii, 1905-1907 gg. Odessa, 1976. pp. 207. *bibliog.*

OESTERREICHISCHER ARBEITER- UND ANGESTELLTENBUND.

MOCK (ALOIS) Für eine menschenwürdige Gesellschaftsordnung: zur Neuauflage des "Wiener Programms" des OAAB. Wien, 1976. pp. 28. (*Österreichischer Arbeiter- und Angestelltenbund. Gesellschaftspolitische Informationen. 13*)

OFFENCES AGAINST PROPERTY

— Netherlands.

NETHERLANDS. Commissie-Vermogensstraffen. 1972. Eindrapport...; (voorzitter, W.C. van Binsbergen) 's-Gravenhage, 1972. pp. 143,30.

OFFENCES AGAINST THE PERSON

— United States — Illinois.

BLOCK (RICHARD) Violent crime: environment, interaction, and death. Lexington, Mass., [1977]. pp. 121. *bibliog.*

OFFICE BUILDINGS.

IRELAND, NORTHERN. Department of Manpower Services. Offices and shop premises: report under the Office and Shop Premises Act (Northern Ireland) 1966. a., 1970, 1971, 1973- Belfast. *Ap 1967/D 1968 [1st] - 1969 included in IRELAND, NORTHERN. Parliament. House of Commons. [Papers].*

OFFICIAL SECRETS

— United Kingdom.

COHEN (STANLEY) and TAYLOR (LAURIE) Prison secrets. London, [1976]. pp. 98.

— United States.

SOCIAL research in conflict with law and ethics; Paul Nejelski, editor. Cambridge, Mass., [1976]. pp. 197. *Papers given at a conference held at the University of Bielefeld, 1974.*

OFFSHORE OIL INDUSTRY

— North Sea.

LEWIS (T.M.) and McNICOLL (IAIN HUGH) North Sea oil and Scotland's economic prospects. London, [1978]. pp. 147. *bibliog.*

ROBINSON (COLIN) and MORGAN (JON) North Sea oil in the future: economic analysis and government policy. London, 1978. pp. 216. *Written under the auspices of the Trade Policy Research Centre.*

OGAREV (NIKOLAI PLATONOVICH).

VERKHOVSKII (IU.) Neizvestnyi Ogarev; [with an appendix: Stikhotvoreniia N.P. Ogareva]. Moskva, 1928. pp. 54.

OGLETHORPE (JAMES EDWARD).

SPALDING (PHINIZY) Oglethorpe in America. Chicago, [1977]. pp. 207.

OIL INDUSTRIES.

BRUSEKER (U.) Unilever, Meneba, Philips en de olieconcerns als inflatiemakers; een bestrijding van de looninflatie-theorie. [Amsterdam], 1974. pp. 133. *bibliog.*

OILSEED PLANTS.

OILSEED PLANTS.

PORTER (K.D.) and McBAIN (B.J.) Final report: oil seeds and wheat, 1961-1963: a cost of production study on 104 farms: central Alberta, Peace River, southern Alberta. [Edmonton], Department of Agriculture, 1964. pp. 54,18.

CANADA. Statistics Canada. Grains and oilseeds review. m., My 1978 (no.1)- Ottawa. *[in English and French]. Supersedes CANADA. Statistics Canada. Coarse grains review, CANADA. Statistics Canada. Oilseeds review and CANADA. Statistics Canada. Wheat review.*

OKANAGAN VALLEY

— Economic conditions.

BRITISH COLUMBIA. Economics and Statistics Branch. 1971. The Okanagan-Shuswap region: a British Columbia regional economic study; originally prepared for the Okanagan Study Committee, Canada-British Columbia Okanagan Basin Agreement. Victoria, 1971. pp. 177.

OLD AGE.

FAMILY, bureaucracy and the elderly; edited by Ethel Shanas and Marvin B. Sussman. Durham, N.C., 1977. pp. 233. *bibliogs. Based on papers at a Conference on Older People, Family and Bureaucracy held at the Quail Roost Conference Center in Rougemont, N.C., in May 1973.*

FONTANA (ANDREA) The last frontier: the social meaning of growing old. Beverly Hills, [1977]. pp. 213. *bibliog.*

AGING into the 21st century: middle-ages today; edited by Lissy F. Jarvik; Helene Kratz, assistant editor. New York, [1978]. pp. 214. *bibliogs.*

— Care and hygiene.

HUTTMAN (ELIZABETH D.) Housing and social services for the elderly: social policy trends. New York, 1977. pp. 293. *bibliog.*

— Transportation — United Kingdom.

NORMAN (ALISON) Transport and the elderly: problems and possible action. London, [1977]. pp. 143.

— Australia — Dwellings.

AUSTRALIA. Department of Housing. States Grants (Dwellings for Aged Pensioners) Act 1969: annual statement. a., 1969/70(1st)- Canberra. *Included in AUSTRALIA. Parliament. [Parliamentary papers].*

— France.

ROSS (JENNIE-KEITH) Old people, new lives: community creation in a retirement residence. Chicago, 1977. pp. 227. *bibliog.*

— Germany — Saarland.

PETER (RUDI) Die soziale Lage der Alten im Saarland: eine repräsentative empirisch-soziologische Erhebung. Saarbrücken, [1973]. pp. 164. *bibliog. (Arbeitskammer des Saarlandes. Schriftenreihe)*

— Japan.

WATANABE (SADAMU) Old people in transitional Japan with activities of gerontology of Japan and mortality trends in selected countries. [Tokyo], 1960. pp. 78. *bibliog.*

— United Kingdom.

ELDER (GLADYS) The alienated: growing old today. London, 1977. pp. 143.

BOSANQUET (NICHOLAS) A future for old age. London, 1978. pp. 166. *bibliog.*

U.K. Social Survey. [Reports. New Series]. 1078. The elderly at home; a survey carried out on behalf of the Department of Health and Social Security; [by] Audrey Hunt. London, 1978. pp. 177.

— — Care and hygiene.

DOWDELL (TIM C.) The role of the social services in the care of the elderly sick. London, [1976]. pp. 16. *(Socialist Medical Association. Discussion Documents)*

ROYAL COLLEGE OF PHYSICIANS OF LONDON. Working Party on Medical Care of the Elderly. Medical care of the elderly. London, 1977. pp. 11.

WICKS (MALCOLM) Old and cold: hypothermia and social policy. London, [1978]. pp. 208. *bibliog.*

— United States.

JONES (ROCHELLE) The other generation: the new power of older people. Englewood Cliffs, [1977]. pp. 264.

AMERICAN ACADEMY OF POLITICAL AND SOCIAL SCIENCE. Annals. vol. 438. Planning for the elderly; special editor of this volume Marvin E. Wolfgang. Philadelphia, 1978. pp. 180.

— — Dwellings.

HUTTMAN (ELIZABETH D.) Housing and social services for the elderly: social policy trends. New York, 1977. pp. 293. *bibliog.*

OLD AGE HOMES

— United States.

HUTTMAN (ELIZABETH D.) Housing and social services for the elderly: social policy trends. New York, 1977. pp. 293. *bibliog.*

MANARD (BARBARA BOLLING) and others. Better homes for the old. Lexington, Mass., [1977]. pp. 152.

OLD AGE PENSIONS

— United Kingdom.

TUTT (SYLVIA) and TUTT (LESLIE) Private pension scheme finance. London, 1976. pp. 316. *Reprint of the 1st ed. of 1971 with a new appendix.*

— United States.

The CRISIS in social security: problems and prospects; Michael J. Boskin, editor. San Francisco, [1977]. pp. 214. *bibliog. (Institute for Contemporary Studies. [Publications])*

INCOME support policies for the aged; edited by G. S. Tolley [and] Richard V. Burkhauser. Cambridge, Mass., [1977]. pp. 194. *bibliogs. Papers presented at a conference held at the University of Chicago in 1976.*

OLDENBURG

— Commerce.

HANSSMANN (GEORG) Lud. Sartorius & Comp., 1777-1977: ein Oldenburger Handelshaus im Wandel der Zeiten. Oldenburg, [1977]. 1 vol. (various pagings).

OLIGOPOLIES.

FRIEDMAN (JAMES W.) Oligopoly and the theory of games. Amsterdam, 1977. pp. 311. *bibliog.*

OLIVE OIL

— Congresses.

UNITED NATIONS. Conference on Olive Oil, Geneva, 1967. Summary of proceedings [of the conference held at Geneva, 28-30 March 1967]. (TD/OLIVE OIL. 3/1). New York, 1967. pp. 14.

UNITED NATIONS. Conference on Olive Oil, Geneva, 1973. Summary of proceedings [of the conference held at Geneva, 19-23 March, 1973]. (TD/OLIVE OIL 5/6/Rev.1). New York, 1973. pp. 20.

O'MALLEY (ERNIE).

O'MALLEY (ERNIE) The singing flame. Dublin, 1978. pp. 312.

OMAN

— History.

PETERSON (JOHN E.) Oman in the twentieth century: political foundations of an emerging state. London, [1978]. pp. 286. *bibliog.*

— Politics and government.

PETERSON (JOHN E.) Oman in the twentieth century: political foundations of an emerging state. London, [1978]. pp. 286. *bibliog.*

OMBUDSMAN

— Canada — New Brunswick.

NEW BRUNSWICK. Office of the Ombudsman. Report. a., 1967/68(1st)- Fredericton. *[in English and French].*

— — Newfoundland.

NEWFOUNDLAND. General Assembly. House of Assembly. Select Committee on the Appointment of an Ombudsman. 1969. Report; [John A. Nolan, chairman]. [St. John's], 1969. 1 vol. (various pagings).

— — Nova Scotia.

NOVA SCOTIA. General Assembly. House of Assembly. Select Committee to consider an Ombudsman type of Official for Nova Scotia. 1970. Report; [Victor Thorpe, chairman]. [Halifax, 1970]. fo. 28. *bibliog.*

NOVA SCOTIA. Ombudsman. Report. a., 1972(2nd)- Halifax.

— — Quebec.

LAVOIE (JOCELYN) Le Protecteur du citoyen du Québec: organisation et fonctionnement. Paris, [1976]. pp. 144. *bibliog. (Paris. Université de Paris II. Travaux et Recherches. Série Science Administrative. 10)*

— — Saskatchewan.

SASKATCHEWAN. Office of the Ombudsman. Annual report. a., 1973(1st)- Regina.

— Europe.

WALKER-SMITH (Sir DEREK) The case for a European Ombudsman. London, 1978. pp. 4. *(Reprinted from The Times, 10 February 1978)*

— Finland.

FINLAND. Eduskunnan Oikeusasiamies. Report: summary and annotations. a., 1975- Helsinki.

— Mauritius.

MAURITIUS. Ombudsman. 1974. Report..., March 1970 to December 1973. Port Louis, 1974. pp. 35. *(Mauritius. Legislative Assembly. Sessional Papers. 1974. No.10)*

ONEIDA COMMUNITY.

WELLS (ORTON) The Oneida community: unique among all human associations, in the highest degree successful commercially, and yet the most splendidly idealistic of them all. [New York?, 1908]. pp. 11. *(Extracted from an article in The Business World, New York, 1st September, 1908)*

THOMAS (ROBERT DAVID) The man who would be perfect: John Humphrey Noyes and the utopian impulse. [Philadelphia], 1977. pp. 199. *bibliog.*

ONTARIO

— Appropriations and expenditures.

AULD (D.A.L.) Fiscal knowledge and preferences in Ontario. Toronto, 1977. 1 vol. (various pagings). *(Ontario. Economic Council. Working Papers. 1977. No. 2)*

— Economic conditions.

BONSOR (N.C.) Transportation rates and economic development in northern Ontario. Toronto, [1977]. pp. 91. *bibliog. (Ontario. Economic Council. Research Studies. 7)*

FOOT (DAVID K.) and others. The Ontario economy, 1977-1987. Toronto, Ontario Economic Council, 1977. pp. 351. *bibliog.*

ONTARIO. Economic Council. 1977. The Ontario economy to 1987. Toronto, 1977. pp. 61. *(Issues and Alternatives, 1977)*

— Economic policy.

ONTARIO JOINT COMMITTEE ON ECONOMIC POLICY. Directions for economic and social policy in Ontario; report; [H.I. Macdonald, chairman of the Steering Committee]. Toronto, [Ministry of Treasury, Economics and Intergovernmental Affairs], 1974. pp. 37. *bibliog.*

ONTARIO. Ministry of Treasury, Economics and Intergovernmental Affairs. Fiscal Policy Division. 1976. Ontario's economic strategy for 1977; presented by W. Darcy McKeough...in the Legislative Assembly of Ontario, November 23, 1976. [Toronto], 1976. fo. 42.

FOOT (DAVID K.) and others. The Ontario economy, 1977-1987. Toronto, Ontario Economic Council, 1977. pp. 351. *bibliog.*

ONTARIO. Economic Council. 1977. The Ontario economy to 1987. Toronto, 1977. pp. 61. *(Issues and Alternatives, 1977)*

— Emigration and immigration.

EMPLOYMENT AND IMMIGRATION REVIEW: ONTARIO (formerly Manpower and immigration review: Ontario region (previously Manpower review: Ontario region [pd. by] Department of Manpower and Immigration, Manpower Information and Analysis Branch, Ontario Regional Office [Canada]. s-a. (formerly q.), (previously bi-m.), 1969 (v.2)- with gaps. Ottawa. *[in English and French] Ja/F 1969 - Jl/Ag 1970 in English only.*

MARR (WILLIAM L.) Labour market and other implications of immigration policy for Ontario. Toronto, 1976. pp. 1-98, 103-241. *bibliog. (Ontario. Economic Council. Working Papers. 1976. No. 1) Pages 99-102 were deleted for reasons of confidentiality.*

— Executive departments.

ONTARIO. Ministry of Health. 1975-76. Organization structure of the Ontario Ministry of Health. [Toronto, 1975-76]. pp. 23.

— Government publications.

BISHOP (OLGA BERNICE) Publications of the government of Ontario, 1867-1900. Toronto, Ministry of Government Services, 1976. pp. 409.

— Population.

ONTARIO POPULATION STATISTICS; [pd. by] Department of Municipal Affairs, Community Planning Branch [Ontario]. a., 1970- Toronto. *Ceased pbln. in 1971.*

ONTARIO. Central Statistical Services Division. 1976. Ontario population trends: a review of implications; based on advance information on preliminary population counts, census of Canada, 1976. [Toronto], 1976. fo. 23.

— Social policy.

ONTARIO JOINT COMMITTEE ON ECONOMIC POLICY. Directions for economic and social policy in Ontario; report; [H.I. Macdonald, chairman of the Steering Committee]. Toronto, [Ministry of Treasury, Economics and Intergovernmental Affairs], 1974. pp. 37. *bibliog.*

ONTOLOGY.

BALLARD (EDWARD GOODWIN) Man and technology: toward the measurement of a culture. Pittsburgh, [1978]. pp. 251.

OPEN AND CLOSED SHOP

— United Kingdom.

MARPLAN LIMITED. Strikes, picketing and the closed shop. [London, 1977]. fo. 7.

WHITEHORN (KATHARINE) Whose news? London, [1978]. pp. 16. *(Unservile State Group. Unservile State Papers. No. 23)*

OPEN UNIVERSITY.

McINTOSH (NAOMI E.) and others. A degree of difference: the Open University of the United Kingdom. New York, 1977. pp. 320. *bibliogs.*

OPERATIONS RESEARCH.

TURNER (JOHN CHRISTOPHER) Modern applied mathematics: probability, statistics, operational research. London, 1970 repr. 1972. pp. 502. *bibliog.*

PAGE (ERIC) Queueing theory in OR. London, 1972. pp. 187. *bibliog.*

HILLIER (FREDERICK STANTON) and LIEBERMAN (GERALD J.) Operations research. 2nd ed. San Francisco, [1974]. pp. 800.

JOHNSON (LYNWOOD A.) and MONTGOMERY (DOUGLAS C.) Operations research in production planning, scheduling, and inventory control. New York, [1974]. pp. xiv,525.

WHITE (DOUGLAS JOHN) and others. Operational research techniques; volume 2. London, 1974. pp. 316.

BEILBY (M.H.) Economics and operational research. London, 1975. pp. 174. *bibliog.*

GUPTA (SHIV KUMAR) and COZZOLINO (JOHN M.) Fundamentals of operations research for management: an introduction to qualitative methods. San Francisco, [1975]. 2 vols. *The second volume consists of Solutions manual with supplementary problems for Fundamentals, etc.*

WAGNER (HARVEY M.) Principles of operations research, with applications to managerial decisions. 2nd ed. London, 1975. pp. 1039. *bibliog.*

WOOLSEY (ROBERT E.D.) and SWANSON (HUNTINGTON S.) Operations research for immediate application: a quick and dirty manual. New York, [1975]. pp. 204.

BAILEY (NORMAN THOMAS JOHN) Mathematics, statistics, and systems for health. Chichester, [1977]. pp. 222. *bibliog. Based on his The mathematical approach to biology and medicine, published in 1967.*

BAUMOL (WILLIAM JACK) Economic theory and operations analysis. 4th ed. Englewood Cliffs, [1977]. pp. 695. *bibliogs.*

A DISCUSSION on the use of operational research and systems analysis in decision-making; [by] R.C. Tomlinson [and others] . London, 1977. pp. 193. *(London. Royal Society of London. Philosophical Transactions. Series A. vol. 287)*

DAELLENBACH (HANS G.) and GEORGE (JOHN A.) Introduction to operations research techniques. Boston, Mass., [1978]. pp. 603. *bibliog.*

OPPOSITION (POLITICAL SCIENCE).

RAINA (PETER K.) Political opposition in Poland, 1954-1977. London, 1978. pp. 584. *bibliog.*

ORAL COMMUNICATION.

CHILD discourse; edited by Susan Ervin-Tripp [and] Claudia Mitchell-Kernan. New York, 1977. pp. 266. *bibliog.*

ORAL HISTORY.

THOMPSON (PAUL) The voice of the past: oral history. Oxford, 1978. pp. 257. *bibliog.*

ORAL TRADITION.

GOSSEN (GARY H.) Chamulas in the world of the sun: time and space in a Maya oral tradition. Cambridge, Mass., 1974. pp. 382. *bibliog.*

ORDER STATISTICS.

GIBBONS (JEAN DICKINSON) and others. Selecting and ordering populations: a new statistical methodology. New York, [1977]. pp. 569. *bibliog.*

ORE DRESSING.

UNITED NATIONS. Interregional Seminar on Ore Concentration in Water-Short Areas, New York, 1966. Proceedings of the...seminar...New York...14-25 February 1966. (ST/TAO/SER.C/95). New York, 1968. pp. 342.

ORE DRESSING PLANTS

— Water supply.

UNITED NATIONS. Interregional Seminar on Ore Concentration in Water-Short Areas, New York, 1966. Proceedings of the...seminar...New York...14-25 February 1966. (ST/TAO/SER.C/95). New York, 1968. pp. 342.

ORGANISATION FOR ECONOMIC COOPERATION AND DEVELOPMENT.

EUROPEAN economic issues: agriculture, economic security, industrial democracy, the OECD. New York, 1977. pp. 263. *(Atlantic Institute. Atlantic Institute Studies. 3)*

ORGANIZATION.

BRUCE-WILLIAMS (MARSHALL) Military and industrial war and the science of organisation. London, 1912. pp. 16.

GLEN (FREDERICK) The social psychology of organizations. London, 1975. pp. 144. *bibliog.*

TABATONI (PIERRE) and JARNIOU (PIERRE) Les systèmes de gestion: politiques et structures. Paris, [1975]. pp. 233.

GASPARINI (GIOVANNI) Tecnologia, ambiente e struttura: temi e modelli per una sociologia dell'organizzazione. Milano, [1976]. pp. 242. *bibliog.*

HERBERT (THEODORE T.) Dimensions of organizational behavior. New York, [1976]. pp. 530.

LAWLER (EDWARD E.) and RHODE (JOHN GRANT) Information and control in organizations. Pacific Palisades, [1976]. pp. 217. *bibliog.*

MANAGEMENT strategy and business development: an historical and comparative study; edited by Leslie Hannah. [London, 1976]. pp. 267. *The present volume has its origins in a conference...held in London on 10 June 1975.*

THOMPSON (VICTOR A.) Bureaucracy and the modern world. Morristown, N.J., [1976]. pp. 141. *bibliogs.*

ABRAHAMSSON (BENGT) Bureaucracy or participation: the logic of organization. Beverly Hills, [1977]. pp. 240. *bibliog. Translation of his Organisationsteori.*

GOODMAN (PAUL S.) and others. New perspectives on organizational effectiveness. San Francisco, 1977. pp. 275. *bibliog.*

ORGANIZATIONAL careers: some new perspectives; edited by John Van Maanen. London, [1977]. pp. 199. *bibliog. Derives from an Industrial Liaison Program Symposium held at M.I.T. in 1974.*

ORGANIZATIONAL choice and constraint: approaches to the sociology of enterprise behaviour; edited by Malcolm Warner. Farnborough, Hants., [1977]. pp. 253. *bibliogs.*

TURK (HERMAN) Organizations in modern life: (cities and other large networks). San Francisco, 1977. pp. 283. *bibliog.*

JORGE (ANTONIO) Competition, cooperation, efficiency, and social organization: introduction to a political economy. Rutherford, [1978]. pp. 89. *bibliog.*

KATZ (DANIEL) and KAHN (ROBERT LOUIS) The social psychology of organizations. 2nd ed. New York, [1978]. pp. 838. *bibliog.*

ORGANIZATION.(Cont.)

MICHELMANN (HANS J.) Organisational effectiveness in a multi-national bureaucracy. Farnborough, Hants., [1978]. pp. 259. *bibliog.*

ORGANIZATION and environment: theory, issues and reality; edited by Lucien Karpik. London, [1978]. pp. 345. *bibliogs. Contributions from the Eighth World Congress of Sociology, Toronto, 1974.*

ORGANIZATION OF AFRICAN UNITY.

ČERVENKA (ZDENEK) The unfinished quest for unity: Africa and the OAU. London, 1977. pp. 251.

CHIME (CHIMELU) Integration and politics among African states: limitations and horizons of mid-term theorizing. Uppsala, 1977. pp. 436.

TUZMUKHAMEDOV (RAIS ABDULKHAKOVICH) Razvivaiushchiesia strany v mirovoi politike: mezhdunarodnye mezhpravitel'stvennye organizatsii razvivaiushchikhsia stran. Moskva, 1977. pp. 207.

ORGANIZATION OF LATIN AMERICAN SOLIDARITY.

ARISMENDI (RODNEY) America Latina: campo de lucha o base de agresion. [Montevideo, 1967]. 1 pamphlet (unpaged).

COLLAZO (ARIEL B.) La OLAS: el camino revolucionario de los trabajadores. [Montevideo, 1968]. pp. 43.

ORGANIZATION OF THE PETROLEUM EXPORTING COUNTRIES.

LUCIANI (GIACOMO) L'OPEC nella economia internazionale. [Torino, 1976]. pp. 136.

The ARAB oil weapon; [compiled] by Jordan J. Paust [and] Albert P. Blaustein, with Adele Higgins. New York, 1977. pp. 370.

BHATTACHARYA (ANINDYA K.) The myth of petropower. Lexington, Mass., [1977]. pp. 108. *bibliog.*

OPEC and the Middle East: the impact of oil on societal development; edited by Russell A. Stone. New York, 1977. pp. 264.

The OPEC market to 1985; [by] Farid Abolfathi [and others]. Lexington, Mass., [1977]. pp. 406. *bibliog.*

MORAN (THEODORE H.) Oil prices and the future of OPEC: the political economy of tension and stability in the Organization of Petroleum Exporting Countries. Washington, D.C., 1978. pp. 102. *(Resources for the Future, Inc. Research Papers. R-8)*

ORGANIZATIONAL BEHAVIOUR.

MANAGEMENT control and organizational democracy; editors Bert King [and others]. Washington, D.C., 1978. pp. 288. *bibliogs. Papers presented at a conference held in Munich in 1976 by the Human Factors Division of the North Atlantic Treaty Organization.*

ORGANIZATIONAL CHANGE.

ORGANIZATIONAL development in the UK and USA: a joint evaluation; edited by Cary L. Cooper. London, 1977. pp. 144. *bibliogs. Based on a symposium held at the annual conference of the US Academy of Management, Kansas City, 1976.*

STJERNBERG (TORBJÖRN) Organizational change and quality of life: individual and organizational perspectives on democratization of work in an insurance company. Stockholm, 1977. pp. 375. *bibliog. A research report of the Programme for Participation and Organization Development, Economic Research Institute, Stockholm School of Economics.*

ZALTMAN (GERALD) and DUNCAN (ROBERT B.) Strategies for planned change. New York, [1977]. pp. 404. *bibliog.*

ORGANIZED CRIME.

McINTOSH (MARY) The organisation of crime. London, 1975. pp. 80. *bibliog.*

ORPHANS AND ORPHAN ASYLUMS

— **France.**

APPLICATION du système de Mettray aux colonies agricoles d'orphelins et d'enfants trouvés. n.p. [185-?]. pp. 7.

— **United Kingdom.**

HOLMES (G.V.) The likes of us. London, [1948]. pp. 192.

ORTHODOX EASTERN CHURCH, ROMANIAN

— **History.**

HITCHINS (KEITH) Orthodoxy and nationality: Andreiu Şaguna and the Rumanians of Transylvania, 1846-1873. Cambridge, Mass., 1977. pp. 332. *bibliog. (Harvard University. Harvard Historical Studies. vol. 94)*

ORTHODOX EASTERN CHURCH, RUSSIAN.

FREEZE (GREGORY L.) The Russian Levites: parish clergy in the eighteenth century. Cambridge, Mass., 1977. pp. 325. *bibliog. (Harvard University. Russian Research Center. Studies. 78)*

OSWESTRY

— **Economic policy.**

DUESBURY (W.K.) Intermediate areas: a non-event?: the case of Oswestry. Birmingham, 1977. pp. 121,xv. *bibliog. (Birmingham. University. Centre for Urban and Regional Studies. Research Memoranda. No. 58)*

OUDH

— **History.**

PEMBLE (JOHN) The Raj, the Indian Mutiny and the kingdom of Oudh, 1801-1859. Rutherford, N.J., [1977]. pp. 303. *bibliog.*

OXFORD

— **City planning.**

LOODMER (PATRICIA SIMONE) A geographical investigation of the social justice content of urban planning decisions, with special reference to the displacement of the population of St. Ebbe's Parish, Oxford, 1951-1961. [1977]. fo. 392. *Typescript. Ph. D. (London) thesis: unpublished. This thesis is the property of London University and may not be removed from the Library.*

— **Hospitals.**

BURROUGH (E.J.R.) Unity in diversity: the short life of the United Oxford Hospitals. Abingdon, [imprint, 1978]. pp. 282. *Privately printed for the author.*

OXFORD UNIVERSITY

— **Merton College.**

OXFORD. Oxford Historical Society. [Publications]. New Series. vol. 24. Registrum annalium Collegii Mertonensis, 1567-1603; edited by John M. Fletcher. Oxford, 1976. pp. 377.

OXFORD UNIVERSITY PRESS.

SUTCLIFFE (PETER H.) The Oxford University Press: an informal history. Oxford, 1978. pp. 303.

OYO

— **Civilization.**

LAW (ROBIN) The Oyo empire, c.1600-c.1836: a West African imperialism in the era of the Atlantic slave trade. Oxford, 1977. pp. 340. *bibliog.*

PACIFIC, THE

— **Commerce.**

RAW materials and Pacific economic integration; edited by Sir John Crawford and Saburo Okita. London, [1978]. pp. 343. *bibliog. A study by the Australia, Japan and Western Pacific Economic Relations Project.*

— **Foreign economic relations — Australia.**

CRAWFORD (Sir JOHN) and OKITA (SABURO) Australia, Japan and western Pacific economic relations: a report to the governments of Australia and Japan. Canberra, Australian Government Publishing Service, 1976. pp. 325.

— — **Japan.**

CRAWFORD (Sir JOHN) and OKITA (SABURO) Australia, Japan and western Pacific economic relations: a report to the governments of Australia and Japan. Canberra, Australian Government Publishing Service, 1976. pp. 325.

— **Foreign relations.**

SHAW (K.E.) and THOMSON (GEORGE G.) The Straits of Malacca: in relation to the problems of the Indian and Pacific Oceans. Singapore, 1973. pp. 174.

— **Population.**

POPULATION HEADLINERS; [pd. by] Division of Population and Social Affairs, Economic and Social Commission for Asia and the Pacific. irreg., current issues only. Bangkok.

— **Statistics.**

EUROPEAN COMMUNITIES. Statistical Office. ACP: statistical yearbook. a., 1970/76 (1st)- Luxembourg. *[in English and French]*

PACIFIC OCEAN

— **Navigation.**

LEMAÎTRE (YVES) Les relations inter-insulaires traditionnelles en Océanie (Tonga): premières données sur l'application d'une méthode mathématique. Paris, [1964?]. fo. 15. *bibliog. (Paris. Ecole Pratique des Hautes Etudes. Centre Documentaire pour l'Océanie. Rapports et Documents. 2)*

PACIFIC SETTLEMENT OF INTERNATIONAL DISPUTES.

SNYDER (GLENN HERALD) and DIESING (PAUL) Conflict among nations: bargaining, decision making, and system structure in international crises. Princeton, N.J., [1977]. pp. 578. *bibliogs.*

PACIFISM

— **Bibliography.**

VAN DEN DUNGEN (PETER) compiler. A bibliography of the pacifist writings of Jean de Bloch. London, 1977. pp. 28.

PAKENHAM (FRANCIS AUNGIER) 7th Earl of Longford.

CRAIG (MARY) Longford: a biographical portrait. London, [1978]. pp. 220.

PAKISTAN.

WEEKLY PAKISTAN NEWS (formerly Pakistan news); [pd. by] Directorate of Films and Publications. w., My 5 1977 (v.1,no.1)- [Islamabad].

— **Constitution.**

PAKISTAN. Information and Broadcasting Division. Directorate of Research, Reference and Publications. 1976. Constitutional amendments: facts and fiction. [Islamabad, 1976?]. pp. 16.

— Constitutional history.

FELDMAN (HERBERT) The end and the beginning: Pakistan, 1969-1971. London, 1975. pp. 210.

ALI (MAHMUD) Quaid-i-Azam as a constitutionalist. Islamabad, National Committee for Birth Centenary Celebrations of Quaid-i-Azam Mohammad Ali Jinnah, 1976. pp. 88. *bibliog.*

— Description and travel.

KUREISHI (RAFIUSHAN) The new Pakistan. London, [1977]. pp. 146.

— Economic conditions.

PAKISTAN. Ministry of Economic Affairs. 1956. Progress of economic development in Pakistan. 2nd ed. Karachi, 1956. pp. 159.

PAKISTAN. Ministry of Information and Broadcasting. Directorate of Research, Reference and Publications. 1976. Partners in prosperity: economic resources and inter-dependence of provinces. [Islamabad, 1976?]. pp. 38.

AHMED (AKBAR S.) Social and economic change in the tribal areas, 1972-1976. Karachi, 1977. pp. 81. *bibliog.*

— Economic history.

PAKISTAN. Economic Adviser to the Government of Pakistan. 1968. Economy of Pakistan, 1948-1968: a summary. [Karachi, 1968]. pp. 58.

— Economic policy.

PAKISTAN. Ministry of Information and Broadcasting. Directorate of Research, Reference and Publications. 1976. Partners in prosperity: economic resources and inter-dependence of provinces. [Islamabad, 1976?]. pp. 38.

PAKISTAN. Ministry of Information and Broadcasting. Directorate of Research, Reference and Publications. 1977. Promises and performance: a report by the government of Pakistan on the implementation of the 1970 manifesto of the Pakistan People's Party. [Islamabad], 1977. pp. 261.

— Foreign relations.

FOREIGN AFFAIRS PAKISTAN; pd. by the Ministry of Foreign Affairs [Pakistan]. m., [Je 1974 (v.1, no.1)]- Islamabad.

FOOT (ROSEMARY JUNE) New areas of tension and great power rivalry: central west Asia and Sino-Soviet relations, 1962-1974. 1976 [or rather 1977]. fo. 353. *bibliog.* Typescript. Ph.D. (London) thesis: unpublished. This thesis is the property of London University and may not be removed from the Library.

PAKISTAN. Ministry of Information and Broadcasting. Directorate of Research, Reference and Publications. 1977. Promises and performance: a report by the government of Pakistan on the implementation of the 1970 manifesto of the Pakistan People's Party. [Islamabad], 1977. pp. 261.

PAKISTAN: the long view; [by] William J. Barnds [and others]; edited by Lawrence Ziring [and others]. Durham, N.C., 1977. pp. 485. *(Duke University. Center for Commonwealth and Comparative Studies. [Publications]. No. 43) A selection of papers from the Wayne Ayres Wilcox Memorial Symposium held in Rougemont, North Carolina, 1974.*

— — East (Near East).

PAKISTAN. President, 1958-1969 (Ayub Khan). 1967. Pakistan's support to the Arabs: speeches and statements by the President and the Foreign Minister of Pakistan, May- July 1967. [Karachi, 1967]. pp. 27.

— — Iran.

PAKISTAN. Information and Broadcasting Division. Directorate of Research, Reference and Publications. 1975. Iran Pakistan friendship. [Islamabad, 1975?]. 1 vol. (unpaged).

— — Mohammedan countries.

PAKISTAN. Ministry of Foreign Affairs. 1977. Pakistan's relations with the Islamic states: a review. [Islamabad], 1977. pp. 34.

— History.

PAKISTAN. National Committee for Birth Centenary Celebrations of Quaid-i-Azam Mohammad Ali Jinnah. 1976. Reminiscences of the day of deliverance. Islamabad, 1976. pp. 114.

KUREISHI (RAFIUSHAN) The new Pakistan. London, [1977]. pp. 146.

— Occupations.

PAKISTAN. Central Statistical Office. Economic Affairs Division. 1965- . Pakistan standard classification of occupations: PSCO. [Karachi, 1965 in progress].

— Politics and government.

JINNAH (MOHAMED ALI) Thus spoke the father: a code of political conduct as prescribed by the Quaid-i-Azam. [Islamabad, Ministry of Information and Broadcasting, Directorate of Research, Reference and Publications, 1966]. pp. 47.

FELDMAN (HERBERT) The end and the beginning: Pakistan, 1969-1971. London, 1975. pp. 210.

PAKISTAN. Information and Broadcasting Division. Directorate of Research, Reference and Publications. 1976. Constitutional amendments: facts and fiction. [Islamabad, 1976?]. pp. 16.

PAKISTAN. Ministry of Information and Broadcasting. Directorate of Research, Reference and Publications. 1977. Promises and performance: a report by the government of Pakistan on the implementation of the 1970 manifesto of the Pakistan People's Party. [Islamabad], 1977. pp. 261.

PAKISTAN. Supreme Court. 1977. Supreme court judgement on Begum Nusrat Bhutto's petition challenging detention of Z.A. Bhutto and others under Martial Law Order 12 of 1977. Lahore, 1977. pp. 120.

PAKISTAN: the long view; [by] William J. Barnds [and others]; edited by Lawrence Ziring [and others]. Durham, N.C., 1977. pp. 485. *(Duke University. Center for Commonwealth and Comparative Studies. [Publications]. No. 43) A selection of papers from the Wayne Ayres Wilcox Memorial Symposium held in Rougemont, North Carolina, 1974.*

PAKISTAN'S western borderlands: the transformation of a political order; edited by Ainslie T. Embree. New Delhi, [1977]. pp. 158. *bibliogs. Based on one of a series of seminars run by the Columbia University Southern Asian Institute, National Seminar on Pakistan.*

PAKISTAN. National Committee. 1978. Bhutto: the truth about his rule and trial. Karachi, [1978]. pp. 59.

PAKISTAN. Statutes, etc. 1977-1978. Martial law regulations. [Islamabad], 1978. pp. 67.

PUNJAB (PAKISTAN). High Court. 1978. Judgment in murder trial: state vs Zulfikar Ali Bhutto and others. [Lahore, 1978]. pp. 134.

QAYYUM (ABDUL) Bhutto and the demands of justice. [Islamabad, 1978]. pp. 15.

— Social policy.

PAKISTAN. Ministry of Information and Broadcasting. Directorate of Research, Reference and Publications. 1977. Promises and performance: a report by the government of Pakistan on the implementation of the 1970 manifesto of the Pakistan People's Party. [Islamabad], 1977. pp. 261.

PAKISTANIS IN THE UNITED KINGDOM.

BIRMINGHAM COMMUNITY DEVELOPMENT PROJECT. People in paper chains; [by Sylvia Whitfield). [Oxford], 1977. pp. 32. *bibliog. (Final Reports. No.3: Immigration and the State)*

PALEOCLIMATOLOGY.

BRYSON (REID A.) and MURRAY (THOMAS J.) Climates of hunger: mankind and the world's changing weather. Madison, 1977. pp. 171. *bibliog.*

PALESTINE

— History.

KIERNAN (THOMAS) Yasir Arafat: the man and the myth. London, 1976. pp. 223.

BOWDEN (TOM) The breakdown of public security: the case of Ireland, 1916-1921 and Palestine, 1936-1939. London, [1977]. pp. 342. *bibliog.*

CAPLAN (NEIL) Palestine Jewry and the Arab question, 1917-1925. London, 1978. pp. 268. *bibliog.*

KAYYALI (ABDUL-WAHHAB) Palestine: a modern history. London, [1978]. pp. 243. *bibliog.*

— — 1917-1948.

COHEN (MICHAEL JOSEPH) Palestine: retreat from the mandate: the making of British policy, 1936-45. London, 1978. pp. 239. *bibliog.*

— Politics and government.

CAPLAN (NEIL) Palestine Jewry and the Arab question, 1917-1925. London, 1978. pp. 268. *bibliog.*

PALESTINIAN ARABS.

BERTELSEN (JUDY S.) The Palestinian Arabs: a non-state nation systems analysis. Beverly Hills, [1976]. pp. 81. *bibliog.*

KAHN (ARTHUR) and MURRAY (THOMAS F.) The Palestinians: a political masquerade. London, [1977]. pp. 40.

OUR roots are still alive: the story of the Palestinian people; written by the Palestine Book Project; Joy Bonds [and others]. San Francisco, 1977. pp. 189. *bibliog.*

TUMA (ELIAS HANNA) and DARIN-DRABKIN (HAIM) The economic case for Palestine. London, [1978]. pp. 126. *bibliog.*

— Israel.

JUREIDINI (PAUL A.) and HAZEN (WILLIAM EDWARD) The Palestinian movement in politics. Lexington, Mass., [1976]. pp. 139. *bibliog.*

— Jordan.

MISHAL (SHAUL) West bank, east bank: the Palestinians in Jordan, 1949-1967. New Haven, 1978. pp. 129.

PANAFRICANISM.

DIOP (CHEIKH ANTA) Les fondements économiques et culturels d'un état fédéral d'Afrique Noire. Paris, [1974]. pp. 126.

MATHURIN (OWEN CHARLES) Henry Sylvester Williams and the origins of the pan-African movement, 1869-1911. Westport, Conn., 1976. pp. 183. *bibliog.*

ASANTE (SAMUEL KINGSLEY BOTWE) Pan-African protest: west Africa and the Italo- Ethiopian crisis, 1934-1941. London, 1977. pp. 243. *bibliog.*

BLACK separatism and social reality: rhetoric and reason; editor Raymond L. Hall. New York, [1977]. pp. 280.

CHIME (CHIMELU) Integration and politics among African states: limitations and horizons of mid-term theorizing. Uppsala, 1977. pp. 436.

RENNIE (RHODA ELIZABETH McKENZIE) Nkrumah, greatest of modern philosophers. New York, [1977]. pp. 125.

PANAMA

PANAMA
— Economic conditions.

GUDEMAN (STEPHEN) The demise of a rural economy: from subsistence to capitalism in a Latin American village. London, 1978. pp. 176. *bibliog.*

— Foreign relations — United States.

RYAN (PAUL B.) The Panama Canal controversy: U.S. diplomacy and defence interests. Stanford, Calif., [1977]. pp. 198. *bibliog. (Stanford University. Hoover Institution on War, Revolution and Peace. Hoover Institution Publications. 187)*

LAFEBER (WALTER FREDERICK) The Panama Canal: the crisis in historical perspective. New York, 1978. pp. xii,248. *bibliog.*

— History.

ALFARO (RICARDO JOAQUIN) Vida del General Tomas Herrera;...prologo de Guillermo Andreve. Barcelona, 1909. pp. 351. *bibliog.*

— Rural conditions.

GUDEMAN (STEPHEN) The demise of a rural economy: from subsistence to capitalism in a Latin American village. London, 1978. pp. 176. *bibliog.*

PANAMA CANAL.

RYAN (PAUL B.) The Panama Canal controversy: U.S. diplomacy and defence interests. Stanford, Calif., [1977]. pp. 198. *bibliog. (Stanford University. Hoover Institution on War, Revolution and Peace. Hoover Institution Publications. 187)*

LAFEBER (WALTER FREDERICK) The Panama Canal: the crisis in historical perspective. New York, 1978. pp. xii,248. *bibliog.*

PANAMERICANISM.

INGENIEROS (JOSE) La universidad del porvenir: America Latina y el imperialismo. Buenos Aires, 1956. pp. 47.

FRANCIS (MICHAEL J.) The limits of hegemony: United States relations with Argentina and Chile during World War II. Notre Dame, [1977]. pp. 292. *(Notre Dame. University. Committee on International Relations. International Studies)*

GASPAR (EDMUND) United States - Latin America: a special relationship? Washington, D.C., [1978]. pp. 90. *(American Institute for Public Policy Research and Stanford University. Hoover Institution on War, Revolution and Peace. AEI-Hoover Policy Studies. 26)*

PAPACY
— History.

POLIAKOV (LEON) Jewish bankers and the Holy See from the thirteenth to the seventeenth century;...translated from the French by Miriam Kochan. London, 1977. pp. 275.

CHADWICK (WILLIAM OWEN) Catholicism and history: the opening of the Vatican archives. Cambridge, 1978. pp. 174. *bibliog. (Oxford. University. Herbert Hensley Henson Lectures. 1976)*

PAPER MAKING AND TRADE
— Canada — British Columbia.

BRITISH COLUMBIA HYDRO AND POWER AUTHORITY. Industrial Development Department. The pulp and paper industry of British Columbia. 2nd ed. Vancouver, 1966. pp. 68.

— United Kingdom.

CHITTY (JEAN) Paper in Devon. Exeter, 1976. pp. 72. *bibliog.*

— Zambia.

ZAMBIA. Central Statistical Office. 1976. Paper, paper products, printing and publishing industries. Lusaka, 1976. fo. 44. *bibliog. (Industry Monographs. No. 4)*

PAPER MONEY
— Argentine Republic.

ARIAS (DAVID M.) Historia e influencia del papel moneda en el desenvolvimiento economico argentino. Buenos Aires, 1912. pp. 116.

PAPIAMENTU.

GOILO (ENRIQUE R.) Papiamentu textbook. Aruba, Netherlands Antilles, [1962]. pp. 150.

PAPUA NEW GUINEA
— Commerce.

PAPUA NEW GUINEA. Bureau of Statistics. Statistical bulletin: export price indexes. q., Je 1977- Port Moresby.

— Constitution.

PAPUA NEW GUINEA. Constitution. 1975. The constitution of the independent state of Papua New Guinea. Port Moresby, 1975. pp. 123.

— Economic policy.

PAPUA NEW GUINEA. Office of the Economic Adviser. 1969. East New Britain draft economic development programme. [Port Moresby?], 1969. 1 vol. (various pagings)

PAPUA NEW GUINEA. Office of the Economic Adviser. 1969. Eastern Highlands district draft economic development programme. [Port Moresby?], 1969. fo. 48.

PAPUA NEW GUINEA. Office of the Economic Adviser. 1969. Madang district draft economic development programme. [Port Moresby?], 1969. 1 vol. (unpaged)

PAPUA NEW GUINEA. Office of the Economic Adviser. 1969. New Ireland draft economic development programme. [Port Moresby?], 1969. pp. 31.

PAPUA NEW GUINEA. Central Planning Office. 1976. The post-independence national development strategy; (Papua New Guinea government white paper). Waigani, 1976. pp. 50.

PAPUA NEW GUINEA. National Planning Office. 1978. The national public expenditure plan 1978-1981. [Port Moresby], 1978. pp. 167.

— Social policy.

PAPUA NEW GUINEA. Office of the Economic Adviser. 1969. East New Britain draft economic development programme. [Port Moresby?], 1969. 1 vol. (various pagings)

PAPUA NEW GUINEA. Office of the Economic Adviser. 1969. Eastern Highlands district draft economic development programme. [Port Moresby?], 1969. fo. 48.

PAPUA NEW GUINEA. Office of the Economic Adviser. 1969. Madang district draft economic development programme. [Port Moresby?], 1969. 1 vol. (unpaged)

PAPUA NEW GUINEA. Office of the Economic Adviser. 1969. New Ireland draft economic development programme. [Port Moresby?], 1969. pp. 31.

PAPUA NEW GUINEA. Central Planning Office. 1976. The post-independence national development strategy; (Papua New Guinea government white paper). Waigani, 1976. pp. 50.

PAPUA NEW GUINEA. National Planning Office. 1978. The national public expenditure plan 1978-1981. [Port Moresby], 1978. pp. 167.

PARA
— Description and travel.

COUDREAU (HENRI) Viagem ao Tapajos;...tradução Eugênio Amado. Belo Horizonte, 1977. pp. 162. *First published, in French, in Paris, 1897.*

COUDREAU (HENRI) Viagem ao Xingu;...tradução Eugênio Amado. Belo Horizonte, 1977. pp. 165. *First published, in French, in Paris, 1897.*

PARA (STATE)
— Social history.

SALLES (VICENTE) O negro no Para: sob o regime da escravidão. Rio de Janeiro, 1971. pp. 336. *bibliog. (Universidade Federal do Para. Coleção Amazônica. Serie Jose Verissimo)*

PARAGUAY
— History.

LÓPEZ (ADALBERTO) The revolt of the comuñeros, 1721-1735: a study in the colonial history of Paraguay. Cambridge, Mass., [1976]. pp. 214. *bibliog.*

— Politics and government.

SOSA JOVELLANOS (FRANCISCO) La revolucion y su ideologia: en memoria de los heroes y martires caidos en holocausto de la revolucion. Asuncion, 1969. pp. 40.

— Population.

CENTRO PARAGUAYO DE ESTUDIOS SOCIOLOGICOS. La poblacion del Paraguay. [Asuncion, 1974]. pp. 196. *bibliog. (Committee for International Coordination of National Research in Demography. C.I.C.R.E.D. Series)*

— Rural conditions.

FOGEL (RAMON) Analisis de una pequeña comunidad rural: estudio de la Colonia Pirareta. Asunción, 1967. pp. 39.

PARAMILITARY FORCES
— Germany.

DIEHL (JAMES M.) Paramilitary politics in Weimar Germany. Bloomington, Ind., [1977]. pp. 406. *bibliog.*

PARENT AND CHILD.

INGLIS (RUTH) Sins of the fathers: a study of the physical and emotional abuse of children. London, 1978. pp. 220. *bibliog.*

PARETO (VILFREDO).

FIOROT (DINO) Politica e scienza in Vilfredo Pareto: contributo alla storia della scienza politica. [Milano, 1975]. pp. 227.

PARETO (VILFREDO) Lo sviluppo economico italiano [a collection of articles]; [with an introductory essay by] Lucio Avagliano. [Salerno, 1975]. pp. 219.

LOMBARDO (ANTONIO) Teorie del potere politico: Mosca e Pareto. Bologna, [1976]. pp. 146.

BUSINO (GIOVANNI) Vilfredo Pareto e l'industria del ferro nel Valdarno: contributo alla storia dell'impreditorialità italiana. Milano, 1977. pp. 922. *(Banco Commerciale Italiana. Studi e Ricerche di Storia Economica Italiana nell'Età del Risorgimento) A considerable appendix of Pareto's letters on the subject.*

CIRILLO (RENATO) The economics of Vilfredo Pareto. London, 1979[or rather 1978]. pp. 148. *bibliog.*

PARIS
— City planning.

ATELIER PARISIEN D'URBANISME. Schéma directeur d'aménagement et d'urbanisme de la ville de Paris: rapport. [Paris, 1977]. 4 pts. (in 1 vol.) *3 folding maps bound at end.*

CHEVALIER (LOUIS) Demographer. L'assassinat de Paris. [Paris, 1977]. pp. 287.

— **Foreign population.**

OGDEN (P.E.) Foreigners in Paris: residential segregation in the nineteenth and twentieth centuries. London, 1977. pp. 71. *bibliog.* (London. University. Queen Mary College. Department of Geography. *Occasional Papers. No. 11*)

— **History.**

WEINBERG (DAVID H.) A community on trial: the Jews of Paris in the 1930s. Chicago, 1977. pp. 239. *bibliog.*

— — **1871, Commune.**

VARLIN (EUGENE) Pratique militante: écrits d'un ouvrier communard; présenté par Paule Lejeune. Paris, 1977. pp. 190.

— — — **Personal narratives.**

[BROCHER (VICTORINE)] Souvenirs d'une morte vivante; [by] Victorine B...; préface de Lucien Descaves. Paris, 1976. pp. 246. *Reprint of 1909 Paris edition with a new introductory note.*

— **Politics and government.**

FRANC (MICHEL) and LECLERC (JEAN PIERRE) Les institutions de la région parisienne: du district à l'Ile-de-France. [n.p., 1977]. pp. 191. *bibliog.*

— **Riot, 1968 — Posters.**

GASQUET (VASCO) Les 500 affiches de mai 68. [Paris], 1978. pp. 220.

— **Social history.**

MOUSNIER (ROLAND) Recherches sur la stratification sociale à Paris aux XVIIe et XVIIIe siècles: l'échantillon de 1634, 1635, 1636. Paris, 1976. pp. 141. *bibliog.* (Paris. Université de Paris IV (Paris-Sorbonne). *Publications. Nouvelle Série. Recherches. 22*)

PARIS (REGION)

— **Economic conditions — Statistics.**

TABLEAUX ECONOMIQUES DE LA REGION PARISIENNE; [pd. by] Institut National de la Statistique et des Etudes Economiques, Direction Régionale de Paris [France]. a., 1972- Paris.

— **Politics and government.**

PICKVANCE (CHRISTOPHER GEOFFREY) Marxist approaches to the study of urban politics: divergences among some recent French studies. Canterbury, 1976. fo. 52. *Paper for the Political Studies Association Conference, Nottingham, 1976.*

PARISHES

— **France.**

TACKETT (TIMOTHY) Priest and parish in eighteenth-century France: a social and political study of the curés in a diocese of Dauphiné, 1750- 1791. Princeton, N.J., [1977]. pp. 350. *bibliog.*

PARLIAMENTARY PRACTICE

— **Australia.**

CONFERENCE OF PRESIDING OFFICERS AND CLERKS OF THE PARLIAMENTS OF AUSTRALIA, FIJI, NAURU, PAPUA NEW GUINEA AND WESTERN SAMOA, 5TH, PERTH, 1972. [Papers and proceedings]. in AUSTRALIA. Parliament. Parliamentary papers, 1972, vol. 7.

PARNAIBA VALLEY

— **Economic conditions.**

DE CASTRO ANDRADE (REGIS) On the relationship between the subsistence sector and the market economy in the Parnaiba Valley (Brazil). Glasgow, 1976. pp. 24. (Glasgow. University. Institute of Latin American Studies. *Occasional Papers. No.22*)

PARNELL (CHARLES STEWART).

LYONS (FRANCIS STEWART LELAND) Charles Stewart Parnell. London, 1977. pp. 704. *bibliog.*

PAROLE

— **United Kingdom.**

HAWKINS (KEITH) compiler. The parole decision: a guide compiled from official sources. Chichester, 1977. pp. 28.

PAROLE: the case for change; [by] Paul Cavadino [and others]. Chichester, [1977?]. pp. 40.

— **United States.**

GOTTFREDSON (DON M.) and others. Guidelines for parole and sentencing: a policy control method. Lexington, Mass., [1978]. pp. 212.

PARSONS (LUCY ELLA).

ASHBAUGH (CAROLYN) Lucy Parsons: American revolutionary. Chicago, 1976. pp. 288. *bibliog.*

PARSONS (TALCOTT).

EXPLORATIONS in general theory in social science: essays in honor of Talcott Parsons; edited by Jan J. Loubser [and others]. New York, [1976]. 2 vols.

PART-TIME EMPLOYMENT

— **Canada — Manitoba.**

MANITOBA. Women's Bureau. Brandon Office. 1976. A study of part-time employment;...written by Joan Simpkins. Brandon, 1976. pp. 39.

PART-TIME FARMING

— **Poland.**

MUSZYŃSKI (MAREK) Transfomacja ludności dwunzawodowej. Warszawa, 1976. pp. 144. *bibliog.* (Polska Akademia Nauk. Instytut Rozwoju Wsi i Rolnictwa. *Problemy Rozwoju Wsi i Rolnictwa*) With Russian and English summaries.

PARTI QUEBECOIS.

MURRAY (VĚRA) Le Parti québécois: de la fondation à la prise du pouvoir. Montréal, [1976]. pp. 242. *bibliog.*

PARTIDO CARLISTA.

BORBON PARMA (CARLOS HUGO DE) La via carlista al socialismo autogestionario: el proyecto carlista de socialismo democratico. Barcelona, 1977. pp. 387.

PARTIDO CARLISTA. Frente Obrero. Asamblea Federal, 1a, 1976. I Asamblea Federal del Frente Obrero del Partido Carlista; [by] Carlos Carnicero [and others]. Madrid, [1977]. pp. 67.

PARTIDO COMUNISTA DEL PERU.

PARTIDO COMUNISTA DEL PERU. Comite Central. Informe politico, VII Conferencia Nacional: sobre el caracter de la sociedad y los problemas de la revolucion peruana. [Lisbon?], 1972. pp. 146.

PARTIDO DEMOCRATA PROGRESISTA.

TORRE (LISANDRO DE LA) Las dos campañas presidenciales, 1916-1931. Buenos Aires, 1939. pp. 255. (*Escritos y Discursos. 1*)

PARTIDO PROVERISTA.

MAYSOUNAVE (MANUEL) Partido Proverista. Bilbao, 1977. pp. 127.

PARTIJ VAN DE ARBEID.

TANS (JEAN GUILLAUME HUBERT) Tans of nooit: een onduidelijke brochure. [Amsterdam, 1967]. pp. 28.

PARTIT NACIONALISTA REPUBLICA D'ESQUERRA.

CULLA I CLARA (JOAN B.) El catalanisme d'esquerra: del Grup de "L'Opinio" al Partit Nacionalista Republica d'Esquerra, 1928-1936. Barcelona, 1977. pp. 428. *bibliog.*

PARTITO COMUNISTA D'ITALIA (MARXISTA-LENINISTA).

Il "QUADERNO dell'attivista": ideologia, organizzazione e propaganda nel PCI degli anni cinquanta; a cura di Marcello Flores. [Milano, 1976]. pp. 219.

PARTITO DI UNITÀ PROLETARIA PER IL COMUNISMO.

PELLEGRINI (ROCCO) and PEPE (GUGLIELMO) Unire è difficile: breve storia del PdUP per il comunismo; (colloqui con V. Foa, etc.). Roma, [1977]. pp. 189.

PARTITO POPOLARE ITALIANO.

SPATARO (GIUSEPPE) De Gasperi e il Partito Popolare Italiano. Roma, [1975]. pp. 118.

MENIS (PIETRO) Dal Partito Popolare Italiano alla Democrazia Cristiana, 1918-1964: memorie di un politico di paese. [Udine, 1977]. pp. 95.

PARTITO RADICALE (ITALY).

AGHINA (GUIDO) and JACCARINO (CLAUDIO) Storia del Partito Radicale. [Milano, 1977]. pp. 158. *With appendix of 32 photographic plates.*

PARTITO SOCIALISTA ITALIANO.

AVOLIO (GIUSEPPE) Agricoltura e sviluppo: la politica agraria del Partito Socialista dal 1973 al 1975. [Venezia, 1976]. pp. 364. *bibliog.*

PARTNERSHIP

— **United States.**

CARY (WILLIAM LUCIUS) Cases and materials on partnership planning: introductory pamphlet. Mineola, N.Y., 1970. pp. 98.

PARTY AFFILIATION

— **Canada.**

SMITH (PATRICK JOSEPH) The sociology of urban party organizations and political behaviour: contemporary party membership with special reference to England and Canada. 1977. fo. 362. *bibliog.* Typescript. Ph.D. (London) thesis: unpublished. *This thesis is the property of London University and may not be removed from the Library.*

— **Finland.**

PESTOFF (VICTOR ALEXIS) Voluntary associations and Nordic party systems: a study of overlapping membership and cross-pressures in Finland, Norway and Sweden. Stockholm, 1977. pp. 200. *bibliog.* (Stockholms Universitet. Statsvetenskapliga Institutionen. *Stockholm Studies in Politics.10*)

— **Norway.**

PESTOFF (VICTOR ALEXIS) Voluntary associations and Nordic party systems: a study of overlapping membership and cross-pressures in Finland, Norway and Sweden. Stockholm, 1977. pp. 200. *bibliog.* (Stockholms Universitet. Statsvetenskapliga Institutionen. *Stockholm Studies in Politics.10*)

— **Russia.**

BRYM (ROBERT J.) The Jewish intelligentsia and Russian Marxism: a sociological study of intellectual radicalism and ideological divergence. London, 1978. pp. 157. *bibliog.*

— **Sweden.**

PESTOFF (VICTOR ALEXIS) Voluntary associations and Nordic party systems: a study of overlapping membership and cross-pressures in Finland, Norway and Sweden. Stockholm, 1977. pp. 200. *bibliog.* (Stockholms Universitet. Statsvetenskapliga Institutionen. *Stockholm Studies in Politics.10*)

PARTY AFFILIATION(Cont.)

— United Kingdom.

SMITH (PATRICK JOSEPH) The sociology of urban party organizations and political behaviour: contemporary party membership with special reference to England and Canada. 1977. fo. 362. *bibliog.* Typescript. *Ph.D. (London) thesis: unpublished. This thesis is the property of London University and may not be removed from the Library.*

— United States.

RAINE (ALDEN S.) Change in the political agenda: social and cultural conflict in the American electorate. Beverly Hills, [1977]. pp. 60. *bibliog.*

PASCAL (PIERRE).

PASCAL (PIERRE) En communisme: mon journal de Russie, 1918-1921. [Lausanne, 1977]. pp. 226.

PASSIVE RESISTANCE.

WAR RESISTERS' INTERNATIONAL. WRI statements: a selection of statements and resolutions from the WRI 1963-July 1972. London, [1972]. pp. 56.

PASSPORTS.

[SCANDINAVIA]. Nordiske Parlamentariske Komité for Friere Samfaerdsel. 1956. Slutbetaenkning. København, 1956. pp. 50. *(Denmark. Betaenkninger. Nr. 166)*

PATENTS

— Australia.

AUSTRALIA. Patent Office. Report. a., 1972/73(1st)- Canberra. *Included in AUSTRALIA. Parliament. [Parliamentary papers].*

PAUL, Saint and Apostle.

LAKE (JOHN W.) Paul: the disowned apostle; a survey of the origin of Christianity. London. 1876. pp. 60.

PEACE.

ARNAUD (EMILE) L'organisation de la paix. Berne, Bureau International de la Paix, 1899. pp. 61.

BAILEY (ALICE ANNE) The coming world order. Bath, 1940. pp. 32.

DONINGTON (ROBERT) ed. Peace aims: a summary of unofficial British opinion expressed since the war; prepared...for the National Peace Council. London, 1940. pp. 67.

YOUNG (NIGEL) On war, national liberation and the state. London, [1971?]. pp. 16. *bibliog.*

JOHNSON (L. GUNNAR) Conflicting concepts of peace in contemporary peace studies. Beverly Hills, [1976]. pp. 63. *bibliog.*

LAMONT (VICTOR) and HIGHFIELD (JOHN) Writer on peace. Hungry for peace. New York, [1976]. pp. 63.

BOGNÁR (JÓZSEF) The fight for a new system of international relations. Budapest, 1977. pp. 28. *(Hungarian Scientific Council for World Economy. [Publications]. Trends in World Economy. No. 21)*

BOLT (ERNEST C.) Ballots before bullets: the war referendum approach to peace in America, 1914-1941. Charlottesville, Va., 1977. pp. 207. *bibliog.*

DECLARATIONS on principles: a quest for universal peace; edited by Robert J. Akkerman [and others]. Leyden, 1977. pp. 403. *bibliog. In honour of Prof. Dr. Bert V. A. Röling.*

INSTITUTE FOR WORLD ORDER. Ten minutes for peace: "you have to begin peace within yourself". 4th ed. New York, [1977?]. 1 pamphlet (unpaged).

ZIEGLER (DAVID W.) War, peace, and international politics. Boston, Mass., [1977]. pp. 444.

AMERICAN thinking about peace and war; [edited by] Ken Booth and Moorhead Wright. Hassocks, 1978. pp. 240. *Proceedings of a Conference held in 1976 by the Department of International Politics, University College of Wales, Aberystwyth, at Gregynog Hall, Powys.*

DOVES and diplomats: foreign offices and peace movements in Europe and America in the twentieth century; edited by Solomon Wank. Westport, Conn., 1978. pp. 303.

PEANUTS

— India.

BULLETIN ON GROUNDNUT STATISTICS IN INDIA: DISTRICT-WISE; [pd. by] Directorate of Economics and Statistics, Ministry of Agriculture and Irrigation. a., 1976(1st)- New Delhi.

PEARL HARBOR, ATTACK ON, 1941.

MELOSI (MARTIN V.) The shadow of Pearl Harbor: political controversy over the surprise attack, 1941-1946. College Station, Tex., [1977]. pp. 183. *bibliog.*

PEARSE (PATRICK).

CARTY (XAVIER) In bloody protest: the tragedy of Patrick Pearse. Dublin, [1978]. pp. 154. *bibliog.*

PEARSON (ANTHONY).

PEARSON (ANTHONY) Journalist. Conspiracy of silence. London, 1978. pp. 179.

PEARSON (LESTER BOWLES).

THORDARSON (BRUCE) Lester Pearson: diplomat and politician. Toronto, 1974. pp. 245. *bibliog.*

PEASANT UPRISINGS

— China.

HOFHEINZ (ROY) The broken wave: the Chinese Communist peasant movement, 1922- 1928. Cambridge, Mass., 1977. pp. 355. *bibliog. (Harvard University. East Asian Research Center. Harvard East Asian Series. 90)*

— Germany.

Die SALPETERER...; herausgegeben von Thomas Lehner. Berlin, [1977]. pp. 125. *bibliog.*

— India.

STOKES (ERIC) The peasant and the Raj: studies in agrarian society and peasant rebellion in colonial India. Cambridge, 1978. pp. 308. *(Cambridge. University. Centre of South Asian Studies. Cambridge South Asian Studies. 23)*

— Yugoslavia — Bosnia.

POPOVIĆ (VASILJ) Agrarno pitanje u Bosni i turski neredi za vreme reformnog režima Abdul-Medžida, 1839-1861. Beograd, 1949. pp. 323. *(Srpska Akademija Nauka i Umetnosti. Posebna Izdanja. knj. 150 [being also] Odeljenje Društvenih Nauka. knj. 59) In Cyrillic.*

PEASANTRY.

PEASANT livelihood: studies in economic anthropology and cultural ecology; Rhoda Halperin [and] James Dow, editors. New York, [1977]. pp. 332. *bibliog.*

— America, Latin.

FEDER (ERNEST) Dr., of the University of Nebraska, ed. La lucha de clases en el campo: analisis estructural de la economia agricola latinoamericana. Mexico, 1975. pp. 520. *bibliogs. (Fondo de Cultura Economica. Lecturas. 14)*

— Asia, Southeast.

SCOTT (JAMES C.) The moral economy of the peasant: rebellion and subsistence in Southeast Asia. New Haven, [1976] repr. 1977. pp. 246.

— Bulgaria.

BELL (JOHN D.) Peasants in power: Alexander Stamboliski and the Bulgarian Agrarian National Union, 1899-1923. Princeton, [1977]. pp. 271. *bibliog.*

— Byzantine Empire.

LAIOU-THOMADAKIS (ANGELIKI E.) Peasant society in the late Byzantine Empire: a social and demographic study. Princeton, [1977]. pp. 332. *bibliog.*

— Chile.

KAY (CRISTOBAL) Chile: an appraisal of Popular Unity's agrarian reform. [Glasgow, 1974]. pp. 21. *(Glasgow. University. Institute of Latin American Studies. Occasional Papers. No.13)*

CASTEX (PATRICK) "Voie chilienne" au socialisme et luttes paysannes: approche théorique et pratique d'une transition capitaliste non révolutionnaire. Paris, 1977. pp. 296.

— Denmark.

ZERLANG (MARTIN) Bøndernes klassekamp i Danmark: agrarsmåborgerskabets sociale og ideologiske udvikling fra landboreformernes tid til systemskiftet. København, 1976. pp. 410.

— Dominican Republic.

SHARPE (KENNETH EVAN) Peasant politics: struggle in a Dominican village. Baltimore, Md., [1977]. pp. 263. *bibliog.*

— France.

GAUTHIER (FLORENCE) La voie paysanne dans la Révolution française: l'exemple de la Picardie. Paris, 1977. pp. 241. *bibliog.*

— Germany.

STRAUB (ALFRED) Das badische Oberland im 18. Jahrhundert: die Transformation einer bäuerlichen Gesellschaft vor der Industrialisierung. Husum, [1977]. pp. 173. *bibliog.*

— India.

SCHWERIN (DETLEF) Graf. Von Armut zu Elend: Kolonialherrschaft und Agrarverfassung in Chota Nagpur, 1858-1908. Wiesbaden, 1977. pp. 551. *bibliog. (Heidelberg. Universität. Südasien-Institut. Beiträge zur Südasienforschung. Band 31) With English summary.*

STOKES (ERIC) The peasant and the Raj: studies in agrarian society and peasant rebellion in colonial India. Cambridge, 1978. pp. 308. *(Cambridge. University. Centre of South Asian Studies. Cambridge South Asian Studies. 23)*

— Italy.

SFRUTTAMENTO e subalternità nel mondo contadino meridionale; ([by] Pino De Angelis [and others]); con un intervento di Luigi M. Lombardi Satriani. Roma, 1975. 1 vol. (unpaged). *Photographs.*

— Malaya.

LIM TECK GHEE Peasants and their agricultural economy in colonial Malaya, 1874- 1941. Kuala Lumpur, 1977. pp. 291. *bibliog.*

— Peru.

COTLER (JULIO) and PORTOCARRERO (FELIPE) Organizaciones campesinas en el Peru. Lima, 1967. pp. 33. *(Instituto de Estudios Peruanos. Los Movimientos Campesinos en el Peru desde Fines del Siglo XVIII hasta nuestros Dias. No. 1)*

COTLER (JULIO) Haciendas y comunidades tradicionales en un contexto de movilizacion politica. Lima, 1968. pp. 29. *(Instituto de Estudios Peruanos. Estudios del Valle de Urubamba. No. 1)*

PADRON CASTILLO (MARIO) and PEASE GARCIA (HENRY) Planificacion rural, reforma agraria y organizacion campesina: programa de promocion campesina en el Valle del Santa 1971-1973. Lima, 1974. 2 vols. (in 1). *(Centro de Estudios y Promocion del Desarrollo. Cuadernos. 4)*

BRUSH (STEPHEN B.) Mountain, field, and family: the economy and human ecology of an Andean valley. Philadelphia, Pa., 1977. pp. 199. *bibliog.*

— Poland.

PRZEMIANY strukturalne w rolnictwie polskim; praca zbiorowa pod redakcją Zdzisława Grochowskiego. Warszawa, 1975. pp. 242.

— Russia.

EMELIAKH (LIUBOV' ISAAKOVNA) Krest'iane i tserkov' nakanune Oktiabria. Leningrad, 1976. pp. 182. *bibliog. (Akademiia Nauk SSSR. Nauchno-Ateisticheskaia Seriia)*

SOBOLEV (PETR NIKIFOROVICH) Uprochenie soiuza rabochikh i krest'ian v pervyi god proletarskoi diktatury. Moskva, 1977. pp. 320.

CRISENOY (CHANTAL DE) Lénine face aux moujiks. Paris, [1978]. pp. 379. *bibliog.*

— — Russia (RSFSR).

BAKLANOVA (ELENA NIKOLAEVNA) Krest'ianskii dvor i obshchina na russkom Severe, konets XVII - nachalo XVIII v. Moskva, 1976. pp. 221.

GRIDNEV (VIKTOR MIKHAILOVICH) Bor'ba krest'ianstva okkupirovannykh oblastei RSFSR protiv nemetsko-fashistskoi okkupatsionnoi politiki, 1941-1944. Moskva, 1976. pp. 231. *bibliog.*

— — Siberia.

KREST'IANSKAIA obshchina v Sibiri XVII - nachala XX v. Novosibirsk, 1977. pp. 287.

— — Ukraine.

BEREZOVCHUK (MYKOLA DANYLOVYCH) Pershi sotsialistychni peretvorennia na seli: pro orhanizatsiï sil's'koï bidnoty ta ïkh rol' u zdiisnenni pershykh sotsialistychnykh peretvoren'. Kyïv, 1976. pp. 149.

— Spain.

WEISSER (MICHAEL R.) The peasants of the Montes: (the roots of rural rebellion in Spain). Chicago, 1976. pp. 143.

— Underdeveloped areas.

See UNDERDEVELOPED AREAS — Peasantry.

— United Kingdom.

BRITTON (EDWARD) The community of the vill: a study in the history of the family and village life in fourteenth-century England. Toronto, [1977]. pp. 291. *bibliog.*

PECCHIO (GIUSEPPE).

PECCHIO (GIUSEPPE) Count. Osservazioni semiserie di un esule sull'Inghilterra; a cura di Giuseppe Nicoletti. Milano, [1976]. pp. 233.

PEDESTRIANS.

TAYLOR (H.) Pedestrian safety: the role of research. Crowthorne, 1977. pp. 33. *bibliog. (U.K. Transport and Road Research Laboratory. Supplementary Reports. 319)*

— New Zealand.

NEW ZEALAND. Valuation Department. Research Papers. 68-6. Pedestrian traffic counts: their role in commercial property valuation. Wellington, 1968. pp. 37.

— United Kingdom.

DAOR (E.) and GOODWIN (P.B.) Variations in the importance of walking as a mode of transport. London, [1976]. pp. 16. *(London. Greater London Council. Research Memoranda. 487)*

PELIKÁN (JIŘÍ).

PELIKÁN (JIŘÍ) Ein Frühling, der nie zu Ende geht: Erinnerungen eines Prager Kommunisten; (aus dem Französischen von Eva Moldenhauer). Frankfurt am Main, [1976]. pp. 332.

PELLOUTIER (FERNAND).

FOULON (MAURICE) Fernand Pelloutier, précurseur du syndicalisme fédéraliste, fondateur des bourses du travail. Paris, [1967]. pp. 189.

PELOPONNESUS

— Economic conditions.

BAXEVANIS (JOHN J.) Economy and population movements in the Peloponnesos of Greece. Athens, National Centre of Social Research, 1972. pp. 86. *bibliog.*

— Population.

BAXEVANIS (JOHN J.) Economy and population movements in the Peloponnesos of Greece. Athens, National Centre of Social Research, 1972. pp. 86. *bibliog.*

PENAL COLONIES

— Russia.

CONQUEST (ROBERT) Kolyma: the arctic death camps. London, 1978. pp. 256. *bibliog.*

PENMANSHIP.

OSLEY (ARTHUR SIDNEY) Mercator: a monograph on the lettering of maps, etc. in the 16th century Netherlands, with a facsmile and translation of his treatise on the italic hand and a translation of Ghim's Vita Mercatoris. London, 1969. pp. 209. *bibliog.*

PENNSYLVANIA

— Economic history.

LINDSTROM (DIANE) Economic development in the Philadelphia region, 1810-1850. New York, 1978. pp. 255. *bibliog.*

— Politics and government.

TULLY (ALAN) William Penn's legacy: politics and social structure in provincial Pennsylvania, 1726-1755. Baltimore, [1977]. pp. 255. *bibliog. (Johns Hopkins University. Studies in Historical and Political Science. Series 95. No. 2)*

— Social history.

TULLY (ALAN) William Penn's legacy: politics and social structure in provincial Pennsylvania, 1726-1755. Baltimore, [1977]. pp. 255. *bibliog. (Johns Hopkins University. Studies in Historical and Political Science. Series 95. No. 2)*

PENNSYLVANIA RAILROAD.

DAVIS (PATRICIA TALBOT) End of the line: Alexander J. Cassatt and the Pennsylvania Railroad. New York, [1978]. pp. 208. *bibliog.*

PENOLOGY.

ALTERNATIVE strategies for coping with crime; edited by Norman Tutt. Oxford, 1978. pp. 230. *bibliog.*

PRISONS past and future; edited for the Howard League for Penal Reform by John C. Freeman. London, 1978. pp. 239.

— Canada — British Columbia.

BRITISH COLUMBIA. Department of the Attorney General. Corrections Branch. 1974. A five-year plan in corrections. Victoria, 1974. pp. 13. *Photocopy.*

— — Manitoba.

MANITOBA. Northern Corrections Committee. 1974. A report on corrections in northern Manitoba. [Winnipeg], 1974. pp. 102.

— United States.

AMERICAN ASSEMBLY. 42nd Assembly, December 1972. Prisoners in America; [edited by Lloyd E. Ohlin]. Englewood Cliffs, N.J., [1973]. pp. 216. *bibliog.*

IN fear of each other: studies of dangerousness in America; [edited by] John P. Conrad [and] Simon Dinitz. Lexington, Mass., [1977]. pp. 141.

PENSION TRUSTS

— Rhodesia — Valuation.

MACPHAIL AND FRASER, Consulting Actuaries. Report...on the valuation of the Southern Rhodesia Pension Fund as at 31st March, 1935. Salisbury, 1937. pp. 20. *(Southern Rhodesia. Legislative Assembly. [Sessional Papers]. 1937. C.S.R.1)*

— United Kingdom.

TUTT (SYLVIA) and TUTT (LESLIE) Private pension scheme finance. London, 1976. pp. 316. *Reprint of the 1st ed. of 1971 with a new appendix.*

PENSIONS.

PENSIONS and inflation: an international discussion [held at Geneva, May 1976]. Geneva, International Labour Office, 1977. pp. 136.

— Canada.

The PENSION fund debate. [Toronto, 1978]. pp. 21. *(Ontario. Economic Council. Discussion Paper Series)*

— United Kingdom.

LABOUR PARTY. 2 pension plans: Labour and Tory plans. London, [1959]. pp. 12.

U.K. Joint Office of Inland Revenue Superannuation Funds Office and Occupational Pensions Board. Memoranda. irreg., Mr 1974(no. 13)- , with gap (1974, nos. 14-17). New Malden.

LUCAS (HARRY) Pensions and industrial relations: a practical guide for all involved in pensions. Oxford, 1977. pp. 191.

PENSIONS, MILITARY

— United Kingdom.

WAR PENSIONS COMMITTEE. A plea for just pensions to the victims of the war. [London, 191-]. s.sh.

PEOPLE'S NATIONAL CONGRESS.

PEOPLE'S NATIONAL CONGRESS. [Pamphlets, including speeches by L.F.S. Burnham]. Georgetown, Guyana, 1961-62. 14 pts.

PERDIGUIER (AGRICOL).

PERDIGUIER (AGRICOL) Mémoires d'un compagnon. Paris, 1977. pp. 419. *bibliog. Reprint of 1854-55 Geneva edition with an introduction by Alain Faure.*

PERFORMANCE.

WRAGG (RICHARD) and ROBERTSON (JAMES) Writer on Employment. Post-war trends in employment, productivity, output, labour costs and prices by industry in the United Kingdom. [London], 1978. pp. 93. *(U.K. Department of Employment. Research Papers. No. 3)*

PERFORMANCE STANDARDS.

MANSIONI e qualifiche dei lavoratori: evoluzione e crisi dei criteri tradizionali: atti delle Giornate di Studio di Pisa, 26-27 maggio 1973. Milano, 1975. pp. 30- . *(Associazione Italiana di Diritto del Lavoro e della Sicurezza Sociale. Annuario di Diritto del Lavoro. N.7)*

PERFUMES.

PERFUMES.

RIMMEL (EUGENE) A lecture on the commercial use of flowers and plants, delivered on the 27th July, 1865, at the Royal Horticultural Society. London, the Author, [1865]. pp. 23.

PERIODICALS

— Abbreviation of titles.

ALKIRE (LELAND G.) compiler. Periodical title abbreviations. 2nd ed. Detroit, [1977]. pp. 436.

— Bibliography.

LUST (JOHN) and WOOD (FRANCES) B.A.(Cantab.) compilers. Catalogue of publications of translation and monitoring services and of periodicals dealing with the People's Republic of China in the library of the School of Oriental and African Studies. London, 1974. pp. 37.

— Indexes.

LETOPIS' ZHURNAL'NYKH STATEI: organ gosudarstvennoi bibliografii SSSR; ([pd. by] Vsesoiuznaia Knizhnaia Palata [Russia]). w., 1957- , with gap (1975, no.26). Moskva.

— Statistics.

WOOTTON (CHRISTOPHER B.) Trends in size, growth and cost of the literature since 1955. London, 1977. pp. 90. *(British Library. Research and Development Department. Reports. 5323)*

PERON (JUAN DOMINGO).

GOMEZ MORALES (ALFREDO) Politica economica peronista. Buenos Aires, [1951]. pp. 230.

DAMONTE TABORDA (RAUL) Ayer fue San Peron: 12 años de humillacion argentina. [Buenos Aires], 1955. pp. 276.

CODOVILLA (VICTORIO) Lo nuevo en la situacion nacional despues de las elecciones: informe presentado al pleno del Comite Central del Partido Comunista, realizado los dias 27 y 28 de marzo de 1965. Buenos Aires, 1965. pp. 39.

GODIO (JULIO) La caida de Peron: de junio a setiembre de 1955. Buenos Aires, 1973. pp. 255.

PERSIAN GULF

— Appropriations and expenditure.

AL-KUWARI (ALI KHALIFA) Oil revenues in the Gulf Emirates: patterns of allocation and impact on economic development; (volume editor Howard Bowen-Jones). Epping, 1978. pp. 218. *bibliog. (Durham. University. Centre for Middle Eastern and Islamic Studies. [Publications. New Series]. 6)*

— Foreign relations.

PRICE (D.L.) Oil and Middle East security. Beverly Hills, [1976]. pp. 84. *bibliog. (Georgetown University. Center for Strategic and International Studies. Washington Papers. vol. 4/41)*

— Politics and government.

CONFLICT and cooperation in the Persian Gulf; edited by Mohammed Mughisuddin. New York, [1977]. pp. 192. *bibliog.*

HALLIDAY (FRED) Mercenaries: "counter-insurgency" in the Gulf. Nottingham, 1977. pp. 80.

PERSONAL PROPERTY

— Russia.

VLADIMIRSKII (EVGENII ALEKSANDROVICH) and PAVLOVA (IRINA PETROVNA) Lichnaia sobstvennost' kak ekonomicheskoe otnoshenie. Leningrad, 1977. pp. 151.

PERSONAL SPACE.

GROWING up in cities: studies of the spatial environment of adolescence in Cracow, Melbourne, Mexico City, Salta, Toluca, and Warszawa; edited by Kevin Lynch from the reports of Tridib Banerjee [and others]. Paris, UNESCO, [1977]. pp. 177. *bibliog.*

PERSONALITY.

JESSUP (GILBERT) and JESSUP (HELEN) Selection and assessment at work. London, 1975. pp. 143. *bibliog.*

RADFORD (JOHN) and KIRBY (RICHARD) The person in psychology. London, 1975. pp. 143. *bibliog.*

AKTIVNOST' lichnosti v sotsialisticheskom obshchestve. Moskva, 1976. pp. 278.

HAAN (NORMA) Coping and defending: processes of self-environment organization. New York, 1977. pp. 346. *bibliog.*

SEVE (LUCIEN) Man in marxist theory and the psychology of personality;... translated from the French by John McGreal. Hassocks, Sussex, 1978. pp. 508.

PERSONALITY, DISORDERS OF.

O'BRIEN (MAJA) The diagnosis of psychopathy: a study of some characteristics in personality and behaviour of "psychopaths" referred for treatment to a therapeutic community. 1976. fo. 446. *bibliog. Typescript. Ph.D. (London) thesis: unpublished. This thesis is the property of London University and may not be removed from the Library.*

PERSONALITY AND CULTURE.

BERRY (JOHN WIDDUP) Human ecology and cognitive style: comparative studies in cultural and psychological adaptation. New York, [1976]. pp. 242. *bibliog.*

SERPELL (ROBERT) Culture's influence on behaviour. London, 1976. pp. 144. *bibliog.*

PIAGETIAN psychology: cross-cultural contributions; edited by Pierre R. Dasen. New York, [1977]. pp. 379. *bibliogs.*

LEARNING non-aggression: the experience of non-literate societies; edited by Ashley Montagu. New York, 1978. pp. 235. *bibliogs.*

PERSONNEL DIRECTORS.

WATSON (TONY J.) The personnel managers: a study in the sociology of work and employment. London, 1977. pp. 246. *bibliog.*

PERSONNEL MANAGEMENT.

In earlier volumes of this Bibliography similar material is entered under EMPLOYMENT MANAGEMENT.

GRANT (JEANNE VALERIE) and SMITH (GEOFFREY JOHN) Personnel administration and industrial relations. 2nd ed. London, 1977. pp. 318. *bibliog.*

LEGGE (KAREN) Power, innovation, and problem-solving in personnel management. London, [1978]. pp. 151. *bibliog.*

— United Kingdom.

ECONOMIC DEVELOPMENT COMMITTEE FOR HOTELS AND CATERING. Employment policy and industrial relations in the hotels and catering industry. London, National Economic Development Office, 1977. pp. 64. *bibliog.*

— United States.

BERG (IVAR E.) and others. Managers and work reform: a limited engagement. New York, [1978]. pp. 316.

PERSONNEL SERVICE IN EDUCATION

— United States.

HARWAY (MICHELE) and ASTIN (HELEN S.) Sex discrimination in career counseling and education. New York, 1977. pp. 154. *bibliog.*

PERSONS (INTERNATIONAL LAW).

INDIVIDUAL rights and the state in foreign affairs: an international compendium; edited by Elihu Lauterpacht [and] John G. Collier. New York, 1977. pp. 743. *Based on a conference of international lawyers held at Bellagio, Italy, in 1972, by the American Society of International Law and the Carnegie Endowment for International Peace.*

PERSONS (LAW)

— Colombia.

PEREZ GAVIRIA (JUAN DAVID) and GARCES HOLGUIN (JULIAN ALBERTO) La suspension artificial de la vida y el derecho. Bogota, 1972. pp. 115. *bibliog.*

— European Economic Community countries.

TOTH (AKOS. G.) Legal protection of individuals in the European Communities. Amsterdam, 1978. 2 vols. *bibliog.*

PERSUASION (PSYCHOLOGY).

REBOUL (OLIVIER) L'endoctrinement. [Paris, 1977]. pp. 198. *bibliog.*

PERU

— Antiquities.

LAVALLEE (DANIELE) and JULIEN (MICHELE) Les établissements Asto à l'époque préhispanique. Lima, 1973. pp. 143. *(Institut Français d'Etudes Andines. Travaux. 15) With Spanish and English summaries.*

— Economic conditions.

VAZQUEZ DIAZ (MANUEL) Crisis economica peruana. Lima, 1969. pp. 47.

THORP (ROSEMARY) and BERTRAM (GEOFFREY) Peru, 1890-1977: growth and policy in an open economy. London, 1978. pp. 475. *bibliog.*

— Economic history.

BONILLA MAYTA (HERACLIO) Guano y burguesia en el Peru. Lima, 1974. pp. 186. *bibliog. (Instituto de Estudios Peruanos. Peru Problema. 11)*

RAMIREZ GASTON (J.M.) 150 años: economia y finanzas en el Peru, 1821-1971 y en el Virreynato, 1544-1824. [Lima, 1974]. pp. 181.

GRAN Bretaña y el Peru: informes de los consules britanicos, 1826-1900; compilador Heraclio Bonilla. Lima, 1975-77. 5 vols. *bibliog. (Instituto de Estudios Peruanos. Estudios Historicos. 2)*

THORP (ROSEMARY) and BERTRAM (GEOFFREY) Peru, 1890-1977: growth and policy in an open economy. London, 1978. pp. 475. *bibliog.*

— Economic policy.

SUNKEL (OSWALDO) Politica nacional de desarrollo y dependencia externa. Lima, 1967. pp. 38. *(Instituto de Estudios Peruanos. Documentos Teoricos. No. 4)*

VAZQUEZ DIAZ (MANUEL) Crisis economica peruana. Lima, 1969. pp. 47.

PERU. Presidencia de la Republica. 1975. Plan nacional de desarrollo 1975-1978: aprobado por Decreto Supremo No. 009-75-PM del 2 de Junio de 1975. [Lima, 1975]. pp. 163.

PERU. Instituto Nacional de Planificacion. 1977. Plan global de desarrollo para 1977 y 1978: aprobado por D.S. No. 008-77-PM del 28 de abril de 1977. [Lima, 1977]. pp. 272.

THORP (ROSEMARY) and BERTRAM (GEOFFREY) Peru, 1890-1977: growth and policy in an open economy. London, 1978. pp. 475. *bibliog.*

— Foreign economic relations — United Kingdom.

GRAN Bretaña y el Peru: informes de los consules britanicos, 1826-1900; compilador Heraclio Bonilla. Lima, 1975-77. 5 vols. bibliog. (Instituto de Estudios Peruanos. Estudios Historicos. 2)

— History.

WERLICH (DAVID P.) Peru: a short history. Carbondale, Ill., [1978]. pp. 434. bibliog.

— — Sources.

GRAN Bretaña y el Peru: informes de los consules britanicos, 1826-1900; compilador Heraclio Bonilla. Lima, 1975-77. 5 vols. bibliog. (Instituto de Estudios Peruanos. Estudios Historicos. 2)

— Politics and government.

BRAVO BRESANI (JORGE) Mito y realidad de la oligarquia peruana. Lima, 1966. pp. 51. (Instituto de Estudios Peruanos. Mesas Redondas y Conferencias. No. 7)

TOWNSEND EZCURRA (ANDRES) Tres años de claudicacion: asi defraudo el belaundismo al pueblo. Lima, 1966. pp. 21.

SANCHEZ (LUIS ALBERTO) La verdad sobre la crisis "politica". [Lima, 1967]. pp. 43.

RAMIREZ NOVOA (EZEQUIEL) Peru: petroleo y revolucion. Buenos Aires, 1969. pp. 45.

PARTIDO COMUNISTA DEL PERU. Comite Central. Informe politico, VII Conferencia Nacional: sobre el caracter de la sociedad y los problemas de la revolucion peruana. [Lisbon?], 1972. pp. 146.

BAELLA TUESTA (ALFONSO) El poder invisible. [Lima, 1977]. pp. 456. Cover subtitle: Los primeros mil dias de la Revolucion peruana.

KLAIBER (JEFFREY L.) Religion and revolution in Peru, 1824-1976. Notre Dame, Ind., [1977]. pp. 259. bibliog. (Notre Dame. University. Committee on International Relations. International Studies)

PEASE GARCIA (HENRY) El ocaso del poder oligarquico: lucha politica en la escena oficial, 1968-1975. Lima, 1977. pp. 313. bibliog.

PHILIP (GEORGE D.E.) The rise and fall of the Peruvian military radicals, 1968-1976. London, 1978. pp. 178. bibliog. (London. University. Institute of Latin American Studies. Monographs. 9)

— Race question.

CUCHE (DENYS) Poder blanco y resistencia negra en el Peru: un estudio de la condicion social del negro en el Peru despues de la abolicion de la esclavitud. Lima, 1975. pp. 203. bibliog.

— Rural conditions.

COTLER (JULIO) Haciendas y comunidades tradicionales en un contexto de movilizacion politica. Lima, 1968. pp. 29. (Instituto de Estudios Peruanos. Estudios del Valle de Urubamba. No. 1)

BRUSH (STEPHEN B.) Mountain, field, and family: the economy and human ecology of an Andean valley. Philadelphia, Pa., 1977. pp. 199. bibliog.

— Social conditions.

STEIN (WILLIAM W.) Modernization and inequality in Vicos, Peru: an examination of the "ignorance of women". Buffalo, 1975. fo. 56. (New York State University. Council on International Studies. Special Studies. No. 73)

ORLOVE (BENJAMIN S.) Alpacas, sheep and men: the wool export economy and regional society in southern Peru. New York, [1977]. pp. 270. bibliog.

— Social history.

SPALDING (KAREN) De indio a campesino: cambios en la estructura social del Peru colonial. Lima, 1974. pp. 258. bibliog. (Instituto de Estudios Peruanos. Historia Andina. 2)

CUCHE (DENYS) Poder blanco y resistencia negra en el Peru: un estudio de la condicion social del negro en el Peru despues de la abolicion de la esclavitud. Lima, 1975. pp. 203. bibliog.

— Social policy.

PERU. Presidencia de la Republica. 1975. Plan nacional de desarrollo 1975-1978: aprobado por Decreto Supremo No. 009-75-PM del 2 de Junio de 1975. [Lima, 1975]. pp. 163.

PERU. Instituto Nacional de Planificacion. 1977. Plan global de desarrollo para 1977 y 1978: aprobado por D.S. No. 008-77-PM del 28 de abril de 1977. [Lima, 1977]. pp. 272.

PÉTAIN (HENRI PHILIPPE BÉNONI OMER JOSEPH).

ISORNI (JACQUES) Je hais ces impostures. Paris, [1977]. pp. 286.

PETALAX

— Population.

WESTER (HOLGER) Innovationer i befolkningsrörligheten: en studie av spridningsförlopp i befolkningsrörligheten utgående från Petalax socken i Österbotten. Uppsala, 1977. pp. 218. bibliog. (Uppsala. Universitet. Historiska Institutionen. Studia Historica Upsaliensia. 93) With English summary.

PETALING JAYA, MALAYSIA

— Population.

SAW (SWEE HOCK) The population survey of Petaling Jaya, 1966. Singapore, 1972. pp. 44.

— Social conditions.

SAW (SWEE HOCK) The population survey of Petaling Jaya, 1966. Singapore, 1972. pp. 44.

PETER I, called the Great, Emperor of Russia.

ANDERSON (MATTHEW SMITH) Peter the Great. London, [1978]. pp. 207. bibliog.

PETROLEUM

— Prices.

MORAN (THEODORE H.) Oil prices and the future of OPEC: the political economy of tension and stability in the Organization of Petroleum Exporting Countries. Washington, D.C., 1978. pp. 102. (Resources for the Future, Inc. Research Papers. R-8)

— Refining — Underdeveloped areas.

See UNDERDEVELOPED AREAS — Petroleum — Refining.

— Taxation — United Kingdom.

HAYLLAR (R.F.) and PLEASANCE (R.T.) UK taxation of offshore oil and gas. London, 1977. pp. 212.

— — United States.

NATIONAL MARINE ENGINEERS BENEFICIAL ASSOCIATION. The multi-billion dollar loopholes. New York, 1974. pp. 8.

PETROLEUM IN SUBMERGED LANDS

— Law and legislation.

INTERNATIONAL OCEAN SYMPOSIUM, 2ND, TOKYO, 1977. (Proceedings): marine technology and law; development of hydrocarbon resources and offshore structures. Kasumigaseki, 1978. pp. 191. With 11 maps and diagrams in end-pocket.

— Asia, Southeast.

SIDDAYAO (CORAZÓN MORALES) The off-shore petroleum resources of south-east Asia: potential conflict situations and related economic considerations. Kuala Lumpur, 1978. pp. 205. bibliog. Part of the research programme of the Institute of Southeast Asian Studies on Oil Discovery and Technical Change in Southeast Asia.

— Canada — Newfoundland.

NEWFOUNDLAND. Department of Mines and Energy. 1977. A white paper and draft regulations respecting the administration and disposition of petroleum belonging to Her Majesty in the right of the province of Newfoundland. [St. John's], 1977. 1 vol. (various foliations).

— North Sea.

OIL over troubled waters: (a report and critique of oil developments in North East Scotland); (written and researched [by] Mark Hill). 2nd ed. Aberdeen, [1976]. pp. 56. (Aberdeen People's Press. Special Reports)

HAYLLAR (R.F.) and PLEASANCE (R.T.) UK taxation of offshore oil and gas. London, 1977. pp. 212.

LEWIS (T.M.) and McNICOLL (IAIN HUGH) North Sea oil and Scotland's economic prospects. London, [1978]. pp. 147. bibliog.

U.K. Working Party on the Financing of North Sea Oil. 1978. The financing of North Sea oil; [A. D. Bain, chairman]. London, 1978. pp. 64. (U.K. Committee to Review the Functioning of Financial Institutions. Research Reports. No. 2)

— United Kingdom — Equipment and supplies.

JOINT STANDING COMMITTEE OF THE SCOTTISH ECONOMIC COUNCIL AND THE OIL DEVELOPMENT COUNCIL FOR SCOTLAND. Scottish industry and offshore markets; (report by the Joint Standing Committee...: summary and government commentary). Edinburgh, H.M.S.O., 1977. pp. 18.

PETROLEUM INDUSTRY AND TRADE.

COMMITTEE OF RETURNED VOLUNTEERS. Gulf Oil Corporation: a study in exploitation. rev. ed. New York, 1971. pp. 48. bibliog.

INTERREGIONAL SEMINAR ON PETROLEUM REFINING IN DEVELOPING COUNTRIES, NEW DELHI, 1973. Report of the Interregional Seminar...[held in] New Delhi, 22 January to 3 February 1973. (ST/TAO/SER.C/146). New York, United Nations, 1973. pp. 34.

BRUSEKER (U.) Unilever, Meneba, Philips en de olieconcerns als inflatiemakers; een bestrijding van de looninflatie-theorie. [Amsterdam], 1974. pp. 133. bibliog.

AL-HAMAD (ABDLATIF Y.) Some aspects of the oil controversy: an Arab interpretation; (address to a seminar organised by the Industrial Development Bank of Japan on oil problems and petrodollar recycling). [Kuwait, Kuwait Fund for Arab Economic Development, 1975] . pp. 13.

AL-HAMAD (ABDLATIF Y.) Towards a reassessment of the recycling problem; (address to the Royal Institute of International Affairs, April 21, 1975). [Kuwait, Kuwait Fund for Arab Economic Development, 1975] . pp. 14.

DIARUNA WAL-ALAM; pd. by Ministry of Finance and Petroleum, Qatar. m., Ag 1977(no. 20)- Doha.

DORAN (CHARLES F.) Myth, oil, and politics: introduction to the political economy of petroleum. New York, [1977]. pp. 226.

PETROLEUM INDUSTRY AND TRADE.(Cont.)

The ENERGY syndrome: comparing national responses to the energy crisis; edited by Leon N. Lindberg. Lexington, Mass., [1977]. pp. 383.

TURNER (LOUIS) Oil companies in the international system. London, 1978. pp. 240. *bibliog.*

— Finance.

BHATTACHARYA (ANINDYA K.) The myth of petropower. Lexington, Mass., [1977]. pp. 108. *bibliog.*

— Government ownership — Venezuela.

PETRAS (JAMES FRANK) and others. The nationalization of Venezuelan oil. New York, 1977. pp. 173.

— Algeria.

SCHLIEPHAKE (KONRAD) Oil and regional development: examples from Algeria and Tunisia; translated by Merrill D. Lyew. New York, 1977. pp. 203. *bibliog.*

— Arab countries.

EURO-Arab cooperation; edited by Edmond Völker. Leyden, 1976. pp. 228. *Papers from a colloquium organized by the University of Amsterdam Europa Instituut in October 1975.*

DIARUNA WAL-ALAM; pd. by Ministry of Finance and Petroleum, Qatar. m., Ag 1977(no. 20)- Doha.

The ARAB oil weapon; [compiled] by Jordan J. Paust [and] Albert P. Blaustein, with Adele Higgins. New York, 1977. pp. 370.

— — Statistics.

ORGANIZATION OF ARAB PETROLEUM EXPORTING COUNTRIES. Economic Department. Statistics Section. Annual statistical report. a., 1974/75(3rd)- Kuwait.

— Argentine Republic.

COMITE UNIVERSITARIO RADICAL. Junta Central. El petroleo argentino: ciclo de conferencias en pro de su nacionalizacion y explotacion por el Estado. [Buenos Aires], 1930. pp. 152.

— Austria.

RAMBOUSEK (HERBERT) Die "ÖMV Aktiengesellschaft": Entstehung und Entwicklung eines nationalen Unternehmens der Mineralölindustrie. Wien, 1977. pp. 225. *bibliog. (Wirtschaftsuniversität Wien. Dissertationen. 23) 2 maps in end pocket.*

— Brazil.

CARVALHO (GETULIO) Petrobras: do monopolis aos contratos de risco. Rio de Janeiro, 1976. pp. 250. *bibliog.*

— Canada.

LOUNSBURY (JOHN PATTON) The demand for Canadian crude and natural gas liquids, 1962-1967. [Toronto?, 1963]. pp. 5. *(Reprint from the Journal of Canadian Petroleum Technology, vol. 2, no. 1)*

BRITISH COLUMBIA. Energy Commission. 1975. Report on matters concerning gasoline marketing in British Columbia, etc. [Vancouver], 1975. pp. 240.

PETRO-CANADA. Annual report. a., 1976(1st)- Ottawa. *[in English and French]*

CANADA. Statistics Canada. Selected petroleum statistics quarterly. q., 1977(v.1, no.1)- Ottawa. *[in English and French].*

— — British Columbia.

BRITISH COLUMBIA. Energy Commission. 1976. Inquiry into matters concerning the production, distribution and sale of liquefied petroleum gas, propane and butane, in British Columbia, etc. [Vancouver], 1976. pp. 211.

BRITISH COLUMBIA. Energy Commission. 1976. Submission on behalf of the Minister Responsible for Energy of the Province of British Columbia...to the National Energy Board in the matter of determining the producibility and domestic demand for oil and related matters. Vancouver, 1976. fo. 66.

— — Newfoundland.

NEWFOUNDLAND. 1977. A White Paper and draft regulations respecting the administration and disposition of petroleum belonging to Her Majesty in right of the Province of Newfoundland. [St. John's], 1977. fo. 61,6.

— — Nova Scotia.

NOVA SCOTIA. Energy Council. Research Division. 1975. Submission to the National Energy Board on petroleum requirements in Nova Scotia 1974-1994. [Halifax], 1975. fo. 36. *Alternative title page reads: Petroleum demand in Nova Scotia 1974-1994.*

— China.

HARRISON (SELIG S.) China, oil, and Asia: conflict ahead? New York, 1977. pp. 317. *Based on a study for the International Fact-Finding Center of the Carnegie Endowment for International Peace.*

— East (Near East).

OPEC and the Middle East: the impact of oil on societal development; edited by Russell A. Stone. New York, 1977. pp. 264.

— Europe, Eastern — Bibliography.

DARLINGTON (T.I.G.) and PARK (J.D.) compilers. Bibliographical guide to the political economy of oil and natural gas in the Soviet Union and Eastern Europe. Stone, Staffs., [1978?]. fo.67.

— European Economic Community countries — Statistics.

EUROPEAN COMMUNITIES. Statistical Office. Petroleum statistics. a., 1976- Luxembourg. *[in Community languages]*

— Indonesia.

CARLSON (SEVINC) Indonesia's oil. Boulder, Colo., 1977. pp. 257. *bibliog. Prepared for the Center for Strategic and International Studies, Georgetown University.*

— Iran.

BHATTACHARYA (ANINDYA K.) The myth of petropower. Lexington, Mass., [1977]. pp. 108. *bibliog.*

— Japan.

WU (YUAN-LI) Japan's search for oil: a case study on economic nationalism and international security. Stanford, [1977]. pp. 116. *(Stanford University. Hoover Institution n War, Revolution and Peace. Hoover Institution Publications. 165)*

— Mexico.

POLITICA PETROLERA: informes del Director General de Petroleos Mexicanos. trien., 1965/1967- Mexico.

LOPEZ PORTILLO Y WEBER (JOSE) El petroleo de Mexico: su importancia, sus problemas. Mexico, 1975. pp. 294.

— Nigeria.

NIGERIA. Department of Petroleum Resources. Monthly petroleum information. m., Ja 1971- Lagos.

NIGERIA. Federal Ministry of Mines and Power. 1972. Nigerians and their oil industry, by P.C. Asiodu. [Lagos, 1972]. pp. 20.

TURNER (TERISA ELAINE) Government and oil in Nigeria: a study of the making and implementation of petroleum policy. 1977. pp. 230. *bibliog. Typescript. Ph.D. (London) thesis: unpublished. This thesis is the property of London University and may not be removed from the Library.*

— Persian Gulf.

AL-KUWARI (ALI KHALIFA) Oil revenues in the Gulf Emirates: patterns of allocation and impact on economic development; (volume editor Howard Bowen- Jones). Epping, 1978. pp. 218. *bibliog. (Durham. University. Centre for Middle Eastern and Islamic Studies. [Publications. New Series]. 6)*

— Peru.

RAMIREZ NOVOA (EZEQUIEL) Peru: petroleo y revolucion. Buenos Aires, 1969. pp. 45.

— Rhodesia.

BINGHAM (THOMAS HENRY) and GRAY (S.M.) Report on the supply of petroleum and petroleum products to Rhodesia. London, H.M.S.O., 1978. pp. 296.

— Romania.

MARGUERAT (PHILIPPE) Le IIIe Reich et le pétrole roumain, 1938-1950: contribution à l'étude de la pénétration économique allemande dans les Balkans à la veille et au début de la Seconde Guerre mondiale. Leiden, 1977. pp. 231. *bibliog. (Geneva. Graduate Institute of International Studies. Collection de Relations Internationales. 6)*

— Russia.

OPTIMIZATSIIA razvitiia i razmeshcheniia neftegazovoi promyshlennosti; otvetstvennye redaktory Iu.I. Maksimov, Z.R. Tsimdina. Novosibirsk, 1977. pp. 181. *bibliog. (Akademiia Nauk SSSR. Sibirskoe Otdelenie. Institut Ekonomiki i Organizatsii Promyshlennogo Proizvodstva. Optimizatsiia Razvitiia i Razmeshcheniia Proizvodstva)*

— — Bibliography.

DARLINGTON (T.I.G.) and PARK (J.D.) compilers. Bibliographical guide to the political economy of oil and natural gas in the Soviet Union and Eastern Europe. Stone, Staffs., [1978?]. fo.67.

— Tunisia.

SCHLIEPHAKE (KONRAD) Oil and regional development: examples from Algeria and Tunisia; translated by Merrill D. Lyew. New York, 1977. pp. 203. *bibliog.*

— United Kingdom.

AIMS FOR FREEDOM AND ENTERPRISE. 1000 a minute: how the oil industry is making Britain richer. London, [1977]. pp. 8.

BAILEY (MARTIN DAWSON) Shell and BP in South Africa. London, 1977. pp. 44.

ARNOLD (GUY) Britain's oil. London, 1978. pp. 388. *bibliog.*

— — Finance.

U.K. Working Party on the Financing of North Sea Oil. 1978. The financing of North Sea oil; [A. D. Bain, chairman]. London, 1978. pp. 64. *(U.K. Committee to Review the Functioning of Financial Institutions. Research Reports. No. 2)*

— — Scotland.

OIL over troubled waters: (a report and critique of oil developments in North East Scotland); (written and researched [by] Mark Hill). 2nd ed. Aberdeen, [1976]. pp. 56. *(Aberdeen People's Press. Special Reports)*

— United States.

TWENTIETH CENTURY FUND. Task Force on the International Oil Crisis. Paying for energy: report...; background paper by Sidney S. Alexander. New York, [1975]. pp. 136.

CONFERENCE ON HORIZONTAL DIVESTITURE IN THE OIL INDUSTRY, WASHINGTON, 1977. Horizontal divestiture; highlights of a conference on whether oil companies should be prohibited from owning nonpetroleum energy resources...; edited by W. S. Moore. Washington, [1977]. pp. 62.

HOBBIE (BARBARA) Oil company divestiture and the press: economic vs. journalistic perceptions. New York, [1977]. pp. 167. *bibliog.*

SUNDER (SHYAM) Oil industry profits. Washington, [1977]. pp. 74. *(American Enterprise Institute for Public Policy Research. AEI Studies. 170)*

— — Alaska.

KRESGE (DAVID T.) and others. Issues in Alaska development. Seattle, [1977]. pp. 223. *Based on studies carried out at the University of Alaska's Institute of Social and Economic Research.*

— Venezuela.

BETANCOURT (ROMULO) Venezuela: dueña de su petroleo. Caracus, 1975. pp. 201.

ALLEN (LORING) Venezuelan economic development: a politico-economic analysis. Greenwich, Conn., [1977]. pp. 310. *bibliog.*

BETANCOURT (RÓMULO) Venezuela's oil. London, [1978]. pp. 275. *bibliog. Translated by Donald Peck.*

PETROLEUM LAW AND LEGISLATION
— Canada — Newfoundland.

NEWFOUNDLAND. Department of Mines and Energy. 1977. A white paper and draft regulations respecting the administration and disposition of petroleum belonging to Her Majesty in the right of the province of Newfoundland. [St. John's], 1977. 1 vol. (various foliations).

— United Kingdom.

HAYLLAR (R.F.) and PLEASANCE (R.T.) UK taxation of offshore oil and gas. London, 1977. pp. 212.

PETROLEUM PRODUCTS
— Prices.

TWENTIETH CENTURY FUND. Task Force on the International Oil Crisis. Paying for energy: report...; background paper by Sidney S. Alexander. New York, [1975]. pp. 136.

— — Canada — Ontario.

ONTARIO. Royal Commission on Petroleum Products Pricing. 1976. [Report]; Claude M. Isbister, commissioner. [Toronto], 1976. pp. 192.

— — India.

INDIA. Working Group on Oil Prices. 1967. Report; [J.N. Talukdar, chairman]. [Delhi, 1967]. pp. 162.

— — United States.

MIERNYK (WILLIAM H.) and others. Regional impacts of rising energy prices. Cambridge, Mass., [1978]. pp. 135. *bibliog.*

— European Economic Community countries.

EUROPEAN COMMUNITIES. Statistical Office. Hydrocarbons: monthly bulletin. m., Ag 1977(no. 8)- Luxembourg. *Supersedes in part EUROPEAN COMMUNITIES. Statistical Office. Quarterly bulletin of energy statistics.*

PETROLEUM REFINERIES
— Nigeria.

NIGERIA. Sessional Papers. 1960. No. 5. Establishment of oil refinery in Nigeria. Lagos, 1960. pp. 6.

PETTY (Sir WILLIAM).

RONCAGLIA (ALESSANDRO) Petty: la nascita dell'economia politica. Milano, [1977]. pp. 133. *bibliog.*

PEUGEOT S.A.

ANGELI (CLAUDE) and BRIMO (NICOLAS) Une milice patronale: Peugeot;...avec la collaboration de Marc- Rémy Donnallin. Paris, 1975. pp. 105.

PAGANELLI (SERGE) and JACQUIN (MARTINE) Peugeot: la dynastie s'accroche. Paris, [1975]. pp. 156.

PHARMACEUTICAL POLICY.

CONTROLLING the use of therapeutic drugs: an international comparison; edited by William M. Wardell. Washington, D.C., [1978]. pp. 263. *(American Enterprise Institute for Public Policy Research. AEI Studies. 178)*

PHARMACEUTICAL RESEARCH
— United States.

SCHWARTZMAN (DAVID) Innovation in the pharmaceutical industry. Baltimore, [1976]. pp. 399.

PHENOMENOLOGY.

SPURLING (LAURIE) Phenomenology and the social world: the philosophy of Merleau- Ponty and its relation to the social sciences. London, 1977. pp. 208. *bibliog.*

PHILADELPHIA
— Economic history.

LINDSTROM (DIANE) Economic development in the Philadelphia region, 1810-1850. New York, 1978. pp. 255. *bibliog.*

— Emigration and immigration.

GOLAB (CAROLINE) Immigrant destinations. Philadelphia, 1977. pp. 246.

— History.

OLTON (CHARLES S.) Artisans for independence: Philadelphia mechanics and the American revolution. Syracuse, N.Y., 1975. pp. 172. *bibliog.*

— Hospitals.

WILLIAMS (WILLIAM H.) America's first hospital: the Pennsylvania Hospital, 1751- 1841. Wayne, [1976]. pp. 186. *bibliog.*

— Riots.

FELDBERG (MICHAEL) The Philadelphia riots of 1844: a study of ethnic conflict. Westport, Conn., 1975. pp. 209. *bibliog.*

PHILIPPINE ISLANDS
— Economic conditions.

VIRATA (CESAR) and others. Restrictions on exports in foreign collaboration agreements in the Republic of the Philippines: by a team of researchers, etc. (TD/B/388). New York, United Nations, 1972. pp. 28.

PERNIA (ERNESTO DEL MAR) Urbanization, population growth, and economic development in the Philippines. Westport, Conn., 1977. pp. 213. *bibliog.*

— Executive departments.

PHILIPPINE ISLANDS. Department of Industry. Report. a., 1976- Manila.

— Foreign relations — United States.

BUSS (CLAUDE ALBERT) The United States and the Philippines: background for policy. Washington, D.C., [1977]. pp. 152. *(American Enterprise Institute for Public Policy Research and Stanford University. Hoover Institution on War, Revolution and Peace. AEI-Hoover Policy Studies. 23)*

— Population.

PERNIA (ERNESTO DEL MAR) Urbanization, population growth, and economic development in the Philippines. Westport, Conn., 1977. pp. 213. *bibliog.*

PHILOSOPHY, MODERN.

— Social policy.

RODGERS (GERRY B.) and others. Population, employment and inequality: BACHUE-Philippines: an application of economic-demographic modelling to development planning. [Farnborough, Hants., 1978]. pp. 434. *bibliog. (A study prepared within the World Employment Programme, International Labour Organisation)*

PHILIPS (FREDERIK).

PHILIPS (FREDERIK) 45 years with Philips: an industrialist's life. Poole, 1978. pp. 280.

PHILIPS GLOEILAMPENFABRIEKEN, N.V.

PHILIPS (FREDERIK) 45 years with Philips: an industrialist's life. Poole, 1978. pp. 280.

PHILLIPS (ALBAN WILLIAM HOUSEGO).

STABILITY and inflation; edited by A.R. Bergstrom [and others]; ...a volume of essays to honour the memory of A.W.H. Phillips. Chichester, [1978]. pp. 323. *bibliogs.*

PHILLIPS CURVE.

STABILITY and inflation; edited by A.R. Bergstrom [and others]; ...a volume of essays to honour the memory of A.W.H. Phillips. Chichester, [1978]. pp. 323. *bibliogs.*

PHILOSOPHICAL ANTHROPOLOGY.

NAVASARDIAN (RAZMIK GAREGINOVICH) Formirovanie marksistskoi kontseptsii cheloveka: nachal'nyi period. Erevan, 1976. pp. 211. *bibliog.*

EATON (GAI) King of the castle: choice and responsibility in the modern world. London, 1977. pp. 219. *bibliog.*

NAUCHNO-tekhnicheskaia revoliutsiia, chelovek, ego prirodnaia i sotsial'naia sreda. Leningrad, 1977. pp. 216.

FLEW (ANTONY GARRARD NEWTON) A rational animal and other philosophical essays on the nature of man. Oxford, 1978. pp. 245. *bibliog.*

PHILOSOPHY.

SKILLEN (ANTHONY) Ruling illusions: philosophy and the social order. Hassocks, Sussex, 1977. pp. 179.

SLOMAN (AARON) The computer revolution in philosophy: philosophy, science and models of mind. Hassocks, 1978. pp. 304.

PHILOSOPHY, AMERICAN.

WHITE (MORTON GABRIEL) The philosophy of the American revolution. New York, 1978. pp. 299.

PHILOSOPHY, FRENCH.

GUIBERT (ELISABETH) Voies idéologiques de la Révolution française. Paris, [1976]. pp. 272. *bibliog.*

Les DIEUX dans la cuisine: vingt ans de philosophie en France. [Paris, 1978]. pp. 251. *Based on articles published in Le Magazine Littéraire, septembre 1977, no. 127-128.*

PHILOSOPHY, GERMAN.

GREGORY (FREDERICK) Scientific materialism in nineteenth century Germany. Dordrecht, [1977]. pp. 279. *bibliog.*

PHILOSOPHY, LATIN AMERICAN.

ZEA (LEOPOLDO) Dependencia y liberacion en la cultura latinoamericana. Mexico, 1974. pp. 119.

PHILOSOPHY, MODERN.

BAUMER (FRANKLIN LE VAN) Modern European thought: continuity and change in ideas, 1600- 1950. New York, [1977]. pp. 541. *bibliog.*

MAKAROV (MIKHAIL GEORGIEVICH) Kategoriia "tsel'" v marksistskoi filosofii i kritika teleologii. Leningrad, 1977. pp. 188.

PHILOSOPHY, MODERN.(Cont.)

ON critical theory; John O' Neill, editor. London, 1977. pp. 265.

BERLIN (Sir ISAIAH) [Selected writings]; edited by Henry Hardy and Aileen Kelly. London, 1978 in progress.

KEUTH (HERBERT) Realität und Wahrheit: zur Kritik des kritischen Rationalismus. Tübingen, 1978. pp. 220. *bibliog.*

MURE (GEOFFREY REGINALD GILCHRIST) Idealist epilogue. Oxford, 1978. pp. 180.

— Dictionaries and encyclopedias.

BULLOCK (ALAN LOUIS CHARLES) Baron Bullock, and STALLYBRASS (OLIVER) eds. The Fontana dictionary of modern thought. London, 1977. pp. 684. *bibliog.*

— History.

HISTORIA i wolność: studia z dziejów ideologii XIX wieku, etc. Warszawa, 1961. pp. 299. *(Polska Akademia Nauk. Instytut Filozofii i Socjologii. Archiwum Historii Filozofii i Myśli Społecznej. 7) With Russian or German summaries.*

MORGAN (MICHAEL J.) Molyneux's question: vision, touch and the philosophy of perception. Cambridge, 1977. pp. 213.

PHILOSOPHY, PRIMITIVE.

GOODY (JOHN RANKINE) The domestication of the savage mind. Cambridge, 1977. pp. 179. *bibliog.*

PHILOSOPHY, WHITE RUSSIAN.

IDEI gumanizma v obshchestvenno-politicheskoi i filosofskoi mysli Belorussii: dooktiabr'skii period; redkollegiia K.P. Buslov [and others]. Minsk, 1977. pp. 279.

PHILOSOPHY, YUGOSLAV.

SHER (GERSON S.) Praxis: Marxist criticism and dissent in socialist Yugoslavia. Bloomington, Ind., [1977]. pp. 360. *bibliog.*

PHILOSOPHY AND RELIGION.

EATON (GAI) King of the castle: choice and responsibility in the modern world. London, 1977. pp. 219. *bibliog.*

PHNOM PENH

— History.

STEINBACH (JERÔME) and STEINBACH (JOCELYNE) Phnom Penh libérée. Paris, [1976]. pp. 165.

PHONETICS.

O'CONNOR (JOSEPH DESMOND) Phonetics. Harmondsworth, 1973. pp. 320. *bibliogs.*

SCHANE (SANFORD A.) and BENDIXEN (BIRGITTE) Workbook in generative phonology. Englewood Cliffs, [1978]. pp. 111.

PHOTOCOPYING SERVICES

— United Kingdom.

PHOTOCOPYING and the law: a guide for librarians and teachers and other suppliers and users of photocopies of copyright works. London, [1970]. pp. 16.

PHYSICAL GEOGRAPHY.

GOUDIE (ANDREW S.) Environmental change. Oxford, 1977. pp. 243. *bibliogs.*

— Africa.

GROVE (ALFRED THOMAS) Africa. 3rd ed. Oxford, 1978. pp. 337. *bibliog.*

— Canada — Quebec.

THORNES (JOHN B.) Some observations on the late-glacial stages in the Coaticook Valley, southern Quebec. Quebec, 1965. pp. 15. *(Reprinted from Cahiers de Géographie de Québec, no. 18, April-September, 1965)*

— United Kingdom.

DURY (GEORGE HARRY) The British Isles: a systematic and regional geography. London, 1961. pp. 503. *bibliog.*

— — Wales.

WALES: a new study; edited by David Thomas; contributors D. Q. Bowen [and others]. Newton Abbot, [1977]. pp. 338. *bibliog.*

PHYSICALLY HANDICAPPED

— Personal narratives.

HERTSLET (MARY) From pain to purpose: the story of Joyce Le Brun as told to Mary Hertslet. Plumstead, South Africs, [1975]. pp. 61.

— Rehabilitation — United Kingdom.

NATIONAL FUND FOR RESEARCH INTO CRIPPLING DISEASES. Working Party on Integration of the Disabled. Integrating the disabled: report of the Snowdon working party. [London, 1976]. pp. 71.

— — United States.

MILIEU rehabilitation for physical and mental handicaps: [by] Robert W. Hyde [and others]. Providence, 1962. pp. 106. *bibliog.*

— South Africa.

HERTSLET (MARY) From pain to purpose: the story of Joyce Le Brun as told to Mary Hertslet. Plumstead, South Africs, [1975]. pp. 61.

— United Kingdom.

OFFICE OF HEALTH ECONOMICS. [Studies in Current Health Problems]. No. 60. Physical impairment: social handicap. London, [1977]. pp. 32. *bibliog.*

PHYSICIAN AND PATIENT.

MEDICAL encounters: the experience of illness and treatment; edited by Alan Davis and Gordon Horobin. London, [1977]. pp. 223. *bibliogs.*

PHYSICIANS

— New Zealand.

MEDICAL COUNCIL OF NEW ZEALAND. The employment of medical practitioners in New Zealand: a report on the 1967 questionnaire survey of the Medical Council of New Zealand. Wellington, 1968. pp. 32. *(Publications. No. 1)*

MEDICAL COUNCIL OF NEW ZEALAND. The employment of medical practitioners in New Zealand: a report on the 1968 questionnaire survey of the Medical Council of New Zealand. Wellington, 1970. pp. 33. *(Publications. No. 2)*

— — Salaries, pensions, etc.

NEW ZEALAND. Superannuation Division. 1971. Superannuation for the medical profession: government superannuation fund, standard scheme for local authorities, national superannuation scheme, annual single premium scheme. [Wellington, 1971]. pp. 20.

— United Kingdom.

GORDON (HARVEY) and ILIFFE (STEVE) Pickets in white: the junior doctors dispute of 1975: a study of the medical profession in transition. London, [1977]. pp. 76.

PHYSICISTS

— Germany.

BEYERCHEN (ALAN D.) Scientists under Hitler: politics and the physics community in the Third Reich. New Haven, 1977. pp. 287. *bibliog.*

PHYSICS

— History.

CLARK (PETER JAMES) Thermodynamics and the kinetic theory in the late nineteenth century: a case study in the methodology of scientific research programmes. [1977]. fo. 393. *bibliog. Typescript. Ph.D.(London) thesis: unpublished. This thesis is the property of London University and may not be removed from the Library.*

— — Sources.

HOLTON (GERALD JAMES) The scientific imagination: case studies. Cambridge, 1978. pp. 382.

— — Germany.

BEYERCHEN (ALAN D.) Scientists under Hitler: politics and the physics community in the Third Reich. New Haven, 1977. pp. 287. *bibliog.*

PHYSIOCRATS.

McLAIN (JAMES J) The economic writings of Du Pont de Nemours. Newark, N.J., [1977]. pp. 244. *bibliog.*

PIACENZA (PROVINCE)

— History.

CHIAPPONI (ANNA) Piacenza nella lotta di liberazione, 1943-1945: testimonianze. Piacenza, 1976. pp. 365. *bibliog.*

PIAGET (JEAN).

AULT (RUTH L.) Children's cognitive development: Piaget's theory and the process approach. New York, 1977. pp. 193. *bibliog.*

PIAGET (JEAN) The essential Piaget; [selections from his works]; edited by Howard E. Gruber and J. Jacques Vonèche. London, 1977. pp. 881. *bibliog.*

PIAGETIAN psychology: cross-cultural contributions; edited by Pierre R. Dasen. New York, [1977]. pp. 379. *bibliogs.*

ROTMAN (BRIAN) Jean Piaget: psychologist of the real. Hassocks, 1977. pp. 200. *bibliog.*

ALTERNATIVES to Piaget: critical essays on the theory; edited by Linda S. Siegel [and] Charles J. Brainerd. New York, [1978]. pp. 262. *bibliogs.*

MAIER (HENRY WILLIAM) Three theories of child development. 3rd ed. New York, [1978]. pp. 292. *bibliogs.*

PICARDY

— Economic conditions — Statistics.

RELAIS: statistiques de l'économie picarde; ([pd. by] Institut National de la Statistique et des Etudes Economiques…Service Régional [de Picardie, France]). bi-m. (formerly q.), S 1971 (no.1)- Amiens.

— History.

GAUTHIER (FLORENCE) La voie paysanne dans la Révolution française: l'exemple de la Picardie. Paris, 1977. pp. 241. *bibliog.*

PICKETING

— United Kingdom.

NATIONAL COUNCIL FOR CIVIL LIBERTIES. Reports. No. 11. Picketing and demonstrations…; briefing papers to the NCCL delegate conference on public order. London, 1975. 1 pamphlet (unpaged).

MARPLAN LIMITED. Strikes, picketing and the closed shop. [London, 1977]. fo. 7.

WARD (GEORGE) Fort Grunwick. London, 1977. pp. 123.

PIECK (WILHELM).

PIECK (WILHELM) Wilhelm Pieck: ein unermüdlicher Streiter für die deutsch- sowjetische Freundschaft: ausgewählte Reden und Schriften... ; eingeleitet und zusammengestellt von Heinz Vosske. Berlin, 1977. pp. 159.

PIERS.

WE WANT THE WEST PIER CAMPAIGN. The West Pier: a second report. Brighton, 1975. pp. 30. *bibliog.*

PIGÜE.

Les AVEYRONNAIS dans la Pampa: fondation, développement et vie de la colonie aveyronnaise de Pigüé-Argentine, 1884-1974; ([by] Jean Andreu [and others]). Toulouse, [1977]. pp. 325.

PISACANE (CARLO).

DOTTI (UGO) I dissidenti del Risorgimento: Cattaneo, Ferrari, Pisacane. Roma, 1975. pp. 117. *bibliog.*

PISTOIA (PROVINCE)

— History.

MORELLI (ALDO) and TOMASSINI (LUIGI) Socialismo e classe operaia a Pistoia durante la prima guerra mondiale. [Milano, 1976]. pp. 218.

PITT (Right Hon. WILLIAM).

REILLY (ROBIN) Pitt the Younger, 1759-1806. London, 1978. pp. 390. *bibliog.*

PITT (WILLIAM) Earl of Chatham.

BROWN (PETER DOUGLAS) William Pitt, Earl of Chatham: the Great Commoner. London, 1978. pp. 448. *bibliog.*

PITTSBURGH

— History.

PITTSBURGH; edited by Roy Lubove. New York, 1976. pp. 294.

— — Sources.

PITTSBURGH; edited by Roy Lubove. New York, 1976. pp. 294.

PIVERT (MARCEAU).

JOUBERT (JEAN PAUL) Révolutionnaires de la S.F.I.O.: Marceau Pivert et le pivertisme. [Paris, 1977]. pp. 296. *bibliog.*

PLAGUE

— United Kingdom.

HATCHER (JOHN) Plague, population and the English economy, 1348-1530. London, 1977. pp. 95. *bibliog. (Economic History Society. Studies in Economic and Social History)*

PLAID CYMRU.

CAVENDISH (RUPERT) Differences and similarities between radical liberalism and Plaid Cymru. Manchester, [1977]. pp. 15.

PLANNING.

SYMPOSIUM ON SOCIAL POLICY AND PLANNING, COPENHAGEN, 1970. Report on the Symposium...[held at] Copenhagen, Denmark, 22 June to 2 July 1970. (ST/TAO/SER.C/128). New York, United Nations, 1971. pp. 26.

EXPERT GROUP MEETING ON PLANNING THE FOREIGN TRADE SECTOR IN RELATION TO OVER-ALL PLANNING, BEIRUT, 1971. Report of the Expert Group Meeting...[in] Beirut, Lebanon, 7 to 11 June, 1971. (ST/TAO/SER.C/135). New York, United Nations, 1971. pp. 16.

SANDBERG (ÅKE) The limits to democratic planning: knowledge, power and methods in the struggle for the future. Stockholm, 1976. pp. 391. *bibliog.*

PRENTICE (RICHARD) The determination of worth: macrorationality in urban and regional planning. Reading, 1977. pp. 30. *bibliog. (Reading. University. Department of Geography. Reading Geographical Papers. No. 61)*

ZALTMAN (GERALD) and DUNCAN (ROBERT B.) Strategies for planned change. New York, [1977]. pp. 404. *bibliog.*

PLANTATION LIFE

— Barbados.

HANDLER (JEROME S.) and others. Plantation slavery in Barbados: an archaeological and historical investigation. Cambridge, Mass., 1978. pp. 368. *bibliog.*

PLANTATIONS

— America, Latin.

HACIENDAS, latifundios y plantaciones en America Latina; coordinacion por Enrique Florescano. Mexico, 1975. pp. 667.

PLASTICS INDUSTRY AND TRADE

— United Kingdom.

HOE (SUSANNA) The man who gave his company away: a biography of Ernest Bader, founder of the Scott Bader Commonwealth. London, 1978. pp. 242. *bibliog.*

PLAY

— United Kingdom.

LLEWELYN-DAVIES WEEKS [AND PARTNERS]. Inner area study: Birmingham: Trinity Arts playvan. [London], Department of the Environment, [1977]. pp. 35.

PLAZA (VICTORINO DE LA).

ALBARRACIN (JOSE MANUEL H.) Victorino de la Plaza y la crisis economica de 1875 a 1880. Buenos Aires, [1950]. pp. 155.

PLEAS (CRIMINAL PROCEDURE).

McCABE (SARAH) and PURVES (ROBERT) By-passing the jury: a study of changes of plea and directed acquittals in higher courts. Oxford, [1972]. pp. 46. *(Oxford. University. Penal Research Unit. Occasional Papers. No. 3)*

PLEYDELL-BOUVERIE (WILLIAM) 3rd Earl of Radnor.

HUCH (RONALD K.) The radical Lord Radnor: the public life of Viscount Folkestone, third Earl of Radnor, 1779-1869. Minneapolis, [1977]. pp. 204. *bibliog.*

PLIUSHCH (LEONID IVANOVICH).

L'AFFAIRE Pliouchtch: dossier rassemblé, annoté et traduit par Tania Mathon et Jean-Jacques Marie. Paris, [1976]. pp. 176.

PLUMBERS

— Norway.

KJELLSTRØM (JOHN) Rørleggernes Fagforening, 1884-1959. Oslo, 1959. pp. 238.

PLURALISM (SOCIAL SCIENCES).

AHMED (RAFIA HASSAN) Ethnic and socio-cultural pluralism in the Sudan: its manifestation and effects on national integration. Khartoum, [Institute of Public Administration], 1975. fo. 40. *(Occasional Papers)*

JACKSON (ROBERT J.) Plural societies and new states: a conceptual analysis. Berkeley, Calif., [1977]. pp. 74. *bibliog. (California University. Institute of International Studies. Research Series. No. 30)*

LIJPHART (AREND) Democracy in plural societies: a comparative exploration. New Haven, 1977. pp. 248.

KELSO (WILLIAM ALTON) American democratic theory: pluralism and its critics. Westport, Conn., 1978. pp. 288. *bibliog.*

SMOOHA (SAMMY) Israel: pluralism and conflict. Berkeley, 1978. pp. 462. *bibliogs.*

PLYMOUTH

— Transit systems.

DEVONSHIRE. County Council and CORNWALL. County Council. Planned transport: Plymouth and environs transportation study. [Plymouth, 1967?]. 1 vol. (unpaged).

SCOTT, WILSON, KIRKPATRICK AND PARTNERS. Plymouth and environs transportation study: (final report). [Basingstoke, 1976?]. pp. 241.

POETRY.

VOLPE (GALVANO DELLA) Critique of taste; translated by Michael Caesar. London, 1978. pp. 272.

POETS

— Biography.

SPENDER (STEPHEN) The thirties and after: poetry, politics, people, 1933-75. Glasgow, 1978. pp. 286.

POINT PROCESSES.

MATTHES (KLAUS) and others. Infinitely divisible point processes. Chichester, [1978]. pp. 532. *bibliog. Translation of Unbegrenzt teilbare Punktprozesse, in which Johannes Kerstan's name appeared first on title page.*

POITOU.

See also POITOU-CHARENTES (REGION).

POITOU-CHARENTES (REGION)

— Economic conditions — Statistics.

RESULTATS STATISTIQUES DU POITOU-CHARENTES: revue trimestrielle; ([pd. by] Institut National de la Statistique et des Etudes Economiques, Direction Régionale de Poitiers [France]). q., Je 1971 (no.1)- Poitiers.

POLAND

— Biography.

KISIELEWSKI (TADEUSZ) Heroizm i kompromis: portret zbiorowy działaczy ludowych. Warszawa, 1977 in progress.

— Colonization.

JAKÓBCZYK (WITOLD) Pruska komisja osadnicza, 1886-1919. Poznań, 1976. pp. 200.

— Constitutional history.

KRAJOWA Rada Narodowa; pod redakcją Andrzeja Burdy. Wrocław, 1976. pp. 250.

ŁOJEK (JERZY) Upadek Konstytucji 3 Maja: studium historyczne. Wrocław, 1976. pp. 333. *Some documents in English or French.*

— Constitutional law.

SIEMIEŃSKI (FELIKS) Prawo konstytucyjne. Warszawa, 1976. pp. 346. *bibliog.*

— Economic conditions.

REPORT on visit to Germany, Polish Corridor and Danzig in September 1928; [by a delegation of Conservatives, led by Sir John Sandeman Allen]. 1928. fo. 6. *Typescript: unpublished.*

KUZIŃSKI (STANISŁAW) Polska na gospodarczej mapie świata. Warszawa, 1976. pp. 144.

POLAND (Cont.)

— — Mathematical models.

GÓRALSKA (H.) and others. Studium struktur gospodarczych Polski; pod redakcją naukową Tadeusza Kasprzaka. Warszawa, 1976. pp. 222. *bibliog. With English and Russian summaries.*

— Economic history.

MODZELEWSKI (KAROL) Organizacja gospodarcza państwa piastowskiego X-XIII wiek. Wrocław, 1975. pp. 296. *With French summary.*

ANDRZEJEWSKI (ROMAN) Proces przebudowy struktury gospodarczej Wielkopolski, 1945-1970. Warszawa, 1978. pp. 135. *bibliog. (Poznań. Urząd Wojewódzki. Wydział Kultury i Sztuki. Biblioteka Kroniki Wielkopolski)*

— Economic policy.

PLICHCIŃSKI (ERWIN) and WOLSKI (MICHAŁ) Organizing the process and changes in methods of planning and administration in Poland's economy. Warszawa, 1970. pp. 56. *(Instytut Gospodarki Krajów Rozwijających Się. Teaching Papers: Advanced Course in National Economic Planning. vol.10)*

PORWIT (KAZIMIERZ) and others. Selected topics on perspective planning in Poland. Warsaw, 1970. pp. 71. *(Instytut Gospodarki Krajów Rozwijających Się. Teaching Papers: Advanced Course in National Economic Planning. vol 8)*

WOLSKI (MICHAŁ) Index tables for construction of economic plans. Warsaw, 1970. pp. 130. *(Instytut Gospodarki Krajów Rozwijających Się. Teaching Papers: Advanced Course in National Economic Planning. vol. 9)*

ZAJCHOWSKI (JÓZEF) The application of input-output analysis to planning. Warszawa, 1970. pp. 38. *bibliog. (Instytut Gospodarki Krajów Rozwijających Się. Teaching Papers: Advanced Course in National Economic Planning. vol.7)*

REGIONALNE zró'znicowanie rozwoju społeczno-gospodarczego Polski. Warszawa, 1976. pp. 131. *bibliog. (Polska Akademia Nauk. Komitet Przestrzennego Zagospodarowania Kraju. Biuletyn. z.89)*

— Emigration and immigration.

BOBIŃSKA (CELINA) ed. Mechanizmy polskich migracji zarobkowych. Warszawa, 1976. pp. 218. *(Powszechny Zjazd Historyków Polskich, 11-y, 1974. Prace. 6)*

— Foreign economic relations — Russia.

POLSKO-Radzieckie stosunki gospodarcze: dokumenty i materialy, 1921-1939; wyboru dokonal i opracowal Stanislaw Lopatniuk. Warszawa, 1976. pp. 655.

— Foreign relations.

BROMKE (ADAM) Polska weltpolitik. Londyn, 1975. pp. 40.

SIKORA (FRANZ) Sozialistische Solidarität und nationale Interessen: Polen, Tschechoslowakei, DDR. Köln, [1977]. pp. 248. *(Bundesinstitut für Ostwissenschaftliche und Internationale Studien. Abhandlungen. Band 31)*

ZARNOWSKI (JANUSZ) ed. Przyjaźnie i antagonizmy: stosunki polski z państwami sąsiednimi w latach 1918-1939, etc. Wrocław, 1977. pp. 253.

— — Treaties.

DUDEK (WIESŁAW) Międzynarodowe aspekty nacjonalizacji w Polsce. Warszawa, 1976. pp. 310. *bibliog. With an appendix of treaties.*

— — Denmark.

CZAPLIŃSKI (WŁADYSŁAW) Polska a Dania XVI-XX w.: studia. Warszawa, 1976. pp. 356.

— — Germany.

ARNDT (CLAUS) Die Verträge von Moskau und Warschau: politische, verfassungsrechtliche und völkerrechtliche Aspekte. Bonn, [1973]. pp. 216.

— — Russia.

BASIŃSKI (EUZEBIUSZ) and WALICHNOWSKI (TADEUSZ) Stosunki polsko-radzieckie, 1944-1974. Warszawa, 1974. pp. 272.

— — United States.

LERSKI (GEORGE JAN) ed. Herbert Hoover and Poland: a documentary history of a friendship. Stanford, 1977. pp. 128. *(Stanford University. Hoover Institution on War, Revolution and Peace. Hoover Institution Publications. 174)*

— Historical geography.

ZIEMIA i ludzie dawnej Polski: studia z geografii historycznej; redaktorzy Adam Galos i Julian Janczak. Wrocław, 1976. pp. 211. *(Wrocław. Wrocławskie Towarzystwo Naukowe. Prace. Seria A. Nr. 179)* One article in Russian. *With French summaries.*

— History.

The RESURRECTION of Poland. 2. For a lasting peace, etc. Paris, 1915. pp. 31.

STROITEL'STVO sotsializma v Pol'skoi Narodnoi Respublike: istoricheskie ocherki. Kiev, 1977. pp. 239.

HALECKI (OSCAR VON) Ritter von Chalecki-Halecki. A history of Poland;...with additional material by A.Polonsky. rev. ed. London, 1978. pp. 407.

— — 1763-1796, Partition period.

ŁOJEK (JERZY) Upadek Konstytucji 3 Maja: studium historyczne. Wrocław, 1976. pp. 333. *Some documents in English or French.*

— — 1795-1830.

KOSIM (JAN) Okupacja pruska i konspiracje rewolucyjne w Warszawie, 1796-1806. Wrocław, 1976. pp. 272. *With French and German summaries.*

— — 1848, Revolution of.

CETERA (BRONISŁAW) Proletariacki nurt rewolucji krakowskiej 1848 roku. Kraków, [1977]. pp. 225. *bibliog.*

— — 1863-1864, Revolution.

UNION DES FEDERALISTES POLONAIS. Manifestation franco-polonaise du centenaire de l'insurrection polonaise de 1863. [Paris], 1963. pp. 48.

— — 1864-1918.

LEBLOND (MARIUS ARY) pseud. [i.e. Georges ATHENAS and Aimé MERLO] La Pologne vivante: Russie, Allemagne, Autriche: une renaissance active sous l'horreur des persécutions, le drame du progrès national, la nationalité, la religion, la langue et la littérature, la vie économique. Paris, 1910. pp. 476.

— — 1905, Revolution.

REWOLUCJA 1905-1907 w Lodzi i okręgu: studia i materiały; pod red. Barbary Wachowskiej. Łódź, [1975]. pp. 302.

— — 1939-1945, Occupation.

POLAND. Polish Information Center, New York. 1940. German destruction of cultural life in Poland. New York, [1940?]. pp. 23. *(Documents relating to the Administration of Occupied Countries in Eastern Europe. No.2)*

POLAND. Polish Information Center, New York. 1940. The German exploitation of Polish forests. New York, [1940?]. pp. 19. *(Documents relating to the Administration of Occupied Countries in Eastern Europe. No.1)*

POLAND. Polish Information Center, New York. 1941. Extermination of the Polish people and Colonization by German nationals. New York, [1941?]. pp. 46. *(Documents relating to the Administration of Occupied Countries in Eastern Europe. Nos.8 and 9)*

POLAND. Polish Information Center, New York. 1941. German organization of distribution in Poland. New York, [1941]. pp. 15. *(Documents relating to the Administration of Occupied Countries in Eastern Europe. No.3)*

POLAND. Polish Information Center, New York. 1941. German persecution of religious life in Poland. New York, [1941?]. pp. 29. *(Documents relating to the Administration of Occupied Countries in Eastern Europe. No.4)*

POLAND. Polish Information Center, New York. 1941. The Soviet occupation of Poland. New York, [1941?]. pp. 46. *(Documents relating to the Administration of Occupied Countries in Eastern Europe. No.5)*

CZAPSKA-JORDAN (WANDA) W[olność] R[ówność] N[iepodległość]: PPS pod okupacją niemiecką, 1939-1945. Londyn, 1976. pp. 40.

KRAJOWA Rada Narodowa; pod redakcją Andrzeja Burdy. Wrocław, 1976. pp. 250.

KROLL (BOGDAN) Opieka i samopomoc społeczna w Warszawie, 1939-1945: Stołeczny Komitet Samopomocy Społecznej i warszawskie agendy Rady Głównej Opiekuńczej. Warszawa, 1977. pp. 342. *bibliog.*

PRZYBYSZ (KAZIMIERZ) Konspiracyjny ruch ludowy na Mazowszu, 1939-1945. Warszawa, 1977. pp. 515. *bibliog.*

— Industries.

KUCIŃSKI (KAZIMIERZ) Przestrzenne zró'znicowanie infrastruktury wsi a uprzemysłowienie: aspekty społeczne. Warszawa, 1977. pp. 148. *bibliog. (Polska Akademia Nauk. Komitet i Zakład Badań Rejonów Uprzemysławianych) With Russian and English summaries.*

— Intellectual life.

POLAND. Polish Information Center, New York. 1940. German destruction of cultural life in Poland. New York, [1940?]. pp. 23. *(Documents relating to the Administration of Occupied Countries in Eastern Europe. No.2)*

— Military policy.

ZALIŃSKI (HENRYK) Towarzystwo Demokratyczne Polskie o władzach powstańczych: z dziejów myśli wojskowej Wielkiej Emigracji. [Warszawa, 1976]. pp. 347. *bibliog.*

— Nationalism.

LEBLOND (MARIUS ARY) pseud. [i.e. Georges ATHENAS and Aimé MERLO] La Pologne vivante: Russie, Allemagne, Autriche: une renaissance active sous l'horreur des persécutions, le drame du progrès national, la nationalité, la religion, la langue et la littérature, la vie économique. Paris, 1910. pp. 476.

PATER (MIECZYSŁAW) Ruch polski na Górnym Śląsku w latach 1879-1893. Wrocław, 1969. pp. 326. *bibliog. (Wrocław. Wrocławskie Towarzystwo Naukowe. Prace. Seria A. Nr.136) With German summary.*

— Politics and government.

SADOWSKI (MICHAŁ) System polityczny Polski Ludowej. Warszawa, 1975. pp. 99.

JARUZELSKI (JERZY) Mackiewicz i konserwatyści: szkice do biografi. Warszawa, 1976. pp. 231.

ZIENKOWSKA (KRYSTYNA) Sławetni i urodzeni: ruch polityczny mieszczaństwa w dobie Sejmu Czteroletniego. Warszawa, 1976. pp. 357.

ASSOCIATION OF POLISH STUDENTS AND GRADUATES IN EXILE. Dissent in Poland: reports and documents in translation, December 1975-July 1977. London, [1977]. pp. 200.

POLITYCZNA organizacja społeczeństwa w Polsce w okresie budowy rozwiniętego społeczeństwa socjalistycznego; praca zbiorowa pod redakcją Mariana Szczepaniaka. Poznań, 1977. pp. 299.

WŁADYKA (WIESŁAW) Działalność polityczna polskich stronnictw konserwatywnych w latach 1926-1935. Wrocław, 1977. pp. 253. *bibliog. With English summary.*

RAINA (PETER K.) Political opposition in Poland, 1954-1977. London, 1978. pp. 584. *bibliog.*

— **Relations (general) with France.**

UNION DES FEDERALISTES POLONAIS. Manifestation franco-polonaise du centenaire de l'insurrection polonaise de 1863. [Paris], 1963. pp. 48.

— **Relations (general) with Russia.**

OCHERKI revoliutsionnykh sviazei narodov Rossii i Pol'shi, 1815-1917; pod redaktsiei V.A. D'iakova [and others]. Moskva, 1976. pp. 602.

SSSR i Pol'sha: internatsional'nye sviazi - istoriia i sovremennost'. Moskva, 1977 in progress.

— **Rural conditions.**

KUCIŃSKI (KAZIMIERZ) Przestrzenne zró'znicowanie infrastruktury wsi a uprzemysłowienie: aspekty społeczne. Warszawa, 1977. pp. 148. *bibliog. (Polska Akademia Nauk. Komitet i Zakład Badań Rejonów Uprzemysławianych) With Russian and English summaries.*

— **Social conditions.**

KRZYWICKI (LUDWIK) Wybór pism: wyboru dokonała i wstępem opatrzyła Henryka Hołda-Róziewicz. Warszawa, 1978. pp. 937.

— **Social history.**

GOŁĘBIOWSKI (BRONISŁAW) and WESOŁOWSKI (WŁODZIMIERZ) Klasy, walka klas i przeobra'zenia struktury społecznej w Polsce Ludowej. [Warszawa], 1969. pp. 79. *bibliog.*

SPOŁECZEŃSTWO Polskiej Rzeczypospolitej Ludowej; pod redakcją Antoniego Czubińskiego. Warszawa, 1977. pp. 285. *(Powszechny Zjazd Historyków Polskich, 11-y, 1974. Prace. 1)*

— **Social life and customs.**

LEWICKI (STANISŁAW) Obyczaje. Warszawa, 1976. pp. 175.

— **Statistics.**

POLAND. Główny Urząd Statystyczny. 1976. Polska 1976 w liczbach. Warszawa, 1976. pp. 170.

POLES IN AUSTRIA.

POLACY w Austrii: materiały międzynarodowego sympozjum naukowego, które odbyło się w Uniwersytecie Jagiellońskim w dniach 20-22 maja 1975 r. [Kraków], 1976. pp. 287. *(Zeszyty Naukowe Uniwersytetu Jagiellońskiego. Prace Polonijne. z.2) With German summaries.*

POLES IN CANADA.

PAMIĘTNIKI imigrantów polskich w Kanadzie: wybór pamiętników nadesłanych na konkurs Kanadyjsko-Polskiego Instytutu Badawczego w 1972 r.; Memoirs of Polish immigrants in Canada; edited by Benedykt Heydenkorn. Toronto, 1975. pp. 279. *(Canadian-Polish Research Institute. Studies. 10)*

POLES IN FOREIGN COUNTRIES.

STAN i potrzeby badań nad zbiorowościami polonijnymi; The present situation of and need for studies on Polonia communities. Wrocław, 1976. pp. 671. *With English table of contents.*

ZALIŃSKI (HENRYK) Towarzystwo Demokratyczne Polskie o władzach powstańczych: z dziejów myśli wojskowej Wielkiej Emigracji. [Warszawa, 1976]. pp. 347. *bibliog.*

POLES IN GERMANY.

MARCHLEWSKI (JULIAN BALTAZAR) Zur Polenpolitik der preussischen Regierung: Auswahl von Artikeln aus den Jahren 1897 bis 1923. Berlin, 1957. pp. 112. *(Institut für Marxismus-Leninismus (Berlin). Beiträge zur Geschichte und Theorie der Arbeiterbewegung. Heft 14)*

DYLIŃSKI (RYSZARD) and others, eds. Z literą "P": polacy na robotach przymusowych w hitlerowskiej Rzeszy, 1939-1945: wspomnienia...; wstęp Czesław Łuczak. Poznań, 1976. pp. 611.

KONIECZNY (ALFRED) and SZURGACZ (HERBERT) eds. Praca przymusowa Polaków pod panowaniem hitlerowskim, 1939-1945. Poznań, 1976. pp. lxx,562. *(Poznań. Instytut Zachodni. Documenta Occupationis. 10) Documents in the original German, with Polish, Russian, English and German introductions.*

KOZIEŁŁO-POKLEWSKI (BOHDAN) Zagraniczni robotnicy przymusowi w Prusach Wschodnich w latach II wojny światowej. Warszawa, 1977. pp. 235. *bibliog. (Ośrodek Badań Naukowych im. Wojciecha Kętrzyńskiego w Olsztynie. Rozprawy i Materiały. nr. 55) With Russian, German and English summaries and tables of contents.*

POLES IN PRUSSIA.

MARCHLEWSKI (JULIAN BALTAZAR) Zur Polenpolitik der preussischen Regierung: Auswahl von Artikeln aus den Jahren 1897 bis 1923. Berlin, 1957. pp. 112. *(Institut für Marxismus-Leninismus (Berlin). Beiträge zur Geschichte und Theorie der Arbeiterbewegung. Heft 14)*

POLES IN SILESIA.

PATER (MIECZYSŁAW) Ruch polski na Górnym Śląsku w latach 1879-1893. Wrocław, 1969. pp. 326. *bibliog. (Wrocław. Wrocławskie Towarzystwo Naukowe. Prace. Seria A. Nr.136) With German summary.*

POLES IN THE UNITED STATES.

SUŁEK (ZDZISŁAW) Polacy w wojnie o niepodległość Stanów Zjednoczonych, 1775-1783. Warszawa, 1976. pp. 277. *bibliog.*

BŁAHIJ (KAZIMIERZ) Lądowanie w Jamestown albo zmyślenia i prawdy o pierwszych Polakach w Ameryce; zebrał i opisał Kazimierz Błahij. Warszawa, 1977. pp. 343.

STASIK (FLORIAN) Adam Gurowski, 1805-1866. Warszawa, 1977. pp. 420. *bibliog.*

See also **POLISH AMERICANS.**

POLICE.

POLICE and society; edited by David H. Bayley. Beverly Hills, [1977]. pp. 257. *bibliog. Essays prepared for a conference held at the Graduate School of International Studies, University of Denver, in 1976.*

BOWDEN (TOM) Beyond the limits of the law: a comparative study of the police in crisis politics. [Harmondsworth, 1978]. pp. 301. *bibliog.*

— **Australia — Australian Capital Territory.**

AUSTRALIAN CAPITAL TERRITORY. Police. Annual report. a., 1969/70[1st]- Canberra. *Included in AUSTRALIA. Parliament. [Parliamentary papers].*

— **Canada.**

KELLY (WILLIAM H.) and KELLY (NORA HICKSON) Policing in Canada. Toronto, [1976]. pp. 704. *bibliog.*

— — **Ontario.**

ONTARIO. Task Force on Policing in Ontario. 1974. Report to the Solicitor General; [Edward B. Hale, chairman]. [Toronto], 1974. pp. 183.

— **Italy.**

REGIONI e polizia locale. Milano, 1975. pp. 173. *(Istituto per la Scienza dell'Amministrazione Pubblica. Quaderni ISAP. 16)*

CANOSA (ROMANO) La polizia in Italia dal 1945 ad oggi. Bologna, [1976]. pp. 413.

— **Norway.**

RASMUSSEN (SIGURD) Norsk Politiforbund gjennom 50 år, 1905-1955. Oslo, 1955. pp. 258.

— **Palestine.**

BOWDEN (TOM) The breakdown of public security: the case of Ireland, 1916-1921 and Palestine, 1936-1939. London, [1977]. pp. 342. *bibliog.*

— **South Africa — Complaints against.**

NAPLEY (Sir DAVID) Steven Biko inquest. [1977]. fo. 26. *Unpublished: photocopy of typescript.*

— **United Kingdom.**

CHRISTIAN ECONOMIC AND SOCIAL RESEARCH FOUNDATION. Occasional Papers. No. 4. The amalgamation of police districts: reconciliation of statistics, 1967-1971. Part B: offences to do with the loading or condition of motor vehicles. London, [1971]. pp. 32.

REPORT [of] independent trade union committee inquiry into events which occurred during the right-to-work march on Friday 19th March 1976; [chairman, Vincent Flynn]. London, 1976. pp. 7.

MANNING (PETER K.) Police work: the social organization of policing. Cambridge, Mass., [1977]. pp. 418. *bibliog.*

PHILIPS (DAVID) Crime and authority in Victorian England: the Black Country, 1835-1860. London, 1977. pp. 321. *bibliogs.*

BOWDEN (TOM) Beyond the limits of the law: a comparative study of the police in crisis politics. [Harmondsworth, 1978]. pp. 301. *bibliog.*

REINER (ROBERT) The blue-coated worker: a sociological study of police unionism. Cambridge, 1978. pp. 295. *bibliog.*

SELLWOOD (ARTHUR VICTOR) Police strike, 1919. London, 1978. pp. 214.

U.K. Home Office. 1978. Evidence to the Royal Commission on Criminal Procedure: memorandum no.1: the background to the work of the Commission; memorandum no.2: the accountability of the police. London, 1978. pp. (72).

— — **Attitudes.**

REINER (ROBERT) The blue-coated worker: a sociological study of police unionism. Cambridge, 1978. pp. 295. *bibliog.*

— — **Complaints against.**

UNDER heavy manners: report of the labour movement enquiry into police brutality and the position of black youth in Islington, held on Saturday July 23, 1977. London, 1977. pp. 23.

— — **Salaries, pensions, etc.**

MARPLAN LIMITED. Survey on policemen's pay. [London], 1977. fo. 7.

— — **Ireland.**

BOWDEN (TOM) The breakdown of public security: the case of Ireland, 1916-1921 and Palestine, 1936-1939. London, [1977]. pp. 342. *bibliog.*

— — **Ireland, Northern.**

EVELEGH (ROBIN) Peace keeping in a democratic society: the lessons of Northern Ireland. London, [1978]. pp. 174.

— **United States.**

FOGELSON (ROBERT M.) Big-city police. Cambridge, Mass., 1977. pp. 374.

MANNING (PETER K.) Police work: the social organization of policing. Cambridge, Mass., [1977]. pp. 418. *bibliog.*

POLICE, POLITICAL AND SECRET

POLICE, POLITICAL AND SECRET

— Germany.

GRÜNBERG (KAROL) SS - czarna gwardia Hitlera. [Warszawa], 1975. pp. 558. *bibliog.*

— Russia.

VEREEKEN (GEORGES) La guépéou dans le mouvement trotskiste. Paris, [1975]. pp. 379.

FOURTH INTERNATIONAL. International Committee. Accomplices of the GPU. London, [1976]. pp. 24.

FOURTH INTERNATIONAL. International Committee. How the GPU murdered Trotsky. London, [1976]. 1 pamphlet (unpaged).

FOURTH INTERNATIONAL. International Committee. Trotsky's assassin at large. London, [1977]. pp. 40.

POLICE, PRIVATE

— France.

ANGELI (CLAUDE) and BRIMO (NICOLAS) Une milice patronale: Peugeot;...avec la collaboration de Marc- Rémy Donnalin. Paris, 1975. pp. 105.

— United Kingdom.

DRAPER (HILARY) Private police. Harmondsworth, 1978. pp. 173.

POLICE POWER

— United Kingdom.

U.K. Home Office. 1978. Evidence to the Royal Commission on Criminal Procedure: memorandum no. 3: the powers of the police to arrest or otherwise stop a person, to search him, to stop and search vehicles, and to enter and search premises. London, 1978. 1 vol. (various pagings).

POLICY SCIENCES.

HANDBOOK of political science;...edited by Fred I. Greenstein [and] Nelson W. Polsby. Reading, Mass., [1975]. 9 vols. *bibliogs.*

SANDBERG (ÅKE) The limits to democratic planning: knowledge, power and methods in the struggle for the future. Stockholm, 1976. pp. 391. *bibliog.*

LINEBERRY (ROBERT L.) American public policy: what government does and what difference it makes. New York, [1977]. pp. 296. *bibliog.*

MAKING public policy: studies in American politics; edited by John Brigham. Lexington, Mass., [1977]. pp. 424. *bibliogs.*

POLICYMAKING in contemporary Japan; edited by T.J. Pempel. Ithaca, 1977. pp. 345. *bibliog. Based in part on papers presented at the 1974 annual convention of the Association for Asian Studies.*

The POLITICS of policy making in America: five case studies; edited by David A. Caputo. San Francisco, [1977]. pp. 189.

SIEGEL (RICHARD L.) and WEINBERG (LEONARD B.) Comparing public policies: United States, Soviet Union, and Europe. Homewood, Ill., 1977. pp. 430.

YATES (DOUGLAS) The ungovernable city: the politics of urban problems and policy making. Cambridge, Mass., [1977]. pp. 219. *(Massachusetts Institute of Technology. MIT Studies in American Politics and Public Policy. 3)*

ALLEN (T. HARRELL) New methods in social science research: policy sciences and futures research. New York, [1978]. pp. 157. *bibliogs.*

EDWARDS (GEORGE C.) and SHARKANSKY (IRA) The policy predicament: making and implementing public policy. San Francisco, [1978]. pp. 336.

HAMBLETON (ROBIN) Policy planning and local government. London, 1978. pp. 268.

POLISH AMERICANS.

GREENE (VICTOR R.) For God and country: the rise of Polish and Lithuanian ethnic consciousness in America, 1860-1910. Madison, Wis., 1975. pp. 202. *bibliog.*

BABIŃSKI (GRZEGORZ) Lokalna społeczność polonijna w Stanach Zjednoczonych Ameryki w procesie przemian. Wrocław, 1977. pp. 207. *bibliog. (Polska Akademia Nauk. Komitet Badania Polonii Zagranicznej. Biblioteka Polonijna. 1) With English summary.*

See also POLES IN THE UNITED STATES.

POLISH LANGUAGE

— Dictionaries — Polyglot.

HEBÁK (PETR) and HUSTOPECKÝ (JIŘÍ) compilers. Šestijazyčný slovník termínů z regresní analýzy: [Czech, Russian, Polish, English, French, German]. Praha, 1978. pp. 211. *With preface and explanatory notes in each language.*

POLISH PERIODICALS.

ZAKRZEWSKI (BOGDAN) Tygodnik Literacki, 1838-1845: zarys monograficny. [Warszawa, 1964]. pp. 237. *(Polska Akademia Nauk. Instytut Badań Literackich. Historia i Teoria Literatury: Studia. Seria Historia Literatury. 5)*

POLITICAL CONVENTIONS.

BYRNE (GARY C.) and MARX (PAUL) Writer on American politics. The great American convention: a political history of presidential elections. Palo Alto, Calif., [1976]. pp. 168. *bibliog.*

POLITICAL CRIMES AND OFFENCES

— Palestine.

BOWDEN (TOM) The breakdown of public security: the case of Ireland, 1916-1921 and Palestine, 1936-1939. London, [1977]. pp. 342. *bibliog.*

— Russia.

CALDWELL (DAVID) Opposition, resistance, and political terror in the Soviet Union. [Coventry], 1976. pp. 19. *(University of Warwick. Department of Politics. Working Papers. No. 11)*

AIMS FOR FREEDOM AND ENTERPRISE. 1917-1977: sixty years of communism: the age of the Gulag. London, [1977]. pp. 13.

— South Africa.

AMNESTY INTERNATIONAL. Political imprisonment in South Africa. London, 1978. pp. 108.

— Spain.

FIESTAS LOZA (ALICIA) Los delitos politicos, 1808-1936. Salamanca, 1977. pp. 345. *bibliog.*

— United Kingdom — Ireland.

BOWDEN (TOM) The breakdown of public security: the case of Ireland, 1916-1921 and Palestine, 1936-1939. London, [1977]. pp. 342. *bibliog.*

— United States.

CORPORATE and governmental deviance: problems of organizational behavior in contemporary society; [edited by] M. David Ermann [and] Richard J. Lundman. New York, 1978. pp. 322.

POLITICAL ETHICS.

BUTTERFIELD (Sir HERBERT) Raison d'état: the relations between morality and government. [Brighton, 1975]. pp. 18. *(Martin Wight Memorial Lectures. 1975)*

ETHICAL perspectives on business and society; edited by Yerachmiel Kugel [and] Gladys W. Gruenberg. Lexington, Mass., [1977]. pp. 135.

RYN (CLAES G.) Democracy and the ethical life: a philosophy of politics and community. Baton Rouge, [1978]. pp. 208.

POLITICAL ORATORY

— France.

GISCARD d'Estaing, Mitterrand: 54,774 mots pour convaincre; by Jean-Marie Cotteret [and others]. Paris, [1976]. pp. 347. *bibliog.*

POLITICAL PARTICIPATION.

BRINTON (MAURICE) The irrational in politics. Montreal, [1974]. pp. 72.

ZAMPETTI (PIER LUIGI) La partecipazione popolare al potere: una nuova alternativa al capitalismo e al socialismo. [Milano, 1976]. pp. 226.

— Canada.

HIGGINS (DONALD J.H.) Urban Canada: its government and politics. Toronto, [1977]. pp. 322. *bibliog.*

— Chile.

ALDUNATE (ADOLFO) Participacion y actitud de los pobladores ante las organizaciones poblacionales: una aproximacion a la heterogeneidad popular. Santiago, Chile, 1971. fo. 103.

— Europe, Eastern.

POLITICAL development in Eastern Europe; edited by Jan F. Triska [and] Paul M. Cocks. New York, 1977. pp. 371.

— France.

Les MILITANTS politiques dans trois partis français: Parti Communiste, Parti Socialiste, Union des Démocrates pour la République, [by] Jacques Lagroye [and others]. [Paris, 1976]. pp. 186. *bibliog. (Bordeaux. Université. Institut d'Etudes Politiques. Centre d'Etude et de Recherche sur la Vie Locale. Série Vie Locale. 5.)*

— Germany.

BUSE (MICHAEL) and others. Determinanten politischer Partizipation: Theorieansatz und empirische Überprüfung am Beispiel der Stadtsanierung Andernach. Meisenheim am Glan, 1978. pp. 410. *bibliog.*

— Hawaiian Islands.

STEINHOFF (PATRICIA G.) and DIAMOND (MILTON) Abortion politics: the Hawaii experience. Honolulu, [1977]. pp. 256.

— India.

ELDERSVELD (SAMUEL JAMES) and AHMED (BASHIRUDDIN) Citizens and politics: mass political behavior in India. Chicago, 1978. pp. 351.

— Japan.

WATANUKI (JOJI) Politics in postwar Japanese society. Tokyo, [1977]. pp. 171. *bibliog.*

— United Kingdom.

KITAMURA (KIMIHIKO) Participation at local level in Sheffield: a case study using the interview technique. [Tokyo, 1974?]. pp. 102. *(Gakushuin Review of Law and Politics. 10)*

MARSH (ALAN JOHN) Protest and political consciousness. Beverly Hills, [1977]. pp. 271. *bibliog.*

— United States.

HARRIS (CARL VERNON) Political power in Birmingham, 1871-1921. Knoxville, Tenn., [1977]. pp. 318. *bibliog.*

LAUDON (KENNETH C.) Communications technology and democratic participation. New York, 1977. pp. 116.

RODGERS (JOSEPH LEE) Citizen committees: a guide to their use in local government. Cambridge, Mass., [1977]. pp. 101. *bibliog.*

KELSO (WILLIAM ALTON) American democratic theory: pluralism and its critics. Westport, Conn., 1978. pp. 288. *bibliog.*

POLITICAL PARTIES.

CARINI (CARLO) Benedetto Croce e il partito politico. Firenze, 1975. pp. 241. *(Pensiero Politico, Il. Biblioteca. 7)*

BLONDEL (JEAN) 1929- . Political parties: a genuine case for discontent? London, 1978. pp. 237. *bibliog.*

— History.

PETRESCU (MIHAI M.) Partide, clase, naţiuni: originea şi rolul istoric al partidelor politice în perspectiva socialismului ştiinţific. Bucureşti, 1977. pp. 255.

— Arab countries.

ISMAEL (TAREQ Y.) The Arab left. Syracuse, N.Y., 1976. pp. 204. *bibliogs.*

— Australia.

The EMERGENCE of the Australian party system; edited by P. Loveday [and others]. Sydney, 1977. pp. 536. *bibliog.*

— Bolivia.

PARTIDO OBRERO REVOLUCIONARIO [BOLIVIA]. Congreso Nacional, 21, 1964. Abstencion electoral para desenmascarar las maniobras del oficialismo: hacia un frente revolucionario de izquierda: tesis politica. [La Paz?], 1964. pp. 34.

— Brazil.

SOUZA (MARIA DO CARMO CARVALHO CAMPELLO DE) Estado e partidos politicos no Brasil, 1930-1964. São Paulo, 1976. pp. 178. *bibliog.*

— Canada.

SMITH (PATRICK JOSEPH) The sociology of urban party organizations and political behaviour: contemporary party membership with special reference to England and Canada. 1977. fo. 362. *bibliog.* Typescript. Ph.D. (London) thesis: unpublished. This thesis is the property of London University and may not be removed from the Library.

— — Bibliography.

HEGGIE (GRACE F.) compiler. Canadian political parties, 1867-1968: a historical bibliography. Toronto, [1977]. pp. 603.

— Europe.

HEERS (JACQUES) Parties and political life in the medieval west. Amsterdam, 1977. pp. 312. *bibliog.* Translated by David Nicholas.

SOCIAL democratic parties in Western Europe; edited by William E. Paterson and Alastair H. Thomas. London, [1977]. pp. 444.

The FOREIGN policies of West European socialist parties; edited by Werner J. Feld. New York, [1978]. pp. 149.

— France.

Les MILITANTS politiques dans trois partis français: Parti Communiste, Parti Socialiste, Union des Démocrates pour la République, [by] Jacques Lagroye [and others]. [Paris, 1976]. pp. 186. *bibliog. (Bordeaux. Université. Institut d'Etudes Politiques. Centre d'Etude et de Recherche sur la Vie Locale. Série Vie Locale. 5.)*

BOURDE (GUY) La défaite du Front populaire. Paris, 1977. pp. 359. *bibliog.*

FREARS (JOHN RUSSELL) Political parties and elections in the French fifth republic. London, [1977]. pp. 292. *bibliogs.*

— Germany.

DOLIVE (LINDA L.) Electoral politics at the local level in the German Federal Republic. Gainesville, 1976. pp. 110. *bibliog. (Florida University. Monographs. Social Sciences. No. 56)*

HEIMANN (NORBERT) Die Schiedsgerichtsbarkeit der politischen Parteien in der Bundesrepublik Deutschland. Bonn, 1977. pp. 305. *bibliog. (Friedrich-Ebert-Stiftung. Forschungsinstitut. Schriftenreihe. Band 128)*

LOPEZ PINA (ANTONIO) ed. La España democratica y Europa. Madrid, [1977]. pp. 195.

— India.

MISRA (BANKEY BEHARI) The Indian political parties: an historical analysis of political behaviour up to 1947. Delhi, 1976. pp. 665. *bibliog.*

— Italy.

PETTA (PAOLO) Ideologie costituzionali della sinistra italiana, 1892-1974. Roma, [1975]. pp. 239.

VALITUTTI (SALVATORE) and CIAURRO (GIAN FRANCO) Contro il finanziamento pubblico dei partiti. [Roma, 1975]. pp. 110.

GAMBINO (SILVIO) Partiti politici e forma di governo: finanziamento pubblico e trasformazione del partito politico. Napoli, 1977. pp. 328. *bibliog.*

HEERS (JACQUES) Parties and political life in the medieval west. Amsterdam, 1977. pp. 312. *bibliog.* Translated by David Nicholas.

MEZZOGIORNO e partiti politici; a cura di Domenico Novacco. [Milan, 1977]. pp. 498. *(Associazione per lo Sviluppo dell'Industria nel Mezzogiorno. Centro per gli Studi sullo Sviluppo Economico. Collana Rodolfo Morandi)*

MUZIO (PIER LUIGI) La crisi politica italiana: verso gli anni ottanta. Milano, [1977]. pp. 416.

— Mexico.

MORENO (DANIEL) Los partidos politicos del Mexico contemporaneo, [1916-1977]. 6th ed. Mexico, 1977. pp. 407. *bibliog.*

— Paraguay.

SOSA JOVELLANOS (FRANCISCO) La revolucion y su ideologia: en memoria de los heroes y martires caidos en holocausto de la revolucion. Asuncion, 1969. pp. 40.

— Russia.

PEARSON (RAYMOND) The Russian moderates and the crisis of tsarism, 1914-1917. London, 1977. pp. 208. *bibliog.*

— South West Africa.

TOETEMEYER (GERHARD) South West Africa/Namibia: facts, attitudes, assessment, and prospects. Randburg, 1977. pp. 323. *bibliog.*

— Spain.

BALDRICH CABALLE (JUAN) Programas agrarios de partidos politicos españoles: alternativa politico-economica para el sector agrario. Madrid, [1977]. pp. 235. *bibliog.*

LOPEZ PINA (ANTONIO) ed. La España democratica y Europa. Madrid, [1977]. pp. 195.

PEREZ CALVO (ALBERTO) Los partidos politicos en el Pais Vasco: approximacion a su estudio. San Sebastian, 1977. pp. 119.

— United Kingdom.

JOURNES (CLAUDE) L'extrême gauche en Grande-Bretagne. Paris, 1977. pp. 229. *bibliog.*

KENYON (JOHN PHILIPPS) Revolution principles: the politics of party, 1689-1720. Cambridge, 1977. pp. 248. *(Oxford. University. Ford Lectures. 1975/76)*

SMITH (PATRICK JOSEPH) The sociology of urban party organizations and political behaviour: contemporary party membership with special reference to England and Canada. 1977. fo. 362. *bibliog.* Typescript. Ph.D. (London) thesis: unpublished. This thesis is the property of London University and may not be removed from the Library.

U.K. Central Office of Information. Reference Division. 1977. Organisation of political parties in Britain. rev. ed. London, 1977. pp. 20. *bibliog.*

— United States.

KIRKPATRICK (JEANE J.) Dismantling the parties: reflections on party reform and party decomposition. Washington, [1978]. pp. 31. *(American Enterprise Institute for Public Policy Research. AEI Studies. 191)*

— — States.

DENT (HARRY S.) The prodigal South returns to power. New York, [1978]. pp. 308.

POLITICAL POSTERS, FRENCH.

GASQUET (VASCO) Les 500 affiches de mai 68. [Paris], 1978. pp. 220.

POLITICAL PRISONERS.

AMNESTY INTERNATIONAL. Summary of proposals to the Fifth United Nations Congress on the Prevention of Crime and the Treatment of Offenders, Toronto, 1-15 September 1975. London, [1975]. pp. 16.

— Argentine Republic.

GRECA (ALCIDES) Tras el alambrado de Martin Garcia. Buenos Aires, 1934. pp. 221.

COMISION ARGENTINA POR LOS DERECHOS HUMANOS. Argentina: proceso al genocidio. Madrid, 1977. pp. 328.

— Greece.

AMNESTY INTERNATIONAL. Torture in Greece : the first torturers' trial, 1975. London, 1977. pp. 98.

— India — Personal narratives.

NARAYAN (JAYAPRAKASH) The essential JP: the philosophy and prison diary of Jayaprakash Narayan; edited by Satish Kumar. Dorchester, 1978. pp. 152.

— Indonesia.

AMNESTY INTERNATIONAL. Indonesia: an Amnesty International report. London, 1977. pp. 146.

— Korea.

AMNESTY INTERNATIONAL. Report of the mission to the Republic of Korea, 27 March-9 April 1975. London, [1976]. pp. 36.

— Malaysia — Personal narratives.

AZIZ ISHAK (ABDUL) Special guest: the detention in Malaysia of an ex-cabinet minister. Singapore, 1977. pp. 210.

— Netherlands.

NETHERLANDS. Centraal Bureau voor de Statistiek. 1976. Onderzoek naar de sterfte onder overlevenden uit concentratiekampen, 1945-1968. 's-Gravenhage, 1976. pp. 63. *With English summary.*

— Nicaragua.

AMNESTY INTERNATIONAL. The republic of Nicaragua;...including the findings of a mission to Nicaragua 10-15 May 1976. London, 1977. pp. 75. *bibliog.*

— Philippine Islands.

AMNESTY INTERNATIONAL. Report of an Amnesty International mission to the Republic of the Philippines, 22 November-5 December 1975. London, [1976]. pp. 60.

POLITICAL PRISONERS.(Cont.)

AMNESTY INTERNATIONAL. Report of an Amnesty International mission to the Republic of the Philippines, 22 November-5 December, 1975. 2nd ed. London, 1977. pp. 95. *Includes reply of Philippine government.*

— **Rhodesia.**

INTERNATIONAL DEFENCE AND AID FUND. Ian Smith's hostages: political prisoners in Rhodesia. London, 1976. pp. 38.

— **Russia.**

L'AFFAIRE Pliouchtch: dossier rassemblé, annoté et traduit par Tania Mathon et Jean-Jacques Marie. Paris, [1976]. pp. 176.

BLOCH (SIDNEY) and REDDAWAY (PETER B.) Russia's political hospitals: the abuse of psychiatry in the Soviet Union. London, 1977. pp. 510.

— **South Africa.**

AMNESTY INTERNATIONAL. Political imprisonment in South Africa. London, 1978. pp. 108.

WOODS (DONALD) Biko. New York, [1978]. pp. 288.

— **Sri Lanka.**

AMNESTY INTERNATIONAL. Report of an Amnesty International mission to Sri Lanka, 9- 15 January 1975. 2nd ed. London, 1976. pp. 51.

— **United Kingdom.**

POLITICAL prisoners and prisoners' unions: conflict or cooperation? [London], 1973. pp. 25.

POLITICAL PSYCHOLOGY.

BRINTON (MAURICE) The irrational in politics. Montreal, [1974]. pp. 72.

CREWE (IVOR) and others. The erosion of partisanship, 1964-1975. [Colchester], 1976. pp. 41. *(University of Essex. Department of Government. British Election Studies)*

EDELMAN (MURRAY JACOB) Political language: words that succeed and policies that fail. New York, [1977]. pp. 164. *(Wisconsin University, Madison. Institute for Research on Poverty. Monograph Series)*

MARSH (ALAN JOHN) Protest and political consciousness. Beverly Hills, [1977]. pp. 271. *bibliog.*

SCHUBERT (GLENDON AUSTIN) Political attitudes and ideologies. Beverly Hills, [1977]. pp. 72. *bibliog.*

ARCHIBALD (WILLIAM PETER) Social psychology as political economy. Toronto, [1978]. pp. 296. *bibliog.*

POLITICAL SATIRE, ITALIAN.

BIAGI (ENZO) Strettamente personale. [Milano, 1977]. pp. 302.

POLITICAL SCIENCE.

COLE (GEORGE DOUGLAS HOWARD) Some relations between political and economic theory. London, 1934. pp. 92. *Based on a course of lectures delivered in Oxford in 1933.*

DAHRENDORF (RALF) Die Regierbarkeit moderner Demokratien...; Vortrag...am 2. Dezember 1974 in München. Frankfurt (Main), [1974]. pp. 3-11. *(Extracted from Nr.13, Deutsche Bank, Beiträge zu Wirtschafts- und Währungsfragen und zur Bankgeschichte)*

GIANNOTTI (DONATO) Opere politiche ([and] Lettere italiane 1526-1571); a cura di Furio Diaz. Milano, [1974]. 2 vols. *bibliog.*

HANDBOOK of political science;...edited by Fred I. Greenstein [and] Nelson W. Polsby. Reading, Mass., [1975]. 9 vols. *bibliogs.*

CORDOVA (ARNALDO) Sociedad y Estado en el mundo moderno. Mexico, 1976. pp. 287.

FILANGIERI (GAETANO) Cavaliere. Scritti; a cura di Franco Venturi. [Torino, 1976]. pp. 139. *bibliog.*

STANKIEWICZ (WLADYSLAW JOZEF) The future of political theory. [London, 1976]. pp. 5. *bibliog.*

RATHENAU (WALTHER) Walther Rathenau-Gesamtausgabe; herausgegeben von Hans Dieter Hellige und Ernst Schulin. München, 1977 in progress.

BALL (TERENCE) ed. Political theory and praxis: new perspectives. Minneapolis, Minn., [1977]. pp. 281. *Essays dedicated to the memory of Hannah Arendt.*

BOSE (ARUN) Political paradoxes and puzzles. Oxford, 1977. pp. 276. *bibliog.*

BOURNE (RANDOLPH SILLIMAN) The radical will: selected writings, 1911-1918; selection and introductions by Olaf Hansen. New York, [1977]. pp. 548. *bibliog.*

BURDEAU (GEORGES) Droit constitutionnel et institutions politiques. 18th ed. Paris, 1977. pp. 690.

FERRARI (GIUSEPPE) Political writer. Scritti politici; a cura di Ernesto Sestan. [Torino, 1977]. pp. 214. *bibliog.*

FOUNDATION of political science: research, methods, and scope; edited by Donald M. Freeman. New York, [1977]. pp. 882. *bibliog.*

HAYEK (FRIEDRICH AUGUST) Drei Vorlesungen über Demokratie, Gerechtigkeit und Sozialismus. Tübingen, 1977. pp. 59. *(Walter Eucken Institut. Vorträge und Aufsätze. 63) German translations of three lectures given in Australia in 1976.*

JACKSON (ROBERT J.) Plural societies and new states: a conceptual analysis. Berkeley, Calif., [1977]. pp. 74. *bibliog. (California University. Institute of International Studies. Research Series. No. 30)*

JAMES (CYRIL LIONEL ROBERT) The future in the present: selected writings. London, 1977. pp. 271.

MELANGES offerts à Georges Burdeau: le pouvoir. Paris, 1977. pp. 1190.

MILNE (ALAN JOHN MITCHELL) Politics and controversy. Durham, 1977. pp. 25. *An inaugural lecture given at Durham University on 25 January 1977.*

MOORHOUSE (FRED) Politics, nonviolence and social justice: an African perspective. New Malden, [1977]. pp. 20. *(Fellowship of Reconciliation. Alex Wood Memorial Lectures. 1977)*

NURMI (HANNU) Rationality and public goods: essays in analytic political theory. Helsinki, 1977. pp. 138. *bibliog. (Societas Scientiarum Fennica. Commentationes Scientiarum Socialium. 9)*

ROUSSEAU (JEAN JACQUES) Du contrat social; précédé de La démocratie selon Rousseau par Jean Pierre Siméon. Paris, [1977]. pp. 317. *bibliog.*

WEINSTEIN (MICHAEL A.) The tragic sense of political life. Columbia, S.C., [1977]. pp. 189.

BAGUENARD (JACQUES) L'univers politique. [Paris, 1978]. pp. 208. *bibliog.*

FERNS (HENRY STANLEY) The disease of government. London, 1978. pp. 148. *bibliog.*

FREY (BRUNO S.) Modern political economy. Oxford, 1978. pp. 166. *bibliogs.*

FROHLICH (NORMAN) and OPPENHEIMER (JOE A.) Modern political economy. Englewood Cliffs, [1978]. pp. 143. *bibliogs.*

JACOBSON (NORMAN) Pride and solace: the functions and limits of political theory. Berkeley, [1978]. pp. 166.

KOLB (EUGENE J.) A framework for political analysis. Englewood Cliffs, [1978]. pp. 338. *bibliog.*

MACKENZIE (WILLIAM JAMES MILLAR) Political identity. [Harmondsworth, 1978]. pp. 185. *bibliog.*

ROSENTHAL (URIEL) Political order: rewards, punishments and political stability. Meppel, 1978. pp. 337. *bibliog. Proefschrift (doctor in de sociale wetenschappen)- Erasmus Universiteit Rotterdam.*

SKILLEN (ANTHONY) Ruling illusions: philosophy and the social order. Hassocks, Sussex, 1977. pp. 179.

SPENCE (LARRY D.) The politics of social knowledge. University Park, Penn., [1978]. pp. 374. *bibliog.*

TUFTE (EDWARD R.) Political control of the economy. Princeton, [1978]. pp. 168.

— **Bibliography.**

CENTRE FOR POLICY STUDIES. Bibliography of freedom. London, 1976. pp. 28.

The COMBINED retrospective index set to journals in political science 1886-1974...; executive editor: Annadel N. Wile. Washington, 1977-78. 8 vols.

— **Decision making.**

CROZIER (MICHEL) The governability of West European societies. Colchester, [1977?]. pp. 15. *(University of Essex. Noel Buxton Lectures. 1977)*

OBLER (JEFFREY L.) and others. Decision-making in smaller democracies: the consociational burden. Beverly Hills, [1977]. pp. 58. *bibliog.*

— **Dictionaries and encyclopedias.**

MICA enciclopedie de politologie. București, 1977. pp. 493. *With English afterword.*

— **History.**

LOCKYER (ANDREW) The traditional approach to the study of the history of political theory. [1976?]. pp. 29. *Unpublished: typescript. Paper presented at the conference of the Political Studies Association, Nottingham, 1976.*

BLUHM (WILLIAM THEODORE) Theories of the political system: classics of political thought and modern political analysis. 3rd ed. Englewood Cliffs, N.J., [1978]. pp. 514. *bibliogs.*

— — **India.**

KARUNAKARAN (KOTTA P.) Indian politics from Dadabhai Naoroji to Gandhi: a study of the political ideas of modern India. New Delhi, 1975. pp. 226. *bibliog.*

— — **Italy.**

LALLA (MANLIO DI) Liberalismo e postfascismo. Roma, [1975]. pp. 291.

LOMBARDO (ANTONIO) Teorie del potere politico: Mosca e Pareto. Bologna, [1976]. pp. 146.

— — **United Kingdom.**

DICKINSON (H.T.) Liberty and property: political ideology in eighteenth-century Britain. London, [1977]. pp. 369.

ECCLESHALL (ROBERT) Order and reason in politics: theories of absolute and limited monarchy in early modern England. Oxford, 1978. pp. 197. *bibliog.*

— — **United States.**

COFFEY (JOHN W.) Political realism in American thought. Lewisburg, [1977]. pp. 217. *bibliog.*

— **Mathematical models.**

NURMI (HANNU) Rationality and public goods: essays in analytic political theory. Helsinki, 1977. pp. 138. *bibliog. (Societas Scientiarum Fennica. Commentationes Scientiarum Socialium. 9)*

— **Methodology.**

MIDDENDORP (C.P.) Progressiveness and conservatism: the fundamental dimensions of ideological controversy and their relationship to social class. The Hague, [1978]. pp. 457. *bibliog.*

— **Periodicals — Indexes.**

The COMBINED retrospective index set to journals in political science 1886-1974...; executive editor: Annadel N. Wile. Washington, 1977-78. 8 vols.

— **Study and teaching.**

The STUDY of politics: a collection of inaugural lectures; edited by Preston King. London, 1977. pp. 322.

— — **Canada.**

JENSON (JANE) and TOMLIN (BRIAN W.) Canadian politics: an introduction to systematic analysis. Toronto, [1977]. pp. 168.

— — **Europe.**

POLITICAL science in Europe. [Colchester, 1976]. 1 vol. (unpaged). *Published by the European Consortium for Political Research.*

— — **United Kingdom.**

POLITICAL education and political literacy; edited by Bernard Crick and Alex Porter. [London, 1978]. pp. 264. *The report and papers of, and the evidence submitted to, the Working Party of the Hansard Society's Programme for Political Education.*

POLITICAL SCIENCE RESEARCH

— **Norway.**

ROKKAN (STEIN) Politisk forskning i Norge: tilbakeblikk og utsyn: foredrag... 15. mars 1973. Bergen, 1974. pp. 20. *(Christian Michelsens Institutt for Videnskap og Åndsfrihet. Beretninger. 37, 2)*

POLITICAL SOCIALIZATION.

ETZIONI-HALEVY (EVA) and SHAPIRA (RINA) Political culture in Israel: cleavage and integration among Israeli Jews. New York, 1977. pp. 249. *bibliog.*

HANDBOOK of political socialization: theory and research; edited by Stanley Allen Renshon. New York, [1977]. pp. 547. *bibliog.*

NIELSEN (H. DEAN) Tolerating political dissent: the impact of high school social climates in the United States and West Germany. Stockholm, [1977]. pp. 138. *bibliog.* *(International Association for the Evaluation of Educational Achievement. IEA Monograph Studies. No. 6)*

SPENCE (LARRY D.) The politics of social knowledge. University Park, Penn., [1978]. pp. 374. *bibliog.*

STACEY (BARRIE G.) Political socialization in western society: an analysis from a life-span perspective. London, 1978. pp. 176. *bibliogs.*

POLITICAL SOCIOLOGY.

COX (GRAHAM) and WOOD (GEOF) Political scientist. State and civil society: an impasse within political sociology? Bath, 1976. pp. 29.

BERGER (PETER L.) Facing up to modernity: excursions in society, politics and religion. New York, [1977]. pp. 233.

EULAU (HEINZ) Technology and civility: the skill revolution in politics. Stanford, Calif., [1977]. pp. 111. *(Stanford University. Hoover Institution on War, Revolution and Peace. Hoover Institution Publications. 167)*

LAPIERRE (JEAN WILLIAM) Vivre sans Etat?: essai sur le pouvoir politique et l'innovation sociale. Paris, [1977]. pp. 380.

LASSWELL (HAROLD DWIGHT) Harold D. Lasswell on political sociology; edited and with an introduction by Dwaine Marvick. Chicago, [1977]. pp. 456. *bibliog.*

LEHMAN (EDWARD W.) Political society: a macrosociology of politics. New York, 1977. pp. 247. *bibliog.*

PAIGE (GLENN D.) The scientific study of political leadership. New York, [1977]. pp. 416. *bibliog.*

ORUM (ANTHONY M.) Introduction to political sociology: the social anatomy of the body politic. Englewood Cliffs, [1978]. pp. 390. *bibliog.*

POWER and the state; edited by Gary Littlejohn [and others]. London, [1978]. pp. 314. *Papers presented at the 1977 Annual Conference of the British Sociological Association.*

SZYMANSKI (ALBERT) The capitalist state and the politics of class. Cambridge, Mass., [1978]. pp. 333.

POLITICIANS

— **Germany.**

HENKELS (WALTER) Neue Bonner Köpfe. 9th ed. Düsseldorf, 1978. pp. 368.

— **United States.**

ALLSWANG (JOHN M.) Bosses, machines, and urban voters: an American symbiosis. Port Washington, 1977. pp. 157. *bibliog.*

COOKE (JACOB E.) Tench Coxe and the early Republic. Chapel Hill, [1978]. pp. 543. *bibliog.*

SCHWENINGER (LOREN) James T. Rapier and reconstruction. Chicago, [1978]. pp. 248. *bibliog.*

POLITICS AND EDUCATION.

— **United Kingdom.**

TAPPER (TED) and SALTER (BRIAN) Education and the political order: changing patterns of class control. London, 1978. pp. 250.

POLITICS AND LITERATURE.

MAURO (WALTER) and CLEMENTELLI (ELENA) eds. La trappola e la nudità: lo scrittore e il potere; [an anthology]. [Milano, 1974]. pp. 269.

POLITICS IN LITERATURE.

MAURO (WALTER) and CLEMENTELLI (ELENA) eds. La trappola e la nudità: lo scrittore e il potere; [an anthology]. [Milano, 1974]. pp. 269.

GATT-RUTTER (JOHN) Writers and politics in modern Italy. London, [1978]. pp. 66. *bibliog.*

MAWBY (JANET) Writers and politics in modern Scandinavia. London, [1978]. pp. 55. *bibliogs.*

POLLUTION.

GENERAL AGREEMENT ON TARIFFS AND TRADE. Studies in International Trade. Geneva, 1971 in progress.

GLADWIN (THOMAS) Environment, planning and the multinational corporation. Greenwich, Conn., [1977]. pp. 295. *bibliog.*

— **Economic aspects.**

BARDE (JEAN PHILIPPE) and GERELLI (EMILIO) Economie et politique de l'environnement. [Paris, 1977]. pp. 210.

ORGANISATION FOR ECONOMIC CO-OPERATION AND DEVELOPMENT. 1977. Emission control costs in the iron and steel industry. Paris, 1977. pp. 175.

PRINGLE (LAURENCE P.) The economic growth debate: are there limits to growth? New York, 1978. pp. 86. *bibliog.*

— — **Canada — British Columbia.**

CONFERENCE ON ECONOMIC INCENTIVES FOR AIR AND WATER POLLUTION CONTROL, VICTORIA, B.C., 1974. The practical application of economic incentives to the control of pollution: the case of British Columbia; edited by James B. Stephenson. Vancouver, [1977]. pp. 446. *(British Columbia Institute for Economic Policy Analysis. Analysis Series. 4)*

— — **United States.**

JOBS, money and pollution; edited by Lester A. Sobel. New York, [1977]. pp. 216. *Based on records compiled by Facts on File.*

— **Law and legislation — Italy.**

GIAMPIETRO (FRANCO) and GIAMPIETRO (PASQUALE) Commento alla legge sull'inquinamento delle acque e del suolo. Milano, 1978. pp. 522.

— **Canada — British Columbia.**

CONFERENCE ON ECONOMIC INCENTIVES FOR AIR AND WATER POLLUTION CONTROL, VICTORIA, B.C., 1974. The practical application of economic incentives to the control of pollution: the case of British Columbia; edited by James B. Stephenson. Vancouver, [1977]. pp. 446. *(British Columbia Institute for Economic Policy Analysis. Analysis Series. 4)*

— **Philippine Islands.**

MARLAY (ROSS) Pollution and politics in the Philippines. Athens, Ohio, 1977. pp. 121. *(Ohio University. Center for International Studies. Papers in International Studies. Southeast Asia Series. No. 43)*

— **United Kingdom.**

FRANKEL (MAURICE) The Social Audit pollution handbook: how to assess environmental and workplace pollution. London, 1978. pp. 210.

— **United States.**

NATIONAL PETROLEUM COUNCIL. Committee on Environmental Conservation. Environmental conservation: the oil and gas industries; volume 1; a summary: a report of the National Petroleum Council's Committee on Environmental Conservation, etc. [Washington], 1971. 1 vol.

The SOCIAL burdens of environmental pollution: a comparative metropolitan data source; Brian J.L. Berry, ed.; contributing authors Susan Caris [and others]. Cambridge, Mass., [1977]. pp. 613. *bibliog.*

POLO (MARCO).

POLO (MARCO) The travels of Marco Polo; translated and with an introduction by Ronald Latham. Harmondsworth, 1958. pp. 351.

POLYBIUS, the Historian.

MOMIGLIANO (ARNALDO) Polybius between the English and the Turks. [Oxford, 1974]. pp. 15. *(Oxford. University. Myres Memorial Lectures. No.7)*

POLYNESIANS IN NEW ZEALAND.

The EDUCATION of non-European children: proceedings of a national in-service course for secondary teachers, held at Lopdell House, 12-16 May, 1969. [Wellington, Department of Education, 1969]. pp. 63.

— **Juvenile literature.**

CHALLIS (R.L.) Pacific islanders in New Zealand;...a bulletin for schools. Wellington, School Publications Branch, 1970. pp. 75.

POLYTECHNIC OF NORTH LONDON.

CAMPBELL (F.J.) Sociologist. High command: the making of an oligarchy at the Polytechnic of North London, 1970-74. [London, 1974]. pp. 132.

POMPIDOU (GEORGES).

LIMAGNE (PIERRE) La Ve République de Charles de Gaulle et Georges Pompidou. Paris, [1978]. pp. 393.

PONCE (ANIBAL).

MARINELLO VIDAURRETA (JUAN) Ocho notas sobre Anibal Ponce. La Habana, [1961]. pp. 45. *(Sobretiro de la revista "Islas", organo de la Universidad Central de las Villas)*

POOR.

MOLLAT (MICHEL) Les pauvres au Moyen Age: étude sociale. [Paris, 1978]. pp. 395. *bibliog.*

POOR. (Cont.)

VEREIN FÜR SOZIALPOLITIK. Schriften. Neue Folge. Band 95. Zur Neuen Sozialen Frage; von Friedrich Buttler [and others]; herausgegeben von Hans Peter Widmaier. Berlin, [1978]. pp. 249.

— Health and hygiene — United States.

DAVIS (KAREN) and SCHOEN (CATHY) Health and the war on poverty: a ten-year appraisal. Washington, D.C., [1978]. pp. 230. *(Brookings Institution. Studies in Social Economics)*

— Medical care — United States.

DAVIS (KAREN) and SCHOEN (CATHY) Health and the war on poverty: a ten-year appraisal. Washington, D.C., [1978]. pp. 230. *(Brookings Institution. Studies in Social Economics)*

LUFT (HAROLD S.) Poverty and health: economic causes and consequences of health problems. Cambridge, Mass., [1978]. pp. 263. *bibliog.*

— Nutrition.

THOMPSON (BENJAMIN) Count Rumford. Essay on food, and particularly on feeding the poor; published in the year 1795, and now reprinted for the Friends of the Poor. Youghal, printed by J.W. Lindsay, 1847. pp. 51.

— Australia.

CHRONIC poverty: city and country families. Canberra, 1975. pp. 122. *(Australia. Commission of Inquiry into Poverty. Research Reports)*

FINANCIAL aspects of rural poverty. Canberra, 1975. pp. 120. *(Australia. Commission of Inquiry into Poverty. Research Reports)*

HILL (KATHLEEN F.) A study of aboriginal poverty in two country towns. Canberra, 1975. pp. 89. *bibliog.* *(Australia. Commission of Inquiry into Poverty. Research Reports)*

TRELOAR (SUSAN) The relationship between poverty and disability in Australia. Canberra, 1977. pp. 72. *(Australia. Commission of Inquiry into Poverty. Social/Medical Aspects of Poverty Series)*

— Belgium.

SENAEVE (PATRICK) De bestrijding van de armoede in België: analyse van het toekennen van een gewaarborgd inkomen en van de hervorming van de COO'S. Leuven, 1977. pp. 615. *(Katholieke Universiteit te Leuven. Instituut voor Sociale Zekerheidsrecht. [Publications]. Nr.27)*

— Byzantine Empire.

PATLAGEAN (EVELYNE) Pauvreté économique et pauvreté sociale à Byzance 4e-7e siècles. Paris, [1977]. pp. 483. *bibliog. (Paris. Ecole des Hautes Etudes en Sciences Sociales. Centre de Recherches Historiques. Civilizations et Sociétés. 48)*

— Canada.

DRAGUSHAN (JEAN L.) To be poor in Canada. Edmonton, [1975]. pp. 85. *bibliog.*

NATIONAL CONFERENCE ON LAW AND POVERTY, OTTAWA, 1971. The law and the poor in Canada; edited by Irwin Cotler and Herbert Marx. Montréal, [1977]. pp. 143.

— Cuba.

LEWIS (OSCAR) and others. Four men: living the revolution: an oral history of contemporary Cuba. Urbana, Ill., [1977]. pp. 538. *bibliog.*

LEWIS (OSCAR) and others. Neighbors: living the revolution: an oral history of contemporary Cuba. Urbana, [1978]. pp. 581. *bibliog.*

— Germany.

VEREIN FÜR SOZIALPOLITIK. Schriften. Neue Folge. Band 95. Zur Neuen Sozialen Frage; von Friedrich Buttler [and others]; herausgegeben von Hans Peter Widmaier. Berlin, [1978]. pp. 249.

— India.

RAKSHIT (GANGADHAR) Poverty and planning in India. Calcutta, 1977. pp. 160. *bibliog.*

— Israel.

HABIB (JACK) Poverty in Israel before and after receipt of public transfers. Jerusalem, 1974. pp. 129. *bibliog. (Israel. National Insurance Institute. Bureau of Research and Planning. Discussion Papers. 4)*

GREENBERG (HAROLD I.) and NADLER (SAMUEL) Poverty in Israel: economic realities and the promise of social justice. New York, 1977. pp. 176. *bibliog.*

— Mexico.

ECKSTEIN (SUSAN) The poverty of revolution: the state and the urban poor in Mexico. Princeton, N.J., [1977]. pp. 300. *bibliog.*

— Netherlands.

EERENBEEMT (H.F.J.M. VAN DEN) Armoede en arbeidsdwang: werkinrichtingen voor "onnutte" Nederlanders in de Republiek, 1760-1795: een mentaliteitsgeschiedenis. 's-Gravenhage, 1977. pp. 231. *bibliog.*

— South Africa.

POTGIETER (J.F.) The household subsistence level in the major urban centres of the Republic of South Africa, April, 1976. Port Elizabeth, 1976. pp. 56. *(University of Port Elizabeth. Institute for Planning Research. Fact Papers. No.16)*

POTGIETER (J.F.) The household subsistence level in the major urban centres of the Republic of South Africa, April, 1977. Port Elizabeth, 1977. pp. 65. *(University of Port Elizabeth. Institute for Planning Research. Fact Papers. No. 21)*

— Spain.

CASADO (DEMETRIO) La pobreza en la estructura social de España. Madrid, [1976]. pp. 176.

— Sweden.

GREVE (JOHN) Low incomes in Sweden;...background paper to Report No. 6: lower incomes. London, 1978. pp. 45. *(U.K. Royal Commission on the Distribution of Income and Wealth, 1974. Background Papers. No. 6) Report No. 6 published as British Parliamentary Paper Cmnd. 7175, Session 1977-78.*

— Underdeveloped areas.

See UNDERDEVELOPED AREAS — Poor.

— United Kingdom.

ALLEN (WILLIAM) F.R.S., of the Society of Friends. Colonies at home: or, Means for rendering the industrious labourer independent of parish relief, and for providing for the poor population of Ireland by the cultivation of the soil;...a new edition with additions. London, Longman, 1832. pp. 52,8.

The CYCLE of deprivation: papers presented to a national study conference, Manchester University, March 1974 [organized by the Child and Family Care Section of the British Association of Social Workers]. Birmingham, [1974?]. pp. 33.

POVERTY, inequality and class structure; edited by Dorothy Wedderburn. Cambridge, 1974, repr. 1975. pp. 247. *Most of these papers were originally written for a meeting of Section N (Sociology) of the British Association meeting at Exeter in 1969.*

ABEL-SMITH (BRIAN) Child poverty; [address given to the annual general meeting of Family Service Units in 1971]. London, [1976]. pp. 22. *(Reprinted from Family Service Units Quarterly, No. 1)*

CLIFF (SHEILA) and FIELD (FRANK) 1942- . "I dread to think about Christmas"; a study of poor families in 1976. London, 1976. pp. 26.

MEANS (ROBIN) Social work and the 'undeserving' poor. Birmingham, 1977. pp. 125. *bibliog. (Birmingham. University. Centre for Urban and Regional Studies. Occasional Papers. No. 37)*

U.K. Equal Opportunities Commission. 1977. Women and low incomes: a report based on evidence to the Royal Commission on Income Distribution and Wealth. [London], 1977. pp. 39.

U.K. Supplementary Benefits Commission. 1977. Low incomes: evidence to the Royal Commission on the Distribution of Income and Wealth. London, 1977. pp. 100. *(Supplementary Benefits Administration Papers. 6)*

DIGBY (ANNE) Pauper palaces. London, 1978. pp. 266. *bibliog.*

WILSON (HARRIETT CHARLOTTE) and HERBERT (GEOFFREY WILLIAM) Parents and children in the inner city. London, 1978. pp. 248. *bibliog.*

— — Ireland.

DUBLIN. Corporation instituted for the Relief of the Poor. Observations on the state and condition of the poor, under the institution, for their relief, in the City of Dublin;... published by order of the Corporation, instituted for the relief of the poor, etc. Dublin, printed by W. Wilson, 1775. pp. 20.

DUBLIN. Association for the Suppression of Mendicity in Dublin. Annual report. a., 1818-1819(1st-2nd). Dublin.

ALLEN (WILLIAM) F.R.S., of the Society of Friends. Colonies at home: or, Means for rendering the industrious labourer independent of parish relief, and for providing for the poor population of Ireland by the cultivation of the soil;...a new edition with additions. London, Longman, 1832. pp. 52,8.

BLACKER (WILLIAM) An essay on the best mode of improving the condition of the labouring classes of Ireland. London, R. Groombridge, 1846. pp. 56. *Revised version of an essay which won the Gold Medal of the Royal Agricultural Improvement Society of Ireland.*

— — Scotland.

NORRIS (GEOFF) Poverty: the facts in Scotland. London, 1977. pp. 65. *(Child Poverty Action Group. Poverty Pamphlets. 30)*

— United States.

WAXMAN (CHAIM I.) The stigma of poverty: a critique of poverty theories and policies. New York, [1977]. pp. 148. *bibliog.*

ANDERSON (MARTIN) Ph.D. Welfare: the political economy of welfare reform in the United States. Stanford, [1978]. pp. 251. *(Stanford University. Hoover Institution on War, Revolution and Peace. Hoover Institution Publications. 181)*

POOR LAWS

— United Kingdom.

RICHARDS (GEORGE) The immoral effects of the poor laws considered in a sermon preached at the Parish Church of Bampton, Oxfordshire, on Monday in Whitsun week, 1818 at the annual meeting of the Friendly Societies of that place. London, F.C. and J. Rivington, 1818. pp. 52.

PLAN for the relief of the agricultural poor, with a view to diminish the poor-rates, and give permanent employment to the labourer, etc. Wycombe, printed by M.C. Morris, 1823. pp. 36.

— — Ireland.

IRISH Poor Law: past, present and future. London, J. Ridgway, 1849. pp. 59.

— — Scotland.

SCOTTISH pauperism: its causes and hints for its cure. [Brechin, 1850]. pp. iii-iv, 5-64. *Title page lacking, p.61-62 mutilated. With the exception of the final pages, previously published in The Brechin Advertiser.*

POPP (ADELHEID).

POPP (ADELHEID) Jugend einer Arbeiterin; hrsg. und eingel. von Hans J. Schütz. Berlin, [1977]. pp. 187.

POPPER (Sir KARL RAIMUND).

KEUTH (HERBERT) Realität und Wahrheit: zur Kritik des kritischen Rationalismus. Tübingen, 1978. pp. 220. *bibliog.*

POPULAR CULTURE.

CULTURA popolare e marxismo; a cura di Raffaele Rauty. Roma, 1976. pp. 267. *bibliog.*

DONAKOWSKI (CONRAD L.) A muse for the masses: ritual and music in an age of democratic revolution, 1770-1870. Chicago, 1977. pp. 435. *bibliog.*

POPULAR FRONTS.

Le NEO-Destour et le Front Populaire en France. [Tunis, 1969]. 2 vols. (in 1). *(Histoire du Mouvement National Tunisien. Documents. 3-4)*

MANTA (L.H. AFONSO) ed. A frente popular antifascista em Portugal: o primeiro esboço da unidade antifascista; documentos da historia do movimento operario português, 1935-1937. Lisboa, [1976]. pp. 206.

BOURDE (GUY) La défaite du Front populaire. Paris, 1977. pp. 359. *bibliog.*

FREDERIK (HANS) Volksfront: der taktische Einsatz der Sowjetunion, um mit Hilfe der Einheitsfrontaktionen zwischen Sozialdemokraten und Kommunisten und der Bündnispolitik mit bürgerlichen Regierungen die materielle und politische Weltordnung des Westens abzulösen. Landshut, 1977. pp. 544.

DRAKE (PAUL W.) Socialism and populism in Chile, 1932-52. Urbana, [1978]. pp. 418. *bibliog.*

POPULATION.

DRYSDALE (CHARLES VICKERY) Can everyone be fed?: a reply to Prince Kropotkin. London, 1913. pp. 14.

NEWSHOLME (HENRY PRATT) The population report and the survival of the Christian family. London, [1949]. pp. 15.

NOBEL SYMPOSIUM, 29TH, STOCKHOLM, 1974. Man, environment, and resources: in the perspective of the past and the future; edited by Torgny Torgnysson Segerstedt and Sam Nilsson. [Stockholm, 1974]. pp. 111.

BROWN (LESTER RUSSELL) World population trends: signs of hope, signs of stress. Washington, 1976. pp. 40. *(Worldwatch Institute. Worldwatch Papers. No. 8)*

PROBLEMY geografii naseleniia i ispol'zovaniia territorii; Problems of the geography of population and land utilization. Tbilisi, 1976. pp. 239. *bibliog. With English table of contents and brief summaries.*

VALUES of growth. Lexington, Mass., [1976]. pp. 161. *(Commission on Critical Choices for Americans. Critical Choices for Americans. vol. 6)*

COLLOQUE NATIONAL DE DEMOGRAPHIE, VIème, 1975. L'analyse démographique et ses applications; (actes du Colloque National...organisé...à Paris du 20 au 11 octobre, 1975); [edited by Paul Clerc]. Paris, 1977. pp. 548. *(Centre National de la Recherche Scientifique. Colloques Nationaux. No. 934)*

MATRAS (JUDAH) Introduction to population: a sociological approach. Englewood Cliffs, N.J., [1977]. pp. 452. *bibliog.*

MILLER (WARREN B.) and GODWIN (R. KENNETH) Psyche and demos: individual psychology and the issues of population. New York, 1977. pp. 332. *bibliog.*

SIMON (JULIAN LINCOLN) The economics of population growth. Princeton, N.J., [1977]. pp. 555. *bibliog.*

The MORE developed realm: a geography of its population; general editor, Glenn T. Trewartha. Oxford, 1978. pp. 275. *bibliogs.*

PRINGLE (LAURENCE P.) The economic growth debate: are there limits to growth? New York, 1978. pp. 86. *bibliog.*

— History.

POPULATION patterns in the past; edited by Ronald Demos Lee [and others]. New York, [1977]. pp. 376. *bibliog.*

— Statistics.

WORLD BANK ATLAS: population, per capita product and growth rates; pd. by International Bank for Reconstruction and Development. [sub-title varies]. a., [1966(1st)]- Washington.

POPULATION FORECASTING.

ASCHER (WILLIAM) Forecasting: an appraisal for policy-makers and planners. Baltimore, [1978]. pp. 239.

— Canada — Nova Scotia.

SELIG (BRIAN M.) and HARVEY (ANDREW S.) Nova Scotia population projections 1972-81 (by age and sex for province, counties and Halifax metro)...; prepared for Economics and Statistics Division, Department of Development. [Halifax], 1975. fo.39. *bibliog.*

— — Quebec.

HENRIPIN (JACQUES) Examen des perspectives de population pour les villes du Québec; [annexe du rapport sur l'urbanisation]. [Québec, Editeur officiel, 1976]. pp. 24. *bibliog.*

— Ireland (Republic).

NATIONAL ECONOMIC AND SOCIAL COUNCIL [EIRE]. Population and employment projections 1986: a reassessment. Dublin, Stationery Office, [1977]. pp. 87. *([Reports]. No. 35)*

— Morocco.

MOROCCO. Division du Plan et des Statistiques. 1965. Projections de population: répercussions sur certains aspects de l'économie du pays et solutions proposées. [Rabat], 1965. pp. 25.

— Netherlands.

NETHERLANDS. Centraal Bureau voor de Statistiek. 1976. De toekomstige demografische ontwikkeling in Nederland na 1975; aansluitend op De toekomstige nederlandse bevolkingsontwikkeling na 1972. 's-Gravenhage, 1976. pp. 127. *With English summary.*

— South West Africa.

SOUTH WEST AFRICA. Census, 1970. Population census, South West Africa, (6 May 1970). Windhoek, 1971. fo. 3. *Includes estimates for May 1975.*

— United Kingdom.

HOLLIS (JOHN) Writer on Population, and others. Population and household projections for London: 1976. London, [1977]. 3 pts. *bibliog. (London. Greater London Council. Research Memoranda. 506-508)*

POPULATION POLICY.

UNITED NATIONS. Department of Economic and Social Affairs. Population Studies. No. 51. Measures, policies and programmes affecting fertility, with particular reference to national family planning programmes. (ST/SOA/SER.A/51). New York, 1972. pp. 162.

WORLD COUNCIL OF CHURCHES. Population policy, social justice and the quality of life: a report from the World Council of Churches. Geneva, 1973. pp. 12. *(Repr. from Study Encounter. vol. 9., no. 4, 1973)*

DEMERATH (NICHOLAS JAY) Birth control and foreign policy: the alternatives to family planning. New York, [1976]. pp. 228. *bibliog.*

DUZA (M. BADRUD) and BALDWIN (C. STEPHEN) Nuptiality and population policy: an investigation in Tunisia, Sri Lanka, and Malaysia. New York, [1977]. pp. 83. *bibliog.*

McNAMARA (ROBERT STRANGE) Accelerating population stabilization through social and economic progress. Washington, 1977. pp. 50. *(Overseas Development Council. Development Papers. 24)*

MILLER (WARREN B.) and GODWIN (R. KENNETH) Psyche and demos: individual psychology and the issues of population. New York, 1977. pp. 332. *bibliog.*

POPULATION RESEARCH

— United Kingdom.

MITCHISON (ROSALIND) British population change since 1860. London, 1977. pp. 99. *bibliog. (Economic History Society. Studies in Economic and Social History)*

POPULATION TRANSFERS.

NEKRICH (ALEKSANDR MOISEEVICH) The punished peoples: the deportation and fate of Soviet minorities at the end of the Second World War; translated from the Russian by George Saunders. New York, [1978]. pp. 238.

POPULISM.

CANOVAN (MARGARET) G. K. Chesterton: radical populist. New York, [1977]. pp. 175. *bibliog.*

— America, Latin.

GERMANI (GINO) Autoritarismo, fascismo e classi sociali. Bologna, [1975]. pp. 306. *bibliog.*

ALMEIDA (CANDIDO ANTONIO MENDES DE) Beyond populism;...translated by L. Gray Cowan. Albany, N.Y., 1977. pp. 112.

— Bolivia.

MITCHELL (CHRISTOPHER) The legacy of populism in Bolivia: from the MNR to military rule. New York, 1977. pp. 167. *bibliog.*

— Chile.

DRAKE (PAUL W.) Socialism and populism in Chile, 1932-52. Urbana, [1978]. pp. 418. *bibliog.*

— Colombia.

SHARPLESS (RICHARD E.) Gaitan of Colombia: a political biography. Pittsburgh, [1978]. pp. 229. *bibliog.*

— Italy.

MATTEUCCI (NICOLA) Dal populismo al compromesso storico. [Roma, 1976]. pp. 194.

— Russia.

MASLIN (MIKHAIL ALEKSANDROVICH) Kritika burzhuaznykh interpretatsii ideologii russkogo revoliutsionnogo narodnichestva. Moskva, 1977. pp. 118. *bibliog.*

— United States.

BLOCKER (JACK S.) Retreat from reform: the prohibition movement in the United States, 1890-1913. Westport, Conn., 1976. pp. 261. *bibliogs.*

GAITHER (GERALD H.) Blacks and the Populist revolt: ballots and bigotry in the "new south". University, Ala., [1977]. pp. 251. *bibliog.*

PORSCHE.

PORSCHE (FERDINAND ANTON ERNST) We at Porsche: the autobiography of Dr. Ing. h.c. Ferry Porsche; with John Bentley. Yeovil, [1976]. pp. 290.

PORT MUHAMMAD BIN QASIM.

BHUTTO (ZULFIKAR ALI) Speech at foundation laying ceremony of Port Muhammad Bin Qasim. [Islamabad, Directorate of Research, Reference and Publications, Ministry of Information and Broadcasting], 1976. pp. 8.

PORT QASIM.

See PORT MUHAMMAD BIN QASIM.

PORTERS

— United States.

HARRIS (WILLIAM HAMILTON) Keeping the faith: A. Philip Randolph, Milton P. Webster and the Brotherhood of Sleeping Car Porters, 1925-1937. Urbana, Ill., [1977]. pp. 252. *bibliog.*

PORTO ALEGRE

— Social conditions.

OLIVEN (RUBEN GEORGE) Urbanization and social change in Brazil: a case study of Porto Alegre. 1977. fo. 424. *bibliog.* Typescript. Ph.D. (London) thesis: unpublished. *This thesis is the property of London University and may not be removed from the Library.*

PORTSMOUTH

— City planning.

HAMPSHIRE. County Council. South Hampshire structure plan for the south east part of the County of Hampshire, City of Portsmouth, City of Southampton; as approved by the Secretary of State for the Environment, March 1977. [Winchester, 1977]. 1 vol. (various pagings). *3 maps in end pocket.*

PORTUGAL

— Armed forces — Political activity.

PORCH (DOUGLAS) The Portuguese armed forces and the revolution. Stanford, [1977]. pp. 273. *bibliog.* (*Stanford University. Hoover Institution on War, Revolution and Peace. Hoover Institution Publications. 188*)

— Colonies.

SPINOLA (ANTONIO SEVASTIAO RIBEIRO DE) Decolonization and democracy; speech delivered by the President of the Republic…10 September 1974. [Lisbon], Ministry of Mass Communication, [1974]. pp. 15.

— Constitution.

CALDEIRA (REINALDO B.) and SILVA (MARIA DO CEU C.) compilers. Constituição politica, 1976. Lisboa, [1976]. pp. 856.

— Economic policy.

KOLM (SERGE CHRISTOPHE) La transition socialiste: la politique économique de gauche. Paris, 1977. pp. 212.

— Foreign relations.

For related heading see EUROPEAN ECONOMIC COMMUNITY — Portugal.

— Government publications — Bibliography.

BIBLIOGRAFIA DAS PUBLICAÇÕES OFICIAIS PORTUGUESAS; ([pd. by] Biblioteca Nacional de Lisboa). a., 1967 [1st issue]- Lisboa.

— History.

PORTUGAL. Secretaria de Estado da Informação e Turismo. Direcção-Geral de Informação. 1972. History of Portugal. [Lisbon, 1972?]. pp. 92.

— — 1974, Revolution.

PORTUGAL: el fracaso del golpe de estado; [by Luis Carandell and others]. Madrid, 1975. pp. 95.

PORCH (DOUGLAS) The Portuguese armed forces and the revolution. Stanford, [1977]. pp. 273. *bibliog.* (*Stanford University. Hoover Institution on War, Revolution and Peace. Hoover Institution Publications. 188*)

HARVEY (ROBERT) Journalist. Portugal: birth of a democracy. [London, 1978]. pp. 151.

— Politics and government.

MITCHELL (ALEX) Writer on socialism. Revolt in Portugal. London, 1974. pp. 96.

SPINOLA (ANTONIO SEVASTIAO RIBEIRO DE) Decolonization and democracy; speech delivered by the President of the Republic…10 September 1974. [Lisbon], Ministry of Mass Communication, [1974]. pp. 15.

MAGALHÃES-GODINHO (VITORINO) Pensar a democracia para Portugal: incomodamente. Lisboa, 1976. pp. 383.

MANTA (L.H. AFONSO) ed. A frente popular antifascista em Portugal: o primeiro esboço da unidade antifascista; documentos da historia do movimento operario português, 1935-1937. Lisboa, [1976]. pp. 206.

REGO (VICTOR CUNHA) and MERZ (FRIEDHELM) eds. Liberdade para Portugal: (documentação coligida e coordenada). Amadora, [1976]. pp. 300.

PORCH (DOUGLAS) The Portuguese armed forces and the revolution. Stanford, [1977]. pp. 273. *bibliog.* (*Stanford University. Hoover Institution on War, Revolution and Peace. Hoover Institution Publications. 188*)

WHEELER (DOUGLAS L.) Republican Portugal: a political history, 1910-1926. Madison, 1978. pp. 340. *bibliog.*

— — 1974- .

HARVEY (ROBERT) Journalist. Portugal: birth of a democracy. [London, 1978]. pp. 151.

— Population.

MENDES (MARIA DE LOURDES) Caracterização estatistica da população jovem portuguesa. Lisboa, 1972. pp. 50. (*Portugal. Ministerio das Corporações e Previdência Social. Serviço de Estatistica. Serie Estatistica. 11*) *With abstracts in English and French.*

— Rural conditions.

CUNHAL (ALVARO) Contribuição para o estudo da questão agraria. Lisboa, 1976. 2 vols. (in 1).

— Social history.

MAGALHÃES-GODINHO (VITORINO) Estrutura da antiga sociedade portuguesa. 2nd ed. Lisboa, 1975. pp. 318. *bibliog.*

— Social policy.

PORTUGAL. Secretaria de Estado da Informação e Turismo. Direcção-Geral de Informação. 1971 Present trends in Portuguese social policy. [Lisbon], 1971. pp. 24.

— Statistics.

ANTUNES (ANTONIO ROQUE) Informação estatistica e desenvolvimento. Lisboa, 1974. pp. 199. (*Portugal. Ministerio das Corporações e Previdência Social. Gabinete de Planeamento. Serie Estudos. 13*) *With abstracts in English, French and German.*

POSITIVISM.

INGRAM (JOHN KELLS) Human nature and morals according to Auguste Comte; with notes illustrative of the principles of positivism. London, 1901. pp. 115.

COMTE (ISIDORE AUGUSTE MARIE FRANÇOIS XAVIER) The religion of humanity…: reprint of the original dedication and final invocation of the positive polity of Auguste Comte… to which is added a translation of the daily prayers of Auguste Comte…; edited by Albert Crompton. Liverpool, 1907. pp. 88.

KUBŮ (LUBOMÍR) Ryzí nauka právní v kontextu buržoazního právního myšlení. Brno, 1977. pp. 102. *bibliog.* *With Russian summary.*

SUTTON (MICHAEL JOHN) Nationalism, positivism and Catholicism: a study of the controversy arising from the proposal of Charles Maurras for a political alliance between positivists and Catholics. [1978]. fo.431. *bibliog.* Typescript. *2 pamphlets in end pocket.* Ph.D. (London) thesis: unpublished. *This thesis is the property of London University and may not be removed from the Library.*

POSTAL SERVICE

— Australia.

AUSTRALIA. Post Office. Post Office prospects and capital programme. a., 1968/69(1st)- Canberra. *Included in* AUSTRALIA. Parliament. *[Parliamentary papers].*

— France — Employees.

NOËL (JEAN FRANÇOIS) Les postiers, la grève et le service public. [Grenoble, 1977]. pp. 198. *bibliog.*

— Netherlands.

OTTENHEIJM (G.C.J.J.) De status van de PTT als staatsbedrijf in historisch perspectief. Den Haag, Staatsbedrijf der Posterijen, Telegrafie en Telefonie, 1974. pp. 179. *bibliogs.* (*Geschiedkundige Uitgaven. 4*)

— Scandinavia.

[SCANDINAVIA]. Nordiske Parlamentariske Komité for Friere Samfaerdsel. 1956. Slutbetaenkning. København, 1956. pp. 50. (*Denmark. Betaenkninger. Nr. 166*)

— — Rates.

[SCANDINAVIA]. Nordiske Parlamentariske Komité for Friere Samfaerdsel. 1954-55. Betaenkning om posttakster i den internordiske udveksling af breve: og Betaenkning om takstsaetningen i den internordiske teletrafik. København, 1954-55. 2 pts. (*Denmark. Betaenkninger. Nr. 105, 118*) *Title of part 2 reads Betaenkning om posttakster i den internordiske udveksling af korsbandsforsendelser, etc.*

— South Africa — Accounting.

SOUTH AFRICA. Parliament. House of Assembly. Select Committee on Posts and Telecommunications. 1977. Report…proceedings and evidence (S.C.3-1977). in SOUTH AFRICA. Parliament. House of Assembly. Select Committee reports.

— United Kingdom.

COLONIAL AND INTERNATIONAL POSTAGE ASSOCIATION. Colonial penny postage: a statement of the facts and arguments presented and discussed at a recent meeting of the Society of Arts. London, 1853. pp. 20.

— United States — Salaries, pensions, etc.

ADIE (DOUGLAS K.) An evaluation of postal service wage rates. Washington, D.C., [1977]. pp. 182. *bibliog.* (*American Enterprise Institute for Public Policy Research. AEI Studies. 166*)

POTATOES

— United Kingdom — Marketing.

U.K. Ministry of Agriculture and Fisheries. Markets Division. 1934. Potato marketing scheme 1933: explanatory memorandum. [London, 1934]. fo.7

POTTERS

— United Kingdom.

SHAW (CHARLES) 1832-1906. When I was a child. Firle, Sussex, 1977. pp. 258. *Facsimile reprint of first edition of 1903 published under the anonym "An Old Potter." Original introduction omitted.*

POUGHKEEPSIE, NEW YORK

— Economic history.

GRIFFEN (CLYDE) and GRIFFEN (SALLY) Natives and newcomers: the ordering of opportunity in mid-nineteenth-century Poughkeepsie. Cambridge, Mass., 1978. pp. 291. (*Harvard University. Harvard Studies in Urban History*)

POUILLY (ALEXANDER MENSDORFF-) Graf.

See MENSDORFF-POUILLY (ALEXANDER) Graf.

POUJADE (PIERRE).

BORNE (DOMINIQUE) Petits bourgeois en révolte?: le Mouvement Poujade..[Paris, 1977]. pp. 250. *bibliog.*

POULTRY INDUSTRY

— Brazil.

BANCO DO NORDESTE DO BRASIL. Departamento de Estudos Econômicos do Nordeste. Mercado consumidor de aves e ovos em Natal. Fortaleza, 1969. pp. 47.

POUND, BRITISH

— Devaluation.

HOLMES (PETER M.) Industrial pricing behaviour and devaluation. London, 1978. pp. 170. *bibliog.*

POVERTY.

EQUITY, income, and policy: comparative studies in three worlds of development; edited by Irving Louis Horowitz. New York, 1977. pp. 293. *bibliogs. Based on a series of panels organised by the American Political Science Association in 1976.*

GARFINKEL (IRWIN) and HAVEMAN (ROBERT H.) Earnings capacity, poverty, and inequality. New York, [1977]. pp. 118. *bibliog. (Wisconsin University, Madison. Institute for Research on Poverty. Monograph Series)*

IMPROVING measures of economic well-being; edited by Marilyn Moon [and] Eugene Smolensky. New York, [1977]. pp. 239. *bibliogs. (Wisconsin University, Madison. Institute for Research on Poverty. Monograph Series)*

WAXMAN (CHAIM I.) The stigma of poverty: a critique of poverty theories and policies. New York, [1977]. pp. 148. *bibliog.*

HOLMAN (ROBERT) Poverty: explanations of social deprivation. [London, 1978]. pp. 302.

POVERTY RESEARCH

— United States.

IMPROVING measures of economic well-being; edited by Marilyn Moon [and] Eugene Smolensky. New York, [1977]. pp. 239. *bibliogs. (Wisconsin University, Madison. Institute for Research on Poverty. Monograph Series)*

POWELL (JOHN ENOCH).

POWELL (JOHN ENOCH) A nation or no nation?: six years in British politics; edited [with a commentary] by Richard Ritchie. London, 1978. pp. 186.

POWER (SOCIAL SCIENCES).

OCAMPO (RODRIGO) Breves anotaciones historicas sobre el poder politico en Colombia. Bogota, 1972. pp. 71. *bibliog.*

MAURO (WALTER) and CLEMENTELLI (ELENA) eds. La trappola e la nudità: lo scrittore e il potere; [an anthology]. [Milano, 1974]. pp. 269.

MAFFESOLI (MICHEL) Logique de la domination. Paris, 1976. pp. 218. *bibliog.*

The ANTHROPOLOGY of power: ethnographic studies from Asia, Oceania, and the New World; edited by Raymond D. Fogelson [and] Richard N. Adams. New York, [1977]. pp. 429. *bibliogs. Based on a conference held under the auspices of the American Association for the Advancement of Science in San Francisco in 1974.*

GARSON (G. DAVID) Power and politics in the United States: a political economy approach. Lexington, Mass., [1977]. pp. 352.

LAPIERRE (JEAN WILLIAM) Vivre sans Etat?: essai sur le pouvoir politique et l'innovation sociale. Paris, [1977]. pp. 380.

McCORD (WILLIAM MAXWELL) and McCORD (ARLINE F.) Power and equity: an introduction to social stratification. New York, 1977. pp. 316.

MELANGES offerts à Georges Burdeau: le pouvoir. Paris, 1977. pp. 1190.

SHARPE (KENNETH EVAN) Peasant politics: struggle in a Dominican village. Baltimore, Md., [1977]. pp. 263. *bibliog.*

KOLB (EUGENE J.) A framework for political analysis. Englewood Cliffs, [1978]. pp. 338. *bibliog.*

POWER RESOURCES.

WORKSHOP ON ALTERNATIVE ENERGY STRATEGIES. Energy demand studies: major consuming countries: analyses of 1972 demand and projections of 1985 demand; first technical report of the Workshop...; Paul S. Basile, editor. Cambridge, Mass., [1976]. pp. 553.

BANKS (FERDINAND E.) Scarcity, energy, and economic progress. Lexington, Mass., [1977]. pp. 200. *bibliog.*

CALDWELL (MALCOLM) The wealth of some nations. London, 1977. pp. 191. *bibliogs.*

INTERNATIONAL studies of the demand for energy: selected papers presented at a conference in the International Institute for Applied Systems Analysis, 2361 Laxenburg, Austria. Amsterdam, 1977. pp. 340.

McKAY (H.A.C.) World energy resources. Harwell, 1977. pp. 17. *(U.K. Atomic Energy Authority. [Research Group. Reports] . AERE-R8856)*

CONANT (MELVIN A.) and GOLD (FERN RACINE) The geopolitics of energy. Boulder, 1978. pp. 224.

EZRA (Sir DEREK JOSEPH) Coal and energy: the need to exploit the world's most abundant fossil fuel. London, 1978. pp. 182.

— Canada — Alberta.

ALBERTA. Energy Resources Conservation Board. 1977. Alberta's energy resources: a summary, 31 December 1976. Calgary, [1977]. pp. 31.

— — British Columbia.

BRITISH COLUMBIA. Energy Commission. 1976. British Columbia's energy outlook, 1976-1991. [Vancouver], 1976. 2 vols. (in 1).

BRITISH COLUMBIA. Energy Commission. 1976. Submission on behalf of the Minister Responsible for Energy of the Province of British Columbia...to the National Energy Board in the matter of determining the producibility and domestic demand for oil and related matters. Vancouver, 1976. fo. 66.

— China.

SMIL (VACLAV) China's energy: achievements, problems, prospects. New York, 1976. pp. 246.

— European Economic Community countries.

EUROPEAN COMMUNITIES. Statistical Office. Overall energy balance-sheets. irreg., 1963/75- Luxembourg.

EUROPEAN COMMUNITIES. Commission. Periodical report on the Community action programme for the rational use of energy...and recommendations of the Council. irreg., 1975(1st)- Brussels.

NETHERLANDS. Centraal Bureau voor de Statistiek. 1975. Ontwikkelingen in de energiesector in Nederland en de Europese Gemeenschap, 1963-1972. 's-Gravenhage, 1975. pp. 48. *With English summary.*

COMITE D'ETUDE DES PRODUCTEURS DE CHARBON D'EUROPE OCCIDENTALE. Energy in western Europe: vital role of coal; a report... prepared in cooperation with the Association for Coal in Europe. [London, National Coal Board], 1977. pp. 42.

— France.

CENTRE D'ETUDES ET DE RECHERCHES ECONOMIQUES SUR L'ENERGIE. Consommations apparentes d'énergie par grand secteur et par branche d'activité industrielle: résultats régionaux et départementaux. a., 1975- Paris. *Supersedes CONSOMMATIONS REGIONALES APPARENTES D'ENERGIE DANS L'INDUSTRIE PAR BRANCHE D'ACTIVITE and CONSOMMATIONS APPARENTES D'ENERGIE PAR SECTEUR.*

— India.

PACHAURI (RAJENDRA KUMAR) Energy and economic development in India. New York, 1977. pp. 185.

— Netherlands.

NETHERLANDS. Centraal Bureau voor de Statistiek. 1975. Ontwikkelingen in de energiesector in Nederland en de Europese Gemeenschap, 1963-1972. 's-Gravenhage, 1975. pp. 48. *With English summary.*

— Sweden.

ODENSTAD (GÖRAN) and HOLMSTRÖM (SVEN J.R.) Energieprisets inverkan på jordbrukets produktionskostnader i Sverige och ett antal andra västeuropeiska länder. Stockholm, 1975. pp. 55. *(Jordbrukets Utredningsinstitut. Meddelanden. 1975. Nr. 2) With English summary.*

— United Kingdom.

U.K. Central Office of Information. Reference Division. Reference Pamphlets. 124. British industry today: energy. 4th ed. London, 1977. pp. 32. *bibliog.*

PRACTICE (PHILOSOPHY).

SAMARSKAIA (ELENA ALEKSANDROVNA) Poniatie praktiki u K. Marksa i sovremennye diskussii: o dialektike ob''ektivnogo i sub''ektivnogo v istoricheskom protsesse. Moskva, 1977. pp. 224.

SÁNCHEZ VÁZQUEZ (ADOLFO) The philosophy of praxis; ...translated by Mike Gonzalez. London, 1977. pp. 387. *bibliog.*

PRAGMATISM.

SMITH (JOHN EDWIN) Purpose and thought. London, 1978. pp. 236.

PRAYER.

ORTHODOX theories of prayer; by a barrister. London, [1874]. pp. 20.

PRECAST CONCRETE CONSTRUCTION.

SEBESTYÈN (GYULA) Use of precast components in masonry building construction. (ST/SOA/116. New York, United Nations, 1972. pp. 128. *bibliog.*

PREDICTION THEORY.

BIBBY (JOHN) and TOUTENBURG (HELGE) Prediction and improved estimation in linear models. Chichester, [1977]. pp. 188. *bibliog. Revised and updated vrsion of Helge Toutenburg's Vorhersage in linearen Modellen.*

PRESCRIPTION (LAW)

— Netherlands.

PITLO (A.) Bewijs en verjaring naar het Nederlands Burgerlijk Wetboek. 5th ed. Groningen, 1968. pp. 255.

PRESS.

HOOD (PETER) Ourselves and the press: a social study of news advertising and propaganda. London, [1939]. pp. 287.

— Argentine Republic.

LIBRO azul y blanco de la prensa argentina; por cincuenta y tres periodistas argentinos. Buenos Aires, 1951. pp. 439.

MIRI (HECTOR F.) Yrigoyen, Peron, Frondizi y el cuarto poder. Buenos Aires, 1959. pp. 111.

PRESS.(Cont.)

— Belgium.

SIMON-RORIVE (MARCELLE) La presse socialiste et révolutionnaire en Wallonie et à Bruxelles de 1918 à 1940. Leuven, 1974. pp. 254. *bibliog. (Centre Interuniversitaire d'Histoire Contemporaine. Cahiers. 75.)*

GÉRIN (PAUL) Presse populaire catholique et presse démocrate chrétienne en Wallonie et à Bruxelles, 1830-1914. Leuven, 1975. pp. ix,362. *bibliog. (Centre Interuniversitaire d'Histoire Contemporaine. Cahiers. 80)*

— France.

LAMBRICHS (NATHALIE) La liberté de la presse en l'an IV: les journaux républicains. Paris, [1976]. pp. 112. *bibliog. (Paris. Université de Paris II. Travaux et Recherches. Série Sciences Historiques. 11)*

BESSON (ALAIN) La presse locale en liberté surveillée: diagnostic et propositions pour les journaux de province. Paris, [1977]. pp. 256.

DAVILLE (DENIS PERIER) La liberté de la presse n'est pas à vendre. Paris, [1978]. pp. 254.

— Poland.

HISTORIA prasy polskiej. Warszawa, 1976 in progress. *bibliog.*

— Russia — Estonia — Statistics.

ESTONIA. Gosudarstvennyi Komitet po Delam Izdatel'stv, Poligrafii i Knizhnoi Torgovli. 1973. Statistika pechati Estonskoi SSR, 1972. Tallinn, 1973. pp. 86.

— — Ukraine — Statistics.

UKRAINE. Knizhnaia Palata. 1976. Presa Ukraïns'koï RSR, 1918-1975: naukovo-statystychnyi dovidnyk. Kharkiv, 1976. pp. 223.

— Spain.

PRENSA y sociedad en España, 1820-1936;...edicion a cargo de Manuel Tuñon de Lara [and others]. Madrid, 1975. pp. 290. *Papers of the 5th Colloquium organized by the Centre de Recherches Hispaniques of the University of Pau.*

— United Kingdom.

CRANFIELD (GEOFFREY ALAN) The press and society: from Caxton to Northcliffe. London, 1978. pp. 242. *bibliog.*

— United States.

HOBBIE (BARBARA) Oil company divestiture and the press: economic vs. journalistic perceptions. New York, [1977]. pp. 167. *bibliog.*

PRESS, CATHOLIC

— Belgium.

GÉRIN (PAUL) Presse populaire catholique et presse démocrate chrétienne en Wallonie et à Bruxelles, 1830-1914. Leuven, 1975. pp. ix,362. *bibliog. (Centre Interuniversitaire d'Histoire Contemporaine. Cahiers. 80)*

— Germany.

HOFMANN (JOSEF) Journalist in Republik, Diktatur und Besatzungszeit: Erinnerungen, 1916-1947; bearbeitet und eingeleitet von Rudolf Morsey. Mainz, [1977]. pp. 236. *(Kommission für Zeitgeschichte. Veröffentlichungen. Reihe A: Quellen. Band 23)*

PRESS, COMMUNIST

— Belgium.

SIMON-RORIVE (MARCELLE) La presse socialiste et révolutionnaire en Wallonie et à Bruxelles de 1918 à 1940. Leuven, 1974. pp. 254. *bibliog. (Centre Interuniversitaire d'Histoire Contemporaine. Cahiers. 75.)*

PRESS, LABOUR

— Italy.

AUDENINO (PATRIZIA) Cinquant'anni di stampa operaia: dall'Unità alla guerra di Libia. [Parma, 1976]. pp. 268.

PRESS AND POLITICS

— France.

DAVILLE (DENIS PERIER) La liberté de la presse n'est pas à vendre. Paris, [1978]. pp. 254.

— Germany.

HALL (ALEX) Scandal, sensation and social democracy: the SPD press and Wilhelmine Germany, 1890-1914. Cambridge, 1977. pp. 267. *bibliog.*

HOLZ (KURT A.) Die Diskussion um den Dawes- und Young-Plan in der deutschen Presse. Frankfurt/Main, [1977]. 2 vols. (in 1). *bibliog.*

— United Kingdom.

MARGACH (JAMES) The abuse of power: the war between Downing Street and the media, from Lloyd George to Callaghan. London, 1978. pp. 199.

— United States.

SMITH (CULVER HAYGOOD) The press, politics, and patronage: the American government's use of newspapers, 1789-1875. Athens, Ga., [1977]. pp. 351. *bibliog.*

PRESS LAW

— Italy.

CARDILLO (ANGELO) Le leggi sulla stampa: codice della stampa e del giornalismo. 2nd ed. Latina, 1977. pp. 430. *bibliog.*

— United Kingdom.

SMITH (ROBIN CALLENDER) Press law. London, 1978. pp. 303.

PRESSURE GROUPS

— Canada.

STANBURY (WILLIAM T.) Business interests and the reform of Canadian competition policy, 1971-1975. Toronto, [1977]. pp. 227.

— European Economic Community countries.

KIRCHNER (EMIL JOSEPH) Trade unions as a pressure group in the European Community. Farnborough, Hants., [1977]. pp. 208. *bibliog.*

— Italy.

VALLAURI (CARLO) I gruppi extraparlamentari di sinistra: genesi e organizzazione. [Roma, 1976]. pp. 134.

— United Kingdom.

ANTI-APARTHEID MOVEMENT. [Selected documents]. 1965. 2 parts (in 1 vol.) *Typescript: unpublished.*

NOYCE (JOHN) Release: its work, with particular reference to its influence on government policy and law reform. [1975?]. pp. 5. *(Release. Documents and Discussions) Unpublished: typescript.*

RYAN (MICK) The acceptable pressure group: inequality in the penal lobby: a case study of the Howard League and RAP. Farnborough, Hants., [1978]. pp. 165. *bibliog.*

— United States.

BERRY (JEFFREY M.) Lobbying for the people: the political behavior of public interest groups. Princeton, [1977]. pp. 311. *bibliog.*

GREENWALD (CAROL SCHIRO) Group power: lobbying and public policy. New York, 1977. pp. 372. *bibliog.*

HARRIS (CARL VERNON) Political power in Birmingham, 1871-1921. Knoxville, Tenn., [1977]. pp. 318. *bibliog.*

ETHNICITY and U.S. foreign policy; edited by Abdul Aziz Said. New York, 1977. pp. 180. *Based on a panel at the annual convention of the International Studies Association in Toronto, 1976.*

PRICE, FORBES AND COMPANY.

AND at Lloyd's: the story of Price, Forbes and Company Limited. London, [1955?]. pp. 71.

PRICE INDEXES.

AFRIAT (S.N.) The price index. Cambridge, 1977. pp. 187. *bibliogs.*

UNITED NATIONS. Statistical Office. Statistical Papers. Series M. No.59. Guidelines on principles of a system of price and quantity statistics. (ST/ESA/STAT/SER.M/59). New York, 1977. pp. 25.

— European Economic Community countries.

EUROPEAN COMMUNITIES. Statistical Office. EC-index of producer prices of agricultural products. a., 1968/75(1st)- Luxembourg. *[in Community languages] 1968/1975 figures included in Methodology of the EC-index of producer prices of agricultural products.*

— Greece.

GREECE. Ethnike Statistike Hyperesia. 1975. Agricultural price indices: 1966 [equals] 100. Athens, 1975. pp. 20. *([Publications]. O. Distribution and Prices. 1) In English and Greek.*

GREECE. Ethnike Statistike Hyperesia. 1976. Analysis of procedures of compiling construction price indices:... price index of the input of new dwelling buildings materials: 1971 [equals] 100. Athens, 1976. pp. 22. *([Publications] Z. Methodological Studies. 11) In English and Greek.*

— Hong Kong.

HONG KONG. Census and Statistics Department. 1976. The household expenditure survey 1973/74 and the consumer price indexes. Hong Kong, [1976]. pp. 143.

— Kenya.

KENYA. Central Bureau of Statistics. 1977. Consumer price indices, Nairobi. [Nairobi], 1977. 1 vol. (various pagings).

— Kuwait.

KUWAIT. Central Office of Statistics. Yearly bulletin of price index numbers: cost of living: wholesale. a., 1975- Kuwait. *[in English and Arabic].*

— Malta.

MALTA. Committee of Users of the Retail Price Index. 1971. The interim index of retail prices: alterations in the vegetables and fruits weighting schedule; report; [G.L. Zammit, chairman]. [Valletta], 1971. pp. 9.

— Papua New Guinea.

PAPUA NEW GUINEA. Bureau of Statistics. Statistical bulletin: export price indexes. q., Je 1977- Port Moresby.

— Singapore.

SINGAPORE. Statistics Department. 1976. The general wholesale price index of Singapore; 1974 equals 100. Singapore, 1976. pp. 26.

SINGAPORE. Statistics Department. 1976. Wholesale price index of imported products; 1974 equals 100. Singapore, 1976. fo. 26.

SINGAPORE. Statistics Department. 1976. Wholesale price index of Singapore manufactured products; 1974 equals 100. Singapore, 1976. fo. 15.

PRICE POLICY

— United Kingdom.

COUTTS (KENNETH J.) and others. Industrial pricing in the United Kingdom. Cambridge, 1978. pp. 147. *bibliog.* *(Cambridge. University. Department of Applied Economics. Monographs. 26)*

PRICE REGULATION.

JORDAN (WILLIAM A.) Ph.D. Some predatory practices under government regulation? Toronto, 1975. fo. 61. *(Toronto. University, and York University (Toronto). Joint Program in Transportation. Research Reports. No. 26) This is an amplified version of papers presented at the Seventh Annual Meeting of the Canadian Economics Association 1973, and at the 49th Annual Conference of the Western Economic Association, 1974.*

— United Kingdom.

U.K. Price Commission. Guidance notes. irreg., 1977(no.1)- London.

WILLOTT (ROBERT) Guide to price controls, 1977-78. London, 1977. pp. 285.

MITCHELL (JOAN) Price determination and prices policy. London, 1978. pp. 215. *bibliogs.*

PRICES.

GYNTHER (REGINALD SYDNEY) Accounting for pricelevel changes: theory and procedures. Oxford, 1966 repr. 1976. pp. 257. *bibliog.*

DELIBANES (DEMETRIOS) The importance of wage and price developments since 1948: internal and external equilibria of individual countries. Athens, 1973. pp. 11. *(Reprint from the Scientific Yearbook of "Panteios", School of Political Sciences Academic Year 1972-1973)*

VICTORIA UNIVERSITY OF WELLINGTON. Department of Accountancy. Annual Seminar on Advanced Accountancy, 22nd, 1974. What is profit?; proceedings of the...Seminar. [Wellington, 1974]. 1 vol. (various pagings). *bibliogs. Bound with papers presented to the Annual Seminar of the Wellington Branch of the New Zealand Society of Accountants in 1974, on The bulls and the bears of price determination.*

HAVEMAN (ROBERT H.) and KNOPF (KENYON A.) The market system: an introduction to microeconomics. 3rd ed. Santa Barbara, [1978]. pp. 272.

RONCAGLIA (ALESSANDRO) Sraffa and the theory of prices. Chichester, [1978]. pp. 176. *bibliog. Translated by Jan A. Kregel.*

— Australia.

NIEUWENHUYSEN (JOHN PETER) and DALY (ANNE ELIZABETH) The Australian Prices Justification Tribunal. [Carlton, Victoria, 1977]. pp. 234. *bibliog.*

— Bahamas.

BAHAMAS. Department of Statistics. Annual review of prices: report. a., 1976(3rd)- Nassau.

— Czechoslovakia.

KYSILKA (HUGO) and ZAHRADNÍČEK (IVAN) Cenová problematika v ČSSR. Praha, 1977. pp. 256. *bibliog.*

— European Economic Community countries.

EUROPEAN COMMUNITIES. Statistical Office. Survey of retail prices. irreg., 1975- Luxembourg. *[in English and French]*

— France.

FRANCE. Centre d'Etude des Revenus et des Coûts. 1977. Connaissances et opinions des Français sur les prix: ce qu'ils savent et pensent des mécanismes de prix; analyse de résultats d'enquêtes, 1970, 1974, 1976. Paris, 1977. pp. 105. *(Documents. No. 33/34)*

— Italy.

I PREZZI d'imperio delle specialità medicinali: atti del Convegno di Pavia del 23 gennaio 1976 ordinati e presentati dai professori A. Grisoli e G. Manera. Padova, 1976. pp. 245. *bibliog. (Pavia. Università. Centro Studi sulle Comunità Europee. Pubblicazioni. 4)*

— New Zealand.

NEW ZEALAND. Office of the Prime Minister. 1976. Incomes and prices. [Wellington], 1976. pp. 33.

— Rhodesia.

RHODESIA. Commission to Inquire into the Extent to which Prices in Rhodesia have changed since the 6th December, 1969. 1976. Report; [Thomas Hugh William Beadle, chairman]. Salisbury, 1976. pp. 5.

— Spain.

BARTHE Y BARTHE (ANDRES) Influencia de los transportes en los mercados y en la baja de los precios: memoria premiada por la Real Academia de Ciencias Morales y Politicas en el concurso ordinario de 1897, tema segundo. Madrid, 1899. pp. 110.

— United Kingdom.

HOLMES (PETER M.) Industrial pricing behaviour and devaluation. London, 1978. pp. 170. *bibliog.*

— United States.

KEMMERER (EDWIN WALTER) High prices and deflation. Princeton, 1920 repr. 1921. pp. 86. *A revision and enlargement of three articles published 1919-1920 by the Bankers' Statistics Corporation of New York City.*

— Yugoslavia.

SISTEM i politika cijena u Jugoslaviji: zbornik priloga i prijedloga; redakcija Marijan Korošić, Dragomir Vojnić. Zagreb, 1976. pp. 237.

PRIME MINISTERS

— Canada.

APEX of power: the prime minister and political leadership in Canada;...Thomas A. Hockin, editor. 2nd ed. Scarborough, Ont., [1977]. pp. 359.

PUNNETT (ROBERT MALCOLM) The prime minister in Canadian government and politics. Toronto, [1977]. pp. 168.

PRINCE EDWARD ISLAND

— Executive departments.

PRINCE EDWARD ISLAND. Environmental Control Commission. Annual report. a., 1973/74 - 1974/75(3rd-4th). Charlottetown. *Superseded by PRINCE EDWARD ISLAND. Department of the Environment. Annual report.*

PRINCE EDWARD ISLAND. Department of the Environment. Annual report. a., 1975/76(2nd)- Charlottetown. *Supersedes PRINCE EDWARD ISLAND. Environmental Control Commission. Annual report.*

PRINTERS

— Germany.

BESTRAFTE Solidarität: Drucker und Journalisten im gewerkschaftlichen Kampf; ([by] Klaus Kräling [and others]). Berlin, [1973]. pp. 139.

— United Kingdom.

BRITISH PRINTING INDUSTRIES FEDERATION. The Master Printers and Allied Trades' Association. London, 1904. pp. 11. *Executive Committee members for 1891-1904 and list of members.*

PRINTING

— History — Malta.

PARNIS (E.) Notes on the first establishment, development and actual state of printing press in Malta. [Valletta], 1916. fo.12.

— Zambia.

ZAMBIA. Central Statistical Office. 1976. Paper, paper products, printing and publishing industries. Lusaka, 1976. fo. 44. *bibliog. (Industry Monographs. No. 4)*

PRINTING, PUBLIC

— Australia.

AUSTRALIA. Parliament. Joint Committee on Publications. 1972. Report relating to departmental publishing activities; third special report; [G.D. Erwin, chairman]. in AUSTRALIA. Parliament. Parliamentary papers, 1972, vol.8.

PRINTING INDUSTRY

— United Kingdom.

BRITISH PRINTING INDUSTRIES FEDERATION. The compositors' agitation, 1900-1, with the arbitrator's award. London, 1901. pp. (18).

BRITISH PRINTING INDUSTRIES FEDERATION. Rules of the Master Printers' and Allied Trades' Association; (revised...1894). London, 1901. pp. 19.

BRITISH PRINTING INDUSTRIES FEDERATION. Profit for printers; or, What is "cost?" London, 1904. pp. 85.

BRITISH PRINTING INDUSTRIES FEDERATION. Rules of the Master Printers' and Allied Trades' Association; (revised...1905). London, 1905. pp. 12.

PRISON RIOTS

— United States.

MORRISON (DERRICK) and WATERS (MARY-ALICE) Attica: why prisoners are rebelling. New York, 1972. pp. 15.

PRISON SENTENCES.

VON HIRSCH (ANDREW) Doing justice: the choice of punishments;...report of the Committee for the Study of Incarceration. New York, 1976. pp. 179.

— United Kingdom.

ADVISORY COUNCIL ON THE PENAL SYSTEM. Sentences of imprisonment: a review of maximum penalties; report; [Baroness Serota, chairman]. London, 1978. pp. 256.

— United States.

TWENTIETH CENTURY FUND. Task Force on Sentencing Policy Toward Young Offenders. Confronting youth crime: report;...background paper by Frankli E. Zimring. New York, [1978]. pp. 120.

PRISONERS

— United Kingdom.

POLITICAL prisoners and prisoners' unions: conflict or cooperation? [London], 1973. pp. 25.

— — Scotland — Personal narratives.

BOYLE (JIMMY) A sense of freedom. London, [1977]. pp. 264.

PRISONERS, IRISH.

See IRISH PRISONERS.

PRISONERS OF WAR.

ROSAS (ALLAN) The legal status of prisoners of war: a study in international humanitarian law applicable in armed conflicts. Helsinki, 1976. pp. 523. *bibliog. (Academia Scientiarum Fennica. Annales. Ser.B. Dissertationes Humanarum Litterarum. 9)*

PRISONS.

PRISONS past and future; edited for the Howard League for Penal Reform by John C. Freeman. London, 1978. pp. 239.

— United Kingdom.

COHEN (STANLEY) and TAYLOR (LAURIE) Prison secrets. London, [1976]. pp. 98.

An EXERCISE in futility: Wandsworth: Wormwood Scrubs: Spring Hill. London, [1977]. fo. 23.

— United States.

AMERICAN ASSEMBLY. 42nd Assembly, December 1972. Prisoners in America; [edited by Lloyd E. Ohlin]. Englewood Cliffs, N.J., [1973]. pp. 216. *bibliog.*

— — Mathematical models.

SALTER (RICHARD G.) A probabilistic procedure for sizing detention facilities. Santa Monica, 1972. pp. 9. *(Rand Corporation. [Papers]. 4926)*

— — Illinois.

JACOBS (JAMES B.) Stateville: the penitentiary in mass society. Chicago, 1977. pp. 281.

PRIVACY, RIGHT OF.

PRIVACY; edited by John B. Young. Chichester, [1978]. pp. 350.

PRIVATE SCHOOLS

— Canada.

GOSSAGE (CAROLYN) A question of privilege: Canada's independent schools. Toronto, [1977]. pp. 301. *bibliog.*

— Portugal.

CORREIA (HERMINIA GALVÃO) and FIALHO (JOSE ANTONIO SOUSA) Inquerito remunerações no ensino particular, 1970. Lisboa, 1972. pp. 52. *(Portugal. Ministerio das Corporações e Previdência Social. Serviço de Estatistica. Serie Estatistica. 13) With abstracts in English and French.*

PRIVATEERING.

ANDREWS (KENNETH R.) The Spanish Caribbean: trade and plunder 1530-1630. New Haven, Conn., 1978. pp. 267.

PRIVILEGES AND IMMUNITIES

— Australia.

McNAIRN (COLIN H.H.) Governmental and intergovernmental immunity in Australia and Canada. Toronto, 1977 repr. 1978. pp. 205.

— Canada.

McNAIRN (COLIN H.H.) Governmental and intergovernmental immunity in Australia and Canada. Toronto, 1977 repr. 1978. pp. 205.

PROBABILITIES.

MEYER (PAUL L.) Introductory probability and statistical applications. 2nd ed. Reading, Mass., 1970 repr. 1977. pp. 367. *bibliog.*

ROSS (SHELDON M.) Applied probability models with optimization applications. San Francisco, [1970]. pp. 198.

TURNER (JOHN CHRISTOPHER) Modern applied mathematics: probability, statistics, operational research. London, 1970 repr. 1972. pp. 502. *bibliog.*

HEATHCOTE (CHRISTOPHER ROBIN) Probability: elements of the mathematical theory. London, 1971. pp. 267.

ZACKS (SHELEMYAHU) The theory of statistical inference. New York, [1971]. pp. 609. *bibliog.*

ROSS (SHELDON M.) Introduction to probability models. New York, [1972]. pp. 272.

CLARKE (L.E.) Random variables. London, 1975. pp. 185. *bibliog.*

ROHATGI (VIJAY K.) An introduction to probability theory and mathematical statistics. New York, [1976]. pp. 684. *bibliog.*

COHEN (JACOB) 1923- . Statistical power analysis for the behavioral sciences. new ed. New York, [1977]. pp. 474. *bibliog.*

COHEN (LAURENCE JONATHAN) The probable and the provable. Oxford, 1977. pp. 363.

MATHAI (A.M.) and PEDERZOLI (G.) Characterizations of the normal probability law. rev. ed. New Delhi, [1977]. pp. 149. *bibliog. Enlarged version of the authors' 1975 monograph.*

EGGLESTON (Sir RICHARD MOULTON) Evidence, proof and probability. London, [1978]. pp. 226.

PROCEDURE (LAW)

— United Kingdom.

LEWIS (JOHN ROYSTON) Civil and criminal procedure. 2nd ed. North Shields, 1976. pp. 210.

PRODUCE TRADE.

JOSLING (TIMOTHY EDWARD) Agriculture in the Tokyo Round negotiations. London, 1977. pp. 42. *(Trade Policy Research Centre. Thames Essays. No. 10)*

PRODUCTION (ECONOMIC THEORY).

L'AMBIVALENCE de la production: logiques communautaires et logique capitaliste. Paris, 1976. pp. 188. *bibliog.*

PASINETTI (LUIGI LODOVICO) Lectures on the theory of production. London, 1977. pp. 285.

— Mathematical models.

HAJRA (S.) and KUMAR (ASHOK) Production function in Indian industry. New Delhi, [1977]. pp. 321. *bibliog.*

PRODUCTION CONTROL.

KING (JOHN RUSSELL) Production planning and control: an introduction to quantitative methods. Oxford, 1975. pp. 403. *bibliogs.*

PRODUCTION MANAGEMENT.

LOCKYER (KEITH GERALD) Factory and production management. 3rd ed. London, 1974 reprinted 1977. pp. 490. *Previous eds. entitled Factory management.*

— Mathematical models.

JOHNSON (LYNWOOD A.) and MONTGOMERY (DOUGLAS C.) Operations research in production planning, scheduling, and inventory control. New York, [1974]. pp. xiv,525.

PRODUCTION PLANNING.

KING (JOHN RUSSELL) Production planning and control: an introduction to quantitative methods. Oxford, 1975. pp. 403. *bibliogs.*

ELLIOTT (DAVID) The Lucas Aerospace workers' campaign. London, 1977. pp. 20. *(Young Fabian Group. Young Fabian Pamphlets. 46)*

PRODUCTIVITY.

JONES (D.T.) and PRAIS (SIGBERT JON) Plant-size and productivity in the motor industry: some international comparisons. London, 1977. pp. 26, 4. *(National Institute of Economic and Social Research. Discussion Papers. No. 8)*

KENDRICK (JOHN W.) Understanding productivity: an introduction to the dynamics of productivity change. Baltimore, [1977]. pp. 141. *bibliog.*

— India.

SATYANARAYANA (Y.) Impact of G[overnment] o[f] I[ndia]'s liberalised licencing policy on industrial output. New Delhi, 1972. pp. 97. *(United States. Agency for International Development. USAID-New Delhi. Economic Affairs Division. Staff Papers)*

— Italy.

D'ANDREA (RITA) Scienza operaia e organizzazione del lavoro: cultura, professionalità e potere dei gruppi operai di fronte al processo produttivo. [Venezia, 1976]. pp. 143. *bibliog.*

— Russia.

ORGANIZATSIONNYE faktory rosta proizvoditel'nosti truda. Kiev, 1977. pp. 280. *bibliog.*

BERGSON (ABRAM) Productivity and the social system: the USSR and the West. Cambridge, Mass., 1978. pp. 256.

— United Kingdom.

FRANKS (BERNARD) The measured day work and productivity deal swindle: how it works and how to fight it. London, 1970. pp. 157. *Articles originally published in the Workers Press, 1970.*

WEST MIDLANDS JOINT MONITORING STEERING GROUP. A developing strategy for the West Midlands: an analysis of manufacturing net output, 1958-68. [Birmingham], 1976. 1 pamphlet (various pagings). *(Technical Reports)*

KRICHIGINA (NATALIIA NIKOLAEVNA) Proizvoditel'nost' truda v obrabatyvaiushchei promyshlennosti Velikobritanii. Moskva, 1978. pp. 165.

WRAGG (RICHARD) and ROBERTSON (JAMES) Writer on Employment. Post-war trends in employment, productivity, output, labour costs and prices by industry in the United Kingdom. [London], 1978. pp. 93. *(U.K. Department of Employment. Research Papers. No. 3)*

— United States.

KATZELL (RAYMOND A.) and others. A guide to worker productivity experiments in the United States, 1971-75. New York, 1977. pp. 186.

KENDRICK (JOHN W.) Understanding productivity: an introduction to the dynamics of productivity change. Baltimore, [1977]. pp. 141. *bibliog.*

BERG (IVAR E.) and others. Managers and work reform: a limited engagement. New York, [1978]. pp. 316.

PRODUCTS LIABILITY

— United Kingdom.

MILLER (CHRISTOPHER JOHN) and LOVELL (PATRICK A.) Product liability. London, 1977. pp. 386.

PROFESSIONAL EDUCATION

— Yugoslavia.

SISTEM kadrologije udruženoga rada; redaktor Jovo Brekić. Zagreb, 1977. pp. 132. *bibliog. (Zagreb. Ekonomski Institut. Centar za Kadrologiju i Poslovodne Kadrove. Kadrologijska Biblioteka. Kolo 5) With English table of contents and summary.*

SISTEM planiranja razvoja kadrova i obrazovanja samoupravno udruženog rada; redaktori Jovo Brekić i M. Jurina. Zagreb, 1977. pp. 305. *bibliog.* *(Zagreb. Ekonomski Institut. Centar za Kadrologiju i Poslovodne Kadrove. Kadrologijska Biblioteka. Kolo 4, svezak 1) With English table of contents and summary.*

PROFESSIONS.

ILLICH (IVAN D.) and others. Disabling professions. London, 1977. pp. 127.

LARSON (MAGALI SARFATTI) The rise of professionalism: a sociological analysis. Berkeley, Calif., [1977]. pp. 309. *bibliog.*

— Canada — Quebec.

QUEBEC (PROVINCE). Office des Professions. 1976. The evolution of professionalism in Quebec. Quebec, 1976. pp. 143. *bibliog.*

— Russia.

PUCHKOV (IGOR' SEMENOVICH) and POPOV (GELII ALEKSANDROVICH) Sotsial'no-demograficheskaia kharakteristika nauchnykh kadrov. Moskva, 1976. pp. 77. *bibliog.*

— United Kingdom.

U.K. Department of Health and Social Security. 1977. Smoking and professional people. [London, 1977]. pp. 10.

U.K. Social Survey. 1977. Smoking and professional people: a survey of some professional groups working in health and education; their smoking habits, knowledge of health hazards and attitudes to anti-smoking education, carried out on behalf of the Department of Health and Social Security; (by Opinion Research Centre). London, 1977. pp. 35.

— — Commonwealth.

COMMONWEALTH FOUNDATION. The first ten years, 1966-1976: a fifth report. [London, 1976]. pp. 97.

— United States.

FURNER (MARY O.) Advocacy and objectivity: a crisis in the professionalization of American social science, 1865-1905. Lexington, Ky., [1975]. pp. 357. *bibliog.*

SARASON (SEYMOUR BERNARD) Work, aging, and social change: professionals and the one life-one career imperative;...with a chapter, The Santa Fe experience; by David Krantz. New York, [1977]. pp. 298. *bibliog.*

— Yugoslavia.

PROJEKCIJA dugoročnog razvoja kadrova do 1985; redaktor Jovo Brekić. Zagreb, 1976. pp. 184. *bibliog. (Zagreb. Ekonomski Institut. Centar za Kadrologiju i Poslovodne Kadrove. Kadrologijska Biblioteka. Kolo 2)*

BREKIĆ (JOVO) and JURINA (MILAN) Razvoj kadrova i organizacije kadrovske funkcije udruženog rada. Zagreb, 1977. pp. 115. *bibliog. (Zagreb. Ekonomski Institut. Centar za Kadrologiju i Poslovodne Kadrove. Kadrologijska Biblioteka. kolo 3)*

PROFIT.

EILON (SAMUEL) On the corporate ethos. [London, 1973]. pp. 4. *(Foundation for Business Responsibilities. Discussion Papers)*

ANDREFF (WLADIMIR) Profits et structures du capitalisme mondial. [Paris, 1976]. pp. 285.

— Accounting.

VICTORIA UNIVERSITY OF WELLINGTON. Department of Accountancy. Annual Seminar on Advanced Accountancy, 22nd, 1974. What is profit?; proceedings of the...Seminar. [Wellington, 1974]. 1 vol. (various pagings). *bibliogs. Bound with papers presented to the Annual Seminar of the Wellington Branch of the New Zealand Society of Accountants in 1974, on The bulls and the bears of price determination.*

GOLDSCHMIDT (YAAQOV) and ADMON (KURT) Profit measurement during inflation: accounting, economic and financial aspects. New York, [1977]. pp. 328. *bibliog.*

— United States.

SUNDER (SHYAM) Oil industry profits. Washington, [1977]. pp. 74. *(American Enterprise Institute for Public Policy Research. AEI Studies. 170)*

PROFIT SHARING

— Sweden.

MEIDNER (RUDOLF) Employee investment funds: an approach to collective capital formation,...with the assistance of Anna Hedborg and Gunnar Fond. London, 1978. pp. 132. *Report of a study commissioned by the Swedish Confederation of Trade Unions (Landsorganisationen i Sverige).*

— United Kingdom.

BLUNDELL, SPENCE AND COMPANY. Gratuities dependent on profits. n.p., [1891]. s.sh.

CONFEDERATION OF BRITISH INDUSTRY. Financial participation in companies: an introductory booklet. London, 1978. pp. 36.

PROGRAMME BUDGETING.

HARTLE (DOUGLAS G.) A theory of the expenditure budgetary process. Toronto, [1976]. pp. 98. *bibliog. (Ontario. Economic Council. Research Studies. 5)*

— United States.

FARQUHAR (JOHN A.) Accountability, program budgeting, and the California educational information system: a discussion and a proposal. Santa Monica, 1971. pp. 28. *(Rand Corporation. [Rand Reports]. 637)*

ROSTKER (BERNARD) Logistics: its planning, programming and budgeting in the Office of the Secretary of Defense, 1968-1970. [Santa Monica, 1972. pp. 15. *(Rand Corporation. [Papers]. 4881)*

PROGRAMMING (ELECTRONIC COMPUTERS).

NAUR (PETER) Concise survey of computer methods. Lund, 1974. pp. 397. *bibliog.*

INTERNATIONAL CONFERENCE ON SOFTWARE ENGINEERING, 2ND, SAN FRANCISCO, 1976. Proceedings. [New York, 1976]. pp. 639. *Sponsored by Association for Computing Machinery [and] IEEE Computer Society.*

SYMPOSIUM ON COMPUTER SOFTWARE ENGINEERING, NEW YORK, 1976. Proceedings of the Symposium on Computer Software Engineering, New York, April 1976. New York, [1976]. pp. 583. *(New York (City). Polytechnic Institute of New York. Microwave Research Institute. Symposium Series. vol.24)*

CURRENT trends in programming methodology. vol. 2. Program validation; Raymond T. Yeh, editor. Englewood Cliffs, [1977]. pp. 322. *bibliog.*

INTERNATIONAL COMPUTING SYMPOSIUM, 5TH, LIEGE, 1977. International computing symposium 1977; proceedings of the... symposium...organized by the European Chapters of the Association for Computing Machinery...; edited by E. Morlet and D. Ribbens. Amsterdam, 1977. pp. 613. *bibliogs.*

CURRENT trends in programming methodology. vol.3. Software modeling; K. Mani Chandy and Raymond T. Yeh, editors. Englewood Cliffs, [1978]. pp. 379. *bibliog.*

CURRENT trends in programming methodology. vol.4. Data structuring; Raymond T. Yeh, editor. Englewood Cliffs, [1978]. pp. 321. *bibliog.*

CYPSER (R.J.) Communications architecture for distributed systems. Reading, Mass., [1978]. pp. 711.

PROGRAMMING (MATHEMATICS).

CARSBERG (BRYAN VICTOR) An introduction to mathematical programming for accountants. London, 1969 repr. 1971. pp. 108.

MITRA (G.) Theory and application of mathematical programming. London, 1976. pp. 214.

WILLIAMS (H.P.) Model building in mathematical programming. Chichester, [1978]. pp. 330. *bibliog.*

PROGRESSIVE PARTY, FOUNDED 1912 (UNITED STATES).

GABLE (JOHN ALLEN) The Bull Moose years: Theodore Roosevelt and the Progressive Party. Port Washington, N.Y., 1978. pp. 302.

PROGRESSIVISM (U.S. POLITICS).

BURROW (JAMES GORDON) Organized medicine in the progressive era: the move toward monopoly. Baltimore, [1977]. pp. 218.

GABLE (JOHN ALLEN) The Bull Moose years: Theodore Roosevelt and the Progressive Party. Port Washington, N.Y., 1978. pp. 302.

GOULD (LEWIS L.) Reform and regulation: American politics, 1900-1916. New York, [1978]. pp. 197. *bibliog.*

LOWITT (RICHARD) George W. Norris: the triumph of a progressive, 1933-1944. Urbana, [1978]. pp. 493. *bibliog.*

MANEY (PATRICK J.) "Young Bob" La Follette: a biography of Robert M. La Follette, Jr., 1895-1953. Columbia, 1978. pp. 338. *bibliog.*

PROHIBITED BOOKS.

HAMON (HERVE) and ROTMAN (PATRICK) L'affaire Alata. Paris, [1977]. pp. 106.

PROHIBITION

— United States.

BLOCKER (JACK S.) Retreat from reform: the prohibition movement in the United States, 1890-1913. Westport, Conn., 1976. pp. 261. *bibliogs.*

CLARK (NORMAN H.) Deliver us from evil: an interpretation of American prohibition. New York, [1976]. pp. 246. *bibliog.*

PROLETARIAT.

CASTORIADIS (CORNELIUS) L'expérience du mouvement ouvrier. [Paris, 1974]. 2 vols.

PERROTTA (COSIMO) La proletarizzazione contemporanea. Lecce, [1975]. 2 vols. (in 1).

NEGRI (ANTONIO) Proletari e stato: per una discussione su autonomia operaia e compromesso storico. Milano, 1976. pp. 67.

CAMMAROTA (ANTONELLA) Proletariato marginale e classe operaia: (un contributo al dibattito sulla cultura e l'unità di classe del proletariato). Roma, [1977]. pp. 156.

PROMOTIONS

SOUTHERN RHODESIA. Commission of Enquiry into Promotions in the Civil Service. 1939. Report; [W.A. Godlonton, chairman]. Salisbury, 1939. pp. 73. *(Legislative Assembly. [Sessional Papers]. 1939. C.S.R. 2)*

PROPAGANDA.

HOOD (PETER) Ourselves and the press: a social study of news advertising and propaganda. London, [1939]. pp. 287.

PROPAGANDA, AMERICAN.

WINKLER (ALLAN M.) The politics of propaganda: the Office of War Information, 1942-1945. New Haven, 1978. pp. 230. *bibliog. (Yale University. Yale Historical Publications. Miscellany. 118)*

PROPAGANDA, BRITISH.

PROPAGANDA, BRITISH.

AUCKLAND (R.G.) Catalogue of British "black" propaganda to Germany 1941-1945. St. Albans, 1977. pp. 32.

PROPAGANDA, CHINESE.

GYÖRGY (IMRE) Cherez prizmu Pekina; perevod s vengerskogo, etc. Moskva, 1975. pp. 284.

PROPAGANDA, COMMUNIST.

AKADEMIIA OBSHCHESTVENNYKH NAUK. Kafedra Teorii i Metodov Ideologicheskoi Raboty. Voprosy Teorii i Metodov Ideologicheskoi Raboty. vyp. 7. Sotsial'no-psikhologicheskie aspekty ideologicheskoi deiatel'nosti. Moskva, 1977. pp. 279.

PROPAGANDA, FRENCH.

KLAITS (JOSEPH) Printed propaganda under Louis XIV: absolute monarchy and public opinion. Princeton, [1976]. pp. 341. *bibliog.*

PROPAGANDA, RHODESIAN.

CATHOLIC COMMISSION FOR JUSTICE AND PEACE IN RHODESIA. Rhodesia: the propaganda war. Salisbury, 1977. 1 pamphlet (unpaged).

PROPERTY.

DICKINSON (H.T.) Liberty and property: political ideology in eighteenth-century Britain. London, [1977]. pp. 369.

MARKETS and morals; edited by Gerald Dworkin [and others]. Washington, [1977]. pp. 206. *bibliogs.* Includes many of the papers presented at a three-day conference beginning May 9, 1974, at the Seattle Research Center of the Battelle Memorial Institute.

FRIEDMAN (DAVID) The machinery of freedom: guide to a radical capitalism. New Rochelle, [1978]. pp. 240. *bibliog.*

MACPHERSON (CRAWFORD BROUGH) ed. Property: mainstream and critical positions; [an anthology] edited, with an introductory and concluding essay, by C. B. Macpherson. Oxford, [1978]. pp. 207.

— Colombia.

MORENO ESCOBAR (BERNABE) Invasiones de predios urbanos: aspectos juridicos. Bogota, 1972. pp. 146. *bibliog.*

— Norway.

NORWAY. Statistiske Centralbyrå. 1977. Formuesstatistikk, 1973, etc. Oslo, 1977. pp. 95. *(Norges Offisielle Statistikk. Rekke A.922)* With English summary. Tables in Norwegian and English.

— Russia — Soviet Central Asia.

KISLIAKOV (NIKOLAI ANDREEVICH) Nasledovanie i razdel imushchestva narodov Srednei Azii i Kazakhstana, XIX - nachalo XX v. Leningrad, 1977. pp. 131. *bibliog.*

— United States.

ACKERMAN (BRUCE A.) Private property and the constitution. New Haven, 1977. pp. 303.

— Yugoslavia.

ARANDJELOVIĆ (SVETISLAV) Pravo svojine u Jugoslaviji. Beograd, 1975. pp. 216. *bibliog.* With Russian and English summaries.

PROPERTY AND SOCIALISM.

WLASNOŚĆ: gospodarka a prawo: studia o marksistowskiej teorii własności; praca zbiorowa pod redakcją Stanisława Kozyra-Kowalskiego. Warszawa, 1977. pp. 545.

PROPERTY TAX.

AUSTRALIA. Commonwealth Treasury. 1974. Net wealth taxes. Canberra, 1974. pp. 26. *(Treasury Taxation Papers. No. 12)*

— Canada — Alberta.

ALBERTA. Provincial-Municipal Finance Council. 1976. A proposal for property tax growth-sharing. [Edmonton, 1976]. fo. 29. *bibliog.*

— — Ontario.

ONTARIO. Provincial-Local Government Committee on Property Tax Reform. 1978. Report; [G. Dean, chairman]. [Toronto], 1978. pp. 110.

— Germany.

GERMANY (BUNDESREPUBLIK). Statistisches Bundesamt. Vermögensteuer. trien., 1972- Wiesbaden. *(Finanzen und Steuern. Reihe 7.4)*

— United Kingdom.

CONFEDERATION OF BRITISH INDUSTRY. Wealth tax: the industry view. London, 1977. pp. 20.

— United States.

METROPOLITAN financing and growth management policies: principles and practice; edited by George F. Break. Madison, 1978. pp. 329. *bibliogs. (Committee on Taxation, Resources and Economic Development. Publications. 9)* Proceedings of a symposium sponsored by the Committee at the University of Wisconsin, Madison, 1974, part of the Thirteenth Annual Conference of the Committee.

PROPORTIONAL REPRESENTATION.

GONZALEZ (JOAQUIN VICTOR) El censo nacional y la Constitucion. Buenos Aires, 1930. pp. 323.

PROSTHESIS.

UNITED NATIONS. Interregional Training Course for Instructors in Prosthetics, Copenhagen, 1969. United Nations...training course...organized...with the cooperation of the International Committee on Prosthetics and Orthotics of the International Society for Rehabilitation of the Disabled, Copenhagen, Denmark 11 August-6 September, 1969. (ST/TAO/SER.C/121). New York, 1971. pp. 126.

— Study and teaching.

UNITED NATIONS. Interregional Seminar on Standards for the Training of Prosthetists, Holte, 1968. Report of the...Seminar...organized by the United Nations and the government of Denmark with the co-operation...of the International Society for Rehabilitation of the Disabled [held at] Holte, Denmark, 1-19 July, 1968. (ST/TAO/SER. C/111). New York, 1969. pp. 238.

PROSTITUTION

— United Kingdom.

BRISTOW (EDWARD J.) Vice and vigilance: purity movements in Britain since 1700. Dublin, 1977. pp. 274. *bibliog.*

PROTEIN METABOLISM.

JOINT FAO/WHO AD HOC EXPERT COMMITTEE ON ENERGY AND PROTEIN REQUIREMENTS. 1973. Energy and protein requirements: report of a...Committee, Rome, 22 March - 2 April 1971. Rome, Food and Agriculture Organization, 1973. pp. 118. *bibliog. (Nutrition Meetings Report Series. No.52)*

PROTEINS.

HOLMSTRÖM (SVEN J.R.) Jordbrukets möjligheter att anpassa sig till nya mönster för proteinförsörjningen. Stockholm, 1975. pp. 32. *(Jordbrukets Utredningsinstitut. Meddelanden. 1975. Nr. 4)* With English summary.

PROTESTANT CHURCHES

— United States.

MOORHEAD (JAMES H.) American apocalypse: Yankee Protestants and the Civil War, 1860-1869. New Haven, 1978. pp. 278. *bibliog.*

PROTESTANTS IN IRELAND.

BOWEN (DESMOND) The Protestant crusade in Ireland, 1800-70: a study of Protestant-Catholic relations between the Act of Union and disestablishment. Dublin, 1978. pp. 412. *bibliog.*

PROUDHON (PIERRE JOSEPH).

LANGLOIS (JACQUES) Défense et actualité de Proudhon. Paris, [1976]. pp. 213. *bibliog.*

PROVENCE-CÔTE D'AZUR

— Economic conditions.

SUD: information économique Provence - Côte d'Azur - Corse: revue trimestrielle; ([pd. by] Institut National de la Statistique et des Etudes Economiques, Direction Régionale de Marseille [France]. q., Jl 1971 (no.1)- Marseille. Jl 1971 - F 1972 as Sud: information économique méditerranéenne; from Ap 1972 information on Languedoc-Roussillon pd. separately as Repères: économie du Languedoc-Roussillon.

PRUSSIA

— Army — History.

DUFFY (CHRISTOPHER) The army of Frederick the Great. Newton Abbot, [1974]. pp. 272. *bibliog.*

— Constitutional history.

JACOBY (JOHANN) Briefwechsel, 1816-1849; herausgegeben und erläutert von Edmund Silberner. Hannover, [1974]. pp. 669. *bibliog. (Institut für Sozialgeschichte Braunschweig. Veröffentlichungen)*

JACOBY (JOHANN) Briefwechsel, 1850-1877; herausgegeben und erläutert von Edmund Silberner. Bonn, [1978]. pp. 715. *(Institut für Sozialgeschichte Braunschweig. Veröffentlichungen)*

— Politics and government.

JACOBY (JOHANN) Briefwechsel, 1816-1849; herausgegeben und erläutert von Edmund Silberner. Hannover, [1974]. pp. 669. *bibliog. (Institut für Sozialgeschichte Braunschweig. Veröffentlichungen)*

GEY (THOMAS) Die preussische Verwaltung des Regierungsbezirks Bromberg, 1871-1920. Köln, [1976]. pp. 344. *bibliog.* Map in end pocket.

JACOBY (JOHANN) Briefwechsel, 1850-1877; herausgegeben und erläutert von Edmund Silberner. Bonn, [1978]. pp. 715. *(Institut für Sozialgeschichte Braunschweig. Veröffentlichungen)*

PSYCHIATRIC HOSPITAL CARE

— France.

GUILBERT (FRANÇOISE) Liberté individuelle et hospitalisation de malades mentaux. Paris, 1974. pp. 381. *bibliog.*

PSYCHIATRIC HOSPITALS.

MAGARO (PETER A.) and others. The mental health industry: a cultural phenomenon: alternate solutions generated from an empirical evaluation of the cultural determinants, vested interests, and treatment effectiveness of the current mental health establishment. New York, [1978]. pp. 272. *bibliog.*

— Russia.

BLOCH (SIDNEY) and REDDAWAY (PETER B.) Russia's political hospitals: the abuse of psychiatry in the Soviet Union. London, 1977. pp. 510.

— **United Kingdom — Statistics.**

DAVIES (HYWEL) Admissions of residents of Greater London to psychiatric hospitals and units, 1973. London, [1976]. pp. 75. *(London. Greater London Council. Research Memoranda. 481)*

U.K. Department of Health and Social Security. 1977. The facilities and services of mental illness and mental handicap hospitals in England, 1975. London, 1977. pp. 130. *(Statistical and Research Report Series. No. 19)*

U.K. Department of Health and Social Security. 1978. In-patient statistics from the mental health enquiry for England, 1975. London, 1978. pp. 138. *(Statistical and Research Report Series. No. 20)*

PSYCHIATRIC PERSONNEL

— **United Kingdom.**

THOMPSON (RICHARD) of the Greater London Council. Staff of local authority residential and day care establishments for the mentally disordered in the London boroughs, 1966-1973. London, [1975]. pp. (80). *(London. Greater London Council. Research Memoranda. 492)*

PSYCHIATRIC RESEARCH.

HARE (ROBERT D.) Psychopathy: theory and research. New York, [1970]. pp. 138. *bibliog.*

PSYCHIATRIC SOCIAL WORK

— **United Kingdom.**

BENDER (M.P.) Community psychology. London, 1976. pp. 144. *bibliog.*

PSYCHIATRY.

LADER (MALCOLM HAROLD) Psychiatry on trial. Harmondsworth, 1977. pp. 202. *bibliog.*

COOPER (DAVID GRAHAM) The language of madness. London, 1978. pp. 182.

PSYCHOANALYSIS.

WACHTEL (PAUL L.) Psychoanalysis and behavior therapy: toward an integration. New York, [1977]. pp. 315. *bibliog.*

SCHAFER (ROY) Language and insight. New Haven, 1978. pp. 208. *bibliog. (London. University. University College. Sigmund Freud Memorial Lectures. 1975-1976)*

PSYCHOBIOLOGY.

PUGH (GEORGE EDGIN) The biological origin of human values. London, 1978. pp. 461. *bibliog.*

PSYCHOLINGUISTICS.

GREENE (JUDITH) Thinking and language. London, 1975 repr. 1977. pp. 144. *bibliog.*

ANDERSON (JOHN ROBERT) Language, memory, and thought. New York, [1976]. pp. 546. *bibliogs.*

LANGUAGE and speech; edited by Edward C. Carterette and Morton P. Friedman. London, 1976. pp. 501. *bibliogs.*

The NEUROPSYCHOLOGY of language: essays in honor of Eric Lenneberg; edited by R.W. Rieber. New York, [1976]. pp. 230. *bibliogs.*

CURTISS (SUSAN) Genie: a psycholinguistic study of a modern-day "wild child". New York, 1977. pp. 288. *bibliog.*

SANDELL (ROLF) Linguistic style and persuasion. London, 1977. pp. 329. *bibliog. (European Association of Experimental Social Psychology. European Monographs in Social Psychology. 11)*

SCHLESINGER (I.M.) Production and comprehension of utterances. Hillsdale, N.J., 1977. pp. 235. *bibliog.*

THINKING: readings in cognitive science; edited by P.N. Johnson-Laird and P.C. Wason. Cambridge, [1977]. pp. 615. *bibliog.*

FOSS (DONALD J.) and HAKES (DAVID T.) Psycholinguistics: an introduction to the psychology of language. Englewood Cliffs, [1978]. pp. 434. *bibliog.*

LINGUISTIC theory and psychological reality; edited by Morris Halle [and others]. Cambridge, Mass., [1978]. pp. 329. *bibliog. (Massachusetts Institute of Technology. M.I.T. Bicentennial Studies. 3)*

SCHAFER (ROY) Language and insight. New Haven, 1978. pp. 208. *bibliog. (London. University. University College. Sigmund Freud Memorial Lectures. 1975-1976)*

The SOCIAL context of language; edited by Ivana Markova. Chichester, [1978]. pp. 241. *Based on a conference on language and the social context sponsored by the Social Section and Scottish Branch of the British Psychological Society held...Jan. 10-11, 1975.*

PSYCHOLOGICAL RESEARCH.

SERPELL (ROBERT) Culture's influence on behaviour. London, 1976. pp. 144. *bibliog.*

STUDIES in cross-cultural psychology;... edited by Neil Warren. London, 1977 in progress. *bibliogs.*

PSYCHOLOGICAL RESEARCH, EXPERIMENTER EFFECTS IN.

EXPERIMENTER effects and the ethnic cueing phenomenon; [by] A. Brah [and others]. Bristol, Social Science Research Council Research Unit on Ethnic Relations, [1977]. pp. 31. *bibliog. (Working Papers on Ethnic Relations. No. 3)*

PSYCHOLOGY.

UNIVERSITY OF SURREY. Centre for Adult Education. Human Potential Research Project. Research report. [1972?]. fo. 17. *bibliog. Unpublished: typescript.*

LEGGE (DAVID) An introduction to psychological science: basic processes in the analysis of behaviour. London, 1975. pp. 144. *bibliog.*

RADFORD (JOHN) and KIRBY (RICHARD) The person in psychology. London, 1975. pp. 143. *bibliog.*

SHOTTER (JOHN) Images of man in psychological research. London, 1975. pp. 144. *bibliog.*

YOU as a product: an essay on the family as the key link between individual structure and socioeconomic reality and changes in family structure, cultural conditioning and sexual repression with economic changes in capitalism; [by members of Newcastle University Socialist Society]. [Newcastle, 1975?]. pp. 76.

ARIETI (SILVANO) The intrapsychic self: feeling and cognition in health and mental illness. New York, [1976]. pp. 350. *bibliog. Abridged version of the 1967 edition.*

HEATHER (NICK) Radical perspectives in psychology. London, 1976. pp. 142. *bibliog.*

WESTLAND (GORDON) Current crises of psychology. London, 1978. pp. 174. *bibliog.*

— **Bibliography.**

KNOCK (ANN) compiler. Library resources in psychology: a directory of libraries in the Greater London area with a specialist interest in psychology, etc. London, 1974. pp. 16. *(London. University. Birkbeck College. Library. Publications. No. 47)*

— **History — United States.**

The ROOTS of American psychology: historical influences and implications for the future; edited by R.W. Rieber and Kurt Salzinger. New York, 1977. pp. 394. *bibliogs. (New York (City). Academy of Sciences. Annals. vol. 291) Based on papers of a conference held by the Academy in 1976.*

— **Methodology.**

RIEGEL (KLAUS F.) Psychology of development and history. New York, [1976]. pp. 263. *bibliog.*

STUDIES in cross-cultural psychology;... edited by Neil Warren. London, 1977 in progress. *bibliogs.*

PSYCHOTHERAPY.

PSYCHOLOGY, APPLIED.

FRANSELLA (FAY) Need to change. London, 1975. pp. 144. *bibliog.*

PSYCHOLOGY, EXPERIMENTAL.

DESPORTES (JEAN PIERRE) Les effets de la présence de l'expérimentateur dans les sciences du comportement. Paris, 1975. pp. 115. *bibliog. (Centre National de la Recherche Scientifique. Monographies Françaises de Psychologie. 31)*

GARDINER (JOHN M.) and KAMINSKA (ZOFIA) First experiments in psychology. London, 1975. pp. 144. *bibliog.*

MILLER (STEPHEN H.) Experimental design and statistics. London, 1975. pp. 142. *bibliog.*

PSYCHOLOGY, FORENSIC.

PSYCHOLOGY and the law: research frontiers; edited by Gordon Bermant [and others]. Lexington, Mass., [1976]. pp. 303. *bibliogs. Includes papers of a conference held June 12-14, 1975 at the Battelle Seattle Research Center and sponsored by the Battelle Memorial Institute.*

PSYCHOLOGY, INDUSTRIAL.

SAINSAULIEU (RENAUD) L'identité au travail: les effets culturels de l'organisation. Paris, [1977]. pp. 487.

STJERNBERG (TORBJÖRN) Organizational change and quality of life: individual and organizational perspectives on democratization of work in an insurance company. Stockholm, 1977. pp. 375. *bibliog. A research report of the Programme for Participation and Organization Development, Economic Research Institute, Stockholm School of Economics.*

SCHULTZ (DUANE P.) Psychology and industry today: an introduction to industrial and organizational psychology. 2nd ed. New York, [1978]. pp. 480. *bibliogs.*

PSYCHOLOGY, MILITARY.

RICHARDSON (FRANK McLEAN) Fighting spirit: a study of psychological factors in war. London, 1978. pp. 189. *bibliog.*

WATSON (PETER) Assistant Editor of New Society. War on the mind: the military uses and abuses of psychology. London, 1978. pp. 534.

PSYCHOLOGY, PATHOLOGICAL.

HARE (ROBERT D.) Psychopathy: theory and research. New York, [1970]. pp. 138. *bibliog.*

ARIETI (SILVANO) The intrapsychic self: feeling and cognition in health and mental illness. New York, [1976]. pp. 350. *bibliog. Abridged version of the 1967 edition.*

O'BRIEN (MAJA) The diagnosis of psychopathy: a study of some characteristics in personality and behaviour of "psychopaths" referred for treatment to a therapeutic community. 1976. fo. 446. *bibliog. Typescript. Ph.D. (London) thesis: unpublished. This thesis is the property of London University and may not be removed from the Library.*

PSYCHOLOGY, PHYSIOLOGICAL.

BLUNDELL (JOHN) Physiological psychology. London, 1975. pp. 144. *bibliog.*

LADER (MALCOLM HAROLD) The psychophysiology of mental illness. London, 1975. pp. 270. *bibliog.*

PSYCHOTHERAPY.

HAHNEMANN SYMPOSIUM, 35TH. Sex and the life cycle: edited by Wilbur W. Oaks [and others]. New York, [1976]. pp. 223.

HARWOOD (ALAN) Rx: spiritist as needed: a study of a Puerto Rican community mental health resource. New York, [1977]. pp. 251. *bibliog.*

WACHTEL (PAUL L.) Psychoanalysis and behavior therapy: toward an integration. New York, [1977]. pp. 315. *bibliog.*

PSYCHOTHERAPY.(Cont.)

MAGARO (PETER A.) and others. The mental health industry: a cultural phenomenon: alternate solutions generated from an empirical evaluation of the cultural determinants, vested interests, and treatment effectiveness of the current mental health establishment. New York, [1978]. pp. 272. *bibliog.*

ROGERS (CARL RANSOM) Carl Rogers on personal power. London, 1978. pp. 305. *bibliog.*

SCHAFER (ROY) Language and insight. New Haven, 1978. pp. 208. *bibliog. (London. University. University College. Sigmund Freud Memorial Lectures. 1975-1976)*

PUBLIC CONTRACTS

— France.

DUPOUX (JEAN) AND grosgeorge (bernard) lES MARCHÉS PUBLICS EN fRANCE. ?pARIS, 1977!. PP. 128. BIBLIOG.

— Mauritania.

BARROT (ANDRE) Les marchés publics en Mauritanie. Nouakchott, Ecole Nationale d'Administration, 1976. fo.70.

— United Kingdom.

BERCUSSON (BRIAN) Fair wages resolutions. London, 1978. pp. 538.

— United States.

TETHER (IVAN J.) Government procurement and operations. Cambridge, Mass., [1977]. pp. 196. *A product of the Energy Conservation Project of the Environmental Law Institute.*

PUBLIC GOODS.

PUBLIC economics and the quality of life; edited by Lowdon Wingo and Alan Evans. Baltimore, [1977]. pp. 327. *bibliogs. Mainly papers evolved from an International Research Conference on Public Policy and the Quality of Life in Cities, New Orleans, 1975, sponsored by Resources for the Future and the Centre for Environmental Studies.*

PUBLIC HEALTH PERSONNEL

— Rhodesia.

RHODESIA. Department of Labour. Manpower Branch. 1973. Public health inspectors. [Salisbury], 1973. pp. [35]. *(Manpower Plans. No. 1)*

PUBLIC HOUSING

— Australia.

CONSUMER groups and their views on welfare services and rented housing. Canberra, 1975. pp. 111. *(Australia. Commission of Inquiry into Poverty. Research Reports)*

— Germany — Finance.

GERMANY (BUNDESREPUBLIK). Statistisches Bundesamt. Bewilligungen im sozialen Wohnungsbau (formerly Bewilligungen im öffentlich geförderten sozialen Wohnungsbau). a., (formerly q.,) 1955/56(1st)- Wiesbaden. *(Bautätigkeit und Wohnungen. Reihe 2).*

— United Kingdom.

KILLICK (ANGELA) Council house blues. London, [1976]. pp. 20.

HOATH (DAVID CHARLES) Council housing. London, 1978. pp. 169.

— — Bibliography.

SCOTT (ANDREW J.C.) compiler. The sale of council houses. London, 1976. pp. 6. *(London. Greater London Council. Research Library. [Research] Bibliographies. No. 75)*

— — London.

BARCLAY (IRENE T.) People need roots: the story of the St. Pancras Housing Association. London, [1976]. pp. 144.

LONDON. Greater London Council. Establishments Department. Behavioural Science Unit. The relationship between the GLC Housing Department, its tenants and the public; by the Behavioural Science Unit and an interdepartmental working party. London, [1977]. pp. 107. *(London. Greater London Council. Research Memoranda. 503)*

TROWBRIDGE (BARRY) Sample survey of borough housing waiting list applicants 1973-76. London, [1978]. 1 vol. (various pagings). *(London. Greater London Council. Research Memoranda. 533)*

— — Manchester.

FLETT (HAZEL) Council housing and the location of ethnic minorities. Bristol, Social Science Research Council Research Unit on Ethnic Relations, [1977]. pp. 52. *(Working Papers on Ethnic Relations. No. 5)*

— United States.

RABUSHKA (ALVIN) and WEISSERT (WILLIAM G.) Caseworkers or police?: how tenants see public housing. Stanford, [1977]. pp. 98. *(Stanford University. Hoover Institution on War, Revolution and Peace. Hoover Institution Publications. 186)*

PUBLIC INSTITUTIONS

— Italy.

Le ISTITUZIONI in Italia: (otto conferenze curate dal Circolo Ottobre di Mantova); [by] Pio Baldelli [and others]. Roma, [1976]. pp. 171. *bibliogs.*

EMILIANI (VITTORIO) L'Italia mangiata: (lo scandalo degli enti inutili). Torino, [1977]. pp. 136.

PUBLIC INTEREST.

WEISBROD (BURTON ALLEN) and others. Public interest law: an economic and institutional analysis. Berkeley, [1978]. pp. 580.

— United States.

BERRY (JEFFREY M.) Lobbying for the people: the political behavior of public interest groups. Princeton, [1977]. pp. 311. *bibliog.*

PUBLIC LAW

— United States.

PUBLIC law and public policy; edited by John A. Gardiner. New York, 1977. pp. 241. *bibliogs.*

PUBLIC LIBRARIES

— Canada.

CANADA. Statistics Canada. Culture statistics: public libraries in Canada. a., 1975(1st)- Ottawa. *[in English and French]*

PUBLIC OPINION

— Europe.

KITZINGER (UWE WEBSTER) The new Europeans: a commentary on products and people, a marketing survey of the European Common Market and Britain, 1963. [London, 1963]. pp. 21.

— Europe, Eastern.

CONNOR (WALTER D.) and GITELMAN (ZVI Y.) Public opinion in European socialist systems. New York, 1977. pp. 196.

— France.

FRANCE. Centre d'Etude des Revenus et des Coûts. 1977. Connaissances et opinions des Français sur les prix: ce qu'ils savent et pensent des mécanismes de prix; analyse de résultats d'enquêtes, 1970, 1974, 1976. Paris, 1977. pp. 105. *(Documents. No. 33/34)*

La FRANCE et les Français en 1938-1939; sous la direction de René Rémond et Janine Bourdin. [Paris, 1978]. pp. 365.

— Germany.

HOLZ (KURT A.) Die Diskussion um den Dawes- und Young-Plan in der deutschen Presse. Frankfurt/Main, [1977]. 2 vols. (in 1). *bibliog.*

— Israel.

ISRAELI MIRROR: what Israelis are saying about themselves; pd. by Middle East International. f. 1973 (nos. 5, 9-16) London.

— United Kingdom.

AIMS FOR FREEDOM AND ENTERPRISE. A bombshell for the Labour Party; report on national opinion survey on trade unions and the Labour Party. London, [1977]. pp. 5.

MARPLAN LIMITED. The Saffron Walden bye-election. [London, 1977]. fo. 11.

MARPLAN LIMITED. Strikes, picketing and the closed shop. [London, 1977]. fo. 7.

MARPLAN LIMITED. Trade union power in Britain today. [London, 1977]. fo. 9.

NEWS INTERNATIONAL. The public view: a look at how the public view some key issues confronting Britain today. London, 1977. pp. 36.

SPARKS (RICHARD FRANKLIN) and others. Surveying victims: a study of the measurement of criminal victimization, perceptions of crime, and attitudes to criminal justice. Chichester, [1977]. pp. 276. *bibliog.*

LORIMER (DOUGLAS A.) Colour, class and the Victorians: English attitudes to the negro in the mid-nineteenth century. Leicester, 1978. pp. 300. *bibliog.*

MARPLAN LIMITED. Britain's leaders. [London, 1978?]. fo. 5.

MARPLAN LIMITED. The state of the family. [London, 1978?]. fo. 12.

POLICING the crisis: mugging, the state, and law and order; [by] Stuart Hall [and others]. London, 1978. pp. 425.

— United States.

CITIZEN preferences and urban public policy: models, measures, uses; edited by Terry Nichols Clark. Beverly Hills, 1976. pp. 142. *Based on papers presented at a meeting of the Public Choice Society, Chicago, 1975, on Preference revelation for public goods.*

KAUFMAN (HERBERT) Fear of bureaucracy: a raging pandemic. Urbana, Ill., [1978]. pp. 30. *(Illinois University. Edmund J. James Lectures on Government. 1978)*

LEONARD (THOMAS C.) Above the battle: war-making in America from Appomattox to Versailles. New York, 1978. pp. 260.

PUBLIC OPINION POLLS.

CONNOR (WALTER D.) and GITELMAN (ZVI Y.) Public opinion in European socialist systems. New York, 1977. pp. 196.

PUBLIC POLICY (LAW)

— United States.

PUBLIC law and public policy; edited by John A. Gardiner. New York, 1977. pp. 241. *bibliogs.*

SIGLER (JAY A.) and BEEDE (BENJAMIN R.) The legal sources of public policy. Lexington, Mass., [1977]. pp. 185.

WEISBROD (BURTON ALLEN) and others. Public interest law: an economic and institutional analysis. Berkeley, [1978]. pp. 580.

PUBLIC PROSECUTORS

— United States.

EISENSTEIN (JAMES) Counsel for the United States: U.S. attorneys in the political and legal systems. Baltimore, [1978]. pp. 264.

PUBLIC RELATIONS

— Police.

MARPLAN LIMITED. Survey on policemen's pay. [London], 1977. fo. 7.

POLICE and society; edited by David H. Bayley. Beverly Hills, [1977]. pp. 257. *bibliog. Essays prepared for a conference held at the Graduate School of International Studies, University of Denver, in 1976.*

UNDER heavy manners: report of the labour movement enquiry into police brutality and the position of black youth in Islington, held on Saturday July 23, 1977. London, 1977. pp. 23.

PUBLIC RELATIONS AS A PROFESSION.

INSTITUTE OF PUBLIC RELATIONS. Interpretation of the code of professional conduct. London, 1973. pp. 10.

PUBLIC UTILITIES

— United States.

PALLEY (MARIAN LIEF) and PALLEY (HOWARD A.) Urban America and public policies. Lexington, Mass., [1977]. pp. 277. *bibliogs.*

PUBLICITY.

LAGNEAU (GÉRARD) La sociologie de la publicité. [Paris, 1977]. pp. 128. *bibliog.*

PUBLISHERS AND PUBLISHING

— Statistics.

WOOTTON (CHRISTOPHER B.) Trends in size, growth and cost of the literature since 1955. London, 1977. pp. 90. *(British Library. Research and Development Department. Reports. 5323)*

— Austria — Bibliography.

SCHROTH (HANS) compiler. Verlag der Wiener Volksbuchhandlung, 1894-1934: eine Bibliographie. Wien, [1977]. pp. 63. *(Ludwig-Boltzmann-Institut für Geschichte der Arbeiterbewegung. Schriftenreihe. 7)*

— Russia.

WALKER (GREGORY) Soviet book publishing policy. Cambridge, 1978. pp. 164. *bibliog. (National Association for Soviet and East European Studies. Soviet and East European Studies)*

— — Siberia.

POSADSKOV (ALEKSANDR LEONIDOVICH) Sibirskaia kniga i revoliutsiia, 1917-1918. Novosibirsk, 1977. pp. 285.

— United Kingdom.

THOMSON ORGANISATION. The Thomson Organisation in Great Britain; [including a statement of Roy Thomson circulated with the report and accounts for the year ended 31 December, 1959]. [London, 1960]. pp. 32.

SOCIETY OF PUBLIC TEACHERS OF LAW. Working Party on Law Publishing. Final report on law publishing and legal scholarship. n.p., 1977. pp. 45.

HODGES (SHEILA) Gollancz: the story of a publishing house, 1928-1978. London, 1978. pp. 256.

— Zambia.

ZAMBIA. Central Statistical Office. 1976. Paper, paper products, printing and publishing industries. Lusaka, 1976. fo. 44. *bibliog. (Industry Monographs. No. 4)*

PUERTO RICANS IN THE UNITED STATES.

HARWOOD (ALAN) Rx: spiritist as needed: a study of a Puerto Rican community mental health resource. New York, [1977]. pp. 251. *bibliog.*

PUERTO RICO.

WAGENHEIM (KAL) Puerto Rico: a profile. 2nd ed. New York, 1975. pp. 294. *bibliog.*

— Economic conditions.

CHARDON (CARLOS E.) Datos que sugieren la integracion economica de una parte de la region del Caribe: la Republica Dominicana y Puerto Rico: informe preliminar. San Juan, Banco Gubernamental de Fomento para Puerto Rico, 1962. fo. 105.

— Politics and government.

PUERTO RICO. Government Development Bank for Puerto Rico. 1962. A special report on the commonwealth of Puerto Rico. San Juan, 1962. pp. 24.

PUERTO RICO. Government Development Bank for Puerto Rico. 1969. A special report on the commonwealth of Puerto Rico. [rev.ed.]. San Juan, 1969. pp. 21.

PUERTO RICO. Bureau of the Budget. 1970. Sinopsis de la organizacion del gobierno del Estado Libre Asociado de Puerto Rico. [San Juan], 1970. pp. 44. *(Boletin de Gerencia Administrativa. Numeros Especiales. 1970. Num. 205)*

PUNISHMENT.

MANNHEIM (HERMANN) ed. Pioneers in criminology. 2nd ed. Montclair, N.J., [1973]. pp. 505.

VON HIRSCH (ANDREW) Doing justice: the choice of punishments;...report of the Committee for the Study of Incarceration. New York, 1976. pp. 179.

POLLOCK (SETON) Law and order: a neglected aspect of penal theory. Birmingham, 1977. pp. 11.

REFORM in corrections: problems and issues; edited by Harry E. Allen [and] Nancy J. Beran. New York, 1977. pp. 129. *bibliogs. Papers presented at the Annual Convention of the American Society of Criminology, in Chicago, 1974.*

— Canada — Newfoundland and Labrador.

NEWFOUNDLAND. Corrections Study Committee. 1973. Report; [Keith Couse, chairman]. [St. John's], 1973. pp. 30.

— Netherlands.

NETHERLANDS. Commissie-Vermogensstraffen. 1972. Eindrapport...; (voorzitter, W.C. van Binsbergen). 's-Gravenhage, 1972. pp. 143,30.

— United Kingdom.

THOMAS (D.A.) The penal equation: derivations of the penalty structure of English criminal law. Cambridge, 1978. pp. 60. *bibliog.*

WOOTTON (BARBARA FRANCES) Baroness Wootton of Abinger. Crime and penal policy: reflections of fifty years' experience. London, 1978. pp. 261.

— United States.

REFORM in corrections: problems and issues; edited by Harry E. Allen [and] Nancy J. Beran. New York, 1977. pp. 129. *bibliogs. Papers presented at the Annual Convention of the American Society of Criminology, in Chicago, 1974.*

PUNJAB (PAKISTAN)

— Rural conditions.

AHMAD (SAGHIR) Class and power in a Punjabi village. New York, [1977]. pp. 174. *bibliogs.*

PURITANS.

MIDDLEKAUFF (ROBERT) The Mathers: three generations of Puritan intellectuals, 1596- 1728. New York, 1971. pp. 440.

QATAR

— Economic conditions.

GRAHAM (HELGA) Arabian time machine: self-portrait of an oil state. London, 1978. pp. 338.

— Social conditions.

GRAHAM (HELGA) Arabian time machine: self-portrait of an oil state. London, 1978. pp. 338.

— Social life and customs.

GRAHAM (HELGA) Arabian time machine: self-portrait of an oil state. London, 1978. pp. 338.

QUALITY CONTROL.

BELBIN (R. MEREDITH) Quality calamities and their management implications. London, [1970]. pp. 16. *bibliog. (British Institute of Management. Occasional Papers. New Series. OPN. 8)*

WETHERILL (GEORGE BARRIE) Sampling inspection and quality control. 2nd ed. London, [1977]. pp. 146. *bibliog.*

QUARRIES AND QUARRYING

— United Kingdom.

NEW CO-OPERATIVE QUARRIES (PIONEER SOCIETY). The New Co-operative Quarries (Pioneer Society), Limited: [prospectus]. [London, 1904?]. pp. (3).

QUEBEC (PROVINCE)

— Boundaries.

QUEBEC (PROVINCE). Commission d'Etude sur l'Intégrité du Territoire du Québec. 1970-71. Rapport; [Henri Dorion, président]. [Québec], 1970-71. 10 vols. (in 5).

— Emigration and immigration.

MANPOWER AND IMMIGRATION REVIEW (formerly Manpower review: Quebec region (previously Québec manpower review); [pd. by] Department of Manpower and Immigration, Manpower Information and Analysis Branch, Québec Region [Canada] q. (formerly bi-m.), Ja/F 1969 (v.2, no.1)- , with gap (My/Je 1969: v.2, no.3). Montreal. *[in English and French] Ja/F 1969 in French only; Mr/Ap 1969 in English only.*

— Government publications — Bibliography.

QUEBEC (PROVINCE). Legislative Library. 1972. Commissions et comités d'enquêtes au Québec depuis 1867. Quebec, 1972. pp. 95. *bibliog. (Bibliographie et Documentation. 1)*

— Languages.

LEBEL (CLEMENT) compiler. Documents de la Commission d'Enquête sur la Situation de la Langue Française et les Droits Linguistiques au Québec, Commission Gendron: bibliographie. Québec, 1974. pp. 206. *(Quebec (Province). Legislative Library. Bibliographie et Documentation. 3)*

QUEBEC (PROVINCE). Statutes, etc. 1974. Official language act. Quebec, 1975. pp. 25. *In English and French.*

— Nationalism.

ALLEMAGNE (ANDRE D') Le R[assemblement pour l'] I[ndépendance] N[ational] de 1960 à 1963: étude d'un groupe de pression au Québec. Montréal, [1974]. pp. 160. *bibliog.*

ARNAUD (NICOLE) and DOFNY (JACQUES) Nationalism and the national question. Montreal, [1977]. pp. 134. *Translated by Penelope Williams.*

PROSPECTS for a socialist Canada; edited by John Riddell and Art Young. Toronto, [1977]. pp. 127.

— Politics and government.

LESAGE (JEAN) Un Québec fort dans une nouvelle confédération. Québec, [Office d'Information et de Publicité du Québec], 1965. pp. 51.

RUMILLY (ROBERT) Honoré Mercier et son temps (1840-1894). Montréal, [1975]. 2 vols.

BERNARD (ANDRE) Québec: elections 1976. Montreal, [1976]. pp. 174. *bibliog.*

QUEBEC (PROVINCE)(Cont.)

MURRAY (VĚRA) Le Parti québécois: de la fondation à la prise du pouvoir. Montréal, [1976]. pp. 242. *bibliog.*

HARBRON (JOHN D.) Canada without Quebec. Don Mills, Ont., [1977]. pp. 159. *bibliog.*

LAXER (JAMES) and LAXER (ROBERT M.) The Liberal idea of Canada: Pierre Trudeau and the question of Canada's survival. Toronto, 1977. pp. 234.

— Religion.

DENAULT (BERNARD) and LEVESQUE (BENÔIT) Eléments pour une sociologie des communautés religieuses au Québec. Sherbrooke, 1975. pp. 220. *bibliog.*

— Social history.

Les TRAVAILLEURS québécois, 1851-1896; par Noël Bélanger [and others]; sous la direction de Jean Hamelin. 2nd ed. Montréal, 1975. pp. 221. *bibliog. (Regroupement de Chercheurs en Histoire des Travailleurs Québécois. Collection Histoire des Travailleurs Québécois. 2)*

QUEENSLAND

— Politics and government.

MURPHY (DENIS J.) T.J. Ryan: a political biography. St. Lucia, Queensland, [1975]. pp. 596. *bibliog.*

QUEUEING THEORY.

PAGE (ERIC) Queueing theory in OR. London, 1972. pp. 187. *bibliog.*

QUINET (EDGAR).

WODZYŃSKA (MARIA) Adam Mickiewicz i romantyczna filozofia historii w Collège de France. Warszawa, 1976. pp. 283. *With French summary.*

RACE.

ISHERWOOD (H.B.) Man's racial nature: an exposure of the false propaganda of the United Nations. Brighton, 1969. pp. 15.

PARTY FOR WORKERS POWER. Racism, intelligence and the working class. Boston, Mass., [1974?]. pp. 71.

ZUR MUEHLEN (PATRIK VON) Rassenideologien: Geschichte und Hintergründe. Berlin, [1977]. pp. 278. *bibliog.*

RACE AWARENESS.

GORDON (CHAD) Looking ahead: self-conceptions, race and family as determinants of adolescent orientation to achievement. Washington, D.C., [197-]. pp. 120. *bibliog. (American Sociological Association. Arnold and Caroline Rose Monograph Series in Sociology)*

ADAMS (HOWARD) Prison of grass: Canada from the native point of view. Toronto, 1975. pp. 238. *bibliog.*

RACE DISCRIMINATION.

GEGEN den Rassismus, Apartheid und Kolonialismus: Dokumente der DDR, 1949-1977; (Dokumentenauswahl und Einführung: Alfred Babing). Berlin, 1978. pp. 703.

— Law and legislation — United Kingdom.

RUNNYMEDE TRUST. Briefing Papers. Review of race relations legislation: comments and proposals. London, 1975. 1 pamphlet (unpaged).

COMMISSION FOR RACIAL EQUALITY. Your rights to equal treatment under the new Race Relations Act 1976: a general guide. [London, 1977]. pp. (8).

COMMISSION FOR RACIAL EQUALITY. Your rights to equal treatment under the new Race Relations Act 1976: housing, education and services. [London, 1977]. pp. 12.

— Canada — Ontario.

HEAD (WILSON A.) The black presence in the Canadian mosaic: a study of perception and the practice of discrimination against blacks in metropolitan Toronto. [Toronto], Ontario Human Rights Commission, 1975. 1 vol. (various pagings). *bibliog.*

— Rhodesia.

RHODESIA. Commission of Inquiry into Racial Discrimination. 1976. Report...; [Sir Vincent Quenet, chairman]. [Salisbury], 1976. pp. 116. *(Rhodesia. [Command Papers]. 1976. Cmd. R.R.6)*

RHODESIA. Prime Minister. 1976. Prime Minister's reply to the debate on the report of the Commission on Racial Discrimination, July 23rd, 1976. [Salisbury], 1976. pp. 8. *(Rhodesia. Ministry of Information, Immigration and Tourism. For the Record. No. 37)*

RHODESIA. Prime Minister. 1977. Removal of racial discrimination: Prime Minister's statement in Parliament, February, 1977. [Salisbury, 1977]. pp. 6. *(Rhodesia. Ministry of Information, Immigration and Tourism. For the Record. No. 40)*

— South Africa.

LEGASSICK (MARTIN) The analysis of racism in South Africa: segregation, the state and the mining economy. [1976?]. 1 pamphlet (unpaged). *bibliog. Unpublished: photocopy of typescript. Paper presented at the Political Studies Association Conference, Nottingham, 1976.*

— United Kingdom.

COOK (DAVE) A knife at the throat of us all: racism and the National Front. London, [1977]. pp. 31. *(Communist Party of Great Britain. Communist Party Pamphlets)*

— United States.

BLACK/brown/white relations: race relations in the 1970's; edited by Charles V. Willie. New Brunswick, N.J., [1977]. pp. 235.

— — Georgia.

DITTMER (JOHN) Black Georgia in the progressive era, 1900-1920. Urbana, [1977]. pp. 239. *bibliog.*

RACE PROBLEMS.

ETHNIC conflict in international relations; edited by Astri Suhrke [and] Lela Garner Noble. New York, 1977. pp. 246.

TINKER (HUGH) Race, conflict and the international order: from empire to United Nations. London, 1977. pp. 157. *bibliogs.*

ZUR MUEHLEN (PATRIK VON) Rassenideologien: Geschichte und Hintergründe. Berlin, [1977]. pp. 278. *bibliog.*

GORDON (MILTON MYRON) Human nature, class and ethnicity. New York, 1978. pp. 302.

RADIATION.

UNITED NATIONS. Scientific Committee on the Effects of Atomic Radiation. 1972. Ionizing radiation: levels and effects; a report...on the effects of atomic radiation to the General Assembly, with annexes. New York, 1972. 2 vols.

RADICAL ALTERNATIVES TO PRISON.

RYAN (MICK) The acceptable pressure group: inequality in the penal lobby: a case study of the Howard League and RAP. Farnborough, Hants., [1978]. pp. 165. *bibliog.*

RADICALISM.

KRAUSE (GUENTER) Das Elend der "Linken": zur Kritik der politischen Ökonomie des Linksrevisionismus. Berlin, 1977. pp. 135. *bibliog.*

RADICALISM in the contemporary age; Seweryn Bialer, editor [and] Sophia Sluzar, associate editor. Boulder, Colo., 1977. 3 vols. *(Columbia University. Research Institute on International Change. Studies) Based on a series of workshops held at the Institute in 1975.*

— Canada.

McCORMACK (ANDREW ROSS) Reformers, rebels, and revolutionaries: the western Canadian radical movement, 1899-1919. Toronto, [1977]. pp. 228. *bibliog.*

— Europe.

TEODORI (MASSIMO) Storia delle nuove sinistre in Europa, 1956-1976. Bologna, [1976]. pp. 694. *bibliog.*

— France.

MERRIMAN (JOHN M.) The agony of the Republic: the repression of the left in revolutionary France, 1848-1851. New Haven, 1978. pp. 298. *bibliog.*

— Germany.

OTTO (KARL A.) Vom Ostermarsch zur APO: Geschichte der ausserparlamentarischen Opposition in der Bundesrepublik, 1960-1970. Frankfurt/Main, [1977]. pp. 230. *bibliog.*

— Italy.

VALLAURI (CARLO) I gruppi extraparlamentari di sinistra: genesi e organizzazione. [Roma, 1976]. pp. 134.

VIOLI (PATRIZIA) I giornali dell'estrema sinistra: (i tranelli e le ambiguità della lingua e dell'ideologia). Milano, 1977. pp. 192.

— Russia.

GORIACHKINA (MARIIA SERGEEVNA) Satira Shchedrina i russkaia demokraticheskaia literatura 60-80-kh godov XIX veka. Moskva, 1977. pp. 175.

PAVLOV (ALEKSEI TERENT'EVICH) Ot dvorianskoi revoliutsionnosti k revoliutsionnomu demokratizmu: ideinaia evoliutsiia A.I. Gertsena. Moskva, 1977. pp. 128. *bibliog.*

— United Kingdom.

BOUCHIER (DAVID LESLIE) The development and containment of radical ideologies in advanced industrial societies: a comparative study of movements in Britain and the United States, 1965-1970. 1976 [or rather 1977]. fo. 355. *bibliog. Typescript. Ph.D. (London) thesis: unpublished. This thesis is the property of London University and may not be removed from the library. Proof article in end pocket.*

CAVENDISH (RUPERT) Differences and similarities between radical liberalism and Plaid Cymru. Manchester, [1977]. pp. 15.

KENT (CHRISTOPHER) Brains and numbers: elitism, Comtism, and democracy in mid- Victorian England. Toronto, [1978]. pp. 212. *bibliog.*

LEWIS (GORDON K.) Slavery, imperialism, and freedom: studies in English radical thought. New York, [1978]. pp. 346. *bibliog.*

— United States.

MAY 1970: birth of the antiwar university. New York, 1971. pp. 62.

MORGAN (ROBIN) Goodbye to all that. Pittsburgh, [1973?]. pp. 7.

BOUCHIER (DAVID LESLIE) The development and containment of radical ideologies in advanced industrial societies: a comparative study of movements in Britain and the United States, 1965-1970. 1976 [or rather 1977]. fo. 355. *bibliog. Typescript. Ph.D. (London) thesis: unpublished. This thesis is the property of London University and may not be removed from the library. Proof article in end pocket.*

GIFFIN (FREDERICK C.) Six who protested: radical opposition to the First World War. Port Washington, N.Y., 1977. pp. 158. *bibliog.*

GOODMAN (PAUL) b. 1911. Drawing the line:...political essays...; edited by Taylor Stoehr. New York, 1977. pp. 272.

RADIO BROADCASTING

— Social aspects — United Kingdom.

BRITISH BROADCASTING CORPORATION. Serving neighbourhood and nation. London, [1977]. pp. 64.

— New Zealand.

SCEATS (LIONEL RALPH) A look to N[ew] Z[ealand] B[roadcasting] C[orporation] 's future role: a transcription of a news conference given by Lionel Sceats, Director-General designate of the NZBC, May 28th 1970. [Wellington], New Zealand Broadcasting Corporation, 1970. pp. (10).

— United Kingdom.

NEWBY (PERCY HOWARD) Broadcasting: a professional view. [London, 1977]. pp. 14. (London. University. Birkbeck College. Haldane Memorial Lectures. 40)

— — Ireland, Northern.

FRANCIS (RICHARD) Broadcasting to a community in conflict: the experience in Northern Ireland. [London], 1977. pp. 16.

RADIO IN PROPAGANDA

— United Kingdom.

CRUICKSHANK (CHARLES GREIG) The fourth arm: psychological warfare, 1938-45. London, 1977. pp. 200. bibliog.

RADIO JOURNALISM

— United Kingdom.

SCHLESINGER (PHILIP RONALD) Putting "reality" together: BBC news. London, 1978. pp. 303. bibliog.

RADIO PROGRAMMES, PUBLIC SERVICE.

GIBSON (GEORGE H.) 1932- . Public broadcasting: the role of the federal government, 1912-76. New York, [1977]. pp. 236.

RADIOGRAPHY.

DE HAMEL (FRANCIS ALEXANDER) An evaluation of a regional mass miniature radiography programme, 1956-67. Wellington, 1970. pp. 43. bibliog. (New Zealand. Department of Health. Special Report Series. 36)

RADISHCHEV (ALEKSANDR NIKOLAEVICH).

A.N. Radishchev i literatura ego vremeni. Leningrad, 1977. pp. 260. (Akademiia Nauk SSSR. Institut Russkoi Literatury. XVIII Vek. sb.12)

RADNOR (WILLIAM PLEYDELL-BOUVERIE) 3rd Earl of.

See PLEYDELL-BOUVERIE (WILLIAM) 3rd Earl of Radnor.

RAILWAY CLEARING HOUSE.

GATTIE (ALFRED WARWICK) How to cheapen transport: a paper read...before the Institute of Builders and the London Master Builders' Association, on 3rd January, 1912. [London, 1912?]. pp. 18.

NEW TRANSPORT COMPANY LIMITED. Economic transport and the goods clearing house system. London, 1913. pp. 10.

RAILWAY LAW

— United States.

REDFIELD (ISAAC FLETCHER) A practical treatise upon the law of railways. 2nd ed. Boston, 1858; New York, 1972. pp. 823. Facsimile reprint.

RAILROAD revitalization and regulatory reform; edited by Paul W. MacAvoy and John W. Snow. Washington, D.C., [1977]. pp. 246. (American Enterprise Institute for Public Policy Research. AEI Studies. 173)

RAILWAYS

— Cars — Construction.

CHARLES ROBERTS AND COMPANY. Charles Roberts and Company Limited, 1856-1956. [Wakefield, 1956]. pp. 52.

— History.

O'BRIEN (PATRICK) The new economic history of the railways. London, [1977]. pp. 121. bibliog.

— Argentine Republic.

ROIGT (HONORIO) Presente y futuro de los ferrocarriles argentinos. Buenos Aires, [1956]. pp. 241.

— Australia — Passenger traffic.

AUSTRALIA. Bureau of Transport Economics. 1977. A study of east-west rail passenger services: the 'Indian Pacific' and 'Trans Australian'. Canberra, 1977. pp. 90.

— Canada — Freight.

CANADA. Transport Commission. Traffic and Tariffs Branch. Commodity flow analysis: Canadian carload all-rail traffic. a., 1974(2nd)- Ottawa. [in English and French]

CANADA. Transport Commission. Traffic and Tariffs Branch. Commodity flow analysis: carload all-rail traffic between Canada and the United States. a., 1974- Ottawa.

— — Passenger traffic.

ALBERTA. Department of Transportation. 1976. Submission...to Canadian Transport Commission in response to notice of public hearings concerning transcontinental passenger train services, Montreal/Toronto-Vancouver. [Edmonton], 1976. pp. 40.

MANITOBA. 1976. Submission of the Province of Manitoba to the Canadian Transport Commission Railway Transport Committee concerning transcontinental passenger train services; presented by the... Minister of Industry and Commerce. Brandon, 1976. fo. 22.

— Finland.

FINNISH STATE RAILWAYS; [pd. by] Rautatiehallitus. a., 1971- Helsinki.

— France — Employees.

MARION (E.) Institutions patronales créées par les grandes compagnies de chemins de fer en faveur de leur personnel. Paris, 1890. pp. 24. (Extrait du Soleil du Dimanche)

— Hong Kong.

HONG KONG. Transport Department. Research and Development Section. 1976. Public transport in the New Territories: Part 2. Development of Kowloon-Canton railway, British section. (Hong Kong], 1974 repr. 1976. pp. 25. (Studies Reports. No. 74/2) Reprint updates to 1976.

— Nigeria — Management.

PALLANT (H.F.) Report on the operating problems of the Nigerian Railway, 1949. Enugu, 1950. pp. 47. (Nigeria. Sessional Papers. 1950. No. 21)

— Rhodesia.

SOUTHERN RHODESIA. Sinoia-Kafue and Beitbridge Railways Enquiry Commission. 1930. Report; [P.E. Potter and R.C. Wallace, commissioners]. Salisbury, 1930. pp. 35. (Legislative Assembly. [Sessional Papers]. 1930. C.S.R. 22)

— — Construction.

JEFFARES (J.L.S.) Report...on Rhodesia-Walvis Bay reconnaissance survey. Salisbury, 1932. pp. 65, 2 maps, 3 diagrams. (Southern Rhodesia. Legislative Assembly. [Sessional Papers]. 1932. C.S.R. 13)

— Russia — Maps.

GLAVNOE UPRAVLENIE GEODEZII I KARTOGRAFII. Atlas skhem zheleznykh dorog SSSR. Moskva, 1976. pp. 101.

— — Lithuania — History.

KOSAKOVSKIS (GERASIMAS) Zheleznye dorogi Litvy. Vil'nius, 1975. pp. 249. bibliog.

— — Russia (RSFSR).

CHERVIAKOV (A.P.) Ekonomicheskie sviazi i razvitie zheleznykh dorog Urala. Moskva, 1976. pp. 87. bibliog. (Akademiia Nauk SSSR. Problemy Sovetskoi Ekonomiki)

— United Kingdom.

WILSON (Sir HAROLD) The future of British transport. London, [1963]. pp. 8. Reprint of the speech in the House of Commons in 1963.

— — Abandonment.

LINDSEY. County Council. Disused railways in Lindsey: policy for after use. Lincoln, 1971. pp. 44.

SMITH (EDWARD) Civil engineer, ed. Better use of railways: comments and rejoinders. Reading, 1978. pp. 89. bibliog. (Reading. University. Department of Geography. Reading Geographical Papers. No. 63)

— — Cost effectiveness.

U.K. British Railways Board. 1978. Measuring cost and profitability in British Rail. [London, 1978]. pp. 30.

— — Employees.

GREAT EASTERN RAILWAY COMPANY. Wages and hours arbitration, 1909: award of...Lord Gorell of Brampton. [London, 1909]. pp. 25.

— — Rates.

CHENG (CHEN-YUEH) State control of railway rates when railways are not nationalised. 1940. fo. 198, 6. bibliog. Typescript.

— — London — Passenger traffic.

WEEKDAY CENSUS AT LONDON TERMINI; [pd. by] Economic Survey Office, (British Rail, Southern [Region]). a., Oc/N 1969 [1st]- London.

— United States.

NEW ENGLAND RAILROADS. Conference of Representatives. The need of the...railroads for remedial legislation by Congress. Boston, 1919. pp. (9).

— — Consolidation.

LOVETT (ROBERT SCOTT) Before the Interstate Commerce Commission: No. 12964 in the matter of the consolidation of the railway properties of the United States into a limited number of systems: statement...at the hearing in San Francisco, April 2nd, 1923. [San Francisco?, 1923]. pp. 59.

— — Rates.

CHENG (CHEN-YUEH) State control of railway rates when railways are not nationalised. 1940. fo. 198, 6. bibliog. Typescript.

— — Ohio — History.

CONDIT (CARL WILBUR) The railroad and the city: a technological and urbanistic history of Cincinnati. Columbus, Ohio, [1977]. pp. 335. bibliog.

RAILWAYS AND OTHER CARRIERS

— United Kingdom.

BROWNE (JOHN HUTTON BALFOUR) The Railway and Canal Traffic Acts. [London, 1897]. pp. 21. (London. Chamber of Commerce. Pamphlet Series. No. 22)

RAILWAYS AND STATE

— Argentine Republic.

GOODWIN (PAUL B.) Los ferrocarriles britanicos y la U.C.R., 1916-1930; traduccion del ingles del original inedito...del profesor Celso Rodriguez. Buenos Aires, [1974]. pp. 320. bibliog.

RAILWAYS AND STATE (Cont.)

— United Kingdom.

HINES (WALKER DOWNER) Railway regulation: the English system contrasted with the demands of the Interstate Commerce Commission, etc. n.p., [191-?]. fo.8.

CHENG (CHEN-YUEH) State control of railway rates when railways are not nationalised. 1940. fo. 198, 6. *bibliog. Typescript.*

— United States.

HINES (WALKER DOWNER) Railway regulation: the English system contrasted with the demands of the Interstate Commerce Commission, etc. n.p., [191-?]. fo.8.

FAYANT (FRANK H.) The government and the railroads. [New York, 1919]. pp. 20. *(Reprinted from The Unpopular Review, April-June, 1919)*

REA (SAMUEL) Statement...presented February 20, 1919 to the Committee on Interstate Commerce of the United States Senate in support of the plan for the future management and regulation of the railroads proposed by the Association of Railway Executives. Philadelphia, [imprint], [1919]. pp. 16.

CHENG (CHEN-YUEH) State control of railway rates when railways are not nationalised. 1940. fo. 198, 6. *bibliog. Typescript.*

RAILROAD revitalization and regulatory reform; edited by Paul W. MacAvoy and John W. Snow. Washington, D.C., [1977]. pp. 246. *(American Enterprise Institute for Public Policy Research. AEI Studies. 173)*

RAIN AND RAINFALL

— Mathematical models.

LONDON. University. London School of Economics and Political Science. Graduate School of Geography. Discussion Papers. No. 59. A stochastic model of daily rainfall simulation in a semi-arid environment; [by] H.M. Scoging. London, 1976. pp. 28. *bibliog.*

RAINER (FERDINAND MARIA JOHANN EVANGELISTA FRANZ HYGINUS)

Erzherzog, 1827-1913.

AUSTRIA. Ministerrat. 1861- . Die Ministerien Erzherzog Rainer und Mensdorff...; bearbeitet von Horst Brettner-Messler, mit einer Einleitung von Friedrich Engel-Janosi. Wien, 1977 in progress. *(Die Protokolle des österreichischen Ministerrates, 1848- 1867. Abteilung 5)*

RAINEY (HENRY THOMAS).

WALLER (ROBERT A.) Rainey of Illinois: a political biography, 1903-34. Urbana, [1977]. pp. 260. *bibliog. (Illinois University. Illinois Studies in the Social Sciences. 60)*

RAJASTHAN

— Industries.

RAJASTHAN. Directorate of Economics and Statistics. 1975. Report on survey of small scale industries in Rajasthan, rural, 1972. Jaipur, [1975]. pp. 56.

RAJASTHAN. Directorate of Economics and Statistics. 1975. Report on survey of small scale industries, urban, 1972-73 in Rajasthan. Jaipur, [1975]. pp. 64.

RAMSDEN FAMILY.

STEPHENSON (CLIFFORD) The Ramsdens and their estate in Huddersfield: the town that bought itself. Almondbury, 1972. pp. 20.

RANDOLPH (ASA PHILIP).

HARRIS (WILLIAM HAMILTON) Keeping the faith: A. Philip Randolph, Milton P. Webster and the Brotherhood of Sleeping Car Porters, 1925-1937. Urbana, Ill., [1977]. pp. 252. *bibliog.*

RANKE (LEOPOLD VON).

KRIEGER (LEONARD) Ranke: the meaning of history. Chicago, 1977. pp. 402. *bibliog.*

RAP.

See RADICAL ALTERNATIVES TO PRISON.

RAPE

— Tasmania.

TASMANIA. Law Reform Commission. 1976. Report and recommendations for reducing harassment and embarrassment of complainants in rape cases. in TASMANIA. Parliament. Journals and Printed Papers. 1976, no.3.

— United States.

HOLMSTROM (LYNDA LYTLE) and BURGESS (ANN WOLBERT) The victim of rape: institutional reactions. New York, [1978]. pp. 293.

RAPE VICTIM SERVICES

— United States.

HOLMSTROM (LYNDA LYTLE) and BURGESS (ANN WOLBERT) The victim of rape: institutional reactions. New York, [1978]. pp. 293.

RAPIER (JAMES T.)

SCHWENINGER (LOREN) James T. Rapier and reconstruction. Chicago, [1978]. pp. 248. *bibliog.*

RAS TAFARI MOVEMENT.

BARRETT (LEONARD E.) The Rastafarians: the dreadlocks of Jamaica. Kingston, Jamaica, 1977. pp. 257. *bibliog.*

RASPAIL (FRANÇOIS VINCENT).

MIRECOURT (EUGENE DE) pseud. [i.e. Charles Jean Baptiste JACQUOT] Raspail. Paris, 1856. pp. 96. *(Les Contemporains)* Bound with his Pierre Leroux, and other works.

RATIONALISM

— Poetry.

[BEVINGTON (LOUISA SARAH)] "Key notes"; by Arbor Leigh [pseud.]. London, 1876. pp. 23. *Poems.*

RAW MATERIALS.

INTERNATIONAL FEDERATION OF TRADE UNIONS. Memorandum on the distribution of raw materials; submitted to the Special International Trades Union Congress, held at London, November 22nd to 28th, 1920. [London?, 1920]. fo. 9.

UNITED NATIONS. Conference on Trade and Development. 1974. Problems of raw materials and development: report by the Secretary-General of UNCTAD prepared for the sixth special session of the General Assembly. (TD/B/488). New York, 1974. pp. 44.

BARON (STEFAN) and others. Internationale Rohstoffpolitik: Ziele, Mittel, Kosten. Tübingen, 1977. pp. 194. *bibliog. (Kiel. Universität. Institut für Weltwirtschaft. Kieler Studien. 150)*

DOBOZI (ISTVÁN) Forecasting structural changes in the international raw materials industries and markets. Budapest, 1977. pp. 85. *(Hungarian Scientific Council for World Economy. [Publications]. Trends in World Economy. No. 22)*

FRANCE, Ministère de la Coopération. Service des Etudes Economiques et des Questions Internationales. 1978. Indices des cours extérieurs et cours des produits tropicaux. Paris, 1978. fo. 38. *(Etudes et Documents. No. 29)*

RANGARAJAN (L.N.) Commodity conflict: the political economy of international commodity negotiations. London, [1978]. pp. 390. *bibliog.*

— Bibliography.

BOLWIG (NIELS GEERT) and THOMSEN (ERIC STØTTRUP) compilers. The economics of raw materials, natural resources, energy, and related topics: a bibliography. Aarhus, [1977]. pp. 282. *(Aarhus. Universitet. Økonomiske Institut. Memos. 1977. 5)*

— Pacific, The.

RAW materials and Pacific economic integration; edited by Sir John Crawford and Saburo Okita. London, [1978]. pp. 343. *bibliog. A study by the Australia, Japan and Western Pacific Economic Relations Project.*

REACTOR FUEL REPROCESSING.

PARKER (Sir ROGER JOCELYN) The Windscale inquiry; report...presented to the Secretary of State for the Environment on 26 January 1978. London, H.M.S.O., 1978. 3 vols.(in 1). *Plan in end pocket.*

— International cooperation.

INTERNATIONAL arrangements for nuclear fuel reprocessing; edited by Abram Chayes and W. Bennett Lewis. Cambridge, Mass., [1977]. pp. 251. *Papers of a symposium held in Racine, Wisconsin, May 24-27, 1976, and sponsored by the Pugwash Conference on Science and World Affairs.*

READERSHIP SURVEYS

— Germany.

HESS (EVA MARIA) Methoden der Leserschaftsforschung. [Munich, 1962]. pp. 263. *bibliog. Inaugural-Dissertation - Ludwig-Maximilians- Universität zu München.*

— United Kingdom.

NEWSPAPER SOCIETY. Regional Readership Surveys among Housewives. No. 4. Southern region. London, 1958. pp. 131-172.

NEWSPAPER SOCIETY. Regional Readership Surveys among Housewives. No. 7. South western region. London, 1959. pp. 257-298.

NEWSPAPER SOCIETY. Regional Readership Surveys among Housewives. No. 9. Eastern region. London, 1959. pp. 341-382.

NEWSPAPER SOCIETY. Regional Readership Surveys among Housewives. No. 10. North Midland region. London, 1959. pp. 383-424.

— — Wales.

READERSHIP survey of Wales; commissioned by the Thomson Organisation Limited and conducted by Marplan Limited. London, 1961. 1 vol (various pagings)

READING, PSYCHOLOGY OF.

GIBSON (ELEANOR JACK) and LEVIN (HARRY) 1925- The psychology of reading. Cambridge, Mass., [1975] repr. 1976. pp. 630. *bibliog.*

READING UNIVERSITY.

HOLT (JAMES CLARKE) The University of Reading: the first fifty years. Reading, 1977. pp. 372. *bibliog.*

REAL ESTATE INVESTMENT.

MARKUSEN (JAMES R.) and SCHEFFMAN (DAVID T.) Speculation and monopoly in urban development: analytical foundations with evidence for Toronto. Toronto, [1977]. pp. 165. *bibliog. (Ontario. Economic Council. Research Studies. 10)*

— South Africa — Mathematical models.

BOADEN (B.G.) The financial evaluation of property development projects: a computer model. Johannesburg, 1977. pp. 29. *bibliog. (Johannesburg. University of the Witwatersrand. Urban and Regional Research Unit. Occasional Papers. No. 16)*

REAL PROPERTY

— New Zealand — Prices.

NEW ZEALAND. Valuation Department. Research Papers. 71-3. The effect of Boeing 737 jet noise on the value of houses near Wellington airport. Wellington, [1971]. fo. 37.

— — Valuation.

NEW ZEALAND. Valuation Department. Research Papers. 68-6. Pedestrian traffic counts: their role in commercial property valuation. Wellington, 1968. pp. 37.

— South Africa — Prices.

BOADEN (B.G.) and HART (T.) Residential land values on the Witwatersrand, 1963 to 1973. Johannesburg, 1975. pp. 31. bibliog. (Johannesburg. University of the Witwatersrand. Urban and Regional Research Unit. Occasional Papers. No. 4)

— United Kingdom.

KOLBERT (COLIN FRANCIS) and MACKAY (NORMAN A.M.) History of Scots and English land law. Berkhamsted, [1977]. pp. 379. (Cambridge. University. Department of Land Economy. Studies in Land Economy) Based on C.D'O. Farran, Principles of Scots and English land law.

— — Valuation.

TURNER (D.M.) An approach to land values. Berkhamsted, [1977]. pp. 223. bibliog.

— — Scotland.

SCOTLAND. Scottish Development Department. 1976. The community land scheme in Scotland: disposal notification areas. [Edinburgh, 1976]. pp. 9.

SCOTLAND. Scottish Development Department. 1976. The community land scheme in Scotland: planning applications and permissions for relevant development. [Edinburgh, 1976]. pp. 19.

REAL PROPERTY TAX.

UNITED NATIONS. Department of Economic and Social Affairs. 1968. Manual of land tax administration including valuation of urban and rural land and improvements. (ST/ECA/103). New York, 1968. pp. 176.

SKOURAS (ATHANASSIOS S.) Land and its taxation in recent economic theory. Athens, [1977]. pp. 214. bibliog. Based on the author's Ph.D. thesis, London, 1975.

— Canada — Ontario.

ONTARIO. Committee on Farm Assessment and Taxation. 1969. Report; [A. N. MacKay, chairman]. [Toronto], 1969. pp. 69.

— Greece.

SKOURAS (ATHANASSIOS S.) Land and its taxation in recent economic theory. Athens, [1977]. pp. 214. bibliog. Based on the author's Ph.D. thesis, London, 1975.

— United Kingdom.

UNITED COMMITTEE FOR THE TAXATION OF LAND VALUES. [Leaflets. Nos.] GE 30,31,32,33,34,35,36, and 37. London, 1929. 8 pts.

MELLOWS (ANTHONY ROGER) Taxation of land transactions. 2nd ed. London, 1978. pp. 582.

REAL-TIME DATA PROCESSING.

FREEDMAN (A.L.) and LEES (ROGER A.) Real-time computer systems. New York, 1977. pp. 277. bibliogs.

REALITY.

RAUCHE (G.A.) The problem of truth and reality in Grisebach's thought. Pretoria, 1966. pp. 122. bibliog. (South Africa. National Council for Social Research. Publication Series. No. 21)

RECABARREN (LUIS EMILIO).

RECABARREN (LUIS EMILIO) Obras; compilacion y prologo de Digna Castañeda Fuertes. La Habana, [1976]. pp. 310. bibliog.

RECEIVERS

— United Kingdom.

KERR (WILLIAM WILLIAMSON) On the law and practice as to receivers; fifteenth edition by Raymond Walton; with a chapter on Extra-territoriality and associated appendices by Muir Hunter. London, 1978. pp. 424.

RECIDIVISTS

— Russia.

SUNDUROV (FEDOR ROMANOVICH) Sotsial'no-psikhologicheskie i pravovye aspekty ispravleniia i perevospitaniia pravonarushitelei. Kazan', 1976. pp. 144.

— — White Russia.

EFIMOV (MIKHAIL ARTEM'EVICH and SHKURKO (VASILII ADAMOVICH) Retsidivnaia prestupnost' i ee preduprezhdenie. Minsk, 1977. pp. 190.

RECIPROCITY.

BAAL (JAN VAN) Reciprocity and the position of women: anthropological papers. Assen, 1975. pp. 128. bibliog.

RECLAMATION OF LAND

— Korea.

UNION OF LAND IMPROVEMENT ASSOCIATIONS OF KOREA. U[nion of] L[and] I[mprovement] A[ssociations] and irrigation works in Korea. Seoul, 1969. pp. 38. In English and Korean.

RECLUS (ELIE).

RECLUS (PAUL) Les frères Elie et Elisée Reclus. Paris, Amis d'Elisée Reclus, 1964. pp. 209. bibliog. Containing Biographie d'Elisée Reclus, par Paul Reclus; Souvenirs personnels sur Elie et Elisée Reclus, par Paul Reclus, etc.

RECLUS (JEAN JACQUES ELISEE).

RECLUS (PAUL) Les frères Elie et Elisée Reclus. Paris, Amis d'Elisée Reclus, 1964. pp. 209. bibliog. Containing Biographie d'Elisée Reclus, par Paul Reclus; Souvenirs personnels sur Elie et Elisée Reclus, par Paul Reclus, etc.

RECLUS (PAUL).

RECLUS (PAUL) Les frères Elie et Elisée Reclus. Paris, Amis d'Elisée Reclus, 1964. pp. 209. bibliog. Containing Biographie d'Elisée Reclus, par Paul Reclus; Souvenirs personnels sur Elie et Elisée Reclus, par Paul Reclus, etc.

RECONSTRUCTION (1914-1939).

FIGHT THE FAMINE AND EUROPEAN RECONSTRUCTION COUNCIL. Economic notes, nos. 3,5,6,7; [with two leaflets: Objects of the. ..Council, and Trade in Central Europe]. London, 1920. 6 pts.

ALLGEMEINER DEUTSCHER GEWERKSCHAFTSBUND. Weltwirtschaftlicher Wiederaufbau: Denkschrift...für die Konferenz in Genua. [Berlin, 1922]. pp. 16.

— Russia.

BRESHKO-BRESHKOVSKAIA (EKATERINA KONSTANTINOVNA) A message to the American people. New York City, 1919. pp. 20.

KUZ'MIN (VALENTIN IVANOVICH) V bor'be za sotsialisticheskuiu rekonstruktsiiu, 1926-1937: ekonomicheskaia politika Sovetskogo gosudarstva. Moskva, 1976. pp. 311.

RECONSTRUCTION (1939-1951)

— Italy.

DANEO (CAMILLO) La politica economica della ricostruzione, 1945-1949. Torino, [1975]. pp. 337.

— Poland.

ANDRZEJEWSKI (ROMAN) Proces przebudowy struktury gospodarczej Wielkopolski, 1945-1970. Warszawa, 1978. pp. 135. bibliog. (Poznań. Urząd Wojewódzki. Wydział Kultury i Sztuki. Biblioteka Kroniki Wielkopolski)

RECONSTRUCTION (UNITED STATES).

HOLT (THOMAS) Black over white: negro political leadership in South Carolina during reconstruction. Urbana, [1977]. pp. 269. bibliog.

SCHWENINGER (LOREN) James T. Rapier and reconstruction. Chicago, [1978]. pp. 248. bibliog.

RECREATION

— France — Apparatus and equipment.

FRANCE. Groupe sectoriel d'Analyse et de Prévision Arts- Création-Loisirs. 1976. Rapport...: préparation du 7e Plan. Paris, [1976]. pp. 95.

— United Kingdom.

CHARLTON (JOHN) and CAMPBELL (LORNA) Preparation and contents of basic data from G[reater] L[ondon] R[ecreation] S[tudy] and S[urvey of] I[nformal] R[ecreation in] S[outh] E[ast] E[ngland]. London, [1977]. pp. 62. bibliog. (London. Greater London Council. Research Memoranda. 523)

LOWERSON (JOHN) and MYERSCOUGH (JOHN) Time to spare in Victorian England. Hassocks, Sussex, 1977. pp. 151. bibliog. Based on a series of talks and conversations for BBC Radio Brighton, under the auspices of the University of Sussex's Centre for Continuing Education.

U.K. Department of the Environment. 1977. Recreation and deprivation in inner urban areas. London, 1977 repr. 1978. pp. 65.

BAILEY (PETER) Leisure and class in Victorian England: rational recreation and the contest for control, 1830-1885. London, 1978. pp. 260. bibliog.

WALVIN (JAMES) Leisure and society, 1830-1950. London, 1978. pp. 181. bibliog.

RECREATION AREAS

— United Kingdom.

LINDSEY. County Council. Disused railways in Lindsey: policy for after use. Lincoln, 1971. pp. 44.

RECYCLING (WASTE, ETC.).

RESOURCE conservation: social and economic dimensions of recycling; edited by David W. Pearce and Ingo Walter. New York, 1977. pp. 383. bibliogs. The outcome of an international symposium held at the Rockefeller Foundation's Study and Conference Center in Bellagio, Italy, in November 1976.

VOGLER (JON) Muck and brass: a domestic waste reclamation strategy for Britain. London, [1978]. pp. 49. bibliog. (Oxfam. Public Affairs Unit. Oxfam Public Affairs Reports)

RED CROSS.

FORSYTHE (DAVID P.) Humanitarian politics: the International Committee of the Red Cross. Baltimore, [1977]. pp. 298.

REFERENCE BOOKS

REFERENCE BOOKS
— Bibliography.

SHEEHY (EUGENE PAUL) and others. Guide to reference books; compiled...with the assistance of Rita G. Keckeissen and Eileen McIlvaine. 9th ed. Chicago, 1976. pp. 1015. *Revised, expanded and updated version of the 8th ed. by C.M. Winchell.*

REFERENDUM
— Bibliography.

QUEBEC (PROVINCE). Legislative Library. 1977. Le référendum: bibliographie sélective et annotée. Québec, 1977. pp. 88. *(Bibliographie et Documentation. 6)*

— United Kingdom.

BRADBURY (FAREL) Electoral reform: V2P: voting for policies as well as for politicians; a political essay. Ross-on-Wye, [1975]. pp. 14.

BRADBURY (PARNELL) Voice of the people: V2P: a plain man's guide to democracy; ...based on an idea by Farel Bradbury featuring the do-it yourself referendum. Ross-on-Wye, 1976. pp. 10.

— United States.

BOLT (ERNEST C.) Ballots before bullets: the war referendum approach to peace in America, 1914-1941. Charlottesville, Va., 1977. pp. 207. *bibliog.*

REFORMATION
— United Kingdom.

CROSS (CLAIRE) Church and people, 1450-1660: the triumph of the laity in the English Church. Hassocks, 1976. pp. 272. *bibliog.*

— — Scotland.

COWAN (IAN B.) Regional aspects of the Scottish Reformation. London, [1978]. pp. 40. *bibliog. (Historical Association. General Series. G.92)*

REFORMATORIES
— France.

APPLICATION du système de Mettray aux colonies agricoles d'orphelins et d'enfants trouvés. n.p. [185-?]. pp. 7.

COCHIN (PIERRE SUZANNE AUGUSTIN) Notice sur Mettray. Tours, [185-?]. pp. 47. *(Extrait des Annales de la charité)* Bound with METTRAY. Colonie Agricole. Rapport annuel...treizième année.

METTRAY. Colonie Agricole. Rapport annuel...treizième année. Paris, 1852. pp. 115. *Bound with COCHIN (PIERRE SUZANNE AUGUSTIN) Notice sur Mettray. Addresses to members of the Société Paternelle pour l'Education Morale et Professionnelle des Jeunes Détenus.*

— United Kingdom.

STRATTA (ERICA WENDY) The educational experience of boys admitted to borstal 1965-1966: a study of their background in relation to their prospects for education as part of borstal training. 1968. fo. 318. *bibliog.* Typescript. Ph.D. (London) thesis: unpublished. This thesis is the property of London University and may not be removed from the Library.

REFORMATORIES FOR WOMEN
— Canada — British Columbia.

BRITISH COLUMBIA. Royal Commission on the Incarceration of Female Offenders. 1978. Report; [Patricia M. Proudfoot, commissioner]. [Vancouver], 1978. pp. 196. *bibliog.*

REFUGEES, AFRICAN.

AFRICAN refugees and the law: [proceedings of a seminar held at Uppsala in October 1977]; edited by Göran Melander [and] Peter Nobel. Uppsala, 1978. pp. 98.

REFUGEES, ARAB.

KARAMEH RECONSTRUCTION SOCIETY. Remember Karameh. Amman, [1970?]. pp. 40.

SHIPTON (SIDNEY L.) The Arab refugee problem. 2nd ed. [London], 1971. pp. 11.

REFUGEES, BANGLADESHI.

PAKISTAN. Department of Films and Publications. 1971. Pakistan welcomes returning citizens. [Karachi, 1971]. pp. 14.

REFUGEES, VIETNAMESE.

KELLY (GAIL PARADISE) From Vietnam to America: a chronicle of the Vietnamese immigration to the United States. Boulder, [1977]. pp. 254. *bibliog.*

REFUGEES IN CANADA.

DIRKS (GERALD E.) Canada's refugee policy: indifference or opportunism? Montreal, 1977. pp. 316.

REFUGEES IN THE UNITED STATES.

KELLY (GAIL PARADISE) From Vietnam to America: a chronicle of the Vietnamese immigration to the United States. Boulder, [1977]. pp. 254. *bibliog.*

REFUSE AND REFUSE DISPOSAL
— Germany — Berlin.

NICKEL (HANS WOLFGANG) Abfallbewirtschaftung in West-Berlin: empirische Untersuchung, etc. Zürich, 1977. pp. 109. *bibliog.* Dissertation - Universität Zürich.

— India.

INDIA. Committee on Urban Wastes. 1976. Report; [B. Sivaraman, chairman]. New Delhi, [1976]. pp. 141.

REGGIO NELL'EMILIA (PROVINCE)
— Social history.

UNITI siamo tutto: il movimento cooperativo delle origini all'esperienza reggiana, 1815-1930; [an anthology]; a cura di Adolfo Zavaroni. Milano, [1977]. pp. 194.

REGIONAL ECONOMICS.

DUESBURY (W.K.) Intermediate areas: a non-event?: the case of Oswestry. Birmingham, 1977. pp. 121,xv. *bibliog. (Birmingham. University. Centre for Urban and Regional Studies. Research Memoranda. No. 58)*

EUROPEAN COMMUNITIES. Commission. 1977. Guidelines for Community regional policy: communication and proposals submitted...to the Council on 3 June 1977. [Brussels], 1977. pp. 44. *(Bulletin of the European Communities. Supplements. [1977/2])*

ORGANISATION FOR ECONOMIC CO-OPERATION AND DEVELOPMENT. 1977. Regional policies: the current outlook. Paris, 1977. pp. 80.

CONTEMPORARY industrialization: spatial analysis and regional development; edited by F.E. Ian Hamilton. London, 1978. pp. 203. *bibliogs. Based on the first conference of the International Geographical Union Working Group on Industrial Geography, held in London in 1974.*

MIERNYK (WILLIAM H.) and others. Regional impacts of rising energy prices. Cambridge, Mass., [1978]. pp. 135. *bibliog.*

REGIONAL economic policy: the Canadian experience; [edited by] N.H. Lithwick. Toronto, [1978]. pp. 368. *bibliog.*

RICHARDSON (HARRY WARD) Regional and urban economics. Harmondsworth, 1978. pp. 416. *bibliog.*

SWIFT (MARK) A regional policy for Europe. London, 1978. pp. 23. *(Young Fabian Group. Young Fabian Pamphlets. 48)*

— Mathematical models.

BARTELS (CORNELIS P.) Economic aspects of regional welfare: income distribution and unemployment. Leiden, 1977. pp. 261. *bibliog.*

PLANQUE (BERNARD) Organisation régionale et intégration spatio-économique. Paris, 1977. pp. 113. *bibliog. (Centre National de la Recherche Scientifique. Actions Thématiques Programmées. No. 20)*

REGIONAL PLANNING.

INTERREGIONAL SEMINAR ON PHYSICAL PLANNING FOR TOURISM DEVELOPMENT, DUBROVNIK, 1970. Report of the...Seminar...[held in] Dubrovnik, Yugoslavia, 19 October to 3 November 1970. (ST/TAO/SER.C/131). New York, United Nations, [1971]. pp. 55.

INTERREGIONAL SEMINAR ON PHYSICAL PLANNING FOR URBAN, REGIONAL AND NATIONAL DEVELOPMENT, BUCHAREST, 1969. Report of the...Seminar...[held in] Bucharest, Romania 22 September to 7 October 1969. (ST/TAO/SER.C/132). New York, United Nations, 1971. pp. 43.

GILLINGWATER (DAVID) Regional planning and social change: a responsive approach. 1976 [or rather 1977]. pp. 331. *bibliog.* Typescript. Ph.D. (London) thesis: unpublished. This thesis is the property of London University and may not be removed from the Library.

LASSEY (WILLIAM R.) Planning in rural environments. New York, [1977]. pp. 257. *bibliog.*

PLANNING in turbulent environments; [edited by] John S. Western [and] Paul R. Wilson. St. Lucia, Queensland, 1977. pp. 206. *bibliogs.*

The REGIONAL planning process; edited by David Gillingwater [and] D.A. Hart. Farnborough, Hants., [1978]. pp. 197.

— Decision making.

DELFT (AD VAN) and NIJKAMP (PETER) Multi-criteria analysis and regional decision-making. Leiden, 1977. pp. 135. *bibliog.*

— Environmental aspects — United States.

LYNCH (KEVIN) Managing the sense of a region. Cambridge, Mass., [1976]. pp. 221. *bibliog.*

— Study and teaching.

FALUDI (ANDREAS K.F.) Essays on planning theory and education. Oxford, 1978. pp. 183. *bibliogs.*

— America, Latin.

INTERREGIONAL SEMINAR ON DEVELOPMENT PLANNING, 3RD, SANTIAGO, 1968. Policies of plan implementation, with special reference to Latin America; report on the...seminar...[held in] Santiago, Chile, 18-29 March 1968. (ST/TAO/SER.C/110). New York, United Nations, 1970. pp. 235.

— Australia.

AUSTRALIA. Department of Urban and Regional Development. Annual report. a., 1972/73(1st)- Canberra. *Included in AUSTRALIA. Parliament. [Parliamentary papers].*

— Brazil.

KATZMAN (MARTIN T.) Cities and frontiers in Brazil: regional dimensions of economic development. Cambridge, Mass., 1977. pp. 255.

— Canada — British Columbia.

BRITISH COLUMBIA. Department of Economic Development. 1975. A summary report on development possibilities in the north east region of British Columbia, etc. [Victoria], 1975. pp. 125.

REGIONAL PLANNING.

— — Manitoba.

INCENTIVES, location and regional development: proceedings of a conference sponsored by the Manitoba Economic Development Advisory Board and the Department of Industry and Commerce, Winnipeg, January 28-29, 1975; edited by Paul Phillips. [Winnipeg, 1975]. pp. 220.

— — New Brunswick.

ALLAIN (GREG) and others. Evaluation of the New Brunswick regional development councils: report submitted to the Agricultural Resources Study. Moncton, N.B., 1976. pp. 244. *bibliog.*

— — Nova Scotia.

NOVA SCOTIA. Department of Municipal Affairs. 1975. Halifax Dartmouth regional development plan, with introduction and analysis. [Halifax, 1975]. 1 vol. (various foliations).

— — Ontario.

ONTARIO. Regional Planning Branch. 1976. Toronto-centred region program statement. [Toronto], 1976. pp. 19.

BOSSONS (JOHN) Reforming planning in Ontario: strengthening the municipal role. [Toronto, 1978]. pp. 231. *(Ontario. Economic Council. Discussion Paper Series)*

— France.

URBANISATION, développement régional et pouvoir politique. [Nice], 1975. pp. 177. *(Nice. Université. Faculté des Lettres et Sciences Humaines. Annales. No. 26)*

— — Mathematical models.

PLANQUE (BERNARD) Organisation régionale et intégration spatio-économique. Paris, 1977. pp. 113. *bibliog. (Centre National de la Recherche Scientifique. Actions Thématiques Programmées. No. 20)*

— Germany.

BLUMENBERG (ROLF) Das System der Raumplanung in der Bundesrepublik Deutschland: eine Organisationsprüfung. Göttingen, 1977. pp. 447. *bibliog. (Münster in Westfalen. Westfälische Wilhelms- Universität. Institut für Verkehrswissenschaft. Beiträge. Heft 83)*

— — Württemberg-Baden.

BACKES (WIELAND) Planung und Raumentwicklung im mittleren Neckarraum: sozioökonomische Determinanten der Lebensbedingungen in einer verdichteten Region, dargestellt unter besonderer Berücksichtigung der Waiblinger Bucht. München, [1978]. pp. 426. *bibliog.*

— Hawaiian Islands.

TOURISM and regional growth: an empirical study of the alternative growth paths for Hawaii; edited by Moheb Ghali; contributors Robert Ebel [and others]. Leiden, 1977. pp. 121.

— India — Madras.

MADRAS. Directorate of Town Planning. 1973. Madras-Chingleput region: a draft regional plan. [Madras, 1973]. pp. 141.

— Italy.

CAFIERO (SALVATORE) La pianificazione regionale in Basilicata: analisi di documenti e di proposte. [Milan], 1975. pp. 67. *(Associazione per lo Sviluppo dell'Industria nel Mezzogiorno. Centro per gli Studi sullo Sviluppo Economico. Collana Francesco Giordani)*

SOCIETÀ ITALIANA DEGLI ECONOMISTI. Riunione Scientifica, 11a, Roma, 1970. La teoria economica di fronte al sistema delle regioni: (atti). Milano, 1975. pp. 171.

MERLONI (FRANCESCO) and URBANI (PAOLO) Il governo del territorio tra regioni e partecipazioni statali. Bari, 1977. pp. 222.

MONTE (ALFREDO DEL) Politica regionale e sviluppo economico: un'analisi teorica ed econometrica degli effetti della politica degli incentivi nel Mezzogiorno, nell'Irlanda del Nord e in Scozia. Milano, [1977]. pp. 277. *(Naples. Università. Centro Studi di Economia Applicata all'Ingegneria. Studi Economici. 3)*

— Netherlands.

ANTI-REVOLUTIONAIRE PARTIJ. College van Advies, and VERBAND VAN VERENIGINGEN VAN ANTIREVOLUTIONAIRE GEMEENTE- EN PROVINCIEBESTUURDERS. Bestuurlijke vormgeving: preadvies van een werkgroep...voor de openbare partijconferentie op 13 oktober 1969. 's-Gravenhage, [1969]. pp. 36.

NETHERLANDS. Ministerie van Economische Zaken. 1977. Nota regionaal sociaal-economische beleid 1977 t/m 1980. ['s-Gravenhage, 1977]. pp. 127.

— Poland.

REGIONALNE zróżnicowanie rozwoju społeczno-gospodarczego Polski. Warszawa, 1976. pp. 131. *bibliog. (Polska Akademia Nauk. Komitet Przestrzennego Zagospodarowania Kraju. Biuletyn. z.89)*

— South Africa.

BROWETT (J.G.) Required and available data for town and regional planning in South Africa. Johannesburg, 1975. fo. 19. *bibliog. (Johannesburg. University of the Witwatersrand. Urban and Regional Research Unit. Occasional Papers. No. 8)*

FAIR (T.J.D.) Some spatial aspects of black homeland development in South Africa. Johannesburg, 1975. pp. 22. *bibliog. (Johannesburg. University of the Witwatersrand. Urban and Regional Research Unit. Occasional Papers. No. 6)*

— United Kingdom.

REGIONAL ECONOMIC REVIEW: ([pd. by] East Anglia Economic Planning Council [U.K.]). a. (formerly s-a.,) Mr 1973- London.

HEREFORDSHIRE. County Planning Department. Herefordshire county structure plan: report of survey. [Hereford, 1973?]. pp. 82.

LEICESTER. City Council, and LEICESTERSHIRE. County Council. Leicester and Leicestershire structure plan: written statement. Leicester, 1974. pp. 109. *Two maps in end pocket.*

WEST SUSSEX. Planning Department. County structure plan: reports [and] Topic reports. [Chichester], 1975-77. 10 pts. (in 1 vol.).

CLEVELAND STRUCTURE PLANS: annual monitoring report; [pd. by] Cleveland County Planning Department. a., 1976- Middlesbrough.

KENT. Planning Department. County structure plan: report of survey; ([with] Supplement). Maidstone, 1976-77. 2 vols. (in 1). *Cover title: Kent structure plan.*

SUFFOLK. County Planning Officer. Suffolk county structure plan: report of survey; [with] Report of survey: public consultation draft. Ipswich, 1976-77. 15 pts. (in 1 vol.).

CUMBRIA. Planning Department, and LAKE DISTRICT SPECIAL PLANNING BOARD. Choices for Cumbria: report of survey; technical analysis of the key issues for the structure plan and review of possible policies. [Kendal], 1976. pp. 244.

HEREFORD AND WORCESTER [COUNTY]. Planning Department. Herefordshire structure plan: written statement. [Worcester, 1976]. pp. 67.

NORTHUMBERLAND. County Planning Department. Northumberland county structure plan: report of survey for consultation. Newcastle upon Tyne, 1976. pp. 264.

PLYMOUTH FRIENDS OF THE EARTH. Towards 2001: the future of the Plymouth sub-region: some observations; submission to Devon and Cornwall County Councils. Plymouth, 1976. fo. 11.

TYNE AND WEAR. County Council. Structure plan: report of survey; [with] Summary report of survey. Newcastle upon Tyne, 1976. 2 vols. (in 1).

CHESHIRE. County Planning Department. County structure plan: report of survey. [Chester], 1977. 13 pts. (in 1 vol.).

DERBYSHIRE. County Council. Derbyshire structure plan: report of survey. [Matlock], 1977. pp. 316.

DERBYSHIRE. County Council. Derbyshire structure plan: written statement. [Matlock], 1977. pp. 341. *2 maps in end pocket.*

DEVONSHIRE. Planning Department. County structure plan: report of the survey. Exeter, 1977. pp. 184.

HAMPSHIRE. County Council. South Hampshire structure plan for the south east part of the County of Hampshire, City of Portsmouth, City of Southampton; as approved by the Secretary of State for the Environment, March 1977. [Winchester, 1977]. 1 vol. (various pagings). *3 maps in end pocket.*

HEREFORD AND WORCESTER [COUNTY]. Planning Department. Herefordshire and Worcestershire structure plans: monitoring statement, July 1977. Worcester, 1977. pp. 119.

MONTE (ALFREDO DEL) Politica regionale e sviluppo economico: un'analisi teorica ed econometrica degli effetti della politica degli incentivi nel Mezzogiorno, nell'Irlanda del Nord e in Scozia. Milano, [1977]. pp. 277. *(Naples. Università. Centro Studi di Economia Applicata all'Ingegneria. Studi Economici. 3)*

NORFOLK. County Council. Norfolk structure plan: written statement. [Norwich], 1977. pp. 170.

NORTHERN REGION STRATEGY TEAM. Strategic plan for the northern region. [Newcastle upon Tyne], 1977. 5 vols. (in 1).

SOUTH YORKSHIRE. County Planning Department. South Yorkshire structure plan: draft written statement. [Barnsley], 1977. pp. 142. *Map in end pocket.*

SOUTH YORKSHIRE. County Planning Department. South Yorkshire structure plan: report of survey. [Barnsley], 1977. 3 vols. (in 1).

SURREY. Planning Department. Structure plan: report of survey. [Kingston upon Thames], 1977. 7 vols. (in 1).

SURREY. Planning Department. Surrey structure plan: written statement: public participation draft. [Kingston upon Thames], 1977. pp. 148,xix.

WEST MIDLANDS JOINT MONITORING STEERING GROUP. (A developing strategy for the West Midlands): development in regional strategic locations, 1971-1975. [Birmingham], 1977. pp. 29. *(Technical Reports)*

WEST MIDLANDS JOINT MONITORING STEERING GROUP. Updating and rolling forward of the West Midlands regional strategy: summary of assessment papers. [London, Department of the Environment], 1977. pp. 87.

WEST SUSSEX. Planning Department. West Sussex: the next 15 years: county structure plan draft written statement. Chichester, 1977. pp. 162.

CHAPMAN (SYDNEY) Conservative. Town and countryside: future planning policies for Britain. London, 1978. pp. 37. *(Conservative Political Centre. [Publications]. No. 619)*

EAST MIDLANDS ECONOMIC PLANNING COUNCIL. East midlands: a forward economic look. 2nd ed. [Nottingham], 1978. pp. 143.

GILG (ANDREW W.) Countryside planning. Newton Abbot, [1978]. pp. 255.

GLASSON (JOHN) An introduction to regional planning: concepts, theory and practice. 2nd ed. London, 1978. pp. 422. *bibliogs.*

UP north: how to unshackle a forgotten people; edited by Paul Temperton. Hebden Bridge, [1978]. pp. 47.

REGIONAL PLANNING.(Cont.)

— — Bibliography.

LAMBERT (CLAIRE M.) compiler. Structure and local plan documents. [2nd ed.]. [London, 1977]. pp. 107. *(U.K. Department of the Environment. Library. Bibliographies. No. 152A)*

— — Citizen participation.

PLANNING EXCHANGE. Development control procedures and inquiries: a discussion paper. Glasgow, [1975]. pp. 27.

DERBYSHIRE. County Council. Derbyshire structure plan: report of consultations. [Matlock], 1977. pp. 286.

NORFOLK. County Council. Norfolk structure plan: statement on public participation and consultation. [Norwich], 1977. pp. 259.

STRINGER (PETER) The press and publicity for public participation. [London], 1977. pp. 24. *(Linked Research Project into Public Participation in Structure Planning. Interim Research Papers. 12)*

— — Mathematical models.

KING (J.F.) and TELFORD (K.) A dynamic simulation model of a regional economy: a case study of the North of England: final report. Peterlee, Co. Durham, 1977. pp. 136. *(IBM United Kingdom Limited. UK Scientific Centre. [Technical Reports]. 0086)*

— — Scotland.

STRATHCLYDE. Regional Council. Department of Physical Planning. Strathclyde structure plan: consultative draft; ([with] Key diagram and schedules). Glasgow, 1977. 2 pts. (in 1 vol.).

— — — Citizen participation.

BURTON (ANTHONY W.) and JOHNSON (ROBINA) Public participation in planning: a review of experience in Scotland. Glasgow, [1976]. pp. 74. *bibliog.*

— — Wales.

U.K. Land Authority for Wales. Land policy statement and rolling programme. a., 1977- [Cardiff].

SOUTH GLAMORGAN. County Council. County of South Glamorgan structure plan. [Cardiff], 1977. pp. 194, xv.

SOUTH GLAMORGAN. County Council. County structure plan: draft written statement. [Cardiff], 1977. pp. 195, xv.

SOUTH GLAMORGAN. County Council. Report of survey instituted by the County Council...pursuant to section 6 of the Town and Country Planning Acts, 1971. [Cardiff], 1977. pp. 190. *bibliog.*

TY TORONTO. Socio-economic Research Group. A socio-economic strategy for the valleys of South Wales; prepared by the Research Group...following the conferences of the Year of the Valleys, 1974. Merthyr Tydfil, [1977]. fo.114.

— — — Citizen participation.

SOUTH GLAMORGAN. County Council. County of South Glamorgan structure plan...: publicity and public participation statement. [Cardiff], 1977. 1 vol. (various pagings).

— United States.

PLANNING the fourth migration: the neglected vision of the Regional Planning Association of America; edited by Carl Sussman. Cambridge, Mass., [1976]. pp. 277. *bibliogs.*

TRI-STATE REGIONAL CONFERENCE, NEW YORK, 1976. Proceedings;...sponsored by Tri-State Regional Planning Commission [and others]. [New York, Tri-State Regional Planning Commission, 1976]. pp. 235.

MARTIN (CURTIS H.) and LEONE (ROBERT ANTHONY) Local economic development: the federal connection. Lexington, Mass., [1972]. pp. 138.

CONNECTICUT. Tri-State Regional Planning Commission. 1978. Regional development guide, 1977-2000. New York, 1978. pp. 49.

WEINSTEIN (BERNARD L.) and FIRESTINE (ROBERT E.) Regional growth and decline in the United States: the rise of the sunbelt and the decline of the northeast. New York, 1978. pp. 151.

— — North Carolina.

HAMMER, GREENE, SILER ASSOCIATES. Investment guidelines for the North Carolina Appalachian region; prepared for...North Carolina Department of Administration...[and] Appalachia Regional Commission. Washington, 1967. pp. 129.

— Yugoslavia.

AMERICAN-YUGOSLAV PROJECT IN REGIONAL AND URBAN PLANNING STUDIES. International collaboration in planning research: summary report of the Ljubljana region demonstration study; general editor John W. Dyckman. Detroit, 1972. pp. 139.

— Zambia.

ZAMBIA. Ministry of Development Planning. Annual report. a., 1975(1st)- Lusaka.

REGIONALISM

— Asia, Southeast.

PAUKER (GUY JEAN) and others. Diversity and development in southeast Asia: the coming decade. New York, [1977]. pp. 190. *bibliog. (Council on Foreign Relations. 1980s Project Studies)*

— Belgium.

ETUDES sur le régionalisme en Belgique et à l'étranger, par A. Fischer [and others]. Bruxelles, 1973. pp. 389. *bibliog.*

— Canada.

CANADA and the burden of unity; edited by David Jay Bercuson. Toronto, [1977]. pp. 191.

— Europe.

ETUDES sur le régionalisme en Belgique et à l'étranger, par A. Fischer [and others]. Bruxelles, 1973. pp. 389. *bibliog.*

CONFERENCE ON ETHNIC PLURALISM AND CONFLICT IN CONTEMPORARY WESTERN EUROPE AND CANADA, ITHACA, 1975. Ethnic conflict in the Western world: [papers presented at the Conference]; edited by Milton J. Esman. Ithaca, 1977. pp. 399. *bibliogs. Sponsored by the Western Societies Program of the Center for International Studies, Cornell University.*

— France.

REGIONS et régionalisme en France du XVIIIe siècle à nos jours; actes publiés par Christian Gras et Georges Livet. [Paris, 1977]. pp. 594. *(Société Savante d'Alsace et des Régions de l'Est. Publications. Tome 13) "Colloque organisé par le Groupe de Recherches d'Histoire Moderne et le Centre de Recherches sur les Sociétés Contemporaines de...l'Université des Sciences humaines de Strasbourg...1974".*

— Italy.

Le REGIONI italiane e l'Europa: atti del convegno internazionale promosso e organizzato dalla Regione Piemonte, Torino, 22-24 Aprile, 1976. Milano, 1976. pp. 399.

AIMO (PIERO) Bicameralismo e regioni. Milano, 1977. pp. 216. *bibliog. (Fondazione Adriano Olivetti. Studi Parlamentari. 3)*

GIZZI (ELIO) La ripartizione delle funzioni tra stato e regioni: il D.P.R.24 luglio 1977 N.616, di attuazione della delega di cui alla legge 22 luglio 1975 N.382. Milano, 1977. pp. 142. *bibliog.*

— United Kingdom.

BIRCH (ANTHONY HAROLD) Political integration and disintegration in the British Isles. London, 1977. pp. 183. *bibliog.*

U.K. Parliament. House of Commons. Library. Research Division. Background Papers. No. 63. The devolution debate: regional statistics, updated. [London, 1978]. pp. 17.

UP north: how to unshackle a forgotten people; edited by Paul Temperton. Hebden Bridge, [1978]. pp. 47.

REGIONALISM (INTERNATIONAL ORGANIZATION).

BENNETT (ALVIN LEROY) International organizations: principles and issues. Englewood Cliffs, [1977]. pp. 440.

REGISTERS OF BIRTHS, ETC.

— India — Gujarat.

INDIA. Office of the Registrar General. Vital Statistics Division. 1976. Report on sample registration system under Kaira project. [Delhi, 1976]. pp. 179. *bibliog.*

— United Kingdom.

LOCAL POPULATION STUDIES and CAMBRIDGE GROUP FOR THE HISTORY OF POPULATION AND SOCIAL STRUCTURE. The first supplement to Original parish registers in record offices and libraries. [Matlock], 1976. pp. 60.

REGRESSION ANALYSIS.

BIBBY (JOHN) and TOUTENBURG (HELGE) Prediction and improved estimation in linear models. Chichester, [1977]. pp. 188. *bibliog. Revised and updated vrsion of Helge Toutenburg's Vorhersage in linearen Modellen.*

SEBER (GEORGE ARTHUR FREDERICK) Linear regression analysis. New York, [1977]. pp. 465. *bibliog.*

— Dictionaries — Polyglot.

HEBÁK (PETR) and HUSTOPECKÝ (JIŘÍ) compilers. Šestijazyčný slovník termínů z regresní analýzy: [Czech, Russian, Polish, English, French, German]. Praha, 1978. pp. 211. *With preface and explanatory notes in each language.*

REHABILITATION.

UNITED NATIONS. Interregional Seminar on Programmes and Administration of Major Rehabilitation Services in Developing Countries, Virum, 1966. Report of the...seminar...[held at] Virum, Denmark, 18 July-5 August 1966. (ST/TAO/SER.C/100). New York, 1967. pp. 181.

— Belgium.

BELGIUM. Fonds National de Reclassement Social des Handicapés. Rapport annuel. a., 1976- Bruxelles. *In 2 pts.*

— Poland.

ILO/UNDP REGIONAL SEMINAR ON THE ORGANISATION AND DEVELOPMENT OF DISABLED PERSONS' CO-OPERATIVES, WARSAW, 1974. ILO/UNDP Regional Seminar...16 September to 5 October 1974... regional Middle East; proceedings, conclusions and recommendations; report, etc. (REM/72/027). Geneva, International Labour Organisation, 1974. pp. 186.

ILO/UNDP REGIONAL SEMINAR ON THE ORGANISATION AND DEVELOPMENT OF COOPERATIVES FOR THE DISABLED, WARSAW, 1977. ILO/ UNDP Regional Seminar...Warsaw, Poland, 4 to 19 October, 1977...: regional Asia; proceedings, conclusions and recommendations, etc. (RAS/75/031). Geneva, International Labour Organisation, 1978. pp. 230.

— Underdeveloped areas.

See UNDERDEVELOPED AREAS — Rehabilitation.

REHABILITATION, RURAL

— European Economic Community countries.

CORRIE (JOHN ALEXANDER) and SCOTT-HOPKINS (JAMES SIDNEY RAWDON) Toward a community rural policy. London, [1978]. pp. 24. *bibliog.*

— Poland.

KUCIŃSKI (KAZIMIERZ) Przestrzenne zró'znicowanie infrastruktury wsi a uprzemysłowienie: aspekty społeczne. Warszawa, 1977. pp. 148. *bibliog.* (Polska Akademia Nauk. Komitet i Zakład Badań Rejonów Uprzemysławianych) *With Russian and English summaries.*

— Underdeveloped areas.

See UNDERDEVELOPED AREAS — Rehabilitation, Rural.

REHABILITATION OF CRIMINALS.

VON HIRSCH (ANDREW) Doing justice: the choice of punishments;...report of the Committee for the Study of Incarceration. New York, 1976. pp. 179.

— Germany.

ALBRECHT (PETER ALEXIS) Zur sozialen Situation entlassener "Lebenslänglicher". Göttingen, [1977]. pp. 449. *bibliog.*

— Russia.

SUNDUROV (FEDOR ROMANOVICH) Sotsial'no-psikhologicheskie i pravovye aspekty ispravleniia i perevospitaniia pravonarushitelei. Kazan', 1976. pp. 144.

REHABILITATION OF JUVENILE DELINQUENTS.

ONTARIO. Ministry of Correctional Services. Planning and Research Branch. 1976. A review of alternatives to the incarceration of the youthful offender. [Toronto], 1976. pp. 80. *bibliogs.*

— United Kingdom.

BURNETT (MARTIN) The delinquent's challenge: trust me if you dare. Chichester, [1978]. pp. 132.

RELATIVITY.

WEINSTEIN (MICHAEL A.) The tragic sense of political life. Columbia, S.C., [1977]. pp. 189.

RELIGION

— Controversial literature.

MOST (JOHANN) La peste réligieuse; traduit de l'Allemand. Amiens, 1905. pp. 16.

— History.

KRYVELEV (IOSIF ARONOVICH) Istoriia religii: ocherki v dvukh tomakh. Moskva, 1975-76. 2 vols.

DONAKOWSKI (CONRAD L.) A muse for the masses: ritual and music in an age of democratic revolution, 1770-1870. Chicago, 1977. pp. 435. *bibliog.*

RELIGION AND HUMOUR.

BRICKER (VICTORIA REIFLER) Ritual humor in highland Chiapas. Austin, [1973]. pp. 257. *bibliog.*

RELIGION AND SCIENCE.

MACKAY (DONALD MACCRIMMON) Science, chance and providence. Oxford, 1976. pp. 67. *(Newcastle-upon-Tyne. University. Riddell Memorial Lectures. 46th Series)*

ZAHAVY (ZEV) Whence and wherefore: the cosmological destiny of man scientifically and philosophically considered. South Brunsick, [1978]. pp. 178. *"Comprising an analysis relating to the significant essay In the centre of immensities, by the distinguished Professor Sir Bernard Lovell, University of Manchester, England".*

RELIGION AND SOCIOLOGY.

BERGER (PETER L.) Facing up to modernity: excursions in society, politics and religion. New York, [1977]. pp. 233.

WINTER (JERRY ALAN) Continuities in the sociology of religion: creed, congregation and community. New York, [1977]. pp. 308. *bibliogs.*

WILSON (JOHN) of Duke University. Religion in American society: the effective presence. Englewood Cliffs, [1978]. pp. 492. *bibliog.*

RELIGION AND STATE

— France.

ROBERT (JACQUES FRÉDÉRIC) La liberté religieuse et le régime des cultes. [Paris, 1977]. pp. 166. *bibliog.*

— India.

GHOUSE (MOHAMMAD) Secularism, society and law in India. Delhi, [1973]. pp. 254. *bibliog.*

— United States.

MALBIN (MICHAEL J.) Religion and politics: the intentions of the authors of the First Amendment. Washington, [1978]. pp. 40. *(American Enterprise Institute for Public Policy Research. AEI Studies. 200)*

RELIGIONS.

EAST comes west: a background to some Asian faiths; [by] Peggy Holroyde [and others]. 2nd ed. London, Community Relations Commission, 1973. pp. 101. *bibliogs.*

— History — Sources.

ELIADE (MIRCEA) ed. From primitives to Zen: a thematic sourcebook of the history of religions. London, 1977. pp. 645. *bibliog.*

RELIGIOUS EDUCATION

— United Kingdom.

The TRUTH about the London School Board and religious education; by Athelstan Riley [and others]. [London, 1895?]. pp. 24. *(Reprinted from the Religious Review of Reviews) Lacking cover.*

SECULAR EDUCATION LEAGUE. The Secular Education League: (manifesto). London, [19--]. pp. (3). *Also lists members of the General Council.*

PROSPECTS and problems for religious education; the report of a seminar held at...Windsor in March 1969. London, H.M.S.O., 1971. pp. 65.

LAQUEUR (THOMAS WALTER) Religion and respectability: Sunday schools and working class culture, 1780-1850. New Haven, 1976. pp. 293. *bibliog.*

RELIGIOUS LIBERTY

— France.

ROBERT (JACQUES FRÉDÉRIC) La liberté religieuse et le régime des cultes. [Paris, 1977]. pp. 166. *bibliog.*

RELIGIOUS THOUGHT

— Russia.

SCHMEMANN (ALEXANDER) ed. Ultimate questions: an anthology of modern Russian religious thought. London, 1977. pp. 310. *bibliog.*

— United States.

HATCH (NATHAN O.) The sacred cause of liberty: republican thought and the millennium in revolutionary New England. New Haven, 1977. pp. 197. *bibliog.*

REMAND HOMES

— United Kingdom.

BURNETT (MARTIN) The delinquent's challenge: trust me if you dare. Chichester, [1978]. pp. 132.

REMSCHEID

— History.

TAUBERT (ROLF) Autonomie und Integration: das Arbeiter-Blatt Lennep: eine Fallstudie zur Theorie und Geschichte von Arbeiterpresse und Arbeiterbewegung, 1848-1850. München, 1977. pp. 215. *bibliog.* (Institut für Zeitungsforschung derStadt Dortmund. Dortmunder Beiträge zur Zeitungsforschung. Band 24)

RENAISSANCE.

PLUMB (JOHN HAROLD) and others. The Penguin book of the Renaissance; with essays by Garrett Mattingly [and others]. Harmondsworth, 1964 repr. 1978. pp. 333. *First published in Britain in 1961 under title The Horizon book of the Renaissance.*

ULLMANN (WALTER) Medieval foundations of renaissance humanism. London, 1977. pp. 212.

RENT

— United Kingdom.

OLDHAM COMMUNITY DEVELOPMENT PROJECT. Fair rents and supplementary benefit rent allowances; or, How the Department of Health and Social Security supports slum landlords from public funds. Oldham, [1976]. 1 pamphlet (various pagings).

ALPREN (LAWRENCE) The causes of serious rent arrears. [London, 1977]. pp. 57. *bibliog.*

FENTON (MIKE) and COLLARD (DAVID) Do coloured tenants pay more?: some evidence. Bristol, Social Science Research Council Research Unit on Ethnic Relations, [1977]. pp. 9. *(Working Papers on Ethnic Relations. No. 1)*

WESTMINSTER RENT ACT WORKING PARTY. The streets where we live: response to the government's Rent Act review. London, 1977. pp. 38.

RENT CONTROL

— United Kingdom.

WAR EMERGENCY: WORKERS' NATIONAL COMMITTEE. Do not pay more rent than the landlord is allowed by law to demand. London, [1917?]. s.sh.

BRITISH PROPERTY FEDERATION. Review of the Rent Acts: submission of evidence in response to Department of Environment consultation paper of January 1977. London, 1977. pp. 34.

PETTIT (PHILIP HENRY) Landlord and tenant under the Rent Act 1977. London, 1978. pp. 317.

— — Ireland, Northern.

IRELAND, NORTHERN. Department of the Environment. 1976. The private rented sector in Northern Ireland: the government's proposals. [Belfast], 1976. pp. 22.

RENT SUBSIDIES

— Germany — North Rhine-Westphalia.

NORTH RHINE-WESTPHALIA. Landesamt für Datenverarbeitung und Statistik. Beiträge zur Statistik des Landes Nordrhein-Westfalen. Heft 392. Wohngeld in Nordrhein-Westfalen, 1975 bis 1977. Düsseldorf, 1978. pp. 37.

— United Kingdom.

OLDHAM COMMUNITY DEVELOPMENT PROJECT. Fair rents and supplementary benefit rent allowances; or, How the Department of Health and Social Security supports slum landlords from public funds. Oldham, [1976]. 1 pamphlet (various pagings).

REPARATION

— United Kingdom.

HOWARD LEAGUE FOR PENAL REFORM. Making amends: criminals, victims and society: compensation, reparation, reconciliation; a discussion paper. Chichester, 1977. pp. 18.

REPARATION(Cont.)

REVIEW of the criminal injuries compensation scheme: report of an interdepartmental working party; [M.J. Moriarty, chairman]. London, H.M.S.O., 1978. pp. 109.

SOFTLEY (PAUL) Compensation orders in magistrates' courts; a Home Office Research Unit report. London, 1978. pp. 38. *bibliog. (U.K. Home Office. Home Office Research Studies. No. 43)*

REPERTORY GRID TECHNIQUE.

FRANSELLA (FAY) and BANNISTER (DONALD) A manual for repertory grid technique. London, 1977. pp. 193. *bibliog.*

REPETTO (NICOLAS).

REPETTO (NICOLAS) Mi paso por la politica: de Roca a Yrigoyen. Buenos Aires, [1956]. pp. 347.

REPRESENTATIVE GOVERNMENT AND REPRESENTATION.

ZAMPETTI (PIER LUIGI) La partecipazione popolare al potere: una nuova alternativa al capitalismo e al socialismo. [Milano, 1976]. pp. 226.

Der MODERNE Parlamentarismus und seine Grundlagen in der ständischen Repräsentation: Beiträge des Symposiums der Bayerischen Akademie der Wissenschaften und der International Commission for [the History of] Representative and Parliamentary Institutions auf Schloss Reisenburg vom 20. bis 25. April 1975;...herausgegeben von Karl Bosl. Berlin, [1977]. pp. 380. *In various languages.*

NAGLE (JOHN DAVID) System and succession: the social bases of political elite recruitment. Austin, [1977]. pp. 273. *bibliog.*

RYN (CLAES G.) Democracy and the ethical life: a philosophy of politics and community. Baton Rouge, [1978]. pp. 208.

— United Kingdom.

HART (VIVIEN) Distrust and democracy: political distrust in Britain and America. Cambridge, 1978. pp. 251. *bibliog.*

— United States.

HART (VIVIEN) Distrust and democracy: political distrust in Britain and America. Cambridge, 1978. pp. 251. *bibliog.*

REPUBLICAN PARTY (FRANCE).

PARTI REPUBLICAIN. Le Projet Républicain: programme du Parti Républicain. [Paris, 1978]. pp. 190.

REPUBLICAN PARTY (UNITED STATES).

HOLT (THOMAS) Black over white: negro political leadership in South Carolina during reconstruction. Urbana, [1977]. pp. 269. *bibliog.*

FAIRLIE (HENRY) The parties: Republicans and Democrats in this century. New York, [1978]. pp. 236.

REPUBLICANISM IN FRANCE.

PARTI REPUBLICAIN. Le Projet Républicain: programme du Parti Républicain. [Paris, 1978]. pp. 190.

RESEARCH.

SCIENCE and technology policy: perspectives and developments; edited by Joseph Haberer. Lexington, Mass., [1977]. pp. 216. *(Policy Studies Organization. Policy Studies Organization Series. 14)*

— Economic aspects.

RESCHER (NICHOLAS) Scientific progress: a philosophical essay on the economics of research in natural science. Oxford, [1978]. pp. 278.

— Australia.

AUSTRALIA. Department of Science. Report. a., 1972/73 (1st)- Canberra. *Included in AUSTRALIA. Parliament. [Parliamentary papers].*

— Belgium.

APERÇU STATISTIQUE SUR LE POTENTIEL SCIENTIFIQUE ET TECHNIQUE DE LA BELGIQUE; [pd. by] Services de Programmation de la Politique Scientifique. a., 1963/71- Bruxelles.

— Canada.

CANADA. Statistics Canada. Annual review of science statistics. a., 1977(1st)- Ottawa. *[in English and French]. Supersedes CANADA. Statistics Canada. Expenditures of provincial non-profit research institutes, CANADA. Statistics Canada. Expenditures on scientific activities by private non-profit organizations, CANADA. Statistics Canada. Federal government activities in the human sciences, CANADA. Statistics Canada. Federal government activities in the natural sciences, CANADA. Statistics Canada. Industrial research and development expenditures in Canada and CANADA. Statistics Canada. Research and development expenditure in Canada.*

McFETRIDGE (D.G.) Government support of scientific research and development: an economic analysis. Toronto, [1977]. pp. 96. *bibliog. (Ontario. Economic Council. Research Studies. 8)*

— European Economic Community countries.

EUROPEAN COMMUNITIES. Commission. 1977. Common policy in the field of science and technology: communication...to the Council of 30 June 1977. [Luxembourg], 1977. pp. 62. *(Bulletin of the European Communities. Supplements. [1977/3])*

— Finland.

FINLAND. Tilastokeskus. Tutkimustoiminta, etc. a., 1975- Helsinki. *[in English, Finnish and Swedish]*

— Norway.

DAHL (HELMER) and others. Forskningspolitikk: tre foredrag...15. mars 1971. Bergen, 1971. pp. 21. *(Christian Michelsens Institutt for Videnskap og Åndsfrihet. Beretninger. 34,2)*

— Romania.

GHIȚĂ (TĂNASE) Reproducția socială, cercetarea și știința. București, 1976. pp. 119. *With English and Russian tables of contents.*

— Scandinavia.

[SCANDINAVIA]. Nordisk Statistisk Skriftserie. 18. Forskningsvirksomhet i Norden i 1967: utgifter og personale, etc. Oslo, 1970. pp. 89. *bibliog. With English and Finnish summaries.*

— United Kingdom.

GASTON (JERRY) The reward system in British and American science. New York, [1978]. pp. 204. *bibliog.*

— United States.

GASTON (JERRY) The reward system in British and American science. New York, [1978]. pp. 204. *bibliog.*

KATZ (JAMES EVERETT) Presidential politics and science policy. New York, 1978. pp. 292. *bibliog.*

RESEARCH, INDUSTRIAL.

RONSTADT (ROBERT) Research and development abroad by U.S. multinationals. New York, [1977]. pp. 127.

— Brazil.

BRAZIL. Instituto de Planejamento Econômico e Social. Instituto de Planejamento. Setor de Industria. 1971. Potencial de pesquisa tecnologica no Brasil;...equipe de trabalho: Francisco Almeida Biato [and others]. Brasilia, 1971. pp. 198. *(Instituto de Planejamento. Relatorios de Pesquisa. No. 5)*

— Germany.

STACHELSKY (FRIEDRICH VON) Aussenwirtschaftliche Bestimmungsfaktoren der staatlichen Forschungspolitik in der Bundesrepublik Deutschland. Berlin, [1978]. pp. 159. *bibliog.*

— Russia.

TAKSIR (KIM ISAEVICH) Nauchno-proizvodstvennye ob"edineniia. Moskva, 1977. pp. 160. *(Akademiia Nauk SSSR. Problemy Sovetskoi Ekonomiki)*

— United Kingdom — Finance.

NATIONAL RESEARCH DEVELOPMENT CORPORATION [U.K.]. Evidence offered to the Committee to review the Functioning of Financial Institutions, the Wilson Committee. London, [1977?]. pp. 28.

NATIONAL RESEARCH DEVELOPMENT CORPORATION [U.K.]. Methods of funding research and development. London, [1977?]. pp. 4. *(Leaflets. 7)*

— United States.

HOLLOMON (JOHN HERBERT) and GRENON (MICHEL) Energy research and development. Cambridge, Mass., 1975. pp. 264. *bibliogs. A report to the Energy Policy Project of the Ford Foundation.*

RESEARCH GRANTS

— Canada.

McFETRIDGE (D.G.) Government support of scientific research and development: an economic analysis. Toronto, [1977]. pp. 96. *bibliog. (Ontario. Economic Council. Research Studies. 8)*

RESEARCH LIBRARIES

— United States.

WRIGHT (LOUIS BOOKER) Of books and men. Columbia, S.C., [1976]. pp. 179.

RESIDENTIAL MOBILITY

— United Kingdom.

DEAKIN (NICHOLAS) and UNGERSON (CLARE) Leaving London: planned mobility and the inner city. London, 1977. pp. 194.

— United States.

NEIGHBORHOOD change: lessons in the dynamics of urban decay; [by] Charles L. Leven [and others]. New York, 1976. pp. 205.

— — New York (City).

BURSTEIN (ABRAHAM C.) Residential mobility in New York City, 1965-1970: movement of population within and into New York City during the period 1965-1970. New York, 1975. 4 vols. (in 3).

RESPONSIBILITY, LEGAL

— Russia.

SHEVCHENKO (IAROSLAVNA NIKOLAEVNA) Pravovoe regulirovanie otvetstvennosti nesovershennoletnikh. Kiev, 1976. pp. 189. *bibliog.*

RESTAURANTS, LUNCHROOMS, ETC.

— Singapore.

SINGAPORE. Statistics Department. 1976. Report on the census of wholesale and retail trades, restaurants and hotels, 1973. Singapore, 1976. pp. 98.

SINGAPORE. Statistics Department. 1978. Report on the census of wholesale and retail trades, restaurants and hotels, 1975. Singapore, 1978. pp. 188.

RESTRAINT OF TRADE.

WARREN-BOULTON (FREDERICK R.) Vertical control of markets: business and labor practices. Cambridge, Mass., [1978]. pp. 213. *bibliog.*

— **European Economic Community countries.**

NEBOLSINE (GEORGE) Die Verteidigungsrechte gegenüber der Kontrolle auf wettbewerbsbeschränkendes Verhalten nach dem Vertrag der Europäischen Wirtschaftsgemeinschaft, etc. Baden-Baden, 1959. pp. 49.

— **India.**

INDIAN INVESTMENT CENTRE. Restrictions on exports in foreign collaboration agreements in India. (TD/B/389). New York, United Nations, 1971. pp. 28.

— **Ireland (Republic).**

EIRE. Restrictive Practices Commission. Annual report. a., 1974- Dublin.

— **Philippine Islands.**

VIRATA (CESAR) and others. Restrictions on exports in foreign collaboration agreements in the Republic of the Philippines: by a team of researchers, etc. (TD/B/388). New York, United Nations, 1972. pp. 28.

— **United Kingdom.**

ZANDER (MICHAEL) Lawyers and the public interest...; notes to bring the book up to date. 1976. fo. 91.

RESTRICTIVE PRACTICES IN INDUSTRIAL RELATIONS.

WARREN-BOULTON (FREDERICK R.) Vertical control of markets: business and labor practices. Cambridge, Mass., [1978]. pp. 213. *bibliog.*

RETAIL TRADE.

UNITED NATIONS. Statistical Office. Statistical Papers. Series F. No.19. Organization and conduct of distributive-trade surveys. (ST/ESA/STAT/SER.F/19). New York, 1977. pp. 165. *bibliog.*

— **Australia.**

AUSTRALIA. Commonwealth Bureau of Census and Statistics. 1975- . Census of retail establishments and selected service establishments, 1973-74: final bulletin. Canberra, 1975 in progress.

— **Colombia.**

COLOMBIA. Departamento Administrativo Nacional de Estadistica. Censos economicos, 1970. Censos economicos 1970: comercio, industria, servicios; datos provisionales. Bogota, [1971?]. pp. 23.

— **European Economic Community countries.**

EUROPEAN COMMUNITIES. Statistical Office. Labour costs in distributive trades, banking and insurance. trien., 1974(2nd)- Luxembourg. *[in Community languages] 1970(1st) included in EUROPEAN COMMUNITIES. Statistical Office. Social statistics, 1972(no. 4).*

EUROPEAN COMMUNITIES. Statistical Office. Special Series: Structure of Earnings in Wholesale and Retail Distribution, Banking and Insurance in 1974. Luxembourg, [1977] in progress.

— **Germany.**

GREIPL (ERICH) Wettbewerbssituation und -entwicklung des Einzelhandels in der Bundesrepublik Deutschland. Berlin, [1978]. pp. 236. *bibliog. (Ifo-Institut für Wirtschaftsforschung. Schriftenreihe. Nr. 96)*

— — **North Rhine-Westphalia.**

NORTH RHINE-WESTPHALIA. Landesamt für Datenverarbeitung und Statistik. Beiträge zur Statistik des Landes Nordrhein- Westfalen. Heft 386. Die Einheitswerte der gewerblichen Betriebe und der Mineralgewinnungsrechte, 1972. Düsseldorf, 1978. pp. 199.

— **New Zealand.**

DISTRIBUTION COUNCIL [NEW ZEALAND]. Role of women in the distribution industry. [Wellington], 1976. pp. 35.

— **Singapore.**

SINGAPORE. Statistics Department. 1976. Report on the census of wholesale and retail trades, restaurants and hotels, 1973. Singapore, 1976. pp. 98.

SINGAPORE. Statistics Department. 1978. Report on the census of wholesale and retail trades, restaurants and hotels, 1975. Singapore, 1978. pp. 188.

— **South Africa.**

COHEN (AARON) and BOADEN (BRUCE G.) The retail structure of the Witwatersrand and the Vaal triangle: a preliminary report. Johannesburg, 1977. pp. 20. *(Johannesburg. University of the Witwatersrand. Urban and Regional Research Unit. Occasional Papers. No. 17)*

SOUTH AFRICA. Bureau of Statistics. 1977. Census of wholesale and retail trade, 1971. [Pretoria, 1977]. 13 pts. (in 4 vols.) *(Reports. Nos.04-41-22 to 04-41-34) In English and Afrikaans.*

— **Zambia.**

ZAMBIA. Central Statistical Office. 1965. Census of distribution in 1962: wholesale, retail trade and selected services. Lusaka, 1965. fo. 22.

RETIREMENT

— **United States.**

SHEPPARD (HAROLD L.) and RIX (SARA E.) The graying of working America: the coming crisis in retirement- age policy. New York, [1977]. pp. 175.

RETIREMENT, PLACES OF

— **France.**

ROSS (JENNIE-KEITH) Old people, new lives: community creation in a retirement residence. Chicago, 1977. pp. 227. *bibliog.*

RETRAINING, OCCUPATIONAL

— **Italy.**

FERRARESI (LUCIANO) and others. Riconversione professionale ed esodo programmato nel mondo agricolo. Milano, [1976]. pp. 181. *bibliog.*

REUNION

— **Economic conditions.**

REUNION. [Secrétariat Général pour les Affaires Economiques. Documentation et Etudes]. Bulletin de conjoncture. q., 4e trimestre 1971 (no.10)- [St. Denis].

— **Statistics.**

REUNION. [Secrétariat Général pour les Affaires Economiques. Documentation et Etudes]. Statistiques et indicateurs économiques. a., 1971 [1st issue]- [St. Denis].

REVENUE

— **Bahamas.**

BAHAMAS. Department of Statistics. 1976. Government revenue and expenditure, 1970-1973. Nassau, [1976]. fo. 18.

— **Persian Gulf.**

AL-KUWARI (ALI KHALIFA) Oil revenues in the Gulf Emirates: patterns of allocation and impact on economic development; (volume editor Howard Bowen- Jones). Epping, 1978. pp. 218. *bibliog. (Durham. University. Centre for Middle Eastern and Islamic Studies. [Publications. New Series]. 6)*

— **United States.**

MACMANUS (SUSAN A.) Revenue patterns in U.S. cities and suburbs: a comparative analysis. New York, 1978. pp. 265. *bibliog.*

REVOLUTIONARY SOCIALIST PARTY (CZECHOSLOVAKIA).

REVOLUTIONARY SOCIALIST PARTY (CZECHOSLOVAKIA). Manifesto. [London], 1970. 1 pamphlet (unpaged).

REVOLUTIONISTS

— **Cuba.**

FONER (PHILIP SHELDON) Antonio Maceo: the "Bronze Titan" of Cuba's struggle for independence. New York, [1977]. pp. 340. *bibliog.*

LLERENA (MARIO) The unsuspected revolution: the birth and rise of Castroism. Ithaca, 1978. pp. 324.

— **France.**

JOUBERT (JEAN PAUL) Révolutionnaires de la S.F.I.O.: Marceau Pivert et le pivertisme. [Paris, 1977]. pp. 296. *bibliog.*

— **Italy.**

ROSSO (SOCCORSO) Brigate Rosse: che cosa hanno fatto, che cosa hanno detto, che cosa se ne è detto. Milano, 1976. pp. 294.

La SINISTRA revoluzionaria in Italia: documenti e interventi delle tre principali organizzazioni: Avanguardia operaia, Lotta continua, PdUP; a cura di Davide Degli Incerti. Roma, [1976]. pp. 320.

— **Russia.**

NAFIGOV (RAFIK IZMAILOVICH) Revoliutsionnye sviazi kazanskogo podpol'ia 80-kh godov, kruzhkov N.E. Fedoseeva. [Kazan'], 1975. pp. 26.

HARDY (DEBORAH) Petr Tkachev, the critic as Jacobin. Seattle, [1977]. pp. 339. *bibliog. (Washington State University. Institute for Comparative and Foreign Area Studies. Publications on Russia and Eastern Europe. No. 8)*

REVOLUTIONISTS, WOMEN.

See **WOMEN REVOLUTIONISTS**.

REVOLUTIONS.

YOUNG (NIGEL) On war, national liberation and the state. London, [1971?]. pp. 16. *bibliog.*

SOCIETY FOR THE LIBERATION OF DAILY LIFE. Daily life. Leeds, [1973?]. pp. 31.

CHÂTELET (FRANÇOIS) and others. La révolution sans modèle. Paris, [1975]. pp. 188.

NCUBE (PATRICK D.) African socialism, imperialism, and a reconsidering of Trotsky's theory of the permanent revolution. Oslo, 1975. pp. 116, viii. *bibliog. (Oslo. Universitet. Instituttet for Sosiologi. Skriftserie. Nr. 29)*

BATALOV (EDUARD IAKOVLEVICH) Philosophie de la révolte: critique de l'idéologie du gauchisme; (traduit du russe). Moscou, [1976]. pp. 332.

SOCIAL REVOLUTION GROUP. Introduction to social revolution. [Aberdeen, 1976]. pp. 12.

BLACKBURN (ROBIN) ed. Revolution and class struggle: a reader in Marxist politics. [London], 1977. pp. 444. *bibliog.*

BURTON (ANTHONY) Revolutionary violence: the theories. London, 1977. pp. 147.

KORSCH (KARL) Karl Korsch: revolutionary theory; edited by Douglas Kellner. Austin, Tex., [1977]. pp. 299.

LINARES (FILADELFO) Die Revolution bei Tocqueville und Marx. Percha am Starnberger See, [1977]. pp. 122.

MARC (ALEXANDRE) Révolution américaine - révolution européenne: message du fédéralisme. Lausanne, 1977. pp. 111. *(Lausanne. Université. Centre de Recherches Européennes. Publications. 2. Le Processus d'Union de l'Europe)*

REVOLUTIONS.(Cont.)

REJAI (MOSTAFA) The comparative study of revolutionary strategy. New York, [1977]. pp. 194. *bibliog. A revised and enlarged version of the author's Strategy of political revolution.*

EISENSTADT (SHMUEL N.) Revolution and the transformation of societies: a comparative study of civilizations. New York, [1978]. pp. 348.

TARIQ ALI. 1968 and after: inside the revolution. London, 1978. pp. 219. *bibliog.*

TRIMBERGER (ELLEN KAY) Revolution from above: military bureaucrats and development in Japan, Turkey, Egypt, and Peru. New Brunswick, [1978]. pp. 196. *bibliog.*

WASSMUND (HANS) Revolutionstheorien: eine Einführung. München, [1978]. pp. 146. *bibliog.*

— America, Latin.

GERASSI (JOHN) Contemporary theories of revolution in Latin America with special reference to Venezuela, Colombia, Guatemala, Uruguay, Brazil and Chile. 1977. fo. 499. *bibliog.* Typescript. Ph.D. (London) thesis: unpublished. *This thesis is the property of London University and may not be removed from the Library.*

— Cuba.

CUBA: revolution and counter-revolution; translated from Acción Libertaria, organ of the Argentine Libertarian Federation, etc. New York, [1961?]. s. sh.

— Ethiopia.

MARKAKIS (JOHN) and AYELE (NEGA) Class and revolution in Ethiopia. Nottingham, 1978. pp. 191.

— Germany.

REVOLUTIONAERER Prozess und Staatsentstehung. Berlin, 1976. pp. 184. *(Akademie der Wissenschaften der DDR. Institut für Theorie des Staates und des Rechts. Staats- und Rechtstheoretische Studien. 2)*

REWARDS (PRIZES, ETC.)

— United Kingdom.

GASTON (JERRY) The reward system in British and American science. New York, [1978]. pp. 204. *bibliog.*

— United States.

GASTON (JERRY) The reward system in British and American science. New York, [1978]. pp. 204. *bibliog.*

RHEGAS, of Velestino.

MANESES (ARISTOBOULOS I.) L'activité et les projets politiques d'un patriote grec dans les Balkans vers la fin du XVIIIe siècle. Thessalonique, 1962. pp. 75-118.

RHIGAS, of Velestino.

See RHEGAS, of Velestino.

RHODESIA

— Commerce.

OTTAWA conference: report of the Committee appointed to investigate and report to the government on certain matters relating to the natural resources and industries of Southern Rhodesia, their present position and future prospects, and their relation to empire and world trade; [H. Bertin, chairman]. Salisbury, 1933. pp. 65. *(Southern Rhodesia. Legislative Assembly. [Sessional Papers]. 1933. C.S.R.1)*

— Constitutional history.

CHANOCK (MARTIN) Unconsummated union: Britain, Rhodesia and South Africa, 1900-45. Manchester, [1977]. pp. 289. *bibliog.*

— Economic conditions.

OTTAWA conference: report of the Committee appointed to investigate and report to the government on certain matters relating to the natural resources and industries of Southern Rhodesia, their present position and future prospects, and their relation to empire and world trade; [H. Bertin, chairman]. Salisbury, 1933. pp. 65. *(Southern Rhodesia. Legislative Assembly. [Sessional Papers]. 1933. C.S.R.1)*

SMITH (IAN DOUGLAS) Prime Minister's speech at the opening of Trade Fair Rhodesia, 1975. [Salisbury], 1975. pp. 10. *(Rhodesia. Ministry of Information, Immigration and Tourism. For the Record. No. 25)*

— Foreign economic relations.

BINGHAM (THOMAS HENRY) and GRAY (S.M.) Report on the supply of petroleum and petroleum products to Rhodesia. London, H.M.S.O., 1978. pp. 296.

STRACK (HARRY R.) Sanctions: the case of Rhodesia. Syracuse, N.Y., 1978. pp. 296. *bibliog.*

— Foreign relations.

STRACK (HARRY R.) Sanctions: the case of Rhodesia. Syracuse, N.Y., 1978. pp. 296. *bibliog.*

— — South Africa.

CHANOCK (MARTIN) Unconsummated union: Britain, Rhodesia and South Africa, 1900-45. Manchester, [1977]. pp. 289. *bibliog.*

— — Zambia.

INTERNATIONAL DEFENCE AND AID FUND. Special Reports. No. 1. The Rhodesia-Zambia border closure. London, 1973. pp. 26.

— Frontier troubles.

INTERNATIONAL DEFENCE AND AID FUND. Special Reports. No. 1. The Rhodesia-Zambia border closure. London, 1973. pp. 26.

— History.

BLAKE (ROBERT NORMAN WILLIAM) Baron Blake. A history of Rhodesia. London, 1977. pp. 430. *bibliog.*

WINDRICH (ELAINE) Britain and the politics of Rhodesian independence. London, [1978]. pp. 283.

— Industries.

RHODESIA. 1974. Policy on decentralization. [Salisbury], 1974. pp. 10. *([Command Papers]. 1974. Cmd. R.R.31)*

— Nationalism.

SITHOLE (NDABANINGI) Letters from Salisbury prison. [Nairobi, 1976]. pp. 186.

RAEBURN (MICHAEL) Black fire!: accounts of the guerrilla war in Rhodesia; ... with an analysis by A.R. Wilkinson. London, 1978. pp. 243.

— Native races.

SOUTHERN RHODESIA. Commission of Enquiry into Certain Sales of Native Cattle in Areas occupied by Natives. 1939. Report; [Robert James Hudson, chairman]. [Salisbury], 1939. pp. 21. *(Legislative Assembly. [Sessional Papers]. 1939. C.S.R. 24)*

— Officials and employees.

SOUTHERN RHODESIA. Commission of Enquiry into Promotions in the Civil Service. 1939. Report; [W.A. Godlonton, chairman]. Salisbury, 1939. pp. 73. *(Legislative Assembly. [Sessional Papers]. 1939. C.S.R. 2)*

— Politics and government.

FRONT FOR THE LIBERATION OF ZIMBABWE. Manifesto; (adopted at the inaugural congress...held...1972). 1972. fo. 3. *Unpublished: photocopy of typescript.*

NGOZI (Z.) and FANIKALO (V.) Zimbabwe: what is to be done now. n.p. [1972?]. pp. 14.

RHODESIA. Prime Minister. 1974. Prime Minister's statement on the constitutional dispute, settlement proposals and African opinion, 19th June, 1974. [Salisbury], 1974. pp. 13. *(Rhodesia. Ministry of Information, Immigration and Tourism. For the Record. No. 23)*

KERSHAW (RICHARD) Prime Minister's interview with Richard Kershaw, B.B.C. "Panorama", May 8th, 1975. [Salisbury], 1975. pp. 16. *(Rhodesia. Ministry of Information, Immigration and Tourism. For the Record. No. 26)*

RHODESIA. Special Court. 1975. Judgement: a judgement concerning the necessity or expediency of continuing the detention of the reverend Ndabaningi Sithole who was the subject of a detention order issued on the 3rd day of March, 1975, [given] 2nd April, 1975. [Salisbury], 1975. pp. 34. *(Rhodesia. Ministry of Information, Immigration and Tourism. For the Record. No. 24)*

SITHOLE (NDABANINGI) In defence of a birthright. [Toronto], 1975. pp. 77.

SMALL (CLIVE) Prime Minister answers questions posed by Clive Small, of the B.B.C., and Dr. L. Meysels, senior editor, Wochenpresse, Vienna. [Salisbury], 1975. pp. 11. *(Rhodesia. Ministry of Information, Immigration and Tourism. For the Record. No. 27)*

SMITH (IAN DOUGLAS) Prime Minister's speech at the opening of Trade Fair Rhodesia, 1975. [Salisbury], 1975. pp. 10. *(Rhodesia. Ministry of Information, Immigration and Tourism. For the Record. No. 25)*

SMITH (IAN DOUGLAS) Prime Minister's statement to Parliament on the Victoria Falls Conference: Tuesday, August 26, 1975. [Salisbury], 1975. pp. 8. *(Rhodesia. Ministry of Information, Immigration and Tourism. For the Record. No. 28)*

INTERNATIONAL DEFENCE AND AID FUND. Fact Papers on Southern Africa. No. 1. "Civilised standards" in Rhodesia: the Law and Order (Maintenance) Act. London, [1976]. pp. 16.

LEWIS (ARTHUR R.) Rhodesia undefeated. Salisbury, 1976, repr. 1977. pp. 16.

RHODESIA. Prime Minister. 1976. Address to the nation...February 6, 1976. [Salisbury], 1976. pp. 7. *(Rhodesia. Ministry of Information, Immigration and Tourism. For the Record. No. 31)*

RHODESIA. Prime Minister. 1976. The new initiative: broadcast to the nation...April 27th, 1976. [Salisbury], 1976. pp. 13. *(Rhodesia. Ministry of Information, Immigration and Tourism. For the Record. No. 35)*

RHODESIA. Prime Minister. 1976. Prime Minister's address to the nation, Friday, 24th September, 1976. [Salisbury], 1976. pp. 6. *(Rhodesia. Ministry of Information, Immigration and Tourism. For the Record. No. 38)*

RHODESIA. Prime Minister. 1976. Prime Minister's statement to Parliament, 20th February, 1976. [Salisbury], 1976. pp. 5. *(Rhodesia. Ministry of Information, Immigration and Tourism. For the Record. No. 32)*

BRITISH COUNCIL OF CHURCHES. Department of International Affairs and CONFERENCE OF BRITISH MISSIONARY SOCIETIES. Rhodesia now : the liberation of Zimbabwe. London, 1977. pp. 20.

CATHOLIC COMMISSION FOR JUSTICE AND PEACE IN RHODESIA. Rhodesia: the propaganda war. Salisbury, 1977. 1 pamphlet (unpaged).

INTERNATIONAL DEFENCE AND AID FUND. Zimbabwe: the facts about Rhodesia. London, 1977. pp. 76.

LAMONT (DONAL) Bishop of Umtali. Speech from the dock. [Leigh-on-Sea, 1977]. pp. 143.

RHODESIA. Ministry of Information, Immigration and Tourism. 1977. Rhodesia and the Anglo-American proposals. [Salisbury], 1977. 2 pts.

RHODESIA. Prime Minister. 1977. Prime Minister announces plans for internal talks, Thursday, 23rd November, 1977. [Salisbury], 1977. pp. 8. *(Rhodesia. Ministry of Information, Immigration and Tourism. For the Record. No. 43)*

RHODESIA. Prime Minister. 1977. Prime Minister's address to the nation, Monday, 18th July, 1977. [Salisbury], 1977. pp. 5. *(Rhodesia. Ministry of Information, Immigration and Tourism. For the Record. No. 42)*

SITHOLE (NDABANINGI) Roots of a revolution: scenes from Zimbabwe's struggle. Oxford, 1977. pp. 142.

HUTSON (HENRY PORTER WOLSELEY) Rhodesia: ending an era. London, [1978]. pp. 198. *bibliog.*

WINDRICH (ELAINE) Britain and the politics of Rhodesian independence. London, [1978]. pp. 283.

— Race question.

LAMONT (DONAL) Bishop of Umtali. Speech from the dock. [Leigh-on-Sea, 1977]. pp. 143.

SITHOLE (NDABANINGI) Roots of a revolution: scenes from Zimbabwe's struggle. Oxford, 1977. pp. 142.

RIANJO

— History.

DURAN (JOSE A.) Historia de caciques, bandos e ideologias en la Galicia no urbana: Rianxo 1910-1914. Madrid, 1972. pp. 387.

— Politics and government.

DURAN (JOSE A.) Historia de caciques, bandos e ideologias en la Galicia no urbana: Rianxo 1910-1914. Madrid, 1972. pp. 387.

RIANXO.

See RIANJO.

RICARDO (DAVID).

RICARDIENS, Keynésiens et Marxistes: essais en économie politique non-néoclassique: actes du colloque de Nice, septembre 1972; (édité par C. Berthomieu [and others]). [Grenoble, 1974]. pp. 405. *bibliogs.*

NEORICARDIANA: Sraffa e Graziadei; a cura di Roberto Finzi. Bologna, [1977]. pp. 258. *(Convegno Nazionale degli Storici del Pensiero Economico, 3, 1974. Atti. vol. 2)*

RICCARDI FAMILY.

MALANIMA (PAOLO) I Riccardi di Firenze: una famiglia e un patrimonio nella Toscana dei Medici. Firenze, 1977. pp. 271. *(Unione Regionale delle Provincie Toscane. Biblioteca de Storia Toscana Moderna e Contemporanea. Studi e Documenti. 15)*

RICE

— Asia.

GABLE (RICHARD W.) and SPRINGER (J. FRED) Administering agricultural development in Asia: a comparative analysis of four national programs. Boulder, Colo., 1976. pp. 398. *bibliog.*

— India — Kerala.

KERALA. State Planning Board. Evaluation Division. 1976. High yielding varieties program in Kerala, virippu paddy 1973-74: an evaluation study. [Trivandrum], 1976. pp. 71. *(Evaluation Series. 24)*

— Japan.

OISHI (TAIZAN) Progressive high productivity and surplus production of rice in Japan: on the background of rice production control. [Tokyo], 1975. pp. 25. *bibliog.* *(Reprinted from Geographical Reports of Tokyo Metropolitan University No. 10, 1975)*

— Malaysia.

CHENG (SIOK-HWA) The rice trade of Malaya. Singapore, [1973]. pp. 44.

HILL (R.D.) Rice in Malaya: a study in historical geography. Kuala Lumpur, 1977. pp. 234. *bibliog.*

RICHARDSON (EVERETT).

CAMERON (SILVER DONALD) The education of Everett Richardson: the Nova Scotia fishermen's strike, 1970-71. Toronto, [1977]. pp. 239.

RIEMANN INTEGRAL.

PFEFFER (WASHEK F.) Integrals and measures. New York, [1977]. pp. 259. *bibliog.*

RIGHT AND LEFT (POLITICAL SCIENCE).

TEODORI (MASSIMO) Storia delle nuove sinistre in Europa, 1956-1976. Bologna, [1976]. pp. 694. *bibliog.*

BRAVO (GIAN MARIO) Critica dell'estremismo: gli uomini, le correnti, le idee del radicalismo di sinistra. Milano, 1977. pp. 438. *bibliog.*

FERRARESI (FRANCO) and KEMENY (PIETRO) Classi sociali e politica urbana: destra e sinistra nelle amministrazioni locali. Roma, 1977. pp. 160.

RIGHT AND WRONG.

FRIED (CHARLES) Right and wrong. Cambridge, Mass., 1978. pp. 226.

RIGHT OF PROPERTY.

DENMAN (DONALD ROBERT) The place of property: a new recognition of the function and form of property rights in land. Berkhamsted, [1978]. pp. 150. *bibliog.* *(Cambridge. University. Department of Land Economy. Studies in Land Economy)*

VEREIN FÜR SOZIALPOLITIK. Schriften. Neue Folge. Band 97. Ökonomische Verfügungsrechte und Allokationsmechanismen in Wirtschaftssystemen; von Rolf Eschenburg [and others]; herausgegeben von Karl-Ernst Schenk. Berlin, [1978]. pp. 205. *bibliogs.*

RIGHT TO COUNSEL

— United States.

HERMANN (ROBERT) and others. Counsel for the poor: criminal defense in urban America. Lexington, Mass., [1977]. pp. 243.

RIGOLA (RINALDO).

CARTIGLIA (CARLO) Rinaldo Rigola e il sindicalismo riformista in Italia. Milano, [1976]. pp. 209.

RINGS (ALGEBRA).

SAMUEL (PIERRE) Anneaux factoriels. São Paulo, 1963. pp. 102. *bibliog.* *(Sociedade de Matematica de São Paulo. Publicações)*

GILMER (ROBERT) Multiplicative ideal theory. New York, 1972. pp. 609. *bibliog.*

RIO DE JANEIRO (CITY)

— Transit systems.

BARAT (JOSEF) Estrutura metropolitana e sistema de transportes: estudo do caso do Rio de Janeiro. Rio de Janeiro, 1975. pp. 292. *bibliog.* *(Brazil. Instituto de Planejamento Econômico e Social. Instituto de Pesquisas. Monografias. No. 20)*

RIO GRANDE DO SUL

— Industries.

OSORIO (IVAN DALL'IGNA) and RAMOS (JOSE HUGO) Rio Grande do Sul: industrialização posta a prova. Pôrto Alegre, 1969. fo. 209. *bibliog.*

RIOTS

— France.

GRIMAUD (MAURICE) En mai, fais ce qu'il te plaît. [Paris, 1977]. pp. 345.

DELALE (ALAIN) and RAGACHE (GILLES) La France de 68. [Paris, 1978]. pp. 238.

— South Africa.

INTERNATIONAL DEFENCE AND AID FUND. Soweto and the uprising of 1976 in South Africa; [pamphlet accompanying] an exhibition of photographs prepared by the...Fund at the Africa Centre...London WC2. London, [1977]. 1 pamphlet (unpaged).

— Spain.

DOMINGUEZ ORTIZ (ANTONIO) Alteraciones andaluzas. Madrid, [1973]. pp. 237.

— United Kingdom.

HAYTER (TONY) The army and the crowd in mid-Georgian England. London, 1978. pp. 239. *bibliog.*

— United States.

BUTTON (JAMES W.) Black violence: political impact of the 1960s riots. Princeton, [1978]. pp. 248. *bibliog.*

RISK.

BEARD (ROBERT ERIC) and others. Risk theory: the stochastic basis of insurance. 2nd ed. London, 1977. pp. 195. *bibliog.*

— Mathematical models.

FOLDES (LUCIEN P.) Optimal saving and risk in continuous time with constant returns. London, 1976. fo. 34. *(Papers on Capital and Risk. No. 1)*

FINANCIAL decision making under uncertainty; edited by Haim Levy and Marshall Sarnat. New York, 1977. pp. 301. *bibliogs.* Based on the 1975 Israel Scientific Research Conference held at Ein Bokek, Israel, by the National Council of Research and Development.

RITES AND CEREMONIES.

SECULAR ritual; edited by Sally F. Moore [and] Barbara G. Myerhoff. Assen, 1977. pp. 293. *bibliog.* Papers presented at a conference held at Burg Wartenstein, Austria, 1974.

RITUALISM.

BENTLEY (JAMES) Ritualism and politics in Victorian Britain: the attempt to legislate for belief. Oxford, 1978. pp. 162. *bibliog.*

RIVADAVIA (BERNARDINO).

FRIZZI DE LONGINI (HAYDEE E.) Rivadavia y la economia argentina. Buenos Aires, 1947. pp. 266. *bibliog.*

RIVERS

— Malaya.

FEDERATED MALAY STATES. Commission appointed to Inquire into and Report upon Certain Matters regarding the Rivers in the Federated Malay States. 1928. Report; [E.C.H. Wolff, chairman]. Kuala Lumpur, 1928. pp. 172. *(Federal Council. Papers to be laid before the...Council, etc. 1928. No. 14)*

ROAD ACCIDENTS

— Statistics.

EUROPEAN MOTOR VEHICLES SYMPOSIUM, BRUSSELS, 1975. Proceedings of the...Symposium and the Seminar on Accident Statistics. Brussels, European Communities, [1977]. 2 vols. (in 1). *bibliogs.*

ROAD ACCIDENTS(Cont.)

— **Ireland (Republic).**

ROAD ACCIDENT FACTS: IRELAND; [pd. by] the National Institute for Physical Planning and Construction Research [Eire]. a., 1968 [1st]- Dublin.

— **Underdeveloped areas.**

See UNDERDEVELOPED AREAS — Road accidents.

ROAD CONSTRUCTION WORKERS

— **Norway.**

VEIVESENETS ARBEIDERFORENING. 75-års beretning: 1900 9. september 1975. [Oslo, 1975]. pp. 126.

ROAD PLANNING

— **Underdeveloped areas.**

See UNDERDEVELOPED AREAS — Road planning.

— **United Kingdom.**

U.K. Advisory Committee on Trunk Road Assessment. 1978. Report...; chairman: Sir George Leitch. London, 1978. pp. 208.

ROAD SAFETY.

TAYLOR (H.) Pedestrian safety: the role of research. Crowthorne, 1977. pp. 33. *bibliog. (U.K. Transport and Road Research Laboratory. Supplementary Reports. 319)*

ROAD TRANSPORT WORKERS

— **Canada.**

CANADIAN LABOUR CONGRESS. Hours of work in the motor transport industry; submission...with respect to the inquiry pursuant to Part III of the Canada Labour Code. Ottawa, 1974. fo. 9.

CANADIAN LABOUR CONGRESS. Submission...to the Motor Vehicle Transport Committee of the Canadian Transport Commission with respect to the submission by Mr. George Smith, doing business as George Smith Trucking Co., Winnipeg, Manitoba. Ottawa, 1974. fo. 8.

ROADS

— **Australia.**

REPORT ON ROADS IN AUSTRALIA; [pd. by] Bureau of Roads. a., 1973- Canberra. *Included in AUSTRALIA. Parliament. [Parliamentary papers].*

— **Macedonia.**

STOJANOVSKI (ALEKSANDAR) Dervendžistvoto vo Makedonija. Skopje, 1974. pp. 362. *bibliog. With Russian and French summaries.*

— **New Zealand.**

NEW ZEALAND. National Roads Board. 1968. Roading in New Zealand: a brief summary. Wellington, 1968. pp. 17.

NEW ZEALAND. National Roads Board. Roads to resources. [Wellington, 1971?]. pp. 24.

— **Puerto Rico.**

PUERTO RICO. Government Development Bank for Puerto Rico. 1971. Highway Authority, Puerto Rico: a special report. San Juan, 1971. pp. 16.

— **Tropics — Bibliography.**

COOPER (L.) compiler. Reports on roads and transport planning in tropical and sub- tropical countries. rev. ed. Crowthorne, 1977. pp. 79. *(U.K. Transport and Road Research Laboratory. Supplementary Reports. 162)*

— **United Kingdom.**

BRITISH ROAD FEDERATION and BRITISH INDUSTRY ROADS CAMPAIGN. Road to Europe: A45: Midlands to East Anglia; a...report. London, [1927]. pp. 12.

MIDLANDS ROAD DEVELOPMENT GROUP. Roads in the Midlands. [London, 1973]. pp. 12.

GILLIVER (IAN) Highway assignment multiflow: a critical appraisal. Reading, 1977. pp. 58. *bibliog. (Reading. University. Department of Geography. Reading Geographical Papers. No.59)*

— — **Bibliography.**

ALLETSON (JOAN) compiler. Roads and transport in rural areas;...edited by Claire M. Lambert. [London], 1976. pp. 23. *(U.K. Department of the Environment. Library. Bibliographies. No. 17B)*

— — **Finance.**

LEBARON (ALLEN) Vehicle taxation and highway development. 1960. 1 vol. (various foliations). *Unpublished: typescript.*

— — **London.**

EAST London river crossing study; report of the Steering Group. [London], Greater London Council, 1975. pp. 32, fo.(11).

— — **Scotland.**

SCOTTISH COUNCIL (DEVELOPMENT AND INDUSTRY). Scotland's roads: a Scottish Council viewpoint. Edinburgh, 1972. fo. 19.

— **United States.**

CONNECTICUT. Tri-State Regional Planning Commission. 1975. The expressway connection. [New York], 1975. pp. 4. *(Regional Profiles. Vol. 3. No.1)*

ROANNE

— **Politics and government.**

PICKVANCE (CHRISTOPHER GEOFFREY) Marxist approaches to the study of urban politics: divergences among some recent French studies. Canterbury, 1976. fo. 52. *Paper for the Political Studies Association Conference, Nottingham, 1976.*

ROCHESTER, NEW YORK

— **History.**

BRIGGS (JOHN WALKER) An Italian passage: immigrants to three American cities, 1890- 1930. New Haven, 1978. pp. 348. *bibliog.*

ROLE CONFLICT.

HAWKINS (PETER JAMES LETHAM) Role conflict and the work study engineer: a study of role consensus in industry. [1977]. fo. 322. *bibliog. Typescript. Ph.D. (London) thesis: unpublished. This thesis is the property of London University and may not be removed from the Library.*

ROMANIA

— **Army — History — Chronology.**

CRONICA participării armatei Române la războiul pentru independență, 1877-1878. București, 1977. pp. xxvi,437. *bibliog.*

— **Civilization.**

PANAITESCU (PETRE P.) Einführung in die Geschichte der rumänischen Kultur; mit einer Vorbemerkung von Stefan S. Gorovei; (aus dem Rumänischen von C. Alfred Alioth). Bukarest, 1977. pp. 338. *bibliog.*

— **Defences.**

APĂRAREA națională a României socialiste: cauză și operă a întregului nostru popor. București, 1974. pp. 258.

— **Economic conditions.**

TITUS (C. MICHAEL) Rebirth of Dacia Felix?: Romania seen from the right angle. London, 1973. pp. 36.

— **Economic policy.**

DANCIU (CONSTANTIN) Coordonate ale conducerii planificate a activității economico- sociale în România. [București], 1976. pp. 226. *bibliog. With Russian and English tables of contents.*

GHIȚĂ (TĂNASE) Reproducția socială, cercetarea și știința. București, 1976. pp. 119. *With English and Russian tables of contents.*

— **Foreign economic relations — Germany.**

MARGUERAT (PHILIPPE) Le IIIe Reich et le pétrole roumain, 1938-1950: contribution à l'étude de la pénétration économique allemande dans les Balkans à la veille et au début de la Seconde Guerre mondiale. Leiden, 1977. pp. 231. *bibliog. (Geneva. Graduate Institute of International Studies. Collection de Relations Internationales. 6)*

— **Foreign relations.**

CEAUȘESCU (NICOLAE) Speeches and writings; selected and introduced by Stan Newens. 2nd ed. Nottingham, 1978. pp. 287.

— — **Egypt.**

BOTORAN (CONSTANTIN) Relațiile româno-egiptene în epoca modernă și contemporană. București, 1974. pp. 302. *bibliog.*

— — **Russia.**

AGAKI (ALEKSEI SOFRONOVICH) Russko-rumynskie mezhgosudarstvennye otnosheniia v kontse XIX- nachale XX v. Kishinev, 1976. pp. 187. *bibliog.*

— **History — 1876-1878, War of Independence.**

CRONICA participării armatei Române la războiul pentru independență, 1877-1878. București, 1977. pp. xxvi,437. *bibliog.*

ROMÂNIA în războiul de independență, 1877-1878. București, 1977. pp. 476. *With English, French and Russian summaries.*

— **Nationalism.**

POLVEREJAN (ȘERBAN) and CORDOȘ (NICOLAE) eds. Mișcarea memorandistă în documente, 1885-1897; cuvînt înainte de Ștefan Pascu. Cluj, 1973. pp. 368. *bibliog. With appendix of photographs.*

— **Politics and government.**

TITUS (C. MICHAEL) Rebirth of Dacia Felix?: Romania seen from the right angle. London, 1973. pp. 36.

MUȘAT (MIRCEA) and ARDELEANU (ION) Viața politică în România, 1918-1921. 2nd ed. București, 1976. pp. 374.

CEAUȘESCU (NICOLAE) Speeches and writings; selected and introduced by Stan Newens. 2nd ed. Nottingham, 1978. pp. 287.

— — **Dictionaries and encyclopedias.**

MICĂ enciclopedie de politologie. București, 1977. pp. 493. *With English afterword.*

— **Relations (general) with Russia.**

STOROZHUK (VLADIMIR PROKOF'EVICH) Rabochee dvizhenie v Rumynii i rumyno-russkie revoliutsionnye sviazi, 1893-1907. Kishinev, 1977. pp. 175. *bibliog.*

— **Rural conditions — Research.**

TEMATICA cercetării realităților contemporane ale localităților rurale șigalorificarea lor în activitatea cultural-educativă; alcătuită de Mihai Deleanu. Reșița, 1975. pp. 98.

— Social conditions.

TITUS (C. MICHAEL) Rebirth of Dacia Felix?: Romania seen from the right angle. London, 1973. pp. 36.

— Social policy.

DANCIU (CONSTANTIN) Coordonate ale conducerii planificate a activității economico- sociale în România. [București], 1976. pp. 226. *bibliog. With Russian and English tables of contents.*

ROMANIANS IN TRANSYLVANIA.

HITCHINS (KEITH) Orthodoxy and nationality: Andreiu Șaguna and the Rumanians of Transylvania, 1846-1873. Cambridge, Mass., 1977. pp. 332. *bibliog. (Harvard University. Harvard Historical Studies. vol. 94)*

ROMANTICISM.

DONAKOWSKI (CONRAD L.) A muse for the masses: ritual and music in an age of democratic revolution, 1770-1870. Chicago, 1977. pp. 435. *bibliog.*

ROME

— Social history.

MOVIMENTO operaio e organizzazione sindacale a Roma, 1860-1960; documenti per la storia della Camera di Lavoro; [by] F. Agostino [and others]. Roma, 1976. 2 vols.

— Suburbs and environs.

BERLINGUER (GIOVANNI) and SETA (PIERO DELLA) Borgate di Roma. 2nd ed. Roma, 1976. pp. 358.

ROME, ANCIENT

— Historiography.

EDWARD Gibbon and the Decline and fall of the Roman Empire; edited by G.W. Bowersock [and others]. Cambridge, Mass., 1977. pp. 257. *Proceedings of a conference held under the auspices of the American Academy of Arts and Sciences, Rome, 1976.*

— History.

CANALI (LUCA) ed. Potere e consenso nella Roma di Augusto: guida storica e critica. Roma, 1975. pp. 276. *bibliog.*

— Nobility.

RANOUIL (PIERRE CHARLES) Recherches sur le patriciat, 509-366 avant J.-C. Paris, 1975. pp. 284. *bibliog.*

ROME UNIVERSITY.

MORDENTI (ADRIANO) Come eravamo: documenti fotografici per una storia della lotte studentesche a Roma, 1966-1972; foto di Adriano Mordenti e Massimo Vergari. Roma, [1975]. pp. 93.

ROOSEVELT (FRANKLIN DELANO) President of the United States.

ROBINSON (EDGAR EUGENE) The Roosevelt leadership, 1933-1945. New York, 1972. pp. 491. *bibliog. Reprint of the first edition, Philadelphia, 1955.*

DORSETT (LYLE W.) Franklin D. Roosevelt and the city bosses. Port Washington, N.Y., 1977. pp. 134. *bibliog.*

TAYLOR (ALAN JOHN PERCIVALE) The war lords. London, 1977. pp. 189. *Transcripts of six lectures delivered on BBC Television in August 1976.*

ROOSEVELT (THEODORE) President of the United States.

GABLE (JOHN ALLEN) The Bull Moose years: Theodore Roosevelt and the Progressive Party. Port Washington, N.Y., 1978. pp. 302.

ROOT CROPS.

REGIONAL MEETING ON THE PRODUCTION OF ROOT CROPS, SUVA, 1975. Collected papers [of the Meeting], (24-29 October, 1975, Suva, Fiji). Noumea, South Pacific Commission, 1977. pp. 213. *(Technical Papers. No.174)*

RØRLEGGERNES FAGFORENING.

KJELLSTRØM (JOHN) Rørleggernes Fagforening, 1884-1959. Oslo, 1959. pp. 238.

ROSAS (JUAN MANUEL DE).

ROSA (JOSE MARIA) Fraudes y adulteraciones documentales en "La caida de Rosas": respuesta a Jose Antonio Soares de Souza. [Buenos Aires, 1969]. pp. 37.

VARELA (FLORENCIO) Rosas y su gobierno: escritos politicos, economicos y literarios. Buenos Aires, 1975. pp. 211. *New edition of work published in 1927 which consisted of material first published in 1859.*

ROSENBERG (ALFRED).

BAUMGAERTNER (RAIMUND) Weltanschauungskampf im Dritten Reich: die Auseinandersetzung der Kirchen mit Alfred Rosenberg. Mainz, [1977]. pp. 272. *bibliog. (Kommission für Zeitgeschichte. Veröffentlichungen. Reihe B: Forschungen. Band 22)*

ROSICKO-OSLAVANSKO

— Economic history.

FRANĚK (OTAKAR) Oslavany obkličují...: kronika prosincové generální stávky na Rosicku-Oslavansku. 2nd ed. Brno, 1976. pp. 143. *bibliog.*

ROSTOV (OBLAST')

— Politics and government.

DEMESHINA (ELENA IVANOVNA) Rabochee dvizhenie na Donu v period imperializma, 1900-1914 gg. Rostov-na-Donu, 1973. pp. 201.

ROTE ARMEE FRAKTION.

BECKER (JILLIAN) Hitler's children: the story of the Baader-Meinhof terrorist gang. Philadelphia, [1977]. pp. 322. *bibliog.*

ROTTERDAM

— Commerce.

MULLER (HENDRIK) Muller: een Rotterdams zeehandelaar Hendrik Muller Szn, 1819-1898. Schiedam, 1977. pp. 467. *(Rotterdam. Historisch Genootschap Roterodamum. [Publications]. 18)*

ROUERGUE

— Social history.

La PIERRE et le seigle; album composé et légendé par Bernard Dufour, précédé d'une étude d'Emmanuel Le Roy Ladurie. [Paris, 1977]. pp. 143.

ROUSSEAU (JEAN JACQUES).

ROUSSEAU (JEAN JACQUES) Du contrat social; précédé de La démocratie selon Rousseau par Jean Pierre Siméon. Paris, [1977]. pp. 317. *bibliog.*

STEINBERG (JULIUS) 1940- . Locke, Rousseau, and the idea of consent; an inquiry into the liberal-democratic theory of political obligation. Westport, 1978. pp. 155. *bibliog.*

ROUSSILLON.

See also LANGUEDOC-ROUSSILLON (REGION).

ROY (MANABENDRA NATH)

— Bibliography.

WILSON (PATRICK) compiler. A checklist of the writings of M.N. Roy. rev. ed. Berkeley, 1957. fo. 14. *(California University. Modern India Project. Bibliographical Studies. No. 1)*

ROYAL SOCIETY OF LONDON.

ANDRADE (EDWARD NEVILLE DA COSTA) A brief history of the Royal Society. London, 1960. pp. 29.

RUBBER INDUSTRY AND TRADE.

UNITED NATIONS. Conference on Trade and Development. 1970. The maritime transportation of natural rubber: report, etc. (TD/B/C.4/60/Rev.1). New York, 1970. pp. 116.

— Malaya.

FEDERATION OF MALAYA. Rural and Industrial Development Authority. Economic and Planning Division. 1959. Report of preliminary investigation on certain economic aspects of Kampong rubber production at Kampong Genting Malik, Ulu Selangor; by Arshad bin Ayub. [Kuala Lumpur, 1959]. 1 pamphlet (various pagings).

— Malaysia.

RUBBER STATISTICS HANDBOOK OF MALAYSIA; [pd. by] Department of Statistics. a., 1973(20th)- Kuala Lumpur. *[in English and Malay]*

RUGBY, TENNESSEE

— Description.

HUGHES (THOMAS) Author of "Tom Brown's School Days". Rugby, Tennessee: being some account of the settlement founded on the Cumberland Plateau by the Board of Aid to Land Ownership, Limited, a company incorporated in England, and authorised to hold and deal in land by act of the legislature of the state of Tennessee. Philadelphia, 1975. pp. 168. *Reprint of the 1881 ed.*

RUHR

— Economic history.

BURKHARD (WOLFGANG) Abriss einer Wirtschaftsgeschichte des Niederrheins: strukturelle Wandlungen in Handel und Industrie in Duisburg und in den Kreisen Wesel und Kleve. Duisburg, 1977. pp. 173. *bibliog.*

HARTMANN (KNUT) Der Weg zur gewerkschaftlichen Organisation: Bergarbeiterbewegung und kapitalistischer Bergbau im Ruhrgebiet, 1851-1889. München, [1977]. pp. 415. *bibliog.*

— History.

AUFSTAND der Bürger: Revolution 1849 im westdeutschen Industriezentrum;...herausgegeben von Klaus Goebel und Manfred Wichelhaus. 3rd ed. Wuppertal, [1974]. pp. 317. *bibliog.*

— Politics and government.

HERLEMANN (BEATRIX) Kommunalpolitik der KPD im Ruhrgebiet, 1924-1933. Wuppertal, [1977]. pp. 339. *bibliog.*

RUKUBA (AFRICAN PEOPLE).

MULLER (JEAN CLAUDE) Chez les Rukuba: parenté et mariage (État Benue- Plateau, Nigeria). Paris, 1976. pp. 206. *bibliog. (Paris. École Pratique des Hautes Études. Section des Sciences Economiques et Sociales. Cahiers de l'Homme. Nouvelle Série. 17) Cover bears title Parenté et mariage chez les Rukuba.*

RULE OF LAW

— Africa, East.

HUMAN rights in a one-party state: international seminar on human rights, their protection and the rule of law in a one-party state; convened by the International Commission of Jurists. London, 1978. pp. 133.

RULE OF LAW(Cont.)

— Germany.

DIETZE (GOTTFRIED) Two concepts of the rule of law. Indianapolis, 1973. pp. 108.

RURAL DEVELOPMENT.

INTERNATIONAL BANK FOR RECONSTRUCTION AND DEVELOPMENT. Sector Policy Papers. Rural development. [Washington], 1975. pp. 89.

JEDLICKA (ALLEN D.) Organization for rural development: risk taking and appropriate technology. New York, 1977. pp. 170.

AZIZ (SARTAJ) Rural development: learning from China. London, 1978. pp. 201. *bibliog.*

— India.

BROEHL (WAYNE G.) The village entrepreneur: change agents in India's rural development. Cambridge, Mass., 1978. pp. 228.

— Italy.

ZAGARI (EUGENIO) Il problema agrario in trent'anni di meridionalismo. Napoli, [1976]. pp. 117.

— Nigeria.

NIGERIA (WESTERN REGION). 1963. White Paper on integrated rural development. [Ibadan], 1963. pp. 31. *(Official Documents. 1963. No. 8)*

— Tanzania.

SENDER (JOHN) Some preliminary notes on the political economy of rural development in Tanzania based on a case-study in the western Usambaras. Dar es Salaam, 1974. pp. 59. *(Dar es Salaam. University. Economic Research Bureau. ERB Papers. 74.5)*

— Thailand.

MURRAY (CHARLES A.) A behavioral study of rural modernization: social and economic change in Thai villages. New York, 1977. pp. 133. *bibliog.*

RURAL POOR

— Asia.

POVERTY and landlessness in rural Asia. Geneva, International Labour Office, 1977. pp. 288.

— Canada — Ontario.

LANGMAN (R.C.) Poverty pockets: a study of the limestone plains of southern Ontario. Toronto, [1975]. pp. 93.

— United Kingdom.

PLAN for the relief of the agricultural poor, with a view to diminish the poor-rates, and give permanent employment to the labourer, etc. Wycombe, printed by M.C. Morris, 1823. pp. 36.

RURAL-URBAN MIGRATION

— Brazil.

COSTA (MANOEL AUGUSTO) Urbanização e migração urbana no Brazil. Rio de Janeiro, 1975. pp. 198. *bibliog. (Brazil. Instituto de Planejamento Econômico e Social. Instituto de Pesquisas. Monografias. No. 21)*

COSTA (MANOEL AUGUSTO) ed. Estudos de demografia urbana. Rio de Janeiro, 1975. pp. 259. *(Brazil. Instituto de Planejamento Econômico e Social. Instituto de Pesquisas. Monografias. No. 18)*

— Germany.

BRUESE (RUDOLF) Mobilität der landwirtschaftlichen Bevölkerung: eine Analyse der Abwanderung und Statuszuweisung in der Bundesrepublik Deutschland. Bonn, 1977. pp. 416. *bibliog. (Forschungsgesellschaft für Agrarpolitik und Agrarsoziologie. [Publications]. 242)*

— Italy.

CERASE (FRANCESCO PAOLO) Sotto il dominio dei borghesi: sottosviluppo ed emigrazione nell'Italia meridionale, 1860-1910. Assisi, [1975]. pp. 164.

L'EMIGRAZIONE italiana negli anni '70: antologia di studi sull'emigrazione; [by Claudio] Calvaruso [and others]. 2nd ed. Roma, 1975. pp. 270.

FERRARESI (LUCIANO) and others. Riconversione professionale ed esodo programmato nel mondo agricolo. Milano, [1976]. pp. 181. *bibliog.*

FORMICA (CARMELO) Lo spazio rurale nel Mezzogiorno: esodo, desertificazione e riorganizzazione. Napoli, [1976]. pp. 173.

MORELLI (UGO) Classi e movimenti migratori. [Roma, 1976]. pp. 101. *bibliog.*

— Liberia.

AKOI (STEPHEN) and HASSELMANN (KARL-HEINZ) Youth and environment: a Liberian case study on food and nutrition in Buzzi-quarter, Monrovia. [Monrovia], 1975. fo. 32. *bibliog. (University of Liberia. Department of Geography. Occasional Research Papers. No. 9)*

— Nigeria.

ADEPOJU (JOHN ADERANTI) Policy implications of migration into medium-sized towns: the case of Abeokuta, Nigeria. Ile-Ife, 1977. pp. 116. *bibliog.*

— Poland.

MUSZYŃSKI (MAREK) Transfomacja ludności dwunzawodowej. Warszawa, 1976. pp. 144. *bibliog. (Polska Akademia Nauk. Instytut Rozwoju Wsi i Rolnictwa. Problemy Rozwoju Wsi i Rolnictwa)* With Russian and English summaries.

— Spain.

SPAIN. Instituto Nacional de Estadistica. 1974. Las migraciones interiores en España, decenio 1961-1970. [Madrid, 1974]. pp. 141.

— Underdeveloped areas.

See UNDERDEVELOPED AREAS — Rural-urban migration.

RURAL WOMEN.

SCARBOROUGH (NEVE) History of the Associated Country Women of the World...and of its member societies. London, 1953. pp. 403.

RURAL YOUTH

— Employment — Ghana.

BOAKYE (KWESI J.A.) Occupational activities of rural youth and their attitudes towards craft training: an exploratory study. Cape Coast, 1973. pp. 64, vii. *(University of Cape Coast. Centre for Development Studies. Research Report Series. Papers. No. 16)*

— Poland.

PAWŁOWSKI (STEFAN) and ZIELIŃSKI (ADAM) Mazowiecki Związek Młodzie'zy Wiejskiej. Warszawa, 1977. pp. 205. *bibliog.*

RUSSIA.

The LAND of Soviets: the country and the people; (a collection of articles translated from the Russian). Moscow, 1957. pp. 256.

— Antiquities.

OCHERKI russkoi kul'tury XVI veka. Moskva, 1977 in progress.

— Appropriations and expenditures.

LEE (WILLIAM THOMAS) The estimation of Soviet defense expenditures, 1955-75: an unconventional approach. New York, 1977. pp. 358. *bibliog.*

— Armed forces.

DEANE (MICHAEL J.) Political control of the Soviet armed forces. London, [1977]. pp. 297.

WARNER (EDWARD L.) The military in contemporary Soviet politics: an institutional analysis. New York, 1977. pp. 314. *bibliog.*

— — Appropriations and expenditures.

LEE (WILLIAM THOMAS) The estimation of Soviet defense expenditures, 1955-75: an unconventional approach. New York, 1977. pp. 358. *bibliog.*

The SOVIET military buildup and U.S. defense spending; [by] Barry M. Blechman [and others]. Washington, [1977]. pp. 61. *(Brookings Institution. Studies in Defense Policy)*

— — History.

TYL Sovetskikh Vooruzhennykh Sil v Velikoi Otechestvennoi voine, 1941-1945 gg.; pod obshchei redaktsiei S.K. Kurkotkina. Moskva, 1977. pp. 559.

VOORUZHENNYE sily Velikogo Oktiabria. Moskva, 1977. pp. 287. *bibliog.*

— Bibliography.

INTERNATIONAL COMMITTEE FOR SOVIET AND EAST EUROPEAN STUDIES. European bibliography of Soviet, East European and Slavonic studies. vol.1. 1975; [editor Thomas Hnik]. Birmingham, 1977. pp. 437. *Compiled by joint Committee representing Birmingham University Library and Centre for Russian and East European Studies, and the Paris École des Hautes Études en Sciences Sociales, Centre d'Études sur l'URSS et l'Europe Orientale.*

— Biography — Bibliography.

ZHITOMIRSKAIA (S.V.) ed. Vospominaniia i dnevniki XVIII-XX vv.: ukazatel' rukopisei, etc. Moskva, 1976. pp. 621.

— Civilization.

OCHERKI russkoi kul'tury XVI veka. Moskva, 1977 in progress.

MIHAJLOV (MIHAJLO) Underground notes. London, 1977. pp. 204. *bibliog.*

CULTURAL revolution in Russia, 1928-1931; edited by Sheila Fitzpatrick. Bloomington, Ind., [1978]. pp. 309. *(Columbia University. Russian Institute. Studies)*

— Commerce.

VNESHNIAIA TORGOVLIA SSSR: statisticheskii obzor: prilozhenie k zhurnaly "Vneshniaia torgovlia"; ([pd. by] Planovo- Ekonomicheskoe Upravlenie, Ministerstvo Vneshnei Torgovli SSSR. a., 1956 [1st issue]- Moskva.

FOREIGN TRADE: (a m. magazine pd. by the U.S.S.R. Ministry of Foreign Trade). m., Jl 1971 (7)- , with gaps (Ja, Oc 1974). Moscow.

PODVIZHENKO (IVAN STEPANOVICH) Optovaia torgovlia: sovershenstvovanie, effektivnost'. Moskva, 1976. pp. 160.

PROTSENKO (OLEG DMITRIEVICH) and SOLOVEICHIK (DAVID IZRAILEVICH) Planirovanie dolgovremennykh khoziaistvennykh sviazei. Moskva, 1976. pp. 143. *bibliog.*

SHIMANSKII (VSEVOLOD PAVLOVICH) and ORLOV (IAKOV L'VOVICH) Torgovlia i blago naroda. Moskva, 1977. pp. 272.

TURPIN (WILLIAM NELSON) Soviet foreign trade: purpose and performance. Lexington, Mass., [1977]. pp. 172. *bibliog.*

— Commercial policy.

PISKULOV (IURII VASIL'EVICH) Torgovlia sblizhaet narody: torgovo-ekonomicheskie otnosheniia SSSR s promyshlenno razvitymi kapitalisticheskimi stranami; pod redaktsiei A.N. Manzhulo. Moskva, 1976. pp. 104.

RUSSIA.

— Constitution.

BEZUGLOV (ANATOLII ALEKSEEVICH) Suverenitet sovetskogo naroda. Moskva, 1975. pp. 199.

BREZHNEV (LEONID IL'ICH) On the draft constitution (fundamental law) of the Union of Soviet Socialist Republics and the results of the nationwide discussion of the draft: report and closing speech at the seventh (special) session of the Supreme Soviet...1977. Moscow, 1977. pp. 32.

RÉVÉSZ (LÁSZLÓ) Menschenrechte in der UdSSR. Bern, [1977]. pp. 320. (Schweizerisches Ost-Institut. Tatsachen und Meinungen. TM 38)

RUSSIA (U.S.S.R.) Constitution, 1977. Constitution (fundamental law) of the Union of Soviet Socialist Republics: adopted at the seventh (special) session of the Supreme Soviet...October 7, 1977. Moscow, 1977. pp. 127.

FUNDAMENTAL law of the socialist state of the whole people. Moscow, 1978. pp. 136. (Social Sciences Today. Supplements) Report presented by L.I. Brezhnev and other documents.

— Constitutional history.

IROSHNIKOV (MIKHAIL PAVLOVICH) Vo glave Sovnarkoma: gosudarstvennaia deiatel'nost' V.I. Lenina v 1917-1922 gg. Leningrad, 1976. pp. 216. (Akademiia Nauk SSSR. Seriia "Istoriia Nashei Rodiny")

ZNAMENSKII (OLEG NIKOLAEVICH) Vserossiiskoe Uchreditel'noe sobranie: istoriia sozyva i politicheskogo krusheniia. Leningrad, 1976. pp. 364.

CHISTIAKOV (OLEG IVANOVICH) Problemy demokratii i federalizma v pervoi Sovetskoi Konstitutsii. Moskva, 1977. pp. 125.

McKEAN (R.B.) The Russian constitutional monarchy, 1907-17. London, [1977]. pp. 47. bibliog. (Historical Association. General Series. G.91)

RAZGON (ANATOLII IZRAILEVICH) VTsIK Sovetov v pervye mesiatsy diktatury proletariata. Moskva, 1977. pp. 335.

— Defences.

The SOVIET military buildup and U.S. defense spending; [by] Barry M. Blechman [and others]. Washington, [1977]. pp. 61. (Brookings Institution. Studies in Defense Policy)

— Description and travel.

KAISER (ROBERT G.) Russia: the people and the power. New York, 1976. pp. 499. bibliog.

— — Views.

RUSSIA in original photographs 1860-1920; [selected by] Marvin Lyons; edited by Andrew Wheatcroft. London, 1977. pp. 211.

— Economic conditions.

INSTITUT EKONOMICHESKIKH ISSLEDOVANII. La situation économique de l'Union Soviétique. Paris, 1926. pp. 185.

KAISER (ROBERT G.) Russia: the people and the power. New York, 1976. pp. 499. bibliog.

ROGACHEV (SERGEI VLADIMIROVICH) and SHEKIR (N.S.) eds. Osobennosti deistviia ekonomicheskikh zakonov v usloviiakh razvitogo sotsializma. Moskva, 1976. pp. 180.

AKHUNDOV (VAID DZHUMSHUDOVICH) Sovershenstvovanie struktury obshchestvennogo vosproizvodstva: voprosy metodologii. Moskva, 1977. pp. 239.

DOBRYNIN (ALEKSANDR IVANOVICH) Regional'nye proportsii vosproizvodstva. Leningrad, 1977. pp. 127.

EKONOMICHESKIE problemy razvitogo sotsialisticheskogo obshchestva. Kiev, 1977. pp. 383.

FAKTORY i tendentsii razvitiia struktury narodnogo khoziaistva SSSR. Moskva, 1977. pp. 392. bibliog. (Akademiia Nauk SSSR. Problemy Sovetskoi Ekonomiki)

MATERIAL'NO-tekhnicheskaia baza kommunizma. Moskva, 1977. 2 vols. bibliog.

SOVIET agriculture: an assessment of its contributions to economic development; edited by Harry G. Shaffer. New York, 1977. pp. 166.

YANOWITCH (MURRAY) Social and economic inequality in the Soviet Union: six studies. London, 1977. pp. 196. bibliog.

LANE (DAVID) Politics and society in the USSR. 2nd ed. London, 1978. pp. 622. bibliogs.

The SOVIET Union since the fall of Khrushchev; edited by Archie Brown and Michael Kaser. 2nd ed. London, 1978. pp. 351.

— — Mathematical models.

ADIRIM (ITSKHOK GIRSHEVICH) Prognozno-planovye modeli ekonomiki respubliki. Riga, 1977. pp. 255. bibliog. With English table of contents.

CHETYRKIN (EVGENII MIKHAILOVICH) Statisticheskie metody prognozirovaniia. 2nd ed. Moskva, 1977. pp. 200. bibliog.

GREEN (DONALD W.) and HIGGINS (CHRISTOPHER I.) A macroeconometric model of the Soviet Union. New York, 1977. pp. 312. bibliog.

— Economic history.

HARRIMAN (WILLIAM AVERELL) Peace with Russia? nEW yORK, 1959. PP. 174.

KUZ'MIN (VALENTIN IVANOVICH) V bor'be za sotsialisticheskuiu rekonstruktsiiu, 1926-1937: ekonomicheskaia politika Sovetskogo gosudarstva. Moskva, 1976. pp. 311.

BETTELHEIM (CHARLES) Les luttes de classes en URSS: deuxième période, 1923-1930. [Paris, 1977]. pp. 605. bibliog.

— — Bibliography.

KAZMER (DANIEL R.) and KAZMER (VERA ULANOWSKI) compilers. Russian economic history: a guide to information sources. Detroit, [1977]. pp. 520.

— — Sources.

DZERZHINSKII (FELIKS EDMUNDOVICH) Izbrannye proizvedeniia, (1897-1926). 3rd ed. Moskva, 1977. 2 vols.

— Economic policy.

XXV s"ezd KPSS: osnovnye napravleniia ekonomicheskogo razvitiia. Kiev, 1977. pp. 208.

BYCHEK (NIKOLAI ROMANOVICH) and CHISTIAKOV (MIKHAIL IVANOVICH) Metodologiia razrabotki piatiletnego plana. Moskva, 1977. pp. 215.

EKONOMICHESKIE zakony sotsializma i ikh ispol'zovanie v praktike kommunisticheskogo stroitel'stva. Minsk, 1977. pp. 271. bibliog.

MAO (TSE-TUNG) A critique of Soviet economics;...translated by Moss Roberts, annotated by Richard Levy, with an introduction by James Peck. New York, [1977]. pp. 157.

MATERIAL'NO-tekhnicheskaia baza kommunizma. Moskva, 1977. 2 vols. bibliog.

ZAKONOMERNOSTI rasshirennogo sotsialisticheskogo vosproizvodstva. Moskva, 1977. pp. 403. (Akademiia Nauk SSSR. Problemy Sovetskoi Ekonomiki)

BERGSON (ABRAM) Productivity and the social system: the USSR and the West. Cambridge, Mass., 1978. pp. 256.

— — Mathematical models.

PROTSENKO (OLEG DMITRIEVICH) and SOLOVEICHIK (DAVID IZRAILEVICH) Planirovanie dolgovremennykh khoziaistvennykh sviazei. Moskva, 1976. pp. 143. bibliog.

ROZANOV (GENNADII VLADIMIROVICH) Statisticheskoe modelirovanie razvitiia otrasli. Moskva, 1976. pp. 167. bibliog.

BERGMANN (THEODOR) The development models of India, the Soviet Union and China: a comparative analysis. Assen, 1977. pp. 255. bibliog. (European Society for Rural Sociology. Publications. 1.)

— Executive departments.

POTASHEV (FEDOR IVANOVICH) Reorganizatsiia Rabkrina i TsKK: tvorcheskoe razvitie i osushchestvlenie Kommunisticheskoi partiei leninskogo plana reorganizatsii Rabkrina. Rostov-na-Donu, 1974. pp. 216.

— Foreign economic relations.

PISKULOV (IURII VASIL'EVICH) Torgovlia sblizhaet narody: torgovo-ekonomicheskie otnosheniia SSSR s promyshlenno razvitymi kapitalisticheskimi stranami; pod redaktsiei A.N. Manzhulo. Moskva, 1976. pp. 104.

SHISHKIN (VALERII ALEKSANDROVICH) V.I. Lenin i vneshneekonomicheskaia politika Sovetskogo. gosudarstva, 1917-1923 gg. Moskva, 1977. pp. 371.

VNESHNEEKONOMICHESKIE sviazi Sovetskogo Soiuza na novom etape; pod redaktsiei V.A. Brykina, B.S. Vaganova. Moskva, 1977. pp. 176.

WOLYNSKI (ALEXANDER) Soviet aid to the third world: strategy before economics. London, 1977. pp. 13. (Institute for the Study of Conflict. Conflict Studies. No. 90)

— — Poland.

POLSKO-Radzieckie stosunki gospodarcze: dokumenty i materialy, 1921-1939; wyboru dokonal i opracowal Stanislaw Lopatniuk. Warszawa, 1976. pp. 655.

— — United Kingdom.

ANAN'ICH (BORIS VASIL'EVICH) Rossiiskoe samoderzhavie i vyvoz kapitalov, 1895-1914 gg.: po materialam Uchetno-ssudnogo banka Persii. Leningrad, 1975. pp. 211.

— Foreign opinion, British.

JONES (BILL) The Russia complex: the British Labour Party and the Soviet Union. Manchester, [1977]. pp. 229. bibliog.

— Foreign relations.

SOWJETUNION: Aussenpolitik...; (Osteuropa-Handbuch); unter Mitarbeit von Heinz Brahm [and others] herausgegeben von Dietrich Geyer. Köln, 1972-76. 3 vols. bibliog.

KHVOSTOV (VLADIMIR MIKHAILOVICH) Problemy istorii vneshnei politiki SSSR i mezhdunarodnykh otnoshenii: izbrannye trudy. Moskva, 1976 in progress.

LEBEDEV (NIKOLAI IVANOVICH) Novyi etap mezhdunarodnykh otnoshenii. Moskva, 1976. pp. 296.

VNESHNIAIA politika Sovetskogo Soiuza: aktual'nye problemy; pod redaktsiei Lebedeva N.I. i Nikol'skogo N.M. Moskva, 1976. pp. 304.

BELETSKII (VIKTOR NIKOLAEVICH) Die Politik der Sowjetunion in den deutschen Angelegenheiten der Nachkriegszeit, 1945-1976; übersetzt von Wolfgang Eckstein [and others]. Berlin, 1977. pp. 429.

EMETS (VALENTIN ALEKSEEVICH) Ocherki vneshnei politiki Rossii v period pervoi mirovoi voiny: vzaimootnosheniia Rossii s soiuznikami po voprosam vedeniia voiny. Moskva, 1977. pp. 367.

RUSSIA.(Cont.)

FREDERIK (HANS) Volksfront: der taktische Einsatz der Sowjetunion, um mit Hilfe der Einheitsfrontaktionen zwischen Sozialdemokraten und Kommunisten und der Bündnispolitik mit bürgerlichen Regierungen die materielle und politische Weltordnung des Westens abzulösen. Landshut, 1977. pp. 544.

GEYER (DIETRICH) Der russische Imperialismus: Studien über den Zusammenhang von innerer und auswärtiger Politik, 1860-1914. Göttingen, 1977. pp. 344. *bibliog.*

SCHWARZ-LIEBERMANN VON WAHLENDORF (HANS ALBRECHT) Positions internationales de la Russie soviétique: tradition et idéologie. Paris, [1977]. pp. 311.

WAJSMAN (PATRICK) L'illusion de la détente. [Paris, 1977]. pp. 288.

CROZIER (BRIAN) Strategy of survival. London, 1978. pp. 224. *bibliog.*

CROZIER (BRIAN) The surrogate forces of the Soviet Union. London, 1978. pp. 20. *(Institute for the Study of Conflict. Conflict Studies. No. 92)*

— — Treaties.

BUTKEVICH (VLADIMIR GRIGOR'EVICH) Sovetskoe pravo i mezhdunarodnyi dogovor. Kiev, 1977. pp. 262. *bibliog.*

— — Asia.

SEN GUPTA (BHABANI) Soviet-Asian relations in the 1970s and beyond: an interperceptional study. New York, 1976. pp. 368.

TAN (SU-CHENG) The expansion of Soviet seapower and the security of Asia. Taipei, 1977. pp. 177. *bibliog.* *(Asia and the World Forum. Asia and the World Monographs. 3)*

— — Bulgaria.

CHICHOVSKA (VESELA) Sobolevata aktsiia. Sofiia, 1972. pp. 109. *bibliog.*

DEVEDJIEV (HRISTO H.) Stalinization of the Bulgarian society, 1949-1953. Philadelphia, [1975]. pp. 216. *bibliog.*

— — China.

[RUSSIA (U.S.S.R.). Soviet Embassy in London. Press Department]. Soviet Booklets. [2nd Series]. No. 120. On internationalism and nationalism; by L. Volodin. London, 1963. pp. 12.

BARNETT (ARTHUR DOAK) China and the major powers in east Asia. Washington, D.C., [1977]. pp. 416.

FOOT (ROSEMARY JUNE) New areas of tension and great power rivalry: central west Asia and Sino-Soviet relations, 1962-1974. 1976 [or rather 1977]. fo. 353. *bibliog.* *Typescript. Ph.D. (London) thesis: unpublished. This thesis is the property of London University and may not be removed from the Library.*

HINTON (HAROLD CLENDENIN) The Sino-Soviet confrontation: implications for the future. New York, [1977]. pp. 71. *(National Strategy Information Center. Strategy Papers. No. 29)*

KERRY (TOM) The Mao myth and the legacy of Stalinism in China. New York, [1977]. pp. 190.

SUTTER (ROBERT G.) China-watch: toward Sino-American reconciliation. Baltimore, [1978]. pp. 155. *bibliog.*

— — East (Near East).

MANGOLD (PETER) Superpower intervention in the Middle East. London, [1978]. pp. 209. *bibliog.*

— — Germany.

ARNDT (CLAUS) Die Verträge von Moskau und Warschau: politische, verfassungsrechtliche und völkerrechtliche Aspekte. Bonn, [1973]. pp. 216.

BELETSKII (VIKTOR NIKOLAEVICH) Die Politik der Sowjetunion in den deutschen Angelegenheiten in der Nachkriegszeit, 1945-1976; übersetzt von Wolfgang Eckstein [and others]. Berlin, 1977. pp. 429.

SCHLESINGER (MORITZ) Erinnerungen eines Aussenseiters im diplomatischen Dienst; aus dem Nachlass herausgegeben und eingeleitet von Hubert Schneider. Köln, [1977]. pp. 315.

— — India.

DRIEBERG (TREVOR) and others. Towards closer Indo-Soviet cooperation. Delhi, [1974]. pp. 182.

— — Iran.

ABDULLAEV (IUSUF NEGMATOVICH) Astrabad i russko-iranskie otnosheniia, vtoraia polovina XIX - nachalo XX v. Tashkent, 1975. pp. 132. *bibliog.*

— — Japan.

DETERRENT diplomacy: Japan, Germany and the USSR 1935-1940: selected translations from Taiheiyo senso e no michi: kaisen gaiko shi; edited by James William Morley. New York, 1976. pp. 363. *bibliog.* *(Columbia University. East Asian Institute. Studies)*

— — Korea.

CHUNG (CHIN O.) Pyongyang between Peking and Moscow: North Korea's involvement in the Sino-Soviet dispute, 1958-1975. University, Ala., [1978]. pp. 230. *bibliog.*

— — Mongolia.

MATERIALY po istorii russko-mongol'skikh otnoshenii. Moskva, 1974 in progress.

— — Poland.

BASIŃSKI (EUZEBIUSZ) and WALICHNOWSKI (TADEUSZ) Stosunki polsko-radzieckie, 1944-1974. Warszawa, 1974. pp. 272.

— — Romania.

AGAKI (ALEKSEI SOFRONOVICH) Russko-rumynskie mezhgosudarstvennye otnosheniia v kontse XIX- nachale XX v. Kishinev, 1976. pp. 187. *bibliog.*

— — United States.

GANELIN (RAFAIL SHOLOMOVICH) Sovetsko-amerikanskie otnosheniia v kontse 1917 - nachale 1918 g. Leningrad, 1976. pp. 202.

The MIDDLE East: critical choices for the United States; Eugene V. Rostow, editor. Boulder, Colo., 1976. pp. 211. *Papers of a symposium convened by the National Committee on American Foreign Policy, Inc.*

SIRACUSA (JOSEPH M.) ed. The American diplomatic revolution: a documentary history of the cold war, 1941-1947. Port Washington, 1977. pp. 265. *bibliog.*

GADDIS (JOHN LEWIS) Russia, the Soviet Union, and the United States: an interpretive history. New York, [1978]. pp. 309. *bibliog.*

— — Yugoslavia.

DRASKOVICH (SLOBODAN M.) Tito, Moscow's Trojan horse. Chicago, 1957. pp. 357.

— Historiography.

SHESTAKOV (SERGEI VASIL'EVICH) Istoriografiia deiatel'nosti bol'shevistskoi partii v period pervoi mirovoi voiny i Fevral'skoi revoliutsii. Moskva, 1977. pp. 296.

VOPROSY metodologii i istorii istoricheskoi nauki. Moskva, 1977. pp. 315.

— History — Sources — Bibliography.

ZHITOMIRSKAIA (S.V.) ed. Vospominaniia i dnevniki XVIII-XX vv.: ukazatel' rukopisei, etc. Moskva, 1976. pp. 621.

— — 1689-1800.

ANDERSON (MATTHEW SMITH) Peter the Great. London, [1978]. pp. 207. *bibliog.*

— — 1800-1899.

GEYER (DIETRICH) Der russische Imperialismus: Studien über den Zusammenhang von innerer und auswärtiger Politik, 1860-1914. Göttingen, 1977. pp. 344. *bibliog.*

— — 1825, Conspiracy of December.

NECHKINA (MILITSA VASIL'EVNA) Griboedov i dekabristy. 3rd ed. Moskva, 1977. pp. 735.

— — 1894-1917.

GEYER (DIETRICH) Der russische Imperialismus: Studien über den Zusammenhang von innerer und auswärtiger Politik, 1860-1914. Göttingen, 1977. pp. 344. *bibliog.*

PEARSON (RAYMOND) The Russian moderates and the crisis of tsarism, 1914-1917. London, 1977. pp. 208. *bibliog.*

SALISBURY (HARRISON EVANS) Black night, white snow: Russia's revolutions, 1905-1917. London, 1978. pp. 746. *bibliog.*

— — — Pictorial works.

FITZLYON (KYRIL) and BROWNING (TATIANA) Before the revolution: a view of Russia under the last Tsar. London, 1977. pp. 205.

— — 1900- .

TREADGOLD (DONALD WARREN) Twentieth century Russia. 4th ed. Chicago [1976]. pp. 573. *bibliog.*

— — 1905, Revolution of.

KHRONIKA revoliutsionnykh sobytii na Odesshchine v gody pervoi russkoi revoliutsii, 1905-1907 gg. Odessa, 1976. pp. 207. *bibliog.*

MOSKOVSKIE bol'sheviki v ogne revoliutsionnykh boev: vospominaniia. Moskva, 1976. pp. 415.

— — 1917, February Revolution.

MOSKOVSKIE bol'sheviki v ogne revoliutsionnykh boev: vospominaniia. Moskva, 1976. pp. 415.

— — 1917- .

L'AVANGUARDIA dopo la rivoluzione: le riviste degli anni Venti nell'URSS: "Il giornale dei futuristi", "L'arte della Comune", "Il Lef", "Il nuovo Lef"; introduzione e cura di Luigi Magarotto. Roma, 1976. pp. 304.

BOFFA (GIUSEPPE) and MARTINET (GILLES) Dialogo sullo stalinismo. [Roma, 1976]. pp. 205.

AIMS FOR FREEDOM AND ENTERPRISE. 1917-1977: sixty years of communism: the age of the Gulag. London, [1977]. pp. 13.

BETTELHEIM (CHARLES) Les luttes de classes en URSS: deuxième période, 1923-1930. [Paris, 1977]. pp. 605. *bibliog.*

SZAMUELY (TIBOR) Socialism and liberty. London, [1977]. pp. 20. *Reprint with postscript of work first published in 1971.*

WODDIS (JACK) How October 1917 changed the world. London, [1977]. pp. 24. *(Communist Party of Great Britain. Communist Party Pamphlets)*

— — 1917-1936.

RUSSIAN NATIONAL UNION. Address to the members of the League of Nations. Paris, 1922. pp. 8.

SOBOLEV (PETR NIKIFOROVICH) Uprochenie soiuza rabochikh i krest'ian v pervyi god proletarskoi diktatury. Moskva, 1977. pp. 320.

RUSSIA.(Cont.)

— — 1917-1921, Revolution.

LA CHESNAIS (PIERRE GEORGET) The defence of the Cossacks against Bolchevism. Paris, 1919. pp. 15.

CHAMBERLIN (WILLIAM HENRY) The Russian revolution 1917-1921. New York, 1965. 2 vols. *bibliog.*

ZNAMENSKII (OLEG NIKOLAEVICH) Vserossiiskoe Uchreditel'noe sobranie: istoriia sozyva i politicheskogo krusheniia. Leningrad, 1976. pp. 364.

ERYKALOV (EFREM FEDOROVICH) and KAMESHKOV (BORIS NIKONOVICH) Leninskii TsK - shtab Velikogo Oktiabria. Leningrad, 1977. pp. 279.

MINTS (ISAAK IZRAILEVICH) Istoriia Velikogo Oktiabria v trekh tomakh. t.1. Sverzhenie samoderzhaviia. 2nd ed. Moskva, 1977. pp. 784.

PIECK (WILHELM) Wilhelm Pieck: ein unermüdlicher Streiter für die deutsch- sowjetische Freundschaft: ausgewählte Reden und Schriften... ; eingeleitet und zusammengestellt von Heinz Vosske. Berlin, 1977. pp. 159.

TYRKOVA-VIL'IAMS (ARIADNA VLADIMIROVNA) From liberty to Brest-Litovsk: the first year of the Russian revolution. Westport, Conn., 1977. pp. 526. *First published by Macmillan, London, in 1919.*

WODDIS (JACK) How October 1917 changed the world. London, [1977]. pp. 24. *(Communist Party of Great Britain. Communist Party Pamphlets)*

— — — Campaigns.

VOORUZHENNYE sily Velikogo Oktiabria. Moskva, 1977. pp. 287. *bibliog.*

— — — Dictionaries and encyclopedias.

VELIKAIA Oktiabr'skaia sotsialisticheskaia revoliutsiia: entsiklopediia; pod redaktsiei G.N. Golikova, M.I. Kuznetsova, etc. Moskva, 1977. pp. 711.

— — — Foreign participation, French.

PASCAL (PIERRE) En communisme: mon journal de Russie, 1918-1921. [Lausanne, 1977]. pp. 226.

— — — Foreign participation, Yugoslav.

DAMJANOVIĆ (P.) and others, eds. Uchastie iugoslavskikh trudiashchikhsia v Oktiabr'skoi revoliutsii i grazhdanskoi voine v SSSR: sbornik dokumentov i materialov. Moskva, 1976. pp. 556.

— — — Foreign public opinion.

ZARODOV (KONSTANTIN IVANOVICH) Tri revoliutsii v Rossii i nashe vremia. 2nd ed. Moskva, 1977. pp. 636.

— — — Historiography.

PARTIIA i Velikii Oktiabr': istoriograficheskii ocherk. Moskva, 1976. pp. 294.

— — — Personal narratives.

MOSKOVSKIE bol'sheviki v ogne revoliutsionnykh boev: vospominaniia. Moskva, 1976. pp. 415.

PASCAL (PIERRE) En communisme: mon journal de Russie, 1918-1921. [Lausanne, 1977]. pp. 226.

— — 1918-1920, Allied Intervention.

KING (JOSEPH) M.P. Why does killing go on in Russia?: a scathing exposure of the Allies' efforts to crush new Russia in the interests of capitalists and financiers. Glasgow, [1919]. pp. 8. *(Reformers' Bookstall. Reformers' Series. No. 26)*

PEOPLE'S RUSSIAN INFORMATION BUREAU. [Leaflets on the civil war]. London, 1919. 6 parts (in 1 vol.).

— — 1925-1953.

STRONG (ANNA LOUISE) The Stalin era. [Belfast], 1976. pp. 77. *First published in 1956.*

— — 1941-1945, German occupation.

PARTIIA vo glave narodnoi bor'by v tylu vraga, 1941-1944 gg. Moskva, 1976. pp. 325.

— Industries.

KORNEICHEVA (TAT'IANA KONSTANTINOVNA) and NAZAROV (VALENTIN KONSTANTINOVICH) Kreditovanie legkoi promyshlennosti. Moskva, 1976. pp. 96.

KOVALENKO (DMITRII ALEKSANDROVICH) Lenin i sotsialisticheskie preobrazovaniia v promyshlennosti Sovetskoi Rossii, 1917-1920 gg. Moskva, 1976. pp. 368. *bibliog.*

NAUCHNO-ISSLEDOVATEL'SKII INSTITUT PLANIROVANIIA I NORMATIVOV. Nauchnye Trudy. Voprosy sovershenstvovaniia planirovaniia promyshlennosti v svete reshenij XXV s"ezda KPSS; pod redaktsiei N.M. Oznobina, A.I. Zalkinda. Moskva, 1976. pp. 182.

DANILENKO (ANATOLII IVANOVICH) and others. Finansovo-kreditnye problemy sotsialisticheskoi promyshlennosti. Kiev, 1977. pp. 260. *bibliog.*

DVOINISHNIKOV (MIKHAIL ALEKSANDROVICH) Rukovodstvo KPSS vosstanovleniem i pazvitiem promyshlennosti v poslevoennyi period. Moskva, 1977. pp. 128.

KHLUSOV (MIKHAIL IVANOVICH) Razvitie sovetskoi industrii, 1946-1958. Moskva, 1977. pp. 280.

— — Mathematical models.

STUDIES in Soviet input-output analysis; edited by Vladimir G. Treml. New York, 1977. pp. 446. *bibliogs.*

— Intellectual life.

SCHWARZ-LIEBERMANN VON WAHLENDORF (HANS ALBRECHT) Positions internationales de la Russie soviétique: tradition et idéologie. Paris, [1977]. pp. 311.

CULTURAL revolution in Russia, 1928-1931; edited by Sheila Fitzpatrick. Bloomington, Ind., [1978]. pp. 309. *(Columbia University. Russian Institute. Studies)*

— Military policy.

FRANK (LEWIS ALLEN) Soviet nuclear planning: a point of view on SALT. Washington, D.C., [1977]. pp. 63. *(American Enterprise Institute for Public Policy Research. AEI Studies. 140)*

TAHTINEN (DALE R.) and LENCZOWSKI (JOHN) Arms in the Indian Ocean: interests and challenges. Washington, D.C., [1977]. pp. 84. *(American Enterprise Institute for Public Policy Research. AEI Studies. 145)*

WARNER (EDWARD L.) The military in contemporary Soviet politics: an institutional analysis. New York, 1977. pp. 314. *bibliog.*

CROZIER (BRIAN) The surrogate forces of the Soviet Union. London, 1978. pp. 20. *(Institute for the Study of Conflict. Conflict Studies. No. 92)*

GALLOIS (PIERRE MARIE) Soviet military doctrine and European defence: NATO's obsolete concepts. London, 1978. pp. 17. *(Institute for the Study of Conflict. Conflict Studies. No. 96)*

— Nationalism.

LENINSKAIA natsional'naia politika i bor'ba protiv ee fal'sifikatorov; redaktsionnaia kollegiia M.B. Mitin [and others]. Ashkhabad, 1975. pp. 423.

— Navy.

TAN (SU-CHENG) The expansion of Soviet seapower and the security of Asia. Taipei, 1977. pp. 177. *bibliog. (Asia and the World Forum. Asia and the World Monographs. 3)*

— Politics and government.

BELOV (GENNADII ANATOL'EVICH) Politicheskie otnosheniia sotsialisticheskogo tipa: politicheskie otnosheniia v sisteme sotsialisticheskikh obshchestvennykh otnoshenii. Moskva, 1976. pp. 184.

SOVETSKAIA demokratiia v period razvitogo sotsializma; otvetstvennyi redaktor D.A. Kerimov. Moskva, 1976. pp. 279.

GOSUDARSTVO, demokratiia i trudovoi kollektiv v razvitom sotsialisticheskom obshchestve. Moskva, 1977. pp. 200.

KOREL'SKII (VIKTOR MIKHAILOVICH) Demokratiia i distsiplina v razvitom sotsialisticheskom obshchestve. Moskva, 1977. pp. 136.

MARCHENKO (MIKHAIL NIKOLAEVICH) Demokraticheskie osnovy politicheskoi organizatsii sovetskogo obshchestva. Moskva, 1977. pp. 199.

ARMSTRONG (JOHN ALEXANDER) Ideology, politics, and government in the Soviet Union: an introduction. 4th ed. New York, [1978]. pp. 240.

ROTHMAN (STANLEY) and BRESLAUER (GEORGE W.) Soviet politics and society. St. Paul, [1978]. pp. 341. *bibliog.*

— — 1800-1899.

BROIDO (VERA) Apostles into terrorists: women and the revolutionary movement in the Russia of Alexander II. New York, 1977. pp. 238. *bibliog.*

— — 1894-1936.

DZERZHINSKII (FELIKS EDMUNDOVICH) Izbrannye proizvedeniia, (1897-1926). 3rd ed. Moskva, 1977. 2 vols.

— — 1894-1917.

VTOROI s"ezd RSDRP i mestnye partiinye organizatsii Rossii. Perm', 1973. pp. 722.

McKEAN (R.B.) The Russian constitutional monarchy, 1907-17. London, [1977]. pp. 47. *bibliog. (Historical Association. General Series. G.91)*

PEARSON (RAYMOND) The Russian moderates and the crisis of tsarism, 1914-1917. London, 1977. pp. 208. *bibliog.*

RAZGON (ANATOLII IZRAILEVICH) VTsIK Sovetov v pervye mesiatsy diktatury proletariata. Moskva, 1977. pp. 335.

SHESTAKOV (SERGEI VASIL'EVICH) Istoriografiia deiatel'nosti bol'shevistskoi partii v period pervoi mirovoi voiny i Fevral'skoi revoliutsii. Moskva, 1977. pp. 296.

— — 1917- .

KING (JOSEPH) M.P. Why does killing go on in Russia?: a scathing exposure of the Allies' efforts to crush new Russia in the interests of capitalists and financiers. Glasgow, [1919]. pp. 8. *(Reformers' Bookstall. Reformers' Series. No. 26)*

TROTSKII (LEV DAVYDOVICH) The basic writings of Trotsky; edited and introduced by Irving Howe. New York, 1976. pp. 427. *Reprint of the ed. published by Random House in 1963.*

ALDWINCKLE (LINDA DENISE) The politics of Novyi Mir, 1950-1970. [1977]. fo.387. Typescript. Ph.D. (London) thesis: unpublished. *This thesis is the property of London University and may not be removed from the Library.*

FRANK (PIERRE) Le stalinisme. Paris, 1977. pp. 221.

HOUGH (JERRY F.) The Soviet Union and social science theory. Cambridge, Mass., 1977. pp. 275. *(Harvard University. Russian Research Center. Studies. 77)*

SCHAPIRO (LEONARD BERTRAM) The government and politics of the Soviet Union. 6th ed. London, 1977. pp. 192. *bibliog.*

RUSSIA.(Cont.)

LANE (DAVID) Politics and society in the USSR. 2nd ed. London, 1978. pp. 622. *bibliogs.*

— 1917-1953.

ANDRUKHOV (NIKOLAI ROMANOVICH) Partiinoe stroitel'stvo v period bor'by za pobedu sotsializma v SSSR, 1917-1937. Moskva, 1977. pp. 375.

STEPHAN (JOHN JASON) The Russian fascists: tragedy and farce in exile, 1925-1945. London, 1978. pp. 450. *bibliog.*

— 1917-1936.

SERGE (VICTOR) pseud. [i.e. Viktor L'vovich KIBAL'CHICH] Le tournant obscur; présentation de Magdeleine Paz; suivi de Pour Victor Serge. Paris, [1972]. pp. 205. *A variant text of his Mémoires d'un révolutionnaire.*

— 1936-1953.

AVTORKHANOV (ABDURAKHMAN) Zagadka smerti Stalina: zagovor Beriia. [Frankfurt, 1976]. pp. 317.

TROTSKII (LEV DAVYDOVICH) Stalin's gangsters. [London, 1977]. pp. 84. *First published as Los gangsters de Stalin, Mexico City, 1940.*

— 1953- .

HARRIMAN (WILLIAM AVERELL) Peace with Russia? nEW yORK, 1959. PP. 174.

MEYER (GERD) Writer on Soviet affairs. Bürokratischer Sozialismus: eine Analyse des sowjetischen Herrschaftssystems. Stuttgart-Bad Cannstatt, 1977. pp. 331. *bibliog. With English summary.*

WARNER (EDWARD L.) The military in contemporary Soviet politics: an institutional analysis. New York, 1977. pp. 314. *bibliog.*

BARRY (DONALD D.) and BARNER-BARRY (CAROL) Contemporary Soviet politics: an introduction. Englewood Cliffs., [1978]. pp. 406. *bibliogs.*

SOLOMON (PETER H.) Soviet criminologists and criminal policy: specialists in policy- making. London, 1978. pp. 253. *bibliog.*

— — 1964- .

KAISER (ROBERT G.) Russia: the people and the power. New York, 1976. pp. 499. *bibliog.*

SOVERSHENSTVOVANIE raboty Sovetov v sovremennykh usloviiakh. Moskva, 1976. pp. 116.

The SOVIET Union since the fall of Khrushchev; edited by Archie Brown and Michael Kaser. 2nd ed. London, 1978. pp. 351.

— Population.

BONDARSKAIA (GALINA ALEKSEEVNA) Rozhdaemost' v SSSR: etnodemograficheskii aspekt. Moskva, 1977. pp. 127. *bibliog.*

CHINN (JEFF) Manipulating Soviet population resources. London, 1977. pp. 163. *bibliog.*

— Princes and princesses.

RAPOV (OLEG MIKHAILOVICH) Kniazheskie vladeniia na Rusi v X - pervoi polovine XIII v. Moskva, 1977. pp. 261.

— Relations (general) with Bulgaria.

PAVLENKO (VIKTORIIA VIKTOROVNA) Solidarnost' trudiashchikhsia Ukrainskoi SSR s revoliutsionnoi bor'boi rabochikh i krest'ian Bolgarii, 1923-1934 gg. Kiev, 1977. pp. 140.

— Relations (general) with Communist countries.

NA putiakh nerushimoi druzhby: materialy vsesoiuznoi nauchnoi konferentsii "Istoricheskoe znachenie ustanovleniia druzhby i sotrudnichestva mezhdu SSSR i sotsialisticheskimi stranami Evropy", g. Moskva, 24-25 fevralia 1975 g. Moskva, 1977. pp. 319.

— Relations (general) with Germany.

FRICKE (DIETER) and SHNEERSON (L.M.) eds. Iz istorii germanskogo rabochego dvizheniia i sovetsko-germanskogo internatsional'nogo sodruzhestva: sbornik statei. Minsk, 1975. pp. 208.

WEILL (CLAUDIE) Marxistes russes et social-démocratie allemande, 1898-1904. Paris, 1977. pp. 254. *bibliog.*

— Relations (general) with Poland.

OCHERKI revoliutsionnykh sviazei narodov Rossii i Pol'shi, 1815-1917; pod redaktsiei V.A. D'iakova [and others]. Moskva, 1976. pp. 602.

SSSR i Pol'sha: internatsional'nye sviazi - istoriia i sovremennost'. Moskva, 1977 in progress.

— Relations (general) with Romania.

STOROZHUK (VLADIMIR PROKOF'EVICH) Rabochee dvizhenie v Rumynii i rumyno-russkie revoliutsionnye sviazi, 1893-1907. Kishinev, 1977. pp. 175. *bibliog.*

— Relations (military) with the United States.

FREEDMAN (LAWRENCE DAVID) US intelligence and the Soviet strategic threat. London, 1977. pp. 235. *bibliog.*

— Religion.

EMELIAKH (LIUBOV' ISAAKOVNA) Krest'iane i tserkov' nakanune Oktiabria. Leningrad, 1976. pp. 182. *bibliog. (Akademiia Nauk SSSR. Nauchno-Ateisticheskaia Seriia)*

— Rural conditions.

SAADANBEKOV (ZHUMAGUL) O sotsial'noi psikhologii sel'skoi intelligentsii. Frunze, 1975. pp. 88.

PUZANEV (VLADIMIR SEMENOVICH) Sel'skii intelligent. Moskva, 1977. pp. 253.

— Social conditions.

AMVROSOV (ANATOLII ALEKSANDROVICH) Sotsial'naia struktura sovetskogo obshchestva. Moskva, 1975. pp. 120.

KAISER (ROBERT G.) Russia: the people and the power. New York, 1976. pp. 499. *bibliog.*

SOTSIOLOGIIA i sovremennost'. Moskva, 1977. 2 vols.

Die SOZIALISTISCHE Gesellschaft: Wesen, Entwicklung, Perspektiven; ([by] R. I. Kossolapow [and others]; Übersetzung [from the Russian]: Wolfgang Eckstein). Frankfurt am Main, 1977. pp. 327.

YANOWITCH (MURRAY) Social and economic inequality in the Soviet Union: six studies. London, 1977. pp. 196. *bibliog.*

BARRY (DONALD D.) and BARNER-BARRY (CAROL) Contemporary Soviet politics: an introduction. Englewood Cliffs., [1978]. pp. 406. *bibliogs.*

LANE (DAVID) Politics and society in the USSR. 2nd ed. London, 1978. pp. 622. *bibliogs.*

ROTHMAN (STANLEY) and BRESLAUER (GEORGE W.) Soviet politics and society. St. Paul, [1978]. pp. 341. *bibliog.*

The SOVIET Union since the fall of Khrushchev; edited by Archie Brown and Michael Kaser. 2nd ed. London, 1978. pp. 351.

— Social history — Pictorial works.

FITZLYON (KYRIL) and BROWNING (TATIANA) Before the revolution: a view of Russia under the last Tsar. London, 1977. pp. 205.

— Social life and customs.

FITZLYON (KYRIL) and BROWNING (TATIANA) Before the revolution: a view of Russia under the last Tsar. London, 1977. pp. 205.

ZUIKOVA (ELIZAVETA MIKHAILOVNA) Byt pri sotsializme. Moskva, 1977. pp. 240. *bibliog.*

— — Pictorial works.

RUSSIA in original photographs 1860-1920; [selected by] Marvin Lyons; edited by Andrew Wheatcroft. London, 1977. pp. 211.

— Social policy.

KORENEVSKAIA (ELENA IGNAT'EVNA) Mestnye Sovety i sotsial'noe planirovanie. Moskva, 1977. pp. 104.

SOCIAL scientists and policy making in the USSR; edited by Richard B. Remnek. New York, 1977. pp. 144.

STRUKOV (EDUARD VLADIMIROVICH) Sotsialisticheskii obraz zhizni: teoreticheskie i ideino-vospitatel'nye problemy. Moskva, 1977. pp. 263. *bibliog.*

— Verkhovnyi Sovet.

VANNEMAN (PETER) The Supreme Soviet: politics and the legislative process in the Soviet political system. Durham, N.C., 1977. pp. 256. *(Consortium for Comparative Legislative Studies. Publications)*

RUSSIAN LANGUAGE

— Dictionaries — Polyglot.

HEBÁK (PETR) and HUSTOPECKÝ (JIŘÍ) compilers. Šestijazyčný slovník termínů z regresní analýzy: [Czech, Russian, Polish, English, French, German]. Praha, 1978. pp. 211. *With preface and explanatory notes in each language.*

RUSSIAN LITERATURE

— History and criticism.

A.N. Radishchev i literatura ego vremeni. Leningrad, 1977. pp. 260. *(Akademiia Nauk SSSR. Institut Russkoi Literatury. XVIII Vek. sb.12)*

GORIACHKINA (MARIIA SERGEEVNA) Satira Shchedrina i russkaia demokraticheskaia literatura 60-80-kh godov XIX veka. Moskva, 1977. pp. 175.

SOTSIALISTICHESKII realizm segodnia: problemy i suzhdeniia. Moskva, 1977. pp. 396.

RUSSIAN NEWSPAPERS.

KUZNETSOV (IVAN VASIL'EVICH) and FINGERIT (EFIM MARKOVICH) Gazetnyi mir Sovetskogo Soiuza, 1917-1970 gg. Moskva, 1972-76. 2 vols.

RUSSIAN PERIODICALS.

L'AVANGUARDIA dopo la rivoluzione: le riviste degli anni Venti nell'URSS: "Il giornale dei futuristi", "L'arte della Comune", "Il Lef", "Il nuovo Lef"; introduzione e cura di Luigi Magarotto. Roma, 1976. pp. 304.

ALDWINCKLE (LINDA DENISE) The politics of Novyi Mir, 1950-1970. [1977]. fo.387. *bibliog. Typescript. Ph.D. (London) thesis: unpublished. This thesis is the property of London University and may not be removed from the Library.*

CHERTKOV (VLADIMIR LAZAREVICH) Avtorskoe pravo v periodicheskoi pechati. Moskva, 1977. pp. 103.

RUSSIAN POETRY.

POSTNOV (IURII SERGEEVICH) Sibir' v poezii dekabristov. Novosibirsk, 1976. pp. 112. *(Akademiia Nauk SSSR. Sibirskoe Otdelenie. Institut Istorii, Filologii i Filosofii. Nauchno-Populiarnaia Seriia)*

RUSSIANS IN ESTONIA.

RIKHTER (ELIZAVETA VLADIMIROVNA) Russkoe naselenie zapadnogo Prichud'ia: ocherki istorii, material'noi i dukhovnoi kul'tury. Tallin, 1976. pp. 292.

RUSSIANS IN FOREIGN COUNTRIES.

STEPHAN (JOHN JASON) The Russian fascists: tragedy and farce in exile, 1925-1945. London, 1978. pp. 450. *bibliog.*

RUTHENIA

— History.

MAGOCSI (PAUL ROBERT) The shaping of a national identity: Subcarpathian Rus', 1848- 1948. Cambridge, Mass., 1978. pp. 640. *bibliog.*

RYAN (THOMAS JOSEPH).

MURPHY (DENIS J.) T.J. Ryan: a political biography. St. Lucia, Queensland, [1975]. pp. 596. *bibliog.*

RYCHLINSKI (STANISLAW).

WÓJCIK (PRZEMYSŁAW) Z rodowodu socjalistycznej polityki społecznej: koncepcje i poglądy Stanisława Rychlińskiego. Warszawa, 1976. pp. 234. *bibliog.*

SABAH

— Appropriations and expenditures.

SABAH. State development budget. a., 1976- Kota Kinabulu. *[in English and Malay]*

SACCHARIN.

The SACCHARIN ban: risks vs. benefits; (a Round Table held on April 21, 1977 and sponsored by the Center for Health Policy Research of the American Enterprise Institute for Public Policy Research [in] Washington); John Charles Daly, moderator, etc. Washington, [1977]. pp. 42. *(American Enterprise Institute for Public Policy Research. Round Tables)*

SACCO (NICOLA).

PORTER (KATHERINE ANNE) The never-ending wrong. London, 1977. pp. 64. *bibliog.*

SAENZ PEÑA (ROQUE).

ARENAS LUQUE (FERMIN V.) Roque Saenz Peña: el presidente del sufragio libre. Buenos Aires, 1951. pp. 292.

SAFES.

CHUBB AND SON'S LOCK AND SAFE COMPANY. Contemporary observations on security from the Chubb collectanea, 1818-1968; [edited by] Noel Currer-Briggs. London, [1970?]. 1 vol. (unpaged).

ŞAGUNA (ANDREIU) Baron.

HITCHINS (KEITH) Orthodoxy and nationality: Andreiu Şaguna and the Rumanians of Transylvania, 1846-1873. Cambridge, Mass., 1977. pp. 332. *bibliog. (Harvard University. Harvard Historical Studies. vol. 94)*

SAHARA.

CRIADO (RAMON) Sahara: pasion y muerte de un sueño colonial. [Paris, 1977]. pp. 303.

SAHEL

— Economic policy.

BERG (ELLIOT J.) The economic impact of drought and inflation in the Sahel. Ann Arbor, 1976. fo. 35. *(Michigan University. Center for Research on Economic Development. Discussion Papers. No. 51)*

— Famines.

MARNHAM (PATRICK) Nomads of the Sahel. London, 1977. pp. 19. *bibliog. (Minority Rights Group. Reports. No. 33)*

ST. ALBANS

— Church history.

CATHEDRAL and city: St. Albans ancient and modern; edited by Robert Runcie. London, 1977. pp. 149. *bibliog.*

SAINT-FLOUR

— Social history.

RIGAUDIERE (ALBERT) L'assiette de l'impôt direct à la fin du XIVe siècle: le livre d'estimes des Consuls de St-Flour pour les annees 1380-1385. Paris, [1977]. pp. 470. *bibliog. (Rouen. Université. Publications. 37)*

ST. KILDA

— Rural conditions.

MACLEAN (CHARLES) Author of Island on the edge of the world. Island on the edge of the world: the story of St. Kilda. rev. ed. Edinburgh, 1977. pp. 160. *bibliog.*

ST. LAWRENCE RIVER.

CANADA. St Lawrence Seaway Authority. The Seaway: operations, outlook, statistics. a., 1977- Ottawa. *[in English and French] Supersedes CANADA. St. Lawrence Seaway Authority. Traffic report of the St. Lawrence Seaway.*

SALARIED EMPLOYEES

— Germany.

KOCKA (JUERGEN) Angestellte zwischen Faschismus und Demokratie: zur politischen Sozialgeschichte der Angestellten: USA, 1890-1940, im internationalen Vergleich. Göttingen, 1977. pp. 556. *bibliog.*

— United States.

KOCKA (JUERGEN) Angestellte zwischen Faschismus und Demokratie: zur politischen Sozialgeschichte der Angestellten: USA, 1890-1940, im internationalen Vergleich. Göttingen, 1977. pp. 556. *bibliog.*

SALAZAR (ROSENDO).

SALAZAR (ROSENDO) Rosendo Salazar: [Las pugnas de la gleba; La Casa del Obrero Mundial; La C.T.M.]. Mexico, 1972. 2 vols.

SALEM, MASSACHUSETTS

— History.

GILDRIE (RICHARD P.) Salem, Massachusetts, 1626-1683: a covenant community. Charlottesville, 1975. pp. 187. *bibliog.*

— Religious life and customs.

GILDRIE (RICHARD P.) Salem, Massachusetts, 1626-1683: a covenant community. Charlottesville, 1975. pp. 187. *bibliog.*

SALES

— United Kingdom.

BENJAMIN (JUDAH PHILIP) Sale of goods; [edited by A.G. Guest and others]. London, 1974. pp. 1287.

SALES TAX.

CNOSSEN (SIJBREN) Excise systems: a global study of the selective taxation of goods and services. Baltimore, [1977]. pp. 192. *bibliog.*

— Poland.

GUTERMANN (CZESŁAW) Tabele podatków obrotowego i dochodowego dla rzemiosła i innej działalności zarobkowej według stanu prawnego na dzień 15 maja 1975 r. Warszawa, 1975. pp. 111.

SALFORD

— Politics and government.

GARRARD (JOHN A.) Leaders and politics in nineteenth century Salford: a historical analysis of urban political power. [Salford, 1977]. pp. 91.

SALINE WATER CONVERSION.

INTERREGIONAL SEMINAR ON THE ECONOMIC APPLICATION OF WATER DESALINATION, NEW YORK, 1965. Proceedings of the Interregional Seminar...[held in] New York, 22 September - 2 October 1965. (ST/TAO/SER. C/90). New York, United Nations, 1967. pp. 367.

UNITED NATIONS. Department of Economic and Social Affairs. 1969. First United Nations desalination plant operation survey: a technical and economic analysis of the performance of desalination plants in operation. (ST/ECA/112). New York, 1969. pp. 122.

UNITED NATIONS. Department of Economic and Social Affairs. 1970. Solar distillation as a means of meeting small-scale water demands. (ST/ECA/121). New York, 1970. pp. 86. *bibliog.*

SALISBURY

— Population.

CONSTABLE (DEREK) Household structure in three English market towns, 1851-1871. Reading, 1977. pp. 63. *(Reading. University. Department of Geography. Reading Geographical Papers. No. 55)*

— Social history.

CONSTABLE (DEREK) Household structure in three English market towns, 1851-1871. Reading, 1977. pp. 63. *(Reading. University. Department of Geography. Reading Geographical Papers. No. 55)*

SALTYKOV-SHCHEDRIN (MIKHAIL EVGRAFOVICH).

GORIACHKINA (MARIIA SERGEEVNA) Satira Shchedrina i russkaia demokraticheskaia literatura 60-80-kh godov XIX veka. Moskva, 1977. pp. 175.

SALVADOR

— Foreign economic relations — Honduras.

JIMENEZ (EDDY E.) La guerra no fue de futbol. La Habana, 1974. pp. 165.

SALVATION ARMY

— Canada.

MOYLES (ROBERT G.) The blood and fire in Canada: a history of the Salvation Army in the Dominion, 1882-1976. Toronto, [1977]. pp. 312. *bibliog.*

SAMPLING (STATISTICS).

CASSEL (CLAES-MAGNUS) and others. Foundations of inference in survey sampling. New York, [1977]. pp. 192. *bibliog.*

NORWAY. Statistiske Centralbyrå. 1977. Prinsipper og metoder for Statistisk Sentralbyrås utvalgsundersøkelser: Sampling methods applied by the Central Bureau of Statistics of Norway. Oslo, 1977. pp. 103. *bibliog. (Samfunnsøkonomiske Studier. 33) With English summary.*

BARNETT (VIC) and LEWIS (TOBIAS) Outliers in statistical data. Chichester, [1978]. pp. 365. *bibliog.*

WILLIAMS (WILLIAM HOWARD) A sampler on sampling. New York, [1978]. pp. 254.

SAN FRANCISCO

— History.

LOTCHIN (ROGER W.) San Francisco 1846-1856: from hamlet to city. New York, 1974. pp. 406.

SAN FRANCISCO (Cont.)

— Social history.

LOTCHIN (ROGER W.) San Francisco 1846-1856: from hamlet to city. New York, 1974. pp. 406.

SAN GIORGIO, ALBANESE

— Rural conditions.

GLASSER (RALPH) The net and the quest: patterns of community and how they can survive progress. London, 1977. pp. 263. *bibliog.*

SANCTIONS (INTERNATIONAL LAW).

STRACK (HARRY R.) Sanctions: the case of Rhodesia. Syracuse, N.Y., 1978. pp. 296. *bibliog.*

SANGER (MARGARET).

SANGER (MARGARET) Woman of the future; including Margaret Sanger: crusader, by Mildred Adams. London, 1934. pp. 32.

SANGUINETTI (GIANFRANCO).

SANGUINETTI (GIANFRANCO) Prove dell'inesistenza di Censor, enunciate dal suo autore. Milano, 1976. pp. 24.

SANTA FE TRAIL.

CONNOR (SEYMOUR V.) and SKAGGS (JIMMY M.) Broadcloth and britches: the Santa Fe trade. College Station, Tex., [1977]. pp. 225. *bibliog.*

SANTIAGO DE CHILE

— Poor.

ALDUNATE (ADOLFO) Participacion y actitud de los pobladores ante las organizaciones poblacionales: una aproximacion a la heterogeneidad popular. Santiago, Chile, 1971. fo. 103.

SÃO PAULO (CITY)

— Poor.

BERLINCK (MANOEL T.) Marginalidade social e relações de classes em São Paulo. Petropolis, 1975. pp. 152. *bibliogs.*

SÃO PAULO (STATE)

— Economic conditions — Statistics.

SÃO PAULO (STATE). Secretaria de Economia e Planejamento. Departamento de Estatistica. Estatisticas economicas. m., Mr 1977-Ag/N 1977. [São Paulo]. *Later data included in SÃO PAULO (STATE). Secretaria de Economia e Planejamento. Coordenadoria de Analise de Dados. Boletim de dados conjunturais.*

SÃO PAULO (STATE). Secretaria de Economia e Planejamento. Coordenadoria de Analise de Dados. Boletin de dados conjunturais. m., Jl 1978 (v. 3, no. 7)- São Paulo. *Includes data previously pd. in SÃO PAULO (STATE). Secretaria de Economia e Planejamento. Departamento de Estatistica. Estatisticas economicas.*

— History — 1932, Revolution.

PICCHIA (MENOTTI DEL) A revolução paulista: atravez de um testemunho, do Gabinete do Governador. São Paulo, 1932. pp. 304.

— Population.

BRAZIL. Conselho Nacional de Estatistica. Laboratorio de Estatistica. 1959. A contribuição das diversas unidades da federação e regiões fisiograficas para a população de São Paulo;... estudo redigido pelo Maria Cascaes Brasil. [Rio de Janeiro, 1959]. fo. 12. *(Estudos Demograficos. No. 246)*

IKEDA (AKIHIRO) and BUENO (LUIZ DE FREITAS) Analise demografica do Estado de São Paulo. São Paulo, 1967. fo. 45. *(Associação Nacional de Programação Econômica e Social. Estudos Anpes. No. 12)*

— Social conditions — Statistics.

SÃO PAULO (STATE). Secretaria de Economia e Planejamento. Coordenadoria de Analise de Dados. Boletin de dados conjunturais. m., Jl 1978 (v. 3, no. 7)- São Paulo. *Includes data previously pd. in SÃO PAULO (STATE). Secretaria de Economia e Planejamento. Departamento de Estatistica. Estatisticas economicas.*

SAÔNE-ET-LOIRE.

FRANCE. Direction de la Documentation. La Documentation Française. Notes et Etudes Documentaires. Nos. 4,356-4, 357-4,358. Les départements français. 71. Saône-et-Loire, Bourgogne; (étude...réalisée...par Daniel Pérault). Paris, 1977. pp. 107.

SARASWATS.

CONLON (FRANK F.) A caste in a changing world: the Chitrapur Saraswat Brahmans, 1700-1935. Berkeley, Calif., [1977]. pp. 255. *bibliog.*

SARAWAK

— Council Negri — Salaries, pensions, etc.

SARAWAK. Council Negri. Sessional Papers. 1963. No.5. Privileges for the Chief Minister and other members of the Supreme Council, the Speaker and members of the Council Negri. [Kuching], 1963. fo.2. *Xerox copy.*

— Economic conditions.

SARAWAK. State Development Office. 1968. Sarawak development progress, 1964-1967. [Kuching, 1968?]. pp. 94.

SARAWAK. State Development Office. 1971. Sarawak development progress, 1968-1970. [Kuching, 1971?]. pp. 167.

— Rural conditions.

GRIJPSTRA (B.G.) Common efforts in the development of rural Sarawak, Malaysia. Assen, 1976. pp. 231. *bibliog. (Studies of Developing Countries. 20)*

— Social conditions.

SARAWAK. State Development Office. 1968. Sarawak development progress, 1964-1967. [Kuching, 1968?]. pp. 94.

SARAWAK. State Development Office. 1971. Sarawak development progress, 1968-1970. [Kuching, 1971?]. pp. 167.

— Supreme Council — Salaries.

SARAWAK. Council Negri. Sessional Papers. 1963. No.5. Privileges for the Chief Minister and other members of the Supreme Council, the Speaker and members of the Council Negri. [Kuching], 1963. fo.2. *Xerox copy.*

SARDINIA

— Economic conditions.

LADU (GIAN PAOLO) La dinamica economica e finanziaria della Sardegna centrale: la provincia di Nuoro, 1951-1971. Milano, 1976. pp. 336. *bibliog.*

— Social conditions.

LADU (GIAN PAOLO) La dinamica economica e finanziaria della Sardegna centrale: la provincia di Nuoro, 1951-1971. Milano, 1976. pp. 336. *bibliog.*

DESSY (UGO) Quali banditi?: controinchiesta sulla società sarda. Verona, [1977]. 2 vols.

— Social life and customs.

PIRA (MICHELANGELO) La rivolta dell'oggetto: antropologia della Sardegna. Milano, 1978. pp. 520. *(Cagliari. Università. Facoltà di Scienze Politiche. Pubblicazioni)*

SARTHE (DEPARTMENT).

FRANCE. Direction de la Documentation. La Documentation Française. Notes et Etudes Documentaires. Nos. 4,384-4, 385-4,386. Les départements français. 72. Sarthe, pays de la Loire; (par Pierre Blayau). [Paris], 1977. pp. 105.

SARTORIUS (LUD.) & COMP.

HANSSMANN (GEORG) Lud. Sartorius & Comp., 1777-1977: ein Oldenburger Handelshaus im Wandel der Zeiten. Oldenburg, [1977]. 1 vol. (various pagings).

SASKATCHEWAN

— Executive departments.

SASKATCHEWAN. Department of Health. Annual report. a., 1976/77- Regina.

— Industries.

SASKATCHEWAN. Department of Industry and Commerce. 1976. Saskatchewan industry today: building for tomorrow. [Regina, 1976]. pp. 27.

— Legislative Assembly — Salaries, pensions, etc.

SASKATCHEWAN. Legislative Assembly. Committee which considered Allowances and Salaries paid to Members of the Legislative Assembly, etc. 1962. Report; [E.M. Culliton, chairman]. Regina, 1962. fo. 13. *(Sessional Papers. 1962. No. 152)*

SASKATCHEWAN. Legislative Assembly. Committee which considered Allowances and Salaries paid to Members of the Legislative Assembly, etc. 1968. Report; [E.M. Culliton, chairman]. Regina, 1968. fo. 16. *(Sessional Papers. 1968. No.139)*

SASKATCHEWAN. Committee on the Role and Remuneration of Members of the Legislative Assembly of Saskatchewan. 1976. Interim report; [Edward N. Hughes, chairman]. [Regina], 1976. fo. 48.

SASKATCHEWAN. Committee on the Role and Remuneration of Members of the Legislative Assebmbly of Saskatchewan. 1976. Second interim report; [Edward N. Hughes, chairman]. [Regina], 1976. fo. 6.

— Statistics.

SASKATCHEWAN. Bureau of Statistics. Monthly statistical review. m., 1975 (v.1)- Regina.

SATIRE, ENGLISH.

The SINECURIST'S creed or belief; as the same can or may be sung or said throughout the kingdom. London, printed and published by R. Carlile, [1817?]. pp. 8. *A parody on the Athanasian Creed. By William Hone?*

SATIRE, FRENCH.

[TICKELL (RICHARD)] La cassette verte de Monsieur de Sartine, trouvée chez Mademoiselle du Thé. 6th ed. La Haye, chez la Veuve Whiskerfeld, 1779. pp. 76.

SATIRE, RUSSIAN.

GORIACHKINA (MARIIA SERGEEVNA) Satira Shchedrina i russkaia demokraticheskaia literatura 60-80-kh godov XIX veka. Moskva, 1977. pp. 175.

SATISFACTION.

LEISS (WILLIAM) The limits to satisfaction: on needs and commodities. London, 1978. pp. 168.

SAUDI ARABIA

— Economic conditions.

LACKNER (HELEN) A house built on sand: a political economy of Saudi Arabia. London, 1978. pp. 224.

— Foreign relations.

LACKNER (HELEN) A house built on sand: a political economy of Saudi Arabia. London, 1978. pp. 224.

— Politics and government.

LACKNER (HELEN) A house built on sand: a political economy of Saudi Arabia. London, 1978. pp. 224.

— Social conditions.

LACKNER (HELEN) A house built on sand: a political economy of Saudi Arabia. London, 1978. pp. 224.

SAUER (PAUL OLIVER).

DE VILLIERS (DIRK CHRISTIAAN) and DE VILLIERS (JOHANNA) Paul Sauer. Kaapstad, 1977. pp. 184.

SAVING AND INVESTMENT.

INTERREGIONAL SEMINAR ON DEVELOPMENT PLANNING, 2ND, AMSTERDAM, 1966. Planning domestic and external resources for investment; report of the...seminar...[held in] Amsterdam, Netherlands, 19-30 September, 1966. (ST/TAO/SER.C/109). New York, United Nations, 1969. pp. 198.

INTERREGIONAL SEMINAR ON THE MOBILIZATION OF PERSONAL SAVINGS IN DEVELOPING COUNTRIES, STOCKHOLM, 1971. Report of the Interregional Seminar...[held in] Stockholm, Sweden, 2 to 11 August 1971. (ST/TAO/SER.C/139). New York, United Nations, 1972. pp. 63.

— Mathematical models.

FOLDES (LUCIEN P.) Martingale conditions for optimal saving: discrete time. London, 1976. pp. 21. *bibliog.* *(Papers on Capital and Risk. No. 2)*

FOLDES (LUCIEN P.) Optimal saving and risk in continuous time with constant returns. London, 1976. fo. 34. *(Papers on Capital and Risk. No. 1)*

— Africa.

MOBILIZATION of household savings: a tool for development; edited by Arnaldo Mauri. Milan, 1977. pp. 219. *(Cassa di Risparmio delle Provincie Lombarde. The Credit Markets of Africa. 14)*

— France.

COTTA (ALAIN) Taux d'intérêt, plus-values et épargne en France et dans les nations occidentales. [Paris, 1976]. pp. 224.

MONNAIE, épargne, investissements. Paris, [1976]. pp. 204. *(Fondation Nationale des Sciences Politiques. Travaux et Recherches de Sciences Economiques. Série "Economie Française". 19)*

— Italy.

FARINA (FRANCESCO) L'accumulazione in Italia, 1959-1972: un'interpretazione della crisi e della ristrutturazione capitalistica. [Bari, 1976]. pp. 188. *bibliogs.*

— Sweden.

MEIDNER (RUDOLF) Employee investment funds: an approach to collective capital formation,...with the assistance of Anna Hedborg and Gunnar Fond. London, 1978. pp. 132. *Report of a study commissioned by the Swedish Confederation of Trade Unions (Landsorganisationen i Sverige).*

— Turkey.

HEPLEVENT (NIMLA) and YASER (BETTY SLADE) Analysis of fiscal performance: Turkey. Ankara, 1973. fo. (27) *(United States. Agency for International Development. USAID-Ankara. Economic Analysis Staff. Discussion Papers. No. 13)*

— Underdeveloped areas.

See UNDERDEVELOPED AREAS — Saving and investment.

— United States.

BARRO (ROBERT J.) The impact of social security on private saving: evidence from the U.S. Time Series...; with a reply by Martin Feldstein. Washington, D.C., [1978]. pp. 47. *(American Enterprise Institute for Public Policy Research. AEI Studies. 199)*

SAVINGS BANKS

— New Zealand.

NEW ZEALAND. Contracts and Commercial Law Reform Committee. 1971. Nominations in respect of savings bank accounts; report... presented to the Minister of Justice in July 1971; [M.F. Chilwell, chairman]. [Wellington], 1971. pp. 10.

— Swaziland.

SWAZILAND DEVELOPMENT AND SAVINGS BANK. Annual report and financial statements (formerly Annual report and accounts). a., 1974(9th), 1976(11th)- Mbabane.

— United Kingdom — Ireland.

HERBERT (HENRY ARTHUR) A few observations upon the defects of the savings' banks system, as illustrated by the frauds committed by the actuaries of the County Kerry banks. London, printed by W.J. Golbourn, 1848. pp. 19.

— United States.

OLMSTEAD (ALAN L.) New York City mutual savings banks, 1819-1861. Chapel Hill, [1976]. pp. 236. *bibliog.*

SAXONY

— Politics and government.

SOZIALDEMOKRATISCHE PARTEI DEUTSCHLANDS. Landesarbeitsausschuss Sachsen. Die sächsische Frage: zur Beurteilung der Ursachen und Wirkungen des sächsischen Parteikonflikts, etc. [Dresden, imprint, 1925]. pp. 32.

SCANDINAVIA

— Biography.

VEM är vem i Norden: biografisk handbok; huvudredaktör: Gunnar Sjöström. Stockholm, [1941]. pp. 1544.

— Economic conditions.

SCANDINAVIA at the polls: recent political trends in Denmark, Norway, and Sweden; edited by Karl H. Cerny. Washington, D.C., [1977]. pp. 272. *(American Enterprise Institute for Public Policy Research. AEI Studies. 143) Based on an AEI conference held in 1975.*

— Foreign relations.

VORONKOV (LEV SERGEEVICH) Severnaia Evropa: obshchestvennost' i problemy vneshnei politiki. Moskva, 1976. pp. 215.

— Neutrality.

VORONKOV (LEV SERGEEVICH) Severnaia Evropa: obshchestvennost' i problemy vneshnei politiki. Moskva, 1976. pp. 215.

— Politics and government.

SCANDINAVIA at the polls: recent political trends in Denmark, Norway, and Sweden; edited by Karl H. Cerny. Washington, D.C., [1977]. pp. 272. *(American Enterprise Institute for Public Policy Research. AEI Studies. 143) Based on an AEI conference held in 1975.*

CASTLES (FRANCIS GEOFFREY) The social democratic image of society: a study of the achievements of Scandinavian social democracy in comparative perspective. London, 1978. pp. 162. *bibliog.*

— Social conditions.

SCANDINAVIA at the polls: recent political trends in Denmark, Norway, and Sweden; edited by Karl H. Cerny. Washington, D.C., [1977]. pp. 272. *(American Enterprise Institute for Public Policy Research. AEI Studies. 143) Based on an AEI conference held in 1975.*

SCANDINAVIAN AIRLINES SYSTEM.

HAGRUP (KNUT) SAS og den internasjonale luftfart. Bergen, 1974. pp. 35. *(Norges Handelshøyskole. Kristofer Lehmkuhl Forelesninger. 1974)*

SCANDINAVIAN LITERATURE

— History and criticism.

MAWBY (JANET) Writers and politics in modern Scandinavia. London, [1978]. pp. 55. *bibliogs.*

SCANDINAVIANISM.

MÅRALD (BERT) Den svenska freds- och neutralitetsrörelsens uppkomst: ideologi, propaganda och politiska yttringar från Krimkriget till den svensk-norska unionens upplösning. Stockholm, [1974]. pp. 314. *bibliog. (Göteborgs Universitet. Studia Historica Gothoburgensia. 14) With English summary.*

SCHAUENSTEIN (CARL FERDINAND VON BUOL-) Graf.

See BUOL-SCHAUENSTEIN (CARL FERDINAND VON) Graf.

SCHEDULING (MANAGEMENT).

BAKER (KENNETH R.) Introduction to sequencing and scheduling. New York, [1974]. pp. 305. *bibliogs.*

SCHELLING (FRIEDRICH WILHELM JOSEPH VON).

HISTORIA i wolność: studia z dziejów ideologii XIX wieku, etc. Warszawa, 1961. pp. 299. *(Polska Akademia Nauk. Instytut Filozofii i Socjologii. Archiwum Historii Filozofii i Myśli Społecznej. 7) With Russian or German summaries.*

SCHELSKY (HELMUT).

FREIHEIT und Sachzwang: Beiträge zu Ehren Helmut Schelskys; herausgegeben von Horst Baier. Opladen, [1977]. pp. 340.

SCHLESINGER (MORITZ).

SCHLESINGER (MORITZ) Erinnerungen eines Aussenseiters im diplomatischen Dienst; aus dem Nachlass herausgegeben und eingeleitet von Hubert Schneider. Köln, [1977]. pp. 315.

SCHMID-AMMANN (PAUL).

SCHMID-AMMANN (PAUL) Unterwegs von der politischen zur sozialen Demokratie: Lebenserinnerungen. Zürich, [1978]. pp. 303.

SCHMIDT (HELMUT) Federal German Chancellor.

SCHOLL (HEINZ) Der Bonze aus Barmbek: Charakter, Karriere und Ideologie des Sozialdemokraten Helmut Schmidt. Euskirchen, [1978]. pp. 111.

SCHOLARLY PERIODICALS.

FRY (BERNARD MITCHELL) and WHITE (HERBERT S.) Publishers and libraries: a study of scholarly and research journals. Lexington, Mass., [1976]. pp. 166. *bibliog.*

SCHOLARLY PUBLISHING

— Costs.

FRY (BERNARD MITCHELL) and WHITE (HERBERT S.) Publishers and libraries: a study of scholarly and research journals. Lexington, Mass., [1976]. pp. 166. *bibliog.*

SCHOOL ATTENDANCE

— United Kingdom.

GRUNSELL (ROB) Born to be invisible: the story of a school for truants. Basingstoke, 1978. pp. 117. *bibliog.*

WHITE (ROGER) and BROCKINGTON (DAVID) In and out of school: the ROSLA community education project. London, 1978. pp. 200.

— — Scotland.

TRUANCY and indiscipline in schools in Scotland; the Pack report; report of a Committee of Inquiry appointed by the Secretary of State for Scotland; chairman: D.C. Pack. [Edinburgh], H.M.S.O., 1977. pp. 139. *bibliog.*

SCHOOL BOARDS

— United Kingdom.

BACON (WILLIAM) Public accountability and the schooling system: a sociology of school board democracy. London, [1978]. pp. 236. *bibliog.*

SCHOOL CHILDREN

— Transportation — Canada — Nova Scotia.

NOVA SCOTIA. Royal Commission on the Safe Transportation of School Pupils. 1964. Report...; C. Roger Rand, commissioner. Yarmouth, 1964. 1 vol.(various foliations).

— — United Kingdom.

JONES (T.S. MERVYN) Young children and their school journey: a survey in Oxfordshire. Crowthorne, 1977. pp. 19. *bibliog.* (U.K. Transport and Road Research Laboratory. Supplementary Reports. 342)

— United States.

ORFIELD (GARY) Must we bus?: segregated schools and national policy. Washington, D.C., [1978]. pp. 470.

— Canada — Manitoba.

SHARP (EMMIT F.) and KRISTJANSON (G. ALBERT) Manitoba high school students and drop-outs. [Winnipeg], Manitoba Department of Agriculture, [1967]. pp. 100. *bibliog.*

MANITOBA. Women's Bureau. 1976. Vocational and educational aspirations of high school youth;... written by Julie Bubnick. Winnipeg, 1976. pp. 218. *bibliog.*

— United Kingdom — Interviews.

EXPERIMENTER effects and the ethnic cueing phenomenon; [by] A. Brah [and others]. Bristol, Social Science Research Council Research Unit on Ethnic Relations, [1977]. pp. 31. *bibliog.* (Working Papers on Ethnic Relations. No. 3)

A REPORT on the development of a standard research instrument for the study of identity structure; [by] R. Miles [and others]. [Bristol, Social Science Research Council Research Unit on Ethnic Relations], 1977. fo. 40. (Research Notes)

RESEARCH strategy in the identity structure research; [by] M. Fuller [and others]. [Bristol, Social Science Research Council Research Unit on Ethnic Relations], 1977. 1 vol. (various foliations). (Research Notes)

— United States.

ENTWISLE (DORIS ROBERTS) and HAYDUK (LESLIE ALEC) Too great expectations: the academic outlook of young children. Baltimore, [1978]. pp. 193. *bibliog.*

SCHOOL DISCIPLINE

— United Kingdom — Scotland.

TRUANCY and indiscipline in schools in Scotland; the Pack report; report of a Committee of Inquiry appointed by the Secretary of State for Scotland; chairman: D.C. Pack. [Edinburgh], H.M.S.O., 1977. pp. 139. *bibliog.*

SCHOOL ENVIRONMENT.

NIELSEN (H. DEAN) Tolerating political dissent: the impact of high school social climates in the United States and West Germany. Stockholm, [1977]. pp. 138. *bibliog.* (International Association for the Evaluation of Educational Achievement. IEA Monograph Studies. No. 6)

SCHOOL INTEGRATION

— United States.

LIMITS of justice: the courts' role in school desegregation; edited by Howard I. Kalodner and James J. Fishman. Cambridge, Mass., [1978]. pp. 655.

ORFIELD (GARY) Must we bus?: segregated schools and national policy. Washington, D.C., [1978]. pp. 470.

— — Georgia.

RODGERS (HARRELL R.) and BULLOCK (CHARLES S.) Coercion to compliance; or, How great expectations in Washington are actually realized at the local level, etc. Lexington, [1976]. pp. 190. *bibliog.*

— — Oregon.

RIST (RAY C.) The invisible children: school integration in American society. Cambridge, Mass., 1978. pp. 289. *bibliog.*

SCHOOL MANAGEMENT AND ORGANIZATION.

RICHARDSON (ELIZABETH) The teacher, the school and the task of management. London, 1973 repr. 1977. pp. 366. *bibliog.*

— United Kingdom.

BACON (WILLIAM) Public accountability and the schooling system: a sociology of school board democracy. London, [1978]. pp. 236. *bibliog.*

— — Isle of Man.

ISLE OF MAN. Commission on the Administration of Education. 1961. The report of the Commission; [S. Wadsworth, chairman]. [Douglas, 1961]. pp. 26.

SCHOOL SOCIAL WORK

— Australia.

ASPECTS of school welfare provision. Canberra, 1977. pp. 129. (Australia. Commission of Inquiry into Poverty. Poverty and Education Series)

SCHOOLS

— France.

TANGUY (LUCIE) Le capital, les travailleurs et l'école: l'exemple de la Lorraine sidérurgique. Paris, 1976. pp. 226.

— United Kingdom.

ST. JOHN-STEVAS (NORMAN ANTHONY FRANCIS) Better schools for all: a Conservative approach to the problems of the comprehensive school. London, 1977. pp. 52. (Conservative Political Centre. [Publications]. No. 617)

WRIGHT (NIGEL) Progress in education: a review of schooling in England and Wales. London, [1977]. pp. 225. *bibliog.*

HOPKINS (ADAM) The school debate. Harmondsworth, 1978. pp. 233.

SCHOONBEKE (GILBERT VAN).

SOLY (HUGO) Urbanisme en kapitalisme te Antwerpen in de 16de eeuw: de stedebouwkundige en industriële ondernemingen van Gilbert van Schoonbeke. [Brussels], 1977. pp. 496. *bibliog.* (Pro Civitate. Collection Histoire. Série in-8°. No. 47) With summary in French.

SCHOPENHAUER (ARTHUR).

HISTORIA i wolność: studia z dziejów ideologii XIX wieku, etc. Warszawa, 1961. pp. 299. (Polska Akademia Nauk. Instytut Filozofii i Socjologii. Archiwum Historii Filozofii i Myśli Społecznej. 7) With Russian or German summaries.

SCIENCE.

INTERNATIONAL CONGRESS OF LOGIC, METHODOLOGY AND PHILOSOPHY OF SCIENCE, 5TH, LONDON, ONTARIO, 1975. Foundation problems in the special sciences: part two of the proceedings...; edited by Robert E. Butts and Jaakko Hintikka. Dordrecht, [1977]. pp. 427. *bibliogs.* (Western Ontario. University. University of Western Ontario Series in Philosophy of Science. 10)

KNELLER (GEORGE FREDERICK) Science as a human endeavor. New York, 1978. pp. 333. *bibliog.*

SLOMAN (AARON) The computer revolution in philosophy: philosophy, science and models of mind. Hassocks, 1978. pp. 304.

— History.

GUSDORF (GEORGES) De l'histoire des sciences à l'histoire de la pensée. 2nd ed. Paris, 1977. pp. 336.

JAKI (STANLEY L.) The road of science and the ways to God. Edinburgh, 1978. pp. 478. (Gifford Lectures. 1974-76)

LAKATOS (IMRE) The methodology of scientific research programmes: Philosophical papers, vol. 1; edited by John Worrall and Gregory Currie. Cambridge, [1978]. pp. 250. *bibliogs.*

— — Germany.

GREGORY (FREDERICK) Scientific materialism in nineteenth century Germany. Dordrecht, [1977]. pp. 279. *bibliog.*

— — Poland.

DZIESIEC lat rozwoju nauki w Polsce Ludowej. [Warszawa], 1956. pp. 725.

— — Russia.

MEDVEDEV (ZHORES ALEKSANDROVICH) Soviet science. New York, [1978]. pp. 262. *bibliog.*

— — United Kingdom.

BERMAN (MORRIS) Social change and scientific organization: the Royal Institution, 1799-1844. London, 1978. pp. 224. *bibliog.*

— Information services.

ORGANISATION FOR ECONOMIC COOPERATION AND DEVELOPMENT. Information Policy Group. 1974. Ireland. Paris, 1974. pp. 82. (Reviews of National Scientific and Technical Information Policy. [No. 2])

ORGANISATION FOR ECONOMIC COOPERATION AND DEVELOPMENT. Information Policy Group. 1974. Spain. Paris, 1974. pp. 170. *bibliog.* (Reviews of National Scientific and Technical Information Policy. [No.3])

— Mathematical models.

ZEEMAN (E.C.) Catastrophe theory: selected papers, 1972-1977. Reading, Mass., 1977. pp. 674. *bibliog.*

— Methodology.

HICKEY (THOMAS J.) Introduction to metascience: an information science approach to methodology of scientific research. Oak Park, Ill., 1976. pp. 74.

INTERNATIONAL CONGRESS OF LOGIC, METHODOLOGY AND PHILOSOPHY OF SCIENCE, 5TH, LONDON, ONTARIO, 1975. Basic problems in methodology and linguistics: part three of the proceedings...; edited by Robert E. Butts and Jaakko Hintikka. Dordrecht, [1977]. pp. 321. *bibliogs.* (Western Ontario. University. University of Western Ontario Series in Philosophy of Science. 11)

INTERNATIONAL CONGRESS OF LOGIC, METHODOLOGY AND PHILOSOPHY OF SCIENCE, 5TH, LONDON, ONTARIO, 1975. Foundation problems in the special sciences: part two of the proceedings...; edited by Robert E. Butts and Jaakko Hintikka. Dordrecht, [1977]. pp. 427. *bibliogs. (Western Ontario. University. University of Western Ontario Series in Philosophy of Science. 10)*

INTERNATIONAL CONGRESS OF LOGIC, METHODOLOGY AND PHILOSOPHY OF SCIENCE, 5TH, LONDON, ONTARIO, 1975. Historical and philosophical dimensions of logic, methodology and philosophy of science: part four of the proceedings...; edited by Robert E. Butts and Jaakko Hintikka. Dordrecht, [1977]. pp. 336. *bibliogs. (Western Ontario. University. University of Western Ontario Series in Philosophy of Science. 12)*

SIMON (HERBERT ALEXANDER) Models of discovery and other topics in the methods of science. Dordrecht, [1977]. pp. 456. *bibliogs. (Boston Colloquium for the Philosophy of Science. Boston Studies in the Philosophy of Science. vol. 54)*

HOLTON (GERALD JAMES) The scientific imagination: case studies. Cambridge, 1978. pp. 382.

LAKATOS (IMRE) The methodology of scientific research programmes: Philosophical papers, vol. 1; edited by John Worrall and Gregory Currie. Cambridge, [1978]. pp. 250. *bibliogs.*

— **Philosophy.**

FILOSOFIIA i nauka. Leningrad, 1975. pp. 192.

LECOURT (DOMINIQUE) Marxism and epistemology: Bachelard, Canguilhem and Foucault; translated from the French by Ben Brewster. London, 1975. pp. 223. *bibliog.*

CAUSEY (ROBERT L.) Unity of science. Dordrecht, [1977]. pp. 185. *bibliog.*

GUSDORF (GEORGES) De l'histoire des sciences à l'histoire de la pensée. 2nd ed. Paris, 1977. pp. 336.

INTERNATIONAL CONGRESS OF LOGIC, METHODOLOGY AND PHILOSOPHY OF SCIENCE, 5TH, LONDON, ONTARIO, 1975. Basic problems in methodology and linguistics: part three of the proceedings...; edited by Robert E. Butts and Jaakko Hintikka. Dordrecht, [1977]. pp. 321. *bibliogs. (Western Ontario. University. University of Western Ontario Series in Philosophy of Science. 11)*

INTERNATIONAL CONGRESS OF LOGIC, METHODOLOGY AND PHILOSOPHY OF SCIENCE, 5TH, LONDON, ONTARIO, 1975. Foundation problems in the special sciences: part two of the proceedings...; edited by Robert E. Butts and Jaakko Hintikka. Dordrecht, [1977]. pp. 427. *bibliogs. (Western Ontario. University. University of Western Ontario Series in Philosophy of Science. 10)*

INTERNATIONAL CONGRESS OF LOGIC, METHODOLOGY AND PHILOSOPHY OF SCIENCE, 5TH, LONDON, ONTARIO, 1975. Historical and philosophical dimensions of logic, methodology and philosophy of science: part four of the proceedings...; edited by Robert E. Butts and Jaakko Hintikka. Dordrecht, [1977]. pp. 336. *bibliogs. (Western Ontario. University. University of Western Ontario Series in Philosophy of Science. 12)*

ROSENKRANTZ (ROGER D.) Inference, method and decision: towards a Bayesian philosophy of science. Dordrecht,[1977]. pp. 262. *bibliogs.*

SIMON (HERBERT ALEXANDER) Models of discovery and other topics in the methods of science. Dordrecht, [1977]. pp. 456. *bibliogs. (Boston Colloquium for the Philosophy of Science. Boston Studies in the Philosophy of Science. vol. 54)*

ACTION and interpretation: studies in the philosophy of the social sciences; edited by Christopher Hookway and Philip Pettit. Cambridge, 1978. pp. 178.

BRONOWSKI (JACOB) The origins of knowledge and imagination. New Haven, 1978. pp. 146. *(Yale University. Silliman Memorial Lectures. 1967)*

The DYNAMICS of science and technology: social values, technical norms and scientific criteria in the development of knowledge; edited by Wolfgang Krohn [and others]. Dordrecht, [1978]. pp. 293.

KNELLER (GEORGE FREDERICK) Science as a human endeavor. New York, 1978. pp. 333. *bibliog.*

LAKATOS (IMRE) Mathematics, science and epistemology: philosophical papers, vol. 2; edited by John Worrall and Gregory Currie. Cambridge, [1978]. pp. 285. *bibliogs.*

LAKATOS (IMRE) The methodology of scientific research programmes: Philosophical papers, vol. 1; edited by John Worrall and Gregory Currie. Cambridge, [1978]. pp. 250. *bibliogs.*

ZAHAVY (ZEV) Whence and wherefore: the cosmological destiny of man scientifically and philosophically considered. South Brunsick, [1978]. pp. 178. *"Comprising an analysis relating to the significant essay In the centre of immensities, by the distinguished Professor Sir Bernard Lovell, University of Manchester, England".*

— **Social aspects.**

FERRARI (LEO C.) Human rights in a changing world; the problem of preserving human values in the upheavals caused by science and technology. Fredericton, New Brunswick Human Rights Commission, 1975. pp. 112.

CORIAT (BENJAMIN) Science, technique et capital. Paris, [1976]. pp. 250.

SOCIOLOGY OF THE SCIENCES: a yearbook. a., 1977(v.1)-Dordrecht.

CARRIER (JAMES GOLDEN) Social influence on the development of scientific knowledge: the case of learning disabilities. 1977. fo. 361. *bibliog.* Typescript. Ph.D. (London) thesis: unpublished. *This thesis is the property of London University and may not be removed from the Library.*

WORLD CONGRESS OF SOCIOLOGY, 8TH, 1974. Scientific-technological revolution: social aspects, with contributions by Ralf Dahrendorf [and others]. London, [1977]. pp. 181. *bibliogs. Papers presented in the first plenary session of the Eighth World Congress of Sociology, held in Toronto in 1974.*

The DYNAMICS of science and technology: social values, technical norms and scientific criteria in the development of knowledge; edited by Wolfgang Krohn [and others]. Dordrecht, [1978]. pp. 293.

KNELLER (GEORGE FREDERICK) Science as a human endeavor. New York, 1978. pp. 333. *bibliog.*

MORLEY (DAVID) The sensitive scientist: report of a British Association [for the Advancement of Science] Study Group [on Science and Ethics]. London, 1978. pp. 131. *bibliogs.*

— — **Europe.**

The SOCIOLOGY of science in Europe; edited by Robert K. Merton and Jerry Gaston. Carbondale, Ill., [1977]. pp. 383. *bibliog.*

— **Africa, Subsaharan.**

NATIONAL RESEARCH COUNCIL Recommendations for strengthening science and technology in selected areas of Africa south of the Sahara; [prepared for the International Cooperation Administration]. Washington, 1959. pp. 108,12. *bibliog.*

— **Canada.**

CANADA. Statistics Canada. Annual review of science statistics. a., 1977(1st)- Ottawa. *[in English and French]. Supersedes CANADA. Statistics Canada. Expenditures of provincial non-profit research institutes, CANADA. Statistics Canada. Expenditures on scientific activities by private non-profit organizations, CANADA. Statistics Canada. Federal government activities in the human sciences, CANADA. Statistics Canada. Federal government activities in the natural sciences, CANADA. Statistics Canada. Industrial research and development expenditures in Canada and CANADA. Statistics Canada. Research and development expenditure in Canada.*

— **European Economic Community countries.**

EUROPEAN COMMUNITIES. Commission. 1977. Common policy in the field of science and technology: communication...to the Council of 30 June 1977. [Luxembourg], 1977. pp. 62. *(Bulletin of the European Communities. Supplements. [1977/3])*

— **Russia.**

SOVIET science and technology: domestic and foreign perspectives; edited by John R. Thomas and Ursula M. Kruse-Vaucienne. Washington, D.C., [1977]. pp. 455. *Based on a workshop held at Airlie House, Virginia, 1976.*

SCIENCE AND ETHICS.

MORLEY (DAVID) The sensitive scientist: report of a British Association [for the Advancement of Science] Study Group [on Science and Ethics]. London, 1978. pp. 131. *bibliogs.*

SCIENCE AND STATE.

COUNCIL FOR SCIENCE AND SOCIETY. Study Group on Scholarly Freedom and Human Rights. Scholarly freedom and human rights: the problem of persecution and oppression of science and scientists. [London], 1977. pp. 63.

SCIENCE and technology policy: perspectives and developments; edited by Joseph Haberer. Lexington, Mass., [1977]. pp. 216. *(Policy Studies Organization. Policy Studies Organization Series. 14)*

— **Australia.**

AUSTRALIA. Department of Science. Report. a., 1972/73 (1st)- Canberra. *Included in AUSTRALIA. Parliament. [Parliamentary papers].*

— **Belgium.**

APERÇU STATISTIQUE SUR LE POTENTIEL SCIENTIFIQUE ET TECHNIQUE DE LA BELGIQUE; [pd. by] Services de Programmation de la Politique Scientifique. a., 1963/71- Bruxelles.

— **Canada.**

ISSUES IN CANADIAN SCIENCE POLICY; [pd. by] Science Council of Canada. irreg., S 1974 (1)- Ottawa.

DALY (D.J.) and GLOBERMAN (S.) Tariff and science policies: applications of a model of nationalism. Toronto, [1976]. pp. 125. *bibliog. (Ontario. Economic Council. Research Studies. 4)*

McFETRIDGE (D.G.) Government support of scientific research and development: an economic analysis. Toronto, [1977]. pp. 96. *bibliog. (Ontario. Economic Council. Research Studies. 8)*

— **India.**

SRINIVAS (MYSORE NARASIMHACHAR) Science, technology and rural development in India. [Poona], 1977. pp. 15. *(Gokhale Institute of Politics and Economics. R.R. Kale Memorial Lectures. 1977)*

— **Russia.**

LECOURT (DOMINIQUE) Lyssenko: histoire réelle d'une "science prolétarienne". Paris, 1976. pp. 257.

— **United States.**

KILLIAN (JAMES RHYNE) Sputnik, scientists, and Eisenhower: a memoir of the first special assistant to the President for science and technology. Cambridge, [1977]. pp. 315. *bibliog.*

KATZ (JAMES EVERETT) Presidential politics and science policy. New York, 1978. pp. 292. *bibliog.*

SCIENTIFIC APPARATUS AND INSTRUMENTS

— Trade and manufacture — United Kingdom — Scotland.

BRYDEN (D. J.) Scottish scientific instrument-makers, 1600-1900. Edinburgh, 1972. pp. 59. *(Royal Scottish Museum. Information Series. Technology. 1)*

SCIENTISTS

— Russia.

PUCHKOV (IGOR' SEMENOVICH) and POPOV (GELII ALEKSANDROVICH) Sotsial'no-demograficheskaia kharakteristika nauchnykh kadrov. Moskva, 1976. pp. 77. *bibliog.*

SCOTLAND.

SCOTTISH GOVERNMENT YEARBOOK, THE (formerly Yearbook of Scottish government). a., 1976/77- Edinburgh.

— Antiquities.

A PREHISTORIC field-boundary from the Black Crofts, North Connel, Argyll; [by] Anna Ritchie [and others]. [Glasgow], 1974. pp. 4. *(Reprinted from Glasgow Archaeological Journal, vol. 3, 1974)*

— Census.

SCOTLAND. Census, 1971. Parliamentary constituency tables, as defined by the Representation of the People Act 1948, as at February 1974: [10 per cent sample figures]. Edinburgh, 1974. pp. 142. *Bound with 100 per cent population and households.*

SCOTLAND. Census, 1971. Parliamentary constituency tables, as defined by the Representation of the People Act 1948, as at February 1974: [100 per cent population and households]. Edinburgh, 1974. pp. 71. *Bound with 10 per cent sample figures.*

SCOTLAND. Census, 1971. Census, 1971: Scotland: economic activity tables, 100 per cent. Edinburgh, 1978. pp. 126.

SCOTLAND. Census, 1971. Census, 1971: Scotland: household composition tables: 100 per cent. Edinburgh, 1978. pp. 69.

SCOTLAND. Census, 1971. Census, 1971: Scotland: migration tables, 100 per cent. Edinburgh, 1978. pp. 154.

SCOTLAND. Census, 1971. Census, 1971: Scotland: qualified manpower tables, 100 per cent. Edinburgh, 1978. pp. 30.

— Economic conditions.

PRATTIS (JAMES IAIN) Economic structures in the Highlands of Scotland. Glasgow, [1977]. pp. 36. *bibliog. (Glasgow. University of Strathclyde. Fraser of Allander Institute. Speculative Papers. No. 7)*

LEWIS (T.M.) and McNICOLL (IAIN HUGH) North Sea oil and Scotland's economic prospects. London, [1978]. pp. 147. *bibliog.*

— — Statistics.

SCOTTISH ECONOMIC BULLETIN; ([pd. by] the Scottish Office [Scotland]). s-a., summer 1971 (no.1)- Edinburgh. *Supersedes in part Digest of Scottish statistics (Ap 1953 - Ap 1971).*

— Economic history.

HUME (JOHN R.) The industrial archaeology of Scotland: 1: the Lowlands and Borders. London, 1976. pp. 279. *bibliog.*

DONNACHIE (IAN) and others. Scotland. Hartington, [1977]. pp. 112. *bibliog.*

— Emigration and immigration.

SCOTLAND. Census, 1971. Census, 1971: Scotland: migration tables, 100 per cent. Edinburgh, 1978. pp. 154.

— History.

MERCER (JOHN) Scotland: the devolution of power. London, 1978. pp. 250. *bibliog.*

MITCHISON (ROSALIND) Life in Scotland. London, 1978. pp. 181.

— Nationalism.

DONALDSON (ARTHUR) Whys of Scottish nationalism. West Calder, Midlothian, 1976. 1 pamphlet (unpaged).

MERCER (JOHN) Scotland: the devolution of power. London, 1978. pp. 250. *bibliog.*

— — Bibliography.

FRASER (KENNETH C.) compiler. A bibliography of the Scottish national movement, 1844-1973. Dollar, 1976. pp. 40.

— Politics and government.

SCOTTISH GOVERNMENT YEARBOOK, THE (formerly Yearbook of Scottish government). a., 1976/77- Edinburgh.

DREVER (JAMES) and others. Scottish universities and devolution. Stirling, 1977. pp. 40. *(University of Stirling. Stirling Educational Monographs. No. 3)*

YOUNG (RONALD GEORGE) The search for democracy: a guide to and polemic about Scottish local government. [Milngavie, 1977]. pp. 135. *bibliog.*

POWER and manoeuvrability; edited by Tony Carty and Alexander McCall Smith. Edinburgh, [1978]. pp. 185.

U.K. Parliament. House of Commons. Library. Research Division. Background Papers. No. 63. The devolution debate: regional statistics, updated. [London, 1978]. pp. 17.

— Population.

SCOTLAND. Census, 1971. Census, 1971: Scotland: migration tables, 100 per cent. Edinburgh, 1978. pp. 154.

— — History.

SCOTTISH population history from the 17th century to the 1930's: [by] Michael Flinn [and others]; edited by Michael Flinn. Cambridge, 1977. pp. 547. *bibliog.*

— Social history.

CAMERON (DAVID KERR) The ballad and the plough: a portrait of the life of the old Scottish farmtouns. London, 1978. pp. 253.

MITCHISON (ROSALIND) Life in Scotland. London, 1978. pp. 181.

MURRAY (NORMAN) The Scottish hand loom weavers, 1790-1850: a social history. Edinburgh, [1978]. pp. 269. *bibliog.*

— Statistics.

SCOTTISH ABSTRACT OF STATISTICS; ([pd. by] the Scottish Office [Scotland]). a., 1971 (no.1)- Edinburgh. *Supersedes in part Digest of Scottish statistics (Ap 1953 - Ap 1971).*

SCOTT BADER COMMONWEALTH LIMITED.

HOE (SUSANNA) The man who gave his company away: a biography of Ernest Bader, founder of the Scott Bader Commonwealth. London, 1978. pp. 242. *bibliog.*

SCOTTISH NATIONAL PARTY.

SCOTTISH NATIONAL PARTY. SNP and you: aims and policy of the Scottish National Party. 5th ed. Edinburgh, 1977. pp. 23.

SEA POWER.

INTERNATIONAL INSTITUTE FOR STRATEGIC STUDIES. Adelphi Papers. No. 139. Sea power and Western security: the next decade; by Worth H. Bagley. London, 1977. pp. 40.

SEALS (NUMISMATICS)

— Poland — Silesia.

TOMCZYK (DAMIAN) Pieczęcie górnośląskich cechów rzemieślniczych z XV- XVIII wieku i ich znaczenie historyczne. Opole, 1975. pp. 188. *bibliog. With English, German and Russian summaries.*

SEAMEN

— Laws and regulations.

INTERNATIONAL LABOUR CONFERENCE. 62nd Session. Reports. 5. Substandard vessels, particularly those registered under flags of convenience: fifth item on the agenda. Geneva, 1975-76. 2 pts.

INTERNATIONAL LABOUR CONFERENCE. 62nd Session. Reports. 2. Holidays with pay for seafarers: second item on the agenda; etc. Geneva, 1976. pp. 45.

INTERNATIONAL LABOUR CONFERENCE. 62nd Session. Reports. 3. The protection of young seafarers: third item on the agenda. Geneva, 1976. pp. 33.

INTERNATIONAL LABOUR CONFERENCE. 62nd Session. Reports. 4. Continuity of employment of seafarers: fourth item on the agenda. Geneva, 1976. pp. 29.

— Salaries, pensions, etc.

INTERNATIONAL LABOUR CONFERENCE. 62nd Session. Reports. 2. Holidays with pay for seafarers: second item on the agenda; etc. Geneva, 1976. pp. 45.

— Poland.

JANISZEWSKI (LUDWIK) Rodzina marynarzy i rybaków morskich: studium socjologiczne. Warszawa, 1976. pp. 363. *bibliog. (Wy'zsza Szkoła Pedagogiczna w Szczecinie. Rozprawy i Studia. t.7) With English summary.*

— United Kingdom.

RASOR (EUGENE L.) Reform in the Royal Navy: a social history of the lower deck, 1850 to 1880. Hamden, Conn., 1976. pp. 210. *bibliog.*

U.K. Working Group on the Employment of Non-Domiciled Seafarers. 1978. Report; [J.N. Archer, chairman]. London, 1978. pp. 67.

SEARS (ROBERT RICHARDSON).

MAIER (HENRY WILLIAM) Three theories of child development. 3rd ed. New York, [1978]. pp. 292. *bibliogs.*

SECESSION.

BUCHHEIT (LEE C.) Secession: the legitimacy of self-determination. New Haven, 1978. pp. 260.

SECONDAT (CHARLES LOUIS DE) Baron de Montesquieu.

HULLIUNG (MARK) Montesquieu and the old regime. Berkeley, Calif., [1976]. pp. 258.

SECRET SERVICE

— United States.

JEFFREYS-JONES (RHODRI) American espionage: from secret service to CIA. New York, [1977]. pp. 276. *bibliog.*

SECTS

— United Kingdom.

TOLMIE (MURRAY) The triumph of the saints: the separate churches of London, 1616- 1649. Cambridge, 1977. pp. 251. *bibliog.*

— United States.

CLARK (ELMER TALMADGE) The small sects in America. rev. ed. New York, [1949]. pp. 256. *bibliog.*

SECULARISM

— India.

GHOUSE (MOHAMMAD) Secularism, society and law in India. Delhi, [1973]. pp. 254. *bibliog.*

SECULARIZATION (THEOLOGY).

MARTIN (DAVID ALFRED) A general theory of secularization. Oxford, [1978]. pp. 353. *bibliog.*

SECURITIES.

ESSLEN (RAINER) The complete book of international investing: how to buy foreign securities and who's who on the international investment scene. New York, [1977]. pp. 368. *Updated and rewritten version of his How to buy foreign securities.*

SECURITIES FRAUD

— United States.

SEIDLER (LEE J.) and others. The Equity Funding papers: the anatomy of a fraud. Santa Barbara, [1977]. pp. 578.

SECURITY (LAW)

— United Kingdom.

GUEST (ANTHONY GORDON) and LOMNICKA (EVA Z.) An introduction to the law of credit and security. London, 1978. pp. 382.

SECURITY, INTERNATIONAL.

CHUBAR'IAN (ALEKSANDR OGANOVICH) Mirnoe sosushchestvovanie: teoriia i praktika. Moskva, 1976. pp. 254.

BROWN (NEVILLE) The future global challenge: a predictive study of world security, 1977-1990. London, 1977. pp. 402.

INTERNATIONAL INSTITUTE FOR STRATEGIC STUDIES. Adelphi Papers. No. 139. Sea power and Western security: the next decade; by Worth H. Bagley. London, 1977. pp. 40.

WAJSMAN (PATRICK) L'illusion de la détente. [Paris, 1977]. pp. 288.

WILKER (LOTHER) Die Sicherheitspolitik der SPD, 1956-1966: zwischen Wiedervereinigungs- und Bündnisorientierung. Bonn-Bad Godesberg, [1977]. pp. 347. *bibliog. (Friedrich-Ebert-Stiftung. Forschungsinstitut. Schriftenreihe. Band 135)*

ASPECTS of conflict; twelve essays by members of the ISC council and senior research fellows...; [by] Sir Louis Le Bailly [and others]. London, 1978. pp. 32. *(Institute for the Study of Conflict. Conflict Studies. No. 100)*

INTERNATIONAL INSTITUTE FOR STRATEGIC STUDIES. Adelphi Papers. Nos. 144, 145. New conventional weapons and East-West security;...papers... given at the nineteenth annual conference of the IISS at Bruges, Belgium, in September 1977. London, 1978. 2 pamphlets.

SEGREGATION IN EDUCATION

— Law and legislation — United States.

LIMITS of justice: the courts' role in school desegregation; edited by Howard I. Kalodner and James J. Fishman. Cambridge, Mass., [1978]. pp. 655.

SEINE-ET-MARNE.

FRANCE. Direction de la Documentation. La Documentation Française. Notes et Etudes Documentaires. Nos. 4,351-4, 352-4,353. Les départements français. 77. Seine-et-Marne, Île-de- France; (étude...réalisée par [Marie Josèphe] Ménard, etc.). Paris, 1977. pp. 133.

SELF-ACTUALIZATION (PSYCHOLOGY).

LEFF (HERBERT L.) Experience, environment, and human potentials. New York, 1978. pp. 523. *bibliog.*

SELF-CONTROL.

CONSCIOUSNESS and self-regulation: advances in research;... edited by Gary E. Schwartz and David Shapiro. London, 1976 in progress. *bibliogs.*

SELF-DEFENCE (INTERNATIONAL LAW).

TUCKER (ROBERT W.) The inequality of nations. New York, [1977]. pp. 214.

SELF-DETERMINATION, NATIONAL.

KALOGEROPOULOS-STRATES (SPYRIDON) Le droit des peuples à disposer d'eux-mêmes. Bruxelles, 1973. pp. 388. *bibliog.*

BUCHHEIT (LEE C.) Secession: the legitimacy of self-determination. New Haven, 1978. pp. 260.

SELF-EVALUATION.

GORDON (CHAD) Looking ahead: self-conceptions, race and family as determinants of adolescent orientation to achievement. Washington, D.C., [197-]. pp. 120. *bibliog. (American Sociological Association. Arnold and Caroline Rose Monograph Series in Sociology)*

SOCIAL comparison processes: theoretical and empirical perspectives; edited by Jerry M. Suls [and] Richard L. Miller. Washington, D.C., [1977]. pp. 371. *bibliogs.*

SELF-HELP GROUPS

— United Kingdom.

ROBINSON (DAVID) 1941- , and HENRY (STUART) Self-help and health: mutual aid for modern problems. London, 1977. pp. 164. *bibliog.*

— United States.

GARTNER (ALAN) and RIESSMAN (FRANK) Self-help in the human services. San Francisco, 1977. pp. 210. *bibliog.*

SEMANTICS.

DILLON (GEORGE L.) Introduction to contemporary linguistic semantics. Englewood Cliffs, [1977]. pp. 150. *bibliog.*

KEMPSON (RUTH M.) Semantic theory. Cambridge, 1977. pp. 216. *bibliog.*

SCHLESINGER (I.M.) Production and comprehension of utterances. Hillsdale, N.J., 1977. pp. 235. *bibliog.*

SEMANTICS (PHILOSOPHY).

KEMPSON (RUTH M.) Semantic theory. Cambridge, 1977. pp. 216. *bibliog.*

HOLDCROFT (DAVID) Words anddeeds: problems in the theory of speech acts. Oxford, 1978. pp. 178. *bibliog.*

SEMICONDUCTORS.

SCIBERRAS (EDMOND) Multinational electronics companies and national economic policies. Greenwich, Conn., [1977]. pp. 328. *bibliog.*

BRAUN (ERNEST) and MACDONALD (STUART) Revolution in miniature: the history and impact of semi-conductor electronics. Cambridge, 1978. pp. 231.

SEMIOLOGY.

ECO (UMBERTO) A theory of semiotics. London, 1977. pp. 354. *bibliog. First published in 1976.*

SEMIOTICS.

GREIMAS (ALGIRDAS JULIEN) Sémiotique et sciences sociales. Paris, [1976]. pp. 219.

SENIOR POWER

— United States.

JONES (ROCHELLE) The other generation: the new power of older people. Englewood Cliffs, [1977]. pp. 264.

SENTENCES (CRIMINAL PROCEDURE)

— United States.

GOTTFREDSON (DON M.) and others. Guidelines for parole and sentencing: a policy control method. Lexington, Mass., [1978]. pp. 212.

TWENTIETH CENTURY FUND. Task Force on Sentencing Policy Toward Young Offenders. Confronting youth crime: report;...background paper by Frankli E. Zimring. New York, [1978]. pp. 120.

SEPARATION OF POWERS

— United States.

BRIDWELL (RANDALL) and WHITTEN (RALPH U.) The constitution and the common law: the decline of the doctrines of separation of powers and federalism. Lexington, Mass., [1977]. pp. 206.

KURLAND (PHILIP B.) Watergate and the constitution. Chicago, [1978]. pp. 261. *(Chicago. University. William R. Kenan, Jr., Inaugural Lectures)*

SERANTINI (FRANCO).

STAJANO (CORRADO) Il sovversivo: vita e morte dell'anarchico Serantini. [Torino, 1975]. pp. 174.

SERFDOM

— Germany.

RABE (HANNAH) Das Problem Leibeigenschaft: eine Untersuchung über die Anfänge einer Ideologisierung...im deutschen Bauernkrieg. Wiesbaden, 1977. pp. 128. *bibliog. (Vierteljahrschrift für Sozial- und Wirtschaftsgeschichte. Beihefte. Nr. 64)*

SERGE (VICTOR) pseud.

SERGE (VICTOR) pseud. [i.e. Viktor L'vovich KIBAL'CHICH] Le tournant obscur; présentation de Magdeleine Paz; suivi de Pour Victor Serge. Paris, [1972]. pp. 205. *A variant text of his Mémoires d'un révolutionnaire.*

SERGIPE

— History.

DANTAS (JOSE IBARÊ COSTA) O tenentismo em Sergipe: da revolta de 1924 a revolução de 1930. Petropolis, 1974. pp. 252. *bibliog.*

SERRAI (PROVINCE)

— History.

KATARDŽIEV (IVAN) Serskiot okrug od Kresnenskoto vostanie do Mladoturskata revolucija: nacionalno-politički borbi. Skopje, 1968. pp. 469. *bibliog.*

SERVANTS

— United Kingdom.

HUGGETT (FRANK E.) Life below stairs: domestic servants in England from Victorian times. London, 1977. pp. 186.

SERVICE, COMPULSORY NON-MILITARY

— Netherlands.

EERENBEEMT (H.F.J.M. VAN DEN) Armoede en arbeidsdwang: werkinrichtingen voor "onnutte" Nederlanders in de Republiek, 1760-1795: een mentaliteitsgeschiedenis. 's-Gravenhage, 1977. pp. 231. *bibliog.*

SERVICE INDUSTRIES

— Classification.

FRANCE. Institut National de la Statistique et des Etudes Economiques. 1974. Regroupements des nomenclatures d'activités et de produits 1973: niveaux 15 et 40. [Paris, 1974?]. pp. 45. *(Nomenclatures et Codes)*

SERVICE INDUSTRIES (Cont.)

FRANCE. Institut National de la Statistique et des Etudes Economiques. 1975. Table de correspondance n.a.e. (nomenclature des activités économiques 1959) - n.a.p. nomenclatures d'activités et de produits 1973. [Paris, 1975?]. pp. 161. *(Nomenclatures et Codes)*

— Australia.

AUSTRALIA. Commonwealth Bureau of Census and Statistics. 1975- . Census of retail establishments and selected service establishments, 1973-74: final bulletin. Canberra, 1975 in progress.

— Colombia.

COLOMBIA. Departamento Administrativo Nacional de Estadistica. Censos economicos, 1970. Censos economicos 1970: comercio, industria, servicios; datos provisionales. Bogota, [1971?]. pp. 23.

— Germany.

OTTO-ARNOLD (CHARLOTTE) Dienstleistungen in der Gesamtwirtschaft. Berlin, 1978. pp. 172. *(Deutsches Institut für Wirtschaftsforschung. Beiträge zur Strukturforschung. Heft 48)*

— — North Rhine-Westphalia.

NORTH RHINE-WESTPHALIA. Landesamt für Datenverarbeitung und Statistik. Beiträge zur Statistik des Landes Nordrhein- Westfalen. Heft 386. Die Einheitswerte der gewerblichen Betriebe und der Mineralgewinnungsrechte, 1972. Düsseldorf, 1978. pp. 199.

— Russia.

PRAVDIN (DMITRII IVANOVICH) Razvitie neproizvodstvennoi sfery pri sotsializme: tempy, proportsii, perspektivy. Moskva, 1976. pp. 158.

— Singapore.

SINGAPORE. Statistics Department. 1977. Report on the census of services, 1974. Singapore, 1977. 2 vols. (in 1).

— United Kingdom.

WEST MIDLANDS JOINT MONITORING STEERING GROUP. A developing strategy for the West Midlands: service industries in the West Midland Region. [Birmingham], 1976. pp. 15. *(Technical Reports)*

MEDLIK (S.) Britain: workshop or service centre to the world? [Guildford, 1977]. pp. 26. *Lecture given at the University of Surrey on 1 June 1977.*

— Zambia.

ZAMBIA. Central Statistical Office. 1965. Census of distribution in 1962: wholesale, retail trade and selected services. Lusaka, 1965. fo. 22.

SERVITUDES

— United Kingdom.

JACKSON (PAUL) The law of easements and profits. London, 1978. pp. 257.

SEVERN

— Barrage.

U.K. Department of Energy. 1977. Tidal power barrages in the Severn estuary: recent evidence on their feasibility. London, 1977. pp. 19. *bibliog. (Energy Papers. No. 23)*

SEVILLE

— History.

COLLANTES DE TERAN SANCHEZ (ANTONIO) Sevilla en la baja Edad Media: la ciudad y sus hombres. Sevilla, 1977. pp. 447. *bibliog.*

— Population.

COLLANTES DE TERAN SANCHEZ (ANTONIO) Sevilla en la baja Edad Media: la ciudad y sus hombres. Sevilla, 1977. pp. 447. *bibliog.*

SEWERAGE

— Puerto Rico.

PUERTO RICO. Government Development Bank of Puerto Rico. 1970. A special report on Puerto Rico Aqueduct and Sewer Authority. [rev. ed.]. San Juan, 1970. pp. 20.

PUERTO RICO. Government Development Bank for Puerto Rico. 1971. Puerto Rico Aqueduct and Sewer Authority: a special report. [rev.ed.]. San Juan, 1971. pp. 20.

SEX.

ROWBOTHAM (SHEILA) and WEEKS (JEFFREY) Socialism and the new life: the personal and sexual politics of Edward Carpenter and Havelock Ellis. London, 1977. pp. 198. *bibliog.*

SEX (PSYCHOLOGY).

REICH (WILHELM) Sex and the class struggle: the best of Wilhelm Reich; selections from his writings edited by Chris Knight. n.p. [1974?]. pp. 47. *bibliog.*

HAHNEMANN SYMPOSIUM, 35TH. Sex and the life cycle: edited by Wilbur W. Oaks [and others]. New York, [1976]. pp. 223.

SEX AND RELIGION.

STOPES (MARIE CARMICHAEL) Sex and religion. London, 1929. pp. 30. *bibliog. Originally published in 1926 as a chapter of the author's Sex and the young.*

PHAYER (J. MICHAEL) Sexual liberation and religion in nineteenth century Europe. London, 1977. pp. 176. *bibliog.*

SEX CRIMES

— United States.

MACNAMARA (DONAL E.J.) and SAGARIN (EDWARD) Sex, crime and the law. New York, [1977]. pp. 291. *bibliog.*

SEX CUSTOMS.

HEATH (GRAHAM) The illusory freedom: the intellectual origins and social consequences of the sexual 'revolution'. London, 1978. pp. 131. *bibliog.*

SEX DIFFERENCES.

EXPLORING sex differences; edited by Barbara Lloyd [and] John Archer. London, 1976. pp. 28. *bibliogs.*

SEX DISCRIMINATION

— Law and legislation — United Kingdom.

MARSHALL (MARGARET) and ALDRED (CHRIS) The Equal Pay and Sex Discrimination Acts: report from Scotland. Aberdeen, [1977]. pp. 25.

— United Kingdom.

U.K. Equal Opportunities Commission. Annual report. a., 1977(2nd)- London. *1st annual report included in British Parliamentary Papers as HC 324, session 1976/77.*

— United States.

HARWAY (MICHELE) and ASTIN (HELEN S.) Sex discrimination in career counseling and education. New York, 1977. pp. 154. *bibliog.*

SEX DISCRIMINATION AGAINST WOMEN

— Peru.

BABB (FLORENCE E.) The development of sexual inequality in Vicos, Peru. Buffalo, 1976. fo.54. *bibliog. (New York State University. State University of New York at Buffalo. Council on International Studies. Special Studies Series. No. 83)*

— United States.

COVERT discrimination and women in the sciences; edited by Judith A. Ramaley. Boulder, Colo., 1978. pp. 123. *bibliogs. (American Association for the Advancement of Science. Selected Symposia Series. 14) Based on a symposium held at the AAAS annual meeting in Denver in 1977.*

SEX DISCRIMINATION IN EDUCATION

— United States.

FISHEL (ANDREW) and POTTKER (JANICE) National politics and sex discrimination in education. Lexington, Mass., [1977]. pp. 159.

SEX DISCRIMINATION IN EMPLOYMENT

— Law and legislation — United Kingdom.

MARSHALL (MARGARET) and ALDRED (CHRIS) The Equal Pay and Sex Discrimination Acts: report from Scotland. Aberdeen, [1977]. pp. 25.

— United States.

BLAU (FRANCINE D.) Equal pay in the office. Lexington, Mass., [1977]. pp. 158. *bibliog.*

COVERT discrimination and women in the sciences; edited by Judith A. Ramaley. Boulder, Colo., 1978. pp. 123. *bibliogs. (American Association for the Advancement of Science. Selected Symposia Series. 14) Based on a symposium held at the AAAS annual meeting in Denver in 1977.*

SEX IN MASS MEDIA.

EYSENCK (HANS JURGEN) and NIAS (D.K.B.) Sex, violence and the media. London, 1978. pp. 306. *bibliog.*

SEX OF CHILDREN, PARENTAL PREFERENCES FOR.

WILLIAMSON (NANCY E.) Sons or daughters: a cross-cultural survey of parental preferences. Beverly Hills, [1976]. pp. 205. *bibliog.*

SEX ROLE.

PINE (FRANCES THERESA) Changes in the division of labour and sex roles among the Akan of Ghana. 1977. fo. 238. *bibliog. Typescript. Ph.D. (London) thesis: unpublished. This thesis is the property of London University and may not be removed from the Library.*

The SEX role system: psychological and sociological perspectives; edited by Jane Chetwynd and Oonagh Hartnett. London, 1978. pp. 184. *bibliog.*

WHYTE (MARTIN KING) The status of women in preindustrial societies. Princeton, 1978. pp. 222. *bibliog.*

SEXUAL DISORDERS.

HAHNEMANN SYMPOSIUM, 35TH. Sex and the life cycle: edited by Wilbur W. Oaks [and others]. New York, [1976]. pp. 223.

SEYCHELLES

— Economic conditions.

SEYCHELLES. Office of the Prime Minister. Economics and Statistics Unit. 1975. A review of the economy. [Victoria, 1975 repr. 1976]. pp. 70, 1 map.

— Population.

NATIONAL SYMPOSIUM ON LABOUR AND FAMILY WELFARE EDUCATION, VICTORIA, MAHE, 1975. National symposium on labour and family welfare education, Seychelles, August 26-30, 1975; organised by the Ministry of Labour and Social Security in collaboration with the International Labour Organisation, etc. Victoria, Mahé, [Government of Seychelles], 1975. pp. 74.

— Statistics.

SEYCHELLES STATISTICAL BULLETIN; prepared by the Chief Statistician. q., My 1976 (no.3)- Mahé.

SHAMANISM.

ELIADE (MIRCEA) Shamanism: archaic techniques of ecstasy; translated from the French by Willard R. Trask. Princeton, [1974]. pp. 610. *bibliog. (Bollingen Foundation. Bollingen Series. 76)*

SHANGHAI

— Economic conditions.

WHITE (LYNN T.) Careers in Shanghai: the social guidance of personal energies in a developing Chinese city, 1949-1966. Berkeley, [1978]. pp. 249. *bibliog.*

— Social conditions.

WHITE (LYNN T.) Careers in Shanghai: the social guidance of personal energies in a developing Chinese city, 1949-1966. Berkeley, [1978]. pp. 249. *bibliog.*

SHAW (CHARLES).

SHAW (CHARLES) 1832-1906. When I was a child. Firle, Sussex, 1977. pp. 258. *Facsimile reprint of first edition of 1903 published under the anonym "An Old Potter." Original introduction omitted.*

SHEEP

— Australia — New South Wales.

AUSTRALIA. Bureau of Agricultural Economics. 1976. Prime lamb production in New South Wales: an economic survey. Canberra, 1976. pp. 70. *(Lamb Research Reports. No. 4)*

AUSTRALIA. Bureau of Agricultural Economics. 1976. Prime lamb production in the Murrumbidgee irrigation area: an economic survey. Canberra, 1976. pp. 44. *(Lamb Research Reports. No. 5)*

— United Kingdom.

MORIMOTO (NAOMI) The sheep farming of Norwich Cathedral Priory in the 13th and 14th centuries. Aichi, [1977]. pp. 37. *(Nagoya Gakuin University. Institute of Industrial Sciences. Discussion Papers. No. 2)*

SHEFFIELD

— Politics and government.

KITAMURA (KIMIHIKO) Participation at local level in Sheffield: a case study using the interview technique. [Tokyo, 1974?]. pp. 102. *(Gakushuin Review of Law and Politics. 10)*

SHERPAS

— Religion.

ORTNER (SHERRY B.) Sherpas through their rituals. Cambridge, 1978. pp. 195. *bibliog.*

SHETLAND ISLANDS

— Constitutional law.

NEVIS INSTITUTE. The Shetland report: a constitutional study; prepared for the Shetland Islands Council by the Nevis Institute under the chairmanship of Lord Kilbrandon. Edinburgh, [1978]. pp. 223.

— Politics and government.

GRØNNEBERG (ROY) Island governments: the experience of autonomous island groups in northern Europe in relation to Shetland's political future. Sandwick, Shetland, 1976. pp. 30. *bibliog.*

SHIFT SYSTEMS.

MAURICE (MARC) Shift work: economic advantages and social costs. Geneva, International Labour Office, 1975. pp. 146. *bibliog.*

SHIPBUILDING

— Argentine Republic.

GONZALEZ CLIMENT (AURELIO) La industria naval en la Argentina. Buenos Aires, [1956]. pp. 180. *(Buenos Aires. Universidad. Facultad de Ciencias Economicas. Instituto de Economia de los Transportes. Publicaciones. 10)*

— France.

FRANCE. Groupe sectoriel d'Analyse et de Prévision Construction Navale. 1976. Rapport...: préparation de 7e Plan. Paris, [1976]. pp. 138.

— Netherlands.

UNGER (RICHARD W.) Dutch shipbuilding before 1800. Assen, 1978. pp. 216. *bibliog.*

— United Kingdom.

TREBILCOCK (CLIVE) The Vickers brothers: armaments and enterprise, 1854-1914. London, [1977]. pp. 181. *bibliog.*

— — Government ownership.

AIMS OF INDUSTRY. Shipbuilding, ship repairing and marine engineering: suppliers' attitudes to nationalization. London, [1974]. pp. 8.

— — Scotland.

JOHNS (STEPHEN) Reformism on the Clyde: the story of UCS. London, [1973]. pp. 128. *(Workers' Revolutionary Party. Pocket Library. No. 7)*

— United States.

GOLDENBERG (JOSEPH A.) Shipbuilding in colonial America. Charlottesville, 1976. pp. 306. *bibliog. (Mariners Museum, [Newport News, Va.]. Museum Publications. No.33)*

SHIPPING

— Australia.

BACH (JOHN) A maritime history of Australia. London, 1976. pp. 481. *bibliog.*

— United Kingdom.

DAVIES (PETER N.) Sir Alfred Jones: shipping entrepreneur par excellence. London, [1978]. pp. 162. *bibliog.*

SHIPS

— Cargo.

INTER-GOVERNMENTAL MARITIME CONSULTATIVE ORGANIZATION. 1977- . International Maritime Dangerous Goods Code. London, 1977 in progress.

— Nationality.

INTERNATIONAL LABOUR CONFERENCE. 62nd Session. Reports. 5. Substandard vessels, particularly those registered under flags of convenience: fifth item on the agenda. Geneva, 1975-76. 2 pts.

— Safety regulations.

INTERNATIONAL LABOUR CONFERENCE. 62nd Session. Reports. 5. Substandard vessels, particularly those registered under flags of convenience: fifth item on the agenda. Geneva, 1975-76. 2 pts.

SHIRAGIAN (ARSHAVIR).

SHIRAGIAN (ARSHAVIR) The legacy: memoirs of an Armenian patriot; translated by Sonia Shiragian. Boston, Mass., 1976. pp. 217.

SHOP ASSISTANTS

— United Kingdom.

POND (CHRIS) Trouble in store: a study of shopwork and low pay. London, 1977. pp. 57. *(Low Pay Unit. Low Pay Pamphlets. No. 8)*

SHOP STEWARDS

— United Kingdom.

KEITHLEY (G.R.) and SAWBRIDGE (D.) The provision of industrial relations training for shop stewards. Durham, 1977. fo. 38. *(Durham. University. Business School. Working Papers. No 2)*

SHOPPING

— South Africa.

DAVIES (WILLIAM J.) A survey of consumer behaviour and shopping patterns amongst Bantu in Port Elizabeth. Port Elizabeth, 1972. fo. 31. *(University of Port Elizabeth. Institute for Planning Research. Information Bulletins. No. 5)*

— — Mathematical models.

COHEN (AARON) and BOADEN (BRUCE G.) The retail structure of the Witwatersrand and the Vaal triangle: a preliminary report. Johannesburg, 1977. pp. 20. *(Johannesburg. University of the Witwatersrand. Urban and Regional Research Unit. Occasional Papers. No. 17)*

SHOPPING CENTRES

— Rhodesia.

SMOUT (M.A.H.) Commercial growth and consumer behaviour in suburban Salisbury, Rhodesia. Salisbury, 1974. pp. 69. *(University of Rhodesia. Series in Social Studies. Occasional Papers. No. 1)*

— South Africa.

COHEN (AARON) and BOADEN (BRUCE G.) The retail structure of the Witwatersrand and the Vaal triangle: a preliminary report. Johannesburg, 1977. pp. 20. *(Johannesburg. University of the Witwatersrand. Urban and Regional Research Unit. Occasional Papers. No. 17)*

— United Kingdom.

CONTINUING survey of the social costs and benefits of shopping centres and precincts;...under the direction of G. Prys Williams and Eve C. Williams. London, 1978. pp. 67. *(Christian Economic and Social Research Foundation. Occasional Papers. Series B, No. 1)*

SHORT TAKE-OFF AND LANDING AIRCRAFT.

KIRKWOOD (T.F.) Effects of a V/STOL commuter transportation system on road congestion in the San Francisco Bay area. Santa Monica, 1972. pp. 25. *bibliog. (Rand Corporation. [Rand Reports]. 1075)*

SHREWSBURY

— Hospitals.

SALOP INFIRMARY. The statutes of the Salop infirmary. 2nd ed. Salop, printed by J. Cotton and J. Eddowes, 1752. pp. 28.

SHUSWAP VALLEY

— Economic conditions.

BRITISH COLUMBIA. Economics and Statistics Branch. 1971. The Okanagan-Shuswap region: a British Columbia regional economic study; originally prepared for the Okanagan Study Committee, Canada-British Columbia Okanagan Basin Agreement. Victoria, 1971. pp. 177.

SIBERIA

— Economic history.

KUZNETSOV (IL'IA INNOKENT'EVICH) Vostochnaia Sibir' v gody Velikoi Otechestvennoi voiny, 1941- 1945. Irkutsk, 1974. pp. 510.

SIBERIA (Cont.)

— History.

DUM vysokoe stremlen'e. Irkutsk, 1975. pp. 335.

NEKOTORYE voprosy rasstanovki klassovykh sil nakanune i v period Velikoi Oktiabr'skoi sotsialisticheskoi revoliutsii: iz istorii Sibiri. Tomsk, 1976. pp. 267.

POSTNOV (IURII SERGEEVICH) Sibir' v poezii dekabristov. Novosibirsk, 1976. pp. 112. *(Akademiia Nauk SSSR. Sibirskoe Otdelenie. Institut Istorii, Filologii i Filosofii. Nauchno-Populiarnaia Seriia)*

— Intellectual life.

BUTORIN (VADIM PETROVICH) Prosveshchenie rabochikh Zapadnoi Sibiri, 1928-1933 gg. Novosibirsk, 1977. pp. 140.

— Population.

MALININ (EVGENII DMITRIEVICH) and USHAKOV (ANATOLII KUZ'MICH) Naselenie Sibiri. Moskva, 1976. pp. 166.

— Rural conditions.

KREST'IANSKAIA obshchina v Sibiri XVII - nachala XX v. Novosibirsk, 1977. pp. 287.

SICILY

— Economic history.

MOTTA (GIOVANNA) Un paraproletariato urbano: proposta per l'identificazione di un modello; per una storia economica della Sicilia, sec. XV. Milano, 1977. pp. 494. *bibliog. (Messina. Università. Istituto di Scienze Economiche. [Publications]. Nuova Serie. 1)*

— History.

MICCICHÈ (GIUSEPPE) Dopoguerra e fascismo in Sicilia, 1919-1927. Roma, 1976. pp. 232.

PERITORE (GIUSEPPE) La Sicilia e la rivoluzione democratico-borghese. Firenze, 1977. pp. 149. *bibliog.*

POTERE e società in Sicilia nella crisi dello stato liberale: per un'analisi del blocco agrario; [by] G. Barone [and others]. Catania, 1977. pp. 400.

— Nationalism.

CASTELLO (FRANCESCO PATERNÒ) Duca di Cárcaci. Il movimento per l'indipendenza della Sicilia: memorie del duca di Cárcaci. Palermo, [1977]. pp. 391.

SICK

— Legal status, laws, etc. — United Kingdom.

PATIENTS ASSOCIATION. Can I insist? London, [1974]. pp. 13.

SIERRA LEONE

— Politics and government.

CARTWRIGHT (JOHN R.) Political leadership in Sierra Leone. London, [1978]. pp. 308.

SIGN LANGUAGE.

ON the other hand: new perspectives on American Sign Language; edited by Lynn A. Friedman. New York, 1977. pp. 245. *bibliog. An outgrowth of a course on the structure of the American Sign Language (ASL) given at U.C. Berkeley in 1975.*

SIGNS AND SYMBOLS.

DE SOLA (RALPH) Abbreviations dictionary. 5th ed. New York, [1978]. pp. 654.

SILESIA

— Economic conditions.

BARTECZEK (ANDRZEJ) Integracyjna funkcja infrastruktury gospodarczej w świetle badań nad Górnośląskim Okręgiem Przemysłowym. Warszawa, 1977. pp. 138. *bibliog. (Polska Akademia Nauk. Komitet Przestrzennego Zagospodarowania Kraju. Studia. t.59) With Russian and English summaries.*

— History.

PATER (MIECZYSŁAW) Ruch polski na Górnym Śląsku w latach 1879-1893. Wrocław, 1969. pp. 326. *bibliog. (Wrocław. Wrocławskie Towarzystwo Naukowe. Prace. Seria A. Nr.136) With German summary.*

DŁUGAJCZYK (EDWARD) Górny Śląsk po powstaniach i plebiscycie. Katowice, 1977. pp. 194. *bibliog.*

— Rural conditions.

KAŃTOCH (F.) and others. Przemiany struktury agrarnej na Górnym Śląsku; Transitions in the agrarian structure in Upper Silesia. Katowice, 1962. pp. 88. *bibliog. (Śląski Instytut Naukowy w Katowicach. Biblioteczka Wiedzy o Śląsku. Seria Rolnicza. Nr.1) With English, French, German and Russian summaries.*

— Social history.

MINCZAKIEWICZ (TADEUSZ) sTOSUNKI SPOŁECZNE NA ŚLĄSKU oPOLSKIM W LATACH 1922-1933. wROCŁAW, 1976. PP. 196. BIBLIOG. wITH rUSSIAN, gERMAN AND eNGLISH SUMMARIES.

SILK MANUFACTURE AND TRADE

— Italy.

GOODMAN (JORDAN) The Florentine silk industry in the seventeenth century. [1977]. fo. 231. *bibliog. Typescript. Ph.D. (London) thesis: unpublished. This thesis is the property of London University and may not be removed from the Library.*

SILVER MINES AND MINING

— Mexico.

TODD (ARTHUR CECIL) The search for silver: Cornish miners in Mexico, 1824-1947. Padstow, [1977]. pp. 192. *bibliog.*

— Peru.

FISHER (JOHN ROBERT) Silver mines and silver miners in colonial Peru, 1776-1824. Liverpool, 1977. pp. 149. *bibliog. (Liverpool. University. Centre of Latin-American Studies. Monograph Series. No. 7)*

— United States — Colorado.

KING (JOSEPH E.) A mine to make a mine: financing the Colorado mining industry, 1859-1902. College Station, Tex., [1977]. pp. 209. *bibliog.*

SIMON (JULES).

BERTOCCI (PHILIP A.) Jules Simon: republican anticlericalism and cultural politics in France, 1848-1886. Columbia, 1978. pp. 247. *bibliog.*

SIMON (JULIUS).

MOERING (MARIA) Julius Simon: Jugend und Wanderjahre. [Hamburg, 1965?]. pp. 24.

SIMON (ULRICH).

SIMON (ULRICH) Sitting in judgement, 1913-1963: an interpretation of history. London, 1978. pp. 166.

SIMONDE DE SISMONDI (JEAN CHARLES LEONARD).

PIĄTKOWSKI (WIESŁAW) J.C.L. Simonde de Sismondi : teoria ekonomiczna. Warszawa, 1978. pp. 320. *bibliog. With English and Russian summaries.*

SIMULA (COMPUTER PROGRAM LANGUAGE).

SIMULA begin; by G.M. Birtwistle [and others]. New York, 1973. pp. 391.

SIMULATION METHODS.

TOCHER (KEITH DOUGLAS) The art of simulation. London, 1963 repr. 1975. pp. 184. *bibliog.*

NAYLOR (THOMAS H.) and others. Computer simulation techniques. New York, [1968]. pp. 352. *bibliog.*

SIND

— Economic policy.

PAKISTAN. Ministry of Information and Broadcasting. Directorate of Research, Reference and Publications. 1977. Achievements of the people's government, 1972-1976: Sind. [Islamabad, 1977?]. pp. 43.

— Politics and government.

PAKISTAN. Ministry of Information and Broadcasting. Directorate of Research, Reference and Publications. 1977. Achievements of the people's government, 1972-1976: Sind. [Islamabad, 1977?]. pp. 43.

— Social policy.

PAKISTAN. Ministry of Information and Broadcasting. Directorate of Research, Reference and Publications. 1977. Achievements of the people's government, 1972-1976: Sind. [Islamabad, 1977?]. pp. 43.

SINDONA (MICHELE).

PANERAI (PAOLO) and DE LUCA (MAURIZIO) Il crack: Sindona, la DC, il Vaticano e gli altri amici. [Milan, 1975]. pp. 264.

SINGAPORE.

SINGAPORE. Ministry of Culture. 1968. Singapore: the island republic. [Singapore, 1968?]. pp. 80.

— Commerce.

SINGAPORE TRADE STATISTICS: imports and exports (formerly SINGAPORE EXTERNAL TRADE STATISTICS; including trade with West Malaysia); compiled by the Department of Statistics, Singapore. m. (formerly q.), 1965- , with gaps. Singapore.

— Economic conditions.

WEE (MON-CHENG) The future of the Chinese in southeast Asia as viewed from the economic angle, and other articles on economic topics. Singapore, 1970 repr. 1972. pp. 116.

SINGAPORE. Ministry of Finance. 1972. Economic pattern in the seventies: text of budget speech by Hon Sui Sen, Minister for Finance, March 7, 1972. [Singapore, 1972?]. pp. 58.

TRENDS in Singapore: proceedings and background paper [of a seminar held in 1974, organized by the Institute of Southeast Asian Studies]; edited by Seah Chee Meow. Singapore, [1975]. pp. 151.

— Emigration and immigration — Personal narratives.

THOMAS (FRANCIS) Memoirs of a migrant. Singapore, 1972. pp. 145.

— Foreign economic relations.

WEE (MON-CHENG) The future of the Chinese in southeast Asia as viewed from the economic angle, and other articles on economic topics. Singapore, 1970 repr. 1972. pp. 116.

— Foreign relations.

TRENDS in Singapore: proceedings and background paper [of a seminar held in 1974, organized by the Institute of Southeast Asian Studies]; edited by Seah Chee Meow. Singapore, [1975]. pp. 151.

— History.

TURNBULL (CONSTANCE M.) A history of Singapore, 1819-1975. Kuala Lumpur, 1977. pp. 384. bibliog.

— Politics and government.

TRENDS in Singapore: proceedings and background paper [of a seminar held in 1974, organized by the Institute of Southeast Asian Studies]; edited by Seah Chee Meow. Singapore, [1975]. pp. 151.

— Population.

SINGAPORE. Family Planning and Population Board. Annual report. a., 1972(7th)- Singapore.

SINGAPORE DEMOGRAPHIC BULLETIN; [pd. by] Statistics Department. m., D 1976- Singapore.

— Social conditions.

THOMAS (FRANCIS) Memoirs of a migrant. Singapore, 1972. pp. 145.

TRENDS in Singapore: proceedings and background paper [of a seminar held in 1974, organized by the Institute of Southeast Asian Studies]; edited by Seah Chee Meow. Singapore, [1975]. pp. 151.

— Statistical services.

SAW (SWEE HOCK) The statistical system of Singapore in 1974. Singapore, 1974. pp. 41. (Singapore National Statistical Commission. Background Papers. No.2)

— Statistics.

SINGAPORE STATISTICAL BULLETIN: a publication of the National Statistical Commission of Singapore. s-a., Je 1972 (v.1, no.1)- Singapore.

— Statistics, Vital.

SINGAPORE DEMOGRAPHIC BULLETIN; [pd. by] Statistics Department. m., D 1976- Singapore.

SINGLE PARENT FAMILY

— Australia.

AUSTRALIA. Social Welfare Commission. 1977. Needs of lone parent families in Australia. Canberra, 1977. pp. 160.

— New Zealand.

NEW ZEALAND. Domestic Purposes Benefit Review Committee. 1977. Report; [J.R.P. Horn, chairman]. in NEW ZEALAND. General Assembly. House of Representatives. Journals…Appendix to journals, 1977, E.28.

— United Kingdom.

ONE-parent families; edited by Dulan Barber. [London, 1978]. pp. 179.

— — Ireland, Northern.

IRELAND, NORTHERN. Inter-departmental Committee on Family Problems. 1977- . Family problems: a guide to progress on the implementation in Northern Ireland of the recommendations of the Finer report on one parent families and of the report of the Select Committee on Violence in Marriage. [Belfast], 1977 in progress. 1 vol. (loose-leaf).

SINGLE PEOPLE.

WILLANS (ANGELA) Alone again. Rugby, 1977. pp. 31.

— Dwellings — United Kingdom.

WAUGH (SARAH) Needs and provision for young single homeless people: a review of information and literature. London, 1976. pp. 56. bibliog.

DRAKE (MADELINE) and BIEBUYCH (TONY) Policy and provision for the single homeless: a position paper; a report to the Personal Social Services Council. [London], Personal Social Services Council, 1977. pp. 49. bibliog.

SINGULARITIES (MATHEMATICS).

LU (YUNG-CHEN) Singularity theory and an introduction to catastrophe theory. New York, [1976]. pp. 199. bibliog.

SINKIANG

— Foreign relations.

NYMAN (LARS-ERIK) Great Britain and Chinese, Russian and Japanese interests in Sinkiang, 1918-1934. [Lund], 1977. pp. 167. bibliog. (Lund. Universitet. Historiska Institutionen. Lund Studies in International History. [No.] 8)

— History.

NYMAN (LARS-ERIK) Great Britain and Chinese, Russian and Japanese interests in Sinkiang, 1918-1934. [Lund], 1977. pp. 167. bibliog. (Lund. Universitet. Historiska Institutionen. Lund Studies in International History. [No.] 8)

SIT DOWN STRIKES

— Italy.

TAKE over the city: community struggle in Italy. London, [1973]. pp. 36. Based on articles in the newspaper of the revolutionary group Lotta Continua (Fight On).

SITHOLE (NDABANINGI).

RHODESIA. Special Court. 1975. Judgement: a judgement concerning the necessity or expediency of continuing the detention of the reverend Ndabaningi Sithole who was the subject of a detention order issued on the 3rd day of March, 1975, [given] 2nd April, 1975. [Salisbury], 1975. pp. 34. (Rhodesia. Ministry of Information, Immigration and Tourism. For the Record. No. 24)

SITHOLE (NDABANINGI) In defence of a birthright. [Toronto], 1975. pp. 77.

SITHOLE (NDABANINGI) Letters from Salisbury prison. [Nairobi, 1976]. pp. 186.

SKIBBEN WINTON CONSTRUCTION LIMITED.

CLARKSON (DEREK JOSHUA) and McKINLAY (KENNETH ALEXANDER) Edward Wood and Company Limited, Skibben Winton Construction Limited: investigations under section 165 of the Companies Act 1948. London, H.M.S.O., 1977. 1 vol. (various pagings).

SKILLED LABOUR.

AD HOC MEETING OF EXPERTS ON THE ROLE OF ADVANCED SKILLS AND TECHNOLOGIES IN INDUSTRIAL DEVELOPMENT. NEW YORK, 1967. Planning for advanced skills and technologies: studies presented at the Ad Hoc Meeting…New York, 22-29 May 1967. (ID/SER.E/3). New York, United Nations, 1969. pp. 225. (United Nations Industrial Development Organization. Industrial Planning and Programming Series. No.3)

— United Kingdom.

EASTWOOD (GERRY) Skilled labour shortages in the United Kingdom with particular reference to the engineering industry. [Washington, D.C.], 1976. pp. 37. (British-North American Committee. Publications. 18)

SLATER (JAMES DERRICK).

SLATER (JAMES DERRICK) Return to go: my autobiography. London, [1977]. pp. 278.

SLAVE TRADE

— Africa, West.

BARKER (ANTHONY J.) The African link: British attitudes to the negro in the era of the Atlantic slave trade, 1550-1807. London, 1978. pp. 263. bibliog.

HAIR (PAUL EDWARD HEDLEY) The Atlantic slave trade and black Africa. London, [1978]. pp. 36. bibliog. (Historical Association. General Series. G. 93)

— United Kingdom.

DRESCHER (SEYMOUR) Econocide: British slavery in the era of abolition. Pittsburgh, [1977]. pp. 279. bibliog.

— West Indies.

DRESCHER (SEYMOUR) Econocide: British slavery in the era of abolition. Pittsburgh, [1977]. pp. 279. bibliog.

SLAVEIKOV (PETKO RACHEV).

PETKO R. Slaveikov, Liuben Karavelov, Khristo Botev, Zakhari Stoianov v spomenite na suvremennitsite si. Sofiia, 1967. pp. 758.

SLAVERY.

LEWIS (GORDON K.) Slavery, imperialism, and freedom: studies in English radical thought. New York, [1978]. pp. 346. bibliog.

SLAVERY IN BARBADOS.

HANDLER (JEROME S.) and others. Plantation slavery in Barbados: an archaeological and historical investigation. Cambridge, Mass., 1978. pp. 368. bibliog.

SLAVERY IN BRAZIL.

SALLES (VICENTE) O negro no Para: sob o regime da escravidão. Rio de Janeiro, 1971. pp. 336. bibliog. (Universidade Federal do Para. Coleção Amazônica. Serie Jose Verissimo)

REIS (JAIME) Abolition and the economics of slaveholding in North east Brazil. Glasgow, [1974]. pp. 24. (Glasgow. University. Institute of Latin American Studies. Occasional Papers. No. 11)

MALHEIRO (PERDIGÃO) A escravidão no Brasil: ensaio historico, juridico, social. Petropolis, 1976. 2 vols. (in 1).

— Antislavery movements.

NABUCO (JOAQUIM) Abolitionism: the Brazilian antislavery struggle;…translated and edited by Robert Conrad. Urbana, Ill., [1977]. pp. 186. bibliog. Translation of O abolicionismo.

SLAVERY IN COLOMBIA.

SHARP (WILLIAM FREDERICK) Slavery on the Spanish frontier: the Colombian Chocó 1680- 1810. Norman, Okla., [1976]. pp. 253. bibliog.

SLAVERY IN INDIA.

CHATTOPADHYAY (AMAL KUMAR) Slavery in the Bengal Presidency, 1772-1843. London, 1977. pp. 178. bibliog.

SLAVERY IN SOUTH AFRICA.

BÖESEKEN (A.J.) Slaves and free blacks at the Cape, 1658-1700. Cape Town, 1977. pp. 208. bibliog.

SLAVERY IN THE UNITED KINGDOM.

BARKER (ANTHONY J.) The African link: British attitudes to the negro in the era of the Atlantic slave trade, 1550-1807. London, 1978. pp. 263. bibliog.

— Antislavery movements.

DRESCHER (SEYMOUR) Econocide: British slavery in the era of abolition. Pittsburgh, [1977]. pp. 279. bibliog.

SLAVERY IN THE UNITED STATES.

SCHLUETER (HERMANN) Lincoln, labor and slavery: a chapter from the social history of America. New York, 1913. pp. 237.

MORGAN (EDMUND SEARS) American slavery, American freedom: the ordeal of colonial Virginia. New York, [1975]. pp. 454. bibliog.

RACE, prejudice and the origins of slavery in America; edited by Raymond Starr and Robert Detweiler. Cambridge, Mass., [1975]. pp. 164. bibliog.

SLAVERY IN THE UNITED STATES. (Cont.)

OWENS (LESLIE HOWARD) This species of property: slave life and culture in the old South. New York, 1976. pp. 291. *bibliog.*

PERSPECTIVES and irony in American slavery; essays by Carl N. Degler [and others]; edited by Harry P. Owens. Jackson, Miss., 1976. pp. 188. *bibliog. Papers read at a conference held by the Department of History of Mississippi University in 1975.*

HALLIBURTON (R.) Red over black: black slavery among the Cherokee Indians. Westport, Conn., [1977]. pp. 218. *bibliog.*

BRUGGER (ROBERT J.) Beverley Tucker: heart over head in the old south. Baltimore, [1978]. pp. 294. *bibliogs. (Johns Hopkins University. Studies in Historical and Political Science. Series 96. No.2)*

HOLT (MICHAEL FITZGIBBON) The political crisis of the 1850s. New York, [1978]. pp. 330. *bibliog.*

— Emancipation.

BERRY (MARY FRANCES) Military necessity and civil rights policy; black citizenship and the constitution, 1861-1868. Port Washington, 1977. pp. 132. *bibliog.*

— Law.

WIECEK (WILLIAM M.) The sources of antislavery constitutionalism in America, 1760-1848. Ithaca, 1977. pp. 309.

SLAVERY IN THE WEST INDIES.

DRESCHER (SEYMOUR) Econocide: British slavery in the era of abolition. Pittsburgh, [1977]. pp. 279. *bibliog.*

SLAVIC AMERICANS.

PRPIC (GEORGE J.) South Slavic immigration in America. Boston, Mass., [1978]. pp. 302. *bibliog.*

SLOPES (PHYSICAL GEOGRAPHY)

— Mathematical models.

THORNES (JOHN B.) Debris slopes as series. [Boulder, Colo.], 1972. pp. 5. *bibliog. (Reprinted from Arctic and Alpine Research, vol. 4, no. 4, 1972)*

SLOVENIA

— Nationalism.

ROGEL (CAROLE) The Slovenes and Yugoslavism, 1890-1914. New York, 1977. pp. 167. *bibliog. (East European Quarterly. East European Monographs. 24)*

SLUMS

— Barbados — Bridgetown.

BARBADOS. Housing Board. 1945. Report on a housing survey of eight slum tenantries in Bridgetown, June 1944-April 1945, with an introductory note from the Office of the Town Planning Adviser to the Comptroller for Development and Welfare in the British West Indies. Bridgetown, [1945]. pp. 47.

BARBADOS. Committee appointed...to Advise on the Utilisation of the Pine Estate for Housing and Slum Clearance. 1947. Report; [L. De Syllas, chairman]. [Bridgetown, 1947]. pp. 11.

— India — Mysore (City).

VENKATARAYAPPA (K.N.) Slums: a study in urban problem. New Delhi, 1972. pp. 105.

— Mexico.

ECKSTEIN (SUSAN) The poverty of revolution: the state and the urban poor in Mexico. Princeton, N.J., [1977]. pp. 300. *bibliog.*

— United Kingdom — Manchester.

FLETT (HAZEL) and PEAFORD (MARGARET) The effect of slum clearance on multi-occupation. Bristol, Social Science Research Council Research Unit on Ethnic Relations, [1977]. pp. 53. *bibliog. (Working Papers on Ethnic Relations. No. 4)*

— — Oldham.

EAST GLODWICK GROUP. Do it our way: a report on the East Glodwick C[ompulsory] P[urchase] O[rder] prepared in conjunction with Oldham Community Development Project. [Oldham, Oldham Community Development Project, 1976]. 1 pamphlet (various pagings).

EAST GLODWICK GROUP. How much longer?: a survey of conditions in the Bowden Street C[ompulsory] P[urchase] O[rder] area; prepared in conjunction with Oldham Community Development Project. [Oldham, Oldham Community Development Project, 1977]. 1 pamphlet (various pagings).

SMALL BUSINESS

— Canada — Nova Scotia.

NOVA SCOTIA. Department of Labour. Economics and Research Division. 1969. Pilot survey: small firm wage rates, salaries and hours of labour, Nova Scotia, 1968: cleaners, laundries and pressers; fish products; general and variety stores; sawmills. Halifax, [1969]. pp. 34.

— China.

AMERICAN RURAL SMALL-SCALE INDUSTRY DELEGATION. Rural small-scale industry in the People's Republic of China. Berkeley, Calif., [1977]. pp. 296.

— Europe.

COUTARELLI (SPIRO A.) Venture capital in Europe. New York, 1977. pp. 164.

— Ghana.

STEEL (WILLIAM F.) Small-scale employment and production in developing countries: evidence from Ghana. New York, 1977. pp. 235. *bibliog.*

— India.

INDIA. Development Commissioner (Small Scale Industries). 1976- . All-India report on the census of small scale industries. [Delhi], 1976 in progress.

NATIONAL SEMINAR ON ENTREPRENEURSHIP DEVELOPMENT IN SMALL SCALE INDUSTRIES, DELHI, 1975. Entrepreneurship development in small scale industries: summary of proceedings, etc. [Delhi, Controller of Publications, 1976]. pp. 188.

— — Maharashtra.

MAHARASHTRA ECONOMIC DEVELOPMENT COUNCIL. Manpower potential and business preferences in a rapidly developing economy: a case-study of Thana Taluka; summary report. Bombay, 1972. pp. 47.

— — Rajasthan.

RAJASTHAN. Directorate of Economics and Statistics. 1975. Report on survey of small scale industries in Rajasthan, rural, 1972. Jaipur, [1975]. pp. 56.

RAJASTHAN. Directorate of Economics and Statistics. 1975. Report on survey of small scale industries, urban, 1972-73 in Rajasthan. Jaipur, [1975]. pp. 64.

— Pakistan.

PAKISTAN. Economic Publicity Wing. 1978. Small scale industry in Pakistan. [Islamabad, 1978]. pp. 24.

— United Kingdom.

BRITISH INSTITUTE OF MANAGEMENT. Management Guides. No.4. Budgetary control for the smaller company. London, [1972]. pp. 31. *bibliog.*

WEST MIDLANDS JOINT MONITORING STEERING GROUP. A developing strategy for the West Midlands: small firms in the West Midlands economy. [Birmingham], 1976. pp. 7. *(Technical Reports)*

CONFEDERATION OF BRITISH INDUSTRY. Smaller Firms Council. Enterprise into the eighties; a...discussion document. London, 1977. pp. 32.

FABIAN SOCIETY. Fabian Tracts. [No.] 453. Think small: enterprise and the economy; [by] Nicholas Falk. London, 1978. pp. 36.

— — Finance.

INSTITUTE OF DIRECTORS. Sources of finance for the smaller company. rev. ed. London, 1978. pp. 128. *bibliog.*

SMALL GROUPS.

ROWAN (JOHN) The power of the group. London, 1976. pp. 212.

SMALL HOLDINGS.

ALLEN (WILLIAM) F.R.S., of the Society of Friends. Colonies at home: or, Means for rendering the industrious labourer independent of parish relief, and for providing for the poor population of Ireland by the cultivation of the soil;...a new edition with additions. London, Longman, 1832. pp. 52,8.

BLACKER (WILLIAM) An essay on the best mode of improving the condition of the labouring classes of Ireland. London, R. Groombridge, 1846. pp. 56. *Revised version of an essay which won the Gold Medal of the Royal Agricultural Improvement Society of Ireland.*

CENTRAL SMALL HOLDINGS SOCIETY. Pamphlets. No. 1. How small holdings may be established by law. [London, 1905?]. s.sh.

NATIONAL LAND AND HOME LEAGUE [Pamphlets]. No. 1. Land and homes for the people. [London, 1911]. s.sh.

NATIONAL LAND AND HOME LEAGUE. [Pamphlets]. No. 4. Small holdings and allotments, and how to get them from the councils. London, 1911. pp. (4).

SMALLPOX

— United Kingdom.

RAZZELL (PETER E.) The conquest of smallpox: the impact of inoculation on smallpox mortality in eighteenth century Britain. Firle, Sussex, 1977. pp. 190. *bibliog.*

SMALLPOX, INOCULATION OF.

RAZZELL (PETER E.) The conquest of smallpox: the impact of inoculation on smallpox mortality in eighteenth century Britain. Firle, Sussex, 1977. pp. 190. *bibliog.*

SMITH (ADAM).

200 Jahre Adam Smith' "Reichtum der Nationen": Internationales Kolloquium vom 30.9. bis 1.10.1975 in Halle, DDR...; Protokoll...; Herausgeber: Peter Thal. Glashütten/Taunus, 1976. pp. 285. *In various languages.*

BAGOLINI (LUIGI) David Hume e Adam Smith: elementi per una ricerca di filosofia giuridica e politica. Bologna, [1976]. pp. 106.

MEEK (RONALD LINDLEY) Smith, Marx and after: ten essays in the development of economic thought. London, 1977. pp. 193.

SMITH (ALBERT EDWARD).

SMITH (ALBERT EDWARD) All my life: an autobiography. Toronto, 1949 repr. 1977. pp. 269.

SMITH (CYRIL).

SMITH (CYRIL) b. 1928. Big Cyril. London, 1977. pp. 245.

SMITH (FREDERICK EDWIN) 1st Earl of Birkenhead.

[ROBERTS (CARL ERIC BECHHOFER)] Lord Birkenhead: being an account of the life of F.E. Smith, first Earl of Birkenhead; by Ephesian. popular ed. London, 1927. pp. 222.

SMOGULEC.

JASSEM (GRA'ZYNA) Majątek smogulecki w latach 1918-1937; das Landgut Smogulec in den Jahren 1918-1937. Poznań, 1976. pp. 185. bibliog. (Poznań. Poznańskie Towarzystwo Przyjaciół Nauk. Wydział Historii i Nauk Społecznych. Badania z Dziejów Społecznych i Gospodarczych. nr. 51) With German summary.

SMOKING.

TOBACCO RESEARCH COUNCIL. Research Papers. 14. Part I. Report on a second retrospective mortality study in north-east England. Part I: Factors related to mortality from lung cancer, bronchitis, heart disease and stroke in Cleveland county, with particular emphasis on the relative risks associated with smoking filter and plain cigarettes. London, 1977. pp. 93. bibliog. Report on the first study published as Research Paper. 8.

U.K. Department of Health and Social Security. 1977. Smoking and professional people. [London, 1977]. pp. 10.

U.K. Social Survey. 1977. Smoking and professional people: a survey of some professional groups working in health and education; their smoking habits, knowledge of health hazards and attitudes to anti-smoking education, carried out on behalf of the Department of Health and Social Security; (by Opinion Research Centre). London, 1977. pp. 35.

SMOLENSKI (WLADYSLAW).

SMOLEŃSKI (WŁADYSŁAW) Mieszczaństwo warszawskie w końcu wieku XVIII; opracowali i wstępem poprzedzili M.H. Serejski i A. Wierzbicki. 2nd ed. Warszawa, 1976. pp. 516. 1st ed. published 1917.

SMOLLETT (TOBIAS).

SEKORA (JOHN) Luxury: the concept in Western thought, Eden to Smollett. Baltimore, [1977]. pp. 340.

SMUGGLING

— United Kingdom.

An ATTEMPT to prove that a free and open trade between the kingdom of Ireland and all the ports of the southern coasts of England would be highly advantageous to both kingdoms:...in a letter to the Worshipful the Mayor and Chamber of the City of Exeter; by a truly impartial hand. Exon, printed by A. Brice and sold by A. Tozer, 1753. pp. 44.

SOBINOV (FEDOR EVGEN'EVICH).

See KOMAROV (NIKOLAI PAVLOVICH) pseud.

SOCCER

— United Kingdom.

INGHAM (ROGER) and others. "Football hooliganism": the wider context. London, 1978. pp. 151. bibliog.

SPORTS COUNCIL. Public disorder and sporting events: a report by a joint panel of the Sports Council and the Social Science Research Council; [Cyril Smith, chairman]. London, [1978]. pp. 60. bibliog.

SOCIAL CASE WORK.

AUSTRALIAN COUNCIL OF SOCIAL SERVICE. Family welfare. Canberra, 1974. fo.48. bibliog. (Australia. Social Welfare Commission. Occasional Papers) Photocopy.

COLLINGRIDGE (ANDREA) and others. Aspects of casework. Nottingham, [1976]. pp. 137. bibliogs. (Nottingham. University. Department of Applied Social Science. Social Work Studies. No. 2)

NATIONAL ASSOCIATION OF PROBATION OFFICERS. West Yorkshire Branch. Risk: an analysis of the problem of risk in social work practice. London, [1977]. pp. 24.

HALMOS (PAUL) The personal and the political: social work and political action. London, 1978. pp. 200.

SOCIAL CHANGE.

GALT (ANTHONY H.) and SMITH (LARRY J.) Models and the study of social change. New York, [1976]. pp. 180. bibliog.

SANDBERG (ÅKE) The limits to democratic planning: knowledge, power and methods in the struggle for the future. Stockholm, 1976. pp. 391. bibliog.

BEYOND the crisis; edited by Norman Birnbaum; with essays by Hans Peter Dreitzel [and others]. London, 1977. pp. 232.

DEVIANCE and social change; edited by Edward Sagarin. Beverly Hills, [1977]. pp. 317. bibliogs.

DIMENSIONS of social change in India; edited by M.N. Srinivas [and others]. Bombay, 1977. pp. 518. bibliogs. Papers presented at a national seminar organized by the Institute for Social and Economic Change, 1972.

GILLINGWATER (DAVID) Regional planning and social change: a responsive approach. 1976 [or rather 1977]. pp. 331. bibliog. Typescript. Ph.D. (London) thesis: unpublished. This thesis is the property of London University and may not be removed from the Library.

GLASSER (RALPH) The net and the quest: patterns of community and how they can survive progress. London, 1977. pp. 263. bibliog.

KOBRIN (STEPHEN JAY) Foreign direct investment, industrialization and social change. Greenwich, Conn., [1977]. pp. 188. bibliog.

PINE (FRANCES THERESA) Changes in the division of labour and sex roles among the Akan of Ghana. 1977. fo. 238. bibliog. Typescript. Ph.D. (London) thesis: unpublished. This thesis is the property of London University and may not be removed from the Library.

ZALTMAN (GERALD) and DUNCAN (ROBERT B.) Strategies for planned change. New York, [1977]. pp. 404. bibliog.

EISENSTADT (SHMUEL N.) Revolution and the transformation of societies: a comparative study of civilizations. New York, [1978]. pp. 348.

The ETHICS of social intervention; edited by Gordon Bermant [and others]. Washington, [1978]. pp. 431. bibliogs. Based on a conference held in 1975 at the Battelle Memorial Institute's Seattle Research Center.

LENSKI (GERHARD EMMANUEL) and LENSKI (JEAN) Human societies: an introduction to macrosociology. 3rd ed. New York, [1978]. pp. 515.

ROBERTSON (JAMES HUGH) The sane alternative: signposts to a self-fulfilling future. London, 1978. pp. 151. bibliog.

SHANKS (MICHAEL) What's wrong with the modern world?: agenda for a new society. London, 1978. pp. 176. bibliog.

STASSINOPOULOS (ARIANNA) The other revolution. London, 1978. pp. 240.

WORLD futures: the great debate; edited by Christopher Freeman and Marie Jahoda. London, 1978. pp. 416. bibliog. Based on a programme of studies at the Science Policy Research Unit, University of Sussex.

SOCIAL CLASSES.

DUMENIL (GERARD) La position de classe des cadres et employés: la fonction capitaliste parcellaire. Grenoble, 1975. pp. 120.

CORDOVA (ARNALDO) Sociedad y Estado en el mundo moderno. Mexico, 1976. pp. 287.

CLASS and class structure; edited...by Alan Hunt. London, 1977. pp. 190. Essays presented at a conference organized by the Sociology Group of the Communist Party of Great Britain held in 1976 in London.

CROMPTON (ROSEMARY) and GUBBAY (JON) Economy and class structure. London, 1977. pp. 248. bibliog.

McCORD (WILLIAM MAXWELL) and McCORD (ARLINE F.) Power and equity: an introduction to social stratification. New York, 1977. pp. 316.

PAPERS on class, hegemony and party; edited by Jon Bloomfield. London, 1977. pp. 125. Papers originally delivered at the Communist University, held in London in 1976.

COXON (ANTHONY PETER MACMILLAN) and JONES (CHARLES L.) The images of occupational prestige. London, 1978. pp. 226. bibliog.

GORDON (MILTON MYRON) Human nature, class and ethnicity. New York, 1978. pp. 302.

WRIGHT (ERIK OLIN) Class, crisis and the state. [London, 1978]. pp. 266. bibliog.

— Economic aspects.

CARCHEDI (GUGLIELMO) On the economic identification of social classes. London, 1977. pp. 224. bibliog.

— Algeria.

LAZREG (MARNIA) The emergence of classes in Algeria: a study of colonialism and socio-political change. Boulder, Colo., 1976. pp. 252. bibliog.

— America, Latin.

SOLARI (ALDO E.) and others. Teoria, accion social y desarrollo en America Latina. Mexico, 1976. pp. 637.

CLASES sociales y crisis politica en America Latina; seminario de Oaxaca;...coordinado por Raul Benitez Zenteno. Mexico, 1977. pp. 454.

IDEOLOGY and social change in Latin America; edited by June Nash [and others]. New York, [1977]. pp. 305. bibliogs.

— Bulgaria.

ATANASOV (ATANAS) and MASHIAKH (ARON) Promeni v sotsialnata prinadlezhnost na zaetite litsa v Bulgariia; Changements dans l'appartenance sociale des personnes occupées en Bulgarie. Sofiia, 1977. pp. 171. bibliog. (Nauchnoizsledovatelski Institut po Statistika. Izdaniia. 3) With Russian and French summaries.

— Canada.

RESNICK (PHILIP) The land of Cain: class and nationalism in English Canada, 1945-1975. Vancouver, [1977]. pp. 297. bibliog.

— Czechoslovakia.

ZÁBRAHOVÁ (LUDOSLAVA) Třídně sociální struktura ve výstavbě socialismu: východiska, kritéria a problémy ČSSR. Praha, 1976. pp. 153.

— East (Near East).

COMMONERS, climbers and notables: a sampler of studies on social ranking in the Middle East; edited by C.A.O. Van Nieuwenhuijze, Leiden, 1977. pp. 412. bibliogs.

— Ethiopia.

MARKAKIS (JOHN) and AYELE (NEGA) Class and revolution in Ethiopia. Nottingham, 1978. pp. 191.

— France.

BERTAUX (DANIEL) Destins personnels et structure de classe: pour une critique de l'anthroponomie politique. [Paris, 1977]. pp. 322.

SOCIAL CLASSES.(Cont.)

GRANOU (ANDRE) La bourgeoisie financière au pouvoir et les luttes de classes en France. Paris, 1977. pp. 306.

— **Germany.**

HANDL (JOHANN) and others. Klassenlagen und Sozialstruktur: empirische Untersuchungen für die Bundesrepublik Deutschland. Frankfurt/Main, [1977]. pp. 275. *bibliog. (Frankfurt am Main. Universität, and Mannheim. Universität. Sozialpolitische Forschergruppe. SPES- Projekt. Schriftenreihe. Band 9)*

HRADIL (STEFAN) Soziale Schichtung in der Bundesrepublik. München, [1977]. pp. 84.

LEISEWITZ (ANDRÉ) Klassen in der Bundesrepublik Deutschland heute. Frankfurt am Main, 1977. pp. 207.

— **Greece.**

MOUZELIS (NICOLAS PANAYIOTOU) Modern Greece: facets of underdevelopment. London, 1978. pp. 222.

— **Italy.**

CORBETTA (PIERGIORGIO) Tecnici, disoccupazione e coscienza di classe. Bologna, [1975]. pp. 227.

TURONE (SERGIO) Sindacato e classi sociali: fra autunno caldo e compromesso storico. [Bari], 1976. pp. 178.

— **Mexico.**

CHANCE (JOHN K.) Race and class in colonial Oaxaca. Stanford, 1978. pp. 250. *bibliog.*

— **Pakistan — Punjab.**

AHMAD (SAGHIR) Class and power in a Punjabi village. New York, [1977]. pp. 174. *bibliogs.*

— **Peru.**

STEIN (WILLIAM W.) Modernization and inequality in Vicos, Peru: an examination of the "ignorance of women". Buffalo, 1975. fo. 56. *(New York State University. Council on International Studies. Special Studies. No. 73)*

— **Poland.**

GOŁĘBIOWSKI (BRONISŁAW) and WESOŁOWSKI (WŁODZIMIERZ) Klasy, walka klas i przeobra'zenia struktury społecznej w Polsce Ludowej. [Warszawa], 1969. pp. 79. *bibliog.*

— **Russia.**

AMVROSOV (ANATOLII ALEKSANDROVICH) Sotsial'naia struktura sovetskogo obshchestva. Moskva, 1975. pp. 120.

— **United Kingdom.**

CONFERENCE OF SOCIALIST ECONOMISTS. Political Economy of Housing Workshop. Housing and class in Britain: a second volume of papers presented at the...Workshop, etc. London, 1976. pp. 104.

WEST MIDLANDS JOINT MONITORING STEERING GROUP. (A developing strategy for the West Midlands): analysis of socio-economic groups. [Birmingham], 1976. pp. 30. *(Technical Reports)*

ENTWISTLE (HAROLD) Class, culture and education. London, 1978. pp. 214. *bibliog.*

LORIMER (DOUGLAS A.) Colour, class and the Victorians: English attitudes to the negro in the mid-nineteenth century. Leicester, 1978. pp. 300. *bibliog.*

PROPERTY, paternalism and power: class and control in rural England; [by] Howard Newby [and others]. London, 1978. pp. 432. *bibliog.*

— **United States.**

BODNAR (JOHN E.) Immigration and industrialization: ethnicity in an American mill town, 1870-1940. Pittsburgh, [1977]. pp. 213. *bibliog.*

EWEN (LYNDA ANN) Corporate power and urban crisis in Detroit. Princeton, [1978]. pp. 312. *bibliog.*

INGHAM (JOHN N.) The iron barons: a social analysis of an American urban elite, 1874-1965. Westport, Conn., 1978. pp. 242. *bibliog.*

ROTHMAN (ROBERT A.) Inequality and stratification in the United States. Englewood Cliffs, [1978]. pp. 243. *bibliogs.*

— **Zambia.**

BHAGAVAN (M.R.) Zambia: impact of industrial strategy on regional imbalance and social inequality. Uppsala, 1978. pp. 76. *(Nordiska Afrikainstitutet. Research Reports. No. 44)*

SOCIAL CONDITIONS

— **Bibliography.**

CENTRE FOR POLICY STUDIES. Bibliography of freedom. London, 1976. pp. 28.

— **Statistics.**

[SCANDINAVIA]. Nordiske Socialministerier. 1951. Samordning af de nordiske landes statistik vedrørende den sociale lovgivning: betaenkning afgivet af den...nedsatte ekspertkomité. 1 Del. Om opstilling af en ensartet oversigt over de sociale udgifter. København, 1951. pp. 36.

SOCIAL CONFLICT.

JAMES (SELMA) and others. Sex, race and class;...with contributions from Barbara Beese, Mala Dhondy, Darcus Howe and correspondents to Race Today. Bristol, 1975. pp. 34.

BONZANINI (ANGELO) and SALERNO (FRANCO) Conflittualità e crisi nella società industriale. [Milano, 1976]. pp. 165.

BLACKBURN (ROBIN) ed. Revolution and class struggle: a reader in Marxist politics. [London], 1977. pp. 444. *bibliog.*

EWEN (LYNDA ANN) Corporate power and urban crisis in Detroit. Princeton, [1978]. pp. 312. *bibliog.*

HADJINICOLAOU (NICOS) Art history and class struggle; translated from the French by Louise Asmal. London, [1978]. pp. 206.

— **Colombia.**

LEYVA DURAN (ALVARO) Centros de integracion y de desarrollo de la comunidad. Bogota, 1972. pp. 139. *bibliog.*

— **Europe.**

CONFLITTI in Europa: lotte di classe; sindacati e stato dopo il '68; a cura di Colin Crouch e Alessandro Pizzorno. Milano, 1977. pp. 438. *bibliogs.*

The RESURGENCE of class conflict in Western Europe since 1968;...edited by Colin Crouch and Alessandro Pizzorno. London, 1978. 2 vols. *bibliogs.*

— **France.**

GRANOU (ANDRE) La bourgeoisie financière au pouvoir et les luttes de classes en France. Paris, 1977. pp. 306.

GUERIN (DANIEL) Class struggle in the first French Republic: bourgeois and bras nus, 1793-1795; translated from the French by Ian Patterson. London, 1977. pp. 295.

— **Israel.**

SMOOHA (SAMMY) Israel: pluralism and conflict. Berkeley, 1978. pp. 462. *bibliogs.*

— **Italy.**

FABBRICA E STATO. No. 13/14. 1974/1975: crisi e lotte proletarie. Bari, 1975. pp. 270.

RESTA (ELIGIO) Conflitti sociali e giustizia. Bari, [1977]. pp. 238.

— **Poland.**

GOŁĘBIOWSKI (BRONISŁAW) and WESOŁOWSKI (WŁODZIMIERZ) Klasy, walka klas i przeobra'zenia struktury społecznej w Polsce Ludowej. [Warszawa], 1969. pp. 79. *bibliog.*

— **Russia.**

BETTELHEIM (CHARLES) Les luttes de classes en URSS: deuxième période, 1923-1930. [Paris, 1977]. pp. 605. *bibliog.*

— **United Kingdom — Ireland, Northern.**

FIELDS (RONA M.) Society under siege: a psychology of Northern Ireland. Philadelphia, 1977. pp. 267.

SOCIAL CONTROL.

YOU as a product: an essay on the family as the key link between individual structure and socioeconomic reality and changes in family structure, cultural conditioning and sexual repression with economic changes in capitalism; [by members of Newcastle University Socialist Society]. [Newcastle, 1975?]. pp. 76.

CROZIER (MICHEL) The governability of West European societies. Colchester, [1977?]. pp. 15. *(University of Essex. Noel Buxton Lectures. 1977)*

DEVIANCE and social control in Chinese society; edited by Amy Auerbacher Wilson [and others]. New York, [1977]. pp. 227. *Proceedings of a preliminary conference held at the International Center of Rutgers University in 1975.*

SOCIAL control in nineteenth century Britain; edited by A.P. Donajgrodzki. London, 1977. pp. 258. *bibliog.*

ZIEGENHAGEN (EDUARD A.) Victims, crime, and social control. New York, 1977. pp. 156.

SOCIAL CREDIT.

WILLIAM Aberhart and social credit in Alberta; edited by Lewis H. Thomas. Vancouver, [1977]. pp. 174. *bibliog.*

SOCIAL DEMOCRATIC PARTY (DENMARK).

SOCIALDEMOKRATISME i 30'ernes Danmark: politisk, kulturelt, litteraert; ([by] Jon Finsen [and others]). [Copenhagen, 1974]. pp. 58. *bibliog. (Københavns Universitet. Institut for Litteraturvidenskab. Skriftraekke. 1)*

BRYLD (CLAUS) Det danske Socialdemokrati og revisionismen: en analyse af socialdemokratisk samfundsforståelse, strategi og taktik før 2. verdenskrig, etc. [Grenå, 1976 in progress]. *bibliog.*

BASTHOLM (ELLEN) Socialdemokratiet som folkeparti: elementer til belysning af Socialdemokratiets revisionisme/reformisme med regeringsperioden 1924-26 som historisk-konkret eksempel. [Århus, 1976]. pp. 159.

LYKKEBO (LARS OLE) Det danske Socialdemokratis militaerpolitiske stilling, 1933-1937. Odense, 1976. pp. 117. *bibliog.*

HANSEN (KARIN) and TORPE (LARS) Socialdemokratiet og krisen i 30'erne. Århus, 1977. pp. 252. *bibliog.*

CASTLES (FRANCIS GEOFFREY) The social democratic image of society: a study of the achievements of Scandinavian social democracy in comparative perspective. London, 1978. pp. 162. *bibliog.*

SOCIAL DEMOCRATIC PARTY (GERMANY).

CRISPIEN (ARTHUR) Eine Abrechnung mit den Rechtssozialisten: Rede...gehalten am 29. Juni 1919 auf der Generalversammlung des Verbandes der Unabhängigen sozialdemokratischen Vereine Berlins und Umgegend. Berlin, [1919]. pp. 32.

NICHTS getan?: die Arbeit seit dem 9. November 1918. [Berlin, 1919]. pp. 32.

SOZIALDEMOKRATISCHE PARTEI
DEUTSCHLANDS. Landesarbeitsausschuss Sachsen. Die sächsische Frage: zur Beurteilung der Ursachen und Wirkungen des sächsischen Parteikonflikts, etc. [Dresden, imprint, 1925]. pp. 32.

OSTERROTH (FRANZ) and SCHUSTER (DIETER) Chronik der deutschen Sozialdemokratie. 2nd ed. Berlin, 1975-78. 3 vols.

LEBER (JULIUS) Schriften, Reden, Briefe; herausgegeben von Dorothea Beck und Wilfried F. Schoeller; mit einem Vorwort von Willy Brandt und einer Gedenkrede von Golo Mann. München, [1976]. pp. 327.

MITTMANN (URSULA) Fraktion und Partei: ein Vergleich von Zentrum und Sozialdemokratie im Kaiserreich. Düsseldorf, [1976]. pp. 455. *bibliog. (Germany (Bundesrepublik). Kommission für Geschichte des Parlamentarismus und der Politischen Parteien. Beiträge zur Geschichte des Parlamentarismus und der Politischen Parteien. Band 59)*

VORWAERTS. Vorwärts, 1876-1976: ein Querschnitt in Faksimiles; herausgegeben von Günter Grunwald und Friedhelm Merz, etc. Berlin, [1976]. pp. 203.

FASSLER (MANFRED) Der Weg zum "roten" Obrigkeitsstaat?: die deutsche Sozialdemokratie zwischen Feudalismus und bürgerlicher Gegenrevolution. Giessen, [1977]. pp. 234. *bibliog.*

FENNER (CHRISTIAN) Demokratischer Sozialismus und Sozialdemokratie: Realität und Rhetorik der Sozialismusdiskussion in Deutschland. Frankfurt/Main, [1977]. pp. 227. *bibliog.*

HALL (ALEX) Scandal, sensation and social democracy: the SPD press and Wilhelmine Germany, 1890-1914. Cambridge, 1977. pp. 267. *bibliog.*

HEBEL-KUNZE (BAERBEL) SPD und Faschismus: zur politischen und organisatorischen Entwicklung der SPD, 1932-1935. Frankfurt am Main, [1977]. pp. 278. *bibliog.*

HOEGNER (WILHELM) Flucht vor Hitler: Erinnerungen an die Kapitulation der ersten deutschen Republik, 1933. München, 1977 repr. 1978. pp. 296.

KOMMUNALPOLITIK und Sozialdemokratie: der Beitrag des demokratischen Sozialismus zur kommunalen Selbstverwaltung; ([edited by] Karl-Heinz Nassmacher). Bonn-Bad Godesberg, [1977]. pp. 256.

KREMENDAHL (HANS) Nur die Volkspartei ist mehrheitsfähig: zur Lage der SPD nach der Bundestagswahl, 1976. Bonn-Bad Godesberg, [1977]. pp. 147.

KUEPPER (JOST) Die SPD und der Orientierungsrahmen '85. Bonn-Bad Godesberg, [1977]. pp. 163. *bibliog.*

LEHNERT (DETLEF) Reform und Revolution in den Strategiediskussionen der klassischen Sozialdemokratie: zur Geschichte der deutschen Arbeiterbewegung von den Ursprüngen bis zum Ausbruch des 1. Weltkriegs. Bonn-Bad Godesberg, [1977]. pp. 318.

MATERIALIEN zum politischen Richtungsstreit in der deutschen Sozialdemokratie;...mit einer Einleitung von Hans Mommsen; (Peter Friedemann, Hrsg.). Frankfurt/M, 1977. 2 vols.

PUMM (GUENTER) Kandidatenauswahl und innerparteiliche Demokratie in der Hamburger SPD, etc. Frankfurt am Main, [1977]. pp. 501. *bibliog.*

Der SPD-Staat; herausgegeben von Frank Grube und Gerhard Richter. München, [1977]. pp. 351.

STEPHAN (CORA) "Genossen, wir dürfen uns nicht von der Geduld hinreissen lassen'": aus der Urgeschichte der Sozialdemokratie, 1862-1878. Frankfurt am Main, [1977]. pp. 390. *bibliog.*

WEILL (CLAUDIE) Marxistes russes et social-démocratie allemande, 1898-1904. Paris, 1977. pp. 254. *bibliog.*

WILKER (LOTHER) Die Sicherheitspolitik der SPD, 1956-1966: zwischen Wiedervereinigungs- und Bündnisorientierung. Bonn-Bad Godesberg, [1977]. pp. 347. *bibliog. (Friedrich-Ebert-Stiftung. Forschungsinstitut. Schriftenreihe. Band 135)*

RABE (BERND) Der sozialdemokratische Charakter: drei Generationen aktiver Parteimitglieder in einem Arbeiterviertel. Frankfurt, [1978]. pp. 202. *bibliog.*

SOCIAL DEMOCRATIC PARTY (HUNGARY).

ERÉNYI (TIBOR) Die Sozialdemokratische Partei Ungarns und die Aussenpolitik der Österreichisch-Ungarischen Monarchie in den Jahren 1908-1914. Budapest, 1970. pp. 397-426. *(Magyar Tudományos Akadémia. Studia Historica. 75)*

SOCIAL DEMOCRATIC PARTY (ITALY).

AVERARDI (GIUSEPPE) I socialisti democratici, da Palazzo Barberini alla scissione del 4 luglio 1969. Milano, [1977]. pp. 478.

SOCIAL DEMOCRATIC PARTY (NORWAY).

CASTLES (FRANCIS GEOFFREY) The social democratic image of society: a study of the achievements of Scandinavian social democracy in comparative perspective. London, 1978. pp. 162. *bibliog.*

SOCIAL DEMOCRATIC PARTY (ROMANIA).

STOROZHUK (VLADIMIR PROKOF'EVICH) Rabochee dvizhenie v Rumynii i rumyno-russkie revoliutsionnye sviazi, 1893-1907. Kishinev, 1977. pp. 175. *bibliog.*

SOCIAL DEMOCRATIC PARTY (RUSSIA).

SUSLOV (IURII PAVLOVICH) Leninskaia agrarnaia programma i bor'ba bol'shevikov Povolzh'ia za ee osushchestvlenie, mart 1917 - mart 1918 gg. Saratov, 1972. pp. 414.

DEMESHINA (ELENA IVANOVNA) Rabochee dvizhenie na Donu v period imperializma, 1900-1914 gg. Rostov-na-Donu, 1973. pp. 201.

MOSKOVSKIE bol'sheviki v ogne revoliutsionnykh boev: vospominaniia. Moskva, 1976. pp. 415.

PARTIIA i Velikii Oktiabr': istoriograficheskii ocherk. Moskva, 1976. pp. 294.

ERYKALOV (EFREM FEDOROVICH) and KAMESHKOV (BORIS NIKONOVICH) Leninskii TsK - shtab Velikogo Oktiabria. Leningrad, 1977. pp. 279.

SHESTAKOV (SERGEI VASIL'EVICH) Istoriografiia deiatel'nosti bol'shevistskoi partii v period pervoi mirovoi voiny i Fevral'skoi revoliutsii. Moskva, 1977. pp. 296.

WEILL (CLAUDIE) Marxistes russes et social-démocratie allemande, 1898-1904. Paris, 1977. pp. 254. *bibliog.*

V.I. Lenin i "Soiuzy bor'by". Moskva, 1978. pp. 303. *bibliog.*

— Congresses.

VTOROI s"ezd RSDRP i mestnye partiinye organizatsii Rossii. Perm', 1973. pp. 722.

SOCIAL DEMOCRATIC PARTY (SWEDEN).

CASTLES (FRANCIS GEOFFREY) The social democratic image of society: a study of the achievements of Scandinavian social democracy in comparative perspective. London, 1978. pp. 162. *bibliog.*

SOCIAL DEMOCRATIC PARTY (SWITZERLAND).

SCHMID-AMMANN (PAUL) Unterwegs von der politischen zur sozialen Demokratie: Lebenserinnerungen. Zürich, [1978]. pp. 303.

SOCIAL ETHICS.

ETHICAL perspectives on business and society; edited by Yerachmiel Kugel [and] Gladys W. Gruenberg. Lexington, Mass., [1977]. pp. 135.

HAWORTH (LAWRENCE) Decadence and objectivity. Toronto, [1977]. pp. 169.

SOCIAL EXCHANGE.

BAAL (JAN VAN) Reciprocity and the position of women: anthropological papers. Assen, 1975. pp. 128. *bibliog.*

SOCIAL GROUP WORK.

GROUP work: learning and practice; edited by Nano McCaughan. London, 1978. pp. 208. *bibliog. (National Institute for Social Work Training. National Institute Social Services Library. No. 33)*

SOCIAL GROUPS.

SEGERSTEDT (TORGNY TORGNYSSON) Gruppen som kommunikationssystem. Uppsala, 1955. pp. 37. *(Uppsala. Universitet. Årsskrifter. 1955: 12)*

SEGERSTEDT (TORGNY TORGNYSSON) Slutna och öppna arbetsgrupper: en studie i social struktur. Uppsala, 1956. pp. 50. *(Uppsala. Universitet. Årsskrifter. 1956: 1)*

PATTERSON (HORACE ORLANDO LLOYD) Ethnic chauvinism: the reactionary impulse. New York, 1977. pp. 346.

SOCIAL HISTORY.

MIĘDZY feudalizmem a kapitalizmem: studia z dziejów gospodarczych i społecznych; prace ofiarowane Witoldowi Kuli. Wrocław, 1976. pp. 428. *Articles in French, English, German or Polish.*

PERCEPTIONS of development; edited by Sandra Wallman. Cambridge, 1977. pp. 210. *bibliog. (McGill University. Centre for Developing-Area Studies. Perspectives on Development. 6)*

DIGGINS (JOHN P.) The bard of savagery: Thorstein Veblen and modern social theory. New York, [1978]. pp. 257.

INDUSTRIELLE Gesellschaft und politisches System: Beiträge zur politischen Sozialgeschichte: Festschrift für Fritz Fischer zum siebzigsten Geburtstag; (Dirk Stegmann [and others], Hrsg.). Bonn, [1978]. pp. 464. *bibliog. (Friedrich-Ebert-Stiftung. Forschungsinstitut. Schriftenreihe. Band 137) In various languages.*

— Bibliography.

GILBERT (VICTOR F.) and HOLMES (COLIN) compilers. Theses and dissertations in economic and social history in Yorkshire universities, 1920-74. 1975. pp. 154. *Typescript: unpublished.*

— Methodology.

MACFARLANE (ALAN DONALD JAMES) and others. Reconstructing historical communities;...in collaboration with Sarah Harrison and Charles Jardine. Cambridge, 1977. pp. 221. *bibliog.*

SOCIAL INDICATORS

— Canada.

McCREADY (GERALD B.) Profile Canada: social and economic projections. Georgetown, Ont., 1977. pp. 413. *bibliog.*

— — Nova Scotia.

NOVA SCOTIA. Department of Development. Economics and Statistics Division. 1976. Perspective Nova Scotia: a compendium of social statistics. [Halifax, 1976?]. pp. 185.

— European Economic Community countries.

SOCIAL INDICATORS FOR THE EUROPEAN COMMUNITY; [pd. by] Statistical Office [European Communities]. irreg., 1960/75(1st)- Luxembourg. *[in Community languages].*

— France.

FRANCE. Groupe de Travail Indicateurs Sociaux et Economiques. 1976. Rapport; (préparation du 7e plan). Paris, [1976]. pp. 101.

SOCIAL INDICATORS(Cont.)

— Germany.

LEBENSBEDINGUNGEN in der Bundesrepublik: sozialer Wandel und Wohlfahrtsentwicklung; (Wolfgang Zapf, Hg.). 2nd ed. Frankfurt/Main, 1978. pp. 947. *bibliog.* (*Frankfurt am Main. Universität, and Mannheim. Universität. Sozialpolitische Forschergruppe. SPES- Projekt. Schriftenreihe. Band 10*)

— Portugal.

PORTUGAL. Instituto Nacional de Estatistica. Indicadores economico-sociais: Social-economic indicators. m., 1973 (ano 1)- Lisboa. *[in Portuguese and English] Supersedes its Indicadores estatisticos a curto prazo (1969-1972)*

— Scandinavia.

ALLARDT (ERIK) On the relationship between objective and subjective predicaments. Helsinki, 1977. pp. 22. *bibliog.* (*Helsinki. Yliopisto. Research Group for Comparative Sociology. Research Reports. No. 16*)

— United Kingdom.

U.K. Department of the Environment. 1976. Ongoing work in the fields of social statistics and social indicators: an information note. London, 1976. pp. 18. *bibliog.*

DINWIDDY (ROBERT) and REED (DEREK) The effects of certain social and demographic changes on income distribution;...background paper to Report No. 5: third report on the standing reference. London, 1977. pp. 168. *bibliog.* (*U.K. Royal Commission on the Distribution of Income and Wealth, 1974. Background Papers. No. 3) Report No. 5 published as British Parliamentary Paper Cmnd. 6999, Session 1977-78.*

WEBBER (RICHARD J.) The national classification of residential neighbourhoods: an introduction to the classification of wards and parishes. London, 1977. pp. 90. *bibliog.* (*Planning Research Applications Group. PRAG Technical Papers. TP 23*)

WEBBER (RICHARD J.) and CRAIG (JOHN) Writer on population. Socio-economic classification of local authority areas. London, 1978. pp. 117. (*U.K. Office of Population Censuses and Surveys. Studies on Medical and Population Subjects. No.35*)

SOCIAL INTERACTION.

GAHAGAN (JUDY) Interpersonal and group behaviour. London, 1975, repr. 1978. pp. 144. *bibliog.*

BLAU (PETER MICHAEL) Inequality and heterogeneity: a primitive theory of social structure. New York, [1977]. pp. 307. *bibliog.*

FISCHER (CLAUDE S.) and others. Networks and places: social relations in the urban setting. New York, [1977]. pp. 229. *bibliog.*

HUMAN services and resource networks; [by] Seymour B. Sarason [and others]. San Francisco, 1977. pp. 201. *bibliog.*

QUESTIONS and politeness: strategies in social interaction; edited by Esther N. Goody. Cambridge, 1978. pp. 324. *bibliog.*

SOCIAL JUSTICE.

LOODMER (PATRICIA SIMONE) A geographical investigation of the social justice content of urban planning decisions, with special reference to the displacement of the population of St. Ebbe's Parish, Oxford, 1951-1961. [1977]. fo. 392. Typescript. Ph. D. (London) thesis: unpublished. *This thesis is the property of London University and may not be removed from the Library.*

SOCIAL justice and preferential treatment: women and racial minorities in education and business; edited by William T. Blackstone and Robert D. Heslep. Athens, Ga., [1977]. pp. 216. *bibliog. Papers presented at a conference held at the University of Georgia, February 13-15, 1975, and sponsored by that university's Dept. of Philosophy and Religion and Dept. of History and Philosophy of Education, together with the Georgia State Committee for the Humanities.*

MOORE (BARRINGTON) Injustice: the social bases of obedience and revolt. London, 1978. pp. 540. *bibliog.*

SOCIAL LEGISLATION

— Italy.

BRANCA (GIORGIO) Legislazione sociale: saggi. Padova, 1977. pp. 329.

— Switzerland.

SCHWEINGRUBER (EDWIN) Sozialgesetzgebung der Schweiz. 2nd ed. Zürich, 1977. pp. 312.

SOCIAL MEDICINE.

JÖNSSON (BENGT) Cost-benefit analysis in public health and medical care. Lund, [1976]. pp. 141. *bibliog.*

TIMIO (MARIO) Classi sociali e malattie: per un nuovo rapporto medico-società. [Roma, 1976]. pp. 136.

KRAUSE (ELLIOTT A.) Power and illness : the political sociology of health and medical care. New York, [1977]. pp. 383.

MEDICAL encounters: the experience of illness and treatment; edited by Alan Davis and Gordon Horobin. London, [1977]. pp. 223. *bibliogs.*

COCKERHAM (WILLIAM C.) Medical sociology. Englewood Cliffs, [1978]. pp. 340. *bibliog.*

The CULTURAL crisis of modern medicine; edited by John Ehrenreich. New York, [1978]. pp. 300.

HORROBIN (DAVID FREDERICK) Medical hubris: a reply to Ivan Illich. Edinburgh, 1978. pp. 109.

— United States.

ENOS (DARRYL D.) and SULTAN (PAUL) The sociology of health care: social, economic, and political perspectives. New York, 1977. pp. 420. *bibliogs.*

KRAUSE (ELLIOTT A.) Power and illness : the political sociology of health and medical care. New York, [1977]. pp. 383.

SOCIAL MOBILITY.

GIROD (ROGER) Inégalité-inégalités: analyse de la mobilité sociale;.. avec un groupe de recherche. Paris, 1977. pp. 183. *bibliog.*

— Bulgaria.

ATANASOV (ATANAS) and MASHIAKH (ARON) Promeni v sotsialnata prinadlezhnost na zaetite litsa v Bulgariia; Changements dans l'appartenance sociale des personnes occupées en Bulgarie. Sofiia, 1971. pp. 171. *bibliog.* (*Nauchnoizsledovatelski Institut po Statistika. Izdaniia. 3) With Russian and French summaries.*

— France.

BERTAUX (DANIEL) Destins personnels et structure de classe: pour une critique de l'anthroponomie politique. [Paris, 1977]. pp. 322.

— Nigeria.

IMOAGENE (OSHOMHA) Social mobility in emergent society: a study of the new elite in western Nigeria. Canberra, 1976. pp. 368. *bibliog.* (*Australian National University. Research School of Social Sciences. Department of Demography. Changing African Family Project Series. 2*)

— Poland.

JANICKA (KRYSTYNA) Ruchliwość międzypokoleniowa i jej korelaty: z badań nad ludnością miejską. Wrocław, 1976. pp. 233.

— United Kingdom.

RICHARDSON (CHARLES JAMES) Contemporary social mobility. London, 1977. pp. 342. *bibliog.*

— United States.

HAUSER (ROBERT MASON) and FEATHERMAN (DAVID L.) The process of stratification: trends and analyses. New York, [1977]. pp. 372. *bibliog.*

DECKER (PETER R.) Fortunes and failures: white-collar mobility in nineteenth-century San Francisco. Cambridge, Mass., 1978. pp. 336.

SOCIAL POLICY.

UNITED NATIONS. Interregional Seminar on Development Policies and Planning in Relation to Urbanization, Pittsburgh, 1966. Report of the...seminar...Pittsburgh, Pennsylvania, 24 October to 4 November, 1966. (ST/TAO/SER.C/97). New York, 1967. pp. 74.

SYMPOSIUM ON SOCIAL POLICY AND PLANNING, COPENHAGEN, 1970. Report on the Symposium...[held at] Copenhagen, Denmark, 22 June to 2 July 1970. (ST/TAO/SER.C/128). New York, United Nations, 1971. pp. 26.

AUSTRALIA. Cities Commission. 1975. Australians' use of time: a contribution of social planning to urban development and land use design. [Canberra], 1975. 1 vol. (unpaged). *Photocopy.*

AU-delà de la crise; ([by] Norman Birnbaum [and others]); présentation par Alain Touraine. Paris, [1976]. pp. 255.

GIL (DAVID G.) Unravelling social policy: theory, analysis, and political action towards social equality. rev. ed. Cambridge, Mass., [1976]. pp. 213.

SANDBERG (ÅKE) The limits to democratic planning: knowledge, power and methods in the struggle for the future. Stockholm, 1976. pp. 391. *bibliog.*

ALTERNATIVES TO GROWTH CONFERENCE, 1ST, HOUSTON, TEXAS, 1975. Alternatives to growth-1: a search for sustainable futures; edited by Dennis L. Meadows. Cambridge, Mass., [1977]. pp. 405. *bibliog. Selection of papers presented at the conference including 4 prize-winning essays submitted to the Mitchell Prize competition.*

AMERICAN ACADEMY OF POLITICAL AND SOCIAL SCIENCE. Annals. vol. 434. Social theory and public policy; special editor of this volume J. Rogers Hollingsworth. Philadelphia, [1977]. pp. 255.

MISHRA (RAMESH) Society and social policy: theoretical perspectives on welfare. London, 1977. pp. 188.

ALLEN (T. HARRELL) New methods in social science research: policy sciences and futures research. New York, [1978]. pp. 157. *bibliogs.*

NATIONAL ECONOMIC AND SOCIAL COUNCIL [EIRE]. Universality and selectivity: strategies in social policy; (by Mike Reddin). Dublin, Stationery Office, [1978]. pp. 115. *bibliog.* (*[Reports]. No. 36*)

WEALE (ALBERT) Equality and social policy. London, 1978. pp. 149. *bibliog.*

— Decision making.

SOCIAL policy research; edited by Martin Bulmer. London, 1978. pp. 373.

— Research.

FAIRWEATHER (GEORGE WILLIAM) and TORNATZKY (LOUIS G.) Experimental methods for social policy research. Oxford, 1977. pp. 420. *bibliog.*

SOCIAL PROBLEMS.

HOYLAND (JOHN SOMERVELL) ed. Experiments in social reconstruction. London, 1937. pp. 125.

HARTJEN (CLAYTON A.) Possible trouble: an analysis of social problems. New York, 1977. pp. 351.

THIS land of promises: the rise and fall of social problems in America; edited by Armand L. Mauss and Julie Camille Wolfe. Philadelphia, [1977]. pp. 452. *bibliogs.*

GRIMOND (JOSEPH) The common welfare. London, 1978. pp. 248.

ROWAN (JOHN) The structured crowd. London, 1978. pp. 157. *bibliogs.*

VEREIN FÜR SOZIALPOLITIK. Schriften. Neue Folge. Band 95. Zur Neuen Sozialen Frage; von Friedrich Buttler [and others]; herausgegeben von Hans Peter Widmaier. Berlin, [1978]. pp. 249.

SOCIAL PSYCHIATRY.

MAGARO (PETER A.) and others. The mental health industry: a cultural phenomenon: alternate solutions generated from an empirical evaluation of the cultural determinants, vested interests, and treatment effectiveness of the current mental health establishment. New York, [1978]. pp. 272. *bibliog.*

SOCIAL PSYCHOLOGY.

GLEN (FREDERICK) The social psychology of organizations. London, 1975. pp. 144. *bibliog.*

WHELDALL (KEVIN) Social behaviour: key problems and social relevance. London, 1975. pp. 144. *bibliog.*

ROWAN (JOHN) The power of the group. London, 1976. pp. 212.

SOCIAL psychology in transition; edited by Lloyd H. Strickland [and others]. New York, [1976]. pp. 361. *bibliogs. Based on a conference held at Carleton University in 1974.*

STACEY (BARRIE B.) Psychology and social structure. London, 1976. pp. 142. *bibliog.*

SYMPOSIUM ON COGNITION, 11TH, CARNEGIE-MELLON UNIVERSITY, 1975. Cognition and social behavior; edited by John S. Carroll [and] John W. Payne. Hillsdale, N.J., 1976. pp. 290. *bibliog.*

PERSPECTIVES on social psychology; edited by Clyde Hendrick. Hillsdale, 1977. pp. 362. *bibliogs.*

SOCIAL comparison processes: theoretical and empirical perspectives; edited by Jerry M. Suls [and] Richard L. Miller. Washington, D.C., [1977]. pp. 371. *bibliogs.*

ULLMANN-MARGALIT (EDNA) The emergence of norms. Oxford, 1977. pp. 206. *bibliog.*

ARCHIBALD (WILLIAM PETER) Social psychology as political economy. Toronto, [1978]. pp. 296. *bibliog.*

DOISE (WILLEM) Groups and individuals: explorations in social psychology. Cambridge, [1978]. pp. 226. *bibliog. Translated by Douglas Graham.*

KATZ (DANIEL) and KAHN (ROBERT LOUIS) The social psychology of organizations. 2nd ed. New York, [1978]. pp. 838. *bibliog.*

NEWMAN (BARBARA M.) and NEWMAN (PHILIP R.) Infancy and childhood: development and its contents. New York, [1978]. pp. 619. *bibliog.*

ROWAN (JOHN) The structured crowd. London, 1978. pp. 157. *bibliogs.*

— Mathematical models.

MATHEMATICAL models for social psychology; edited by Wilhelm F. Kempf [and] Bruno H. Repp; with contributions by Erling B. Andersen [and others]. Chichester, 1977. pp. 283. *bibliogs. First published in 1976 under title: Some mathematical models for social psychology. A rev. and augmented translation of Probabilistische Modelle in der Sozialpsychologie.*

— Methodology.

The SOCIAL contexts of method; edited by Michael Brenner [and others]. London, [1978]. pp. 261. *bibliogs.*

SOCIAL REFORMERS

— United Kingdom.

PIKE (EDGAR ROYSTON) Pioneers of social change. [London, 1963]. pp. 218.

— United States.

DIGGINS (JOHN P.) The bard of savagery: Thorstein Veblen and modern social theory. New York, [1978]. pp. 257.

SOCIAL ROLE.

COULTER (IAN DOUGLASS) A philosophical and theoretical criticism of "homo sociologicus" in twentieth century sociology. [1977]. fo. 524. *bibliog. Typescript: (unpublished.) Ph.D. (London) thesis. This thesis is the property of London University and may not be removed from the Library.*

HARTMAN (TOR) Uppsatser om alienation och kärlek: (three essays on alienation and love). Helsinki, 1977. pp. 62. *(Helsinki. Yliopisto. Research Group for Comparative Sociology. Research Reports. No.13) In Swedish, with English summaries.*

SOCIAL SCIENCE RESEARCH.

BATSCHA (ROBERT) The effectiveness of dissemination methods for social and economic development research. Paris, Organisation for Economic Co-operation and Development, 1976. pp. 201. *bibliog.* (Development Centre. Technical Papers)

FAIRWEATHER (GEORGE WILLIAM) and TORNATZKY (LOUIS G.) Experimental methods for social policy research. Oxford, 1977. pp. 420. *bibliog.*

— Directories.

UNITED NATIONS EDUCATIONAL, SCIENTIFIC AND CULTURAL ORGANIZATION. World Social Science Information Services. 2. World directory of social science institutions. Paris, 1977. pp. 262. *In English and French.*

— Angola.

EGERO (BERTIL) Mozambique and Angola: reconstruction in the social sciences. Uppsala, 1977. pp. 78. *(Nordiska Afrikainstitutet. Research Reports. No. 42)*

— Ireland (Republic) — Registers.

ECONOMIC AND SOCIAL RESEARCH INSTITUTE. Register of research projects in the social sciences in progress in Ireland, February 1974; compiled by Maria Maher. Dublin, 1974. fo. 21.

— Italy.

FIORAVANTI (LUCIANO) La Fondazione Agnelli: cultura e potere nella strategia neo-capitalistica italiana. Rimini, 1976. pp. 162.

— Mozambique.

EGERO (BERTIL) Mozambique and Angola: reconstruction in the social sciences. Uppsala, 1977. pp. 78. *(Nordiska Afrikainstitutet. Research Reports. No. 42)*

— Netherlands.

NETHERLANDS. Verkenningscommissie Sociaal Onderzoek. 1975. Sociaal-wetenschappelijk onderzoek en beleid: rapport. ['s-Gravenhage], 1975. pp. 83. *bibliog.*

— South Africa.

HUMANITAS: tydskrif vir navorsing in die geesteswetenskappe: jl. for research in the human sciences: (pd. by the South African Human Sciences Research Council). 2 a 'yr., 1971 (v.1)- , with gap (1971, v.1, no.2). Pretoria. *[articles in Afrikaans or English, with a summary in the alternative language]*

— United Kingdom.

SOCIAL policy research; edited by Martin Bulmer. London, 1978. pp. 373.

— United States.

SOCIAL research in conflict with law and ethics; Paul Nejelski, editor. Cambridge, Mass., [1976]. pp. 197. *Papers given at a conference held at the University of Bielefeld, 1974.*

SOCIAL SCIENCES.

SOCIAL SCIENCE JOURNAL; [pd. by] Korean National Commission for Unesco. a., 1973 [1st]- Seoul.

EXPLORATIONS in general theory in social science: essays in honor of Talcott Parsons; edited by Jan J. Loubser [and others]. New York, [1976]. 2 vols.

HOUGH (JERRY F.) The Soviet Union and social science theory. Cambridge, Mass., 1977. pp. 275. *(Harvard University. Russian Research Center. Studies. 77)*

INTERNATIONAL CONGRESS OF LOGIC, METHODOLOGY AND PHILOSOPHY OF SCIENCE, 5TH, LONDON, ONTARIO, 1975. Foundation problems in the special sciences: part two of the proceedings...; edited by Robert E. Butts and Jaakko Hintikka. Dordrecht, [1977]. pp. 427. *bibliogs. (Western Ontario. University. University of Western Ontario Series in Philosophy of Science. 10)*

SPURLING (LAURIE) Phenomenology and the social world: the philosophy of Merleau-Ponty and its relation to the social sciences. London, 1977. pp. 208. *bibliog.*

WEINSTEIN (MICHAEL A.) The tragic sense of political life. Columbia, S.C., [1977]. pp. 189.

ACTION and interpretation: studies in the philosophy of the social sciences; edited by Christopher Hookway and Philip Pettit. Cambridge, 1978. pp. 178.

HAYEK (FRIEDRICH AUGUST) New studies in philosophy, politics, economics and the history of ideas. London, 1978. pp. 314.

[WEBER (MAX)] Max Weber: selections in translation; edited by W.G. Runciman. Cambridge, 1978. pp. 398. *bibliog.*

— Bibliography.

INTERNATIONAL LABOUR OFFICE. Library. 1978. International labour documentation: cumulative edition, 1972-1976. Boston, Mass., 1978. 5 vols.

— Dictionaries.

READING (HUGO F.) A dictionary of the social sciences. London, [1976]. pp. 231.

— History — United Kingdom.

SOFFER (REBA N.) Ethics and society in England: the revolution in the social sciences, 1870-1914. Berkeley, Calif., [1978]. pp. 325.

— — United States.

HASKELL (THOMAS L.) The emergence of professional social science: the American Social Science Association and the nineteenth-century crisis of authority. Urbana, [1977]. pp. 276. *bibliog.*

WARD (DWAYNE) Toward a critical political economics: a critique of liberal and radical economic thought. Santa Monica, Calif., [1977]. pp. 334. *bibliog.*

— Information services — Congresses.

INTERNATIONAL COMMITTEE FOR SOCIAL SCIENCE INFORMATION AND DOCUMENTATION. Réunion du Bureau, 7 et 8 mai 1962, Moscou: compte rendu. Paris, 1962. pp. 13.

INTERNATIONAL CONFERENCE ON INFORMATION AND DOCUMENTATION IN SOCIAL SCIENCES, MOSCOW, 1977. Papers of the International Conference...[held at] Moscow, June, 1977; by the European Coordination Centre for Research Documentation in Social Sciences. Moscow, Unesco, 1977. 2 vols.

— Mathematical models.

COATS (R.B.) and PARKIN (ANDREW) Computer models in the social sciences. London, 1977. pp. 184. *bibliogs.*

LATENT variables in socio-economic models; edited by D.J. Aigner and A.S. Goldberger. Amsterdam, 1977. pp. 383. *bibliogs.*

ZEEMAN (E.C.) Catastrophe theory: selected papers, 1972-1977. Reading, Mass., 1977. pp. 674. *bibliog.*

SOCIAL SCIENCES.(Cont.)

— Methodology.

BOGUE (DONALD JOSEPH) and BOGUE (ELIZABETH J.) Essays in human ecology: 1. Chicago, [1976]. pp. 138. *bibliogs*. *(Chicago. University. Community and Family Study Center. Community and Family Monographs)*

GALT (ANTHONY H.) and SMITH (LARRY J.) Models and the study of social change. New York, [1976]. pp. 180. *bibliog*.

COATS (R.B.) and PARKIN (ANDREW) Computer models in the social sciences. London, 1977. pp. 184. *bibliogs*.

FADEN (ARNOLD M.) Economics of space and time: the measure-theoretic foundations of social science. Ames, 1977. pp. 703.

GASTIL (RAYMOND D.) Social humanities. San Francisco, 1977. pp. 314. *bibliog*.

LATENT variables in socio-economic models; edited by D.J. Aigner and A.S. Goldberger. Amsterdam, 1977. pp. 383. *bibliogs*.

PÖRN (INGMAR) Action theory and social science: some formal models. Dordrecht, [1977]. pp. 129. *bibliog*.

ACTION and interpretation: studies in the philosophy of the social sciences; edited by Christopher Hookway and Philip Pettit. Cambridge, 1978. pp. 178.

ALLEN (T. HARRELL) New methods in social science research: policy sciences and futures research. New York, [1978]. pp. 157. *bibliogs*.

ELSTER (JON) Logic and society: contradictions and possible worlds. Chichester, [1978]. pp. 235. *bibliog*.

— Philosophy.

GASTIL (RAYMOND D.) Social humanities. San Francisco, 1977. pp. 314. *bibliog*.

— Societies.

MAYENCE (SERGE) L'IPSSA à 25 ans: contribution à l'histoire de l'Institut et réflexions sur l'avenir des sciences sociales appliquées. [Marcinelle, 1970]. pp. 72. *bibliog*.

UNITED NATIONS EDUCATIONAL, SCIENTIFIC AND CULTURAL ORGANIZATION. World Social Science Information Services. 2. World directory of social science institutions. Paris, 1977. pp. 262. *In English and French*.

— Statistical methods.

MAYES (DAVID G.) Projects in economic and social statistics. Exeter, 1976. pp. 141.

COHEN (JACOB) 1923- . Statistical power analysis for the behavioral sciences. new ed. New York, [1977]. pp. 474. *bibliog*.

PINE (VANDERLYN R.) Introduction to social statistics. Englewood Cliffs, [1977]. pp. 415.

WEISBERG (HERBERT F.) and BOWEN (BRUCE D.) An introduction to survey research and data analysis. San Francisco, [1977]. pp. 243. *bibliog*.

— Study and teaching.

INTERREGIONAL COURSE ON SOCIAL PLANNING, 1ST, GENEVA, 1968. Interregional course...[held at] Geneva, Switzerland, 30 September to 9 November 1968. (ST/TAO/SER.C/107). New York, United Nations, 1969. pp. 10.

INTERREGIONAL COURSE ON SOCIAL PLANNING, 2ND, AMSTERDAM, 1970. Interregional course...[held in] Amsterdam, 23 March to 9 May, 1970. (ST/TAO/SER.C/122). New York, United Nations, 1971. pp. 10.

JAROLIMEK (JOHN) Social studies competencies and skills; learning to teach as an intern. New York, [1977]. pp. 272. *bibliog*.

JAROLIMEK (JOHN) Social studies in elementary education. 5th ed. New York, [1977]. pp. 369. *bibliogs*.

— — Mongolia.

OBSHCHESTVENNYE nauki v MNR. Moskva, 1977. pp. 227. *bibliog*.

— — Russia — Tajikistan.

RADZHABOV (ZARIF SHARIPOVICH) Ocherki istorii kul'turnogo stroitel'stva v Tadzhikistane; pod redaktsiei...G.A. Ashurova. Dushanbe, 1976. pp. 135.

SOCIAL SCIENTISTS

— Europe, Eastern.

SOCIAL scientists and policy making in the USSR; edited by Richard B. Remnek. New York, 1977. pp. 144.

— Russia.

SOCIAL scientists and policy making in the USSR; edited by Richard B. Remnek. New York, 1977. pp. 144.

— United States.

FURNER (MARY O.) Advocacy and objectivity: a crisis in the professionalization of American social science, 1865-1905. Lexington, Ky., [1975]. pp. 357. *bibliog*.

SOCIAL SECURITY.

In earlier volumes of this Bibliography, similar material is entered under INSURANCE, SOCIAL.

BEYME (KLAUS VON) Sozialismus oder Wohlfahrtsstaat?: Sozialpolitik und Sozialstruktur der Sowjetunion im Systemvergleich. München, [1977]. pp. 144.

INTERNATIONAL LABOUR OFFICE. 1977. Social security for migrant workers. Geneva, 1977. pp. 154. *bibliog*.

PENSIONS and inflation: an international discussion [held at Geneva, May 1976]. Geneva, International Labour Office, 1977. pp. 136.

— America, Latin.

MEXICO. Instituto Mexicano del Seguro Social. 1977. Conferencia Interamericana de Seguridad Social: aportaciones a la XI Asamblea General. [Mexico, 1977]. 2 vols.

— Australia.

ESSAYS on law and poverty: bail and social security. Canberra, 1977. pp. 92. *(Australia. Commission of Inquiry into Poverty. Law and Poverty Series)*

— Bahamas.

INTERNATIONAL LABOUR OFFICE. Development Programme. Technical Assistance Sector. [Bahamas]. R.2. Report to the Government of the Commonwealth of the Bahamas on the financial and actuarial aspects of the national insurance scheme. (ILO/TAP/Bahamas/R.2.). Geneva, 1973. pp. 124.

— Denmark.

STORM (SUSANNE) A comparison between the administration of supplementary benefits in England and public assistance in Denmark with special reference to the exercise of discretion. 1977. fo. 313. *Typescript. Ph.D. (London) thesis: unpublished. This thesis is the property of London University and may not be removed from the Library.*

— European Economic Community countries.

FERREIRA (MARIA MARGARIDA PONTE) Alguns aspectos da segurança social na C.E.E. Lisboa, 1973. pp. 30. *(Portugal. Ministerio das Corporações e Previdência Social. Gabinete de Planeamento. Serie Relatorio e Analises. 1) With abstracts in English and French*.

EUROPEAN COMMUNITIES. Social Security for Migrant Workers. Guides. No. 1. Guide...concerning the rights and obligations with regard to social security of employed persons going to work in...[European Economic Community countries]. Brussels, 1975. 9 parts (in 1 vol.)

— — Accounting.

EUROPEAN COMMUNITIES. Statistical Office. Social accounts: accounts of social protection in the EC. a., 1970/75- Luxembourg. *[in Community languages]*

— France.

FRANCE. Ministère de la Santé Publique et de la Sécurité Sociale. Bulletin de statistiques de santé et de sécurité sociale. bi-m., Ja/F 1972 (no.1)- Paris.

— Germany.

BETHUSY-HUC (VIOLA VON) Gräfin. Das Sozialleistungssystem der Bundesrepublik Deutschland. 2nd ed. Tübingen, 1976. pp. 346. *bibliog*.

— Guatemala.

GARCIA LAGUARDIA (JORGE MARIO) Antecedentes del seguro social en Guatemala: la responsibilidad civil y los infortunios del trabajo. Guatemala, 1964. pp. 195. *bibliog*. *(Universidad de San Carlos de Guatemala. [Publications]. vol. 49)*

— Israel.

GREENBERG (HAROLD I.) and NADLER (SAMUEL) Poverty in Israel: economic realities and the promise of social justice. New York, 1977. pp. 176. *bibliog*.

— Italy.

CHERUBINI (ARNALDO) Storia della previdenza sociale in Italia, 1860-1960. Roma, 1977. pp. 435.

— Japan.

JAPAN. Ministry of Health and Welfare. 1977. Guide to health and welfare services in Japan. Tokyo, 1977. pp. 59.

JAPAN. Ministry of Health and Welfare. 1977. Health and welfare services in Japan. Tokyo, 1977. pp. 170.

WOODSWORTH (DAVID E.) Social security and national policy: Sweden, Yugoslavia, Japan. Montreal, 1977. pp. 156. *bibliog*.

— Mexico.

MEXICO. Instituto Mexicano del Seguro Social. 1977. Conferencia Interamericana de Seguridad Social: aportaciones a la XI Asamblea General. [Mexico, 1977]. 2 vols.

— Netherlands.

NETHERLANDS. Ministerie van Sociale Zaken. 1974. Interim rapport 1973 inzake de unificatie en codificatie der soziale zekerheidswetgeving: inventorisatierapport. 's-Gravenhage, 1974. pp. 174. *bibliog*. *(Verslagen en Rapporten: Sociale Zaken. 1974.8)*

BAKKER (VINCENT) Uw geld en uw leven: het verzekeringsbedrijf ontmaskerd. Bussum, 1978. pp. 272.

— New Zealand.

NEW ZEALAND. Social Security Department. 1969. Rates and conditions of benefits and pensions since inception; supplement to first background paper. Wellington, 1969. fo. 47.

NEW ZEALAND. Social Security Department. 1969. Social security cash benefits in New Zealand. Wellington, 1969. pp. 39.

NEW ZEALAND. Department of Social Welfare. 1972. Guide to the reciprocal agreement on social security between New Zealand and the United Kingdom. Wellington, [1972]. pp. 15.

NEW ZEALAND. Domestic Purposes Benefit Review Committee. 1977. Report; [J.R.P. Horn, chairman]. in NEW ZEALAND. General Assembly. House of Representatives. Journals...Appendix to journals, 1977, E.28.

— Russia.

BEYME (KLAUS VON) Sozialismus oder Wohlfahrtsstaat?: Sozialpolitik und Sozialstruktur der Sowjetunion im Systemvergleich. München, [1977]. pp. 144.

— Spain.

ALDAZ ISANTA (JUAN) and FERNANDEZ SANCHEZ (JOSE LUIS) Libro verde de la Seguridad Social: analisis critico economico- financiero de la seguridad social española. [Madrid, 1977]. pp. 497.

— Sweden.

WOODSWORTH (DAVID E.) Social security and national policy: Sweden, Yugoslavia, Japan. Montreal, 1977. pp. 156. *bibliog.*

— United Kingdom.

SOCIAL SECURITY STATISTICS; [pd. by] Department of Health and Social Security [U.K.]). a., 1972 (1st)- London.

MILSOM (PENNY) Unsupported mothers on social security. London, [1972]. pp. 9. *(Mothers in Action. Study Pamphlets. No.2)*

NEW ZEALAND. Department of Social Welfare. 1972. Guide to the reciprocal agreement on social security between New Zealand and the United Kingdom. Wellington, [1972]. pp. 15.

SOCIALIST WORKER. Pamphlets. Know your rights: social security for strikers. [London, 1973]. 1 pamphlet (unpaged).

SBC NOTES AND NEWS; issued by the Supplementary Benefits Commission. irreg., S 1974(no.1)- London.

HOWELL (RALPH FREDERIC) Low pay and taxation. London, 1976. fo. 9. *(Low Pay Unit. Low Pay Papers. No. 8)*

CHILD BENEFITS NOW CAMPAIGN. The great child benefit robbery. London, 1977. pp. 32.

CLAIMANTS' UNION MOVEMENT. Claimants' Union guidebook; (a handbook from the Claimants' Union Movement). Birmingham, 1977. pp. 45.

LISTER (RUTH) Patching up the safety net?;...evidence to the review of the supplementary benefits scheme. London, 1977. pp. 88. *(Child Poverty Action Group. Poverty Pamphlets. 31)*

STORM (SUSANNE) A comparison between the administration of supplementary benefits in England and public assistance in Denmark with special reference to the exercise of discretion. 1977. fo. 313. *Typescript. Ph.D. (London) thesis: unpublished. This thesis is the property of London University and may not be removed from the Library.*

TUNNARD (JO) and WHATELY (CLARE) Rights guide for home owners. 2nd ed. London, 1977. pp. 80.

U.K. Supplementary Benefits Commission. 1977. Low incomes: evidence to the Royal Commission on the Distribution of Income and Wealth. London, 1977. pp. 100. *(Supplementary Benefits Administration Papers. 6)*

U.K. Supplementary Benefits Commission. 1977. Supplementary benefits handbook: a guide to claimants' rights. 5th ed. London, 1977. pp. 115. *(Supplementary Benefits Administration Papers. 2)*

CALVERT (HARRY) Social security law. 2nd ed. London, 1978. pp. 549.

— — Law and legislation.

OGUS (ANTHONY IAN) and BARENDT (ERIC MARTIN) The law of social security. London, 1978. pp. 714.

PARTINGTON (MARTIN) Claim in time: a study of the time limit rules for claiming social security benefits. London, 1978. pp. 195.

— — Ireland, Northern.

IRELAND, NORTHERN. Department of Health and Social Services. 1976. Family benefits and pensions in Northern Ireland. [3rd ed.] [Belfast], 1976. pp. 48.

— United States.

BROWN (JAMES DOUGLAS) Essays on social security. Princeton, 1977. pp. 121. *(Princeton University. Department of Economics and Sociology. Industrial Relations Section. Research Report Series. No.123)*

FLOWERS (MARILYN R.) Women and social security: an institutional dilemma. Washington, [1977]. pp. 41. *(American Enterprise Institute for Public Policy Research. AEI Studies. 161)*

INCOME support policies for the aged; edited by G. S. Tolley [and] Richard V. Burkhauser. Cambridge, Mass., [1977]. pp. 194. *bibliogs. Papers presented at a conference held at the University of Chicago in 1976.*

BARRO (ROBERT J.) The impact of social security on private saving: evidence from the U.S. Time Series...; with a reply by Martin Feldstein. Washington, D.C., [1978]. pp. 47. *(American Enterprise Institute for Public Policy Research. AEI Studies. 199)*

— Yugoslavia.

WOODSWORTH (DAVID E.) Social security and national policy: Sweden, Yugoslavia, Japan. Montreal, 1977. pp. 156. *bibliog.*

SOCIAL SECURITY TAXES

— Ireland (Republic).

NATIONAL ECONOMIC AND SOCIAL COUNCIL [EIRE]. Integrated approaches to personal income taxes and transfers; (by Brendan Dowling). Dublin, Stationery Office, [1977]. pp. 100. *bibliog. ([Reports]. No. 37)*

SOCIAL SERVICE.

GENG (J.M.) Mauvaises pensées d'un travailleur social. Paris, [1977]. pp. 207.

KADUSHIN (ALFRED) Consultation in social work. New York, 1977. pp. 236. *bibliog.*

— Dictionaries and encyclopedias.

CLEGG (JOAN) Dictionary of social services: policy and practice. 2nd ed. London, 1977. pp. 147. *bibliog.*

— Finance.

PETERSEN (JØRN HENRIK) Co-ordination of the use of financial resources at and between central and local levels within the public sector. Odense, [1975?]. 1 vol. (various pagings). *(Odense Universitet. Institut for Historie og Samfundsvidenskab. Skrifter. No. 20) Paper presented at United Nations Seminar on Problems of Policy, Administration and Coordination in the Financing of the Social Services, Killarney, Ireland, 1975.*

— Philosophy.

PHILOSOPHY in social work; edited by Noel Timms and David Watson. London, 1978. pp. 209. *bibliog.*

— Team work.

KADUSHIN (ALFRED) Consultation in social work. New York, 1977. pp. 236. *bibliog.*

— Australia.

BENJAMIN (C.) and MORTON (J.) A model for welfare service planning and delivery. Canberra, 1975. pp. 118. *(Australia. Commission of Inquiry into Poverty. Research Reports)*

CONSUMER groups and their views on welfare services and rented housing. Canberra, 1975. pp. 111. *(Australia. Commission of Inquiry into Poverty. Research Reports)*

GRIFFITHS (DAVID) Emergency relief: a report prepared for the Social Welfare Commission. [Canberra?], 1975. pp. 71. *bibliog.*

WELFARE of migrants. Canberra, 1975. pp. 184. *bibliogs. (Australia. Commission of Inquiry into Poverty. Research Reports)*

COMMUNITY services: four studies. Canberra, 1976. pp. 178. *(Australia. Commission of Inquiry into Poverty. Research Reports)*

— — South Australia.

DUIGAN (M.G.) A study of the Hindmarsh, South Australia, community. Canberra, 1975. pp. 61. *(Australia. Commission of Inquiry into Poverty. Research Reports)*

— Belgium.

ANTWERP. Commissie van Openbare Onderstand. Vijftig jaar Commissie van Openbare Onderstand Antwerpen 1915-1975. [Antwerp, 1975]. pp. 225.

— Germany.

GERMANY (BUNDESREPUBLIK). Statistisches Bundesamt. Sozialhilfe. a., 1970- Wiesbaden. *(Sozialleistungen. Reihe 2)*

BETHUSY-HUC (VIOLA VON) Gräfin. Das Sozialleistungssystem der Bundesrepublik Deutschland. 2nd ed. Tübingen, 1976. pp. 346. *bibliog.*

— Germany, Eastern.

POLICIES which put people first: life and social welfare in the G.D.R.; [written by Dr. Karl-Heinz Arnold]. Berlin, [1976]. pp. 96. *Based on policies outlined at the 9th Congress of the Socialist Unity Party of Germany, May 1976.*

— Israel.

HABIB (JACK) Poverty in Israel before and after receipt of public transfers. Jerusalem, 1974. pp. 129. *bibliog. (Israel. National Insurance Institute. Bureau of Research and Planning. Discussion Papers. 4)*

— Italy.

TERRANOVA (FERDINANDO) Il potere assistenziale. [Roma, 1975]. pp. 264.

— Japan.

JAPAN. Ministry of Health and Welfare. 1977. Guide to health and welfare services in Japan. Tokyo, 1977. pp. 59.

JAPAN. Ministry of Health and Welfare. 1977. Health and welfare services in Japan. Tokyo, 1977. pp. 170.

— Malaysia.

FEDERATION OF MALAYSIA. Ministry of Welfare Services. 1970. Social welfare services in Malaysia. Kuala Lumpur, [1970]. pp. 76.

— Netherlands.

HUELSTER (MICHAEL) Strukturwandel der Sozialarbeit: dargestellt am Zusammenschluss katholischer, protestantischer und humanistischer sozialer Dienste in den Niederlanden. Frankfurt/Main, [1976]. pp. 273. *bibliog.*

— New Zealand.

NEW ZEALAND COUNCIL OF SOCIAL SERVICE. Roles of central government, local authority and voluntary agency in social welfare. [Wellington], 1976. 1 vol. (various foliations).

— Pacific, The.

FOX (MORRIS G.) Social welfare services and development planning in the Pacific islands: principal English-speaking areas served by the South Pacific Commission, etc. Noumea, South Pacific Commission, 1976. pp. 182. *bibliogs. (Technical Papers. No.173)*

SOCIAL SERVICE.(Cont.)

— Poland.

KROLL (BOGDAN) Opieka i samopomoc społeczna w Warszawie, 1939-1945: Stołeczny Komitet Samopomocy Społecznej i warszawskie agendy Rady Głównej Opiekuńczej. Warszawa, 1977. pp. 342. *bibliog.*

— — Cracow (Province) — Finance.

PAWLIK (JAN) Wydatki rad narodowych na usługi socjalno-bytowe na terenach o ró'znym charakterze gospodarczym i o ró'znym tempie rozwoju gospodarczego na przykładzie Województwa Krakowskiego. Kraków, 1964. pp. 199. *bibliog. (Zeszyty Naukowe Uniwersytetu Jagiellońskiego. Prace Prawnicze. zeszyt 16) With English and Russian summaries.*

— Scandinavia.

[SCANDINAVIA]. Nordiske Socialministerier. 1951. Samordning af de nordiske landes statistik vedrørende den sociale lovgivning: betaenkning afgivet af den...nedsatte ekspertkomité. 1 Del. Om opstilling af en ensartet oversigt over de sociale udgifter. København, 1951. pp. 36.

UUSITALO (HANNU) Education and welfare: some findings from the Scandinavian survey. Helsinki, 1977. pp. 28. *bibliog. (Helsinki. Yliopisto. Research Group for Comparative Sociology. Research Reports. No. 15) Paper prepared for the European Seminar on Measuring the Economic and Social Effects of Educational Inequalities held in Sigriswil in 1976.*

— South Africa.

SOCIAL WELFARE AND PENSIONS: (official half-yearly jl. of the Department of Social Welfare and Pensions [South Africa]) . s-a., Je 1971 (v.6, no.1)- Pretoria. *[in English and Afrikaans]*

— United Kingdom.

CRAWFORTH (JOHN) and others. Working in the community. Nottingham, [1975]. pp. 109. *bibliogs. (Nottingham. University. Department of Applied Social Science. Social Work Studies. No. 1)*

COLLINGRIDGE (ANDREA) and others. Aspects of casework. Nottingham, [1976]. pp. 137. *bibliogs. (Nottingham. University. Department of Applied Social Science. Social Work Studies. No. 2)*

DOWDELL (TIM C.) The role of the social services in the care of the elderly sick. London, [1976]. pp. 16. *(Socialist Medical Association. Discussion Documents)*

PERSONAL SOCIAL SERVICES COUNCIL [U.K.]. Complaints procedures in the personal social services: a discussion paper. [London], 1976. pp. 17.

PERSONAL SOCIAL SERVICES COUNCIL [U.K.]. Personal social services: basic information. [London], 1976. pp. 23.

ROMIJN (JAN) Tabu: Uganda Asians: the old, the weak, the vulnerable; a report on...work with the elderly and handicapped among the Uganda Asian evacuees in London...together with the LCSS's recommendations and suggestions for further action. London, 1976. pp. 41.

BAUGH (WILLIAM E.) Introduction to the social services. 3rd ed. London, 1977. pp. 204. *bibliogs.*

BROWN (MURIEL) Introduction to social administration in Britain. 4th ed. London, 1977. pp. 253. *bibliogs.*

ROSE (HILARY) Social welfare and the inner city. [Bradford, 1977?]. pp. 24. *An inaugural lecture delivered at the University of Bradford on 1st February 1977.*

U.K. Central Office of Information. Reference Division. Reference Pamphlets. 3. Social services in Britain. 11th ed. London, 1977. pp. 81. *bibliog.*

WELFARE in action; edited by Mike Fitzgerald [and others] at the Open University. London, 1977. pp. 232. *bibliogs.*

COMMITTEE ON VOLUNTARY ORGANISATIONS. The future of voluntary organisations: report of the Wolfenden Committee. London, [1978]. pp. 286. *bibliogs. Commissioned by the Joseph Rowntree Memorial Trust and the Carnegie United Kingdom Trust.*

DIGBY (ANNE) Pauper palaces. London, 1978. pp. 266. *bibliog.*

HALMOS (PAUL) The personal and the political: social work and political action. London, 1978. pp. 200.

JUDGE (KEN) Rationing social services: a study of resource allocation and the personal social services. London, 1978. pp. 212.

PRITCHARD (COLIN) and TAYLOR (RICHARD K.S.) Social work: reform or revolution? London, 1978. pp. 162. *bibliogs.*

U.K. Department of Health and Social Security. 1978. Health and personal social services in England: DHSS planning guidelines for 1978/79. [London, 1978]. pp. 26.

— — Bibliography.

HUSTWIT (JANE) and WEBLEY (MAUREEN) compilers. Information in social welfare: a survey of resources. London, 1977. pp. 95. *bibliog. (National Institute for Social Work. Papers. No. 6)*

— — Statistics.

HEALTH AND PERSONAL SOCIAL SERVICES STATISTICS FOR ENGLAND (formerly Digest of health statistics for England and Wales); ([pd. by] Department of Health and Social Security [U.K.]) . a., 1969 [1st]- London.

— — Ireland, Northern.

VIOLENCE and the social services in Northern Ireland; edited by John Darby [and] Arthur Williamson. London, 1978. pp. 205. *bibliog.*

— — Scotland.

SCOTLAND. Standing Consultative Council on Youth and Community Service. Newsletter. s-a., Ja 1972 (1)- Edinburgh.

— — — Statistics.

SCOTTISH SOCIAL WORK STATISTICS; ([pd. by] Social Work Services Group [and] Scottish Education Department). a., 1971 (1st)- Edinburgh.

— — Wales — Statistics.

HEALTH AND PERSONAL SOCIAL SERVICES STATISTICS FOR WALES; ([pd. by] Welsh Office [U.K.]). a., 1974 (no.1)- London.

— United States.

The DIVERSE society: implications for social policy; Pastora San Juan Cafferty and Leon Chestang, editors. Washington, [1976]. pp. 176.

GROSSER (CHARLES F.) New directions in community organization: from enabling to advocacy. [2nd ed.]. New York, 1976. pp. 286.

MYRDAL (GUNNAR) Race and class in a welfare state; introductory lecture to a symposium in a series entitled The national purpose reconsidered, 1776-1976 at Columbia University, October 28, 1976. 1976. pp. 57. *Unpublished: photocopy of typescript.*

GILBERT (NEIL) and SPECHT (HARRY) Coordinating social services: an analysis of community, organizational, and staff characteristics. New York, 1977. pp. 84.

RABUSHKA (ALVIN) and WEISSERT (WILLIAM G.) Caseworkers or police?: how tenants see public housing. Stanford, [1977]. pp. 98. *(Stanford University. Hoover Institution on War, Revolution and Peace. Hoover Institution Publications. 186)*

SOCIAL SERVICE AND RACE PROBLEMS.

The DIVERSE society: implications for social policy; Pastora San Juan Cafferty and Leon Chestang, editors. Washington, [1976]. pp. 176.

SOCIAL STABILITY.

ROSENTHAL (URIEL) Political order: rewards, punishments and political stability. Meppel, 1978. pp. 337. *bibliog. Proefschrift (doctor in de sociale wetenschappen)- Erasmus Universiteit Rotterdam.*

SOCIAL STATUS.

BLAU (PETER MICHAEL) Inequality and heterogeneity: a primitive theory of social structure. New York, [1977]. pp. 307. *bibliog.*

SOCIAL STRUCTURE.

STACEY (BARRIE B.) Psychology and social structure. London, 1976. pp. 142. *bibliog.*

BLAU (PETER MICHAEL) Inequality and heterogeneity: a primitive theory of social structure. New York, [1977]. pp. 307. *bibliog.*

MALNUTRITION, behavior, and social organization; edited by Lawrence S. Greene. New York, 1977. pp. 298. *bibliogs. Based on a symposium held at the Annual Meeting of the American Association for the Advancement of Science in 1976.*

PERIN (CONSTANCE) Everything in its place: social order and land use in America. Princeton, [1977]. pp. 291. *bibliog.*

ROSS (JENNIE-KEITH) Old people, new lives: community creation in a retirement residence. Chicago, 1977. pp. 227. *bibliog.*

ROTHMAN (ROBERT A.) Inequality and stratification in the United States. Englewood Cliffs, [1978]. pp. 243. *bibliogs.*

SOCIAL SURVEYS.

QUESTIONNAIRE and code book of the comparative Scandinavian welfare survey in 1972. [Helsinki, 1977]. pp. XLVIII, 69. *(Helsinki. Yliopisto. Research Group for Comparative Sociology. Research Reports. No. 14)*

WEISBERG (HERBERT F.) and BOWEN (BRUCE D.) An introduction to survey research and data analysis. San Francisco, [1977]. pp. 243. *bibliog.*

HOINVILLE (GERALD) and JOWELL (ROGER) Survey research practice;...in association with Colin Airey [and others]. London, 1978. pp. 228. *bibliogs.*

— Russia.

SHLIAPENTOKH (VLADIMIR EMMANUILOVICH) Problemy reprezentativnosti sotsiologicheskoi informatsii: sluchainaia i nesluchainaia vyborki v sotsiologii. Moskva, 1976. pp. 214. *bibliog.*

— United Kingdom.

SOCIAL SCIENCE RESEARCH COUNCIL SURVEY ARCHIVE. Catalogue; (with booklet, How to use the catalogue). 3 a yr. Colchester. *Current issue only kept, as each supersedes the previous one. File includes current issue of Inventory.*

SOCIAL VALUES.

BOUHDIBA (ABDELWAHAB) A la recherche des normes perdues. [Tunis, 1973]. pp. 271.

KMIECIAK (PETER) Wertstrukturen und Wertwandel in der Bundesrepublik Deutschland: Grundlagen einer interdisziplinären empirischen Wertforschung mit einer Sekundäranalyse von Umfragedaten. Göttingen, [1976]. pp. 699. *bibliog. (Kommission für Wirtschaftlichen und Sozialen Wandel. Schriften. 135)*

RUCHKA (ANATOLII ALEKSANDROVICH) Sotsial'nye tsennosti i normy: nekotorye teoreticheskie i prikladnye voprosy sotsiologicheskogo analiza. Kiev, 1976. pp. 152. *bibliog.*

FOSS (DENNIS C.) The value controversy in sociology. San Francisco, 1977. pp. 131. *bibliog.*

HAWORTH (LAWRENCE) Decadence and objectivity. Toronto, [1977]. pp. 169.

The ETHICS of social intervention; edited by Gordon Bermant [and others]. Washington, [1978]. pp. 431. *bibliogs. Based on a conference held in 1973 at the Battelle Memorial Institute's Seattle Research Center.*

SOCIAL WORK ADMINISTRATION.

GILBERT (NEIL) and SPECHT (HARRY) Coordinating social services: an analysis of community, organizational, and staff characteristics. New York, 1977. pp. 84.

— **United Kingdom.**

U.K. Social Work Service. Development Group. 1977. Records in social services departments; a Development Group project report. London, 1977. pp. 34.

SOCIAL WORK AS A PROFESSION.

CORRIGAN (PAUL) and LEONARD (PETER TERRANCE) Social work practice under capitalism: a marxist approach. London, 1978. pp. 161.

STATHAM (DAPHNE) Radicals in social work. London, 1978. pp. 121.

SOCIAL WORK EDUCATION.

INTERNATIONAL CONGRESS OF SCHOOLS OF SOCIAL WORK, 18TH, SAN JUAN, PUERTO RICO, 1976. Social realities and the social work response: the role of social work; proceedings of the...Congress. New York, [1977]. pp. 173.

SEMINAR ON SOCIAL WORK EDUCATION AND HUMAN SETTLEMENTS, VANCOUVER, 1976. People and places: social work education and human settlements. New York, [1977]. pp. 174. *Papers of a seminar sponsored by the International Association of Schools of Social Work.*

— **United Kingdom.**

KLEIN (JOSEPHINE) Training for the new helping professions: community and youth work. London, 1973. pp. 16. *(London. University. Goldsmiths' College. Occasional Papers on Community and Youth Work. No. 1)*

GROUP ON WORK WITH CHILDREN AND YOUNG PEOPLE AND THE IMPLICATIONS FOR SOCIAL WORK EDUCATION [U.K.]. Good enough parenting; report; [Reg Wright, chairman]. London, Central Council for Education and Training in Social Work, 1978. pp. 192. *bibliogs. (Studies. 1)*

— — **Scotland.**

SCOTLAND. Standing Consultative Council on Youth and Community Service. Newsletter. s-a., Ja 1972 (1)- Edinburgh.

SOCIAL WORK WITH CHILDREN

— **United Kingdom.**

INTERMEDIATE treatment: 28 choices: a collection of papers on the projects described during the two seminars on intermediate treatment activities at Oxford and Clacton-on-Sea, November/December 1976. [London], Department of Health and Social Security, 1977. pp. 308.

GROUP ON WORK WITH CHILDREN AND YOUNG PEOPLE AND THE IMPLICATIONS FOR SOCIAL WORK EDUCATION [U.K.]. Good enough parenting; report; [Reg Wright, chairman]. London, Central Council for Education and Training in Social Work, 1978. pp. 192. *bibliogs. (Studies. 1)*

SOCIAL WORK WITH DELINQUENTS AND CRIMINALS

— **United Kingdom.**

INTERMEDIATE treatment: 28 choices: a collection of papers on the projects described during the two seminars on intermediate treatment activities at Oxford and Clacton-on-Sea, November/December 1976. [London], Department of Health and Social Security, 1977. pp. 308.

FOWLES (A.J.) Prison welfare: an account of an experiment at Liverpool; a Home Office Research Unit report. London, 1978. pp. 31. *bibliog. (U.K. Home Office. Home Office Research Studies. No. 45)*

SOCIAL WORK WITH THE AGED

— **Israel.**

HANDELMAN (DON) Work and play among the aged: interaction, replication and emergence in a Jerusalem setting. Amsterdam, 1977. pp. 193. *bibliog.*

— **United States.**

HUTTMAN (ELIZABETH D.) Housing and social services for the elderly: social policy trends. New York, 1977. pp. 293. *bibliog.*

SOCIAL WORK WITH YOUTH

— **United Kingdom.**

REDFERN (MARGARET) Brooks House: an experiment in the provision of accommodation for young people at risk. [Liverpool, 1977]. pp. 76.

TYLER (MARY) Writer on Counselling. Advisory and counselling services for young people. London, 1978. pp. 93. *bibliog. (U.K. Department of Health and Social Security. Research Reports. No. 1)*

— **United States.**

LIPSITZ (JOAN) ed. Growing up forgotten: a review of research and programs concerning early adolescence. Lexington, Mass., [1977]. pp. 267. *bibliog. A report to the Ford Foundation.*

SOCIAL WORKERS.

GENG (J.M.) Mauvaises pensées d'un travailleur social. Paris, [1977]. pp. 207.

— **United Kingdom.**

THOMAS (DAVID NICHOLAS) and WARBURTON (R. WILLIAM) Community workers in a social services department: a case study. [London], Personal Social Services Council, 1977. pp. 91. *bibliog.*

CORRIGAN (PAUL) and LEONARD (PETER TERRANCE) Social work practice under capitalism: a marxist approach. London, 1978. pp. 161.

GRACE (CLIVE) and WILKINSON (PHILIP) Negotiating the law: social work and legal services. London, [1978]. pp. 85.

SOCIALISM.

SOCIALIST LEAGUE ?1885-94!. A straight talk to working-men. [London, 1886?]. pp. 3.

FELIX (CELESTIN JOSEPH) Le socialisme devant la société: conférences prononcées à Notre-Dame de Grenoble dans le Carême de 1878. 2nd ed. Paris, 1890. pp. 315.

HERVE (GUSTAVE) La muraille: recueil in-extenso des articles publiés par Gustave Hervé dans la "Guerre Sociale" du 1er février 1915 au 1er mai 1915. Paris, [1916]. pp. 331.

FOREL (AUGUSTE) Der wahre Sozialismus der Zukunft; autorisierte Übersetzung aus dem Französischen von Paul Chr. Plottke. Berlin, 1926. pp. 22.

JUSTO (JUAN BAUTISTA) El socialismo...: conferencia dada en el Salon "Unione e Benevolenza", de Buenos Aires, el 17 de agosto de 1902. [Buenos Aires?, 1956]. pp. 47.

YOUNG PEOPLES' SOCIALIST LEAGUE. The defence of man: (an introduction to democratic socialism). New York, [1963?]. pp. 4.

SOCIETY FOR THE LIBERATION OF DAILY LIFE. Daily life. Leeds, [1973?]. pp. 31.

REICH (WILHELM) Sex and the class struggle: the best of Wilhelm Reich; selections from his writings edited by Chris Knight. n.p. [1974?]. pp. 47. *bibliog.*

BATALOV (EDUARD IAKOVLEVICH) Philosophie de la révolte: critique de l'idéologie du gauchisme; (traduit du russe). Moscou, [1976]. pp. 332.

COLLOQUE DE LA FEDERATION DE PARIS DU PARTI SOCIALISTE, 1976. Socialisme et multinationales. Paris, [1976]. pp. 189. *bibliog.*

LOMBARDI (RICCARDO) L'alternativa socialista; intervista a cura di Carlo Vallauri. [Cosenza, 1976]. pp. 121.

MESMER (BEATRIX) Steuerreform als Übergangsmassnahme: die Rezeption der Forderung nach progressiver Besteuerung in den frühsozialistischen Programmen. Bern, [1976]. pp. 239. *bibliog.*

MOLNAR (THOMAS) Le socialisme sans visage: l'avènement du tiers modèle. [Paris, 1976]. pp. 187.

SOCIAL REVOLUTION GROUP. Introduction to social revolution. [Aberdeen, 1976]. pp. 12.

BUBER (MARTIN) Utopie et socialisme; traduit de l'allemand par Paul Corset et François Girard. Paris, [1977]. pp. 261.

ELGOZY (GEORGES) Le bourgeois socialiste; ou, Pour un post-libéralisme. [Paris, 1977]. pp. 310.

FILLOUX (JEAN CLAUDE) Durkheim et le socialisme. Genève, 1977. pp. 388. *bibliog.*

GREBING (HELGA) Der Revisionismus: von Bernstein bis zum "Prager Frühling". München, [1977]. pp. 281. *bibliogs.*

INTERNATIONAL SCIENTIFIC SEMINAR ON THE JUCHE IDEA, ANTANANARIVO, 1976. Juche: the banner of independence. Pyongyang, 1977. pp. 326.

JAMES (CYRIL LIONEL ROBERT) The future in the present: selected writings. London, 1977. pp. 271.

JUCHE idea: the current thought of our present time. Pyongyang, 1977. pp. 265.

LEMAITRE (JACQUES) Le chaos ou la troisième voie: ni capitalisme, ni socialisme étatiques, un système totalement différent: le libérisme. Paris, [1977]. pp. 324.

LITSCHAUER (HANS) Kein Respekt vor Ideologen: Notizen eines pragmatischen Sozialdemokraten. Wien, [1977]. pp. 122.

PETITFILS (JEAN CHRISTIAN) Les socialismes utopiques. [Paris, 1977]. pp. 211. *bibliog.*

SEDGEMORE (BRIAN) The how and why of socialism. Nottingham, 1977. pp. 88.

SHAFAREVICH (IGOR' ROSTISLAVOVICH) Le phénomène socialiste; traduit du russe par Jacques Michaut. Paris, 1977. pp. 351. *bibliog.*

ŠIK (OTA) Pour une troisième voie; traduit de l'allemand par Marcel Chabernaud. [Paris, 1978]. pp. 254.

SOZIALISMUS in Theorie und Praxis: Festschrift für Richard Löwenthal zum 70. Geburtstag am 15. April 1978; herausgegeben von Hannelore Horn [and others]. Berlin, 1978. pp. 687. *bibliog. In various languages.*

TARIQ ALI. 1968 and after: inside the revolution. London, 1978. pp. 219. *bibliog.*

— **Caricatures and cartoons.**

CRANE (WALTER) Cartoons for the cause: designs and verses for the socialist and labour movement, 1886-1896. London, 1976. 1 pamphlet (unpaged). *Reprint of pamphlet first published in 1896.*

— **Chronology.**

SOCIAL-DEMOCRATIC FEDERATION. Almanac for 1905. [London, 1905]. s.sh.

— **History.**

LOUIS (PAUL) La puissance ouvrière. Paris, 1946. pp. 183.

SOCIALISM.(Cont.)

— Societies.

DONNEUR (ANDRE) Histoire de l'Union des partis socialistes pour l'action internationale, 1920-1923. [Geneva], 1967. pp. 434. *bibliog*. Thèse (docteur ès sciences politiques)- Université de Genève.

— Study and teaching.

INDEPENDENT LABOUR PARTY and FABIAN SOCIETY. Joint Committee. Socialist educational classes: syllabus, second session, 1914-15. London, [1914?]. pp. 24.

SOCIALISM, CHRISTIAN.

CHRISTIAN SOCIAL UNION. Oxford University Branch. Leaflets. Nos. 1-29, 33-35, 38,45, 49-51, 54,57, 59-62, 64,66,68,70,71. [Oxford, 1895-1913]. 48 pts.

GIRARDI (GIULIO) Chrétiens pour le socialisme: contradictions, problèmes, perspectives; traduit de l'italien par Marie-Claude Ryckebusch et revu par l'auteur. Paris, 1976. pp. 206.

SOCIALISM AND ART.

SCOTT (MAUREEN) and BAKER (MIKE) Essays on art and imperialism [and] art and socialism [based on lectures given in the 1972 lecture programme of the League of Socialist Artists]. London, [1976]. pp. 26.

SOCIALISM AND CATHOLIC CHURCH.

FELIX (CELESTIN JOSEPH) Le socialisme devant la société: conférences prononcées à Notre-Dame de Grenoble dans le Carême de 1878. 2nd ed. Paris, 1890. pp. 315.

ZUNINO (PIER GIORGIO) La questione cattolica nella sinistra italiana, 1919-1939. [Bologna, 1975]. pp. 503.

GIRARDI (GIULIO) Chrétiens pour le socialisme: contradictions, problèmes, perspectives; traduit de l'italien par Marie-Claude Ryckebusch et revu par l'auteur. Paris, 1976. pp. 206.

MONDO cattolico e alternativa socialista: [papers given at a conference organized by the Comitato Regionale Lombardo del PSI at Monza, 1976]. Milano, [1976]. pp. 180.

SOCIALISM AND JUDAISM.

KRIEGEL (ANNIE) Les Juifs et le monde moderne: essai sur les logiques d'émancipation. Paris, [1977]. pp. 255.

LEVIN (NORA) Jewish socialist movements, 1871-1917; while Messiah tarried. London, 1978. pp. 554.

SOCIALISM AND SOCIETY.

LEWIS (GORDON K.) Slavery, imperialism, and freedom: studies in English radical thought. New York, [1978]. pp. 346. *bibliog*.

SOCIALISM AND YOUTH

— Singapore.

SINGAPORE. Sessional Papers. 1956. Cmd. 53. Singapore Chinese Middle Schools Students' Union. Singapore, 1956. pp. 22.

SOCIALISM IN AFRICA.

NCUBE (PATRICK D.) African socialism, imperialism, and a reconsidering of Trotsky's theory of the permanent revolution. Oslo, 1975. pp. 116, viii. *bibliog*. (Oslo. Universitet. Instituttet for Sosiologi. Skriftserie. Nr. 29)

SOCIALISM IN ALGERIA.

LAZREG (MARNIA) The emergence of classes in Algeria: a study of colonialism and socio-political change. Boulder, Colo., 1976. pp. 252. *bibliog*.

SOCIALISM IN ARAB COUNTRIES.

ISMAEL (TAREQ Y.) The Arab left. Syracuse, N.Y., 1976. pp. 204. *bibliogs*.

SOCIALISM IN BELGIUM.

MAHIEU-HOYOIS (FRANÇOISE) L'évolution du mouvement socialiste borain. Leuven, 1972. pp. xvi, 92. *bibliog*. (Centre Interuniversitaire d'Histoire Contemporaine. Cahiers. 68)

POTY (FRANCIS) Histoire de la démocratie et du mouvement ouvrier au Pays de Charleroi. Bruxelles, [1975 in progress]. *bibliog*.

SOCIALISM IN CANADA.

IMPERIALISM, nationalism, and Canada: essays from the Marxist Institute of Toronto;...edited by Craig Heron. Toronto, [1977]. pp. 206.

McCORMACK (ANDREW ROSS) Reformers, rebels, and revolutionaries: the western Canadian radical movement, 1899-1919. Toronto, [1977]. pp. 228. *bibliog*.

PROSPECTS for a socialist Canada; edited by John Riddell and Art Young. Toronto, [1977]. pp. 127.

SOCIALISM IN CHILE.

RECABARREN (LUIS EMILIO) Obras; compilacion y prologo de Digna Castañeda Fuertes. La Habana, [1976]. pp. 310. *bibliog*.

CASTEX (PATRICK) "Voie chilienne" au socialisme et luttes paysannes: approche théorique et pratique d'une transition capitaliste non révolutionnaire. Paris, 1977. pp. 296.

DRAKE (PAUL W.) Socialism and populism in Chile, 1932-52. Urbana, [1978]. pp. 418. *bibliog*.

SOCIALISM IN CHINA.

SINGH (AJIT) Political economy of socialist development in China since 1949. Cambridge, 1974. 1 pamphlet (unpaged). (Cambridge. University. Department of Applied Economics. Reprint Series. No. 395) Reprinted from Economic and Political Weekly, vol. 8. No. 47, November 24, 1973.

SOCIALISM IN CZECHOSLOVAKIA.

PRINZ (FRIEDRICH) Beneš, Jaksch und die Sudetendeutschen. Stuttgart, 1975. pp. 76.

SOCIALISM IN EASTERN EUROPE.

BAHRO (RUDOLF) Die Alternative: zur Kritik des real existierenden Sozialismus. Köln, 1977. pp. 543.

SOCIALISM IN EUROPE.

CLAUDIN (FERNANDO) Eurocommunism and socialism; translated by John Wakeham. London, 1978. pp. 168.

— Bibliography.

SILBERNER (EDMUND) compiler. Western European socialism and the Jewish problem (1800-1918) : a selective bibliography. Jerusalem, 1955. pp. 61.

SOCIALISM IN FRANCE.

GAGNEUR (LOUISE MIGNEROT) La part du feu: les terreurs du bourgeois Prudence et de son ami Furibus; par M.-L. Gagneur. Magny en Vexin, [imprint, 1872]. pp. 36.

MASQUARD (EUGENE DE) Aux électeurs de la 1re circonscription de Nîmes/Gard. Montreux, 1893. pp. (4).

JULLIARD (JACQUES) Contre la politique professionnelle. Paris, [1977]. pp. 164.

LEFRANC (GEORGES) Le mouvement socialiste sous la Troisième République. 2nd ed. Paris, [1977]. 2 vols. *bibliog*.

LINDENBERG (DANIEL) and MEYER (PIERRE ANDRE) Lucien Herr: le socialisme et son destin. [Paris, 1977]. pp. 318.

ROSANVALLON (PIERRE) and VIVERET (PATRICK) Pour une nouvelle culture politique. Paris, [1977]. pp. 158.

TAÏX (GABRIEL) Monsieur Mitterrand vous n'êtes pas socialiste. Paris, 1977. pp. 179.

PARTI SOCIALISTE. Le programme commun de gouvernement de la gauche: propositions socialistes pour l'actualisation. [Paris, 1978]. pp. 128.

SOCIALISM IN GERMANY.

CRISPIEN (ARTHUR) Eine Abrechnung mit den Rechtssozialisten: Rede...gehalten am 29. Juni 1919 auf der Generalversammlung des Verbandes der Unabhängigen sozialdemokratischen Vereine Berlins und Umgegend. Berlin, [1919]. pp. 32.

NICHTS getan?: die Arbeit seit dem 9. November 1918. [Berlin, 1919]. pp. 32.

OSTERROTH (FRANZ) and SCHUSTER (DIETER) Chronik der deutschen Sozialdemokratie. 2nd ed. Berlin, 1975-78. 3 vols.

BUONFINO (GIANCARLO) La politica culturale operaia da Marx e Lassalle alla rivoluzione di novembre, 1859-1919. Milano, 1975. pp. 211.

GAREWICZ (JAN) Między marzeniem a wiedzą: początki myśli socjalistycznej w Niemczech. Warszawa, 1975. pp. 325. *With German summary*.

LEBER (JULIUS) Schriften, Reden, Briefe; herausgegeben von Dorothea Beck und Wilfried F. Schoeller; mit einem Vorwort von Willy Brandt und einer Gedenkrede von Golo Mann. München, [1976]. pp. 327.

VORWAERTS. Vorwärts, 1876-1976: ein Querschnitt in Faksimiles; herausgegeben von Günter Grunwald und Friedhelm Merz, etc. Berlin, [1976]. pp. 203.

ABENDROTH-Forum: Marburger Gespräche aus Anlass des 70. Geburtstags von Wolfgang Abendroth; herausgegeben von Frank Deppe [and others]. Marburg, [1977]. pp. 443. (Studiengesellschaft für Sozialgeschichte und Arbeiterbewegung, Marburg. Schriftenreihe für Sozialgeschichte und Arbeiterbewegung. Band 6) Papers and discussion of four symposia held in May and June of 1976.

ARBEITERBEWEGUNG, Erwachsenenbildung, Presse: Festschrift für Walter Fabian zum 75. Geburtstag;...herausgegeben von Anne-Marie Fabian. Köln, [1977]. pp. 240.

FENNER (CHRISTIAN) Demokratischer Sozialismus und Sozialdemokratie: Realität und Rhetorik der Sozialismusdiskussion in Deutschland. Frankfurt/Main, [1977]. pp. 227. *bibliog*.

LEHNERT (DETLEF) Reform und Revolution in den Strategiediskussionen der klassischen Sozialdemokratie: zur Geschichte der deutschen Arbeiterbewegung von den Ursprüngen bis zum Ausbruch des 1. Weltkriegs. Bonn-Bad Godesberg, [1977]. pp. 318.

STILLER (KARL THEODOR) Gewerkschaftspolitik und Bewegungen in der Arbeiterschaft, 1914 bis 1920. Offenbach, 1977. pp. 111. *bibliog*.

SOCIALISM IN GUINEA-BISSAU.

AABY (PETER) The state of Guinea-Bissau: African socialism or socialism in Africa? Uppsala, 1978. pp. 35. *bibliog*. (Nordiska Afrikainstitutet. Research Reports. No. 45)

SOCIALISM IN IRELAND.

RONALD, pseud. Freedom's road for Irish workers. Cork, 1975. pp. 12. (Cork Workers' Club. Historical Reprints. No. 14) Reprint of pamphlet first published in 1917.

SOCIALISM IN ITALY.

ROSSELLI (CARLO) Socialismo liberale; a cura di John Rosselli. [Torino, 1973]. pp. 532. (Opere. vol. 1)

MANACORDA (GASTONE) Rivoluzione borghese e socialismo: studi e saggi. Roma, 1975. pp. 403.

MORETTI (PAOLO) I due socialismi: la scissione di Palazzo Barberini e la nascita della socialdemocrazia. [Milano, 1975]. pp. 223. *bibliog*.

PETTA (PAOLO) Ideologie costituzionali della sinistra italiana, 1892-1974. Roma, [1975]. pp. 239.

CICCHITTO (FABRIZIO) La questione socialista: dall'autunno caldo all'alternativa. Venezia, [1976]. pp. 147.

GRAMSCI (ANTONIO) Scritti 1915-1921: (inediti dal Grido del Popolo e dall' Avanti...); a cura di Sergio Caprioglio. [Milano, 1976]. pp. 411.

GUIDUCCI (ROBERTO) La società dei socialisti. Milano, [1976]. pp. 206.

LUSSO (EMILIO) Essere a sinistra: democrazia, autonomia e socialismo in cinquant'anni di lotte; a cura del Collettivo Emilio Lussu di Cagliari. Milano, [1976]. pp. 287.

MONDO cattolico e alternativa socialista: [papers given at a conference organized by the Comitato Regionale Lombardo del PSI at Monza, 1976]. Milano, [1976]. pp. 180.

MORELLI (ALDO) and TOMASSINI (LUIGI) Socialismo e classe operaia a Pistoia durante la prima guerra mondiale. [Milano, 1976]. pp. 218.

NENNI (PIETRO) Storia di quattro anni, 1919-1922. 4th ed. Milano, [1976]. pp. 254. *bibliog.*

RAGIONERI (ERNESTO) Il movimento socialista in Italia, 1850-1922. Milano, 1976. pp. 140. *Bound with Cronologia del movimento operaio italiano by Franco Pedone.*

BENOT (YVES) L'autre Italie, 1968-1976: problèmes de la dictature du prolétariat. Paris, 1977. pp. 319.

LAVAGNA (CARLO) Costituzione e socialismo. Bologna, [1977]. pp. 100.

SOCIALISM IN KOREA.

INTERNATIONAL SCIENTIFIC SEMINAR ON THE JUCHE IDEA, ANTANANARIVO, 1976. Juche: the banner of independence. Pyongyang, 1977. pp. 326.

SOCIALISM IN PORTUGAL.

OLIVEIRA (CESAR) O socialismo em Portugal, 1850-1900: contribuição para o estudo da filosofia política do socialismo em Portugal na segunda metade do seculo XIX. Porto, 1973. pp. 404. *bibliog.*

SOCIALISM IN ROMANIA.

MOSHANU (ALEKSANDR KONSTANTINOVICH) Sotsialisticheskoe dvizhenie v Rumynii, seredina 70-kh - nachalo 90-kh gg. XIX v. Kishinev, 1977. pp. 272.

SOCIALISM IN RUSSIA.

PUTNAM (GEORGE F.) Russian altervatives to Marxism: Christian socialism and idealistic liberalism in twentieth-century Russia. Knoxville, [1977]. pp. 233. *bibliog.*

SOCIALISM IN SPAIN.

ANDRES-GALLEGO (JOSE) El socialismo durante la dictadura, 1923-1930. Madrid, [1977]. pp. 636. *bibliog.*

BORBON PARMA (CARLOS HUGO DE) La via carlista al socialismo autogestionario: el proyecto carlista de socialismo democratico. Barcelona, 1977. pp. 387.

MALUQUER DE MOTES BERNET (JORDI) El socialismo en España, 1833-1868. Barcelona, [1977]. pp. 410. *bibliog.*

SOCIALISM IN SWEDEN.

BÄCKSTRÖM (KNUT) Arbetarrörelsen i Sverige, etc. new ed. [Stockholm], 1977. 2 vols. (in 1). *bibliogs.*

SOCIALISM IN SWITZERLAND.

NIEDER mit dem Marxismues. [Bern?, 1933?]. pp. 48. *(Separatdruck aus der Schweiz. Metallarbeiter-Zeitung)*

KRAMER (HUGO) Was soll werden?: Gedanken zur wirtschaftlichen Erneuerung der Schweiz. [Zürich], 1941. pp. 80. *(Sozialdemokratische Partei der Schweiz. Kultur und Arbeit)*

SOCIALISM IN TANZANIA.

CLARK (W. EDMUND) Socialist development and public investment in Tanzania, 1964-73. Toronto, [1978]. pp. 319. *bibliog.*

SOCIALISM IN THE NETHERLANDS.

TANS (JEAN GUILLAUME HUBERT) Tans of nooit: een onduidelijke brochure. [Amsterdam, 1967]. pp. 28.

JAARBOEK VOOR DE GESCHIEDENIS VAN SOCIALISME EN ARBEIDSBEWEGING IN NEDERLAND. a., 1976- Nijmegen.

FRIESWIJK (JOHAN) Socialisme in Friesland, 1880-1900. Amsterdam, 1977. pp. 270. *bibliog. (International Institute of Social History. De Nederlandse Arbeidersbeweging. 2)*

SOCIALISM IN THE SOMALI REPUBLIC.

DECRAENE (PHILIPPE) L'expérience socialiste somalienne. [Paris, 1977]. pp. 219. *bibliog.*

SOCIALISM IN THE UNITED KINGDOM.

BESANT (ANNIE) A selection of the social and political pamphlets of Annie Besant; with a preface and bibliographical notes by John Saville. New York, 1970. 1 vol. (various pagings). *bibliog. Originally published between 1877 and 1891.*

WORKERS ILLUSTRATED NEWS. D. 13 1929 (vol. 1, no. 1) London.

HILL (DOUGLAS) ed. Tribune 40: the first forty years of a socialist newspaper. London, 1977. pp. 214.

HODGSON (GEOFF) Socialism and parliamentary democracy. Nottingham, 1977. pp. 183. *bibliog.*

JENKINS (PETER) The Labour Party and the politics of transition. Leeds, [1977]. pp. 24. *(Labour Party. Labour Party Discussion Series. No.1)*

JOURNES (CLAUDE) L'extrême gauche en Grande-Bretagne. Paris, 1977. pp. 229. *bibliog.*

ROWBOTHAM (SHEILA) and WEEKS (JEFFREY) Socialism and the new life: the personal and sexual politics of Edward Carpenter and Havelock Ellis. London, 1977. pp. 198. *bibliog.*

WYATT (WOODROW LYLE) What's left of the Labour Party? London, 1977. pp. 183.

LEWIS (GORDON K.) Slavery, imperialism, and freedom: studies in English radical thought. New York, [1978]. pp. 346. *bibliog.*

McSHANE (HARRY) and SMITH (JOAN) Harry McShane: no mean fighter. London, 1978. pp. 282.

RICHARDS (VERNON) The impossibilities of social democracy. London, 1978. pp. 142.

SOCIALISM IN THE UNITED STATES.

SOCIALIST LABOR PARTY OF AMERICA. Records, 1877-1906. Madison, Wis., 1970. 42 vols. *This microfilm edition is produced by the State Historical Society of Wisconsin under the sponsorship of the National Historical Publications Commission.*

SOCIALIST LABOR PARTY OF AMERICA. Records of the Socialist Labor Party of America: guide to a microfilm edition; F. Gerald Ham [and others], editors. Madison, Wis., 1970. pp. 28. *(State Historical Society of Wisconsin. Guides to Historical Resources)*

GARLIN (SENDER) John Swinton, American radical (1829-1901). New York, 1976. pp. 47. *bibliog.(American Institute for Marxist Studies. Occasional Papers. No. 20)*

CANNON (JAMES PATRICK) The struggle for socialism in the "American century": (writings and speeches, 1945-47). New York, [1977]. pp. 480.

FONER (PHILIP SHELDON) American socialism and black Americans: from the age of Jackson to World War II. Westport, Conn., 1977. pp. 462. *bibliog.*

The LESSER evil?: the Left debates the Democratic Party and social change; [by] Michael Harrington, [and others]. New York, 1977. pp. 128.

SOCIALISM IN TRANSYLVANIA.

CICALĂ (I.) Mişcarea muncitorească şi socialistă din Transilvania, 1901-1921. Bucureşti, 1976. pp. 289.

SOCIALISM IN UNDERDEVELOPED AREAS.

See UNDERDEVELOPED AREAS — Socialism.

SOCIALISM IN VIETNAM.

LE DUAN. This nation and socialism are one: selected writings...; edited with an introduction by Tran Van Dinh. Chicago, 1976. pp. 261. *bibliog.*

SOCIALISM IN YUGOSLAVIA.

SOCIALISM IN YUGOSLAV THEORY AND PRACTICE: collection of conferences; [organized by] Medjunarodni Univerzitetski Centar za Društvene Nauke, Univerzitet [Belgrade]. irreg. (formerly a.), 1969(1st), 1972(4th), 1974(6th), 1976(8th)- Beograd. *[in English and French].*

SOCIALIST LABOR PARTY OF AMERICA.

SOCIALIST LABOR PARTY OF AMERICA. Records, 1877-1906. Madison, Wis., 1970. 42 vols. *This microfilm edition is produced by the State Historical Society of Wisconsin under the sponsorship of the National Historical Publications Commission.*

SOCIALIST LABOR PARTY OF AMERICA. Records of the Socialist Labor Party of America: guide to a microfilm edition; F. Gerald Ham [and others], editors. Madison, Wis., 1970. pp. 28. *(State Historical Society of Wisconsin. Guides to Historical Resources)*

The FORMATION of the Workingmen's Party of the United States; proceedings of the union congress held at Philadelphia, July 19-22, 1876; edited by Philip S. Foner. New York, 1976. pp. 38. *(American Institute for Marxist Studies. Occasional Papers. No. 18)*

SOCIALIST PARTIES.

SOCIAL democratic parties in Western Europe; edited by William E. Paterson and Alastair H. Thomas. London, [1977]. pp. 444.

BRYM (ROBERT J.) The Jewish intelligentsia and Russian Marxism: a sociological study of intellectual radicalism and ideological divergence. London, 1978. pp. 157. *bibliog.*

The FOREIGN policies of West European socialist parties; edited by Werner J. Feld. New York, [1978]. pp. 149.

SOCIALIST PARTY (ARGENTINE REPUBLIC).

REPETTO (NICOLAS) Mi paso por la politica: de Roca a Yrigoyen. Buenos Aires, [1956]. pp. 347.

DICKMANN (EMILIO) La conduccion politica del Partido Socialista. [Buenos Aires, 1964]. pp. 45.

SOCIALIST PARTY (AUSTRIA).

MAGAZINER (ALFRED) Ein Sohn des Volkes: Karl Maisel erzählt sein Leben. Wien, [1977]. pp. 123.

POPP (ADELHEID) Jugend einer Arbeiterin; hrsg. und eingel. von Hans J. Schütz. Berlin, [1977]. pp. 187.

SOCIALIST PARTY (BELGIUM).

PARTI SOCIALISTE BELGE. Statuts. n.p. n.d. s.sh.

SOCIALIST PARTY (FINLAND).

SOCIAL DEMOCRATIC PARTY [FINLAND]. Report. n.p., [1909?]. pp. 42. *Lacking title page.*

SOCIALIST PARTY (FRANCE).

D'ERAMO (MARCO) Rinascita di un partito: i socialisti francesi, 1971-1975. [Cosenza, 1976]. pp. 254. *bibliog.*

Les MILITANTS politiques dans trois partis français: Parti Communiste, Parti Socialiste, Union des Démocrates pour la République, [by] Jacques Lagroye [and others]. [Paris, 1976]. pp. 186. *bibliog. (Bordeaux. Université. Institut d'Etudes Politiques. Centre d'Etude et de Recherche sur la Vie Locale. Série Vie Locale. 5.)*

CITOYEN dans sa commune: propositions municipales socialistes. Paris, [1977]. pp. 159.

JOUBERT (JEAN PAUL) Révolutionnaires de la S.F.I.O.: Marceau Pivert et le pivertisme. [Paris, 1977]. pp. 296. *bibliog.*

Les SOCIALISTES et le Tiers Monde: éléments pour une politique socialiste de relations avec le Tiers Monde. [Paris, 1977]. pp. 251.

PARTI SOCIALISTE. Le programme commun de gouvernement de la gauche: propositions socialistes pour l'actualisation. [Paris, 1978]. pp. 128.

SOCIALIST PARTY (GERMANY).

TALLEN (HERMANN) Die Auseinandersetzung über [Paragraph] 218 StGB: zu einem Konflikt zwischen der SPD und der Katholischen Kirche. München, 1977. pp. 376. *bibliog.*

SOCIALIST PARTY (ITALY).

BASSO (LELIO) Il Partito Socialista Italiano. Milano, [1958]. pp. 175.

PARTITO SOCIALISTA ITALIANO. Conferenza Nazionale di Organizzazione, 1975. Il Partito Socialista: struttura e organizzazione:atti. Venezia, 1975. pp. 366.

L'ALTERNATIVA socialista: autogestione e riforme di struttura; [by] Claudio Signorile [and others], prefazione di Riccardo Lombardi. [Milano, 1976]. pp. 154.

MARTELLI (CLAUDIO) Socialisti a confronto. Milano, [1976]. pp. 103. *Partito Socialista Italiano. Congresso Nazionale, 40, 1976.*

RIOSA (ALCEO) Il sindicalismo rivoluzionario in Italia e la lotta politica nel Partito socialista dell'età giolittiana. Bari, [1976]. pp. 390.

TAMBURRANO (GIUSEPPE) ed. Pietro Nenni: intervista sul socialismo italiano. Roma, 1977. pp. 170.

TRENT'anni di politica socialista, 1946-1976: atti del Convegno organizzato dall'Istituto Socialista di Studi Storici, Parma, gennaio 1977. [Rome, 1977]. pp. 261. *(Istituto Socialista di Studi Storici. Biblioteca Storica)*

SOCIALIST PARTY (POLAND).

CZAPSKA-JORDAN (WANDA) W[olność] R[ówność] N[iepodległość]: PPS pod okupacją niemiecką, 1939-1945. Londyn, 1976. pp. 40.

PAWŁOWSKI (IGNACY) Geneza i działalność organizacji Spiskowo-Bojowej PPS, 1904-1905. Wrocław, 1976. pp. 156. *(Opole. Opolskie Towarzystwo Przyjaciół Nauk. Wydział Nauk Historyczno-Społecznych. Prace)*

HOLZER (JERZY) PPS: szkic dziejów. Warszawa, 1977. pp. 221. *bibliog.*

SOCIALIST PARTY (PORTUGAL).

REGO (VICTOR CUNHA) and MERZ (FRIEDHELM) eds. Liberdade para Portugal: (documentação coligida e coordenada). Amadora, [1976]. pp. 300.

SOCIALIST PARTY (SPAIN).

MARTINEZ DE SAS (MARIA TERESA) El socialismo y la España oficial: Pablo Iglesias, diputado a Cortes. Madrid, [1975]. pp. 358. *bibliog.*

GONZALEZ (FELIPE) and GUERRA (ALFONSO) Partido Socialista Obrero Español. Bilbao, 1977. pp. 135.

SOCIALIST PARTY (TUNISIA).

BOURGUIBA (HABIB) Articles de presse, 1929-1934. [Tunis, 1967]. pp. 388. *(Histoire du Mouvement National [Tunisien. Documents.])*

Le NEO-Destour et le Front Populaire en France. [Tunis, 1969]. 2 vols. (in 1). *(Histoire du Mouvement National Tunisien. Documents. 3-4)*

Le NEO-Destour face à la première épreuve, 1934-36. [Tunis, 1969]. pp. 274. *(Histoire du Mouvement National Tunisien. Documents)*

Le NEO-Destour face à la deuxième épreuve, 1938-1943. [Tunis, 1970]. 3 vols. (in 1) *(Histoire du Mouvement National Tunisien. Documents. 7-9)*

POUR préparer la troisième épreuve...; textes réunis et commentés par Mohamed Sayah. [Tunis, 1972-74). 3 vols. (in 1). *(Histoire du Mouvement National Tunisien. Documents. 10-12)*

SOCIALIST WORKERS' PARTY (UNITED STATES).

CANNON (JAMES PATRICK) The struggle for socialism in the "American century": (writings and speeches, 1945-47). New York, [1977]. pp. 480.

SOCIALISTS

— Italy.

DEGL'INNOCENTI (MAURIZIO) Il socialismo italiano e la guerra di Libia. [Roma, 1976]. pp. 341. *bibliogs.*

SOCIALIZATION.

MARTI (CASIMIRO) Socializacion: que dice la Iglesia?. Barcelona, [1964]. pp. 51.

BOOTH (TONY) Growing up in society. London, 1975. pp. 144. *bibliog.*

AKTIVNOST' lichnosti v sotsialisticheskom obshchestve. Moskva, 1976. pp. 278.

BANDURA (ALBERT) Social learning theory. Englewood Cliffs, [1977]. pp. 247. *bibliog.*

CULTURE and infancy: variations in the human experience; edited by P. Herbert Leiderman [and others]. New York, [1977]. pp. 615. *bibliogs. Based on a conference held in 1973 by the Wenner-Gren Foundation for Anthropological Research.*

LASCH (CHRISTOPHER) Haven in a heartless world: the family besieged. New York, [1977]. pp. 230.

WHITE (GRAHAM E.) Socialisation. London, 1977. pp. 147.

SOCIALLY HANDICAPPED

— Canada.

NEW BRUNSWICK. Human Rights Commission. 1968. A study of the socially disadvantaged. Fredericton, [1968]. pp. 17.

— Denmark.

SOCIALPOLITISK FORENING. Sommermøde, 1976. De oversete: restgrupperne i samfundet; (fra Askovmødet, 1976). [Copenhagen, 1977]. pp. 76. *(Socialpolitisk Forening. Småskrifter. Nr.49)*

— Scandinavia.

ALLARDT (ERIK) On the relationship between objective and subjective predicaments. Helsinki, 1977. pp. 22. *bibliog. (Helsinki. Yliopisto. Research Group for Comparative Sociology. Research Reports. No. 16)*

— United Kingdom.

LLEWELYN-DAVIES WEEKS [AND PARTNERS]. Inner area study: Birmingham: circumstances of families. [London], Department of the Environment, [1977]. pp. 140.

U.K. Department of the Environment. 1977. Recreation and deprivation in inner urban areas. London, 1977 repr. 1978. pp. 65.

SOCIALLY HANDICAPPED CHILDREN.

CORDIER (JEAN) Une anthropologie de l'inadaptation: la dynamique de l'exclusion sociale. Bruxelles, [1975]. pp. 240. *bibliog. (Brussels. Université Libre. Institut de Sociologie. Sciences Pédagogiques et Sociologie de l'Education)*

— Education — United Kingdom.

LLEWELYN-DAVIES WEEKS [AND PARTNERS]. Inner area study: Birmingham: educational action projects. [London], Department of the Environment, [1977]. 2 vols.

— Education (Secondary) — United States.

MIDDLE start: an experiment in the educational enrichment of young adolescents; [by] J. Milton Yinger [and others]. Cambridge, 1977. pp. 134. *bibliog. (American Sociological Association. Arnold and Caroline Rose Monograph Series in Sociology)*

SOCIOBIOLOGY.

SAHLINS (MARSHALL DAVID) The use and abuse of biology: an anthropological critique of sociobiology. London, 1977. pp. 120. *bibliog.*

SOCIOLINGUISTICS.

RABOTIN (MAURICE) Le vocabulaire politique et socio-ethnique à Montréal de 1839 à 1842. Montréal, [1975]. pp. 123. *bibliog.*

DITTMAR (NORBERT) Sociolinguistics: a critical survey of theory and application. London, 1976. pp. 307. *bibliog.*

EDELMAN (MURRAY JACOB) Political language: words that succeed and policies that fail. New York, [1977]. pp. 164. *(Wisconsin University, Madison. Institute for Research on Poverty. Monograph Series)*

MACAULAY (RONALD K.S.) Language, social class, and education: a Glasgow study. Edinburgh, [1977]. pp. 179. *bibliog. Revised version of a report to the Social Science Research Council.*

HUDSON (KENNETH) The language of modern politics. London, 1978. pp. 167. *bibliog.*

MUNBY (JOHN) Communicative syllabus design: a sociolinguistic model for defining the content of purpose-specific language programmes. Cambridge, 1978. pp. 232. *bibliog.*

The SOCIAL context of language; edited by Ivana Markova. Chichester, [1978]. pp. 241. *Based on a conference on language and the social context sponsored by the Social Section and Scottish Branch of the British Psychological Society held...Jan. 10-11, 1975.*

SOCIOLINGUISTIC patterns in British English; edited by Peter Trudgill. London, 1978. pp. 186. *bibliog.*

SOCIOLOGICAL JURISPRUDENCE.

IAKOVLEV (ALEKSANDR MAKSIMOVICH) Pravo i sotsiologiia: krizis zakonnosti v SShA. Moskva, 1975. pp. 112.

BLACK (DONALD J.) The behavior of law. New York, [1976]. pp. 175. *bibliog.*

PSYCHOLOGY and the law: research frontiers; edited by Gordon Bermant [and others]. Lexington, Mass., [1976]. pp. 303. *bibliogs. Includes papers of a conference held June 12-14, 1975 at the Battelle Seattle Research Center and sponsored by the Battelle Memorial Institute.*

CANOSA (ROMANO) Diritto e rivoluzione. Milano, [1977]. pp. 168.

CONFERENCE ON THE SOCIOLOGY OF LAW, 1976. (Proceedings): sociology of law and legal sciences; edited and introduced by Kálmán Kulcsár. Budapest, 1977. pp. 380.

FREIHEIT und Sachzwang: Beiträge zu Ehren Helmut Schelskys; herausgegeben von Horst Baier. Opladen, [1977]. pp. 340.

FRIEDMAN (LAWRENCE MEIR) Law and society: an introduction. Englewood Cliffs, [1977]. pp. 177. *bibliog.*

HOERNER (HANS) Anton Menger: Recht und Sozialismus. Frankfurt am Main, [1977]. pp. 217.

TIGAR (MICHAEL E.) and LEVY (MADELEINE R.) Law and the rise of capitalism. New York, [1977]. pp. 346. *bibliog.*

HUNT (ALAN) The sociological movement in law. London, 1978. pp. 185. *bibliog.*

LAW and society: the crisis in legal ideals; edited by Eugene Kamenka [and others]. London, 1978. pp. 137.

LAW in social context: Liber Amicorum honouring Professor Lon L. Fuller; edited by Thomas W. Bechtler. Deventer, 1978. pp. 227. *bibliog.*

REASONS (CHARLES E.) and RICH (ROBERT M.) eds. The sociology of law: a conflict perspective; [a collection of essays]. Toronto, [1978]. pp. 475.

SOCIOLOGICAL RESEARCH.

DOING sociological research; edited by Colin Bell and Howard Newby. London, 1977. pp. 186. *bibliog.*

ECKHARDT (KENNETH W.) and ERMANN (M. DAVID) Social research methods: perspective, theory, and analysis. New York, [1977]. pp. 410. *bibliogs.*

— **Russia.**

SHLIAPENTOKH (VLADIMIR EMMANUILOVICH) Problemy reprezentativnosti sotsiologicheskoi informatsii: sluchainaia i nesluchainaia vyborki v sotsiologii. Moskva, 1976. pp. 214. *bibliog.*

SOCIOLOGISTS.

KLASSIKER des soziologischen Denkens;...herausgegeben von Dirk Käsler. München, [1976-78]. 2 vols. *bibliogs.*

— **Germany.**

HARDIN (BERT L.) The professionalization of sociology: a comparative study: Germany - USA. Frankfurt, [1977]. pp. 196. *bibliog.*

— **Poland.**

WÓJCIK (PRZEMYSŁAW) Z rodowodu socjalistycznej polityki społecznej: koncepcje i poglądy Stanisława Rychlińskiego. Warszawa, 1976. pp. 234. *bibliog.*

— **United States.**

HARDIN (BERT L.) The professionalization of sociology: a comparative study: Germany - USA. Frankfurt, [1977]. pp. 196. *bibliog.*

SOCIOLOGISTS, AFRO-AMERICAN

See AFRO-AMERICAN SOCIOLOGISTS.

SOCIOLOGY.

WAXWEILER (EMILE) Recueil de textes sociologiques d'Émile Waxweiler, 1906-1914. Bruxelles, 1974. pp. 680.

COSER (LEWIS ALFRED) and ROSENBERG (BERNARD) eds. Sociological theory: a book of readings. 4th ed. New York, [1976]. pp. 651. *bibliogs.*

NISBET (ROBERT ALEXANDER) Sociology as an art form. London, [1976, repr. 1977]. pp. 145.

STAPLES (ROBERT) Introduction to black sociology. New York, [1976]. pp. 338. *bibliogs.*

FOSSAERT (ROBERT) La société. Paris, 1977 in progress.

BERGER (PETER L.) Facing up to modernity: excursions in society, politics and religion. New York, [1977]. pp. 233.

FOSS (DENNIS C.) The value controversy in sociology. San Francisco, 1977. pp. 131. *bibliog.*

FREIHEIT und Sachzwang: Beiträge zu Ehren Helmut Schelskys; herausgegeben von Horst Baier. Opladen, [1977]. pp. 340.

HOLZER (HORST) Gesellschaft als System: makrosoziologische Systemtheorie in der Soziologie der USA und der BRD. Frankfurt am Main, 1977. pp. 104.

OFSHE (RICHARD J.) compiler. The sociology of the possible. 2nd ed. Englewood Cliffs, [1977]. pp. 381.

PACHOLSKI (MAKSYMILIAN) Florian Znaniecki: społeczna dynamika kultury. Warszawa, 1977. pp. 307. *bibliog. With English table of contents.*

PARSONS (TALCOTT) Social systems and the evolution of action theory. New York, [1977]. pp. 420.

SCHMALENBACH (HERMAN) Herman Schmalenbach on society and experience; selected papers edited, translated and with an introduction by Günther Lüschen and Gregory P. Stone. Chicago, 1977. pp. 280. *bibliog.*

SOTSIOLOGIIA i sovremennost'. Moskva, 1977. 2 vols.

WARREN (CAROL A.B.) Sociology: change and continuity. Homewood, Ill., 1977. pp. 427. *bibliog.*

WEBER (MAX) Critique of Stammler;...translated, with an introductory essay, by Guy Oakes. New York, [1977]. pp. 184.

WORSLEY (PETER MAURICE) and others. Introducing sociology. 2nd ed. Harmondsworth, 1977. pp. 605. *bibliog.*

COTGROVE (STEPHEN FREDERICK) The science of society: an introduction to sociology. 4th ed. London, 1978. pp. 302. *bibliogs.*

ELIAS (NORBERT) What is sociology?: translated by Stephen Mennell and Grace Morrissey. London, 1978. pp. 187.

FROMM (ERICH) To have or to be? London, 1978. pp. 215. *bibliog.*

KRZYWICKI (LUDWIK) Wybór pism: wyboru dokonała i wstępem opatrzyła Henryka Hołda-Róziewicz. Warszawa, 1978. pp. 937.

LENSKI (GERHARD EMMANUEL) and LENSKI (JEAN) Human societies: an introduction to macrosociology. 3rd ed. New York, [1978]. pp. 515.

MODERN sociology: introductory readings: selected readings; edited by Peter Worsley. 2nd ed. Harmondsworth, 1978. pp. 675.

ORGANIZATION and environment: theory, issues and reality; edited by Lucien Karpik. London, [1978]. pp. 345. *bibliogs. Contributions from the Eighth World Congress of Sociology, Toronto, 1974.*

ROBERTSON (ROLAND) Meaning and change: explorations in the cultural sociology of modern societies. Oxford, [1978]. pp. 284.

[WEBER (MAX)] Max Weber: selections in translation; edited by W.G. Runciman. Cambridge, 1978. pp. 398. *bibliog.*

— **Bibliography.**

BONO (ANNA) and others, compilers. Bibliografia della sociologia italiana, 1969-1971. Milano, [1978]. pp. 266. *(Turin. Università. Istituto di Scienze Politiche. Archivio Italiano di Sociologia. 1)*

The COMBINED retrospective index set to journals in sociology 1895-1974...; executive editor: Annadel N. Wile. Washington, 1978. 6 vols.

— **Dictionaries and encyclopedias.**

WOERTERBUCH der Soziologie; von Günter Hartfiel. 2nd ed. Stuttgart, [1976]. pp. 715.

WOERTERBUCH der marxistisch-leninistischen Soziologie; herausgegeben von Georg Assmann [and others]. Berlin, 1977. pp. 758.

GALLINO (LUCIANO) Dizionario di sociologia. Torino, [1978]. pp. 820. *bibliogs.*

— **History — Germany.**

ABENDROTH-Forum: Marburger Gespräche aus Anlass des 70. Geburtstags von Wolfgang Abendroth; herausgegeben von Frank Deppe [and others]. Marburg, [1977]. pp. 443. *(Studiengesellschaft für Sozialgeschichte und Arbeiterbewegung, Marburg. Schriftenreihe für Sozialgeschichte und Arbeiterbewegung. Band 6) Papers and discussion of four symposia held in May and June of 1976.*

HOLZER (HORST) Gesellschaft als System: makrosoziologische Systemtheorie in der Soziologie der USA und der BRD. Frankfurt am Main, 1977. pp. 104.

— — **Hungary.**

WORLD CONGRESS OF SOCIOLOGY, 8TH, 1974. Sociology in Hungary: recent issues and trends; ...Sociologie en Hongrie: sujets et tendances récents, etc. Budapest, 1974. pp. 176. *bibliog. (Magyar Tudományos Akadémia. Szociológia. 5. Supplement)*

— — **Russia — Bibliography.**

MATTHEWS (MERVYN) and JONES (THOMAS ANTHONY) compilers. Soviet sociology, 1964-75: a bibliography. New York, 1978. pp. 268.

— — **United States.**

HOLZER (HORST) Gesellschaft als System: makrosoziologische Systemtheorie in der Soziologie der USA und der BRD. Frankfurt am Main, 1977. pp. 104.

— **Methodology.**

BECKER (H.A.) Simulatie en sociologie: rede uitgesproken bij het aanvaaden van het ambt van hoogleraar in de sociologie...aan de Rijksuniversiteit te Utrecht op 2 Juni 1969. 's-Gravenhage, 1969. pp. 23.

EXPLORATIONS in general theory in social science: essays in honor of Talcott Parsons; edited by Jan J. Loubser [and others]. New York, [1976]. 2 vols.

ECKHARDT (KENNETH W.) and ERMANN (M. DAVID) Social research methods: perspective, theory, and analysis. New York, [1977]. pp. 410. *bibliogs.*

KALENSKII (VALERII GEORGIEVICH) Gosudarstvo kak ob"ekt sotsiologicheskogo analiza: ocherki istorii i metodologii issledovaniia; otvetstvennyi redaktor V.E. Guliev. Moskva, 1977. pp. 182.

BAILEY (KENNETH D.) Methods of social research. New York, [1978]. pp. 478. *bibliog.*

— **Periodicals — Indexes.**

The COMBINED retrospective index set to journals in sociology 1895-1974...; executive editor: Annadel N. Wile. Washington, 1978. 6 vols.

— **Philosophy.**

CHELOVEK kak ob"ekt sotsiologicheskogo issledovaniia; pod redaktsiei L.I. Spiridonova i Ia.I. Gilinskogo. Leningrad, 1977. pp. 197.

COULTER (IAN DOUGLASS) A philosophical and theoretical criticism of "homo sociologicus" in twentieth century sociology. [1977]. fo. 524. *bibliog. Typescript: (unpublished.) Ph.D. (London) thesis. This thesis is the property of London University and may not be removed from the Library.*

FREIHEIT und Sachzwang: Beiträge zu Ehren Helmut Schelskys; herausgegeben von Horst Baier. Opladen, [1977]. pp. 340.

— **Societies, etc.**

NATIONAL ASSOCIATION FOR THE PROMOTION OF SOCIAL SCIENCE. National Association for the Promotion of Social Science... 1865-6. London, [1865?]. pp. 47.

SOCIOLOGY.(Cont.)

— Statistical methods.

MATHEMATICAL models for social psychology; edited by Wilhelm F. Kempf [and] Bruno H. Repp; with contributions by Erling B. Andersen [and others]. Chichester, 1977. pp. 283. *bibliogs. First published in 1976 under title: Some mathematical models for social psychology. A rev. and augmented translation of Probabilistische Modelle in der Sozialpsychologie.*

HANDEL (JUDITH D.) Introductory statistics for sociology. Englewood Cliffs, [1978]. pp. 387.

— Study and teaching — America, Latin.

SOLARI (ALDO E.) and others. Teoria, accion social y desarrollo en America Latina. Mexico, 1976. pp. 637.

— — Brazil.

FERNANDES (FLORESTAN) A sociologia no Brasil: contribuição para o estudo de sua formação e desenvolvimento. Petropolis, 1977. pp. 270.

— France — Bibliography.

NANDAN (YASH) The Durkheimian school: a systematic and comprehensive bibliography. Westport, [1977]. pp. 458.

SOCIOLOGY, CHRISTIAN.

GILL (ROBIN) Theology and social structure. London, 1977. pp. 153.

MALHERBE (ABRAHAM J.) Social aspects of early Christianity. Baton Rouge, [1977]. pp. 98. *(Rice University. Rockwell Lectures on Religion. 1975)*

MARTIN (DAVID ALFRED) A general theory of secularization. Oxford, [1978]. pp. 353. *bibliog.*

— Catholic.

DENAULT (BERNARD) and LEVESQUE (BENÔIT) Eléments pour une sociologie des communautés religieuses au Québec. Sherbrooke, 1975. pp. 220. *bibliog.*

GREELEY (ANDREW M.) No bigger than necessary: an alternative to socialism, capitalism and anarchism. New York, [1977]. pp. 181.

SOCIOLOGY, MILITARY.

BACHMAN (JERALD G.) and others. The all-volunteer force: a study of ideology in the military. Ann Arbor, [1977]. pp. 210. *bibliog.*

FELD (MAURY D.) The structure of violence: armed forces as social systems. Beverly Hills, [1977]. pp. 203.

GOODPASTER (ANDREW JACKSON) and HUNTINGTON (SAMUEL PHILLIPS) Civil-military relations. Washington, D.C., [1977]. pp. 84. *(American Enterprise Institute for Public Policy Research. AEI Studies. 141) Based on a symposium sponsored by the University of Nebraska at Omaha and the AEI in 1976.*

TRIMBERGER (ELLEN KAY) Revolution from above: military bureaucrats and development in Japan, Turkey, Egypt, and Peru. New Brunswick, [1978]. pp. 196. *bibliog.*

SOCIOLOGY, RURAL.

INTERREGIONAL SEMINAR ON PHYSICAL PLANNING FOR URBAN, REGIONAL AND NATIONAL DEVELOPMENT, BUCHAREST, 1969. Report of the...Seminar...[held in] Bucharest, Romania 22 September to 7 October 1969. (ST/TAO/SER.C/132). New York, United Nations, 1971. pp. 43.

INTERNATIONAL perspectives in rural sociology; edited by Howard Newby. Chichester, [1978]. pp. 220. *bibliogs.*

SOCIOLOGY, URBAN.

GANS (HERBERT J.) People and plans: essays on urban problems and solutions. New York, [1968]. pp. 395.

FINLAYSON (JAMES) Urban devastation: the planning of incarceration. Oxford, [1976]. pp. 25. *(Solidarity (Oxford). Pamphlets. No. 2)*

FISCHER (CLAUDE S.) The urban experience. New York, [1976]. pp. 309. *bibliog.*

MICHELSON (WILLIAM) Man and his urban environment: a sociological approach. rev. ed. Reading, Mass., [1976]. pp. 273. *bibliog.*

URBAN ethnic conflict : a comparative perspective edited by Susan E. Clarke and Jeffrey L. Obler. Chapel Hill, 1976. pp. 257. *bibliogs. Proceedings of a conference held in Chapel Hill in 1975 by the University of North Carolina Institute for Research in Social Science.*

FISCHER (CLAUDE S.) and others. Networks and places: social relations in the urban setting. New York, [1977]. pp. 229. *bibliog.*

TURK (HERMAN) Organizations in modern life: (cities and other large networks). San Francisco, 1977. pp. 283. *bibliog.*

WHITE (MORTON GABRIEL) and WHITE (LUCIA) The intellectual versus the city: from Thomas Jefferson to Frank Lloyd Wright. Oxford, 1977. pp. 270.

CASTELLS (MANUEL) City, class and power; translation supervised by Elizabeth Lebas. London, 1978. pp. 198.

ISSUES in urban society; edited by Ross Davies and Peter Hall. Harmondsworth, 1978. pp. 299. *bibliogs.*

KIRK (GWYNETH) Sociology of land use planning: Southwark's redevelopment plans. 1977 [or rather 1978]. pp. fo.537. *bibliog. Typescript. Ph.D. (London) thesis: unpublished. This thesis is the property of London University and may not be removed from the Library.*

— Abstracts.

URBAN ABSTRACTS; (compiled in the Research Library of the Greater London Council). m., Ap 1974 (no.1)- London. *Supersedes Planning and transportation abstracts (Ag 1970 - F/Mr 1974, with gap)*

SOCIOLOGY AS A PROFESSION.

HARDIN (BERT L.) The professionalization of sociology: a comparative study: Germany - USA. Frankfurt, [1977]. pp. 196. *bibliog.*

SOCRATES.

BLUM (ALAN F.) Socrates: the original and its images. London, 1978. pp. 227.

SOILS

— Malawi.

MALAWI. Agro-Economic Survey. 1976. Agro-economic survey: report no. 20: soil types and land suitability for coffee in the northern region of Malawi. Lilongwe, 1976. fo. 58. *bibliog.*

— New Zealand.

GRIFFITHS (E.) Soils of part of the Port Hills and adjacent plains, Canterbury, New Zealand. Wellington, 1974. pp. 36. *(New Zealand. Soil Bureau. Bulletins. No.35) 3 charts and 1 map in end pocket.*

SOKOLSKY (GEORGE EPHRAIM).

COHEN (WARREN I.) The Chinese connection: Roger S. Greene, Thomas W. Lamont, George E. Sokolsky and American-East Asian relations. New York, 1978. pp. 322. *(Columbia University. East Asian Institute. Studies)*

SOLAR ENERGY

— United Kingdom.

LONG (GEOFFREY) Solar energy: its potential contribution within the United Kingdom; a report prepared for the Department of Energy;... with contributions from J.D. Garnish [and others]. London, 1976. pp. 81. *bibliog. (U.K. Department of Energy. Energy Papers. No. 16)*

SOLAR STILLS.

UNITED NATIONS. Department of Economic and Social Affairs. 1970. Solar distillation as a means of meeting small-scale water demands. (ST/ECA/121). New York, 1970. pp. 86. *bibliog.*

SOLDIERS

— Education, Non-military — Austria.

KOERNER (THEODOR) Bundespräsident. Auf Vorposten: ausgewählte Schriften, 1928-1938; herausgegeben und kommentiert von Ilona Duczynska. Wien, [1977]. pp. 299.

— United Kingdom.

WORKERS' AND SOLDIERS' COUNCIL. Provisional Committee. Constitution of local councils. London, [192-?]. pp. (4).

— United States.

BACHMAN (JERALD G.) and others. The all-volunteer force: a study of ideology in the military. Ann Arbor, [1977]. pp. 210. *bibliog.*

SOLZHENITSYN (ALEKSANDR ISAEVICH).

BARKER (FRANCIS) Solzhenitsyn: politics and form. London, 1977. pp. 112.

SOMALI REPUBLIC

— History.

DECRAENE (PHILIPPE) L'expérience socialiste somalienne. [Paris, 1977]. pp. 219. *bibliog.*

— Languages.

LAITIN (DAVID D.) Politics, language, and thought: the Somali experience. Chicago, [1977]. pp. 268. *bibliog.*

SOMOZA FAMILY.

MILLETT (RICHARD) Guardians of the dynasty. Maryknoll, [1977]. pp. 284. *bibliog.*

SONORA

— History.

AGUILAR CAMIN (HECTOR) La frontera nomada: Sonora y la Revolucion mexicana. Mexico, 1977. pp. 450. *bibliog.*

SORBS.

In earlier volumes of this Bibliography similar material is entered under WENDS.

GESCHICHTE der Sorben: Gesamtdarstellung;...Gesamtredaktion: Jan Šolta [and others]. Bautzen, 1974 in progress. *bibliogs. (Akademie der Wissenschaften der DDR. Institut für Sorbische Volksforschung in Bautzen. Schriftenreihe. 39-41)*

SOREL (GEORGES).

FURIOZZI (GIAN BAGIO) Sorel e l'Italia. Firenze, [1975]. pp. 377.

SOUTH AFRICA

— Appropriations and expenditures.

SOUTH AFRICA. Department of the Auditor-General. Report of the Auditor-General. a., 1950/51- Pretoria. *[in English and Afrikaans]. Included in SOUTH AFRICA. Parliament. House of Assembly. Votes and proceedings [with Printed annexures]. In 3 pts.*

SOUTH AFRICA

— Biography.

FELDBERG (LEON) compiler. South African Jewry: a survey of the Jewish community: its contribution to South Africa: directory of communal institutions: and a who's who of leading personalities. 3rd ed. Johannesburg, 1976-77. pp. 529.

— Census.

SOUTH AFRICA. Census, 1970. Population census, 1970: [Bantu national units]. [Pretoria, 1976-77]. 12 pts. (in 2 vols.). *(Bureau of Statistics. Reports. Nos.02-02-03 to 02-02-14) In English and Afrikaans.*

SOUTH AFRICA. Census, 1970. Population census, 1970: metropolitan area[s]. [Pretoria, 1977 in progress]. *(Bureau of Statistics. Reports. Nos. 02-05-13, etc.) In English and Afrikaans.*

SOUTH AFRICA. Census, 1970. Population census, 1970: home language. [Pretoria, 1977]. pp. 526. *(Bureau of Statistics. Reports. No. 02-01-09) In English and Afrikaans.*

— Commerce.

VAN RENSBURG (W.C.J.) and PRETORIUS (DESMOND A.) South Africa's strategic minerals: pieces on a continental chess board. Johannesburg, 1977. pp. 156. *bibliogs.*

— Constitutional history.

CHANOCK (MARTIN) Unconsummated union: Britain, Rhodesia and South Africa, 1900-45. Manchester, [1977]. pp. 289. *bibliog.*

— Economic conditions.

FAIR (T.J.D.) Polarisation, dispersion and decentralisation in the South African space economy. Johannesburg, 1975. pp. 22. *bibliog. (Johannesburg. University of the Witwatersrand. Urban and Regional Research Unit. Occasional Papers. No. 7)*

CHANGE, reform and economic growth in South Africa; editors Lawrence Schlemmer [and] Eddie Webster. Johannesburg, 1978. pp. 244. *bibliogs. Based on a workshop held in the Centre for Applied Social Sciences at the University of Natal in 1974.*

— Economic policy.

FAIR (T.J.D.) Some spatial aspects of black homeland development in South Africa. Johannesburg, 1975. pp. 22. *bibliog. (Johannesburg. University of the Witwatersrand. Urban and Regional Research Unit. Occasional Papers. No. 6)*

BUTLER (JEFFREY ERNEST) and others. The black homelands of South Africa: the political and economic development of Bophuthatswana and KwaZulu. Berkeley, Calif., [1977]. pp. 250. *bibliog.*

LOMBARD (JOHANNES ANTHONIE) Freedom, welfare and order: thoughts on the principles of political co-operation in the economy of southern Africa. Pretoria, Bureau for Economic Research, Bantu Development, 1978. pp. 192. *bibliog.*

— Executive departments.

SOUTH AFRICA. Department of Information. Report. a., 1976. Pretoria. *These reports not for general distribution.*

— Foreign relations.

SOUTH Africa: the next 15 years: a microcosm of world problems; three of the papers delivered at the US-SALEP symposium on Southern Africa...in March 1976; edited by E.A. Kraayenbrink. Johannesburg, 1976. pp. 39.

BISSELL (RICHARD E.) Apartheid and international organizations. Boulder, Colo., 1977. pp. 231. *bibliog.*

METROWICH (F.R.) South Africa's new frontiers. Sandton, [1977]. pp. 160.

See also UNITED NATIONS — South Africa.

— — Malawi.

MALAWI. Department of Information. 1970. Pioneers in inter-African relations: (speeches by the President of Malawi and the Prime Minister of South Africa at State House, Zomba, 20 May 1970). [Blantyre, 1970]. pp. 18.

— — Rhodesia.

CHANOCK (MARTIN) Unconsummated union: Britain, Rhodesia and South Africa, 1900-45. Manchester, [1977]. pp. 289. *bibliog.*

— — United Kingdom.

CHANOCK (MARTIN) Unconsummated union: Britain, Rhodesia and South Africa, 1900-45. Manchester, [1977]. pp. 289. *bibliog.*

WINDRICH (ELAINE) Britain and the politics of Rhodesian independence. London, [1978]. pp. 283.

— — United States.

The UNITED States and South Africa: three South African perspectives; [by] Percy Qoboza [and others]. Johannesburg, 1977. pp. 15. *(South African Institute of International Affairs. Occasional Papers) Panel discussion held in Johannesburg in 1977.*

— Languages.

SOUTH AFRICA. Census, 1970. Population census, 1970: home language. [Pretoria, 1977]. pp. 526. *(Bureau of Statistics. Reports. No. 02-01-09) In English and Afrikaans.*

— Manufactures.

NATTRASS (JILL) and BROWN (RICHARD P.C.) Capital intensity in South African manufacturing. Durban, 1977. pp. 44. *(Natal University. Department of Economics. Black/White Income Gap Project. Interim Research Reports. No. 4)*

— Military policy.

BARNABY (CHARLES FRANK) Nuclear proliferation and the South African threat. Geneva, [1977]. pp. 22.

— Native races.

SOUTH AFRICA. Bureau of Statistics. Report on Bantu deaths in selected magisterial districts (formerly Bantu deaths in selected magisterial districts). a., 1968/71- Pretoria. *[in English and Afrikaans].*

SOUTH AFRICA. Department of the Auditor General. Report...on the accounts of the South-Western Cape Area Bantu Affairs Administration Board. a., 1973/75(1st)- Pretoria. *[in English and Afrikaans] Included in SOUTH AFRICA. Parliament. House of Assembly. Votes and proceedings (with Printed annexures).*

BALDWIN (ALAN) and HALL (ANTHONY) A place called Dimbaza: a case study of a rural settlement township in South Africa. London, 1973. pp. 29. *(Africa Publications Trust. Studies in the Mass Removal of Population in South Africa. [No. 1])*

SOUTH AFRICA. Department of the Auditor General. Report...on the accounts of the Northern Cape Area Bantu Affairs Administration Board. a., 1975/76- Pretoria. *[in English and Afrikaans] Included in SOUTH AFRICA. Parliament. House of Assembly. Votes and proceedings [with Printed annexures].*

SOUTH AFRICA. Census, 1970. Population census, 1970: [Bantu national units]. [Pretoria, 1976-77]. 12 pts. (in 2 vols.). *(Bureau of Statistics. Reports. Nos.02-02-03 to 02-02-14) In English and Afrikaans.*

ROGERS (BARBARA) Divide and rule: South Africa's Bantustans. London, 1976. pp. 86.

The THERON Commission report: an evaluation and early reactions to the report and its recommendations; edited by O.D. Wollheim. Johannesburg, [1977]. pp. 39.

— Parliament — Elections.

SCHOEMAN (B.M.) Parlementêre verkiesings in Suid-Afrika, 1910-1976. Pretoria, 1977. pp. 513.

— Politics and government.

BLACKWELL (LESLIE) Farewell to Parliament: more reminiscences of bench, bar, Parliament and travel. Pietermaritzburg, 1946. pp. 239.

[VAN LINGEN (J.)] Race policies. Johannesburg, 1965. pp. 60.

INTERNATIONAL UNIVERSITY EXCHANGE FUND. Summary of the so-called Schlebusch Committee's final report on the National Union of South African Students (NUSAS).... Geneva, 1975. 1 vol. (various pagings).

SOUTH Africa: the next 15 years: a microcosm of world problems; three of the papers delivered at the US-SALEP symposium on Southern Africa...in March 1976; edited by E.A. Kraayenbrink. Johannesburg, 1976. pp. 39.

DE ST. JORRE (JOHN) A house divided: South Africa's uncertain future. New York, [1977]. pp. 136.

DE VILLIERS (DIRK CHRISTIAAN) and DE VILLIERS (JOHANNA) Paul Sauer. Kaapstad, 1977. pp. 184.

HITCHCOCK (BOB) Flashpoint South Africa. London, 1977. pp. 212.

NAPLEY (Sir DAVID) Steven Biko inquest. [1977]. fo. 26. *Unpublished: photocopy of typescript.*

— Population.

HART (T.) and LOURENS (I.K.) The demographic structure of black and white populations in the Witwatersrand metropolitan region, 1970. Johannesburg, 1977. pp. 30. *bibliog. (Johannesburg. University of the Witwatersrand. Urban and Regional Research Unit. Occasional Papers. No. 18)*

— Race question.

ANTI-APARTHEID MOVEMENT. [Selected documents]. 1965. 2 parts (in 1 vol.) *Typescript: unpublished.*

[VAN LINGEN (J.)] Race policies. Johannesburg, 1965. pp. 60.

BALDWIN (ALAN) and HALL (ANTHONY) A place called Dimbaza: a case study of a rural settlement township in South Africa. London, 1973. pp. 29. *(Africa Publications Trust. Studies in the Mass Removal of Population in South Africa. [No. 1])*

INTERNATIONAL UNIVERSITY EXCHANGE FUND. Summary of the so-called Schlebusch Committee's final report on the National Union of South African Students (NUSAS).... Geneva, 1975. 1 vol. (various pagings).

LEGASSICK (MARTIN) and HEMSON (DAVID) Foreign investment and the reproduction of racial capitalism in South Africa. London, 1976. pp. 16. *(Anti-Apartheid Movement. Foreign Investment in South Africa. No. 2)*

BISSELL (RICHARD E.) Apartheid and international organizations. Boulder, Colo., 1977. pp. 231. *bibliog.*

COUNTER INFORMATION SERVICES. Anti-Reports. No. 17. Black South Africa explodes. London, [1977]. pp. 63. *bibliog.*

A GUIDE to multi-racial contact prepared by a member of the legal profession. Johannesburg, [1977]. pp. 4.

HITCHCOCK (BOB) Flashpoint South Africa. London, 1977. pp. 212.

McGRATH (M.D.) Racial income distribution in South Africa. Durban, 1977. pp. 31. *(Natal University. Department of Economics. Black/White Income Gap Project. Interim Research Reports. No. 2)*

SHEPHERD (GEORGE W.) the Younger. Anti-apartheid: transnational conflict and western policy in the liberation of South Africa. Westport, Conn., 1977. pp. 246.

STEPHAN (KLAUS) Südafrika: Weg in die Tragödie. München, [1977]. pp. 192.

The THERON Commission report: an evaluation and early reactions to the report and its recommendations; edited by O.D. Wollheim. Johannesburg, [1977]. pp. 39.

SOUTH AFRICA (Cont.)

RACE and politics in South Africa; edited by Ian Robertson and Phillip Whitten. New Brunswick, [1978]. pp. 270.

WOODS (DONALD) Biko. New York, [1978]. pp. 288.

— Relations (general) with Malawi.

MALAWI. Department of Information. 1968. Speeches by G.W. Kumtumanji, Minister of Local Government, Health and Education, and H. Muller, the South Africa's Foreign Minister, made at Ryall's Hotel, Blantyre, during his visit to the Republic of Malawi, August 27, 1968. Blantyre, [1968]. pp. 7,8.

— Statistics, Vital.

SOUTH AFRICA. Bureau of Statistics. Report on Bantu deaths in selected magisterial districts (formerly Bantu deaths in selected magisterial districts). a., 1968/71- Pretoria. *[in English and Afrikaans].*

SOUTH AFRICAN WAR, 1899-1902.

STOP-THE-WAR COMMITTEE. What is now being done in South Africa: the testimony of British soldiers at the front. [London, 1900]. pp. 4.

— Finance, commerce, confiscations, etc.

CLAIM against the imperial government in the matter of the specie commandeered by the government of the late South African Republic from British banks: further correspondence between the Colonial Office and the banks. [London?, 1904]. pp. 13.

— Personal narratives.

RUIJSSENAERS (LEENDERT CORSTIAAN) Krijgsgevangenschap...1899-1902; geredigeer en geannoteer deur O. J.O. Ferreira. Pretoria, 1977. pp. 237. *bibliog. (Instituut vir Geskiedenisnavorsing. Bronnepublikasies. Nr. 6)*

— Prisoners and prisons.

RUIJSSENAERS (LEENDERT CORSTIAAN) Krijgsgevangenschap...1899-1902; geredigeer en geannoteer deur O. J.O. Ferreira. Pretoria, 1977. pp. 237. *bibliog. (Instituut vir Geskiedenisnavorsing. Bronnepublikasies. Nr. 6)*

SOUTH AUSTRALIA

— Politics and government.

JAENSCH (DEAN HAROLD) The government of South Australia. St. Lucia, Queensland, [1977]. pp. 203.

SOUTH CAROLINA

— Politics and government.

HOLT (THOMAS) Black over white: negro political leadership in South Carolina during reconstruction. Urbana, [1977]. pp. 269. *bibliog.*

SOUTH-EAST ASIA TREATY ORGANIZATION.

SOUTH-EAST ASIA TREATY ORGANIZATION. 1977. SEATO record: 1954-1977; a survey of the activities of the South-East Asia Treaty Organization. Bangkok, 1977. 1 vol. (various pagings).

SOUTH GLAMORGAN

— Economic conditions.

SOUTH GLAMORGAN. County Council. Report of survey instituted by the County Council...pursuant to section 6 of the Town and Country Planning Acts, 1971. [Cardiff], 1977. pp. 190. *bibliog.*

— Economic policy.

SOUTH GLAMORGAN. County Council. County of South Glamorgan structure plan. [Cardiff], 1977. pp. 194, xv.

SOUTH GLAMORGAN. County Council. County of South Glamorgan structure plan...: publicity and public participation statement. [Cardiff], 1977. 1 vol. (various pagings).

SOUTH GLAMORGAN. County Council. County structure plan: draft written statement. [Cardiff], 1977. pp. 195, xv.

— Social conditions.

SOUTH GLAMORGAN. County Council. Report of survey instituted by the County Council...pursuant to section 6 of the Town and Country Planning Acts, 1971. [Cardiff], 1977. pp. 190. *bibliog.*

— Social policy.

SOUTH GLAMORGAN. County Council. County of South Glamorgan structure plan. [Cardiff], 1977. pp. 194, xv.

SOUTH GLAMORGAN. County Council. County of South Glamorgan structure plan...: publicity and public participation statement. [Cardiff], 1977. 1 vol. (various pagings).

SOUTH GLAMORGAN. County Council. County structure plan: draft written statement. [Cardiff], 1977. pp. 195, xv.

SOUTH WEST AFRICA

— Census.

SOUTH WEST AFRICA. Census, 1970. Population census, 6 May 1970: South-West Africa: geographical distribution of the population. Pretoria, 1971. pp. 8. *(South Africa. Bureau of Statistics. Statistical News Releases. No. 64) In English and Afrikaans.*

SOUTH WEST AFRICA. Census, 1970. Population census, South West Africa, (6 May 1970). Windhoek, 1971. fo. 3. *Includes estimates for May 1975.*

— Economic policy.

RUBIN (NEVILLE) Labour and discrimination in Namibia. Geneva, International Labour Office, 1977. pp. 126.

— History.

VIGNE (RANDOLPH) A dwelling place of our own: the story of the Namibian nation. London, 1973. pp. 52. *bibliog.*

— Nationalism.

VIGNE (RANDOLPH) A dwelling place of our own: the story of the Namibian nation. London, 1973. pp. 52. *bibliog.*

— Politics and government.

The FUTURE of South West Africa/Namibia; a symposium; [by] John Barratt [and others]. Johannesburg, 1977. pp. 14. *(South African Institute of International Affairs. Occasional Papers) Papers given at a symposium in Johannesburg in 1977.*

TOETEMEYER (GERHARD) South West Africa/Namibia: facts, attitudes, assessment, and prospects. Randburg, 1977. pp. 323. *bibliog.*

BRITISH COUNCIL OF CHURCHES. Department of International Affairs. Namibia. London, [1978]. pp. 23. *bibliog.*

— Race question.

GORDON (ROBERT J.) Ph.D. Mines, masters and migrants: life in a Namibian mine compound. Johannesburg, [1977]. pp. 276. *bibliog. Based on a dissertation submitted at the University of Illinois.*

SOUTH YORKSHIRE

— Economic conditions.

SOUTH YORKSHIRE. County Planning Department. South Yorkshire structure plan: report of survey. [Barnsley], 1977. 3 vols. (in 1).

— Economic history.

ABELL (PAUL HENRY) Transport and industry in South Yorkshire. Barnsley, [1977]. pp. 84. *bibliog.*

— Economic policy.

SOUTH YORKSHIRE. County Planning Department. South Yorkshire structure plan: draft written statement. [Barnsley], 1977. pp. 142. *Map in end pocket.*

SOUTH YORKSHIRE. County Planning Department. South Yorkshire structure plan: report of survey. [Barnsley], 1977. 3 vols. (in 1).

— Industries.

ABELL (PAUL HENRY) Transport and industry in South Yorkshire. Barnsley, [1977]. pp. 84. *bibliog.*

— Social conditions.

SOUTH YORKSHIRE. County Planning Department. South Yorkshire structure plan: report of survey. [Barnsley], 1977. 3 vols. (in 1).

— Social policy.

SOUTH YORKSHIRE. County Planning Department. South Yorkshire structure plan: draft written statement. [Barnsley], 1977. pp. 142. *Map in end pocket.*

SOUTH YORKSHIRE. County Planning Department. South Yorkshire structure plan: report of survey. [Barnsley], 1977. 3 vols. (in 1).

SOUTHAMPTON

— City planning.

HAMPSHIRE. County Council. South Hampshire structure plan for the south east part of the County of Hampshire, City of Portsmouth, City of Southampton; as approved by the Secretary of State for the Environment, March 1977. [Winchester, 1977]. 1 vol. (various pagings). *3 maps in end pocket.*

— History — Sources.

SOUTHAMPTON. University. Southampton Records Series. vol. 21. The Southampton mayor's book of 1606-1608; edited by W.J. Connor. Southampton, 1978. pp. 127.

— Politics and government.

SOUTHAMPTON. University. Southampton Records Series. vol. 21. The Southampton mayor's book of 1606-1608; edited by W.J. Connor. Southampton, 1978. pp. 127.

SOUTHWARK

— City planning.

SOUTHWARK. Borough Council. Towards a community plan. [London], 1977. 8 pts. (in 1 vol.).

KIRK (GWYNETH) Sociology of land use planning: Southwark's redevelopment plans. 1977 [or rather 1978]. pp. fo.537. *bibliog. Typescript. Ph.D. (London) thesis: unpublished. This thesis is the property of London University and may not be removed from the Library.*

— Economic history.

UNION PLACE COMMUNITY RESOURCE CENTRE. Nine days 1926: the General Strike in Southwark. London, 1976. pp. 52. *bibliog.*

— Politics and government.

DAVIS (ALAN) and others. The management of deprivation: final report of Southwark Community Development Project. [London, 1977]. pp. 100.

— Social conditions.

SOUTHWARK. Borough Council. Towards a community plan. [London], 1977. 8 pts. (in 1 vol.).

— Social policy.

SOUTHWARK. Borough Council. Towards a community plan. [London], 1977. 8 pts. (in 1 vol.).

SOUTHWEST, NEW

— Commerce.

CONNOR (SEYMOUR V.) and SKAGGS (JIMMY M.) Broadcloth and britches: the Santa Fe trade. College Station, Tex., [1977]. pp. 225. bibliog.

— History.

CONNOR (SEYMOUR V.) and SKAGGS (JIMMY M.) Broadcloth and britches: the Santa Fe trade. College Station, Tex., [1977]. pp. 225. bibliog.

SOVEREIGNTY.

KALOGEROPOULOS-STRATES (SPYRIDON) Le droit des peuples à disposer d'eux-mêmes. Bruxelles, 1973. pp. 388. bibliog.

BEZUGLOV (ANATOLII ALEKSEEVICH) Suverenitet sovetskogo naroda. Moskva, 1975. pp. 199.

FRANKLIN (JULIAN HAROLD) John Locke and the theory of sovereignty: mixed monarchy and the right of resistance in the political thought of the English revolution. Cambridge, 1978. pp. 146. bibliog.

SOVIET NORTH

— Economic conditions.

PROBLEMY razvitiia raionov s ekstremal'nymi prirodnymi usloviiami; (Problems of developing districts with extremal natural conditions). Irkutsk, 1976. pp. 193. bibliog. With English foreword, summaries and table of contents.

— Politics and government.

VO glave bor'by trudiashchikhsia za diktaturu proletariata i sotsialisticheskogo stroitel'stva: iz istorii partiinykh organizatsii Severo-Zapada RSFSR. Petrozavodsk, 1975. pp. 190.

SOVIETS.

RENTSCH (NIKLAUS B.) Das System der Räte. Bern, [1976]. pp. 199.

— Germany.

Der JUELICHER Arbeiter- und Soldatenrat im November 1918: eine Dokumentation; ([edited by] Günter Bers). Jülich, 1974. pp. 31.

STILLER (KARL THEODOR) Gewerkschaftspolitik und Bewegungen in der Arbeiterschaft, 1914 bis 1920. Offenbach, 1977. pp. 111. bibliog.

— Russia.

SOVERSHENSTVOVANIE raboty Sovetov v sovremennykh usloviiakh. Moskva, 1976. pp. 116.

SOWETO.

SIKAKANE (JOYCE) A window on Soweto. London, 1977. pp. 80.

VENTER (PAUL C.) Soweto: shadow city. Johannesburg, [1977]. pp. 193.

SOYA-BEANS.

The DEVELOPMENT and production of soy-ogi, a corn based complete protein food; [by] I.A. Akinrele [and others]. Lagos, Federal Ministry of Industries, 1970. pp. 63. bibliog. (Federal Institute of Industrial Research [Nigeria]. Research Reports. No.42)

SPACE AND TIME.

HALL (EDWARD TWITCHELL) The hidden dimension. Garden City, N.Y., 1969. pp. 217. bibliog.

AUSTRALIA. Cities Commission. 1975. Australians' use of time: a contribution of social planning to urban development and land use design. [Canberra], 1975. 1 vol. (unpaged). Photocopy.

INTERNATIONAL CONGRESS OF AMERICANISTS. 42nd Congress. Actes du XLIIe Congrès International des Américanistes: Congrès du Centenaire, Paris, 2-9 septembre 1976. volume II. Paris, 1977. pp. 623. bibliogs.

SPACE IN ECONOMICS.

BERRY (BRIAN JOE LOBLEY) Geography of market centers and retail distribution. Englewood Cliffs, [1967]. pp. 145.

FAIR (T.J.D.) Polarisation, dispersion and decentralisation in the South African space economy. Johannesburg, 1975. pp. 22. bibliog. (Johannesburg. University of the Witwatersrand. Urban and Regional Research Unit. Occasional Papers. No. 7)

FADEN (ARNOLD M.) Economics of space and time: the measure-theoretic foundations of social science. Ames, 1977. pp. 703.

BOYCE (RONALD R.) The bases of economic geography. 2nd ed. New York, [1978]. pp. 433. bibliogs.

SPACE LAW.

GOROVE (STEPHEN) Studies in space law: its challenges and prospects. Leyden, 1977. pp. 228. (Mississippi University. Law Center. L.Q.C. Lamar Society of International Law. Monograph Series. No. 2)

SPACE PERCEPTION.

HALL (EDWARD TWITCHELL) The hidden dimension. Garden City, N.Y., 1969. pp. 217. bibliog.

SPAIN.

SPAIN TODAY: politics, economics and development: (the review of the present); (pd. by Spanish Information Service). m., Mr 1970 (no.1)- Madrid.

— Civilization.

ALEN LASCANO (LUIS C.) Hispanoamerica en el pensamiento de Yrigoyen. Buenos Aires, [1959]. pp. 88. bibliog.

— Colonies — Administration.

SPALDING (KAREN) De indio a campesino: cambios en la estructura social del Peru colonial. Lima, 1974. pp. 258. bibliog. (Instituto de Estudios Peruanos. Historia Andina. 2)

JORNADAS AMERICANISTAS DE LA UNIVERSIDAD DE VALLADOLID, 3AS, 1974. Estudios sobre politica indigenista española en America. Valladolid, 1975-77. 3 vols.

ANDREWS (KENNETH R.) The Spanish Caribbean: trade and plunder 1530-1630. New Haven, Conn., 1978. pp. 267.

— Commerce.

INFORMACION COMERCIAL ESPANOLA: boletin semanal; [pd. by] Ministerio de Comercio [Spain]. w., My 15 1947 (año 1, num.6)- , with gaps. Madrid.

— Cortes.

GONZALEZ MUÑIZ (MIGUEL ANGEL) Los asturianos y la politica: de las Cortes de Cadiz a nuestros dias. Salinas, Asturias, [1976]. pp. 231. bibliog.

GARRORENA MORALES (ANGEL) Autoritarismo y control parlamentario en las Cortes de Franco: apuntes para un analisis critico. Murcia, 1977. pp. 428. bibliog. (Universidad de Murcia. Departamento de Derecho Politico. Monografias. 1)

— Economic conditions.

TAMAMES GOMEZ (RAMON) La oligarquia financiera en España. Barcelona, 1977. pp. 262.

SPAIN.

— Economic history.

BARTHE Y BARTHE (ANDRES) Influencia de los transportes en los mercados y en la baja de los precios: memoria premiada por la Real Academia de Ciencias Morales y Politicas en el concurso ordinario de 1897, tema segundo. Madrid, 1899. pp. 110.

BARTHE Y BARTHE (ANDRES) El aumento de la riqueza en España desde 1795. Madrid, 1907. pp. 47.

ECONOMIA y sociedad en los siglos XVIII y XIX; [by] Pierre Vilar [and others]. [New York, 1975?]. pp. 132. (Historia Iberica. 1)

NADAL OLLER (JORGE) El fracaso de la revolucion industrial en España, 1814-1913. Barcelona, 1975 repr. 1977. pp. 315. bibliog.

PANIAGUA (FRANCISCO JAVIER) La ordenacion del capitalismo avanzado en España, 1957-1963. Barcelona, [1977]. pp. 272. bibliog.

— Emigration and immigration.

VILAR RAMIREZ (JUAN BAUTISTA) Emigracion española a Argelia, 1830-1900: colonizacion hispanica de la Argelia francesa. Madrid, 1975. pp. 537. bibliog.

— History — 1868-1931.

MARTINEZ DE SAS (MARIA TERESA) El socialismo y la España oficial: Pablo Iglesias, diputado a Cortes. Madrid, [1975]. pp. 358. bibliog.

— — 1900- .

LACOMBA AVELLAN (JUAN ANTONIO) La crisis española de 1917. Madrid, [1970]. pp. 571. bibliog.

— — 1931-1939, Republic — Bibliography.

SECO SERRANO (CARLOS) Los testimonios de primer plano en la crisis española de 1931 a 1939: acotaciones bibliográficas. Santander, 1967. pp. 40. (Universidad Internacional Menendez Pelayo. Publicaciones. 28)

— — 1936-1939, Civil War.

SPAIN illustrated: a year's defence of democracy...; articles by J.B.S. Haldane [and others]. London, [1973]. 1 pamphlet (unpaged).

HERNANDEZ (JESUS) Negro y rojo: los anarquistas en la revolucion española. Mexico, D.F., 1946. pp. 557.

GUERRA y revolucion en España, 1936-1939; [elaborada por una comision presidida por Dolores Ibarruri e integrada por Manuel Azcarate [and others]]. Moscu, 1966-71. 3 vols.

CRUELLS PIFARRE (MANUEL) El separatisme catala durant la guerra civil. Barcelona, 1975. pp. 248. bibliog.

ROMERO (LUIS) El final de la guerra. Barcelona, [1976]. pp. 470.

SONADELLAS (CONCEPCIO) Clase obrera y revolucion social en España, 1936-1939. Madrid, 1977. pp. 181. bibliog.

— — — Foreign participation.

BREDEL (WILLI) Spanienkrieg...; herausgegeben von Manfred Hahn. Berlin, 1977. 2 vols.

— — — Personal narratives.

BREDEL (WILLI) Spanienkrieg...; herausgegeben von Manfred Hahn. Berlin, 1977. 2 vols.

— — — Refugees.

TORRE BLANCO (JOSE) Uno de tantos: un medico republicano español refugiado en Mexico. Mexico, 1976. pp. 386.

— — — Secret Service.

PAZ (ARMANDO) Los servicios de espionaje en la guerra civil española, 1936-1939. Madrid, [1976]. pp. 234.

SPAIN.(Cont.)

— — 1939-1975.

YGLESIAS (JOSE) The Franco years. Indianapolis, [1977]. pp. 274.

ROA VENTURA (AGUSTIN) Agonia y muerte del franquismo: una memoria. [Barcelona], 1978. pp. 427.

— Kings and rulers.

LOPEZ RODO (LAUREANO) La larga marcha hacia la monarquia. Barcelona, 1977. pp. 694.

— Politics and government.

FEDERACION IBERICA DE JUVENTUDES LIBERTARIAS. Para una estrategia revolucionaria en España. Bruxelles, [1969]. pp. 30.

JUAN CARLOS, King of Spain. Por España, con los españoles. Madrid, 1973. pp. 280.

UGARANA LARRUN (ANDONI) La agonia del Franquismo: no hay mal que dure cien años. Saint Jean de Luz, 1975. pp. 208.

DEMOCRACIA 2.000. Radiografia politica española: octubre, el adios a la democracia organica. [Madrid, 1976]. pp. 168.

TARRAGO (JAIME) La monarquia que quiso Franco. Madrid, 1976. pp. 159.

AREILZA (JOSE MARIA DE) Conde de Motrico. Diario de un Ministro de la monarquia. Barcelona, 1977 repr. 1978. pp. 222.

MARAVALL (JOSE ANTONIO) Dictatorship and political dissent: workers and students in Franco's Spain. London, 1978. pp. 199. *bibliog.*

— Population.

SPAIN. Instituto Nacional de Estadistica. 1976. Panoramica demografica: analisis, estructura y proyecciones de la poblacion española; (with Anexos). Madrid, 1976. 3 vols.

— Rural conditions.

CONFEDERACION REGIONAL DE ARAGON, RIOJA Y NAVARRA. Comarcal de Valderrobres, Teruel: sus luchas sociales y revolucionarias. [Royan, 1971?]. pp. 165.

La CUESTION agraria en la España contemporanea; [by] Manuel Tuñon de Lara [and others]; (edicion a cargo de Jose Luis Garcia Delgado). Madrid, 1976. pp. 565. *Papers of the 6th Colloquium organized by the Centre de Recherches Hispaniques of the University of Pau.*

— Social conditions.

CASADO (DEMETRIO) La pobreza en la estructura social de España. Madrid, [1976]. pp. 176.

YGLESIAS (JOSE) The Franco years. Indianapolis, [1977]. pp. 274.

— Social history.

SANCHEZ (MARIA HELENA) Los gitanos españoles:[el periodo borbonico]. [Madrid, 1977]. pp. 554. *Map in end pocket.*

— Social policy.

CAMPO URBANO (SALUSTIANO DEL) and NAVARRO (MANUEL) Critica de la planificacion social española, 1964-1975. Madrid, [1976]. pp. 157.

— Statistics.

SPAIN. Instituto Nacional de Estadistica. Boletin mensual de estadistica. m. (formerly q.), 1923-1932, with gaps; 1939- Madrid.

SPAIN. Instituto Nacional de Estadistica. 1975. España: panoramica social, 1974. [Madrid, 1975]. pp. 485.

SPANIARDS IN ALGERIA.

VILAR RAMIREZ (JUAN BAUTISTA) Emigracion española a Argelia, 1830-1900: colonizacion hispanica de la Argelia francesa. Madrid, 1975. pp. 537. *bibliog.*

SPANIARDS IN MEXICO.

TORRE BLANCO (JOSE) Uno de tantos: un medico republicano español refugiado en Mexico. Mexico, 1976. pp. 386.

SPANIARDS IN THE DOMINICAN REPUBLIC.

LLORENS (VICENTE) Memorias de una emigracion: Santo Domingo, 1939-1945. Barcelona, [1975]. pp. 214.

SPANISH GUINEA.

BAGUENA CORELLA (LUIS) Guinea. Madrid, 1950. pp. 160. *bibliog. (Instituto de Estudios Africanos. Manuales del Africa Española. 1)*

SPANISH LITERATURE

— History and criticism.

LECUYER (M.C.) and SERRANO (C.) La guerre d'Afrique et ses répercussions en Espagne: idéologies et colonialisme en Espagna, 1859-1904. Paris, [1976]. pp. 389. *bibliog.*

SPANISH-MOROCCAN WAR, 1859-1860.

LECUYER (M.C.) and SERRANO (C.) La guerre d'Afrique et ses répercussions en Espagne: idéologies et colonialisme en Espagna, 1859-1904. Paris, [1976]. pp. 389. *bibliog.*

SPANISH SAHARA

— Nationalism.

MISKE (AHMED BABA) Front Polisario: l'âme d'un peuple. Paris, 1978. pp. 383.

— Politics and government.

PRICE (D.L.) Morocco and the Sahara: conflict and development. London, 1977. pp. 16. *bibliog. (Institute for the Study of Conflict. Conflict Studies. No. 88)*

SPECIAL ASSESSMENTS

— America, Latin.

MACON (JORGE) and MERINO MAÑON (JOSE) Financing urban and rural development through betterment levies: the Latin American experience. New York, 1977. pp. 147. *bibliog.*

SPECIAL DRAWING RIGHTS.

DREYER (JACOB S.) Composite reserve assets in the international monetary system. Greenwich, Conn., [1977]. pp. 191. *bibliog.*

SPECTATOR CONTROL.

INGHAM (ROGER) and others. "Football hooliganism": the wider context. London, 1978. pp. 151. *bibliog.*

SPECULATION.

PANERAI (PAOLO) and DE LUCA (MAURIZIO) Il crack: Sindona, la DC, il Vaticano e gli altri amici. [Milan, 1975]. pp. 264.

PEYRELEVADE (JEAN) L'économie de spéculation. Paris, [1978]. pp. 308.

SPEECH.

LANGUAGE and speech; edited by Edward C. Carterette and Morton P. Friedman. London, 1976. pp. 501. *bibliogs.*

SPEECH, DISORDERS OF.

The NEUROPSYCHOLOGY of language: essays in honor of Eric Lenneberg; edited by R.W. Rieber. New York, [1976]. pp. 230. *bibliogs.*

DALTON (PEGGY) and HARDCASTLE (W.J.) Disorders of fluency and their effects on communication. London, 1977. pp. 161. *bibliog.*

SENTENCE production: developments in research and theory; edited by Sheldon Rosenberg. Hillsdale, N.J., [1977]. pp. 323. *bibliogs.*

SPEECH AND SOCIAL STATUS.

MACAULAY (RONALD K.S.) Language, social class, and education: a Glasgow study. Edinburgh, [1977]. pp. 179. *bibliog. Revised version of a report to the Social Science Research Council.*

SPEECH DISORDERS IN CHILDREN.

INGRAM (DAVID) Lecturer in linguistics. Phonological disability in children. London, 1976. pp. 167. *bibliog.*

CURTISS (SUSAN) Genie: a psycholinguistic study of a modern-day "wild child". New York, 1977. pp. 288. *bibliog.*

SPENCER (HERBERT).

WILTSHIRE (DAVID) The social and political thought of Herbert Spencer. Oxford, 1978. pp. 269. *bibliog.*

SPENDER (STEPHEN).

SPENDER (STEPHEN) The thirties and after: poetry, politics, people, 1933-75. Glasgow, 1978. pp. 286.

SPIES.

SKILLITER (S.A.) William Harborne and the trade with Turkey, 1578-1582: a documentary study of the first Anglo-Ottoman relations. London, 1977. pp. 291. *bibliog.*

SPIRITUAL LIFE.

STUDENT CHRISTIAN MOVEMENT. Movement Pamphlets. No. 28. Ways of the spirit. London, [1976?]. pp. 23.

SPITSBERGEN.

See SVALBARD.

SPORTS

— Canada — Newfoundland.

NEWFOUNDLAND. Commission on the Disposition of Canada Summer Games Facilities. 1978. Report...; Geoffrey L. Steele, commissioner. St. John's, 1978. 1 vol. (various foliations)

— United Kingdom.

SPORTS DEVELOPMENT BULLETIN; [produced by the Sports Council, U.K.]. q., Oc 1967 (no.1)- London.

SPORTS AND STATE

— United Kingdom.

SPORTS COUNCIL. Capital grants for sports facilities. London, 1971. pp. 8.

SPORTS COUNCIL. Sport in the seventies: making good the deficiencies: the need for a planned programme of capital investment on sports facilities. [London, 1971]. pp. 15, 1 map.

— United States.

PRO sports: should government intervene?; (an [AEI] Round Table held on February 22, 1977...[in] Washington]; John Charles Daly, moderator, etc. Washington, [1977]. pp. 42. *(American Enterprise Institute for Public Policy Research. Round Tables)*

SQUATTERS

— Colombia.

MORENO ESCOBAR (BERNABE) Invasiones de predios urbanos: aspectos juridicos. Bogota, 1972. pp. 146. *bibliog.*

— Malaysia.

WEGELIN (EMIEL A.) Urban low-income housing and development: a case study in Peninsular Malaysia. Leiden, 1978. pp. 347. *bibliog.*

— Mexico.

ECKSTEIN (SUSAN) The poverty of revolution: the state and the urban poor in Mexico. Princeton, N.J., [1977]. pp. 300. *bibliog.*

— United Kingdom.

NATIONAL COUNCIL FOR CIVIL LIBERTIES. Reports. No. 11. Picketing and demonstrations...; briefing papers to the NCCL delegate conference on public order. London, 1975. 1 pamphlet (unpaged).

KINGHAN (MIKE) Squatters in London; (commissioned by the Department of the Environment). [London], 1977. pp. 89.

— — Bibliography.

FAWKES (S.) and HARGREAVES (J.) compilers. Squatting. London, 1976. pp. 9. *(London. Greater London Council. Research Library. Research Bibliographies. No. 77)*

SRAFFA (PIERO).

NEORICARDIANA: Sraffa e Graziadei; a cura di Roberto Finzi. Bologna, [1977]. pp. 258. *(Convegno Nazionale degli Storici del Pensiero Economico, 3 , 1974. Atti. vol. 2)*

RONCAGLIA (ALESSANDRO) Sraffa and the theory of prices. Chichester, [1978]. pp. 176. *bibliog. Translated by Jan A. Kregel.*

SRI LANKA

— Administrative and political divisions.

SRI LANKA. Delimitation Commission. 1976. Report; [N. Tittawella, chairman]. Colombo, 1976. pp. 378. *(Sri Lanka. Parliament. Sessional Papers. 1976. No.1)*

— Census.

SRI LANKA. Department of Census and Statistics. Census. 1971. Census of population, 1971. Colombo, 1975 in progress.

SRI LANKA. Department of Census and Statistics. Census, 1971. Census of population 1971, Sri Lanka: general report. [Colombo, 1978]. 1 vol. (various pagings).

— Economic conditions.

CENTRAL BANK OF CEYLON. Review of the economy. a., 1975- Colombo. *Formerly included in CENTRAL BANK OF CEYLON. Monetary Board. Annual report.*

— Economic policy.

AMARASEKERA (ANIL) The crisis in Sri Lanka. [Colombo, 1975]. pp. 18.

— Officials and employees — Salaries, allowances, etc.

SRI LANKA. Salaries and Cadres Commission. 1974. Report. pt. 1, vols. 1-3; [L.B. de Silva, chairman]. Colombo, 1974. pp. 679. *(Sri Lanka. Parliament. Sessional Papers. 1974. No.3)*

— Parliament — Elections.

SRI LANKA. Elections Department. 1978. Report on the general election to the second National State Assembly of Sri Lanka, eighth parliamentary general election, 21st July, 1977. Colombo, 1978. pp. 115. *(Sri Lanka. Parliament. Sessional Papers. 1978. No. 4)*

— Politics and government.

MILITANT: for labour and youth. Pamphlets. Which way forward for the workers and peasants of Ceylon?: a Marxist analysis of the insurrection. London, [1972?]. pp. 5.

JUPP (JAMES) Sri Lanka: third world democracy. London, 1978. pp. 423. *bibliog.*

STABILITY.

ROUCHE (NICOLAS) and others. Stability theory by Liapunov's direct method. New York, [1977]. pp. 396. *bibliog.*

STACK (AUSTIN).

GAUGHAN (J. ANTHONY) Austin Stack: portrait of a separatist. Mount Merrion, Co. Dublin, [1977]. pp. 408. *bibliog.*

STAFFORDSHIRE

— Social history.

SHAW (CHARLES) 1832-1906. When I was a child. Firle, Sussex, 1977. pp. 258. *Facsimile reprint of first edition of 1903 published under the anonym "An Old Potter." Original introduction omitted.*

STAGNATION (ECONOMICS).

DALY (HERMAN E.) Steady-state economics: the economics of biophysical equilibrium and moral growth. San Francisco, [1977]. pp. 185. *bibliogs.*

STALIN (IOSIF VISSARIONOVICH).

FISCHER (RUTH) Stalin und der deutsche Kommunismus: der Übergang zur Konterrevolution; (translated from the English by H. Langerhans). Frankfurt am Main, [1950]. pp. 844.

STRONG (ANNA LOUISE) The Stalin era. [Belfast], 1976. pp. 77. *First published in 1956.*

AVTORKHANOV (ABDURAKHMAN) Zagadka smerti Stalina: zagovor Beriia. [Frankfurt, 1976]. pp. 317.

BOFFA (GIUSEPPE) and MARTINET (GILLES) Dialogo sullo stalinismo. [Roma, 1976]. pp. 205.

BOFFA (GIUSEPPE) and MARTINET (GILLES) Dialogue sur le stalinisme; traduit de l'italien par Tamara Thorgevsky. [Paris, 1977]. pp. 252.

FRANK (PIERRE) Le stalinisme. Paris, 1977. pp. 221.

MAO (TSE-TUNG) A critique of Soviet economics;...translated by Moss Roberts, annotated by Richard Levy, with an introduction by James Peck. New York, [1977]. pp. 157.

TAYLOR (ALAN JOHN PERCIVALE) The war lords. London, 1977. pp. 189. *Transcripts of six lectures delivered on BBC Television in August 1976.*

TROTSKII (LEV DAVYDOVICH) Stalin's gangsters. [London, 1977]. pp. 84. *First published as Los gangsters de Stalin, Mexico City, 1940.*

STAMBOLIISKI (ALEKSANDUR STOIMENOV).

BELL (JOHN D.) Peasants in power: Alexander Stamboliski and the Bulgarian Agrarian National Union, 1899-1923. Princeton, [1977]. pp. 271. *bibliog.*

STAMMLER (RUDOLF).

WEBER (MAX) Critique of Stammler;...translated, with an introductory essay, by Guy Oakes. New York, [1977]. pp. 184.

STANDARDIZATION

— European Economic Community countries — Congresses.

STANDARDS and Community technical directives; report of a conference presented by the Confederation of British Industry, 21 January 1974. London, 1974. pp. 40.

STANLEY (EDWARD GEORGE GEOFFREY SMITH) 14th Earl of Derby.

[RICH (Sir HENRY)] Yes or no? London, J. Ridgway, 1852. pp. 13.

STANLEY (EDWARD HENRY SMITH) 15th Earl of Derby.

STANLEY (EDWARD HENRY SMITH) 15th Earl of Derby. Disraeli, Derby and the Conservative Party: journals and memoirs of Edward Henry, Lord Stanley, 1849-1869; edited by John Vincent. Hassocks, 1978. pp. 404.

STARE DECISIS

— United Kingdom.

CROSS (Sir RUPERT) Precedent in English law. 3rd ed. Oxford, 1977. pp. 242. *bibliog.*

STATE, THE.

MOLNÁR (KÁLMÁN) Niederschlag der Staatstheorien im positiven Verfassungsrecht. Pécs, 1938. pp. 15. *(Reprinted from Pannonia, 1938)*

BUTTERFIELD (Sir HERBERT) Raison d'état: the relations between morality and government. [Brighton, 1975]. pp. 18. *(Martin Wight Memorial Lectures. 1975)*

L'ETAT contemporain et le marxisme; [by] J.-M. Vincent [and others]. Paris, 1975. pp. 235.

GIORGIANNI (VIRGILIO) Studio sul concetto di stato. Milano, 1975. pp. 323. *(Trieste. Università. Facoltà di Scienze Politiche. [Publications]. 1)*

CORDOVA (ARNALDO) Sociedad y Estado en el mundo moderno. Mexico, 1976. pp. 287.

COX (GRAHAM) and WOOD (GEOF) Political scientist. State and civil society: an impasse within political sociology? Bath, 1976. pp. 29.

MOLNAR (THOMAS) Le socialisme sans visage: l'avènement du tiers modèle. [Paris, 1976]. pp. 187.

NEGRI (ANTONIO) Proletari e stato: per una discussione su autonomia operaia e compromesso storico. Milano, 1976. pp. 67.

REVOLUTIONAERER Prozess und Staatsentstehung. Berlin, 1976. pp. 184. *(Akademie der Wissenschaften der DDR. Institut für Theorie des Staates und des Rechts. Staats- und Rechtstheoretische Studien. 2)*

BUCHANAN (JAMES B.) Freedom in constitutional contract: perspectives of a political economist. College Station, Tex., [1977]. pp. 311. *bibliog. (Texas A and M University. Texas A and M University Economics Series. 2)*

BULL (HANS PETER) Die Staatsaufgaben nach dem Grundgesetz. 2nd ed. Kronberg, [1977]. pp. 468.

FABRE (JEAN) and others. Les communistes et l'état. Paris, [1977]. pp. 253. *bibliog.*

IANNI (OCTAVIO) El Estado capitalista en la epoca de Cardenas; [translated from the Portuguese by] Ana Maria Palos. Mexico, 1977. pp. 146.

KALENSKII (VALERII GEORGIEVICH) Gosudarstvo kak ob"ekt sotsiologicheskogo analiza: ocherki istorii i metodologii issledovaniia; otvetstvennyi redaktor V.E. Guliev. Moskva, 1977. pp. 182.

LAPIERRE (JEAN WILLIAM) Vivre sans Etat?: essai sur le pouvoir politique et l'innovation sociale. Paris, [1977]. pp. 380.

LOJKINE (JEAN) Le marxisme, l'état et la question urbaine. [Paris, 1977]. pp. 362.

Il RUOLO dello Stato nel pensiero degli economisti; a cura di Roberto Finzi. Bologna, [1977]. pp. 249. *(Convegno Nazionale degli Storici del Pensiero Economico, 3 , 1974. Atti. vol.1)*

SETON-WATSON (GEORGE HUGH NICHOLAS) Nations and states: an enquiry into the origins of nations and the politics of nationalism. London, 1977. pp. 563. *bibliog.*

STATO e accumulazione del capitale; [by] Elmar Altvater [and others]; a cura di Alberto Martinelli. Milano, [1977]. pp. 287.

STATE, THE.(Cont.)

ORIGINS of the state: the anthropology of political evolution; edited by Ronald Cohen and Elman R. Service. Philadelphia, [1978]. pp. 233. *bibliogs.*

POGGI (GIANFRANCO) The development of the modern state: a sociological introduction. Stanford, 1978. pp. 175.

POWER and the state; edited by Gary Littlejohn [and others]. London, [1978]. pp. 314. *Papers presented at the 1977 Annual Conference of the British Sociological Association.*

ROSENBLUM (NANCY L.) Bentham's theory of the modern state. Cambridge, Mass., 1978. pp. 169.

STATE and capital: a Marxist debate; edited by John Holloway and Sol Picciotto. London, 1978. pp. 220. *bibliog.*

WRIGHT (ERIK OLIN) Class, crisis and the state. [London, 1978]. pp. 266. *bibliog.*

STATE ENCOURAGEMENT OF SCIENCE, LITERATURE AND ART

— United Kingdom.

LEWES (FREDERICK MARTIN MEREDITH) and MENNELL (STEPHEN) Leisure, culture and local government: a study of policies and provision in Exeter. Exeter, [1976]. pp. 75.

LABOUR PARTY. The arts and the people: Labour's policy towards the arts. London, 1977. pp. 69.

— United States.

PENKOWER (MONTY NOAM) The Federal Writers' Project: a study in government patronage of the arts. Urbana, Ill., [1977]. pp. 266. *bibliog.*

STATE FARMS

— Russia.

VINOGRADOV (IVAN IVANOVICH) Politotdely MTS i sovkhozov v gody Velikoi Otechestvennoi voiny, 1941-1943 gg. Leningrad, 1976. pp. 128.

STATE GOVERNMENTS

— United States.

AMICK (GEORGE) The American way of graft: a study of corruption in state and local government, how it happens, and what can be done about it. Princeton, [1976]. pp. 245.

STATE SUCCESSION.

PAPADOPOULOS (ANDRESTINOS N.) La pratique chypriote en matière de succession d'états aux traités. Nicosie, 1976. pp. 240. *bibliog. Thèse (docteur en droit) - Université de Genève.*

POWER and manoeuvrability; edited by Tony Carty and Alexander McCall Smith. Edinburgh, [1978]. pp. 185.

STATELESSNESS.

MUTHARIKA (A. PETER) The regulation of statelessness under international and national law: text and documents. Dobbs Ferry, 1977. pp. 262. *Loose-leaf binder.*

STATES, NEW.

JANOWITZ (MORRIS) Military institutions and coercion in the developing nations. Chicago, 1977. pp. 211. *Expanded edition of The military in the political development of new nations.*

STATES, SMALL.

PLISCHKE (ELMER) Microstates in world affairs: policy problems and options. Washington, D.C., [1977]. pp. 153. *(American Enterprise Institute for Public Policy Research. AEI Studies. 144)*

REICHOLD (HELMUT) Bismarcks Zaunkönige: Duodez im 20. Jahrhundert: eine Studie zum Föderalismus im Bismarckreich. Paderborn, [1977]. pp. 320. *bibliog.*

POWER and manoeuvrability; edited by Tony Carty and Alexander McCall Smith. Edinburgh, [1978]. pp. 185.

STATESMEN

— Africa, Subsaharan.

VAN RENSBURG (ARRIE P.J.) The tangled web: leadership and change in Southern Africa. Cape Town, 1977. pp. 225. *bibliog.*

— France.

MENDES-FRANCE (PIERRE) La vérité guidait leurs pas. [Paris, 1976]. pp. 261.

— Poland.

KISIELEWSKI (TADEUSZ) Heroizm i kompromis: portret zbiorowy działaczy ludowych. Warszawa, 1977 in progress.

— Spain.

GONZALEZ MUÑIZ (MIGUEL ANGEL) Los asturianos y la politica: de las Cortes de Cadiz a nuestros dias. Salinas, Asturias, [1976]. pp. 231. *bibliog.*

— United Kingdom.

WILSON (Sir HAROLD) A prime minister on prime ministers. London, [1977]. pp. 334.

MARPLAN LIMITED. Britain's leaders. [London, 1978?]. fo. 5.

— — Ireland.

MALCOMSON (A.P.W.) John Foster: the politics of the Anglo-Irish ascendancy. Oxford, 1978. pp. 504. *bibliog.*

STATICS AND DYNAMICS (SOCIAL SCIENCES).

KLEIN (BURTON H.) Dynamic economics. Cambridge, Mass., 1977. pp. 289.

EQUILIBRIUM and disequilibrium in economic theory: proceedings of a conference organized by the Institute for Advanced Studies, Vienna, Austria, July 3-5, 1974; edited by Gerhard Schwödiauer. Dordrecht, [1978]. pp. 736. *bibliogs.*

STATISTICAL DECISION.

FERGUSON (THOMAS SHELBURNE) Mathematical statistics: a decision theoretic approach. New York, 1967. pp. 396. *bibliog.*

EPSTEIN (RICHARD A.) The theory of gambling and statistical logic. rev.ed. New York, [1977]. pp. 450.

STATISTICAL SERVICES.

UNITED NATIONS. Statistical Office. Statistical Papers. Series F. No. 21. The organization of national statistical services: a review of major issues. (ST/ESA/STAT/SER.F/21). New York, 1977. pp. 23.

STATISTICS.

EUROPEAN COMMUNITIES. Statistical Office. Special Series: Structure of Earnings in Wholesale and Retail Distribution, Banking and Insurance in 1974. Luxembourg, [1977] in progress.

SMITH (T.M. FRED) Statistics: a universal discipline. Southampton, 1977. pp. 27. *Inaugural lecture delivered at University of Southampton on 3rd March 1977.*

HANDEL (JUDITH D.) Introductory statistics for sociology. Englewood Cliffs, [1978]. pp. 387.

— Charts, tables, etc.

NEAVE (HENRY R.) Statistics tables for mathematicians, engineers, economists and the behavioural and management sciences. London, 1978. pp. 88.

— Congresses.

[SCANDINAVIA]. Nordisk Statistisk Skriftserie. 17. Det 11. nordiske statistikermøte i Oslo, 1967, etc. Oslo, 1970. pp. 107.

— History.

POUR une histoire de la statistique. [Paris], Institut National de la Statistique et des Etudes Economiques, [1977 in progress].

— — France.

POUR une histoire de la statistique. [Paris], Institut National de la Statistique et des Etudes Economiques, [1977 in progress].

— — Spain.

SANCHEZ-LAFUENTE FERNANDEZ (JUAN) Historia de la estadistica como ciencia en España, 1500-1900. Madrid, Instituto Nacional de Estadistica, [1975]. pp. 296.

— Theory, methods, etc.

STATISTICAL STUDIES; ([pd. by] Centraal Bureau voor de Statistiek, Netherlands). irreg., Ag 1953 (no.1)- Utrecht.

GUMBEL (EMIL JULIUS) Statistics of extremes. New York, [1958]. pp. 375. *bibliog.*

BROWNLEE (KENNETH ALEXANDER) Statistical theory and methodology in science and engineering. 2nd ed. New York, [1965]. pp. 590. *bibliogs.*

SNEDECOR (GEORGE WADDEL) and COCHRAN (WILLIAM GEMMELL) Statistical methods. 6th ed. Ames, Iowa, 1967 reprinted 1976. pp. 593.

TURNER (JOHN CHRISTOPHER) Modern applied mathematics: probability, statistics, operational research. London, 1970 repr. 1972. pp. 502. *bibliog.*

KMENTA (JAN) Elements of econometrics. New York, [1971]. pp. 655. *bibliog.*

MOOD (ALEXANDER McFARLANE) and others. Introduction to the theory of statistics. 3rd ed. New York, [1974]. pp. 564. *bibliog.*

PLACKETT (ROBERT LEWIS) The analysis of categorical data. London, 1974. pp. 159. *bibliog.*

LINDGREN (BERNARD WILLIAM) Statistical theory. 3rd ed. New York, [1976]. pp. 614.

KENDALL (Sir MAURICE GEORGE) and STUART (ALAN) The advanced theory of statistics;...in three volumes. 4th ed. London, [1977 in progress]. *bibliog.*

CHETYRKIN (EVGENII MIKHAILOVICH) Statisticheskie metody prognozirovaniia. 2nd ed. Moskva, 1977. pp. 200. *bibliog.*

HUNTSBERGER (DAVID V.) and BILLINGSLEY (PATRICK) Elements of statistical inference. 4th ed. Boston, Mass., [1977]. pp. 385.

PALUMBO (DENNIS JAMES) Statistics in political and behavioral science. rev. ed. New York, 1977. pp. 469. *bibliogs.*

UNITED NATIONS. Statistical Office. Statistical Papers. Series F. No.19. Organization and conduct of distributive-trade surveys. (ST/ESA/STAT/SER.F/19). New York, 1977. pp. 165. *bibliog.*

UNITED NATIONS. Statistical Office. Statistical Papers. Series M. No.59. Guidelines on principles of a system of price and quantity statistics. (ST/ESA/STAT/SER.M/59). New York, 1977. pp. 25.

UNITED NATIONS. Statistical Office. Statistical Papers. Series M. No.60. Provisional international guidelines on the national and sectoral balance-sheet and reconciliation accounts of the system of national accounts. (ST/ESA/STAT/SER.M/60). New York, 1977. pp. 117.

UNITED NATIONS. Statistical Office. [Statistical Papers.] Series. M. No.61. Provisional guidelines on statistics of the distribution of income, consumption and accumuation of households. (ST/ESA/STAT/SER.M/61). New York, 1977. pp. 97.

ANDERSON (THEODORE WILBUR) and SCLOVE (STANLEY L.) An introduction to the statistical analysis of data. Boston, [Mass., 1978]. pp. 704.

COX (DAVID ROXBEE) and HINKLEY (DAVID VICTOR) Problems and solutions in theoretical statistics. London, 1978. pp. 193. *bibliog.*

FREEDMAN (DAVID) and others. Statistics. New York, [1978]. pp. 506, 83.

LAPIN (LAWRENCE L.) Statistics for modern business decisions. 2nd ed. New York, [1978]. 1 vol. (various pagings).

STEAM-ENGINES

— History.

VON TUNZELMANN (GEORGE NICHOLAS) Steam power and British industrialization to 1860. Oxford, [1978]. pp. 344. *bibliog.*

STEEL INDUSTRY AND TRADE

— France.

FRITSCH (PIERRE) Les Wendel: rois de l'acier français. Paris, [1976]. pp. 280. *bibliog.*

— India.

INDIA. Department of Steel. 1976. White paper on steel industry. [Delhi], 1976. pp. 81.

— Italy.

BONELLI (FRANCO) Lo sviluppo di una grande impresa in Italia: la Terni dal 1884 al 1962. [Torino, 1975]. pp. 360. *bibliog.*

— United Kingdom.

JONES (KEITH LLOYD) The growth and development of white collar trade unionism in the British steel industry. [1977]. fo. 238. *bibliog. Typescript.* Ph.D. (London) thesis: unpublished. This thesis is the property of London University and may not be removed from the Library.

STEELTON, PENNSYLVANIA

— Social history.

BODNAR (JOHN E.) Immigration and industrialization: ethnicity in an American mill town, 1870-1940. Pittsburgh, [1977]. pp. 213. *bibliog.*

STEFCZYK (FRANCISZEK).

GURNICZ (ANTONI) Franciszek Stefczyk: 'zycie, poglądy, działalność. Warszawa, 1976. pp. 204. *bibliog.*

STEPHEN SIMPSON (FIRM).

SIMPSON (STEPHEN) History of the firm of Stephen Simpson, 1829-1929. Preston, [1929]. pp. 74.

STEPPES.

MAGAKIAN (GEORGII LUK'IANOVICH) Step' i voda: novoe v geografii irrigatsii v SSSR. Moskva, 1977. pp. 191.

STERN (MIKHAIL).

STERN (MIKHAIL) defendant. The USSR versus Dr. Mikhail Stern: an "ordinary" trial in the Soviet Union; edited by August Stern; translated from the Russian by Marco Carynnyk. London, 1978. pp. 267.

STOCHASTIC PROCESSES.

KARLIN (SAMUEL) and TAYLOR (HOWARD M.) A first course in stochastic processes. 2nd ed. New York, [1975]. pp. 557. *bibliogs.*

BERTSEKAS (DIMITRI P.) Dynamic programming and stochastic control. New York, 1976. pp. 397. *bibliog.*

KALLENBERG (OLAV) Random measures. Berlin, 1976. pp. 104. *bibliog.*

BEARD (ROBERT ERIC) and others. Risk theory: the stochastic basis of insurance. 2nd ed. London, 1977. pp. 195. *bibliog.*

ROZANOV (IURII ANATOL'EVICH) Innovation processes. Washington, D.C., 1977. pp. 136.

KOLCHIN (VALENTIN FEDOROVICH) and others. Random allocations; translation editor A.V. Balakrishnan. Washington, D.C., 1978. pp. 262. *bibliog.*

STOCK AND STOCK BREEDING

— Africa, Subsaharan.

KONCZACKI (ZBIGNIEW A.) The economics of pastoralism: a case study of sub-Saharan Africa. London, 1978. pp. 185.

— Argentine Republic.

PANETTIERI (JOSE) La crisis ganadera: ideas en torno a un cambio en la estructura economica y social del pais, 1866-1871. La Plata, [1965]. pp. 123. *bibliog.* (La Plata. Universidad Nacional. Facultad de Humanidades y Ciencias de la Educacion. Departamento de Historia. Monografias y Tesis. 6)

— Bangladesh.

BANGLADESH. Directorate of Livestock Services. 1966. Livestock wealth in East Pakistan. [Dacca, 1966]. pp. 110. *bibliog.*

— Hungary.

GAÁL (L.) and GUNST (PETER) Animal husbandry in Hungary in the 19th-20th centuries. Budapest, 1977. pp. 411.

— India.

INDIA. Ministry of Agriculture. Directorate of Economics and Statistics. 1974. Indian livestock census, 1966. [Delhi, 1974 in progress].

INDIA. Ministry of Agriculture and Irrigation. Directorate of Economics and Statistics. 1977- . Indian livestock census, 1972. [Delhi, 1977 in progress].

STOCK COMPANIES

— Germany.

NORTH RHINE-WESTPHALIA. Landesamt für Datenverarbeitung und Statistik. Beiträge zur Statistik des Landes Nordrhein- Westfalen. Heft 391. Die Kapitalgesellschaften in Nordrhein-Westfalen, 1971 bis 1976. Düsseldorf, 1978. pp. 217.

STOCK EXCHANGE.

FAMA (EUGENE F.) Foundations of finance: portfolio decisions and securities prices. Oxford, 1977. pp. 395. *bibliog.*

STOCKHOLDERS

— United Kingdom.

MINNS (RICHARD) and THORNLEY (JENNIFER) State shareholding: the role of local and regional authorities. London, 1978. pp. 159.

STOCKS

— Mathematical models.

FAMA (EUGENE F.) Foundations of finance: portfolio decisions and securities prices. Oxford, 1977. pp. 395. *bibliog.*

— Prices.

FIRTH (MICHAEL A.) The valuation of shares and the efficient-markets theory. London, 1977. pp. 184.

STOIANOV (ZAKHARI).

PETKO R. Slaveikov, Liuben Karavelov, Khristo Botev, Zakhari Stoianov v spomenite na suvremennitsite si. Sofiia, 1967. pp. 758.

STOLYPIN (PETR ARKAD'EVICH).

HENNESSY (RICHARD) The agrarian question in Russia, 1905-1907: the inception of the Stolypin reform. Giessen, 1977. pp. 203. *bibliog.* (Marburg. Universität. Arbeitsgemeinschaft für Osteuropaforschung. Marburger Abhandlungen zur Geschichte und Kultur Osteuropas. Band 16)

LIPINSKII (LEONID PAVLOVICH) Stolypinskaia agrarnaia reforma v Belorussii. Minsk, 1978. pp. 223.

STONEHOUSE, LANARKSHIRE.

SCOTLAND. Scottish Development Department. 1972. New Towns, Scotland, Act, 1968: draft new town, Stonehouse, designation order, 1972: memorandum by the Secretary of State for Scotland. Edinburgh, [1972]. pp. 15.

STORE LOCATION.

BERRY (BRIAN JOE LOBLEY) Geography of market centers and retail distribution. Englewood Cliffs, [1967]. pp. 145.

STORES, RETAIL.

NEW ZEALAND. Valuation Department. Research Papers. 68-6. Pedestrian traffic counts: their role in commercial property valuation. Wellington, 1968. pp. 37.

IRELAND, NORTHERN. Department of Manpower Services. Offices and shop premises: report under the Office and Shop Premises Act (Northern Ireland) 1966. a., 1970, 1971, 1973- Belfast. Ap 1967/D 1968 [1st] - 1969 included in IRELAND, NORTHERN. Parliament. House of Commons. [Papers].

STRAITS OF MALACCA.

See MALACCA, STRAIT OF.

STRATEGY.

KOERNER (THEODOR) Bundespräsident. Auf Vorposten: ausgewählte Schriften, 1928-1938; herausgegeben und kommentiert von Ilona Duczynska. Wien, [1977]. pp. 299.

STRATHCLYDE

— Economic policy.

STRATHCLYDE. Regional Council. Department of Physical Planning. Strathclyde structure plan: consultative draft; ([with] Key diagram and schedules). Glasgow, 1977. 2 pts. (in 1 vol.).

— Social policy.

STRATHCLYDE. Regional Council. Department of Physical Planning. Strathclyde structure plan: consultative draft; ([with] Key diagram and schedules). Glasgow, 1977. 2 pts. (in 1 vol.).

STRAUSS (DAVID FRIEDRICH).

WHEELWRIGHT (G.) The "Edinburgh Review" and Dr. Strauss. London, 1873. pp. 14.

STREAM MEASUREMENTS

— Canada.

CANADA. Inland Waters Directorate. 1972. Historical streamflow summary to 1970. Ottawa, 1972. 7 pts. (in 2 vols.). *Volume for Quebec out of print.*

STREICHER (JULIUS).

HAHN (FRED) Lieber Stürmer: Leserbriefe an das NS-Kampfblatt, 1924 bis 1945: eine Dokumentation aus dem Leo-Baeck-Institut, New York; Bearbeitung der deutschen Ausgabe von Günther Wagenlehner. Stuttgart, [1978]. pp. 263. *bibliog.* (Studiengesellschaft für Zeitprobleme. Zeitpolitik. 19)

STRESEMANN (GUSTAV).

STRESEMANN (GUSTAV) Schriften; mit einem Vorwort von Willy Brandt; herausgegeben von Arnold Harttung. Berlin, [1976]. pp. 438.

STRESEMANN (GUSTAV).(Cont.)

HIRSCH (FELIX EDWARD) Stresemann: ein Lebensbild. Göttingen, [1978]. pp. 335. *bibliog.*

STRIKES AND LOCKOUTS.

GERMANY (BUNDESREPUBLIK). Statistisches Bundesamt. Streiks und Aussperrungen im Ausland. a., 1975- Wiesbaden. *(Statistik des Auslandes. Reihe 1.3) Formerly included in GERMANY (BUNDESREPUBLIK). Statistisches Bundesamt. Arbeitnehmerverdienste im Ausland.*

— Bolivia.

AGUILAR PEÑARRIETA (ANIBAL) Revolucion y derecho de huelga: debe irse a la huelga en las minas nacionalizadas? La Paz, [1960?]. pp. 23.

— Czechoslovakia — Czech Republic.

FRANĚK (OTAKAR) Oslavany obkličují...: kronika prosincové generální stávky na Rosicku-Oslavansku. 2nd ed. Brno, 1976. pp. 143. *bibliog.*

— Denmark.

MEIDELL (BJØRN) DKP og storstrejkerne i 1956. København, [1976]. pp. 106.

— France.

NOËL (JEAN FRANÇOIS) Les postiers, la grève et le service public. [Grenoble, 1977]. pp. 198. *bibliog.*

— Germany.

BESTRAFTE Solidarität: Drucker und Journalisten im gewerkschaftlichen Kampf; ([by] Klaus Kräling [and others]). Berlin, [1973]. pp. 139.

KLESSMANN (CHRISTOPH) and FRIEDEMANN (PETER) Streiks und Hungermärsche im Ruhrgebiet, 1946-1948. Frankfurt/Main, [1977]. pp. 163. *bibliog.*

— Iran.

JALIL (T.) Workers say no to the Shah: labour law and strikes in Iran. London, 1977. pp. 136.

— Netherlands.

BINNEVELD (JOHANNES MARTINUS WOUTER) De Rotterdamse metaalstaking van 1965. Amsterdam, 1977. pp. 175. *bibliog. Revised version of his De stakingen in de Rotterdamse metaalindustrie in 1965.*

— Spain.

LUCHAS obreras en España. Lausanne, [1974]. pp. 177.

RIERA (IGNASI) and BOTELLA (JOSE) El Baix Llobregat: 15 años de luchas obreras. Barcelona, 1976. pp. 187.

SOLIDARITY (LONDON). Motor Bulletins. No. 5. Spain: struggle at SEAT Barcelona. London, 1976. pp. 12.

MIGUELEZ (FAUSTINO) La lucha de los mineros asturianos bajo el franquismo; prologo de Gerado Iglesias. Barcelona, 1977. pp. 309.

— United Kingdom.

TRANSPORT AND GENERAL WORKERS' UNION. To the members of the London Bus Section, Central Area. London, 1937. pp. 6.

JOHNS (STEPHEN) Victimization at Cowley. London, 1974. pp. 111. *(Workers' Revolutionary Party. Pocket Library. No. 11)*

GENNARD (JOHN) Financing strikers. London, 1977. pp. 184. *bibliog.*

GLENDON (ALECK IAN) The participant observer and groups in conflict: a case study from industry. 1977. 2 vols. *bibliog. Typescript. Ph.D. (London) thesis: unpublished. This thesis is the property of London University and may not be removed from the Library.*

MARPLAN LIMITED. Strikes, picketing and the closed shop. [London, 1977]. fo. 7.

PRAIS (SIGBERT JON) The strike-proneness of large plants in Britain. London, 1977. pp. 28. *(National Institute of Economic and Social Research. Discussion Papers. No. 5)*

SEARBY (PETER) Coventry in crisis 1858-1863: ribbon factory, free trade and strike. Coventry, 1977. pp. 17. *bibliog. (Historical Association. Coventry Branch. Coventry and Warwickshire History Pamphlets. No. 10)*

WARD (GEORGE) Fort Grunwick. London, 1977. pp. 123.

SELLWOOD (ARTHUR VICTOR) Police strike, 1919. London, 1978. pp. 214.

— — Social aspects.

BATSTONE (ERIC) and others. The social organization of strikes. Oxford, [1978]. pp. 236. *bibliog. (Warwick Studies in Industrial Relations)*

— United States.

FONER (PHILIP SHELDON) The great labor uprising of 1877. New York, [1977]. pp. 288. *bibliog.*

STRUCTURAL ANTHROPOLOGY.

SAHLINS (MARSHALL DAVID) Culture and practical reason. Chicago, 1976. pp. 252. *bibliog.*

STRUCTURALISM.

SCHAFF (ADAM) Structuralism and Marxism. Oxford, 1978. pp. 205.

STUDENT-ADMINISTRATOR RELATIONSHIPS.

COWEN (DENIS VICTOR) Academic freedom in our time: the rights and responsibilities of students in a modern university. [Durban, 1968]. pp. 26. *(Natal University. E.G. Malherbe Academic Freedom Lectures. 1968)*

STUDENT AID

— Canada — Ontario.

MEHMET (OZAY) Who benefits from the Ontario University system: a benefit- cost analysis by income groups. [Toronto, 1978]. pp. 62. *(Ontario. Economic Council. Occasional Papers. 7)*

— United States.

DAVIS (JAMES ALLAN) and others. Stipends and spouses: the finances of American arts and science graduate students. Chicago, 1962. pp. 294.

AMERICAN ENTERPRISE INSTITUTE FOR PUBLIC POLICY RESEARCH. Legislative Analyses. 95th Congress. No. 27. Tuition tax credits and alternatives. Washington, D.C., 1978. pp. 50.

STUDENT COUNSELLORS.

STUDENT problems and performance in higher education; proceedings of a conference organized by the Department of Higher Education, University of London Institute of Education. London, [1970]. pp. 40.

STUDENT UNIONS.

SINGAPORE. Sessional Papers. 1956. Cmd. 53. Singapore Chinese Middle Schools Students' Union. Singapore, 1956. pp. 22.

— United States.

SCHNELL (RODOLPH LESLIE) National activist student organizations in American higher education, 1905-1944. Ann Arbor, 1976. pp. 258. *bibliog. (Michigan University. School of Education. Social Foundations of Education Monograph Series. No. 7)*

STUDENTS.

ANTISTUDENT PAMPHLET COLLECTIVE. Antistudent. London, [1972]. pp. 37. *bibliog.*

— Political activity.

MEHNERT (KLAUS) Twilight of the young: the radical movements of the 1960s and their legacy. New York, 1977. pp. 428. *bibliog. (Stanford University. Hoover Institution on War, Revolution and Peace. Hoover Institution Publications. 182)*

— Argentine Republic — Political activity.

GONZALEZ (JULIO V.) La reforma universitaria. Buenos Aires, 1927. 2 vols.

— Belgium.

De GROOTE Stooringe 1875: historische bijdrage tot de geschiedenis van de Vlaamse studenten-beweging; een realisatie van het Instituut Klein Seminarie te Roeselare). Gent, [1975?]. pp. 431.

— Canada — Ontario.

MEHMET (OZAY) Who benefits from the Ontario University system: a benefit- cost analysis by income groups. [Toronto, 1978]. pp. 62. *(Ontario. Economic Council. Occasional Papers. 7)*

— Denmark — Political activity.

SCHOU (HANS OLUF) and others. Om studenterbevaegelsen, 1968-1976: en tematiseret gennemgang af den århusianske studenterbevaegelses udvikling fra radikal- demokratisk til socialistisk kamp. [Århus, 1976]. pp. 330. *bibliog.*

— Europe — Political activity.

The DYNAMICS of university protest; [by] Donald Light and John Spiegel, [and others]. Chicago, [1977]. pp. 198. *bibliog.*

— France — Political activity.

GRIMAUD (MAURICE) En mai, fais ce qu'il te plaît. [Paris, 1977]. pp. 345.

BAYNAC (JACQUES) Mai retrouvé: contribution à l'histoire du mouvement révolutionnaire du 3 mai au 16 juin 1968. Paris, [1978]. pp. 301.

— Germany.

GERMANY (BUNDESREPUBLIK). Statistisches Bundesamt. Studenten an Hochschulen. s-a., 1975- Wiesbaden. *(Bildung und Kultur. Reihe 4.1)*

— — Attitudes.

NIELSEN (H. DEAN) Tolerating political dissent: the impact of high school social climates in the United States and West Germany. Stockholm, [1977]. pp. 138. *bibliog. (International Association for the Evaluation of Educational Achievement. IEA Monograph Studies. No. 6)*

— — Political activity.

BAUSS (GERHARD) Die Studentenbewegung der sechziger Jahre in der Bundesrepublik und Westberlin: Handbuch. Köln, [1977]. pp. 353. *bibliog.*

MOSLER (PETER) Was wir wollten, was wir wurden: Studentenrevolte, zehn Jahre danach. Reinbek bei Hamburg, [1977]. pp. 301. *bibliog.*

— Greece — Political activity.

NATIONAL UNION OF STUDENTS. Greece: students in struggle, April 1967 to September 1973. [London], [1974?]. 1 pamphlet (unpaged).

— Italy — Political activity.

CAMBONI (GIANFRANCO) and SAMSA (DANILO) PCI e movimento degli studenti, 1968-1973: ceti medi e strategi delle riforme. Bari, [1975]. pp. 208. *bibliog.*

MORDENTI (ADRIANO) Come eravamo: documenti fotografici per una storia della lotte studentesche a Roma, 1966-1972; foto di Adriano Mordenti e Massimo Vergari. Roma, [1975]. pp. 93.

ASOR ROSA (ALBERTO) and others. PCI, classe operaia e movimento studentesco; a cura di Gregorio Paolini e Walter Vitali. [Rimini, 1977]. pp. 250.

Il MOVIMENTO degli studenti medi in Italia, 1970-76: analisi e documenti di AO, LC, PdUP, PCI-FGCI; a cura di Marcello Sarno e Marino Sinibaldi. [Roma, 1977]. pp. 256.

— Mexico — Political activity.

TUOHY (WILLIAM S.) and AMES (BARRY) Mexican university students in politics: rebels without allies? Denver, [1970]. pp. 45. (Denver. University. Social Science Foundation and Graduate School of International Studies. Monograph Series in World Affairs. vol. 7, no. 3)

— Nigeria — Attitudes.

BECKETT (PAUL) Political scientist and O'CONNELL (JAMES) Education and power in Nigeria: a study of university students. London, [1977]. pp. 224.

— Poland — Political activity.

ASSOCIATION OF POLISH STUDENTS AND GRADUATES IN EXILE. Dissent in Poland: reports and documents in translation, December 1975-July 1977. London, [1977]. pp. 200.

— Russia.

PAS'KO (NINA IVANOVNA) Sotsiologicheskie problemy kommunisticheskogo vospitaniia studencheskoi molodezhi. Kiev, 1977. pp. 191. bibliog.

— Singapore — Political activity.

SINGAPORE. Sessional Papers. 1956. Cmd. 53. Singapore Chinese Middle Schools Students' Union. Singapore, 1956. pp. 22.

— South Africa — Political activity.

INTERNATIONAL UNIVERSITY EXCHANGE FUND. Summary of the so-called Schlebusch Committee's final report on the National Union of South African Students (NUSAS).... Geneva, 1975. 1 vol. (various pagings).

— Spain — Political activity.

MARAVALL (JOSE ANTONIO) Dictatorship and political dissent: workers and students in Franco's Spain. London, 1978. pp. 199. bibliog.

— Sri Lanka.

SRI LANKA. Commission of Inquiry into "Ragging" at Vidyalankara Campus of the University of Sri Lanka. 1975. Report; [V.W. Kularatne, commissioner]. Colombo, 1975. pp. 114. (Sri Lanka. Parliament. Sessional Papers. 1975. No. 11)

SRI LANKA. Commission appointed to Inquire into the Incidents at the Peradeniya Campus of the University of Sri Lanka on 11th and 12th November, 1976. 1977. Report; [D. Wimalaratne, commissioner]. Colombo, 1977. pp. 107. (Sri Lanka. Parliament. Sessional Papers. 1977. No. 1)

— Trinidad and Tobago.

TRINIDAD AND TOBAGO. Central Statistical Office. Report on enrolment in educational institutions. a., 1973/74(1st)- Port of Spain. Data previously included in TRINIDAD AND TOBAGO. Central Statistical Office. Digest of statistics on education.

— United Kingdom.

NATIONAL BOOK LEAGUE. Conference, London, 1975. Books and undergraduates; proceedings...; edited by Peter H. Mann. London, 1976. pp. 132.

ASSOCIATION OF UNIVERSITY TEACHERS. University student numbers. London, [1977]. pp. 11.

— — Political activity.

CAMPBELL (F.J.) Sociologist. High command: the making of an oligarchy at the Polytechnic of North London, 1970-74. [London, 1974]. pp. 132.

— United States — Attitudes.

NIELSEN (H. DEAN) Tolerating political dissent: the impact of high school social climates in the United States and West Germany. Stockholm, [1977]. pp. 138. bibliog. (International Association for the Evaluation of Educational Achievement. IEA Monograph Studies. No. 6)

— — Political activity.

MAY 1970: birth of the antiwar university. New York, 1971. pp. 62.

SCHNELL (RODOLPH LESLIE) National activist student organizations in American higher education, 1905-1944. Ann Arbor, 1976. pp. 258. bibliog. (Michigan University. School of Education. Social Foundations of Education Monograph Series. No. 7)

The DYNAMICS of university protest; [by] Donald Light and John Spiegel, [and others]. Chicago, [1977]. pp. 198. bibliog.

— — Religious life.

CAPLOVITZ (DAVID) and SHERROW (FRED) The religious drop-outs: apostasy among college graduates. Beverly Hills, [1977]. pp. 199.

STUDENTS, FOREIGN

— Statistics.

UNITED NATIONS EDUCATIONAL, SCIENTIFIC AND CULTURAL ORGANIZATION. Office of Statistics. 1976. Statistics of students abroad, 1969-1973. Paris, 1976. pp. 345. (Statistical Reports and Studies. No. 21) In English and French.

STUDENTS' SOCIO-ECONOMIC STATUS

— Nigeria.

LAGOS. University. Human Resources Research Unit. Research Project No. 1. Employment aspirations and prospects of Nigerian university undergraduates and graduates. Research Bulletins. [No. 1]. Socio-economic background of Nigerian university students. Lagos, [1973?]. fo. 17.

— United States.

ENTWISLE (DORIS ROBERTS) and HAYDUK (LESLIE ALEC) Too great expectations: the academic outlook of young children. Baltimore, [1978]. pp. 193. bibliog.

STURZO (LUIGI).

VASALE (CLAUDIO) Democrazia e pluralismo nella sociologia storicista di Luigi Sturzo. [Roma, 1975]. pp. 118.

STUTTERING.

DALTON (PEGGY) and HARDCASTLE (W.J.) Disorders of fluency and their effects on communication. London, 1977. pp. 161. bibliog.

STUTTGART

— History.

BOHN (WILLI) Stuttgart: geheim!: Widerstand und Verfolgung, 1933-1945. 3rd ed. Frankfurt am Main, [1978]. pp. 207. bibliog.

SUBCULTURE.

BRAKE (MICHAEL DAVID) Hippies and skinheads: sociological aspects of subcultures of working class and middle class youth. [1977]. fo. 324. bibliog. Typescript. Ph.D. (London) thesis: unpublished. This thesis is the property of London University and may not be removed from the Library.

SUBSIDIES.

MALMGREN (HARALD B.) International order for public subsidies. London, 1977. pp. 74. bibliog. (Trade Policy Research Centre. Thames Essays. No. 11)

INTERNATIONAL trade and industrial policies: government intervention and an open world economy; edited by Steven J. Warnecke. [London, 1978]. pp. 245.

— Puerto Rico.

PUERTO RICO. Statutes, etc. 1963-68. Industrial Incentive Act of 1963; (with Addenda of amendments up to June 28, 1968). [San Juan, 1963-68]. 1 vol. (various pagings).

— United Kingdom.

BRITISH ROAD FEDERATION. Who pays the fares?: the transport subsidy labyrinth. London, [1977]. pp. 8.

ENGLISH TOURIST BOARD. Investing in tourism: aid to tourist projects in England's development areas, 1971-76. London, [1977]. pp. 40.

— United States.

TAX FOUNDATION. Research Publications. New Series. No. 29. Federal grants: the need for reform. New York, [1973]. pp. 44.

SUBURBAN SCHOOLS

— United States.

WYNNE (EDWARD A.) Growing up suburban. Austin, [1977]. pp. 237.

SUBURBS

— Sweden.

POPENOE (DAVID) The suburban environment: Sweden and the United States. Chicago, [1977]. pp. 275.

— United States.

KAPLAN (SAMUEL) The dream deferred: people, politics and planning in suburbia. New York, 1977. pp. 242. bibliog.

POPENOE (DAVID) The suburban environment: Sweden and the United States. Chicago, [1977]. pp. 275.

The SUBURBAN economic network: economic activity, resource use, and the great sprawl; edited by John E. Ullmann. New York, 1977. pp. 251.

BURROWS (LAWRENCE B.) Growth management: issues, techniques and policy implications. New Brunswick, N.J., [1978]. pp. 141. bibliog.

SUBVERSIVE ACTIVITIES.

CROZIER (BRIAN) The surrogate forces of the Soviet Union. London, 1978. pp. 20. (Institute for the Study of Conflict. Conflict Studies. No. 92)

— Chile.

HIRSCH (FRED) and FLETCHER (RICHARD) The CIA and the labour movement. Nottingham, 1977. pp. 71.

— United States.

McAULIFFE (MARY SPERLING) Crisis on the left: cold war politics and American liberals, 1947-1954. Amherst, 1978. pp. 204. bibliog.

WEINSTEIN (ALLEN) Perjury: the Hiss-Chambers case. New York, 1978. pp. 674. bibliog.

SUCCESS.

KINOMETRICS: determinants of socioeconomic success within and between families; editor, Paul Taubman. Amsterdam, 1977. pp. 324. bibliogs.

SUDAN

— Census.

SUDAN. Census, 1955/56. First population census of Sudan, 1955/1956: final report, vol. 1. Khartoum, 1961. pp. 141, 1 map.

— Commerce — Statistics.

BANK OF SUDAN. Statistics Department. Foreign trade statistical digest. a., 1976(v. 9)- Khartoum.

BANK OF SUDAN. Statistics Department. Foreign trade statistical digest. q., Ja/Mr 1977(v.10,no.1)- Khartoum.

SUDAN (Cont.)

— Economic conditions.

BARNETT (TONY) The Gezira scheme: an illusion of development. London, 1977. pp. 192. *bibliog.*

SUDAN PROGRESS: a m. report on the economic development of the Sudan; [pd. by] Ministry of Culture and Information. m., current issues only. Khartoum.

— — Statistics.

BANK OF SUDAN. Statistics Department. Economic and financial statistics review. q., Ja/Mr 1977 (v. 18, no. 1)- Khartoum.

— Economic policy.

EL MILIGI (IBRAHIM SAAD) National policies for computer applications in developing countries: a case study of the Sudan. 1977. fo. 317. *bibliog.* Typescript. Ph.D. (London) thesis: unpublished. This thesis is the property of London University and may not be removed from the Library.

— Nationalism.

AHMED (RAFIA HASSAN) Ethnic and socio-cultural pluralism in the Sudan: its manifestation and effects on national integration. Khartoum, [Institute of Public Administration], 1975. fo. 40. *(Occasional Papers)*

— Politics and government.

DENG (FRANCIS MADING) Africans of two worlds: the Dinka in Afro-Arab Sudan. New Haven, 1978. pp. 244.

— Rural conditions.

BRAUSCH (GEORGES) and others. Bashaqra area settlements, 1963: a case study in village development in the Gezira scheme. Khartoum, 1964. pp. 172. *bibliog.*

— Social conditions.

BARNETT (TONY) The Gezira scheme: an illusion of development. London, 1977. pp. 192. *bibliog.*

SUEZ CANAL.

GEORGES-PICOT (JACQUES) The real Suez crisis: the end of a great nineteenth century work; translated from the French by W. G. Rogers. New York, [1978]. pp. 200.

SUFFICIENT STATISTICS.

BARNDORFF-NIELSEN (OLE) Information and exponential families in statistical theory. Chichester, [1978]. pp. 238. *bibliog.*

SUFFOLK

— Economic conditions.

SUFFOLK. County Planning Officer. Suffolk county structure plan: report of survey; [with] Report of survey: public consultation draft. Ipswich, 1976-77. 15 pts. (in 1 vol.).

— Social conditions.

SUFFOLK. County Planning Officer. Suffolk county structure plan: report of survey; [with] Report of survey: public consultation draft. Ipswich, 1976-77. 15 pts. (in 1 vol.).

SUFFRAGE

— Argentine Republic.

VILLAFAÑE (BENJAMIN) La ley suicida. Buenos Aires, 1936. pp. 157.

SUGAR

— Congresses.

UNITED NATIONS. Sugar Conference, Geneva, 1968. Summary of proceedings [of the conference held at Geneva, 17 April to 1 June and 23 September to 24 October, 1968]. (TD/SUGAR. 7/12). New York, 1968. pp. 75.

— Manufacture and refining — Cuba.

MORENO FRAGINALS (MANUEL) The sugarmill: the socioeconomic complex of sugar in Cuba, 1760-1860;...translated by Cedric Belfrage. New York, [1976]. pp. 182.

— — Malawi.

AMER (JOHN) and HUTCHESON (ALEXANDER MACGREGOR) The Nchalo sugar estate: a major agricultural development in Malawi. [Zomba], Malawi Information Department, 1966. pp. 24, 1 map. *bibliog.*

— — United Kingdom.

HUGILL (ANTONY) Sugar and all that: a history of Tate and Lyle. London, 1978. pp. 320. *bibliog.*

— Prices.

CANADA. Food Prices Review Board. 1974. Sugar prices and policies. [Ottawa], 1974. pp. 59, 63. *In English and French.*

HAGELBERG (G.B.) Variations in world sugar prices. Berlin, 1977. pp. 32. *bibliog. (Berlin. Technische Universität Berlin- Charlottenburg. Institut für Zuckerindustrie. Forschungsberichte. 8)*

SUGAR GROWING

— Argentine Republic.

SCHLEH (EMILIO J.) El azucar en la Argentina: reseña informativa de la industria azucarera en todos sus aspectos. Buenos Aires, 1953. pp. 134.

— Brazil.

FREYRE (GILBERTO DE MELLO) A presença do açucar na formação brasileira. Rio de Janeiro, 1975. pp. 212.

— Cuba.

ROCA (SERGIO) Cuban economic policy and ideology: the ten million ton sugar harvest. Beverly Hills, [1976]. pp. 70. *bibliog.*

— Malawi.

AMER (JOHN) and HUTCHESON (ALEXANDER MACGREGOR) The Nchalo sugar estate: a major agricultural development in Malawi. [Zomba], Malawi Information Department, 1966. pp. 24, 1 map. *bibliog.*

SUGAR MACHINERY.

MORENO FRAGINALS (MANUEL) The sugarmill: the socioeconomic complex of sugar in Cuba, 1760-1860;...translated by Cedric Belfrage. New York, [1976]. pp. 182.

SUGAR TRADE.

CANADA. Food Prices Review Board. 1974. Sugar prices and policies. [Ottawa], 1974. pp. 59, 63. *In English and French.*

— Argentine Republic.

SCHLEH (EMILIO J.) El azucar en la Argentina: reseña informativa de la industria azucarera en todos sus aspectos. Buenos Aires, 1953. pp. 134.

— Cuba.

MORENO FRAGINALS (MANUEL) The sugarmill: the socioeconomic complex of sugar in Cuba, 1760-1860;...translated by Cedric Belfrage. New York, [1976]. pp. 182.

BRUNNER (HEINRICH) 1945- . Cuban sugar policy from 1963 to 1970; translated by Marguerite Borchardt and H.F. Broch de Rothermann. Pittsburgh, [1977]. pp. 163. *bibliog.*

SUICIDE.

ALBERTA. Task Force on Suicides. 1976. Report...to the Minister of Social Services and Community Health...; Menno Boldt, chairman. [Edmonton], 1976. pp. 360. *bibliog.*

ATKINSON (J. MAXWELL) Discovering suicide: studies in the social organization of sudden death. London, 1978. pp. 225. *bibliog.*

— Canada.

MANITOBA. Department of Health and Social Development. Statistics Section. 1977. Suicide and suicide attempts. [Winnipeg], 1977. pp. 104.

— — Alberta.

ALBERTA. Task Force on Suicides. 1976. Report...to the Minister of Social Services and Community Health...; Menno Boldt, chairman. [Edmonton], 1976. pp. 360. *bibliog.*

SUMATRA

— Statistics.

INDONESIA. Kantor Sensus dan Statistik Propinsi Sumatera Utara. Statistical year book [of North Sumatra]. a., 1974- Medan. *[in English and Indonesian].*

SUMMER HOMES

— United Kingdom — Wales.

HOLIDAY homes; by Steffan Allison [and others]. Cardiff, [1972]. 1 pamphlet (various pagings). *(Cwmni Gwasg Rydd Caerdydd. Reports. No. 3) In English and Welsh.*

SUNDAY LEGISLATION

— United Kingdom.

SOCIETY FOR PROMOTING THE DUE OBSERVANCE OF THE LORD'S DAY. The municipal elector: a guide to voters at the municipal elections, 1925. London, the Society, 1925. pp. 4.

SUNDAY-SCHOOLS.

LAQUEUR (THOMAS WALTER) Religion and respectability: Sunday schools and working class culture, 1780-1850. New Haven, 1976. pp. 293. *bibliog.*

SUPPLEMENTARY EMPLOYMENT

— Poland.

MUSZYŃSKI (MAREK) Transformacja ludności dwunzawodowej. Warszawa, 1976. pp. 144. *bibliog. (Polska Akademia Nauk. Instytut Rozwoju Wsi i Rolnictwa. Problemy Rozwoju Wsi i Rolnictwa) With Russian and English summaries.*

— United Kingdom — Mathematical models.

JOSHI (HEATHER) Secondary workers in the cycle: married women and older workers in employment fluctuations, Great Britain 1961-74. London, Department of Health and Social Security, 1978. pp. 38. *bibliog. (Government Economic Service Working Papers. No. 8)*

SUPPLY AND DEMAND.

LLUCH (CONSTANTINO) and others. Patterns in household demand and saving; with contributions by Roger R. Betancourt [and others]; published for the World Bank. New York, [1977]. pp. 280. *bibliog.*

SCHULTZE (CHARLES L.) The public use of private interest. Washington, [1977]. pp. 93. *Revised and expanded version of the Godkin lectures delivered at the John F. Kennedy School of Government, Harvard University in Nov. and Dec. 1976.*

DEMAND management; edited by Michael Posner. London, 1978. pp. 242. *(National Institute of Economic and Social Research. Economic Policy Papers. 1) Proceedings of a conference held in London in 1977.*

HAVEMAN (ROBERT H.) and KNOPF (KENYON A.) The market system: an introduction to microeconomics. 3rd ed. Santa Barbara, [1978]. pp. 272.

— **Mathematical models.**

RAY (RANJAN) Utility maximisation and consumer demand with an application to the United Kingdom, 1900-1970. 1977. fo. 174. *bibliog.* Typescript. Ph.D. (London) thesis: unpublished. *This thesis is the property of London University and may not be removed from the Library.*

SURGERY.

SELZER (RICHARD) Mortal lessons: notes on the art of surgery. New York, [1974]. pp. 219.

SURREALISM.

LE BRETON (ANDRE) Position politique du surréalisme. Paris, 1971. pp. 32. *(Bibliothèque Volante, La. No.2)*

SURREY

— **Economic conditions.**

SURREY. Planning Department. Structure plan: report of survey. [Kingston upon Thames], 1977. 7 vols. (in 1).

— **Economic policy.**

SURREY. Planning Department. Surrey structure plan: written statement: public participation draft. [Kingston upon Thames], 1977. pp. 148,xix.

— **Social conditions.**

SURREY. Planning Department. Structure plan: report of survey. [Kingston upon Thames], 1977. 7 vols. (in 1).

— **Social policy.**

SURREY. Planning Department. Surrey structure plan: written statement: public participation draft. [Kingston upon Thames], 1977. pp. 148,xix.

SUSSEX

— **Social history.**

LOWERSON (JOHN) and MYERSCOUGH (JOHN) Time to spare in Victorian England. Hassocks, Sussex, 1977. pp. 151. *bibliog. Based on a series of talks and conversations for BBC Radio Brighton, under the auspices of the University of Sussex's Centre for Continuing Education.*

SUTTER (JOSEPH ANTON).

TRIET (MAX) Der Sutterhandel in Appenzell Innerrhoden, 1760-1829: ein Beitrag zur Geschichte der politischen Unruhen in der Schweiz des Ancien Régime. Appenzell, 1977. pp. 279. *bibliog.*

SVALBARD

— **Economic conditions.**

ØSTRENG (WILLY) Politics in high latitudes: the Svalbard Archipelago;... translated by R.I. Christophersen. London, [1977]. pp. 134. *bibliog.*

— **International status.**

ØSTRENG (WILLY) Politics in high latitudes: the Svalbard Archipelago;... translated by R.I. Christophersen. London, [1977]. pp. 134. *bibliog.*

SVERDLOV (IAKOV MIKHAILOVICH).

PLOTNIKOV (IURII PAVLOVICH) Ia.M. Sverdlov v turukhanskoi ssylke. Krasnoiarsk, 1976. pp. 112.

SWABIANS IN HUNGARY.

SPIRA (THOMAS) German-Hungarian relations and the Swabian problem: from Károlyi to Gömbös, 1919-1936. New York, 1977. pp. 382. *bibliog. (East European Quarterly. East European Monographs. 25)*

SWAZILAND

— **Economic policy.**

SWAZILAND. 1969. Post independence development plan. Mbabane, 1969. pp. 73.

SWAZILAND. 1973. Second national development plan, 1973-1977. Mbabane, [1973?]. pp. 251.

— **Social policy.**

SWAZILAND. 1969. Post independence development plan. Mbabane, 1969. pp. 73.

SWAZILAND. 1973. Second national development plan, 1973-1977. Mbabane, [1973?]. pp. 251.

— **Statistics.**

SWAZILAND. Central Statistical Office. Quarterly digest of statistics (formerly Statistical news and economic indicators). q., Ag 1971(no. 24)- , with gap (1972, no. 26) Mbabane. *Not pd. Je 1975 (no. 37)*

SWEATING SYSTEM.

SHAH (SAMIR) Immigrants and employment in the clothing industry: the rag trade in London's East End. London, 1975. fo.42

SWEDEN

— **Commerce — China.**

LARSSON (JAN) Diplomati och industriellt genombrott: svenska exportsträvanden på Kina, 1906-1916. Uppsala, 1977. pp. 212. *bibliog. (Uppsala. Universitet. Historiska Institutionen. Studia Historica Upsaliensia. 94) With English summary.*

— **Commercial policy.**

LARSSON (JAN) Diplomati och industriellt genombrott: svenska exportsträvanden på Kina, 1906-1916. Uppsala, 1977. pp. 212. *bibliog. (Uppsala. Universitet. Historiska Institutionen. Studia Historica Upsaliensia. 94) With English summary.*

— **Emigration and immigration.**

FROM Sweden to America: a history of the migration; editors Harald Runblom and Hans Norman. Minneapolis, 1976. pp. 391. *(Uppsala. Universitet. Historiska Institutionen. Acta Universitatis Upsaliensis. 74)*

— **Foreign relations.**

PALME (OLOF) World peace, super powers and national independence. [Stockholm, 1974]. pp. 35.

— — **Germany.**

KARLSSON (RUNE) Så stoppades tysktågen: den tyska transiteringstrafiken i svensk politik, 1942-1943. Stockholm, 1974. pp. 363. *bibliog. With English summary.*

DRANGEL (LOUISE) Den kämpande demokratin: en studie i antinazistisk opinionsrörelse, 1935-1945. Stockholm, 1976. pp. 287. *bibliog. With English summary.*

— **History.**

SCOTT (FRANKLIN DANIEL) Sweden: the nation's history. Minneapolis, [1977]. pp. 654. *bibliog.*

— — **1905- .**

KARLSSON (RUNE) Så stoppades tysktågen: den tyska transiteringstrafiken i svensk politik, 1942-1943. Stockholm, 1974. pp. 363. *bibliog. With English summary.*

DRANGEL (LOUISE) Den kämpande demokratin: en studie i antinazistisk opinionsrörelse, 1935-1945. Stockholm, 1976. pp. 287. *bibliog. With English summary.*

— **Neutrality.**

KARLSSON (RUNE) Så stoppades tysktågen: den tyska transiteringstrafiken i svensk politik, 1942-1943. Stockholm, 1974. pp. 363. *bibliog. With English summary.*

MÅRALD (BERT) Den svenska freds- och neutralitetsrörelsens uppkomst: ideologi, propaganda och politiska yttringar från Krimkriget till den svensk-norska unionens upplösning. Stockholm, [1974]. pp. 314. *bibliog. (Göteborgs Universitet. Studia Historica Gothoburgensia. 14) With English summary.*

— **Officials and employees.**

SWEDEN. Statistiska Centralbyrån. Statsanställda (formerly Statstjänsteman). a., 1975- Stockholm. *[in Swedish with English summary and table headings]*

— **Population policy.**

MYRDAL (ALVA) and MYRDAL (GUNNAR) Kris i befolkningsfrågan. 7th ed. Stockholm, [1935]. pp. 403.

SWEDES IN FINLAND.

BJÖRKQVIST (HEIMER) Handelsflottan och dess betydelse för sysselsättningen i de svensk-österbottniska städerna åren 1815-1858. Åbo, 1970. pp. 195-240. *(Åbo. Akademi. Handelshögskolan. Nationalekonomiska Institutionen. Meddelanden. Nr. 17) (Särtryck ur Österbotten 1970)*

SWEDISH LITERATURE.

KJELLGREN (JOSEF) Jag är tusenden. [Stockholm, 1975]. pp. 88. *bibliog.*

SWINDON

— **Population.**

CONSTABLE (DEREK) Household structure in three English market towns, 1851-1871. Reading, 1977. pp. 63. *(Reading. University. Department of Geography. Reading Geographical Papers. No. 55)*

— **Social history.**

CONSTABLE (DEREK) Household structure in three English market towns, 1851-1871. Reading, 1977. pp. 63. *(Reading. University. Department of Geography. Reading Geographical Papers. No. 55)*

SWINE

— **Rhodesia.**

SOUTHERN RHODESIA. Committee of Enquiry into Certain Aspects of the Dairy and Pig Industries. 1936. Report; [William Purdie Currie, chairman]. Salisbury, 1936. pp. 40. *(Legislative Assembly. [Sessional Papers]. 1936. C.S.R. 4)*

SWINTON (JOHN).

GARLIN (SENDER) John Swinton, American radical (1829-1901). New York, 1976. pp. 47. *bibliog.(American Institute for Marxist Studies. Occasional Papers. No. 20)*

SWITZERLAND

— **Constitutional history.**

VIAL (JEAN CLAUDE) Fribourg et la révision de la constitution fédérale de 1872. Fribourg, 1977. fo. 259. *bibliog.*

— **Economic conditions.**

BEGUELIN (JEAN PIERRE) Indicateurs statistiques de la conjoncture suisse: essai sur la signification conjoncturelle des statistiques économiques suisses. Berne, 1976. 1 vol. (various pagings). *bibliog. Thèse (docteur ès sciences économiques et sociales) - Université de Genève.*

— **Economic history.**

BERGIER (JEAN FRANÇOIS) Problèmes de l'histoire économique de la Suisse: population, vie rurale, échanges et trafics. Berne, [1968]. pp. 95. *bibliog. (Allgemeine Geschichtforschende Gesellschaft der Schweiz. Monographien zur Schweizer Geschichte. Band 2)*

— **Economic policy.**

KRAMER (HUGO) Was soll werden?: Gedanken zur wirtschaftlichen Erneuerung der Schweiz. [Zürich], 1941. pp. 80. *(Sozialdemokratische Partei der Schweiz. Kultur und Arbeit)*

LIBERALSOZIALISTISCHE PARTEI DER SCHWEIZ. 25 Jahre später: zur Abstimmung über die Kaufkraft-Initiative vom 15. April 1951. Zürich, 1976. pp. 28.

SWITZERLAND (Cont.)

SCHWEIZERISCHE Wirtschaftspolitik zwischen gestern und morgen: Festgabe zum 65. Geburtstag von Hugo Sieber; herausgegeben von Egon Tuchtfeldt. Bern, [1976]. pp. 493. *bibliog.*

La POLITIQUE économique de la Suisse: mélanges en l'honneur de Jean Valarché...; sous la direction de Gaston Gaudard [and others]. Fribourg, 1977. pp. 326. *bibliog. Articles in German or French.*

— **Emigration and immigration.**

L'IMMIGRAZIONE in Svizzera: il lavoro straniero in Svizzera dalle origini ad oggi, con particolare riferimento all'immigrazione italiana; di S. Soldini [and others]. Milano, 1970 repr. 1975. pp. 202. *bibliog.*

— **Foreign economic relations.**

La SUISSE et la diplomatie multilatérale; [by] Franz A. Blankart [and others]; sous la direction de Jacques Freymond. Genève, 1976. pp. 302.

BRODMANN (ROMAN) Der Un-Schweizer: was machen Eidgenossen mit einem Dissidenten?: vom "Fall Ziegler" zum Fall Schweiz. Darmstadt, [1977]. pp. 126.

— **Foreign relations.**

La SUISSE et la diplomatie multilatérale; [by] Franz A. Blankart [and others]; sous la direction de Jacques Freymond. Genève, 1976. pp. 302.

— **Industries.**

SWITZERLAND. Bureau Fédéral de Statistique. 1977. Recensement fédéral des entreprises, 1975: Industrie, arts et métiers, services. Berne, 1977. 5 vols. (in 1). *(Statistiques de la Suisse. 605e-609e fasc.) Vols. 3-5 in French and German.*

— **Politics and government.**

LIBERAL-DEMOKRATISCHE UNION DER SCHWEIZ. Congrès, 1974. La socialisation à froid: résumé des rapports présentés au Congrès...à Pully le 9 février 1974. [Bern], 1974. pp. 37. *In French or German.*

BRODMANN (ROMAN) Der Un-Schweizer: was machen Eidgenossen mit einem Dissidenten?: vom "Fall Ziegler" zum Fall Schweiz. Darmstadt, [1977]. pp. 126.

OBLER (JEFFREY) and others. Decision-making in smaller democracies: the consociational burden. Beverly Hills, [1977]. pp. 58. *bibliog.*

THUT (ROLF) and BISLIN (CLAUDIA) Aufrüstung gegen das Volk: (Staat und Staatsschutz in der Schweiz; zur Entwicklung der "inneren Sicherheit"). Zürich, [1977]. pp. 245. *bibliog.*

SCHMID-AMMANN (PAUL) Unterwegs von der politischen zur sozialen Demokratie: Lebenserinnerungen. Zürich, [1978]. pp. 303.

— **Social conditions.**

LIBERAL-DEMOKRATISCHE UNION DER SCHWEIZ. Congrès, 1974. La socialisation à froid: résumé des rapports présentés au Congrès...à Pully le 9 février 1974. [Bern], 1974. pp. 37. *In French or German.*

SYMBIONESE LIBERATION ARMY.

BEAL (MARY F.) Safe house: a casebook study of revolutionary feminism in the 1970's. [Eugene, Or.], 1976. pp. 153. *bibliog.*

SYMBOLISM.

HUNT (EVA) The transformation of the hummingbird: cultural roots of a Zinacantecan mythical poem. Ithaca, 1977. pp. 312. *bibliog.*

The SOCIAL use of metaphor: essays on the anthropology of rhetoric; edited by J. David Sapir and J. Christopher Crocker. Philadelphia, [1977]. pp. 249. *bibliog. Based on papers presented at a symposium held at the 1970 annual meetings of the American Anthropological Association.*

SYMBOLS and sentiments: cross-cultural studies in symbolism; edited by Ioan Lewis. London, 1977. pp. 300. *bibliogs.*

SYNDICALISM.

LEHNING (ARTHUR) Anarcho-syndikalisme: (tekst van een op November 1926 gehouden inleiding; [with] Anton Constandse, Syndikalisme en bedrijf, uit Grondslagen van het anarchisme...1938). Amsterdam, [197-]. pp. 31.

— **Belgium.**

VERHOEVEN (JOSEPH) C.S.C., qui es-tu?: révolutionnaire dans l'évolution. Bruxelles, 1976. pp. 196.

— **France.**

FOULON (MAURICE) Fernand Pelloutier, précurseur du syndicalisme fédéraliste, fondateur des bourses du travail. Paris, [1967]. pp. 189.

— **Italy.**

CARTIGLIA (CARLO) Rinaldo Rigola e il sindicalismo riformista in Italia. Milano, [1976]. pp. 209.

RIOSA (ALCEO) Il sindicalismo rivoluzionario in Italia e la lotta politica nel Partito socialista dell'età giolittiana. Bari, [1976]. pp. 390.

SYSTEM ANALYSIS.

An INTRODUCTION to linear analysis; [by] Donald L. Kreider [and others]. Reading, Mass., [1966]. pp. 773. *bibliog.*

BOEHM (B.W.) Computer systems analysis, methodology: studies in measuring, evaluating, and simulating computer systems. Santa Monica, 1970. pp. 42. *bibliog. (Rand Corporation. [Rand Reports]. 520)*

FISHMAN (GEORGE S.) Concepts and methods in discrete event digital simulation. New York, [1973]. pp. 385. *bibliog.*

BAILEY (NORMAN THOMAS JOHN) Mathematics, statistics, and systems for health. Chichester, [1977]. pp. 222. *bibliog. Based on his The mathematical approach to biology and medicine, published in 1967.*

COMPUTING system design: proceedings of the joint IBM- University of Newcastle-upon-Tyne seminar held in the University Computing Laboratory, 7th-10th September 1976; edited by B. Shaw. Newcastle-upon-Tyne, 1977. pp. 260.

A DISCUSSION on the use of operational research and systems analysis in decision-making; [by] R.C. Tomlinson [and others]. London, 1977. pp. 193. *(London. Royal Society of London. Philosophical Transactions. Series A. vol. 287)*

SHAPIRA (EDGAR) Systems analysis of clinical decision-making: a suggested approach. 1977. fo. 155. *bibliog. Typescript. Ph.D. (London) thesis: unpublished. This thesis is the property of London University and may not be removed from the Library.*

CLIFTON (HAROLD DENNIS) Business data systems: a practical guide to systems analysis and data processing. Englewood Cliffs, [1978]. pp. 336. *bibliogs.*

CYPSER (R.J.) Communications architecture for distributed systems. Reading, Mass., [1978]. pp. 711.

LILIENFELD (ROBERT) The rise of systems theory: an ideological analysis. New York, [1978]. pp. 292.

— **Study and teaching.**

BASIC training in systems analysis; edited by Alan Daniels and Donald Yeates. 2nd ed. London, 1971 repr. 1977. pp. 301. *bibliog.*

SYSTEM THEORY.

AOKI (MASANAO) Optional control and system theory in dynamic economic analysis. New York, [1977]. pp. 400. *bibliog.*

LILIENFELD (ROBERT) The rise of systems theory: an ideological analysis. New York, [1978]. pp. 292.

— **Anecdotes, facetiae, satire, etc.**

GALL (JOHN) Systemantics: how systems work and especially how they fail. New York, [1975]. pp. 111. *bibliog.*

SYSTEMS ENGINEERING.

BOEHM (B.W.) Computer systems analysis, methodology: studies in measuring, evaluating, and simulating computer systems. Santa Monica, 1970. pp. 42. *bibliog. (Rand Corporation. [Rand Reports]. 520)*

TAHITI

— **History — Sources.**

CHASTENET DE GÉRY (J.) Les derniers jours de la Troisième République à Tahiti, 1938-1940: souvenirs d'un gouverneur. Paris, 1975. pp. 75. *(Reprinted from Bulletin de la Société des Etudes Océaniennes, Dec. 1974, no. 187-189)*

TAIPING REBELLION, 1850-1864.

HAKE (ALFRED EGMONT) Events of the Taeping Rebellion, being reprints of Mss. copied by General Gordon, C.B. in his own handwriting. London, 1891. pp. 531. *Includes Reminiscences by one who served with Gordon in China [i.e. F.L. Story]*

TAITAS

— **Religion.**

HARRIS (GRACE GREDYS) Casting out anger: religion among the Taita of Kenya. Cambridge, 1978. pp. 193. *bibliog.*

TAIWAN

— **Commerce — New Zealand.**

NEW ZEALAND ECONOMIC AND GOODWILL MISSION TO JAPAN AND TAIWAN. Report...October 1965. Wellington, Department of Industries and Commerce, [1966]. pp. 25.

— **Economic conditions.**

CENTRAL BANK OF CHINA. Economic Research Department. Graphical survey of the economy of Taiwan, the Republic of China [for 1975]. [Taipei], 1976. pp. 35.

CENTRAL BANK OF CHINA. Economic Research Department. Graphical survey of the economy of Taiwan, the Republic of China [for 1976]. [Taipei], 1977. pp. 35.

HO (SAMUEL P.S.) Economic development of Taiwan, 1860-1970. New Haven, 1978. pp. 461. *bibliog. (Yale University. Economic Growth Center)*

— **Economic policy.**

PRYBYLA (JAN S.) The societal objective of wealth, growth, stability and equity in Taiwan. [Baltimore] 1978. pp. 31. *(Maryland University. School of Law. Occasional Papers/Reprints Series in Contemporary Asian Studies. No. 4)*

— **Foreign economic relations — United States.**

CONFERENCE ON LEGAL ASPECTS OF UNITED STATES-REPUBLIC OF CHINA TRADE AND INVESTMENT, 1977. Proceedings...; editors: Hungdah Chiu and David Simon. Baltimore, 1977. pp. 217. *bibliog. (Maryland. University. School of Law. Occasional Papers/Reprints Series in Contemporary Asian Studies. No. 10)*

— **Foreign relations — Malawi.**

FORMOSA. Ministry of Foreign Affairs. 1968. Press conferences made by the Chinese Vice-Minister for Foreign Affairs, H.K. Yang, on his arrival and before his departure, at Chileka airport on August 25-27, 1968. Blantyre, Malawi Department of Information, [1968]. pp. 4, 2.

— **Religious life and customs.**

AHERN (EMILY M.) The cult of the dead in a Chinese village. Stanford, Calif., 1973. pp. 280. *bibliog.*

— Social policy.

PRYBYLA (JAN S.) The societal objective of wealth, growth, stability and equity in Taiwan. [Baltimore] 1978. pp. 31. *(Maryland University. School of Law. Occasional Papers/Reprints Series in Contemporary Asian Studies. No. 4)*

TAJIKISTAN

— Economic history.

ISKANDAROV (BUKHODOR ISKANDAROVICH) Iz istorii proniknoveniia kapitalisticheskikh otnoshenii v ekonomiku dorevoliutsionnogo Tadzhikistana, vtoraia polovina XIX v.; otvet. redaktor Kh. Saidmuradov. Dushanbe, 1976. pp. 143.

— Learned institutions and societies.

RADZHABOV (ZARIF SHARIPOVICH) Ocherki istorii kul'turnogo stroitel'stva v Tadzhikistane; pod redaktsiei...G.A. Ashurova. Dushanbe, 1976. pp. 135.

— Politics and government.

PROBLEMY istoricheskogo materializma...: nekotorye zakonomernosti razvitiia bazisa i nadstroiki etapa razvitogo sotsializma: tematicheskii sbornik. Dushanbe, 1975. pp. 179. *(Dushanbinskii Gosudarstvennyi Pedagogicheskii Institut. Uchenye Zapiski. t.96)*

TALES, MAYAN.

CAMBRIDGE. University. Centre of Latin American Studies. Working Papers. No.19. Ethnographic notes on the Maya of Belize, Central America; [by] J.C.H. King. Cambridge, [1974]. pp. 43. *bibliog.*

TALL BUILDINGS

— Fires and fire prevention — Bibliography.

GOMERSALL (ALAN) compiler. Fire in high-rise buildings. London, 1977. pp. 8. *(London. Greater London Council. Research Library. Research Bibliographies. No. 78)*

TALLEYRAND-PERIGORD (CHARLES MAURICE DE) Prince.

SCHUMANN (MAURICE) Talleyrand, prophet of Entente Cordiale. Oxford, 1977. pp. 22. *(Oxford. University. Zaharoff Lectures. 1976-77)*

TANAKA (SHOZO).

STRONG (KENNETH) Ox against the storm: a biography of Tanaka Shozo, Japan's conservationist pioneer. Tenterden, Kent, 1977. pp. 232. *bibliog.*

TANZANIA.

TANZANIA NEWS REVIEW; [pd. by] Information Services Division. bi-m., Ja/F 1978(v. 2, no. 2)- Dar es Salaam.

— Economic conditions.

RASILIMALI: Tanzania investment outlook; [pd. by] Tanzania Investment Bank. 2 a yr., [1972 (no.1)]- Dar es Salaam.

— Economic history.

HALL (PETER KENNETH) African economic initiative and response in British Tanganyika. 1977 [or rather 1978]. fo.457. *bibliog.* Typescript. Ph.D. (London) thesis: unpublished. This thesis is the property of London University and may not be removed from the Library.

— Economic policy.

JENGA: magazine of the National Development Corporation [Tanzania]. irreg. (formerly bi.m.,) [Je?] 1969 (no.3)- Dar es Salaam.

BLUE (RICHARD N.) and WEAVER (JAMES H.) A critical assessment of the Tanzanian model of development. New York, 1977. pp. 19. *bibliog.* *(Agricultural Development Council. Reprints. No. 30)*

— Emigration and immigration.

UNITED REPUBLIC OF TANZANIA. Bureau of Statistics. Migration statistics. a., 1969- Dar es Salaam.

— Population.

UNITED REPUBLIC OF TANZANIA. Bureau of Statistics. 1976. 1973 national demographic survey of Tanzania. [Dar es Salaam, 1976?]. 4 vols. (in 1)

— Public works.

CLARK (W. EDMUND) Socialist development and public investment in Tanzania, 1964-73. Toronto, [1978]. pp. 319. *bibliog.*

— Rural conditions.

CONNELL (JOHN) 1946- . The evolution of Tanzanian rural development. Brighton, [1973]. pp. 21. *bibliog.* *(Brighton. University of Sussex. Institute of Development Studies. Communications. 110)*

— Social policy.

BLUE (RICHARD N.) and WEAVER (JAMES H.) A critical assessment of the Tanzanian model of development. New York, 1977. pp. 19. *bibliog.* *(Agricultural Development Council. Reprints. No. 30)*

TARASHKEVICH (BRANISLAU ADAMAVICH).

BERGMAN (ALEKSANDRA) Rzecz o Bronisławie Taraszkiewiczu. Warszawa, 1977. pp. 243.

TARASZKIEWICZ (BRONISLAW)

See TARASHKEVICH (BRANISLAU ADAMAVICH).

TARIFFS.

KOLASA (JAN) Law-making and law-enforcing for international trade: some reflections on the GATT experience. Princeton, 1976. pp. 37. *(Princeton University. Center of International Studies. World Order Studies Program. Occasional Papers. No. 3)*

CLINE (WILLIAM R.) and others. Trade negotiations in the Tokyo Round: a quantitative assessment. Washington, D.C., [1978]. pp. 314.

— Canada.

DALY (D.J.) and GLOBERMAN (S.) Tariff and science policies: applications of a model of nationalism. Toronto, [1976]. pp. 125. *bibliog.* *(Ontario. Economic Council. Research Studies. 4)*

WILLIAMS (JAMES RALLA) The Canadian-United States tariff and Canadian industry: a multisectoral analysis. Toronto, [1978]. pp. 174. *bibliog.*

— European Economic Community countries.

EUROPEAN COMMUNITIES. [Commission]. Practical guide to the use of the European Communities' scheme of generalized tariff preferences. a., current issue only. Brussels.

— Mediterranean.

TOVIAS (ALFRED) Tariff preferences in Mediterranean diplomacy. London, 1977. pp. 153. *bibliogs.*

— Peru.

ATTIA (MONA FOUAD) Tariff protection and growth in developing countries: a multisectoral analysis applied to Peru. Rotterdam, 1976. pp. 251. *bibliog.*

— Scandinavia.

[SCANDINAVIA]. Nordiske Parlamentariske Komité for Friere Samfaerdsel. 1956. Slutbetaenkning. København, 1956. pp. 50. *(Denmark. Betaenkninger. Nr. 166)*

— Singapore — Terminology and classification.

SAW (SWEE HOCK) The use of the Brussels tariff nomenclature in Singapore. Singapore, 1974. pp. 31. *bibliog.* *(Singapore. National Statistical Commission. Background Papers. No. 1)*

— Underdeveloped areas.

See UNDERDEVELOPED AREAS — Tariffs.

— United States.

WILLIAMS (JAMES RALLA) The Canadian-United States tariff and Canadian industry: a multisectoral analysis. Toronto, [1978]. pp. 174. *bibliog.*

TASHKENT

— History.

NABIEV (R.N.) Tashkentskoe vosstanie 1847 g. i ego sotsial'no-ekonomicheskie predposylki. Tashkent, 1966. pp. 80.

TASMANIA

— Commerce — East (Near East).

TASMANIA. Trade Mission of 1976 to Iran and the Arabian Peninsula. 1976. Report; [S.C.H. Frost, leader]. in TASMANIA. Parliament. Journals and Printed Papers. 1976, no. 51.

TATARS IN THE CRIMEA.

FISHER (ALAN W.) The Crimean Tatars. Stanford, [1978]. pp. 264. *bibliog.* *(Stanford University. Hoover Institution on War, Revolution and Peace. Hoover Institution Publications. 166)*

TATE AND LYLE LIMITED.

HUGILL (ANTONY) Sugar and all that: a history of Tate and Lyle. London, 1978. pp. 320. *bibliog.*

TAX ADMINISTRATION

— Africa.

SEMINAR ON ADMINISTRATION OF INCOME TAX IN AFRICAN COUNTRIES, DAKAR, 1968. Report of the Seminar...[held at] Dakar, Senegal, 25 March to 5 April 1968. (ST/TAO/SER.C/104). New York, United Nations, 1968. pp. 33. *bibliog.*

— Brazil.

BRAZIL. Secretaria da Receita Federal. 1969. General plan for the administration of federal taxes, 1969/70/71. [Rio de Janeiro, 1969?]. pp. 112.

TAX COLLECTION

— Canada.

INSIDE TAXATION; [pd. by Department of National Revenue, Canada]. a. Ottawa. *[in English and French] Current issue only kept.*

— United Kingdom — Isle of Man.

ISLE OF MAN. Income Tax Commission. 1957. Third interim report; [W.P. Cowley, chairman]. [Douglas, 1957]. pp. 7.

ISLE OF MAN. Income Tax Commission. 1964. Eighth interim report; [J.B. Bolton, chairman]. [Douglas, 1964]. pp. 8.

TAX CREDITS.

AUSTRALIA. Commonwealth Treasury. 1974. Negative income tax and tax credit systems. Canberra, 1974. pp. 18. *(Treasury Taxation Papers. No. 8)*

TAX CREDITS.(Cont.)

— United States.

AMERICAN ENTERPRISE INSTITUTE FOR PUBLIC POLICY RESEARCH. Legislative Analyses. 95th Congress. No. 27. Tuition tax credits and alternatives. Washington, D.C., 1978. pp. 50.

RISING costs in education: the federal response?; (a Round Table held on March 20, 1978...); John Charles Daly, moderator, etc. Washington, [1978]. pp. 44. *(American Enterprise Institute for Public Policy Research. Public Policy Forums. 17)*

TAX INCIDENCE

— Ireland (Republic).

DOWLING (BRENDAN R.) The income sensitivity of the personal income tax base in Ireland, 1947-1972. Dublin, 1977. pp. 82. *bibliog. (Economic and Social Research Institute. Papers. No. 86)*

TAX LIENS

— United States — Iowa.

SWIERENGA (ROBERT P.) Acres for cents: delinquent tax auctions in frontier Iowa. Westport, Conn., 1976. pp. 262. *bibliog.*

TAX PLANNING

— United Kingdom.

POTTER (DONALD CHARLES) and MONROE (HUBERT HOLMES) Tax planning with precedents; eighth edition by D.C. Potter and A.R. Thornhill. London, 1978. pp. 387.

TAX REFUNDS

— European Economic Community countries.

La RESTITUTION de taxes perçues indûment par l'état: colloque de droit européen et de droit administratif comparé; organisé conjointement par le Centre...et la Section de Droit Public de la Faculté de Droit de Genève. Genève, 1976. pp. 254. *(Institut für Europäisches und Internationales Wirtschafts- und Sozialrecht, and Centre d'Etudes Juridiques Européennes. Schweizerische Beiträge zum Europarecht. Band 18) In various languages.*

TAX-SALES

— United States — Iowa.

SWIERENGA (ROBERT P.) Acres for cents: delinquent tax auctions in frontier Iowa. Westport, Conn., 1976. pp. 262. *bibliog.*

TAXATION.

EXPERT GROUP ON TAX REFORM PLANNING. Tax reform planning: report of the...Group. (ST/ECA/135). New York, United Nations, 1971. pp. 16.

PETRETTO (ALESSANDRO) La teoria dell'ottima tassazione in economie di second best. Napoli, 1976. pp. 176. *bibliogs. (Istituto di Studi per lo Sviluppo Economico. Quaderni d'Istituto. 4)*

ARMEES et fiscalité dans le monde antique; (actes du colloque national...organisé...à Paris, les 14-16 octobre, 1976). Paris, 1977. pp. 478. *(Centre National de la Recherche Scientifique. Colloques Nationaux. No. 936) In French, Italian, or English.*

— History.

MESMER (BEATRIX) Steuerreform als Übergangsmassnahme: die Rezeption der Forderung nach progressiver Besteuerung in den frühsozialistischen Programmen. Bern, [1976]. pp. 239. *bibliog.*

— Mathematical models.

LLUCH SANZ (CAMILO) El esfuerzo fiscal de España. Madrid, 1977. pp. 185. *bibliog.*

— America, Latin.

PORZECANSKI (ARTURO C.) ed. Politica fiscal en America Latina: seleccion de textos. Mexico, 1977. pp. 558.

— Australia.

AUSTRALIA. Commonwealth Treasury. 1974. Commonwealth taxation of goods and services. Canberra, 1974. pp. 46. *(Treasury Taxation Papers. No. 5)*

AUSTRALIA. Commonwealth Treasury. 1974. The level and composition of taxation in Australia. Canberra, 1974. pp. 16. *(Treasury Taxation Papers. No. 2)*

AUSTRALIA. Commonwealth Treasury. 1974. Summary of issues. Canberra, 1974. pp. 11. *(Treasury Taxation Papers. No. 13)*

AUSTRALIA. Commonwealth Treasury. 1974. Taxation reform: problems and aims. Canberra, 1974. pp. 27. *(Treasury Taxation Papers. No. 1)*

— Canada.

MANITOBA. 1967. Submission of the government of Manitoba to the Federal Minister of Finance on the Carter Royal Commission on Taxation. [Winnipeg], 1967. fo. 36. *Photocopy.*

— France.

UNITED NATIONS. Department of Economic and Social Affairs. 1971. Interaction between the French tax system and those of developing countries. (ST/ECA/149). New York, 1971. pp. 64.

FRANCE. Direction de la Documentation. La Documentation Française. Notes et Etudes Documentaires. Nos. 4,306-4, 307. Un essai de mesure anti-inflationniste: le prélèvement conjoncturel; par Jean-Paul Courthéoux. Paris, 1976. pp. 61. *bibliog.*

RIGAUDIERE (ALBERT) L'assiette de l'impôt direct à la fin du XIVe siècle: le livre d'estimes des Consuls de St-Flour pour les années 1380-1385. Paris, [1977]. pp. 470. *bibliog. (Rouen. Université. Publications. 37)*

— Germany — Law.

JENETZKY (JOHANNES) System und Entwicklung des materiellen Steuerrechts in der wissenschaftlichen Literatur des Kameralismus von 1680-1840, etc. Berlin, 1978. pp. 298. *bibliog.*

— — Hesse.

HESSE. Statistiches Landesamt. Beiträge zur Statistik Hessens. Neue Folge. No. 89. Das steuerpflichtige Vermögen und die betrieblichen Einheitswerte am 1. Januar 1972: Ergebnisse der Vermögensteuer-und Einheitswertstatistik, 1972. Wiesbaden, 1978.

— India.

LAKDAWALA (DANSUKHLAL TULSIDAS) Taxation and the plan. Bombay, 1956. pp. 211.

— Ireland (Republic).

LLEWELLYN (G.E.J.) The potential for growth in Irish tax revenues. Dublin, Stationery Office, [1977]. pp. 140. *bibliog. (National Economic and Social Council [Eire]. [Reports]. No. 31)*

— — Law.

EIRE. Statutes, etc. 1921- . The taxes acts: income tax acts, corporation tax acts, Capital Gains Tax Act, 1975; with indices. Dublin, 1977 in progress. 3 vols. (loose-leaf).

— Italy — Lombardy.

KLANG (DANIEL M.) Tax reform in eighteenth century Lombardy. Boulder, Colo., 1977. pp. 110. *bibliog. (East European Quarterly. East European Monographs. 27)*

— Mauritania.

BARROT (ANDRE) Le recouvrement de l'impôt direct en Mauritanie. Nouakchott, Ecole Nationale d'Administration, 1975. fo. 139.

— Norway.

CHRISTIANSEN (VIDAR) and JANSEN (EILEV S.) Implicit social preferences in the Norwegian system of indirect taxation. Oslo, 1977. pp. 88. *bibliog. (Oslo. Universitet. Socialøkonomiske Institutt. Memoranda)*

— Spain.

BARTHE Y BARTHE (ANDRES) Reformas en los presupuestos. Madrid, 1902. pp. 65.

CRONICA TRIBUTARIA; [pd. by] Ministerio de Hacienda, Instituto Estudios Fiscales [Spain]. 3 a yr., 1972 (no.1)- , with gap (1974, no.8). Madrid.

LLUCH SANZ (CAMILO) El esfuerzo fiscal de España. Madrid, 1977. pp. 185. *bibliog.*

— Underdeveloped areas.

See UNDERDEVELOPED AREAS — Taxation.

— United Kingdom.

CONFEDERATION OF BRITISH INDUSTRY. The Finance Act, 1976: an explanatory guide. London, 1976. pp. 34.

HOWELL (RALPH FREDERIC) Low pay and taxation. London, 1976. fo. 9. *(Low Pay Unit. Low Pay Papers. No. 8)*

BRACEWELL-MILNES (JOHN BARRY) Short measure from Whitehall: how CSO statistics understate the British tax burden. London, 1977. pp. 8.

BURGESS (RONALD) Full employment and public spending. London, [1977]. pp. 19. *bibliog.*

CONFEDERATION OF BRITISH INDUSTRY. The Finance Act, 1977: an explanatory guide. London, 1977. pp. 40.

FERNS (HENRY STANLEY) Galloping bureaucracy and taxation: the radicalism the case requires. London, [1977]. pp. 9.

KAY (JOHN A.) and KING (MERVYN A.) The British tax system. Oxford, 1978. pp. 275. *bibliog.*

The STRUCTURE and reform of direct taxation: report of a committee chaired by Professor J.E. Meade. London, 1978. pp. 533. *A committee set up by the Institute for Fiscal Studies.*

— — Law.

LEWIS (MERVYN) British tax law: income tax, corporation tax, capital gains tax. Plymouth, 1977. pp. 528.

TILEY (JOHN) Revenue law. 2nd ed. London, 1978. pp. 1307,27.

— — Statistics.

INLAND REVENUE STATISTICS; (prepared by the Statistics and Intelligence Division of the Board of Inland Revenue [U.K.]) a., 1970 [1st issue]- London.

— United States.

FELLNER (WILLIAM JOHN) Problems to keep in mind when it comes to tax reform. Washington, [1977]. pp. 26. *(American Enterprise Institute for Public Policy Research. AEI Studies. 167)*

TAX cuts and tax reform: the quest for equity; (an [AEI] Round Table held on February 27, 1978...) John Charles Daly, moderator, etc. Washington, D.C., [1978]. pp. 43. *(American Enterprise Institute for Public Policy Research. Round Tables)*

— — Law.

WOLFMAN (BERNARD) and others. Dissent without opinion: the behavior of Justice William O. Douglas in Federal tax cases. Philadelphia, [1975]. pp. 204. *bibliog.*

TAXATION, EXEMPTION FROM

— Puerto Rico.

PUERTO RICO. Statutes, etc. 1963-68. Industrial Incentive Act of 1963; (with Addenda of amendments up to June 28, 1968). [San Juan, 1963-68]. 1 vol. (various pagings).

TAXATION OF ARTICLES OF CONSUMPTION.

CNOSSEN (SIJBREN) Excise systems: a global study of the selective taxation of goods and services. Baltimore, [1977]. pp. 192. *bibliog.*

TAXATION OF BONDS, SECURITIES, ETC.

— United Kingdom.

ORHNIAL (ANTONY J.H.) and FOLDES (LUCIEN P.) Estimates of marginal tax rates for dividends and bond interest in the United Kingdom 1919-1970. London, 1976. pp. 33. *bibliog. (Papers on Capital and Risk. No. 4)*

TAXICABS

— Hong Kong.

HONG KONG. Transport Department. Research and Development Section. 1977. New Territories taxi availability survey, 1977. [Hong Kong], 1977. 1 vol. (various pagings). *(Studies Reports. No. 77/5)*

TAYLOR (MOSES).

HODAS (DANIEL) The business career of Moses Taylor: merchant, finance capitalist, and industrialist. New York, 1976. pp. 356. *bibliog.*

TEA

— Bangladesh.

REHABILITATION project for the Bangladesh tea industry: report of a Mission financed by the British Overseas Development Ministry. [London, Ministry of Overseas Development], 1977. 3 vols. (in 1). *bibliogs.* Map in end pocket.

— Malawi.

MALAWI. Agro-Economic Survey. 1976. Agro-economic survey: report no. 19: smallholder tea growers in Mulanje; a farm economic survey of smallholder tea growers in the southern part of Mulanje district, Malawi. Lilongwe, 1976. fo. 151.

TEA TRADE.

SINGH (SHAMSHER) and others. Coffee, tea, and cocoa: market prospects and development lending. [Washington], International Bank for Reconstruction and Development, [1977]. pp. 129. *(World Bank Staff Occasional Papers. No. 22.)*

TEACHERS.

COMPARATIVE perspectives on the academic profession; edited by Philip G. Altbach. New York, 1977. pp. 214. *bibliogs.*

— Supply and demand — United Kingdom.

TEACHERS' ACTION COLLECTIVE. Education cuts and teacher unemployment: a strategic analysis. London, [1976]. pp. 15.

— Tenure — United Kingdom.

SAVILLE (JOHN) The Wakstein case at the University of Liverpool. London, [1973]. pp. 12.

— Australia.

AUSTRALIA. Commonwealth Teaching Service. Annual report. a., 1972(1st)- Canberra. *Included in AUSTRALIA. Parliament. [Parliamentary papers].*

— Canada — Salaries, pensions, etc.

CANADA. Statistics Canada. Teachers in universities: salaries related to experience. a., 1972-73/1974-75 to date. Ottawa. *[in English and French]. Supersedes in part CANADA. Statistics Canada. Salaries of teachers in degree granting institutions.*

— France.

NORVEZ (ALAIN) Le corps enseignant et l'évolution démographique: effectifs des enseignants du second degré et besoins futurs; préface d'Alain Girard. [Paris], 1977. pp. 206. *bibliog.(France. Institut National d'Etudes Démographiques. Travaux et Documents. Cahiers. No. 82)*

— Germany.

GERMANY (BUNDESREPUBLIK). Statistisches Bundesamt. Personal an Hochschulen. a., 1976- Wiesbaden. *(Bildung und Kultur. Reihe 4.4.)*

— — Political activity.

KUEPPERS (HEINRICH) Der Katholische Lehrerverband in der Übergangszeit von der Weimarer Republik zur Hitler-Diktatur: zugleich ein Beitrag zur Geschichte des Volksschullehrerstandes. Mainz, [1975]. pp. 201. *bibliog. (Kommission für Zeitgeschichte. Veröffentlichungen. Reihe B: Forschungen. Band 18)*

— Portugal — Salaries, pensions, etc.

CORREIA (HERMINIA GALVÃO) and FIALHO (JOSE ANTONIO SOUSA) Inquerito remunerações no ensino particular, 1970. Lisboa, 1972. pp. 52. *(Portugal. Ministerio das Corporações e Previdência Social. Serviço de Estatistica. Serie Estatistica. 13)* With abstracts in English and French.

— United Kingdom.

RICHARDSON (ELIZABETH) The teacher, the school and the task of management. London, 1973 repr. 1977. pp. 366. *bibliog.*

— — Salaries, pensions, etc.

NATIONAL UNION OF TEACHERS. Salaries Department. The bitter lesson. [No. 1]. Teacher turnover and the London allowance: a sample survey. London, [1973]. pp. 22.

NATIONAL UNION OF TEACHERS. Salaries Department. The bitter lesson. No. 2. The decline in teachers' pay. London, [1973]. pp. 16.

— — Scotland — Salaries, pensions, etc.

SCOTLAND. Arbitral Body on the Salaries of Registered Teachers in Primary and Secondary Schools and Teachers in Further Education Centres, Scotland. 1972. Report. Edinburgh, 1972. pp. 39.

TEACHERS, TRAINING OF

— United Kingdom.

ASSOCIATION OF TEACHERS IN TECHNICAL INSTITUTIONS. Comments of the executive committee on training for the future. London, 1972. pp. 5.

BROCK (MICHAEL) "We must educate our masters". Exeter, 1978. pp. 19. *A public lecture delivered in the University of Exeter on 13 March 1978.*

— United States.

JAROLIMEK (JOHN) Social studies competencies and skills; learning to teach as an intern. New York, [1977]. pp. 272. *bibliog.*

TEACHING

— Bibliography.

DENNIS (HAMLYN) compiler. School learning: a literature survey. [Watford], Engineering Industry Training Board, 1976. pp. 30. *(Library. Literature Survey Series. No. 1976/3)*

TEACHING, FREEDOM OF.

COWEN (DENIS VICTOR) Academic freedom in our time: the rights and responsibilities of students in a modern university. [Durban, 1968]. pp. 26. *(Natal University. E.G. Malherbe Academic Freedom Lectures. 1968)*

KERR (CLARK) Universities: open to truth and to merit. Johannesburg, 1976. pp. 27. *(Johannesburg. University of the Witwatersrand. Chancellors' Lectures. No. 5)*

— United Kingdom.

BACKGROUND papers [to a] conference...[in] 1970 [held by the] Council for Academic Freedom; [by] David Page [and others]. [London, 1970?]. pp. 2,2,4,2.

FREEDOM of speech in tertiary education;...background papers [for] a conference...held in...London...[in] 1974. 1974. pp. 58. *Unpublished: typescript.*

— — Ireland, Northern.

DOWNING (JOHN DEREK HALL) Nothing to hide: the Boehringer case and academic freedom in Northern Ireland. London, [1975?]. pp. 19.

TECHNICAL ASSISTANCE.

UNITED NATIONS. Conference on Trade and Development. 1972. Guidelines for the study of the transfer of technology to developing countries: a study, etc. (TD/B/AC.11/9). New York, 1972. pp. 59. *bibliog.*

STRUGSTAD (OSCAR) Noen tanker om det private naeringslivs rolle i overføringen av teknologi til utviklingslandene. Bergen, 1976. pp. 26. *(Norges Handelshøyskole. Kristofer Lehmkuhl Forelesninger. 1976)*

UNITED NATIONS INDUSTRIAL DEVELOPMENT ORGANIZATION. Development and Transfer of Technology Series. New York, 1977 in progress.

TECHNICAL ASSISTANCE, AMERICAN.

DEMERATH (NICHOLAS JAY) Birth control and foreign policy: the alternatives to family planning. New York, [1976]. pp. 228. *bibliog.*

TECHNICAL ASSISTANCE IN AFRICA

— Bibliography.

AFRICAN BIBLIOGRAPHIC CENTER. Special Bibliographic Series. vol. 1, no. 2. A select bibliographical listing on technical assistance in Africa, 1961-1962. Washington, D.C., 1963. fo. 12.

TECHNICAL EDUCATION

— Australia — Finance.

AUSTRALIA. Department of Education and Science. States Grants (Technical Training) Act 1971: report. a., 1971/72(1st)- Canberra. *Included in AUSTRALIA. Parliament. [Parliamentary papers].*

— Barbados.

BARBADOS. Select Committee on Vocational and Technical Training. 1950. Report...with special reference to the part-time training of apprentices. [Bridgetown, 1950?]. pp. 55.

— Brazil.

OSORIO (IVAN DALL'IGNA) and RAMOS (JOSE HUGO) Rio Grande do Sul: industrialização posta a prova. Pôrto Alegre, 1969. fo. 209. *bibliog.*

— New Zealand.

ADVISORY COUNCIL ON EDUCATIONAL PLANNING [NEW ZEALAND]. Technical and industrial academic awards; report of a working party; [P.L. Laing, chairman]. [Wellington, Government Printer], 1971. pp. 60.

— Nigeria.

THORP (W.H.) and HARLOW (FREDERICK JAMES) Report on a technical college organisation for Nigeria. Lagos, 1950. pp. 46. *(Nigeria. Sessional Papers. 1950. No. 11)*

TECHNICAL EDUCATION (Cont.)

— Rhodesia.

RHODESIA. Commission of Inquiry into Further Education in the Technical and Commercial Fields. 1974. Report...; [John Douglas Cameron, chairman]. [Salisbury], 1974. pp. 30.

— Zambia.

ZAMBIA. Department of Technical Education and Vocational Training. Annual report. a., 1974(2nd)- Lusaka

TECHNICIANS IN INDUSTRY.

CORBETTA (PIERGIORGIO) Tecnici, disoccupazione e coscienza di classe. Bologna, [1975]. pp. 227.

TECHNOLOGICAL FORECASTING.

KUL'BOVSKAIA (NINA KARPOVNA) Prognozirovanie i izmerenie nauchno-tekhnicheskogo progressa. Moskva, 1976. pp. 120. *(Akademiia Nauk SSSR. Problemy Sovetskoi Ekonomiki)*

ASCHER (WILLIAM) Forecasting: an appraisal for policy-makers and planners. Baltimore, [1978]. pp. 239.

JONES (HARRY) b. 1911 and TWISS (BRIAN CHARLES) Forecasting technology for planning decisions. [London, 1978]. pp. 263. *bibliogs.*

TECHNOLOGICAL INNOVATIONS.

CHESTNUT (HAROLD) Influence of technology on modern world evolution and use of dynamic models of macro-economic systems in development planning. Roma, 1976. pp. 61. *Paper read at a conference held at the Accademia Nazionale dei Lincei in Rome in 1972.*

CORIAT (BENJAMIN) Science, technique et capital. Paris, [1976]. pp. 250.

NAUCHNO-tekhnicheskaia revoliutsiia: obshcheteoreticheskie problemy. Moskva, 1976. pp. 207. *bibliog.*

AQUINO (ANTONIO) Technical progress and international specialization in manufactures, 1951-1974. 1977. fo. 373. *bibliog. With two previously published articles by the author. Typescript. Ph.D. (London) thesis: unpublished. This thesis is the property of London University and may not be removed from the Library.*

RESEARCH, technological change, and economic analysis; edited by Bela Gold. Lexington, Mass., [1977]. pp. 240. *bibliogs.*

MEACCI (FERDINANDO) La teoria del capitale e del progresso tecnico. Padova, 1978. pp. 379. *(Padua. Università. Facoltà di Giurisprudenza. Pubblicazioni. 80)*

— Social aspects.

SOTSIOLOGIIA i sovremennost'. Moskva, 1977. 2 vols.

— — Australia.

AUSTRALIA. Department of Labour and National Service. 1970. National survey (of the employment effects of technological change): stage one: textiles, metal products, pulp and paper. Melbourne, 1970. pp. 32. *(Employment and Technology. No. 8)*

AUSTRALIA. Department of Labour and National Service. 1971. National survey of the employment effects of technological change: stage two. Melbourne, 1971. pp. 44. *(Employment and Technology. No. 9)*

AUSTRALIA. Department of Labour and National Service. 1971. National survey of the employment effects of technological change: stage three. Melbourne, 1971. pp. 52. *(Employment and Technology. No.11)*

AUSTRALIA. Department of Labour. 1973. National survey of the employment effects of technological change: stage four. Melbourne, 1973. pp. 53. *(Employment and Technology. No. 14)*

AUSTRALIA. Department of Labour and Immigration. 1974. National survey of the employment effects of technological change: stage five. Melbourne, 1974. pp. 81. *(Employment and Technology. No.15)*

— — Canada — Nova Scotia.

NOVA SCOTIA. Department of Labour. Economics and Research Division. 1967. Technological change provisions in the manufacturing industry in Nova Scotia. Halifax, [1967]. pp. 17.

— — Australia.

AUSTRALIA. Department of Labor and Immigration. 1975. Studies of displacement. Canberra, 1975. pp. 44. *(Employment and Technology. No. 16)*

— — Communist countries.

EKONOMICHESKIE problemy nauchno-tekhnicheskoi revoliutsii pri sotsializme. Moskva, 1975. pp. 263.

PROBLEMY effektivnosti i nauchno-tekhnicheskogo progressa: materialy rabochego soveshchaniia, Sofiia, 22-27 sentiabria 1975 g. Sofiia, 1976. pp. 131.

TECHNOLOGY and communist culture: the socio-cultural impact of technology under socialism; edited by Frederic J. Fleron. New York, 1977. pp. 518. *Papers presented at the conference held at Bellagio in 1975 under the auspices of the American Council of Learned Societies Planning Group on Comparative Communist Studies.*

— — Europe.

MILLER (ROGER EMILE) Entreprises et innovation: étude comparative de seize entreprises sidérurgiques européennes et américaines. Grenoble, 1975. pp. 124. *bibliog.*

— — Germany.

WEBER (WOLFHARD) Innovationen im frühindustriellen deutschen Bergbau und Hüttenwesen: Friedrich Anton von Heynitz. Göttingen, 1976. pp. 309. *bibliog. (Fritz Thyssen Stiftung. Neunzehntes Jahrhundert. Studien zu Naturwissenschaft, Technik und Wirtschaft im Neunzehnten Jahrhundert. Band 6)*

— — Romania.

GHIŢĂ (TĂNASE) Reproducţia socială, cercetarea şi ştiinţa. Bucureşti, 1976. pp. 119. *With English and Russian tables of contents.*

— — Russia.

ALEKSEEV (NIKOLAI SERGEEVICH) Nauchno-tekhnicheskii progress i pravo. Leningrad, 1976. pp. 40. *bibliog.*

IVANOVA (ROZA KONSTANTINOVNA) Nauchno-tekhnicheskaia revoliutsiia i razvitie obshchestvennogo truda v SSSR. Moskva, 1976. pp. 189. *(Akademiia Nauk SSSR. Problemy Sovetskoi Ekonomiki)*

NAUCHNO-tekhnicheskaia revoliutsiia i material'noe proizvodstvo. Leningrad, 1976. pp. 120. *(Leningrad. Universitet. Problemy Istoricheskogo Materializma. vyp.4)*

SHTEINGAUZ (VIKTORIIA GEORGIEVNA) Ekonomicheskie problemy realizatsii nauchno-tekhnicheskikh razrabotok. Moskva, 1976. pp. 136. *(Akademiia Nauk SSSR. Problemy Sovetskoi Ekonomiki)*

HEWER (ULRICH) Zentrale Planung und technischer Fortschritt: Probleme seiner Organisation und Durchsetzung am Beispiel der sowjetischen Industrie. Berlin, 1977. pp. 225. *bibliog. (Giessen. Universität. Zentrum für Kontinentale Agrar- und Wirtschaftsforschung. Giessener Abhandlungen zur Agrar- und Wirtschaftsforschung des Europäischen Ostens. Band 84) With English summary.*

LUSHCHIK (IVAN ALEKSEEVICH) Nauchno-tekhnicheskaia revoliutsiia i obobshchestvlenie proizvodstva. L'vov, 1977. pp. 178. *bibliog.*

— — United States.

MILLER (ROGER EMILE) Entreprises et innovation: étude comparative de seize entreprises sidérurgiques européennes et américaines. Grenoble, 1975. pp. 124. *bibliog.*

TECHNOLOGY.

AD HOC MEETING OF EXPERTS ON THE ROLE OF ADVANCED SKILLS AND TECHNOLOGIES IN INDUSTRIAL DEVELOPMENT. NEW YORK, 1967. Planning for advanced skills and technologies: studies presented at the Ad Hoc Meeting...New York, 22-29 May 1967. (ID/SER.E/3). New York, United Nations, 1969. pp. 225. *(United Nations Industrial Development Organization. Industrial Planning and Programming Series. No.3)*

— History — United States.

AMERICA's wooden age: aspects of its early technology; edited by Brooke Hindle. Tarrytown, [1975]. pp. 218. *bibliog.*

— Information services.

ORGANISATION FOR ECONOMIC COOPERATION AND DEVELOPMENT. Information Policy Group. 1974. Ireland. Paris, 1974. pp. 82. *(Reviews of National Scientific and Technical Information Policy. [No. 2])*

ORGANISATION FOR ECONOMIC COOPERATION AND DEVELOPMENT. Information Policy Group. 1974. Spain. Paris, 1974. pp. 170. *bibliog. (Reviews of National Scientific and Technical Information Policy. [No.3])*

— Philosophy.

The DYNAMICS of science and technology: social values, technical norms and scientific criteria in the development of knowledge; edited by Wolfgang Krohn [and others]. Dordrecht, [1978]. pp. 293.

— Social aspects.

BECK (ANATOLE) The technological society. [College Park, Md., 1972?]. fo. 21.

FERRARI (LEO C.) Human rights in a changing world; the problem of preserving human values in the upheavals caused by science and technology. Fredericton, New Brunswick Human Rights Commission, 1975. pp. 112.

CHESTNUT (HAROLD) Influence of technology on modern world evolution and use of dynamic models of macro-economic systems in development planning. Roma, 1976. pp. 61. *Paper read at a conference held by the Accademia Nazionale dei Lincei in Rome in 1972.*

EULAU (HEINZ) Technology and civility: the skill revolution in politics. Stanford, Calif., [1977]. pp. 111. *(Stanford University. Hoover Institution on War, Revolution and Peace. Hoover Institution Publications. 167)*

GEORGE (FRANK HONYWILL) Machine takeover: the growing threat to human freedom in a computer-controlled society. Oxford, 1977. pp. 193. *bibliog.*

LOVINS (AMORY BLOCH) Soft energy paths: towards a durable peace. Harmondsworth, 1977. pp. 231.

NAUCHNO-tekhnicheskaia revoliutsiia, chelovek, ego prirodnaia i sotsial'naia sreda. Leningrad, 1977. pp. 216.

WORLD CONGRESS OF SOCIOLOGY, 8TH, 1974. Scientific-technological revolution: social aspects, with contributions by Ralf Dahrendorf [and others]. London, [1977]. pp. 181. *bibliogs. Papers presented in the first plenary session of the Eighth World Congress of Sociology, held in Toronto in 1974.*

The DYNAMICS of science and technology: social values, technical norms and scientific criteria in the development of knowledge; edited by Wolfgang Krohn [and others]. Dordrecht, [1978]. pp. 293.

— Africa, Subsaharan.

NATIONAL RESEARCH COUNCIL Recommendations for strengthening science and technology in selected areas of Africa south of the Sahara; [prepared for the International Cooperation Administration]. Washington, 1959. pp. 108,12. *bibliog.*

— **European Economic Community countries.**

EUROPEAN COMMUNITIES. Commission. 1977. Common policy in the field of science and technology: communication...to the Council of 30 June 1977. [Luxembourg], 1977. pp. 62. *(Bulletin of the European Communities. Supplements. [1977/3])*

— **Germany.**

LITTLE (ARTHUR D.) INCORPORATED. New technology-based firms in the United Kingdom and the Federal Republic of Germany: a report prepared for the Anglo-German Foundation for the Study of Industrial Society. [London], 1977. pp. 323.

— **Russia.**

SOVIET science and technology: domestic and foreign perspectives; edited by John R. Thomas and Ursula M. Kruse-Vaucienne. Washington, D.C., [1977]. pp. 455. *Based on a workshop held at Airlie House, Virginia, 1976.*

The TECHNOLOGICAL level of Soviet industry; edited by Ronald Amann [and others]. New Haven, 1977. pp. 575. *Essays prepared by an inter-university group of scholars based on the Centre for Russian and East European Studies, University of Birmingham.*

— **Underdeveloped areas.**

See UNDERDEVELOPED AREAS — Technology.

— **United Kingdom.**

LITTLE (ARTHUR D.) INCORPORATED. New technology-based firms in the United Kingdom and the Federal Republic of Germany: a report prepared for the Anglo-German Foundation for the Study of Industrial Society. [London], 1977. pp. 323.

TECHNOLOGY AND CIVILIZATION.

DUPUY (JEAN PIERRE) and ROBERT (JEAN) La trahison de l'opulence. [Paris, 1976]. pp. 256. *bibliog.*

KAHN (HERMAN) and others. The next 200 years: a scenario for America and the world. New York, 1976. pp. 241. *bibliog.*

SMALL comforts for hard times: humanists on public policy; Michael Mooney and Florian Stuber, editors. New York, 1977. pp. 402. *Papers from a conference series conducted under the auspices of Columbia's program of University Seminars.*

TECHNOLOGY AND ETHICS.

BALLARD (EDWARD GOODWIN) Man and technology: toward the measurement of a culture. Pittsburgh, [1978]. pp. 251.

TECHNOLOGY AND LAW.

ALEKSEEV (NIKOLAI SERGEEVICH) Nauchno-tekhnicheskii progress i pravo. Leningrad, 1976. pp. 40. *bibliog.*

TECHNOLOGY AND STATE.

EULAU (HEINZ) Technology and civility: the skill revolution in politics. Stanford, Calif., [1977]. pp. 111. *(Stanford University. Hoover Institution on War, Revolution and Peace. Hoover Institution Publications. 167)*

SCIENCE and technology policy: perspectives and developments; edited by Joseph Haberer. Lexington, Mass., [1977]. pp. 216. *(Policy Studies Organization. Policy Studies Organization Series. 14)*

— **Europe — Citizen participation.**

NELKIN (DOROTHY) Technological decisions and democracy: European experiments in public participation. Beverly Hills, [1977]. pp. 110. *bibliog.*

— **India.**

SRINIVAS (MYSORE NARASIMHACHAR) Science, technology and rural development in India. [Poona], 1977. pp. 15. *(Gokhale Institute of Politics and Economics. R.R. Kale Memorial Lectures. 1977)*

— **United Kingdom.**

CLARKE (Sir RICHARD WILLIAM BARNES) Mintech in retrospect - I. Oxford, 1973. pp. 40. *bibliog. Reprinted from Omega, vol. 1. no.1, 1973.*

— **United States.**

KILLIAN (JAMES RHYNE) Sputnik, scientists, and Eisenhower: a memoir of the first special assistant to the President for science and technology. Cambridge, [1977]. pp. 315. *bibliog.*

KATZ (JAMES EVERETT) Presidential politics and science policy. New York, 1978. pp. 292. *bibliog.*

TECHNOLOGY TRANSFER.

UNITED NATIONS. Conference on Trade and Development. 1972. Guidelines for the study of the transfer of technology to developing countries: a study, etc. (TD/B/AC.11/9). New York, 1972. pp. 59. *bibliog.*

HAYDEN (ERIC W.) Technology transfer to East Europe: U.S. corporate experience. New York, 1976. pp. 134. *bibliog.*

TEECE (DAVID J.) The multinational corporation and the resource cost of international technology transfer. Cambridge, Mass., [1976]. pp. 129. *bibliog.*

UNITED NATIONS INDUSTRIAL DEVELOPMENT ORGANIZATION. Development and Transfer of Technology Series. New York, 1977 in progress.

EL MILIGI (IBRAHIM SAAD) National policies for computer applications in developing countries: a case study of the Sudan. 1977. fo. 317. *bibliog. Typescript. Ph.D. (London) thesis: unpublished. This thesis is the property of London University and may not be removed from the Library.*

JEDLICKA (ALLEN D.) Organization for rural development: risk taking and appropriate technology. New York, 1977. pp. 170.

RONSTADT (ROBERT) Research and development abroad by U.S. multinationals. New York, [1977]. pp. 127.

— **Europe.**

UDIS (BERNARD) From guns to butter: technology organizations and reduced military spending in western Europe. Cambridge, Mass., [1978]. pp. 368.

TEESDORF

— **Economic history.**

KORP (ANDREAS) Der Konsumverein Teesdorf: ein Beitrag sur Frühgeschichte des österreichischen Genossenschaftswesens. Wien, [1977]. pp. 56. *bibliog.*

TEESSIDE

— **Social policy.**

BATLEY (RICHARD) and others. An evaluation of two neighbourhood schems in Liverpool and Teesside. Leeds, [1975?]. fo. 96. *(Centre for Environmental Studies. Working Papers)*

TELECOMMUNICATION

— **Australia.**

AUSTRALIA. Post Office. Post Office prospects and capital programme. a., 1968/69(1st)- Canberra. *Included in AUSTRALIA. Parliament. [Parliamentary papers].*

— **Europe.**

JEQUIER (NICOLAS) Les télécommunications et l'Europe. Lausanne, 1976. pp. 118. *(Lausanne. Université. Centre de Recherches Européennes. Publications. 6. Etudes Sectorielles)*

— **France — Apparatus and supplies.**

FRANCE. Groupe sectoriel d'Analyse et de Prévision Biens d'Equipement Electronique, Informatique et Télécommunications. 1976. Rapport...: préparation du 7e Plan. Paris, [1976]. pp. 62.

— **Netherlands.**

OTTENHEIJM (G.C.J.J.) De status van de PTT als staatsbedrijf in historisch perspectief. Den Haag, Staatsbedrijf der Posterijen, Telegrafie en Telefonie, 1974. pp. 179. *bibliogs. (Geschiedkundige Uitgaven. 4)*

— **Nigeria.**

NIGERIAN EXTERNAL TELECOMMUNICATIONS LIMITED. Annual report. a., 1963/64(1st)- , with gaps. Lagos.

— **South Africa — Accounting.**

SOUTH AFRICA. Parliament. House of Assembly. Select Committee on Posts and Telecommunications. 1977. Report...proceedings and evidence (S.C.3-1977). in SOUTH AFRICA. Parliament. House of Assembly. Select Committee reports.

— **United States — Employees.**

BROOKS (THOMAS R.) Communications workers of America: the story of a union. New York, 1977. pp. 257. *bibliog.*

TELEGRAPH

— **Scandinavia — Rates.**

[SCANDINAVIA]. Nordiske Parlamentariske Komité for Friere Samfaerdsel. 1954-55. Betaenkning om posttakster i den internordiske udveksling af breve: og Betaenkning om takstsaetningen i den internordiske teletrafik. København, 1954-55. 2 pts. *(Denmark. Betaenkninger. Nr. 105, 118) Title of part 2 reads Betaenkning om posttakster i den internordiske udveksling af korsbandsforsendelser, etc.*

TELEOLOGY.

MAKAROV (MIKHAIL GEORGIEVICH) Kategoriia "tsel'" v marksistskoi filosofii i kritika teleologii. Leningrad, 1977. pp. 188.

TELEVISION

— **United States — Psychological aspects.**

BELSON (WILLIAM A.) Television violence and the adolescent boy. Farnborough, Hants., [1978]. pp. 529.

TELEVISION ADVERTISING.

BARNOUW (ERIK) The sponsor: notes on a modern potentate. New York, 1978. pp. 220.

BARCUS (FRANCIS EARLE) Children's television: an analysis of programming and advertising; (with Rachel Wolkin). New York, 1977. pp. 218.

PALETZ (DAVID L.) and others. Politics in public service advertising on television. New York, 1977. pp. 123.

TELEVISION AND CHILDREN.

HARPER (D.) and others. Social and personality factors associated with childrens' tastes in television viewing: summary of study. London, [1974]. fo. 13.

BARCUS (FRANCIS EARLE) Children's television: an analysis of programming and advertising; (with Rachel Wolkin). New York, 1977. pp. 218.

DUNN (GWEN) The box in the corner: television and the under-fives: a study. London, 1977. pp. 160. *bibliog.*

MARPLAN LIMITED. Children of the box. [London, 1978?]. fo. 11, 8.

TELEVISION AND YOUTH.

TELEVISION AND YOUTH.

BELSON (WILLIAM A.) Television violence and the adolescent boy. Farnborough, Hants., [1978]. pp. 529.

TELEVISION AUDIENCES

— United Kingdom.

ASSOCIATED TELEVISION. Media and Marketing Surveys. 4. Media and marketing survey of the London T.V. area. London, [1960]. pp. 158.

ASSOCIATED TELEVISION. Media and Marketing Surveys. 5. Media and marketing survey of the Midlands T.V. area; prepared for Associated Television Limited. London, [1960]. pp. 192.

HARPER (D.) and others. Social and personality factors associated with childrens' tastes in television viewing: summary of study. London, [1974]. fo. 13.

TELEVISION BROADCASTING

— Social aspects — United States.

BARNOUW (ERIK) The sponsor: notes on a modern potentate. New York, 1978. pp. 220.

— New Zealand.

SCEATS (LIONEL RALPH) A look to N[ew] Z[ealand] B[roadcasting] C[orporation] 's future role: a transcription of a news conference given by Lionel Sceats, Director-General designate of the NZBC, May 28th 1970. [Wellington], New Zealand Broadcasting Corporation, 1970. pp. (10).

— United Kingdom.

INDEPENDENT BROADCASTING AUTHORITY. IBA notes. irreg., Oc 1963 - Jl 1974 (2 - 29), with gaps (4,5,14); ceased pbln. London.

NEWBY (PERCY HOWARD) Broadcasting: a professional view. [London, 1977]. pp. 14. *(London. University. Birkbeck College. Haldane Memorial Lectures. 40)*

— — Ireland, Northern.

FRANCIS (RICHARD) Broadcasting to a community in conflict: the experience in Northern Ireland. [London], 1977. pp. 16.

TELEVISION BROADCASTING OF NEWS

— United Kingdom.

SCHLESINGER (PHILIP RONALD) Putting "reality" together: BBC news. London, 1978. pp. 303. bibliog.

TELEVISION IN HIGHER EDUCATION

— Italy.

DELL'ACQUA (CESARE) Università, televisione e decentramento regionale: profili costituzionale e organizzativi. Napoli, 1974. pp. 157.

TELEVISION IN POLITICS.

BLUMLER (JAY G.) and others. The challenge of election broadcasting. Leeds, 1978. pp. 91. bibliog. *Report of an enquiry by the Centre for Television Research, University of Leeds.*

— United Kingdom.

TRACEY (MICHAEL) The production of political television. London, 1977[or rather 1978]. pp. 283. bibliog.

TELEVISION INDUSTRY

— United Kingdom.

THOMSON ORGANISATION. The Thomson Organisation in Great Britain; [including a statement of Roy Thomson circulated with the report and accounts for the year ended 31 December, 1959]. [London, 1960]. pp. 32.

TELEVISION PROGRAMMES

— United States.

BARNOUW (ERIK) The sponsor: notes on a modern potentate. New York, 1978. pp. 220.

TELEVISION PROGRAMMES, PUBLIC SERVICE.

GIBSON (GEORGE H.) 1932- . Public broadcasting: the role of the federal government, 1912-76. New York, [1977]. pp. 236.

TELEVISION PROGRAMMES FOR CHILDREN

— United States.

BARCUS (FRANCIS EARLE) Children's television: an analysis of programming and advertising; (with Rachel Wolkin). New York, 1977. pp. 218.

TENENTISMO.

DANTAS (JOSE IBARÊ COSTA) O tenentismo em Sergipe: da revolta de 1924 a revolução de 1930. Petropolis, 1974. pp. 252. bibliog.

SANTA ROSA (VIRGINIO) O sentido do tenentismo. São Paulo, 1976. pp. 127. *Reprint, with new preface, of work first published in 1933.*

TENNESSEE VALLEY AUTHORITY

— Officials and employees.

BROOKSHIRE (MICHAEL L.) and ROGERS (MICHAEL D.) Collective bargaining in public employment: the TVA experience. Lexington, Mass., [1977]. pp. 245.

TERENO INDIANS.

OLIVEIRA (ROBERTO CARDOSO DE) Do indio ao bugre: o processo de assimilação dos Terêna. Rio de Janeiro, 1976. pp. 149. bibliog. *Reprint of O processo de assimilação dos Terêna, published in 1960, with new preface.*

TERNI.

— Industries.

BONELLI (FRANCO) Lo sviluppo di una grande impresa in Italia: la Terni dal 1884 al 1962. [Torino, 1975]. pp. 360. bibliog.

TERNI (FIRM).

BONELLI (FRANCO) Lo sviluppo di una grande impresa in Italia: la Terni dal 1884 al 1962. [Torino, 1975]. pp. 360. bibliog.

TERRITORIAL WATERS

— Laws and legislation.

FOOD AND AGRICULTURE ORGANIZATION. Legislative Series. No. 8. Limits and status of the territorial sea, exclusive fishing zones, fishery conservation zones and the continental shelf, with particular reference to fisheries. Rome, 1969. pp. 32.

TERRORISM.

PARRY (ALBERT) Terrorism from Robespierre to Arafat. New York, [1976]. pp. 624. bibliog.

LEACH (Sir EDMUND RONALD) Custom, law and terrorist violence. Edinburgh, 1977. pp. 37. *(Edinburgh. University. Munro Lectures on Anthropology and Prehistoric Archaeology. 1977)*

ROCK (MARTIN) Anarchismus und Terror: Ursprünge und Strategien. Trier, 1977. pp. 105.

BELL (J. BOWYER) A time of terror: how democratic societies respond to revolutionary violence. New York, [1978]. pp. 292. bibliog.

CLUTTERBUCK (RICHARD LEWIS) Kidnap and ransom: the response. London, [1978]. pp. 192. bibliog.

— East (Near East).

JUREIDINI (PAUL A.) and HAZEN (WILLIAM EDWARD) The Palestinian movement in politics. Lexington, Mass., [1976]. pp. 139. bibliog.

PALESTINIAN impasse: Arab guerrillas and international terror; edited by Lester A. Sobel. New York, [1977]. pp. 282. *Based on records compiled by Facts on File.*

— Germany.

BECKER (JILLIAN) Hitler's children: the story of the Baader-Meinhof terrorist gang. Philadelphia, [1977]. pp. 322. bibliog.

— Italy.

ROSSO (SOCCORSO) Brigate Rosse: che cosa hanno fatto, che cosa hanno detto, che cosa se ne è detto. Milano, 1976. pp. 294.

— Rhodesia.

RHODESIA. Special Court. 1975. Judgement: a judgement concerning the necessity or expediency of continuing the detention of the reverend Ndabaningi Sithole who was the subject of a detention order issued on the 3rd day of March, 1975, [given] 2nd April, 1975. [Salisbury], 1975. pp. 34. *(Rhodesia. Ministry of Information, Immigration and Tourism. For the Record. No. 24)*

RHODESIA. Ministry of Information, Immigration and Tourism. 1976. Harvest of fear: a diary of terrorist atrocities in Rhodesia. [Salisbury, 1976]. pp. 31.

— United Kingdom — Ireland, Northern.

CONNOLLY (COLM) Herrema: siege at Monasterevin. Dublin, [1977]. pp. 116.

EVELEGH (ROBIN) Peace keeping in a democratic society: the lessons of Northern Ireland. London, [1978]. pp. 174.

TESOS

— Social life and customs.

KARP (IVAN) Fields of change among the Iteso of Kenya. London, [1978]. pp. 186. bibliog.

TEUTONIC RACE.

BRYN (HALFDAN) Der nordische Mensch: die Merkmale der nordischen Rasse mit besonderer Berücksichtigung der rassischen Verhältnisse Norwegens. München, 1929. pp. 166. bibliog.

TEXAS

— Race question.

WOOLFOLK (GEORGE RUBLE) The free negro in Texas, 1800-1860: a study in cultural compromise. Ann Arbor, 1976. pp. 240. bibliog.

— Social conditions.

WOOLFOLK (GEORGE RUBLE) The free negro in Texas, 1800-1860: a study in cultural compromise. Ann Arbor, 1976. pp. 240. bibliog.

TEXTBOOKS

— United Kingdom.

PUBLISHERS' ASSOCIATION. Educational Group. Schoolbook Expenditure Committee. Schoolbook expenditure. London, 1969. pp. 15.

TEXTILE FIBRES, SYNTHETIC

— Mediterranean.

INDUSTRIE des fibres synthétiques: délocalisation en Méditerranée: conséquences pour Fos-Etang de Berre; [by] Yvon le Moal and others'. (Marseille), (Organisation d'Etudes d'A menagement de L'Aire Metropolitaine Provence-Côte d'Azur), 1973. FO.94. bibliog.

TEXTILE INDUSTRY AND FABRICS.

INTERNATIONAL FEDERATION OF COTTON AND ALLIED TEXTILE INDUSTRIES. Directory. 7th ed. Zürich, 1975. pp. 44.

— Canada — Bibliography.

LYN (D.E.) and McDONALD (L.) compilers. A selective bibliography on the clothing and textile industry in Canada. [Toronto], Ontario Ministry of Labour Research Library, 1973. fo. 5.

— India.

MEHTA (RATILAL) The story of Khadi. Bombay, Directorate of Publicity and People's Education, Khadi and Village Industries Commission, 1974. pp. 39.

— Italy.

SULL'industria tessile: interventi di Franco Rivolta [and others]; prefazione e cura di Giuseppe Turani. Milano, 1976. pp. 279.

— United States.

GREGORY (FRANCES W.) Nathan Appleton, merchant and entrepreneur, 1779-1861. Charlottesville, Va., 1975. pp. 358. bibliog.

— Zambia.

ZAMBIA. Central Statistical Office. 1975. Textile, wearing apparel and leather industries. Lusaka, 1975. pp. 61. bibliog. (Industry Monographs. No. 2)

TEXTILE WORKERS

— Belgium.

De GENTSE textielarbeiders in de 19e. en 20e. eeuw; [by] G. Avondts [and others]. Brussel, [1976]. 3 vols. (in 1). bibliogs.

— Canada — Nova Scotia.

NOVA SCOTIA. Department of Labour. Economics and Research Division. 1967. Cosmos Imperial Mills: a case study in labour force recruitment and training. [Halifax, 1967]. pp. 12.

— United Kingdom.

SEARBY (PETER) Coventry in crisis 1858-1863: ribbon factory, free trade and strike. Coventry, 1977. pp. 17. bibliog. (Historical Association. Coventry Branch. Coventry and Warwickshire History Pamphlets. No. 10)

THAELMANN (ERNST).

THAELMANN (ERNST) Zwischen Erinnerung und Erwartung: autobiografische Aufzeichnungen, geschrieben in faschistischer Haft, etc. Frankfurt am Main, [1977]. pp. 111. bibliog.

THAILAND

— Commerce — China.

VIRAPHOL (SARASIN) Tribute and profit: Sino-Siamese trade, 1652-1853. Cambridge, Mass., 1977. pp. 419. bibliog. (Harvard University. East Asian Research Center. Harvard East Asian Monographs. 76)

— Economic conditions.

TRENDS in Thailand II: proceedings with background and commentary papers [of a seminar held in 1976 organized by the Institute of Southeast Asian Studies]; edited by Somporn Sangchai and Lim Joo-Jock. Singapore, [1976]. pp. 164.

DONNER (WOLF) The five faces of Thailand: an economic geography. London, [1978]. pp. 930. bibliog.

— Economic policy.

THAILAND DEVELOPMENT REPORT; [pd. by the Information Bureau, Office of the Under-Secretary of State, Ministry of National Development, Thailand]. irreg., Ap 1966 (v.1, no.1)- Bangkok.

— Executive departments.

BUNNAG (TEJ) The provincial administration of Siam, 1892-1915: the Ministry of the Interior under Prince Damrong Rajanubhab. Kuala Lumpur, 1977. pp. 322. bibliog.

— Foreign relations.

FOREIGN AFFAIRS BULLETIN; [pd. by] Information Department, Ministry of Foreign Affairs...Thailand. bi-m., Ag/S 1969 (v.9, no.1)- Bangkok.

TRENDS in Thailand II: proceedings with background and commentary papers [of a seminar held in 1976 organized by the Institute of Southeast Asian Studies]; edited by Somporn Sangchai and Lim Joo-Jock. Singapore, [1976]. pp. 164.

— History.

ELLIOTT (DAVID) Thailand: origins of military rule. London, [1978]. pp. 190. bibliog.

— Politics and government.

TRENDS in Thailand II: proceedings with background and commentary papers [of a seminar held in 1976 organized by the Institute of Southeast Asian Studies]; edited by Somporn Sangchai and Lim Joo-Jock. Singapore, [1976]. pp. 164.

ELLIOTT (DAVID) Thailand: origins of military rule. London, [1978]. pp. 190. bibliog.

— Rural conditions.

MURRAY (CHARLES A.) A behavioral study of rural modernization: social and economic change in Thai villages. New York, 1977. pp. 133. bibliog.

— Social conditions.

TRENDS in Thailand II: proceedings with background and commentary papers [of a seminar held in 1976 organized by the Institute of Southeast Asian Studies]; edited by Somporn Sangchai and Lim Joo-Jock. Singapore, [1976]. pp. 164.

THAMES, RIVER.

EAST London river crossing study; report of the Steering Group. [London], Greater London Council, 1975. pp. 32, fo.(11).

— Bridges — Bibliography.

HAMLYN (PENNY) compiler. Thames bridges in the Greater London area. 2nd ed. London, 1976. pp. 22. (London. Greater London Council. Research Library. [Research] Bibliographies. No. 45)

THATCHER (MARGARET).

COSGRAVE (PATRICK) Margaret Thatcher: a Tory and her party. London, 1978. pp. 224.

THEATRE AND STATE

— Netherlands.

PROLOOG en de overheiden: een voorbeeld van konfessionele politiek; samenstelling: Jan Smeets en Richard van Dijk. Den Bosch, 1974. pp. 44.

THEOLOGY.

GILL (ROBIN) Theology and social structure. London, 1977. pp. 153.

— 20th century.

SIMON (ULRICH) Sitting in judgement, 1913-1963: an interpretation of history. London, 1978. pp. 166.

THEORY (PHILOSOPHY).

CAUSEY (ROBERT L.) Unity of science. Dordrecht, [1977]. pp. 185. bibliog.

ON critical theory; John O' Neill, editor. London, 1977. pp. 265.

THERAPEUTIC COMMUNITY.

SUGARMAN (BARRY) Daytop village: a therapeutic community. New York, [1974]. pp. 134. bibliog.

THINGS (LAW)

— Netherlands.

PITLO (A.) and BOLWEG (M.F.H.J.) Het zakenrecht naar het Nederlands Burgerlijk Wetboek. 6th ed. Groningen, 1972. pp. 528.

THOMAS (FRANCIS).

THOMAS (FRANCIS) Memoirs of a migrant. Singapore, 1972. pp. 145.

THORNETT (ALAN).

JOHNS (STEPHEN) Victimization at Cowley. London, 1974. pp. 111. (Workers' Revolutionary Party. Pocket Library. No. 11)

THOUGHT AND THINKING.

ANDERSON (JOHN ROBERT) Language, memory, and thought. New York, [1976]. pp. 546. bibliogs.

THINKING: readings in cognitive science; edited by P.N. Johnson- Laird and P.C. Wason. Cambridge, [1977]. pp. 615. bibliog.

TICINO

— Emigration and immigration.

MONDADA (GIUSEPPE) Commerci e commercianti di Campo Valmaggia nel Settecento, dalle lettere dei Pedrazzini e di altri conterranei attivi in Germania e in Italia. Lugano, 1977. pp. 247.

TIDAL POWER.

U.K. Department of Energy. 1977. Tidal power barrages in the Severn estuary: recent evidence on their feasibility. London, 1977. pp. 19. bibliog. (Energy Papers. No. 23)

TIETGEN (CARL FREDERIK).

SCHOVELIN (JULIUS) Tidens Hjul og Tietgen, 1857-1897. København, 1929. pp. 671.

TIMBER

— Sri Lanka.

SRI LANKA. Committee of Inquiry on the Establishment of the Wood Working Complex and the Proposals to Exploit the Sinharaja Forest. 1975. Report; [G. Rajapakse, chairman]. Colombo, 1975. pp. 94. (Sri Lanka. Parliament. Sessional Papers. 1974. No. 15)

TIME AND ECONOMIC REACTIONS.

MELANGES offerts à Henri Guitton: le temps en économie, les mathématiques et l'économie, recherches pluridisciplinaires. [Paris, 1976]. pp. 503. bibliog.

BRESSON (YOLAND) Le capital-temps: pouvoir, répartition et inégalités. [Paris, 1977]. pp. 218.

RAMB (BERND THOMAS) Zeitentwicklungsanalyse: eine ökonometrische Methode für die Untersuchung der zeitlichen Entwicklung makroökonomischer Zusammenhänge, etc. Berlin, [1977]. pp. 241. bibliog.

TIME SERIES ANALYSIS

— Methodology.

CHATFIELD (CHRISTOPHER) The analysis of time series: theory and practice. London, 1975 repr. 1978. pp. 263. bibliog.

TIMOR

— History.

JOLLIFE (JILL) East Timor: nationalism and colonialism. St. Lucia, Queensland, [1978]. pp. 362.

TIN.

TIN.

INTERNATIONAL TIN COMMITTEE. International tin control and buffer stocks. London, [1944?]. pp. 38.

— Congresses.

UNITED NATIONS. Tin Conference, Geneva, 1970. Summary of proceedings [of the conference held at Geneva, 13 April to 15 May, 1970]. (TD/TIN.4/7/Rev.1). New York, 1970. pp. 31.

TIN INDUSTRY.

ALLEN (H.W.) How the tin agreement works. London, [1971]. pp. 6. *(Reprinted from Tin International November 1971)*

TITMUSS (RICHARD MORRIS).

REISMAN (DAVID ALEXANDER) Richard Titmuss: welfare and society. London, 1977. pp. 192.

TITO (JOSIP BROZ).

DRASKOVICH (SLOBODAN M.) Tito, Moscow's Trojan horse. Chicago, 1957. pp. 357.

BOROWIEC (ANDREW) Yugoslavia after Tito. New York, 1977. pp. 122. *bibliog.*

TKACHEV (PETR NIKITICH).

HARDY (DEBORAH) Petr Tkachev, the critic as Jacobin. Seattle, [1977]. pp. 339. *bibliog. (Washington State University. Institute for Comparative and Foreign Area Studies. Publications on Russia and Eastern Europe. No. 8)*

TOBACCO

— Australia.

AUSTRALIA. Bureau of Agricultural Economics. 1976. The Australian tobacco growing industry: report on an economic survey 1970-71 to 1972-73. Canberra, 1976. pp. 154.

— Netherlands.

ROESSINGH (HENDRIK KAREL) Inlandse tabak: expansie en contractie van een handelsgewas in de 17e en 18e eeuw in Nederland. Zutphen, 1976. pp. 594. *bibliog.*

TOBACCO MANUFACTURE AND TRADE

— Australia.

AUSTRALIA. Bureau of Agricultural Economics. 1976. Labour and technology in the Australian tobacco growing industry. Canberra, 1976. pp. 95. *bibliog. (Industry Economics Monographs. No. 16)*

— United Kingdom.

FOOD, DRINK AND TOBACCO INDUSTRY TRAINING BOARD [U.K.]. The Board's views on Training for vital skills. Gloucester, 1976. pp. 2. *(FDT News. Special Issues. November 1976)*

— Zambia.

ZAMBIA. Central Statistical Office. 1975. Food, beverages and tobacco industries. Lusaka, 1975. fo. 67. *bibliog. (Industry Monographs. No. 1)*

TOBACCO WORKERS

— Australia.

AUSTRALIA. Bureau of Agricultural Economics. 1976. Labour and technology in the Australian tobacco growing industry. Canberra, 1976. pp. 95. *bibliog. (Industry Economics Monographs. No. 16)*

— India.

INDIA. Labour Bureau. 1971. Report on survey of labour conditions in bidi factories in India, 1965-66. [Delhi, 1971]. pp. 73.

TOGLIATTI (PALMIRO).

GRANDI (BLASCO) Togliatti y los suyos en España. Madrid, 1954. pp. 45.

TOGLIATTI e il comunismo antirivoluzionario; a cura di Benedetto Spriola. Roma, [1975]. pp. 143. *bibliog.*

PARTITO DI UNITÀ PROLETARIA PER IL COMUNISMO. Federazione Milanese. Gruppo di Lavoro Teoria e Controinformazione. Convegno, Maggio 1975. Da Togliatti alla nuova sinistra: (atti). [Roma, 1976]. pp. 290.

SPALLONE (MARIO) Vent'anni con Togliatti. Milano, [1976]. pp. 165.

TOGO

— Population.

LUCIEN-BRUN (B.) La colonisation des terres neuves du Centre-Togo par les Kabrè et les Losso. [Bondy], Office de la Recherche Scientifique et Technique Outre-Mer, [1974]. fo. 293. *bibliog. Maps in end pocket.*

— Rural conditions.

LUCIEN-BRUN (B.) La colonisation des terres neuves du Centre-Togo par les Kabrè et les Losso. [Bondy], Office de la Recherche Scientifique et Technique Outre-Mer, [1974]. fo. 293. *bibliog. Maps in end pocket.*

TOKYO ROUND, 1973-1977.

CLINE (WILLIAM R.) and others. Trade negotiations in the Tokyo Round: a quantitative assessment. Washington, D.C., [1978]. pp. 314.

TOLEDO (PROVINCE)

— Rural conditions.

WEISSER (MICHAEL R.) The peasants of the Montes: (the roots of rural rebellion in Spain). Chicago, 1976. pp. 143.

TOLERATION.

MURA (VIRGILIO) Cattolici e liberali nell'età giolittiana: il dibattito sulla toleranza. [Bari, 1976]. pp. 271.

TOLL BRIDGES

— United Kingdom — Ireland.

LONDONDERRY BRIDGE TRUST. Report of the trustees of the Londonderry Bridge. Londonderry, 1852. pp. 13.

TONGA

— Economic policy.

TONGA. Central Planning Office. 1976. Third development plan 1975-1980: policy objectives, programmes and strategies for social and economic progress. Nuku'alofa, 1976. pp. 421. *bibliog.*

— Social policy.

TONGA. Central Planning Office. 1976. Third development plan 1975-1980: policy objectives, programmes and strategies for social and economic progress. Nuku'alofa, 1976. pp. 421. *bibliog.*

TONGANS.

LEMAÎTRE (YVES) Les relations inter-insulaires traditionnelles en Océanie (Tonga): premières données sur l'application d'une méthode mathématique. Paris, [1964?]. fo. 15. *bibliog. (Paris. Ecole Pratique des Hautes Etudes. Centre Documentaire pour l'Océanie. Rapports et Documents. 2)*

TOPOLOGY.

LIPSCHUTZ (SEYMOUR) Schaum's outline of theory and problems of general topology. New York, [1965]. pp. 239.

EISENBERG (MURRAY) Topology. New York, [1974]. pp. 427. *bibliog.*

THOM (RENÉ) Structural stability and morphogenesis: an outline of a general theory of models; translated...by D.H. Fowler. Reading, Mass., 1975. pp. 348.

AUBIN (JEAN PIERRE) Applied abstract analysis; translated by Carole Labrousse. New York, [1977]. pp. 263.

TORNAU (FEDOR FEDOROVICH).

DZIDZARIIA (GEORGII ALEKSEEVICH) F.F. Tornau i ego kavkazskie materialy. Moskva, 1976. pp. 130. *bibliog.*

TORONTO

— Politics and government.

ONTARIO. Royal Commission on Metropolitan Toronto. 1977. Report...; John P. Robarts, commissioner. [Toronto], 1977. 2 vols.(in 1)

— Social conditions.

MAXWELL (THOMAS R.) The invisible French: the French in metropolitan Toronto. [Waterloo, Ont., 1977]. pp. 174. *bibliog.*

TORRE (LISANDRO DE LA).

TORRE (LISANDRO DE LA) Las dos campañas presidenciales, 1916-1931. Buenos Aires, 1939. pp. 255. *(Escritos y Discursos. 1)*

TORRE BLANCO (JOSE).

TORRE BLANCO (JOSE) Uno de tantos: un medico republicano español refugiado en Mexico. Mexico, 1976. pp. 386.

TORTS

— United Kingdom.

JAMES (PHILIP SEAFORTH) and BROWN (DAVID JAMES LATHAM) General principles of the law of torts. 4th ed. London, 1978. pp. 505.

TORTURE.

AMNESTY INTERNATIONAL. Summary of proposals to the Fifth United Nations Congress on the Prevention of Crime and the Treatment of Offenders, Toronto, 1-15 September 1975. London, [1975]. pp. 16.

RUTHVEN (MALISE) Torture: the grand conspiracy. London, 1978. pp. 342.

— Argentine Republic.

COMISION ARGENTINA POR LOS DERECHOS HUMANOS. Argentina: proceso al genocidio. Madrid, 1977. pp. 328.

— Brazil.

RUSSELL TRIBUNAL II ON REPRESSION IN BRAZIL, CHILE AND LATIN AMERICA. The Bertrand Russell Tribunal on Brazil and Repression in Latin America; sponsored by the Bertrand Russell Peace Foundation. Nottingham, [1973]. pp. 43. *Reprint of first 3 issues of the Tribunal Bulletin.*

— Europe.

LANGBEIN (JOHN H.) Torture and the law of proof: Europe and England in the ancien régime. Chicago, [1977]. pp. 229.

— Greece.

AMNESTY INTERNATIONAL. Torture in Greece: the first torturers' trial, 1975. London, 1977. pp. 98.

— Nicaragua.

AMNESTY INTERNATIONAL. The republic of Nicaragua;...including the findings of a mission to Nicaragua 10-15 May 1976. London, 1977. pp. 75. *bibliog.*

— Philippine Islands.

AMNESTY INTERNATIONAL. Report of an Amnesty International mission to the Republic of the Philippines, 22 November-5 December 1975. London, [1976]. pp. 60.

AMNESTY INTERNATIONAL. Report of an Amnesty International mission to the Republic of the Philippines, 22 November-5 December, 1975. 2nd ed. London, 1977. pp. 95. *Includes reply of Philippine government.*

— South Africa.

AMNESTY INTERNATIONAL. Political imprisonment in South Africa. London, 1978. pp. 108.

— United Kingdom.

LANGBEIN (JOHN H.) Torture and the law of proof: Europe and England in the ancien régime. Chicago, [1977]. pp. 229.

TOTTENHAM

— Social conditions.

TOTTENHAM COMMUNITY PROJECT. A better place. London, 1977. pp. 77.

TOUCH.

MORGAN (MICHAEL J.) Molyneux's question: vision, touch and the philosophy of perception. Cambridge, 1977. pp. 213.

TOURIST TRADE.

UNITED NATIONS. Conference on Trade and Development. 1971. Guidelines for tourism statistics. (TD/B/C.3/86). New York, 1971. pp. 50.

UNITED NATIONS. Conference on Trade and Development. 1973. Elements of tourism policy in developing countries: report, etc. (TD/B/C.3/89/Rev.1). New York, 1973. pp. 60.

HOSTS and guests: the anthropology of tourism; Valene L. Smith, editor. Oxford, 1978. pp. 254. *bibliog. Based on a symposium held in Mexico City in 1974 in conjunction with the meetings of the American Anthropological Association.*

MATTHEWS (HARRY G.) International tourism: a political and social analysis. Cambridge, Mass., [1978]. pp. 99. *bibliog.*

— Mathematical models.

ARCHER (BRIAN H.) The uses and abuses of multipliers. Bangor, 1973. pp. 26. *(Wales. University. University College of North Wales. Economics Research Unit. Tourist and Recreational Research Division. Tourist Research Papers. TUR 1)*

ARCHER (BRIAN H.) and SHEA (SHEILA) Gravity models and tourist research. Bangor, 1973. pp. 17. *bibliog. (Wales. University. University College of North Wales. Economics Research Unit. Tourist and Recreational Research Division. Tourist Research Papers. TUR 2)*

ARCHER (BRIAN H.) The anatomy of a multiplier. Bangor, 1974. pp. 14. *bibliog. (Wales. University. University College of North Wales. Institute of Economic Research . Tourist and Recreational Research Division. Tourist Research Papers. TUR 5)*

— America, Latin.

SEMINARIO REGIONAL SOBRE EL DESARROLLO DE LOS RECURSOS HUMANOS Y EL TURISMO OIT/PNUD, BUENOS AIRES, 1976. Seminario Regional..., 15-19 noviembre de 1976: Latino- America Regional; discusiones, conclusiones y recomendaciones, etc. (RLA/74/037). Geneva, International Labour Orginisation, 1977. pp. 163.

— Australia.

AUSTRALIA. Department of Tourism and Recreation. 1975. Development of tourism in Australia. Canberra, 1975. pp. 36.

— Barbados.

BARBADOS. Development Board. 1959. Barbados hotel development survey, 1958. [Bridgetown, 1959?]. pp. 11.

— Brazil.

BRAZIL. Superintendência do Desenvolvimento da Região Sul. 1971. Plano regional de turismo: palestra proferida pelo Engenheiro Paulo Affonso de Freitas Melro, Superintendente da SUDESUL, no plenario da Assembleia Legislativa do Estado do Rio Grande do Sul, a 6 de outubro de 1971. Pôrto Alegre, 1971. fo. 23.

— Canada — British Columbia.

BRITISH COLUMBIA. Department of Industrial Development, Trade and Commerce. 1973. Investment potential in the British Columbia travel industry. [Victoria], 1973. pp. 141.

— Hawaiian Islands.

TOURISM and regional growth: an empirical study of the alternative growth paths for Hawaii; edited by Moheb Ghali; contributors Robert Ebel [and others]. Leiden, 1977. pp. 121.

— New Zealand.

NEW ZEALAND. Tourist Facilities - Transport Working Party. Air Sub-Committee. 1968. Air transport development applicable to the non-resident tourist; report. [Wellington], 1968. fo. 14.

TOURIST DEVELOPMENT CONFERENCE, WELLINGTON, 1969. Record of conference proceedings and documents, 12-14 March 1969. Wellington, [1969]. 28 pts. (in 1 vol.).

TOURIST DEVELOPMENT CONFERENCE, WELLINGTON, 1969. [Reports of working parties and steering committee]. Wellington, [1969]. 7 pts. (in 1 vol.).

NEW ZEALAND. Tourist and Publicity Department. Development and Research Division. 1970. Survey of overseas visitor expenditure patterns in New Zealand. Wellington, 1970. pp. 23.

NEW ZEALAND. Tourist and Publicity Department. 1971. Invest in the New Zealand tourist industry. Wellington, 1971. pp. 36.

NEW ZEALAND. Tourist and Publicity Department. Development and Research Division. 1973. The national travel survey 1970-1971. Wellington, [1973]. 1 vol. (unpaged).

— Pakistan.

PAKISTAN. Central Statistical Office. Economic Affairs Division. 1967. Tourist statistics of Pakistan, 1956-1966. [Karachi, 1967]. pp. 46.

— Solomon Islands.

SOLOMON ISLANDS. Statistics Service. 1975. Tourism, 1970-1974. Honiara, 1975. 1 vol. (unpaged).

— Tanzania — Statistics.

UNITED REPUBLIC OF TANZANIA. Bureau of Statistics. Migration statistics. a., 1969- Dar es Salaam.

— Trinidad and Tobago.

TRINIDAD AND TOBAGO. Central Statistical Office. 1975. Report of tourism surveys, 1972-1974. Port of Spain, 1975. pp. 25.

— Underdeveloped areas.

See **UNDERDEVELOPED AREAS — Tourist trade.**

— United Kingdom.

BRITISH TOURIST AUTHORITY. Digest of tourist statistics. a., 1976 (no. 6)- London.

ENGLISH TOURIST BOARD. Investing in tourism: aid to tourist projects in England's development areas, 1971-76. London, [1977]. pp. 40.

TOURISM IN ENGLAND: the magazine of the English Tourist Board. q. London. *Current issues only kept.*

— — Wales.

ARCHER (BRIAN H.) and SHEA (SHEILA) The importance of length of stay in tourist studies. Bangor, 1974. pp. 8. *bibliog.* (Wales. University. University College of North Wales. Institute of Economic Research. Tourist and Recreational Research Division. Tourist Research Papers. TUR 6)

— Western Samoa.

WESTERN SAMOA. Department of Statistics. Migration report. a., 1976(1st)- Apia.

— Yugoslavia.

INTERREGIONAL SEMINAR ON PHYSICAL PLANNING FOR TOURISM DEVELOPMENT, DUBROVNIK, 1970. Report of the...Seminar...[held in] Dubrovnik, Yugoslavia, 19 October to 3 November 1970. (ST/TAO/SER.C/131). New York, United Nations, [1971]. pp. 55.

— Zambia — Statistics.

ZAMBIA. Central Statistical Office. Migration statistics: immigrants and visitors. a., 1965- Lusaka.

TOWARZYSTWO DEMOKRATYCZNE POLSKIE.

ZALIŃSKI (HENRYK) Towarzystwo Demokratyczne Polskie o władzach powstańczych: z dziejów myśli wojskowej Wielkiej Emigracji. [Warszawa, 1976]. pp. 347. *bibliog.*

TRADE AND PROFESSIONAL ASSOCIATIONS

— United Kingdom.

NATIONAL ASSOCIATION OF MERCHANTS AND MANUFACTURERS. National Association of Merchants and Manufacturers to Resist Interference with Trade. [London, 192-?]. pp. 4.

— United States.

HASKELL (THOMAS L.) The emergence of professional social science: the American Social Science Association and the nineteenth-century crisis of authority. Urbana, [1977]. pp. 276. *bibliog.*

TRADE REGULATION

— European Economic Community countries.

COMPETITION policy in the U.K. and EEC; edited by Kenneth D. George [and] Caroline Joll. Cambridge, 1975. pp. 220. *Papers presented at a Social Science Research Council conference held at Somerville College, Oxford in 1974.*

— United Kingdom.

COMPETITION policy in the U.K. and EEC; edited by Kenneth D. George [and] Caroline Joll. Cambridge, 1975. pp. 220. *Papers presented at a Social Science Research Council conference held at Somerville College, Oxford in 1974.*

— United States.

DEREGULATING American industry: legal and economic problems; edited by Donald L. Martin [and] Warren F. Schwartz. Lexington, Mass., [1977]. pp. 120. *Papers of a conference sponsored by the Law and Economics Center, University of Miami School of Law, in May 1976.*

The INTERACTION of economics and the law: [lectures given at the University of San Diego School of Law]; edited by Bernard H. Siegan. Lexington, Mass., [1977]. pp. 175.

TRADE ROUTES.

TRADE ROUTES.

PARRY (JOHN HORACE) The age of reconnaissance. 2nd ed. London, 1966 repr. 1973. pp. 366. *bibliog.*

TRADE UNIONS.

RAMIREZ DIAZ (LUIS JORGE) El sindicalismo en el mundo moderno. Bogota, 1972. pp. 207. *bibliog.*

DEUTSCHER VEREIN FÜR INTERNATIONALES SEERECHT. Schriften. Reihe A: Berichte und Vorträge. Heft 26. Schiffahrtsfreiheit und Gewerkschaften: Vortrag von Ingo von Münch gehalten am 29. Januar 1976. Hamburg, 1976. pp. 23, iii.

INTERNATIONAL COMMUNIST CURRENT. Pamphlets. No.1. Unions against the working class. London, [1976]. pp. 52.

EDWARDS (ROBERT) Multinational companies and the trade unions. Nottingham, 1977. pp. 70.

ERSTLING (JAY A.) The right to organise: a survey of laws and regulations relating to the right of workers to establish unions of their own choosing. Geneva, International Labour Office, 1977. pp. 82.

HORKE (GERTRAUDE) Soziologie der Gewerkschaften. Wien, [1977]. pp. 448.

MULVEY (CHARLES) The economic analysis of trade unions. Oxford, 1978. pp. 159. *bibliog. (Glasgow. University. Social and Economic Research Studies. 5)*

— Elections.

GERNIGON (BERNARD) Tenure of trade union office. Geneva, International Labour Office, 1977. pp. 112.

— Government employees — United States.

UNIONIZING the armed forces; edited by Ezra S. Krendel and Bernard Samoff. [Philadelphia], 1977. pp. 198.

— Law.

INTERNATIONAL LABOUR OFFICE. 1972. Eligibility for trade union office. Geneva, 1972. pp. 86.

— Officials and employees.

INTERNATIONAL LABOUR OFFICE. 1972. Eligibility for trade union office. Geneva, 1972. pp. 86.

GERNIGON (BERNARD) Tenure of trade union office. Geneva, International Labour Office, 1977. pp. 112.

— Argentine Republic.

CODOVILLA (VICTORIO) El movimiento sindical y la union nacional; tercera parte del informe rendido al Comite Central del Partido Comunista, el 12 de septiembre de 1942. Buenos Aires, 1942. pp. 38.

ISCARO (RUBENS) Algunas cuestiones ideologicas del movimiento sindical. [Buenos Aires], 1968. pp. 45.

ISCARO (RUBENS) Por un movimiento sindical orientado en los principios de clase, de independencia y unidad para conquistar los derechos obreros y restaurar la democracia. Buenos Aires, 1968. pp. 31.

— Austria.

MAGAZINER (ALFRED) Ein Sohn des Volkes: Karl Maisel erzählt sein Leben. Wien, [1977]. pp. 123.

— Bolivia.

LORA (GUILLERMO) A history of the Bolivian labour movement, 1848-1971;...edited and abridged by Laurence Whitehead; translated by Christine Whitehead. Cambridge, 1977. pp. 408. *bibliog.*

— Brazil.

VIANNA (LUIZ WERNECK) Liberalismo e sindicato no Brasil. Rio de Janeiro, 1976. pp. 288.

— — Political activity.

ERICKSON (KENNETH PAUL) The Brazilian corporative state and working-class politics. Berkeley, Calif., [1977]. pp. 225. *bibliog.*

— Bulgaria — Bibliography.

TSOLOV (IVAN) and others, compilers. Revoliutsionnoto profsuiuzno dvizhenie v Bulgariia, 1878- 1944: bibliografiia. [Sofiia], 1968. pp. 811. *Contains material published before Jan. 1967.*

— Canada.

INDUSTRIAL unionism in Kitchener, 1937-47; researched and written by students in the Department of History, Wilfrid Laurier University; edited by Terry Copp. Elora, Ont., [1976]. pp. 129.

— — Political activity.

McCORMACK (ANDREW ROSS) Reformers, rebels, and revolutionaries: the western Canadian radical movement, 1899-1919. Toronto, [1977]. pp. 228. *bibliog.*

— — Nova Scotia.

FERGUSSON (CHARLES BRUCE) The labour movement in Nova Scotia before confederation. Halifax, 1964. pp. 36. *(Nova Scotia. Public Archives. Bulletins. No. 20)*

— — Quebec.

DUPONT (PIERRE) and TREMBLAY (GISELE) Les syndicats en crise: un dossier de Pierre Dupont. Montréal, [1976]. pp. 152. *bibliog.*

— China.

KHOR'KOV (VIKTOR IVANOVICH) Nankinskii gomin'dan i rabochii vopros, 1927-1932. Moskva, 1977. pp. 158. *bibliog.*

— Colombia.

RAMIREZ DIAZ (LUIS JORGE) El sindicalismo en el mundo moderno. Bogota, 1972. pp. 207. *bibliog.*

— Denmark.

JERN- OG METALINDUSTRIARBEJDSMAENDENES FAGFORENING. Århus Afdeling. Jern og metal igennem 75 år. [Århus, 1972]. pp. 44.

LOGUE (JOHN) Trade unions in the corporate state: the effects of corporatism on party competition, contract referenda and internationalism in Danish trade unions. Gothenburg, 1976. pp. 65. *(Goteborgs Universitet. Historiska Institutionen. Research Section Post-War History. Publications. No. 5)*

CHRISTENSEN (ERIK) Historian. Fagforeninger og lokalsamfund: en beskrivelse og analyse af 4 vestjyske fagforeninger. Esbjerg, 1977. pp. 384. *bibliog.*

— Europe.

CONFLITTI in Europa: lotte di classe; sindacati e stato dopo il '68; a cura di Colin Crouch e Alessandro Pizzorno. Milano, 1977. pp. 438. *bibliogs.*

— European Economic Community countries.

KIRCHNER (EMIL JOSEPH) Trade unions as a pressure group in the European Community. Farnborough, Hants., [1977]. pp. 208. *bibliog.*

— France.

CAILLE (MARCEL) Les truands du patronat. Paris, 1977. pp. 307. *bibliog.*

— Germany.

FUGGER (KARL) Geschichte der deutschen Gewerkschaften. Berlin, 1947. pp. 55. *bibliog.*

GEWERKSCHAFTEN am Kreuzweg: ausgewählte Beiträge aus den "Arbeitsheften der Sozialwissenschaftlichen Vereinigung"; herausgegeben von Adolf Brock. Berlin, [1973]. pp. 259. *bibliog.*

NEJEDLO (BERND) Föderalismus oder Zentralismus: Alternativen der Gewerkschaftsreform?. Berlin, [1973]. pp. 60. *bibliog.*

KRUSCHE (REINHARD) and PFEIFFER (DAGMAR) Betriebliche Gewerkschaftsorgane und Interessenvertretung: zur Betriebsräte- und Vertrauensleutepolitik der IG Metall. Berlin, [1975]. pp. 158. *bibliog.*

EISNER (FREYA) Das Verhältnis der KPD zu den Gewerkschaften in der Weimarer Republik. Köln, [1977]. pp. 271. *bibliog. (Otto Brenner Stiftung. Schriftenreihe. 8)*

GESCHICHTE der deutschen Gewerkschaftsbewegung; mit Beiträgen von Frank Deppe [and others]; (Frank Deppe [and others], Hrsg.). Köln, 1977. pp. 475. *bibliog.*

GEWERKSCHAFTLICHE Politik: Reform aus Solidarität: zum 60. Geburtstag von Heinz O. Vetter; herausgegeben von Ulrich Borsdorf [and others]. Köln, [1977]. pp. 650.

GRUNDLAGEN der Einheitsgewerkschaft: historische Dokumente und Materialien; (Ulrich Borsdorf [and others], Hrsg.). Köln, 1977. pp. 336.

HARTMANN (KNUT) Der Weg zur gewerkschaftlichen Organisation: Bergarbeiterbewegung und kapitalistischer Bergbau im Ruhrgebiet, 1851-1889. München, [1977]. pp. 415. *bibliog.*

LINK (WERNER) Deutsche und amerikanische Gewerkschaften und Geschäftsleute, 1945-1975: eine Studie über transnationale Beziehungen. Düsseldorf, [1978]. pp. 296. *bibliog.*

— — Law.

GERHARDT (MICHAEL) Das Koalitionsgesetz: verfassungsrechtliche Überlegungen zur Neuregelung des Rechts der Gewerkschaften und der Arbeitgeberverbände. Berlin, [1977]. pp. 328. *bibliog.*

— — Berlin.

BESTRAFTE Solidarität: Drucker und Journalisten im gewerkschaftlichen Kampf; ([by] Klaus Kräling [and others]). Berlin, [1973]. pp. 139.

— Germany, Eastern.

WARNKE (HERBERT) Gewerkschaften: Sachwalter der Arbeiterinteressen: ausgewählte Reden und Aufsätze, 1971-1975; [edited by Alfred Förster and others]. Berlin, 1977. pp. 560.

— Hungary.

STUDIES on the history of the Hungarian trade-union movement; edited by E. Kabos and A. Zsilák; (translated from the Hungarian by Alex Bandy). Budapest, 1977. pp. 308.

— Italy.

La DEMOCRAZIA nel sindacato; ([by] Guido Romagnoli [and others]). Milano, [1975]. pp. 133.

MERCATO del lavoro, politiche sindacali, inflazione; a cura di Giancarlo Mazzocchi. Milano, 1975. pp. 252. *(Milan. Università Cattolica del Sacro Cuore. Pubblicazioni. Scienze Economiche. 2)*

CARTIGLIA (CARLO) Rinaldo Rigola e il sindacalismo riformista in Italia. Milano, [1976]. pp. 209.

MANCINI (GIUSEPPE FEDERICO) Costituzione e movimento operaio. Bologna, [1976]. pp. 281.

MARGIOTTA (UMBERTO) La formazione dei lavoratori italiani: premesse, condizioni, prospettive. Roma, [1976]. pp. 254.

MOVIMENTO operaio e organizzazione sindacale a Roma, 1860-1960; documenti per la storia della Camera di Lavoro; [by] F. Agostino [and others]. Roma, 1976. 2 vols.

ROMAGNOLI (GUIDO) Consigli di fabbrica e democrazia sindacale. [Milano, 1976]. pp. 284.

TURONE (SERGIO) Sindacato e classi sociali: fra autunno caldo e compromesso storico. [Bari], 1976. pp. 178.

TRADE UNIONS.

ABRATE (MARIO) Lavoro e lavoratori nell'Italia contemporanea. Milano, [1977]. pp. 108.

ROMAGNOLI (UMBERTO) and TREU (TIZIANO) I sindacati in Italja: storia di una strategia, 1945-1976. Bologna, [1977]. pp. 300.

— — **Political activity.**

SINDACATO e sistema democratico; a cura del Centro Studi CISL. Bologna, [1975]. pp. 251. *Papers of a seminar organised by the Centro.*

— **Mexico.**

SALAZAR (ROSENDO) Rosendo Salazar: [Las pugnas de la gleba; La Casa del Obrero Mundial; La C.T.M.]. Mexico, 1972. 2 vols.

— **Netherlands.**

De BEHEERSTE vakbeweging: het NVV tussen loonpolitiek en loonstrijd, 1959-1973; ([by] Kees van Doorn [and others]). Amsterdam, 1976. pp. 568.

COOMANS (PAUL) and others. De Eenheidsvakcentrale (EVC), 1943-1948. Groningen, 1976. pp. 507. *bibliog.(Rijksuniversiteit te Utrecht. Instituut voor Geschiedenis. Historische Studies. 30)*

— **New Zealand.**

CAMPBELL (ROB) The only weapon: the history of the Wellington Drivers Union. Wellington, 1976. pp. 110.

— **Norway.**

OUSLAND (GUNNAR) Norsk Treindustriarbeiderforbund 50 år. [Oslo, 1954]. pp. 438.

RASMUSSEN (SIGURD) Norsk Politiforbund gjennom 50 år, 1905-1955. Oslo, 1955. pp. 258.

KJELLSTRØM (JOHN) Rørleggernes Fagforening, 1884-1959. Oslo, 1959. pp. 238.

HANOA (ROLF) Fagbevegelsen og arbeidsmiljøet. [Oslo, 1974]. pp. 111.

VEIVESENETS ARBEIDERFORENING. 75-års beretning: 1900 9. september 1975. [Oslo, 1975]. pp. 126.

— **Peru.**

COTLER (JULIO) and PORTOCARRERO (FELIPE) Organizaciones campesinas en el Peru. Lima, 1967. pp. 33. *(Instituto de Estudios Peruanos. Los Movimientos Campesinas en el Peru desde Fines del Siglo XVIII hasta nuestros Dias. No. 1)*

MEJIA (JOSE MANUEL) and DIAZ SUAREZ (ROSA) Sindicalismo y reforma agraria en el valle de Chancay. Lima, 1975. pp. 151. *bibliog. (Instituto de Estudios Peruanos. Proyecto de Estudios Etnologicos del Valle de Chancay. Monografias. No. 5)*

— **Romania — Congresses.**

UNIUNEA GENERALĂ A SINDICATELOR DIN REPUBLICA SOCIALISTĂ ROMÂNIA. Congresul, 1976. Congresul Uniunii Generale a Sindicatelor din Republica Socialistă România, 26-28 aprilie, 1976. București, 1976. pp. 205.

— **South Africa.**

STARES (RODNEY) Black trade unions in South Africa: the responsibilities of British companies. London, 1977. pp. 82. *bibliog.*

— **Spain.**

ZAGUIRRE (MANUEL) and HOZ (JOSE M. DE LA) eds. Presente y futuro del sindicalismo. Barcelona, 1976. pp. 217.

ACTAS de la Union General de Trabajadores de España;... prologo y notas por Amaro del Rosal. Barcelona, 1977 in progress. *Photographic copies of original minutes.*

— **Sweden.**

ADAMS (ROY J.) The growth of white-collar unionism in Britain and Sweden: a comparative investigation. Madison, Wis., 1975. pp. 63. *(Wisconsin University, Madison. Industrial Relations Research Institute. Monograph Series)*

BÄCKSTRÖM (KNUT) Arbetarrörelsen i Sverige, etc. new ed. [Stockholm], 1977. 2 vols. (in 1). *bibliogs.*

— **Switzerland.**

TRABER (ALFRED) Geschichte des V[erbandes des] P[ersonals] O[effentlicher] D[ienste], Sektion Zürich, städtische Arbeiter und Angestellte, 1893-1953. [Zürich, 1953]. pp. 229.

LOERTSCHER (CLIVE) Le Parti communiste suisse et les syndicats, 1920-1921: stratégie de front unique en Suisse. Lausanne, 1977. pp. 219. *bibliog.*

VETTERLI (RUDOLF) Industriearbeit, Arbeiterbewusstsein und gewerkschaftliche Organisation; dargestellt am Beispiel der Georg Fischer AG, 1890-1930. Göttingen, 1978. pp. 344. *bibliog.*

— **United Kingdom.**

NORTHUMBERLAND. Northumberland Miners' Mutual Confident Association. Rules...[1911]. Newcastle-upon-Tyne, 1911. pp. 54.

NATIONAL UNION OF DISTRIBUTIVE AND ALLIED WORKERS. Circulars 1925-(1946). Manchester, 1925-46. 2 loose-leaf binders.

PETCH (ARTHUR W.) Branch administration and arrears. [Manchester, 1929]. pp. 12. *Paper read at a conference of branch secretaries of the National Union of Distributive and Allied Workers at Leicester on February 3rd, 1929.*

UNION OF SHOP, DISTRIBUTIVE AND ALLIED WORKERS. Circulars, 1962-1965. Manchester, 1962-65. 1 loose-leaf binder.

MURPHY (JOHN THOMAS) The workers' committee: an outline of its principles and structure;...introduction by James Hinton. London, [1972?]. pp. v, 12.

ADAMS (ROY J.) The growth of white-collar unionism in Britain and Sweden: a comparative investigation. Madison, Wis., 1975. pp. 63. *(Wisconsin University, Madison. Industrial Relations Research Institute. Monograph Series)*

ROWE (PAULINE) and BOUKEROU (MARGARET) What's wrong with the unions?; two trade unionists...write from their own experience. London, [1975?]. pp. 4. *(Socialist Current. Specials)*

ADVISORY, CONCILIATION AND ARBITRATION SERVICE [U.K.]. Trade union recognition [under the] Employment Protection Act 1975, Section 12. Reports. irreg., [S 1976] (no.1)- [London].

U.K. Certification Office for Trade Unions and Employers' Associations. Anuunual report of the Certification Officer. a., 1976(1st)- London.

HUMPHRIES (BARBARA) The Tolpuddle martyrs: victims of the rich man's law. London, [1976]. pp. 8.

ADVISORY, CONCILIATION AND ARBITRATION SERVICE [U.K.]. Time off for trade union duties and activities. [London, 1977]. pp. 8. *(Codes of Practice. 3)*

AIMS FOR FREEDOM AND ENTERPRISE. A bombshell for the Labour Party; report on national opinion survey on trade unions and the Labour Party. London, [1977]. pp. 5.

CLINTON (ALAN) The trade union rank and file: trades councils in Britain, 1900- 40. Manchester, [1977]. pp. 262. *bibliog.*

DEMOCRACY at work: a book for active trade unionists. London, 1977. pp. 184. *Accompanies a series of ten Trade Union Studies programmes shown on BBC television.*

HOWIE (WILL) B.Sc., C. Eng., M.I.C.E. Trade unions and the professional engineer. London, 1977. pp. 76.

JONES (KEITH LLOYD) The growth and development of white collar trade unionism in the British steel industry. [1977]. fo. 238. *bibliog. Typescript. Ph.D. (London) thesis: unpublished. This thesis is the property of London University and may not be removed from the Library.*

LATHAM (PETER) Labour historian. Rank and file movements in building 1910-1920. London, 1977. pp. 27. *(Communist Party of Great Britain. History Group. Our History. No. 69)*

MARPLAN LIMITED. Trade union power in Britain today. [London, 1977]. fo. 9.

MILES (R.) and PHIZACKLEA (A.) The TUC, black workers and new Commonwealth immigration, 1954- 1973. Bristol, Social Science Research Council Research Unit on Ethnic Relations, [1977]. pp. 44. *(Working Papers on Ethnic Relations. No. 6)*

RADICE (GILES) The industrial democrats: trade unions in an uncertain world. London, 1978. pp. 241.

REINER (ROBERT) The blue-coated worker: a sociological study of police unionism. Cambridge, 1978. pp. 295. *bibliog.*

TAYLOR (ROBERT) Journalist. The fifth estate: Britain's unions in the seventies. London, ;978. pp. 368. *bibliog.*

TRADE unions: public goods or public 'bads'?...; [by] Lord Robbins [and others], etc. London, 1978. pp. 132. *(Institute of Economic Affairs. Readings. 17)*

ADVISORY CONCILIATION AND ARBITRATION SERVICE [U.K.]. Press notices. irreg., current issues only. London.

— — **Congresses.**

WORKING MEN'S ASSOCIATION. Conference of Trades' Delegates, London, 1867. Report of the trades conference. London, [1867?] pp. 32.

— — **Handbooks, manuals, etc.**

PETCH (ARTHUR W.) A manual of branch administration; prepared and issued by authority of the Executive Council for the guidance of N.U.D.A.W. branch officials ([with] Supplement). Manchester, 1925. pp. 117.

— — **Officials and employees.**

TRADES UNION CONGRESS. Paid release for union training. [London, 1978]. pp. 23.

— — **Political activity.**

HEMINGWAY (JOHN) Conflict and democracy: studies in trade union government. Oxford, 1978. pp. 184.

— — **Ireland, Northern — Directories.**

IRELAND, NORTHERN. Ministry of Health and Social Services. Industrial Relations Division. 1973. Directory of principal organisations of employers and workpeople in Northern Ireland. 17th ed. Belfast, 1973. pp. 39.

IRELAND, NORTHERN. Department of Manpower Services. Industrial Relations Division. 1975. Directory of principal organisations of employers and workpeople in Northern Ireland. 18th ed. Belfast, 1975. pp. 39.

— **United States.**

LEWIS (JOHN LLEWELLYN) Papers, 1879-1969. Madison, Wis., 1970. Microfilm: 4 reels. With printed guide to the microfilm edition.

LEWIS (JOHN LLEWELLYN) Papers of John L. Lewis: guide to a microfilm edition; edited by Eleanor Niermann. Madison, Wis., 1970. pp. 12. *bibliog. (State Historical Society of Wisconsin. Guides to Historical Resources)*

FRANK W. PIERCE MEMORIAL CONFERENCE, CORNELL UNIVERSITY, 1973. Union power and public policy; David B. Lipsky, editor. Ithaca, N.Y. 1975. pp. 131.

KERPER (MICHAEL) The international ideology of U.S. labor, 1941-1975. Gothenburg, 1976. pp. 42. *(Göteborgs Universitet. Historiska Institutionen. Research Section Post-War History. Publications. No. 6)*

TRADE UNIONS.(Cont.)

AMERICAN FEDERATION OF LABOR AND CONGRESS OF INDUSTRIAL ORGANIZATIONS. Executive Council. Statements and reports, 1956-1975; edited, with an introduction, by Gary M. Fink. Westport, Conn., 1977. 5 vols.

BROOKS (THOMAS R.) Communications workers of America: the story of a union. New York, 1977. pp. 257. *bibliog.*

HARRIS (WILLIAM HAMILTON) Keeping the faith: A. Philip Randolph, Milton P. Webster and the Brotherhood of Sleeping Car Porters, 1925-1937. Urbana, Ill., [1977]. pp. 252. *bibliog.*

LABOR unions; editor-in-chief Gary M. Fink. Westport, Conn., 1977. pp. 520.

OUT of the sweatshop: the struggle for industrial democracy; edited by Leon Stein. New York, [1977]. pp. 367.

REES (ALBERT) The economics of trade unions. 2nd ed. Chicago, [1977]. pp. 200. *bibliog.*

JENNINGS (KENNETH M.) and others. Labor relations in a public service industry: unions, management, and the public interest in mass transit. New York, 1978. pp. 323. *bibliog.*

LINK (WERNER) Deutsche und amerikanische Gewerkschaften und Geschäftsleute, 1945-1975: eine Studie über transnationale Beziehungen. Düsseldorf, [1978]. pp. 296. *bibliog.*

RAMIREZ (BRUNO) When workers fight: the politics of industrial relations in the Progressive era, 1898-1916. Westport, [1978]. pp. 241. *bibliog.*

— — **Bibliography.**

WOODBRIDGE (MARK E.) compiler. American Federation of Labor and Congress of Industrial Organizations pamphlets, 1889-1955: a bibliography and subject index to the pamphlets held in the AFL-CIO library. Westport, Conn., 1977. pp. 73.

— — **Officials and employees — Biography.**

WHO's who in labor. New York, 1976. pp. 807.

— — **Political activity.**

HOROWITZ (RUTH L.) Political ideologies of organized labor. New Brunswick, N.J., [1978]. pp. 260. *bibliog.*

RA (JONG OH) Labor at the polls: union voting in Presidential elections, 1952- 1976. Amherst, 1978. pp. 182. *bibliog.*

— — **Minnesota.**

DOBBS (FARRELL) Teamster bureaucracy. New York, 1977. pp. 304.

— **Uruguay.**

MOVIMIENTO DE IZQUIERDA REVOLUCIONARIA [URUGUAY]. Por un sindicalismo al servicio de la revolucion Uruguaya. [Montevideo?, 1969]. 1 pamphlet (unpaged). (*Documentos marxista-leninistas para la construccion del partido de la clase obrera Uruguaya. No. 1*)

TRADE UNIONS, CATHOLIC

— **Austria.**

MOCK (ALOIS) Für eine menschenwürdige Gesellschaftsordnung: zur Neuauflage des "Wiener Programms" des OAAB. Wien, 1976. pp. 28. (*Österreichischer Arbeiter- und Angestelltenbund. Gesellschaftspolitische Informationen. 13*)

— **Germany.**

BRACK (RUDOLF) Deutscher Episkopat und Gewerkschaftsstreit, 1900-1914. Köln, 1976. pp. 448. *bibliog.*

TRADE UNIONS AND COMMUNISM.

KOMMUNISTY i profsoiuzy: bor'ba revoliutsionnogo avangarda za ukreplenie i edinstvo mezhdunarodnogo profsoiuznogo dvizheniia. Moskva, 1977. pp. 335.

WILLIAMS (DAVID) Writer on communism. The Kremlin's world trade union links. London, [1977?]. fo. 29.

— **Germany.**

EHRENBERG (ERNST N.) Die Bündnispolitik der Deutschen Kommunistischen Partei mit dem Deutschen Gewerkschaftsbund. Gerbrunn bei Würzburg, [1977]. pp. 306. *bibliog.*

EISNER (FREYA) Das Verhältnis der KPD zu den Gewerkschaften in der Weimarer Republik. Köln, [1977]. pp. 271. *bibliog.* (*Otto Brenner Stiftung. Schriftenreihe. 8*)

SCHOECK (EVA CORNELIA) Arbeitslosigkeit und Rationalisierung: die Lage der Arbeiter und die kommunistische Gewerkschaftspolitik, 1920-28. Frankfurt, [1977]. pp. 280. *bibliog.*

— **Switzerland.**

LOERTSCHER (CLIVE) Le Parti communiste suisse et les syndicats, 1920-1921: stratégie de front unique en Suisse. Lausanne, 1977. pp. 219. *bibliog.*

— **United Kingdom.**

STEWART-SMITH (DUDLEY GEOFFREY) Not to be trusted: left wing extremism in the Labour and Liberal Parties. Richmond, Surrey, 1974. pp. 24.

— **United States.**

COCHRAN (BERT) Labor and communism: the conflict that shaped American unions. Princeton, N.J., [1977]. pp. 394. (*Columbia University. Research Institute on International Change. Studies*)

TRAFFIC ASSIGNMENT

— **Mathematical models.**

GILLIVER (IAN) Highway assignment multiflow: a critical appraisal. Reading, 1977. pp. 58. *bibliog.* (*Reading. University. Department of Geography. Reading Geographical Papers. No.59*)

TRAFFIC ENGINEERING.

LEBARON (ALLEN) Vehicle taxation and highway development. 1960. 1 vol. (various foliations). *Unpublished: typescript.*

TRAFFIC ESTIMATION

— **United Kingdom.**

TANNER (JOHN CURNOW) Car ownership trends and forecasts. Crowthorne, 1977. pp. 117. *bibliog.* (*U.K. Transport and Road Research Laboratory. Reports. LR 799*)

U.K. Advisory Committee on Trunk Road Assessment. 1978. Report...; chairman: Sir George Leitch. London, 1978. pp. 208.

TRAFFIC OFFENCES

— **United Kingdom.**

CHRISTIAN ECONOMIC AND SOCIAL RESEARCH FOUNDATION. Occasional Papers. No. 4. The amalgamation of police districts: reconciliation of statistics, 1967-1971. Part B: offences to do with the loading or condition of motor vehicles. London, [1971]. pp. 32.

TRAFFIC REGULATIONS

— **United Kingdom.**

U.K. Department of the Environment. 1976. A study of some methods of traffic restraint: summary report. [London, 1976]. pp. 20. (*Research Reports. 15*) Full report published as Research Report 14.

TRAFFIC SURVEYS.

UNITED NATIONS. Economic Commission for Europe. 1967. Census of motor traffic on main international traffic arteries, 1965, etc. Geneva, 1967. 10 maps. *Title and map legends in English and French.*

— **United Kingdom — London.**

KINLOCK (A.G.) and NESS (M.P.) Greater London transportation survey: screenline validation. London, [1976]. pp. 35. (*London. Greater London Council. Research Memoranda. 308*)

TRAMPS

— **United Kingdom.**

PROD (PRESERVATION OF THE RIGHTS OF DOSSERS) Seven nights at the fire; [by] Ted Eagle [and others]. London, 1976. pp. 11.

TRAMWAYS

— **Argentine Republic.**

JALIKIS (MARINO) Historia de los medios de transporte y de su influencia en el desarrollo urbano de la ciudad de Buenos Aires. Buenos Aires, 1925. pp. 65.

— **United Kingdom.**

McKAY (JOHN P.) Tramways and trolleys: the rise of urban mass transport in Europe. Princeton, [1976]. pp. 266. *bibliog.*

TRANSHUMANCE

— **Romania.**

CONSTANTINESCU-MIRCEŞTI (C.) Păstoritul transhumant şi implicaţiile lui în Transilvania şi Ţara Românească în secolele XVIII- XIX. Bucureşti, 1976. pp. 170. (*Academia de Stiinţe Sociale şi Politice a Republicii Socialiste România. Biblioteca Istorică. 44*)

TRANSKEI.

TRANSKEI. Department of Foreign Affairs. Information Division. 1976. The republic of Transkei. Johannesburg, 1976. pp. (295).

— **Politics and government.**

LAURENCE (PATRICK) The Transkei: South Africa's politics of partition. Johannesburg, 1976. pp. 137.

TRANSPORT WORKERS

— **New Zealand.**

CAMPBELL (ROB) The only weapon: the history of the Wellington Drivers Union. Wellington, 1976. pp. 110.

— **United States.**

JENNINGS (KENNETH M.) and others. Labor relations in a public service industry: unions, management, and the public interest in mass transit. New York, 1978. pp. 323. *bibliog.*

— — **Minnesota.**

DOBBS (FARRELL) Teamster bureaucracy. New York, 1977. pp. 304.

TRANSPORTATION.

PUSHKAREV (BORIS SERGEEVICH) and ZUPAN (JEFFREY MICHAEL) Public transportation and land use policy. Bloomington, Ind., [1977]. pp. 242. *bibliog.*

— **Cost of operation.**

BRUNET (ANDRE) compiler. The problem of cost in the inland transport industry: a conspectus of the work of the costing experts. (ME/533/55). [Geneva?], United Nations, [1955?]. 2 vols. (in 1)

— **Argentine Republic.**

LOPEZ MAYER (ADOLFO) Transportes en la Argentina. [Rosario, Arg.], 1946. pp. 269. *bibliog.*

— **Australia.**

TRANSPORT OUTLOOK CONFERENCE, CANBERRA, 1975. Papers and proceedings. Canberra, Australian Government Publishing Service, 1976. pp. 252.

— **Canada — Passenger traffic.**

ALBERTA. Department of Transportation. 1976. Submission...to Canadian Transport Commission in response to notice of public hearings concerning transcontinental passenger train services, Montreal/Toronto-Vancouver. [Edmonton], 1976. pp. 40.

— — **Alberta.**

ALBERTA. Department of Transportation. 1976. Re-organization study, November 1976. [Edmonton], 1976. 1 vol. (unpaged)

— — **Ontario — Rates.**

BONSOR (N.C.) Transportation rates and economic development in northern Ontario. Toronto, [1977]. pp. 91. bibliog. *(Ontario. Economic Council. Research Studies. 7)*

— **Europe.**

SEIDENFUS (HELLMUTH STEFAN) Ostverkehr: das Eindringen der östlichen Staatshandelsländer in die Verkehrswirtschaft der westlichen Welt. Berlin, [1977]. pp. 81. *(Adolf-Weber-Stiftung. Wirtschaftspolitische Kolloquien)*

— **Europe, Eastern.**

SEIDENFUS (HELLMUTH STEFAN) Ostverkehr: das Eindringen der östlichen Staatshandelsländer in die Verkehrswirtschaft der westlichen Welt. Berlin, [1977]. pp. 81. *(Adolf-Weber-Stiftung. Wirtschaftspolitische Kolloquien)*

— **European Economic Community countries — Statistics.**

EUROPEAN COMMUNITIES. Statistical Office. Monthly tables of transport. m., Jl/Ag 1977(no. 7/8)- Luxembourg. *[in Community languages]*

— **France.**

PROSPECTIVE des transports de 1975 à 1990. Paris, [1977]. pp. 284. *(France. Commissariat Général du Plan. Economie et Planification)*

— **Germany — Cost of operation.**

GERMANY (BUNDESREPUBLIK). Statistisches Bundesamt. Kostenstruktur des gewerblichen Güterkraftverkehrs, der Speditionen und Lagereien, der Binnenschiffahrt: Güterbeförderung und der See- und Küstenschiffahrt (formerly Gewerblicher Güterkraftverkehr Spedition und Lagerei Binnenschiffahrt: Güterbeförderung See- und Küstenschiffahrt). quadrennial. 1971- Wiesbaden. *(Unternehmen und Arbeitsstätten. Reihe 1.5.2.)*

— **Hong Kong.**

HONG KONG. Census, 1976. 1976 by-census: transport characteristics. [Hong Kong], 1978. pp. 98.

— **Netherlands.**

BEZ (KHAGESWAR) Demand for energy for transportation in the Netherlands. [Rotterdam, 1978]. pp. 93. bibliog. *Proefschrift (doctor) - Erasmus Universiteit Rotterdam. With summary in Dutch.*

— **New Zealand.**

NEW ZEALAND. Ministry of Transport. Economics Division. 1974. The effects of regional development on transport. Wellington, 1974. fo. 32.

NEW ZEALAND. Ministry of Transport. Information Section. 1975. Transport in New Zealand. Wellington, 1975. pp. 44.

— **Poland — Silesia.**

BARTECZEK (ANDRZEJ) Integracyjna funkcja infrastruktury gospodarczej w świetle badań nad Górnośląskim Okregiem Przemysłowym. Warszawa, 1977. pp. 138. bibliog. *(Polska Akademia Nauk. Komitet Przestrzennego Zagospodarowania Kraju. Studia. t.59) With Russian and English summaries.*

— **Russia.**

MARKOVA (ANNA NIKOLAEVNA) Transport SSSR i osnovnye etapy ego razvitiia. Moskva, 1977. pp. 232. *(Akademiia Nauk SSSR. Problemy Sovetskoi Ekonomiki)*

RAZVITIE edinoi transportnoi seti SSSR v desiatoi piatiletke; pod redaktsiei V.L. Stanislaviuka. Moskva, 1977. pp. 126. bibliog.

TSCHIERSKY (HORST) Zentrale Leitung und Planung des Transportwesens in der UdSSR. Berlin, [1977]. pp. 188. bibliog.

— — **Russia (RSFSR).**

VOPROSY razvitiia transportnoi seti krupnogo raiona. Sverdlovsk, 1976. pp. 69.

— **Scandinavia — Laws and regulations.**

[SCANDINAVIA]. Nordiske Parlamentariske Komité for Friere Samfaerdsel. 1952. Betaenkning om lettelser i toldbehandlingen af rejsende i den internordiske trafik: og Betaenkning om valutamaessige lettelser i rejsetrafikken mellem de nordiske lande. København, 1952. pp. 27,16.

[SCANDINAVIA]. Nordiske Parlamentariske Komité for Friere Samfaerdsel. 1955. Betaenkning om samordning af de nordiske landes faerdselslovgivning m.m. [Copenhagen], 1955. pp. 155. *(Denmark. Betaenkninger. Nr. 138)*

— **Spain.**

BARTHE Y BARTHE (ANDRES) Influencia de los transportes en los mercados y en la baja de los precios: memoria premiada por la Real Academia de Ciencias Morales y Politicas en el concurso ordinario de 1897, tema segundo. Madrid, 1899. pp. 110.

— **United Kingdom.**

WILSON (Sir HAROLD) The future of British transport. London, [1963]. pp. 8. *Reprint of the speech in the House of Commons in 1963.*

FREEMAN FOX AND ASSOCIATES. Nottingham and environs transportation study: the preferred transportation system; [commissioned by Nottinghamshire County Council and Derbyshire County Council]. London, 1975. pp. 30. *Bound with their Nottingham and environs transportation study.*

FREEMAN FOX AND ASSOCIATES. Nottingham and environs transportation study, [commissioned by Nottinghamshire County Council and Derbyshire County Council]. London, 1976. 2 vols. (in 1).

MERSEYSIDE. County Council. Joint Transportation Unit. Transport policies and programme. a., 1977/78- Liverpool. *File includes annual supplement and appendices.*

OXFORDSHIRE. County Council. Transport policy and programme: submission to the Department of the Environment for Transport Supplementary Grant. a., 1977/78- Oxford.

ABELL (PAUL HENRY) Transport and industry in South Yorkshire. Barnsley, [1977]. pp. 84. bibliog.

BIRMINGHAM COMMUNITY DEVELOPMENT PROJECT. Driven on wheels. [Oxford], 1977. pp. 52. *(Final Reports. No. 1: the Transport Industry)*

FOWLER (NORMAN) The right track: a paper on Conservative transport policy. London, 1977. pp. 38. *(Conservative Political Centre. [Publications]. No. 612.*

TRADE and transport: essays in economic history in honour of T.S. Willan; W.H. Chaloner [and] Barrie M. Ratcliffe, editors. Manchester, [1977]. pp. 293.

HERTFORDSHIRE. County Council. Transport policies and programmes: submission. a., 1978/79(4th)- [Hertford].

HUMBERSIDE. County Council. Transport policy and programme: submission. a., 1978/79- [Beverley].

KENT. County Council. Transport policies and programme: submission. a., 1978/79(4th)- Maidstone.

SHROPSHIRE. County Council. Transport policies and programme: submission. a., 1978/79(4th)- [Shrewsbury].

SURREY. County Council. Transport policies and programme. a., 1978/79- [Kingston upon Thames].

SMITH (EDWARD) Civil engineer, ed. Better use of railways: comments and rejoinders. Reading, 1978. pp. 89. bibliog. *(Reading. University. Department of Geography. Reading Geographical Papers. No. 63)*

— — **Fares.**

BRITISH ROAD FEDERATION. Who pays the fares?: the transport subsidy labyrinth. London, [1977]. pp. 8.

— — **Finance.**

BRITISH ROAD FEDERATION. Who pays the fares?: the transport subsidy labyrinth. London, [1977]. pp. 8.

— — **Fuel.**

ADVISORY COUNCIL ON ENERGY CONSERVATION [U.K.]. Freight transport: short and medium term considerations. London, H.M.S.O., 1977. pp. 22. *(Papers. 6)*

ADVISORY COUNCIL ON ENERGY CONSERVATION [U.K.]. Energy for transport: long-term possibilities. London, H.M.S.O., 1978. pp. 20. bibliog. *(Papers. 8)*

— — **Passenger traffic.**

SOUTH YORKSHIRE TRANSPORT; annual report of South Yorkshire County Council and South Yorkshire Passenger Transport Executive and accounts of South Yorkshire Passenger Transport Executive. a., 1974/75(1st)- Sheffield.

PEOPLE and their settlements: aspects of housing, transport and strategic planning in the U.K.; papers for a conference held in London in January 1976, organised by the National Council of Social Service...as a contribution to the NGO Forum on Habitat, Vancouver, June 1976. London, [1976]. pp. 107.

BRITISH ROAD FEDERATION. Who pays the fares?: the transport subsidy labyrinth. London, [1977]. pp. 8.

— — — **Bibliography.**

ALLETSON (JOAN) compiler. Roads and transport in rural areas;...edited by Claire M. Lambert. [London], 1976. pp. 23. *(U.K. Department of the Environment. Library. Bibliographies. No. 17B)*

— — **Ireland, Northern — Passenger traffic.**

NORTHERN IRELAND PASSENGER SURVEY; [pd. by] Northern Ireland Tourist Board, Research and Planning Department. s-a., Ap/S 1973- Belfast.

— **United States.**

CONNECTICUT. Tri-State Regional Planning Commission. 1973. 1970 workplaces and work travel. New York, 1973. 1 pamphlet (unpaged). *(Regional Profiles. Vol. 2. No. 4)*

TRANSPORTATION, AUTOMOTIVE

— **Environmental aspects — United Kingdom.**

MORTON-WILLIAMS (JEAN) and others. Road traffic and the environment; (survey of attitudes to road traffic sponsored by the Office of Population Censuses and Surveys on behalf of the Department of Transport). London, [1978]. 1 vol. (various pagings). bibliog.

— **Taxation.**

LEBARON (ALLEN) Vehicle taxation and highway development. 1960. 1 vol. (various foliations). *Unpublished: typescript.*

TRANSPORTATION, AUTOMOTIVE (Cont.)

— Europe — Freight.

U.K. Department of Transport. 1977. International road haulage permits; a report. [London], 1977. pp. (40).

— Italy.

CECCHINI (DOMENICO) Trasporto stradale e struttura insediativa nel Mezzogiorno. [Milano, 1975]. pp. 191. *(Associazione per lo Sviluppo dell'Industria nel Mezzogiorno. Centro per gli Studi sullo Sviluppo Economico. Collana di Monografie)*

— Puerto Rico.

PUERTO RICO. Government Development Bank for Puerto Rico. 1971. Highway Authority, Puerto Rico: a special report. San Juan, 1971. pp. 16.

— Russia.

FILIPPOV (VITALII KONSTANTINOVICH) Razvitie avtomobil'nogo transporta obshchego pol'zovaniia. Moskva, 1965. pp. 110.

— Underdeveloped areas.

See UNDERDEVELOPED AREAS — Transportation, Automotive.

— United Kingdom — Freight.

U.K. Department of Transport. 1977. International road haulage permits; a report. [London], 1977. pp. (40).

— — Government ownership.

McPARTLAN (H.) A dissertation on nationalised road transport. 1955. fo. 161. *Unpublished: typescript.*

TRANSPORTATION AND STATE

— New Zealand.

NEW ZEALAND. Ministry of Transport. 1968. Why a Ministry of Transport. Wellington, [1968?]. pp. 6. *(News Backgrounders)*

— Rhodesia.

SOUTHERN RHODESIA. Commission appointed to Inquire into the Control and Co-ordination of Transport in Southern Rhodesia. 1940. Report; [Robert James Hudson, chairman]. Salisbury, 1940. pp. 23, 1 map. *(Legislative Assembly. [Sessional Papers]. 1940. C.S.R. 27)*

— United Kingdom.

BRITISH ROAD FEDERATION. Who pays the fares?: the transport subsidy labyrinth. London, [1977]. pp. 8.

TRANSPORTATION NOISE.

NELSON (JON P.) Economic analysis of transportation noise abatement. Cambridge, Mass., [1978]. pp. 264. *bibliog.*

TRANSPORTATION PLANNING.

RALLIS (TOM) Intercity transport: engineering and planning. London, 1977. pp. 232.

— Tropics — Bibliography.

COOPER (L.) compiler. Reports on roads and transport planning in tropical and sub-tropical countries. rev. ed. Crowthorne, 1977. pp. 79. *(U.K. Transport and Road Research Laboratory. Supplementary Reports. 162)*

— United Kingdom.

PEAT, MARWICK, MITCHELL AND COMPANY. An initial report on minimum levels of service for rural public transport; prepared for the National Bus Company. [London], 1977. fo. 124,(5). *bibliog.*

— United States.

CONNECTICUT. Tri-State Regional Planning Commission. 1975. Maintaining mobility: the plan and program for regional transportation through 2000. [New York], 1975. pp. 47.

CONNECTICUT. Tri-State Regional Planning Commission. 1976. Maintaining mobility: the plan and program for regional transportation through 2000. 2nd ed. [New York], 1976. pp. 53.

TRANSYLVANIA

— History.

HITCHINS (KEITH) Orthodoxy and nationality: Andreiu Şaguna and the Rumanians of Transylvania, 1846-1873. Cambridge, Mass., 1977. pp. 332. *bibliog.* *(Harvard University. Harvard Historical Studies. vol. 94)*

— — Sources.

POLVEREJAN (ŞERBAN) and CORDOŞ (NICOLAE) eds. Mişcarea memorandistă în documente, 1885-1897; cuvînt înainte de Ştefan Pascu. Cluj, 1973. pp. 368. *bibliog.* With *appendix of photographs.*

— Politics and government.

CICALĂ (I.) Mişcarea muncitorească şi socialistă din Transilvania, 1901-1921. Bucureşti, 1976. pp. 289.

TRAVEL

— Mathematical models.

DETERMINANTS of travel choice; edited by David A. Hensher and Quasim Dalvi. Farnborough, Hants., [1978]. pp. 394. *bibliogs.* A contribution to the US National Academy of Sciences Transportation Research Board Sub-Committee on the Value of Travel Time.

TRAVEL COSTS.

NATIONAL ASSOCIATION FOR THE WELFARE OF CHILDREN IN HOSPITAL. The fares enquiry; a NAWCH report prepared by Barbara Browse. London, 1972-73. pp. 25.

TREASON.

WEST (Dame REBECCA) pseud. [i.e. Cicily Isabel ANDREWS]. The meaning of treason. New York, 1947. pp. 307.

TREATIES.

PAPADOPOULOS (ANDRESTINOS N.) La pratique chypriote en matière de succession d'états aux traités. Nicosie, 1976. pp. 240. *bibliog.* Thèse (docteur en droit) - Université de Genève.

NAPOLETANO (GUIDO) Violenza e trattati nel diritto internazionale. Milano, 1977. pp. 608. *(Rome. Università. Istituto di Diritto Internazionale. Pubblicazioni. 14)*

TREATY-MAKING POWER

— Russia.

BUTKEVICH (VLADIMIR GRIGOR'EVICH) Sovetskoe pravo i mezhdunarodnyi dogovor. Kiev, 1977. pp. 262. *bibliog.*

TREVISO (PROVINCE)

— Politics and government.

TREVISO (PROVINCE). Amministrazione Provinciale. La provincia de Treviso, 1970-1975: una politica per il rinnovamento dei poteri locali. Treviso, 1975. pp. 40.

TRIALS (BLASPHEMY)

— United Kingdom.

WALTER (NICOLAS) Blasphemy in Britain: the practice and punishment of blasphemy and the trial of Gay News. London, 1977. pp. 16.

TRIALS (CONSPIRACY)

— United Kingdom.

CONSPIRACY: notes; [by] Chris Bott [and others]. [London?, 1971?]. pp. 20.

TRIALS (HERESY)

— United Kingdom.

CAMDEN SOCIETY. [Publications]. 4th Series. vol. 20. Heresy trials in the diocese of Norwich 1428-31; edited for the Royal Historical Society from Westminster Diocesan Archives MS.B.2 by Norman P. Tanner. London, 1977. pp. 233.

TRIALS (MURDER)

— United States.

PORTER (KATHERINE ANNE) The never-ending wrong. London, 1977. pp. 64. *bibliog.*

TRIALS (POLITICAL CRIMES AND OFFENCES)

— Austria-Hungary.

POLVEREJAN (ŞERBAN) and CORDOŞ (NICOLAE) eds. Mişcarea memorandistă în documente, 1885-1897; cuvînt înainte de Ştefan Pascu. Cluj, 1973. pp. 368. *bibliog.* With *appendix of photographs.*

— Greece.

AMNESTY INTERNATIONAL. Torture in Greece : the first torturers' trial, 1975. London, 1977. pp. 98.

— Russia.

STERN (MIKHAIL) defendant. The USSR versus Dr. Mikhail Stern: an "ordinary" trial in the Soviet Union; edited by August Stern; translated from the Russian by Marco Carynnyk. London, 1978. pp. 267.

— United States.

BELKNAP (MICHAL R.) Cold war political justice: the Smith Act, the Communist Party, and American civil liberties. Westport, Conn., 1977. pp. 322. *bibliog.*

WEINSTEIN (ALLEN) Perjury: the Hiss-Chambers case. New York, 1978. pp. 674. *bibliog.*

TRIALS (SEDITION)

— United Kingdom.

ALDRED (GUY ALFRED) Dogmas discarded;...revised [sic], extended, and, in parts abridged from an autobiographical fragment published in 1908, author's trial for sedition affixed. London, 1913. pp. 31. *(Revolt Library. No. 6)*

TRIALS (TREASON)

— United Kingdom.

WEST (Dame REBECCA) pseud. [i.e. Cicily Isabel ANDREWS]. The meaning of treason. New York, 1947. pp. 307.

TRIBES AND TRIBAL SYSTEM

— Africa, Subsaharan.

SYLLA (LANCINE) Tribalisme et parti unique en Afrique noire: esquisse d'une théorie générale de l'intégration nationale. [Paris, 1977]. pp. 392.

TRINIDAD AND TOBAGO

— Economic conditions.

CENTRAL BANK OF TRINIDAD AND TOBAGO. Quarterly economic bulletin. q., S 1977(v. 2, no. 3)- Port of Spain.

— — Statistics.

CENTRAL BANK OF TRINIDAD AND TOBAGO. Statistical digest. m., F 1978(v. 11, no. 2)- Port of Spain.

— Parliament — Elections.

TRINIDAD AND TOBAGO. Elections Commission. 1972. Report on the parliamentary general elections, 1971. [Port of Spain], 1972. pp. 95.

TRINIDAD AND TOBAGO. Elections and Boundaries Commission. 1977. Report on the parliamentary general elections, 1976. [Port of Spain], 1977. pp. 202.

TRIPURA

— Population.

INDIA. Census, 1971. Series 20. Tripura: a portrait of population; [by] A.K. Bhattacharyya. [Delhi, 1975]. pp. 200.

TROPICAL CROPS.

FRANCE, Ministère de la Coopération. Service des Etudes Economiques et des Questions Internationales. 1978. Indices des cours extérieurs et cours des produits tropicaux. Paris, 1978. fo. 38. (Etudes et Documents. No. 29)

TROTSKII (LEV DAVYDOVICH).

TROTSKII (LEV DAVYDOVICH) The basic writings of Trotsky; edited and introduced by Irving Howe. New York, 1976. pp. 427. Reprint of the ed. published by Random House in 1963.

NCUBE (PATRICK D.) African socialism, imperialism, and a reconsidering of Trotsky's theory of the permanent revolution. Oslo, 1975. pp. 116, viii. bibliog. (Oslo. Universitet. Instituttet for Sosiologi. Skriftserie. Nr. 29)

VEREEKEN (GEORGES) La guépéou dans le mouvement trotskiste. Paris, [1975]. pp. 379.

FOURTH INTERNATIONAL. International Committee. Accomplices of the GPU. London, [1976]. pp. 24.

FOURTH INTERNATIONAL. International Committee. How the GPU murdered Trotsky. London, [1976]. 1 pamphlet (unpaged).

FOURTH INTERNATIONAL. International Committee. Trotsky's assassin at large. London, [1977]. pp. 40.

JENKINS (PETER) Where Trotskyism got lost: the restoration of European democracy after the Second World War. Nottingham, [1977]. pp. 23. (Spokesman, The. Pamphlets. No. 59)

MARIE (JEAN JACQUES) Le trotskysme. [Paris, 1977]. pp. 192. bibliog.

PAYNE (PIERRE STEPHEN ROBERT) The life and death of Trotsky. New York, [1977]. pp. 498. bibliog.

TROTSKII (LEV DAVYDOVICH) Portraits: political and personal. New York, [1977]. pp. 237.

HOWE (IRVING) Trotsky. [Hassocks, 1978]. pp. 186. bibliog.

KNEI-PAZ (BARUCH) The social and political thought of Leon Trotsky. Oxford, 1978. pp. 629. bibliog.

VAN HEIJENOORT (JEAN) With Trotsky in exile: from Prinkipo to Goyoacán. Cambridge, Mass., 1978. pp. 164.

TRUDEAU (PIERRE ELLIOTT).

BOM (PHILIP C.) Trudeau's Canada: truth and consequences. St. Catharines, Ont., [1977]. pp. 173. bibliog.

LAXER (JAMES) and LAXER (ROBERT M.) The Liberal idea of Canada: Pierre Trudeau and the question of Canada's survival. Toronto, 1977. pp. 234.

ZINK (LUBOR J.) Viva Chairman Pierre. Toronto, 1977. pp. 150.

TRUMAN (HARRY S.) President of the United States.

DONOVAN (ROBERT JOHN) Conflict and crisis: the presidency of Harry S. Truman, 1945- 1948. New York, [1977]. pp. 473.

CAUTE (DAVID) The great fear: the anti-communist purge under Truman and Eisenhower. New York, [1978]. pp. 697. bibliog.

TRUST TERRITORIES.

LOUIS (WILLIAM ROGER) Imperialism at bay, 1941-1945: the United States and the decolonization of the British Empire. Oxford, 1977. pp. 595.

TRUSTS, INDUSTRIAL.

WARREN-BOULTON (FREDERICK R.) Vertical control of markets: business and labor practices. Cambridge, Mass., [1978]. pp. 213. bibliog.

— Law.

See ANTITRUST LAW.

TRUSTS AND TRUSTEES

— Australia.

HARDINGHAM (IAN JAMES) and BAXT (ROBERT) Discretionary trusts. Sydney, 1975. pp. 235. bibliog.

— New Zealand.

NEW ZEALAND. Property Law and Equity Reform Committee. 1970. Trustees' statutory powers of investment; report; [C.P. Hutchinson, chairman]. [Wellington, 1970]. pp. 24.

— United Kingdom.

MAUDSLEY (RONALD HARLING) and BURN (EDWARD HECTOR) Trusts and trustees: cases and materials. 2nd ed. London, 1978. pp. 673.

OAKLEY (ANTHONY JAMES) Constructive trusts. London, 1978. pp. 142.

TRUTH.

RAUCHE (G.A.) The problem of truth and reality in Grisebach's thought. Pretoria, 1966. pp. 122. bibliog. (South Africa. National Council for Social Research. Publication Series. No. 21)

STEINER (GEORGE) Has truth a future? London, 1978. pp. 18. (British Broadcasting Corporation. Bronowski Memorial Lectures. 1978)

TSINAN

— History.

BUCK (DAVID D.) Urban change in China: politics and development in Tsinan, Shantung, 1890-1949. [Madison, 1978]. pp. 296.

TUAREGS.

KEENAN (JEREMY) The Tuareg: people of Ahaggar. London, 1977. pp. 385. bibliog.

TUCKER (NATHANIEL BEVERLEY).

BRUGGER (ROBERT J.) Beverley Tucker: heart over head in the old south. Baltimore, [1978]. pp. 294. bibliogs. (Johns Hopkins University. Studies in Historical and Political Science. Series 96. No.2)

TUCSON

— History.

DOBYNS (HENRY F.) Spanish colonial Tucson: a demographic history. Tucson, [1976]. pp. 246. bibliog.

— Population.

DOBYNS (HENRY F.) Spanish colonial Tucson: a demographic history. Tucson, [1976]. pp. 246. bibliog.

TUEBINGEN UNIVERSITY.

ADAM (UWE DIETRICH) Hochschule und Nationalsozialismus: die Universität Tübingen im Dritten Reich. Tübingen, 1977. pp. 240. bibliog. (Tübingen. Universität. Contubernium. 23)

TUNISIA

— Economic conditions.

SCHLIEPHAKE (KONRAD) Oil and regional development: examples from Algeria and Tunisia; translated by Merrill D. Lyew. New York, 1977. pp. 203. bibliog.

— Economic policy.

TUNIS. 1973. IVe plan de développement économique et social, 1973-1976. [Tunis, 1973?]. pp. 302.

— Politics and government.

BOURGUIBA (HABIB) Articles de presse, 1929-1934. [Tunis, 1967]. pp. 388. (Histoire du Mouvement National [Tunisien. Documents.])

Le NEO-Destour et le Front Populaire en France. [Tunis, 1969]. 2 vols. (in 1). (Histoire du Mouvement National Tunisien. Documents. 3-4)

Le NEO-Destour face à la première épreuve, 1934-36. [Tunis, 1969]. pp. 274. (Histoire du Mouvement National Tunisien. Documents)

Le NEO-Destour face à la deuxième épreuve, 1938-1943. [Tunis, 1970]. 3 vols. (in 1) (Histoire du Mouvement National Tunisien. Documents. 7-9)

POUR préparer la troisième épreuve...; textes réunis et commentés par Mohamed Sayah. [Tunis, 1972-74]. 3 vols. (in 1). (Histoire du Mouvement National Tunisien. Documents. 10-12)

— Population.

TUNIS. Institut National de la Statistique. 1972. Les sources de la démographie tunisienne à l'époque contemporaine: tableau méthodologique. Tunis, 1972. pp. 120. bibliog. (Etudes et Enquêtes de l'I.N.S. No 3)

— Social conditions.

TUNIS. Secrétariat d'État à la Jeunesse, aux Sports et aux Affaires Sociales. 1967. (10 ans de promotion sociale, 1956/1966). 1. La protection sociale; 2. La jeunesse et les sports; 3. Le travail: la formation professionelle et l'emploi. [Tunis, 1967?]. pp. 121.

BOUHDIBA (ABDELWAHAB) A la recherche des normes perdues. [Tunis, 1973]. pp. 271.

— Social policy.

TUNIS. 1973. IVe plan de développement économique et social, 1973-1976. [Tunis, 1973?]. pp. 302.

— Statistics, Vital.

TUNIS. Institut National de la Statistique. 1972. Les sources de la démographie tunisienne à l'époque contemporaine: tableau méthodologique. Tunis, 1972. pp. 120. bibliog. (Etudes et Enquêtes de l'I.N.S. No 3)

TURATI (FILIPPO).

VALERI (NINO) Turati e la Kuliscioff. Firenze, 1974. pp. 214. bibliog.

TURGOT (ANNE ROBERT JACQUES) Baron de l'Aulne.

TURGOT (ANNE ROBERT JACQUES) Baron de l'Aulne. The economics of A.R.J. Turgot; edited and translated...by P.D. Groenewegen. The Hague, 1977. pp. 194.

TURIN

— Economic history.

GEC (ENRICO GIANERI) Storia di Torino industriale: il miracolo della Ceronda. Torino, [1977?]. pp. 324.

— History.

GIOVANA (MARIO) Torino: la città e i "signori Fiat". Milano, [1977]. pp. 208.

TURIN (Cont.)

— Industries.

GEC (ENRICO GIANERI) Storia di Torino industriale: il miracolo della Ceronda. Torino, [1977?]. pp. 324.

— Politics and government.

GRAMSCI (ANTONIO) Sotto la mole, 1916-1920. Torino, 1960 repr. 1971. pp. 509. (*Opere. 10*)

TURIN UNIVERSITY.

BONGIOVANNI (BRUNO) and LEVI (FABIO) L'Università di Torino durante il fascismo: le facoltà umanistiche e il Politecnico. Torino, 1976. pp. 236. (*Turin. Università. Istituto di Storia. Collana. 9*)

TURKEY.

TURKISH DIGEST; pd. by the State Information Organisation of Turkey. m. Ankara. *Current issues only kept.*

— Commerce — United Kingdom.

SKILLITER (S.A.) William Harborne and the trade with Turkey, 1578-1582: a documentary study of the first Anglo-Ottoman relations. London, 1977. pp. 291. *bibliog.*

— Economic conditions — Abstracts.

KEY TO TURKISH SCIENCE: industrial management (formerly: applied economics); (pd. by) Turkish Scientific and Technical Documentation Centre (Türdok). irreg., Ap 1969 (v.1, no.1)- Ankara.

— Foreign relations.

EREN (NURI) Turkey, NATO and Europe: a deteriorating relationship? Paris, [1977]. pp. 54. (*Atlantic Institute. Atlantic Papers. No. 34*)

See also NORTH ATLANTIC TREATY ORGANIZATION — Turkey.

TURKMENISTAN

— History.

ISTORIIA Sovetskogo Turkmenistana. ch.1. 1917-1937. Ashkhabad, 1970. pp. 469.

TURKS IN BOSNIA.

POPOVIĆ (VASILJ) Agrarno pitanje u Bosni i turski neredi za vreme reformnog režima Abdul-Medžida, 1839-1861. Beograd, 1949. pp. 323. (*Srpska Akademija Nauka i Umetnosti. Posebna Izdanja. knj. 150 [being also] Odeljenje Društvenih Nauka. knj. 59*) In Cyrillic.

TWENTIETH CENTURY

— Forecasts.

HACKETT (Sir JOHN WINTHROP) and others. The Third World War: a future history. London, 1978. pp. 368.

HIGGINS (RONALD) The seventh enemy: the human factor in the global crisis. London, [1978]. pp. 303.

TWENTY-FIRST CENTURY

— Forecasts.

LAGOS MATUS (GUSTAVO) and GODOY (HORACIO H.) Revolution of being: a Latin American view of the future. New York, [1977]. pp. 226.

TYNE AND WEAR

— Economic conditions.

TYNE AND WEAR. County Council. Structure plan: report of survey; [with] Summary report of survey. Newcastle upon Tyne, 1976. 2 vols. (in 1).

— Social conditions.

TYNE AND WEAR. County Council. Structure plan: report of survey; [with] Summary report of survey. Newcastle upon Tyne, 1976. 2 vols. (in 1).

TZOTZIL INDIANS

— Language.

GOSSEN (GARY H.) Chamulas in the world of the sun: time and space in a Maya oral tradition. Cambridge, Mass., 1974. pp. 382. *bibliog.*

— Religion and mythology.

HUNT (EVA) The transformation of the hummingbird: cultural roots of a Zinacantecan mythical poem. Ithaca, 1977. pp. 312. *bibliog.*

— Rites and ceremonies.

BRICKER (VICTORIA REIFLER) Ritual humor in highland Chiapas. Austin, [1973]. pp. 257. *bibliog.*

VOGT (EVON ZARTMAN) Tortillas for the gods: a symbolic analysis of Zinacanteco rituals. Cambridge, Mass., [1976]. pp. 234. *bibliog.*

UELAND (OLE GABRIEL GABRIELSEN).

BERGSGÅRD (ARNE) Ole Gabriel Ueland og bondepolitikken. Oslo, 1932. 2 vols.

UGANDA

— Armed forces — Political activity.

HANSEN (HOLGER BERNT) Ethnicity and military rule in Uganda: a study of ethnicity as a political factor in Uganda, based on a discussion of political anthropology and the application of its results. Uppsala, 1977. pp. 144. (*Nordiska Afrikainstitutet. Research Reports. No. 43*)

— Boundaries.

AMIN DADA (IDI) The shaping of modern Uganda and administrative divisions; documents 1900-76. [Entebbe, Government Printer, 1976?]. pp. 75.

— Church history.

PIROUET (M. LOUISE) Black evangelists: the spread of Christianity in Uganda, 1849- 1914. London, 1978. pp. 255. *bibliog.*

— Economic conditions — Statistics.

UGANDA. Ministry of Planning and Economic Development. Statistics Division. Quarterly economic and statistical bulletin. q., D 1969- Entebbe. *Not pd. S, D 1972; Ja 1973. Formerly Uganda quarterly digest, of which the Library has no file.*

— Economic policy.

AMIN DADA (IDI) The shaping of modern Uganda and administrative divisions; documents 1900-76. [Entebbe, Government Printer, 1976?]. pp. 75.

UGANDA. Ministry of Planning and Economic Development. 1977. The action programme: a three-year economic rehabilitation plan, 1977/78-1979/80. Entebbe, [1977]. pp. 193.

— Foreign relations.

UGANDA: (foreign affairs bulletin; [pd. by] Ministry of Foreign Affairs [Uganda]). q., Ja 1974 (v.1, no.1)- Kampala.

AMIN DADA (IDI) The shaping of modern Uganda and administrative divisions; documents 1900-76. [Entebbe, Government Printer, 1976?]. pp. 75.

— History.

AMIN DADA (IDI) The shaping of modern Uganda and administrative divisions; documents 1900-76. [Entebbe, Government Printer, 1976?]. pp. 75.

— Politics and government.

HANSEN (HOLGER BERNT) Ethnicity and military rule in Uganda: a study of ethnicity as a political factor in Uganda, based on a discussion of political anthropology and the application of its results. Uppsala, 1977. pp. 144. (*Nordiska Afrikainstitutet. Research Reports. No. 43*)

— Social policy.

AMIN DADA (IDI) The shaping of modern Uganda and administrative divisions; documents 1900-76. [Entebbe, Government Printer, 1976?]. pp. 75.

UGANDA. Ministry of Planning and Economic Development. 1977. The action programme: a three-year economic rehabilitation plan, 1977/78-1979/80. Entebbe, [1977]. pp. 193.

UKRAINE

— Commerce.

The UKRAINE within the USSR: an economic balance sheet; edited by I.S. Koropeckyj. New York, 1977. pp. 316. *bibliogs. Proceedings of a conference held in Cambridge, Mass., in 1975, sponsored by the Committee on Research and Development of the American Association for the Advancement of Slavic Studies.*

— Economic conditions.

The UKRAINE within the USSR: an economic balance sheet; edited by I.S. Koropeckyj. New York, 1977. pp. 316. *bibliogs. Proceedings of a conference held in Cambridge, Mass., in 1975, sponsored by the Committee on Research and Development of the American Association for the Advancement of Slavic Studies.*

— Economic policy.

The UKRAINE within the USSR: an economic balance sheet; edited by I.S. Koropeckyj. New York, 1977. pp. 316. *bibliogs. Proceedings of a conference held in Cambridge, Mass., in 1975, sponsored by the Committee on Research and Development of the American Association for the Advancement of Slavic Studies.*

— History.

ISTORIIA Ukraïns'koï RSR u vos'my tomakh, desiaty knyhakh. Kyïv, 1977 in progress. *bibliog.*

— — 1917-1921, Revolution.

PALIJ (MICHAEL) The anarchism of Nestor Makhno, 1918-1921: an aspect of the Ukrainian revolution. Seattle, [1976]. pp. 428. *bibliog.* (*Washington State University. Institute for Comparative and Foreign Area Studies. Publications on Russia and Eastern Europe. No. 7*)

The UKRAINE, 1917-1921: a study in revolution; Taras Hunczak, editor. Cambridge, Mass., 1977. pp. 424. (*Harvard University. Harvard Ukrainian Research Institute. Monograph Series*) *Based on a conference held in New York in 1968.*

— Industries.

PROMYSHLENNOST' i rabochii klass Ukrainskoi SSR, 1933-1941: sbornik dokumentov i materialov v dvukh chastiakh. Kiev, 1977. 2 vols.

— Politics and government.

JEUNE UKRAINE, LA; revue trimestrielle publiée par le Comité National Ukrainien. q. 1921 (No. 5) Paris.

— Rural conditions.

BEREZOVCHUK (MYKOLA DANYLOVYCH) Pershi sotsialistychni peretvorennia na seli: pro orhanizatsiï sil's'koï bidnoty ta ïkh rol' u zdiisnenni pershykh sotsialistychnykh peretvoren'. Kyïv, 1976. pp. 149.

UKRAINIANS IN ALBERTA.

POTREBENKO (HELEN) No streets of gold: a social history of Ukrainians in Alberta. Vancouver, 1977. pp. 311. *bibliog.*

UL'IANOV (ALEKSANDR IL'ICH)

— Bibliography.

BARANOVSKAIA (I.E.) compiler. Aleksandr Ul'ianov: rekomendatel'nyi ukazatel' literatury; (pod obshchei redaktsiei Zh.A. Trofimova). Ul'ianovsk, 1967. pp. 19.

UNCERTAINTY.

NATURAL resources, uncertainty, and general equilibrium systems: essays in memory of Rafael Lusky; edited by Alan S. Blinder [and] Philip Friedman. New York, [1977]. pp. 255. *bibliogs.*

— Mathematical models.

MOSSIN (JAN) The economic efficiency of financial markets. Lexington, Mass., [1977]. pp. 158. *bibliogs.*

UNDERDEVELOPED AREAS.

[NESTLÉ]. A Swiss firm and its activities in developing countries: Nestlé's experience. [Lausanne, 1963]. 1 pamphlet (unpaged).

MYINT (MAUNG HLA) The economics of the developing countries. 4th ed. London, 1973 repr. 1977. pp. 160. *bibliog.*

PAKISTAN INSTITUTE OF INTERNATIONAL AFFAIRS. Zulfikar Ali Bhutto and the third world's struggle for new economic order. Karachi, 1976. pp. 32.

SACHS (IGNACY) The discovery of the third world. [Cambridge, Mass., 1976]. pp. 287.

SOTSIAL'NO-ekonomicheskie problemy razvivaiushchikhsia stran: materialy Vsesoiuznoi nauchnoi konferentsii, sostoiavsheisia 14-16 aprelia 1975 g. Moskva, 1976. pp. 157.

SEWELL (JOHN WILLIAMSON) The United States and world development: agenda 1977. New York, 1977. pp. 245. *Written under the auspices of the Overseas Development Council.*

SFEIR-YOUNIS (ALFREDO) and BROMLEY (DANIEL W.) Decision making in developing countries: multiobjective formulation and evaluation methods. New York, [1977]. pp. 200. *bibliog.*

SINGH (JYOTI SHANKAR) A new international economic order: toward a fair redistribution of the world's resources. New York, 1977. pp. 135. *bibliog.*

— Agriculture.

INTERNATIONAL BANK FOR RECONSTRUCTION AND DEVELOPMENT. Sector Policy Papers. Rural development. [Washington], 1975. pp. 89.

ASKARI (HOSSEIN) and CUMMINGS (JOHN THOMAS) Agricultural supply response: a survey of the econometric evidence. New York, 1976. pp. 443. *bibliog.*

SHAPIRO (KENNETH H.) Efficiency differentials in peasant agriculture and their implications for development policies. Ann Arbor, 1976. pp. 13. *bibliog. (Michigan University. Center for Research on Economic Development. Discussion Papers. No. 52)*

TRADITION and dynamics in small-farm agriculture: economic studies in Asia, Africa, and Latin America; edited by Robert D. Stevens. Ames, Iowa, 1977. pp. 266. *bibliogs.*

MORGAN (WILLIAM BASIL) Agriculture in the Third World: a spatial analysis. Boulder, 1978. pp. 290. *bibliog.*

YOSHIDA (TSUNEAKI) Applicability of project appraisal for developing countries with special reference to agricultural projects. 1977 [or rather 1978]. fo.115. *Typescript. M.Phil. (London) thesis: unpublished. This thesis is the property of London University and may not be removed from the Library.*

— Banks and banking.

ABDI (ALI ISSA) Commercial banks and economic development: the experience of eastern Africa. New York, 1977. pp. 148. *bibliog.*

— Bibliography.

LAMBERT (CLAIRE M.) compiler. Development studies, 1966-1976; a select list of the writings on third world development by members of the Institute of Development Studies at the University of Sussex. [Brighton], 1976. pp. 88.

— Birth control.

DEMERATH (NICHOLAS JAY) Birth control and foreign policy: the alternatives to family planning. New York, [1976]. pp. 228. *bibliog.*

— Brain drain.

GLASER (WILLIAM ARNOLD) and HABERS (G. CHRISTOPHER) The brain drain: emigration and return: findings of a UNITAR multinational comparative survey of professional personnel of developing countries who study abroad. Oxford, [1978]. pp. 324. *bibliogs. (United Nations Institute for Training and Research. Research Reports. 22)*

— Broadcasting.

KATZ (ELIHU) and WEDELL (EBERHARD GEORGE) Broadcasting in the Third World: promise and performance. Cambridge, Mass., 1977. pp. 305.

— Building materials industry.

WORKSHOP ON ORGANIZATIONAL AND TECHNICAL MEASURES FOR THE DEVELOPMENT OF BUILDING MATERIALS, MOSCOW, 1968. Report of the Workshop...organized jointly by the United Nations and the Government of the Union of Soviet Socialist Republics, Moscow, 25 September to 18 October, 1968. (ST/TAO/SER.C/123). New York, United Nations, 1970. pp. 130.

— City planning.

MOHAN (RAKESH) Urban land policy, income distribution and the urban poor. [Princeton], 1974. pp. 76. *bibliog. (Princeton University and Brookings Institution. Project on Income Distribution in Less Developed Countries)*

AD HOC GROUP OF EXPERTS ON INDICATORS OF THE QUALITY OF URBAN DEVELOPMENT, [NEW YORK], 1975. Report of the meeting of the Ad Hoc Group...held at United Nations Headquarters from 8 to 12 December 1975. (ST/ESA/56). New York, United Nations, 1977. pp. 47.

— Civil rights.

CHOMSKY (NOAM) 'Human rights' and American foreign policy. Nottingham, 1978. pp. 90.

— Commerce.

UNITED NATIONS. Conference on Trade and Development. 1974. Problems of raw materials and development: report by the Secretary-General of UNCTAD prepared for the sixth special session of the General Assembly. (TD/B/488). New York, 1974. pp. 44.

MURRAY (TRACY) Trade preferences for developing countries. London, 1977. pp. 172. *bibliog.*

CABLE (VINCENT) Developments in international trade policy and their implications for developing countries; paper. London, 1978. pp. 35.

COMMONWEALTH SECRETARIAT. Multilateral trade negotiations and relevant trends in international trade policy; paper. London, 1978. pp. 23.

GOLT (SIDNEY) Developing countries in the GATT system. London, 1978. pp. 36. *(Trade Policy Research Centre. Thames Essays. No. 13)*

— Commercial policy.

BRUTON (HENRY J.) Industrialization policy and income distribution. [Princeton], 1974. pp. 96. *bibliog. (Princeton University and Brookings Institution. Project on Income Distribution in Less Developed Countries)*

— — Mathematical models.

PORTER (RICHARD C.) and STAELIN (CHARLES P.) On the rationality of "cascaded" export subsidies and taxes. Ann Arbor, 1974. pp. 11. *bibliog. (Michigan University. Center for Research on Economic Development. Discussion Papers. No. 34)*

UNDERDEVELOPED AREAS.

— Cost and standard of living.

YUGOSLAVIA. Savezni Zavod za Statistiku. Studije, Analize i Prikazi. 80. Socio-ekonomski nivo i profil razvijenih zemalja i zemalja u razvoju u 1970. godini; Niveau et socio-économique [sic] des pays développés et [sic] voie de développement en 1970; [by] Branislav Ivanović. Beograd, 1976. pp. 75. *With French summary.*

— Debts, External.

SMITH (GORDON W.) The external debt prospects of the non-oil-exporting developing countries: an econometric analysis. Washington, 1977. pp. 49. *bibliog. (Overseas Development Council. Monographs. No. 10)*

PARSONS (CHRISTOPHER) Finance for development or survival?: the debt crisis of developing countries. London, 1978. pp. 27. *(Fabian Society. Research Series. [No.] 336)*

— Drug trade.

HELLER (TOM) Poor health, rich profits: multinational drug companies and the Third World. Nottingham, 1977. pp. 76.

— Economic conditions.

TEMMAR (HAMID) Approche structurelle du phénomène du sous-développement: la structure de l'économie sous-développée. Alger, 1973. pp. 128. *bibliog.*

La PLURALITE des mondes: théorie et pratiques du développement. [Genève, 1975]. pp. 139.

UNION GENERALE DES TRAVAILLEURS SENEGALAIS EN FRANCE. Qui est responsable du sous-développement. Paris, 1975. pp. 85.

BIONDI (JEAN PIERRE) Le tiers-socialisme: essai sur le socialisme et le "Tiers-Monde". [Paris, 1976]. pp. 187.

AMIN (SAMIR) Imperialism and unequal development. Hassocks, [1977]. pp. 267. *Translation of his L'impérialisme et développement inégal.*

BURNELL (PETER) Absorptive capacity and development. [Coventry], 1977. pp. 21. *(University of Warwick. Department of Politics. Working Papers. No. 14)*

ECONOMIC development, poverty, and income distribution; edited by William Loehr and John P. Powelson. Boulder, 1977. pp. 307. *bibliogs. Papers presented at a conference in 1976 sponsored by the Institute of Behavioral Science, University of Colorado.*

KANGA (RUSTOM ADI) Economic evaluation of computer systems for developing countries. 1977. fo. 372,(73). *bibliog. Typescript. Ph.D. (London) thesis: unpublished. This thesis is the property of London University and may not be removed from the Library.*

MENON (BHASKAR P.) Global dialogue: the new international economic order. Oxford, 1977. pp. 110.

PEASANT livelihood: studies in economic anthropology and cultural ecology; Rhoda Halperin [and] James Dow, editors. New York, [1977]. pp. 332. *bibliog.*

RESHAPING the world economic order: symposium 1976, ([held at] Institut für Weltwirtschaft an der Universität Kiel; edited by Herbert Giersch. Tübingen, [1977]. pp. 291.

UNITED NATIONS. Centre for Development Planning, Projections and Policies. 1977. Economic and social progress in the second development decade: assessment of progress made in the implementation of the international development strategy...; report of the Secretary- General. (E/5981)(ST/ESA/68). New York, 1977. pp. 114.

WORLD DEVELOPMENT REPORT; [pd. by] International Bank for Reconstruction and Development. a., 1978 (1st)- Washington.

LATHAM (ANTHONY JOHN HEATON) The international economy and the undeveloped world, 1865-1914. London, [1978]. pp. 217. *bibliog.*

UNDERDEVELOPED AREAS.(Cont.)

LEAN (GEOFFREY) Rich world, poor world. London, 1978. pp. 352. *bibliog.*

THIRLWALL (ANTHONY PHILIP) Growth and development: with special reference to developing economies. 2nd ed. London, 1978. pp. 398. *bibliog.*

DEVELOPMENT DIRECTIONS; [pd. by] Canadian International Development Agency. 9 a yr., Current issues only. Hull, Québec. *Supersedes COOPERATION CANADA.*

— — Statistics.

YUGOSLAVIA. Savezni Zavod za Statistiku. Studije, Analize i Prikazi. 80. Socio-ekonomski nivo i profil razvijenih zemalja i zemalja u razvoju u 1970. godini; Niveau et socio-économique [sic] des pays développés et [sic] voie de développement en 1970; [by] Branislav Ivanović. Beograd, 1976. pp. 75. *With French summary.*

— Economic policy.

BONGOMA (JACQUES DANIEL) Indépendance économique et révolution. Kinshasa, [1969]. pp. 187. *bibliog.*

INTERREGIONAL SEMINAR ON DEVELOPMENT PLANNING, 4TH, ACCRA, 1968. Development prospects and planning for the coming decade, with special reference to Africa: report on the...Seminar...[held in] Accra, Ghana, 4 to 13 December 1968. (ST/TAO/SER.C/116) . New York, United Nations, 1970. pp. 38.

ROBSON (PETER) Fiscal compensation and the distribution of benefits in economic groupings of developing countries. (TD/B/322/Rev.1). New York, United Nations, 1971. pp. 39.

LARABI (HACHEMI) Opinions sur l'économie algérienne, suivies de notes de voyages. Alger, 1973. pp. 269.

DIA (MAMADOU) Emancipation des économies captives. Paris, 1976 in progress.

INTERNATIONAL BANK FOR RECONSTRUCTION AND DEVELOPMENT. Sector Policy Papers. Development finance companies. Washington, 1976. pp. 65.

SINGER (PAUL ISRAEL) Dinâmica populacional e desenvolvimento: o papel do crescimento populacional no desenvolvimento econômico. São Paulo, 1976. pp. 250. *bibliog.*

BURNELL (PETER) Political commitment to economic development. [Coventry], 1977. pp. 66. *(University of Warwick. Department of Politics. Working Papers. No. 13)*

Der DIALOG Nord-Süd: Informationen zur Entwicklungspolitik;... ([edited by] Jan Tinbergen). Frankfurt am Main, [1977]. pp. 227.

FROEBEL (FOLKER) and others. Die neue internationale Arbeitsteilung: strukturelle Arbeitslosigkeit in den Industrieländern und die Industrialisierung der Entwicklungsländer. Reinbek bei Hamburg, 1977. pp. 654.

JEDLICKA (ALLEN D.) Organization for rural development: risk taking and appropriate technology. New York, 1977. pp. 170.

MOBILIZATION of household savings: a tool for development; edited by Arnaldo Mauri. Milan, 1977. pp. 219. *(Cassa di Risparmio delle Provincie Lombarde. The Credit Markets of Africa. 14)*

THEORY and practice of development in the third world; edited by Jozsef Nyilas. Leyden, 1977. pp. 298. *Part of a study undertaken by the Department of World Economy, Karl Marx University of Economics, Budapest, based on vol. 3 of Korunk Világgazdasága.*

WELLONS (P.A.) Borrowing by developing countries on the euro-currency market. Paris, Organisation for Economic Co-operation and Development, 1977. pp. 449. *(Development Centre. Studies)*

MEHMET (OZAY) Economic planning and social justice in developing countries. London, [1978]. pp. 282.

VEREIN FÜR SOZIALPOLITIK. Schriften. Neue Folge. Band 94. Wachstum, Einkommensverteilung und Beschäftigung in Entwicklungsländern; von Michael Bohnet [and others]; herausgegeben von Winfried von Urff. Berlin, [1978]. pp. 175.

YOSHIDA (TSUNEAKI) Applicability of project appraisal for developing countries with special reference to agricultural projects. 1977 [or rather 1978]. fo.115. Typescript. M.Phil. (London) thesis: unpublished. *This thesis is the property of London University and may not be removed from the Library.*

— — Mathematical models.

BERENDSEN (BERNARDUS STEPHANUS MARIA) Regional models of trade and development. Leiden, 1978. pp. 252. *bibliog.*

— Education.

HARBISON (FREDERICK HARRIS) The connection between education and income distribution. [Princeton], 1974. pp. 36, 27. *(Princeton University and Brookings Institution. Project on Income Distribution in Less Developed Countries)*

— Education (Higher).

THOMPSON (KENNETH WINFRED) and FOGEL (BARBARA R.) Higher education and social change: promising experiments in developing countries; volume 1: reports. New York, 1976. pp. 224.

THOMPSON (KENNETH WINFRED) and others, eds. Higher education and social change: promising experiments in developing countries; volume 2: case studies. New York, 1977. pp. 564.

— Energy policy.

HAYES (DENIS) Environmentalist. Energy for development: third world options. Washington, 1977. pp. 43. *(Worldwatch Institute. Worldwatch Papers. No. 15)*

— Environmental policy.

PEARSON (CHARLES S.) and PRYOR (ANTHONY) Environment: north and south: an economic interpretation. New York, [1978]. pp. 355. *bibliog.*

— Export premiums — Mathematical models.

PORTER (RICHARD C.) and STAELIN (CHARLES P.) On the rationality of "cascaded" export subsidies and taxes. Ann Arbor, 1974. pp. 11. *bibliog. (Michigan University. Center for Research on Economic Development. Discussion Papers. No. 34)*

— Finance.

HARBERGER (ARNOLD CARL) Fiscal policy and income redistribution. [Princeton], 1974. pp. 23,5. *(Princeton University and Brookings Institution. Project on Income Distribution in Less Developed Countries)*

NEWLYN (WALTER TESSIER) The financing of economic development. Oxford, 1977. pp. 374. *bibliog.*

STEINBERG (ELEANOR B.) and YAGER (JOSEPH A.) New means of financing international needs; (with Gerard M. Brannon). Washington, D.C., [1978]. pp. 256.

— Finance — Accounting.

UNITED NATIONS. Interregional Seminar on Government Accounting and Financial Management, Beirut, 1969. Report of the...Seminar...[held at] Beirut, Lebanon, 8-19 December, 1969. (ST/TAO/SER.C/117). New York, 1970. pp. 31. *bibliog.*

— Financial institutions.

INTERNATIONAL BANK FOR RECONSTRUCTION AND DEVELOPMENT. Sector Policy Papers. Development finance companies. Washington, 1976. pp. 65.

— Food supply.

CROSSON (PIERRE R.) and FREDERICK (KENNETH D.) The world food situation: resource and environmental issues in the developing countries and the United States. Washington, D.C., [1977]. pp. 174. *bibliog. (Resources for the Future, Inc. Research Papers. R-6)*

— Foreign economic relations.

ACP-EEC COUNCIL OF MINISTERS. Annual report [and] Commission report...on the administration of financial and technical aid. a., 1976/77- Suva.

HAQ (MAHBUB UL) The third world and the international economic order. Washington, 1976. pp. 56. *(Overseas Development Council. Development Papers. 22)*

SUTTON (MARY) The EEC and the developing world: a changing relationship. Dublin, 1976. pp. 59. *bibliog. (Trócaire and Irish Commission for Justice and Peace. Joint Development Education Programme)*

Der DIALOG Nord-Süd: Informationen zur Entwicklungspolitik;... ([edited by] Jan Tinbergen). Frankfurt am Main, [1977]. pp. 227.

ECONOMIC relations between socialist countries and the third world; edited by Deepak Nayyar. London, 1977. pp. 265.

ISSUES and prospects for the new international order; edited by William G. Tyler. Lexington, Mass., [1977]. pp. 195. *Derived from a conference organised by the International Studies Association/South held in Virginia in 1976.*

KODACHENKO (ALEKSANDR SERGEEVICH) Vneshneekonomicheskaia politika imperializma i razvivaiushchiesia strany. Moskva, 1977. pp. 311.

The NEW international economic order: the North-South debate; Jagdish N. Bhagwati, editor. Cambridge, Mass., [1977]. pp. 390. *bibliogs. (Massachusetts Institute of Technology. M.I.T. Bicentennial Studies) Based largely on a workshop held at MIT in May 1976.*

SHARP (ROBIN) and WHITTEMORE (CLAIRE) Europe and the world without: policies and programmes of the European Community and their impact on world poverty. London, [1977]. pp. 49. *bibliog. (Oxfam. Public Affairs Unit. Oxfam Public Affairs Reports. 3)*

Les SOCIALISTES et le Tiers Monde: éléments pour une politique socialiste de relations avec le Tiers Monde. [Paris, 1977]. pp. 251.

WOLYNSKI (ALEXANDER) Soviet aid to the third world: strategy before economics. London, 1977. pp. 13. *(Institute for the Study of Conflict. Conflict Studies. No. 90)*

COMMONWEALTH SECRETARIAT. Review of progress in the implementation of recommendations of the report of the Commonwealth Experts' Group, Towards a new international economic order; paper. London, 1978. pp. 47.

RICH and poor nations in the world economy; [by] Albert Fishlow [and others]. New York, [1978]. pp. 262. *bibliog. (Council on Foreign Relations. 1980's Project Studies)*

ROTHSTEIN (ROBERT L.) The weak in the world of the strong: the developing countries in the international system. New York, 1977. pp. 384.

— Foreign relations.

FOREIGN policy making in developing states: a comparative approach; edited by Christopher Clapham. Farnborough, Hants., [1977]. pp. 184. *bibliogs.*

PLISCHKE (ELMER) Microstates in world affairs: policy problems and options. Washington, D.C., [1977]. pp. 153. *(American Enterprise Institute for Public Policy Research. AEI Studies. 144)*

TUZMUKHAMEDOV (RAIS ABDULKHAKOVICH) Razvivaiushchiesia strany v mirovoi politike: mezhdunarodnye mezhpravitel'stvennye organizatsii razvivaiushchikhsia stran. Moskva, 1977. pp. 207.

CHOMSKY (NOAM) 'Human rights' and American foreign policy. Nottingham, 1978. pp. 90.

UNDERDEVELOPED AREAS.(Cont.)

ROTHSTEIN (ROBERT L.) The weak in the world of the strong: the developing countries in the international system. New York, 1977. pp. 384.

— **Full employment policies.**

STEEL (WILLIAM F.) Small-scale employment and production in developing countries: evidence from Ghana. New York, 1977. pp. 235. *bibliog.*

— **Government ownership.**

CAUAS (JORGE) and SELOWSKY (MARCELO) Potential distributive effects of nationalization policies: the economic aspects;...revised version of an earlier paper prepared for the Research Workshop on Income Distribution in Less Developed Countries, Princeton University, November 13, 1973. [Princeton], 1974. pp. 41. *(Princeton University and Brookings Institution. Project on Income Distribution in Less Developed Countries)*

— **Health planning.**

MANPOWER and primary health care: guidelines for improving/expanding health service coverage in developing countries; edited by Richard A. Smith. Honolulu, [1968]. pp. 189.

— **Housing.**

SEMINAR ON THE USE OF WOOD IN HOUSING, VANCOUVER, 1971. Report of the Seminar...with the emphasis on the needs of developing countries; organized jointly by the United Nations and the Government of Canada, [held in] Vancouver, Canada, 3-16 July 1971. (ST/TAO/SER.C/137). New York, United Nations, 1972. pp. 32. *bibliog.*

INTERNATIONAL BANK FOR RECONSTRUCTION AND DEVELOPMENT. Sector Policy Papers. Housing. [Washington], 1975. pp. 74.

MABOGUNJE (AKIN L.) and others. Shelter provision in developing countries: the influence of standards and criteria. Chichester, [1978]. pp. 94. *(International Council of Scientific Unions. Scientific Committee on Problems of the Environment. SCOPE Reports. 11)*

— **Hygiene, Public.**

OFTEDAL (OLAV T.) and LEVINSON (F. JAMES) Health, nutrition and income distribution. [Princeton], 1974. pp. 70. *bibliog. (Princeton University and Brookings Institution. Project on Income Distribution in Less Developed Countries)*

INTERNATIONAL BANK FOR RECONSTRUCTION AND DEVELOPMENT. Sector Policy Papers. Health. [Washington], 1975. pp. 83.

— **Income distribution.**

CAUAS (JORGE) and SELOWSKY (MARCELO) Potential distributive effects of nationalization policies: the economic aspects;...revised version of an earlier paper prepared for the Research Workshop on Income Distribution in Less Developed Countries, Princeton University, November 13, 1973. [Princeton], 1974. pp. 41. *(Princeton University and Brookings Institution. Project on Income Distribution in Less Developed Countries)*

CLINE (WILLIAM R.) Policy instruments for rural income redistribution. [Princeton, 1974?]. pp. 71. *bibliog. (Princeton University and Brookings Institution. Project on Income Distribution in Less Developed Countries)*

FRANK (CHARLES R.) and WEBB (RICHARD CHARLES) Income distribution and growth in less developed countries: some reflections on theory and policy. [Princeton], 1974. pp. 44, 21. *bibliog. (Princeton University and Brookings Institution. Project on Income Distribution in Less Developed Countries)*

HARBERGER (ARNOLD CARL) Fiscal policy and income redistribution. [Princeton], 1974. pp. 23,5. *(Princeton University and Brookings Institution. Project on Income Distribution in Less Developed Countries)*

HARBISON (FREDERICK HARRIS) The connection between education and income distribution. [Princeton], 1974. pp. 36, 27. *(Princeton University and Brookings Institution. Project on Income Distribution in Less Developed Countries)*

MOHAN (RAKESH) Urban land policy, income distribution and the urban poor. [Princeton], 1974. pp. 76. *bibliog. (Princeton University and Brookings Institution. Project on Income Distribution in Less Developed Countries)*

OFTEDAL (OLAV T.) and LEVINSON (F. JAMES) Health, nutrition and income distribution. [Princeton], 1974. pp. 70. *bibliog. (Princeton University and Brookings Institution. Project on Income Distribution in Less Developed Countries)*

WEBB (RICHARD CHARLES) Wage policy and income distribution in developing countries. [Princeton], 1974. pp. 58. *(Princeton University and Brookings Institution. Project on Income Distribution in Less Developed Countries)*

ECONOMIC development, poverty, and income distribution; edited by William Loehr and John P. Powelson. Boulder, 1977. pp. 307. *bibliogs.* Papers presented at a conference in 1976 sponsored by the Institute of Behavioral Science, University of Colorado.

INCOME distribution and growth in the less-developed countries; Charles R. Frank and Richard C. Webb, editors. Washington, D.C., [1977]. pp. 641. *bibliog.* Based on a project carried out by the Brookings Institution and the Woodrow Wilson School of Public and International Affairs at Princeton University.

— — **Mathematical models.**

BRUTON (HENRY J.) Industrialization policy and income distribution. [Princeton], 1974. pp. 96. *bibliog. (Princeton University and Brookings Institution. Project on Income Distribution in Less Developed Countries)*

ADELMAN (IRMA) and ROBINSON (SHERMAN) Income distribution policy in developing countries: a case study of Korea. Stanford, 1978. pp. 346. *bibliog.*

— **Industrial promotion.**

UNITED NATIONS INDUSTRIAL DEVELOPMENT ORGANIZATION. Development and Transfer of Technology Series. New York, 1977 in progress.

— **Industries.**

BRUTON (HENRY J.) Industrialization policy and income distribution. [Princeton], 1974. pp. 96. *bibliog. (Princeton University and Brookings Institution. Project on Income Distribution in Less Developed Countries)*

GIRVAN (NORMAN PAUL) Corporate imperialism: conflict and expropriation: transnational corporations and economic nationalism in the Third World. White Plains, N.Y., 1976. pp. 241. *bibliog.*

UNITED NATIONS INDUSTRIAL DEVELOPMENT ORGANIZATION. Development and Transfer of Technology Series. New York, 1977 in progress.

— **Industry and state.**

BIONDI (JEAN PIERRE) Le tiers-socialisme: essai sur le socialisme et le "Tiers-Monde". [Paris, 1976]. pp. 187.

— **Inflation.**

JUD (G. DONALD) Inflation and the use of indexing in developing countries. New York, 1978. pp. 220. *bibliog.*

— **Information services.**

STAMPER (RONALD) Learning from the developing world. [London], 1975. pp. 5. *(Reprinted from Computer Weekly, Nov. 27th, 1975)*

— **International business enterprises.**

GIRVAN (NORMAN PAUL) Corporate imperialism: conflict and expropriation: transnational corporations and economic nationalism in the Third World. White Plains, N.Y., 1976. pp. 241. *bibliog.*

HELLER (TOM) Poor health, rich profits: multinational drug companies and the Third World. Nottingham, 1977. pp. 76.

— **Investments.**

YOSHIDA (TSUNEAKI) Applicability of project appraisal for developing countries with special reference to agricultural projects. 1977 [or rather 1978]. fo.115. Typescript. M.Phil. (London) thesis: unpublished. *This thesis is the property of London University and may not be removed from the Library.*

— **Investments, Foreign.**

KOBRIN (STEPHEN JAY) Foreign direct investment, industrialization and social change. Greenwich, Conn., [1977]. pp. 188. *bibliog.*

— **Labour supply.**

DASGUPTA (BIPLAB KUMAR) and others. Village society and labour use:...a study prepared for the International Labour Office, within the framework of the World Employment Programme, etc. Delhi, 1977. pp. 229. *bibliog. (Brighton. University of Sussex. Institute of Development Studies. Village Studies Programme).*

STUDIES of urban labour market behaviour in developing areas; edited by Subbiah Kannappan. Geneva, International Institute for Labour Studies, 1977. pp. 234. *bibliogs.*

SINCLAIR (STUART W.) Urbanisation and labour markets in developing countries. London, [1978]. pp. 115.

— **Land use.**

MOHAN (RAKESH) Urban land policy, income distribution and the urban poor. [Princeton], 1974. pp. 76. *bibliog. (Princeton University and Brookings Institution. Project on Income Distribution in Less Developed Countries)*

— **Loans, Foreign.**

WELLONS (P.A.) Borrowing by developing countries on the euro-currency market. Paris, Organisation for Economic Co-operation and Development, 1977. pp. 449. *(Development Centre. Studies)*

— **Local transit.**

FOURACRE (P.R.) Intermediate public transport in developing countries. Crowthorne, 1977. p. 18. *bibliog. (U.K. Transport and Road Research Laboratory. Reports. LR 772)*

— **Medical care.**

INTERNATIONAL BANK FOR RECONSTRUCTION AND DEVELOPMENT. Sector Policy Papers. Health. [Washington], 1975. pp. 83.

NEWELL (KENNETH W.) ed. Health by the people. Geneva, World Health Organization, 1975. pp. 206. *bibliogs.*

MANPOWER and primary health care: guidelines for improving/expanding health service coverage in developing countries; edited by Richard A. Smith. Honolulu, [1968]. pp. 189.

— **Medical personnel.**

MANPOWER and primary health care: guidelines for improving/expanding health service coverage in developing countries; edited by Richard A. Smith. Honolulu, [1968]. pp. 189.

— **Milk trade.**

MULLER (MIKE) The baby killer: a War on Want investigation into the promotion and sale of powdered baby milks in the Third World. London, 1974. pp. 19.

— **Mineral industries.**

UNITED NATIONS. Department of Economic and Social Affairs. Resources and Transport Division. 1972. Small-scale mining in the developing countries. (ST/ECA/155). New York, 1972. pp. 171. *bibliog.*

BOSSON (REX) and VARON (BENSION) The mining industry and the developing countries. Washington, International Bank for Reconstruction and Development, 1977. pp. 292. *bibliog.*

UNDERDEVELOPED AREAS.(Cont.)

— — Taxation.

GILLIS (MALCOLM) and others. Taxation and mining: nonfuel minerals in Bolivia and other countries. Cambridge, Mass., [1978]. pp. 358.

— National income.

PYATT (FRANK GRAHAM) and ROE (ALAN R.) Social accounting for development planning with special reference to Sri Lanka. Cambridge, [1977]. pp. 190. *bibliog.* Based on an International Labour Office World Employment Programme Research Branch mission to Sri Lanka in 1973.

— Natural resources.

GIRVAN (NORMAN PAUL) Corporate imperialism: conflict and expropriation: transnational corporations and economic nationalism in the Third World. White Plains, N.Y., 1976. pp. 241. *bibliog.*

— Nutrition.

OFTEDAL (OLAV T.) and LEVINSON (F. JAMES) Health, nutrition and income distribution. [Princeton], 1974. pp. 70. *bibliog. (Princeton University and Brookings Institution. Project on Income Distribution in Less Developed Countries)*

REUTLINGER (SHLOMO) and SELOWSKY (MARCELO) Malnutrition and poverty: magnitude and policy options. [Washington], International Bank for Reconstruction and Development, [1976]. pp. 82. *(World Bank Staff Occasional Papers. No. 23)*

— Peasantry.

SHAPIRO (KENNETH H.) Efficiency differentials in peasant agriculture and their implications for development policies. Ann Arbor, 1976. pp. 13. *bibliog. (Michigan University. Center for Research on Economic Development. Discussion Papers. No. 52)*

TRADITION and dynamics in small-farm agriculture: economic studies in Asia, Africa, and Latin America; edited by Robert D. Stevens. Ames, Iowa, 1977. pp. 266. *bibliogs.*

— Petroleum — Refining.

INTERREGIONAL SEMINAR ON PETROLEUM REFINING IN DEVELOPING COUNTRIES, NEW DELHI, 1973. Report of the Interregional Seminar...[held in] New Delhi, 22 January to 3 February 1973. (ST/TAO/SER.C/146). New York, United Nations, 1973. pp. 34.

— Politics and government.

SEBRELI (JUAN JOSE) Tercer mundo: mito burgues. Buenos Aires, [1975]. pp. 252.

BURNELL (PETER) Political commitment to economic development. [Coventry], 1977. pp. 66. *(University of Warwick. Department of Politics. Working Papers. No. 13)*

JACKSON (ROBERT J.) Plural societies and new states: a conceptual analysis. Berkeley, Calif., [1977]. pp. 74. *bibliog. (California University. Institute of International Studies. Research Series. No. 30)*

LIJPHART (AREND) Democracy in plural societies: a comparative exploration. New Haven, 1977. pp. 248.

CLARK (ROBERT P.) Power and policy in the Third World. New York, [1978]. pp. 159. *bibliogs.*

— Poor.

LEWIS (JOHN PRIOR) Designing the public-works mode of antipoverty policy. [Princeton], 1974. pp. 64. *(Princeton University and Brookings Institution. Project on Income Distribution in Less Developed Countries)*

MOHAN (RAKESH) Urban land policy, income distribution and the urban poor. [Princeton], 1974. pp. 76. *bibliog. (Princeton University and Brookings Institution. Project on Income Distribution in Less Developed Countries)*

— Population.

SINGER (PAUL ISRAEL) Dinâmica populacional e desenvolvimento: o papel do crescimento populacional no desenvolvimento econômico. São Paulo, 1976. pp. 250. *bibliog.*

STAMPER (B. MAXWELL) Population and planning in developing nations: a review of sixty development plans for the 1970s. New York, [1977]. pp. 265. *bibliog.*

— Public works.

LEWIS (JOHN PRIOR) Designing the public-works mode of antipoverty policy. [Princeton], 1974. pp. 64. *(Princeton University and Brookings Institution. Project on Income Distribution in Less Developed Countries)*

— Rehabilitation.

UNITED NATIONS. Interregional Seminar on Programmes and Administration of Major Rehabilitation Services in Developing Countries, Virum, 1966. Report of the...seminar...[held at] Virum, Denmark, 18 July-5 August 1966. (ST/TAO/SER.C/100). New York, 1967. pp. 181.

MEETING OF EXPERTS ON THE PLANNING, ORGANIZATION AND ADMINISTRATION OF NATIONAL PROGRAMMES FOR THE REHABILITATION OF THE DISABLED IN DEVELOPING COUNTRIES, GENEVA, 1971. Report of...[the] Meeting...[held at] Geneva, 27 September-6 October 1971. (ST/SOA/115). New York, United Nations, 1972. pp. 25.

— Rehabilitation, Rural.

CLINE (WILLIAM R.) Policy instruments for rural income redistribution. [Princeton, 1974?]. pp. 71. *bibliog. (Princeton University and Brookings Institution. Project on Income Distribution in Less Developed Countries)*

— Road accidents.

JACOBS (G.D.) and BARDSLEY (MARGUERITE N.) Road accidents as a cause of death in developing countries. Crowthorne, 1977. pp. 18. *bibliog. (U.K. Transport and Road Research Laboratory. Supplementary Reports. 277)*

— Road planning.

BOVILL (D.I.N.) and others. A guide to transport planning within the roads sector; for developing countries. London, H.M.S.O., 1978. pp. 43. *bibliog.*

— Rural conditions.

NEWELL (KENNETH W.) ed. Health by the people. Geneva, World Health Organization, 1975. pp. 206. *bibliogs.*

DASGUPTA (BIPLAB KUMAR) and others. Village society and labour use:...a study prepared for the International Labour Office, within the framework of the World Employment Programme, etc. Delhi, 1977. pp. 229. *bibliog. (Brighton. University of Sussex. Institute of Development Studies. Village Studies Programme).*

— Rural development.

See RURAL DEVELOPMENT.

— Rural-urban migration.

SINCLAIR (STUART W.) Urbanisation and labour markets in developing countries. London, [1978]. pp. 115.

— Saving and investment.

INTERREGIONAL SEMINAR ON THE MOBILIZATION OF PERSONAL SAVINGS IN DEVELOPING COUNTRIES, STOCKHOLM, 1971. Report of the Interregional Seminar...[held in] Stockholm, Sweden, 2 to 11 August 1971. (ST/TAO/SER.C/139). New York, United Nations, 1972. pp. 63.

MOBILIZATION of household savings: a tool for development; edited by Arnaldo Mauri. Milan, 1977. pp. 219. *(Cassa di Risparmio delle Provincie Lombarde. The Credit Markets of Africa. 14)*

— Social conditions.

BURNELL (PETER) Absorptive capacity and development. [Coventry], 1977. pp. 21. *(University of Warwick. Department of Politics. Working Papers. No. 14)*

DISARMAMENT and world development; edited by Richard Jolly. Oxford, [1978]. pp. 185. *bibliog.* Based on a conference held by the UK Section of the United Nations Association and the Society for International Development.

MEHMET (OZAY) Economic planning and social justice in developing countries. London, [1978]. pp. 282.

— Social policy.

INTERREGIONAL COURSE ON SOCIAL PLANNING, 1ST, GENEVA, 1968. Interregional course...[held at] Geneva, Switzerland, 30 September to 9 November 1968. (ST/TAO/SER.C/107). New York, United Nations, 1969. pp. 10.

INTERREGIONAL COURSE ON SOCIAL PLANNING, 2ND, AMSTERDAM, 1970. Interregional course...[held in] Amsterdam, 23 March to 9 May, 1970. (ST/TAO/SER.C/122). New York, United Nations, 1971. pp. 10.

AZIZ (SARTAJ) Rural development: learning from China. London, 1978. pp. 201. *bibliog.*

— Socialism.

BIONDI (JEAN PIERRE) Le tiers-socialisme: essai sur le socialisme et le "Tiers-Monde". [Paris, 1976]. pp. 187.

— Tariffs.

ATTIA (MONA FOUAD) Tariff protection and growth in developing countries: a multisectoral analysis applied to Peru. Rotterdam, 1976. pp. 251. *bibliog.*

MURRAY (TRACY) Trade preferences for developing countries. London, 1977. pp. 172. *bibliog.*

— Taxation.

EXPERT GROUP ON TAX REFORM PLANNING. Tax reform planning: report of the...Group. (ST/ECA/135). New York, United Nations, 1971. pp. 16.

UNITED NATIONS. Department of Economic and Social Affairs. 1971. Interaction between the French tax system and those of developing countries. (ST/ECA/149). New York, 1971. pp. 64.

UNITED NATIONS. Department of Economic and Social Affairs. 1972. Tax treatment of private investment in developing countries by the United Kingdom of Great Britain and Northern Ireland. (ST/ECA/163). New York, 1972. pp. 13.

UNITED NATIONS. Department of Economic and Social Affairs. 1972. Taxation of private investments in developing countries by the Federal Republic of Germany. (ST/ECA/164). New York, 1972. pp. 45.

— — Mathematical models.

PORTER (RICHARD C.) and STAELIN (CHARLES P.) On the rationality of "cascaded" export subsidies and taxes. Ann Arbor, 1974. pp. 11. *bibliog. (Michigan University. Center for Research on Economic Development. Discussion Papers. No. 34)*

— Technology.

UNITED NATIONS INDUSTRIAL DEVELOPMENT ORGANIZATION. Development and Transfer of Technology Series. New York, 1977 in progress.

JEDLICKA (ALLEN D.) Organization for rural development: risk taking and appropriate technology. New York, 1977. pp. 170.

— Tourist trade.

INTERREGIONAL SEMINAR ON PHYSICAL PLANNING FOR TOURISM DEVELOPMENT, DUBROVNIK, 1970. Report of the...Seminar...[held in] Dubrovnik, Yugoslavia, 19 October to 3 November 1970. (ST/TAO/SER.C/131). New York, United Nations, [1971]. pp. 55.

UNITED NATIONS. Conference on Trade and Development. 1973. Elements of tourism policy in developing countries: report, etc. (TD/B/C.3/89/Rev.1). New York, 1973. pp. 60.

SADLER (PETER G.) and ARCHER (BRIAN H.) The economic impact of tourism in developing countries. Bangor, 1974. pp. 23. *(Wales. University. University College of North Wales. Institute of Economic Research. Tourist and Recreational Research Division. Tourist Research Papers. TUR 4)*

— Transportation, Automotive.

BOVILL (D.I.N.) and others. A guide to transport planning within the roads sector; for developing countries. London, H.M.S.O., 1978. pp. 43. *bibliog.*

— Unemployed.

STUDIES of urban labour market behaviour in developing areas; edited by Subbiah Kannappan. Geneva, International Institute for Labour Studies, 1977. pp. 234. *bibliogs.*

— Urban transportation policy.

INTERNATIONAL BANK FOR RECONSTRUCTION AND DEVELOPMENT. Sector Policy Papers. Urban transport. [Washington], 1975. pp. 103.

— Villages.

DASGUPTA (BIPLAB KUMAR) and others. Village society and labour use:...a study prepared for the International Labour Office, within the framework of the World Employment Programme, etc. Delhi, 1977. pp. 229. *bibliog. (Brighton. University of Sussex. Institute of Development Studies. Village Studies Programme).*

— Wage-price policy.

WEBB (RICHARD CHARLES) Wage policy and income distribution in developing countries. [Princeton], 1974. pp. 58. *(Princeton University and Brookings Institution. Project on Income Distribution in Less Developed Countries)*

UNDEREMPLOYMENT

— United States.

SULLIVAN (TERESA A.) Marginal workers, marginal jobs: the underutilization of American workers. Austin, [1978]. pp. 229. *bibliog.*

UNDERGROUND LITERATURE

— Russia.

Une OPPOSITION socialiste en Union Soviétique aujourd'hui: (samizdat Vingtième siècle); introduction d'E. Bérard. Paris, 1976. pp. 205.

— United States.

LEAMER (LAURENCE) The paper revolutionaries: the rise of the underground press. New York, [1972]. pp. 220. *bibliog.*

UNEMPLOYED.

VALENTEI (DMITRII IGNAT'EVICH) Die Arbeitslosigkeit: der unvermeidliche Gefährte des Kapitalismus; (übersetzt [from the Russian] von Leon Nebenzahl). Berlin, 1953. pp. 286.

FROEBEL (FOLKER) and others. Die neue internationale Arbeitsteilung: strukturelle Arbeitslosigkeit in den Industrieländern und die Industrialisierung der Entwicklungsländer. Reinbek bei Hamburg, 1977. pp. 654.

GARRATY (JOHN ARTHUR) Unemployment in history: economic thought and public policy. New York, [1978]. pp. 273.

ILLICH (IVAN D.) The right to useful unemployment and its professional enemies. London, [1978]. pp. 95.

— Mathematical models.

BARTELS (CORNELIS P.) Economic aspects of regional welfare: income distribution and unemployment. Leiden, 1977. pp. 261. *bibliog.*

— Australia.

AUSTRALIA. Commonwealth Bureau of Census and Statistics. Persons looking for work. irreg., My 1976- Canberra.

AUSTRALIA. Commonwealth Bureau of Census and Statistics. 1977. Survey of persons registered with the C[ommonwealth] E[mployment] S[ervice] as unemployed, March 1977. Canberra, 1977. pp. 23.

— Canada — Quebec.

BARBE (JEAN MICHEL) Les chômeurs du Québec. [Montréal, 1977]. pp. 166. *bibliog.*

— Germany.

DAEUBLER-GMELIN (HERTA) Frauenarbeitslosigkeit; oder, Reserve zurück an den Herd'. Reinbek bei Hamburg, 1977. pp. 218.

— India — Kerala.

KERALA. Committee on Unemployment in Kerala. 1971. Report. Part 1. Trivandrum, 1971. pp. 113.

— Italy.

CORBETTA (PIERGIORGIO) Tecnici, disoccupazione e coscienza di classe. Bologna, [1975]. pp. 227.

LAUREATI e disoccupati; a cura di R. Barbaresi [and others]. [Firenze, 1975]. pp. 249.

— Norway.

HANISCH (TED) Hele folket i arbeid: et essay om sysselsettingspolitikken i Norge. Oslo, 1977. pp. 108. *bibliog.*

— Underdeveloped areas.

See UNDERDEVELOPED AREAS — Unemployed.

— United Arab Republic.

[PLANCK (ULRICH)] Rural employment problems in the United Arab Republic. Geneva, International Labour Office, 1969. pp. 165. *bibliog. (Employment Research Papers)*

— United Kingdom.

MANCHESTER COUNCIL OF ACTION FOR THE DEFENCE OF TRADE UNIONISM. How to fight unemployment. [Manchester], [1972?]. pp. 24.

SMITH (BARBARA M.D.) Employment opportunities in the inner area study part of Small Heath, Birmingham, in 1974: report of an inquiry for the Llewelyn-Davies, Weeks, Forestier-Walker and Bor inner area study. Birmingham, 1974. pp. 104. *(Birmingham. University. Centre for Urban and Regional Studies. Research Memoranda. No. 38)*

OAKESHOTT (J.J.) Unemployment in London. London, [1975]. pp. 48. *(London. Greater London Council. Research Memoranda. 499)*

BIRMINGHAM COMMUNITY DEVELOPMENT PROJECT. Youth on the dole; (by R. Dicker and A. Cochrane). [Oxford], 1977. pp. 24. *(Final Reports. No.4: Young Workers)*

MANPOWER SERVICES COMMISSION [U.K.] Young people and work: report on the feasibility of a new programme of opportunites for unemployed young people. London, 1977. pp. 63.

FULL employment; edited by Michael Barratt Brown [and others]. Nottingham, 1978. pp. 144. *bibliog. Based on a seminar held at Leicester University in July 1977, organised by the Institute for Workers' Control.*

LISTER (RUTH) and FIELD (FRANK) 1942- . Wasted labour: a call for action on unemployment. London, 1978. pp. 86. *(Child Poverty Action Group. Poverty Pamphlets. 33)*

MANPOWER SERVICES COMMISSION [U.K.]. Young people and work; research studies commissioned and managed by Maureen Colledge, Geoffrey Llewellyn and Vernon Ward. London, H.M.S.O., 1978. pp. 79. *bibliog. (Manpower Studies. No. 19781)*

ROBERTS (JENNIFER ANN) Economic aspects of the unemployment policy of the government, 1929- 1931. 1977 [or rather 1978]. fo. 505. *bibliog.* Typescript. Ph.D. *(London) thesis: unpublished. This thesis is the property of London University and may not be removed from the Library.*

SWANN (BRENDA AUDREY SWANTON) and TURNBULL (MAUREEN) Records of interest to social scientists, 1919 to 1939: employment and unemployment. London, 1978. pp. 590. *(U.K. Public Record Office. Handbooks. No. 18)*

— — Ireland, Northern.

IRELAND, NORTHERN. Redundancy Fund account, together with the report of the Comptroller and Auditor-General thereon. a., 1971/72- Belfast. *D 6 1965/Mr 31 1966[1st]- 1970/71 included in IRELAND, NORTHERN. Parliament. House of Commons. [Papers].*

— United States.

SHERMAN (HOWARD JAY) Stagflation: a radical theory of unemployment and inflation. New York, [1976]. pp. 252. *bibliogs.*

HALLMAN (HOWARD W.) Emergency employment: a study in federalism. University, Ala., [1977]. pp. 207.

AMERICAN ENTERPRISE INSTITUTE FOR PUBLIC POLICY RESEARCH. Legislative Analyses. 95th Congress. No. 21. Full Employment and Balanced Growth Act: an update. Washington, D.C., 1978. pp. 27.

UNEMPLOYMENT, TECHNOLOGICAL

— Australia.

AUSTRALIA. Department of Labour and National Service. 1970. National survey (of the employment effects of technological change): stage one: textiles, metal products, pulp and paper. Melbourne, 1970. pp. 32. *(Employment and Technology. No. 8)*

AUSTRALIA. Department of Labour and National Service. 1971. National survey of the employment effects of technological change: stage two. Melbourne, 1971. pp. 44. *(Employment and Technology. No. 9)*

AUSTRALIA. Department of Labour and National Service. 1971. National survey of the employment effects of technological change: stage three. Melbourne, 1971. pp. 52. *(Employment and Technology. No.11)*

AUSTRALIA. Department of Labour. 1973. National survey of the employment effects of technological change: stage four. Melbourne, 1973. pp. 53. *(Employment and Technology. No. 14)*

AUSTRALIA. Department of Labour and Immigration. 1974. National survey of the employment effects of technological change: stage five. Melbourne, 1974. pp. 81. *(Employment and Technology. No.15)*

UNGARLAENDISCHE DEUTSCHE VOLKSPARTEI.

SENZ (INGOMAR MANFRED) Die nationale Bewegung der ungarländischen Deutschen vor dem Ersten Weltkrieg: eine Entwicklung im Spannungsfeld zwischen Alldeutschtum und ungarischer Innenpolitik. München, 1977. pp. 306. *bibliog. (Südostdeutsche Historische Kommission. Buchreihe. Band 30)*

UNIDAD POPULAR.

TEORIA y praxis internacional del gobierno de Allende; [by] Leopoldo González Aguayo [and others]. Mexico, 1974. pp. 238. *bibliog. (Mexico City. Universidad Nacional Autonoma de Mexico. Centro de Relaciones Internacionales. Cuadernos. Nueva Epoca. 3)*

UNILEVER LIMITED.

UNILEVER LIMITED.

COUNTER INFORMATION SERVICES and TRANSNATIONAL INSTITUTE. Unilever's world. London, [1975?]. pp. 103. *bibliog. (Counter Information Services. Anti-Reports. No. 11)*

UNION CIVICA.

UNION CIVICA: su origen, organizacion y tendencias; publicacion oficial. Buenos Aires, 1890. pp. 415.

VEDIA Y MITRE (MARIANO DE) La revolucion del 90: origen y fundacion de la Union Civica; causas, desarrollo y consecuencias de la revolucion de julio. Buenos Aires, 1929. pp. 271.

UNION CIVICA RADICAL.

PERALTA (WILFRIDO R.) and BLANCO (A.) Historia de la Union Civica Radical: su origen, su vida, sus hombres; estudio politico, 1890 y 1916. Buenos Aires, 1917. pp. 175.

CALLE (JORGE) Los iluminados: su encumbramiento y su fracaso en la politica argentina. Buenos Aires, 1922. pp. 339.

PONSSA (JOSE M.) Principios y orientaciones del radicalismo. Cordoba, Argentine Republic, 1925. pp. 139.

BIANCO (JOSE) La doctrina Radical. Buenos Aires, 1927. pp. 508.

ETKIN (ALBERTO M.) Bosquejo de una historia y doctrina de la Union Civica Radical. Buenos Aires, 1928. pp. 356.

GUTIERREZ DIEZ (A.) Nuestro radicalismo. Buenos Aires, 1930. pp. 141.

HERRERA (MARIO A.) El Coronel Blanco: de la tradicion Radical, 1856-1919. Buenos Aires, 1930. pp. 422.

MAINO (ALEJANDRO) La funcion social de la Union Civica Radical: escuelas economicas, el comunismo y la libertad; el plan Radical. Buenos Aires, 1932. pp. 151.

OYHANARTE (RAUL F.) Radicalismo de siempre; exegesis doctrinaria por Adolfo Korn Villafañe. La Plata, 1932. pp. 108.

ATENEO RADICAL "BERNARDINO RIVADAVIA". El radicalismo americanista de Hipolito Yrigoyen. Buenos Aires, 1933. pp. 75.

CATALANO (LUCIANO R.) Plan constructivo del radicalismo: el libro de las masas productoras. Buenos Aires, 1933. pp. 238. *bibliogs.*

TOLEDO (ANTONIO B.) Accion y doctrina radical. Buenos Aires, 1933. pp. 309.

RABUFFETTI (LUIS ERNESTO) El dogma radical. Buenos Aires, 1943. pp. 350.

UNION CIVICA RADICAL. Comite Nacional. Congreso Agrario de la Union Civica Radical: "tierra y libertad". Buenos Aires, [1950]. pp. 126.

OLGUIN (DARDO) Lencinas, el caudillo radical: historia y mito. Mendoza, Argentine Republic, 1961. pp. 566.

GOODWIN (PAUL B.) Los ferrocarriles britanicos y la U.C.R., 1916-1930; traduccion del ingles del original inedito...del profesor Celso Rodriguez. Buenos Aires, [1974]. pp. 320. *bibliog.*

UNION CIVICA RADICAL INTRANSIGENTE.

GRANCELLI CHA (NESTOR) De la crisis al desarrollo nacional; la UCRI y la realidad economica. [Buenos Aires, 1961]. pp. 134.

UNION DES DEMOCRATES POUR LA REPUBLIQUE.

Les MILITANTS politiques dans trois partis français: Parti Communiste, Parti Socialiste, Union des Démocrates pour la République, [by] Jacques Lagroye [and others]. [Paris, 1976]. pp. 186. *bibliog. (Bordeaux. Université. Institut d'Etudes Politiques. Centre d'Etude et de Recherche sur la Vie Locale. Série Vie Locale. 5.)*

UNION DES PARTIS SOCIALISTES POUR L'ACTION INTERNATIONALE.

See INTERNATIONAL WORKING UNION OF SOCIALIST PARTIES.

UNION DOUANIERE ET ECONOMIQUE DE L'AFRIQUE CENTRALE.

LANGHAMMER (ROLF J.) Die Zentralafrikanische Zoll- und Wirtschaftsunion: Integrationswirkungen bei Ländern im Frühstadium der industriellen Entwicklung. Tübingen, [1978]. pp. 268. *bibliog. (Kiel. Universität. Institut für Weltwirtschaft. Kieler Studien. 151)*

UNION GENERAL DE TRABAJADORES DE ESPAÑA.

ACTAS de la Union General de Trabajadores de España;... prologo y notas por Amaro del Rosal. Barcelona, 1977 in progress. *Photographic copies of original minutes.*

UNION OF SHOP, DISTRIBUTIVE AND ALLIED WORKERS.

UNION OF SHOP, DISTRIBUTIVE AND ALLIED WORKERS. Circulars, 1962-1965. Manchester, 1962-65. 1 loose-leaf binder.

UNIONIST PARTY (UNITED KINGDOM).

NATIONAL UNION OF CONSERVATIVE AND UNIONIST ASSOCIATIONS. [Leaflets. 1909]. No.738. The Unionist position in educational politics. rev. ed. London, 1909. pp. 24.

UNITED ARAB EMIRATES

— History.

ABDULLAH (MUHAMMAD MORSY) The United Arab Emirates: a modern history. London, 1978. pp. 365. *bibliog.*

ZAHLAN (ROSEMARIE SAID) The origins of the United Arab Emirates: a political and social history of the Trucial States. London, 1978. pp. 278. *bibliog.*

— Politics and government.

ZAHLAN (ROSEMARIE SAID) The origins of the United Arab Emirates: a political and social history of the Trucial States. London, 1978. pp. 278. *bibliog.*

— Statistics.

GERMANY (BUNDESREPUBLIK). Statistisches Bundesamt. Länderkurzberichte: Vereinigte Arabische Emirate. a., 1975- Wiesbaden.

UNITED ARAB REPUBLIC

— Rural conditions.

[PLANCK (ULRICH)] Rural employment problems in the United Arab Republic. Geneva, International Labour Office, 1969. pp. 165. *bibliog. (Employment Research Papers)*

UNITED KINGDOM

— Air Force.

POWERS (BARRY D.) Strategy without slide-rule: British air strategy, 1914-1939. London, [1976]. pp. 295. *bibliog.*

— Antiquities.

MEDIEVAL moated sites; edited by F.A. Aberg. London, 1978. pp. 93. *bibliog. (Council for British Archaeology. Research Reports. No. 17)*

— Appropriations and expenditures.

BURGESS (RONALD) Full employment and public spending. London, [1977]. pp. 19. *bibliog.*

CLARK (STEVE) Who benefits?: a study of the distribution of public expenditure on housing; evidence to the House of Commons expenditure sub- committee submitted on behalf of Shelter...by the Housing Research Group. London, 1977. pp. 34. *bibliog.*

— — Mathematical models.

ROY (ANDREW DONALD) A Bayesian approach to the control of expenditure. [London], Department of Health and Social Security, 1978. pp. 13. *(Government Economic Service Working Papers. No. 9)*

— Army.

EVELEGH (ROBIN) Peace keeping in a democratic society: the lessons of Northern Ireland. London, [1978]. pp. 174.

— — History.

BAYLEY (CHARLES CALVERT) Mercenaries for the Crimea: the German, Swiss, and Italian legions in British service, 1854-1856. Montreal, 1977. pp. 197. *bibliog.*

HAYTER (TONY) The army and the crowd in mid-Georgian England. London, 1978. pp. 239. *bibliog.*

— — Supplies and stores.

U.K. War Office. Contracts Department. 1916. Report on local purchases for the British expeditionary force in France; by E.M.H. Lloyd and G.U. Yule. [London, 1916]. pp. 44.

— Census.

LOCAL AUTHORITIES MANAGEMENT SERVICES AND COMPUTER COMMITTEE. Computer Panel. Census analysis. London, 1974. pp. 30.

GLASS (DAVID VICTOR) and TAYLOR (PHILIP ARTHUR MICHAEL) Population and emigration. Dublin, [1976]. pp. 125. *bibliogs.*

U.K. Office of Population Censuses and Surveys. OPCS Monitor. 1981 Census. irreg., Mr 1978(no.1)- London.

— — History.

The CENSUS and social structure: an interpretative guide to nineteenth century censuses for England and Wales; edited by Richard Lawton. London, 1978. pp. 330.

— — 1971.

U.K. Census, 1971. Census, 1971: England and Wales: index of place names. London, 1977. 2 vols.

U.K. Census, 1971. Census, 1971: England and Wales: migration regional report[s], 10 per cent sample..., as constituted on 1st April 1974. London, 1978 in progress.

U.K. Office of Population Censuses and Surveys. 1978. 1971 census: income follow-up survey. London, 1978. pp. 25. *(Studies on Medical and Population Subjects. No. 38)*

— Church history.

CROSS (CLAIRE) Church and people, 1450-1660: the triumph of the laity in the English Church. Hassocks, 1976. pp. 272. *bibliog.*

MACHIN (GEORGE IAN THOM) Politics and the churches in Great Britain, 1832 to 1868. Oxford, 1977. pp. 438. *bibliog.*

— Commerce.

[CAREW (GEORGE) Esq.] Severall considerations, offered to the Parliament concerning the improvement of trade, navigation, and comerce, more especially the old draperies and other woolen manufactures of England: by G.C. a Louer, of his country. [London, 1675]. pp. 8. *Wing C551.*

UNITED KINGDOM

POSTLETHWAYT (MALACHY) Selected works. Farnborough, [1968]. 2 vols. *Originally published between 1745 and 1759. Facsimile reprints.*

IMPORTS into the United Kingdom of food and animal feeding stuffs: annual average, 1934/38. [London, 1946]. pp. 171.

TRADE AND INDUSTRY; (pd....for the Departments of Trade, Industry, and Prices and Consumer Protection [U.K.]). w., Oc 21 1970 (v.1, no.1)- London. *Incorporates Board of Trade jl. (1886 - Oc 14 1970, v.1- 199, with gaps).*

BANKS and the British exporter; based on the seminar held at... Cambridge, 11-16 September, 1977. London, 1977. pp. 86. *bibliog.*

GRIFFITHS (Sir PERCIVAL) A history of the Inchcape Group. London, 1977. pp. 211.

TRADE and transport: essays in economic history in honour of T.S. Willan; W.H. Chaloner [and] Barrie M. Ratcliffe, editors. Manchester, [1977]. pp. 293.

HOLMES (PETER M.) Industrial pricing behaviour and devaluation. London, 1978. pp. 170. *bibliog.*

YOGEV (GEDALIA) Diamonds and coral: Anglo-Dutch Jews and eighteenth-century trade. Leicester, 1978. pp. 360. *bibliog.*

— — **Mathematical models.**

HIBBERD (JIM) and WREN-LEWIS (SIMON) A study of U.K. imports of manufactures. London, Treasury, 1978. pp. 38,4. *bibliog. (Government Economic Service Working Papers. No. 6)*

— — **Africa, West.**

DAVIES (PETER N.) Sir Alfred Jones: shipping entrepreneur par excellence. London, [1978]. pp. 162. *bibliog.*

— — **India.**

TOMLINSON (JAMES DAVID) Anglo-Indian economic relations, 1913 to 1928, with special reference to the cotton trade. [1977]. fo. 233. *bibliog. Typescript: unpublished. Ph.D. (London) thesis. This thesis is the property of London University and may not be removed from the Library.*

— — **Japan.**

JAPAN. Japanese Embassy, London. Information Centre. 1977. British trade with Japan. [London], 1977. pp. 33. *bibliog.*

— — **Turkey.**

SKILLITER (S.A.) William Harborne and the trade with Turkey, 1578-1582: a documentary study of the first Anglo-Ottoman relations. London, 1977. pp. 291. *bibliog.*

— **Commercial policy.**

[RICH (Sir HENRY)] Yes or no? London, J. Ridgway, 1852. pp. 13.

FEDERAL TRUST FOR EDUCATION AND RESEARCH. Research Committee. Britain in Europe: viewpoint for the labour movement. London, [1958]. pp. (11).

COMPETITION policy in the U.K. and EEC; edited by Kenneth D. George [and] Caroline Joll. Cambridge, 1975. pp. 220. *Papers presented at a Social Science Research Council conference held at Somerville College, Oxford in 1974.*

— **Constitution.**

HARVEY (JACK) and BATHER (LESLIE) The British constitution. 4th ed. Basingstoke, 1977. pp. 648. *bibliogs.*

HOGG (QUINTIN McGAREL) Baron Hailsham. The dilemma of democracy: diagnosis and prescription. London, 1978. pp. 238.

RICHARDS (S.G.) Introduction to British government. London, 1978. pp. 237. *bibliogs.*

— **Constitutional law.**

STREET (HARRY) Freedom, the individual and the law. 4th ed. Harmondsworth, 1977. pp. 346.

— **Courts and courtiers.**

SHERWOOD (ROY) The court of Oliver Cromwell. London, [1977]. pp. 194. *bibliog.*

— **Defences.**

LABOUR PARTY. Study Group on Defence Expenditure, the Arms Trade and Alternative Employment. Sense about defence: the report of the...Study Group; [Ian Mikardo, chairman]. London, 1977. pp. 163.

— **Description and travel.**

DURY (GEORGE HARRY) The British Isles: a systematic and regional geography. London, 1961. pp. 503. *bibliog.*

— **Economic conditions.**

COATES (BRYAN ELLIS) and RAWSTRON (ERIC MITCHELL) Regional variations in Britain: studies in economic and social geography. London, 1971 reprinted 1972. pp. 304. *Reprinted with minor revisions.*

REGIONAL ECONOMIC REVIEW: ([pd. by] East Anglia Economic Planning Council [U.K.]). a. (formerly s-a.,) Mr 1973- London.

BROWN (C.J.F.) and SHERIFF (T.D.) Problems of medium term assessments: a postmortem on The British economy in 1975. London, 1977. pp. 89. *(National Institute of Economic and Social Research. Discussion Papers. No.11)*

GRANT (ALEXANDER THOMAS KINGDOM) Economic uncertainty and financial structure. London, 1977. pp. 234.

MACKINTOSH (JOHN PITCAIRN) Britain's malaise: political or economic? Southampton, 1977. pp. 26. *(Southampton. University. Fawley Foundation. Lectures. 23)*

MEDLIK (S.) Britain: workshop or service centre to the world? [Guildford, 1977]. pp. 26. *Lecture given at the University of Surrey on 1 June 1977.*

BACON (ROBERT WILLIAM) and ELTIS (WALTER ALFRED) Britain's economic problem: too few producers. 2nd ed. London, 1978. pp. 255.

NOSSITER (BERNARD D.) Britain: a future that works. London, 1978. pp. 224.

— — **Mathematical models.**

NATIONAL INSTITUTE OF ECONOMIC AND SOCIAL RESEARCH. Discussion Papers. No.7. A listing of National Institute Model III, May 1977 review. London, [1977]. pp. 49,11.

— — **Statistics.**

AIMS FOR FREEDOM AND ENTERPRISE. Economic facts for business spokesmen. London, 1977. pp. 28.

ORMEROD (P.A.) The effects of revisions to Central Statistical Office data for the U.K. economy. London, 1977. fo. 14. *(National Institute of Economic and Social Research. Discussion Papers. No. 12)*

U.K. Central Statistical Office. 1977. New contributions to economic statistics: eighth series. London, 1977. pp. 146. *(Studies in Official Statistics. No. 28) Reprinted from Economic Trends, January 1974-February 1975.*

U.K. Central Statistical Office. 1977. New contributions to economic statistics: ninth series. London, 1977. pp. 154. *(Studies in Official Statistics. No.33) Reprinted from Economic Trends, March 1975 - December 1976.*

— **Economic history.**

CLARKE (JOHN J.) The price of progress: Cobbett's England 1780-1835. London, 1977. pp. 200. *bibliog.*

HATCHER (JOHN) Plague, population and the English economy, 1348-1530. London, 1977. pp. 95. *bibliog. (Economic History Society. Studies in Economic and Social History)*

STEVENSON (JOHN) Historian, and COOK (CHRISTOPHER PIERS) The slump: society and politics during the depression. London, 1977. pp. 348. *bibliog.*

CALVOCORESSI (PETER) The British experience, 1945-75. London, 1978. pp. 253.

LANE (PETER) The industrial revolution: the birth of the modern age. London, [1978]. pp. 292. *bibliog.*

O'BRIEN (PATRICK) and KEYDER (CAGLAR) Economic growth in Britain and France, 1780-1914: two paths to the twentieth century. London, 1978. pp. 205.

THIRSK (JOAN) Economic policy and projects: the development of a consumer society in early modern England. Oxford, 1978. pp. 199. *(Oxford. University. Ford Lectures. 1975)*

VON TUNZELMANN (GEORGE NICHOLAS) Steam power and British industrialization to 1860. Oxford, [1978]. pp. 344. *bibliog.*

WEALTH and power in Tudor England: essays presented to S.T. Bindoff; edited by E.W. Ives [and others]. London, 1978. pp. 248. *bibliog.*

— — **Sources.**

SURTEES SOCIETY. Publications. vol. 189. Commercial papers of Sir Christopher Lowther, 1611-1644; edited by D.R. Hainsworth. Gateshead, 1977. pp. 250.

— **Economic policy.**

LABOUR PARTY. Go-ahead Britain. [London], 1965. pp. 16.

NATIONAL AND LOCAL GOVERNMENT OFFICERS ASSOCIATION. NALGO economic review, 1976: a background to the present situation and future prospects. [London], 1976. pp. 27.

SANDEMAN (E.K.) S.O.S. Britain: appeal to the International Monetary Fund. Hindhead, 1976. pp. 3,3,3. *Photocopy of typescript.*

BRITTAN (SAMUEL) The economic consequences of democracy. London, 1977. pp. 298. *bibliogs.*

BURGESS (RONALD) Full employment and public spending. London, [1977]. pp. 19. *bibliog.*

The CASE against the social contract: the story of the worst bargain of all time; by a group of independent socialists. [Liverpool?, 1977]. 1 pamphlet (unpaged).

COUNTER INFORMATION SERVICES. Anti-Reports. No.18. Paying for the crisis. London, [1977]. pp. 46. *bibliog.*

DUESBURY (W.K.) Intermediate areas: a non-event?: the case of Oswestry. Birmingham, 1977. pp. 121,xv. *bibliog. (Birmingham. University. Centre for Urban and Regional Studies. Research Memoranda. No. 58)*

FERNS (HENRY STANLEY) Galloping bureaucracy and taxation: the radicalism the case requires. London, [1977]. pp. 9.

HILTON (ANDREW JOHN BOYD) Corn, cash, commerce: the economic policies of the Tory governments, 1815-1830. Oxford, 1977. pp. 338. *bibliogs.*

MACKINTOSH (JOHN PITCAIRN) Britain's malaise: political or economic? Southampton, 1977. pp. 26. *(Southampton. University. Fawley Foundation. Lectures. 23)*

MEDLIK (S.) Britain: workshop or service centre to the world? [Guildford, 1977]. pp. 26. *Lecture given at the University of Surrey on 1 June 1977.*

UNITED KINGDOM (Cont.)

MONTE (ALFREDO DEL) Politica regionale e sviluppo economico: un'analisi teorica ed econometrica degli effetti della politica degli incentivi nel Mezzogiorno, nell'Irlanda del Nord e in Scozia. Milano, [1977]. pp. 277. *(Naples. Università. Centro Studi di Economia Applicata all'Ingegneria. Studi Economici. 3)*

NORTHERN REGION STRATEGY TEAM. Strategic plan for the northern region. [Newcastle upon Tyne], 1977. 5 vols. (in 1).

ROBENS (ALFRED) Baron Robens of Woldingham. Managing Great Britain Limited. [Berkhamsted, 1977]. pp. 19. *(Ashridge Management College. Ashridge Lectures. 1976)*

BACON (ROBERT WILLIAM) and ELTIS (WALTER ALFRED) Britain's economic problem: too few producers. 2nd ed. London, 1978. pp. 255.

BEESON (TREVOR) Britain today and tomorrow. [London], 1978. pp. 284.

BUCHANAN (JAMES McGILL) and others. The consequences of Mr. Keynes: an analysis of the misuse of economic theory for political profiteering, with proposals for constitutional disciplines. London, 1978. pp. 88. *bibliog. (Institute of Economic Affairs. Hobart Papers. 78)*

BUDD (ALAN) The politics of economic planning. [London, 1978]. pp. 172. *bibliog.*

DEMAND management; edited by Michael Posner. London, 1978. pp. 242. *(National Institute of Economic and Social Research. Economic Policy Papers. 1) Proceedings of a conference held in London in 1977.*

FABIAN SOCIETY. Fabian Tracts. [No.] 458. Labour and the social contract; [by] Robert Taylor. London, 1978. pp. 24.

JEWKES (JOHN) A return to free market economics?: critical essays on government intervention. London, 1978. pp. 249.

LITTLECHILD (STEPHEN CHARLES) The fallacy of the mixed economy: an Austrian critique of conventional mainstream economics and of British economic policy. London, 1978. pp. 83. *bibliog. (Institute of Economic Affairs. Hobart Papers. 80)*

ROBERTS (JENNIFER ANN) Economic aspects of the unemployment policy of the government, 1929- 1931. 1977 [or rather 1978]. fo. 505. *bibliog. Typescript. Ph.D. (London) thesis: unpublished. This thesis is the property of London University and may not be removed from the Library.*

SANDFORD (CEDRIC T.) Economics of public finance: an economic analysis of government expenditure and revenue in the United Kingdom. 2nd ed. Oxford, 1978. pp. 301. *bibliog.*

STEWART (MICHAEL) Politics and economic policy in the UK since 1964: the Jekyll and Hyde years. Oxford, 1978. pp. 272. *bibliog.*

WALTERS (ALAN A.) Economists and the British economy. London, 1978. pp. 31. *(Institute of Economic Affairs. Occasional Papers. 54)*

WHAT'S wrong with Britain?; edited by Patrick Hutber. London, 1978. pp. 112.

— **Emigration and immigration.**

BARBADOS. 195-. Information booklet for intending emigrants to Britain. [Bridgetown, 195-]. pp. 24.

U.K. Office of Population Censuses and Surveys. International migration: migrants entering or leaving the United Kingdom. a., 1974(1st)- London. *Supersedes in part Registrar General's statistical review of England and Wales.*

MONCK (ELIZABETH M.) and LOMAS (GLENYS BARBARA GILLIAN) The employment and socio-economic conditions of the coloured population. London, 1975. pp. 33. *(Centre for Environmental Studies. Research Papers. 21)*

GLASS (DAVID VICTOR) and TAYLOR (PHILIP ARTHUR MICHAEL) Population and emigration. Dublin, [1976]. pp. 125. *bibliogs.*

BIRMINGHAM COMMUNITY DEVELOPMENT PROJECT. People in paper chains; (by Sylvia Whitfield). [Oxford], 1977. pp. 32. *bibliog. (Final Reports. No.3: Immigration and the State)*

JOINT COUNCIL FOR THE WELFARE OF IMMIGRANTS. The numbers game:...evidence to the Select Committee on Race Relations and Immigration. London, 1977. pp. 13.

MILES (R.) and PHIZACKLEA (A.) The TUC, black workers and new Commonwealth immigration, 1954- 1973. Bristol, Social Science Research Council Research Unit on Ethnic Relations, [1977]. pp. 44. *(Working Papers on Ethnic Relations. No. 6)*

DEMUTH (CLARE) Immigration: a brief guide to the numbers game. London, 1978. fo. 11. *(Runnymede Trust. Briefing Papers. 1978, No. 1)*

IMMIGRANTS and minorities in British society; edited by Colin Holmes. London, 1978. pp. 208. *bibliog.*

— **Executive departments.**

CLARKE (Sir RICHARD WILLIAM BARNES) Mintech in retrospect - I. Oxford, 1973. pp. 40. *bibliog. Reprinted from Omega, vol. 1. no.1, 1973.*

U.K. Health and Safety Commission. Report. a., 1974/76 (1st)- London.

ADAMS (PETER) Fatal necessity: British intervention in New Zealand, 1830- 1847. Auckland, 1977. pp. 308. *bibliog.*

BRACEWELL-MILNES (JOHN BARRY) Short measure from Whitehall: how CSO statistics understate the British tax burden. London, 1977. pp. 8.

MIDDLETON (CHARLES RONALD) The administration of British foreign policy, 1782-1846. Durham, N.C., 1977. pp. 364. *bibliog.*

— **Famines.**

APPLEBY (ANDREW B.) Famine in Tudor and Stuart England. Stanford, 1978. pp. 250.

— **Foreign economic relations.**

See also EUROPEAN ECONOMIC COMMUNITY — United Kingdom.

— — **Ghana.**

MILBURN (JOSEPHINE F.) British business and Ghanaian independence. London, [1977]. pp. 156.

— — **India.**

ALL INDIA CONGRESS COMMITTEE. Select Committee on the Financial Obligations between Great Britain and India. Report. vol.1. Bombay, [1931]. pp. 70,ix,ii.

— — **Peru.**

GRAN Bretaña y el Peru: informes de los consules britanicos, 1826-1900; compilador Heraclio Bonilla. Lima, 1975-77. 5 vols. *bibliog. (Instituto de Estudios Peruanos. Estudios Historicos. 2)*

— — **Russia.**

ANAN'ICH (BORIS VASIL'EVICH) Rossiiskoe samoderzhavie i vyvoz kapitalov, 1895-1914 gg.: po materialam Uchetno-ssudnogo banka Persii. Leningrad, 1975. pp. 211.

— **Foreign population.**

KOHLER (DAVID F.) Ethnic minorities in Britain: statistical data. 6th ed. London, Community Relations Commission, 1976. pp. 21.

KHAN (VERITY SAIFULLAH) Bilingualism and linguistic minorities in Britain: developments, perspectives. London, 1977. fo. 13. *(Runnymede Trust. Briefing Papers. 1977, No. 4)*

KOHLER (DAVID F.) Immigration and race relations. London, 1977. pp. 10. *bibliog. (Liberal Publication Department. Study Papers. No. 7)*

IMMIGRANTS and minorities in British society; edited by Colin Holmes. London, 1978. pp. 208. *bibliog.*

— — **Bibliography.**

BUSH (MARTHA) compiler. Immigrant housing. London, 1976. pp. 15. *(London. Greater London Council. Research Library. [Research] Bibliographies. No. 74)*

— **Foreign relations.**

HUME (MARTIN ANDREW SHARP) The great Lord Burghley (William Cecil): a study in Elizabethan statecraft. London, 1906. pp. 511.

FRY (MICHAEL GRAHAM) Lloyd George and foreign policy. Montreal, 1977 in progress.

LUCE (RICHARD) and RANELAGH (JOHN) Human rights and foreign policy. London, 1977. pp. 31. *(Conservative Political Centre. [Publications]. No. 614)*

STEINER (ZARA SHAKOW) Britain and the origins of the First World War. London, 1977. pp. 305. *bibliog.*

ELDRIDGE (C.C.) Victorian imperialism. London, [1978]. pp. 248. *bibliogs.*

FEST (WILFRIED) Peace or partition: the Habsburg monarchy and British policy, 1914-1918. London, 1978. pp. 276. *bibliog.*

See also EUROPEAN ECONOMIC COMMUNITY — United Kingdom.

— — **Austria.**

FEST (WILFRIED) Peace or partition: the Habsburg monarchy and British policy, 1914-1918. London, 1978. pp. 276. *bibliog.*

— — **East (Far East).**

NYMAN (LARS-ERIK) Great Britain and Chinese, Russian and Japanese interests in Sinkiang, 1918-1934. [Lund], 1977. pp. 167. *bibliog. (Lund. Universitet. Historiska Institutionen. Lund Studies in International History. [No.] 8)*

— — **Egypt.**

MELLINI (PETER) Sir Eldon Gorst: the overshadowed proconsul. Stanford, [1977]. pp. 315. *bibliog. (Stanford University. Hoover Institution on War, Revolution and Peace. Hoover Colonial Studies)*

— — **France.**

JORDAN (W.M.) Great Britain, France, and the German problem, 1918-1939: a study of Anglo-French relations in the making and maintenance of the Versailles settlement. London, 1971. pp. 234. *Reprint of the 1943 edition, originally issued under the auspices of the Royal Institute of International Affairs.*

SCHUMANN (MAURICE) Talleyrand, prophet of Entente Cordiale. Oxford, 1977. pp. 22. *(Oxford. University. Zaharoff Lectures. 1976-77)*

— — **Germany.**

ASPEKTE der deutsch-britischen Beziehungen im Laufe der Jahrhunderte: Ansprachen und Vorträge zur Eröffnung des Deutschen Historischen Instituts London: Aspects of Anglo- German relations through the centuries...; herausgegeben von Paul Kluke und Peter Alter. Stuttgart, 1978. pp. 83. *(Deutsches Historisches Institut. Veröffentlichungen. Band 4) In German or English.*

UNITED KINGDOM (Cont.)

KRIEGER (WOLFGANG) Labour Party und Weimarer Republik: ein Beitrag zur Aussenpolitik der britischen Arbeiterbewegung zwischen Programmatik und Parteitaktik, 1918-1924. Bonn, [1978]. pp. 450. *bibliog.* (*Friedrich-Ebert-Stiftung. Forschungsinstitut. Schriftenreihe. Band 136*)

— — Greece.

KOLIOPOULOS (JOHN S.) Greece and the British connection, 1935-1941. Oxford, 1977. pp. 315. *bibliog.*

— — New Zealand.

ADAMS (PETER) Fatal necessity: British intervention in New Zealand, 1830-1847. Auckland, 1977. pp. 308. *bibliog.*

— — South Africa.

CHANOCK (MARTIN) Unconsummated union: Britain, Rhodesia and South Africa, 1900-45. Manchester, [1977]. pp. 289. *bibliog.*

WINDRICH (ELAINE) Britain and the politics of Rhodesian independence. London, [1978]. pp. 283.

— — United States.

LOUIS (WILLIAM ROGER) Imperialism at bay, 1941-1945: the United States and the decolonization of the British Empire. Oxford, 1977. pp. 595.

THORNE (CHRISTOPHER) Allies of a kind: the United States, Britain and the war against Japan, 1941-1945. London, 1978. pp. 772. *bibliog.*

— Foreign relations administration.

MIDDLETON (CHARLES RONALD) The administration of British foreign policy, 1782-1846. Durham, N.C., 1977. pp. 364. *bibliog.*

— Full employment policies.

BURGESS (RONALD) Full employment and public spending. London, [1977]. pp. 19. *bibliog.*

— Gazetteers.

U.K. Census, 1971. Census, 1971: England and Wales: index of place names. London, 1977. 2 vols.

— Gentry.

EMMISON (FREDERICK GEORGE) Elizabethan life: wills of Essex gentry and merchants proved in the Prerogative Court of Canterbury. Chelmsford, 1978. pp. 361. (*Essex. Records Committee. Essex Record Office Publications. No. 71*)

— Government publications.

BRACEWELL-MILNES (JOHN BARRY) Short measure from Whitehall: how CSO statistics understate the British tax burden. London, 1977. pp. 8.

— — Indexes.

AVON. County Library. British government reports, 1971-1975: indexes of chairmen and subjects; (compiled by John Kite). [Bristol], 1977. pp. 39.

U.K. Department of the Environment. 1978. Town and country planning: development plans, development control and associated matters, including community land scheme and land transactions: index to departmental circulars and other relevant publications as at 15 May 1978. London, 1978. 1 pamphlet (unpaged).

— History.

REBELS and their causes: essays in honour of A.L. Morton; edited by Maurice Cornforth. London, 1978. pp. 224.

— — Bibliography.

NICHOLLS (DAVID) compiler. Nineteenth-century Britain, 1815-1914. Folkestone, 1978. pp. 170. *bibliog.*

— — 1066-1485, Medieval period.

MEDIEVAL settlement: continuity and change; edited by P.H. Sawyer. London, 1976. pp. 357. *bibliog.* Based on a colloquium held at the University of Leeds in July 1974.

— — 1485-1603, Tudors.

HUME (MARTIN ANDREW SHARP) The great Lord Burghley (William Cecil): a study in Elizabethan statecraft. London, 1906. pp. 511.

APPLEBY (ANDREW B.) Famine in Tudor and Stuart England. Stanford, 1978. pp. 250.

— — 1603-1714, Stuarts.

APPLEBY (ANDREW B.) Famine in Tudor and Stuart England. Stanford, 1978. pp. 250.

FRANKLIN (JULIAN HAROLD) John Locke and the theory of sovereignty: mixed monarchy and the right of resistance in the political thought of the English revolution. Cambridge, 1978. pp. 146. *bibliog.*

— — 1642-1649, Civil War.

MANNING (BRIAN S.) The English people and the English revolution, 1640-1649. London, 1976. pp. 390.

— — 1649-1660, Commonwealth and Protectorate.

DAMPIER (Sir WILLIAM CECIL DAMPIER) The restoration of Charles the Second; edited by Edith H. Whetham. Exeter, [imprint], 1960. pp. 64. *bibliog.*

JONES (JAMES REES) Country and court: England, 1658-1714. London, 1978. pp. 377. *bibliog.*

— — 1660-1714.

JONES (JAMES REES) Country and court: England, 1658-1714. London, 1978. pp. 377. *bibliog.*

— — 1714-1760.

SPECK (WILLIAM ARTHUR) Stability and strife: England, 1714-1760. London, 1977. pp. 311. *bibliog.*

— — 1760-1820.

HARVEY (A.D.) Britain in the early nineteenth century. London, [1978]. pp. 395. *bibliog.*

— — 1800-1899 — Sources.

CROMWELL (VALERIE) compiler. Revolution or evolution: British government in the nineteenth century. London, 1977. pp. 230. *bibliog.*

— — 1837-1901.

CLAYDEN (PETER WILLIAM) England under Lord Beaconsfield;...new introductory note by E. J. Feuchtwanger. Richmond, Surrey, 1971. pp. 542. *Reprint of original edition published in London in 1880 with subtitle: The political history of six years from the end of 1873 to the beginning of 1880.*

YOUNG (GEORGE MALCOLM) Portrait of an age: Victorian England; annotated edition by George Kitson Clark, with a biographical memoir by Sir George Clark. London, 1977. pp. 423.

— — — Sources.

LEEDS. University. Library. Handlists. 34. Political correspondence (1884-1897) of Louis Henry Hayter. [Leeds], 1977. pp. 16.

STOREY (RICHARD A.) and MADDEN (LIONEL) Primary sources for Victorian studies: a guide to the location and use of unpublished materials. London, 1977. pp. 81.

STANLEY (EDWARD HENRY SMITH) 15th Earl of Derby. Disraeli, Derby and the Conservative Party: journals and memoirs of Edward Henry, Lord Stanley, 1849-1869; edited by John Vincent. Hassocks, 1978. pp. 404.

— — 1900- .

BARTLETT (CHRISTOPHER JOHN) A history of postwar Britain, 1945-1974. London, 1977. pp. 360. *bibliog.*

ADAMS (R.J.Q.) Arms and the wizard: Lloyd George and the Ministry of Munitions, 1915-1916. London, [1978]. pp. 252.

WALKER (MARTIN) Daily sketches:...a cartoon history of twentieth century Britain. London, 1978. pp. 192. *bibliog.*

— History, Local — Sources.

WILLIAMS (GLANMOR) The general and common sort of people, 1540-1640. Exeter, 1977. pp. 32. (*Exeter. University. Harte Memorial Lectures in Local History. 1975*)

— History, Military.

BRITISH defence policy in a changing world; edited by John Baylis. London, [1977]. pp. 295. *bibliog.*

— History, Naval.

LEUTZE (JAMES R.) Bargaining for supremacy: Anglo-American naval collaboration, 1937-1941. Chapel Hill, [1977]. pp. 328. *bibliog.*

— — Sources.

GUIDE to the manuscripts in the National Maritime Museum; edited by R.J.B. Knight. London, 1977 in progress.

— Industries.

LONDON. University. London School of Economics and Political Science. Seminar on Problems in Industrial Administration. Papers. Nos. 1-452. London, 1946-73. 19 vols. (including index vol.).

TRADE AND INDUSTRY; (pd....for the Departments of Trade, Industry, and Prices and Consumer Protection [U.K.]). w., Oc 21 1970 (v.1, no.1)- London. *Incorporates Board of Trade jl. (1886 - Oc 14 1970, v.1- 199, with gaps).*

CONFEDERATION OF BRITISH INDUSTRY. National Conference. Proceedings. irreg., 1977(1st)- London.

COMMUNITY DEVELOPMENT PROJECT. The costs of industrial change. London, 1977. pp. 96.

CONFEDERATION OF BRITISH INDUSTRY. Industry and the city; the first-stage CBI evidence to the Committee to Review the Functioning of Financial Institutions (the Wilson Committee). London, 1977. pp. 40.

ESSAYS in British business history; edited for the Economic History Society by Barry Supple. Oxford, 1977. pp. 267.

NATIONAL ECONOMIC DEVELOPMENT OFFICE. Financial statistics on manufacturing industry: suggestions for improvement; (Statistical Users Conference, 1977: financial statistics: [paper]). [London, 1977]. pp. 11.

NATIONAL ENTERPRISE BOARD [U.K.]. Investment potential in the north east and north west of England; report. [London, 1977]. fo. 17.

KRICHIGINA (NATALIIA NIKOLAEVNA) Proizvoditel'nost' truda v obrabatyvaiushchei promyshlennosti Velikobritanii. Moskva, 1978. pp. 165.

MUSSON (ALBERT EDWARD) The growth of British industry. London, 1978. pp. 396. *bibliog.*

WRAGG (RICHARD) and ROBERTSON (JAMES) Writer on Employment. Post-war trends in employment, productivity, output, labour costs and prices by industry in the United Kingdom. [London], 1978. pp. 93. (*U.K. Department of Employment. Research Papers. No. 3*)

UNITED KINGDOM (Cont.)

— Intellectual life.

BESANT (ANNIE) A selection of the social and political pamphlets of Annie Besant; with a preface and bibliographical notes by John Saville. New York, 1970. 1 vol. (various pagings). *bibliog. Originally published between 1877 and 1891.*

COLE (GEORGE DOUGLAS HOWARD) Samuel Butler. London, 1952. pp. 52. *bibliog. (British Book News. Bibliographical Series of Supplements: Writers and their Work. No. 30)*

KENT (CHRISTOPHER) Brains and numbers: elitism, Comtism, and democracy in mid- Victorian England. Toronto, [1978]. pp. 212. *bibliog.*

KNIGHTS (BEN) The idea of the clerisy in the nineteenth century. Cambridge, [1978]. pp. 274. *bibliog.*

SOFFER (REBA N.) Ethics and society in England: the revolution in the social sciences, 1870-1914. Berkeley, Calif., [1978]. pp. 325.

— Kings and rulers.

UPTON (W. PRESCOTT) The King's Protestant declaration: why it must not be altered. London, 1910. pp. 16. *(Church Association. [Publications]. No. 404)*

COMMUNIST PARTY OF GREAT BRITAIN. London District Committee. Royal wedding. London, 1934. pp. 4.

COMMUNIST PARTY OF GREAT BRITAIN. London District Committee. Royal jubilee: 25 years of war and starvation. London, 1935. pp. 4.

ECCLESHALL (ROBERT) Order and reason in politics: theories of absolute and limited monarchy in early modern England. Oxford, 1978. pp. 197. *bibliog.*

— — Caricatures and cartoons.

JONES (MICHAEL WYNN) A cartoon history of the monarchy. London, 1978. pp. 207.

— Manufactures.

THIRSK (JOAN) Economic policy and projects: the development of a consumer society in early modern England. Oxford, 1978. pp. 199. *(Oxford. University. Ford Lectures. 1975)*

— Military policy.

BRITISH defence policy in a changing world; edited by John Baylis. London, [1977]. pp. 295. *bibliog.*

— Militia.

SUGGESTIONS for the reorganisation of the militia; respectfully submitted for the consideration of the Royal Commission by a Lieutenant-Colonel of militia and retired officer of the line. n.p., 1859. pp. 12.

— Moral conditions.

BRISTOW (EDWARD J.) Vice and vigilance: purity movements in Britain since 1700. Dublin, 1977. pp. 274. *bibliog.*

— Nationalism.

BIRCH (ANTHONY HAROLD) Political integration and disintegration in the British Isles. London, 1977. pp. 183. *bibliog.*

— Navy.

HALSTED (EDWARD PELLEW) The Navy unarmed still: an appeal to both Houses of Parliament, in a series of letters to the Daily News. [London], 1865. pp. 86.

— — History.

RASOR (EUGENE L.) Reform in the Royal Navy: a social history of the lower deck, 1850 to 1880. Hamden, Conn., 1976. pp. 210. *bibliog.*

ROSKILL (STEPHEN WENTWORTH) Churchill and the admirals. London, 1977. pp. 351.

— Nobility.

RICHARDSON (R.J.) of Manchester. The red book; or, A peep at the peers!! shewing the salaries, sinecures, pensions, and emoluments, derived by the peers and their families out of the public taxes, the offices they likewise hold in the army, navy, law, court, church and state, and local departments: their patronage and influence in the House of Commons: it is also a complete peerage for the people up to the present date. London, 1841. pp. 94.

LUDOVICI (ANTHONY MARIO) A defence of aristocracy: a text book for Tories. London, 1915. pp. 459.

— Occupations.

PRESTON (BRIAN) Occupations of father and son in mid-Victorian England. Reading, 1977. pp. 40. *(Reading. University. Department of Geography. Reading Geographical Papers. No. 56)*

— Officials and employees.

CSD MANPOWER PLANNING NEWSLETTER; [pd. by Civil Service Department, U.K.]. s-a., Ja 1974 (no.1)- London.

— Parliament.

LATCHFORD (HENRY) The wit and wisdom of Parliament. London, [1881]. pp. 192.

PEOPLE and Parliament: edited by John P. Mackintosh. Farnborough, Hants., [1978]. pp. 214.

— — Elections.

BRADBURY (FAREL) Electoral reform: V2P: voting for policies as well as for politicians; a political essay. Ross-on-Wye, [1975]. pp. 14.

BRADBURY (PARNELL) Voice of the people: V2P: a plain man's guide to democracy; ...based on an idea by Farel Bradbury featuring the do-it yourself referendum. Ross-on-Wye, 1976. pp. 10.

HOLMES (GEOFFREY) The electorate and the national will in the first age of party. Lancaster, [1976]. pp. 33. *An inaugural lecture delivered on 26 November 1975.*

CRAIG (FREDERICK WALTER SCOTT) ed. Britain votes, 1: a handbook of parliamentary election results, 1974-1977. Chichester, 1977. pp. 273. *Supplements British parliamentary election results, 1832-1970.*

HARRINGTON (WILLIAM) and YOUNG (PETER) Public relations consultant. The 1945 revolution. London, 1978. pp. 218.

— — House of Commons — Resolutions.

BERCUSSON (BRIAN) Fair wages resolutions. London, 1978. pp. 538.

— Politics and government.

POLITICS for the working man. Norwich, 1885. s.sh *(Reprinted from the Norfolk Chronicle)*

RUSSELL (GEORGE WILLIAM ERSKINE) Politics and personalities, with other essays. London, 1917. pp. 368.

COALITIONS in British politics; edited by David Butler: essays by Robert Blake [and others]. London, 1978. pp. 128.

CROSS (MARTIN) and MALLEN (DAVID) Local government and politics. [London, 1978]. pp. 144. *bibliog. (Politics Association. Political Realities)*

IN defence of freedom; edited by Dr. K.W. Watkins; essays by Winston S. Churchill, M.P. [and others]. London, 1978. pp. 180.

RICHARDS (S.G.) Introduction to British government. London, 1978. pp. 237. *bibliogs.*

— — Bibliography.

SHELLEY (IVOR D.) British works on public administration since 1963. London, 1971. 2 pts. *(Extracted from British Book News, May and July, 1971)*

The RADICAL right and patriotic movements in Britain: [a collection of primary source material]; a bibliographical guide: an author, title and chronological index...; compiled by William Pidduck. Hassocks, 1978 in progress.

— — 1603-1714.

FACTION and Parliament: essays on early Stuart history; edited by Kevin Sharpe. Oxford, 1978. pp. 292.

— — 1660-1714.

HOLMES (GEOFFREY) The electorate and the national will in the first age of party. Lancaster, [1976]. pp. 33. *An inaugural lecture delivered on 26 November 1975.*

NENNER (HOWARD) By colour of law: legal culture and constitutional politics in England, 1660-1689. Chicago, 1977. pp. 251. *bibliog.*

— — 1700-1799.

DICKINSON (H.T.) Liberty and property: political ideology in eighteenth-century Britain. London, [1977]. pp. 369.

KENYON (JOHN PHILIPPS) Revolution principles: the politics of party, 1689-1720. Cambridge, 1977. pp. 248. *(Oxford. University. Ford Lectures. 1975/76)*

— — 1714-1756.

HOLMES (GEOFFREY) The electorate and the national will in the first age of party. Lancaster, [1976]. pp. 33. *An inaugural lecture delivered on 26 November 1975.*

SPECK (WILLIAM ARTHUR) Stability and strife: England, 1714-1760. London, 1977. pp. 311. *bibliog.*

— — 1756-1837.

JUNIUS, pseud. [Author of the "Letters"]. The letters of Junius; edited by John Cannon. Oxford, 1978. pp. 643. *bibliog.*

— — 1800-1899.

CROMWELL (VALERIE) compiler. Revolution or evolution: British government in the nineteenth century. London, 1977. pp. 230. *bibliog.*

— — 1837-1901.

[RICH (Sir HENRY)] Yes or no? London, J. Ridgway, 1852. pp. 13.

BESANT (ANNIE) A selection of the social and political pamphlets of Annie Besant; with a preface and bibliographical notes by John Saville. New York, 1970. 1 vol. (various pagings). *bibliog. Originally published between 1877 and 1891.*

CLAYDEN (PETER WILLIAM) England under Lord Beaconsfield;...new introductory note by E. J. Feuchtwanger. Richmond, Surrey, 1971. pp. 542. *Reprint of original edition published in London in 1880 with subtitle: The political history of six years from the end of 1873 to the beginning of 1880.*

LIFE of Joseph Chamberlain; by Rt. Hon. Viscount Milner [and others]. [London, 1914?]. pp. 320.

LEEDS. University. Library. Handlists. 34. Political correspondence (1884-1897) of Louis Henry Hayter. [Leeds], 1977. pp. 16.

— — 1900- .

LEE (JOHN MICHAEL) Reviewing the machinery of government 1942-1952: an essay on the Anderson Committee and its successors. n.p., 1977. pp. 176.

MILLER (WILLIAM L.) Electoral dynamics in Britain since 1918. London, 1977. pp. 242.

WALKER (MARTIN) Daily sketches:...a cartoon history of twentieth century Britain. London, 1978. pp. 192. *bibliog.*

WILSON (Sir DUNCAN) and EISENBERG (JOE) Leonard Woolf: a political biography. London, 1978. pp. 282. *bibliog.*

UNITED KINGDOM (Cont.)

—— 1901-1945.

[ROBERTS (CARL ERIC BECHHOFER)] Lord Birkenhead: being an account of the life of F.E. Smith, first Earl of Birkenhead; by Ephesian. popular ed. London, 1927. pp. 222.

FRY (MICHAEL GRAHAM) Lloyd George and foreign policy. Montreal, 1977 in progress.

—— 1901-1918.

LIFE of Joseph Chamberlain; by Rt. Hon. Viscount Milner [and others]. [London, 1914?]. pp. 320.

—— 1918-1945.

STEVENSON (JOHN) Historian, and COOK (CHRISTOPHER PIERS) The slump: society and politics during the depression. London, 1977. pp. 348. *bibliog.*

—— 1945- .

LABOUR PARTY. The men who failed: the story of the Westminster dunces. London, [1956]. pp. 27.

LABOUR PARTY. 2 pension plans: Labour and Tory plans. London, [1959]. pp. 12.

LABOUR PARTY. The Tory swindle 1951-1959. London, [1959]. 1 pamphlet (unpaged).

LABOUR RESEARCH DEPARTMENT. Unfit to govern: the record of the Tory government. London, 1974. pp. 23.

AXFORD (BARRIE) and BRIER (ALAN) Interpretations of the British crisis. Nottingham, 1976. pp. 27. *Paper presented to the Political Studies Association Conference, Nottingham, 1976.*

AMIS (KINGSLEY) ed. Harold's years: impressions from the New Statesman and the Spectator. London, 1977. pp. 175.

BIFFEN (JOHN) Political office or political power?; six speeches on national and international affairs. London, 1977. pp. 46.

JOHNSTON (W.B.) Church of Scotland minister, and others. Devolution and the British churches;...report to the spring 1977 assembly of the British Council of Churches. London, 1977. pp. 55.

MACKINTOSH (JOHN PITCAIRN) Britain's malaise: political or economic? Southampton, 1977. pp. 26. *(Southampton. University. Fawley Foundation. Lectures. 23)*

STEEL (DAVID) 1938- . Militant for the reasonable man; addresses...at the Brighton assembly, 1977. London, [1977]. pp. 23.

THATCHER (MARGARET) Let our children grow tall; selected speeches, 1975-1977. London, 1977. pp. 114.

The RADICAL right and patriotic movements in Britain: [a collection of primary source material]. Hassocks. [1978 in progress]. *Microfiche. Microfiches 1a and 1b contain a bibliographical guide to 2-129. For a printed version of the guide see next card.*

BEESON (TREVOR) Britain today and tomorrow. [London], 1978. pp. 284.

CLUTTERBUCK (RICHARD LEWIS) Britain in agony: the growth of political violence. London, 1978. pp. 335. *bibliog.*

DIVIDED loyalties: British regional assertion and European integration; edited by Martin Kolinsky, assisted by David Scott Bell. Manchester, 1978. pp. 216.

HOGG (QUINTIN McGAREL) Baron Hailsham. The dilemma of democracy: diagnosis and prescription. London, 1978. pp. 238.

MARSH (Sir RICHARD WILLIAM) Off the rails: an autobiography. London, 1978. pp. 214.

NOSSITER (BERNARD D.) Britain: a future that works. London, 1978. pp. 224.

PENROSE (BARRIE) and COURTIOUR (ROGER) The Pencourt file. London, 1978. pp. 423.

POLICY and politics: essays in honour of Norman Chester, Warden of Nuffield College, 1954-1978; edited by David Butler and A.H. Halsey. London, 1978. pp. 214. *bibliog.*

POWELL (JOHN ENOCH) A nation or no nation?: six years in British politics; edited [with a commentary] by Richard Ritchie. London, 1978. pp. 186.

RIGHT turn: eight men who changed their minds; essays by Reg Prentice [and others]...; edited by Patrick Cormack. London, 1978. pp. 104.

TRENDS in British politics since 1945; edited by Chris Cook and John Ramsden. [London, 1978]. pp. 197.

WHAT'S wrong with Britain?; edited by Patrick Hutber. London, 1978. pp. 112.

— Population.

POPULATION TRENDS; ([pd. by] Office of Population Censuses and Surveys, [U.K.]). q., S 1975 (no.1)- London.

GLASS (DAVID VICTOR) and TAYLOR (PHILIP ARTHUR MICHAEL) Population and emigration. Dublin, [1976]. pp. 125. *bibliogs.*

CRAIG (JOHN) Writer on population. Grid references of centres of population, Great Britain, 1971. [London?], 1977. pp. 39. *(U.K. Office of Population Censuses and Surveys. Occasional Papers. 1)*

DAVIES (E.M.) A classification of urban populations in England and Wales, 1951- 1971. [Birmingham], 1977. pp. 298.

DINWIDDY (ROBERT) and REED (DEREK) The effects of certain social and demographic changes on income distribution;...background paper to Report No. 5: third report on the standing reference. London, 1977. pp. 168. *bibliog. (U.K. Royal Commission on the Distribution of Income and Wealth, 1974. Background Papers. No. 3) Report No. 5 published as British Parliamentary Paper Cmnd. 6999, Session 1977-78.*

HATCHER (JOHN) Plague, population and the English economy, 1348-1530. London, 1977. pp. 95. *bibliog. (Economic History Society. Studies in Economic and Social History)*

MITCHISON (ROSALIND) British population change since 1860. London, 1977. pp. 99. *bibliog. (Economic History Society. Studies in Economic and Social History)*

U.K. Office of Population Censuses and Surveys. 1978. Demographic review: a report on population in Great Britain. London, 1978. pp. 102. *bibliog. ([Publications]. Series DR. No.1)*

— Population, Rural.

LEVINE (DAVID) of the Ontario Institute for Studies in Education. Family formation in an age of nascent capitalism. New York, [1977]. pp. 194. *bibliog.*

— Race question.

NEW COMMUNITY: jl. of the Community Relations Commission [U. K.]. q., Oc 1971 (v.1, no.1)- London. *Supersedes Community: q. jl. of Community Relations Commision [U.K.].*

COMMUNITY RELATIONS COMMISSION. Some of my best friends...: a report on race relations attitudes. London, [1976]. pp. 45.

NEW EQUALS; [pd. by] Commission for Racial Equality. bi-m., N/D 1977 (v. 1, no. 1)- London. *Supersedes EQUALS. File includes supplement.*

FENTON (MIKE) and COLLARD (DAVID) Do coloured tenants pay more?: some evidence. Bristol, Social Science Research Council Research Unit on Ethnic Relations, [1977]. pp. 9. *(Working Papers on Ethnic Relations. No. 1)*

KOHLER (DAVID F.) Immigration and race relations. London, 1977. pp. 10. *bibliog. (Liberal Publication Department. Study Papers. No. 7)*

MILES (R.) and PHIZACKLEA (A.) The TUC, black workers and new Commonwealth immigration, 1954- 1973. Bristol, Social Science Research Council Research Unit on Ethnic Relations, [1977]. pp. 44. *(Working Papers on Ethnic Relations. No. 6)*

U.K. Commission for Racial Equality. 1977. sTRATEGY STATEMENT: A PROGRAMME FOR ACTION. lONDON, 1977. PP. 11.

U.K. Commission for Racial Equality. Education journal. bi-m., Ap/My 1978 (v.1, no. 1)- London.

LORIMER (DOUGLAS A.) Colour, class and the Victorians: English attitudes to the negro in the mid-nineteenth century. Leicester, 1978. pp. 300. *bibliog.*

— Relations (general) with Africa.

HETHERINGTON (PENELOPE) British paternalism and Africa, 1920-1940. London, 1978. pp. 196. *bibliog.*

— Relations (general) with Germany.

GROSSBRITANNIEN und Deutschland: europäische Aspekte der politisch-kulturellen Beziehungen beider Länder in Geschichte und Gegenwart: (Festschrift für John W.P. Bourke, München; herausgegeben von Ortwin Kuhn, Berlin). München, [1974]. pp. 691. *bibliogs. In German or English.*

The BRITISH in Germany: educational reconstruction after 1945; edited by Arthur Hearnden. London, 1978. pp. 335. *Based on papers delivered at a conference held at St. Edmund Hall, Oxford in January 1975.*

PILLARS of partnership...; edited by Rolf Breitenstein. London, [1978]. pp. 103.

— Relations (general) with Japan.

MAUGHAN (T.J.) An introduction to the market for British books and journals in Japan and South Korea, etc. Tokyo, 1976. pp. 255.

— Relations (general) with Korea.

MAUGHAN (T.J.) An introduction to the market for British books and journals in Japan and South Korea, etc. Tokyo, 1976. pp. 255.

— Religion.

MARX (ROLAND) Religion et société en Angleterre de la Réforme à nos jours. [Paris, 1978]. pp. 208.

— Rural conditions.

NATIONAL LAND AND HOME LEAGUE. [Pamphlets]. No.3. The revival of country life. London, 1911. s.sh.

— Social conditions.

BESANT (ANNIE) A selection of the social and political pamphlets of Annie Besant; with a preface and bibliographical notes by John Saville. New York, 1970. 1 vol. (various pagings). *bibliog. Originally published between 1877 and 1891.*

LUDOVICI (ANTHONY MARIO) A defence of aristocracy: a text book for Tories. London, 1915. pp. 459.

COMMUNIST PARTY OF GREAT BRITAIN. London District Committee. Royal jubilee: 25 years of war and starvation. London, 1935. pp. 4.

COATES (BRYAN ELLIS) and RAWSTRON (ERIC MITCHELL) Regional variations in Britain: studies in economic and social geography. London, 1971 reprinted 1972. pp. 304. *Reprinted with minor revisions.*

NOBLE (TREVOR) Modern Britain: structure and change. London, 1975. pp. 348. *bibliog.*

AMIS (KINGSLEY) ed. Harold's years: impressions from the New Statesman and the Spectator. London, 1977. pp. 175.

BROWN (MURIEL) Introduction to social administration in Britain. 4th ed. London, 1977. pp. 253. *bibliogs.*

NORTON (MICHAEL) Community. London, 1977. pp. 250. *(The Directory of Social Change. vol.2)*

UNITED KINGDOM (Cont.)

WEBBER (RICHARD J.) The national classification of residential neighbourhoods: an introduction to the classification of wards and parishes. London, 1977. pp. 90. *bibliog. (Planning Research Applications Group. PRAG Technical Papers. TP 23)*

COLMER (JOHN) Coleridge to Catch-22: images of society. [London, 1978]. pp. 240.

CRANFIELD (GEOFFREY ALAN) The press and society: from Caxton to Northcliffe. London, 1978. pp. 242. *bibliog.*

The DEVELOPMENT of the British welfare state, 1880-1975; [edited by] J.R. Hay. London, 1978. pp. 116. *bibliog.*

HALSEY (ALBERT HENRY) Change in British society. Oxford, 1978. pp. 191. *bibliog. (British Broadcasting Corporation. Reith Lectures. 1977)*

NOSSITER (BERNARD D.) Britain: a future that works. London, 1978. pp. 224.

WEBBER (RICHARD J.) and CRAIG (JOHN) Writer on population. Socio-economic classification of local authority areas. London, 1978. pp. 117. *(U.K. Office of Population Censuses and Surveys. Studies on Medical and Population Subjects. No.35)*

WORK, urbanism and inequality: UK society today; edited by Philip Abrams. London, [1978]. pp. 310. *bibliog.*

— **Bibliography.**

WESTERGAARD (JOHN HARALD) and others, compilers. Modern British society: a bibliography. 2nd ed. London, 1977. pp. 199.

— — **Statistics.**

SOCIAL TRENDS: a pbln. of the Government Statistical Service (Central Statistical Office [U.K.]). a., 1970 (no.1)- London.

U.K. Department of the Environment. 1976. Ongoing work in the fields of social statistics and social indicators: an information note. London, 1976. pp. 18. *bibliog.*

— **Social history.**

PIKE (EDGAR ROYSTON) Pioneers of social change. [London, 1963]. pp. 218.

PECCHIO (GIUSEPPE) Count. Osservazioni semiserie di un esule sull'Inghilterra; a cura di Giuseppe Nicoletti. Milano, [1976]. pp. 233.

ANGLO-DUTCH HISTORICAL CONFERENCE, 6TH, 1976. Britain and the Netherlands:...war and society: papers delivered to the...Conference; edited by A.C. Duke and C.A. Tamse. The Hague, 1977. pp. 256.

BRITTON (EDWARD) The community of the vill: a study in the history of the family and village life in fourteenth-century England. Toronto, [1977]. pp. 291. *bibliog.*

CLARKE (JOHN J.) The price of progress: Cobbett's England 1780-1835. London, 1977. pp. 200. *bibliog.*

MEACHAM (STANDISH) A life apart: the English working class, 1890-1914. London, [1977]. pp. 272. *bibliog.*

PRESTON (BRIAN) Occupations of father and son in mid-Victorian England. Reading, 1977. pp. 40. *(Reading. University. Department of Geography. Reading Geographical Papers. No. 56)*

A WIDENING sphere: changing roles of Victorian women; edited by Martha Vicinus. Bloomington, [1977]. pp. 326.

WILLIAMS (GLANMOR) The general and common sort of people, 1540-1640. Exeter, 1977. pp. 32. *(Exeter. University. Harte Memorial Lectures in Local History. 1975)*

YOUNG (GEORGE MALCOLM) Portrait of an age: Victorian England; annotated edition by George Kitson Clark, with a biographical memoir by Sir George Clark. London, 1977. pp. 423.

CALVOCORESSI (PETER) The British experience, 1945-75. London, 1978. pp. 253.

CAMPLIN (JAMIE) The rise of the plutocrats: wealth and power in Edwardian England. London, 1978. pp. 340.

DAVIES (R.R.) Lordship and society in the March of Wales, 1282-1400. Oxford, 1978. pp. 512. *bibliog.*

EMMISON (FREDERICK GEORGE) Elizabethan life: wills of Essex gentry and merchants proved in the Prerogative Court of Canterbury. Chelmsford, 1978. pp. 361. *(Essex. Records Committee. Essex Record Office Publications. No. 71)*

HALSEY (ALBERT HENRY) Change in British society. Oxford, 1978. pp. 191. *bibliog. (British Broadcasting Corporation. Reith Lectures. 1977)*

HARRINGTON (WILLIAM) and YOUNG (PETER) Public relations consultant. The 1945 revolution. London, 1978. pp. 218.

REBELS and their causes: essays in honour of A.L. Morton; edited by Maurice Cornforth. London, 1978. pp. 224.

— — **Bibliography.**

WESTERGAARD (JOHN HARALD) and others, compilers. Modern British society: a bibliography. 2nd ed. London, 1977. pp. 199.

— — **Sources.**

WILLIAMS (GLANMOR) The general and common sort of people, 1540-1640. Exeter, 1977. pp. 32. *(Exeter. University. Harte Memorial Lectures in Local History. 1975)*

WINTER (GORDON) The golden years, 1903-1913: a pictorial survey of the most interesting decade in English history, recorded in contemporary photographs and drawings. Harmondsworth, 1977. pp. 112.

The DEVELOPMENT of the British welfare state, 1880-1975; [edited by] J.R. Hay. London, 1978. pp. 116. *bibliog.*

— — **Statistics.**

DINWIDDY (ROBERT) and REED (DEREK) The effects of certain social and demographic changes on income distribution;...background paper to Report No. 5: third report on the standing reference. London, 1977. pp. 168. *bibliog. (U.K. Royal Commission on the Distribution of Income and Wealth, 1974. Background Papers. No. 3) Report No. 5 published as British Parliamentary Paper Cmnd. 6999, Session 1977-78.*

— **Social life and customs.**

SAMBROOK (GEORGE ARTHUR) ed. English life in the eighteenth century. London, 1940 repr. 1946. pp. 304.

SAMBROOK (GEORGE ARTHUR) ed. English life in the nineteenth century. London, 1942 repr. 1946. pp. 269.

— **Social policy.**

LABOUR PARTY. Go-ahead Britain. [London], 1965. pp. 16.

BRIGGS (HAROLD W.) Building a society fit for drop-outs to live in. Reading, 1977. pp. 63.

BROWN (MURIEL) Introduction to social administration in Britain. 4th ed. London, 1977. pp. 253. *bibliogs.*

NORTHERN REGION STRATEGY TEAM. Strategic plan for the northern region. [Newcastle upon Tyne], 1977. 5 vols. (in 1).

ROSE (HILARY) Social welfare and the inner city. [Bradford, 1977?]. pp. 24. *An inaugural lecture delivered at the University of Bradford on 1st February 1977.*

U.K. Central Office of Information. Reference Division. Reference Pamphlets. 3. Social services in Britain. 11th ed. London, 1977. pp. 81. *bibliog.*

BEESON (TREVOR) Britain today and tomorrow. [London], 1978. pp. 284.

EEKELAAR (JOHN M.) Family law and social policy. London, [1978]. pp. 335. *bibliog.*

FABIAN SOCIETY. Fabian Tracts. [No.] 458. Labour and the social contract; [by] Robert Taylor. London, 1978. pp. 24.

FABIAN SOCIETY. Fabian Tracts. [No.] 459. Deserting the middle ground: Tory social policies. London, 1978. pp. 16.

JONES (KATHLEEN) and others. Issues in social policy. London, 1978. pp. 176.

JUDGE (KEN) Rationing social services: a study of resource allocation and the personal social services. London, 1978. pp. 212.

The ORIGINS of British social policy; edited by Pat Thane. London, [1978]. pp. 209. *Essays presented to a conference on the history of British social policy, 1870-1945, held at Manchester University in 1976.*

ROACH (JOHN PETER CHARLES) Social reform in England 1780-1880. London, 1978. pp. 254. *bibliog.*

SOCIAL policy, 1830-1914: individualism, collectivism, and the origins of the welfare state; edited by Eric J. Evans. London, 1978. pp. 302. *bibliogs.*

SOCIAL policy research; edited by Martin Bulmer. London, 1978. pp. 373.

WHAT'S wrong with Britain?; edited by Patrick Hutber. London, 1978. pp. 112.

— **Statistical services.**

U.K. Business Statistics Office. Report. a., 1977 (1st)- Newport.

— **Statistics.**

U.K. Central Statistical Office. 1971. Profit from facts. [London, 1971]. pp. 36.

BRACEWELL-MILNES (JOHN BARRY) Short measure from Whitehall: how CSO statistics understate the British tax burden. London, 1977. pp. 8.

— **Statistics, Vital.**

POPULATION TRENDS; ([pd. by] Office of Population Censuses and Surveys, [U.K.]). q., S 1975 (no.1)- London.

WATERS (W.E.) Matters of life and death. Southampton, 1977. pp. 26. *bibliog. An inaugural lecture given at Southampton University on 12 May 1977.*

U.K. Office of Population Censuses and Surveys. 1978. Trends in mortality, 1951-1975. London, 1978. pp. 44. *bibliog. ([Publications]. Series DH1. No.3)*

— **Commonwealth — Bibliography.**

LONDON. University. Institute of Commonwealth Studies. Theses in progress in Commonwealth studies; a cumulative list. London, 1977. pp. 19.

— — **Economic policy.**

AMBIRAJAN (SRINIVASA) Classical political economy and British policy in India. Cambridge, 1978. pp. 301. *bibliog. (Cambridge. University. Centre of South Asian Studies. Cambridge South Asian Studies. 21)*

— — **Finance.**

BROCK (LESLIE V.) The currency of the American colonies, 1700-1764: a study in colonial finance and imperial relations. New York, 1975. pp. 602. *bibliog. Originally presented as a thesis, University of Michigan, 1941.*

— — **Foreign relations.**

LOUIS (WILLIAM ROGER) Imperialism at bay, 1941-1945: the United States and the decolonization of the British Empire. Oxford, 1977. pp. 595.

— — History.

EGERTON (HUGH EDWARD) The origin and growth of greater Britain; an introduction to Sir C.P. Lucas's Historical geography. Oxford, 1920. pp. 242. *bibliogs. Previously published as The origin and growth of the English colonies and of their system of government.*

McINTYRE (WILLIAM DAVID) The Commonwealth of Nations: origins and impact, 1869-1971. Minnesota, 1977. pp. 596. *bibliog.*

POWELL (J.M.) Mirrors of the New World: images and image-makers in the settlement process. Folkestone, 1977. pp. 207. *bibliog.*

ELDRIDGE (C.C.) Victorian imperialism. London, [1978]. pp. 248. *bibliogs.*

— — Officials and employees.

BARR (PAT) Taming the jungle: the men who made British Malaya. London, 1977. pp. 172. *bibliog.*

U.K. Foreign and Commonwealth Office. 1977. Colonial regulations: part 1: public officers. London, [1977]. pp. 30.

— — Politics and government.

U.K. Foreign and Commonwealth Office. 1977. Colonial regulations: part 2: public business. London, [1977]. pp. 58.

HETHERINGTON (PENELOPE) British paternalism and Africa, 1920-1940. London, 1978. pp. 196. *bibliog.*

— — Social policy.

HETHERINGTON (PENELOPE) British paternalism and Africa, 1920-1940. London, 1978. pp. 196. *bibliog.*

— — Societies, etc.

COMMONWEALTH SECRETARIAT. Information Division. Commonwealth organisations: a handbook of official and unofficial organisations active in the Commonwealth. London, 1977. pp. 113. *bibliog.*

UNITED NATIONS.

GEGENWARTSPROBLEME der Vereinten Nationen: Vorträge gehalten im Rahmen der vom Institut für Völkerrecht der Universität Göttingen..vom 25 bis 29 Oktober in Göttingen veranstalteten Seminarwoche über die Vereinten Nationen. Göttingen, [1955]. pp. 198. *(Göttingen. Universität. Institut für Völkerrecht. Göttinger Beiträge für Gegenwartsfragen. Band 10)*

TANDON (YASHPAL) A comparative analysis of the executive organs of the United Nations, and their contribution to international peace and security. 1968. fo. 304. *bibliog. Typescript. Ph.D. (London) thesis: unpublished. This thesis is the property of London University and may not be removed from the Library.*

UNITED NATIONS. Disarmament Affairs Division. 1970. The United Nations and disarmament, 1945-1970. New York, 1970. pp. 515.

EICHELBERGER (CLARK MELL) Organizing for peace: a personal history of the founding of the United Nations. New York, [1977]. pp. 317.

ORBACH (WILLIAM W.) To keep the peace: the United Nations condemnatory resolution. Lexington, [1977]. pp. 155.

STONE (JULIUS) Conflict through consensus: United Nations approaches to aggression. Baltimore, 1977. pp. 234.

HILL (WILLIAM MARTIN) The United Nations system: coordinating its economic and social work: a study prepared under the auspices of the United Nations Institute for Training and Research (UNITAR). Cambridge, 1978. pp. 252. *A revised, enlarged and updated version of his Towards greater order, coherence and coordination in the United Nations system.*

THANT, U. View from the UN. Newton Abbot, 1978. pp. 508.

— Bibliography.

UNITED NATIONS. Library. 1978. United Nations sales publications 1972-1977: cumulative list with indexes. (ST/LIB/SER.B/27). New York, 1978. pp. 149. *([Bibliographical Series. No. 27])*

— Indexes.

UNITED NATIONS. Library. 1972. Index to resolutions of the General Assembly 1946-1970. (ST/LIB/SER.H/1). New York, 1972. 2 parts (in 1 vol.) *(Indexes to Resolutions. No.1)*

UNITED NATIONS. Library. 1973. Index to resolutions and other decisions of the United Nations Conference on Trade and Development and of the Trade and Development Board, 1964-1972. (ST/LIB/SER.H/2). New York, 1973. pp. 57. *(Indexes to Resolutions. No.2)*

UNITED NATIONS. Library. 1973. Index to resolutions of the Security Council 1946-1970. (ST/LIB/SER.H/3). New York, 1973. pp. 39. *(Indexes to Resolutions. No. 3)*

— Information services.

INTER-ORGANIZATION BOARD FOR INFORMATION SYSTEMS. 1978. Directory of United Nations information systems and services. Geneva, 1978. pp. 267.

— Bangladesh.

OLIVER (THOMAS W.) The United Nations in Bangladesh. Princeton, [1978]. pp. 231.

— China.

ORBACH (WILLIAM W.) To keep the peace: the United Nations condemnatory resolution. Lexington, [1977]. pp. 155.

— Israel.

ORBACH (WILLIAM W.) To keep the peace: the United Nations condemnatory resolution. Lexington, [1977]. pp. 155.

— Kashmir.

PAKISTAN. Department of Films and Publications. 1966. Kashmir in the Security Council: (a compilation of the texts of various resolutions tabled at the Security Council since 1948 until 5th November, 1965). [Karachi, 1966?]. pp. 49.

— Korea.

UNITED NATIONS. General Assembly. 1975. The question of Korea at the 30th session of the U.N. General Assembly: [collection of General Assembly documents]. Seoul, Republic of Korea Ministry of Foreign Affairs, 1975. 2 vols.(in 1).

— Malawi.

MALAWI. Prime Minister. 1964. Malawi admitted to United Nations: address to the General Assembly by the Prime Minister, Ngwazi Dr. Kamuzu Banda, December 2nd 1964. [Blantyre, 1964]. pp. 12.

MALAWI. Prime Minister. 1965. Speech of the Prime Minister of Malawi, Ngwazi Dr. Kamuzu Banda, to the General Assembly of the United Nations, delivered by Hon. A.M. Nyasulu, M.P., on September 27, 1965. [Blantyre, 1965]. pp. 10.

MALAWI. Delegation to the 23rd Session of the General Assembly of the United Nations. 1968. An address to the 23rd session of the General Assembly, 1968: Malawi and the United Nations; (delivered by the Hon. Alec Nyasulu on the behalf of the President of Malawi). [Blantyre, 1968]. pp. (5).

— South Africa.

ORBACH (WILLIAM W.) To keep the peace: the United Nations condemnatory resolution. Lexington, [1977]. pp. 155.

— United States.

DMITRICHEV (TIMUR FEDOROVICH) Amerikanskaia diplomatiia v OON. Moskva, 1977. pp. 255.

UNITED NATIONS CONFERENCE ON TRADE AND DEVELOPMENT.

TANNER (JOHN) The tide has turned: a first-hand report on the outcome of UNCTAD 4. London, [1976]. pp. 28.

BEHRMAN (JERE R.) International commodity agreements: an evaluation of the UNCTAD integrated commodity programme. [Washington], 1977. pp. 93. *(Overseas Development Council. Monographs. No. 9)*

UNITED NATIONS ECONOMIC COMMISSION FOR LATIN AMERICA.

PINEDO (FEDERICO) La CEPAL y la realidad economica en America Latina. Buenos Aires, 1963. pp. 79.

— Bibliography.

UNITED NATIONS. Economic Commission for Latin America. Library. 1973- . Bibliografia de la CEPAL, 1948-1972; ([with] Suplemento[s]). Santiago, 1973 in progress.

UNITED NATIONS EDUCATIONAL, SCIENTIFIC AND CULTURAL ORGANIZATION.

UNITED NATIONS EDUCATIONAL, SCIENTIFIC AND CULTURAL ORGANIZATION. Committee for the Furtherance of the Medium-Term Plan of Unesco. Bulletin. irreg., [1977, (no. 1)]- Paris.

UNITED NATIONS UNIVERSITY.

UNU NEWSLETTER; [pd. by] United Nations University. irreg., current issues only. Tokyo.

UNITED STATES

— Antiquities.

PADDOCK (JOHN) Pristine urbanism in Mesoamerica and the forgotten man. Mitla, Mexico, [1973]. pp. 27.

— Armed forces.

BACHMAN (JERALD G.) and others. The all-volunteer force: a study of ideology in the military. Ann Arbor, [1977]. pp. 210. *bibliog.*

BETTS (RICHARD K.) Soldiers, statesmen, and cold war crises. Cambridge, Mass., 1977. pp. 292. *bibliog.*

GOODPASTER (ANDREW JACKSON) For the common defense. Lexington, Mass., [1977]. pp. 174.

GOODPASTER (ANDREW JACKSON) and HUNTINGTON (SAMUEL PHILLIPS) Civil-military relations. Washington, D.C., [1977]. pp. 84. *(American Enterprise Institute for Public Policy Research. AEI Studies. 141) Based on a symposium sponsored by the University of Nebraska at Omaha and the AEI in 1976.*

LEVITAN (SAR A.) and ALDERMAN (KAREN CLEARY) Warriors at work: the volunteer armed force. Beverly Hills, [1977]. pp. 215.

— — Appropriations and expenditures.

The SOVIET military buildup and U.S. defense spending; [by] Barry M. Blechman [and others]. Washington, [1977]. pp. 61. *(Brookings Institution. Studies in Defense Policy)*

— Biography.

WHO's who in labor. New York, 1976. pp. 807.

— Census.

UNITED STATES. Census, 1860. Population schedules of the eighth census of the United States, 1860. [various places], 1860. *Microfilm.*

UNITED STATES. Census, 1870. Population schedules of the ninth census of the United States, 1870. [various places], 1870. *Microfilm.*

UNITED STATES. Census, 1880. 10th census, 1880: [population schedules]. [various places], 1880. *Microfilm.*

UNITED STATES (Cont.)

— Civilization.

CARTER (PAUL ALLEN) Another part of the twenties. New York, 1977. pp. 229.

— Commerce.

WEISSKOPF (THOMAS E.) American economic interests in foreign countries: an empirical survey. Ann Arbor, 1974. pp. 56. *(Michigan University. Center for Research on Economic Development. Discussion Papers. No.35)*

THIMM (ALFRED L.) Business ideologies in the reform-progressive era, 1880-1914. University, Ala., [1976]. pp. 264. *bibliog.*

— — America, Latin.

STEWARD (DICK) Trade and hemisphere: the good neighbor policy and reciprocal trade. Columbia, Ma., 1975. pp. 307. *bibliog.*

— — Europe, Eastern.

ATLANTIC COUNCIL OF THE UNITED STATES. Committee on East-West Trade. East-West trade: managing encounter and accommodation. Boulder, 1977. pp. 194.

— — Japan.

SANDERSON (FRED HUGO) Japan's food prospects and policies. Washington, D.C., [1978]. pp. 99. *bibliog. Published under the auspices of the Brookings Institution.*

— Commercial policy.

BROOKSTONE (JEFFREY M.) The multinational businessman and foreign policy: entrepreneurial politics in east-west trade and investment. New York, 1976. pp. 183. *bibliog.*

ATLANTIC COUNCIL OF THE UNITED STATES. Committee on East-West Trade. East-West trade: managing encounter and accommodation. Boulder, 1977. pp. 194.

SEWELL (JOHN WILLIAMSON) The United States and world development: agenda 1977. New York, 1977. pp. 245. *Written under the auspices of the Overseas Development Council.*

WARES (WILLIAM A.) The theory of dumping and American commercial policy. Lexington, Mass., [1977]. pp. 130. *bibliog.*

— Congress.

BIOGRAPHICAL directory of the United States executive branch, 1774-1977; Robert Sobel, editor in chief. Westport, 1977. pp. 503.

— — Elections.

CLEM (ALAN L.) ed. The making of Congressmen: seven campaigns of 1974; with associates Donald M. Austern [and others]. North Scituate, Mass., [1976]. pp. 275. *bibliog.*

— — Rules and practice.

RALPH NADER CONGRESS PROJECT. Ruling Congress: how the House and Senate rules govern the legislative process; [edited by] Ted Siff and Alan Weil, directors. [Harmondsworth, 1977]. pp. 299.

— — Senate — Committees.

DASH (SAMUEL) Chief counsel: inside the Ervin committee: the untold story of Watergate. New York, [1976]. pp. 275.

— Constitution.

KRASNER (MICHAEL A.) and others. American government: structure and process. New York, [1977]. pp. 390. *bibliogs.*

FOTHERINGHAM (PETER) and others. American government and politics. rev. ed. London, 1978. pp. 363. *bibliogs.*

— — Amendments.

BERRY (MARY FRANCES) Military necessity and civil rights policy; black citizenship and the constitution, 1861-1868. Port Washington, 1977. pp. 132. *bibliog.*

— — 1st-10th Amendments.

MALBIN (MICHAEL J.) Religion and politics: the intentions of the authors of the First Amendment. Washington, [1978]. pp. 40. *(American Enterprise Institute for Public Policy Research. AEI Studies. 200)*

— — 14th Amendment.

BERGER (RAOUL) Government by judiciary: the transformation of the Fourteenth Amendment. Cambridge, Mass., 1977. pp. 483. *bibliog.*

— Constitutional history.

WIECEK (WILLIAM M.) The sources of antislavery constitutionalism in America, 1760-1848. Ithaca, 1977. pp. 309.

SIMPSON (WILLIAM O.) Vision and reality: the evolution of American government. London, [1978]. pp. 243. *bibliog.*

— Constitutional law.

ACKERMAN (BRUCE A.) Private property and the constitution. New Haven, 1977. pp. 303.

BEDAU (HUGO ADAM) The courts, the constitution, and capital punishment. Lexington, Mass., [1977]. pp. 165.

BRIDWELL (RANDALL) and WHITTEN (RALPH U.) The constitution and the common law: the decline of the doctrines of separation of powers and federalism. Lexington, Mass., [1977]. pp. 206.

JACOBSOHN (GARY J.) Pragmatism, statesmanship, and the Supreme Court. Ithaca, 1977. pp. 214. *bibliog.*

KURLAND (PHILIP B.) Watergate and the constitution. Chicago, [1978]. pp. 261. *(Chicago. University. William R. Kenan, Jr., Inaugural Lectures)*

— Council of Economic Advisers.

NORTON (HUGH STANTON) The Employment Act and the Council of Economic Advisers, 1946-1976. Columbia, S.C., 1977. pp. 348. *bibliog.*

— Defences.

COMMITTEE FOR ECONOMIC DEVELOPMENT. Research and Policy Committee. Nuclear energy and national security. New York, 1976. pp. 80.

PFALTZGRAFF (ROBERT L.) and DAVIS (JACQUELYN K.) The cruise missile: bargaining chip or defense bargain? Cambridge, Mass., 1977. pp. 53. *(Institute for Foreign Policy Analysis. Special Reports)*

RYAN (PAUL B.) The Panama Canal controversy: U.S. diplomacy and defence interests. Stanford, Calif., [1977]. pp. 198. *bibliog. (Stanford University. Hoover Institution on War, Revolution and Peace. Hoover Institution Publications. 187)*

The SOVIET military buildup and U.S. defense spending; [by] Barry M. Blechman [and others]. Washington, [1977]. pp. 61. *(Brookings Institution. Studies in Defense Policy)*

— Description and travel.

FINCH (MARIANNE) An Englishwoman's experience in America. [London], 1853; New York, 1969. pp. 386. *Facsimile reprint.*

HAMMOND (GEORGE PETER) The adventures of Alexander Barclay, mountain man...: a narrative of his career, 1810-1855, his memorandum diary, 1845 to 1850. Denver, Colo., 1976. pp. 246.

— Diplomatic and consular service.

ETZOLD (THOMAS H.) The conduct of American foreign relations: the other side of diplomacy. New York, 1977. pp. 159. *bibliog.*

— Economic conditions.

AGLIETTA (MICHEL) Régulation et crises du capitalisme: l'expérience des Etats-Unis. [Paris, 1976]. pp. 334.

KAHN (HERMAN) and others. The next 200 years: a scenario for America and the world. New York, 1976. pp. 241. *bibliog.*

CONNECTICUT. Tri-State Regional Planning Commission. 1977. Metromonitor: a regional review of social and economic trends. New York, 1977. pp. 10.

CONTEMPORARY economic problems, 1977; William Fellner, editor. Washington, D.C., [1977]. pp. 428. *(American Enterprise Institute for Public Policy Research. AEI Studies)*

KLEIN (BURTON H.) Dynamic economics. Cambridge, Mass., 1977. pp. 289.

POSNER (RICHARD A.) Economic analysis of law. 2nd ed. Boston, Mass., [1977]. pp. 572.

ALTERNATIVE directions in economic policy; edited by Frank J. Bonello and Thomas R. Swartz. Notre Dame, [1978]. pp. 179.

MELLOAN (GEORGE) and MELLOAN (JOAN) The Carter economy. New York, [1978]. pp. 312.

MIERNYK (WILLIAM H.) and others. Regional impacts of rising energy prices. Cambridge, Mass., [1978]. pp. 135. *bibliog.*

ROSTOW (WALT WHITMAN) Getting from here to there. New York, [1978]. pp. 271.

WEINSTEIN (BERNARD L.) and FIRESTINE (ROBERT E.) Regional growth and decline in the United States: the rise of the sunbelt and the decline of the northeast. New York, 1978. pp. 151.

— — Mathematical models.

HOUSE (PETER WILLIAM) and WILLIAMS (EDWARD R.) The carrying capacity of a nation: growth and the quality of life. Lexington, Mass., [1976]. pp. 356. *bibliog.*

— Economic history.

FLAMANT (MAURICE) Histoire économique et sociale contemporaine. Paris, [1976]. pp. 647. *bibliog.*

HEILBRONER (ROBERT LOUIS) The economic transformation of America;...in collaboration with Aaron Singer. New York, [1977]. pp. 276. *bibliog.*

The MANY-faceted Jacksonian era: new interpretations; edited by Edward Pessen. Westport, Conn., 1977. pp. 331. *bibliog.*

NORTON (HUGH STANTON) The Employment Act and the Council of Economic Advisers, 1946-1976. Columbia, S.C., 1977. pp. 348. *bibliog.*

RANSOM (ROGER L.) and SUTCH (RICHARD) One kind of freedom: the economic consequences of emancipation. Cambridge, 1977. pp. 409. *bibliog.*

— Economic policy.

COMMITTEE FOR ECONOMIC DEVELOPMENT. Research and Policy Committee. Fighting inflation and promoting growth. [New York], 1976. pp. 96.

SHERMAN (HOWARD JAY) Stagflation: a radical theory of unemployment and inflation. New York, [1976]. pp. 252. *bibliogs.*

CONTEMPORARY economic problems, 1977; William Fellner, editor. Washington, D.C., [1977]. pp. 428. *(American Enterprise Institute for Public Policy Research. AEI Studies)*

GARSON (G. DAVID) Power and politics in the United States: a political economy approach. Lexington, Mass., [1977]. pp. 352.

NORTON (HUGH STANTON) The Employment Act and the Council of Economic Advisers, 1946-1976. Columbia, S.C., 1977. pp. 348. *bibliog.*

UNITED STATES (Cont.)

PINE (R. DEAN) Beginning the third century: the liberal-led march to communism. New York, [1977]. pp. 68.

SHULTZ (GEORGE PRATT) and DAM (KENNETH W.) Economic policy beyond the headlines. New York, [1977]. pp. 225. *bibliog.*

ALTERNATIVE directions in economic policy; edited by Frank J. Bonello and Thomas R. Swartz. Notre Dame, [1978]. pp. 179.

MELLOAN (GEORGE) and MELLOAN (JOAN) The Carter economy. New York, [1978]. pp. 312.

— Emigration and immigration.

HIGHAM (JOHN) Send these to me: Jews and other immigrants in urban America. New York, 1975. pp. 259.

FROM Sweden to America: a history of the migration; editors Harald Runblom and Hans Norman. Minneapolis, 1976. pp. 391. *(Uppsala. Universitet. Historiska Institutionen. Acta Universitatis Upsaliensis. 74)*

GOLAB (CAROLINE) Immigrant destinations. Philadelphia, 1977. pp. 246.

— Executive departments.

ROSTKER (BERNARD) Logistics: its planning, programming and budgeting in the Office of the Secretary of Defense, 1968-1970. [Santa Monica], 1972. pp. 15. *(Rand Corporation. [Papers]. 4881)*

ETZOLD (THOMAS H.) The conduct of American foreign relations: the other side of diplomacy. New York, 1977. pp. 159. *bibliog.*

KAUFMAN (HERBERT) Red tape: its origins, uses, and abuses. Washington, D.C., [1977]. pp. 100.

WEAVER (SUZANNE) Decision to prosecute: organization and public policy in the Antitrust Division. Cambridge, Mass., [1977]. pp. 196. *(Massachusetts Institute of Technology. MIT Studies in American Politics and Public Policy. 2)*

FEDERAL reserve policies and public disclosure; edited by Richard D. Erb. Washington, D.C., [1978]. pp. 108. *(American Enterprise Institute for Public Policy Research. AEI Symposia. 78B) Papers from a conference held in 1977.*

WINKLER (ALLAN M.) The politics of propaganda: the Office of War Information, 1942-1945. New Haven, 1978. pp. 230. *bibliog. (Yale University. Yale Historical Publications. Miscellany. 118)*

— Foreign economic relations.

BECSKY (GYÖRGY) The international monetary situation and the global economic strategy of the USA; translated by George Hajdu. Budapest, 1972. pp. 46. *(Hungarian Scientific Council for World Economy. [Publications]. Trends in World Economy. No. 8)*

La CRISE de l'impérialisme et la troisième guerre mondiale; [by] Noam Chomsky [and others]. Paris, 1976. pp. 282.

COHEN (STEPHEN D.) The making of United States international economic policy: principles, problems, and proposals for reform. New York, 1977. pp. 208.

CONTEMPORARY economic problems, 1977; William Fellner, editor. Washington, D.C., [1977]. pp. 428. *(American Enterprise Institute for Public Policy Research. AEI Studies)*

DEWITT (R. PETER) The Inter-American Development Bank and political influence, with special reference to Costa Rica. New York, 1977. pp. 197. *bibliog.*

HUDSON (MICHAEL) Ph.D. Global fracture: the new international economic order. New York, [1977]. pp. 296.

McALISTER (ANDREW MCDONALD) Overseas economic relations and foreign policy in the administration of President Kennedy, 1961-1963. [1977]. fo. 356. *bibliog.* Typescript. Ph.D. (London) thesis: unpublished. *This thesis is the property of London University and may not be removed from the Library.*

WHITMAN (MARINA VON NEUMANN) Sustaining the international economic system: issues for U.S. policy. Princeton, 1977. pp. 56. *bibliog. (Princeton University. Department of Economics and Sociology. International Finance Section. Essays in International Finance. No. 121)*

— — America, Latin.

STEWARD (DICK) Trade and hemisphere: the good neighbor policy and reciprocal trade. Columbia, Ma., 1975. pp. 307. *bibliog.*

— — Asia.

SHAH (S.A.) ed. U.S. imperialism in modern Asia. Montreal, 1972. pp. 65. *bibliogs. (Afro-Asian-Latin American Peoples' Solidarity Committee. Pamphlet Series. No. 2)*

— — Brazil.

COMMITTEE OF RETURNED VOLUNTEERS. Brazil: who pulls the strings?: or, Alliance for repression. Chicago, [1970?]. pp. 82.

— — Germany.

LINK (WERNER) Deutsche und amerikanische Gewerkschaften und Geschäftsleute, 1945-1975: eine Studie über transnationale Beziehungen. Düsseldorf, [1978]. pp. 296. *bibliog.*

— — Japan.

JAPAN-U.S. ASSEMBLY, 1975. The Japan-U.S. Assembly. vol.2. Proceedings of a conference on the threat to the world economic order. Washington, D.C., [1976]. pp. 151. *Annual meeting of the Conference Board on U.S.-Japan Economic Policy in co-operation with the American Enterprise Institute for Public Policy Research.*

— — Taiwan.

CONFERENCE ON LEGAL ASPECTS OF UNITED STATES-REPUBLIC OF CHINA TRADE AND INVESTMENT, 1977. Proceedings...; editors: Hungdah Chiu and David Simon. Baltimore, 1977. pp. 217. *bibliog. (Maryland. University. School of Law. Occasional Papers/Reprints Series in Contemporary Asian Studies. No. 10)*

— Foreign population.

IMMIGRANTS and religion in urban America; edited by Randall M. Miller and Thomas D. Marzik. Philadelphia, 1977. pp. 170. *Based on a series of symposia held at Saint Joseph's College, Philadelphia, during the academic year 1975-1976.*

IMMIGRANTS in industrial America, 1850-1920; edited by Richard L. Ehrlich. Charlottesville, 1977. pp. 218. *Papers of a conference organised by the Eleutherian Mills-Hagley Foundation and the Balch Institute of Philadelphia and held in 1973.*

— Foreign relations.

HOROWITZ (DAVID) The free world colossus: a critique of American foreign policy in the cold war. rev. ed. New York, 1971. pp. 465. *bibliog.*

The NEW era in American foreign policy; John H. Gilbert, editor. New York, [1973]. pp. 214. *Based on papers presented at a symposium held in 1972 at North Carolina State University.*

AMERICAN FOREIGN RELATIONS: a documentary record; [pd. by] Council on Foreign Relations. a., 1974- New York. *Incorporates DOCUMENTS ON AMERICAN FOREIGN RELATIONS and UNITED STATES IN WORLD AFFAIRS.*

JOHANSEN (ROBERT C.) The Vladivostok accord: a case study of the impact of U.S. foreign policy on the prospects for world order reform. Princeton, 1976. pp. 114. *(Princeton University. Center of International Studies. World Order Studies Program. Occasional Papers. No. 4)*

MARKEL (LESTER) and MARCH (AUDREY) Global challenge to the United States: a study of the problems, the perils, and the proposed solutions involved in Washington's search for a new role in the world: summary and analysis. Rutherford, [N.J.], [1976]. pp. 241. *(Fairleigh Dickinson University. Leverton Lecture Series) Report on project conducted by the Graduate Institute of International Studies, Fairleigh Dickinson University.*

BETTS (RICHARD K.) Soldiers, statesmen, and cold war crises. Cambridge, Mass., 1977. pp. 292. *bibliog.*

DMITRICHEV (TIMUR FEDOROVICH) Amerikanskaia diplomatiia v OON. Moskva, 1977. pp. 255.

ETZOLD (THOMAS H.) The conduct of American foreign relations: the other side of diplomacy. New York, 1977. pp. 159. *bibliog.*

GERLACH (HERIBERT) Die Berlinpolitik der Kennedy-Administration: eine Fallstudie zum aussenpolitischen Verhalten der Kennedy- Regierung in der Berlinkrise, 1961. Frankfurt/Main, [1977]. pp. 325. *bibliog.*

HAENDEL (DAN) The process of priority formulation: U.S. foreign policy in the Indo-Pakistan war of 1971. Boulder, 1977. pp. 428. *bibliog.*

ISAAK (ROBERT A.) American democracy and world power. New York, [1977]. pp. 216. *bibliog.*

LISKA (GEORGE) Quest for equilibrium: America and the balance of power on land and sea. Baltimore, [1977]. pp. 254. *(Johns Hopkins University. Washington Center of Foreign Policy Research. Studies in International Affairs)*

McALISTER (ANDREW MCDONALD) Overseas economic relations and foreign policy in the administration of President Kennedy, 1961-1963. [1977]. fo. 356. *bibliog.* Typescript. Ph.D. (London) thesis: unpublished. *This thesis is the property of London University and may not be removed from the Library.*

REICH (BERNARD) Quest for peace: United States-Israel relations and the Arab- Israeli conflict. New Brunswick, [1977]. pp. 495. *bibliog. (Tel-Aviv. University. Shiloah Center for Middle Eastern and African Studies. Monograph Series)*

SEWELL (JOHN WILLIAMSON) The United States and world development: agenda 1977. New York, 1977. pp. 245. *Written under the auspices of the Overseas Development Council.*

SPENCER (DONALD S.) Louis Kossuth and Young America: a study of sectionalism and foreign policy, 1848-1852. Columbia, Miss., 1977. pp. 203. *bibliog.*

CHOMSKY (NOAM) 'Human rights' and American foreign policy. Nottingham, 1978. pp. 90.

ETHNICITY and U.S. foreign policy; edited by Abdul Aziz Said. New York, 1977. pp. 180. *Based on a panel at the annual convention of the International Studies Association in Toronto, 1976.*

HUGHES (BARRY B.) The domestic context of American foreign policy. San Francisco, [1978]. pp. 240.

KENNAN (GEORGE FROST) The cloud of danger: some current problems of American foreign policy. London, 1978. pp. 234.

MAJOR problems in American foreign policy: documents and essays; edited by Thomas G. Paterson. Lexington, Mass., [1978]. 2 vols. *bibliogs.*

ROSE (LISLE ABBOTT) The long shadow: reflections on the Second World War era. Westport, Conn., 1978. pp. 224. *bibliog.*

SAFFORD (JEFFREY J.) Wilsonian maritime diplomacy, 1913-1921. New Brunswick, [1978]. pp. 282. *bibliog.*

SZULC (TAD) The illusion of peace: foreign policy in the Nixon years. New York, 1978. pp. 822.

See also UNITED NATIONS — United States.

UNITED STATES (Cont.)

— — Treaties.

ENRIQUEZ COYRO (ERNESTO) El tratado entre Mexico y los Estados Unidos de America sobre rios internacionales: una lucha nacional de noventa años. Mexico, [1976]. 2 vols. (in 1). *(Mexico City. Universidad Nacional Autonoma de Mexico. Facultad de Ciencias Politicas y Sociales. Serie Estudios. 47-48)*

— — Africa, Subsaharan.

COHEN (BARRY) The black and white minstrel show: Carter, Young and Africa. Nottingham, 1977. pp. 21. *(Spokesman, The. Pamphlets. No. 58)*

— — America, Latin.

The AMERICAS in a changing world: a report of the Commission on United States-Latin American Relations...; selected papers by Kalman H. Silvert [and others]. New York, [1975]. pp. 248.

THEBERGE (JAMES DANIEL) and FONTAINE (ROGER W.) Latin America: struggle for progress. Lexington, Mass., [1977]. pp. 205. *(Commission on Critical Choices for Americans. Critical Choices for Americans. vol. 15)*

GASPAR (EDMUND) United States - Latin America: a special relationship? Washington, D.C., [1978]. pp. 90. *(American Institute for Public Policy Research and Stanford University. Hoover Institution on War, Revolution and Peace. AEI-Hoover Policy Studies. 26)*

— — Argentine Republic.

CIRIA (ALBERTO) Estados Unidos nos mira. Buenos Aires, [1973]. pp. 258.

FRANCIS (MICHAEL J.) The limits of hegemony: United States relations with Argentina and Chile during World War II. Notre Dame, [1977]. pp. 292. *(Notre Dame. University. Committee on International Relations. International Studies)*

— — Asia.

SHAH (S.A.) ed. U.S. imperialism in modern Asia. Montreal, 1972. pp. 65. *bibliogs. (Afro-Asian-Latin American Peoples' Solidarity Committee. Pamphlet Series. No. 2)*

ASIA AND THE WORLD FORUM. Forum on the U.S. and east Asia [held in 1977: proceedings] . Taipei, 1977. pp. 157. *(Asia and the World Forum. Asia and the World Monographs. 7)*

HARRISON (SELIG S.) The widening gulf: Asian nationalism and American policy. New York, [1978]. pp. 468. *bibliog.*

— — Asia, Southeast.

FEDULOVA (NADEZHDA GEORGIEVNA) SSha: politika v Iugo-Vostochnoi Azii: sotsial'no- ekonomicheskie aspekty. Moskva, 1975. pp. 223.

BLAUFARB (DOUGLAS S.) The counterinsurgency era: US doctrine and performance, 1950 to the present. New York, [1977]. pp. 356. *bibliog.*

— — Canada.

SWANSON (ROGER FRANK) Intergovernmental perspectives on the Canada-U.S. relationship. New York, 1978. pp. 278.

— — Chile.

MARIN (GERMAN) Una historia fantastica y calculada: la CIA en el pais de los chilenos. Mexico, 1976. pp. 280.

FRANCIS (MICHAEL J.) The limits of hegemony: United States relations with Argentina and Chile during World War II. Notre Dame, [1977]. pp. 292. *(Notre Dame. University. Committee on International Relations. International Studies)*

— — China.

WHITAKER (URBAN GEORGE) ed. The foundations of U.S. China policy; contributors, George E. Taylor [and others]. Berkeley, Calif., [1959]. pp. 136. *Transcript of a radio programme, 1959.*

VARG (PAUL A.) The closing of the door: Sino-American relations, 1936-1946. [East Lansing, Mich.], 1973. pp. 300.

THOMSON (JAMES C.) An anatomy of Chinese-American relations. Braamfontein, 1976. pp. 11. *(South African Institute of International Affairs. Occasional Papers)*

BARNETT (ARTHUR DOAK) China and the major powers in east Asia. Washington, D.C., [1977]. pp. 416.

ASPECTS of Sino-American relations since 1784; edited by Thomas H. Etzold. New York, 1978. pp. 173. *bibliogs.*

COHEN (WARREN I.) The Chinese connection: Roger S. Greene, Thomas W. Lamont, George E. Sokolsky and American-East Asian relations. New York, 1978. pp. 322. *(Columbia University. East Asian Institute. Studies)*

SUTTER (ROBERT G.) China-watch: toward Sino-American reconciliation. Baltimore, [1978]. pp. 155. *bibliog.*

— — Colombia.

RANDALL (STEPHEN J.) The diplomacy of modernization: Colombian-American relations, 1920-1940. Toronto, [1977]. pp. 239. *bibliog.*

— — East (Near East).

The MIDDLE East: critical choices for the United States; Eugene V. Rostow, editor. Boulder, Colo., 1976. pp. 211. *Papers of a symposium convened by the National Committee on American Foreign Policy, Inc.*

MANGOLD (PETER) Superpower intervention in the Middle East. London, [1978]. pp. 209. *bibliog.*

PRIMAKOV (EVGENII MAKSIMOVICH) Anatomiia blizhnevostochnogo konflikta. Moskva, 1978. pp. 374.

— — Europe.

MENIL (LOIS PATTISON DE) Who speaks for Europe?: the vision of Charles de Gaulle. London, [1977]. pp. 232. *bibliog.*

WESTERN Europe: the trials of partnership; edited by David S. Landes. Lexington, Mass., [1977]. pp. 406. *(Commission on Critical Choices for Americans. Critical Choices for Americans. vol. 8)*

WILLIAMS (GEOFFREY LEE) The permanent alliance: the European-American partnership, 1945-1984. Leyden, 1977. pp. 407. *bibliog.*

— — France.

[TICKELL (RICHARD)] La cassette verte de Monsieur de Sartine, trouvée chez Mademoiselle du Thé. 6th ed. La Haye, chez la Veuve Whiskerfeld, 1779. pp. 76.

— — Indian Ocean Region.

BEZBORUAH (MONORANJAN) U.S. strategy in the Indian Ocean. New York, 1977. pp. 268. *bibliog.*

— — Indochina.

BRITISH CAMPAIGN FOR PEACE IN VIETNAM. Vietnam, Laos, Cambodia: Nixon get out!. Alkrington, Nr. Manchester, [1971?]. pp. (10).

— — Israel.

DRINAN (ROBERT F.) Honor the promise: America's commitment to Israel. Garden City, N.Y., 1977. pp. 250.

REICH (BERNARD) Quest for peace: United States-Israel relations and the Arab- Israeli conflict. New Brunswick, [1977]. pp. 495. *bibliog. (Tel-Aviv. University. Shiloah Center for Middle Eastern and African Studies. Monograph Series)*

SAFRAN (NADAV) Israel: the embattled ally. Cambridge, Mass., 1978. pp. 633. *bibliog.*

— — Italy.

BRANCOLI (RODOLFO) Gli USA e il PCI. Milano, 1976. pp. 197.

— — Japan.

COHEN (WARREN I.) The Chinese connection: Roger S. Greene, Thomas W. Lamont, George E. Sokolsky and American-East Asian relations. New York, 1978. pp. 322. *(Columbia University. East Asian Institute. Studies)*

— — Korea.

DOCUMENTS on Korean-American relations, 1943-1976; editor Se-Jin Kim. Seoul, [1976]. pp. 558.

The US imperialists started the Korean war. Pyongyang, 1977. pp. 308.

— — Mexico.

SCHOONOVER (THOMAS DAVID) Dollars over dominion: the triumph of liberalism in Mexican- United States relations, 1861-1867. Baton Rouge, [1978]. pp. 316. *bibliog.*

— — Panama.

RYAN (PAUL B.) The Panama Canal controversy: U.S. diplomacy and defence interests. Stanford, Calif., [1977]. pp. 198. *bibliog. (Stanford University. Hoover Institution on War, Revolution and Peace. Hoover Institution Publications. 187)*

LAFEBER (WALTER FREDERICK) The Panama Canal: the crisis in historical perspective. New York, 1978. pp. xii,248. *bibliog.*

— — Philippine Islands.

BUSS (CLAUDE ALBERT) The United States and the Philippines: background for policy. Washington, D.C., [1977]. pp. 152. *(American Enterprise Institute for Public Policy Research and Stanford University. Hoover Institution on War, Revolution and Peace. AEI-Hoover Policy Studies. 23)*

— — Poland.

LERSKI (GEORGE JAN) ed. Herbert Hoover and Poland: a documentary history of a friendship. Stanford, 1977. pp. 128. *(Stanford University. Hoover Institution on War, Revolution and Peace. Hoover Institution Publications. 174)*

— — Russia.

GANELIN (RAFAIL SHOLOMOVICH) Sovetsko-amerikanskie otnosheniia v kontse 1917 - nachale 1918 g. Leningrad, 1976. pp. 202.

The MIDDLE East: critical choices for the United States; Eugene V. Rostow, editor. Boulder, Colo., 1976. pp. 211. *Papers of a symposium convened by the National Committee on American Foreign Policy, Inc.*

SIRACUSA (JOSEPH M.) ed. The American diplomatic revolution: a documentary history of the cold war, 1941-1947. Port Washington, 1977. pp. 265. *bibliog.*

GADDIS (JOHN LEWIS) Russia, the Soviet Union, and the United States: an interpretive history. New York, [1978]. pp. 309. *bibliog.*

— — South Africa.

The UNITED States and South Africa: three South African perspectives; [by] Percy Qoboza [and others]. Johannesburg, 1977. pp. 15. *(South African Institute of International Affairs. Occasional Papers) Panel discussion held in Johannesburg in 1977.*

— — United Kingdom.

LOUIS (WILLIAM ROGER) Imperialism at bay, 1941-1945: the United States and the decolonization of the British Empire. Oxford, 1977. pp. 595.

THORNE (CHRISTOPHER) Allies of a kind: the United States, Britain and the war against Japan, 1941-1945. London, 1978. pp. 772. *bibliog.*

UNITED STATES (Cont.)

— Foreign relations administration.

ETZOLD (THOMAS H.) The conduct of American foreign relations: the other side of diplomacy. New York, 1977. pp. 159. *bibliog.*

HAENDEL (DAN) The process of priority formulation: U.S. foreign policy in the Indo-Pakistan war of 1971. Boulder, 1977. pp. 428. *bibliog.*

SWANSON (ROGER FRANK) Intergovernmental perspectives on the Canada-U.S. relationship. New York, 1978. pp. 278.

— Full employment policies.

WALLACE (HENRY AGARD) Sixty million jobs. London, 1946. pp. 155.

LEVITAN (SAR A.) and BELOUS (RICHARD S.) Shorter hours, shorter weeks: spreading the work to reduce unemployment. Baltimore, [1977]. pp. 94.

AMERICAN ENTERPRISE INSTITUTE FOR PUBLIC POLICY RESEARCH. Legislative Analyses. 95th Congress. No. 21. Full Employment and Balanced Growth Act: an update. Washington, D.C., 1978. pp. 27.

— Government publications — Indexes.

KANELY (EDNA A.) compiler. Cumulative subject guide to U.S. government bibliographies 1924-1973; (with Superintendent of Documents classification number index to the...guide, etc.). Arlington, Va., [1976-77]. 7 vols.

— Historiography.

LOEWENBERG (BERT JAMES) American history in American thought: Christopher Columbus to Henry Adams. New York, 1973. pp. 731. *bibliog.*

RUSSO (DAVID J.) Families and communities: a new view of American history. Nashville, Tenn., [1974]. pp. 322. *bibliog.*

AMERICAN history - British historians: a cross-cultural approach to the American experience; David H. Burton, editor. Chicago, [1976]. pp. 322. *bibliog.*

The POLITICAL economy of the American Revolution; Nancy B. Spannaus and Christopher White, editors. New York, [1977]. pp. 470.

— History.

BAILEY (THOMAS ANDREW) Probing America's past: a critical examination of major myths and misconceptions. Lexington, Mass., [1973]. 2 vols. (in 1). *bibliogs.*

AMERICAN history - British historians: a cross-cultural approach to the American experience; David H. Burton, editor. Chicago, [1976]. pp. 322. *bibliog.*

CARROLL (PETER N.) and NOBLE (DAVID W.) The free and the unfree: a new history of the United States. Harmondsworth, 1977. pp. 448. *bibliog.*

POLE (JACK RICHON) The pursuit of equality in American history. Berkeley, [1978]. pp. 380. *An expanded version of his Jefferson Memorial Lectures, 1971.*

SIMPSON (WILLIAM O.) Vision and reality: the evolution of American government. London, [1978]. pp. 243. *bibliog.*

— — Bibliography.

SAUTTER (UDO) Americana, 1964-1976: Literaturbericht über Neuerscheinungen zur Geschichte der Vereinigten Staaten von Amerika; (herausgegeben von Walther Kienast). München, 1978. pp. 276. *(Historische Zeitschrift. Sonderhefte. 6)*

— — 1607-1783, Colonial period.

GOLDENBERG (JOSEPH A.) Shipbuilding in colonial America. Charlottesville, 1976. pp. 306. *bibliog. (Mariners Museum, [Newport News, Va.]. Museum Publications. No.33)*

SIMMONS (R.C.) The American colonies: from settlement to independence. London, 1976. pp. 438.

— — 1775-1783, Revolution.

OLTON (CHARLES S.) Artisans for independence: Philadelphia mechanics and the American revolution. Syracuse, N.Y., 1975. pp. 172. *bibliog.*

SOCIETY, freedom, and conscience: the American revolution in Virginia, Massachusetts, and New York; [by] Jack P. Greene [and others]; edited by Richard M. Jellison. New York, [1976]. pp. 233. *(Miami University (Ohio). McClellan Lectures. 1973, 1974, 1975)*

SUŁEK (ZDZISŁAW) Polacy w wojnie o niepodległość Stanów Zjednoczonych, 1775-1783. Warszawa, 1976. pp. 277. *bibliog.*

TRADITION, conflict, and modernization: perspectives on the American Revolution; edited by Richard Maxwell Brown [and] Don E. Fehrenbacher. New York, [1977]. pp. 130. *Revised papers presented at a Bicentennial conference held at the Institute of American History, Stanford University, 1976.*

The POLITICAL economy of the American Revolution; Nancy B. Spannaus and Christopher White, editors. New York, [1977]. pp. 470.

— — — Humour, caricatures, etc.

JONES (MICHAEL WYNN) The cartoon history of the American Revolution. London, 1977. pp. 191. *bibliog.*

— — — Personal narratives — British.

The LOST war: letters from British officers during the American revolution; edited and annotated by Marion Balderston and David Syrett. New York, [1975]. pp. 237.

— — — Sources.

The LOST war: letters from British officers during the American revolution; edited and annotated by Marion Balderston and David Syrett. New York, [1975]. pp. 237.

— — 1783-1865 — Sources.

WEBSTER (DANIEL) The papers of Daniel Webster: correspondence...; Charles M. Wiltse, editor; Harold D. Moser, associate editor. Hanover, N.H., 1974 in progress.

— — 1800-1899.

STASIK (FLORIAN) Adam Gurowski, 1805-1866. Warszawa, 1977. pp. 420. *bibliog.*

— — 1861-1865, Civil War — Afro-Americans.

BERRY (MARY FRANCES) Military necessity and civil rights policy; black citizenship and the constitution, 1861-1868. Port Washington, 1977. pp 132. *bibliog.*

— — — Religious aspects.

MOORHEAD (JAMES H.) American apocalypse: Yankee Protestants and the Civil War, 1860-1869. New Haven, 1978. pp. 278. *bibliog.*

— — 1900- .

ROBINSON (EDGAR EUGENE) The Roosevelt leadership, 1933-1945. New York, 1972. pp. 491. *bibliog. Reprint of the first edition, Philadelphia, 1955.*

BOLT (ERNEST C.) Ballots before bullets: the war referendum approach to peace in America, 1914-1941. Charlottesville, Va., 1977. pp. 207. *bibliog.*

— History, Local.

RUSSO (DAVID J.) Families and communities: a new view of American history. Nashville, Tenn., [1974]. pp. 322. *bibliog.*

— History, Military.

LEONARD (THOMAS C.) Above the battle: war-making in America from Appomattox to Versailles. New York, 1978. pp. 260.

— History, Naval.

LEUTZE (JAMES R.) Bargaining for supremacy: Anglo-American naval collaboration, 1937-1941. Chapel Hill, [1977]. pp. 328. *bibliog.*

— Industries.

CHANDLER (ALFRED D.) The visible hand: the managerial revolution in American business. Cambridge, Mass., [1977] repr. 1978. pp. 608.

— Intellectual life.

WHITE (MORTON GABRIEL) The philosophy of the American revolution. New York, 1978. pp. 299.

— Military policy.

BETTS (RICHARD K.) Soldiers, statesmen, and cold war crises. Cambridge, Mass., 1977. pp. 292. *bibliog.*

BLAUFARB (DOUGLAS S.) The counterinsurgency era: US doctrine and performance, 1950 to the present. New York, [1977]. pp. 356. *bibliog.*

FREEDMAN (LAWRENCE DAVID) US intelligence and the Soviet strategic threat. London, 1977. pp. 235. *bibliog.*

GOODPASTER (ANDREW JACKSON) For the common defense. Lexington, Mass., [1977]. pp. 174.

GOODPASTER (ANDREW JACKSON) and HUNTINGTON (SAMUEL PHILLIPS) Civil-military relations. Washington, D.C., [1977]. pp. 84. *(American Enterprise Institute for Public Policy Research. AEI Studies. 141) Based on a symposium sponsored by the University of Nebraska at Omaha and the AEI in 1976.*

KINNARD (DOUGLAS) President Eisenhower and strategy management: a study in defense politics. Lexington, Ky., [1977]. pp. 169. *bibliog.*

The LIMITS of military intervention; edited by Ellen P. Stern. Beverly Hills, [1977]. pp. 399. *Based on papers presented at two conferences held in 1976.*

STRATEGIES, alliances, and military power: changing roles; with contributions by the Faculty and Staff of the Strategic Studies Institute at the United States Army War College, etc. Leyden, 1977. pp. 372. *bibliogs. (United States Army War College. Strategic Studies Institute. Studies in U.S. National Security.1) Published proceedings of the annual Security Issues Symposium, 1976.*

TAHTINEN (DALE R.) and LENCZOWSKI (JOHN) Arms in the Indian Ocean: interests and challenges. Washington, D.C., [1977]. pp. 84. *(American Enterprise Institute for Public Policy Research. AEI Studies. 145)*

— National security.

GOODPASTER (ANDREW JACKSON) For the common defense. Lexington, Mass., [1977]. pp. 174.

McAULIFFE (MARY SPERLING) Crisis on the left: cold war politics and American liberals, 1947-1954. Amherst, 1978. pp. 204. *bibliog.*

— Officials and employees.

SMITH (SHARON P.) Equal pay in the public sector: fact or fantasy. Princeton, N.J., 1977. pp. 177. *bibliog. (Princeton University. Department of Economics and Sociology. Industrial Relations Section. Research Report Series. No. 122)*

— Politics and government.

DOLBEARE (KENNETH M.) and EDELMAN (MURRAY JACOB) American politics: policies, power, and change. 3rd ed. Lexington, Mass., [1977]. pp. 564. *bibliogs.*

FERGUSON (JOHN HENRY) and McHENRY (DEAN EUGENE) The American system of government. 13th ed. New York, [1977]. pp. 644. *bibliogs.*

GARSON (G. DAVID) Power and politics in the United States: a political economy approach. Lexington, Mass., [1977]. pp. 352.

UNITED STATES (Cont.)

KAUFMAN (HERBERT) Red tape: its origins, uses, and abuses. Washington, D.C., [1977]. pp. 100.

LINEBERRY (ROBERT L.) American public policy: what government does and what difference it makes. New York, [1977]. pp. 296. *bibliog.*

FOTHERINGHAM (PETER) and others. American government and politics. rev. ed. London, 1978. pp. 363. *bibliogs.*

MALEK (FREDERIC V.) Washington's hidden tragedy: the failure to make government work. New York, [1978]. pp. 292.

ROSE (RICHARD) What is governing?: purpose and policy in Washington. Englewood Cliffs, [1978]. pp. 173.

SIMPSON (WILLIAM O.) Vision and reality: the evolution of American government. London, [1978]. pp. 243. *bibliog.*

WATSON (RICHARD A.) Promise and performance of American democracy. 3rd ed. New York, [1978]. pp. 650.

—— 1607-1783, Colonial period.

DINKIN (ROBERT J.) Voting in provincial America: a study of elections in thirteen colonies, 1689-1776. Westport, Conn., 1977. pp. 284. *bibliog.*

HEALE (MICHAEL JOHN) The making of American politics, 1750-1850. London, 1977. pp. 263. *bibliog.*

PETERSON (MERRILL DANIEL) Adams and Jefferson: a revolutionary dialogue. Oxford, 1978. pp. 146. *(Mercer University. Eugenia Dorothy Blount Lamar Memorial Lectures. No. 19)*

—— 1783-1865.

McDONALD (FORREST) The presidency of Thomas Jefferson. Lawrence, Kan., [1976]. pp. 201. *bibliog.*

HEALE (MICHAEL JOHN) The making of American politics, 1750-1850. London, 1977. pp. 263. *bibliog.*

SMITH (CULVER HAYGOOD) The press, politics, and patronage: the American government's use of newspapers, 1789-1875. Athens, Ga., [1977]. pp. 351. *bibliog.*

COOKE (JACOB E.) Tench Coxe and the early Republic. Chapel Hill, [1978]. pp. 543. *bibliog.*

CUNNINGHAM (NOBLE E.) The process of government under Jefferson. Princeton, [1978]. pp. 357. *bibliog.*

PETERSON (MERRILL DANIEL) Adams and Jefferson: a revolutionary dialogue. Oxford, 1978. pp. 146. *(Mercer University. Eugenia Dorothy Blount Lamar Memorial Lectures. No. 19)*

—— 1815-1861.

The MANY-faceted Jacksonian era: new interpretations; edited by Edward Pessen. Westport, Conn., 1977. pp. 331. *bibliog.*

REMINI (ROBERT VINCENT) Andrew Jackson and the course of American empire, 1767-1821. New York, [1977]. pp. 502.

SPENCER (DONALD S.) Louis Kossuth and Young America: a study of sectionalism and foreign policy, 1848-1852. Columbia, Miss., 1977. pp. 203. *bibliog.*

HOLT (MICHAEL FITZGIBBON) The political crisis of the 1850s. New York, [1978]. pp. 330. *bibliog.*

—— 1865-1898.

GAITHER (GERALD H.) Blacks and the Populist revolt: ballots and bigotry in the "new south". University, Ala., [1977]. pp. 251. *bibliog.*

WALLER (ROBERT A.) Rainey of Illinois: a political biography, 1903-34. Urbana, [1977]. pp. 260. *bibliog. (Illinois University. Illinois Studies in the Social Sciences. 60)*

—— 1898-1945.

DORSETT (LYLE W.) Franklin D. Roosevelt and the city bosses. Port Washington, N.Y., 1977. pp. 134. *bibliog.*

MELOSI (MARTIN V.) The shadow of Pearl Harbor: political controversy over the surprise attack, 1941-1946. College Station, Tex., [1977]. pp. 183. *bibliog.*

WALLER (ROBERT A.) Rainey of Illinois: a political biography, 1903-34. Urbana, [1977]. pp. 260. *bibliog. (Illinois University. Illinois Studies in the Social Sciences. 60)*

GABLE (JOHN ALLEN) The Bull Moose years: Theodore Roosevelt and the Progressive Party. Port Washington, N.Y., 1978. pp. 302.

GOULD (LEWIS L.) Reform and regulation: American politics, 1900-1916. New York, [1978]. pp. 197. *bibliog.*

LOWITT (RICHARD) George W. Norris: the triumph of a progressive, 1933-1944. Urbana, [1978]. pp. 493. *bibliog.*

—— Bibliography.

GREENSTEIN (FRED I.) and others, compilers. Evolution of the modern presidency: a bibliographical survey. Washington, D.C., [1977]. 1 vol. (unpaged). *(American Enterprise Institute for Public Policy Research. Studies. 153)*

—— 1900- .

ROBINSON (EDGAR EUGENE) The Roosevelt leadership, 1933-1945. New York, 1972. pp. 491. *bibliog.* Reprint of the first edition, Philadelphia, 1955.

CHILDS (MARQUIS WILLIAM) Witness to power. New York, [1975]. pp. 277.

FAIRLIE (HENRY) The parties: Republicans and Democrats in this century. New York, [1978]. pp. 236.

—— 1945- .

LUBELL (SAMUEL) The hidden crisis in American politics. New York, [1970]. pp. 306.

LOWI (THEODORE JAY) The politics of the second republic of the United States. Urbana-Champaign, [1976]. pp. 26. *(Illinois University. Edmund J. James Lectures on Government. 1976)*

MYRDAL (GUNNAR) A worried America. 1976. fo. 21. Unpublished: typescript. Address at the annual meeting of the Lutheran Council in the United States, Philadelphia, March 11th 1976.

PARMET (HERBERT S.) The Democrats: the years after FDR. New York, 1977. pp. 371. *bibliog.* First published in 1976.

CAMPAIGN for president: the managers look at '76; edited by Jonathan Moore [and] Janet Fraser. Cambridge, Mass., [1977]. pp. 194. *A project of the Institute of Politics, John Fitzgerald Kennedy School of Government, Harvard University. Proceedings of a conference held in Cambridge, Mass., in 1976.*

DONOVAN (ROBERT JOHN) Conflict and crisis: the presidency of Harry S. Truman, 1945-1948. New York, [1977]. pp. 473.

FINN (CHESTER E.) Education and the presidency. Lexington, Mass., [1977]. pp. 167.

FISH (HAMILTON) An American manifesto of freedom in answer to the manifesto on communism, 1848. New York, [1977]. pp. 209. *bibliog.*

JOHNSON (ROBERT H.) Managing interdependence: restructuring the U.S. government. Washington, 1977. pp. 23. *(Overseas Development Council. Development Papers. 23)*

KRASNER (MICHAEL A.) and others. American government: structure and process. New York, [1977]. pp. 390. *bibliogs.*

McGOVERN (GEORGE STANLEY) Grassroots: (the autobiography of George McGovern). New York, [1977]. pp. 307.

MAKING public policy: studies in American politics; edited by John Brigham. Lexington, Mass., [1977]. pp. 424. *bibliogs.*

The POLITICS of policy making in America: five case studies; edited by David A. Caputo. San Francisco, [1977]. pp. 189.

SHOGAN (ROBERT) Promises to keep: Carter's first hundred days. New York, [1977]. pp. 300.

WITCOVER (JULES) Marathon: the pursuit of the presidency, 1971-1976. New York, 1977. pp. 684.

BUTTON (JAMES W.) Black violence: political impact of the 1960s riots. Princeton, [1978]. pp. 248. *bibliog.*

CAUTE (DAVID) The great fear: the anti-communist purge under Truman and Eisenhower. New York, [1978]. pp. 697. *bibliog.*

CROSBY (DONALD F.) God, church, and flag: Senator Joseph R. McCarthy and the Catholic church, 1950-1957. Chapel Hill, [1978]. pp. 307. *bibliog.*

DENT (HARRY S.) The prodigal South returns to power. New York, [1978]. pp. 308.

KELSO (WILLIAM ALTON) American democratic theory: pluralism and its critics. Westport, Conn., 1978. pp. 288. *bibliog.*

McAULIFFE (MARY SPERLING) Crisis on the left: cold war politics and American liberals, 1947-1954. Amherst, 1978. pp. 204. *bibliog.*

—— Bibliography.

GREENSTEIN (FRED I.) and others, compilers. Evolution of the modern presidency: a bibliographical survey. Washington, D.C., [1977]. 1 vol. (unpaged). *(American Enterprise Institute for Public Policy Research. Studies. 153)*

— Population.

JONES (ROCHELLE) The other generation: the new power of older people. Englewood Cliffs, [1977]. pp. 264.

LITTLEWOOD (THOMAS B.) The politics of population control. Notre Dame, [1977]. pp. 232. *bibliog.*

MORGAN (DAVID J.) Patterns of population distribution: a residential preference model and its dynamic. Chicago, 1978. pp. 200. *bibliog. (Chicago. University. Department of Geography. Research Papers. No. 176)*

—— Mathematical models.

DAVANZO (JULIE) A family choice model of U.S. interregional migration based on the human capital approach. Santa Monica, 1972. pp. 57. *bibliog. (Rand Corporation. [Papers]. 4815)*

— Presidents.

McCONNELL (GRANT) The modern presidency. 2nd ed. New York, [1976]. pp. 131. *bibliog.*

BIOGRAPHICAL directory of the United States executive branch, 1774-1977; Robert Sobel, editor in chief. Westport, 1977. pp. 503.

A DISCUSSION with Gerald R. Ford: the American Presidency. Washington, 1977. pp. 19. *(American Enterprise Institute for Public Policy Research. AEI Studies. 159)*

HECLO (HUGH) Studying the Presidency: (a report to the Ford Foundation). [New York], 1977. pp. 53.

KATZ (JAMES EVERETT) Presidential politics and science policy. New York, 1978. pp. 292. *bibliog.*

—— Bibliography.

GREENSTEIN (FRED I.) and others, compilers. Evolution of the modern presidency: a bibliographical survey. Washington, D.C., [1977]. 1 vol. (unpaged). *(American Enterprise Institute for Public Policy Research. Studies. 153)*

UNITED STATES (Cont.)

— — Election.

BYRNE (GARY C.) and MARX (PAUL) Writer on American politics. The great American convention: a political history of presidential elections. Palo Alto, Calif., [1976]. pp. 168. *bibliog.*

CAMPAIGN for president: the managers look at '76; edited by Jonathan Moore [and] Janet Fraser. Cambridge, Mass., [1977]. pp. 194. *A project of the Institute of Politics, John Fitzgerald Kennedy School of Government, Harvard University. Proceedings of a conference held in Cambridge, Mass., in 1976.*

DIAMOND (MARTIN) The electoral college and the American idea of democracy. Washington, [1977]. pp. 22. *(American Enterprise Institute for Public Policy Research. AEI Studies. 163)*

SHOGAN (ROBERT) Promises to keep: Carter's first hundred days. New York, [1977]. pp. 300.

WITCOVER (JULES) Marathon: the pursuit of the presidency, 1971-1976. New York, 1977. pp. 684.

HESS (STEPHEN) The presidential campaign: an essay. rev. ed. Washington, D.C., [1978]. pp. 123. *bibliog. Published under the auspices of the Brookings Institution.*

RA (JONG OH) Labor at the polls: union voting in Presidential elections, 1952- 1976. Amherst, 1978. pp. 182. *bibliog.*

— — Nomination.

RANNEY (AUSTIN) Participation in American presidential nominations, 1976. Washington, [1977]. pp. 37. *(American Enterprise Institute for Public Policy Research. AEI Studies. 149)*

— — Succession — Bibliography.

TOMPKINS (DOROTHY LOUISE CAMPBELL) compiler. Selection of the vice president; [a bibliography]. Berkeley, 1974. pp. 26. *(California University. Institute of Governmental Studies. Public Policy Bibliographies. No.6)*

— Race question.

RACE, prejudice and the origins of slavery in America; edited by Raymond Starr and Robert Detweiler. Cambridge, Mass., [1975]. pp. 164. *bibliog.*

The DIVERSE society: implications for social policy; Pastora San Juan Cafferty and Leon Chestang, editors. Washington, [1976]. pp. 176.

MYRDAL (GUNNAR) A worried America. 1976. fo. 21. *Unpublished: typescript. Address at the annual meeting of the Lutheran Council in the United States, Philadelphia, March 11th 1976.*

SCOTT (JOSEPH WALTER) The black revolts: racial stratification in the U.S.A.: the politics of estate, caste, and class in the American society. Cambridge, Mass., [1976]. pp. 182. *bibliog.*

BLACK/brown/white relations: race relations in the 1970's; edited by Charles V. Willie. New Brunswick, N.J., [1977]. pp. 235.

BLAIR (THOMAS LUCIEN VINCENT) Retreat to the ghetto: the end of a dream? New York, 1977. pp. 263. *bibliog.*

BUCHANAN (ALBERT RUSSELL) Black Americans in World War II. Santa Barbara, Calif., [1977]. pp. 148. *bibliog.*

COX (OLIVER CROMWELL) Race relations: elements and social dynamics. Detroit, 1976. pp. 337. *bibliog.*

FONER (PHILIP SHELDON) American socialism and black Americans: from the age of Jackson to World War II. Westport, Conn., 1977. pp. 462. *bibliog.*

RABINOWITZ (HOWARD N.) Race relations in the urban south, 1865-1890. New York, 1978. pp. 441. *bibliog.*

WILSON (WILLIAM JULIUS) The declining significance of race: blacks and changing American institutions. Chicago, 1978. pp. 204. *bibliog.*

— Relations (general) with Arab countries.

CAN cultures communicate?; (an AEI Round Table held on September 23, 1976...); Edward Stewart, moderator, etc. Washington, 1976. pp. 33. *(American Enterprise Institute for Public Policy Research. Round Tables)*

— Relations (general) with Canada.

RESNICK (PHILIP) The land of Cain: class and nationalism in English Canada, 1945-1975. Vancouver, [1977]. pp. 297. *bibliog.*

— Relations (general) with Europe.

ATLANTIS lost: U.S.-European relations after the Cold War; edited by James Chace and Earl C. Ravenal. New York, 1976. pp. 273.

— Relations (general) with India.

KAMATH (MADHAV V.) The United States and India, 1776-1976. Washington, Embassy of India, [1976]. pp. 226. *bibliog.*

— Relations (general) with New Zealand.

HARLAND (W. BRYCE) New Zealand's relations with the United States of America: text of an address...at the fifth Foreign Policy School, University of Otago, Department of University Extension, Dunedin, 15-19 May 1970. [Wellington, Ministry of Foreign Affairs, 1970]. pp. 16. *(Reprinted from Foreign Affairs Review, May 1970)*

— Relations (general) with Nicaragua.

MILLETT (RICHARD) Guardians of the dynasty. Maryknoll, [1977]. pp. 284. *bibliog.*

— Relations (general) with other countries.

HEALD (MORRELL) and KAPLAN (LAWRENCE SAMUEL) Culture and diplomacy: the American experience. Westport, Conn., [1977]. pp. 361.

— Relations (general) with the Argentine Republic.

LIBRO azul y blanco de la prensa argentina; por cincuenta y tres periodistas argentinos. Buenos Aires, 1951. pp. 439.

— Relations (military) with Russia.

FREEDMAN (LAWRENCE DAVID) US intelligence and the Soviet strategic threat. London, 1977. pp. 235. *bibliog.*

— Religion.

CLARK (ELMER TALMADGE) The small sects in America. rev. ed. New York, [1949]. pp. 256. *bibliog.*

IMMIGRANTS and religion in urban America; edited by Randall M. Miller and Thomas D. Marzik. Philadelphia, 1977. pp. 170. *Based on a series of symposia held at Saint Joseph's College, Philadelphia, during the academic year 1975-1976.*

WILSON (JOHN) of Duke University. Religion in American society: the effective presence. Englewood Cliffs, [1978]. pp. 492. *bibliog.*

— Rural conditions.

RURAL U.S.A.: persistence and change; edited by Thomas R. Ford. Ames, Iowa, 1978. pp. 255. *bibliog.*

— Social conditions.

MYRDAL (GUNNAR) A worried America. 1976. fo. 21. *Unpublished: typescript. Address at the annual meeting of the Lutheran Council in the United States, Philadelphia, March 11th 1976.*

BLACK/brown/white relations: race relations in the 1970's; edited by Charles V. Willie. New Brunswick, N.J., [1977]. pp. 235.

CLARK (JOHN G.) and others. Three generations in twentieth century America: family, community, and nation. Homewood, 1977. pp. 529. *bibliog.*

CONNECTICUT. Tri-State Regional Planning Commission. 1977. Metromonitor: a regional review of social and economic trends. New York, 1977. pp. 10.

EDELMAN (MURRAY JACOB) Political language: words that succeed and policies that fail. New York, [1977]. pp. 164. *(Wisconsin University, Madison. Institute for Research on Poverty. Monograph Series)*

GOIST (PARK DIXON) From Main Street to State Street: town, city, and community in America. Port Washington, N.Y., 1977. pp. 180. *bibliog.*

JONES (ROCHELLE) The other generation: the new power of older people. Englewood Cliffs, [1977]. pp. 264.

PERIN (CONSTANCE) Everything in its place: social order and land use in America. Princeton, [1977]. pp. 291. *bibliog.*

STEIN (HOWARD F.) and HILL (ROBERT F.) The ethnic imperative: examining the new white ethnic movement. University Park, Pa., [1977]. pp. 308.

THIS land of promises: the rise and fall of social problems in America; edited by Armand L. Mauss and Julie Camille Wolfe. Philadelphia, [1977]. pp. 452. *bibliogs.*

ROTHMAN (ROBERT A.) Inequality and stratification in the United States. Englewood Cliffs, [1978]. pp. 243. *bibliogs.*

— Social history.

CLARK (NORMAN H.) Deliver us from evil: an interpretation of American prohibition. New York, [1976]. pp. 246. *bibliog.*

CARTER (PAUL ALLEN) Another part of the twenties. New York, 1977. pp. 229.

The MANY-faceted Jacksonian era: new interpretations; edited by Edward Pessen. Westport, Conn., 1977. pp. 331. *bibliog.*

BLUM (JOHN MORTON) The burden of American equality. Oxford, 1978. pp. 22. *An inaugural lecture delivered before the University of Oxford on 26 April 1977.*

POLE (JACK RICHON) The pursuit of equality in American history. Berkeley, [1978]. pp. 380. *An expanded version of his Jefferson Memorial Lectures, 1971.*

— Social policy.

GROSSER (CHARLES F.) New directions in community organization: from enabling to advocacy. [2nd ed.]. New York, 1976. pp. 286.

MYRDAL (GUNNAR) Race and class in a welfare state; introductory lecture to a symposium in a series entitled The national purpose reconsidered, 1776-1976 at Columbia University, October 28, 1976. 1976. pp. 57. *Unpublished: photocopy of typescript.*

GARVEY (GERALD) Nuclear power and social planning: the city of the second sun. Lexington, Mass., [1977]. pp. 159. *bibliog.*

ANDERSON (MARTIN) Ph. D. Welfare: the political economy of welfare reform in the United States. Stanford, [1978]. pp. 251. *(Stanford University. Hoover Institution on War, Revolution and Peace. Hoover Institution Publications. 181)*

LILIENFELD (ROBERT) The rise of systems theory: an ideological analysis. New York, [1978]. pp. 292.

PASSELL (PETER) and ROSS (LEONARD) State policies and federal programs: priorities and constraints. New York, [1978]. pp. 168. *A Twentieth Century Fund Report.*

— Territorial expansion.

REMINI (ROBERT VINCENT) Andrew Jackson and the course of American empire, 1767-1821. New York, [1977]. pp. 502.

UNITIZED CARGO SYSTEMS.

UNITIZED CARGO SYSTEMS.

UNITED NATIONS. Interregional Seminar on Containerization and other Unitized Methods for the Intermodal Movement of Freight, London, 1967. Report on the...seminar...[held in] London, England, 1-12 Máy 1967. (ST/TAO/SER.C/102). New York, 1968. pp. 61.

BUNCE (J.A.) and LYNAM (D.A.) The significance of intermodal transfer techniques in inland container transport. Crowthorne, 1976. pp. 77. bibliog. (*U.K. Transport and Road Research Laboratory. Supplementary Reports. 243*)

UNIVERSITIES AND COLLEGES.

KERR (CLARK) Universities: open to truth and to merit. Johannesburg, 1976. pp. 27. (*Johannesburg. University of the Witwatersrand. Chancellors' Lectures. No. 5*)

EDWARDS (EDWARD GEORGE) The relevant university. Bradford, [1977]. pp. 27.

— Administration.

BAILEY (FREDERICK GEORGE) Morality and expediency: the folklore of academic politics. Oxford, [1977]. pp. 230. *bibliog.*

— Congresses.

HAZARDS of learning: an international symposium on the crisis of the university; [edited by] G.R. Urban. La Salle, Ill., [1977]. pp. 294. *Thirteen dialogues commissioned and broadcast by Radio Free Europe in 1973 and 1974.*

— Directories.

INTERNATIONAL ASSOCIATION OF UNIVERSITIES. International handbook of universities and other institutions of higher education; (edited by H.M.R. Keyes [and others]). 7th ed. Paris, 1978. pp. 1182.

— Law and legislation — Argentine Republic.

DOMINGORENA (HORACIO O.) Articulo 28: universidades privadas en la Argentina; sus antecedentes. Buenos Aires, 1959. pp. 159.

— Teachers.

See TEACHERS.

— Africa, Subsaharan.

The FUTURE of the university in southern Africa; (edited by Hendrik W. Van der Merwe and David Welsh). Cape Town, 1977. pp. 302. *bibliogs. Proceedings of a conference held in 1976 at the Centre for Intergroup Studies, Cape Town University.*

— America, Latin.

INGENIEROS (JOSE) La universidad del porvenir: America Latina y el imperialismo. Buenos Aires, 1956. pp. 47.

ALBORNOZ (ORLANDO) La universidad latinoamericana: la crisis del desarrollo. Santiago de Chile, 1971. pp. 63. (*Instituto Latinoamericano de Investigaciones Sociales. Estudios y Documentos.10*)

— Argentine Republic.

GONZALEZ (JULIO V.) La reforma universitaria. Buenos Aires, 1927. 2 vols.

— Australia.

AUSTRALIA. Universities Commission. Report. irreg., 1958/63[1st]- Canberra. *Included in AUSTRALIA. Parliament. [Parliamentary papers].*

— Bolivia.

VISCARRA (FELIPE N.) Mision de la universidad boliviana en el desarrollo y formacion de la nacionalidad. La Paz, 1966. pp. 17.

— Canada — Ontario.

CAMERON (DAVID M.) The northern dilemma: public policy and post-secondary education in northern Ontario. [Toronto, 1978]. pp. 198. (*Ontario. Economic Council. Discussion Paper Series*)

MEHMET (OZAY) Who benefits from the Ontario University system: a benefit- cost analysis by income groups. [Toronto, 1978]. pp. 62. (*Ontario. Economic Council. Occasional Papers. 7*)

— Germany.

DAHRENDORF (RALF) Zur Entstehungsgeschichte des Hochschulgesamtplans für Baden- Württemberg, 1966/67: auch ein Beitrag zum Thema des Verhältnisses von Wissenschaft und Politik in Deutschland. Stuttgart, [1974]. pp. 138-63. (*Sonderdruck aus Bildungspolitik mit Ziel und Mass*)

— — Baden-Württemberg.

DAHRENDORF (RALF) Zur Entstehungsgeschichte des Hochschulgesamtplans für Baden- Württemberg, 1966/67: auch ein Beitrag zum Thema des Verhältnisses von Wissenschaft und Politik in Deutschland. Stuttgart, [1974]. pp. 138-63. (*Sonderdruck aus Bildungspolitik mit Ziel und Mass*)

— India — Examinations.

INDIA. University Grants Commission. 1976. Principles and mechanics of the system of grading in the universities; based on the recommendations of the zonal workshops. New Delhi, 1976. pp. 8.

— Italy.

TORTORELLA (ALDO) and CHIARANTE (GIUSEPPE) Per la riforma universitaria. [Roma, 1976]. pp. 96.

— — Administration.

DELL'ACQUA (CESARE) Università, televisione e decentramento regionale: profili costituzionale e organizzativi. Napoli, 1974. pp. 157.

CLARK (BURTON R.) Academic power in Italy: bureaucracy and oligarchy in a national university system. Chicago, 1977. pp. 205. *bibliog.*

— Pakistan.

PAKISTAN. University Grants Commission. 1975. Projects and activities of the University Grants Commission. Islamabad, [1975?]. pp. 31.

— — Admissions.

PAKISTAN. University Grants Commission. 1975. A note on the proposals for a new admission policy for the universities. Islamabad, [1975?]. fo. 14.

— Romania.

DINAMICA socială a învăţămîntulu i universitar: studiu pe modelul Universităţii din Craiova; coordonator... Aculin Cazacu. Craiova, 1973. pp. 278.

— South Africa.

The FUTURE of the university in southern Africa; (edited by Hendrik W. Van der Merwe and David Welsh). Cape Town, 1977. pp. 302. *bibliogs. Proceedings of a conference held in 1976 at the Centre for Intergroup Studies, Cape Town University.*

— United Kingdom.

COMMITTEE OF VICE-CHANCELLORS AND PRINCIPALS OF THE UNIVERSITIES OF THE UNITED KINGDOM. Report on the period 1972-76. [London, 1976]. pp. 74.

SOCIETY FOR RESEARCH INTO HIGHER EDUCATION. Annual Conference, 11th, 1975. Power and authority in higher education; edited by Colin Flood Page and Mary Yates. Guildford, 1976. pp. 94.

CONFERENCE OF UNIVERSITY ADMINISTRATORS. Group on Forecasting and University Expansion. Interim report 1977. Glasgow, [1977]. pp. 62.

— — Administration.

CAMPBELL (F.J.) Sociologist. High command: the making of an oligarchy at the Polytechnic of North London, 1970-74. [London, 1974]. pp. 132.

ORTON (FRANCIS J.) Resource allocation within universities; based on a seminar held on 27 February 1974. London, [1976?]. pp. 19. (*London. University. Institute of Education. Staff Development in Universities Programme. Occasional Papers. 3*)

— — Scotland.

GRANT (NIGEL) and MAIN (ALEX) Scottish universities: the case for devolution. [Edinburgh, 1976]. pp. 24.

DREVER (JAMES) and others. Scottish universities and devolution. Stirling, 1977. pp. 40. (*University of Stirling. Stirling Educational Monographs. No. 3*)

— United States — Administration.

GOVERNMENT regulation of higher education; edited by Walter C. Hobbs. Cambridge, Mass., [1978]. pp. 117. *Revised versions of papers presented to a conference held in 1977 by the Department of Higher Education at the State University of New York at Buffalo.*

UNIVERSITY OF THE NORTH.

TURMOIL at Turfloop: a summary of the reports of the Snyman and Jackson commissions of inquiry into the University of the North; compiled by J.G.E. Wolfson. Johannesburg, 1976. pp. 99. *bibliog.*

UNMARRIED COUPLES.

The COUPLE; edited by Marie Corbin. Harmondsworth, 1978. pp. 248.

UNMARRIED MOTHERS

— United Kingdom.

GILL (DEREK) Illegitimacy, sexuality and the status of women. Oxford, [1977]. pp. 362. *bibliog.*

UNTOUCHABLES.

AMBEDKAR (BHIMARAO RAMJI) Mr. Gandhi and the emancipation of the untouchables. Jullundur, Punjab, [1943]. pp. 56.

UOMO QUALUNQUE, L'.

SETTA (SANDRO) L'Uomo Qualunque, 1944-1948. [Roma], 1975. pp. 342.

UPPER CLASSES

— France.

HUPPERT (GEORGE) Les bourgeois gentilshommes: an essay on the definition of elites in Renaissance France. Chicago, 1977. pp. 237.

— Switzerland — Lucerne (Canton).

MESSMER (KURT) and HOPPE (PETER) Luzerner Patriziat: sozial- und wirtschaftsgeschichtliche Studien zur Entstehung und Entwicklung im 16. und 17. Jahrhundert; mit einer Einführung von Hans Conrad Peyer. Luzern, 1976. pp. 561. *bibliog.* (*Lucerne (Canton). Staatsarchiv. Luzerner Historische Veröffentlichungen. Band 5*)

UPPER VOLTA

— Economic policy.

MÉTHODE de planification du développement rural: compte rendu du séminaire de Ouagadougou 2-5 mars 1976. Paris, 1977. pp. 100. (*France. Ministère de la Coopération. Méthodologie de la Planification. No. 11*)

UPPSALA

— Population.

BOSAEUS (BJÖRN) Uppsala city: demographic and occupational structure and development of the population. Uppsala, 1960. pp. 16.

— Social conditions.

BOSAEUS (BJÖRN) Uppsala city: demographic and occupational structure and development of the population. Uppsala, 1960. pp. 16.

URAL REGION

— Industries.

PROMYSHLENNOST' v khoziaistvennom komplekse Urala. Sverdlovsk, 1975. pp. 100.

URANIUM

— Isotopes.

MOORE (THOMAS GALE) Uranium enrichment and public policy. Washington, [1978]. pp. 64. (*American Enterprise Institute for Public Policy Research and Stanford University. Hoover Institution on War, Revolution and Peace. AEI-Hoover Policy Studies. 25*)

URBAN ECONOMICS.

SINGER (PAUL ISRAEL) Economia politica de la urbanizacion; traduccion de Stella Mastrangelo. Mexico, 1975. pp. 178.

AD HOC GROUP OF EXPERTS ON INDICATORS OF THE QUALITY OF URBAN DEVELOPMENT, [NEW YORK], 1975. Report of the meeting of the Ad Hoc Group...held at United Nations Headquarters from 8 to 12 December 1975. (ST/ESA/56). New York, United Nations, 1977. pp. 47.

NATIONAL CONFERENCE ON NEIGHBORHOOD COMMERCIAL REVITALIZATION, 2ND, 1976. Neighborhoods in the urban economy: the dynamics of decline and revitalization; edited by Benjamin Goldstein [and] Ross Davis. Lexington, Mass., [1977]. pp. 160.

RICHARDSON (HARRY WARD) The new urban economics: and alternatives. London, [1977]. pp. 266. *bibliog.*

SHAFER (THOMAS W.) Urban growth and economics. Reston, Va., [1977]. pp. 233. *bibliogs.*

SMITH (BARBARA M.D.) The inner city economic problem: a framework for analysis and local authority policy. Birmingham, 1977. pp. 104, xxii. (*Birmingham. University. Centre for Urban and Regional Studies. Research Memoranda. No. 56*)

ISSUES in urban society; edited by Ross Davies and Peter Hall. Harmondsworth, 1978. pp. 299. *bibliogs.*

MARXISM and the metropolis: new perspectives in urban political economy; edited by William K. Tabb and Larry Sawers. New York, 1978. pp. 376. *bibliogs. Based on a conference held in 1975 in New York City by the Union for Radical Political Economics.*

RICHARDSON (HARRY WARD) Regional and urban economics. Harmondsworth, 1978. pp. 416. *bibliog.*

TOWNS in societies: essays in economic history and historical sociology; edited by Philip Abrams [and] E.A. Wrigley. Cambridge, 1978. pp. 344. *bibliog. Papers of a Conference held in 1975 by the Past and Present Society, together with articles from Past and Present.*

URBANIZATION and conflict in market societies; edited by Kevin Cox. [London, 1978]. pp. 255. *Contains four papers originally presented at the World Congress of the International Political Science Association in Edinburgh in 1976.*

WILSON (HARRIETT CHARLOTTE) and HERBERT (GEOFFREY WILLIAM) Parents and children in the inner city. London, 1978. pp. 248. *bibliog.*

URBAN HOMESTEADING

— United States.

CLARK (ANNE) and RIVIN (ZELMA) Homesteading in urban U.S.A. New York, 1977. pp. 179. *bibliog.*

URBAN RENEWAL.

URBAN environmental indicators. Paris, Organisation for Economic Co-operation and Development, 1978. pp. 274.

— Australia.

TARRANT (VALERIE) and LYNE (ALEX) Conserving Australia. London, 1974. pp. 64. *bibliog.*

— United Kingdom.

RIGHTER (ROSEMARY) Save our cities; [a report on the Save Our Cities Conference organized by the Calouste Gulbenkian Foundation and the Sunday Times in Bristol in 1977]. London, 1977. pp. 52.

— United States.

GILBERT (NEIL) and SPECHT (HARRY) Dynamics of community planning. Cambridge, Mass., [1977]. pp. 183.

NATIONAL CONFERENCE ON NEIGHBORHOOD COMMERCIAL REVITALIZATION, 2ND, 1976. Neighborhoods in the urban economy: the dynamics of decline and revitalization; edited by Benjamin Goldstein [and] Ross Davis. Lexington, Mass., [1977]. pp. 160.

The FUTURE of urban centers: what are the policy options?; (a Round Table held on January 27, 1978...); John Charles Daly, moderator, etc. Washington, [1978]. pp. 38. (*American Enterprise Institute for Public Policy Research. Public Policy Forums. 15*)

URBAN TRANSPORTATION.

URBAN transportation planning: current themes and future prospects; edited by Peter Bonsall [and others]. [Tunbridge Wells, 1977]. pp. 386.

— Australia.

AUSTRALIA. Commonwealth Bureau of Roads. 1976. An approach to developing transport improvement proposals. [Melbourne], 1976. pp. 128. *bibliog. (Occasional Papers. No.2)*

— Canada — Quebec.

OUELLET (ANDRE) Le transport urbain au Québec; [annexe du rapport sur l'urbanisation]. [Québec, Editeur officiel, 1976]. pp. 55. *bibliog.*

— Europe.

McKAY (JOHN P.) Tramways and trolleys: the rise of urban mass transport in Europe. Princeton, [1976]. pp. 266. *bibliog.*

— United Kingdom.

DEVONSHIRE. County Council and CORNWALL. County Council. Planned transport: Plymouth and environs transportation study. [Plymouth, 1967?]. 1 vol. (unpaged).

FREEMAN FOX AND ASSOCIATES. Nottingham and environs transportation study: the preferred transportation system; [commissioned by Nottinghamshire County Council and Derbyshire County Council]. London, 1975. pp. 30. *Bound with their Nottingham and environs transportation study.*

FREEMAN FOX AND ASSOCIATES. Nottingham and environs transportation study, [commissioned by Nottinghamshire County Council and Derbyshire County Council]. London, 1976. 2 vols. (in 1).

SCOTT, WILSON, KIRKPATRICK AND PARTNERS. Plymouth and environs transportation study: (final report). [Basingstoke, 1976?]. pp. 241.

ABELL (APUL HENRY) Transport and industry in Greater Manchester. Barnsley, 1978. pp. 84. *bibliog.*

— United States.

ZEHNER (ROBERT B.) Access, travel, and transportation in new communities. Cambridge, Mass., [1977]. pp. 217. *bibliog. (North Carolina University. Center for Urban and Regional Studies. New Communities Research Series)*

URBAN TRANSPORTATION POLICY.

PUSHKAREV (BORIS SERGEEVICH) and ZUPAN (JEFFREY MICHAEL) Public transportation and land use policy. Bloomington, Ind., [1977]. pp. 242. *bibliog.*

— Underdeveloped areas.

See UNDERDEVELOPED AREAS — Urban transportation policy.

— United Kingdom.

GRANT (JOHN) 1946- . The politics of urban transport planning. London, 1977. pp. 164.

— United States.

TAEBEL (DELBERT A.) and CORNEHLS (JAMES V.) The political economy of urban transportation. Port Washington, N.Y., 1977. pp. 218. *bibliog.*

URBANIZATION.

INTERREGIONAL SEMINAR ON THE FINANCING OF HOUSING AND URBAN DEVELOPMENT, COPENHAGEN, 1970. Report of the...Seminar...[held in] Copenhagen, 25 May to 10 June 1970. (ST/TAO/SER.C/134). New York, United Nations, 1972. pp. 94.

FRIEDMANN (JOHN REMBERT PETER) and WULFF (ROBERT) The urban transition: comparative studies of newly industrializing societies. London, 1976. pp. 96. *bibliog.*

MEDAM (ALAIN) Conscience de la ville. Paris, 1977. pp. 302.

POLSKA AKADEMIA NAUK. Instytut Geografii. Geografia Polonica. 37. Urbanization and settlement: proceedings of the second Soviet- Polish geographical seminar, Moscow and Leningrad, June 1974. Warsaw, 1977. pp. 224. *bibliog.*

SHAFER (THOMAS W.) Urban growth and economics. Reston, Va., [1977]. pp. 233. *bibliogs.*

THEMES de recherches sur les villes antiques d'occident; (actes du colloque international, Strasbourg, 1er-4 octobre, 1971). Paris, 1977. pp. 429. (*Centre National de la Recherche Scientifique. Colloques Internationaux. No. 542*) *In French, English, Italian or German.*

SYSTEMS of cities: readings on structure, growth, and policy; edited by L.S. Bourne and J.W. Simmons. New York, 1978. pp. 565. *bibliogs.*

URBANIZATION and conflict in market societies; edited by Kevin Cox. [London, 1978]. pp. 255. *Contains four papers originally presented at the World Congress of the International Political Science Association in Edinburgh in 1976.*

— Africa.

CAIRO DEMOGRAPHIC CENTRE. Urbanization and migration in some Arab and African countries. Cairo, 1973. pp. 528. *bibliogs. (Research Monograph Series. No. 4)*

— Africa, West.

GUGLER (JOSEF) and FLANAGAN (WILLIAM G.) Urbanization and social change in West Africa. Cambridge, 1978. pp. 235. *bibliog.*

— America, Latin.

SINGER (PAUL ISRAEL) Economia politica de la urbanizacion; traduccion de Stella Mastrangelo. Mexico, 1975. pp. 178.

ASENTAMIENTOS humanos, urbanismo y vivienda: cometido del poder publico en la segunda mitad del siglo XX; [by] Jesus Silva- Herzog Flores [and others]. Mexico, 1977. pp. 788.

ROBERTS (BRYAN REES) Cities of peasants: the political economy of urbanization in the Third World. London, 1978. pp. 207. *bibliog.*

URBANIZATION.(Cont.)

— Arab countries.

CAIRO DEMOGRAPHIC CENTRE. Urbanization and migration in some Arab and African countries. Cairo, 1973. pp. 528. *bibliogs.* (*Research Monograph Series. No. 4*)

— Brazil.

COSTA (MANOEL AUGUSTO) Urbanização e migração urbana no Brazil. Rio de Janeiro, 1975. pp. 198. *bibliog.* (*Brazil. Instituto de Planejamento Econômico e Social. Instituto de Pesquisas. Monografias. No. 21*)

COSTA (MANOEL AUGUSTO) ed. Estudos de demografia urbana. Rio de Janeiro, 1975. pp. 259. (*Brazil. Instituto de Planejamento Econômico e Social. Instituto de Pesquisas. Monografias. No. 18*)

KATZMAN (MARTIN T.) Cities and frontiers in Brazil: regional dimensions of economic development. Cambridge, Mass., 1977. pp. 255.

OLIVEN (RUBEN GEORGE) Urbanization and social change in Brazil: a case study of Porto Alegre. 1977. fo. 424. *bibliog.* Typescript. Ph.D. (London) thesis: unpublished. *This thesis is the property of London University and may not be removed from the Library.*

— Canada — Alberta.

ALBERTA. Task Force on Urbanization and the Future. 1975. Task Force activities 1971-1974. Edmonton, [1975?]. fo. 19. *bibliog.*

— — Quebec.

QUEBEC (PROVINCE). Groupe de Travail sur l'Urbanisation. 1976. L'urbanisation au Québec: rapport...; Claude Castonguay, président. Quebec, 1976. pp. 347.

— Colombia.

PEELER (JOHN A.) Urbanization and politics. Beverly Hills, [1977]. pp. 56. *bibliog.*

— Europe, Eastern.

POPULATION and migration trends in eastern Europe; edited by Huey Louis Kostanick. Boulder, Colo., 1977. pp. 247. *Proceedings of the Conference on Demography and Urbanization in Eastern Europe held in Los Angeles in 1976 and sponsored by the Center for Slavic and East European Studies of the University of California at Los Angeles.*

— France.

URBANISATION, développement régional et pouvoir politique. [Nice], 1975. pp. 177. (*Nice. Université. Faculté des Lettres et Sciences Humaines. Annales. No. 26*)

LOJKINE (JEAN) Le marxisme, l'état et la question urbaine. [Paris, 1977]. pp. 362.

— Netherlands.

KNAAP (GIJSBERTUS ADRIANUS VAN DER) A spatial analysis of the evolution of an urban system: the case of the Netherlands. Utrecht, [1978]. pp. 242. *bibliog.*

— Philippine Islands.

PERNIA (ERNESTO DEL MAR) Urbanization, population growth, and economic development in the Philippines. Westport, Conn., 1977. pp. 213. *bibliog.*

— Poland.

POLSKA AKADEMIA NAUK. Instytut Geografii. Geografia Polonica. 37. Urbanization and settlement: proceedings of the second Soviet- Polish geographical seminar, Moscow and Leningrad, June 1974. Warsaw, 1977. pp. 224. *bibliog.*

— Rhodesia.

GARGETT (ERIC) The administration of transition: African urban settlement in Rhodesia. Gwelo, 1977. pp. 104.

— Russia.

POLSKA AKADEMIA NAUK. Instytut Geografii. Geografia Polonica. 37. Urbanization and settlement: proceedings of the second Soviet- Polish geographical seminar, Moscow and Leningrad, June 1974. Warsaw, 1977. pp. 224. *bibliog.*

— United States.

GOIST (PARK DIXON) From Main Street to State Street: town, city, and community in America. Port Washington, N.Y., 1977. pp. 180. *bibliog.*

BERG (BARBARA J.) The remembered gate: origins of American feminism: the woman and the city, 1800-1860. New York, 1978. pp. 334. *bibliog.*

— — Pennsylvania.

WOLF (STEPHANIE GRAUMAN) Urban village: population, community and family structure in Germantown, Pennsylvania 1683-1800. Princeton, N.J., [1976]. pp. 361. *bibliog.*

— Venezuela.

PEELER (JOHN A.) Urbanization and politics. Beverly Hills, [1977]. pp. 56. *bibliog.*

URUGUAY

— Economic conditions.

PARTIDO SOCIALISTA [URUGUAY]. Los caminos de la izquierda uruguaya. [Montevideo?], 1964. pp. 24.

— Economic policy.

HERRERA VARGAS (JULIO) Como se agrava la crisis nacional, etc. Montevideo, 1968. pp. 55.

— Foreign relations — Germany.

MARQUEZ (JOAQUIN C.) Informe relativo a la reclamacion entablada ante el Gobierno de la Republica Oriental del Uruguay por las Compañias propietarias de los vapores alemanes requisados en 1917. Montevideo, 1922. pp. 36.

— History.

CARDOZO (NEBIO ARIEL) De paysandu a Cerro Cora, o el genocidio de los "civilizadores". [Montevideo?, 1970]. pp. 32. *bibliog.* (*Centro de Estudios Revisionistas "Mariscal Francisco Solano Lopez". Cuadernos de la Patria Grande. 1*)

— — Sources.

MARIANI (ALBA) Fuentes para la historia economica del Uruguay moderno, 1852-1914. Montevideo, 1969. pp. 43. (*Montevideo. Universidad. Facultad de Humanidades y Ciencias. Fuentes para la Historia Social y Economica del Rio de la Plata. Fichas de Referencia. 2*)

— Politics and government.

PARTIDO SOCIALISTA [URUGUAY]. Los caminos de la izquierda uruguaya. [Montevideo?], 1964. pp. 24.

MOVIMIENTO DE IZQUIERDA REVOLUCIONARIA [URUGUAY]. Por un sindicalismo al servicio de la revolucion Uruguaya. [Montevideo?, 1969]. 1 pamphlet (unpaged). (*Documentos marxista-leninistas para la construccion del partido de la clase obrera Uruguaya. No. 1*)

[PARTIDO COMUNISTA DEL URUGUAY]. Congreso, 17, 1958. Declaracion programatica y plataforma politica inmediata del Partido Comudocumento aprobado por XVII Congreso, 15-17 de Agosto de 1958. Montevideo, 1969. pp. 29.

— Rural conditions.

MONTEVIDEO. Universidad. Departamento de Extension Universitaria. Los rancherios y su gente: tareas, costumbres, historias de vida. Montevideo, [1968]. pp. 101. (*Montevideo. Universidad. Departamento de Publicaciones. Coleccion Nuestra Realidad. 4*)

MONTEVIDEO. Universidad. Departamento de Extension Universitaria. Los rancherios y su gente: viviendas y familias. Montevideo, [1968]. pp. 115. (*Montevideo. Universidad. Departamento de Publicaciones. Coleccion Nuestra Realidad. 8*)

— Social life and customs.

MONTEVIDEO. Universidad. Departamento de Extension Universitaria. Los rancherios y su gente: tareas, costumbres, historias de vida. Montevideo, [1968]. pp. 101. (*Montevideo. Universidad. Departamento de Publicaciones. Coleccion Nuestra Realidad. 4*)

USURY LAWS

— New Zealand.

NEW ZEALAND. Contracts and Commercial Law Reform Committee. 1971. Working paper on the reform of the Moneylenders Act 1908. Wellington, [1971]. pp. (68). *bibliog.*

UTICA, NEW YORK

— History.

BRIGGS (JOHN WALKER) An Italian passage: immigrants to three American cities, 1890- 1930. New Haven, 1978. pp. 348. *bibliog.*

UTILITARIANISM.

LONG (DOUGLAS G.) Bentham on liberty: Jeremy Bentham's idea of liberty in relation to his utilitarianism. Toronto, [1977]. pp. 294. *bibliog.*

UTILITY THEORY.

RAY (RANJAN) Utility maximisation and consumer demand with an application to the United Kingdom, 1900-1970. 1977. fo. 174. *bibliog.* Typescript. Ph.D. (London) thesis: unpublished. *This thesis is the property of London University and may not be removed from the Library.*

UTOPIAS.

STIFFONI (GIOVANNI) Utopia e ragione in Gabriel Bonnot de Mably. Lecce, [1975]. pp. 391.

HAYDEN (DOLORES) Seven American utopias: the architecture of communitarian socialism, 1790-1975. Cambridge, Mass., [1976]. pp. 401. *bibliog.*

BUBER (MARTIN) Utopie et socialisme; traduit de l'allemand par Paul Corset et François Girard. Paris, [1977]. pp. 261.

ERASMUS (CHARLES JOHN) In search of the common good: Utopian experiments past and future. New York, [1977]. pp. 424.

MALUQUER DE MOTES BERNET (JORDI) El socialismo en España, 1833-1868. Barcelona, [1977]. pp. 410. *bibliog.*

PETITFILS (JEAN CHRISTIAN) Les socialismes utopiques. [Paris, 1977]. pp. 211. *bibliog.*

STUDI sull'Utopia; raccolti da Luigi Firpo. Firenze, 1977. pp. 368.

THOMAS (ROBERT DAVID) The man who would be perfect: John Humphrey Noyes and the utopian impulse. [Philadelphia], 1977. pp. 199. *bibliog.*

GOODWIN (BARBARA) Social science and utopia: nineteenth century models of social harmony. Hassocks, 1978. pp. 220. *bibliog.*

UTRECHT

— Foreign population.

GRIEKSE junta in Nederland: rapport n.a.v. de bezetting van de ruimte van de Griekse arbeidskommissie in Utrecht op 26-11-1973. Amsterdam, 1974. pp. 48.

UZBEKISTAN

— Rural conditions.

KUL'TURA sela Uzbekistana v usloviiakh razvitogo sotsializma. Tashkent, 1977. pp. 199.

— Social history.

KADYROV (ASADULLA ABDULLAEVICH) Stanovlenie i razvitie sovetskogo zdravookhraneniia v Uzbekistane; pod redaktsiei...B.D. Petrova. Tashkent, 1976. pp. 133. *bibliog.*

V-1 BOMB.

GARLIŃSKI (JÓZEF) Hitler's last weapons: the underground war against the V1 and V2. London, 1978. pp. 244. *bibliog.*

V-2 ROCKET.

GARLIŃSKI (JÓZEF) Hitler's last weapons: the underground war against the V1 and V2. London, 1978. pp. 244. *bibliog.*

VACATION SCHOOLS

— United States.

MIDDLE start: an experiment in the educational enrichment of young adolescents; [by] J. Milton Yinger [and others]. Cambridge, 1977. pp. 134. *bibliog.* (*American Sociological Association. Arnold and Caroline Rose Monograph Series in Sociology*)

VALDERROBRES

— Politics and government.

CONFEDERACION REGIONAL DE ARAGON, RIOJA Y NAVARRA. Comarcal de Valderrobres, Teruel: sus luchas sociales y revolucionarias. [Royan, 1971?]. pp. 165.

VALENCE.

FRANCE. Direction de la Documentation. La Documentation Française. Notes et Etudes Documentaires. Nos. 4,372-4, 373-4, 374. Les villes françaises: Valence; par Catherine Mestre. [Paris], La Documentation Française, 1977. pp. 87. *bibliog.*

VALENCIA, SPAIN (REGION)

— Industries.

PICO LOPEZ (JOSEP) Empresario e industrializacion: el caso valenciano. Madrid, [1976]. pp. 184. *bibliog.*

VALLE DEL SANTA

— Economic policy.

PADRON CASTILLO (MARIO) and PEASE GARCIA (HENRY) Planificacion rural, reforma agraria y organizacion campesina: programa de promocion campesina en el Valle del Santa 1971-1973. Lima, 1974. 2 vols. (in 1). (*Centro de Estudios y Promocion del Desarrollo. Cuadernos. 4*)

VÄLLINGBY, STOCKHOLM

— Social conditions.

POPENOE (DAVID) The suburban environment: Sweden and the United States. Chicago, [1977]. pp. 275.

VALUE.

MARX (KARL) Karl Marx on value:...comments on Adolph Wagner's "Lehrbuch der politischen Ökonomie"...; translated by Angela Clifford. Belfast, 1971. pp. 37.

BORELLI (GIANFRANCO) Teoria del valore e crisi sociale: sul concetto di capitale in generale. Napoli, [1975]. pp. 168.

LARIONOV (IGOR' KONSTANTINOVICH) Stoimostnye rychagi v krugooborote fondov sotsialisticheskogo predpriiatiia. Moskva, 1976. pp. 151.

LUNGHINI (GIORGIO) La crisi dell'economia politica e la teoria del valore. [Milano, 1977]. pp. 77. *bibliog. Text of the report to the sixteenth scientific meeting of the Società Italiana degli Economisti, 1975.*

VALUE ADDED TAX

— European Economic Community countries.

GUIEU (PIERRE JOSEPH FELICIEN) The sixth Council directive on value added tax, uniform basis of assessment: comments and text. Deventer, 1977. pp. 133.

— United Kingdom.

VAT NEWS; [pd. by] Her Majesty's Customs and Excise. q., F 1974 (no.1)- London. *Supersedes its VAT bulletin (Ag 1972 - N 1973).*

MAINPRICE (HUGH) Value added tax. London, 1978. pp. 301.

VALUES.

In earlier volumes of this Bibliography similar material is entered under WORTH.

HAYEK (FRIEDRICH AUGUST) The three sources of human values. London, 1978. pp. 40. (*London. University. London School of Economics and Political Science. Hobhouse Memorial Trust Lectures. No. 44*)

PUGH (GEORGE EDGIN) The biological origin of human values. London, 1978. pp. 461. *bibliog.*

VANCOUVER

— Suburbs and environs.

LOWER MAINLAND REGIONAL PLANNING BOARD OF BRITISH COLUMBIA. The urban frontier. New Westminster, 1963. 2 pts. *Supplementary studies 1 and 4 to Land for living.*

VAN HEIJENOORT (JEAN).

VAN HEIJENOORT (JEAN) With Trotsky in exile: from Prinkipo to Goyoacán. Cambridge, Mass., 1978. pp. 164.

VANZETTI (BARTOLOMEO).

PORTER (KATHERINE ANNE) The never-ending wrong. London, 1977. pp. 64. *bibliog.*

VARGAS (GETULIO).

SANTOS (FRANCISCO MARTINS DOS) 1903- . O fato moral e o fato social da decada Getuliana. Rio de Janeiro, 1941. pp. 142.

VARIABLES (MATHEMATICS).

CLARKE (L.E.) Random variables. London, 1975. pp. 185. *bibliog.*

VARLIN (EUGENE).

VARLIN (EUGENE) Pratique militante: écrits d'un ouvrier communard; présenté par Paule Lejeune. Paris, 1977. pp. 190.

VATICAN

— Archivio vaticano.

CHADWICK (WILLIAM OWEN) Catholicism and history: the opening of the Vatican archives. Cambridge, 1978. pp. 174. *bibliog.* (*Oxford. University. Herbert Hensley Henson Lectures. 1976*)

VEBLEN (THORSTEIN).

DIGGINS (JOHN P.) The bard of savagery: Thorstein Veblen and modern social theory. New York, [1978]. pp. 257.

VECTOR-VALUED MEASURES.

DIESTEL (JOSEPH) Geometry of Banach spaces: selected topics. Berlin, 1975. pp. 282. *bibliogs.*

VEGETABLES

— Canada.

CANADA. Department of Agriculture. Marketing Service. Annual unload report of fresh fruits and vegetables on 12 Canadian markets. a., 1977- Ottawa. *[in English and French]*

— Kenya — Marketing.

WILSON (FRANK A.) Some economic aspects of the structure and organization of small scale marketing systems: a discussion of the research findings of a study into the marketing of fruit and vegetables in Kenya. 1973. fo. 21. *Unpublished: photocopy of typescript.*

VEGETARIANISM.

SINGER (PETER) Animal liberation: towards an end to man's inhumanity to animals. London, 1977. pp. 285. *bibliog.*

VEIVESENETS ARBEIDERFORENING.

VEIVESENETS ARBEIDERFORENING. 75-års beretning: 1900 9. september 1975. [Oslo, 1975]. pp. 126.

VENEZIA EUGANEA

— History.

MARCO (MAURIZIO DE) Il Gazzettino: storia di un quotidiano. Venezia, 1976. pp. 223. *bibliog.*

VENEZUELA

— Boundaries — Guyana.

PARTIDO SOCIALCRISTIANO "COPEI". Fracción Parlamentaria. Frente al acuerdo de Ginebra. Caracas, 1966. pp. 948-960. (*Publicaciones. No. 38*)

— Commerce — Statistics.

ESTADISTICAS DEL COMERCIO EXTERIOR DE VENEZUELA: resumen anual; [pd. by] Direccion General de Estadistica. a., 1970/1971- Caracas.

ESTADISTICAS DEL COMERCIO EXTERIOR DE VENEZUELA: exportacion; [pd. by] Direccion General de Estadistica. a., 1972/73- Caracas.

ESTADISTICAS DEL COMERCIO EXTERIOR DE VENEZUELA: importacion: articulo y pais; [pd. by] Direccion General de Estadistica. a., 1972- Caracas. *File includes anexo Cuadros resumenes de importacion.*

ESTADISTICAS DEL COMERCIO EXTERIOR DE VENEZUELA: Boletin mensual; [pd. by] Direccion General de Estadistica. m., Ja 1974- Caracas.

— Economic conditions.

ALLEN (LORING) Venezuelan economic development: a politico-economic analysis. Greenwich, Conn., [1977]. pp. 310. *bibliog.*

CONTEMPORARY Venezuela and its role in international affairs; edited by Robert D. Bond. New York, 1977. pp. 267. *Based on a series of discussions held at the Council on Foreign Relations during 1975-76.*

— Economic history.

MALAVE MATA (HECTOR) Formacion historica del antidesarrollo de Venezuela. [La Habana, 1974]. pp. 275.

LOSADA ALDANA (RAMON) La tierra venezolana en la dialectica del subdesarrollo. Caracas, 1976. 2 vols. (in 1). *bibliog.*

— Economic policy.

ALLEN (LORING) Venezuelan economic development: a politico-economic analysis. Greenwich, Conn., [1977]. pp. 310. *bibliog.*

— Foreign economic relations — Colombia.

NATHAN (ROBERT R.) ASSOCIATES. La integracion economica de Colombia y Venezuela...1967. Bogota, 1970. pp. 110.

VENEZUELA (Cont.)

— Foreign relations — Cuba.

CASTRO RUZ (FIDEL) Criticas a la direccion del Partido Comunista de Venezuela. Montevideo, Nativa Libros, 1967. pp. 39.

— History.

PARDO (ISAAC J.) Esta tierra de gracia: imagen de Venezuela en el siglo XVI. 3rd ed. Caracas, 1975. pp. 181.

— — 1830- .

RANGEL (DOMINGO ALBERTO) Gomez: el amo del poder. Valencia, Venezuela, 1975. pp. 411. *bibliog.*

— Industries.

VENEZUELA. Direccion General de Estadistica. Boletin trimestral de estadisticas industriales. q., Ja/Mr 1967-Ja/Je 1968 (años 27-28, nos. 27-30) Caracas. *Supersedes in part and continues numbering of VENEZUELA. Direccion General de Estadistica. Boletin mensual estadistica.*

— Politics and government.

CONTEMPORARY Venezuela and its role in international affairs; edited by Robert D. Bond. New York, 1977. pp. 267. *Based on a series of discussions held at the Council on Foreign Relations during 1975-76.*

PEELER (JOHN A.) Urbanization and politics. Beverly Hills, [1977]. pp. 56. *bibliog.*

VENEZUELA: the democratic experience; edited by John D. Martz [and] David J. Myers. New York, 1977. pp. 401. *bibliog.*

— Population.

UNIVERSIDAD DEL ZULIA. Centro de Investigaciones Economicas. La poblacion de Venezuela. [Caracas, 1975?]. pp. 167. *(Committee for International Coordination of National Research in Demography. C.I.C.R.E.D. Series)*

— Relations (general) with foreign countries.

CONTEMPORARY Venezuela and its role in international affairs; edited by Robert D. Bond. New York, 1977. pp. 267. *Based on a series of discussions held at the Council on Foreign Relations during 1975-76.*

— Social conditions — Statistics.

VENEZUELA. Direccion General de Estadistica. Boletin trimestral de estadisticas demograficas y sociales. q., Ja/Mr 1967 (año 27, no. 28)- Caracas. *Supersedes in part VENEZUELA. Direccion General de Estadistica. Boletin mensual estadistica.*

— Statistics, Vital.

VENEZUELA. Direccion General de Estadistica. Boletin trimestral de estadisticas demograficas y sociales. q., Ja/Mr 1967 (año 27, no. 28)- Caracas. *Supersedes in part VENEZUELA. Direccion General de Estadistica. Boletin mensual estadistica.*

VENICE

— History — Sources.

VENICE. Comune. 1943-1945: Venezia nella Resistenza: testimonianze; a cura di Giuseppe Turcato e Agostino Zanon Dal Bo. Venezia, 1976. pp. 609.

— Politics and government.

VENEZIA: prospettive di sviluppo e politiche di governo; a cura di Donatella Calabi. Venezia, 1976. pp. 153. *(Rinnovamento Veneto. Quaderni)*

VENTURE CAPITAL

— Europe.

COUTARELLI (SPIRO A.) Venture capital in Europe. New York, 1977. pp. 164.

VERBAND DES PERSONALS ÖFFENTLICHER DIENSTE.

TRABER (ALFRED) Geschichte des V[erbandes des] P[ersonals] O[effentlicher] D[ienste], Sektion Zürich, städtische Arbeiter und Angestellte, 1893-1953. [Zürich, 1953]. pp. 229.

VERONA (PROVINCE)

— Rural conditions.

TURRI (EUGENIO) Villa veneta. Verona, [1977]. pp. 209.

VERSAILLES, TREATY OF, JUNE 28, 1919 (GERMANY).

U.K. Foreign Office. 1925. The treaty of peace between the allied and associated powers and Germany, with amendments, and other treaty engagements, signed at Versailles, June 28, 1919; together with the reply of the allied and associated powers to the observations of the German delegation on the conditions of peace. London, 1925. pp. 353.

JORDAN (W.M.) Great Britain, France, and the German problem, 1918-1939: a study of Anglo-French relations in the making and maintenance of the Versailles settlement. London, 1971. pp. 234. *Reprint of the 1943 edition, originally issued under the auspices of the Royal Institute of International Affairs.*

VERTICALLY RISING AIRCRAFT.

KIRKWOOD (T.F.) Effects of a V/STOL commuter transportation system on road congestion in the San Francisco Bay area. Santa Monica, 1972. pp. 25. *bibliog.* *(Rand Corporation. [Rand Reports]. 1075)*

VICKERS FAMILY.

TREBILCOCK (CLIVE) The Vickers brothers: armaments and enterprise, 1854-1914. London, [1977]. pp. 181. *bibliog.*

VICKERS LIMITED.

TREBILCOCK (CLIVE) The Vickers brothers: armaments and enterprise, 1854-1914. London, [1977]. pp. 181. *bibliog.*

VICOS

— Social conditions.

BABB (FLORENCE E.) The development of sexual inequality in Vicos, Peru. Buffalo, 1976. fo.54. *bibliog.* *(New York State University. State University of New York at Buffalo. Council on International Studies. Special Studies Series. No. 83)*

VICTIMS OF CRIME.

ZIEGENHAGEN (EDUARD A.) Victims, crime, and social control. New York, 1977. pp. 156.

— United Kingdom.

SPARKS (RICHARD FRANKLIN) and others. Surveying victims: a study of the measurement of criminal victimization, perceptions of crime, and attitudes to criminal justice. Chichester, [1977]. pp. 276. *bibliog.*

— United States.

HINDELANG (MICHAEL J.) and others. Victims of personal crime: an empirical foundation for a theory of personal victimization. Cambridge, Mass., [1978]. pp. 324. *bibliog.*

— — Illinois.

BLOCK (RICHARD) Violent crime: environment, interaction, and death. Lexington, Mass., [1977]. pp. 121. *bibliog.*

VICTOR, LE SAUVAGE DE L'AVEYRON.

LANE (HARLAN) The wild boy of Aveyron. London, 1977. pp. 351. *bibliog.*

VIETNAM.

OBJECTIVE; issued by the Information Centre of the Republic of Vietnam in the South Pacific...New Zealand. irreg., [S?] 1970 Ja/F1973 (v.1, no.1, v.4, no. 1/2)- Wellington.

VIETNAM NEWS; issued by the Information Centre of the Republic of Vietnam in the South Pacific...New Zealand. m., [Ag?] 1971 (no.8) - D 1972 (no.12). Wellington.

— Economic policy.

REES (DAVID) Vietnam since "liberation": Hanoi's revolutionary strategy. London, 1977. pp. 24. *(Institute for the Study of Conflict. Conflict Studies. No. 89)*

— Foreign economic relations — France.

FRONT SOLIDARITE INDOCHINE. Documents. No. 7. Le néo-colonialisme français: la France complice de Thieu. Paris, 1973. pp. 38. *bibliog.*

— Foreign relations.

VIETNAM FOREIGN AFFAIRS REVIEW; [pd. by] Ministry of Foreign Affairs, Republic of Vietnam. 2 a yr., N 1973 (v.1, no.1)- Saigon.

— — Korea.

KOREA (REPUBLIC). Ministry of Public Information. 1965. Why do we send our troops to Vietnam? [Seoul], 1965. pp. 26. *(Korean Information: Foreign Publicity Material Series. No. 4)*

— — New Zealand.

NEW ZEALAND. 1966. Vietnam: questions and answers. [Wellington], 1966. pp. 40.

— History.

LE DUAN. This nation and socialism are one: selected writings...; edited with an introduction by Tran Van Dinh. Chicago, 1976. pp. 261. *bibliog.*

— Politics and government.

LACOUTURE (JEAN) Hô Chi Minh. Paris, [1977]. pp. 253. *bibliog.*

REES (DAVID) Vietnam since "liberation": Hanoi's revolutionary strategy. London, 1977. pp. 24. *(Institute for the Study of Conflict. Conflict Studies. No. 89)*

VIETNAMESE WARS, 1945-1975.

NEW ZEALAND. 1966. Vietnam: questions and answers. [Wellington], 1966. pp. 40.

OBJECTIVE; issued by the Information Centre of the Republic of Vietnam in the South Pacific...New Zealand. irreg., [S?] 1970 Ja/F1973 (v.1, no.1, v.4, no. 1/2)- Wellington.

VIETNAM NEWS; issued by the Information Centre of the Republic of Vietnam in the South Pacific...New Zealand. m., [Ag?] 1971 (no.8) - D 1972 (no.12). Wellington.

VIETNAM FOREIGN AFFAIRS REVIEW; [pd. by] Ministry of Foreign Affairs, Republic of Vietnam. 2 a yr., N 1973 (v.1, no.1)- Saigon.

GOLLAN (JOHN) Victory in Vietnam: the struggle and its lessons. London, [1975]. pp. 30. *(Communist Party of Great Britain. Communist Party Pamphlets)*

INDOCHINA: perspectives for reconciliation; edited...by Peter A. Poole. Athens, Ohio, 1975. pp. 84. *(Ohio University. Center for International Studies. Papers in International Studies. Southeast Asia Series. No.36).*

LAMB (HELEN BOYDEN) Studies on India and Vietnam. New York, [1976]. pp. 267.

NGUYEN THI DINH. No other road to take; memoir...translated by Mai Elliott. Ithaca, N.Y., 1976. pp. 77. *(Cornell University. Department of Asian Studies. Southeast Asia Program. Data Papers. No. 102)*

DAWSON (ALAN) 55 days: the fall of South Vietnam. Englewood Cliffs, [1977]. pp. 366.

WARNER (DENIS ASHTON) Not with guns alone. London, 1977. pp. 286.

CHARLTON (MICHAEL) and MONCRIEFF (ANTHONY) Many reasons why: the American involvement in Vietnam. London, [1978]. pp. 250. *Based on the radio programs broadcast in 1977 by the BBC.*

— Campaigns.

VAN-TIEN-DUNG. Our great spring victory: an account of the liberation of South Vietnam. New York, [1977]. pp. 275. *Translated by John Spragens, Jr.*

— Personal narratives, Vietnamese.

VAN-TIEN-DUNG. Our great spring victory: an account of the liberation of South Vietnam. New York, [1977]. pp. 275. *Translated by John Spragens, Jr.*

— Refugees.

KELLY (GAIL PARADISE) From Vietnam to America: a chronicle of the Vietnamese immigration to the United States. Boulder, [1977]. pp. 254. *bibliog.*

VILCANOTA VALLEY

— Economic conditions.

GADE (DANIEL W.) Plants, man and the land in the Vilcanota Valley of Peru. The Hague, 1975. pp. 240. *bibliog.*

VILLAGE COMMUNITIES

— India.

ISHWARAN (KARIGOUDAR) A populistic community and modernization in India. Leiden, 1977. pp. 122.

— Russia — Russia (RSFSR).

BAKLANOVA (ELENA NIKOLAEVNA) Krest'ianskii dvor i obshchina na russkom Severe, konets XVII - nachalo XVIII v. Moskva, 1976. pp. 221.

— — Siberia.

KREST'IANSKAIA obshchina v Sibiri XVII - nachala XX v. Novosibirsk, 1977. pp. 287.

VILLAGES

— India — Maharashtra.

PUNEKAR (S.D.) and GOLWALKAR (ALKA R.) Rural change in Maharashtra: an analytical study of change in six villages in Konkan. Bombay, 1973. pp. 138.

— — West Bengal.

KLASS (MORTON) From field to factory: community structure and industrialization in West Bengal. Philadelphia, [1978]. pp. 264. *bibliog.*

— Malaysia — Sarawak.

GRIJPSTRA (B.G.) Common efforts in the development of rural Sarawak, Malaysia. Assen, 1976. pp. 231. *bibliog. (Studies of Developing Countries. 20)*

— Nigeria.

REHFISCH (FARNHAM) The social structure of a Mambila village. Zaria, 1972. pp. 197. *bibliog. (Ahmadu Bello University. Sociology Department. Occasional Papers. No. 2)*

— Pakistan — Punjab.

AHMAD (SAGHIR) Class and power in a Punjabi village. New York, [1977]. pp. 174. *bibliogs.*

— Panama.

GUDEMAN (STEPHEN) The demise of a rural economy: from subsistence to capitalism in a Latin American village. London, 1978. pp. 176. *bibliog.*

— Sudan.

BRAUSCH (GEORGES) and others. Bashaqra area settlements, 1963: a case study in village development in the Gezira scheme. Khartoum, 1964. pp. 172. *bibliog.*

— Tanzania.

CONNELL (JOHN) 1946- . The evolution of Tanzanian rural development. Brighton, [1973]. pp. 21. *bibliog. (Brighton. University of Sussex. Institute of Development Studies. Communications. 110)*

— Thailand.

POTTER (JACK M.) Thai peasant social structure. Chicago, 1976. pp. 249. *bibliog.*

MURRAY (CHARLES A.) A behavioral study of rural modernization: social and economic change in Thai villages. New York, 1977. pp. 133. *bibliog.*

— Underdeveloped areas.

See UNDERDEVELOPED AREAS — Villages.

— United Kingdom.

MEDIEVAL settlement: continuity and change; edited by P.H. Sawyer. London, 1976. pp. 357. *bibliog. Based on a colloquium held at the University of Leeds in July 1974.*

VILLEFRANCHE-DE-ROUERGUE.

La PIERRE et le seigle; album composé et légendé par Bernard Dufour, précédé d'une étude d'Emmanuel Le Roy Ladurie. [Paris, 1977]. pp. 143.

VIOLENCE.

SOCIETY OF FRIENDS. Friends Peace and International Relations Committee. Violence and oppression: a Quaker response. London, 1972. pp. 16.

WAR RESISTERS' INTERNATIONAL. WRI statements: a selection of statements and resolutions from the WRI 1963-July 1972. London, [1972]. pp. 56.

BURTON (ANTHONY) Revolutionary violence: the theories. London, 1977. pp. 147.

O'BRIEN (CONOR CRUISE) Herod: reflections on political violence. London, 1978. pp. 236.

— America, Latin — Bibliography.

SABLE (MARTIN HOWARD) compiler. The guerrilla movement in Latin America since 1950: a bibliography. Milwaukee, [1977]. pp. 57. *(Wisconsin University, Milwaukee. Center for Latin American Studies. Center Special Studies Series. No. 3)*

— France.

FRANCE. Comité d'Etudes sur la Violence, la Criminalité et la Délinquance. 1977. Réponses à la violence: rapport du Comité...présidé par Alain Peyrefitte. [Paris, 1977]. 2 vols. (in 1)

— United Kingdom.

ROSE (J.S.) A study of violence on London Transport. [London], Greater London Council Establishments Department, Behavioural Science Unit, 1976. 1 vol.(various pagings). *bibliog.*

MARSH (ALAN JOHN) Protest and political consciousness. Beverly Hills, [1977]. pp. 271. *bibliog.*

CLUTTERBUCK (RICHARD LEWIS) Britain in agony: the growth of political violence. London, 1978. pp. 335. *bibliog.*

— — Ireland, Northern.

EVELEGH (ROBIN) Peace keeping in a democratic society: the lessons of Northern Ireland. London, [1978]. pp. 174.

VIOLENCE and the social services in Northern Ireland; edited by John Darby [and] Arthur Williamson. London, 1978. pp. 205. *bibliog.*

— United States.

IN fear of each other: studies of dangerousness in America; [edited by] John P. Conrad [and] Simon Dinitz. Lexington, Mass., [1977]. pp. 141.

— — Bibliography.

MANHEIM (JAROL B.) and WALLACE (MELANIE) compilers. Political violence in the United States, 1875-1974: a bibliography. New York, 1975. pp. 116.

VIOLENCE IN MASS MEDIA.

EYSENCK (HANS JURGEN) and NIAS (D.K.B.) Sex, violence and the media. London, 1978. pp. 306. *bibliog.*

VIOLENCE IN MOTION PICTURES.

BRODY (STEPHEN) Screen violence and film censorship: a review of research; a Home Office Research Unit report. London, 1977. pp. 176. *bibliog. (U.K. Home Office. Home Office Research Studies. No. 40)*

VIOLENCE IN TELEVISION.

STRINGER (GILBERT HENRY) Violence and the responsibility of broadcasting: an address given to the Carterton Rotary Club on March 9th, 1970, by the Director-General of the N[ew Z[ealand] B[roadcasting] C[orporation]. [Wellington, New Zealand Broadcasting Corporation, 1970]. pp. 7.

BELSON (WILLIAM A.) Television violence and the adolescent boy. Farnborough, Hants., [1978]. pp. 529.

VIRGINIA

— Biography.

BRUGGER (ROBERT J.) Beverley Tucker: heart over head in the old south. Baltimore, [1978]. pp. 294. *bibliogs. (Johns Hopkins University. Studies in Historical and Political Science. Series 96. No.2)*

— History.

MORGAN (EDMUND SEARS) American slavery, American freedom: the ordeal of colonial Virginia. New York, [1975]. pp. 454. *bibliog.*

GAVINS (RAYMOND) The perils and prospects of southern black leadership: Gordon Blaine Hancock, 1884-1970. Durham, N.C., 1977. pp. 221. *bibliog.*

— Politics and government.

SOCIETY, freedom, and conscience: the American revolution in Virginia, Massachusetts, and New York; [by] Jack P. Greene [and others]; edited by Richard M. Jellison. New York, [1976]. pp. 233. *(Miami University (Ohio). McClellan Lectures. 1973, 1974, 1975)*

VISUAL PERCEPTION.

KAUFMAN (LLOYD) Sight and mind: an introduction to visual perception. London, 1974. pp. 580. *bibliog.*

MORGAN (MICHAEL J.) Molyneux's question: vision, touch and the philosophy of perception. Cambridge, 1977. pp. 213.

VOCATIONAL EDUCATION.

ZYMELMAN (MANUEL) and others. The economic evaluation of vocational training programs. [Washington], International Bank for Reconstruction and Development, [1976]. pp. 122. *bibliog. (World Bank Staff Occasional Papers. No. 21)*

— Australia.

AUSTRALIA. Working Party on the Transition from Secondary Education to Employment. 1976. Report; [J.W. Mather then B.C. Milligan, chairman]. Canberra, 1976. pp. 139.

VOCATIONAL EDUCATION.(Cont.)

— Barbados.

BARBADOS. Select Committee on Vocational and Technical Training. 1950. Report...with special reference to the part-time training of apprentices. [Bridgetown, 1950?]. pp. 55.

— Ethiopia.

TRAINING OF MANPOWER IN ETHIOPIA, THE; (pd. by) Employment and Manpower Division. a., 1974/75(7th)- Addis Ababa.

— European Economic Community countries.

EUROPEAN COMMUNITIES. Education Committee. 1977. From education to working life: resolution of the Council and of the Ministers of Education...concerning measures to be taken to improve the preparation of young people for work and to facilitate their transition from education to working life, etc. [Brussels, 1977]. pp. 63. (*Bulletin of the European Communities. Supplements. [1976/12]*)

— France.

FRANCE. Groupe Technique de Prévision Emploi-Formation. 1976. Rapport; (Préparation du 7e plan). Paris, [1976]. pp. 395. *bibliogs*.

— Germany.

GERMANY (BUNDESREPUBLIK). Statistisches Bundesamt. Lehrer an Schulen der beruflichen Aus- und Fortbildung. a., 1975. Wiesbaden. (*Bildung und Kultur. Reihe 2.3*) *Superseded by* GERMANY (BUNDESREPUBLIK). Statistisches Bundesamt. Berufliches Schulwesen.

GERMANY (BUNDESREPUBLIK). Statistisches Bundesamt. Berufliches Schulwesen. a., 1976- Wiesbaden. (*Bildung und Kultur. Reihe 2*). *Supersedes* GERMANY (BUNDESREPUBLIK). Statistisches Bundesamt. Schulen der beruflichen Fortbildungen, GERMANY (BUNDESREPUBLIK). Statistisches Bundesamt. Schulen der beruflichen Ausbildung *and* GERMANY (BUNDESREPUBLIK). Statistisches Bundesamt. Lehrer an Schulen der beruflichen Aus- und Fortbildung.

— United Kingdom.

O'BRIEN (RICHARD) 1920- . Education, industry and people. [Birmingham, 1978]. pp. 16. (*Birmingham. University. Sir Josiah Mason Centenary Memorial Lectures. 1977*)

— United States.

LECHT (LEONARD ABE) Occupational choice and training needs: prospects for the 1980's. New York, 1977. pp. 203.

— Zambia.

ZAMBIA. Department of Technical Education and Vocational Training. Annual report. a., 1974(2nd)- Lusaka.

VOCATIONAL GUIDANCE.

HARWAY (MICHELE) and ASTIN (HELEN S.) Sex discrimination in career counseling and education. New York, 1977. pp. 154. *bibliog*.

— Australia.

AUSTRALIA. Working Party on the Transition from Secondary Education to Employment. 1976. Report; [J.W. Mather then B.C. Milligan, chairman]. Canberra, 1976. pp. 139.

— China.

WHITE (LYNN T.) Careers in Shanghai: the social guidance of personal energies in a developing Chinese city, 1949-1966. Berkeley, [1978]. pp. 249. *bibliog*.

— Nigeria.

NIGERIA. Federal Ministry of Labour. Occupational Monographs . [Lagos, 1971 in progress].

— United Kingdom.

BRIGHTON. University of Sussex. Appointments Advisory Service. The occupational choices of Sussex graduates. Brighton, 1972. pp. 20, 9.

MILLER (RUTH) Equal opportunities: a careers guide for women and men. rev. ed. Harmondsworth, 1978. pp. 476.

— United States.

HARRIS (NORMAN C.) and GREDE (JOHN F.) Career education in colleges. San Francisco, 1977. pp. 419. *bibliog*.

VOCATIONAL GUIDANCE FOR WOMEN

— Canada — Manitoba.

MANITOBA. Women's Bureau. 1976. Counselling service: profile and follow-up;...written by Joan Simpkins. Winnipeg, 1976. pp. 15.

VOCATIONAL INTERESTS

— United Kingdom.

KIRTON (MICHAEL J.) Career knowledge of sixth form boys;...with K.M. Miller [and others]. [London], Careers and Occupational Information Centre, Employment Service Agency, [1976]. pp. 102. *bibliog*. (*Careers Information Briefs*)

VOLGA BASIN

— Economic history.

SUSLOV (IURII PAVLOVICH) Leninskaia agrarnaia programma i bor'ba bol'shevikov Povolzh'ia za ee osushchestvlenie, mart 1917 - mart 1918 gg. Saratov, 1972. pp. 414.

VOLOGDA (OBLAST')

— Economic history.

BAKLANOVA (ELENA NIKOLAEVNA) Krest'ianskii dvor i obshchina na russkom Severe, konets XVII - nachalo XVIII v. Moskva, 1976. pp. 221.

VOLPE (GALVANO DELLA).

GIANNANTONI (GABRIELE) Il marxismo di Galvano della Volpe. [Roma, 1976]. pp. 167. *bibliogs*.

FRASER (JOHN) 1939- . An introduction to the thought of Galvano della Volpe. London, 1977. pp. 320.

VOLTA RIVER

— Bibliography.

COCHRANE (T.W.) compiler. Bibliography of the Volta river project and related matters; (with Supplement). Accra, Volta River Authority, 1971-72. 2 pts.

VOLUNTARY HEALTH AGENCIES

— Nigeria — Finance.

NIGERIA (WESTERN STATE). Review Committee on Grants-in-Aid to Voluntary Agency Hospitals in Western Nigeria. 1969. Report; [T.O. Ogunlesi, chairman]. [Ibadan, 1969]. pp. 94.

VOLUNTEER WORKERS IN EDUCATION.

CARIBBEAN ECONOMIC DEVELOPMENT CORPORATION. Final report, C[aribbean] E[ducational] S[ervices] CO[ops] project. Hato Rey, 1968. 1 vol. (various pagings).

VOLUNTEER WORKERS IN SOCIAL SERVICE

— United Kingdom.

LANSLEY (JOHN) Voluntary reorganisation: progress and problems of response to local government change; [second interim report to the Community Councils Development Group]. Liverpool, 1974. pp. 46. *bibliog*.

DARVILL (GILES) Bargain or barricade?: the role of the social services department in meeting social need through involving the community. Berkhamsted, [1977]. pp. 31. *bibliog*.

DAVIES (MARTIN) Support systems in social work. London, 1977. pp. 132. *bibliog*.

COMMITTEE ON VOLUNTARY ORGANISATIONS. The future of voluntary organisations: report of the Wolfenden Committee. London, [1978]. pp. 286. *bibliogs*. *Commissioned by the Joseph Rowntree Memorial Trust and the Carnegie United Kingdom Trust*.

HOLME (ANTHEA) and MAIZELS (JOAN) Social workers and volunteers. London, 1978. pp. 222. *bibliog*.

VOORTMAN (A.)-N.V. TEXAS.

De GENTSE textielarbeiders in de 19e. en 20e. eeuw; [by] G. Avondts [and others]. Brussel, [1976]. 3 vols. (in 1). *bibliogs*.

VORSTER (BALTHAZAR JOHANNES).

D'OLIVEIRA (JOHN) Vorster: the man. Johannesburg, 1977. pp. 292.

VOTERS, REGISTRATION OF.

MANITOBA. Law Reform Commission. 1977. Working paper on voter registration: the alternatives to enumeration. Winnipeg, 1977. pp. 34.

VOTING

— Germany.

SCHAUFF (JOHANNES) Das Wahlverhalten der deutschen Katholiken im Kaiserreich und in der Weimarer Republik: Untersuchungen aus dem Jahre 1928... ; herausgegeben und eingeleitet von Rudolf Morsey. Mainz, [1975]. pp. 214. (*Kommission für Zeitgeschichte. Veröffentlichungen. Reihe A: Quellen. Band 18*)

WAEHLERBEWEGUNG in der deutschen Geschichte: Analysen und Berichte zu den Reichstagswahlen, 1871-1933; bearbeitet und herausgegeben von Otto Büsch [and others]. Berlin, [1978]. pp. 672. *bibliog*. (*Historische Kommission zu Berlin. Einzelveröffentlichungen. Band 20*)

— Italy.

ANCISI (ALVARO) La cattura del voto: sociologia del voto di preferenza; presentazione di Luciano Pellicani. [Milano, 1976]. pp. 282. *bibliog*.

— Jamaica.

STONE (CARL) Electoral behaviour and public opinion in Jamaica. [Kingston, Jamaica], 1974. pp. 107.

— United Kingdom.

CREWE (IVOR) and others. The erosion of partisanship, 1964-1975. [Colchester], 1976. pp. 41. (*University of Essex. Department of Government. British Election Studies*)

MARPLAN LIMITED. The Saffron Walden bye-election. [London, 1977]. fo. 11.

MILLER (WILLIAM L.) Electoral dynamics in Britain since 1918. London, 1977. pp. 242.

— United States.

RAINE (ALDEN S.) Change in the political agenda: social and cultural conflict in the American electorate. Beverly Hills, [1977]. pp. 60. *bibliog*.

RA (JONG OH) Labor at the polls: union voting in Presidential elections, 1952- 1976. Amherst, 1978. pp. 182. *bibliog*.

VOYADZIS (VASILIOS TH.).

DELIBANES (DEMETRIOS) Vasilios Th. Voyadzis, 1901-1970. Thessaloniki, 1973. pp. xxv-xxxvii. *In German*.

VOYAGES AND TRAVELS.

POLO (MARCO) The travels of Marco Polo; translated and with an introduction by Ronald Latham. Harmondsworth, 1958. pp. 351.

— Mathematical models.

LEMAÎTRE (YVES) Les relations inter-insulaires traditionnelles en Océanie (Tonga): premières données sur l'application d'une méthode mathématique. Paris, [1964?]. fo. 15. bibliog. (Paris. Ecole Pratique des Hautes Etudes. Centre Documentaire pour l'Océanie. Rapports et Documents. 2)

VUGHT

— Foreign population.

SMEETS (HENK) Lunetten, kroniek van een failliet beleid: het overheidsbeleid ten aanzien van de Molukse gemeenschap in Vught. Vught, 1977. pp. 207.

WAGE PAYMENT SYSTEMS

— Australia.

AUSTRALIA. Commonwealth Bureau of Census and Statistics. 1976. Frequency of pay, August 1976. Canberra, 1976. pp. 5.

— Hungary.

HARASZTI (MIKLÓS) Salaire aux pièces: ouvrier dans un pays de l'est; traduit du hongrois par Judit Svaradja et Joël Aizac. Paris, [1976]. pp. 188.

HARASZTI (MIKLÓS) A worker in a worker's state: piece-rates in Hungary; translated by Michael Wright; with...a note about the author and a transcript of the author's trial. Harmondsworth, 1977. pp. 175.

WAGE-PRICE POLICY

— Canada.

CANADIAN LABOUR CONGRESS. Submission to the Committee on Finance, Trade and Economic Affairs on Bill C-73 (An Act to Provide for the Restraint of Profit Margins, Prices, Dividends and Compensation in Canada). [Ottawa], 1975. fo. 6.

CANADIAN LABOUR CONGRESS. Analysis of the Anti-Inflation Act regulations with respect to part 4 "compensation". [Ottawa], 1976. pp. 25.

CANADIAN LABOUR CONGRESS. Collective bargaining and the appeal procedures under the anti- inflation programme. [Ottawa], 1976. pp. 8,12.

CANADIAN LABOUR CONGRESS. Memorandum to the government of Canada...March 22, 1976. Ottawa, 1976. pp. 42. *In English and French.*

WHICH way ahead?: Canada after wage and price control; contributors include Thomas Courchene [and others]; Michael Walker, editor. [Vancouver], 1977. pp. 291, 32.

— — Ontario.

ONTARIO. Ministry of Treasury, Economics and Intergovernmental Affairs. 1976. Anti-inflation program: the first six months. [Toronto], 1976. fo. 16.

ONTARIO. Ministry of Treasury, Economics and Intergovernmental Affairs. 1976. Anti-inflation program: the first year. [Toronto], 1976. fo. 16.

—Underdeveloped areas.

See UNDERDEVELOPED AREAS — Wage-price policy.

— United Kingdom.

KLINE (ROGER) Anti freeze: a handbook for trade unionists. [London, 1973]. pp. 8.

U.K. Construction Panel. 1974. Final report; [K.J. Johnson, chairman]. [London, 1974]. pp. 29.

CONFEDERATION OF BRITISH INDUSTRY. The future of pay determination: a discussion document. London, 1977. pp. 56.

JOHNSTON (THOMAS LOTHIAN) Incomes policy: the long view and the short. Glasgow, [1977]. pp. 20. *bibliog.* (Glasgow. University of Strathclyde. Fraser of Allander Institute. Speculative Papers. No. 6)

MARPLAN LIMITED. The future of incomes policy. [London, 1977]. fo. 5.

POND (CHRIS) For whom the pips squeak: differentials in the pay policy. London, 1977. fo. 12. (Low Pay Unit. Low Pay Papers. No. 15)

LABOUR RESEARCH DEPARTMENT. Guide to the pay policy: phase 4. London, 1978. pp. 12.

— United States.

NATIONAL BUREAU OF ECONOMIC RESEARCH. Conference on Research in Income and Wealth. Studies in Income and Wealth. vol. 42. Analysis of inflation, 1965-1974: [papers presented in 1974]; Joel Popkin, editor. Cambridge, Mass., 1977. pp. 487. *bibliogs. Proceedings of a Conference held in 1974 in Bethesda, Md. Tables on microfiche (1 card)*

CURING chronic inflation; Arthur M. Okun and George L. Perry, editors. Washington, D.C., [1978]. pp. 297. *Based on a special conference of the Brookings Panel on Economic Activity held in 1978.*

WEBER (ARNOLD R.) and MITCHELL (DANIEL J.B.) The Pay Board's progress: wage controls in Phase II. Washington, D.C., [1978]. pp. 454. *(Brookings Institution. Studies in Wage-Price Policy)*

WAGES.

GERMANY (BUNDESREPUBLIK). Statistisches Bundesamt. Tariflöhne und -gehälter im Ausland (formerly Tariflöhne und Löhnindizes, previously Tariflöhne und Löhnindizes in ausgewählten Ländern). a. (formerly irreg.) 1950/58- Wiesbaden. *(Statistik des Auslandes. Reihe 4.2)*

POMPEI (GIULIANA) Wages for housework: with contributions from the feminist conference organised in Padova on the theme of wages for domestic work, in April 1972; translated by Joan Hall. Cambridge, [1972]. pp. 6.

DELIBANES (DEMETRIOS) The importance of wage and price developments since 1948: internal and external equilibria of individual countries. Athens, 1973. pp. 11. *(Reprint from the Scientific Yearbook of "Panteios", School of Political Sciences Academic Year 1972-1973)*

VELASCO (GUSTAVO R.) Labor legislation from an economic point of view; edited...by B.A. Rogge. Indianapolis, [1973]. pp. 65. *bibliog.*

— Cost-of-living-adjustments -- Canada.

CANADIAN LABOUR CONGRESS. Analysis of the Anti-Inflation Act regulations with respect to part 4 "compensation". [Ottawa], 1976. pp. 25.

— Minimum wage — Canada.

AYKROYD (COLIN) A survey of recent Canadian minimum wage research;...prepared on behalf of the Statistics and Research Committee of the C[anadian] A[ssociation of] A[dministration of] L[abour] L[egislation]. [Victoria], Ministry of Labour, 1976. pp. 60. *bibliog.*

— — — British Columbia.

BRITISH COLUMBIA. Board of Industrial Relations. 1971. Summary of orders and regulations made pursuant to Male Minimum Wage Act, Female Minimum Wage Act, Annual and General Holidays Act, Hours of Work Act, Payment of Wages Act; compiled as at February 1, 1971. [Victoria], 1971. pp. 43.

RHODES (FRANK A.) A study of the impact of minimum wage revisions on selected business establishments in British Columbia. Victoria, Research Branch, Department of Labour, 1973. pp. 74.

— — Uganda.

UGANDA. Minimum Wages Advisory Board. 1971. Report; [A.G. Bazanyamaso, chairman]. Entebbe, [1971]. pp. 19.

— — United Kingdom.

WINYARD (STEVE) The weak arm of the law?: an assessment of the new strategy of minimum wage enforcement. London, 1976. fo. 16. *(Low Pay Unit. Low Pay Papers. No. 13)*

— — United States.

AMERICAN ENTERPRISE INSTITUTE FOR PUBLIC POLICY RESEARCH. Legislative Analyses. 95th Congress. No. 7. Minimum wage legislation. Washington, 1977. pp. 32.

— Australia.

AUSTRALIA. Commonwealth Bureau of Census and Statistics. 1975. Earnings and hours of employees: distribution and composition, May 1975. Canberra, 1975. pp. 31.

AUSTRALIA. Department of Labor and Immigration. 1975. Labour's share of the national product: the post-war Australian experience: a discussion paper. Canberra, 1975. pp. 54. *bibliog.*

— Belgium.

De GENTSE textielarbeiders in de 19e. en 20e. eeuw; [by] G. Avondts [and others]. Brussel, [1976]. 3 vols. (in 1). *bibliogs.*

— Canada.

CANADA. Department of Labour. Labour data: wage developments resulting from major collective bargaining settlements. q., 1977 (no. 3)- Ottawa. *[in English and French]*

CANADA. Department of Labour. Wage developments...resulting from major collective bargaining settlements, construction industry excluded: (annual review). a., 1977 (incorporating 1976 revision)- Ottawa. *[in English and French]*

— — Nova Scotia.

NOVA SCOTIA. Department of Labour. Economics and Research Division. 1969. Pilot survey: small firm wage rates, salaries and hours of labour, Nova Scotia, 1968: cleaners, laundries and pressers; fish products; general and variety stores; sawmills. Halifax, [1969]. pp. 34.

— European Economic Community countries.

EUROPEAN COMMUNITIES. Statistical Office. Hourly earnings: hours of work. s-a., 1975(no. 1)- Luxembourg. *[in Community languages]*

— Germany.

ALLGEMEINER DEUTSCHER GEWERKSCHAFTSBUND. Weltwirtschaftlicher Wiederaufbau: Denkschrift...für die Konferenz in Genua. [Berlin, 1922]. pp. 16.

GERMANY (BUNDESREPUBLIK). Statistisches Bundesamt. Index der Tariflöhne und -gehälter. q., Ja 1977-Wiesbaden. *(Löhne und Gehälter. Reihe 4.3)*

GERMANY (BUNDESREPUBLIK). Statistisches Bundesamt. Tarifgehälter. s-a., Ap 1977- Wiesbaden. *(Löhne und Gehälter. Reihe 4.2)*

GERMANY (BUNDESREPUBLIK). Statistisches Bundesamt. Tariflöhne. s-a., Ap 1977- Wiesbaden. *(Löhne und Gehälter. Reihe 4. 1)*

ROBAK (BRIGITTE) Industriezweigstruktur und übertarifliche Entlohnung: zur Differenz von Tarif- und Effektivlöhnen in der westdeutschen Industrie. Berlin, [1978]. pp. 232. *bibliog.*

WAGES.(Cont.)

— — Statistics.

GERSS (WOLFGANG) Lohnstatistik in Deutschland: methodische, rechtliche und organisatorische Grundlagen seit der Mitte des 19. Jahrhunderts. Berlin, [1977]. pp. 332. *bibliog.*

— India.

INDIA. Labour Bureau. 1974- . Report on second occupational wage survey, 1963-65. [Delhi, 1974 in progress].

MADAN (BALKRISHNA) The real wages of industrial labour in India. New Delhi, 1977. pp. 64. *bibliog. (Management Development Institute. Monographs. 1)*

WARREN (BILL) Inflation and wages in underdeveloped countries: India, Peru and Turkey, 1939-1960. London, 1977. pp. 285. *bibliog.*

— Italy.

SALARIO e crisi economica: dalla "ricetta Modigliani" al dopo- elezioni; interventi di [Nino] Andreatta [and others]; introduzione e cura di Ezio Tarantelli. Roma, [1976]. pp. 192.

— Netherlands.

De BEHEERSTE vakbeweging: het NVV tussen loonpolitiek en loonstrijd, 1959-1973; ([by] Kees van Doorn [and others]). Amsterdam, 1976. pp. 568.

— New Zealand.

NEW ZEALAND. Court of Arbitration. 1966. General wage order of Court of Arbitration amending awards and industrial agreements, dated 10/11/66. [Wellington, 1966]. pp. 51.

— Nigeria.

NIGERIA. Federal Ministry of Pensions. Federal Establishment Office. 1960. 1960 revision of salaries and wage rates in the federal public service; (with Review of salaries and wage rates in the federal public service, 1959: distribution and amendment). [Lagos], 1960. 1 vol. (various foliations). *(Circulars. No. 1960/20-21)*

NIGERIA. Federal Ministry of Information. 1971. Better conditions for you: twenty questions and answers on Adebo report and government decisions. [Lagos, 1971]. pp. 12.

— Peru.

WARREN (BILL) Inflation and wages in underdeveloped countries: India, Peru and Turkey, 1939-1960. London, 1977. pp. 285. *bibliog.*

— Portugal.

FUNDO DE DESENVOLVIMENTO DA MÃO-DE-OBRA. Nucleo de Remunerações. Analise de salarios medios diarios, por profissoes, em alguns ramos de actividade economica, nas cidades de Lisboa e Porto. Lisboa, [1971]. pp. 83. *(Fundo de Desenvolvimento da Mão-de-Obra. Colecção Elementos para uma Politica de Emprego. Serie B. Remunerações. No. 2) With abstracts in English and French.*

FERREIRA (MARIA CECILIA CAMPOS) and PAU-PRETO (MARIA DE LOURDES) Indices de salarios profissionais em alguns ramos de actividade ao nivel do continente. [Lisbon, 1972?]. pp. (58). *(Portugal. Instituto Nacional de Estatistica. Estudos. 42) With summaries in English and French.*

— South Africa.

STARES (RODNEY) Poverty wages in South Africa: a review of the effectiveness of self-regulation and voluntary disclosure. London, [1976]. pp. 31, 16.

SOUTH AFRICAN INSTITUTE OF RACE RELATIONS. Earnings and employment in various sectors of the economy, second quarter, 1976. Johannesburg, [1977]. pp. 8.

— Spain.

BARTHE Y BARTHE (ANDRES) Le salaire des ouvriers en Espagne. Madrid, 1896. pp. 63.

— Sri Lanka.

SRI LANKA. Salaries and Cadres Commission. 1974. Report. pt. 1, vols. 1-3; [L.B. de Silva, chairman]. Colombo, 1974. pp. 679. *(Sri Lanka. Parliament. Sessional Papers. 1974. No.3)*

— Sweden.

SVENSKA ARBETSGIVAREFÖRENINGEN. Technical Department. Pay reform in Sweden: (report on new payment systems). [Stockholm, 1977]. pp. 84.

— Turkey.

WARREN (BILL) Inflation and wages in underdeveloped countries: India, Peru and Turkey, 1939-1960. London, 1977. pp. 285. *bibliog.*

— United Kingdom.

The FRAMEWORK knitters and handloom weavers: their attempts to keep up wages; eight pamphlets, 1820-1845. New York, 1972. 1 vol.(various pagings). *Facsimile reprints.*

UNITED COMMITTEE FOR THE TAXATION OF LAND VALUES. Leaflets. No. 60. An illustration from the "Lusitania": the reward of monopoly and the wages of labour; a contrast. London, [1912]. s.sh.

NEW EARNINGS SURVEY; [pd. by] Department of Employment [U.K.] a., 1968 [1st issue]- London. *Not pd. 1969.*

ERLAM (ANDREW) and BROWN (MARIE) Catering for homeless workers: a study of low pay and homelessness amongst casual catering workers [produced by the Low Pay Unit and the Campaign for the Homeless and Rootless]. [London, 1975]. fo. 13.

JAROSZEK (J.) Earnings in relation to employment changes. London, [1975]. pp. 42. *(London. Greater London Council. Research Memoranda. 500)*

TRINDER (CHRIS) A stitch in time?: a proposal for the reform of the clothing wages councils. London, 1975. fo. 9. *(Low Pay Unit. Low Pay Papers. No. 4)*

TRINDER (CHRIS) and WINYARD (STEVE) A new deal for farmworkers: the case for an independent inquiry into the pay of farmworkers. London, 1975. fo. 7. *(Low Pay Unit. Low Pay Papers. No. 5)*

WINYARD (STEVE) Who will protect the low paid?; a submission to the Commission of Inquiry on the proposed abolition of the Industrial and Staff Canteen Undertakings Wages Council. London, 1975. fo. 8. *(Low Pay Unit. Low Pay Papers. No. 7)*

HOWELL (RALPH FREDERIC) Low pay and taxation. London, 1976. fo. 9. *(Low Pay Unit. Low Pay Papers. No. 8)*

JORDAN (DAVID) Writer on wages. The wages of uncertainty: a critique of wages councils' orders. London, 1977. pp. 60. *(Low Pay Unit. Low Pay Pamphlets. No. 6)*

POND (CHRIS) Trouble in store: a study of shopwork and low pay. London, 1977. pp. 57. *(Low Pay Unit. Low Pay Pamphlets. No. 8)*

WINYARD (STEVE) From rags to rags: low pay in the clothing industry. London, 1977. pp. 52. *(Low Pay Unit. Low Pay Pamphlets. No.7)*

BERCUSSON (BRIAN) Fair wages resolutions. London, 1978. pp. 538.

— United States.

CURTIN (RICHARD T.) Income equity among U.S. workers: the bases and consequences of deprivation. New York, [1977]. pp. 152. *bibliog.*

WAGNER (ADOLPH).

WAGNER (ADOLPH) Briefe, Dokumente, Augenzeugenberichte, 1851-1917; ausgewählt und herausgegeben von Heinrich Rubner. Berlin, [1978]. pp. 452. *With English summary.*

WAIBLINGEN

— City planning.

BACKES (WIELAND) Planung und Raumentwicklung im mittleren Neckarraum: sozioökonomische Determinanten der Lebensbedingungen in einer verdichteten Region, dargestellt unter besonderer Berücksichtigung der Waiblinger Bucht. München, [1978]. pp. 426. *bibliog.*

WAITANGI, TREATY OF, 1840.

ADAMS (PETER) Fatal necessity: British intervention in New Zealand, 1830- 1847. Auckland, 1977. pp. 308. *bibliog.*

WAKSTEIN (CHARLES).

SAVILLE (JOHN) The Wakstein case at the University of Liverpool. London, [1973]. pp. 12.

WALES

— Administrative and political divisions.

U.K. Local Government Boundary Commission for Wales. 1976- . Boundary review[s]: draft proposals. [Cardiff, 1976 in progress]. *In English and Welsh.*

U.K. Local Government Boundary Commission for Wales. 1977- . Boundary review[s]; report[s] and proposals. [Cardiff, 1977 in progress]. *In English and Welsh.*

— Boundaries.

DAVIES (R.R.) Lordship and society in the March of Wales, 1282-1400. Oxford, 1978. pp. 512. *bibliog.*

— Economic conditions.

TY TORONTO. Socio-economic Research Group. A socio-economic strategy for the valleys of South Wales; prepared by the Research Group...following the conferences of the Year of the Valleys, 1974. Merthyr Tydfil, [1977]. fo.114.

WALES: a new study; edited by David Thomas; contributors D. Q. Bowen [and others]. Newton Abbot, [1977]. pp. 338. *bibliog.*

— — Statistics.

WELSH ECONOMIC TRENDS; (prepared by the Welsh Office [U.K.]). a., 1974 (no.1)- Cardiff.

— Economic history.

HOWELL (DAVID W.) Land and people in nineteenth-century Wales. London, 1978. pp. 207. *bibliog.*

— Economic policy.

TY TORONTO. Socio-economic Research Group. A socio-economic strategy for the valleys of South Wales; prepared by the Research Group...following the conferences of the Year of the Valleys, 1974. Merthyr Tydfil, [1977]. fo.114.

WELSH COUNCIL. The operation of the European Regional Development Fund in Wales; report. [Cardiff], 1977. pp. (38).

— History.

DAVIES (R.R.) Lordship and society in the March of Wales, 1282-1400. Oxford, 1978. pp. 512. *bibliog.*

— Politics and government.

U.K. Welsh Office. 1977. Guidelines for the industrial investment functions of the Welsh Development Agency. [Cardiff], 1977. pp. 8.

OSMOND (JOHN) Creative conflict: the politics of Welsh devolution. Llandysul, 1978. pp. 305.

U.K. Parliament. House of Commons. Library. Research Division. Background Papers. No. 63. The devolution debate: regional statistics, updated. [London, 1978]. pp. 17.

— Rural conditions.

HOWELL (DAVID W.) Land and people in nineteenth-century Wales. London, 1978. pp. 207. *bibliog.*

— Social conditions.

TY TORONTO. Socio-economic Research Group. A socio-economic strategy for the valleys of South Wales; prepared by the Research Group...following the conferences of the Year of the Valleys, 1974. Merthyr Tydfil, [1977]. fo.114.

WALES: a new study; edited by David Thomas; contributors D. Q. Bowen [and others]. Newton Abbot, [1977]. pp. 338. *bibliog.*

SOCIAL and cultural change in contemporary Wales; edited by Glyn Williams. London, 1978. pp. 282. *bibliogs. Based on a conference held in 1976.*

— — Statistics.

WELSH SOCIAL TRENDS; [pd.by] Welsh Office. a., 1977(no.1)- Cardiff.

— Social history.

DAVIES (R.R.) Lordship and society in the March of Wales, 1282-1400. Oxford, 1978. pp. 512. *bibliog.*

— Social policy.

TY TORONTO. Socio-economic Research Group. A socio-economic strategy for the valleys of South Wales; prepared by the Research Group...following the conferences of the Year of the Valleys, 1974. Merthyr Tydfil, [1977]. fo.114.

WALLONIA

— Economic policy.

SEMAINE SOCIALE WALLONNE. 57me Semaine. Emploi et politique de développement en Wallonie, [by] A. Carton [and others]. Bruxelles, [1976]. pp. 135.

WALLOON MOVEMENT.

FRANCIS (JEAN) Lettre ouverte à trois millions cent quatre-vingt mille cent dix- huit Wallons. [Bruxelles], 1974. pp. 71.

WALRAS (LEON).

MORISHIMA (MICHIO) Walras' economics: a pure theory of capital and money. Cambridge, 1977. pp. 212.

WAPPING

— Social conditions.

EAST END DOCKLANDS ACTION GROUP. Down Wapping. London, 1974. 1 pamphlet (unpaged). *Consists of photographs.*

WAR.

STUDII social-politice asupra fenomenului militar contemporan. [București, 1971]. pp. 212. *With Russian, French and English summaries and tables of contents.*

COLLOQUE DES INTELLECTUELS JUIFS DE LANGUE FRANÇAISE. 16ième Colloque, 1975. La conscience juive face à la guerre: données et débats...; textes introduits, présentés et revus par Jean Halpérin et Georges Levitte. Paris, [1976]. pp. 163.

LIDER (JULIAN) On the nature of war. Westmead, [1977]. pp. 409. *bibliog. (Utrikespolitiska Institutet. Swedish Studies in International Relations. 8)*

SMOKE (RICHARD) War: controlling escalation. Cambridge, Mass., 1977. pp. 419. *bibliogs.*

ZIEGLER (DAVID W.) War, peace, and international politics. Boston, Mass., [1977]. pp. 444.

AMERICAN thinking about peace and war; [edited by] Ken Booth and Moorhead Wright. Hassocks, 1978. pp. 240. *Proceedings of a Conference held in 1976 by the Department of International Politics, University College of Wales, Aberystwyth, at Gregynog Hall, Powys.*

HOWARD (MICHAEL ELIOT) War and the liberal conscience. London, 1978. pp. 143. *(Cambridge. University. Trevelyan Lectures. 1977)*

WALZER (MICHAEL) Just and unjust wars: a moral argument with historical illustrations. [London, 1978]. pp. 361.

— Economic aspects.

SANGUINETTI (JULIO) Nuestro potencial economico industrial y la defensa nacional. Buenos Aires, 1946. pp. 323. *bibliog. (Circulo Militar. Biblioteca del Oficial. vol. 331)*

— Environmental aspects.

WESTING (ARTHUR H.) Weapons of mass destruction and the environment. London, 1977. pp. 95. *bibliog.*

— Moral aspects.

SOCIETY FOR THE PROMOTION OF PERMANENT AND UNIVERSAL PEACE. The wars and war system of Europe, 1903-4. London, [1904?]. pp. 8.

— Psychological aspects.

WATSON (PETER) Assistant Editor of New Society. War on the mind: the military uses and abuses of psychology. London, 1978. pp. 534.

— Public opinion.

LEONARD (THOMAS C.) Above the battle: war-making in America from Appomattox to Versailles. New York, 1978. pp. 260.

WAR (INTERNATIONAL LAW).

NAPOLETANO (GUIDO) Violenza e trattati nel diritto internazionale. Milano, 1977. pp. 608. *(Rome. Università. Istituto di Diritto Internazionale. Pubblicazioni. 14)*

WAR, COST OF.

SOCIETY FOR THE PROMOTION OF PERMANENT AND UNIVERSAL PEACE. The wars and war system of Europe, 1903-4. London, [1904?]. pp. 8.

WAR AND MORALS.

WALZER (MICHAEL) Just and unjust wars: a moral argument with historical illustrations. [London, 1978]. pp. 361.

WAR AND RELIGION.

LAMONT (VICTOR) and HIGHFIELD (JOHN) Writer on peace. Hungry for peace. New York, [1976]. pp. 63.

WAR AND SOCIALISM.

BERGER (MARTIN) 1942- . Engels, armies, and revolution: the revolutionary tactics of classical marxism. Hamden, Conn., 1977. pp. 239. *bibliog.*

WAR AND SOCIETY.

ANGLO-DUTCH HISTORICAL CONFERENCE, 6TH, 1976. Britain and the Netherlands:...war and society: papers delivered to the...Conference; edited by A.C. Duke and C.A. Tamse. The Hague, 1977. pp. 256.

SMALL comforts for hard times: humanists on public policy; Michael Mooney and Florian Stuber, editors. New York, 1977. pp. 402. *Papers from a conference series conducted under the auspices of Columbia's program of University Seminars.*

WAR CRIMES

— Trials — Germany.

MASER (WERNER VIKTOR) Nürnberg: Tribunal der Sieger. Düsseldorf, 1977. pp. 702. *bibliog.*

WESTPHAL (SIEGFRIED) Der deutsche Generalstab auf der Anklagebank: Nürnberg, 1945- 1948; mit einer Denkschrift von Walther von Brauchitsch [and others]. Mainz, [1978]. pp. 152. *bibliog.*

WAR FINANCE.

ARMEES et fiscalité dans le monde antique; (actes du colloque national...organisé...à Paris, les 14-16 octobre, 1976). Paris, 1977. pp. 478. *(Centre National de la Recherche Scientifique. Colloques Nationaux. No. 936) In French, Italian, or English.*

WAR IN LITERATURE.

LEONARD (THOMAS C.) Above the battle: war-making in America from Appomattox to Versailles. New York, 1978. pp. 260.

WAR RELIEF.

FORSYTHE (DAVID P.) Humanitarian politics: the International Committee of the Red Cross. Baltimore, [1977]. pp. 298.

WARD (GEORGE).

WARD (GEORGE) Fort Grunwick. London, 1977. pp. 123.

WARD (LESTER FRANK).

SCOTT (CLIFFORD H.) Lester Frank Ward. Boston, Mass., [1976]. pp. 192. *bibliog.*

WAREHOUSES.

WANHILL (S.R.C.) The appraisal of port warehouse extensions. Bangor, [1973?]. fo. 7. *(Wales. University. University College of North Wales. Economic Research Papers. REG 7)*

WARRANTS (LAW)

— United Kingdom.

U.K. Home Office. 1978. Evidence to the Royal Commission on Criminal Procedure: memorandum no. 3: the powers of the police to arrest or otherwise stop a person, to search him, to stop and search vehicles, and to enter and search premises. London, 1978. 1 vol. (various pagings).

WARSAW

— Economic history.

WIELKIE zakłady przemysłowe Warszawy. Warszawa, 1978. pp. 860.

— History.

KOSIM (JAN) Okupacja pruska i konspiracje rewolucyjne w Warszawie, 1796-1806. Wrocław, 1976. pp. 272. *With French and German summaries.*

SMOLEŃSKI (WŁADYSŁAW) Mieszczaństwo warszawskie w końcu wieku XVIII; opracowali i wstępem poprzedzili M.H. Serejski i A. Wierzbicki. 2nd ed. Warszawa, 1976. pp. 516. *1st ed. published 1917.*

— — 1944, Uprising of.

ZAWODNY (JANUSZ K.) Nothing but honour: the story of the Warsaw Uprising, 1944. London, 1978. pp. 328. *bibliog.*

— Industries.

WIELKIE zakłady przemysłowe Warszawy. Warszawa, 1978. pp. 860.

— Social history.

KROLL (BOGDAN) Opieka i samopomoc społeczna w Warszawie, 1939-1945: Stołeczny Komitet Samopomocy Społecznej i warszawskie agendy Rady Głównej Opiekuńczej. Warszawa, 1977. pp. 342. *bibliog.*

WARSAW (PROVINCE)

— Economic conditions.

KUCIŃSKI (KAZIMIERZ) Przestrzenne zró'znicowanie infrastruktury wsi a uprzemysłowienie: aspekty społeczne. Warszawa, 1977. pp. 148. *bibliog.* (*Polska Akademia Nauk. Komitet i Zakład Badań Rejonów Uprzemysławianych*) *With Russian and English summaries.*

WASHINGTON, D.C.

— City planning — History.

UNITED STATES. National Capital Planning Commission. 1977. Worthy of the nation: the history of planning for the national capital, [by] Frederick Gutheim. Washington, D.C., [1977]. pp. 415. *bibliog.*

WASHINGTON, DURHAM

— City planning.

POUNTNEY (MELVILLE TREVOR) Planning and the concept of community: a brief assessment of the theory of community and the practice of community building in the setting of Washington New Town. Watford, [1978]. pp. 26. (*Building Research Establishment [U.K.]. Current Papers. 78/2)*

WATER

— Electrolysis.

LONDON. University. London School of Economics and Political Science. Graduate School of Geography. Discussion Papers. No. 62. Water and cation movement in a tropical rainforest environment: I. Objectives, experimental design and preliminary results; [by] S. Nortcliff and J.B. Thornes. London, [1977]. pp. 30. *bibliog.*

— Laws and legislation.

TECLAFF (LUDWIK A.) Abstraction and use of water: a comparison of legal régimes. (ST/ECA/154). New York, United Nations, 1972. pp. 254. *bibliog.*

WATER, UNDERGROUND

— Africa.

UNITED NATIONS. Department of Economic and Social Affairs. 1973. Ground water in Africa. (ST/ECA/147). New York, 1973. pp. 170. *Map in end pocket.*

— New Zealand.

GRANT-TAYLOR (THOMAS LUDOVIC) Groundwater in New Zealand. [Wellington, 1967]. pp. 15, 2 maps. *bibliogs.* (*New Zealand. Geological Survey Branch. Reports. No. 24*)

WATER CONSUMPTION

— United Kingdom.

U.K. Central Water Planning Unit. 1977. Public water supply in 1975 and trends in consumption. Reading, 1977. pp. 13. (*Technical Notes. No. 19*)

WATER DISTRICTS

— United Kingdom.

SEVERN-TRENT WATER AUTHORITY. Report and accounts. a., 1974/75(1st)- Birmingham.

YORKSHIRE WATER AUTHORITY. Annual report and accounts. a., 1974/75(1st)- [Leeds].

SOUTH WEST WATER AUTHORITY. Annual report and accounts. a., 1975/76 (2nd)- Exeter.

THAMES WATER AUTHORITY. Annual report and accounts. a., 1975/76(2nd)- London.

ANGLIAN WATER AUTHORITY. Annual report and accounts. a., 1976/77(3rd)- Huntingdon.

WATER POWER

— United States.

AMERICA's wooden age: aspects of its early technology; edited by Brooke Hindle. Tarrytown, [1975]. pp. 218. *bibliog.*

WATER POWER ELECTRIC PLANTS

— Australia.

SNOWY MOUNTAINS COUNCIL. Annual report. a., 1972/73 (15th)- Canberra. *Included in* AUSTRALIA. *Parliament. [Parliamentary papers].*

WATER QUALITY MANAGEMENT

— United States — Finance.

CAPITAL markets and water quality needs, 1975-1985...; [report of] a conference held...1975...New York City; (prepared for publication by Leonard Lund); a report from the Conference Board in cooperation with the National Commission on Water Quality. New York, [1975]. pp. 78. (*National Industrial Conference Board. Conference Board Reports. No. 673*)

WATER RESOURCES DEVELOPMENT.

UNITED NATIONS. Water Resources Development Centre. 1971. Triennial report on water resources development 1968-1970. (ST/ECA/143). New York, 1971. pp. 202. *bibliog.*

UNITED NATIONS WATER CONFERENCE, MAR DEL PLATA, 1977. Report of the...Conference..., 14-25 March, 1977. (E/CONF. 70/29). New York, United Nations, 1977. pp. 181.

— Social aspects — Mexico.

BARABAS (ALICIA) and BARTOLOME (MIGUEL) Hydraulic development and ethnocide: the Mazatec and Chinantec people of Oaxaca, Mexico. Copenhagen, 1973. pp. 20. *bibliog.* (*International Work Group for Indigenous Affairs. Documents. 15*)

— Canada.

CANADA. Department of the Environment. The Canada Water Act: annual report. a., 1973/74 [2nd]- Ottawa. *[in English and French]*

— China.

VERMEER (E.B.) Water conservancy and irrigation in China: social, economic and agrotechnical aspects. Leiden, 1977. pp. 350. *bibliog.*

— United Kingdom.

WATER: jl. of the National Water Council [U.K.]. q., Oc 1974 - N 1976 (nos.1-11). London.

— — Wales.

WELSH NATIONAL WATER DEVELOPMENT AUTHORITY. Annual report, including the annual accounts and annual report of the Water Quality Panel. a., 1975/76(2nd)- Brecon.

WATER RIGHTS.

MAASS (ARTHUR AARON) and ANDERSON (RAYMOND LLOYD) ... And the desert shall rejoice: conflict, growth, and justice in arid environments. Cambridge, Mass., [1978]. pp. 447.

WATER SUPPLY.

WATER needs for the future: political, economic, legal, and technological issues in a national and international framework; edited by Ved P. Nanda. Boulder, Colo., 1977. pp. 329. *Based on essays presented at a conference sponsored by the University of Denver College of Law in 1976.*

— Kuwait.

KUWAIT. Ministry of Guidance and Information. 1963. The story of water in Kuwait. Kuwait, 1963. pp. 42.

— Nigeria.

NIGERIA (LAGOS STATE). Information Service. 1974. Water supply in Lagos State. [Apapa, 1974?] pp. 15.

— Puerto Rico.

PUERTO RICO. Government Development Bank of Puerto Rico. 1970. A special report on Puerto Rico Aqueduct and Sewer Authority. [rev. ed.] San Juan, 1970. pp. 20.

PUERTO RICO. Government Development Bank for Puerto Rico. 1971. Puerto Rico Aqueduct and Sewer Authority: a special report. [rev.ed.] San Juan, 1971. pp. 20.

— United Kingdom.

SEVERN-TRENT WATER AUTHORITY. Report and accounts. a., 1974/75(1st)- Birmingham.

YORKSHIRE WATER AUTHORITY. Annual report and accounts. a., 1974/75(1st)- [Leeds].

SOUTH WEST WATER AUTHORITY. Annual report and accounts. a., 1975/76 (2nd)- Exeter.

THAMES WATER AUTHORITY. Annual report and accounts. a., 1975/76(2nd)- London.

ANGLIAN WATER AUTHORITY. Annual report and accounts. a., 1976/77(3rd)- Huntingdon.

WELSH NATIONAL WATER DEVELOPMENT AUTHORITY. Annual report, including the annual accounts and annual report of the Water Quality Panel. a., 1975/76(2nd)- Brecon.

WATERGATE AFFAIR, 1972- .

DASH (SAMUEL) Chief counsel: inside the Ervin committee: the untold story of Watergate. New York, [1976]. pp. 275.

HALDEMAN (HARRY R.) and DIMONA (JOSEPH) The ends of power. London, 1978. pp. 326.

KURLAND (PHILIP B.) Watergate and the constitution. Chicago, [1978]. pp. 261. (*Chicago. University. William R. Kenan, Jr., Inaugural Lectures*)

— Fiction.

EHRLICHMAN (JOHN) The company. London, 1976. pp. 313.

WAXWEILER (EMILE).

WAXWEILER (EMILE) Recueil de textes sociologiques d'Émile Waxweiler, 1906-1914. Bruxelles, 1974. pp. 680.

WEALTH.

BOSELLINI (CARLO) Opere complete; a cura di Miriam Rotondò Michelini. Torino, 1976. 2 vols. (*Fondazione Luigi Einaudi. Scrittori Italiani di Politica, Economia e Storia*)

EYRE (SAMUEL ROBERT) The real wealth of nations. London, [1978]. pp. 220. *bibliog.*

— France.

BABEAU (ANDRE) and STRAUSS-KAHN (DOMINIQUE) La richesse des Français: épargne, plus-value, héritage: enquête sur la fortune des Français. [Paris, 1977]. pp. 287. *bibliog.*

— United Kingdom.

ATKINSON (ANTHONY BARNES) and HARRISON (ALAN JAMES) Distribution of personal wealth in Britain. Cambridge, 1978. pp. 330. *bibliog.*

— United States.

BRITTAIN (JOHN A.) Inheritance and the inequality of material wealth. Washington, D.C., [1978]. pp. 102. (*Brookings Institution. Studies in Social Economics*)

WEALTH TAX.

See PROPERTY TAX.

WEATHER.

REGIMES for the ocean, outer space, and weather; ([by] Seyom Brown [and others]). Washington, D.C., [1977]. pp. 257.

WEAVERS

— United Kingdom.

The FRAMEWORK knitters and handloom weavers: their attempts to keep up wages; eight pamphlets, 1820-1845. New York, 1972. 1 vol.(various pagings). *Facsimile reprints.*

— — Scotland.

MURRAY (NORMAN) The Scottish hand loom weavers, 1790-1850: a social history. Edinburgh, [1978]. pp. 269. *bibliog.*

WEBB (BEATRICE).

ARCHIVE ARRANGEMENT ROUTLEDGE ASSOCIATES. Index to the diary of Beatrice Webb, 1873-1943. Cambridge, [1978]. 1 vol. (unpaged). *Published in association with the London School of Economics and Political Science.*

WEBB (SIDNEY) 1st Baron Passfield and WEBB (BEATRICE) The letters of Sidney and Beatrice Webb; edited by Norman MacKenzie. Cambridge, 1978. 3 vols. *Published in co-operation with the London School of Economics and Political Science.*

WEBB (SIDNEY) 1st Baron Passfield.

WEBB (SIDNEY) 1st Baron Passfield and WEBB (BEATRICE) The letters of Sidney and Beatrice Webb; edited by Norman MacKenzie. Cambridge, 1978. 3 vols. *Published in co-operation with the London School of Economics and Political Science.*

WEBSTER (DANIEL).

WEBSTER (DANIEL) The papers of Daniel Webster: correspondence...; Charles M. Wiltse, editor; Harold D. Moser, associate editor. Hanover, N.H., 1974 in progress.

WEBSTER (MILTON P.)

HARRIS (WILLIAM HAMILTON) Keeping the faith: A. Philip Randolph, Milton P. Webster and the Brotherhood of Sleeping Car Porters, 1925-1937. Urbana, Ill., [1977]. pp. 252. *bibliog.*

WEEKLY REST-DAY.

CANADIAN LABOUR CONGRESS. Submission...to the Motor Vehicle Transport Committee of the Canadian Transport Commission with respect to the submission by Mr. George Smith, doing business as George Smith Trucking Co., Winnipeg, Manitoba. Ottawa, 1974. fo. 8.

WEHNER (HERBERT).

HERBERT Wehner: Beiträge zu einer Biographie; herausgegeben von Gerhard Jahn, etc. Köln, [1976]. pp. 302. *Published to commemorate Wehner's 70th birthday.*

FREUDENHAMMER (ALFRED) and VATER (KARLHEINZ) Herbert Wehner: ein Leben mit der Deutschen Frage. München, [1978]. pp. 400. *bibliog.*

WELFARE ECONOMICS.

BOHM (PETER) Social efficiency: a concise introduction to welfare economics. London, 1973 repr. 1977. pp. 150. *bibliog.*

SETTLE (TOM) In search of a third way: is a morally principled political economy possible? Toronto, [1976]. pp. 208. *bibliog.*

WOODSWORTH (DAVID E.) Social security and national policy: Sweden, Yugoslavia, Japan. Montreal, 1977. pp. 156. *bibliog.*

WORCESTER (DEAN A.) and NESSE (RONALD) Welfare gains from advertising: the problem of regulation. Washington, D.C., [1978]. pp. 134. *(American Enterprise Institute for Public Policy Research. AEI Studies. 188)*

— Mathematical models.

MOSSIN (JAN) The economic efficiency of financial markets. Lexington, Mass., [1977]. pp. 158. *bibliogs.*

WELFARE RIGHTS MOVEMENT

— United States.

PIVEN (FRANCES FOX) and CLOWARD (RICHARD A.) Poor people's movements: why they succeed, how they fail. New York, [1977]. pp. 381. *bibliogs.*

WELFARE STATE.

MISHRA (RAMESH) Society and social policy: theoretical perspectives on welfare. London, 1977. pp. 188.

WELFARE WORK IN INDUSTRY

— France.

MARION (E.) Institutions patronales créées par les grandes compagnies de chemins de fer en faveur de leur personnel. Paris, 1890. pp. 24. *(Extrait du Soleil du Dimanche)*

WELLINGTON DRIVERS UNION.

CAMPBELL (ROB) The only weapon: the history of the Wellington Drivers Union. Wellington, 1976. pp. 110.

WELSH LANGUAGE

— Grammar, Generative.

AWBERY (G.M.) The syntax of Welsh: a transformational study of the passive. Cambridge, 1976. pp. 243. *bibliog.*

— Voice.

AWBERY (G.M.) The syntax of Welsh: a transformational study of the passive. Cambridge, 1976. pp. 243. *bibliog.*

WENDEL FAMILY.

FRITSCH (PIERRE) Les Wendel: rois de l'acier français. Paris, [1976]. pp. 280. *bibliog.*

WENDS.

See SORBS.

WEST, THE

— Commerce.

LAMAR (HOWARD ROBERTS) The trader on the American frontier: myth's victim. College Station, Tex., [1977]. pp. 53.

WEST INDIANS IN THE UNITED KINGDOM.

GILES (RAYMOND H.) The West Indian experience in British schools: multi-racial education and social disadvantage in London. London, [1977]. pp. 170.

WEST MIDLANDS STANDARD REGION (UNITED KINGDOM)

— Economic policy.

WEST MIDLANDS JOINT MONITORING STEERING GROUP. Updating and rolling forward of the West Midlands regional strategy: summary of assessment papers. [London, Department of the Environment], 1977. pp. 87.

— Industries.

WEST MIDLANDS JOINT MONITORING STEERING GROUP. A developing strategy for the West Midlands: an analysis of manufacturing net output, 1958-68. [Birmingham], 1976. 1 pamphlet (various pagings). *(Technical Reports)*

— Social conditions.

WEST MIDLANDS JOINT MONITORING STEERING GROUP. (A developing strategy for the West Midlands): analysis of socio-economic groups. [Birmingham], 1976. pp. 30. *(Technical Reports)*

WEST SUSSEX

— Economic conditions.

WEST SUSSEX. Planning Department. County structure plan: reports [and] Topic reports. [Chichester], 1975-77. 10 pts. (in 1 vol.).

— Economic policy.

WEST SUSSEX. Planning Department. County structure plan: reports [and] Topic reports. [Chichester], 1975-77. 10 pts. (in 1 vol.).

WEST SUSSEX. Planning Department. West Sussex: the next 15 years: county structure plan draft written statement. Chichester, 1977. pp. 162.

— Social conditions.

WEST SUSSEX. Planning Department. County structure plan: reports [and] Topic reports. [Chichester], 1975-77. 10 pts. (in 1 vol.).

— Social policy.

WEST SUSSEX. Planning Department. County structure plan: reports [and] Topic reports. [Chichester], 1975-77. 10 pts. (in 1 vol.).

WEST SUSSEX. Planning Department. West Sussex: the next 15 years: county structure plan draft written statement. Chichester, 1977. pp. 162.

WESTERN SAMOA

— Census.

WESTERN SAMOA. Census, 1971. Census of population and housing 1971. Apia, [1972?]. pp. 612.

— Economic policy.

WESTERN SAMOA. Department of Economic Development. Annual development plan. a., 1977(1st)- Apia.

WESTERN SAMOA. Department of Economic Development. 1977. Review of the progress of development projects in the third five- year plan, January 1975-March 1977. [Apia], 1977. fo. 130.

— Emigration and immigration.

WESTERN SAMOA. Department of Statistics. Migration report. a., 1976(1st)- Apia.

— Industries.

WESTERN SAMOA. Department of Statistics. 1971. Survey of business activities, 1968, Western Samoa. Apia, 1971. fo. 26.

WESTERN SAMOA. Department of Statistics. 1977. Survey of business activities, 1972, Western Samoa. Apia, 1977. pp. 34.

— Population.

WESTERN SAMOA. Department of Statistics. Migration report. a., 1976(1st)- Apia.

— Social policy.

WESTERN SAMOA. Department of Economic Development. Annual development plan. a., 1977(1st)- Apia.

WESTERN SAMOA. Department of Economic Development. 1977. Review of the progress of development projects in the third five- year plan, January 1975-March 1977. [Apia], 1977. fo. 130.

— Statistics, Vital.

WESTERN SAMOA. Department of Statistics. 1976. Vital statistics sample survey report, 1975. Apia, [1976]. pp. 31.

WESTPHAL (SIEGFRIED).

WESTPHAL (SIEGFRIED) Der deutsche Generalstab auf der Anklagebank: Nürnberg, 1945- 1948; mit einer Denkschrift von Walther von Brauchitsch [and others]. Mainz, [1978]. pp. 152. *bibliog.*

WHALING.

JAPAN WHALING ASSOCIATION. Whales and the Japanese. Tokyo, 1973. pp. 11.

JACKSON (GORDON) The British whaling trade. London, 1978. pp. 310. *bibliog.*

— New Zealand.

GASKIN (DAVID EDWARD) The whaling potential of the New Zealand sub-region. [Wellington, Marine Department, 1967]. pp. 28. *bibliog. (Fisheries Technical Reports. No. 16)*

WHEAT.

— Congresses.

INTERNATIONAL WHEAT CONFERENCE, ROME, 1967. International Wheat Conference [held in Rome, 12 July to 18 August, 1967]. (TD/WHEAT. 4/1). New York, United Nations, 1967. pp. 26.

UNITED NATIONS. Wheat Conference, Geneva, 1971. [Summary of proceedings of the conference held at Geneva, 18 January to 20 February, 1971]. (TD/WHEAT.5/9). New York, 1971. pp. 30.

— Canada — Alberta.

PORTER (K.D.) and McBAIN (B.J.) Final report: oil seeds and wheat, 1961-1963: a cost of production study on 104 farms: central Alberta, Peace River, southern Alberta. [Edmonton], Department of Agriculture, 1964. pp. 54,18.

WHITE COLLAR CRIMES

— United States.

CONKLIN (JOHN E.) Illegal but not criminal: business crime in America. Englewood Cliffs, [1977]. pp. 153.

WHITE-collar crime: offenses in business, politics and the professions; edited, with introduction and notes, by Gilbert Geis and Robert F. Meier. 2nd ed. New York, [1977]. pp. 356. *bibliog.*

CORPORATE and governmental deviance: problems of organizational behavior in contemporary society; [edited by] M. David Ermann [and] Richard J. Lundman. New York, 1978. pp. 322.

WHITE COLLAR WORKERS

— Sweden.

ADAMS (ROY J.) The growth of white-collar unionism in Britain and Sweden: a comparative investigation. Madison, Wis., 1975. pp. 63. *(Wisconsin University, Madison. Industrial Relations Research Institute. Monograph Series)*

— United Kingdom.

ADAMS (ROY J.) The growth of white-collar unionism in Britain and Sweden: a comparative investigation. Madison, Wis., 1975. pp. 63. *(Wisconsin University, Madison. Industrial Relations Research Institute. Monograph Series)*

JONES (KEITH LLOYD) The growth and development of white collar trade unionism in the British steel industry. [1977]. fo. 238. *bibliog.* Typescript. Ph.D. (London) thesis: unpublished. This thesis is the property of London University and may not be removed from the Library.

— United States.

DECKER (PETER R.) Fortunes and failures: white-collar mobility in nineteenth-century San Francisco. Cambridge, Mass., 1978. pp. 336.

WHITE RUSSIA

— Constitutional law.

SLOBODCHIKOV (NIKOLAI AFANAS'EVICH) Sovet Narodnykh Komissarov BSSR v 1920-1936 gg.: pravovye voprosy organizatsii i deiatel'nosti. Minsk, 1977. pp. 166. *bibliog.*

— Industries.

WHITE RUSSIA. Tsentral'noe Statisticheskoe Upravlenie. 1976. Promyshlennost' Belorusskoi SSR: statisticheskii sbornik. Minsk, 1976. pp. 478.

— Politics and government.

VOPROSY istorii KPSS: nekotorye voprosy organizatsionnoi i ideologicheskoi deiatel'nosti KPSS: mezhvedomstvennyi sbornik 8. Minsk, 1977. pp. 167.

WHOLESALE TRADE

— Colombia.

COLOMBIA. Departamento Administrativo Nacional de Estadistica. Censos economicos, 1970. Censos economicos 1970: comercio, industria, servicios; datos provisionales. Bogota, [1971?]. pp. 23.

— European Economic Community countries.

EUROPEAN COMMUNITIES. Statistical Office. Special Series: Structure of Earnings in Wholesale and Retail Distribution, Banking and Insurance in 1974. Luxembourg, [1977 in pr0gress].

— Germany.

GERMANY (BUNDESREPUBLIK). Statistisches Bundesamt. Beschäftigte und Umsatz im Grosshandel: Messzahlen (formerly Umsätze und Beschäftigte: Messzahlen). a., 1971- Wiesbaden. *(Handel, Gastgewerbe, Reiseverkehr. Reihe 1.1)*

— — North Rhine-Westphalia.

NORTH RHINE-WESTPHALIA. Landesamt für Datenverarbeitung und Statistik. Beiträge zur Statistik des Landes Nordrhein- Westfalen. Heft 386. Die Einheitswerte der gewerblichen Betriebe und der Mineralgewinnungsrechte, 1972. Düsseldorf, 1978. pp. 199.

— New Zealand.

DISTRIBUTION COUNCIL [NEW ZEALAND]. Role of women in the distribution industry. [Wellington], 1976. pp. 35.

— Russia.

PODVIZHENKO (IVAN STEPANOVICH) Optovaia torgovlia: sovershenstvovanie, effektivnost'. Moskva, 1976. pp. 160.

— Singapore.

SINGAPORE. Statistics Department. 1976. Report on the census of wholesale and retail trades, restaurants and hotels, 1973. Singapore, 1976. pp. 98.

SINGAPORE. Statistics Department. 1978. Report on the census of wholesale and retail trades, restaurants and hotels, 1975. Singapore, 1978. pp. 188.

— South Africa.

SOUTH AFRICA. Bureau of Statistics. 1977. Census of wholesale and retail trade, 1971. [Pretoria, 1977]. 13 pts. (in 4 vols.) *(Reports. Nos.04-41-22 to 04-41-34)* In English and Afrikaans.

— Zambia.

ZAMBIA. Central Statistical Office. 1965. Census of distribution in 1962: wholesale, retail trade and selected services. Lusaka, 1965. fo. 22.

WICKSELL (JOHAN GUSTAF KNUT)

— Bibliography.

KNUDTZON (ERIK J.) compiler. Knut Wicksells tryckta skrifter, 1868-1950; utg. av Torun Hedlund-Nyström. Lund, 1976. pp. 108. *(Lund. Universitet. Acta Universitatis Lundensis. Sectio 1. Theologica, Juridica, Humaniora. 25)*

WIESNER (ERICH).

WIESNER (ERICH) Man nannte mich Ernst: Erlebnisse und Episoden aus der Geschichte der Arbeiterjugendbewegung. 4th ed. Berlin, 1978. pp. 316.

WIFE BEATING.

BATTERED women: a psychosociological study of domestic violence; edited by Maria Roy. New York, [1977]. pp. 334.

VIOLENCE and the family; edited by J.P. Martin. Chichester, [1978]. pp. 369. *bibliogs.*

— United Kingdom.

PAHL (JANICE MARY) A refuge for battered women: a study of the rôle of a women's centre. London, H.M.S.O., 1978. pp. 81.

WILD LIFE, CONSERVATION OF

— Russia.

KONSTANTINIDI (STAVRO SAVEL'EVICH) Okhrana zhivotriogo mira: pravovye voprosy. Alma-Ata, 1975. pp. 119.

WILLIAM I, Prince of Orange.

SWART (KOENRAAD WOLTER) William the Silent and the revolt of the Netherlands. London, [1978]. pp. 40. *bibliog. (Historical Association. General Series. G. 94)*

WILLIAMS (HENRY SYLVESTER).

MATHURIN (OWEN CHARLES) Henry Sylvester Williams and the origins of the pan-African movement, 1869-1911. Westport, Conn., 1976. pp. 183. *bibliog.*

WILLS

— New Zealand.

NEW ZEALAND. Maori and Island Affairs Department. 1968. Estates and wills of Maoris. [Wellington, 1968]. pp. (6).

— United Kingdom.

EMMISON (FREDERICK GEORGE) Elizabethan life: wills of Essex gentry and merchants proved in the Prerogative Court of Canterbury. Chelmsford, 1978. pp. 361. *(Essex. Records Committee. Essex Record Office Publications. No. 71)*

WILSON (Sir HAROLD).

AMIS (KINGSLEY) ed. Harold's years: impressions from the New Statesman and the Spectator. London, 1977. pp. 175.

ROTH (ANDREW) Sir Harold Wilson: Yorkshire Walter Mitty. London, 1977. pp. 338.

WILSON (MALCOLM).

NEW YORK (STATE). Governor, 1973- .(Wilson). Public papers of Malcolm Wilson, fiftieth Governor of the State of New York. 1973- . [Albany, 1975 in progress].

WILSON (Sir ROBERT).

GLOVER (MICHAEL) A very slippery fellow: the life of Sir Robert Wilson, 1777- 1849. Oxford, [1977]. pp. 224. *bibliog.*

WILSON (THOMAS WOODROW) President of the United States.

SAFFORD (JEFFREY J.) Wilsonian maritime diplomacy, 1913-1921. New Brunswick, [1978]. pp. 282. *bibliog.*

WILTON-FIJENOORD N.V.

BINNEVELD (JOHANNES MARTINUS WOUTER) De Rotterdamse metaalstaking van 1965. Amsterdam, 1977. pp. 175. *bibliog. Revised version of his De stakingen in de Rotterdamse metaalindustrie in 1965.*

WIND POWER.

ATOMIC ENERGY RESEARCH ESTABLISHMENT [U.K.]. Energy Technology Support Unit. The prospects for the generation of electricity from wind energy in the United Kingdom; a report prepared for the Department of Energy by J. Allen and R.A. Bird. London, 1977. pp. 67. *bibliog. (U.K. Department of Energy. Energy Papers. No. 21)*

WINNIPEG

— Politics and government.

MANITOBA. Law Reform Commission. 1972. Report on The City of Winnipeg Act, S.M. 1971, Cap. 105; [Francis C. Muldoon, chairman]. [Winnipeg], 1972. pp. 43. *(Reports. 7)*

WIRE INDUSTRY

— United Kingdom.

STONES (FRANK) The British ferrous wire industry, 1882-1962. Sheffield, 1977. pp. 418.

WISCH

— Population.

SAMSON (MIKE L.) Population mobility in the Netherlands 1880-1910: a case study of Wisch in the Achterhoek. Uppsala, 1977. pp. 180. *bibliog. (Uppsala. Universitet. Historiska Institutionen. Studia Historica Upsaliensia. 87) Doctoral dissertation, University of Uppsala, 1977.*

WISCONSIN

— History.

LESY (MICHAEL) Wisconsin death trap. New York, [1973]. 1 vol. (unpaged).

— Social history.

LESY (MICHAEL) Wisconsin death trap. New York, [1973]. 1 vol. (unpaged).

WITCHCRAFT.

BARANOWSKI (BOHDAN) Najdawniejsze procesy o czary w Kaliszu. Lublin, 1951. pp. 66. *(Polskie Towarzystwo Ludoznawcze. Archiwum Etnograficzne. nr.2)*

WITNESSES

— Australia.

GREENWOOD (IVOR JOHN) and ELLICOTT (ROBERT JAMES) Parliamentary committees: powers over and protection afforded to witnesses. in AUSTRALIA. Parliament. Parliamentary papers, 1972, vol. 6.

WITWATERSRAND

— Economic conditions.

FAIR (T.J.D.) The Witwatersrand: its major socio-economic and land use trends, problems and prospects. Johannesburg, 1976. pp. 25. *(Johannesburg. University of the Witwatersrand. Urban and Regional Research Unit. Occasional Papers. No.12)*

— Social conditions.

FAIR (T.J.D.) The Witwatersrand: its major socio-economic and land use trends, problems and prospects. Johannesburg, 1976. pp. 25. *(Johannesburg. University of the Witwatersrand. Urban and Regional Research Unit. Occasional Papers. No.12)*

WOLF CHILDREN.

LANE (HARLAN) The wild boy of Aveyron. London, 1977. pp. 351. *bibliog.*

WOMEN.

BIRMINGHAM. University. Centre for Contemporary Cultural Studies. Women's Studies Group. Women take issue: aspects of women's subordination. London, 1978. pp. 210. *bibliog.*

— Bibliography.

ARMSTRONG (DOUGLAS) and DWORACZEK (MARIAN) compilers. Women: a bibliography of materials held in the Research Library. Toronto, Ontario Ministry of Labour Research Library, 1974. pp. 81.

— Congresses.

WORLD CONFERENCE OF THE INTERNATIONAL WOMEN'S YEAR, MEXICO CITY, 1975. Report of the...Conference...[held at] Mexico City, 19 June-2 July 1975. (E/CONF.66/34). New York, United Nations, 1976. pp. 199.

— Economic conditions.

BOULDING (ELISE) Women in the twentieth century world. New York, [1977]. pp. 264. *bibliog.*

— Employment.

The FERTILITY of working women: a synthesis of international research; edited by Stanley Kupinsky. New York, 1977. pp. 398. *bibliogs.*

— — Austria.

BEIRAT FÜR WIRTSCHAFTS- UND SOZIALFRAGEN. [Publikationen. 25]. Frauenbeschäftigung in Österreich. Wien, 1974. pp. 130.

POPP (ADELHEID) Jugend einer Arbeiterin; hrsg. und eingel. von Hans J. Schütz. Berlin, [1977]. pp. 187.

— — Canada.

ROBERTS (WAYNE) Honest womanhood: feminism, femininity and class consciousness among Toronto working women, 1893 to 1914. Toronto, [1976]. pp. 60.

— — — Manitoba.

MANITOBA. Planning and Priorities Committee. Women in the Manitoba civil service. [Winnipeg], 1973. pp. 124.

MANITOBA. Women's Bureau. Brandon Office. 1976. A study of part-time employment;...written by Joan Simpkins. Brandon, 1976. pp. 39.

— — — Nova Scotia.

HALIFAX WOMEN'S BUREAU. Women at work in Nova Scotia. Halifax, 1973. pp. 47. *bibliog.*

— — — Quebec.

BARRY (FRANCINE) Le travail de la femme au Québec: l'évolution de 1940 à 1970. Montréal, 1977. pp. 80.

— — Germany.

DAEUBLER-GMELIN (HERTA) Frauenarbeitslosigkeit; oder, Reserve zurück an den Herd'. Reinbek bei Hamburg, 1977. pp. 218.

LANGKAU (JOCHEM) Bestimmungsgründe regionaler Unterschiede in der Frauenarbeit und Ansätze für eine regionale Förderung: ein Beitrag zur Regionalisierung der Sozialpolitik. Bonn-Bad Godesberg, [1977]. pp. 327,148. *bibliog. (Friedrich-Ebert-Stiftung. Forschungsinstitut. Schriftenreihe. Band 133)*

PINL (CLAUDIA) Das Arbeitnehmerpatriarchat: die Frauenpolitik der Gewerkschaften. Köln, [1977]. pp. 166. *bibliog.*

— — India.

INDIA. Labour Bureau. 1964. Women in employment. [Delhi, 1964]. pp. 146. *(Pamphlet Series. No. 8)*

— — Italy.

PISELLI (FORTUNATA) La donna che lavora: la condizione femminile fra arretratezza e società industriale. [Bari, 1975]. pp. 396.

OCCUPAZIONE e sottoccupazione femminile in Italia; ([by] Luigi Frey [and others]). Milano, [1976]. pp. 150.

PER la salute delle lavoratrici. Milano, [1976]. pp. 215. *Proceedings of a conference organised by the Federazione provinciale di Milano of CGIL, CISL, UIL, July 1974.*

— — Netherlands.

BLOK (ELS) Loonarbeid van vrouwen in Nederland, 1945-1955. Nijmegen, [1978]. pp. 192. *bibliog.*

— — New Zealand.

ROMANOVSKY (P.C.) The education and employment of women graduates in New Zealand: the application of statistical and mechanical models to social structure studies. Wellington, 1975. pp. 36. *(Victoria University of Wellington. Industrial Relations Centre. Industrial Relations Research Monographs. No. 2)*

DISTRIBUTION COUNCIL [NEW ZEALAND]. Role of women in the distribution industry. [Wellington], 1976. pp. 35.

— — Russia — Kazakstan.

MAILYBAEVA (GUL'SHAT AKHMETOVNA) Zhenshchina i obshchestvennoe proizvodstvo: na materialakh Kazakhstana. Alma-Ata, 1975. pp. 86.

— — United Kingdom.

COMMUNIST PARTY OF GREAT BRITAIN. Communist Party Pamphlets. Women at work. London, [1977]. pp. 7.

CHASSERIAUX (E.) and REILLY (E.) Women working in London. London, 1978. pp. 87. *bibliog. (London. Greater London Council. Research Memoranda. 532)*

— — United States.

BLAU (FRANCINE D.) Equal pay in the office. Lexington, Mass., [1977]. pp. 158. *bibliog.*

The FACTORY girls; edited by Philip S. Foner. Urbana, [1977]. pp. 360.

OUT of the sweatshop: the struggle for industrial democracy; edited by Leon Stein. New York, [1977]. pp. 367.

SIMCICH (TINA L.) Women and minorities in banking: shortchanged/update. New York, 1977. pp. 173. *bibliog. A survey of the Council on Economic Priorities.*

— Health and hygiene — Italy.

PER la salute delle lavoratrici. Milano, [1976]. pp. 215. *Proceedings of a conference organised by the Federazione provinciale di Milano of CGIL, CISL, UIL, July 1974.*

— History.

A WIDENING sphere: changing roles of Victorian women; edited by Martha Vicinus. Bloomington, [1977]. pp. 326.

— Legal status, laws, etc.

LAW and the status of women: an international symposium; edited by the Columbia Human Rights Law Review, Columbia University School of Law. New York, Centre for Social Development and Humanitarian Affairs, United Nations, 1977. pp. 371. *bibliogs. Originally published in Columbia Human Rights Law Review, vol.8, no.1.*

— America, Latin.

LERET DE MATHEUS (MARIA GABRIELA) La mujer, una incapaz como el demente y el niño: segun las leyes latinoamericanas. Mexico, 1975. pp. 333. *bibliog.*

WOMEN.(Cont.)

— — Canada — Manitoba.

MANITOBA. Women's Bureau. 1975. Women's place in Manitoba: their legal rights;...researched and written by Julie Bubnick. Winnipeg, 1975. pp. 27. *bibliog.*

— — — Saskatchewan.

SASKATCHEWAN. Task Force on the Status of Women. 1973. Saskatchewan women '73: Task Force report on the status of women in Saskatchewan; prepared by Arleen N. Hynd [and] Mary Rocan. [Regina], 1973. fo. 54, xxiv.

— — Italy.

REMIDDI (LAURA) I nostri diritti: manuale giuridico per le donne. [Milan], 1976. pp. 215.

CANOSA (ROMANO) Il giudice e la donna: cento anni di sentenze sulla condizione femminile in Italia. Milano, [1978]. pp. 153.

— — Poland.

LESIŃSKI (BOGDAN) Stanowisko kobiety w polskim prawie ziemskim do połowy XV wieku. Wrocław, 1956. pp. 210. *bibliog.* *(Polska Akademia Nauk. Instytut Nauk Prawnych. Studia nad Historią Państwa i Prawa. Seria 2, t.4)*

— — United Kingdom.

COOTE (ANNA) and GILL (TESS) Women's rights: a practical guide. 2nd ed. Harmondsworth, 1977. pp. 499. *bibliogs.*

— — United States.

WOMEN into wives: the legal and economic impact of marriage; edited by Jane Roberts Chapman and Margaret Gates. Beverly Hills, [1977]. pp. 320. *bibliogs.*

— Pensions — United States.

FLOWERS (MARILYN R.) Women and social security: an institutional dilemma. Washington, [1977]. pp. 41. *(American Enterprise Institute for Public Policy Research. AEI Studies. 161)*

— Psychology.

BROWN (GEORGE WILLIAM) Ph.D. and HARRIS (TIRRIL) Social origins of depression: a study of psychiatric disorder in women. London, 1978. pp. 399. *bibliog.*

MILLER (JEAN BAKER) Toward a new psychology of women. [Harmondsworth, 1978]. pp. 147.

— Services for — United Kingdom.

PAHL (JANICE MARY) A refuge for battered women: a study of the rôle of a women's centre. London, H.M.S.O., 1978. pp. 81.

— Social conditions.

BAAL (JAN VAN) Reciprocity and the position of women: anthropological papers. Assen, 1975. pp. 128. *bibliog.*

BOULDING (ELISE) Women in the twentieth century world. New York, [1977]. pp. 264. *bibliog.*

NEWLAND (KATHLEEN) Women and population growth: choice beyond childbearing. Washington, 1977. pp. 32. *(Worldwatch Institute. Worldwatch Papers. No. 16)*

A WIDENING sphere: changing roles of Victorian women; edited by Martha Vicinus. Bloomington, [1977]. pp. 326.

WHYTE (MARTIN KING) The status of women in preindustrial societies. Princeton, 1978. pp. 222. *bibliog.*

— Societies and clubs.

SCARBOROUGH (NEVE) History of the Associated Country Women of the World...and of its member societies. London, 1953. pp. 403.

— Suffrage.

JACOBS (ALETTA HENRIETTE) Herinneringen...; met een voorwoord van...J. Oppenheim. Amsterdam, 1924; Nijmegen, 1978. pp. 318.

— — United Kingdom.

BECKER (LYDIA ERNESTINE) The franchise for women. Manchester, A. Ireland, [1867]. pp. 15. *(Reprinted from the Contemporary Review for March 1867)*

HARRISON (BRIAN HOWARD) Separate spheres: the opposition to women's suffrage in Britain. London, [1978]. pp. 274. *bibliog.*

— — United States.

STEVENS (DORIS) Jailed for freedom. New York, [1976]. pp. 388. *Reprint, with a new introduction, of the 1920 ed.*

— America, Latin — Bibliography.

KNASTER (MERI) compiler. Women in Spanish America: an annotated bibliography from pre- conquest to contemporary times. Boston, Mass., [1977]. pp. 696.

— Australia.

AUSTRALIAN INFORMATION SERVICE. The status of women. [Canberra], 1973. pp. 22. *(Reference Papers)*

AUSTRALIA. Prime Minister. 1974. International women's year: priorities and considerations; statement prepared for the information of Parliament and tabled by the Prime Minister...4 December 1974. Canberra, 1974. pp. 23.

— Canada.

MOTHER was not a person; compiled by Margret Andersen. Montreal, [1972]. pp. 253. *bibliog. An anthology of writings by Montreal women as the result of a course on Women in Modern Society at Loyola of Montreal.*

— — Manitoba.

MANITOBA. Women's Bureau. 1975. Women in the community;...by Helen Balderstone [and others]. Winnipeg, 1975. pp. 28, 98.

— — — Bibliography.

OUT from the shadows: a bibliography of the history of women in Manitoba; researched and compiled by Pam Atnikov [and others]. [Winnipeg], Manitoba Human Rights Commission, 1975. pp. 64.

— — New Brunswick.

NEW BRUNSWICK. Interdepartmental Committee on the Role of Women in the New Brunswick Economy and Society. 1975. Report; [R.P. Campbell, chairman]. [Fredericton, 1975]. pp. 169.

— — Quebec.

BARRY (FRANCINE) Le travail de la femme au Québec: l'évolution de 1940 à 1970. Montréal, 1977. pp. 80.

— — Saskatchewan.

SASKATCHEWAN. Task Force on the Status of Women. 1973. Saskatchewan women '73: Task Force report on the status of women in Saskatchewan; prepared by Arleen N. Hynd [and] Mary Rocan. [Regina], 1973. fo. 54, xxiv.

— Cuba.

LEWIS (OSCAR) and others. Four women: living the revolution: an oral history of contemporary Cuba. Urbana, [1977]. pp. 443. *bibliog.*

— Europe.

BRANCA (PATRICIA) Women in Europe since 1750. London, [1978]. pp. 233. *bibliog.*

— Hungary.

VÖLGYES (IVÁN) and VÖLGYES (NANCY) The liberated female: life, work, and sex in socialist Hungary. Boulder, Colo., 1977. pp. 240. *bibliog.*

— India.

INDIA. Committee on the Status of Women in India. 1975. Towards equality; report. New Delhi, 1975. pp. 480.

— Japan.

WOMEN in changing Japan; edited by Joyce Lebra [and others]. Stanford, 1978. pp. 322. *bibliog.*

— Netherlands.

VAN moeder op dochter: de maatschappelijke positie van de vrouw in Nederland vanaf de franse tijd; onder redactie van W.H. Posthumus-van der Goot en Anna de Waal. 3rd ed. Nijmegen, 1968 repr. 1977. pp. 427. *Includes a postscript written in 1977.*

— New Zealand.

NEW ZEALAND. [General Assembly]. House of Representatives. Select Committee on Women's Rights. 1975. The role of women in New Zealand society: report; [N.V. Douglas, chairman]. Wellington, 1975. pp. 108. *Cover title.*

— Poland.

TRYFAN (BARBARA) Rola kobiety wiejskiej. Warszawa, 1976. pp. 166.

— Russia.

LAPIDUS (GAIL WARSHOFSKY) Women in Soviet society: equality, development, and social change. Berkeley, [1978]. pp. 381. *bibliog.*

STITES (RICHARD) The women's liberation movement in Russia: feminism, nihilism and bolshevism, 1860-1930. Princeton, [1978]. pp. 464. *bibliog.*

WOMEN in Russia; edited by Dorothy Atkinson [and others]. Hassocks, 1978. pp. 410. *Based on a conference held by the Stanford University Center for Russian and East European Studies in 1975.*

— — Azerbaijan.

MAMEDOV (SABIR SULEIMANOVICH) Put' k progressu. Baku, 1975. pp. 70.

— Singapore.

WONG (ALINE K.) and others. Women in modern Singapore. Singapore, [1975]. pp. 144.

— Thailand.

POTTER (SULAMITH HEINS) Family life in a northern Thai village: a study in the structural significance of women. Berkeley, [1977]. pp. 137. *bibliog.*

— United Kingdom.

WOMEN'S NATIONAL COMMISSION [U.K.]. International Women's Year Co-ordinating Committee. International Women's Year, 1975 in the United Kingdom; (with Part 2: activities arranged...in London and throughout the United Kingdom); [Barbara Castle and Joan Boulind, co- chairmen]. [London, 1976]. 2 pts.

— — Congresses.

UNION OF WOMEN FOR LIBERATION. Lessons of Skegness; a brief account of the proceedings of the Women's National Co-ordinating Committee Conference at Skegness (October 15-17, 1971) and an exposure of the dirty role of the Trotskyites, revisionists and feminists. Hemel Hempstead, [1971]. pp. 60.

— — Economic conditions.

U.K. Equal Opportunities Commission. 1977. Women and low incomes: a report based on evidence to the Royal Commission on Income Distribution and Wealth. [London], 1977. pp. 39.

— United States.

MORGAN (ROBIN) Goodbye to all that. Pittsburgh, [1973?]. pp. 7.

BERG (BARBARA J.) The remembered gate: origins of American feminism: the woman and the city, 1800-1860. New York, 1978. pp. 334. *bibliog.*

— **Vietnam.**

BERGMAN (ARLENE EISEN) Women of Viet Nam. rev. ed. San Francisco, [1975]. pp. 255. *bibliog.*

WOMEN, MOHAMMEDAN.

ABDUL-RAUF (MUHAMMAD) The Islamic view of women and the family. New York, [1977]. pp. 171. *bibliog.*

WOMEN AND SOCIALISM.

KOLLONTAI (ALEKSANDRA MIKHAILOVNA) International women's day; translated by Alix Holt [from a pamphlet written in 1920]. [London, 1972?]. pp. 6. *(North London Socialist Woman. Socialist Woman Specials)*

UNION OF WOMEN FOR LIBERATION. Lessons of Skegness; a brief account of the proceedings of the Women's National Co-ordinating Committee Conference at Skegness (October 15-17, 1971) and an exposure of the dirty role of the Trotskyites, revisionists and feminists. Hemel Hempstead, [1971]. pp. 60.

UNION OF WOMEN FOR LIBERATION. Feminism and the women's liberation movement. [Hemel Hempstead, 1972?]. pp. 35.

UNION OF WOMEN FOR LIBERATION. Forward to a proletarian revolutionary women's movement: an answer to the reactionary Selma James. [Hemel Hempstead, 1972]. pp. 46.

ROBERTS (SABINA) Revolutionary dynamics of women's liberation. London, [1974?]. pp. 36.

TISO (AIDA) I comunisti e la questione femminile. Roma, 1976. pp. 151. *bibliog.*

KOLLONTAI (ALEKSANDRA MIKHAILOVNA) Selected writings...; translated with an introduction and commentaries by Alix Holt. London, [1977]. pp. 335. *bibliog.*

CAPITALIST patriarchy and the case for socialist feminism; edited by Zillah R. Eisenstein. New York, [1979 or rather 1978]. pp. 389.

CROLL (ELISABETH) Feminism and socialism in China. London, 1978. pp. 363.

HAMILTON (ROBERTA) The liberation of women: a study of patriarchy and capitalism. London, 1978. pp. 117. *bibliog.*

WOMEN BANKERS

— **United States.**

SIMCICH (TINA L.) Women and minorities in banking: shortchanged/update. New York, 1977. pp. 173. *bibliog.* *A survey of the Council on Economic Priorities.*

WOMEN FARMERS.

BOMMERT (WILFRIED) Bestimmungsgründe der Weiterbildungsbereitschaft von Landfrauen: Befunde einer repräsentativen Befragung, etc. Bonn, 1977. pp. 185. *bibliog. (Forschungsgesellschaft für Agrarpolitik und Agrarsoziologie. [Publications]. 245)*

WOMEN GRADUATE STUDENTS

— **New Zealand.**

ROMANOVSKY (P.C.) The education and employment of women graduates in New Zealand: the application of statistical and mechanical models to social structure studies. Wellington, 1975. pp. 36. *(Victoria University of Wellington. Industrial Relations Centre. Industrial Relations Research Monographs. No. 2)*

WOMEN IN AGRICULTURE

— **Botswana.**

BOND (C.A.) Women's involvement in agriculture in Botswana. [Gaborone, Ministry of Agriculture], 1974. fo. 66.

— **Poland.**

TRYFAN (BARBARA) Rola kobiety wiejskiej. Warszawa, 1976. pp. 166.

WOMEN IN BUSINESS

— **Bibliography.**

HAIST (DIANNE) compiler. Women in management: a selected bibliography, 1970-1975. [Toronto], 1976. pp. 18. *(Ontario. Ministry of Labour. Research Library. Bibliography Series. No. 4)*

WOMEN IN LITERATURE.

FERNANDO (LLOYD) "New women" in the late Victorian novel. University Park, Pa., [1977]. pp. 168.

AUERBACH (NINA) Communities of women: an idea in fiction. Cambridge, Mass., 1978. pp. 222.

WOMEN IN TRADE UNIONS

— **Germany.**

PINL (CLAUDIA) Das Arbeitnehmerpatriarchat: die Frauenpolitik der Gewerkschaften. Köln, [1977]. pp. 166. *bibliog.*

— **United Kingdom.**

SOLDON (NORBERT C.) Women in British trade unions, 1874-1976. Dublin, 1978. pp. 226. *bibliog.*

— **United States.**

The FACTORY girls; edited by Philip S. Foner. Urbana, [1977]. pp. 360.

WOMEN PRISONERS

— **Canada — British Columbia.**

BRITISH COLUMBIA. Royal Commission on the Incarceration of Female Offenders. 1978. Report; [Patricia M. Proudfoot, commissioner]. [Vancouver], 1978. pp. 196. *bibliog.*

WOMEN REVOLUTIONISTS

— **Russia.**

BROIDO (VERA) Apostles into terrorists: women and the revolutionary movement in the Russia of Alexander II. New York, 1977. pp. 238. *bibliog.*

WOMEN SCIENTISTS.

COVERT discrimination and women in the sciences; edited by Judith A. Ramaley. Boulder, Colo., 1978. pp. 123. *bibliogs. (American Association for the Advancement of Science. Selected Symposia Series. 14) Based on a symposium held at the AAAS annual meeting in Denver in 1977.*

WOMEN'S HEALTH SERVICES.

The CULTURAL crisis of modern medicine; edited by John Ehrenreich. New York, [1978]. pp. 300.

WOMEN'S RIGHTS.

SANGER (MARGARET) Woman of the future; including Margaret Sanger: crusader, by Mildred Adams. London, 1934. pp. 32.

UNION OF WOMEN FOR LIBERATION. Forward to a proletarian revolutionary women's movement: an answer to the reactionary Selma James. [Hemel Hempstead, 1972]. pp. 46.

DIURISI (MARIA) Mary Wollstonecraft e la rivendicazione dei diritti della donna. [Lecce], 1975. pp. 93. *bibliog.*

LAW and the status of women: an international symposium; edited by the Columbia Human Rights Law Review, Columbia University School of Law. New York, Centre for Social Development and Humanitarian Affairs, United Nations, 1977. pp. 371. *bibliogs. Originally published in Columbia Human Rights Law Review, vol.8, no.1.*

— **Netherlands.**

JACOBS (ALETTA HENRIETTE) Herinneringen...; met een voorwoord van...J. Oppenheim. Amsterdam, 1924; Nijmegen, 1978. pp. 318.

— **New Zealand.**

NEW ZEALAND. [General Assembly]. House of Representatives. Select Committee on Women's Rights. 1975. The role of women in New Zealand society: report; [N.V. Douglas, chairman]. Wellington, 1975. pp. 108. *Cover title.*

— **United Kingdom.**

COOTE (ANNA) and GILL (TESS) Women's rights: a practical guide. 2nd ed. Harmondsworth, 1977. pp. 499. *bibliogs.*

— **United States.**

WOMEN into wives: the legal and economic impact of marriage; edited by Jane Roberts Chapman and Margaret Gates. Beverly Hills, [1977]. pp. 320. *bibliogs.*

DUBOIS (ELLEN CAROL) Feminism and suffrage: the emergence of an independent women's movement in America, 1848-1869. Ithaca, [1978]. pp. 220. *bibliog.*

WOMEN'S ROYAL NAVAL SERVICE.

MASON (URSULA STUART) The Wrens, 1917-77: a history of the Women's Royal Naval Service. Reading, 1977. pp. 160. *bibliog.*

WOOD-PULP INDUSTRY

— **Canada — British Columbia.**

BRITISH COLUMBIA HYDRO AND POWER AUTHORITY. Industrial Development Department. The pulp and paper industry of British Columbia. 2nd ed. Vancouver, 1966. pp. 68.

WOOD-USING INDUSTRIES

SEMINAR ON THE USE OF WOOD IN HOUSING, VANCOUVER, 1971. Report of the Seminar...with the emphasis on the needs of developing countries; organized jointly by the United Nations and the Government of Canada, [held in] Vancouver, Canada, 3-16 July 1971. (ST/TAO/SER.C/137). New York, United Nations, 1972. pp. 32. *bibliog.*

— **France.**

FRANCE. Groupe sectoriel d'Analyse et de Prévision Industries du Bois, de l'Ameublement et du Papier. 1976. Rapport...: préparation du 7e Plan. [Paris, 1976]. pp. 158.

— **Sri Lanka.**

SRI LANKA. Committee of Inquiry on the Establishment of the Wood Working Complex and the Proposals to Exploit the Sinharaja Forest. 1975. Report; [G. Rajapakse, chairman]. Colombo, 1975. pp. 94. *(Sri Lanka. Parliament. Sessional Papers. 1974. No. 15)*

— **Zambia.**

ZAMBIA. Central Statistical Office. 1976. Wood, wood products and furniture industries. Lusaka, 1976. fo. 46. *bibliog. (Industry Monographs. No. 3)*

WOODS (DONALD).

WOODS (DONALD) Biko. New York, [1978]. pp. 288.

WOODWORKERS

— **Norway.**

OUSLAND (GUNNAR) Norsk Treindustriarbeiderforbund 50 år. [Oslo, 1954]. pp. 438.

WOODWORKING INDUSTRIES

WOODWORKING INDUSTRIES

— United States.

AMERICA's wooden age: aspects of its early technology; edited by Brooke Hindle. Tarrytown, [1975]. pp. 218. *bibliog.*

WOOL TRADE AND INDUSTRY.

PHILPOTT (BRYAN PASSMORE) and others. The structure of wool and wool textile production, trade and consumption, 1948-68. Christchurch, N.Z., 1969. pp. 41. *(Christchurch, New Zealand. University of Canterbury. Lincoln College. Agricultural Economics Research Unit. Research Reports. No.55)*

— Czechoslovakia.

FREUDENBERGER (HERMAN) of Tulane University. The industrialization of a central European city: Brno and the fine woollen industry in the 18th century. Edington, 1977. pp. 220. *bibliog.*

— Peru.

ORLOVE (BENJAMIN S.) Alpacas, sheep and men: the wool export economy and regional society in southern Peru. New York, [1977]. pp. 270. *bibliog.*

— United Kingdom.

[CAREW (GEORGE) Esq.] Severall considerations, offered to the Parliament concerning the improvement of trade, navigation, and comerce, more especially the old draperies and other woolen manufactures of England: by G.C. a Louer, of his country. [London, 1675]. pp. 8. *Wing C551.*

The SINKING state of the woollen exportation-trade, and therein the landed as well as trading interest in general: with the cause thereof; humbly represented by the British woollen-manufacturers, to the honourable the Members of Parliament, etc. London, 1737. pp. 16.

An ATTEMPT to prove that a free and open trade between the kingdom of Ireland and all the ports of the southern coasts of England would be highly advantageous to both kingdoms:...in a letter to the Worshipful the Mayor and Chamber of the City of Exeter; by a truly impartial hand. Exon, printed by A. Brice and sold by A. Tozer, 1753. pp. 44.

WOOLF (LEONARD SIDNEY).

WILSON (Sir DUNCAN) and EISENBERG (JOE) Leonard Woolf: a political biography. London, 1978. pp. 282. *bibliog.*

WORCESTERSHIRE

— Economic policy.

HEREFORD AND WORCESTER [COUNTY]. Planning Department. Herefordshire and Worcestershire structure plans: monitoring statement, July 1977. Worcester, 1977. pp. 119.

— Social policy.

HEREFORD AND WORCESTER [COUNTY]. Planning Department. Herefordshire and Worcestershire structure plans: monitoring statement, July 1977. Worcester, 1977. pp. 119.

WORK.

RODGERS (DANIEL T.) The work ethic in industrial America 1850-1920. Chicago, 1978. pp. 300.

— Psychological aspects.

DAVIES (DAVID ROY) and SHACKLETON (V.J.) Psychology and work. London, 1975. pp. 144. *bibliog.*

JESSUP (GILBERT) and JESSUP (HELEN) Selection and assessment at work. London, 1975. pp. 143. *bibliog.*

STAMMERS (ROBERT) and PATRICK (JOHN) The psychology of training. London, 1975. pp. 144. *bibliog.*

MURRELL (KENNETH FRANK HYWEL) Motivation at work. London, 1976. pp. 144. *bibliog.*

GILBERT (JAMES BURKHART) Work without salvation: America's intellectuals and industrial alienation, 1880-1910. Baltimore, [1977]. pp. 240.

SAINSAULIEU (RENAUD) L'identité au travail: les effets culturels de l'organisation. Paris, [1977]. pp. 487.

SIMON (MARTIN) Youth into industry: a study of young people's attitudes to work at a large Midlands factory. Leicester, [1977]. pp. 69.

WORK DESIGN.

MILANACCIO (ALFREDO) and RICOLFI (LUCA) Lotte operaie e ambiente di lavoro: Mirafiori, 1968-1974. [Torino, 1976]. pp. 196.

WORK MEASUREMENT.

FRANKS (BERNARD) The measured day work and productivity deal swindle: how it works and how to fight it. London, 1970. pp. 157. *Articles originally published in the Workers Press, 1970.*

WORKINGMEN'S PARTY OF THE UNITED STATES.

See SOCIALIST LABOR PARTY OF AMERICA.

WORKMEN'S COMPENSATION

— Australia.

AUSTRALIA. Office of the Commissioner for Employees' Compensation. Report. a., 1971/72[1st]- Canberra. *Included in AUSTRALIA. Parliament. [Parliamentary papers].*

— Singapore.

SINGAPORE. Ministry of Labour. 1975. The workmen's compensation guide. Singapore, 1975. pp. 22.

— United States.

CHELIUS (JAMES ROBERT) Workplace safety and health: the role of workers' compensation. Washington, [1977]. pp. 97. *(American Enterprise Institute for Public Policy Research. AEI Studies. 174)*

WORKS COUNCILS

— Germany.

Die BETRIEBSRAETE in der Weimarer Republik: von der Selbstverwaltung zur Mitbestimmung; ([edited by] R. Crusius [and others]). Berlin, [1978]. 2 vols. *vol. 1 contains documents originally published 1919-1931; vol. 2 consists of the reprint of Das Betriebsräteproblem by Kurt Brigl-Matthiass, originally published in Berlin in 1926.*

— Italy.

La DEMOCRAZIA nel sindacato; ([by] Guido Romagnoli [and others]). Milano, [1975]. pp. 133.

LA VALLE (DAVIDE) Le origini della classe operaia alla Fiat: salario e forza- lavoro dalla fondazione ai consigli di fabbrica. Roma, 1976. pp. 182.

ROMAGNOLI (GUIDO) Consigli di fabbrica e democrazia sindacale. [Milano, 1976]. pp. 284.

— Yugoslavia.

SAMOUPRAVLJANJE u Jugoslaviji, 1950-1976: dokumenti razvoja. Beograd, 1977. pp. 367.

SISTEM kadrologije udruženoga rada; redaktor Jovo Brekić. Zagreb, 1977. pp. 132. *bibliog. (Zagreb. Ekonomski Institut. Centar za Kadrologiju i Poslovodne Kadrove. Kadrologijska Biblioteka. Kolo 5) With English table of contents and summary.*

SISTEM planiranja kadrova i obrazovanja samoupravno udruženog rada; redaktori Jovo Brekić i M. Jurina. Zagreb, 1977. pp. 305. *bibliog. (Zagreb. Ekonomski Institut. Centar za Kadrologiju i Poslovodne Kadrove. Kadrologijska Biblioteka. Kolo 4, svezak 1) With English table of contents and summary.*

WORLD COUNCIL OF CHURCHES.

SMITH (BERNARD) Monday Club member. The fraudulent gospel: politics and the World Council of Churches. Petersham, 1977. pp. 99.

WORLD COUNCIL OF INDIGENOUS PEOPLES.

SANDERS (DOUGLAS ESMOND) The formation of the World Council of Indigenous Peoples. Copenhagen, 1977. pp. 27. *(International Work Group for Indigenous Affairs. Documents. 29)*

WORLD JEWISH CONGRESS.

FRAENKEL (JOSEF) The history of the British section of the World Jewish Congress. London, [1977?]. pp. 10.

WORLD POLITICS.

HAYA DE LA TORRE (VICTOR RAUL) Carta a los jovenes de Indoamerica que me escriben: un documento trascendental. [Lima, 1968]. pp. 23.

WAR RESISTERS' INTERNATIONAL. WRI statements: a selection of statements and resolutions from the WRI 1963-July 1972. London, [1972]. pp. 56.

PALME (OLOF) World peace, super powers and national independence. [Stockholm, 1974]. pp. 35.

SALAMON (BENJAMIN) Nuclear power plants and international politics. [1975] fo.57. *Photocopy of typescript: unpublished.*

SEBRELI (JUAN JOSE) Tercer mundo: mito burgues. Buenos Aires, [1975]. pp. 252.

ANTONICELLI (FRANCO) La pratica della libertà: documenti, discorsi, scritti politici, 1929-1974. Torino, 1976. pp. 257.

BERLIA (GEORGES) Le maintien de la paix: doctrines et problèmes, 1919-1976. Paris, [1976]. pp. 341, vi.

CĂTRE o nouă ordine internațională; coordonator Nicolae Ecobescu, cu un cuvînt înainte de Ștefan A. Andrei. București, 1976. pp. 542. *With English, French, German and Russian tables of contents.*

CHUBAR'IAN (ALEKSANDR OGANOVICH) Mirnoe sosushchestvovanie: teoriia i praktika. Moskva, 1976. pp. 254.

MAYER (PIERRE) Le monde rompu. [Paris, 1976]. pp. 310.

CALVOCORESSI (PETER) World politics since 1945. 3rd ed. London, 1977. pp. 458.

COLBERT (EVELYN SPEYER) Southeast Asia in international politics, 1941-1956. Ithaca, 1977. pp. 372. *bibliog.*

DONOVAN (ROBERT JOHN) Conflict and crisis: the presidency of Harry S. Truman, 1945- 1948. New York, [1977]. pp. 473.

GATI (CHARLES) and GATI (TOBY TRISTER) The debate over detente. New York, 1977. pp. 63. *bibliog. (Foreign Policy Association. Headline Books. No. 234)*

HILLGRUBER (ANDREAS) Deutsche Grossmacht- und Weltpolitik im 19. und 20. Jahrhundert. Düsseldorf, [1977]. pp. 389. *bibliog. Selected essays and articles originally published between 1964 and 1976.*

The IMPACT of the cold war: reconsiderations; edited by Joseph M. Siracusa and Glen St. John Barclay. Port Washington, 1977. pp. 207. *bibliog.*

KUNERT (DIRK) Wars of national liberation, the super-powers and the Afro-Asian ocean region. Braamfontein, 1977. pp. 68. *(South African Institute of International Affairs. Special Studies)*

LUCE (RICHARD) and RANELAGH (JOHN) Human rights and foreign policy. London, 1977. pp. 31. *(Conservative Political Centre. [Publications]. No. 614)*

WORLD WAR, 1939-1945.

NOLTE (ERNST) Marxismus, Faschismus, Kalter Krieg: Vorträge und Aufsätze, 1964-1976. Stuttgart, [1977]. pp. 400. *bibliog.*

SMITH (ARTHUR LEE) 1927- . Churchill's German army: wartime strategy and cold war politics, 1943-1947. Beverly Hills, [1977]. pp. 158. *bibliog.*

SNYDER (GLENN HERALD) and DIESING (PAUL) Conflict among nations: bargaining, decision making, and system structure in international crises. Princeton, N.J., [1977]. pp. 578. *bibliogs.*

TINKER (HUGH) Race, conflict and the international order: from empire to United Nations. London, 1977. pp. 157. *bibliogs.*

UNOFFICIAL diplomats; Maureen R. Berman and Joseph E. Johnson, editors. New York, 1977. pp. 268. *Based on a conference held at Bellagio, Italy, in 1973 by the Communications Institute.*

ZARODOV (KONSTANTIN IVANOVICH) Sotsializm, mir, revoliutsiia: nekotorye voprosy teorii i praktiki mezhdunarodnykh otnoshenii i klassovoi bor'by. Moskva, 1977. pp. 303.

ZARODOV (KONSTANTIN IVANOVICH) Tri revoliutsii v Rossii i nashe vremia. 2nd ed. Moskva, 1977. pp. 636.

ASPECTS of conflict; twelve essays by members of the ISC council and senior research fellows...; [by] Sir Louis Le Bailly [and others]. London, 1978. pp. 32. *(Institute for the Study of Conflict. Conflict Studies. No. 100)*

CONANT (MELVIN A.) and GOLD (FERN RACINE) The geopolitics of energy. Boulder, 1978. pp. 224.

GARVEY (Sir TERENCE) Bones of contention: an enquiry into East-West relations. London, 1978. pp. 203. *bibliog.*

INNOCENTI (MARCO) Atlante politico: (principi e vassali; USA, URSS, CEE, Cina e Terzo Mondo). Milano, [1978]. pp. 172.

ROSE (LISLE ABBOTT) The long shadow: reflections on the Second World War era. Westport, Conn., 1978. pp. 224. *bibliog.*

— Congresses.

AFRO-ASIAN-LATIN AMERICAN PEOPLES' SOLIDARITY CONFERENCE, HAVANA, 1966. Première Conférence de Solidarité des Peuples d'Afrique, d'Asie, d'Amérique Latine: documents. Paris, [1966?]. fo. 27.

WORLD WAR, 1939-1945.

La SECONDA guerra mondiale nella prospettiva storica a trent'anni dall'epilogo: [proceedings of a conference organised by the Comité International d'Histoire de la 2e Guerre Mondiale at Como, 1975]. Como, 1977. pp. 555.

— Afro-Americans.

BUCHANAN (ALBERT RUSSELL) Black Americans in World War II. Santa Barbara, Calif., [1977]. pp. 148. *bibliog.*

— Atrocities.

POLAND. Polish Information Center, New York. 1941. Extermination of the Polish people and Colonization by German nationals. New York, [1941?]. pp. 46. *(Documents relating to the Administration of Occupied Countries in Eastern Europe. Nos.8 and 9)*

POLAND. Polish Information Center, New York. 1941. German persecution of religious life in Poland. New York, [1941?]. pp. 29. *(Documents relating to the Administration of Occupied Countries in Eastern Europe. No.4)*

— Biography.

TAYLOR (ALAN JOHN PERCIVALE) The war lords. London, 1977. pp. 189. *Transcripts of six lectures delivered on BBC Television in August 1976.*

— Campaigns — Russia.

VOROB'EV (FEDOR DANILOVICH) and KRAVTSOV (VIKTOR MIKHAILOVICH) Velikaia Otechestvennaia voina Sovetskogo Soiuza, 1941-1945 gg. : kratkii voenno-istoricheskii ocherk. Moskva, 1961. pp. 456.

BAGRAMIAN (IVAN KHRISTOFOROVICH) Tak nachinalas' voina. Kiev, 1975. pp. 510.

BAGRAMIAN (IVAN KHRISTOFOROVICH) Tak shli my k pobede. Moskva, 1977. pp. 608.

— Catholic Church.

MASSARA (MASSIMO) La Chiesa cattolica nella seconda guerra mondiale, dallo scatenamento delle aggressioni hitleriane alla capitolazione della Francia, 1935-1940. Legnano, [1977]. pp. 377. *bibliog.*

— Causes.

ADAMTHWAITE (ANTHONY P.) France and the coming of the Second World War, 1936-1939. London, 1977. pp. 434. *bibliog.*

MELOSI (MARTIN V.) The shadow of Pearl Harbor: political controversy over the surprise attack, 1941-1946. College Station, Tex., [1977]. pp. 183. *bibliog.*

— Collaborationists — Belgium.

DEGRELLE (LEON) Lettres à mon Cardinal. [Bruxelles, 1975]. pp. 341.

— — France.

ORY (PASCAL) Les collaborateurs, 1940-1945. Paris, [1976]. pp. 320. *bibliog.*

— Conscript labour — Germany.

DYLIŃSKI (RYSZARD) and others, eds. Z literą "P": polacy na robotach przymusowych w hitlerowskiej Rzeszy, 1939-1945: wspomnienia...; wstęp Czesław Łuczak. Poznań, 1976. pp. 611.

KONIECZNY (ALFRED) and SZURGACZ (HERBERT) eds. Praca przymusowa Polaków pod panowaniem hitlerowskim, 1939-1945. Poznań, 1976. pp. lxx,562. *(Poznań. Instytut Zachodni. Documenta Occupationis. 10) Documents in the original German, with Polish, Russian, English and German introductions.*

POŁOMSKI (FRANCISZEK) Aspekty rasowe w postępowaniu z robotnikami przymusowymi i jeńcami wojennymi III Rzeszy, 1939-1945. Wrocław, 1976. pp. 130. *bibliog. (Wrocław. Wrocławskie Towarzystwo Naukowe. Prace. Seria A. Nr. 185) With English summary.*

KOZIEŁŁO-POKLEWSKI (BOHDAN) Zagraniczni robotnicy przymusowi w Prusach Wschodnich w latach II wojny światowej. Warszawa, 1977. pp. 235. *bibliog. (Ośrodek Badań Naukowych im. Wojciecha Kętrzyńskiego w Olsztynie. Rozprawy i Materiały. nr. 55) With Russian, German and English summaries and tables of contents.*

— Diplomatic history.

CHICHOVSKA (VESELA) Sobolevata aktsiia. Sofiia, 1972. pp. 109. *bibliog.*

DETERRENT diplomacy: Japan, Germany and the USSR 1935-1940: selected translations from Taiheiyo senso e no michi: kaisen gaiko shi; edited by James William Morley. New York, 1976. pp. 363. *bibliog. (Columbia University. East Asian Institute. Studies)*

Das "ANDERE Deutschland" im Zweiten Weltkrieg: Emigration und Widerstand in internationaler Perspektive: The "Other Germany" in the Second World War...; herausgegeben von Lothar Kettenacker. Stuttgart, 1977. pp. 258. *(Deutsches Historisches Institut in London. Veröffentlichungen. Band 2) In German or English, with summaries in the alternative language.*

FRANCIS (MICHAEL J.) The limits of hegemony: United States relations with Argentina and Chile during World War II. Notre Dame, [1977]. pp. 292. *(Notre Dame. University. Committee on International Relations. International Studies)*

LEUTZE (JAMES R.) Bargaining for supremacy: Anglo-American naval collaboration, 1937-1941. Chapel Hill, [1977]. pp. 328. *bibliog.*

SIRACUSA (JOSEPH M.) ed. The American diplomatic revolution: a documentary history of the cold war, 1941-1947. Port Washington, 1977. pp. 265. *bibliog.*

TOLSTOY (NIKOLAI) Victims of Yalta. London, [1977]. pp. 496.

GENERAL staffs and diplomacy before the Second World War; edited by Adrian Preston. London, [1978]. pp. 138. *Essays originally read to the Fourth Annual Military History Symposium held at the Royal Military College of Canada in 1977.*

ROSE (LISLE ABBOTT) The long shadow: reflections on the Second World War era. Westport, Conn., 1978. pp. 224. *bibliog.*

THORNE (CHRISTOPHER) Allies of a kind: the United States, Britain and the war against Japan, 1941-1945. London, 1978. pp. 772. *bibliog.*

— Economic aspects — Poland.

POLAND. Polish Information Center, New York. 1941. German organization of distribution in Poland. New York, [1941]. pp. 15. *(Documents relating to the Administration of Occupied Countries in Eastern Europe. No.3)*

— — Russia.

VINOGRADOV (IVAN IVANOVICH) Politotdely MTS i sovkhozov v gody Velikoi Otechestvennoi voiny, 1941-1943 gg. Leningrad, 1976. pp. 128.

— — — Russia (RSFSR).

ANISKOV (VIKTOR TIKHONOVICH) S polei kolkhoznykh na polia srazhenii: partiino-organizatorskaia deiatel'nost' v iaroslavskoi i kostromskoi derevne v gody Velikoi Otechestvennoi voiny. Iaroslavl', 1975. pp. 208. *bibliog.*

— — — Siberia.

KUZNETSOV (IL'IA INNOKENT'EVICH) Vostochnaia Sibir' v gody Velikoi Otechestvennoi voiny, 1941- 1945. Irkutsk, 1974. pp. 510.

— Forced repatriation.

TOLSTOY (NIKOLAI) Victims of Yalta. London, [1977]. pp. 496.

— Jews.

DRUKS (HERBERT) The failure to rescue. New York, [1977]. pp. 108. *bibliog.*

— Naval operations, British.

ROSKILL (STEPHEN WENTWORTH) Churchill and the admirals. London, 1977. pp. 351.

— Occupied territories.

GRÜNBERG (KAROL) SS - czarna gwardia Hitlera. [Warszawa], 1975. pp. 558. *bibliog.*

SCOTTI (GIACOMO) "Bono taliano": (gli italiani in Yugoslavia, 1941-43). Milano, [1977]. pp. 167.

— Peace.

OVERESCH (MANFRED) Gesamtdeutsche Illusion und westdeutsche Realität: von den Vorbereitungen für einen deutschen Friedensvertrag zur Gründung des Auswärtigen Amts der Bundesrepublik Deutschland, 1946-1949/51. Düsseldorf, [1978]. pp. 204. *bibliog.*

— Personal narratives, British.

TRORY (ERNIE) Imperialist war: further recollections of a communist organiser. Brighton, 1977. pp. 242. *bibliog.*

ZUCKERMAN (SOLLY) Baron Zuckerman. From apes to warlords: the autobiography, 1904-1946. London, 1978. pp. 447.

WORLD WAR, 1939-1945.(Cont.)

— Personal narratives, Italian.

FORNASIERO (FLAVIO) Cantavamo l'Internazionale. Milano, [1977]. pp. 159.

— Prisoners and prisons.

TOLSTOY (NIKOLAI) Victims of Yalta. London, [1977]. pp. 496.

— Propaganda.

AUCKLAND (R.G.) Catalogue of British "black" propaganda to Germany 1941-1945. St. Albans, 1977. pp. 32.

CRUICKSHANK (CHARLES GREIG) The fourth arm: psychological warfare, 1938-45. London, 1977. pp. 200. *bibliog.*

HEARTFIELD (JOHN) Photomontages of the Nazi period. London, 1977. pp. 143. *bibliog.*

WINKLER (ALLAN M.) The politics of propaganda: the Office of War Information, 1942-1945. New Haven, 1978. pp. 230. *bibliog. (Yale University. Yale Historical Publications. Miscellany. 118)*

— Science.

JONES (REGINALD VICTOR) Most secret war. London, 1978. pp. 556.

— Secret service — Germany.

KAHN (DAVID) Hitler's spies: German military intelligence in World War II. New York, [1978]. pp. 671. *bibliog.*

— — United Kingdom.

JONES (REGINALD VICTOR) Most secret war. London, 1978. pp. 556.

LEWIN (RONALD) Ultra goes to war: the secret story. London, 1978. pp. 398. *bibliog.*

— Sources.

MAYER (S.L.) and KOENIG (W.J.) The two world wars: a guide to manuscript collections in the United Kingdom. London, 1976. pp. 317.

— Supplies.

TYL Sovetskikh Vooruzhennykh Sil v Velikoi Otechestvennoi voine, 1941-1945 gg.; pod obshchei redaktsiei S.K. Kurkotkina. Moskva, 1977. pp. 559.

— Technology.

JONES (REGINALD VICTOR) Most secret war. London, 1978. pp. 556.

— Transportation.

TYL Sovetskikh Vooruzhennykh Sil v Velikoi Otechestvennoi voine, 1941-1945 gg.; pod obshchei redaktsiei S.K. Kurkotkina. Moskva, 1977. pp. 559.

— Underground literature — Denmark.

SNITKER (HANS) Det illegale Frit Danmark: bladet och organisationen. Odense, 1977. pp. 190. *(Odense Universitet. Studies in History and Social Sciences. vol. 42)*

— Underground movements.

GARLIŃSKI (JÓZEF) Hitler's last weapons: the underground war against the V1 and V2. London, 1978. pp. 244. *bibliog.*

— — Denmark.

HAESTRUP (JØRGEN) Secret alliance: a study of the Danish resistance movement, 1940-45. Odense, 1976-77. 3 vols. *(Odense Universitet. Studies in History and Social Sciences. vols. 35, 37, and 41)*

SNITKER (HANS) Det illegale Frit Danmark: bladet och organisationen. Odense, 1977. pp. 190. *(Odense Universitet. Studies in History and Social Sciences. vol. 42)*

— — France.

DANK (MILTON) The French against the French: collaboration and resistance. London, 1978. pp. 365. *bibliog.*

KEDWARD (HARRY RODERICK) Resistance in Vichy France: a study of ideas and motivation in the southern zone, 1940-1942. Oxford, [1978]. pp. 311. *bibliog.*

— — Italy.

FERRARI AGGRADI (MARIO) La svolta economica della resistenza: primi atti della politica di programmazione. [Bologna, 1975]. pp. 202.

ANTONICELLI (FRANCO) La pratica della libertà: documenti, discorsi, scritti politici, 1929-1974. Torino, 1976. pp. 257.

CHIAPPONI (ANNA) Piacenza nella lotta di liberazione, 1943-1945: testimonianze. Piacenza, 1976. pp. 365. *bibliog.*

COLARIZI (SIMONA) Classe operaia e ceti medi. [Venezia, 1976]. pp. 172.

VENICE. Comune. 1943-1945: Venezia nella Resistenza: testimonianze; a cura di Giuseppe Turcato e Agostino Zanon Dal Bo. Venezia, 1976. pp. 609.

POLCRI (ANDREA) Le cause della resistenza italiana. [Milano, 1977]. pp. 171. *bibliog.*

— — Norway.

MEZ (LUTZ) Ziviler Widerstand in Norwegen: Untersuchung zu Organisation und Form der sozialen Bewegung, etc. Frankfurt/Main, [1976]. pp. 376. *bibliog.*

— — Poland.

CZAPSKA-JORDAN (WANDA) W[olność] R[ówność] N[iepodległość]: PPS pod okupacją niemiecką, 1939-1945. Londyn, 1976. pp. 40.

SYZDEK (BRONISŁAW) ed. Działalność PPR na ziemi Rzeszowskiej: szkice, opracowania, wspomnienia: zbiór. Warszawa, 1976. pp. 435.

WOJTAS (ANDRZEJ) Kryzys programu i polityki "Rocha": powstanie SL "Wola Ludu", 1943-1944. [Warszawa], 1976. pp. 179.

PRZYBYSZ (KAZIMIERZ) Konspiracyjny ruch ludowy na Mazowszu, 1939-1945. Warszawa, 1977. pp. 515. *bibliog.*

ZAWODNY (JANUSZ K.) Nothing but honour: the story of the Warsaw Uprising, 1944. London, 1978. pp. 328. *bibliog.*

— — Russia.

PARTIIA vo glave narodnoi bor'by v tylu vraga, 1941-1944 gg. Moskva, 1976. pp. 325.

— — — Russia(RSFSR).

GRIDNEV (VIKTOR MIKHAILOVICH) Bor'ba krest'ianstva okkupirovannykh oblastei RSFSR protiv nemetsko-fashistskoi okkupatsionnoi politiki, 1941-1944. Moskva, 1976. pp. 231. *bibliog.*

— — Yugoslavia.

KOMUNISTIČKA partija Jugoslavije u ratu i revoluciji: istina o narodno oslbodilačkoj [sic] borbi. [München], 1975. pp. 128.

SCOTTI (GIACOMO) "Bono taliano": (gli italiani in Yugoslavia, 1941-43). Milano, [1977]. pp. 167.

— Denmark.

BONVIG CHRISTENSEN (ARNE) Invasion i Danmark?: Danmark i det tyske invasionsforsvar under Den anden Verdenskrig. Odense, 1976. pp. 197. *bibliog. (Odense Universitet. Studies in History and Social Sciences. vol.36)With German summary.*

— Germany.

DEUTSCHLAND im zweiten Weltkrieg; von einem Autorenkollektiv unter Leitung von Wolfgang Schumann [and others];... Herausgeberkollegium: Walter Bartel [and others]. Berlin, 1974 in progress.

Das "ANDERE Deutschland" im Zweiten Weltkrieg: Emigration und Widerstand in internationaler Perspektive: The "Other Germany" in the Second World War...; herausgegeben von Lothar Kettenacker. Stuttgart, 1977. pp. 258. *(Deutsches Historisches Institut in London. Veröffentlichungen. Band 2) In German or English, with summaries in the alternative language.*

GARLIŃSKI (JÓZEF) Hitler's last weapons: the underground war against the V1 and V2. London, 1978. pp. 244. *bibliog.*

— India.

BHUYAN (ARUN CHANDRA) The quit India movement: the Second World War and Indian nationalism. New Delhi, [1975]. pp. 262. *bibliog.*

— Japan.

THORNE (CHRISTOPHER) Allies of a kind: the United States, Britain and the war against Japan, 1941-1945. London, 1978. pp. 772. *bibliog.*

— Poland.

POLAND. Polish Information Center, New York. 1940. German destruction of cultural life in Poland. New York, [1940?]. pp. 23. *(Documents relating to the Administration of Occupied Countries in Eastern Europe. No.2)*

POLAND. Polish Information Center, New York. 1940. The German exploitation of Polish forests. New York, [1940?]. pp. 19. *(Documents relating to the Administration of Occupied Countries in Eastern Europe. No.1)*

POLAND. Polish Information Center, New York. 1941. Extermination of the Polish people and Colonization by German nationals. New York, [1941?]. pp. 46. *(Documents relating to the Administration of Occupied Countries in Eastern Europe. Nos.8 and 9)*

POLAND. Polish Information Center, New York. 1941. German persecution of religious life in Poland. New York, [1941?]. pp. 29. *(Documents relating to the Administration of Occupied Countries in Eastern Europe. No.4)*

— Russia.

MOLOTOV (VIACHESLAV MIKHAILOVICH) Russia and the war: Molotov's speech to the Supreme Soviet of the Soviet Union, October 31st, 1939. London, 1939. pp. 19.

— — Siberia — Bibliography.

SOBOLEVA (ELENA VLADIMIROVNA) and LEBEDEVA (A.N.) compilers. Zapadnaia Sibir' v Velikoi Otechestvennoi voine, 1941-1945 gg.: bibliograficheskii ukazatel'. Novosibirsk, 1973. pp. 167. *bibliog.*

— Sweden.

KARLSSON (RUNE) Så stoppades tysktågen: den tyska transiteringstrafiken i svensk politik, 1942-1943. Stockholm, 1974. pp. 363. *bibliog. With English summary.*

DRANGEL (LOUISE) Den kämpande demokratin: en studie i antinazistisk opinionsrörelse, 1935-1945. Stockholm, 1976. pp. 287. *bibliog. With English summary.*

— United Kingdom.

DONINGTON (ROBERT) ed. Peace aims: a summary of unofficial British opinion expressed since the war; prepared...for the National Peace Council. London, 1940. pp. 67.

— United States.

MELOSI (MARTIN V.) The shadow of Pearl Harbor: political controversy over the surprise attack, 1941-1946. College Station, Tex., [1977]. pp. 183. *bibliog.*

WORTH.

See VALUES.

WRIGHT (FRANK LLOYD).

FISHMAN (ROBERT) Urban utopias in the twentieth century: Ebenezer Howard, Frank Lloyd Wright and Le Corbusier. New York, [1977]. pp. 332. *bibliog.*

WU (P'EI-FU).

WOU (ODORIC YING-KWONG) Militarism in modern China: the career of Wu P'ei-Fu, 1916- 39. Folkestone, 1978. pp. 346. *bibliog. (Columbia University. East Asian Institute. Studies)*

XIKRIN INDIANS.

VIDAL (LUX BOELITZ) Morte e vida de uma sociedade indigena brasileira: os Kayapo- Xikrin do Rio Catete. São Paulo, 1977. pp. 268. *bibliog.*

YAGNOB RIVER.

MADALIEV (NARIMON) Nedra Iagnoba - na sluzhbu narody. Dushanbe, 1976. pp. 130.

YAROSLAVL' (OBLAST')

— Economic history.

ANISKOV (VIKTOR TIKHONOVICH) S polei kolkhoznykh na polia srazhenii: partiino-organizatorskaia deiatel'nost' v iaroslavskoi i kostromskoi derevne v gody Velikoi Otechestvennoi voiny. Iaroslavl', 1975. pp. 208. *bibliog.*

YONNE (DEPARTMENT).

FRANCE. Direction de la Documentation. La Documentation Française. Notes et Etudes Documentaires. Nos. 4,326-4, 327-4,328. Les départements français. 89. Yonne, Bourgogne; (étude...rédigée...par Catherine Johanet). Paris, 1976. pp. 120.

YORK

— History.

YORK ARCHAEOLOGICAL WEEKEND, 4TH, YORK, 1976. Viking age York and the north; [proceedings of the weekend]; edited by R.A. Hall. London, 1978. pp. 73. *bibliog. (Council for British Archaeology. Research Reports. No. 27)*

YORKSHIRE

— Antiquities.

YORK ARCHAEOLOGICAL WEEKEND, 4TH, YORK, 1976. Viking age York and the north; [proceedings of the weekend]; edited by R.A. Hall. London, 1978. pp. 73. *bibliog. (Council for British Archaeology. Research Reports. No. 27)*

YORKSHIRE, SOUTH.

See SOUTH YORKSHIRE.

YORUBAS.

IMOAGENE (OSHOMHA) Social mobility in emergent society: a study of the new elite in western Nigeria. Canberra, 1976. pp. 368. *bibliog. (Australian National University. Research School of Social Sciences. Department of Demography. Changing African Family Project Series. 2)*

YOUNG COMMUNIST LEAGUE

— Russia.

VSESOIUZNYI LENINSKII KOMMUNISTICHESKII SOIUZ MOLODEZHI. Tsentral'nyi Komitet. Dokumenty TsK VLKSM, 1976. Moskva, 1977. pp. 351.

— — Latvia.

ISTORIIA komsomola Latvii v dokumentakh, 1917-1975. Riga, 1977. pp. 527.

— — White Russia.

VOPROSY istorii KPSS: nekotorye voprosy organizatorskoi i ideologicheskoi deiatel'nosti KPSS: mezhvedomstvennyi sbornik 8. Minsk, 1977. pp. 167.

— Yugoslavia.

CVETKOVIĆ (SLAVOLJUB) Napredni omladinski pokret u Jugoslaviji, 1919-1928. [Beograd, 1966]. pp. 284. *bibliog. (Institut Društvenih Nauka. Odeljenje za Istorijske Nauke. Serija 1: Monografije. 7)* With Russian and English summaries.

YOUTH.

BRAKE (MICHAEL DAVID) Hippies and skinheads: sociological aspects of subcultures of working class and middle class youth. [1977]. fo. 324. *bibliog.* Typescript. Ph.D. (London) thesis: unpublished. *This thesis is the property of London University and may not be removed from the Library.*

— Employment — Australia.

AUSTRALIA. Working Party on the Transition from Secondary Education to Employment. 1976. Report; [J.W. Mather then B.C. Milligan, chairman]. Canberra, 1976. pp. 139.

— — Belgium.

DU LAING (M.) and MARIVOET (M.) Situationele benadering van de werkende jongeren in Vlaanderen. Leuven, 1976. 2 vols. (in 1). *bibliog.*

— — Canada — Ontario.

HALL (OSWALD) and CARLTON (RICHARD) Basic skills at school and work: the study of Albertown, an Ontario community. [Toronto, 1977]. pp. 326. *bibliog. (Ontario. Economic Council. Occasional Papers. 1)*

— — European Economic Community countries.

EUROPEAN COMMUNITIES. Commission. 1977. Communication...to the Council on youth employment of 17 October 1977. [Luxembourg], 1977. pp. 35. *(Bulletin of the European Communities. Supplements. [1977/4])*

EUROPEAN COMMUNITIES. Education Committee. 1977. From education to working life: resolution of the Council and of the Ministers of Education...concerning measures to be taken to improve the preparation of young people for work and to facilitate their transition from education to working life, etc. [Brussels, 1977]. pp. 63. *(Bulletin of the European Communities. Supplements. [1976/12])*

— — United Kingdom.

ACTION against youth unemployment; [by] Chris Allinson [and others]; [edited by Jeremy Harrison]. London, 1976. pp. 36.

BIRMINGHAM COMMUNITY DEVELOPMENT PROJECT. Youth on the dole; (by R. Dicker and A. Cochrane). [Oxford], 1977. pp. 24. *(Final Reports. No.4: Young Workers)*

MANPOWER SERVICES COMMISSION [U.K.] Young people and work: report on the feasibility of a new programme of opportunites for unemployed young people. London, 1977. pp. 63.

SIMON (MARTIN) Youth into industry: a study of young people's attitudes to work at a large Midlands factory. Leicester, [1977]. pp. 69.

MANPOWER SERVICES COMMISSION [U.K.]. Young people and work; research studies commissioned and managed by Maureen Colledge, Geoffrey Llewellyn and Vernon Ward. London, H.M.S.O., 1978. pp. 79. *bibliog. (Manpower Studies. No. 19781)*

— — United States.

WILLIAMS (WALTER E.) Youth and minority employment. Stanford, [1977]. pp. 44. *(Stanford University. Hoover Institution on War, Revolution and Peace. Hoover Institution Studies. 61)*

— Religious life.

BERAR (PETRU) Tineretul şi religia. Bucureşti, 1974. pp. 120.

— Australia.

AUSTRALIAN NATIONAL COMMISSION FOR UNESCO. Youth Research Project Sub-Committee. Youth work in Australia. Canberra, 1974 repr. 1976. pp. 57.

AUSTRALIA. Study Group on Youth Affairs. 1977. Report. Canberra, 1977. pp. 36.

— — Victoria.

AUSTRALIA. Department of Immigration. Survey Section. 1967. Survey of youth in Victoria. Canberra, 1967. fo. 230.

— Belgium.

DU LAING (M.) and MARIVOET (M.) Situationele benadering van de werkende jongeren in Vlaanderen. Leuven, 1976. 2 vols. (in 1). *bibliog.*

— Canada.

TUTTLE (GEORGE) Youth organizations in Canada: a reference manual...prepared for the Canadian Youth Commission. Toronto, 1946. pp. 110.

— China.

BERNSTEIN (THOMAS P.) Up to the mountains and down to the villages: the transfer of youth from urban to rural China. New Haven, 1977. pp. 371. *bibliog.*

— Germany — Political activity.

WIESNER (ERICH) Man nannte mich Ernst: Erlebnisse und Episoden aus der Geschichte der Arbeiterjugendbewegung. 4th ed. Berlin, 1978. pp. 316.

— Ghana — Attitudes.

BOAKYE (KWESI J.A.) Occupational activities of rural youth and their attitudes towards craft training: an exploratory study. Cape Coast, 1973. pp. 64, vii. *(University of Cape Coast. Centre for Development Studies. Research Report Series. Papers. No. 16)*

— Italy.

RADI (LUCIANO) Il voto dei giovani. Torino, [1977]. pp. 190.

— Liberia.

AKOI (STEPHEN) and HASSELMANN (KARL-HEINZ) Youth and environment: a Liberian case study on food and nutrition in Buzzi-quarter, Monrovia. [Monrovia], 1975. fo. 32. *bibliog. (University of Liberia. Department of Geography. Occasional Research Papers. No. 9)*

— Portugal.

MENDES (MARIA DE LOURDES) Caracterização estatistica da população jovem portuguesa. Lisboa, 1972. pp. 50. *(Portugal. Ministerio das Corporações e Previdência Social. Serviço de Estatistica. Serie Estatistica. 11)* With abstracts in English and French.

— United Kingdom — Attitudes.

BOYSON (RHODES) Youth and the image of free enterprise. London, [1973]. pp. 6. *(Aims of Industry. The Future of Capitalism.)*

SIMON (MARTIN) Youth into industry: a study of young people's attitudes to work at a large Midlands factory. Leicester, [1977]. pp. 69.

— — Dwellings.

WAUGH (SARAH) Needs and provision for young single homeless people: a review of information and literature. London, 1976. pp. 56. *bibliog.*

REDFERN (MARGARET) Brooks House: an experiment in the provision of accommodation for young people at risk. [Liverpool, 1977]. pp. 76.

YOUTH.(Cont.)

— — Political activity.

REVOLUTIONARY WORKERS PARTY (TROTSKYIST). The role of the Labour Party Young Socialists and the need to use the YS annual conference to prepare the LPYS to act as a revolutionary tendency in the Labour Party. London, 1974. pp. 11.

— United States.

FASS (PAULA S.) The damned and the beautiful: American youth in the 1920's. New York, 1977. pp. 497.

— — Political activity.

SEAGULL (LOUIS M.) Youth and change in American politics. New York, 1977. pp. 160. *bibliog.*

YOUTH VOLUNTEERS IN COMMUNITY DEVELOPMENT

— United Kingdom.

COMMUNITY work through a community newspaper; by YVFF workers in Stoke-on-Trent, John Armstrong, Peter Hudson, Michael Key and independent evaluators, John Whittaker and Marian Whittaker. London, [1976]. pp. 48. *(Young Volunteer Force Foundation. Community and Youth Work Papers)*

YOUTH VOLUNTEERS IN SOCIAL SERVICE

— United Kingdom.

BALL (MOG) Young people as volunteers. Berkhamsted, [1976]. pp. 60. *bibliog.*

COMMUNITY work through a community newspaper; by YVFF workers in Stoke-on-Trent, John Armstrong, Peter Hudson, Michael Key and independent evaluators, John Whittaker and Marian Whittaker. London, [1976]. pp. 48. *(Young Volunteer Force Foundation. Community and Youth Work Papers)*

YUCATAN PENINSULA

— History.

ANTHROPOLOGY and history in Yucatán; edited by Grant D. Jones. Austin, Tex., [1977]. pp. 344. *bibliog.*

YUGOSLAVIA

— Bibliography.

TERRY (GARTH M.) compiler. Yugoslav studies: an annotated list of basic bibliographies and reference works. Twickenham, Middx., 1977. pp. 89. *bibliogs.*

— Commerce.

YUGOSLAVIA. Savezni Zavod za Statistiku. Studije, Analize i Prikazi. 82. Medjusobni odnosi privrednih delatnosti SFR Jugoslavije u 1972. godini: uvoz po delatnostima porekla i namene; Inter-industry relations of the economy of the SFRY in 1972: imports by industries of origin and destination. Beograd, 1976. pp. 51. *With English summary.*

CHITTLE (CHARLES R.) Industrialization and manufactured export expansion in a worker- managed economy: the Yugoslav experience. Tübingen, [1977]. pp. 168. *bibliog.* *(Kiel. Universität. Institut für Weltwirtschaft. Kieler Studien. 145)*

— Constitutional history — Sources.

SAMOUPRAVLJANJE u Jugoslaviji, 1950-1976: dokumenti razvoja. Beograd, 1977. pp. 367.

— Economic conditions.

SOTSIALISTICHESKAIA Federativnaia Respublika Iugoslaviia; redaktsionnaia kollegiia L.A. Nikiforov [and others]. Moskva, 1975. pp. 180. *(Akademiia Nauk SSSR. Institut Ekonomiki Mirovoi Sotsialisticheskoi Sistemy. Ekonomika i Politika Zarubezhnykh Stran Sotsializma)*

AKTUELNI problemi privrednih kretanja i ekonomske politike Jugoslavije: prilozi za Savjetovanje Saveza ekonomista Jugoslavije, Opatija, studeni 1976. Zagreb, 1976. pp. 212.

HORVAT (BRANKO) The Yugoslav economic system: the first labor-managed economy in the making. White Plains, [1976]. pp. 285. *bibliog.* *An expansion and revision of his Yugoslav economic policy in the post-war period.*

AKTUELNI problemi privrednih kretanja i ekonomske politike Jugoslavije: prilozi za Savjetovanje Saveza ekonomista Jugoslavije, Opatija, studeni 1977; redakcija P. Jurković [and others]. Zagreb, 1977. pp. 298.

— — Statistics.

YUGOSLAVIA. Savezni Zavod za Statistiku. Studije, Analize i Prikazi. 81. Medjusobni odnosi privrednih delatnosti SFR Jugoslavije u 1972. godini; Inter-industry relations of the economy of the SFRY in 1972. Beograd, 1976. pp. 118. *With English summary.*

— Economic policy.

AKTUELNI problemi privrednih kretanja i ekonomske politike Jugoslavije: prilozi za Savjetovanje Saveza ekonomista Jugoslavije, Opatija, studeni 1976. Zagreb, 1976. pp. 212.

YUGOSLAVIA. Statutes, etc. Zbirka Saveznih Propisa. Društveni plan Jugoslavije za period od 1976. do 1980. godine. Beograd, 1976. pp. 139. *In Cyrillic.*

AKTUELNI problemi privrednih kretanja i ekonomske politike Jugoslavije: prilozi za Savjetovanje Saveza ekonomista Jugoslavije, Opatija, studeni 1977; redakcija P. Jurković [and others]. Zagreb, 1977. pp. 298.

CHITTLE (CHARLES R.) Industrialization and manufactured export expansion in a worker- managed economy: the Yugoslav experience. Tübingen, [1977]. pp. 168. *bibliog.* *(Kiel. Universität. Institut für Weltwirtschaft. Kieler Studien. 145)*

— Foreign relations.

NINČIĆ (MOMČILO) Spoljna politika Kraljevine Srba, Hrvata i Slovenaca u god. 1922-1924: govori i ekspoze u Narodnoj Skupštini. Beograd, 1924. pp. 147. *In Cyrillic*

RA'ANAN (GAVRIEL D.) Yugoslavia after Tito: scenarios and implications. Boulder, 1977. pp. 206. *bibliog.*

— — Communist countries.

SUKOB s Informbiroom; priredili Maroje Mihovilović, Mario Bošnjak, Sead Saračević. Zagreb, 1976. pp. 145.

— — Russia.

DRASKOVICH (SLOBODAN M.) Tito, Moscow's Trojan horse. Chicago, 1957. pp. 357.

— History — 1941, Coup d'état.

27 mart: "narodni ustanak" ili zavera protiv države. Paris, 1951. pp. 39.

ISTINA o 25. i 27. martu. Paris, 1951. pp. 39.

— Industries.

CHITTLE (CHARLES R.) Industrialization and manufactured export expansion in a worker- managed economy: the Yugoslav experience. Tübingen, [1977]. pp. 168. *bibliog.* *(Kiel. Universität. Institut für Weltwirtschaft. Kieler Studien. 145)*

— Nationalism.

ROGEL (CAROLE) The Slovenes and Yugoslavism, 1890-1914. New York, 1977. pp. 167. *bibliog.* *(East European Quarterly. East European Monographs. 24)*

— Occupations.

PROJEKCIJA dugoročnog razvoja kadrova do 1985; redaktor Jovo Brekić. Zagreb, 1976. pp. 184. *bibliog.* *(Zagreb. Ekonomski Institut. Centar za Kadrologiju i Poslovodne Kadrove. Kadrologijska Biblioteka. Kolo 2)*

BREKIĆ (JOVO) and JURINA (MILAN) Razvoj kadrova i organizacije kadrovske funkcije udruženog rada. Zagreb, 1977. pp. 115. *bibliog.* *(Zagreb. Ekonomski Institut. Centar za Kadrologiju i Poslovodne Kadrove. Kadrologijska Biblioteka. kolo 3)*

SISTEM kadrologije udruženoga rada; redaktor Jovo Brekić. Zagreb, 1977. pp. 132. *bibliog.* *(Zagreb. Ekonomski Institut. Centar za Kadrologiju i Poslovodne Kadrove. Kadrologijska Biblioteka. Kolo 5) With English table of contents and summary.*

SISTEM planiranja razvoja kadrova i obrazovanja samoupravno udruženog rada; redaktori Jovo Brekić i M. Jurina. Zagreb, 1977. pp. 305. *bibliog.* *(Zagreb. Ekonomski Institut. Centar za Kadrologiju i Poslovodne Kadrove. Kadrologijska Biblioteka. Kolo 4, svezak 1) With English table of contents and summary.*

— Politics and government.

BOROWIEC (ANDREW) Yugoslavia after Tito. New York, 1977. pp. 122. *bibliog.*

RA'ANAN (GAVRIEL D.) Yugoslavia after Tito: scenarios and implications. Boulder, 1977. pp. 206. *bibliog.*

SAMOUPRAVLJANJE u Jugoslaviji, 1950-1976: dokumenti razvoja. Beograd, 1977. pp. 367.

YUGOSLAVS IN SWEDEN.

EK (ÅKE) Aspekter på den jugoslaviska invandringen till Sverige. Lund, [1974]. pp. 45. *bibliog.*

ZAIRE.

ZAIRE. Bureau du Président. 1975. 500 visages du Zaire. [Kinshasa, 1975]. pp. 320.

— Description and travel.

DROOGMANS (HUBERT) Le Congo: quatre conférences publiques. Bruxelles, [1895]. pp. 122.

— Economic conditions.

DROOGMANS (HUBERT) Le Congo: quatre conférences publiques. Bruxelles, [1895]. pp. 122.

— Politics and government.

MPINGA-KASENDA. L'administration publique du Zaïre: l'impact du milieu socio- politique sur sa structure et son fonctionnement. Paris, [1973]. pp. 316. *bibliog.* *(Bordeaux. Université. Centre d'Etude d'Afrique Noire. Bibliothèque. Série Afrique Noire. 3)*

ZAIRE UNIVERSITY.

PROBLEMES de l'enseignement supérieur et de développement en Afrique centrale: recueil d'études en l'honneur de Guy Malengreau; [edited by Roman Iakemchuk]. [Paris, 1975]. pp. 227.

ZAMBIA.

Z MAGAZINE (formerly Z: international ed.): pd. m. by Zambia Information Services. m., Je 1969 (no.1)- Lusaka.

— Census.

ZAMBIA. Census, 1974. Sample census of population, 1974: preliminary report. Lusaka, 1975. fo. 10.

— Economic conditions.

HARVEY (CHARLES) Macroeconomics for Africa: the elementary theory of the working of present-day African economics, illustrated by examples taken mainly from the economy of Zambia. London, 1977. pp. 240.

— Economic policy.

ZAMBIA. Ministry of Development Planning. Annual report. a., 1975(1st)- Lusaka.

SHAW (TIMOTHY M.) Dependence and underdevelopment: the development and foreign policies of Zambia. Athens, Ohio, 1976. pp. 60. *bibliog.* *(Ohio University. Center for International Studies. Papers in International Studies. Africa Series. No. 28)*

HARVEY (CHARLES) Macroeconomics for Africa: the elementary theory of the working of present-day African economics, illustrated by examples taken mainly from the economy of Zambia. London, 1977. pp. 240.

— **Emigration and immigration.**

ZAMBIA. Central Statistical Office. Migration statistics: immigrants and visitors. a., 1965- Lusaka.

— **Executive departments.**

ZAMBIA. Department of Technical Education and Vocational Training. Annual report. a., 1974(2nd)- Lusaka.

ZAMBIA. Division of Provincial Administration, National Guidance and Culture. Annual report. a., 1974- Lusaka.

ZAMBIA. Ministry of Development Planning. Annual report. a., 1975(1st)- Lusaka.

— **Foreign relations.**

SHAW (TIMOTHY M.) Dependence and underdevelopment: the development and foreign policies of Zambia. Athens, Ohio, 1976. pp. 60. *bibliog. (Ohio University. Center for International Studies. Papers in International Studies. Africa Series. No. 28)*

— — **Rhodesia.**

INTERNATIONAL DEFENCE AND AID FUND. Special Reports. No. 1. The Rhodesia-Zambia border closure. London, 1973. pp. 26.

— **Frontier troubles.**

INTERNATIONAL DEFENCE AND AID FUND. Special Reports. No. 1. The Rhodesia-Zambia border closure. London, 1973. pp. 26.

— **History.**

ROTBERG (ROBERT IRWIN) Black heart: Gore-Brown and the politics of multiracial Zambia. Berkeley, [1977]. pp. 359. *bibliog.*

— **Industries.**

BHAGAVAN (M.R.) Zambia: impact of industrial strategy on regional imbalance and social inequality. Uppsala, 1978. pp. 76. *(Nordiska Afrikainstitutet. Research Reports. No. 44)*

— **Population.**

ZAMBIA. Division of Provincial Administration, National Guidance and Culture. Annual report. a., 1974- Lusaka.

ZAMBIA. Central Statistical Office. 1975. Fertility data from census questions and from pregancy histories: a comparison. Lusaka, 1975. fo. 30. *bibliog. (Population Monographs. No. 1)*

ZAMBIA. Central Statistical Office. 1975. Inter-regional variations in fertility in Zambia. Lusaka, 1975. fo. 24. *bibliog. (Population Monographs. No. 2)*

— **Social policy.**

ZAMBIA. Ministry of Development Planning. Annual report. a., 1975(1st)- Lusaka.

ZANARDELLI (GIUSEPPE).

CORTI (PAOLA) ed. Inchiesta Zanardelli sulla Basilicata. [Torino, 1976]. pp. 175. *bibliog.*

ZANZIBAR

— **History.**

BENNETT (NORMAN R.) A history of the Arab state of Zanzibar. London, 1978. pp. 304. *bibliog.*

ZASULICH (VERA IVANOVNA).

GEIERHOS (WOLFGANG) Vera Zasulič und die russische revolutionäre Bewegung. München, 1977. pp. 314. *bibliog.*

ZAWADZKI (ALEKSANDER).

WYSZOMIRSKA-KUŹMIŃSKA (OTILDA) Aleksander Zawadzki. Warszawa, 1977. pp. 93.

ZERO-BASE BUDGETING.

WHOLEY (JOSEPH S.) Zero-base budgeting and program evaluation. Lexington, Mass., [1978]. pp. 157.

ZIEGLER (JEAN).

BRODMANN (ROMAN) Der Un-Schweizer: was machen Eidgenossen mit einem Dissidenten?: vom "Fall Ziegler" zum Fall Schweiz. Darmstadt, [1977]. pp. 126.

ZINACANTÁN

— **Religion.**

VOGT (EVON ZARTMAN) Tortillas for the gods: a symbolic analysis of Zinacanteco rituals. Cambridge, Mass., [1976]. pp. 234. *bibliog.*

— **Social life and customs.**

VOGT (EVON ZARTMAN) Tortillas for the gods: a symbolic analysis of Zinacanteco rituals. Cambridge, Mass., [1976]. pp. 234. *bibliog.*

ZJEDNOCZONE STRONNICTWO LUDOWE.

WOJTAS (ANDRZEJ) Kryzys programu i polityki "Rocha": powstanie SL "Wola Ludu", 1943-1944. [Warszawa], 1976. pp. 179.

PRZYBYSZ (KAZIMIERZ) Konspiracyjny ruch ludowy na Mazowszu, 1939-1945. Warszawa, 1977. pp. 515. *bibliog.*

ZNANIECKI (FLORIAN WITOLD).

PACHOLSKI (MAKSYMILIAN) Florian Znaniecki: społeczna dynamika kultury. Warszawa, 1977. pp. 307. *bibliog. With English table of contents.*

ZONING

— **United States.**

BURROWS (LAWRENCE B.) Growth management: issues, techniques and policy implications. New Brunswick, N.J., [1978]. pp. 141. *bibliog.*

ZOROASTRIANISM.

BOYCE (MARY) A Persian stronghold of Zoroastrianism. Oxford, 1977. pp. 284. *bibliog. (Oxford. University. Ratanbai Katrak Lectures. 1975)*

ZUCKERMAN (SOLLY) Baron Zuckerman.

ZUCKERMAN (SOLLY) Baron Zuckerman. From apes to warlords: the autobiography, 1904-1946. London, 1978. pp. 447.

ZUERICH (CITY)

— **Officials and employees.**

TRABER (ALFRED) Geschichte des V[erbandes des] P[ersonals] O[effentlicher] D[ienste], Sektion Zürich, städtische Arbeiter und Angestellte, 1893-1953. [Zürich, 1953]. pp. 229.

ZULUS.

NGUBANE (HARRIET) Body and mind in Zulu medicine: an ethnography of health and disease in Nyuswa-Zulu thought and practice. London, 1977. pp. 184. *bibliog.*

List of subject headings used
in the Bibliography
arranged under topics

TABLE OF SUBJECT SUB-DIVISIONS

SUBJECT SUB-DIVISIONS UNDER NAMES OF CONTINENTS, COUNTRIES, STATES OR TOWNS

Works on the following subjects, if confined to a particular geographical area, are entered not under subject, but under the name of the country, etc., with the subject sub-division.

Administrative and political divisions
Air force
Annexation
Antiquities
Appropriations and expenditures
Armed forces
Army

Bibliography
Bio-bibliography
Biography
Boundaries

Capital
Census
Centennial celebrations, etc
Charters, grants, privileges
Church history
City planning
Civilization
Claims
Climate
Clubs
Colonies
Colonization
Commerce
Commercial policy
Commercial treaties
Constitution
Constitutional conventions
Constitutional history
Constitutional laws
Courts and courtiers

Defences
Description and travel
Dictionaries and encyclopaedias
Diplomatic and consular service
Directories
Discovery and exploration

Economic conditions
Economic history
Economic integration
Economic policy

Emigration and immigration
Executive departments
Exiles

Fairs
Famines
Foreign economic relations
Foreign opinion
Foreign population
Foreign relations
Foreign relations — Treaties
Foreign relations administration

Gazeteers
Genealogy
Gentry
Government property
Government publications
Government vessels
Governors

Historic houses, etc.
Historical geography
History
History, Local
History, Military
History, Naval

Industries
Intellectual life
International status

Kings and rulers

Languages
Learned institutions and societies

Manufactures
Maps
Military policy
Militia
Moral conditions

Nationalism
Native races

Navy
Neutrality
Nobility

Occupations
Officials and employees

Parliament (Congress, Nationalrat, etc.)
Peerage
Politics and government
Population
Presidents
Public buildings
Public lands
Public works

Race question
Registers
Relations (general) with (country)
Relations (military) with (country)
Religion
Religion and mythology
Rural conditions

Sanitary affairs
Seal
Semi-centennial celebrations, etc.
Social conditions
Social history
Social life and customs
Social policy
Statistics
Statistics, Medical
Statistics, Vital
Surveys

Territorial expansion
Territories and possessions
Tornadoes

Vice-Presidents
Voting registers

Year-books

SUBJECT SUB-DIVISIONS USED ONLY UNDER NAMES OF CITIES OR TOWNS

Works on the following matters, if confined to a particular region or country, are entered under the subject, with local sub-division; if confined to a particular city or town, under the name of the city or town, with subject sub-division.

Almshouses and workhouses
Ambulance service
Amusements

Benevolent and moral institutions and societies
Bridges
Buildings

Cemeteries
Charities
Civic improvement
Clubs

Description
Docks

Earthquake
Evening and continuation schools
Exhibitions
Fires and fire prevention

Fortifications

Gilds
Growth

Harbour
Hospitals
Hotels, taverns, etc.

Libraries
Lodging-houses

Markets
Massacre
Music-halls (Variety-theatres, cabarets, etc.)

Office buildings

Parks
Police
Poor
Port

Porters
Prisons and reformatories
Public laundries

Rapid transit
Recreation areas
Recreational activities
Riots

Schools
Sewerage
Stock Exchange (Beurs, Bourse, etc.)
Street cleaning
Streets
Suburbs and environs
Synagogues

Theatres
Transit systems

Water-supply

BIOGRAPHY

AGRICULTURE (including ANIMAL AND PLANT INDUSTRIES)

General.

AERIAL PHOTOGRAPHY IN AGRICULTURE
AFFORESTATION
AGRICULTURAL ADMINISTRATION
AGRICULTURAL ASSISTANCE.
AGRICULTURAL COLONIES
AGRICULTURAL CREDIT.
AGRICULTURAL GEOGRAPHY.
AGRICULTURAL INDUSTRIES
AGRICULTURAL INNOVATIONS.
AGRICULTURAL LAWS AND LEGISLATION
AGRICULTURAL MACHINERY
AGRICULTURAL PRICE SUPPORTS
AGRICULTURAL PRICES
AGRICULTURAL SOCIETIES
AGRICULTURAL WAGES
AGRICULTURE.
AGRICULTURE, COOPERATIVE.
AGRICULTURE AND STATE
ALLOTMENTS
ANIMAL INDUSTRY.
BRITISH COTTON GROWING ASSOCIATION.
CATTLE TRADE
CONSOLIDATION OF LAND HOLDINGS.
COOPERATIVE MARKETING OF FARM PRODUCE
COTTON GROWING
CROPS AND CLIMATE
DAIRY LAWS
DAIRY PRODUCTS.
DAIRYING
DRAINAGE.
FARM INCOME
FARM LIFE
FARM MANAGEMENT.
FARM MECHANIZATION.
FARM PRODUCE
FARM TENANCY
FARMS
FARMS, SIZE OF
FEEDS
FERTILIZER INDUSTRY.
FOREST MANAGEMENT
FOREST PRODUCTS
FOREST SURVEYS
FORESTS AND FORESTRY
FRUIT CULTURE
FRUIT TRADE
FUR TRADE.
HACIENDAS
IRRIGATION.
IRRIGATION CANALS AND FLUMES.
LAND REFORM.
LAND TENURE.
LAND USE, RURAL
LATIFUNDIO
MACHINE TRACTOR STATIONS
MILK SUPPLY
PART TIME FARMING
PLANTATIONS
POULTRY INDUSTRY
PRODUCE TRADE.
ROOT CROPS.
SMALL HOLDINGS.
SOILS
STATE FARMS
STOCK AND STOCK BREEDING
SUGAR GROWING
TROPICAL CROPS.
WOMEN IN AGRICULTURE

Particular animals and animal products.

BACON.
BEEF
BEEF CATTLE
EGGS
GUANO.
MEAT.
MILK
MUTTON
SHEEP
SWINE

Particular crops and plant products.

CITRUS FRUITS
COCOA
COFFEE
FRUIT
GRAIN.
MAIZE.
MARIHUANA.
OILSEED PLANTS.
OLIVE OIL
PEANUTS
PERFUMES.
POTATOES
RICE
SOYA BEANS.
SUGAR
TEA
TIMBER
TOBACCO
VEGETABLES
WHEAT.

Fisheries.

FISH-CULTURE.
FISHERIES
FISHERY LAW AND LEGISLATION.
FISHERY MANAGEMENT.
FISHERY MANAGEMENT, INTERNATIONAL.
WHALING.

BIBLIOGRAPHY AND GENERAL WORKS.

ABBREVIATIONS.
ACCADEMIA D'ITALIA.
ACQUISITIONS (LIBRARIES).
ACRONYMS.
ARCHIVES
BIBLIOGRAPHY
BIBLIOGRAPHY, NATIONAL
BOOKS
BOOKS AND READING.
CATALOGUES, BOOKSELLERS'.
CATALOGUES, LIBRARY.
CATALOGUING IN PUBLICATION.
CIPHERS.
DIARIES
GOVERNMENTAL INVESTIGATIONS
HISTORICAL LIBRARIES
INCUNABULA
INFORMATION NETWORKS.
INFORMATION SERVICES.
INFORMATION STORAGE AND RETRIEVAL SYSTEMS.
INTERNATIONAL FEDERATION OF LIBRARY ASSOCIATIONS.
LIBRARIES
LIBRARIES, PRIVATE
LIBRARIES, UNIVERSITY AND COLLEGE
LIBRARIES AND PUBLISHING.
LIBRARIES AND STUDENTS.
LIBRARY FINANCE
MANUSCRIPTS
MANUSCRIPTS, AZTEC.
MONASTIC LIBRARIES
MUSEUMS
NATIONAL MARITIME MUSEUM.
NEWSPAPER READING.
NORSKE VIDENSKAPS-AKADEMI I OSLO.
PENMANSHIP.
PERIODICALS
PHOTOCOPYING SERVICES
PRINTING
PRINTING, PUBLIC
PUBLIC LIBRARIES
PUBLISHERS AND PUBLISHING
READERSHIP SURVEYS
REFERENCE BOOKS
RESEARCH LIBRARIES
SCHOLARLY PERIODICALS.
SCHOLARLY PUBLISHING
SIGNS AND SYMBOLS.

BIOGRAPHY.

ABERHART (WILLIAM).
ACHEAMPONG (IGNATIUS KUTU).
ACTON FAMILY.
ADAMS (HOWARD).
ADAMS (JOHN) President of the United States.
ADENAUER (KONRAD).
ADORNO (THEODOR WIESENGRUND).
AISHWARYA RAJYA LAXMI DEVI, Crown Princess of Nepal.
ALATA (JEAN PAUL).
ALDRED (GUY ALFRED).
ALEM (LEANDRO NICEFORO).
ALEMAN VALDES (MIGUEL).
ALICATA (MARIO).
ALLENDE (SALVADOR).
ALPHAND (HERVE).
ALVEAR (MARCELO TORCUATO DE).
ANSART (GUSTAVE).
ANTONICELLI (FRANCO).
APPLETON (NATHAN).
ARAFAT (YASIR) pseud.
AREILZA (JOSE MARIA DE) Conde de Motrico.
ARISTOTLE.
ARNOLD (STANISŁAW).
ASQUITH (HERBERT HENRY) 1st Earl of Oxford and Asquith.
AVILA CAMACHO (MANUEL).
AZIZ ISHAK (ABDUL).
BAADER (ANDREAS).
BACHELARD (GASTON).
BACKHOUSE (Sir EDMUND TRELAWNY).
BADER (ERNEST).
BAGRAMIAN (IVAN KHRISTOFOROVICH).
BAIN (JOE STATEN).
BAKUNIN (MIKHAIL ALEKSANDROVICH).
BALFOUR (JABEZ SPENCER).
BALZAC (HONORÉ DE).
BARCLAY (ALEXANDER).
BARTELS (ADOLPHE).
BARTH (KARL).
BECHER (JOHANN JOACHIM).
BENEŠ (EDVARD).
BENTHAM (JEREMY).
BERIIA (LAVRENTII PAVLOVICH).
BERLINGUER (ENRICO).
BERNSTEIN (EDUARD).
BHUTTO (ZULFIKAR ALI).
BIERMANN (WOLF).
BIKO (STEVEN).
BIRENDRA BIR BIKRAM SHAH DEVA, Crown Prince of Nepal.
BISMARCK SCHOENHAUSEN (OTTO EDUARD LEOPOLD VON) Prince.
BLACKWELL (LESLIE).
BLANC (JEAN JOSEPH LOUIS).
BLANCO (ANGEL SATURNINO).
BLANQUI (LOUIS AUGUSTE).
BLOCH (JAN).
BLUM (LEON).
BOEHRINGER (GILL HALE).
BOFFI (LUIS LEOPOLDO).
BOLIVAR (SIMON).

385

BIOGRAPHY (Cont.)

BONNOT DE MABLY (GABRIEL).
BORDEN (Sir ROBERT LAIRD).
BORMANN (MARTIN).
BOTEV (KHRISTO).
BOTTAI (GIUSEPPE).
BOYLE (JIMMY).
BRETT FAMILY.
BROCHER (VICTORINE).
BROOKES (EDGAR HARRY).
BROWN (MARY ANNE DAY).
BUOL-SCHAUENSTEIN (CARL FERDINAND VON) Graf.
BUSONI (JAURÈS).
BUTLER (SAMUEL) Philosophical writer.
CABRERA (LUIS).
CAFFI (ANDREA).
CANGUILHEM (GEORGES).
CANNON (JAMES PATRICK).
CANTIMORI (DELIO).
CAPODISTRIA (JOHN) Count.
CARDENAS (LAZARO).
CARPENTER (EDWARD).
CARTER (JAMES EARL) President of the United States.
CASSATT (ALEXANDER JOHNSTON).
CASSIODORUS (MAGNUS AURELIUS).
CASTELLO BRANCO (HUMBERTO DE ALENCAR).
CASTRO RUZ (FIDEL).
CATTANEO (CARLO).
CEAUSESCU (NICOLAE).
CECIL (ROBERT ARTHUR TALBOT GASCOYNE) 3rd Marquess of Salisbury
CECIL (WILLIAM) Baron Burghley.
CHAMBERLAIN (JOSEPH).
CHAMBERS (WHITTAKER).
CHANG (TSO-LIN).
CHASTENET DE GERY (J.)
CHEGARAY (THOMAS and PIERRE ANTOINE).
CHESTERTON (GILBERT KEITH).
CHILDERS (ERSKINE).
CHILDS (MARQUIS WILLIAM).
CHOU (EN-LAI).
CHURCHILL (Sir WINSTON LEONARD SPENCER).
CLARKE (JOHN SMITH).
CLAUSEWITZ (CARL VON).
CLEREL DE TOCQUEVILLE (CHARLES ALEXIS HENRI MAURICE) Comte.
COBBETT (WILLIAM).
CODOVILLA (VICTORIO).
COEUR (JACQUES).
COLBY (WILLIAM EGAN).
COLLINS (LEWIS JOHN).
COMTE (ISIDORE AUGUSTE MARIE FRANÇOIS XAVIER).
CONNOLLY (JAMES).
COXE (TENCH).
CROCE (BENEDETTO).
CROMWELL (OLIVER) Lord Protector.
CROMWELL (THOMAS) 1st Earl of Essex.
CUMMINGS (EDWARD ESTLIN).
DALADIER (EDOUARD).
DASH (SAMUEL).
DEBRAY (REGIS).
DEGRELLE (LEON).
DELČEV (GOCE).
DELORS (JACQUES).
DENNIS (PEGGY).
DESCARTES (RENE).
DIAZ (PORFIRIO).
DIETZGEN (JOSEPH).
DISRAELI (BENJAMIN) 1st Earl of Beaconsfield.
DJILAS (MILOVAN).
DOUGLAS (WILLIAM ORVILLE).
DU BOIS (WILLIAM EDWARD BURGHARDT).
DULLES (JOHN FOSTER).
DULLES FAMILY.
DUNANT (JEAN HENRI).

DUPONT (PIERRE SAMUEL).
DURKHEIM (EMILE).
DZERZHINSKII (FELIKS EDMUNDOVICH).
EBAN (ABBA SOLOMON).
EHLERS (ADOLF).
EILDERMANN (WILHELM).
EINAUDI (LUIGI).
EISENHOWER (DWIGHT DAVID) President of the United States.
EL SADAT (ANWAR).
ELDER (GLADYS).
ELIZABETH I, Queen of England.
ELLIS (HENRY HAVELOCK).
ENGEL (CORNELIS J.M.).
ENGELS (FRIEDRICH).
ERHARD (LUDWIG).
ERIKSON (ERIK HOMBURGER).
EUGENE FRANCIS, Prince of Savoy.
FABIAN (WALTER).
FACERIAS (JOSE LLUIS).
FAULKNER (ARTHUR BRIAN DEANE) Baron Faulkner.
FEDOSEEV (NIKOLAI EVGRAFOVICH).
FERRARI (GIUSEPPE).
FERREIRA DA SILVA (VIRGOLINO) known as Lampião.
FEUERBACH (LUDWIG ANDREAS).
FLATHER (HORACE).
FORD (GERALD RUDOLPH) President of the United States.
FOSTER (JOHN) 1740-1828.
FOUCAULT (MICHEL).
FOURIER (FRANÇOIS CHARLES MARIE).
FRANKLIN (BENJAMIN).
FREDERICK II, King of Prussia.
FRIGERIO (ROGELIO).
FUENTES (CARLOS).
GAITAN (JORGE ELIECER).
GALLEANI (LUIGI).
GANDHI (INDIRA).
GANDHI (MOHANDAS KARAMCHAND).
GARFIELD (JAMES ABRAM) President of the United States.
GARIBALDI (GIUSEPPE).
GASPERI (ALCIDE DE).
GAULLE (CHARLES DE).
GEDDES (Sir PATRICK).
GEISEL (ERNESTO).
GEORGE (DAVID LLOYD) 1st Earl Lloyd George.
GERTSEN (ALEKSANDR IVANOVICH).
GIANNOTTI (DONATO).
GIBBON (EDWARD).
GILL (ARTHUR ERIC ROWTON).
GISCARD D'ESTAING (VALERY).
GODWIN (MARY).
GODWIN (WILLIAM).
GOKHALE (GOPAL KRISHNA).
GOLLANCZ (Sir VICTOR).
GOMEZ (JUAN GUALBERTO).
GOMEZ (JUAN VICENTE).
GONZI (MICHAEL) Archbishop of Malta.
GOODMAN (PAUL).
GORDON (CHARLES GEORGE).
GORDON (WALTER LOCKHART).
GORE-BROWN (Sir STEWART).
GORST (Sir ELDON).
GOULD (JULIUS).
GRAMSCI (ANTONIO).
GRAZIADEI (ANTONIO).
GRECO (JUAN).
GREEN (THOMAS HILL).
GREENE (ROGER SHERMAN).
GREGORY I, Saint, surnamed the Great, Pope.
GRIBOEDOV (ALEKSANDR SERGEEVICH).
GRISEBACH (EBERHARD).
GROOTE (NICHOLAS DE).
GUEVARA (ERNESTO).
GUROWSKI (ADAM).
HANCOCK (GORDON BLAINE).
HARASZTI (MIKLÓS).
HARBORNE (WILLIAM).

HARDIE (JAMES KEIR).
HARRISON (FREDERIC).
HARTSHORNE (CHARLES).
HAYA DE LA TORRE (VICTOR RAUL).
HAYEK (FRIEDRICH AUGUST).
HAYTER (LOUIS HENRY).
HEGEL (GEORG WILHELM FRIEDRICH).
HEINEMANN (GUSTAV WALTER).
HEINITZ (FRIEDRICH ANTON VON) Freiherr.
HELMER (JEF).
HERBST (STANISŁAW).
HEREN (LOUIS).
HERON (HUGH).
HERR (LUCIEN).
HERREMA (TIEDE).
HERRERA (TOMAS).
HESS (MOSES).
HEYDRICH (REINHARD).
HISS (ALGER).
HITLER (ADOLF).
HÔ CHI MINH.
HODGSKIN (THOMAS).
HOEGNER (WILHELM).
HOFMAIER (KARL).
HOFMANN (JOSEF).
HOFMANNSTHAL (HUGO VON).
HOLMES (G.V.).
HOOVER (HERBERT CLARK) President of the United States.
HOWARD (Sir EBENEZER).
HUGENBERG (ALFRED).
HUGO (VICTOR MARIE) Vicomte.
HUME (DAVID).
HUSÁK (GUSTÁV).
IAROSLAVSKII (EMEL'IAN MIKHAILOVICH).
IGLESIAS POSSE (PABLO).
IKONOMOV (TODOR).
ILLICH (IVAN D.).
IRIGOYEN (BERNARDO DE).
IRIGOYEN (HIPOLITO).
JACKSON (ANDREW) President of the United States.
JACKSON (GEORGE LESTER).
JACOBS (ALETTA HENRIETTE).
JACOBY (JOHANN).
JAKSCH (WENZEL).
JANSSON (ERIK).
JEFFERSON (THOMAS) President of the United States.
JENSEN (ARTHUR R.).
JEVONS (WILLIAM STANLEY).
JINNAH (MOHAMED ALI).
JOHNSON (HARRY GORDON)
JONES (Sir ALFRED LEWIS).
JONES (REGINALD VICTOR).
KAISEN (WILHELM).
KAMITZ (REINHARD).
KARAMZIN (NIKOLAI MIKHAILOVICH).
KARAVELOV (LIUBEN).
KELSEN (HANS).
KENNEDY (JOHN FITZGERALD) President of the United States
KENNEDY (ROBERT FRANCIS).
KEYNES (JOHN MAYNARD) 1st Baron Keynes.
KHAMA (BOIKANYO) Chief of the Ngwato.
KILLIAN (JAMES RHYNE).
KIM (IL-SUNG).
KING (MARTIN LUTHER).
KIREEVSKII (IVAN VASIL'EVICH).
KISSINGER (HENRY ALFRED).
KOLLEK (TEDDY).
KOLLONTAI (ALEKSANDRA MIKHAILOVNA).
KOMAROV (NIKOLAI PAVLOVICH) pseud.
KORSCH (KARL).
KOSSUTH (LAJOS).
KOT (STANISŁAW).
KROGMANN (CARL VINCENT).
KROPOTKIN (PETR ALEKSEEVICH) Prince.

BIOGRAPHY (Cont.)

KUBITSCHEK DE OLIVEIRA (JUSCELINO).
KULA (WITOLD)
KULISHEVA (ANNA MIKHAILOVNA).
LA FOLLETTE (ROBERT MARION) the Younger.
LAMBTON (JOHN GEORGE) 1st Earl of Durham.
LAMONT (DONAL) Bishop of Umtali.
LAMONT (THOMAS WILLIAM).
LARKIN (JAMES JOSEPH).
LASKI (HAROLD JOSEPH).
LASSALLE (FERDINAND JOHANN GOTTLIEB).
LEBER (JULIUS).
LE BRUN (JOYCE).
LE CORBUSIER ( ) pseud. [i.e. Charles Edouard JEANNERET].
LE MERCIER DE LA RIVIERE (PIERRE FRANÇOIS JOACHIM HENRI).
LENCINAS (JOSE NESTOR).
LENIN (VLADIMIR IL'ICH).
LEOPOLD I, Emperor of Germany.
LEROUX (PIERRE) Socialist.
LE ROY LADURIE (EMMANUEL).
LEWIS (JOHN LLEWELLYN).
LIBELT (KAROL).
LIEBKNECHT (WILHELM PHILIPP MARTIN CHRISTIAN LUDWIG).
LINCOLN (ABRAHAM) President of the United States.
LIVINGSTONE (DAVID).
LOCKE (JOHN).
LORER (NIKOLAI IVANOVICH).
LOUGHLIN (ANNE).
LOWTHER (Sir CHRISTOPHER).
LUSSO (EMILIO).
LYSENKO (TROFIM DENISOVICH).
McCARTHY (JOSEPH RAYMOND).
MACCHIAVELLI (NICCOLÒ).
MACEO (ANTONIO).
McGOVERN (GEORGE STANLEY).
MACKIEWICZ (STANISŁAW).
McSHANE (HARRY).
MAISEL (KARL).
MAKHNO (NESTOR).
MALRAUX (ANDRE).
MANDEVILLE (BERNARD DE).
MANNHEIM (KARL).
MAO (TSE-TUNG).
MARSH (Sir RICHARD WILLIAM).
MARX (KARL).
MATHER (COTTON).
MATHER (INCREASE).
MATHER (RICHARD).
MATTEI (ENRICO).
MAURRAS (CHARLES MARIE PHOTIUS).
MEDICI FAMILY.
MEDVEDEV (ROI ALEKSANDROVICH).
MEES (WILLEM CORNELIS).
MEINHOF (ULRIKE MARIE).
MENDÈS-FRANCE (PIERRE).
MENGER (ANTON).
MENSDORFF-POUILLY (ALEXANDER) Graf.
MERCATOR (GERARDUS).
MERCIER (HONORE).
MICHELET (JULES).
MICKIEWICZ (ADAM).
MISES (LUDWIG VON).
MITRIONE (DAN).
MITTERRAND (FRANÇOIS).
MOLYNEUX (WILLIAM).
MONTESSORI (MARIA).
MOORE (CHARLES GARRETT PONSONBY) 11th Earl of Drogheda.
MORGAN (Sir CHARLES).
MORLEY (JOHN) Viscount Morley of Blackburn.
MORO (ALDO).
MORRIS (WILLIAM).
MORRISON (GEORGE ERNEST).
MOSCA (GAETANO).

MUCKERMANN (FRIEDRICH JOSEPH).
MUELLER VON NITERSDORF (ADAM HEINRICH).
MULDOON (ROBERT DAVID).
MULLAN (JOHN PAT).
MUÑOZ (ERASMO).
MUSSOLINI (BENITO).
NA'INI (MIRZA MUHAMMAD HUSAYN).
NAPOLEON I, Emperor of the French.
NARAYAN (JAYAPRAKASH).
NASSER (GAMAL ABDEL).
NENNI (PIETRO).
NGUYEN THI DINH.
NIELSEN (FRITZ WALTER).
NIETZSCHE (FRIEDRICH WILHELM).
NIN (ANDREU).
NIXON (RICHARD MILHOUS) President of the United States.
NKRUMAH (KWAME).
NORRIS (GEORGE WILLIAM).
NOYES (JOHN HUMPHREY).
O'BRIEN (CONOR CRUISE).
O'BRIEN (EDNA).
OCAMPO (MELCHOR).
OGAREV (NIKOLAI PLATONOVICH).
OGLETHORPE (JAMES EDWARD).
O'MALLEY (ERNIE).
PAKENHAM (FRANCIS AUNGIER) 7th Earl of Longford.
PARETO (VILFREDO).
PARNELL (CHARLES STEWART).
PARSONS (LUCY ELLA).
PARSONS (TALCOTT).
PASCAL (PIERRE).
PAUL, Saint and Apostle.
PEARSE (PATRICK).
PEARSON (ANTHONY).
PEARSON (LESTER BOWLES).
PECCHIO (GIUSEPPE).
PELIKÁN (JIŘÍ).
PELLOUTIER (FERNAND).
PERDIGUIER (AGRICOL).
PERON (JUAN DOMINGO).
PÉTAIN (HENRI PHILIPPE BÉNONI OMER JOSEPH).
PETER I, called the Great, Emperor of Russia.
PETTY (Sir WILLIAM).
PHILIPS (FREDERIK).
PHILLIPS (ALBAN WILLIAM HOUSEGO).
PIAGET (JEAN).
PIECK (WILHELM).
PISACANE (CARLO).
PITT (Right Hon. WILLIAM).
PITT (WILLIAM) Earl of Chatham.
PIVERT (MARCEAU).
PLAZA (VICTORINO DE LA).
PLEYDELL-BOUVERIE (WILLIAM) 3rd Earl of Radnor.
PLIUSHCH (LEONID IVANOVICH).
POLO (MARCO).
POLYBIUS, the Historian.
POMPIDOU (GEORGES).
PONCE (ANIBAL).
POPP (ADELHEID).
POPPER (Sir KARL RAIMUND).
POUJADE (PIERRE).
POWELL (JOHN ENOCH).
PROUDHON (PIERRE JOSEPH).
QUINET (EDGAR).
RADISHCHEV (ALEKSANDR NIKOLAEVICH).
RAINER (FERDINAND MARIA JOHANN EVANGELISTA FRANZ HYGINUS) Erzherzog, 1827-1913.
RAINEY (HENRY THOMAS).
RAMSDEN FAMILY.
RANDOLPH (ASA PHILIP).
RANKE (LEOPOLD VON).
RAPIER (JAMES T.).
RASPAIL (FRANÇOIS VINCENT).
RECABARREN (LUIS EMILIO).
RECLUS (ELIE).

RECLUS (JEAN JACQUES ELISEE).
RECLUS (PAUL).
REPETTO (NICOLAS).
RHEGAS, of Velestino.
RICARDO (DAVID).
RICCARDI FAMILY.
RICHARDSON (EVERETT).
RIGOLA (RINALDO).
RIVADAVIA (BERNARDINO).
ROOSEVELT (FRANKLIN DELANO) President of the United States.
ROOSEVELT (THEODORE) President of the United States.
ROSAS (JUAN MANUEL DE).
ROSENBERG (ALFRED).
ROUSSEAU (JEAN JACQUES).
ROY (MANABENDRA NATH)
RYAN (THOMAS JOSEPH).
RYCHLIŃSKI (STANISŁAW).
SACCO (NICOLA).
SAENZ PEÑA (ROQUE).
ŞAGUNA (ANDREIU) Baron.
SALAZAR (ROSENDO).
SALTYKOV-SHCHEDRIN (MIKHAIL EVGRAFOVICH).
SANGER (MARGARET).
SANGUINETTI (GIANFRANCO).
SAUER (PAUL OLIVER).
SCHELLING (FRIEDRICH WILHELM JOSEPH VON).
SCHELSKY (HELMUT).
SCHLESINGER (MORITZ).
SCHMID-AMMANN (PAUL).
SCHMIDT (HELMUT) Federal German Chancellor.
SCHOONBEKE (GILBERT VAN).
SCHOPENHAUER (ARTHUR).
SEARS (ROBERT RICHARDSON).
SECONDAT (CHARLES LOUIS DE) Baron de Montesquieu.
SERANTINI (FRANCO).
SERGE (VICTOR) pseud.
SHAW (CHARLES).
SHIRAGIAN (ARSHAVIR).
SIMON (JULES).
SIMON (JULIUS).
SIMON (ULRICH).
SIMONDE DE SISMONDI (JEAN CHARLES LEONARD).
SINDONA (MICHELE).
SITHOLE (NDABANINGI).
SLATER (JAMES DERRICK).
SLAVEIKOV (PETKO RACHEV).
SMITH (ADAM).
SMITH (ALBERT EDWARD).
SMITH (CYRIL).
SMITH (FREDERICK EDWIN) 1st Earl of Birkenhead.
SMOLEŃSKI (WŁADYSŁAW).
SMOLLETT (TOBIAS).
SOCRATES.
SOKOLSKY (GEORGE EPHRAIM).
SOLZHENITSYN (ALEKSANDR ISAEVICH).
SOMOZA FAMILY.
SOREL (GEORGES).
SPENCER (HERBERT).
SPENDER (STEPHEN).
SRAFFA (PIERO).
STACK (AUSTIN).
STALIN (IOSIF VISSARIONOVICH).
STAMBOLIISKI (ALEKSANDUR STOIMENOV).
STAMMLER (RUDOLF).
STANLEY (EDWARD GEORGE GEOFFREY SMITH) 14th Earl of Derby.
STANLEY (EDWARD HENRY SMITH) 15th Earl of Derby.
STEFCZYK (FRANCISZEK).
STERN (MIKHAIL).
STOIANOV (ZAKHARI).
STOLYPIN (PETR ARKAD'EVICH).
STRAUSS (DAVID FRIEDRICH).

BIOGRAPHY (Cont.)

STREICHER (JULIUS).
STRESEMANN (GUSTAV).
STURZO (LUIGI).
SUTTER (JOSEPH ANTON).
SVERDLOV (IAKOV MIKHAILOVICH).
SWINTON (JOHN).
TALLEYRAND-PERIGORD (CHARLES MAURICE DE) Prince.
TANAKA (SHOZO).
TARASHKEVICH (BRANISLAU ADAMAVICH).
TAYLOR (MOSES).
THAELMANN (ERNST).
THATCHER (MARGARET).
THOMAS (FRANCIS).
THORNETT (ALAN).
TIETGEN (CARL FREDERIK).
TITMUSS (RICHARD MORRIS).
TITO (JOSIP BROZ).
TKACHEV (PETR NIKITICH).
TOGLIATTI (PALMIRO).
TORNAU (FEDOR FEDOROVICH).
TORRE (LISANDRO DE LA).
TORRE BLANCO (JOSE).
TROTSKII (LEV DAVYDOVICH).
TRUDEAU (PIERRE ELLIOTT).
TRUMAN (HARRY S.) President of the United States.
TUCKER (NATHANIEL BEVERLEY).
TURATI (FILIPPO).
TURGOT (ANNE ROBERT JACQUES) Baron de l'Aulne.
UELAND (OLE GABRIEL GABRIELSEN).
UL'IANOV (ALEKSANDR IL'ICH)
VAN HEIJENOORT (JEAN).
VANZETTI (BARTOLOMEO).
VARGAS (GETULIO).
VARLIN (EUGENE).
VEBLEN (THORSTEIN).
VICKERS FAMILY.
VICTOR, LE SAUVAGE DE L'AVEYRON.
VOLPE (GALVANO DELLA).
VORSTER (BALTHAZAR JOHANNES).
VOYADZIS (VASILIOS TH.).
WAGNER (ADOLPH).
WAKSTEIN (CHARLES).
WALRAS (LEON).
WARD (GEORGE).
WARD (LESTER FRANK).
WAXWEILER (EMILE).
WEBB (BEATRICE).
WEBB (SIDNEY) 1st Baron Passfield.
WEBSTER (DANIEL).
WEBSTER (MILTON P.).
WEHNER (HERBERT).
WENDEL FAMILY.
WESTPHAL (SIEGFRIED).
WICKSELL (JOHAN GUSTAF KNUT)
WIESNER (ERICH).
WILLIAM I, Prince of Orange.
WILLIAMS (HENRY SYLVESTER).
WILSON (Sir HAROLD).
WILSON (MALCOLM).
WILSON (Sir ROBERT).
WILSON (THOMAS WOODROW) President of the United States.
WOODS (DONALD).
WOOLF (LEONARD SIDNEY).
WRIGHT (FRANK LLOYD).
WU (P'EI-FU).
ZANARDELLI (GIUSEPPE).
ZASULICH (VERA IVANOVNA).
ZAWADZKI (ALEKSANDER).
ZIEGLER (JEAN).
ZNANIECKI (FLORIAN WITOLD).
ZUCKERMAN (SOLLY) Baron Zuckerman.

COMMERCE AND INDUSTRY.

General.

ACCOUNTING.
ACCOUNTING AND PRICE FLUCTUATIONS.
ADVERTISING.
ADVERTISING, CORRECTIVE.
ADVERTISING, PUBLIC SERVICE.
ADVERTISING AGENCIES
ALCOHOLISM AND EMPLOYMENT.
APPRENTICES
ARBITRATION, INDUSTRIAL
AUDITING.
BIG BUSINESS
BUDGET IN BUSINESS.
BUSINESS.
BUSINESS AND POLITICS
BUSINESS CYCLES.
BUSINESS EDUCATION
BUSINESS ETHICS.
BUSINESS RELOCATION
BUSINESS TRAVEL.
BUYING.
CENTRAL AMERICAN COMMON MARKET.
CENTRAL BUSINESS DISTRICTS
CHAMBERS OF COMMERCE.
COMMERCE.
COMMERCIAL POLICY.
COMMERCIAL PRODUCTS
COMMERCIAL TREATIES.
COMMODITY CONTROL.
COMMODITY EXCHANGES.
COMMUNICATION IN ORGANIZATIONS.
CONSOLIDATION AND MERGER OF CORPORATIONS
CONSUMER EDUCATION
CONSUMER PROTECTION
CONSUMERS.
CONSUMERS' PREFERENCES.
COOPERATION.
COOPERATIVE SOCIETIES.
CORPORATE DIVESTITURE.
CORPORATE PLANNING.
CORPORATION REPORTS
CORPORATIONS.
CORPORATIONS, AMERICAN.
CORPORATIONS, BRITISH
CORPORATIONS, CANADIAN
CORPORATIONS, FOREIGN
CORPORATIONS, NON-PROFIT.
CORPORATIONS, PUBLIC
CORPORATIONS, SWISS
DANGEROUS GOODS
DUMPING (COMMERCIAL POLICY).
EAST-WEST TRADE (1945-).
EFFICIENCY, INDUSTRIAL.
EMBARGO.
EMPLOYEE OWNERSHIP
EMPLOYEE RIGHTS
EMPLOYEES, DISMISSAL OF
EMPLOYEES, RATING OF.
EMPLOYEES, RELOCATION OF
EMPLOYEES, TRAINING OF.
EMPLOYEES' REPRESENTATION IN MANAGEMENT.
EMPLOYERS' ASSOCIATIONS
EMPLOYMENT FORECASTING
ENTREPRENEUR.
EUROPEAN COAL AND STEEL COMMUNITY.
EUROPEAN ECONOMIC COMMUNITY.
EXECUTIVE ABILITY.
EXPORT CREDIT.
EXPORT MARKETING.
EXPORT PREMIUMS.
FACTORIES.
FACTORY MANAGEMENT.
FACTORY SYSTEM
FIRMS.
FOOD PRICES
FOREIGN TRADE PROMOTION.
FOREIGN TRADE REGULATION.
FRANCHISES (RETAIL TRADE).
GOVERNMENT ADVERTISING.
GOVERNMENT BUSINESS ENTERPRISES
HOLDING COMPANIES.
HUMAN CAPITAL.
HYDROGEN AS FUEL.
IMPORT SUBSTITUTION
INCENTIVES IN INDUSTRY
INDUSTRIAL ACCIDENTS
INDUSTRIAL CONCENTRATION.
INDUSTRIAL EQUIPMENT
INDUSTRIAL HOUSING
INDUSTRIAL HYGIENE
INDUSTRIAL MANAGEMENT.
INDUSTRIAL NOISE
INDUSTRIAL ORGANIZATION.
INDUSTRIAL PROJECT MANAGEMENT.
INDUSTRIAL PROMOTION
INDUSTRIAL PROPERTY
INDUSTRIAL RELATIONS.
INDUSTRIAL SAFETY
INDUSTRIAL STATISTICS.
INDUSTRIALIZATION.
INDUSTRIES, LOCATION OF.
INDUSTRIES, SIZE OF.
INDUSTRY.
INDUSTRY AND STATE.
INFLATION (FINANCE) AND ACCOUNTING.
INTERNATIONAL BUSINESS ENTERPRISES.
INVENTORY CONTROL.
KONSUMVEREIN TEESDORF.
LATIN AMERICAN FREE TRADE ASSOCIATION.
LEGA NAZIONALE DELLE COOPERATIVE E MUTUE.
LICENCES
LOMÉ, CONVENTION OF.
MACHINERY IN INDUSTRY.
MANAGEMENT.
MANAGEMENT INFORMATION SYSTEMS.
MANAGEMENT RIGHTS.
MANAGERIAL ACCOUNTING.
MANUAL TRAINING
MANUFACTURES.
MARKET SURVEYS
MARKETING.
MARKETING BOARDS.
MARKETING MANAGEMENT.
MARKETING RESEARCH
MARKS OF ORIGIN.
MEDIATION AND CONCILIATION, INDUSTRIAL
METHODS ENGINEERING.
METRIC SYSTEM.
MOTIVATION RESEARCH (MARKETING).
NONTARIFF TRADE BARRIERS.
OCCUPATIONAL MOBILITY
OCCUPATIONAL TRAINING
OCCUPATIONS
OFFICE BUILDINGS.
OPERATIONS RESEARCH.
ORGANIZATION OF THE PETROLEUM EXPORTING COUNTRIES.
PATENTS
PERSONNEL MANAGEMENT.
POWER RESOURCES.
PRECAST CONCRETE CONSTRUCTION.
PRODUCTION CONTROL.
PRODUCTION MANAGEMENT.
PRODUCTION PLANNING.
PRODUCTIVITY.
PROFESSIONS.
PROMOTIONS
PUBLIC CONTRACTS
PUBLIC UTILITIES
PUBLICITY.
QUALITY CONTROL.
RAW MATERIALS.

COMMERCE AND INDUSTRY

RESEARCH, INDUSTRIAL.
RESTRICTIVE PRACTICES IN INDUSTRIAL RELATIONS.
RETAIL TRADE.
ROLE CONFLICT.
SANTA FE TRAIL.
SCHEDULING (MANAGEMENT).
SERVICE INDUSTRIES
SHOPPING
SHOPPING CENTRES
SMALL BUSINESS
STANDARDIZATION
STORE LOCATION.
STORES, RETAIL.
TECHNICIANS IN INDUSTRY.
TOKYO ROUND, 1973-1977.
TRADE REGULATION
UNITED NATIONS CONFERENCE ON TRADE AND DEVELOPMENT.
VOCATIONAL GUIDANCE.
VOCATIONAL GUIDANCE FOR WOMEN
VOCATIONAL INTERESTS
WELFARE WORK IN INDUSTRY
WHOLESALE TRADE
WOMEN IN BUSINESS
WORK.
WORK DESIGN.
WORK MEASUREMENT.
WORKMEN'S COMPENSATION

Occupations and professions.

ACCOUNTANTS.
AGRICULTURAL LABOURERS
AGRICULTURISTS
ARTISANS
AUTOMOBILE INDUSTRY WORKERS
BANK EMPLOYEES
BLACKSMITHS
BUSINESSMEN
CAPITALISTS AND FINANCIERS
CLOTHING WORKERS
COAL MINERS
COMMERCIAL AGENTS
CONSTRUCTION WORKERS
CORONERS
CRIMINOLOGISTS
DAY CARE AIDES
DENTAL HYGIENISTS
DIPLOMATS.
DIPLOMATS, FRENCH
DIRECTORS OF CORPORATIONS
DOCK WORKERS
ELECTRONIC DATA PROCESSING PERSONNEL
ENGINEERS
EXECUTIVES.
FARMERS
FARMERS' WIVES
FISHERMEN
GOLD MINERS
HOSIERY WORKERS
IRON AND STEEL WORKERS
JOURNALISTS
JUDGES
LAWYERS
MEDICAL PERSONNEL
MERCHANTS
METAL WORKERS
MIDWIVES
MIGRANT AGRICULTURAL LABOURERS
MINERS
NURSES AND NURSING.
PERSONNEL DIRECTORS.
PHYSICIANS
PHYSICISTS
PLUMBERS
POETS
POLITICIANS
PORTERS
POTTERS

PRINTERS
PSYCHIATRIC PERSONNEL
PUBLIC HEALTH PERSONNEL
PUBLIC PROSECUTORS
PUBLIC RELATIONS AS A PROFESSION.
ROAD CONSTRUCTION WORKERS
ROAD TRANSPORT WORKERS
SCIENTISTS
SEAMEN
SERVANTS
SHOP ASSISTANTS
SOCIAL WORK AS A PROFESSION.
SOCIAL WORKERS.
SOCIOLOGY AS A PROFESSION.
TEACHERS.
TEXTILE WORKERS
TOBACCO WORKERS
TRANSPORT WORKERS
WEAVERS
WOMEN BANKERS
WOMEN FARMERS.
WOODWORKERS

Particular firms, trades and industries.

AEROSPACE INDUSTRIES
ALUMINIUM INDUSTRY AND TRADE
ART INDUSTRIES AND TRADE
ATOMIC ENERGY INDUSTRIES
ATOMIC POWER INDUSTRY
ATOMIC POWER-PLANTS
AUTOMOBILE INDUSTRY AND TRADE.
BAKERS AND BAKERIES
BEER.
BEVERAGES.
BOOK INDUSTRIES AND TRADE
BOOTS AND SHOES
BREAD
BREEDER REACTORS.
BREWING INDUSTRIES
BUILDING FAILURES.
BUILDING MATERIALS.
BUILDING MATERIALS INDUSTRY.
BUILDING TRADES
BUILDINGS, PREFABRICATED.
CANNING AND PRESERVING
CARPETS.
CATERERS AND CATERING
CATTLE TRADE
CEMENT INDUSTRIES
CEREAL PRODUCTS.
CEREALS AS FOOD.
CHARLES ROBERTS AND COMPANY.
CHEMICAL INDUSTRIES.
CHUBB AND SON'S LOCK AND SAFE COMPANY.
CIVIL ENGINEERING
CLOCK AND WATCH MAKING
CLOTHING TRADE
COAL
COAL MINES AND MINING.
COAL TRADE
COCOA TRADE.
COFFEE TRADE.
CONSTRUCTION EQUIPMENT
CONSTRUCTION INDUSTRY
COPPER INDUSTRY AND TRADE.
COPPER MINES AND MINING
CORAL INDUSTRY AND TRADE
COTTAGE INDUSTRIES
COTTON MANUFACTURE
COTTON TRADE
DANISH BACON COMPANY.
DE GROOTE (FIRM).
DIAMOND INDUSTRY AND TRADE
DOWLAIS IRON COMPANY.
DRUG TRADE.
DYES AND DYEING.
EDWARD WOOD AND COMPANY.
ELECTRIC INDUSTRIES.
ELECTRIC MACHINERY INDUSTRY

ELECTRIC POWER PRODUCTION.
ELECTRIC POWER-PLANTS
ELECTRICITY SUPPLY.
ELECTRONIC APPARATUS AND APPLIANCES.
ELECTRONIC DATA PROCESSING.
ELECTRONIC DIGITAL COMPUTERS.
ELECTRONIC INDUSTRIES.
ENGINEERING
EQUITY FUNDING CORPORATION OF AMERICA.
FERTILIZER INDUSTRY.
FIREARMS INDUSTRY AND TRADE
FOOD INDUSTRY AND TRADE.
FOOD SUPPLY.
FORD MOTOR COMPANY.
FOUNDRIES
FRUIT TRADE
FUR TRADE.
FURNITURE INDUSTRY AND TRADE
GARDEN CITIES
GAS
GAS, NATURAL
GAS INDUSTRY
GEORGE BRETTLE AND COMPANY.
GLASHUETTE SCHMIDSFELDEN.
GLASS INDUSTRY AND TRADE
GOLD MINES AND MINING
GRAIN TRADE.
GULF OIL CORPORATION.
HOHENLOHE-WERKE, AKTIENGESELLSCHAFT.
HOSIERY INDUSTRY
HOTELS, TAVERNS, ETC.
INCHCAPE GROUP.
INTERNATIONAL FEDERATION OF COTTON AND ALLIED TEXTILE INDUSTRIES.
IRON INDUSTRY AND TRADE.
KRUPP (FRIEDRICH) AKTIENGESELLSCHAFT.
LEATHER INDUSTRY AND TRADE.
LINEN
LOCKS AND KEYS
LONAUERHAMMERHUETTE.
LYLE SHIPPING COMPANY.
MACHINERY
MASCHINENFABRIK ESSLINGEN AG.
MEAT INDUSTRY AND TRADE
MECHANICAL ENGINEERING
METAL TRADE
METALLURGY.
METALS
MILK, DRIED.
MILK SUPPLY
MILK TRADE
MINERAL INDUSTRIES.
MINES AND MINERAL RESOURCES.
MINING CORPORATIONS
MINING INDUSTRY AND FINANCE
MOELVEN BRUG, AKSJESELSKAPET.
MONSANTO COMPANY.
MULLER SZN. (HENDRIK).
MUNITIONS.
NESTLÉ.
NEW CO-OPERATIVE QUARRIES (PIONEER SOCIETY).
NEWSPAPER PUBLISHING
NICHOLAS INTERNATIONAL LIMITED.
NIGERIAN EXTERNAL TELECOMMUNICATIONS LIMITED.
NIGERIAN STEEL DEVELOPMENT AUTHORITY.
NONFERROUS METALS
NONMETALLIC MINERALS
OFFSHORE OIL INDUSTRY
OIL INDUSTRIES.
ORE DRESSING PLANTS
OXFORD UNIVERSITY PRESS.
PAPER MAKING AND TRADE
PETROLEUM
PETROLEUM IN SUBMERGED LANDS

COMMERCE AND INDUSTRY (Cont.)

PETROLEUM INDUSTRY AND TRADE.
PETROLEUM PRODUCTS
PETROLEUM REFINERIES
PEUGEOT S.A.
PHILIPS GLOEILAMPENFABRIEKEN, N.V.
PLASTICS INDUSTRY AND TRADE
PORSCHE.
PRICE, FORBES AND COMPANY.
PRINTING INDUSTRY
PRODUCE TRADE.
PUBLISHERS AND PUBLISHING
QUARRIES AND QUARRYING
REACTOR FUEL REPROCESSING.
RESTAURANTS, LUNCHROOMS, ETC.
RUBBER INDUSTRY AND TRADE.
SAFES.
SARTORIUS (LUD.) & COMP.
SCOTT BADER COMMONWEALTH LIMITED.
SEMICONDUCTORS.
SHIPBUILDING
SILK MANUFACTURE AND TRADE
SILVER MINES AND MINING
SKIBBEN WINTON CONSTRUCTION LIMITED.
STEAM-ENGINES
STEEL INDUSTRY AND TRADE
STEPHEN SIMPSON (FIRM).
SUGAR MACHINERY.
SUGAR TRADE.
TATE AND LYLE LIMITED.
TEA TRADE.
TELEVISION ADVERTISING.
TELEVISION INDUSTRY
TELEVISION PROGRAMMES
TERNI (FIRM).
TEXTILE FIBRES, SYNTHETIC
TEXTILE INDUSTRY AND FABRICS.
TIN.
TIN INDUSTRY.
TOBACCO MANUFACTURE AND TRADE
TOURIST TRADE.
UNILEVER LIMITED.
URANIUM
VICKERS LIMITED.
VOORTMAN (A.)-N.V. TEXAS
WATER DISTRICTS
WATER POWER ELECTRIC PLANTS
WILTON-FIJENOORD N.V.
WIRE INDUSTRY
WOOD-PULP INDUSTRY
WOOD-USING INDUSTRIES
WOODWORKING INDUSTRIES
WOOL TRADE AND INDUSTRY.

ECONOMICS.

See also AGRICULTURE; COMMERCE AND INDUSTRY; FINANCE; TRANSPORT

ABSENTEEISM (LABOUR)
AGE AND EMPLOYMENT
AIMS FOR FREEDOM AND ENTERPRISE.
ALIEN LABOUR.
ALIEN LABOUR, AFRICAN
ALIEN LABOUR, TURKISH
AMERICAN FEDERATION OF LABOR AND CONGRESS OF INDUSTRIAL ORGANIZATION
ANDEAN GROUP
AUSTRIAN SCHOOL OF ECONOMISTS.
BOYCOTT
BROTHERHOOD OF SLEEPING CAR PORTERS.
CAPITALISM.
CHRISTIANITY AND ECONOMICS.
CHURCH AND LABOUR.
CIVIL SERVICE PENSIONS
COLLECTIVE BARGAINING.
COLLECTIVE LABOUR AGREEMENTS
COMMONWEALTH FUND FOR TECHNICAL CO-OPERATION.
COMPAGNONNAGES.
COMPETITION.
COMPETITION, UNFAIR
CONFÉDÉRATION DES SYNDICATS CHRÉTIENS DE BELGIQUE
CONSUMPTION (ECONOMICS).
CONTRACT SYSTEM (LABOUR)
CONVICT LABOUR
COPARTNERSHIP.
COST AND STANDARD OF LIVING
COST EFFECTIVENESS.
COSTS, INDUSTRIAL
COUNCIL FOR MUTUAL ECONOMIC ASSISTANCE.
CRISES.
DISCRIMINATION IN EMPLOYMENT.
DISTRIBUTION (ECONOMIC THEORY).
DIVISION OF LABOUR.
DOMESTIC ECONOMY
DRUG ABUSE AND EMPLOYMENT.
ECONOMIC ASSISTANCE.
ECONOMIC ASSISTANCE, ARAB
ECONOMIC ASSISTANCE, AUSTRALIAN.
ECONOMIC ASSISTANCE, BRITISH
ECONOMIC ASSISTANCE, CANADIAN.
ECONOMIC ASSISTANCE, DOMESTIC
ECONOMIC ASSISTANCE, EUROPEAN.
ECONOMIC ASSISTANCE, NEW ZEALAND.
ECONOMIC ASSISTANCE, NORWEGIAN.
ECONOMIC ASSISTANCE, RUSSIAN.
ECONOMIC ASSISTANCE IN COSTA RICA.
ECONOMIC ASSISTANCE IN GUATEMALA.
ECONOMIC CONDITIONS.
ECONOMIC COUNCILS
ECONOMIC DEVELOPMENT.
ECONOMIC FORECASTING.
ECONOMIC HISTORY.
ECONOMIC INDICATORS
ECONOMIC LEGISLATION
ECONOMIC POLICY.
ECONOMIC STABILIZATION
ECONOMIC ZONING
ECONOMICS.
ECONOMICS, COMPARATIVE.
ECONOMICS, MATHEMATICAL.
ECONOMICS, PRIMITIVE.
ECONOMISTS
EENHEIDSVAKCENTRALE.
EMPLOYMENT (ECONOMIC THEORY)
ENERGY
ENERGY CONSERVATION.
ENERGY CONSUMPTION.
ENERGY POLICY.
ENVIRONMENTAL POLICY.
ENVIRONMENTAL POLICY RESEARCH
ENVIRONMENTAL PROTECTION.
EQUAL PAY FOR EQUAL WORK.
EQUILIBRIUM (ECONOMICS).
EXTERNALITIES (ECONOMICS).
FAMILY ALLOWANCES
FERTILITY, HUMAN.
FOOD CONSUMPTION
FOUR-DAY WEEK
FREE TRADE AND PROTECTION.
FUEL.
GENERAL AGREEMENT ON TARIFFS AND TRADE.
GENERAL STRIKE, UNITED KINGDOM, 1926.
GENERAL STRIKE, UNITED STATES, 1877.
GEOGRAPHY, ECONOMIC.
GILDS
GOVERNMENT OWNERSHIP.
GOVERNMENT PURCHASING OF REAL PROPERTY
GROSS NATIONAL PRODUCT.
GRUNWICK STRIKE, 1976.
HOME LABOUR
HOME OWNERSHIP.
HOURS OF LABOUR.
HOUSING.
HOUSING, COOPERATIVE
HOUSING, RURAL
HOUSING MANAGEMENT.
HOUSING POLICY
INCOME
INCOME DISTRIBUTION.
INCOME MAINTENANCE PROGRAMMES
INDEXATION (ECONOMICS).
INDUSTRIEGEWERKSCHAFT DRUCK UND PAPIER.
INDUSTRIEGEWERKSCHAFT METALL FÜR DIE BUNDESREPUBLIK DEUTSCHLAND.
INFLATION (FINANCE) AND UNEMPLOYMENT.
INTEREST AND USURY.
INTERINDUSTRY ECONOMICS.
INTERNATIONAL ECONOMIC INTEGRATION.
INTERNATIONAL ECONOMIC RELATIONS.
INTERNATIONAL LABOUR ACTIVITIES.
INTERNATIONAL LABOUR CONFERENCE.
INTERNATIONAL LABOUR ORGANISATION.
JERN- OG METALINDUSTRIARBEJDSMAENDENES FAGFORENING.
JOB EVALUATION.
JOB SATISFACTION
JOB VACANCIES
LABOUR AND LABOURING CLASSES.
LABOUR BUREAUS.
LABOUR COSTS
LABOUR DISPUTES
LABOUR ECONOMICS.
LABOUR EXCHANGES
LABOUR MOBILITY.
LABOUR POLICY
LABOUR SUPPLY.
LABOUR TURNOVER.
LAISSEZ-FAIRE.
LAND, NATIONALIZATION OF
LAND REFORM.
LAND SETTLEMENT.
LAND SUBDIVISION.
LAND TENURE.
LAND USE.
LAND USE, URBAN.
LUXURY.
MALTHUSIANISM.
MANPOWER
MANPOWER POLICY.
MARGINAL UTILITY.
MARXIAN ECONOMICS.
MEDICAL CARE, COST OF
MEDICAL ECONOMICS.
METAYER SYSTEM
MIGRANT LABOUR
MIGRATION, INTERNAL.
MILK CONSUMPTION
MONOPOLIES.
NATIONAL UNION OF DISTRIBUTIVE AND ALLIED WORKERS.
NEDERLANDS VERBOND VAN VAKVERENIGINGEN.
NIGHT LABOUR.
NOISE CONTROL
NORSK POLITIFORBUND.
NORSK TREINDUSTRIARBEIDERFORBUND.
NORTHUMBERLAND MINERS' MUTUAL CONFIDENT ASSOCIATION.
OESTERREICHISCHER ARBEITER- UND ANGESTELLTENBUND.
OLIGOPOLIES.
OPEN AND CLOSED SHOP
ORGANISATION FOR ECONOMIC COOPERATION AND DEVELOPMENT.

EDUCATION

PART-TIME EMPLOYMENT
PENSION TRUSTS
PENSIONS.
PENSIONS, MILITARY
PERFORMANCE.
PERFORMANCE STANDARDS.
PERSONAL PROPERTY
PHYSIOCRATS
PICKETING
PLAGUE
POLLUTION.
POPULATION.
POPULATION POLICY.
POPULATION RESEARCH
PRICE INDEXES.
PRICE POLICY
PRICE REGULATION.
PRICES.
PRODUCTION (ECONOMIC THEORY).
PROFIT.
PROFIT SHARING
PROLETARIAT.
PROPERTY.
PROPERTY AND SOCIALISM.
PUBLIC GOODS.
PUBLIC HOUSING
REAL PROPERTY
RECYCLING (WASTE, ETC.)
REGIONAL ECONOMICS.
RENT
RENT CONTROL
RENT SUBSIDIES
RESIDENTIAL MOBILITY
RESTRAINT OF TRADE.
RETIREMENT
RETRAINING, OCCUPATIONAL
RIGHT OF PROPERTY.
RØRLEGGERNES FAGFORENING.
RURAL DEVELOPMENT.
SALARIED EMPLOYEES
SALINE WATER CONVERSION.
SATISFACTION.
SERVICE, COMPULSORY NON-MILITARY
SEX DISCRIMINATION AGAINST WOMEN
SEX DISCRIMINATION IN EMPLOYMENT
SHIFT SYSTEMS.
SHOP STEWARDS
SIT DOWN STRIKES
SKILLED LABOUR.
SOLAR ENERGY
SPACE IN ECONOMICS.
STAGNATION (ECONOMICS).
STATICS AND DYNAMICS (SOCIAL SCIENCES).
STRIKES AND LOCKOUTS.
SUBSIDIES.
SUPPLEMENTARY EMPLOYMENT
SUPPLY AND DEMAND.
SWEATING SYSTEM.
SYNDICALISM.
TECHNICAL ASSISTANCE.
TECHNICAL ASSISTANCE, AMERICAN.
TECHNICAL ASSISTANCE IN AFRICA
TENNESSEE VALLEY AUTHORITY
TIME AND ECONOMIC REACTIONS.
TRADE AND PROFESSIONAL ASSOCIATIONS
TRADE UNIONS.
TRADE UNIONS, CATHOLIC
TRADE UNIONS AND COMMUNISM.
TRUSTS, INDUSTRIAL.
UNCERTAINTY.
UNDERDEVELOPED AREAS.
UNDEREMPLOYMENT
UNEMPLOYED.
UNEMPLOYMENT, TECHNOLOGICAL
UNION DOUANIERE ET ECONOMIQUE DE L'AFRIQUE CENTRALE.
UNION GENERAL DE TRABAJADORES DE ESPAÑA.
UNION OF SHOP, DISTRIBUTIVE AND ALLIED WORKERS.

UNITED NATIONS ECONOMIC COMMISSION FOR LATIN AMERICA.
URBAN ECONOMICS.
URBAN HOMESTEADING
URBAN RENEWAL.
UTILITY THEORY.
VALUE.
VEIVESENETS ARBEIDERFORENING.
VERBAND DES PERSONALS ÖFFENTLICHER DIENSTE.
WAGE PAYMENT SYSTEMS
WAGE-PRICE POLICY
WAGES.
WAR, COST OF.
WATER RIGHTS.
WEALTH.
WEEKLY REST-DAY.
WELFARE ECONOMICS.
WELFARE RIGHTS MOVEMENT
WELLINGTON DRIVERS UNION.
WHITE COLLAR WORKERS
WIND POWER.
WOMEN IN TRADE UNIONS
WORKS COUNCILS

EDUCATION.

General.

ABILITY GROUPING IN EDUCATION.
AFRICAN STUDIES.
AFRO-AMERICAN COLLEGE GRADUATES.
AFRO-AMERICAN STUDIES.
BRAIN DRAIN.
BUSINESS EDUCATION
CATHOLIC SCHOOLS
CHILDREN OF ALIEN LABOURERS
CHILDREN OF IMMIGRANTS
COMMUNISM AND EDUCATION.
COMMUNIST EDUCATION
COMMUNIST TEACHERS
COMMUNITY AND SCHOOL.
COMMUNITY SCHOOLS
CURRICULUM PLANNING.
DISCRIMINATION IN EDUCATION
DISSERTATIONS, ACADEMIC
DROPOUTS
EDUCATION.
EDUCATION, COMPARATIVE.
EDUCATION, COOPERATIVE
EDUCATION, ELEMENTARY
EDUCATION, HIGHER
EDUCATION, HUMANISTIC.
EDUCATION, PRESCHOOL.
EDUCATION, SECONDARY
EDUCATION, URBAN
EDUCATION AND STATE
EDUCATION OF ADULTS.
EDUCATION OF PRISONERS.
EDUCATION OF WOMEN
EDUCATIONAL ACCOUNTABILITY
EDUCATIONAL ANTHROPOLOGY.
EDUCATIONAL ASSISTANCE, BRITISH
EDUCATIONAL ASSISTANCE, CANADIAN.
EDUCATIONAL ASSISTANCE, NEW ZEALAND.
EDUCATIONAL ASSOCIATIONS
EDUCATIONAL EQUALIZATION.
EDUCATIONAL INNOVATIONS.
EDUCATIONAL LAW AND LEGISLATION
EDUCATIONAL PLANNING.
EDUCATIONAL PSYCHOLOGY.
EDUCATIONAL RESEARCH
EDUCATIONAL SOCIOLOGY.
EDUCATORS
EXAMINATIONS
FEDERAL AID TO EDUCATION
GRADING AND MARKING (STUDENTS).
GRADUATES
HEALTH ATTITUDES.
HOME AND SCHOOL.

HUMANITIES
ILLITERACY.
INTERCULTURAL EDUCATION
ISRAELI STUDENTS IN THE UNITED STATES.
KATHOLISCHER LEHRERVERBAND DES DEUTSCHEN REICHES.
LAW SCHOOLS
LEARNING, PSYCHOLOGY OF.
LEARNING AND SCHOLARSHIP
LIBRARIES AND STUDENTS.
MANUAL TRAINING
MENTALLY HANDICAPPED CHILDREN
MUSEUMS IN EDUCATION.
NURSERY SCHOOLS.
PERSONNEL SERVICE IN EDUCATION
POLITICS AND EDUCATION.
PRIVATE SCHOOLS
PROFESSIONAL EDUCATION
RELIGIOUS EDUCATION
SCHOOL ATTENDANCE
SCHOOL BOARDS
SCHOOL CHILDREN
SCHOOL DISCIPLINE
SCHOOL ENVIRONMENT.
SCHOOL INTEGRATION
SCHOOL MANAGEMENT AND ORGANIZATION.
SCHOOL SOCIAL WORK
SCHOOLS
SEGREGATION IN EDUCATION
SEX DISCRIMINATION IN EDUCATION
SOCIAL WORK EDUCATION.
STUDENT-ADMINISTRATOR RELATIONSHIPS.
STUDENT AID
STUDENT COUNSELLORS.
STUDENT UNIONS.
STUDENTS.
STUDENTS, FOREIGN
STUDENTS' SOCIO-ECONOMIC STATUS
SUBURBAN SCHOOLS
TEACHERS, TRAINING OF
TEACHING
TEACHING, FREEDOM OF.
TECHNICAL EDUCATION
TELEVISION IN HIGHER EDUCATION
TEXTBOOKS
UNITED NATIONS EDUCATIONAL, SCIENTIFIC AND CULTURAL ORGANIZATION.
UNIVERSITIES AND COLLEGES.
VACATION SCHOOLS
VOCATIONAL EDUCATION.
VOLUNTEER WORKERS IN EDUCATION.
WOMEN GRADUATE STUDENTS

Educational institutions.

BELFAST UNIVERSITY.
BIRMINGHAM UNIVERSITY.
BOROUGH ROAD COLLEGE.
BOSTON UNIVERSITY.
BRIGHTON FREE SCHOOL.
BRISTOL UNIVERSITY.
CORNELL UNIVERSITY
CRAIOVA UNIVERSITY.
LEIDEN UNIVERSITY
LIVERPOOL UNIVERSITY.
LONDON UNIVERSITY
MEXICO UNIVERSITY.
OPEN UNIVERSITY.
OXFORD UNIVERSITY
POLYTECHNIC OF NORTH LONDON.
READING UNIVERSITY.
ROME UNIVERSITY.
TUEBINGEN UNIVERSITY.
TURIN UNIVERSITY.
UNITED NATIONS UNIVERSITY.
UNIVERSITY OF THE NORTH.
ZAIRE UNIVERSITY.

FINANCE

FINANCE.

General.

AGRICULTURAL CREDIT.
ASIAN DOLLAR MARKET.
ASSESSMENT
BALANCE OF PAYMENTS.
BANK DEPOSITS
BANK HOLDING COMPANIES
BANK INVESTMENTS.
BANK LOANS.
BANK-NOTES.
BANKRUPTCY
BANKS AND BANKING.
BANKS AND BANKING, AMERICAN
BANKS AND BANKING, CENTRAL
BANKS AND BANKING, FOREIGN
BANKS AND BANKING, INTERNATIONAL.
BROKERS
BUDGET.
BUILDING AND LOAN ASSOCIATIONS
BUSINESS TAX
CAPITAL.
CAPITAL ASSETS PRICING MODEL.
CAPITAL GAINS TAX.
CAPITAL INVESTMENTS.
CAPITAL LEVY.
CLEARING-HOUSE
COINAGE
CONSUMER CREDIT
COST ACCOUNTING.
COUNTERFEITS AND COUNTERFEITING
CREDIT.
CUSTOMS ADMINISTRATION
CUSTOMS UNIONS.
DEBTS, EXTERNAL
DEBTS, PUBLIC.
DEFICIT FINANCING
DEVELOPMENT BANKS
DEVELOPMENT CREDIT CORPORATIONS
DIVIDENDS
DOLLAR.
EMIGRANT REMITTANCES
EURODOLLAR MARKET.
EUROPEAN REGIONAL DEVELOPMENT FUND.
EXPENDITURES, PUBLIC.
EXPORT CREDIT.
FEDERAL RESERVE BANKS.
FINANCE.
FINANCE, PERSONAL.
FINANCIAL INSTITUTIONS.
FINANCIAL STATEMENTS.
FLOW OF FUNDS.
FOREIGN EXCHANGE.
FRIENDLY SOCIETIES
FUND RAISING
GOLD.
GOVERNMENT SPENDING POLICY.
GRANTS-IN-AID.
IMPERIAL PREFERENCE.
INCOME TAX
INFLATION (FINANCE).
INFLATION (FINANCE) AND ACCOUNTING.
INFLATION (FINANCE) AND UNEMPLOYMENT.
INHERITANCE AND TRANSFER TAX
INSURANCE.
INSURANCE, AGRICULTURAL
INSURANCE, AUTOMOBILE
INSURANCE, EXPORT CREDIT
INSURANCE, FIRE
INSURANCE, HEALTH
INSURANCE, LIFE
INSURANCE, MARINE
INSURANCE, UNEMPLOYMENT.
INSURANCE COMPANIES
INTERGOVERNMENTAL FISCAL RELATIONS.
INTERGOVERNMENTAL TAX RELATIONS
INTERNATIONAL FINANCE.
INTERNATIONAL MONETARY FUND.
INVESTMENT ANALYSIS.
INVESTMENT OF PUBLIC FUNDS.
INVESTMENTS.
INVESTMENTS, AMERICAN.
INVESTMENTS, AUSTRALIAN
INVESTMENTS, BRITISH
INVESTMENTS, EUROPEAN.
INVESTMENTS, FOREIGN.
INVESTMENTS, GERMAN.
INVESTMENTS, JAPANESE.
INVESTMENTS, NORWEGIAN.
INVESTMENTS, SWEDISH.
INVESTMENTS, SWISS
LOANS, FOREIGN.
LOCAL FINANCE
LOCAL TAXATION
MEDICAL FEES
METROPOLITAN FINANCE
MONETARY POLICY.
MONETARY UNIONS.
MONEY.
MONEY SUPPLY.
MORTGAGE LOANS
MORTGAGES
MUNICIPAL BONDS
MUNICIPAL FINANCE
NATIONAL INCOME.
NEGATIVE INCOME TAX
PAPER MONEY
PHILLIPS CURVE.
POUND, BRITISH
PROGRAMME BUDGETING.
PROPERTY TAX.
REAL ESTATE INVESTMENT.
REAL PROPERTY TAX.
RESEARCH GRANTS
REVENUE
RISK.
SALES TAX.
SAVING AND INVESTMENT.
SAVINGS BANKS
SEALS (NUMISMATICS)
SECURITIES.
SOCIAL SECURITY TAXES
SPECIAL ASSESSMENTS
SPECIAL DRAWING RIGHTS.
SPECULATION.
STOCK COMPANIES
STOCK EXCHANGE.
STOCKHOLDERS
STOCKS
TARIFFS.
TAX ADMINISTRATION
TAX COLLECTION
TAX CREDITS.
TAX INCIDENCE
TAX LIENS
TAX REFUNDS
TAX-SALES
TAXATION.
TAXATION, EXEMPTION FROM
TAXATION OF ARTICLES OF CONSUMPTION.
TAXATION OF BONDS, SECURITIES, ETC.
VALUE ADDED TAX
VENTURE CAPITAL
WAR FINANCE.
WATER QUALITY MANAGEMENT
ZERO-BASE BUDGETING.

Banks, exchanges, etc.

AFRICAN DEVELOPMENT BANK.
BANCO DE LA PROVINCIA DE BUENOS AIRES.
BANK VAN DE NEDERLANDSE ANTILLEN.
BANK ZWIĄZKU SPÓŁEK ZAROBKOWYCH.
INTER-AMERICAN DEVELOPMENT BANK.
INTERNATIONAL BANK FOR RECONSTRUCTION AND DEVELOPMENT.
NEDERLANDSCHE BANK.

GEOGRAPHY, GEOLOGY AND METEOROLOGY.

General.

AGRICULTURAL GEOGRAPHY.
ANTHROPOGEOGRAPHY.
ARCTIC REGIONS.
ARID REGIONS.
ARTIFICIAL SATELLITES.
ATLASES.
CENTRAL PLACES.
CITIES AND TOWNS.
CLIMATIC CHANGES.
COASTAL ZONE MANAGEMENT
COASTS
COLD REGIONS.
COMMONS.
COMMUNISM AND ECOLOGY.
CONSERVATION OF NATURAL RESOURCES.
CONTINENTAL SHELF.
CROPS AND CLIMATE
DESERTS.
DISCOVERIES (IN GEOGRAPHY).
DROUGHTS.
EARTHQUAKES
ECOLOGY.
EUROPEAN ECONOMIC COMMUNITY ASSOCIATED COUNTRIES.
FLOOD CONTROL.
GAS, NATURAL, IN SUBMERGED LANDS
GEOGRAPHICAL PERCEPTION.
GEOGRAPHY.
GEOGRAPHY, ECONOMIC.
GEOGRAPHY, POLITICAL.
GEOLOGY
GEOLOGY, STRATIGRAPHIC.
GEOMORPHOLOGY.
GEOTHERMAL RESOURCES.
GRIDS (CARTOGRAPHY)
HISTORICAL GEOLOGY.
HUMAN ECOLOGY.
MARINE POLLUTION
MARINE RESOURCES.
MEDICAL GEOGRAPHY.
MINES AND MINERAL RESOURCES.
MOHAMMEDAN COUNTRIES
MOUNTAIN ECOLOGY
NATIONAL PARKS AND RESERVES
NATURAL RESOURCES.
NEW TOWNS
OCEANOGRAPHIC RESEARCH.
PALEOCLIMATOLOGY.
PHYSICAL GEOGRAPHY.
PIERS.
RAIN AND RAINFALL
RECLAMATION OF LAND
RIVERS
SLOPES (PHYSICAL GEOGRAPHY)
SOILS
SPACE AND TIME.
SPACE PERCEPTION.
STEPPES.
STREAM MEASUREMENTS
TIDAL POWER.
VOYAGES AND TRAVELS.
WATER
WATER, UNDERGROUND
WATER CONSUMPTION
WATER RESOURCES DEVELOPMENT.

GEOGRAPHY, GEOLOGY AND METEOROLOGY

WATER SUPPLY.
WEATHER.

Rocks, minerals, etc.

BAUXITE
CLAY
COPPER ORES.

Individual countries and places

Africa

ABEOKUTA
AFRICA
AFRICA, CENTRAL
AFRICA, EAST
AFRICA, NORTH.
AFRICA, NORTHEAST
AFRICA, SUBSAHARAN
AFRICA, WEST
ALGERIA
ANGOLA
ARAB COUNTRIES.
BANTU HOMELANDS, SOUTH AFRICA.
BOPHUTHATSWANA
BOTSWANA
BURUNDI
CAIRO
CAMEROUN
CAPE MACLEAR
CAPE TOWN
CAPE VERDE ISLANDS
CHAD
DIMBAZA
EGYPT
ETHIOPIA
FERNANDO POO
FRENCH WEST AFRICA.
GABON
GAMBIA
GBARNGA
GHANA.
GUINEA (REPUBLIC)
IVORY COAST
KAMPALA
KANO (STATE)
KAYES.
KENYA
KUMASI
KWAZULU
LAGOS
LESOTHO
LIBERIA
LIBYA
LOGONE BASIN.
MADAGASCAR
MALAWI
MALI (REPUBLIC)
MAURITANIA.
MAURITIUS
MOROCCO
MOZAMBIQUE
NIGER
NIGERIA.
NUBIA
OYO
REUNION
RHODESIA
SAHARA.
SAHEL
SEYCHELLES
SIERRA LEONE
SOMALI REPUBLIC
SOUTH AFRICA
SOUTH WEST AFRICA
SOWETO.
SPANISH GUINEA.
SPANISH SAHARA
SUDAN
SWAZILAND
TANZANIA.
TOGO
TRANSKEI.
TUNISIA
UGANDA
UPPER VOLTA
VOLTA RIVER
WITWATERSRAND
ZAIRE.
ZAMBIA.
ZANZIBAR

America, Latin.

AMAZON VALLEY
AMERICA
AMERICA, LATIN.
ANTIOQUIA
ARGENTINE REPUBLIC
BAHAMAS
BARBADOS
BELIZE.
BOLIVIA
BRAZIL
BRITISH VIRGIN ISLANDS
BUENOS AIRES
CALI
CARACAS
CARIBBEAN AREA
CAYMAN ISLANDS.
CHANCAY VALLEY
CHILE
CHOCÓ, COLOMBIA
CIUDAD GUAYANA
COLOMBIA
CORRIENTES (PROVINCE)
COSTA RICA
CUBA.
DISTRITO FEDERAL, BRAZIL
DOMINICAN REPUBLIC
DUTCH GUIANA
ECUADOR
GUADALAJARA, MEXICO
GUATEMALA
GUYANA.
HAITI
HONDURAS
HUALLAGA VALLEY
JAMAICA
MEDELLIN, COLOMBIA
MENDOZA (PROVINCE)
MEXICO.
MINAS GERAIS
MONTERREY, MEXICO
NATAL, BRAZIL
NETHERLANDS ANTILLES
NICARAGUA
OAXACA
PANAMA
PARA
PARA (STATE)
PARAGUAY
PARNAIBA VALLEY
PERU
PIGÜE.
PORTO ALEGRE
PUERTO RICO.
RIO DE JANEIRO (CITY)
RIO GRANDE DO SUL
SALVADOR
SANTIAGO DE CHILE
SÃO PAULO (CITY)
SÃO PAULO (STATE)
SERGIPE
SONORA
TRINIDAD AND TOBAGO
URUGUAY
VALLE DEL SANTA
VENEZUELA
VICOS
VILCANOTA VALLEY
YUCATAN PENINSULA
ZINACANTÁN

America, North.

ALASKA
ALBERTA
AMERICA
APPALACHIAN MOUNTAINS
BERMUDA
BIRMINGHAM, ALABAMA
BOSTON, MASSACHUSETTS
BRITISH COLUMBIA
BROOKLYN
BUCHANS
BUFFALO
CALIFORNIA
CANADA
CHICAGO
CINCINNATI
COATICOOK VALLEY.
COLORADO
DETROIT
GEORGIA (UNITED STATES)
GERMANTOWN, PENNSYLVANIA
GREENLAND
GREENWICH VILLAGE, NEW YORK CITY.
HOLLAND MARSH
ILLINOIS
IOWA
KANSAS CITY, MISSOURI
KITCHENER
LEVITTOWN, PENNSYLVANIA
LOS ANGELES
MANITOBA
MASSACHUSETTS
MILLEDGEVILLE
MISSOURI
MONTREAL
NEW BRUNSWICK
NEW HARMONY
NEW HAVEN
NEW YORK (CITY)
NEW YORK (STATE)
NEWFOUNDLAND
NORTH CAROLINA
NORTH WEST TERRITORIES
NOVA SCOTIA
NYACK, NEW YORK
OKANAGAN VALLEY
ONTARIO
PENNSYLVANIA
PHILADELPHIA
PITTSBURGH
POUGHKEEPSIE, NEW YORK
PRINCE EDWARD ISLAND
QUEBEC (PROVINCE)
ROCHESTER, NEW YORK
RUGBY, TENNESSEE
ST. LAWRENCE RIVER.
SALEM, MASSACHUSETTS
SAN FRANCISCO
SASKATCHEWAN
SHUSWAP VALLEY
SOUTH CAROLINA
SOUTHWEST, NEW
STEELTON, PENNSYLVANIA
TEXAS
TORONTO
TUCSON
UNITED STATES
UTICA, NEW YORK
VANCOUVER
VIRGINIA
WASHINGTON, D.C.
WEST, THE
WINNIPEG
WISCONSIN

GEOGRAPHY, GEOLOGY AND METEOROLOGY (Cont.)

Asia.

AFGHANISTAN
AMBOINA
ARAB COUNTRIES.
ARMENIA
ARUNACHAL PRADESH
ASIA
ASIA, SOUTHEAST
ASTRABAD
AZAD KASHMIR
BAHRAIN
BALI
BALUCHISTAN
BANGLADESH
BENGAL, WEST
BHUTAN
BIHAR
BUKHARA
BURMA
CAMBODIA
CHIANG MAI, THAILAND (PROVINCE)
CHINA.
CHOTA NAGPUR
CYPRUS
DELHI (UNION TERRITORY)
EAST (FAR EAST)
EAST (NEAR EAST)
GOA, DAMAN AND DIU
GUJARAT
HONG KONG
INDIA.
INDIAN OCEAN REGION.
INDOCHINA
INDONESIA
IRAN
IRAQ
ISRAEL
JAMMU AND KASHMIR
JAPAN
JERUSALEM
JORDAN
KAMCHATKA
KAZAKSTAN
KELANTAN
KERALA
KHIVA KHANATE
KIRGHIZIA
KOREA
KOSI RIVER
KURUSU
KUWAIT
LEBANON
MADRAS
MAHARASHTRA
MALACCA, STRAIT OF.
MALAYA.
MALAYSIA
MANCHURIA
MEGHALAYA
MONGOLIA
MYSORE
MYSORE (CITY)
NEPAL.
OMAN
OUDH
PAKISTAN.
PALESTINE
PERSIAN GULF
PETALING JAYA, MALAYSIA
PHILIPPINE ISLANDS
PHNOM PENH
PORT MUHAMMAD BIN QASIM.
PUNJAB (PAKISTAN)
QATAR
RAJASTHAN
RUSSIA.
SABAH
SARAWAK
SAUDI ARABIA
SHANGHAI
SIBERIA
SIND
SINGAPORE.
SINKIANG
SOVIET NORTH
SRI LANKA
SUMATRA
TAIWAN
TAJIKISTAN
TASHKENT
THAILAND
TIMOR
TRIPURA
TSINAN
TURKEY.
TURKMENISTAN
UNITED ARAB EMIRATES
UNITED ARAB REPUBLIC
UZBEKISTAN
VIETNAM.
YAGNOB RIVER.

Australia and Oceania.

ADELAIDE
AUCKLAND
AUSTRALIA
BRISBANE
CANBERRA
FIJI.
FREDERIK-HENDRIK ISLAND.
GILBERT AND ELLICE ISLANDS COLONY
GILBERT ISLANDS.
HAWAIIAN ISLANDS
HEIDELBERG, VICTORIA
HINDMARSH
MAPOON
NEW GUINEA
NEW ZEALAND.
NIUE
OCEANIA
PACIFIC, THE
PACIFIC OCEAN
PAPUA NEW GUINEA
QUEENSLAND
SOUTH AUSTRALIA
TAHITI
TASMANIA
TONGA
WESTERN SAMOA

Europe.

ABKHAZIA
ADZHARIA
ALTOPASCIO
AMSTERDAM
ANDALUSIA
ANDERNACH
ANDRYCHÓW
ANTWERP
APPENZELL-INNERRHODEN (CANTON).
AQUITAINE
ARNO VALLEY
ASTURIAS
AUGSBURG
AUSTRIA
AUSTRIA-HUNGARY
AUVERGNE
AZERBAIJAN
BADEN
BADEN-WUERTTEMBERG
BALKAN STATES
BALTIC, THE.
BALTIC STATES
BARCELONA
BASILICATA
BASQUE PROVINCES
BAVARIA
BELGIUM
BERLIN
BERN (CANTON)
BESSARABIA
BOLOGNA
BORINAGE
BRAȘOV
BREMEN
BRITTANY
BRNO
BULGARIA
BYDGOSZCZ (PROVINCE)
CADIZ
CAEN.
CALABRIA
CAPITANATA
CATALONIA
CAUCASUS
CHAMPAGNE
CHAMPAGNE-ARDENNE
CHARLEROI
CLARE
CORK (COUNTY)
CORRÈZE
CORSICA
CRACOW (CITY)
CRACOW (PROVINCE)
CROATIA
CZECHOSLOVAKIA
DENMARK
DORTMUND
DUBLIN
DUISBURG
ESSEN
ESSLINGEN
ESTONIA.
EUROPE.
EUROPE, EASTERN.
EUROPEAN ECONOMIC COMMUNITY
   COUNTRIES
FINLAND
FLORENCE
FOS
FRANCE.
FRANCHE-COMTE
FRANKFURT AM MAIN
FREIBURG (CANTON)
FRIESLAND
FRIULI
FRIULI-VENEZIA GIULIA
GALICIA (EASTERN EUROPE)
GALICIA (SPAIN)
GDANSK
GDAŃSK (PROVINCE)
GENOA
GEORGIA
GERMANY
GERMANY, EASTERN.
GIESSEN
GREECE
HAMBURG
HANOVER
HAUENSTEIN
HESSE
HUNGARY.
ICELAND
ILE-DE-FRANCE
IRELAND (REPUBLIC)
ITALY
IVANOVO (OBLAST')
JUELICH
JURA
JUTLAND
KALISZ
KATOWICE (PROVINCE)
KAZAN'
KOSTROMA (OBLAST')
KRASNODAR (KRAI)
LANGUEDOC-ROUSSILLON (REGION)
LA ROCHELLE.
LATVIA
LIMOUSIN
LITHUANIA
LÓDZ

HISTORY

ŁÓDŹ (PROVINCE)
LOMBARDY
LUCCA
LUXEMBOURG
LYONS
MACEDONIA
MALTA
MANNHEIM
MEDITERRANEAN.
MIDI-PYRENEES
MOLDAVIAN REPUBLIC
MOSCOW
MURCIA
MURMANSK (OBLAST')
NAPLES
NETHERLANDS
NIEVRE.
NIKOLAEV (OBLAST')
NORMANDY
NORTH RHINE-WESTPHALIA
NORWAY
NORWEGIAN SEA REGION.
ODESSA
OLDENBURG
PARIS
PARIS (REGION)
PELOPONNESUS
PETALAX
PIACENZA (PROVINCE)
PICARDY
PISTOIA (PROVINCE)
POITOU-CHARENTES (REGION)
POLAND
PORTUGAL
PROVENCE-CÔTE D'AZUR
PRUSSIA
REGGIO NELL'EMILIA (PROVINCE)
REMSCHEID
RIANJO
ROANNE
ROMANIA
ROME
ROSICKO-OSLAVANSKO
ROSTOV (OBLAST')
ROTTERDAM
ROUERGUE
RUHR
RUSSIA.
RUTHENIA
SAINT-FLOUR
SAN GIORGIO, ALBANESE
SAÔNE-ET-LOIRE.
SARDINIA
SARTHE (DEPARTMENT).
SAXONY
SCANDINAVIA
SEINE-ET-MARNE.
SERRAI (PROVINCE)
SEVILLE
SICILY
SILESIA
SLOVENIA
SMOGULEC.
SPAIN.
STUTTGART
SVALBARD
SWEDEN
SWITZERLAND
TEESDORF
TERNI.
TICINO
TOLEDO (PROVINCE)
TRANSYLVANIA
TREVISO (PROVINCE)
TURIN
UKRAINE
UPPSALA
URAL REGION
UTRECHT
VALDERROBRES
VALENCE.
VALENCIA, SPAIN (REGION)

VÄLLINGBY, STOCKHOLM
VENEZIA EUGANEA
VENICE
VERONA (PROVINCE)
VILLEFRANCHE-DE-ROUERGUE.
VOLGA BASIN
VOLOGDA (OBLAST')
VUGHT
WAIBLINGEN
WALLONIA
WARSAW
WARSAW (PROVINCE)
WHITE RUSSIA
WISCH
YAROSLAVL' (OBLAST')
YONNE (DEPARTMENT).
YUGOSLAVIA
ZUERICH (CITY)

United Kingdom.

ANGUS.
BEDFORD PARK, LONDON
BELFAST
BINBROOK
BIRMINGHAM
BISLEY, GLOUCESTERSHIRE
BOSTON
BRADFORD
CAMBRIDGE
CAMDEN
CHESHIRE
CLAYBROOKE
CLEATOR MOOR
CLEVELAND, UNITED KINGDOM
CORNWALL
COVENTRY
CUMBERLAND
CUMBRIA
DERBY
DERBYSHIRE
DEVONSHIRE
DURHAM (COUNTY)
EAST ANGLIA
EAST MIDLANDS STANDARD REGION
    (UNITED KINGDOM).
EXETER
EXMOOR NATIONAL PARK.
GATESHEAD
GLASGOW
GUERNSEY
HAMPSHIRE
HARINGEY
HAYFIELD
HEREFORDSHIRE
HORSHAM
HUDDERSFIELD
IRELAND
IRELAND, NORTHERN
ISLE OF MAN
ISLINGTON
JERSEY
KENT
LAMBETH
LANCASHIRE
LEICESTER
LEICESTERSHIRE
LINCOLNSHIRE
LIVERPOOL
LONDON.
LONDONDERRY
MANCHESTER
MEDWAY VALLEY
MERTHYR TYDFIL
MILTON KEYNES
NORFOLK
NORTHUMBERLAND
NORWICH (DIOCESE)
OSWESTRY
OXFORD
PLYMOUTH

PORTSMOUTH
ST. ALBANS
ST. KILDA
SALFORD
SALISBURY
SCOTLAND.
SEVERN
SHEFFIELD
SHETLAND ISLANDS
SHREWSBURY
SOUTH GLAMORGAN
SOUTH YORKSHIRE
SOUTHAMPTON
SOUTHWARK
STAFFORDSHIRE
STONEHOUSE, LANARKSHIRE.
STRATHCLYDE
SUFFOLK
SURREY
SUSSEX
SWINDON
TEESSIDE
THAMES, RIVER.
TOTTENHAM
TYNE AND WEAR
UNITED KINGDOM
WALES
WAPPING
WASHINGTON, DURHAM
WEST MIDLANDS STANDARD REGION
    (UNITED KINGDOM)
WEST SUSSEX
WORCESTERSHIRE
YORK
YORKSHIRE

HISTORY.

General.

ANTISEMITISM.
ARCHIVES
CHURCH HISTORY.
CHURCH RECORDS AND REGISTERS
CITIES AND TOWNS, ANCIENT.
CITIES AND TOWNS, MEDIEVAL.
CIVILIZATION.
CIVILIZATION, ARAB.
CIVILIZATION, MODERN.
COLONIZATION
CONSTITUTIONAL HISTORY.
EARTHWORKS (ARCHAEOLOGY)
EAST AND WEST.
ECONOMIC HISTORY.
EIGHTEENTH CENTURY.
ENLIGHTENMENT.
FEUDALISM.
GILDS
HISTORIANS
HISTORICAL GEOLOGY.
HISTORICAL LIBRARIES
HISTORICAL LINGUISTICS.
HISTORICISM.
HISTORIOGRAPHY.
HISTORY.
HISTORY, MODERN
MIDDLE AGES
MILITARY HISTORY, MODERN.
ORAL HISTORY.
PEASANT UPRISINGS
RIOTS
SERFDOM
SOCIAL HISTORY.
TWENTIETH CENTURY
TWENTY-FIRST CENTURY
WILLS

International (including wars).

CHANGKUFENG INCIDENT, 1938.

HISTORY (Cont.)

CRIMEAN WAR, 1853-1856.
DARDANELLES.
EUROPEAN WAR, 1914-1918.
INDIA-PAKISTAN CONFLICT, 1971.
ISRAEL-ARAB CONFLICT, 1948- .
ISRAEL-ARAB WAR, 1967.
ISRAEL-ARAB WAR, 1973.
ITALO-ETHIOPIAN WAR, 1935-1936.
KOREAN WAR, 1950-1953.
LITTLE ENTENTE, 1920-1939.
MONTREUX, SWITZERLAND, TREATY OF, 1936.
MUNICH FOUR POWER AGREEMENT, 1938.
NORTH ATLANTIC TREATY, 1949.
PEARL HARBOR, ATTACK ON, 1941.
RECONSTRUCTION (1914-1939).
RECONSTRUCTION (1939-1951)
SOUTH AFRICAN WAR, 1899-1902.
SPANISH-MOROCCAN WAR, 1859-1860.
VERSAILLES, TREATY OF, JUNE 28, 1919 (GERMANY).
VIETNAMESE WARS, 1945-1975.
WAITANGI, TREATY OF, 1840.
WORLD WAR, 1939-1945.

African territories

ANTHROPOMETRY

American territories.

AMERICAN LOYALISTS.
FREEDMEN IN TEXAS.
FRONTIER AND PIONEER LIFE
FRONTIER THESIS.
GENERAL STRIKE, UNITED STATES, 1877.
NEW GRANADA (VICEROYALTY)
NEW SPAIN (VICEROYALTY)
RECONSTRUCTION (UNITED STATES).

Asiatic territories.

ARMENIAN QUESTION.
KASHMIR QUESTION.
KOREAN RESISTANCE MOVEMENTS, 1905-1945.
KOREAN REUNIFICATION QUESTION (1945-).
LONG MARCH, 1934-1935.
TAIPING REBELLION, 1850-1864.

European territories.

ANSCHLUSS MOVEMENT, 1918-1938.
BERLIN QUESTION (1945-).
BYZANTINE EMPIRE
CONCENTRATION CAMPS
EASTERN QUESTION (BALKAN).
FRONDE.
GERMAN REUNIFICATION QUESTION (1949-).
GREECE, ANCIENT
HOLOCAUST, JEWISH (1939-1945).
MACEDONIAN QUESTION.
MANORS
PARISHES
RENAISSANCE.
ROME, ANCIENT

United Kingdom.

ALMANACS, ENGLISH.
ALMANACS, IRISH.
ARCHAEOLOGY, INDUSTRIAL
CHARTISM
CROWDS.
GENERAL STRIKE, UNITED KINGDOM, 1926.
HOME RULE
INCLOSURES.
IRISH QUESTION.
LOLLARDS.
MOATS.
PLAGUE
REFORMATION

Colonial companies.

NIGER COMPANY.

LANGUAGE, LITERATURE AND THE ARTS.

Language.

ANTHROPOLOGICAL LINGUISTICS.
BILINGUALISM
CASE GRAMMAR.
COMPETENCE AND PERFORMANCE (LINGUISTICS).
CREOLE DIALECTS.
CZECH LANGUAGE
ENGLISH LANGUAGE
FRENCH LANGUAGE
FRENCH LANGUAGE IN CANADA.
GENERATIVE GRAMMAR.
GERMAN LANGUAGE
GRAMMAR, COMPARATIVE AND GENERAL.
HINDI LANGUAGE
HISTORICAL LINGUISTICS.
IRISH LANGUAGE
ITALIAN LANGUAGE
LANGUAGE AND LANGUAGES.
LANGUAGES
LANGUAGES, MODERN
LINGUISTIC ANALYSIS (LINGUISTICS).
LINGUISTIC CHANGE.
LINGUISTIC GEOGRAPHY.
LINGUISTICS.
METAPHOR.
PAPIAMENTU.
PHONETICS.
POLISH LANGUAGE
PSYCHOLINGUISTICS.
RUSSIAN LANGUAGE
SEMANTICS.
SEMIOLOGY.
SEMIOTICS.
SOCIOLINGUISTICS.
SPEECH.
WELSH LANGUAGE

Literature.

AMERICAN FICTION
AMERICAN LITERATURE
AUTHORS, ENGLISH.
BIOGRAPHY.
BULGARIAN LITERATURE
CATALAN NEWSPAPERS.
CITIES AND TOWNS IN LITERATURE.
COMMUNISM AND LITERATURE.
COMMUNITY NEWSPAPERS
CRITICISM.
ECONOMICS IN LITERATURE.
ENGLAND IN LITERATURE.
ENGLISH FICTION.
ENGLISH LITERATURE
ENGLISH NEWSPAPERS.
ENGLISH PERIODICALS
FICTION
FRENCH LITERATURE
FUTURISM (LITERATURE).
GERMAN LITERATURE
GERMAN NEWSPAPERS.
GERMAN PERIODICALS.
INDIANS IN LITERATURE.
IRISH LITERATURE.
ITALIAN LITERATURE
ITALIAN NEWSPAPERS.
JOURNALISM
LABOUR AND LABOURING CLASSES IN LITERATURE.
LITERARY FORGERIES.
LITERATURE.
LITERATURE AND POLITICS.
LITERATURE AND REVOLUTIONS.
LITERATURE AND SOCIETY.
MEXICAN FICTION
NEWSPAPERS
POETRY.
POLISH PERIODICALS.
POLITICS AND LITERATURE.
POLITICS IN LITERATURE.
PRESS.
PROHIBITED BOOKS.
RADIO JOURNALISM
RUSSIAN LITERATURE
RUSSIAN NEWSPAPERS.
RUSSIAN PERIODICALS.
RUSSIAN POETRY.
SATIRE, ENGLISH.
SATIRE, FRENCH.
SATIRE, RUSSIAN.
SCANDINAVIAN LITERATURE
SPANISH LITERATURE
SWEDISH LITERATURE.
UNDERGROUND LITERATURE
UOMO QUALUNQUE, L'.
WAR IN LITERATURE.
WOMEN IN LITERATURE.

The Arts.

AESTHETICS.
ARCHITECTURE
ARCHITECTURE AND SOCIETY.
ART
ART AND SOCIETY.
ART PATRONAGE.
ARTS
ARTS AND SOCIETY
CARICATURES AND CARTOONS
FUTURISM (ART).
MUSIC
MUSIC, POPULAR (SONGS, ETC.)
POPULAR CULTURE.
ROMANTICISM.
SOCIALISM AND ART.
STATE ENCOURAGEMENT OF SCIENCE, LITERATURE AND ART
THEATRE AND STATE

LAW (including INTERNATIONAL LAW).

General.

APPELLATE PROCEDURE
BAIL
COMMON LAW.
COMMUNIST TRIALS
CONFIDENTIAL COMMUNICATIONS
COURT RECORDS
COURT RULES
COURTS
CUSTOMARY LAW.
EQUALITY BEFORE THE LAW.
EVIDENCE (LAW).
EVIDENCE, DOCUMENTARY
GOVERNMENT ATTORNEYS
GOVERNMENT LAWYERS
GOVERNMENT LITIGATION
JUDICIAL POWER
JUDICIAL REVIEW

MATHEMATICS AND STATISTICS

JUDICIAL STATISTICS
JURISDICTION
JURISPRUDENCE.
JUSTICE, ADMINISTRATION OF.
JUSTICES OF THE PEACE
JUVENILE COURTS
JUVENILE JUSTICE, ADMINISTRATION OF
LAW.
LAW, COMPARATIVE.
LAW AND ETHICS.
LAW AND SOCIALISM.
LAW REFORM
LAW REPORTS, DIGESTS, ETC.
LAW SCHOOLS
LEGAL AID
LEGAL ETHICS
MOTIVE (LAW)
NATURAL LAW.
PROCEDURE (LAW)
RESPONSIBILITY, LEGAL
RIGHT TO COUNSEL
RULE OF LAW
SOCIAL LEGISLATION
SOCIOLOGICAL JURISPRUDENCE.
STARE DECISIS
TECHNOLOGY AND LAW.
WARRANTS (LAW)
WITNESSES

Public law.

ADMINISTRATIVE COURTS
ADMINISTRATIVE DISCRETION
ADMINISTRATIVE LAW
ADMINISTRATIVE PROCEDURE
ADMINISTRATIVE REMEDIES
ADMINISTRATIVE RESPONSIBILITY
AGRICULTURAL LAWS AND LEGISLATION
ALIENS.
ARREST
BILL DRAFTING.
BIRTH CONTROL.
CENSORSHIP.
CITY PLANNING AND REDEVELOPMENT LAW
COMPENSATION (LAW)
CONSTITUTIONAL LAW.
DAIRY LAWS
DETENTION OF PERSONS
ECONOMIC LEGISLATION
EDUCATIONAL LAW AND LEGISLATION
ELECTION LAW
EMIGRATION AND IMMIGRATION LAW
EMINENT DOMAIN
ENVIRONMENTAL LAW
FISHERY LAW AND LEGISLATION.
FOOD ADDITIVES.
FOOD LAW AND LEGISLATION.
GENETICS.
HIGHWAY LAW
IMPEACHMENTS
LEGISLATION.
LITTER (TRASH)
MARTIAL LAW
MEDICAL LAWS AND LEGISLATION
MENTAL HEALTH LAWS
MILITARY LAW
NARCOTIC LAWS
POLITICAL CRIMES AND OFFENCES
POOR LAWS
PRESS LAW
PRIVILEGES AND IMMUNITIES
PUBLIC INSTITUTIONS
PUBLIC INTEREST.
PUBLIC LAW
PUBLIC POLICY (LAW)
RAILWAY LAW
SEGREGATION IN EDUCATION
SERVITUDES
WATER
WILD LIFE, CONSERVATION OF

Civil law and procedure.

ALIMONY.
CHARITABLE USES, TRUSTS AND FOUNDATIONS
CIVIL LAW
CIVIL PROCEDURE
CLASS ACTIONS (CIVIL PROCEDURE)
DECEDENTS' ESTATES
DIVORCE.
DOMESTIC RELATIONS
DOMESTIC RELATIONS COURTS
ESTATE PLANNING
FENCES
ILLEGITIMACY
INHERITANCE AND SUCCESSION
LAND TITLES
LANDLORD AND TENANT.
LEASES
LIABILITY FOR ANIMALS
LIBEL AND SLANDER
MARRIAGE LAW
NEGLIGENCE
PERSONS (LAW)
PRESCRIPTION (LAW)
SECURITY (LAW)
TAX PLANNING
THINGS (LAW)
TORTS
TRUSTS AND TRUSTEES

Commercial, industrial and labour laws.

AGENCY (LAW)
ANTITRUST LAW
ARBITRATION AND AWARD
BANKING LAW
BANKRUPTCY
COMMERCIAL CRIMES
COMMERCIAL LAW
CONCESSIONS
CONTAINERS
CONTRACTS
COPYRIGHT
CORN LAWS
CORPORATION LAW
DELIVERY OF GOODS (LAW)
HANDICRAFT
INDUSTRIAL LAWS AND LEGISLATION.
INSURANCE LAW
LABOUR LAWS AND LEGISLATION.
LAYAWAY PLAN
LEGACIES
MASTER AND SERVANT
MERCANTILE SYSTEM.
MINERAL WATERS
MINES, SUBMARINE.
MINING LAW.
NEGOTIABLE INSTRUMENTS
PARTNERSHIP
PETROLEUM LAW AND LEGISLATION
PRODUCTS LIABILITY
PUBLIC CONTRACTS
RECEIVERS
SALES
USURY LAWS

Criminal law and procedure.

ACQUITTALS
ARREST
CAPITAL PUNISHMENT
CRIMINAL COURTS
CRIMINAL INVESTIGATION.
CRIMINAL JUSTICE, ADMINISTRATION OF.
CRIMINAL LAW
CRIMINAL PROCEDURE
DEFENCE (CRIMINAL PROCEDURE)
FORGERY
HOMICIDE
OBSCENITY (LAW).
OFFENCES AGAINST PROPERTY
OFFENCES AGAINST THE PERSON
PLEAS (CRIMINAL PROCEDURE).
RAPE
SENTENCES (CRIMINAL PROCEDURE)
SEX CRIMES
TRIALS (BLASPHEMY)
TRIALS (CONSPIRACY)
TRIALS (HERESY)
TRIALS (MURDER)
TRIALS (POLITICAL CRIMES AND OFFENCES)
TRIALS (SEDITION)
TRIALS (TREASON)

Ecclesiastical law.

ECCLESIASTICAL COURTS

Foreign law.

LAW, BANTU.
LAW, PRIMITIVE.

Conflict of laws, civil and criminal.

CONFLICT OF LAW.

International law.

AGGRESSION (INTERNATIONAL LAW).
ALIENS.
CIVIL RIGHTS (INTERNATIONAL LAW).
COURT OF JUSTICE OF THE EUROPEAN COMMUNITIES.
EQUALITY OF STATES.
FAVOURED NATION CLAUSE.
FREEDOM OF THE SEAS.
GOVERNMENT LIABILITY (INTERNATIONAL LAW).
INTERNATIONAL AND MUNICIPAL LAW
INTERNATIONAL LAW.
INTERVENTION (INTERNATIONAL LAW).
LABOUR LAWS AND LEGISLATION, INTERNATIONAL.
MARITIME LAW.
OCEAN BOTTOM (MARITIME LAW).
PASSPORTS.
PERSONS (INTERNATIONAL LAW).
PRISONERS OF WAR.
SANCTIONS (INTERNATIONAL LAW).
SELF-DEFENCE (INTERNATIONAL LAW).
SPACE LAW.
STATELESSNESS.
TERRITORIAL WATERS
TREATIES.
TREATY-MAKING POWER
WAR (INTERNATIONAL LAW).
WAR CRIMES

MATHEMATICS AND STATISTICS.

ABELIAN GROUPS.
ALGEBRA.
ALGEBRA, ABSTRACT.
ALGEBRAS, LINEAR.
ALGORITHMS.
ANALYSIS OF VARIANCE.
AUTOMATA.
AUTOMATION
BANACH SPACES.

MATHEMATICS AND STATISTICS (Cont.)

BAYESIAN STATISTICAL DECISION THEORY.
BURROUGHS B1726 (COMPUTER).
CALCULUS.
CALCULUS, DIFFERENTIAL.
CALCULUS, INTEGRAL.
CATASTROPHES (MATHEMATICS).
COBOL (COMPUTER PROGRAM LANGUAGE).
COMBINATORIAL ANALYSIS.
COMPUTABLE FUNCTIONS.
COMPUTER ARCHITECTURE.
COMPUTER NETWORKS.
COMPUTER PROGRAMS
COMPUTER SIMULATION.
COMPUTER STORAGE DEVICES.
COMPUTERS.
CONTINGENCY TABLES.
CONTROL THEORY.
CONVEX FUNCTIONS.
CURVES, ALGEBRAIC.
CYBERNETICS.
DATA BASE MANAGEMENT.
DATA STRUCTURES (COMPUTER SCIENCE).
DATA TRANSMISSION SYSTEMS.
DECIMAL SYSTEM.
DEMOGRAPHY
DIFFERENTIAL EQUATIONS.
DIFFERENTIAL EQUATIONS, LINEAR.
DIFFERENTIAL MAPPINGS.
DIFFERENTIAL TOPOLOGY.
DISTRIBUTION (PROBABILITY THEORY).
DUALITY THEORY (MATHEMATICS).
DYNAMIC PROGRAMMING.
ECONOMICS, MATHEMATICAL.
ESTIMATION THEORY.
EXPERIMENTAL DESIGN.
FIELD EXTENSIONS (MATHEMATICS).
FIELDS, ALGEBRAIC.
FILE ORGANIZATION (COMPUTER SCIENCE).
FUNCTIONAL ANALYSIS.
FUNCTIONAL DIFFERENTIAL EQUATIONS.
FUNCTIONAL EQUATIONS.
FUNCTIONS.
FUNCTIONS, EXPONENTIAL.
FUNCTIONS OF COMPLEX VARIABLES.
GALOIS THEORY.
GAMES, THEORY OF.
GAMES OF CHANCE (MATHEMATICS).
GASP (COMPUTER PROGRAM LANGUAGE).
GRAPH THEORY.
IDEALS (ALGEBRA).
INDUSTRIAL STATISTICS.
INTEGRALS, GENERALIZED.
JUDICIAL STATISTICS
LIAPUNOV FUNCTIONS.
LIFE SPAN, PRODUCTIVE.
LINEAR PROGRAMMING.
MARKOV PROCESSES.
MATHEMATICAL ANALYSIS.
MATHEMATICAL MODELS.
MATHEMATICAL OPTIMIZATION.
MATHEMATICAL STATISTICS.
MATHEMATICS.
MATRICES.
MEASURE THEORY.
MEDICAL STATISTICS.
METRIC SPACES.
MODULES (ALGEBRA).
MORTALITY
MULTIVARIATE ANALYSIS.
NETWORK ANALYSIS (PLANNING).
NONPARAMETRIC STATISTICS.
OPERATIONS RESEARCH.
ORDER STATISTICS.
POINT PROCESSES.
POPULATION FORECASTING.
PREDICTION THEORY.
PROBABILITIES.
PROGRAMMING (ELECTRONIC COMPUTERS).
PROGRAMMING (MATHEMATICS).
QUEUEING THEORY.
REAL-TIME DATA PROCESSING.
REGISTERS OF BIRTHS, ETC.
REGRESSION ANALYSIS.
RIEMANN INTEGRAL.
RINGS (ALGEBRA).
SAMPLING (STATISTICS).
SIMULA (COMPUTER PROGRAM LANGUAGE).
SIMULATION METHODS.
SINGULARITIES (MATHEMATICS).
STABILITY.
STATISTICAL DECISION.
STATISTICAL SERVICES.
STATISTICS.
STOCHASTIC PROCESSES.
SUFFICIENT STATISTICS.
SYSTEM ANALYSIS.
SYSTEM THEORY.
SYSTEMS ENGINEERING.
TIME SERIES ANALYSIS
TOPOLOGY.
VARIABLES (MATHEMATICS).
VECTOR-VALUED MEASURES.

MILITARY AND NAVAL SCIENCE.

AERONAUTICS, MILITARY
AIR POWER.
ARMAMENTS.
ARMED FORCES.
ARMIES
ARMS CONTROL
ATOMIC WEAPONS.
BIOLOGICAL WARFARE.
BOMBING, AERIAL.
BORDER PATROLS
CHEMICAL WARFARE.
CIVIL SUPREMACY OVER THE MILITARY.
CIVILIAN DEFENCE
COUNTERINSURGENCY.
EMERGENCY COMMUNICATION SYSTEMS
EMERGENCY TRANSPORTATION.
EVACUATION OF CIVILIANS.
EXSERVICEMEN
GUERRILLA WARFARE.
GUIDED MISSILES.
IMAGINARY WARS AND BATTLES.
LOGISTICS.
MERCENARY TROOPS.
MILITARISM
MILITARY ART AND SCIENCE.
MILITARY ASSISTANCE, AMERICAN.
MILITARY ASSISTANCE, NEW ZEALAND
MILITARY DISCIPLINE
MILITARY GEOGRAPHY
MILITARY GOVERNMENT.
MILITARY HISTORY, MODERN.
MILITARY INTELLIGENCE.
MILITARY LAW
MILITARY SERVICE, COMPULSORY
MILITARY SERVICE, VOLUNTARY
MILITARY UNIONS
MUNITIONS.
MUTINY
NAVAL STRATEGY.
PARAMILITARY FORCES
PENSIONS, MILITARY
PRISONERS OF WAR.
PRIVATEERING.
PSYCHOLOGY, MILITARY.
SEA POWER.
SOCIOLOGY, MILITARY.
SOLDIERS
STRATEGY.
V-1 BOMB.
V-2 ROCKET.
WAR.
WOMEN'S ROYAL NAVAL SERVICE.

PHILOSOPHY AND RELIGION.

Philosophy.

ACT (PHILOSOPHY).
BUSINESS ETHICS.
COSMOLOGY.
DIALECTIC.
ETHICS.
ETHICS, GREEK.
EVOLUTION.
FREE WILL AND DETERMINISM.
HUMANISM.
IDEALISM.
IDENTITY.
IDEOLOGY.
IMAGINATION.
KNOWLEDGE, SOCIOLOGY OF.
KNOWLEDGE, THEORY OF.
LAW AND ETHICS.
LEGAL ETHICS
LOGIC.
LOGIC, SYMBOLIC AND MATHEMATICAL.
MATERIALISM.
MEANING.
MEANING (PHILOSOPHY).
MEDICAL ETHICS.
MIND AND BODY.
MOVEMENT (PHILOSOPHY).
ONTOLOGY.
PHENOMENOLOGY.
PHILOSOPHY.
PHILOSOPHY, AMERICAN.
PHILOSOPHY, FRENCH.
PHILOSOPHY, GERMAN.
PHILOSOPHY, LATIN AMERICAN.
PHILOSOPHY, MODERN.
PHILOSOPHY, PRIMITIVE.
PHILOSOPHY, WHITE RUSSIAN.
PHILOSOPHY, YUGOSLAV.
PHILOSOPHY AND RELIGION.
POLITICAL ETHICS.
POSITIVISM.
PRACTICE (PHILOSOPHY).
PRAGMATISM.
RATIONALISM
REALITY.
RIGHT AND WRONG.
SCIENCE AND ETHICS.
SEMANTICS (PHILOSOPHY).
SOCIAL ETHICS.
STRUCTURALISM.
SURREALISM.
TECHNOLOGY AND ETHICS.
TELEOLOGY.
THEORY (PHILOSOPHY).
TRUTH.
UTILITARIANISM.
WAR AND MORALS.

Religion.

AFRICAN METHODIST EPISCOPAL CHURCH IN ZAMBIA.
ALBIGENSES.
ANCESTOR WORSHIP
ANTICLERICALISM
APOLOGETICS.
APOSTASY.
ATHANASIAN CREED.
ATHEISM.
BIBLE
BISHOPS
BUDDHA AND BUDDHISM
CATHOLIC CHURCH
CATHOLIC CHURCH AND CIVIL RIGHTS.

POLITICAL SCIENCE, POLITICS AND GOVERNMENT

CATHOLIC CHURCH IN CANADA.
CATHOLIC CHURCH IN FRANCE.
CATHOLIC CHURCH IN GERMANY.
CATHOLIC CHURCH IN ITALY.
CATHOLIC CHURCH IN PERU.
CATHOLIC CHURCH IN POLAND.
CATHOLIC CHURCH IN SPAIN.
CATHOLIC CHURCH IN THE UNITED STATES.
CATHOLIC SCHOOLS
CATHOLICS IN FRANCE.
CATHOLICS IN ITALY.
CATHOLICS IN NORTHERN IRELAND.
CATHOLICS IN THE UNITED STATES.
CHRISTIAN LIFE.
CHRISTIAN PILGRIMS AND PILGRIMAGES.
CHRISTIANITY.
CHRISTIANITY AND ECONOMICS.
CHRISTIANITY AND INTERNATIONAL AFFAIRS.
CHRISTIANITY AND POLITICS.
CHRISTIANS IN CHINA.
CHURCH AND LABOUR.
CHURCH AND RACE PROBLEMS.
CHURCH AND SOCIAL PROBLEMS.
CHURCH AND STATE
CHURCH AND STATE IN FRANCE.
CHURCH AND STATE IN GERMANY.
CHURCH AND STATE IN MALTA.
CHURCH AND STATE IN MEXICO.
CHURCH AND STATE IN PERU.
CHURCH AND STATE IN RUSSIA.
CHURCH AND STATE IN SPAIN.
CHURCH AND STATE IN THE UNITED KINGDOM.
CHURCH HISTORY.
CHURCH OF ENGLAND.
CHURCH RECORDS AND REGISTERS
CLERGY
COMMUNISM AND CHRISTIANITY.
COMMUNISM AND RELIGION.
CONVERTS, CATHOLIC.
COUNCILS AND SYNODS.
DISSENTERS, RELIGIOUS
DUKHOBORS.
FAITH-CURE AND SPIRITUALISM.
FRANCISCANS IN BRAZIL.
FRIENDS, SOCIETY OF.
GOD.
HERESIES AND HERETICS
HUTTERITES.
JANSONISM.
JESUITS IN MEXICO.
JEWISH CHRISTIANS.
LAITY
LIBERALISM (RELIGION)
LIBERTY OF CONSCIENCE.
LOLLARDS.
MASOWE APOSTLES.
MENNONITES IN IOWA.
MESSIAH
MESSIANISM.
MESSIANISM, AMERICAN.
MESSIANISM, BRAZILIAN.
MILLENNIUM
MISSIONS
MOHAMMEDANS AND SOCIAL PROBLEMS
MOHAMMEDANS IN MALAYSIA.
MONASTERIES
MONASTIC LIBRARIES
MONASTICISM AND RELIGIOUS ORDERS
NATURAL THEOLOGY.
ONEIDA COMMUNITY.
ORTHODOX EASTERN CHURCH, ROMANIAN
ORTHODOX EASTERN CHURCH, RUSSIAN.
PAPACY
PARISHES
PHILOSOPHY AND RELIGION.

PRAYER.
PRESS, CATHOLIC
PROTESTANT CHURCHES
PROTESTANTS IN IRELAND.
PURITANS.
RAS TAFARI MOVEMENT.
REFORMATION
RELIGION
RELIGION AND HUMOUR.
RELIGION AND SCIENCE.
RELIGION AND SOCIOLOGY.
RELIGION AND STATE
RELIGIONS.
RELIGIOUS EDUCATION
RELIGIOUS LIBERTY
RELIGIOUS THOUGHT
RITUALISM.
SALVATION ARMY
SECTS
SECULARISM
SECULARIZATION (THEOLOGY).
SEX AND RELIGION.
SHAMANISM.
SOCIALISM, CHRISTIAN.
SOCIALISM AND CATHOLIC CHURCH.
SOCIALISM AND JUDAISM.
SOCIOLOGY, CHRISTIAN.
SPIRITUAL LIFE.
SUNDAY LEGISLATION
SUNDAY-SCHOOLS.
THEOLOGY.
TOLERATION.
TRADE UNIONS, CATHOLIC
VATICAN
WAR AND RELIGION.
WOMEN, MOHAMMEDAN.
WORLD COUNCIL OF CHURCHES.
ZOROASTRIANISM.

POLITICAL SCIENCE, POLITICS AND GOVERNMENT.

General.

ADMINISTRATION.
ADMINISTRATIVE AGENCIES
ADMINISTRATIVE AND POLITICAL DIVISIONS
AFFIRMATIVE ACTION PROGRAMMES
AGRICULTURE AND STATE
ALLEGIANCE.
ANARCHISM AND ANARCHISTS.
ANTICOMMUNIST MOVEMENTS
ARISTOCRACY.
ASSASSINATION
ATOMIC WEAPONS AND DISARMAMENT.
ATROCITIES
AUTHORITARIANISM.
AUTONOMY.
BALANCE OF POWER.
BOUNDARIES.
BRIBERY.
BUREAUCRACY.
BUSINESS AND POLITICS
CABINET MINISTERS
CAMPAIGN FUNDS.
CATHOLIC CHURCH AND CIVIL RIGHTS.
CENTRE PARTIES
CHRISTIANITY AND INTERNATIONAL AFFAIRS.
CHRISTIANITY AND POLITICS.
CHURCH AND STATE
CHURCH AND STATE IN FRANCE.
CHURCH AND STATE IN GERMANY.
CHURCH AND STATE IN MEXICO.
CHURCH AND STATE IN PERU.
CHURCH AND STATE IN RUSSIA.
CHURCH AND STATE IN SPAIN.
CHURCH AND STATE IN THE UNITED KINGDOM.
CITIZENS' ASSOCIATIONS

CITIZENSHIP, LOSS OF
CIVICS, AMERICAN.
CIVICS, RUSSIAN.
CIVIL RIGHTS.
CIVIL SERVICE
CIVIL SUPREMACY OVER THE MILITARY.
COALITION (SOCIAL SCIENCES).
COALITION GOVERNMENTS
COLONIES.
COLONIES IN AFRICA.
COLONIES IN ASIA.
COMMUNICATION IN POLITICS.
COMMUNISM.
COMMUNISM AND CHRISTIANITY.
COMMUNISM AND CULTURE.
COMMUNISM AND ECOLOGY.
COMMUNISM AND EDUCATION.
COMMUNISM AND INTELLECTUALS.
COMMUNISM AND LITERATURE.
COMMUNISM AND MASS MEDIA.
COMMUNISM AND RELIGION.
COMMUNISM AND SOCIETY.
COMMUNIST EDUCATION
COMMUNIST REVISIONISM.
COMMUNIST STATE.
COMMUNIST STRATEGY.
COMMUNIST TEACHERS
COMMUNIST TRIALS
COMMUNISTIC SETTLEMENTS
COMMUNITY LEADERSHIP.
COMMUNITY POWER.
CONSCIENTIOUS OBJECTORS.
CONSENSUS (SOCIAL SCIENCES).
CONSERVATISM.
CONSTITUTIONAL HISTORY.
CORPORATE STATE.
CORRUPTION (IN POLITICS)
COUPS D'ETAT.
CROWN LANDS
DECENTRALIZATION IN GOVERNMENT
DELEGATED LEGISLATION
DEMOCRACY.
DEMONSTRATIONS
DETENTE.
DICTATORSHIP OF THE PROLETARIAT.
DISARMAMENT.
DISCIPLINARY POWER
DISCRIMINATION
DISSENTERS
EDUCATION AND STATE
ELECTIONS.
ELITE.
EMIGRATION AND IMMIGRATION.
ESPIONAGE, GERMAN
EUROPEAN FEDERATION.
EXECUTIVE POWER
EXECUTIVE PRIVILEGE (GOVERNMENT INFORMATION).
FASCISM.
FEDERAL GOVERNMENT.
FREEDOM OF ASSOCIATION.
FREEDOM OF INFORMATION
GEOGRAPHY, POLITICAL.
GOVERNMENT, COMPARATIVE.
GOVERNMENT, PRIMITIVE.
GOVERNMENT, RESISTANCE TO.
GOVERNMENT ADVERTISING.
GOVERNMENT AND THE PRESS
GOVERNMENT CONSULTANTS
GOVERNMENT EXECUTIVES, TRAINING OF
GOVERNMENT PUBLICITY
GRAFFITI
GRAND JURY
GUERRILLAS
HIGHWAY DEPARTMENTS
HISTORICAL MATERIALISM.
HOME RULE
IMPEACHMENTS
IMPERIALISM.
INDIVIDUALISM.
INDUSTRY AND STATE.

POLITICAL SCIENCE, POLITICS AND GOVERNMENT (Cont.)

INSURGENCY
INTELLECTUALS
INTELLIGENCE SERVICE
INTERNAL SECURITY
INTERNATIONAL AGENCIES.
INTERNATIONAL BROADCASTING.
INTERNATIONAL COOPERATION.
INTERNATIONAL OFFICIALS AND EMPLOYEES.
INTERNATIONAL ORGANIZATION.
INTERNATIONAL RELATIONS.
INTERNATIONALISM.
ISLANDS.
JURY
KIDNAPPING
LAW AND SOCIALISM.
LEADERSHIP.
LEGISLATIVE BODIES.
LEGISLATORS.
LEGITIMACY OF GOVERNMENTS.
LIBERALISM.
LIBERTY.
LIBERTY OF SPEECH.
LIBERTY OF THE PRESS.
LITERATURE AND POLITICS.
LITERATURE AND REVOLUTIONS.
LOBBYING
LOCAL ELECTIONS
LOCAL GOVERNMENT
LOCAL GOVERNMENT OFFICIALS AND EMPLOYEES
MARXISM.
MAYORS
METROPOLITAN GOVERNMENT
MILITARISM
MILITARY GOVERNMENT.
MINORITIES.
MONARCHY.
MUNICIPAL GOVERNMENT.
MUNICIPAL OFFICIALS AND EMPLOYEES
MUNICIPAL OWNERSHIP
MUNICIPAL SERVICES
NATIONALISM.
NATIONALISM AND SOCIALISM.
NATIONALITIES, PRINCIPLE OF.
NATIVISM.
NATURALIZATION
NIHILISM.
NOMINATIONS FOR OFFICE
NONVIOLENCE.
OMBUDSMAN
OPPOSITION (POLITICAL SCIENCE).
PACIFIC SETTLEMENT OF INTERNATIONAL DISPUTES.
PACIFISM
PARLIAMENTARY PRACTICE
PARTY AFFILIATION
PASSIVE RESISTANCE.
PEACE.
PEASANT UPRISINGS
PICKETING
POLICE, POLITICAL AND SECRET
POLICY SCIENCES.
POLITICAL CONVENTIONS.
POLITICAL CRIMES AND OFFENCES
POLITICAL ETHICS.
POLITICAL ORATORY
POLITICAL PARTICIPATION.
POLITICAL PARTIES.
POLITICAL PRISONERS.
POLITICAL PSYCHOLOGY.
POLITICAL SCIENCE.
POLITICAL SCIENCE RESEARCH
POLITICAL SOCIALIZATION.
POLITICAL SOCIOLOGY.
POLITICS AND EDUCATION.
POLITICS AND LITERATURE.
POPULAR FRONTS.
POPULATION TRANSFERS.
POPULISM.
POWER (SOCIAL SCIENCES).
PRESS, COMMUNIST

PRESS, LABOUR
PRESS AND POLITICS
PRESSURE GROUPS
PRIME MINISTERS
PRIVACY, RIGHT OF.
PROPAGANDA.
PROPERTY AND SOCIALISM.
PROPORTIONAL REPRESENTATION.
RADICALISM.
RADIO IN PROPAGANDA
RADIO PROGRAMMES, PUBLIC SERVICE.
RAILWAYS AND STATE
REFERENDUM
REFUGEES, AFRICAN.
REFUGEES, ARAB.
REFUGEES, BANGLADESHI.
REFUGEES, VIETNAMESE.
REGIONALISM
REGIONALISM (INTERNATIONAL ORGANIZATION).
RELATIVITY.
RELIGION AND STATE
RELIGIOUS LIBERTY
REPRESENTATIVE GOVERNMENT AND REPRESENTATION.
REVOLUTIONISTS
REVOLUTIONS.
RIGHT AND LEFT (POLITICAL SCIENCE).
RIOTS
SCIENCE AND STATE.
SECESSION.
SECRET SERVICE
SECURITY, INTERNATIONAL.
SELF-DETERMINATION, NATIONAL.
SEPARATION OF POWERS
SEX.
SOCIALISM.
SOCIALISM, CHRISTIAN.
SOCIALISM AND ART.
SOCIALISM AND CATHOLIC CHURCH.
SOCIALISM AND JUDAISM.
SOCIALISM AND SOCIETY.
SOCIALISM AND YOUTH
SOCIALISTS
SOVEREIGNTY.
SOVIETS.
SPIES.
SPORTS AND STATE
STATE, THE.
STATE GOVERNMENTS
STATE SUCCESSION.
STATES, NEW.
STATES, SMALL.
STATESMEN
SUBVERSIVE ACTIVITIES.
SUFFRAGE
SUNDAY LEGISLATION
TECHNOLOGY AND STATE.
TELEVISION IN POLITICS.
TERRORISM.
THEATRE AND STATE
TORTURE.
TRADE UNIONS AND COMMUNISM.
TRUST TERRITORIES
UTOPIAS.
VIOLENCE.
VOTERS, REGISTRATION OF.
VOTING
WAR.
WAR AND SOCIALISM.
WAR RELIEF.
WOMEN AND SOCIALISM.
WOMEN REVOLUTIONISTS
WORLD POLITICS.

Particular countries, nationalities, parties, organizations, etc.

AFRO-ASIAN PEOPLES' SOLIDARITY ORGANIZATION.

AFRO-ASIAN-LATIN AMERICAN PEOPLES' SOLIDARITY CONFERENCE, HAVANA, 1966.
ALIANZA POPULAR REVOLUCIONARIA AMERICANA.
AMERICAN LOYALISTS.
AMNESTY INTERNATIONAL
ANTINAZI MOVEMENT.
ASSOCIAZIONE NAZIONALISTA ITALIANA.
BLACK POWER.
BULGARSKI ZEMEDELSKI NARODEN SUIUZ.
BUND.
COMMUNIST COUNTRIES
COMMUNIST PARTIES.
COMMUNIST PARTY
COMMUNISTS
CONGRESS OF THE PEOPLES OF THE EAST, BAKU, 1920.
CONSERVATIVE PARTY (CANADA).
CONSERVATIVE PARTY (UNITED KINGDOM).
COOPERATIVE COMMONWEALTH FEDERATION.
COUNCIL OF EUROPE.
DECEMBRISTS.
DEMOCRATIC PARTY (UNITED STATES).
DEUTSCHE DEMOKRATISCHE PARTEI.
DEUTSCHE VOLKSPARTEI.
DEUTSCHNATIONALE VOLKSPARTEI.
EUROPEAN COMMISSION OF HUMAN RIGHTS.
EUROPEAN COMMUNITIES.
EUROPEAN CONVENTION ON HUMAN RIGHTS.
EUROPEAN ECONOMIC COMMUNITY.
EUROPEAN PARLIAMENT.
FABIAN SOCIETY.
FLEMISH MOVEMENT.
FREIE DEMOKRATISCHE PARTEI.
FRONT DE LIBERATION QUEBECOIS.
INDIAN NATIONAL CONGRESS.
INTERNATIONAL, THE.
INTERNATIONAL WORKING UNION OF SOCIALIST PARTIES.
JEWISH-ARAB RELATIONS.
JEWISH QUESTION.
KUOMINTANG.
LABOUR PARTY
LEAGUE OF ARAB STATES.
LEAGUE OF NATIONS.
LIBERAL PARTY
LIGUE DE LA PATRIE FRANÇAISE.
MONARCHY, SPANISH.
MOVIMIENTO DE LA IZQUIERDA REVOLUCIONARIA.
MOVIMIENTO NACIONALISTA REVOLUCIONARIO.
NATIONAL FRONT.
NATIONAL SOCIALISM.
NATIONALDEMOKRATISCHE PARTEI DEUTSCHLANDS [BUNDESREPUBLIK].
NEW COMMUNIST PARTY OF BRITAIN.
NEW GUARD.
NORTH ATLANTIC TREATY ORGANIZATION.
OCCITANE MOVEMENT.
ORGANIZATION OF AFRICAN UNITY.
ORGANIZATION OF LATIN AMERICAN SOLIDARITY.
PANAFRICANISM.
PANAMERICANISM.
PARTI QUEBECOIS.
PARTIDO CARLISTA.
PARTIDO COMUNISTA DEL PERU.
PARTIDO DEMOCRATA PROGRESISTA.
PARTIDO PROVERISTA.
PARTIJ VAN DE ARBEID.
PARTIT NACIONALISTA REPUBLICA D'ESQUERRA.

PUBLIC HEALTH AND MEDICINE

PARTITO COMUNISTA D'ITALIA (MARXISTA-LENINISTA).
PARTITO DI UNITÀ PROLETARIA PER IL COMUNISMO.
PARTITO POPOLARE ITALIANO.
PARTITO RADICALE (ITALY).
PARTITO SOCIALISTA ITALIANO.
PEOPLE'S NATIONAL CONGRESS.
PLAID CYMRU.
POLITICAL POSTERS, FRENCH.
POLITICAL SATIRE, ITALIAN.
PROGRESSIVE PARTY, FOUNDED 1912 (UNITED STATES).
PROGRESSIVISM (U.S. POLITICS).
PROPAGANDA, AMERICAN.
PROPAGANDA, BRITISH.
PROPAGANDA, CHINESE.
PROPAGANDA, COMMUNIST.
PROPAGANDA, FRENCH.
PROPAGANDA, RHODESIAN.
RED CROSS.
REFUGEES IN CANADA.
REFUGEES IN THE UNITED STATES.
REPUBLICAN PARTY (FRANCE).
REPUBLICAN PARTY (UNITED STATES).
REPUBLICANISM IN FRANCE.
REVOLUTIONARY SOCIALIST PARTY (CZECHOSLOVAKIA).
SCANDINAVIANISM.
SCOTTISH NATIONAL PARTY.
SOCIAL DEMOCRATIC PARTY (DENMARK).
SOCIAL DEMOCRATIC PARTY (GERMANY).
SOCIAL DEMOCRATIC PARTY (HUNGARY).
SOCIAL DEMOCRATIC PARTY (ITALY).
SOCIAL DEMOCRATIC PARTY (NORWAY).
SOCIAL DEMOCRATIC PARTY (ROMANIA).
SOCIAL DEMOCRATIC PARTY (RUSSIA).
SOCIAL DEMOCRATIC PARTY (SWEDEN).
SOCIAL DEMOCRATIC PARTY (SWITZERLAND).
SOCIALISM IN AFRICA.
SOCIALISM IN ALGERIA.
SOCIALISM IN ARAB COUNTRIES.
SOCIALISM IN BELGIUM.
SOCIALISM IN CANADA.
SOCIALISM IN CHILE.
SOCIALISM IN CHINA.
SOCIALISM IN CZECHOSLOVAKIA.
SOCIALISM IN EASTERN EUROPE.
SOCIALISM IN EUROPE.
SOCIALISM IN FRANCE.
SOCIALISM IN GERMANY.
SOCIALISM IN GUINEA-BISSAU.
SOCIALISM IN IRELAND.
SOCIALISM IN ITALY.
SOCIALISM IN KOREA.
SOCIALISM IN PORTUGAL.
SOCIALISM IN ROMANIA.
SOCIALISM IN RUSSIA.
SOCIALISM IN SPAIN.
SOCIALISM IN SWEDEN.
SOCIALISM IN SWITZERLAND.
SOCIALISM IN TANZANIA.
SOCIALISM IN THE NETHERLANDS.
SOCIALISM IN THE SOMALI REPUBLIC.
SOCIALISM IN THE UNITED KINGDOM.
SOCIALISM IN THE UNITED STATES.
SOCIALISM IN TRANSYLVANIA.
SOCIALISM IN VIETNAM.
SOCIALISM IN YUGOSLAVIA.
SOCIALIST LABOR PARTY OF AMERICA.
SOCIALIST PARTIES.
SOCIALIST PARTY (ARGENTINE REPUBLIC).
SOCIALIST PARTY (AUSTRIA).
SOCIALIST PARTY (BELGIUM).
SOCIALIST PARTY (FINLAND).
SOCIALIST PARTY (FRANCE).
SOCIALIST PARTY (GERMANY).
SOCIALIST PARTY (ITALY).
SOCIALIST PARTY (POLAND).
SOCIALIST PARTY (PORTUGAL).
SOCIALIST PARTY (SPAIN).
SOCIALIST PARTY (TUNISIA).
SOCIALIST WORKERS' PARTY (UNITED STATES).
SOUTH-EAST ASIA TREATY ORGANIZATION.
TENENTISMO.
TOWARZYSTWO DEMOKRATYCZNE POLSKIE.
UNGARLAENDISCHE DEUTSCHE VOLKSPARTEI.
UNIDAD POPULAR.
UNION CIVICA.
UNION CIVICA RADICAL.
UNION CIVICA RADICAL INTRANSIGENTE.
UNION DES DEMOCRATES POUR LA REPUBLIQUE.
UNIONIST PARTY (UNITED KINGDOM).
UNITED NATIONS.
WALLOON MOVEMENT.
WATERGATE AFFAIR, 1972- .
WORLD JEWISH CONGRESS.
YOUNG COMMUNIST LEAGUE
ZJEDNOCZONE STRONNICTWO LUDOWE.

PSYCHOLOGY.

ADAPTABILITY (PSYCHOLOGY).
ADJUSTMENT (PSYCHOLOGY).
ADOLESCENT PSYCHOLOGY.
AGE (PSYCHOLOGY).
AGGRESSIVENESS (PSYCHOLOGY).
ALTRUISM.
ARTIFICIAL INTELLIGENCE.
ATTITUDE (PSYCHOLOGY).
AUDITORY PERCEPTION.
AUTONOMY (PSYCHOLOGY).
BEHAVIOUR THERAPY.
BEREAVEMENT.
CHILD PSYCHIATRY
CHILD PSYCHOLOGY.
CHILD STUDY.
CLINICAL PSYCHOLOGY.
COGNITION.
COGNITION (CHILD PSYCHOLOGY).
COGNITIVE STYLES.
COMMUNITY PSYCHOLOGY.
CONFESSION
CONSCIOUSNESS.
CREATIVE ABILITY.
CRIMINAL PSYCHOLOGY.
DECISION-MAKING.
DEPRESSION, MENTAL.
DEPTH PERCEPTION.
DEVELOPMENTAL PSYCHOBIOLOGY.
DEVELOPMENTAL PSYCHOLOGY.
DISSONANCE (PSYCHOLOGY).
EDUCATIONAL PSYCHOLOGY.
EGO (PSYCHOLOGY).
ENVIRONMENTAL PSYCHOLOGY.
ESCAPE (PSYCHOLOGY).
FANTASY.
GENETIC PSYCHOLOGY.
GRIEF.
GROWTH.
HUMAN BEHAVIOUR.
HUMAN INFORMATION PROCESSING.
HYPNOTISM.
IDENTITY (PSYCHOLOGY).
INDIVIDUALITY.
INFANT PSYCHOLOGY.
INTELLECT.
INTERPERSONAL ATTRACTION.
INTERPERSONAL COMMUNICATION.
INTERVIEWING.
LEARNING, PSYCHOLOGY OF.
MEMORY.
MENTAL TESTS.
MOTIVATION (PSYCHOLOGY).
MOVEMENT, PSYCHOLOGY OF.
NEGOTIATION.
PERSONALITY.
PERSONALITY, DISORDERS OF.
PERSONALITY AND CULTURE.
PERSUASION (PSYCHOLOGY).
POLITICAL PSYCHOLOGY.
PSYCHIATRIC RESEARCH.
PSYCHIATRIC SOCIAL WORK
PSYCHIATRY.
PSYCHOANALYSIS.
PSYCHOBIOLOGY.
PSYCHOLINGUISTICS.
PSYCHOLOGICAL RESEARCH.
PSYCHOLOGICAL RESEARCH, EXPERIMENTER EFFECTS IN.
PSYCHOLOGY.
PSYCHOLOGY, APPLIED.
PSYCHOLOGY, EXPERIMENTAL.
PSYCHOLOGY, FORENSIC.
PSYCHOLOGY, INDUSTRIAL.
PSYCHOLOGY, MILITARY.
PSYCHOLOGY, PHYSIOLOGICAL.
PSYCHOTHERAPY.
READING, PSYCHOLOGY OF.
REPERTORY GRID TECHNIQUE.
SELF-ACTUALIZATION (PSYCHOLOGY).
SELF-CONTROL.
SELF-EVALUATION.
SEX (PSYCHOLOGY).
SEX DIFFERENCES.
SOCIAL PSYCHOLOGY.
SPEECH, DISORDERS OF.
SPEECH DISORDERS IN CHILDREN.
THOUGHT AND THINKING.
TOUCH.
VALUES.
VISUAL PERCEPTION.
WORK.

PUBLIC HEALTH AND MEDICINE.

ABORTION
AIR
ALCOHOLISM.
AMBULATORY MEDICAL CARE.
APHASIA.
BIRTH CONTROL CLINICS
BLINDNESS
BLOOD BANKS
BODY, HUMAN
BREAST FEEDING.
BRONCHITIS.
BUILDING
CANCER
CHARITIES, MEDICAL
CHILD PSYCHIATRY
CHILDBIRTH.
CHOLERA, ASIATIC
CHRONICALLY ILL
CLUTTERING (SPEECH PATHOLOGY).
COMMUNICABLE DISEASES.
COMMUNICATIVE DISORDERS.
COMMUNITY HEALTH SERVICES
COMMUNITY MENTAL HEALTH SERVICES.
CONTRACEPTIVES
CRYONICS.
DEATH.
DISEASES
DRUG UTILIZATION.
DRUGS.
EMERGENCY MEDICAL SERVICES.
EPIDEMICS
EPIDEMIOLOGY.
EUTHANASIA.
HEALTH ATTITUDES.
HEALTH EDUCATION

PUBLIC HEALTH AND MEDICINE (Cont.)

HEALTH MAINTENANCE ORGANIZATIONS.
HEALTH SERVICES ADMINISTRATION
HOME ACCIDENTS
HOSPITAL CARE
HOSPITAL PHARMACIES.
HOSPITALS
HOSPITALS, GYNAECOLOGIC AND OBSTETRIC.
HUNGER.
HYGIENE, PUBLIC.
HYPNOTISM.
HYPOTHERMIA.
INDUSTRIAL ACCIDENTS
INDUSTRIAL HYGIENE
INDUSTRIAL SAFETY
INFANTS
LUNGS
MALNUTRITION.
MALNUTRITION IN CHILDREN.
MATERNAL AND INFANT WELFARE
MEDICAL APPOINTMENTS AND SCHEDULES.
MEDICAL CARE.
MEDICAL CARE, COST OF
MEDICAL CENTRES
MEDICAL ECONOMICS.
MEDICAL ETHICS.
MEDICAL FEES
MEDICAL GEOGRAPHY.
MEDICAL LAWS AND LEGISLATION
MEDICAL PERSONNEL AND PATIENT
MEDICAL POLICY.
MEDICAL RESEARCH
MEDICAL SOCIETIES
MEDICAL STATISTICS.
MEDICINE
MEDICINE, CLINICAL
MEDICINE, PRIMITIVE
MEDICINE, STATE
MEDICINES, PATENT, PROPRIETARY, ETC.
MENTAL HEALTH LAWS
MENTAL HEALTH SERVICES.
MENTAL ILLNESS.
MENTALLY HANDICAPPED
MENTALLY ILL
NARCOTIC ADDICTS
NARCOTIC HABIT
NURSES AND NURSING.
NURSING HOME ACCIDENTS
NURSING HOMES
NUTRITION.
NUTRITION POLICY.
OCCUPATIONAL DISEASES.
OCCUPATIONAL THERAPY.
PHARMACEUTICAL POLICY.
PHARMACEUTICAL RESEARCH
PHYSICALLY HANDICAPPED
PHYSICIAN AND PATIENT.
PROSTHESIS.
PROTEIN METABOLISM.
PROTEINS.
PSYCHIATRIC HOSPITAL CARE
PSYCHIATRIC HOSPITALS.
PSYCHIATRY.
PSYCHOLOGY, PATHOLOGICAL.
PSYCHOLOGY, PHYSIOLOGICAL.
PSYCHOTHERAPY.
RADIATION.
RADIOGRAPHY.
ROAD ACCIDENTS
SACCHARIN.
SEXUAL DISORDERS.
SICK
SMALLPOX
SMALLPOX, INOCULATION OF.
SMOKING.
SOCIAL MEDICINE.
SOCIAL PSYCHIATRY.
STUTTERING.
SURGERY.
VOLUNTARY HEALTH AGENCIES
WOMEN'S HEALTH SERVICES.

SCIENCE AND TECHNOLOGY.

ACCEPTANCE SAMPLING.
ARTIFICIAL INTELLIGENCE.
ATOMIC ENERGY.
ATOMIC POWER.
BIOLOGICAL WARFARE.
BIOLOGY
BIOMETRY.
BOTANY
BRITISH EMPIRE EXHIBITION, 1924-1925.
CATIONS.
CHEMICAL WARFARE.
COMMUNICATION IN SCIENCE.
DIGITAL COMPUTER SIMULATION.
ENVIRONMENTAL IMPACT ANALYSIS.
EXPLOSIVES
FIREARMS
FOOD ADDITIVES.
FOOD RESEARCH.
FORECASTING.
HEREDITY.
HUMAN ENGINEERING.
HUMAN GENETICS.
HYDROCARBONS.
INFORMATION SCIENCE.
INFORMATION STORAGE AND RETRIEVAL SYSTEMS.
INTERNATIONAL ATOMIC ENERGY AGENCY.
MAN-MACHINE SYSTEMS.
METHODOLOGY.
MORPHOGENESIS
NOISE CONTROL
ORE DRESSING.
PHYSICS
REFUSE AND REFUSE DISPOSAL
RELIGION AND SCIENCE.
RESEARCH.
REWARDS (PRIZES, ETC.)
ROYAL SOCIETY OF LONDON.
SCIENCE.
SCIENCE AND ETHICS.
SCIENCE AND STATE.
SCIENTIFIC APPARATUS AND INSTRUMENTS
SEWERAGE
SOLAR STILLS.
TECHNOLOGICAL FORECASTING.
TECHNOLOGICAL INNOVATIONS.
TECHNOLOGY.
TECHNOLOGY AND CIVILIZATION.
TECHNOLOGY AND ETHICS.
TECHNOLOGY AND LAW.
TECHNOLOGY AND STATE.
TECHNOLOGY TRANSFER.
WATER POWER
WOMEN SCIENTISTS.

SOCIOLOGY, ANTHROPOLOGY AND ETHNOLOGY.

General.

ABORTION
ACCULTURATION.
ADOLESCENCE.
ADOLESCENT BOYS.
AFRO-AMERICAN SOCIOLOGISTS.
AGE GROUPS.
AGING.
ALBANY PRISON.
ALCOHOL AND YOUTH
ALCOHOLISM.
ALIENATION (SOCIAL PSYCHOLOGY).
ANIMALS, TREATMENT OF.
ANTHROPOLOGICAL LINGUISTICS.
ANTHROPOLOGY.
ANTISEMITISM.
APARTMENT HOUSES
ARCHITECTURE AND SOCIETY.
ART AND SOCIETY.
ARTS AND SOCIETY
ASSIMILATION (SOCIOLOGY).
ASSISTANCE IN EMERGENCIES
ASSOCIATED COUNTRY WOMEN OF THE WORLD.
ASSOCIATIONS, INSTITUTIONS, ETC.
AUTISM.
BEGGING
BIRTH CONTROL.
BLACK NATIONALISM
BLACK POWER.
BOHEMIANISM
BOYS
BRIGANDS AND ROBBERS
BRITISH BROADCASTING CORPORATION.
CASTE
CHARITIES
CHARITIES, MEDICAL
CHILD ABUSE
CHILD DEVELOPMENT.
CHILD WELFARE.
CHILDREN
CHILDREN, FIRST BORN.
CHILDREN OF WORKING MOTHERS.
CHURCH AND RACE PROBLEMS.
CHURCH AND SOCIAL PROBLEMS.
CITIES AND TOWNS.
CITIZENSHIP
CITY CHILDREN.
CITY PLANNING.
CITY PLANNING AND THE PRESS.
CLANS AND CLAN SYSTEM.
CLASSIFICATION OF CRIMES.
COMMUNES (CHINA).
COMMUNICATION.
COMMUNICATION IN MARRIAGE.
COMMUNICATION IN THE SOCIAL SCIENCES.
COMMUNISM AND CULTURE.
COMMUNISM AND INTELLECTUALS.
COMMUNISM AND MASS MEDIA.
COMMUNISM AND SOCIETY.
COMMUNISTIC SETTLEMENTS
COMMUNITY.
COMMUNITY AND SCHOOL.
COMMUNITY ANTENNA TELEVISION
COMMUNITY CENTRES
COMMUNITY DEVELOPMENT.
COMMUNITY DEVELOPMENT CORPORATIONS
COMMUNITY LIFE.
COMMUNITY ORGANIZATION.
COMMUNITY SCHOOLS
COMMUNITY-BASED CORRECTIONS
CONFORMITY.
CONJUGAL VIOLENCE.
CONSANGUINITY.
COUNSELLING.
CRIME AND CRIMINALS.
CRIME AND THE PRESS.
CROSS CULTURAL STUDIES.
CRUELTY TO CHILDREN.
CULTURAL RELATIONS.
CULTURE.
CULTURE CONFLICT.
CUSTODY OF CHILDREN
DAY NURSERIES
DEAF
DEVIANT BEHAVIOUR.
DIFFUSION OF INNOVATIONS.
DIRECT ACTION
DISASTER RELIEF.
DISASTERS.
DISCONTENT.
DISCRIMINATION IN HOUSING
DRUG ABUSE.
DURKHEIMIAN SCHOOL OF SOCIOLOGY

SOCIOLOGY, ANTHROPOLOGY AND ETHNOLOGY

DWELLINGS
ELITE.
ENCOMIENDAS (LATIN AMERICA).
ENDOWMENTS.
EQUALITY.
ETHNIC ATTITUDES.
ETHNICITY.
ETHNOCENTRISM.
ETHNOLOGY.
ETHNOPSYCHOLOGY.
EUGENICS.
EVACUATION OF CIVILIANS.
EVALUATION RESEARCH (SOCIAL ACTION PROGRAMMES).
EXPERIENCE.
EXSERVICEMEN
FAMILY.
FAMILY LIFE EDUCATION.
FAMILY RESEARCH.
FAMILY SIZE.
FAMILY SOCIAL WORK
FAMINES.
FATHER AND CHILD.
FEMINISM.
FERTILITY, HUMAN.
FESTIVALS
FIELD THEORY (SOCIAL PSYCHOLOGY).
FOLK LORE.
FOLK LORE, BLACK
FONDAZIONE GIOVANNI AGNELLI.
FOOD (IN RELIGION, FOLK-LORE, ETC.)
FOOD HABITS
FOOD RELIEF.
FORCED LABOUR
FOSTER DAY CARE.
FOSTER HOME CARE
FOUNDLINGS
FREEDMEN IN TEXAS.
FUNCTIONAL ANALYSIS (SOCIAL SCIENCES).
GAMBLING.
GOVERNMENT AND THE PRESS
GOVERNMENT PUBLICITY
GROUP RELATIONS TRAINING.
GUARANTEED ANNUAL INCOME
HALFWAY HOUSES.
HANDICAPPED
HANDICAPPED CHILDREN
HEROIN HABIT.
HOLIDAYS.
HOMELESSNESS
HOMOSEXUALITY
HOOLIGANS
HORSE RACING
HOWARD LEAGUE FOR PENAL REFORM.
HUMAN ECOLOGY.
HURRICANE PROTECTION
HYPOTHERMIA.
ILLEGITIMACY
INDIANS, TREATMENT OF.
INDUSTRIAL SOCIOLOGY.
INFORMATION THEORY IN SOCIOLOGY.
INSANE, CRIMINAL AND DANGEROUS.
INSTITUT PROVINCIAL DES SCIENCES SOCIALES APPLIQUEES.
INSTITUTIONAL CARE
INTELLECTUALS
INTELLIGENCE LEVELS.
INTERCULTURAL COMMUNICATION.
INTERNATIONAL RELIEF
INTERPERSONAL RELATIONS.
IRISH PRISONERS
JUVENILE COURTS
JUVENILE DELINQUENCY.
JUVENILE JUSTICE, ADMINISTRATION OF
KINSHIP
LAND USE, URBAN.
LANDLORD AND TENANT.
LEADERSHIP.
LEARNING ABILITY.
LEISURE

LIFE IMPRISONMENT
LIQUOR PROBLEM
LITERATURE AND SOCIETY.
LOVE.
LYNCHING
MALNUTRITION IN CHILDREN.
MAN.
MARIHUANA.
MARRIAGE.
MARRIED PEOPLE.
MARRIED WOMEN
MASS MEDIA.
MASS SOCIETY.
MATERNAL AND INFANT WELFARE
MEDICINE, PRIMITIVE
MENTALLY HANDICAPPED CHILDREN
METROPOLITAN AREAS.
MIDDLE CLASSES.
MOBILE HOMES
MOHAMMEDANS AND SOCIAL PROBLEMS
MOTHER AND CHILD.
MOTHERS
MOVING PICTURE JOURNALISM
MOVING PICTURES
MUGGING
MURDER
MUSIC AND SOCIETY.
MUSIC FESTIVALS.
MYTHOLOGY.
NARCOTIC ADDICTS
NARCOTIC HABIT
NATIONAL PARKS AND RESERVES
NATIVE RACES.
NEIGHBOURHOOD.
NEW TOWNS
NEWSREEL
NOMADS
OCCUPATIONAL PRESTIGE.
OFFICIAL SECRETS
OLD AGE.
OLD AGE HOMES
OLD AGE PENSIONS
ORAL COMMUNICATION.
ORAL TRADITION.
ORGANIZATION.
ORGANIZATIONAL BEHAVIOUR.
ORGANIZATIONAL CHANGE.
ORGANIZED CRIME.
ORPHANS AND ORPHAN ASYLUMS
PARENT AND CHILD.
PAROLE
PEASANTRY.
PENAL COLONIES
PENOLOGY.
PERSONAL SPACE.
PERSONALITY AND CULTURE.
PHILOSOPHICAL ANTHROPOLOGY.
PLANNING.
PLANTATION LIFE
PLAY
PLURALISM (SOCIAL SCIENCES).
POLICE.
POLICE, PRIVATE
POLICE POWER
POLITICAL SOCIALIZATION.
POLITICAL SOCIOLOGY.
POOR.
POPULAR CULTURE.
POVERTY.
POVERTY RESEARCH
POWER (SOCIAL SCIENCES).
PRISON RIOTS
PRISON SENTENCES.
PRISONERS
PRISONS.
PROHIBITION
PROSTITUTION
PSYCHIATRIC SOCIAL WORK
PUBLIC HOUSING
PUBLIC INSTITUTIONS
PUBLIC OPINION

PUBLIC OPINION POLLS.
PUBLIC RELATIONS
PUNISHMENT.
RACE.
RACE AWARENESS.
RACE DISCRIMINATION.
RACE PROBLEMS.
RADICAL ALTERNATIVES TO PRISON.
RAPE
RAPE VICTIM SERVICES
RECIDIVISTS
RECIPROCITY.
RECREATION
RECREATION AREAS
REFORMATORIES
REFORMATORIES FOR WOMEN
REGIONAL PLANNING.
REHABILITATION.
REHABILITATION, RURAL
REHABILITATION OF CRIMINALS.
REHABILITATION OF JUVENILE DELINQUENTS.
RELIGION AND HUMOUR.
RELIGION AND SOCIOLOGY.
REMAND HOMES
REPARATION
RETIREMENT, PLACES OF
RITES AND CEREMONIES.
ROTE ARMEE FRAKTION.
RURAL POOR
RURAL WOMEN.
RURAL YOUTH
RURAL-URBAN MIGRATION
SCHOOL SOCIAL WORK
SECURITIES FRAUD
SELF-HELP GROUPS
SENIOR POWER
SEX AND RELIGION.
SEX CUSTOMS.
SEX DISCRIMINATION
SEX DISCRIMINATION AGAINST WOMEN
SEX IN MASS MEDIA.
SEX OF CHILDREN, PARENTAL PREFERENCES FOR.
SEX ROLE.
SIGN LANGUAGE.
SINGLE PARENT FAMILY
SINGLE PEOPLE.
SLAVE TRADE
SLAVERY.
SLAVERY IN BARBADOS.
SLAVERY IN BRAZIL.
SLAVERY IN COLOMBIA.
SLAVERY IN INDIA.
SLAVERY IN SOUTH AFRICA.
SLAVERY IN THE UNITED KINGDOM.
SLAVERY IN THE UNITED STATES.
SLAVERY IN THE WEST INDIES.
SLUMS
SMALL GROUPS.
SMUGGLING
SOCCER
SOCIAL CASE WORK.
SOCIAL CHANGE.
SOCIAL CLASSES.
SOCIAL CONDITIONS
SOCIAL CONFLICT.
SOCIAL CONTROL.
SOCIAL CREDIT.
SOCIAL ETHICS.
SOCIAL EXCHANGE.
SOCIAL GROUP WORK.
SOCIAL GROUPS.
SOCIAL HISTORY.
SOCIAL INDICATORS
SOCIAL INTERACTION.
SOCIAL JUSTICE.
SOCIAL LEGISLATION
SOCIAL MOBILITY.
SOCIAL POLICY.
SOCIAL PROBLEMS.
SOCIAL PSYCHIATRY.

SOCIOLOGY, ANTHROPOLOGY AND ETHNOLOGY (Cont.)

SOCIAL PSYCHOLOGY.
SOCIAL REFORMERS
SOCIAL ROLE.
SOCIAL SCIENCE RESEARCH.
SOCIAL SCIENCES.
SOCIAL SCIENTISTS
SOCIAL SECURITY.
SOCIAL SERVICE.
SOCIAL SERVICE AND RACE PROBLEMS.
SOCIAL STABILITY.
SOCIAL STATUS.
SOCIAL STRUCTURE.
SOCIAL SURVEYS.
SOCIAL VALUES.
SOCIAL WORK ADMINISTRATION.
SOCIAL WORK EDUCATION.
SOCIAL WORK WITH CHILDREN
SOCIAL WORK WITH DELINQUENTS AND CRIMINALS
SOCIAL WORK WITH THE AGED
SOCIAL WORK WITH YOUTH
SOCIALISM AND SOCIETY.
SOCIALISM AND YOUTH
SOCIALIZATION.
SOCIALLY HANDICAPPED
SOCIALLY HANDICAPPED CHILDREN.
SOCIOBIOLOGY.
SOCIOLINGUISTICS.
SOCIOLOGICAL JURISPRUDENCE.
SOCIOLOGICAL RESEARCH.
SOCIOLOGISTS.
SOCIOLOGY.
SOCIOLOGY, CHRISTIAN.
SOCIOLOGY, MILITARY.
SOCIOLOGY, RURAL.
SOCIOLOGY, URBAN.
SPECTATOR CONTROL.
SPEECH AND SOCIAL STATUS.
SPORTS
SPORTS AND STATE
SQUATTERS
STATE ENCOURAGEMENT OF SCIENCE, LITERATURE AND ART
STRUCTURAL ANTHROPOLOGY.
SUBCULTURE.
SUBURBS
SUCCESS.
SUICIDE.
SUMMER HOMES
SYMBIONESE LIBERATION ARMY.
SYMBOLISM.
TALES, MAYAN.
TALL BUILDINGS
TELEVISION
TELEVISION AND CHILDREN.
TELEVISION AND YOUTH.
TELEVISION AUDIENCES
TELEVISION BROADCASTING
TELEVISION BROADCASTING OF NEWS
TELEVISION PROGRAMMES FOR CHILDREN
TERRORISM.
THERAPEUTIC COMMUNITY.
TRAMPS
TRANSHUMANCE
TREASON.
TRIBES AND TRIBAL SYSTEM
UNDERDEVELOPED AREAS.
UNMARRIED COUPLES.
UNMARRIED MOTHERS
UNTOUCHABLES.
UPPER CLASSES
URBAN RENEWAL.
URBANIZATION.
VEGETARIANISM.
VICTIMS OF CRIME.
VILLAGE COMMUNITIES
VILLAGES
VIOLENCE.
VIOLENCE IN MASS MEDIA.
VIOLENCE IN MOTION PICTURES.
VIOLENCE IN TELEVISION.

VOLUNTEER WORKERS IN SOCIAL SERVICE
WAR AND SOCIETY.
WELFARE STATE.
WHITE COLLAR CRIMES
WIFE BEATING.
WITCHCRAFT.
WOLF CHILDREN.
WOMEN.
WOMEN, MOHAMMEDAN.
WOMEN AND SOCIALISM.
WOMEN PRISONERS
WOMEN'S RIGHTS.
WORLD COUNCIL OF INDIGENOUS PEOPLES.
YOUTH.
YOUTH VOLUNTEERS IN COMMUNITY DEVELOPMENT
YOUTH VOLUNTEERS IN SOCIAL SERVICE
ZONING

Particular races, tribes and nationalities.

AFRICANS IN FRANCE.
AFRICANS IN THE UNITED KINGDOM.
AFRO-AMERICAN CRIMINALS.
AFRO-AMERICAN FAMILIES.
AFRO-AMERICANS.
AKANS (AFRICAN PEOPLE).
AKWE-SHAVANTE INDIANS.
ALGERIANS IN FRANCE.
ANTAISAKA.
APINAGE INDIANS.
ARABS.
ARAUCANIAN INDIANS.
ARMENIANS IN SYRIA.
ARMENIANS IN TURKEY.
ASIATICS IN THE UNITED KINGDOM.
ASTO INDIANS.
AUSTRALIAN ABORIGINES.
AYMARA INDIANS
AZTECS.
BANTUS.
BLACKS
BORORO INDIANS.
BRITISH IN INDIA.
BRITISH IN NEW ZEALAND.
BUBE (AFRICAN TRIBE).
BULGARIANS IN RUSSIA.
CARIB INDIANS.
CHEROKEE INDIANS.
CHINANTEC INDIANS.
CHINESE AMERICANS.
CHINESE IN CUBA.
CHINESE IN MALAYSIA.
CHINESE IN SOUTHEAST ASIA.
COLOURED PEOPLE (SOUTH AFRICA).
CORNISHMEN IN MEXICO.
COSSACKS.
CUIVA INDIANS.
DINKAS.
DJUKAS.
DUTCH IN CANADA.
EAST INDIANS IN EAST AFRICA.
EAST INDIANS IN FIJI.
EAST INDIANS IN SOUTH AFRICA.
EAST INDIANS IN THE UNITED KINGDOM.
EAST INDIANS IN UGANDA.
ESKIMOS
ESTONIANS IN RUSSIA.
FRENCH CANADIANS.
FRENCH IN RUSSIA.
FRENCH IN THE ARGENTINE REPUBLIC.
FULAHS.
GAUCHOS.
GERMAN AMERICANS.
GERMANS IN CZECHOSLOVAKIA.
GERMANS IN ESTONIA.
GERMANS IN FOREIGN COUNTRIES.

GERMANS IN HUNGARY.
GERMANS IN LATVIA.
GERMANS IN POLAND.
GERMANS IN ROMANIA.
GERMANS IN RUSSIA.
GERMANS IN SILESIA.
GERMANS IN THE ARGENTINE REPUBLIC.
GIPSIES
GREEKS IN CANADA.
GREEKS IN THE NETHERLANDS.
HUASTEC INDIANS.
HUNGARIANS IN ROMANIA.
INDIANS.
INDIANS OF CENTRAL AMERICA
INDIANS OF MEXICO.
INDIANS OF NORTH AMERICA
INDIANS OF SOUTH AMERICA.
IRISH AMERICANS.
ITALIAN AMERICANS.
ITALIANS IN CANADA.
JAPANESE AMERICANS.
JAPANESE IN BRAZIL.
JAPANESE IN CANADA.
JEWISH AMERICANS.
JEWS.
JEWS IN FRANCE.
JEWS IN GERMANY.
JEWS IN ITALY.
JEWS IN PALESTINE.
JEWS IN POLAND.
JEWS IN RUSSIA.
JEWS IN SOUTH AFRICA.
JEWS IN THE UNITED KINGDOM.
JIVARO INDIANS.
KABRE (AFRICAN PEOPLE).
KAMAIURA INDIANS.
KOOROKO (AFRICAN PEOPLE).
KURDS IN ISRAEL.
LITHUANIAN AMERICANS.
MALAY RACE.
MAORIS.
MAROONS.
MATACO INDIANS.
MAYAS.
MAZATEC INDIANS.
MEHINACU INDIANS
MEXICAN AMERICANS.
MEXICANS IN THE UNITED STATES.
MIAO PEOPLE.
MOLUCCANS IN THE NETHERLANDS.
MOSSI (AFRICAN PEOPLE).
NAHUAS.
NAUDEBA (AFRICAN PEOPLE).
NEW ZEALANDERS IN THE UNITED KINGDOM.
NICARAO INDIANS
NORTH AFRICANS IN FRANCE.
NSO (AFRICAN PEOPLE).
PAKISTANIS IN THE UNITED KINGDOM.
PALESTINIAN ARABS.
POLES IN AUSTRIA.
POLES IN CANADA.
POLES IN FOREIGN COUNTRIES.
POLES IN GERMANY.
POLES IN PRUSSIA.
POLES IN SILESIA.
POLES IN THE UNITED STATES.
POLISH AMERICANS.
POLYNESIANS IN NEW ZEALAND.
PUERTO RICANS IN THE UNITED STATES.
ROMANIANS IN TRANSYLVANIA.
RUKUBA (AFRICAN PEOPLE)
RUSSIANS IN ESTONIA.
RUSSIANS IN FOREIGN COUNTRIES.
SARASWATS.
SHERPAS
SLAVIC AMERICANS.
SORBS.
SPANIARDS IN ALGERIA.
SPANIARDS IN MEXICO.

TRANSPORT AND COMMUNICATIONS

SPANIARDS IN THE DOMINICAN REPUBLIC.
SWABIANS IN HUNGARY.
SWEDES IN FINLAND.
TAITAS
TATARS IN THE CRIMEA.
TERENO INDIANS.
TESOS
TEUTONIC RACE.
TONGANS.
TUAREGS.
TURKS IN BOSNIA.
TZOTZIL INDIANS
UKRAINIANS IN ALBERTA.
WEST INDIANS IN THE UNITED KINGDOM.
XIKRIN INDIANS.
YORUBAS.
YUGOSLAVS IN SWEDEN.
ZULUS.

TRANSPORT AND COMMUNICATIONS.

General.

AERONAUTICS
AERONAUTICS, COMMERCIAL.
AEROPLANES
AIR LINES.
AIR TRAFFIC CONTROL.
AIRPORT NOISE
AIRPORTS
ARTIFICIAL SATELLITES IN TELECOMMUNICATION.
AUTOMOBILE OWNERSHIP.
AUTOMOBILE PARKING
AUTOMOBILES
BROADCASTING
BROADCASTING POLICY
BUSINESS TRAVEL.
CHOICE OF TRANSPORTATION
CITY TRAFFIC.
COASTWISE SHIPPING.
COMMUNICATION AND TRAFFIC
COMMUTING
CONCORDE (JET TRANSPORTS).
DANGEROUS GOODS
EMERGENCY COMMUNICATION SYSTEMS
EMERGENCY TRANSPORTATION.
FERRIES.
FREIGHT AND FREIGHTAGE.
HARBOURS.
HIGHWAY LAW
INLAND NAVIGATION
INLAND WATER TRANSPORTATION.
JET PLANES
LOCAL TRANSIT.
MERCHANT MARINE
MOTOR BUS LINES
MOTOR BUSES
MOTOR VEHICLES
NATIONAL MARITIME MUSEUM.
PEDESTRIANS.
POSTAL SERVICE
RADIO BROADCASTING
RADIO PROGRAMMES, PUBLIC SERVICE.
RAILWAY CLEARING HOUSE.
RAILWAYS
RAILWAYS AND OTHER CARRIERS
RAILWAYS AND STATE
ROAD ACCIDENTS
ROAD PLANNING
ROAD SAFETY.
ROADS
SHIPPING
SHIPS
SHORT TAKE-OFF AND LANDING AIRCRAFT.
TAXICABS
TELECOMMUNICATION
TELEGRAPH
TELEVISION PROGRAMMES, PUBLIC SERVICE.
TOLL BRIDGES
TRADE ROUTES.
TRAFFIC ASSIGNMENT
TRAFFIC ENGINEERING.
TRAFFIC ESTIMATION
TRAFFIC OFFENCES
TRAFFIC REGULATIONS
TRAFFIC SURVEYS.
TRAMWAYS
TRANSPORTATION.
TRANSPORTATION, AUTOMOTIVE
TRANSPORTATION AND STATE
TRANSPORTATION NOISE.
TRANSPORTATION PLANNING.
TRAVEL
TRAVEL COSTS.
UNITIZED CARGO SYSTEMS.
URBAN TRANSPORTATION.
URBAN TRANSPORTATION POLICY.
VERTICALLY RISING AIRCRAFT.
WAREHOUSES.

Individual undertakings, etc.

BAIKAL-AMUR RAILWAY.
CHANNEL TUNNEL.
INTEROCEANIC RAILWAY OF MEXICO.
PANAMA CANAL.
PENNSYLVANIA RAILROAD.
SCANDINAVIAN AIRLINES SYSTEM.
SUEZ CANAL.

APR 9 1980

Z
7161
L84
v.36
1978